THE

PROBLEM OF

DELINQUENCY

Edited by

SHELDON GLUECK

Roscoe Pound Professor of Law

Harvard University

HOUGHTON MIFFLIN COMPANY · BOSTON

The Riverside Press Cambridge

To

DR. WILLIAM HEALY

and

DR. AUGUSTA BRONNER,

creative organizers and directors of the clinic of

the Judge Baker Foundation, to the late

JUDGE FREDERICK PICKERING CABOT

of the Boston Juvenile Court,

and to the late

HANS WEISS,

probation officer of the Boston Juvenile Court,

dedicated servants of children and of justice

PREFACE

been quite successful in aiding students in the delinquency problem whole, to note its ramifications, to assess its legal implications, and to develop some facility in financing a wide variety of technical vocabularies derived not alone from the legal decisions but also from the points of view of psychology, psychiatry, sociology

With so much professional and public concern centered on the delinquency problem nowadays, the time has arrived for putting together a set of materials which will reflect the intricacies of the problem and assist in training prospective prosecutors, judges, probation and parole officers, clinicians, social workers, and others in an appreciation of its ramifications and implications.

Several good textbooks and one or two compilations of materials already exist; but what has long been needed is a set of materials that is eclectic and far-ranging in respect to the causes of delinquency, its treatment and prevention, and at the same time takes account of the legal problems inherent in society's efforts to cope with its maladjusted youngsters. For the targets that must be borne in mind are both welfare and justice.

That is the twofold aim of the present book.

I have made every effort to include all relevant points of view, since I have long been convinced that no single discipline can supply all or even most of the fundamental answers. A basic weakness of criminology has been the tendency of certain textbook writers to "stake out a claim" for some particular discipline, such as anthropology or sociology or psychiatry or psychoanalysis, and to promote that discipline as either exclusively explanatory or primarily significant in the understanding, treatment, and prevention of delinquency. This professional parochialism has sometimes reached absurd results. It has led to a neglect or an unfair appraisal of research findings that run counter to the pet "theory" of some "school of thought." It has bedeviled the efforts of sober investigators to study a many-caused social problem by a many-faceted approach.

To the lawyer and judge who would cope with the "purely legal" issues involved in the heart-rending and dangerous social problem of delinquency, a mere glance at the table of contents with its wide-ranging sweep of materials relevant to the delinquency problem ought to stimulate intellectual reorientation. To the sociologist and cultural anthropologist who see the world largely in terms of environmental conditioning, an examination of the psychologic and psychiatric materials should prove enlightening. To the physical anthropologist and biologist, who tend to minimize the role of sociocultural conditioning, the articles involving environmental influences should give ground for thought. In a word, what has long been badly needed in examining the problem of delinquency in all its facets is a convenient chart and compass for wider horizons. Modest as may be the success of the present effort to supply such tools of thought and action in the delinquency field, it at least emphasizes a crucial need. Selections in assignments can of course be readily made to emphasize the individual instructor's chief interest.

This book is, then, designed to give a presentation of the multiple forces and factors that must be considered in any realistic approach to the delinquency problem. The materials are taken largely from articles in a wide variety of periodicals, American and foreign, some of them difficult of access. Some fifty decisions, involving the basic legal problems that have arisen, are included. Extracts from books have been limited essentially to works of the joint authorship of Dr. Eleanor Touroff Glueck and myself.

In a volume of this kind there will always be questions as to why some particular article was included or excluded. My aim has been to bring together materials that are not only sound in content but which lend themselves most readily to the art of pedagogy. I have tried out many of the items in this compilation for two years in my seminar on The Problem of Delinquency at the Harvard Law School, attended by a group of third-year and postgraduate law students. I believe the seminar has been quite successful in aiding students to see the delinquency problem whole, to note its ramifications, to assess its legal implications, and to develop some facility in managing a wide variety of technical vocabularies derived not alone from the legal decisions but also from the points of view of psychology, psychiatry, sociology, social work, and anthropology. It is the semantic problem, in addition to certain professional prejudices, that creates difficulties in the process of delving deeply into the issues presented by juvenile delinquency. It is, therefore, especially gratifying to record that with the progress of the discussions of the materials assembled in this book, the students gained an improved facility in crossing bridges between the various disciplines. Indeed, the well-equipped lawyer has always felt the need of keeping in touch with other disciplines. As far back as 1886, Mr. Justice Holmes, in his imaginative lecture on "The Profession of the Law," advised his youthful listeners at Harvard in these words:

> And your business as thinkers is to make plainer the way from some thing to the whole of things; to show the rational connection between your fact and the frame of the universe. If your subject is law, the roads are plain to anthropology, the science of man, to political economy, the theory of legislation, ethics, and thus by several paths to your final view of life . . . To be master of any branch of knowledge, you must master those which lie next to it.

It is pleasant to record that the Harvard Law School has long striven to instill in its students the point of view expressed by Holmes.

For the rest, the injunction of Francis Bacon, in his well-known essay, "Of Studies," might well be borne in mind by teacher and student alike: "Read not to contradict and confute; nor to believe and take for granted; nor to find talk and discourse; but to weigh and consider."

As to the pedagogical method that is suited to the type of wide mixture of legal and extralegal materials herein assembled, I suggest the procedure I have found useful in my seminar on The Problem of Delinquency at the Harvard Law School: Each student is appointed *Rapporteur* for several articles or legal decisions. The student presents a digest of the materials, along with his own comments on them. The other students, having also read the assigned materials, participate in the discussion. The instructor interjects comments, from time to time, and gives a brief summing up at the end of the session. However, some instructors may prefer not to have a special student be responsible for each assignment. Others may prefer to have a team of specialists give the course: a lawyer, a psychiatrist or psychologist, and a sociologist; or, experts can be invited to participate in certain sessions. Law school professors may choose to begin the course with the legal decisions which comprise the major portion of Part Two: The Juvenile Court and the Law.

The original intention in assembling and organizing the materials was to provide intellectual meat and drink for advanced law students whose vision went so far beyond the narrow issues presented in the legal decisions as to embrace the various criminogenic influences which brought the child to the court, and the processes that might counteract those influences, return him to the family and the community as a happy, law-abiding junior citizen, and reduce the number of potential delinquents. But the book is so designed that I believe it can be of pedagogical value not only in law schools, but in university departments of sociology, psychology, psychiatry, education or government, and schools of social work.

Primarily, however, I hope that the appearance of this teaching instrument will stimulate law schools throughout the country to introduce into their curricula seminars or courses on the mountingly serious problem of child delinquency. That the time is ripe for this is shown, among other evidence that might be marshalled, by the fact that at the 1957 Conference of the National Council of Juvenile Court Judges — an organization comprising 1500 of the 3000 juvenile court judges in the country — a resolution was passed that (1) law schools throughout America include in their curricula "adequate courses" on the philosophy and procedure of juvenile courts, and (2) that bar examiners include questions on this subject in their admittance examinations.

Like all teachers, I owe a debt to my pupils. I am particularly indebted to John C. Howell, James P. Felstiner, and Professor J. J. Rappeport, students in my first experimental seminars on juvenile delinquency, for aid in selecting materials and especially for helping me to determine student reaction to the subject matter.

I am also deeply grateful to my secretary, Mrs. Esther Churchill Ghostlaw, for typing the manuscript and for skillfully attending to the thousand and one details involved in gaining permission to include the various articles and gathering biographical materials. I am especially indebted to Mrs. Ghostlaw for assisting me in reading the proof of this large book.

My special appreciation is due the authors and publishers of these materials. The biographies of the authors and the names of the publishers are set out in appropriate places in the book.

With deep appreciation and on behalf of student users of this book as well as myself, I record the fact that the Ella Lyman Cabot Trust and the Field Foundation, Inc., as well as another foundation and a public spirited friend both of whom prefer to remain anonymous have made possible the sale of this book at a price much lower than would otherwise have been necessary.

My thanks are also due to Dean Emeritus Roscoe Pound and to Dean Erwin N. Griswold of the Harvard Law School for their encouragement.

Finally, my deepest gratitude is due my devoted wife, Dr. Eleanor T. Glueck, wise and dedicated partner in many researches.

Harvard Law School   SHELDON GLUECK.
Cambridge, Mass.
December 16, 1958.

CONTENTS

Part One: Incidence and Causation

Part Two: The Juvenile Court and the Law

Section I

History and Organization

Section II

Basic Legal Issues

Part Three: Treatment

Section I

Types of Disposition and Treatment

Chapter 21. FORMS OF TREATMENT: PROBATION AND ITS ADJUNCTS

Chapter 22. FORMS OF TREATMENT: FOSTER HOME CARE

Chapter 23. FORMS OF TREATMENT: INSTITUTIONAL CARE

Chapter 24. FORMS OF TREATMENT: HOSPITAL CARE

Part Four: Prevention of Delinquency

Section I

Early Recognition of Potential Delinquents

Section II

Preventive Action

PART ONE

Incidence

and Causation

Chapter 1

Incidence and Measurement of Delinquency

AT THE VERY THRESHOLD of a problem such as delinquency one is met with the difficulty of obtaining accurate statistics regarding its incidence and fluctuation. First, there are variations in the definition of the term itself, both legally and psychiatrically. "Delinquency," depending on the provisions of a particular statute, may include not merely the serious offenses which when committed by adults are denominated crimes, and not only such deviant childhood behavior as truancy, running away from home, "stubbornness," disobedience and similar conduct compendiously referred to as "incorrigibility" or "waywardness," but also more general and vague attitudes of an antisocial flavor or tendency, such as hostility, aggressiveness and even guilt feelings leading to some form of deviant behavior deemed potentially dangerous to the child and to society. Influenced by an understandable zeal for anticipatory preventive action, some courts may accept, as cases legitimately within the scope of their competence although not necessarily involving the need of an official hearing and a formal legal finding of a status of delinquency, situations in which overt antisocial action, much less downright criminal behavior, would be hard to prove.[1]

But apart from the problem of definition of the content of the term delinquency, there are other obstacles to a trustworthy assessment of its incidence and variations. There are differences in the policies and practices of police organizations, schools, other social agencies, as well as juvenile courts themselves, in respect to "screening" practices and to the types of cases to be dealt with officially. Obviously, to compare the incidence of delinquency in any region over a period of time, or as between two or more regions, requires a reasonable uniformity in the definition of the phenomenon under comparison and in the policies and practices of selection.

All this is illustrated in an official report on delinquency in California from which the following quotation is taken:

> Then there is another element of definition. What are some of the possible levels of detection or treatment of antisocial juvenile conduct which might serve as a focal point for an index of juvenile delinquency? In theory, juveniles coming within the following categories might be considered:
> (1) Those coming within a legal definition.
> (2) Those reprimanded by parents or teachers.
> (3) Those interrogated by the police.
> (4) Those arrested.
> (5) Those referred to probation departments.
> (6) Those retained by probation departments for court hearings or for informal supervision. (Conversely, those not dismissed immediately, or shortly following an initial contact.)

---

[1] For a thought-provoking discussion of the problem of definition of delinquency, see P. W. Tappan, *Juvenile Delinquency*, New York, McGraw-Hill Book Co., Inc., 1949, 21–36.

(7) Those who are subjects of petitions for juvenile court hearings.

(8) Those declared wards of the juvenile courts and placed under the supervision of probation departments for probationary or custodial treatment.

(9) Those committed to state institutions.[2]

At the first United Nations Congress on the Prevention of Crime and the Treatment of Offenders, held in Geneva in 1955, there was a great deal of futile discussion about the definition of delinquency. It did not seem to occur to some of the delegates that a definition depends on the aim of the inquiry and that often a clear definition must be postponed until thorough discussion of several tentative ones clarifies the aim. For example, in a well-known research project that has stimulated considerable discussion and research, the concept of delinquency was deliberately defined as follows:

> Actually, any child who commits even a single minor act in violation of the law is technically a delinquent. In Massachusetts, for example, a "delinquent child" is one "between seven and seventeen who violates any city ordinance or town by-law or commits an offense not punishable by death." A "wayward child" is one "between seven and seventeen years of age who habitually associates with vicious or immoral persons, or who is growing up in circumstances exposing him to lead an immoral, vicious or criminal life."
>
> For the purposes of the present study, however, delinquency refers to repeated acts of a kind which when committed by persons beyond the statutory juvenile court age of sixteen are punishable as crimes (either felonies or misdemeanors) — except for a few instances of persistent stubbornness, truancy, running away, associating with immoral persons, and the like. Children who once or twice during the period of growing up in an excitingly attractive milieu steal a toy in a ten-cent store, sneak into a subway or motion picture theatre, play hooky, and the like, and soon outgrow such peccadilloes are not true delinquents even though they have violated the law. Indeed, it is now recognized that a certain amount of petty pilfering occurs among many children around the age of six or seven and is to be expected as part of the process of trying their wings. Children appear to be no worse for very occasional and slight experimental deviations from socially acceptable norms of conduct. Since they soon voluntarily abandon such behavior, their misconduct cannot be deemed either habitual or symptomatic of deep-rooted causes.[3]

Yet the authors of the work from which the quotation is taken have been chided by some reviewers for not including single petty-offense delinquents and others. It has not been recognized that the definition of "delinquent" in the research in question was taken "in order to arrive at the clearest differentiation of disease and health," a comparison "between the unquestionably pathologic and the normal." It has not been recognized that the definition, if it results in certain findings of a significant variation between the experimental group and the control group may be regarded as an hypothesis, the testing of which can come only when the prediction tables derived from the comparison are applied to other samples of delinquents and non-delinquents.[4] It has been dogmatically stated that the prediction tables developed on the basis of the traits and background factors of the sample of delinquents as defined above in comparison with those of a carefully determined sample of non-delinquents of similar age, ethnico-racial derivation, general intelligence and residence in economically and culturally underprivileged urban areas, could not possibly predict delinquency at an early age.

---

[2] *Delinquency and Probation in California,* State of California Department of Justice Division of Criminal Law and Enforcement, 1954, pp. 18–19.

[3] Reprinted by permission of the publishers and The Commonwealth Fund from *Unraveling Juvenile Delinquency,* Sheldon and Eleanor T. Glueck, Cambridge, Mass.: Harvard University Press, Copyright, 1950, by The Commonwealth Fund. Pages 13–14.

[4] See Articles 116–117, 171–173 of this volume.

So, in attempting to determine the incidence of delinquency, there is need, first, to establish a definition of the concept for the purpose in question and, secondly, to assure a reasonable degree of fixity and uniformity of major influences of selection [5] that may affect the outcome when making statistical comparisons of incidence of delinquency (as defined for the purpose in question) as between periods of time in any one locality or as between various regions.

A typical news item regarding the rise of delinquency is the following from the respected periodical, *Children*, published under the auspices of the Children's Bureau:

> Provisional findings by the Children's Bureau indicate that in 1956 juvenile-court delinquency cases increased in the United States by about 20 percent over the number handled by the courts in 1955. The child population of juvenile-court age (generally 10 through 17) increased by only 3 percent for the country. The 1955–1956 increase was more than twice as great as that for 1954–1955, which was 9 percent.
>
> On the basis of the juvenile-court statistics, the Bureau estimates that roughly 2 percent of the 20.6 million children of juvenile-court age in the United States were referred to the courts in delinquency cases in 1956. Many more children than come to the attention of juvenile courts for delinquency — perhaps two or three times as many — are dealt with by the police for misbehavior without referral to court.[6]

To point to the matters that must be borne in mind in drawing conclusions from this type of statement, the following quotation is given:

> Our report measures a human problem in terms of figures by the formula consistently used in our city for the past several years . . . that of boys and girls who come into contact with the Police for unlawful behavior.
>
> Care must be exercised in any comparisons. Some cities take delinquency rates only on youth actually appearing in courts . . . a convenient tabulation, but one which minimizes rather than emphasizes youth problems. Other cities count offenses by an age group, say 10 through 16, but on a ratio to the entire youth population, age 1 through 16. This is convenient, too, but tends to artificially reduce the problem's extent.[7]

The articles in this chapter are designed to bring out some of the relevant issues on this matter of the bases for reliable statistical accounting of the incidence and fluctuations of delinquency.

The first article, by Perlman, discusses the measurability of delinquent behavior and considers the various statistical indices and state and local reporting. Murphy, Shirley and Witmer take up the matter presenting the hardest problem in the assessment of the delinquency rate: the incidence of "hidden delinquency."

---

[5] On the difficulties inherent in this matter, see S. M. Robison, *Can Delinquency Be Measured?* New York, Columbia University Press, 1936.

[6] 5 *Children*, 36–37.

[7] *Youth Offenders*, Detroit 1956, City of Detroit Commission on Children and Youth, Preface.

1

Reporting Juvenile Delinquency *

I. Richard Perlman

The reporting of juvenile delinquency is "woefully inadequate."

"Juvenile delinquency statistics do not measure juvenile delinquency at all; they reflect only the adequacy or efficiency of law-enforcement agencies. Add more policemen and more delinquency shows up."

"Juvenile delinquency is influenced by newspaper publicity and public hysteria on the subject. The more the newspapers and magazines write about such things, the more delinquency goes up."

These are comments you hear or read in the press. Some of them are hard to disprove. How can we tell, for example, whether or not newspaper stories have influenced the data?

The mounting trend in delinquency as shown by the statistics began back in 1949, some time before the tremendous public and newspaper interest in it had built up to present heights. Newspaper publicity and public concern and pressure, since the rise began, may have resulted in even greater increases. But can we be sure? How can we measure their influence? Obviously here we can only guess — and one guess may be as good as another.

Similarly, the statement that increasing the strength of a law enforcement agency causes an increase in delinquency is very hard to prove — or disprove. Many factors would have to be

* Reprinted from 3 NPPA Journal (1957), 242–249. Used by permission of the author and the publisher. See, also, O. M. Wilson, "How to Measure the Extent of Juvenile Delinquency," 41 J. Crim. L. and Criminology (1950), 435–438; I. Richard Perlman, "The Meaning of Juvenile Delinquency Statistics," 13 Federal Probation (1949), 63–67; F. L. Roth, "Juvenile Cases: Simplified System for Reporting," 14 Conn. Bar J. (1940), 337–360. — Ed.

controlled in any study that attempted to do so. The number on the police force may correlate positively with an increase in reported delinquency; indeed, one very good community study reports this. But other communities, experimenting with heavy police patrols in certain areas, report decreases in delinquency and crime as a result. So, again, we have no answer.

But one thing is clear — the criticisms do indicate that all is not well, and that we should look more closely at current juvenile delinquency statistics to get a better understanding of why they are being reported, what they show, what they mean, and what they imply.

Various kinds of statistical data relate in one way or another to juvenile delinquency. For example, there are series of data on children arrested by the police; on children referred to juvenile courts for delinquency; on children committed and resident in institutions for delinquents. These series of data are gathered by various agencies for specific purposes, generally for their own administrative use or for public information. As such, they are valuable and serve their specific purposes quite well.

But difficulties do arise when these reported statistics are misinterpreted by people who vary the definition of delinquency on which the specific statistics are based, or who use them for purposes for which they were not intended.

CAN DELINQUENCY BE MEASURED?

One of the most popular uses of delinquency-related statistics is in showing whether "delinquency" has gone up or down and how good or bad present-day children are in comparison with previous generations. This use creates a good deal of misunderstanding and controversy and involves two basic questions: Do juvenile delinquency statistics actually measure juvenile delinquency? Can delinquency really be measured? We would all agree that juvenile delinquency, to be measured, must mean the same to those who collect the data and those who interpret it.

At present, juvenile delinquency is variously defined. One group holds that a delinquent is a child who has violated the law and has been adjudged delinquent by a court. According to this definition juvenile court statistics would measure delinquency *if* they were adequately collected.

Others say that referral to a juvenile court is often influenced by chance factors — that the circumstances under which delinquency is adjudicated vary with the laws, the administrative procedures, the philosophy of the police and the courts, and even with differences in community attitudes toward the police and the courts. In fact, many children committing delinquent acts are handled by police without referral to court. Many children referred to courts are handled unofficially, without a formal court hearing or adjudication of delinquency. For these reasons, some hold that police statistics provide a better measure of juvenile delinquency than court statistics. Police reporting, they point out, cuts down the number of arbitrary procedural steps influencing the data.

Two obvious conditions must be met before police or court statistics can be collected: (1) the child must commit an act regarded as delinquent, and (2) he must come to the attention of a law-enforcement agency. And the second of these conditions provokes objection by another group to police and juvenile court data as a measure of delinquency. This group holds that a delinquent is any child committing a delinquent act whether or not he comes to the attention of legal authorities. Delinquency is defined by them as any juvenile misconduct which *could* be dealt with under the law.

To measure delinquency by this definition, we would need to know not only the number of delinquent children handled by social agencies, child guidance clinics, schools, law-enforcement agencies, and others, but also the number who do not come to the attention of any agency — those who are not apprehended. Delinquency defined in this way is practically impossible to measure, though it is the simplest and most complete definition. Those statistics that *can* be gathered — on children dealt with by law-enforcement agencies and courts — do, however, represent a portion of all children whose misconduct could, if detected, be dealt with by the law, and trends in their number and characteristics probably reflect changes occurring in the entire group.

National Reporting

The two series of national data most frequently cited are the juvenile court statistics collected by the Children's Bureau and the police arrest data collected by the Federal Bureau of Investigation.

Certain other national data collected by other federal agencies are related to juvenile delinquency — notably those on federal juvenile offenders reported by the Federal Bureau of Prisons; those on children in institutions for delinquent children, now being collected annually by the Children's Bureau and collected by the Bureau of the Census in its 1950 decennial census. These last two series, however, are less frequently used in statistics of juvenile delinquency than are juvenile court and police arrest data, since they deal with so small a portion of the total group of delinquent children.

1. *Juvenile court statistics.* In 1926 the Children's Bureau first worked out a plan for the uniform reporting by juvenile courts of a few essential statistics. Back of this reporting plan lay the recognition of the need for uniform statistical data on juvenile courts' volume of work in dealing with delinquents. From the beginning, the reporting has been voluntary.

Reporting procedures and content have been modified several times, primarily to make collection and tabulation easier and to increase the usefulness of the data. Originally, the Bureau tabulated individual data cards sent in directly by the courts. Now reports come to the Children's Bureau in the form of a summary from the state agency that collects and tabulates the data of its courts. To encourage an increasing number of courts to report, the amount of detailed information requested has been greatly reduced. Formerly, such items as age of child, reason for referral to court, place of detention care, and type of disposition were included. Now the reports are limited to a simple count of cases of children referred to juvenile courts for delinquency, dependency, or neglect, and of cases involving special proceedings, whether handled officially or unofficially (without the filing of a petition).

Although juvenile court statistics are not perfect measures of delinquency, they do have some assets as close estimates. First, they include that group of children whose delinquencies were considered important enough to refer to a court. They approximate more closely than do other series of data the definition of those who consider a child delinquent only when the courts have so adjudicated.

Second, these statistics do not include children whose misbehavior is handled by the police without referral to court. Nationally, three out of every four cases are handled this way. Most such police cases are for minor offenses. Therefore, their omission from the court count somewhat meets the objection that juvenile court statistics are inadequate as delinquency data because they include many minor infractions which are not delinquencies at all.

Third, national juvenile court statistics have been collected and published in the Children's Bureau Statistical Series for quite some time. This means that uniform reporting definitions and concepts have been developed with the cooperation of the courts; as a result, there is some stability in these statistics.

The Children's Bureau is constantly trying to improve its juvenile court statistics. These statistics, because they are limited to a simple count of delinquency cases handled by the courts, tell us nothing about the reasons for which children are referred to courts. Therefore, they tell nothing about what types of offenses are increasing or decreasing, nor do they indicate what disposition is made of the cases referred to court.

Reporting by the courts is voluntary and not all courts in the country participate. Some regions of the country are overrepresented; others underrepresented. Thus, the statistics are incomplete both in items reported and geographical representation.

To fill in some of these gaps, the Children's Bureau recently initiated a plan for collecting data from a national sample of 502 juvenile courts. This will supplement the present system of collecting data. The new national sample, designed with technical assistance from the Bureau of the Census, has been selected as representative of the country as a whole.

In devising the sample, the United States was first divided into about 2,000 primary sampling units, each consisting of a county or a number of contiguous counties, such as those in a standard metropolitan area. The 2,000 primary sampling units were then grouped into 230 strata, each consisting of a set of units as much alike as possible in such characteristics as regional location, population density, rate of growth, percent of nonwhite population, principal industry, type of agriculture, etc. From each

stratum, a single primary sample unit was selected at random. This resulted in 230 sampling units in which there were 502 courts.

Reports for 1955, the first year of the plan, have been received from about 83 per cent of the sample courts. The Bureau anticipates that all 502 courts will volunteer to participate. For 1956, the Children's Bureau hopes to be able to issue reports based on this national sample.

The data from the national sample will provide a basis for national estimates that have a degree of reliability that is known, and higher than has ever been possible before. Once the sample plan is fully working, the Bureau will collect, efficiently, reliable national information not only on the number of juvenile court cases but also on certain characteristics of children referred to court and on court activities such as reason for referral, type of service rendered, and disposition.

2. *Police arrest data.* The only source of federally collected statistics on police arrest of children is the uniform crime-reporting plan of the Federal Bureau of Investigation. Until 1952, data regarding arrests of juveniles were obtained from fingerprint records — the only records which showed the age of persons arrested. The Federal Bureau of Investigation had long recognized that data for juveniles based on fingerprint records were inadequate, since many jurisdictions do not fingerprint children who are arrested. For this reason, in 1952, the Federal Bureau of Investigation undertook to remedy this inadequacy by obtaining data on the age, sex, and race of persons arrested, whether or not they were fingerprinted.

The coverage of this reporting has increased steadily each year. By 1955, 1,477 cities, representing 46.8 per cent of the urban population, were reporting. But, as in juvenile court statistics, certain regions of the country and types of cities are overrepresented; some are underrepresented.

The Federal Bureau of Investigation also points out that its data does not include instances of nonpolice detention of juveniles under circumstances amounting to technical arrest. Thus these arrest figures, though far more complete than data obtained from fingerprint arrest records, are probably still conservative in the lower-age groups. These data appear in *Uniform Crime Reports,* annual bulletins pub-

Figure 1

Comparison of Delinquency Cases Disposed of by Juvenile Courts, with
Police Arrests of Children Under 18 Years of Age, 1940–1951

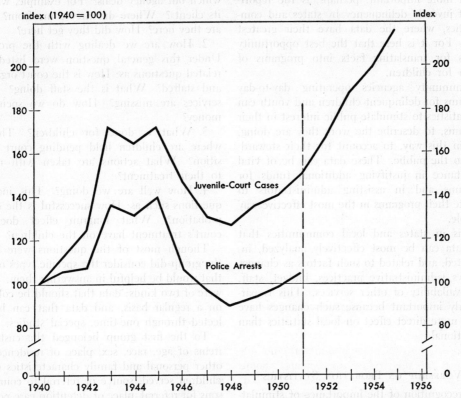

Sources: Police-arrest data from section on fingerprint arrest records in *Uniform
Crime Reports* (annual bulletins) issued by the Federal Bureau of Investigation;
juvenile-court data from *Statistical Series No. 37* issued by the Children's Bureau.

lished by the Federal Bureau of Investigation.

3. *Arrest and court statistics compared.*
Despite the fact that neither the police arrest
data nor the juvenile court statistics are complete
in extent of coverage, geographic representation,
and other factors; despite the fact that neither
is a completely accurate measurement of juvenile delinquency; and despite their divergent
units of count, these two statistical series show
a remarkable similarity in their trends, as indicated in the graph above.

Police arrest data are shown in the graph
only through 1951, since the data for 1952 and
subsequent years are not comparable to data
for prior years due to the revision of fingerprint
record procedure described above. (Even after
this revision, the trends revealed by the two
series of data appear fairly similar. The revised

police arrest data show, for example, an 11 per
cent increase between 1954 and 1955; the
juvenile court data, an increase of 9 per
cent.)

The striking similarity between these two
trends suggests that they are each influenced
by some common determining factor, perhaps
"delinquency," however defined. The similarity
cannot be accounted for on the grounds that
police arrest data include a large proportion of
the cases referred to court, for police fingerprint arrest records embrace only a small proportion of those cases referred to juvenile court.
From this similarity in trends we can have some
confidence that national data on juvenile delinquency do show the general direction of the
volume of delinquency, even though the extent
of the change is not precise.

STATE AND LOCAL REPORTING

The practical use of national data is limited. Much more important, perhaps, is the reporting of juvenile delinquency by states and communities, where the data have their greatest value. For it is here that the best opportunity occurs for translating facts into programs of action for children.

Community agencies operating day-to-day programs for delinquent children and youth can use statistics to stimulate public interest in their programs, to describe the work they are doing, and, in this way, to account for their stewardship to the public. These data can be of vital importance in justifying additional funds for programs and in assisting administrators to operate their programs in the most effective way possible.

It is in states and local communities that the data can be most effectively analyzed, interpreted, and related to such factors as changes in laws, administrative practices, budget, staff, and availability of other services. This is particularly important because such changes have much more direct effect on local statistics than on national.

WORKSHOP ON PROBATION STATISTICS

In recognition of the importance of stimulating and improving state and local reporting of juvenile delinquency, the Children's Bureau recently called together a small group of state and local probation practitioners to explore: (1) the questions administrators need to answer in assigning staff and work, in evaluating work performance, in planning and budgeting, and in aiding community interpretation, (2) the statistical data most useful in answering these questions, and (3) some of the problems of obtaining the data, together with some possible solutions. The Children's Bureau was convinced that data administratively useful to local courts, if developed in a uniformly acceptable way, would provide a reservoir of information useful for local, state, and federal planning and research.

Most of the participants in the workshop agreed that the questions administrators of local courts need to answer covered all phases of court services — intake, social study, detention, and supervision. The following questions were formulated:

1. What is the nature of the problem with which our agency deals? For example, who are its clients? Where did they come from? Why are they here? How did they get here?

2. How are we dealing with the problem? Under this general question were listed such related questions as: How is the court organized and staffed? What is the staff doing? What services are missing? How do we spend our money?

3. What is done for children? That is, where are children held pending court disposition? What actions are taken with respect to their treatment?

4. How well are we doing? This included questions such as: How successful is the child's probation? What longrun effect does the court's treatment have on the children?

Though most of the questions were broad, the group did consider the specific types of data that would be helpful in answering them. These were of two kinds: data that should be collected on a regular basis, and data that can be collected through one-time, special studies.

To the first group belonged the customary items of age, race, sex, place of residence, and other personal and family characteristics of the children served, source of referral to court, reasons for referral, place of detention care pending court hearing, disposition, etc. In the second group were studies of the success of children on probation, follow-up of children who have been discharged from court, time studies which would have bearing on staff assignment and the evaluation of work performance, cost studies, etc.

Throughout the workshop, the members of the group emphasized the desirability of developing uniform definitions and reporting procedures. They agreed that some local courts and state agencies had excellent reports and record-keeping systems. At the same time, for the sake of uniformity, they urged that the Children's Bureau develop a manual outlining the types of data to be maintained by courts and setting forth definitions and procedures to be used in obtaining them. This manual would be aimed primarily at data to be collected on a regular basis. Regarding special one-time studies, the group suggested that the Bureau undertake several demonstration studies in selected courts and then so describe the study method that it could be duplicated by other courts.

The Bureau views the workshop as an important first step toward strengthening and improving reporting on juvenile delinquency at the local level — where it is most needed and most useful.

Juvenile court and police arrest data give a count of the number of children coming to the attention of these law-enforcement agencies. They are the best statistics relating to juvenile delinquency now available and, as such, give some insight into delinquency trends.

Current efforts to improve these data are salutary and will unquestionably increase their value. Although these two series will never measure juvenile delinquency to the complete satisfaction of everyone, they can, if extended and improved, define more accurately the size of the problem with which communities and agencies must deal. They can provide much more information than we now have about the children — why they were referred to court and how their cases were handled; the number, qualifications, and salaries of staff; the availability of detention and diagnostic facilities; a basis for studying the effectiveness of treatment.

Even with such imperfect measures as we have, we know enough to take some action now. We know there are thousands of delinquent children coming to the attention of the police and the juvenile courts for whom we can plan treatment. We can provide proper facilities for the care of the 100,000 or so delinquent children held in jails each year pending official action. We can begin to set up probation services for juveniles in the more than half of the counties in the country where they are not now available. We can take steps to improve the training of probation officers (more than four out of ten lack college training) who now deal with delinquent children.

Along with attempts to improve the statistics should go a concerted effort to help the public interpret and use these statistics as constructively as possible. Then perhaps our ultimate aim — the benefits that could accrue to children — will be realized.*

* For an excellent set of recommendations for improving the gathering and interpretation of criminal statistics, see Uniform Crime Reports for the United States, Special Issue, 1958, Appendix III. — Ed.

2

The Incidence of Hidden Delinquency *

Fred J. Murphy,[1] Mary M. Shirley, and Helen L. Witmer

Mental hygienists have always been concerned, on the one hand, that many a youthful violator of the law goes unprosecuted and even undetected until a delinquent pattern becomes deeply ingrained; and on the other, that many a lad receives a juvenile court record for a

* Reprinted from 16 Am. J. Orthopsychiatry (1946), 686–696. Used by permission of Fred J. Murphy, Helen L. Witmer, and the publisher. See, also, T. Sellin, "The Significance of Records of Crime," 67 L. Q. Rev. (1951), 489–504, and "The Uniform Criminal Statistics Act," 40 J. Crim. L. and Criminology (1950), 679–700; A. L. Porterfield, "Hidden Delinquency," 37 J. Crim. L. and Criminology (1946–47), 425–426; E. H. Stullken, "Misconceptions about Juvenile Delinquency," 46 J. Crim. L., Criminology and Police Science (1956), 833–842; E. E. Schwartz, "Statistics of Juvenile Delinquency in the United States," 261 Annals (1949), 9–20; R. L. Rowland, and I. R. Perlman, "Statistical Reporting of Probation Services in Juvenile Courts," Dept. of Health, Education and Welfare, Social Security Administration, Children's Bureau, Washington, D. C., 1957. Essentially, the changes advocated by Perlman (in the preceding article), Schwartz and others have been made in recent years. For example, the police reports now received list the ages of all arrested persons. In 1929 the Committee on Uniform Crime Records of the International Association of Chiefs of Police published "Uniform Crime Reporting," a comprehensive manual of instructions for use of police officers in making out reports. For an authoritative assessment of the current extent of institutional treatment of juvenile delinquents, see "Some Facts about Public State Training Schools for Juvenile Delinquents," Children's Bureau Statistical Series No. 33, U. S. Dept. of Health, Education and Welfare, Social Security Administration, Children's Bureau, 1956. For a county project in gathering statistics on delinquency, see J. Martin, "A County-Wide Delinquency Recording System," 47 J. Crim. L., Criminology and Police Science (1957), 628–687. — Ed.

[1] Presented as a thesis in social work at Boston University.

relatively innocent misdemeanor. Students of juvenile delinquency have long suspected that juvenile court statistics do not reflect adequately the extent of youthful misconduct and that a considerable number of violations and violators never find their way into official court records. Hitherto, research workers have been baffled as to how to get at this pool of hidden delinquency. The Cambridge–Somerville Youth Study, which has maintained an intimate contact with a large group of boys throughout their adolescent years, has afforded a unique opportunity to arrive at some measure of the amount of juvenile lawbreaking that is hidden from public view. From our case records, it is possible to make a minimum estimate of how frequently the group of boys under study committed acts that *could* have brought them into court if someone in the community had wanted to register a court complaint.

This program of character-building and delinquency-prevention sponsored by the late Dr. Richard Cabot directed its efforts chiefly toward underprivileged boys who lived amidst the congestion and squalor of high delinquency areas. The plan of treatment involved close contact with the subjects and their parents by case workers who became trusted friends and were consequently afforded the boys' confidences. In the course of work the case workers acquired a great deal of information concerning misdeeds that had never become a matter of official court complaint.

Before extracting the pertinent data from the case histories, certain terms had to be understood and procedures developed and explained. The General Laws of Massachusetts define a delinquent as "A child between seven and seventeen years who violates any city ordinance or town by-law or commits an offense not punishable by death, or by imprisonment for life." Our classification as to an unofficial or official delinquent depended upon whether or not a court complaint had been granted for an offense. The distinction was arbitrarily established at this point because Juvenile Court statistics are computed upon the basis of the number of court complaints issued. This step was decided upon in collaboration with an official of the Boston Juvenile Court, now Justice John J. Connelly, a recognized authority on delinquency.

Because the length of a period of probation or the term of institutional commitment for juvenile offenses do not serve as an adequate measure of the seriousness of an act, three groupings by nature of offenses were formulated with the assistance of the aforementioned authority. The three categories as developed in the order of seriousness were:

(1) *Violations of city ordinances*, such as shining shoes or vending without a license, street ball playing, hopping street cars, swimming and/or fishing in forbidden places, and curfew laws.

(2) *Minor offenses*, of the nature of truancy, petty stealing (5 and 10¢ stores), trespassing, running away, stubborn child, sneaking into movies.

(3) *More serious offenses*, involving such acts as breaking and entering, larceny, assault, drunkenness, sex offenses.

The comprehensive list of approximately 50 offenses was drawn up on individual work sheets which provided space for identifying material on the boy and columns for tabulating his law violations.

A group consultation with the case workers, later to be interviewed individually, was held. This was done to avoid confusion and to assure consistency in the workers understanding the procedure. The project was thoroughly explained and their advice sought particularly in reference to the tabulation of the frequency of unofficial acts wherein it did not always make for accurate enumeration. Case workers often knew that a boy had repeatedly committed a certain infraction during a given period, but they would have been at a loss to enumerate the individual occurrences. Hence, it was decided to use — *rarely, occasionally* and *frequently* — giving to each a range of numerical value which would represent the number of violations in a given year of a boy's life. *Rarely* denoted a frequency span of from one to three offenses per year; *occasionally*, from four to nine, and *frequently*, ten and over. By this method it was obvious that we would have to be satisfied in most instances with a numerical approximation of a youth's unofficial offenses. This was termed a "score" of law infractions.

In the process of tabulating a boy's offenses, the case worker and I (F.J.M.) jointly reviewed each page of the case record. Any uncertainty as to whether an offense had been committed, either because the record was vague or because it seemed possible that the boy was entertaining his case worker with a story of fantasied misdeeds, always resulted in his being given the benefit of the doubt, and no tally was recorded. Likewise, in totaling the number of misdemeanors of a boy in a given year, we conservatively employed the lowest weighting; i.e., *rarely* was given a weight of 1, *occasionally*, 4, and *frequently*, 10. When an incident might have two possible interpretations, the less serious was utilized. For example, one little culprit disturbed a theater manager no end by dropping a lighted match into his pocket. This situation never reached the court, but if it had, we speculated that one of two complaints could have been made — a charge of malicious mischief, or a more serious one of assault and battery. In this instance we used the former label. As the result of these precautions, our estimate of the number of violations and of their seriousness is a very conservative one.

In order to obtain uniformity in the delinquency scores, it was necessary to select an age span that could be consistent for all cases. From a survey of the entire case load, it was found that the majority had received service throughout the age span from 11 to 16 years. A total of 114 boys had been given service throughout this five-year period, and the present study is based upon their analyses.

To the workers' knowledge, only 13 of the boys had never committed an offense for which a complaint might have been made in court. The rest had all been more or less serious juvenile offenders; 40 designated as official delinquents because complaints were registered in court, and 61 as unofficial delinquents because they "got by" without court complaint.

The numerical scores hereafter referred to as "number of violations" represent the minimum

number of law infractions committed by these boys between their eleventh and sixteenth years. At our conservative estimate, these boys had committed a minimum of 6,416 infractions of the law during the five-year period; while only 95 of their violations had become a matter of official complaint. In other words, authorities took official action in less than 1½ per cent of the infractions. Approximately 1,400 of these infractions were violations of city ordinances, none of which became a matter of court complaint. Of 4,400 minor offenses, only 27 (.60%) were prosecuted. Of 616 serious offenses, 68 (11%) were prosecuted.

Lest the small proportion of infractions resulting in court complaints should lead to the inference that law enforcement was lax in these communities, it must be explained that during the period covered by this study there was a policy of handling a large proportion of juvenile offenders informally. Hence, many of our boys were apprehended and warned by police but no complaint was registered in court. Furthermore, lest it be thought that CSYS case workers were protecting the boys from court involvement, it must be mentioned that, in many instances the boys revealed their delinquencies months or even years after they had occurred. In reminiscing on their activities, they often owned up to earlier law violations hitherto unsuspected.

Analysis of the type of infractions for which court complaints were registered indicated that larceny, and breaking and entering were the charges of highest frequency. Truancy and school offenses were a matter of official court complaint only rarely in comparison to the frequency with which these were committed. This suggests that school authorities manifest a con-

Table 1 Comparison of Violations for Unofficial and Official Delinquents (Based on Records of 114 Boys, Ages 11–15) *

VIOLATION	UNOFFICIAL DELINQUENTS	OFFICIAL DELINQUENTS	BOTH
	N 61	N 40	N 101
City Ordinance	739	655	1394
Minor Offenses	1913	2493	4406
Serious Offenses	174	442	616
Total	2826	3590	6416

* Of 114 boys, 13 had no violations to the case workers' knowledge.

Table 2   Number and Proportion of Violations Resulting in Court Complaints

TYPE OF VIOLATION	NO. COURT COMPLAINTS	OFFICIAL DELINQUENTS	BOTH GROUPS
City Ordinance	0	0.00%	0.00
Minor Offenses	27	1.08	.61
Serious Offenses	68	15.39	11.04
Total	95	2.72	1.47

siderable degree of tolerance of such juvenile offenses and tend to handle them by their own methods rather than to call upon the help of the court.

In the main, the transgressions of the official offenders were more frequent and more serious than those of the unofficial group. The total scores of violations for the officials ranged from 5 to 323 with a median of 79; whereas the unofficials ranged from 0 to 266 with a median of 30. Furthermore, the median official delinquent over the five-year period scored 10 city ordinance infractions, 53 minor acts, and 6 more serious offences; whereas the median unofficial delinquent had scored 0 on city ordinance violations, only 20 on minor offenses, and 0 on serious offenses. There were, however, a number of exceptions because 5 boys having official records had total scores less than 30, the median of the unofficials; and 13 unofficials equaled or exceeded in minor and more serious offenses the median score of the official delinquents. In computing the percentiles for the scores of delinquent acts for the two respective groups, it was found that for the most part from year to year, 11 through 16, the pattern of asocial behavior was fairly even and consistent. The amount of delinquency exhibited in the eleventh year remained surprisingly constant in the ensuing four years.

Relevant to the bearing that intelligence might have as a differentiating factor between the two groups, we at first speculated that perhaps higher mental endowments enabled the unofficial delinquents to remain out of court. However, upon compiling the figures, it was found that there was no appreciable difference. The official offenders had IQ's on the revised Stanford-Binet ranging from a low of 59 to a high of 117 with a median of 93.25, as compared

to a median of 93.70 for the unofficials who ranged from 65 to 149. Thus, our study seems to substantiate the present more or less accepted contention that law violators, known officially by the courts and authorities, do not differ markedly from the general population.

We were interested further in ascertaining what the case records revealed concerning the personalities of these boys, especially insofar as these enabled us to judge whether the delinquencies seemed to spring from a neurotic basis or whether they resulted largely from the boys' acquiescence to the prevailing juvenile pattern of their communities. It was also hoped that the records might throw light on why some relatively law-abiding boys had court records and why some of the chronic offenders escaped court action. We therefore studied the case records of the five official delinquents who had low scores and the 13 unofficial delinquents with high scores. It appeared that three of the five official delinquents were dull, passive boys, who had considerable security within their own families and were not particularly troublesome in the community. For these three, court involvement seemed to be a piece of ill luck. Two were perhaps the victims of police vigilance directed toward their entire families.

Ned, one of the boys, had always been a quiet stay-at-home, but regularly throughout Ned's childhood the father had been arrested for drunkenness and assault, and the older brother had been sent to a correctional school on a charge of larceny. Hence, when Ned was discovered with a "borrowed" bicycle, the police being aware of the hazards surrounding children in this family, brought him into court and he was placed on probation. The other two, with a small number of violations, gave the impression of being greatly disturbed, with neurotic

Table **3** *Percentile Scores for Unofficial and Official Delinquents*

PERCENTILE	UNOFFICIAL DELINQUENTS *				OFFICIAL DELINQUENTS *			
	CO	MO	SO	All	CO	MO	SO	All
First	0	0	0	0	0	0	0	5
Tenth	0	1	0	2	0	12	0	27
Twenty-fifth	0	8	0	10	0	30	1	39
Fiftieth	0	20	0	30	10	53	6	79
Seventy-fifth	14	48	0	71	24	70	16	102
Ninetieth	50	84	5	107	40	118	32	194
Hundredth	88	134	44	266	90	187	46	323

* Type of offense: CO = City Ordinance; MO = Minor Offenses; SO = Serious Offenses.

trends springing largely from difficult home relationships. Henry's father regarded his wife as his inferior; he constantly belittled his son, and remarked openly that the boy took after his mother's family and would sooner or later end up in a penal institution. The mother was ambivalent toward the boy, occasionally indulging him but more often railing at him. As he grew into adolescence, Henry's toleration of this treatment lessened, and the case worker believed that his removal from the home would be the only way of safeguarding him from an aggressive attack upon his parents or from some serious delinquency outside. The parents were eager to have him placed out, but were not willing to have the placement go through court. The placement agency was reluctant to accept the boy without a court order. While placement negotiations were under way, Henry was summoned to a police station to give testimony concerning a sex pervert of whom he had been a victim, but he was led to believe that he would not be implicated. Upon learning of this private hearing, the placement worker, in an effort to obtain court custody, started a rumor that Henry was being protected in his delinquencies. When this rumor, much enlarged, reached the ears of the officer he was disturbed, had Henry reappear and prosecuted him on a charge of lewdness. Embittered by what he considered as "being framed," Henry walked out of court muttering "I'll show that officer what I can do"; whereupon he entered a haberdashery, stole a pair of braces from the counter, was apprehended by the store detective and again handed over to the police.

Percy, the last of these five boys, seems to

have had a delinquency score that was spuriously low, due to the fact that he was in foster homes in rural villages during much of his eleventh to sixteenth years. Prior to CSYS contact he and his brothers had been sent out by their mother to steal. Her desertion led to breaking up of the home and to placement of the children in areas that either presented fewer temptations or were more tolerant of youthful misdemeanors. On the other hand, the foster mothers may have been less willing to recount to the case worker, at his infrequent visits, all of Percy's bad deeds lest their own status as worthy foster mothers be questioned. Percy was in and out of foster homes and correctional schools throughout the entire period, and his inability to settle down and accept the advantages of a good placement, when such was provided, was indicative of his general instability.

Of greater interest are the personalities of the 13 who avoided court records in spite of having committed a larger number of minor or serious infractions than the median official delinquent. These likewise could be grouped in a general way into two categories — gregarious, fairly well-adjusted boys whose delinquencies seemed free from a neurotic component; and emotionally disturbed boys whose asocial behavior seemed primarily the outgrowth of tension or friction within the home. There were five boys in the first group; eight in the second.

The four most frequent and most serious of these offenders gave no evidence of being poorly adjusted, in that their behavior reflected the mores of their particular group. Marcus whose minor infractions totaled 134 and whose 44 serious offenses included larceny from parked cars, assault, picking the pockets of a service man, and breaking and entering, was a confirmed gang member from early childhood. Although his mother was psychotic and was hospitalized a good part of the period under consideration, her illness and absence from the home seemed to have little effect on the boy's pleasant, outgoing personality and his popularity with the gang with whom he roved the neighborhood. His infractions increased from begging on the streets at age 11 and peddling Christmas wreaths stolen from front doors, to the mysterious possession of a seaman's wallet containing more than $200 at the age of 14. In this last escapade, his accomplice was a boy on probation through whom the incident became known to the probation officer. The boys declared they had found the wallet on the floor of a theater. Since no loss was reported they got by with their story, Marcus's father having first salted the money away in war bonds and hired an attorney to discuss his rights with a probation officer. On some of their other larcenies the gang's activities were known and Marcus was warned by the police. Often he tended to drop out when he believed serious mischief was in the wind. While he has never manifested particular strengths, he has maintained good standing with his friends throughout and now seems to be making an adequate adjustment in the Merchant Marine.

Denny, with a score of 84 minor offenses and 25 serious ones, manifested considerable strength and independence in the management of his own life when his home was broken up by the accidental death of his besotted stepmother. Reviewing this period of his life later with his case worker, he told how his gang had taken a bike here and there until they had so many of them they didn't know what to do. He told that he had often stolen food, and when he was ill-shod in winter he and a pal had snatched a purse containing $40. "Every now and then I see that woman on the street and it makes me feel pretty mean," he added. While some of these early larcenies seemed prompted by a desire for excitement, many seemed to the case worker to have been directed toward survival. Though only 14 when his home dissolved, Denny took things into his own hands, obtaining working papers and making his way back

and forth to the home of a friendly Vermont farmer each summer. Winters, he lived either with his aunt or with his employer, an ash hauler. Denny demonstrated his ability to fend for himself at an early age, and he kept himself out of trouble with the law by being very streetwise.

Al, with a score of 96 minor infractions, seemed an independent, self-sufficient boy, with inner strengths that fortified him against the more contaminating influences of a highly delinquent neighborhood. On the whole, his family life was one of harmony and integration. During the early years, he had the companionship of his grandfather which seemed to have represented a character-building force in his life. His case worker observed that his gang membership seemed in a peripheral capacity so far as group activities went, but that he had a close enough association with each of the members to obtain a companion in a dual project — one for swimming and another for bicycle trips. Thus, the gang did not have sway over his activities for he knew what he wanted and always had command of the situation. His most frequent offenses were street fighting, sneaking into movies, swimming in forbidden places, and shining shoes without a license. Only occasionally did he engage in petty stealing, and never in more serious larceny.

Jerry, with a score of 108 minor offenses, was a passive, lackadaisical boy, who tended to go along with the gang in their less serious infractions and to avoid becoming involved in more serious episodes. This seemed a sign of weakness and cowardice, and was all of a pattern with his tendency to give up school at the slightest difficulty, and to postpone until tomorrow or next week or until he was 16, appointments for job interviews arranged for him. He was, in fact, a quitter, and his avoidance of serious law infractions was not a matter of ego strength. In spite of these signs of weakness, Jerry showed no symptoms of deep, underlying anxieties. He lived on the surface, and made as little effort as possible, following perhaps the pattern of his two ne'er-do-well brothers rather than that of his steady, hard-working father.

John, the last of these five reasonably well-adjusted boys, had a score of 61 minor infractions, and was once warned by the police for trespassing during a realistic game of commandos. Temper outbursts during his early school years were perhaps suggestive of some emotional disturbance, but these had been overcome by the time he was 11. He was a favorite with his teachers and had friends among the boys in the neighborhood. John's father was given to drunken sprees, during which his mother seemed to lean on John as the eldest of her three boys. He accepted this responsibility in a rather mature way. Throughout the years, the case workers tried to draw him out on the subject of family relationships, thinking he well might feel considerable hostility toward his father. They were never able to elicit anything except matter-of-fact comments and occasional genuine admiration of his father's athletic prowess, and concluded that he felt no resentment and really took the father's drunkenness and periodic upsets in the home in his stride.

In contrast to these five, the other eight unofficial delinquents all seemed to be suffering to some degree from neurotic difficulties springing largely from discord within the home.

Between Mrs. B. and her eldest son, Herbert, a cordial hatred existed, stemming perhaps from the paternal grandparents' belief that their son had married beneath him. They compensated for their dislike of the mother by indulging Herbert, encouraging him to seek haven in their home when he and his mother came to blows, which sometimes occurred. Herbert's 104 minor offenses consisted largely of aggression and profanity directed toward the mother. His eight serious offenses were composed of occasional physical assaults on his mother and some sex play with one of his sisters. Since his infractions were for the most part confined to aggression within the home, it is understandable that they did not come to the attention of the police.

Edwin, whom the police had warned because his mother complained that he was stubborn and sometimes assaulted her, had adequate provocation for attacks on his mother. This childish widow never stopped lamenting that her only child had not been a girl, and never ceased to nag for every little fault, from failure to brush his hair to ripping a button from his shirt at play. She constantly harped on her own imaginary ailments and upon her many sacrifices for her son. She tried her best to train him into girlish behavior, and to some extent succeeded,

so that he was considered a sissy by his contemporaries. Small wonder that his response to all these frustrations developed from childish pinching and pommeling of his mother to adolescent attacks with a chair, and finally, to bitter cursing and turning away. His mother often expressed to the case worker her wonderment that she, being such a good woman, could have such a bad boy. She often threatened to have him sent to a correctional school, but it was apparent that she could not part with him, nor could he emancipate himself from her.

Dan, a colored boy whose father had deserted during Dan's infancy, had close physical contact with his mother, even sleeping with her until late childhood. Many of his aggressions seemed to have a sexual basis, his most serious offense being that of assaulting white girls. In the opinion of the case worker, they were only girls who were sexually promiscuous with colored boys. The worker summarized Dan's record by saying "Certain antisocial problems exist not because of any conflict between Dan and his environment, but because Dan is so akin to his environment."

The most neurotic boy of all this group early exhibited traits suggestive of Levy's "affect hunger" cases. Andy's mother had died in his infancy. The father placed him and his much older brother in various boarding homes where they suffered a good deal of neglect and abuse. When Andy was three, the father married a rather young woman who later claimed that her love of children and the knowledge that she would never have any of her own had entered into her decision to marry Mr. T. and bring up his motherless boys. At the beginning of the study, Andy was a disturbing element in the primary grades, being unable to concentrate on his lessons and annoying the teachers and other children. His parents also found him a problem at home, and the father controlled him with very strict discipline. The stepmother worked, thus leaving the elder brother to enforce the stringent rules laid down by the father.

Andy's attitude toward his case worker was that of teasing and begging for little gifts and for trips and excursions. The worker recognized him as a very disturbed child and sought the help of a child guidance clinic. There Andy and his mother received treatment for several months, with little improvement in his behavior. Eventually, he was removed from his home, which shortly after placement was dissolved, leaving the boy entirely without anchorage. He was resentful at being sent to a boarding school for difficult children and ran away twice. Andy's delinquencies consisted mainly of truancy, school offenses, and stubborn, unruly behavior. He engaged in petty stealing only twice, and in breaking and entering once. The depth of his emotional disturbance was indicated by his failure to use the help of either his CSYS case worker or of the psychiatrist in a constructive way. He has developed into a youth that borders on the psychopathic personality.

The chief contribution of this study is that we have been able to arrive at a minimal estimate of the amount of unofficial delinquency that takes place among a sizeable group of underprivileged boys. Both official and unofficial delinquents commit numerous infractions of juvenile laws which do not become a matter of official record. Although both groups differ somewhat in the frequency and seriousness of offenses, there is much overlapping between the two.

While it has not been within the scope of this paper to make a comprehensive analysis of factors which may perhaps differentiate the official and unofficial delinquents, some marked similarities between the two groups have been found. Both have a wide range in intelligence as measured by standard tests, and show no difference in this respect. Both groups contain boys who are socially well adjusted to the pattern of life within their particular subcultures and whose asocial acts could not be considered as springing from emotional conflict or turmoil within themselves. These boys seem to commit most of the violations of property rights, such as larceny, breaking and entering, and destruction of property. Both groups also contain boys whose offenses seem to arise out of deep neurotic disturbance within themselves. These boys, with a neurotic component in their delinquencies, tend to commit aggressions directed toward the home or school in greater frequency than they commit violations against property rights. This observation is consistent with the findings of other students of delinquency and is what one would be led to except from psychological theory. It is hoped that further anal-

ysis of the material will reveal factors that differentiate between the groups of official and unofficial delinquents.

Discussion

Helen Witmer, Ph.D.: It seems to me that these findings have important implications for research in regard to social maladjustment. It has long been said that statistics of juvenile delinquency are unreliable indices of the amount of juvenile misconduct or of variations in it from year to year, and it has been suspected that delinquency records are not a satisfactory means of judging the social adjustment of individual children. These findings, however, provide a factual check and show that the situation (so far as research is concerned) is even worse than suspected.

First, consider the matter from its collective aspect. The figures presented here show that court statistics are wholly inadequate as a measure of the amount of youthful illegal behavior in the community. In fact, so frequent are the misdeeds of youth that even a moderate increase in the amount of attention paid to it by law enforcement authorities could create the semblance of a "delinquency wave" without there being the slightest change in adolescent behavior. The same considerations throw doubt on the validity of court statistics as an *index* to change in amount of juvenile misconduct from time to time, for it is doubtful that such figures bear a consistent relationship to the unascertainable total. From the collective angle, then, court statistics appear as valuable to the administration of courts, but as not too useful to students of children's behavior.

Second, is the individual aspect of the matter. The study again shows that an adolescent's court record even if he lives in an "underprivileged area" is a very inadequate measure of the amount of his antisocial conduct; and that, moreover, absence of a court appearance is far from an indication that he is free from misconduct. The figures do show that on the average, official delinquents somewhat more frequently commit serious offenses than do unofficial delinquents, but there is much variation in even this from case to case.

Such findings cast very serious doubt on research workers' practice of using court records as an index of social adjustment. Not only do these records appear to be an inadequate measure of individual behavior, but it also seems doubtful that they provide a valid basis for comparisons of one adolescent with another. This is a matter that calls for careful study.

All in all, then, consideration of the figures presented suggests that the term "delinquency" is of little more value than the term "insanity" so far as orthopsychiatric research is concerned. Both of these terms are legal ones and useful in the proper context. For our purposes, however, they are only misleading. In judging an individual's adjustment, consideration must be given to many aspects of his life. We obtain nothing but spurious accuracy if much reliance is put on the incidence of court appearances.

Chapter 2

Cause and Effect in Biosocial Problems Involving Delinquency

IN RECENT YEARS there has been a steadily increasing attack on "barren empiricism" in the study of crime causation and a correlative insistence that research be "guided by a theory," as in the physical sciences. It has been pointed out that one is never certain whether the data turned up in criminologic causal research are comprehensive enough to "explain" the antisocial behavior.

This does not mean that etiologic research is useless without having been buttoned in to some single *a priori* theory. It should, besides, be pointed out that much causal research *is* derived from a theoretical framework, implicit if not explicit. For example, the research behind the findings in *Unraveling Juvenile Delinquency* [1] was not a haphazard putting together of scraps from some grab-bag. It involved two basic theoretical assumptions: first, that etiology is multiple and varied, that is, that numerous "causes" participate to bring about the end-result of the variety of acts legally comprised under "delinquency" and that the same product — delinquency — can be derived from a varied series of preceding influences; secondly, that certain areas, techniques and tests give special promise of yielding causal involvements; namely, anthropologic measurements and classifications, psychiatric interviews, the Rorschach test, the Wechsler-Bellevue test, investigation of the parent–child relationships, examination of the boys' school history, study of the neighborhood influences. To say that this research was not guided by any theories simply because its directors did not include in the printed report a sentence or two spelling out such theories when they were perfectly obvious, is to indulge in a fallacy.

The fact that a prediction table based on such a theoretical approach has been found to "work" successfully in nine-tenths of the cases — prospective, as well as retrospective — of several diverse samples to which it has been applied since the publication of the table [2] would seem to be strong evidence that the "causal theory" behind the research was sound. For in this field, the old adage about "the proof of the pudding" is especially apt.

Another point needs to be stressed in this connection: There are degrees of refinement in the descriptions of reality. The science of chemistry was able to achieve wonders long before a basic assumption on which it worked — that the atom was the ultimate particle and unsplittable — was shown to be erroneous. Malaria was satisfactorily

---

[1] S. and E. T. Glueck, New York, The Commonwealth Fund, 1950; and Cambridge, Harvard University Press, 1951.
[2] See Articles 171–173 of this volume.

managed by the application of quinine long before the discovery that the basic cause of malaria was the presence of certain parasites in the red blood cells.

There can therefore be but one crucial test of the validity of a causal pattern in connection with delinquency: can the delinquent behavior be successfully predicted from the presence of the supposed criminogenic pattern and, relatedly, does it disappear when that pattern, or its major constituents, are blotted out?

Learned preoccupation with vague and lofty "theory" in the field of criminology has thus far yielded pitifully barren results [3]; on the other hand, a wide-ranging empirical eclecticism — not blind, but guided by reasonable assumptions — has produced, among other values, a very useful product: the workable prediction device. If American criminologists were more preoccupied with the tough and tedious task of gathering carefully defined and expertly verified raw materials and less intoxicated with the spinning of speculative theories, progress in the understanding and management of the delinquency problem would be markedly enhanced.

The materials in this section are concerned with fundamental concepts of etiology. A great deal has been written about the imperfection of the social sciences generally and of criminology in particular, in that these disciplines do not have, and seemingly can never hope to have, the precision, and the "controls," the possibility of experimental verification, and the predicability of the natural or "pure" sciences. The materials in this section are designed to raise this fundamental issue and to provide certain insights into the possibility of improving research methods with a view to obtaining greater precision, accuracy and reliability in the exploration of the causal problem.

The first item in the present chapter, by Cantor, raises some important issues regarding criminology as a discipline, through comparison of the social sciences in general and criminology in particular, with the natural sciences. Cantor brings out vividly the relationship of individual physical and psychological attributes to cultural influences, and makes an arguable distinction between the objectives of the natural and social sciences and between the methods of the two. Some readers will doubtless differ with Cantor in his emphasis upon the fundamental importance of the economic order in the control of crime.

The second piece in this chapter, by Carr, emphasizes the distinction between "cause-mindedness" and "myth-mindedness," and points to the dangerous consequences of the latter in public opinion and legislative attitudes. Written in a popular style, this article has been included as part of a realistic conception of the practical issues in coping with delinquency and as offering a contrast between the causal approach and the quasi-magical approach to the understanding of the problem.

The third item in the present chapter, also by Cantor, begins with a brief historical sketch of the search for physical laws in natural phenomena and relates crime causation studies to the fundamental attitudes of such thinkers as Aristotle, Galileo and Freud. The author makes some searching observations on the concept of causation, with emphasis on the "organismic" approach, the importance of the way in which the individual reacts to the environment, and the "transformations" that occur in him at the given moment preceding the offense.

The fourth article, by the Editor, points out the difficulties inherent in the study of cause and effect in such an individual-social phenomenon as delinquency.

The fifth item in the present chapter, by Sheldon and Eleanor Glueck, goes more deeply into the idea of cause-and-effect in general and in the study of human behavior in particular. It emphasizes the need of looking at the problem from the point of view of statistical probabilities.

The sixth item, also by the Gluecks, from their *Physique and Delinquency*, draws a distinction between statistical association and the concept of cause.

---

[3] See Article 41, and G. B. Vold, *Theoretical Criminology*, N.Y., Oxford University Press, 1958.

3

Criminology as a Social Science *

Nathaniel Cantor

1. CRIMINOLOGY AND SCIENTIFIC METHOD

Modern criminology must adopt the general methods of natural science if it, too, is to rank as one of the "social sciences."

Even at best, those human relations termed economic, moral, religious, educational and political are far from being reduced to a scientific system. For the most part, the processes and mechanisms involved in human affairs are neither clearly understood nor intelligently guided. The laws of learning involved in education, for example, are not quite clear. Yet no profound changes in controlling experimental education may be accepted as final until such laws are definitively established. The tragic waste of economic effort may be minimized, provided changed economic procedure is desired and a knowledge of economic laws acquired. Again, the political problems of the public are not even formulated, let alone solved. The technique of fashioning public opinion in the future waits upon a better understanding of its present operation and growth. The multiplication of similar instances would merely illustrate the need for knowledge rather than opinion in human affairs.

The so-called social sciences are, strictly speaking, not sciences. Historically these social disciplines developed much later than the physical and biological sciences. They are still in embryonic form. One is not quite sure where social psychology ends and sociology begins, nor where sociology ends and anthropology begins. The lines between government and economics blur. To be sure, the situation is not strange to the natural sciences of chemistry,

physics, biology, physiology, neurology and so forth. Yet, in the latter, agreement upon fundamental postulates and experimental procedure is the rule. This is not true of the social sciences. We find psychologists, sociologists, anthropologists, economists and educationalists concerned to this day with defining the scope of their respective subject matter, their fundamental concepts, their methods.

These remarks apply with greater force to the field of criminology. The methods of science have not been rigidly applied to criminology. The nature of the problems has not even been made clear.

2. THE SUBJECT MATTER OF CRIMINOLOGY

Apart from the historical explanation underlying the slower development of the social sciences, there are inherent difficulties in constructing sciences of human relations. A statement of the difficulties in subject matter, goal and method between the natural and the social sciences will make clear some of the major difficulties in the development of criminology, the new-born among the social sciences.

First, then, as to the subject matter of the social sciences. Social science deals with *culture*. This is not to deny the physical basis of human activity. Attention is called to the distinctive roles that purpose and meaning play in social science. To insist that war hysteria is based solely upon the flow of the individual's adrenalin is to ignore the role of social "ideals," true or false, in that individual's experience, or of the economic institutions in the lives of the people. A lover's kiss ends neurologically in muscle and gland, but socially in babies and infant wear. Social acts, in brief, must be regarded not only as events, as physical facts are, but also as problems. *This problematic character of social events is irrelevant in physical inquiry.* The fact that a man suffers from a glandular disturbance does not disprove that he is a dangerous criminal. Medical diagnosis ends with labeling the patient a dementia praecox. Penology, however, is faced with the problem of where to place the defendant so as best to protect society and at the same time to serve the prisoner.

Again, in the physical sciences, explanation rests upon the microscopic analysis of individual events. *Social* phenomena, on the other hand, can neither be predicated upon nor ex-

---

* Reprinted from *Crime, Criminals and Criminal Justice*, New York, Henry Holt & Company, 1932, 21–30. Used by permission of the author and the publisher.

plained by individual behavior. The "causes" of *social* crime cannot be understood through an analysis of a particular criminal's motives. The cause of typhoid, however, was discovered and explained by the isolation of the bacillus. The incidence of typhoid is safely predictable upon discovery of the presence of bacilli. In short, the *meaning* of human events, their purposes, the traditions and desires of human beings are distinctive of social science. It follows that social science must necessarily deal with social life.

The significance of this discussion for criminology becomes, it is hoped, obvious. A scientific criminology and penology will deal not only with the individual criminal and institutional prison but must consider the social aspects of crime, its environmental roots, the influence of prison life on the inmate, the desirability of one penal philosophy as against another, the preventive measures. In short, the *modification* of conditions generating crime and leading to criminals is as much the proper concern of the sciences of criminology and penology as is the analysis of individual criminal behavior and the causes of crime.

3. THE TASK OF CRIMINOLOGY

The social sciences are distinguished from the natural sciences not only by their subject matter but also by their objective. The aim in natural science is the reduction of its propositions to a series of mathematically related laws. Whether or not the implications of relativity mathematics are good or bad for Christian morals is beside the point. The Quakerish tinge of Mr. Eddington's religion receives treatment in a text distinct from his volume on *The Nature of the Physical Universe*. The light that comes to Michelson, the deist, differs in character from the beams in the Michelson-Morley ether experiment. The social scientist cannot remain so neutral in his inquiries. His task is predetermined by his *social* interests, whether they be explicitly alleged or subconsciously implied.

To be sure, the physical scientist, too, has some hypothesis governing his procedure. But that hypothesis is related to the general goal of natural science, the subsumption of his results under a more general principle or law. Einstein's newer field theory is precisely such an achievement.

The goal of the social scientist is of a different character. His *ultimate* aim is to interpret the data, which may be objectively gathered, and *modify social life*. Prison statistics, for example, may be objectively compiled. What follows? Either a contribution to anthropometrics or an understanding of how *better* to classify prison inmates. In one case, criminal statistics would fall in the category of physical science; in the other, it would align itself with social science.[1] The point is that social scientists are committed to a program of social interpretation by the very nature of the subject matter, even though they maintain neutrality in their immediate investigations.

Particularly in criminology and penology, emphasis is shifted to the individual criminal or inmate. Physical science, as a rule, deals with statistical averages. The chemist, astronomer or physicist is not interested in the behavior of any one particular molecule or atom. The conglomerate activity of group atoms comprising the event is his object of interest and investigation. Physical laws and principles relate to mass activity, average behavior. While this holds for criminological surveys as well, the final purpose of criminological and penological principles is the prevention of *individual* crime careers and the reformation of *individual* inmates. And since each individual differs, the application of the derived principles must be modified to the individual requirements.

Within the present structure of society, the application of rigid method to the prevention of *individual* criminal careers, the treatment and care of the *individual* criminal, remains an ideal. *So long as the Western European economic order remains fundamentally unaltered, there is little likelihood of controlling in any large measure the complex factors generating crime and criminals.*[2]

On the other hand, without classification and analysis of these complex causal factors, no improvement in the present conditions generating crime is possible. The remoteness of the

---

[1] The so-called applied sciences fall somewhere between the "pure" physical sciences and the social sciences. The civil engineer, for example, has as his task the construction of a bridge or a Holland Tunnel. He had better remain neutral in his trigonometric calculations. Yet the blessed bridge prevents the New Jersey purgatory for wandering motorists.

[2] See Chapter XXV, sec. 9 [of Cantor's book].

goal does not destroy the need for a guiding principle.

A rigid physical science would not deal with the individual criminal and his surrounding circumstances; that is, the whole situation. It would isolate several of the elements and concentrate on some phase of the problem. Similarly, a scientific criminology would concern itself with the underlying principles which specifically control criminal behavior. Individual situations not strictly related to a particular crime would be irrelevant. The individual criminal, however, receives as much, if not more, attention than the concentrated analysis of specific causal factors of crime. The criminologist must be both critical and wise; critical in grasping general principles and wise in applying them to the individual case where so many factors remain unknown or undetermined.

A third distinction between the social and natural sciences must be pointed out: the difference in the method of research. The failure to observe this difference is in part responsible for the irreconcilable views so often met with in the writings of legalists and students of criminology.

The sociologists insist upon rigid scientific method in the study of crime and prison reform. They call for radical revision of our criminal codes, rules of procedure and a scrapping of our penal system. They support these demands by pointing out the anachronistic basis of our criminal forms and institutions, and by calling attention to our present knowledge of human nature. The professional jurists and legislators ignore or scoff at such demands, insisting that the criminologists and sociologists fail to appreciate the administrative and legal problems involved. They charge the psychological and psychiatric experts with setting up mechanisms of human behavior upon which they themselves cannot agree. Prison authorities, with the familiarity of the expert, all but ignore the plea for new architectural prison planning and modified or radically altered institutional life. They *know* the material which must be handled, the problems which arise and the treatment therefor.

4. DIFFERENCES IN METHOD BETWEEN THE SOCIAL AND NATURAL SCIENCES

It is submitted that a number of careful analyses of the differences in methods of research between the social sciences and the physical or natural sciences will make for closer coordination between these points of view.

Prior discussion of the differences in method between the social sciences *in general* and the physical sciences will enable us to appreciate more clearly the difficulties involved in meeting the legal and penal problems.

The complexity of social phenomena as compared with the relative systematizing of physical data is obvious. What, for example, are the effects of the sex segregation of prison inmates? We may answer *generally* that homosexualism is found more frequently in penal institutions than in the general population. If we insist upon *accurate* information, we must proceed more critically. We should have to repeat the experiment several times, set up identical kinds of institutions, the same administrative personnel, the same prison population. We should have to observe these practices directly. We should want to make sure the situations do not vary. And in order to know precisely the effects of this sex segregation of the inmates, it would be necessary to isolate and vary one factor at a time to learn the effects of all or any of the elements in the situation. The absurdity of this procedure makes it none the less necessary if the essentials of scientific method as used in the physical sciences are to be followed.

If the social sciences or criminology and penology cannot adopt these rigid methods because of the complexity of the data, they can at least employ this method generally and *as far as possible* approach the care and caution of the laboratory scientists. The scientific criminologist must not ask or be asked for mathematical formulae. The activity of men and women cannot be so readily and minutely observed, so easily repeated or made uniform, or the individual factors so easily isolated from the behavior context as hydrogen in its relation to oxygen. Sociological data are unamenable to such precise measurement. Calculus cannot readily be employed in human conduct.

The complexity of social events is matched by their variability. A calorie, a volt, a circle are numerically determined units. Agreement as to their meaning is universal among scientists. In the fields of criminology and penology, or for that matter in any of the social sciences, there are few units, if any, which carry identical implications for the investigators. Intelligence tests multiply. They are employed in school, factory and business. Well, what is "intelligence?" What is an "instinct," an "emotion?" What is the precise meaning of an economic "value?" The classic use of the concept of "supply and demand" has been modified by critical economists. The annual meetings of the social scientists are in part given over to a consideration of the proper subject matter of their respective sciences, let alone the determination of their units.

Criminology fares even worse. The term "criminal" is often indiscriminately applied to many types of criminals differing in age, sex, nativity, degree of recidivism and seriousness of offence. Is a crime determined by an act or by the arrest and conviction of the actor? The concept "crime" covers a multitude of sins. The intent of these remarks is not to disparage any effort to determine more sharply the underlying concepts of crime in general. The purpose is rather to indicate how inevitably variable these social situations are as compared to the controlled laboratory situations artificially established by the physical scientist.

A third factor distinguishing the methods of the natural and social sciences is the element of time. Under set laboratory conditions, an experiment may be repeated at will. A comparison of the common elements in the complete series of experiments is possible. The principle or law deduced therefrom will operate within that system at any time. Sodium and chlorine will combine under proper conditions to give salt regardless of time.

The data of social science, on the other hand, are historically continuous. Violence is done to facts if historical sequence is ignored.[3]

At best, a comparison of social data can be of similar but not of identical situations. The social elements will never appear twice quite alike. The comparative method, when applied to human relations, may result in tendencies, but not laws. The infinite number of possible human situations together with the infinite number of permutations and combinations makes a closed system of any social science quite unlikely. The "causes" of crime cannot be determined once and for all, as can the "causes" for the appearance of the rainbow. The causes of crime in the United States in the first quarter of the twentieth century are not the causes of crime in the United States during the seventeenth century. Nor are the causes of crime among the Bukaua of New Guinea, either in the first quarter of the twentieth century or in the early part of the nineteenth century, the same as the causes of crime in the United States at any time. The unique *history* of each situation is of vital importance in determining the causes of crime *at that time*.[4]

Strict scientific method can never be applied to methods of criminology and penology. The complexity of the subject matter, the aims of the science and the methods of inquiry necessarily modify the degree of caution, the deliberateness of control and the comparatively simple fields of inquiry which prevail in the physical sciences. Psychiatrists, psychologists and sociologists dealing with the problems of crime and prison reform must recognize these limitations. They must appreciate that unlimited freedom of experimentation in criminology and legal procedure would lead to an anarchic state of affairs; that easy experimentation at the cost of life and property is dangerous to the general security of society; that legislation requires security and uniformity; that no criminal system can progress unless the public is first educated to sympathize with the newer suggestions. These students do recognize that *multiplying* statutes and *modifying* existing practice does not significantly affect the fundamental matters.

Even if judicial, administrative, procedural and penal problems are not reducible to ironclad formulae, they are nevertheless amenable to a more orderly arrangement than that which prevails in our American courts, prisons and state legislatures. Granting the inconclusiveness of academic solutions of crime prevention or prison reform, there remains an array of established psychological and psychiatrical data which could be profitably assimilated by the

[3] Astronomy is the one mathematical physical science in which an historical series is present. Here nature sets a laboratory. The trajectories of the planets do present a time series without significantly affecting either the deduction of astronomical laws or the prediction of planetary movement. Geology, too, illustrates a nonduplicable historical series of stratifications.

[4] The method of research in the social sciences is further modified by the meaning attached to social "causation." This will be more appropriately discussed in Ch. V. [of Cantor's book].

state legislators, prison administrators and the legal profession generally.

If these data will not permanently solve many of the seemingly hopeless problems arising out of crime, they will most certainly make possible more rational principles of treatment. The least that may be hoped for is a recognition by the state legislatures and bar associations of a need for the application of *more* critical method in criminological inquiry.

The problems of delinquency, probation, parole, police, prison management, crime detection, conviction, prevention, judicial administration, psychological and psychiatrical treatment, each of which gives rise to special conditions must be met by special methods. The statistical approach may be required in one instance, the case method in another, personal supervision in still another, psychological and psychiatrical analysis in some cases, the survey or historical methods in others. At the same time, co-ordination between these processes is essential, if clarity of purpose is to be attained and a definite penal philosophy established.

The last ten years have witnessed increasing interest in more critical method on the part of many state legislatures, bar associations and municipalities. The interest, however, has been of a general nature.

An attempt will be made in the subsequent chapters to indicate how far more critical methods may be applied to several of the specific problems arising in criminology and penology.

4

Cause-Mindedness *

Lowell J. Carr

Ever since the coming of the machine more and more men more and more of the time have had to acquire causal clarity in their dealings

* Reprinted from *Delinquency Control* (Revised Edition), New York, Harper and Brothers, 1950, 11–17, 19. Used by permission of the author and the publisher.

with material things. Not only have they had to give up thinking in terms of "spirits" and "will" in their dealings with binders and punch presses and railroad engines and motor cars and radio sets, but they have had to learn to seek actual specific causes for actual specific events. Veblen long ago called attention to this tendency. But the expected carry-over to social situations has hardly even begun. For dealing with the physical world — for starting a furnace fire, building a bridge, removing an abdominal pain — the average man behaves neither on the level of superstition nor on that of myth-mindedness, but on a purely modern level, *cause-mindedness*. He assumes that the road to mastery lies in (1) positing the dependability of the world, (2) discovering specific cause-and-effect relationships, (3) inventing methods of utilizing those relationships, and (4) then applying the methods. That is the taken-for-granted pattern of behavior for physical situations. But it is the rare and exceptional pattern for social situations, the almost unheard-of pattern for dealing with crime. Why?

Probably there are two reasons: (1) the seductive plausibility of traditional, myth-minded answers, and (2) the formidable obscurity of causation itself in personal and social situations.

Consider, first, the seductive plausibility of traditional, myth-minded answers. For generations culture has had to "explain" why children behave as they do. At any given time these "explanations" express the prevalent world view. When superstition was the dominant mind set, chronic misbehavior was the outcome of witchcraft, possession by the devil, or similar unlucky contacts with the spirit world. Later, emotionally rebellious boys like Johnny came to be regarded as "naturally mean," or "just stubborn," or marked by the characteristics of some disreputable relative — "just exactly like his good-for-nothing Uncle Jake." All this, of course, implied a tacit recognition of some kind of causal relationship between the objectionable behavior and something else. So in a general way, partly because such explanations did become traditional and partly because they seemed to supply a frame of reference that made sense according to the ideas of the time, they were accepted; they became part of the myth-mind. And because more specific causal relationships had not been made clear they passed muster as the small change, so to speak, of common-sense give-and-take. They could pass all the more readily because of the obscurity of causal relationships.

Now consider the formidable obscurity of causation itself in personal and social situations. When your car stopped it was easy for any expert mechanic to demonstrate the connection between the faulty timer and the stoppage: all he had to do was to readjust the timer and your engine "ticked" once more. But when Johnny began to disobey, no such simple one-to-one demonstration was possible. Suppose you had guessed that possibly your placing of the boy in his grandmother's home was responsible for his misbehavior, and suppose you had brought him back to his own home. Now unlike the faulty timer, Johnny has a certain inner momentum, or drive, of his own. Restoring him to his own home might have quieted that inner drive for the time being or it might merely have stimulated it to test your new attitude. Instead of accepting the new situation at face value — "ticking" again as your motor did — Johnny might have set out deliberately to find out whether you really wanted him home or not. Thus instead of restoring everything to normal, as the readjustment of the timer restored your motor, your "readjustment" of Johnny's living arrangements to what once had been normal might very well have created a whole new series of "boy failures." So obviously causation in personal and social situations is not so simple as it is in mechanical matters.

Nevertheless, causal relationships still exist in such situations and it is the business of the so-called social sciences to determine what those relationships are. The fact that this task is at present more difficult than the task of the physical scientist in most physical situations does not relieve the ordinary person from the mental obligation to face his social world with the modern rather than the myth-minded, traditional point of view. That scientists themselves are not primarily concerned with causation as such but take it for granted is here beside the point.[1] Scientists are seeking objective uniformities in the phenomena about

them. Described in words or mathematical symbols, these uniformities are called scientific laws. Two kinds of scientific laws can be distinguished: *positive laws*, or invariant relationships between phenomena, and *statistical laws*, or statements of probability. That any physical body falling freely in a vacuum moves at a speed which has a definite relationship to the time during which it has been in motion is an invariant uniformity that may be expressed in a positive law. But that any child picked at random between the ages of ten and seventeen will be taken to court as a delinquent during the next twelve months cannot be expressed as a positive uniformity of any kind. The best we can do is to say that on the average the chances are about one in a hundred that such a youngster will be taken in as a delinquent during the next year. We can only state a degree of probability, not an invariant certainty. Unquestionably this complicates the scientific task in social situations, *but it does not eliminate the obligation to think causally with reference to such situations.* Because family troubles, economic pressures, neighborhood associates, personality handicaps, and other variables in a behavior situation interact in such complicated ways that no invariant relationship between any one of them and the ultimate behavior can be established — all this does not not in any way eliminate these variables as factors conditioning and controlling that ultimate behavior. We shall deal with this more in detail in Chapter VI when we discuss the question, "Why maladjustment and delinquency?" For the present the point remains: The obscurity of causation in personal and social situations may be part of the reason why myth-mindedness with reference to such situations persists. But it is no reason why educated people, people whose entire lives are posited on the dependability of the universe, on the *necessity* of uniformities, should continue as "philosophical schizoids." Philosophically it is positively indecent to accept causality for motor cars and radio sets and to try to ignore it in the handling of our children.

THE MENACE OF THE MYTH-MIND

The first step, then, in applying the scientific technology to crime control must be the conscious, deliberate step up from myth-mindedness to cause-mindedness. We must realize

---

[1] Karl Pearson in *The Grammar of Science* long ago pointed out that causation is a philosophical problem. What scientists study is "concomitant variations," i.e., things that vary together.

that myth-mindedness is as out of date as belief in witches. But because it is so prevalent and so completely dominates our thinking about social matters, myth-mindedness is vastly more important than superstition. It is vastly more dangerous.[2] A few centuries ago when people still believed in human sacrifice or in the disease-discouraging potency of a dead man's bones it was a matter of vital importance to human progress that superstition be conquered. The cause-mind has accomplished that conquest. Outside of the backwaters of our culture, superstition is no longer a menace. But the myth-mind still is. Men are willing to advocate capital punishment, the legalization of prostitution, the continuance of child labor, and a hundred other measures without actually knowing anything whatever about cause and effect in such matters. With complete ignorance of the crucial facts, with utter intellectual irresponsibility, — i.e., no sense that opinions *should* be based on knowledge; — with only a strong emotional urge to action and a traditional belief that has never been critically examined, with nothing, in short, but a muddle-headedness of which he is blissfully unaware, the average man is perfectly willing to invoke measures that vitally affect the lives and happiness of hundreds or thousands or even millions of human beings.

If this were a unique reaction confined to a few persons or to a single issue, no great harm would be done. But it is typical of the way in which millions of Americans respond not merely to crime but to any social problem. On the basis of common sense only (which means almost complete ignorance of the crucial facts — as shown, for example, by a straw vote that approved the legalization of prostitution to control syphilis), with no appreciation of their own ignorance and no saving sense that in the words of Cromwell, "By the bowels of Christ, gentlemen, bethink ye that ye may be wrong," they are perfectly willing to "treat prisoners rough," "crush" strikes, "dictate to employers," "put Negroes in their place," advocate popular referenda on foreign policy, and settle a hundred other issues involving the welfare of actual human beings. Can there be any question that this kind of behavior is every whit as disreputable as superstition? That under modern conditions, when any fool can aim a machine gun or propound a new nostrum to save the world, it is vastly more dangerous? Superstition has been driven into the slums and backwaters of civilization, but myth-mindedness flourishes in every Rotary Club, PTA, and meeting of the Bar. It is the current, everyday frame of mind of the average American facing his social world. As compared with superstition, which once slew its millions, myth-mindedness by perpetuating crime, poverty, and war seems in a fair way to slay its tens of millions, yes, even civilization itself. If the cause-mind could make superstition ridiculous, it is high time it made myth-mindedness impossible too.

Listen to the Senate of the United States considering whether to spend tax dollars for the scientific study of man as well as for the study of the atom. Atomic science is respectable. It has produced a bomb that can kill more people quicker than anything man ever had in his hands before. But social science — what is social science anyway? Stuart Chase reproduces some of the answers:

Senator Fulbright: I asked an able scientist yesterday if he would define social science. He said: "In the first place I would not call it science. What is commonly called social science is one individual or group, telling another group how they should live."

Senator Hart: The fact is that social studies and basic science are not sufficiently alike either to be joined in the same legislation or to be administered by the same organization. . . . No agreement has been reached with reference as to what social science really means. It may include philosophy, anthropology, all the racial questions, all kinds of economics, literature, perhaps religion, and various kinds of ideology.

Senator Smith: I should like to see social science given aid, but I think their problem is such a different one that the two should not be joined in this bill. . . . We are trying to subsidize pure science, the discovery of truth. This has nothing to do with the theory of life . . . nothing to do with sociology.[3]

---

[2] See, for example, an article in a serious magazine blaming the contemporary "increase" in juvenile delinquency — *the postwar decrease was actually under way* (see Fig., p. 109 [of magazine article]) — on "sociologists," i.e., social workers and "sentimentalists." Robert E. Coulson, "Little Donald Took an Axe," *Harper's*, May, 1948, pp. 385–393.

---

[3] Stuart Chase, *The Proper Study of Mankind*, New York, Harper, 1948, pp. 7–8.

And so on for hours. The burden of the refrain, as George A. Lundberg later pointed out in the *Scientific Monthly*, was that *we really know the solutions to all our social problems already.* "If we would but listen to the philosophers, the seers, and the writers of great books down the ages and search our souls, we would find the answers. What we really need to do — and this came out repeatedly in the testimony — is to *educate* people so they will read and listen. Not research, not new knowledge, but education in old knowledge is the key."

This, remember, is not the Ladies Aid Society of Possum Creek in the Gay Nineties. This is the Senate of the United States in the Year of Our Lord 1947. Two years after the failure of man's most extensive effort — to date — to exterminate himself, the most august legislative body in the nation, facing the solemn decision whether to include the social sciences within the charmed circle of those to be subsidized by the government, cannot even define social science *except in terms of traditional ignorance!*

Is there no menace, then, left in the myth-mind? Is there no menace in statesmen, who, surrounded by mounting crime bills, by millions of their fellow citizens living in slums and rookeries, by hordes of social problems leering in at them through every window, can yet find no answer except an appeal to the past? No menace in myth-minds who can calmly contemplate the expenditure of billions for the research to produce bigger and better obliteration bombs and with equal calmness deny even the possibility of the scientific study of man? No menace in men who say "we already know what to do about social problems" — the very same social problems that they are so persistently bungling or refusing to face at all? . . .

. . . If your son were to die of diphtheria after you had refused antitoxin in favor of a rabbit's foot, your superstitious belief would make you guilty of something closely resembling manslaughter. Without the shadow of a doubt, in most states, you could be prosecuted for neglect or something worse. But if your son merely became delinquent and wound up as a master criminal because you had been clinging to some outworn belief about filial duty and the power of exhortation, you could

escape scotfree. There are even good people who would agree with you that you had done your best but "the Lord had given you too heavy a burden to bear!" It is time such twaddle should be recognized for what it is — twaddle.

A parent's failure to obtain expert guidance in such a case — *if expert guidance is available* — is merely the old reliance on the rabbit's foot, with tradition now playing the role of magic. At least one great service of magic in primitive life was that it provided a definite action-pattern for the relief of tense emotions in critical situations. Concerned about the healing of a wound, you dunked the offending arrow in the creek *to keep the fever down.* The dunking had no physical effect on the fever, but at the moment it made you feel better. You had *done* something. In the same way, when you are stirred up about the behavior of your son or your daughter, it makes you feel better to *do* something, and the traditional patterns tell you what to do. Disobeyed by a youngster, it is much easier as a parent "to assert one's authority," for example, than to find out *why* the disobedience in the first place.

And it is much easier for a community to feel righteous and effective by merely enforcing traditional laws or enacting savage new ones, than to find out scientifically why the laws are being violated in the first place and then to take the difficult and costly measures necessary for controlling, in so far as possible, the incidence of those causes in the community. . . .

5

Dynamics of Delinquency *

Nathaniel Cantor

One of the reasons little progress has been made in understanding the causes of delin-

* Reprinted from 10 *Am. J. Orthopsychiatry* (1940), 789–793. Used by permission of the author and the publisher.

quency is due, I believe, to a false emphasis on what is meant by scientific method. This essay points out wherein the error lies and indicates in a general way how it may be corrected.

Until Galileo's time the search for physical laws followed the "line" laid down by Aristotle. For Aristotle, only those things or events were lawful which occurred frequently and without exception. This implied that if a thing or event happened only once it was due to "chance" and could not be explained *lawfully*. Aristotle's view of scientific law followed from his views of the nature of Being. He believed that the nature (the essence) of an object or event was determined by the class of objects or events to which it belonged; that is, classes of objects, the sum total of all the common characteristics of entire groups of objects or events, were realities which alone made any individual member of the class intelligible and lawful. An illustration will make his position clear. We recognize John Jones, Richard Smith, Socrates and Plato as men because they possess the common characteristics of the class Man. If we did not know what it meant to be Man we could not speak about or recognize any individual male. So far so good.

Now suppose that John Jones does something which no other man has ever done. This unique act is not common to other men and hence, Aristotle would say, it is accidental to the Man Jones, it is mere chance and not subject to lawful understanding.

Furthermore, Aristotle believed not only that the essential nature of a thing was determined by the abstractly defined class to which it belonged but he also maintained that behavior and development was determined in advance by its very nature. Jones, Smith, Socrates and Plato developed from infancy to manhood because it is the nature of Boy to become Man.

Modern physical research, which started with Galileo, has repudiated this point of view. Galileo believed that every occurrence was lawful, whether it happened once or a million times. The unique behavior of John Jones occurred for definite reasons. In other words, Galileo maintained that frequency and similarity of occurrence were no test of lawfulness. Galileo did not believe there were fixed abstract classes or essences which alone defined the nature and determined the development of

the individual members of the class. The nature and development of an event is characterized by the individuality of the total situation at any one moment, even if such event will never occur again. John Jones' unique act occurred when and why it did because of the exact "situation" in which John Jones found himself. He behaved as he did not only because he belonged to the class of objects known as Man, and because of an Environment, but because of the concrete environmental situation under the specific needs, tensions and meanings of a particular moment.

Aristotle would say that unless one could refer the act of Jones to the larger possible historical collection of frequent repetitions of similar acts it could not be explained. It is a chance occurrence and out of the realm of law. For Aristotle the general laws which described the causal relationships of events were based upon those factors only which were observed under all circumstances in any and every situation. For him the direction and the kind of changes which took place were determined in advance by the nature of the object or situation concerned.

For modern physics the historical and temporal antecedents of an object and its inherent nature provide the conditions for something to happen. They are not the cause.[1] The way events are related is not determined by reference to the abstract average of as many historically given cases as possible but by noting the full concreteness of the particular situation being investigated.[2]

In the living world of men and women there are no actual "average" situation, "average" people or "average behavior." "Average" is an abstract mathematical term which refers to common factors abstracted from living situations and which ignores the vital unique differences that make the particular situation just what it is. The "average" number of children in families of college graduates may be 1.8 but it would be an event of years to see a cooing .8 child.

Galileo's great service to scientific research was to have recognized that there are no rigidly

---

[1] See Hook, "A Pragmatic Critique of the Historico-Genetic Method," *Essays in Honor of John Dewey*, 156; also, Lamprecht, "Causality," *ibid.*, 191.

[2] See Lewin, *A Dynamic Theory of Personality*, Ch. I.

defined classes of physical objects; that events are in fluid transition and that to be understood they must be studied functionally and not structurally. In other words, a physical event was to be understood in the light of what took place at the particular moment and in the particular situation. Regularity or uniformity of occurrence were no test of lawfullness. All events, uniform and unique, were lawful. What Aristotle called a "chance" occurrence meant only that the event was not understood, *not* that it could not be understood.

What Galileo did for physical science, Sigmund Freud did for the field of psychology. All behavior, Freud declared, was lawful whether it was "normal" (average) or "abnormal."

This point of view is not widely accepted in social research although it is the prevailing point of view in modern physical science. In economics, sociology, education, psychology, and especially in criminology, the search is made for general laws which purport to explain "average" or uniform behavior. Why, for example, do certain offenders commit crime? Because so and so many come from broken homes and slum areas; so many have had bad associates and poor use of their leisure time, and so on (uniformity and frequency of occurrence).

Until recent times almost all studies in crime causation have been made from the Aristotelian viewpoint. Investigators have been seeking uniform and similar traits which characterize offenders. The assumption is implicit that unless such frequent occurrence of similar conditions is discernible, no laws of crime causation can be stated. The contrary view being maintained is that the search for uniformity of behavior is precisely what distorts an understanding of the actual factors which cause particular individuals to commit crime. The more we know about all criminals the less will we understand why any one offender commits crime. The key to an understanding of crime causation in any specific case is to discover why a particular person commits a particular crime at a particular time. The fact that this is a complex and difficult approach is irrelevant to whether it is sound.

This "organismic" conception of how events are related to each other emphasizes the process of growth and development rather than the measurement of structures and formal aspects.

The formal causes are surrendered for the study of efficient causes. Instead of solely analyzing for common factors one observes the peculiarities of actual organic behavior.[3]

This does not mean that the prior history or present environment of the offenders should not be studied. It means that emphasis must be given to the way in which the individual in a given situation selectively responds to the situation. The background of the offender, i.e., his home life, education, religious, social, economic and medical history and the present environment provide merely the conditions for what will take place. They provide the stimulus or energy release. Whether the offender will react, and to what stimuli, depends primarily upon his present needs, tensions and interests. The transformations in the offender set off by the stimuli are the focal point of the search for crime causation.[4]

The lack of progress in discovering the facts of crime causation is in large measure due, it seems to me, to preoccupation with the analytical problem of correlating abstracted uniformities in the lives and environments of criminals. Most research workers recognized early that no single cause of crime was satisfactory. As soon as a particular cause was set forth it was shown that the same factor was found and no criminal behavior followed. Thus broken homes were found associated with a large number of delinquents. However, many non-delinquents came from broken homes. It became necessary, therefore, to seek additional factors. Perhaps broken homes plus truancy? And so the theory of multiple causation was supported. By stating that there was no single cause of crime the difficulty was not solved, but made greater. Instead of relating abstract "crime" and the abstracted

---

[3] Frank states this view as follows: "The so-called cause may be defined as 'an event which delivers energy to another event in distinction from a limitation' thereby releasing or initiating energy transformations in the organism that exhibits the so-called effect. But this 'effect' is not the product of the 'cause'; it is the alteration in structure-function of the organism touched off by the energy of that 'cause'." "Structure and Growth" (Apr. 1935), 2 *Phil. of Science*, 230. See also Frank, "Causation: An Episode in the History of Thought" (Aug. 1934), 31 *J. of Phil.*, 421.

[4] This organismic view is widely accepted by research workers in cytology, physiology and biology. See, for example, Carrel, "The New Cytology" (1931), *Science* 73: 298; "Physiological Time" (1931), *Science* 74: 618.

concept of "broken home" the attempt is now made to correlate many more abstract variables. The organic unified total situations of different individuals committing particular offences are shredded into artificial concepts which leave out and ignore that which is most significant in understanding the criminal behavior, the peculiarly individual processes of change and adjustment in a dynamic, developing situation.

Neither the study of individual case histories nor correlations of crime and environmental factors will yield the facts of individual crime causation. At best such data will show what the conditions are which provide the limitations of what can or can not happen. What will happen depends upon the dynamic configurations of the total situation. An active adjusting individual differentially selects from the many stimuli of his personality-environment those which aid him in present adjustment.

In the light of what has been said, a general answer can be given to what has been a set of perplexing questions. Delinquency has been attributed to broken homes, bad associates, poverty and so on. The questions often raised are, why, then, do not all children who come from broken homes commit crime? Why do not all poor people and why do some rich people commit crime? The general answer, which points to the area of inquiry, is that native disposition, training and environmental circumstances set the limitations or sufficient conditions which may or may not eventuate in crime. Whether or not crime will be committed depends upon how the individual reacts to and with the environment. This depends upon the particular kind of individual who is a living, conflicting, behaving, growing, changing, adjusting organism. It is the transformations which occur at any moment that are significant in understanding the causes of crime. *The transformations themselves constitute the causal factors.*

Furthermore, there are kinds of transformations which vary in degree of efficiency and in quality of influence. The attempt to correlate the different kinds of transformations will lead to error. Such effort is futile. Correlation means measurement. A feeble minded youngster, let us say, commits rape. How intelligible is the question, what is the correlation between the amount of feeble-mindedness and the amount of sex urge? A bank teller employed by the same bank for thirty years embezzles funds to send his children to college. He is superintendent of the community's religious school. An opportunity to falsify the books presents itself. Transformations occur. What happens to life-long ethical attitudes, thirty years' loyalty to his employers, the regard for his wife and children, his own sense of financial inadequacy? The various systems of habit interact on different levels. They have developed at different rates.[5] It is in the realm of the meanings and purposes (means-end relationships) of the individual that explanations are to be sought for the particular behavior which follows.

In conclusion, it should be stated clearly that the organismic approach is not the only approach to gathering and discovering the facts of crime causation. It is the most promising approach in the study of the individual offender. The discovery of facts common to all criminals (the formal or material causes of crime) will help to establish general principles. Environmental studies and intensive case histories will show and have revealed common denominators. How the general conclusions are modified, only the study of the special cases, i.e., every individual offender, will show. Each individual represents a special law of crime causation.

There can be as many different kinds of data and explanations as the investigators have techniques for discovering. Knowledge is desirable no matter through what methods obtained. If certain and complete knowledge cannot be obtained through accepted and tested methods, then one should attempt other methods which will give some clues even though the knowledge be incomplete and uncertain. The final test of whether we understand the causes of crime is the ability to predict whether any one will commit crime.* All the research on criminal behavior taken together could not predict that Richard Roe will or will not commit crime. If such prediction is possible only the psychiatrist or one who "knows" and deals intensively with an individual can make it with some success.

The mental hygiene approach to the study of the individual represents, then, an additional and promising method of discovering the efficient causes of crime. It assumes that discover-

---

[5] This view has much in common with the principle of "the functional autonomy of motives" described by G. Allport in *Personality, A Psychological Interpretation*, Ch. VII (1937).
* See articles 116–117, 171–173. — *Ed.*

ing what experience means to the individual, how he feels and thinks, is the key to the problem of crime causation.

6

On the Causes of Crime *

Sheldon Glueck

"The cause of crime is feeblemindedness. . . . The cause of crime is poverty." These and similar dogmatisms are not infrequently expressed when people, even very intelligent people, pontificate about crime. Newspapers print summaries of statistical compilations about certain characteristics of prisoners, and editorial writers proceed to draw a moral and adorn a tale, without always taking into consideration indispensable fundamentals as to the very concept of criminality or the notion of causation. To call attention to some of these fundamentals as a basis for future interpretations of crime statistics by the intelligent lay public is the chief aim of this article.

I

First of all, are we always quite clear as to the meaning of crime itself? From a legal point of view, a crime is any act or failure to act that is prohibited by law for the protection or supposed welfare of the public, and punishable by politically organized society in a formal judicial proceeding initiated in the name of the state. But when we say that the act is prohibited by law, that is an imperfect description. This law, it must be pointed out, is only the legislation of a *particular time and place*. In other words, crime is a *relative* concept — relative to the society in which the act is prohibited and relative to the time at which it is prohibited.

Certain acts that in some civilized countries are designated by the laws of those societies as criminal, may not be such in other regions. Certain acts that at some periods in any particular country are designated as crimes may not be criminal at other periods. Infanticide and patricide have not been regarded as criminal among certain primitive peoples. The prohibition of the manufacture, sale or transportation of liquor of a specified alcoholic content rendered certain acts criminal in our own country at one time and not at another. Gold hoarding was lawful only a short time ago; today it is punishable.

This relativity of crime to place and time makes it difficult to indulge in sound generalizations about it. But despite that inherent obstacle to the analysis of criminality, some useful description of it is still possible. For there are certain acts which have been quite generally condemned and punished by all developed societies through their laws and other repressive instrumentalities. Treason, a very uncommon crime, is one of these; murder, a much more frequent offense, is another. In most modern civilized communities, also, certain takings of property without the consent of the owner are stigmatized as criminal.

These illustrations lead to the important clue that, as Parmalee puts it, there are probably "certain types of individuals who are very likely to become criminal under *any* social system." They are so organized innately as to find it very difficult to conform their behavior to even the minimal requirements of orderly, peaceful living together in any modern society. "In every community are to be found intractable, rebellious, and unadaptable persons who are sure to react against any form of social control. . . . Consequently, while the personnel of the criminal class at any time and place is determined in part . . . by the kinds of acts which are criminal, it is also determined in part . . . by the traits" which enter into the composition of those persons who find it difficult, sometimes impossible, to become "socialized."

Hence, if we can determine the characteristic traits of modern American criminals who commit offenses which have long been prohibited as criminal, our findings will require but little qualification on the score of variations in acts deemed criminal at different times and places.

II

But no sooner have we dealt with this difficulty than another and more serious one arises. *A completely valid sample of criminals cannot*

---

* Reprinted from 29 *American Mercury* (1933), 430–436. Used by permission of the publisher.

be obtained. The human beings we can subject to study are not the criminal class in general, but only a selected group of that class; as a rule only those incarcerated in prison or jails.

This difficulty is too often ignored even in official reports, yet it is inherent in practically all criminologic research. For example, it is impossible to know exactly how many of the New York City population commit crimes at any time. For much that is violative of the law is done secretly and does not come to the attention of the authorities; and other crimes are winked at by public opinion and the police. No matter how far back we reach into the rake's progress, we cannot unwind the whole story.

Shall we begin with the first available record, crimes reported to the police? This will not give us a complete picture, because it is impossible to say what fraction of crimes is never reported to the police. And who can describe the characteristics of those offenders whose crimes are not reported? Shall we take, then, statistics of arrests as our point of departure? This is still worse, for a high percentage of the crimes reported to the police do not result in arrests.

Shall we turn, then, to statistics of convictions? It is difficult to say how many persons who have certainly committed crimes are not brought to trial or are acquitted on trial. How can we know their characteristics, unless they are willing to subject themselves to study? And if we take persons actually convicted as our point of departure, we run into still another difficulty. For most of our existing research materials on the mental and social factors in criminality deal with persons sent to prison; and among convicts only a fraction are thus dealt with.

So at best we can have only an imperfect picture of the makeup of offenders, even when we gather together the most reliable evidence thus far thrown up in the researches. Moreover, it is conceivable that our picture, however painstakingly we draw it, will be biassed; particularly when we realize the power of political influence and money in keeping many higher-ups out of the toils of the law and allowing many lower-downs to "take the rap."

But our troubles do not end there by any means. Let us assume that we can obtain a valid sample of offenders and that we can subject them to painstaking study, case by case.

If our objective be to throw light on crime *causation,* we shall soon run into even greater involvements than those I have rehearsed. They arise from the fact of the puzzling complexity of crime causation. In order to appreciate the difference in the task of the modern criminalist and that of criminologists of the past, it will be helpful to look backward upon some of the chief crime-causation notions of the days gone by.

Medieval and early modern theories of crime causation were characterized by a simplicity as naïve as it was brutal. In the Middle Ages it was simply assumed that crime was the handiwork of the Devil, operating on the inborn depravity of the individual. That view accounted, in large measure, for the fierce, sadistic brutality with which criminals were treated in the olden times. Not only hanging, but hanging, drawing and quartering were freely indulged in. Boiling, pressing, breaking on a wheel were other methods of expiation and deterrence.

Moreover, many more offenses (some of them relatively insignificant) were punishable capitally in the past than are so treated today. Pike, the historian of crime, described conditions at the end of the Middle Ages by passages like the following:

The gibbet, with a robber hanging in chains, was one of the objects most frequently presented to the eye. A petty thief in the pillory, a scold on the ducking-stool, a murderer drawn to the gallows on a hurdle, were spectacles as familiar when Henry VII ascended the throne as a messenger from the telegraph office is to ourselves.

It was in protest against this brutality and the arbitrariness and irresponsibility of judges that, in 1764, Beccaria, an Italian humanitarian, published his epoch-making essay, "Crimes and Punishments." This little book took Europe by storm, coming as it did when the great humanitarian movement of the Eighteenth Century was swiftly gathering momentum. The essay soon passed into numerous editions and languages. Among other reforms, Beccaria recommended that judges should be strictly confined to presiding at trials and to imposing the exact punishments prescribed in advance by the legislature to fit crimes of various degrees of severity. The crime-causation theory back of this so-called Classical system (and basically it is still in force) is the dogma that every person is able to exercise a completely free will, that this inborn capacity makes him a free moral agent, and that therefore he is responsible and punishable for acts which the law prohibits.

The rigor of the Classical School soon had to be relaxed somewhat in the case of two types of persons whose patent condition ran contrary to the initial dogma of absolute freedom of will; namely, the extremely insane or feeble-minded, and children of tender years. Hence, exceptions to the general concept of responsibility grew up for these two classes of cases, in the form of legal rules or standards which (with certain modifications) are still with us.

But this invasion of absolute freedom of will did not suggest to the law-makers that, having opened the door a few inches on the basis of evidence patently contrary to their dogma, they might be asked to open it still farther in the light of further evidence. In other words, it does not seem to have occurred to them that there is a multiplicity of influences — organic and social — involved in human behavior and its motivations. Who can say with any claim to precision that irresponsible conduct, in any rational sense, is more due to mental disorder than to the pulls and pressures of socio-economic forces?

It was not until the Nineteenth Century that there was anything more than a flank attack on the simple free-will theory of crime causation. It came through the development of the positive, scientific method in the physical and biologic disciplines. In the field of criminology, this movement had its first fruits in the publication of a series of books by Cesare Lombroso, beginning in 1878 and running to the end of the century, based on clinical investigations into the anthropologic and psychiatric (and later, also, the sociologic) factors in criminality. The Lombrosian School will always be credited with one very important contribution: instead of speculating about human freedom versus determinism and spinning out theories of crime causation and criminal responsibility in the abstract, the Lombrosians went to the prisoner for the evidence.

Lombroso contended that the criminal "reproduces in civilized times characteristics not only of primitive savages but of still lower types." His hypothesis, too enthusiastically promoted, was that the biologic process of atavism, or throw-back to a distant ancestral type, accounts for the existence of what he called the "criminal type." Toward the end of his career, he concluded that not all offenders are born criminals, but only a fourth or a third; and that offenders "form a graduated scale leading from the born criminal to the normal individual." Among the latter ranks social and cultural influences predominate in the complex of causative forces.

III

Though the modern approach to the study of crime stresses the complexity of causation, there still exist pronounced biasses in favor of the social factors in crime causation on the one hand, and the organic (largely psychiatric and psychologic) on the other. The difficulties involved may be illustrated by taking up the question from several typical points of view.

In many recent sociologic researches, for example, it has been emphasized that the rate of delinquency in a city varies with the type of area involved. This concept is by no means a new one. It was carefully worked out at least as far back as 1897 in Alfredo Niceforo's monograph on "Delinquency in Sardinia," but it has received more refined statistical treatment in recent years. It is demonstrated by the sociologists that the highest incidence of delinquency is customarily found in so-called "interstitial" areas. These are regions usually characterized by a transition from a residential to a business or manufacturing use, and by such unwholesome social conditions as crowded, unattractive housing, vice, desertion, anti-social cultural traditions handed down from group to group, gang life, and the like. Frequently, as one proceeds from such regions outward, the rate of delinquency becomes less and less.

This is a very useful concept. But let us examine its implications, which the sociologists do not as yet seem to have taken sufficiently into account. Suppose it is found that in delinquency areas as high a proportion as, say, 15% of all children are arrested for delinquencies, whereas in other areas, where the enumerated bad conditions prevail to a lesser degree, only 2% of the children are so treated. Granting, for the sake of argument, that policing and other necessary conditions in the two areas are quite similar, how can we account for the correlative and equally significant fact that even in such "interstitial" areas 85% of the children are *not* delinquent? The most we can assume, from researches of the type mentioned, is that in delinquency areas there is a complex of unhealthy social and cultural conditions which probably operate, to some degree, in a criminogenic way. But even this assumption must be greatly qualified. Standing alone, it does not explain why it is that these same adverse socio-economic and cultural conditions apparently did not "cause" the delinquency in the far larger proportion of cases.

But the psychiatrist and psychologist also indulge in methodologic and logical fallacies. They naturally have tended to stress the biologic elements in the complex situation that is crime. Suppose a psychiatrist should find that in New York City 15% of the psychotic, psychopathic, psychoneurotic and feebleminded population are criminal, whereas only 2% of the mentally sound population indulge in crime. Could he thereby conclude that mental abnormality is "the cause" or even the principal cause of crime in New York? How could he have a rounded conception of the truth if, staring him in the face, was the tough fact that 85% of the mentally ill do *not* commit crimes?

Thus far we have considered this matter by taking offenders in the mass and treating them statistically. Let us now look at an illustration or two of individual cases. X and Y are neighbors. Both were reared in the worst possible delinquency area. The entire "kingdom of evils" was their realm in childhood, and adolescence. I met X in prison, where he finally landed with a stiff sentence after numerous exploits of burglary, robbery, shooting at cops, and the like. The social and cultural factors in his career were so markedly unwholesome that any reasonable student of the case history would conclude, without more ado, that of course X turned out to be a bad man because of the woefully unfavorable environmental conditions. But unfortunately for the comprehensiveness and conclusiveness of this assumption, Y, who was subjected to practically the same conditions, has turned out to be a sober, law-abiding and successful citizen.

Take another case. A is in prison for burglary. On examination, the psychiatrist triumphantly informs us that A is not only a long-standing burglar, but what is more important, a "psychopathic personality," and, in addition, a chronic alcoholic already showing signs of nervous and mental deterioration. The psychiatrist points out that his diagnosis is well supported by the developmental history of A. From very early childhood, he was regarded by teachers and parents as a problem child. He was very difficult to manage; he constantly revolted against all forms of authority. The history shows, further, that these patterns of temperament and behavior were systematically operative in A's later social relationships, — in the various places where he was employed and discharged for heatedly resenting orders of the foremen, in his relations with his wife and children, in his other companionships. Such is the psychiatrist's diagnosis. But the sociologist triumphantly insists that A is the person we know him to be today because since earliest childhood he and his family have lived in the direst poverty, and resided in the vilest tenements of the most marked delinquency area; that A has eagerly imbibed the "anti-social cultural traditions" of corner gangs for the past twenty years.

The psychiatrist and sociologist now desire to synthesize their information and obtain a more rounded and convincing account of the etiology of A's criminalism. But they soon find themselves enmeshed in a series of vicious circles and spirals, arguing over what is the cart and what the horse, and whether the cart always goes after the horse or sometimes, as supposedly in this case, precedes. Has A's criminality been caused by his drunkenness, or have both his alcoholism and his misconduct been caused by his psychopathic personality? Did A become a drunkard because he could not stand his family's miserable situation, or was its economic insufficiency the result of A's alcoholism? Or have both the alcoholism and criminality been caused by A's supposedly innate constitutional inferiority?

These sequences, and many more, may have occurred at different stages in the career of A, in a series of vicious action-reaction mechanisms. But even by the closest scrutiny of his developmental history with the means thus far available to criminologists it would be found difficult to assign *primacy* to any of the factors involved. Naturally, one would be inclined to place the constitutional or innate inadequacy first; but often it cannot be said conclusively that any particular factor or condition is innate; and even if it could be done it is conceivable that an innate defect, such as psychopathic personality or mental deficiency, standing alone, would not have brought about the anti-social conduct.

IV

The illustrations given suggest a number of fruitful ideas about crime causation that are too often ignored. First, whether considered in the mass, statistically, or in the individual case, criminalistic etiology is extremely complex. That is why it is so easy for special pleaders to seize upon one element or group of factors that happens to interest them and assign to it exclusive or at any rate primary causative force.

Secondly, it is very difficult, even by the use of refined mathematical statistics, to assign relative weights to different elements in the causation complex. And this is true even when we study the individual case with great thoroughness. The most we can talk about is probabilities.

Thirdly, it is very difficult to assign primacy to any of the arcs in the series of vicious circles so often found in the careers of criminals.

Fourthly, just because we find a biologic or social condition existing in the career of one criminal that has been reasonably proved to be criminogenic in another, is no reason for jumping to the conclusion that it was also causative of the misconduct in the first, or if causative, that it operated to the same degree of intensity. To state the matter differently, we must not ignore the fact that individuals differ in the degree of *permeability* to the social and cultural milieu in which they find themselves, and that social factors vary in the degree to which they affect people as a whole. As Dr. Bernard Glueck puts it, "a factor, whether personal or situational, does not become a cause unless and until it first becomes a motive." Some unfavorable social conditions are thrown off by certain people like water off a duck's back; other unfavorable social conditions, far from dragging particular individuals down, serve as an added stimulus to effort and ambition. In brief, the actual interplay of personal and social factors in the individual case is the bridge one must try to cross before arriving at conclusions regarding the causation of crime.

Finally, it should be clear from what has gone before that in criminal conduct, as in most other forms of human expression, every person has his individual resistance-point or, if you will, breaking-point. It is difficult for *all* members of any society at any one time to lead a socially acceptable existence, involving a subordination of the natural impulses to the alleged general welfare. But *most* persons are able (natively and through elaborate education) to meet the ordinary requirements of the legal standard of the age and place wherein they live.

If that society raises its demands, or through social stress such as long-standing unemployment makes it more difficult to adhere to the rules of the game, it thereby taps a deeper layer of persons who will violate the law; because it has in this way brought further pressure to bear on those whose resistance-capacity is at present stretched almost to the breaking-point. Thus the criminal act occurring at any given time is the outcome of constitutional and acquired, personal and social forces, and shows only that the individual's power of resistance has been over-balanced by the strength of the other circumstances.[1]

Despite the researches of the past decade, it is in my opinion as yet premature to make any well-grounded statement as to the relative participation of these social and biologic factors in crime causation. This does not mean, however, that a reasonable knowledge of the mental and physical characteristics, as well as social background, of prisoners is as yet unavailable. It means only that the transition from a description of the *traits* of existing delinquents and criminals to conclusions as to *causation* should not too readily be made.

A study of the traits of offenders is extremely useful for the practical correctional purposes of classification, education, trade instruction, mental therapy and the like. Having ascertained them, we shall in part be engaged in a

---

[1] I have developed these views in detail in pages 13–19 of the chapter on "Housing and Delinquency," written by a committee under the chairmanship of Clifford Shaw, in "Housing and the Community," edited by John M. Gries and James Ford. Several criminologies have mistakenly attributed the above ideas to Clifford Shaw. See, for example, P. V. Young, *Social Treatment in Probation and Delinquency*, New York, McGraw-Hill, 1937, 120; H. A. Bloch, and F. T. Flynn, *Delinquency: The Juvenile Offender in America Today*, New York, Random House, 1956, 75, 78. — *Ed.*

symptom therapy, in part in a causal therapy. For the welfare of society, inasmuch as the vast majority of offenders are sooner or later to be returned to freedom, all measures looking to improvements in their mental and physical health, their educational and industrial equipment, their deep-rooted attitudes, may be regarded as a sound investment of the public funds. Moreover, intensive preoccupation with programmes of control and therapy will most likely lead us nearer and nearer to the secret citadel of crime causation.

7

The Meaning of "Cause" *

Sheldon and Eleanor T. Glueck

Let us first be clear as to what is meant by causation — something that seems simple enough but that is fraught with perplexing difficulties. Several issues have to be examined:
1. *Is there such a thing as cause-and-effect?* This may strike the reader as a superfluous question; but there has long been debate among philosophers and scientists as to the meaning, and even the reality, of the very concept of cause-and-effect. It is often urged that causal connection is only *inferential* in character rather than something that can be directly perceived by the senses. "What we perceive is *sequence* of events; and it is from their sequence that we feel justified in *inferring* their causal connection, provided certain conditions are satisfied." [1]

* Reprinted from *Delinquents in the Making*, New York, Harper and Brothers, 1952, 164–169. Used by permission of the publisher. See, also, *International Review of Criminal Policy*, ST/SOA/Ser. M/7–8, United Nations, Nos. 7–8 (January–July), 1950, 23–30. For an example of an attempt to track down the cause of a sharp increase in boys picked up for felonious or aggravated assault, see W. W. Wattenberg and J. B. Moir, "A Phenomenon in Search of a Cause," 48 *J. Crim. L., Criminology and Police Science* (1957), 54–58. — Ed.

[1] 5 *Encyclopaedia Britannica* (1942), 62 (italics for "inferring" supplied).

Along similar lines James Bryant Conant, discussing the difference between biologic phenomena and those of chemistry and physics, says: "If repeated observation shows that event A always precedes event B, we accept as a matter of common sense that A is the cause, B the effect, although we realize that there is possible a long argument as to whether some earlier event was not the 'real' cause of B, or perhaps of both A and B. A boy throws a stone through a neighbor's window. What is the cause of the broken glass? The stone, the boy, the friend who put him up to the defiant act? The important point is the sequence of events in time. Except in a moving picture run backwards we do not observe in common life such a series of events as broken window, unbroken window, stone near the window, stone in boy's hand, etc. Biological phenomena are events in time not unlike the simple case just cited." [2]

While recognizing the fundamental significance to the idea of cause-and-effect of *sequence in time*, we can rationally assume, further, that if such sequence occurs consistently in a definite order from the presence of a certain combination of factors to the presence of persistent delinquency, then these "successive events not only *follow*, but *follow from* one another." [3] In other words, we can legitimately assume, for practical purposes, the existence of a system of cause-and-effect in the generally accepted sense. We can, moreover, test it by experiments designed to modify or eliminate the conditions that have been found to precede delinquency in one sample of cases so that we may check on whether or not the subsequent result in the new sample turns out to be delinquency or non-delinquency.

This matter of causal sequence is important, further, because it dictates that in marshaling the factors which have proved to differentiate delinquents from non-delinquents, our causal conception requires that we eliminate from consideration such factors, for example, as membership in gangs, which occurred, in the vast majority of instances among our delinquents, *after* they had become delinquent, and could not therefore have been causal in the above-

[2] J. B. Conant, *Science and Common Sense*, New Haven, Yale University Press, 1951, 238.
[3] *Encyclopaedia Britannica, op. cit.*, 62.

described sense. It will be recalled that the onset of persistent misbehavior tendencies was at the early age of seven years or younger among 48% of our delinquents, and from eight to ten in an additional 39%, making a total of almost nine-tenths of the entire group who showed delinquent tendencies before the time when boys generally become members of organized boys' gangs. The leading authorities on the subject recognize the gang as "largely an adolescent phenomenon." [4] For example, of some 1,200 cases of gang membership studied in Chicago, only 1.5% of the boys were six–twelve years old, while 63% were classified as adolescents.[5]

Basically, then, it is important in considering causal factors in the biosocial field not to put the cart before the horse.

2. *"Cause" requires a totality of conditions necessary to the result.* "As a rule a cause is complex — it consists of a number of conditions each of which is only a part of the cause." [6] It is very doubtful whether, standing alone, any *single* factor that we have disentangled in the preceding chapters would be sufficient to account for persistent delinquency. Take, for example, the fact that twice as many delinquents as non-delinquents were found to be of the closely knit, muscular, athletically inclined (mesomorphic) type. The very fact that 30% of the *non*-delinquent lads also were of this physique immediately contradicts any conclusion that *mesomorphy* inevitably "causes" persistent delinquency. Or, consider such a trait as *defiance*, which one would naturally regard as closely related to delinquent behavior tendencies. True, 50% of the delinquents had this characteristic, but 12% of the non-delinquents also had it; and the very fact that half the delinquent group did *not* display this trait further reveals the inadequacy of conclusions about causation derived from a single factor.

Thus, a single factor (or even a small group

of factors) may be involved, even frequently involved, in delinquent behavior and yet each one may not of itself be of sufficient weight or potency to tip the scales among boys who remain non-delinquent. In other words, "the cause of a certain effect is that *totality* of conditions that is sufficient to produce it." [7]

3. *A variety of causal patterns can account for a similar result.* The fact above noted that as many as half the delinquent group were *not* characterized by the trait of *defiance* is but one illustration of the absence among a considerable group of delinquents of characteristics which are present in some other large group of delinquents. It reveals the usually unrecognized truism that persistent delinquency can be the result of not only *one specific* combination or pattern of factors that markedly differentiate delinquents from non-delinquents, but of each of several *different* combinations. This is the concept of *"Plurality of Causes,* or the view that the same kind of effect may in different instances be produced by different kinds of causes." [8] Just as the fact of a boy's death, although always the *same terminal event,* may nonetheless be the result of *various preceding sequences* of conditions, so the terminal event of persistent delinquency may have in its causal background a variety of different sequences leading to the same ultimate result. For we are dealing with a complex aggregation of many internal and external conditions which are associated with socially maladjusted, unlawful behavior, and not all of them may always be *indispensable* to the result.

In criminal conduct, as in most other forms of human expression, every person has his individual resistance point or breaking point. It is difficult for all members of any society at any one time to conform to the requirements and prohibitions of socially acceptable conduct, because this involves a subordination of the natural impulses of sex expression, aggression, and the like, to those conduct norms which the law has declared necessary to the general welfare. But most persons are able (through various combinations of numerous factors of native endowment and elaborate conditioning in home, school, and society) to meet the ordinary requirements of the major legal standards of the age and place wherein they live. If a boy per-

---

[4] F. M. Thrasher, *The Gang,* Chicago, University of Chicago Press, 1936, 2nd Rev. Ed., p. 36. "The lure of the gang is undoubtedly due in part to the fact that the gang boy is in the adolescent stage which is definitely correlated with gang phenomena. Although this period has no exact limits for any individual, it includes broadly for the boy the years from twelve to twenty-six."

[5] *Ibid.,* p. 74.

[6] *Encyclopaedia Britannica, op. cit.,* p. 63.

[7] *Ibid.*   [8] *Ibid.*

sists in delinquency, it means that his power of resistance to natural impulse, or his desire to obey socio-legal mandates, has been over-balanced by the strength of the other circumstances that incline to antisocial behavior.

These circumstances can consist of any combination of factors, so long as they add up sufficiently to that "totality of conditions" necessary to overbalance inhibitions.[9] That is why there can be a "plurality of causes" in delinquency. The present *general,* or mass, comparison of data analyzed in the preceding chapters does not involve any differentiation of a possible *variety* of causal patterns or syndromes each of which is sufficient to turn the scales in favor of persistent antisocial maladjustment. In this book the delinquents are treated as a single group. In subsequent volumes we plan to describe several different patterns of factors each of which, probably, would be of sufficient weight to incline boys to persistent delinquency.

4. *"Cause-and-effect" in the sense of high probability of persistent delinquency.* Closely related to the preceding concept is the matter of *probability.* Even the physical sciences, nowadays, state their generalizations in terms not of absolute inevitability but only of high probability. The statistical method of comparing delinquents, as a group, with non-delinquents, as

---

[9] When a certain individual influence (X) in a complex of causes is removed from the life of a delinquent, it does not necessarily follow that he will reform, for several reasons: (a) the amount of causal pressure exerted by X may have been so low originally that the remainder of influence is still enough to keep him delinquent. (b) Some of the remaining influences may even operate more strongly through the removal of X, since the influence of X may partially have counteracted the influence of the other factors in the causal pressure complex. (c) A new causal influence may take the place of the eliminated X; for instance, habituation in antisocial behavior. (d) The effect of increased age and its accompanying physiologic and temperamental changes, may have, in the interim, reshuffled the influence of the original causal pressures.

When a factor, such as residence in an "interstitial" or high delinquency area is shown to be statistically more frequent among delinquents than non-delinquents but is itself found in only a relatively small proportion of the totality of delinquents (e.g., 10%–15%), it means that in only relatively few instances is that factor causally involved; that is, it is a fringe factor rather than a core factor. However, this does not necessarily mean that that factor may not play a predominant part in the few cases in which it *is* involved. — *Ed.*

a group, is not designed to bring out any point-to-point causal sequence that will always hold good for each and every case. It is rather intended to disclose whether or not an entire group having a certain cluster of factors in its make-up and background will much more probably turn out to be delinquent than a group of boys not so loaded down; or, to put it differently, whether the "typical" or "average" delinquent is likely to be the result of such a concatenation of factors.

In other words, we are concerned with the discovery of a general relationship between certain preceding factors and a tendency to a specific subsequent course of conduct. Having discovered even such a general relationship, we have at hand some of the crucial information necessary as a guide to experimental programs of therapy and prevention, for we can now attack, singly or in groups, those factors which have been found to contribute most frequently and most heavily to the tendency in question.

8

"Association" and "Causation" *

Sheldon and Eleanor T. Glueck

Before closing this chapter, a few words are in order regarding the concepts of *association* and *causation.*

Those who have worked in any field of human behavior realize how extremely difficult it is to clarify causal implications.

When a significant relationship between two facts emerges, there is statistical "association," but not necessarily "causation" in the sense of an *influence of one trait or factor upon the other.* If, for example, some research disclosed a high association between fluctuations in the length of women's skirts in Paris over a certain

---

* Reprinted from *Physique and Delinquency,* New York, Harper and Brothers, 1956, 40–43. Used by permission of the publisher.

period and fluctuations in the political parties which had control of the United States Congress during the same period, one would be hard put to it to explain the *etiologic* interrelationship of the two phenomena. At best, it would be remote, indirect, and tied in with a great many other subtle influences. An association found statistically, even by the most sensitive mathematical formulae, must have some basis in experience or reason. The associations in our tables (i.e., the significant differences in trait-incidence between delinquents and non-delinquents and those between the various body types) do have such a basis.

It is also essential for the concept of "causation," as opposed to the broader and more indefinite "association," that the phenomena involved be related in temporal sequence. One must avoid the familiar cart-before-the-horse fallacy. Both in *Unraveling* [1] and in the present study we have laid aside traits and factors which did not meet this sequence-in-time test. Thus, as has been pointed out, we have eliminated from consideration the factor *membership in gangs* as an influence in originating delinquency because we found that, in the vast majority of instances among our delinquents, gang membership occurred *after* the onset of delinquency and it could not therefore have been causal in the above sense. The onset of persistent delinquency occurred before the age of eight among 48% of our delinquents, and in the eighth to the tenth years in an additional 39%, making a total of almost nine-tenths of the entire group who showed delinquent tendencies before the time when the gang, "largely on adolescent phenomenon," played a part in the life of some of our boys.

Where temporal sequence does occur consistently in a definite order from the presence of a certain factor or group of factors to the presence of a tendency to delinquency, we can rationally assume that these successive events not only follow each other but follow *from* each other. In other words, we can legitimately assume, for practical purposes, the existence of a system of cause-and-effect in the generally accepted sense; that is to say, we have, in such a situation, not merely association but *etiologic*

association. Moreover, we can test it by experiments designed to modify or eliminate the conditions that have been found to precede delinquency in one sample of cases in order to check on whether or not the subsequent result in a new sample turns out to be delinquency or non-delinquency.

Where the interacting elements are of such nature as to indicate clearly that the horse comes before the cart, relatively clean-cut causal sequence is then traceable. This is true, for example, in the relationship of a somatotype to a personality trait, on the obvious assumption that body type precedes sociocultural conditioning. But even in such sequences reciprocal influences may sometimes be at work. Certainly, in the case of parent-child, child-sibling, and child-companion relationships, we are dealing with a complex process of *interstimulation* and *interresponse* in which it is sometimes difficult to establish the temporal sequence of events.

The concept of temporal sequence does not exclude the fact that two or more interrelated traits or factors may in turn be the product of a third or fourth influence which is often not clearly apparent on the surface. There are degrees of directness or indirectness in the causal association of traits and factors with delinquency or physique type. Such a trait, for example, as *sensitivity* (Table 51) is not directly implicated in the criminogenic complex, as is shown by the fact that it fails to distinguish delinquents from non-delinquents either as a whole or within any body type. Yet in the case of both delinquents and non-delinquents there is a much greater incidence of the trait among ectomorphs than among mesomorphs; and it may well be that this trait is indirectly related to delinquency in being associated with other traits that do distinguish delinquents from non-delinquents or in effecting a special reaction to certain environmental stimuli on the part of ectomorphs. The interrelationship of causal forces is so complex that ordinarily one can be certain of little more than that an association between two variables is probably not due to chance.

It must also be borne in mind that etiologic influence is typically multiple and complex, consisting of numerous traits and factors of which each is but a part of the causal nexus. It is very doubtful whether, standing alone, any single trait or factor analyzed in this study would be

---

[1] S. and E. T. Glueck, *Unraveling Juvenile Delinquency*, Cambridge, Mass.: Harvard University Press, Copyright, 1950, by The Commonwealth Fund. — *Ed.*

sufficient to account for delinquency. Moreover, while "cause" requires a totality of influences indispensable to the result, it cannot be exactly determined how much weight each of the traits contributes to any theoretical total causal influence.

Another important point (already mentioned in Chapter 1) is that a *variety* of combinations of specific factors or causal patterns can account for a uniform result in terms of antisocial behavior. Just as death, although always the same terminal event, is nonetheless the result of a variety of preceding sequences of influence, so the end product of persistent delinquency, or of some trait of personality or character, may have in its etiologic background a variety of different sequences leading to the same ultimate result.

Finally, it must be kept in mind that we are not attempting the clinical task of analyzing causal sequences in individual cases, but are rather approaching the problem via *mass* comparisons of delinquents and non-delinquents. In dealing with problems of human behavior in society we must be content with accepting "cause-and-effect" to signify, not a hundred per cent relationship, but rather a high *probability* of relationship. Even in the physical sciences, generalizations are not stated in terms of absolute inevitability in each and every instance, but only of high probability in the mass. The statistical method of comparing delinquents as a group with non-delinquents as a group is not designed to bring out any point-to-point causal tie-in that will always hold good for each and every case. It is rather intended to disclose whether or not the general run of cases possessing a certain cluster of traits is much more likely to be delinquent than a group not so loaded down or impelled.

Chapter 3

Anthropologic-Biologic (Hereditary-Constitutional) Aspects of Delinquency

THE NEXT SEVERAL CHAPTERS comprise an examination of influences believed, at one time or another, to be fundamentally involved in criminogenesis. While it is incontestable that delinquency is the product of the interplay of many internal and external influences, the nature of the problem makes it necessary to examine each of the major areas of influence separately.

The first field of inquiry presented is the biologic one. In the United States today this approach to the etiologic problem is not popular, the sociologic and cultural explanations of delinquency holding sway in the textbooks. Because of the decline of Lombrosianism in the twentieth century, any research involving possible hereditary implications is frowned upon. However, a distinction must be made between Lombroso's inadequately supported theory of the "born criminal" as a product of hereditary "atavism" and/or epilepsy, and the intercorrelation of carefully derived modern somatotype data with psychiatric, psychologic and sociocultural data, as illustrated by the extracts from *Physique and Delinquency*.[1]

The chapter begins with a brief statement by Tappan, warning against the ignoring of hereditary influences. On the anthropologic aspects, the Editor would have preferred the inclusion of original source material from Lombroso, in expounding the theory of the Italian school; but available data by the famous Italian anthropologist-psychiatrist did not lend themselves to editing as well as did material from the book by Lombroso's daughter, Gina Lombroso Ferrero and by Parmelee. An extract from Goring's critique of Lombrosianism is included.

Following upon a passage from the Gluecks' *Physique and Delinquency*, giving light on the role of constitution in the complex network of antisocial maladjustment, there is an article by Podolsky suggestive of the possible relationship of physiologic (chemical) influences to the problem of delinquent and criminal behavior.

The final item is an extract from *Unraveling Juvenile Delinquency* consisting of a summary of the chapter in that work which deals with the physical condition of delinquents and non-delinquents. As in other summaries from *Unraveling*, the student is advised to read the original chapter in order to note the statistical support for the summary.

---

[1] S. and E. T. Glueck, *Physique and Delinquency*, New York, Harper and Brothers, 1956.

9

Hereditary Influences *

Paul W. Tappan

The point has been made, and quite appropriately, that one does not inherit delinquency or criminalism. Too often an erroneous inference has been that heredity is therefore an irrelevant matter in the study of delinquent behavior. Heredity *is* related to antisocial behavior as it is, indeed, to all behavior. That is not to say, however, that the old familiar studies of the Jukes, Kallikaks, Namms, and identical twins, or the Lombrosian and more recent Hooton researches really prove their point on hereditary causation. The matter is not so simple as a direct and complete hereditary etiology, since quite obviously influences of the social environment occupy an important part of the situation in which the defectives and maladjusted personalities develop. This denial of hereditary determinism, however, makes out no case for the inclination among some students to attach their faith to an equally oversimplified and absurd social determinism. The fact is, in reality, that man's physiological traits are a consequence of his genes as these and their somatic products in the body have responded to a continuous succession of milieux, chemical, physical, and social. The hereditary process is, then, an initial and limiting force in the ultimate development of the individual. It is only a partial determinant, since it is associated inextricably with the numerous conditioning influences that are necessary to its effects, but it is far too important a factor to be neglected in any realistic consideration of human behavior. Just as hered-

ity represents a class of significant influences upon constitutional traits, so the latter partly determine behavior, since conduct is a result of the response of the organism to the continuum of environing influences, external and internal, to which it is exposed. Obviously, the behavior varies not only with circumstances but with the physiological characteristics that are at work, and in some of these the initiatory role of heredity is important. Other organic influences, too, play an important part in delinquency, which have not come out of the heredity but which have been induced by accident, disease, or conditioning. Unfortunately, from a diagnostic point of view, it is impossible to determine what the role of heredity is in any precise way in a particular case, since the individuals studied reflect — even from birth — the environmental circumstances to which they have reacted. However, it is as absurd to deny heredity as it is to attach to it a specified weight as a factor in behavior.[1]

10

Introduction to *Criminal Man* *

Cesare Lombroso

[Professor Lombroso was able before his death to give his personal attention to the volume prepared by his daughter and collaborator, Gina Lombroso Ferrero (wife of the distinguished historian), in which is presented a summary of the conclusions reached in the great treatise by Lombroso on the causes of criminality and the treatment of criminals. The preparation of the Introduction to this volume was the last literary work which the distin-

---

* By permission from *Juvenile Delinquency*, by Paul W. Tappan. Copyright, 1949. McGraw-Hill Book Company, New York, 120–121. Used by permission of the author and the publisher. A summary of the various twin studies was made by M. F. Ashley-Montagu, who opines that "there is not the slightest evidence to believe that anyone ever inherits a tendency to commit criminal acts. Crime is a social condition, not a biological condition." "The Biologist Looks at Crime," 217 *Annals* (1941), 55. — *Ed.*

[1] For an excellent analysis of the relationship between heredity, constitutional factors, and social and cultural influences on behavior and adjustment, see Kimball Young, *Personality and Social Adjustment*, Part I, 1940.

* Reprinted from Cesare Lombroso's Introduction to *Criminal Man*, by Gina Lombroso Ferrero, New York, G. P. Putnam, 1911, xi–xx. Used by permission of the publisher.

guished author found it possible to complete during his final illness.]

It will, perhaps, be of interest to American readers of this book, in which the ideas of the Modern Penal School, set forth in my work, *Criminal Man*, have been so pithily summed up by my daughter, to learn how the first outlines of this science arose in my mind and gradually took shape in a definite work — how, that is, combated by some, the object of almost fanatical adherence on the part of others, especially in America,[1] where tradition has little hold, the Modern Penal School came into being.

On consulting my memory and the documents relating to my studies on this subject, I find that its two fundamental ideas — that, for instance, which claims as an essential point the study not of crime in the abstract, but of the criminal himself, in order adequately to deal with the evil effects of his wrongdoing, and that which classifies the congenital criminal as an anomaly, partly pathological and partly atavistic, a revival of the primitive savage — did not suggest themselves to me instantaneously under the spell of a single deep impression, but were the offspring of a series of impressions. The slow and almost unconscious association of these first vague ideas resulted in a new system which, influenced by its origin, has preserved in all its subsequent developments the traces of doubt and indecision, the marks of the travail which attended its birth.

The first idea came to me in 1864, when, as an army doctor, I beguiled my ample leisure with a series of studies on the Italian soldier. From the very beginning I was struck by a characteristic that distinguished the honest soldier from his vicious comrade: the extent to which the latter was tattooed and the indecency of the designs that covered his body. This idea, however, bore no fruit.

The second inspiration came to me when on one occasion, amid the laughter of my colleagues, I sought to base the study of psychiatry

on experimental methods. When in '66, fresh from the atmosphere of clinical experiment, I had begun to study psychiatry, I realised how inadequate were the methods hitherto held in esteem, and how necessary it was, in studying the insane, to make the patient, not the disease, the object of attention. In homage to these ideas, I applied to the clinical examination of cases of mental alienation the study of the skull, with measurements and weights, by means of the esthesiometer and craniometer. Reassured by the result of these first steps, I sought to apply this method to the study of criminals — that is, to the differentiation of criminals and lunatics, following the example of a few investigators, such as Thomson and Wilson; but as at that time I had neither criminals nor moral imbeciles available for observation (a remarkable circumstance since I was to make the criminal my starting-point), and as I was skeptical as to the existence of those "moral lunatics" so much insisted on by both French and English authors, whose demonstrations, however, showed a lamentable lack of precision, I was anxious to apply the experimental method to the study of the diversity, rather than the analogy, between lunatics, criminals, and normal individuals. Like him, however, whose lantern lights the road for others, while he himself stumbles in the darkness, this method proved useless for determining the differences between criminals and lunatics, but served instead to indicate a new method for the study of penal jurisprudence, a matter to which I had never given serious thought. I began dimly to realise that the *a priori* studies on crime in the abstract, hitherto pursued by jurists, especially in Italy, with singular acumen, should be superseded by the direct analytical study of the criminal, compared with normal individuals and the insane.

I, therefore, began to study criminals in the Italian prisons, and, amongst others, I made the acquaintance of the famous brigand Vilella. This man possessed such extraordinary agility, that he had been known to scale steep mountain heights bearing a sheep on his shoulders. His cynical effrontery was such that he openly boasted of his crimes. On his death one cold grey November morning, I was deputed to make the *postmortem*, and on laying open the skull I found on the occipital part, exactly on the spot where a spine is found in the normal skull, a distinct depression which I named *median*

---

[1] The opposite has been the case in America during the past four decades. There are still some adherents to Lombroso's ideas, or to neo-Lombrosianism, in South America and on the European continent. Evidence has been presented that there have been precursors of Lombroso whom most scholars seem to have ignored. See Lindersmith and Levin, "The Lombrosian Myth in Criminology," 42 *Am. J. of Soc.* (1937–38), 653–671. — *Ed.*

occipital fossa, because of its situation precisely in the middle of the occiput as in inferior animals, especially rodents. This depression, as in the case of animals, was correlated with the hypertrophy of the *vermis,* known in birds as the middle cerebellum.

This was not merely an idea, but a revelation. At the sight of that skull, I seemed to see all of a sudden, lighted up as a vast plain under a flaming sky, the problem of the nature of the criminal — an atavistic being who reproduces in his person the ferocious instincts of primitive humanity and the inferior animals. Thus were explained anatomically the enormous jaws, high cheek-bones, prominent superciliary arches, solitary lines in the palms, extreme size of the orbits, handle-shaped or sessile ears found in criminals, savages, and apes, insensibility to pain, extremely acute sight, tattooing, excessive idleness, love of orgies, and the irresistible craving for evil for its own sake, the desire not only to extinguish life in the victim, but to mutilate the corpse, tear its flesh, and drink its blood.

I was further encouraged in this bold hypothesis by the results of my studies on Verzeni, a criminal convicted of sadism and rape, who showed the cannibalistic instincts of primitive anthropophagists and the ferocity of beasts of prey.

The various parts of the extremely complex problem of criminality were, however, not all solved hereby. The final key was given by another case, that of Misdea, a young soldier of about twenty-one, unintelligent but not vicious. Although subject to epileptic fits, he had served for some years in the army when suddenly, for some trivial cause, he attacked and killed eight of his superior officers and comrades. His horrible work accomplished, he fell into a deep slumber, which lasted twelve hours and on awakening appeared to have no recollection of what had happened. Misdea, while representing the most ferocious type of animal, manifested, in addition, all the phenomena of epilepsy, which appeared to be hereditary in all the members of his family. It flashed across my mind that many criminal characteristics not attributable to atavism, such as facial asymmetry, cerebral sclerosis, impulsiveness, instantaneousness, the periodicity of criminal acts, the desire for evil for evil's sake, were morbid characteristics common to epilepsy, mingled with others due to atavism.

Thus were traced the first clinical outlines of my work which had hitherto been entirely anthropological. The clinical outlines confirmed the anthropological contours, and vice versa; for the greatest criminals showed themselves to be epileptics, and, on the other hand, epileptics manifested the same anomalies as criminals. Finally, it was shown that epilepsy frequently reproduced atavistic characteristics, including even those common to lower animals.

That synthesis which mighty geniuses have often succeeded in creating by one inspiration (but at the risk of errors, for a genius is only human and in many cases more fallacious than his fellow-man) was deduced by me gradually from various sources — the study of the normal individual, the lunatic, the criminal, the savage, and finally the child. Thus, by reducing the penal problem to its simplest expression, its solution was rendered easier, just as the study of embryology has in a great measure solved the apparently strange and mysterious riddle of teratology.

But these attempts would have been sterile, had not a solid phalanx of jurists, Russian, German, Hungarian, Italian, and American, fertilised the germ by correcting hasty and one-sided conclusions, suggesting opportune reforms and applications, and, most important of all, applying my ideas on the offender to his individual and social prophylaxis and cure.

Enrico Ferri was the first to perceive that the congenital epileptoid criminal did not form a single species, and that if this class was irretrievably doomed to perdition, crime in others was only a brief spell of insanity, determined by circumstances, passion, or illness. He established new types — the occasional criminal and the criminal by passion, — and transformed the basis of the penal code by asking if it were more just to make laws obey facts instead of altering facts to suit the laws, solely in order to avoid troubling the placidity of those who refused to consider this new element in the scientific field. Therefore, putting aside those abstract formulae for which high talents have panted in vain, like the thirsty traveller at the sight of the desert mirage, the advocates of the Modern School came to the conclusion that sentences should show a decrease in infamy and ferocity proportionate to the increase in length and social safety. In lieu of infamy they substituted a longer period of segregation, and for cases in which alienists were unable to decide between criminality and insanity, they advocated an intermediate institution, in which merciful treatment and social security were alike considered. They also emphasized the importance of certain measures which hitherto had been universally regarded as a pure abstraction or an unattainable desideratum — measures for the prevention of crime by tracing it to its source, divorce laws to diminish adultery, legislation of an anti-alcoholistic tendency to prevent crimes of violence, associations for destitute children, and co-operative associations to check the tendency to theft. Above all, they insisted on those regulations — unfortunately fallen into disuse — which indemnify the victim at the expense of the aggressor, in order that society, having suffered once for the crime, should not be obliged to suffer pecuniarily for the detention of the offender, solely in homage to a theoretical principle that no one believes in, according to which prison is a kind of baptismal font in whose waters sin of all kinds is washed away.

Thus the edifice of criminal anthropology, circumscribed at first, gradually extended its walls and embraced special studies on homicide, political crime, crimes connected with the banking world, crimes by women, etc.

But the first stone had been scarcely laid when from all quarters of Europe arose those calumnies and misrepresentations which always follow in the train of audacious innovations. We were accused of wishing to proclaim the impunity of crime, of demanding the release of all criminals, of refusing to take into account climatic and racial influences and of asserting that the criminal is a slave eternally chained to his instincts; whereas the Modern School, on the contrary, gave a powerful impetus to the labors of statisticians and sociologists on these very matters. This is clearly shown in the third volume of *Criminal Man*, which contains a summary of the ideas of modern criminologists and my own.

One nation, however — America — gave a warm and sympathetic reception to the ideas of the Modern School which they speedily put into practice, with the brilliant results shown by the Reformatory at Elmira, the Probation System, Juvenile Courts, and the George Junior Republic. They also initiated the practice, now in general use, of anthropological co-operation in every criminal trial of importance. . . .

11

The Theory of the Born Criminal *

Maurice Parmelee

Lombroso's conception of the born criminal grew out of his anatomical and physiological researches. He found certain malformations of the skeleton and of the viscera and several abnormalities in the physiological processes unusually prevalent among the criminals he examined, and he arrived at the conclusion that they constituted the traits of a distinct biological and anthropological type which is prone to become criminal. He also concluded, as a result of a study of the equivalents of crime among animals and among primitive men and of the traits and conduct of children, that this congenital criminal type is to a large extent an atavistic type. That is to say, he thought that many of the distinctive traits of this type are atavistic in the sense that they revert to earlier human types and to pre-human ancestors of man.

Furthermore, Lombroso studied the mental traits of this type, and arrived at the conclusion that the born criminal is morally insane or a moral imbecile (*fou moral*). It is difficult to ascertain from the terminology used by him whether he had in mind insanity or imbecility. But inasmuch as he recognized a distinct type of insane criminal, it is probable that he con-

* Reprinted from *Criminology*, New York, The Macmillan Company, 1918, 128–131. Footnotes omitted. Used by permission of the author and The Macmillan Company. See, also, C. Lombroso, *Crime, Its Causes and Remedies* (trans. by Horton), The Modern Criminal Science Series, Boston, Little, Brown & Company, 1912; E. A. Hooton, *The American Criminal*, Cambridge, Harvard University Press, 1939; *Crime and the Man*, Cambridge, Harvard University Press, 1939; E. H. Sutherland, Review of Hooton's basic study, 29 *J. Crim. L. and Criminology* (1939), 911–914; R. K. Merton and M. F. A. Montagu, "Crime and the Anthropologist," 42 *Am. Soc. Rev.* (1940), 254; W. B. Tucker, "Is There Evidence of a Physical Basis for Criminal Behavior?" 31 *J. Crim. L. and Criminology* (1940), 427–437. — Ed.

sidered the born criminal a moral imbecile. According to his theory, this moral defectiveness arises principally out of the weak sensibility of the born criminal, which makes it difficult for this type of criminal to feel sympathetically. He also concluded that many born criminals are epileptic, and that probably all of them are at least epileptoid in the sense that the disease is latent in them and may become active under favorable conditions. He then attempted to connect the moral imbecility and the epileptic tendency with the atavistic anatomical and physiological traits.

Lombroso's theory of the born criminal has created an enormous amount of discussion, criticism, and difference of opinion, which there is not the space to review here. I shall be able merely to point out some of the main defects in the theory.

To begin with, it is obvious that there can be no "born" criminal in the literal sense of that term. No person is a criminal in the strict legal sense of the term until he has committed a criminal act, and no one could commit such an act until several years after birth. Furthermore, no person is predestined from birth to become a criminal on account of his congenital traits, because criminality depends in part upon environment and social status. So that an individual with all of the distinctive traits of the "born" criminal may be born a king who is legally incapable of committing any crime, or even doing any wrong!

On the other hand, it is doubtless true that some persons are born with traits which make them peculiarly prone to commit crimes if their environment is conducive to criminal conduct, and part of the criminal class is recruited from this group. In recognition, therefore, of these powerful congenital forces for crime, there is a measure of truth in calling them born criminals. There are, however, several egregious errors in Lombroso's theory.

Lombroso seems to have been rather ignorant of the modern science of biology, and especially of the theory of heredity. This is indicated by the loose way in which he used the term "atavism." Biologists recognize that atavism, or reversion, as they usually call it, takes place when there reappears in an individual of the present day a trait of an earlier type, provided that this reappearance is due to hereditary forces. That is to say, if primitive traits which have long re-

mained dormant reassert themselves in the germ plasm at the time of conception, there is a true case of reversion. But a perusal of Lombroso's writings shows that many of the criminal traits which he calls atavistic are not hereditary in their origin, but are cases of arrested development either before or after birth. For example, this is the case when he speaks of degeneracy as a form of atavism, for most if not all of the traits he includes under this term are not congenital. The fact that the individual has them at birth does not indicate necessarily that they are congenital, for they may be the result of arrested development during the prenatal period of the life of the individual. In other cases he characterizes as atavistic certain habits which have been transmitted by social agencies. For example, he seems to regard the habit of tattooing as an atavistic trait, though tattooing is obviously a habit which could not possibly be transmitted by hereditary means.

In fact, Lombroso's exposition of his theory of the born criminal indicates that he probably believed in the hereditary transmission of acquired traits, though he nowhere explicitly states his opinion on this point. But he again and again speaks as if habits or the effects of habits are transmitted by hereditary means. The consensus of opinion among biologists today is that no acquired traits can be transmitted by hereditary means. Consequently, Lombroso was seriously in error in this respect, and this grave scientific mistake greatly vitiated the value of his theory.

Lombroso apparently believed that moral imbecility is a distinct morbid entity. This could not be so since morality is in part a social trait, but certain kinds of feeblemindedness are prone to give rise to immoral conduct. So that there is no distinct congenital immoral type, the existence of which he implied. Furthermore, he exaggerated the closeness of the relationship between epilepsy and moral imbecility, and overestimated the amount of epilepsy among criminals.

The theory of the born criminal as a biological, anthropological type is the most characteristic feature of Lombroso's classification of criminals. It is evident that there is not and could not be any such type in the strict sense of the term, and Lombroso committed some grave scientific errors in expounding his theory. However, his theory has performed a useful service in emphasizing some of the powerful hereditary factors for criminal conduct which have been overlooked by many of the writers on this subject.[1]

12

A Critique of Lombrosianism *

Charles Goring

The ends of criminological science, of all social science, must be approached across facts, and facts only. The collecting of opinion, the exercising of dialectical ingenuity, the referring to authority, the quoting of illustrative cases — these uncharted ways of the old descriptive sociologists have led only to confusion, dogma, and superstition: they must be abandoned. The discoveries of the explorer cannot be recognised until he produces a verifiable map of his journey; if the goal, professed to have been reached by the sociological pioneer, is to be accepted, he must show that the path he has pursued is one which others may follow.

[1] It should not be overlooked that Lombroso, especially in his latest works, took account of environmental influences on crime. See, for example, his *Crime, Its Causes and Remedies, op. cit.* — Ed.

* Reprinted from the Conclusion of *The English Convict*, London, H. M. Stationery Office, 1913, 370–378. British Crown Copyright. Used by permission of Her Britannic Majesty's Stationery Office. "Although, as Haeckel pointed out, Lombroso's ideas on inherited criminality would lead directly, if social Darwinian doctrine were applied, to the use of the death penalty on a grand scale as a means of freeing the human species from its malefactors by artificial selection, Lombroso held the death penalty to be the last resource in the repression of crime. He favored instead methods of readaptation of the criminals and advocated the doctrine of the symbiosis of crime, by which society would utilize the serviceable qualities and aptitudes of the malefactors." — C. B. de Quiros, *Cesare Lombroso*, 9 *Encyc. Soc. Sciences* (1933), 604. See, also, C. Goring, "The Aetiology of Crime," 64 *J. Mental Science* (1918), 129–146; E. D. Driver, "Pioneers in Criminology XIV — Charles Buckman Goring (1870–1919)," 47 *J. Crim. L., Criminology and Police Science* (1957), 515–525. — Ed.

Now, the road we have attempted to shape, during the past eight years, is paved with statistical facts; each of which, within the limits of our search, we believe to be indestructible by controversy. The credentials of our every statement will be found in the scheduled data, in the tables of analysed data, in the figures resulting from these analysed data; and, by their aid, our path may be re-traced step by step, its bearings tested, and its direction criticised. If we have gone astray anywhere, the fault can be logically demonstrated by the critic pointing the error in our data, or in the analysis of these data, or in their interpretation. But he must not dismiss our results because they may be opposed to his opinion, or to current opinion: he must enforce any condemnation he may make by the production of statistics more representative than ours, and related to a more exhaustive and accurate observation.

Let us resume our results. What is the final point of view we have attained? We need not recapitulate all the qualifying details, and minor issues, explicitly set forth at the close of every chapter. It is sufficient to restate certain broad relations, which appear to underline the genesis of crime; certain fundamental conclusions, connected with the origin of the criminal: and to contrast these with the current doctrines of criminologists.

In the first place, we were confronted with the notion of a distinct anthropological criminal type: with the idea of the criminal being such in consequence of an hereditary element in his psychic organisation, and of certain physical and mental peculiarities, which stigmatised him as predestined to evil, and which differentiated him from the morally well-conditioned person. In accordance with this notion, every individual criminal is an anomaly among mankind, by inheritance; and can be detected by his physical malformations, and mental eccentricities: the inevitable deduction being that any attempt at his reform must prove vain.

The preliminary conclusion reached by our inquiry is that this anthropological monster has no existence in fact. The physical and mental constitution of both criminal and law-abiding persons, of the same age, stature, class, and intelligence, are identical. There is no such thing as an anthropological criminal type. But, despite this negation, and upon the evidence of our statistics, it appears to be an equally indisputable fact that there is a physical, mental, and moral type of normal person who tends to be convicted of crime: that is to say, our evidence conclusively shows that, on the average, the criminal of English prisons is markedly differentiated by defective physique — as measured by stature and body weight; by defective mental capacity — as measured by general intelligence; and by an increased possession of wilful anti-social proclivities [1] — as measured apart from intelligence, by length of sentence to imprisonment.

Reviewing the general trend of our results, it would seem that the appearances, stated by anthropologists of all countries to be peculiar to criminals, are thus described because of a too separate inspection, and narrow view of the facts, by these observers. They cannot see the wood for the trees. Obsessed by preconceived beliefs, small differences of intimate structure have been uncritically accepted by them, and exaggerated to fit fantastic theories. The truths that have been overlooked are that these deviations, described as significant of criminality, are the inevitable concomitants of inferior stature and defective intelligence: both of which are the differentia of the types of persons who are selected for imprisonment. The thief, who is caught thieving, has a smaller head and a narrower forehead than the man who arrests him: but this is the case, not because he is more criminal, but because, of the two, he is the more markedly inferior in stature. The incendiary is more emotionally unstable, more lacking in control, more refractory in conduct, and more dirty in habits, etc. than the thief; and the thief is more distinguished by the above peculiarities than the forger; and all criminals display these qualities to a more marked extent than does the law-abiding public: not because any one of these classes is more criminal than another, but because of their inter-differentiation in general intelligence. On statistical evidence, one assertion can be dogmatically made: it is, that the criminal is differentiated by inferior stature, by defective intelligence and, to some extent, by his anti-social proclivities; but that, apart from these broad differences, there are no physical, mental, or moral characteristics peculiar to the inmates of English prisons. We need not re-

capitulate the social, economic, and legal selective processes which, without drawing upon theories of degeneracy or atavism, have seemed to us sufficient simple explanation of the criminal's physical and mental distinctions. The following figure, however, may assist the imagination in realising the nature and proportions of this differentiation. We may take it that 1 in 13 persons of the general population are convicted at some time of life for indictable offences. If the total adult population were made to file by in groups of 13, and, out of each group, one person was selected, who happened to be the smallest there in stature, or the most defective in intelligence, or who possessed volitional anti-social proclivities to a more marked degree than his fellows in the group — the band of individuals resulting from this selection would, in physical, mental, and moral constitution, approximate more closely to our criminal population than the residue.

The second conclusion resulting from our inquiry defines the relative importance of constitutional and environmental factors in the etiology of crime. The criminal anthropologists assert that the chief source of crime lies in the personal constitution. His physical and mental stigmata, they argue, while showing the anomalous biological origin of the lawbreaker, prove also the existence in him of a peculiar constitutional psychic quality: by reason of which he is destined from birth to do evil, and will become criminal, however favourable or unfavourable his circumstances may be. On the other hand, the criminal sociologists say that the source of crime must be sought, not in the constitution of the malefactor, but in his adverse social and economic environment. He is not born, but is made, criminal, it is contended: his physical, mental, and moral characteristics, and the ultimate fate of imprisonment these entail, are products of unfavourable circumstances; in the absence of which, even inborn criminal tendencies will fail to develop.

We have traced and measured the relation of conviction for crime in a variety of constitutional and environmental conditions: and while, with many of the former, high degrees of association have been revealed, with practically none of the latter do we discover any definite degree of relationship. Thus, as already stated, we find close bonds of association with defective

[1] We find that it is the most intelligent recidivists who are guilty of the most serious acquisitive offences.

physique and intelligence; and, to a less intimate extent, with moral defectiveness, or wilful anti-social proclivities — as demonstrated by the fact that it is the most intelligent recidivists who are guilty of the most serious acquisitive offences. We find, also, that crimes of violence are associated with the finer physique, health and muscular development, with the more marked degrees of ungovernable temper, obstinacy of purpose, and inebriety, and with the greater amount of insane and suicidal proclivity, of persons convicted of these offences; and that tall persons are relatively immune from conviction for rape; and that fraudulent offenders are relatively free from the constitutional determinants which appear to conduce to other forms of crime. Alcoholism, also, and all diseases associated with alcoholism; venereal diseases, and all conditions associated with venereal diseases; epilepsy, and insanity — appear to be constitutional determinants of crime: although, upon the evidence of our data, it would seem that these conditions, in their relation to conviction, are mainly accidental associations, depending upon the high degree of relationship between defective intelligence and crime. On the other hand, between a variety of environmental conditions examined, such as illiteracy, parental neglect, lack of employment, the stress of poverty, etc., etc., including the states of a healthy, delicate, or morbid constitution *per se*, and even the situation induced by the approach of death [2] — between these conditions and the committing of crime, we find no evidence of any significant relationship. Our second conclusion, then, is this: that, relatively to its origin in the constitution of the malefactor, and especially in his mentally defective constitution, crime is only to a trifling extent (if to any) the product of social inequalities, of adverse environment, or of other manifestations of what may be comprehensively termed the force of circumstances . . .

The fact that conviction for crime is associated, as our figures have shown, mainly with constitutional, and scarcely to any appreciable extent with circumstantial, conditions, would make the hypothesis a plausible one that the force of heredity plays some part in determining the fate of imprisonment. We have seen that the principal constitutional determinant of crime is mental defectiveness — which, admittedly, is a heritable condition; and scarcely less than 8 per cent of the population of this country are convicted for indictable offences — which could only be possible on the assumption that crime is limited to particular stocks of the community:[3] from these facts the conclusion seems inevitable that the genesis of crime, and the production of criminals, must be influenced by heredity. Our family histories of convicts bear testimony to this truth; and the fifth and final conclusion emerging from our biometric inquiry is as follows: that the criminal diathesis, revealed by the tendency to be convicted and imprisoned for crime, is influenced by the force of heredity in much the same way, and to much the same extent, as are physical and mental qualities and conditions in man . . .

Let us remember — it is nearly always forgotten — that heredity is not a spectre to be disregarded, an enemy to be dreaded; it is a universal and natural force, to be studied and measured, so that, when understood, it can be consciously directed to the welfare of human beings. The force itself is neither modifiable nor extinguishable. The force of gravity does not cease to operate when the balloon flies upward; nor is the mode of action of the wind annihilated when a ship sails in its teeth. And, similarly, the force of heredity is not extinguished when, isolated on a Pacific island, the tubercular escape the penalties of their inheritance; nor, when by appropriate physical culture, the stature of man may be increased by inches. Assuming that by the segregation of all criminals, crime might be reduced to nothing: yet parents with the least social proclivities would still go on begetting offspring who, on the average, would commit the greatest number of anti-social offences; just as, despite of physical culture exercised by everybody, the tallest offspring would, in the long run, be begotten by the tallest parents.

Yet no rational definition of the hereditary nature of crime supposes the criminal's pre-

---

[2] At all ages of life up to fifty-five the death rates of prisoners are practically identical with the general population rates.

[3] If persons convicted, at some time of life, for indictable offences, were distributed at random, every other family in the land would produce a criminal member.

destination to inevitable sin. Our own statement is that degrees of the criminal tendency possessed, to some degree, by all people, are inherited in the same way as other conditions and tendencies in men are inherited: which is to say that, in regard to constitutional qualities — feeble-mindedness, inebriety, ungovernable temper, etc., etc., — tending to affect conviction for crime, there is a degree of parental resemblance of much the same intensity as there is between parents and offspring in regard to their tendency to become diseased, or to develop, under the influence of a common environment, to a certain grade of stature. But this fact of resemblance does not argue absence of the influence of environment in the development of human beings. It is as absurd to say that, because criminal tendency is heritable, a man's conviction for crime cannot be influenced by education, as it would be to assert that, because mathematical ability is heritable, accomplishment in mathematics is independent of instruction; or that, because stature is heritable, growth is independent of nutriment and exercise. Our correlations tell us that, despite of education, heritable constitutional conditions prevail in the making of criminals; but they contain no pronouncement upon the extent to which the general standard of morality may have been raised by education. We know that to make a law-abiding citizen, two things are needed — capacity and training. Within dwells the potentiality for growth; but without stands the natural right of each child born into the world — the right to possess every opportunity of growing to his full height.

The crusade against crime may be conducted in three directions. The effort may be made to modify inherited tendency by appropriate educational measures; or else to modify opportunity for crime by segregation and supervision of the unfit; or else — and this is attacking the evil at its very root — to regulate the reproduction of those degrees of constitutional qualities — feeble-mindedness, inebriety, epilepsy, deficient social instinct, etc. — which conduce to the committing of crime. But, into whichever field we take our battle, it is of paramount importance that we should have accurate notions of the purpose of the strife, and a clear idea of the nature of the evil we are contesting. And this knowledge can be attained by facts, and by facts only . . .

13

The Role of Constitution *

Sheldon and Eleanor T. Glueck

MESOMORPHS AND DELINQUENCY

Introductory. Having reviewed the traits and factors that underlie the delinquency of all our boys — irrespective of physique type — we are now ready to integrate by physique type those influences that play a special role in the delinquency of the various body types. We recognize the tentative nature of these conclusions pending a check against other samples.

This chapter is devoted to the mesomorphs who, because of their large proportion in the total of delinquents, may be deemed the "core" of the delinquent group. In arriving at this integration we will focus on (a) the traits that have been found to differentiate the non-delinquent mesomorphs from the other body types, these comprising what may be called, in one sense, their *delinquency potential;* (b) the traits that exert a special influence on the delinquency of the mesomorphs in contrast with the other body types; (c) the sociocultural factors that exert a special influence on the delinquency of the mesomorphs as compared with their effect on the delinquency of the other physique types.

This tripartite analysis will also be applied in the succeeding chapters dealing with endomorphs, ectomorphs, and the balanced type. Although the resultant portraits will necessarily be imperfect because of the limitations of the inquiry to a selected group of traits assembled originally for the more general purposes of *Unraveling Juvenile Delinquency* without thought of a later breakdown of the data by body types, the findings should be at least suggestive concerning the implications of body structure in the prevention and control of juvenile delinquency.

Traits Distinguishing Mesomorphs from Other Physique Types. Mesomorphy, says

* Reprinted from *Physique and Delinquency*, New York, Harper and Brothers, 1956, 217–248. Used by permission of the publisher.

Exhibit 1 Traits Distinguishing Non-Delinquent Mesomorphs from Other Physique Types

TRAITS	HIGHEST (H) OR LOWEST (L) AS COMPARED WITH		
	Endo-morphs	Ecto-morphs	Balanced Type
Susceptibility to Contagion		L	
Tremors		L	
Genital Under-development	L	L	
Strength of Hand Grip	H	H	H
Tendency to Phantasy		L	L
Social Assertiveness	H		
Marked Submissiveness	L		
Fear of Failure and Defeat			H
Destructiveness		L	
Destructive-Sadistic Trends		L	
Sensitivity		L	L
Inadequacy		L	L
Uninhibited Motor Responses to Stimuli	H	H	H
Emotional Instability		L	
Aestheticism		L	
Sensuousness	L		
Conventionality	L		H
Practicality			H
Emotional Conflicts		L	

Sheldon, "means relative predominance of muscle, bone, and connective tissue. The mesomorphic physique is normally heavy, hard, and rectangular in outline. Bone and muscle are prominent and the skin is made thick by a heavy underlying connective tissue. The entire bodily economy is dominated, relatively, by tissues derived from the *mesodermal* embryonic layer." [1]

This description of the mesomorphic body type or norm suggests physical strength. Has evidence of this emerged from our inquiry?

As far as clinical indications permit, it is reasonable to infer that mesomorphs are in fact more vigorous than the other body types. This conclusion is based on the fact that, as compared with other physiques, mesomorphs are as a group found to have been less susceptible to contagion in childhood, less burdened by disorders of which tremors are symptomatic, have better developed genitals, and have more strength in their hands. Certain of their char-

acteristics are, then, in accord with the underlying organismal pattern of this physique type.

Turning to psychologic traits (some derived from Rorschach Tests and some from psychiatric interviews), it is evident from Exhibit 1 that mesomorphic non-delinquents are strikingly different from one or more of the other physique types. They are less sensitive, less aesthetic, and less sensuous; they have less of a tendency to phantasy, suffer less from feelings of inadequacy, and are less destructive and destructive-sadistic. Further, they are more practical, more socially assertive, markedly less submissive to authority, and not as convention-bound as the endomorphs, but less so than the ectomorphs, and they are more fearful of failure and defeat than boys of balanced physique.

In dynamisms, mesomorphic non-delinquents as opposed to one or more of the other physique types are found to be less unstable emotionally, less burdened by emotional conflicts, and less inhibited in motor responses to stimuli (i.e., more likely to express their tensions in action rather than to bottle them up). In this latter regard they differ from all the other body types.

[1] W. H. Sheldon, *The Varieties of Human Physique*, New York, Harper and Brothers, 1940, p. 5.

It should already be somewhat obvious that unless channeled toward socially acceptable goals, such traits might well furnish the strength, daring, and enterprise, together with the dynamic tendency to unrestrained action, that are involved in much delinquency, and may hence explain the high proportion of mesomorphs in our delinquent group. In brief, the mesomorphs apparently have a higher delinquency *potential* than the other body types.

Traits Contributing Selectively to Delinquency of Mesomorphs. The reader is reminded that a determination of the body types on which a particular trait has a greater delinquency-propelling force than on another was arrived at by comparing the quantum of difference in percentages of the incidence of a particular trait between the delinquents and the non-delinquents of each body type (by the method of multiple comparisons, described on pp. 33, 278–83).

There are in fact 9 traits in all among the 67 we studied that have been found to exert a greater influence on the delinquency of mesomorphs than on that of one or more of the other body types: susceptibility to contagion, low verbal intelligence, feeling of not being taken care of, destructiveness, destructive-sadistic trends, receptive trends, feelings of inadequacy, emotional instability, and emotional conflicts.

Exhibit 2 makes it evident at a glance that, in the considerable majority of instances, the greater impact of certain traits on the conduct of the sturdy mesomorphs contrasts most sharply with their lesser impact on the delinquency of the fragile ectomorphs. In fact, in only one trait — receptive trends (the more or less unconscious expectation that others — people, society, God — will take care of one) — is the contrast exclusively with another physique type, the balanced, while in the feeling of not being taken care of, it is with all three of the other body types.

Comparison of Exhibit 2 with Exhibit 1 reveals six of the nine traits though significantly *less* characteristic of *non-delinquent* mesomorphs than of one or more of the other body types (largely ectomorphs), emerge now as more markedly associated with the delinquency of mesomorphs. Susceptibility to the contagious diseases of childhood is one such trait. It constitutes more of a danger signal of delinquency when atypically occurring in mesomorphs than in ectomorphs. Destructiveness (the tendency

Exhibit 2 *Traits Contributing Selectively to Delinquency of Mesomorphs*			
TRAITS	**HIGHEST (H) OR LOWEST (L) AS COMPARED WITH**		
	Endo-morphs	Ecto-morphs	Balanced Type
Susceptibility to Contagion		H	
Extreme Restlessness in Early Childhood		L	
Cyanosis	L		
Dermographia		L	
Strength of Hand Grip			L
Low Verbal Intelligence		H	
High Performance Intelligence	L		L
Ambivalence to Authority	L		
Feeling of Not Being Taken Care of	H	H	H
Good Surface Contact with Others	L		
Destructiveness		H	
Feeling of Being Able to Manage Own Life	L		
Receptive Trends			H
Destructive-Sadistic Trends		H	
Inadequacy		H	
Emotional Instability		H	
Emotional Conflicts		H	

to hurt, to destroy) and destructive-sadistic drives, both of which are likewise *less* characteristic of mesomorphic youngsters than of ectomorphs, are also more likely to result in antisocial behavior when occurring in mesomorphs than in ectomorphs. This is the case, too, as regards feelings of inadequacy, emotional instability, and emotional conflicts. All six traits are *less* characteristic of non-delinquent mesomorphs than of one or more of the other body types, notably of ectomorphs, yet exert a greater criminogenic influence.

A reasonable hypothesis to account for the excessive association of such traits with the delinquency of mesomorphs would appear to be that traits *atypical of this constitutional "host,"* when they do exist in mesomorphs, tend to bring about some sort of internal disharmony. This (together with traits that are generally criminogenic) leads reactively or indirectly to delinquency. Some such hypothesis is worthy of exploration on larger samples of cases of each physique type.

So much for the six traits that are typical of the mesomorphic norm.

The greater involvement of the three remaining traits in the delinquency of mesomorphs than in that of one or another body type, namely, low verbal intelligence, feeling of not being taken care of, and receptive (oral) trends, is less readily explained. These traits, unlike the six just described, are not found to vary in incidence among the body types of the non-delinquents despite their dominant criminogenic impact on the mesomorphs.

Expectedly, a defect of intellect (reflected in low verbal intelligence) is more likely to embroil in delinquency youngsters of the energetic, outlet-seeking body type than other boys.

As for the feeling of not being taken care of, this seems to have a more profound effect on delinquency among mesomorphs than on any other body type. This trait reflects a lack of active interest on the part of others (especially of parents) in situations in which the child feels himself entitled to such interest. It should be pointed out that this feeling plays far less of a role in the delinquency of all the other body types. Why it operates so heavily on mesomorphs we can only surmise. It seems reasonable to assume, however, that mesomorphs, who are normally energetic and dynamic, tend to seek active outlets for the tensions and frustra-

tions that are engendered in them by the feeling of parental neglect.

Finally, as to receptive (oral) trends, the greater role of this trait in the delinquency of mesomorphs (as contrasted with boys of balanced physique) may be clarified if we remember that the expression of receptive trends as a typical mode of satisfaction reflects a more or less unconscious expectation that one will somehow be taken care of by others and therefore need not make any effort to assume responsibilities. This tendency, according to Schachtel (*Unraveling*, p. 235) may take a passive form or it may take a more active form leading to outwardly expressed greed or to attempts to secure the desired object without effort (stealing) or without assuming any obligations. It could reasonably be postulated that because of the great need of mesomorphs for energy outlets they are less likely to be passive than other boys not so endowed, and that receptive trends in this physique habitus are more likely to seek an *active* expression.

In connection with such speculative explanations of the impact of certain traits on the delinquency of a particular physique type, it must of course be borne in mind that persistent delinquency cannot be attributed to any single trait, be it one of ideation, attitude, feeling, or emotional mechanism. There is always an interplay of numerous influences in the misconduct of both the individual delinquent and of groups of delinquents. It is the piling up of such pressures to a degree where they over-balance the internal and external monitors and inhibitors of antisocial conduct which results in prohibited action. It must not be forgotten, further, that those traits which have not been found, by statistical computation, to exert a significantly diverse influence among the body types but which do significantly distinguish delinquents from non-delinquents as a whole, are also involved in the total dynamic interplay of organism and environment that results in delinquency.

It should be noted (Exhibit 3) that of the nine traits found to exert a significantly heavier criminogenic impact on mesomorphs than on one or another of the remaining physique types, four or more were found to be present in 75 per cent of the delinquent mesomorphs in contrast with only 19 per cent of the non-delinquent mesomorphs; and three or more of the traits characterize 88 per cent of the delinquent

Exhibit **3**   *Distribution of Nine Traits Having Greater*
Delinquency-Inducing Impact on Mesomorphs

NUMBER OF DELINQUENCY INDUCING TRAITS PRESENT	139 DELINQUENT MESOMORPHS			70 NON-DELINQUENT MESOMORPHS		
	Number	% of Total		Number	% of Total	
		Actual	Cumulative		Actual	Cumulative
9	0	0.00%	0.00%	0	0.00%	0.00%
8	3	2.16	2.16	0	0.00	0.00
7	11	7.91	10.07	0	0.00	0.00
6	27	19.42	29.49	1	1.43	1.43
5	40	28.78	58.27	4	5.71	7.14
4	23	16.55	74.82	8	11.43	18.57
3	18	12.95	87.77	13	18.57	37.14
2	7	5.04	92.81	17	24.29	61.43
1	8	5.75	98.56	11	15.71	77.14
0	2	1.44	100.00	16	22.86	100.00

mesomorphs as compared with 37 per cent of the non-delinquent mesomorphs. Evidently, therefore, the greater effect of the traits in question on the delinquency of mesomorphs depends, ordinarily, on the cumulative impact of at least three traits.

Sociocultural Factors Contributing Selectively to Delinquency of Mesomorphs. Exhibit 4 again reveals the phenomenon previously noted of a sharp contrast between mesomorphs and ecto-

morphs, this time in respect to differences in the sociocultural forces that affect their behavior. Yet there is a striking difference; for while certain traits have an excessive influence on the delinquency of mesomorphs, the factors of home and family life have more of an effect on the antisocial behavior of ectomorphs than of mesomorphs.

Of the 42 sociocultural factors included in the present work, only three are found to have

Exhibit **4**   *Sociocultural Factors Contributing Selectively to*
Delinquency of Mesomorphs

SOCIOCULTURAL FACTORS	HIGHEST (H) OR LOWEST (L) AS COMPARED WITH		
	Endomorphs	Ectomorphs	Balanced Type
Emotional Disturbance in Father		L	
Gainful Employment of Mother		L	
Careless Household Routine	H		
Lack of Cultural Refinement in Home		L	
Broken Home		L	
Rearing by Parent Substitute		L	
Low Conduct Standards of Family		L	
Incompatibility of Parents		L	
Family Group Recreations Lacking	H		
Meager Recreational Facilities in Home	H		
Lack of Family Cohesiveness		L	
Mother Not Attached to Boy		L	
Siblings Not Attached to Boy		L	
Careless Supervision by Mother		L	

a greater influence on the delinquency of meso-morphs (in contrast to endomorphs only): careless household routine, lack of family group recreations, and meagerness of recreational facilities in the home. It seems reasonable to attribute this outcome to the fact that meso-morphs, who are usually of healthy, vigorous body build, and are dynamic and outgoing in their impulses, are more likely than other boys (especially endomorphs) to overreact to a lack of recreational facilities in disordered homes and, because of their greater vigor and energy, to seek adventure and recreation elsewhere.

It should be noted (Exhibit 5) that of the three sociocultural factors found to exert a significantly heavier criminogenic impact on mesomorphs than on one or another body type, at least two were present in 74 per cent of the delinquent mesomorphs as contrasted with 39 per cent of the non-delinquent mesomorphs.

But certain aspects of their home environ-ment have *less* of an effect on the delinquency of mesomorphs than on that of ectomorphs (the fragile, sensitive body type): emotional dis-turbance in the father, working mothers, care-less supervision of boy by mother, indifference or hostility of mothers and/or of brothers and sisters to the boy, lack of cultural refinement in the home, broken homes, rearing by substitute parents, low conduct standards in the family, quarrelsome parents, disharmony in the family group.

Clearly, these provocations to childhood anx-iety and insecurity, with their resultant dep-rivation of affection and their building up of a feeling of isolation, do not exert nearly as po-tent an influence on mesomorphs as on ecto-morphs. The more rugged constitution of meso-morphs and their generally hardier temperamen-tal makeup are evidently powerful enough to withstand many of the assaults on emotional life which exert a more damaging influence on the fragile, sensitive, overreactive ectomorphs.

Mesomorphic Constitution and Delinquency. In considering the evidence regarding the role of body structure in the delinquency of the pre-dominantly mesomorphic physique, there is a permeative difficulty that must be kept in mind. Apart from the fact that the inquiry covers only a relatively modest number of traits and factors that are more or less involved in the totality of criminogenic influences, it should be pointed out that there is probably no exact point-to-point "stimulus–response" nexus between any par-ticular criminogenic trait, or even small group of traits, and any specific sociocultural element or group of elements. It is the *total organism* in its morphologic, temperamental, and charac-terial aspects that is involved in the antisocial reaction of any physique type to a battery of external influences. Hence, not only the rela-tively few traits which have been found to have a *greater* association with the delinquency of mesomorphs than of one or more of the re-maining physique types, but also the ones that are quite *uniformly* causal, and even the traits found to characterize the *"normal"* (i.e., the non-delinquent) mesomorphs must be taken into account in assessing the behavioral response of the predominantly mesomorphic type to the threats, tensions, and unwholesome provoca-tions of home and family life.

It remains true, nevertheless, that our data per-mit of at least tentative answers to two questions: (*a*) How account for the finding in *Unraveling* that there is a 60 per cent incidence of meso-morphs among the delinquents in comparison with only 12–14 per cent of each of the other

Exhibit **5** *Distribution of Three Sociocultural Factors Having Greater Impact on Delinquency of Mesomorphs*

NUMBER OF DELINQUENCY INDUCING FACTORS PRESENT	289 DELINQUENT MESOMORPHS			146 NON-DELINQUENT MESOMORPHS		
	Number	% of Total		Number	% of Total	
		Actual	Cumula-tive		Actual	Cumula-tive
3	121	41.87%	41.87%	28	19.18%	19.18%
2	92	31.83	73.70	29	19.86	39.04
1	49	16.96	90.66	48	32.88	71.92
0	27	9.34	100.00	41	28.08	100.00

body types? (*b*) Why do some mesomorphs become delinquent, others not?

(*a*) Regarding the reason for the excess of mesomorphs among our delinquents, the current inquiry has revealed that this physique type is more highly characterized by traits particularly suitable to the commission of acts of aggression (physical strength, energy, insensitivity, the tendency to express tensions and frustrations in action), together with a relative freedom from such inhibitions to antisocial adventures as feelings of inadequacy, marked submissiveness to authority, emotional instability, and the like.

It must further be kept in mind that although recognizing the greater delinquency potential of mesomorphs, the admixture of the *uniformly* criminogenic ("common ground") traits with those affecting the physique types variously, may result in more widespread delinquency among mesomorphs than in other body types. For example, a trait such as adventurousness, when it occurs in boys of the strong, energetic, and uncontrolled mesomorphic physique, may well have more of a bearing on their behavior than when occurring in the less dynamic endomorph; emotional conflict may well have a different destiny in the dynamic mesomorph than in the sensitive but inhibited ectomorph.

(*b*) As for the question of which boys among mesomorphs actually become delinquent, the striking finding is that most of the traits that have a special impact on the delinquency of mesomorphs are *not usually typical of that physique*. It would seem reasonable to postulate that those mesomorphs in whom traits alien to the constitutional host are present are the ones more likely to be selected for delinquency. But in large measure, the uniformly criminogenic ("common ground") traits of course also exert an influence in selecting from among all mesomorphs those who will become delinquent, as they do in the case of the other physique types.

ENDOMORPHS AND DELINQUENCY

Introductory. In the prior chapter we brought into focus the traits that distinguish the non-delinquent mesomorphs from one or another body type and also the traits and socio-cultural factors that contribute selectively to the delinquency of the mesomorphs. As the mesomorphs have proven to be the "core type" among the delinquents, it is of major interest to determine how the other physique types compare with them.

Traits Distinguishing Endomorphs from Other Physique Types. Unlike mesomorphy, in which there is an emphasis on bone and musle, "*Endomorphy* means relative predominance of soft roundness throughout the various regions of the body. When endomorphy is dominant the digestive viscera are massive and tend relatively to dominate the bodily economy. The digestive viscera are derived principally from the *endodermal* embryonic layer." [2]

First of all, what evidence is there of difference between the "norm" of this body type and the mesomorphic?

As regards physical endowment, Exhibit 6 shows that genital underdevelopment is more characteristic of endomorphs than of mesomorphs; and that endomorphs do not have as much strength of hand as do mesomorphs.

As regards traits of temperament, endomorphs are found to be less socially assertive and more submissive to authority than mesomorphs. Further, they are more inhibited in motor responses to stimuli, that is, less likely than mesomorphs to resolve their tensions in action. Although endomorphs are more sensuous than mesomorphs (and than all the other body types) they are also more conventional in their ideas and behavior.

These distinguishing characteristics appear consistent with the soft, round endomorphic physique as opposed to the muscular, outgoing mesomorphic type and would seem to provide a lower delinquency *potential* among the endomorphs as contrasted with the mesomorphs.

The contrast in respect to some of these traits of the endomorphic norm is not only with mesomorphs but with other physique types. Thus they are, as a group, not only less well developed genitally than mesomorphs, but also than boys of balanced physique. Not only are they more markedly submissive to authority, more sensuous, and more conventional than mesomorphs, but, in these respects, they are likewise more so than ectomorphs. And it is to be especially noted that endomorphs are more sensuous and more conventional than boys of *all* the other body types.

It seems clear then that lesser energy, greater inhibition, greater submissiveness to authority,

---

[2] *Ibid.*

Exhibit **6** *Traits Distinguishing Non-Delinquent Endomorphs from Other Physique Types*

TRAITS	HIGHEST (H) OR LOWEST (L) AS COMPARED WITH		
	Meso-morphs	Ecto-morphs	Balanced Type
Susceptibility to Contagion		L	
Cyanosis		L	
Tremors		L	
Genital Under-development	H		H
Strength of Hand Grip	L		
Social Assertiveness	L	L	
Marked Submissiveness	H	L	L
Fear of Failure and Defeat			
Destructiveness		L	
Marked Dependence on Others			H
Masochistic Trends			H
Destructive-Sadistic Trends		L	
Vivacity		L	L
Sensitivity		L	L
Uninhibited Motor Responses to Stimuli	L		
Emotional Instability		L	
Aestheticism		L	
Sensuousness	H	H	H
Acquisitiveness		L	
Conventionality	H	H	H

and a greater tendency to conventional modes of thinking and acting, are characteristics providing, at the outset, a lower *delinquency potential* among endomorphs than among mesomorphs.

Which traits are, however, in fact found to exert a special criminogenic impact on endomorphs in contrast with mesomorphs?

Traits Contributing Selectively to Delinquency of Endomorphs. Examination of Exhibit 7 reveals a significant difference in the impact of six characteristics on the delinquency of endomorphs as contrasted with mesomorphs: cyanosis, high performance intelligence, ambivalence to authority, feeling of being able to manage own life, good surface contact with others, feeling of not being taken care of.

In respect to cyanosis (impaired oxygenization of the blood probably reflecting some neurological imbalance), this condition occurring in endomorphs appears to constitute more of a danger signal of delinquency than when it exists in mesomorphs, despite the fact that endomorphs are not found to be normally (i.e., among non-

delinquents) more cyanotic as a group than mesomorphs.

Regarding the ability to manipulate concrete things (high performance intelligence), this too has more of a bearing on the delinquency of endomorphs than of mesomorphs. It will be recalled from Chapter XI that, on the contrary, low verbal intelligence rather than high performance intelligence is more likely to embroil *mesomorphs* in delinquency.

As to temperamental and emotional traits, ambivalence to authority in endomorphs plays more of a role in their delinquent behavior than when it occurs in mesomorphs. This is true also of the feeling of being able to manage one's own affairs.

There is one other trait which exerts a greater influence on the delinquency of endomorphs than of mesomorphs — good surface contact with others.

However, the feeling of not being taken care of, has *less* of an influence on the delinquency of endomorphs than of mesomorphs.

Thus there are five traits which are found to

Exhibit **7**   *Traits Contributing Selectively to Delinquency of Endomorphs*

TRAITS	HIGHEST (H) OR LOWEST (L) AS COMPARED WITH		
	Meso-morphs	Ecto-morphs	Balanced Type
Cyanosis	H		
High Performance Intelligence	H		
Ambivalence to Authority	H		
Feeling of Not Being Taken Care of	L		
Fear of Failure and Defeat			L
Good Surface Contact with Others	H	H	
Marked Dependence on Others			L
Feeling of Being Able to Manage Own Life	H		

exert an excessive influence on the delinquency of endomorphs as contrasted with mesomorphs. Of these (Exhibit 8), four or five are present in 48 per cent of the *delinquent* endomorphs and 11 per cent of the *non-delinquent* endomorphs; at least three in 68 per cent of the delinquent endomorphs as compared with their presence in 40 per cent of the non-delinquent endomorphs. Evidently, therefore, the criminogenic influence of the traits in question does not depend on the presence of any one trait but rather on the cumulative impact of at least three traits.

With one exception (cyanosis), the traits that have a distinctive bearing on the delinquency of endomorphs as contrasted with mesomorphs are not found to differ significantly in incidence among *non-delinquent* endomorphs and mesomorphs.

It is to be noted from Exhibits 2 and 7 that the traits which contribute selectively to the delinquency of the endomorphs are not the same as those which exert a special criminogenic influence on mesomorphs. Also, Exhibit 6 reveals that what might be called *temperamental disharmony* is less related to the delinquency of endomorphs than of mesomorphs.

Sociocultural Factors Contributing Selectively to Delinquency of Endomorphs as Contrasted with Mesomorphs. Consultation of Exhibit 9 strikingly reveals that, in contrast to the mesomorphs, on whom three factors of home and family exert a greater delinquency-inducing influence than they do on the endomorphs, not one of the sociocultural factors studied is found to have more influence on the delinquency of endomorphs than of mesomorphs. On the con-

Exhibit **8**   *Distribution of Five Traits Having Greater Delinquency Inducing Impact on Endomorphs*

NUMBER OF DELINQUENCY INDUCING TRAITS PRESENT	31 DELINQUENT ENDOMORPHS			35 NON-DELINQUENT ENDOMORPHS		
	Number	% of Total		Number	% of Total	
		Actual	Cumulative		Actual	Cumulative
5	4	12.90%	12.90%	0	0.00%	0.00%
4	11	35.48	48.38	4	11.43	11.43
3	6	19.35	67.73	10	28.57	40.00
2	8	25.81	93.54	13	37.14	77.14
1	1	3.23	96.77	7	20.00	97.14
0	1	3.23	100.00	1	2.86	100.00

Exhibit **9** *Sociocultural Factors Contributing Selectively to Delinquency of Endomorphs*

SOCIOCULTURAL FACTORS	HIGHEST (H) OR LOWEST (L) AS COMPARED WITH		
	Meso-morphs	Ecto-morphs	Balanced Type
Gainful Employment of Mother		L	
Careless Household Routine	L		
Incompatibility of Parents		L	
Family Group Recreations Lacking	L		
Meager Recreational Facilities in Home	L		
Lack of Family Cohesiveness		L	
Siblings Not Attached to Boy			H
Unsuitable Discipline by Father		L	

trary, the fat, soft endomorphs *underreact* to certain unwholesome conditions in their home life which have a special influence on the delinquency of the mesomorphs: namely, a hit-or-miss routine in the household, absence of family group recreations, and insufficient provision of recreational opportunities in the home.

However, lack of attachment of brothers and sisters to them is more involved in the delinquency of endomorphs than of boys of balanced type. The reason for this is obscure. It may be speculated that the endomorphs are excessively in need of affection; and in seeking companionship to substitute for that denied by brothers and sisters, they are likely to get into trouble.

Endomorphic Constitution and Delinquency. What conclusions can be drawn from the foregoing analysis of traits and sociocultural factors having a special influence on the delinquency of endomorphs in contrast (largely) with mesomorphs?

As in the case of mesomorphs, it is not possible to arrive at definitive answers solely on the basis of the small number of traits found within the limitations of this inquiry to exert a special influence on the delinquency of endomorphs. The distinctive traits of the endomorphic *non-delinquents* must be taken into account, for these enter as *potentials* in the total dynamic system that ultimately determines the much lower incidence of delinquency among endomorphs than among mesomorphs. These endomorphic traits, as opposed to those present in the mesomorphic norm, would not appear to be useful in delinquent activity.

For example, the more marked tendency of endomorphs to submit to authority is inconsistent with the enterprise and daring required for so much of delinquent activity. Their greater tendency to conventional modes of thinking and behaving are bulwarks against antisocial activity. Their lesser assertiveness and lesser tendency to work off their emotional tensions in action would also account for the far lower participation of endomorphs than of mesomorphs in delinquent activity. While endomorphs are the most sensuous (self-indulgent) of all the physique types, this might at times impel them to theft for the satisfaction of appetites but is not consistent with the more dangerous delinquent escapades.

These traits are, in a nutshell, *not conducive to a career of criminalistic aggression.* They are better suited to one of law-abidingness. Endomorphs, in other words, have a *lower delinquency potential* than mesomorphs, who are typically energetic and outgoing.

It should be emphasized that this explanation is more in the nature of a reasonable hypothesis than a definitive conclusion, based as it necessarily is on incomplete evidence. There is enough probative value in it, however, to make it well worth pursuing further on a much larger sample of cases.

As for the traits that are found to have a distinctive bearing on the delinquency of endomorphs, they are not numerous — five in all; and they all play more of a role in the delinquency of endomorphs than of mesomorphs. But not one of the factors of home and family which exert a special impact on delinquency in other body types is especially involved in impelling endomorphs to delinquency as compared with mesomorphs. On the contrary, the three factors of home and family life which are influential in the delinquency of mesomorphs exert a distinctly *lesser* influence on the endomorphs.

In brief, the relatively low incidence of endomorphic delinquents in contrast with mesomorphic delinquents is attributable essentially to the characteristics that are typical of the soft, round, easy-going endomorphic norm and which by their very nature preclude excessive delinquency. It is rather to the traits and factors that furnish the "common ground" of delinquency-inducing influences described in Chapter X to which we must look for explanation of such delinquency as does exist among endomorphs.

ECTOMORPHS AND DELINQUENCY

Introductory. We turn now to the ectomorphs, whom we have already noted as contrasting most sharply with mesomorphs not only in their general characteristics, but in the traits and sociocultural factors that have a bearing on their delinquency. We are interested to throw light on why they constitute only 14.4 per cent of the delinquent group as contrasted with 60.1 per cent of mesomorphic delinquents.

Traits Distinguishing Ectomorphs from Other Physique Types. Ectomorphy has been defined as involving "relative predominance of linearity and fragility . . . In proportion to his mass, the ectomorph has the greatest surface area and hence relatively the greatest sensory exposure to the outside world. Relative to his mass he also has the largest brain and central nervous system. In a sense, therefore, his bodily economy is relatively dominated by tissues derived from the *ectodermal* embryonic layer." [3]

Such a fragile constitutional type would hardly be likely to have many traits shown to distinguish mesomorphs from other body types, but would on the contrary be likely to possess traits not generally associated with the robust, energetic mesomorphic type.

What picture of the normal (i.e., *non-delinquent*) ectomorphic body type emerges from the analysis of the tables?

In Exhibit 10 will be found not only significant contrasts in the characteristics of ectomorphs and mesomorphs but also between the ectomorphs and endomorphs and, to a far lesser extent, the balanced physique.

First, in regard to clinical findings, ectomorphs are as a group more likely to be subject to tremors than mesomorphs. They are more susceptible to the contagious diseases of childhood than all other body types. Their genitalia (like those of the endomorphs) are less fully developed than those of mesomorphs. And (like the endomorphs) they do not as a group have as great strength of hand grip as mesomorphs.

So far, then, the picture suggests less physical sturdiness than in the mesomorphs.

The temperamental traits of the ectomorphic norm suggest a more delicately organized innate system than in mesomorphs. Thus, ectomorphs are more inclined to phantasy than mesomorphs; they are more sensitive and more aesthetic and have a greater tendency to feel inadequate than mesomorphs. They are less stable emotionally, not only than mesomorphs but than the other two physique types; and a greater proportion of them than of mesomorphs are prone to emotional conflict. Ectomorphs are, further, more inhibited in motor responses to stimuli, tending to "bottle up" their impulses instead of resolving their tensions in action as do the mesomorphs. Ectomorphs are less conventional in ideas and conduct than mesomorphs. As a group, ectomorphs are also more destructive and sadistic than mesomorphs. Finally, ectomorphs are not as practical as mesomorphs.

While the basic contrast is between ectomorphs and mesomorphs, secondary contrasts exist differentiating ectomorphs from endomorphs and from the balanced type.

As distinguished from *endomorphs*, ectomorphs are more susceptible to contagion, more cyanotic, and more prone to conditions of which tremors are symptomatic. Apart from these clinical signs, ectomorphs are psychologically different from endomorphs in that they are more sensitive and aesthetic and less sensuous. They are more destructive and sadistic. They are less stable emotionally. They are less conventional in their ideas and behavior than endomorphs and more acquisitive. Ectomorphs are more socially assertive and more vivacious than endomorphs and not as markedly submissive.

³ *Ibid.,* 5–6.

Exhibit **10** *Traits Distinguishing Non-Delinquent Ectomorphs from Other Physique Types*

TRAITS	HIGHEST (H) OR LOWEST (L) AS COMPARED WITH		
	Meso-morphs	Endo-morphs	Balanced Type
Susceptibility to Contagion	H	H	H
Cyanosis		H	
Tremors	H	H	
Genital Under-development	H		
Strength of Hand Grip	L		
Tendency to Phantasy	H		
Social Assertiveness		H	
Marked Submissiveness		L	
Fear of Failure and Defeat			H
Destructiveness	H	H	
Destructive-Sadistic Trends	H	H	
Vivacity		H	
Sensitivity	H	H	
Inadequacy	H		
Uninhibited Motor Responses to Stimuli	L		
Emotional Instability	H	H	H
Aestheticism	H	H	
Sensuousness		L	H
Acquisitiveness		H	H
Conventionality	L	L	
Practicality	L		
Emotional Conflicts	H		H

In contrast with the *balanced* type, ectomorphs are more susceptible to childhood contagions, more sensuous (albeit less so than endomorphs), more acquisitive, more unstable emotionally, more fearful of failure and defeat, and more prone to emotional conflicts.

The sketch of the non-delinquent ectomorphs reflects characteristics that contrast largely with those of mesomorphs and endomorphs. In the ectomorphic body type there appears to be less vitality, greater sensitivity and aestheticism; a greater tendency to emotional disturbance; greater acquisitiveness; less conventionality in ideas and behavior particularly in contrast with the mesomorphs. The general impression is gained of a *less smooth functioning and less well-integrated organism, one more susceptible to "the slings and arrows of outrageous fortune" and finding outlets for frustrations not in action but in internal emotional tension with resultant neurotic symptoms.* While there are only six traits that distinguish mesomorphs from one or another of the physique types, there are 17

which distinguish the ectomorphs from the others.

Certainly, *the traits that are more characteristic of the ectomorphic norm (non-delinquents) than of the mesomorphic are, by and large, not of a kind involving the vigor, daring, enterprise, and "acting out" of impulse necessary for adventures in delinquency.* It may be concluded, therefore, that the *delinquency potential* of the ectomorphic physique type is much lower than that of mesomorphs. This probably explains, in part, not only the lesser incidence of delinquency in this body type than in the mesomorphic, but also the finding in *Unraveling* that the ectomorphic is the only body type in which the proportion of delinquents was substantially *lower* than among the non-delinquent controls.

In the light of these findings we are ready to consider the syndrome of traits that have in fact been found to exert a greater influence on the delinquency of ectomorphs than on that of other body types.

Traits Contributing Selectively to Delinquency

Exhibit **11** *Traits Contributing Selectively to Delinquency of Ectomorphs*

TRAITS	HIGHEST (H) OR LOWEST (L) AS COMPARED WITH		
	Meso-morphs	Endo-morphs	Balanced Type
Susceptibility to Contagion	L		L
Extreme Restlessness in Early Childhood	H		
Dermographia	H		
Low Verbal Intelligence	L		
Feeling of Not Being Taken Care of	L		
Good Surface Contact with Others		L	
Destructiveness	L		
Receptive Trends			H
Destructive-Sadistic Trends	L		
Inadequacy	L		
Emotional Instability	L		
Sensuousness			L
Emotional Conflicts	L		

of Ectomorphs. From Exhibit 11 it becomes evident that extreme restlessness in early childhood, when occurring in boys of ectomorphic physique, is more likely to be a forerunner of delinquency than when it occurs in mesomorphs. The same is true of the clinical sign of skin sensitivity (dermographia). These are the only two traits which contribute significantly more to the delinquency of ectomorphs than of mesomorphs. The physical conditions reflected in these two traits, together with the overly sensitive temperament of ectomorphs, render them somehow especially vulnerable.

On the other hand, it is to be noted that, by and large, the traits that have a greater bearing on the delinquency of mesomorphs than on one or more of the other body types, have *less* to do with the delinquency of ectomorphs: namely, susceptibility to contagious diseases, low verbal intelligence, the feeling of not being taken care of, destructiveness, destructive-sadistic trends, feelings of inadequacy, emotional instability, emotional conflicts. With only two exceptions (low verbal intelligence and feeling of not being taken care of) *ectomorphs as a group normally are more often than mesomorphs characterized by the very traits that contribute so heavily to the delinquency of mesomorphs.*

Turning now to a comparison of ectomorphs with endomorphs and boys of balanced type, despite the fact that ectomorphs differ as mark-

edly from endomorphs (the soft, round physique) as from mesomorphs (the physique heavily endowed with bone and muscle), not one trait among the 67 studied is found to contribute significantly more to the delinquency of ectomorphs than of endomorphs. But receptive (oral) trends (a tendency often expressed in a more or less unconscious expectation that others — people, society, God — will take care of one) seem to have more of a part in the delinquency of ectomorphs than in that of boys of balanced type.

Of the three traits found to exert a greater criminogenic impact on ectomorphs than on one or another body type (Exhibit 12) — extreme restlessness in early childhood, dermographia, receptive trends — two or three were present in 61 per cent of the delinquent ectomorphs in contrast with 24 per cent of the non-delinquent ectomorphs.

Sociocultural Factors Contributing Selectively to Delinquency of Ectomorphs. Turning to the criminogenic influence on ectomorphs of what must be regarded as unfavorable environmental conditions (largely in home and family life), it becomes strikingly clear from Exhibit 13 that *overreactivity* is the keynote to the antisocial response of this more fragile and sensitive physique type to unfavorable family conditions, in contrast, largely, with the lesser effect of these same circumstances and conditions on the de-

Exhibit **12** *Distribution of Three Traits Having Greater Delinquency Inducing Impact on Ectomorphs*

NUMBER OF DELINQUENCY INDUCING TRAITS PRESENT	64 DELINQUENT ECTOMORPHS			168 NON-DELINQUENT ECTOMORPHS		
	Number	% of Total		Number	% of Total	
		Actual	Cumulative		Actual	Cumulative
3	9	14.06%	14.06%	4	2.38%	2.38%
2	30	46.88	60.94	37	22.02	24.40
1	20	31.25	92.19	89	52.98	77.38
0	5	7.81	100.00	38	22.62	100.00

linquency of mesomorphs. All but three of the fifteen factors that have been found to have a varied influence on the delinquency of boys of the four body types exert a selective criminogenic impact of ectomorphs largely in contrast with their significantly *lesser* involvement in the delinquency of mesomorphs.

Thus, ectomorphs are more likely than mesomorphs to become delinquent if they are the sons of emotionally disturbed fathers and/or working mothers, of mothers who give them little personal supervision; if they are reared in homes lacking cultural refinement and in which the conduct standards are low; if they have grossly incompatible parents; if they belong to families not unified in deed and spirit; if they are deprived of warm affection from their mothers and brothers and sisters: if their homes

are broken, by death, separation, or desertion of parents; if they are reared by parent substitutes.

All such unwholesome influences of hearth and home are more likely to be conducive to delinquency in the more delicately structured ectomorphs than in the sturdier mesomorphs.

Apart from this major contrast, the ectomorphs were also found to respond differently than the endomorphs to certain potentially injurious home influences. Ectomorphs are evidently more likely to become delinquents than are endomorphs if subjected to paternal discipline which is not firm and kindly; and they have a greater tendency to misbehavior than endomorphs (and mesomorphs) if their mothers work, if they are reared in discordant homes, and

Exhibit **13** *Sociocultural Factors Contributing Selectively to Delinquency of Ectomorphs*

SOCIOCULTURAL FACTORS	HIGHEST (H) OR LOWEST (L) AS COMPARED WITH		
	Meso-morphs	Endo-morphs	Balanced Type
Emotional Disturbance in Father	H		
Gainful Employment of Mother	H	H	
Lack of Cultural Refinement in Home	H		
Broken Home	H		
Rearing by Parent Substitute	H		
Low Conduct Standards of Family	H		H
Incompatibility of Parents	H	H	H
Lack of Family Cohesiveness	H	H	
Mother Not Attached to Boy	H		
Siblings Not Attached to Boy	H		H
Careless Supervision by Mother	H		
Unsuitable Discipline by Father	H		

Exhibit **14**   *Distribution of Twelve Sociocultural Factors Having Greater Impact on Delinquency of Ectomorphs*

NUMBER OF DELINQUENCY INDUCING FACTORS PRESENT	58 DELINQUENT ECTOMORPHS			141 NON-DELINQUENT ECTOMORPHS		
	Number	% of Total		Number	% of Total	
		Actual	Cumula-tive		Actual	Cumula-tive
12	2	3.45%	3.45%	0	0.00%	0.00%
11	6	10.34	13.79	0	0.00	0.00
10	7	12.07	25.86	1	0.71	0.71
9	17	29.31	55.17	2	1.42	2.13
8	6	10.34	65.51	8	5.67	7.80
7	10	17.24	82.75	10	7.09	14.89
6	5	8.62	91.37	15	10.64	25.53
5	3	5.17	96.54	16	11.35	36.88
4	1	1.73	98.27	7	4.96	41.84
3	1	1.73	100.00	19	13.47	55.31
2				30	21.28	76.59
1				28	19.86	96.45
0				5	3.55	100.00

if they are reared by parents who are not well mated.

Ectomorphs are also more prone to delinquency than boys of balanced physique if reared in families of low conduct standards, by parents who are incompatible, and when surrounded by sisters and brothers who are not attached to them.

Of the twelve sociocultural factors exerting a greater influence on the delinquency of ectomorphs than on one or another body type (Exhibit 14), it is to be noted that at least seven were present among 83 per cent of the delinquents as contrasted with 15 per cent of the non-delinquents.

Ectomorphic Constitution and Delinquency. Despite the heavier impact on their delinquency of unwholesome influences of home and family life, only 14 per cent of the delinquents were of ectomorphic physique as contrasted with 60 per cent of the mesomorphic body type. A reasonable explanation of this is *a greater deficiency among ectomorphs generally of energy, drive, and outflowing motor tendency, coupled with an excess of such curbing traits as a tendency to phantasy, emotional instability, emotional conflict, and feelings of inadequacy.* The basic finding appears to be that the traits of the ectomorph naturally tend to a bottling up of aggressive impulse, while the traits of the mesomorph naturally tend to an acting out of impulse. However, the *overreactivity in terms of delinquent behavior of the ectomorphic physique type to the pressures and tensions of family life is a major finding of the analysis, made intelligible by the basic constitutional makeup, especially the sensitivity, of this body type which renders it especially vulnerable to environmental influences.*

BALANCED TYPE AND DELINQUENCY

Introductory. We have completed a description of the mesomorphs, endomorphs, and ectomorphs and turn now to the balanced physique which comprises about equal elements of all three body structures. Delinquents of this body type encompass 13.5 per cent of our delinquent group.

Traits Distinguishing Balanced Type from Other Physique Types. The balanced physique type is assessed by anthropologists as having a "mid-range physical endowment in which none of the three traits assumes dominance over the other two in any marked degree." [4] Because of this we shall depart from our usual practice of first comparing the "norm" of each body type with the mesomorphs, but will rather compare the balanced physique with all the other body types.

[4] S. and E. T. Glueck, *Unraveling Juvenile Delinquency,* Cambridge, Harvard University Press, Copyright 1950 by The Commonwealth Fund, 342.

Exhibit 15 *Traits Distinguishing Non-Delinquents of the Balanced Type from Other Physique Types*

TRAITS	HIGHEST (H) OR LOWEST (L) AS COMPARED WITH		
	Meso-morphs	Endo-morphs	Ecto-morphs
Susceptibility to Contagion			L
Genital Under-development		L	
Strength of Hand Grip	L		
Tendency to Phantasy	H		
Social Assertiveness		H	
Fear of Failure and Defeat	L	L	L
Marked Dependence on Others		L	
Masochistic Trends		L	
Vivacity		H	
Sensitivity	H	H	
Inadequacy	H		
Uninhibited Motor Responses to Stimuli	L		
Emotional Instability			L
Sensuousness		L	L
Acquisitiveness			L
Conventionality		L	
Emotional Conflicts			L

Exhibit 15 shows that in respect to indicia of physical health, boys of the balanced type do not have as strong a hand grip as mesomorphs; they are less susceptible to contagion than ectomorphs; they have better genital development than endomorphs.

As regards traits of temperament, boys of balanced type have a greater tendency to phantasy than mesomorphs; they are more sensitive than both mesomorphs and endomorphs, and feel less adequate than do mesomorphs. They are less likely to seek outlets for their tensions in action than are mesomorphs. Boys of balanced type are more assertive socially than endomorphs, less dependent on others and less self-punishing (masochistic). They are also more vivacious (lively) than endomorphs. Boys of balanced type are less conventional in their attitudes and behavior than endomorphs.

In contrast with ectomorphs, boys of balanced type are more stable emotionally and tend less than ectomorphs to have emotional conflicts. They are not as sensuous as either ectomorphs or endomorphs, and they are not as acquisitive as ectomorphs.

It is to be especially noted, however, that they are less fearful of failure and defeat than all the other physique types, this being the only trait in which the balanced physique contrasts with all the others.

We certainly do not get as clear a picture of the balanced type or of its delinquency potential as in the case of the other body types. This is probably attributable to the nature of this physique which is poised, as it were, in the middle of three more or less conflicting constitutional tendencies.

Traits Contributing Selectively to Delinquency of Balanced Physique. There are six traits in all (see Exhibit 16) that have a significantly *greater* impact on the delinquency of boys of balanced physique than on that of one or another body type: susceptibility to contagion, strong hand grip, high performance intelligence, fear of failure and defeat, marked dependence on others, and sensuousness. There are two traits that are *less* influential in the delinquency of boys of balanced physique than among one or more of the other body types: feeling of not being taken care of and receptive trends.

In contrast with *mesomorphs,* only four traits among the 20 that were found to exert a varied influence on the delinquency of one or another body type contribute selectively (excessively or in lesser degree) to the delinquency of boys of balanced type.

Exhibit **16**   *Traits Contributing Selectively to Delinquency of the Balanced Type*

TRAITS	HIGHEST (H) OR LOWEST (L) AS COMPARED WITH		
	Meso-morphs	Endo-morphs	Ecto-morphs
Susceptibility to Contagion			H
Strength of Hand Grip	H		
High Performance Intelligence	H		
Feeling of Not Being Taken Care of	L		
Fear of Failure and Defeat		H	
Marked Dependence on Others		H	
Receptive Trends	L		L
Sensuousness			H

Strength of hand grip is more markedly involved in the delinquency of boys of balanced physique than in that of mesomorphs (who, normally, i.e., among non-delinquents, have a stronger hand grip than boys of all other body types). High performance intelligence when existing in boys of balanced type has more of a bearing on their delinquency than when it occurs in mesomorphs (in this regard they are like the endomorphs).

The feeling of not being taken care of has *less* of an influence on the delinquency of boys of balanced type than when it occurs in boys of predominantly mesomorphic physique (in this regard they are also like the endomorphs and the ectomorphs). Receptive (oral) trends in boys of this body type have *less* to do with their being delinquent than when they occur in mesomorphs.

As contrasted with *endomorphs*, only two traits have more of a bearing on the delinquency of boys of balanced type — fear of failure and defeat and marked dependence on others.

As contrasted with *ectomorphs*, susceptibility to contagion and sensuousness have more to do with the delinquency of boys of balanced physique, while receptive (oral) trends have *less* of a bearing on their delinquency.

At least three of the six traits which impel the balanced type to delinquency (Exhibit 17) were present in 43 per cent of the delinquents as contrasted with 26 per cent of the non-delinquents. One or two such traits in a boy of balanced physique do not exert a sufficient delinquency-inducing pressure, since 64 per cent of boys of balanced type who remained non-delinquent had one or two such traits as contrasted with 77 per cent of those who became delinquent.

Sociocultural Factors Contributing Selectively to Delinquency of Balanced Type. It will immediately be noted from Exhibit 18 that not one factor was found to exert a greater influence on the delinquency of the balanced type as contrasted with the mesomorphs. In the few differentiative factors involved, their special impact on the delinquency of boys of balanced type is rather in contrast with endomorphs and ectomorphs.

Indifference or hostility of brothers and sisters to boys of balanced type has less to do with their delinquency than it does with that of endomorphs. And boys of balanced type are less likely than ectomorphs to become delinquent if reared in homes in which the conduct standards are low, the parents constantly bickering, and brothers and sisters are not attached to the boy.

Balanced Constitution and Delinquency. It is impossible to discern any consistent pattern of special criminogenic involvement either in the traits or in the sociocultural influences involving the balanced type.

The considerably lower incidence of delinquents of the balanced constitution than of mesomorphic delinquents may be attributable to the relative scarcity of this physique type in the general population from which our samples were drawn and/or to their lower criminalistic potential, as indicated, for example, by such

Exhibit **17** *Distribution of Six Traits Having Greater Delinquency Inducing Impact on Boys of Balanced Type*

NUMBER OF DELINQUENCY INDUCING TRAITS PRESENT	53 DELINQUENTS OF BALANCED TYPE			58 NON-DELINQUENTS OF BALANCED TYPE		
	Number	% of Total		Number	% of Total	
		Actual	Cumulative		Actual	Cumulative
6	0	0.00%	0.00%	0	0.00%	0.00%
5	0	0.00	0.00	0	0.00	0.00
4	6	11.32	11.32	1	1.73	1.73
3	17	32.08	43.40	14	24.14	25.87
2	18	33.96	77.36	22	37.93	63.80
1	8	15.09	92.45	15	25.86	89.66
0	4	7.55	100.00	6	10.34	100.00

Exhibit **18** *Sociocultural Factors Contributing Selectively to Delinquency of the Balanced Type*

SOCIOCULTURAL FACTORS	HIGHEST (H) OR LOWEST (L) AS COMPARED WITH		
	Mesomorphs	Endomorphs	Ectomorphs
Low Conduct Standards of Family			L
Incompatibility of Parents			L
Siblings Not Attached to Boy	L		L

traits as their greater sensitivity, greater feeling of inadequacy, and lesser tendency to seek outlets for emotional tension in action than is characteristic of mesomorphs.

14

The Chemical Brew of Criminal Behavior *

Edward Podolsky

"The universe," says the physicist, "is a problem in geometry."

* Reprinted from 45 J. Crim. L., Criminology and Police Science (1955), 675–678. Used by permission of the author and the publisher.

"Human behavior," says the biochemist, "is a problem in body chemistry."

The biochemist is a bit too dogmatic in his statement. Not all human behavior is chemically determined, yet there are some rather interesting instances where chemical factors are of great importance. Life, in the final analysis, is a series of chemical reactions: the heart beats because the appropriate chemical stimulants are constantly present in the heart muscle; the brain functions because it has a favorable internal chemical environment.

The great French physiologist, Claude Bernard, in 1860 stated that there are two environments for all living beings — a general environment which is the same for inanimate objects and which surrounds the organism as a whole, and an internal environment in which the living elements of the body are to be found and which exert just as profound an influence on the behavior and character of the individual as does the external environment. Later he spoke of both the plasma and lymph. Finally, he regarded the internal environment as "the totality of the circulating fluids of the organism." Today the internal environment is regarded as the totality of all the chemical materials that go into the composition of the body.

"It is the fixity of the *milieu interieur* which is the condition of free and independent life," Bernard wrote, and "all the vital mechanisms, however varied they may be, have only one object, that of preserving constant the conditions of life in the internal environment." Bernard listed oxygen, water, temperature and nutrient materials (including salts, fats and sugar) as the necessary constants which free the organism from the limitations set by the external world. Today many more factors are included.

For some years past it has been known that there is an intimate relationship between the amount of sugar present in the blood and man's social behavior. J. Wilder has compiled from the literature a list of crimes and other infractions of law committed either under the influence of insulin or in a state of spontaneous hypoglycemia (decrease of normal amount of sugar in the blood). The list includes: disorderly conduct, assault and battery, attempted suicide and homicide, cruelty against children and spouse, various sexual perversions and aggressions, false fire alarms, drunkenness, embezzlement, petty larceny, willful destruction of property, arson, slander, violation of traffic regulations.

Some problem children and delinquents have been found to have a tendency to hypoglycemia. The lower the sugar level falls the greater is the tendency to commit a criminal act. The normal amount of sugar is from 90 to 110 milligrams per 100 cubic centimeters.

Of course not all physiological processes are always maintained at their proper level. Our blood sugar varies from hour to hour and there are times when it is below normal. As a rule crimes and offenses are committed not in the minor attacks of sugarlessness but in the medium or major attacks. A pronounced fall in blood sugar is manifested by weakness, perspiration, tremor, hunger and certain typical physiological changes.

Among the special criminal acts attempted and committed repeatedly in medium as well as major states of hypoglycemia the following are particularly frequent:

1. Theft, violence, petty larceny in connection with the frantic attempt to secure food, especially sweets. This is chemically motivated by the state of sugarlessness.

2. Violations of traffic regulations. In connection with this there are clashes with traffic policemen or serious accidents. Hypoglycemia in such instances results in impairment of judgment, sensory perception and motor reaction. There is also a release of primitive aggressiveness which further aggravates the original offense.

Aggressiveness is an outstanding characteristic of hypoglycemic generated criminality. A man whose blood sugar fell so low that he began to perspire, also became so violent that he attacked the doorman of his house for no reason whatever. Following this outbreak, during which he was pummeled himself, his anger rose, so did his blood sugar, and he calmed down.

Some cases of homicide for no apparent reason have been explained on the basis of hypoglycemia. A hunter returning with a rifle on his shoulder shot a woman sleeping in a car. When asked why he had done so he said that an impulse came over him to commit the crime. He did not know the woman but the urge to kill was so great that he had to yield to it. An examination of his blood sugar showed a marked depression. Similarly, a diabetic who took too large a dose of insulin picked up a revolver and shot his brother dead for no apparent reason.

Parents who suffer from attacks of hypoglycemia are inclined to cruelty to their children. A woman suffering from such a condition beat her son unmercifully without provocation in one of her attacks. A father almost strangled his daughter during one of these sugarless episodes.

The case is on record of a woman who for years had hysterical attacks in which she felt herself extremely weak, incoherent and emotionally upset. During these attacks she threw dishes and other objects at her husband. Also during these spells she had a great desire for sweets. Many cases of domestic discord are due to undetected hypoglycemia.

One of the most thoroughly investigated subjects ever tried in court, acquitted after the connection between his crime and hypoglycemia could be satisfactorily proved was reported by Hill and Sargent in 1943.

A twenty year old man, living alone with his mother, stabbed her to death with a kitchen knife, inflicting many wounds on her body. In the five days preceding the murder he had worked hard and had had but irregular meals. Also, there had been some quarreling with his mother over money. On the morning of the day of the murder he struck her, a very unusual act for which he apologized. He ate poorly on that day. He had his last carbohydrate meal at noon. Between 9 and 10:30 P.M. he drank four pints of mild ale. At 11 P.M. there was again a quarrel with his mother over money and she pushed him out of her room. At this moment he suddenly felt thirsty, went to the kitchen to get a bottle opener, saw a knife, and then "something came over" him: "I was like a homicidal maniac." He stabbed his mother to death, then realized what he had done, wiped the knife for fingerprints, washed and dressed, and left the house. There is a gap in his memory for seven hours following the crime. The next day, he gave himself to the police and made a full statement.

After the patient's arrest, his family physician notified the defense that two years prior to the crime a sugar tolerance curve had shown a tendency to hypoglycemia. Hill and Sargent performed a number of tests which showed that the prisoner was definitely suffering from hypoglycemia. They expressed the opinion that his blood at the time of the crime must have been below 100 mgm. and that his brain at that time was functioning abnormally; and that his judgment was impaired at the time. The verdict was: "Guilty but insane."

The relationship between excitement and hypoglycemia is of great importance. Impulsive crimes are often committed in a state of excitement. It is not always easy to say whether the excitement was adequate to the cause or not. The hypoglycemic impulsive crime is also committed in an excited state.

A few of the psychologic traits of hypoglycemia are: impairment of will-power, hazy thinking, loss of associations, impairment of moral sense, impairment of abstractive thinking, irritability, negativism, strengthening of aggressive and sexual drives, imperative hunger, etc. Of all these features, the early loss of spontaneity seems to be the most interesting feature in the psychology of hypoglycemia. Hypoglycemia offers the unusual opportunity of experimentation in criminology.

The first suspicion of hypoglycemia as the cause of criminal behavior appears when the criminal offense does not seem psychologically

motivated; when there is amnesia for the whole incident or for single details, or for the time prior to the incident. In addition there are physical symptoms like striking perspiration, tremor and other symptoms of hypoglycemia, such as deep sleep following the criminal offense.

Lack of calcium is another condition productive of antisocial attitudes and actions. Many high strung, very emotionally unstable individuals are victims of calcium starvation. One who is deficient in calcium is deeply affected by environmental changes, temperature variations and noise.

The calcium starved individual cannot stand opposition and criticism. A word of admonition or fault-finding or even a glance or attitude denoting this will cause such a person to react violently. Quite often violent tempers have their roots in calcium deprivation.

It has been noted that the person whose lime level is below normal has a tendency to shout and scream and strike. He throws things about and attacks his aggressor without any sense of judgment arising to inhibit these rapid changes.

One such person, during an interval of extreme calcium deprivation, threw his sister out of the window because of some disparaging remark she had made. Another shot at a group of schoolmates with a gun that was handy at the moment.

The calcium-starved personality is always on edge. At home, a harsh word from any member of the family, at the table, for instance, would result in a plate or knife or some other utensil being hurled at the aggressor. In school a blow, a shout, or a curse would be hurled at a fellow student, or even at the teacher.

Calcium starved individuals have many points in common, such as stature, bodily features and biochemical conditions. It has been found that these individuals form an actual group which can be differentiated by certain stigmas, both physically and biochemically. All such persons, both children and adults, show extreme muscle irritability, and are quite likely to have twitchings of the face and neck.

It has been shown that a decrease in the supply of calcium in the blood results in increased reaction of nerve tissue to an induction current. It is possible that the same factors that bring about muscle irritability also bring about untoward reactions in the nervous system. That is to say, reaction follows stimulus so rapidly that the overt act is committed before reason and judgment can come into play for purposes of inhibition.

There is also a close relationship between endocrine gland activity and aggressive and antisocial activity.[1] The endocrine glands, through their hormones, influence personality by their effects upon all the organs and parts of the body in general and the brain and nervous system in particular. It is generally agreed that behavior, normal and abnormal, is mediated through the brain and nervous system. Thus, thyroxin, parathyrin, adrenalin and cortin as well as the estrogens and androgens, all glandular secretions, have very definite effects on the brain and therefore on the behavior of the individual.

Thus the thyroid and thyroxin increases the excitability and nervousness of the individual; while a lack of it produces a slowing down of thinking and action, a sort of stupidity. A lack of parathyrin causes an increase in sensitivity; the person thus affected is annoyed by sounds and other stimuli. In time he becomes irritable and angry and prone to commit aggressive deeds at the least provocation.

Several years ago a series of interesting observations were carried out by several psychiatrists at Sing Sing Prison. The chemical background of the various types of criminal behavior was investigated. It was found that in cases of robbery and burglary the prisoners usually lacked pituitrin and parathyrin in their bodily chemistry. In criminal actions involving grand larceny there was a lack of parathyrin and pituitrin, but there was an increase in thyroxin and thymus hormones. In petty larceny there was a lack of parathyrin and pituitrin but an

increase in thymus secretion. Murderers usually had a decrease in the amount of parathyrin, but there was an abnormal increase in thymus, adrenalin and thyroxin.

Further studies revealed that in fraud there was an increase in thyroxin but a decrease in pituitrin and parathyrin. In forgery there was too much thyroxin and thymus and too little parathyrin. Rapists were found to have an overwhelming supply of thyroxin and estrogens and too little pituitrin. Those prisoners who had been sentenced for assault and battery were found to have too much adrenalin, too much thyroxin and too little pituitrin and the estrogens. When the blood of the Sing Sing inmates was analyzed it was found that the great majority of them had an excessive amount of non-protein nitrogen in the blood; their blood sugar level was too low, their uric acid and cholesterol levels were always above normal.

The biochemical evaluation of the criminal personality and of criminal behavior is still in its infancy. It seems destined to become, in the not too distant future, a very important methodology in the understanding and treatment of criminal actions.

15

Physical Condition of Delinquents and Non-Delinquents *

Sheldon and Eleanor T. Glueck

Summarizing the findings (in *Unraveling Juvenile Delinquency*) of the medical examination of the delinquents and non-delinquents, we see that the view that delinquents are in poorer

---

[1] Cf. statement by M. F. Ashley-Montagu: ". . . I should venture the opinion that not one of the reports on the alleged relation between glandular dysfunctions and criminality has been carried out in a scientific manner, and that all such reports are glaring examples of the fallacy of *false cause* . . . The fact is that as far as the endocrine system and its relation to personality and behavior are concerned, we are still almost completely in a world of the unknown, and that to resort to that system for an explanation of criminality is merely to attempt to explain the known by the unknown." "The Biologist Looks at Crime," 217 *Annals* (1941), 55–56. — *Ed.*

---

* Reprinted by permission of the publishers and The Commonwealth Fund from *Unraveling Juvenile Delinquency*, Sheldon and Eleanor T. Glueck, Cambridge, Mass.: Harvard University Press, Copyright 1950, by The Commonwealth Fund. Pages 181–182. This statement consists of the summary of Chapter XIV of *Unraveling*; it is recommended that the student read the entire chapter. — *Ed.*

health than non-delinquents receives no support. Very little, if any, difference exists between the physical condition of the two groups as a whole.

First, as regards their health as infants and young children, no differences between the two sets of boys have been revealed from careful inquiry of their mothers and consultation of early medical records, except that a considerably higher proportion of the delinquents are reported to have been enuretic [1] and extremely restless children. As regards their susceptibilities to disease and infection and their immunity to contagious diseases, they resemble each other.

Certain differences emerging from the medical examination are worth emphasizing:

Slightly greater strength of grip among the delinquents, though it does not quite reach the level of statistical significance adopted in this research, may be evidence of more basic vitality on their part.

Although there is no over-all difference between the two groups as regards palatal abnormalities, a significantly lower proportion of the delinquents have prognathous jaws (believed to be a frequently-found characteristic of the "criminal type"), and a significantly higher proportion have low-arched palates, though the numbers involved here are small. The possible significance of these findings is that they may relate to differences in types of physique among the two groups.

A significantly lower proportion of the delinquents than the non-delinquents have neurological handicaps.

Although there is no over-all difference between the two groups in observable evidences of functional deviations, a few differences in the incidence of certain of these deviations should be noted: Tics and ambidexterity are more prevalent among the non-delinquents, while extreme nail-biting is more characteristic of the delinquents, although this latter does not quite reach the level of statistical significance. The first two differences may be associated with the fact already noted that a higher proportion of the non-delinquents have neurotic characteristics, in general; and the latter difference with the probability that, in greater measure than the control group, the delinquents tend to be of the oral-erotic type (see Table XVIII–35 of *Unraveling Juvenile Delinquency*).[2]

---

[1] Considering a great excess of enuresis in 146 psychopathic personalities, 32 "psychiatric behavior problems," and 100 delinquents, as compared to "normals," Michaels believes "there is a similar fundamental disorder in that type of delinquent who has been persistent in his enuresis, the delinquency and enuresis both reflecting deep disturbances of the personality at different levels. One might offer as an interesting hypothesis that the absence of 'sphincter morality,' as phrased by Ferenczi — expressed in persistent enuresis — is the physiological precursor of the later deficiency in 'social morality' which is so apparent in the delinquent." J. J. Michaels, "The Incidence of Enuresis and Age of Cessation in One Hundred Delinquents and One Hundred Sibling Controls," *American Journal of Orthopsychiatry*, VIII (1938), 460, 464. See, also, J. J. Michaels and A. Steinberg, "Persistent Enuresis and Juvenile Delinquency," 3 *British J. Delinquency* (1952–53), 114–123. — Ed.

[2] For a brief analysis of the oral stage of psychosexual development, see O. S. English and G. H. J. Pearson, *Common Neuroses of Children and Adults*, New York, Norton, 1937, pp. 21–27.

Chapter 4

Psychologic Aspects of Delinquency

DURING THE EARLY PART of the century, it was common practice to attribute delinquency largely to mental defect. In the first excitement over the newly discovered Binet-Simon tests of supposedly native intelligence, there was great enthusiasm for the study of the role of mental defect in various forms of deviant behavior; and delinquency was deemed the most fertile for that purpose.

The exaggerated attribution of antisocial behavior to mental defect began to lessen, however, with the development of criticisms of the tests themselves and with the recognition of the influence of sociocultural factors on intelligence and of the role of selective influences in determining which children will be screened out of the general stream and committed to schools for the feebleminded and which will be sent, as *delinquents*, to industrial schools and reformatories.

One of the basic weaknesses of researches in this respect as in others has been not only the failure to identify clearly the sample of human beings under test study but also the failure to employ relevant control groups. With the use of adequate controls it began to be evident that while the early enthusiasts had greatly exaggerated the role of mental defect in antisocial behavior,[1] the opposite error — failure to give any weight at all to this influence — must also be avoided.

The first item in this chapter, by Shulman, is a careful review of the status of the mental deficiency studies as related to delinquent behavior, while the materials from *Unraveling Juvenile Delinquency* show that there are measurable differences in certain constituents of general intelligence between delinquents and non-delinquents who had been previously matched as to I.Q. They indicate, also, that there are statistically significant differences between delinquents and the control group as to various intellectual traits and tendencies of a qualitative and dynamic nature, as determined through application of the Rorschach Test.

---

[1] It will be recalled that Goring, in his criticism of Lombroso, nevertheless placed great emphasis on a rather crude form of intelligence classification to conclude that "the principal constitutional determinant of crime is mental defectiveness." See p. 51 *supra*.

16

Intelligence and Delinquency *

Harry M. Shulman

The study of the relationship of intelligence and delinquency began with the early 19th century neo-classical criminal justice doctrine that since crime was a rational choice of conduct, mental defectives in common with infants and the insane, were not legally responsible for their actions. While the medical differentiation of mental defectives from the insane was accomplished during the early part of the 19th century, it was not until the late 19th century that scientific standards were established for the measurement of degrees of mental ability and for the determination of mental defect, despite man's observation since time immemorial of the individual variability in mental ability. These were tests for general intelligence, the product of research by a whole school of psychologists, but attributable directly to the researches of Alfred Binet, of France.

The application of these early crude intelligence tests to samplings of institutionalized offenders in prisons, reformatories and juvenile training schools and the finding that a very large proportion of those tested could be diagnosed as mental deficients, led to the single-factor theory of mental deficiency as the greatest cause of delinquent conduct. Thus Harry H. Goddard, one of America's most distinguished adherents of the psychological school of crime causation, was impelled to state, as late as 1919, that "It is no longer to be denied that the greatest single cause of delinquency and crime is low-grade mentality, much of it within the limits of feeble-mindedness." A similar declaration was made by Dr. William Healy, while Dr. Charles Goring, the English investigator into Lombroso's claims, declared more conservatively that defective in-

telligence was a vital constitutional factor in the aetiology of crime.[1]

While there was substantial agreement as to the facts, there was considerable divergence as to the interpretation of the test findings, leading to such theories as: (1) the mental defective is a type of "born criminal," i.e., the "moral idiot"; (2) feeble-mindedness is a hereditary unit-character following Mendel's law, accounting for the preponderance of male defective offenders; (3) the feeble-minded characteristically commit dangerous crimes of assault and sex assault; (4) feeble-minded individuals commit crimes, in the absence of inhibiting social factors, because they lack the capacity to grasp the social values of their culture, including its social and legal definitions of right and wrong; (5) the feeble-minded cannot foresee the consequences of their actions, hence cannot be deterred by the threat of punishment laid down for crimes; (6) feeble-minded are suggestible, and so respond to the criminal leadership of brighter persons; (7) feeble-mindedness in individuals reared in families and neighborhoods where delinquent example is common, leads to delinquency.

Thus the elaborations of proponents of this single-factor theory ranged from the biological to the bio-social. The biological concept of the mental defective as a moral idiot or a Mendelian criminal type preceded in historical sequence the bio-social view of the mentally deficient offender as a product of social interaction. During the early decades of the 20th century there was still a predisposition to think fatalistically of mental deficiency, delinquency and dependency as inevitably associated phenomena. Even Sumner, in his brilliant source-book on the *Folkways*, published in 1906, was willing to associate these three groups as the submerged tenth at the bottom of the social class ladder.

Today, the concept that mental deficiency is necessarily a product of a tainted heredity is no longer accepted as wholly true. Evidence exists that perhaps one-half of all mental deficiency is the effect of non-germinal toxic and mechanical damage during the intra-uterine period and at birth.[2] Mental deficients are found among

* Reprinted from 41 *J. Crim. L. and Criminology* (1951), 763–781. A contribution to the International Congress of Criminology in Paris in 1950. Used by permission of the author and the publisher. See, also, L. D. Zeleny, "Feeble-Mindedness and Criminal Conduct," 38 *Am. J. Sociol.* (1932–33), 564–576. — *Ed.*

[1] See H. H. Goddard, *Feeble-Mindedness*, 1914.
[2] Negley H. Teeters and John Otto Reinemann, *The Challenge of Delinquency*, New York, 1950, p. 91.

all social classes and in every parental occupational and educational level.[3] Nor is the concept any longer accepted that mental deficients
must necessarily be behavior risks. Together
with the awareness that mental deficiency occurs in all levels of the population, it has been
discovered that under proper conditions of
child rearing and supervision, the mental defective may become a docile and obedient
personality, with useful occupational potentialities. A perhaps contrary trend of thought is
seen, however, in the growth in many American
jurisdictions, of the practice of voluntary sterili-
zation of defective delinquents, and in the
spread of legislation authorizing this practice.[4]

Despite a changing outlook upon the relationship between mental defect and delinquency
there remain a number of questions regarding
which it is essential to have scientific evidence,
such as: (1) The proportion of mental defectives among delinquents compared to the general population; (2) significant differences in
general mental ability between delinquents and
the general population; (3) criminal patterns
and tendencies toward recidivism among defectives compared to non-defective offenders;
(4) the relationship between level of intelligence and treatability. We will consider these
matters in the following sections. First, however, we shall seek a somewhat clearer view of
the nature of general intelligence, of mental
deficiency, and of the concepts and procedures
involved in their measurement.

The Testing of General Intelligence

Whereas no adequate concept of the nature
of intelligence has yet been constructed, owing
to a conflict among psychologists as to the
priority of general intelligence or of specific in-
telligences (such as social, mechanical, musical
intelligence, etc.) there is agreement that general intelligence is the capacity to learn from
experience. Binet constructed a scale to test
the growth in this ability, based on the observation that in childhood and youth growth in
learning ability parallels physical growth. In the
absence of any objective criteria for the measurement of learning growth, Binet depended
upon empirical trial and error, devoting fifteen
years to the discovery of a scale of mental

tests of increasing difficulty, correlated with the
chronological age of his subjects.[5]

Out of this experimentation came the year-
level general intelligence scale. Tests were assigned to a year-level when 75 per cent of the
subjects in an age-group successfully performed
the tests. By assigning a given number of subtests to each year-level, and a given amount of
year-level credit to each sub-test, it became
possible to establish a *mental age*, consisting of
the basal mental age below which all tests were
passed, plus year-level credit for all succeeding
tests passed. By comparing the mental age
with the chronological age of the child and
multiplying this ratio by 100, it became possible to establish an intelligence quotient, or
IQ. Thus a child of 12 years, chronological
age, with a mental age of nine years, had an
IQ of 9/12 x 100 or 75, while a child of the
same age with a mental age of 15 years, had an
IQ of 15/12 x 100 or 125.

Successive tests of child population samplings
by other psychologists disclosed that tested general intelligence assumed a normal or bell-
shaped curve, with half of the IQ's falling within the range of 90 and 110, the remainder being
almost equally divided above and below this
range. Terman classified intelligence ratings
into the following mental ability levels: Above
140, "near" genius or genius; 120–140, very
superior; 110–120, superior; 90–110, normal or
average; 80–90, dull; 70–80, borderline mental
deficiency; below 70, mental deficiency.[6]

Problems in the Testing of Intelligence

Despite the proliferation of individually applied verbal tests for general intelligence, their
standardization in nearly every tongue and
their application to millions of school children,
certain fundamental problems in intelligence
testing remain unsolved. Among these are:
(*a*) the nature of the normal learning curve,
(*b*) the constancy of the IQ and (*c*) the nature
of the mental functions which the tests presume to measure.

The form of the learning curve is related both
to the constancy of the IQ and to the determination of a mental growth cessation point, to

[3] *Ibid.*
[4] *Ibid*, p. 96.

[5] A. Binet et Th. Simon, "Le development de
l'intelligence chez les enfants," *Année Psychologie*,
1908, Vol. 14, pp. 1–94.
[6] Lewis M. Terman, *The Measurement of Intelligence*, Boston, 1916, p. 79.

serve as the enumerator of the equation for the determining of the IQ among children above that chronological age. The determination of that point is of very real significance in the diagnosis of mental defect, especially when mental deficiency must be established as a legal entity for purposes of differentiated social treatment. There is evidence that the growth curve in learning ability reaches its maximum somewhere between the fourteenth and sixteenth year, and then declines sharply. Thus examiners have variously taken chronological ages between 14 and 16 to represent adulthood, for intelligence testing purposes. As a result, a given mental age will fluctuate in IQ according to the adult year level chosen. Until there is arbitrary uniformity in defining this mental growth cessation point, the percentages of mental deficiency established for either general populations or delinquent samplings will be noncomparable. It was suggested by many psychologists that 15 years be arbitrarily set to represent adulthood for mental growth purposes, and the majority of child guidance clinics now adhere to this standard.

The labeling of children as to their mental ability by means of the IQ assumes the constancy of the IQ; that, is that the future mental growth of a child is predictable in terms of his rate of mental growth up to the time of testing. The evidence to date is that within a probable error of perhaps 2.5 points in either direction, *under conditions of constant cultural stimulation,* the IQ does not vary with age. But such factors as serious illness, or irregularity in exposure to learning situations, or other factors that affect opportunity for learning, do appear to affect the learning growth rate, and the IQ. Thus, there is evidence that children transferred from inferior to superior cultural environments appreciate in their learning rate, and gain in IQ, and that children returned from superior to inferior cultural environments tend to regress in learning rate and in IQ to the level previously established in the inferior social environment.[7]

The product of learning growth known as "native" general intelligence is thus not alone dependent upon nature, but on nature and nurture. As a result, general intelligence must be viewed as a product of bio-social interaction. This introduces the problem of the significance of cultural differences in the determination of intelligence levels. This factor is of significance for the relation between intelligence and delinquency. Since the accurate measurement of general intelligence is dependent upon constancy of cultural stimulation, factors tending to differentiate the cultural background levels of delinquents and non-delinquents would lead to the under-estimation or over-estimation of the intelligence of one group or the other. Thus a finding as to the relative mental status of delinquents and non-delinquents requires holding constant the factor of cultural stimulation. Since this has not usually been done, a finding that delinquents are inferior in tested general intelligence to non-delinquents does not necessarily prove that intelligence and delinquency are causally related but only that the same antecedent factors that contributed an inferior nurture to the group from which the preponderance of delinquents were drawn, also led to the preponderance of that culture level in juvenile court arraignments.

The desirability of disentangling the functions of nurture and nature in learning potential, so that "native" potential may be measured, has led to the suggestion that culture-free mental tests be devised. Whether culture-free tests, if they could be devised, would successfully elicit the full measurement of intelligence potential is questionable. Motivation has ordinarily strong cultural reference, and especially for delinquents, the necessity of arousing full response to an intellectual situation probably involves the utilization of culturally familiar motivations, since among delinquents there is a disproportion of emotionally disturbed children.[8, 9]

---

[7] Frank N. Freeman, K. J. Holzinger and others, *The Influence of Environment on Intelligence.* Yearbook of National Society for the Study of Education, 27:103–217 (1928). See also Robert S. Woodworth, "Heredity and Environment," Bulletin 47, Social Science Research Council, New York, 1941.

[8] Furthermore, the emotional tensions accompanying the usual situations within which delinquents are psychologically tested — prior to court adjudication or upon admission to a juvenile training school — probably lead often to blocking of full participation in the test situation.

[9] The desirability of having a common instrument for the testing of all children, regardless of culture origin, has led some criminologists to suggest the establishment of an International Commission under the United Nations to establish standards of international psychological examination. C. Nony, of the

A final comment on the role of culture in the testing of general intelligence must stress the desirability of the homogeneity of culture backgrounds among delinquents compared with non-delinquents for mental status. Since delinquents are drawn disproportionately from urban areas, from among industrial groupings that include disproportionate numbers of children of ill-educated, bi-lingual and low-socio-economic status parentage, they should be compared in general intelligence, not to the whole child population, nor even to the total urban child population, but to samplings drawn from the same races, ethnic origins, socio-economic levels, and residence areas. These fundamental needs must be kept in mind in evaluating the available evidence on the intelligence of delinquents.

THE GENERAL INTELLIGENCE OF JUVENILE DELINQUENTS

We have said that the earliest studies of the general intelligence of juvenile delinquents emphasized their retarded mentality as a class. Studies of more than 200 American samples of institutionalized delinquent children, on a literal translation of the original Binet-Simon scale, in connection with the knowledge that practically no institutionalized feeble-minded rated above twelve years in mental age, led to the conclusion that at least one-half of juvenile delinquents were mental defectives.[10, 11]

Institute de Psychologie, Sorbonne, Paris, abstractor for the psychological section of the Second International Congress of Criminology, Paris, 1950, has made this suggestion in correspondence with the writer. The problem of culture effect on motivation, in the absence of culture-free tests based on fundamental human drives, would be a problem such a commission would have to solve.

[10] H. H. Goddard, *Human Efficiency and Levels of Intelligence*, Princeton, 1920, pp. 73–74.

[11] Mental retardation has been referred to by two terms, *feeble-mindedness* and *mental deficiency*, each having a somewhat different meaning. Mental deficiency refers only to mental test level. Feeble-mindedness refers to an inadequacy in personal social adjustment — to get along in school, make an independent living, manage one's own affairs, etc. — without special assistance or supervision. An individual may be mentally deficient as defined by test, yet capable of self-support and adequate social adjustment in a congenial social environment, and hence, not feeble-minded. The writer recalls a juvenile training school graduate who by test was mentally deficient, yet who out of his experience in the institution powerhouse, invented a fuse with a handle that mini-

Recent examinations, however, have tended to a reduction in the proportion of alleged mental defect among juvenile delinquents, in part as a result of newer tests having a higher mental age "ceiling," that permitted the testing of superior individuals, in part the greater skill of examiners and the use of more effective techniques for achieving motivation, and in part the extension of tests to broader samplings of juvenile delinquents to include non-committed as well as committed cases.

A study in 1928–29, of all the mental tests reported on criminals and delinquents, comprising some 350 reports on approximately 150,000 offenders, showed a decrease from an average of 50 per cent of delinquents diagnosed as feeble-minded in the period 1910–1914 to an average percentage of 20 per cent in the period 1925–1928. The wide variation in test results was regarded as reflecting differences in test methods and scoring rather than differences in mental abilities of offenders.[12]

THE INTELLIGENCE OF JUVENILE DELINQUENTS AND TOTAL JUVENILE POPULATION

Attention has been directed during the two past decades to a comparison of the intelligence levels of juvenile delinquents as compared to the general juvenile population. Samples of juvenile delinquents, drawn for the most part from court-arraigned cases, have been found to be lower in tested general intelligence that the child population series upon which the major intelligence tests were standardized. Terman, in standardizing the revised Binet, found that approximately 50 per cent of his one thousand unselected American school children fell between an IQ of 93 and 108 and that the remainder fell above and below in equal proportion. Only .3 per cent had IQ's below 65 and only 2.6 per cent had IQ's below 75. In comparison, Healy and Bronner, in their 1926 court sample, reported 13.5 per cent of their cases as mentally deficient, Burt reported 8 per cent of a London, England, court sample

---

mized the danger of shock, and established a paying manufacturing enterprise around his invention. (See Maud A. Merrill, *Problems of Child Delinquency*, Boston, 1947, pp. 160–161.)

[12] Edwin H. Sutherland, *Mental Deficiency and Crime*, Ch. XV in Kimball Young (Editor), *Social Attitudes*, 1931, pp. 357–375.

as mentally deficient, and Merrill reported 23 per cent of 1,731 Los Angeles court delinquents as mentally deficient with IQ's below 70. Merrill, however, pointed out that her sample contained an unknown proportion of Mexican-born and Mexican ethnic stock children of presumed bi-lingual backgrounds. In a second California court sample of 500 cases from a territory having a more homogeneous ethnic stock, she reported 11.6 per cent as mentally deficient.[13]

Relatively similar findings have been reported for other delinquency samplings, some more selective and others less selective than total court intake. Kvaraceus reported 10.4 per cent of all public school problem children referred for guidance care as mentally deficient, with IQ's below 70. Sheldon and Eleanor Glueck reported 13.1 per cent of a sample referred by the Boston juvenile court to the Judge Baker foundation clinic for diagnostic study as mentally deficient. The New Jersey Juvenile Commission found 13 per cent of New Jersey children committed to juvenile training schools to have IQ's under 70.[14]

Zeleny, after equating the procedures of different examiners, concluded that the ratio of delinquents and general child population in respect to mental deficiency was about 1.2 to 1.[15]

Somewhat similar findings were reported for differences in *average intelligence* among delinquents and non-delinquents. Kvaraceus found an average intelligence quotient of 103 among unselected Passaic, New Jersey school children compared to an average IQ of 89 among 761 problem children referred by schools to a central guidance service. Eleanor Glueck, comparing 1,000 clinic-referred juvenile delinquents with 3,638 school children, found that only 41.6 per cent of the delinquents had average

intelligence or better (IQ's over 90) compared to 79 per cent of the school children.[16]

INTELLIGENCE OF GROUPS OF DELINQUENTS GIVEN SELECTIVE TREATMENT

Whereas contemporary interest in the relation of general intelligence and delinquency has continued unabated, instead of seeking a causal explanation of delinquency in intellectual inferiority, the tendency has been to explain the established test differences between delinquents and non-delinquents as a product of social selection.[17] That is, inferior mentality is coming to be viewed as one of a series of attributes that characterize children whom society has selected out for formal adjudication as delinquents through the differential operation of the machinery of juvenile justice.

There is evidence that not only are juvenile delinquents non-representative of the whole child population for social status, but that the selectivity of the delinquent group increases proportionately with the degree of authority applied to their handling. Thus they are found to be drawn in disproportionate numbers from (*a*) lower socio-economic groups, (*b*) Negroes, (*c*) foreign-born parentage, (*d*) groups disproportionately high in indices of mental disorder, dependency and adult crime.[18] Those dealt

[13] William Healy and Augusta Bronner, *Delinquents and Criminals*, 1926. Cyril Burt, *The Young Delinquent*, D. Appleton & Co., 1925. Maud Merrill, *ibid*.

[14] William C. Kvaraceus, *Juvenile Delinquency and the School*, Yonkers, 1945, pp. 122–123. New Jersey Juvenile Commission, *Justice and the Child in New Jersey*, 1939, p. 82. Sheldon and Eleanor Glueck, *One Thousand Juvenile Delinquents*, Cambridge, 1934, p. 102.

[15] L. D. Zeleny, "Feeble-mindedness and Criminal Conduct," *American Journal of Sociology*, 38:564–578, January, 1933.

[16] Kvaraceus, *ibid*. Glueck, *ibid*.

[17] A recently annotated bibliography of 972 articles dealing with juvenile delinquency included 243 or approximately one-quarter that referred to some aspect of the relationship between intelligence and delinquency. See P. S. de Q Cabot, *Juvenile Delinquency: A Critical Annotated Bibliography*, New York, 1946.

[18] Clifford Shaw, in *Delinquency Areas*, and in succeeding publications, found that a significantly higher proportion of court-arraigned delinquents were drawn from central residence areas characterized by low rentals, dependency and tenancy, than from outlying residence areas characterized by home ownership and higher rentals. This finding has been corroborated by other investigators, including Elmer, Schmidt, and Burt. For the higher proportion of official delinquency arraignments among Negro children, see reports on juvenile statistics of the Federal Children's Bureau, Federal Security Agency, especially for 1939; U. S. Department of Labor, Children's Bureau, 1939, p. 12. For Negro juvenile delinquency in selected urban areas see J. B. Maller, "Juvenile Delinquency in New York City," *Journal of Psychology*, 3, 1–25, November, 1936, and New Jersey Juvenile Commission, "Justice and The Child in New Jersey," 1939, p. 80. For the disproportion of juvenile delinquency among children of foreign-born

with unofficially, either through the courts or through the public and private child guidance facilities of schools and community appear to represent a group from higher socio-economic status than those officially arraigned or committed to juvenile training schools.

There is further evidence that the selective social characteristics of the officially arraigned delinquency group are accompanied by differential tested intelligence; and that as more selective screening takes place among the arraigned group, in terms of the severity of the subsequent controls applied, the greater the tested intelligence differential. Thus Kvaraceus, in New Jersey, reported an unselected sampling of Passaic school children as having an average IQ of 103, and all public school children referred to a special service division of the Board of Education for child guidance care as having an average IQ of 89. Merrill, in California, reported an unselected sampling of 2,904 children in the general child population as having an average IQ of 101.8 and a court sampling from the same area of 500 consecutive arraignments as having an average IQ of 92.5.[19]

As one progresses from court arraignment to training school commitments, the average IQ drops. Merrill cites evidence that with the 1916 Stanford Revision of the Binet scale, the average IQ of court samples reported in the literature is around 85, and for institutional commitments, around 82.[20]

There are two possible interpretations of these findings: (a) that greater maladjustment accompanies lower intelligence, resulting in the application of more extreme social controls; (b) that the greater maladjustment and the lower

tested intelligence among official cases are both dependent upon inferior antecedent cultural backgrounds of delinquents as compared to general population samples.

The first interpretation leads to the conclusion that since a disproportionate number of severely maladjusted institutionalized delinquents tend to be dullards there is a correlation between mental backwardness and the social conditions within which delinquency is encouraged. From this conclusion it is an easy step to the view that mental dullness and social breakdown, as measured by such terminal indices as dependency, delinquency and crime, are closely related phenomena.

The cultural interpretation rejects the adequacy of the initial findings, arguing that the very tests used for the measurement of general intelligence are discriminatory against the delinquent group. They are not culture-free tests, but tests depending largely upon skill in language expression, vocabulary, breadth of reading, exposure to conceptualized discussion, etc., involving a high level of training in the use of written and spoken English, and presuming an exposure to comparable linguistic cultural material in the family, among both delinquents and non-delinquents. But since we already know that a disproportionately large number of delinquents are of low socio-economic status, whose parents suffer from the handicaps of limited schooling, partial or total illiteracy, and bilingual or foreign language speech, it may be inferred that their social backgrounds are not comparable to those of the general child population. Hence the general intelligence test results are not explicable by any fancied relation between intelligence and delinquency, but by a real relationship between court arraignment and low socio-economic and culture status.

Research evidence bearing upon both types of interpretation is at hand from studies of the differential intelligence levels of public school children in high and low delinquency areas. Shulman has shown, for New York City, that the tested intelligence of children in high delinquency areas tends to be lower than that of school children in low delinquency areas. In a recalculation of data from a series of group intelligence tests conducted among public school pupils by the Board of Education, he found that in five public schools in high delinquency areas, the median IQ's ranged from 88.5 to

parentage see Thorsten Sellin, "Culture Conflict and Crime," Social Science Research Council, Bulletin 41, 1938, pp. 78–107. For the concurrence of official juvenile delinquency and adult crime see such case study researches as Sheldon and Eleanor Glueck, *One Thousand Juvenile Delinquents*, Cambridge, 1934, p. 79 (in which 86.7 per cent of the known total of families contained members, other than the juvenile delinquent himself, who were delinquent or criminal), and such area studies as those by Halpern, Stanislaus and Botein, *Slums and Crime*, New York, 1931, in which the areas of greatest juvenile delinquency and of adult crime were shown to be similar.

[19] William C. Kvaraceus, *Juvenile Delinquency and the School*, New York, 1945, p. 123. Maud A. Merrill, *Problems of Child Delinquency*, Boston, 1947, p. 167.
[20] Maud Merrill, *ibid.*, p. 164.

98.5, with an average median of 91.5, while in seven public schools in low delinquency areas, the medians ranged from 95 to 115.5, with an average median of 103.5. Thus between the low delinquency areas and the high delinquency areas there was an IQ difference averaging 12 points favoring the low delinquency areas. Similar findings, based upon extensive restudy of the same source data were reported by Maller.[21, 22]

More pertinent to a cultural interpretation were the findings of Allison Davis, who devised a test for the measurement of untaught responses to problems in daily life outside of school. In an experimental study of school children from varying socio-economic backgrounds, on standard intelligence tests, and on the test for daily life problems, he found that whereas on ten standard tests there was an average difference of nearly 8 points in IQ between the high and the low socio-economic groups, favoring the former, these differences vanished when the tests for daily life problems were applied.[23] He concluded that the standard tests did not truly measure the problem-solving potentialities of children from low socio-economic backgrounds.

DELINQUENTS AND MATCHED CONTROL SAMPLES

Whereas apparently significant tested intelligence differences, usually without calculation of statistical significance, have been found between arraigned delinquents and the general child population, the controversy as to the role of native and cultural factors in the results has led some authorities to suggest that comparisons of delinquents and non-delinquents in samplings in which socio-economic status is held constant might be helpful in resolving this problem.

In this connection, Lichtenstein and Brown are reported to have found among 658 grade school children from a high delinquency area, 10 percent with IQ's below 70. Use of this figure as a control percentage for the general population in a high delinquency area would not be unfavorable to the theory that delinquents are of the same tested mental potential as non-delinquents when equated for socio-economic background. Some of Merrill's findings lend additional weight to this theory. Among 300 delinquents of both sexes compared to 300 non-delinquent controls from the same communities and public schools, she found an average IQ for the controls only slightly and not significantly higher (89.3–86.7) but on the other hand she found among the delinquents almost twice as many IQ's below 70 as among the controls.[24]

However, the findings of other investigators controvert this point of view. Burt's delinquents and controls from the same districts and public schools in London showed differences favoring the controls, with 1.2 per cent in the defective group (IQ's 50–70) compared to 7.6 per cent in the delinquents, a ratio of better than six to one; and IQ's above 115 among only 2.5 per cent of the delinquents and 8.5 per cent of the controls, a reverse ratio of better than three to one.[25] Charles, comparing Kuhlman-Anderson IQ's for 528 reform school boys with a public school group of the same socio-economic status found that among delinquents, 29.5 per cent of white boys and 47.3 per cent of Negro boys, had IQ's under 70, compared to 1.16 per cent and 3.48 per cent, respectively, for the public school groups.[26]

A difficulty in equating culture backgrounds in terms of socio-economic status or area of residence is that within the same area of residence, as pointed out elsewhere by the writer, or within the same income group, there are significant familial variations in culture level.[27] A stricter measure of cultural homogeneity is afforded when delinquents and non-delinquents within the same families are compared for general intelligence. Healy and Bronner, in 105 court-arraigned delinquency cases, compared to a like number of non-delinquent siblings matched closely for age and usually for sex, found differences slightly favoring the non-delinquents. Their data sought to

[21] Harry Manuel Shulman, A Study of Problem Boys and Their Brothers, New York State Crime Commission, Albany, 1929, pp. 18–22.
[22] Julius Maller, "Juvenile Delinquency in New York City," Journal of Psychology, 1937, 3, 1–25.
[23] From New York Times, March 23, 1950.

[24] For Lichtenstein and Brown, see Milton Metfessel and Constance Lovell, "Recent Literature on Individual Correlates of Crime," Psychological Bulletin, 1942, 34, 153–160. Merrill, ibid., pp. 169–170.
[25] Cyril Burt, ibid.
[26] M. F. Metfessel and Constance D. Lovell, opus cit.
[27] Harry Manuel Shulman, Slums of New York, New York, 1938, p. 107.

exclude mental defectives and were therefore valid only for IQ's above 70. Their findings (figures for delinquents given first) were: IQ above 110, 13–17 per cent; 90–110, 52–57 per cent 72–90, 30.8–22.6 per cent.[28] These differences were not calculated for significance. Shulman, in a smaller matched sample of siblings, found that for 28 pairs, delinquents averaged IQ 75 and non-delinquents IQ 86.[29] Thus, both studies favored the theory that delinquents tend toward lower tested intelligence than non-delinquents, when equated for culture level. It is suggested that in the interest of a resolution of this question of the relation of intelligence and delinquency, further studies concern themselves with the intelligence of delinquent and non-delinquent siblings, with emphasis upon the analysis of those physical and emotional factors that might affect learning, mental growth and motivation to maximum test output.

GENERAL INTELLIGENCE AND TYPE OF OFFENSE

Since the publication of Goring's study on the English convict, there has been an interest in the relation of intelligence and type of offense. Forgery and fraud have been associated with higher levels of intelligence and crimes of violence with lower levels. Findings of this type, based on adult samplings, are as pointed out by Merrill, of limited significance for juvenile delinquency, since legal offenses are not always descriptive of juvenile behavior. Thus, in 500 cases of children's offenses, she found only eight cases of forgery. It could also be pointed out that many other forms of offense have their origin in the economic and cultural roles of adult life and their presence in adult criminal statistics affords no basis for use of similar categories in dealing with children.

Merrill has traced certain relationships between type of juvenile offense and intelligence level. She found intelligence positively correlated with forgery, lack of parental control and malicious mischief; and negatively correlated with sex offenses, truancy and vagrancy. Stealing, comprising a majority of the cases in her sampling, was found to have no significant

relation to intelligence. It is possible, however, that a refinement of the categories of theft, to reveal differential theft patterns, would have been productive of more significant results.[30]

Luton Ackerson, in a sampling comprising nearly 5,000 cases, found that for children ages five to 12.9 years, the offenses of stealing, fire-setting, forgery or check-raising, incorrigibility, truancy and escape from an institution, increased with IQ increase. However, since his entire sample had a low median IQ, the results are not too significant. Certain of his findings were very interesting. He found a greater tendency to gang membership among IQ's from 40 to 99 than among problem children with IQ's over 99. He found, among girls ages 13–17.9 years, a high proportion of sex delinquency, including unmarried motherhood, among low IQ's. It should be pointed out that since none of his correlations exceeded .30 they are not statistically significant, even though suggestive of further avenues of exploration.[31] Ackerson's findings on the sex offender may be taken together with those of Tendler, that on a test for impulsiveness (the Porteus Maze) unmarried female sex offenders who did not become pregnant, achieved scores superior to those who became unwed mothers. Thus the young unwed mother is described by these findings as tending toward lower general intelligence and greater impulsiveness than either the sex delinquent girl who avoids pregnancy or the non-delinquent girl.[32]

Qualitative distinctions have been made between the offenses of individuals of different intelligence levels. Abrahamsen, speaking without specific reference to children, has remarked that the offense chosen is typical of the individual who commits it; thus an individual with a low IQ will usually commit a simple theft such as breaking in through a window and taking some insignificant object, or stealing a car, leaving it and running away.[33]

John Levy made the observation that bright children tend toward personality problems and dull children toward conduct disorders. Among more than 700 children with IQ's above 80

[28] William Healy and Augusta Bronner. *New Light on Delinquency and Its Treatment*, New Haven, 1936, p. 75.

[29] Harry Manuel Shulman, *A Study of Problem Boys and Their Brothers*, New York State Crime Commission, Albany, 1929, p. 61.

[30] Maud Merrill, *ibid.*, p. 171.

[31] Luton Ackerson, *Children's Behavior Problems*, Chicago, 1931.

[32] Alexander Tendler, unpublished.

[33] David Abrahamsen, *Crime and the Human Mind*, New York, 1944, p. 22.

referred to a child guidance clinic, personality problems increased with IQ from 25 to 53 per cent, and conduct problems decreased from 32 to 12 per cent. He sought to equate out the socio-economic factor by comparing 50 bright children (IQ's over 110) from the lowest socio-economic group with 70 dull children (IQ's 80–90) from the highest socio-economic group and found that socio-economic differences did not modify the trend of his findings.[34]

In this connection, the findings of Davis and Havighurst are significant, that middle-class families tend to rear their children more rigidly than do lower-class families and that differences in socio-economic status are more important in rearing than those of race. Thus the rearing practices of middle-class Negro mothers tended to approximate the tightness of control by middle-class white mothers as opposed to the relative permissiveness of the lower socio-economic group of mothers in both races.[35]

It is possible that the common factor operating in both the Levy and Davis-Havighurst findings was differential general intelligence, with higher parental intelligence tending to be correlated with strictness of rearing and lower parental intelligence with permissiveness in rearing. If this were so, the anxieties resulting from the frustrations of strict rearing might have explained the greater number of personality problems in bright children, and the contact with delinquency attitudes and experiences that would result from laxness in rearing in lower socio-economic areas might have explained the greater number of cases of conduct disorder among dull children.

The writer has pursued this line of reasoning further, pointing out that the differences in types of adult crime characteristic of lower and middle classes — the former tending to assault and theft, and the latter to fraud — may be in part a function of differences in childhood rearing. The lower-class child, reared permissively, but frustrated in his status aspiration in a democratic society, and subjected to temperamental

and culture clashes in his family environment, may react to his frustrations by conduct disorder, while the middle class child, reared strictly, but with less frustration of his status aspirations, may react to frustrations in opportunity for self-expression and to temperamental and culture clashes in his family environment by anxiety and personality problems. Thus the lower class child may behave as though the social order has many loopholes and few restrictions, and the middle-class child as though society has few loopholes and many restrictions. Such behavior would be consistent with differential criminal behavior in adult life, with the poor tending toward crimes involving outbursts of hostility and aggression — thefts and assaults — and the middle-class tending toward crimes involving tension maintenance and the application of an extensive range of conventional protective practices — namely, fraud.[36]

INTELLIGENCE AND RECIDIVISM

The relationship of intelligence and recidivism, *i.e.*, repetition of offenses, has been given some attention. In the United States, roughly one-quarter of all children arraigned as juvenile delinquents have previous arraignments. This proportion is much higher among Negro children. The proportion for girls is roughly one-half the rate for boys of the same race.

Criminologists have reported that among adults, low IQ's contribute an excessive proportion of offenders who tend to become recidivist about as frequently as other offenders and to be as successful on parole. The findings for children are inconclusive. Mann and Mann found among 428 children recidivists lower IQ's (average IQ 78) than among 1,731 unselected delinquents (average IQ 84) arraigned in the Los Angeles juvenile court.[37] The Gluecks found recidivists to deviate in the same direction.[38] But Merrill found no significant difference be-

[34] John Levy, "A Quantitative Study of the Relationship Between Intelligence and Economic Status as a Factor in the Etiology of Children's Behavior Problems." *American Journal of Orthopsychiatry*, 1, pp. 152–162, Jan. 1931.

[35] Allison Davis and Robert J. Havighurst, *Social Class and Color Differences in Child-Rearing*, *American Sociological Review*, December, 1946.

[36] Harry Manuel Shulman, "The Family and Juvenile Delinquency," *Annals American Academy of Political and Social Science*, Vol. 261, January, 1949, p. 30.

[37] Cecil W. Mann and Helene Powner Mann, "Age and Intelligence of a Group of Juvenile Delinquents," *Journal of Abnormal and Social Psychology*, 1939, 34, 351–360.

[38] Eleanor Glueck, "Mental Retardation and Juvenile Delinquency," *Mental Hygiene*, 1935, 19, 549–572. Merrill, *ibid*.

tween recidivists and single arraignments, while Lane and Witty found no difference.[39]

The problem of recidivism has been approached by some investigators in terms of the normal curve for intelligence. Haggerty, among others, has reported that while deviants from the normal curve, *i.e.*, both superior and dull children, tend to higher incidences of behavior disorder than children of average intelligence, the bright group tend to "unlearn" much of their maladjusted behavior between the ages of 9 and 13 years, whereas the dull either continue or increase in the extent of their maladjustment with age increase. In this connection, the finding by Tendler is pertinent, that in a psychiatric child guidance clinic, among matched groups of children, the bright group responded to case work treatment more effectively than the dull group.[40]

Ackerson has studied the effect of intelligence on frequency of offense at different age groups. He found the same results as Haggerty, that bright children tended to a reduction in the frequency of their offenses, compared to dull children. He reported that among pre-adolescents under the age of 13, there was an increase with IQ (to IQ 110–120) of frequency in 154 types of problem incident, but among adolescents ages 13–18 years, the increase in frequency of problem incidents was only among the low IQ's, 70–80, particularly with respect to conduct disorder.[41] Thus the findings of Haggerty, Tendler and Ackerson, while each having a somewhat different orientation, all indicate that bright children tend toward a reduction in their behavior problems with age increase, with or without treatment, while dull children tend toward an increase in behavior problems with age.

SOCIAL INTELLIGENCE AND DELINQUENCY

The material up to this point deals with the relation of *general* intelligence and delinquency. General intelligence has been thought by many psychologists to be a poor indicator of social adjustment. The tendency has been to limit the prognostic use of tests of general intelligence to the prediction of educability through formal classroom instruction in the content of academic education, and to seek the prediction of social adjustment through other tests. Thus Miss Chassell, in an extensive survey of the literature on the relation of intelligence and morality, found correlations between plus 0.10 and plus 0.39, none high enough for statistical significance. Such findings do not wholly thrust aside a relation between intelligence and morality, since the findings demonstrate a positive relationship, but the correlation is too low to be predictive.

The term *social intelligence* refers to the capacity for social adjustment and maturity in social relationships as differentiated from the ability to learn from experience. That is to say, an intelligent person may through his general intelligence learn to profit from experience, but not necessarily in the direction of benefit to society. The adequate study of social intelligence has been retarded by a lack of research in this area, resulting in a lack of well-standardized tests for social intelligence. In part, this has been due to a lack of reference points for the measurement of social development. Child psychology has been relatively successful in tracing the social development of the preschool age group, but beyond this age our knowledge of the individual process in social development is extremely sketchy and based very largely upon doctrinaire speculative theories.

Chief among the very few social intelligence scales is the Vineland Social Maturity scale, a year-level scale standardized for the estimation of level of social performance through the observation of social behavior in the areas of personal hygiene, household duties, purchasing, employment, social relations and civic life. In the belief that this scale might disclose delinquents to be socially immature, in the light of their ego-centricity, it has been used by some investigators. The scanty evidence is conflicting, and not helpful. For example, Springer, testing 80 white and 50 Negro delinquents, found that social maturity level tended to be correlated with IQ, so that bright delinquents tended to be socially mature as measured by the scale. The social maturity of first offenders and recidivists was related to their mental levels. Thus,

[39] R. A. Lane and P. A. Witty, "The Mental Ability of Delinquent Boys," *Journal Juvenile Research*, 1935, 19, pp. 1–12.

[40] Alexander Tendler, "Role of Intelligence and Emotion in Maladjusted Children," *Proceedings and Papers, Ninth International Congress of Psychology*, Princeton, N. J., Psychol. Review Co., p. 425.

[41] Luton Ackerson, *ibid*.

from this study, it would appear that any tendency toward social immaturity among juvenile delinquents would be a function of their tendency to vary from the normal for general intelligence. This area will have to be studied much more before adequate generalizations can be made.[42]

It may prove to be necessary to treat statistics of delinquents in more qualitatively descriptive categories than merely *first offenders* and *recidivists*, for purposes of social intelligence research. The primary behavior disorder, the personality disorder, the assaultive group, and the matured predatory group, may have varying levels of social intelligence corresponding to the varying degrees of social participation involved in different types of delinquent activity. There is a possibility that training school admissions are heavily loaded with predatory offenders whose anti-social experience has included considerable group association and delinquent gang membership. Such delinquents may have had considerably greater experience in group participation than others, and may test higher on tests for social intelligence than isolate offenders.

MECHANICAL INTELLIGENCE AND DELINQUENCY

In addition to general and social intelligence, psychologists have distinguished a number of others in the hierarchy of capacities, of which for our purposes perhaps the most important is mechanical intelligence. This series of qualities, which includes the capacities for form perception, effective hand-eye co-ordination, and an understanding of mechanical relations, is of prime importance in a technical society. A number of tests, some involving actual manipulation of mechanical objects, and others requiring only paper and pencil responses, have been standardized, including the Stenquist Mechanical Assembly Test, the McQuarrie, the Minnesota, the O'Rourke, etc. In addition, numerous tests exist for the measurement of specific motor performances. These tests have demonstrated that general intelligence and mechanical ability are largely independent capacities, the correlation between them rarely rising above plus .40.

Early tests on delinquents gave rise to the hope that here was a quality in which the problem individual might find compensating superiority to the well-adjusted child, and thus a basis for constructive education and training. Several experimenters found delinquents slightly superior to non-delinquents in mechanical ability, and others found no significant differences between the two groups. Slawson found the performance of delinquent boys at the House of Refuge and the Hawthorne school practically on a par with that of New York City school children, on a paper-and-pencil group form of the Stenquist. The writer, on a small sample of 22 pairs of delinquents and their non-delinquent brothers, found the delinquents as a group superior to their brothers, as well as to unselected school children, on a mechanical assembly form of the Stenquist, although they were inferior to their brothers on the average, for general intelligence and school achievement.[43, 44]

Belief in the relative adequacy of delinquents in mechanical ability, as compared to general intelligence and academic school achievement led to a movement during the '20's for the use of trade and vocational education as a delinquency rehabilitation program. School problem youths together with other academic failures were shunted into trade and vocational schools. This program has been generally abandoned, with recognition among educators that competence in trade and vocational careers calls for good intelligence, stable temperamental and personality characteristics, and adequacy in mathematical and language skills, in addition to good mechanical ability. The frequent mental dullness, emotional instabilities, and reading and writing disabilities of a large proportion of delinquents make them poor risks for industrial training. Today, delinquents are recommended for trade and vocational education only on the basis of individual diagnostic study and counselling.

[42] N. N. Springer, "The Social Competence of Adolescent Delinquents; A Comparative Study of White and Negro First Offenders and Recidivists," *The Journal of Social Psychology*, 14, 337–348, 1941.

[43] John Slawson, *The Delinquent Boy*, Boston, 1926.
[44] Harry Manuel Shulman, *Problem Boys and Their Brothers*, Albany, 1929, pp. 64–66.

17

Intelligence and Delinquency *

Sheldon and Eleanor T. Glueck

In view of the fact that the delinquents and non-delinquents were matched as to total intelligence quotient (allowing not more than a ten-point difference), we have been concerned to determine what differences there are, if any, in the components of their intelligence as revealed in the verbal and performance aspects of the Wechsler-Bellevue Scale.

On the whole, the delinquents average less in verbal intelligence than do the non-delinquents, but the two groups resemble each other closely in performance intelligence.

A comparison of the delinquents and non-delinquents in their attainment of the Vocabulary test and the five subtests of the Wechsler-Bellevue verbal battery reveals that the delinquents show less aptitude in Vocabulary, Information, and Comprehension, but that they resemble the non-delinquents in their scores on Similarities, Arithmetic Reasoning, and Memory Span for Digits.

It should be pointed out that the Vocabulary test, although a good indicator of general intelligence, is particularly affected by the amount of actual schooling. In Chapter XII, we have already seen that the delinquents are more retarded in school than the non-delinquents and that they have truanted excessively. The Information test, although likewise a very good indicator of intellectual capacity, is also considerably affected by educational opportunities and the cultural atmosphere of the home. (In the latter respect it has been seen in Chapter XI that the delinquents were less advantaged than

---

* Reprinted by permission of the publishers and The Commonwealth Fund from *Unraveling Juvenile Delinquency*, Sheldon and Eleanor T. Glueck, Cambridge, Mass.: Harvard University Press, Copyright, 1950, by The Commonwealth Fund. Summaries of Chapters XVI and XVII, pages 206–207, 214. Students may wish to consult the detailed statistical findings in *Unraveling.* — Ed.

the non-delinquents.) Success in the Comprehension test, on the other hand, depends upon possession of practical information and the ability to evaluate past experience; and in this test poor verbalizers tend to make lower scores.

Despite the resemblance between the delinquents and non-delinquents on the scores they attain in the performance aspect of the Wechsler-Bellevue Scale, a comparison of their accomplishment on the subtests of this battery shows that the delinquents have less aptitude than the non-delinquents on the Digit Symbol test, but a little more on the Block Design and Object Assembly tests. However, the two groups resemble each other in their accomplishment on the Picture Completion and the Picture Arrangement tests. In assaying the differences in these aspects of performance intelligence, we must keep in mind that the Digit Symbol test, on which the delinquents average less than the non-delinquents, involves concentration and persistency of effort, and is therefore a test in which impulsive, emotionally labile persons would not perform as well as those who are more stable. It will be seen in Chapter XVIII that the delinquents as a group are more labile emotionally than the non-delinquents. The slight superiority of the delinquents over the non-delinquents in the Block Design and Object Assembly tests, although in the latter test the difference between the two groups merely approaches the level of statistical significance, may reflect a greater skill in motor capacity.

It appears, therefore, that the delinquents are, on the whole, somewhat superior in those intellectual tasks in which the approach to meaning is by direct physical relationships (Block Design, and, probably, Object Assembly tests), with a minimum dependence on a structure of intermediary symbols; while the generalizing and abstract thinking of the non-delinquents is through the conventionally accepted intermediate means (symbols). The delinquents apparently do not accumulate a large repertoire of symbols (Vocabulary test) or of symbolized content (Information test). Their generalizations are closely, even though not directly, geared to concrete realities.

We see also that, both as a group and as individuals, the delinquents are more variable than the non-delinquents in their accomplishment on the verbal subtests, but do not manifest any greater variability on the performance sub-tests.

Briefly summarizing the findings presented in Chapter XVII concerning the qualitative and dynamic aspects of intelligence derived through the Rorschach Test, we see that the delinquents and non-delinquents resemble each other in originality, creativity, banality, intuition, phantasy, and over-verbalizing intelligence. The delinquents have somewhat lesser powers of observation, however, and show less potential capacity for objective interests; and significantly larger proportions of them than of the non-delinquents are unrealistic thinkers, lack common sense, and are unsystematic in their approach to the mastery of mental problems or tasks.

Reflection upon these findings suggests that the differences between the delinquents and non-delinquents are concerned with intellectual tendencies that are interwoven with emotional dynamics, and that they are, therefore, of a kind that are likely to be involved, not only in the ability to cope with school tasks, but also in the general process of socialization or maladjustment.

Chapter 5

Psychiatric and Psychoanalytic Aspects
of Delinquency

As is true of proponents of other disciplines, psychiatrists have tended to make exaggerated claims for the role of psychiatry in the understanding and treatment of delinquency. Valuable contributions have been made to the study of the incidence of various types of mental illness among prisoners, beginning with the famous study of inmates of Sing Sing Prison by Dr. Bernard Glueck [1] near the beginning of the century, a research that spearheaded the movements for the establishment of classification centers in correctional institutions as well as court clinics. Some contributions have been made by Sigmund Freud, Franz Alexander, William Healy, Gregory Zilboorg, Robert Lindner and Kate Friedlander, to name but a few, to an understanding of the deeper dynamics of causation of delinquency and criminalism from a psychoanalytic point of view. But it cannot be said that solid progress has been achieved in the development of a body of materials susceptible of verification by familiar techniques of scientific investigation.

Nevertheless, in the Editor's opinion, dynamic psychiatry offers the greatest promise of any single discipline for the elucidation of the subtle and complex motivations of delinquency and crime. For this approach deals with the blended products of the *interplay* of nature and nurture, instead of, as the old criminal anthropology did, tending grossly to overemphasize the innate, or, as typical sociologic criminology does, tending grossly to overemphasize the external environmental, and the too vague and general cultural, influences. At the same time, it is possible that the causes of emotional malaise — whether such illness results in delinquency or not — will ultimately be traced to disturbances of bodily chemical function and that cures will come not from the psychoanalytical couch but from the physical and chemical laboratories. There is reason to believe that psychoanalytic psychiatry deals more with the smoke than with the fire. It is impossible, within the compass of a book of this kind, which has to bring together contributions from several disciplines, to do justice to this difficult subject. The selections are intended to give students an orientation and to indicate the practical applications rather than to enter into subtle and involved discussions of psychoanalytic theories.

The first paper, by Bernard Glueck, Sr., discusses similarities of therapeutic needs and techniques among non-criminal and criminal patients, and provides the basic framework of general psychoanalytic thinking in respect to the development of personality and character structure as these are related to delinquency.

Glueck's general presentation is followed by an important analysis by Jenkins and Hewitt on "Types of Personality Structure in Child Guidance Clinics." This schematic presentation indicates the dynamic relationship of various personality traits and environmental influences among three fundamental types of children found by Jenkins and his co-workers: the overinhibited, internal conflicting, neurotic personality structure; the uninhibited hostile, unsocialized aggressive type; the pseudosocial type. This article

---

[1] B. Glueck, "Clearing Houses and Classification of Institutions as Aids to Institutional Work," New York City Conf. on Char. and Corr., 1917, 158–166.

is significant for the leads inductively arrived at through reflection upon clinical experience, — insights suggestive of fruitful further research of a kind that should tend to integrate, into patterns meaningful for understanding and therapy, the disparate traits and sociocultural factors (especially those of parent-child relationships) involved in undifferentiated "delinquency." Jenkins and his colleagues have been developing their basic concepts in further significant research.

After distinguishing four types of antisocial behavior corresponding to the natural age-periods, Blau, in the third article of this chapter, emphasizes the basic role of parent–child relationships in the taming of instinct and the development of personality and character. Lack of parental affection and understanding is stated to be the fundamental cause of antisocial maladjustment and "the great injustice hidden within most delinquent histories" — conclusions the Editor and his co-researcher, Dr. Eleanor T. Glueck, had reached previously through intensive statistical study of many hundreds of delinquents and non-delinquents. In Blau's clinical experience, "the child misbehaves because he is unhappy, and he has discovered this means of maintaining his emotional balance."

The fourth article, by Blau and Hulse, deals with anxiety neurosis as a cause of behavior disorders in children. The thesis developed is "that a large number of so-called primary behavior disorders in children are childhood instances of anxiety ('actual') neurosis and that its symptoms are all derivatives of persistent, direct anxiety expressed in the peculiar and special ways open to a child." An attempt is made to fit into a "logical dynamic pattern" the symptomatology, the child's immaturity, his apparent lack of guilt feeling, the threatening and depriving role of the parents, and the technique of treatment. A differential diagnosis is provided, distinguishing anxiety or "actual" neurosis from psychoneurosis (symptomatic and character neuroses) and from neurotic traits and habit disorders.

Gardner's article discusses the relationship of the youthful offender's act to the other acts of children, normal or neurotic, and emphasizes how valuable is the study of both the delinquent act and the child offender to an understanding of normal child behavior at various stages of development. He lists and discusses seven significant propositions, relative to neurotic behavior, which he deems equally applicable to delinquent conduct. He is of the opinion that "our present-day concepts of human behavior will allow us . . . to include the child's delinquent behavior — all delinquent behavior — within the framework of the neuroses . . . The delinquent act is but a special type — a syndrome, if you will — within the group designated 'the neuroses,' " a view not dissimilar to that of Blau and other psychoanalytically oriented psychiatrists. Gardner contributes a thought-provoking analysis of "aggressive, incorporative behavior," and of the resistance to a recognition of the great significance of the primitive, unconscious dynamisms in theft, the most frequent type of delinquency. Stealing, Gardner insists, is usually an instinctual act of "wrenching away" the stolen object from the person of another with whom the object is identified. Thus, he regards the aggressive-destructive impulse, as the deepest causal source — that is, the fundamental pleasurable motivation — of stealing. An equally suggestive analysis, contained in Gardner's article on the aggressive-destructive impulses in the sex offender, was omitted for lack of space.[2]

The final item in this chapter, from Unraveling Juvenile Delinquency, shows the incidence of various aspects of mental pathology among 500 true delinquents and 500 boys found, after long and intensive investigation, to be non-delinquents.

---

[2] This is to be found in 34 Mental Hygiene (1950), 44–63.

18

Analytic Psychiatry and
Criminology *

Bernard Glueck

I

It may be worth while to preface this paper by a reference to two types of predictions which are justified by the current state of affairs in the respective fields of psychiatry and criminology.

On the one hand, the current admission rate into hospitals for the mentally diseased entirely justifies the conclusion that there are today a round number of 1,000,000 boys and girls, young men and young women in our homes, schools, colleges, shops and factories who are destined to become patients in hospitals for the mentally ill in the course of their lives. On the other hand, such criminal statistics as are available in this country justify the opinion that of every one hundred men and women, children and adults of our population there is at least one individual who at some time in his life will be sentenced to a fine or imprisonment, and that about five out of every hundred of the population will be subject to arrest in the course of their life span. Now if by some happy turn of events it were possible to institute a dependable enterprise which would carry the promise of preventing the prodigious amount of suffering, maladjustment and waste in one of the above fields, would such an enterprise require very much modification to render it equally effective in the other field?

If we were to learn how to prevent the criminalism to which such a large proportion of our population is apparently destined and really

had the opportunity and means for setting into operation an adequate machinery for such prevention, would we then have to learn very much that is new? Would we require a very different equipment to achieve similar results in connection with the preventable forms of neuroticism and mental disorder?

The answer one might give to these queries is likely to define one's attitude regarding the relationship of psychiatry to criminology.

There is no particular advantage in restating here the traditional views which dominated both of these fields until several decades ago. Suffice it to say, first, that a useful and constructive cooperation between them was made possible only when criminalism came to be considered as a form of conduct *subject to the same laws which apply to all other forms of conduct,* and, secondly, when psychiatry and psychiatrists ceased to confine their interest to the frankly psychotic or defective individual and reached out to study and understand the imperfectly designated "border-line cases" of mental malaise. Such reorientation toward the problem of criminalism is also indispensable to truly effective work on the part of those who, as judges, institutional workers, probation or parole officers, are entrusted with the pressing tasks of coping with criminal conduct.

II

In order to make this point of view clear to the probation officer and others concerned with the treatment of that form of aberrant conduct which the laws of civilized communities designate criminal, a brief sketch of some fundamentals of psychoanalytic psychology is necessary.

The recognition that every infant comes into the world as an unadjusted, egocentric and narcissistic [1] creature, wholly devoid of any concern about social requirements, which psychoanalytic psychology made possible, is of equal significance for psychiatry and criminology. It com-

---

* Reprinted from S. Glueck (Editor), *Probation and Criminal Justice,* New York, The Macmillan Company, 1933, 197–220. Used by permission of The Macmillan Company. See, also, K. Friedlander, *The Psycho-analytical Approach to Juvenile Delinquency,* New York, International Universities Press, Inc., 1947, 1949, 67–73; J. J. Michaels, "Delinquency and Control," 24 *Am. J. Orthopsychiatry* (1954), 258–265. — *Ed.*

[1] Narcissism, "love of self," is an important concept in psychoanalytic theory and technique, relating to a condition the existence of which has been borne out by a vast fund of clinical evidence. The erotic impulses of early childhood become more or less integrated with the growth of the individual and are normally focussed on the self either during a certain stage of development or practically throughout life, depending on the emotional economy of the individual. — *Ed.*

pels the inference that so-called normal, socially acceptable and ethically correct conduct is a hard-won achievement which only follows the successful taming, transformation and socialization of the original instinctual equipment in response to environmental pressures and demands for adjustment. Any experience in the life of the new individual — especially during the important period from birth to the age of five or six — which facilitates or hinders this socializing process is of significance for personality and conduct, irrespective of the type of personality or the type of conduct — criminal or otherwise — one happens to be dealing with.

It would seem, therefore, that any discussion of the relation of psychiatry to criminology and of the technique of the psychiatrically trained worker to that of the probation officer must first of all stress the common background in human nature and in certain universal experiences attending the process of socialization of the original nature of man that underlies all human conduct. *Whether a given child will develop into a normal, healthy and decent citizen, or into a mentally diseased, inadequate or criminal individual, depends more upon this common background of human nature and experience than upon all the special noxious agents of a physical or social nature that have been stressed from time to time as causes of inadequacy, maladjustment and criminalism. The same holds good for those frank mental diseases which are still among the most prevalent today, the schizophrenias* [2] *and manic-depressive disorders.* [3] Similarly, there is no reason to assume that those techniques which have

proved themselves to be effective in the management of the problems that belong to the field of psychiatry require a radical modification when applied to the problems associated with criminal conduct. This is certainly true of the field of probation. That the prevalent approach to the problems of crime (particularly that outside the domain of juvenile delinquency) still reflects an almost complete failure to take advantage of this fact is due to causes which do not in the least invalidate the correctness of the above thesis.

III

In a communication before the Annual Conference of the National Probation Association in 1923, I endeavored to outline the reasons for the difficulty of carrying over into the field of criminology of the techniques and points of view of dynamic psychiatry. It is pertinent to the object of this book to repeat what I then said concerning the expectations of the probation movement on the part of those of us of the medical profession who had become associated with the field of criminology. I then characterized the probation movement as the bridge over which might be carried some of the idealism and some of the scientific spirit of modern medicine and modern social service into the dark recesses of the traditional processes of the criminal law; for unlike these, the probation process does imply a clearly defined meliorative aim and is carried on in the normal environmental setting rather than behind walls and bars. In the same address I drew certain comparisons between the fields of mental medicine and criminology with the view of indicating some of the reasons, at least, for the difficulties in the way of a more effective cooperation between psychiatry and criminology.

Notwithstanding the fact that much progress has been made in some sections of the United States in promoting and refining this cooperation, the issues I stressed in 1923 still apply with equal force and will bear restatement.

The medical sciences, and particularly psychiatry, owe their relatively greater success in the management of their problems as compared with the achievements in attacking the problems of crime, first of all, to their *clarity of purpose.* The medical sciences have never compromised with the principle that disease is an enemy of mankind and is to be eradicated.

[2] "A group of mental disorders arising on a basis of autistic or schizoid temperament [i.e., self-absorption, detachment from the environment, preoccupation with internal rumination]; in its most marked manifestations it constitutes dementia praecox; in it, however, are also included more recoverable conditions such as acute halucinoses, delusional states, some psychotic episodes seen in cases of mental deficiency, in psychopathic personalities, and even in some conditions with a toxic or organic etiology." A. J. Rosanoff, *Manual of Psychiatry*, 6th Ed., 1927, p. 691. — *Ed.*

[3] "A group of constitutional mental disorders in which the disturbances are mainly in the sphere of the emotions. They are characterized by attacks of excitement, or depression, or of mixtures of both; each attack terminates in recovery, but leaves behind a tendency toward recurrence." Rosanoff, *op. cit.*, p. 681. — *Ed.*

Having thus clearly defined the objective, the medical sciences proceeded to devote their energies to the discovery and the perfection of a technique for its attainment. Finally, progress in the field of medicine depended to a very large extent upon the deliberate and intelligent cultivation of public sentiment in favor of the eradication of the enemies to health.

Thus clarity of purpose, a scientific and workable technique and the backing of an enlightened public opinion have always been indispensable conditions for progress in the medical sciences. The history of medicine records many an obstacle to the achievement and maintenance of these conditions, and even today medical progress is impeded by many hindrances among which are those of ignorance, prejudice and special privilege, familiar enough ghosts in the field of criminology. But in spite of these difficulties the clarity of purpose, individual and social, which characterizes the medical profession is a substantial guarantee of the ultimate attainment of those of its objectives which are at all attainable.

What is the situation in these respects in the field of criminology? It did not require the elaborate and costly enterprise of the much-discussed Wickersham Commission to prove how radically different the situation is here. By no stretch of the imagination can "clarity of purpose" for the eradication of the evils of crime be discerned in the contemporary American scene. Security to life and property is becoming more and more a matter of pure chance in most of our centers of population instead of something which every citizen of a civilized community has a right to expect. Law enforcement and any deliberate attempt at the cultivation of a respect for the law are becoming increasingly impossible in a society where it has become so difficult to determine what the *mores* really are that govern its conduct. The general public apathy toward the problem which is bred on the one hand by a loss of faith in the integrity of our political, social and industrial leadership, and on the other by a most ominous and historically unprecedented intimidation of the law-abiding elements of the community, render more or less futile any attempt at the cultivation of an enlightened public opinion in favor of the eradication of the evils of crime. While it is true that in a certain sense these questions have little to do specifically with a

discussion of the relation of psychiatry to criminology, the fact remains that whatever benefits might accrue to criminology from its association with psychiatry must continue to be limited to the occasional, sporadic contact of psychiatrist and individual criminal as long as the conditions described above persist.

The outstanding exception to this general state of affairs is to be found in the field of probation. The offender who is selected for this type of management could, theoretically at any rate, at once become identified with any other maladjusted individual requiring scientific and purposeful understanding and help, irrespective of the fact that his particular maladjustment expressed itself, among other things, in criminal conduct. Indeed, every psychiatrist is called upon to deal with types of difficulties of personality and conduct which are antisocial and could legally be designated as criminal. He does not, on this account, feel compelled to resort to any special techniques unless the element of safety to the individual or society enters the situation. When this is the case he is obliged to have recourse to any one of a variety of psychiatric institutions designed to meet the requirements of safety alike to the patient and the community. But because he has to resort to this additional measure of security it does not mean that he has to modify any of the essential elements of the technique for the amelioration or cure of human maladjustments. His choice of method of treatment is determined first and last by the type of individual he has to deal with and the type of disorder responsible for the maladjustment. In the case of the dangerously and incurably insane, for instance, he does not hesitate to insist upon permanent segregation in a proper institution, virtually a sentence to life imprisonment. But this type of decision, regrettable as it is from the point of view of sentiment, is based always on the findings of objective, unprejudiced, scientific inquiry into all the elements entering a given situation. Moreover, it is always a provisional decision and subject to modification as soon as the application of new discoveries in understanding and treatment calls for a different procedure. Thus, less than a decade or so ago patients suffering from paresis [4] were

---

[4] Paresis, or "general paralysis," is a "disease of the brain due to invasion of the nervous tissues by the

considered incurable and were managed as incurables. The newer therapy of this condition compels an entirely different procedure for this type of patient.

IV

Assuming then that there really exists a genuine honesty of purpose and a sufficient clarity of objective behind the probation movement, all that is needed to assure the adequately selected probationer a fair chance of successful rehabilitation is the provision of instrumentalities within the ambit of criminal law administration of a kind which approximate as nearly as possible the existing techniques of psychiatry and social service.[5] Both of these disciplines have become very much enriched in the past several decades through the contributions of psychoanalytic psychology, and a very important element of this enrichment is the greater applicability of both psychiatry and social service to problems of human maladjustment which are not definable in strictly somatic or psychopathological terms. Psychoanalysis has made possible a conception of the human personality which opened the way to a more specifically *causal* therapy and intelligent guidance in matters of human relationship than has been possible ever before. Whereas, before the advent of Freud's teachings, problems of adjustment and maladjustment, of health and disease, were viewed very largely and often entirely so, as problems in the relationship between the individual and his environment, the new vistas concerning the nature of man's subjective or internal environment which psychoanalysis made possible present a radically different and more promising orientation.

The more minute investigation of the deeper structures of the human personality revealed man as the carrier, from the moment of birth, of opposing and conflicting forces which strive for mastery and which expose him to a con-

tinuous and difficult struggle to achieve and maintain some sort of workable adjustment between these contending forces within himself. Any deliberate undertaking in guidance and treatment must take account of this conception of the human personality. Otherwise the fundamental and compelling motives in the conduct of the individual we are attempting to influence will surely escape our scrutiny, and we will be engaged in the bankrupt gestures of punishing or "treating" mere symptoms.

The judge, probation officer and any other official dealing with criminals should therefore have a clear picture of the structure of personality. They have to take cognizance, first of all, of the conscious, the socially oriented and visible self, the self which is in continuous contact with the realities of the external world. This is the self of brain and brawn, of education and experience, the initiator and executor of conscious purposes and the spearhead of man's impacts with the world about him. It is obvious that whatever the forces may be which enter into the determination of attitude and conduct they must function through this conscious self, since it alone has direct access to man's equipment for dealing with the requirements of life. In the final analysis, it is the strength or weakness of this conscious self which decides the issues of adaptation. It requires no profound psychological insight to appreciate that this "self" of which we are speaking, and which is psychoanalytically designated the "ego," is not co-equal with the "somatic-self," the disorders of which constitute the domain of medicine and surgery. It is all that is accessible to us from ordinary observation of what constitutes the human personality, which even the most stubborn somatist is obliged to consider as beyond understanding on purely somatic grounds. Nevertheless, this conscious self — this perceptive, reasoning and executive organ of the human personality and the only accessible object of influence to ordinary methods of education, guidance and therapy — is largely the servant *of forces which are inaccessible by these methods of influence.*

We are able to obtain a glimpse of what the moving forces of human attitude and human conduct are that lie outside of this conscious self when we observe what happens in the case of the insane patient. Here the conscious self abandons control and submits to forces which

germ of syphilis (parenchymatous invasion), characterized by progressive mental and physical deterioration, resisting treatment, and generally terminating fatally within a few years." Rosanoff, *op. cit.*, p. 673. Dr. Rosanoff's definition, published as recently as 1927, containing the opinion that this disorder resists treatment, makes Dr. Glueck's illustration all the more pointed. — *Ed.*

[5] On the role of modern social work in the rehabilitation of offenders, see particularly the articles by Mr. Weiss and Mr. Ferris. — *Ed.*

were hitherto unsuspected by ordinary observation. The delusions and misinterpretations of the insane, their bizarre distortions of reality and their symbolic actions, speak a language unfamiliar to us from observation of the ego of the average normal individual. Whence arise these strange attitudes and actions, these queer symbolizations and distortions?

This brings me to a consideration of a second self that enters into the constitution of the human personality, the "instinctual self." The expression of this aspect of the personality in pure form in adult life is strictly limited to certain organic cravings for satisfaction, but it comes to expression more freely in connection with the dream and in certain pathological states, particularly the psychosis. In the course of individual development this self has to be subjected to a complicated and difficult process of taming, transformation and socialization before it can be utilized in the service of the adaptive requirements of man. It is the self which is identical with the psychoanalytic concept of the "*id*," a hypothetical reservoir of primitive, egocentric and unadjusted strivings reflecting man's kinship to the lower forms of life. The conscious self, on the other hand, is the product of rearing, education and culture; it reflects the impress upon the asocial and amoral and unadjusted infant of his social environment; it is the evidence of the moulding influence which the social milieu has exercised upon the developing individual. Now the central objective of this environmental influence is the weaning of the developing individual from the lures and attractions of the egocentric, selfish and asocial aspects of the instinctual self with the view of adjusting it to the requirements of living in association with others.

Recognition of the relationship of the two aspects of the personality thus far discussed is basically important if not, indeed, indispensable, to a lasting, rather than superficial, therapy. Yet the major concern of traditional psychiatry and psychology — and thus far only these have been called upon by crime-treating agencies — has been with the constitution and difficulties of the conscious self, whereas psychoanalytic theory and practice concern themselves primarily with the developmental vicissitudes and destiny of the instinctual self and its relation to the conscious manifestations of human life.

But psychoanalysis, under the pressure of a vast fund of clinical experience, has defined a third major aspect of the personality. For a long time after the advent of the psychoanalytic conception of the personality, the sources of the conflicts at the root of human maladjustment were considered to have been covered by the antagonism between the instinctual and conscious selves. This antagonism is in the nature of a striving for the control of the conscious personality of two sets of forces, those of instinct or nature on the one hand, and those of nurture and culture on the other. Excessive domination of the conscious self by either of these forces is bound to lead to conflict and maladjustment, while so-called normal conduct reflects the achievement of a satisfactory compromise between them. Thus excessive repression and checking of the claims of instinct brings in its wake no less serious effects than does failure to restrict and adapt adequately the life of instinct to the requirements of normally healthy and effective living.

The third aspect of the personality formulated as the result of further experience with psychoanalysis as an instrument of research and therapy is what has been conveniently designated the *super-self*, the so-called "super-ego" of psychoanalytic terminology. It is conceived of as a part of the conscious self which becomes differentiated in the very earliest stages of individual development, is gradually internalized through the process of introjection [6] and continues to develop as the subjective and unconscious aspect of what we consciously know as "conscience." The super-ego gradually develops into the subjective regulator or monitor of conduct, or, to put it differently, the means of the ego's management of the claims of instinct. For instance, an impulse to cruelty which if permitted free rein would lead the conscious self to the commission of a cruel act, is subjected, as are all other instinctual drives, to the scrutiny of this super-ego; and the destiny of this impulse, that is, whether it is to be checked or sublimated,[7] or permitted expression

---

[6] Introjection or mental assimilation, is a term of art used by psychoanalysts to describe the unconscious tendency of the ego, as soon as it begins to have need of the external world, to incorporate the environment, as it were, into the personality — *Ed*.

[7] "Sublimation is the exchange of infantile sexual aims for interests or modes of pleasure-finding which

in direct action, is determined by the relationship, on the one hand, between the super-ego and ego and, on the other, by the quality of these functions in a given personality.

This bare outline of the psychoanalytic conception of the nature of the human personality naturally fails to do justice to the requirements for a complete and comprehensive sketch of psychoanalytic theory and practice. It is not the purpose of this paper to restate what has been so adequately and fully written in the extensive literature on the subject. It is given here to probation officers and others in simple terms as a background for the working hypothesis which is increasingly dominating psychiatric and social procedure. The claims and aims of psychoanalysis do not in the least invalidate the significance of toxic, traumatic or degenerative factors in psychopathology. These noxious agents are estimated in the light of their capacity to influence the conscious self, or ego, in the performance of its role in the total adaptive requirements of the personality, internal as well as external. The psychoanalytic approach does not in the least call for a neglect of those therapeutic endeavors of a chemical, physical or social nature which have the capacity of benefiting the *conscious self*. It merely calls attention to the one-sidedness and necessarily restricted range of applicability of these methods. The great majority of socially maladjusted individuals, as well as those who belong to the categories of psycho-neurotics [8] and so-called psychopathic [9] and neurotic characters, do not suffer from disabilities which the traditional methods of chemical, physical and social therapy are capable of benefitting, although a certain number of them do. In the great majority of them the difficulties or failures to meet successfully the requirements of social living are due to unsolved conflicts of

a subjective nature, initiated and kept alive by factors which are the common heritage of mankind. The same is certainly true of certain types of so-called confirmed criminals as well as of those who rarely or in some exceptionally specific way give expression in conduct to primitive anti-social impulses.

I am taking it for granted that any enlightened medical, psychiatric or social procedure of which the probationary process may have occasion to avail itself in connection with the individual probationer will strive to employ every possibility of diagnosis and treatment which might throw light on the difficulty and offer ways for correcting it. But intimate contact with problems of personality and conduct, including those of crime and delinquency for a period of twenty years and more, has convinced me that the traditional methods of a chemical, physical and social nature have but a very limited applicability in matters of this sort, particularly in the field of criminology. It is a great pity that after twenty years of contact with criminology I cannot truthfully say that these aids, limited though they are, have anywhere been given the kind of complete and adequate opportunity to function within the machinery of the criminal law that is considered an indispensable minimum in the field of medicine and psychiatry.[10] There exist in the main a great deal of lip service and perfunctory gesture and an expectancy of results of which the kind of practice which existing opportunities make possible is totally incapable.

When we come to the strictly psychological approaches in connection with problems of crime and delinquency we are faced with the same situation which confronts even today the field of psychological medicine. Those who ignore the teachings of the psychoanalytic school and limit their approach to efforts at influencing the conscious personality can of necessity have recourse only to methods of persuasion, suggestion and reëducation. No one can have any quarrel with these methods as long as the condition which one attempts to influence is accessible to such techniques. Nevertheless it has become an axiom of modern psychiatric practice at its best to strive for a kind of treatment which is not limited to the removal of symp-

---

are no longer directly sexual although psychically related, and which are on a higher social level." William Healy, A. F. Bronner, and A. M. Bowers, *The Structure and Meaning of Psychoanalysis as Related to Personality and Behavior*, New York, 1930, p. 248. — *Ed.*

[8] Psychoneuroses are disorders "characterized by nervous symptoms produced by psychic causes and through psychic mechanisms." Rosanoff, *op. cit.*, p. 689. — *Ed.*

[9] Psychopathic means "psychically abnormal in ways other than those of mental deficiency, epilepsy, the psychoses, psychoneuroses, and alcohol and drug addictions." Rosanoff, *Id.* — *Ed.*

[10] But see Part Three, especially Chapters 27–28, of this book. — *Ed.*

toms but which aims at ridding the patient of the need for *symptom formation*.

Surely a similar objective can be no less desirable in the treatment of the individual delinquent. Even the most conscientious sort of application of the methods of suggestion, persuasion and reëducation is apt to fall short of the desired result unless a clear conception is had of the moving forces behind a specific bit of conduct. And these forces, as we have already indicated, are not confined to the sphere of the conscious self and are therefore not accessible to scrutiny and influence by methods applicable only to the conscious self. This view is gaining recognition in an ever wider sphere of psychiatric and social practice. Whenever practical conditions of accessibility and economic status permit, patients suffering from various types of psychological or conduct disorder, in some instances even those suffering from certain forms of frank mental disease, seek, by preference, psychoanalytic treatment. The logic for preferring this type of treatment to the traditional psychological methods mentioned above is irresistible, once the psychoanalytic formulations concerning the nature of man — formulations not based on mere speculation but much clinical experience and therapeutic success — are accepted.

So-called normality, in the light of this conception, is a relative and not an absolute concept and depends, as do the various deviations from normal, upon the interrelations between the various selves sketched above which enter into the constitution of the human personality. The so-called normal personality reflects the successful achievement of a satisfactory and workable compromise between the forces contending for the control of personality and conduct. It is entirely in accord with actual clinical experience to see in the various forms of personality maladjustment, from the mildest to the most severe, differing degrees of deviation from the above-mentioned norm. These deviations will depend either on some special qualities of the different selves which we outlined above or upon some disturbance in the relation between them. To begin with, individuals undoubtedly differ as regards the original strength, intensity or plasticity of their instinctual heritage. Clinical experience with the psychoanalytic instrument renders inescapable the assumption of such primary differences in in-

stinctual equipment. Individuals undoubtedly differ as regards native capacity for sublimatory management of their instinctual equipment. The same is true of the strength and quality of the conscious self; and differences in early experiences are bound to lead to differences in the composition of the "super-ego." It is well known to what lengths psychoanalytic theory has gone in the emphasis of experiences in the early years of life as conditioners of personality and conduct.

V

Having given this general formulation of the psychoanalytic view of the personality, it will be of some service to survey at this point, briefly to be sure, the various forms of pathological deviation as seen by the psychoanalytic school of psychology, with the view of determining to what extent the clinical manifestations of criminalism might be brought within the framework of psychoanalytic theory. At one end of the scale are found the so-called transference neuroses,[11] at the other end the narcissistic neuroses. Between these extremes there is to be found a very important group of patients, the so-called "neurotic characters," whose difficulties of adjustment are of great social and criminologic significance.

When we speak of the *transference neuroses* we have in mind the various forms of hysteria and compulsion and obsessional neuroses. These concern individuals who suffer because of an unmanageable intrapsychic conflict and

---

[11] "The field of psychoanalytic therapy has been limited mainly to what are known as the Transference Neuroses (Hysteria, Anxiety neurosis, Obsessional neurosis), that is, the symptoms are all substitutive libidinous gratifications, and transference is the center of the cure. In contradistinction to these are the Narcistic Neuroses in which the capacity for transference is little or none, and the physician is rejected with indifference; such individuals have been considered practically inaccessible to psychoanalytic efforts. Freud's recent conception of three mental systems (the Id, Ego, Super-Ego) has opened up new possibilities for exploring both the narcistic neuroses and the psychoses. Much stress is now being laid on the Super-ego, and Freud says that its attitude should be taken into account in all forms of mental disease. On the basis of these new dynamic conceptions, he defines the transference neurosis as a conflict between the Ego and the Id; the narcissic neurosis as a conflict between the Ego and the Super-ego; and the psychosis as a conflict between the Ego and reality." Healy, Bronner and Bowers, *op. cit.*, p. 458. — *Ed.*

in whom the symptoms reflect an effort at a symbolic or substitutive gratification of instinctual drives which are tabooed and prohibited by the super-ego. The conscious or socially oriented self has not undergone any appreciable weakening or disintegration, but it is inhibited or interfered with to a greater or less degree because of its subjugation to a too severe inhibitory influence from the side of the super-ego. The conscious self still possesses insight into the fact that something is wrong and is capable of a considerable degree of auto-criticism. But it is incapable of dealing adequately with the intrapsychic conflict. Its integrity is threatened because, as Ernest Jones says, "for the maintenance of this integrity it needs, on the one hand, secure possession of certain sexual impulses, or their derivatives, and on the other hand, a secure relation to external reality."

There are significant differences of etiology between the hysterias and the compulsion neuroses which need not concern us here. But it is true of all forms of psychoneuroses that in a general way the claims of instinct or nature have experienced an unnecessarily excessive denial and restriction, in response to excessive taboos imposed upon the individual by that side of his nature which reflects the claims of culture or nurture. Since even the mildest case of transference-neurosis is a problem of the personality as a whole, and affects therefore the behavior and responses of the total personality, it is bound to carry with it difficulties of adaptation and frictions with the environment. But in order to avoid serious fallacies of treatment, it is important to recognize that no matter how severe these frictions with the environment may be they cannot have any *causal* bearing upon the disorder. The cause of the psychoneurosis lies in the intrapsychic conflict. In so far as the claims of society or culture constitute an element of this conflict, they have become internalized and to all intents and purposes are now part of the nature of the individual. They have acquired in the course of time a degree of significance and power equal to the significance and power of instinct itself. Hence the futility of so much treatment that is directed primarily or solely to changes of environmental conditions.[12]

The next large category of personality maladjustment embraces the various forms of *psychosis* or mental disease (*narcissistic neuroses*). Here the situation might be said to be quite the reverse of what happens in the psychoneuroses. This need not in the least invalidate the conception that basically the same forces are at work here as in the psychoneuroses. But in the case of the psychoses the claims of instinct assume ascendency and are given free play to the extent of the degree of ego disintegration. Through the abandonment of the sense of reality and of auto-criticism the claims of culture are increasingly ignored. Psychotic thinking and behavior reflect a regression of libido [13] to the earliest narcissistic phases. The difficulty here is primarily with the ego, or the conscious, socially oriented self; and it opens the way for a helpful definition of the relation of psycho-

---

of a mechanical nature, dealing with "interstitial areas" in cities, is indicated by personality analysis of individual criminals. Simplest logic should have pointed out to the active researchers into the extremely crude and far-removed cause-and-effect relationship between gross environmental conditions in city neighborhoods and individual or mass delinquency that while, as has often been pointed out in their studies, a higher percentage of delinquents are found in "interstitial areas" than in other neighborhoods, the fact remains that over 90 per cent of children living even in the extremest of such delinquency regions *do not become delinquent*. The probable reason for this, as Dr. Glueck above implies, has nothing to do with conditions dealt with by ordinary sociological methods, and has much to do with what goes on in the deeper mental life of people. In studying the etiologic factors in many cases of criminality, the significant data are not so much the objectively discernible and measurable conditions of a delinquency area as the nature and management of the introjected materials the personality absorbs from without. Not only is this concept important from the point of view of criminologic research but from that of the practical treatment of delinquents and criminals. — Ed.

[13] No term has precipitated more heated attack on psychoanalysis than libido. While Freud says, "that force by which the sexual instinct is represented in the mind, we call libido," it must be remembered that his conception of sexual force is so broad as to embrace other instinctual energy. Freud somewhere says: "Our one-sidedness is like that of the chemist who traces all compounds back to the force of chemical attraction. In doing so, he does not deny the force of gravity; he leaves that to the physicist to reckon with." For a comprehensive analysis of libido and such analogous or related concepts as Bergson's "*élan vital*" and McDougall's "*hormé*," see Healy, Bronner and Bowers, *op. cit.*, pp. 2–6. — Ed.

---

[12] The great gap between the realities of the problem and the elaborate recent sociological researches

analytic doctrine to organic or toxic etiology when we observe that the same state of affairs obtains whether the damage to the ego is due to organic or toxic agents, or to psychologic developmental vicissitudes. In the case of the psychotic the conflict is between the ego and reality.

There exists still another, fairly well differentiated category of personality maladjustment which has received very illuminating consideration psychoanalytically — the so-called *"neurotic character."* In this class belong many of the cases formerly designated as "psychopathic personalities" and constitutionally inferior, as well as certain forms of perversion and addiction.

In endeavoring to define what the play of forces is in the neurotic character we are obliged to approach our discussion from a different angle. If we are correct in our assumption that this internal conflict to which we have repeatedly referred is the inevitable destiny of every human being, is it not permissible to look upon ontogenetic development in general as a defence against this natural impediment? The problem which confronts every new-born infant is that of bringing under the control of a weak, poorly organized and inexperienced ego the forces of instinctual drive which are supported by all the phylogenetic background of human evolution. The development of the conscious self, of the ego, is in itself a defensive construction against the threat of being overwhelmed by the force of instinct which is bound to lead to friction with reality, a consequence which the infant and young child can but poorly endure.

Normal character has been defined as "a set of organized behavior reactions founded on and tending to preserve a stable equilibrium between Id tendencies and submission to reality; they are characterized by more or less satisfactory adaptation along lines of displacement." [14] Normal character itself is an adequate defence against the internal sources of conflict. In the psychoneuroses, as we have seen, the socially

oriented part of the self, the ego, protects itself against being overwhelmed by the claims of instinct through the release of substitutive gratification, the symptom. The disorder itself is a defensive construction. In the psychoses, the socially oriented part of the self is overwhelmed by instinctual pressure and yields more or less completely to its sway. Regression [15] is a defeat, temporary or permanent as the case may be.

What happens in the case of the neurotic character? Provisionally we may assume that the original conflict here has the same source. May we go a step further and say that the character traits which in various combinations constitute the neurotic character are also in the nature of a defence? According to Edward Glover, who has contributed considerably to the elucidation of the neurotic character, this type of individual is deficient, as is the psychotic, in a sense of reality; but while the psychotic distorts reality through projection,[16] the neurotic character makes social situations and conventions fit in with his distorted notions of reality. These individuals lack adequate defence mechanisms against instinctual impulses which are condemned by the super-ego. In contradistinction to the psycho-neurotic, who deals with unmanageable instinctual tensions by symptom formation, the neurotic characters "act out" their symptoms in daily life. They embroil their environment in their fight against their sense of guilt, making serious blunders in connection with the most important and decisive moments of their lives. They are usually subject to the domination of their unconscious instinctual tendencies, a fact reflected in senseless, irrational behavior. They live out their impulses and at the same time manage to get themselves punished, as it were, by the cruelty of "fate" or "chance." The neurotic character may be conceived of as standing between the neurotic and the healthy personality.

---

[14] Displacement is "the mechanism by which an emotion appropriate to one group of ideas becomes attached to a logically inappropriate idea, but quite appropriate as seen in the unconscious." Martin W. Peck, *The Meaning of Psychoanalysis* (Introduction by Bernard Glueck, M.D.), New York, 1931, p. 272. — *Ed.*

[15] Regression is "the act of backward coursing of the libido to an early fixation because the individual is unable to function at a higher level." Peck, *op. cit.*, p. 271. — *Ed.*

[16] Projection "is a defensive process under sway of the pleasure principle whereby the Ego thrusts forth on the external world unconscious wishes and ideas which, if allowed to penetrate into consciousness, would be painful to the Ego." Healy, Bronner and Bowers, *op. cit.*, 230. — *Ed.*

Now the human being has always been subject to the types of distorted management of his nature that we have described above, certainly since the beginnings of civilization. He has always resorted to various measures for the relief of the discomforts and the inadequacies which failure to manage the intrapsychic conflict brought in its wake. To review even very briefly the history of man's efforts to deal with the difficulties of his own nature and bring it into accord with the requirements of reality would carry us considerably beyond the scope of this paper. It would involve a review of his experimentations with magic and religion and with the early groping after a more disciplined psychological medicine. But whatever these methods might have been, whether suggestion, persuasion, hypnosis, or reëducation, none could have as its objective anything beyond the removal of existing symptoms. They all ignored the unconscious sources of human motivation and their influence was limited to the conscious self. With the exception of Freud's employment of hypnosis for affect-discharge purposes during the early stages of the psychoanalytic movement, they never reached unconscious sources of difficulty. The advent of psychoanalysis brought with it a radical shift of aim; the aim of therapy became the ridding of the individual of the need for symptom formation. A successfully completed psychoanalysis not only rids the patient of his symptoms but brings about a degree of extension of conscious or ego control over unconscious impulses which eliminates the *need for pathological methods* of dealing with the internal conflict.

What has been said thus far naturally applies first of all to well-defined issues in psychopathology and psychiatry. To be sure, in all of these issues questions of human attitudes and human conduct occupy the center of the stage. The relation which this discussion up to now may be said to bear to the definition and management of the problems of criminalism will, as I have indicated early in this paper, depend upon the point of view one entertains with respect to the nature of criminal conduct. It is a well-established and readily discernible fact, however, that a truly enlightened criminal procedure always reflects a recognition of the close relationship between criminology and psychiatry.

VI

Alexander and Staub [17] undertook in a recent book a preliminary systematic presentation of the psychoanalytic approach to the criminal problem. Having in mind the desirability of a causal therapy in this field they divided the recidivists in crime into three classes etiologically.

(1) The neurotic criminal, whose hostile activity against society is a result of an intrapsychic conflict between the social and antisocial components of his personality; this conflict, like that of a psycho-neurosis, comes from impressions of earliest childhood and from circumstances of later life. (Psychological etiology.)

(2) The normal criminal, whose psychic organization is similar to that of the normal individual, except that he identifies himself with criminal prototypes. (Sociological etiology.)

(3) The criminal whose criminality is conditioned by some pathological process of organic nature. (Biological etiology.)

After referring to various types of acute or isolated criminalism they go on to say: "All these classes and forms of criminality which we have just outlined fall between two extreme types of personality which occupy the opposite poles of our scheme and which are conceivable only theoretically. On the one end we find the pure criminal who had not formed any superego to represent the demands of society within him; this criminal, when and if he does restrict his antisocial tendencies, does so without any inner urge and unwillingly; he does it merely because he is afraid of the outside authorities. At the other extreme end of our scheme we should find the perfectly adjusted social individual, who without any inner conflict considers the interests of the community before he considers his own; in other words his super-ego and ego would be fused into one. In reality it is impossible to find these conflict-less individuals; only intermediary types can be found. These intermediary types (every single civilized individual belongs to one of the intermediary types) do not possess a homogeneous psychological organization; they always experience a certain ten-

---

[17] F. Alexander, and H. Staub, *The Criminal, the Judge and the Public, A Psychological Analysis,* Trans. from the German by G. Zilboorg, N. Y., 1931.

sion between the primitive and socialized parts of the psychic apparatus." [18]

Some such type of etiological classification has been the aim of every scientific approach to the problems of crime. In considering the recidivist, however, it is necessary to stress the causative importance, if not in the original conditioning of a criminal career, at any rate in its maintenance, of the *repeated experiences of contact with the law*. In no discussion of recidivism has the etiologic role or contact with the machinery of the criminal law and with prison life in creating and fixing the antisocial habits of the recidivist been adequately stressed.

The character of the population which a given prison harbors is affected materially by the social vision of the community served by that prison. As the technique and vision of the various community enterprises for the medico-social treatment of the individual offender improve, especially those which deal with the juvenile offender, one should expect the prison to become more and more restricted to the needs of a type of individual who, because of some constitutional incapacity, has failed to respond to the efforts of these various community enterprises. The prison of the future will acquire more than ever the character of a custodial institution for the refractory cases of recidivism. It is this fact which will force the necessary vital changes in the nature of the prison, namely, the elimination of those of its features that are of a positively detrimental nature to the normal functioning of the individual. The prison of the future will have to be purged of those features of its atmosphere which constitute positive insults to the morale, the self-respect and the social-self generally of inmates, *keepers as well as prisoners*. Leaving out of consideration for the moment the fact that the character and conduct of a certain number of the habitually criminal are determined by fixations [19] at asocial and purely egoistic phases of

emotional development, the insults above referred to might be looked upon as experiences which favor regression to, and reanimation of, those early unsocialized tendencies of man.

In this fundamental reorganization, both as regards the selection of the type of the offender who will require prison treatment and the purging of the prison atmosphere of its noxious elements, an enlightened probation system can be of great help. In the first place, the wholly unjustified legal fiction of the preferential status of the "first offender," *qua* first offender, must be eliminated entirely. Similarly, the *a priori* and tragic odium which attaches to recidivism, *qua* recidivism, must likewise be modified. The lines which these modifications must pursue are clear enough to every enlightened criminologist. Procedure must be guided by scientific estimation of all the facts surrounding a given criminal act. Only then can criminology aspire to a truly causal therapy and hope to eliminate gradually the criminogenic elements, individual and social.

The public apathy toward the problem of crime to which we alluded earlier in this paper does not alter the ominous fact that criminalism as a method of adaptation to life is not only gaining in popularity among all classes of society, but the very manner of its expression, has become more brutally antisocial and more devoid of any concern over consequences. When one takes into consideration the reckless brutality of society's retaliatory measure, as reflected, for instance, in the growing popularity of some of the Baumes laws; or, when one stops to consider the real significance for contemporary American civilization of the veritable witches' dance of the "prohibition movement" with the attending flagrant and deliberate traumatization of the "sense of justice," a sacred and indispensable attribute of every human being, savage or civilized, one wonders what the ultimate outcome is going to be of this battle between the contending forces of good and evil. The criminal tendency seems to be gaining the upper hand over the equally universal tendency of man to free himself of his sadistic and selfish dispositions. If probation is ever to realize the aims of the conscientious and decent men and women who have labored as pioneers in this movement, it must increasingly identify itself with the scientific and humane purposes of modern mental medicine.

---

[18] *Ibid.*, pp. 54–55.

[19] "Fixation may be defined as a halting of some part of the libido during the course of its development at one or other of its somatic positions or zones. In other words, one (or several) of the infantile 'sexual aims' or modes of pleasure-finding has not been relinquished, that is, adequately desexualized or sublimated." Healy, Bronner, Bowers, *op. cit.*, p. 116.

19

Types of Personality Structure Encountered in Child Guidance Clinics *

R. L. Jenkins and Lester Hewitt

Scientific progress in child psychiatry depends, as in other fields, upon reducing the infinite variety of problems through some broad conceptualization. It goes without saying that any schematization involves some oversimplification and hence some distortion. The justification for any scheme depends upon the aid it gives to understanding the phenomena represented. In presenting our scheme of personality structure, we believe we are emphasizing concepts which are useful and valuable in child psychiatry. We are fully aware that our scheme is not exhaustive, that all cases cannot be fitted into the scheme and that a tremendous amount of significant material about the individual case is ignored. Our description of these types is a compounding of tendencies that are typical. No case may fit the scheme perfectly. The case is a particular reality and the scheme is an abstraction. One should never make the mistake of treating the scheme as a reality. Rather, the scheme should aid in understanding the reality of the individual case. If this scheme contributes to the understanding of many maladjusted children, it will have accomplished its purpose.

While major elements in the scheme are frankly taken over from Freud, the concepts here presented are in themselves in no sense sectarian and will, it is hoped, be intelligible to all who work in this field regardless of the question of sectarian identification.

* Reprinted from 14 *Am. J. Orthopsychiatry* (Jan. 1944), 84–94. Used by permission of the authors and the publishers. See, also, R. L. Jenkins and Sylvia Glickman, "Patterns of Personality Organization among Delinquents, 6 *Nervous Child* (1947), 329–339, and R. L. Jenkins, "Adaptive and Maladaptive Delinquency," 11 *Nervous Child* (1955), 9–11. — Ed.

The personality is conceived as having a central core of primitive impulses. Primitive is here used in the sense of spontaneous and socially undisciplined, or instinctual in the Freudian terminology. Around this core of primitive impulse there is in the adult or in the older child a shell of inhibition which prevents free expression of the impulses. This corresponds somewhat with the Freudian concept of superego, while the core of primitive impulses represents the Freudian concept of the id. This shell represents repressing forces which keep the primitive impulses unconscious and prevent them from coming into action, except as modified through social discipline.

The surface zone of the personality is the ego — conscious, socialized, discriminating, and choosing. It is our thesis that the three major types of personality structure encountered in child psychiatry may be illustrated by the three diagrams in Figure 1.

In Type I we see an individual who has an excessive development of the shell of inhibition. As a result of this the primitive impulses are denied adequate expression. Tension mounts within the personality and strong pressures develop in the struggle between the primitive impulses and the repressive forces. This individual is chronically in a state of internal conflict. Here we have the over-inhibited individual likely to react to these internal conflicts by developing terror dreams or anxiety attacks, or by developing physical symptoms of illness through conversion hysteria, or to defend himself from them by compulsive rituals. We do not, as a rule, see such well developed neurotic symptoms in the child, but we see the milder over-inhibited symptoms of shyness, seclusiveness, fears, clinging, tics, sleep disturbances, nail biting, and other common evidences of tension and anxiety with which the child guidance worker is familiar. The essential points are to recognize that the person with severe internal conflict is, as a rule, the over-inhibited individual.

Type II represents the opposite of Type I. Type II represents the individual with an inadequate shell of internal inhibitions. As a result the primitive impulses come not only into consciousness but into expression very directly, providing there are no external pressures which check them. Such an individual is unsocialized and aggressive in his actions and is continually

Figure 1

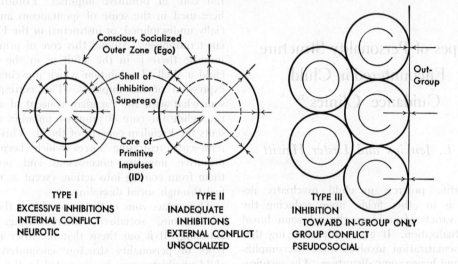

coming in conflict with others — the authorities and the police — as a result of his freely giving vent to his primitive impulses. This represents a type of personality totally different from Type I, although many workers who use terms loosely will speak of this unsocialized, aggressive type of individual as neurotic. It is our belief that such a usage leads to a confusion of thinking and of treatment and that the expression should not be used for this type of personality which allies itself rather with the psychopathic personality of asocial and amoral character.

Type III represents a more nearly normal type of personality structure than either of the foregoing. There is a normal shell of inhibition toward members of an in-group. Toward members of any out-group there is a deficit in the inhibitions, no sense of obligation and a free expression of the primitive impulses. In child guidance we see here the pseudosocial boy, the loyal gang member, the good comrade of the delinquent subculture who is socialized — often highly socialized — within a delinquent group but regards the rest of the world as fair prey. The same character has been well exemplified by the Japanese soldier in many instances. The Japanese soldier in Japan in contact with other Japanese is a socialized individual. The Japanese soldier in China has typically, or at least very frequently, a gross deficit in inhibitions of the expression of primitive impulses toward the Chinese civilian population — as the rape of Nanking so well exemplified. Conflict occurs

at the margins of the group and here we have a third type — group conflict.

Our study of these types of personality structure is supported by an extensive and detailed statistical analysis of 500 cases examined at the Michigan Child Guidance Institute. The data cannot be presented here, and it will be necessary simply to indicate the general outline with a few bold strokes.

The overinhibited personality structure is extremely familiar to mental hygienists. Typically, it develops in an atmosphere of parental repression. The parents are likely to be cold and unsocial, the mother compensating for some rejection by overprotection and overrestriction, the father perfectionistic and intolerant. Both parents are inconsistent in methods of discipline. Both parents are restrained, socially disciplined persons. They are typically of a social stratum and a level of education above the clinic average. The mother is likely frequently to be ill from one affliction or another. The child himself is likely to have experienced an unusual amount of illness which contributes to his insecurity and dependence. He is likely to be jealous of his siblings in their relation to the parents, feeling his own relation less secure.

In order to understand such a personality structure, we need only to consider the dynamics of personality development. The young child obtains his sense of security from his parents; he has no other source of security. He is utterly dependent upon the parents, and there is no frequent childhood fear which produces such chronic anxiety as the fear of loss of the parents, or the fear of loss of parent love. Just as the parent is the fundamental source of security to the young child, fear of loss of the parents is the fundamental source of insecurity and of anxiety. This fact is so simple and obvious it is often overlooked.

Here we are dealing with the unsociable, cold, distant parent lacking in warmth. The child lacks the assurance, through close emotional contact with the parents, of acceptance and affection. These are parents whose approval (and presumably whose love) can be won only by very good, very conforming, very inhibited behavior. Any violation of parental taboos is met by disapproval which this insecure child feels or fears means rejection. There is deeply implanted, as the result of this experience, the pervading fear that if he is not a good child his parents will not love him. As a result, any aggressive act by the child throws him into a panic of anxiety. He can feel secure only by being excessively good, by being excessively inhibited. To protect himself he screws down the safety valve on his central core of primitive impulses, and the pressure there mounts to produce an acute situation of internal conflict, which may be relieved by neurotic disorders.

The Type II personality pattern is really simpler than Type I and might well have been presented first but for the fact that psychiatric and mental hygiene circles are more familiar with the overinhibited personality than with the unsocialized, aggressive type represented in Type II.

This child's problem centers around his uninhibited hostile treatment of others. He is cruel, defiant, prone deliberately to destroy the property of others as well as violently to attack their persons. He shows little feeling of guilt or remorse.[1] He is seldom able to get along with other children, but is always quarreling, fighting or engaging in mischievous annoying tricks. He is inclined to bully and boss, and is boastful, selfish and jealous. He is rude or defiant toward persons in authority, openly antagonistic toward his teachers and has outbursts of temper when crossed. He will deceive others and refuses to accept the blame for his own mis-

behavior. Because of his personality makeup, he has few close friends, if any.

Even if others attempt to become friendly, this boy does not respond with friendship, for he is suspicious and reacts negatively. He is noncommittal and evasive when questioned and usually appears sullen. He seeks vengeance against those he dislikes. In our small series we find even arson and murder. Frequent petty thieving at home or at school sometimes results from the same vengeful attitude. His language is profane and obscene. He displays an unusually overt interest in sex, and *is known* to indulge in masturbation.

Typically, this boy lives in a deteriorated neighborhood, either in the country or at the edge of town. His troubles, however, did not begin in this neighborhood or even in this particular home, for his life has been very unstable. He has carried his troubles with him since birth and their origins even preceded this unhappy event, in the pre-marital experience of his parents. His mother's own home life in particular has been unhappy. It is likely that she left home at an early age to get away from her own parents and met the child's father. The child is likely to have been illegitimate.

In any event neither parent wanted the pregnancy and the mother was probably under considerable emotional strain during that period. Labor may have been prolonged or exceedingly difficult and, if so, the suffering the mother experienced only served to increase any existing tendency to reject the child. Both parents, but particularly the mother, denied this child affection from the beginning. Even if the parents married, desertion or divorce is likely to have broken the relationship, with the child being subsequently placed either temporarily or permanently with relatives or strangers or being shuttled from one parent to the other. If the parents remained together, their relationship was fraught with bitterness and disharmony. The mother is likely to have been very unstable, a characteristic not entirely foreign to her husband, who was also deceptive in his dealings with others. Both parents were probably violent tempered and abusive toward each other or the children. The mother, possibly of low intelligence, may also have been addicted to the use of alcohol. She may have been and perhaps still is quite unwilling to accept the responsibilities of motherhood, and has frequently been

---

[1] Lombroso noted the absence of remorse in his "born criminal" type. — *Ed.*

involved in illicit sex affairs with various men. The family itself is regarded with disfavor by the neighbors and may be known unfavorably throughout the community.

No other relationships between the members of the family are encouraging to the development of a healthy social attitude on the part of the child. Rarely is authority in this family reasonably divided between the parents. One of them is usually extremely dominating and the other assumes little direct responsibility. The parents quarrel or engage in open fights and what loyalty exists between members of the family is split between opposing factional units. Sexual relationships between the parents are unsatisfactory and contribute to conflict. The status of the child in the home is also a source of conflict. The parents disagree on methods of discipline in which the father particularly is likely to be inconsistent.

The mother, and to a greater extent the father, will brook no interference from the outside, frequently shielding the child from the charges of school and community authorities. Neither parent, however, is affectionate toward him. They are at most indifferent in their attitudes and the mother is most likely to be openly hostile or rejecting. Little wonder then that he feels unwanted in the home and is ambivalent toward his parents or openly expresses hostility to parents and siblings alike.

In view of the mother's behavior, it is not surprising that other children in the home may also have engaged in unconventional sex behavior, and it is probable that one or more is officially known to the juvenile court as a delinquent on other counts. As a final note of emphasis, the picture presented is essentially one of generalized and continual parental rejection, and particularly overt maternal rejection, beginning at or before the birth of the child.

The product of this background is a child of bottomless hostilities and endless bitterness, who feels cheated in life, views himself as the victim although he is constantly the aggressor, is grossly defective in his social inhibitions, or if you prefer, in his superego, and is grossly lacking in guilt sense over his misconduct. We may think of his hostility as springing from three sources. First, there is the hostility of the individual who has a need for and, by common judgment, a right to expect love from his parents and receives none. Even adults who have

developed a good deal of social restraint often become hostile and sometimes even violent when they find themselves rejected in a love relationship, and certainly the reaction of resentment and bitterness is natural to a child who is rejected by his mother. Secondly, this child has lacked an effective affectional tie to any adult through which he could incorporate standards of behavior or from whom he could develop a superego. In the third place, the example of behavior this child sees before him is one which is highly selfish and inconsiderate and, by our conventional standards, objectionable if not delinquent. This background has developed a hostile, uninhibited personality, tending to act with direct violence at any provocation or desire. He has cause for insecurity and cause for anxiety, but the anxiety usually leads him to attack.

Our third type of personality structure is not quite on a level with the other two, for it is the result of tendencies which developed at a higher level of differentiation. This is the pseudo-social boy — the loyal gang member, the good comrade of a delinquent subculture. Within his own group he is commonly a socialized and adjusted individual. It is only in relation to the larger group that he can be considered maladjusted and antisocial.

While his behavior bears certain resemblances to that of the unsocialized, aggressive boy, there are important differences. These are related to the fact that he is socialized in his own group and loyal to his comrades. This boy also is deceptive and defiant toward authority. When possible he avoids self-incrimination by not accepting the blame for his own acts and he feels little guilt over his delinquent depredations. On the other hand, should he violate the code of his group, as by informing on his companions when caught, he would feel deeply guilty. Even more than the unsocialized, aggressive boy, he engages in petty stealing at home or school, but this behavior would appear to be motivated more by acquisitiveness than by a desire for revenge. He also is extremely antagonistic toward school attendance, but expresses this antagonism chiefly in truancy. This antagonism to school is not due to lack of friends there, for compared with the average child seen at the clinic, this boy is popular.

He is engaged in a good deal of furtive stealing, either alone or in the company of others and is likely to have engaged in aggressive stealing as well. He is quite likely to be a member of some rather well-organized adolescent gang, and invariably is known to be associating with companions whom others consider to be undesirable and delinquent. He remains on the street late at night or may neglect to come home at all. He may be an inveterate smoker and probably has some experience in sex relations with girls. Among his own group he is "hail-fellow-well-met," but to the good people of the dominant society from whom he dissociates himself, he is a menace to law and order.

His home is located in a downtown, deteriorated neighborhood where traditions of delinquency and disrespect for law are most likely to flourish. His family is held in disrepute even among such neighbors and offers little in the way of constructive training in conformity to rules of the larger society. His home is physically inadequate in every respect. The family is obliged to accept outside financial aid, or at least to confine its spending to bare necessities. The house is sadly in need of repair; it is crowded among other buildings so that little space is available for safe and supervised play at home. The interior of the house may be inadequately equipped with sanitary and other household facilities, and is in all probability unkempt. The family is a large one and four or more persons may be obliged to sleep in the same room — possibly three or more occupying the same bed. The boy is aware of and sensitive to the unfavorable contrast which his circumstances present in comparison with those of other children he knows.

Contrasted with the uninhibited aggressive boy, who represents a failure particularly of maternal function, expressed in overt maternal rejection, the pseudosocial boy represents typically a failure in paternal function — the neglect of supervision, training and control for the older child. The father's own childhood is much more likely to have been markedly unpleasant than is the mother's, and it is the father more than the mother in this case who has expressed subsequent unwillingness to accept family responsibilities. Both parents are inclined to be alcoholic, violent tempered or abusive. The father may also have a reputation for dishonesty. The chronic illness or physical impairment which he may suffer reduces his

effectiveness both as a breadwinner and as a parent. The siblings are likely to be known either officially or unofficially to the court as delinquents.

Between the members of the family there is likely to be disharmony which on the surface appears similar to that within the family of the rejected child. Both the expressions and implications of this disharmony, however, differ in a number of respects. There may be mutual indifference between the members of the family and little feeling of common interest or loyalty — there may be split loyalties with the possibility that the delinquent boy allies himself with the mother against the abusiveness and neglect of her husband. If the parents quarrel, it is most likely over the boy himself, or it may be over the functional inadequacies or cultural standards of one of the parents rather than over unsatisfactory sex relations which loom large in the previous picture. The children too may quarrel constantly among themselves, but with little evidence of the consistent sibling rivalry and jealousy characteristic of both the unsocialized, aggressive child and the over-inhibited child.

The father's general indifference toward family responsibilities is further exemplified in his greater tendency to be lax in his methods of discipline and in his more openly expressed attitude of indifference toward this particular boy. It is the mother moreover who most frequently shields the boy from responsibility for his own acts. Both parents, however, may be extremely harsh in their attempts to secure discipline, using violent physical punishment and extreme measures of deprivation. The mother, in fact, may express a currently rejective attitude toward her wayward son much as does the mother of the unsocialized, aggressive boy. It should be noted, however, that maternal rejection in this case is of comparatively recent origin and may presumably have developed in her despair over the trouble caused by her delinquent offspring. This child was not unwanted at birth, and whatever parental rejection developed shortly thereafter was displayed by the father rather than by the mother. Hence one should not be surprised to find this boy most resentful toward the father and, like the unsocialized, aggressive boy, feeling rejected by and hostile toward both parents. Once more the gross behavior may appear similar in both cases, but it arises from different circumstances and carries different implications. Furthermore, the significant pressure in the family toward deviant behavior in this case would appear to come from the father rather than from the mother.

In brief, the pseudosocial boy was typically given an adequate fundamental socialization in his relationship with his mother. Later, as a result of this socialization, the failure of paternal function, and the neighborhood deviation pressures, he fell under the influence of the delinquent gang and reached his adolescent socialization within a delinquent group.

RELATION OF PERSONALITY STRUCTURE TO CULTURE

As a generalization, we are prepared to defend the following hypotheses:

A culture imposing little self-discipline is typically marked by a high incidence of overt external conflicts and a high incidence of primitive aggressive behavior. Competition for dominance is direct, undisguised, and primitive. The incidence of internal conflict and neuroticism is relatively low. As an example we would cite the lower-class American Negro community.

A culture imposing much self-discipline is typically marked by a low incidence of overt external conflicts and a low incidence of primitive aggressive behavior. Competition for dominance is canalized, disciplined, and often masked. The incidence of internal conflict and neuroticism is high. As an example we cite the American Jewish community.

As an instance related to differences in cultures, we would point out that women live under stronger social inhibitions than do men. It is therefore not surprising that they show a lower incidence of overt aggressive behavior, a competition for dominance which is more disguised and subtle, and a higher incidence of neuroticism.

PSYCHOTHERAPY

The type of therapy needed is determined by the type of personality deviation with which we are dealing. First, let us consider the therapy of the over-inhibited, neurotic individual. This has been relatively well worked out. Indeed in the thinking of a vast number of people in psychiatry and mental hygiene the concept of psychiatric treatment is limited to the treatment

appropriate for this particular type of problem, and to them nothing else is psychotherapy. With the first type of personality structure we are dealing with an individual in whom the shell of inhibition is too thick and too impenetrable. Obviously the treatment must be directed to canalize this shell of inhibition so that the primitive impulses may find some expression in a socially acceptable way. The manner in which this is done will depend upon the setting, but the same fundamental elements will be present whether one is dealing with an individual in a classroom relationship, in a foster home placement, or in intensive psychotherapy in the psychiatrist's office.

This method of therapy has been developed in its most elaborate form in the Freudian psychoanalysis. Here the therapist develops an essentially parental relationship to the patient. The parental nature of this relationship is recognized in the term which Freud applied to the patient's attitude toward his therapist — transfer. This expression is used because the patient's feeling for his therapist is recognized as a transfer of feelings which he previously had toward his parent. The psychoanalyst then proceeds to analyze the superego, essentially to take apart and canalize this shell of repression. To accomplish this purpose he puts his patient under a certain discipline — which is more or less parentally enforced. The requirement is that the patient shall freely associate, shall tell the therapist everything which comes into his mind. In this way the therapist is gradually able to bring the patient to relate those things of which he is conscious but of which he is ashamed. The therapist does not condemn the patient for these revelations, but is likely directly or indirectly to convey the impression that other people, too, think of such things, and to accept them as not shocking or unexpected. By the method of free association, by the interpretation of dreams, more and more of the unconscious repressed material is gradually brought to light. The patient may be shocked and distressed, but the therapist is not. He continues to accept the patient and, in this living therapeutic relationship, the patient gradually has the experience that here is a "parent" who does not reject him because of his secret nonconforming or "evil" desires.

The therapist definitely leads the patient toward certain interpretations of his dreams and of his behavior. These interpretations are at least exceedingly likely to include a desire of the patient to violate the two most fundamental taboos of our culture — to kill his father and to have incestuous relations with his mother. We need not enter into the question of how frequently these interpretations may be justified. Interpretations do not *necessarily* have to be correct to be therapeutic, and one is not justified in arguing that an interpretation is necessarily correct because the patient accepts it with benefit. It should be apparent that when the patient has accepted such interpretations, and believes that he has these desires, and that his therapist believes that he has these desires and still does not reject him or regard him as wicked, then something has happened to reduce the insecurity responsible for his excessive shell of repression. The repression itself is not as tight and impenetrable as it was before. The primitive impulses can more readily find some overt and, we hope, not too unsocialized expression, and the inner conflict is in great part abated. The anxieties disappear and the neurotic symptoms are no longer needed to solve a conflict which is at least reduced in its intensity. The therapy is successful — at least to a degree. The patient improves.

This method of therapy is not adapted to the unsocialized, aggressive child. This point cannot be emphasized too strongly, as there is a widespread tendency to believe that if the analysis just goes deep enough a cure will inevitably result. Such a child as is represented in Type II does not have too much superego; he has too little. His behavior results not from inner conflict, but from a lack of it. One does not need to analyze a superego, rather it is necessary to synthesize one. One does not seek to relieve guilt-anxiety. One seeks to create it. This is done in essentially the way that taboos are planted at any time of life, whether in the early training period of childhood when the process is normally most intense or in later life readjustments as upon induction into the army. It requires the use of authority, firmness, planned limitation, and at times, punishment.

What is necessary for success is first of all a warm accepting attitude on the part of the parent or parent substitute. This is particularly important with the unsocialized, aggressive child who feels rejected and expects to be rejected. Until one has convinced such an individual of a fundamental interest in his welfare, therapy is not likely to be successful. It often requires an exceptional personality to be able to develop and maintain a high degree of personal warmth for some of these aggressive, unsocialized individuals whom most people are able to describe only in zoological metaphors.

Having established such a relationship, the next step is to establish and effectively maintain pressure toward required kinds of behavior and against certain objectionable types of behavior. This must be done step by step, often in very small steps. While an effort should be made to develop and exploit personal loyalty to one or more socialized adults, it must be recognized that this child's capacity for loyalty and identification is definitely feeble. The appeal must consequently be oriented in great part in terms of self-interest. Privileges which are abused must be withdrawn and returned step by step. For this reason older children and adolescents who are of the unsocialized, aggressive make-up usually cannot be effectively treated outside of an institution, because adequate control is impossible in the open democratically organized community. Constant reassurance of personal interest and warmth is necessary while particular patterns of behavior are disapproved. The reason that certain requirements are set upon the individual must be explained over and over again and the requirements must be made effective. Authoritative management and limitation which will be experienced and interpreted as punishment are essential portions of the treatment.

If one attempts to treat the unsocialized aggressive child by the methods suitable for the overinhibited, neurotic, withdrawn child, his behavior will typically get worse. Encouragement of the free expression of aggressiveness does not lead to improvement. An overinhibited person or a person of adequate inhibitions, who in a particular situation has developed special tension, may so relieve his feelings by a cathartic discharge of verbal hostilities, or acted out hostilities, as to be able to function effectively under the control only of his own conscience. This is not true of the child who lacks guilt feelings or any effective conscience. When treatment is undertaken by methods of play analysis, for example, if the therapist encourages more and more outpourings of the aggression, he will find that the well of hostility is bottomless. The therapeutic sessions may be made more frequent, but the hostile, aggressive, wild behavior only intensifies.

It must be recognized that the unsocialized, aggressive individual will frequently seek to protect himself from developing an attachment for anyone, and may respond negatively when he begins to feel himself becoming attached. This must be accepted as one of the problems of treatment.

As has been stated, treatment of the adolescent will usually need to be carried out in an institution, the major portion of it by someone who is in contact with the child much of the day. The social situation needs to be simplified by contact with fewer adults and with stable, mature, even-tempered and strong personalities. The maximum simplification should occur at the start, with a step-by-step increase in freedom and responsibility as the child is able to manage them. Psychotherapy has a place, but it is a very different type of psychotherapy than that employed with the overinhibited, neurotic, withdrawn individual. Psychotherapy here will be directed toward helping the patient recognize that his substitute parent is interested in his welfare, is not hostile, but is simply enforcing reasonable restrictions and that the wise course is to take advantage of the constructive opportunities the situation affords. This will have to be repeated over and over again and in different ways. There is an advantage in having a therapist not responsible (in the eyes of the child) for the authoritative decisions, participate or carry major responsibility for this psychotherapy. If this is criticized as superficial treatment, we would respond that it is as much of an error to use deep level therapy in a case requiring superficial treatment as it is to use only superficial treatment in a case which calls for deep level therapy.

The results of the treatment will be to develop somewhat the inadequate shell of inhibition, to stimulate foresight and an enlightened self-interest, and to develop certain patterns of conformity. If in addition skills are acquired, the prospect for an individual reasonably able to take his place in society may be good. In some extreme instances, only an improvement in the capacity for institutional adjustment may be realized.

The socialized delinquent or pseudosocial boy (typically this child is a boy) presents still an-other problem of treatment and one less "psychiatric" in that it is much closer to the ordinary techniques of influencing normal adults. This problem has been well discussed by Ruth Topping.[2] We are dealing with a child who had a fundamental socialization and then became a part of an aggressive minority group. He is a socialized person who resonates over too limited a scale. His fundamental socialization is expressed in his outstanding capacity for loyalty and this capacity, with the corresponding response to being given what he recognizes as a "break," plus his capacity to identify with and pattern himself after a masculine, socialized adult, are the major elements upon which one must depend.

The process of establishing rapport constitutes a major problem with the boy who is suspicious toward and well armored against adults related in his mind to authority. If rapport is established, loyalty can be built by "giving him a break" or otherwise showing real interest and confidence in him. The circumstances should be such that he interprets the generous act or "break" as a result of personal interest and personal confidence, not as a result of weakness, fear, or an effort to "buy him off," for this boy typically despises weakness. The process of treatment then becomes a process of enlarging his concept of his in-group through the skillful development and utilization of his loyalty. Since he is part of a closely knit group it is necessary for success effectively to separate him from this group, to neutralize its influence, or effectively to treat the whole group. Particularly suited for work with this group are strong masculine personalities with capacity for warmth of response, generosity of feeling, utter fairness, and for uncompromising fixity of purpose. It should be delinquents of this group who would be most responsive to methods such as are employed by Clifford Shaw and his associates in the Area Projects in Chicago.

As a final comment, it is our hope that these considerations may stimulate the more discriminating thinking which is needed to resolve the conflicts between the educator often faced with the need to implant inhibitions, and the mental hygienist often faced with the need to reduce them.

[2] Ruth Topping, "The Treatment of the Pseudosocial Boy," this Journal, April 1943. [Article 147.]

20

Childhood Behavior Disorders and Delinquency *

Abram Blau

Of all the cases referred by the schools to the Bureau of Child Guidance, the outstanding group is that of childhood behavior disorders and pre-delinquency. Many people are not aware of the close correlation that exists between these two conditions and adult crime as well. It is now a well-established fact that most criminals are repeaters and that crime usually has its beginnings in early youth. In fact, one goal in the development of child-guidance clinics has been to prevent crime, and the course of this development has revealed a chain of antisocial disorders from the infant to the adult. Antisocial behavior is now recognized as a biological, psychological, and sociological problem. We now know that its solution must be sought through coöperation in all these fields, with emphasis on its evolutionary development from childhood.

We can differentiate four types of antisocial behavior — infantile misbehavior, childhood behavior disorder, delinquency, and crime, corresponding, respectively, to the natural age periods of the pre-school period, the school period, adolescence, and maturity. All have the common feature of a failure to meet the prescribed behavior generally required for social living at the age period in question. They differ only in variations of complexity, corresponding to the age involved and the relative degree of experience, sophistication, and responsibility.

At the outset, we find that there is nothing inherently bad in antisocial behavior. It is only behavior that is wrong at a particular time. One and the same act may be condemned in one set of circumstances and approved in others. As an extreme example, let us take the killing of a human being. Murder is unanimously claimed a crime; but killing in war is praised; in self-defense, it is condoned; and when committed during the heat of understandable emotion, it is sometimes forgiven. The act must always be weighed with its attendant circumstances. Therein lies the great psychological problem of determining culpability in the courts of law. Responsibility changes with age, and even the law is not fixed. Not so long ago, truancy was regarded merely as undesirable, but nowadays, with our compulsory-education laws, it is an act of delinquency.

But one positive feature is outstanding in all antisocial behavior — it is aggressively self-indulgent and rebellious. To illustrate, the following cases may be cited:

Robert, a six-year-old, with an I.Q. of 141, was referred because he was restless, annoying, uncooperative, careless, and untidy. He sucked his fingers, and pinched and slapped other children. His mother confirmed these complaints and added that he was a fussy eater and a bed-wetter.

Howard, nine years old and of average intelligence, was described as quarrelsome, bossy, obscene, overactive, insolent, lazy.

Joseph, eleven years, also of normal intelligence, was defiant, destructive, argumentative, disturbing, stubborn, untrustworthy. He played truant from school, bit his nails, and stole small articles.

Constance, a bright, overgrown, eleven-year-old girl, was disobedient, ill-tempered, untidy, unfriendly, untruthful, sexually precocious, and conceited, and habitually sucked her tongue.

Oliver, aged fourteen and of superior intelligence, was unstable, noisy, restless, boastful, and disrespectful to teachers, and had frequent temper tantrums.

Thomas, fifteen years old, was talkative, insolent, and rude, and rebelled at discipline. He would desert his home for days, played truant from school, was irritable with other children, and used abusive language.

The cases become repetitious in the obvious recurrence of a direct, free, impulsive expression of personal desires contrary to the standards set by the world in which these children live. Their behavior reminds one of the little child

* Reprinted from 27 *Mental Hygiene* (1943), 261–266. Used by permission of the author and the publisher. Presented at the Tenth Anniversary Conference of the Bureau of Child Guidance, Board of Education, New York City, October 18, 1941.

who wants what he wants at once — with no sense of restraint.

In fact, infantile behavior may be taken as the prototype of criminality. Here we see the naked original desires, the inborn biological elements, that form the basis of all later human activity, whether good or bad, social or anti-social, moral or immoral. It may be said that the human being enters the world as a delin-quent — that is, socially unadjusted. The in-fant is wild, uncivilized, untrained, and undo-mesticated. In the first years he is dominated mostly by those instinctual urges that impul-sively seek satisfaction and that are unbridled by any sense of the rights or needs of others.

This state of undisciplined instinct gratifica-tion cannot last long, however. Partly through his own contacts with impersonal dangerous situations such as fire, height, climate, and so on, and partly through the teachings of his guardians, the child soon becomes aware that some control of his desires must be brought about in order that he may adapt to life. Of course, the solution of this universal problem can only be a compromise. A certain measure of emotional gratification is biologically essential to every one. This need must be met in one way or another, whether through normal, neu-rotic, perverse, or delinquent channels. The normal child learns how to curb his primitive impulses, to postpone their satisfaction, and to modify them along socially acceptable lines. The socially unadjusted child is a child who is failing in this development.

Education for social living is thus a two-sided problem. The individual must learn, on the one hand, how to obtain proper gratifica-tion of hereditary instinctual urges, and on the other, how to control them adequately. But what, we may ask, motivates the child to learn these adjustments? For our reply we must turn to the age-old educational principles of pleasure and pain, of reward and punishment. Well-chosen or approved ways of satisfaction are en-couraged, and reprehensible patterns are cen-sored. This process of learning is obviously so like Darwin's law of natural selection and so well-known that we need spend little time on it.

One aspect of learning gained during per-sonality growth deserves special attention, how-ever, because it is so closely related to the prob-lem of socialization. This is the acquisition of a sense of right and wrong, a private moral and ethical code. The pre-school child has little understanding of how and why to supervise himself. He curbs naughtiness mainly because he fears the loss of the approval of grown-ups. In most children, however, at about the age of five or six years, we begin to find that they can be trusted with some management of their own affairs. Incidentally, it is significant that pedagogues have empirically chosen this age for the beginning of formal education. The child now shows some self-critical concern about his behavior even when alone or when his mis-deeds would not be discovered. The elements of a conscience and of ambition become ap-parent, and discipline and drive become in part self-imposed undertakings. By the process of repeated parental encouragement and direction, the parental point of view is gradually, yet so thoroughly, taken over that it becomes incor-porated into the newly forming personality as an integral part of the child himself.

Later, after the child has gone out from the family circle, he is similarly influenced by his teachers and other authoritative and respected persons. This inner capacity for discipline re-mains for the rest of his life as the great ally of the outer authority in the moral, ethical, and social guidance of his behavior.

There is no doubt to-day that the basic groundwork for personality growth is laid down in the early pre-school years while the child is under parental influences. From time imme-morial, pedagogues have maintained that char-acter is made at home. Modern psychological research only substantiates and elaborates the truth of this idea. The foundations and es-sential framework of all the later character traits are established during the plastic period of early childhood through the precepts and the ex-ample of mother and father. The most sig-nificant education begins at home; the school only supplements from then on. It is in large part the identifications, conscious and uncon-scious, formed in those early years that deter-mine the specific individual features of adult character. These experiences decide the degrees of moral stringency, self-sacrifice, idealism, and repression that are the basis of the relationships of later life. In one person the inner authority is excessive, and he may become either a rigid, inflexible type, an impractical idealist, or a psy-choneurotic. At the other extreme, this inner authority may be inadequate, and the person will defy social customs with no sense of guilt.

Just how the characters of the criminal, of the delinquent, and of the child who manifests a behavior disorder are related to the love and discipline of the family circle is disclosed by comprehensive child-guidance studies. Because his need for protection, love, and the good opinion of his guardians is greater than his desire to satisfy his instinctual tensions, the child becomes willing to make social concessions. In every one of the cases I have cited, and in many more that have been studied, the outstanding factor in the child's life was the lack of parental affection. Either the parents actually did not love the child, or because of the death or the desertion of his parents, he had never found love or understanding in his home. There was not only a temporary deprivation of some desired gratification, but a continued lack of many of the basic needs of early life. And the more severe the antisocial behavior, the more complete and long-standing the emotional deficiencies are found to be.

This is the great injustice hidden within most delinquent histories. It is far more significant than any other environmental privations, and it accounts for the occurrence of antisocial behavior among both rich and poor. The parents frequently blame the child for their rejecting attitude. They do not realize that the child's misbehavior is the effect rather than the cause of their failure to give him adequate attention.

In the light of all these facts, one final note of caution must be stressed for those who work with maladjusted children. Since so much of the child's behavior is motivated by a multitude of remote forces, instinctual and learned, conscious and forgotten, many of which he has never even recognized, can he then be held responsible for his misdeeds? The answer must be "no" and "yes." We cannot agree with the traditional concepts of "free will" because the child is as a rule quite ignorant of the real sources of his misconduct. To a large extent he is impotent in its control and is in great part merely the expression of his biological, cultural, and educational background. Really to know why he is misbehaving, we must thoroughly examine the child and his setting and evaluate them objectively. Yet, despite these considerations, we must demand a degree of responsibility from the child because it is our only means of influencing him. Al-

though this requirement does not have complete scientific validity, it has a practical and tactical justification. As in the case of the principal who is said to be fully liable for his school, but who cannot be held really accountable for every neglect or mistake of each teacher, the rôle of responsibility is necessary and reasonable on grounds of efficiency. Thus, only for practical purposes, we require that the individual must have the duty of responsibility for his behavior, even though we must always bear in mind his actual inner limitations.

To recapitulate, the child misbehaves because he is unhappy, and he has discovered this means of maintaining his emotional balance. Abnormal though it is, it becomes his way of obtaining satisfaction and of asserting himself. The painful price of punishment seems to him worth the gain. At least he gets some attention and is retaliating at a seemingly unjust world. The outside world has failed for him. But despite the apparent arrogance and lack of guilt, within himself he actually feels weak, fearful, deserted, anxious — all these feelings being magnified tenfold by his immature and fantastic imagination. Misbehavior in a child is thus a plea for help and a signal of distress. And relief must be given as soon as possible, before the pattern becomes habitual and fixed, and the child progresses from childhood behavior disorder to adolescent delinquency, to adult crime.

The aim of child guidance is to discover the true causal deficiencies in each situation and to introduce measures for their correction. The causes are usually numerous and may be medical, social, emotional, intellectual, educational, or economic. Moreover, since antisocial behavior is a relative condition, we must not only weigh the nature of the noxious influences within and without the child; we must also consider their extent at the special time and place, and in connection with the potentialities and make-up of the particular individual as well. Often the parents can readjust to meet the child's needs, but sometimes parental surrogates — teacher, social worker, doctor, psychiatrist — must be called upon to compensate for the failures at home.

In the final analysis, we must grant that antisocial behavior is an extremely complex problem, and its ultimate solution, if this is ever attained, will require the combined efforts of biologist, sociologist, pedagogue, jurist, and psychiatrist. Cost cannot enter the question because the community always remains liable for delinquency and crime, either at its inception or at its end stages. And regardless of how it is reckoned, prevention is always more economical than cure.

21

Anxiety ("Actual") Neuroses as a Cause of Behavior Disorders in Children *

Abram Blau and Wilfred C. Hulse

One of the most common psychiatric disorders of children is that designated as "Primary Behavior Disorders in Children" with subgroups of "Habit Disturbance," "Conduct Disturbance," and "Neurotic Traits." The adjective "primary" distinguishes this syndrome from other behavior disturbances secondary to psychoneurotic, psychotic, psychopathic, mentally defective, neurotic character and organic cerebral disorders. The terms "behavior disorder" and "conduct disorder" are simply descriptive and do not offer any etiologic suggestions, as is generally expected from scientific medical diagnoses; "habit disturbance" at least expresses some fault in development, education, or training; and only "neurotic traits" points to possible psychopathological etiology. In the recently revised standard nomenclature published by the American Psychiatric Association,[1] the syndrome was renamed "Transient Situational Personality Disturbance, Adjustment Reaction of Childhood" and the three subgroups were retained. This is an improvement in that psychodynamic ideas are introduced to point to a

conflict with the environment and a failure of the child to cope with it.

A comprehensive study of primary behavior disorders in children was presented by Van Ophuijsen [2] in 1945. The great majority of cases are boys. The classical symptomatology is running away, tantrums, over-aggressiveness, destructiveness, disobedience, disrespectfulness, lying, truancy, stealing, fighting, excessive sexual activities, general unmanageableness at home and at school, and difficulties with peers and siblings. The onset dates to an early age, three years or earlier, with contrary and rebellious behavior; at school the child is a disruptive element, fights with other children, is defiant to the teacher, and inattentive to the work. The parents complain that they suffer from the child's condition, that it has become progressively worse and that no amount of discipline has any effect in improving his behavior. In contrast, the child seems to show no sense of remorse or guilt, and even worse, presents a conceited grandiosity — a narcissistic self-evaluation as Van Ophuijsen calls it. The child appears to think of himself as exceptional, great, strong, and has no respect for authority and the limitations of the environment with its laws, customs, and moral code.

It is generally accepted that the cause of primary behavior disorders is to be found in some disharmony in the family. At least one inadequate or severely disturbed parent has mismanaged the emotional aspects of the rearing process. Van Ophuijsen explains how the hostile rejecting attitude of the parent and the lack of love prevent the internalization of aggression which is necessary for the child to form an adequate superego. The development of proper object relationships is disturbed. This tends to leave the child narcissistic and aggressively rebellious. Van Ophuijsen divided treatment into three stages: first, to serve the patient as an instrument of his narcissism in order to gain his cooperation; then gradually to lead him to the development of an object-love relationship with the therapist; and finally, to use this relationship toward the internalization of aggression and the development of a superego.

* Reprinted, with adaptation of footnotes, from 26 *Am. J. Orthopsychiatry* (1956), 108–114. Used by permission of the authors and the publisher.
[1] *Diagnostic and Statistical Manual: Mental Disorders*, American Psychiatric Assoc., Washington, 1952.

[2] J. A. W. Van Ophuijsen, "Primary Conduct Disturbances," in *Modern Trends in Child Psychiatry* (N. D. C. Lewis and B. L. Pacella, Eds.), Internat. Univ. Press, New York, 1945.

We agree with Van Ophuijsen's excellent description of the symptomatology, the course of its development from earliest infancy, and its etiology from disturbed parental influences. However, the delineation of the child's emotional disturbance seems incomplete in that the nature of the impulsiveness behind the acting-out behavior is not sufficiently explored. Moreover, the diagnosis is inadequate for a clear classification of the syndrome in the framework of dynamic psychiatric nosology made up of the well-known generic syndromes of anxiety neuroses, psychoneuroses, psychoses, and character psychopathology.

Our thesis is that a large number of so-called primary behavior disorders in children are childhood instances of anxiety ("actual") neurosis and that its symptoms are all derivatives of persistent, direct anxiety expressed in the peculiar and special ways open to a child. We will attempt to show how the nature of the symptomatology, the child's immaturity, the apparent lack of guilt, the role of the parents as threatening and depriving agents, and our rationale for treatment all fit together into a logical dynamic pattern. Although we originally planned to include several clinical cases as illustrations, this seems unnecessary because such cases are very common and well-known.[3, 4] We are therefore limiting ourselves to a discussion of the syndrome on the premise that all persons in the field are very familiar with its manifestations.

Let us first review briefly the nature of anxiety ("actual") neurosis. This generic syndrome was described by Freud [5] in 1894, but has not received adequate recognition. A general discussion of the syndrome was recently presented by one of us.[6] Freud delineated anxiety neurosis as a functional physiologic disturbance in which anxiety and its direct derivatives are the major symptoms. It is part of the group of neurophysiologic disorders which Beard [7] designated

as neurasthenia, and must be differentiated from the functional psychoneuroses and psychoses which are essentially psychologic defense reactions against anxiety. Freud called the condition an "actual" neurosis because it is primarily a direct response to real conflict and its symptoms are not amenable to psychologic analysis as are those of psychoneuroses. The differentiation of this syndrome was a significant achievement, and it is aside from our present problem that Freud, in those pioneer days, speculated that anxiety actual neuroses were caused by biochemical disturbances due to sexual frustration.

Anxiety per se is not abnormal — only when it is excessive or inappropriate is it so. When a person is faced with a real, serious problem and becomes anxious, this is natural. Any conflict, frustration or insecurity can lead to anxiety. The anxiety is manifested in many direct physiologic and psychologic disturbances, especially when it is sustained and prolonged. Physiologic effects include palpitation, increased perspiration, respiratory and intestinal disturbances, tension, inability to relax, tremors, restlessness and increased motor activity. The direct psychologic expression of anxiety in children takes the form of the varied symptoms of behavior disorder (running away, tantrums, destructiveness, etc.) which we have already listed.

Anxiety is expressed by the human organism from the moment of birth. However, infants and children differ considerably from adults in what causes anxiety, their ways of showing it, and its effects. Immediately after birth, anxiety is manifested by visceral adrenosympathetic changes, as well as crying and wild mass movements of the limbs and whole body. Crying, restlessness, and impulsive acting-out behavior continue to a great extent to be the way of expressing anxiety in childhood. After the ego has developed, various anger reactions, defiance and opposition become other ways of showing dissatisfaction. The infant and child are limited in the capacity to handle threats to their security by their weakness and dependency, their immature egos, and the restrictions of the environment. Direct acting out becomes one of the main outlets for anxiety. We have shown elsewhere [8] how anxiety in infants may cause

[3] A. Blau, "Childhood Behavior Disorders and Delinquency," Ment. Hyg., 27: 261, 1943.

[4] ———, "In Support of Freud's Syndrome of 'Actual' Anxiety Neurosis," Int. J. Psychoanal., 33: 363, 1952.

[5] S. Freud, "The Justification for Detaching from Neurasthenia a Particular Syndrome: The Anxiety Neurosis" (1894), in Collected Papers, International Psycho-Analytical Press, London, 1924.

[6] Int. J. Psychoanal., op. cit.

[7] G. M. Beard, "Neurasthenia or Nervous Exhaustion," Boston Med. and Surg. J., 3: 1869.

[8] A. Blau, and W. C. Hulse. "Preventive Psychiatry in the Care of the Newborn and Infant." Presented

inhibition of natural expression, disorganization and retardation of intellectual and emotional growth, and fixations at immature levels. These reactions, however, are expressions of defeat and failure on the part of the child. The hyperkinetic aggressiveness of the behavior disorder, though faulty, is an advance from the disorganized, tantrumlike action of the infant and is also a primitive attempt toward organization beyond the early acting-out impulsivity of the infant.

Thus, the pattern of behavior disorder is from the child's viewpoint a healthier one than that of retardation or inhibition. In the behavior disorder one sees that the child has not submitted with a sense of failure and hopelessness but is fighting to save himself as an individual, despite the tremendous odds that he faces. The opposition is in many ways fantastic, unrealistic and futile, but it still means that he has not given up the ghost to save himself. From this angle, more sympathetic to the child, one can better understand the apparent lack of a sense of guilt and the forthright pugnacious attitude. It is only from the adult moralistic standpoint of the parents that a sense of guilt seems appropriate, not from that of the child whose interests and needs are frustrated. Rather than being an unfavorable sign, this attitude shows that the ego is asserting itself. If directed properly and not against such overwhelming odds, the ego may be encouraged to develop more constructive and social forms of expression for aggressiveness.[9]

The etiology of childhood anxiety neurosis with behavior disorder is, in our experience, also found to be related to a rejecting hostile attitude in the parental atmosphere. However, by the time the case comes to clinical attention, this noxious influence may be obscured by many factors. The rejecting parental attitude is often unconscious and covered by reaction formations which take the form of overprotection and overconcern.[10] Frequently, immature ambivalent attitudes by the mother in her early relations with the child

are the original provocation. Some of these mothers are content to follow rigid procedures of upbringing, like scheduled feeding, long periods of crying, lack of caressing, cold distant attitudes to avoid spoiling, and other methods which compensate for their ambivalence and at the same time permit them to enjoy the reassurance of authoritative backing for their rejecting attitude. In any case, the disturbed development of the child soon gives them additional reasons for a negative relationship. Undoubtedly, an anxious unhappy child can test the patience of even the best-intentioned parent, and a vicious cycle is established. The fact is that these mothers usually suffer from marked personality disturbances with psychoneurotic or psychotic characters and the child's behavior disturbance is generally intimately involved with their own unconscious conflicts.

The significant point regarding the etiology of anxiety neurosis is that it is a reaction to real provocation, and in the case of childhood anxiety neurosis, this is the lack of parental care. A child needs the direction, support and loving care of a parent as much as he needs other essentials for life, growth and development. In order to grow out of his disorganized infantile state, the child must be in contact with a supporting, loving, and adequately organized parent or surrogate. Lacking as yet an adequate ego organization of his own, he depends upon the outside one which promotes his own ego by identification, direction and support. Without these supporting influences, he is truly deprived and threatened. The resulting anxiety and behavior are a direct reaction to real noxious neglect and any treatment is wanting if it is short of recognizing this provocative factor. Thus, it is generally fruitless to attempt treatment of the anxiously disturbed child without concurrent treatment of the other members of the family, especially the mother, who is the essential pivot in a child's life. For this reason, the optimum treatment for childhood anxiety neurosis is the team approach which includes not only the different disciplines (psychiatry, social casework, psychology) for the diagnosis, but also a number of therapists working together in the individual treatment of the mother and father as well as the child.[11]

at the Annual Meeting of the American Psychiatric Assoc., Los Angeles, California, May 1953.

[9] W. C. Hulse, R. Whitfield, and M. D. Vergara, "'On the Spot' Psychotherapy in a Children's Institution," *Psychiatric Quart. Suppl.*, 28: Part I, 121–130, 1954.

[10] D. M. Levy, *Maternal Protection*, Columbia Univ. Press, New York, 1943.

[11] W. C. Hulse, "Psychotherapy with Parents and Children," Sauvegarde de l'Enfance, Paris, 1951, p. 181.

In the treatment of the child, it is not quite exact to regard what we do as narcissistic indulgence. The anxiously disturbed child is really in trouble and he really needs sympathy and help. The therapist, in identifying with the child's interests and often siding against the rejecting parent, is not merely carrying out a technique of therapy to obtain his cooperation. He is really helping the child out of a "blind alley" situation of unfair odds by adults who do not understand his needs. The child's bravado and apparent conceit must be understood as a puny defense by his weak ego, very much like the grandiose delusions of the manic patient. Indeed, if we manage to break through this superficial façade of the arrogant child, it becomes very apparent that he is really anxious, afraid and depressed. Direct support of the child enhances his ego by joining it temporarily with that of the therapist. Moreover, as he begins to sense a change in the parental and home atmosphere as a result of therapy with the mother, his ego begins to flourish, object relations become meaningful, a happier and stronger child emerges and the misbehavior recedes. Then more normal socialized behavior appears and true psychoneurotic reaction may develop. In other words, the anxiety "actual" neurosis is relieved so that the child can go on to develop normally or to take the direction of a psychoneurosis with an internalization of the psychic conflict. In the latter instance, the child is then ready for psychoanalytic psychotherapy in which he can develop a transference neurosis and work through his psychoneurotic problems. Thus, the further development of proper object relationships is a matter separate from the problem of anxiety neurosis, as is also that of the symptoms of habit disorders and neurotic traits. In the milieu of the better, less anxious parent-child relations, a true object relationship develops naturally. The positive realistic relationship of the child with the therapist contributes further opportunities for good identifications and cooperative constructive material for superego development.

The habit disorders are different from behavior disorders. Masturbation, enuresis, soiling, thumb-sucking, nail-biting, are infantile fixations or arrests in development conditioned by the anxiety of the child and faulty upbringing. These manifestations have somewhat the nature of perversions, as direct expressions of libidinal drives. Neurotic traits, like phobias, tics, stammering, are also in a different class from the behavior disturbances and are examples of true psychoneurotic symptoms. These more elaborate symptoms are psychologic distortions derived from repression and unconscious defenses against an inner conflict and anxiety. To the extent that the psychoneurotic mechanisms are successful, to that degree is the anxiety lessened, but at the price of a limitation of the ego's freedom. For example, the child with a school phobia has succeeded in localizing and circumscribing his anxiety in the phobia, and as long as he can avoid school, he enjoys relative comfort; however, by this psychoneurotic defense for his anxiety, his freedom of action is limited. Moreover, the psychoneurotic symptom must be differentiated from the psychoneurotic trait — the former is felt by the patient as an extraneous foreign body while the latter is more at one with the total personality. The trait has been incorporated and accepted within the personality as part of the self-image.

These points of differential diagnosis of habit disorders and neurotic traits from childhood anxiety neurosis with behavior disorder are important because each requires a different line of treatment. However, it must also be recognized that childhood anxiety neurosis with behavior disorder, if left untreated, can continue into adolescence and adulthood and take the more serious form of delinquency and crime.[12] Childhood misbehavior is a frequent antecedent in the history of delinquents. In these unrelieved anxiety neuroses with behavior disorders, the unbearable anxiety is successfully denied and the acting-out behavior becomes part of the deviant character development.

In summary the thesis is presented that the common childhood syndrome of primary behavior disorder is a form of anxiety "actual" neurosis and must be differentiated from habit disorders, neurotic traits and psychoneuroses (symptomatic and character neuroses).

The differentiation is important because each requires different approaches for treatment, and it also permits the inclusion of primary behavior disorder of childhood in the general psychodynamic nosology of anxiety neuroses, psychoneuroses, psychoses and character disturbances.

---

12 Blau, *op. cit.*

22

The Community and
the Aggressive Child *

George E. Gardner

The problem of the aggressive child in the community brings all of us face to face with the much larger and more inclusive problem of juvenile delinquency. It is, I think, in a consideration of this more inclusive community problem that the origins and significance of aggressive acts in childhood can be brought out most clearly.

First of all, I wish to discuss the relationship of the juvenile-criminal *act*, particularly of an aggressive nature, to other acts of children called either (1) normal or (2) neurotic. And, secondly — contrary to the usual procedure of telling what psychiatry and medicine and sociology have contributed to the solution of this very vexing problem — I wish to point up and emphasize that the study of the delinquent act and of the delinquent youth can contribute to our knowledge of normal child behavior and of the child's stages and phases of development.

If the study of the neurotic — in the pure sense of the term — has contributed to our knowledge of human motivation, the study of delinquent behavior has contributed to an equal or greater degree — and bids fair, I believe, to make even more important contributions in the future. As to the distinctions between these two labels, "neurotic" and "delinquent," we are led immediately to our first problem — namely, the relationship of the juvenile-criminal act to normal and to neurotic behavior in childhood.

---

* Reprinted from 33 *Mental Hygiene* (1949), 537–550. Used by permission of the author and the publisher. This is the first of two papers on "The Community and the Aggressive Child." The second "The Aggressive-Destructive Impulses in the Sex Offender," appeared in the January, 1950, issue of *Mental Hygiene*. A brief summarization of the two papers was presented at the International Congress on Mental Health, held in London, August, 1948.

It has always seemed to me unfortunate that psychiatrists have attempted to differentiate between the motivations, purposes, and techniques of the so-called neurotic and the non-neurotic delinquent. Such a dichotomy, I am sure, is not in the least conducive to better understanding of the delinquent act — better, that is, from the point of view of the only worth-while object and purpose, that of enabling us to apply a better therapeutic approach or technique — and it has, I fear, in the second place, made us less appreciative of the lessons that the anatomy of the delinquent act can and will teach us about other neurotic syndromes and about normal behavior.

Hence, we probably should not approach the juvenile delinquent *diagnostically* with the question in mind: Is this a "neurotic" delinquent or is it a "non-neurotic" delinquent? Is this "neurotic" aggression or "non-neurotic" aggression? Of course, I know that all who work at close quarters with these problems in juvenile sessions, faced as they are with expanding case loads and inadequate psychiatric help, do their best to determine which cases must be — and should be — sent to the psychiatrist. All of us have urged this practical diagnostic approach to probation officers and judges for many years. But except in those cases in which the *material* lacks and needs are so outstandingly prominent and predominant that it is obvious that secondary gains and not primary (internal neurotic) gains are of paramount importance in causing the delinquency, I no longer think that such a distinction is fruitful.

This artificial distinction between the neurotic and the non-neurotic is, I think, less fruitful not only in the matter of our theoretical concepts of behavior, both the known and the to-be-known; it also continues to foster and to perpetuate in the minds of non-professionals that particularly reactionary and unrealistic point of view that a segment of our delinquents need diagnosis and individual treatment because they are neurotic, but that an even larger number do not need treatment — or, worse, need only discipline and punishment — because they are *not* neurotic.

What, then, are the possible theoretical bases for a concept of juvenile delinquency as neurotic behavior upon which we can all agree, and that will eliminate for us at least this unsatisfactory differentiation? And in our discussion of this concept, the problem of childhood aggression as it relates to the community, in the most frequently encountered types of delinquency will be seen in a clearer light (I will take up later the question why we have been unable or unwilling to accept these concepts; and in that phase of our discussion I think you will see what I mean when I suggest that we note what the study of aggression in delinquent behavior has to contribute to our better understanding of motivations in normal behavior).

I shall list some seven propositions or conceptions relative to neurotic behavior which are equally applicable to delinquent behavior, and in doing so I shall rely quite heavily upon the formulations of the psychoanalytic school in psychiatry.

1. All behavior — normal, neurotic, psychotic, or delinquent — is designed to fulfill some biological need of the organism.

2. In as much as the instantaneous and complete fulfillment of biological needs is impossible in most human communities, the individual in his development is subjected to blocks and frustrations to and delays in their fulfillment. Hence the behavioral result that is allowed expression is a compromise between the instinctual biological needs and the demands of communities of other human beings.

3. Thus there are only two criteria with which we measure human behavior — i.e., these compromises — whether we look upon it biologically, socially, economically, psychiatrically, or spiritually: Is the behavior both (1) satisfying to the organism and (2) satisfactory to the community?

4. Now from the restricted area of our fields — psychiatrically — we label that behavior which is both satisfying and satisfactory as typical for society and culture, non-neurotic, non-psychotic, non-criminal. And behavior that is either unsatisfying or unsatisfactory, or both, we call either atypical, or neurotic, or psychotic, or criminal (in the case of an adult), or "delinquent" (if in a child below seventeen years of age). And, of course, our labels vary throughout the centuries.

5. And part and parcel of this concept is the added concept that such neurotic or delinquent behavior is in some degree disabling.

6. So much for a bit of behavior viewed cross-sectionally, or at the instant it is carried out as an isolated act or segment. But we have an equally important concept which we apply in our appraisal of behavior, and that is the concept inherent in our basic genetic approach. In other words, we must view behavior, too, in its longitudinal or developmental aspects, if it is to ever have real meaning for us, and we establish certain norms — age-span norms, if you will — within which span of, say, a few months at three or four years, or perhaps a span of a year or more between ages six and eight, we expect certain developmental steps to be taken, certain types of behavior to be manifested; but after the age span in question is passed, we expect these forms of behavior to be discarded and laid aside in favor of more satisfactory expressions of wants and needs.

If, however, these developmental phases, stages, segments, or components of our earlier life's development are not superseded, in the course of the educative process, by other and "better" compromises, but persist in their expression, we say that our child or adult is atypical, infantile, immature; and depending upon the specific nature of the persisting immature behavior, we say that he is neurotic or psychotic.

It is our thesis that this same genetic concept is applicable to all aggressive, delinquent, and criminal acts — and definitely should be applied if we are to have any uniform consistency in our own personal and workable theory of human behavior, or any self-assurance in our professional attack upon the problem of crime and the problem of the treatment of the delinquent child.

7. It follows then, finally, that the disabling feature or element of neurotic or delinquent behavior is the persistence into a later stage of development of a type of behavior — or manner of fulfilling a need, of attaining a pleasure — that was at an earlier stage "normal," but that should, under the community's demands, have been supplanted long since by a more acceptable expression of the need. Such "emotional rests" or "vestigial behavior" are characterized by their irrationality and by the compulsive chronicity or periodicity in their expression.

Our present-day concepts of human behavior will allow us, I believe, to include the child's delinquent behavior — all delinquent behavior — within the framework of the neuroses. I do not believe we violate any of the well-accepted criteria of the typically neurotic act if we do so, for I feel quite confident that the delinquent act is but a special type — a syndrome, if you will — within the group designated "the neuroses." Delinquent behavior can be seen to fulfill all of the criteria of this group. I say *"can"* be seen to do so because it is now our task to see wherein it does; wherein and to what extent we ourselves (I am talking now only about us in psychiatry and social work) have been unable to accept this notion; and why we have tended to be content with our older differentiated "neurotic" and "non-neurotic" categories.

Our primary difficulty, I feel, has been our inability or our unwillingness to apply the instinct theory in our consideration of the delinquent, as we have been able and willing to do in dealing with the neurotic. By "instinct theory" we are all aware that we mean that all behavior has, as its ultimate root and driving force, certain inborn predispositions to act or biological needs to fulfill, the fulfillment of which gives the individual pleasure, the frustration of which causes pain. We have in our psychoanalytic theories approached human behavior as if it were motivated by two such forces — the sex instinct and the *instinct of aggression.*

Now we come upon what is to me a very interesting — and illuminating — paradox. Although we have always noted the great opposition to an acceptance of Freud's concepts of the sexual drive — particularly infantile sexuality — having noted it, we have gone ahead bravely and scientifically and applied those theories and accumulated more and more data. And in the field of delinquency — though there has been (and still is) some reluctance in some quarters to assume that sexual deviations are *neurotic* manifestations of the sexual instincts, rather than just punishable misdemeanors — nevertheless, we have considered them as neurotic, and have pushed and pleaded for the professional diagnosis and treatment of delinquents so afflicted.

But, to return to our theme, here is our paradox: Although we have accepted and applied the knowledge of the *sex* instinct to delinquency, we have not been able — or, I suspect, we have not wished — to apply the instinctivist approach, and the rigid, but very useful criteria outlined above, when we are faced in our child with obvious demonstrations of the *instinct of aggression.* When we do this — *i.e.,* when we *can* do this — I think we will see that the division, neurotic and non-neurotic delinquents, is of little practical use — is, in fact, a definite hindrance to our treatment programs. It is obvious to all of us, of course, that the behavior of the delinquent, in 90 or more per cent of the cases, has seemingly nothing to do with the expression of the sex instinct, but has much — or everything — to do with acting *aggressively* toward the person or the property of another.

But why have we been loath to face this problem of aggression as dispassionately as we have learned to deal with what we have always *felt* to be a much more "unwholesome" drive — namely, the sexual impulse? It must be — if our analytic theories of resistance are of any validity at all — that we have not *wished* to consider the problem of aggression — whether it be in the delinquent or in any one else — because we are bothered by its deep, underlying, unconscious implications. In other words, we know full well that such a "blind spot" or "scotoma" in our thinking must be due to a serious fear of or distaste for the real meaning of the data or observations rejected — a meaning that threatens us with a possible loss of self-esteem as human individuals, causing us to make further modifications of the assumed rationality of our behavior and thinking. As a matter of fact, it should — if our suppositions are at all correct — have an even more serious connotation for us than our modern scientific concepts regarding sexuality. (And here we approach what I feel can be one of the contributions of the data gleaned in the study of juvenile delinquency to our fundamental knowledge of *normal* behavior — and particularly of aggression.)

If the delinquent act 90 per cent of the time is concerned not with the expression of the sex drive, but rather with the expression of the aggressive instincts, what is the exact nature or form of this expression as it is observed in our boys and girls before the courts? Superficially, it is easy to answer this question, because from 70 to 90 per cent of such behavior, in any series of cases reported, has to do with *stealing* — general or specialized stealing — of property belonging to some one else. And may I say also that any one who at the present time proposes to deal in articles or books with the problem of the juvenile delinquent and does *not* concentrate practically his sole attention on the possible dynamic factors inherent in this most prevalent of all delinquent acts — stealing — simply is not professionally realistic. It would be comparable, for example, to a clinical pathologist's dealing with anæmia without a primary concern for the disturbed functions of the red cells.

Has this most frequent affront to the community's well-being — stealing — as an act, anything to do with aggression, and, if so, what? And, further, if stealing can be considered an aggressive act, can it always be justly labeled "neurotic" in that it satisfies all of the criteria of a neurotic act? Finally, what does this mean in relation to normal behavior?

In answer to the first question, I will state again that I have become more and more convinced that all of us have a tendency, when talking about aggression, to forget the deeper, unconscious, primitive — biological, if you will — significance of this act. I am afraid that we are accustomed — because we wish it so — to consider "aggression" more or less as a mere brushing aside of *external* objects that get in our way, of neutralizing *external* forces that thwart and hamper us, instead of regarding it as what it really is — a vital, *internal*, instinctive drive clamoring incessantly for repeated expression, expression that in itself must be pleasurable and thus is difficult to modify or repress.

The aggressive act in its simpler expressions is in reality a *destructive* act, and our first aggressive acts are of a distinctly destructive nature in that we act either to eliminate (destroy) an external object that confronts us, or to incorporate it and by so doing also eliminate (destroy) it. I am not referring here merely to the so-called "*counter*-aggression" that is alleged to be a response to some frustration instigated by some one else; rather, I refer here to *primary* aggression — a biologically grounded instinct, manifested by unicellular as well as multicellular organisms, to incorporate and destroy — "destroy" in the sense that the material is taken up unto ourselves, made a *part* of ourselves through transformations that render it no longer completely a part of the environment external to us. This destructive (or "aggressive") impulse exists, and its presence is open to our citation and interpretation, at *all* levels of functioning in living organisms, from the strictest biological or even chemical functions of the cells to the myriad complexities of individual or even group behavior.

Stealing — the major element of all delinquent behavior — seems to us to be just such a *destructive* act in that it does symbolically involve the taking up unto ourselves and the transformation for our own use of that object or thing which *was a part of* — "belonged to," we say — some other person. This extension of ownership (and note the word!) is a destructive act in a double sense: it incorporates the object taken, and it to some degree symbolically destroys (mutilates, injures, or strips) the *person* of another. The power to steal is the power to destroy, and stealing is in essence a destructive act.

To pursue this concept further, property is conceived of in the unconscious as a part of some one — of some *person* beyond the self — and stealing it symbolizes unconsciously the *destructive* taking of it — wrenching it away from the person of another.

It is not possible, it seems to me, to account (1) for the stealing of boys who have everything material in this world that they need or want, or (2) for the *absence* of stealing in boys who live in the most undesirable neighborhoods, subjected to the most severe material deprivations, even lack of the barest necessities of life, by any theory that does not ultimately place this act in its proper meaning relative to the unconscious identity of property — all property — with the body of some person. Psychotherapy must start with this assumption.

All other "causes" of stealing — and the "causes," as the textbooks tell us, are multiple (poor training, deprivation, rejection, symbolic fetishistic stealing, desire to demonstrate physical prowess, and so on) — have their fullest meaning and relative significance for us only in the light of this concept.

As to the pleasurable aspects of this instinctual expression — not only in the simple incorporation of food and drink, but also in the complex destructive crimes against property — such aspects cannot be denied. We are sometimes puzzled, I think, in dealing with a delinquent boy, at the great patience and the vast, painstaking expenditure of energy often involved in the formulation, planning, and execution of an act of stealing. In spite of our common concept that stealing is a lazy man's way of making a living, I am sure that had we an accurate measure of energy output for such acts, from their inception to their successful or unsuccessful termination, we should find that the delinquent really *works* at his delinquency.

And we may note also that all this planning, all this scheming, is in itself a *pleasurable* output of energy. I have faith enough in the pleasure-pain principle as a working hypothesis to be convinced that were all this work *not* pleasurable, it would not be pursued. This pleasure, both in anticipation and in its eventual realization, is, I submit, the pleasure derived from the destructive (aggressive) instinct of man. And just as in the expression of the sexual instinct, the fore-pleasure becomes in itself an end to be sought — and sought for the pleasure derived over and above that inherent in the actual commission of the sexual act itself — just so, in the expression of man's destructive impulses in the stealing act, or in any other mode of expression selected, the pleasure in detailed preparation and planning constitutes the fore-pleasure of the destructive act and can, and often does, become the chief motivation of, or even a substitute for, the actual value of the thing to be stolen or the pleasure involved in actually depriving another of his ownership.

So much for the *instinctive drive* — the aggressive-destructive impulse — which we propose as the motivation in stealing, our most frequent of all juvenile delinquencies. Without some such formulation as this, I cannot see how we can ever begin to view the cases of delinquency in our everyday practice in clinic and agency with any degree of psychiatric sophistication at all. We will have to continue to content ourselves with essentially a non-dynamically oriented approach, except in those very few — comparatively, very few — cases of deviations in the expression of the *sex* impulses in which we already admit that the dynamic interpretations are the only helpful ones in our understanding of the individual case.

Let us return now to our criteria of a neurotic act — constructed through the years mainly as a result of consideration of the *sexual* instinct — and very briefly note whether stealing, as an expression of the aggressive-destructive instinct, fulfills these criteria.

1. In the first place, destructive incorporation of material associated directly or indirectly, actually or symbolically, with the person of another is a mode of behavior designed to fulfill a bio-logical need of the organism. In fact, we can argue that such aggressive-destructive impulses, through incorporation, subserve the very existence or life of the organism itself.

2. Because of the demands of society — at first represented by the parents, then by the community — the immediate, continued, unchecked, and unmodified gratification of this instinctive impulse is not condoned. Hence the human organism must get the best *compromise* (between gratification and denial) it can for the attainment of this pleasure.

3. Such compromises with our pleasurable aggressive-destructive impulses have to be both satisfying and satisfactory in relation to our biological make-up, on the one hand, and in relation to cultural insistences on the other.

4. That aggressive-destructive behavior which is either *not* satisfying or *not* satisfactory (or both) we may label neurotic or delinquent — and, to be completely accurate, it is *definitely* neurotic, with the added descriptive term "delinquent," if we do not desire to place it in relation to *other* types of neurotic expression, such as phobias, and so on.

5. Delinquent behavior, just like other neurotic manifestations of needs, *is* disabling to the organism in some degree. It is disabling either because of the destructive (retaliative, punitive) impulses that it invites from the external sources attacked, or because in the child it definitely prevents a normally orderly future development, since it prevents the formation of a strong and healthy ego mechanism.

6. When the individual is considered in a *developmental* sense (genetically), unrestricted destructive incorporation *is* a type of behavior that is normal and expected in earliest infancy, and in its execution and its initial frustration it becomes indissolubly linked to the presence of and "ownership" by some one beyond the baby itself. As development proceeds year after year toward adolescence, these aggressive impulses are modified, and each modification becomes an expected stage or phase in mature (for that age) behavior, which in turn is modified in the interest of more serviceable, more efficient, more socialized, or more moral behavior, as regards the expression of the child's instinct of aggression in the form of stealing.

7. Finally, then, the disabling or inefficient "neurotic" feature of the delinquent act of stealing is the *persistence* beyond seven or ten or

fourteen — or whatever developmental age or stage we wish to select — of aggressive, incorporative behavior, the components of which should have been modified or repressed at an earlier stage of development. The fulfillment of this need was once efficient and permissible, but at a later date it is inefficient and prohibited. It is, again, an "emotional rest," a demand or need the infantile, primitive, or immature nature of which makes it just as irrational as it is compelling and insistent upon periodic expression.

And, parenthetically, it is just as much our task in therapy to uncover and expose in so far as we can this unverbalized — or, if you prefer, unconscious — destructive aggression inherent in the stealing act of the delinquent boy, as it is to bring to light the sexual motivations in any other neurosis of childhood. The more insight we can help the child to attain through this therapeutic procedure, the greater will be his ability to deal with these impulses as they repeat their demands. For here, too, you must replace an imperfectly understood "id" demand with meaning accessible to the ego, and hence subject to its control. And it follows, of course, that the more disabling the behavior, the more the need for intensive psychiatric treatment.

In the above discussion, then, through a shift in emphasis from the sex to the aggressive instincts, the undeniably neurotic characteristics of the act we call delinquent — and, in particular, of that most prevalent of all our delinquent acts, stealing — have been outlined. There is one other problem, however, which immediately comes to mind when the destructive features of delinquent behavior are emphasized, whether such behavior occurs in the neurotic or in the normal child — and that is the problem of passivity.

You will recall, if you think for a moment, that a large percentage of our writings on juvenile delinquency — and notably those that have dealt with stealing — have been concerned with what *seems* to the writers at first glance to be the essential passivity or "passive oral receptivity" of the person who repeatedly engages in the thieving act. It is emphasized again and again that the child in stealing is trying "to get something for nothing" — that he is trying to recapture a state of blissful oral receptivity and passivity wherein gifts — symbolic of food and love and attention — are obtained *without an*

output of energy or "a giving of himself" in return for such pleasures. It is, we have stressed, a sort of reactivation or continuation of that pleasurable, passive, parasitic stage or phase of development so characteristic of early infancy.

Somehow the continued actual study and observation of these cases do not seem to bear out these formulations in the theoretical sense, and proceeding along these lines in the practical aspects of therapy has never led to helpful or conclusive structuralization of the meaning of the child's stealing. The oral passivity theory always seems to be too "pat," and, once voiced, it closes the door on the question what is the child to do about it, with an implied (and incidentally too often expressed) "So what?"

Again, the observations that we can make daily in these cases I am sure bear out my previous suggestions that boys and girls in stealing — like Gilbert and Sullivan's policeman when he is "poleecing" — work hard at their delinquency. There seems to be little that is passive about the act itself, and in the light of our previous examination of this act, there is nothing passive either in the motivations, drives, aims, intentions, or purposes that give this act its so all-consuming power. This impulse is repeatedly carried out by children in the very face of and in spite of the *intellectually* appreciated fact that they have but about one chance in ten of not getting caught and, if caught, may face very severe punishments and losses of privileges and even of freedom itself.

To be sure, there are many delinquents who are described accurately as passive when their *total* personalities are considered. They do *not* respond to the admonitions of parents and other adults. There is often not a single instance wherein their behavior can be called "aggressive" in the usually accepted sense of this term. They have suffered marked and prolonged deprivations, rejection, and frustration in early life, but counter-aggression does not seem to take the form of striking back with physical abuse and hostile defiance. On the contrary, they may be quiet, undisturbed, and undisturbable.

To account for such delinquencies by a theory of aggressive-destructive motivation, one may have to give some of our theories regarding passivity in people in general a severe wrench. It has always seemed to me that the so-called passive, oral, recipient delinquents were responding with the most deadly, most upsetting, and most impenetrable (therapeutically) type of *aggression* that they or any one can resort to in their fight against parents, colleagues, teachers, law-enforcement agencies, psychiatrists — namely, the aggression so aptly expressed by the passive response.

This heretical explanation of the rôle of passivity in human behavior is suggested not just to save a theoretical notion about the aggressive determinants in stealing, but because of two relevant and compelling observations. The first is that it is difficult to fit the commonly accepted theory into one's notions as to how organisms behave in their own best interests biologically by the use of a passive stage of inaction. Doing something — reactivity — is a basic attribute that distinguishes all living matter. That being so, the use of passivity at all would seem to be, not a waiting, static acceptance, as a defensive maneuver, till a more propitious moment arises, but rather in itself an aggressive response. Certainly an abundance of clinical material of the use of passivity in this fashion could be amassed to demonstrate this quality in the behavior of predominantly passive patients.

My second bit of evidence for the unconscious aggressive elements in an assumed passivity is the very definite *counter*-aggression that is aroused in most people when faced with an individual who resorts to such tactics. With our delinquent youngsters, such passive behavior almost never fails to arouse the anger of the parents, the court, the teacher, the probation officer, and all others who are endeavoring to understand and help the child. In other words, it is as if we, through *our own* unconscious motivations, understood full well the aggressive nature of our clients' or patients' superficially non-aggressive intentions. And, of course, that is exactly what happens if we do not watch and guard our responses, and it is my feeling that just such unconscious responses on the part of well-intentioned (consciously) people have led to some pretty bad theories as to the true origins, meanings, and necessary treatment of such boys and girls.

At any rate, to leave this particular phase of our discussion, I hope that, though we *do* note the alleged "oral parasitic passivity" of many delinquents and criminals, there is considerable justification for the interpretation of

such behavior as being, in reality, aggressive in nature. And here, again, I feel that such observations as these on delinquent children will enable us to make some contribution to the allied theories of human behavior regarding both normal and traditionally considered neurotic responses.

23

Mental Pathology *

Sheldon and Eleanor T. Glueck

Although the description of the basic characteristics, behavior tendencies, and goals of strivings of the delinquent and non-delinquent boys as derived from the Rorschach Test does not indicate the extent to which they occur in particular combinations or syndromes, it is possible, without arriving statistically at such syndromes, to determine roughly the mental patterns of the boys as summarized in a psychiatric diagnosis of each case made by the Rorschach analysts. The extent and nature of mental pathology among the delinquents and non-delinquents is shown in Table XVIII–43. (Although provision was made for determination of paranoia and epilepsy, no such cases were ultimately found, and therefore these particular conditions are not defined or discussed.)

It is apparent that there is a statistically valid difference between the two groups in the extent and nature of their mental pathology. A slightly higher proportion of the delinquents than of the non-delinquents (51.4% : 44.3%) are found to have mental abnormality of one kind or another, and many more delinquents than controls (16.9% : 5.9%) are described by the Rorschach analysts as "poorly adjusted, or asocial, or poorly adapted, or primitive."

Organic disturbances — "cerebral (cortical-

---

* Reprinted by permission of the publishers and The Commonwealth Fund from *Unraveling Juvenile Delinquency*, Sheldon and Eleanor T. Glueck, Cambridge, Mass.: Harvard University Press, Copyright 1950, by The Commonwealth Fund. Pages 239–243.

Table XVIII-43 *Mental Pathology*

DESCRIPTION	DELINQUENTS		NON-DELINQUENTS		DIFFERENCE
	Number	Per Cent	Number	Per Cent	Per Cent
No conspicuous mental pathology	241	48.6	276	55.7	−7.1
Asocial, "primitive," poorly adjusted, unstable	84	16.9	29	5.9	11.0
Organic disturbances	4	0.8	1	0.2	0.6
Psychotic trends	2	0.4	8	1.6	−1.2
Neuroticism	122	24.6	177	35.8	−11.2
Marked	16	3.2	25	5.1	−1.9
Mild	81	16.3	115	23.2	−6.9
Trends	25	5.1	37	7.5	−2.4
Psychopathy	36	7.3	2	0.4	6.9
Undifferentiated pathology	7	1.4	2	0.4	1.0
Total	496	100.0	495	100.0	

$$X^2 = 77.85; P < .01$$

subcortical) and non-cerebral disturbances of the central nervous system" — are evident in 4 of the delinquents and 1 of the non-delinquents. As for psychoses, 2 delinquents and 8 non-delinquents are diagnosed by the Rorschach analysts as having disorders of the schizophrenic type. This does not include paranoia, which is characterized by systems and ideas of a delusional nature.

Marked neuroticism is found in 3.2% of the delinquents and in 5.1% of the non-delinquents. This is defined as "a condition in which the individual suffers from more than average insecurity and anxiety (conscious or unconscious) against which he develops protective devices differing quantitatively or qualitatively from the culturally accepted ones and leading to conflicts which are, as a rule, not solvable by him for the time being. If the neurosis interferes with efficient adaptation, the boy is classified as a marked neurotic."

Mild neurotics, "in whom the neurosis does not prevent the individual from efficient adaptation," also appear in lower proportion among the delinquents than among the non-delinquents (16.3% : 23.2%). In addition to those diagnosed as marked or mild neurotics are boys who cannot be clearly placed in one or the other category but who show distinct neurotic trends. Here too we find a lower proportion of delinquents than of non-delinquents (5.1% : 7.5%). Totaling all the boys who are diagnosed as marked or mild neurotics or as having

neurotic trends, we see (Table XVIII–43) that there is neuroticism in some degree among 24.6% of all the delinquents and 35.8% of all the non-delinquents.

Although it is often assumed that many delinquents are psychopathic or show marked trends towards psychopathy, only 36 of the 500 delinquents are thus characterized by the Rorschach analysts. *Psychopathy* is not a uniform and definite concept; it here refers (following Bleuler and others) to "all marked mental and emotional deviations that do not clearly belong in any one of the other diagnostic groupings. Often a difference in degree of a disorder rather than of kind places a person in this category. This may be illustrated by saying that the psychopath is less ill than the psychotic and more ill than the neurotic. He is distinguished from the neurotic also by the fact that he is much more often openly destructive and antisocial or asocial. He is also usually less amenable than the neurotic to therapeutic or educative efforts. The most important trait of the psychopath is the fleeting, non-integrative, superficial quality of his personal relations." A comparison of the presence of psychopathy in the two groups shows (Table XVIII–43) that 7.3% of the delinquents and only 0.4% of the control group can be thus described. Unlike neuroticism, therefore, psychopathy is more markedly present among the delinquents than among the non-delinquents.

As for *undifferentiated pathology,* which refers to all those cases "that are considered mentally and/or emotionally pathological and that either do not belong in any of the other categories, or in which a differential diagnosis on the basis of the Rorschach record is not possible," there are 7 such among the delinquents and 2 among the non-delinquents (1.4% : 0.4%).

To summarize briefly, a statistically significant difference exists between the delinquents and the non-delinquents in the incidence of mental pathology, which largely derives from the higher proportion of asociality or primitiveness and of psychopathy among the delinquents, and the greater neuroticism of the non-delinquents.[1]

SUMMARY

The traits in the character structure that most sharply differentiate the delinquents and non-delinquents as derived from the Rorschach protocols have already become apparent.

---

[1] Although we realized in designing the research that a diagnosis made by the psychiatrist as the result of one interview with a boy and derived from a behavioristic level of personality structure could not be conclusive, we nevertheless felt that as experienced a child psychologist as Dr. Bryant E. Moulton would be able to make reliable diagnostic classifications for purposes of comparing and supplementing the diagnoses arrived at by the Rorschach analyst.

When the two series of examinations were entirely completed, we ourselves compared the two sets of diagnoses, keeping in mind the somewhat different concepts that were used in making the classifications by each method. Wherever significant differences were found, Dr. Schachtel was asked to resolve them after we had made available to him the full psychiatric report. As Dr. Moulton was at this time no longer connected with the research, the materials were not submitted to him.

We found what seemed to be inconsistencies between the two sets of diagnoses in only 74 cases, and these were examined by Dr. Schachtel in the following manner: "In examining the differences between the psychiatric and Rorschach diagnoses, a distinction has been made between diagnosis proper and personality description. This has been done merely for the sake of presentation and in full awareness of the fact that these two factors are really inseparable and that diagnosis constitutes essentially a very generalized, highly abstract summary of certain aspects of the personality description.

"In comparing the diagnoses the fact must be kept

Considering first those traits in which the delinquents as a group significantly exceed the non-delinquents, we have observed that they are to a much greater degree socially assertive,

---

in mind that some of the psychiatrist's categories of diagnostic classification have not been used for the Rorschach diagnoses and some of the Rorschach classifications have not been used by the psychiatrist, and furthermore that the definitions of some of the diagnostic categories (especially of the term neurotic) differ as between the psychiatric and Rorschach materials.

"For these reasons the apparent differences in diagnostic classification often may not be real, but merely differences in terminology. Perhaps the most frequent seeming, but not real, differences arise from the fact that the psychiatrist does not seem to use the concept of character-neurosis and that the Rorschach does not use the concept, constitutionally inferior. Most of the cases classified as neurotic in the Rorschach diagnosis suffer from character-neurosis.

"In view of these differences in diagnostic terminology, in all cases where the diagnoses seem to differ markedly I have primarily compared the personality descriptions and ratings. Where these are not contradictory or markedly different from each other in essential respects, I have generally assumed agreement and noted that the seeming difference in diagnosis is the result of the definition."

The following results were achieved by Dr. Schachtel's study of the 74 cases:

In 20 cases he found that the differences resulted from differences in definitions or in terminology. For example, Case No. 11: Rorschach diagnosis: *marked neurotic.* Psychiatric diagnosis: *no conspicuous mental pathology.* "Psychiatrist mentions the 'distinct impression that this boy has definite conflicts,' is non-confiding, has extreme compensatory tendencies, is stubborn and suspicious. This fits well with the Rorschach description and forms the basis for the Rorschach classification of *neurotic.*" Case No. 38: Rorschach diagnosis: *psychopathic.* Psychiatric diagnosis: *no conspicuous mental pathology.* "The material in the psychiatric interview makes it much more likely, to my mind, that this boy has marked pathological features than that he has none. The psychiatrist states that he is very suggestible, has marked inferiority feelings, and was rejected or deserted at a very early age by both parents. The last circumstance almost inevitably would lead to serious disturbances and is typical in the life-history of many psychopaths. The boy must have resented this desertion deeply. Also, the final statement of the psychiatrist that even under the most favorable conditions the boy will be a poor risk and will need guidance all his life speaks for the likelihood of the Rorschach diagnosis." Case No. 511: Rorschach diagnosis: *marked neurotic.* Psychiatric di-

defiant and ambivalent to authority; they are more resentful of others, and far more hostile, suspicious, and destructive; the goals of their drives are to a much greater extent receptive

(oral) and destructive–sadistic; they are more impulsive and vivacious, and decidedly more extroversive in their behavior trends.

At the same time, the delinquents are far

---

agnosis: *no conspicious mental pathology.* "Essentially, both the Rorschach materials and the psychiatric materials agree on submissive attitude toward authority and lack of self-confidence. There is disagreement only as to the degree of these traits. According to the Rorschach analysis, they are so marked that they make this boy quite repressed and dependent."

In 43 cases, although the diagnoses were apparently different, the personality description (made by the psychiatrist in the text of his report) was in the direction of substantiating the Rorschach classification. For example, Case No. 108: Rorschach diagnosis: *no conspicuous mental pathology.* Psychiatric diagnosis: *psychoneurotic tendencies.* "I doubt that this is a disagreement. The wording of the psychiatric diagnosis seems to indicate that the psychiatrist does not want to classify him as acutely, out-and-out neurotic, but only as tending in that direction. There are some neurotic trends, as described also in the Rorschach Test. They did not seem sufficiently strong to classify the boy as neurotic. If there is any difference between the psychiatrist and the Rorschach analysts it is a question of estimating degree of trends rather than of assuming or not assuming a characteristic diagnostic picture; difference of degree rather than of kind." Case No. 265: Rorschach diagnosis: *between neurotic and psychopathic.* Psychiatric diagnosis: *no conspicuous mental pathology.* "The psychiatrist mentions unconscious conflict and sense of inadequacy. This would easily be compatible with the assumption of neurosis. The type of stealing, for immediate use, goes well with the assumption of oral-receptive trends." Case No. 624: Rorschach diagnosis: *marked neurotic.* Psychiatric diagnosis: *no conspicuous mental pathology.* "No evidence of definite disagreement. Outstanding in the psychiatric interview is the impression that the boy does not really talk freely and that one does not quite know what he is like and what his motivations are. The psychiatrist also notices indications of compensatory processes. This could very well be compatible with an underlying structure such as the Rorschach analysis points to."

In 4 cases the differences were due to the fact that the particular category used by the psychiatrist could not be derived through the Rorschach Test. This refers especially to epileptic personality. For example, Case No. 328: Rorschach diagnosis: *no conspicuous mental pathology.* Psychiatric diagnosis: *epilepsy.* "Epilepsy is not among the Rorschach categories since quite often it cannot be seen on the basis of the Rorschach record. This boy's Rorschach Test shows none of the outstanding epilepsy symptoms,

but this might merely mean that his epilepsy is not apparent in the Rorschach, which happens quite often. His intensive feeling reaction, mentioned by the psychiatrist, also shows in the Rorschach."

In one case the comparison could not be made because the data were not sufficiently clear.

Finally, in only 6 cases was there frank disagreement between the Rorschach and the psychiatric diagnosis. We cite them all: Case No. 236: Rorschach diagnosis: *no conspicuous mental pathology.* Psychiatric diagnosis: *abnormal personality, unstable, neurotic.* "The Rorschach record does give a less unstable picture than the psychiatric. The life history of this boy would lead one to expect that he is unstable and neurotic. The psychiatrist's diagnosis is the more likely. The two diagnoses agree on the lack of spontaneity and insecurity." Case No. 713: Rorschach diagnosis: *marked neurotic (?).* Psychiatric diagnosis: *no conspicuous mental pathology.* "Disagreement in personality description. According to the psychiatric record, the boy is unattractive, has a stiff knee joint that is the cause of an awkward limp. The psychiatrist feels surprised that the boy does not seem to have any intense conflicts. The Rorschach analysis quite definitely points to an unstable, pathological personality and to destructive-sadistic trends such as often develop on the basis of physical or other handicaps." Case No. 725: Rorschach diagnosis: *psychopathic.* Psychiatric diagnosis: *no conspicious mental pathology.* "Disagreement. The Rorschach picture is definitely that of a quite egocentric, unstable personality tending toward impulsiveness. The destructive trends, assumed in the Rorschach analysis, may be questionable. The only symptoms mentioned by the psychiatrist that may point to some disturbance are tenseness, a tendency to stutter, and insecurity." Case No. 314: Rorschach diagnosis: *no conspicuous mental pathology.* Psychiatric diagnosis: *unstable — on organic basis.* "The Rorschach record definitely does not indicate any organic disturbance of the central nervous system. Whether there are any other organic disturbances cannot be seen from the Rorschach record. On his unstableness the two diagnoses agree." Case No. 466: Rorschach diagnosis: *psychopathic trends.* Psychiatric diagnosis: *no conspicuous mental pathology.* "The Rorschach analysis stresses impulsiveness and rebellious-destructive trends more than the psychiatrist and gives a more pathological picture. This seems to be more than a difference in emphasis." Case No. 478: Rorschach diagnosis: *marked neurotic.* Psychiatric diagnosis: *no conspicuous mental pathology.* "Disagreement in diagnosis and in personality picture."

less submissive to authority; they suffer far less than the non-delinquents from fear of failure and defeat; they are considerably less cooperative with and dependent upon others, and markedly less conventional in their ideas, feelings, and behavior; they are also noticeably less masochistic and self-controlled.

It is clear that the delinquent group is strikingly different from the non-delinquent in respect to those traits and dynamisms of personality-character structure and function which the Rorschach Test is designed to reveal. It is also obvious that the differences in incidence of such characteristics are not altogether haphazard but tend to fall into a general, meaningful pattern, although there is some evidence that subpatterns also exist. Moreover, even a simple review of the traits and tendencies under consideration shows that they are of a nature to facilitate uncontrolled, antisocial self-expression.

A preliminary synthesis of the differentiae of the delinquents and non-delinquents as related to other findings of this study is presented in Chapter XXI [of *Unraveling*]. Further and deeper exploration of the meaning of the findings of the Rorschach Test must await a subsequent volume, in which we expect to make systematic statistical correlations of the data with somatotypes on the one hand,[2] and the significant sociologic findings, on the other.

Although the major purpose of this research project is to focus attention upon the differences between delinquents and non-delinquents in or-

der to arrive at the dynamic pattern of crime causation, we cannot leave the comparison of the traits in the basic character structures of the delinquents and non-delinquents without adverting to a number of them in which the incidence in *both* groups, although not always similar, is nevertheless very high. This is true of the *presence* of general vague or unconscious feelings of insecurity and/or anxiety (89.2% : 95.7%), of the feeling of not being wanted or loved (84.3% : 88%), and of markedly good surface contact with others (91.7% : 96.7%); and the *absence* of self-assertion (93.7% : 97.8%), of an overcompetitive attitude (94% : 92.3%), of a feeling of resignation (94.9% : 97.3%), of depressive trends (96.3% : 98.6%), of an attitude of kindliness and trust (95.8% : 92.9%), of spontaneity (91.7% : 94.5%), and of a preponderance of introversive trends (72.7% : 75.5%).

To give an adequate explanation of the high incidence or marked absence of these traits would require correlation between them and other factors in the research. It would seem, however, that the traits which highly characterize both delinquents and non-delinquents are more attributable to the process of environmental–cultural conditioning than they are to constitutional roots, since they are markedly present in both groups despite the differences in the constitutional make-up of the boys.*

---

[2] See Article 13 of this volume. The Gluecks are in the process of analyzing the intercorrelations of sociocultural data with somatotypes. — *Ed.*

---

* This summary includes not merely the diagnosis of mental pathology but also various traits arrived at through psychiatric interviews. For want of space, the materials regarding traits have been omitted. It is advisable for the student to read Chapter XVIII in *Unraveling*. — *Ed.*

Chapter 6

Family Life and Delinquency

ANALYSIS AND SYNTHESIS of the wide variety of factors entering into the causation of delinquency make it abundantly clear that we cannot simply regard human beings as fundamentally and naturally good though corrupted and made antisocial through evil environmental influences. Rather, we come closer to biologic and psychologic reality if we recognize that the child is essentially a bundle of elemental, egoistic impulses and needs and that throughout life — but especially during the first few years — the individual must struggle to tame, discipline, redirect or sublimate these primitive tendencies in accordance with social demands and tabus. Any influence within or without the family group which aids the growing youngster to manage his primitive inclinations without resort to the adjustive escape into antisocial behavior or into psychoneurosis or psychosis is, therefore, fundamentally a preventive of delinquency. *Per contra*, the more that the instructive, protective and supportive social institutions (the home, the school, the church, the neighborhood, society in general) disintegrate and thereby lose their power to socialize instinct, the more will the natural impulses toward selfish, asocial, dissocial or antisocial expression tend to flow into action. Such resultant loss of power is one reason for the increase of delinquency and crime during or shortly after periods of social crisis, such as long-standing economic depressions, famines, wars, etc. Only in such times of widespread social malaise and strain does the role of social and cultural forces tend to predominate over the more delicate internal character structure developed in individuals during the first few years of life. The family is without question the chief school of character for the child and the chief source of example; its members symbols of "identification" and emulation.

The article by Shulman summarizes the findings in some of the most reliable researches involving the role of the family in delinquency.

The extracts from *Unraveling Juvenile Delinquency* demonstrate the types of family differences which emerge when comparing a carefully selected sample of delinquents from an urban, underprivileged area with a sample of true non-delinquents from a similar sociocultural background.

Gardner's article throws light on the emotional ties between parents and children, with special reference to the child's concept of self; and that of Schwarz and Ruggieri vividly illustrates the relationship of morbid parental attitudes to the evolution of antisocial practices in children.

24

The Family and
Juvenile Delinquency *

Harry M. Shulman

Juvenile delinquency is more than a formal breach of the conventions; it is indicative of an acute breakdown in the normal functions of family life. The loss of parental control represented in the formal breach of the law is usually the culmination of a period of heightened tensions arising from severe conflict over patterns of rearing — disagreement over duties, restrictions and limitations, standards of education and training, selection of associations and places of association, and so forth — culminating in a breakdown of emotional attachment between parent and delinquent child, and leading often to a break in essential communication of attitudes between the generations.

Juvenile delinquency is thus a circumstance of acute emotional disturbance both to parent and to problem child, involving usually several aspects; among them, the parent's sense of helplessness in the situation, his ambivalent desires to protect the errant child and at the same time to injure it physically for rejecting the parental protection, and the shame and sense of social degradation that accompany the exposure of family incompetence. The shock is often productive of complete emotional rupture and of rejection of the wayward child, although unconscious emotional rejection of the child may have long preceded the outward break in relationships.

FACTORS IN FAMILY INFLUENCE

The family fulfills at least three major functions: it provides organic sustenance and habit-training in survival patterns; it affords primary group association for the experiencing of social-

---

* Reprinted from 261 *Annals* (1949), 21–31. Used by permission of the author and the publisher. See, also, G. H. Barker, "Family Factors in the Ecology of Juvenile Delinquency," 30 *J. Crim. L. and Criminology* (1940), 681–691. — *Ed.*

izing interpersonal relationships; and it is a major source for the transmission of the values and knowledge of the culture. We shall therefore have to consider the influence of aspects of each of these upon juvenile delinquency.

Among the conditions which we shall consider are physical factors such as family size and crowding; economic and social factors such as the economic status of the house and the structure of the family; sociopsychological factors such as transmission of delinquent attitudes and the role of discipline; and cultural factors such as the role of social class in patterns of rearing, and the influence of ethnic group upon the solidarity of family structure. The importance of any single one of these as an agency in juvenile delinquency may be minimal; it is the cumulative impact of a large number of these factors that constitutes the multiple causation pattern and, at the same time, the complex treatment problem of the delinquent situation.

SELECTIVE NATURE OF COURT CASES

A major research difficulty in evaluating family influences upon misconduct lies in the selective nature of the court arraignments from which are drawn most of the data upon the home backgrounds of delinquents. Court arraignments are selective from the delinquent population in terms of age, sex, race, nationality, rural-urban residence, and socioeconomic level, as well as in terms of offense category. Court cases are drawn more characteristically from urban industrial communities, and the children represented in disproportionate numbers are Negroes or first-generation white Americans of European or Latin American backgrounds. They include a disproportionate number of boys of the adolescent age group drawn from families of lower socioeconomic status.

Court cases emphasize property offenses, particularly among boys, as contrasted to the problems in educational and interpersonal adjustment that constitute the bulk of child guidance clinic referrals. Fully three-quarters of court arraignments of boys are by police complaint, whereas the majority of clinic referrals are directly by parents; thus the court intake includes a larger proportion of parents who have been unaware of their inadequate guardianship, if not actually protective of their children's misconduct, whereas clinic intake includes a larger proportion of parents who have been made aware of their own inadequacies in coping with adjustment problems. Among this group there may possibly be a larger number of parents whose acts of referral represent emotional rejection of the child. Hence in discussing the role of family influences upon juvenile delinquency, the reader should remain fully aware of the selective nature of much of the data upon which discussion of this type must be based.

PHYSICAL FACTORS

In the earlier history of juvenile delinquency research there was preoccupation with the physical and economic concomitants of delinquency. Several studies of family size indicated that a disproportionate number of delinquents spring from large families. Merrill, in a very recent matched control study, verified this point for her sampling. But it has been pointed out that family size is related directly to socioeconomic status in terms of per capita income, and that the child from a very large, poverty-stricken family may become delinquent not necessarily because of size, *per se*, but because of the crowding, poor housing conditions, bad neighborhood, and early cessation of education and early beginning of employment that accompany the living conditions of such families.[1]

Adverse economic conditions in the home appear to have, in combination with other influences, some relationship to delinquency. The majority of studies of court samples of arraigned delinquents bring out the low socioeconomic status of the families and the fact that a large proportion of them have been recipients of aid from public and private social welfare agencies. Burt, in his London study, discovered more poverty in the homes of his delinquents than in those of his control group of nondelinquents from the same neighborhoods and schools. Merrill also found sharp differences in economic status among a sample of delinquents carefully matched against a control group of nondelinquents.[2] There is the possibility that family economic status is entirely an outcome of skewness of court intake; as against this interpretation is the finding of Glueck and Glueck, that among their "juvenile delinquents grown up" there were marked differences in the economic status of the parents of the delinquents who succeeded compared to those who failed following treatment.

The occupation of the parents is important in relation to economic status. Studies of the occupational backgrounds of fathers of court-arraigned delinquents indicate an excess number with slight skills or unskilled, and relatively fewer in semiskilled and skilled occupations. This is indicative of the greater occupational precariousness, the less secure income, and the lower social status of many of the parents of delinquents. Similarly, most studies of delinquents bring out the greater extent of total unemployment among parents and the greater number of families in which the mother is the sole support or where both parents are employed. In the latter case, there is a marked effect upon the capacity of the parents for supervision of the children.

Crowding, as determined by the number of persons per room, has been shown in several studies to be greater in families of delinquents than of nondelinquents in congested areas. Shulman, in his New York State Crime Commission study on truants, discovered that the median number of persons per room was 1.7 as against an estimated housing congestion of approximately one-half of that amount in congested areas generally.[3] Crowding, while an effect of large family size and economic marginality, has its own significant social and psychological effects in contributing to a lack of privacy, to breakdown of barriers to sex experience within the family, and to limitations of activity, leading to quarreling and to the flight of children and adolescents from the home to the street or to public and commercial centers for recreation and companionship.

RESEARCH REGARDING BROKEN HOMES

The most systematic research on the role of the family in juvenile delinquency has been on the so-called broken family, defined by a majority of investigators as one in which one or both parents are absent owing to death, desertion,

---

[1] Mapheus Smith in Walter C. Reckless and Mapheus Smith, *Juvenile Delinquency*, New York, 1932, 122.

[2] Family economically comfortable: delinquents 11.5 per cent, non-delinquents 31.5 per cent. Maud A. Merrill, *Problems of Child Delinquency*, Boston, 1947, 77.

[3] Harry M. Shulman, *From Truancy to Crime, a Study of 251 Adolescents*, New York State Crime Commission, Albany, 1928, 49.

separation or divorce, or commitment to an institution. A major hypothesis has been that a complete family, consisting of father, mother, and children, is essential to the development of a balanced and socially adjusted personality. Evidence favoring the causal significance of the broken home in juvenile delinquency should reveal a higher incidence of broken homes among delinquents as compared to nondelinquents.

Among the hindrances to scientific research on this point is the fact that no data for the United States as a whole give the proportion of broken homes for the whole population, and studies emphasizing the influence of the broken home on delinquency, such as Shideler's in 1918, have been based on estimates of the extent of broken homes in the general population.[4]

Separate data are available as to the separation and divorce of married couples, but the number of children in the United States whose parents are living apart because of desertion, divorce, separation, or annulment is not known.[5] Nor are data available as to the number of families with children that are broken by the death of one or both parents. A Chicago study of unpublished census data indicated that one-seventh of the families studied were broken by death, desertion, separation, or divorce.[6] A special census enumeration conducted by the United States Department of Labor in New York City in 1936, based on 1,749,000 families comprising the total family population of New York City, reported that 17 per cent of the families were broken.[7]

Data on the proportion of juvenile delinquents from broken homes are based largely on reports of juvenile courts; and since a break in the family may itself determine that there shall be a court handling of the problem rather than unofficial or private handling, these figures do not indicate the average amount of family breakdown among problem children in the United States. Nevertheless, since court arraignments may represent what are considered within the values of our culture to be the more serious types of conduct disorder, data on broken families may throw some light on the association between that factor and certain types of offense.

BROKEN HOMES OF DELINQUENTS

Breckinridge and Abbott, reporting on 13,000 cases studied between 1899 and 1909, found 34 per cent from broken homes.[8] The United States Children's Bureau, in successive reports, has indicated high percentages of broken homes among court cases. In 1939 it reported broken homes in 36 per cent of boys' cases and 50 per cent of girls' cases disposed of in sixty-four courts in 1936.[9]

Among children committed to institutions there has been an even higher proportion from broken homes. In 1923 the United States Bureau of Census reported that 56 per cent were from broken homes.[10] In Wisconsin 63.5 per cent of girls committed to correctional schools were from broken homes.[11] The factor of the family break may have influenced judges in the direction of institutional commitment; but this must be taken together with the fact that institutional commitments usually represent either severer offenses or more persistent offenders, especially in urban jurisdictions, from which the bulk of systematic court reports originate.

Thus, the increase in the frequency of the broken home as we progress from court arraignment to commitment may be taken as one evidence of a relationship between family disorganization and delinquency. In general, percentages of broken families among children arraigned in juvenile courts appear to be higher than for known samples of the general population.

---

[4] E. H. Shideler, "Family Disintegration and the Delinquent Boy in the United States," *Journal of Criminal Law and Criminology*, Vol. 8 (1917–18), pp. 709–32. He estimated that 25% of all children in the United States were from broken homes, compared to percentages ranging from 40 to 70 in various groups of delinquents.

[5] James H. S. Bossard, *The Sociology of Child Development*, New York: Harper and Brothers, 1948, p. 366.

[6] Monroe Day, *Chicago Families, a Study of Unpublished Census Data*, Chicago, 1932.

[7] Consumer's Bureau, U.S. Department of Labor, *Broken Homes and Income in New York City*, Washington, 1938.

[8] S. P. Breckinridge and Edith Abbott, *The Delinquent Child and the Home*, New York, 1912, 91–92.

[9] Children's Bureau, U.S. Department of Labor, *Juvenile Court Statistics*, Publication No. 245, Washington, 1939, 49.

[10] Bureau of the Census, *Children Under Institutional Care*, Washington, 1927, 322.

[11] Katherine Du Pre Lumpkin, "Parental Conditions of Wisconsin Girl Delinquents," *American Journal of Sociology*, Vol. 37, No. 2 (Sept. 1932), 232–39.

Collateral evidence on this point is available from private researches based on individual case study. In a study of 966 cases presenting special problems of diagnosis, referred by the Boston Juvenile Court to Dr. William Healy and his associates at the Judge Baker Foundation, Sheldon and Eleanor Glueck found that 48 per cent came from broken homes.[12] The same authors, in their earlier study of the family backgrounds of 500 youths committed to the Massachusetts Reformatory for serious offense reported 60 per cent from broken families.[13]

ETHNIC BACKGROUNDS AND BROKEN HOMES

The point has been made that measures of the extent of broken homes among juvenile delinquents should take into consideration the ethnic backgrounds of delinquents, since the incidence of broken homes varies markedly by race and nationality. For example, the New York City census by the United States Labor Department [14] found that its average of 17 per cent of broken families in that city represented a range, by ethnic group, from 14 per cent to 31 per cent as follows: foreign-born whites, 14 per cent; foreign-born Negroes, 16 per cent; native-born whites, 20 per cent; native-born Negroes, 31 per cent.

Sophia Robison has demonstrated that the proportion of problem children known to the courts varies by ethnic groups; hence the general child population is not unselectedly represented in court intake, for ethnic background. Jewish problem children, with a low broken-home incidence, tend to be underrepresented in some jurisdictions, because of the provision of private facilities for their care; and Negro problem children, with a high broken-home incidence, are overrepresented, owing to a lack of private facilities for their care. Thus, the disproportionate number of broken families among court cases may be a result of the ethnic distribution of court cases.

FINDINGS DIFFER

Shaw and McKay, in a Chicago study, sought to minimize the influence of broken homes, through equating the broken-home rates for court cases and unselected school children, by establishing norms of broken-home incidence among 7,000 Chicago schoolboys chosen from 29 schools in the entire range of neighborhoods classified in terms of incidence of juvenile delinquency. When nationality and age were held constant, the nondelinquents had a broken-home incidence of 36.1 per cent, compared to 42.5 per cent among 1,600 delinquents — a difference too slight to be considered significant. The authors do point out that their delinquent sample consisted largely of serious gang offenders, and that a group of boys with personality problems might present a very different family disorganization pattern.

It should be pointed out that the significance of the Shaw and McKay study derives not from a lower incidence of broken homes among delinquents, for their proportion of 42.5 per cent was similar to the findings of other investigators, but rather from a high incidence of broken homes among their nondelinquent control group. Since their general population sample had a broken-home incidence, uncorrected for age and nationality, of 29 per cent, compared to the 14 per cent incidence reported by Day [15] and the 17 per cent incidence reported in the New York study of the United States Labor Department, it is possible either that their schoolboy sample was a skewed one for incidence of broken homes, or that their method of obtaining data through unverified school interviews with pupils ranging in age from 10 to 17 years did not produce as accurate results as census enumerations.[16]

Other controlled studies, in which the rates for family organization have been equated for ethnic factors, do not support Shaw's position. Cyril Burt, in his distinguished London study of juvenile delinquents, although not seeking to equate the ethnic factor, used delinquent and nondelinquent samplings of the same culture group, same age, and same social class, living usually on the same streets and attending the same schools. He found that broken homes accounted for 61.3 per cent of families of delinquents contrasted to 25.1 per cent of families

[12] Sheldon and Eleanor Glueck, *One Thousand Juvenile Delinquents*, Cambridge, Mass., Harvard University Press, 1934, 75–77.

[13] Sheldon and Eleanor Glueck, *500 Criminal Careers*, New York, 1930, 116–18.

[14] *Op. cit.* note 7 *supra*.

[15] *Op cit.* note 6 *supra*.

[16] Clifford R. Shaw and Henry D. McKay, *Report on the Causes of Crime*, Vol. II, Washington: National Commission on Law Observance and Enforcement, 1931, 261–84.

of nondelinquents — a difference of 2.4 times.[17] Miss Merrill, in a recent study of three hundred consecutive juvenile court arraignments matched for age, sex, and nationality against an equal number of nondelinquents, found a proportion of 50.7 per cent of broken families in her delinquent sample compared to 26.7 per cent in the matched control group — a difference that, measured by the size of the critical ratio, was statistically significant.[18]

LIMITED SIGNIFICANCE OF BROKEN HOMES

In general, then, the majority of research studies are in agreement with official court reports, that the incidence of broken homes is higher for delinquents than for nondelinquents, even when such factors as age and ethnic background are taken into account. This does not necessarily prove a causal relation, but strongly suggests one.

Significant as the hypothesis of the broken home may be for the objectives of a broad social welfare program of delinquency prevention, its framework is too broadly conceived to be useful as a guide in the study of the dynamics of individual delinquency in the family setting. The role of the family in juvenile delinquency involves discussion of at least two other areas — the family as culture transmission group and as a matrix of socialization.

DELINQUENCY AND THE VALUE SYSTEM

What differentiates juvenile delinquency from personality disorders is that, in addition to a similar set of interpersonal maladjustments, delinquency involves deviation from an officially stated value system. Actually, all deviations in conduct are at the same time deviations in interpersonal relationships; that is, disagreements as to what constitutes proper behavior toward other persons in a defined situation. But in juvenile delinquency, treatment involves not only a series of adjustments in interpersonal relations to ease the tensions that underlie breaks in communication and understanding, but the development of a sharpened sensitivity to the rights and welfare of other persons as officially defined within the culture. Thus the treatment

of juvenile delinquency involves inquiry into the value systems of delinquents over against the value system of the culture as officially defined.

We have come to recognize that "guilt," as constituting breach of an official value system, is not necessarily the responsibility of the delinquent child, but may be a reflection of the value system within which he has been reared. Delinquency codes fall short in that they attempt to generalize for all children the value systems of parts of the culture. We have come to recognize that differences in ethical training and clashes in ethical definition among different families in our multicultural society contribute to culture conflict and to juvenile delinquency itself. We recognize the existence of demoralized families in which the value system is a debased one, in which children have an example of lewdness and crime. We recognize the existence of families whose parents deny their conventional responsibilities toward their offspring, as revealed in excessive cruelty and neglect. We recognize the existence of families in which parent and child generations are torn with the dissensions of parent adherence to one code and culture pattern, and adherence of the children to another code and culture pattern characteristic of a social group of which they aspire to be accepted as members.

THE FAMILY PATTERN

In this connection, a hypothesis recently advanced and now widely held is that delinquency is learned experience similar to any other learned experience, and requires direct contact with other delinquents for the acquisition of delinquent attitudes and skills. Sutherland has formulated a concept of professionalism in delinquency as being the outcome of differential association.[19]

This hypothesis deserves testing within the framework of the family setting. Since the family is the most effective transmitter of attitudes, the hypothesis should be sustained by evidence that delinquency is transmitted as a family behavior pattern. That evidence is to some extent available. The Gluecks reported that 84.8 per cent of the young offenders released from the Massachusetts Reformatory were from families

---

17 Cyril Burt, The Young Delinquent, New York, D. Appleton and Company, 1925, 60–98.
18 Op. cit. note 2 supra, 77.

19 E. H. Sutherland, Principles of Criminology, 4th ed.; Chicago, 1947, 6–9. Cf. Glueck, "Theory and Fact in Criminology" (Article 41). — Ed.

in which other members were delinquent,[20] and that 86.7 per cent of the juvenile delinquents and 80.7 per cent of the women delinquents studied in other samplings were exposed to delinquent example at home.

This does not say that the child directly copied the delinquent conduct of the parent or elder sib, but it indicates that breach of the law did not begin with the offender under study, and that the families of these offenders had not been galvanized by earlier misconduct of other members into energetic action to prevent future misconduct.

There is evidence that increase in the severity of the conduct of delinquents is associated with increased severity of conduct among other members of the family. Shulman, in his Crime Commission study of 251 truants, six to eight years after release from a school for truants, found that 43 per cent of those who were not further delinquent came from families that had criminal records; that 50 per cent of those who had subsequent records of juvenile delinquency, 66 per cent of those subsequently charged with misdemeanors, and 83 per cent later charged with felonies, had been reared in such families.[21]

The hypothesis that differential association is a prime process in delinquency maturation raises the question of the relative strength of vertical transmission from parent to child versus lateral transmission from sib to sib. In Shulman's study, based on a sampling composed largely of native-born children of foreign-born parents, the findings pointed to the greater importance of delinquency transmission within the same generation, for the police records of brothers increased sharply with the increase in severity of subsequent misconduct of the truants.

There are evidences that the delinquent home and the broken home overlap. Miss Elliott found that 67 per cent of the broken homes of delinquent girls had records of immoralities of one or both parents, as compared to 44 per cent of the unbroken homes of delinquent girls.[22] Miss Lumpkin found that 82 per cent of the broken homes and 61 per cent of the unbroken homes of delinquent girls were socially defec-

tive, in that they involved alcoholism, sexual irregularities, or mental or physical disabilities.[23]

INCIDENCE OF DELINQUENTS IN FAMILIES

On the other hand, there is little evidence that where there is one delinquent in a family, the other children are necessarily delinquent. On the contrary, many studies indicate that families ordinarily contain both delinquents and nondelinquents; Healy has estimated the incidence of delinquents in families to be 1.2. This important fact forces us to inquire into the differential factors both within the family and outside of it making for the delinquency of one child and not for that of the other.

Burt made a comparison of the incidence, among families containing delinquents and nondelinquents, of four family influences: poverty and its concomitants, defective family relationships, defective discipline, and viciousness (unethical example). He discovered a greater frequency of association of defective discipline and vicious example with delinquency, than of poverty and defective family relationships (broken homes). Thus Burt turns our attention to the importance of dynamic aspects of personal relationship in family life.[24]

DELINQUENCY AND FAMILY DISCORD

The interpersonal conditions of family relationship leading to delinquent behavior stand out as more important than general background factors. Numerous studies have shown that uncongenialities, tensions, marital triangles and sexual breaches, frictions over income and expenditure, projections of frustrated ambitions, losses of authority and standing, and many other broken threads in the tangled skein of family relationships are as important as, if not more important than, physical breaks in family structure, are usually antecedent to physical breaks, and contribute largely to delinquency. Clinical experience has demonstrated that rarely does a child become delinquent where the members of a family have successfully maintained love and affection for one another. The treatment of delinquency involves the treatment not of the individual but of the whole family constellation.

Carl Rogers, in a discussion of the Smith Col-

20 Op. cit. note 13 supra, 111–13.
21 Op. cit. note 3 supra, 52–55.
22 Mable A. Elliott, Correctional Education and the Delinquent Girl, Harrisburg, 1928, 26–28.

23 Op. cit. note 11 supra.
24 Cyril Burt, op. cit. note 17 supra, 60–98.

lege studies based on 197 case records from the Institute of Child Guidance in New York City, has pointed out that Miss Witmer and her associates, in studying the factors associated with success and failure in treatment, both at the time of disposition and several years later, reported negative findings for such items as the child's age at the time of clinic study, sex, school placement, ordinal position in family, even the child's symptomatic behavior, and but slight significance for such factors as intelligence, economic status of home, and family size. What did have a striking relation to the clinic's success in dealing with children were the marital adjustments of parents, the emotional tone of the home, and the behavior and attitudes of parents toward the child.[25]

The adjustment of parents to each other was alone significantly related to successful treatment, distinctly better results having been achieved where parents were living together in a satisfactory relation than where they were definitely dissatisfied with their marital life. Intermediate results were obtained in homes where the parents were divorced or separated or where they had a resigned or neutral attitude toward the frictions of their married life. From these results Rogers concludes that so far as children's behavior is concerned, a broken home is probably less injurious than the tensions of a home in which the parents are deeply dissatisfied with each other.[26]

PARENT–CHILD RELATIONSHIP

The most striking relation in family life bearing on the prognosis of behavior outcome, in the Witmer findings, was the parent–child relationship. Rogers states in this connection:

If we were to gamble on the outcome of treatment in the case of a problem child or delinquent and had to base our gamble on one item alone, we would do best to disregard the child entirely and investigate simply the way in which the parents behave toward the youngster and the attitudes which they hold toward him.[27]

In subsequent studies, Miss Witmer's students have corroborated the importance of parental attitudes. Among clinic cases where there was an extreme lack of affection for the child on the part of the parents there was no improvement in 64 per cent of the cases, compared to improvement or completed adjustment in 97 per cent of the cases where a normal affectional relationship existed and where the faults consisted in inadequate handling.[28]

The definition of the interpersonal situation is just as important at the hands of the problem child as his parents, according to studies conducted by Drs. William Healy and Augusta Bronner. In a study of 105 delinquents and a like number of nondelinquent brothers and sisters, usually of near age and same sex, no fewer than 91 per cent of the delinquents gave clear evidence of being or having been very unhappy and discontented in their life circumstances or extremely disturbed because of emotion-provoking situations or experiences. In great contradistinction, similar evidences of inner stresses were found at the most in only 13 per cent of the controls.

Among the symptoms of the delinquents suffering from emotional disturbances were: (a) feeling keenly either rejected, deprived, insecure, not understood in affectional relationship, unloved or that love had been withdrawn — 46 cases; (b) deep feelings of being thwarted other than affectionally — 28 cases; (c) feeling real or fancied inadequacies in home life, school, etc. — 46 cases; (d) intense feelings of discomfort regarding family harmony, parental misconduct, conditions of family life, or parental errors in management and discipline — 34 cases; (e) bitter feelings of jealousy toward one or more siblings or feelings of being markedly discriminated against — 31 cases; (f) confused unhappiness over mental conflicts — 17 cases; (g) sense of guilt over previous delinquencies — 9 cases.[29]

SOCIAL DIFFERENCES

Findings which place emotional frustration at the root of juvenile delinquency have for the most part been based on studies of clinic and court samples drawn from lower socioeconomic

---

[25] Carl Rogers, *Clinical Treatment of the Problem Child*, Boston, 1939, 179–80.

[26] *Ibid.*, 181–82.

[27] *Ibid.*

[28] Helen Witmer and students, *The Outcome of Treatment in a Child Guidance Clinic*, Smith College Studies in Social Work, Vol. 3, June 1933, 370.

[29] William Healy and Augusta Bronner, *New Light on Delinquency and Its Treatment*, New Haven, 1936, 128–29.

levels. New light recently shed on different patterns of child training in different social classes in American society suggests that these differences may have their effects on patterns of social behavior, including delinquency. They suggest that a stricter regimen with more frustration of direct pleasure impulses is distinctly a middle-class characteristic, and that in contradistinction lower-class rearing is distinctly permissive in its practices. Thus middle-class parents tend to initiate tensions in child-rearing patterns earlier and sustain them longer than poor parents. Habits of sphincter control and weaning are established earlier and more rigidly among the middle class, and later and more permissively among the poor. Middle-class children are more closely supervised than children of the poor. They are expected to participate in home duties more frequently.[30] These facts raise a question.

If frustration is closely allied to delinquent behavior, and if middle-class rearing involves sustaining of many tensions, why do these tensions not result in frustrations leading to officially recorded delinquency? The answers may lie along at least three lines of reasoning:

(1) The frustration patterns in middle and lower classes appear to be differently organized. The middle-class child is forced to maintain tensions leading to discipline, learning and utilization of skills, and is concomitantly guarded against early pleasure behavior of unapproved type. The lower-class child is less restricted in his range and choice of activities, being permitted greater freedom with regard to distance allowed from home, choice of companionships and recreation, and time of entering upon both part-time after-school and full-time posteducational employment. The child of lower socioeconomic background more frequently has earlier heterosexual experience.[31]

Thus, the frustrations of the lower-class child are not in relation to severe checks upon his freedom. He achieves the partial independence of a wage-earning status earlier, whereas middle-class children remain in school and economically dependent on their parents longer. Middle-class rearing delays social maturation longer, while establishing parental authority earlier. The middle-class child appears to accept his frustrations more philosophically as part of his life pattern. The pattern differences, one may suggest, lie in the earlier onset and greater consistency in establishment and maintenance of tensions in middle-class rearing. The middle-class child accepts his harness of tension patterns on a habitual basis because he has been less indulged and less subjected to ambiguous and inconsistent rearing practices.

To the middle-class child, frustration involves obedience which gives him a status, as inheritor of the parental status, to which he may aspire. The child of the poor, if obedient, has a status as inheritor of his parental status, to which, in our culture, he usually does not aspire. Thus tensions are endured by the middle-class child more consistently because they lead to a goal acceptable in our culture, but are less consistently endured by children of the poor as leading to an unacceptable goal.

(2) The delinquencies of the lower-class child arise from the conditions of his rearing — greater deprivation of material means to pleasure, and greater clash of temperaments in family life owing to the inconsistencies and lack of discipline in rearing. His offenses (among boys) consist largely of various types of stealing, and (in girls) of waywardness and ungovernability — behavior for which the penal code and its counterpart in children's court acts have well-defined statutes and rulings. In contrast, and in the absence of scientific data, we may speculate from scanty evidence that the characteristic offenses of middle-class children consist of malicious mischief occurring under group stimulus, and sex offenses that are privately dealt with.

(3) The characteristic offenses of the middle class do not show up in criminal statistics until adult life, and are then occupationally differentiated from the offenses of the poor, tending toward fraud, in contrast to assault and theft among the poor. Aside from occupational opportunities, it may be pointed out that the personality structure involved in successful fraud is wholly consistent with middle-class education and training, depending not on a single successful attack or raid, as in the case of assault or theft, but on a more carefully controlled aggression involving knowledge and application

---

[30] Allison Davis and Robert J. Havighurst, "Social Class and Color Differences in Child-Rearing," *American Sociological Review*, Dec. 1946.

[31] Alfred C. Kinsey, Wardell B. Pomeroy, and Clyde E. Martin, *Sexual Behavior in the Human Male*, Philadelphia, 1948, 387–550.

of a wide range of technical skills and patience and fortitude in planning and carrying out extensive frauds as nearly within the letter of the law as technical skill will permit. This suggests that the middle-class child who in later life resorts to crime does so in the light of earlier experience which has taught him that the social order has few loopholes and many restrictions; whereas the poor child resorts to types of crime which suggest that earlier experience has taught him that the social order has many loopholes and few restrictions.

25

Family Life and Delinquency *

Sheldon and Eleanor T. Glueck

The foregoing analysis [from *Unraveling Juvenile Delinquency*] has shown that the parents of the delinquents and non-delinquents both stem from a background similar in the size of the families in which they grew up and similar in economic circumstances, the limited education of their parents, and the incidence of serious physical ailments in their family group. On the other hand, the paternal and maternal families of the delinquents were to a greater extent characterized by mental retardation, emotional disturbance, drunkenness, and criminality. Whether these undesirable conditions are to be regarded as largely hereditary or largely environmental in origin is difficult to say without more information; but they

---

* Reprinted by permission of the publishers and The Commonwealth Fund from *Unraveling Juvenile Delinquency*, Sheldon and Eleanor T. Glueck, Cambridge, Mass.: Harvard University Press, Copyright 1950, by The Commonwealth Fund. Pages 107; 115–116; 133. This article consists of summaries of Chapters IX, X, and XI of *Unraveling*; it is recommended that the student read each of these entire chapters. See, also, S. and E. T. Glueck, *One Thousand Juvenile Delinquents*, Cambridge, Harvard University Press, Second Edition, 1934, 80–83. — *Ed.*

must have had their adverse influence upon the parents of the boys who, in their turn, had to assume the responsibilities of marriage and the care of children.

As to the ability of the boys' parents to assume their family responsibilities, it has been revealed that although both sets of parents were married at an equally early age, and although there is no greater disparity between the ages of the fathers and mothers of the delinquents than that of the fathers and mothers of the non-delinquents, they differed in other respects. More of the parents of the delinquents made forced marriages. The parents of the delinquents were more burdened with serious physical ailments, mental retardation, emotional disturbances, drunkenness, and criminalism. This is likewise true of the brothers and sisters of the delinquents.

The families of the delinquents were to a greater extent than those of the non-delinquents dependent for financial assistance upon relief agencies or relatives. Reflective of their lesser ability to manage their affairs without propping from social agencies is the fact that many more agencies had to provide, in addition to financial relief, services of one kind or another for them, services necessitated by domestic difficulties, improper care of children, problems of physical and mental health, need for recreational outlets, and vocational difficulties.

The difference in the caliber of the two sets of families is strikingly revealed by the fact that unforeseeable conditions, such as economic depression and seasonal unemployment, were the bases of the need for financial assistance among the largest proportion of the families of the non-delinquents who had to resort to outside aid; while in the families of the delinquents unwillingness of the principal breadwinners to assume their responsibilities to support their families constituted the main reason for financial assistance. A further difference in the quality of the two sets of families is reflected in the far lower proportion of fathers of the delinquents having *good* work habits.

By these simple yet fundamental yardsticks, it is clear that the families in which the delinquents were reared were more inadequate than those in which the non-delinquents grew up. This basic finding is abundantly supported in the chapters that follow. . . .

The poorer quality of the family life of the delinquents is clearly reflected in a number of striking findings: There was less planning of household routine and a less refined cultural atmosphere. Their families were less self-respecting than the families of the non-delinquents and less ambitious to improve their status or that of their children. Standards of conduct were likewise much poorer in the homes in which the delinquents grew up.

Nor was the quality of the family life of the delinquents as good as that of the non-delinquents in aspects more intimately related to child welfare. This is the case as regards the relationship between the parents, the supervision of the children, provision for recreational outlets in or outside the home, and finally the cohesion of the family as a group.

Obviously the environment in which the delinquent boys grew up was less conducive to the wholesome rearing of healthy, happy, and law-abiding children than that in which the non-delinquent boys grew up.

Since the two sets of boys had been carefully matched at the outset — not only in respect to age and general intelligence (factors involving only the boys themselves), but also with reference to ethnic–racial derivation and, pointedly, residence in underprivileged neighborhoods, the differences between the families of the delinquents and those of the non-delinquents that have emerged in this and other extensive portions of the analysis are all the more impressive. They indicate strikingly how inadequate to any fundamental analysis of the cultural influences involved in the causation of delinquency is any study which is limited to comparison of the external and crude factors comprising the neighborhood or residential area. Without consideration of the under-the-roof culture there can be no explanation of the differential influence of similar neighborhoods. . . .

We have seen that as to certain situational factors that are involved in the formation of parent-child relationships, the delinquents and non-delinquents resembled each other: in the age of their parents at the birth of the boys, in potentials for culture conflict, and in the frequency of the advent of children. The delinquents came from somewhat larger families than the non-delinquents, but fewer of them were among those generally deemed more vulnerable to emotional trauma in their intrafamily relations, that is, only children, first-born, or youngest children in the family.

With reference to a more dynamic pattern of parent-child relationship, the delinquents, as a group, were to a greater extent the victims not only of less stable households but of broken homes. To a far greater extent than the non-delinquents they had substitute parents, that is, foster or step-parents, or lived with relatives.

As regards affectional relations between the parents and the boys, on which so much of the development of personality and character depend, the delinquents were much more the victims of the indifference or actual hostility of their fathers and mothers, and were, in turn, less attached to their parents. Not only did they derive less affection from their mothers and fathers, but they were also regarded with less warmth by their brothers and sisters. This greater emotional deprivation is further reflected in a greater feeling on the part of the delinquent boys that their parents were not concerned about their welfare. Whether as a result of this or of other elements in the family life, the delinquents did not identify themselves with or seek to emulate their fathers nearly as much as did the non-delinquents.

How much this, in turn, has to do with the more erratic discipline imposed on the delinquent boys by their fathers and the fathers' far greater resort to physical punishment can only be surmised. The mothers of the delinquents, though not as erratic in their discipline, were, however, much more lax than the fathers. Fewer of both the mothers and fathers of the delinquents were consistent and kindly in their disciplinary practices.

It seems clear, therefore, that the delinquent boys, far more than the non-delinquents, grew up in a family atmosphere not conducive to the development of emotionally well-integrated, happy youngsters, conditioned to obedience to legitimate authority.*

* See, also, the recent article, "Juvenile Delinquency in Cardiff," by H. C. Wilson, 9 *British J. of Delinquency*, 1958, 94–105. For a thoughtful recent attempt to introduce greater precision into the study of family relationships from a psychiatric point of view, see E. Chance, "Measuring Pathogenic Family Relationships," 4 *Internat J. of Social Psychiatry*, 1958, 10–17.

26

Separation of the Parents and the Emotional Life of the Child *

George E. Gardner

In this paper I shall confine myself to the effects on the emotional development of the child of the prolonged and essentially permanent absence of one parent from the home, and comment only to a limited degree upon those even more unfortunate situations where both natural parents are absent, presumably permanently so. I shall consider only those situations, too, where the absent parent, though away from home, is still living and may or may not be accessible to the child at stated intervals. Furthermore, because of the fact that in 75 to 90 per cent of any series of broken homes coming to our attention it is the father of the child who is absent, my remarks will be primarily

---

* Reprinted from 40 *Mental Hygiene* (1956), 53–64. Used by permission of the author and the publisher. Presented at the Massachusetts Conference of Social Work. See also, M. E. Bonney, "Parents as the Makers of Social Deviates," 20 *Social Forces* (1941), 77–87. As to the role of ordinal rank of children in connection with delinquency, the following is of interest: "Only children, first children, and youngest children are thought to be especially vulnerable to the development of behavior difficulties, because they receive preferential treatment. It is of interest, therefore, to see how the delinquents and non-delinquents compared in rank order among their brothers and sisters. Table XI–5 shows that, contrary to general expectation, lower proportions of the delinquent boys were only children, first children, or youngest children. Although the families are as yet incompleted, resemblance of the delinquents and non-delinquents in age distribution makes this finding significant." S. and E. T. Glueck, *Unraveling Juvenile Delinquency*, New York, The Commonwealth Fund, 1950, and Cambridge, Harvard University Press, 1951, p. 120. For an intensive analysis of this problem, see J. P. Lees, and L. J. Newson, "Family or Sibship Position and Some Aspects of Juvenile Delinquency," 5 *British J. Delinquency* (1954), 46–64. For another aspect of parent–child relationships involved in some cases of delinquency, see D. M. Levy, *Maternal Overprotection*, New York, Columbia University Press, 1943. — *Ed.*

directed to the effect of his absence on the child's development. To be sure, a certain percentage of mothers do desert their children, or their children are taken from them by direction, and when this happens the basic problems set for the child vary in kind and in intensity; to these I shall lend some emphasis. Yet the prototype of the broken home is that where the father is absent and the mother has the sole care of the children. In the fourth place, I shall not attempt, except tangentially, to outline the different effects of the absent parent on boys and on girls as such. Rather I would select for our consideration some universal effects upon children regardless of sex and some fundamental problems in emotional development that are affected by the absence of the parent.

Specifically, I shall speak of the effects of parental separation upon:

The child's developing "concept of self" — the ingredients that go to establish his own inner sense of separateness, integrity, worthwhileness, and security as an individual.

The child's "concept of human beings" that comprise his outer world — human objects to which he must make a definite feeling orientation and to which he is expected to respond, as a child and later as an adult, in an acceptable and an efficient way. (To the technically minded perhaps it is correct to say that I am directing my attention to the possible effects of parent absence on the ego development of the child.)

We shall begin our discussion by a glance for a moment at what the parent is to the child; *i.e.*, what are some of the most important attributes of the parent as far as the child is concerned and as he or she is seen through children's eyes and feelings at various stages of development. In the light of these many parental rôles (and they are many and complex), we ourselves shall be better able to appreciate the effect of deviations from these rôles which are brought about when a parent leaves. To the child at any age — and particularly in earliest childhood — the parent (both parents) is the source of life itself in the form of food and clothes — the one single factor of basic significance in establishing within him a sense of security and in indicating probable continuing survival. He predicates his physical integrity, including later his sense of anatomical integrity, upon the presence of parents who will care for his bodily needs and will protect him from aggressive and mutilative attacks by others.

To this basic feeling of security of body and its associated concept in the child's mind that parents through their presence alone will maintain it are added other elements in the child's over-all estimate of his parents. They are the givers of gifts that may be used as objects for gratification and the givers of love in and by itself or as symbolized by these gifts. They are in great measure the omniscient givers of information that explains his world and omnipotently protects him in it. In their seeming omniscience and omnipotence also they control his life, direct his behavior, and emphasize ideals of conduct in individual and group living.

These are the elements of the fundamental concept of the parent as it exists in the mind of the young child. Obviously many modifications of this biological or strictly "dependency-need" concept of the parents must take place as the child advances toward the establishment of a necessary concept of himself as an independently (relatively independently, of course) behaving individual or "self," at which point he is expected to refer his behavior to inculcated or incorporated mental images of these parents which, for good or ill, are to be the most powerful models that he will have within him.

It should be emphasized, too, that these parental concepts will in large part determine what the child's notions of human beings as a whole in his world of the present and the future will be like. The human objects to which he will direct, or from which he will withhold, his love in the expectation of gratifying and satisfying experiences will be determined in large part by his infant and childhood concept of the parent figures. These are models of the human love objects in his environment.

On the other hand, it is not difficult to conjecture that the child's basic concept of self is also determined by the variations in behavior on the part of his parents as they relate to the security feelings mentioned above. His worthwhileness and his intrinsic value of himself as an individual is first, and hence most crucially, demonstrated to him by the expression of his parents' own love, care, attention, protection, gifts, companionship, etc., through their presence (in the earliest years almost omnipresence) in his vicinity. One's concept of one's worth of self is inevitably a product of another's expressed need or want.

If these hypotheses and assumptions of the importance to the child of these parental relationships in the formation of both his concept of self and his concept of human beings are correct, it is possible to examine and outline the effect upon the child of any and all deviations of parents from the most efficient model for which we could hope.

We have selected for consideration one trauma, the deleterious effect of a prolonged or permanent parent absence upon these concepts. These varying effects in varying situations are brought to our attention through numberless clinical observations.

Let us start, first of all, with the child whose parent left the home before the child was two or three years of age. He has, let us say, never seen the father or cannot remember ever seeing him. It is natural for such children, at four or five and thereafter, to note the difference in their own homes; and their questions as to "Where is my father?" or, more pointedly, "Who is my father?" are either answered evasively or are virtually ignored by the remaining parent. Naturally the mother is in a very difficult position because she is caught in a conflict which she knows she has, in part, and which, regardless of what she answers, she is going to transmit with full force on the child. If she tells the child that the father left because he did not love them, the child himself feels — just as does she — for the first time a sense of worthlessness. He feels that he must have been (and still is) of little worth or his father would never have left. There is, too, a questioning of the absolute worth of his mother, for she too was left. If the mother states that she left the father because they "could not get along together" — thereby trying to minimize the shortcomings of the father in the eyes of the child — the child may very well feel that perhaps his father was all right, perhaps even better than mother really, that mother is keeping his father from him, and that the latter really would like to be home if mother would only let him. In this situation the child's concept of the mother is that she is in some part a depriving mother — depriving him of the love and companionship of a father, not because he, the child, is at fault, but because the mother and father didn't like *each other*.

Assume for a moment that the mother tries to soften the blow by taking it out of the realm of personalities or of likes or dislikes and placing it instead in the area of economics. She states, for example, that father left "because he could not support us," really meaning of course in many situations that "he *would* not support us." Immediately the child's concept of his father, of fathers in general, and of men in general is that they are unable to care for mothers or children and that under such circumstances men in general may leave their children or — even worse — ladies may leave or abandon the fathers of their children. To go beyond this rumination of the child: in the clinical setting it is not unusual for a further equation to be arrived at, namely, if mothers can so easily abandon husbands, they perhaps may at some time, if provoked enough, just as easily abandon the small prototype of husband, the male child, *i.e.*, himself. And this certainly does not add to the child's sense of security, nor does it add to his estimate of his own worth in a world populated by human love objects.

Another explanatory device is based on the assumption that all such feelings may be prevented if the child is led to believe, through either expressed or unexpressed hints, that the absent parent is dead. This is a solution used more often than one would suppose. By such a technique the remaining parent escapes an expression of her feelings only temporarily, and the child does not escape for long either. Almost inevitably the child learns or has to be told that the absent parent is not really dead; and the acute, drastic, and painful modifications that he must make at that time are equally traumatic, if not more traumatic than the changes in concepts and feelings that must occur in the light of the other explanations commented on above. They involve, too, a marked change in his estimation of the trustworthiness of all human beings. If a parent can lie about a thing so important to him, the parent certainly cannot be trusted in all other explanations which he has received or in the future expects to receive on demand.

There is a specific anxiety that is aroused in the child as he grows older — and particularly in adolescence — following a spurious explanation that the absent parent is dead. As the child begins to doubt this explanation or as he is later given indirect or direct inklings as to the truth, he is tortured by the possibility that he is an illegitimate child: that his father left before he was born because his father and mother were never married or that he was illegitimately conceived and the marriage took place merely "to give him a name." This is a very logical deduction on his part when the remaining parent attempts to correct the original falsehood by explaining that the father disappeared before the child was born or shortly thereafter.

Finally, there is the possible deduction too — in separations taking place in the child's infancy and earliest years — that his father and mother got along reasonably well and lived together until he was born. In this situation it is very easy for the child to assume that if he hadn't been born the parents would be together — that he was the *cause* of the separation. They wanted each other but did not want *him*. One can estimate the child's own sense of worth as an individual human being in the midst of such logical ruminations. And such ruminations are the only logical ones the child can make in the light of the information that he is allowed to receive in many broken homes.

As I stated above, the mother's position following a separation in the early life of the child is a difficult one when she is asked to explain to the child the absence of the father. My thesis is that there is no explanation that will not have an adverse effect on the developing self-concept and human-being concept of the child. These effects may be and should be minimized, but they probably cannot be entirely eliminated.

Let us turn now to the effects on the child of a separation of the parents at a later stage in his development, placing the separation at a time after the child has received the benefits of an unbroken home and has had the opportunity of forming positive relationships with and concepts of both a father and a mother. I need not tell you that there is usually a long period of strife and discord in the family to which the child is subjected before the separation actually becomes a fact. He has formed to a certain degree a working relationship with both parents; both have satisfied his needs to some extent as love objects, and with respect to each he has formed a definite concept of his own self-worth and also a notion of the worth to him of father and mother — and of the value and worth of adult male and adult female human beings.

The positive aspects of both of these self and not-self concepts come under severe attack during the distressful times preceding parental separation. If the child is inclined to believe or take sides with his mother perforce in her continued and severe devaluations of his father, he may acquiesce, but he does so with poignant feelings of guilt because of the necessary modification of the concept of himself as one who must show expected love of and devotion to his father. The same arousal of guilt is caused as he listens to his father's complaint of his mother and to the citing of her deficiencies as a mother. The "good child" picture of himself that he has constructed for himself as the best source of security obtainable in this world demands that — if he is to remain a "good child" — he must retain his love for both parents. Circumstances just won't allow him to do this.

Even worse for the child is the feeling that his basic and fundamental security may be in large part swept away if either parent leaves him. Both parents are necessary to take care of his needs, the satisfaction of which he has ascribed as being particularly and peculiarly the rôle of one and not the other parent. Despite repeated attempts at reassurance on the part of the parent who is to remain with him, he is rarely convinced that that parent alone has the power to supply all his needs — and, of course, this intuitive feeling of the child is essentially a correct one and is so proved in time.

When we turn at this time to the other aspect of our discussion, namely, the effect of these devaluative maneuvers and strife between parents on the child's concept of human beings as a whole, we again note some necessary modifications in his estimations of human worth. These are serious and can be far-reaching. For the child the behavior and worth of parents are the models for his evaluation of the behavior and worth of all men and women. Particularly do they constitute the only closely and intimately available model of the expected love of one human being for another and of one man for one woman. The expected and hoped-for stability of love relationships of all persons — including those directed by and directed toward him — must be drastically modified at this period. Love relationships with human beings no longer appear sufficiently stable — they may

be hazardous and lead to eventual hatred and abandonment. At least the child will henceforth be forced to consider them extremely conditional and capricious, and his reluctance to enter himself into such relationships and his attitudes toward them when he does may be patternized at the time of his parents' separation and lead to considerable future distress.

In short, if one has the opportunity to study a child intensively just before, during, and after parental separation, one is struck by the similarity of the child's reaction to the well-known "grief reaction." He tries desperately to withdraw the emotional investment he heretofore had in the now absent parent and struggles to place it elsewhere in other persons, objects, or interests in his environment. He cannot allow such positive feelings to persist or he feels guilty in respect to his negative feelings or hate for the *remaining* parent. His normal ambivalence toward the parent who has left him is heightened and his guilt becomes greater. To acquire any kind of security and peace he must get rid of both his positive and his negative feelings regarding the latter — and this process, like the mourning process, is a long and painful one.

Following the essentially permanent separation of the parents, other problems arise which in the main are more or less directly related to the possibly changed attitudes toward him on the part of his parents and to the difficulties involved in his attempts to maintain a desirable relationship with both of them — with the present parent in his everyday life and with the absent parent whom it may be possible (or expected of him) to see at stated intervals.

Assume for a moment that the child stays with his mother. Any number of changes may take place in her attitude toward him, and they are easily detectable.

1. For example, he may become to the mother — and he may sense that he has become — a burden. He may be regarded as an economic burden making it necessary for the mother to work both outside and inside the home. Or the fact of his existence and his presence may become to the mother a definite block to her desire for social relationships with adults of both sexes, or to her desire to marry again, or to the carrying out of a previously desired career that had been thwarted by her marriage in the first place.

2. The presence of the child may be a continuing example to the mother of her own deficiencies —

notably her failure in her attempt to maintain a home, to satisfy a husband, to be a completely adequate wife and mother. Doubts concerning her abilities along these lines may have existed before her marriage, and its breakup may have confirmed them. The child in turn is a continual reminder and reactivator of these long-existing doubts and fears.

3. Directly associated with these changed attitudes toward the child on the part of the mother is the tendency for her to identify the child with the absent husband, and particularly to identify the child with all the bad and undesirable aspects of the father's make-up. This may happen whether the child is a boy or a girl, though obviously it occurs more often when the child is a boy. Here again the causes may reflect the mother's deep, unconscious, and unrecognized feelings about all males and only secondarily her feelings concerning a particular one — the child's father.

In short, the child may have become an economic burden, a social burden, and an emotional burden to the mother and he begins to realize it. In this situation the child necessarily fears that he is in danger of being abandoned, deserted a second time, this time by the mother. His feelings and his responses when he is seen clinically are those of the terribly insecure and fear-ridden child who in his behavior is attempting all the maneuvers that he can to attain or to maintain what to him seems to be a security position. He may try docility, passivity, and quiet withdrawal to make himself into the "good child" that the mother must love. More often he will fight back with hyperaggressiveness, hostility, and insubordination. He may attempt a regressive move to the behavioral levels of infancy when, he remembers, he was really loved and wanted, or resort to frequent feigned illnesses to regain an attentive response of love and care. Whichever one of these security tactics he may try — and any given child will usually attempt all of them in turn — he usually is unsuccessful in meeting these newly expressed hostile attitudes on the part of the mother.

On the other hand, it sometimes happens that the mother's changed attitude is one of increased positiveness and devotion to the child — and overwhelmingly so. The mother, in her attempts to demonstrate that she is an adequate mother in the face of a separation from the father (with all that this involves concerning her estimate of her own worth) may become extremely oversolicitous and overprotective of the child. His every wish has to be satisfied and his every need gratified in order that her child may appear before the world as a happy and contented youngster. He is figuratively smothered with love and gifts so that the mother may prove to herself and to him that she has not failed and will not fail in her rôle as a mother. In the absence of the father the child becomes the single, all-inclusive libidinal investment that the mother makes, to the exclusion of an investment of any part of herself in other people or other interests. I need not emphasize the harmful effects that such an excessively overprotective attitude on the part of the mother has on the child because, in the first place, of the impossibility of complete reciprocity of feeling toward the mother on his part. Such reciprocity is not possible in the case of the child in the intact home, nor is it possible when one parent is permanently absent.

You are aware too, I am sure, of the harmful effects of such maternal behavior in relation to the orderly development of the child — to the necessity for eventual separateness and individuality and to the initiation and beneficial completion of those maturity thrusts that depend on the widest possible association of the child with other human beings, both children and adults. And, finally, there is always to be considered the deviated and unrealistic conception of self-worth and self-value that is inculcated within the child when he is the sole object of the mother's love and overprotectiveness.

In short, when this becomes the relationship of the mother and child, the mother's needs rather than those of the child become the real motivating factors in maternal behavior.

There are additional problems set for the child whose parents are separated which, though I shall mention them but briefly, are extremely important in that they may involve the child in acute conflicted feelings resulting in guilt and a consequent modification of his internal notion of his own worth.

The child of the broken home feels "different" from other children. He is continually asked by his colleagues to explain the absence of the parent, to answer the question as to where the parent is, to give judgments to them as to which parent he feels is or was at fault, and to declare which of them he likes the more. In addition to his not knowing the answers to all these factual questions, he is not able without considerable guilt to express his true feelings in the matter. Children in general are particularly curious about broken homes and the causes of them, their curiosity arising, of course, from the possibility — however remote it may actually be in reality — that such a fate may befall their own homes. The child of separated parents is a source of information for them about facts and feelings that they hope may lead to their own reassurance and security, and they can be unwittingly cruel in their approach. At any rate, the child is made to feel "different."

Then there are the conflicted feelings that arise at the time of necessary visits to the absent parent: the child feels guilty if he leaves his remaining parent and he feels particularly guilty if he feels he had a better time there than he ever has at home. On the other hand, if he does not wish to visit the absent parent, he also feels he is a sinful child. Unfortunately he is subjected many times by both parents — by the one at home and by the one he visits — to expressed or unexpressed hostility toward, and devaluation of, the other parent. He becomes an instrument for each parent to prove that he is the better parent, that he loves the child more, that the other parent's care of him is inadequate and the cause of all his unhappiness and deficiencies in conduct or attainments. The child attempts, if he can, a double, mutually exclusive attitude of love and devotion to both parents, in order to prove to himself that he has two good parents who love him; but he rarely succeeds in this and his attempts are usually transitory and are inevitably guilt-laden.

Such visits to absent parents — their time and duration — are sometimes set by law and occasionally they are badly set. One suggestion that I might make in this respect is that visits, if demanded at all, should not be restricted to occasional single days or week-ends or to one or two holidays a year. Such short visits merely result in compulsion on the part of the parent to shower the child with innumerable gifts, and with attendance at a score of entertainments of various sorts to try to indicate to the child that this is the kind of idyllic life he would lead if he lived there all the time — a much happier existence than he now has in his permanent residence. The child returns home with little or no real appreciation of the real worth of this parent and with no feeling that the parent really loves him for his own sake. Visits should be long enough for the child to appreciate both, and particularly for him to maintain a feeling of really belonging somewhat to the other parent and to feel that there can be a meaningful continuity of this relationship.

In summary, then, I have tried to sketch some of the effects of the separation of parents on the emotional state and on the emotional development of the child. I have confined my remarks at this time solely to the effects of parental separation of any kind where the permanently absent parent is still living, believing that these are some of the universal feelings of children thrust into such circumstances, regardless of the fine type imbedded in various legal documents.

I have stressed the ill-effects of such separations upon the all-important adequate and efficient "concept of self" and "concept of human beings" that we wish to see formulated in the minds of our children as they mature. For over and above our concern about the immediate insecurity and conflicted feelings of children whose parents are separated should be our equally great concern for a predictable constancy and stability in the love relationships of all people, one for the other.

27

Morbid Parent–Child Passions in Delinquency *

Berthold E. Schwarz and Bartholomew A. Ruggieri

Youthful vandalism and criminality have been variously attributed to the comics, school conditions and an inadequate number of patrolmen. Many observers say that it is the parents' responsibility to see that their children learn to act as law-abiding citizens. However, aside from non-controversial broad generalizations

* Reprinted from 3 *J. Social Therapy* (1957), 180. Used by permission of the authors and the publisher.

and platitudes that find ready acceptance, all too few observers have spelled out the specific manner in which parents are responsible for the specific delinquency. Thus it would seem important to know of some recent investigations [1,2,3] which pinpoint parental responsibility for juvenile delinquency in a highly specific manner and relegate the other factors to a more minor role.

These concepts are a result of a fact-finding medical project extending over the last fifteen years and consisting of a painstaking and difficult technique of collaborative study and treatment. By this technique, two or more physicians undertake the simultaneous treatment of the parent and child and possibly other members of the family and then, at frequent intervals, meet and compare in infinite detail all the material from their respective interviews. In this way the specific delinquency in any given child has been found to stem in a definite manner from highly specific emotional problems in the parent. As these facts have become more well known, this method of study and treatment has become widely accepted in leading medical centers.

Much has been said about juvenile gangs and the squalor, poverty and cultural complexion of the neighborhoods in which they breed. Although these factors are important, it should be remembered that in the worst slum areas, where gang delinquency and gang wars are an everyday occurrence, there are many families of "underprivileged" cultural and economic status with children who remain immune to delinquency and later criminality. It should also be emphasized that individual cases of delinquency are also common in the "best of families" in which all the material needs of life are abundantly supplied. Individual rather than gang delinquents have comprised the majority of cases of juvenile delinquency studied by this new technique, which has revealed the constant relationship between the particular delinquency

in the child and the covert emotional illness in the parent. Admitting the importance of the cultural and economic factors in the environment of the gang delinquent, the same underlying antecedent-warped parent-child relationships that have been found in the individual delinquents have also been found to exist in those gang delinquents studied by the same intensive technique.

The child is born with no predetermined tendency to be good or bad. His concept of right or wrong and what should and should not be done are learned from his parents in his early formative years, to become indelibly imprinted on his mind. He will learn to respond to situations as he himself was treated in similar situations. If he has received love, he will be able to give love in return; if he has seen lying, he will learn to lie; if he has seen dishonesty, he will learn dishonesty; and if he has received hate, he will learn to hate. Thus, in later years, when he is away from his parents, he will respond to situations and temptations as though the parents were still with him.

In acquiring these values he will detect and respond to a parent's true underlying feelings of what may lie on the surface. In fact, observers have called the child a "natural psychiatrist" who possesses an uncanny skill at sensing the various nuances of his parents' feelings.[4] The child will dimly recognize for what they really are any parental double talk, two-facedness, evasiveness, excessive interest, preoccupations and dishonesty. For instance, it is hardly giving when strings are attached; the child will know when he is being cheated in this way. Marital discords will be recognized by the child regardless of the parents' attempts to hide their disagreements from him. The child will sense the bias when the parents have favorites among their children or select one child as the scapegoat for their own warped passions. This bias becomes doubly unhealthy when the parents deny its existence and insist "We treat you all alike."

However, being small, helpless and inarticulate, the child cannot react as reality might demand. He is forced, by his dependence, to deny the validity of his own senses and accept

[1] A. Johnson and S. A. Szurek, "Etiology of Antisocial Behavior in Delinquents and Psychopaths," J.A.M.A. 154:814 (March) 1954.

[2] B. E. Schwarz and B. A. Ruggieri, "Parent–Child Tensions," Philadelphia, J. B. Lippincott and Company (in press).

[3] M. E. Giffin, A. M. Johnson, and E. M. Litin, "Specific Factors Determining Antisocial Acting Out," Am. J. Orthopsychiat. 24:668 (October) 1954.

[4] Sandor Ferenczi, "Confusion of Tongues Between the Adult and the Child," Internat. J. of Psychoanalysis 30:225–230 (1949).

as real the façade of excuses, outright lies and distorted reasons his parents may present to him. This is highly confusing to the child. From repeated exposure to such distortions, the child's ability to test and accept the reality of his senses becomes compromised and the unity of his personality becomes disorganized as "splitting" occurs. This pattern of behavior then becomes a stereotyped inappropriate response to all later situations that are reminiscent of these earlier ones.

Seldom if ever does one incident determine a child's personality; rather it is the constant exposure to a set pattern of parental feelings and behavior, manifested by these repeated everyday trivialities and undercurrents, that in their aggregate build the child's character. In this way the parents' values gradually become a vital part of the child. When the parents' feelings are healthy, the child will have similar healthy feelings. And, no matter how healthy parents may be in all their daily activities, if there are particular situations in which they have doubts, equivocations or laxities, even if not apparent to themselves, the child will acquire the same crippling defects for similar situations.

The tragedy is that the child, without even knowing what was going on, has to follow the pattern determined by the warped feelings of his parents, as the latter had had to follow similar paths laid out by their parents before them. The sick emotions of one generation are passed on to the next. Each is driven on by a devil beyond his ken; nor is he even aware that he is sick. But life is a constant give and take, and the past imperceptibly merges with the present as new experiences constantly modify existing relationships. It has been seen how the child responds to his parents' feelings, but it is also important to realize that the parents in turn react to their child. Cause and effect become blurred in the complexities of this ever-changing situation, especially so since neither parent nor child fully understands his particular role.

Thus, it is a fundamental fact that, before one can love, one must first have received love.

Fifteen-year-old Harry, a handsome, strapping six-footer with unkempt long blond hair, matter-of-factly described the hold-up to the physician. His detailed account of previous crimes included beating younger children for the few coins they might have had in their pockets, stealing money from his mother, consorting with prostitutes and committing acts of vandalism on a church. It is true that Harry came from an underprivileged minority group in his town, but none of his brothers had got into trouble with the law. Harry showed no sign of remorse or concern. He was callous, arrogant and suspicious. He had boasted to his brothers that we would "get that lousy cop who put the handcuffs on [him]". At no point in his study did the physician have the feeling of "getting through" to him. Harry blandly called himself the "bad seed." He expressed no concern over his future, despite his father's repeated prophecies that he would die in the electric chair. When the physician asked Harry about his parents' reaction to his predicament, he said, "They were glad I got probation."

At the age of 15, Harry was already a hardened criminal. He was completely diffident about the personal or social consequences of his delinquent behavior. He had committed repeated acts of violence and said he was "out to get" the cop. Threats of the electric chair did not deter him. His parents' only reaction to his serious trouble was not righteous indignation and alarm because of his criminal acts, but relief that he had been put on probation.

When Harry was 7, he would steal a dollar a week from his mother's rent money. Neither Harry nor his parents mentioned this thievery until one day ten dollars was missing. His mother confronted him with the theft, saying that she could tolerate his taking one dollar but not ten dollars. Later that day, when his father came home from work, he subjected Harry to an all-night inquest. Harry at first vehemently denied the stealing and finally admitted to what both he and his mother already knew to be true when his father promised not to punish him if he told "the honest truth."

What was wrong with the mother's sense of values that she would permit her young son to steal one dollar but not ten? If the child is to be taught that stealing is wrong and therefore forbidden, there can never be any exceptions. The father entered the mother's duplicity and undermined the authority of both by his bizarre method of handling Harry. With all three having complete knowledge of the stealing, the father nevertheless interrogated a recalcitrant Harry for hours and then finally made a deal with him. He did not punish his son, nor did he insist on repentance. The parents were satisfied with the empty words of a pallid confession. They never drew a line and said "no." This incident is symptomatic of the distorted sick relationships among all three: father, mother and son.

The only time during the interview that Harry's face glowed with excitement was when he described how he and his friends "beat up queers for the fun of it." Harry recalled that on many occasions his father had told him that, from his own early experiences, "you can always beat up a queer and the cops will never bother you." On one recent occasion, following such an episode, the police came to the house, asking for the driver of a car that had been abandoned in someone's driveway. The father fabricated a story satisfactory to the police about why he himself had left the car there. After the police left, the father told Harry it was stupid to have left the car in that way since Harry did not yet have a driver's license. When Harry told his father he had "used the car to beat up some queers," his father said merely: "I don't care. You should be more careful with the car."

At an age when many boys play baseball, football and other competitive sports, Harry prowled the neighborhood "to beat up queers." The permission and frank encouragement for such violence came from his father. As in stealing, the same parental double standards with the same corrupting influence on the developing conscience were found here. The young boy was told that violence, as long as it is directed against queers, would not be punished by either the father or the police. The father was less interested in prohibiting violence than he was in finding means for his son to evade punishment for such acts. What was there about the emotional makeup of the father and son that both derived enjoyment from such cruelties? What was it within themselves that almost compelled them to focus on "queers"? By his father's lying to the police in Harry's presence and by his father's own concluding remarks about the car, Harry knew that his father practiced and condoned what was wrong. Come what may, Harry knew that he had a secret ally.

The first time Harry mentioned his mother was when the physician asked him to whom he turned for advice. He said he was very close to his mother and frequently lay on the bed with her at night discussing his "problems." He told her of his wanton experiences and even discussed his lewd girl friends. His mother often implied to him that she was dissatisfied with the physical aspects of her own marital relationship. There was no shame in this household. Obscene language and frequent references to sexual matters were commonplace. In their sleeping, bathing and dressing habits, neither mother nor son showed any mutual respect for their privacy.

The only time Harry mentioned his mother was to describe his very unusual relationship with her. One might wonder about the obviously unhealthy implications of a grown boy lying on a bed with his mother while both discussed in intimate detail highly charged sexual material. The mother described to her son her own marital problems and then apparently derived a warped gratification by hearing of her son's erotic exploits. The complete lack of household modesty compounded the existing unnatural and confused family relationships. Harry had no warmth, tenderness or friendliness toward any member of the opposite sex. From the unnaturally close relationship with his mother he had learned only the unhealthy values of an obscene and contemptuous attitude toward women.

The father was seen separately by the physician. He needed the aid of two canes as he hobbled into the office in a hunched-over stiff-legged gait. Although still a young man with an alert mind, he had been badly crippled with arthritis since shortly before Harry's birth. With an air of resignation about his son's bleak future, his first words were: "Is it hopeless, Doc? I'm very worried. Will he end up like the sex maniac who raped and shot the girl in [a neighboring town]?"

He then wondered whether he and his wife might not have been at least partly responsible for Harry's predicament. As one example of his own ineffectiveness and inconsistency, the father described how Harry would come into the house at any time and leave at any time despite the 9 o'clock curfew. There was one revealing occasion when the father lectured Harry with some force and at length about some infraction and then "sentenced" him to his room after supper for a week. However, after the first night, Harry left the house anyway and his father could only remark: "What could I do with him; it has always been that way." As a further example of his ineffectiveness, it developed that the father was often a passive witness to Harry's temper tantrums, when he would smash his fist through the wall, throw furniture at the television set and rip his clothes to shreds. Despite Harry's being too young to have a driver's license and despite his taking out the family car without a license, the father bought him a "hot rod" on which he might tinker in the back yard. And, despite Harry's all too apparent destructiveness, the father bought him a shotgun for his birthday. The mother, alarmed, had objected, "I'm afraid he'll shoot some children."

There were many additional examples of the father's inability to set limits to his son's destructive predations and therefore unwittingly directing his son closer to destruction. As more facts were elicted, the father's role in the formation of Harry's defective conscience began to emerge. Cut down in the prime of life by a crippling disease, this unfortunate man became even more vulnerable to any emotional problems he might already have had. His own increasing physical disabilities might have been poignantly brought home to him by the sharp contrast with the strong, healthy body of his growing son. This combination of circumstances, in addition to the burdensome knowledge of his sexual inadequacy, might well have led to increased emotional tension as he looked bleakly and angrily at the world that had dealt him so cruel a blow. Harry passed through infancy into adolescence totally dependent upon such a father for his physical and emotional needs. The father's sense of personal doom eclipsed his son's future by tainting their relationship and affecting his ability to support and guide his son toward a healthy emotional development.

Later in the interview, the father described his wife as having a very violent temper. When the physician reminded him of his earlier description of Harry's temper, the father paused. "Huh! I never thought of that," he replied. "They're both alike. But my wife's trouble was with her father. You can't blame her. He was a heavy drinker." With the idea of determining how well the father really understood the role of the family in causing Harry's delinquency, the physician asked what the father thought might be the cause. The father quickly blamed bad companions and the change in the character of the neighborhood.

The father had always nurtured the dream of opening a large toy store on the boardwalk at the seashore. He estimated the cost at $30,000. Knowing this, Harry tempted his father with the statement, "If you really want this, I can get it for you; you just have to know the right people."

The father could see the possible relationship between his wife's temper and her trouble with an alcoholic father, and he had a brief glimpse of his own role in Harry's delinquency. However, he could not take the next step of clearly relating his son's delinquencies to his own and his wife's distorted values. Instead he resorted to blaming a number of extraneous factors. This incident confirmed the physician in his opinion that the family was scarcely motivated to seek treatment and that any psychiatric efforts directed toward these deep and longstanding emotional problems would meet with parental resistance.

It might be recalled that Harry was a delinquent while his brothers were not and that even Harry thought of himself as the "bad seed" of the family. Careful collaborative studies reveal many reasons why only some families in a given neighborhood and only some children in a given family are afflicted when the same environmental conditions appear to exist for all.[5, 6] The choice of the specific type of delinquency, as well as the particular child in the family who becomes delinquent, is determined by specific emotional factors in the parents' emotional backgrounds. Without appreciating exactly how this all comes about, society is often content to apply the following colloquialisms: scapegoat, fall-guy, skeleton in the closet, black sheep, whipping boy, his father's son, bad heredity and bad seed. And there the matter often rests, as though these slogans were the last word in explaining the delinquency.

Marie had repeatedly been caught stealing, and was brought to the physician's office at the request of the school principal. The reason for the problem and the mother's inability to cope with it was clarified by a study of the mother's

5 Johnson and Szurek, op. cit.
6 Schwarz and Ruggieri, op. cit.

past. Marie's mother, Jane, had been the youngest child of a large farm family. Jane's own mother had been so busy that she had largely delegated the rearing of Jane to the eldest sister. The latter bitterly resented this burden because she also had many other necessary farm chores while her brothers were permitted much time for going into town. The sister provided well for Jane's material needs. However, at the same time she took out her rage on Jane by constant criticism and merciless punishment. Jane married early to escape this hateful situation. Soon after her marriage, she first met her husband's great-aunt, the family "black sheep," who had a lifelong "weakness" for stealing things. Marie, the eldest of Jane's four children, became the outlet for this mother's years of smouldering rage against the cruel elder sister who had raised her. And the knowledge of the great-aunt's kleptomania provided the unwitting means by which Jane's old score with her sister could be settled. The physician, having collected all these background facts, was not hoodwinked into agreeing with the mother that heredity was to blame. After the physician discussed with them some of these tragic emotional factors in an understanding manner, the mother decided that both she and her daughter should seek psychiatric help.

Another example of delinquency was Stan, who was brought to the physician because he had recently attempted to set fire to a stack of newspapers in a neighbor's basement. He had terrorized his neighborhood with many previous fire-setting activities. The first thing Stan's mother said was that she herself liked to play with matches as a child until she accidentally started a fire that burned down the house. Her baby sister died in the fire and the father was badly burned trying to rescue her. Thereafter, whenever she did anything wrong, her father, whose face was still scarred by the old burns, punished her by reminding her how she had "killed her sister." Her elder brother had tormented her in a similar manner. In later years, whenever her brother visited her after her marriage and Stan's birth, the brother would bring up the subject of the old tragedy. Stan's mother said: "When Stan began to play with matches, I was worried he'd take after me. But my brother told me not to worry, Stan would outgrow it just as I did."

Further study revealed that this mother had much submerged understandable rage toward her own father and brother. She found release from this bottled-up tension by acting out through her son, whom she confused with her father and brother in her deepest feelings. Her own significant life experience with fire-setting determined her choice of delinquency for her son. By implicating heredity she had a convenient excuse. In thus finding surcease from her inner tensions through the unwitting destruction of her son, there was no need for her other children, who were daughters, to be affected.

As shown in the above examples, heredity and bad companions are often blamed for an individual's delinquency. In the case of the child who has been adopted by parents who themselves are emotionally disturbed, the excuse of a tainted heredity can be even more readily implicated, since the heredity that is blamed is that of the child but not of the adoptive parents.

Sam was in serious trouble because he had threatened to stab his foster mother. Despite her own disturbed emotional background and the questions raised by her encouraging Sam to collect knives, guns, bayonets and whips, and in the face of numerous previous threats and even assaults upon herself, this mother was convinced that her son's destructive tendencies stemmed from his natural parents.

Another scapegoat mechanism becomes available when a child has had an illness or injury, especially when this involves the head. It is true that in some instances of illness or injury of the brain, defective intelligence and emotional instability may develop. Such cases can usually be identified by special diagnostic techniques. In such cases the parent's sick emotions may increase the child's handicap or may create a handicap where none otherwise existed. Such parents often find in the child's illness or injury a conveniently plausible explanation for the child's antisocial behavior.

Thirteen-year-old Len was very belligerent, was always in fights and was doing poorly in school. This behavior began shortly after a diagnosis of epilepsy had been established. The history revealed that he had been having the symptoms of epilepsy for many years prior to the diagnosis. Len's mother attributed his difficulties to the epilepsy. In her deepest inner self she confused her feelings toward Len with the feelings she had had as a young girl toward her older brother, who was demented, assaultive and unable to attend to his body needs following a severe auto accident. Len's mother had lost out in the play, pleasures and frivolities of youth as she spent much of her early girlhood nursing this brother.

Operations and hospitalizations may be incorrectly held responsible in a similar manner.

It is common knowledge that individuals with a physical disability, deformity or illness may understandably develop associated emotional reactions. For example, one may recall the extreme anxiety of a patient who has sustained a severe and possibly disfiguring cut on the face, or the patient who faces a possible amputation. In all illnesses the mind and the body are inseparably meshed together. Emotions in turn can lead to physical body changes; everyone is aware of the tachycardia and palpitations that may follow sudden fright and the temporary anorexia that may accompany melancholy. In more complex fashion, long-standing emotional conflicts of which the patient may not even be aware may lead to such psychosomatic illnesses as asthma, eczema, migraine, peptic ulcer, colitis and deforming arthritis. As one example of the frequency of emotional disturbance in the families of delinquents, the physician commonly finds many psychosomatic problems. A great number of these are disturbances in sexual adjustments between the parents.

It is unfortunately true that these maladjustments almost invariably leave their mark on the children. In such situations the child is often drawn too closely in an unnatural manner to the parent of the opposite sex, with the tacit permission if not encouragement of the other parent. Many of the ways in which the child is brought too closely to the parent of the opposite sex may at first glance appear to be harmless. Under the guise of "modern frankness" the physician often finds the parent bathing and showering with a child of the opposite sex until the latter is well into the teens; parents and children dressing with no respect for one another's privacy; the parent sleeping with a child of the opposite sex until the latter is well into manhood and womanhood; day in and day out family chattering with countless improvisations and variations on the subject of sex; prolonged and insinuating fondlings, embraces and caresses between the parent and a child of the opposite sex through adolescence and beyond. In a word,

parent and child exchange feelings of a type that should be reserved for the relationship between the parents themselves. By these means the parent derives vicarious gratification through the child as a substitute for that which is lacking in the marital relationship.[7, 8] Being totally dependent upon his parents, the child can do nothing but react appropriately to these manifestations of his parents' warped love.[9] As a result, the child acquires the parents' own distorted attitudes toward sex. By being kept in such an unnaturally close attachment to the parent, the child's chances of developing a mature healthy relationship with someone of the opposite sex are forfeited. In these ways the child will become a perennial "mama's boy" or a "daddy's girl," who will always think of "love" in the same infantile overdependent terms. These same unnatural early relationships also often account for men and women who are never quite comfortable with members of the opposite sex.

What purpose was served by the mother's taking a shower with her 10-year-old son immediately after a heated argument with her husband? Why did the stepmother persist in lying on the couch in her flimsy nightgown under the goggle-eyed stare of her 15-year-old son although she had received repeated complaints that he molested girls? Why did the daughter often sleep in the same bed with her father when the mother had not done so for the previous eight months because of his "awful snoring"? What was the effect on the 12-year-old girl when her father shared with his daughter lurid jokes and neighborhood gossip with frank sexual overtones?

An example of such unhealthy parent-child relationships was the case of Al, a 17-year-old high school senior of old colonial stock who came from a "good home" and moderate economic circumstances. He was arrested for molesting girls. He told the physician: "I've been doing this for a long time, and now that I'm caught I'm glad. The devil is in me . . . I'm full of violence — afraid I'll murder . . .

---

[7] E. M. Litin, M. E. Giffin, and A. M. Johnson, "Parental Influence in Unusual Sexual Behavior in Children," Psychoanalyt. Quart. XXV:37, 1956.

[8] B. E. Schwarz, "The Man Who Was Married 55 Times," J. of Nerv. and Ment. Dis., 124:287 (Sept.) 1956.

[9] Ferenczi, op. cit.

she makes me feel so guilty." Later statements revealed he was referring to his mother.

This boy revealed that, in addition to his mugging, he had strong impulses toward violence and even murder. These destructive designs upon others also meant that ever-present danger of his own destruction by a society bent on retaliation. Now that he was caught, not only society but he himself might be saved from the devil within him. It is no wonder, then, that as in many such cases his first feeling on being caught was relief. And why did Al mention his mother in almost the same breath as sex and violence?

Al's father was a brutal alcoholic who habitually went on weekend rampages in his house with his shotgun or pistol. It was a common occurrence for his father to beat and kick Al. The father, in blind rage, often impulsively picked up a whip and flailed at the terrified boy while shouting obscenities and railing at his son's alleged stupidity. The father frequently pitted his children against one another for his own perverse amusement. The mother was ineffectual in defending her children against violent physical and verbal abuse by the husband.

As a child, Al had received many lessons in impulsiveness, lack of restraint, sadism and violence. Left unprotected in this hostile and threatening environment, he stored up a full measure of fear and hate, which could later find an outlet through the means taught him by his father.

Al's relationship with his mother was just as unhealthy. He said: "She tries to buy my love by filling my plate full of food and then being offended if I don't stuff myself. It used to burn my insides out . . . she makes me feel unsure of myself . . . whenever she touches me, I feel something strange from her. When I'm going to bed, I can hear her. She never closes the door between us. She comes in and sits on my bed . . . sometimes I get so mad that I can put my fist through the door . . . she always worries about who I'll marry . . . she's jealous of my girl friends. She's old . . . resents their youth . . . they're about to live; she never did live. I hate her."

Whenever Al was sick, his mother would take him to bed with her. This continued until he was 14 years old. She also bathed him until the same time, when she noticed he was becoming a man, and he said, "Don't you think I can take care of myself by now?" The mother often commented on newspaper articles about "sex maniacs" and would tell her son that she hoped he would never be like her cousin, Louis, who had been sent to jail for raping a little girl. Al's mother felt that "it was a put-up job." Being separated from his wife, Louis was living with his mother. His wife's best friend sent her little daughter to spend the weekend with Louis' mother. During the stay the little girl slept with Louis. Her family then tried to "squeeze money out of him," and in the resulting imbroglio Louis was accused and convicted of rape.

As Al told his story, there was in his mind a close connection between his hate and violence and his unnaturally close and warped relationship with his mother. Was this outlet for his anger being subtly suggested to him by her own behavior with him, her intense interest in crimes of sex violence and the oft-recounted story of her cousin? And why did this mother have to repeat so often her hope that Al would not be like her cousin? Might she not in this manner have communicated to her son her own doubts about his moral conduct? Such early fusion of warped love and hate between a mother and her son are often the ingredients for later crimes of violence.

In fact, Al summarized all this when he said as he was leaving the physician's office: "They [mother and father] too lost their temper when they did such things [violence.] Why shouldn't I? What's the difference?"

Fifteen-year-old Julie was a strikingly attractive girl with a social poise beyond her years. In contrast, her mother was a middle-aged overweight woman who was sloppily dressed, used no make-up and spoke in a harsh, low-pitched voice. "She's always running around and chasing out . . . She goes around with a blonde who's had a couple of fathers and whose mother is a drunk . . . she has boys on the mind all of the time . . . already in trouble with the police. I want to check and find out what she's doing. I went through her correspondence . . . she tells how she took a boy away from her best girl friend . . . she's just clever . . . she even smoked marijuana . . . I know. I went through her purse . . . now she's going with a boy who once went to jail for rape . . . She thinks her nails and her face will carry her through life . . . . She seems to get money somehow . . . She has no sense of fairness . . . just thinks of herself."

Julie's mother had had a hard life. She was the eldest girl in a large, struggling farm family. After working her way through high school, she worked in a factory for a few years to save enough money to enroll in a business college in the city. During this time she seldom went out with boys and described these few experiences as "a couple of horrible blind dates to take me out in the park . . . I never had any chance." Finally she married a man twenty-three years her senior who was very bashful and retiring and had had no dates prior to meeting her. Unable to have children, they adopted Julie when she was four months old. They did not go through any regular adoption agency and had had to pay about $1,500 to settle all the legal difficulties they had with Julie's true parents. When Julie was 10, her adoptive father had a stroke and was completely paralyzed on one side, lost the power of speech and needed continual nursing care. Despite a pension, the mother went back to work to earn money for Julie's college education. Julie got along well in these changed circumstances until the body changes of early womanhood appeared. Her good looks and vivacious personality made her popular with the boys, who began to gather at her house at all hours. At this point in her description, the mother commented, "I never had it myself." Gradually and imperceptibly the mother became more and more disturbed. Despite Julie's continuing good school grades, the mother insisted that she should spend less time with the boys and concentrate on her studies. She became very curious about Julie's dates. She would ask many detailed questions about where she was, who she was with and what she did. The mother repeatedly warned Julie and told her to be careful. "How horrible boys are! They learn too much too young. They're just out for what they can get. No man can be trusted."

Julie's assets of beauty and brains, which in other circumstances might have led to a fuller and happier life, were subverted to sexual promiscuity and her eventual undoing. She became the means by which her mother unwittingly achieved vicarious gratification for all that a life of hardship and tragedy had denied her. Having been forced to swallow all the disappointments that life had dealt her, Julie's mother had had to hold her peace and continue to struggle for a living. All too well aware of the difference in the physical appearance between her daughter and herself, the mother could not help but feel at least a little envious of her daughter's comeliness and popularity. Therefore, the appearance of Julie's womanhood became the occasion for her own undoing and the relief of her pent-up tensions through her daughter. By the mother's repeated queries, her highly suggestive insinuations and warnings and her dishonest intrusion on her daughter's privacy by checking her purse and correspondence, the mother showed her own unhealthy doubts and attitudes, which would be further revealed in numerous other day-to-day occurrences. The mother unwittingly revealed to her daughter a course of behavior quite divergent from a strictly moral one, a course of behavior that the mother felt Julie might well follow.

RECOMMENDATIONS

It is hoped that the preceding discussion has shown the connection between the child's specific delinquency and the specific emotional problems of his parents. Rather than the broad generalization that "the parent is responsible for his child's behavior," there exists between the two a complex, often subtle emotional relationship that is usually concealed from their conscious awareness. It would seem that this relationship is the nucleus of the problem of delinquency rather than the more peripheral but oft-incriminated and related socio-economic factors. As the child mirrors all the aspirations, yearnings and secret desires of his parents in health, so does he reflect the parental attitudes in disease. Therefore the delinquent child cannot be considered apart from the warped passions, conscience defects, unconscious hostilities and past and current life experiences of his parents. These attitudes in turn become part of the child's total character.

Admitting society's need to protect itself from its undesirable elements by prisons, reform schools and the like, it would seem more to the point for society to orient itself toward the prevention of delinquency and the later criminality.[10] In many instances parents may lack the simple information that would help them

[10] Ralph S. Banay, "We Call Them Criminals," Appleton-Century-Crofts, 1957, New York.

direct their children toward later emotional health and maturity.

Parents should remember that they cannot expect their children to be honest in all activities unless the parents themselves set the correct example in their dealings with all people, including the child. There cannot be one set of standards for the parents and a different set for the child. It is important for the parent to realize that the child will be more comfortable with himself and with his fellow men if he knows what he can and cannot do. And this knowledge comes from his recognition of his parents' feelings and his observation of his parents' actions. Therefore the child cannot learn to curb his own violent impulses if he sees his parents do otherwise. If the child is to grow emotionally and learn to respect society, its codes and its members, he must first have been shown respect by his parents. Although a child should be permitted to express his own feelings and opinions, even when they are opposed to those of the parents, such permission never means that the child should be allowed to strike his parents, injure any individual or destroy their property.

Another important way of preventing delinquency and later criminality with its frequent sexual core is the elimination of the so-called modern frankness with its household nudity. Sleeping, bathing and dressing practices that may be appropriate for infancy and babyhood are often extended well beyond the ages during which such practices are really necessary. Aside from simple parental lack of knowledge, such practices too often stem from the parents' own marital problems and are not carried out simply to satisfy the needs of the child. Such pernicious habits undermine the child's individuality by keeping him close to the parent in an unnatural way. This warped love is nothing less than a seduction of the child. The far-reacting effects are well recognized by physicians and have been seen to contribute heavily to delinquency and criminality as well as to many mental illnesses and psychosomatic conditions.

These facts must first be recognized for what they are. Then delinquency may be prevented or treatment begun soon enough to insure a restoration to health of both the delinquent parent and the child.

Chapter 7

School Influences and Delinquency

THE SECOND SOCIAL INSTITUTIONAL CIRCLE of influences that the growing child is subjected to — after the home — is the school. Here he must meet the test of acceptance by his peers and the test of competition before judges who, unlike his parents, are not biased in his favor.

It is a fact discovered in numerous researches that school maladjustment — ranging from misbehavior for the purpose of attracting attention, to truancy and vandalism — is a frequent precursor of more serious forms of delinquency.

The first item in the present chapter is a summary taken from *Unraveling Juvenile Delinquency*, of the findings in respect to children's school attitudes and behavior regarding their studies. The interested student should turn to the appropriate chapter in that work for specific details. The article by Stullken relates the school as an educational and social institution to the delinquency problem and presents some useful principles concerning wholesome practices that take account of the mental hygiene aspects of the child-in-school situation and serve to make the school climate friendly, attractive and constructive. Discussions of this article by Binford and Roser, have been included.

The materials illustrate the difficulty of tearing the school situation out of its contextual relationship to the home, at one end, and the general community at the other.

In Chapter 33, on Prevention, there are included some school experiments in the prophylactic and therapeutic approaches to aberrant behavior of children.

28

The Boy in School *

Sheldon and Eleanor T. Glueck

Despite the original matching of the boys in age and general intelligence and despite the similarity of the two groups in the age at which they entered the first grade, the delinquents were definitely more retarded educationally than were the non-delinquents.

---

* Reprinted by permission of the publishers and The Commonwealth Fund from *Unraveling Juvenile Delinquency*, Sheldon and Eleanor T. Glueck, Cambridge, Mass.: Harvard University Press, Copyright 1950, by The Commonwealth Fund. Pages 153–154. This statement is a summary of Chapter XII; it is recommended that the student read the entire chap-

This finding is no doubt partly explainable by the greater moving about that the delinquents did with their families; by their placement in foster homes following the disruption of the parental home; and by commitments to correctional institutions. However, such factors do not completely account for the excessive repetition of grades and marked backwardness in terms of achievement in relation to age and grade placement.

Fewer delinquents than non-delinquents expressed preference for certain subjects in the curriculum, and half of each group markedly disliked some subjects. In similar proportions the delinquents and non-delinquents preferred manual training and disliked verbal disciplines; however, there was a more prevalent distaste among the delinquents not only for subjects

---

ter. See, also, the thoughtful intensive study of the role of the school, both in contributing to and coping with delinquency, by W. C. Kvaraceus, *Juvenile Delinquency and the School*, World Book Company, Yonkers-on-Hudson, New York, 1945. — Ed.

requiring strict logical reasoning and persistency of effort, but also for those dependent upon good memory.

To a much greater extent than the non-delinquents, the delinquents expressed violent dislike for school, resentment at its restrictions, lack of interest in school work. The few non-delinquents who disliked school, on the other hand, did so largely because they were unable to learn and felt intellectually inferior.

The school attainment of the delinquents was far below that of the non-delinquents, even less than might be expected in the light of their achievements as measured by the Stanford tests in reading and arithmetic. This would seem to indicate a greater degree of maladaptation to school. Although the delinquents showed less ability than the non-delinquents in reading and arithmetic, the differences between them were not as great as has been generally supposed. The delinquents, however, were somewhat more variable in their school accomplishment as determined by their achievement in these two tests.

As to their academic ambitions, a markedly higher proportion of the delinquents expressed a desire to stop school at once while many more non-delinquents planned to go on to high school, trade school, or beyond.

In vocational ambitions, likewise, the delinquents differed from the non-delinquents, a higher proportion of them expressing childish notions about what they wanted to do in life, or inclining to adventurous occupations and to work requiring little training, instead of to trades and intellectual pursuits.

In their interpersonal relationships with schoolmates the delinquents were more unfriendly and pugnacious.

Marked differences between the two groups were also noted in respect to school conduct. More than nine-tenths of the delinquents seriously or persistently misbehaved in school at one time or another as compared to less than a fifth of the non-delinquents, their misbehavior running the entire gamut of school offenses. Truancy was the first and most frequent manifestation of maladjustment among the 478 delinquents who misbehaved in school.

The various indications of maladaptation and misconduct occurred at a much earlier age among the delinquents than among the very small group of 86 non-delinquents who misbe-

haved, indicating the relative deep-rootedness of the emotional difficulties of the delinquents.

It is evident that the traits and tendencies involved in the form of social maladaptation which the law, representing society in general, calls delinquency are also found in excess among the delinquents in maladaptation to the code of behavior governing the smaller society, the school.

29

The Schools and the Delinquency Problem *

Edward H. Stullken

The title assigned for this paper may seem to imply that the problem of delinquency is peculiar to schools. Again some may assume that delinquency is a separate and distinct problem; that is, that delinquency must be viewed as a social disorder, or disease, which must be eradicated by the schools. Still others may assume that if schools do something about the problem then delinquent behavior can be corrected. There is no doubt some truth in each assumption. Moreover, the problem should be considered from a positive rather than a negative approach, from the prevention rather than treatment angle; and to do this certain basic considerations should be kept in mind.

BASIC CONSIDERATIONS

Purpose of Modern Education. The first of these principles is that schools are institutions established to help young people realize their best potentialities and to develop into wholesome personalities and useful citizens. Public

* Reprinted from 43 J. Crim. L., Criminology, and Police Science (1953), 567–574. Used by permission of the author and the publisher. See, also, M. Roser, "The Role of the Schools in Heading Off Delinquency," Gary Public Schools, 1953; W. C. Kvaraceus, Juvenile Delinquency and the School, New York, World Book Company, 1945; A. J. Kahn, "Who Are Our Truants?" 15 Federal Probation (1951), 35–40. — Ed.

schools are instruments of the state, organized so that all the children of all the people can receive a good common school education. This implies that schools deal in education, a process by which the behavior of people is improved so that they may think, feel, and act differently than they did before. In America, we expect schools to serve each child according to his capacity regardless of his race, religion, national background, social and economic conditions of life, or handicapping conditions of any kind. The school, today, is concerned with helping students to guide their conduct by reason, to use intelligence in reaching decisions rather than blind obedience, habit, or prejudice, and to acquire a knowledge of self and an understanding of the consequences of behavior. The schools today must aim to develop young people physically, spiritually, and morally as well as intellectually so that they can take a competent and effective part in daily life, contribute to the welfare of others and make their own lives happy and good. The schools, therefore, must recognize and integrate all those aspects of life — moral, ethical, economic, civil, social — in which people need to exercise intelligence and understanding. Schools therefore are concerned with all the problems of life, the delinquency problem included; but their concern is primarily one of dealing with all children in such a way that delinquent behavior will not likely result on the part of individual children.

Delinquency Is a Symptom. The second principle to be kept in mind is that delinquency is not a distinct or separate problem. Delinquency should not be considered as we consider a disease but rather as the symptom of a disease. Delinquency, like truancy or incorrigibility, is but a symptom picture of underlying conditions the roots of which may be found in the family life, the school adjustment, or the environmental background in the community, and sometimes in physiological or psychological aspects of the child's personality. In dealing with the delinquency problem, from the standpoint of the school or any other agency, one deals with the problem of a symptom which may have any one or more of many different causes. Moreover in dealing with delinquency or any other symptom one does not correct the problem until fundamental causes are found and corrected or alleviated, even though some measures may temporarily allay the symptom.

The Point-of-View Is Important. A third fact to be considered when studying the relation of the schools to delinquency is the need to recognize all possible attitudes and points of view. Delinquent behavior is complex and has many different meanings in different social contexts. To the judge and policeman, stealing, for example, is contrary to criminal law and the child who steals is a delinquent; to the psychologist, interested in the theory of learning, the child has learned to steal, something that society as a whole wishes he had not learned; to the psychiatrist stealing may be viewed as a way of resolving some emotional conflict or tensions which have arisen from the child's inability to cope with life situations; to the citizen who owned the property stolen, the child is a threat to the safety of property and should be punished; to the parent the child's stealing may be viewed as the work of the devil, as a mental disorder, as an act of rebellion, as an attempt to ruin the family reputation, as a bad habit, or even as an act of carelessness about getting caught which the child should avoid the next time he steals. To the child's playmates, stealing may be an act in an exciting and dangerous drama to be judged by whether he lives up to their code, shares with them or refuses to tell on those who have stolen with him. And of course it is most important to know what stealing means to the child himself. From the educator's point of view delinquency is learned, and the teacher in looking for conditions that give rise to delinquency finds many that are common to other kinds of poor learning development — broken home, poverty, emotional conflicts in family life, retarded mental development, poor neighborhood background, etc. It is necessary for the school to study these conditions; to discover how some children learn delinquency in these conditions, and how other children in the same home, school, and neighborhood, often with the same intelligence and basis for emotional conflict learn socially acceptable behavior; to discover how children can unlearn delinquent behavior; and most of all the school must study to know how more desirable social behavior can be learned.

The School Is an Important Agency. The school, as a part of society, and together with all other agencies in society, has the responsibility to help adjust school and society to the needs of the individual child so that he may build up self-respect, self-confidence, and a hopeful orientation to his life. Healy and Bronner in their lifetime experience of working intimately with thousands of delinquent boys and girls have clarified causes in a way to help schools focus attention on conditions that can be remedied, and among these are changes in the school atmosphere, procedures of instruction, and modification of school attendance laws. In this conclusion it must be pointed out that the school is related to juvenile delinquency in three ways; it may produce delinquency, it may help to prevent delinquency, and it may deal with delinquent behavior that is encountered within its walls. The schools hold a central place among all the agencies that affect the ideas and activities of children. Delinquents are or ought in most cases to be in school and so schools can play a major role in preventing delinquency. They will accomplish this end by better understanding of and provision for the intellectual, educational, social and emotional needs of every child enrolled. In many cases schools will need the help of special services provided by other disciplines such as psychology, psychiatry, social work, as well as improved educational service. In some cases they will need to make special school provisions for some children who need intensive care. An awareness and an understanding by all school administrators of the nature, extent, and seriousness of the delinquency problem is necessary before schools can help solve it.

THE SCHOOL'S PROGRAM

Schools and teachers to-day are professionally concerned with individual children and their problems. They are becoming increasingly democratic in their dealings with children, giving them practice in democratic citizenship and in learning ways of living together in an acceptable manner. In common with the home, the church, and the social-service agencies, the school is directing its efforts toward the building of character in youth more than it did a generation or two ago when it was primarily concerned with the intellectual development of a child. Surveys of current practices for children who are delinquent or in danger of becoming so in the better schools reveal several general levels of operation. These modes of attack on the problem from the simplest to the most complex type include the following personnel and services; (a) the work and responsibility of the regular classroom teacher in preventing and correcting social maladjustment, (b) the employment of school counselors, school psychologists, school social workers, and medical consultants, whose specialized services aid and assist teachers in helping prevent and treat cases of maladjustment, and (c) the organization of special classes and schools where different techniques are employed and where specialized services are concentrated upon the more serious cases of maladjustment.

Services of Regular Classroom Teachers. Almost every teacher faces the responsibilities from time to time of dealing with a maladjusted or delinquent child. Every teacher can have a part in helping to identify (See Articles 171–173, — Ed.) these children since many of them remain in regular classrooms before their problems are recognized and many will remain there even after recognition. The regular teacher can do much to give maladjusted children a chance to develop into good citizens, to learn the meaning of civic responsibility, to cultivate good social relationships and to acquire a measure of economic competence. It is the business of every teacher not only to teach children what they otherwise would not know and to help them acquire skills which they otherwise would not acquire but also to help them behave in a way that society expects them to behave. Since the interpersonal relations between teachers and pupils are significant in helping maladjusted children the personality of the regular teacher is very important. If teachers themselves are not well adjusted they help produce maladjusted children instead of preventing maladjustment.

Must Prepare to Deal with Problem Children. They must realize that disorderly behavior is likely to occur in some degree in every teacher's career and that the teacher must avoid losing self-control and must avert actions or words which render later adjustments difficult. Wholesome human relationships are important for pupil growth. The total emotional climate of the classroom is very important in the prevention and control of maladjustment in children. Teachers must be objective; that is, be able to view the behavior of children for what it is and not be confused or distracted by their own feelings. Teachers must avoid resentment or self-reference in regard to what a delinquent may do in the classroom or elsewhere. If the teacher can distinguish between the child and the behavior, he has the key to his own salvation in the situation. Teachers need to understand the significance of the symptoms and problems which children in school present.

The regular school can do much to prevent maladjustment and delinquency and to help build wholesome personalities if it meets the basic needs of all children. Every child has the need for affection and a feeling of belonging, so teachers must be able to accept every child, classroom procedures should help children who lack friends and school administrators should provide assistance to teachers and parents who need help in giving pupils a sense of emotional security.

Every child has a need for a sense of achievement and an opportunity for creative expression. Therefore, the school must provide a learning situation where he can succeed and can express himself. Teachers must encourage pupils who feel defeated, classrooms should be operated so that all children do not need to learn the same things at the same rate or even the same things at the same age. School work should make it possible for each pupil to express his own individuality even though pupils vary widely in interests and abilities.

Every child likes to have some part in deciding what his activities are to be, make his own decisions and solve his own problems. They want to make choices and make their opinions count and they want to find answers rather than to be told. Teachers must give pupils a chance to do these things and administrators must be able to handle conflicts between student opinion and teachers' wishes in a way that respects the pupils' as well as the teacher's individualities. Wise guidance in making choices is one of the best ways in which schools can help build good character.

Every child needs freedom from fear and from feelings of guilt. Fear at times has a protective function but excessive fears can produce maladjustment. Some children have been threatened and reproached so much and have been made to feel so guilty that they come to feel that they are "bad." Teachers must be able to reject a child's behavior while making it clear that they are not rejecting the child himself.

Every child has a need for discipline. Schools must develop the child's sense of responsibility and capacity for self-discipline. Teachers must use methods which will transform imposed discipline into self-discipline and students should be provided with opportunities to learn from experience in student government.

Every child has physical and economic needs and many children suffer when these needs are not met. Many more problem children and delinquents come from the ranks of the underprivileged, from those who lack medical and dental care, from those who wear poor clothes, from those who cannot buy the things that other children buy, and from those who suffer from the economic insecurity of their homes than from among those who come from better conditioned circumstances. Schools must discover such pupils, classroom procedures should avoid embarrassment of needy pupils and school administrators should make provision for their care.

The basic needs enumerated above are typical of many that affect the social adjustment of pupils but they are fundamental factors which, if properly met, help the school in doing its share to prevent delinquency.

The organization and work of the regular classroom and the challenge it presents to the interests, activities, and loyalties of children and youth are important factors in the way schools deal with the delinquency problem. For example, if dull or slow-learning children must meet fixed curriculum requirements before promotion, and if they are held back year after year until they are social misfits, truancy, incorrigibility, or delinquency is apt to follow. On the other hand, if more individual instruction and better teaching methods are employed; if schools employ skill in guiding better group experiences of all children; if suitable, worthwhile, activities are used; and if constructive leadership in the classroom is present, then much delinquency is prevented. Excessive teacher loads and the availability of special services to help regular teachers are other factors which must be considered in the regular classroom program for dealing with problems of maladjustment such as delinquency.

Use of Specialized Services. Even though every classroom had a well qualified and adequately prepared teacher, there would still be cases of delinquency and behavior problems among children with which the teachers would need help from specialists. Actually, many teachers now employed in schools need much more than assistance with a few complex behavior problems. Because they have not been adequately prepared for child-guidance work, they need in-service training in child study and counseling and in techniques of work with groups. Thus, special school services that supplement and facilitate the work of the regular teacher make an important contribution to the school's attempt to solve the delinquency problem.

By specialized services are meant the services of those departments, bureaus, divisions, or other organized services in a school or school system which provide direct assistance to pupils, or to their teachers and parents. Among such school organizations are child study departments, child guidance clinics, psychological bureaus, pupil personnel divisions and others. They employ pediatricians, psychiatrists, psychologists, school social workers, home and school visitors, and attendance supervisors. All these services supplement and support the instructional program and the activities of the regular classroom or school.

Child study departments and psychological bureaus usually assist with problems arising from learning difficulties, personality problems, and family maladjustments. The school psychologist is particularly concerned with the adjustment of the curriculum to the mental capacities of problem children and with teaching techniques that will facilitate learning.

Home–school visitors and school social workers try to bring homes and schools closer together in the effort to understand and to serve children who are becoming problems. This type of pupil personnel service co-ordinates the social worker's case-work techniques and the teacher's point of view and knowledge of the school program. Through specialized training in social service, the school service worker is prepared to help with the child's social and emotional problems. They must know the techniques of interviewing, building case histories, and counseling.

The counselor in a school program for dealing with problem cases deals with the child as a whole, in the situation as a whole, and has a co-ordinating function in bringing into relationship all the specialized information which psychologists, psychiatrists, and physicians can contribute to the school, its teachers, and to the home and the parents. They can help identify the influences in the school, home, and community that contribute to delinquency. The counselor must help the child too by making him an active participant in the process of identifying his own problems and in working out his own solutions.

All special services should provide the facilities which teachers need to help children realize their maximum potentialities. Basic to any successful pupil personnel program is a continuous census of all the children of a district providing information concerning age, handicaps, and any other special problems. Attendance officers, the first pupil personnel workers to appear in schools, were concerned primarily with enforcement of attendance laws; and while some need for this service still exists, they are being replaced by professionally trained school social workers who are interested not only in attendance but also in determining the reasons for absence and in removing its causes. The school doctor, dentist, and nurse are concerned primarily with the physical aspects of the maladjusted child's development while the psychiatrist concentrates his efforts on emotional growth.

All the large school systems provide something in the way of child study bureaus, attendance departments, and psychological services to aid teachers and administrators in dealing with problem children, and to aid in the in-service training of all teachers.

Special Classes and Schools. In every large school system, and even in many small ones, there will be found a sizeable number of delinquent and severe problem cases who fail to respond to the work of the best teachers, the most modern school programs, and the efforts of specialized services provided by school systems to help teachers prevent maladjustment. One reason is that the symptoms of their disturbances are too severe or too upsetting to other children. The regular school can do little for the habitual truant who rarely attends classes, neither can he be helped by specialists when he cannot be reached by their services. Another reason some children cannot be retained in regular grades is because schools must operate with 25 to 35 and even more pupils per teacher. No teacher has the right to take from the great majority of his pupils an unreasonable amount of time which may be necessary to deal with an extremely difficult case in his room. As long as schools must educate children in groups as large as those found in many systems this factor will be in evidence in dealing with the problem of delinquency. Children who are well started on the road to delinquency cannot be reached effectively with the regular group work in ordinary classrooms. Many such children cannot profit by regular class activities until they have undergone a personal re-orientation through counseling, psychotherapy, or remedial work done in small groups.

For such children as those described above the special class or special school is often provided in the larger school systems. While at first thought it might seem that the behavior problems of such children would be intensified by transfer to a special school, it has been the experience of the better special schools that serious types of misbehavior are diminished. Moreover, segregation as commonly defined is not a necessary concomitant of the special education of problem children because a problem child may be more harmfully segregated when kept in a regular class which cannot meet his needs than when assigned to a special class which does meet his needs better. This is no doubt due to the fact that the special school concentrates on remedial measures, gives more attention to physical and mental health, and maintains a competent staff of teachers of remedial reading, social workers, psychologists, and other adjustment workers. The special educational program is adapted to the particular needs of maladjusted individuals, with emphasis upon activities that prove an effective antidote for emotional disturbances. Special schools for social adjustment usually enroll only pupils who are so maladjusted as to need careful mental and physical examinations. These schools make it possible for the maladjusted to enjoy success in school work instead of experiencing the accumulation of feelings of failure which characterized their work in the regular schools where their unusual needs could not be met. Such schools should not be called "truant schools," or "disciplinary schools" or "industrial schools." The last title does not properly describe the function of the special day school. At least industrial courses should not be emphasized to the exclusion of regular academic work. Such schools should be located so that they can be reached conveniently from all parts of the city and should not be placed in unfavorable neighborhoods. School transfer rather than court commitment should govern admission. Placement should not be considered as punishment; rather, the decision to place a child in a special school should be based upon the fact that the evidence indicates that such placement will be of material benefit to him.

Special schools should provide a variety of curriculum offerings. Academic work is needed in English, mathematics, science, and social studies. Courses in woodwork, general metal work, electric shop, automotive and print shop, crafts laboratory, cartooning, and general mechanics are usually offered for boys. Homemaking, hairdressing, personal grooming, sewing, cooking and typing are usually offered in the special school for girls. Other courses found in both boys' and girls' schools are music, art, and physical training. Teachers in such schools should have special training, wholesome personalities, and ability as instructors. Excellent craftsmanship should be a requirement for those who teach shop courses. All such schools must make provision for vocational, educational, and personal guidance. In fact, the special school for the socially maladjusted should be a combination of a special school and a child guidance clinic.

The weakest point in most special school programs is the lack of proper placement procedures and adequate follow-up of the pupils after they leave the school. Discipline in the better schools is no different than that found in the best elementary or secondary schools. Systems of penalties and merits or credits as bases for determining the length of stay in a special school are of no value because they imply placement in the school as a punishment for wrongdoing. In addition to the regular and remedial work in school subjects and the special services for emotionally disturbed children, all special schools need more systematic provision for the rehabilitation of the pupils, more study of the variety of causative factors that produce maladjustment, truancy, and delinquency, and better provision for the child's re-entry into the normal life of society, including his return to the regular school. No special school can do these things if it does not make curriculum modifications, provide special equipment, including proper clinical office space, and keep adequate cumulative records of the work and interests of those enrolled.

The special school is an important provision

which must be made for the more severely emotionally disturbed children and for those children with the more fixed patterns of bad behavior. They should be created in all communities containing a sizeable number of emotionally disturbed or delinquent children. An early diagnosis and identification of those children needing this special service is a factor in the success of the special school in solving the problem of juvenile delinquency.

PRINCIPLES OF GOOD PRACTICE

In developing the school's program to meet the problem of juvenile delinquency, experience has shown that certain principles should be followed. Some of these have been suggested in the preceding pages and they are restated here for the sake of emphasis. They should be considered whenever the relationship of the schools to the delinquency problem is under discussion.

1. All children must have the right to develop into self-respecting, useful citizens by the process of public education, and that right must not be abridged by a handicap of any kind which can be eliminated or mitigated through the facilities and resources of the schools.

2. No program for problem children is sound unless it recognizes the fact that the behavior of such children is symptomatic and purposive. An objective attitude on the part of school workers toward children's behavior may serve to prevent problem cases from developing.

3. Problem children differ from normal children more in degree than in kind. There is no hard and fast line between normal and abnormal adjustment.

4. School systems should provide for early identification and early diagnosis of children who are maladjusted.

5. The education of problem children requires a broader basis than that of mere intellectual development. These children often have warped personalities, and, consequently, their feelings and attitudes are the object of more concern than their academic attainments. Children who are deviates because of social maladjustment need a chance to develop emotional stability; they need personal, educational, and vocational guidance; they need to experience the sense of security that goes with a socially acceptable personality.

6. Schools must recognize the fact that a problem child is one who may be normal within himself but yet be exceptional because of antisocial home and community influences.

7. The special education program for problem children should be a part of and not apart from the general educational program. The same objectives for educating normal children hold for educating socially maladjusted children. The tendency to substitute specific trade training for courses in general education is no more justifiable for problem children than it is for normal children.

8. In organizing and administering a program of education for the problem child, school administrators must maintain a balance between the interests of pupils needing placement in special groups and the interests of the great majority of the school population. While these interests often conflict, the conflict must be resolved for the best interests of all concerned. In general, placement of any child in a special group should not be made if that child may receive as good or better training in a normal group, even though it may be necessary to give special help and additional services over and above those which are usually provided. The exception to this rule is found whenever the detriment to the normal pupils outweighs the benefits to the handicapped individual from his association with the regular group.

9. Any program of education for the socially maladjusted will be conditioned by the selection of properly qualified and trained personnel, both those who work in the program, and those who administer and direct it.

DISCUSSION

Jessie F. Binford, Superintendent, Juvenile Protective Association, Chicago: I can think of no one in Chicago as well qualified as Mr. Stullken, to speak on this subject. I had the privilege of serving on Mr. Bogan's (Superintendent of Schools) Committee in 1929, which considered the special problems of children in our schools.

We selected Mr. Stullken to visit schools in many different states and cities. The Montefiore School was opened as a result of one of our recommendations and Mr. Stullken appointed as the Principal. For 20 years he has had the most realistic experience with these problems.

I believe he would agree with me that the subject of this meeting is misleading and the term "delinquency" limits our discussion for it excludes the large number of children who need, as do the comparatively few whom we could classify as "delinquent," all the services we are considering tonight.

Mr. Stullken emphasizes first, as a basic consideration, the purpose of Modern Education. Only as we keep this purpose in mind and as it is understood by the members of our Boards of Education, our City Officials who approve our School Budgets, our Legislators who pass our educational laws and appropriate state funds and the citizens who pay taxes, can we expect them to institute and support the services which are regarded by many as non-educational.

Mr. Stullken says that "the schools are concerned with all the problems of life, delinquency included, but their concern is primarily one of dealing with all children in such a way that delinquent behavior will not result on the part of individual children."

Here again, I think the term "delinquency" limits our consideration. The primary concern of the schools is rather one of understanding the problems of each child, physical, mental, emotional and conduct, whether these problems become apparent through delinquency or not. Who knows just what problems will lead to delinquency?

Not only delinquency, but all the problems which affect and limit a child's potentialities for education are of course "symptoms" of deep underlying conditions in a child's personality, his family life and the community.

The school is the first institution outside of the home which has the opportunity to perceive and analyze the problems of children. Parents accept the school to which they entrust their children while they are still very young and that fact increases its opportunities and importance.

It goes without saying that all teachers should be so trained that they can perceive and understand the physical, intellectual, educational, social and emotional needs of every child.

Last Friday I talked with one of the most able members of our Board of Education about this program. She said that we should first emphasize additional special training for every classroom teacher and secondly, a reduction in the number of children in each room or class. If that were done, she believes, the individual teacher would be able to understand and meet problems for which now they are asked to pro-

vide so many special departments and schools.

Many schools today have already included in their programs, Child Study departments with special psychologic and psychiatric services, counseling services, social workers and special schools. We have seen great progress on the part of individual teachers and school programs in the recognition of problems and the impossibility of meeting them under our present school system.

How far can the schools go in providing the services needed when the problems are obvious and beyond the ability or the time of the teacher to meet?

Should our schools become social service agencies and carry through all the case-work which a child's family and the consideration of community conditions which are contributing to the problems reflected in the child at school?

How much of a medical program shall be assumed by our schools? Shall it be only the examinations necessary to detect physical conditions which affect the child's education, or a program to carry out any recommendations which the parents are unable to or neglect to carry out?

Or shall all these services be reported to private and public agencies in the community?

If the schools are to refer these problems, as they do more and more at the present time, then the Welfare Council and the Community Fund must provide and finance greatly increased resources in social and medical agencies.

The reports from the Child Study Department in Chicago include not only recommendations for the teachers but for services in the child's home and community generally.

Whether the schools include all these services or refer some of them to agencies outside the school, those who are responsible for them must be specially trained.

I believe all the school personnel in departments of counseling, of visiting teachers — call them what you will, should have not only the education and training required of teachers and some experience in that profession, but also training in social service. This will add greatly to the time and expense of preparation, as well as higher salaries probably for such personnel.

Mr. Stullken raises the question of special schools, like the Montefiore and Moseley and Washington Schools here in Chicago. I am convinced that we need them for the reasons so well stated by Mr. Stullken, but there is a great difference of opinion in Chicago today among those who administer our Board of Education and the principals of our schools. Some of the objections to them have developed because principals have regarded it as a failure on their part if they had to transfer a child to a special school.

For this reason they wait so long to make the transfer that the child's problems and conduct have so developed that it is too late for him to profit from all the special school has to offer, and when he fails there the special school is held responsible.

The mechanics of transfer are too cumbersome. It now takes 30 days to transfer a child and during that time he is out of school altogether.

To those of us who were on Mr. Bogan's Committee to which Mr. Stullken made such an important contribution, great emphasis was given to the recommendation for a continuous census of school children in Chicago. No one knows how many children are completely lost in our school system. Only by such a census can we be sure that all of Chicago's children have the opportunity to be educated.

We must always remember the many great fundamental problems, social and economic which so affect the lives of children before they enter school and all through their years of being educated. No school system, however perfect, can completely counteract them or prevent their effects.

I am certain that in our schools many children for the first time in their lives find security and understanding and an opportunity to grow up and develop normally.

Mark C. Roser, Child Welfare Department, Gary, Indiana Public Schools: I'm extremely reassured by the fact that the Academy of Criminology considers this important topic, because its ramifications are very little known. Dr. Stullken, in a very scholarly and able fashion, has drawn a large perspective around the many factors of the problem of delinquency and schools.

His comments about the application and realization of the over-all philosophy of education are extremely important. Treatment of every child according to his own needs would go a long way to reduce, not only juvenile delinquency but adult crime as well. For example, research has indicated that schools without

facilities to help individual children contribute the largest percentage of referrals to Juvenile Court. School truancy is the first symptom of the unadjusted school child. The majority of these school truants in our Juvenile Courts are found to be slow learners. With the rigid curriculum and without special help such children are unsuccessful in meeting the requirements of the normal curriculum, and become frustrated, hostile and quite naturally begin to express themselves in delinquent behavior.

The Gluecks, in "Unraveling Juvenile Delinquency," have found that the outstanding characteristic of juvenile delinquents is a dislike for school. We could say that a child who is learning in school and is accepted by his group, by that degree, is protected from the pattern of juvenile delinquency. A child who is a rejectee in his school group, and who experiences school failure easily develops patterns of delinquency. A rejection of school learning means rejection of authority and community standards. It is not surprising then to find from research that most of our so-called non-readers are boys. And in this group of boys, they are not particularly limited by their intelligence. Learning and emotional health are linked very closely together.

Dr. Stullken has stressed the main outlines for a successful school program to meet the needs of deviant children, with one exception. That exception is the problem of controlling the psycho-social tensions caused by children of varying class structures. For example, any classroom that has representatives of upper-class, middle-class, and low-income group children, will exhibit classroom tension. Many teachers can do miracles with such a classroom, but this is not the average situation. Usually there is tension, rejection, hostility flowing between the children of the higher class structures and those of the lower end of the scale. Unfortunately the teacher has to struggle in the middle ground. Schools with mixed social class structures will be full of tension, and the need for special education, special services and special counseling is very apparent here.

I am sure that the point will be made about these proposals of Dr. Stullken that his program is expensive. Where do the schools stop, in terms of these services? It is expensive to educate the crippled child, to give him the physical care that he needs. I maintain, however, that the costs are not excessive to change the curriculum to meet the needs of deviant children.

How much it costs a community is always a relative question. For example, the U.S. Attorney General in 1947 said it costs on the average $247,000 to send one boy to the Boys' Training School. That is on the assumption that ultimately such a boy goes to the Reformatory and later to the State Prison. For these boys, special help and special schools will offset the delinquency pattern. With special help in schools, social case work and curriculum adjustments, etc., school truancy could be completely eliminated as a Court problem. Rigid schools, rigid curriculums increase rather than lower juvenile delinquency. Special schools, such as this paper describes, make a real contribution to the prevention of juvenile delinquency.

Chapter 8

Sociocultural Aspects of Delinquency

OF ALL THE SOURCES of character-molding, habit-formation and deterrence, American criminologic research has tended in recent years to emphasize the neighborhood — the "delinquency area" [1] and, more recently, the "delinquent sub-culture" [2] — as the most influential. Yet, living in the same underprivileged areas and the same sub-culture, the great majority of children somehow manage to grow up without resort to a persistently delinquent way of life. The regions from which both the non-delinquents and the delinquents included in *Unraveling Juvenile Delinquency* were chosen for study presented very similar temptations, suggestions, cultural traditions and opportunities for evil companionships and antisocial attitudes to both sets of boys. It was possible to find 500 truly non-delinquent boys in the very same neighborhoods from which the 500 persistent delinquents came. It cannot be said, therefore, that the major causes of delinquency spring from the sub-culture of the underprivileged urban area. This provides merely the locale and opportunity for enactment of the drama of aggressive or furtive misconduct. The cultural milieu of an area has a differential, not a uniform, influence on various types of persons. Most of the structure of personality and character in the child has been built in the home and therefore precedes, rather than follows, the impact of the antisocial traditions of the delinquent sub-culture or "area."

There is an inherent confusion in the thinking and writing of certain sociologists between the undoubted advantage of community-wide effort to cope with delinquency and the assumption that the basic causal influences of delinquency are indubitably community or national sociocultural forces. The first is an opinion in the realm of practical administration of community facilities focused on a specific social problem; the second is an opinion in the realm of the scientific study of the causes of delinquency.

One cannot be greatly impressed by the contributions so far made by the "behavioral sciences" to an understanding of human conduct. The Editor ventures the opinion that a basic reason for this is that researchers have emphasized environment and in so doing they have taken hold of the wrong end or of but one end of the stick: instead of defining their fields of interest as the behavioral sciences, they should have called them the *motivational* disciplines. For environment plays no role in conduct unless and until it is introjected and becomes part of the motive force in an individual.

Although the milieu of the home, and the emotional relations between parents and children have been found to be of prime significance, even in the atmosphere of the home it is evident that the environment does not affect equally all persons living within it. To understand "culture" one must examine the makeup of the various types of persons subjected to it; and this means a study of the varieties of somatic constitution and temperamental equipment. There are many strands of the cultural

---

[1] The outstanding works in this field are: C. R. Shaw and H. D. McKay, *Juvenile Delinquency in Urban Areas*, Chicago, University of Chicago Press, 1942; C. R. Shaw and H. D. McKay, *Social Factors in Juvenile Delinquency*, Vol. II of National Commission on Law Observance and Enforcement, Report on the Causes of Crime, Washington, U.S. Govt. Printing Office, 1931.

[2] See A. K. Cohen, *Delinquent Boys, The Culture of the Gang*, Glencoe, Ill., The Free Press, 1955; B. Lander, *Towards an Understanding of Juvenile Delinquency: A Study of 8,464 Cases of Juvenile Delinquency*, New York, Columbia University Press, 1954.

web which ensnare individuals *selectively*, as well as those which operate quite generally. Persons differ in the elements of any culture, even the under-the-roof culture, which they tend to select or to which they tend to succumb because those elements are naturally more congenial or more closely related to their particular vulnerability.

Individuals vary in somatic constitution, temperament, strength of instinctual drives, and the degree of integrative and inhibitory capacity they possess. These differences are the result not only of early conditioning in the home, but also, to an as yet unmeasurable extent, heredity.[3] Especially when the educative and supportive social agencies are inadequate or in process of rapid change, does the reaction of different individuals subjected to a similar culture vary. Some find it impossible to inhibit their primitive impulses in the absence or even in the presence of the deterrent influence of external force; others have so effectively "internalized" the psychologic accompaniments of various forms of authority that they have an efficient superego (conscience) which, despite major changes in cultural controls, still enables them to "toe the mark."

Yet certain textbooks on crime and delinquency keep emphasizing community cultural forces out of all proportion to their true significance in the total picture. There are several crucial statistics that cast doubt upon the views held by some sociologists that (*a*) gang membership, or (*b*) neighborhood culture, or (*c*) the wider general culture comprises the most potent cause of delinquency.

As to gang membership, it has been established, in *Unraveling Juvenile Delinquency*, that almost nine-tenths of the delinquent youths had already shown clear signs of antisocial behavior when they were under eleven years of age; and the typical "gang age" is well beyond that period, in adolescence.

As to neighborhood culture, even in the most marked "delinquency area" of our cities not more than a small fraction of the boys (say 10 or 15 per cent) become delinquent. It seems unreasonable, therefore, to emphasize the role of neighborhood influences on the small percentage of boys who become delinquent and utterly ignore the fact that the vast majority of the boys, in the same neighborhoods, somehow manage not to follow an antisocial path.

As to the wider general culture, the New York City Youth Board has established that in America's leading urban center no fewer than 75 per cent of the delinquents are contributed by only 1 per cent of the families.

If the neighborhood or general cultural values were as permeatively antisocial as they are said to be and if these values were as powerful in their criminogenic influence as is claimed, how account for these figures?

One can most clearly assess the role of such environmental factors as residence in an area of high delinquency rates or in a cultural milieu with unconventional values by considering a simple example.

Suppose ten youths go out in a boat on a lake. The boat springs a leak and fills with water. Two boys drown; the other eight successfully reach shore. It happens that one of the drowned boys did not know how to swim and the second could swim but had a weak heart which could not stand the excessive exertion; the other eight were good swimmers in good physical condition.

Under the circumstances, what is the more rational procedure: to focus primarily and (according to some) even exclusively, upon the composition of the water in the lake or, while not ignoring the lake as the setting of the deaths to be explained, to concentrate on the relevantly varying characteristics of the individuals subjected to the very same hazard but with such widely differing results?

What was the chief cause of the drowning of the first two boys? Was the water the cause? This cannot be so because, despite the fact that two of the youths drowned, eight others, who had been subjected to the same "cause," managed to survive. The

---

[3] See Articles 9 and 13 of this volume.

water is equivalent to the "delinquency sub-culture"; of ten persons subjected to a like external influence, only two succumbed. The condition that affected them is general; it is equivalent to the existence of the institution of property and of laws against theft: all men are subject to such a general condition, but the vast majority of them do not commit larceny.

The eight youths were saved, not because the water, in their case, was less deep or less wet, but because they could swim and were in good physical condition. The first boy was drowned, not because the water, in his case, was different from that of the others, but because he could not swim. The second lad was drowned, not because the general "cause" brought about his drowning, but because, although he could swim he did not have the necessary strength to swim the required distance to shore.

Now suppose that this same little drama were enacted on the high seas, where the environmental forces are much stronger than in a lake. All youths are by this *force majeure* reduced to a similar state. True, the first two boys drown earlier than the others, but the general environmental condition with which all the boys have to struggle is so overpowering as to make a difference in *individual* capacity or equipment virtually irrelevant.

Of course, the analogy is not perfect; the characteristics of a culture medium are much more subtle and complex than are the properties of a lake, as is also the dynamic interplay between the culture and the human organism. But the basic principle illustrated by the foregoing example is similar, as an explanatory device, to the principle involved in assessing the role in criminogenesis of the special sub-culture of gang life, or of the "interstitial area," or of the "working class," or of the process of "differential association" — favorite explanations of delinquency advanced by certain criminologists.

It cannot be denied that despite the many unwholesome and antisocial features of our culture the great majority of people are, in normal times, relatively law-abiding. In times of exceptional crisis, such as a widespread depression, some of them who have been treading a precarious zone between law-abidingness and criminalism go over or are pushed over into antisocial territory; but even in such times the great majority of them remain law-abiding. Yet they have been swimming about in the same culture as those who become delinquent or criminals. To insist, therefore, that in such a situation cultural influences are the most satisfactory explanation of the incidence of delinquency and crime is seriously to distort the picture. Environmental or cultural forces are only *potential* or *possible* causes of delinquency; persons of varied innate nature and early parent–child relationships select those elements of the culture which they wish, or are impelled, to introject. As pointed out, general cultural influences are no more causal of delinquency in any realistic sense than is the existence of property and the criminal law which prohibits theft and other crimes.

It will be noted, moreover, that neither gang membership, nor the neighborhood matrix, nor the general culture or "delinquent sub-culture" can be used as efficient *predictive* devices: the first, because, as was indicated, children are delinquent long before the gang age (besides which, only about half the delinquents in *Unraveling Juvenile Delinquency* ever became members of gangs); the second, because any set of factors that influences, even in the most tainted delinquency area, only a minor fraction of the boys, can obviously not be used to predict the behavior of all boys; the third, because, in addition to the fact that the general cultural influences evidently incline to delinquency only a small proportion of all children, they cannot be clearly enough defined to be used as factors in a predictive table.

But in contrast to the failure, as fundamental explanatory principles of delinquency, of the gang, the neighborhood, and the delinquent or working-class sub-culture or the wider general culture of the times, there is impressive evidence that other factors *do* explain the origins of delinquency and successfully predict its presence or absence very early in the life of the child. This evidence comes from *Unraveling Juvenile Delinquency* and from the successful validations of the Social Prediction Table presented in that volume and derived from the systematic comparison of a representative sample of delinquents with a representative sample of non-delinquents, both coming from the economically and culturally sub-standard areas of Greater Boston.

All this does not mean that group contacts, neighborhood impacts, the "delinquent sub-culture" and the more general cultural influences play no role whatsoever in criminogenesis. The issue is one of *primacy, weight, penetrability* and *permeability* of the various factors suggested as criminogenic in the case of children.

There can be little doubt, for example, that certain cultural clashes, especially those arising out of too rapid and ruthless an uprooting from a relatively unified and simple culture and a deposit into a more complex, exciting and freedom-granting culture, aggravate the mechanisms leading to delinquency. Witness the recent violent delinquency in certain New York City schools with high Puerto Rican and Negro increments of students. But even in these cases, the crucial and ultimate source of aggressive maladaptation can be traced to the breakdown of family unity, affection and discipline — a situation which reliable predictive studies has shown to be highly premonitory of delinquent behavior.[4]

Consideration of the types of approach suggested in the articles in this chapter, especially those by McKay and Clinard, is important, however, because of the fact that personality and character are not developed in a social vacuum but in a cultural milieu. It must be borne in mind that the process of "identification" of youngsters with adult ego-ideal figures is directed not alone at their own parents or at historic figures — Washington, Lincoln — but at persons in the news who symbolize cultural values. Repeated evidence of blatant corruption and evident immunity from prosecution among public officials, heads of labor union aggregates, big business men, and neighborhood gangsters; and the constant feeding to children of exciting acts of violence through modern means of mass communication such as television, motion pictures and comics, present both consciously conceived and subliminal patterns of illegality and aggression to impressionable children. That may be a fundamental reason why one reads so often nowadays of vandalism and violence to the point of murder on the part of youth. To be sure, corruption in high place is as old as government. But two of its more significant features in the modern scene — its frequency and the awareness of it by millions of people — are essentially recent phenomena, in historic perspective. Corruption, malfeasance and violence are continually pressing to invade the neighborhood and the body politic generally in competition with more virtuous standards and behavior. Such pressure is bound to have a seriously erosive effect on the authority of government and law in the minds of certain people. The memory of the public may be short-lived but, if one may make a novel application of a familiar psychoanalytic concept, the emotional effects of continuous shocks of disclosures of corruption and the continuous dinning into the eyes and ears of youngsters of scenes and acts of violence and immorality persist in the social "unconscious," breeding in many cynicism and disrespect or, in the case of less sophisticated youth, at least a set of confused and conflicting mores. When Al Capone is idealized above Al Smith, the ego ideal has become seriously tarnished. It would appear that too few men in high place realize the special duty they owe: to serve as father-ideals to the youth of America.

But, fortunately, the time is still distant when it can be maintained that the majority of American youth are adversely affected by the corrupting and divisive cultural in-

---

[4] See Articles 171–173 of this volume.

fluences of the neighborhood or the nation to the point of becoming persistent delinquents or criminals.

The first piece in the present chapter is a summary from *Unraveling Juvenile Delinquency* which brings out contrasts between delinquents and non-delinquents in neighborhood activities, and hints at the possible reasons for selectivity of response to the general cultural climate of a region. The next article, by Wattenberg and Balistrieri, is an experimental analysis of the relationship of gang formation to various factors in home and environment. The next item, by Shaw and McKay, summarizes their well-known views of the cultural influences of urban areas on the generation of delinquency, and the implications of their theory for prevention and treatment. An article by McKay follows which analyzes the effect of neighborhood influences on child behavior. Clinard presents, next, his views regarding the broader and more permeative influences on delinquency of the general culture comprehended under the term, "secondary community influences," and emphasizes the role of adult criminalism in inciting youth to delinquency. The description by Waldner, of delinquency in the newly established special community of Oak Ridge and, by Eisenstadt, of delinquency group formation among immigrant youth in Israel suggests impressively both the significance and the inadequacy, because of its incompleteness, of a purely sociocultural explanation of delinquent behavior.

The final piece — a United Nations contribution — is significant in that it gives clues to the development of delinquency in countries of varied cultures, ranging from simple, agrarian societies to highly complex industrial ones. Only by a multinational, but carefully conducted, study of the forces involved in generating antisocial behavior in lands of varied stages of social evolution can it be ultimately determined which influences are general and which are attributable largely to the peculiar characteristics of any particular society and culture.

It is hoped that the materials in this chapter will caution the reader that the weakness of the overemphasis of the cultural explanation of delinquency in any single region is that it deals almost exclusively with but one possible infective agent and tells us little or nothing about any of the others that may be more potent or more widespread, or about varying degrees of human susceptibility to culture.

30

The Boy in the Community*

Sheldon and Eleanor T. Glueck

It is clear that the impact of the socio-cultural matrix on the two sets of boys varied. We

* Reprinted by permission of the publishers and The Commonwealth Fund from *Unraveling Juvenile Delinquency*, Sheldon and Eleanor T. Glueck, Cambridge, Mass.: Harvard University Press, Copyright 1950, by The Commonwealth Fund. Pages 167–168. It is advisable for the student to read the data in the chapter from *Unraveling* (XIII) of which the above is but a summary. — *Ed.*

have seen that the delinquents moved about more than the non-delinquents and therefore had less opportunity to strike root in any one neighborhood. They were also subjected to many more changes of environment, the changes stemming in part at least from their antisocial behavior.

Large numbers of both groups worked after school or during vacations, a considerably higher proportion of the delinquents engaging in street trades, while more non-delinquents were in jobs in which some supervision was provided. Whether or not the delinquents preferred street trades because they provided greater freedom and excitement, we do not know, but it is clear that as a group they inclined more to adventurous activities. This is further reflected in the greater frequency with which they went to the movies, and also in more truck-hopping, ride-stealing, keeping late hours, smoking and drinking at an early age, sneaking into theatres, committing destructive mischief, running away from home, bunking out, gambling, begging, setting fires, and the like.

Further evidence of their craving for excitement and adventure is found in the far larger proportion of delinquents who hung around street corners; sought their recreations in neighborhoods distant from their homes; played in vacant lots, on waterfronts, and in railroad yards; frequented cheap poolrooms, dance halls, and the like. By contrast, many more non-delinquents found at least some of their recreations at home or in playgrounds.

Regarding the companionships of the two groups of boys, the delinquents were much more inclined to gang membership, while the non-delinquents avoided gangs almost entirely, preferring a few intimates, very largely non-delinquents like themselves. The delinquents, however, not only chummed largely with other delinquents but gravitated towards older boys.

While almost all the boys had some contact with boys' clubs, settlement houses, and other agencies of supervised recreation, far less initiative in seeking such outlets was shown by the delinquents, and they attended less frequently and spontaneously. Almost twice as many delinquents expressed a marked dislike for supervised recreation.

Finally, the delinquent boys attended church with far less regularity than the non-delinquents; but only a few of either group neglected their religious duties entirely.

When these facts are reflected upon, it becomes clear that in order to understand the impact of the milieu on those who live and act therein, findings regarding the varying rates of delinquency in different zones or areas of a city are of little illumination. For, given the same general culture, the response to some of its elements is uniform, to others different and selective. In this chapter we have derived some hints of the possible reasons for this selectivity of response to the general culture of a region. Other hints may come from other parts of the study. In the meantime it is clear that in addition to the marked disadvantages already shown to exist among the delinquents in respect to their parental and home background, the influences of the larger social environment have played their part.

31

Gang Membership and Juvenile Misconduct*

*William W. Wattenberg
and James J. Balistrieri*

There has long been a fascination about those young people, mostly in their teens, who form groups which challenge society. Popular interest is evidenced by the avid consumption of highly dramatized articles on gang life and gang warfare. Scientifically, there is a puzzle to be solved: How can we account for those young people who prove able to make a seemingly fine social adjustment in groups of their peers but nevertheless get in trouble with the larger social organizations? There have been quite a few attempts to work out theoretical structures of the dynamics involved, but very few good research studies have appeared.

OPINIONS OF RESEARCHERS

A number of workers tackle the problem first by assuming that membership in groups is a sign that something is wrong in the lives of the boys or girls concerned. There is no agreement as to who or what should be blamed. In *Street Corner Society*, W. F. Whyte points out that home plays a very small part in the daily routine of a full-fledged gang member. In a study of Mexican-American gangs in Los Angeles, E. S. Bogardus attributed gang formation to a sense of differences due to language difficulties, academic problems in school, contrasts in child-control methods, race discrimination, and low economic status. C. Himber is inclined to blame broken homes and weak religious ties, as well as social conditions. Going somewhat more deeply into personal factors found in gang leaders, M. Van Waters sees rejection in school, church and social clubs as putting youngsters in the position where the gang is their only

* Reprinted from 15 *Am. Soc. Rev.* (1950), 744–752. Used by permission of the authors and the publishers.

road to prestige and status. The other gang members are likely to fill or give promise of filling psychological needs not met by the adolescent's own parents.

The larger proportion of writers either explicitly or implicitly assume that it is normal for pre-adolescents and adolescents to join groups. F. Redl goes even further and states that pre-adolescents have a deep need to form cliques and gangs among themselves. As a sociologist, C. B. Spaulding sees the gang as necessary to satisfy wishes for response and security. In accord with practitioners of group therapy, P. Rosenthal found that the gang setting permitted disturbed youngsters to work out some of their conflicts.

On the question as to why gang members go in for misconduct, the differences are very wide. A. S. Beckham, for example, believes that suggestibility is higher in such groups, due to such factors as broken or disturbed homes. Retardation in school, he feels, increases their willingness to accept suggestions of truancy. S. M. Robison, N. Cohen, and M. Sachs attribute such phenomena as gang warfare to aggressive tendencies arising out of homes where there was hardly any family life but where there was fear of the parents. An answer more typical of sociologists has been given by D. B. Harris who states that delinquent gangs arise in areas in ecological transition and largely take on the standards prevalent in such areas.

Simple and appealing as this sociological explanation may be, a number of child-guidance workers and psychiatrists are emphatic in the belief that it is far from the whole story. W. Healy and A. Bronner point to their findings on delinquents who came from families in which there were non-delinquent siblings, which reveal that the delinquent in 91 per cent of the cases was extremely disturbed emotionally, largely because of poor relationships within the family. They regard the delinquent's lack of social restraints as a product of poor ego-ideal formation, due to lack of affectional identification with a good parent.

R. Topping has given a somewhat fuller picture of what she calls the "pseudosocial boy." She regards gang membership as possibly an attempt to compensate for a sense of effeminacy or of physical or mental inadequacy. On the basis of clinical experience she declares that many such boys show a lack of warm, whole-some attachment to other members of the family. Specifically, she notes there is often a dependent attitude toward the mother and an indifference or resentment toward the father. The causative situation within the family is held to be sufficient family acceptance to promote socialization but insufficient supervision and adult influence to build a strong sense of values. She further notes the possibility that such gang members may come from large families.

FINDINGS FROM OBJECTIVE RESEARCH

Those studies which are built around reports of more or less objective research, as contrasted with the ones which are primarily speculative or are based on clinical experience, show almost as wide a range of findings, which are supplementary rather than contradictory. The best known study, that of F. M. Thrasher, documents the sociological viewpoint. He came to the conclusion that delinquent gang membership was the outgrowth of a situation-complex involving inadequate family life, poverty, deteriorating neighborhoods, ineffective religion, poor education, and inadequate recreation. The gang was held to arise to fill the needs thus left unmet; the social setting determined the nature of the activity. As a statement of position, Thrasher's work was admirable; as a compilation of evidence, disappointing. The methodology is vague and the documentation weak, if delightful. One even runs across such romantic footnotes as "unpublished study of an experienced boys' worker in gangland," and "interview with a railroad detective."

Somewhat less inclusive are the manipulations of statistical data more familiar to the pedestrian psychologists. W. C. Kvaraceus found that in a group of 761 delinquents referred to the Children's Bureau of the Passaic Board of Education only 23 per cent of the boys and 33 per cent of the girls engaged in solitary misdemeanors. He found that only 7.9 per cent of the total group, however, had any affiliation with any recognized recreational activity. Working with 100 boys, aged 12 to 16, on their first commitment to the Indiana School for Boys, B. S. Atwood and E. H. Shideler found that delinquents had a higher degree of social participation than non-delinquents. A study of activities rated by six judges gave rise to the conclusion that those boys were more extrovertive.

The techniques of multiple-factor analysis were used by Hart, Jenkins, Axelrad and Sperling in a study of personality traits of 300 delinquent boys. They found a factor which they labeled "street gang activity." The elements in the factor pattern which they presumed to be causative were neglect by parents and the disorganization often associated with immorality of the parents.

HEWITT AND JENKINS REPORT

In many ways, the most promising report is that which L. E. Hewitt and R. L. Jenkins made (*Fundamental Patterns of Maladjustment*, 1946) on the basis of trained observers' analyses of 500 child-guidance clinic case histories. These were reduced to ratings on a series of items, and the degree of association between the items determined by tetrachoric correlation. The correlations were further studied to determine the existence of clusters or syndromes. One of these they called "socialized delinquent," and pointed out its similarity to Topping's "pseudo-social boy." A tetrachoric correlation of .63 ± .07 with a situational cluster of parental negligence plus exposure to delinquent conduct was found. In this pattern there was often physical inadequacy in the homes; the houses needed repair; the families were large; one of the parents was dead; there was parental alcoholism; and, above all, a general lack of supervision. In their discussion of this finding, Hewitt and Jenkins parallel Topping as well as Healy and Bronner in their use of psychoanalytical dynamics. They see the boys as coming out of the family situation with a weak superego structure and ready to identify with the delinquent patterns found among their older siblings or playmates.

Hypotheses. As their major hypothesis the authors accepted the position that the combination of a home typified by weak supervision or discipline and a surrounding neighborhood having a high delinquency rate or its concomitants was a primary causative influence in shaping the personality structure of adolescent boys who would engage in unlawful actions and, at the same time, make a good adjustment in gangs of their peers. If one were to use the adjective "antisocial" in relation to their conduct, the group under study would be antisocial toward larger social entities but not primary peer groups. From the basic hypothesis, the following corollaries which could be subjected to statistical test were derived.

1. In a group of boys, all having police records, those belonging to gangs would show a higher proportion coming from poorly supervised homes and from unfavorable socioeconomic conditions. It is assumed as amply demonstrated that in large American cities neighborhoods which have populations low in the socioeconomic scale generally have high delinquency rates. Level on the socioeconomic scale would be indicated by such objective criteria as condition of housing, family income, and family possession of automobiles. The strength of home supervision could be evaluated in terms of such direct or indirect indices as a boy's grooming, the measures by which he was given spending money, and the extent of parental participation in his recreation.

2. The differentials between gang and non-gang boys on items reflecting socioeconomic conditions and home supervision would be sharper among boys repeatedly in trouble than among those whose police records were limited to a single incident. It is assumed that repetition of a course of conduct is an indication of strength of the personality structure leading to the behavior. Accordingly, boys who are repeatedly in trouble can be considered more delinquent than those who showed no such consistency in "misconduct." Just as the degree of delinquency is a variable, so are the other factors under study. If a causal relationship exists, then we would expect to find that the differences between indices to home situations and neighborhood conditions for gang members would be sharper among seriously delinquent boys than those whose tendencies in that direction were light.

3. Items reflecting weak home supervision and poor neighborhood conditions would be more highly predictive of repeating among gang boys than non-gang boys. If a factor is causative, then its presence should be predictive. Thus in a group of boys arrested for the first time, those who belonged to gangs and showed most evidence of coming from weak homes and bad neighborhoods would be more likely to become repeaters. Moreover, such items should have a higher predictive value for gang boys than for those in whose behavior patterns other factors are operative.

Procedure. To test these propositions, use

was made of the records of some 5,878 boys between the ages of 10 and 16, inclusive, who were "interviewed on complaint" by Detroit police officers in 1946 and 1947. When a complaint was lodged against a boy, he was interviewed and his home visited by specially designated Crime Prevention Bureau officers. On the information thus obtained, a "history sheet" containing some fifty items on home conditions, neighborhood situations and other matters of interest was completed. The data were coded and punched on IBM cards so as to be available for statistical manipulation.

Among the facts recorded for each boy was whether or not he was a member of a neighborhood gang. This was considered to be a group of four or more boys who spent their spare time regularly with each other. The police officers' judgment on this matter was based not only on interviews but also on such observations as they made in the course of precinct duties. On the basis of their recorded judgment, therefore, it was possible to divide the population on the basis of gang membership into two groups: 2,737 gang members and 3,141 nonmembers. This cannot be considered a simon pure dichotomy. What can be said with confidence is that our gang member group is more highly saturated with boys having a strong tendency to take part in gang behavior than the nonmember group.

The records available covered the last five months of 1946 and all of 1947. The 1946 group could be divided into two groups according to whether or not they were in trouble again in 1947. On this basis a three-way classification of the entire population could be made: 1,462 boys with records only in 1946; 670 repeaters with records in both years; and 3,746 new offenders in 1947. Here, again, the grouping was not a pure one. However, we can safely assume that the 1946 repeater group is more highly saturated with serious delinquents than either the 1946 non-repeaters or the 1947 new offenders.

To test the several corollaries to the principal hypothesis these groups were paired in different combinations. For each item recorded on the history sheets, a table was prepared and submitted to the chi-square test. Both this procedure and the data had been previously tested, as reported in other studies and found to be useful. Three sets of pairings were made. To test Corollary 1, all gang boys were compared with

all non-members. To test Corollary 2, a similar pairing was made within the 1946 non-repeaters, 1946 repeaters, and 1947 new offenders, and the three sets of results compared with each other. To test Corollary 3, a comparison was made between the results of a 1946 repeater vs. non-repeater pairing for gang members and for non-members. In all, some 354 chi-square computations were made. Of these, 104 permitted rejection of the null hypothesis at a one per cent level of confidence.

In making the analyses, where a table showed statistical significance at the one per cent level it was further broken down to determine which cells contributed a total of 6 or more to the chi-square total. In effect, this meant that such a cell if incorporated as one of the four in a two-by-two-fold table would give rise to a statistically reliable result. In this way we could list not only the items which had a statistically reliable association with either gang membership or repeating, whichever was under study at the time, but also could point out which categories in that item had contributed to the result.

In preparing all tables, the "not stated" category was treated as any other. That is to say, failure of the police to secure an answer was considered as a category within each item. This had the statistical effect of increasing by one the degrees of freedom and thereby raising the chi-square total required to reach any given level of P. At first glance this may appear to cause an overly conservative evaluation of the results. However, previous experience with these data had indicated that the "not stated" categories could be psychologically significant. As will be seen, in this study they proved repeatedly to be of value.

Findings. The results of the over-all comparison between gang members and non-members are given in Table 1. Only those items on which a statistically significant relationship was found are reported. For each of these, all categories yielding a contribution of 6 to the chi-square total are listed in the second column if they are associated with gang membership and in the third column if with non-membership.

It should be noted that the factor of repeating is not included in the table. The item was submitted to the chi-square test and for it the null hypothesis could not be rejected with confidence (P was greater than 0.30). In view of the size of the population under study, this

Table 1   *Items Showing Relationship with Gang Membership at One Per Cent Level of Confidence*

ITEM	CATEGORY ASSOCIATED WITH:	
	Gang Membership	Non-Membership
Parental participation in boy's recreation	Occasional	
Marital status of parents	Marriage Intact	Separated, both dead
Boy's chores around home	Few	Occasional
Allowance	Money given "on request"	None given, "Not stated"
Boy permitted to drive family car		"Not stated"
When parents are at home	Evenings	"Not stated"
Alcoholism in family	Father	"Not stated"
Chronic illness in family		"Not stated"
Congeniality of family		"Not stated"
Boy's expressed attitude toward mother		Disliked, "Not stated"
Boy's expressed attitude toward father		"Not stated"
Boy's appearance		Neat and clean
Boy's recreational equipment		Not comparable to playmates
Father's age	Over 45	Under 45
Mother's age	Over 45	Under 45
General rating of neighborhood	Average	Good
Condition of home	Substandard	Modern
Racial homogeneity of neighborhood	Mixed	
Type of home	Flat	Rooming house
Nature of nearest recreational facility		Vacant area
Parents' employment		"Not stated"
Parents' income		"Not stated"
Type of entertainment boy prefers	Shows and sports	
Nickname	Has one he doesn't resent	
Attitude toward adult neighbors	Poor, Indifferent	
Attitude toward police in interview as judged by police		"Honest"
Attitude of parents toward police	Antagonistic	

can be taken to mean that these two variables are substantially unrelated.

Inspection of Table 1 reveals a pattern somewhat different from what one would expect if the major hypothesis and the first corollary were adequate. The items and categories distinguishing gang boys in general do not fit a picture of weak supervision or poor home relations so much as they would one of normality. On only three items do we find evidence of poor or inadequate home ties: (1) The boys receive funds on a hit-or-miss basis rather than as a definite allowance or as compensation for work done around the home; (2) the boys are required to

perform few chores; and (3) the fathers were more likely to be alcoholics.

By contrast, the non-gang group shows distinct evidence of disturbed family relationships. Most striking is the highly differentiating significance of "not stated" replies. These would indicate either an emotional blocking on the item or a defensive secrecy. All told, the non-members showed a statistically significant tendency to be high on "not stated" replies for ten family items ranging from expressed attitudes towards parents to policy regarding use of the family car. There was also direct evidence of emotional tension in the homes: (1) This group was high in number of separated parents, and (2) boys who openly expressed dislike for their mothers. In addition, there was a picture of some deprivation: more boys in this group (1) received no money from their parents and (2) had less recreational equipment than their friends.

On indices of socioeconomic status the evidence somewhat more closely approximates the predicted situation. The gang members were more likely to come from substandard homes and racially mixed neighborhoods, which at the time of this study in Detroit (before the Supreme Court ruling on restrictive covenants) tended to be less well-to-do. The non-gang group had a higher proportion of youngsters living in good neighborhoods. The group living in rooming houses was 170, of whom 116 belonged to no gang.

On those items representing a rating of attitudes and peer group activity the gang boys conformed to the popular stereotype. They seemed to be out-going individuals who enjoyed popular commercial recreation, boasted nicknames, were hostile to adult neighbors and evasive with the police. In this latter attitude they appeared to have some support at home from their parents.

For several relationships stressed in other publications the results were inconclusive. Failing to pass the chi-square test at a one per cent level of confidence were such items as size of family, number of brothers, and frequency of church attendance.

In a second series of tabulations, a similar comparison between the gang and non-gang groups was made separately for each of three classifications of boys: (1) 1946 non-repeaters; (2) 1946 repeaters; and (3) 1947 new offenders. According to our second corollary, differences on items reflecting neighborhood conditions and family supervision should have been more marked among the 1946 repeaters than either of the other groups, which were weighted more heavily with mildly delinquent boys. The results however, were inconclusive, if not negative. There was not a single interview item that discriminated at a one per cent level of confidence between gang members and non-members among the 1946 repeaters which was not an equally clear indicator for the 1946 non-repeaters, 1947 new offenders or both. By contrast, there were several items which attained a

one per cent level of confidence in distinguishing gang members from non-members in both of the mildly delinquent groups but not in the repeaters. In view of the strong influence of N in the calculation of chi-squares and the fact that the 1946 repeaters were considerably smaller in number than either of the other groups, some such effect could be expected. To discount this influence of group size, we arbitrarily ruled out all instances where the P for the repeaters was less than .50. There still remained six items which were significantly related to gang membership among both the 1946 non-repeaters and 1947 new offenders but not among 1946 repeaters. On one of these, even the sign of the differences was reversed: more gang members than non-members among 1946 repeaters lived in rooming houses, although the reverse was true for the other groups. For the remaining five items, the direction of observed differences was the same in all three groups, although too slight among repeaters to approach statistical reliability. These five items were: father's age, boy's appearance, allowance, type of entertainment preferred by boy, and racial homogeneity of neighborhood.

It will be noted that none of these items is central to the major factors being studied, although three (boy's appearance, allowance, and racial homogeneity) are considered indirect indices.

On the third series of comparisons, the results were much more clear cut and interesting. Taking the gang members and the non-members as separate populations, we studied the phenomenon of repeating. For each population we compared the 1946 non-repeaters with the repeaters. Theoretically, if different causal factors were operating, the list of items predictive of repeating would not be the same for gang members as for non-members. As a glance at Tables 2 and 3 will show, this was definitely true. There were only two items which reliably predicted repeating among gang members but which failed of reliability for the non-gang boys. Both of these are clearly indications of poverty and low socioeconomic level.

A striking contrast is the list of eight items which although not reliably predictive for the gang boys were statistically significant for the non-gang boys. Of these the following six are clearly related to family conditions: number of sisters, boy's attitude toward his father, his ap-

Table 2 *Items Predictive of Repeating at One Per Cent Level of Confidence for Gang Members but not Non-Members*

ITEM	CATEGORY ASSOCIATED WITH:	
	Repeating	Non-Repeating
Size of Home	Inadequate	
Parent's Income	Inadequate	

pearance, his willingness to talk about the amount of money received from his parents, their participation in his activities, and alcoholism in the family. The seventh item, regularity in church attendance, may also be linked to family morale. Only one item, living in a racially mixed neighborhood, is definitely socioeconomic. This one item may be of considerable theoretical interest.

Discussion. The results of this study indicate that the initial hypothesis was not wholly adequate. This is not too surprising when we recollect that the statistics and observations from which it was formulated were all based on youngsters who turned up either at child-guidance clinics, juvenile courts, or correctional institutions. By contrast, the population included in the present study is relatively normal. Only about ten per cent of the group were referred to the juvenile court. The boys covered in this study did belong to gangs and did engage in misconduct but not in as extreme a degree. Also, they were a more representative sample than boys who go before juvenile courts or are sent for clinic treatment. The latter group is selected or, rather, is the residue left after parents have used their influence, neighbors have relented, or youngsters have appealed to arresting officers. That findings in the population now under study differ somewhat from those in a residue group is to be expected in the same way that a study of factors linked with "intelligence" might be different in a relatively normal group as contrasted with one limited to feeble-minded children. This may account especially for the failure of the second corollary.

The main modification of the initial hypothesis seems to be in the evaluation of the family influence. The socioeconomic factors held up

well. However, the family picture of the gang boys is less like neglect and more like low-tension or easy-goingness. More significant, the way in which the non-gang boys appeared to show evidence of emotional upset due to strong tensions or deprivations at home suggests that the two sets of influence, familial and socioeconomic, are not equal in effect but are dynamically related. It looks as though the social forces are limited in their play upon the individuals by the previous effects of the family factors.

An attempt to construct a theoretical formulation of the dynamics which could account for the findings runs head-on into difficulties in interpretation. The picture of the family life of many of the gang boys has been described as easy-going. The question which must be settled, and upon which the data cannot throw light, is whether or not this picture is objective truth on the one hand or is merely the manifestation of some defense mechanism, or both. For example, it is within the realm of probability that boys who had won emancipation would not be aware of family tensions. In this case, part of the differences between the groups would be symptoms or reflections of deeper but unde-

Table 3 *Items Predictive of Repeating at One Per Cent Level of Confidence for Non-Members but not Gang Members*

ITEM	CATEGORY ASSOCIATED WITH:	
	Repeating	Non-Repeating
Number of sisters	Three or more	
Attitude toward father	Dislikes	
Boy's appearance	Slovenly	Neat and clean
Church attendance ..		Regular
Money received from parents	"Not stated"	
Racial homogeneity of neighborhood ..	Mixed	
Participation of parents in boy's activities		Regular
Family addiction to alcohol		None

fined present personality differences. The predictive value of those symptoms could remain prognostically valid, in the same sense that an intelligence test score or a Rorschach response can be a good indicator even though its full psychological import is debatable.

If one could assume that the data may be taken at face value, it is possible to account for them if we assume that those segments of personality structure which result from the interaction of the growing child with his parents would be more likely to be characterized by tension if the family itself was under high tensions. The resultant rigidity in this portion of his psychological life space would strengthen the barriers within it and impede locomotion. Consequently his activities would be relatively more influenced by such an area of strong boundaries and high tensions than by the less developed areas. The predictive value of the family influences would therefore be great. An incidental finding adds weight at this point. It will be recalled that the only social index included in the list of factors which predicted repeating by non-gang boys but not by gang boys was a racially mixed neighborhood. E. Frenkel-Brunswik has demonstrated that ethno-centrism is linked with that type of rigidity which is also correlated with the presence of anxiety and a past history of being subjected to child-raising methods involving use of fear techniques. The findings for the gang boys would give the reverse of the dynamics. The sectors of personality structure formed by low-tension family interactions would have relatively weak boundaries and great flexibility; the development of the individual would be more free in the direction of social, peer relations. The effect of immediate situations would have relatively greater weight in determining action patterns than the carry-over of past family situations. Therefore, the socioeconomic influences could be expected to have higher predictive value.

It must be emphasized that the basic data in this study are mass statistics and the findings deal with differences between groups in which there is considerable overlap. Therefore, it would be wildly inaccurate to assume that dynamic patterns such as those described above typify all gang boys or all non-gang boys. Undoubtedly there are many other factors operating in each specific case. At best, the patterns described might be assumed to be the common elements for the portions of each group which gave rise to the differences.

Practical Implications. The results of this study, if verified by others dealing with the same phenomena, have certain very important practical implications. There is the possibility that the difference in pattern of predictive factors might call for a new approach to prediction in criminology. As L. E. Ohlin and O. D. Duncan have pointed out, current formulae used by parole boards and others yield results little better than chance expectation. It may be that this is because all such formulae are applied without modification to an undifferentiated group. To use an old analogy, they may be trying to use the same set of measures to evaluate the ripeness of oranges and watermelons. Possibly it will be necessary to construct several different prediction tables to use with delinquents and criminals having different dynamic patterns. Dichotomization based on gang membership is not being suggested here, but rather a fuller study based on factors which underlie the patterns we have found and others which might be indicated by work along the lines of Hewitt and Jenkins.

There is also the possibility that these findings might provide a clue to treatment strategies. It would seem offhand that where delinquency could be traced to tensions arising out of early family history, individual psychotherapy would be indicated and an environmental attack contra-indicated. On the other hand, where delinquency resulted from a too free interaction with the peer culture or a poor neighborhood subculture, the unit of treatment or prevention would appear to be the social group or the neighborhood.

Summary. This study dealt with the records of some 5,878 adolescent boys contacted on complaint by Detroit police. Those boys who belonged to gangs differed from non-gang boys in showing evidence of coming from easy-going homes and living in socioeconomically low neighborhoods. The non-gang boys displayed indications of coming from tense or depriving families. In predicting repeating by these boys, socioeconomic indices had greater value in the case of gang members, and family indices in the case of non-members.

SELECTED REFERENCES

1. Tappan, Paul W., *Juvenile Delinquency* (New York: McGraw-Hill Book Co., 1949), Chapter 7:

"Causes and Conditions of Delinquency — Social Variables in the Etiology of Delinquency."

In this discussion, attention is called to the fact that exposure to unwholesome companions who carry habits and attitudes of law violation may easily spread delinquency patterns. Gang war incidents are related in dramatic manner.

2. Ellingston, John R., *Protecting Our Children from Criminal Careers* (New York: Prentice-Hall, 1948), Chapter 2: "The Social Roots of Crime."

The pervasive influence of a lawless society is advanced as a partial explanation for much unlawful behavior of youth as well as the major role played by the delinquency area.

3. Neumeyer, Martin H., *Juvenile Delinquency in Modern Society* (New York: D. Van Nostrand Co., 1949), Chapter 7: "Companionship and Juvenile Gangs."

In addition to a comprehensive presentation of the importance of gangs as viewed sociologically, Neumeyer's analysis of the "Zoot-suiter" is one of the best in the literature.

4. Thrasher, Frederic M., *The Gang* (Chicago: University of Chicago Press, 1927).

This study, over many years, was concerned with 1313 gangs containing about 25,000 members and is a "classic" in the field of juvenile delinquency.

5. Whyte, William Foote, *Street Corner Society* (Chicago: University of Chicago Press, 1943).

6. Von Hentig, Hans, *The Criminal and His Victim* (New Haven: Yale University Press, 1948).

32

Urban Areas and Delinquency*

C. Shaw and H. D. McKay

Year after year, decade after decade, large cities — and especially certain areas in large cities — send to the courts an undiminished line of juvenile offenders. Year after year, decade after decade, likewise, society continues to organize or construct new agencies or institutions designed to reduce the number of these offenders and to rehabilitate those who have already offended against the law. Perhaps the unsatisfactory results of these treatment and

prevention efforts have been due, in part at least, to the fact that our attention has been focused too much upon the individual delinquent and not enough upon the setting in which delinquency arises.

James S. Plant, on the basis of many years' experience in a psychiatric clinic, arrives at somewhat the same conclusion. He states:

Society is, and has been, aroused over its misfits and the mass of human breakdown that is in the wake of its progress. It has erected every conceivable type of agency to study, salvage, or merely sweep up this debris. As the wreckage mounts, new agencies are demanded or "better standards of service" asked of those existing. The folly of believing that happiness and goodness can be fabricated by machinery (agencies) will be exposed only when we understand that the ills, corruptions, and hypocrisies of a cultural pattern flow into the child and man and "become a part of him for the day, for the year, or for stretching cycles of years." If it is true that the triumphs and tragedies of the street flow into and become a part of the child, then all programs of personality change must manage somehow to change the street.[1]

Whether or not we care to admit it, most delinquent boys reflect all too accurately what they have learned in the process of living in their own communities. If we wish to have fewer delinquents, or if we wish to modify the mode of life of those who already are delinquent, a way must be found to modify those aspects of the community life which provide the appropriate setting for delinquency careers and which give to these careers the sanction and approbation on which all social behavior depends.

It may be said, therefore, that the existence of a powerful system of criminal values and relationships in low-income urban areas is the product of a cumulative process extending back into the history of the community and of the city. It is related both to the general character of the urban world and to the fact that the population in these communities has long occupied a disadvantageous position. It has developed in somewhat the same way as have all social traditions, that is, as a means of satisfying certain felt needs within the limits of a particular social and economic framework.

It should be observed that, while the tradition of delinquency and crime is thus a powerful

* Reprinted, with change in order of paragraphs, from *Juvenile Delinquency and Urban Areas*, Chicago, University of Chicago Press, 1942, 446, 440–441. Used by permission of the authors and the publisher. — Ed.

[1] *Personality and the Cultural Pattern* (New York: Commonwealth Fund, 1937), p. 18.

force in certain communities, it is only a part of the community's system of values. As was pointed out previously, the dominant tradition in every community is conventional, even in those having the highest rates of delinquents. The traditionally conventional values are embodied in the family, the church, the school, and many other such institutions and organizations. Since the dominant tradition in the community is conventional, more persons pursue law-abiding careers than careers of delinquency and crime, as might be expected.

In communities occupied by Orientals, even those communities located in the most deteriorated sections of our large cities, the solidarity of Old World cultures and institutions has been preserved to such a marked extent that control of the child is still sufficiently effective to keep at a minimum delinquency and other forms of deviant behavior. As Professor Hayner has pointed out in his chapter on five cities of the Pacific Northwest, the close integration of the oriental family, the feeling of group responsibility for the behavior of the child, and the desire of these groups to maintain a good reputation in American communities have all been important elements in preserving this cultural solidarity.

It is the assumption of this volume that many factors are involved in determining whether a particular child will become involved in delinquency, even in those communities in which a system of delinquent and criminal values exists. Individual and personality differences, as well as differences in family relationships and in contacts with other institutions and groups, no doubt influence greatly his acceptance or rejection of opportunities to engage in delinquent activities. It may be said, however, that if the delinquency tradition were not present and the boys were not thus exposed to it, a preponderance of those who become delinquent in low-income areas would find their satisfactions in activities other than delinquency.

In conclusion, it is not assumed that this theoretical proposition applies to all cases of officially proscribed behavior. It applies primarily to those delinquent activities which become embodied in groups and social organizations. For the most part, these are offenses against property. They comprise a very large proportion of all the cases of boys coming to the attention of the courts.

IMPLICATIONS FOR PREVENTION AND TREATMENT

The theoretical formulation set forth in the preceding pages has certain definite implications with regard to the task of dealing with the problem of delinquency in large American cities. Some of the more important may be stated as follows:

1. Any great reduction in the volume of delinquency in large cities probably will not occur except as general changes take place which effect improvements in the economic and social conditions surrounding children in those areas in which the delinquency rates are relatively high.

2. Individualized methods of treatment probably will not be successful in a sufficiently large number of cases to result in any substantial diminution of the volume of delinquency and crime.

3. Treatment and preventive efforts, if they are to achieve general success, should increasingly take the form of broad programs which seek to utilize more effectively the constructive institutional and human resources available in every local community in the city. Tannenbaum states this point vividly: "The criminal is a product of the community, and his own criminal gang is part of the whole community, natural and logical to it; but it is only part of it. In that lies the hope that the rest of the community can do something with the gang as such."

33

The Neighborhood and Child Conduct*

Henry D. McKay

The introduction of cause-and-effect explanations into the field of children's behavior has thus far brought about only a partial meta-

* Reprinted from 261 *Annals* (1949), 32–41. Used by permission of the author and the publisher.

morphosis in thinking habits. It has long been recognized that the child's attitudes, habits, and mode of life are natural products of his experience, and that not much is gained by blaming him for being a problem. What has happened, however, is that the blame has been transferred. During the past decade or more, the practice of blaming the parents for the misconduct of their children has been very prevalent. Now, in turn, there are some signs that this practice is being challenged, and that some other object of blame is being sought.

This discussion is not an attempt to replace the parents with another scapegoat. The neighborhood is not to be blamed for the misbehavior of youth. Just as first blaming the individual and later the parents proved to be futile, so it would be futile to place the blame elsewhere, because blame is not a concept of science and understanding. Instead, an effort will be made to describe the roles of the neighborhood and leisure-time activity in the whole education and socialization process. In keeping with the subject matter of this issue of The Annals, particular emphasis will be given to the process through which the child becomes a delinquent, and its counterpart, the process through which he is remade into a conventional citizen. For emphasis, in this discussion the neighborhood and leisure-time activities will be considered separately, although it is recognized that they are inseparable parts of the same situation.

THE AREA OF PARTICIPATION

The term "neighborhood" is used here as a general concept to describe the world of the child exclusive of his family on the one hand, and of the radio, newspapers, and other symbols of the larger community on the other. It is essentially the area known to him through participation — it is the area in which he works and plays.

The activities of the child in the neighborhood tend to be organized around basic institutions and groupings such as the church, the school, the playgrounds, and perhaps the movie theater. In addition it may include participation in teams, clubs, or other groups organized on the basis of interests, talents, or accomplishment. Collectively these groups may represent the most meaningful part of the child's social world. The neighborhood of the child includes also institutions and activities in which he does

not participate but with which he is familiar. Thus local lodges, taverns, clubs, and adult sport organizations are part of his world in a very real sense. In many but not all neighborhoods, other institutions and activities, such as picnics, carnivals, fights, weddings, funerals, and celebrations in which persons of all ages participate, are integral parts of the social life.

In short, everything that happens on a groupwise basis constitutes part of the setting for the neighborhood stage on which the drama of socialization and education is played.

The importance of the neighborhood in the conduct of the child is seen most clearly in an examination of the educational process. Formal education outside of the home takes place in the school where the child spends approximately one-sixth of his waking hours. But education in the broad sense goes on continuously, either in the home or in the neighborhood, during the remaining five-sixths of his waking hours. It is with this informal, continuous, educative process that we are primarily concerned here.

The basic task of the school is instruction, but it is involved directly in conduct problems also. If the school is well integrated in the neighborhood life, if the values of the teachers coincide with the values of the parents, and if there are no status or communication barriers between teachers and pupils, the effect of the school in the area of moral instruction may be very great. But if there is a cleavage between the school and the neighborhood, and if teachers exhibit attitudes of superiority or intolerance, the influence of the school upon individuals or on the moral tone of the neighborhood is greatly reduced.

Even when the school is effective, a large part of the child's moral education is acquired outside its walls; and when it is ineffective, the role of the informal and noninstitutional aspects of neighborhood life in the educational program is proportionately greater. In this situation the child takes over whatever the neighborhood has to offer — its traditional leisure-time activities, its standards of sportsmanship, its characteristic way of expressing anger, pleasure, or hostility, its philosophy of life, its moral codes, and its language. These come not only from the institutions in which the child participates directly, but also from his vicarious participation in all the activities which the neighborhood encourages or tolerates.

It is not possible to evaluate precisely the relative importance, in the education of the child, of the influence of the neighborhood on the one hand, and the influence of movies, radio, printed matter, and other contacts with the world outside of the neighborhood on the other. Each is part of his world and each must have some influence. But it is felt that the personal contact and participation in the neighborhood groups make neighborhood education more dynamic and significant than the education which is acquired more indirectly from the outside.

As a result of the relatively large amount of time spent at the movies, listening to serials or murder mysteries on the radio, or reading comic books, the modern child can imitate a machine gun, shoot or be shot with appropriate histrionics, anticipate the plots of murder mysteries, or play the role of superman. But there is reason to believe that these are just forms of play, without much meaning or significance in the formation of conduct patterns. Basic attitudes and values, it is felt, are not effectively transmitted through these more impersonal media of communication.

IMPORTANCE OF THE PLAY GROUP

On the other hand, it is known that attitudes and values are transmitted effectively through the personal relationships of the play group. Impersonal communication must depend upon abstract symbols, but direct personal communication is augmented by the immediate sensory impressions of four of the five senses. Moreover, the communication of the personal groups has emotional overtones which arise out of identification with the group, and the communication of meanings is facilitated by the successive responses of each person to each of the other participating persons. And it is just because this communication is so effective that the group is so important in the educational process.

The play group, in addition, is able to enforce conformity. Its sanction is more openly sought, and its disapprobation more carefully avoided, than is that of other groups. The family may decide how the child shall dress, but the verdict on whether the form of dress is satisfactory depends upon play-group reaction. The accepted standards in speech, clothing,

manners, relationships with the other sex, and entertainment, all are decided by this same group. If these decisions do not coincide with those of the home, the church, and the school, the resulting conflict often reveals that the sanction of the play group is more important to the child than is the sanction of any other group or institution. When this is true, the conventional neighborhood institutions may find that they are relatively ineffective in their efforts to regulate conduct.

NEIGHBORHOOD TYPES AND DELINQUENCY RATES

Since the child reflects the influences of the neighborhood, it follows that if there are differences in the adequacy of neighborhoods, these differences should be reflected in variations in rates of law violations. Or, stated conversely, variations in rates of law violations should indicate discernible differences among neighborhoods or areas. The data on the number of juvenile offenders are so variable that valid comparisons cannot be made between rates for rural and urban areas or among cities, but within the same judicial area or city, defensible comparisons can be and have been made.

Rates of official delinquents based on several different kinds of indexes vary widely among areas in Chicago and other large American cities.[1] Every city has its sections where the rates of delinquents are high and its sections where the rates are low, with the areas of intermediate rates spread out over the wide range between these two extremes. Rates of school truants, young adult and adult offenders, and female offenders, all are distributed about the same as rates of delinquents. Likewise, studies of rates for widely separated periods of time indicate that areas of high rates tend to remain areas of high rates, and vice versa.

Studies of areas within the city reveal also that the distribution of other community problems resembles the distribution of delinquents. The areas of high rates of delinquents also are the areas of highest rates of morbidity, infant mortality, mortality, dependency, and physical deterioration. And the areas of highest rates in one city have external characteristics in com-

---

[1] See Clifford R. Shaw and Henry D. McKay, *Juvenile Delinquency and Urban Areas*, Chicago: University of Chicago Press, 1942.

mon with areas of high rates in other cities. There is little question that rates of delinquents vary with types of neighborhood situations.

The only other possibility would be the association of high rates of delinquents with particular nativity, nationality, or racial groups. Studies in Chicago have revealed, however, that the variations in rates among areas within nativity, nationality, or racial groups are as great as the variations in total rates. Moreover, in the same types of areas the different groups have approximately the same rates. This point is further reinforced by the fact that in Chicago different nationality and nativity groups have succeeded one another in the areas of high rates of delinquents without any appreciable change in the relative magnitude of the rates. Thus it appears that nativity or nationality does not explain the difference in rates among areas, and that the social life of the neighborhood should be examined in somewhat greater detail.

Conflicting Values

Areas of high rates of delinquents are areas of conflicting values — areas in which alternative educational processes are in operation. Part of the social life with which the child comes in contact is conventional and part of it is non-conventional. The result is that he may be educated in either or in both of these lines of activity. This is described by Sutherland as differential participation in conventional and non-conventional group activities.

An adequate explanation for the lack of consensus in the areas of high rates of delinquents is not easily found. The problem is: Under what conditions do alternative value systems come into existence in an area, and why are they not driven out by groups representing the dominant conventional values? It is suggested here that these alternative values arise most frequently in the struggle for position or status where the institutional organization is inadequate. If the institutional arrangements were completely adequate, the competition and conflicts through which persons and groups establish their status would be regularized. But in the absence of such adequacy, alternative devices for making a living and for getting ahead develop and are tolerated. A few of the conditions which seem to be favorable for such developments will be discussed briefly.

The alternative devices for the acceleration

of the process of upward mobility outside of the traditional institutional arrangements have been developed most openly in the areas of low economic status in large cities. But many elements common to other types of situations are involved in the process. Among them are the traditions of a fluid status structure in which the possession of material goods is the symbol of power and prestige; free competition for the acquisition of goods; the weakening of traditional controls through the organization of society on an impersonal basis; and the presence of obstacles to the acquisition of the technical skills or education which are so important in the status struggle. Implicit also in our literature, radio programs, and advertising is the assumption that all persons have access to the luxury pattern of life, and that if the person does not have access he is being deprived of what he justly deserves. It is when these elements are coupled with the institutional weakness of inner city areas that the competitive process is most likely to take on new forms. And where it does take alternative illegal forms, the child is exposed to illegal modes of behavior.

Leisure-Time Problem

Another element which complicates the education of the child in the neighborhood of high rates of delinquents is the problem of leisure time. In the Old World or in rural America the leisure-time problem for children was not serious because the child was part of the economy. He did his share of the family work and by so doing earned his share of the family income. But in the city he is not part of the income-earning group, and as a result he is free from income-procuring activity a large proportion of the time.

Since the problem did not exist before arrival in the city, no institutional forms were brought by the groups in the inner city areas to meet these particular needs. Likewise, the city has not developed adequate institutions for this purpose, since the large city in America is itself comparatively new. The result has been that children, especially boys, do not have any meaningful or acceptable way of employing their leisure time. And in gaining leisure time they have lost the devices through which, historically, they have established themselves in the neighborhood. Children now have freedom, but they are not important in the economy. As the late Professor Reuter has pointed out, the lack of any real function leaves the urban adolescents in a position of tolerated parasitism.[2]

INDIGENOUS INSTITUTIONS

In this situation where the traditional institutional arrangements do not control the status struggle or provide for the needs of young people, new native or indigenous institutions come into existence. Some of these institutions are conventional and some are either criminal or quasi criminal. Examples of the former are ethnic group organizations and social-athletic clubs. The ethnic group organizations are concerned both with welfare problems in the narrower sense and with efforts to improve the position of the group in the total society. Social-athletic clubs, it would seem, are perfect illustrations of natural institutions which have arisen to meet the social and recreational needs of young men in the inner areas of large cities.

Examples of nonconventional institutions are organized crime (often designated as the syndicate) and delinquent boys' gangs. The power and prestige of the former guarantees that the boys in the area of operation will have access, in their education, to knowledge of this mode of getting on in the world. The presence of the delinquent gang means in addition that some boys will have an opportunity to participate in illegal activities. Delinquent gangs, as differentiated from play groups, encompass only some of the boys in a neighborhood; none of the boys can escape the influence of the presence of adult organized crime.

The other type of institution which comes into existence in the areas where the institutional arrangements are inadequate are the superimposed or nonindigenous welfare institutions such as boys' clubs or social settlements. These can be distinguished from local institutions by the fact that they are developed, controlled, operated, and financed largely from outside the neighborhood. It is quite clear that the addition of these institutions on the side of conventionality has not materially reduced the operation of illegal or quasi-legal devices for making a living, nor has it resulted in the child's

being insulated or protected from these influences. Gangs prosper in the very shadow of these institutions, and rates of delinquents continue to be high in spite of efforts to reduce them.

When examined from the point of view of the education of the child in the neighborhood, however, these nonindigenous institutions could hardly be expected to bring about important changes. Their number is small in the total number of neighborhood institutions, and participation in their activities represents only a segment of the child's total participation in the life of the neighborhood. Moreover, these institutions have the disadvantage of being "foreign" to the area where they are located, with all that is implied by that term. Although this does not prevent children from engaging in the activities of these institutions, it does reduce their value for the purpose of moral instruction.

RECREATION AND DELINQUENCY COMPARED

As forms of activity, recreation and delinquency have many qualities in common. In its early stages, delinquency is clearly a form of play. It is easy to see that running away from home, stealing pies from a pie wagon, or driving a stolen car may satisfy some of the basic needs or desires that are satisfied conventionally by baseball, pleasure riding, or going on a camping trip. In fact, it is easy to see that for those involved in them, many forms of delinquency, although costly to the community, may satisfy more of the immediate needs and wishes of children than are satisfied by more conventional forms of recreation. And this competition between the two types of activity is further complicated if the delinquency becomes financially profitable.

Both delinquency and recreation are essentially group activities. Each can be participated in alone, but in the more prevalent and meaningful forms, two or more persons usually are involved. Each type of activity has a tradition. Children's groups are the recipients and bearers of tradition governing rules, regulations, and mode of play of a great variety of games and means of entertainment, ranging from the rhymes which are sung while skipping rope to the techniques for playing third base. Similarly, in those neighborhoods where there are delin-

[2] E. B. Reuter, "The Sociology of Adolescence," *American Journal of Sociology*, Vol. 43 (Nov. 1937), pp. 414–427.

quent groups, the members are the recipients and bearers of a tradition on such subjects as how to break into a car, shoplift from a store, or avoid a policeman. The latter groups may be the recipients, also, of the conventional traditions.

In spite of these similarities, from the point of view of the larger community, these two forms of group activity are widely different. One is destructive, the other is constructive; one is dangerous, the other is desirable; one is law violation, the other is recreation. Even random play-group activity, which in its beginnings is inherently neither delinquent nor recreational, becomes one or the other in terms of whether or not the culmination of the activity is acceptable to the community. Thus a visit to an old house may be defined as an adventure; but if there is destruction it may be defined as law violation. In this connection it should be noted that the likelihood that random behavior will become destructive or malicious probably varies with the extent to which the neighborhood has provided for the needs of children along conventional lines.

Not only are recreation and delinquency both group activities, but in areas of high rates of delinquents the groups resemble each other in terms of physical characteristics, mental abilities, economic status, and family situations. Both delinquent and play groups have in their membership large boys and small boys, smart boys and dull boys, boys from broken homes and boys from integrated homes, and boys from families economically deprived and boys from families economically self-sufficient. In fact, with reference to these and similar characteristics, both kinds of groups are cross sections of the membership of the neighborhoods from which they are drawn.

The importance of this point is that there is no inherent reason why one group engages in delinquent activity and the other in recreation. The delinquent boys might just as well be limiting their activities to conventional games, and vice versa. The important variable is to be found, not in the boys, but in the variations in the educational process in the neighborhood. Of course after habits of delinquency have been established, it may not be easy to substitute less exhilarating conventional activities. It is not easy to satisfy a champagne taste with Coca-Cola.

ORGANIZED RECREATION NOT A PREVENTIVE

If the rate of delinquency in an area is high, often it is assumed that there is a dearth of organized recreation, and that if more organized recreation were introduced, the rate of delinquents would show a reduction. Probably neither one of these propositions is completely valid. They are true to the extent that a child engaging in organized recreation cannot at the same time be involved in delinquency. They are false to the extent that it is assumed that participation in organized recreation makes it unlikely that the child will engage in delinquency.

Organized recreation and delinquency are not mutually exclusive activities. In the summary of the findings of a study of recreation and delinquency in Chicago the following proposition is set forth: "In all of the areas studied, of those children who took part in recreation activities, delinquent boys spent more time in such activities than did nondelinquent boys."[3] These findings based on five areas in Chicago may or may not hold true for all of Chicago or for other cities, but they do establish, at least, that participation in one of these types of activity does not preclude participation in the other.

Another reason why recreation programs will not, by themselves, prevent delinquency is that participation in organized recreation represents such a small proportion of the total life experience of the child. In the study just mentioned, it was pointed out that during any one three-month season, between one-third and one-half of the recreation participants took part in supervised programs for less than ten hours, that a smaller proportion of boys over fourteen years took part in such activities, and that twice as much time was spent by boys in the movies as in supervised recreational activities. Thus it is clear that even for those who do participate, organized recreation consumes but a small part of their total leisure time.

The fact that organized recreation does not eliminate delinquency has little to do with its value. It is suggested here that it is a mistake to attempt to justify recreation in terms of delinquency or any other such activity. Actually,

---

[3] Ethel Shanas, "Recreation and Delinquency," Chicago Recreation Commission, 1942.

recreation needs no such justification. A chance to engage in leisure-time activities through which energies and creative urges are satisfied and which are not harmful to the neighborhood should be the heritage of every child, regardless of where he lives. Moreover, play has a defensible role in the socialization process. To suggest, however, that a boy will not be delinquent because he plays ball is no more valid than to say that he will not play ball because he is delinquent. He may do either, neither, or both.

Basis of Prevention Programs

Implicit or explicit in every program for the prevention of delinquency is some conception of the nature of the problems. Thus, if delinquency were assumed to be caused by mosquitoes, the prevention program would be mosquito abatement; or if the cause were assumed to be inadequate diets, the treatment program would be diet improvement. By the same logic, if it is assumed that the delinquent is a neighborhood product, a program of prevention must be related to the life of the neighborhood.

Prevention means that something is kept from happening which might otherwise have happened. As applied to delinquency in the community, this means that the probability of education for delinquency must be reduced or eliminated, and that the probability of education for conventional behavior must be increased. In some neighborhoods, where the rates of delinquents are low, education for accepted behavior need only be maintained; but in other areas, where rates of delinquents are high, some characteristics of the neighborhood must actually be changed.

Real achievement in this direction involves several kinds of endeavors. The first is the recognition of the need for the satisfaction of human needs and desires within the framework of conventional life. If the institutions and organizations are not available for this purpose, prevention may require their development. Another necessary step is the elimination of conflicting elements in the neighborhood. If delinquency is to be prevented, alternatives to conventional behavior cannot be tolerated. As was indicated earlier, organized crime, delinquent gangs, fences, and other illegal or quasi-legal activities are indications that the child is being subjected to alternative systems of values. It is evident that the influence of these alternatives must be reduced if delinquency is to be prevented.

Another kind of conflict which makes for appearance in court, if not for actual delinquency, is the conflict between the court and the local community in the way behavior is defined. If children are taken to court for engaging in practices which are tolerated or considered to be acceptable in the local neighborhood, they are the victims of such conflicts. Shoeshining, junking, and picking up coal along the railroad are examples of the types of behavior which the neighborhood may endorse, but which the police and the court, representing the attitudes of the wider community, may define as illegal. Attempts to remove or reconcile such variations of definitions are in themselves attempts at prevention.

Stigma of Delinquency

An entirely different kind of prevention program can be directed at a reduction in the number of children defined as problems or as delinquents either by neighborhood action or by experience in legal agencies. Technically a child is a delinquent only when so defined by a court, but he may come to conceive of himself as a delinquent either through official action or by being pointed out as a delinquent in the neighborhood. This neighborhood definition, which may result in ostracism or exclusion from participation, has far-reaching consequences. Surely if it interferes with participation, it interferes with the normal socialization process and also may drive children who are rejected or ostracized into groups which furnish their own sanction and approval for retaliatory acts against the neighborhood.

Similarly, when children are arrested for relatively minor offenses, the treatment accorded them in the police station, the detention home, or the court may provide the basis for their coming to conceive of themselves as offenders or as delinquents. From this point of view it may be seen that neighborhood reaction or the action of neighborhood or community officials may be part of the process through which the minor offender is made into a delinquent. Thus efforts to prevent misbehavior may be the efforts through which it is created.

Prevention of delinquency, so conceived, would involve such action or restraint from action in the neighborhood as would keep children from being defined as problems or delinquents. Keeping good little boys from playing with Johnny, the bad boy, may be justified from the point of view of righteous citizens, but it is also part of the process through which Johnny is cast permanently in the role of a bad boy. Similarly, calling the police and sending boys to the station because they have been playing ball in the streets may be the beginning of the process through which they may become real offenders.

TREATMENT

Effective treatment means that the offender who has been devalued, ostracized, or incarcerated, must be helped to establish himself in a satisfactory role in the conventional community. This proposition has few exceptions; for if the offender is not re-established in conventional activity, it is probable that once more he will re-establish himself in the world of the delinquent. The alternative is that temporarily he may belong to some groups in both the delinquent and the conventional world without being fully incorporated into either. Such a person is a potential candidate for either conventionality or delinquency, and, as such, is a good subject for treatment.

This fact brings to the foreground the dilemma of treatment. It is: How can the society which casts out the offender because he has violated its laws be induced to accept him again for the purpose of treatment? "Casting out" the offender, either actually or symbolically, has been accepted practice throughout the written history of man. At the present time with juveniles our "casting out" usually takes the form of a sentence to a training school, followed by a period during which the offender is designated either as a delinquent or as a criminal and treated with suspicion and hostility both by the ordinary citizen and by our representatives of the law and order. Yet as a logical proposition this offender must be reincorporated into conventional groups before it can be said that he has been successfully treated. Therein lies the problem.

Treatment, like prevention, must be formulated with reference to a theory of causation. If it is assumed that delinquency and crime are products of education in situations where there are alternative systems of values and ways of getting ahead in the world, then treatment involves getting the person to be treated to accept the values and mode of life of the conventional group. This must be accomplished either in opposition to the conflicting values or through their elimination.

Treatment programs not involving major changes in the community include attempts to introduce nondelinquent types of activity into the delinquent groups and attempts to induce the offenders being treated into conventional groups. The process is facilitated through the use of persons of prestige in the world of the offender, and it is encouraged by sympathetic understanding and the avoidance of evidence of moral indignation or recrimination. Only when the person has been incorporated into conventional groups long enough to have experienced a re-education in terms of conventional values can the treatment be said to have been complete. Such a program applies, of course, to children who are physically and mentally normal.

Finally, neighborhood treatment, like prevention, is more likely to succeed if the opportunities for participation in delinquent activities are reduced and the opportunities for satisfactory participation in conventional activities are increased. This cannot be accomplished by enacting harsher laws or selecting a new chief of police. It might come, however, from neighborhood action. If illegal activities meet with organized neighborhood opposition they may be driven out or closed. Likewise, organized activity on the part of adults may strengthen the conventional aspects of neighborhood life both through participation in constructive neighborhood activities and through the stimulation of such goals. To the extent that these activities create consensus and uniform values, they are changing the community and increasing the probability that the offender will be re-educated in terms of conventional conduct.

RECAPITULATION

The neighborhood furnishes the setting in which the child is educated either for conventional or for delinquent behavior. If the values of the neighborhood are consistent, this consistency is likely to be reflected in conventional behavior. If, however, conventional institutions are not completely adequate, and illegal institutions and activities develop and persist in the neighborhood, the conflict of values is likely to be reflected in high rates of violation of the conduct norms. Such neighborhoods are found in the inner areas of large cities.

Both recreation and delinquency are group activities, and although one is legal and the other illegal, both satisfy many of the same basic needs in the child. Recreation is not a cure for delinquency, although it can be defended in its own right as a socializing agency. Delinquency prevention involves the elimination of conflicting values from the neighborhood and the protection of the child from definition as a delinquent. Successful treatment of delinquents necessitates the reincorporation of the offender into conventional groups. Such a program clearly requires some type of neighborhood action.

34

Secondary Community Influences and Juvenile Delinquency*

Marshall B. Clinard

Despite the fact that there is increasing evidence to link the problem of the juvenile with the adult world through the larger community in which both juveniles and adults participate in the standards of the culture as a whole, many writers in the field persist in regarding the delinquent as a product almost exclusively of personal maladjustment. The delinquency of the juvenile is explained with little reference to the social and cultural realities or to the fact that there are indications of widespread social disorganization in the general adult society.

Most of those with this belief write of maladjusted personality traits.[1] and a few who are Freudian psychoanalysts invent a mystical world of innate animal drives, Oedipus and various other guilt complexes to explain the delinquent. Others tend to look chiefly at the family as though it were the sole source of value judgments. Still additional writers seem to concentrate their analyses, with much more validity, on the boys' associates to the exclusion of the larger outside world, either in the form of the neighborhood in which the gang functions or, in turn, the over-all society and culture whose standards are reflected and found in the behavior of the family, the gang, and the neighborhood.

THE POINT OF ATTACK

The results of such one-sided emphases are seen in the panaceas that are recommended. Those who look at the individual personality believe that testing and clinical guidance programs in our schools should be stressed. Many stress more and better psychiatrists, psychoanalysts, and psychologists who, by diagnosing and treating the deviations and stresses and strains of youth, will put them soundly on the road to social health. Some who regard the family as the basic cause stress family training and counseling, while the more radical believe that the parents should be punished. Those who see the nexus of the problem in the boys gang believe that organized recreation and the diverting of the delinquent group into more acceptable social patterns will offer a complete solution. Co-ordinating councils and neighborhood councils have been offered in turn as the most adequate means of dealing with problems of delinquency at the neighborhood level.[2]

While the evidence seems to indicate that the neighborhood, particularly in more socially deteriorated areas, is a more logical basis for an attack on delinquency, it is well for us not to

* Reprinted from 261 Annals (1949), 42–54. Used by permission of the author and the publisher. For an assessment of the contribution of sociology to criminology, see, also, M. B. Clinard, "Sociologists and American Criminology," 41 J. Crim. L. and Criminology (1950–51), 549–577. See, also, "The Climate of Justice," Chapter I of S. Glueck, Crime and Justice, Boston, Little, Brown & Company, 1936; Cambridge, Harvard University Press, 1945. — Ed.

[1] For a recent example of this approach see Maud A. Merrill, Problems of Child Delinquency, Boston: Houghton Mifflin Co., 1947.

[2] One recent volume, while partially recognizing other influences, is built almost entirely around institutional changes as well as this theme as the solution to delinquency. See John R. Ellingston, Protecting Our Children from Criminal Careers, New York: Prentice-Hall, Inc., 1948.

confine our efforts solely in this direction.[3] The larger society, as it impinges on the community and also upon the adult and the juvenile alike, must be dealt with in any realistic analysis of juvenile delinquency. Moreover, the attempt to draw a line between the world of juveniles and young adults (as seen in the current enthusiasm for Youth Correction Authorities) and the larger adult world is theoretically indefensible, for both secure their values within the social framework of our culture. In fact, such a position of separating the behavior of certain age groups from that of others resembles the attempt of persons formerly to see only problems of the individual rather than of society.[4]

In general, secondary influences such as the police, judges and penal institutions, the schools, the newspapers, the movies, radio programs, and comic books are largely administered or controlled by forces outside the immediate local community or neighborhood. To evaluate and deal effectively with these secondary influences [5] requires a much broader perspective than the family, the gang, or the immediate neighborhood. In fact, the behavior of almost the entire adult world, whether in the neighborhood or not, constitutes a moral hazard to the juvenile.[6]

POLICE, COURTS, AND PENAL INSTITUTIONS [7]

Numerous studies have indicated that the police and other agencies of law enforcement

constitute, in many communities, one of the chief moral hazards to both juveniles and adults. It is doubtful, however, that in terms of typical adult standards, such agencies are any different from what the public deserves. The employment of police personnel and the election of judges who in no way exemplify the type of conduct required of juveniles add both directly and indirectly to the production of delinquency. A great many police officers, both urban and rural, are still political appointees, intellectually unfit, inefficient, frequently willing to accept bribes even from juveniles, and brutal in making arrests and securing evidence, whether of juveniles or adults.[8] Their attitude is not one to encourage respect for law or to aid in the rehabilitation of the juvenile.

Similarly, many judges do not deserve the respect of juveniles, for both their attitude on the bench and the general demeanor of the courtroom seem to indicate a lack of understanding. This is understandable when we realize that neither law schools nor the legal system itself provides adequate, if any, training for juvenile rehabilitation work by jurists. The fact that a middle-class jurist has children of his own does not necessarily provide him with an adequate comprehension of juvenile delinquency problems. Experience achieved by mistakes made in dealing with innumerable delinquents is a process costly to society.

Recently a police judge in Newark, for example, pleaded guilty to stealing over $630,000 through a rigged-up series of fictitious mortgages. The money was used to cover his losses in horserace bets. The really serious injury to society in this case, as in the many others like it, was the effect such disobedience of law must have had on the majority of potential delinquents or those already delinquent residing not only in Newark but perhaps elsewhere.

The failure in most communities to provide separate juvenile detention facilities of an acceptable type and the tendency to incarcerate juveniles with adults in our local jails represent a serious hazard to any juvenile placed in

---

[3] One study that has recognized this interrelationship of the local community and the outside world is William F. Whyte, *Street Corner Society*, Chicago: University of Chicago Press, 1943.

[4] No better refutation of this separation has been made, nor a clearer statement of the relation of culture and personality, than that by Lawrence K. Frank, *Society as the Patient*, New Brunswick: Rutgers University Press, 1948.

[5] The term is employed here to refer to influences which are impersonal, nonintimate, and categoric in nature. It is recognized that in some instances these influences may be primary and personal. In general, they can be distinguished from the family, companions, the gang, and the intimate neighborhood.

[6] The discussion here, due to space limitations, centers on the negative, disorganizing aspects of secondary contacts. In each instance there are usually some positive, organizing forces in operation, as, for example, the work of trained juvenile officers specializing in preventive work.

[7] The term "penal" is employed deliberately, for few such institutions today are correctional with no regard to punishment.

[8] See, for example, John L. Gillin, *Criminology and Penology* (3d ed., New York: D. Appleton-Century Co., 1945), pp. 268–74. It is recognized that these relationships are not always secondary, but may be intimate and personal. Moreover, the local community may not only tolerate but may sometimes support this behavior.

them. Our jails are one of the most disgraceful aspects of our society, most of them being unable to receive a satisfactory evaluation in terms of minimum human welfare standards from state or Federal inspectors.[9] It is fortunate that our Nation is not judged by its jails and by its treatment of the tens of thousands of juveniles incarcerated in them. Although not affecting as large a number, the so-called boys and girls schools for delinquents are, for the most part, little more than junior prisons, and the boys who enter leave marked as much by its education in crime and by the stigma of society as any criminal released from a penal institution.

All these agencies, police courts and penal institutions, are still largely staffed with untrained persons, filled with prejudice and folk knowledge. The evidence is so overwhelming on all these scores that social scientists are frequently faced with the dilemma of either delinquency unapprehended and untreated or delinquency apprehended but made worse by the social situation of arrest and incarceration. The public must sometime come to the conclusion that all persons dealing with human beings in a preventive or corrective capacity must be trained in the social sciences, whether they be police, judges, or correctional officers, as otherwise they frequently constitute a menace to juveniles. Such training is now chiefly in techniques of criminal identification and apprehension, in the technicalities of the law, or in custodial care which too often emphasizes confinement, at the same time sacrificing rehabilitative treatment.

The School and Truancy

It is a curious commentary on our modern world, which emphasizes education, that the school is a large contributing factor in delinquency. Truancy, for example, constitutes a considerable proportion of delinquency in itself, and if we recognize that it in turn is related to stealing and sex delinquency, it becomes even more important.[10] By definition, truancy implies that school is an unsatisfactory experience.

Schools are generally not operated with the purpose of developing interested, creative minds with some degree of individuality. Most professional educators would agree that in reality schools are places where juveniles, during a process of several hours a day, are routinized, bored, crushed in their individuality, and thrown into needless competition with others rather than aided in the development of co-operation.[11] The preoccupation with competitive grades, beginning at the first grade, is illustrative of this.

Many schools are staffed by persons who inspire neither creative intelligence nor respect for the values of our society. The influences of the school and the teacher may sometimes be personal, but in general, at least in many urban areas, they are secondary, nonintimate, and categoric.

The school situation is a social situation; and the learning process takes place in a situation of personal interaction. Not a few of those selected to educate the young are themselves maladjusted, teaching being, if anything, a neurotic adjustment to life. Wickman demonstrated that those behavior elements which the majority of our teachers feared most were precisely those regarded by mental hygiene experts as least likely to result in behavior disorders.[12] But our teachers act as if their fears were well founded; and the inquisitive, creative student is silenced by the demands for obedience. It is no wonder that part of the function of juvenile gangs engaging in delinquency is to furnish new experience, the thrill of the cleverly executed act of vandalism or auto theft.

The Newspaper

The style and contents of many newspaper stories represent a continual glorification of and preoccupation with crime, the delinquent, and the criminal. By continually playing up crime it is likely that newspapers are important in making us a crime-centered culture. They make crime seem probably more frequent than it is. The treatment is such as to imply adventure and excitement, and in many cases indirectly the

---

[9] U. S. Department of Justice, Bureau of Prisons, *Federal Prisons: 1944*, p. 87. Also see Merrill Conover, "Children in Jail," *The Child*, Vol. 7, No. 10, April 1943.

[10] Walter C. Reckless and Mapheus Smith, *Juvenile Delinquency* (New York: McGraw-Hill Book Co., 1932), pp. 174-76.

[11] "Education for Our Time," Special issue of *Survey Graphic*, XXXVI, Nov. 1947.

[12] E. K. Wickman, *Children's Behavior and Teacher's Attitudes*, New York: The Commonwealth Fund, 1928. See also F. V. Mason, "A Study of Seven Hundred Maladjusted School Teachers," *Mental Hygiene*, Vol. 15 (1931), p. 579.

glorification of the criminal participant is achieved. Pictures and stories of juveniles and criminals apprehended in crime give publicity and status; perhaps to some juveniles these resemble the folk tales of frontier bad men. They provide vicariously emotional thrills not provided by home or school. In some the vicarious becomes the real. The newspapers also furnish knowledge of techniques of committing crime, although this is probably not too important.

Unusual events are newsworthy and gain ready access to the printed page, for the urban American reader is little concerned with the ordinary happenings in everyday life. Only the unusual, the different, the new, can attract his attention. He dotes on war, rape, murder, crime. The breaking of the law is an event that can capture reader interest. The amount and prominence of space devoted to crime in the newspapers, and the amount of conversation based on these stories, must present a bewildering picture of immorality even to a delinquent child.

Though the line is difficult to draw, there is a difference between reporting verifiable facts about an event, such as crime, and loading the story with emotionally charged words that convey to the reader but one impression.[13] Crime is given a specific prominence in our newspapers through the amount of space given its reporting, as well as through the position of the news stories on the front page. The total percentage of crime stories is not an adequate basis for comparison, for the front page sells the paper. Even a juvenile on his way to the comic section of the paper cannot help noticing front-page crime stories and pictures. If he misses them there, he is sure to hear them included in the dinner-table conversation.

Under the guise of supplying what the reader demands, crime is not merely made prominent, but is supplied to the reader in colorful exposition and frequently with on-the-scene lurid photographs.[14] A person is not merely murdered or slain, he is brutally slain with a blunt instrument. The suspect does not merely attempt to escape capture; the desperate killer, his cunning

increased by his emotional stimulation, gives the inept police a terrific run for their money.

There is general indifference in newspapers to the serious moral implication of the offense or to the necessity for bulwarking society against such behavior. Admittedly, this statement raises the problem of the function of the newspapers. On the one hand, the conception of "free enterprise" condones the collection of sordid tales as a valuable vehicle for selling advertisements; on the other, the conception of social responsibility suggests that these newspapers should be re-evaluated in terms of the role they play in determining human behavior.

Unfortunately, the actual effect of the newspaper on delinquency, while giving an impression of a crime-centered society, has not been accurately ascertained. Probably the crime emphasis has only a minor direct influence, for considerable delinquency starts before the reading of newspapers, other than comics, becomes frequent. While not conclusive, William Healy, some twenty-five years ago, after studying one thousand delinquents, reported:

> In no one single case can we in the least show that the reading of newspapers was a strong cause of criminality. We have inquired about mental influence in many hundreds of cases, and, while other factors stand out clearly as affecting mental processes, this one does not.[15]

Like the motion picture and the radio, the important influence of newspapers is that they furnish rationalizations for deviant conduct learned in the gang or by other personal associations. This is not to underestimate the importance of the newspaper in making some positive contributions to crime control. The point to be made here is that crime stories both reflect and further influence the general culture. It is hoped that the newspaper may be able to develop sufficient professional ethics to compromise the desire to sell more papers for profit by playing up crime stories, and recognize the interests of the general public welfare which is now of secondary importance in this connection.

MOTION PICTURES, RADIO, AND COMIC BOOKS

The great interest of juveniles in motion pictures, the radio, and comic books has caused

---

[13] Kimball Young, *Social Psychology* (2d ed., New York: F. S. Croft & Co., 1944), pp. 460–80.
[14] Lawrence G. Brown, *Social Pathology* (New York: F. S. Croft & Co., 1942), Chap. XXXII, "The Press in Social Disorganization."

[15] William Healy, *The Individual Delinquent* (Boston: Little, Brown and Co., 1920), p. 302.

some persons to overestimate their importance, while others in their explanations of delinquency tend to discount them. It is conceivable that were all three media to disappear from our culture, we would still probably have almost as much delinquency. Certainly we had delinquency and crime before any of the three were considered of consequence. Yet today there is a great wave of public indignation against so-called and misnamed "comic" books for their emphasis on the morbid aspects of life and particularly on their vicious crime content.[16] It is reported that nearly fifty cities have taken steps to ban objectionable comic books. The same acute public interest was and still is to a less degree centered on the crime stories on the radio and before that on the motion picture, and if we go still further back, on dime novels.

All these entertainment forms probably have some effect, with the motion picture, due to its visual imagery, probably having the most.[17] There is no question that the motion picture often presents a version of our culture emphasizing wealth, materialism, and immoral conduct, both crime and sex, which, as far as juveniles are considered, furnishes to them approved models conducive to delinquency. Research indicates that while both delinquents and nondelinquents attend the movies, the delinquents attend more often and exhibit greater interest in them. In some recent studies marked differences were noted between delinquents and their control groups in this regard. While this may have significant implications,[18] yet careful additional study would be required to ascertain them. The radio, the motion picture, and comic books tend, on the whole, to glorify the criminal or immoral girl.[19] All three offer knowledge of techniques of how to execute crime or delinquency.

It has long been noted by both lay and professional publics that the growing child needs an outlet for imaginative thinking. In answer to accusations of the harmful effects of the radio thrill drama and the sordid comic books, some people are prone to point out that a generation ago the children acted out much the same roles in a play world, and the radio and the comic book, it is alleged, give a vicarious experience in these comparable situations. One need, however, only observe children listening to or reading such stories to note a significant difference. The child listening to the exploits of his favorite hero can only sit and squirm as his emotional tensions are aroused, for in guiding his imaginative process along perilous routes and all sorts of dangers the radio program leaves the juvenile's tensions unsolved. It is conceivable that overt physical activity of a delinquent type may result in some cases, provided there is a prior pattern of deviant behavior.

Limited Influence. A realistic appraisal of these forms of entertainment indicates that while there are cases in which they may be important, on the whole their direct influence on the juvenile is either almost nil or serves only to aggravate already existent attitudes and personality traits.[20] Blumer and Hauser found in their study of some fifteen years ago, which is still our chief source of information, that motion pictures were one of the factors that was important in only about one out of ten of the delinquent males and one out of four girls.[21]

Present evidence seems to indicate that the process of acquiring conduct norms, both deviant and conventional, is primarily through intimate association with others and personal experiences of a face-to-face nature. Delinquents who have already had differential association through companions with deviant norms may be further stimulated by bad motion pictures, by certain radio programs, or by comic books. In his study of 1,313 gangs in Chicago, Thrasher found that comic strips influenced these groups and their activities. Not only did many of the gangs obtain their names from the comic strip, but suggestions for vandalism and other destruc-

---

[16] A psychiatrist has recently stated that he feels that "comic" books produce a great deal of serious delinquency. Frederic Wertham, "The Comics — Very Funny!" *The Saturday Review of Literature,* May 29, 1948.

[17] It is conceivable that television may sometime compete with the motion picture in furnishing deviant visual imagery.

[18] See Maud A. Merrill, *op. cit.* note 1 *supra,* p. 91. Also see William Healy and Augusta F. Bronner, *New Light on Delinquency and Its Treatment* (New Haven: Yale University Press, 1936), p. 72.

[19] Arthur Mann, "The Children's Hour of Crime," *Scribners,* Vol. 93 (May 1933), pp. 313–15.

[20] See also Edwin H. Sutherland, *Principles of Criminology* (4th ed., New York: J. B. Lippincott, 1947), p. 184.

[21] Herbert Blumer and Philip M. Hauser, *Movies, Delinquency and Crime* (New York: Macmillan Co., 1933), p. 198.

tive activities were directly traceable to this source.[22] In fact, such sources may even furnish rationalizations for deviant behavior. Similarly, persons with abnormal psychogenic traits may be morbidly influenced by such media.

It is doubtful that many cases can be found where, even though there was no evidence of prior deviant behavior, it occurred as a result of such contacts of a secondary nature. Much of this material represents a world of impersonal fantasy rather than having personal reality. Nondelinquents are not likely to succumb to such influences, any more than the average adult readers' attitudes are too greatly changed by editorials in newspapers as compared with the opinions of their friends. The problem is chiefly one of differential response.

Lack of Data. In general, we may agree with Reckless in saying:

At any rate, no one would gainsay the fact that agencies of mass impression are carriers of behavior models, culture patterns, and fashions as well as news and propaganda. Because of their growing accessibility to larger and larger audiences, they may soon take their place alongside the family and companions in importance in influencing behavior.[23]

So far, however, there have not been many actual scientific investigations of the influence of such forms of entertainment on juvenile delinquency. Certainly there has been only limited investigation of the millions of nondelinquent juveniles who avidly attend crime movies, listen nightly to several radio broadcasts dealing with criminal cases, and read one or two comic books a week. Children from the upper socioeconomic groups probably have the most of these contacts but also the least delinquency.

This is important because, while many may agree that such media should be censored for political opinions, religious antagonisms, and sometimes sexual display, it is unfair to concentrate on one medium of communication without dealing with the others. In most cases such preoccupation of the public with the menace of, for example, comic books is to release feelings that something should be done.

The public does not wish to face the deeper questions of why juveniles are so interested in such entertainment, because it would involve its own interests in similar material. Likewise it marks a reluctance on the part of the public to deal effectively with basic factors such as general disobedience to law, the presence of disorganizing influences in local neighborhoods, political corruption, and certain emphases in our culture such as materialism and extreme individuality. The question of delinquent boys' gangs is a more important and more difficult immediate problem than the movies, the radio, or comic books; but the public does not wish to assume the local responsibility necessary to attack it. The tendency of the public mind in dealing with social difficulties is to take the easiest course.

OTHER AGENCIES OF MORAL RISK

There is much public discussion but little research on taverns and roadhouses and their relation to delinquency. Reckless has termed places of this type "agencies of moral risk" and has included also poolrooms, pawnshops, junk yards, criminal fences, dens of vice, gambling parlors, and cheap dance halls.[24] While some of them may be located in the immediate neighborhood, some are at considerable distance from it and beyond its immediate control. It is doubtful whether taverns and roadhouses constitute a very serious problem as far as alcoholic beverages are concerned, since these may be secured by other means; but rather they may serve as centers for the dissemination of deviant value systems because of their anonymity and, in the case of roadhouses, freedom from the social control of the family and the neighborhood. This may be the result of the attraction to them of juveniles and adults who previously possess these attitudes, or it may be that the owners of these concerns are themselves persons of ill repute and with an unsavory past. Certainly, while the chief influence of these places is probably impersonal, in the hands of deviant persons their influence may be that of a personal relationship.

Such establishments do perform a function for the juvenile as social gathering places, and by providing recreation varying from pinball machines to dancing. Realistic thinking must rec-

[22] Frederic M. Thrasher, *The Gang* (Chicago: University of Chicago Press, 1927), p. 113.

[23] Walter C. Reckless, *The Etiology of Delinquent and Criminal Behavior* (New York: Social Science Research Council, 1943), p. 42.

[24] *Ibid.*, p. 40.

ognize this fact, and society should closely supervise them and their management or else it must provide alternative social situations. In rural areas as well as many urban areas, it is likely that taverns and roadhouses exert far more influence on the lives of many juveniles and young adults than traditional organizations, including the church.

In a nation-wide rural opinion survey, the question was asked: "Which of the following are doing the greatest harm to young farm people: liquor, tavern dances, gambling, petting?" Some six million farm neighbors were of the opinion that liquor was the most important, and a strong second was tavern dances. Interestingly enough, the opinion of farm youth itself was more lenient toward tavern dances, yet still ranked them second to liquor.[25] Curiously, rural sociology works contain virtually no mention of such agencies. Rather the discussion centers around Four-H clubs and church groups. The author is now engaged in a study of taverns and roadhouses as factors in social disorganization but with potentialities for social reorganization.

THE ADULT WORLD

Studies of peoples living in folk or provincial types of society have so far brought in limited but rather consistent evidence that juvenile delinquency, crime, suicide, chronic alcoholism, and many other forms of disorganization among us, while not nonexistent, are relatively rare.[26] This furnishes considerable but not conclusive evidence that juvenile delinquency is not a product of personal inadequacy. Further evidence has been furnished by studies of disorganization among some people living under varying types of society, such as the Negro or Polish people. Thomas and Znaniecki conducted a monumental study of the Polish people which had, in addition to a theoretical interest, a practical purpose in examining the validity of discriminatory immigration laws. The authors showed clearly that juvenile delinquency, for example, was rare in peasant vil-

lages, moderate in Polish cities, and high in Chicago.[27]

Inconsistent Value Patterns. There are several factors in the patterns of these societies of different types to account for this, including a minimum amount of individualism and impersonality in social relations, which our society stresses, emphasis on kinship, other status values than materialism, and less mobility both spatial and mental. One of the most important factors, however, is the general consistency in their value structure, a relative absence of differential attitudes on basic social relationships among most members of the society.[28] This is not to say that there are no differences, but that these differences are neither numerous nor as pronounced on important questions of conduct.

But what is most important is that either there are not pronounced differences in acceptable conduct between the different age groups in the society, or the society carefully prescribes the behavior and takes it for granted that everyone will eventually assume certain rights and obligations with increasing maturity. In our society, on the other hand, there is great inconsistency between the behavior of a child and of an adult, these differences not being clearly defined as a correlate of age. In fact, as will be indicated shortly, an adult is permitted increasing transgressions of the conduct norms, while juveniles are expected to obey even the ideals.

In many simple societies the situation is reversed, for it is the juveniles that have considerable freedom, whereas the behavior of adults is one of rigid conformity.[29] The inconsistent value patterns of the adult world constitute one of the chief moral hazards to the juvenile in the modern world.

The term "delinquency," in fact, refers to prohibited forms of conduct ranging from behavior ordinarily designated as crime, includ-

---

[25] "The Farmer Speaks," *Successful Farming*, Vol. XXXVII (1939), p. 12.

[26] See particularly references in Robert E. L. Faris, *Social Disorganization*, New York: The Ronald Press, 1948; and for crime, in Walter C. Reckless, *Criminal Behavior*, New York: McGraw-Hill, 1940.

[27] W. I. Thomas and Florian Znaniecki, *The Polish Peasant in Europe and America*, Chicago: University of Chicago Press, 1918.

[28] Robert Redfield, "The Folk Society," *American Journal of Sociology*, Vol. 52 (May 1947), pp. 293–309; Louis Wirth, "Urbanism as a Way of Life," *American Journal of Sociology*, Vol. 44, No. 1 (July 1938), pp. 1–24.

[29] For example, see Margaret Mead, *Coming of Age in Samoa*, New York: William Morrow & Co., Inc., 1928, and the works of Bronislaw Malinowski on the Trobriand Islanders.

ing theft, to such as truancy, being ungovernable or beyond parental control, late hours, malicious mischief and destruction of property, intoxication, gambling, sexual misconduct, and violations of the traffic laws. The relation between the differing degrees of latitude allowed in the behavior norms of the adult world and the juvenile can best be illustrated by the fact that if we were to insist on the same or comparable behavior standards among our adults, neither the police, the jails, nor the courts could possibly deal with the consequent avalanche of cases that would ensue. There are few adults, certainly very few in large urbanized areas, who in their conduct approach the standards set by that ideal for juveniles, the Boy Scout code.

Flagrant law violation. The wholesale flouting of many of these taboos by the general adult population, including labor, farmers, and business and professional men, is self-evident. The Kinsey report, for example, even if the sample were only partially representative, shows that sexual misconduct is both extensive and flagrant among all sections of the adult population.[30] There is considerable indication both from government reports and from a limited number of research studies that there are extensive violations of law not only by adults of the lower socioeconomic groups but among business and professional men and politicians as well.[31]

Crimes committed by the latter groups include the sale of fraudulent securities, black market activities, sale of adulterated and misbranded foods and drugs, violations of the antitrust Federal trade and labor relations laws, fraudulent income tax returns, fee-splitting in medicine, illegal abortions, and bribery. The crimes committed by these groups are both flagrant and willful, and the social and monetary damage to society far exceeds that of ordinary crime. Most important is the damage to general law obedience through violations of laws by white collar criminals, since they occupy positions of trust and public importance.

An illustration of adult noncompliance with law was the flagrant disregard for law by businessmen exhibited in the black market during World War II,[32] in which over half chose to violate the law and in which the government found over 1,000,000 violations and imposed serious penalties upon more than 200,000 businessmen. Although many have failed to see the connection, black market activities for individual material gain, as well as other white collar crimes, are intimately tied up with the problem of juvenile delinquency in our society.

The typical apprehended criminal is usually between 14 and 20 years of age, and over one million juveniles and youths come annually to the attention of the police. The tendency at present is to approach the problem by asking what is wrong with youth and trying to study them without reference to the behavior of the larger social world.

Following the Adult Model. Conversations with many young offenders readily reveal the fact that they do not regard their actions as different from the behavior displayed by many ordinary citizens, politicians, businessmen, and other professional groups. A large number can recite cases they know or have read of in the newspapers. Some perhaps were learned around the dinner table where a father may have bragged about how he defrauded the government either on the black market, his income tax, or some other regulation, Federal or otherwise. It is obviously impossible to rear law-abiding children in a world where their adult models disobey the law.

One may suggest that there is a difference between political and business crimes and the more overt acts that are commonly committed by juveniles. It appears, however, from social-psychological experimentation that children and young adults frequently do not distinguish between similar situations which may appear to an adult as different or as actually representing a distinction in kind.

"Do as I say but not as I do" is an attitude that is responsible for many problems that arise in the

[30] Alfred C. Kinsey, Wardell B. Pomeroy, and Clyde E. Martin, *Sexual Behavior in the Human Male*, Philadelphia: W. B. Saunders Co., 1948.

[31] See any standard textbook in criminology, particularly Edwin H. Sutherland, *Principles of Criminology* (4th ed., Chicago: J. B. Lippincott, 1947), pp. 29–46. Also see his articles, "White Collar Criminality," *American Sociological Review*, Vol. 5 (Feb. 1940), pp. 1–12; and "Crime and Business," *The Annals of the American Academy of Political and Social Science*, Vol. 217 (Sept. 1941), pp. 112–18.

[32] See Marshall B. Clinard, "Criminological Theories of Violations of Wartime Regulations," *American Sociological Review*, Vol. XI, No. 3, June 1946.

lives of teen age boys and girls as they seek to adjust to social relationships. "Don't smoke, don't drink, don't go to night clubs and roadhouses. Don't stay out late, don't be late for appointments, don't choose wrong companions, don't spend too much time at motion picture houses." Don't! Don't! Don't!

However, many of adults who thus attempt to direct the conduct of young people go blithely along in their own behavior practices, giving satisfaction to their immediate urges, prejudices and desires with no regard for the effect of their conduct upon the lives of others.[33]

One might question whether juveniles are familiar with the delinquent or criminal activity of adults. It is true that juveniles may not be actually as aware as an observer might think, but we would still be reasonably safe in assuming that the effect of adult criminality, at least in the form of rationalizations, is considerable. Certainly there was extensive knowledge among all age groups of the existence of a black market. The arrest of police, judges, or prominent politicians for corruption soon reaches the attention of most people, young or old. Criminal behavior in the sports world, especially among leading contenders, becomes common knowledge. And in the case of a juvenile play model, such as the Air Forces, the arrest and conviction of a high-ranking officer such as General Meyers may create a serious moral hazard in the community.

In stating this there is no intention to deny that delinquency, like crime, is primarily the outgrowth of personal association with those having deviant standards, but rather to point out that such delinquency among adults furnishes rationalizations both for the delinquent group and for the individual delinquent, to support, probably unconsciously, their deviant behavior. The conclusion is obvious that no successful program for dealing with delinquency can leave out the larger adult world.[34]

Public attitudes. In addition to the example of law violation, the adult world furnishes juveniles with patterns in the general public attitude toward law obedience and toward the agents of the law, the police.[35] This attitude is either that all laws except those dealing with very serious offenses should be violated if one can get away with it, or that laws should be selectively obeyed according to one's interests. The first can be seen in the public attitude toward intoxication, taxes, gambling, traffic law, and general disorderly conduct. The second can be seen in the selective obedience to laws by labor, business, and the farmer. Laws governing labor, such as injunctions against strikes or the prohibition of violence in picketing, can be violated by labor; laws governing the conduct of commerce, ranging from the securities laws to prices and rationing in wartime, can be violated by business; and farmers may use violence to dump milk trucks to keep up prices. In each instance the group requires obedience to the laws by all other groups. The juvenile likewise is expected by all groups to obey the regulations of society even though some of these rules may furnish controls over peculiarly juvenile aspects, such as school attendance and recreation in the form of malicious mischief.

Linked with this differential morality of adults which at the same time requires almost ideal behavior by the juvenile, is the lack of extensive generation interaction which we term the adolescent conflict. The person from age 12 to 18 has a vague role of duties and obligations in our society. The result is a separate culture of adolescents.[36] This failure of the adult to encourage the participation of adolescents in the larger world, keeping them half adult and half child, results frequently in the diversion of their activities into unconventional patterns. To this extent the social controls of the adult world are weakened and the violations of conduct norms are frequently seen out of context by the adolescent, who witnesses the adult world deprived of intimate knowledge and adult responsibilities.

Adult attitudes of the larger community toward minority groups, particularly racial groups, add to the difficulties in dealing with juveniles

[33] Lester D. Crow and Alice Crow, *Our Teen Age Boys and Girls* (New York: McGraw-Hill Book Co., Inc., 1945), p. 251.

[34] Some research studies have uncovered situations in which both juveniles and adults participate in the same violation of community norms. See, for example, Elbert L. Hooker, "The Urban Tourist Camp," *Studies in Sociology*, Sociology Department, Southern Methodist University, Vol. 1, No. 1, Summer 1936.

[35] For an excellent discussion of crime as a product of American culture, see Donald Taft, *Criminology*, New York: The Macmillan Co., 1945.

[36] E. B. Reuter, "The Sociology of Adolescence," *American Journal of Sociology*, Vol. 43, November 1937, pp. 414-27.

from these groups, particularly where the boys delinquent gang, consisting of members of a minority group, secures for its members status and material gain.[37] The segregation of minority groups in areas fostering delinquency is a problem of the larger adult world, and must be dealt with as much on this level as in the immediate neighborhood where the group resides. Certainly the individual delinquent or family is not the proper unit.

CONCLUSIONS

There is no question that those who in studying delinquency concentrate almost exclusively on the personality characteristics of the juvenile or on the influence of the family are in an extremely vulnerable position theoretically. Although not nearly to as great an extent, the same error of limited perspective is made by those who see the exclusive cause of delinquency in the companions and gang associates of the juvenile. Even those approaching the problem of delinquency entirely through the local neighborhood are faced by social forces emanating from beyond this small world.

While agreeing that delinquency is chiefly a product of personal contacts, the world of secondary relationships can by no means be completely eliminated from an investigation of delinquency. Such secondary contacts may furnish models and rationalizations which become part of the set of beliefs of the juvenile delinquent as he sees the world. Among those contacts having a possible influence, there is no question about the police, courts, penal institutions, and the school. While the relationship seems obvious, there is only limited evidence to indicate that the newspaper, magazines, movies, the radio, comic books, and various agencies of moral risk produce delinquency. Similarly, the immorality of the general adult population, its extensive violation of law while at the same time it requires model behavior of juveniles, must not only be bewildering but must have a relation to delinquent behavior.

Most of the very few studies which have been made of secondary influences either represent findings which have not been substantiated by other studies or are more than fifteen years old and do not necessarily embody improved research techniques. Considering the seriousness of the problem of delinquency, the amount of largely scientifically unsupported public discussion of the relation of secondary contacts and the large financial investment in such media as the movies and the radio, it is surprising that there is not more valid evidence of relationship today. One reason for this is that research problems have been set up to look only for certain factors, with the obvious result that if secondary contacts are not included in the research, no evidence of their relationship is found.

Perhaps if more research were done, this important problem would be taken out of the realm of speculation into the scientific world of fact, process, understanding, and control. Of primary concern to such research is the question of the extent of contact of nondelinquents with each of these influences.[38] Certainly no definite conclusion can be reached as to causation by confining ourselves to delinquents and not including as well the frequency of the same experience among those who have not engaged in delinquency.

35

Juvenile Delinquency at Oak Ridge*

Paul F. Waldner

Oak Ridge, as the origin of the atomic bomb, is universally known, Oak Ridge as a community has had little publicity, it has been taken for granted that it undoubtedly had all the problems of any urban community.

---

[37] For a discussion of the concept "conduct norm," as well as conflicts of conduct norms, particularly among immigrant groups and their children, see Thorsten Sellin, *Culture Conflict and Crime*, Bulletin 41, Social Science Research Council, 1938.

[38] This point of view applies to all research on delinquency. See W. I. Thomas and Dorothy S. Thomas, *The Child in America* (New York: Alfred A. Knopf, 1928), p. 573.

* Reprinted from 11 *Federal Probation* (1947), 3–8. Used by permission of the author and the publisher.

Probably there have been few cities that have offered a parallel opportunity to observe and attempt to correct social and physical maladjustment in all its phases, as a constructive part of the over-all planning for community living, as existed here. The discussion of delinquency among the juvenile residents of Oak Ridge that will be presented here is but one of the many phases of the development.

CHARACTERISTIC OF OAK RIDGE

Before any discussion can be made of the problem of the maladjusted or delinquent child in Oak Ridge it is important to understand the background and characteristics of the city. Production and research in nuclear energy have been, and to a large extent still are, the keynote of life in this war-created city. Every thought, every effort was bent toward this goal. It was a city with a mission, a job to do. It is well known that few of its residents were aware of the nature of the mission. Each worker, except those few who know the over-all plan, had some small part to play but could not discuss any aspect of his work with his co-workers, friends, and neighbors. The tensions that all these factors could create were obvious.

From its inception Oak Ridge has been a community that has followed a definite plan. It grew from a draftsman's blueprint to a city of 75,000 persons in a matter of months. Housing was hastily erected and ranged from comfortable permanent-type units and dormitories to demountable prefabricated houses, barracks, hutments, and trailers. The workers and their families had the interesting, and at times trying, experience of living through the birthpangs of a frontier town, 20th century version. They lived through the creation, recognition, and eventual solution or modification of innumerable community problems. As many of these problems had not and could not have been foreseen, the necessary agencies and facilities to meet the various needs of the community were organized or directed to be organized by the Army Engineers who were responsible for the administration of the town.

Such agencies as a psychiatric clinic, an American Red Cross Chapter, a Family Service Bureau and a Juvenile Department were organized for the over-all welfare of the workers and their families, solely in the interest of production. Emotional upsets, family break-

downs, delinquency — anything that contributed to absenteeism — were enemies that had to be conquered. In addition to these agencies which met problems after the fact, as it were, others were established to meet recognized needs and on a high level. Outstanding of the latter were a progressive school system with its Guidance Division of psychologists and visiting teachers and a comprehensive recreational association which conducted an elaborate program on both the adult and juvenile level.

To date no one has ventured to describe Oak Ridge as being a normal community in the true sense of the word. It invariably has been and is described as "unique" and the descriptive adjective "different" has been overworked. However, many of its characteristics do tend to make it somewhat different from the more established communities. For security reasons the entire townsite, as well as the production areas, is isolated by fences and a river — the Clinch, which winds 35 miles around part of the project. Entrance and exit are achieved only through gates manned by armed guards. The population is a true cross section of the country. There are no blighted or slum areas in the city, although the large trailer camps presented many problems and pressures that are generally associated with inferior housing. Family housing units are assigned to employees on the basis of size of family as well as type of work. Consequently, with everything else being equal, a man with four children will be eligible for a large housing unit while a co-worker with only one child will, in turn, be considered only for certain of the smaller type units. The end result is that a certain uniqueness is present and certainly the city is more "controlled" than the average community. Such is the setting of the delinquencies upon which the observations and conclusions of this paper will be based.

NO ORGANIZED CRIME AT OAK RIDGE

At no time has there been organized crime — either adult or juvenile — in Oak Ridge. In the city's 3½ years of existence no armed robbery involving a commercial or business establishment has been committed. The reasons for this are logical. It can be assumed that no professional criminal would consider a major crime which would, naturally, involve a planned escape, in a setting where the success or failure of the venture would greatly depend on his ability to "clear a gate" 7 or 8 miles from the scene of the crime. Since employment is a prerequisite of residence in the town, any unemployed male adult would be an early subject of investigation. Prior to employment each prospective employee is carefully investigated and the administration, as well as the personnel departments of the various companies, is particularly alert to any derogatory information. The town and the plants are heavily guarded and these forces are augmented by a police department that has in its short existence already been commended by the Federal Bureau of Investigation.

Law enforcement rapidly became a serious community problem during the construction and organizational days of the project. This fact necessitated the early development of the police department. For many months this organization was kept busy combating such crimes as gambling, assaults, bootlegging, and the like, which were in their incidence out of proportion to the size of the community. The large number of unattached construction workers was significant here. Offenses on the part of adults have ranged from murder down to petty larcenies. The over-all crime rate is now well below the average for a community of its size.

TYPES OF BEHAVIOR PROBLEMS

Oddly enough, these deterrents have not greatly influenced, in many categories, the incidents of juvenile behavior that come under the category of "delinquency" and rise out of behavior problems and emotional conflicts produced by family breakdowns as well as school and community influences. Primarily, the antisocial behavior of the youth in Oak Ridge has been expressed in such acts as vandalism, petit larceny, truancy, running away, breaking and entering, and incorrigibility. Most cases of residential breaking and entering have been attributed to juveniles and a good percentage of cars stolen on the area is also the act of minors. These two categories of offenses have been by far the most common of the more serious delinquencies committed by youngsters in the community.

The age range of the approximately 1,000 cases of delinquency and neglect known to the Juvenile Department since its organization in December, 1944, provides considerable material for speculation. About 85 percent of the delinquencies have been committed by youngsters whose ages range from 10 to 15 years. A considerable number of these cases could be classified more properly as predelinquent behavior. This group, however, did commit the majority of the major delinquencies. The 16 to 18-year-olds rarely have been involved in acts which might be deemed felonies and their offenses have been generally in the realm of disorderly conduct, drunkenness, and vandalism. One possible explanation for this lack of delinquency in the above mentioned group is that the median age of the population of Oak Ridge is 30 years. Parents are young. Those families having children over 16 are in the minority. Another might be the fact that many enlisted in the armed services and thus escaped apprehension by the police for crimes still carried as unsolved, or closed without results. The perpetual manpower shortage opened many avenues for employment of the 16- to 18-year-old group, at a substantial wage that cut down the amount of free time and interest in nonconformance.

BACKGROUND OF YOUTH IN RELATION TO SOCIAL ADJUSTMENT

Oak Ridge has drawn its population from every state in the Union and from every size and type of community. Hence, the backgrounds of the youth have presented a wide variety of experiences. A study of the backgrounds of the delinquents known to us has shown that their life experience prior to coming to Oak Ridge had, to a great degree, a causative relationship with the problems found upon investigation. The cases generally have fallen into one of the following three categories: (1) those from urban settings; (2) those with rural backgrounds; and (3) those with a migratory background. We feel that the reactions of each of these groups in turn to the experience of being abruptly removed from their usual and familiar surroundings are significant, in that there has followed, for the most part, a definite pattern or trend.

It has been our observation that the child coming from the urban areas makes the adjustment to life in this new community more readily and successfully than did his contemporary from the small town or farm. The rural youngster had particular difficulty in adjusting to the more impersonal relationships inherent in the new situation. The new school setting was foreign and intimidating. In many cases of truancy in this group it was found that the boy or girl just could not accept being one of hundreds after being accustomed to small teaching and social groups. They missed the close relationships with both teachers and classmates that are traditional in the small school. Dissatisfaction and rebellion resulted. Often only nominal success was encountered in our efforts to effect a successful school adjustment with and for this group. Special efforts of the teachers and the social worker functioning as a probation officer to individualize the child in the school and recreational setting were met with suspicion and distrust by child and parent as well. The latter were also quite insecure in this new setting as their rural patterns and customs were not always applicable or acceptable in this semi-urban setting. This maladjustment was not confined to the school setting, as, almost to a man, these youngsters admitted to an over-all dissatisfaction with life in such a "big" place. Authoritative efforts on the part of school and juvenile authorities to force attendance met with overt rebellion, continued truancy, and in some cases outright defiance from the child and his family as well. These situations occasionally led to antisocial acts upon the part of the truant in the form of petty thievery, vandalism, and the like. The most common solution finally resorted to in these situations was placement away from Oak Ridge in either their former homes or in settings comparable to what they had known prior to coming to Oak Ridge.

THE URBAN CHILD

The city-bred adolescent, trained and experienced in urban ways and mores, also had his particular problems. For the most part, the school and community setting was not much of a novelty to him. His rebellion and resentment, in addition to those created by family tensions well known as contributing factors to delinquency, were aroused in part by his hostility toward Oak Ridge, itself. He wanted to know why he had to come to Oak Ridge and more specifically why did the family have to leave home. The answers his parents gave to these questions were necessarily vague either for reasons of security or ignorance as to the object of the project. Because of this the

youngster could not or would not accept the necessity for his being separated from his friends and from his familiar surroundings in a well-established and organized city for the rigors of life in a new town, possibly physically ugly to him, certainly lacking in many of the facilities and advantages, to him at least, to which he had become accustomed. The focal point of his dissatisfaction was the town. He didn't like it and he wanted to go home. The release of the news of the atomic bomb has instilled some semblance of civic pride in most of the youngsters. However, in many cases those who have remained are having a rather hard time accepting Oak Ridge as a home.

The behavior of this group also has followed a rather definite pattern. First to be observed was an intensified degree of continuous misbehavior and failure to accept and pay attention to parental authority and counsel. This was ordinarily followed by a marked lack of interest in school accompanied by truancy and prolonged absences from home. In general, this truancy was not attributable to the school or its curriculum, although many were resentful of the many snags encountered in organizing and staffing a complete school system in a very short time. Generally, this behavior was culminated by the act of running away. This particular category of offense has been by far the most common of our delinquencies and it is known that not all such cases were reported to us or to the police. Of particular interest has been the fact that very few of these youngsters returned to their home towns. If anything, they generally headed in the opposite direction. Investigation of the family situation after their return generally resulted in finding that the runaway was not running away to something but was running away from something. The something, in the majority of cases, proved to be Oak Ridge. This group responded much more readily to efforts to resolve their emotional conflicts. Their behavior patterns were modified much more readily than were those of their rural counterparts.

CHILDREN OF MIGRATORY FAMILIES

The children of the migratory and semi-migratory construction workers provided an interesting departure from the above mentioned patterns. The delinquency rate of this group, in our experience, proved to be very low. Seemingly, the constant moving from project to project, job to job, covering the length and breadth of the nation, conditioned these children to change. They readily adjusted themselves to the new situation and had little feeling about moving on. What delinquency did occur was generally on the nuisance level or at best petty stealing. Investigation showed that the majority of the delinquents encountered in this group had established their antisocial attitudes and behavior patterns prior to their coming to Oak Ridge. In the other two groups it was a very rare experience to encounter delinquents who had previously resorted to such behavior. The interdependence and loyalty within this group as a whole amounted to almost a tribal pattern that was unusual.

In considering the causal relationship of all the factors and patterns described above, a logical question that we have considered at length, both on an individual and group basis, has been the question whether or not it was due primarily to the experiences in the new setting of a war-created community or whether it was due to environmental and emotional factors experienced prior to their coming to Oak Ridge, or finally, whether a combination of these factors contributed to the delinquency act. If the parents of these youngsters were to be believed, every child reported to us came to this new setting just about perfect. It was a very rare case indeed when the workers failed to have the parents comment on the fact that they were confused and upset by their children's behavior primarily because they had never been in trouble prior to the family arrival in Oak Ridge and had always been good children. The parents were quick to seize the opportunity of rationalizing their offsprings' delinquency on a very convenient source outside the home. It must be stated, however, that investigation in many cases would establish their allegations as being true. Again a definite pattern has developed. Johnny achieved his adolescence just prior to, or immediately after, his arrival in Oak Ridge. We found many youngsters who readily stated that their family life had not been what they would have liked with all the classic problems of marital discord, rejecting parents, broken homes, and like factors contributing to their unhappiness. Johnny had just never gotten around to doing anything about it and the pressures of life in a war-created com-

munity on both an adult and juvenile level resulted in action. As mentioned, Johnny quite frequently ran away as a result of the above, but this situation was found in many cases of outright delinquency which involved a more overt violation of law. In many cases the most precipitating factor that could be found was that of "homesickness." Families that provided adequate physical and emotional care and had always worked for their children's happiness were unable to combat the youngster's desire for "home." In a good percentage of the cases it was found that the social situation in the family and home was such that, regardless of the whereabouts of the family, delinquent behavior could logically be expected unless corrective steps were taken. In like manner, these many problems had existed long before the transition from home to Oak Ridge had occurred. As a result, the two sets of contributing factors had to be taken into consideration in working with most of our delinquents because it became more and more obvious that the roots of the social pathology in the situation extended far beyond the Oak Ridge experience.

Further analysis of the reaction of the various age groups known to us has resulted in our feeling that the lack of anything more than a nominal delinquency rate in the 16 to 18-year-old group is indicative of an ability of these youngsters to effect an adjustment to a changing reality situation at a relatively mature level. This statement must be made with reservations. Such factors as the absence of blighted and slum areas and the lack of organized crime, together with an adequate recreational program and the deterrents to crime previously mentioned, must be taken into consideration. Our experience with this group has been reasonably successful with only a very small percentage of such youngsters having resorted to the more aggressive and serious types of crime and delinquency.

The 12 to 15-year-old group has, in our experience, proved to be our most seriously disturbed children and has reacted in an overt manner to the social pathology which was present in their life situation prior to their coming to Oak Ridge, as well as whatever tensions and pressures were created by the new experience. This group obviously does not possess the ability to adjust as evidenced in our experience with the older group. Further observations involving children whose background and Oak Ridge experience were very similar, but who have not been known to us as delinquents or in any way inclined toward delinquency, have made it rather apparent that a child's reaction to a new experience is or will be influenced primarily by his previous life experience. Happy, secure, and well-adjusted children will have a better chance of effecting a socially acceptable adjustment to a completely new situation than will those children who have been exposed to social pathological situations.

Establishment of Juvenile Department

The source of the above information might prove of interest. Following a wave of delinquencies it was soon recognized by those authorities responsible for law enforcement that some provisions would have to be made other than those used in the disposition of adult offenders. Accordingly, the Juvenile Department was established with the prime responsibility of screening all cases of delinquency and any situation involving child welfare for the purpose of ascertaining which offenders should be turned over to the local authorities for prosecution. The Juvenile Department was to function more or less as the referee for the county court which has jurisdiction over delinquents. Appropriate referral procedures were devised with community authorities and such agencies as the police, the guard force, and the school system. The office was to function more or less as a juvenile court but without the legal authority of a court. Our authority was purely administrative and, of course, certain limitations in function were inherent in the setup. However, the procedures followed were not unlike those followed by most progressive courts and involved informal hearings with the offender, his parents, and other interested adults with appropriate social investigations having been made.

Every attempt was made to effect a satisfactory adjustment without resorting to the County Court and to date only 18 youngsters have been turned over for formal prosecution and all but 2 of these were institutionalized.

Use of Probation

Probation was the most common technique and disposition made in our cases. Because of limitations of staff and the unique characteristics of the community, certain modifications in the accepted probational techniques were used. No definite period of time was designated as being the duration of probation. Instead, the youngster was told that termination of probation was dependent entirely upon his attitudes and progress in adjusting. This was augmented by our practice of concentrating the probational interviews wherein the youngster was seen weekly and on occasion biweekly. It was our feeling that it was preferable to develop a close working relationship with the youngster as soon as possible with the twofold purpose in mind of being in a position to know intimately his personality and his over-all situation, as well as being able to analyze the known situation for the purpose of determining just what should be done and how long it would be necessary for probation to continue. We felt that extended probation often became meaningless to the probationer and that unjustifiable continuance fostered resentment to the point where little good could be recognized in the situation by either the offender or the probation officer. Accordingly, we tried to make probation a meaningful experience to each youngster consistent in his mind, as well as the community's, as being justifiable in the light of his offense. We tried as best we could to base our decisions as to the ultimate disposition of a given case on the kind of a youngster we had rather than what he had done.

It was interesting to find that in approximately 35 per cent of our probationary cases it was found necessary to work intensively over extended periods with youngsters who had been referred to us for very nominal offenses. Accordingly, we have decided that there is not necessarily a definite correlation between the offense committed and the duration of probation. Our experience has been that the amount of corrective and rehabilitative work with a lad found guilty of larceny of $1.00 will possibly far exceed that necessary in working with a lad guilty of the larceny of an automobile.

We found early that it was to the advantage of our agency as well as the probationer for us to make extensive use of collateral resources. Those most commonly used were the guidance offices of the various schools and the child guidance clinic, as well as the family agency. Quite frequently the entire supervision of a youngster would be turned over to one of the outside agencies with our workers maintaining a behind-the-scenes and administrative role. This technique was resorted to primarily in situations where the behavior pattern was the prime problem and the delinquency could be definitely attributed to an emotionally disturbed or insecure child who had in reality done little wrong in the eyes of the law. These youngsters proved to be overly sensitive and since they were already in overt rebellion it was felt that nothing really could be gained on either an individual or community basis if they were forced to report regularly to a probation officer. It is obvious that a high degree of selectivity must be used in deciding to use this technique and it must be part of a definite plan on the part of the probation officer consistent with his knowledge of the probationer and indicated by the needs of the youngster.

RELATIONS WITH THE POLICE

We have found that the success or failure of our program has depended to a large degree upon the maintenance of a sound, practical, and mutually acceptable working relationship with the police. Initially, procedures in working agreements were by necessity confined to the administrative level. However, it shortly became evident that staff participation and interest was by far the most important. Accordingly, our staff has worked very closely with the police, both in individual cases and on an interpretive basis, to explain such things as the philosophy of the agency regarding delinquency; social, emotional, and personality factors that have to be taken into consideration in either disposing of or working with problems of delinquency; and finally, in detail, how we worked with children and why.

It has been interesting to note that many cases have been handled in a very satisfactory manner by detectives and patrolmen working in conjuction with members of our staff. The problem was met and solved in the field by staff members to the benefit of the youngster involved who, together with his family, was spared a needless "court" experience. We found that unless the police were advised of plans for a child known to them as well as the progress made, or lack of progress, they did not possess or maintain an understanding of the many social pathological conditions that were being faced by the child. On the other hand, our policy of keeping them advised before, during, and after

disposition of a given case has resulted in creased co-operation and understanding on their part. Our staff agrees that it has been time well spent.

CONCLUSION

Our experience in working with children in this setting has shown, in our opinion, that delinquent behavior does definitely have its roots in the early family life. The mass migration of families to Oak Ridge created individual problems which, in some cases, fostered family and personality breakdowns. We also have found that youngsters can be conditioned to change as evidenced by our observations of the children of known migratory workers. The average youngster seems to resent change, particularly a change from a rural to an urban setting, or from an urban to a rural environment. The capacity to adjust and accept such an experience seems to be determined by personality strengths, emotional growth and maturity, and finally, age. However, with the possible exception of the problems inherent in this migrant situation, we have found little difference in the nature, etiology, treatment, and disposition of delinquents in our community when contrasted with those found in the more "normal" communities.

36

Delinquent Group-Formation Among Immigrant Youth *

S. N. Eisenstadt

The purpose of this paper is to analyse some sociological aspects of the incidence of juvenile delinquency and especially of delinquent (youth) group-formation among immigrants. Most of the material is based on statistical data and research carried out in Israel,[1] but compara-

* Reprinted from 2 British J. Delinquency (1951–52), 34–45. Used by permission of the author and the publisher.
[1] Most of the investigations on which this paper is based have been carried out at the Sociological

tive studies from other countries, particularly the United States, have also been used. The paper is concerned mainly with the influence on family life and adolescence of the social processes connected with migration. It does not touch on either biological or psychological aspects of the ætiology and typology of delinquents. This should not be interpreted as claiming any monopoly for sociological interpretation. On the contrary, it is hoped that the limits and inherent inadequacies of the purely sociological approach will be clearly emphasized.

The high incidence of juvenile delinquency among immigrant families, especially in the second generation, has long been stressed in the literature of the subject (especially in America) (1). This incidence has been usually ascribed to different "causes," most of which are in line with the current sociological explanations of juvenile delinquency. The following main factors have been emphasized: (a) broken homes, existing among those immigrants who could not adapt themselves to conditions in the new country; (b) bad economic conditions, usually connected with (a); (c) conflict of cultural elements, norms, habits, etc., consequent on living in two different worlds; and (d) conflict between parents and children, due mainly to (c). Although these explanations do, of course, account in varying degrees for the different manifestations of juvenile delinquency, they seem to us rather inadequate. They have unduly emphasized those aspects of modern migratory movements which are related to social disorganization, conflict, etc., and correspondingly the relation between immigration and juvenile delinquency became an obvious, too obvious, one. This undue emphasis does not always enable us to see the problems of juvenile delinquency in proper perspective and does not take into account the full context of social forces bearing on them.

Our investigations suggest that a somewhat fuller understanding of the problem could be arrived at if two more general sociological characteristics of the processes of adaptation and

Research Seminar of the Hebrew University, Jerusalem, unless otherwise specified. All the references to interviews are from the files of the Seminar. The sample on which this paper is based is derived from three different research projects mentioned in Footnote 3, and totals about 300 families and 450–500 adolescents (ages thirteen to nineteen).

absorption of new immigrants were taken into account. These characteristics are: (1) diminution of the family's effective capacity to satisfy an *organized hierarchy* of needs and aspirations of its members, and especially of children and adolescents; and (2) limitation of the social sphere and functions of the family, leading to the emergence of specific "youth-groups" and "youth-culture."

(1) The process of adaptation to a new country necessarily transforms both the internal structure of the family and the whole field of social participation of its members. In the first phases of adaptation a shrinkage in the field of effective social participation of the immigrants usually takes place. Large amounts of energy have to be expended in various activities connected with economic problems and in making fresh orientations in the new country, the usual result of which is that the old family roles cannot be fully sustained. This feeling of the inadequacy of their new family set-up has been spontaneously expressed by about 80 per cent. of the new immigrants observed by us, and is generally recognized in the literature on immigrants. Such a situation quite frequently gives rise to undue emphasis on some basic needs — food, shelter, sexual relations — and apathy in relation to other, broader social "needs" and problems. It has sometimes even been found that the family ceases almost entirely to function as a social unit. In most cases, anyhow, it is only gradually that the new immigrant extends his participation to broader fields of the new social structure. This process involves many points of tension as the new immigrant must learn not only new "techniques" of behaviour, but must rearrange his whole hierarchy of needs and activities, and re-define his conception of himself, his social status, etc. This process, which is in any case difficult, is rendered still more difficult by the various dislocations connected with immigration (2). The lack of integration of needs, etc., may affect, in various degrees, the ability of the family to orient the children and adolescents towards their future social roles and to give them the wider social perspective and values that are essential.

(2) Along with this transitory process we find in most modern industrial immigration countries a more basic one which has more permanent, structural results. In almost all these countries, the immigrants' adaptation in-

volves a diminution and limitation of the social functions performed by the family. This is due to a large extent to the fact that the immigrants come from "familial" communities (usually peasant or artisan) and find themselves in more individualistic societies, based on a high degree of economic specialization and "universal" citizenship. The family does not constitute, in the countries of absorption, the basic unit of the social division of labour, and many social roles have to be performed by the individual independently of his role and status within the family. The limitation of the sphere of the family and the undermining of the "traditional"-familial scale of values always gives rise in varying degrees to "peer-groups" formed at different age-levels by children and adolescents.[2] These groups, which emerge in almost any industrial, urbanized society fill the social "vacuum" between the family and the community. The predisposition towards formation of age-groups is largely intensified among immigrants, especially, as has been rightly emphasized in the literature among the second generation of immigrants. This is due, firstly, to the differences of tradition and cultural orientation between the different generations of immigrants; secondly, to the speed of dislocation from a "familial" to a "non-familial" setting and the consequent inability of the families to orient their children towards performing extra-familial roles. For this reason the "peer-group" type of behaviour seems to be more prevalent among the different ethnic groups in the United States than in European industrial countries (3).

The decreasing scope of the family does not diminish, however, its crucial importance for the understanding of our problem. The family remains, of course, the main and primary socializing agency and its relation to the total social structure becomes perhaps even more crucial and important — from the point of view of the social development of children — than in a "familial" society. From the above statement, it should be clear, however, that it is not the internal structure of the family which

is most important, but the relations between this structure and the total new social field (4).

In the Jewish community in Palestine these specific youth-groups prevail, in different forms, in almost all sections of the social structure (5). We may distinguish between the following main types: (a) organized, legitimate "youth-movements," some of them linked with different "pioneering" movements, others mostly of a recreational character; (b) relatively unorganized, or loosely-organized cliques, recreational groups of children of a given neighbourhood, school, etc.; (c) "delinquent groups," which engage in pilfering, smuggling and other illegal practices. It has been estimated that about 30 per cent. of urban and semi-urban youths are organized within the first type, and many more have passing contact with them. Even more participate, of course, in the unorganized groups, of which no detailed statistical accounts exist. Although in principle the different types can be distinguished one from the other, in actual fact they overlap and intermingle to some extent. While the structural difference between, on the one hand, the legitimate, accepted youth movements, whose activities are in varying degrees oriented towards the realization of the basic values of the community, and, on the other, the delinquent, deviant youth-groups is very large, their common background makes comparison between them both easier and more interesting.

All this brings us to our main problem, namely: Which family types and types of new environment give rise to socially adapted youth-groups and which to delinquent groups? The common process of migration, with its dislocations can, perhaps, account for the general emergence of "youth-groups," but not for variations in type. We must therefore compare the internal structure of these two main youth-groups, and, then analyse the different family constellations and environmental influences under which they emerge.[3]

---

[2] The correlation between a "non-familial" division of labour and the emergence of specific "youth-groups" has been verified by us in a small "cross-cultural" survey of a sample of about fifty societies. We hope to publish the results of the investigation shortly.

[3] This analysis is based on three different research-projects conducted by us at the Research Seminar in Sociology of the Hebrew University. These projects are: (1) The problems of Oriental Jews in Palestine, completed in 1947; (2) The Absorption of New Immigrants since 1948; and (3) Problems of Youth Movements — the latter two still being carried out. As no specific, thorough, statistical investigations of this problem have been undertaken, the

Our investigations showed that all these types of youth-groups have some common characteristics, associated mainly with the needs they fulfil. Interviews, observation and analysis of the internal literature of the movement indicated fairly clearly a number of motivations, varying in intensity in the different groups. These were as follows: (a) Acquirement of various social skills, especially in the sphere of spontaneous competitive behaviour, which are not fully developed at home. (b) The possibility of achieving not-too-distant goals (play, recreation, etc.) in contrast to the more distant ones towards which most of their activities at home are orientated. (c) Acquisition of a fuller, more independent status within a group, in contrast to their dependent status at home, school, and in the occupational field (if there is any status at all in the latter). (d) Identification with a small primary (nuclear) group, with the members of which one shares the same experiences. (e) More direct experience of social activities and values which are outside the scope of the family and school and which give to the youngsters a feeling of fuller and more direct participation in the community.

It is interesting to note that these factors have been equally emphasized by members of the socially adapted and the delinquent groups: no significant difference could be found among them from this point of view. In each group-formation these functions were fulfilled by different sets of activities, or, to put it another way, the activities of each type of youth-group were organized in different ways and oriented towards different goals and values.

When differences between these two types of groups were investigated it was discovered that they did not lie mainly in the nature of these activities, e.g. sports, recreations, excursions, attending the cinema, reading, etc. In these respects, the differences between the groups were not significant. The main difference seemed to lie in the structure and organization of the group. The most important factors were found to be the following:

A. *Stability, organization and solidarity of the group.* In all these respects a very marked

difference existed, the delinquent groups in every case ranking lowest. In fact, the stability of any delinquent group and its component members was as a rule extremely low. The youths changed their groups very often and the group had only a minimal degree of organization. There scarcely existed any permanent goal towards which its activities were directed. Groups would shift their attention from one direction to another, from pilfering to going to the cinema, etc., each shift involving a change in membership and in organization. There existed scarcely any fixed types of rôle and the youths' relations with one another changed frequently, following, however, a leader-follower pattern in which physical aggression played a major part. In contrast to this, the socially adapted groups showed a higher degree of stability and organization.

B. *Degree of organization of the different goals in a definite hierarchy.* This is, of course, closely connected with the above. Among the delinquent groups it was found that the different goals toward which their activities were directed were not to any large extent arranged in any definite hierarchy, involving some patterning of priorities and ordering in time. They were more or less unrelated to one another, and, with constant shifts among them, each of them would acquire a temporary priority, only to be forgotten when the next goal came within their field of perception. A concomitant characteristic was the great stress laid on the *immediacy of attainment* of a goal and a minimal ability to see it in a somewhat longer temporal perspective, and to be able to arrange other activities as steps towards this attainment. This characteristic gives rise in the delinquent groups to many tensions, as it does not enable them to gain any of the adult social aims towards which they aspire. By contrast, in the socially adapted groups, the aims and activities of the members are well-organized in definite patterns and in a means-ends sequence. Even here the "temporal" span is always shorter than that accorded to the children within the orbit of adult society (home, school, etc.). Importance is attached to a fuller and quicker achievement of status within the peer-group, but all these goals and activities are organized in more or less definite patterns and hierarchies.

C. *Communication and identification with the general community and its values.* We

conclusions are necessarily tentative, but they seem to converge into some definite pattern. They are based on about 300 families and comparative analysis of several youth movements.

have seen earlier that one of the main functions of the youth group is to provide its members with a channel of communication with those aspects and values of community life towards which the family does not orient them in an effective way, and to give them the feeling of a fuller participation in the community. This explains why in all these groups — social adapted and delinquent alike — considerable emphasis is laid on goals and "virtues" which symbolize the adult world and status, and certain of its aspects from which children may be excluded at home and in school: competitive behaviour, full physical prowess and strength, independence in a spontaneity of recreation, social and political problems, activities, etc. This common orientation towards the adult community, however, takes entirely different directions in the two types of youth groups. The main difference lies in the fact that in the socially adapted groups there is a gradual and more or less orderly preparation for socially sanctioned adult rôles whereas in the delinquent groups emphasis is mainly on "symbolic" goals, which do not lead to such accepted adult rôles, and on a more "vicarious" type of identification with the values of the community. The marked emphasis on immediate attainment of different external symbols of full social status — clothes, spending money, frequenting various recreational (and/or vice) resorts — is a manifestation of this tendency. This difference between the two types of group is also manifest in their communication with the adult world. In the socially accepted groups, with the gradual extension of new social perspectives, attempts to establish more intensive, regular and organized communication with the adult world are almost always made, and the tensions between the generations do not have a "rebellious" and totally negative character. In the delinquent groups these tensions are only rarely overcome and neither effective communication with the adult world, nor extension of participation in regular and recognized common social situations, roles and identifications develop to any large extent.

This difference in the attitude towards the adult world can be well illustrated by comparing the following examples quoted from interviews with members of an organized, socially accepted youth movement and of a semidelinquent gang respectively:

"I think that we are all very interested to learn many of those things that adults do, and to be able to understand the adult's world. It is true that many of them are very dull and do not interest me, but it is not true of all of them. I think we can learn from grown-ups, especially from those who understand us and do not try to be very remote. I think my father is really such a man and so is also the "madrich" (leader, guide) in the movement. I like to spend my time with them although they sometimes irritate me."

". . . All the grown-ups do is make constant demands on one and pretend to be very important or a different race of men. They grab all the good things that are to be had and they don't allow anyone to take these things from them. . . . Of course, I want to be like them. I want to have as much money as they, nice clothes, to play around with girls and women, but I do not think they will let me have all this when I want it — only when I am an old man and unable to enjoy it. That is why I hate them so much. . . ."

D. *Incidence of internal and external aggression.* The instability of delinquent groups and lack of attainment of full social roles gives rise among them to a higher incidence of internal and external aggression. Internally, this aggression is usually connected with the constant changing of roles and the strong emphasis on force and physical prowess. In external relations, the feeling of insecurity of their own status quite often gives rise to verbal or physical aggression, the main aim of which is to emphasize their full "status." This is, for instance, very frequently seen in their behaviour towards waiters in coffeehouses or cinema attendants.

These characteristics of the socially accepted and delinquent youth groups respectively show us that the basic difference between them lies in the way they solve the psychological and sociological problems arising from the discontinuity between the family and the community — a discontinuity which exists in any modern industrial society and which is emphasized among immigrants. From the sociological point of view, the main characteristic of the delinquent group is that it does not provide its members with effective channels of communication with the adult community and its values, and that it constitutes an uneven and disorderly field of social activity and perception through which only very few stable, recognized social roles can be learnt and performed (6).

Our next problem is to consider under what conditions the formation of these groups takes place. For reasons of space, only the briefest outline of the conclusions arrived at during our investigations can be given. From the outset it was clear that the usual "objective" socioeconomic indices could not fully account for the formation of the two different types of group. We had to look for more specific, and, at the same time, dynamic factors. Those were mostly related to some dynamic relations between the family structure and the "absorbing" environments. While only about 50 per cent. of the children belonging to the type of family to be described took part in the delinquent groups, about 85 to 90 per cent. of the children participating in these groups belonged to such families. This emphasizes, on the one hand, the need to elaborate our formula, and on the other, the possible inadequacy of purely sociological explanation.

The most universal condition under which delinquent youth-formation took place was absence of identification and presence of intensive conflict between the family (especially the head of the family) and the new country and social structure. It should be emphasized that we are not alluding here to "mere" differences in norms, values, etc., which are quite prevalent among the most different types of immigrant. Of much greater importance than the "objective" difference and discrepancy is the attitude taken by the immigrants towards this difference; in other words, their (and the absorbing population's) social definition of this difference. Whenever immigrants establish a positive identification with the new social structure and its values, and whenever this identification is not blocked by the "absorbing" environment, the cultural and social differences only rarely give rise to a high incidence of delinquent group-formations among the children and adolescents. Even when the parents are apathetic towards the new social structure, the incidence of delinquent group-formation is rather low, although higher than in the former case. In our example (which is not, of course, representative of the whole immigrant population, new and old) only about 5 per cent. of children from the first type of family, and only 15 per cent. of the second (apathetic) type were involved in some delin-

quent groups. On the other hand, about 50 per cent. of the children from families where parents did not identify themselves with the new social setting were involved in such activities. The explanation of this fact seems to be the following: those parents who identify themselves with the social system and its values tend to transfer this identification to their children and to orient the children towards the new environment and its social demands. Even if they themselves cannot effectively teach the children the new skills and roles, they do not hinder, and may even encourage, such acquisitions. As one of the parents put it in an interview: "I do not understand many of these things which I see around me, and sometimes they are quite strange to me, and not always can I say what is good and what is bad. But this is our country, and all this is a part of it, and I want my children to know all this better than I do. That is why I do not interfere with them very much and sometimes even help them. I want only to see that they have good comrades and instructors — that is what is important." Of course, conflicts and disagreements do occur, but these develop only very seldom into a definite, emotional upheaval. In the case of more apathetic parents a positive orientation towards the new social structure is absent but the relative lack of interest of the parents ensures at least that no intense conflict will be generated. In such cases it seems that the adequacy of the "absorbing" conditions is the crucial factor in the predisposition to delinquent group-formation. What are the main manifestations of this negative identification? The following seem to be the most important ones:

(1) *Incongruity in conceptions of social status.* One of the most frequent manifestations — or causes — of the negative identification is that among the parents there exists a very great rigidity in their conception of their own status, which was mainly influenced by their old social and cultural setting. Any change means loss of status, and correspondingly any emergence of new types of demands on the children — whether in schooling, leisure-time activities, etc. — is greeted with hostility. Pressure — physical, emotional, etc. — is exerted on the children not to perform the new social roles or to satisfy the new "needs."

Take, for instance, the following typical interview with a middle-aged father, an immigrant from central Europe. "I do not want my children to go wild and to behave in a manner in which they should not. I must always remember my education and my previous position, even if I have not yet got it here, and even if some clever people make fun of it, and even my own children do not really understand it. Here, almost all children are wild — they shout, are neither polite nor obedient, are not interested in working — only in playing and excursions. They do not dress properly; boys and girls mix too freely. I have many difficulties with my children and sometimes have to beat them; otherwise they will not become real men. . . . Here, at least, in my home, I must have some authority. . . ." One of his children summed up thus: "Father still lives in the past and thinks himself very important. But really he does not understand very much here. He makes life very hard for us, and we cannot get any fun with him. He gets terribly angry if we have some fun on our own. . . . But never mind, we shall do what we like and he will be very sorry for it."

It is among the children from these families that the highest rates of truancy from school, absenteeism from work, etc., are found. The result of this is, of course, that the children find it more and more difficult to establish for themselves a recognized social status according to the criteria of the new social structure, while the "old" status of their families lacks any reality in the new setting. Such a situation may develop — either in extreme cases or in thorough and prolonged undermining of the family structure — into a complete disruption of family life and of its ability to achieve any status at all. In such cases we witness the exclusive emphasis on a few basic biological needs and satisfactions and a lack of any stable roles and social relations. The relations between the parents and children become based more and more on sheer physical force which is not backed by any social participation or orientation. While among children of these "extreme" families, the various indices of delinquent group-behavior are usually intensified, it may quite often be found that they are unable to form any group relations at all, as the degree of organization of their personalities is minimal and their ability to perform *any* stable social roles undeveloped.

(2) *Conflicts of conceptions of authority.* This problem has been most widely emphasized in the literature on delinquency among immigrants (7). The stable and effective transmission of social and cultural orientations from the parents to the children is dependent on the acceptance of the parents' authority by the children. This is undermined whenever the conception of authority in the new social setting is different from the old and transmitted to the children through the "wider, non-familial" environment. In these cases the children's ability to perform new social roles and achieve full status within the new environment is jeopardized to the extent that the old authority norms are enforced on them, and the ensuing conflict predisposes the youths toward delinquent group formation. The emergence of such conflict is, of course, related to the difference of norms between familial-patriarchal and industrial-individualistic societies, but is not a necessary outcome of this difference. It is the degree of insistence on the old authority-dependence relations in the new environment which is the predominant factor. This attitude also can be illustrated from our interview material. The following excerpts are from an interview with an immigrant from North Africa: "I cannot really understand what happens here with parents and children. I do not think that what they do here is right and really it is a great sin. . . . At home we knew our place with our father, and he would not allow any disobedience. He knew what was right for us. But here children are becoming wild and unruly . . . they think that they should not obey their parents, that they are much wiser than the father and mother. They tell me openly that I do not understand what is good here. . . . It is the school, their teachers, and their 'groups' that teach them all this. Whoever has heard that children should have groups of their own and not obey the elders? . . . I try, always, to assert my authority and if they will not accept it, I shall throw them out. . . ."

(3) *Discrepancy between the parents' level of aspiration in the new country and the possibility of its realization.* This applies mainly to those immigrants who were initially more predisposed to change their social roles and to orient their aspirations towards the new social setting, but did not succeed in realizing them. It is in this context that cultural differences become of greater dynamic importance, since the lack of various skills and knowledge which are necessary for the performance of these new rôles

may seriously impede their realization. As one of them put it: "I have always thought that here I should begin a new life, become more prosperous and more influential. But these were vain hopes. The people here are hard and jealous and do not like to give me a chance. They always say that I do not know this or that and so on, as if they were the only wise people in the world. And so I am here, as you can see, in such conditions. What makes me really very angry is that now my children go out and play there with their children; they imitate them and they also think that all wisdom is there. I am very angry at them and I think we do not understand one another any longer. . . . They live in a world apart and are not interested in me. . . . I have really got no influence over them. . . ." Although no exact comparisons can be made, it seems that among children of these families a more intensive manifestation of the different delinquent symptoms can be found.

These main manifestations of a negative identification and conflict with the new social structure have been found to exist — although in different proportions — among all ethnic groups and socio-economic strata. They could not be attributed either to cultural heritage or to socioeconomic positions, but mainly to other factors, such as motives for immigration to Palestine, types of Jewish life and identification, consciousness and degree of social security as Jews in the countries of origin, etc. These causes were analysed by us in great detail in connection with the project of absorbing new immigrants, but are outside the scope of this paper.

In conclusion we must mention the type of conditions in the country of immigration which intensify the discontinuity and tensions between the family setting and the community. Although no full-scale analysis can be given in this short paper, some general indications should be mentioned. It has been found that generally this discontinuity is increased in so far as (a) the new immigrants are put in undefined and unorganized settings in which no clearly defined rights and duties are assigned them and in which their own inclination to emphasize only the basic, biological needs is intensified; (b) they encounter their new social setting mainly through bureaucratic channels and institutions in which they perform merely passive and subordinate roles; (c) they cannot fully participate in informal, face-to-face groups and relations with the old inhabitants and are mainly confined to formal relations in which only minimal mutual identification can develop; and (d) they are discriminated against by the old inhabitants. This last condition is, however, rare.

In other words, the predisposition towards delinquent group formation is minimized where the new immigrants (and specially the children and adolescents) can find or are enabled to acquire new, permanent and recognized social rôles and to participate in close personal relations with the old inhabitants. The existence of personal channels through which the immigrants can be introduced to the new social setting is the prerequisite of absorption. In many cases, the existence of such channels mitigates the results of unfavourable family settings, and the identification fostered through them may sometimes overcome the negative identification between the families and the community.

REFERENCES

1. P. W. TAPPAN, "Juvenile Delinquency." New York, 1949, pp. 139–40.

   H. v. HENTIG, "The Criminal and His Victim." Yale Univ. Press, 1948, pp. 259–97.

   W. RECKLESS, "The Crime Problem." New York, 1950, pp. 71–3.

   TH. SELLIN, "Culture Conflict and Crime." New York, 1938.

   S. N. EISENSTADT, "The Sociological Structure of the Jewish Community in Palestine." *Jewish Social Studies*, January, 1948.

   S. N. EISENSTADT, "Oriental Jews in Palestine." *Jewish Social Studies*, July, 1950.

   C. FRANKENSTEIN, "Juvenile Delinquency" (in Hebrew). Jerusalem, 1947.

   A. N. POLIAK, "The Jewish Community at the End of the Second World War" (in Hebrew). Tel-Aviv, 1946.

2. W. THOMAS, and F. ZNANIECKI, "The Polish Peasant in Europe and America." New York, 1927.

3. J. BOSSARD, "Sociology of Child Development." New York, 1949, pp. 493–520.

4. H. D. McKAY, "The Neighbourhood and Child Conduct," *Annals of the American Academy of Political and Social Science*, January, 1949, **261**, pp. 32–42.

5. S. N. EISENSTADT, "Youth Culture and Social Structure." (To be published in the *British Journal of Sociology*.)

6. S. N. EISENSTADT, "Unstructured Social Behaviour in a Situation of Culture Contact." Proceedings of the 14th International Congress of Psychology, Edinburgh, 1948.

7. IRVIN L. CHILD, "Italian or American, the Second Generation in Conflict." Yale Univ. Press, 1943. (See also (1) above.)

*   *   *

The Sociological point of view . . . has a regrettable tendency to beg the question. It takes for granted that, by definition, the crime is an attempt against social organization. Led on by this prejudicial statement, it emphasizes its destructive and negative aspects, and pays little attention to its positive functions as a factor of reform and progress. 'Aussi est il inutile d'observer les moeurs, puisque on peut les déduire des lois psychologiques' says Marcel Proust. We may trust to the words of this oracle. — Hanns Sachs: "Masks of Love and Life." (Sci-Art Publishers, Cambridge, Mass., 1948.)

37

A Brief Outline of Factors Influencing Delinquent Behavior*

United Nations

A brief summary of some of the various factors which are felt to play a part in the development of juvenile delinquency will be presented next, in order to provide background for the discussion of delinquency prevention. Various methods have been used to ascertain these factors ranging from observation by people working in the field to such research methods as the statistical method, case history method, use of life histories, participant observers, control groups, etc. It should be emphasized that most of the factors elicited from researches are based on information from Western nations. It should be stressed that not until carefully planned cross-cultural research is carried out will it be possible to know if causative factors felt to be useful with respect to delinquent behaviour in one part of the world are as useful in other parts of the world. Delinquent be-

haviour is not an isolated phenomenon and cannot be dealt with in a manner unrelated to the social matrix.

In the discussion on the extent of juvenile delinquency throughout the world it was brought out that in a few areas of the world the incidence of juvenile delinquency is low or almost non-existent, in other areas juvenile delinquency has become a problem within recent years or is now becoming one and in still other areas the problem has been cause for considerable concern for a long period of time. A brief analysis of some of the characteristics of these various types of societies,[1] as well as of the mechanisms for social control operating in each type, will now be set forth. This may help in understanding some of the factors which are important in the development or lack of development of juvenile delinquency.

In the first type — that where there is little delinquency — the family and the community are the primary agencies for social control. In some of these societies the tribe or clan plays a powerful role. There is little need for extensive use of legal codes, police, institutions, etc. Patterns of behaviour are well defined and each member of the society knows what is expected of him and in turn what he can expect of others. Norms of behaviour are inculcated into the personality of each member of the group and except for rare instances, most of the people conform and are adjusted to a patterned way of living. Children and young people have distinct functional roles in the society and participate closely with adults in daily activities.

The Non-Self-Governing Territory of American Samoa might be cited as an example of an area where formal control exists but where little is needed in handling juvenile delinquents, as they can be entrusted to the care of the family or clan. The United States Government reports the following:

"Juvenile delinquency . . . presents no problem of any consequence . . . in these islands; no more than two or three offenses, on an average, committed by juveniles, are reported per year. These almost invariably are instances of petty pilfering. In each such case, a notice is sent to the matai (patriarchal head

---

* Reprinted, with abridgment of footnotes, from "A Brief Outline of Various Factors Believed to Influence Delinquent Behavior and the Need for Research," International Review of Criminal Policy, No. 7–8 (ST/SOA/Ser. M/7–8), United Nations, January–July, 1955, pp. 25–29. Used by permission of the publishers. — Ed.

---

[1] When speaking of "types of societies" it should be understood that there are no societies which fit these artificial classifications exactly. This division is for the purpose of analysis.

of a clan) of the family involved to bring the offending juvenile or juveniles and their parents to the headquarters of the Government. This notice is usually sent by letter and does not involve an arrest or other police action. The family or families affected then go before the Chief Justice of the High Court of American Samoa in the privacy of the Judge's chambers. The Chief Justice proceeds to inquire into the matters complained of and delivers whatever corrective warning or instructions to the persons concerned as may appear to be appropriate. In conclusion, the juveniles involved are promptly returned to their homes. Their matai and parents [are] charged with the responsibility of ensuring the future good conduct of the young offenders. There is no arrest, no jail sentence and no record kept to embarrass the juvenile in the future. The Judge's admonition constitutes the whole proceeding."

The second type of society (where juvenile delinquency is just becoming or has only recently become a problem) is characterized by social change. In these areas industrialization is increasing, urban centres are developing, customs, traditions, and old values are disappearing and are being supplemented or intertwined with the new. Conflicts in values between the old and the new are often responsible for creating personal disorganization. This latter point is brought in a recent report of UNESCO entitled "Contribution of the Social Sciences to the Study of Social Conditions in the African Non-Self-Governing Territories":

"Although the westernized groups are still a small minority in Africa, the number of those who share in varying degrees in both cultures is constantly increasing. From the psychological standpoint, this means that the individual, while freeing himself of obligations to his parents, family group or tribe and seeking integration with other groups, is ultimately exposed to two sets of values and subjected to two kinds of pressure."

Parents are leaving the home to work outside and children are very often left to fend for themselves. Members of the new urban communities do not have the same close relationship that existed in the old rural way of life, and the community cannot exercise the same influence on young people that it once did. Legislation for controlling the actions of individuals is being introduced and social agencies established, thus replacing some of the functions that formerly were entrusted to the family and the community. With the development of in-dustrialization, consumer goods become available, and new desires for these goods become apparent.

In some areas, widespread immigration is felt to be an important factor with respect to juvenile delinquency. In Israel, for example, large scale immigration of children who either had no parents or whose parents failed to provide properly for them is reflected in the statistics of juvenile delinquency as well as those of juvenile vagrancy. Most of these children were brought up during the years of World War II and had little or no education. Many of them had grown up in a world whose people, in many respects, had abandoned the accepted values of civilized living. They had hidden or had spent years in concentration camps. These and other related factors are felt to have contributed to Israel's problem of juvenile delinquency.

While little scientific research exists on juvenile delinquency in these areas undergoing rapid change, observations by experts in the field, as well as findings of scattered researches, allow for the positing of some assumptions with respect to possible causative factors in various regions.

In a report of the Department of Social Welfare and Community Development (1946–1951) in the Gold Coast, for example, the following statement presents some ideas for consideration in relation to factors that might be responsible for delinquency among young people:

"The causes of crime among the very young is a question beyond the scope of this report. Very little is known at the moment of any difference that there might be in the reasons for criminal tendencies between, for example, the British and the Gold Coast child. Here there is room for very valuable research and it is hoped that in the not far distant future it will be possible to report some progress. Certain lines of thought do emerge, however, and they are of interest.

"Interviews with boys undergoing institutional training have elicited the fact that in the child's mind there is often a general unsettled feeling. So many of them live not with their parents but with a relative and it is more usual than not to find a lad in court with only one natural parent, the other partner having left the family or died. This cannot but have a harmful effect upon the child who is subjected to the added strain of modern urban life.

"Again, the question of continuous moving from one home to another seems to give the child a life lacking in security. There is one point of difference between Gold Coast family structure and that of the United Kingdom. It is possible that this difference does have a deep effect upon children. Inheritance in the Akan tribes (Ashanti and part of the Colony) is through the mother's family. On the death of the father, the property passes over to his eldest sister and her children as does the responsibility for the children. This, in the past, in small rural communities did not affect the children seriously, since the custom was adhered to completely, was well known and tended to be something of an insurance policy. In the modern town, and with educated people, where custom is receding, the responsibility of taking on children is sometimes not willingly accepted. It is understandable that a family living in already overcrowded conditions will not gladly receive an extra young nephew who has got to be accommodated. Children are in some cases tolerated only and the natural effect can be very harmful to young lives. Yet again it is not uncommon to find a youngster dissatisfied with life as it is, and running away to find a brave new world armed with nothing except his youth. We see the results of a transitional stage where the inequalities of opportunity, which rest on whether a lad has been to school or not, are upsetting his whole outlook on life and producing a desire to learn, or to receive at least the material benefits available to those who have had that opportunity, even though he may not have had it himself . . . the worries and an unsettled state of mind in a youngster are apt to drive him to want to fill his day so that they are excluded from his thoughts — and the day is spent in the streets with his young friends who form youthful gangs and pass the time in their own forms of excitement. In addition to this, in the towns, we are finding an alarming number of children who are leaving school before their time. Sometimes this is due to a lack of money or to transfer of parents or guardians, but too often it would seem to be due to the children themselves being impatient or unsettled, and truancy seems to be on the increase, the children doing little except idling in the town."

In many countries of Asia and the Far East, Latin America, the Middle East and other areas, juvenile delinquency has been increasing and similar factors are found to be of importance. In Asia and the Far East, for example, there exists a high incidence of offences against property and it is felt that this may "be attributable to the process of urbanization taking place . . . with its consequent disorganization of family life and with the resultant problems of personality and economic adjustment."

In Latin America, where the incidence of juvenile delinquency is high in the larger cities,

"children are suffering from the consequences of the disorganization of family life, which is spreading to every class of society . . ."

While industrialization and the development of urban centres are important factors with respect to the problem of juvenile delinquency, the effects of these phenomena upon young people living in rural areas must not be overlooked. In some areas, young people, hearing of the life in the towns and cities, are leaving their rural homes to seek employment and adventure in urban centres. In the Gold Coast, for example, it is stated that young people have migrated to the industrialized sea port of Sekondi Takoradi to obtain employment.

"There are a number of hardened youths and youngsters . . . who are grown up well beyond and live on the flotsam of this tropical sea-port during the time they cannot obtain employment as painters or as gang labourers, by pilfering stores from the docks or by catering for the needs of seamen who come to the town. They pick up the language and habits of the visiting seamen of all nationalities, and seem to earn a precarious living of a far higher standard than that which would accrue from their casual dock earnings."

Another point to be considered in relation to the industrialization process, and one which is often overlooked, is the transfer of rural customs to urban living sometimes resulting in undesirable consequences. This point has been recently stated in relation to underdeveloped countries:

". . . child labour in factories may be regarded as a continuation of the much less harmful rural custom of child labour on the farm; and urban slums often reveal a carry-over to cities of rural methods of house construction, refuse disposal, use of water, and so on. In fact, many — perhaps most — of the undesirable social consequences of industrialization are more properly regarded as results of failure to deal with the problems of social transition that inevitably arise from so basic a change in economic and social organization."

Finally, it should be realized that even in these regions which are feeling the impact of vast social changes, most of the population still live in predominently rural areas. In the survey on Asia and the Far East it has been stated that urbanization is not the only factor to be considered in relation to juvenile delinquency and the fact that "most of the juveniles, whether delinquent or neglected and ill-treated in Ceylon, Burma, India, Pakistan and the Philippines, come from poverty-stricken families and from slum areas indicates, however, that economic maladjustment is a very important factor in the causation of juvenile delinquency. The proverbial poverty and the chronic indebtedness of the agricultural and industrial labourers in India are certainly contributory factors to this problem."

Many of these less-developed regions have expressed concern over the paucity of studies relating to the determining factors of juvenile delinquency. With respect to Asia and the Far East, it has been stated that "special studies dealing with the relationship of juvenile delinquency to the cultural, social and economic conditions of the countries are extremely rare . . . Due to the limitations in the number and scope of . . . special studies, it is difficult to draw any conclusions with regard to the relationship of juvenile delinquency to the cultural, social and economic conditions which are prevalent in the region . . ." A recommendation of the Middle East Seminar on the Prevention of Crime and the Treatment of Offenders states, *inter alia*, that "A special centre devoted exclusively to scientific and practical research on the problem of juvenile delinquency should . . . be established in order to discover the causes of and methods for treating delinquency in the light, so far as possible, of living conditions in the Middle East."

In the third type of society to be discussed — where the problem of juvenile delinquency has been cause for considerable concern for a long period of time — much of the control which once rested with the family and the community has been or is being taken over by other agencies.

In a report of this type it is not necessary to describe at length the modern industrial societies of the United States, some parts of Europe and certain other countries of the world, nor is it possible or worth while to present a detailed account of the researches carried out in these societies which relate to the problem of juvenile delinquency. A brief description of the industrial, urban society as well as a short presentation of the direction that research with respect to juvenile delinquency is taking will be presented, however, to serve as a setting for the subsequent discussion of preventive programmes being attempted.

These areas have emerged through the processes of industrialization and urbanization into complex, urban societies. Here we find that values, which once were understood by nearly everyone in the society, are no longer consistent, that controls which once were executed by the family and through the face to face relationships of the small community are now weakened. In such countries the rates of delinquency are higher than anywhere in the world, yet, paradoxically, the standard of living and the existence of social services are also higher. There are no easy answers to the questions raised in relation to this situation. With respect to the United States of America it has been stated:

"The problems of law violation run deeper into the conflicts, complexity and competition of American culture, the materialism and superficiality in family values, the deterioration in traditional standards and values. All of these spell the loss of the personal integrity and loyalties upon which stable relationships are predicated. The problem then appears to arise with the development of mass urban society and its overpowering impact upon those whose personal deficiencies, family experience and group associations render them peculiarly pregnable to moral and social deterioration. While police, juvenile courts, agency services, foster homes and institutions have come to focus attention on these individuals, they appear not to have overcome in any significant measure the disorganizing influences of the community and the culture."

In an attempt to discover more explicitly what factors exist and in what manner they operate with respect to those "individuals whose personal deficiencies, family experience and group associations" make them deviate from the laws and norms of society, various types of research have been carried out in these areas. The findings of these researches, although by no means definitive, can serve as guides in the planning of programmes for the prevention of juvenile delinquency and the treatment of juvenile delinquents, as well as enriching the field of the behaviour sciences.

Much of the early research utilized the single cause approach, discussed above. Emphasis was placed on studying such factors as economic conditions, delinquency areas, gangs, culture conflict, constitutional factors, psychological and emotional factors as well as various other phenomena.

Although such studies have contributed to the knowledge of juvenile delinquency and have provoked further research, they have also assisted in giving the impression that the factors studied in a particular research are more important in producing juvenile delinquency than factors found in other studies. This has led to the establishment of elaborate and expensive programmes of prevention, which perhaps do no harm, but which are not necessarily useful in preventing juvenile delinquency.

In recent years the trend has been toward multidiscipline research and emphasis has been placed on studying factors relating to the individual delinquent and his environment as well as on comparable control groups of non-delinquents. While the findings of these researches are as yet limited, and methods used need to be greatly refined, certain interesting and useful data have been elicited.

An example of recent research using the participating of several sciences and a comparative sample of delinquents and non-delinquents is that of Sheldon and Eleanor Glueck,[2] which was carried out in Massachusetts, U.S.A. In this study 500 persistently delinquent boys (ranging in ages from eleven to seventeen) were compared with 500 non-delinquent boys. The boys were matched by age, ethnic derivation, intelligence, and neighbourhood residence. The two groups were compared on several hundred different factors. Results showed that the pattern which emerged with respect to delinquent behaviour was "neither exclusively biologic nor exclusively socio-cultural, but evidently deriving from an interplay of somatic, temperamental, intellectual, and socio-cultural conditions."[3]

With respect to the findings, the Gluecks have stated:

"Taken in the mass, if boys in underprivileged urban areas have in their make-up and early background a substantial number of the factors we have found markedly to differentiate delinquents from non-delinquents, they are very likely to turn out to be delinquent. In this general sense, then, a causal relation-ship has been established. Various subpatterns of factors, each sufficient to be causal of persistent delinquency, remain to be analyzed out of this general complex of factors."[4]

This study was presented merely as an example of one type of research that can be carried out in the attempt to ascertain the determining factors with respect to juvenile delinquency. More extensive research needs to be done because as yet our knowledge of behaviour is far too imperfect to predict with any degree of accuracy what the behaviour of a *particular* individual will be. The findings of such research can help not only those who are attempting to establish effective programmes of prevention and treatment on a group basis, but those who are working with individuals.

Research in areas of the world which are just now facing the problem of juvenile delinquency also needs to be carried out, taking into account the characteristics particular to the region. Methods of research used must be appropriate to the problems inherent in a given region. In a recent report on sociological surveys in the Non-Self-Governing Territories, it has been stated that too often such surveys "have been based on principles established in industrialized countries and have consequently proved unsuited to the realities of the colonial situation."

As was previously stated, knowledge with respect to causation is richer now than it was years ago, but much of this knowledge obtained from research is not being transmitted to practitioners. This often results in haphazard planning of prevention and treatment programmes based on easy explanations of what people *think* are the determining factors of juvenile delinquency. On the other hand, many valuable observations of practitioners, which could be useful to those doing research, are not properly communicated. The limitations in knowledge relating to causation, however, need not discourage those who on the basis of the findings are responsible for establishing prevention and treatment programmes, as long as they recognize the existing limitations and proceed in a realistic manner.*

---

[2] For details of this research see Sheldon and Eleanor T. Glueck, *Unraveling Juvenile Delinquency*, Cambridge, Mass.: Harvard University Press, 1950; also, *Delinquents in the Making*, New York: Harper and Brothers, 1952.

[3] *Delinquents in the Making, op. cit.*, pp. 183, 184.
[4] *Ibid.*, 186.
* Compare Chapter 33 of this volume. — Ed.

Chapter 9

Theories of Delinquency Causation

DEALING WITH VARIOUS THEORIES of delinquency causation and with the fundamental problem of the role of theory in criminologic research, this chapter might well have preceded the chapters on causation. It was felt, however, that after the student had a grounding in the major lines of etiologic investigation, he would be in a better position to assess the role and accomplishments of theoretical constructs in guiding and interpreting factual investigations.

The urge of criminologists to emulate the physical scientists in formulating basic etiologic thought in terms of some particular theory is understandable and commendable. The difficulty lies in the fact that the theories thus far formulated have not fulfilled the fundamental benefits of a theory; namely, the subsuming of a variety of disparate findings under a succinct and fruitful generalization which synchronizes various lines of empirical knowledge and which, in turn, leads to more relevant investigations in further fulfillment or modification of the formula. A favorite criticism advanced by certain criminologists is that the detailed, time-consuming and persistent preoccupation of a few investigators with the gathering of hard facts has been virtually useless. That this is a gross exaggeration, not consistent with the history of research criminology, can readily be proved. To cite but one example, the researches of the Editor and his wife have, among other values, turned up workable prediction tables [1]; and it is still true that a crucial test of scientific method is the capacity to make predictions. By contrast, the predictive, and indeed the explanatory, aspects of contributions to criminologic literature which claim to be based on some single, all-embracing theory have not been notable for their illumination. It may be conceded that perhaps, if it were possible, the effectiveness of the predictive instruments thus far developed could have been enhanced had the researches in question been guided (or misguided) at the outset by some all-embracing theory; but this remains to be proved. In the meantime, the predictions achieved by the methods employed are remarkably accurate.

Besides, as already mentioned in a previous connection, it is not true that follow-up and causal investigations have just been haphazard, grab-bag affairs in which no theoretical reflection about the research design had previously entered. In *Unraveling Juvenile Delinquency*,[2] for example, the research plan embraced a statistical comparison of a representative sample of true delinquents with a representative sample of proved nondelinquents. The two groups were matched, pair by pair, in terms of general intelligence, age, ethnic derivation and residence in an economically and culturally underprivileged urban area, and then compared in detail. The lines of comparison — anthropologic, psychiatric, psychologic, sociocultural (involving home, school and neighborhood) — were predicated on the assumption that the causes of human behavior are exceedingly complex, that they implicate both biologic and sociocultural factors, that delinquency, like death, is probably the result of a variety of etiologic chains, and that a forward step might be taken in understanding causation and predicting behavior

---

1 See Chapter 20, Articles 116–117, and Chapter 32 of this book.
2 By S. and E. T. Glueck, New York, The Commonwealth Fund, 1950; and Cambridge, Harvard University Press, 1951.

by determining which of several hundred traits and factors suggested by sound prior research into human behavior and its aberrations distinguish delinquents from non-delinquents with statistical significance. Those who question the findings of that study should attempt a similar one with equal care and see if the outcomes turn out to be alike. It is difficult to see that some pre-existent, single theory would have yielded results more illuminative and practical than those which were obtained. Suppose, for example, the research into delinquency causation had been limited to neighborhood influences. We know, by the fact that we also studied intrafamily life and that this proved to be of high significance in differentiating delinquents from non-delinquents, that concentration on a single theory — Shaw's "interstitial area," or Sutherland's "differential association" theory, or the delinquency subculture conception which has recently gained popularity, or the older Lombrosian theory of the "born criminal" — we would have missed a vitally crucial field of causation and prediction.

Claude Bernard has formulated a safe rule: "When you meet with a fact opposed to a prevailing theory, you should adhere to the fact and abandon the theory, even when the latter is supported by great authorities and generally adopted."

The articles in the present chapter raise some of the relevant issues in respect to causal philosophy as related to practice.

The first, by Weinberg, aims at the appraisal of group and individual approaches to the understanding of criminal behavior, in order to relate this understanding to the prediction problem and to develop a theory designed to reconcile differences. The author discusses the variations in thought on delinquency in the light of a broad historical-intellectual setting. He points to the weakness in the sociological acculturation theory in that it fails to explain individual variations in response to the delinquent subculture. He suggests, however, that the individual psychological explanations are, in turn, weak in not differentiating adequately "the antisocial person and the criminal," a fault attributable to the alleged dismissal or minimizing of the learning process. (This leaves out of consideration the question of who taught the first teachers of delinquent youth.) Weinberg arrives at a thoughtful synchronization of the two fundamental lines of etiologic thought. He concludes with a list of what he deems to be the crucial items to be used as predictors in a cultural approach to delinquency, as well as a list of predictors reflecting the intersection of the psychiatric and sociologic approaches "in the discontinuity between the family and peer group." The questions he leaves unanswered are how the delinquent sub-culture originated in the first place, and why such cultural factors should be used in prediction devices, when those involving family relations (the under-the-roof culture) have been proved to be adequate to prediction of delinquency at a very early period in life — long before the "gang age" or serious emotional attachment to a peer group.

Beeley's theoretical formulation runs along somewhat different lines. First, he takes account of the fact that, considering his anthropologic inheritance, mankind is "basically prone to theft and violence." This fact is then assessed in the light of the ineffectiveness, in modern urban cultures, of the traditional moral sanctions, partly because the social institutions which define and enforce them — such as the law — tend to become complex and therefore to lose their monolithic potency to control antisocial tendencies. To this is added "the criminological illiteracy" of the majority of the people regarding causes and control of crime, especially the most widespread fallacy that there is one single cause — deliberate evil design. Beeley takes as axiomatic the ideas that causes of crime are complex, plural, concurrent and/or contributory rather than exclusive, that "delinquency" is a generic term comparable to "sickness" and therefore analogous to "symptom" and not to "disease," and that — since delinquency is the result of many different antecedents — the causal factors are interchangeable. He distinguishes between the legal and the behavioristic answer to the question, Why do persons commit offenses? He concludes (a fact indicated, by the way, in the

Glueck researches) that "the social conduct of a person at any one time represents an equilibrium or balance between (1) the *expressive* force of his own impulses, and (2) the *repressive* force of social control . . . In the case of the offender a negative imbalance exists between (1) and (2)." Beeley then divides etiologic influences into those which enfeeble self-control and those which enfeeble social control, and lists a series of findings from various researches that fit into this dichotomy.

The article by the Editor, an address before the National Probation Association, indicates the difficulties involved in the analysis of the concept of causation, points to some crucial gaps in certain sociologic theories, and criticizes a typical social-psychologic theory. It ends with some practical suggestions to the probation officer investigating a case for a court, distinguishing between the mere presence of an alleged criminogenic factor and proof of its operative significance in the case. It is in determining the dynamic links between specific factors and behavior that the assessing of the degrees or the weight of the relationship between various factors in the matrix of causation and the varied responses of human beings in whose life these factors are operative, become of prime importance; and this is a basic contribution of the prediction technique to cause, treatment and prevention.

The final article in this chapter — "Theory and Fact in Criminology" — also by the Editor — poses some fundamental issues in the thought-content of theorizers and practical researchers. It is essentially a critique of a very popular American sociologic theory — that of "differential association." — and the Editor is not aware that satisfactory replies have thus far been made to his criticism of this frequently advanced theory.

38

Theories of Criminality and Problems of Prediction *

S. Kirson Weinberg

The aims of this paper are 1) to appraise the group and individual approaches to criminal behavior, 2) to seek a tentative theory of criminal behavior which reconciles these differences and 3) to relate theories of criminal behavior to the prediction of criminal behavior.

Although sometimes overlooked in actuarial studies, theory and prediction have an integral relationship in a scientific endeavor. The func-

* Reprinted from 45 *J. Crim. L., Criminology and Police Science* (1954), 412, 424. Used by permission of the author and the publisher. See, also, M. B. Clinard, "Research Frontiers in Criminology," 7 *Brit. J. Del.* (1956–57), 110–122. — *Ed.*

tion of theory is to explain the processes which contribute to or cause criminal behavior. The function of prediction is to test the theory by relating the processes to outcome for a series of cases. Since different theories emphasize diverse processes in the causation of crime, prediction studies should be able to test these theories. But many prediction studies have been so separated from theory that they have not been concerned with testing specific theories. In order to relate prediction to theory we shall first elaborate on the varying theories of criminal behavior, see to what extent these theories have been tested by prediction techniques and how these theories can aid in predicting criminal behavior.

Of the various theories of criminal behavior, we shall consider 1) the sociological version which deals with criminality as a product of learning and acculturation, and 2) the individualistic versions which explain criminality in terms of distinct personality traits.

I

Modern sociological theories of criminal behavior arose during the decline of social Darwin-ism. Human behavior was explained by learning and acculturation, and explanations based upon instincts and innate characteristics were repudiated.[1] The person generally was defined as a subjective aspect of his culture and as a cultural type.[2] The criminal, from this perspective was viewed as a product of a deviant subculture within the urban community.[3] The criminal, was a deviant type who became acculturated to a special behavior system in a learning process by association with other criminals.

Sociologists drew these inferences primarily from delinquents in high rate delinquency areas, and from confirmed adult offenders. Later they extended these theories to upper-class and middle-class persons, specifically to white-collar criminals.[4] The delinquents who were studied were in urban areas where the criminal culture was dominant, and where a network of relations extended from adult criminals to pre-delinquent children.[5] The other subjects, who were usually confirmed criminals, were also characterized as having a minimal opportunity to select conventional orientations. Although these inquiries have demonstrated conclusively that criminality is learned instead of inborn behavior, sociologists left unanswered why the individual selected, accepted, and executed his criminal behavior, except for certain delinquents in very high rate areas where conventional alternatives of behavior are few. But this left open the well-known questions why non-delinquents exist in very high delinquency areas where alternatives for conventional behavior are few; or why in low-rate delinquency areas, where the middle class conventional peer group and culture predominate, the juvenile seeks and selects delinquent associates. These aspects of criminal development are integral aspects of a total learning process. Despite the voluminous literature on delinquency and crime, these questions have not been answered adequately, except for two

studies. One study has shown that many non-delinquents are actually undetected delinquents; the other study has sifted out the pre-schizophrenics who were dominated by their mothers and who were too timid to participate in delinquent peer groups.[6]

Seemingly, this limitation in the sociological theory of crime resulted from a limiting theory of personality. First, since the individual reflected his culture or his role in the group, the dynamisms as to why he selected or did not select a singular organization of attitudes and meanings, were not explained adequately, and, in some instances, were not considered necessary for explanation. Hence singular motives, meanings, and aspirations of the criminal were muted in these descriptions in order to emphasize the shared behavior of the criminal as a cultural participant. Second, the process of selecting criminal or conventional norms of behavior was analyzed in terms of preferring one alternative from a series of alternatives as a means of renewing interrupted or disrupted action. This preference process, in turn, was explained by the theory of differential associations. Third, this theory of differential association was based upon a rational psychology, reminiscent of utilitarian psychology, and it conceived of preferred alternatives of behavior in terms of quantity and rational deliberation. From this approach, a given person would accept criminality because his contacts and definitions favoring violating the law exceeded his definitions and contacts favoring conforming to the law.[7]

But it is evident that the attachments and aversions, the diffuse and focused kinds of hostility, are acquired from past relations and experiences, and can affect contemporary decisions. In this respect, an individual may select criminal associates for reasons which he does not understand and of which he is unaware. This point is too frequently dismissed by claiming a fortuitous or adventitious theory of crime based upon chance association or upon chance combination of circumstances. The process of decid-

[1] Fay B. Karpf: *American Social Psychology*, 1932. Ellsworth Faris: *The Nature of Human Nature*, 1937.

[2] See William I. Thomas, and Florian Znaniecki: *The Polish Peasant in Europe and America*, 1927.

[3] Clifford R. Shaw, Editor: *The Natural History of a Delinquent Career*, 1931. Edwin H. Sutherland: *Principles of Criminology*, 4th ed., 1947.

[4] Edwin H. Sutherland: *White Collar Crime*, 1949. Mabel A. Elliott: *Crime in Modern Society*, 1952.

[5] Clifford R. Shaw, et al., editors: *Brothers in Crime*, 1938.

[6] Solomon Kobrin, "The Conflict of Values in Delinquency Areas," *Amer. Sociol. Rev.*, 16, October, 1951, pp. 653–661. Dunham H. Warren, "The Social Personality of the Catatonic Schizophrene," *Amer. Jour. of Sociol.* 12, May, 1944, pp. 574–576.

[7] Edwin H. Sutherland: *Principles of Criminology*, 4th ed. 1947, pp. 6–9.

ing upon, accepting, and incorporating criminal behavior means that an individual has internalized certain norms because of attachments to one or a series of persons who might be called reference points or reference groups.[8] These interpersonal attachments and the needs for social approval as bases for selecting and accepting motives and ideas, are not functions of frequency of association, and are not fortuitous, but are based upon emotional security, feelings of self-enhancement, or upon expressive behavior and conflict solution.

For example, one aspect of delinquent behavior during the 1920's concerned American born delinquents who rejected their parents' immigrant culture as inferior and who accepted their American peer culture as status-enhancing and superior.[9] This rejection of the parents' values by the children sometimes meant also rejecting the parents as role-models and hence accepting delinquents as role-models. Although the parents of many contemporary delinquents are natives, still the juveniles prefer the youth culture because of its prestige in our youth-oriented society. In the discontinuity of generations between parents and children, conformity to adults becomes mitigated by the peer group. Schachtel found that defiance of adult authority was one crucial symptom of delinquent behavior. He stated:[10]

The most important consideration in answering (whether a boy would or would not become delinquent) was whether or not the boy showed much dependence on or fear of authority. The more such fear and dependence has become part of the character structure and the prohibitions of the significant authoritative adults had been internalized, the more likely it seemed to me that the boy would not become delinquent.

It might also be pointed out the potential schizophrenics from high rate delinquency areas identify with the adult culture and tend to reject the peer culture or are rejected by their peers. In fact, in the Glueck study many indicators seem to point to some non-delinquents

in their control group as potential schizophrenics: they were extremely ectomorphic, dependent upon others, had vague feelings of anxiety and felt overwhelmed and helpless.[11]

Clearly when youths are more attached to an adult conventional culture than to a peer delinquent culture they will not necessarily resort to delinquent behavior even though they have learned delinquent techniques and experienced some relationships with delinquents. Healy and Bronner have specified that the criminal ideology is very pervasive and that the individual should have slight difficulty in acquiring criminal techniques.[12] But sociologists have, for this very reason, emphasized that criminal influences stem from direct association with other delinquents.[13] Hence they have stressed that delinquency usually arises from this direct association and not from indirect sources. Consistent with the reference group theory, however, association is necessary but is not sufficient as an explanation for accepting delinquent behavior; for the individual internalizes the types of behavior from persons with whom he has definite rapport and to whom he is attracted and frequently attached emotionally. The mode of relationships with a given person in a total content of a person's modes of relationships will indicate the direction of his influences towards delinquent or towards conventional behavior.

In this respect, parent–child conflict means not only displaced hostility from a parent to another person but also the possible rejection of the parent as a role-model and the search for other approving role-models. Frequently, these other role-models can be delinquents or criminals. Also, the individual who has ambivalent attitudes towards his parents, may have certain guilt-ridden reactions to crime which are residual from past attachments. Thus, the selection of delinquent values is a resultant process of social relations.[14]

In short, the sociologists have isolated delin-

[8] Theodore M. Newcomb: *Social Psychology*, 1950, pp. 240–243. Herbert J. Zucker: "Affectional Identification and Delinquency," *Archives of Psychology*, 286, 1943.

[9] See Thorsten Sellin, *Culture Conflict and Crime*, 1938.

[10] Quoted in Sheldon and Eleanor Glueck: *Unraveling Juvenile Delinquency*, 1950, p. 217.

[11] Sheldon and Eleanor Glueck: *Unraveling Juvenile Delinquency*, 1950. pp. 193, 221, 222, 224, 225.

[12] William Healy and Augusta Bronner: *New Light on Delinquency and Its Treatment*, 1936, pp. 135, 136.

[13] Edwin H. Sutherland: *Principles of Criminology*, 1947, pp. 6–9.

[14] Walter Reckless: *The Etiology of Delinquent and Criminal Behavior*, 1943. S. Kirson Weinberg: *Society and Personality Disorders*, 1952, pp. 290–295.

quents and criminals as cultural types. They have limited their explicit theories either to persistent juvenile offenders or to systematic adult property criminals. They have demonstrated that this behavior is learned in an acculturation process by association with other criminals. They have stressed the shared techniques and attitudes which the criminal expresses in the criminal culture. But they have not explicitly integrated the rise of criminal behavior of the singular person with the individualized meanings which go into the selection and acceptance of criminal behavior. Sometimes, the person has been analyzed as a passive rather than as a dynamic participant, by the contention of the fortuitous nature of his crime, and second, by the theory of culture conflict in which the individual is described as being pulled by two forces which create polar influences that he can not dispel or resolve.[15] But the active phase of individual selection emerges from accepting the attitudes of those persons to whom one becomes attracted and attached. The incomplete part in this learning process is that personal attachment was not acknowledged as affecting the acceptance of one set of attitudes and practices in preference to another set of attitudes and practices.[16] The cultural approach has explained one dimension of delinquency and adult crime. It has explained one type of delinquent or criminal who has experienced a minimal set of alternatives in selecting his criminal behavior. Thus the sociologists have formulated a framework for understanding the development of crime as learned behavior. They have made this causal formulation from subjects who were already delinquents and criminals. But these processes which lead to delinquent and criminal behavior, as we shall see, can also be used as predictors of potential criminals.

II

The gap which pertains to the development of criminal behavior has been supplemented by studies of the criminal as an individual. Nonetheless, these clinical studies have not answered these questions within a theoretical framework

of learning and acculturation and inter-personal relations. Aichhorn recognized the gap of development in criminality when he stated: [17]

When I ask parents how they account for the dissocial behavior of their children, I usually receive the answer that it is the result of bad company and running around on the streets. To a certain extent this is true, but thousands of other children grow up under the same unfavorable circumstances and still are not delinquent. There must be something in the child himself which the environment brings out in the form of delinquency.

The Gluecks have been more explicit when they said: [18]

They (the Sociologists) do not explain why the deleterious influences of even the most extreme delinquency area fail to turn the great majority of its boys into persistent delinquents. They do not disclose whether the children who do not succumb to the evil and disruptive neighborhood influences differ from those who become delinquents, and, if so, in what respects.

Healy and Bronner, among others, have recognized these facets of delinquent behavior as points of departure, although this does not necessarily mean that they have produced a conclusive answer.[19]

Since both personality maturation and character structure theories seek something physically, tempcramentally, or emotionally distinctive in the delinquent's or criminal's personality make-up, then how does the person acquire these distinctive characteristics which lead to criminal activity?

The biopsychological maturation theorists, such as Sheldon, Seltzer, and Glueck, emphasized the constitution-temperament trait couplet as predisposing the youths to selecting and to accepting criminal behavior.[20] The individual with a tightly-knit muscular, predominantly

---

[15] This "fortuitous process" would be very difficult to verify.

[16] For a discussion of role-taking and learning, see George H. Mead: Mind, Self and Society, 1935, pp. 73–81.

[17] August Aichhorn: Wayward Youth, 1939, pp. 39, 40.

[18] Sheldon and Eleanor Glueck: Unraveling Juvenile Delinquency, 1950, p. 5.

[19] William Healy and Augusta Bronner: New Light on Delinquency and Its Treatment, 1936, pp. 68, 69.

[20] William H. Sheldon: Varieties of Delinquent Youth, 1949. C. C. Seltzer "Body Disproportions and Dominant Personality Traits," Psychosomatic Medicine, 8, 1946, pp. 75–79. Sheldon and Eleanor Glueck: Unraveling Juvenile Delinquency, 1950, Chapters 15, 21, Appendix C.

mesomorphic constitution, has an aggressive, outgoing temperament, and will be attracted to activities that may defy or oppose conventional constraints. Hence he becomes delinquent because his mode of expression differs from that of the non-delinquent who, at the extreme, predominates as an ectomorphic body-type. Of course, physical anthropologists and constitutional biologists do not explain why so many conventional children with similar physiques and temperament do not become delinquent. This approach may impute to constitutional factors what also is a product of a particular peer culture. The constitution-temperament trait-couplet seems to imply a built-in kind of delinquent potential. It does not explain the manner in which selection of the delinquent or criminal norms of behavior occurs, although it does show that the majority of delinquents, fit this body type. In brief, does body-type and temperament have a bearing upon predicting criminal behavior?

The clinicians who advocate indirect learning and fixation in early life as the basis of a potential delinquent character structure, have tried to show that these roots of personality difficulties are the antisocial tendencies. The most pervasively distinct characteristic in these studies has been the outgoing aggressive behavior among delinquents in contrast to non-delinquents. They minimize the effects of learning from the delinquent peer-group in a tolerant neighborhood situation. When they preclude the probability of a stable person becoming delinquent, they make criminality coincide with character disorders, such as Abrahamsen or, Healy and Bronner who specifically assert that delinquency results from "thwarted wishes in early life" or the Gluecks who conclude that delinquency is a "character disease." They see in these early predispositions the bases for selecting and accepting delinquent behavior.[21] While the Healy and Bronner study does not specify the given community areas, the Gluecks' study did identify the high rate delinquency areas.

But the clinicians have difficulty in differentiating between the antisocial person and the criminal. The characteristics of outgoing hostility, defiance, destructiveness, and impulsive aggression, are not the same as criminal behavior. An antisocial person may engage in random acting-out behavior, and still not violate the law — or he may engage in stealing. This view errs in dismissing the learning process in criminal behavior or in appraising it as of slight importance. Boys who are behavior problems in conventional middle-class areas do not necessarily become delinquents or criminals, but boys in lower-class areas frequently become delinquents. This approach somehow attributes an inevitability to the selection of delinquent associates and to the learning of crime when the early frustrations and subsequent hostility are present. But connecting the sequence between predisposition towards and acceptance of delinquent behavior remains to be demonstrated. On the other hand, it must be recognized too that the process of social definition is important. The lower-class juveniles may be defined and arrested as delinquent, whereas middle-class boys for somewhat similar activities, might be spared from arrest.[22]

The theory of character disorders as the crucial causal basis of behavior does not explain the different distribution of delinquents and criminals in different areas of the city by diverse childhood training techniques, or even by constitutional temperamental types. Seemingly, the most plausible explanation is the concentration of delinquent traditions in these areas of the urban community. Since lower-class juvenile and adolescent males participate in perhaps one of the most unrestrained and aggressive peer sub-cultures of any society in the world, if rated by unrestrained individual fighting as well as by unsupervised inter-group fighting, then an emotionally normal boy who associates with his peers would become aggressive by sheer participation in the group.[23] Hence a person's aggression can be explained by one of three levels. Some boys become very aggressive, defiant and destructive from the influence of their

---

[21] William Healy and Augusta Bronner: *New Light on Delinquency and Its Treatment*, 1936, p. 133. Sheldon and Eleanor Glueck: *Unraveling Juvenile Delinquency*, 1950, p. 289. David Abrahamsen: *Who Are the Guilty?* 1952, pp. 26–28. K. R. Eissler: "General Problems of Delinquency," *Searchlights on Delinquency*, edited by K. R. Eissler, 1949, pp. 3–25.

[22] Austin L. Porterfield and C. Stanley Clifton: *Youth in Trouble*, 1946.
[23] Allison Davis and John Dollard: *Youth in Bondage*, 1940. S. Kirson Weinberg: "Occupational Culture of the Boxer," *Amer. Jour. of Sociol.*, 57, March, 1952, pp. 460–469.

peers. Other boys become very aggressive as a defensive formation from the helplessness and guilt in anxiety neurosis. Still other boys become very aggressive from psychopathic tendencies and minimal guilt. Seemingly, there has been no satisfactory differentiation of these levels of aggression in terms of their relevance to criminal behavior.

Aggressive behavior which is so pervasive among lower class boys cannot be explained satisfactorily by early child training except in a very general way. One difficulty in assessing the aggression as well as other traits of the delinquent boy results from the methods in the individualistic clinical inquiry. It does not see the boy as an integral part of his cultural context. Instead, it sees a series of actions which are abstracted away from the cultural context. Thus, it imputes certain rash actions as personality difficulties when these may possibly be expected reactions in the given cultural context. Frequently the clinician has a middle class bias in evaluating the behavior of the lower-class delinquent boy, particularly when his interpretations are based upon interviews. Furthermore, the boy's behavior acquired by participation in the peer group may resemble superficially behavior resulting from personality difficulties. As we shall see, these discrepant interpretations affect the kinds of predictors used in forecasting potential delinquent behavior.

A gang member may have the same lack of empathy for an out-group enemy that a psychopath has for another person. He may show the same lack of guilt by peer identification that the psychopath has. Many activities of delinquents which have been attributed to temperament or to early frustrations can be explained too by participation in and by learning from the peer group of lower-class boys in slum areas. What is considered early frustrated training may, in some instances, be the acquisition of the motivational emphases of a gang in a neighborhood milieu.

But from another vantage point, the individualistic clinical approach to criminal behavior has complemented the collective approach in the following ways: It has dealt with individualized meanings as distinct from shared attitudes. Hence criminal behavior has been viewed as symptomatic of, and as a defensive formation from, personality conflicts which are distinct from the shared norms and practices of a deviant group. Delinquents satisfied their individual needs and also responded to shared norms of behavior by their delinquent behavior. This means then that delinquency is a response not only to the social control of a deviant group but also is the activity stemming from private emotional needs.

Both sociologists and psychiatrists have recognized that delinquents become attracted to each other and cultivate socially intimate relations. Perhaps delinquents have certain predisposing attitudes which make for a certain inter-personal rapport among themselves and which non-delinquents do not share because they have different personal needs to satisfy in their social relationships. Still we cannot conceive of delinquents and non-delinquents as arrayed in two neat, separate rows as some of the matched studies of experimental and control samples implicitly and explicitly may lead one to believe. In some high rate delinquency areas, the two groups may mingle but their relationships do not become sustained. These subtle aspects of the communicative process in social interaction must be considered along with the cultural view as a medium for transmitting and imparting criminal norms and techniques.

For the sociologists have emphasized the conjunctive relations among delinquent associates as tutelage media in transmitting crime. They have seen delinquency as a positive and rewarding form of behavior either in terms of thrill, peer group approval, or status enhancement, which reinforced the learned delinquent patterns of behavior. The psychiatrists have emphasized the disjunctive relations in the family as instrumental to delinquency; have seen delinquency as a negative form of behavior either in terms of residual hostility acquired from inter-personal relations in the family, or as compensatory association for parental or familial rejection or indifference. Thus the two views emphasize diverse aspects of learning. The sociologists, from a cultural approach, regard the criminal as acquiring and sharing symbols and actions in a variant sub-culture. Clinicians have emphasized the individual manner in which the criminal learns to execute his actions, to confront his difficulties, to relate with people, and to solve his conflicts, either as private defenses against anxiety or as the forms of hostility and of other perverse traits persisting from childhood. For example, two individuals may learn to drive an automobile, which is a new technique. One person may never have an accident; the other may have repeated accidents. Two individuals may learn to steal. One may never get caught. The other may get caught repeatedly. The mere learning of new behavior on a shared, rational level does not tell us how the individual will execute his knowledge in terms of the private meanings it has for him as an individual. These individualized meanings have been the preoccupation of the psychiatrists and psychologists who approached the delinquent as a unique person rather than as a cultural participant or as a social type. And these individualized meanings which may be witting and unwitting affect the manner in which the individual will learn and use his skills and socialized values. Thus the delinquent or criminal who conforms to a given socially deviant value system on a group level also uses these values as symptoms or as defenses to solve his personal conflicts on an individual level.

III. Types of Theories

These diverse approaches to criminality describe different aspects of crime and place diverse emphases upon the factors which can predict criminal behavior. Since the first or cultural approach regards systematic crime as an acquisition by social participation, the criminal is viewed in a benign way in terms of his similarity to the conventional person: Both learn their behavior and abide by the norms peculiar to their respective groups. Both have similar goals — such as money, prestige, success. Although criminal and conventional norms differ, insofar as the criminal has acquired his behavior by social participation, he is basically not different in degree of stability or maturity than the conventional person. Hence the advocates of this approach stress the normality of the criminal, and disregard the personality differences as an explanation of crime. It is not surprising, then, that in one critical review of the studies of personality attributes among criminal and conventional persons, the authors concluded that personality traits are distributed in the criminal population in about the same way as in the general population.[24] They write:[25]

When the (test) results are considered chronologically, there is nothing to indicate that the personality components of criminal behavior are being established by this method. On the contrary, as often as not the evidence favored the view that personality traits are distributed in the criminal population in about the same way as in the general population.

The advocates of the individual approach who regard crime as deviant and nonconforming, view the criminal as an antisocial individual who cannot be restrained by conventional norms and who has a distinctive personality. Hence they search for the combination of personality traits which cause his deviation, and depict the criminal negatively as one who cannot participate successfully in conventional society.

Seemingly, these two images of the criminal as it has been thus far depicted have resulted from different implicit questions. The sociologists have asked: "Why does systematic criminality exist?" And their answer is that it is a group and cultural process that cannot be explained by individual differences. Then, how does the individual become a criminal? They answer: By learning. The psychiatrists and psychologists, as clinicians, have asked: "Why do individuals become criminals and not remain law-abiding persons?" Their answer is that the criminal has distinct traits, stemming, either from personality maturation or early conditioning which differ from the traits of the conventional person.

IV. Bases for an Integrated Hypothesis of Criminality

From the foregoing discussion, can we synthesize the group and individual versions of delinquent behavior — as limited to systematic property offenses — within an integrated frame of reference? This does not mean arriving at a coordinate eclecticism in which diverse variables are juxtaposed to each other, but rather seeking an analysis of behavior within an integrated theoretical scheme.

If we begin with social relations as a way of learning new behavior, we would have to investigate the function of social relations upon the group and individual aspects of behavior. First, social relations vary by meanings, form, and motives. Thus, the meaning of social relations as pertinent to delinquency would vary for children who become delinquents and for adults

[24] Karl F. Schuessler and Donald R. Cressey: "Personality Characteristics of Criminals," *Amer. Jour. of Sociol.*, 55, March, 1950, pp. 476–484.

[25] *Ibid.* p. 483.

who become criminals. The boy who values the companionship of his delinquent associates may steal to retain the approval of his companions rather than to get the monetary gain. On the other hand, the adult may consider the gain as foremost in his relationship with other criminals. Thus the salience — that is, the peripheral or central importance — of the attitudes in forming and retaining the relationship, varies for the two age-groups.

Second, the positions of the interactants in their relationships must be considered. Although an individual learns to become a criminal by the influence of his social relations, the criminal also can learn to become a conventional person by his relations with conventional persons. Thus the role of the person in the association process must be explicitly defined. From the available evidence, it appears that the novitiate in crime tends to be emotionally dependent upon the criminal. Were the dependence upon a conventional person, such as a therapist, the influence would flow towards a conventional orientation.

Third, the individualized satisfactions in the inter-personal process lead to the attraction and rapport of persons whose needs are similar. These needs which may be verbalized and unverbalized, pertain to the selection of delinquent associates apparently by persons who seem to come from families and other groups that fail to provide these juveniles with definite feelings of personal security and that do not create the kinds of relationships by which the juvenile internalizes deep attitudes towards conventional behavior.

Fourth, when these juveniles encounter accessible delinquent associates, they seem to prefer them as companions to more conventional persons, because these delinquents satisfy verbalized and unverbalized emotional needs. In this association process, the individual becomes responsive to accepting and sharing delinquent techniques and practices. But the situations leading to acceptance of crime vary considerably. The 6 year old boy who is initiated into crime by his older brothers has an entirely different problem of selection than the 16 year old boy who leaves conventional friends in his neighborhood to associate with delinquents in another neighborhood.

Fifth, when the delinquent group is not accessible, or when delinquent companions do not gratify the juvenile's individualized needs, then he will seek conventional outlets in a process of dynamic selection.

In short, we might suggest that criminal behavior as manifested among juveniles, arises when, for individualized purposes of emotional security, self-enhancement, or conflict-resolution, they seek and select accessible associates from whom they learn, accept, and express criminal attitudes.

By assessing the varying theories of delinquent and criminal behavior and by presenting a unified theory of criminal behavior, we shall have some gauges for checking the implicit and explicit theories in the prediction studies. From the individualistic approach, the emphasis would be upon the body-type, temperament, family relations, early personality development and personality structure of the potential delinquent. From the group approach, the emphasis would be upon the type of neighborhood, the kinds of accessible peers and perhaps the family relations. The unified approach would combine personality organization with accessible peer relations in a given cultural context.

V. THEORY AND PREDICTION

The studies of prediction pertain not only to the potential delinquency of children but also to the reformation or recidivism of delinquents on probation and of adult criminals on parole. The methods used in formulating the theories of causation and those applied to prediction provide a commentary on the devious ways in which social science works.

The theories of causation are based mainly upon inductive analysis and typology. Thus Sutherland, Shaw and McKay, Cressey, Healy and Bronner, Abrahamsen among others state their theories in a manner which account for all cases and which explain one level of reality whether it be the cultural, the social or the personal.[26]

[26] Edwin H. Sutherland: *Principles of Criminology*, 4th ed., 1947, pp. 6–9. Clifford R. Shaw and Henry D. McKay: "Social Factors in Juvenile Delinquency," *Report on the Causes of Crime*, II, 13, 1931, pp. 222–257. D. R. Cressey: *Other Peoples' Money*, 1953. William Healy and Augusta Bronner: *New Light on Delinquency and Its Treatment*, pp. 273–282. David Abrahamsen: *Who Are the Guilty?* 1952, pp. 66–72.

The pertinent findings of prediction are based upon probability analysis and upon the testing of specified items of multi-dimensional levels by the actual outcome for a given sample of subjects. The theories of criminal behavior are usually within the scope of pure theory because they are non-utilitarian in purpose. The findings of prediction are designed usually for administrative purposes and are within the scope of applied theory. Theories of causation usually consider arrest or detection as superfluous in understanding criminal behavior. The findings of prediction — with the exception of work on potential delinquency — operate within the policy framework of probation or parole. Hence detection or arrest may be crucial. Also the predictive instrument does not always test personality dynamics and social dynamics but becomes a function of empirical trial and error outcome for specified items in terms of a given criterion, whether it be arrest or violation of parole or other action. Frequently, these items are taken from records in the files and have been recorded for purposes other than prediction. Hence these items become direct or indirect indexes at best of the pertinent behavioral dynamics of criminality. On the other hand, there has been an increasing recognition of the need to use items derived from a consistent theory and then applied to predictive tests.

Of the two types of theories of crime, namely crime as deviant behavior and crime as learned behavior, the theory of crime as deviant behavior is implicit or explicit in most predictive studies. Also, personality differences which are ignored or considered unimportant in the cultural approach to crime are considered relevant in most prediction instruments whether devised by clinicians or by sociologists. For example, Reiss has emphasized that delinquent recidivism is the result of failure of personal and/or social controls, whether in the family or in the local community.[27] But from a learning viewpoint of delinquency, the emphasis would have been upon accessibility to delinquent associates and upon the continued influence by delinquents as against conventional persons.

To illustrate the impact of personality differences upon potential delinquency in predictive

inquiry, we find that the Hathaway-Monachesi studies of delinquency are based upon the scores of the items in the Minnesota Multiphasic Inventory.[28] Thus the subjects with high scores in the "psychopathic deviate" category of behavior would portend a high probability of potential delinquency. In fact, almost twice as many subjects with high scores in the psychopathic deviate items were later arrested for delinquency than were the group as a whole.

Perhaps the most consistent attempts to apply sociological theory in which crime is regarded as a form of acquisition have been the Ohlin-Glaser studies of prediction of paroled criminals.[29] This theory is based upon the process of differential identification which has been derived from Sutherland's theory of differential association. Since the Sutherland theory of differential association applies to the systematic property offender, this theory too would also pertain to the systematic property offender, and would not include other offenders, specifically sex offenders, whose crimes result from personality difficulties.[30] Furthermore, the theory of differential association does not admit of individual differences in the causation of crime. Still in one item, called "social development pattern," the "respected citizen" category had 6.0 percent violators while the "socially maladjusted person" category had 60.6 percent violators.[31] Does this mean that personality differences are of slight importance in the causation of crime but are of decided importance in the renewal of crime? This may mean that the type of personality does influence the selectivity of associations in the process of reformation or recidivism. Indeed, it is difficult to see how the process of selective identification would work without considering the

[27] Albert Reiss, Jr.: "Delinquency As The Failure of Personal and Social Controls," *Amer. Sociol. Rev.* 16, April, 1951, pp. 196–206.

[28] Starke Hathaway and Elio D. Monachesi: "The Prediction of Juvenile Delinquency Using the Minnesota Multiphasic Inventory," *Amer. Jour. of Psychiatry*, 108, 1951, pp. 469–473.
[29] Loyd E. Ohlin: *Selection for Parole*, 1951. Loyd E. Ohlin and R. A. Lawrence: "Alternative Methods of Parole Prediction," *Amer. Sociol. Rev.* 17, June, 1952, pp. 268–274.
[30] Daniel Glaser: "A Reconsideration of Some Parole Factors," *Amer. Sociol. Rev.* 19, June, 1954, pp. 335–341.
[31] Daniel Glaser: *Report on Pontiac Parole Prediction Study* (Mimeographed). Both percentages were very significant and as such had a high degree of selectivity.

individualized needs of the person who does the selecting. Thus the theory of differential identification would perhaps be influenced by personality type, situational context or both in different degrees. The sensitivity of this point might possibly require further data from questionnaires as well as from information recorded in the files.

The Glueck study had the advantage of devising a prediction table based upon data gathered in a field study to verify certain specific hypotheses. From these data, the components of a multi-dimensional causal hypothesis were evolved and some of the components were used in a prediction study. In fact, they emphasize a multi-disciplinary inquiry, including constitutional, intellectual, emotional and social components, but devise a prediction table based upon the psychiatric aspects of personality only. Does this mean that a coordinate interdisciplinary approach to delinquency does not enhance the demonstration of predictive outcome for the factors considered? Seemingly, this study does not answer this question directly, but in predicting potential delinquency, it states that the constitutional approach is still controversial for ascertaining behavior of young children and that peer group influences do not begin in early childhood. Hence the Glueck study orients its predictive table about parent–child relations, and the formative character structure which emerges from these relations.[32] Their findings are highly consistent — causally considered — with the Healy-Bronner study. Both studies, emphasize the deviance theory of criminality and consider such character traits as defiance, suspicion, social assertion, aggression and outgoing destructiveness as indicative of potential delinquency. Still these traits may also be the learned and expected behavior of boys in lower-class gangs. Thus in some cases the behavior that is acquired from residually hostile relations in the family may also be acquired in the adjustment to peers in lower class areas.

From a cultural approach to delinquency, the crucial items which might predict potential delinquency would include: 1) the boy's capacity for group participation and for acceptance by other boys, 2) his relative accessibility to criminally-oriented boys and to conventionally-ori-

ented boys, 3) his satisfaction or dissatisfaction with conventional interests and activities, 4) his attachment or aversion to conventional role-models, particularly in the family, 5) his need for being accepted by his peers even when their behavioral practices are delinquent.

Seemingly, the psychiatric and sociological approaches intersect in the discontinuity between the family and the peer group. In a synthesis of these approaches, the predictors of potential delinquency would include 1) the independent variables of family relations, capacity for peer relations, and accessibility of delinquent or conventional peers, and 2) the intervening variables of satisfaction or dissatisfaction with conventional role-models and of the search for delinquent or conventional companions or outlets, while 3) the dependent variable would be the uniformly specified criterion of property offences. In this manner, perhaps the use of interdisciplinary theory of the behavioral dynamics of delinquency could be tested concertedly by prediction of outcome.

39

A Sociopsychological Theory of Crime and Delinquency*

Arthur L. Beeley

This paper reports an attempt to formulate a working hypothesis aimed at synthesizing the empirical knowledge of crime causation. As ground work for the theory, the logic of crime causation is first examined and restated. The sociopsychological theory outlined here is designed as a framework, within which to organize and relate the observed data of criminology, and also to indicate the gaps for further investi-

---

* Reprinted from "A Socio-Psychological Theory of Crime and Delinquency: A Contribution to Etiology," 45 J. Crim. L., Criminology and Police Science (1954), 391–399. Used by permission of the author and the publisher. This is an expansion of a paper read by the author at the 31st Annual Meeting of the American Orthopsychiatric Association, New York City, March 11, 1954. — Ed.

---

32 Sheldon and Eleanor Glueck: Unraveling Juvenile Delinquency, 1950, pp. 259–269, 273–282.

gation. The implications of the theory for criminology and crime control are then briefly set forth.

A. The Logic of Crime Causation

The chain of reasoning which constitutes the logic and argument supporting the theory is set forth in four propositions, as follows:

1. Experience has shown that human beings are basically prone to theft and violence. In a pre-civilized society men prey upon each other, individually or as members of a group. All civilized societies, however, sooner or later evolve sanctions which forbid and punish predatory behavior. These mores are calculated to protect the individual in his right to the ownership of property, and to the inviolability of his personality.[1]

2. In complex urban cultures, such as those of the West — especially societies like ours which experience periods of rapid social change — the traditional moral sanctions and the social institutions which define and enforce them tend to become ineffective in controlling the antisocial tendencies of their members. Consider, for example, the constitutional guarantees still accorded a gangster in a modern American city, e.g., the late Al Capone of Chicago. These provisions in the organic law of the several states were never intended to protect lawbreakers of this variety. They are, in fact, a historical vestige of the English Bill of Rights of 1689, originally drawn up as a bulwark against the tyranny of the Stuart kings.

3. The perennial failure to cope effectively with the increasing amount and the manifold forms of lawlessness in America is due to two things. First, the widening gap between our material culture, i.e., our systems of communication and transportation which accelerate social mobility and increase anonymousness, and our adaptive culture, i.e., our law and government, based, as they are, upon medieval conceptions of conduct and moral responsibility. This disparity between the two main divisions of our total culture tends to produce social disorganization, and its counterpart, disorganization of personality.

A second reason for this failure is the criminological illiteracy, so to speak, of the vast majority of people regarding the nature, causes, and control of crime. Consider briefly just a few of the antiquated beliefs of the typical layman:[2]

(a) the fallacy that all crime is equally serious, and its corollary, that all prisoners are criminals, *per se.* That fact is that the vast majority of all offenses are minor infractions of the law, legally defined as *mala prohibita;* that is, quasi-crimes, which, for the most part, are the prohibitions embodied in local ordinances, calculated to control vice, regulate traffic, promote safety, sanitation, etc. This large group differs qualitively from all other offenses, legally classified as *mala in se;* that is, such crimes as larceny, rape, homicide, etc. Even in this latter category, the great bulk of offenses are petty crimes and minor misdemeanors, which together far outweigh in number all other forms of essential crime. In fact, this phenomenon can be expressed as a simple criminological axiom: the seriousness of an offense tends to vary inversely as its frequency.[3] Furthermore, it is little known by the public that a very large number of inmates in city and county jails at any one time are petty offenders, committed to prison for their inability to pay even a small fine.

(b) another fallacy is the belief that crime is a product of an "evil design," the expression of "an abandoned and malignant heart," notwithstanding a mass of scientific evidence to the contrary. This belief is a vestige of the English common law, and the dubious metaphysics of atonement, retribution, and vengeance which were the prevailing beliefs during the formative period of Anglo-American criminal law. This view naively imputes complete "freedom of will" to all offenders, except children, the feebleminded, and the psychotic.

---

[1] The bulk of offenses comprise what in law are called (a) crimes against property, and (b) crimes against the person. There are, of course, other crimes of a qualitatively different nature; but these two categories constitute the two largest groups.

[2] See also Arthur L. Beeley, "Fact and Fiction in Criminology," *The Sci. Mo.,* Vol. LXXIV, No. 1, Jan., 1952, pp. 45–50.
[3] A. L. Beeley, "Delinquency: Its Forms, Causes, and Prevention," *Character Education,* U. S. Bureau of Education Bulletin No. 7, 1926, pp. 59–60. From a tabulation of 1,585,560 cases dealt with in the Municipal Court of Chicago during the ten-year period, 1915–24, incl., the following appeared:

Felonies 5.9
Misdemeanors 23.7
Quasi-crimes 70.4

(c) the Lombrosian fallacy of the born criminal is still widely cherished and has been commercially exploited in our time by the mass media of communication, with the result that it has become a rigid stereotype in the minds of the masses, including many public officials who are responsible for the administration of criminal justice. Equally fallacious, although repeatedly disproved by controlled experimentation is the belief that all offenders are mentally defective, psychotic, or psychoneurotic. To add to the confusion, there has appeared in recent years a wide range of uncritical conjectures advanced by preachers, lawyers, judges, and reformers, singling out such isolated factors as impiety, alcoholism, immigration, parental neglect, etc., as the sole cause of crime or delinquency.

(d) a cross-section of American public opinion reveals, therefore, what is perhaps the most widespread of all the fallacies, namely: the popular misconception that there is one single cause of crime, with the naive inference that if each of these malevolent factors could be controlled or stamped out, crime and delinquency could be well-nigh eradicated, or, at least, reduced to a negligible minimum. This is the fallacy most difficult to eradicate; first, because the layman is culturally conditioned to the notion of personal and moral responsibility for human conduct, whereas the relatively new science of criminology [4] must perforce deal with the entire problem along strictly deterministic lines in an endeavor to isolate and measure the naturalistic rather than the super-naturalistic nexus between cause and effect; secondly, the findings of this new science, unlike those in medicine and engineering, are sometimes negative. Consider, for instance, the painstaking scientific work of Goring, who first laid the ghost of Lombroso's "criminal man." He concluded that there is no such thing an an anthropological criminal type; ". . . this anthropological monster has no existence, in fact." [5]

Moreover, many conclusions are unspectacular, albeit profound; as for example, the experimental studies of Burt, who compared delinquent and non-delinquent children in London and finally concluded that it is either the number of factors or their combination that renders delinquency a probable result. "On an average," he said, "each delinquent child is the product of nine or ten subversive circumstances, one as a rule preponderating and all conspiring to draw him into crime." [6]

Thirdly, public opinion and public policy in our democracy are largely formed and enforced by laymen, rarely by the criminologist. (The findings of the New Jersey Commission on the habitual sex offender are an exception to this generalization.[7])

4. As a final proposition or thesis, three axioms of criminology are here formulated as more or less self-evident truths:

(a) there is clear proof that the causes of crime (or delinquency) are complex rather than simple, plural rather than singular, concurrent and/or contributory rather than exclusive;

(b) the words "crime" and "delinquency" are generic terms comparable to the word "sickness" in the field of medicine. They are, therefore, analogous to the concept "symptom," and not the concept "disease" (syndrome);

(c) that crime (or delinquency) is the uniform consequent of many different antecedents; the causative factors are, therefore, interchangeable.

B. A Sociopsychological Theory of Crime and Delinquency

In the light of the foregoing, it is argued that the criminologist has an obligation, not only to his science, but also to the social control of crime and delinquency, to formulate an inclusive theory of causation which attempts to synthesize the wide range of empirical findings now available from many lines of independent and unrelated inquiry, and thus to indicate fruitful lines of further research and investigation.

At the outset it would be well to define the

---

[4] There were few, if any, scientific studies of crime, criminals, and the administration of criminal justice prior to about 1900.

[5] Charles Goring, The English Convict, A Statistical Study; London: H. M. Stationery Office, 1919, p. 269.

[6] Cyril Burt, The Young Delinquent: New York: Appleton and Co., 1930, p. 577.

[7] The Habitual Sex Offender, Report and Recommendations as formulated by Dr. Paul W. Tappan, Trenton, N. J., 1950.

terms used throughout this discussion: (a) causation, and (b) crime and delinquency.

As used here, the word "causation" means simply the antecedent(s) of an event. As in the case of most other sciences, we are concerned only with the proximate rather than the ultimate causes of the phenomena considered. One of the common mistakes of everyday thinking about crime and delinquency, as with many other problems, is the uncritical assumption that because one thing follows another, there must somehow be a causal connection between them, thus illustrating the common fallacy, *post hoc, ergo propter hoc*.

The usually accepted definition of a crime is that it is an act, either of omission or commission, specifically forbidden by public law. Definitions of delinquency, on the other hand, are less explicit, for the reason, of course, that in most Western societies the public takes a more charitable view of youthful offenders and their wrong-doings. However, there is general agreement to the effect that a delinquent is a person who, while under age, is nevertheless guilty of an anti-social act which constitutes an infraction of public law.

For purposes of the theory advanced here, however, it would seem more appropriate to define crime and delinquency in socio-psychological terms and say that crime (or delinquency) is, in effect, the violation of a group's legalized taboos (mores) by any person who is presumed by age or status to be a more or less responsible member of that group.

The central question then becomes clear, namely: Why do persons commit offenses? First, we must distinguish clearly between the legal question and the behavioristic one. The primary concern of society, as illustrated by the role and function of the trial court, is to establish a single fact, namely: Is the defendant guilty or not? In sociopsychological terms a criminal court then is an institution whose primary, if not sole function is "to define the situation" in strictly legalistic terms. So that in the common law and also in most statutory law, the question of "why" the accused committed the crime is irrelevant. Only since about 1900, with the establishment of juvenile courts, is the behavioristic question raised as to the offender's motivation and the causative factors responsible for his misconduct. Herein lies the fundamental difference between the approach of the criminologist and that of the jurist.

Pursuing the subject further, it is now necessary to make the following general assumption regarding human behavior: human beings possess many native traits or original tendencies, which, when uncontrolled or allowed free expression, are inimical to the welfare of other human beings in the same society. In order, therefore, to achieve what advanced societies regard as a civilized life for the greatest number, the expression of these anti-social impulses must of necessity be curbed. These taboos, or checks, ultimately take the form of our penal codes.

On this basis, therefore, the social conduct of a person at any one time represents an equilibrium or balance between (1) the *expressive* force of his own impulses, and (2) the *repressive* force of social control. For the majority of law-abiding persons in a given society, these two forces are in a positive equilibrium; but in the case of the offender, a negative imbalance exists between (1) and (2). This division of all persons into two such categories is admittedly hypothetical. On the theory of probability it would, of course, be more exact to assume that the social behavior of human beings ranges on a continuum, i.e., from the extreme of obedience on the one hand, to the opposite extreme of lawlessness on the other. Obviously, there are all degrees of conformity and nonconformity to the rules of social living. What is implied in the hypothesis, however, is the notion that there is a theoretical point beyond which a society will not tolerate infractions of its laws.

The final question now becomes: What factors, singly or in combination, produce this negative imbalance, and, therefore, constitute the antecedent causes of crime and delinquency?

Assuming the plausibility of such a theory, the next step is to categorize the range and variety of empirical factors into a simple, orderly scheme. The following plan is proposed:

1. factors which enfeeble self-control.
2. factors which enfeeble social-control.

With this dichotomy as the framework, the etiological literature of criminology was thoroughly re-examined and found to yield itself readily to the proposed classification.

The separate factors are grouped into general categories, each one containing two or more specific examples, as follows:

CLASSIFICATION OF THE CAUSES OF CRIME AND DELINQUENCY, ACCORDING TO THE AUTHOR'S SOCIO-PSYCHOLOGICAL THEORY OF CAUSATION.

(N.B. The numbers in brackets ( ) refer to pertinent, representative titles in the List of References at the end of this article.)

1. FACTORS WHICH ENFEEBLE SELF-CONTROL
   a. Inherited or acquired physical and physiological handicaps (13). e.g., in physique (35), stature, deformities, and defects.
   b. Physical injury or disease (10). e.g., accidents, occupational (or other), tuberculosis, syphilis.
   c. Inherited or acquired mental handicaps. e.g., feeble-mindedness (40), psychopathic personality (21), epilepsy.
   d. Mental and psycho-somatic disorders. e.g., psychoses (11), psycho-neuroses, mental conflicts (16, 25), emotional disturbances (1), (31).
   e. Personal disorganization from excesses (17), (19). e.g., sex, alcohol (3), narcotics (26), gambling.
   f. Character structure (12). e.g., ignorance, naivete, inadequate life-organization.

2. FACTORS WHICH ENFEEBLE SOCIAL CONTROL
   a. "Sick" societies. e.g., Great Britain and its mining community (14).
   b. Inherent defects in the economic order. e.g., poverty, unemployment (42), depression (32), exploitation (37).
   c. Urbanization (7). e.g., mobility, anonymous life in cities (36).
   d. Changing mores and group conflict (43). e.g., with regard to sex, use of alcohol, tobacco.
   e. Family disorganization (20). e.g., death of parent, divorce, non-support, faulty discipline (24), incompatibility, internal conflict (23).
   f. Community and neighborhood disorganization. e.g., depressed areas, poor housing, unwholesome companionships (34), lawless gangs (39).
   g. Overlapping and conflicting governments (29). e.g., municipal, county, state, federal.
   h. Inherent limitations of the criminal law, substantive and adjective (30). e.g., obsolete, unenforceable, and conflicting laws.
   i. Maladministration of criminal justice. e.g., the breakdown of law enforcement (27), prosecution (4), and the courts (8), incompetent prison administration (2), corruption in parole administration (6), (41), organized crime and racketeering (22).
   j. Inadequate educational activities. e.g., amount, quality, and rigidity of secular (18), religious (9), and vocational instruction.
   k. Inadequate avocational facilities. (28). e.g., unwholesome leisure interests, commercialized amusements.
   l. Opinion-making and control. e.g., press (15), film (5), radio, television.
   m. Interpersonal and intergroup conflict (33). e.g., ethnic (38), religious, economic.

C. SOME IMPLICATIONS OF THE THEORY

The implications of this theory are many and far-reaching. A few of the more pertinent inferences are briefly formulated, as follows:

— 1 —

The validity of a sociopsychological theory of crime causation stems from the currently accepted view as to the nature and scope of social psychology itself. While there is by no means complete agreement on all points as to just what contemporary social psychology encompasses, there is, nevertheless, a general consensus on three important points: (a) that the central problem is the human personality, its structure, genesis, dynamics, patterning, pathology, etc.; (b) that from the viewpoint of etiology, the environmental factors are, theoretically, equal in importance to the biological ones; and (c) that human behavior is a function of interaction, not alone between the organism and its environment, but also between persons, groups, and cultures.

Since all offenders are persons, the analysis of their behavior is, therefore, most effectively approached from the standpoint of social psychology; that is, in terms of the integrated knowledge drawn from all the behavior sciences. Dr. Bernard Glueck, formerly psychiatric consultant at Sing Sing Prison, once observed profoundly: "The criminal act in every instance is the resultant of the interaction between a particularly constituted personality and a particular environment." This generalization by an eminent criminologist is, of course, an etiological principle couched in sociopsychological terms.

— 2 —

Some of the prolific lines of further study and investigation of crime and delinquency will no doubt have occurred to the reader already. Six suggestions, however, are offered here and grouped under (a) studies of offenders, (b) the criminogenic environment, and (c) the machinery of crime control.

(a) *Studies of offenders.* The primary and most fruitful scientific approach is, of course, the comparative case-study of the offender.

What empirical criminology needs is more personality studies by all the behavioristic disciplines working together, in order to determine the etiological relationship between crime and such specific conditions as the psychosomatic disorders, epilepsy, narcotic addiction, and the compulsion neuroses, e.g., pyromania, kleptomania, dipsomania, etc. Ideally, such studies could be made while the offender is in custody, although they could be made even while he is on probation.

Likewise, there is need for more intensive studies of hostility and aggression in young and old offenders, especially during the early stages of their incarceration in a prison or a reformatory, in order to reveal in magnification the dynamic interpersonal relationships affecting the human personality.

(b) *The criminogenic environment.* It has been repeatedly proved that the social environment, when in a state of rapid social change, tends to become criminogenic. A recent case in point is the exposure of a new pattern of lawlessness with far-reaching ramifications, namely: syndicated racketeering, as brought out in a nationwide investigation by the Senate Committee to Investigate Organized Crime in Interstate Commerce. Similarly, the new and virulent forms of gangsterism recently manifested on the New York City water-front.

Another illustration of potential criminogenesis in the social environment is the accelerating gravitation of persons to cities and urban environments. In such a *milieu* the person tends to become anonymous, losing his status, and with it, a sense of social responsibility. It is an axiom of social psychology that intimacy in a small group is the most effective system of social control, and that personality thrives best in the matrix of normal family life. To what extent then are law-breakers persons who have never had or may have been prematurely deprived of normal family life? Here is an admirable problem for further controlled experimentation, comparing offenders and non-offenders identically.

(c) *The machinery of crime control.* It is argued here that if and when the institutions of crime control are ineffective, as they too often are, the decrepit machinery of criminal justice administration is *per se* a contributory cause of crime and delinquency. Especially is this true on the state and local levels, as illustrated

by the overlapping and uncoordinated machinery for the apprehension, trial, imprisonment, and parole of offenders. A specific example of the clumsy machinery of local law enforcement is the case of Los Angeles County, with its 46 separate bodies, most of which function independently. This same anomaly exists in Cook County, Illinois, and in many other metropolitan areas.

Another instance is the obsolescent county jail system and the need for a re-examination of its role in crime control. The county jail is the prototype of all American prisons and exceeds in number and influence all other prisons put together. Its continued use in its present form is self-defeating, to say the least.

— 3 —

The theory here advanced amply attests the scientific soundness of the current trend in penology, namely: the principle of individualization in the diagnosis and treatment of the offender.

— 4 —

Perhaps the most far-reaching implication of this theory of crime causation is the conclusion that we can no longer hope to find a universal panacea or a palliative. Crime cannot be dealt with intelligently *en bloc* any more than disease can be effectively treated or wholly prevented *en bloc*. Progress in treatment and prevention will probably be achieved in much the same way it was achieved in the field of medicine and public health, that is, by the isolation and control of specific patterns or symptom-complexes.

REFERENCES: REPRESENTATIVE TITLES

1. ACKERLY, SPAFFORD, "Rebellion and Its Relation to Delinquency and Neurosis in 60 Adolescents," *Amer. Jour. Orthopsych.*, 3: 147–60, April, 1933.
2. AMERICAN ACADEMY OF POLITICAL AND SOCIAL SCIENCE, "Prisons of Tomorrow," *The Annals*, Vol., 157, Sept., 1931 (Ed. by E. H. Sutherland and Thorsten Sellin).
3. BANAY, RALPH S., "Alcoholism and Crime," *Quart. Jour. Studies in Alcohol*, 2: 686–716, March, 1942.
4. BEELEY, ARTHUR L., *The Bail System in Chicago*, Univ. of Chicago Press, 1927.
5. BLUMER, HERBERT, AND HAUSER, PHILIP, *Movies, Delinquency and Crime*, New York, 1933.
6. BRUCE, A. A., BURGESS, E. W., AND HARNO, A.

J., *The Working of the Indeterminate Sentence Law and the Parole System in Illinois*, Springfield, Ill., 1928.

7. CLINARD, MARSHALL B., "The Process of Urbanization and Criminal Behavior," *Am. Jour. Sociol.*, 48: 202–13, Sept., 1942.

8. *Criminal Justice in Cleveland*, Part III, *The Criminal Courts*, Cleveland: Cleveland Foundation, 1922.

9. DODSON, DAN W., *The Role of Institutionalized Religion in Ethnic Groups of Dallas*, M. A. Thesis, So. Methodist Univ., 1937.

10. FERNALD, MABLE R., HAYES, M. H. S., et al., *A Study of Women Delinquents in New York State*, New York: Century Co., 1920.

11. GLUECK, BERNARD, "A Study of 608 Admissions to Sing Sing Prison," *Mental Hygiene*, Vol. 2: 85–151, 1918.

12. GLUECK, SHELDON AND ELEANOR, *Unraveling Juvenile Delinquency*, New York: Commonwealth Fund, 1950, Chapter XVIII, "Character and Personality Structure."

13. GORING, CHARLES, *The English Convict, A Statistical Study*, London: H. M. Stationery Office, 1919.

14. HALLIDAY, JAMES L., *Psychosocial Medicine* (A Study of the Sick Society), New York: Norton & Co., 1948.

15. HARRIS, FRANK, *The Presentation of Crime in the Newspapers*, Hanover, N. H. Sociological Press, 1932.

16. HEALY, WILLIAM, *Mental Conflicts and Misconduct*, Boston: Little, Brown, & Co., 1917.

17. HEALY, WILLIAM, *The Individual Delinquent*, Boston: Little, Brown, & Co., 1915.

18. HEALY, WILLIAM, AND BRONNER, AUGUSTA, "How Does the School Produce or Prevent Delinquency?" *Jour. Educ. Sociol.*, 6: 450–70, April, 1933.

19. HEALY, WILLIAM, AND BRONNER, AUGUSTA, *Judge Baker Foundation Case Studies*, Series No. 1, New York: Knopf, 1929.

20. HEALY, WILLIAM, AND BRONNER, AUGUSTA, *New Light on Delinquency and Its Treatment*, New Haven: Yale University Press, 1936.

21. KARPMAN, BEN, *Case Studies in the Psychopathology of Crime*, Washington, 1933.

22. Kefauver's Crime Committee Report, *Special Committee to Investigate Organized Crime in Interstate Commerce*, Third Interim Report, U. S. Senate 82nd Congress, Report No. 307, Washington, 1951.

23. LEVY, DAVID M., "Studies in Sibling Rivalry," Monograph Series No. 2, *Amer. Jour. of Orthopsychiat.*, 1937.

24. LEVY, JOHN, "A Quantitative Study of Behavior Problems in Relation to Family Constellations," *Amer. Jour. Psychiat.*, 10: 637–654, 1931.

25. LEWIS, NOLAN D. C., AND YARNELL, HELEN,

Pathological Firesetting (Pyromania), New York: Nervous & Mental Disease Monographs, No. 82, 1951.

26. LINDESMITH, A. R., "A Sociological Theory of Drug Addiction," *Amer. Jour. Sociol.*, 43: 593–609, January, 1938.

27. *National Commission on Law Observance & Enforcement*, No. 14, 1931, *The Police*, Washington: U. S. Govt. Printing Office.

28. NEUMEYER, MARTIN H., AND ESTER S., *Leisure and Recreation*, New York: Barnes & Co., 1936 and 1949.

29. New York Legislature, *Report of Joint Committee on the Government of the City of New York* (Hofstadter and Seabury Committee), 5 Vols. in 2, New York, 1932.

30. POUND, ROSCOE, *Criminal Justice in America*, New York: Henry Holt & Co., 1930.

31. REDL, FRITZ, AND WINEMAN, DAVID, *Children Who Hate*, Glencoe, Ill.: The Free Press, 1951.

32. SELLIN, THORSTEN, *Crime in the Depression*, New York: Social Science Research Council, 1937.

33. SELLIN, THORSTEN, *Culture Conflict and Crime*, Bulletin 41, New York: Social Science Research Council, 1938.

34. SHAW, CLIFFORD, AND MCKAY, HENRY, "Social Factors in Juvenile Delinquency," *National Commission on Law Observance and Enforcement*, No. 13, June 26, 1931, Report on the Causes of Crime, Vol. II, Part II and III, Washington: U. S. Govt. Printing Office.

35. SHELDON, WILLIAM H., *Varieties of Delinquent Youth*, An Introduction to Constitutional Psychiatry, New York: Harpers, 1949.

36. STUART, JOHANNES, "Mobility and Delinquency," *Amer. Jour. Orthopsychiat.*, 6: 486–493, October, 1936.

37. SUTHERLAND, EDWIN H., *White Collar Crime*, New York: Dryden Press, 1949.

38. THOMAS, W. I., AND ZNANIECKI, F., *The Polish Peasant in Europe and America*, New York: Knopf, 1927, Vol. II.

39. THRASHER, FREDERICK M., *The Gang: A Study of 1313 Gangs in Chicago*, Chicago: University of Chicago Press, 1927.

40. TULCHIN, SIMON H., *Intelligence and Crime, A Study of Penitentiary and Reformatory Offenders*, Chicago: University of Chicago Press, 1939.

41. U. S. ATTORNEY GENERAL, "Parole," *Survey of Release Procedures*, Vol. IV, Washington, D. C., 1939, pp. 545–659.

42. WINSLOW, EMMA A., "Relationships Between Employment and Crime Fluctuations as Shown by the Massachusetts Statistics," *Natl. Com. on Law Obs. and Enf.*, No. 13, Vol. I, 1939, pp. 257–333, op. cit.

43. WIRTH, LOUIS, "Culture Conflict and Delinquency," *Amer. Jour. of Sociol. Forces*, 9: 484–492, June, 1931.

Note: Some of my contemporaries have made admirable contributions to the etiological theory of crime and delinquency. The following are noteworthy:

SELLIN, THORSTEN, "A Sociological Approach to the Study of Crime Causation," *Culture Conflict and Crime*, Bulletin 41, Chapter II, New York: Social Science Research Council, 1938.
SUTHERLAND, EDWIN H., "A Theory of Criminology," *Principles of Criminology*, (4th Edition), Chapter 1, New York: Lippincott Co., 1947.
TAPPAN, PAUL W., "The Problem of Cause," *Juvenile Delinquency*, Chapter III, New York: McGraw-Hill Co., 1949. — The author.

40

Crime Causation*

Sheldon Glueck

In the brief time at my command, I propose to discuss a few matters about which you have perhaps thought at one time or another but which deserve emphasis: first, the attempt to construct a general theory of crime causation; second, analysis of some problems in the dynamics of crime causation; third, some obstacles to the fruitful study of the causes of crime; and last, some suggestions regarding the scope of the case history from a causal point of view.

In considering a topic of such complexity, it is important at the outset to define the field. What do we mean by *crime*? In one aspect it is a term covering behavior which some particular society at some specified time and place has chosen to forbid, by means of laws the infringement of which is supposed to result in the punishment of violators. But even if we remain on a purely legal plane, such a defini-

* Reprinted from *Probation and Parole Progress*, National Probation Association Yearbook, 1941, New York, 86–108. Used by permission of the publisher.

tion is too general to have much meaning. For the patterns of legally prohibited behavior may range all the way from the buying of a drink to the killing of a human being. And the mental states involved may vary all the way from lack of intention to violate the law (in crimes not requiring proof of a "criminal intent") to a deliberate and premeditated intention to commit a murder. Moreover, under certain conditions, a person may commit even a homicide and yet not be guilty of a crime, as in accidental killing not amounting to criminal negligence, or legitimate self-defense.

Despite these troublesome complications of what ought to be a clear concept, we may legitimately limit our discussion of the problem of crime causation to that group of acts which for a long time and in most civilized communities have been prohibited under threat of punishment — the familiar property crimes and crimes against the person. Our conclusions regarding crime causation may or may not be valid for exceptional statutory crimes. We are not concerned with an abstraction so lofty that it will cover all possible prohibited acts done with every conceivable state of mind, in every politically organized society that ever existed anywhere. A crime causation theory covering all this would be so thin as to have very little theoretical value and certainly no practical value.

But it is not enough to limit our vision to the act and the criminal intent or "guilty mind" of the law, if our object be to look into the causes of misconduct. When we step behind these oversimplified conceptions to the individuals who usually commit crimes, we see at once that the motives behind, and the circumstances surrounding different types of delinquent and criminal behavior vary markedly; and more, that the persons committing crimes are as different in their mental makeup as are noncriminals. Most important, we see that many persons have been subjected to very much the same temptations and social pressures as have delinquents and criminals, and yet have managed somehow to remain noncriminal.

A HIERARCHY OF CAUSAL INFLUENCES

How can we account for this puzzling state of affairs?

Let us look at the concept of *cause* in the realm of human behavior. At the outset it must be recognized that we are faced with a hierarchy of causal influences, some of them very remote from the individual human being's theater of thought and action, others closer, still others right on the stage, as it were. Thus it has been shown by graphs based on statistical correlations that climate and weather have some influence on human behavior, considered in the mass. It is a familiar historical fact that geographic conditions exert an effect on human behavior. It has been demonstrated that fluctuations in economic conditions, unemployment and like phenomena of a broad societal nature are more or less related to such changes in human behavior as the rise and fall of the crime rate, particularly that of property crimes. It has also been established that the conflict of cultures in a community or a family bears some relationship to the incidence of delinquency and criminality. Coming to the individual himself, it has been shown that mental makeup is related to patterns of behavior, including antisocial behavior.

Broad general theories of crime causation may be of some value as a basis for broad, general social reforms, such as programs for reducing unemployment or projects for changes in a criminal code. They may also be of value in suggesting leads for more specific inquiries. But in order to do so, these general theories must not be so far removed from the scene of action as to be almost meaningless in their abstractness. At the same time, every such theory must cover and account for *all* the relevant evidence that its formula is supposed to summarize. With these requisites in mind, let us first examine a recently advanced general theory of crime causation, and then descend to more specific and tangible mechanisms of causal significance in the individual case.

CRITIQUE OF A CURRENT THEORY

There is a natural urge among thinkers to find one beautifully simple explanation for a multiplicity of complex factors and forces. They seek intellectual security and aesthetic symmetry; they search for a philosopher's stone. But while this attitude may have resulted in the brilliant theories of Newton and Einstein, I doubt whether this search for the very highest abstraction in a hierarchy of causal forces will produce much of value in the study of crime, or indeed in the study of any important social phenomenon involving the behavior of human beings. Yet this attempt to explain everything by one thing is a marked feature of the activities of criminologists since men began to speculate about "*the* cause" of crime, or of sin, or of man's inhumanity to man.

Now considering the great variation in the kind of behavior patterns the law condemns as criminal, it would be strange indeed to discover but one underlying cause — whether it be the law's classic concept of guilty intent, behind which lies the unproved assumption of a completely free will; or Lombroso's theory that criminals are, by reason of a combination of epilepsy, atavism and degeneration, predestined from birth to become criminals; [1] or the theories of the earlier psychologists and psychiatrists that crime is largely caused by mental defect or disease; or the theory of certain modern sociologists who insist that the "interstitial" or slum area is the chief cause of delinquency; or most recently, the rediscovery by them that "social disorganization" is the basic cause of "systematic criminal behavior."

At the present stage of our investigation into cause, it seems to me wholly unwarranted to attribute exclusive or even major causal significance to any one of these factors. The desire to do so has led to putting one's scientific faith in a theory so remote from the dynamic realities of the individual offender's intellectual and emotional life as to be almost meaningless. To urge, for example, that all systematic criminal behavior is basically caused by social disorganization is to advance our thinking little further beyond the equally valid observation that the basic reason why people become criminals is the fact that they were born; had they never come into this world, they would never have become criminal.

Theories of this kind are too abstract and too far removed from the relevant operative mechanisms of conduct and misconduct in the individual case, or even in types or classes of cases, to throw much light on the problem either theoretically or practically. Besides, they are fatally incomplete in the light of the available evidence. One has only to state the proposition that the basic cause of crime is "social disorganization" to see how unfinished an explana-

[1] In his more mature writings Lombroso limited the application of his theory to only one-third of all criminals. G. L. Ferrero, *Criminal Man*, Putnam, New York, 1911, p. 100.

tion of the facts it is. For it leaves out of account two crucial questions: Why do so many persons *not* become criminal even under a high degree of social disorganization? And what distinguishes the kind of person who, when each of the socially-disintegrating influences becomes more and more operative, steps across the thin line separating law-abidingness from criminality, from the kind who remains noncriminal? Such theorizing, in other words, omits from consideration, or does not sufficiently take into account, the crucial area of causal mechanism — the *nexus* between the social forces and the particular individual's bodily and mental makeup. For obviously, whatever be the element of social disintegration we are concerned with, its influence makes itself felt only on a *selected group of individuals*. It must therefore be the physical and mental makeup of offenders, as compared with nonoffenders, that presents the crucial and practical issue in the study of crime causation.[2]

In recent years some criminologists have been celebrating the demise of biological theories of crime causation. They have tended to overlook the role played by the structure and functions of the individual's mind in originating, selecting and resisting different forms of behavior. To read some of their writings, one would think that practically all there is by way of explanation of the varieties of human conduct is the fluctuation in so-called social forces, which fluctuation arises by reason of causes not at all clearly explained. In fact, these criminologists have gone so far as to insist that the notion that mental defect or disease or distortion has anything appreciable to do with bringing about crime is as dead as the dodo. It is all due to these mysterious social forces, or societal disintegration, or the blind clash of cultures. The fact

that crime has existed as long as recorded history, among civilizations of widely varied states of social disorganization is ignored. The fact that the criminalistic "culture" in the "interstitial areas," into which boys move and to which they allegedly succumb by becoming delinquent, had to come from somewhere in the first place gives them little concern. The fact that even in the most marked interstitial area nine-tenths of the children do *not* become delinquent is lightly passed over. Indeed, from their lyrical insistence upon social factors as the sole or at least the determining influences one would almost conclude that human beings have nothing to do with crime and that the state of intelligence, instinctual drives and emotional–inhibitory mechanisms of the individual are almost wholly irrelevant to the problems of crime causation!

A good illustration of this point of view is the opinion held by many sociologists of the fundamental significance of the concept of attitudes. By trying to get away from the quest for "the innate and universal tendencies" of man's makeup, such as instincts, to the less fixed aspects of man's mind as influenced by social experience, they have thrown the baby out with the bath.[3] In their eagerness to kill the instinct theory as a basis for social psychology and sociology, they seem to have ignored the fact that though "social attitudes of individuals are but the specific instances in individuals of the collective phenomena"[4] of society as a whole, individuals do differ in the kind of attitudes they acquire, even though subjected to the same social influences. It is no answer to this criticism to say that many individuals within the same social group have the same attitudes. The crucial question is, why do so many other individuals *not* acquire those attitudes, if it be not largely because of innate differences in the organization and strength of their fundamental drives? The only other explanation could be chance, and this explanation requires too long a stretching of the "long arm of coincidence."

The prejudiced attitude of some sociologists

---

[2] In describing the general theory of crime causation to which I largely have reference in the above remarks, Edwin H. Sutherland (*Principles of Criminology*, Lippincott, 3rd ed., 1939, p. 7) illustrates: "A child who is not wanted at home may be emotionally upset, but the significant thing is that this condition may drive him away from the home and he may therefore come into contact with delinquents." I submit that the more significant thing is that many children who are unwanted, do not because of that leave home, and that many of those who do leave home and do come into contact with delinquents do not themselves become, or remain, delinquent.

[3] This is the chief criticism I would make of the otherwise admirably instructive collection of essays *Social Attitudes*, edited by Kimball Young, Holt, New York, 1931. See Ellsworth Faris' "The Concept of Social Attitudes," Chapter 1.
[4] *Ibid*, p. 5.

toward the concept of attitudes is illustrated by the following quotation from Professor Faris, a leader of this school of thought: "Institutions are not produced by the instincts. Warfare makes men warlike and churches make men religious." [5] Professor Faris neatly avoids committing himself on the question of whether it has required the institution of marriage to make man sexual. It is difficult to have patience with these extreme environmentalists. They talk as if it is the easiest thing in the world to make a human being out of a gorilla by simply "conditioning" the ape from early apehood. And as for making a silk purse out of a sow's ear — that seems to be mere child's play.

A passage from a lecture by Freud will show how unreal are the theorizings of these extremists. Speaking of Marxism, Freud said that by it: [6]

A whole collection of correlations and causal sequences was . . . discovered which had hitherto been almost completely disregarded. But it cannot be assumed that economic motives are the only ones which determine the behavior of men in society. The unquestionable fact that different individuals, races and nations behave differently under the same economic conditions in itself proves that the economic factor cannot be the sole determinant. It is quite impossible to understand how psychological factors can be overlooked where the reactions of living human beings are involved; for not only were such factors already concerned in the establishment of these economic conditions, but even in obeying these conditions men can do no more than set their original instinctual impulses in motion — their self-preservative instinct, their love of aggression, their need for love and their impulse to attain pleasure and to avoid pain. . . . If anyone were in a position to show in detail how these different factors — the general human instinctual disposition, its racial variations and its cultural modifications — behave under the influence of varying social organization, professional activities and methods of subsistence, how these factors inhibit or aid one another — if, I say, anyone could show this, then he would . . . have made [Marxism] into a true social science. For sociology, which deals with the behavior of man in society, can be nothing other than applied psychology. Strictly speaking, indeed, there are only two sciences — psychology, pure and applied, and natural science.

If a general theory of crime causation is needed, it ought to be formulated to take account both of social pressures and individual differences. It is true that there exists a dynamic pattern of repression and reaction in the relationship between the system of social pressures defined as society, and the system of innate and acquired forces within an individual defined as personality. Given a certain standard of social pressures — economic, legal, religious, educational or any other forces comprising the core of culture — then a certain percentage and variety of delinquency and crime are naturally to be expected, and will be found at any specific time in any population of a specific ethnic and psychologic composition. These societal forces bear a definite relation to the personal forces, whether we are talking about Boston in 1941 or England in Queen Elizabeth's time.

The proportion of persons who violate the laws or taboos of the particular society at any one time depends upon the extent and force of the pressures and the makeup of those subjected to them. If the pressure of one or more of these external forces decreases or increases and the ethnic and psychologic composition of the population remains essentially the same, we ought to be able to predict the amount and nature of the increase or decrease in crime that will result. For example, during the Boston police strike there was an immediate rise in the quantity of crime in our community. A certain amount of police pressure having been lifted from the total dynamic situation, it followed that a definite quantum of deterrence through fear of arrest had been removed. When this happened, a number of persons who needed just that extra pressure to prevent them from committing crime, stepped across the line between law-abidingness and criminality.

But notice that only a small number of persons did so. Evidently the other would require a more radical or different change in the system of external pressures before they would commit crime. As was pointed out, statistics quite uniformly disclose, for instance, that in periods of long-standing unemployment and attendant poverty there is a rise in crime, particularly in property crime. But once more, not all by far of the persons in any community subjected to the added pressure of unemployment and poverty become criminal. Again, in a predominantly religious community, after a

[5] Young, op. cit., pp. 5–6.
[6] Sigmund Freud, New Introductory Lectures on Psycho-analysis, translated by Sprett, Norton, New York, 1933, pp. 228–229.

long-standing period of irreligion, there is likely to be an increase in criminality, owing to the removal of a system of forces which with others had participated in determining the general level of law-abidingness in that region.

Why do not all, or more, become criminal?

Clearly, if an organized society has a certain system of laws and taboos, it requires, on pain of punishment, the possession of a certain minimum adaptive capacity on the part of its members. If there are persons in that society who because of mental defect, disease, or distortion, or other inadequate biological equipment do not have sufficient adaptive capacity to carry on their lives within the confines of these taboos and laws, they will commit crimes, and their crimes will be essentially attributable to their inadequate biological equipment. The social pressure or social disorganization was there, but the adaptive capacity could not withstand it. Were such persons members of a more primitive society, some of them might, by their very substandard equipment, not only *not* become criminals but even be selected as leaders and heroes. But in such a society the adaptive equipment necessary is different from that required by our highly complex society which involves numerous delicate social and legal pressures, and requires a high degree of adaptive capacity on the part of its members. Surely in so complex an environment there must be many people who simply cannot "make the grade" in conforming their behavior to the demands of socially-tamed living. Their intelligence may be too faulty to enable them to grasp the necessary distinctions made by the criminal laws; their instinctual equipment may be too strong for control in the light of existing taboos; their emotional life may be topsy turvey because of varying degrees of mental abnormality or temporary or permanent derangement.

All this does not of course mean that equally thorough study should not be given to the social forces involved in bringing about the end result of criminal conduct. If a number of children are exposed to smallpox infection, and only certain of them develop the disease, we must study both the nature of the infective force and the nature of the children who, subjected to it, succumbed and those who, equally subjected to it, did not succumb. In such a study that which is constant, that to which both groups of children were subjected, is the force of smallpox infection; while that which is crucial to our thinking and doing, that which is concerned with the problem why some of these children were infected while others were not, is the makeup of the two sets of children. If we stop with a study of the nature of the infective agent, we have only half the picture; in fact, we cannot fully determine even the nature of the infective force unless we analyze and explain its tendency to selectivity in influence — why it is operative on some persons and not on others. And in order to do that, we are forced to study the composition of those whom it affects and those whom it passes over.

To put it differently, all of us are subjected to certain social pressures and to social disorganization. The great issue in crime causation is, why do some of us succumb to them and continue to do so, while others do not? And to answer that question it is necessary to answer a prior question, how do those who become criminal when these pressures operate, differ from those who do not? These differences can be determined only by a careful and detailed comparison of the bodily, intellectual and emotional-inhibitory traits of both groups.

OBSTACLES AND DIFFICULTIES

Now there are many obstacles to such a study. In order to know what is abnormal one must know what is normal. Here the researcher is immediately up against difficulties. There exists no reliable sample of the noncriminal population which embraces social and economic conditions, bodily build, grade of intelligence, emotional-inhibitory makeup and numerous other detailed factors that ought to be carefully compared. The census figures are not always classifiable for reliable comparisons even as to very crude factors; they are very meager, containing data of only superficial significance to our problem, much of it unverified. Individual studies of special classes of the population in terms of mental age or economic status exist, but again these investigations are usually not comparable with the factors in our criminal population. Certainly little or no comparative materials are available regarding the more subtle personality structures and mechanisms which seem likely to be of really crucial significance. Moreover, it is very difficult to construct the desired biosocial yardstick which will represent the norm of the noncriminal population.

However, by carefully comparing an adequate sample of delinquents with nondelinquents, or criminals with noncriminals, certain differences will emerge. We cannot jump to the conclusion that all of these differences are causally relevant either to the mass of cases or to any specific case. But we can conclude that among all the differences, certain factors so markedly differentiate criminals from noncriminals and influence them in a manner so rationally to be expected, that they must somehow be entangled in the causal complex in many individual cases, and probably in the one we are concerned with at any one time. We cannot tell just how, because the mass method we are using is incapable of showing us exactly how these forces play their parts on the stage of the individual offender's mind. Our findings should be useful, however, not only in giving us valid theories about the involvement of certain factors in criminality looked at in terms of whole masses of offenders, but also in helping us to overcome the first obstacle to the effective clinical analysis of any individual case: namely, the ascertainment of relevant factors.

This brings me to a major difficulty encountered in the intensive study of the actually operative mechanisms of causation in the individual case. The great number and complex interplay of the factors and forces entangled in any one criminal career are well known to all of you. You cannot even be certain whether you have assembled all the possibly relevant factors in any case. Further, it is difficult to determine which ones, among the numerous factors you have gathered and systematized in a case history, actually have anything to do with the case. Poverty may have been present in the home but it may not necessarily have had any influence in making your client delinquent. To get at the role played by poverty in this particular instance you are compelled to trace the exact dynamic relationship between the external poverty and the internal change of attitude and motivation in the life of your client. You may discover that his brother, brought up in the same poverty-stricken home, far from going under because of it, used that very poverty as an incentive and a stepping stone to legitimate ambition and law-abiding success.

Suppose again you find that your client's life was spent in a slum area subject to the numerous unwholesome influences and the un-

desirable cultural traditions of such a region. The discovery of this system of forces in the youth's life situation, and the setting of it down in a case history, are far from ending the job of explanation of cause. You are compelled to determine if, how and why this social situation turned this particular youth's behavior in a criminalistic direction. For clearly, thousands of boys living in slum areas are not delinquents. If they were, Horatio Alger would never have had such widespread popularity.

Suppose you find your client to be more on the dull than the normal side of intelligence. The discovery and the setting down of that fact are only the beginning of the exploration that must be made to bridge the gap between a situation and a course of behavior. It must be shown just how and why this intellectual defect got this particular offender into trouble when so many people of dull intelligence manage to get along without resort to delinquency or crime.

And so with numerous other factors that enter into the typical case history. The materials looked for and entered in the record are those which have long been advanced as factors affecting conduct adversely. We really do not know whether they did or did not have such influence in any individual case until we take the next step and determine whether they were introjected into the person's mental life and thereafter became a dynamic force tending to misconduct on his part. We must bridge the gap between the factor and the personality; and then bridge the gap between the changed personality and the changed behavior. It cannot be too often repeated that *a factor is not a cause unless and until it first becomes a motive.*[7]

One lesson to be drawn by the practical student of crime causation is, therefore, that any one who seeks to understand the whys and wherefores of an offender's antisocial behavior must not be satisfied with a mere setting down of factors claimed at one time or another to be important in bringing about delinquency or criminality. He must, rather, consciously focus his attention on discovering and describing the *exact operative connections* of these factors with the particular offender's self-expression through misbehavior.

7 Dr. Bernard Glueck's formulation of the problem.

SOME SUGGESTIONS ON CONTENT OF EXAMINATION

Time does not permit a detailed exposition of the possible contents of a case history that will be meaningful for the intricate problem of crime causation, but here are a few suggestions based on the points just discussed. Assuming that it provides the familiar sociologic data about the neighborhood, the home, economic status, industrial history and the like, the case history, from a causal point of view, should contain the results of systematic probing of at least four levels or aspects of the offender's mental structure and dynamics.

First, what are the evidently *fixed points or limits* of this particular offender's mental organization, judged both by a detailed review of his childhood history and an analysis of his present equipment? It is a common error to assume that the balance of the instinctual-inhibitory mechanisms, the attitude-formations and the ideational preoccupations of any group, such as delinquents in a slum area, are all alike. We speak, for instance, of attitudes without realizing that the typical attitudes a person is capable of, have in the first place been more or less fixed by nature as well as affected by culture. The kind of effort any particular offender is capable of has been more or less fixed at birth by nature's endowing him with a certain energy system. So also, the richness of barrenness, the sophistication or primitiveness of any particular person's ideational system depend, basically, on his general intelligence and on special abilities and disabilities rather than on the mental food that is fed him. We should not, therefore, overlook the fact that in every case there are certain limits of effective correctional action which have been set at birth. We ought to try to determine what are the limits of any particular client's original mental endowment.

I need hardly remind you, in passing, that there are also limits to the individual's physical equipment, and that a meaningful report on the offender's bodily structure and tendency to certain diseases is called for. This is necessary not only for the health aspects of the probation officer's plan of action, but because of the evident interplay between physical defects and mental stresses and strains. The simplest and most familiar of these is of course the compensatory mental mechanism that arises to balance unpleasant feelings accompanying some physical inferiority; but there are many others.

In defining the limits of effort dictated by nature, there is one difficult problem upon which our recent researches have thrown a little light, namely, the effect of an individual's lack of maturation commensurate to the norm for the particular age. In defining the limits of effective correctional action, one must bear in mind that individuals differ in the rate at which their mental and physical functions grow and integrate to bring about a mature, self-managing personality. The worker should take this fact into account in his tentative setting down of the boundaries of possible constructive effort with the individual. Adaptive capacity changes with degree of maturation achieved. We have recommended the construction of a "maturation quotient" which would be a composite of the degree to which the individual has achieved the requisite norm for his age in each phase of mental activity as well as physical development;[8] but such an "M.Q." device has still to be constructed and tested out.

While in our researches we have stressed the role of inadequate maturation as an interferer with the reform of offenders, it seems to have important implications also for the original causation of delinquent trends of conduct. For instance, it was found that it is not so much the arrival at a certain age, such as twenty-one or forty, that impels many offenders to abandon their criminalistic careers, as the arrival at a certain distance in years from the time of the origin of their delinquent tendencies. From this evidence it seems reasonable to infer that the beginning of consistent trends of delinquent behavior is a sign of the individual's failure, at that stage of his development, to have achieved a degree of maturity sufficient for adaptation to society's demands from persons of his age and status, without resort to prohibited behavior, whether it be in the home, school, factory or world at large. Instead of the familiar expression, "X has reached years of discretion," we should rather say, "X has achieved a stage of socially adequate maturity," that is, adequate to meet

---

[8] Sheldon and E. T. Glueck, *Juvenile Delinquents Grown Up,* The Commonwealth Fund, New York, 1940, p. 270.

the responsibilities commensurate to his age and status and to do so without violating laws. And we should bear in mind that there are not a few X's who, despite all the efforts of probation, prison, parole, in addition to those of the home, school, church and other social organizations, never achieve sufficient maturity and integration to adapt lawfully to the high requirements set by our complex system of customary and legal taboos.

Further research will be needed to establish these theories solidly or to disprove them; but in the meantime, the probation officer cannot go wrong in taking into account the evidence of individual differences in the rates of growth toward the goal of socially acceptable maturity when he is estimating the limits of effective correctional action in the particular case.

Setting down tentatively the mental and physical limits of effective action is a guide to systematic and economical reconstructive efforts. It points out to all concerned what is feasible and what cannot reasonably be expected; and it helps to define what is meant by success and failure of the worker's efforts in any particular case.

The second type of psychologic data that should go into a case history to make it meaningful from a causal point of view is an inventory, with illustrations from a sufficiently extensive vertical sample of the offender's life span, of his typical attitudes. An attitude is a person's usual disposition or slant toward general modes of response rather than toward specific acts of response. For example, "an attitude of devotion to one's mother is something that can be investigated and concerning which confident and demonstrable assertions can be made in particular cases. But we cannot know what particular act will be performed toward one's mother on account of the existence of this attitude." [9] The probation officer is interested in his client's typical slant toward his family as a unit, toward his father, mother, wife, or particular children; toward God, toward churchgoing; toward authority as symbolized by the teacher, shop foreman, fellow-worker, policeman, probation officer, and others with whom he has dealings; toward working for a living or loafing for a living.

Numerous useful tests of attitudes have been evolved to show how the individual rates when compared with the norm; but even without formal testing techniques, the systematic search for the client's attitudes regarding basic social values can give much insight into the kind of person the probation officer has to deal with. Moreover, systematic exploration of other people's attitudes should give the probation officer considerable insight into his own, and should make him wary of any prejudices he may import into his work of dealing with others. Further, since attitudes, or typical tendencies toward action, can be at least roughly defined, they give concrete points of attack to the probation officer in his effort to change undesirable attitudes. Indeed, so promising was the attitude approach to the understanding of human nature deemed a few years ago that a new school of treatment, that of "attitude therapy," was invented.

The third type of personality data that should go into a case history if one wants to dig down to causal roots, is an inventory of the offender's typical conflict problems. All of us have conflicts, both between ourselves and the various aspects of our environment, and within ourselves. By externalizing and setting down these conflicts, the probation officer can begin to see the reasons for what, on the surface, seem to be irrational attitudes and bits of behavior.

The fourth type of personality data that should enter into a case history if one wants to understand causal dynamics is a systematic inventory of the client's typical ideas. What's his head filled with? If you start him off on a little verbalized ideational trip, to which one or two landmarks of subject matter does he usually return — some particular ambition, or his personal appearance, or his athletic prowess, or women, or "ganging," or some other system of ideas? "Ideas," we have been vividly reminded, "are weapons." Whole peoples have been hypnotized, betrayed and enslaved through the systematic pumping into their heads of ideologies of the most absurd kind. Ideas are dynamic. By analyzing the offender's conversations with you, you will begin to get at the things with which your client is typically preoccupied. By setting down this person's most beloved ideas, you not only gain insight into what he's like, but obtain clues to changing him by exposure to more desirable ideas.

---

[9] Faris in Young, *op. cit.*, p. 8.

In all these difficult and delicate explorations and probings it would be advantageous for a probation officer to have the aid of a psychiatrist or psychologist with a broad training in both biology and sociology, so as to counteract a natural tendency to allow himself to be hypnotized by the conceptual lingo of any one-sided, or copyrighted, picture of Man or Society. As to some of them, particularly the last three, devices like the Rorschach test will be found instructive. Ideally, such thorough explorations into mental structure and dynamics should be made in all cases; but practically, considering the pressures of time and case load, probation officers will be forced to limit such systematic mental analyses to but a small proportion of cases. But what they thereby learn ought to be useful not alone in understanding and dealing with those cases, but in gaining new insight into all their cases.

At all events it seems to me that ascertainment of the mental factors mentioned should furnish some, at least, of those stepping stones between the outer and inner worlds of the offender which have been indicated as indispensable to any real grappling with causal mechanism.

A Long Look Ahead

I have raised a number of points to be considered in dealing with the intricate problem of crime causation. Clearly, the process of analyzing the impact of social pressures upon mental makeup and the reissuance of the new product into antisocial behavior is difficult. It challenges the thought of every worker with delinquents and criminals. It requires the constant interchange of experience and ideas between the practical worker on the firing line and the speculative and research worker. The determination of clearly defined, specific mechanisms of causation will take a long time. Does this therefore mean that the complexity of crime causation must entail the indefinite postponement of preventive, therapeutic and rehabilitative methods and points of view until such time as a mature science and art of criminology can be built up? Must we, in the meantime, rely only upon the simplistic conceptions of criminal intent and absolutely unhampered freedom of will as the sole causal forces we have to deal with? Must we put our faith once more in pain-inflicting punishment? I can best give the answer to these important questions by repeating

a passage from the introduction to *Preventing Crime*,[10] which Mrs. Glueck and I edited a few years ago:

"We know enough about the conditioning factors of delinquency and criminality in a general way to justify any efforts that give reasonable promise of success. For example, we know that a large proportion of delinquents and criminals come from homes that are either in dire poverty or in constant hazard of becoming so. It is true that many poor people do not commit crimes and that, therefore economic insecurity is not always a cause of wrongdoing. Still, given poverty plus some other condition such as mental deficiency, the chances are multiplied that this pattern will become causative of delinquency and criminality. And given poverty, plus mental deficiency, plus residence in a crowded slum area with ample opportunity for wrongdoing and a tradition of antisocial conduct, the chances are still further multiplied. And so with the cumulation of other factors frequently present in the careers of offenders.

"In other words, we know that a complex of factors is usually associated with criminality, although we may not know the exact interaction of elements in the complex. We are therefore justified in assuming that if we made a many-sided attack on the factors commonly found in the careers of offenders, our efforts would reduce the number of recruits to the criminal army. This is true even though it be granted at the outset that if such a many-sided attack on the mass of factors associated with delinquency and crime did result in a reduction of wrongdoing, it would be difficult to say which one of the destroyed factors, or which element in the preventive program, has contributed the most to the happy outcome.

"[Considering] the analogy to fire prevention, most of the places where inflammables are stored will never burn, and in many instances an intervening influence between the inflammables and the conflagration is necessary. But where combustibles are present the danger of fire is greatly increased. The implication for crime preventive efforts seems clear. The more 'inflammables' (such as poverty, broken and distorted home life, badly occupied leisure time, culture conflict, and the like) that can be removed from the environment of childhood and youth, the less possibility is there of criminalistic conflagration. The exact manner of the relationship of such factors to misconduct cannot always be determined. The relationship may not necessarily be either inevitable or direct, but merely one that is several steps removed from the factor which is the direct source of criminal-

---

[10] Sheldon and E. T. Glueck (editors), *Preventing Crime*, McGraw-Hill, New York, 1936, pp. 2–3.

istic behavior. But such facts, while rendering crime preventive efforts more difficult and wasteful than they would be if we knew more about causation, do not make them hopeless."

But while such encouraging words may be enough for the practical worker, they may not sufficiently satisfy the scientist. To his despair at how little we as yet know about the mechanisms of crime causation, I can only interpose the statement of a very wise man. In his brilliant lecture on *A Philosophy of Life*,[11] Freud, answering criticisms leveled against science, reminds us of something we are too prone to overlook:

The reproaches made against science for not having solved the riddle of the universe are unfairly and spitefully exaggerated. Science has had too little time for such a tremendous achievement. It is still very young, a recently developed human activity. Let us bear in mind, to mention only a few dates, that only about three hundred years have passed since Kepler discovered the laws of planetary movement; the life of Newton, who split up light into colors of the spectrum, and put forward the theory of gravitation, came to an end in 1727, that is to say a little more than two hundred years ago; and Lavoisier discovered oxygen shortly before the French Revolution. I may be a very old man today, but the life of an individual man is very short in comparison with the duration of human development, and it is a fact that I was alive when Charles Darwin published his work on the origin of species. In the same year, 1859, Pierre Curie, the discoverer of radium, was born. And if you go back to the beginnings of exact natural science among the Greeks, to Archimedes or to Aristarchus of Samos (*circa* 250 B.C.), the forerunner of Copernicus, or even to the tentative origins of astronomy among the Babylonians, you will only be covering a very small portion of the period which anthropology requires for the evolution of man from his original ape-like form, a period which certainly embraces more than a hundred thousand years. And it must not be forgotten that the last century has brought with it such a quantity of new discoveries and such a great acceleration of scientific progress that we have every reason to look forward with confidence to the future of science.

Let us therefore take heart. You and I are dealing with the most complex of all problems, the riddle of man's motives and actions. Under no fond illusion that we shall be able to solve that riddle the day after tomorrow, let us still carry on with intelligence and faith.

[11] Freud, *op. cit.*, pp. 221–222.

41

Theory and Fact in Criminology*

Sheldon Glueck

I

Before and after Lombroso published his theory of the "born criminal" in 1897, there have been attempts to attribute crime to some unilateral cause. Intellectual defect as an exclusive or major explanation followed atavism, degeneracy and epilepsy; mental disease followed intellectual defect; the psycho-analytic concept of criminalism "from a sense of guilt" followed traditional psychiatric explanations. The older unilateral sociological explanations in terms of poverty, movements of the business cycle and the like, were succeeded by the over-emphasis of residence in economically under-privileged and culturally conflicting "interstitial" urban areas.

In more recent years, the theory of "differential association" has been put forward by the late Professor E. H. Sutherland,[1] a distinguished criminologist, and elaborated in Professor D. R. Cressey's new edition of Sutherland's popular text-book on criminology. This theory plays a prominent part in American criminological circles.[2] The proponents of this view disclaim that they, like their forerunners, are resorting to a unilateral explanation of crime; they do not call differential association a "cause" but rather a "theory." The theory is alleged to explain crime not in terms of a single etiological influence but rather in terms of many variables which it supposedly "organizes and relates."

It is the thesis of this paper that the theory of differential association supported by its related concept of "definitions of the situation,"

* Reprinted from 7 *British J. Delinquency* (1956), 92–109. Used by permission of the publisher.
[1] For the latest elaboration of this theory, see Sutherland, E. H., "*Principles of Criminology*," 5th edition, revised by D. R. Cressey, J. B. Lippincott Company, 1955, Chapter IV.
[2] Virtually all criminological text-books published in the United States during the past three decades are by dedicated sociologists.

fails to organize and integrate the findings of respectable research and is, at best, so general and puerile as to add little or nothing to the explanation, treatment and prevention of delinquency.

Simply stated, the theory explains criminality as the result of an excess of "definitions favourable to violation of the law over definitions unfavourable to violation of the law," [3] learned by the prospective offender in social interaction with existing criminals. However, as stated in the text-books the theory is not too clear. One form of explanation (in the quotation that follows) seems to emphasize the individual rather than the *milieu*, and to include, thereby, early childhood experiences and perhaps even original natural endowment of the offender in the bringing about of delinquent behaviour; but, if this be so, the theory adds nothing but the excess baggage of confusing terminology to what is already well known and explainable without the benefit of the theory:

In another sense, a psychological or sociological sense, the situation is not exclusive of the person, for the situation which is important is the situation as defined by the person who is involved. That is, some persons define a situation in which a fruitstand owner is out of sight as a "crime-committing" situation, while others do not so define it. Furthermore, the events in the person-situation complex at the time a crime occurs cannot be separated from the prior life experiences of the criminal. This means that the situation is defined by the person in terms of the inclinations and abilities which the person has acquired up to date. For example, while a person could define a situation in such a manner that criminal behaviour would be the inevitable result, his past experiences would for the most part determine the way in which he defined the situation. . . . . The following paragraphs state such a genetic theory of criminal behaviour on the assumption that a criminal act occurs when a situation appropriate for it, as defined by the person, is present.[4]

While it is true that a person's "inclinations and abilities," and his prior experiences influence his latest experience, it is difficult to see what is added to understanding by all this talk about "definitions of the situation." It comes down to saying that if a person's make-up and experiences are such as to incline him to criminalism he will consciously become a criminal — some-

thing with which nobody can quarrel except for the unwarranted exclusion of the subconscious and unconscious influences in behavior. Why place major emphasis on a "definition of the situation" which the prospective offender supposedly goes through? The important question is what makes him a delinquent, or, if we must pay tribute to the sociological formula, what makes him define a situation as conducive to criminalism?

But another form of exposition of the differential association theory emphasizes the influence of the *milieu*. We are informed, first, of the discovery that "criminal behaviour is *learned*" and that "Negatively, this means that criminal behaviour is not inherited, as such; also, the person who is not already trained in crime does not invent criminal behaviour, just as a person does not make mechanical inventions unless he has had training in mechanics." [5]

Consider the first part of this statement. Does anybody nowadays believe that criminal behaviour "as such" is inherited? Did even Lombroso believe so? Those criminologists who call attention to variations in the strength of different hereditary drives and controlling mechanisms do not claim that criminalism *per se* is inherited, but merely point to the too often sociologically underemphasized if not ignored biological fact that, in the eyes of nature, all men are not created equal and that some, because of certain traits useful to the kind of activities involved in criminal behaviour, probably have a higher delinquency *potential* than others.[6]

Consider, now, the second part of the quotation, to the effect that a person cannot invent criminal behaviour or commit crime without training. This is so contrary to obvious fact that it is surprising to see it seriously advanced. It attributes all criminal conduct to indoctrination by other criminals or contagion by crimi-

[3] Sutherland–Cressey, *op. cit.*, p. 78.
[4] *Ibid.*, p. 77.

[5] Sutherland–Cressey, *op. cit.*, p. 77. "The differential association theory, which is considered by most sociologists as the best formulation to date of a general theory of criminality, holds, in essence, that criminality is learned in interaction with others in a process of communication." D. R. Cressey, "The Differential Association Theory and Compulsive Crimes," *J. of Crim. Law, Criminology and Police Science*, Vol. 45 (May–June, 1945), p. 29.
[6] See *Physique and Delinquency*, by Sheldon and Eleanor Glueck, New York, Harper and Brothers, 1956.

nalistic "patterns" and utterly ignores such primitive impulses of aggression, sexual desire, acquisitiveness, and the like, which lead children to various forms of anti-social conduct before they have learned it from others. What is there to be learned about simple lying, taking things that belong to another, fighting and sex play? Do children have to be taught such natural acts? If one takes account of the psychiatric and criminological evidence that involves research into the early childhood manifestations of anti-social behaviour, one must conclude that it is not delinquent behaviour that is learned; that comes naturally. It is rather *non*-delinquent behaviour that is learned. Unsocialized, untamed and uninstructed, the child resorts to lying, slyness, subterfuge, anger, hatred, theft, aggression, attack and other forms of asocial behaviour in its early attempts at self-expression and ego formation. What he is normally forced to learn in his earliest struggles with the adult environment, in order to develop a personality and win the affection and sense of security and approval he craves, is not the non-conforming behaviour of egoism and delinquency but the conventional behaviour of altruism and non-delinquency; not the expression of natural asocial, dissocial or anti-social impulses and desires, but how to tame these primitive tendencies sufficiently to win parental love and approval. Law-abiding character formation is a hard-won process.

If, as the proponents of the "differential association" theory insist, "the person who is not already trained in crime does not invent criminal behaviour just as a person does not make mechanical inventions unless he has had training in mechanics," how account for a basic finding in *Unraveling Juvenile Delinquency*,[7] that the onset of delinquent behaviour occurred at the tender age of seven years or less in 44.4 per cent. of the delinquents and at ten years or less in 87.6 per cent.?[8] These are not theoretical speculations but carefully verified facts.[9] Just where and when did these very young children "differentially associate" with delinquents or criminals in order to learn how to commit their delinquencies? True, another finding of *Unraveling* was that 56 per cent of the delinquents, compared to only three individuals among the non-delinquents, became members of boy gangs;[10] but since nine-tenths of the delinquents were, as has been indicated, committing offences at under eleven years of age, and since the gang is an adolescent phenomenon,[11] it cannot be said that the delinquents learned their anti-social behaviour from the gang.

If what is meant by the proponents of the "crime is learned" school is that most criminals consolidate their anti-social attitudes in contact with others, or learn *techniques* of various crimes from others, there is less objection (although this does not account for the *origins* of misconduct); but even this is exaggerated. We found little evidence in our numerous solidly grounded follow-up studies involving (in addition to the 500 delinquents reported on in *Unraveling*) 1,000 juvenile delinquents and 500 adult reformatory offenders studied over a period of 15 years, as well as 500 female offenders, that the great majority of these criminals would have failed to pass from juvenile delinquency to adult criminalism had it not been for "differential association," or that they learned their techniques from each other.[12]

By way of further elucidation of the differential association concept, the crux of this theory is presented in the following words:

The specific direction of motives and drives is learned from definitions of the legal codes as favour-

---

[7] S. and E. T. Glueck, *Unraveling Juvenile Delinquency*, New York, The Commonwealth Fund, 1950.

[8] *Unraveling, op. cit.*, p. 28.

[9] For a detailed account of method, see *Unraveling, op. cit.*, Chaps. II-VII.

[10] *Unraveling*, p. 163.

[11] "The lure of the gang is undoubtedly due in part to the fact that the gang boy is in the adolescent stage which is definitely correlated with gang phenomena. Although this period has no exact limts for any individual, it includes broadly for the boy the years from twelve to twenty-six." F. M. Thrasher, *The Gang*, Chicago, University of Chicago Press, 1936, 2nd Rev. Ed., p. 36. Of some 1,200 cases of gang membership studied in Chicago, only 1.5 per cent. of the boys were six to twelve years old, while 63 per cent. were classified as adolescents. Thrasher, *op. cit.*, p. 74.

[12] *500 Criminal Careers*, 1930, New York, Alfred Knopf; *One Thousand Juvenile Delinquents*, 1934, Boston, Harvard University Press; *Five Hundred Delinquent Women*, 1934, New York, Alfred Knopf; *Later Criminal Careers*, 1937, New York, The Commonwealth Fund; *Criminal Careers in Retrospect*, 1943, New York, The Commonwealth Fund; *After-Conduct of Discharged Offenders*, 1945, New York and London, Macmillan Co.

able or unfavourable. In some societies an individual is surrounded by persons who invariably define the legal codes as rules to be observed, while in others he is surrounded by persons whose definitions are favourable to the violation of the legal codes. In our American society these definitions are almost always mixed, with the consequence that we have culture conflict in relation to the legal codes. A person becomes delinquent because of an excess of definitions favourable to violation of law over definitions unfavourable to violation of law. This is the principle of differential association.[13]

The ratio between such definitions and others unfavourable to law violation determines whether or not a person becomes criminal.[14]

Consider these statements. In the first place, has anybody actually counted the number of definitions favourable to violation of law and definitions unfavourable to violation of law, and demonstrated that in the predelinquency experience of the vast majority of delinquents and criminals, the former exceed the latter? [15]

---

[13] Sutherland–Cressey, *op. cit.*, p. 78.

[14] D. R. Cressey, "Application and Verification of the Differential Association Theory," *J. of Crim. Law, Criminology and Police Science*, Vol. 43 (1952–53), p. 43.

[15] The only systematic check-up I know of, by Cressey himself (and that not involving a count of "definitions"), resulted in the conclusion that the theory will hardly stand up. Reporting on 65 prisoners in the Illinois State Penitentiary at Joliet, 20 in the California Institution for Men at Chino, and 40 in the United States Penitentiary at Terre Haute, Indiana, who were "questioned in detail about the acquisition of the techniques and rationalizations" pertaining to their common offence of criminal trust violation, Cressey says: "On the basis of evidence found in interview materials gathered from these men, the first hypothesis, that the techniques are learned in association with identifiable criminal behaviour patterns, was rejected." A second hypothesis was supposedly established (partially) on the following reasoning: "Since a rationalization that one is 'borrowing' rather than 'stealing' or 'embezzling' the entrusted funds, for example, must be learned, it is inconceivable that it could be present unless the individual using it had been in contact with persons who presented it to him or had been in contact with some other cultural source which gave him a general acquaintance with it. . . . It is not possible for trust violators to use rationalizations in the manner indicated without first having come into contact with definitions of situations which to a greater or less degree sanction the criminal violation of financial trust." . . . However, "rather than naming a specific source, the subjects referred directly or indirectly to rather general cultural ideolo-

Indeed, it is highly probable that, by the very extent, frequency and intensity of conventional home and school and church influences, and the very early stage of the development of character at which these influences operate, there is an excess of "definitions *un*favourable to violation of law" even in the case of most of those who become delinquent and criminal.

In the second place, the theory in question, by emphasizing a quantitative excess of "definitions," ignores the patent fact that the individual influences of the human and physical environment to which persons are subjected vary in their impact. But more seriously, it fails to take account of obvious differences in the somatic, temperamental and characterological make-up of individuals subjected to a superficially similar environment.

Those sociological criminologists who have taken up the ideas of W. I. Thomas are not as discerning as was the master. For right at the threshold of Thomas's significant *Primitive Behaviour*, he points out that conditioning is only half the process, the other half being the varied natures of those conditioned; and that these involve both experience and original endowment:

The reaction of different individuals in the same culture to identical cultural influences will depend partly on their different trains of experience and partly on their biochemical constitutions and unlearned psychological endowments. Local, regional, nationalistic and racial groups are in turn conditioned, in the formation of their behavior patterns and habits, by their several trains of experience and conceivably by their particular biochemical and psychological constitutions.[16]

He includes, among the problems of individual and group adjustment, the "capacity and opportunity of the individual to be adjusted (*constitutional* factors, incentives, social position)." [17]

---

gies with which they had informal contact at some vague period in their lives. For this reason, that portion of the second hypothesis which pertains to the identification of the specific sources of the rationalizations was rejected, and a calculation of the differential association ratio could not be attempted." Cressey, *op. cit.*, pp. 45, 47, 48, 49. It is submitted that the proponents of the differential association theory can derive little comfort from this experiment.

[16] W. I. Thomas, *Primitive Behavior, An Introduction to the Social Sciences*, New York, McGraw-Hill Book Co., 1937, p. 1.

[17] *Ibid.*, p. 2. Italics supplied.

But by emphasizing the *number* or *ratio* of "definitions" as controlling, the differential association theory treats all persons as *equally* influenced by stimuli of one kind or another — something patently contrary to elementary biology and psychology. If the quantitative emphasis of the theory is sound, then, to press it to its logical conclusion, the biggest criminals of all would be professors of criminology, prison guards, and prison chaplains! They certainly spend a great deal of time and effort in numerous instances of "differential association" with criminals. These persons are not criminal but essentially law-abiding, because of their original endowment and early home influences and training; and to say they "define the situation" differently from criminals is to add no insight whatsoever to the understanding of delinquency and non-delinquency, but to state, in pseudo-scientific language, the fact that they are not criminally inclined or do not wish to be criminals.

However, the proponents of this theory want to have it both ways. They also tell us that "differential associations vary in frequency, duration, priority, and intensity." If these influences vary in these different ways, how can one say that it is a mere numerical excess of definitions favourable to criminality that determines the issue? In discussing "intensity," Professor Cressey says that "intensity" is not precisely defined but it has to do with such things as the prestige of the source of a criminal or anti-criminal pattern and with *emotional reactions related to the associations*." [18] (Italics supplied.) But if this be so, it is not the *stimulus* of the "differential association" that is crucial but rather the *response* in terms of the emotional reaction of the individual to such stimulus; and this response obviously must vary with differences in the biopsychologic structure of those who make it. What is added to this by the *deus ex machina* of "definitions of the situation"? How much more illuminating is Dr. Bernard Glueck's formulation: "A factor is not a cause unless and until it becomes a motive."

There remains the mention of a significant phenomenon which the "differential association" and "definition of the situation" theory fails to explain, and which is rationally explainable on other grounds; namely, the phenomenon

of fluctuations in criminality and recidivism with age. Cressey states, among other features, that "the age of maximum general criminality is probably during or shortly before adolescence," that it varies with type of crime, that "in general . . . criminal behaviour varies widely with age and sex," that "the age of concentration of the more violent types of crimes, such as burglary and robbery, has remained relatively constant for several centuries," that "the crime rate decreases regularly and steadily from the age of maximum criminality until the end of life." [19]

By way of explanation of such phenomena, Cressey considers certain biological views, as follows:

One of the theories presented as an explanation of the age ratios in crime is that they are due directly to biological traits such as physical strength and vigour: crimes are committed frequently by persons who are strong and active and infrequently by persons who are weak and passive. Another biological theory is that crimes are concentrated in three periods, ages three to six, fourteen to sixteen, and forty-two to forty-five, and that these periods are products of libidinal tides due to changes in the instincts of sex and aggression and to changes in the ego strength. A third biological theory is that inheritance is the direct cause.[20]

He does not discuss these views. He disposes of them by this simple *ipse dixit*: "These biological theories *obviously* [sic] provide no explanation of many of the variations in the age ratios in crime; indeed, it may be said that they do not explain even one of the facts outlined above when that fact is considered in its ramifications. On the other hand, all of these facts are consistent with the general theory that crime is a product of social experiences and social interaction." [21] But where is the evidence that the number and/or "duration, priority, and intensity" of "definitions favourable to crime" fluctuates with age, so as to explain the ebb and flow of crime at various biological stages? Cressey claims that "the general conclusion from this survey of the facts regarding physical and physiological conditions is that these conditions have not in any case been demonstrated to be a direct force in the production of crime or delinquency. On the contrary, it is *apparent* [sic]

---

18 Sutherland–Cressey, *op. cit.*, pp. 78–9.

19 *Ibid.*, pp. 108–9.
20 *Ibid.*, pp. 110–11.
21 *Ibid.*, p. 11. Italics supplied.

that these conditions are related to crime only as they are socially defined and interpreted."[22] How apparent? To whom apparent?

Nobody claims any direct or exclusive relationship between physical characteristics and crime. The difference between the eclectic criminologist and the type of sociological criminologist whose reasoning is reflected above is that the latter evidently argues that original nature means nothing, that all is sociocultural conditioning, that you can make a silk purse out of a sow's ear; while the former, basing his views on carefully validated data from biological as well as sociocultural sources, attributes the end-product of criminality to an interplay of various more or less well-defined increments of nature and nurture.

Even well-recognized social processes are dogmatically shaped to fit into the prejudices of the pre-existing theory of "differential association." For example, in discussing culture conflict between foreign-born parents and native-born children, Cressey adverts to the following facts:

Psychiatrists and social workers find these conflicts within the home to be highly significant in emotional disturbances of children, and they feel that the emotional disturbances are conducive to delinquency. Levy has reported that differences in language, manners, methods of discipline, and ideals presented by the parents are important factors in the maladjustment of children.[23]

Is this satisfactory? No. These clear findings which reasonably explain certain behaviour must be forced into the theory of differential association. The quoted passage is followed by this: "However, it is likely that culture conflict is significant to delinquency principally as it determines differential associations with behaviour patterns sanctioning violation of American laws pertaining to delinquency."[24] Proof?

We are told that "a test of the theory is how well it accounts for all the variations in the values of the variables"[25] involved in the etiology of delinquency. Only by assuming the basic fact which the proponents of the differential association theory have not proved — namely, that in the life of all or the vast majority of delinquents and criminals there is an

excess of "definitions of the situation" favourable to criminality — and by assuming that all people react uniformly to the same sociocultural stimuli — something that is patently not true — can this theory be upheld.

Cressey repeats Sutherland's not very persuasive dogma that "It is not necessary, at this level of explanation, to explain why a person has the associations which he has; this certainly is a complex of many things . . . ."[26] It most assuredly is necessary to explain it, if "this level of explanation" is to descend from the clouds; for the "complex of many things," disposed of in such cavalier fashion, is the very essence of the issue. Without ventilation of this fundamental matter, the theory of differential association as the basic explanation of delinquency is a roof without a base. Here are a few items in this "complex of many things": We have shown, in Unraveling, that 98.4 per cent. of the delinquents sought out other delinquents as companions, while only 7.4 per cent. of the nondelinquents, who lived in similar neighbourhoods, often in the same block and sometimes in the very same house as the delinquents, had companions among delinquents.[27] We found that the delinquents had many temperamental and personality traits and early childhood home experiences in common, as well as similar interests distinguishing them clearly from the control group. It is this combination of influences that led them to chum with other delinquents. To

---

[22] Ibid., p. 115. Italics supplied.
[23] Ibid., p. 92.
[24] Ibid., pp. 92–3.
[25] Ibid., p. 61.

[26] Ibid., p. 79. A similar avoidance of the basic issue is found in another exponent of this theory, Clinard: "Many here might say, why does one and why not another person engage in delinquent or criminal behaviour when most all persons have been exposed to some contact with deviant norms. At this stage all we can say is something like Sutherland's answer that criminal behaviour varies according to the frequency, intensity, priority, and continuousness of such associations. In the balance of contacts of pushes and pulls one individual may be drawn toward crime and another away from it." M. B. Clinard, "Criminal Behaviour is Human Behaviour," Federal Probation, Vol. XIII, No. 1 (March, 1949), p. 24. If all that can be said in explanation of criminalistic behaviour "at this stage" is the foregoing, one cannot avoid the conclusion that the differential association-definition of the situation theory is "at this stage," in a half-baked stage. It rests on unproven assumptions; and even if they were proven they would deal with but a single minor influence in a complex totality of biocultural influences.

[27] Unraveling, op. cit., p. 163.

say that they were non-delinquents before and only became delinquents because of differential association with other delinquents and because they had "an excess of definitions favourable to delinquency" is, factually, to put the cart before the horse and to ignore proved relevant differences between the delinquents and controls in favour of guesses that the former became delinquent because of differential association and an excess of unfavourable "definitions."

Incidentally, elsewhere in his text-book, Cressey states that "practically all juveniles commit delinquencies," [28] an assumption requiring the conclusion that virtually *all* children "differentially associate" with delinquents and are subjected to an excess of "definitions" favourable to misconduct.[29] If he means that they are delinquent *before* they "differentially associate" he is contradicting the Sutherland–Cressey theory.

II

In order to contrast the superficiality of the "differential association" theory with the facts of life among delinquents as determined by intensive, verified and relevant biological and sociocultural research data, let me indicate those traits and factors (among many others) in *Unraveling Juvenile Delinquency* which were so highly differentiative of delinquents from non-delinquents as to be usefully embodied in three prediction tables, one of which, that dealing with factors of family life, has thus far been subjected to validation through its application to several other and varied samples of cases, and found to have remarkably high discriminative

power.[30] The predictive traits derived from the Rorschach ("ink-blot") Test, applied to delinquents and non-delinquents, are the following: *social assertiveness, defiance, suspiciousness, destructiveness* and *emotional lability.* The traits derived from psychiatric examination of the delinquents and non-delinquents are the following: *adventurousness, extroversiveness, suggestibility, stubbornness* and *emotional instability.* The factors derived from the social investigation of the homes of both the delinquents and non-delinquents are: *discipline of the boy by the father, supervision of the boy by his mother, affection of the father for the boy, affection of the mother for the boy, family cohesiveness.*

In order to show how strikingly these traits and factors distinguish delinquents from non-delinquents and are therefore (at least indirectly) causally involved in anti-social behaviour, a few illustrations may be given. 91 per cent. of all the boys whom the Rorschach Test showed to have in their make-up a *marked degree of defiance* were delinquents, while of those in whom this trait was absent only 35 per cent. were delinquents; [31] 83 per cent. of those who were shown by psychiatric examination to be *markedly stubborn* were delinquents, compared to only 39 per cent. in whom this trait was absent; 72 per cent. of the boys whose paternal discipline of them was *overstrict or erratic* were

[28] Sutherland–Cressey, *op. cit.*, p. 110.

[29] In response to the obvious fact that the "ecologic characteristics of the interstitial area" could not be the major influence in the etiology of delinquency because even in the worst possible "delinquency area" of the urban slums the great majority of boys somehow manage *not* to become delinquents, the answering tactic of the extreme environmentalists seems to be to throw all ballast overboard and claim that the great majority, if not *all*, boys are in fact delinquents — a *reductio ad absurdum* clearly without proof to support it and contrary to the published findings of Clifford Shaw and his associates. In *Unraveling Juvenile Delinquency*, Sheldon and Eleanor Glueck were able to find hundreds of *truly non-delinquent* boys residing in the same underprivileged "interstitial" areas in which the delinquents resided. This is fact, verified by intensive check and re-check from many sources, and not guesswork.

[30] Richard E. Thompson, "A Validation of the Glueck Social Prediction Scale for Proneness to Delinquency," *J. of Crim. Law, Criminology and Police Science,* Vol. 43 (November–December, 1952), pp. 451–70; S. Axelrad and S. J. Glick, "Application of the Glueck Social Prediction Table to 100 Jewish Delinquent Boys," *The Jewish Social Quarterly,* Vol. XXX (Winter, 1953), pp. 127–36; Ralph W. Whelan, "An Experiment in Predicting Delinquency," *J. of Crim. Law, Criminology and Police Science,* Vol. 45, No. 4, November–December, 1954; "Predicting Juvenile Delinquency," *Research Bulletin,* No. 124, April, 1955, published by Department of Institutions and Agencies, Trenton, New Jersey. Two other validations, one on *adult sex offenders* studied in Sing Sing Prison, reported on by Mrs. I. Brandon, another involving a follow-up of children treated at the clinic of the London County Council, reported on by Dr. Augusta Bonnard, were presented at the meeting of the Third International Congress of Criminology in London, summer of 1955, and will doubtless be published in due course.

[31] The tests were given by a group of psychologists in Boston and interpreted by two Rorschach experts in New York, without the latter knowing which test protocols came from delinquents and which from non-delinquents.

delinquents, compared to only 9 per cent. of those who were guided by *firm but kindly discipline*; 97 per cent. of the boys who came from *unintegrated families* were delinquents as compared to only 21 per cent. of those who came from *cohesive families*. These are only a few illustrations. Wide distinctions in the incidence of traits and factors were also found in respect to a great many other influences in the make-up and background of the boys in this research.

Can the differential association theory make such meaningful discriminations between delinquents and non-delinquents? Can it be used as a predictive factor?

And just how does the differential association theory account for, integrate and reconcile such established biological differences between delinquents and non-delinquents in the Glueck researches as the statistically significant predominance of mesomorphs in the former and ectomorphs in the latter? Or such temperamental–characterial variations between delinquents and non-delinquents as the predominance in the former of aggressiveness, defiance, emotional lability, impulsivity, to name but a few; or the vital differences in the emotional parent–child relationships of the first few years, such as the lack of parental affection, hostile or erratic disciplinary practices, lack of supervision, family disunity, and other faulty parent–child relationships which were found to be indubitably much more numerous in the families of our delinquents than in those of the control group?

The only integration and reconciliation that the theory under discussion can make of these diverse influences which highly differentiate delinquents and criminals from control groups and some of which vary in their relative weights in different circumstances, times and places is to ascribe everything to differential association and an excess of crime-inducing definitions over law-abiding ones. Just what does such a formula add to understanding? Does it say more than that, if conditions and desires are favourable to crime, persons will resort to crime?

In the *Preface* to his book, Cressey says: "The differential association theory and alternative theories of crime causations are evaluated in the light of their comparative capacity to 'make sense' of the facts." [32] Applying this test, is it not more in accordance with facts, clinical experience and common sense to attribute delinquency to a patterned concatenation of various combinations of the above-listed traits and factors which markedly distinguish delinquents from non-delinquents than to advance as an over-all explanation the view that among the boys included in the research in question only those who just happened to have learned the ways of crime from association with other delinquents, or who somehow or other acquired or were subjected to an excess of anti-social "definitions of the situation," became offenders while the others did not?

The multiple factor method of assigning causal power to a combination of traits and factors which in fact demonstrably distinguishes the vast majority of delinquents from non-delinquents is criticized by the proponents of the differential association theory as not involving a "theoretical framework." But as successful validations of the statistical prediction tables based on combinations of relevant factors demonstrate, this approach is unquestionably more realistic and revealing of etiologic involvements than is the cloudy adumbration of a "theory" the proponents of which are so eager to establish the pre-eminence of nurture in the causal complex as to leave out of account fundamental variations in nature. [33] In attacking the multiple factor theory, it is claimed that researchers who have followed that method presume that each factor is "independent of all other factors." [34] In the Gluecks' researches on delinquency, this is not true. Not only their synthesis of the most discriminative factors into prediction tables but the following summary of *Unraveling Juvenile Delinquency* proves that the authors in question fully recognize the *interdependence* of the factors involved:

It will be observed that in drawing together the more significant threads of each area explored, we have not resorted to a theoretical explanation from the standpoint, exclusively, of any one discipline. It has seemed to us, at least at the present stage of our reflections upon the materials, that it is premature and misleading to give exclusive or even primary significance to any one of the avenues of interpretation. On the contrary, the evidence seems

---

32 Sutherland–Cressey, *op. cit.*, p. v.

33 One notable exception is Donald Taft. See his intelligent appraisal of Sutherland's theory, D. R. Taft, *Criminology*, New York, The Macmillan Co., 1942, pp. 284–86.
34 Sutherland–Cressey, *op. cit.*, p. 62.

to point to the participation of forces from several areas and levels in channeling the persistent tendency to socially unacceptable behaviour . . .

We are impelled to such a multidimensional interpretation because, without it, serious gaps appear. If we resort to an explanation exclusively in terms of somatic constitution, we leave unexplained why most persons of mesomorphic tendency do *not* commit crimes; and we further leave unexplained how bodily structure affects behaviour. If we limit ourselves to a sociocultural explanation, we cannot ignore the fact that sociocultural forces are selective; even in underprivileged areas most boys do *not* become delinquent and many boys from such areas do not develop into persistent offenders. And, finally, if we limit our explanation to psychoanalytic theory, we fail to account for the fact that the great majority of non-delinquents, as well as of delinquents, show traits usually deemed unfavourable to sound character development, such as vague feelings of insecurity and feelings of not being wanted; the fact that many boys who live under conditions unfavourable to the development of a wholesome superego do not become delinquents, but do becomes neurotics.

If, however, we take into account the dynamic interplay of these various levels and channels of influence, a tentative causal formula or law emerges, which tends to accommodate these puzzling divergencies so far as the great mass of delinquents is concerned:

The delinquents as a group are distinguishable from the non-delinquents: (1) physically, in being essentially mesomorphic in constitution (solid, closely knit, muscular); (2) temperamentally, in being restlessly energetic, impulsive, extroverted, aggressive, destructive (often sadistic) — traits which may be related more or less to the erratic growth pattern and its physiologic correlates or consequences; (3) in attitude, by being hostile, defiant, resentful, suspicious, stubborn, socially assertive, adventurous, unconventional, non-submissive to authority; (4) psychologically, in tending to direct and concrete, rather than symbolic, intellectual expression, and in being less methodical in their approach to problems; (5) socioculturally, in having been reared to a far greater extent than the control group in homes of little understanding, affection, stability, or moral fibre by parents usually unfit to be effective guides and protectors or, according to psychoanalytic theory, desirable sources of emulation and the construction of a consistent, well-balanced, and socially normal supergo during the early stages of character development . . .

In the exciting, stimulating, but little-controlled and culturally inconsistent environment of the underprivileged area, such boys readily give expression to their untamed impulses and their self-centered desires by means of various forms of delinquent behaviour.

Their tendencies toward uninhibited energy-expression are deeply anchored in soma and psyche and in the malformations of character during the first few years of life.

This "law" may have to be modified after more intensive, microscopic study of the atypical cases. . . . "A scientific law must always be considered as a temporary statement of relationships. As knowledge increases this law may require modification. Even the natural sciences state all generalizations in terms of probability." [35]

Thus the enigmatic question of whether one factor or another "causes" delinquency is shown to be an unsound one; for, given certain surrounding conditions, internal or external, various combinations of biologic or social factors referred to by criminologists in the past can precipitate antisocial behaviour. A *variety* of causal syndromes can bring about the very same criminalistic behaviour. In one case certain biological ones predominate, in another certain sociocultural ones, in the sense that they apparently contribute the most *weight* in the combination of internal and external forces that culminates in antisocial expression.

Hence, there should be substituted for the notion of specificity or unity of causation (or of cause thinly disguised as "theory") the concept of internal and external pressures and inhibitions. If the total weight of pressures to antisocial behaviour exceeds the total strength of inhibitory forces, the person commits crime. Theoretically, say, twenty factors of minor pressure (weight) are just as likely to conduce to criminal behaviour as four or five factors of heavy pressure. By substituting this concept of varied forces or energy reaching a point of antisocial discharge, for the insistence upon a certain specific theory or factor, or even syndrome, as inevitably and always conducing to delinquency, we arrive at a conception of *interchangeability* of etiologic traits and factors and thus at a realistic and relatively accurate doctrine of causation. At any time, the person is poised between a natural tendency to egoistic anti-social behaviour and a habit-disciplined tendency to conform to the socio-legal taboos. Biosocial pressures of one sort or another tend to turn the scales in one direction or another. (Of course, the relationship between energy pressure and inhibitory tendency is not usually simple or direct; there are, as a rule, complex

[35] *Unraveling, op. cit.,* pp. 281–82.

intermediary processes.) Consequently, it is not mesomorphic constitution, or strong instinctual impulse, or an hereditary aggressive tendency, or weak inhibitory mechanism, or low intelligence, or excessive emotional lability, or marked suggestibility, or an unresolved Oedipus situation, or residence in a poverty-stricken "delinquency area" or in a region with a tradition of delinquency, or "differential association" with those already criminal, or an excess of anti-social "definitions of the situation" or any other biological, social or cultural factor that *inevitably* conduces to delinquent behaviour. Any of these factors alone or in various combinations may or may not bring about delinquency, depending on the balance of energy tendencies at a particular time, in the particular individual involved. In times of great crisis, emergency, poverty, unemployment and the like, many persons will commit crimes who, under normal conditions, would not.

However, as was shown in *Unraveling Juvenile Delinquency*, certain factors in combination are found to occur so frequently in the constitution and developmental history of delinquents and so seldom among non-delinquents, that we may legitimately conclude that the *weight* they contribute to the causal scales is very excessive, and usually so, in comparison to that of other influences. This is a realistic conception of causation; for by isolating the biosocial syndromes most *usually* operative in the lives of delinquents and most usually absent in the lives of non-delinquents, it not only adds to understanding of cause and effect but it highlights the traits, factors and areas *most relevant* to prediction, to therapeutic effort in the individual case and to prophylactic effort in general.

It may be that some day variations in the way people conduct themselves will be explainable in the more ultimate terms of differences in endocrine gland structure and function, or of microscopic physico-chemical reactions. However, we can in the meantime reasonably speak of cause-and-effect when we disentangle even the cruder forces at play in inclining persons to one course of behaviour or another, just as chemistry and physics opened the doors to the solution of many problems of nature even before the dawn of nuclear science. The question is, whether such an explanation in the field of our concern brings us closer to an understanding of delinquency and therefore to its control. If

it does, then, even though we are dealing with forces which may some day be reduced to more subtle constituents, we have made a stride forward in the understanding and possible management of delinquent behaviour.

III

So much for the contrast between the differential association–definition of the situation theory and our eclectic approach to causation.

What now of the recommendations for the prevention of delinquency that flow from the "differential association–definition of the situation" theory? They consist essentially of a call for "local community organization" to cope with the problem! We are told, preliminarily, that "the policy implied in the earlier chapters . . . is that control of delinquency lies principally in the personal groups within the local community." [36] We are told that "it was *shown* [sic] that delinquency is explained principally by an excess of delinquent associations over anti-delinquent associations." [37] (Where is the proof that this has been shown?) We are told that "moreover it was *shown* [sic] that the factor in these local and personal groups which had the greatest significance was the definition of behaviour as desirable or undesirable." [38] (Where is the proof of this showing?) We are then solemnly assured that "the closest approximation to a formula for the control of delinquency that can be made at present is that delinquency must be defined as undesirable by the personal groups in which a person participates." [39] Surely a minuscule mouse, brought forth after all the mountainous labours of "differential association" and "definitions of the situation"!

How are these "definitions" of delinquency as "undesirable" to be brought about? Will not this process require a probing into original endowment and parent–child relationships in early childhood, and the moral re-education of adults? Just how helpful in all this are the formulæ of "differential association" and "definitions of the situation"? Do they say anything except the obvious fact that people must somehow be made to desire to be good?

The sum and substance of advice regarding crime prevention is stated by Cressey in these words:

[36] Sutherland–Cressey, *op. cit.*, p. 609.
[37], [38] *Ibid*. Italics supplied.
[39] *Ibid*.

Policies for prevention of delinquency and crime, therefore, should be directed primarily at these personal groups [the family, school and neighbourhood groups, work or recreational groups, religious groups, or others]. In this sense, control of delinquency and crime lies within the local community. This means, first, that the local community must be the active agency in reducing its own delinquency. The personal groups can be modified through the efforts of local organizations such as the school, the church, the police, welfare agencies, and civic groups; they also can be modified through the efforts of laymen.[40]

There is nothing in these well-worn generalizations about crime prevention that is attributable, as a novel discovery, to the theory of differential association—definitions of the situation. By contrast, reliable researches, with their solidly verified factual foundations, indicate much more pointedly and specifically the how and why of participation of community institutions in delinquency prevention programmes [41] and in addition indicate the rôle of various forms of psychotherapy and group therapy in a preventive programme, as well as other approaches *relevant to the facts* revealed in the intensive study of several samples of delinquents and criminals and non-delinquents.

All the agencies and methods of crime prevention discussed in the work by Sutherland–Cressey have been suggested by other writers, without benefit of the illumination of the theory of differential association and definitions of the situation. The theory has not enhanced, in the slightest, understanding of the methods of delinquency prevention. It has the demerit, in comparison with views derived from the researches which meticulously compare the incidence of biopsychological traits and sociocultural factors in the make-up and background of delinquents and non-delinquent matched controls, of *not* integrating and *not* reconciling the variety of delinquency-etiologic elements and at the same time of being so abstract and cloudy as not to be useful either in explaining or in controlling delinquent behaviour.

There can be no doubt that science advances most rapidly through the discovery of theories or systems which account for a variety of facts already known and lead in turn to the discovery of new ones. But how does the theory under consideration compare in these crucial respects with Einstein's theory of relativity, or with the Copernican system, or the Newtonian generalization, or the Darwinian insight into the processes of natural selection? One has only to put the question to see how absurdly deficient is the elaborately adumbrated theory of differential association and its accompanying definitions of the situation.

There are evidently criminologists who find such a "theory" helpful in their thinking. To me it is a superficial and superfluous generalization. The multiple factor approach is much more illuminating and much more in accord with the variety of original natures involved in crime, the variety in kind and intensity of human and physical environmental influences involved in crime, the variety in the behaviour patterns of the acts and mental states and mechanisms embraced in the single legal concept of "crime." For this not only recognizes the evident fact of a wide variation in influences, weights and combinations of traits and factors in crime causation; it recognizes, too, that while there is a "core type" of offender, there is also a variety of subtypes or fringe types. It recognizes that just as the fact of a boy's death, although always the same terminal event, may nonetheless be the result of various preceding sequences of conditions, so the terminal event of persistent delinquency may have in its etiologic background a variety of different sequences leading to the same ultimate result. It recognizes that all behaviour is conditioned by both biological and sociocultural influences.

The foregoing analysis leads to the conclusion that a *wise eclecticism*, guiding research in which investigations, examinations and tests are thorough, and sociocultural data are carefully verified and collated, is still the only promising and sensible credo for the modern criminologist. At all events, neither "differential association" nor an inadequate conception of human psychology and motivation reflected in the mechanical totting up of the number of "definitions of the situation favourable to delinquency" as opposed to the number unfavourable to delinquency can satisfy the researcher who has ob-

[40] *Ibid.*, pp. 609–10.
[41] See, for example, S. and E. T. Glueck, *Delinquents in the Making*, New York, Harper and Bros., 1952, Chap. XVI, "Paths to Prevention"; *Unraveling Juvenile Delinquency, op. cit.*, pp. 285–89; *Preventing Crime* (Editors), New York, McGraw-Hill, 1936; *One Thousand Juvenile Delinquents*, Harvard University Press, 1934, pp. 272–84; *500 Criminal Careers*, New York, Knopf, pp. 335–9, and others.

served again and again that it is the dynamic interplay of certain discernible, and more or less measurable elements of nature and nurture that best accounts for the phenomena of delinquency and crime. Penetrating theories, which summarize and integrate existing reliable findings and which lead in turn to further discoveries, are highly desirable. But premature theorizings can only act as blinders, excluding or grossly under-emphasizing facts that do not fit into preconceptions and ending up with a thin abstraction that neither integrates nor explains.[42]

POSTSCRIPT

After the above piece was written, Glaser's recent paper, "Criminality Theories and Behavioral Images," [43] appeared. This attempts to save the differential association theory through assuming that "association" includes "identification." It sets forth a "differential identifica-

[42] Compare Albert Morris's critique of the theory that the crime rate is a function of the differential between frustration and expectancy of punishment: "This, and other all-encompassing theories, seem to me of modest value and analagous to trying to develop a theory of ill-health in terms of a high incidence of germs and a low expectancy of sanitary engineering." A. Morris, *Homicide: An Approach to the Problem of Crime,* University Lecture, April 14, 1955. Boston Univ. Press, 1955, p. 4.

[43] D. Glaser, "Criminality Theories and Behavioral Images," *The American Journal of Sociology,* Vol. LXI, No. 5, March, 1956, pp. 433–44.

tion" theory as a "reconceptualization" of Sutherland's theory. Although more sophisticated, this theory has all the weaknesses of the differential association theory. Like differential association, it is a roof without a house, with little furniture and that little barren. It does not account for the early delinquency of children nor for the criminalism of those adults who steal, commit assaults, rapes or murders on the spur of the moment or "in the heat of passion." It does not explain the participation of the numerous biological and sociocultural influences involved in delinquency and criminalism nor account for the variety of causal syndromes which multidisciplinary research shows to be involved in the various types of anti-social behaviour.

The theory of "differential identification" can be of little practical help in predicting delinquency or recidivism because, standing alone, it does not adequately differentiate between offenders and non-offenders; because there is no proof that most criminals begin their careers by deliberate identification with criminal patterns; and because, in the case of a criminal career, by the time such a person has completely identified with the criminal culture he is already a criminal. Thus the theory is at best tautological.

The theory is inadequate for treatment and preventive purposes, since where identification does play a rôle, it is not so much the fact of identification as the reasons and conditions of identification that are relevant.

PART TWO

The Juvenile Court

and the Law

PART TWO

The Juvenile Court and the Law

Chapter 10

The Juvenile Court: Historical Background

IT IS SOMETIMES TAKEN for granted that the well-known pioneering juvenile court statute of Illinois (1899) originated the history of the law's special concern with delinquent children. But there were much earlier indications, in the case of dependent and neglected children, which might have foretold the development of juvenile court ideas with reference to delinquents as well.

This chapter begins with a brief historical *résumé* from *One Thousand Juvenile Delinquents*.[1] There follow a few early decisions which foreshadowed the reasoning of the framers of the Illinois statute and of courts passing on the constitutionality of its provisions and those of similar enactments later.

Subsequent chapters deal with the philosophy and organization of juvenile courts and with the basic legal decisions in the field.

I have not included the Federal Juvenile Delinquency Act[2] because its basic features are set out in *Shioutakon* v. *District of Columbia* (Article 58 of this book).

42

Historical and Legislative Background of the Juvenile Court*

Sheldon and Eleanor T. Glueck

1. HISTORY OF JUVENILE COURT MOVEMENT†

The Role of Massachusetts in Juvenile Correctional Work. It is most fitting that Boston should furnish the locale of this research. Massachusetts has long been a center of experimentation in methods of dealing with delin-

quency and crime. Not infrequently it has been the initiator of movements for the better understanding of youth and the amelioration of its conditions.

The humanitarian note in the treatment of juvenile delinquents was originally sounded in the creation of "houses of refuge" for children. Though the first of these in America was the New York House of Refuge (1825), the Boston institution followed a year later.[1] The first state reform school for juvenile offenders was established in Massachusetts in 1847, the early correctional reformers being more concerned with the treatment of youthful offenders after their

---

[1] By S. and E. T. Glueck, Cambridge, Harvard University Press, 1934.

[2] The Federal Act is ably discussed in H. A. Bloch and F. T. Flynn, *Delinquency*, New York, Random House, 1956, 473–486.

* Reprinted by permission of the publishers from Sheldon and Eleanor T. Glueck, *One Thousand Juvenile Delinquents*, Cambridge, Mass.: Harvard University Press, Copyright, 1934, by the President

and Fellows of Harvard College, pages 9–27, with abridgement of footnotes.

† For good accounts of the early history of the treatment of child offenders, see W. H. S. Garnett, *Children and the Law*, London, Murray, 1911; F. J. Ludwig, *Youth and the Law*, Foundation Press, New York, 1955. — *Ed.*

[1] For a penetrating contemporary account of such institutions and the motives leading to their establishment, see the interesting report by G. de Beaumont and A. de Tocqueville, *Du Système Pénitentiaire aux Etats Unis* (1833). This book has been translated into English and German.

conviction than with modifications in the processes of arrest, detention, trial, and the like.
Improvement in the procedural and administrative handling of juvenile delinquents before
correctional treatment is imposed was a later development.

Gradually the interest of reformers that had,
as it were, been directed at first to the wrong
end — treatment of juvenile offenders *after* conviction — shifted to needed reforms in the procedure *preceding* punishment or correction. And
here again Massachusetts was among the
pioneers. The reforms took the shape of special
personnel, social investigations, and the gradual
relaxation of the strict, technical criminal procedure when applied to child offenders. Thus
an 1869 statute provided for the presence in
court of a "state agent" or his deputy "whenever application is made for the commitment
of any child to any reformatory maintained by
the Commonwealth" — a provision still in
force.[2] The agent and his deputies were also
charged with the finding of suitable homes for
children whose interests would better be promoted by placement in a family or by indenture
than by incarceration in a reformatory, and with
the periodic visiting of such children. A law
of 1870[3] required that, in the Suffolk County
courts, cases against children under sixteen
should be heard "separate from the general and
ordinary criminal business," while elsewhere the
"hearing" should be held before probate courts
instead of criminal tribunals. Here also was the
germ of the modern elaborate procedure for
social investigations in the requirement that the
agent for the juveniles or an assistant "shall have
an opportunity to investigate the case, attend
the trial and protect the interest of, or otherwise provide for, such child."[4]

The provision for separate trials was extended
to all pertinent courts in the state in 1872,[5] the
Governor and Council designating and com-
missioning the necessary number of justices of
the peace, or municipal, district, and police
court justices, "to try juvenile offenders." These
justices were given concurrent jurisdiction with
the judges of probate courts in cases of juvenile
offenders under seventeen. They were to be

known as "trial justices of juvenile offenders."[6]
A few years later (1877) a separate "session for
juvenile offenders" was provided for, with its
own court records and docket.[7]

At about the same time (1878) Massachusetts contributed still another element to the
humanitarian movement in the treatment of
offenders. In that year the Mayor of Boston
was authorized to appoint a probation officer
with investigative and visitorial powers in relation to probationers.[8] In 1891 power of appointment was transferred to the judges and
was made mandatory; and the duties of probation officers were more specifically set forth.[9]
Thus probation, probably the most promising,
and certainly the most flexible, instrument at
the command of juvenile as well as adult courts,
owes its inception to Massachusetts.

Toward the close of the last century, a number of states adopted many of these features
or contributed still others to the general movement to humanize justice which culminated in
the juvenile court. Thus in 1892 New York
provided that juvenile cases involving such violations of the penal code as fell within the jurisdiction of a police court or court of special sessions might "be heard and determined by such
court, at suitable times to be designated therefor by it, separate and apart from the trial of
other criminal cases."[10] A separate docket and
record were to be established. Rhode Island, in
1898, provided for the segregation of children
under sixteen awaiting trial, for their separate

---

[2] Laws of Massachusetts, 1869, chap. 453, sec. 4.
[3] *Ibid.*, 1870, chap. 359, sec. 7.
[4] *Ibid.*, sec. 8.
[5] *Ibid.*, 1872, chap. 358.

[6] *Ibid.*, sec. 3.
[7] *Ibid.*, 1877, chap. 210, sec. 5.
[8] *Ibid.*, 1878, chap. 198. Curiously, the law placed
the probation officer under control of the chief of
police, and provided that the officer should be appointed either from the police force or from the
citizenry at large.
The elements of probation go back much farther
than 1878. See F. W. Grinnell, "Probation as an
Orthodox Common Law Practice in Massachusetts
Prior to the Statutory System," *Massachusetts Law
Quarterly*, II (1917), 591; S. Glueck, "The Status
of Probation," *Mental Hygiene*, XV (1931), 290; J.
Augustus, A *Report of the Labors of John Augustus
for the Last Ten Years in Aid of the Unfortunate*
(Boston, 1852).
[9] Laws of Massachusetts, 1891, chap. 356. See
also Laws of Massachusetts, 1898, chap. 511, which
granted authority to the Superior Court to appoint
probation officers.
[10] Laws of New York, 1892, chap. 217, sec. 7.

arraignment and trial, for a special docket and record, and for the presence of public and private agents at the proceedings "to take care of the interests of said children." There were provisions also for the protective safekeeping of children under thirteen held for examination or trial.[11] Other illustrations from American and European practice[12] might be mentioned, all making their contributions toward the establishment of the present-day juvenile court.

All these contributions to the general modification of procedure and administration in children's cases were primarily stimulated by a growing humanitarianism, and only secondarily and more recently by a scientific attitude toward misbehavior and its motivations. They deal, as we have shown, with such matters as separate confinement of children preceding trial, separate trial, special dockets, the use of probation and of placement of children in private homes under the aegis of the court, confinement in special children's institutions, and the like. In the inception of almost all of them Massachusetts has played a prominent role.

The First Specialized Court for Juvenile Delinquents. The first tribunal created to deal specifically with the problems of juvenile delinquency was the Juvenile Court of Cook County, Illinois, established in 1899.[13] The statute creating it was a comprehensive one dealing with jurisdiction over and treatment of dependent, neglected, and delinquent children. It clearly was the precipitate of the various humanitarian elements that, both in America and abroad, were "in the air." Considering the fact that it established the pioneer juvenile court, its provisions are remarkably liberal and far-seeing, as may be gathered from the following paragraph pertaining to the legal construction of the act:

This act shall be liberally construed, to the end that its purpose may be carried out, to-wit: That the

care, custody and discipline of a child shall approximate as nearly as may be that which should be given by its parents, and in all cases where it can properly be done the child be placed in an improved family home and become a member of the family by legal adoption or otherwise.[14]

In respect to the attitude of the court and others concerned with the child, therefore, this important law provided that the delinquent child should be treated the same as the neglected or dependent one; thereby it took the significant step of recognizing officially that, whatever the immediate act or situation may be that brings a child into the custody of a court, the issues presented are, in essence, problems requiring understanding, guidance, and protection rather than those involving such concepts as "criminal responsibility," "guilt," "punishment." As nearly as possible, the suggestion of formal, contentious criminal proceedings was eliminated from this law.[15] All essential elements of the modern juvenile court were present: petition instead of complaint; summons instead of warrant; informal hearing instead of formal trial; specially designated (though not necessarily specially qualified) judges; special juvenile court-room and separate "juvenile record"; probation officers for investigations, in order "to represent the interests of the child" and to have custody over it, when necessary; supervision of the child; provision for allowing the juvenile to remain in its own home, "subject to the visitation of the probation officer"; placement of the child in a family "subject to the friendly supervision of such probation officer"; boarding it "in some suitable family home"; committing it, when necessary, to some appropriate institution; discharge therefrom by the court on recommendation of the board of managers; [16] segregation of children sentenced to an adult institution; re-

---

11 Acts and Resolves of Rhode Island, 1898, chap. 581, secs. 2, 3, 5, 7.

12 Especially the English Juvenile Offenders' Act of 1847 and the Summary Jurisdiction Act of 1879; also the practice in South Australia of having children's courts under a ministerial order (1889), later (1895) legalized in the State Children Act, which provided for separate hearing of cases against children under eighteen in a separate room, and for probation.

13 Laws of Illinois, 1899, p. 131.

14 *Ibid.*, p. 137, sec. 21.

15 A remnant of traditional criminal procedure was embodied, however, in the requirement that "in all trials under this act any person interested therein may demand a jury of six, or the judge of his own motion may order a jury of the same number, to try the case." (*Ibid*, sec. 2.) Perhaps this was included to meet possible objections on the grounds of unconstitutionality.

16 This has an advantage over the procedure in most states, where children are discharged from industrial schools either by a separate parole board or, as in Massachusetts, by a parole committee of the

quirement of reports to the court from both private and public child-caring institutions receiving children from the court; appointment by the court of boards of visitation to institutions and organizations receiving children; and other provisions in like spirit. Before long other courts having several or all of these new features were established, until by 1932 there were at least 633 independent juvenile courts and 2255 juvenile sessions of regular criminal, probate, equity, or other courts in the United States.[17] One of the earliest separate juvenile courts to be established was that in Boston, but before examining the legislation governing the functions of this court we may consider a question frequently raised regarding the parentage of the juvenile court.

2. COMMON LAW OR EQUITY ORIGIN OF COURT?

In the literature on the beginnings of the juvenile court there is considerable debate as to whether the court owes its origin to an extension of the common law or of equity. A recent investigator of this problem correctly informs us that when American "courts of last resort have been called upon to construe the laws, through which the state assumed its rights to control the custody of the child, they have almost uniformly upheld these rights on the broad principle that the courts as agents of the state, are exercising a power derived from the court of chancery of England, which held from early times that such rights existed where the welfare or property of the child was at stake." [18] On the other hand, it must be remembered that the English courts of equity never presumed to have jurisdiction over children because they violated the *criminal*

law. Hence American decisions purporting to find in English chancery authority the justification for the power of juvenile courts over delinquent, as opposed to neglected or dependent, children seem to be partially *ex post facto* legal rationalizations of practices of certain humanitarian judges in criminal cases involving juveniles.[19] The most that may be claimed, in giving equity the credit for the juvenile court idea, seems to be that much the same general motive that gave rise to equity itself in the history of English law is involved in the origin of the juvenile court.[20] One feature of equity, as op-

---

[19] See R. Pound, *Interpretations of Legal History* (Cambridge, 1923), p. 134. Dean Pound cites the origin of the juvenile court as an instance of "judicial empiricism," which creates law not "cautiously from case to case with an occasional creative generalization," but by establishing a new legal institution "almost at a stroke."

"The Juvenile Court," says Dean Pound, "is due to the initiative of a few definitely known socially-minded judges, who had the large vision to see what was required and the good sense not to be hindered in doing it because there had never been such things before. Today we find a legal basis for it in the jurisdiction of chancery over infants. We reconcile it with legal-historical dogmas on this basis. But the jurisdiction of equity over infants was not a factor in creating it. It arose on the criminal side of the courts because of the revolt of those judges' consciences from legal rules that required trial of children over seven as criminals and sentence of children over fourteen to penalties provided for adult offenders." He cites the well-known article of Judge Julian W. Mack, one of the pioneers in the juvenile court movement, "The Juvenile Court," *Harvard Law Review*, XXIII (1909), 104; Flexner and Baldwin, *Juvenile Courts and Probation* (New York, 1915), pp. 1–7; T. D. Eliot, *The Juvenile Court* (New York, 1914), pp. 1–2.

[20] Such a conclusion can be deduced from an examination into the nature of equity practices as opposed to those of the common law. "The Common Law became, to a great extent, a *lex scripta*, positive and inflexible; so that the rule of justice could not accommodate itself to every case according to the exigency of right and justice." (George Spence, *The Equitable Jurisdiction of the Court of Chancery* [London, 1846], I, 322.) The accommodation of "the rule of justice" to the individual case is in effect the "individualization" attempted by juvenile courts. T. E. Holland summarizes the *rationale* of equity clearly: "As old rules become too narrow, or are felt to be out of harmony with advancing civilization, a machinery is needed for their gradual enlargement and adaptation to new views of society. One mode of accomplishing this object on a large scale, without appearing to disregard existing law, is the introduction, by the prerogative of some high

---

board of managers or trustees of such institutions; for under the Illinois provision, the same tribunal that originally prescribed the treatment has the authority to modify it by discharge of the child from the institution, albeit only on recommendation of the board of managers. Generally speaking, it is not wise for too many "doctors" to be involved in the treatment process, which is a continuing one.

[17] Information obtained from the Children's Bureau, Washington, D. C. An independent juvenile court is not necessarily more efficient than a juvenile session of a regular court. Court personnel is the primary consideration.

[18] H. H. Lou, *Juvenile Courts in the United States* (Chapel Hill, N. C., 1927), p. 4. Lou has conveniently collected most of the leading legal authorities.

posed to common law, is its relative flexibility. Its processes and general temper are more suited to individualization of justice than are those of the traditional criminal law. Equity is the vehicle of the attempt of English law to soften the rigors of a too severe, as well as too mechanical, administration of justice.

But while the equity analogy seems to have played a role at least in the rationalization of juvenile court practices if not in their origin, the fact remains that criminal law concepts have also participated. For instance, "both crime and delinquency are based upon intent, for the juvenile court has retained that element at least in the distinction between delinquency and dependency or neglect." [21] The new ingredient in the situation, however, and the basically significant one, is that the procedure of the developed juvenile court — the summons instead of the warrant, the informal interviews with child, parents, and other witnesses rather than the strait-jacketing of the testimony within too technical rules of evidence, the absence of a jury, the social and personal investigation of the background and physical and mental health of the delinquent — all this does not comprise the typical criminal trial.[22] The procedure in the true juvenile court (and more than one in America is so largely in name) is motivated differently from that in criminal courts. Its keynote is protection based on understanding rather than punishment based on the establishment of a technical status of guilt.*

---

functionary, of a more perfect body of rules, discoverable in his judicial conscience, which is to stand side by side with the law of the land, overriding it in case of conflict . . . but not purporting to repeal it. Such a body of rules has been called 'Equity.' It consists in reality of such of the principles of received morality as are applicable to legal questions, and commend themselves to the functionary in question." (*Elements of Jurisprudence* [9th ed., Oxford, 1900], pp. 66–67.)

[21] Lou, *op. cit.*, p. 7.

[22] This interpretation is the typical answer to objections to juvenile court procedure on constitutional grounds. See the leading decisions collected by B. Flexner and R. Oppenheimer, *The Legal Aspect of the Juvenile Court*, United States Department of Labor, Children's Bureau, Publication No. 99, 1922, and Lou, *op. cit.*, p. 10, n. 1. The oft-quoted case on the constitutionality of the juvenile court is Commonwealth *v.* Fisher, 213 Pa. 48 (1905).

* See Chapters 12–15, *infra.* — Ed.

43

Ex parte Crouse*

This was a *habeas corpus* directed to the keeper and managers of the "House of Refuge," in the county of Philadelphia, requiring them to produce before the Court one Mary Ann Crouse, an infant, detained in that institution. The petition for the *habeas corpus* was in the name of her father.

By the return to the writ it appeared, that the girl had been committed to the custody of the managers by virtue of a warrant under the hand and seal of Morton M'Michael, Esq., a justice of the peace of the county of Philadelphia, which recited that complaint and due proof had been made before him by Mary Crouse, the mother of the said Mary Ann Crouse, "that the said infant by reason of vicious conduct, has rendered her control beyond the power of the said complainant, and made it manifestly requisite that from regard to the moral and future welfare of the said infant she should be placed under the guardianship of the managers of the House of Refuge"; and the said alderman certified that in his opinion the said infant was "a proper subject for the said House of Refuge." Appended to the warrant of commitment were the names and places of residence of the witnesses examined, and the substance of the testimony given by them respectively, upon which the adjudication of the magistrate was founded.

The House of Refuge was established in pursuance of an act of assembly passed on the 23rd day of March, 1826. The 6th section of that act declared that the managers should, "at their discretion, receive into the said House of Refuge, such children who shall be taken up or committed as vagrants, or upon any criminal charge, or duly convicted of criminal offences, as may be in the judgment of the Court of Oyer and Terminer, or of the Court of Quarter Sessions of the peace of the county, or of the Mayor's Court of the city of Philadelphia, or of any alderman or justice of the peace, or of the managers of

---

* Ex parte Crouse, Supreme Court of Pennsylvania, 1838, 4 Wharton (Pa.) 2.

the Alms-house and house of employment, be deemed proper objects." By a supplement to the act passed on the 10th day of April 1835, it was declared, that in lieu of the provisions of the act of 1826, it should be lawful for the managers of the House of Refuge "at their discretion, to receive into their care and guardianship, infants, males under the age of twenty-one years, and females under the age of eighteen years, committed to their custody in either of the following modes, viz. First: infants committed by an alderman or justice of the peace on the complaint and due proof made to him by the parent, guardian or next friend of such infant, that by reason of incorrigible or vicious conduct such infant has rendered his or her control beyond the power of such parent, guardian or next friend, and made it manifestly requisite that from regard for the morals and future welfare of such infant, he or she should be placed under the guardianship of the managers of the House of Refuge. Second: infants committed by the authority aforesaid, where complaint and due proof have been made that such infant is a proper subject for the guardianship of the managers of the House of Refuge, in consequence of vagrancy, or of incorrigible or vicious conduct, and that from the moral depravity or otherwise of the parent or next friend in whose custody such infant may be, such parent or next friend is incapable or unwilling to exercise the proper care and discipline over such incorrigible or vicious infant. Third: infants committed by the Courts of this commonwealth in the mode provided by the act to which this is a supplement."

PER CURIAM. — The House of Refuge is not a prison, but a school.* Where reformation, and not punishment, is the end, it may indeed be used as a prison for juvenile convicts who would else be committed to a common gaol;

and in respect to these, the constitutionality of the act which incorporated it, stands clear of controversy. It is only in respect of the application of its discipline to subjects admitted on the order of the court, a magistrate, or the managers of the Alms-house, that a doubt is entertained. The object of the charity is reformation, by training its inmates to industry; by imbuing their minds with principles of morality and religion; by furnishing them with means to earn a living; and, above all, by separating them from the corrupting influence of improper associates. To this end, may not the natural parents, when unequal to the task of education, or unworthy of it, be superseded by the *parens patriæ*, or common guardian of the community? It is to be remembered that the public has a paramount interest in the virtue and knowledge of its members, and that, of strict right, the business of education belongs to it. That parents are ordinarily entrusted with it, is because it can seldom be put into better hands; but where they are incompetent or corrupt, what is there to prevent the public from withdrawing their faculties, held, as they obviously are, as its sufferance? The right of parental control is a natural, but not an unalienable one. It is not excepted by the declaration of rights out of the subjects of ordinary legislation; and it consequently remains subject to the ordinary legislative power, which, if wantonly or inconveniently used, would soon be constitutionally restricted, but the competency of which, as the government is constituted, cannot be doubted. As to abridgment of indefeasible rights by confinement of the person, it is no more than what is borne, to a greater or less extent, in every school; and we know of no natural right to exemption from restraints which conduce to an infant's welfare. Nor is there a doubt of the propriety of their application in the particular instance. The infant has been snatched from a course which must have ended in confirmed depravity; and, not only is the restraint of her person lawful, but it would be an act of extreme cruelty to release her from it.

Remanded.

---

* At the time of this decision, the *fact* was that ". . . the Philadelphia House of Refuge was surrounded by a high wall, and within that wall the most repressive routine was the rule." N. Teeters, and J. O. Reinemann, *The Challenge of Delinquency*, New York, Prentice-Hall, Inc., 1950, p. 442. — Ed.

44

People *ex rel.*
O'Connell *v.* Turner*

By the order of this court, the writ of *habeas corpus* was issued, commanding Robert Turner, superintendent of the reform school of the city of Chicago, to show cause for the caption and detention of Daniel O'Connell.

The petition of Michael O'Connell represents, that he is the father of Daniel, a boy between fourteen and fifteen years of age, and that he is restrained of his liberty contrary to the law, without conviction of crime, and under color of the following mittimus:

STATE OF ILLINOIS, } ss. { Superior Court of Cook county. Of the Sept. Term, A.D. 1870.

The People of the State of Illinois to the Superintendent of the Reform School of the City of Chicago: Greeting:

We do hereby command you, that you take the body of Daniel O'Connell, a boy above the age of six and under the age of sixteen years, who, upon due examination by the Hon. Wm. A. Porter, one of the judges of the Superior Court of Cook county, has been found, by competent evidence, to be a proper subject for commitment in the said reform school, and whose moral welfare and the good of society require that he should be sent to said school for instruction, employment and reformation, and that you confine the said Daniel O'Connell within the said reform school, according to the statute in such cases made and provided, and for so doing, this shall be your sufficient warrant.

To the sheriff of Cook county to execute.

Witness, Augustus Jacobson, clerk of our said Superior Court, and the seal thereof, this ninth day of September, A.D. 1870.

A. JACOBSON, Clerk.

---

* *The People of the State of Illinois,* ex rel. *Michael O'Connell* v. *Robert Turner,* Superintendent of the Reform School of the City of Chicago, Supreme Court of Illinois, 1872, 55 Ill. 280.

The return is, that the boy had been detained by authority of the mittimus.

It is admitted, that the relator is the father of the boy, alleged to be restrained of his liberty, and that he is of the age stated.

The only question for determination, is the power of the legislature to pass the laws, under which this boy was arrested and confined.

The first act, in relation to this "reform school," is a part of the charter of the city of Chicago, approved February 13, 1863, and the second is entitled, "an act in reference to the reform school of the city of Chicago," approved March 5, 1867.

The first section establishes "a school for the safe keeping, education, employment and reformation of all children between the ages of six and sixteen years, who are destitute of proper parental care, and growing up in mendicancy, ignorance, idleness or vice."

Section four, of the act of 1867, provides, that "whenever any police magistrate, or justice of the peace, shall have brought before him any boy or girl, within the ages of six or sixteen years, who he has reason to believe is a vagrant, or is destitute of proper parental care, or is growing up in mendicancy, ignorance, idleness or vice," he shall cause such boy or girl to be arrested, and, together with the witnesses, taken before one of the judges of the superior or circuit court of Cook county. The judge is empowered to issue a summons, or order in writing, to the child's father, mother, guardian, or whosoever may have the care of the child, in the order named, and if there be none such, to any person, at his discretion, to appear, at a time and place mentioned, and show cause why the child should not be committed to the "reform school," and upon return of due service of the summons, an investigation shall be had. The section then directs, "if, upon such examination, such judge shall be of opinion that said boy or girl is a proper subject for commitment to the reform school, and that his or her moral welfare, and the good of society, require that he or she should be sent to said school for employment, instruction and reformation, he shall so decide, and direct the clerk of the court of which he is judge, to make out a warrant of commitment to said reform school; and such child shall thereupon be committed."

Section nine, of the act of 1863, directs, that all persons between six and sixteen years of age, convicted of crime punishable by fine or imprisonment, who, in the opinion of the court, would be proper subjects for commitment, shall be committed to said school.

Section ten authorizes the confinement of the children, and that they "shall be kept, disciplined, instructed, employed and governed," until they shall be reformed and discharged, or shall have arrived at the age of twenty-one years; and that the sole authority to discharge shall be in the board of guardians.

The warrant of commitment does not indicate that the arrest was made for a criminal offense. Hence, we conclude that it was issued under the general grant of power, to arrest and confine for misfortune.

The contingencies enumerated, upon the happening of either of which the power may be exercised, are vagrancy, destitution of proper parental care, mendicancy, ignorance, idleness or vice. Upon proof of any one, the child is deprived of home, and parents, and friends, and confined for more than half of an ordinary life. It is claimed, that the law is administered for the moral welfare and intellectual improvement of the minor, and the good of society. From the record before us, we know nothing of the management. We are only informed that a father desires the custody of his child; and that he is restrained of his liberty. Therefore, we can only look at the language of the law, and the power granted.

What is proper parental care? The best and kindest parents would differ, in the attempt to solve the question. No two scarcely agree; and when we consider the watchful supervision, which is so unremitting over the domestic affairs of others, the conclusion is forced upon us, that there is not a child in the land who could not be proved, by two or more witnesses, to be in this sad condition. Ignorance, idleness, vice are relative terms. Ignorance is always preferable to error, but, at most, is only venial. It may be general or it may be limited. Though it is sometimes said, that "idleness is the parent of vice," yet the former may exist without the latter. It is strictly an abstinence from labor or employment. If the child performs all its duties to parents and to society, the State has no right to compel it to labor. Vice is a very comprehensive term. Acts, wholly innocent in the estimation of many good men, would, according to the code of ethics of others, show fearful depravity. What is the standard to be? What extent of enlightenment, what amount of industry, what degree of virtue, will save from the threatened imprisonment? In our solicitude to form youth for the duties of civil life, we should not forget the rights which inhere both in parents and children. The principle of the absorption of the child in, and its complete subjection to the despotism of, the State, is wholly inadmissible in the modern civilized world.

The parent has the right to the care, custody and assistance of his child. The duty to maintain and protect it, is a principle of natural law. He may even justify an assault and battery, in the defense of his children, and uphold them in their law suits. Thus the law recognizes the power of parental affection, and excuses acts which, in the absence of such a relation, would be punished. Another branch of parental duty, strongly inculcated by writers on natural law, is the education of children. To aid in the performance of these duties, and enforce obedience, parents have authority over them. The municipal law should not disturb this relation, except for the strongest reasons. The ease with which it may be disrupted under the laws in question; the slight evidence required, and the informal mode of procedure, make them conflict with the natural right of the parent. Before any abridgment of the right, gross misconduct or almost total unfitness on the part of the parent, should be clearly proved. This power is an emanation from God, and every attempt to infringe upon it, except from dire necessity, should be resisted in all well governed States. "In this country, the hope of the child, in respect to its education and future advancement, is mainly dependent upon the father; for this he struggles and toils through life; the desire of its accomplishment operating as one of the most powerful incentives to industry and thrift. The violent abruption of this relation would not only tend to wither these motives to action, but necessarily, in time, alienate the father's natural affections."

But even the power of the parent must be exercised with moderation. He may use correction and restraint, but in a reasonable manner. He has the right to enforce only such discipline, as may be necessary to the discharge of his sacred trust; only moderate correction and temporary confinement. We are not governed by the twelve tables, which formed the Roman law.

The fourth table gave fathers the power of life and death, and of sale, over their children. In this age and country, such provisions would be atrocious. If a father confined or imprisoned his child for one year, the majesty of the law would frown upon the unnatural act, and every tender mother and kind father would rise up in arms against such monstrous inhumanity.* Can the State, as *parens patriæ*, exceed the power of the natural parent, except in punishing crime?

These laws provide for the "safe keeping" of the child; they direct his "commitment," and only a "ticket of leave," or the uncontrolled discretion of a board of guardians, will permit the imprisoned boy to breathe the pure air of heaven outside his prison walls, and to feel the instincts of manhood by contact with the busy world. The mittimus terms him "a proper subject for commitment"; directs the superintendent to "take his body," and the sheriff endorses upon it, "executed by delivering the body of the within named prisoner." The confinement may be from one to fifteen years, according to the age of the child. Executive clemency can not open the prison doors, for no offense has been committed. The writ of *habeas corpus*, a writ for the security of liberty, can afford no relief, for the sovereign power of the State, as *parens patriæ*, has determined the imprisonment beyond recall. Such a restraint upon natural liberty is tyranny and oppression. If, without crime, without the conviction of any offense, the children of the State are to be thus confined for the "good of society," then society had better be reduced to its original elements, and free government acknowledged a failure.

In cases of writs of *habeas corpus* to bring up infants, there are other rights beside the rights of the father. If improperly or illegally restrained, it is our duty, *ex debito justitiæ*, to liberate. The welfare and rights of the child are also to be considered. The disability of minors does not make slaves or criminals of them. They are entitled to legal rights, and are under legal liabilities. An implied contract for necessaries is binding on them. The only act which they are under a legal incapacity to perform, is the appointment of an attorney. All their other acts are merely, voidable or confirmable. They are

liable for torts, and punishable for crime. Lord Kenyon said, "If an infant commits an assault, or utters slander, God forbid that he should not be answerable for it, in a court of justice." Every child over ten years of age may be found guilty of crime. For robbery, burglary or arson, any minor may be sent to the penitentiary. Minors are bound to pay taxes for the support of the government, and constitute a part of the militia, and are compelled to endure the hardship and privation of a soldier's life, in defense of the constitution and the laws; and yet it is assumed, that to them, liberty is a mere chimera. It is something of which they may have dreamed, but have never enjoyed the fruition.

Can we hold children responsible for crime; liable for their torts; impose onerous burdens upon them, and yet deprive them of the enjoyment of liberty, without charge or conviction of crime? The bill of rights declares, that "all men are, by nature, free and independent, and have certain inherent and inalienable rights — among these are life, liberty, and the pursuit of happiness." This language is not restrictive; it is broad and comprehensive, and declares a grand truth, that "all men," all people, everywhere, have the inherent and inalienable right to liberty. Shall we say to the children of the State, you shall not enjoy this right — a right independent of all human laws and regulations? It is declared in the constitution; is higher than constitution and law, and should be held forever sacred.

Even criminals can not be convicted and imprisoned without due process of law — without a regular trial, according to the course of the common law. Why should minors be imprisoned for misfortune? Destitution of proper parental care, ignorance, idleness and vice, are misfortunes, not crimes. In all criminal prosecutions against minors, for grave and heinous offenses, they have the right to demand the nature and cause of the accusation, and a speedy public trial by an impartial jury. All this must precede the final commitment to prison. Why should children, only guilty of misfortune, be deprived of liberty without "due process of law?"

It can not be said, that in this case, there is no imprisonment. This boy is deprived of a father's care; bereft of home influences; has no freedom of action; is committed for an uncertain time; is branded as a prisoner; made subject

---

* See the case of *Fletcher et al.* v. *The People*, holding that the father may be indicted and punished for inhuman treatment of his child.

to the will of others, and thus feels that he is a slave. Nothing could more contribute to paralyze the youthful energies, crush all noble aspirations, and unfit him for the duties of manhood. Other means of a milder character; other influences of a more kindly nature; other laws less in restraint of liberty, would better accomplish the reformation of the depraved, and infringe less upon inalienable rights.

It is a grave responsibility to pronounce upon the acts of the legislative department. It is, however, the solemn duty of the courts to adjudge the law, and guard, when assailed, the liberty of the citzen. The constitution is the highest law; it commands and protects all. Its declaration of rights is an express limitation of legislative power, and as the laws under which the detention is had, are in conflict with its provisions, we must so declare.

It is therefore ordered, that Daniel O'Connell be discharged from custody.

Discharged

45

In re Ferrier*

APPEAL from the County Court of Cook county; the Hon. MASON B. LOOMIS, Judge, presiding.

Appellee filed a petition in the county court of Cook county, under section 3 of "An act to aid industrial schools for girls," approved May 29, 1879. (Laws 1879, p. 309.) The petition set forth that Winifred Breen, the appellant, was a girl nine years old; had repeatedly been picked up by the police and others while wandering about the streets at night; was a truant from school, and had not proper parental care, and was in imminent danger of ruin and harm, etc.

Three witnesses testified as to the character and habits of the girl, Winifred Breen, stating that she was without proper parental care; that

---

* *Petition of Ferrier,* Supreme Court of Illinois, 1882, 103 Ill. 367.

she wandered upon the streets of Chicago at all hours of the day and night; that she had been frequently picked up by the policemen of the city, late at night and miles away from her usual place of abode, and had been confined all night in police stations; that she kept bad company, and was in great danger of being ruined; that the mother of the child is weak-minded, and at times insane, having on one occasion attempted to hang Winifred; that she was unfit to have the control of the child, and incapable of managing her; that the step-father is poor and an invalid, earning only a small salary, and is compelled to be absent from his home the entire day, and he found it impossible to control the girl, and that she had been guilty of thefts and falsehood. The fourth witness, Mrs. Beveridge, stated that she was president of the Industrial School for Girls; that the school is situated in Evanston, in Cook county, on a five-acre tract of beautiful rolling ground, over which the inmates have free range as a play-ground; that there is no more restraint upon their liberty than that imposed upon children in an ordinary family or institution of learning; that they are taught ordinary household duties, sewing, and the ordinary branches of English education; that parents are permitted to visit their children when they desire, and that children are given places in private families whenever suitable places can be procured, but not without their and their parents' consent. The girl herself testified that she sometimes ran away; that her mother tried to hang witness, and then tried to hang herself; that she was afraid of her mother; that she knew about this industrial school and wanted to go there. The father of the child, if still living, appears to have been a worthless character, — a professional thief; — who when last heard from, three years ago, was at the Bridewell, and the mother was divorced from him.

The jury returned a verdict that Winifred Breen was a dependent girl, and that the facts set forth in the petition were true, and thereupon the county judge entered an order that said Winifred should be committed to said Industrial School for Girls, and appointed Mrs. Ellen Woodward, one of the vice-presidents of the school, guardian of the child, in accordance with a provision of the act. The county attorney, whom the court had appointed counsel for the girl, and who appeared for her, took an appeal to this court.

Section 3 of the act under which this proceeding was taken, is as follows: "Any responsible person who has been a resident of any county in this State one year next preceding the time at which the petition is presented, may petition the county court of said county to inquire into the alleged dependency of any female infant then within the county, and every female infant who comes within the following description shall be considered a dependent girl, viz: Every female infant who begs or receives alms while actually selling or pretending to sell any article in public, or who frequents any street, alley or other place for the purpose of begging or receiving alms, or who, having no permanent place of abode, proper parental care or guardianship, or sufficient means of subsistence, or who for other cause is a wanderer through streets and alleys, and in other public places, or who lives with or frequents the company of, or consorts with, reputed thieves or other vicious persons, or who is found in a house of ill-fame, or in a poor house." The petition is to be verified by oath, and notice is to be given to the parents and guardian. The female infant is brought before the court, and if without counsel, it is made the duty of the court to assign counsel for her, and a trial is had before a jury of six. Section 2 declares: "The object of industrial schools for girls shall be to provide a home and proper training school for such girls as may be committed to their charge. . . ."

MR. JUSTICE SHELDON delivered the opinion of the Court:

It is insisted that the law under which the proceding was had is unconstitutional — first, as being in violation of the Bill of Rights as to personal liberty, in respect of the provision that no person shall be deprived of life, liberty or property without due process of law, and *The People* v. *Turner*, 55 Ill. 280, is relied upon as being a decisive authority in favor of appellant in this respect. That was an application by the father of a boy for a writ of *habeas corpus* to the superintendent of the "reform school" of Chicago, to free the boy from an alleged illegal restraint of his liberty, and it was held that the law providing for the commitment to that "re-

form school" was unconstitutional. That school was established under a statute different and much less careful in its provisions, and nearer in its approach to a criminal enactment, than the one in question. The judge was the only one to decide in the matter. Criminals between six and sixteen years of age, convicted of crime punishable by fine or imprisonment, were confined there. That institution was regarded in that case as a place of confinement, and for punishment, and the commitment to it was regarded as imprisonment.

In the statute now under consideration, anxious provision is made for the due protection of all just rights. To begin, there must be the petition of a responsible person, verified by oath, setting forth the facts, and if there be a parent or a guardian, it must also show that the parent or guardian is not a fit person to have the custody of the infant, there must be notice to the parents, the child must be brought before the court, there is a trial as to the facts by six jurymen, defense by counsel is provided, proof is made before a court of record of the facts alleged, there is the verdict of a jury of six men, and if, by the 4th section, after the verdict of the jury the judge is of the opinion that the girl should be sent to the industrial school, then he may order that she be committed there. Provision is made for a discharge from the school, when proper, through the managers, and the Governor may at any time order a discharge. This institution is not a prison, but it is a school, and the sending of a young female child there to be taken care of, who is uncared for, and with no one to care for her, we do not regard imprisonment. We perceive hardly any more restraint of liberty than is found in any well regulated school. Such a degree of restraint is essential in the proper education of a child, and it is in no just sense an infringement of the inherent and inalienable right to personal liberty so much dwelt upon in the argument.

The power conferred under the act in question upon the county court is but of the same character of the jurisdiction exercised by the court of chancery over the persons and property of infants, having foundation in the prerogative of the Crown, flowing from its general power and duty, as *parens patriæ*, to protect those who have no other lawful protector. (2 Story's Eq. Jur. sec. 1333.) That jurisdiction extends to the care and person of the infant, so far as is necessary for his protection and education, and upon this ground that court interferes with the ordinary rights of parents in regard to the custody and care of their children, for although, in general, parents are intrusted with the custody of the persons and the education of their children, yet this is done upon the natural presumption that the children will be properly taken care of, and will be brought up with a due education. But whenever this presumption is removed, and the parent is grossly unfit and fails in this respect, the court of chancery will interfere, and deprive him of the custody of his children, and appoint a suitable person to act as guardian, and to take care of them, and to superintend their education. (*Ibid.*, sec. 1341.) The statute in question provides that if the court finds that the parent is not a fit person to have the custody of the infant, the court may appoint the president, or any one of the vice-presidents, of such industrial school the guardian of the infant, and such guardian shall permit such infant to be placed under the care and in the custody of such industrial school, and the court here accordingly made such appointment of guardian. It is a statute making provision for the needed control and care of female infants which they are found to be destitute of, and which parents should bestow, and when the superintendence in this respect, which is required, is assumed on the part of the State, there should be in the agency which the State makes use of, the same power of needful restraint in the child's care and education as belonged to the parent. The right to liberty which is guaranteed is not that of entire unrestrainedness of action. Civil government in itself implies an abridgement of natural liberty. "Civil liberty, which is that of a member of society, is no other than natural liberty, so far restrained by human laws (and no farther) as is necessary and expedient for the general welfare." (1 Black. Com. 125.) It is not natural but civil liberty of which a person may not be deprived without due process of law. There are restrictions imposed upon personal liberty which spring from the helpless or dependent condition of individuals in the various relation of life, among them being those of parent and child, guardian and ward, teacher and scholar. There are well recognized powers of control in each

of these relations over the actions of the child, ward or scholar, which may be exercised. These are legal and just restraints upon personal liberty which the welfare of society demands, and which, where there is no abuse, entirely consist with the constitutional guaranty of liberty. See Cooley's Const. Lim. 339, 342.

We find here no more than such proper restraint which the child's welfare and the good of the community manifestly require, and which rightly pertains to the relations above named, and find no such invasion of the right to personal liberty as requires us to pronounce this statute to be unconstitutional. The decision in 55 Ill. as to the reform school, we do not think should be applied to this industrial school. The courts in other States have sustained similar laws. . . . [citations omitted. — *Ed.*]

It is objected that there was not reasonable notice given. The statute provides merely that notice to the parents shall be given. There was here written notice served upon the mother, with a copy of the petition, on the day before the trial. The step-father appeared. We think there was notice in compliance with the statute. There was opportunity to be present, and to apply for further time if not ready for the investigation.

A jury of twelve men was demanded and denied, and it is insisted there was error in this denial. The statute provides for a jury of only six. The constitutional provision that "the right of trial by jury, as heretofore enjoyed, shall remain inviolate," does not apply. This is not a proceeding according to the course of the common law, in which the right of a trial by jury is guaranteed, but the proceeding is a statutory one, and the statute, too, enacted since the adoption of the constitution. There was not, at the time of such adoption, the enjoyment of a jury trial in such a case. In reference to this subject generally, Judge Cooley, in his work on Constitutional Limitations, p. 319, remarks: "But in those cases which formerly were not triable by jury, if the legislature provide for such a trial now, they may doubtless create for the purpose a statutory tribunal composed of any number of persons, and no question of constitutional power or right could arise." And see *Ross* v. *Irving*, 14 Ill. 171.

The act requires the payment of $10 per month by the county for each girl sent from any county. It is insisted that this is in violation of the provision of the constitution that "the General Assembly shall not impose taxes upon municipal corporations, or the inhabitants or property thereof, for corporate purposes," etc. This is a minor independent feature of the act, which, if invalid, would not affect the other distinct portions of the act, and hence its consideration is not necessary in this case. It will be time to consider it when the country makes resistance and presents the question for determination.

The judgment of the county court will be affirmed.

Judgment affirmed.

MR. JUSTICE WALKER: I dissent to this opinion and judgment.

Chapter 11

The Juvenile Court:
Its Philosophy and Organization

THE PURPOSE OF THIS CHAPTER is to give the student a preliminary and general impression of some of the sociolegal problems that have arisen in the development of the juvenile court movement. Later chapters deal specifically with the technical problems as considered in legal decisions.

Judge Schramm's article affords insight into the underlying theory of the juvenile court as related to its origins and to the functions it must perform on the modern scene. He discusses the reasons why he believes it would be impractical to limit the court's function to a determination of status and to assign the treatment and supervisory functions to other social agencies. He defines the concept of "individualized justice," especially in given cases involving several children, and shows how necessary it is for the court to deal not only with the errant child but with the family and other parties who are related to the situation that brought the delinquent into court. He makes clear the meaning of "the socialization of justice," and emphasizes the obligation of the court to exert leadership in coordinating the relevant community resources. He points to three basic premises inherent in the juvenile court idea irrespective of variations in the administrative areas involved: the court's residual powers to fill gaps in the community's resources for aiding troubled children; its giving of status to auxiliary arts and disciplines relevant to the basic functions of protection, treatment and restoration of children in trouble; its role as a suggestor of equivalent reforms in the management of the adult offender.

Killian's article traces the difficulties that have been encountered in juvenile court administration as well as judicial decision to a "conflict of norms" involving "a sharper delineation between behavior circumstance and treatment consequence than perhaps was first contemplated." He introduces some order into the situation by detailed analysis of "structural norms, substantive norms, and procedural norms," these being involved in making decisions throughout the process of juvenile court activity, from "intake" policy, through the judicial hearing, to dispositional policy once the status of delinquency has been lawfully established. A basic need discussed is a clearer differentiation of the judicial function from the case work function — a problem of confusion between legal jurisdictional requirements and the intake practices. Although Killian's article is about a decade old, it presents issues regarding juvenile court structure and function that are still urgent and still require solution.

Problems involving the territorial scope of the court's activities are considered in Bander's piece on area jurisdiction in juvenile courts. Municipal, county, regional and statewide organizations are discussed. Distinction is drawn between the local jurisdictional limits of a court and the supplementary clinical and therapeutic facilities, which may be statewide.

The two pieces by Tappan reflect the concern of some authorities on juvenile delinquency who are both law-trained and sociology-trained, with the development of "socialized" processing of children charged with delinquency — devices which are, as Tappan puts it, "largely a hybrid product of court and case work methods." Tappan alludes to the dangers inherent in such practices as "unofficial" probation or remand without prior formal judicial hearing and of judicial procedures in which, in lieu of determination of "guilt" of some specific offense, the case of the juvenile is legally disposed of on the basis of an assessment of "personality factors" or of "the total situation."

Tappan sets down what he conceives to be minimal protections of due process which existing practices deny children charged with being delinquent. Such problems will be explored later, both in the editor's note preceding the chapters dealing with the law governing juvenile delinquency and in the judicial decisions therein presented. In the meantime, serious students of juvenile practice can profit from Tappan's analysis, especially his critique of "omnibus statutes," which define the basis of the delinquency status so broadly that they lead to confusion and abuse, and his distinction between what he conceives to be the court's legitimate sphere of operation and the field of social work. This defining of the types of situations which are legitimately within the purview of courts and those which might better be left to other community welfare agencies is carried further in Tappan's second article, "Unofficial Delinquency." His point of view is perhaps summarized in the following passage: "In relation to delinquency, there is an issue of policy even more vital than is true in other channels of child welfare: an issue of justice itself. Because court adjudication and authoritarian treatment are entailed, the difference between being a 'delinquent' and being a 'problem child' of some other sort is momentous." Tappan cites evidence of the widespread prevalence of "unofficial delinquency" — itself a vague and confusing concept differing in its application in various courts and their auxiliary services — and concludes with a summary of the dangers inherent in practices that have become not merely "unofficial" but loose.

The Editor believes that the sort of discussion contributed by Tappan and a few other students of juvenile court proceedings is a wholesome corrective of a situation that has developed without sufficient consideration of its implications and ramifications; for, however lofty may be the intentions and motives of the proponents of "socialization," there is some danger of procedures designed to reduce stigma and trauma giving rise to other evils that smack too much of arbitrariness.

Judge Waite's frequently cited article, although written years ago, is still helpful in defining the issues regarding constitutional and other safeguards to be observed in juvenile court proceedings. The questions he raises are discussed in the collection of legal decisions that follow.

By way of contrast and as a basis for comparison, there are included in the present chapter a digest of extracts from the statute and rules and orders governing juvenile court procedure in England as well as an article by Pihlblad on juvenile offender proceedings in Norway. There are two major aspects of the apparatus for coping with juvenile maladjustment in Scandinavian countries that deserve intensive investigation by Americans interested in reform: first, the employment of Welfare Committees or Councils instead of, or (in the case of older delinquents) in cooperation with, courts; secondly, the development of a great variety of small institutions and homes for the study and treatment of different types of delinquents, thus providing both a much needed flexibility of method and an opportunity for more intimate understanding and treatment. Whether it be advisable to substitute wholly administrative for judicial proceedings in juvenile cases is thus not a completely closed question. Dean Pound has well stated the case for the Anglo-American type of procedure:

> There are . . . special advantages in a juvenile court as a judicial tribunal rather
> than a purely administrative agency, such as a board of children's guardians, which
> was at one time much advocated as a substitute. Although there was for a time
> a cult of the administrative in this country, experience is making us appreciate the
> importance of the ethics of judicial adjudication, of hearing both sides, fully, of

acting on evidence of logical probative force, and of not combining the function of accuser, prosecutor, advocate of the complaint, and judge; of a record from which it can be seen what has been done and how and on what basis; and of possibility of review before a bench of judges in order to save fundamental constitutional and legal rights — something we must not forget our American constitutional polity was set up to maintain. The juvenile court as a means of dealing with juvenile delinquency is better adapted than a purely administrative agency to keep the balance between justice and security.[1]

The extent to which there are differences between the procedures described in the foregoing passage and the administrative procedures in Scandinavian countries is well exemplified in the article by Pihlblad.[2] The Editor regrets that two excellent reports to the Fifth International Congress for Social Defence, one by P. Tappan and the other by E. Bexelius, debating the issue of juvenile courts versus child welfare boards as the competent authority to cope with legal and social-psychiatric problems of delinquency and child neglect, were not available at the time this book was prepared. The attention of students is directed to these two valuable reports which are now in print.[3]

46

Philosophy of the Juvenile Court*

Gustav L. Schramm

Fifty years ago in Chicago, American children received the advantage of the first juvenile court. It was created to protect and guide them, to correct them and help them to grow into useful, happy, and desirable citizens. According to Roscoe Pound, this was the most significant advance in the administration of justice

since the Magna Charta was signed in 1215. In the document of Runnymede, Dean Pound points out, the principles of human freedom were set forth. In Chicago, in 1899, a group of Chicago lawyers outlined the first philosophy and objectives of the juvenile court. They set forth the principles of personalized justice.

Fifty years have passed since some thoughtful people launched the first juvenile court in America. They have been eventful years. Men and women have changed their attitudes, habits, and occupations. Nations have changed positions in the international scene. In fifty years we have experienced two world wars and an unprecedented economic depression. Our world is emerging with new problems. Fifty years of scientific and technological development have introduced many innovations in living, transportation, and communication. What was once two hemispheres, seven continents, and many nations has become one world.

During this half-century, however, the ideal of personalized justice, first embodied in Chicago, has been reinforced repeatedly. Courts have changed in attitudes, in application of methods, and in techniques and resources in their practices. Fifty years of experience have reaffirmed the principles adopted by that Chicago group. Today this strengthened philosophy of personalized justice and the principle of freedom from oppression stand as two of America's most cherished traditions, to be used by all the world as mankind seeks to live in peace and good will. All about us is the evidence of force,

[1] R. Pound, "The Juvenile Court and the Law," in M. Bell (Ed.), *Cooperation in Crime Control,* 1944 Yearbook, National Probation Association, 1945, 14–15.

[2] See also the thoroughgoing article on Swedish procedure by T. Sellin, "Sweden's Substitute for the Juvenile Court," 261 *Annals* (1949), 137–149. See, further, O. Nyquist, "How Sweden Handles Its Juvenile and Youth Offenders," 20 *Federal Probation* (1956), 36–42; *The Prevention of Juvenile Delinquency in Selected European Countries,* Institute for the Study and Treatment of Delinquency, London, 1955, United Nations, Department of Economic and Social Affairs, Bureau of Social Affairs.

[3] "The Competent Authorities," General Reports to Fifth International Congress for Social Defence, by P. Tappan and E. Bexelius, Stockholm, 25–30 August, 1958.

* Reprinted from 261 *Annals* (1949), 101–108. Used by permission of the author and the publisher.

fear, and confusion, but in this land a child's court leads to a better understanding of human dignity, of the growth of personality, of opportunities, and of appreciation of the wants and needs of others. It is a child's court that has led to change in attitudes and in methods of justice.

COURT OF EQUITY

To some, the Chicago doctrine was a strange one. The juvenile court was to act for the state according to the legal philosophy of *parens patriae*. It was not to be a court of "an eye for an eye." The court, acting for the state as a parent, was to recognize the individuality of the child and adapt its orders accordingly. There was legal precedent for this basic idea in the English tradition of the court of equity. A duty of such court was (and always should be) to see that neglected and abused children were given a chance under protection of the court to grow into useful citizenship.

Functions of the court were broadened logically and wisely. The age when a child is capable of responsibility was studied. If children under seven years were considered under the old Common Law as incapable of criminality, then why not those of eight, nine, or ten years of age? Was it not obvious that criminal courts, which were designed for adults, were not the proper ones to treat children in their growing years? Hence this group of delinquent children could be added to the others already protected by equity courts, the dependent and neglected children.

The men of Chicago therefore decided that such a court, the court of the king's conscience or equity court, was the logical one to assume responsibility for the delinquent child. It would reinforce its older, fundamentally sound responsibility to those already in its charge, the neglected children of the community. It recognized the principle that children could not in practice be held accountable for their behavior as adults for the simple but valid reason that they are not adults.[1]

---

[1] "The fundamental idea of the [juvenile court] law is that the state must step in and exercise guardianship over a child found under such adverse social or individual conditions as develop crime. . . . It proposes a plan whereby he may be treated, not as a criminal, or legally charged with crime, but as a ward of the state, to receive practically the care, cus-

At one time in our Anglo-American civilization it was believed that a child over seven could perform all the manual skills necessary for financial independence. At that time the age of legal responsibility was seven. Today, because we understand more about the social, ethical, and technological preparation that is necessary for a person to become legally responsible, most of the states define a child as being a person under the age of eighteen. In this step toward a better understanding of the maturing process and its length, the original tenets of the first juvenile court have led the way.

PUTTING PHILOSOPHY INTO PRACTICE

The first juvenile court stimulated thinking about the need of children for legal protection. It brought about new developments in court administration and in function. It began serving children not for prescribed periods of time but for whatever length of time was necessary to help the child. It created administrative machinery for service which would be fluid in that it would change services and adjust them to changing conditions and needs of the children in its charge.

It seems almost self-evident to declare that the juvenile court, protector of children needing help, should follow through in providing this help. Yet there are some who would restrict the juvenile court to a role of "legal determination" and would give executive bodies the administrative responsibilities. Applying such thinking to the functions of any court of equity reveals a lack of understanding of them. What would happen to the orphans' court, a court of equity? In settlements of estates, especially of minors, an orphans' court may function over a considerable period of time, as much as twenty years. Any limitation of the orphans' court to a mere legally determining body would add confusion and would jeopardize the financial interests of children. Such a limitation upon the juvenile court would nullify this dynamic, positive force in modern jurisprudence. It would add nothing but confusion and would jeopardize the children themselves.

---

tody and discipline that are accorded the neglected and dependent child, and which, as the act states, 'shall approximate as nearly as may be that which should be given by its parents.'" Report of the Committee of the Chicago Bar, 1899.

Much of the difference in opinion concerning juvenile courts and their proper functions and spheres of activity stems from lack of understanding that this court has the same approach and philosophy as any other equity court. People try to judge the changing pattern of juvenile procedure according to the old yardstick of "an eye for an eye." "Why shouldn't children pay in kind for the grief, anxiety, pain, and inconvenience suffered by others whom they wrong?" they ask. Punishment is the remedy, they argue, not realizing that a juvenile court does not mete out mere punishment, but it corrects children as a parent would. There is no conflict between the state and the child. The state accepts the child into its protection and seeks to help the child to grow into a useful citizen.

During the fifty years since the founding of the juvenile court movement courts have changed in attitudes, skills, and effectiveness. All juvenile courts are not alike. This is as true as the platitude that people differ. Individuals are different in attitudes, cultural levels, mental capacities, and economic status. These differences prevail among courts. There are courts rich in tradition, in philosophy, and in skill, and there are courts impoverished by legislation, inadequate staffs, lack of facilities, and absence of community cooperation and support. In such latter instances the children suffer as they do when serious defects prevail in homes.

INDIVIDUALIZATION RECOGNIZES HUMAN DIFFERENCES

The idea that people are different is the very foundation of the philosophy represented by the juvenile court. We call that philosophy personalized and individualized justice. Each person is an entity within himself, having basic rights and privileges as do all children, but having different needs according to circumstance and personality. In all juvenile court procedure there is nothing more difficult than properly to identify this difference, to explore it to its conclusion, and to set forth a course of treatment that will be most effective.

In a juvenile court the phrase "individualized justice" means "individualized treatment." It is exactly the opposite to the panacea or elixir viewpoint of one medicine for all suffering from a disease, the medicine given in the same quantity and at the same time. In juvenile court,

Tommy and Johnny differ in reaction and in absorption of the treatment prescribed. It does not mean that the court ignores, from case to case, certain general considerations such as procedure, channels, institutions, or social obligations. It means that in the systematic consideration of each problem, co-ordination of resources and skills in behalf of the child must and does follow.

Individualization means that the problems of Tommy and Johnny, although the boys were referred to the court on identical complaints, must be separated when considered by the court. The judge also must adapt himself to each personality in "countenance, speech and tone of voice." [2] Individualization means that the court will not generalize, or ridicule, or abuse or arbitrarily display its power; but will seek to elicit from family and child a willingness to work out with the court and its representatives the difficulties confronting them. When justice is translated in a child's mind into the relationship between "me and the judge," and when the interest of the court is demonstrated in the personal interest of a man who represents the court and its authority and, in the larger sense, society itself, the entire process becomes humanized.

This approach demands that the court make definite impressions on all parties who have been gathered in the interest of a child. Each person who is in court represents the community, a social interest. Each must carry back to the community an impression that what he contributed was recognized as important by the court; that the judge gave his point of view consideration. We feel that each person who appears in court should carry out with him positive impressions of good faith; faith as evidenced by the discussion and uncovering of all the facts; faith as exemplified by trust in the judicial and ethical integrity of the court's personnel; faith in the court even when decisions are contrary to the interested party's wishes. The public must carry away the impression that decisions are not made routinely or arbitrarily, nor are they made in haste or anger. It is our hope that they take with them the impression that the court's decision is in the best interests

---

[2] Gustav L. Schramm, "The Judge Meets the Boy and His Family," 1945 *Yearbook National Probation Association*, pp. 182–94.

of the child; that the findings represent an opportunity for improvement rather than a means for despair.

Group cases, where several children have been apprehended by the police for having participated in one or a series of illegal acts, are one of the most frequent challenges to this individualized approach. Group cases do not evolve into group decisions. Proper variations in the court's findings are accepted when the differences are analyzed in terms of *this* child's needs, *its* personality, *its* social and moral environment. Such differences would be difficult if the emphasis of the court were on the offenses rather than on the troubled children, on their past rather than on their future.

Community Responsibility and Opportunity

The socialization of justice, as Roscoe Pound has propounded in many articles [3] and lectures, not only looks for the common good but also seeks remedies, skills, and resources outside of the courts which may be used in the fulfillment of these objectives. The word "socialization" takes on its traditional, semantic meaning of group participation as well as that of group use. The labels — juvenile delinquency, dependency, and neglect — are tools and devices used to initiate the proceedings and to focus the problem. But an accompaniment to this court's procedures goes not only to the resources of the court for investigation of factors that led to the present problems, but also to the mobilization of all skills whose aim it is to revitalize the community and its members.

The juvenile court is in a position to accept leadership in co-ordinating various community resources. It has a strategic role in the logistics of a society's battle for the less fortunate youth in trouble before the public. The medical profession, the psychologists and the psychiatrists, the sociologists and the social workers, the group and recreational leaders, the ministers, the educators, and the policemen [4] all have something

to contribute which will be positive from their point of view. Only in the juvenile court can their individual contributions be integrated and strengthened.

In the juvenile courts of today, after the facts of a child's problems have been established, the analysis of causes and the evaluation of remedies take the foreground. Only the most naïve and credulous will accept the theories of unit causation of crime and delinquency. The social scientists have thoroughly discredited the singular explanation of behavior problems. Johnny isn't truant because. . . . An examination of even the simplest case will show that behavior, whether socially approved or not, is colored by every experience of the individual from the time of his birth to the present.

Many people, particularly zealots who are promoting some pet idea of social control, will advance unit cures and panaceas. A playground, a course in manual training, mental examinations for all, the erection of better housing, fishing trips, the creation of another committee, a juvenile night club, and innumerable other devices have many advocates and promoters. The writer has approved most of these as projects, but they are single approaches to prevention and rehabilitation. We know that many people persist in their beliefs in panaceas in spite of evidence to the contrary. Lags in knowledge of scientific findings and their application seem to be inevitable.

Parens Patriae

The juvenile court's function is to protect children when their own parents have not done so. The Latin phrase *parens patriae* used in the Law, as we have previously said, means that the juvenile court acting for the state must, to the extent of the default of the child's real parents, assume their parental responsibilities.

Let us make another analogy between real parents and the court acting as a protective substitute parent. What, generally, are a real parent's responsibilities to his child? Statistically, the normal or average family consists of two parents and two children living in one household. Parents are required not only by the mores and customs but also by law to provide for the physical needs of their children. Fathers and mothers are actually required by society to give more than physical sustenance to their children. Society expects them to

[3] Roscoe Pound, "The Rise of Socialized Criminal Justice," 1942 *Yearbook National Probation Association*, pp. 1–22; "The Juvenile Court and the Law," 1944 *Yearbook National Probation Association*, pp. 1–22; "The Future of Socialized Justice," 1946 *Yearbook National Probation Association*, pp. 6–18.

[4] Gustav L. Schramm, "Police–Juvenile Court Teamwork in Pittsburgh, Pa.," *FBI Law Enforcement Bulletin*, July 1948, pp. 7–9.

instill some ethics into children in their relation to other people, some acceptance of the
prevailing customs, cultural forms, and institutions, and some awareness of their physical, social, and educational potentialities.

To realize these goals, parents may use the
facilities and the knowledge represented by the
schools. They may appeal and subscribe to the
inspiration and teachings of their church. They
may ask for the authority of the law. They
may demand the protection of the state. When
a child is ill, if a mother cannot minister to its
needs, she will call for the advice of a neighbor
or for the skill of a physician. When a child
is having difficulties in the classroom, a mother
may discuss his problems with his teachers and
his school principal, perhaps even with the
child guidance clinic. When her boy seems to
be drifting with undesirable companions, she
may discuss her problems with the minister,
the policeman on the beat, or the playground
director. All those persons whose help is solicited
on an individual basis by parents may also be
asked to help children in whom the court is
interested.

Basic Importance of the Juvenile Court

A juvenile court is an integral part of any
community program of services to children. The
exact relationship may vary with the community resources, the experience of the community, and the effectiveness of the co-operation
between groups. While the administrative area
of the court need not be duplicated exactly in
any two communities, there are three basic
premises that are universally applicable.

1. The court has residual powers. It is
charged by the law to protect the state as well
as to determine the best interests of a child in
trouble. Wherever there are gaps the court
should attempt directly or indirectly to see that
needed service is provided. Wherever adequate
facilities are available the court should be careful not to duplicate but to make full and profitable use of them. The court should be as alert
as a resourceful parent to make the most of
what the community has to offer to meet *this*
child's problems.

For example, despite the large number of
cases of neglect, few cases of dependency come
into many juvenile courts today. The public assistance program provides society's channel for
financial aid to the needy in their own homes.

Here and there executive machinery categorically administering such a law fails a particular
child. The court, however, with the broad discretion inherent in a court of equity, can meet
this need.

As another example, private agencies are indispensable in a modern community's service
to children. In a democracy they are the life-
blood of private initiative, resourcefulness, and
discrimination. Where, however, there is inadequate or no coverage because of temporary or
permanent limitation of funds, staff, or function,
again the juvenile court, acting for the whole
of the community, has power and responsibility
for action. No petition for care, guidance,
and control of any child can be disregarded.

2. As a court, the juvenile court carries with
it broad public support for its ideals. It can
therefore give status to the specialized branches
of the arts and sciences whose skill the court
needs. Social work, psychiatry, psychology, and
sociology, as they contribute to the solution
of a child's problems, receive through the court
public encouragement and support. Such professional groups are neither minimized nor belittled because of their aid, since in their demonstration of co-operation and in the proof of
their integration they can justify the public
support they receive. There should be no rival-
ries. The juvenile court as a court of equity is
not a competitor, but society's lawful integrator
of skills for public service to troubled children.

Courts are generally called upon to settle
legal disputes of two parties, plaintiff and
defendant. Courts of equity functioning within
the judicial process have been able over the
centuries to develop the techniques of determining many-sided problems. Their administrative
arm has enabled them to follow through in all
directions needed and for as long as necessary
to come to an equitable conclusion. Juvenile
courts, as courts of equity, are thus uniquely
fitted by experience and by authority to meet
the public demand for fair dealing under the
law for all concerned in the welfare of a child
— the community, the parents, and the child.[5]

---

[5] It is in such connections that the law, which has
grown up out of experience of how to adjust relations so as to take account of all the interests involved, so far as possible by general precepts, shows
itself superior to administration which tends to treat
each case as unique and so to lose sight of or to ignore
some of the interests to be affected. From this stand-

For example, the placement of children under public foster care can be safeguarded by continuous court sanction. The administration of such care may be carried out directly by the court staff or by the staff of a court-appointed citizens board working closely with the court. In such a setup, professional and community resources can be developed and focused upon the needs of a child deprived of the natural advantages of its own home.

3. The juvenile court has, in the half-century of its existence, amply demonstrated to the informed community the wisdom and the advantages of personalized justice for children. These same principles will be more and more accepted until they are adapted to adults as well. Such developments in the adult field as indeterminate sentence, probation, behavior clinics, and pre-sentence investigations owe their acceptance to the demonstration made by the juvenile court. Just as in other areas, such as our labor laws, "a little child shall lead them."

THE YOUTH AUTHORITY

A word of caution is in order. Today there is enthusiasm for what is called "Youth Authority," utilizing with the older youth in criminal court the experience gained in the juvenile court field. This is good. However, some proponents go so far as to advocate that juvenile courts lose their jurisdiction of 16- and 17-year-old youths and have them placed within the Youth Authority's jurisdiction.

This is indeed an absurd proposal when it is recalled that the Youth Authority functions only after a *criminal court conviction*. In other words, such youths, recognized as still growing up, still immature, and still nonadults, would first be branded criminals for life in order to receive the benefits of corrective treatment! Another suggestion, obviously not well thought out, is to have established an "adolescent or youth court." Would it be a juvenile court,

or a criminal court? Would it be fish, or fowl? We hope no loose thinking will mar the progress of the juvenile court to serve to the full those entitled to its service. Let us not retrogress.

THE NEWCOMER IN JURISPRUDENCE

Juvenile courts are the least understood and the most misunderstood of the courts of our land. Their unique philosophy, procedures, and approach are features that not all segments of the population, even of the legal profession and the bench, have fully perceived as yet. In our traditional courts the emphasis is on "Did you or did you not?"; not on "Why, under what circumstances, and what can be done to help?"

It is only half a century since the Chicago group launched the juvenile court movement in the United States. In this period every state in the Union has made statutory provisions based on the fundamentals propounded by the originators. It is in the day-to-day carrying out of those fundamentals that much yet remains undone. Some courts by implementations have kept pace with experience and have brought about progressive changes; some have been able to incorporate the findings of many fields of social and medical science into their processes of treatment and diagnosis. There are up-to-date models, aging models, and obsolescent ones.

We who work in the field of personalized justice have many responsibilities to the past and to the future. Our juvenile courts are far from perfect. They are changing as experience accumulates. New discoveries and techniques in diagnosis, prediction, and treatment will modify our practices. Those of us responsible for administration of justice realize that our responsibilities do not rest solely with our actions within our courts or derive from the specialists in the community who give us help and co-operation. We have a great obligation to tell and retell to the public what we are doing, what we have done, and what we hope to do. We have the duty to point up community weaknesses and to co-operate in overcoming them.

It is the right of the public to expect us to make an accounting. They should know our effectiveness in dealing with children, our methods, and our objectives. Likewise, it is the right of the public to demand that we be willing to learn; that we constantly improve ourselves to

point it was especially fortunate that equity, judicially administered, was taken as the basis of the jurisdiction of the juvenile court from the beginning. The flexibility of equity procedure, the ability of equity to deal with numerous parties who have conflicting or overlapping interests in one proceeding, and its power of molding relief to the facts of the case in hand, are decisive." Roscoe Pound, "The Juvenile Court and the Law," *1944 Yearbook National Probation Association*, p. 16.

the end that every child shall gain by it. In the field of interpretation we should approach the public with pride for the past, with strength for the present, and with hope for the future. In humility we should remember that we act as custodians of this heritage, since it was first pronounced in Chicago. In humility we must seek to inform the public so that this heritage may have its fullest use and effect upon children and, in due time, upon mankind generally.

Science seems to be annihilating time and space. The amazing progress of man in the field of natural science poses serious questions for us all. Can man match that progress with his own? Will he instead risk annihilating civilization? Upon the answer may well depend the future of mankind. It is not too much to say that the humane newcomer — the juvenile court — in its personalized justice for troubled youth will be a significant factor in determining that answer.

47

The Juvenile Court as an Institution[*]

Frederick W. Killian

With the establishment of the juvenile court, approximately fifty years ago,[1] a policy design was put into operation in which the idea of public security with reference to the offenses, neglect, and dependency of children was to be implemented through a separate, special, and sometimes exclusive jurisdiction. This was the first recognition by the law of a separate area of legal control for a distinct field of behavior. Implicit in this policy design, unlike the criminal court emphasis, *treatment consequence* was to predominate rather than *behavior circum-*

stance,[2] and the norms and standards of common law and equity, as well as of social and administrative necessity, were to find an operating relation in a new synthesis of experience.[3] The laws establishing these courts have, as policy designs, been hypotheses for action and experimentation.

THE CONFLICT OF NORMS

During fifty years of experience, these factors have led to a sharper delineation between behavior circumstance and treatment consequence than perhaps was first contemplated, certainly more than in any other court, and have even effected a change in the predominance of behavior circumstances in the criminal courts. From the juvenile court come also theories for the newly established youth authorities or commissions.[4]

The conflict of norms [5] and standards is the court's bane today; it has been apparent both within the court itself and between the court and other community agencies. The policy design of the court has necessarily brought it nearer to other agencies, correlating its work with theirs in implementing the public security with reference to children. This sharpens conflict, as the norms and standards of courts and of agencies are still in the stage of formulation.

The court, established in 1899, graced by charity, reform, and progress, each too vague and speculative to provide more than an atmos-

---

[*] Reprinted from 261 *Annals* (1949), 89–100. Used by permission of the author and the publisher.

[1] The Illinois law (L. 1899, p. 131) was the first; for dates of other laws, see Gilbert Cosulich, *Juvenile Court Laws of the United States* (New York: National Probation Association, 1939), pp. 9–12.

[2] For elaboration, see Jerome Hall, "Criminology and a Modern Penal Code," *Journal of Criminal Law and Criminology*, Vol. 27, No. 1, May-June, 1936; also Paul W. Tappan, *Delinquent Girls in Court* (New York: Columbia University Press, 1947), *passim.*

[3] As used by Roscoe Pound, who connects the term with the concept "social control"; see *Social Control Through Law* (New Haven: Yale University Press, 1942), pp. 111–12, *passim*; also Huntington Cairns, *Law and the Social Sciences* (New York: Harcourt, Brace, 1935), pp. 147–57.

[4] Established by various names — California 1941, Minnesota and Wisconsin 1947, Massachusetts 1948; in other states, bills not carried. See John Barker Waite, "The Youth Correction Authority Act," *Law and Contemporary Problems*, Vol. 9, No. 4 (Autumn 1942), pp. 600–616.

[5] For the investigation see Thorsten Sellin, *Culture Conflict and Crime* (New York: Social Science Research Council, Bulletin 41, 1938), Chap. IV, "The Conflict of Conduct Norms."

phere of good will and good intentions, each increasingly to be rejected, therefore fell somewhat short of expectations, and too often worked, and still does, behind a façade of hope, looking for new idealogical supports in a fuller development of the social disciplines and of social work.

The limitations as well as the advantages of each normative system embodied in its structure have come to be more apparent in the struggle for equilibration. Case work functions and judicial functions vie with each other.[6] Active, or potentially active, in the court's ideology are doctrines and hypotheses concerning the nature of law or of some control area, as well as their specialized terminologies, and confusion results. New logical applications are being sought for the analysis, formulation, and reformulation of norms and doctrines of substance, procedure, court structure, and operation.[7] The emphasis on treatment demands clarification between judicial function and case work function as old legalities and new inductive concepts pervade the court's operation on all levels.

For the purpose of analysis, it seems advisable to classify the norms as structural norms, substantive norms, and procedural norms. The first includes form, arrangement of components, and the court's connection with the judicial system; the second, the norms of behavior or conduct which may be applied to particular situations; and the last, the procedures for making the applications of substantive norms. The purpose behind the adoption and use of a norm of conduct and of the procedure for its application will ultimately determine the norms of structure; all normative levels are interrelated in operation.

What, then, has been the experience of this court, and what does it offer as experience?[8] The selection of norms and standards as the unit of attention reduces the analysis to an operational level which will therefore proceed from intake to disposition, after certain preliminary considerations have been examined.

---

[6] See Thomas D. Eliot, "Case Work Function and Judicial Functions" *Coping With Crime* (Marjorie Bell, Ed.), New York: National Probation Association, 1937.

[7] Paul W. Tappan, *op. cit.*, note 2 *supra*.

[8] For a review of the court from 1899 to 1927, see Harbert H. Lou, *Juvenile Courts in the United States*, Chapel Hill: University of North Carolina Press, 1927.

STRUCTURE AND WORK OF THE COURT

Students of the court will find considerable differences from place to place in the organization of the courts, in the emphasis on various stages of procedure, in the competence of staff, judge, and officials, and also in tone and atmosphere.

The Court's Structure. For purposes of discussion and to give a general picture of this special jurisdiction, its organization may be classified[9] under four general heads:

1. Independent courts with jurisdiction over children: with city, county, or state-wide jurisdiction and with probation services supplied by the court or by city, county, or state agencies; mostly in large urban centers (or state-wide courts, as in Connecticut and Rhode Island).

2. Family courts with jurisdiction over specified offenses and relations and over specified types of family conflict, including jurisdiction over children; services attached or separate; urban centers largely. (Of 33 family and domestic relations courts listed in *The Book of the States*, only 19 possess divorce jurisdiction.)

3. Juvenile and domestic relations courts: independent or parts of courts with more general jurisdiction; rarely having jurisdiction over divorce and separation; services attached or independent; in urban centers largely.

4. Juvenile courts as sections or parts of courts with more general jurisdiction: judges of the court holding juvenile parts of divisions by designation sometimes in rotation (usually probate, county, circuit, or common pleas courts); services attached or separate; more common in nonurban centers.

Operation for all these courts could easily be uniform from a normative point of view; indeed, they largely resemble one another as to the jurisdiction conferred over children, the differences being largely due to community needs, understanding, and resources, which determine good or poor operations, functionaries, and facilities.

Sources of Intake. To all of these courts,

---

[9] See Cosulich, *op. cit.* note 1 *supra*, pp. 14–20; brought to date in National Probation (now National Probation and Parole) Association Yearbooks, sections entitled "Legislation and Decisions." For family and domestic relations courts, see *The Book of the States, 1945–46* (Chicago: Council of State Governments), pp. 346–47.

children come on petitions alleging delinquency, dependency, or neglect. Generally, parents or any interested person, including the police, school officials, or social agencies, may make a petition informally alleging the offense or difficulty. Children may be brought directly to the court by the police; if arrested after court hours, they are taken first to a detention home (where such exists).

Very many delinquency cases come to the court through the police. Police departments, including juvenile aid bureaus, where properly organized, furnish indispensable aids to the court in sifting out those cases that need court action; many complaints — particularly of neighbors, watchmen, janitors, foremen, railroad guards, and others to whom other people's children are a nuisance, often whether good or bad — indicate little if any need for special treatment, but rather for recreation and play facilities or for a warning. This service, as the New York City and Detroit experiences show, saves the court many valuable intake interviews in disposing of such cases. Most of these cases come from low income families and areas of the city [10] — the juvenile court being primarily an urban institution with a population heavy in this category.

Indispensable to the court, its functions centered around the intake process, is the detention home.[11] Sometimes an independent service and sometimes under probation direction (as in the Toledo juvenile court), it serves the court in and out of hours as a protection for neglected and dependent children as well as for serious or questionable cases of delinquency where the child cannot be released to a parent's or relative's custody. It furnishes a first view of the child, his needs and temperament, and the conditions of his difficulty. This home is by no means a jail substitute, but a treatment-initiating and study center, and relations between it and the court must be highly integrated through proper procedures.

The schools rely on the courts for truancy

control, for cases of unmanageable children, and sometimes in cases where further schooling seems inadvisable. The authoritarian setting of the court and the quasi-authoritarian setting of the school tend toward a common emphasis (often that of functional autonomy) on discipline and responsibility, but may conflict because attention is to different values.[12] The schools referring children to a court too often expect it to achieve in a week, by some mysterious operation, what it, with more extensive facilities, could not do in years. Good schools and good courts alone, through the conference method, can define a proper relation.[13]

Procedures. All of what has been said suggests the importance of formulating procedures to define the methods of work between the court and other agencies and between divisions of the court itself. These should be made, cooperatively, in a conference of qualified agency representatives. This is a procedural norm perfected in social work, through which referrals based on cooperative and overlapping functions are defined. The trained social worker assumes the necessity; the judge tends to regard it as a matter for authoritarian attention — is he not superordinate? The answer is, No. This function is nonjudicial; it relates to treatment consequence, to intake, to agency relations, and not to jurisdiction. However, the judge should participate in such conferences. In this process the judge waives no prerogative, as here he performs an administrative function. Too frequently court procedures are established (and procedures are very few) [14] by judicial directives,

---

[10] Delinquency does not stop here; it is common knowledge that much unreported delinquency occurs in rural and suburban areas. See George B. Vold, "Crime in City and Country Areas," *The Annals of the American Academy of Political and Social Science,* Vol. 217 (Sept. 1941), pp. 38–45.

[11] See Sherwood Norman in this volume.

[12] Arnold Green, "The Concept of Responsibility," *Journal of Criminal Law and Criminology,* Vol. 33, No. 5 (Jan.-Feb. 1943), pp. 392–94. For the great disparity in the values stressed, see Paul H. Landis, *Social Policies in the Making* (Boston: Heath, 1947), Wickman's chart showing teacher's ratings v. mental hygienist's ratings on relative seriousness of behavior in children, pp. 168–69.

[13] See L. Wallace Hoffman, "Court-School Relations," *Federal Probation,* Vol. 9, No. 3 (July-Sept. 1945), pp. 27–30.

[14] Four good manuals of procedures were carefully worked out by this method in: Domestic Relations and Juvenile Court, Lucas County (Toledo), Ohio; The Family Court for New Castle County (Wilmington), Del.; and the Connecticut and San Francisco juvenile courts. This need is pressing; see Walter Reckless, "Juvenile Institutions and the Courts and Their Relationships," *Probation,* April 1947, pp. 113–18, at p. 118.

either as parts of rules of the court or as temporary instructions.

The Judge — Focal Norm of the Court. All lines of operation in the court either lead to or emanate from the judge. No court can rise above its judge — particularly a separate and independent court. He is chief administrator, adjudicator, policy maker; also the public relations man for the court, and the reconcilor of disputes. It cannot be too plainly asserted that no condition — of selection, or preparation for office, of tenure, of salary — is favorably defined for the judge of this court.

His education, legal,[15] and general, has probably been of little use. Criminal law, a short one-year course, is usually a formalistic study of remedial categories, not of normative development. Juvenile court judges more than others must learn on the job and acquire judgment with respect to the exacting application of legal and social norms, and experience in a dawning sense of the law in relation to the social disciplines.[16]

Judges are generally selected by election or by appointment.[17] Both are hazardous, and separate effort is always essential to obtain a qualified judge. By either method, demands of politics enter into the selection and later into the judge's work. Nor is performance of work for one or more terms necessarily a guarantee of re-election or re-appointment.[18]

Relegated to the lowest level of the judicial hierarchy in an inferior court,[19] the office does not, as a rule, attract men of maturity or ability. Pressure is insistent at the lower levels, and selection for quality is more difficult because public sensitivity tends to be directed to higher offices. Nor is this work regarded as adequate preparation for the coveted status of a judgeship on the superior or appellate benches, but rather as specialized and not demanding extensive legal experience.

In courts of mixed jurisdiction, judges frequently avoid assignment to the juvenile division as unprofitable, particularly in terms of promotion and legal achievement; only a few prefer it. Rotation of work is therefore often resorted to in order that no judge shall be deprived of common law or equity experience. Several such judges may have to learn the trade, so to speak. Generally they will not regard it worth while to make this effort, and, in any event, such experience will be spotty and discontinuous.

The fact that this judge may practice law in many jurisdictions, mostly outside the large urban centers, indicates a lack of community resources or of awareness of job demands, or both. This is closely correlated with salaries, which range from under $1,000 in rural areas to generally fair competences of $10,000 and over in large cities, as in New York.[20]

Short tenures do not encourage men of ability to seek this inferior position. Five-year terms (in New Jersey, for instance) have demonstrated that no sooner is a judge in command of the situation than his office may be filled by a novice. In short, the judge of this court is now faced with an impossible definition of the situation.

Intake, Jurisdiction and Power. The sources of intake and referral above described are preludes to entry into the court. But before the court can begin to function, two norms of procedure must be given weight — intake and jurisdiction — each fixing its own standards for

---

[15] The present status and future of legal education are of prime importance in new areas of formal control; space prevents discussion here, but the subject has not been neglected. See Alfred Z. Reed, *Training for the Public Profession of the Law* (New York: Carnegie Foundation for the Advancement of Teaching, 1921); Wesley Newcomb Hohfeld, in *Fundamental Legal Conceptions* (Walter Wheeler Cook, Ed., New Haven: Yale University Press, 1923), Chap. VIII; Harold D. Lasswell, *The Analysis of Political Behavior* (New York: Oxford University Press, 1947), Chap. III (With Myres S. McDougal) — includes excellent bibliography on legal education.

[16] Paul W. Alexander, "Of Juvenile Court Justice and Judges," *Redirecting the Delinquent* (Marjorie Bell, Ed., New York: National Probation Association Yearbook, 1947), pp. 187–205.

[17] See Cosulich, *op. cit.* note 1 *supra*, Chap. XIII, on "Selection." He describes other methods (pp. 80–84), but it is difficult to measure their effectiveness for lack of adequate documentation.

[18] This admits of exceptions, as judges have been and are carefully selected, by election and otherwise. See issues of *Journal of the American Judicature Society* (Ann Arbor, Mich.), 32 vols., *passim*; reviews all methods of judicial selection, with bibliographies.

[19] Legally speaking, "inferior" refers to judicial review. The word, *qua* word, has a deflating tendency.

[20] On salary and tenure, see Cosulich, *op. cit.* note 1 *supra*, p. 83; also various salary surveys made from time to time by National Probation Association, 1790 Broadway, New York City; also *The Book of the States, 1945–46* (Chicago: Council of State Governments), pp. 448–49.

admission to the court. Unity between them is found in the concept of "public security," a concept of social control. The two definitions were formulated in different areas of control at different times — jurisdiction out of the King's peace, intake as a limit of services in a social-agency policy-design; both out of experience. Each is organized around its own principle of authority, with jurisdiction superordinate; a norm carried over from criminal law emphasizing behavior circumstance.

The social worker sees ordering and commanding as attendant upon the requirements of treatment consequence, a norm of case work, based on service, which in the court, therefore, tends to function to the limits of this definition, which is its own.[21] Judges may tend to refrain from power exercise as a concession, in lieu of punishment — "giving another chance," an expression which is anathema to the trained social worker.

Thus intake and jurisdiction are too often irreconcilable, each operating as a unit of taught and of operational experience and conditioning. Each exercises a sifting function designed to protect its respective area of operation — intake, the social; jurisdiction, the legal. Jurisdiction, in certain respects a substitute for self-help, defines the exercise and limits of power applied from ideas of behavior circumstance and is concerned with rights and duties, largely with a mechanical application thereof,[22] while intake defines the client need in relation to agency resources. These norms operate simultaneously and tend to be mechanically related, and in most courts the judicial process dominates, as none is present to dissent.

In the better courts having trained staff, it is unlikely that judge and case worker can, in the foreseeable future, possess an identity of taught and of operating experience;[23] and here responsibility falls heavy on the judge, while the case worker often overemphasizes professionalization.

From Intake to Disposition. From whatever source, the child entering the court is handled by a staff [24] which in good courts consists of skilled professional workers, chiefly trained in social work techniques and supported by medical, psychological, and psychiatric services. The interjection into the case of any such service, including the judicial process, should be made only at stated intervals and through channels established by carefully prepared procedures. When treatment is being emphasized, the case work process must be the predominant norm, subject only to considerations of public security. Unusual circumstances may demand a departure from a defined process sequence.

Sometimes the procedures themselves call for revision; and in good courts, procedures will be continually evaluated in terms of experience, and all unnecessary interference with the case work process eliminated. Staff conferences in better courts help to interpret these definitions. In a properly organized juvenile court, probation workers and staff can clear most matters of interpretation, legalities, jurisdiction, and so forth informally, as parties to the proceedings rarely insist on the observance of strictly technical forms.

Social agencies insist upon skilled and tested workers for intake; in the court, the intake worker should have all the skills of the case worker in addition to a comprehensive knowledge of the court's jurisdiction. This requires continual training, and is only one reason why training-on-the-job conferences — another case work norm — are imperative and are held in good courts at least monthly.[25]

However, in the great majority of courts

---

[21] See Kenneth L. M. Pray, "The Place of Social Case Work in the Treatment of Delinquency," *The Social Service Review*, Vol. XIX, No. 2, June, 1945.

[22] Heavily saturated with ideas of natural law; see Roscoe Pound, *Interpretations of Legal History* (New York: Macmillan, 1923), *passim*; the reason for the mechanical application presented, pp. 5–6. For new ideas and applications of natural law, see Pound, *Social Control Through Law, op. cit.* note 3 *supra*, pp. 3–4, 6, 8.

[23] The contemplated revision of the Standard Juvenile Court Act (New York: National Probation Association, 1943, latest revision) may help here by essential reformulations of norms in conflict.

[24] Part of the court or a separate service, the personnel are known as probation officers or counselors — a preferable term. See Thorsten Sellin, "Adult Offenders," for quality of probation service; also Alice Scott Nutt, "Juvenile and Domestic Relations Courts," *Social Work Year Book* (New York: Russell Sage Foundation, 1947), pp. 38, 274, respectively.

[25] In the Probation Department of Essex County, New Jersey, the conference method has been particularly well worked out by the chief probation officer and has been in operation for many years, as in several other probation offices, but in most cases very poorly, if at all.

throughout the United States, intake, in any technical sense, is almost completely neglected; even clerks of the court, frequently miserable hacks, are sometimes allowed to hold first interviews. Clerks, bailiffs, and uniformed attendants have no place in a juvenile court. Even in many common law and equity courts, certain clerks have for some time had legal training and are in a sense, judicial administrators and professional employees. In this sense, a clerk is a useful official.

Treatment consequence, if stressed, must begin at intake and continue as defined, with the few exceptions made necessary by serious offenses, for instance, homicides and adult-linked larcenies. In these cases it may be essential, and actually advisable and appropriate, initially to emphasize the public security by bringing the child directly before the judge. He may then make a referral to intake, as is frequently done in good courts, if behavior circumstance, in his estimation, need not be emphasized at that stage of the proceedings to meet the needs of public security.

Actually, this method, thoughtfully used, may strengthen a later case work process, and it interrupts no process begun. For many judges, the hardest lesson to learn is that an undefined interjection into the case disrupts treatment; for many social workers, that their norms of process must be flexible in an authoritarian agency.

At intake the case begins to fall into one of two categories — official cases and unofficial cases (used by almost all courts).[26] No uniform definition of these terms can be stated, as a considerable difference of opinion prevails from person to person and from place to place as to whether an offense belongs in the area dominated by behavior circumstance or by treatment consequence. The definition of delinquency, rarely specific,[27] influences all that happens to a child from intake, through hearing to disposi-

tion, and later in treatment. Someone, either the judge himself or a staff member, must determine whether an adjudication shall be made with treatment to follow (official) or whether adjudication is unnecessary, the child to be carried for treatment (unofficial) or the case dismissed. This reflects a conflict of norms which will be discussed shortly, but a view of the hearing and disposition stages is essential for the analysis.

If a case is not designated as unofficial, and if behavior circumstance marks it for the judge's attention at some stage, it is docketed for the court.[28] In good courts the judge hears the case on a staff report with the worker present together with parents, very occasionally legal counsel, and interested parties. Medical, psychological, and psychiatric reports may be included, or, if needed, may be required by the judge and the case may be continued. School and recreational experiences are included. But hearings in these courts vary from strictly legal exhibitions to careful studies — sometimes sixty or seventy children or more herded through the court in a single day.

Referees. In about one-third of the courts, referees are provided for by statute. In other courts they are designated, in lieu of such provision, under the judge's power (as chancellor) to designate masters in chancery; but a wide variety of referee use, mostly poor is found to exist. A well-developed use of the referee system is found in the Toledo court,[29] where the judge, also possessing divorce and domestic relations jurisdiction, sits in juvenile cases on rehearings from a referee's decision; in that court, the staff is of the highest quality in training and education. In the vast majority of cases in that court such rehearings are not demanded. The Standard Juvenile Court Act (§10) provides a

---

[26] On this question see Paul Tappan, "Treatment Without Trial," *Social Forces,* Vol. 24, No. 3 (March 1946), pp. 306–11. [Article 49 hereof. — *Ed.*]

[27] See 1943, latest edition Standard Juvenile Court Act, §3(1)(b), (c), (d); §3(2); §13, where specific definitions have been eliminated. Note that several members of the drafting committee, including Judge Paul Alexander and Judge Ricks, favored their retention. This is a most important question; see Tappan, *Delinquent Girls in Court, op. cit.* note 2 *supra,* p. 184.

[28] The laws provide for separate, private, and simplified hearings and for flexible rules of evidence (certain limits have been stated, for instance in *People* v. *Lewis,* 260 N.Y. 171); few require juries (there are notable exceptions here); essential legal processes are defined. See Cosulich, *op. cit.* note 1 *supra,* Chap. VII; also Standard Juvenile Court Act, §§ 13–16; § 19, on hearing, eliminates the jury. This being a court of equity, there is no necessity for jury trials, but they may result from appellate interpretations. See, for instance, *In re Mei,* 121 N.J. Eq. 123, 122 N.E. Eq. 124; and *In re Daniecki,* 117 N.J. Eq. 527, 119 N.J. Eq. 359. [See Chapter 12 hereof. — *Ed.*]

[29] Ohio Code Annotated, §§1639–21, referee's power defined.

definition for the use of referees correlating judicial with case work functions, allowing flexibility and inventiveness.[30]

It is not too much to say that the referee system, contemplating highly trained and carefully selected functionaries, will in the final analysis prove to be the most promising device for resolving the conflict of norms in this court and for overcoming the difficulties facing juvenile court judges. This device has the advantages of reducing political pressures, providing for career service, retaining the essential legal safeguard of judicial review, and ultimately allowing an appeal on questions of law.[31]

Seen as part of Dean Pound's proposal for a unified court system [32] (now in effect in New Jersey under the new constitution), the referee system holds a place for juvenile, domestic relations, and family jurisdictions within a unified court structure but with a separately defined area for the indispensable administrative and case work functions. In this way a member of the bench of a unified court could be assigned to a part of that court dealing with family matters,[33] with reasonable assurance that the difficulties now impeding juvenile court judges, as above described, would be eliminated in great measure.

A judge cannot perform all functions. If he hears all or nearly all cases in courts where the referee system is not developed, he is actually involved in administrative work. Since present-day legal education does not measurably deal with behavior problems, and since a new type of

legal-social mind and approach is needed, it would seem that the referee function, institutionalized, might more easily provide it than a re-education of judges.

Trials, in a more formal sense, are sometimes necessary in juvenile courts for older children involved in serious offenses in terms of behavior circumstance or (and this seldom occurs) where a child denies having committed the offense alleged. Some laws provide for such trials, and some for transfer of such cases to adult courts.[34]

Disposition. Because a child is not charged with crime in this court, disposition of the case is not necessarily a terminal stage, and of course does not impose on the child any civil disabilities, nor does it, legally speaking, work against his interests, the theory being treatment in which discipline, where needed, is related to estimated needs. The disposition favored is to keep children in their own homes, if possible, under probation supervision if necessary. It is also generally possible for the courts to commit to designated guardians (foster homes placement) or to public or private institutions, which are rarely satisfactory, or to order treatment which is deemed to be to the best interests of the child.[35]

But it is obvious that the decision, whatever it be, cannot be mechanical or, as is more general in the criminal law, move directly from behavior circumstance to a particular penalty. The laws neither define a penalty nor a necessary, specific consequence following a stated and determined offense. Disposition is a function of clinical judgment, of which treatment is the consequence. Notwithstanding, in many courts, (how many, it would be difficult to document), probation and institutionalization are mechanically and impatiently applied with little or no thought, induced through careful study, given to human needs. Moreover, institutional and foster home resources are often meager, and where the child's own home is not to be considered but action must be taken, a devil's advocate argument often determines the decision.

[30] *The Report of the New Jersey Juvenile Delinquency Commission* (Trenton, 1939), an excellent, detailed study of delinquency control, advocates their extensive use (see pp. 20, 143), recommending that appointments of unqualified persons be avoided, including local magistrates, as the latter have not proved useful in that capacity.

[31] For appeals (juvenile court), see Cosulich, *op. cit.* note 1 *supra*, Chap. XII.

[32] See Roscoe Pound, *Organization of Courts* (Boston: Little, Brown and Co., 1940).

[33] For a far-reaching proposal along these lines, which, with further development of youth authority measures, may well revolutionize the field of socialized justice, see Reginald Heber Smith, Paul W. Alexander, *et al.* (as members of an American Bar Association Committee), *Report to National Conference on Family Life,* March 1948 (White House Conference) — the recommendations on divorce, new jurisdiction, and so forth adopted by the Conference May 7, 1948.

[34] Frequently fixed by age limits. See Cosulich, *op. cit.* note 1 *supra,* Chap. V. The Standard Act (§ 6) makes provision for transfer.

[35] Cosulich, *op. cit.* note 1 *supra,* Chap. IX; Standard Act, § 20.

FUTURE DIRECTION

Four urgencies now press for attention and for solution, and may be thus stated:

1. Should the juvenile court continue to provide complete services for dependent and neglected children (including placement)?

2. Should it continue to provide treatment for delinquent children after (and before) adjudication?

3. Should the definition of delinquency be made more specific?

4. What form of organization should the juvenile court seek to follow in the future?

It should now be apparent that each of these questions is related to the other; that each is dependent on the factors stated in the suggestive analysis above. Because space is limited and because the present interest is to suggest possible solutions, these questions will be considered within certain established trends bearing on the juvenile court and, for convenience, will be handled in reverse.

Three developments, all bearing upon the juvenile court and affecting its work, are materializing: (1) the youth correction system; (2) a growing demand and trend toward a new separate and special jurisdiction over divorce, separation, and family matters; and (3) the gradual acceptance of unified state-wide court systems.[36]

It is not difficult to see that family matters as heretofore handled, children's cases, divorce and separation (as suggested that they be handled), and youth matters, all lend themselves to the referee device. As now operating or as proposed, much of this work will be administrative, most of it an incident of equity jurisdiction, and all of it needs protection by judicial review and by appeal on matters of law.

Three separate areas of behavior stand out here: youth, child, and adult family. However, in a real sense, all are family subdivisions. Maybe the proper line of thought for organization utilizing the best that experience has to offer, as well as contemporary needs, will lead to a plan for allocating all these jurisdictions within the framework of a court of general

jurisdiction with administrative and service areas fixed in referee divisions of the court, these divisions responsible to a judge presiding over a division of such court. The advantages seem to be many as Dean Pound has observed.[37]

Services of the Court. Concerning the other questions raised: in the early days of the juvenile court, it was necessary for the court to develop services for children.[38]

Social services have now expanded outside the courts, and where such agencies serving dependent and neglected children are now well developed and adequate (including foster home placement) and where proper definitions can be worked out between courts and agencies, it appears the better practice to divorce any extensive work in this field from the court. There should be reserved to it, of course, the hearing of petitions for changing guardians (natural or otherwise), for removing children from homes, for institutionalization, and for incidental relief.

Social services should be rendered by private or public agencies, the private agencies being frequently better equipped than the court for this purpose. In this respect the court would retain its strictly judicial function on an informed social basis, with the agency protected by proper procedures of operation.

Study Needed. The second and third problems are actually difficult and will need detailed and careful consideration before any action taken. This much is certain — they will not be satisfactorily settled without better documentation than now exists. The fact is that since Lou's book [39] no general study of the juvenile court has been made bringing together the chief types of experience. Most of the critical and pressing questions arising since his study (1927) are reviewed in materials cited herein.

Many particular practices, devices, and forms need summarizing. Moreover, no recent, fully scientific, objective study of particular courts and court types has been made. We badly need such detailed studies (not made by special

---

[36] See New Jersey Constitution, effective January 1, 1948; judicial section effective September 15, 1948; also Pound, *Organization of Courts, op. cit.*, note 32 *supra*.

[37] Roscoe Pound, *Organization of the Courts, op. cit.* note 32 *supra*.

[38] Alice Scott Nutt, "The Responsibility of the Juvenile Court and the Public Welfare Agency in the Child Welfare Program," *Redirecting the Delinquent* (Marjorie Bell, Ed., New York: National Probation and Parole Association, Yearbook, 1947). pp. 206–23.

[39] Lou, *op. cit.* note 8 *supra*.

arrangement for the purpose of immediate improvement of some one court) as Professor Tappan's work on an adolescent court for girls — the only thoroughly competent, scientific, and wholly objective treatise concerning a special jurisdiction based on a separate control area. How a reformulation of normative factors can be made without such studies is difficult to see.[40]

Definition of Delinquency. Inadequacies are apparent in the definition of delinquency. Professor Tappan points out [41] that, with a vague definition of delinquency, judges and probation officers are allowed scope (harmful in proportion to their lack of skill, training, and knowledge) for moralizing. Thus, what offense will, as an offense, require treatment (perhaps actually lead to an unreasoning and even diabolic reaction) may vary from judge to judge, from officer to officer, from court to court.

Tappan's point is well taken and carefully documented for the court he studied; empirical observations of juvenile courts in operation tend to confirm it. It is certain at least that behavior circumstance has been neglected. It is not suggested that a predetermined result should follow a particular offense, but rather that the offenses which symbolize the conduct desired to be prevented or modified be carefully defined, weighed, and seen as part of what Dr. Jenkins, for instance, calls behavior syndromes.[42]

Children, and often adults, do not comprehend the meaning of metaphysical designations such as felony, even of terms like larceny, or the various degrees of crime. The present classification of crimes is totally inapplicable to this court's task; in fact, is outworn in criminal courts.[43]

The juvenile court has been thinking in terms of the child's interest and welfare. This is a fine purpose, but does not offer much for adjudication. Determinations of welfare may vary considerably. More intelligent is the concept "course of conduct," which Tappan expounds.[44] It has the advantage of representing concrete behavior as an identifiable area of psychological experience related to the public security, and thus ties in the Jenkin's behavior syndromes [45] as relatively predictable patterns implicit in which is *the* treatment reflecting *the* disorder.

Bringing the petition for entering this court to the level of behavior-circumstance language and, with it, using a common name to designate the offense or conduct, a specific, meaningful statement of the reasons for court attention could be made. Course of conduct also should be retained as a reason for exerting jurisdiction, and can be illuminated by the syndrome descriptions. In passing, the terms "wayward child" and "minor" are vague and, for that reason, useless.

As Tappan shows from the adolescent court experience, vagueness in jurisdictional terms leads to vagueness in the exercise and the results of jurisdiction, and thus, for reasons stated above, affects intake policy adversely; but intake and jurisdiction must center on the same norms for initiating court activity. The full extent of moralizing to a disposition-conclusion in juvenile courts is perhaps little understood. A wealth of experience from the criminal law bears on this subject,[46] and, aside from that, it is common experience to one familiar with juvenile court proceedings. New formulations of policy design cannot escape this problem; its partial solution is implicit in a referee system, which itself depends on high quality staff.

Psychiatric, most often psychological and medical, services are furnished the court on a part-time basis; in some places, by city or county units. Urban centers have largely established child guidance clinics, and many hospital facilities and special services are at the court's disposal.[47] It is generally convenient to utilize

[40] The American Law Institute's policy design for a Youth Correction Act (June 22, 1940) had no body of experience to draw from except juvenile and domestic relations courts.

[41] *Op. cit.* note 2 *supra*, pp. 161–66, *passim*.

[42] Richard L. Jenkins, "A Psychiatric View of Personality in Children" (Marjorie Bell, Ed., New York: National Probation Association Yearbook, 1943), pp. 199–217. [See, also, Article 19 hereof. — Ed.]

[43] Jerome Hall, *Theft, Law and Society* (Boston: Little, Brown and Company, 1935), p. 301.

[44] Tappan, *Delinquent Girls in Court, op. cit.* note 2 *supra*, pp. 98–106.

[45] Jenkins, *op. cit.* note 42 *supra*; also (with Sylvia Glickman) "Common Syndromes in Child Psychiatry," *American Journal of Orthopsychiatry,* April 1946.

[46] See John Lewis Gillin, *Criminology and Penology* (3d ed., New York: Appleton, 1945), Part III.

[47] J. P. Shalloo, "Understanding Behavior Problems of Children," *The Annals of the American Academy of Political and Social Science,* Nov. 1940, pp. 194–201.

such services by referral, conference, and definition. This would certainly be so if the court included no treatment staff consequent upon adjudication.

Social agencies — family societies, public welfare units, boys and girls clubs — work closely with the court, particularly in urban centers. The growth of the council of social agencies, or community council, has stimulated a definition and practice of total community need expressed as community organization.

Continuation Services. The question is now asked whether the court should continue to service children on probation, and the answer has been in part suggested through the analysis in terms of the conflict of norms. Ideally, probably it should not; but, retaining a diagnostic staff, presently handled unofficial cases could be referred to other agencies (many could be handled in juvenile aid bureaus), and later, upon adjudication when course of conduct or public security violation was determined, cases could be referred to separate, specialized treatment agencies or to institutions. But this is an ideal projection, as much still remains to be accomplished in securing proper institutions as well as new service areas.

What may be regarded as semantic confusion — the question whether adjudication should follow or precede investigation — is referred to by Professor Tappan. In the New York Children's Court (New York City) and the Boston Juvenile Court it is insisted that an adjudication be first made. In most courts this is not the theory of operation; and in terms of a balance between treatment consequence and behavior circumstance as applied to the offenses of children, investigation first would seem to be the sound procedure, depriving no child of any right but rather illuminating obligations of society to children. This confusion of procedure has not been adequately discussed.

It would seem, too, that probation departments find a more acceptable definition of operations apart from the court, and, continuing to supply intake personnel or working close to intake (which must remain at the court), could expand into adequate treatment services. This seems to be agreeable to certain structural arrangements now present in the courts, and certainly to the idea of the juvenile court as part of a uniform jurisdiction including the referee system.

The conflict of norms is now in process of accommodation, with the separate jurisdiction over children certain to remain, however, related or reorganized.

48

Problems of Area [1] Jurisdiction in Juvenile Courts*

Edward J. Bander

Since the birth of the first juvenile court in Cook County, Illinois,[2] the county as a political sub-division has continued to lead the field in fathering this youngest judicial offspring. Nevertheless, the past fifty years have witnessed offshoots on the family tree, some juvenile courts branching out to be encompassed by entire states, others whittled down to city districts. Legal and social scientists, pulling sometimes together and as often apart, maintain the struggle to determine the area unit best suited to harbor this vital structure, which is still undergoing its growing pains in this country.

Frederick B. Sussman's "Law of Juvenile Delinquency"[3] contains a state by state breakdown of juvenile courts[4] which illustrates the complete lack of uniformity, not only among states but within the same state, with respect to the area

---

[1] For purposes of this article "area" and "political" are interchangeable terms as regards jurisdiction. This discussion gravitates around the state, the country, and the city as the unit of operation for a juvenile court. Each of these units constitutes an area, though actual size or bigness is immaterial. Each of these units is also political; the city having a certain identifiable structure and having problems similar to other cities — as do the county and state.

* Reprinted from 45 *J. Crim. L.*, *Criminology and Police Science* (1955), 668–674. Used by permission of the author and the publisher.

[2] For a description of this "birth" see "The Child, The Clinic and The Court," *New Republic, Inc.,* New York, 1925, a group of selected papers, pp. 267–330. See also Grace Abbott, *The Child and the State,* Volume II, University of Chicago Press, 1938, pp. 330–331.

[3] Oceana Publications, New York, 1950.

[4] *Ibid.,* pp. 67–79.

jurisdiction problem. Boston[5] has a separate juvenile court for its populous in-town area, with delinquencies occurring elsewhere in the city presided over by the city's district court judges in juvenile sessions. Baltimore offers a court which handles the entire city's delinquency.[6] A county juvenile court is maintained in Cleveland. Florida provides by state law that counties may combine to deal with the problem. Three states — Connecticut, Rhode Island and Utah — have organized juvenile courts on a state-wide basis. Except for the state-wide courts, variations in political areas are frequent, as, for example, Pennsylvania, where the Municipal Court of Philadelphia houses a juvenile court while a county juvenile court prevails in Alleghany County (Pittsburgh).

What reasons are there for Boston, Baltimore and Cleveland, cities of similar population, to require a different area set-up? What could have been the factors leading to Connecticut legislating a state-wide court, Ohio a county court system and Massachusetts contenting itself with smaller area units? One purpose of this article is to appraise the areas utilized for juvenile courts. Another is to determine how much of a factor and what consideration has been given to area in determining the effectiveness of a juvenile court.

That area should be a factor is indicated by the concern the legal and social authorities have accorded it. Roscoe Pound's reasoning, very likely guided by his conception of judicial organization, has expressed a wariness of those who feel that the remedy for every social ill is a new court.[7] This eminent legal authority, a past president of the National Probation and Parole Association, was convinced that the juvenile court should be a branch of the court of general jurisdiction of first instance.[8] "Specialist judges rather than specialized courts,"[9] he has insisted, is the most practical and efficient approach. This implies a reliance on the county area,[10] upon which basis most states are judicially organized.[11]

Those whose thinking is more aligned with social work theory veer not only away from the county as a unit, but conventional court systems as a whole. While Mr. Pound regards the Juvenile Court as a natural growth of the prevalent court systems, not a departure from them, others see in it such a sweeping change in emphasis [12] that not only a separate court but a state boundary is their goal. Charles L. Chute, late honorary vice-president of the N. P. P. A., concluded in advocating a state court; "separation from control by any other court is the best system."[13]

Two other solutions to the area problem have notable backing. The multi-county proponents suggest an apparent compromise, that counties band together to organize regional juvenile courts. Another group, seeming to believe that the juvenile court should serve a limited function, recommends no further alteration in the already existing courts than that they have separate sessions for juveniles, and permit other agencies, public and private, to perform all other duties.

One question is vital to any consideration of the geographic unit to be adopted: Does the juvenile court differ radically in approach and function from the regular court system? Legally, the answer is "No." In theory, the juvenile court is but an extension of our common law inheritance[14] — its foundation in the equitable

---

[5] For further information as to particular juvenile courts mentioned in this article see their respective Annual Reports.

[6] See the *Yearbook*, National Probation Association (hereafter referred to as N.P.A.), 1945, p. 257.

[7] Roscoe Pound, "The Juvenile Court and the Law," *Yearbook*, National Probation and Parole Association (N.P.P.A., hereafter), 1944, pp. 1–22 at p. 10.

[8] *Ibid.*, pp. 10–11.

[9] Roscoe Pound, "The Juvenile Court in the Service State," *Yearbook*, N.P.P.A., 1949, pp. 21–43 at p. 37.

[10] Roscoe Pound, *Organization of Courts*, Little, Brown and Co., Boston, 1940, p. 283–284.

[11] Negley K. Teeters, and John Otto Reinemann, *The Challenge of Delinquency*, Prentice-Hall, Inc., New York, 1950, p. 292. See also Herbert H. Lou, *Juvenile Courts in the United States*, University of North Carolina Press, 1927, p. 36.

[12] Sol Rubin, "State Juvenile Court: A New Standard," *Focus*, July 1951, pp. 103–107.

[13] Charles L. Chute, "Fifty Years of the Juvenile Court," *Yearbook*, N.P.P.A., 1949, pp. 1–20, at p. 7.

[14] Bernard Flexner and Reuben Oppenheimer, "The Legal Aspect of the Juvenile Court," Children's Bureau Publication No. 99, Government Printing Office, Washington, D. C., 1922, p. 1. See also Roger J. Waybright, "A Proposed Juvenile Court Act for Florida," *University of Florida Law Review*. Spring 1950 (reprint of article). And also Helen D. Pigeon, *Probation and Parole in Theory and Practice*, N.P.A., New York, 1942, pp. 54–55.

principle of *parens patriae* is secure, and many of its procedures have been adopted by other courts.[15] Fundamentally, it is organized as are all courts, to maintain the general security.[16]

Socially, however, the answer to the question posed above might well be "Yes." The juvenile court diverges widely in practice from any other court. It concentrates more and more on rehabilitation, and places less emphasis upon formal court room proceedings.[17] No juvenile court receives a favorable evaluation today unless it has ready access to facilities for psychological testing, psychiatric and medical examinations, probation officers with master's degrees in social work, and a professionally supervised detention home. One judge goes so far as to analogize the court's work to that of a hospital.[18] The issue, in part, is whether the answers to the above question should in fact affect the choice of a geographic or political area for a juvenile court, as is so frequently the case. An examination of the geographic settings in which the juvenile court functions today may do much to clarify this area problem.

THE COUNTY COURT

As Lou points out, "The coincidence of the area of jurisdiction with the taxing and governing unit is a great financial benefit"; moreover, other agencies, social and private, are generally organized on a county basis.[19] Many advocate family or domestic relations courts which would include a juvenile court.[20] It would be a much simpler matter for the juvenile court to join in the area of jurisdiction which handles divorce, guardianship, non-support, paternity, etc., cases, than to persuade these courts to join the juvenile court on a different geographic basis.[21] Before recommending any alteration in the existing judicial pattern the juvenile court should be soundly tested upon the level where most courts do operate.[22]

From a social point of view, delinquency is first a family problem, then a community responsibility and so on in ever increasing ripples. The farther away the authority, the less its influence upon the delinquent. The county, particularly in urban areas, is sufficiently local to comprehend the nature of its youth problem, and sufficiently populated and financed to provide the means of rehabilitation. Such reasoning does not prohibit the state from establishing minimum standards for juvenile courts as many states do; it does imply that a county willing to provide as well as possible for its youth, would not be leveled down to what a state legislature will compromise to for all its counties.

The criticism that a delinquent does not receive the same attention and treatment which an adjoining county would accord him, making the county unit an inequitable one, could as well be directed against adjoining state-wide systems, and no one yet has advocated a Federal Juvenile Court.

The county court recognizes that it should render unto Caesar that which is Caesar's. When it is economically unsound for a county to provide certain desirable services, it is not unusual for the state to organize a program to meet the need. Ohio has recently expanded its Bureau of Juvenile Research, which provides for examination, observation and classification of

---

[15] Teeters and Reinemann, *op. cit.*, see Chapter X.

[16] For a general discussion of the Juvenile Court, in this regard, see Lou, *op. cit.*, p. 32 and following.

[17] Joseph E. Lady, "Some Aspects of the Juvenile Court Hearing, Youth Morality A Public Concern," National Council of Juvenile Court Judges, May 1952, pp. 54–57. See also Gustav L. Schramm, "The Court Hearing As Part of the Treatment Process," *Yearbook*, N. P. P. A., 1949, pp. 44–56. As to evidence in the Juvenile Court, see Irving I. Goldsmith, Legal Evidence in the New York Children's Courts, *Brooklyn Law Review*, October 1933 (reprint of article).

[18] Paul Alexander, "Of Juvenile Court Justice and Judges," *Yearbook*, N.P.P.A., 1947, pp. 187–205. But see John F. Perkins, *Common Sense and Bad Boys*, published and copyrighted by the Citizenship Training Group, Inc. of the Boston Juvenile Court, 1946, particularly p. 78 and following.

[19] Lou, *op. cit.*, p. 36.

[20] Paul W. Alexander, "The Family Court of the Future," *Journal of the Amer. Judicature Soc.*, August, 1952, pp. 38–46. Also in *Federal Probation*, Dec. 1952, pp. 24–31.

[21] The problem whether a juvenile court should be part of a family court or operated exclusively for juveniles is not pertinent here. However, I do feel it important that the reader be made aware, at this point, that such a problem does exist.

[22] The Glueck study of 1934 had the effect of casting shadows on the value of the Juvenile Court *per se* let alone its extension. See Abbott, *op. cit.*, p. 334 and following, particularly p. 338. But see the original study, Sheldon Glueck, and Eleanor Glueck, *One Thousand Juvenile Delinquents*, Harvard University Press, 1934, particularly pp. 232–233. And see also the Glueck–Eastman debate on this subject, *Yearbook*, N.P.A., 1934, pp. 63–103. Also Perkins, *op. cit.*, p. 11 and following.

delinquents from counties where the population is less than 40,000.[23] Ohio also has statistical data organized on intensive local and comprehensive state levels.[24] New Jersey has developed a state agency program which seeks, in part, to raise the standards of its juvenile courts.[25] The Youth Conservation Commission in Minnesota and Wisconsin's Youth Service Commission are organized on state-wide levels, providing probationary, and other services, to the local courts.[26] In this manner home rule is preserved, no extensive changes in judicial structure are necessitated, and where services for children vary within states the more enlightened can establish a pattern for others to imitate.

THE STATE COURT

The N.P.P.A. has recently included in its Standard Juvenile Court Act an alternate section dealing with the creation of state courts.[27] The Association is aware that most counties do not have specially appointed judges and trained juvenile court personnel[28] and many could not afford them. Where a state court is provided, the state can be divided into districts according to area, population and other determining factors, with a view to maintaining adequate services and eliminating such duplication and waste as arises from 134 municipal court judges, 115 probate court judges, and 500 Justices of the Peace handling delinquency cases — a situa-

tion which existed in Connecticut prior to the founding of a state juvenile court.[29]

In a state court, probation services, detention and clinical facilities, and research activities could be established on an efficient, effective and adequately financed level. Civil service standards could be set up to help eliminate political appointments (the danger here to youth's rehabilitation cannot be over-estimated!), and salaries commensurate with the vital duties performed could be, and are,[30] paid.

County courts are predominantly big city courts, many rural areas having only the form without the substance of the juvenile court function. As a Children's Bureau pamphlet points out, delinquency is not essentially a big city problem:[31] the significance of a state court's radii into hitherto unreached areas is manifest. The greater finances of a state court are believed to be an assurance that new resources can be more quickly developed and assimilated. Moreover, children's agencies would have one court to deal with rather than a maze of courts, each with a different personality and policy.

THE MULTI-COUNTY COURT

The Multi-County Court has at least two eminent supporters, though they limit their support to rural areas where only a combination of counties could afford the facilities necessary for an effective court. Judge Schramm has suggested[32] that if a single county cannot afford a full-time judge it should consider a regional juvenile court in collaboration with neighboring counties; he also discusses the advantages of good local administration. L. J. Carr asks,[33] "Why not combine counties to provide enough work for one well-equipped, technically competent court in place of half a dozen or a dozen

[23] See Bureau of Juvenile Research Reception Center, Public Welfare in Ohio Today, Sept. 1953, p. 16.

[24] See the *Annual Reports* of the Cuyahoga County Juvenile Court and also the Ohio State reports.

[25] Douglas H., MacNeil, "Two and One-Half Years of State-Local Collaboration in Delinquency Prevention," *Yearbook*, N.P.P.A., 1948, pp. 252–262 at p. 257.

[26] See Teeters and Reinemann, *op. cit.*, p. 395. Also George J. Reed, "Minnesota's Youth Conservation Commission Program," *Focus*, March 1953, pp. 49–51; and Richard T. Smith, "Statewide Organization of Probation Services," *Yearbook*, N.P.P.A., 1950, pp. 130–138.

[27] See "A Standard Juvenile Court Act," N.P.P.A., revised edition, 1949.

[28] But see Martin F. Nilan, "It's Different in the Country," *Focus*, March 1951, pp. 40–42. Also, Samuel Haig Jameson, "Experiment in Developing a Small County Juvenile Delinquency Program," *Federal Probation*, January–March 1943, pp. 38–40.

[29] William N. MacKay, "The Juvenile Court as a State Responsibility," *Yearbook*, N. P. P. A., 1951, pp. 114–128.

[30] While Wisconsin does not have a state court, its state run probation department is an indication of the efforts a state can put forth in acquiring a competent staff. See Russell G. Oswald, "Professionalizing Services," *Yearbook*, N. P. P. A., 1950, pp. 139–145.

[31] "Some Facts About Juvenile Delinquency," Children's Bureau Publication, U. S. Department of Health, Education and Welfare, 1953.

[32] Gustav L. Schramm, "The Juvenile Court Idea," *Federal Probation*, Sept. 1949, pp. 19–23.

[33] "Most Courts Have to be Substandard," *ibid.*, pp. 29–33.

of the imitations that we now have." [34] This type of court is somewhat of a compromise between the two already discussed, but its advocacy, we should reiterate, is restricted to rural areas.

THE LESS THAN COUNTY COURT

Such a court may be seen in operation in the city courts of Baltimore and Philadelphia, the in-town court of Boston, and the many areas where local and/or inferior courts receive the delinquency case assignment. Where state probation services are provided for the local courts, as in Wisconsin and New Hampshire, there is an apparent belief that the problem of rehabilitation (disposition) is one best left to less authoritative agencies, and that consequently there is no need to radically alter the existing court system.[35] Such reasoning is indicative of a visible trend to limit the juvenile court's function to the mere determination of delinquency.[36] If the features within various states on this level were combined, they would present this kind of picture: No investigation prior to an adjudication of delinquency;[37] if detention home facilities are necessary, the youngster is sent to a regional detention home;[38] if the court adjudicates the child a delinquent, he is assigned to a separate bureau which will determine the best plan for him.[39] The bureau[40]

may decide upon probation and if so, a state probation officer is assigned;[41] or the youngster may be sent by the bureau to a state institution. Thus, where actual court function is so restricted, there is no need to alter the existing court system in any way, since other independent agencies will do all accommodating beyond delinquency determination.

CONCLUSION

The above area groupings exhaust the possibilities. The favorable aspects of each have been presented; they, in turn, suggest the liabilities of the others. Conclusions as to which system is best immediately incurs the hazard of blacklisting all others by endorsing one, when in fact the county court has proved successful in many areas, the state court has eliminated much waste and duplication, the multi-county court has a limited practicality, and the idea of making the court itself subordinate to rehabilitation has obvious value. The best summation may be Miss Lenroot's opinion that there is really no such thing as a model court, that community interest and initiative are paramount in the success or failure of any court structure.[42] This does suggest that before making a geographical boundary for the juvenile court other than that in effect for the general court system, the advantages of doing so should clearly outweigh not only what can be gained by maintaining the status quo but the disadvantage implicit in organizing a new institution.

In attempting to determine an area most suitable to our growing delinquency problem, one point should be clear. The juvenile court, while it is a vital adjunct to our court system, is neither the most nor by any means the least

[34] *Ibid.*, p. 31. But see note 28.

[35] Wisconsin does not have a Children's Court in Milwaukee County.

[36] See William Draper Lewis, "The Treatment of the Adolescent Offender," *Yearbook*, N. P. P. A., 1940, pp. 79–92 at p. 86. One judge believes that if placement is to be in an institution not under juvenile court control then the court should merely adjudicate delinquency; Nochem S. Winnet, "Fifty Years of the Juvenile Court: An Evaluation," 36 *Amer. Bar Assoc. Jour.* May 1950, pp. 363–366. See also Alfred J. Kahn, *A Court For Children*, Columbia University Press, New York, 1953, p. 275. For a general treatment of this subject see Teeters and Reinemann, *op. cit.*, pp. 338–342, particularly p. 341.

[37] John J. Connelly, "Postadjudication Techniques in the Boston Juvenile Court, Youth Morality A Public Concern," National Council of Juvenile Court Judges, May 1952, pp. 58–64 at p. 59.

[38] See *Focus*, Sept. 1953, p. 151.

[39] The stricture of Roscoe Pound against administrative agencies usurping the judicial function may well be pertinent here, though it should be borne in mind that under this procedure only the dispositioning power is taken away from the judge, not the power to adjudicate delinquency. But see Pound,

"The Juvenile Court and the Law," *op. cit.*, at p. 5. See also Perkins, *op. cit.*, p. 86 and following. And see also Alfred J. Kahn, *op. cit.*, at p. 305: ". . . well-selected judges, working together with well-prepared probation officers and provided with necessary resources and community facilities, can very effectively indeed arrive at an initiate case dispositions." Mr. Kahn discusses this topic at page 135, and read also pp. 301 and following. For a general discussion see Teeters and Reinemann, *op. cit.*, pp. 354 and following.

[40] See "Bureau of Juvenile Research Reception Center," *op. cit.*

[41] Smith, *op. cit.*

[42] "The Child, the Family and the Court," *Yearbook*, N.P.A., 1928, pp. 102–123 at p. 116.

important structure in any judicial scheme of things. Just as no obese person would unwittingly select a diet designed to eliminate excess weight at the risk of bodily health, so one could not intelligently advocate a juvenile court system which no legislature would consider, should it appear injurious or unsound in terms of over-all whole. We should recognize and keep the ideal clearly in mind, but work toward it with practical means.

49

Treatment Without Trial *

Paul W. Tappan

During the past generation there have developed in the court procedures of this country a series of novel institutional devices breaking with legal tradition and looking toward a more "socialized" processing of offenders. These devices are largely a hybrid product of court and case work methods. Some of them it is the purpose of this paper to consider. In general they are characterized by one or both of the following: (1) informal, unofficial probation supervision or institutional remand before a hearing is held, and (2) hearings in which there is no determination as to guilt of an offense, where personality factors and the "total situation" determine adjudication.

The purposes behind the emerging procedural methods appear fairly clear and, on their face at least, "progressive" and laudable. The desire is to avoid the stigma which grows out of court contact and adjudication and, particularly where the offense involved is of no great seriousness, to prevent the sentencing to an offender's status and to formal correction. The aim, too, is to break with the legal approach of adjudging defendants on the proof of a given criminal act, holding it more scientifically appropriate to determine through social and biological information whether a case needs treat-

ment and, if so, what sort is required. To the socially-minded it may appear absurd to concentrate attention upon a criminal act when it is itself merely a symptom or end product of character drives conditioned through extended experience. The need, it may be claimed, is to view rather the area of true significance — the defendant's total personality — in order to deal correctly with the case. Statutes which define the elements of a crime and establish a fixed penalty conceived by a legislature as punishment appropriate to the seriousness of that act appear as absurd relics of a classical criminology in an age when social science points toward individualization, prevention, and rehabilitation. Furthermore, the experimental courts of today rest largely on the shoulders of probation departments which have fostered the development of the new procedures. They would extend the philosophy and practice of case work in dealing with what are basically conduct problems, avoiding the "legal technicalities" which may slow or prevent the application of needed therapy based on social diagnosis and prescription for the peculiar needs of the case. The prevailing philosophy of these courts has been expressed ably by its advocates.[1]

The growth of an idea and its institutional entrenchment are well illustrated by the continuing crystallization in our courts of these new procedures. The methods used are rather numerous and varied in detail, but they fall into one or the other of the two general categories referred to above. For the most part they have originated in non-statutory or extra-legal procedures, avoiding therefore the hazard of invalidation by appellate decisions. Some have received statutory formulation. By and large, however, the legal specifications under which the experimental courts operate do not sanction that full flowering of novel procedure which case work philosophy has brought into actual court custom. Indeed, under the statutes many of the existing practices are invalid; some of the informal administrative procedures are clearly violative of due process.

Let us review briefly the evolution of some of these devices employed to circumvent the traditional methods of criminal trial (wherein the

---

* Reprinted from 24 Social Forces (March, 1946), 306–311. Used by permission of the author and the publisher.

[1] See, for example, Pauline V. Young, Social Treatment in Probation and Delinquency (1937); Herbert H. Lou, Juvenile Courts in the United States (1927); Belle B. Beard, Juvenile Probation (1934).

issue of guilt is determined by the court and penalties are graded to the offense). Their origins lie in the children's court movement in which has developed a series of peculiarities in processing, today quite generally diffused throughout the country at this level of tribunal. Their emergence may be understood in part as a result of the rationalizing principle of the state as *parens patriae*, protector to the child, associated with the belief that deprivation of procedural rights is unimportant when the court is attempting to treat and protect the child. Its purpose is clinical and rehabilitative. There has been small danger of defendant's contesting the validity of the procedural methods employed: neither the naive child nor his distraught parent are wont to challenge the procedures and no attorney or prosecutor is present generally to raise the issue. If the right of review is permitted, it is discouraged and often condemned as a legal device to undo the progressive work of the court.[2] Chiefly the following differentiating characteristics mark the children's court methodology:

1. *Intake.* Basic information is sought by a probation officer at intake on the background of the case — family data; educational, economic and recreational history; conduct of the child; and other germane matters.

2. *Unofficial Treatment.** Probation personnel (known in the New York Children's Court as the Adjustment Bureau) may apply informal supervision to cases in which the intake officer believed that social therapy was needed but which did not appear to require court hearing and adjudication. (It should be noted that an extremely elastic discretion may be employed at intake in directing the case to unofficial treatment or to court. When — as is the widely prevailing condition today — the operative philosophy or probation department favors informal case work without a hearing, this "treatment without trial" becomes a popular practice.)

3. *Pre-adjudication Investigation.* Reversing the procedure traditional in our criminal courts, at the juvenile level a social investigation on each case is undertaken by a probation officer *prior* to a hearing and the information obtained therefrom is made available later at the hearing. This is unorthodox procedure in two chief respects: It applies to all cases whether or not the defendant is later adjudicated. (It tends, of course, to lead to adjudication in commonly establishing the foundation therefor in the discovery of social problems deemed to need treatment.) Also, in preceding the hearing, it allows in evidence matters which would be considered prejudicial, incompetent, and irrelevant for purposes of proof in the usual criminal trial.

4. *Interim Dispositions.* During the period of social investigation a temporary disposition of the case must be made by adjourning to a later date and either paroling the defendant to home or agency or remanding him to an institution. The period of interim disposition is usually several weeks. In effect it constitutes a phase of treatment without trial when the child is either incarcerated (often with others already found to be delinquent, sometimes with convicted adult criminals[3]) or held under the restricted liberty of probation-scrutiny.

5. *Adjudication Based on the Total Situation.* As noted above, the information from reports of probation investigation is available at the hearing. Thereby social data come to determine not only the treatment methods to be employed (as in the criminal court) but very largely whether or not the defendant is to be adjudicated a delinquent. Hence his guilt of a specific offense comes to be considered irrelevant, court decision being predicated upon the social and personal problems appearing in the history of the defendant and his family.

6. *Omnibus Statutes.* The wide latitude of discretion possible in adjudication is supported and extended by the statutes defining the recalcitrant child so broadly as to facilitate the easy status-fixing of delinquency.[4] Where, in

---

[2] See Benedict S. Alper, "Forty Years of the Juvenile Court," *American Sociological Review* (April, 1941), p. 230.

* For the extent of resort to "unofficial delinquency" techniques, see P. W. Tappan, "Unofficial Delinquency," Article 50 *infra.* — Ed.

[3] See Leonard V. Harrison and Pryor M. Grant, *Youth in the Toils* (1938).

[4] Under the Federal Juvenile Court Act which has now been in operation for six years, such pre-hearing investigations are also conducted and reports submitted to the court at the hearing. As in the state courts, the procedures used are largely extra-legal in permitting adjudication based in part upon untested hearsay of probation reports. In the federal courts, however, many protections to the defendant's interests exist which are absent in the courts of the States.

accordance with the provisions of the statutes, a hearing is held before treatment is applied, it is scarcely a "trial" in the usual sense since guilt of specific enumerated offenses need not be proven to adjudicate. Rather, rumor of the needs of the defendant and/or his family may be a matter of primary moment to the children's court's decision. Again it is treatment without trial.

The procedures which evolved in the children's courts have come to be applied in the more recently emerging tribunals for adolescents. The variations in age-coverage of the children's court statutes in different jurisdictions is significant here. A large proportion of the States provide for children's court control over the delinquent up to the age of 18, some as high as 21. A few, including New York, end jurisdiction at 16. The trend has been generally upward throughout the country.

The result has been a drive to develop special facilities for the adolescent who otherwise must traverse the trial routes taken by adult criminals. New York City in its Adolescent Courts in Brooklyn and Queens, its citywide Wayward Minor Court for girls and its Youthful Offender divisions of the County Courts, has provided special tribunals and methods of processing for the recalcitrant youth over 16. Similarly Chicago, Philadelphia, and other cities have established courts to deal particularly with young offenders over the juvenile age.[5] For the most part these tribunals apply procedures comparable to those previously developed in the children's courts and they justify their use by analogy. It should be noted in passing, however, that there are several clear differences, which should distinguish adolescent from juvenile procedures: The children's courts are often — as in New York — civil, whereas the adolescent courts are a part of the criminal court system. Also, the same standards of behavior cannot justifiably be applied to adolescent and child. Too, the facilities of the children's courts for treatment are generally more numerous, varied, and qualitatively superior to those of the adolescent courts — a significant matter in determining the sorts of cases in which jurisdiction should be taken by a court.

These courts for adolescents, too, operate under broad statutes which define the recalcitrant or wayward youth in most general fashion, thus facilitating adjudication when the court may wish to apply treatment to the case before it.[6] Pre-hearing investigations, interim procedures — often with temporary institutional disposition — and adjudication based on general hearsay information concerning personality and social background appear again at this level — though somewhat more fearfully than in the children's courts. Here the individuals processed are adults under the criminal law and the large variations from due process could more easily lead to invalidation of the court methods. "Consent" of the defendant to the investigation before hearing has usually been required. There is formal statutory enunciation of defendant's rights, including the provision that his statements during investigation may not be used against his interest at the trial. Yet these matters are taken as a most pro forma matter. Indeed, under the new Wayward Minor Act in New York the requirement of consent for interim remands of two weeks has been abandoned so that such commitments may be made automatically. In some of the experimental courts the adolescent's consent to investigation and special hearing virtually assures adjudication of the status of offender but with more lenient treatment than could be expected from the criminal court to which the case would otherwise go. Thus the defendant is presented with a choice of consenting to an investigation by an officer of the court on the basis of which adjudication is most probable, to be followed by probation supervision; or, protesting his innocence, he risks conviction in an ordinary criminal court where the judge may impose a harsher penalty of commitment. This selection would test severely the preferences of many defendants innocent of law-violation.

These recent experimental methods of treatment without trial outlined above which have

---

[5] See particularly the following: *Young People in the Courts of New York State*, Leg. Doc. 55 (1942); Paul W. Tappan, *Court for Wayward Girls* (1946); Worthington and Topping, *Specialized Courts Dealing with Sex Delinquency* (1925).

[6] See New York Statutes: the Wayward Minor Act, chapter 873, laws of 1945, recently expanding the terms of the original statute and permitting, particularly, remands without consent. See also the Youthful Offender Act, chapter 549, laws of 1943, recently repealed in its application to the Special Sessions Court, chapter 873, laws of 1945.

taken hold at the children's level and entered the adolescent range somewhat tentatively have come to appear in our adult criminal courts as well. Here they have emerged in at least two forms. The idea of "pre-adjudication conciliation" has been applied unofficially in the Magistrates' Courts of New York City, though never very largely used. It has been chiefly a matter of attempting informal probation treatment of social problems and conciliatory efforts between defendants and complainants when the offense alleged was minor and/or no complaint would issue. Considerably more formalized has been the device adopted elsewhere of applying probation where certain offenses are alleged without the requirement of arraignment or of adjudication.[7] The accused party is confronted with an option not unlike that of the defendant in the adolescent courts: he may accept unofficial treatment, without however going through trial and conviction for an offense at all, or he may stand trial with the danger of conviction and possible incarceration. One would dislike to be "taken in" "on suspicion" and confronted with this choice.

These various methods of applying court treatment without a full and fair judicial trial of the issue of guilt of a particular offense, despite their seductive rationale, appear to the writer to be peculiarly hazardous and unnecessary. Though criticism of methods used in experimental courts has sometimes been attacked as "technical" and reactionary, nevertheless the techniques which develop crescively through unthoughtful adoption in our social institutions do need careful inspection to test their effectiveness and their wider consequences. Novel experimental devices must be tried to be sure, yet permanent crystallization is to be avoided of methods which are based on error or which lead to excessive injustice. Existing or developing institutions may be "progressive" or "reactionary" depending upon the directions of their development and their effects.

In general denial of the validity of the current procedures, the writer maintains that they resemble too closely in some respects the philosophy of the Star Chamber.* For their greatest

fault is in failing to give to the defendant some of the most basic protection of due process which inhere in our modern legal system. Under our constitutions and laws the defendant deserves at very least (1) a definite charge of a particular offense, (2) the right be confronted by the witnesses from whom is derived the evidence on which he is convicted, (3) a (real) right to counsel and appeal, and (4) conviction only upon a preponderance of credible, competent, relevant evidence. (In a criminal court such evidence should, of course, be convincing beyond a reasonable doubt.) These rights are assured even in the administrative tribunals of today; their disappearance from our criminal and quasi-criminal courts should not be tolerated.

The view is expressed by some criminologists that the issue of a particular criminal act is unimportant, particularly in dealing with the young where the general objective is to accomplish preventive and rehabilitative results; that general conduct, personality, and social problems are sufficient to justify adjudication and/or treatment at this level; and that broad statutes are needed to give the necessary latitude, the free play to court discretion. The difficulties with this approach are basic: Where no specific and clear-cut offense categories are established most anyone can be adjudicated to a status carrying stigma and potentially damaging treatment by the correctional agencies of criminal and quasi-criminal courts. The utmost of discretion is left in the hands of judicial and probation personnel unhampered by statutory defini-

---

[7] See *Attorney General's Survey of Release Procedures*, Vol. II, p. 113–5, for the development of assorted practices of this sort under the statutes of Massachusetts, Rhode Island, Kentucky, and Maine.

* "By a convenient but highly misleading sophistry, it is maintained that the child is not charged with a 'crime,' 'convicted' as a 'criminal,' nor 'sentenced to a punishment.' Rather, he is merely 'adjudicated' under a 'petition' as a 'delinquent,' studied to determine how he may be 'saved,' and then 'treated' in his own best interest. The slightest inspection of the characteristic methodology and personnel of the children's court, the detention facility, or the training school, should disillusion any but the most ingenuous about these euphemisms. Unfortunately most people never scrutinize these facilities critically and are led quite readily to confuse what juvenile courts are with what interested parties wishfully imagine their becoming." From P. W. Tappan, "Unofficial Delinquency," Article 50 of this volume. See, also, Tappan's thoughtful *Delinquent Girls in Court*, New York, Columbia University Press, 1947, and *Comparative Survey on Juvenile Delinquency*, North America, United Nations, Department of Social Affairs, 1952. — *Ed.*

tions or limitations, undirected save by a very general principle of treating, reforming, rehabilitating. Unfortunately the personnel of our courts cannot be omniscient or omnicompetent. Indeed, they vary tremendously in their views on conduct, morality, treatment methods, and in their personal biases. Too they tend to lean toward punitive and correctional treatment and, in the experimental courts, toward broadening their functions to treat all manner of social problems. The result may often be damaging when individuals innocent of any serious wrongdoing or real law violation are subject to the rather crude tools of correctional treatment such as those available to our courts. As the author has said elsewhere:

. . . the court system is not designed to deal with problems which are not directly associated with law violation. The philosophies of courts, commitment institutions and probation bureaus are preponderately correctional and punitive. Their rôles have been clearly assigned in the mind and reactions of the defendant by the stereotypes of the cop, the criminal court, the reform school, and the probation officer. Similarly the public attitude toward these institutions and the adolescents subjected to them renders it wholly unrealistic for the courts to attempt to operate as general social agencies: they bear the indelible stamp of public stigma and ostracism. *Thus the frame of reference within which the court may legitimately and effectively operate is narrowly limited by public and institutional definition.* Attempts therefore at comprehensive social work are sheer folly; the problems of domestic relations, psychological pathology, occupational maladjustments, etc. are not within the sphere of appropriate function. This is the more obviously true when no offense has been shown — haphazard manipulation by the unskilled or partially trained probation officer in areas of specialized therapy adds misapplied treatment to the injustice of court and institutional contact. Even when an offense has been proven, far greater success in treatment could be achieved by the referral of problems requiring trained and non-correctional specialized assistance to proper public and private agencies. (Yet, the adolescent courts are far from attaining a nice integration with the varied social agencies of the city, though the fault is not wholly their own.) In addition to the inappropriateness of crimino-legal handling of general social problems, the absurdity of this trend is enhanced by the insufficiency of personnel in the courts. Where, for optimum results, they should work experimentally and intensively on a carefully selected sample of favorable probation risks to insure creative individualization and reformation, the expansive drive in some courts toward problem-solving for all-comers has resulted in attenuated, inexact, and ineffectual service. The proper sphere of social agencies and behavior clinics should not be usurped by the courts, however benevolent the motivation. It appears clear that the work of crime prevention must be performed, if at all, *before* court contact and by non-court agencies. *The personnel of correctional court and institution is not equipped to do a non-correctional job.*[8]

Within the present limitations of our knowledge in the fields of psychology, sociology, and biology, our guesses must be quite tentative concerning treatment methods. Nevertheless we can and should use the training of specialists in these fields to recommend and apply therapy to the unadjusted who go through our courts. It is a different matter entirely, however, to attempt to apply these still-infantile sciences through non-specialists, who make up our court personnel for the most part, to determine on the basis of personality or total situation whom the court should adjudicate, whom it should treat. The idea that the function of law is to provide officials with convenient and general tools by which they may convict and treat those known to be criminals, or believed to require treatment, is a very cynical notion. Held by a few officials of our criminal courts, it is even more out of place at the children's or adolescent's level. The best and safest criterion justifying court action is the commission of an act in violation of a rule of law specifically defining the conduct to be avoided. Such a criminal act expresses — as no vague standard of recalcitrance or "moral depravity" can — a clear, definite, and relevant foundation for court action. It may well be argued that the offense categories should be increased to include specific forms of misconduct appearing in youth which, if untreated, would lead into crime of a more serious nature. If so, these must come into legal definition and delimitation so as to avoid the injustices flowing from an uninstructed judicial latitude. The present law and practice encourage abuse by the generality and variability of principles applied. The result is that these experimental courts appear either to operate on a presumption of guilt or to assume guilt to be irrelevant. A most progressive step, then, for

8 Paul W. Tappan, *The Adolescent in Court* (1946).

the courts desiring to deal as effectively as possible with the young would be the clear statutory enunciation of the conduct-categories to be tabooed. This would mean that adjudication should occur only if and when such conduct is clearly shown by legitimate evidence.

Closely associated with the problem of the general statutes and free discretion which now obtain in these courts is the method so widely used of holding pre-adjudication investigations with reports to the court at the hearing. If adjudication of the offender status should be based — as the author has maintained — on proof of guilt of a particular offense, there is no sound reason for requiring an investigation until after the hearing — and then, of course, only for those cases which are adjudicated. This more traditional procedure would provide at least three distinct advantages over the present method:

1. It would save from court correctional devices those cases which do not merit adjudication legally, cases which are now treated with inappropriate methods due to the expansionist drives within these tribunals toward general social problem-solving.

2. It would make unnecessary the use of parole and remand during rather extended periods of social investigation when no hearing has been held. It is certainly impossible in good law or sound sense to assume a defendant to be guilty of an unproven charge or to justify his treatment without trial during an interim disposition. Errors can be and frequently are made in these courts, as in adult criminal courts, through arrests of and complaints against innocent parties. Too, often when the complaint is made by parents, the fault and problem lies with them not their child; in these cases to impose institutional remands or to adjudicate, as we often do, and apply treatment that is at least partially correctional, punitive, and non-specialized does unnecessary injustice.

3. It would result in a considerably more efficient utilization of the all-too-limited probation resources available in these courts. Under the suggested procedure numerous investigations would not be required: the time thus saved could be devoted to the more creative and rehabilitative work of supervision in cases that had been carefully selected by legal process for social treatment. To reiterate, social investigations should be made *after* adjudication in order

that the court may apply therapy as nicely adjusted to the individual requirements of the cases as possible. To be sure, the suggested change in procedure would require that more witnesses be used at hearings to determine the relevant facts and adjudication would be made more difficult. However, difficulty in eliciting proof of specific offenses is no justification for holding as offenders all who are brought into court. Rather, the elimination of many who do not deserve adjudication could be a great positive gain in preventing that development of delinquencies which occurs so often among the young who have been exposed to the correctional facilities of our courts.

Since the adoption in our adolescent courts of the procedures referred to has been rationalized by their prior institutionalization at the children's court level, it is significant to note that these devices have come under serious criticism by the judiciary of that children's court system. Chief Justice W. B. Cobb of the Domestic Relations Court in New York City has recently attacked with vehemence the unofficial treatment of the adjustment bureau, the use of pre-hearing investigations for purposes of adjudication, and extended remands without a hearing. He condemns them as legally and socially invalid.[9] The reasoning which denounces them must apply as vigorously in the adolescent and adult courts where mild misconduct or complete innocence may lead today to criminal court treatment.

In conclusion it should be noted that our system of law as it is constituted today and within its appropriate methods of application does permit of full and sound individualization of treatment based on the findings and theories of the social sciences. Just treatment of the alleged offender requires this sort of processing: (1) The charge of a specific, statutorily defined offense; (2) A hearing of the issue at the earliest meeting of the court at which witnesses may be summoned with full protection of the defendant's rights of due process (including an attorney, relevant and competent testimony in his presence, adjudication only on convincing proof, and appeal); (3) Where court contact with a case indicates that the individual is not

---

[9] W. Bruce Cobb, Address Delivered on February 6, 1945 before a Joint Meeting of the Committees of the Court of Domestic Relations, of the Association of the Bar, and the County Lawyers Association.

guilty of an offense but does require treatment, he should be referred to those public or private social agencies which may deal in a specialized way with his problem, thereby assuring most effective treatment without stigma. Much of this could be done at Intake. (Indeed, one of the most useful functions of these specialized tribunals could well be to act as agencies of referral to more specialized social facilities in order that individual and community problems may be met more effectively.); (4) A probation investigation into the background of the adjudicated offender to determine on the basis of his prior history, conduct, and character what methods of therapy may best be applied to recondition him and protect society; (5) In the case of adjudicated offenders after receipt of the probation report and any other information available which is relevant to disposition, the court should dispose of the case with careful attention to adjusting treatment methods to the needs of the case, avoiding institutionalization wherever possible.†

50

Unofficial Delinquency*

Paul W. Tappan

Much has been written in recent years concerning the nature and content of delinquency. Today the substance of unofficial delinquency is coming to be recognized as a matter of at least equally important concern. Definitional questions are involved here of more than academic significance, in part because the student and researcher in the field are interested to

† For a more recent analysis of fundamental reforms needed in the juvenile court, see H. Nunberg, "Problems in the Structure of the Juvenile Court" (a paper written for the seminar on the Problem of Juvenile Delinquency conducted by the Editor at the Harvard Law School), 48 *J. Crim. L., Criminology and Police Science.* 500–516. — Ed.

* Reprinted from 29 *Nebraska L. Rev.* (1950), 547–558. Used by permission of the author and the publisher.

measure the frequency and trends of juvenile law violation and to inquire into the relative seriousness of the problem under differing circumstances. More important than measurement, however, is the need to define the limits of these terms in the interest of an equitable handling of the needs of children. In essence the question is this: how should youngsters with specified deviations in behavior, personality, or social situation be treated in order best to meet their requirements and, at the same time, to utilize community resources most effectively? It is with this broader problem, rather than the semantic question that the present paper proposes to deal. The point of particular emphasis here is that if child-care efforts are to rise above the level of a vague, generalized benevolence, fortuitous and sporadic in its expression, one must come to differentiate the functional areas of service to children in order to handle the diversity of their problems. This means defining the situations in which a given community resource, court or otherwise, should function. And it is in this connection that the problem of delinquency, official and unofficial, arises.

OFFICIAL DELINQUENCY

In relation to delinquency, there is an issue of policy even more vital than is true in other channels of child welfare: an issue of justice itself. Because court adjudication and authoritarian treatment are entailed, the difference between being a "delinquent" and being a "problem child" of some other sort is momentous. Delinquency is an irrevocable status with treatment implications that are uniquely different from those evoked by other classifications of child deviation. As the Supreme Court of Virginia, in a decision handed down in 1947, put the matter:

The judgment against a youth that he is a delinquent is a serious reflection upon his character and habits. The stain against him is not removed merely because the statute says no judgment in this particular proceeding shall be deemed a conviction for crime or so considered. The stigma of conviction will reflect upon him for life. It hurts his self-respect. It may, at some inopportune, unfortunate moment, rear its ugly head to destroy his opportunity for advancement and blast his ambition to build up a character and reputation entitling him to the esteem and respect of his fellow men. . . .
There is nothing in the record to suggest that the

accused were inherently vicious or incorrigible. To classify an infant as delinquent because of a youthful prank, or for a mere single violation of a misdemeanor statute or municipal ordinance, not immoral per se, in this day of numberless laws and ordinances is offensive to our sense of justice and to the intendment of the law. We cannot reconcile ourselves to the thought that the incautious violation of a motor-vehicle law, a single act of truancy, or a departure from an established rule of similar slight gravity is sufficient to justify the classification of the offender as a 'delinquent,' and require the supervision of a probation officer. We can but reflect that if this were so, there would be an inclusion of so many in the classification that the word would lose its accepted meaning.[1]

The writer has maintained elsewhere that at the child's level the experience of a delinquency adjudication in the juvenile court, its treatment consequences, and its effects on his reputation and his self-esteem are as severe — very often more so — as criminal conviction is to an adult. In spite of this, the insensitive perceptions of an adult world, what appears to be a self-deception induced by benign but misdirected motives, persists in viewing the court handling of the child as an innocuous or even a generally constructive experience. This illusion has been particularly common, perhaps, among persons who have been affiliated with courts and their servicing agencies: people whose daily experience in authoritarian roles, in which they are determined to "help the child," has blunted them to any real appreciation of his reactions. To many of these people the court becomes, in a modern miracle of transmutation, a "parent substitute" or an administrative agency designed to "save the child." [2]

By a convenient but highly misleading sophistry, it is maintained that the child is not charged with a "crime," "convicted" as a "criminal," nor "sentenced to a punishment." Rather, he is merely "adjudicated" under a "petition" as a "delinquent," studied to determine

how he may be "saved," and then "treated" in his own best interest. The slightest inspection of the characteristic methodology and personnel of the children's court, the detention facility, or the training school, should disillusion any but the most ingenuous about these euphemisms. Unfortunately most people never scrutinize these facilities critically and are led quite readily to confuse what juvenile courts are with what interested parties wishfully imagine their becoming.

EXPANSION OF JUVENILE COURT CONTROL

A limited introduction into the juvenile court field of the methods and terminology of voluntary case work has done much to popularize the misconceptions of what the court is, what it should and can do. This transfusion has come mainly by way of some probation officers' very partial and shallow exposure to social case work through brief in-service programs and the reading of over-simplified treatises that cannot possibly accomplish the educational or training purposes for what is, after all, a complicated craft of case work. The combination of crude empiricism with hortatory moralizations so often found in the juvenile court obviously does not spell out case work. Nor does an occasional fragment of Freudian jargon insinuated into case records. There are in fact serious hazards in the efforts of untrained or undertrained personnel to employ subtle skills requiring extensive and carefully supervised development. A gravest consequence lies in the unrealistic effort to translate certain functions of voluntary case work directly to an official court setting. The treatment of a rejected, neglected, or anti-social child by an authoritarian agency cannot be equated to the family or psychiatric case work that a client seeks from a more highly specialized social agency.

The current fashion of euphemistic description of the juvenile court and of the social agency role it would aspire to play are briefly recounted here because with them are associated to a great extent the drives toward an extension of court function and toward a growing imprecision in defining what delinquency is. In fact it is from these roots that the whole province of unofficial delinquency has burgeoned. Before considering that term specifically, however, it may be well briefly to analyze the concept of juvenile delinquency itself.

[1] Jones et al v. Commonwealth, 185 Va. 335, 38 S.E.2d 444 (1947).
[2] See Commonwealth v. Fisher, 213 Pa. 48, 62 Atl. 198 (1905): "It (the Children's Court Act) is not for the punishment of offenders, but for the salvation of children, and points out the way by which the state undertakes to save, not particular children of a special class, but all children under a certain age, whose salvation may become the duty of the state in the absence of proper parental care or disregard of it by wayward children."

Delinquency, it appears, may be identified *procedurally* on the basis of the child's attributed status as an offender, ensuing from a court conviction. The number of delinquents through court adjudication is rather precisely determinable, at least within the limits of formal court reporting and recording. In some respects, however, this adminstrative definition of delinquency may be inadequate. It does not inform as to the kinds of conduct that are delinquent, nor does it even approximate the numbers of cases of actual delinquency that have remained unreported or unprosecuted. Moreover, the procedural determination of law violation is itself founded upon normative definitions: the kinds of conduct that are taboo or the situations which justify a court in taking hold. One is led back necessarily, therefore, to the substantive problem of what is forbidden. Under the traditions of Anglo-American justice, it is generally conceived essential before one may be tried by a court that the behavior of the individual in question should be sufficiently dangerous to the community (or otherwise reprehensible) to bring it under legislative prohibition and to warrant subjecting the individual to the unusual treatment measures established by the state.

Thus one may describe the delinquent either procedurally as a court-adjudicated child or substantively as one who has violated some specification of the children's court statutes. The latter province is in part quite specific, as in the type of provision of the law that a delinquency is any act "which, if committed by an adult, would be a crime." However, unlike most phases of ordinary criminal law, many of the norms established in juvenile court statutes are quite nonspecific and unclear, as, for example, in the description of the delinquent as one "who is incorrigible, ungovernable, or habitually disobedient and beyond the control of his parents, guardian, or other lawful authority" or one "who, without just cause and without the consent of his parent, guardian, or other custodian, deserts his home or place of abode." The most generic concept of delinquency is expressed in the New York statute in these terms: one ". . . who so deports himself as wilfully to injure or endanger the morals or health of himself or others. . . ."[3] The determination of what delinquency is is

left here actually to the widely varying discretion of the magistrates and the equally variable predilections of particular probation officers. In line with the trends toward the enlargement of the area of court control, as the court comes to conceive itself an administrative social agency or a general instrument of child welfare, definitions of delinquency become less and less precise. In some jurisdictions no statutory definition is attempted at all, (viz., California and the District of Columbia). In many quarters there is, moreover, a strong drive to eliminate even the term, delinquent, itself because of the unsavory implications it carries. All this serves to facilitate the expansion of court power. More particularly, it has encouraged experimental tribunals to deal with all those cases in which there appears in the child's background to be either a pathological social situation or some form of personal unadjustment, whether or not any real delinquent conduct is involved.

UNOFFICIAL DELINQUENCY

It is from this trend toward the court handling of any youngster who "needs help" that unofficial delinquency has been born. Undoubtedly a recognition of the injurious consequences of court adjudication, in spite of numerous judicial pronouncements to the contrary, has also played a part. Beginning with its 1946 reports of juvenile court statistics, the Federal Security Agency has reported unofficial along with official cases, recognizing the importance of the former:

A large part of the work of the 220 courts for which data are included in this report (91,851 cases) did not require formal judicial action. Less than half of all cases were disposed of officially; 46 per cent of the delinquency cases and 59 per cent of the other cases were disposed of in this manner. . . . Courts vary in the percentage of all cases they dispose of officially. For example, of the courts serving areas of 100,000 or more population, two courts reported that they had disposed of all cases officially. At the other extreme, the courts serving two counties in Texas reported that they had disposed of only 9 per cent of their cases in this manner.

The state of New York, in its most recent report of the Department of Correction, inquired into the status of unofficial delinquency in the court procedures there:

In an effort to learn more about the extent to which the courts are handling such cases in a man-

---

[3] N.Y. Penal Law § 483 (b), (d), (j).

ner they term 'unofficial' or 'informal' a check was made of the annual reports received from forty of the fifty-seven counties outside New York City. In twenty-two reports no mention was made of 'unofficial cases' though it was learned from discussion with clerks that this did not necessarily mean there had been no cases so handled. Some courts believed there should be no record of them. In the remaining eighteen courts the number of unofficial cases reported varied from a small number to several hundred. One of the larger counties classified some of its unofficial cases as delinquency, and from the figures given 57.0 percent of the delinquency cases were about evenly divided between those reported as 'formal' and 'informal'; and in the third largest county in this group about 40.0 percent of the delinquency cases were reported as 'unofficial.' Thus it is obvious that this practice can materially change the delinquency picture with regard to adjudicated delinquents.[4]

The hazard of the practice of court handling of unofficial delinquency is implicit in these recent reports. A child's need for help, leading to unofficial court treatment, may be determined by the mere fact of a petition being entered in his behalf. The tendency today to handle a large proportion of cases informally without court adjudication is undoubtedly due in large part to a recognition of the injustice implicit in attributing the delinquency status to youngsters who have done no injury to the community. It also reflects a recognition of the harm that may be done to a child through formal court handling and treatment and through the role he then assumes in the public mind. But, recognizing the vice that is inherent in the official court adjudication of cases that are essentially nondelinquent in the conduct involved, these courts often fail to note the danger of authoritarian handling of these children by the same methods and personnel employed in ordinary delinquency cases.

As a result of all this, while juvenile delinquency has become increasingly difficult to delimit conceptually, the task of definition has become virtually impossible for unofficial delinquency. This latter creature, begotten from a liaison of court and quasi-case work, is not defined procedurally with any nicety, for there is no regularized method of determining that condition: there is not necessarily a court hearing at all; there is no finding or adjudication of

a recognized status; there are no uniformly established treatment methods. Even less clearly ascertainable are the substantive criteria of what constitutes unofficial delinquent conduct.

Despite the vague character of the term, it may be profitable to give more detailed consideration to unofficial delinquency, its procedures, agencies handling it, treatment methods, and types of conduct involved. As to procedural methods of determination, the concept may be applied to all cases that come to court intake regardless of their subsequent handling: this connotation would include all cases of petitions filed with a clerk of the court. More narrowly, the concept may refer to those youngsters who are handled without a court hearing by the probation department or some auxiliary division of that department, such as a clinic or adjustment bureau. Alternatively, it may denote those individuals who are brought to a formal court hearing but who are not adjudicated. The judge, after a hearing of the petitioner's testimony, may hold a decision in abeyance during the child's good behavior, with the implicit or explicit threat of adjudication in the event of his failure to cooperate. The "deferred prosecution" technique now employed by the federal government in many juvenile cases is a variant of this method.

To confound confusion, the term "agency delinquency" and sometimes "unofficial delinquency" has come to be applied to cases that do not go to court at all. For example, juvenile bureaus in police departments throughout the country are handling a large number of children's cases without court referral, sometimes directly by specifically assigned policemen, sometimes more or less informally by a police magistrate. In some communities a clear cut policy has been worked out to avoid either formal arrest or court appearance. The result of this trend in cutting down the statistical visibility of delinquency is clear, whatever may be its effect on the actual frequency of juvenile misconduct. As the Children's Bureau has stated the matter:

Many children whose behavior may be classed as delinquent are not represented in juvenile-court statistics, either because they are not apprehended or because they are not dealt with by the police, social agencies, schools, public or private youth-serving agencies, or other resources in the community and are not referred to a court. For example, the

---

[4] Annual Report of the Department of Correction for 1947, State of New York, 141–142 (1948).

Table 1   *Children Registered for Specific Reasons for Reference by*
All Agencies and By the Juvenile Court [5]

REASON FOR REFERENCE	CHILDREN REGISTERED BY ALL AGENCIES	CHILDREN REGISTERED BY JUVENILE COURT	PER CENT
Traffic violations	591	585	99
Stealing	1,870	1,487	80
Assault, injury to person	187	148	79
Acts of carelessness or mischief	951	733	77
Being ungovernable	456	244	54
Sex offense	258	61	24
Truancy	3,488	177	5
Running away	819	16	2

decline between 1943 and 1944 in the number of cases disposed of by the St. Louis (city) court, 40 percent, and by the Polk County (Des Moines) court, 24 percent, reflect the effects of the establishment of juvenile divisions in the police departments that made it unnecessary for some children involved in delinquent behavior to appear in court.[6]

Agencies other than the police, both public and private, also handle innumerable cases of children whose conduct and social situations are not significantly different from those dealt with in the juvenile courts of the same communities. In a study conducted in the District of Columbia to determine the total volume of delinquency as reflected in the cases of public social agencies as well as the juvenile court, it was found that a substantial proportion of "delinquency" cases were handled by non-court resources, as shown in Table 1.

Such public resources as welfare departments, schools and specifically children's aid agencies receive and usually attempt insofar as they can, to deal with many cases involving juvenile recalcitrance. Similarly, private or voluntary social agencies, neighborhood houses, and the like take many cases in which child behavior problems and deprived children are involved. Most private agencies are less inclined, however, to work with the youngster who has had police or court contacts in his social history. In all these forms of agency delinquency there is an attempt for the most part to avoid the term, delinquency.

TREATMENT METHODS

The treatment methods applied to the unofficial delinquent are similarly diverse. Within the court setting the child is most frequently exposed to some measure of informal treatment: he may be submitted to unofficial probation for a definite period of time or during good behavior. In the alternative, cases brought to a hearing may be filed or a decision held in abeyance, with or without any real efforts at supervisory treatment. Often these terms euphemistically describe a period of inaction, or at most only brief remonstrations, threats, or other minatory devices designed to convince the youngster of the dire consequences should he fail to behave. The supposition that a contact with court authority is in itself a therapeutic and deterrent influence to shock the child into conformity is a widely prevalent notion, too often employed indiscriminately as a quick and simple expedient. Not uncommonly more heroic measures are employed, measures that are potentially more hazardous as well. Thus, "temporary" detention may be utilized, pending a court hearing or decision, with a similar shock thesis that an opportunity to reflect upon his ways may "bring the child around" and, if he makes a proper show of penitence, he can then be released unadjudicated.[7] In many communities such temporary incarceration may last for weeks or even months! And the *locus peni-*

---

[5] Schwartz, Community Experiment in Delinquency Measurement, National Probation Association Yearbook 173 (1945).

[6] Juvenile Court Statistics for 1945, Federal Security Agency (1947).

[7] It has been suggested in the materials of the Children's Bureau that "the high proportion of dismissals, especially in boys' cases (46%) may mean that many children are being brought into court needlessly or that they need services other than those the courts are equipped to provide."

tentiae is generally either an ordinary jail (some 25 percent of detained children, at least, are held each year in jail) or in its very similar junior equivalent. Quaintly this detention is not looked upon as punishment. A less extensive but still quite common practice is the "voluntary" placement of children in institutions, to which extreme the parents have been induced by the simple expedient of posing to them as an alternative the formal adjudication and commitment of their children. Private institutional resources to which both official and unofficial delinquents may be committed are most often used for such voluntary placements. More rarely than the methods related above, youngsters may be referred to a clinic or social agency for treatment instead of being subjected to formal court handling. Such facilities, however, are lacking or inadequate in most communities. Adjustment clinics are attached to only a minority of courts. But, to use New York City as an example, where such a bureau has existed for a number of years, the personnel who conduct treatment are mainly students-in-training from a local school of social work. They handle only a limited number of cases.

Outside the framework of unofficial court delinquency, there are widely diverse patterns of social agency treatment of children with conduct problems. These methods vary to a great extent with the type of agency involved. Some employ simple stereotyped panaceas, such as recreation, religion, threats, or moralization. Others, particularly child clinics and case work agencies, may utilize numerous therapeutic methods, designed to meet the individualized requirements of the particular case. The level and proficiency of care a youngster receives as well as the accompanying status that accrues to him depend, more than anything else, upon the sort of treatment facility to which chance may expose him.

Conduct of Unofficial Delinquents

Unfortunately, as we turn now to the problem of the types of conduct implied by unofficial delinquency, it must be noted that the nature of the child's problems and needs play all too little role in the usual case in determining the sort of agency to which he may be brought for treatment. Unless he has committed a serious law violation — in which instance an official delinquency adjudication

is more likely — the child's handling depends on the frequently irrelevant and sometimes incongruous referrals that happen to bring him to the attention of one resource rather than another or, indeed to none at all.[8] With the trend for juvenile courts to handle cases of unofficial delinquency, children may frequently travel through authoritarian channels with little relation to the kind or severity of the behavioral or situational problems in their histories. And with equally small regard to the adequacy of court resources to respond to their needs.

Let us consider then the varieties of unofficial delinquency. What is the substantive content of this term? It may be clear from what has already been said that it has no precise boundaries. Yet different levels of meaning may be delineated in a rough way.

Most narrowly construed, unofficial delinquency may be taken to include only cases of criminal law violation. Here the situation is substantively identical to that of official delinquency, but the child is spared an adjudication to the status. More rigorous practice would apply the unofficial techniques only where the youngster is a first offender and/or where the offense is inconsequential. A far broader scope of effort is implied in those courts that conceive it desirable, in the interest of "delinquency prevention," to deal with conduct problems broadly, though no real law violation at all is shown. It may be noted that "ungovernable behavior" is the chief reason for which girls' cases are referred to court (about forty-five percent of all cases) and that for boys, next to stealing, "acts of carelessness or mischief" are the forms of conduct most frequently complained of (some twenty percent of the male cases). These are the sorts of mild misconduct, much of it in reality behavior quite normal to childhood, that may lead the child either to court and often official adjudication, to some other treatment

---

[8] The Department of Correction in the State of New York has indicated, in this connection, that "another factor in the delinquency story is the degree to which the community social agencies, the school and the police carry on their preventive work. As one illustration, it is possible for the schools in one county to handle nearly all of their truancy problems through visiting teachers, attendance officers and school courts, while in another county there is the tendency to bring all truancy cases into court without first attempting to handle them as school problems." *Op. cit. supra* note 4, at 142.

resource of the community, or to no public attention at all.

The Children's Bureau has pointed up this anomaly of conduct and its treatment consequence in these terms: "Because in the juvenile court laws delinquency is so loosely defined that it covers the whole gamut of undesirable behavior, many of the acts for which children are referred to juvenile courts are obviously of a very different character from what is usually considered law-breaking. Reasons for referral may range from ungovernable behavior to assault, from using obscene language to stealing large sums of money; from hitching on street cars to unlawful entry; from riding a bicycle on the sidewalk to robbery." [9] Negativistic, aggressive, or some other troublesome behavior may be considered sufficient to warrant intervention. Apparently distorted personality situations are also used to rationalize the unofficial handling of the youngster. Thus, the troubled or disturbed child, or one suffering from inadequacy feelings or frustration, may be brought under court control.

Even though a child may himself present no obvious problem, court supervision may nevertheless be assumed on the grounds of his surrounding circumstances, where there appear to be parental, domestic, neighborhood, school or other deficiencies. This is facilitated, of course, by the legal power of many juvenile court jurisdictions over neglected and dependent children. The trend is carried to its most logical but absurd conclusion, a direction toward which some court and probation philosophy clearly tends, in the assumption that any case coming to the attention of the court authorities is a proper case for treatment efforts. The rationale for this is that "the child would not be here if he did not need help." It is this sort of seemingly truistic assertion, loaded with false assumptions, that can do much to prevent the function of juvenile courts.

We have considered in a brief way some of the more important aspects of unofficial delinquency: the status feature, and procedural methods, its treatment implications, and finally the substantive connotations of the term. It may be well finally to generalize from the relation of these several factors. One clear and distinctive

[9] Juvenile Court Statistics for 1940–1942, Children's Bureau (1943).

virtue inheres in the unofficial method of handling juveniles: it avoids the attribution of a stigmatic and injurious legal status to the child. It represents a kind of circumvention of delinquency that may be quite helpful in many cases. In a more positive sense, the development of unofficial methods has implied in some courts a greater amount of experimentalism and more effort to refer cases not requiring official attention to specialized non-court agencies. The latter is a particularly desirable but not very widespread development. If more of a favorable nature may be said of unofficial delinquency, it is that the method does reflect the abundant good intentions of our children's courts.

DANGERS IN THE UNOFFICIAL DELINQUENT APPROACH

On the other side of the picture, however, a number of serious difficulties must be faced. Long experience has shown that good intentions, taken alone, are quite inadequate in the field of child care. It is essential to improve and diversify our treatment resources and to fit these facilities to the cases needing help so as to produce the most effective results. To repeat what has already been suggested, our juvenile courts cannot themselves employ either the approach or the resources of a well-staffed administrative social agency, so as to handle all manner of unadjusted children wisely and well. The court must be limited and specialized in its roles and methods. The major vice in unofficial delinquency is that no technique is provided to regularize the discretion of those who employ the device. Almost universally our children's court personnel lack training for the discriminate use of the unlimited power that the unofficial approach implies. As a result, endless numbers of children may be treated in or through the court who require no treatment at all and may be disserved by authoritarian handling. Others who do need help may often receive the wrong sorts of treatment through the court, or be foreclosed because of official contacts from the agency assistance they require.

These problems of unofficial delinquency would be resolved to a great extent if the emphasis, wherever possible, were put upon careful court intake and referral for treatment to specialized community resources. Unfortunately, the court's jealousy of its power and autonomy, together with the commonly uncooperative responses of social agencies have tended to keep and extend court control in areas where the result for the child is at best inefficient and at worst disastrous.

In conclusion, it should be emphasized, perhaps, that the sociological jurisprudence of the juvenile court is a vital area in contemporary administration of justice, too much neglected both by lawyers and by sociologists. Our children's courts feed too generously into our criminal courts and adult correctional institutions to justify complacency. It behooves us to inspect thoughtfully the fast developing trends in the work of the courts in child care, a sphere where so large a proportion of unadjusted youngsters go today. To quote the words of Dean Pound:

The powers of the Star Chamber were a trifle in comparison with those of our juvenile court and courts of domestic relations. The latter may bring about a revolution as easily as did the former. It is well known that too often the placing of a child in a home or even in an institution is done casually or perfunctorily or even arbitrarily. Moreover, effective preventive work through these courts requires looking into much more than the bad external conditions of a household, such as poverty or neglect or lack of discipline. Internal conditions, a complex of habits, attitudes, and reactions, may have to be dealt with and this means administrative treatment of the most intimate affairs of life. Even with the most superior personnel, these tribunals call for legal checks.[10]

51

How Far Can Court Procedure Be Socialized Without Impairing Individual Rights?*

Edward F. Waite

What do we mean by "socializing" court procedure? †

Measuring time by standards appropriate to the development of human institutions, it may be said that until very recently the courts were concerned almost wholly with the adjustment of conflicting claims of individuals and groups against each other, and procedure was meticulously guarded to prevent unjust advantage, for precisely the same reasons that dictated the details of the code duello. The modern tendency toward what is termed the socialization of the courts has produced new tribunals and evolved new functions of older ones in which the aim is not so much the adjudication of private rights as the performance of what are conceived to be community obligations. This tendency chiefly interests the lawyer as it has enlarged the use of the police power to secure the general welfare. It interests the social worker chiefly as it brings directly and conveniently to his aid the judicial machinery through which alone, according to the traditions of free peoples, the state may exercise its ultimate authority in time of peace.

The working out of this tendency toward broader functions and a more human emphasis and aim has involved a more liberal procedure or method of transacting the business of the courts, or at least, of certain courts in which

ference on Juvenile Courts held under the joint auspices of the Federal Children's Bureau and the National Probation Association, Milwaukee, June 21–22, 1921.

† It is a long time since the article by Judge Waite was written. A number of articles and law review notes on the same theme have appeared since, but there has been little improvement on the assessment of the basic issues. Among the more recent articles that have appeared are: "Determination of Delinquency in the Juvenile Court: An Appraisal and Suggested Approach," by J. J. Rappeport, 1958 Wash. U.L.Q. (1958), 123–166, Article 104 hereof (a class paper prepared for the seminar on juvenile delinquency conducted by Professor Sheldon Glueck at the Harvard Law School); "Fairness to the Juvenile Offender," by M. G. Paulsen, 41 Minn. L. Rev. (1957); "The Rights of Juvenile Delinquents: An Appraisal of Juvenile Court Procedures," by L. Diana, 47 J. Crim. L., Criminology and Police Science (1957), 561–569; Note: "Juvenile Courts: Applicability of Constitutional Safeguards and Rules of Evidence to Proceedings: In re Holmes," by T. W. Cashel, 41 Cornell L.Q. (1955), 147–154; "Protecting the Child in the Juvenile Court," by S. Rubin, 43 J. Crim. L., Criminology and Police Science (1952), 425–440; "Juvenile Justice: Treatment or Travesty?," by F. E. Ellrod, Jr., and D. H. Melany, 11 U. Pitt. L. Rev. (1950), 277–287. — Ed.

10 Young, Social Treatment in Probation and Delinquency, xxvii (1937), foreword by Roscoe Pound.
* Reprinted from 12 J. Crim. L. and Criminology (1921–22), 339–347. Used by permission of the author and the publisher. Presented at the Con-

the socializing process has made substantial headway. When a court is acting not as an arbiter of private strife but as the medium of the state's performance of its sovereign duties as *parens patriae* and promoter of the general welfare, it is natural that some of the safeguards of judicial contests should be laid aside. This corollary to the main tendency to which we have referred may be fitly styled the socialization of court procedure.

I assume that by "individual rights" in our subject is meant those personal rights recognized by the common law as adopted in the United States and established by constitutions, national and state.

On the basis of these definitions let us consider the following subdivisions of the general subject proposed by those who have prepared the program:

1. Exclusion of public.
2. Representation by attorneys.
3. Swearing of witnesses.
4. Methods of taking testimony and conformity with rules of evidence.
5. Weight of evidence.
6. Jury trials.
7. Investigation into circumstances of offense.
8. Testimony of probation officers.
9. Use of referee in girls' cases.

The discussion will relate solely to so-called juvenile courts, and my contribution is untechnical, summary and suggestive. So far as I state legal principles I shall undertake to be correct according to interpretations that prevail in my own state, Minnesota. Even were my learning sufficient I could not differentiate here between the several states on points where they do not agree.

I have said "so-called juvenile courts" advisedly. I do not reflect upon those communities where the legislature has not made the radical change from the criminal to the non-criminal type of court in dealing with delinquent children. But has not the time come to reform our terminology in the interests of clear thinking? The court which must direct its procedure even apparently to do something *to* a child because of what he *has done,* is parted from the court which is avowedly concerned only with doing something *for* a child because of what he *is* and *needs,* by a gulf too wide to be bridged by any humanity which the judge may introduce into his hearings, or by the habitual use of corrective rather than punitive methods after conviction. I suspect that the theory of the juvenile court which stresses the moving forward of the common law age of criminal responsibility involves some bad psychology and is responsible for some bad law. Has not the time arrived when no tribunal should claim the title of juvenile court, implying in its origin and major application a jurisdiction and procedure founded wholly on the parental idea, without distinction in aim and essential method between delinquent, dependent and neglected wards of the state, unless this is in its real character? Let other courts be styled what they are — police or criminal courts for children.

But I should not be warranted in excluding courts of the latter sort from this discussion. Therefore, having thus filed my protest, I shall adopt the current nomenclature and refer to all children's courts as juvenile courts.

Another comment, to clear the ground: One too often sees departure from these traditional safeguards of the individual which are familiar in Anglo-Saxon jurisprudence explained and justified by the parental attitude of the juvenile court. Some looseness prevails in this regard, even in the opinions of appellate courts. It should not be forgotten that the performance of judicial functions always involves two processes: the first, to determine whether jurisdiction assumed for the purpose of an inquiry should be retained for the application of a remedy; the second, application of the remedy. The first seeks the facts; the second applies the law to the facts as ascertained. Is it not obvious that the rights of the individual who holds the state at arm's length and says: "The matters charged are false; government has no call to interfere with me" should be more strictly regarded during the first process than the second, when his status as a person with whom public interference is warranted has been established? Otherwise all that is necessary to justify a despotism is to make sure it intends to be benevolent.

Taking up now the suggested sub-topics:

1. *Exclusion of Public.* One who is accused of crime has a constitutional right to a public trial. As to what a public trial is, the courts have differed. If a juvenile court is organized as a criminal court for children, any child who comes before it charged with an offense is en-

titled to a public trial. If the court that deals with him is exercising chancery jurisdiction, no such constitutional right exists; and for the purpose of this discussion non-criminal courts with purely statutory jurisdiction over children will be classed, though not with technical exactness, as courts of chancery jurisdiction. To a mind, "not warped," as somebody has said, "by study and practice of the law" it may seem absurd that the hearing in the case of Johnny Jones must be public if he is charged in a criminal court with stealing, and need not be so if he is charged in a non-criminal court with being delinquent because he stole. I shall not now defend this seeming inconsistency. If it is constitutional law it is binding on the courts and legislatures, and can be changed only by constitutional amendments.

There is no constitutional right to a public hearing when dependency or neglect is the issue; and the court has no right to deny it in cases of "contributing," since here it acts always as a criminal court, whether or not it has also chancery jurisdiction.

Even when the right to a public trial exists much discretion is allowed the judge in the matter of excluding idle onlookers in the interest of public decency or the good order of the court proceedings. Probably no reasonable exercise of this discretion would ever be questioned by or on behalf of a juvenile delinquent, for the protection of whose sensibilities and reputation it is commonly exercised. Indeed, all doubtful questions that have arisen in my own experience have had reference to *inclusion* rather than *exclusion*. I have sometimes found it puzzling to know how far it was just to children and their parents to permit their troubles to be heard even by qualified social observers who wished to use the clinical opportunities afforded by court sessions. The smaller the court room, by the way, the simpler the problem both ways.

2. *Representation by Attorneys.* Here also the nature of the proceeding is the proper basis for distinctions. In prosecutions for crime, even children, representation by counsel is a constitutional right. In non-criminal proceedings, however, courts of conciliation and small claims have made us familiar with the idea that legal rights are not necessarily violated by the elimination of attorneys. But is it not a moot question? Is not the experience of other judges like

my own, that in most cases it is easily possible to make the lawyer who comes into the juvenile court an ally of the court, and interest him in securing the real welfare of those for whom he appears? The absence of antagonistic claims of personal rights makes this the more feasible. I refer, of course, to cases immediately involving children. In "contributing" cases appearance of counsel must be permitted, and in my judgment should be encouraged.

3. *Swearing of Witnesses.* I fancy most judges exercise wide discretion in this regard and are not conscious of any danger to personal rights. I can hardly conceive that if desired by the parties concerned all witnesses would not be sworn. Sometimes essential facts are within the knowledge of a child so young that to put him on oath would seem unreasonable. An obvious corollary to this situation would be the conclusion that his testimony would be unreliable. This would be true in general; and yet skilful questioning by an impartial judge might elicit important and well accredited truth. The discretion to determine the competency of a child to testify has always lain with the court. Would it be any violation of rights for the judge to determine also whether or not to administer the oath? I think not. The greater discretion includes the less.

4. (a) *Methods of Taking Testimony and* (b) *Conformity with Rules of Evidence.*

(*a*) There can be no question of impairing rights in determining whether to receive testimony from the witness stand or the floor in front of the judge's table; or whether and to what extent the judge himself shall interrogate witnesses. These and others of like sort are questions of taste and convenience, and the preference of any person fit to act as judge ought to be a safe reliance. As between criminal and non-criminal proceedings interrogation by the court is much more limited in the former, according to usage in the United States.

(*b*) More serious questions arise in respect to conformity with the rules of evidence. Speaking generally, rules of evidence throughout the United States are the rules of the English common law, variously modified by local statutes, and uniform in their application to all courts deriving authority from the same source — the state or the nation. I do not happen to know of any legislative rule of evidence peculiar to juvenile courts except a Minnesota statute permitting findings upon the written reports of official investigators with like effect as upon testimony received in open court, in "county allowance" or "mothers' pension" cases. Rules of ancient origin, approved or at least tolerated by the community for generations, encountered by the citizen whenever he resorts to other legal forums to assert or defend his rights, should not lightly be set aside in juvenile courts. The only safe practice is to observe them. If hearsay, for example, has not been found justly admissible in civil disputes and criminal trials, it is no better in juvenile court proceedings. Exceptions should be made when appropriate, and informal short cuts will often be found agreeable to all concerned; but the exception should always be recognized as an exception. No judge on any bench has need to be more thoroughly grounded in the principles of evidence and more constantly mindful of them than the judge of a juvenile court. The boy against whom it is proposed to make an official record of misconduct, involving possible curtailment of his freedom at the behest of strangers, has a right to be found delinquent only according to law. The father, however unworthy, who faces a judicial proceeding, the event of which may be to say to him — "This child of your loins is henceforth *not* your child: the state takes him from you as finally as though by the hand of death" — that father may rightfully demand that the tie of blood shall be cut only by the sword of constitutional justice. Surely, those substantial rules of evidence which would protect the boy if the state called its interference "punishment" instead of "protection," and would safeguard the father in the possession of his dog, should apply to issues which may involve the right of the boy to liberty within the family relationship, and the right of the father to his child. The greater the conceded discretion of the judge, the freer he is from the vigilance of lawyers, the less likely he is to have his mistakes corrected on appeal, so much the more careful should he be to base every judicial conclusion on evidence proper to be received in any court of justice. Otherwise the state's parental power which he embodies is prostituted; the interpreter of the law degenerates into the oriental kadi, and the juvenile court falls into suspicion and disrepute.

5. *Weight of Evidence.* Shall the standard be preponderance of evidence or proof beyond a reasonable doubt? The latter, surely, whenever the proceeding is a criminal one; the former — technically, at least — in dependency and neglect cases. I say "technically," for while a jury would be so instructed, it is certain that the average juror, regardless of instructions, will require something more than a mere tipping of the balance before he will agree to a verdict that may separate protesting parents from their child. And when, as in most cases, the duty to pass upon disputed facts falls to the fallible intelligence of a single person, any judge who realizes his responsibility will insist upon clear proof.

When delinquency cases are heard in non-criminal courts I suppose the true rule to be preponderance of evidence. But here I, at least, must plead guilty to judicial legislation, and I suspect I am not alone in this. When we have minimized the stigma of an adjudication of delinquency in every way that kindly ingenuity may devise, it remains true that in the mind of the child, his family and his acquaintances who know about it, it is practically equivalent to conviction of a criminal offense. In the face of this fact legal theory should give way, and no less evidence should be required than if the hearing were a criminal trial. In the rare instances when I have juries in the juvenile court I instruct them to this effect, and I apply the same test to my own mind in reaching judicial conclusions.

6. *Jury Trials.* It appears to be well settled that in none of the cases heard in non-criminal juvenile courts is there a constitutional right to trial by jury. In Minnesota when juvenile court functions are exercised by the district court, which is the court of general jurisdiction, a jury trial may be demanded. This, however, is a privilege granted, rather than a right confirmed, by the legislature; and the privilege is rarely claimed. Doubtless this situation is typical. When, however, the court is so organized that a child is prosecuted for a criminal violation of a state law, I think it is generally understood that a jury must be called unless specifically waived. The same is true in "contributing" cases, especially when, as in Minnesota, the act or omission is made a misdemeanor.

7. *Investigation Into Circumstances of Of-*

fense. If there is a question here it must be as to the use to be made of information obtained rather than as to the propriety of a preliminary investigation through agents of the court. The value of such an investigation in suggesting inquiry at the hearing is obvious. But when there are issues of fact to be tried it seems to me equally plain that statements made to an investigator out of court should have no standing as evidence when they are disputed by parties in interest, who by the implications of their denial demand the same right to be confronted with the witnesses against them that is freely recognized in other judicial proceedings. Without attempting a discussion of "due process of law," considerations of public policy seem conclusive. The undisciplined minds of the juveniles and most of the parents who come before the court cannot make clear distinctions between proceedings that are really friendly and paternal and those that are hostile, when the results may be alike in depriving them of liberty of action which they had before they came into court and are unwilling to surrender. Public opinion, too, looks askance upon any abandonment of traditional barriers against governmental interference with the citizen. However wise the judge and kind his purpose, he must have regard to both the individual and the community sense of justice; and Americans have an ingrained conviction that nothing, however well meant, ought to be forced upon them on the basis of information obtained behind their backs.

Let it be observed that I am now discussing policy rather than constitutional rights. As respects non-criminal proceedings, I am not prepared to set limits to the power of the legislature to enlarge and adapt to modern conditions the ancient methods of official inquisition. Professor Wigmore speaks of an increasing need "for the more liberal recognition of an authority such as would make admissible various sorts of reports dealing with matters seldom disputable and only provable otherwise at disproportionate inconvenience and cost." "This policy," he says, "when judiciously employed, greatly facilitates the production of evidence without introducing loose methods." (Evidence, Vol. III, Sec. 1672.)

It is probable that as socialization of the courts proceeds the tendency toward the use of this form of evidence will grow stronger; but popular prejudices must be reckoned with, and procedural convenience will be dearly bought if the cost be impairment of the general confidence in the administration of justice.

When, however, the adjudication is made the situation changes. It has been lawfully determined that the facts warrant the interference of the court. The nature and extent of that interference is discretionary with the judge within the limits set by the law. In exercising his discretion he may rely upon anything that brings conviction to his mind, and the parties concerned have no legal right to question the sources of his information. Here official investigation is a proper and valuable aid, whether made before or after the adjudication.

8. *Testimony of Probation Officers.* No legal right seems to be involved: the question is rather one of expediency. In my judgment the probation officer should not appear as a hostile factor in court proceedings. The friendly relations with child and family that are essential to his corrective and constructive work would thus be jeopardized in advance. Should adverse information after probation is ordered be disclosed to the court? By all means if it is important. No confidences should be received on condition of concealment. The probation officer is the eyes and ears of the court. What he sees and hears is a part of the court's knowledge of the case, and ought to be so regarded by all concerned.

9. *Use of Referee in Girls' Cases.* Once more a distinction must be made between criminal and non-criminal proceedings. Probably no one would suggest the reference of a criminal case against an adult. Then why of a criminal case against a juvenile? But in non-criminal matters, masters in chancery and statutory referees have familiarized us with the idea of delegation by the court of some part of its judicial authority. I think there is no constitutional reason why a court exercising chancery powers as a juvenile court may not be authorized to appoint a referee not only to examine and recommend but to hear and determine. Masters of discipline in Colorado, juvenile commissioners in North Dakota and referees in Missouri are instances where statutes have expressly authorized such procedure. Other examples are referees in girls' cases. I have never heard a suggestion

that rights were thus violated. On the contrary, girls and their parents are likely to deem it an advantage to have both inquiry and action in a woman's hands. Doubtless it is the experience of every man who acts as judge in cases of sex delinquency on the part of girls that, even if he has not the assistance of an official referee, a woman probation officer relieves him of embarrassing investigation and virtually determines the appropriate action.

We may state three general conclusions:

1. In criminal proceedings the child has, before conviction, all the legal rights of the adult. Here the field of socialization is practically limited to treatment of the child after conviction.

2. In non-criminal proceedings there may be, either with or without express legislative authorization, according to the nature of the court, the broad latitude customarily exercised by courts of chancery jurisdiction, this being appropriate and necessary to the full use of parental functions. Here no constitutional provisions relating to criminal prosecutions apply, and socialization of procedure may have wide scope. There are limits, however, of which the judge should never be unmindful.

3. In adopting this broader practice courts should have regard to the popular sense of justice, even when it is not supported by established principles of constitutional law.

Do not these conclusions point toward wider powers, freer action, better and more thoroughly socialized judges for the true juvenile court, and speedy evolution of the criminal court for children into the broader type? This process spells, I think, the liberal development of the family court idea.

Furthermore, while they seem to me in no wise at variance with the growing tendency toward transfer to the public schools of administrative details after adjudication, do they not negative conclusively the assumption by any other agency than a court of justice of the task of adjudicating disputed facts? *

---

* See, also, Roscoe Pound, "The Rise of Socialized Criminal Justice," *Social Defenses Against Crime*, N.P.P.A. Yearbook, 1942, 1–22, and Paul W. Alexander, "Of Juvenile Court Justice and Judges," *Redirecting the Delinquent*, N.P.P.A. Yearbook, 1947, 187–205. — Ed.

52

Juvenile Court Procedure in England*

GENERAL PROVISIONS AS TO PROCEEDINGS IN COURT

36. *Prohibition against children being present in court during the trial of other persons.* No child (other than an infant in arms) shall be permitted to be present in court during the trial of any other person charged with an offense, or during any proceedings preliminary thereto, except during such time as his presence is required as a witness or otherwise for the purposes of justice; and any child present in court when under this section he is not permitted to be so shall be removed:

Provided that this section shall not apply to messengers, clerks, and other persons required to attend at any court for purposes connected with their employment.

37. *Power to clear court while child or young person is giving evidence in certain cases.* (1) Where, in any proceedings in relation to an offence against, or any conduct contrary to, decency or morality, a person who, in the opinion of the court, is a child or young person is called as a witness, the court may direct that all or any persons, not being members or officers of the court or parties to the case, their counsel or solicitors, or persons otherwise directly concerned in the case, be excluded from the court during the taking of the evidence of that witness:

Provided that nothing in this section shall authorise the exclusion of bona fide representatives of a newspaper or news agency.

(2) The powers conferred on a court by this section shall be in addition and without

---

* Extracted by J. J. Rappeport from *Statute and Rules*, Children and Young Persons Act (1933), 23 Geo. 5, Ch. 12. See, also, E. Younghusband, "The Juvenile Court and the Child," 7 *Brit. J. Del.* (1956–57), 181–194; W. E. Cavenagh, "Justice and Welfare in Juvenile Courts," *Id.*, 196–205. — Ed.

prejudice to any other powers of the court to hear proceedings in camera.

38. *Evidence of child of tender years.* Where (1) in any proceedings against any person for any offence, any child of tender years called as a witness does not in the opinion of the court understand the nature of an oath, his evidence may be received, though not given upon oath, if, in the opinion of the court, he is possessed of sufficient intelligence to justify the reception of the evidence, and understands the duty of speaking the truth; and his evidence, though not given on oath, but otherwise taken and reduced into writing in accordance with the provisions of this Act shall be deemed to be a deposition within the meaning of that section and that Part respectively:

Provided that where evidence admitted by virtue of this section is given on behalf of the prosecution the accused shall not be liable to be convicted of the offence unless that evidence is corroborated by some other material evidence in support thereof implicating him.

(2) If any child whose evidence is received as aforesaid willfully gives false evidence in such circumstances that he would, if the evidence had been given on oath, have been guilty of perjury, he shall be liable on summary conviction to be dealt with as if he had been summarily convicted of an indictable offence punishable in the case of an adult with imprisonment.

39. *Power to prohibit publication of certain matter in newspapers.* (1) In relation to any proceedings in any court which arise out of any offence against, or any conduct contrary to, decency or morality, the court may direct that

(a) no pewspaper report of the proceedings shall reveal the name, address or school, or include any particulars calculated to lead to the identification of any child or young person concerned in the proceedings, either as being the person against or in respect of whom the proceedings are taken, or as being a witness therein;

(b) no picture shall be published in any newspaper as being or including a picture of any child or young person so concerned in the proceedings as aforesaid; except in so far (if at all) as may be permitted by the direction of the court.

(2) Any person who publishes any matter in contravention of any such direction shall on summary conviction be liable in respect of each offence to a fine not exceeding fifty pounds.

41. *Power to proceed with case in absence of child or young person.* Where in any proceedings with relation to any of the offences mentioned in the First Schedule to this Act, the court is satisfied that the attendance before the court of any child or young person in respect of whom the offence is alleged to have been committed is not essential to the just hearing of the case, the case may be proceeded with and determined in the absence of the child or young person.

42. *Extension of power to take deposition of child or young person.* (1) Where a justice of the peace is satisfied by the evidence of a duly qualified medical practitioner that the attendance before a court of any child or young person in respect of whom any of the offences mentioned in the First Schedule to this Act is alleged to have been committed would involve serious danger to his life or health, the justice may take in writing the deposition of the child or young person on oath, and shall thereupon subscribe the deposition and add thereto a statement of his reason for taking it and of the day when and place where it was taken, and of the names of the persons, if any, present at the taking thereof.

(2) The justice taking any such deposition shall transmit it with his statement

(a) if the deposition relates to an offence for which any accused person is already committed to trial, to the proper officer of the court for trial at which the accused person has been committed; and

(b) in any other case, to the clerk of the court before which proceedings are pending in respect of the offence.

43. *Admission of deposition of child or young person in evidence.* Where, in any proceedings in respect of any of the offences mentioned in the First Schedule of this Act, the court is satisfied by the evidence of a duly qualified medical practitioner that the attendance before the court of any child or young person in respect of whom the offence is alleged to have been committed would involve serious danger to his life or health, any deposition of the child or young person taken under the Indictable Offences Act, 1848, or this Part of this Act, shall be admissible in evidence either for or against the accused person without further proof thereof if it purports to be signed by the justice by or before whom it purports to be taken:

Provided that the deposition shall not be admissible in evidence against the accused person unless it is proved that reasonable notice of the intention to take the deposition has been served upon him and that he or his counsel or solicitor had, or might have had if he had chosen to be present, an opportunity of cross-examining the child or young person making the deposition.

44. *General considerations.* (1) Every court in dealing with a child or young person who is brought before it, either as being in need of care or protection or as an offender or otherwise, shall have regard to the welfare of the child or young person and shall in a proper case take steps for removing him from undesirable surroundings, and for securing that proper provision is made for his education and training.

(2) A court shall not order a child under the age of ten years to be sent to an approved school unless for any reason, including the want of a fit person of his own religious persuasion who is willing to undertake the care of him, the court is satisfied that he cannot suitably be dealt with otherwise.

STATUTORY RULES AND ORDERS, 1933

PART I — *Juvenile Offenders:*

4. This Part of these Rules shall apply in the case of a child or young person brought before a court charged with an offence and, so far as applicable, in the case of any child or young person dealt with in pursuance of section 65 of the Act.

5. (1) The court shall, except in any case where the child or young person is legally represented, allow his parent or guardian to assist him in conducting his defence, including the cross-examination of witnesses for the prosecution.

(2) Where the parent or guardian cannot be found or cannot in the opinion of the court reasonably be required to attend, the court may allow any relative or other responsible person to take the place of the parent or guardian for the purposes of this Part of these Rules.

6. The court shall explain to the child or young person the substance of the charge in simple language suitable to his age and understanding.

7. Subject to the provisions of Rule 8, the court shall then ask the child or young person whether he admits the charge.

8. (1) When a young person is charged with an indictable offence other than homicide and

the court at any time during the hearing of the case is satisfied that it is expedient to deal with the case summarily, the court shall put to the young person the following or similar question, telling him that before replying he may consult his parent or guardian, if present:

"Do you consent to be tried by this court or do you wish to be tried by a jury?"

and the court shall explain the difference between summary trial and trial by jury and state at what court and place the trial by jury would be held.

(2) If the young person consents to be dealt with summarily, the court shall then ask him whether he admits the charge.

9. (1) If the child or young person does not admit the charge the court shall hear the evidence of the witnesses in support of the charge. At the close of the evidence-in-chief of each witness the witness may be cross-examined by or on behalf of the child or young person.

(2) If in any case where the child or young person is not legally represented or assisted in his defence as provided by Rule 5, the child or young person, instead of asking questions by way of cross-examination, makes assertions, the court shall then put to the witness such questions as it thinks necessary on behalf of the child or young person and may for this purpose question the child or young person in order to bring out or clear up any point arising out of any such assertions.

10. If it appears to the court that a prima facie case is made out, the child or young person shall be told that he may give evidence or make a statement and the evidence of any witnesses for the defence shall be heard.

11. Where the child or young person is found guilty of an offence, whether after a plea of guilty or otherwise

(i) he and his parent or guardian, if present, shall be given an opportunity of making a statement;

(ii) the court shall, except in cases which appear to it to be of a trivial nature, obtain such information as to the general conduct, home surroundings, school record and medical history of the child or young person as may enable it to deal with the case in his best interests, and shall if such information is not fully available consider the desirability of remanding the child or young person for such enquiry as may be necessary:

(iii) the court shall take into consideration any report which may be furnished by a probation officer or by a local authority in pursuance of section 35 of the Act;

(iv) any written report of a probation officer, local authority, or registered medical practitioner may be received and considered by the court without being read aloud:

Provided that

(a) the child or young person shall be told the substance of any part of the report bearing on his character or conduct which the court considers to be material to the manner in which he should be dealt with;

(b) the parent or guardian, if present, shall be told the substance of any part of the report which the court considers to be material as aforesaid and which has reference to his character or conduct, or the character, conduct, home surroundings, or health of the child or young person; and

(c) if the child or young person or his parent or guardian, having been told the substance of any part of any such report, desires to produce evidence with reference thereto, the court, if it thinks the evidence material, shall adjourn the proceedings for the production of further evidence, and shall, if necessary, require the attendance at the adjourned hearing of the person who made the report; and

(v) if the court acting in pursuance of this Rule considers it necessary in the interests of the child or young person, it may require the parent or guardian or the child or young person, as the case may be, to withdraw from the court.

12. The court shall thereupon, unless it thinks it undesirable to do so, inform the parent or guardian, if present, of the manner in which it proposes to deal with the child or young person and allow the parent or guardian to make representations.

13. Where a child or young person has been remanded, and the period of remand is extended in his absence in accordance with section 48 of the Act, notice shall be given to him and his sureties (if any) of the date at which he will be required to appear before the court.

PART II — *Juveniles in need of care or protection.*

14. This part of these Rules shall apply in the case of a child or young person dealt with

in pursuance of sections 61, 62 and 63 of the Act and shall apply also in the case of a child or young person dealt with in pursuance of section 64 or section 66 of the Act, subject to the modifications in Rules 23 or 24 as the case may be.

15. Where a child or young person is to be brought before the court otherwise than by way of summons or warrant as provided by Rule 16 and an application is to be made to the court in respect of the child or young person for an order under sections 61, 62 and 63 of the Act, the person or authority intending to make the application (hereinafter called the applicant) shall, subject to the provisions of section 34 of the Act, serve a notice on the parent or guardian of the child or young person, if he can be found, specifying the grounds upon which the child or young person is to be brought before the court, and the time and place at which the court will sit: and in any case shall send a notice to the clerk of the court, who shall thereupon enter the particulars of the case in the register:

16. (1) Where the child or young person has not been removed to a place of safety, a summons may, if necessary, be issued requiring him to attend before the court, and the provisions of section 1 of the Summary Jurisdiction Act, 1848 (a) shall apply as if the application were by way of complaint for an order.

(2) If anyhow it appears necessary to a justice of the peace he may (whether or not a summons has previously been issued) grant a warrant in accordance with the provisions of section 2 of the Summary Jurisdiction Act, 1848 (a) subject to the modification that the warrant shall direct that the child or young person shall be brought before a juvenile court and unless he is released on bail, shall be detained in a place of safety until he can be so brought.

17. Before proceeding with the hearing the court shall inform the child or young person of the nature of the application.

18. (1) Where the application is made under sections 61, 62 and 63 of the Act, the court shall, except in a case where the child or young person is legally represented, allow his parent or guardian, if present, to conduct the case in opposition of the application.

(2) Where the parent or guardian cannot be found or cannot in the opinion of the court reasonably be required to attend, the court may allow any relative or other responsible person

to take the place of the parent or guardian for the purposes of this part of these Rules.

19. (1) The court shall proceed in accordance with section 15 of the Summary Jurisdiction Act, 1848, (a) to hear the evidence tendered by or on behalf of the applicant.

(2) Where the nature of the case, or the evidence to be given, is such that in the opinion of the court it is in the interests of the child or young person that the evidence, other than any evidence relating to the character or conduct of the child or young person, should not be given in his presence, the court may hear any part of such evidence in his absence; and in that event his parent or guardian shall be permitted to remain in court during the absence of the child or young person.

(3) The court may exclude the parent or guardian of the child or young person while he gives evidence or makes a statement, if the court is satisfied that in the special circumstances it is proper to do so:

Provided that the court shall inform the parent or guardian of the substance of any allegation made by the child or young person, and shall give him an opportunity of meeting it by calling evidence or otherwise.

20. If it appears to the court after hearing the evidence in support of the application that a prima facie case is made out, it shall tell the child or young person and his parent or guardian, if present, that they may give evidence or make a statement, and call witnesses.

21. Where the court is satisfied that the child or young person comes within the description mentioned in the application, or, in the case of an application under section 64 of the Act, that the parent or guardian is unable to control the child or young person

(i) the court shall obtain such information as to the general conduct, home surroundings, school record and medical history of the child or young person as may enable it to deal with the case in his best interests; and shall, if such information is not fully available, consider the desirability of adjourning the case for such enquiry as may be necessary or of making an interim order under section 67 of the Act:

(ii) the court shall take into consideration any report which may be furnished by a probation officer or local authority in pursuance of section 35 of the Act;

(iii) any written report of a probation officer,

local authority, or registered medical practitioner may be received and considered by the court without being read aloud:

Provided that

(a) the child or young person shall be told the substance of any part of the report bearing on his character or conduct which the court considers to be material to the manner in which he should be dealt with;

(b) the parent or guardian, if present, shall be told the substance of any part of the report which the court considers to be material as aforesaid and which has reference to his character or conduct, or the character, conduct, home surroundings, or health of the child or young person, and

(c) if the child or young person or his parent or guardian, having been told the substance of any part of such report, desires to produce evidence with reference thereto, the court, if it thinks the evidence material, shall adjourn the proceedings for the production of further evidence and shall, if necessary, require the attendance at the adjourned hearing of the person who made the report; and

(iv) if the court acting in pursuance of this Rule considers it necessary in the interests of the child or young person, it may require the parent or guardian or the child or young person, as the case may be, to withdraw from the court.

22. The court shall thereupon, unless it thinks it undesirable to do so, inform the parent or guardian, if present, of the manner in which it proposes to deal with the child or young person and allow his parent or guardian to make representations.

23. In the application of this Part of these Rules to the case of a child or young person brought before the court under section 64 of the Act the following modifications shall have effect:

(i) Rules 15 and 18 shall not apply.

(ii) The clerk of the court shall enter the particulars of the case in the register, and the court before dealing with the application shall, unless it is satisfied that the local authority has already been informed, cause notification in writing to be sent to the local authority within whose area the child or young person is resident.

24. In the application of this Part of these Rules to the case of a child or young person brought before a court under section 66 (1) of

the Act the following modifications shall have effect:

(i) In addition to the notice required to be served on the parent or guardian pursuant to Rule 15 the person responsible for bringing the child or young person before the court shall serve notice on the local authority in the same manner as if section 35 of the Act were applicable and reports furnished by a probation officer or local authority shall be taken into consideration as if they were furnished in accordance with that section.

(ii) Rule 18 shall apply in like manner as it applies in the case of an application under sections 61, 62 and 63 of the Act.

(iii) Rule 21 shall apply where the court is satisfied that a prima facie case has been made out for the making of an Order under the said section.

53

The Juvenile Offender in Norway*

C. Terence Pihlblad

At approximately the same time as the Juvenile Court movement had its inception in the United States, there grew up in the Scandinavian countries a somewhat different type of agency for dealing with the child offender. This was the Child Welfare Council first established

* Reprinted from 43 *J. Crim. L., Criminology and Police Science* (1955), 500–511. Used by permission of the author and the publisher. See, also, Aulie and Halvorsen, "A New Approach to the Treatment of Young Offenders in Norway," 2 *Int'l. Rev. of Crim. Policy* (U. N.), 1952, 115; H. Goransson, "The Treatment of Criminals and Other Asocial Individuals (Sweden), 197 *Annals* (1938) and "The Treatment of Offenders in Sweden," 8 *Howard Journal* (1949–1953), 21; O. Kinberg, "Criminal Policy in Sweden during the Last Fifty Years," 24 *J. Crim. L. and Criminology* (1933), 313; C. M. Craven, "The Child Welfare Boards of Sweden," 8 *Howard Journal* (1949), 10; O. Nyquist, "How Sweden Handles Its Juvenile and Youth Offenders," 20 *Federal Probation* (1956), 36; and (especially important), T. Sellin, "Sweden's Substitute for the Juvenile Court," 261 *Annals* (1949), 137. — *Ed.*

in Norway and later imitated in all the Scandinavian countries. The councils were organized in Norway to carry out the provisions of a law of 1896 which provided that the term "neglected child" should be extended to cover not only children who because of the parents' or foster parents' depravity or negligence are found to be neglected, ill treated or morally depraved, deprived of educational opportunity or otherwise neglected, but also should include children who "have committed any punishable act showing depravation of morals or neglect." [1] By this act the delinquent child was entirely removed from the jurisdiction of the criminal courts, where he had been treated as a law breaker, and placed under the guardianship of the Child Welfare Council to be protected, reared and educated as might seem best in light of his own interest and those of the community.

This was essentially the same philosophy which motivated the establishment of the juvenile court in the United States. In the Scandinavian countries, however, the care and protection of the delinquent was entirely removed from the courts and made an administrative function, divested completely of the judicial punitive legalistic point of view which still permeates the operation of many juvenile courts in the United States.

The law provided for the establishment in each municipality or commune of at least one Council, although more than one may be provided for in larger communities such as Oslo, where there are four. In 1950 there were 744 Councils in the country, 680 in rural municipalities and 64 in towns and cities. As constituted prior to July 1, 1954, each Council consisted of seven members. Two of these, a local judge and the parish clergyman, served ex officio; the other five members were elected by the Commune Council (municipal legislative body) with the provision also that at least one member must be a physician and at least one must be a woman. Terms of service were for two years and service was regarded as a public duty which could not be refused and which was not compensated. In lieu of the local judge, the Government could appoint a permanent chairman with

[1] Hanne-Marie Tjensvoll, *The Treatment in Norway of Neglected and Refractory Children and Young Offenders*, Norwegian Joint Committee on International Social Policy, Ministry of Social Affairs, Oslo, 1950.

the qualifications of a judge who would serve as permanent administrative officer. This was commonly done in larger municipalities, such as Oslo, where the Council occupies permanent quarters and has the services of a trained probation staff and a corps of clerical workers. In smaller communes, with much less business, investigation and supervision is done by the members of the Council itself or with the assistance of volunteer workers.

In 1947–1953 the Child Welfare Council system has gone through the first radical overhauling since the adoption of the plan at the turn of the century.[2] The new law provides for the abolishment of the Child Welfare Councils, and the establishment in their place of Child Welfare Committees to exercise considerably wider functions. The Committees are to have extended functions in the protection of all classes of children in need of special care. Jurisdiction extends to age 18. These will include, not only delinquent and neglected children but those who present health problems, assistance cases, handicapped children and other categories for which other agencies have hitherto had responsibility. The following classes are mentioned specifically in the law as wards of the Committee:

1) children who are so treated or live under such conditions that their health (mental or physical) is likely to be impaired;
2) those who, thru breaking the law or other conduct, exhibit such lack of adjustment to their environment that special measures seem necessary;
3) children who have no one to support them or whose parents are unable to support them properly, and who are not otherwise properly cared for;
4) children who are sick or physically, mentally or otherwise handicapped and which do not have the care and treatment which they need.

The new Child Welfare Committees are to consist of five members, both men and women, chosen by the Communal authority, from among persons with a special understanding and interest in child welfare. Persons chosen are under obligation to serve unless over 60 years of age, or have already served one term of office.

In all cases involving custody, withdrawal of parental power and like matters the district-court or town judge shall sit ex officio as member of the Committee. Provision is also made for a local official in each County responsible for child welfare matters. The new law provides also that local administration of the Child Welfare law shall be supervised by the Ministry of Social Affairs. A State Child Welfare Council, of not less than five members, is to be appointed by the King to advise the Ministry in such affairs. Regulations and rules governing the placement of children, the inspection and supervision of children's institutions, supervision of foster homes are spelled out in the law. Jurisdiction over children who violate the law is essentially the same as that formerly enjoyed by the Child Welfare Councils.

As in most American juvenile courts, procedure is entirely informal and private. Members of the Council or Committee, under the guidance of the Chairman, question witnesses or direct queries to members of the probation staff familiar with the case. The child or his parents may be present, as the Council thinks wise. Parents have the legal right to appear, before the Council. Often the hearing takes the form of a sort of family council (as observed by the writer) with the parents seated on one side of the table, the child standing behind them, and the members of the Council seated on the other side. Parents are encouraged to ask questions both with respect to their assessment of the problem as well as to the decision and proposed plan. The family may retain counsel if they wish but there is little function for him to perform, since the hearing is in no sense a trial. The Council has powers of subpoena and may compel the attendance of witnesses. Under certain circumstances, parents or other relatives may be excused from giving evidence which might appear to be self incriminating.[3]

Records of the Council must be adequately kept and provision made for the collection of social, psychological and psychiatric data. Decisions of the Council must be preceded by the

---

2 *Instilling fra Barnevernkomiteen, I, Lov Om Barnevern*, Oslo, 1951 (Report of Child Welfare Committee, Law Relative to Child Care) Act of 17th July, 1953, respecting Child Welfare. Trans. by United Nations.

3 This is consistent with the principle in Norwegian law that no defendant nor an accomplice is allowed to give evidence under oath, nor is any child under 15 allowed to take an oath. The same rule applies to any witness whose weak intellect or retarded development might make clear understanding of the nature of the oath doubtful.

opinion on which they are based. If decision is made to remove the child from the home notice in writing must be served on the parents who may also express their opinion, either orally or in writing. Appeals from the decision of the Council may be had to the Ministry but not to the courts.

Problems of delinquency or neglect may come to the Council in a variety of ways. The police must refer all children under age 14 who come into their hands to the Council. If he believes it in the public interest the Prosecutor may waive prosecution of any person under 18, a practice which is almost universal between 14 and 16, and common up to age 18. Children may also be referred to the Council by the schools, the Public Health Councils, Public Assistance Boards, by employers, neighbors and, most often by parents themselves, who come to the Council for aid. The schools may refer refractory or unmanageable children who are a threat to the safety or welfare of other pupils or who seriously disturb the orderly school routine. Jurisdiction, once taken, extends to age 21 unless surrendered to some other child welfare or educational agency.

After a case is referred, investigation procedures are started. In the larger city Councils this function is performed by probation officers, both men and women, who visit the home and school, relatives, neighbors or others in a position to provide information. Complete physical examination is provided as a matter of routine. If the case warrants the child may be referred for either or both psychological or psychiatric observation. These professional services may be obtained from the school psychologists or psychiatrists or from the clinics supported by the Commune or the State as a part of the public health service. During the period while investigation is under way the child may be left in his own home, if this seems wise, placed in a boarding home or temporarily committed to the local "Observation School," or even left in the Psychiatric Division of the National Hospital. No disposition of the case is made until investigation is complete. It should be noted, of course, that complete examinations and investigations tend to be achieved only in those areas where facilities are available. In rural districts, and in the more isolated regions, members of the Councils do much of their own social investigation and must rely on local medical resources

for the physical examinations. Where psychiatric service is patently necessary, cases may be referred to Oslo or to other urban centers for specialized study. Since the major share of the population resides in the south third of the country, which contains almost all the larger urban centers, most of the children who need specialized service get it.

In dealing with the children several courses are open to the Council. The simplest, and the most common, is a warning to the child and to the parents. The warning generally takes the form of an oral admonition to the child and parents given by the Chairman of the Council in the presence of other members. The Chairman points out to the parents and the child the dangers of the course being followed and the penalties and consequences ultimately likely to flow from it. Promises of closer supervision from parents, and improvement in conduct from the child are commonly forthcoming and the case is closed unless reopened by future misconduct. One gets the impression that these "warnings" are primarily in the nature of a lecture with little done positively to make it possible for parents to carry out promises or children to keep out of mischief. The Chairman of the Oslo Council, however, reports that less than ten percent of the cases to whom warnings are administered ever again come to the attention of the Council. In a substantial number of cases no action is taken.

Where the nature of the offense calls for something more than a warning, or where the home and family situation warrant, the child may be placed on probation and left in his own home. In this event periodic home visits, counseling by the probation officer with the parents in seeking a solution for the child's problems, enlisting the aid of other agencies, securing public assistance when necessary, consultation with school authorities and other steps may be taken. Probation may continue as long as the Council feels necessary or up to age 21.

It is in connection with investigation and, especially with respect to supervision, that the Council feel themselves handicapped. As in the United States, funds are often lacking to permit the employment of sufficient staff to maintain adequate supervision. Case loads are often too heavy and "follow up" is neglected. Another difficulty is the scarcity of trained social workers and probation officers even if the funds for paying them were forthcoming. The latter difficulty is gradually being corrected as social work becomes established as a profession and as graduates of the State School of Social Work become available to fill the positions. In the rural areas, however, a great deal of the work of investigation and supervision falls on the members of the local Councils themselves or on the volunteers whom they can enlist as aids.

In many cases, however, the child cannot safely be left in his own home. This may grow out of the inadequacy and incompetence of the parents in dealing with the child or because the home itself imposes serious moral risks. In these cases probation is often accompanied with placement in either a foster home or in boarding homes. Such homes are selected only after careful investigation and approval by the Council. Homes of relatives, if suitable, are preferred and often used. Maintenance of family unity and responsibility is regarded as of supreme importance and use of the homes of grandparents or other relatives is believed to further this end. Where necessary small subventions, in homes where means are limited, are often granted by the Council to foster parents. Most normal children, who present no serious behavior problems, are provided for in this way. Later, if and when conditions warrant, the child may be returned to his own home. In Oslo, often the children who come to the Councils, are youngsters of parents who have recently moved into the city from the surrounding rural regions. In many cases grandparents, residing in the home communities, provide a resource for the care and protection of children whose parents are having a hard "go" of it in the city. Serious housing shortage and almost incredible overcrowding in the cities, both during and since the German occupation, have imposed great strains on the family.

Another interesting contrast with American attitudes and practices may be noted with respect to the use of public funds for securing home or institutional care for wards of the Councils. It seems to be taken for granted that Council funds should be used for boarding homes or for payments to foster parents, or even for payments to private institutions such as children's and youth "pensions," or children's homes. The Council may make payments to foster parents, to relatives such as grandparents, or even to parents, in cases where economic need

makes necessary employment of mothers outside the home, and where such employment might be inconsistent with the child's best interest.

In the event that home placement is not feasible resort must be had to institutional care. There are two kinds of institutions available to the Council, the coercive school and the school home. Placement in the institution is provided for in the Child Welfare Councils Act when the child "is so morally depraved that it would submit other children to harmful influence if it attended the ordinary school." [4]

The coercive school is designed for those children who present particularly difficult behavior problems. There are three of these institutions, two of them in Oslo, and one in Bergen. One in Stavanger has not been rebuilt since it was destroyed by fire in 1948. Originally conceived as disciplinary institutions, these schools are now developing into study centers where children may be placed for extended periods for careful study and observation as the basis for treatment. In Oslo the school for boys is now called Observation School. The number of boys has been reduced from 40 to 25. All are accepted entirely on the basis that they need expert study. The Superintendent of the institution is a specialist in behavior problems, thoroughly familiar with the literature in this field as evidenced by the extensive library with which his study was equipped, and quite conversant with trends in child welfare in the United States, England as well as other countries. A psychologist, nurses, teachers and matrons make up the staff which also has medical and psychiatric service from the Royal Hospital. The physical resources of the institution are not impressive; buildings are old, and the plant inadequate but there was a family atmosphere in the informal relations which prevailed between staff and the children which seemed to more than compensate for the lack of modern play ground or school and workshop. The role of father, in the Superintendent's relation to the boys, was illustrated in the interruption of our conference by a breathless and tousle-headed ten year old who had an immediate problem on which he needed advice and counsel from the Superintendent. Great emphasis is placed on keeping the school small, in creating as far as possible a family atmosphere, the avoidance of formal rules and

---

[4] H. M. Tjensvoll, *op. cit.*, p. 1.

resort to coercion only in the form which it would normally take in a family situation. In striking contrast with the situation in American institutions, was the calm way in which the runaway was dealt with. The only concern seemed to be to see to it that the lad should come to no harm, to secure his early return, and to diagnose the difficulties which were behind the running away. Children are committed to these institutions up to the age of 15, the folk school leaving age, but ordinarily do not remain for more than a year. The observation schools are operated and administered by the local Councils.

The school homes are designed for children without serious behavior problems but for whom special treatment and education is desirable. Many of them are backward children who seem to show more aptitude for acquiring manual and vocational skills than they do for the more literary type of training in the traditional school curriculum. Emphasis is placed on such subjects as agriculture, dairying, market gardening, carpentry, metal work and seamanship. The ordinary school curriculum is also included and, in cases where it seems desirable, the children may attend neighborhood schools. Learning proceeds at a more leisurely pace than in the ordinary schools and, since the school leaving age has been extended to 21, trade training can more readily be combined with the traditional school curriculum.

The school homes are administered and supervised by the Directorate of School Homes in the Ministry of Education and Ecclesiastical Affairs. In the 1953–54 session of the Parliament, however, a proposal to place control of these institutions in the Directorate of Special Schools was adopted. This will combine their administration with that for the schools for deaf, blind, feebleminded and otherwise handicapped children.

Some of the School Homes are operated by the State, one by a County, two by municipalities and one under private auspices. All are subject to inspection by the State Authority to see that standards are maintained. Since 1950 there has been a tendency to reduce the number of children cared for in these institutions and to divert the facilities toward other purposes. One of the two private school homes for boys has been closed as has one of the State Schools, and the total accommodations have been reduced from nearly six hundred to 420, 250 places for

boys and 170 for girls. The tendency also has been to reduce the number of pupils in each institution in keeping with a policy of creating a home rather than an institutional atmosphere. It should be noted that once a child is committed to a School Home the Council surrenders jurisdiction which passes to the Directorate of School Homes.

Finally, it is possible to place the child in a children's home. These institutions are designed, primarily, to care for normal children who have been neglected in their own homes, where homes have been broken by death or separation of parents, or where other conditions preclude care in the child's home or, temporarily while awaiting placement in a foster home. Between fifteen and twenty of these homes are supported by the Oslo Commune and nearly forty are managed under various auspices; by the Red Cross, The Norwegian Women's Public Health Association, by various religious denominations and by private individuals. All receive some support from public sources. The number of children per home varies from less than 10 to 80, although most of them have less than 30 children. Ages range from infancy to 21, with some homes caring for only very young children, others receiving youngsters of all ages. In many of the smaller homes it is the deliberate policy to take children of widely varying age to create a normal home situation in so far as possible. The homes are commonly operated by a middle aged couple who play the role of parents. Children attend neighborhood schools, the older ones help with household tasks, caring for younger children and contributing to a common enterprise. While less commonly used for the care of delinquent children, in cases where the child shows no serious behavior problems, is unlikely to disturb the routine of the home and seems likely to profit by its program, it may be placed in a home of this type. These homes are operated by the Child Welfare Agency of the Commune or receive partial support and are subject to its inspection.

No current data are available to reveal the present operations of the Child Welfare Councils. A 1950 report, prepared for the Norwegian Joint Committee on International Social Policy, supplies some information for 1947.[5] About 70 per cent of the 1244 cases dealt with by the

---

[5] *Ibid.*, pp. 12–18.

Councils for that year were referred for misconduct while 519 were referred as neglected. While it is impossible to separate the delinquent from the neglected children with respect to their treatment, about 140 or approximately 20 per cent of the delinquents, were committed to observation schools or school homes. More than two thirds appear to have been dealt with simply by warnings and admonitions.

A better picture of the operations of the Councils, as well as the outcome of various treatment policies has been presented in a number of studies.[6] The latest and most elaborate of these studies reports the results of a follow-up study of 1863 children, 668 girls and 1195 boys who were dealt with by the Councils in the five year period 1929 to 1933.[7] These children were followed to Dec. 1, 1948 with respect to later conduct as well as status in 1948. Records from the Child Welfare Council, the Folk-register, records of the Department of Justice, the records of fines from the Oslo Police Department and the Social Register of persons receiving any form of public aid, were utilized. It should be kept in mind that the study shows a pre-war and pre-depression record with respect to the measures adopted by the Councils and would not be representative of current policies.

The cases were almost evenly divided into two groups; a delinquent group and a neglected group. About one fourth of the delinquent group were removed from their homes of which the major share were committed to institutions, one fourth were left to the schools to deal with, and in about one third no more serious measures than a warning were followed. A considerably larger proportion of the neglected than the delinquent were removed from their own homes and a larger proportion of those removed were placed in foster homes rather than institutions.

The results of the follow-up study are not essentially different from the results of similar investigations in the United States [8] and give no great support for the notion that the Councils have solved the delinquency problem. In 1947–1948, the young adults who had been the wards of the Councils in 1929 to 1933, as compared with comparable sex and age groups of the city of Oslo were disproportionately concentrated in unskilled labor, were less frequently married, more frequently divorced, had been more frequently fined and imprisoned and were more frequently recipients of public assistance. Of the delinquent group two thirds approximately, had been fined, imprisoned or received public assistance. Of the neglected group the corresponding percentage was forty. The institutionalized children showed a far higher proportion of persons committed to penal or correctional institutions than was true for the ones who had been left in their own homes. Whether or not the large proportion of the subjects with "negative criteria of adjustment" (to use the author's phrase) was due to the selective influence of institutional commitment or to the results of the separation from home and family is not revealed.

The authors conclude their study with the suggestion that the creation of a single child welfare authority, with responsibility for all kinds of child welfare problems, could better serve the needs of children and be more completely removed from the punitive connotations which still, in the public mind, surround the Child Welfare Council. As mentioned above such an authority has now been created in the Child Welfare Committee which on July 1, 1954 took over all responsibility for the care and protection of children who are the special concern of the community.

In addition to attendance at meetings of the Council the author also had the opportunity for extended conferences with the Chairman and a number of members of the probation staff. He also was given permission for extended study of the case records of the Council. From the material so gathered the following brief account of a group of six related cases may illustrate more concretely than statistical studies can do, both the kinds of problems with which the Council (now the Committee) deals as well as the

---

[6] Signy Arctander and Sigurd Dahlstrom, *How Do the Council Children Fare* (Hvordan går det våre verjerådsbarn?) Oslo 1932. Signy Arctander, *Child Welfare Council Measures and their Results* (Verjeradsbehandlingen og dens resultater), Statsökonomisk Tidskrift, 1936 (S.97–294).

[7] Max Petersen and Egil Nilsen, *Results of Child Welfare Council Measures with Special Reference to Children's Environmental Background* (Verjeradsbehandlingens resultater I Forhold Til Barnas Miljöbakgrund) Oslo Commune, 1950.

[8] See studies by Sheldon and Eleanor Glueck, William Healy and Augusta Bronner, Belle Boone Beard.

methods resorted to and the community resources upon which it can rely.

THE RUSELKEN GANG

All the boys are involved as a group in a series of thefts covering a two year period. They vary in age from 8 to 13. A definite gang relationship with strong loyalty ties, group stealing, considerable skill and technique, division of the spoils, leader and follower relationships are reminiscent of delinquent behavior probably more common in America than in Scandinavian cities. The boys have been engaged for more than two years in stealing candy and cigarettes from kiosks, purses from women's bags in shopping centers and at sales. Pleasure boats lying in the harbor often have provided rich loot as have lockers in the public baths where wrist watches, purses and other goods have been stolen. The valuables have been sold or pawned and the money used for movies, cigarettes, rides in the amusement park and other childish pleasures. The boys have been referred to the Council by the police. The youngsters all attend the same public school and are all residents of the same neighborhood, an old and rather deteriorated section of the city in the harbor district, probably the poorest section of the city although hardly a slum area by American standards.

Case No. 1. The first boy, Leif S., is twelve years old. He lives with his mother, an older sister and her three children, an older brother and two younger children in an incredibly overcrowded four-room apartment. The father is employed outside the city and is seldom at home. The mother has a job as a washer woman on board ships in the harbor and is away from home a great deal.

The boy is described as small for his age, infantile in physical development and emotionality. He is easily led by other boys. The boy has had rheumatic fever and has spent some time in a "fresh air school." The mother suggests that he be placed with relatives at Vardal but the Council feels that he needs the systematic care and ordered regimen which can be provided at an "approved school" and orders him to be placed in the Orkeröd School for Boys.

At the institution the boy has made a good adjustment. He is very fond of his mother and writes to her often. He has visited at home several times. In the meantime his own home situation has considerably improved as the married sister has found quarters for her own family. Mother and other children are eager for Leif to return home. Decision of the council is to return the boy to his home, place him in a public school in a different part of the city, see to it that he receives special assistance in school in correcting deficiencies in arithmetic, and keep him under medical supervision. If protected he should do well.

Case No. 2. The second boy is Erland S., also twelve years old. His offences are essentially the same as those of the others; snatching purses in the underground station, rifling women's handbags, shop lifting, etc.

The parents are separated and the boy lives with his mother in a small apartment. The father is a carpenter but works only sporadically. He is a chronic alcoholic and has been arrested numerous times for drunkenness, and peace disturbance. A psychiatrist reports no psychosis although mental illness feigned to escape prosecution; emotional instability. Mother vacillates in attitude toward the boy between indifference and extreme overprotection with a belittling of the boy's offences as mere mischief. She wishes the boy placed with relatives who reside in a nearby suburban community.

The school reports the boy as aggressive and brutal toward other children, very poor student, not stupid but completely indifferent to his studies. The boy smokes habitually, is often truant from school, stays out late, absents himself for long weekends which he spends with grandparents. He is further described in the school report as "crafty, sly and a mischief maker." The mother works outside the home and is gone much of the time. She has failed to report for conference with school authorities when requested to do so and seems indifferent to the welfare of her son.

The critical nature of the case and lack of any home resources forced a decision to commit the boy immediately to the Geitmyra Observation School for study and treatment. At the Observation School the boy does well in making social adjustment although his limited intelligence (I.Q. 86) handicaps him in his school work. While often exhibiting aggressive tendencies, contact with him is quite easily established. The roots of his trouble seem to lie in the conflict between loyalties. He defends his drunken father against the mother's criticism. He responds well to friendship, accepts discipline when he feels himself at fault but protests vociferously if he feels unfairly treated. The Superintendent recommends that he should be allowed to return home and resume his studies at the local school.

During the year conditions in the home have greatly improved. The father has discontinued drinking and works steadily as does the mother. The apartment is clean and well kept. The boy has visited at home on a number of occasions. He has rejected advances from his old associates. The council, however, feels that return home may be premature and, at the mother's suggestion, decides to place the boy with maternal grandparents in a rural village on the outskirts of Oslo. The grandparents live on a small "gaard" (farm). They appear devoted to the boy who has often visited with them and are willing to accept responsibility for his care. A contract with the council is drawn, the grandfather is appointed foster father, an agreed payment established, and the boy is moved to the home. Here he does well for a time, especially in connection with the activities of the farm, the care of animals and other farm chores. School adjustment, however, is a different matter; progress is slow and painful and the boy is unhappy, the traditional curriculum is unsuited to a boy with limited intelligence and the upshot of the matter is a request from the boy himself to be transferred back to the Observation School, a step which is ordered by the council. Here the record leaves him.

Case No. 3. The third boy is Olaf N., also thirteen years old. He lives with his father and step mother in a neatly furnished apartment in a middle class neighborhood. The father is occupied as a legal counselor, income is adequate to provide a stable economic foundation for the family; family relationships appear to be congenial. The boy is described as tall, overgrown and lanky; lazy in disposition, easily led by other boys. He is a failure in school where he is also reported as a nuisance.

The sources of the boy's difficulty are not clear. Some years earlier the father had been involved in some kind of shady deal which had resulted in a conviction and three-year suspended prison sentence. It is not known to what extent this circumstance may have influenced the boy. School failure seems related to low intelligence, lack of interest in "literary" subjects and arithmetic and revolt against the monotony and routine of the school.

After consultation there is agreement with the parents to place the boy on a nearby farm home. An interest in farm animals and liking for the country seems to have been the principal reason for placement. The foster parents are middle-aged people with a boy of their own of approximately the same age as Olaf. At last report (about a year after referral) the boy seems to be doing well in so far as home adjustment goes. He is liked by the foster parents, assumes responsibility for tasks about the farm and is, himself, satisfied. In school work, however, he is deficient and backward. The teacher recommends placement in a "help class" but such facilities are lacking in the village school.

Case No. 4. Gustaf A. is ten years old. He has been stealing from boats in the harbor with the other boys. The family consists of father, mother and two sisters, aged eleven and thirteen. The father works steadily as a machinist and makes a good living. He is a stern disciplinarian, completely disgusted with the boy and quite willing that he be punished. The mother appears to be a cowed and weak character, is extremely protective of the boy against his father, belittles the boy's offenses and blames associates for his behavior.

In school Gustaf is described as "the worst boy in his class"; insolent, disobedient, cruel to other children and completely beyond control. School authorities request his removal.

There is sentiment in the council for placement in the Observation School, but the mother's pleas are allowed to prevail and the boy is finally placed in a "fresh air school" in the environs of the city. No adequate explanation is made for the decision. Rather scanty records indicate reasonably satisfactory progress.

Case No. 5. Sven E., boy No. 5, is only nine years of age. Delinquencies are the same as those of the others. School authorities report him as a most difficult case. He is backward in his studies, a disturbing element in the school, group leader in all sorts of mischief, steals from other children, failure in all subjects. Removal is recommended.

The family situation is most unfavorable. Both parents have been arrested for drunkenness. At the time of referral the parents are separated as they have done numerous times in the past. The child has shifted about between parents and relatives, although at the time of report he is living in one room with the mother who is employed. Psychological and psychiatric examination report low normal intelligence but emotionally unstable. Projective tests show much insecurity, fear and hostility, lively fantasy life, poor powers of abstraction. Worry over father's imprisonment has contributed to boy's insecurity. Mother and relatives reluctantly agree to temporary placement in children's home.

Three months later parents propose a new plan. Father and mother have been reconciled and will rent a small apartment. Father promises to discontinue drinking, and has obtained steady employment as a waiter in a first class restaurant. Mother will discontinue outside employment and make a home for the boy. The boy himself is overjoyed at the prospects, especially in light of the bicycle he has been promised. Reluctantly the council agrees to go along with the plan although the child welfare worker fears it has been specially concocted to get the boy out of the home. In spite of misgivings, however, the plan works out well. A report three months after the move reports the boy doing well, the father has worked steadily and has had only one drink with his pals at Easter time. The boy is back in his own school. His teacher reports a complete transformation which is attributed to improvement in conditions at home. No further difficulties, either at home or at school, appear in the case record.

Case No. 6. The last case is Jan K., thirteen years of age. Jan presents the most difficult problem of all. He appears to have been the leader of the gang and seems to present even more serious difficulties than those apparent in the other cases. Immediate placement in the Observation School, pending study and investigation of both boy and home situation, is the first step.

The father is, at present, at sea. He presents a whole train of problems: alcoholism, stomach ulcers, emotional instability. He leaves home for prolonged periods, has tried numerous jobs and failed at all, is off to sea with each family crisis. Life is just too much to cope with. The mother is a serious and conscientious person, deeply religious and greatly concerned over the boy who is just too much for her. She has held a series of unskilled jobs and at time of report was employed as scrubwoman in one of the large banks of the city. The family moved into Oslo from a rural district about ten years ago. Besides Jan, there are two older brothers, neither of whom has ever been in any trouble.

Jan is described as hostile, defiant, boasts of his misdeeds, proclaims his intention to run away from any school where he may be placed. Psychological tests show an I.Q. of 76 and mental age of 9.7. Personality described as impulsive, defiant and aggressive.

In his reaction to placement Jan has fulfilled his threats. He ran away from the Observation School the same day he was first placed there. Tried out in the Fresh Air School he created so much disturbance that his removal was requested. His next placement was in a home for boys (Children's Pension) privately operated. From this institution he has run away several times. He does poor work in his class, is jealous toward other children, an attitude which he has exhibited toward his brothers in his own home. Parents of other children at the home fear his influence over their children and have asked his transfer. While at this institution he is under care of a psychiatrist whom he sees each week. The last entry reports transfer to an Approved School. No progress. Prognosis poor.

The cases described above give us some insight into the kinds of behavior problems with which the council is faced and the institutions and agencies on which it relies for care and guidance in the treatment program. Probably those chosen represent more difficult problems than the average case would present. They do illustrate the relatively non-punitive atmosphere in which the Child Welfare Council operates, the flexibility with which it may experiment with various kinds of treatment programs, the wide use of psychological–psychiatric service, and medical services, and the different types of institutions available for temporary as well as permanent care.

SECTION II — BASIC LEGAL ISSUES

NOT ONLY IN ITS EARLY HISTORY but also in more recent years has the juvenile court movement been subjected to criticism on the ground that its procedures, although designedly benign and motivated by the lofty aim of protecting and rehabilitating, rather than punishing, the endangered child, too readily invite abuse. The proceedings in a juvenile court are alleged in the statutes to be non-criminal [1]; yet there is a serious problem whether even a child in court for protection and therapy rather than retributive punishment should be deprived of certain basic constitutional and procedural protections. Among the questions that have arisen in the decisions are the following:

(a) How specific should the law be in defining the types of antisocial behavior which constitute delinquency? Shall all types of "delinquency" be similarly processed in the courts?

(b) How specific should the petition initiating delinquency proceedings be?

(c) Should the child be afforded the familiar constitutional protections of a criminal trial, especially the privilege against self-incrimination?

(d) What shall be the nature of the "hearing" to prove the status of delinquency (or neglect)?

(e) Shall hearsay evidence be admissible, considering that it is a judge, rather than a jury, who ordinarily is the trier of fact in juvenile cases? For example, shall the judge be permitted to consult, *prior to or during* the hearing on delinquency status, the previous delinquency record of the child and the probation officer's investigation report?

(f) How shall fairness in the disposition (treatment) phase be assured?

(g) What about the court practice of supervising delinquents "unofficially"?

(h) Shall the delinquent be afforded both the right and the opportunity of counsel?

Such questions do not of course exhaust the crucial issues involved in juvenile court proceedings. In connection with all of them, is it sufficient for the court to take it for granted that, because the statutory aim is protective and therapeutic rather than punitive, the pursuit of that aim has in fact been implemented by sound institutions and by dedicated and informed personnel? For the protective devices in the proceedings ought partly to be influenced by the *consequences* of an adjudication of delinquency. Is the

---

[1] Bloch and Flynn, among others, have formulated the basic differences between the juvenile court and adult criminal court procedures: summons instead of warrant; petition on behalf of the child as opposed to indictment or information; detention separate from adults or in a specialized children's institution, instead of in jail (or release on bail); hearing to establish state's right to intervene on behalf of the child, as opposed to trial on specific charge to determine guilt; infrequent use of counsel, versus usual employment of counsel; infrequent participation of prosecuting attorney, versus invariable presentation of state's case by prosecutor; private hearing as opposed to public trial; informal hearing, at which both social and legal data are used and proof is by preponderance, as opposed to trial under strict rules of evidence with requirement of proof beyond a reasonable doubt; very infrequent use of jury, as opposed to right to jury trial; occasional consultation of social investigation report before hearing, as opposed to use of investigation report only after establishment of guilt; disposition aimed at treatment, as opposed to sentence which not infrequently has a punitive aim; emphasis on need of aid to and guidance of child in contrast with emphasis on protection of society. H. A. Bloch, and F. T. Flynn, *Delinquency: The Juvenile Offender in America Today*, New York, Random House, 1956, pp. 340–341.

average "correctional school," for example, in fact a place of understanding, therapy and rehabilitation, or is it more like a "junior prison"? [2]

These and similar questions have been raised in recent decisions and comments.[3] Such issues are sharpened and made realistic in the cases assembled in this section.

Let us consider some of them, not dogmatically but to set the stage for the cases that follow:

(a) Perhaps much of the disagreement and inefficiency in juvenile court administration is attributable to the basic confusion in the *legislative definitions* of the types of behavior patterns to be embraced in juvenile court jurisdiction. These vary from acts which, if committed by adults, would be crimes, to conditions or states of undesirable behavior on the part of children (such as associating with bad companions), to repetitive or habitual conduct deemed undesirable (such as frequent truanting), to actions against parents and other adults for neglect or abuse of children or contributing to their delinquency. In the background of this admixture is the desire to operate in the atmosphere and with the aim of the historic juvenile court: to employ kindly, non-adversary, non-traumatic, informal procedures, and to exercise at all stages the protective and anticipatory instruments of preventive justice — an intervention in the life of the child at a point when serious damage to personality, character, and status can be avoided or repaired.

But however benevolent the motives may be, the basic requirement of justice — adequate proof of the state's right to intervene — cannot and should not be ignored.

Juvenile court statutes can be classified into those which resort to detailed enumeration of the specific prohibited acts proof of which will result in a finding of delinquency, and those which, in more vague terms, emphasize habituation in truancy from school or home, lack of controllability, incorrigibility, chronic disobedience, habitual deportment in a way to endanger morals, etc. Both types, of course, also include violations of state, county or town laws which would be crimes if committed by adults; but the former goes into considerable detail regarding specific acts or courses and locales of behavior that should be proved, while the latter (and to some extent the former, as well) couches its prohibitions of childhood misconduct in such broad terms as to allow considerable flexibility of proof. Yet reasonable specificity in the definition of prohibited behavior is generally deemed indispensable to fair play and due process of law; and vagueness is a temptation to intervene for a child's presumed good, even without proof of delinquency.

(b) Apart from the statute, it has been urged by some that laxity of procedure and proof in juvenile courts is traceable largely to looseness, in the *petition*, of the allegations describing specific offenses or a course of endangering conduct or of misconduct.[4]

---

[2] "There are things going on, methods of discipline being used in the state training schools of this country, that would cause the warden of Alcatraz to lose his job if he used them on his prisoners. There are practices that are a daily occurrence in some of our state training schools that are not permitted in the prisons or penitentiaries of the same states. There are many states in which the discipline is more humane, more reasonable, in the prison than it is in the state training school." A. MacCormick, "The Essentials of a Training School Program," *Matching Scientific Advance with Human Progress*, National Council of Juvenile Court Judges, Pittsburgh Conference, May 1–3, 1950, 15. See, also, Articles 128, 129, 133 hereof.

[3] The latest and one of the most adequate articles on the subject, prepared as a student exercise in the Editor's seminar on the Problem of Juvenile Delinquency, is by J. J. Rappeport and is entitled "Determination of Delinquency in the Juvenile Court: Suggested Approach," 1958 *Wash. U.L.Q.* (1958), 124–166. For an extract thereof, see Article 104 *infra*. For other good articles discussing the major issues, see M. G. Paulsen, "Fairness to the Juvenile Offender," 41 *Minnesota L.R.* (1957), 547–576; S. Rubin, "Protecting the Child in the Juvenile Court," 43 *J. Crim. L., Criminology and Police Science* (1952), 425–440. *Compare A Standard Juvenile Court Act*, N.P.P.A., 1949.

[4] "Without a definite charge of a particular offense, rules of relevancy of evidence become impossible to apply; anything that the juvenile may be alleged to have done that would reflect badly on his character becomes 'relevant' to such vague standards. Without a specific charge

A great pioneer in the juvenile court movement, the late Judge Julian W. Mack, stated, in respect to the earliest juvenile court statute, that "The problem for determination by the judge is not, Has this boy or girl committed a specific wrong, but What is he, how has he become what he is, and what had best be done in his interest and in the interest of the State to save him from a downward career." [5] However, experience has shown that to put the problem of the judge as a choice between the above two alternatives is an oversimplification; for, regardless of the rehabilitative aims of juvenile court proceedings, fair play demands that the act or course of behavior which the law defines as delinquency be clearly stated and reasonably proved in the individual case, *before* the benign therapeutic influences of the court are brought into play.

(c) One difficulty with juvenile court adjudications is the fact that, despite the existence of special tribunals for children for over half a century, there is still some difference of opinion, from jurisdiction to jurisdiction, regarding the extent and the details of constitutional safeguards. Some jurisdictions accept as their chart and compass the liberal provisions of the pioneering Pennsylvania *Fisher* case [6] to the effect that a bare minimum of constitutional protections of the kind assured to adults accused of crime is called for in the juvenile court. The familiar argument of the decisions is that usual constitutional guaranties are superfluous since such a tribunal acts for the state as *parens patriae* and its aim is not the ascertainment of "guilt," with infliction of retributive punishment, but rather the determination of a status dangerous (or even only potentially hazardous) to the welfare of the child, with the goals of prevention, protection, education and rehabilitation. Other jurisdictions are much more sensitive to familiar rights of due process of law, a preoccupation that seems to have gained momentum in recent years. The writers of certain recent decisions (*e.g.*, the Iowa *Breon* case [7] [1952], the District of Columbia *Poff* case [8] [1955], and several strong dissenting opinions in *People* v. *Lewis*,[9] and *In re Holmes* [10] are disturbed that some judges tend to ignore the fact that, irrespective of the noble ideals expressed in statutes and decisions, there is in truth some stigma attached to a finding of delinquency by a juvenile court; that commitment of a child to an institution is a serious matter for himself and for his parents, and that it can and does result in a very real and sometimes lengthy deprivation of a child's freedom; that therefore the adjudication of even the non-criminal status of delinquency should be based on the observance of most, if not all, of the constitutional protections enjoyed by adults accused of crime.

One example of criticism has been that leveled against the practice of ignoring the privilege against self-incrimination by not notifying the child that he cannot be compelled to testify at the hearing. This example illustrates how difficult it is to choose among alternatives. It is a question of balancing values. Normally, the warning to a child that he need not tell the judge about the act or course of behavior alleged in the petition can do more harm than good when it is borne in mind that the motivation of the whole proceeding is the protection of the child; that he is not on criminal trial; that the petition is not an indictment charging him with crime but a document which will be used to determine whether he falls into a class that the court is set up to protect and rehabilitate. It must be borne in mind that, historically, the privilege against self-incrimination derives from the accusatorial, adversary type of proceeding. Moreover, the child who testifies cannot later be indicted for a crime because of information he

---

the juvenile has no opportunity to know with what accusations he is charged and hence is deprived of the right to marshal evidence in his defense. Further, in states where a delinquency adjudication is appealable, his rights on appeal are diluted since the vagueness of these terms is such as to convey an indeterminate discretion on trial judges applying them." S. M. Hermans, 48 *J. Crim. L., Criminology and Police Science* (1958), 594. See Article 83 of this book.

[5] J. Mack, "The Juvenile Court," 23 *Harv. L. Rev.* (1909), 104.

[6] Article 54 in this book.   [7] Article 79 in this book.   [8] Article 57 in this book.
[9] Article 55 in this book.   [10] Article 77 in this book.

freely gave at a juvenile court hearing. If, however, the statute provides that the juvenile can later be remanded to an adult criminal court, or if he can be punished after the juvenile authorities have surrendered control, it would seem preferable to afford him the privilege against self-incrimination.[11]

(d) Some critics have been blunt about the failure of certain courts, in their understandable zeal for the "social approach," to assure the familiar trial protections to *hearings* involving delinquents and their parents. Thus, former Chief Justice Cobb of the New York City Court of Domestic Relations, decried the tendency in the following caustic words in a speech in 1945 before the Court of Domestic Relations, the Association of the Bar, and the County Lawyers' Association:

> Become legalistic for the occasion, the supporters of the unrestricted social processes in a court of law for children and their parents, have embraced the catchwords *parens patriae* and *chancery* as something equivalent to little or no legal restraint so that they may cast the beneficent safeguards of due process of law into the limbo of forgotten things. Nothing could be more fallacious . . . Children must be duly adjudicated before a children's court can assume authority . . .
>
> The appallingly perverted doctrine of *parens patriae*, so specious that it has wheedled the judiciary and even cast its spell over some courts of appeal, has in it the germ of case-work domination. It has led to the legal baptism by legislatures of youths up to voting age as children, and has made a rubber stamp in some states of the judicial function to the point that it has well nigh surrendered to social processes in the guise of "probation," instead of jealously protecting both child and parent from infringement of their constitutional rights and personal privileges. Both children and insane are wards of the state, but are they to be prejudged by determining them to be such without regard to forms of law? [12]

And Arthur T. Vanderbilt, the late Chief Justice of the Supreme Court of New Jersey, has said in a similar vein:

> In their zeal to care for children neither juvenile judges nor welfare workers can be permitted to violate the Constitution, especially the Constitutional provisions as to due process that are involved in moving a child from its home. The indispensable elements of due process are: first, a tribunal with jurisdiction; second, notice of a hearing to the proper parties; and finally, a fair hearing. All three must be present if we are to treat the child as an individual human being and not to revert, in spite of good intentions, to the more primitive days when he was treated as a chattel.[13]

---

[11] It should be pointed out that strict adherence to the privilege is not necessarily indispensable to fair play. Thus Cardozo, J. in Palko v. Connecticut, 1937, 302 U.S. 319, 58 S. Ct. 149, 82 L. Ed. 288 (holding that the protections of the Fourteenth Amendment do not necessarily embrace the prohibition of double jeopardy in the Fifth Amendment) points out: "Few would be so narrow or provincial as to maintain that a fair and enlightened system of justice would be impossible without them. What is true of jury trials and indictments is true, also, as the cases show, of the immunity from compulsory self-incrimination. This too might be lost, and justice still be done. Indeed, today as in the past there are students of our penal system who look upon the immunity as a mischief rather than a benefit, and who would limit its scope, or destroy it altogether. No doubt there would remain the need to give protection against torture, physical or mental. Justice, however, would not perish if the accused were subject to a duty to respond to orderly inquiry."

[12] Cobb, "Social and Legal Aspects of the Children's Court" (mimeographed), quoted in P. Tappan, *Comparative Survey on Juvenile Delinquency*, Part I, North America, United Nations Department of Social Affairs, Division of Social Welfare, ST/SOA/1/Rev. 1, New York, 1958, p. 117.

[13] A. T. Vanderbilt, in foreword to Maxine B. Virtue's *Basic Structure of Children's Services in Michigan*, Ann Arbor, Mich.: The American Judicature Society, 1953, p. x. See, also, F. E. Ellrod, Jr., and D. H. Melany, "Juvenile Justice: Treatment of Travesty?", 11 *U. Pitt. L. Rev.* (1950), 277–287; T. W. Cashel, Note: "Juvenile Courts: Applicability of Constitutional Safeguards and Rules of Evidence to Proceedings: *In re Holmes*," 379 Pa. 599, 109 A. 2d 523 (1954), 41 *Cornell L.Q.* (1955), 147–154.

Regarding the requisite of a "fair hearing," the outstanding authority on the law of evidence, Wigmore, puts the situation in these words:

> The procedure devised for juvenile courts is apt and enlightened. Nevertheless, the promoters of that legislation in their enthusiasm for its benefits and their determination to eliminate the conditions of the usual criminal court, have gone to the borderline of prudence in their iconoclasm. In the most advanced type of statute, the orthodox rules of trial evidence have been riddled as with a reformative machine-gun. The record of conviction in such a court can never be used elsewhere . . . The record of moral delinquencies can be examined and used for determining his present guilt . . . The hearsay reports of probation officers and others can be used without calling them to be examined . . . The courtroom may be closed and the hearing held in private . . . The party may be subjected to a physical and mental examination . . . The child may be compelled to answer as to his own crimes, past and present . . . And, finally, the *testimony can be heard in the child's absence.*
>
> . . . And for all of these measures a good deal can be said, — for some of them, everything . . . A technical enforcement of the orthodox rule for every detail of the proof need not be urged. But that the judge should have the *power* to commit to long detention any person without giving the person *any opportunity to hear the substance of the testimony against him,* is fundamentally unsound and practically dangerous. That provision should be eliminated from those statutes, and no judge in practice should allow himself to employ it.[14]

Elsewhere Wigmore points out that

> logically and practically, it [a juvenile court] is not bound in law to observe the jury-trial rules of Evidence.[15] Nevertheless, it deals with adults in their relation to dependent and delinquent children, and must therefore at times employ repressive or compulsory measures which approach the border line of penalty. For this reason, and because the responsibilities involve serious need of caution, it becomes a question how far the judge should consider himself morally bound to observe at least the fundamental framework of the jury-trial rules. There is constant pressure from lay advisers to eliminate "technicalities." On the other hand, since the juvenile-court methods are due to be extended gradually to adult offenders in some fields, it is needful to build up a system that will not depart too radically from accepted traditions of criminal procedure.[16]

Wigmore suggests that there has been relatively little adjudication of the issue of exactly and specifically how far the proceedings in a juvenile court can be "socialized," and that "legislatures have been slow to intervene by statutes." Moreover, the legislation is very vague. One example Wigmore cites is a clause in the laws of the Dominion of Canada to the effect that juvenile court proceedings "may be as informal as the circumstances will permit, consistently with a due regard for the administration of justice." A provision is quoted from Puerto Rico, to the effect that any case "may in the discretion of the Court be conducted informally." The illustration from North Carolina is that the court shall "determine the case in a summary manner," but may make "rules to regulate the procedure," while an extract from Rhode Island legislation

---

[14] J. Wigmore, *A Treatise on the Anglo-American System of Evidence in Trials at Common Law,* Third Edition, Boston, Little, Brown and Co., 1940, Vol. V, p. 145.

[15] Citing Mary E. Richmond's famous *Social Diagnosis,* Wigmore includes a quotation by her of Flexner and Baldwin: "The best interests of the child make it necessary for the court to consider hearsay and other evidence of a more or less informal kind which would ordinarily under strict rules of evidence be excluded. It is of the utmost importance that the court should avail itself of just the kind of evidence that the investigator [the probation officer] presents. If it should finally be determined that the laws as drawn do not permit the introduction of such evidence, express provision should be inserted in the statutes allowing its use." Wigmore, *op. cit.,* Vol. I, p. 113.

[16] *Ibid.,* Vol. I, p. 101.

provides that the juvenile court "need not be bound by the technical rules of evidence in receiving or admitting testimony." More specifically, a Missouri provision is that in proceedings governing delinquents when charged with crime, "the practice and procedure . . . for criminal cases shall govern," otherwise the procedure "customary in proceedings in equity." [17]

Thus there is a variety of provisions, most of them not too clear as to where the line should be drawn between traditional adversary criminal court proceedings and the "informal hearing" concept of the juvenile court. A wise judge can get at the truth while conducting a fair hearing, and an experienced judge may be assumed to be trained in making allowances for the limited value of weak proof, — something to which a jury would ordinarily not be so sensitive.[18] But the decisions show that serious problems nevertheless continue to arise.

(e) A major ground of criticism by lawyers has been the practice, in a number of courts, of using the social investigation report, an unsworn statement, as a basic source of information on which to determine the issue of delinquency.[19] In the case of neglect, this may be desirable, since the social investigation is intended to be a comprehensive report of the parent–child relationships, the parents are competent to state their side of the matter, and it would be too difficult and time-consuming to require first-hand testimony on many details of parent–child relationships. But in the case of delinquency, use of the report as the chief source of information can be unfair to the child. *In re Mantell* [20] presents the issue. Other cases illustrate different varieties of hearsay.

Loftiness of the motives of a juvenile court can be an insufficient exchange for hearsay or neighborhood gossip or the inability of the child to examine the witnesses from whom the social investigator obtained his information. This is especially true where the basis of delinquency is not some specific offense but a vague, general standard such as "waywardness" or "incorrigibility," involving a course of behavior the interpretation of which entails much subjective judgment. Usually, there is other evidence in addition to the probation officer's or clinician's report; but the danger of exclusive or major reliance on reports of this kind is shown by cases (e.g., *In re Mantell* [21] in which the appellate court reversed the finding of delinquency when the juvenile court did not have before it other reliable evidence.

It may be that a distinction should be drawn between two basic types of delinquency: that which involves proof of an act which, had an adult been charged with it, would be a felony, and the other, vaguer types of "delinquency" encountered in the statutory definitions, such as being "incorrigible," or "ungovernable," or "habitually disobedient and beyond the control of parents," or "repeated runaway from home," "habitual truancy," "habitual use of profane language," etc. It is true that both the

---

[17] Recent legislation distinguishes between counties with a population under 50,000, which may establish their own rules, and those over 50,000 wherein courts are bound to follow criminal procedure in cases in which the delinquent is charged with violating a criminal statute, and equity proceedings in other cases. Mo. Ann. Stat. 211:340, 211: 020 (1947). Outside of the matter of convenience, it is difficult to justify this kind of distinction based on a population differential.

[18] Some states may, a few must, provide a jury in children's cases when asked. Sec. 17 of the *Standard Juvenile Court Act* provides that there shall be no jury.

[19] Such material is, of course, of the utmost importance in the constructive disposition of the case and in designing a treatment plan, once the delinquency *status* has been lawfully established; it can be unfair at the stage prior to the finding of delinquency. For the distinction between these stages in adult criminal cases, see *Williams* v. *New York*, 337 U.S. 241, 69 S. Ct. 1079, 93 L. Ed. 1337 (1949). It can, of course, also be unfair even at the disposition stage, if the pre-sentence investigation is based largely on unverified data or neighborhood gossip. The report should be open to consultation by counsel or parents, under court control.

[20] Article 80 in this book. For other faulty proof involving hearsay, see Article 77 hereof.

[21] Article 80. See, also, 43 A.L.R. 2d 1128, 1141–43 (1955); *Ford* v. *State*, 122 Ind. App. 315, 104 N.E. 406 (1952) (custody).

delinquency status and the plan of treatment decided upon can be the same in the two types of cases; but perhaps the manner of proof ought to be different. For the first category — that involving commission of a specific act which would be a crime if committed by an adult, and therefore more stigmatic, — more formal proceedings, yet of a kind to be readily interpreted to the child and his parents (as is the case in English practice),[22] might be required, involving, primarily, the exclusion from consideration on the instant case of the investigation report by the probation officer and including, in situations where this is demanded, a modified form of jury trial. For the second category, which often involves questions of parental supervision and essentially social material, the report might well form an important source of proof of delinquency status involving habituation in a course of prohibited, or endangering, but not criminalistic, behavior.

It may be true that some such differentiation is made at present by certain judges who have had considerable experience in coping with varieties of juvenile delinquency.

The above suggestion regarding the procedural separation of that form of delinquency which is based on a serious antisocial act from the other forms may not be acceptable. The idea involves a seeming inconsistency between, on the one hand, the "legalistic" conception of delinquency which, more superficially, emphasizes the particular criminal act, and the social and psychiatric, which regards the behavior as "symptomatic." However, the inconsistency exists only if we assume that the legal point of view, which stresses the importance of constitutional and procedural safeguards against abuse of power exercised even with the finest motives of prevention, protection and rehabilitation, must necessarily be the same as the clinical point of view, which looks upon the particular act as but one symptom of a deeper and more permeative personal and social disharmony. The legal emphasis is necessary as a convenient and fair basis for determining the authority of the state to intervene in the first place. On the other hand, the data in the more penetrating and widespread (yet more impressionistic than precise) social and psychiatric reports do not readily lend themselves to the type of sharp and limited definition and proof necessary in a legal proceeding; and they can best come into play once delinquency has been established by fair legal process.

There is also a tendency in the thinking of some outstanding juvenile court authorities as well as social workers to foster the abolition of the legal distinction between the delinquent child and the neglected child, both groups of children having in common the fundamental need of care by and protection of the state. In the 1949 Standard Juvenile Court Act and in a few state statutes it is provided the petition simply allege that the child comes within the purview of the Juvenile Court Act, detailing the facts (whether, in other jurisdictions, these spell out "delinquency" or "neglect") which bring him within the ambit of the statute. It is argued by those who favor consolidation of these forms of status and conduct which come to the attention of a juvenile court, that the sharp separation of delinquent from neglected children arose at a time when knowledge of the causes of maladjustment was limited and therefore it was assumed that there is a basic difference between delinquent and neglected children, a distinction that has been reflected both in court procedures and in the specialization of institutional facilities for delinquent, or for neglected, children. Much modern thinking inclines to the belief that ordinarily the acts comprising delinquency are, fundamentally, manifestations of parental neglect.

Historically, however, the English decisions cited in support of the court's acting as *parens patriae* for the Crown did not involve the commission, on the part of the child, of acts which were criminal. But apart from historical considerations, some authorities insist on retention of the distinction between a charge of delinquency (which involves

---

[22] On English procedure, see Article 52 in this book, and consult J. A. F. Watson, *The Child and the Magistrate, J. Cape,* London, 1950, pp. 55–70; see, also, the 1933 English Children's and Young Persons Act, 23 Geo. 5, Ch. 12.

the conduct of a child) and a petition alleging neglect (which is directed against its parents [23]). Basic needs in neglect cases are, unfortunately, not supplied or suppliable at present in many juvenile courts; namely, constructive family casework, psychotherapeutic aid and wholesome child-placement facilities. Where such social resources do exist, it would seem better that they be left to trained social-work administrative direction than conducted by a court.

Perhaps the troubles of proof derive from the failure of judges to draw a sharp enough line between the delinquency-determining aspect of the proceedings and the sentencing aspect. The motive for this is understandable: many judges have tended to adopt a sort of clinical attitude which is in harmony with the best thought in the psychiatric and other behavioral fields; namely, that the single act which, had it been performed by an adult would have been deemed a crime, should properly be regarded as only symptomatic of deeper-lying personality and character involvements. Such juvenile court judges, in assessing the issue of delinquency or non-delinquency, therefore wish to take account of a great deal of social, psychologic and psychiatric data throwing light on what is believed to be the underlying problem that brought the boy into court. On the other hand, certain critics contend that it is elementarily unfair for a judge, without a jury, to determine the fundamental issue of the boy's delinquency status — the issue on which rests its authority to deprive him of his freedom and his parents of his custody in the first place — on the basis of a great deal of information, including the boy's past delinquencies, which may affect the judge's decision on whether the boy really committed the act or pursued the course of conduct complained of in the *instant* case, and which involves matter that would be excluded at a criminal trial in a court for adults.

A sharp separation of the status-determining aspect from the dispositional aspect of juvenile court procedure clarifies the evidential issue. In the former, the adjudication of the fact of delinquency is involved. Where the act on which the delinquency status is predicated is admitted — which is usually the case — the judge can readily pass to the second phase, in which social and psychiatric data are relevant to the disposition and the treatment plan. Where, however, the delinquent act is denied (or there is a question of whether the parents' behavior constitutes the "neglect" envisaged by the statute), an opportunity should be afforded for a reasonable proof of the basic issue. The evidence should be at least of the probative force required in a civil proceeding; and, unlike the situation in a criminal trial, it would seem adequate in this type of fact-determination that the measure of proof should be a fair preponderance instead of proof beyond a reasonable doubt, with opportunity for appeal from findings of fact as well as law.

But such a generalization does not specify just how the line between a criminal trial and a juvenile court delinquency hearing should be drawn; and herein arises a major difficulty and source of complaint. For example, in *In re Holmes* [24] the Supreme Court of Pennsylvania went so far as to state that, "Even from a purely technical standpoint hearsay evidence, if it is admitted without objection and is relevant and material to the issue, is to be given its natural probative effect and may be received as direct evidence." True; but the court overlooked the fact that a child is in no position to "object" and, typically, a child in court on a delinquency hearing is not represented by counsel.

---

[23] The *Standard Juvenile Court Act*, Sec. 18(4), provides that in support of its order or decree the court may require the custodian of the child, or any other person who has been found to be causing or contributing to its delinquency, to do or omit acts required or forbidden by law which are necessary for the child's welfare, on pain of contempt of court for failure to comply. It should be borne in mind, however, that although the right of the parents to custody is involved in neglect cases and the compulsive authority of the court may be needed, the children who are the subject of the neglect may themselves be placed in an institution as part of the court's order in the case.

[24] Article 77 in this book.

Because of the wide discretion they are entrusted with, judges with a highly developed sense of fairness are especially needed in the juvenile court. Even a remote suggestion of bias,[25] however lofty the ultimate aim of aiding the child, should be avoided.

(f) There are other problems involved in juvenile court procedure,[26] among them the important question of fairness in the disposition and treatment plan decided upon, once there has been a finding of delinquency. A number of decisions in this collection, notably *Petition of Morin, In re Weintraub,* and *In re Smith,* are concerned with various aspects of this matter and show the value of appellate review of disposition.[27]

(g) However, one of the chief sources of criticism of juvenile court proceedings is the practice that has grown up of taking control of cases "unofficially," [28] that is, without the filing of a petition and without a hearing and an official finding of delinquency. This is based on the authority given most juvenile courts to make a preliminary inquiry to determine if the public interest or that of the child calls for more formal proceedings. Chief Justice Vanderbilt complained in the following words about such informal management of the life of a child:

> Without a formal petition before it, the court, of course, has no jurisdiction to act at all. It is said that it is difficult to get formal complaints made but there is no basis in fact for any such alleged difficulty in view of the secrecy that universally attaches to juvenile court proceedings. In line with this illegal and constitutionally unwarranted procedure of assuming jurisdiction gratuitously is the practice in some juvenile courts of proceedings without notice to the child's parents or the persons standing in the place thereof and, even worse, of turning the child over to a criminal court for trial without the benefit of counsel. Finally, an "unofficial probation" of short or long duration is widely used in these "unofficial cases" involving children who are not delinquents, dependents, or neglected, and accordingly not within the jurisdiction of the juvenile court.[29]

The use of "unofficial probation" is not necessarily an unmitigated evil. Often, boys accused of some form of offense which would result in an official finding of delinquency, admit the offense to the police and the probation officer, and, because of unfavorable home circumstances which account for the boy's misbehavior, the officer may recommend to the judge that the case be continued under unofficial oversight. The chief object is to prevent the boy from having an official record which may arise to plague him at some later stage in his career, as when he applies for admission to the armed forces. It would seem advisable that such unofficial handling of cases should be specifically provided for in the statute and that the individual case receive the judge's or referee's attention before it is decided not to make it official through the filing of a delinquency petition and a finding of delinquency status after proof at a hearing.

(h) Finally, permeating the entire situation, is the extent to which a child brought into a juvenile court is afforded the right and the opportunity of counsel: for without a trained advocate the juvenile is not aware of many of the rights he may be entitled to. *Shioutakon v. District of Columbia* and *Arizona State Department of Public Welfare v. Barlow et al.,* among other cases, deal with the problem.[30] Yet it must be confessed that the majority of lawyers know very little about the aims and procedures in juvenile courts, and some of them have been a hindrance instead of a help.

---

[25] Such an inference could arise, for example, from the practice of reading a prepared, typed statement of the decision as soon as the testimony is in. See *In re Church,* 204 S.W. 2d 126 (1947).

[26] To mention some, there is the matter of a public trial, the questioning of adult witnesses and the child without administration of an oath (Article 78 of this book), the recording of the proceedings for purposes of appeal, the finding of delinquency solely on the child's confession.

[27] Chapter 15.

[28] See Articles 49 and 50, by Tappan, in this volume.

[29] Vanderbilt, *op. cit.*

[30] Articles 58, 102 of this book.

The weaknesses and dangers inherent in juvenile court practices have not gone un-heeded by standard-setting agencies.

A commendable attempt has been made by the United States Children's Bureau in cooperation with the National Probation and Parole Association and the National Council of Juvenile Court Judges, to take account, in the *Standards* drafted under the auspices of these organizations, of the importance of retaining fundamental legal protections while providing for the necessary clinical point of view in the dispositional and treatment aspects of the proceedings. It has been emphasized that "while a court must have reasonable discretion to act in the best interests of the child, and must have facilities necessary for study, care and treatment," certain principles "appear to be gen-erally applicable even to the most progressive courts, and should be recognized as an essential part of individualized justice by all coming into contact with the court." [31] These provisions are:

> The conditions under which the State seeks to intervene should be "specifically and clearly delineated in the statutes," the State being required to show both that the conditions exist and that its intervention is necessary. The State should not interfere with parental rights solely "on the generalized assumption that the child is in need of the care or protection of the State," or because it disagrees with the parents regarding the "best course to pursue in rearing a child," or because a proba-tion officer or judge believes a child can be better provided for as a ward of the State.
> The child and parents are entitled to know and to rebut the bases on which the State seeks to intervene. "This means that rules of evidence calculated to assure proceedings in accordance with due process of law should be applicable." However, these rules should be "especially designed" to "protect the informality of the hear-ing and avoid the needless legalism of the rules of evidence customarily applicable to judicial hearings . . . The court should give clear reasons for its decision" both as to the finding and in respect to any order "for treatment, care or protection."
> The statute should authorize the court to take specific actions in relation to certain causes rather than allow it unlimited discretion to make any disposition or to order any treatment that it may think advisable. It must, however, have wide discre-tion within the range of specific actions authorized.
> There should be certain procedural safeguards established for the protection of the rights of parents and children.[32]

These principles are enlarged upon in the Children's Bureau publication; and it is rightly observed that "the real effectiveness and democratic nature of the process will not depend alone upon written standards or procedures or facilities available but also upon the wisdom, humility, understanding, sympathy, fairness, and devotion of every person concerned with the care and treatment of children." [33]

It is fair to assume that the publication of the *Standards* has exerted and will continue to exert a helpful influence in the juvenile court judicial process, as well as on new legislation. But many of the major legal problems are as yet not solved or are settled uneasily.

---

[31] *Standards for Specialized Courts Dealing with Children*, prepared by Children's Bureau, in cooperation with National Probation and Parole Association, National Council of Juvenile Court Judges, Washington, U. S. Government Printing Office, 1954, pp. 6–7.

[32] It will be observed that while the *Standards* recognize the problem of modifying rules of evidence in children's court cases, they leave the line still to be drawn. See, also, the rather vague Sec. 17 of the *Standard Juvenile Court Act*, 1949.

[33] *Standards for Specialized Courts Dealing with Children, op. cit.*, p. 8. A Committee to Revise the Standard Juvenile Act, including a roster of distinguished judges, representatives of the U. S. Children's Bureau, National Council of Juvenile Court Judges, the legislative committee of the Board of Trustees and two staff members of the National Probation and Parole Association is presently (1957) engaged in revising the Standard Juvenile Court Act of 1949, and in that

The series of decisions included in this section bring out, realistically and dramatically, how serious can be the consequences to the child and his parents of a carelessness regarding fundamental legal protections, and how puzzling are the problems involved.

It is easy to generalize about the juvenile court needing to have a "liberal" procedure; but how and where to draw the line is no easy matter; and legislation, including even model drafts, has not made this line any too clear.

The insistence upon certain basic procedural safeguards does not imply a return to the cruder devices developed in the administration of criminal justice in adult cases. The problem is one of a wise differentiation between what is required for the minimizing of the highly technical adversary-proceeding aspects of the adult criminal court and the "hearing" device of the juvenile court with its attendant protective, non-traumatic and therapeutic aims. The issue is well put in the following assessment:

> Much in the customary criminal court procedure is well eliminated in children's court. Formalism, jury trials, fines, jail detention, definite terms of imprisonment, public trial, indictment, bail, formal prosecution, the labels of "crime" and "convict," assumptions of moral responsibility, and perhaps some other incidents of criminal trial should be abandoned in dealing with children. To this both the legal and the administrative exponents will agree. Where dissension arises is on the issue of how much of normal trial procedure in addition may safely and justifiably be stripped from the children's court in keeping with its purposes.[34]

In Chapter 17 are presented sketches of proposed reforms of juvenile court procedure; but the thoughtful student will first pass through his mind the outstanding problems as reflected in a fair sample of the judicial decisions which are presented in Chapters 12 to 16. The cases in the next four chapters are not intended to be exhaustive of all the important legal issues that have arisen; and certainly it was not the Editor's aim to total up the number of jurisdictions that follow one line of reasoning or another. The aim was rather to give a fair and varied sample of the practical legal problems that have arisen in the administration of juvenile court statutes. Inductive analysis shows that, despite some overlap, it is reasonable to classify the decisions into the following categories: (a) Constitutional Protections, (b) Jurisdictional and Related Problems, (c) Problems of Proof, (d) Problems of Disposition. A few cases involving custody, neglect, and dependency proceedings have also been included.

However, in addition to decisions (and legislation) pertaining to juvenile delinquency proper, there are various legal pronouncements regarding supplementary or auxiliary issues, such as labor law provisions pertaining to juveniles, statutes regarding the education of children, laws pertaining to traffic, health, safety and to such special problems as alcoholism and certain sex offenses, commitment of the feebleminded and other special groups, etc., which it was obviously impossible to include in a compilation of this sort, that must be limited to the core problems. Auxiliary and borderline legislation and decisions pertaining to children must be left to student exploration and report in class exercises and papers.

A major aim of assembling the decisions in the next few chapters has been to indicate the conflict of points of view on fundamental issues and the inherent variation in the legal and social–psychiatric approaches to a similar problem.

Wherever possible the decisions used are those of courts of last resort; but in this

---

connection is considering the spelling out in greater detail of the qualifications — legal, extra-legal and those involving personality and character — of the juvenile court judge. The Committee is also concerned with the manner of selecting judges.

[34] Tappan, P. W. *Juvenile Delinquency*, New York, McGraw-Hill Book Co., Inc., 1949, pp. 211–212.

field it appears that many cases have gone no farther in adjudication than the first stage of appellate review.

Finally, there is the policy question as to whether certain forms of deviant childhood behavior, such as truancy,[35] and certain instances of neglect in which there is little likelihood of the court having to remove the child from custody of its parents for its welfare, belong properly in a juvenile court. With the great development of various family and child welfare agencies since the establishment of the juvenile court, there is little advantage and there may be some loss, in taking such cases into the juvenile court, except in extreme instances, where compulsion must replace persuasion. The statutory redefinition of various categories of child and family malaise is a problem for the immediate future; in the meantime, judges might rethink their experience in the types of cases mentioned with a view to developing more efficient and rational intake policies. Parts of Chapter 19 are relevant to the intake problem.

---

[35] "If the school is flexible and adequately staffed, truancy is not a legal problem to refer to a court, but a matter of overcoming any child's resistance to learning by individual diagnosis and treatment. As a result of this point of view, the Gary school system does not use the juvenile court for problems of truancy. As facilities have been increased and trained staff made available, referral of truants to the juvenile court has been reduced from an average of 350 cases per year out of an enrollment of 23,000 to zero. Insofar as we can determine, the rates of school attendance have not been lowered." Mark Roser, "The Role of the Schools," *The Community and the Correctional Process*, 1951 Yearbook, N.P.P.A., 182.

Chapter 12

Constitutional Protections

54

Commonwealth *v.* Fisher*

BROWN, J. In a proceeding conducted in the court of quarter sessions of the county of Philadelphia under the provisions of the act of April 23, 1903 (P. L. 274), Frank Fisher, the appellant, was committed by that court to the House of Refuge. From the order so committing him an appeal was taken to the superior court, which affirmed it. *Commonwealth* v. *Fisher*, 27 Pa. Super. Ct. 175. The constitutionality of the act of 1903 was the sole question before the court in that case, and is renewed here. The objections of the appellant to the constitutionality of the act, as presented by counsel, are: (*a*) Under its provisions the defendant was not taken into court by due process of law. (*b*) He was denied his right of trial before a

---

* *Commonwealth* v. *Fisher*, Supreme Court of Pennsylvania, 1905, 213 Pa. 48, 62 Atl. 198, 5 Ann., Cas. 92. It has been pointed out that Justice Brown, who wrote this opinion, eight years later showed "a decided ability to ignore his own words, when speaking for the majority, he wrote an opinion which denied juveniles the right to attend the local public school when these children had been found to be 'dependent' or 'incorrigible' by a juvenile court and had been placed in a foster home in a borough in which their natural parents did not reside. In order to reach that result, Justice Brown found it necessary to write, '. . . the relation, established by the order of the Juvenile Court . . . is really penal in its nature. . . . Such of these children as are 'incorrigible' are quasi-criminals. They have been apprehended for wrongs committed by them. All of these children are, in effect, prisoners.' And these were not even delinquent children." J. Felstiner, "The Legal Precepts Involved in the Institutional Treatment of Juvenile Delinquents," unpublished class paper in seminar on Juvenile Delinquency, Harvard Law School, 1957, commenting on *Black* v. *Graham*, 238 Pa. 381, 385, 86 A. 266, 267 (1913). Cf. Article 84 of this book. — *Ed.*

jury on the charge of the felony for which he had been arrested. (*c*) The tribunal before which he appeared, and which heard the case and committed him to the House of Refuge, was an unconstitutional body, and without jurisdiction. (*d*) The act provides different punishments for the same offense by a classification of individuals according to age. (*e*) The act contains more subjects than one, some of which are not expressed in the title. In considering these objections, the order in which they are made will not be followed.

The act is entitled "An act defining the powers of the several courts of quarter sessions of the peace, within this commonwealth, with reference to the care, treatment and control of dependent, neglected, incorrigible and delinquent children, under the age of 16 years, and providing for the means in which such power may be exercised." By this title notice of the purpose of the act is distinctly given. It is a single one. It is to define what powers the state, as the general guardian of all of its children, commits to the several courts of quarter sessions in exercising special guardianship over children under the age of 16 years needing the substitution of its guardianship for that of parents or others. This purpose is expressed in the title in as few words as are consistent with clearness. No one, from reading the title, can possibly misunderstand the purpose of the act that follows, and article 3, § 3, of the Constitution is not offended, if, in passing to the body of the act, nothing is there found but this one single purpose. The preamble to it is a recital that, as the welfare of the state requires that children should be guarded from association and contact with crime and criminals, and as those who, from want of proper parental care or guardianship, may become liable to penalties which ought not to be imposed upon them, it is important that the powers of the court, in respect to the care, treatment, and control of dependent, neglected, delinquent, and incorrigible children, should be clearly distinguished from those exercised by it in the administration of the criminal law. After defining the powers of the court the act proceeds to direct how they are to be exercised in giving effect to its purpose. Nothing in the first nine sections can be read as relating or germane to any other purpose than the one named; and there can be no surer test than this of compliance with the constitutional requirement of the singleness of purpose of an act of assembly.

The objection that "the act offends against a constitutional provision in creating, by its terms, different punishments for the same offense by a classification of individuals," overlooks the fact, hereafter to be noticed, that it is not for the punishment of offenders but for the salvation of children, and points out the way by which the state undertakes to save, not particular children of a special class, but all children under a certain age, whose salvation may become the duty of the state, in the absence of proper parental care or disregard of it by wayward children. No child under the age of 16 years is excluded from its beneficent provisions. Its protecting arm is for all who have not attained that age and who may need its protection. It is for all children of the same class. That minors may be classified for their best interests and the public welfare has never been questioned in the legislation relating to them. Under the act of 1887, the classification of females under 16 years of age means felonious rape, with its severe penalties for what may be done one day, though on the next it remains simple fornication, to be expiated by a mere fine. Other acts forbid the employment of minors under 12 years of age in mills; of any boy under 14, or any female, in anthracite coal mines; of minors under 14 in and about elevators; of a boy under 12, or any female, in bituminous coal mines. Others make it a misdemeanor to furnish intoxicating drinks, by sale, gift, or otherwise, to one under 21, and forbid the admission of any minor into certain places of amusement. Such classification is not prohibited by the Constitution, and what has not been therein prohibited the Legislature may enact. Shortly after the adoption of our present Constitution, we said, in the leading case, Wheeler v. The City of Philadelphia, 77 Pa. 338: "In like manner other subjects, trades,

occupations, and professions may be classified; and not only things, but persons, may be so divided. The genus homo is a subject within the meaning of the Constitution. Will it be contended that as to this there can be no classification? No laws affecting the personal and property rights of minors as distinguished from adults? Or of males as distinguished from females? Or, in the case of the latter, no distinction between a feme covert and a single woman? What becomes of all our legislation in regard to the rights of married women, if there can be no classification? And where is the power to provide any future safeguards for their separate estate? These illustrations might be multiplied and indefinitely, were it necessary."

No new court is created by the act under consideration. In its title it is called an act to define the powers of an already existing and ancient court. In caring for the neglected or unfortunate children of the commonwealth, and in defining the powers to be exercised by that court in connection with these children, recognized by the state as its wards requiring its care and protection, jurisdiction is conferred upon that court as the appropriate one, and not upon a new one created by the act. The court of quarter sessions is not simply a criminal court. The Constitution recognizes it, but says nothing as to its jurisdiction. Its existence antedates our colonial times, and by the common law and statutes, both here and in England, it has for generations been a court of broad general police powers in no way connected with its criminal jurisdiction. Innumerable statutes upon our own books during the last two centuries attest this. With its jurisdiction unrestricted by the Constitution, it is for the Legislature to declare what shall be exercised by it as a general police court; and, instead of creating a distinctively new court, the act of 1903 does nothing more than confer additional powers upon the old court and clearly define them. On this point nothing can be profitably added to the following from the opinion of the superior court: "No new court is created, and the ancient court of quarter sessions, which is older than all the Constitutions of Pennsylvania, is given thereby not greater, but different, powers from those previously exercised. The court of quarter sessions has for many years exercised jurisdiction over the settlement of paupers, over the relation of a man to his wife and children in desertion cases, in surety of the peace cases, in the granting of liquor licenses, and in very many of the ways in which the public welfare is involved, where there is neither indictment nor trial by jury. It might as well be said that the court of quarter sessions is not a court of quarter sessions, because it keeps a separate road docket, or, for convenience, a separate docket for desertion cases, or appoints days in which it will hear a certain class of cases, or, as it is said in popular parlance, will hold a 'license court.' In the latter class of cases, where there is more than one court of common pleas within a county, it is usual for the courts themselves to designate the judges who shall hold what is known as the 'license court.' It has never been claimed, so far as we know — certainly not successfully claimed — that such designation was in any sense unconstitutional, or that, because of the designation, a separate court was created. It is no more so in the case under consideration than in any of the cases spoken of above." It is a mere convenient designation of the court of quarter sessions to call it, when caring for children, a "juvenile court"; but no such court, as an independent tribunal, is created. It is still the court of quarter sessions before which the proceedings are conducted, and though that court, in so conducting them, is to be known as the "juvenile court," the records are still those of the court of quarter sessions.

In pressing the objection that the appellant was not taken into custody by due process of law, the assumption, running through the entire argument of the appellant, is continued that the proceedings of the act of 1903 are of a criminal nature for the punishment of offenders for crimes committed, and that the appellant was so punished. But he was not, and he could not have been without due process of law; for the constitutional guaranty is that no one charged with a criminal offense shall be deprived of life, liberty, or property without due process of law. To save a child from becoming a criminal, or from continuing in a career of crime, to end in maturer years in public punishment and disgrace, the Legislature surely may provide for the salvation of such a child, if its parents or guardian be unable or unwilling to do so, by bringing it into one of the courts of the state without any process at all, for the purpose of subjecting it to the state's guardianship and protection. The natural parent needs no process to temporarily deprive his child of its liberty by confining it in his own home, to save it and to shield it from the consequences of persistence in a career of waywardness; nor is the state, when compelled, as *parens patriæ*, to take the place of the father for the same purpose, required to adopt any process as a means of placing its hands upon the child to lead it into one of its courts. When the child gets there, and the court, with the power to save it, determines on its salvation, and not its punishment, it is immaterial how it got there. The act simply provides how children who ought to be saved may reach the court to be saved. If experience should show that there ought to be other ways for it to get there, the Legislature can, and undoubtedly will, adopt them, and they will never be regarded as undue processes for depriving a child of its liberty or property as a penalty for crime committed.

The last reason to be noticed why the act should be declared unconstitutional is that it denies the appellant a trial by jury. Here again is the fallacy that he was tried by the court for any offense. "The right of trial by jury shall remain inviolate," are the words of the Bill of Rights, and no act of the Legislature can deny this right to any citizen, young or old, minor or adult, if he is to be tried for a crime against the commonwealth. But there was no trial for any crime here, and the act is operative only when there is to be no trial. The very purpose of the act is to prevent a trial, though, if the welfare of the public require that the minor should be tried, power to try it is not taken away from the court of quarter sessions; for the eleventh section expressly provides that nothing in the preceding sections "shall be in derogation of the powers of the courts of quarter sessions and oyer and terminer to try, upon an indictment, any delinquent child, who, in due course, may be brought to trial." This section was entirely unnecessary, for without it a delinquent child can be tried only by a jury for a crime charged but, as already stated, the act is not for the trial of a child charged with a crime, but is mercifully to save it from such an ordeal, with the prison or penitentiary in its wake, if the child's own good and the best interests of the state justify such salvation. Whether the child deserves to be saved by the state is no more a question for a jury than whether the father, if able to save it, ought to save it. If the latter ought to save, but is powerless to do so, the former, by the act of 1903, undertakes the duty; and the Legislature, in directing how that duty is to be performed in a proper case, denies the child no right of a trial by a jury, for the simple reason that by the act it is not to be tried for anything. The court passes upon nothing but the propriety of an effort to save it, and, if a worthy subject for an effort of salvation, that effort is made in the way directed by the act. The act is but an exercise by the state of its supreme power over the welfare of its children, a power under which it can take a child from its father and let it go where it will, without committing it to any guardianship or any institution, if the welfare of the child, taking its age into consideration, can be thus best promoted. "The true rule is 'that the courts are to judge upon the circumstances of the particular case, and to give their directions accordingly.'" This was said in habeas corpus proceedings in Rex v. Sir Francis Blake Delaval et al., 3 Burr. 1434, by Lord Mansfield, in discharging Anne Catley, a minor. And he further said: "In the present case there is no reason for the court to deliver her to her father. She has sworn 'to have received ill usage from him before she was at all put out apprentice'; and, whilst she was with Bates, her master, it appears that her father seldom or never came near her, or ever gave her either advice or reprimand. It is even suspicious 'whether the father and mother were not parties to the conspiracy,' and whether the father does not carry on this prosecution in hopes of extorting money from the defendants. Let the girl, therefore, be discharged from all restraint, and be at liberty to go where she will." . . .

[The Court here refers to and quotes from the opinion in *Ex parte Crouse*, pp. 259–260, *infra.* — Ed.]

. . . Appellate courts of other states have expressed this same view. Among the cases which might be cited is Wisconsin Industrial School for Girls v. Clark County, 103 Wis. 651, 79 N. W. 422, where it is said: "The power to place children under proper guardianship has been exercised by chancellors and judges exer-

cising chancery powers from time immemorial. Said Lord Redesdale, in 1828, in Wellesley v. Wellesley, 2 Bligh (N. S.) 124, the right of a chancellor to exercise such power has not been questioned for 150 years. Such a proceeding is not a trial for an offense requiring a common law, or any jury. It was never so regarded in England, nor has it been in this country in but few instances, notably cases in New Hampshire and in People ex rel. O'Connell v. Turner, 55 Ill. 280, 8 Am. Rep. 645. That case was in effect overruled by later cases, and is not now considered as authority. Petition of Ferrier, 103 Ill. 367, 43 Am. Rep. 10; McLean County v. Humphreys, 104 Ill. 378. As said, in substance, in the Ferrier Case, the proceeding is not one according to the course of the common law, in which the right of trial by jury is guarantied, but a mere statutory proceeding for the accomplishment of the protection of the helpless, which object was accomplished before the Constitution without the enjoyment of a jury trial. There is no restraint upon the natural liberty of children contemplated by such a law, none whatever, but rather the placing of them under the natural restraint, so far as practicable, that should be, but is not, exercised by parental authority. It is the mere conferring upon them that protection to which, under the circumstances, they are entitled as a matter of right. It is for their welfare and that of the community at large. The design is not punishment, nor the restraint imprisonment, any more than is the wholesome restraint which a parent exercises over his child. The severity in either case must necessarily be tempered to meet the necessities of the particular situation. There is no probability, in the proper administration of the law, of the child's liberty being unduly invaded. Every statute which is designed to give protection, care, and training to children, as a needed substitute for parental authority and performance of parental duty, is but a recognition of the duty of the state, as the legitimate guardian and protector of children where other guardianship fails. No constitutional right is violated, but one of the most important duties which organized society owes to its helpless members is performed, just in the measure that the law is framed with wisdom and is carefully administered. The conclusions above expressed are in accordance with adjudications elsewhere, with but very few exceptions. . . . [Citations omitted. — Ed.]

None of the objections urged against the constitutionality of the act can prevail. The assignments of error are therefore all overruled, and the order of the superior court, affirming the commitment below, is affirmed.[†]

55

People v. Lewis*

CROUCH, J.

This is a juvenile delinquency proceeding under chapter 393 of the Laws of 1930, known as the Children's Court Act of the State of New York. Its proper title is not "The People of the State of New York against Arthur L. Lewis," as printed on the record and briefs. It was commenced and carried to judgment under the correct title of "In the Matter of Arthur Lewis, a child under the Age of Sixteen Years." Section 10. The distinction is not without significance.

Arthur Lewis, fifteen years old, in company with a younger boy, broke into a store in Binghamton and stole $12. Afterward the two boys, together with two other boys, made their way to Buffalo by means of three automobiles stolen in succession. Brought home, each boy, in separate proceedings, was charged in Children's Court with juvenile delinquency. In this particular case the charge was based upon the theft of the money. No fault is found with the proceedings had prior to the hearing. The hearings in the four cases were held in succession on the same day. Each boy was ex-

amined separately in his own proceeding in the presence of his parents, relatives, and friends. When so examined the other boys were not in the room. The entire testimony thus taken was apparently deemed evidence in each case. The course of the hearing in this case, then, was as follows: The boy, in company with his mother, sister, and the family clergyman, appeared and their appearances were noted. They were advised by the judge that they might have the aid of counsel if they so desired. The boy was then questioned by the judge. The other boys were thereafter examined in the manner above stated. All the testimony thus given appears in the record by question and answer. Each boy told substantially the same story. The testimony sustains the charge beyond any doubt. Indeed, there was full admission and no attempt at denial. The judge then inquired if any one desired to speak on behalf of the boy. There was no answer. The boy was thereupon adjudged a delinquent child and was committed to the State Industrial and Agricultural School at Industry, N. Y.

Upon appeal to the Appellate Division, the judgment was reversed. The decision is placed upon the ground that the specific act upon which the delinquency charge is based would be a felony if committed by an adult and must be proved in substantially the same manner. The judgment, it is said, is supported by no evidence received in the boy's presence, and hence rests solely upon his own confession made without a warning against self-incrimination.

Even in a criminal trial the confession which requires corroboration to sustain conviction is only the extrajudicial confession, not the admission made in open court on the witness stand. 16 C. J. 735, § 1514. If the hearing here had been a criminal trial, its sole defect would have been the failure to warn against self-incrimination. But it was not a criminal trial and there was no defect.

The decision of this court in People v. Fitzgerald, 244 N. Y. 307, 155 N. E. 584, is cited by respondent as conclusive authority. That case arose under the provisions (since repealed) of chapter 385 of the Laws of 1925, relating to the Children's Court, so called, of Buffalo. As the opinion points out, that act was little, if any, different in substance and effect from section 486 of the Penal Law. Broadly speak-

† Accord: Cinque v. Boyd, 99 Conn. 70, 121 Atl. 678 (1923) (collects and cites cases). See also Juvenile Court v. State, 139 Tenn. 549, 201 S. W. 771, Ann. Cas. 1918D, 752 (1918). Compare State ex rel. Cave v. Tincher, 258 Mo. 1, 166 S. W. 1028, Ann. Cas. 1915D, 696 (1914). On validity of juvenile court acts, see 45 L. R. A. (N. S.) 908; on restraint of freedom of child as impairment of child's constitutional rights, 18 L. R. A. (N. S.) 886. — Ed.

* People v. Lewis, Court of Appeals of New York, 1932, 260 N. Y. 171, 183 N. E. 353, 86 A. L. R. 1001, certiorari denied, 289 U. S. 709, 77 L. Ed. 1464; 53 Sup. Ct., 1933.

ing, it did little more than to set up a separate local court to administer existing law in cases falling under that section. As the opinion also points out, a distinction existed under both statutes between children who fell within the neglect and delinquency provisions not involving acts of a criminal nature, and children who had committed specific acts which had always been and were still regarded as criminal. That distinction was a recognized if not an adjudicated one under section 291 of the Penal Code, which was the forerunner of section 486 of the Penal Law. In the one case, the proceeding was not regarded as criminal in its nature; rather, it was said to be benign and protective. In the other, though often resulting in a commitment to a reformatory instead of to a prison, the proceeding was one to punish for crime; the child was a "defendant" standing "in the attitude of a criminal duly convicted of crime." In re Knowack, 158 N. Y. 482, 487, 53 N. E. 676, 677, 44 L. R. A. 699.

The Buffalo statute by its express terms established a Children's Court with "criminal jurisdiction." Section 344-a. The judge was vested with discretion to consider the child either as upon trial for the commission of a crime, or as one in need of the care and protection of the state. Section 344-x. If he took the latter view, he might suspend the trial, inquire into all the facts and surrounding circumstances and then, in lieu of proceeding with the trial, deal with the child in the manner provided in section 486 of the Penal Law in the case of a child without proper guardianship. If the trial proceeded, it might, upon "competent evidence," eventuate in a judgment of "conviction" whereby, among other things, a fine might be imposed. Section 344-x. A judgment upon conviction was appealable to the County Court as prescribed in title 3 of part 5, of the Code of Criminal Procedure (section 749 et seq.), which is entitled "Of Proceedings in Courts of Special Sessions and Police Courts." The record in the Fitzgerald Case shows that the proceeding was begun by the filing of a petition, also called an information, charging juvenile delinquency by the commission of burglary and larceny. Upon the trial the "charge" was "burglary," not delinquency. The "plea" was "not guilty." Defendant was "informed of his constitutional rights." A judgment of "conviction" resulted, which was

affirmed by the County Court and reversed by this court because the trial was a criminal trial in fact and in law, and the conviction rested not on competent evidence as required by the statute under which the proceeding was had, but on grossly incompetent evidence.

The proceeding here is under a widely different statute, which clearly and unmistakably abolishes the distinction referred to above between the two classes of children. The concept of crime and punishment disappears. To the child delinquent through the commission of an act criminal in its nature, the state extends the same aid, care, and training which it had long given to the child who was merely incorrigible, neglected, abandoned, destitute, or physically handicapped. All suggestion and taint of criminality was intended to be and has been done away with. The legislative intent is made as plain as language can make it. The statute (section 45) says:

"No adjudication under the provisions of this act shall operate as a disqualification of any child subsequently to hold public office or as a forfeiture of any right or privilege or to receive any license granted by public authority; and no child shall be denominated a criminal by reason of such adjudication, nor shall such adjudication be denominated a conviction. Neither the fact that a child has been before the children's court for hearing, nor any confession, admission or statement made by him to the court or to any officer thereof while he is under the age of sixteen years, shall ever be admissible as evidence against him or his interests in any other court."

"All provisions of the penal law or code of criminal procedure or other statutes inconsistent with or repugnant to any of the provisions of this act shall be considered inapplicable to the cases arising under this act."

The final mandate of the statute is that: "This act shall be construed to the end that the care, custody and discipline of the children brought before the court shall approximate as nearly as possible that which they should receive from their parents, and that as far as practicable they shall be treated not as criminals but as children in need of aid, encouragement and guidance."

So much has been written, judicially and extrajudicially, about the sociological and legal aspects of juvenile delinquency, and about the public policy which underlies such statutes as the one in question, that a detailed discussion here would be trite. For the purposes of this case, the fundamental point is that the proceeding was not a criminal one. The state was not seeking to punish a malefactor. It was seeking to salvage a boy who was in danger of becoming one. In words which have been often quoted, "the problem for determination by the judge is not, Has this boy or girl committed a specific wrong, but What is he, how has he become what he is, and what had best be done in his interest and in the interest of the State to save him from a downward career." 23 Harvard Law Review, 104, "The Juvenile Court," by Julian W. Mack.

The evidence of his specific acts was relevant as an aid in answering those questions. Since the proceeding was not a criminal one, there was neither right to nor necessity for the procedural safeguards prescribed by constitution and statute in criminal cases. Many cases in many jurisdictions so hold. . . . [Citations omitted. — Ed.]

Whatever the power of the Legislature may be in the case of adults (cf. Lawton v. Steele, 119 N. Y. 226, 233, 23 N. E. 878, 7 L. R. A. 134, 16 Am. St. Rep. 813), there is no doubt about its power to say that an act done by a child shall not be a crime. No act or omission is a crime except as prescribed by statute. Penal Law, § 22; People v. Knapp, 206 N. Y. 373, 380, 99 N. E. 841, Ann. Cas. 1914B, 243.

In the administration of Children's Courts there is evidence of a tendency to confuse the procedure usual in mere dependency cases with that necessary in delinquency cases involving an issue of fact. To serve the social purpose for which the Children's Court was created, provision is made in the statute for wide investigation before, during and after the hearing. But that investigation is clinical in its nature. Its results are not to be used as legal evidence where there is an issue of fact to be tried. When it is said that even in cases of lawbreaking delinquency constitutional safeguards and the technical procedure of the criminal law may be disregarded, there is no implication that a purely socialized trial of a specific issue may properly or legally be had. The contrary is true. There must be a reasonably definite charge. The customary rules of evidence shown by long experience as essential to getting at the truth with reasonable certainty in civil trials must be adhered to. The finding of fact must rest on the preponderance of evidence adduced under those rules. Hearsay, opinion, gossip, bias, prejudice, trends of hostile neighborhood feeling, the hopes and fears of social workers, are all sources of error and have no more place in Children's Courts than in any other court.[1] People v. Pikunas, 260 N. Y. 72, 182 N. E. 675. Cf. U. S. Children's Bureau Publication No. 97 (1922), "How Far Can Court Procedure be Socialized Without Impairing Individual Rights," Judge Edward F. Waite. . . . [Some citations omitted. — Ed.]

The rights of the child and of the parents are thus amply safeguarded, for the statute provides not only for appeals (section 43), but it also provides (section 25) that in delinquency cases, such as this, the court on its own motion or upon application by any interested person may set aside or arrest judgment or grant a new hearing in the exercise of its powers of protection over the child, either before or after final adjudication or commitment. Moreover, though it is not now necessary so to hold, it may be that the Supreme Court has power, under its general chancery jurisdiction, to intervene in any given case. In re Knowack, supra.

The judgment of the Appellate Division should be reversed, and that of the Children's Court affirmed.

CRANE, J. (dissenting).

Do the Constitution of the United States and the Constitution of the State of New York apply to children or only to adults? By the Fifth Amendment to the Federal Constitution, applicable to federal courts, no person

---

[1] Commenting on this statement, Wigmore says: "Now, if the learned judge meant to say that *all* 'the customary rules,' as applied in civil trials are 'essential to getting at the truth,' then this opinion must be classed as committing itself to an anachronistic view, which no jurist today would be expected to defend; and, in so far as the implication is made that 'bias' and 'prejudice' are eliminated from all testimony by those rules, the implication is obviously erroneous; this opinion, in so far as it may seem to condemn the usual materials of inquiry used in juvenile courts, should be given no force, while awaiting a more reflective judicial treatment of this question." J. Wigmore, A *Treatise on the Anglo-American System of Evidence in Trials at Common Law*, Third Edition, Boston, Little, Brown and Company, 1940, Vol. 1, note, pp. 102–103. — Ed.

shall be compelled in a criminal case to be a witness against himself, nor deprived of his liberty, without due process of law. The latter provision, by the Fourteenth Amendment, is made binding on all the States.

These provisions are also in the New York State Constitution. Article 1, § 6, says that no person shall be compelled in any criminal case to be a witness against himself nor deprived of his liberty without due process of law. Again, I ask the question, do these protections and safeguards, found necessary against arbitrary and abusive power, apply only to grown-ups, or do our children share the protection? May a child be incarcerated and deprived of his liberty in a public institution by calling that which is a crime by some other name; and if so, at what age may the Legislature take from him the constitutional right? Again, let me put this more concretely, that we may realize just what we are doing. A man charged with burglary or larceny cannot be compelled to be a witness against himself. He cannot be forced to testify and then be convicted on his own statement. This law is as old as our Constitution. Can a child be deprived of his liberty, taken from his home and parents, and incarcerated in an institution for a term of years, by changing the name of the offense from "burglary" or "larceny" to "juvenile delinquency?" If the Legislature can thus wipe out the constitutional protection by changing a name, the substance and reality remaining the same, at what age of an accused does this power begin and end? May the Legislature call forgery, larceny, burglary, assault, "moral delinquency," and send a person twenty years of age to Elmira Reformatory, or some other correctional institution, on his own confession, wrung from him by an inquisitorial process in court, compelling him to be a witness against himself? If this legislative power exists regarding a boy fifteen years of age, why is it not also possible to do the same thing to a young man twenty years of age? At what age do the constitutional safeguards and protections begin? The Constitution of this state and the Federal Constitution, in so far as it is applicable, cannot be nullified by a mere nomenclature, the evil of the thing itself remaining the same.

In this case, young Arthur L. Lewis, a boy fifteen years of age, was charged with violating section 486 of the Penal Law, by willfully, wrongfully, and unlawfully forcibly breaking and entering a building, to wit, the Grand Union grocery store, situated at 126 Schubert street in the city of Binghamton, N. Y., and stealing and carrying away therefrom lawful money of the United States. Section 486 of the Penal Law provides that a child over seven, and under sixteen years of age, is a delinquent, who commits an act, which, if committed by an adult, would be a crime, not punishable by death or life imprisonment. *This is the only act of delinquency charged against young Lewis.* If he had been sixteen years of age, the act charged would have been a crime.

Under the provisions of the Constitution, above mentioned, he could not be forced to be a witness against himself, which means that the charge could not be proved by questioning him about it as a witness in court.

Other provisions of the Code of Criminal Procedure would also apply to him, such as the inability to convict him on his own confession, without corroboration and the right to be confronted with witnesses and to cross-examine them. We brush these aside for the present, and deal only with the constitutional provision, which the Legislature cannot undermine. Therefore, Lewis, if he were sixteen years of age, would be charged with a crime, and the crime would have to be proved in accordance with the restrictions and prohibitions of the Constitution; he could not be compelled to be a witness against himself, or convicted and sent away on such testimony. Lewis being under sixteen years of age, all these safeguards have been brushed aside; the Constitution means nothing. The acts committed are exactly the same for a boy over sixteen as for a boy under sixteen, but the Legislature has called the one a "crime" and the other "juvenile delinquency." Changing the name for the same series of acts, the Legislature permits and authorizes a judge to question the accused in his court or in his chambers on the charge made against him; can compel him to be a witness against himself, and on his sworn or unsworn statement unsupported by any other evidence, send him to an institution until he is twenty-one years of age. This court should be very slow in sustaining any such arbitrary power.

We fully realize that all these measures

were adopted in behalf of the infant, and out of so-called charitable considerations for his welfare. The motives behind all our reform movements are probably commendable and beyond criticism. Some are ever on the lookout to improve civic conditions and the morals of the individual by the force of law, and yet we must be careful that in these endeavors to correct others, we do not exceed well-recognized principles of municipal government. Absolute power in the hands of a careful and just man may be a benefit, but most of our Constitutions have been adopted out of experience, with human nature as it is, and is apt to be in the future. We must minimize the chance of abuse and place limitations even upon those who have the best of purposes and the most benevolent dispositions. To send a young man to prison for a crime is a serious matter for him and his family. To take a young lad, filled with the wild dreams of childhood, from his parents and his home and incarcerate him in a public institution until he is twenty-one years of age, is equally as serious, and the consequences are not lessened by the emollient term, "juvenile delinquency."

The Children's Court Act of the State of New York (Laws of 1930, c. 393) provides that a delinquent child is a person less than sixteen years of age who commits any act which, if committed by an adult, would be a crime, not punishable by death or life imprisonment. This is the part we are dealing with here in this case, but the act provides much more. It deals mainly with those children who are incorrigible, ungovernable, habitually disobedient, and beyond the control of their parents, those who are habitually truant, and repeatedly desert their home, or who associate with unmoral and vicious persons, or who habitually use obscene or profane language or beg or solicit alms or money in public places. Juvenile delinquency is the commission by a child of any of the offenses enumerated in the foregoing, none of which are crimes if committed by adults or by anybody else. These charges are more or less informal, although records of the proceedings must be kept and sufficient evidence must be produced to prove the condition covered by the act. We are dealing here, however, with a charge of a crime, or that which would be a crime in an adult; it is a single act, not a continuing one. The doing of the deed

constitutes the offense which this law calls "juvenile delinquency," and which in a child a year older would be called "a crime." It is such acts and deeds, call them what you will, which lead to the consequences or punishment; permit incarceration in a protective institution. When the *only* charge is one of crime — called out of charity "juvenile delinquency" — it must be surrounded in prosecution by the safeguards and limitations of the Constitution. This fundamental document of our State government, if it protects a boy sixteen years of age, must also protect a boy fifteen years of age. Once remove the barriers and where will we stop? If we say sixteen years of age is the limit to-day, the next Legislature may say twenty. Wise it is for this court to follow the Constitution as it is written, for even under it the field remains wide open for all experiments in the upbringing and development of our citizenry.

The Children's Court Act refers to neglected children and abandoned and destitute children and those physically handicapped. Surely here the Children's Court, as established, performs a most humane function in caring for these unfortunates. In dealing with this subject, even at the expense of repetition, we must be careful to note that we are here touching upon only one minor portion of this progressive legislation, and that is, the juvenile delinquency existing solely upon the charge of an offense which in an adult would be a crime. That recognized procedure is to be followed as far as the circumstances permit is evidenced by section 14 of the Children's Court Act, which reads: "Where the method of procedure in a case or proceeding in which the court has jurisdiction is not provided in this act, such procedure shall be the same as provided by law, or by rules formally adopted by the court within the scope of this act, but the court may hear and determine causes in which it has jurisdiction with or without a jury, in the discretion of the court. If there be a jury, the number of jurors shall be six and the jury shall be drawn and a trial had in the same manner as obtains in the trial of criminal actions in the county court of said county, and the jury shall be in charge of the county officers the same as though said trial was in fact held in the county court."

Section 22 also provides that upon the

return of a summons after a child has been taken into custody, the court shall proceed "to hear and determine the case, * * * and inquire into the habits, surroundings, conditions and tendencies of the child." *The judge made no such inquiry.* What did the judge do in this case?

Arthur Lewis, a boy fifteen years of age, was, as already stated, charged with willfully, wrongfully, and unlawfully breaking and entering a building and stealing money; that is, he was charged with acts which would constitute burglary and larceny if he had been one year older. The record shows that the boy appeared before the judge and was questioned by him. Whether he was sworn does not appear. The recital in the judgment of conviction says that the judge advised the boy and his mother that they might have the aid of counsel if they so desired. He at least must have had an idea that the proceedings were in the nature of a judicial inquiry. The questions put by the judge and the answers given by the boy have been written out and form the *sole* record of the proceeding. The boy confessed and the judge sent him to the State Industrial and Agricultural School at Industry, N. Y., to stay there until he was twenty-one years of age, unless sooner discharged. No other evidence was taken and no other proof given outside the confession. The accused having been forced to be a witness against himself, was sent away to be locked up on his own testimony. This was in direct violation of the Constitution of this state, and the Appellate Division was right in reversing the judgment.

We had this same question before us in People v. Fitzgerald, 244 N. Y. 307, 313, 155 N. E. 584, 587, and while it arose under the Children's Court Act of Buffalo (Laws 1925, c. 385), in essence there is no difference. This court was unanimous in saying: "Where, therefore, a child is arrested and charged with being a delinquent child because it has committed an offense which would be a crime in an adult, that offense must be proved, and proved by competent evidence. If our own good sense and judgment did not tell us this, the act itself creating the Children's Court of Buffalo would remind us of it. Section 344-x of the act notes the difference between a trial for an offense requiring competent proof before conviction and the other

informal hearings whereby children may be provided with homes or proper guardianship. This section says:

"'Upon the return of the summons * * * after any child has been taken into custody, and at the time set for the hearing, the court shall proceed to hear and determine the case. The court from time to time may adjourn the hearing and inquire into the habits, surroundings, conditions and tendencies of the child.'"

These are the identical words as now found in section 22 of the Children's Court Act of the State of New York (Laws 1930, c. 393).

Reference may again be made to the caution suggested by Judge Andrews in People ex rel. Van Riper v. New York Catholic Protectory, 106 N. Y. 604, 609, 13 N. E. 435, in dealing with this summary jurisdiction for the disposition of children. It was quoted at length in the Fitzgerald Case.

The judgment of the Appellate Division should be affirmed.

POUND, C. J., and LEHMAN, O'BRIEN, and HUBBS, JJ., concur with CROUCH, J.

CRANE, J., dissents in opinion in which KELLOGG, J., concurs.†

Judgment accordingly.

56

Dendy *et al.* v. Wilson *et al.**

SHARP, Justice.

This is a proceeding against Billy Dendy and L. W. King, Jr., instituted by petition of John W. Wilson, probation officer of Lubbock County, under the provisions of Article 2338 — 1, Vernon's Annotated Civil Statutes, Acts 48th Leg., 1943, p. 313, ch. 204, known as the Juvenile Delinquency Act. Upon a hearing in the Juvenile Court of Lubbock County, judgment was rendered declaring Billy Dendy and L. W. King, Jr., to be delinquent children and committing them to the State School for Boys

---

† *Cf. In re Hill,* 78 Cal. App. 23, 247 Pac. 591 (1926). — *Ed.*

* *Dendy* et al. v. *Wilson* et al., Supreme Court of Texas, 1944, 142 Tex. 460, 179 S. W. 2d 269, (Rehearing Denied April 26, 1944).

at Gatesville, Coryell County, Texas, for an indeterminate period, not to extend beyond each child's twenty-first birthday. Upon appeal to the Court of Civil Appeals at Amarillo, the judgment was reversed and the cause remanded. 175 S.W.2d 297.

Separate petitions were filed, but inasmuch as the act alleged to constitute delinquency appeared to be the same, the juvenile court consolidated the cases, over the objection of counsel for the children, and heard them together. The petitions alleged that Billy Dendy and L. W. King, Jr., were delinquent children by reason of their taking an automobile belonging to C. B. Conditt, and both children were alleged to be over the age of ten years and under the age of seventeen years. Notices were served on the parents of the children, and motions to dismiss the petitions, which asserted that the Act authorizing the proceeding was unconstitutional, were overruled by the court. Said children asked to be tried by a jury, but the trial court held that since a jury was not demanded in the manner and as required in other civil cases, the right to a jury trial had been waived. Thereupon the hearing proceeded before the court with the general public excluded, over the objection of counsel for the children.

It was stipulated by and between counsel for the children and counsel for the petitioner that "the juveniles were taken into custody by the Sheriff of Dawson County, Texas, in possession of the car in question in Dawson County." Both children were required to testify, over the objection of their counsel, to the effect that they took the car in question from a car lot belonging to C. B. Conditt and C. J. Reynolds, and they were taken into custody in possession of the car near Lamesa, in Dawson County. On examination by the court, Billy Dendy testified to having served a term in the Boys Reformatory at Gatesville. The owners of the car testified that they knew the boys, that one of them worked for them, and that they had not given them permission to take the car.

The court found the children to be delinquent children within the meaning of the Act, and ordered them committed to the State School for Boys at Gatesville for an indeterminate period, subject to modification or revocation from time to time. In their appeal to the

Court of Civil Appeals the boys attacked the constitutionality of the Act in numerous respects. The court sustained the validity of the Act generally, but held that the juvenile court erred in failing to allow the boys a jury trial and in compelling them to testify against themselves.

It is quite obvious that the tendency of modern legislation is to radically change the method of procedure in the trial of juveniles. The underlying thought in our early criminal laws was to punish the offender, and this rule applied to children and adults alike. Prior to the enactment of the law now under consideration, the Legislature of this State had enacted laws applicable to the trial of juveniles. See Articles 1083 to 1093, inclusive, Code of Criminal Procedure, and Articles 2329 to 2338, inclusive, Vernon's Annotated Civil Statutes. In Article 1093, Code of Criminal Procedure, it was provided that the prosecution and conviction of a juvenile shall be regarded as a criminal case, and an appeal of such case had to be taken to the Court of Criminal Appeals. The Court of Criminal Appeals had occasion to construe Article 1083 et seq., Code of Criminal Procedure, and held that they were designed for the protection and reformation of juvenile offenders. It also held that the law was corrective, not punitive. In the case of Phillips v. State, Tex.Cr.App., 20 S.W.2d 790, 791, it was said: "In order that the beneficent purpose of the act may be effectuated, it should be construed liberally, except in so far as it purports to restrain the liberty of the child, in which case it should be strictly construed." See also Davis v. State, 113 Tex.Cr.R. 429, 21 S.W.2d 1068; Morgan v. State, 114 Tex.Cr.R. 434, 25 S.W.2d 842.

In 1943 the Legislature enacted the Act under consideration. It is quite long, and we shall refer only to the parts thereof essential to this opinion.

Section 1 of Article 2338 — 1 states the underlying purpose of this Act as follows:

"Section 1. The purpose of this Act is to secure for each child under its jurisdiction such care, guidance and control, preferably in his own home, as will serve the child's welfare and the best interest of the state; and when such child is removed from his own family, to secure for him custody, care and discipline as nearly as possible equivalent to that which should have been given him by his parents. * * *"

Section 3 reads as follows:

"Sec. 3. The word 'court' means the 'Juvenile Court.' The word 'Judge' means the Judge of the Juvenile Court. The term 'delinquent child' means any female person over the age of ten (10) years and under the age of eighteen (18) years and any male person over the age of ten (10) years and under the age of seventeen (17) years:

"(a) who violates any penal law of this state of the grade of felony;

"(b) or who violates any penal law of this state of the grade of misdemeanor where the punishment prescribed for such offense may be by confinement in jail;

"(c) or who habitually violates any penal law of this state of the grade of misdemeanor where the punishment prescribed for such offense is by pecuniary fine only;

"(d) or who habitually violates any penal ordinance of a political subdivision of this state;

"(e) or who habitually violates a compulsory school attendance law of this state;

"(f) or who habitually so deports himself as to injure or endanger the morals or health of himself or others;

"(g) or who habitually associates with vicious and immoral persons."

Section 4 defines how juvenile courts may be established.

Section 5 reads as follows:

"Sec. 5. The Juvenile Court shall have exclusive original jurisdiction in proceedings governing any delinquent child, and such court shall be deemed in session at all times.

"Nothing contained herein shall deprive other courts of the right to determine the custody of children upon writs of habeas corpus, or when such custody is incidental to the determination of causes pending in such courts.

"When jurisdiction shall have been obtained by the court in the case of any child, such child shall continue under the jurisdiction of the court until he becomes twenty-one (21) years of age, unless discharged prior thereto; such continued jurisdiction shall, however, in no manner prejudice or constitute a bar to subsequent or additional proceedings against such child under the provisions of this Act."

Section 6 describes how a transfer of cases may be made.

Sections 7, 7-A, 8, 9, and 10 describe how an information may be filed, where the venue of the case is, the method and service of summons, the punishment for failure to obey such summons, and the issuance of a warrant.

Section 11 provides how a child taken into custody may be released.

Section 13 reads as follows:

"Sec. 13. The Judge may conduct the hearing in an informal manner and may adjourn the hearing from time to time. In the hearing of any case the general public may be excluded. All cases involving children shall be heard separately and apart from the trial of cases against adults.

"If no jury is demanded, the Judge shall proceed with the hearing. When the proceeding is with a jury, the verdict shall state whether the juvenile is a 'delinquent child' within the meaning of this Act, and if the Judge or jury finds that the child is delinquent, or otherwise within the provisions of this Act, the court may by order duly entered proceed as follows:

"(1) place the child on probation or under supervision in his own home or in the custody of a relative or other fit person, upon such terms as the court shall determine;

"(2) commit the child to a suitable public institution or agency, or to a suitable private institution or agency authorized to care for children; or to place them in suitable family homes or parental homes for an indeterminate period of time, not extending beyond the time the child shall reach the age of twenty-one (21) years;

"(3) make such further disposition as the court may deem to be for the best interest of the child, except as herein otherwise provided.

"No adjudication upon the status of any child in the jurisdiction of the court shall operate to impose any of the civil disabilities ordinarily imposed by conviction, nor shall any child be deemed a criminal by reason of such adjudication, nor shall such adjudication be deemed a conviction, nor shall any child be charged with or convicted of a crime in any court. The disposition of a child or any evidence given in the court shall not be admissible as evidence against the child in any case or proceeding in any other court other than another

Juvenile Court, nor shall such disposition or evidence operate to disqualify a child in any future civil service examination, appointment, or application.

"Whenever the court shall commit a child to any institution or agency, it shall transmit with the order of commitment, a summary of its information concerning such child and give in the order of commitment the birth date of the child or attach thereto a certified copy of the birth certificate."

Section 14 provides for the modification of a judgment and the return of the child to its parents.

Section 17 reads as follows:

"Sec. 17. No female person over the age of ten (10) years and under the age of eighteen (18) years, or any male person over the age of ten (10) years and under the age of seventeen (17) years, shall be placed or committed to any compartment of any jail or lock-up in which persons over juvenile age are incarcerated or detained; but shall be placed in a room or ward separate and apart from that occupied by adults. The proper authorities of all counties shall provide suitable place of detention for such juveniles separate and apart from any jail or lock-up in which adults are confined. Said detention place may be in the same building housing adults, or in a building separate and apart from that where adults are confined."

Section 21 provides that an appeal may be taken by any party aggrieved to the Court of Civil Appeals, and the case may be carried to the Supreme Court.

Section 24 repealed Articles 2329 and 2338 of the Revised Civil Statutes, and Articles 1083 to 1093 of the Code of Criminal Procedure, and all conflicting laws or parts of laws.

Petitioners contend that this law is unconstitutional, and that the trial court erred in the following matters: (1) That the trial court erred in consolidating the two cases as civil cases for trial, when in fact they were criminal cases; (2) that the trial court erred in refusing to allow said children a public trial; (3) that the trial court erred in refusing the minor children a trial by jury; and (4) that the trial court erred in compelling the children to testify, over their objections, against themselves, in violation of the Fifth Amendment to the United States Constitution and Section 10 of Article I of the Texas Constitution, Vernon's Ann.St.

The State complains of the holding of the Court of Civil Appeals that the trial court erred in not permitting a jury trial.

The harsh rule that was applied to children in former laws has been abolished in this Act. As stated, in Section 1 of Article 2338 — 1, the dominant purpose of the Act is to throw around the child the care and guidance of a good home life, if such is available, and if not available to place such child in such surroundings as would as nearly as possible be equivalent thereto. Section 13 in part provides that, "No adjudication upon the status of any child * * * shall operate to impose any of the civil disabilities ordinarily imposed by conviction, nor shall any child be deemed a criminal by reason of such adjudication, nor shall such adjudication be deemed a conviction, nor shall any child be charged with or convicted of a crime in any court." It further provides that "The disposition of a child or any evidence given in the court shall not be admissible as evidence against the child in any case or proceeding in any other court other than another Juvenile Court, nor shall such disposition or evidence operate to disqualify a child in any future civil service examination, appointment, or application."

This Act does not undertake to convict and punish a child for the commission of a crime. It defines a "delinquent child," and this definition furnishes the basis for proceedings against such a child under the Act. The only issue to be determined at the trial is whether the juvenile is a "delinquent child" within the meaning of the Act.

The Act created juvenile courts with special jurisdiction over delinquent children. A juvenile court is not a criminal court. It is a special court created by statute, and the statute specifically provides what disposition may be made of a "delinquent child" until he or she reaches the age of 21 years. The purpose of the statute is to get away from the old method of handling minors charged with offenses, and to place such minors with suitable persons or in suitable institutions or agencies authorized to take care of minors, for a certain period of time.

The power to make laws is vested through the Constitution in the Legislature. This power gives the Legislature the right to define crimes and the punishment therefor, and this is done by statute. 12 Tex.Jur. p. 213, § 7; p. 223, § 14. However, the Legislature does not have the power to enact any law contrary to the provisions of the Constitution. If any law, or part thereof, undertakes to nullify the protection furnished by the Constitution, such law, or part thereof, that conflicts with the Constitution is void.

It is quite clear that the Legislature intended by this Act to radically change the law relating to minors. It specifically states that the Act shall be liberally construed to accomplish the purposes sought therein. We think from the language used that the Legislature made it plain that the juvenile courts are invested with exclusive original jurisdiction over children *within the age limits prescribed by the law*. In Section 5 we find this language: "*The Juvenile Court shall have exclusive original jurisdiction in proceedings governing any delinquent child, and such court shall be deemed in session at all times.*" (Italics ours.) In Section 12 is found the following: "If during the pendency of a criminal charge or indictment against any person in any other court than a Juvenile Court, it shall be ascertained that said person is a female over the age of ten (10) years and under the age of eighteen (18) years, or is a male person over the age of ten (10) years and under the age of seventeen (17) years *at the time of the trial for the alleged offense*, it shall be the duty of such court to transfer such case immediately together with all papers, documents and testimony connected therewith to the Juvenile Court of said county." (Italics ours.) This section of the Act makes it the duty of any other court to transfer such a case to the juvenile court upon ascertaining that the accused is within the statutory age limits. No discretion is vested in the other court, as was the case under an early statute. Ex parte Thomas, 56 Tex.Cr.R. 66, 118 S.W. 1053; Ragsdale v. State, 61 Tex.Cr.R. 145, 134 S.W. 234. Furthermore, the Act repeals by specific mention certain articles of both the civil statutes and the Code of Criminal Procedure, and all laws or parts of laws in conflict therewith. The Act provides for a jury trial when a jury is demanded, and authorizes the trial court to order a jury on its own motion. Nothing is said about the payment of a jury fee. The Act does not require a minor to

testify against himself in a proceeding under same, and it does not require the trial court to follow the rules of civil procedure in taking testimony in the trial of such cases. We think, however, that the whole Act discloses that the Legislature intended that proceedings instituted thereunder should be governed, as far as practicable, by the rules relating to civil procedure. The trial court construed the Act as giving it power to compel the minors to testify against themselves.

This Act gives broad powers to the trial court in the handling of cases arising thereunder. The law does not specifically authorize the trial court to consolidate two cases, but in view of the purposes of the law we see no sound reason to hold that in the exercise of its sound discretion the trial court erred in consolidating the two cases. The law also authorizes the trial court to exclude the general public from a hearing of any case, if it thinks proper to do so. This saves the minor from embarrassment, and also permits the court to avoid the publicity that often surrounds the trial of a case. Since the proceedings under this Act must be governed largely by rules governing civil actions, the trial court did not err in excluding the general public from the trial.

It has been repeatedly held by other courts, in construing acts similar to the one under consideration, that such statutes are not criminal in nature, and where their purpose is for the education and reformation of the minor, and the institution to which he or she is committed is not penal in nature, the denial of the right of a jury trial is not a violation of the Constitution. [Citations omitted. — Ed.]

This law provides for a trial by jury,* and a person tried thereunder is entitled to a jury if properly demanded. No jury was properly demanded in this instance, and under the facts the trial court did not err in proceeding with the trial without a jury. Nor did the trial court abuse its discretion in consolidating the two cases. The Court of Civil Appeals erred in

---

* The decisions differ regarding the right to jury trial, dependent upon the wording of the state constitution and statute. Cf. *Application of Banschbach*, _____ Mont. _____, 323 P2d. 1112 (1958) (jury an essential part of tribunal); *contra, Bryant* v. *Brown*, 151 Miss. 398, 118 So. 184 (1928).

holding that the case should have been tried with the aid of a jury.

The State also contends that the Court of Civil Appeals erred in reversing the trial court for compelling the minors to testify against themselves.*

Certain provisions in both the Federal and the State Constitutions bear upon this contention. [Sentence omitted. — Ed.] In Section 10 of Article I of the Constitution of the State of Texas it is provided: "In all criminal prosecutions the accused * * * shall not be compelled to give evidence against himself * * *."

In passing upon the question whether these minors could have been legally compelled to testify as to the transaction, we must necessarily inquire whether they were granted complete immunity from prosecution under the general criminal law for the act concerning which they testified. At the outset, it is to be noted that the Act itself does not purport to repeal the provisions of the Penal Code with respect to offenses committed by minor children. Repeal of laws by implication is not favored. . . . [Citations omitted. — Ed.] In Wintermann v. McDonald, supra [129 Tex. 275, 102 S.W. 2d 171], it was said: "In the absence of an express repeal by statute, where there is no positive repugnance between the provisions of the old and new statutes, the old and new statutes will each be construed so as to give effect, if possible, to both statutes." The Court of Criminal Appeals held that Article 5143a, Section 1, Vernon's Annotated Civil Statutes, which defined the age of a delinquent child the same as in this Act, did not expressly repeal Article 30 of the Penal Code. Flannery v. State, 135 Tex.Cr.R. 235, 117 S.W.2d 1111.

The Constitution of Texas gives the Court of Criminal Appeals appellate jurisdiction of all criminal cases. Section 5 of Article V of the Constitution. That court has not construed this Act, and this court is compelled to construe same in the light of the opinions of the Court of Criminal Appeals.

Section 12 of the Act provides that a pending criminal case shall be transferred to the juvenile court when it appears that the defendant is within the statutory age limits *at the time of trial*; thus implying that if the defendant is above the statutory age limit at the time of trial, even though the act upon which the prosecution is based was committed while the defendant was within the age limits, the courts can try him for crimes.* This interpretation of the language of the Act is fortified by the fact that the Court of Criminal Appeals has always held that the age at the time of the trial is controlling. . . . [Citations omitted. — Ed.] The reason for the rule is illustrated by this language from McLaren v. State, 85 Tex. Cr.R. 370, 116 S.W. 806:

"It could hardly be seriously contended that one who had committed a heinous crime, as, for instance, murder, while 15 or 16 years of age, and who was not apprehended or indicted until past 21, would, by reason of such lapse, go absolutely unwhipped of justice, unless the language of the law were such as that it was reasonably susceptible of no other construction than one which produced such result. And that is true whether such lapse resulted from an act of the accused or of another, for neither his resistance to or avoidance of prosecution, nor the state's failure or refusal to prosecute, could add to or take from the force of the law as written."

The argument is made on behalf of the State that the Act provides express immunity to those who testify. We find no such immunity in the Act. It merely provides that evidence given in the juvenile court shall be inadmissible in another proceeding. Under the settled law, that is not sufficient. . . . [Citations omitted. — Ed.]

In keeping with the general rule that a witness cannot be compelled to give testimony against himself in a criminal case, it has been held that a witness cannot be compelled to give evidence that will tend either directly or indirectly to incriminate himself, either in a civil case or in a criminal case. . . . [Citations omitted. — Ed.]

A good illustration of the result that would be accomplished under the construction contended for by the State is made by the case of McLaren v. State, supra. That case holds that when a

---

* See *Ex parte Tahbel*, 46 Cal. A. 755, 189 Pac. 804 (1920) holding that a court cannot commit a juvenile solely on the ground of his refusal to answer incriminating questions. — Ed.

* *U. S. v. Jones*, 141 Fed. Supp. 641 (1956) holds that under the Federal Juvenile Delinquency Act, the age at time of the offense is determinative. — Ed.

case is reversed on appeal and remanded for a new trial at a time when the defendant is above the upper age limit, the trial must be as for crime, even though the crime was committed at a time when the defendant would have had the right to be proceeded against under the statutes relating to juvenile delinquents. But if the theory of complete immunity from criminal prosecution were adopted, a person whose case was identical on the facts with the McLaren case would escape any consequences of his act. See the recent case of Hardie v. State, supra. This result would follow because the juvenile court has jurisdiction only over delinquent children, and that term is defined in Section 3 of the Act so as to exclude males over seventeen years of age and females over eighteen years. In our judgment a reading of the Act will not justify the holding that the Legislature intended any such result. Unless this Act extends absolute immunity to those who are forced to give testimony thereunder in any court other than a juvenile court, the Constitution protects the minors from being compelled to testify against themselves.

It is contended that the provision of Section 13 which states that no child shall "be charged with or convicted of a crime in any court" repeals the articles of the Penal Code relating to offenses committed by minors. This presents a very serious question. If a minor under this Act cannot be convicted of any crime, then is it possible for him to testify in any case in the face of the provisions of Section 5 of Article I of the Constitution, which provides that "all oaths * * * shall be taken subject to the pains and penalties of perjury"? Article 30 of the Penal Code reads:

"No person shall be convicted of any offense committed before he was nine years old except perjury, and for that only when it shall appear by proof that he had sufficient discretion to understand the nature and obligation of an oath; nor of any other offense committed between the age of nine and thirteen, unless it shall appear by proof that he had discretion sufficient to understand the nature and illegality of the act constituting the offense."

Former Article 34 of the Penal Code of 1895 provided that no person could be convicted of an offense committed before he was of the age of nine years, and it was held that children under that age were not competent

witnesses, in view of Section 5 of Article I of the Constitution, requiring oaths to be taken subject to the pains and penalties of perjury. Freasier v. State, Tex.Cr.App., 84 S.W. 360. As a result of that decision the statute was amended so as to except perjury from its operation (see Penal Code 1925, Article 30), thereby authorizing children under the age of nine years to testify. See 44 Tex.Jur. p. 1004, § 55, and cases cited in footnotes, and 12 Tex.-Jur. p. 272, § 44. Furthermore, Section 10 of Article I of the Constitution provides that "no person shall be held to answer for a criminal offense, unless on an indictment of a grand jury, except in cases [where] the punishment is by fine or imprisonment, otherwise than in the penitentiary, * * *." If a person can be prosecuted for a felony after he gets beyond the age limit prescribed in this Act, then such prosecution must be under an indictment of a grand jury.

If this court were to say that the trial court had the right to compel these children to testify, then it would have to hold that the Act itself extends immunity from future prosecution to them. In effect, that decision would be a holding that the entire Penal Code has been repealed by implication, in so far as it deals with acts committed by persons within the statutory age limits. In the absence of a clear manifestation of the legislative intent to reach that result, and in the face of expressed intent to the contrary in Section 12, this court will not so hold, regardless of the social desirability of obtaining testimony from delinquent children themselves.

It will here be noted that Section 5 of this Act provides: "The Juvenile Court shall have exclusive original jurisdiction in proceedings governing any delinquent child, * * *," and that, "When jurisdiction shall have been obtained by the court in the case of any child, such child shall continue under the jurisdiction of the court until he becomes twenty-one (21) years of age, unless discharged prior thereto; * * *." As already pointed out by us, under the decisions of the Court of Criminal Appeals one who commits a criminal offense while a juvenile can be tried and punished therefor provided the trial takes place after the juvenile has reached the age of 18 years if a female, and 17 years if a male. Whether this law prevents the criminal trial from being had until the juvenile has reached the age of 21 years is a matter we leave to the decision of the Court of Criminal Appeals, the court of last resort in criminal cases in this State. We content ourselves with saying that when the criminal trial may take place makes no difference as regards the principles of law we have announced with reference to the right to compel the juvenile to testify against himself.

No opinion is expressed as to the effectiveness of a tender of immunity by the prosecuting attorney with the approval of the court, since that question is not before this court. See 44 Tex.Jur., pp. 976, 977, and authorities cited.

Many other States have passed similar legislation dealing with minors. There is a division of opinion among the courts in construing such legislation, and we cite some of the opinions, pro and con, as follows: Ex parte Mei, 122 N.J.Eq. 125, 192 A. 80, 110 A.L.R. 1080, and annotations; People of the State of New York v. Lewis, 260 N.Y. 171, 183 N.E. 353, 86 A.L.R. 1001, and annotations; Commonwealth v. Fisher, 213 Pa. 48, 62 A. 198, 5 Ann.Cas. 92; Cinque v. Boyd, 99 Conn. 70, 121 A. 678; State v. Elbert, 115 Conn. 589, 162 A. 769; People v. Fitzgerald, 244 N.Y. 307, 155 N.E. 584; Hampton v. State, 167 Ala. 73, 52 So. 659; Ex parte Januszewski, C.C., 196 F. 123; Lindsay v. Lindsay, 257 Ill. 328, 100 N.E. 892, 45 L.R.A.,N.S., 908, Ann.Cas. 1914A, 1222; Ex parte Daedler, 194 Cal. 320, 228 P. 467; Marlowe v. Commonwealth, 142 Ky. 106, 133 S.W. 1137; Re Sharp, 15 Idaho 120, 96 P. 563, 18 L.R.A.,N.S., 886; Mill v. Brown, 31 Utah 473, 88 P. 609, 120 Am.St.-Rep. 935; Bryant v. Brown, 151 Miss. 398, 118 So. 184, 60 A.L.R. 1325; Wissenberg v. Bradley, 209 Iowa 813, 229 N.W. 205, 67 A.L.R. 1075; 31 Amer.Jur. 786, and cases cited; 1 Wharton, Crim.Law, 11th Ed., § 370, note 2.

To come under the provisions of this Act, a reasonable and definite charge must be filed against the minor. The minor is entitled to have his rights fully safeguarded, and to have adequate process for his witnesses. If the objects of the Act are to be accomplished, the proceedings thereunder must necessarily be civil in nature, and while in some respects the orders or the judgment of the court may have the characteristics of a judgment in a criminal

case, the customary rules of evidence in civil cases, developed through long experience as essential in arriving at the truth with reasonable certainty, must be followed. The Act confers on the trial court certain powers to carry into effect its judgment. This, too, is absolutely essential if the law is to accomplish the purposes for which it was enacted. By the enactment of this law the Legislature was earnestly endeavoring to pass a law which would be for the benefit of the minor, and possibly save him from a career of crime and enable him to become a worthy citizen. And while safeguarding the rights of the minor, the Legislature was trying to protect the public as well.

Section 23 of the Act provides: "If any section, sub-division or clause of this Act shall be held to be unconstitutional or invalid, such decision shall not affect the validity of the remaining portions of the Act."

We find no constitutional provision which prohibited the Legislature from passing this Act, and unless some provision of the Constitution is pointed out clearly condemning the Act, it is the duty of courts to sustain it. 39 Tex.Jur. p. 251, § 133, and 9 Tex.Jur. p. 475, § 58. It is true that this law is a radical departure from the laws heretofore existing which it seeks to repeal, and we are not unmindful of the serious objections presented against the validity of this law. That the law is valid by the narrowest of margins will not justify courts to strike it down. Many cases could be cited which uphold the constitutionality of laws by a narrow margin. This court has repeatedly declared that a legislative enactment will not be held unconstitutional unless it is absolutely necessary to so hold, and in the case of Smith v. Patterson, 111 Tex. 535, 242, S.W. 749, 750 this court quoted with approval the rule laid down by Mr. Justice Ramsey in Solon v. State, 54 Tex.Cr.R. 261, 114 S.W. 349, as follows: "The rule is universal that the courts will not declare an act of the Legislature unconstitutional, unless such infirmity and vice clearly appears. Indeed this rule is necessary, and evidences that respectful regard in which the judicial should hold the legislative department of our government." See also Koy v. Schneider, 110 Tex. 369, 218 S.W. 479, 221 S.W. 880; Cooley on Const. Lim., 8th Ed., pp. 371, 372.

We hold that the Act under consideration

is valid; and the Court of Civil Appeals was correct in so holding, and in holding that it was error for the trial court to compel the minors to testify against themselves.

The judgment of the Court of Civil Appeals, reversing the judgment of the trial court, is affirmed, and this cause is remanded to the trial court for further proceedings consistent with this opinion.

57

In re Poff *

CURRAN, District Judge.

Four petitions were filed in the Juvenile Court of the District of Columbia representing that John Lawrence Poff, aged sixteen, was within the jurisdiction of the Juvenile Court. One petition, number 15–535–J, filed March 28, 1953, alleged that Poff, on January 30, 1953, used an automobile without the permission of the owner. A second petition, number 15–540–J, filed March 20, 1953, alleged that between February 8, 1953 and February 9, 1953 Poff used an automobile without the permission of the owner. A third petition, number 15–545–J, filed March 23, 1953, alleged that on December 10, 1952, Poff took, without right, property belonging to three separate persons. A fourth petition, number 15–558–J, filed March 24, 1953, alleged that between February 8, 1953 and February 9, 1953, Poff used an automobile without the permission of the owner.

The records of the Juvenile Court disclose, as to the first three above described petitions, that Poff appeared with his mother in the Juvenile Court on April 3, 1953 and acknowledged the allegations of the three petitions. As to the fourth petition, the record discloses that Poff appeared with his mother and after a hearing in the Juvenile Court, was found to be involved. The record further discloses that as to all four petitions filed, disposition was made on April 10, 1953 when, in all four instances, Poff was found and adjudged to have violated a law and, being under the age of eighteen, he was ordered, in number 15–535–J, to be committed to the National Training School for Boys of the District of Columbia until he was twenty-one years of age. The same commitment was ordered in number 15–540–J, number 15–545–J and number 15–558–J, said commitments to run concurrently with the commitment in number 15–535–J. The specific violation alleged in number 15–535–J, was unauthorized use of a motor vehicle. Poff was confined in Natural Bridge Camp, Virginia until November 3, 1954, at which time he was released on parole. In March 1955 petitioner was arrested in the District of Columbia for petit larceny, which charge was dismissed by the United States Attorney, and the petitioner was taken before the United States Parole Board, charged with a violation of his parole.

Petitioner now comes before this Court for a writ of habeas corpus praying that the sentence imposed by the Juvenile Court was unconstitutional inasmuch as he was not advised of his right to counsel, a right guaranteed him under the Sixth Amendment.

The Government urges upon this Court that the constitutional guarantee of the right to the assistance of counsel in all criminal prosecutions is not applicable to proceedings before the Juvenile Court to determine the delinquency of a child, and relies upon the decision reached in the case of Shioutakon v. District of Columbia, 114 A.2d 896, 898, decided June 24, 1955 in the Municipal Court of Appeals for the District of Columbia. The distinguished and learned Judge of that Court, writing for the Court, states:

" * * * The purpose of the proceedings is not to determine the question of guilt or innocence, but to promote the welfare of the child and the best interests of the state by the strengthening of family ties where possible, and, when necessary, to remove the child from custody of his parents for his welfare or the safety or protection of the public * * *." Citing Thomas v. United States, 74 App.D.C. 167, 121 F.2d 905, 908.

The Thomas case is authority for the principle that the procedure in the Juvenile Court in

* *In re Poff*, United States District Court, District of Columbia, 1955, 135 F. Supp. 224 (Dist. Ct., Dist. Col.). See note in 54 *Mich. L. Rev.* (1956), 1000–1003. See, also, *In re Poulin*, 129 A. 2d. (N. H., 1957) 672. — *Ed.*

making the adjudication is non-criminal in character and such adjudication "is in no sense the counterpart of a conviction in a criminal court." But I cannot overlook the ultimate function of the Juvenile Court to determine the guilt or innocence of the individual in order to make an adjudication of whether he is a delinquent.

The original Juvenile Court Act enacted in the District of Columbia in 1906, March 19, 1906, 34 Stat. 73, Ch. 960, § 1, D.C.Code 1951, § 11–901 et seq., was devised to afford the juvenile protections in addition to those he already possessed under the Federal Constitution. Before this legislative enactment, the juvenile was subject to the same punishment for an offense as an adult. It follows logically that in the absence of such legislation, the juvenile would be entitled to the same constitutional guarantees and safeguards as an adult. If this be true then the only possible reason for the Juvenile Court Act was to afford the juvenile safeguards *in addition to those* he already possessed. The legislative intent was to enlarge, *not to diminish* these protections.

The humanitarian tendency of modern legislation towards infants is best evidenced by the statutory enactments, providing that certain acts committed by certain infants, which in cases of adults would be crimes, shall be considered as constituting juvenile delinquency only. 43 C.J.S., Infants, § 98, p. 232. The validity of such legislation has been repeatedly upheld, except as it conflicts with constitutional limitations. State ex rel. Cave v. Tincher, 258 Mo. 1, 166 S.W. 1028, Ann.Cas.1915D, 696. Juvenile statutes should be construed liberally in favor of the welfare of the child. In re Powell, 6 Okl.Cr. 495, 120 P. 1022; McClain 1. Chelan County Super.Ct. 112 Wash. 260, 191 P. 852.

"In order that the beneficial purpose of the act may be effectuated, it should be construed liberally, except in-so-far as it purports to restrain the liberty of the child, in which case it should be strictly construed." Phillips v. State, Tex.Cr. App. 20 S.W.2d 790, 791. See also In re Lundy, 82 Wash. 148, 143 P. 885.

The question boils down simply to whether the legislature could deprive, had it so intended, a youth of these constitutional rights. This Court believes it could not for in so doing it would be contrary to all principles that only by amendment may the Congress depart from the Federal Constitution. If this deprivation were extended to cover certain crimes committed by adults, it would be condemned by the Courts. Yet by some sort of rationalization, under the guise of protective measures, we have reached a point where rights once held by a juvenile are no longer his. Have we now progressed to a point where a child may be incarcerated and deprived of his liberty during his minority by calling that which is a crime by some other name? If so, at what age is the Congress limited to legislate on behalf of the juvenile? May a child be deprived of his liberty and incarcerated in an institution until he reaches the age of twenty-one years merely by changing the name of the offense from unauthorized use of a motor vehicle to juvenile delinquency? In other words, has the Congress wiped out the constitutional protection by changing a name, the substance remaining the same? This Court stands steadfast in the belief that the Federal Constitution insofar as it is applicable "cannot be nullified by a mere nomenclature, the evil or the thing itself remaining the same." See dissenting opinion of Judge Crane in People v. Lewis, 260 N.Y. 171, 183 N.E. 353, 356, 86 A.L.R. 1001, which contains reasoning closely analogous to that of Dendy v. Wilson, 1944, 142 Tex. 460, 179 S.W.2d 269, 151 A.L.R. 1217.

The Government states that the rights guaranteed by the Sixth Amendment to persons accused of crime are not available to petitioner because he was not charged with a crime and the proceedings before the Juvenile Court resulting in his commitment to the Department of Public Welfare was not a criminal prosecution.

In Dendy v. Wilson, supra, the Texas Supreme Court held that minor children against whom proceedings were pending in the Juvenile Court could not be compelled over their objections to give testimony which might incriminate them under the protective provisions respecting self-incrimination in the Federal and State Constitutions, and the provision of the statute creating the Juvenile Court that evidence given in that Court should be inadmissible in another proceeding did not afford sufficient immunity to void the constitutional prohibitions. In California, Section 736 of the Welfare and Institutions Code, provides that "An order adjudging a person to be a ward of the juvenile court shall not be deemed to be a conviction of crime." In the case of In re Contreras, 109 Cal.App.2d 787, 241 P.2d 631, 633, the District Court of Appeals, Second District, Division 1, State of California, said:

"While the juvenile court law provides that adjudication of a minor to be a ward of the court shall not be deemed to be a conviction of crime, nevertheless, for all practical purposes, this is a legal fiction, presenting a challenge to credulity and doing violence to reason."

The Court further went on to say:

"True, the design of the Juvenile Court Act is intended to be salutary, and every effort should be made to further its legitimate purpose, but never should it be made an instrument for the denial to a minor of a constitutional right or of a guarantee afforded by law to an adult."

The Court further stated that the motion to vacate and set aside the order committing the minor to the Youth Authority of California "should have been granted thereby enabling said minor, *with the aid of counsel,* to properly prepare and present a defense to the charges preferred against him."

The opinion of the learned Judge in the Shioutakon case, supra, is interesting and not without authority, but not convincing. There is no unanimity of opinion among the various courts as to whether or not constitutional guarantees are applicable to juvenile offenders. The position is best stated in an annotation at 151 A.L.R. 1229:

"Such suggestions as may be gathered from cases discussing the general question of constitutional guaranties as applicable to juvenile offenders * * * in juvenile court proceedings, indicate unsettled and conflicting views,"

and further the opinions of some courts

"respecting the constitutional issues presented, or which may, upon proper presentment, become directly involved, illustrates the existence of a sharp divergence of views as to the applicability of constitutional limitations to juvenile courts."

I recognize that the Juvenile Court was created for the disposition of delinquent children and is not a criminal court. I also recognize that a hearing in the Juvenile Court is an

adjudication upon the status of a child in the nature of a guardianship imposed by the State as *parens patriae* to provide the care and guidance that, under normal circumstances, would be furnished by the natural parents. I hold only that where the child commits an act, which act if committed by an adult would constitute a crime, then due process in the Juvenile Court requires that the child be advised that he is entitled to the effective assistance of counsel, and this is so even though the Juvenile Court in making dispositions of delinquent children is not a criminal court.

In other words, in the District of Columbia, where the charge in the Juvenile Court is one of crime which, because of charitable considerations for the welfare of the child, is called "juvenile delinquency," then it must be surrounded by the guarantees and limitations of the Federal Constitution.

It is interesting to note that the distinguished Chief Judge of the Municipal Court of Appeals for the District of Columbia, in a most recent case, Gaddis v. Hongell, 117 A.2d 230, 231, said

"As is well known and understood, the procedures established for the small claims court were designed to make the services and protection of that court available to every litigant, plaintiff or defendant, without a lawyer. But as ought to be equally well understood, it was never intended that lawyers be barred from that court or that there be any interference with their traditional functions when they appear there."

This certainly is true and the same principle is applicable here. The Congress, in enacting the Juvenile Court Act, which designated certain crimes when committed by a child to be juvenile delinquency, never intended that the child be barred from the protection of the Federal Constitution, but rather intended, out of charitable considerations for the child's welfare, that an additional protection be granted to the child by forbidding the stigma of the word "crime" to be attached to a person under the age of eighteen years.

One more matter deserves comment. It is not disputed, aside from the constitutional considerations, that petitioner would have been entitled to a jury trial. This being so, who is to make the decision as to whether or not a jury trial should be demanded? Is a sixteen year old boy capable of deciding whether he should be tried by a jury or tried by a Judge? I do not think so.

Chief Judge Edgerton of the United States Court of Appeals for the District of Columbia Circuit said in Williams v. Huff, 79 U.S.App. D.C. 31, 142 F.2d 91, 92:

"It seems to me to follow as a matter of law that a boy of seventeen cannot competently waive his right to counsel in a criminal case."

Courts should not brush aside lightly the guarantees of the Federal Constitution on some highly technical theory, and until the United States Court of Appeals for the District of Columbia Circuit has directed that the rights guaranteed by the Sixth Amendment are not available to the petitioner. I must grant the relief sought. The petitioner shall be released and counsel shall prepare an appropriate order not inconsistent with this memorandum.

58

Shioutakon v. District of Columbia*

Before PRETTYMAN, BAZELON and BASTIAN, Circuit Judges.

BAZELON, Circuit Judge.

This juvenile delinquency proceeding was instituted by a petition charging our 15-year old appellant with having used an automobile without the owner's consent.[1] At the hearing before the Juvenile Court, he admitted the charge and was committed to a training school.[2]

---

* Shioutakon v. District of Columbia, United States Court of Appeals District of Columbia Circuit, 1956, 236 F. 2d 666.

[1] The Juvenile Court Act, D.C.Code, § 11–901 et seq. (1951), as amended (Supp. 1954), applies, inter alia, to "any person under the age of 18 years — (1) Who has violated any law; or who has violated any ordinance or regulation of the District of Columbia * * *." D.C.Code, § 11–906 (a) (1951). D.C.Code, § 11–908 (1951) provides for filing of a petition.

[2] D.C.Code, § 11–915 (1951), as amended (Supp. 1954).

He was not represented by counsel, nor did the judge advise him or his mother, who was present,[3] that he might be represented by counsel. About three months later, counsel appeared for him and filed a motion to vacate and set aside the court's judgment on the ground that he had been deprived of his constitutional right to counsel. Denial of this motion was appealed to the Municipal Court of Appeals which affirmed.[4] This court allowed a petition for leave to appeal because the question presented is important to the fair administration of justice.

One of the aims of the 1938 revision of the Juvenile Court Act[5] was to eliminate the formalities of a criminal proceeding which emphasizes "punishment and retribution," and to provide in its place a more informal procedure designed to enhance the protective and rehabilitative features which have come to be associated with modern juvenile courts.[6]

To this end the Act authorizes the Director of Social Work to investigate any complaint "to determine whether the interests of the public or of the child require that further action be taken."[7] Congress clearly intended, in this section, to encourage the disposition of cases on a social rather than legal basis. In the event such disposition is deemed unwise, "further action" may be taken, as in the present case, by the filing of a petition which requires a court hearing.[8]

But even where a petition is filed, the proceedings are meant to be non-criminal and non-formal in nature.[9] Instead of an indictment

---

[3] His father's whereabouts were unknown.

[4] Shioutakon v. District of Columbia, D.C. Mun.-App.1955, 114 A.2d 896.

[5] 52 Stat. 596 (1938), D.C.Code, § 11–902 (1951).

[6] S.Rep. No. 530, 75th Cong., 1st Sess., 4 (1937); H.R.Rep. No. 177, 75th Cong., 1st Sess. 3 (1937).

[7] D.C.Code, § 1–908 (1951).

[8] Out of 4412 complaints received by the court in the year ending June 30, 1955, 1318 were informally disposed of by the juvenile section either through dismissal or referral to social agencies. Petitions were filed on 3094 complaints. Annual Report, Juvenile Court of the District of Columbia 1954–55. In the year ending June 30, 1954, 1205 out of 5211 complaints were informally terminated; petitions on 4006 were filed. Annual Report 1954. Out of a total of 5351 complaints in the year ending June 30, 1953, 1440 were informally terminated, and 3911 went to hearing. Annual Report 1953.

[9] D.C.Code, § 11–908 (1951).

or information, there is a petition entitled " 'In the matter of —————— * * *.' " The hearing itself may be conducted in an "informal manner,"[10] that is, without the "technicalities which are not essential to justice and which tend to confuse or intimidate a child."[11] The court is not open to the general public.[12] In the event an adjudication of delinquency results, the court is authorized to place the child on probation in his parents' custody, to commit him to the Board of Public Welfare or to a training school, or to "make such further disposition" as it deems in the child's "best interests."[13] The statute's aim is to avoid the stigmatizing effects of a criminal conviction.[14]

In recognizing and approving the laudable

---

[10] D.C.Code, § 11–915 (1951). Nevertheless it appears that "the atmosphere of formality which surrounds the hearings [in the District] is equal to or greater than that in hearings in adult courts." Report of a Committee Composed of Representatives From United Community Services, Department of Justice, Children's Bureau, Department of Health, Education and Welfare 29 (1951) (hereinafter referred to as "Survey Report"). The courtroom has "all the physical attributes of an adult court," including raised benches and equipment for the prosecuting attorney. The judge wears the usual black robe, the court clerk and corporation counsel are present, announcements are made in a formal manner by a marshal, and the child sits in an enclosure without his parents. The charges are read out loud to the child and he is asked to admit or deny them. He is put under oath if he testifies. *Ibid.*

Such procedure is, in most respects, contrary to that generally recommended for, and observed by juvenile courts. Standards for Specialized Courts Dealing With Children, Children's Bureau, Department of Health, Education and Welfare 54–55 (1954) (hereinafter referred to as "Standards for Specialized Courts"); Survey Report 28. No change in courtroom procedure has been made since the 1951 survey. Hearings on Juvenile Delinquency in the District of Columbia Before the Subcommittee to Investigate Juvenile Delinquency of the Senate Committee on the Judiciary, 83d Cong., 1st and 2d Sess., Exh. 15(b), pp. 247–48 (1953–54).

[11] Standards for Specialized Courts 54 (1954), quoting Lou, Juvenile Courts in the United States 129 (1927).

[12] D.C.Code, § 11–915 (Supp.1954).

[13] D.C.Code, § 11–915 (1951), as amended (Supp.1954).

[14] The adjudication does not impose civil disabilities. The child is not "deemed a criminal" nor is any adjudication deemed a conviction of a crime. D.C.Code, § 11–915 (1951). See Thomas v. United States, 1941, 74 App.D.C. 167, 169–170, 121 F.2d 905, 907–908.

objectives of this system of "individualized justice,"[15] we may not overlook the fact that the status and rights of the child as well as rights of the parents are involved.[16] That fact inheres in the court's power to deprive the child of liberty and the parents of custody.[17] And where, as here, the exercise of this power rests upon an alleged violation of law, the court must find, from evidence in a hearing, whether the child has in fact committed an unlawful act.

The serious nature and effect of this adjudication suggests that Congress could not have been unaware of the need for effective assistance of counsel.[18] Although the Act in terms neither recognizes nor withholds such assistance, the legislative history reflects congressional understanding that alleged delinquents would be represented by counsel.[19] That there is a need for such representation to protect the child's interests is apparent, for example, from a realistic view of § 11–915's provision for "hearing." The "right to be heard" when personal liberty is at stake requires the effective assistance of counsel in a juvenile court quite as much as it does in a criminal court.[20] The need is also apparent from the provision for

---

[15] Standards for Specialized Courts 1.

[16] Id. at 1–8, 53–58. Increasing concern for protecting the child in juvenile courts has been expressed by commentators. E. g., Rubin, Protecting the Child in the Juvenile Court, 43 J.Crim.L. 425 (1952); Tappan, Juvenile Delinquency 188–223 (1949).

[17] D.C.Code, § 11–915 (1951), as amended (Supp.1954). In the year ending June 30, 1955, delinquency cases resulted in the commitment of 144 boys to the National Training School and 380 to the Department of Public Welfare. Annual Report, Juvenile Court of the District of Columbia 3 (1954–55).

[18] Courts have found such need in deportation cases where, as here, deprivation of personal liberty is involved in proceedings that are civil rather than criminal. [Citations omitted. — Ed.] These cases recognize the right to counsel as an essential element of due process. In the present case, however, we do not reach consideration of due process requirements since our holding rests on our view of the statute.

[19] H.R.Rep. No. 177, 75th Cong., 1st Sess. 3 (1937); S.Rep. No. 530, 75th Cong., 1st Sess. 4 (1937); 81 Cong.Rec. 1004 (1937). See also Standards for Specialized Courts 56–58.

[20] See e. g., Powell v. Alabama, 1932, 287 U.S. 45, 68–69, 53 S.Ct. 55, 77 L.Ed. 158, quoted in Johnson v. Zerbst, 1938, 304 U.S. 458, 463, 58 S.Ct. 1019, 82 L.Ed. 1461.

a jury on demand.[21] Clearly a child cannot, without the aid of counsel, competently decide whether he should exercise this right.

Rights afforded by the rules of the Juvenile Court would also be meaningless without legal assistance. Under Rule VIII, demand for a jury trial must be made *in writing* within five days of arraignment. If a jury is demanded, the juvenile may exercise peremptory challenges (Rule IX) and prepare written requests for instructions (Rule X). He is allowed to make written motion for a new trial or in arrest of judgment (Rule XII). Appeals to the Municipal Court of Appeals and to this court are available.

Since an intelligent exercise of the juvenile's rights under the Act and the Rules clearly requires legal skills not possessed by the ordinary child under 18, it is plain that, as appellee, the District of Columbia, concedes, a juvenile is entitled to be represented by counsel if he or his parents or guardian choose to furnish one. Appellee contends, however, that the court is not required to advise a juvenile of that right, or to assure itself that the right has been intelligently waived.* It also contends that the court is not required to appoint counsel where there is no such waiver or where the juvenile's family is indigent. We think these contentions are unsound.

Appellee in effect would have us accept the proposition that protection of a child's rights hinges on whether he is either something of a genius or a member of a family which can afford counsel. Obviously the intelligence quotient of the child or the economic position of his family cannot be controlling.[22] Our concern for the fair administration of justice [23]

impels us to hold that, in this and in similar cases in the future,[24] the juvenile must be advised that he has a right to engage counsel or to have counsel named on his behalf.[25] And, where that right exists, the court must be assured that any waiver of it is intelligent and competent.[26]

We are in full accord with the objectives of the Act to enable the court to deal with children in an informal manner and to encourage dispositions, on the basis of all relevant social data, looking toward treatment rather than punishment. Requiring the court to inform an alleged delinquent like appellant, against whom a petition has been filed, that he has a right to counsel is not, we think, incompatible with these objectives.[27]

It follows from the foregoing discussion that the court erred in denying appellant's motion to vacate the judgment of commitment.

Reversed and remanded for further proceedings required by this opinion.

BASTIAN, Circuit Judge, concurs in the result.*

---

[21] D.C.Code, § 11–915 (1951).

* "Where the court finds for any reason the minor is not capable of a waiver the parent may so waive provided the court also finds there is no conflict of interest between them; and of course the waiver by the parent must be an intelligent, knowing act." McBridge v. Jacobs, 1957, 236 F.2d, 666 (D.C. Cir. 1957). — *Ed.*

[22] Cf. Griffin v. Illinois, 1956, 351 U.S. 12, 76 S.Ct. 585.

[23] Griffin v. United States, 1949, 336 U.S. 704, 717–718; Fisher v. United States, 1946, 328 U.S. 463, 476, 66 S.Ct. 1318, 90 L.Ed. 1382; McNabb v. United States, 1943, 318 U.S. 332, 340–341, 63 S.Ct. 608, 87 L.Ed. 819; Kelly v. United States, 1952, 90 U.S.App.D.C. 125, 127, 194 F.2d 150, 152.

[24] Durham v. United States, 1954, 94 U.S.App.-D.C. 228, 240, 14 F.2d 862, 874, 45 A.L.R.2d 1430. Cf. Mr. Justice Frankfurter's opinion, concurring in Griffin v. Illinois, 351 U.S. at pages 25–26, 76 S.Ct. at page 593, with respect to the prospective application of a constitutional right.

[25] We do not hold that counsel is essential in the preliminary stages before a petition is filed.

[26] That question should be resolved as one of fact "in the light of [the child's] age, education, and information, and all other pertinent facts * * *." Williams v. Huff, 1944, 79 U.S.App.D.C. 31, 32, 142 F.2d 91, 92.

The court would be well advised to consult the child's parents or guardian where their interests are not adverse.

[27] See Rubin, Protecting the Child in the Juvenile Court, 43 J.Crim.L. 425, 440 (1952); Standards for Specialized Courts 56.

* For the conflict of views regarding the right of counsel in delinquency proceedings, see "Right to and appointment of counsel in juvenile court proceedings," 60 ALR 2d 691 (1958). The care with which judges should examine the question of waiver is shown in a case in which the court concluded that a fourteen-year-old girl could make an effective waiver on the questionable grounds that since the girl had recently been married it could be inferred that she knew what she was doing and because she told the judge: "I don't want no lawyers or anyone representing me." State v. Cronin, 220 La. (1951) 233, 241, 56 So. 2d 242, 245. — *Ed.*

59

In re Singer *

THE COURT. — Upon petition of Herbert L. Singer and wife, parents of Sharon Singer, for a writ of habeas corpus on behalf of their daughter, a writ was issued directed to David Bogan, superintendent of Juvenile Hall of the County of Los Angeles. A return has been filed by said respondent and a hearing has been held, upon which it was stipulated that the petition and supplemental petition be treated as a traverse to the return. The allegations of the petition and supplemental petition insofar as they have not been placed in issue by the return will be taken as true. . . . [Citations omitted. — Ed.]

The facts bearing upon the detention of Sharon Singer by the authorities are the following. The minor, 8 years of age, was residing with her parents in a fit and proper home and was receiving proper and sufficient parental care, support, supervision and control; her parents were fit and proper persons to have custody of the minor and her home environment was unobjectionable. On June 23, 1955, at about 8 p.m., the minor was taken into custody and placed in juvenile hall and she remained in the custody of the superintendent of juvenile hall until she was released to the custody of her parents under order of this court on July 7. No petition that the minor be made a ward of the juvenile court was filed until on or about June 29, 1955, when the judge of the juvenile court granted a writ of habeas corpus for said minor and set the same for hearing at 9:30 a.m., June 30, and at that time proceeded to conduct a hearing "for the purpose of determining the reasons for the necessity of the detention of the minor," (Welf. & Inst. Code, § 729.5), and a hearing on the writ of habeas corpus; that no notice of the hearing was given to the parents of said minor; the court then discharged the writ of habeas corpus, ordered the minor to be detained in said juvenile hall and set for hearing on July 13 the petition to have said minor made a ward of the juvenile court.

---

* In re Singer, District Court of California, Second Dist., Div. Three, 1955, 134 C. A. 2d, 547.

During said detention of the minor neither her parents nor their attorney have been allowed to speak privately with her. At the hearing on June 30 an officer having charge of the minor prevented the parents from speaking with her and when she signaled a greeting to them, removed her from the room. On July 7 at the time this court issued its writ of habeas corpus, the court also made an order for the release of said minor to the custody of her parents upon their written agreement to produce said minor before this court upon the hearing of the writ.

It has been made to appear to the satisfaction of this court that the sole purpose of the detention of said minor and of the filing of the petition to have her made a ward of the juvenile court and all proceedings had thereunder was and is to keep her in custody for use as a witness in a criminal action against David Ely Singer, the paternal grandfather of the minor, who was accused by complaint filed June 24 of an offense committed against said minor in violation of section 288 of the Penal Code while the child was visiting her grandparents. On July 1 said minor did testify as a witness at the preliminary hearing of said accused on said charge and upon the conclusion of said hearing said minor was retained in custody by juvenile court authorities, was placed in a private home under their jurisdiction, and the parents of said minor were denied all information as to the place where said minor was retained and as to the identity of the person or persons in whose custody she was held. It is alleged in the petition and not denied that a deputy district attorney has threatened to cause said minor to be detained in custody by placing a "District Attorney's Hold" against her with the superintendent of juvenile hall and that such "hold" orders have been and will be accepted by said superintendent as authority for holding juveniles in custody solely as witnesses and subject to the orders of the district attorney.

In reaching our conclusions as to the lawfulness of the detention of said minor and the purposes and motives of the authorities involved, we have taken into consideration certain additional facts which are known to the court, namely, when this court in conference decided to issue a writ of habeas corpus, the court was advised of the fact that said minor had been placed in the custody of a person or persons and in a home unknown to the petitioners and the court made inquiries of the superintendent of juvenile hall and requested that the court be advised as to the person or persons having custody of said minor at that time; said inquiries met with delay, evasion, opposition and lack of cooperation.

From all the facts made known to the court, this court has concluded that the pending proceeding purporting to be one to have said minor declared a ward of the juvenile court was instituted as a mere device and means to retain said minor in custody solely for the purpose of separating her from her parents, the petitioners, and keeping her available as a witness at the trial of said David Ely Singer.

Section 700 of the Welfare and Institutions Code sets forth the conditions and circumstances in which any person under the age of 21 years is within the jurisdiction of the juvenile court. The described conditions are 14 in number and need not be enumerated. Suffice it to say that it appears from the facts divulged to the court that the detention of said minor as related above has not been and is not based upon the existence of any of the conditions specified in section 700 of the code. The same is true with respect to the conditions under which a person under the age of 21 years may be declared free from the custody and control of either or both parents as specified in section 701 of the code.

Section 726 of the code requires that upon the filing of such a petition, a citation shall issue directing the parents etc., to appear at a time and place for which a hearing has been set and that such citation be served at least 24 hours before the time set for the hearing. Section 729 specifies the conditions in which a probation officer or peace officer may take temporary custody of a minor to be detained at juvenile hall or other suitable place designated by the juvenile court "when such custody or detention is a matter of immediate and urgent necessity for the protection of the welfare of the child." Throughout the proceedings above related no claim has been advanced or pretention made that the custody or detention of the minor was a matter of immediate or urgent necessity or for the protection of her welfare. Sections 729.5 and 730 read as set out in the margin.[1] Authority of law is not vested in any

court, official, officer or authority to seize the person of a minor and to incarcerate and detain said minor for the sole purpose of keeping said minor available for use as a witness in a criminal proceeding or any other proceeding. No court, official, officer or authority responsible for the detention of the minor, Sharon Singer, has had any right or authority over the person of said minor other than is conferred by the provisions of the Welfare and Institutions Code which we have cited. The taking of said minor into custody and her detention was illegal unless the same was a matter of immediate and urgent necessity for the protection of the welfare of the child. The facts as known to us refute the existence of any such condition. The detention of said minor for more than 48 hours without the filing of a petition in accordance with subdivision (a) of section 720, or the filing of a criminal complaint, was illegal. The district attorney has no shadow of authority to cause a minor to be wrested from his or her home or the custody of parents or legal custodian and incarcerated or detained for the sole purpose of using such minor as a witness. It manifestly appears from the facts which are known to the court that the actions and proceedings that have been had for the incarceration of said minor were illegal and void *ab initio* and that the further incarceration of said minor has been

---

officer or probation officer, such minor shall be released within forty-eight hours after having been taken into custody, excluding Sundays and nonjudicial days, unless within said period of time a petition in accordance with subdivision (a) of Section 720 concerning him is filed with the clerk of the superior court or a criminal complaint against him is filed in a court of competent jurisdiction. If the minor remains in the custody of any peace officer or probation officer, within twenty-four hours, excluding Sundays and non-judicial days, after the filing of the petition, the judge of the juvenile court shall conduct a hearing for the purpose of determining the reasons for the necessity of the detention of the minor. If within said period such a hearing has not been held then the minor shall be released from custody."

"§ 730. Whenever a petition has been filed in the juvenile court alleging that a person comes within the provisions of Section 700 or 701 of this code and praying for a hearing thereon or whenever any subsequent petition has been filed praying for a further hearing in the matter of said person, said person, pending the hearing of any of said petitions, or during the continuance thereof, may be retained by the person having charge of said person or the court may order that said person be detained in the detention home or in some other suitable place."

---

[1] "§ 729.5. Whenever a minor under the age of eighteen years is taken into custody by any peace

and is for an illegal purpose and in violation of the rights of said minor and her parents, the petitioners herein.

It is ordered that said minor be discharged from the custody of the juvenile court and the probation officer of the county of Los Angeles

and that her custody remain with her parents, the petitioners herein.*

---

* For other examples of abuse of juvenile court proceedings, see *Ex parte Moilanen*, 104 Cal. A 2d 835, 233 P2d 91 (1951); *Application of Jacobsen*, 278 App. Div. 945, 104 N. Y. S. 2d 949 (1951). — *Ed.*

Chapter 13

Jurisdictional and Related Problems

60

Commonwealth *v.* Mead *

Indictment for being a common seller of intoxicating liquors.

At the trial in the superior court before BRIGHAM, J., the Commonwealth proved several sales made by the defendant within the time named in the indictment, and offered no other evidence. It was proved on the part of the defendant that she was a daughter of Eliza Mead, and at the time of said sales was under twelve years of age, living with her parents, and that the sales were made by her in the dwelling-house of her parents, and under and by direction of her mother, to whom the liquors belonged. The defendant also put in evidence a license granted to her mother to sell liquors, under the internal revenue acts of the United States.

The defendant requested the court to instruct the jury that if she, at the time of making the sales, was under twelve years of age, and if the sale were made under the general direction of the mother, in the dwelling-house of the parents of the defendant, then she could not be convicted under this indictment. The judge declined so to rule, and instructed the jury that the license was no defence, if the sales were made in violation of the statutes of Massachusetts; and that if the defendant did, in the dwelling-house of her parents, and while she lived with them, and by direction of her mother, and while under twelve years of age, make three or more separate sales of her mother's intoxicating liquors within the time alleged in the indictment, they should find her guilty.

The jury returned a verdict of guilty, and the defendant alleged exceptions.

---

* *Commonwealth* v. *Mead*, Supreme Judicial Court of Massachusetts, 1865, 10 Allen 398.

BIGELOW, C. J. The question of the legal competency of the defendant to commit the offence charged in the indictment was distinctly raised in the present case by the fact proved at the trial, that she was under twelve years of age. The rule of the common law is perfectly well settled, that a child between the ages of seven and fourteen is not presumed to be *doli capax*, and the question whether, in committing an offence, such child in fact acted with intelligence and capacity, and an understanding of the unlawful character of the act charged, is to be determined by the jury upon the evidence, and in view of all the circumstances attending the alleged criminal transaction. [Citations omitted. — Ed.] This rule is uniformly applied in cases where children under fourteen and above seven years of age are charged with murder or other felonies.* A *fortiori*, it is applicable where they are accused of lesser offences, or with the commission of acts coming within the class of *mala prohibita*. These do not so violently shock the natural moral sense or instinct of children, and would not be so readily recognized and understood by them to be wrong, or a violation of duty, as the higher crimes of murder, arson, larceny, and the like.†

Although the attention of the judge at the trial was drawn to the fact that the defendant was of tender years, so that no presumption of legal capacity to commit crime existed, he wholly omitted to give any instructions from which the jury could be led to infer that it was their duty to find that the defendant knew the unlawful character of the act with which she was charged, before they could render a verdict of guilty against her. For aught that we can

---

* A recent attempt to have the court take into account the common law presumption despite existence of the Federal Juvenile Court Act was blocked in *United States* v. *Borders*, 154 F. Supp. 214 (1957); aff'd *Borders* v. *United States*, 256 F. 2d 458 (1958). — Ed.

† Cf. French Code Pénal, Art. 69. — Ed.

see, the verdict was rendered without any consideration of the legal competency of the defendant to commit the offence alleged in the indictment. The case was one which seems to us to have required an explicit instruction on this point. It is true that it was not necessary to show actual knowledge by the defendant of the unlawfulness of the act, if sufficient legal capacity to commit crime was otherwise proved. If capacity is established, knowledge may be presumed. Nor is it necessary to offer direct evidence of capacity. It may be inferred from the circumstances under which the offence was committed. But nevertheless it is to be established as a distinct fact. We are unable to see anything in the facts set out in the exceptions which tend to prove that the defendant was cognizant of the illegal character of the act which she committed. She seems to have made the illegal sale in the presence of and in obedience to the express command of her mother. This fact of itself had some tendency to show that the child did not understand that the act which she was told by her parent to commit was wrong, and, in connection with the request for instructions which was made by the defendant's counsel, required the judge to give full and explicit instructions on the subject of legal competency to commit crime. The omission of such instructions was an error, which, in our judgment, renders it necessary that there should be a new trial of the case.

Exceptions sustained.[1]

---

[1] In many states the common-law age of irresponsibility has been raised above seven years. See, for instance, *Allen v. United States,* 150 U.S. 551; 14 Sup. Ct. Rep. 196; FULLER, C. J., said: "The age of irresponsibility has been changed in many of the states by statute, and among others, in Arkansas, where it is provided that 'an infant under twelve years of age shall not be found guilty of any crime or misdemeanor.' Ark. Stat. Dig. 1884, 425, c. 45, § 1498, it being held, however, that the common law presumption that a person between the ages of twelve and fourteen is incapable of discerning good from evil, until the contrary is affirmatively shown, still prevails. *Dove v. State,* 37 Arkansas, 261." The courts have also been faced with the problem of whether the age incapacity applies to both mental and chronologic ages. Generally, it has been held to apply only to chronologic age. See *State v. Schabert,* 222 Minn. 261, 24 N. W. 2d 846 (1946); *State v. Gardner,* 219 S.C. 97, 64 S.E. 2d 130 (1951); *State v. Schilling,* 95 N. J. L. 145, 112 A. 400 (1920). — *Ed.*

61

In re Mont *

RHODES, President Judge.

On this appeal, Arnold Mont, an alleged delinquent, questions the validity and legality of a finding of delinquency and of the commitment to a reform school made by the Municipal Court of Philadelphia, Juvenile Division, under The Juvenile Court Law of June 2, 1933, P.L. 1433, as amended, 11 P.S. § 243 et seq. Some of the questions involved are identical with those raised in Re Holmes, Pa.Super., 103 A.2d 454. The two appeals, although not otherwise related, were argued together.

Briefly, the evidence in this case discloses that Mont, aged 15, and a companion, obtained a 22 caliber rifle, and Mont, while shooting at objects in the street from a roof top, shot and killed Robert Morgan, Jr., aged 11, who happened suddenly to emerge from around the corner of a building into the path of the rifle fire.

On September 23, 1952, a petition was filed in the Municipal Court of Philadelphia, Juvenile Division, alleging the delinquency of Mont based on charges of homicide and burglary. On the same day, after hearing, Mont was held by Judge Propper, sitting as a committing magistrate, without bail for the grand jury on a charge of murder. Thereafter, the grand jury returned true bills on indictments for murder and manslaughter. Subsequently, on January 28, 1953, the Commonwealth had entered a nolle prosequi on the murder bill. The charges of manslaughter remained pending in the Court of Quarter Sessions of Philadelphia County, which then transferred the proceedings to the Juvenile Court.

A hearing was held before Judge Propper in the Juvenile Court on February 16, 1953, at which time counsel appeared for Mont. At this hearing Detective McGurk gave testimony as to the police investigation of the shooting, and read in evidence the apparently voluntary statement of Mont to the effect that Mont hit Robert Morgan, who came into view from around the

---

* In re Mont, Superior Court of Pennsylvania, 1954, 175 Pa. Super. 150, 103 A. 2d 460.

corner of a house, while Mont was aiming at a tin can in the street from a position on a roof top. A representative from the Board of Education testified Mont was absent from school 87 days out of a school year. A probation officer of the Juvenile Court testified to Mont's oral statement that Mont had "pulled the trigger" and shot the deceased boy. Over counsel's claim of privilege against self-incrimination on behalf of Mont, appellant was examined and corroborated his former statements as to the manner of obtaining the rifle and the circumstances surrounding the killing of Robert Morgan. Mont's mother and father were called and examined by the court and counsel for Mont. Mont's attorney also placed upon the record of this hearing the fact that he had attempted to secure a court order for prehearing inspection of the entire record of the Mont proceeding in the Juvenile Court, including the reports of investigators. The court permitted inspection of the record but excluded therefrom what it considered confidential reports of its investigators. On the basis of the testimony the court formally adjudged Arnold Mont a delinquent, and giving consideration to his past record, ordered him committed to Glen Mills School For Boys. According to the court records, as set forth in the court's opinion, Mont was arrested July 10, 1951, for delinquency based on larceny of a bicycle, aggravated assault and battery, highway robbery, and malicious mischief. Apparently no formal hearing was had, nor was any finding made on these alleged delinquencies. Further, the court in its opinion states: "On June 22, 1952 Arnold Mont was placed on probation for delinquency involving an arson charge. On September fifth, 1952 the juvenile court judge who heard the instant case placed Arnold Mont on probation because of delinquencies involving an incorrigibility charge made by his mother and a disorderly conduct charge."

On appeal Mont's attorney contends that the jurisdiction of the juvenile court is limited to unlawful acts other than murder and hence the court lacked jurisdiction or power to find the child delinquent and commit him on what was in substance a murder charge. Clearly, under general principles and under the express provisions of the Law, the juvenile court has no authority or jurisdiction to conduct a criminal trial of a child on a murder indictment. The Law makes certain exceptions in the case of

murder. Cf. In re Edwards, 54 Pa.Dist. & Co. 601. Section 14, as amended, 11 P.S. § 256, requires the court of quarter sessions or oyer and terminer in all pending criminal charges involving children under 16 to transfer such cases other than murder to the juvenile court. So, also, in section 18, 11 P.S. § 260, where a child above 14 is held for any offense other than murder, punishable by imprisonment in a state penitentiary, the judge of the juvenile court having jurisdiction may, if the interests of the state require it, certify the case to the district attorney for formal criminal prosecution. Neither of these sections says or implies that the act of unlawful homicide may not constitute, under proper circumstances, the basis for the jurisdiction of the juvenile court, and the ground for adjudication and commitment of the minor as a delinquent. In the present case it was entirely proper and lawful for a nol. pros. to be entered on the murder charge and to remit the case to the juvenile court for action. While under the Law the juvenile court has no jurisdiction over a charge for murder where a true bill has been found and is pending, it must of necessity considering the fundamental purposes of The Juvenile Court Law, have jurisdiction to base a determination of delinquency upon acts which would otherwise constitute murder or unlawful homicide under the criminal law. Any other interpretation of the Law would mean that a child whose unlawful acts in substance amounted to unlawful homicide, the most serious violation of law known, would be exempted from the beneficent provision of the Law. The framers of the Law intended no such anomaly. There is as much, if not more, reason for applying the Law to such a child as to one whose delinquency arises from less serious violations.

Here disposition was made of the formal indictment for murder before the case was referred to the Juvenile Court. It would appear to be equally permissible that a juvenile court exercise jurisdiction in a case of unlawful homicide where no murder or formal criminal prosecution has been instituted. Cf. In re Edwards, supra, 54 Pa.Dist. & Co. 601; In re Clifford, 55 Pa.Dist. & Co. 238. Judge Propper having originally held the child for the grand jury upon a formal charge of murder, and a nol. pros. having been entered on the murder indictment, there was no such conclusive disposition of the case in the criminal court as would preclude on remission further proceeding in the Juvenile Court. Cf. In re Trignani's Case, 150 Pa.Super. 491, 28 A.2d 702.

Appellant's next assertion is that a juvenile has a constitutional right to a speedy and final disposition of the murder indictment. The adjudication of delinquency and the commitment under The Juvenile Court Law is not a criminal trial but an action looking to treatment, reformation, and rehabilitation of the child. Com. v. Fisher, 213 Pa. 48, 62 A. 198. Under its express provisions, The Juvenile Court Law does not take away the right of the courts of quarter sessions and of oyer and terminer to try a child on an indictment for any offense where the interests of the state demand such trial. Section 18, 11 P.S. § 260. But where, as here, the authorities decide that a criminal trial is unnecessary, the violation of law by the child may constitute the child a delinquent in proceedings under The Juvenile Court Law.* A child who has been adjudicated delinquent under the Law, rather than prosecuted for a criminal offense, has no inherent constitutional or legal right to ask that the juvenile court proceedings be set aside and that he be proceeded against criminally. It was stated in Com. v. Carnes, 82 Pa. Super. 335, 339, that: "The purpose of the act is reformation, not punishment. The State as *parens patriae* has the right to save a child from prosecution and punishment and, as against this right, neither the child nor its parents can insist that the child shall be tried for a criminal offense with which he may have been charged. The right to trial by jury vouchsafed to us by constitutional guarantees is the right to be tried in that manner, if tried. The Constitution has never been held to guarantee to the citizen the right to insist that he be tried for a crime if the State determines that it is to the interest of the citizen and the State that he shall be saved from such an ordeal." There has been no violation of any constitutional right which appellant might have to a speedy trial. The matter of trial is not involved in the absence of any proceeding on the indictment.

It is argued on behalf of appellant that he was adjudicated delinquent and committed on hearsay testimony in violation of the fundamental rules of evidence. Appellant freely admitted

facts showing his violation of law and his delinquency, and the court's finding of delinquency is therefore supported by competent evidence of record. It was not necessary to rely upon hearsay testimony to support the basic finding of delinquency, and it does not appear that hearsay testimony or ex parte reports were used by the court in making its determination and adjudication. As the basic finding of delinquency was supported by competent evidence, the admission of hearsay testimony would not constitute reversible error. Our statements in Re Holmes, supra, Pa.Super., 103 A.2d 454, regarding the applicability of the rules of evidence to juvenile court proceedings and the use of hearsay evidence are relevant here.

In this appeal, also, counsel contends that the juvenile's constitutional right against self-incrimination was violated. Appellant was called, interrogated by the court, and freely admitted acts constituting a violation of law and forming the basis of the delinquency adjudication. For reasons set forth at length in the Holmes Appeal, there was no infringement in this proceeding of any privilege guaranteed the juvenile against self-incrimination.

What we said in the Holmes Appeal is controlling on the question of the right of appellant's attorney to inspect the court record and files dealing with the juvenile. In the present case the parents of the juvenile had notice of the proceeding; they were present and were examined as witnesses at the court hearing at which the delinquency charge was established.

The order of the court below is affirmed.

WOODSIDE, J., absent.

62

State *v.* Monahan *et al.**

JACOBS, J.

Prompted by mid-Twentieth Century sociological precepts, our Legislature has directed

---

* In State v. *Interest of Lindsey*, 78 Ida. 241, 300 P2d 491 (1956) it was held that under the Idaho

constitution a juvenile has the right to demand a jury trial. — *Ed.*

* State v. *Monahan* et al., Supreme Court of New Jersey, 1954, 15 N. J. 34, 104 A. 2d 21, 48 A.L.R. 2d 641. For the aftermath of this opinion, see *Ex parte Johnson*, 31 N. J. Super. 382, 106 A2d 560

that children under 16 who commit any offenses which would be criminal if committed by adults, shall not be triable in criminal proceedings but shall be dealt with exclusively by our specialized juvenile courts. The legal issue presented to us is whether this clear statutory mandate may be judicially disregarded to enable a first degree murder trial in the County Court of a 15-year-old boy who participated in a robbery with his father during which his father killed two persons.

In April 1953 Eugene Monahan and his 15-year-old son Michael were indicted for the murder of William Diskin and Sebastian Weilandics. Eugene Monahan has been tried, convicted and sentenced to death and his appeal is pending before this court. The State concedes that the victims were killed by the father and not the son but asserts that since the homicides occurred during a robbery in which the son participated, the son was equally triable for murder in the first degree, punishable by death unless there is a recommendation of life imprisonment. See N.J.S. 2A:113–1, N.J.S.A.; N.J.S. 2A:113–2, N.J.S.A. A motion was made for transfer of the proceeding against the son to the Juvenile and Domestic Relations Court on the ground that under N.J.S. 2A:85–4, N.J.S.A., and N.J.S. 2A:4–14, N.J.S.A., it was cognizable exclusively in that court. The motion was denied and an appeal was taken. Cf. R.R. 1:10–1(b); R.R. 2:2–3(a) (3); R.R. 2:2–4; R.R. 2:12; R.R. 3:5–5(b) (6) (a). Although several preliminary procedural matters have been raised by the State, we shall pass them and proceed with the determination of the meritorious issue presented. It is of public concern, it has been fully briefed and argued, and its expeditious determination is required in the interests of complete justice. . . . [Citations omitted. — Ed.]

The principle of removing or mitigating the criminal responsibility of children has ancient origins. In the early case of State v. Aaron, 4 N.J.L. 231, 244 [Reprint 269, 277] (Sup.Ct. 1818), Chief Justice Kirkpatrick restated the settled common law doctrine, adapted from earlier Roman law, that since a child under seven "cannot have discretion to discern between good and evil" he is incapable of com-

mitting crime; between the ages of seven and 14 he is subject to a rebuttable presumption of incapacity; and after 14 he is presumptively capable. See Clark & Marshall, A Treatise on the Law of Crimes, (5th ed.1952), pp. 125–128. Although the common law rule precluded criminal convictions of many young offenders, there are instances in which it failed to do so, with shocking consequences. Blackstone cites cases in which children of very tender age were drastically condemned as adult criminals; he refers to the hanging of an eight-year-old for maliciously burning some barns; to the hanging of a ten-year-old who had killed one of his companions; and to the burning of a girl of 13 who had killed her mistress. 4 Bl.Comm. (13th ed.1800), 23. Similar illustrations in our own State are not lacking. In 1818 a boy of 11 was tried for murder (State v. Aaron, supra), and in 1828 a boy of 13 was hanged for an offense which he committed when he was 12. State v. Guild, 10 N.J.L. 163 (Sup.Ct.1828). During most of the Nineteenth Century, child and adult offenders were treated alike although intermittent steps were taken towards their separate confinement. It was not until the turn of the century that modern concepts really began to take form; they embodied the upward movement in the child's age of criminal responsibility, the extended recognition of society's obligation as *parens patriae* to care for delinquent children, and the creation of independent juvenile courts. [Citations omitted. — Ed.]

The first juvenile court in this country was established in Cook County, Illinois, by an 1899 act which provided that the child offender was to be considered a ward of the state under control of the juvenile court; proceedings were there to be conducted informally with rehabilitative supervision rather than retributive punishment in mind, and without public indictment, trial by jury and other incidents of criminal causes. Thereafter the other states adopted legislation which was comparable though specific provisions varied. Attacks on the legislation based on the absence of indictment, trial by jury and the other constitutional guarantees applicable to criminal proceedings were quickly rejected. See Commonwealth v. Fisher, 213 Pa. 48, 62 A. 198 (Sup.Ct.1905). . . . [Some citations omitted. — Ed.]

In the Fisher case [213 Pa. 48, 62 A. 200] the Supreme Court of Pennsylvania pointed out

(1954), aff'd *sub. nom. Johnson v. State*, 18 N. J. 422, 114 A2d 1 (1955) and "Recent Cases," 10 Rutgers L. R. 448 (1956). — *Ed.*

that the juvenile court proceeding is not "the trial of a child charged with a crime, but is mercifully to save it from such an ordeal, with the prison or penitentiary in its wake, if the child's own good and the best interests of the state justify such salvation." In the Lindsay case [257 Ill. 328, 100 N.E. 894] the Supreme Court of Illinois noted that the "prerogative of the state, arising out of its power and duty, as *parens patriae*, to protect the interest of infants, has always been exercised by courts of chancery" and has not been questioned for generations. In the Lewis case [260 N.Y. 171, 183 N.E. 354] the New York Court of Appeals stated that there is no doubt about the power of the legislature "to say that an act done by a child shall not be a crime." And in the recent Morin case [95 N.H. 518, 68 A.2d 670] the Supreme Court of New Hampshire, in rejecting an attack on its statute relating to delinquent children, said:

"We think it sufficiently plain that the act in question is designed to permit the exercise of the powers of the state as 'parens patriae,' for the purpose of rehabilitating minor children, and not of punishing them for the commission of a crime. 'It is generally held that the purpose of such statutes is not penal, but protective. It is not that the child shall be punished for breach of a law or regulation, but that he shall have a better chance to become a worthy citizen.' . . ." [Citations omitted. — *Ed.*]

During colonial days and the early Nineteenth Century, our State dealt with child and adult offenders in identical fashion. See Justice and the Child in New Jersey, Report of the New Jersey Juvenile Delinquency Commission, 35 (1939). In 1850 legislative steps were first taken towards the separate confinement of children (L.1850, p. 125; L.1852, p. 476) although it was not until 1867 that the State Reform School for Juvenile Delinquents at Jamesburg was opened. Shortly thereafter the State Industrial School for Girls at Trenton was established. Finally there was legislative recognition that children do not have that degree of intellectual and emotional development which should subject them to adult responsibility and that the child and adult offenders should therefore be differentiated before trial rather than after conviction. In 1903 county courts for juvenile offenders, consisting of the judges of the Courts of Common Pleas, were created. L.1903, c. 219. In 1912 courts manned by spe-

cial juvenile court judges were set up in first class counties. L.1912, c. 353. In 1928 the Juvenile and Probation Study Commission, headed by Vice-Chancellor Bentley, recommended the adoption of new legislation based on the Standard Juvenile Court Act which had been prepared for the National Probation Association by a committee of judges from various states; pursuant thereto a comprehensive statutory revision was adopted in 1929 establishing juvenile and domestic relations courts and defining their jurisdiction over children under 16 years. L.1929, c. 157; R.S. 9:18-1 et seq., N.J.S.A. Although the 1903 and 1912 acts had expressly excluded the crimes of murder and manslaughter from juvenile court jurisdiction, the 1929 revision contained no comparable exclusion.

In In re Daniecki, by Ratner, 117 N.J.Eq. 527, 177 A. 91, 92, (Ch.1935), affirmed 119 N.J.Eq. 359 183 A. 298 (E. & A.1936), Vice-Chancellor Backes had occasion to deal with the issue of whether a 15-year-old boy, charged with murder, was triable in the same manner as an adult in the Court of Oyer and Terminer. The vice chancellor held that he was, expressing the sweeping view that the Legislature had no power "to vest jurisdiction in the juvenile court to try the crime of murder (or any other indictable offense) without a jury." He did not consider any of the many cases to the contrary throughout the states and if his view had ultimately prevailed it would have struck a mortal blow to the juvenile court movement in our State. Fortunately, it was later rejected in State v. Goldberg, 124 N.J.L. 272, 11 A.2d 299, 302, (Sup.Ct.1940), affirmed 125 N.J.L. 501, 17 A.2d 173 (E. & A.1940), where the court, while recognizing that assault with intent to kill was indictable at common law (cf. State v. Maier, 13 N.J. 235, 277, 99 A.2d 21 (1953)), held that, when committed by a 15-year-old, it was cognizable exclusively in the juvenile court. In the course of his opinion Justice Case noted that the goal of saving "erring children to their own better selves and to orderly, law-abiding society, is beyond criticism," and that juvenile court proceedings are not "by way of punishment but by way of reformation, education and parental care, intended to save children from the consequences of wrongful conduct which in an older person would merit indictment, conviction and punishment, and are in the nature of ascertaining what the conduct of a child under sixteen years has been and whether restraint and care from the public authorities should in larger degree be substituted for that which the child would ordinarily receive from its parents." In the recent case of In re Lewis, 11 N.J. 217, 224, 94 A.2d 328, 331, (1953), Justice Brennan, in an opinion delivered for the entire court, similarly pointed out "that the statutory policy for the treatment of juvenile offenders is directed to their rehabilitation for useful citizenship through reformation and education and not to their punishment, even when the offense underlying the adjudication of juvenile delinquency is of a kind which when committed by an older person would merit indictment, conviction and punishment."

Immediately after Vice-Chancellor Backes had rendered his decision in the Daniecki case, holding that the 15-year-old boy before him was triable for murder in the same manner as an adult, the Legislature took affirmative steps to obviate its effects. It provided in L.1935, c. 285, that a person under the age of 16 shall be deemed incapable of committing a crime under the common law or statute law of this State; and in L.1935, c. 284, in defining delinquency cognizable exclusively in the juvenile court, it included conduct which, if committed by any one 16 or over, would constitute a felony, high misdemeanor, misdemeanor or other offense. The statutory language was unmistakable in design; it appropriately embodied the clear legislative wishes as expressed in the following statements by Senator Wolber (later Judge), who was the introducer of S. 330 and S. 331 which later became L.1935, cc. 284, 285 (Board of National Missions of Presbyterian Church in the United States v. Neeld, 9 N.J. 349, 358, 88 A.2d 500 (1953)):

"The purpose of the two bills is to vest exclusive jurisdiction in juvenile and domestic relations courts over all children who, while under the age of sixteen years, commit any offense which would constitute crime under the law as it now stands.

"A recent decision of the New Jersey Court of Chancery declares the existing provisions having the same purpose, unconstitutional because they deprive the defendant of the right to indictment and jury trial. These bills eliminate the objection by providing that the juvenile delinquency does not constitute crime and the penalties for crime cannot be imposed.

"The purpose is to effectuate the social policy already expressed in the juvenile and domestic relations court law of confining the handling of juvenile delinquents to specialists in the field. These bills merely correct a possible technical defect in the existing act, pointed to by the Chancery decision. This act was drawn by the New Jersey Crime Commission pursuant to a resolution adopted by the New Jersey State Conference on Crime."

In In re Mei, 122 N.J.Eq. 125, 192 A. 80, 83, 110 A.L.R. 1080 (E. & A.1937), the question was again raised as to whether a 15-year-old was triable for murder in the same manner as an adult; the court held that he was notwithstanding the express terms of L.1935, cc. 284, 285. It did not suggest that the Legislature intended to exclude murder from its comprehensive enactments; nor did it adopt the sweeping view of unconstitutionality expressed in the Daniecki case and later rejected in the Goldberg case. Instead, it rested on the unprecedented ground that since the charge of murder is "so horrible in fact and in the contemplation of society" it must remain "a crime within the purview of the Constitution, whatever name and whatever treatment may be appended to it by the legislature." This ground would be equally applicable to cases involving children of very tender age and the records at State Prison disclose that as late as 1944 it was applied in Camden County to a youngster of 13 who was tried, convicted and sentenced to life imprisonment for a murder committed when he was 12. See also State v. Smigelski, 137 N.J.L. 149, 58 A.2d 780 (Sup.Ct.1948), appeal dismissed, 1 N.J. 31, 61 A.2d 583 (1948). Viewed strictly as a legal ground it has no supporting basis whatever since the Constitution makes no pertinent mention of murder and the guarantees, when applicable, govern murder and other indictable common law offenses with like force. Viewed strictly as an emotional ground it concededly may not be given any controlling effect.

In approximately half the states the jurisdiction of the juvenile court over children under 16 is exclusive, even where the offense would constitute murder if committed by an adult. See Juvenile Delinquency, 261 Annals 129 (1949); United Nations Comparative Survey on Juvenile Delinquency 26 (1952). The Standard Juvenile Court Act as revised in 1949 likewise vests exclusive jurisdiction in the juvenile court over all children under 16. It also provides for jurisdiction over children from 16 to 18 but states that if the child is 16 or over and is charged "with an offense which would be a felony if committed by an adult" the juvenile court may, in its discretion, certify the child for criminal proceedings. To remove any doubts, it expressly directs that "no child under sixteen years of age shall be so certified." Judicial opinions sustaining such legislation are now legion and the Mei decision stands alone in its notion that a child of seven or over, charged with murder, must be tried in the same manner as an adult regardless of what the Legislature says on the subject. Although the decision is devoid of supporting reason and authority, the suggestion is advanced that since it was rendered many years ago it should be permitted to stand until altered by the Legislature. This approach might have some merit if the Mei decision turned on a matter of statutory construction but the fact is that the court there asserted an absence of constitutional power which no amount of legislation could supply. See Snyder v. State, 189 Md. 167, 55 A.2d 485, 487 (Sup.Ct.1947). In any event, the pertinent legislative enactments after the Mei case clearly reaffirm the plain statutory purpose to vest in the juvenile court, exclusive jurisdiction over children under 16 regardless of the severity of their offenses. See L.1943, c. 97; L.1946, c. 77; L.1948, c. 284. In 1946 the Legislature, in dealing with juvenile court jurisdiction over persons between the ages of 16 and 18, expressly stated that the juvenile court may refer the matter to the prosecutor for criminal trial where the offense was of a "heinous nature." L.1946, c. 77; N.J.S. 2A:4–15, N.J.S.A. See State v. Vaszorich, 13 N.J. 99, 110, 98 A.2d 299 (1953). No comparable provision was ever adopted with respect to children under 16, thus evidencing the legislative purpose of preserving the exclusive jurisdiction of the juvenile court in such instances. See R.R. 6:9–7. When our statutes relating to civil and criminal justice were recently revised, the Legislature re-enacted its comprehensive declarations that a person under the age of 16 shall be deemed incapable of committing a crime (N.J.S. 2A:85–4, N.J.S.A.) and that juvenile delinquency shall include any act which, if committed by an adult, would constitute a felony, high misdemeanor, misdemeanor or other offense. N.J.S. 2A:4–14, N.J.S.A. And at the same time it reasserted the broad powers of the juvenile court, including authority for extended institutional commitment of offenders in appropriate instances. N.J.S. 2A:4–37, N.J.S.A. In Re Lewis, supra, this authority was invoked to sustain a reformatory commitment of a juvenile who had wantonly driven an automobile killing a pedestrian.

Until recently the legislative policy in our neighboring state of New York was to exclude designated crimes such as murder from the jurisdiction of the juvenile court. Thus its statute [McK.Consol.Laws N.Y., c. 40, Penal Law, § 2186], had provided that where a child under 16 committed an offense which would be "a crime not punishable by death or life imprisonment" if committed by an adult, he was not to be deemed guilty of any crime but was to be dealt with as a juvenile offender. Notwithstanding the express exclusionary language, the New York Court of Appeals held that a person under 16 who was charged, not with premeditated murder, but with participating in a robbery which resulted in a killing, was to be treated as a juvenile offender. See People v. Roper, 259 N.Y. 170, 181 N.E. 88, 90, (1932), reargument denied, 259 N.Y. 635, 182 N.E. 213 (1932); People v. Porter, 54 N.Y.S.2d 3, 5 (Cty.Ct.1945). As expressed in the Porter case, "although an adult may be convicted of first degree murder on proof that a killing occurs in the course of a felony upon which he is engaged, a fifteen year old youth may not be so adjudged, unless there is proof that he intended to kill." In the Mei case the child was accused of having committed a premeditated murder. In the case before us the 15-year-old Michael Monahan is not accused of having committed premeditated murder or any act with intent to kill; he is charged with having participated in a robbery with his father during which his father killed two persons. Under the statutory provisions and policy sustained by the Court of Errors and Appeals in the Goldberg case he is not triable as an adult for the robbery which he committed, yet the State contends that he is triable as an adult for the killing which he did not commit. If, as the statute directs, he is to be deemed legally incapable of robbery, it is difficult to see how he can be tried for murder during a robbery in the course of which another killed.

The problems presented by juvenile offenders are admittedly most serious in nature and are rightly receiving intensive study by legislative and administrative agencies at both federal and state levels. Our national hopes and destinies rest with our children and, fortunately, they are born both free and with promise for good. If along the way their freedom is lost and their goodness is not realized, society itself may be largely to blame. See John Edgar Hoover, Juvenile Delinquency, 4 Syracuse L.Rev. 179, 184 (1953):

"Criminal behavior is learned behavior. The child and the adolescent are impressionable, and their active minds develop codes of morality no higher than those to which they are exposed. The environment which the adult community provides its growing children is the most important factor underlying the behavior patterns cultivated by the normal child."

Centuries of history indicate that the pathway lies not in unrelenting and vengeful punishment, but in persistently seeking and uprooting the causes of juvenile delinquency and in widening and strengthening the reformative process through socially enlightened movements. Cf. A.L.I. Draft, Youth Correction Authority Act, § 16 (1940) [See Article 106 of this book. — Ed.] Amongst the states, New Jersey has long been in the forefront in its recognition and development of this pathway; that it intends to retain its position is well evidenced by recent activities at the New Jersey State Diagnostic Center and the Highfields Experimental Treatment Project. See Henry, The Right to be Good, The Welfare Reporter (Dec. 1953) p. 1; Life Magazine, Helping Bad Boys, A Plan Pays off for New Jersey (March 15, 1954), pp. 24, 97.

There remain, nevertheless, strongly conflicting opinion as to how juveniles should be dealt with in cases involving homicide and other heinous misconduct. Some simply content themselves with expressions which couple their natural outrage and lack of sympathy for the juvenile court movement; they fail to suggest any alternative except, perhaps, the return to the barbarous days when eight and ten-year-old boys and a 13-year-old girl were tried and executed for arson and murder. Others take the view that although the juvenile court movement is soundly based and should be strengthened, it should nevertheless be confined to non-heinous offenses, at least when older children are concerned; in other words, errant children should receive supervision and correction but only so long as they have not erred too greatly. Still others, however, urge both the strengthening and widening of the juvenile court movement, pointing out that the grossness of the child's misconduct intensifies rather than lessens the need for corrective supervision under the jurisdiction of a specialist judge, empowered to protect fully both the interests of the child and the public at large. In any event, the determination as to what is the wise and acceptable approach from society's viewpoint clearly rests with the other branches of government. Matters of statutory policy are the exclusive concern of the legislative and executive branches which are fully accountable to the electorate acting at the polls; and statutory enactments may not properly be nullified in whole or in part simply because the judicial branch thinks them unwise. It is well that we ever remind ourselves that in our democracy the executive and legislative branches of government are the "ultimate guardians of the liberties and welfare of the people in quite as great a degree as the courts." Holmes, J. in Missouri, Kansas, & Texas Ry. Co. of Texas v. May, 194 U.S. 267, 270, 24 S.Ct. 638, 639, 48 L.Ed. 971, 973 (1904).

A majority of the court is satisfied that our present legislation lawfully vests exclusive jurisdiction in the juvenile court over misconduct by children under 16, including misconduct which would constitute murder or other heinous crime if committed by an adult. Accordingly, the order entered below is set aside and the matter is remanded to the Juvenile and Domestic Relations Court of Union County for further proceedings in accordance with the governing statutes and rules of court.

HEHER, J., concurring in result.

For reversal: Justices HEHER, BURLING, JACOBS and BRENNAN — 4.

For affirmance: Chief Justice VANDERBILT, and Justices OLIPHANT and WACHENFELD — 3.

HEHER, J. (concurring).

The Legislature in clear and indubitable terms admitting of no doubt of the purpose has decreed, as a prime and compelling measure of social policy, that a child under the age of 16 shall be deemed incapable of committing a crime, any and all offenses entailing criminal consequences under the common law or the statute law of this State when perpetrated by an adult, irrespective of the gravity of the misconduct, whether a capital or other heinous offense, or any of the lesser evil deeds comprised within the category of crime, but rather that such misconduct shall be treated as "juvenile delinquency" when done by a child under 16 years subjecting the offender to protective custody, guidance and correctional treatment; and I, too, entertain the view that such an ordinance is within the legislative competency if it is in fact that and not in reality a punitive and criminal measure under a new and euphemistic label and a procedure that disregards the constitutional safeguards against arbitrary action in restraint of individual liberty, more especially the presentment process and the right of trial by jury.*

The question is basically one of constitutional power and statutory construction, to be considered in the context of criminal responsibility and its essential nature.

A child is not criminally responsible at common law for his acts or omissions if he is of such tender years as to be incapable of distinguishing between right and wrong, and of understanding the nature of the particular act. At common law (1) under the age of seven years the presumption of incapacity is conclusive; (2) between the ages of seven and 14 years there is a rebuttable presumption of incapacity; and (3) above the age of 14 years there is a rebuttable presumption of capacity.

With some exceptions, a child is accountable for his torts in a civil action to the same degree as in an adult, for the object is to redress the personal injury by compensation, and not to punish the child, and so his mental capacity is generally immaterial. But when it is proposed to hold a child amenable to the criminal law, the *mens rea* is of the essence. At common law, a crime is a combination of a criminal act and a criminal intent. The maxim is *actus non facit reum, nisi mens sit rea*. A wrongful act and a wrongful intent must concur. Reg. v. Tolson, 23 Q.D. 168 (1889); Levet's Case, Cro. Car. 538 (1793); 1 Hale P.C. 474 (1778); [Some citations omitted. — *Ed.*] This was early deemed a principle of natural justice. Fowler v. Padgett, 7 T.R. 509, 514 (1798). It is a rule of justice discernible by right reason. Lord Abiger said, in Rex v. Allday, 8 Car. and P. 136 (1837),

173 Eng.Rep. 431: "It is a maxim older than the laws of England that no man is guilty unless his mind is guilty." And St. Augustine, speaking of perjury as a sin, said: "It is a sinful mind that makes a sinful tongue." This conception of divine law has influenced the common-law principle of criminal responsibility. Pollard [*sic.*] and Maitland, History of English Law, II, 476 (1895).

Under the common law, a child is not criminally responsible "unless he is old enough, and intelligent enough, to be capable of entertaining a criminal intent; and to be capable of entertaining a criminal intent he must be capable of distinguishing between right and wrong as to the particular act." Clark and Marshall, Crimes (5th ed.1952), sections 38, 76; Kean, The History of the Criminal Liability of Children, 53 Law Quar.Rev. 364 (1937); Woodbridge, Physical and Mental Infancy in the Criminal Law, 87 U. of Pa. Law Rev. 426 (1939).

Children under the age of seven years are, by an arbitrary rule of the common law, conclusively presumed to be *doli incapax*, or incapable of entertaining a criminal intent, and no evidence at all can be received to show capacity in fact. This rule applies to both common-law and statutory offenses. . . . [Citations omitted. — *Ed.*]

The presumption of such incapacity as to children between the ages of seven and 14 is not conclusive, as in cases of children under the age of seven, but rebuttable in the particular case by a showing of sufficient intelligence to distinguish between right and wrong, and to understand the nature and illegality of the particular act, or, as it is sometimes said, that he was possessed of "a mischievous discretion." 1 Hale P.C. 26, 27 (1778); 4 Blackstone's Comm. 23 (1800). The burden of proving capacity in this latter age group is upon the state; and capacity must be shown beyond any reasonable doubt. Reg. v. Smith, cited supra; State v. Aaron, 4 N.J.L. 231 (Sup.Ct.1818); 4 Blackstone's Comm. 24 (1800).

Children over the age of 14 are presumed to be *doli capax*, and therefore responsible, but the presumption is rebuttable, with the burden on the accused to satisfy the jury that he did not have sufficient intelligence to understand the nature and consequences of his act, and to know that he was doing wrong. Clark and

---

* *Homicide by Juvenile*, the annotation in 48 A.L.R. 2d, 663, gives a survey of the extent of juvenile court jurisdiction in homicides, under various statutes and decisions. — *Ed.*

Marshall, Crimes (5th ed.1952), section 77, 78, 79.

But in historical perspective we find, in the treatment of juvenile delinquents, evidences of unreasoning justice, expiative and retributive, a vengeful justice, in utter disregard of the physical fact of criminal capacity and the promptings of a humane and understanding psychology and sound sociology in the handling of behavior-problem children. In York's Case, Fost. C.L. 70 (1791), a boy of ten years, who, after killing a little playmate, concealed the body, was convicted of murder, and executed; it was considered that the circumstances showed a consciousness of guilt, and a knowledge of right and wrong. In another English case, a child of eight was convicted of arson. Emlyn on 1 Hale P.C. 25, note. In 1819 and 1821, these sentences were pronounced by English judges: on a 14-year old boy who stole a cotton gown, value two shillings, "Seven years transportation"; on a 13-year old girl for stealing a hat, "To be imprisoned six months"; on two boys, 11 and 13, accused of stealing about 17 shilling, "Guilty-Death." Thurston's Concerning Juvenile Delinquency, 3 (1942). And in our own State a boy of 13 was convicted and hanged for a killing when he was 12. State v. Guild, 10 N.J.L. 163 (Sup.Ct.1828).

In criminal law, "intent" signifies a state of mind "which willingly consents to the act that is done, or free will, choice, or volition in the doing of an act"; it means that the act "is voluntary, that it proceeds from a mind free to act in distinction from an act done without mental capacity to understand its nature, or under circumstances which sufficiently show that it was the result of involuntary forces and against the will." Neither an act alone nor an intent alone can constitute a crime; therefore, an "actual intent to commit a crime may long precede its commission, but no predetermined intent is necessary for any length of time in connection with any crime, because if the will is simultaneous with the act it is sufficient." Burdick, Law of Crimes, sections 113, 115 (1946). Yet a criminal intent is not necessarily an intent to do wrong; the voluntary doing of a forbidden act may be enough. At common law, the mental element required in every crime is the "voluntary exercise of the will, that faculty of the human mind which has the power of choice, and in the exercise

of that power wishes, desires, determines or intends. The criminal law forbids and commands various things. If one chooses not to obey, and voluntarily carries that choice, or will, into effect by some act, the two necessary elements of crime are present, and the liability to punishment is incurred. This voluntary choice of doing what the law has declared to be crime constitutes what the law calls a bad or evil intent, otherwise called malice." *Ibid*, sections 112, 129, 129(a), 129(b), and 129(c). The Legislature may make the doing of the prohibited act criminal or penal, regardless of a corrupt or criminal purpose or even knowledge of the illegal character of the act; and in such case only the doing of the proscribed act need be shown. State v. Labato, cited supra.

Blackstone, affirming the views of Coke and Hawkins, says: "Infancy is a defect of the understanding, and infants under the age of discretion, ought not to be punished by any criminal prosecution whatever." 4 Blackstone's Comm. 21 (1800); 1 Coke's Inst. 247(h) (1629); 1 Hawk. P.C. (Curw. ed.1787), 2.

We have here an enlightened concept of justice that equates intelligence and moral responsibility with criminal culpability, not always the rule in practice. But the age of discretion varies with the individual; and there is a twilight zone in which discretion and understanding vary in degree and render objective judgment difficult and uncertain. There is no absolute age at which it may be said, to use the words of Hawkins, that the individual is no longer "under a natural disability of distinguishing between good and evil." Burdick, Law of Crimes, section 154. But if incompetent minors are to be saved the penal consequences of their irresponsible acts, an age of discretion and criminal accountability fairly grounded in the teachings and fruits of experience must needs be established by law, not alone to insure the essence of justice to the individual child, but to effect the salvation of children of tender years and unripened understanding for the ultimate good of society itself. This in its very nature involves the exercise of a reasonable legislative discretion, directed by the common experiential knowledge of mankind. Considered in relation to the individual case, a rule establishing the age of discretion is perforce arbitrary; but it is sustainable as a measure of prime social import for the care and protection of irresponsible youth rather than punishment for a knowing and understanding criminal act.

Under the Roman law, the age of puberty was the age of discretion. The earlier jurists were not in agreement concerning the legal age of puberty, some insisting it should correspond in each case to the physical fact, others that it should be fixed uniformly by law. Justinian accepted the latter view and established the age of discretion at 14 in boys and 12 in girls. Justinian's Inst. 1, 22 pr. The common law followed the Roman law and set 14 years as the age of full criminal capacity. 1 Coke's Inst. 247(b); 1 Hale P.C. 28; 4 Blackstone's Comm. 23. See Burdick, Law of Crime, sections 155, 156.

But new concepts of the criminal capacity of youth have come from the crucible of human experience, in a complex society that has undergone great structural change; and New Jersey, in common with other states, has accepted the thesis that a person under the age of 16 is to be deemed incapable of committing a crime. N.J.S. 2A:85–4, N.J.S.A. whose genesis is L. 1935, c. 285.

There can be no doubt that this age limitation in relation to criminal capacity is within the legislative province. It is in accord with proved and generally accepted principles of sociology * * * a measure that bears a rational relation to the basic interests of society itself. History, as we have seen, is not without its instances of the criminal prosecution of children of tender years seemingly for wholly punitive purposes, irrespective of the existence of the mental qualities which are of the very essence of criminal responsibility. Under a system that made the physical fact the test of criminal accountability in the particular case, miscarriages of justice were all too frequent, more especially in the complex of our present-day social organism. But above and beyond the danger of administrative mischance, failure and frustration, there is the undoubted fundamental consideration that children of such tender years, in the formative period of life, physically and psychologically are peculiarly susceptible to the sympathetic approach and the regenerative processes that make for individual uplift and social adjustment and integration. The humanitarian principle activates a modern socioeconomic philosophy designed to serve the primary purpose of criminal justice as an instrument of society's protection against crime * * * not as a means of vengeance and retribution, but rather the furtherance of social justice and the general welfare. Erring youth offers a fertile field for remedial effort; and the obvious aim of this statutory policy is correction according to the science of human behavior, in the fulfillment of a primary social responsibility.

Child delinquency is largely due to broken homes and parental irresponsibility and default, and unfavorable environmental and associated factors, involving pressures that are ofttimes beyond the child's control, and the State, as *parens patriae*, undertakes by such means to provide for the wayward victims protective custody, care, discipline, and correctional treatment to fit them, psychologically and physically, for a useful social life. Once the status is established, the delinquent is treated much the same as the dependent or neglected child. Such concepts as "criminal responsibility," "guilt," "punishment," and the like, have no place here; custody and control are exercised for protective and correctional purposes * * * protection and treatment based on understanding rather than punishment based on a technical status of guilt. The policy is both preventive and reformative. The philosophy of the juvenile policy involved in statutes that render youths of tender years incapable of crime is child-protective and child-corrective. I would refer to Professor and Mrs. Glueck's One Thousand Juvenile Delinquents, pp. 12, 13, 14, 16, 76, 241. The end in view is not criminal but social justice. Wayward children are a community problem; adult behavior ofttimes has its roots in childhood experiences. The redemptive process concerns diagnostic techniques and child therapy, by psychologic, psychiatric and other modes and methods which are not of immediate intent. There are those who would question the wisdom and efficacy of sociological techniques. But, once the legislative field of action is conceded, the legislative policy is not a justifiable issue.

Yet, in this, as in all other spheres of action, the Legislature is controlled by specific constitutional limitations.

In State v. Goldberg, 124 N.J.L. 272, 11 A.2d 299 (Sup.Ct.1940), affirmed 125 N.J.L. 501, 17 A.2d 173 (E. & A.1940), I had occasion to dissent from the holding that the then Juvenile Court Act, R.S.1937, 9:18–1 et seq.,

N.J.S.A., constitutionally deprived the old Court of Oyer and Terminer of jurisdiction to try a 15-year old boy on an indictment charging assault with intent to kill and carrying concealed weapons. The dissent was rested upon the thesis that it is beyond the power of the Legislature to term either murder or an assault with intent to kill "juvenile delinquency," and then proceed to an adjudication of guilt without regarding the constitutional safeguards applicable to criminal prosecutions, and impose upon such adjudication the penalty prescribed for the specific criminal offense thus branded juvenile delinquency. I read the then existing statute as purporting to do that very thing.

R.S.1937, 9:18–30, N.J.S.A., authorized, upon such adjudication, the imposition of "the penalty provided by law" * * * one that was established as in consonance with the criminal concept of the particular transgression against society. For a specific offense, termed a crime when committed by a person of the age of 16 years or more, so it was provided, the court "may" impose the same penalty prescribed by the law in the case of an adult, although "on proper cause shown," it "may" direct that the child be placed on "probation" or committed (1) "to a public institution established for the care, custody, instruction and reform of juvenile offenders," or (2) "to any other like institution commitment to which may be authorized by law," or (3) "to the care, custody and control of the state board of children's guardians as provided by law." This seemed to be the plain sense and significance of the legislative terms. The use of the permissive verb "may" in relation to these alternative courses of action could have no other meaning. The statute, R.S.1937, 9:18–29, N.J.S.A., directed the Juvenile Court to "hear and determine all cases of children arising under" its provisions "without a jury," but secured a jury trial where an adult was charged with an offense triable by that mode, upon demand made. It is requisite that there be careful drafting of a statute of this class to distinguish between a delinquency and a criminal proceeding, both in procedure and treatment after the status is determined. One Thousand Juvenile Delinquents, cited supra, pp. 12, 17, where the Massachusetts and Illinois acts are analyzed. But it is not necessary to pursue the inquiry as to constitutional sufficiency. I would refer to the majority opinion

in the Goldberg case and to In re Mei, 122 N.J.Eq. 125, 192 A. 80, 110 ALR. 1080 (E. & A.1937), and In re Daniecki, by Ratner, 117 N.J.Eq. 527, 177 A. 91 (Ch.1935), affirmed 119 N.J.Eq. 359, 183 A. 298 (E. & A.1935). It suffices to say that I held to the view that the difference in nomenclature did not alter the essential character of the act thus given judicial cognizance, and the infant could not be deprived of the constitutional procedures where conviction subjected him to the same penal consequences as the conviction of an adult.

But, beginning in 1943, there came a series of amendments of R.S.1937, 9:18–12, N.J.S.A., eventuating in N.J.S. 2A:4–14, N.J.S.A., and 2A:4–15, N.J.S.A., which renders the validity of this hypothesis academic. By the amendment of 1943, the Juvenile Court was given exclusive jurisdiction over all cases of "juvenile delinquency," defined as the commission by a child under 16 years of age of any act which committed by a person "of the age of sixteen years or over" would constitute "a felony, high misdemeanor, misdemeanor, or other offense," these among others. The court was given exclusive jurisdiction to hear and determine "all cases of persons between the ages of sixteen and eighteen who shall commit any" of the enumerated offenses, "if the complaint in such cases shall be certified by the grand jury with the approval of the prosecutor of the pleas, or by the prosecutor of the pleas, or by a judge of the court of quarter sessions or special sessions," to the judge of the Juvenile Court, after investigation and report made by the chief probation officer of the county. It was directed that the Juvenile Court's hearings in such case "shall be separate from those involving juveniles under the age of sixteen years"; and the court was empowered, "at any time before final adjudication," to "return" the complaint whence it came "if, in its judgment upon the facts disclosed at the hearings, the complaint should not be adjudicated" in the Juvenile Court, or thereafter for a violation of the conditions of probation, and thereupon "jurisdiction shall be resumed by the grand jury, prosecutor of the pleas, the court of quarter sessions or special sessions, as the case may be, as if said complaint had not in the first instance been certified" to the Juvenile Court. L.1943 c. 97.

There were amendments in 1946, c. 77, and

in 1948, c. 284, and then came N.J.S. 2A:4–15, N.J.S.A., in 1953, defining "juvenile delinquency" as the commission by a child under 18 years of age of any act which when committed by a person of the age of 18 years or over would constitute a felony, high misdemeanor, misdemeanor, or other offense, and providing that if it shall appear to the satisfaction of the Juvenile Court that "a case of juvenile delinquency," as thus defined, committed by any juvenile of the age of 16 or 17 years "should not be dealt with by the court, either because of the fact that the person is an habitual offender, or has been charged with an offense of a heinous nature, under circumstances which may require the imposition of a sentence rather than the disposition permitted by this chapter for the welfare of society, then the court may refer such case to the county prosecutor," and a juvenile of the age of 16 or 17 years "may demand a presentment and trial by jury and, in such case, when this act is made known to the court, such case" shall be "referred to the county prosecutor," and thereafter "be dealt with in exactly the same manner as a criminal case."

There is determining significance in this classification that resolves the constitutional problem I found in the earlier statute considered in State v. Goldberg, cited supra. The subjection of youthful delinquents of 16 or 17 years to a "sentence" rather than the "disposition" permissible under the act "for the welfare of society," where the delinquent is "an habitual offender" or the offense charged is of a "heinous nature, under circumstances" requiring the "imposition of a sentence," and the recognition of the constitutional rights of presentment and trial by jury in such cases, make manifest a legislative purpose to exonerate delinquents under 16 years of age from the essentially penal consequences of acts that would be criminal if perpetrated by persons above that age, and to subject them to society's care, protection, and corrective custody for the individual's social uplift and the common good.

Intent would seem to be an ingredient of juvenile delinquency also; but it is not criminal intent, penal rather than correctional in its consequences when the wrongful act occurs.

But, by the same token, there is no statutory distinction in this regard between "capital" and "noncapital" acts or offenses. A delinquent of 16 or 17 years is made criminally responsible in the given circumstances, but under the safeguard of all constitutional guaranties, rather than the object of reformative measures merely under the Juvenile Act. Delinquents under the age of 16 years are wholly incapable of crime, no matter what the nature or gravity of the act when done by one of criminal capacity, and are amenable only to protective care and custody and the rehabilitative process for the social good as well as their own interest. This by certain and unequivocal terms. There being in the contemplation of the law the absence of punitive fault, the delinquent behavior and waywardness cannot entail punitive consequences. Delinquency in its statutory connotation suggests the psychological rather than the judicial attitude toward the offender. Such is plainly within the competency of the State, as *parens patriae*.

The Legislature is the forum for those who would quarrel with the wisdom of this concept of moral and social responsibility. The constitutional doctrine of separation of powers forbids judicial superintendence of legislative policy. One of the primary functions of the judiciary is to confine the coordinate legislative and executive departments of government within their respective spheres of action, but it must be certain that in this process of containment it maintains the balance against excesses and intrusions of its own.

Thus it is that I cannot subscribe to the view that murder is a crime *sui generis* that remains a crime within the purview of the Constitution, and as such is not subject to different legislative classification such as we have here, following In re Mei and State v. Goldberg, cited supra.

Even on that hypothesis, the indictment for murder is not sustainable against this 15-year-old boy unless it be shown that he entertained a criminal intent to commit robbery; and under the holding in the Goldberg case he is by the statute incapable of robbery. The criminal offense laid against him is murder in the perpetration of a robbery; and where there is criminal capacity, the killing in such circumstances is murder in the first degree, even though not a wilful, deliberate and premeditated killing. R.S.1937, 2:138–1, 2, N.J.S. 2A:113–1, 2, N.J.S.A. The intent to commit the crime of robbery is an essential element of the statutory offense of murder in the first degree; and of this the infant defendant was incapable as a matter of law. I would refer in this regard to the dissent in State v. Grillo, 11 N.J. 173, 93 A.2d 328 (1952).

In People v. Roper, 259 N.Y. 170, 181 N.E. 88 (Ct.App.1932), the New York Court of Appeals considered a felony murder in relation to a statute providing that only a child under seven years is incapable as matter of law of committing a crime, though a child "of the age of seven years, and under the age of twelve years, is presumed to be incapable of crime, but the presumption may be removed by proof that he had sufficient capacity to understand," and "a child of more than seven and less than sixteen years of age, who shall commit any act or omission which, if committed by an adult, would be a crime not punishable by death or life imprisonment, shall not be deemed guilty of any crime, but of juvenile delinquency."

Pointing out that under the statute, a child of 15 years may be guilty of murder in the first degree, Lehman, J., said:

"When guilt of a crime has been established, its penal consequences are the same for child and adult criminal. But guilt cannot be established without proof of every essential element of the crime, and, since a felonious intent is an essential element of the crime of murder, guilt of a defendant can never be established without proof of such intent. Thus, the guilt of a defendant charged with murder in the first degree may depend upon his capacity to form the felonious intent. Then the fact that a defendant is under the age of sixteen may carry legal consequences. There can be no murder without evidence of malice and felonious intent and a depraved mind. The indictment was sufficient in form when it simply accused defendant of having killed the deceased 'willfully, feloniously, and with malice aforethought.' On the trial it was necessary to prove such malice and willful and felonious conduct, and this necessity was satisfied in accordance with the provision of the statute by showing that the homicide occurred while the defendant was engaged in the commission of another felony. * * * The crime of murder charged in the indictment is a single crime, whether committed by design or during the commission of an independent felony; 'the independent felony like the deliberate and premeditated intent being established solely for the purpose of characterizing the degree of the crime so charged, the evil mind or purpose inherent in the killing.' People v. Lytton, 257 N.Y. 310, 315, 178 N.E. 290, 292 [79 A.L.R. 503]. The defendant may

have participated in the robbery; but, unless that participation was with felonious intent, he was not guilty of the felony, and, if he was not guilty of the independent felony, participation does not evince 'the evil mind or purpose inherent in the killing,' * * * The defendant can be convicted of murder in the first degree only upon a finding of 'felonious intent.' The verdict of the jury imports a finding that the defendant participated in the commission of a robbery, as defined by the statute, for the trial judge charged that without such finding the verdict must be not guilty. Upon the trial of a defendant over the age of sixteen years, a finding of participation in a robbery, as defined by the statute, would import a finding of 'felonious intent,' for robbery, in every degree, is a felony. Upon the trial of a child under the age of sixteen, the participation of a child in a robbery, or at least in a robbery in the second or third degrees, would not establish the guilt of a felony, but only of a minor offense characterized as juvenile delinquency. Hence, it is plain that the defendant's conviction rests upon no finding of guilt of a felony, and thus no finding of felonious intent, and the judgment must be reversed. * * * Upon the new trial this defendant may be tried for murder in the first or second degrees committed through the killing of a human being with intent to effect his death. Such an action may be impelled by 'evil mind' and felonious intent as evidenced by the criminal acts of the child, but not by acts which the Legislature has declared are not criminal when committed by a child. A person who with evil mind commits a crime may, in the interests of society, be punished, even by death for the undesigned and unforeseen result of the crime. No person, certainly no child under the age of sixteen, is subject to death or life imprisonment because of the calamitous though undesigned result of acts which are not criminal in their inception."

Here, guilt of the murder laid to the accused child by the indictment can be predicated only of the commission of a crime of which by the statute he is incapable, and so the requisite felonious intent would be wanting. The illogic of the converse of this hypothesis would seem to be incontestable; and if it is not good logic, it is not good law, for it is to be presumed that the Legislature intended the logical consequence of the declared policy.

I concur in the reversal of the order and the remand of the cause to the Juvenile and Domestic Relations Court.

OLIPHANT, J. (dissenting).

I find myself compelled to dissent in this

case because I differ basically with the approach and reasoning of the majority opinion.

In In re Mei, 122 N.J.Eq. 125, 192 A. 80, 110 A.L.R. 1080 (E. & A.1937), it was held that the provisions of N.J.S. 2A:85–4, N.J. S.A., and R.S. 9:18–12, N.J.S.A., did not deprive the grand jury or the courts in finding a murder indictment against the defendant under the age of 16 years and trying it. In that case it was held that the accused, who was 15 years and 4 months of age when the crime was committed, could not be held under a charge of murder by the Juvenile and Domestic Relations Court because "a charge * * * of murder cuts so deeply into human emotions, collides so violently with life's experiences and fair expectations, and is so horrible in fact and in the contemplation of society, that it remains a crime within the purview of the Constitution, whatever name and whatever treatment may be appended to it by the legislature."

This observation goes to the very heart of the problem in attempting to bring the crime of murder within the statutory definition of "juvenile delinquency" over which subject the Juvenile and Domestic Relations Court is vested with jurisdiction by the statute. N.J.S. 2A:85–4, N.J.S.A., merely re-enacted the provisions of L.1935, c. 285, which was passed in conjunction with L.1935, c. 284, defining juvenile delinquency. Both statutes became effective June 27, 1935, two years prior to the decision in the Mei case. The Mei case turned on the question of constitutional power and not of policy.

The legislative enactments subsequent to the Mei case, L.1943, c. 97; L.1946, c. 77 and L. 1948, c. 284, were likewise prior to the decision in State v. Smigelski, 137 N.J. L. 149, 58 A.2d 780 (Sup.Ct.1948), appeal dismissed 1 N.J. 31, 61 A.2d 583 (1948). I discern no clear-cut legislative intention in these statutes to ignore the flat holding in the Mei case that murder was beyond the purview of the jurisdiction of the Juvenile and Domestic Relations Court. I am compelled to follow the established rule that where a statute has been construed by the courts and this construction has been supported by long acquiescence on the part of the Legislature or by continued use of the same language, or by failure to amend the statute with respect to the particular question, that this is evidence that such construction is in accordance with the legislative intent. Commissioner of Banking & Insurance v. Moresh, 122 N.J.L. 77, 3 A.2d 638 (E. & A.1939); Barringer v. Miele, 6 N.J. 139, 77 A.2d 895 (1951); Miller v. Board of Chosen Freeholders, 10 N.J. 398, 91 A.2d 729 (1952). Therefore, I conclude that the holding in the Mei case is still controlling and that the Juvenile and Domestic Relations Court is without jurisdiction to try a charge of murder as defined by N.J.S. 2A: 113–1, 2, N.J.S.A.

The majority, however, have in effect overruled the holding in the Mei case and assert that under the *parens patriae* doctrine, both on psychological and sociological grounds, the State and the Legislature have the power to treat such a crime when committed by an infant on a psychological or sociological basis and bring it within the definition of juvenile delinquency as set forth in the statute.

The right of punishing malefactors derives its origin from that which every individual originally had in the society of nature to repel the injuries committed against himself, or against members of the society; a right that has been yielded and transferred to the State. The principal end of punishment is the welfare of society, but there are many various means of arriving at this end according to varying circumstances, and the State in inflicting punishment may propose different and particular views consistent with the welfare of society. In the words of Grotius, "In punishments we must either have the good of the criminal in view, or the advantage of him whose interest it was that the crime should not have been committed, or the good of all indifferently." So it is universally acknowledged that if the State proposes to correct the criminal and impose a punishment, the punishment, if the criminal is reformed by it, tends to the public good. But punishment ought to be strictly subordinate to the principal end of criminal processes; namely, the safety of the public. Prudence dictates that the justice established for the preservation of society should not be exercised in such a manner as to subvert the State. Within this general ambit the action of the Legislature is free from judicial restraint under our doctrine of the separation of the powers, and whether punishment for a crime should be solely punitive or correctional or a combination of both is strictly within the Legislative province.

But the nub of the problem here presented revolves around the statutory provision, N.J.S. 2A:85–4, N.J.S.A., which provides:

"A person under the age of 16 years is deemed incapable of committing a crime." *

This provision seemingly ignores the fundamental fact of the law of nature as applied to man and facts of everyday existence which are of common knowledge and public notice.

I cannot comprehend the reasoning that suggests that marauding gangs of little hoodlums armed with guns, knives, switch knives or other lethal weapons are to be considered as a matter of law incapable of committing the crime of murder. Infants under the age of 21 years, according to statistics, perpetrate a high percentage of the heinous crimes committed throughout the country, and the situation has reached such serious proportions that it is a threat to the public welfare and safety of the law-abiding citizen. In one instance it reached the alarming situation where a confirmed criminal had organized a gang of teenagers "to murder and rob" while he himself never took physical part in the crimes. This gang of little hoodlums committed 50 holdups and burglaries in a period of eight months with weapons supplied by the confirmed criminal. Murder by an individual criminal is bad enough but when it appears that a confirmed criminal has organized a group of teenagers for the sole purpose to murder and rob, then the time has come to examine the underlying philosophy of the treatment of juvenile offenders particularly where the crime of murder is involved.

Homicide or the killing of any human creature is of three kinds: justifiable, excusable and felonious. The first has no share of guilt at all, the second very little, but the third is the highest crime against the law of nature that man is capable of committing. 2 Chitty's Blackstone *178.

The constituents of a criminal offense are an evil intention and an unlawful act, State v. Labato, 7 N.J. 137, 80 A.2d 617 (1951), so that the effect of the legislative declaration above quoted is that any infant who is mentally capable of forming an evil intent and commits the overt act of homicide is not guilty or cannot be found guilty of the highest crime

against nature, because he is incapable of a criminal intent merely because of his age.

The principal end of civil government on society is to secure to mankind all their natural advantages, and especially their lives. Of all the natural rights the preeminent one is the right to life. Man is not a master of his own life nor can he voluntarily accede to the proposition that the State is master of his life except in two situations: (1) in the indirect manner for the defense of the State, and (2) in the direct manner for the punishment of crimes. His right to life is based upon a natural law; otherwise he would be the creature of the State, he would have no rights based upon his own nature as a rational being except the rights given to him by the State. What rights the State might give to him it could take away from him, and if this were so the word "unalienable" as used in Article I of the Constitution of 1947 would become another synonym for "expendable."

Article I of our Constitution provides:

"All persons are by nature free and independent, and have certain natural and unalienable rights, among which are those of enjoying and defending life and liberty, of acquiring, possessing, and protecting property, and of pursuing and obtaining safety and happiness."

Thus there is reserved to the individual citizen his unalienable rights, including that of life and liberty.

Natural liberty is the right, which nature gives to all mankind, of disposing of their persons and property after the manner they judge most convenient to their happiness, on condition of their acting within limitation of the law the nature and of their not abusing it to the prejudice of their fellowman. To this reciprocal right of liberty there is a reciprocal corresponding obligation, by which the law of nature binds all mankind to respect the liberty of other men and not to disturb them in the use they make of it so long as they do not abuse it.

Civil liberty, on the other hand therefore, is nothing more than natural liberty so far restrained by positive law as is necessary for the preservation of human rights and the maintenance of peace and order in society. Civil liberty is natural liberty, regulated by such laws as are necessary for the maintenance of justice and attended with the right of every citizen and person of insisting that the government shall make the proper use of its authority, and the security that this unalienable right of natural and civil liberty shall be respected and protected. Thus it is that the highest duty of the State is to protect the life of man. Man as a citizen of the State has a right to insist that the positive law of the State discharge this duty. He and his children have rights in this respect that are superior to those of the child malefactor.

In every civilized society in history murder has been considered to be naturally and inherently wrong. It is *malum per se* because from the very nature of the transaction it violates the highest natural right of man. Every civilization or society has considered murder the highest offense against the law when committed by a rational human being, and it has never been questioned that murder is wrong and *malum per se*. This principle of the natural law is immutable and indisputable and was well understood by the founding fathers, and the mere fact it is not specifically mentioned in the Constitution is of no moment in view of the general guarantees of unalienable rights of man found in Article I.

As is stated in the Mei case, the mere restatement of this proposition as part of the positive law adds nothing to the turpitude of the crime of murder. In murder by a felonious act the right of life is wiped out, and if this can be done with impunity or lack of guilt on a psychological or sociological basis, then the other unalienable rights, among which are the right to personal liberty, to freedom of speech, to liberty of conscience and to private property, would be utterly futile and sterile. All attempts to protect and defend them in the judicial forum would be without meaning or purpose if the right to life is not inviolable and by legislative fiat the positive law can say that an infant mentally capable of criminal intent is incapable of committing the crime of murder. Man, including children, is a rational animal, a psychophysical being capable of rational thought and free will. Unless he is mentally incompetent and thus irrational, there comes a point in the life of each when he becomes capable of distinguishing between right and wrong. This is in the nature of man himself, although the point at which it is reached depends upon the type of society or civilization in which he lives and will also vary somewhat with each individual.

At the common law and in this State, insofar as a crime is concerned, the inability to form a criminal intent is a matter of defense. As to children under the age of seven years there is a conclusive presumption that the child was *doli incapax,* or incapable of entertaining a criminal intent, and no evidence can or should be received to show capacity in fact. Between the ages of seven and 14 the presumption is rebuttable, but the State or prosecution has the burden of showing that the infant has sufficient intelligence to distinguish between right and wrong and to understand the nature and illegality of the particular act. Over the age of 14 children were and are presumed to be *doli capax* and therefore responsible. The presumption is rebuttable but the burden of proof is upon the defendant to establish that he did not have sufficient intelligence to understand the nature and consequences of his act. These rules are consistent with the nature of man and the natural use of his faculties of intellect and will, and his freedom to acquire the necessary knowledge to make the distinction between right and wrong. They are rules to determine the ultimate fact of the ability of an individual to distinguish between right and wrong. The point in life when a person is capable of making this distinction may vary, but once it is reached that person, whether it be an adult or a child, is capable of criminal intent.

The trial and conviction for a crime is strictly within the judicial province and the determination of the ultimate fact of criminal intent is likewise within the judicial province. And this being so, as I see it, the constitutional guarantees with respect to indictment and trial are applicable. Once an indictment is found, the trial of the ultimate fact of criminal intent, which is the most important element in a charge of murder, must be tried by a jury.

The views expressed here were of sufficient moment to induce the Legislatures in many states to remove the charge of murder from the field of juvenile delinquency. It is indeed a curious anomaly that in this country, where civilization in some respects has reached its highest peak insofar as the welfare and comfort of an individual is concerned and where the educational opportunities are practically unlimited for a child, we are brought face to face with a statute that in effect denies that the normal child is not a rational human being insofar as the highest crime against nature is concerned. I doubt that even in the primitive state of civilization there is any society that subscribes to such a proposition. Bluntly, the statute practically says that a child, within defined age limits, is not a rational being but merely an animal without the will or mind to control its baser animal instincts.

The appellant makes the argument that all previous pertinent decisions of the court of last resort in this State, In re Daniecki, by Ratner, 117 N.J.Eq. 527, 177 A. 91 (Ch. 1935), affirmed 119 N.J.Eq. 359, 183 A. 298 (E. & A.1936); In re Mei, supra; State v. Smigelski, supra, are cases in which the infant defendant was a wilful, deliberate, premeditated killer or was the actual killer in the perpetration of a robbery or other felony. He refers to such murders as "designed murders." He contends that these cases are not in point here where the infant defendant was not the actual killer and that there is no case in this State involving "a felony murder" by an infant where the criminal intent or scienter is predicated upon the commission of crimes listed in N.J.S. 2A:113–1, 2, N.J.S.A.

Murder, by statute, is defined as follows, N.J.S. 2A:113–1, N.J.S.A.:

"If any person, in committing or attempting to commit arson, burglary, kidnapping, rape, robbery, sodomy or any unlawful act against the peace of this state, of which the probable consequences may be bloodshed, kills another, or if the death of anyone ensues from the committing or attempting to commit any such crime or act; or if any person kills a judge, magistrate, sheriff, coroner, constable or other officer of justice, either civil or criminal, of this state, or a marshal or other officer of justice, either civil or criminal, of the United States, in the execution of his office or duty, or kills any of his assistants, whether specially called to his aid or not, endeavoring to preserve the peace or apprehend a criminal, knowing the authority of such assistant, or kills a private person endeavoring to suppress an affray, or to apprehend a criminal, knowing the intention with which such private person interposes, then such person so killing is guilty of murder."

The degrees of murder and the punishments are fixed by N.J.S. 2A:113–2, N.J.S.A., which reads:

"Murder which is perpetrated by means of poison, or by lying in wait, or by any other kind of willful, deliberate and premeditated killing, or which is committed in perpetrating or attempting to perpetrate arson, burglary, kidnapping, rape, robbery or sodomy, is murder in the first degree. Any other kind of murder is murder in the second degree. A jury finding a person guilty of murder shall designate by their verdict whether it be murder in the first degree or in the second degree."

The statutes make no distinction between those who do the actual killing and those who do not where the killing occurs in the commission or attempt to perpetrate any of the crimes enumerated therein. Under these sections one who aids, abets, counsels or procures another to commit murder provided he is near enough to render assistance, is a principal and not an accessory. State v. Giberson, 99 N.J.L. 85, 122 A. 724 (E. & A.1924); State v. Mule, 114 N.J.L. 384, 177 A. 125 (E. & A.1935).

The appellant further argues that the commission of the crime, in this instance robbery, provided the criminal or felonious intent for the crime of murder and that under the provisions of N.J.S. 2A:85–4, N.J.S.A., the defendant is deemed incapable of committing the crime of robbery. He relies principally upon the case of People v. Roper, 259 N.Y. 170, 181 N.E. 88 (Ct.App.1932), and many other cases in other jurisdictions not dealing with the crime of murder.

But our law is to the contrary. In State v. Mowser, 92 N.J.L. 474, 479, 483, 106 A. 416, 4 A.L.R. 695 (E. & A.1919), it is held that the heinous offense is the killing and the crime of robbery, while it is an essential and integral part of the principal offense, is not a distinct affair but grows out of the same transaction. All murder at the common law was a capital offense and there was no grading of murder or definition of degrees of the crime, and such is the situation in England today. The reason for grading or fixing degrees of murder is to provide different punishments in different situations, and I do not challenge the legislative competency in this respect. The history of legislation of this type is discussed at some length in 22 Fordham L.Rev. 274.

Our Legislature, following this theory, set up two classifications of murder, murder of the first degree and murder of the second degree and it made the crime of robbery a constituent element of murder in the first degree where death results from the perpetration or the attempt to perpetrate a robbery. In so doing it reiterated the doctrine of the common law that if death results in the prosecution of a felonious intent or in its consequences naturally tended to bloodshed, it will be murder. 4 Chitty's Blackstone *193. It made murder in the first degree a capital offense punishable by death unless the jury recommends life imprisonment. N.J.S. 2A:113–4, N.J.S.A. We have but two capital offenses in this State; they are murder in the first degree, N.J.S. 2A:113–1, 2, 4, N.J. S.A., and treason, N.J.S. 2A:148–1, N.J.S.A.

Whether in the matter of punishment of murder the Legislature feels it desirable to place children in a different classification is purely a matter of public policy and within the legislative power. But insofar as guilt for the commission of the crime of murder is concerned I cannot disregard the enormity of the offense by fine spun legal reasoning and agree that it can be treated as mere juvenile delinquency.

I am unable to subscribe to nor can I find support for the legal theory by which the Legislature can declare that those young in years but old in crime and depravity are incapable of committing the crime of murder. Many such are experienced criminals. A prominent jurist recently said: "The whole problem of juvenile and adolescent delinquency has become worse and is now a scandal."

A peaceful citizen has the right to be protected by his government and to have a spade called a spade, and if young hoodlums are mentally incapable of a criminal intent they should be put to the burden of establishing that proposition in a court of law under established rules and are only entitled as a matter of right to the constitutional guarantees afforded to other citizens.

I would affirm the order of the court below in denying the motion for the transfer of the indictments to the Juvenile and Domestic Relations Court.

WACHENFELD, J. (dissenting).

Over the many years our present procedure in reference to these matters has worked out quite satisfactorily. No hue or cry of great injustice has been heard, nor is there a single case the disposition of which has offended the public's sense of essential fairness.

The method of disposing of these cases has now been changed, not by legislative enactment, where the power admittedly resides, but by a new judicial interpretation. In re Mei, 122 N.J.Eq. 125, 192 A. 80, 110 A.L.R. 1080 (E. & A.1937), which has stood for 17 years, is overruled and is no longer the law.

Up until now, all who committed murder, whether old or young, were held strictly accountable to the law. If the offender appreciated the difference between right and wrong, he was answerable in a court of law for the highest crime known, the taking of another's life.

Today's youth is more precocious than yesterday's. His aggressiveness has not been diminished, and the record unfortunately shows his propensity for going out of bounds has not decreased. The child who flouts authority is becoming too prevalent, and the seriousness of these infractions is becoming increasingly grim. Juvenile delinquency is still one of our foremost problems, and its solution is being vainly sought by educator, legislator and many public agencies.

How, then, will this change in the law affect the dilemma confronting us? Will it help or hinder? Those of tender age who are likely to commit the crime involved will certainly not be additionally deterred by the knowledge that the punishment for it has practically been abolished and the worst that can befall them for committing a felony murder under the new rule is confinement in a reformatory or correctional institution for the term fixed by the trustees, not to exceed in any case a few years.

Erring youth indeed offers a fertile field for remedial effort, but I doubt if in this instance we are making much of a contribution.

The police now cannot keep track of those they have apprehended and referred to the Juvenile Court. The disposition there is confidential and secret and makes better law enforcement by those responsible for it more difficult. To the classification of the offenses so processed we now add the crime of murder. I have grave fears of its consequences.

I cannot embrace many of the expressions in Justice OLIPHANT's dissent, but I feel obligated to state briefly the reasons why I would adhere to the decision in In re Mei, supra, and therefore affirm the judgment below.

63

State v. Elbert*

. . . MALTBIE, C. J. The defendant was arrested under a warrant issued at the direction of the Superior Court, upon an information by the State's Attorney charging him with the crime of rape. The information was later amended by the addition of other counts, eight charging him with the crime of burglary, one with the crime of attempt to rape, and one, the tenth, with the crime of rape. He pleaded to the jurisdiction of the court upon the ground that at the time of the commission of the crimes alleged he was under the age of sixteen, that consequently he was within the provisions of the Juvenile Court Act, General Statutes, Chapter 95, §§ 1854–1872, and that the Superior Court was therefore without jurisdiction to hear and determine the case. To this plea the State demurred and the trial court sustained the demurrer. The State's Attorney thereafter elected to try the defendant upon the tenth count and at the trial the defendant again raised in various ways the question whether he was amenable to trial in the ordinary process of criminal procedure in the Superior Court, but the trial court overruled his claims, found him guilty and sentenced him to the reformatory. The question before us is whether the Superior Court had jurisdiction to try the defendant for the crimes with which he was charged and to find him guilty and sentence him for the crime alleged in the tenth count of the amended information, in view of the provisions of the Juvenile Court Act.†

The Act defines a child as any person under sixteen years of age, and then goes on to define the meaning as used in it of the words "dependent child," "uncared-for child," "neglected child," "defective child" and "delin-

quent child." In the definition of the last it includes several classes, but we are concerned only with the first, a child who "violates any law of the state or local ordinance." Juvenile Courts are established in all cities, towns and boroughs having City, Police, Town or Borough Courts, the Juvenile Courts to be distinct from, but to be conducted by the same officials as, the other courts designated. In any town where there is no City, Police, Town or Borough Court, each justice of the peace or probate judge having jurisdiction therein has the same powers and duties in relation to any child who may be brought before him as a delinquent child or as having committed a crime or misdemeanor, as are conferred and imposed upon the officials of such courts as officers of the Juvenile Courts under the Act. "The several Juvenile Courts shall exercise exclusive original jurisdiction over all proceedings concerning uncared-for, neglected, dependent and delinquent children within the territory over which their respective jurisdictions extend, except in matters of guardianship and adoption and all other matters affecting property rights of any child over which the Probate Court has jurisdiction." The filing of petitions for action by Juvenile Courts by a parent or guardian or any one of several officials designated, including prosecuting officers, the proceedings upon such petitions, and the temporary custody and detention of the child concerned are all provided for. It is stated that nothing in the terms of the Act shall prevent the arrest of a child with or without a warrant, with certain limitations, but it is required that "whenever a child shall be brought before a judge of a City, Police, Borough or Town Court, such judge shall immediately transfer such case to the Juvenile Court having jurisdiction over it and direct that the child be forthwith delivered to such Juvenile Court or into the custody of the probation or other officer of such court. . . . Upon the arrest of any child by any officer, such officer shall immediately turn him over to the probation or other officer of the Juvenile Court, if such course be practical." The court, after hearing the case, is authorized to commit the child to any public or private institution or agency which is permitted by law to care for children or to any suitable person, or to permit him to remain at home subject to supervision by the probation officer. An appeal is

---

* *State* v. *Elbert*, Supreme Court of Errors, Connecticut, 1932, 115 Conn. 589, 162 A. 769.

† For a list of the jurisdictional variations in the different statutes, see Table IV, "Juvenile and Criminal Court Jurisdiction over Delinquency Cases," in P. W. Tappan, *Comparative Survey of Juvenile Delinquency*, Part I, North America, United Nations, 1958, ST/SOA/SD/1/Rev. 1, pp. 28–29. — *Ed.*

allowed from any order of the court to the next criminal term of the Court of Common Pleas, or if there be no such court in the county having criminal jurisdiction, to the next criminal term of the Superior Court. The Act also contains these provisions: "No child shall be prosecuted for an offense before a Juvenile Court, nor shall the adjudication of such court that a child is delinquent in any case be deemed a conviction of crime." "The disposition of any child under the provisions of this chapter, evidence given in such cases, except evidence of crime which, if committed by a person of sufficient age, would be punishable by imprisonment in the state prison, and all orders therein, shall be inadmissible as evidence in any criminal proceedings against such child."

The Act was before this court in *Cinque v. Boyd*, 99 Conn. 70, 121 Atl. 678, and *Amato v. Erskine*, 100 Conn. 497, 123 Atl. 836. In the first of these cases we sustained its constitutionality against the attacks then made upon it and pointed out that the proceedings under it did not constitute a criminal prosecution but a civil inquiry to determine whether in a greater or less degree some child should be taken under the direct care of the State to safeguard and foster its adolescent life. In the second case we held that when an information is presented to the Superior Court and the claim is made that the defendant is under the age of sixteen the Superior Court has jurisdiction to determine the question, and we expressly pointed out that the disposition of the appeal did not make it necessary to determine the question whether the Juvenile Court Act made all juvenile offenders under sixteen years of age incapable of committing a crime.

In the present case the State claims that, in so far as the Act attempts to oust our criminal courts of jurisdiction over the prosecution and punishment of crime, the legislature has transgressed the bounds of its constitutional functions and invaded those of the judiciary, because it has in effect made the fact that a person is under sixteen years of age conclusive that he cannot be found guilty of crime. If it be conceded, as the defendant claims, that the effect of the Act is to make any person under that age incapable of committing crime, and thus to make, as to such a person, an exception to the broad terms of our criminal statutes, the legislature is really only exercising its unques-

tioned power to define the elements necessary to constitute a crime. *State v. Lanyon*, 83 Conn. 449, 451, 76 Atl. 1095; *State v. Pape*, 90 Conn. 98, 102, 96 Atl. 313. The age of one who has committed a particular act forbidden by law has always been an element necessary to make that act a crime. Thus, at common law a child under seven could not commit a crime, and while this rule is sometimes stated in the form of a conclusive presumption, in contradistinction to the rule that a child between the ages of seven and fourteen was deemed prima facie not to be capable of committing crime, it in fact established an incapacity. 2 Swift's Digest, p. 361; 4 Black. Comm. p. 23; 1 Wharton, Criminal Law (11th Ed.) § 85. The age below which that incapacity exists has been varied in several of the States. See, for example, *Angelo v. People*, 96 Ill. 209; *Ford v. State*, 100 Ga. 63, 25 S. E. 845; *Gardiner v. State*, 33 Tex. 692. In our own State the legislature has specifically made the age of the defendant a necessary element in certain crimes. Thus, a woman under the age of forty-five who is epileptic, imbecile or feeble-minded is forbidden to marry or, when she is under that age, to consent to carnal knowledge by any man who is so afflicted. General Statutes, §§ 6275, 6277. It is also made a criminal offense for any minor under the age of sixteen to use tobacco in a public place. General Statutes, § 6284. The power of the legislature to make the age of a person who violates the prohibition of a statute a necessary element in making his act a crime, so far as our research goes, has never been questioned save in one instance involving the constitutionality of a Juvenile Court Act, and there the power was upheld. *State v. Burnett*, 179 N. C. 735, 743, 102 S. E. 711. That the effect of Juvenile Court Acts in certain of the States was to render a child under the age designated in the Act incapable of committing crime has, however, been asserted in several decisions. *State v. Coble*, 181 N. C. 554, 557, 107 S. E. 132; *Ex parte Parnell*, 19 Okl. Crim. 273, 281, 200 Pac. 456; *State v. Malone*, 156 La. 617, 619, 100 So. 788. In the last case it is succinctly stated "It is clear that what in an adult would be a crime, yet when done by a juvenile is a delinquency and punishable not as in the case of an adult but in a manner" provided in the Juvenile Court Act. That the legislature has power to provide that no child under the age of sixteen can be convicted of crime but shall be dealt with only under the provisions of a law such as that establishing our Juvenile Courts, we do not deem open to question.

The State claims, however, that, even though the legislature might constitutionally do this, it has not sufficiently evinced such an intent in the Act. It is perhaps fortunate that the exigencies of this case do not require us to attempt a solution of the problem so presented. The Act does not in terms state that no child under sixteen may be prosecuted for crime; and the State points particularly to the provision in the Act already quoted, which provides that the disposition of a child under its terms, orders made in the case and evidence given in it, except evidence of crime which, if committed by a person of sufficient age, would be punishable by imprisonment in state prison, should not be admissible "in any criminal proceedings against such child," a provision not easy to explain if under no circumstances can any child under sixteen be amenable to criminal process. Moreover, there is among our criminal statutes one which expressly makes a child under sixteen liable to a fine. General Statutes, § 6284. It is difficult to attribute to the legislature an intent that every offender under the age of sixteen, though he may have committed murder, rape, robbery or other serious crime and however hardened he may be in iniquity, merely because he has not reached that age though it be but a matter of days, must necessarily be immune from criminal proceedings, to be dealt with only as are those boys or girls who have committed some slight offense or are classed in the Act as "delinquent" merely because they are growing up in idleness, ignorance or vice, or are truants from their homes and wanderers by night without any lawful purpose, or engaged in some practice or occupation prejudicial to their normal development, physically, mentally or morally. The defendant not only committed a heinous offense, at a time when he fell short of the age of sixteen by but a few weeks, but the long series of serious crimes with which he is charged at least suggests that he is thoroughly depraved and irresponsible. The thought of remitting the disposition of proceedings against such an offender to the Juvenile Court arouses

a natural reluctance. That such a course would not accord with the general feeling of mankind is indicated by the fact that in most of the Juvenile Court Acts in the various States some provision is made for the disposition of such cases, either by excepting certain of the more serious offenses or by giving to some tribunal the power to determine whether the Juvenile Court or the criminal court should take cognizance of them. Moreover, to draw an arbitrary line of distinction at the age of sixteen, without regard to the character or history of the offender or the circumstances of the offense is hardly cognizant with that individualization of punishment which has become one of the fundamentals of modern penology.

On the other hand, the legislature, at the same session at which the Act was passed and at the succeeding session, made other changes in related statutes which, carried to their logical result in the Revision of 1930, would, if any child under the age of sixteen is to be held subject to criminal prosecution, bring about a most unfortunate situation. Public Acts, 1921, Chap. 356, § § 2, 5; Public Acts, 1923, Chap. 184, § 1. It is now provided that only Juvenile Courts have power to commit girls to Long Lane Farm or boys to the Connecticut School for Boys; General Statutes, § § 1812, 1848; and only such courts and Courts of Probate have power to commit children to county temporary homes or other institutions. General Statutes, § § 1876, 1886. Other statutes provide that no child under sixteen may be sent to jail, General Statutes, § 1895; that no boy under sixteen may be committed to the Connecticut Reformatory, General Statutes, § 1830; and that no girl under sixteen may be committed to the State Farm for Women. General Statutes, § 1800. It is true that in the present case, the trial court deferred sentence after conviction for a few days, during which the defendant became sixteen years of age, and then sentenced him to the Connecticut Reformatory; but, whatever might be said as to the correctness of that procedure in this particular case, a practice of thus deferring sentence for any more than a brief period would not be proper; and, generally speaking at least, upon conviction of a boy under sixteen in a criminal court, as the statutes now exist, he could not be committed to the reformatory. The necessary result is that, upon conviction in the criminal court of a child under sixteen, only two courses are open, either to commit him or her to a state prison or to place him or her upon probation. General Statutes, § 6518. The former course would be beyond the jurisdiction of justices of the peace and of most, if not all, of the City, Police, Town and Borough Courts, so that no justice of the peace and few, if any, of these courts now have power to punish children under sixteen by imprisonment of any kind. Even the Superior Court and Courts of Common Pleas have not that power unless the child is found guilty of a crime for which the statute provides a penalty of more than a year of imprisonment. General Statutes, § 6508. Probation, if legally possible in cases where the court has no power to imprison, necessarily lacks the sanction of punishment for its breach. Even where the court could impose a sentence of imprisonment in a state prison, it would have no discretion in the case of the conviction of one under sixteen save to fix a sentence of more than a year in such institution, if it deemed imprisonment necessary. To put the trial court in such a position as would follow if the State's position in this case is correct would be contrary to the policy of our statutes which have tended more and more to broaden the discretion of courts in determining the disposition of one found guilty of crime, a tendency which well accords with that individualization of punishment to which we have referred.

We have pointed out some of the difficulties created by the present state of our law in the thought that a solution of the problem not freighted with so many possibilities of ill may be evolved. The decision of the present case may rest upon narrow grounds. Section 1856, quoted above, provides that Juvenile Courts shall exercise "exclusive original jurisdiction" over all proceedings concerning delinquent children, save in the excepted cases. This provision is to be read in conjunction with those of § 1855, in which it is provided that, where there is no City, Police, Town or Borough Court, and therefore criminal proceedings against a child would, save in exceptional cases where original informations might be filed in the Superior Court or Courts of Common Pleas, be inaugurated before some justice of the peace, he is given the same power and subjected to the same duties as are imposed upon such courts, "in relation to any child who may be brought before him . . . as having committed a crime or misdemeanor." It is also provided with reference to City, Police, Town and Borough Courts, which in cities and towns where they exist are courts of original criminal jurisdiction, that whenever a child is brought before a judge thereof, he shall immediately transfer the case to the Juvenile Court and direct the child to be delivered to that court or one of its officers; and that "upon the arrest of any child by any officer, the officer shall immediately turn him over to the probation or other officer of the Juvenile Court." It thus appears that save in such cases as might be begun in the Superior Court or Courts of Common Pleas, all proceedings against children under sixteen who have violated any law of the State or local ordinance must, unless the terms of the Act are to be violated, be conducted, at least in the first instance, in the Juvenile Courts. Proceedings inaugurated in the Superior Court or the Courts of Common Pleas upon information by State's Attorneys or Prosecuting Attorneys involve the exercise of "original jurisdiction" of the offenses by such courts . . . [Citations omitted. — Ed.] . . . and if these courts could exercise such a jurisdiction, at least before proceedings are had in the Juvenile Courts, then the latter would not have that "exclusive original jurisdiction" with which the Act purports to invest them. It necessarily follows that proceedings against any child within the class of delinquents as defined in the Act must, in the first instance at least, be taken in the Juvenile Court and until that court has acted the Superior Court can have no jurisdiction. If the Superior Court might in any event take jurisdiction of the offense charged against the defendant, a question which we do not decide, it could only do so after proceedings had first been taken against him in the Juvenile Court. The demurrer to the plea to the jurisdiction should have been overruled and that plea sustained.

There is error and the case is remanded with direction to dismiss the information against the accused.

In this opinion the other judges concurred.

64

Harris *et ux. v.* Souder *et al.**

EMMERT, Judge.

This is an appeal from a judgment of the Hendricks Circuit Court for the appellees, who were defendants to a complaint for a writ of habeas corpus. Appellants' motion for a new trial, which charged that the finding was not sustained by sufficient evidence and was contrary to law, was overruled, and this ruling is here assigned as error.

The complaint for the writ charged that appellants were the father and mother of Exel Harris,[1] aged 16 years, and were entitled to his custody; that said son was illegally restrained by the Superintendent and Trustees of the Indiana Boys' School by reason of a pretended commitment of the Johnson Circuit Court issued on a judgment of said court which was illegal and void for reasons later discussed in this opinion. As an exhibit to this complaint, the appellants set out the following order book entry of criminal order book No. 4:

"State of Indiana
VS   No. 5984
Axel Harris

*   *   *   *   *   *   *

"Comes now the State of Indiana by the Prosecuting Attorney and comes also the defendant into open court and after being advised of his constitutional rights he is duly arraigned and for his plea says that he is guilty of Contributing to the delinquency of a minor, as charged. And this cause being now at issue, the same is submitted to the court for trial, finding and judgment without the intervention of a jury. And the court after hearing the evidence and being fully advised in the premises, now takes the same under advisement until March 12, 1953 at 9:30 A. M., when the defendant is ordered to appear.

"And afterwards, to-wit: On the 12th day of March, 1953, the same being the 10th Judicial day of the March Term 1953, of said court, before the same Honorable Judge thereof, the following further proceedings were had herein, to-wit:

---

* *Harris* et ux. v. *Souder* et al., Supreme Court of Indiana, 1954, 233 Ind. 287, 119 N.E. 2d 5.

[1] The certified copy of the proceedings in the Johnson Circuit Court show the juvenile's Christian name as "Axel."

"Comes now the State of Indiana by the Prosecuting Attorney, and comes also the defendant in person, and comes also the court, and the court having heretofore taken said cause under advisement, and after giving the same careful consideration in all things, now finds the defendant is sixteen years of age; that he be sentenced to the custody of the Trustees of Indiana Boys School until he arrives at the age of twenty-one years or is released by them.

"It is therefore ordered, adjudged and decreed by the court that the defendant is guilty as charged; that he is sixteen years of age; that he be sentenced to the custody of the Trustees of the Indiana Boys School until he arrives at the age of twenty-one years or is released by them."

This was the only part of the intrinsic record of the Johnson Circuit Court introduced by the appellants. The appellees introduced a certified copy of the commitment to the Indiana Boys' School. The commitment was in substantial compliance with § 13–916, Burns' 1942 Replacement, and § 9–3215(5), Burns' 1942 Replacement Supp., neither of which require a copy of the judgment.

The action here for the writ was a collateral attack upon the judgment of the Johnson Circuit Court. Appellants sought to challenge the court's jurisdiction over the person of the juvenile, and of the subject matter of the action. If either be lacking the judgment is void, and the commitment can be no better than the judgment that supports it. In determining these questions, we are limited to the court's intrinsic record, and matters dehors such record are not in issue. Dinkla v. Miles, 1934, 206 Ind. 124, 188 N.E. 577; Witte v. Dowd, Warden, 1951, 230 Ind. 485, 102 N.E. 2d 630; State ex rel. Eggers v. Branaman, 1932, 204 Ind. 238, 183 N.E. 653.

Under §§ 9–3209 and 9–3210, Burns' 1942 Replacement (Supp.), appellants were entitled to have a summons served upon them. As parents, they had an interest in the custody and welfare of their child, and in the absence of waiver or statutory exceptions, without summons the court acquired no jurisdiction over the juvenile or his parents. In Ford v. State, 1952, 122 Ind.App. 315, 104 N.E.2d 406, the Appellate Court held that lack of notice under § 9–3209, Burns' 1942 Replacement Supp., made the judgment void. We agree with this construction.

But the record here does not affirmatively disclose no summons was issued or served. The

Johnson Circuit Court is a court of superior and general jurisdiction under § 4–303, Burns' 1946 Replacement. It exercises general civil, criminal and probate jurisdiction. Under Chapter 347 of the 1945 Acts, § 9–3102, Burns' 1942 Replacement Supp., it exercises juvenile jurisdiction.[2] No additional court was created for Johnson County, and the court or judge thereof in exercising juvenile jurisdiction is not acting as a separate court. See Lindsay v. Lindsay, 1913, 257 Ill. 328, 333, 100 N.E. 892, 45 L.R.A.,N.S., 908. Different considerations on jurisdiction may be involved if we were deciding such issues coming from a special statutory juvenile court under § 9–3101, Burns' 1942 Replacement Supp., and we decide nothing as to such courts. [Citation omitted. — Ed.]

When a judgment of a court of general jurisdiction is attacked in a collateral proceedings, and the record does not affirmatively show lack of jurisdiction of the person, the presumption is that such court had jurisdiction of the person of the defendant. In a collateral attack, Indiana has followed the rule that this presumption cannot be rebutted by evidence dehors the record. Friebe v. Elder, 1914, 181 Ind. 597, 105 N.E. 151. The court's intrinsic record determines the issue of jurisdiction in an action for habeas corpus. [Some citations omitted. — Ed.]

The plea of guilty by the juvenile was wholly void, and did not place the cause at issue. The juvenile was being proceeded against for a juvenile offense and not for a criminal offense. The jurisdiction of the court to commit the juvenile to the Indiana Boys' School was a statutory extension of the ancient right of the sovereign, acting as a *parens patriae* through a court of chancery, to protect infants. [Some citations omitted. — Ed.] In the absence of express statutory authority, neither the infant, nor his guardian *ad litem*, can waive issuance and service of process, nor may either admit an issue against the infant in a suit at law or in equity. . . . [Citations omitted. — Ed.]

However, the record in this case affirmatively shows that the trial judge did hear evidence, and we will presume that he acted upon the evidence and not the plea.

The record also recites that the juvenile pleaded guilty to contributing to the delinquency of a minor. There is no such juvenile offense as this. However, we do not have a full record before us and we are unable to know what the charge was. If he had been originally charged with a crime and it was ascertained under § 9–3213, Burns' 1942 Replacement Supp., that he was a juvenile, the proceedings could have been transferred to the juvenile records and the finding and judgment should have been, if guilty, that he was guilty of delinquency. Under § 9–3207(b), Burns' 1942 Replacement Supp., when such a transfer is made no new charge is required, but when transferred the charge is then for a juvenile offense, to-wit delinquency.

A matter of statutory public policy is disclosed by the certificate of the clerk to the effect that the records certified were from the criminal order book. Proceedings against juveniles should not be in the civil or criminal order books, which are public records open to the inspection of the public. It has been the practice in this state for circuit courts to have separate juvenile minute books and separate juvenile order books. Section 9–3114, Burns' 1942 Replacement Supp., provides, "Such records shall be open only by order of the court to persons having a legitimate interest." Section 9–3215, Burns' 1942 Replacement Supp., requires only such persons be admitted at the hearing as have a direct interest in the case, and prohibits the use of the evidence given in any case or proceeding in any other court. The fact that the record was made in an improper order book, however, does not affect the jurisdiction of the court. . . . [Citations omitted. — Ed.] . . . Appellants by proper action could compel the trial court to place the proceedings in the proper records, but in a collateral attack by way of habeas corpus we have no jurisdiction to correct the records by our mandate.

Judgment affirmed.

DRAPER, C. J., and GILKISON, FLANAGAN and BOBBITT, JJ., concur.†

---

[2] "In all other counties except as may be provided by law otherwise, the circuit court and the judge thereof shall have and possess all the powers and shall perform the duties by law conferred on the juvenile court and the judge thereof." [Acts 1945, ch. 347, § 2, p. 1647; 1949, ch. 20, § 1, p. 37] § 9–3102, Burns' 1942 Replacement Supp.

† See *State ex rel. Knutson* v. *Jackson*, 249 Minn. 246, 82 N.W. 2d 234 (1957) holding that notice is

65

State ex rel. White v. District Court of Milwaukee County et al.*

On November 16, 1951, a complaint was filed with the clerk of the respondent district court of the county of Milwaukee (hereinafter referred to as the district court) against the relator Frank D. White, Jr., and one Charles Verace, charging them with the violation of sec. 340.39, Stats., the crime charged being assault and theft while armed, and having been committed on said 16th day of November, 1951. Criminal warrants for the arrest of the relator and Verace were issued by the respondent district judge, and they were taken into custody.

On November 17, 1951, the relator and Verace were brought before the district judge for a preliminary hearing, but the hearing was adjourned until December 3, 1951, at the request of counsel. On December 3, 1951, the preliminary hearing was again adjourned at the request of counsel for Verace until December 27, 1951.

The relator was born on December 8, 1933, and therefore was not eighteen years of age when the crime with which he was charged was committed, but he would have reached the age of eighteen before the adjourned date of hearing on December 27, 1951. On December 3, 1951, after the adjournment of the scheduled preliminary hearing for that date, the judge of the Children's Court of Milwaukee county (which is the juvenile court for that county) was given information which tended to show that the relator was a delinquent child and said judge authorized a petition to be filed in the juvenile court pursuant to sec. 48.06, Stats.,

which petition was verified by one of the relator's counsel. This petition alleged that relator was a delinquent child because he had violated sec. 340.39, Stats., and further, being wayward or habitually disobedient, was uncontrolled by his parents. The judge of the juvenile court set the hearing on the petition for December 6, 1951, and a summons was issued and served on the relator's parents.

At the hearing in the juvenile court on December 6, 1951, a special assistant district attorney for Milwaukee county appeared for the state of Wisconsin, pursuant to notice given by the judge of the juvenile court, and he presented an argument in opposition to the exercise of jurisdiction by the juvenile court. The argument of such assistant district attorney was overruled, and after a full hearing, the juvenile court entered a judgment on said 6th day of December, 1951, material parts of which judgment are:

"I, John J. Kenney, the Judge before whom the proceedings were had, do find that Frank D. White, Jr., is a delinquent child in that he violated a law of the state in that he participated in assault and armed robbery in violation of Wisconsin Statute 340.39; also, by reason of being wayward or habitually disobedient, is uncontrolled by his parents; that the legal settlement is in Rockford, Illinois. State-at-large charge.

"Therefore It Is Adjudged That said Frank D. White, Jr. be and hereby is committed to the care and custody of State Department of Public Welfare, Madison, Wisconsin."

Pursuant to said judgment, the State Department of Public Welfare placed the relator in the Wisconsin School for Boys at Waukesha, where he now is.

On December 11, 1951, after the district judge learned of the juvenile court judgment, he issued an order requiring the State Department of Public Welfare to produce the relator before the district judge at the preliminary hearing scheduled for December 27, 1951, and caused the same to be served on the superintendent of the Wisconsin School for Boys. On December 15, 1951, a petition for an alternative writ of mandamus and prohibition directed to the respondents district court and district judge was presented to the circuit court for Milwaukee county by relator's counsel.

---

a jurisdictional requisite and that failure to serve parents would invalidate any order. See, also, *In re Florance*, 47 Cal. 2d 25, 300 P 2d 825 (1956) holding that notice to the minor is not necessary but, under statute, it must be given to parents. — *Ed.*

* *State* ex rel. *White* v. *District Court of Milwaukee County* et al., Supreme Court of Wisconsin, 1952, 262 Wis. 139, 54 N.W. 2d 189.

The prayer of said petition prayed that the circuit court issue its writ of mandamus and prohibition requiring the respondents district judge and district court to dismiss the criminal complaint against relator, rescind the criminal warrant, release the bail posted, discharge petitioner as a matter of record in the proceedings before the district judge, rescind the order of the district judge of December 11, 1951, and desist and refrain from any further proceedings until the hearing and determination of the petition. An alternative writ, dated December 17, 1951, was served on respondents. The respondents moved to quash the petition, which motion to quash was granted in an order of the circuit court, entered February 1, 1952. The relator has appealed from said order. . . .

CURRIE, Justice.

The question presented on this appeal is whether a criminal court had jurisdiction over relator by reason of the issuance of a warrant and the setting of a date for preliminary hearing at the time the juvenile court assumed jurisdiction and entered its judgment of December 6, 1951.

Under the provision of the statutes hereinafter quoted, criminal courts and the juvenile court are given concurrent jurisdiction over "children between the ages of sixteen and eighteen who have committed a crime." In a case in which two courts are given concurrent jurisdiction over a particular subject matter, and one of such courts has assumed jurisdiction, it is reversible error for the other to also assume jurisdiction. Kusick v. Kusick, 1943, 243 Wis. 135, 9 N.W.2d 607; and Cawker v. Dreutzer, 1928, 197 Wis. 98, 129, 221 N.W. 401. Therefore, if the prior proceedings before the district judge did constitute an assumption of jurisdiction by a criminal court, it was a reversible error for the juvenile court to thereafter assume jurisdiction and enter its judgment of December 6, 1951, committing relator to the State Department of Public Welfare. On the other hand, if the proceedings before the district judge did not constitute a proceeding in a criminal court, the juvenile court would then have been the first court to assume jurisdiction and the judgment of December 6, 1951, would be a bar to any further proceedings by the respondents district judge or district court.

The portions of the pertinent statutes ap-plicable to the point in issue are:

(1) Sec. 48.01(1)(c) — "The words 'delinquent child' shall mean any child under the age of 18 years who has violated any law of the state or any county, city, town or village ordinance; or who by reason of being wayward or habitually disobedient, is uncontrolled by his parent, guardian or custodian; or who is habitually truant from school or home; or who habitually so deports himself as to injure or endanger the morals or health of himself or others; * * *."

(2) Sec. 48.01(5)(am) — " * * * In all cases of delinquent children over 16 years of age, the criminal courts shall have concurrent jurisdiction with the juvenile court * * *."

(3) Sec. 48.07(3) — "No adjudication upon the status of any child in the jurisdiction of the juvenile court shall operate to impose any of the civil disabilities ordinarily imposed by conviction, nor shall any child be deemed a criminal by reason of such adjudication, nor shall such adjudication be deemed a conviction, nor shall any child be charged with or convicted of a crime in any court, except as provided in section 48.11.* * *."

Sec. 48.11, referred to in sec. 48.07(3), supra, contains no exception applicable to the present case. Therefore, if it was not reversible error for the juvenile court to have entered its order of December 6, 1951, adjudging relator a delinquent child by reason of having committed the identical crime of which he was charged in the warrant issued by the respondent district judge, such judgment of the juvenile court would, under the provisions of sec. 48.07 (3), bar further criminal proceedings before the respondent district judge. Counsel for relator contend that even though such judgment of the juvenile court might have been erroneously entered, it, nevertheless, would bar any further criminal proceedings until directly attacked and reversed on appeal; but we find it unnecessary to determine such latter point in order to arrive at our decision herein.

The district court of Milwaukee county has jurisdiction to hear, try, and determine charges of violations of ordinances of the city of Milwaukee; misdemeanors committed in Milwaukee county; and felonies committed within the county which are punishable by not more than one year's imprisonment or a fine of not more than $1,000, or both. The municipal court of Milwaukee county is the only court which possesses the general criminal jurisdiction to hear, try, and determine the offense for which the relator was charged in the warrant issued by the district judge because the minimum punishment therefor is three years' imprisonment. However, sec. 5 of the District Court Act of Milwaukee county, confers the following authority and jurisdiction upon the district judge with respect to such offenses:

" * * * authority and jurisdiction to issue warrants for the apprehension of persons charged with the commission of offenses in said county of Milwaukee, and not triable before a justice of the peace of said county; and exclusive jurisdiction to examine said alleged offenders and commit or hold them to bail, the same as a justice of the peace might otherwise do."

Counsel for the respondents contends that because the foregoing quoted portion of sec. 5 of the District Court Act is preceded by the words "said court" (referring to the district court) the authority to isssue warrants, hold preliminary examinations, and to commit or hold offenders to bail, is vested in the district court, rather than the district judge acting as a magistrate. However, sec. 6 of the District Court Act, makes it clear that said authority is vested in the judge, rather than the court, the pertinent provision of sec. 6 being as follows:

"No justice of the peace, court commissioner, police justice or other committing magistrate in said county of Milwaukee, shall exercise any jurisdiction in any criminal cases, except as hereinafter provided, but all such jurisdiction is vested in said district judge * * *."

The functions of issuing warrants, conducting preliminary examinations or adjourning them, and committing or holding to bail are functions only conferred upon and exercised by certain persons or officers known to the law and designated by statute in Wisconsin as "magistrates." Secs. 354.01 and 354.05, Stats.

When the legislature provided in sec. 48.01(5)(am), Stats., that "criminal courts shall have concurrent jurisdiction with the juvenile court" in all cases of delinquent children over sixteen years of age, did its use of the term *"criminal courts"* have reference to a

court exercising criminal jurisdiction over the offender as a court, to the exclusion of a situation in which a judge of a criminal court functions as a magistrate? Considerable light in answering this question is provided by the following language used in sec. 48.07(1)(d), Stats.:

"In any case involving a male minor between eighteen and twenty-one years of age *where the criminal court shall have waived jurisdiction* in favor of the juvenile court as provided in paragraph (a) of subsection (5) of section 48.01 the court may place such minor on probation, as provided in this section, until twenty-five years of age or commit him to such institution and for such term as he might have been committed to by the criminal court."

An examining magistrate, such as the district judge in the instant case, has no power to sentence an offender charged with an offense triable in the municipal court for a term, or place him on probation. Therefore, the use of the term "criminal courts" in sec. 48.07(1)(d) had reference to a court functioning as a court, and not to the judge thereof functioning as a magistrate. We do not believe that the legislature intended to use the term "criminal courts" in sec. 48.07(1)(d) as not including a judge functioning as a magistrate, and to have used the same words in sec. 48.01(5) (am) as including a judge functioning as a magistrate. The conclusion would seem to be inescapable that the legislature's intended meaning of the term "criminal courts" as used throughout ch. 48 was consistent, and that the term does not include a situation of a judge, court commissioner, or justice of the peace, functioning as a magistrate.

This conclusion is further fortified by the fact that sec. 48.01(5)(am) provides that in a case of certain sex offenses committed by a male minor child between eighteen and twenty-one years of age, the *"criminal court having jurisdiction thereof"* may in a proper case waive jurisdiction in favor of the juvenile court. We doubt very much if the legislature intended to vest such a discretion in a justice of the peace, or a court commissioner, who had issued the warrant or was conducting the preliminary examination of such a sex offender, which would be the case if it included magistrates.

State v. Friedl, 1951, 259 Wis. 110, 47 N.W.2d 306, 307, is directly in point. In that case the state appealed from an order of Herman W. Sachtjen, circuit judge, at the conclusion of a preliminary examination of the defendants, who were charged with having committed two misdemeanors and two felonies, by which order the criminal complaints against the defendants were dismissed. The order was in the form of an order of the court, having been entered "By the court, Herman W. Sachtjen, judge." The state requested and was granted permission to appeal, and defendants moved to dismiss the appeal on the ground that an order entered by a magistrate is not an order of the court, and therefore not appealable. This court in its decision stated:

"The question here presented is whether Judge Sachtjen was acting as a court or as a magistrate.

"Ch. 354, Wis.Stats., provides the procedure for the arrest and examination of persons charged with crime. Sec. 354.01 authorizes certain officials, including judges of courts of record, to issue criminal process and designates all such as magistrates. Sec. 354.02(5) provides in part: ' * * * It [the warrant] shall command that the defendant be arrested and brought before the magistrate.'

"Sec. 354.04 requires that every person arrested upon a warrant shall be taken before the magistrate before whom it is returnable.

"There can be no doubt that in issuing the warrant Judge Sachtjen was functioning as a magistrate. The nature of the proceedings and not the form of the order must determine his capacity in entering it.

" 'Proceedings for the arrest and examination of offenders, and commitment for trial, under chapter 195, Rev. St. [now Chapter 354], are not, technically or properly speaking, proceedings in any court. They are proceedings before certain officers, known to the law as "magistrates," for the purpose of carrying out the provisions of this chapter; and these are "the judges of the several courts of record, — in vacation as well as in term time, — court commissioners, and all justices of the peace" who are authorized to issue process to carry it into execution. Rev. St. § 4775.' State v. Sorenson, 1893, 84 Wis. 27, 31, 53 N.W. 1124, 1125.

" 'But a proceeding before an examining magistrate is not a judicial trial. It is a mere judicial inquiry, as before indicated, for the purpose of determining whether an offense has been committed and there is a probability that the accused is guilty thereof and should be placed on trial therefor. No plea or issue is necessary.* * * The doctrine of res adjudicata

does not apply so that the result of one inquiry will preclude another. It is a proceeding that was unknown to the common law, — a mere statutory creation, a personal privilege which the accused must be accorded unless he waives it.' State ex rel. Durner v. Huegin, 1901, 110 Wis. 189, 239, 85 N.W. 1046, 1058, 62 L.R.A. 700."

The relator has never been and is not now before the district court or the district judge in connection with any charge which either of them has jurisdiction to hear, try and determine; because the offense with which he is charged is one punishable by imprisonment for not less than three years. The municipal court of Milwaukee county is the only court which possesses the criminal jurisdiction to hear, try and determine such offenses. In State ex rel. Wojtycski v. Hanley, 1945, 248 Wis. 108, 113, 20 N.W.2d 719, 721, this court held:

"Jurisdiction to try an offender for a crime of which the court has jurisdiction is obtained by his appearance in court, and by pleading guilty or not guilty, jurisdiction of his person is conferred on the court."

In the case at bar a preliminary hearing has not been held or waived; therefore, an information cannot be presented. Sec. 355.18, Stats. If an information cannot yet be presented, the general jurisdiction of the municipal court has not attached to the offense with which the relator is charged.

Therefore, no criminal court had as yet assumed jurisdiction over relator at the time the juvenile court issued its judgment of December 6, 1951, adjudging relator a delinquent child because of his having committed the crime charged in the warrant issued by the district judge, and committing him to the State Department of Public Welfare. Such judgment under the provisions of sec. 48.07(3), Stats., is a bar to any further criminal proceedings against relator for the same offense.

Order reversed and cause remanded with directions to issue the writ of mandamus and prohibition prayed for in relator's petition.

FRITZ, C. J., dissenting.

FAIRCHILD, J., not participating.*

---

* See, also, Whitman v. State, 96 Ga. App. 730, 101 S.E. 2d 621 (1957). — Ed.

66

State *ex. rel.* Jones *v.* Geckler *

FANSLER, Judge.

This is an original action by which the relator seeks a mandate requiring the respondent to sustain his motion for a change of judge. An alternative writ has issued.

It appears that the relator is a boy under the age of sixteen years; that a proceeding was begun against him in the Juvenile Court of Marion County, by affidavit charging that he "did then and there commit an act of delinquency in this, to wit: * * * "; that he committed a specified assault and battery. The cause was set for trial. The relator filed a verified motion for a change of judge, which is in the usual form used in criminal procedure, and is upon the ground of bias and prejudice. The change of judge was denied upon the theory, as we are advised by the respondent, that the action is not an adversary criminal proceeding, but merely a proceeding to determine whether the relator is a delinquent child as described by the statute, and that, for that reason, he is not entitled to a change of judge.

Respondent suggests that the relator, being an infant, cannot maintain this action in his own name; that it can be maintained only by a next friend or guardian in his behalf. If the proceeding is adversary, and in the nature of a prosecution of a criminal charge against the relator, the latter position is not well taken, since it is well recognized that infants, when charged with crime, plead in their own names, and that they may appeal in their own names.

The statute, section 9–2803, Burns' Ann. St.1933, section 5697, Baldwin's Ind.St.1934, defines a delinquent child as "any boy under the full age of sixteen (16) years and any girl under the full age of eighteen (18) years: Who shall violate any law of this state or any ordinance of a city"; or who shall be guilty of doing any one of a number of specified acts, all of which are commonly recognized as constituting misconduct on the part of young people. The section then continues: "Any boy

* State ex rel. *Jones* v. *Geckler,* Supreme Court of Indiana, 1938, 214 Ind. 574, 16 N.E. 2d 875. By

under the full age of sixteen (16) years or any girl under the full age of eighteen (18) years who shall commit any of the acts herein specified shall be deemed a delinquent child and shall be proceeded against as such in the manner provided by law for the prosecution of persons charged with misdemeanors, and upon conviction thereof, may be released on probation or may be dealt with by the court in such manner as may appear to be for the best interest of the child." Section 9–2814, Burns' Ann.St1933, section 1761, Baldwin's Ind.St.1934, provides that a warrant may issue for a child against whom complaint has been filed, and that: "If, upon the trial of any child, it shall appear to the judge of the juvenile court, or the judge thereof sitting in vacation, that such child is guilty of the offense charged he may withhold judgment," or order the child placed under public or private guardianship, or he "may impose a fine with costs"; and there is a further provision that: "If any child is found guilty of the offense charged against it or appears to be wilfully wayward and unmanageable, the court may commit him or her to the Indiana boys' school, the industrial school for girls, or to any other state, penal or reformatory institution authorized by law to receive such boy or girl." It is provided that, when a child is sentenced to confinement in an institution to which adult convicts are sentenced, he shall not be confined in the same building or yard with the adult convicts; and: "That in every trial of any such child he shall be entitled to a trial by jury of twelve persons if he shall so elect."

The statute (section 9–2803, Burns' AnnSt. 1933, section 5697, Baldwin's Ind.St.1934, supra) provides that if a boy or girl commits any of the acts specified in the statute, such child "shall be deemed a delinquent child and shall be proceeded against as such in the manner provided by law for the prosecution of persons charged with misdemeanors." Persons charged with misdemeanors are entitled to a change of judge, and the statute, section 9–1301, Burns' Ann.St.1933, section 2222, Baldwin's Ind.St.1934, does not restrict the right to a change to any court or jurisdiction. Not only the expressions, but the necessary implications of the act as a whole require the conclusion that, when a child is charged with delinquency, some specific act or conduct must be charged as constituting the delinquency; that the truth of the charge shall be determined in an adversary proceeding; and that the child shall be entitled to a trial under the rules prescribed for the trial of prosecutions for the commission of misdemeanors. It must follow that the child charged is entitled to a change of judge.

The respondent relies upon Dinson v. Drosta, 1907, 39 Ind.App. 432, 80 N.E. 32, and Heber et al. v. Drake et al., 1918, 68 Ind.App. 448, 118 N.E. 864. In the first case we have examined the record and the briefs. The proceedings were had, not in a juvenile court, but in a circuit court, under a statute enacted at the same session, but prior to the enactment of the juvenile court law, providing procedure for the admission of girls to the Indiana Industrial School for Girls. The complaint did not charge the eleven year old girl with being a delinquent. It did charge that, because of incorrigibility and vicious conduct, she was a proper subject for the guardianship of the Indiana Industrial School for Girls, and that her parents were depraved, and incapable of and unwilling to exercise care or discipline over the child. The court found that the girl was a suitable person to be committed to the instruction and discipline of the institution, and she was ordered committed. There is no finding or judgment that the child was delinquent, vicious, or incorrigible, nor was there any evidence of such facts. There was evidence from which the court might have concluded that the parents were not proper persons to have the custody of the child, although there is no express finding or judgment to that effect. In view of this record, it is reasonable to conclude that the court, in writing its opinion, treated the judgment as one against the parents only, depriving them of the custody of the child, and not as a judgment against the child. The other case involved a proceeding to remove a child from the custody of its parents. There was no charge that the child was delinquent or that it had done any wrong. The case is not in point.

The alternative writ heretofore issued is made absolute, and the respondent is ordered to grant the relator's motion for a change of judge.

Acts of 1945, Chaps. 347, 356, Indiana revised its juvenile court law, among other matters doing away with the provision dealt with in this decision. The case is retained as raising an interesting problem. — Ed.

67

Gatlin *et al. v.* State *

HALL, Justice.

Appellants are admittedly guilty of the larceny of $1,100 in currency. They are fifteen and fourteen years of age, respectively. Upon their apprehension a proceeding was instituted in the Youth Court seeking to have them adjudged delinquent and dealt with under the provisions of the Youth Court Act, Chapter 207, Laws of Mississippi of 1946. Upon the hearing, they were adjudged delinquent, but instead of imposing a sentence upon them the Youth Court certified them for proper criminal proceedings to the Circuit Court of Newton County, the order reciting that the offense committed by them would be a felony if committed by an adult.

In the Circuit Court they were indicted, tried, convicted and sentenced to a term of five years each in Oakley Training School at Oakley, Mississippi, from which they appeal.

It is contended by appellants that the Youth Court first obtained jurisdiction of this matter, that the Circuit Court was wholly without jurisdiction, and that consequently its judgment is void and should be reversed.

Section 3 of the Youth Court Act confers original jurisdiction in that court concerning any delinquent or neglected child "except as otherwise provided herein." Section 9 provides that the Youth Court may terminate its jurisdiction over such child; and Section 15 provides: "If a child thirteen years of age or older is charged with an offense which would be a felony if committed by an adult, the court, after full investigation, may, in its discretion, retain jurisdiction and proceed with the case as a delinquency case, or certify such child for proper criminal proceedings to any court which would have trial jurisdiction of such an offense if committed by an adult, and may fix the amount of bail, except that the circuit court shall have exclusive jurisdiction of such child if he be charged with any crime which, upon conviction, is punishable by life imprisonment or death."

* *Gatlin* et al. v. *State*, Supreme Court of Mississippi, in Banc., 1949, 207 Miss. 588, 42 So. 2d 774.

Section 19 of said Act provides that upon conviction of such child in the Circuit Court, the trial judge may, in his discretion, and in lieu of other statutory punishment, commit such child to any state institution now or hereafter established for delinquents.

It will at once be seen from the foregoing sections of the Act that it fully authorizes everything that was done in this case. The Circuit Court was not deprived of its jurisdiction by virtue of the fact that appellants were first brought into the Youth Court, since the latter court, as it was fully authorized to do, certified them over to the Circuit Court for appropriate proceedings against them. The appeal is, therefore, without merit.

The Attorney General has filed an able and lengthy brief assailing the constitutionality of numerous provisions of the Youth Court Act, and has asked that we declare the whole act, or at least a goodly portion of it, unconstitutional. It will be noted that this case has been disposed of without reaching the constitutional question. It is well-settled that this Court will not pass upon the constitutionality of a statute unless such decision is necessary to dispose of the case. Numerous cases to this effect are collated in 4 West's Miss. Dig., Constitutional Law, 46.

Affirmed.†

68

Seibert v. Ferguson *

SMITH, Justice.

This is an original petition for habeas corpus. The respondent filed his return, whereupon the

---

† Compare *Wheeler* v. *Shoemaker*, 213 Miss. 374, 57 So. 2d 267 (1952), where it was held that a child is entitled to his freedom under habeas corpus when tried and convicted in a criminal proceeding by a circuit court, without having first been given a youth court hearing. *Accord Lee* v. *State*, 214 Miss. 740, 59 So. 2d 338 (1952). Regarding such a transfer in Pennsylvania, the court in In re Holmes, pp. 422–433 *infra*, observed in a dictum that "such a certification could not be made after the Juvenile Court had made an adjudication of delinquency nor, perhaps, after any self-incriminatory examination of the child." — *Ed.*

* *Seibert* v. *Ferguson*, Supreme Court of Kansas, 1949, 167 Kan. 128, 205 Pac. 2d 484.

parties stipulated that the facts as set out in the petition and the return were the actual facts. The case was submitted for final determination on the petition for a writ and the respondent's return.

Petitioner, Robert Dean Seibert, was born May 7, 1934. At the time the events with which we are interested transpired he was fourteen years of age. He was found to be a juvenile delinquent in the juvenile court of Sherman county, Kansas, on August 4, 1948, and on that date was committed to the Boys' Industrial School at Topeka, to which he was admitted August 12, 1948. He remained at that school until October 15, 1948. On October 15, 1948, he escaped from the Boys' Industrial School and together with three other inmates rode a freight train to Kansas City, Kansas; in the railroad yards there the next morning he, together with his companions, was taken into custody by the police; they admitted they had escaped from the Boys' Industrial School the day before, whereupon the police delivered them to the custody of the probation officer of the probate court of Wyandotte county early in the morning of October 16, 1948. The probation officer advised the superintendent of the school by phone, was told that these boys had escaped and the probation officer told the superintendent they would be held in the custody of that officer until Monday or Tuesday of the following week, when they would be returned to the school. Sometime during October 17, 1948, one Gertrude Hutchison, the matron of the Detention Home, where petitioner was being held, was murdered by being strangled with a scarf. On October 18 a complaint charging petitioner with the crime of murder was filed in the city court of Kansas City, Kansas, by the county attorney of Wyandotte county. A warrant was duly issued for the arrest of petitioner and he was arrested. He was arraigned in the city court and ordered held without bond and at the same time an order appointing two reputable attorneys, members of the bar of Wyandotte county, were appointed by the court to defend him. He was ordered held in the custody of the jailer of Wyandotte county, Kansas, until discharged by due course of law. On October 26, his preliminary hearing was continued until November 9, 1948. On that date the judge of the city court of Kansas City, Division No. 2, ordered him held for trial for the crime charged in the warrant and complaint without bond, those orders being made after his attorneys had announced in open court they desired to waive a preliminary hearing. The commitment was thereupon issued directing the jailer of Wyandotte county jail to hold petitioner in his custody until discharged by law. On November 18 an information was filed in the district court of Wyandotte county, Kansas, charging petitioner with murder in the first degree. On November 24, the case was continued until the December, 1948 term upon request of counsel for petitioner. On December 7, 1948, the district court appointed the same two attorneys who had represented petitioner at the preliminary hearing to represent him in district court, pursuant to G.S.1947 Supp. 62–1304. On December 18, 1948, counsel for petitioner filed a motion in the district court challenging the jurisdiction of that court to try the cause and asking the court to remand it to the juvenile court for determination. On December 30, 1948, the judge of the district court, before whom the case was pending, denied this motion and continued the case to the March, 1949 term. March 4, 1949, an amended information was filed by the county attorney of Wyandotte county, Kansas, and on March 7, 1949, the case was set for trial. The answer of respondent sets out some details as to the circumstances surrounding the murder of Gertrude Hutchison. We are not concerned with those details here since the only question with which we are concerned is the jurisdiction of the district court to try petitioner and that turns altogether upon our construction of the statutes.

Counsel for petitioner filed this petition for a writ. On account of the youth of petitioner we entertained the petition for a writ rather than permit the trial to proceed and leave the question of jurisdiction to be raised on appeal.

Counsel for petitioner argue that on account of the age of the petitioner the only tribunal before which he could be tried is the juvenile court of Wyandotte county. They base this argument upon the provisions of what is known as our juvenile court law, being G.S.1935, 38–401 to 38–432, inc. This chapter inaugurated a new policy in Kansas as to the manner with which juvenile delinquents should be dealt. We considered the general purpose of the act in

Burris v. State Board of Administration, 156 Kan. 600, 134 P.2d 649, 651. There we said:

"This state has long been among the leaders in humanitarian approach to the problems of juvenile delinquents. Nor is this to say that there are not, perhaps, other forward steps which might well be taken. In 1879 the legislature provided for the erection of a 'state reform school' building. Ch. 170, Laws of 1879. In 1881 was enacted the first organic act relating to this 'state reform school.' Ch. 129, Laws of 1881. Though the name of the school was subsequently changed to 'Boys' Industrial School' fundamental provisions of the original act have been retained. The institution is fundamentally parental and educational in character. Boys are committed to it who are under sixteen years of age and who have committed offenses or found to be incorrigible. Sections 76–2104, 76–2105, G.S.1935. Boys so committed remain until they are twenty-one years old, unless sooner discharged as provided by statute. Section 76–2109, G.S.1935. A similar institution for girls — Girls' Industrial School — was established in 1889. At these schools every characteristic of penal institutions is avoided as far as possible. There are no stout enclosures, no armed guards, no provisions for control by force. To set up those instrumentalities would destroy the very atmosphere and spirit with which the state seeks to surround the boys. Schooling, including occupational and trade courses, and other helpful training is provided. Most of the boys prove amenable to its care and discipline and the school is justly proud of the many fine citizens who received constructive training within its walls and on its campus."

The first section of the act, Chapter 190, Laws 1905, now G.S.1935, 38–401, made the judge of the probate court in each county the juvenile court judge in that county and gave it jurisdiction over all cases concerning "dependent, neglected and delinquent" children. The second section, G.S.1935, 38–402, defined "dependent" child and "neglected" child and amongst these definitions we find it provided that the words "delinquent" child should include "any child under the age of sixteen years who violates any law of this state or any city, town or village ordinance." The third section, G.S.1935, 38–403, provided for the appointment of probation officers and defined their authority. The fourth section, G.S.1935, 38–

404, provided for the filing of petitions calling the court's attention to any "delinquent" or "dependent" child. The fifth section, G.S.1935, 38–405, provided for a hearing and for notice. The sixth section, G.S.1935, 38–406, provided for a continuance of the hearing and for the child being held in the custody of some person other than the jailer. The seventh section, G.S. 1935, 38–407, provided for awarding the custody of the child to some reputable citizen or industrial school as provided by law. The eighth section, G.S.1935, 38–408, provided that where the child be awarded to the care of any association or individual it should become a ward and subject to the guardianship of the association or individual. The ninth section, G.S.1935, 38–409, provided the case might be continued from time to time and the child held in the control of the probation officer or permitted to remain at home. This section also provided, in part, as follows:

"Or the court may commit the child to a suitable institution for the care of delinquent children: Provided, That no child under the age of sixteen years shall be committed to the state reformatory, and in no case shall a child be committed beyond his or her minority."

The tenth section, G.S.1935, 38–410, provided for the court causing a child who has been committed to an institution or individual to be brought before it from time to time. The eleventh section, G.S.1935, 38–411, provided that when a child under the age of sixteen was arrested instead of being taken before the justice of the peace or police magistrate or judge heretofore having jurisdiction of the offense he must be taken before the juvenile court or if he has been taken before a magistrate that magistrate must transfer the case to the juvenile court. The twelfth section, G.S.1935, 38–412, provided for children appealing from any order of commitment to the district court. The thirteenth section, G.S.1935, 38–413, made it the duty of the county attorneys to aid the probation officers in the performance of their duties. The fourteenth section, G.S. 1935, 38–414, was as follows:

"All punishments and penalties imposed by law upon persons for the commission of offenses against the laws of the state, or imposed by city ordinances for the violation of such ordinances, in the case of delinquent children under the age of sixteen years, shall rest in the discretion of the judge of the juvenile court, and execution of any sentence may be suspended or remitted by said court."

The fifteenth section, G.S.1935, 38–415, provided that the act should be liberally construed. The sixteenth section, G.S.1935, 38–416, provided that all acts in conflict with the act or inconsistent therewith should be repealed. Petitioner pointed to the language of that chapter, especially that which has been quoted, and argues that under its provisions on account of the fact that he was only fourteen years of age when he is alleged to have murdered Mrs. Hutchison neither the city court of Kansas City, Kan., nor the district court of Wyandotte county had any jurisdiction to try him and the only tribunal which did have such jurisdiction was the juvenile court of Wyandotte county. He asks us to hold by granting this writ. At the outset of the consideration of this argument we will take note of a provision in G.S.1935, 38–402, between section 2 of chapter 190 of the Laws of 1905. That provision is —

"This act shall apply only to children under the age of sixteen years, not now or hereinafter inmates of any state institution or any industrial school for boys or industrial school for girls."

Counsel for respondent realizes the possible effect of this provision. They state in their brief as follows:

"It would appear from the foregoing statutes that the only tribunal to try said petitioner for said offense is the juvenile court of Wyandotte county, Kansas, unless it be held under section 38–401 of the juvenile court act that at the time of the commission of the offense he was an inmate of a state institution or industrial school for boys."

They then proceed to argue petitioner was not an inmate of the Boys' Industrial School when he is charged to have committed the crime of murder because he had escaped from that institution. They couple this with an argument based on G.S.1935, 21–2001, a statute that provides for trial in district court and punishment of persons confined in the State Reform School, the name once borne by the Boys' Industrial School. G.S.1935, 21–2001, provides as follows:

"Any person confined in the state industrial school for boys or in the state industrial school for girls, who shall attempt to set fire to any building belonging to either of such institutions, or to any combustible matter for the purpose of setting fire to any such building, or who shall willfully and forcibly resist the lawful authority of any officer of either of such institutions, or shall incite or attempt to incite others to do so, or shall by gross or habitual misconduct exert a dangerous and pernicious influence over other persons confined in either of such institutions, or shall commit a felonious assault upon any officer, attendant, employee or inmate of either of such institutions, or shall in any manner willfully burn or otherwise destroy property of the value of more than twenty dollars belonging to either of such institutions, or shall run away or escape from either of such institutions, or from the lawful authorities thereof, shall be deemed guilty of a felony, and upon conviction thereof in the district court of the county wherein such offense shall have been committed shall be punished as follows: If the person so convicted is confined in the state industrial school for boys, he shall be sentenced and committed to the Kansas State Industrial Reformatory for a term of not less than one year nor more than three years; and if the person so convicted is confined in the state industrial school for girls, such person shall be sentenced and committed to the state penitentiary for a term of not less than one year nor more than three years: Provided, that for running away or escaping from either of such institutions the person so offending shall be deemed guilty of a violation of this act only upon the second or subsequent offense."

The above with a change in the name of the institution is Section 1 of Chapter 172 of the Laws of Kansas for 1901. It will be noted it provides that any person confined in either the state reform school, which is now the Boys' Industrial School, and the state industrial school for girls, should be punished by trial in the district court where the offense was committed for certain offenses, that is, setting fire to a building, resisting authority of an officer, by conduct exercising a dangerous or pernicious influence over other persons, felonious assault upon an officer, destruction of property and running away from the institution. We construed that statute in Burris v. State Board of Administration, supra.

In that case a boy fourteen years old had been committed to the Boys' Industrial School. While there he escaped several times and while

at large committed other crimes. He was finally tried and convicted of escaping, in violation of G.S.1935, 21–2001, and sentenced to be confined at the State Reformatory at Hutchinson. While there he filed a petition for a writ of habeas corpus alleging that under the provisions of G.S.1935, 30–401 to 38–432, he on account of his age could not be regarded as a criminal but only as a delinquent child. He relied strongly on G.S.1935, 38–409, where it is provided, in part, that —

"No child under the age of sixteen years shall be committed to the state reformatory."

We referred to the portion of G.S.1935, 38–402, which has already been quoted in this opinion, where it is provided that —

"This act shall apply only to children under the age of sixteen years, not now or hereafter inmates of any state institution or any industrial school for boys."

We held that the section meant what it said and the petitioner had been an inmate when he escaped and the juvenile court act did not apply to him and he could be prosecuted in district court for a violation of G.S.1935, 21–2001. In the syllabus we said:

"The classification established by section 38–402, G.S.1935, whereby the juvenile court act is made inapplicable to inmates of certain institutions, is valid insofar, at least, as it relates to inmates of the Boys' Industrial School."

To meet this situation petitioner argues that at the time of the commission of the offense with which he is charged he was not an inmate of the Boys' Industrial School on account of the fact that he had escaped therefrom and that he was not "confined" in the Boys' Industrial School, as contemplated by G.S.1935, 21–2001, for the same reason — hence neither of the provisions of the above statutes, that is, G.S.1935, 21–2001, nor the exception in G.S.1935, 38–402, applies to him.

We find it unnecessary to decide whether petitioner at the time the crime with which he is charged was committed was "confined" in the Boys' Industrial School since he is not charged with a violation of G.S.1935, 21–2001, but is charged with murder, as provided in the general crimes act, murder not being one of the crimes covered by G.S.1935, 21–2001. We must, however, give attention to this argument that he was not at the time of the commission of the offense with which he was charged an "inmate" of the Boys' Industrial School. We hold by escaping from the school he did not cease to be an inmate of it. This wrongful act of escape subjected him to be punished under the provisions of G.S.1935, 21–2001, as well as the general crimes act. Furthermore, under the terms of G.S.1935, 76–2111, any sheriff, constable or policeman had the power to arrest petitioner and return him to the school. As a matter of fact upon his arrest in Kansas City the superintendent of the school had been advised of his arrest and the superintendent asked the authorities in Kansas City to hold him for the officers from the school. He was actually in the custody of the school at the time he is charged with the commission of the crime though the probation officer of Kansas City, Kansas, was exercising the actual physical restraint. To hold otherwise would be to hold that when a group of these boys from the Boys' Industrial School are taken some distance from the school for the purpose of taking part in some athletic event or some other function while they are away from the grounds immediately surrounding the school they are not inmates thereof. Such was not the intention of the legislature. The general rule is stated at 18 C.J.S., Convicts, § 9, page 109, as follows:

"The legislature has full power to pass statutes relative to the custody, care, and control of persons convicted of crime. When a convict is serving a penal sentence, he is in the custody of the state or its authorities, and he remains constructively in such custody even though he may be released on parole. * * * A person convicted of felony and sentenced to confinement in the state prison is in contemplation of law in prison until he serves his term or is pardoned, although he may have been hired out to work for a contractor for convict labor, for the state cannot surrender its police power over convicts. A prisoner who has been convicted of a crime by a federal court and is confined in a state prison, with the consent of that state, is deemed to be in the custody of the federal authorities."

Once we have arrived at the conclusion that petitioner never ceased to be an inmate of the Boys' Industrial School from the time he escaped we have then only to consider the effect of the exception in G.S.1935, 38–402. It provides, in part, that the act, that is, the juvenile court act, shall apply only to children under the age of sixteen not then or thereafter inmates

of any industrial school for boys. The question is settled against the argument of the petitioner by Burris v. State Board of Administration, supra. Up to the time of the passage of that act in 1905 boys under sixteen could be prosecuted under the provisions of G.S.1935, 76–2104. That section was formerly section 3 of chapter 129 of the Laws of 1881. It provides, as follows:

"Whenever any boy under the age of sixteen years shall be convicted of any offense known to the laws of this state, and punishable by imprisonment, the court or justice, as the case may be, before whom such conviction shall be had, may at its discretion sentence such boy to the state industrial school for boys, or to such punishment as is now provided by law for the same offense; and if the sentence shall be to the state industrial school for boys, then it shall be in the alternative to the state industrial school for boys, or to such punishment as would have been awarded if this act had not been passed."

It will be noted the section provides for boys under the age of sixteen and that they may be sentenced under the general crimes act or in the discretion of the court to the state industrial school for boys.

It also gave the courts before which he should be arraigned, which would include at that time the district court, the power with the consent of the accused to arrest any proceedings and commit the boy to the reform school, now the industrial school. The provision with which we are concerned is that any court before whom the boy was arraigned had the discretion to sentence the boy to be an inmate of the industrial school for boys or to the punishment provided in the general crimes act. It was a matter of discretion for the court. It was our first step in the handling of what we now term juvenile delinquents, that is, a more intelligent, enlightened method than formerly followed of sentencing boys of tender years to a penal institution.

It has been brought to our attention that G.S.1935, 21–117, provides that when any person under the age of sixteen years shall be convicted of any felony he shall be sentenced to imprisonment in a county jail not exceeding one year instead of confinement and hard labor, as prescribed by the preceding sections of the crime act. The section has been in our statute books ever since 1868. At the time it was enacted there were only county jails and the penitentiary at Lansing. It is suggested that the section was the one the legislature had reference to in enacting G.S.1935, 76–2104, and the district court would in this case only have authority to sentence petitioner to serve a year in the county jail of Wyandotte county for a year or to the Boys' Industrial School. We have considered this section and the other sections, to which reference is made in this opinion, and hold that G.S.1935, 21–117, has been repealed by implication and is no longer in effect. In this connection we have considered what we held in State v. Hewes, 60 Kan. 765, 57 P. 959. If petitioner should be found guilty under the information filed against him he may be given an indeterminate sentence to the state industrial reformatory at Hutchinson, pursuant to G.S.1935, 76–2306.

We have in 1901 the act we have just discussed providing for boys confined in the Boys' Industrial School being sentenced to the reformatory at Hutchinson for the commission of certain offenses having to do with the institution. Then we see in 1905 the juvenile court act being passed, which has come down from that time to this, just about intact for the further intelligent handling of the affairs of juvenile delinquents, both boys and girls, with the proviso, however, that it should not apply to children who are inmates of an institution at the time they commit the crime with which they were charged.

Petitioner cites and relies on Swehla v. Malone, 114 Kan. 712, 220 P. 299; State v. Dubray, 121 Kan. 886, 250 P. 316; State v. O'Keith, 136 Kan. 283, 15 P.2d 443. In all these cases we held generally that offenses committed by children under sixteen years of age were under the exclusive jurisdiction of the juvenile court. In none of them, however, did we consider a case where the child charged with the offense was an inmate of the industrial school for boys or some other institution at the time the offense with which he was charged was committed.

The conclusion seems inescapable that the proviso was intended by the legislature to make it possible for boys or girls who had shown themselves to be so incorrigible that they violated some state statute, to be dealt with as criminals and not as mere juvenile delinquents,

as they had been up to the time of the commission of their crime. This must be so. The Boys' Industrial School and the industrial school for girls at Beloit are neither one of them penal institutions. The social ideas of the state have progressed from year to year in this connection. Much effort has been made to bring it about that these two schools shall be utterly devoid of the atmosphere of a penal institution. To do this there must be an absence of restraint, no walls, no high fences, no barred windows, no armed guards. The whole theme of the institution is that of education and rehabilitation. Now if we are going to insist that boys who, once inmates there, have shown themselves unfit subjects for that type of influence and treatment by committing some serious crime, such as murder, then we would break down the whole philosophy of the school. For the benefit of the other inmates of these institutions that should not be the law as the legislature evidently intended.

The writ is denied.

69

People v. Scherbing *

PETERS, Presiding Justice.

Appellant was convicted of a violation of § 4502 of the Penal Code. He appeals from the judgment of conviction and from the order denying his motion for a new trial.

Section 4502 provides that "Every prisoner committed to a State prison who, while at such State prison * * * possesses or carries upon his person * * * any dirk or dagger or sharp instrument, * * * is guilty of a felony and shall be punishable by imprisonment in a State prison for a term not less than five (5) years." The uncontradicted evidence shows that appellant, while an inmate of San Quentin under what purports to be a commitment from the Youth Authority, was found to possess a homemade sharp-pointed knife with a five and one-half

* *People* v. *Scherbing*, District Court of Appeal, First District, Division 1, California, 1949, 93 Cal. App. (2d) 736, 209 P. 2d 796.

inch blade sharpened along one side. Appellant does not attack the sufficiency of the evidence. His basic contentions are that he was not lawfully committed to San Quentin, and that only one who has been lawfully committed to a state prison can violate § 4502.

The basic facts are not in dispute. In 1946, when appellant was 18 years of age, he was convicted, after a plea of guilty, of second degree burglary and sentenced to one year in the county jail. Execution of the sentence was suspended and appellant was formally "committed" to the Youth Authority. Section 1732, Welfare and Institutions Code. This was in May, 1946. Under the then existing law, both the commitment and the judgment erroneously refer to the offense as a felony. See 1947 amendment to § 17 of the Penal Code for the present law on this subject. Under date of August 27, 1946, the Youth Authority issued its "commitment" which states that, upon the recommendation of its diagnostic clinical officer, the Authority "orders" and "adjudges" that appellant be committed to San Quentin Prison. Appellant was received at the prison by virtue of this document and has been confined there ever since. He was so confined on July 5, 1947, the date upon which he admittedly possessed a knife in violation of § 4502, if that section is applicable to him.

The theory of appellant is that, on the date in question, he was not a prisoner "committed" to a state prison within the meaning of § 4502. He argues that the Legislature has used the term "commitment" in that and other sections of the Penal Code to refer only to action by a court or judicial body, and has not used the term to refer to action by any administrative agency such as the Youth Authority.* Therefore, so he contends, the commitment under which he was being detained was void, he was being unlawfully held in San Quentin, and therefore could not violate § 4502.

These arguments are fallacious. A "commitment," in the legal sense, may be issued, lawfully, by other than a judicial body. The Penal Code clearly provides that the Youth Authority and the Adult Authority may make orders transferring prisoners under their supervision from one state institution to another. Such

orders of transfer are lawful, and the prisoner confined pursuant to such order is lawfully committed to the new prison. *People v. Howard*, 120 Cal. App. 45, 8 P.2d 176; *People v. French*, 61 Cal. App. 275, 214 P. 1003. Section 5077 of the Penal Code expressly confers on the Adult Authority the power of "commitment of a prisoner to a particular State prison." Section 1767 of the Welfare and Institutions Code provides that the power of the Youth Authority to make orders "committing to an institution" any person under the control of the Authority may not be delegated. These sections demonstrate that the Legislature has not used the word "commitment" to refer solely to judicial action.

Next, appellant urges that he was not lawfully committed because he was only convicted of a misdemeanor, and misdemeanants, according to appellant, may not be confined lawfully in the state prison. He also contends that, in any event, the Youth Authority has no power to confine a youthful offender in the state prison. The respondent concedes that appellant was convicted only of a misdemeanor. Such concession is undoubtedly in accordance with the law here applicable. See § 17 of the Penal Code as it read prior to the 1947 amendment. On these points the argument is that, traditionally, misdemeanors have never been punishable in a state prison in California. See § 17, 18 and 19, Penal Code, *Ex parte Arras*, 78 Cal. 304, 20 P. 683; *Ex parte Ah Cha*, 40 Cal. 426. It is then contended that, in enacting the Youth Authority Act, the Legislature could not have intended to modify this well-settled procedure by permitting youthful misdemeanants to be confined in a state prison while continuing to prohibit like punishment for adult misdemeanants. It is pointed out that the main purpose of the Youth Authority Act was to protect society by substituting for retributive punishment of youthful offenders "training and treatment directed toward the correction and rehabilitation of young persons." § 1700, Welfare and Institutions Code. Appellant argues that youths cannot be corrected and rehabilitated by confining them with hardened and adult offenders.

These arguments are interesting but unsound. We agree that it is the purpose of the Youth Authority Act to rehabilitate youthful offenders, and that all the provisions of the Act should be

---

* For a discussion of the California Youth Authority, see Article 106 of this book. — *Ed.*

construed in view of this main purpose. To accomplish this main purpose the Authority is given the broadest powers in the broadest terms to utilize all state institutions and facilities. Thus, § 1766 of the Welfare and Institutions Code gives the Authority power to confine all offenders committed to its charge "under such conditions as it believes best designed for the protection of the public." Section 1753 provides that "For the purpose of carrying out its duties, the Authority is authorized to make use of law enforcement, detention, probation, parole, medical, educational, correctional, segregative and other facilities, institutions and agencies, whether public or private, within the State." These sections make no distinction between youthful offenders who are convicted of a misdemeanor and those convicted of a felony. The sections empower the Authority to use all state institutions, including prisons, for any person within its control, whether felon or misdemeanant. See, also, § 1742(f) and 1772 of the Welfare and Institutions Code, specifically referring to offenders under control of the Authority who have been placed in state prisons. While under § 1737.1 of the Welfare and Institutions Code as amended in 1945, Stats. 1945, Chap. 781, p. 1470, the Authority, when it finds a youthful offender to be incorrigible, "may return him to the committing court" and such court may "commit" the offender to the state prison or county jail in accordance with law, such section is not exclusive. The purpose of the act was to give the Authority flexible powers in the handling of its charges. Only when the case is one that, in the opinion of the Authority, is completely hopeless, would resort be had to § 1737.1. That is so because if the Authority returns the offender to the Court, the offender would then have to serve the minimum term fixed for the offense and could not be discharged or placed under less stringent control.

It thus appears that, under the terms of the statutes involved, the Authority had legislative power to commit appellant to San Quentin. But, says appellant, if the statutes be so construed they are unconstitutional, either because they result in an unlawful delegation of judicial power, or because, so construed, they deny equal protection of the laws to youthful misdemeanants by permitting them to be confined in state prisons.

These arguments are unsound. Once it is determined that the Legislature did not intend the term "commit" to be limited to judicial action, the law is well settled that the Legislature may authorize an administrative agency such as the Youth Authority to "commit" or transfer charges within its control to state prisons. See annotation on this subject in 95 A.L.R. p. 1455. The treatment of youthful offenders, differently from adult offenders, even where such treatment results in a longer confinement of youthful offenders than could be imposed on adult offenders for the same offense, has been upheld in this state. Thus, under the Act, a misdemeanant committed to the Authority, may be kept under its control until the person so committed reaches the age of 23. § 1770, Welfare and Institutions Code. The fact that a youthful offender may thus be restrained of his liberty for a longer period than an adult could be for the same offense, does not render the Act unconstitutional. *In re Herrera*, 23 Cal. 2d 206, 143 P.2d 345; *Ex parte Nichols*, 110 Cal. 651, 43 P. 9; *Ex parte Liddell*, 93 Cal. 633, 29 P. 251; see annotation in 3 A.L.R. p. 1614. Appellant, while recognizing the rule of these cases, nevertheless urges that the juvenile has been deprived of equal protection when he is subjected to a harsher punishment than that imposed on adults, namely, confinement in a state prison, when an adult misdemeanant must be confined in a county jail. The argument goes that such a classification has no substantial, just and reasonable relation to the object of the legislation; that longer detention of juveniles and their segregation are reasonably related to their peculiar need for and adaptability to reform, education and rehabilitation, but that no such justification exists for placing adults in county jails and juveniles in a state prison where they will come into contact with hardened offenders; that legislation that singles out the youth for such purposes cannot be justified on reformation grounds and therefore cannot be upheld. The basic premise of this argument is that there is a better chance of rehabilitation in the county jail than exists in state prisons. In view of the well-known fact that no rehabilitative efforts at all are made in many of the county jails, this basic premise may well be questioned. Moreover, the basic theory of the Act is to empower the Authority to make its treatment fit the individual offender rather than to be predicated on the crime committed. There are vicious, hardened youthful offenders who are extremely dangerous to society. The Legislature has determined that the Authority should have power to imprison such offenders in a state prison. Such a classification is not unreasonable, and, in our opinion, is valid.

There is another complete answer to the points raised by appellant. Even if the various provisions of the Youth Authority Act here under attack were unconstitutional (which they are not), it would not result in a reversal of the conviction. Appellant was confined under a commitment in the state prison. While so confined he unlawfully possessed a knife. It is no defense to a prosecution for unlawfully possessing a knife in prison under § 4502 of the Penal Code, that the statute under which the inmate is confined is unconstitutional. The statute was passed to protect the guards and other inmates of the prison. It is a reasonable regulation. The fact that the particular inmate may be unlawfully confined certainly does not confer upon him the right to possess weapons denied to other inmates. If the purpose of the statute is to be achieved, and obviously the purpose is a sound one, it makes no difference why the prisoner has been confined, or that he may be legally entitled to release. While an inmate, necessity requires that the prisoner submit to prison regulations, and certainly § 4502 is a reasonable regulation.

We think that appellant was lawfully confined in San Quentin. But even if the statutes so providing were unconstitutional, he cannot raise that defense to a prosecution under § 4502 of the Penal Code.

The judgment and order appealed from are affirmed. BRAY, J., concurs.

WARD, Justice.

I concur, as held in effect in the main opinion, that any inmate lawfully or unlawfully confined in a state prison does not possess the right "while at such State prison" to possess a dirk or dagger. Pen. Code § 4502. In my opinion a discussion of other points is not necessary to decide the merits of this appeal.†

---

† Cf. *Sheehan v. Supt. of Concord Reformatory*, 254 Mass. 342, 150 N.E. 231 (1926) (upholding transfer of delinquent from industrial school to reformatory). — Ed.

70

Collins v. Robbins *

NULTY, Justice.

Habeas corpus proceedings from Knox County Supreme Judicial Court in vacation and brought forward to this court on report upon facts agreed, R.S. 1944, Chap. 91, Sec. 14, and certified for immediate decision by agreement of Counsel. Wade v. Warden of State Prison, 145 Me. —, 73 A.2d 128. The facts disclosed by the record are:

Dennis Collins, a minor, brought a petition for a writ of habeas corpus against Allan L. Robbins, Warden of the Maine State Prison, in usual form on July 24, 1951, and, on said petition the writ of habeas corpus was ordered to issue forthwith. On the same day the Warden produced the body of Dennis Collins before the court and made the usual return, attaching thereto a certified copy of the mittimus under which said Dennis Collins was detained. A brief hearing was had in which Dennis Collins testified that at the time of his indictment for the murder of his father he was thirteen years old and that the date of his birth was February 23, 1937.

The record as reported includes the petition for the writ, the writ, the return of the writ by the Warden of the State Prison, with a certified copy of the mittimus, the record of the original case in Knox County Superior Court and the facts taken out at the hearing. It also includes a stipulation that said Dennis Collins was arraigned in the Rockland Municipal Court on October 30, 1950, on the charge of murder and that he was bound over to the grand jury of the Superior Court, November Term, Knox County, 1950.

The Knox County records of the Superior Court for the November Term, 1950, disclose that the grand jury indicted Dennis Collins for murder and that Counsel was appointed by the court to represent said Dennis Collins. Upon arraignment said Dennis Collins pleaded guilty to the crime of manslaughter which plea the

---

* *Collins v. Robbins*, Supreme Judicial Court of Maine, 1951, 147 Me. 163, 84 A. 2d 536.

court accepted and sentenced him to be confined to hard labor in the State Prison at Thomaston for the term of not less than five years and not more than ten years and a mittimus for his commitment was duly issued and said Dennis Collins was duly committed under said mittimus.

The petition for the writ of habeas corpus alleges in the usual form that the petitioner, Dennis Collins, is now unlawfully imprisoned in the Maine State Prison at Thomaston, and the Petitioner, Dennis Collins, now contends that the Superior Court for the County of Knox, when it accepted his plea of manslaughter to the indictment charging murder, was without jurisdiction to impose sentence because judges of municipal courts within their respective jurisdictions have exclusive original jurisdiction of all offenses, except for a crime the punishment for which may be imprisonment for life or any term of years committed by children under the age of 17 years. Thus, the petitioner's claim involves the construction of the second paragraph of R.S.1944, Chap. 133, Sec. 2, as amended by Chap. 334 of the Public Laws of 1947, the pertinent part, as amended, reading as follows: "Judges of municipal courts within their respective jurisdictions shall have exclusive original jurisdiction over all offenses, except for a crime the punishment for which may be imprisonment for life or for any term of years, committed by children under the age of 17 years, and when so exercising said jurisdiction shall be known as juvenile courts. Any adjudication or judgment under the provisions of sections 4 to 7, inclusive, shall be that the child was guilty of juvenile delinquency, and no such adjudication or judgment shall be deemed to constitute a conviction for crime." No question is raised by the petitioner as to the jurisdiction of the Superior Court of Knox County over the crime of murder for which he was charged in the indictment found by the grand jury at the November 1950 Term. This court recently declared in Wade v. Warden of State Prison, supra, that murder was an offense clearly excepted from the jurisdiction of the juvenile courts and set forth at length in that exhaustive opinion the interpretation of Revised Statutes and Public Laws last cited with respect to the respective jurisdictions of the Superior and Municipal Courts over a juvenile charged with the crime of manslaughter. In other words, the petitioner's claim now is that he could not be legally sentenced after his accepted plea of manslaughter to an indictment charging him with murder because the Superior Court of Knox County by its action in accepting his plea of manslaughter was without jurisdiction over the offense being by law vested in the Judges of the Municipal Courts.

The petitioner, Dennis Collins, was charged with murder. He was first taken before the Rockland Municipal Court, arraigned and bound over to the grand jury for the November 1950 Term of Knox County Superior Court. At that time the Superior Court of Knox County had exclusive original jurisdiction of this particular crime of murder, it being excepted in the act granting jurisdiction to the judges of the municipal courts over offenses committed by children under the age of seventeen years. See R.S.1944, Chap. 133, Sec. 2, as amended, supra. We, therefore, hold that the Superior Court of Knox County has exclusive original jurisdiction of the crime of murder. Therefore, at the time of the arraignment of the petitioner, Dennis Collins, for the crime of murder on the indictment found by the grand jury of said Knox County the jurisdiction of the Superior Court with respect to the crime charged was the same as if the so-called juvenile court laws referred to and cited herein had not been enacted. In other words, the jurisdiction of said Superior Court was in no way changed. See State v. Rand and Henry, 1934, 132 Me. 246, 250, 169 A. 898.

The question now before us seems to be, was the Superior Court for Knox County without jurisdiction to impose sentence when it accepted the petitioner's plea of guilty of manslaughter to the indictment charging murder?

It has long been accepted as a well known principle of law that "the jurisdiction of a court depends upon the state of affairs existing at the time it is invoked, and if the jurisdiction once attaches to the person and subject matter of the litigation, the subsequent happening of events, though they are of such a character as would have prevented jurisdiction from attaching in the first instance, will not operate to oust the jurisdiction already attached. This is the statement of the rule that subsequent events will never defeat jurisdiction already acquired." 12 Encyclopedia of Pleading and Practice, Page 171. The Supreme Court of Missouri, in State v. Wear, 1898 145 Missouri, 162, 205, 46 S.W.

1099, 1112, said, in speaking of jurisdiction: "The pendency of a cause in a court where jurisdiction exists, and has been acquired in a lawful manner, is a test of the continuance of such jurisdiction, and of its valid exercise until final disposition is made of the cause, no matter how flagrant may be the errors which attend the exercise of such jurisdiction, nor how numerous and obvious may be the errors with which the record abounds, because, the jurisdiction to decide right, being once conceded, such concession necessarily embraces the power to decide wrong, and a wrong decision, though voidable, and though it may be avoided, yet until avoided is equally as binding as a right one. It cannot be attacked collaterally. The only way its binding force can be escaped or avoided is by appeal or writ of error." The Court of Appeals of Kentucky, in Stewart, Pros.Atty. et al. v. Sampson, Judge et al., 1941, 285 Ky. 447, 148 S.W.2d 278, 280, 281, said in speaking of jurisdiction:

"The term (jurisdiction) applies to both the litigant in the cause and to its subject matter, by which is meant that a court, before it may exercise judicial power to determine a cause pending before it, must have authority to deal with and determine the questions relating to the subject matter of the litigation, and also must in some way have the litigant whose interest is involved in the subject matter properly brought into court, and which is usually designated as 'jurisdiction of the person.' Therefore (employing the usual terms with reference thereto), a court may not proceed to determine a matter before it unless it has 'jurisdiction of the person' as well as 'jurisdiction of the subject matter.'

"To begin with, it should be borne in mind that the term 'jurisdiction,' as applied to judicial tribunals, emanates exclusively from the constitution and legally enacted statutes of the sovereignty of the forum. 14 Am.Jur. 368, § 169.

*   *   *

"Technical jurisdiction, therefore, is the power and authority on the part of the court to hear and judicially determine and dispose of the cause pending before it, and which power and authority must be conferred in the manner hereinbefore stated." The Supreme Court of Florida in Tidwell v. Circuit Court of De Soto County et al., 1942, 151 Fla. 333, 9 So.2d 630,

said in speaking of jurisdiction where the claim was made in connection with the charge of a felony which by operation of a statute was reduced to a misdemeanor, the petitioner claiming that the circuit court had no jurisdiction because of the reduced grade of crime, said the following: "The gravity of the offense was fixed at the time of its commission and the voluntary act on the part of the defendant in making restoration to the person whose property was stolen has no influence upon the nature of the crime or the jurisdiction of the court in which the matter should be tried, but only serves to diminish the character of the punishment if the defendant is eventually convicted." To the same effect see Harmon v. State, 1913, 8 Ala.-App. 311, 62 So. 438, and Koppel v. Heinrichs, 1847, 1 Barb., N.Y., 449.

In 16 Corpus Juris, Criminal Law, Par. 247, Page 182, in speaking of a conviction of an offense below jurisdiction or within jurisdiction of the lower court, we find the following statement: "Where the court has jurisdiction of the crime for which accused is indicted, it is not lost if on the evidence he is convicted of a crime of an inferior grade of which it would not have jurisdiction originally, * * *." See cases cited in note. See also, 22 C.J.S., Criminal Law, § 169. To the same effect, see 22 C.J.S., Criminal Law, § 169, Page 264.

In Carson, Petition of, 1944, 141 Me. 132, 39 A.2d 756, we had occasion to consider whether the accused in an indictment charging a substantive offense could be legally convicted and sentenced for an attempt to commit the crime charged and if so whether the attempt to commit the crime is a lesser crime included in the greater one. We decided in that case that the accused could and that an attempt to commit a particular crime is not only necessarily included in but is also substantially charged by an indictment alleging the crime itself has been committed, and that R.S.1944, Chap. 132, § 10, aptly provides for such a situation if, according to the wording of the statute, the residue of the charged crime is substantially charged in the indictment under which the prosecution is conducted. See also State v. Ham et al., 1866, 54 Me. 194, and State v. Leavitt, 1894, 87 Me. 72, 32 A. 787. In State v. Waters, 1854, 39 Me. 54, 65, cited in Carson, Petitioner, supra, we declared: "The jury may acquit the defendant of part and find him guilty of the residue. 1

Chit.C.L. 637. Where the accusation includes an offense of an inferior degree, the jury may discharge the defendant of the higher crime and convict him on the less atrocious. 2 Hale, 203. This rule applies in all cases where the minor offense is necessarily an elemental part of the greater, and when proof of the greater necessarily establishes the minor."

In the instant case the petitioner was charged with murder. Under our law the crime of murder includes manslaughter. State v. Conley, 1854, 39 Me. 78, 87. In fact, it has been held from the earliest days that upon an indictment for murder a conviction may be had for manslaughter. 1 Hale, 449; 2 Hale, 302. There are a great many instances where defendants have been found guilty of the lesser offense embraced or included in the larger charge and these have been sustained by the authorities. See State v. Webster, 1859, 39 N.H. 96, 99, where the court said: "The evidence failing to substantiate the greater offense, the jury, under the instructions of the court, returned a verdict for an assault and battery. * * * It is a verdict for a lesser offense embraced in a larger one, and as such is sustained by the authorities; * * *." The New Hampshire Court goes on to say, 39 N.H. at page 100, in speaking of higher offenses which involved the construction of a New Hampshire statute relating to the jurisdiction of justices of the peace under the statute: "It does not apply to higher offenses, (enumerating them). An indictment may be found in all such cases without any preliminary examination before a magistrate; and if upon the trial the evidence fails to sustain the indictment to the full extent, the court are not thereby ousted of their jurisdiction. The grand jury find the matter as it appears before them, and present to the court an indictment for an offense, which requires no preliminary proceedings before a justice of the peace, and of which the court have jurisdiction in the first instance; and having that jurisdiction it is not in any way affected by the result of the trial." The cases cited and commented upon up to this point indicate that the accused has been found guilty of the lesser or included offense by the jury but it is a well settled principle of law requiring no citation of authorities that the accused may plead guilty or confess to an inferior or lesser crime provided the court having jurisdiction is willing for good cause shown to accept the plea and there is no reason why an

indictment charging murder which necessarily includes the lesser offense of manslaughter and contains everything essential to establish the guilt of the petitioner, would not have the legal effect, if the petitioner were permitted to plead guilty to manslaughter, of acquitting the petitioner of the charge of murder. See Carson, petitioner, supra.

The petitioner through his counsel strongly urges that this court adopt the holding of the Louisiana Court in State v. Dabon, 1927, 162 La. 1075, 111 So. 461, which held that the conviction of manslaughter of a juvenile charged with murder and who had not previously been before the juvenile court could not be sustained and amounted only to a verdict of not guilty of murder, and that the child was still subject to proceedings before the juvenile court based upon manslaughter as juvenile delinquency. The contrary result was reached by the Tennessee Court in Howland v. State, 1924, 151 Tenn. 47, 268 S.W. 115, which holds that if a juvenile is properly indicted for murder, that crime not being within the jurisdiction of the juvenile court, the jurisdiction of the criminal court having properly attached, it attached for all purposes and the conviction of the juvenile of manslaughter was correct.

As a result of our examination of the authorities and cases cited herein we are of the opinion that the Tennessee Rule is the correct rule and we, therefore, hold and declare that the jurisdiction of the Superior Court of Knox County was in no way changed when it accepted from the petitioner, a juvenile under the age of seventeen years, a plea of guilty of manslaughter to an indictment charging murder and we further hold and declare that jurisdiction as we have defined it in this opinion cannot be lost or ousted under such circumstances as are described herein, and once having attached it continues until the final disposition of the cause.

We said in Wallace v. White, 1916, 115 Me. 513, 519, 521, 99 A. 452, 454:

"If a court has jurisdiction of the person and cause, the fact that the sentence is excessive or otherwise erroneous is not ground for discharge on habeas corpus. A writ of habeas corpus can not reach errors or irregularities which render proceedings voidable merely, but only such defects in substance as render the judgment or process absolutely void."

"It is the judgment of the court which authorizes detention. * * * The judgment is the real thing; * * *. The important question on habeas corpus is: Is the prisoner in the custody where the judgment commanded him to be put? * * *." See also Cote v. Cummings, 1927, 126 Me. 330, 332, 138 A. 547.

We hold that the commitment of the petitioner was properly made under a valid judgment. It necessarily follows that the mandate will be

Writ discharged. Petitioner remanded to the custody of the Warden of Maine State Prison in execution of sentence.†

71

People v. Lattimore *

Mr. Justice Herrick delivered the opinion of the court:

The defendant, Susie Lattimore, on her trial in the criminal court of Cook county before that court, a jury having been waived, was found guilty of murder. She was sentenced upon such finding to imprisonment for twenty-five years in the Illinois State Reformatory for Women at Dwight. A review of such judgment is here sought by the defendant.

The facts show that the defendant was guilty of an atrocious murder, and that at the time of the commission of the crime, and at her trial, she was between fifteen and sixteen years of age. It was stipulated that the defendant for some misconduct not connected with the present charge, was, more than four months prior to the trial on the indictment here, declared delinquent in the juvenile court of Cook county. In the criminal court the defendant contended that such court was without jurisdiction to proceed with the trial of the cause

---

† This problem is now before the Supreme Judicial Court of Massachusetts, in Metcalf v. Massachusetts, Law no. 57472. — Ed.

* People v. Lattimore, Supreme Court of Illinois, 1935, 362 Ill. 206, 199 N.E. 275. See, also, People ex rel. Malec v. Lewis, 362 Ill. 229, 199 N.E. 276, in which habeas corpus was denied juvenile seeking discharge from reformatory on same grounds as in Lattimore case. Stone, C. J., dissenting without opinion, as in Lattimore case. — Ed.

and that the criminal court should transfer the cause to the juvenile court. The criminal court decided that issue adversely to the defendant. The sole question presented here for decision is whether the defendant, a ward of the juvenile court, who had been indicted for murder, can on such indictment be tried in the criminal court without the consent of the juvenile court.

Section 9a of chapter 23, (Smith's Stat. 1933, par. 199, p. 288; Cahill's Stat. 1933, par. 328, p. 272); relating to the juvenile court, provides: "The court may in its discretion in any case of a delinquent child permit such child to be proceeded against in accordance with the laws that may be in force in this State governing the commission of crimes or violations of city, village, or town ordinance. In such case the petition filed under this act shall be dismissed."

Among the definitions given to the term "delinquent child" by section 2 [1] of chapter 23, (Smith's Stat. 1933, par. 190, p. 285; Cahill's Stat. 1933, par. 319, p. 269); is, any male child who while under the age of seventeen years or any female child who while under the age of eighteen years, violates any law of this State," etc.

In support of her position the defendant urges that under the provisions of section 9a of chapter 23 the juvenile court had the judicial discretion to determine whether the defendant here, "a delinquent child," might be proceeded against on the indictment for murder pending against her in the criminal court of Cook county, and that by reason of such lack of consent by the juvenile court the criminal court of Cook county was precluded from trying her on such indictment.

Article 6 of the constitution of 1870 created our judicial system. By section 26 of that article the criminal court of Cook county was established and its jurisdiction defined. While the circuit court is a court of general jurisdiction, yet the jurisdiction of the circuit court of Cook county is not necessarily the same in all respects as the circuit courts of other counties of the State. It does not have concurrent jurisdiction with the criminal court of Cook county of criminal causes, but jurisdiction of criminal cases is by section 26 of our constitution placed in the criminal court of Cook county. (People v. Feinberg, 348 Ill. 549; People v. Warren, 260 id. 297.) The juvenile court is a court of limited jurisdiction. The legislature is without authority to confer upon an inferior court the power to stay a court created by the constitution from proceeding with the trial of a cause jurisdiction of which is expressly granted to it by the constitution. Nor, in our opinion, was it the legislative intent to attempt to confer such power upon the juvenile court. Provision is made by section 4 of chapter 23 for the filing of a petition to have a child declared delinquent. Other sections provide for summons and a hearing on the issue as to whether the child named is a "delinquent child" within the purview of the act. Some meaning must be given the clause italicized in section 9a. That clause manifestly could not refer to the dismissal of a petition whereon a final judgment had been entered finding that the child named in the petition was delinquent but necessarily refers to a then pending, undetermined proceeding in that court. The section granting the discretion to the juvenile court clearly refers to a case where a child capable, under the law, of committing a criminal offense is named in the petition and his or her status is the subject of the inquiry. If the facts developed by the hearing show a criminal offense has been committed by such child, the juvenile court, in its discretion, may refuse to take custody of the child as a delinquent, dismiss the petition and direct the child to be delivered to the proper authorities for trial on the criminal charge. It was not intended by the legislature that the juvenile court should be made a haven of refuge where a delinquent child of the age recognized by law as capable of committing a crime should be immune from punishment for violation of the criminal laws of the State, committed by such child subsequent to his or her being declared a delinquent child.

The criminal court of Cook county had jurisdiction of the person of the defendant and of the cause on which she was placed on trial.

The judgment of the criminal court is affirmed.

Judgment affirmed.

MR. CHIEF JUSTICE STONE, dissenting.*

---

* See, also, *Contrell* v. *State*, 190 Tenn. 64, 227 S.W. 2d 772 (1950); *Dearing* v. *State*, 151 Tex. Crim. 6, 204 S.W. 2d 983 (1947). — Ed.

72

People v. Roper *

LEHMAN, J. A little before two o'clock in the morning of January 20th, 1931, two youths or men, with handkerchiefs covering their faces and armed with pistols, entered a negro restaurant on Seventh avenue in New York city. At the point of the pistol, one of them compelled the people in the restaurant to go to the rear and took some money from their persons. The same youth shot and killed William Groce, a customer of the restaurant. The other bandit took money from the cash register. Then both escaped.

The robbery and shooting were promptly reported to the police. Those who had been present in the restaurant were examined at the precinct station house in the presence of a stenographer. Thorp, the manager, gave a description of the general appearance and build of the masked bandits. They were, so he said, both negroes of dark complexion. One was tall and one was short. "He had a soft face, well dressed, this tall fellow. Short fellow had a rough face." Promptly the police sent out a general police alarm for the apprehension of these men. The description of the men wanted was of necessity meagre. One of them has never been apprehended. A few nights after the robbery the defendant Roper was arrested on the street, after being shot by police officers. On the chance that Roper might be one of the robbers, Thorp was summoned to look at the defendant while the defendant was in the operating room of the hospital awaiting surgical treatment for his wounds. Before the magistrate and at the trial Thorp positively identified the defendant as the tall robber with a "soft face" who had shot William Groce.

The indictment of the defendant and one "John Doe" for murder in the first degree charges, in common-law form, that the "said

---

* *People* v. *Roper*, Court of Appeals of the State of New York, 1932, 259 N. Y. 170, 181 N. E. 88. Motion for reargument denied, 259 N. Y. 635. — Ed.

defendants in the County of New York * * * with force and arms, in and upon one William Groce * * * willfully, feloniously and of their malice aforethought did make an assault, * * * giving unto him * * * one mortal wound of which * * * the said William Groce * * * did die." Thorp was the only eye witness of the crime who was produced by the prosecution. The People frankly admit that none of the others, if produced, could identify the defendant as one of the men whose faces were concealed by handkerchiefs while they robbed the restaurant. Thorp explained that at one time the handkerchief which covered the defendant's face slipped down and that thus he had opportunity to see the defendant's features while the handkerchief was being hurriedly readjusted.

The trial was conducted with eminent fairness, and we find no reversible error in the admission or exclusion of evidence or in the charge, if the case was tried and submitted to the jury on the proper theory. Perhaps there may be doubt as to Thorp's identification of the defendant. On that question the defendant has had a fair trial, and none of his substantial rights have been infringed by excess of zeal or fault of police, prosecuting attorney or trial judge. A majority of the court, at least, find that the verdict of the jury is not against the weight of evidence upon the issue presented to the jury. We confine discussion in this opinion to the question whether the jury's finding of guilt on these issues supports the defendant's conviction of the crime of murder in the first degree.

Thorp's testimony establishes that a negro, whom he identified as the defendant on trial, shot and killed William Groce while he and another negro were engaged in taking money at the point of a pistol from the cash register of the restaurant and from the persons of those who were present in the restaurant. The defendant's age at the time of the homicide was not determined in the manner provided by section 817 of the Penal Law. Upon the preliminary examination of the jurors, the assistant district attorney stated to them: "The defendant Louis Roper at the time of the alleged commission of the crime by him was between fifteen and sixteen years of age." Testimony that the defendant was under the age of sixteen was uncontradicted. The case was tried and submitted to the jury upon the assumption that the fact that the defendant was at the time of the homicide

under the age of sixteen carries no legal consequences in a trial for murder in the first degree. We are called upon to test the validity of that assumption in this case.

Only a child under the age of seven years is incapable as matter of law of committing a crime (Penal Law, § 816), though a child "of the age of seven years, and under the age of twelve years, is presumed to be incapable of crime, but the presumption may be removed by proof that he had sufficient capacity to understand" (§ 817). Even so, not every act or omission which, if committed by an adult, would be a crime, is a crime when committed by a child, for the Legislature has expressly decreed that "a child of more than seven and less than sixteen years of age, who shall commit any act or omission which, if committed by an adult, would be a crime not punishable by death or life imprisonment, shall not be deemed guilty of any crime, but of juvenile delinquency" (Penal Law, § 2186). Murder in the first degree is punishable by death. Therefore, it is clear that a child of fifteen may be guilty of the crime of murder in the first degree. When guilt of a crime has been established, its penal consequences are the same for child and adult criminal. But guilt cannot be established without proof of every essential element of the crime and, since a felonious intent is an essential element of the crime of murder, guilt of a defendant can never be established without proof of such intent. Thus, the guilt of a defendant charged with murder in the first degree may depend upon his capacity to form the felonious intent. Then the fact that a defendant is under the age of sixteen may carry legal consequences.

"There can be no murder without evidence of malice and of a felonious intent and a depraved mind. The indictment was sufficient in form when it simply accused defendant of having killed the deceased 'willfully, feloniously and with malice aforethought.' On the trial it was necessary to prove such malice and willful and felonious conduct, and this necessity was satisfied in accordance with the provisions of the statute by showing that the homicide occurred while the defendant was engaged in the commission of another felony (*People* v. *Conroy*, 97 N. Y. 62, 68, 69; *People* v. *Giblin*, 115 N. Y. 196)." (*People* v. *Nichols*, 230 N. Y. 221, 226.)

Here, as in that case, the conviction rests upon a finding of the jury that a human being was killed by a person "engaged in the commission of another felony." True, the evidence is sufficient to support a finding that the homicide was committed by the defendant "from a deliberate and premeditated design to effect the death of the person killed," and a homicide committed in that way also would constitute murder in the first degree (Penal Law, § 1044) and might be proven under an indictment in common-law form. The jury, if such question had been presented to it, might have found that the defendant formed such a deliberate design, though under the age of sixteen; but the jury here made no such finding, for no such question was presented to it. If the trial judge in his charge had left that question to the jury, he would have been bound to charge on the degrees of homicide, and the jury would have been free to find a verdict of guilt in lesser degree than murder in the first degree. He chose to do otherwise. He charged the jurors that they were concerned only with the question of whether a human being was killed during the commission of a felony in which the defendant was a guilty participant, and that their verdict must be either guilty of murder in the first degree or not guilty.

"We may not 'sustain a conviction erroneously secured on one theory on the conjecture that it would have followed just the same if the correct theory had been applied.' (HISCOCK, Ch. J., in *People* v. *Smith*, 232 N. Y. 239, 244.) A criminal, however shocking his crime, is not to answer for it with forfeiture of life or liberty till tried and convicted in conformity with law." (*People* v. *Moran*, 246 N. Y. 100, 105.) Certainly we may apply no other rule where the defendant, though perhaps a hardened offender, is still of tender age. The judgment may be sustained only if, in spite of his youth, the defendant's participation in a felony establishes his guilt of murder in the first degree.

The charge of the trial judge was fair and accurate, if the defendant's participation was with felonious intent. The crime of murder charged in the indictment is a single crime, whether committed by design or during the commission of an independent felony; "the independent felony like the deliberate and premeditated intent, being established solely for the purpose of characterizing the degree of the

crime so charged, the evil mind or purpose inherent in the killing." (*People* v. *Lytton*, 257 N. Y. 310, 315.) The defendant may have participated in the robbery; but unless that participation was with felonious intent he was not guilty of the felony, and if he was not guilty of the independent felony, participation does not evince "the evil mind or purpose inherent in the killing." (See *People* v. *Koerber*, 244 N. Y. 147.)

Sometimes a spirit of innocent mischief, sometimes evil associations, not of his own choice but forced upon him by family conditions, impel a child under the age of sixteen to commit acts which constitute felonies as defined by law. The State has adopted a humane policy in its treatment of a child under the age of sixteen who commits such acts. It does not, upon proof of guilt, fasten upon him the ineffaceable stain of conviction of guilt of a felony, nor subject him to imprisonment with adult offenders. For the child's benefit, as well as for the benefit of the State, it treats a child who commits acts which, if committed by an adult would constitute a felony, not punishable by death or life imprisonment, merely as a juvenile delinquent, an unfortunate ward of the State rather than a criminal. The law, in its mercy, demands that a child should be subject to such correction as may tend to remove the causes which have led the child to commit acts inimical to society; where it might demand that an adult committing the same acts should be visited with punishment of deterrent effect.

Doubtless at times the causes which have led a child into "juvenile delinquency" are too deep-seated to be removed by such corrective treatment as the State now offers. Perhaps at times "innate depravity" is more than a fiction. The Penal Law is not concerned with such abstractions. It decrees that the acts of a child shall, in all cases other than acts constituting a felony punishable by death or life imprisonment, be treated as if done without the "evil mind" which characterizes felonious intent, and each child must be given the opportunity to benefit by corrective treatment though he be unable or unwilling to avail himself of the benefit. The law does not say that a criminal under the age of sixteen is not subject to punishment for a crime; it says that proof of acts which would establish guilt of crime if committed by an older person does not establish the guilt of a child under the age of sixteen years, of any crime, but only of juvenile delinquency.

These considerations must lead to a reversal in this case. The defendant can be convicted of murder in the first degree only upon a finding of "felonious intent." The verdict of the jury imports a finding that the defendant participated in the commission of a robbery, as defined by the statute, for the trial judge charged that without such finding the verdict must be not guilty. Upon the trial of a defendant over the age of sixteen years a finding of participation in a robbery, as defined by the statute, would import a finding of "felonious intent"; for robbery, in every degree, is a felony. Upon the trial of a child under the age of sixteen, the participation of a child in a robbery, or at least in a robbery in the second or third degrees, would not establish the guilt of a felony but only of a minor offense characterized as juvenile delinquency. Hence, it is plain that the defendant's conviction rests upon no finding of guilt of a felony and thus no finding of felonious intent, and the judgment must be reversed. (*People* v. *Moran, supra.*) That is true even though no exception was taken to the charge which raises such question. A child under sixteen can be guilty of murder in the first or second degrees where he kills a man with felonious intent, but such felonious intent is not established without both proof and finding of intent to kill or of *guilt of an independent felony* during which the homicide occurred.

The question of whether the defendant's participation in a robbery in the first degree might establish guilt of a felony is not now presented; for the trial judge charged the jury that they were not concerned with degrees of robbery, since robbery in every degree is a felony. It might arise upon a new trial. At the time of the homicide and of the trial, robbery in the first degree and burglary in the first degree were punishable by imprisonment for not less than a specified term of years, and *no limit of the duration of the punishment was declared* in the statute. In such case the "court authorized to pronounce judgment upon conviction may, in its discretion, sentence the offender to imprisonment during his natural life, or for any number of years not less than the amount prescribed." (Penal Law, § 2191.) Perhaps crimes "punishable by death or life imprisonment," as those words are used in section 2186 of the Penal Law, applying to juvenile offenders, include any crime where a judge authorized to pronounce sentence may *in his discretion* sentence the offender to imprisonment for life. Doubtless similar words in other sections of the Penal Law were used by the Legislature with that intention. We do not now decide whether considerations of public policy and complications arising from the fact that upon trial for burglary or robbery in the first degree a jury may convict of a lesser degree of crime, punishable only by imprisonment for a limited term, and constituting crimes of which a child cannot be guilty, might dictate a different construction of those words as used in section 2186. That question has now become academic, for by chapter 275 of the Laws of 1932, amending Penal Law, sections 407, 2125, a "limit of the duration of imprisonment is declared" in the punishment for burglary or robbery in the first degree.

Thus at the present time, even if not at the time of the original trial, proof that a child under the age of sixteen years participated in a robbery in the first degree cannot establish the child's guilt of a felony. Change in the punishment for that crime has the indirect result of removing the crime of robbery in the first degree from the category of crimes of which a child can be guilty if it ever was within that category. The effect is the same as if the Legislature had expressly declared that no child under the age of sixteen years can be guilty of robbery in any degree, and that upon the trial of such child for murder in the first degree, "felonious intent" may not be predicated upon guilt of robbery. In the absence of a clause excluding from its provisions offenses previously committed, the law as amended applies in all trials held thereafter, even for offenses previously committed. (Cf. *Hartung* v. *People,* 22 N. Y. 95; same case, 26 N. Y. 167, and 28 N. Y. 400.)

Upon the new trial this defendant may be tried for murder in the first or second degrees committed through the killing of a human being with intent to effect his death. Such an action may be impelled by "evil mind" and felonious intent as evidenced by the criminal acts of the child, but not by acts which the Legislature has declared are not criminal when committed by a child. A person who with evil mind commits a crime may, in the interests of society, be punished even by death for the undesigned and unforeseen result of the crime. No person, certainly no child under the age of sixteen, is subject to death or life imprisonment because of the calamitous though undesigned result of acts which are not criminal in their inception.

The judgment of conviction should be reversed and a new trial ordered. (See 259 N. Y. 635.)

POUND, Ch. J. CRANE, KELLOGG, O'BRIEN and HUBBS, JJ., concur.

Judgment reversed, etc.

73

Tilton v. Commonwealth *

EGGLESTON, J., delivered the opinion of the court.

This writ of error brings to us for review a final judgment of the court below by which Lanvee Irby Tilton, aged seventeen, and Grover Willie Newman, aged twenty-three, were sentenced to death by electrocution after each had pleaded guilty to an indictment for murder. The determination of the questions presented requires a full statement of the proceedings below, as well as the undisputed underlying facts.

On the afternoon of February 10, 1954, T. Eldridge Bunn was found shot to death in his store near Hillsville in Carroll County. Suspicion was directed toward Tilton and Newman and they were arrested the same afternoon and lodged in jail. At first they denied their guilt, but during the night they separately confessed to the sheriff and the Commonwealth's attorney that pursuant to their prearranged plan they went to the store for the purpose of shooting and robbing Bunn. Each was armed with a .22 rifle. Upon entering the store Newman "set his gun down beside the door" while Tilton held his rifle. As Bunn was in the act of placing on the counter some articles of merchandise which the defendants had ordered, Tilton shot

---

* *Tilton* and *Newman* v. *Commonwealth*, Supreme Court of Appeals of Virginia, 1955, 196 Va. 774.

him twice in the face and again in the head. The defendants took a total of $33 from the cash drawer and the billfold on Bunn's body.

On the day following the killing separate warrants were procured for the defendants and served on them in jail. Upon examination the trial justice held the two defendants for the grand jury. Separate indictments were found against them at the March, 1954, term. On March 15 the two indictments were heard together, the defendants being represented by counsel of their choosing. Two motions were made on behalf of the defendants:

(1) That the indictment against Tilton be quashed "because he had not been tried before the Trial Justice of Carroll County, sitting as the Juvenile and Domestic Relations Court Judge"; and

(2) That each defendant be "examined by one or more physicians skilled in the diagnosis of insanity in accordance with section 19–202."

The court overruled the first motion and counsel for the defendant, Tilton, excepted, as the order states, on the ground that there had been no compliance with Code, §§ 63–268, 63–273, and 63–288.

In support of the second motion the defendant, Tilton, offered as a witness the sheriff, C. I. Jackson, who testified that "Tilton told me on one occasion that he had seen a little devil in his cell. He was kindly (*sic*) laughing about it. He had been in a cell away from the other prisoners and after this I moved him to another cell and put Newman in the cell Tilton had been in. I heard nothing further from him. This did not indicate to me that he was mentally ill. It appears to me a fairly normal reaction after the crime that he had committed." There was no evidence in support of the motion on behalf of Newman.

In overruling the motion for mental examinations of the two defendants the order recites that "the court is of opinion that Tilton is sane and that there is no reason to believe that he is mentally ill or for any reason incapable of being tried." The order recites no finding as to the defendant, Newman.

On the same day the case came on to be tried on the merits. Each defendant, after having consulted with and been advised by counsel, pleaded guilty to the indictment and waived trial by jury. (*Cf.* Const., § 8.) Thereupon the court heard the evidence, including the confessions of the two defendants, the testimony of the coroner that death was caused by the rifle bullets which had been fired into Bunn's head, and the testimony of an agent of the Federal Bureau of Investigation that the two bullets taken from the body of the deceased had been fired by Tilton's rifle.

Tilton's mother testified that he was seventeen years old on the day of the trial.

Upon consideration of the evidence the court found both defendants guilty of murder in the first degree, as charged in the indictments. Pursuant to Code, § 53-278.1 (as amended by Acts 1952, ch. 233, p. 319), upon motion of the defendants, before fixing punishment or imposing sentence, the court directed its probation officer "to thoroughly investigate and report upon the history of both of the accused, * * * and any and all relevant facts to the end that the court may be fully advised as to the appropriate and just sentence to be imposed."

On March 30 the probation officer appeared in open court and read his written report in the presence of the two defendants and delivered a copy thereof to their counsel. Counsel for the defendants was given the right, but declined, to cross-examine the probation officer as to any matters contained in the report.

In his report the officer found no "extenuating circumstances" on behalf of either defendant. Their only excuse for the crime was that they wanted the money which they expected to receive from the robbery. The report shows that Tilton was reared by a widowed mother. He "was almost 17 years of age at the time this offense was committed, seems to be a fairly intelligent boy. He was old enough and intelligent enough to know right from wrong and to realize the seriousness of the offense he committed."

After considering the evidence and probation report the court sentenced both defendants to death by electrocution. Whereupon Newman remarked to the court, "May you die with your boots on, you God damn son of a bitch." Upon the pronouncement of sentence Tilton remained mute.

The sufficiency of the evidence to establish the finding that the defendants were guilty of murder in the first degree is not challenged. It shows beyond doubt a "wilful, deliberate and premeditated killing" within the statutory definition of that offense (Code, § 18-30), for which the extreme penalty may be exacted. Code, § 18-31.

[1] The only assignment of error applicable to Newman is that "the court abused its discretion in refusing an order for each defendant to be examined by one or more physicians skilled in the diagnosis of insanity, in accordance with section 19-202." At the time of the trial [1] Code, § 19-202, read:

"*When question of sanity raised, commitment before trial* — If, prior to the time for trial of any person charged with crime, either the court or attorney for the Commonwealth has reason to believe that such person is in such mental condition that his confinement in a hospital for the insane or a colony for the feeble-minded is necessary for proper care and observation, the court or the judge thereof may, after hearing evidence on the subject, commit such person, if a white person, to any State hospital for the insane best adapted to meet the needs of the case * * *, pending the determination of his mental condition. In any such case the court, in its discretion, may appoint one or more physicians skilled in the diagnosis of insanity, or other qualified physicians, and when any person is alleged to be feeble-minded may likewise appoint persons skilled in the diagnosis of feeble-mindedness, not to exceed three, to examine the defendant before such commitment is ordered, make such investigation of the case as they may deem necessary and report to the court the condition of the defendant at the time of their examination. * * * "

In *Wood* v. *Commonwealth*, 146 Va. 296, 135 S. E. 895, we pointed out that this section places no obligation upon the trial court to appoint a commission for the examination of an accused except where the court or attorney for the Commonwealth has reason to believe that the accused is in such mental condition that his confinement in a hospital for the insane, or colony for the feeble-minded, for proper care and observation is necessary to attain the ends of justice. Moreover, we said that while the appellate court has the power to review the action of the trial court in refusing to commit persons pursuant to this section, it will not disturb the trial court's ruling unless it plainly appears that there has been an abuse of discretion. (146

---

[1] This section was amended by Acts of 1954, ch. 229, p. 267, which became effective after the trial.

Va., at page 305.) See also, *Delp v. Commonwealth*, 172 Va. 564, 571, 200 S. E. 594, 596.

Here there was no showing that the court or attorney for the Commonwealth had reason to believe that either defendant was in such mental condition that his confinement in an institution for care and observation was necessary to attain the ends of justice. Indeed, as has been said, there was no evidence at all in support of the motion on behalf of Newman. On behalf of Tilton, a single witness, the sheriff, merely testified that Tilton told him in a joking manner that on one occasion "he had seen a little devil in his cell." Clearly, then, there is no basis for the assignment that the trial court abused its discretion in refusing to order a mental examination of the defendants under this section.

[2] The other errors assigned on behalf of the defendant, Tilton, are:

(1) That he "was not tried before the Trial Justice of Carroll County sitting as a Juvenile and Domestic Relations Court Judge"; and

(2) That "the court failed to require a full and complete investigation of the physical, mental and social condition and personality of Lanvee Irby Tilton and the facts surrounding the violation of the law which is the cause of his being before the court," under the "mandatory" provisions of Code, § 16-172.42.

The argument under the first point is that the trial court, under the provisions of Code, 1952 Cum. Supp., § 16-172.41, should have transferred the case to the trial justice sitting as the juvenile court for disposition. This section reads:

"*Transfer from other courts.* — If during the pendency of a criminal or quasi-criminal proceeding against any person in any other court it shall be ascertained that the person was under the age of eighteen years at the time of committing the alleged offense, such court shall forthwith transfer the case, together with all papers, documents and evidence connected therewith, to the juvenile court of the city or county having jurisdiction, *provided if such is pending in a court of record, the judge thereof, in his discretion, may continue with the trial thereof.* The court making the transfer shall order the child or minor to be taken forthwith to the place of detention, designated by the juvenile court or by the transferring court, or release on bail or otherwise the child or minor to be brought

before the juvenile court at the time designated." Acts 1950, p. 677. (Italics supplied.)

This provision came into our statute law as section 39 of House Bill 520, Acts of 1950, ch. 383, p. 677. As introduced, the section made mandatory the transfer of a pending criminal proceeding against a person under the age of eighteen years from a court of record to the juvenile court. It was designed to change the holding in *Mickens v. Commonwealth*, 178 Va. 273, 16 S. E. (2d) 641, that under the former statutes such transfer was not mandatory.

The report of the Virginia Advisory Legislative Council, dated November 30, 1949, on the proposed bill carried this comment: "Another striking weakness in our present law appears to be the question of jurisdiction. This was brought to the fore in a recent case involving an aggravated crime, when upon appeal to the Supreme Court of Appeals it was held that a child could be indicted and tried without the necessity of any proceedings of a preliminary nature in the Juvenile and Domestic Relations Court." (Sen. Doc. No. 9, 1950 Sess., p. 5.) To correct this situation, the report says, the proposed bill "provides for the transfer from other courts to the juvenile court of cases that might through error, or for some other reasons, have originated in another court." (Sen. Doc. No. 9, 1950 Sess., p. 8.)

However, the General Assembly did not adopt this suggestion and amended section 39 (§ 16-172.41) by the addition of the italicized proviso. Thus, in its form as enacted, such transfer is not mandatory and the judge of the court of record in which such a case is pending, "in his discretion, may continue with the trial thereof." We find, then, no merit in this assignment.

[3] The main contention urged on behalf of the defendant, Tilton, is that the court erred in not requiring prior to trial the examination provided for in the final sentence of Code, 1952 Cum. Supp., § 16-172.42. The section as it stood at the time of trial [2] read thus:

"*Transfers to other courts.* — If a child fourteen years of age or over is charged with an offense which, if committed by an adult, could be punishable by confinement in the penitentiary the court after full investigation and hear-

---

[2] This section was amended by Acts of 1954, ch. 599, p. 768, which became effective after the trial.

ing may, in its discretion, retain jurisdiction or certify such child for proper criminal jurisdiction of such offenses if committed by an adult; provided, however, that in the event the juvenile court does not so certify a child fourteen years of age or over, charged with an offense which, if committed by an adult, would be punishable by death or confinement in the penitentiary for life or a period of twenty years or more, the Commonwealth's attorney of the city or county, if he deems it to the public interest, may present the case to the grand jury of the proper court of record. If the grand jury returns a true bill upon such indictment the jurisdiction of the juvenile court as to such case shall terminate. In no case shall any child under the age of fourteen be so certified, nor shall any such child be indicted or tried under the criminal laws of this State. The ages specified in this section refer to the age of the child or minor at the time of the alleged commission of the offense. *In all cases under this section, the court shall require a full and complete investigation of the physical, mental and social condition and personality of the child or minor and the facts and circumstances surrounding the violation of the law which is the cause of his being before the court.*" [3] Acts 1950, p. 678; 1952, p. 707. (Italics supplied.)

So far as the record discloses this provision of the law was not brought to the attention of the trial court. It was urged there that an examination should be had under Code, § 63–288. That section provides: "The court, in its discretion, either before or after a hearing, may cause any child within its jurisdiction to be given a physical and mental examination by a competent physician or physicians or an approved mental examiner, to be designated by the court having jurisdiction of such child, * * *."

As has been said, it was also urged in the trial court that the indictment be quashed on the ground that the "proceedings" against this defendant had not been commenced in accordance with the provisions of section 63–268, and that his parent had not been "notified," as required by section 63–273, of the pendency

---

[3] By the Acts of 1950, p. 678, the italicized provision was put in section 41 (§ 16–172.43), but made applicable to "all cases under the next preceding section." By Acts of 1952, p. 707, it was put in its present logical position in § 16–172.42.

of the warrant against him in the trial justice court. The order overruling the motion recites that since the mother of this defendant knew of the pendency of the warrant the requirements of section 63–273 had been met.

Thus, both counsel and the trial court overlooked the fact that sections 63–288, 63–268 and 63–273 had been repealed by Acts of 1950, ch. 383, p. 690, and superseded by the provisions of that chapter as amended by Acts of 1952, ch. 419, p. 702. (Code, 1952 Cum. Supp., § 16–172.1 *ff.*) Plainly the applicable statutes in force governing the trial of juveniles were not brought to the attention of the trial court.

The 1950 Act, providing for a state-wide system of juvenile and domestic relations courts and the trial of juveniles, was enacted by the General Assembly after a careful study and report by the Virginia Advisory Legislative Council. (Sen. Doc. No. 9, 1950 Sess., *supra.*) In the Act directing such study the General Assembly said: "The public policy of Virginia has been to provide for the correction of youthful offenders rather than to rely upon punitive methods." Acts 1948, ch. 390, p. 766.

With respect to the "purpose and intent" of the statute which was enacted the General Assembly said: "This law shall be construed liberally and as remedial in character; and the powers hereby conferred are intended to be general to effect the beneficial purposes herein set forth. It is the intention of this law that in all proceedings concerning the disposition, custody or control of children coming within the provisions hereof, the court shall proceed upon the theory that the welfare of the child is the paramount concern of the State * * *." Code, 1952 Cum. Supp., § 16–172.1; Acts 1950, p. 665, 1952, p. 703.

Section 16–172.42 deals with the transfer of cases from juvenile courts "to other courts." Under its provisions if a child fourteen years of age or over is charged with an offense "punishable by confinement in the penitentiary," the juvenile court "after full investigation and hearing" may retain jurisdiction of the child or certify him "to the appropriate court of record having criminal jurisdiction of such offenses if committed by an adult." But should the offense be punishable by death or confinement in the penitentiary for life or a period of twenty years or more, and the child is not certified to

JURISDICTIONAL AND RELATED PROBLEMS

the court of record, the Commonwealth's attorney "may present the case to the grand jury of the proper court of record." If a true bill is returned upon such indictment "the jurisdiction of the juvenile court as to such case shall terminate." That was the procedure followed in the present case.

The section closes with the provision requiring, "In all cases under this section, the court shall require a full and complete investigation of the physical, mental and social condition and personality of the child," etc.

The Attorney General argues that the juvenile court alone is charged with the duty of requiring this investigation, and that since under the terms of the section, upon the finding of a true bill upon the indictment, the jurisdiction of the juvenile court is terminated, the provision requiring the investigation becomes inoperative.

This argument violates the elementary rule of statutory construction that every provision in or part of a statute shall be given effect if possible. Clearly the section charges some court with the duty of carrying out the provision. The language embraces "all cases under this section," including those which like the present case are commenced by an indictmnt in a court of record, as well as those which are certified to it by the juvenile court and those which are retained by the juvenile court. The direction is mandatory for the language is the court "shall require" the specified "full and complete investigation."

It may be noted in passing that if the juvenile court alone is charged with the duty of making the required investigation, then the court of record is charged with the duty of referring the case to the juvenile court for that purpose. Otherwise a vital provision in the statute cannot be given effect.

But we do not agree with the argument that "in all cases" the juvenile court alone is charged with the duty of executing the provision. The basis for that argument is the statutory definition in section 16–172.3 which reads: "When used in this law, *unless the context otherwise requires:* (1) 'The court' or the 'juvenile court' means the juvenile and domestic relations court of each county or city; * * *." Acts 1950, p. 666. (Italics supplied.) But the qualifying italicized words are significant, and there are many instances in the 1950 Act,

as amended, in which the context shows that "the court" was not intended to mean the juvenile court. We think that under the proper interpretation of section 16–172.42 the court having jurisdiction of the case, whether it be the juvenile court or the court of record, is charged with the duty and responsibility of requiring the investigation. When, as in the present case, the prosecution against a child has been commenced by an indictment in a court of record that court is charged with the duty of executing the provision.

This view is supported by the fact that the provision requiring such investigation "in all cases" is placed in section 16–172.42 following the direction for the termination of the jurisdiction of the juvenile court upon the finding of a true bill upon an indictment "in a court of record." To require an investigation in the juvenile court whose jurisdiction has terminated is, of course, meaningless.

The history of this provision requiring the investigation supports the same view. The report of the Virginia Advisory Legislative Council says that this provision "follows § 1913." (Sen. Doc. 9, *supra*, p. 22.) Section 1913 of Michie's Code of 1942 provides: "The court, in its discretion, either before or after a hearing, may cause any child within its jurisdiction to be given a physical and mental examination by a competent physician or physicians or an approved mental examiner to be designated *by the court having jurisdiction of such child,* * * *." (Italics supplied.)

This provision originated in the Acts of 1914, ch. 350, p. 698, which provided: "Every child coming within the provisions of this act may be subjected to a physical and mental examination by a competent physician or physicians or other mental diagnostician, to be appointed by *the court, judge or justice having jurisdiction of the case,* * * *." (Italics supplied.) The provision became section 1910 of the Code of 1919.

By Acts of 1922, ch. 481, p. 825, section 1910 of the Code of 1919 was rewritten and became section 1913 of Michie's Code of 1942. Section 1913 became section 63–288 of the Code of 1950, the Code Commission having changed the provision for appointment of a physician "by the court, judge or justice having jurisdiction of the case" to read "by the court having jurisdiction of such child."

Thus, the history of the provision shows that the authority to require the investigation is lodged in the court "having jurisdiction of the case" or "jurisdiction of such child." Hence, if the case is pending before the juvenile court such authority and duty are lodged with the judge of that court. If, on the other hand, the jurisdiction of the juvenile court has terminated, the authority and duty to require such investigation are lodged with the "proper court of record" having jurisdiction of the case.

But it should be observed that whereas in the former statutes the authority to require such examination was *discretionary*, the requirement under section 16–172.42 is *mandatory*.

We are of opinion that both the context and the history of the provision show that under the circumstances of this case the duty of requiring the investigation under section 16–172.42 devolved upon the circuit court below. This view gives full effect to the provision and accords with the legislative direction that the statute "shall be construed liberally." (§ 16–172.1).

[4] The reason for requiring such investigation appears in section 16–172.41 and 16–172.43. Under the provisions of section 16–172.41, *supra*, the judge of the "court of record" may transfer a pending criminal proceeding against a juvenile to the juvenile court, or "in his discretion, may continue with the trial thereof."

Section 16–172.43 prescribes the "procedure in transfer cases." The last paragraph of that section reads: "In the hearing and disposition of cases properly before a court having general criminal jurisdiction the court may sentence or commit the juvenile offender in accordance with the criminal laws of this State or may in its discretion deal with the juvenile in the manner prescribed in this law for the hearing and disposition of cases in the juvenile court." Acts 1950, p. 678; 1952, p. 707.

In this paragraph the "court having general criminal jurisdiction" is given the authority either to "sentence or commit the juvenile offender in accordance with the criminal laws of this State," or "in its discretion deal with the juvenile in the manner prescribed in this law for the hearing and disposition of cases in the juvenile court."

Under sections 16–172.41 and 16–172.43 the discretion lodged in the court of record is a sound judicial discretion, to be exercised not arbitrarily or willfully, but based upon knowledge of facts upon which the discretion may properly operate. "[A] full and complete investigation of the physical, mental and social condition and personality of the child or minor and the facts and circumstances surrounding the violation of the law which is the cause of his being before the court," whether made under the direction of the court of record or the juvenile court, will give the court of record information upon which to exercise its judicial discretion in determining whether, under the provisions of section 16–172.41, the case should be transferred to the juvenile court or the trial proceeded with in the court of record. Likewise, after such investigation the court of record will be in a position to exercise its sound judicial discretion in determining whether, under the provisions of section 16–172.43, the case should be disposed of "in accordance with the criminal laws of this State," or the juvenile dealt with "in the manner prescribed in this law for the hearing and disposition of cases in the juvenile court."

As has been said, these related provisions of the law were not brought to the attention of the trial court, they were not complied with, and this child who was sixteen years of age at the time of the commission of the offense, was put on trial for his life as if he had been an adult.

[5] The provision for the required investigation in section 16–172.42 was not satisfied by the investigation and report of the probation officer which were had and made in the present case, after trial and conviction, pursuant to section 53–278.1, as amended. The investigation and report under section 53–278.1 are directed to be made after a plea of guilty or conviction, as the statute says, "to the end that the court may be fully advised as to the appropriate and just sentence to be imposed." The investigation required under section 16–172.42 has the additional and broader purpose of furnishing information from which the court may determine, in cases of aggravated offenses, whether the child should be tried as a juvenile or as an adult, and in what tribunal.

Section 8 of the Virginia Constitution guarantees to an accused, whether guilty or innocent, that "He shall not be deprived of life or liberty, except by the law of the land * * *." In the trial of the defendant, Newman, this provision has been fully satisfied, and as to him the judgment is affirmed. In the trial of the defendant, Tilton, the constitutional provision has not been satisfied, in that he was denied the benefit of the investigation required by section 16–172.42. Accordingly, the judgment against the defendant, Tilton, is reversed, the order of conviction set aside, and the case remanded for a new trial.

Affirmed in part; reversed in part and remanded.

74

Matter of Jones v. Rochester S.P.C.C.*

WITMER, J. This is a habeas corpus proceeding instituted by "Helen Jones," the mother of "Ann Brown," fifteen years old, for the release of said minor from detention by the respondent, the Rochester Society for the Prevention of Cruelty to Children, Inc., which society is acting under an order of detention by Monroe County Children's Court.

Petitioner charges that the order of detention was improperly made because it was founded solely upon the petition of an individual whose allegations are made only upon information and belief. The allegations are that "by reason of immorality and depravity" this petitioner's husband, stepfather of the minor, "is unfit to properly care for said child in that he has committed immoral acts against said child * * * which have endangered and corrupted the morals of said child," and that the minor's mother, petitioner herein, "with whom said child resides, having knowledge of said improper acts against said child, has condoned same or * * * (has done) nothing to prevent same. That said child is now at the S.P.C.C. and * * * (affiant) believes that the welfare of said child requires that her custody be immediately assumed by the Court."

Upon the issuance of the order of detention a summons was also issued and served upon this petitioner and her husband under section 11 of the Children's Court Act, requiring them to appear in Children's Court and show cause why the court should not deal with said minor according to the provisions of the Children's Court Act. They have appeared in that proceeding in Children's Court by the same attorney who is representing petitioner herein, and have asked for and secured repeated adjournments of the hearing in that court.

It also appears that the District Attorney presented to the Grand Jury in this county evidence against the stepfather concerning his alleged acts which are the basis of the Children's Court proceeding, and that the Grand Jury has indicted the stepfather, charging him with the crime of rape, second degree, in two counts. Petitioner's attorney herein represented the stepfather in this court last month in unsuccessful efforts to secure dismissal of the indictment and to examine the Grand Jury minutes.

Upon the return of the writ herein this court spoke privately with the minor, "Ann Brown," and she advised the court that she is being well treated by respondent society, and desires to remain with the society pending the determination of the Children's Court proceeding; and she does not join with her mother, petitioner herein, in this application for a writ of habeas corpus.

This court is disturbed by the informality of the proceeding in Children's Court, at least to the extent of the failure to reveal therein what is orally acknowledged to be the fact, namely, that petitioner therein, Doris M. Adkins, is an officer of the respondent society to whom the minor originally complained of her stepfather, and the failure to have an affidavit of fact by some person possessed of direct knowledge concerning the charges to support the petition. (See Children's Court Act, § 10.) It is acknowledged that in a criminal case a mere allegation upon information and belief is insufficient to support a warrant of arrest (*People v. Bertram*, 302 N. Y. 526), but it is asserted in behalf of respondent that this is a civil, not criminal, proceeding, as indeed it is (*People v. Lewis*, 260 N. Y. 171), and hence it is contended that an allegation upon information and belief is sufficient. (See *Hammond v.*

---

* *Matter of Jones v. Rochester S.P.C.C.*, Supreme Court of New York, 1954, 206 Misc. R. N. Y. 557.

Citizens Nat. Bank of Potsdam, 260 App. Div. 374, and 3 Carmody-Wait on New York Practice, § 22, p. 451.) But it seems to me that the fact that the proceeding is civil and not criminal is not determinative of the question of the necessity for direct allegations of fact. It has frequently been held that in cases of civil arrest and in civil cases wherein nonpersonal jurisdiction is sought, the supporting papers must contain direct allegations of fact. . . . [Citations omitted.]

The arrest or detention of an individual against his will is a serious business, and may not be done except upon the direct knowledge of the arresting officer or of an affiant in support of a warrant of arrest. (See *People* v. *Belcher,* 302 N. Y. 529.) Hence I think the petition would be insufficient to support an order to take the minor into custody against her will. In many, if not most, situations it is the will of the parental guardian with which we should be concerned. But the circumstances here justify the court considering the will of the minor, temporarily, as against that of her parent.

The court is not unmindful that if this application were granted, presumably one of the witnesses before the Grand Jury could make an affidavit which would afford a basis for jurisdiction of this minor by Children's Court. That, it seems, would be the simple way of avoiding the question now presented. But that has not been done, and the court must determine whether or not Children's Court may act *summarily* to give custody and protection to a complaining minor, pending due hearing of charges affecting the welfare of the child in her home.

Special facts exist in this case. If the serious charges against petitioner's husband and herself are true, the minor should not be released to return to them. Although the court may not assume the charges to be true, it cannot rightly overlook the fact that they have been accepted by the Grand Jury which indicted the stepfather thereon. Furthermore, counsel for petitioner openly states that his clients wish the minor released so that they can talk with her alone. The hearing of the matter in Children's Court has been delayed by them for this purpose; and it is apparent that the proceeding herein is part of the plan of the defense of the stepfather upon his trial under the indictment. Moreover, the minor originally went to the respondent society with her charges against the stepfather and voluntarily sought the protection of the society in Children's Court. The court need not be blind to the patent fact that there is, temporarily at least, a diversity of interest between the minor and her mother, and that this proceeding is not in reality brought on behalf of the minor, but is on behalf of the mother and her husband.

If, as petitioner contends, this minor is recalcitrant and is merely seeking revenge upon her stepfather for having disciplined her, the hearing of the charges in Children's Court should be sufficient remedy. That proceeding will undoubtedly be conducted with all of the usual safeguards of court procedure. (*People* v. *Lewis,* 260 N. Y. 171, 178, *supra.*)

The salient fact in this proceeding is that the minor has asked and still asks for the protection of the court, and is only temporarily "detained." The Children's Court Act contemplates that a judge of that court may act summarily for the temporary protection of such a minor (Children's Court Act, § 20), pending due notice of hearing and due hearing of the issues involved. Petitioner makes no claim that Children's Court has delayed action in the proceeding. For that reason and because the minor has voluntarily placed herself in the protection of the respondent society and Children's Court, as well as for other reasons, *Matter of Jacobsen* (278 App. Div. 945) and *Matter of Post* (280 App. Div. 268) are not in point.

With respect to another child it was said, "She is not, within the meaning of the constitutional provisions relied upon, deprived of her liberty at all, but rather, for her own welfare, she is intrusted temporarily to the care and custody of a society organized for such and kindred purposes and recognized as a State agency." (*People ex rel. Bolt* v. *Society,* 48 Misc. 175, 177, and see *People* v. *Lewis,* 260 N. Y. 171, 178–179, *supra.*)

Children's Court having lawful custody of this minor, the petition is sufficient to support the proceeding to determine the merits of the charges. (Cf. *People* v. *Belcher,* 302 N. Y. 529, 533, *supra.*)

The writ is, therefore, dismissed, and said minor is remanded to the custody and control of the respondent society, subject to the further direction of Monroe County Children's Court.

Chapter 14

Problems of Proof

75

People *v.* Pikunas *

APPEAL, by permission, from a judgment of the Appellate Division of the Supreme Court in the second judicial department, entered July 19, 1932, which affirmed a judgment of the Nassau County Children's Court committing the defendant as a delinquent child to the New York State Training School for Girls. . . .

POUND, Ch. J. The record in this case is not a satisfactory one on which to deprive a fifteen-year old child of her liberty, with proper regard for due legal process. Juvenile delinquency is not a crime and the acts charged here do not involve any crime. (Children's Court Act [L. 1922, ch. 547, as amd. L. 1930, ch. 393], § 45; Penal Law, § 2186.) The strict rules of criminal procedure for the protection of parties accused of crime are, therefore, inapplicable to the proceedings. Full and complete records must be kept. (Children's Court Act, § 45.) Some degree of informality is to be expected. (*People* v. *Fitzgerald*, 244 N. Y. 307, 312.) It is, however, reasonable to require that some form or forms of juvenile delinquency be charged in the complaint,† established by

* *People* v. *Pikunas*, Court of Appeals of New York, 1932, 260 N. Y. 72, 182 N.E. 675.

† *Cf. Robinson* v. *State*, 204 S.W. 2d 981, where the court reversed a finding of delinquency under a complaint which charged a boy to be delinquent because of "5 cases of arson," without specifying owners or location of burned property, or times of commission of alleged arsons, although recognizing the proceedings to be non-criminal. "While it was not essential that the petition allege an offense with the particularity of a criminal indictment still 'a reasonable and definite charge must be filed against the minor.'" — Ed.

the evidence and found by the court before the child may be committed to a disciplinary institution, so that it may appear that it is the law which determines the commitment and not the ukase of the magistrate, however wise and judicious he may be.

The gist of the charge against appellant is that she deserted her home without good or sufficient cause in violation of section 486 of the Penal Law. It was on this charge alone that she was adjudged delinquent and committed to an institution; but this clause of the Penal Law is inapplicable as it is inconsistent with the Children's Court Act. (Children's Court Act, § 45.) The Children's Court Act (L. 1930, ch. 393, § 2, par. 2 [d]) defines "delinquent child," in this connection, as a child "who, without just cause and without the consent of his parent, parents, guardians or other custodian, *repeatedly* deserts his home or place of abode," and thus applies to habitual truancy and not to a single act of truancy. The evidence in this case, so far as set forth in the record, indicates but one absence from home, accompanied, it is true, by an act or acts of sexual intercourse with a man who, defendant says, forced her to stay in a car with him. A child who is forced into a car and taken away from home without her consent cannot be said to "desert her home without good and sufficient cause" and one such act in its worst aspect is not to be described as *repeatedly* deserting one's home. If she went willingly and actually if not legally consented to sexual intercourse, she might be regarded as delinquent and a proper object for commitment to a suitable institution, but on this record the finding is merely that she deserted her home without good and sufficient cause.

The Children's Court Act, § 22, provides that the court after hearing and determining the case if satisfied that the child is in need of the care, discipline and protection of the State, may adjudicate the child to be delinquent, and commit the child to a suitable institution.

Proper regard for the rights of the child requires that the court should hear and determine some charged act or acts of juvenile delinquency as defined in the Children's Court Act, § 2, and not decide, to the judge's own satisfaction merely, that "she should have some correction," without regard to the nature of the charge or the proof. Arbitrary action in this case was perhaps a matter of form rather than substance but we think that the ends of justice require that a more complete record (Children's Court Act, § 45) be made the basis of an adjudication under the Children's Court Act so that it will clearly appear that such adjudication is legal.

The judgment should be reversed and a new trial ordered.

CRANE, LEHMAN, KELLOGG, O'BRIEN, HUBBS and CROUCH, JJ., concur.

Judgment reversed, etc.

76

Jones *et al. v.* Commonwealth *

SPRATLEY, Justice.

Upon separate petitions filed by a probation officer, the defendants, William Jones and George Patrick, infants under the age of eighteen years, respectively ———— years and fifteen years, were summoned to appear before the Juvenile and Domestic Relations Court of the city of Bristol, Virginia, to answer complaints that they were delinquent children within the meaning of chapter 78, Virginia Code 1942 (Michie).

Upon trial, the Juvenile and Domestic Relations Court found each of them guilty of throwing stones at a dwelling in the nighttime. Separate judgments were entered declaring each a delinquent child. They were placed under the supervision of a probation officer, but allowed to remain in the care and custody of their parents. "As punishment for the offense

---

* *Jones* et al. v. *Commonwealth*, Supreme Court of Appeals of Virginia, 1946, 185 Va. 335, 38 S. E. 2d 444.

committed," it was ordered that each defendant pay a fine of $25 and $3 costs out of their own individual earnings at gainful employment.

In each judgment there were seven additional conditions of probation imposed, depriving the defendants of certain normal privileges and rights for one year. One directed that they be at home each evening by 9:30 and remain there the rest of the night, unless escorted from the home by an adult. A second deprived them of the right to drive an automobile or motor vehicle for pleasure. Another ordered that each boy "attend Sunday School and Church each Sunday hereafter for a period of one year, and present satisfactory evidence of such attendance at the conclusion of each month to the Probation Officer."

Appeals were taken to the Corporation Court of Bristol, where, by agreement, trial by jury being waived, the cases were tried together and heard on the same evidence before the judge. Upon this trial, the judgments of the Juvenile and Domestic Relations Court were affirmed in all respects. The same fines and the same conditions of probation were imposed on the defendants. Hence this appeal.

The defendants contend that the judgments are without evidence to support them, and that they are illegal, unreasonable, and contrary to public policy, and in violation of the laws of Virginia and of the Federal and State Constitutions.

The material evidence in the cases may be summarized as follows:

Mrs. Edith Reed testified that she lived in a one-story house fronting on West Mary street, Bristol (an humble section of the city occupied by white and colored residents). The rear of her lot was vacant and ran back to Piedmont street. On the vacant portion of the lot, near her bedroom window, was located a metal sign of some kind, a billboard or signboard, placed at an angle to Piedmont street. About 8:30 o'clock on Friday night, March 2, 1945, she heard some rocks hitting the rear of her house. She looked out of her window and saw a boy a short distance therefrom, wearing white and tan slippers, standing in front of the billboard. The boy ran to a street light on Piedmont street, and three more boys came from behind the billboard to join him. She holloed to them, pleading that no more rocks be thrown or she would call the police. While the first boy was running to the light more rocks were thrown toward her home by some unseen person or persons. She thought these rocks came from behind the billboard. She only saw four boys. One of the four wore a green sweater. She did not actually see any one of these boys throw a rock or stoop down to get a rock. She called the police.

Mrs. Belle Justice testified that she came to the house of her mother, Mrs. Reed, just as some rocks were being thrown. She heard her mother tell a boy not to peep in her window. She thought this boy had on white and tan shoes; but she did not see his shoes until he had gotten on Piedmont street. She also saw three other boys come from behind the billboard and a girl who subsequently joined the four boys under the street light. One boy had on a green sweater and another wore a jacket. She did not see any one throw a rock.

Much of the above evidence of the two witnesses is taken from the whole of their testimony, which is vague and confused in some respects and contradictory in others.

Another witness for the Commonwealth, Ella Hardy, who lived in the immediate neighborhood, heard some one throwing rocks, either against the billboard or near the house of Mrs. Reed. She raised her window and saw a boy with white and tan shoes, accompanied by a boy wearing a brown jacket, both on the sidewalk of Piedmont street, near the hedge close to the lot of Pearl Roberts. Subsequently two other boys came along and joined the first two under the street light. Some rocks were thrown by some unseen person while the boy in the white shoes was within her vision. Subsequently a boy and girl joined the other four boys under the light. She stated positively that none of the boys threw a rock while she looked, and that neither of the defendants raised his hands, although rocks were then being thrown by some one else.

Pearl Roberts heard Ella Hardy call out that some rocks were being thrown. She looked out of her window and saw a boy with white shoes and another boy with a jacket "about the color of a felt mattress." She then observed four boys come down the street and stop under the street light, where they were joined later by a girl and another boy. They stood there talking for two or three minutes, and then went on their respective ways. She further stated that

when she saw the boys none of them was engaged in throwing rocks. She went upstairs after Ella Hardy told her that the boys they saw were not doing anything.

The evidence of the defendants' witnesses was as follows:

At the time of the rock-throwing episode, William Jones and George Patrick, in company with Allan Clark and Guy Fuller, Jr., were walking down Piedmont street, on their direct route to a moving picture show. The four boys, all high school students, had been on an automobile ride, and had just gotten out of the automobile on Euclid avenue. Jones and Patrick walked in front. About 25 feet behind them were Clark and Fuller. Walking behind the latter, about 20 or 25 feet distant, were two other high school students, Richard McKenzie and Miss Dolly Sopigoti. When the defendants reached the hedge that separated the property of Pearl Roberts from the vacant lot of Mrs. Reed, upon which is located the billboard, the four boys heard the rocks being thrown. Some one called out in protest, but they did not know what was said. Patrick immediately ran down to a street light at the next corner. He was followed by Jones, who hastened to join him under the street light. Both defendants heard some rocks thrown after they started towards the street light. Clark and Fuller heard the rocks in both instances as they came up and joined the first two boys. They were followed to the same place by McKenzie and Miss Sopigoti. Standing together they speculated among themselves as to what had happened, and who had thrown the stones. After exchanging a few words, they separated, McKenzie and Miss Sopigoti proceeding to one theater and the four boys to another. The four boys walked down Piedmont street towards Scott street. A police car passed them going towards the Roberts' home. When the defendants and the two boys had reached Scott street, the police car turned around and came back, and the police officers took the boys into custody and carried them to the scene of the rock-throwing.

William Jones wore a tan jacket, and George Patrick had on white and tan shoes. Guy Fuller, Jr., wore a green sweater.

When the four boys were brought before Mrs. Reed and Mrs. Justice, they undertook to identify Patrick as the boy they saw wearing the white and tan shoes, Guy Fuller, Jr., as the lad with the green sweater, and Jones as the wearer of the brown jacket.

The defendants testified that they did not leave the sidewalk of Piedmont street. They denied positively that either of them threw a single rock. The other three boys and the young miss testified that the defendants were in full view during their entire passage down Piedmont street, and that neither one of the defendants, nor any one in the party of the six young persons, threw a rock. All six of these witnesses were acquainted with each other (being students in the same high school), but they were in no wise engaged in the same enterprise or occupation on the night of March 2d.

The evidence further discloses that there were other persons traveling Piedmont street that night about the time in question. On the far side of that street, opposite the home of Mrs. Reed, there is a high bank, from which rocks could have been thrown by an unseen person. This was actually suggested by McKenzie in the conversation which he had with the defendants under the street light.

The testimony of the police officers related only to what they were told by the witnesses for the Commonwealth.

The testimony of each of the defendants and their witnesses was direct, straightforward, and positive. The action of Jones and Patrick in proceeding directly to the most exposed place for discovery, under a street light, after the rocks had been thrown, is not indicative of any sense of guilt on their part. Further opposed to the inference of their guilt, drawn from the description of their clothes, is the positive evidence of their innocence.

Eleven character witnesses, among them leading and prominent citizens of Bristol and neighbors of the defendants, testified positively that each of the defendants bore a good reputation for truth and veracity.

The judgment against a youth that he is delinquent is a serious reflection upon his character and habits. The stain against him is not removed merely because the statute says no judgment in this particular proceeding shall be deemed a conviction for crime or so considered. The stigma of conviction will reflect upon him for life. It hurts his self-respect. It may, at some inopportune, unfortunate moment, rear its ugly head to destroy his opportunity for

advancement, and blast his ambition to build up a character and reputation entitling him to the esteem and respect of his fellow man. Nor is the implication that he has wilfully sworn to a falsehood to prevent conviction to be disregarded lightly. Guilt should be proven by evidence which leaves no reasonable doubt. Inferences must give way when in conflict with facts established by positive proof.

The provisions of chapter 78, Virginia Code 1942 (Michie), sections 1905–1922, are protective, not penal. Proceedings thereunder are of a civil nature, not criminal. They are intended for the protection of the child and society, to save the child from evil tendencies and bad surroundings, and to give it more efficient care and training that it may become a worthy and useful member of society.

Mr. Justice Hudgins in Mickens v. Commonwealth, 178 Va. 273, 279, 16 S. E.2d 641, 643, succinctly stated the powers of the juvenile courts under chapter 78. Said he:

"No power is given to the juvenile courts to convict any child of any crime, either misdemeanor or felony, or to commit any child to any penal institution. Such court may only adjudge a child a delinquent and commit him, not to a penal institution, but to the State Board of Public Welfare, which board is given power to make proper disposition of the child. Sec. 1910.

"It is thus seen that the matters over which the juvenile courts are given exclusive original jurisdiction are the 'disposition, custody or control of delinquent, dependent or neglected children,' but not their trial and punishment for the offense which they have committed.

"The trial and punishment of minor offenders follows the regular criminal procedure, modified, in certain respects, by the statutes setting up juvenile and domestic relations courts. These statutes have established a system whereby most juvenile offenders are first subjected to the jurisdiction of the juvenile courts for proceedings therein designed to subject such offenders to the supervision and control of the State in a manner in which the delinquent ways of the child will be corrected and he be made to lead a correct life."

In view of what we have said, it is unnecessary to discuss the severity of the punishment for the supposed offense of the two infants.

The statute, section 1922, provides that it

"shall be liberally construed in order to accomplish the beneficial purposes herein set forth." There is nothing in the record to suggest that the accused were inherently vicious or incorrigible. To classify an infant as delinquent because of a youthful prank, or for a mere single violation of a misdemeanor statute or municipal ordinance, not immoral per se, in this day of numberless laws and ordinances is offensive to our sense of justice and to the intendment of the law. We cannot reconcile ourselves to the thought that the incautious violation of a motor vehicle traffic law, a single act of truancy or a departure from an established rule of similar slight gravity, is sufficient to justify the classification of the offender as a "delinquent," and require the supervision of a probation officer. We can but reflect that if this were so, there would be an inclusion of so many in the classification that the word would lose its accepted meaning.

The next question is whether the requirement in the judgments that the defendants "attend Sunday School and Church each Sunday" for the period of a year violates their constitutional guaranty of religious freedom.

Nothing is more fully set forth or more plainly expressed than the determination of our forefathers to establish and perpetuate in the several States of the Union complete religious liberty. No State has more jealously guarded and preserved the questions of religious belief and religious worship as questions between each individual man and his Maker than Virginia. See Pirkey Brothers v. Commonwealth, 134 Va. 713, 114 S.E. 764, 29 A.L.R. 1290.

The Virginia Bill of Rights, adopted June 12, 1776, contains the first declaration of the people of Virginia, in convention assembled, relating to religious freedom. With language unchanged, it became, and is now, section 16 of the Constitution of Virginia.

"16. That religion or the duty which we owe to our creator, and the manner of discharging it, can be directed only by reason and conviction, not by force or violence and, therefore all men are equally entitled to the free exercise of religion, according to the dictates of conscience and that it is the mutual duty of all to practise Christian forbearance, love and charity towards each other."

Jefferson's great statute of Religious Freedom, enacted December 16, 1785, retained in its original form in every revision of the laws from that time until now, constitutes section 34 of our Code, again declared and re-affirmed in section 35.

The preamble of this statute, after recognizing religion, morality, and knowledge as essential to good government and to the happiness of the people, proceeds to declare and proclaim: "[That] no man shall be compelled to frequent or support any religious worship, place, or ministry, whatsoever, nor shall be enforced, restrained, molested or burthened in his body or goods, nor shall otherwise suffer on account of his religious opinions or belief; but that all men shall be free to profess and by argument to maintain their opinions in matters of religion, and [that] the same shall in no wise diminish, enlarge, or affect, their civil capacities."

This language, unchanged, has been incorporated as a part of our present Constitution, section 58.

The first amendment to the Constitution of the United States provides that "Congress shall make no law respecting an establishment of religion, or prohibiting the free exercise thereof; * * *."

Thus, in these statutes and constitutional provisions are contained the fundamental principles of the separation of church and state. There is preserved and assured to each individual the right to determine for himself all questions which relate to his relation with the Creator of the Universe. No civil authority has the right to require any one to accept or reject any religious belief or to contribute any support thereto. The growth of religion is not made dependnt on force or alliance with the state. Its support is left to moral and spiritual forces.

Mr. Cooley in his great work on Constitutional Limitations, 8th Ed., Volume 2, page 968, forcefully states the compelling reasons for our statutes and constitutional provisions.

"Whoever is not led by choice or a sense of duty to attend upon the ordinances of religion is not to be compelled to do so by the State. It is the province of the State to enforce, as far as it may be found practicable, the obligations and duties which the citizen may be under or may owe to his fellow-citizens or to society; but those which spring from the relations between himself and his Maker are to be enforced by the admonitions of the conscience, and not by the penalties of human laws. Indeed, as all real worship must essentially and necessarily consist in the free-will offering of adoration and gratitude by the creature to the Creator, human laws are obviously inadequate to incite or compel those internal and voluntary emotions which shall induce it, and human penalties at most could only enforce the observance of idle ceremonies, which, when unwillingly performed, are alike valueless to the participants and devoid of all the elements of true worship."

For the foregoing reasons, we are of opinion to reverse and annul each of the judgments complained of, and to dismiss the proceedings against each of the defendants.

Reversed and proceedings dismissed.

77

In re Holmes *

HORACE STERN, Chief Justice.

We allowed an appeal in this case from the order of the Superior Court, 175 Pa. Super. 137, 103 A.2d 454, because appellant's petition asserted that questions of his constitutional rights were involved.

Appellant, Joseph Holmes, had been in trouble with the authorities several times before the proceedings which gave rise to the present appeal. In 1949, when he was 13 years of age, he was adjudged delinquent by the Juvenile Division of the Municipal Court of Philadelphia on a petition alleging that he was involved in a highway robbery, and he was then placed on probation. He was later accused of participation in a burglary, but that offense was not proved; however, he failed to attend school for long periods of time and in 1951 his proba-

tion was continued. He continued to be a persistent truant from school, and, in August, 1952, being charged with participation in a highway robbery and assault and battery, he was committed to Pennypack House and remained there until November of that year when he was again placed on probation.

This brings us to the hearing before the Juvenile Court on January 7, 1953, the delinquency petition alleging larceny of an automobile, operating an automobile without the owner's consent, and operating an automobile without a driver's license. There was definite evidence that the automobile had been stolen and appellant admitted driving it without a license but he denied guilty knowledge of the theft of the car. The Juvenile Court adjudged him delinquent on the charge of operating a motor vehicle without a license. Five days later a delinquency petition was filed alleging his participation in the armed robbery of a church. At a hearing on that charge held on January 23, 1953, the court revoked his probation and committed him to the Pennsylvania Industrial School at White Hill, basing this action on his prior record, his present activities, the failure of his parents to control him, and the desirability of his receiving the training provided in such an institution. Counsel for appellant thereupon intervened and requested a rehearing, which was held on March 6, 1953, and at which additional testimony was taken.[1] The court repeated its adjudication of delinquency and ordered Holmes remanded to White Hill. On appeal to the Superior Court this order was affirmed.

Appellant's able counsel have urged upon us as upon the Superior Court, many claims of illegality and deprivation of constitutional rights in connection with the proceedings before the Municipal Court. Such claims, however, entirely overlook, in our opinion, the basic concept of a Juvenile Court. The proceedings in such a court are not in the nature of a criminal trial but constitute merely a civil inquiry or action looking to the treatment, reformation and rehabilitation of the minor child. Their purpose

---

* In re Holmes, Appeal of Holmes, Supreme Court of Pennsylvania, 1954, 379 Pa. 599, 109 A. 2d 523. Certiorari denied, March 28, 1955. In re Joseph Holmes, an Alleged Delinquent Minor, 348 U. S. 973, 75 S. Ct. 535, 99 L. Ed. 757. Noted, 41 Cornell L. Q. (1955), 147. — Ed.

[1] Section 15 of the Juvenile Court Law evidently presupposed that additional testimony may be received at a rehearing because it provides that such testimony shall be taken down and transcribed by an official stenographer and made a part of the record in the case.

is not penal but protective, — aimed to check juvenile delinquency and to throw around a child, just starting, perhaps, on an evil course and deprived of proper parental care, the strong arm of the State acting as *parens patriae*. The State is not seeking to punish an offender but to salvage a boy who may be in danger of becoming one, and to safeguard his adolescent life. Even though the child's delinquency may result from the commission of a criminal act the State extends to such a child the same care and training as to one merely neglected, destitute or physically handicapped. No suggestion or taint of criminality attaches to any finding of delinquency by a Juvenile Court.

The conception that children are regarded as wards of the State is not one of recent origin; indeed from the very earliest times children in England were regarded as the wards of Chancery, and the Chancellor exercised the prerogatives of the Crown in acting for the care, treatment and protection of unfortunate minors and placing them under proper guardianship.[2] The first Juvenile Court was established in 1899. In our own Commonwealth the Juvenile Court Act of June, 2, 1933, P.L. 1433, section 8, 11 P.S. § 250, gave to the judges of the Municipal Court in Philadelphia the duty, after an inquiry of the facts at a hearing, to determine whether the best interests and welfare of a child and the State required the care, guidance and control of such child, and to make an order accordingly; by the amendatory Act of June 15, 1939, P.L. 394, the word "child," as used in the Act, is defined to mean a minor under the age of 18 years.

One of the principal contentions made by appellant is that he was improperly compelled to answer a question, the answer to which involved self-incrimination, namely, whether he had a license to drive an automobile, to which

he answered "No." Article I, Section 9, of the Constitution, P.S., provides that "In all *criminal* prosecution the accused * * * cannot be compelled to give evidence against himself." But since, as pointed out, Juvenile Courts *are not criminal courts*, the constitutional rights granted to persons accused of *crime* are not applicable to children brought before them, as was definitely held in the elaborate opinion of Mr. Justice Brown in Commonwealth v. Fisher, 213 Pa. 48, 62 A. 198, which held the Act of April 23, 1903, P.L. 274, 11 P.S. § 71 et seq., the forerunner of the present Juvenile Court Act, constitutional. It may be added that appellant was not "compelled" to testify; he was questioned in the same manner and in the same spirit as a parent might have acted, for whom, under the theory of juvenile court legislation, the State was substituting. It is true that section 18 of the Juvenile Court Act provides that if the child had been held by a magistrate or justice of the peace for any offense, other than murder, punishable by imprisonment in a State penitentiary, the judge of the Juvenile Court might, if in his opinion the interests of the State required a prosecution of such case on an indictment, certify the same to the district attorney of the county, who should thereupon proceed with the case in the same manner as though the jurisdiction of the Juvenile Court had never attached. But such a certification could not be made after the Juvenile Court had made an adjudication of delinquency nor, perhaps, after any self-incriminatory examination of the child. That question is not here involved, but it may be noted that section 19 of the Act provides that "The disposition of a child or any evidence given in a juvenile court shall not be admissible as evidence against the child in any case or proceeding in any other court."

Appellant complains that the court received certain hearsay testimony in regard to the charge that he was implicated in the armed robbery of the church. It seems that one of the two men who were convicted of that crime had confessed to having committed it, and a detective testified at appellant's hearing as to the substance of that confession and that it implicated appellant. It is true that subsequently the man who had made the confession repudiated it and now stated that appellant did not participate in the robbery, but of course the judge was

[2] There will be recalled the famous proceeding in which Lord Chancellor Eldon in 1817 deprived Shelley of the custody of his two children on the ground that he had deserted his wife, Harriet, (who had shortly before committed suicide) and thereafter unlawfully cohabited with Mary Godwin (whom he subsequently married); also on the ground that he apparently intended to inculcate in his offspring his own atheistic and antisocial opinions. The chancellor appointed a curator to take charge of the children. The proceedings are reported in Jacob's Chancery Reports, p. 266, sub. nom. Shelley v. Westbrooke, the Westbrooke being Harriet's father.

not obliged to believe his retraction. He admitted that he had made the confession and the fact that the testimony of the detective was technically "hearsay" was therefore wholly unimportant. Moreover, from the very nature of the hearings in the Juvenile Court it cannot be required that strict rules of evidence should be applied as they properly would be in the trial of cases in the criminal court. Although, of course, a finding of delinquency must be based on sufficient competent evidence, the hearing in the Juvenile Court may, in order to accomplish the purposes for which juvenile court legislation is designed, avoid many of the legalistic features of the rules of evidence customarily applicable to other judicial hearings. Even from a purely technical standpoint hearsay evidence, if it is admitted without objection and is relevant and material to the issue, is to be given its natural probative effect and may be received as direct evidence: Harrah v. Montour R. Co., 321 Pa. 526, 184 A. 666; Sledzianowski Unemployment Compensation Case, 168 Pa.Super. 37, 76 A.2d 666. Moreover, there is nothing in the record to indicate that the judge who presided in the Juvenile Court acted in the final disposition of appellant's case on the basis of any conclusion that appellant had in fact participated in the armed robbery of the church.

Counsel for appellant demanded of the court the right to inspect the records of the proceedings in connection with appellant's case, claiming to be entitled thereto by virtue of the provision of section 3 of the Juvenile Court Act, 11 P.S. § 245, which provided that such records should be kept in a docket and should be open to inspection by the parent or other representative of the person concerned. The court granted this request as far as the notes of testimony were concerned but refused it as to the reports of probation officers. As the Superior Court properly held, the records referred to in the statute are obviously the ordinary petitions, docket entries, notes of testimony and court orders; the reports received by the court from probation officers are not entered in the docket as a part of the "records of the proceedings." It is true that ex parte information received by the court and not publicly disclosed cannot properly be made the basis of a finding of delinquency in the Juvenile Court any more than of any important adverse finding in a trial be-

fore a judge in any other court.[3] However, this rule does not apply in connection with the determination of a *sentence* in a criminal court and, all the more, should not apply to the disposition of a case in a Juvenile Court. In Williams v. New York, 337 U.S. 241, 69 S.Ct. 1079, 93 L.Ed. 1337, the court pointed out that, as distinguished from the situation where the question for consideration is the *guilt* of a defendant, it has always been the right of a court in sentencing to consider information concerning the defendant's past life, health, habits, conduct, and mental and moral propensities, even though such information is obtained outside the courtroom from persons whom the defendant has not been permitted to confront or cross-examine. The court said, 337 U.S. at page 247, 69 S.Ct. at page 1083. "Highly relevant — if not essential — to his selection of an appropriate sentence is the possession of the fullest information possible concerning the defendant's life and characteristics. And modern concepts individualizing punishment have made it all the more necessary that a sentencing judge not be denied an opportunity to obtain pertinent information by a requirement of rigid adherence to restrictive rules of evidence properly applicable to the trial." And further, 337 U.S. at page 249, 69 S.Ct. at page 1084: "Under the practice of individualizing punishments, investigational techniques have been given an important role. Probation workers making reports of their investigations have not been trained to prosecute but to aid offenders. Their reports have been given a high value by conscientious judges who want to sentence persons on the best available information rather than on guesswork and inadequate information." If all this is true as applicable to a criminal court it is certainly a fortiori true in regard to proceedings in the Juvenile Court.

---

[3] As to ordinary criminal and civil courts: Commonwealth v. Johnson, 348 Pa. 349, 35 A.2d 312; Commonwealth ex rel. Ritter v. Ritter, 91 Pa.Super. Ct. 563; Commonwealth ex rel. Mark v. Mark, 115 Pa.Super. 181, 175 A. 289; Commonwealth ex rel. McClenen v. McClenen, 127 Pa.Super. 471, 193 A. 83; Commonwealth ex rel. Knode v. Knode, 145 Pa.Super. 1, 20 A.2d 896; Commonwealth ex rel. Oncay v. Oncay, 153 Pa.Super. 569, 34 A. 2d 839; Commonwealth ex rel. Balick v. Balick, 172 Pa.Super. 196, 92 A.2d 703.

Counsel for appellant makes much of the contention that the hearings of January 23 and March 6, 1953, could not properly have been for the purpose of determining whether appellant's probation should be revoked because section 12 of the Juvenile Court Act, 11 P.S. § 254, provides that any amendment of an order made by it should be upon motion of the district attorney or a probation officer or upon petition of any other person in interest after notice both to the district attorney and a probation officer, and it is claimed that here there was no such motion made or petition presented. It is, however, wholly immaterial whether those hearings were initiated for the purpose of passing upon the revocation of appellant's probation or considering an adjudication of delinquency. Neither the district attorney nor any probation officer complains of any lack of notice. At the January hearing the court had revoked appellant's probation, and while, at the rehearing, it again adjudged appellant delinquent, the order remanding him to White Hill was in effect merely a reäffirmation of the revocation of the probation.

Complaint is made of the fact that it does not affirmatively appear from the record that notices of the hearings were given to appellant's parents. The parents of a child involved in a Juvenile Court proceeding should certainly be notified in regard to what ought to be to them a matter of supreme importance. It has been held to be "an abuse of discretion for a [juvenile] court to go into such hearing and adjudication without notice to the persons having custody of the child, and without an opportunity for them to be heard, unless imperious reasons exist therefor." In re Rose Child Dependency Case, 161 Pa.Super. 204, 207, 208, 54 A.2d 297, 298. However, the record definitely indicates a total lack of interest on the part of appellant's parents rather than any absence of notification to them on the part of the court. After counsel appeared in the case it must be assumed that he was in touch with them and that, if they had wanted to be present they would have been there instead of the uncle and aunt who did appear. Appellant's repeated derelictions are proof positive of the fact either that his parents were indifferent to his bad behavior or were unable to control him.

A final complaint is urged in regard to the court's commitment of appellant to White Hill on the alleged ground that the inmates of that institution are not restricted to delinquent juveniles but may include also persons convicted of crime in a criminal court, and that the purpose of the Juvenile Court Act is to guard children from association and contact with crime and criminals. Section 8 of the Juvenile Court Act, as amended by the Act of June 15, 1939, P.L. 394, provides that the court may "Commit any child over the age of sixteen years to any state industrial school or home for the reformation and correction of youths above the age of sixteen." The fact that the Act of July 29, 1953, P.L. 1447, provides that minors between the ages of fifteen and twenty-one who were sentenced in the criminal court may be committed to the Pennsylvania Industrial School if not known to have been previously sentenced to a State penitentiary, does not make that institution a prison; the Act merely extends the benefits of reformatory treatment to minors even though convicted in the criminal court instead of being adjudged delinquent in the Juvenile Court. Commitments by the Juvenile Court to such institution are therefore proper and have been supported by the courts without question.[4]

The order of the Superior Court is affirmed.

BELL, J., absent.

MUSMANNO, Justice.

In upholding the commitment of Joseph Holmes, a minor, to the Pennsylvania Industrial School at White Hill, a reformatory, the Majority uses an argument similar to that employed down though the centuries by Spartan parents, namely, that disciplinary treatment is administered to a child only for his own good. But this approach to the problem before us completely misses the target of inquiry. The question is not *how* Joseph Holmes should be treated, but whether he should be "treated" at all.

There are two phases to every Juvenile Court proceeding: (1) Determination as to whether the juvenile involved is delinquent or not; (2)

---

[4] In re Trignani's Case, 150 Pa.Super. 491, 28 A.2d 702; Weintraub's Appeal, 166 Pa.Super. 342, 71 A.2d 823; Commonwealth ex rel. Perino v. Burke, 175 Pa.Super. 291, 104 A.2d 163; Commonwealth ex rel. O'Donnell v. Prasse, 84 Pa.Dist. & Co. 306.

Decision as to whether the juvenile is to be returned to his home, placed in a foster home, or committed to a reform institution. It is the first phase with which we are most concerned in this appeal.

How is the presence or absence of guilt to be ascertained? In all civilized countries it is determined by following a certain organized procedure which assures to the accused an opportunity to assert his innocence, face his accusers, call witnesses in his behalf, obtain the services of counsel and be adjudged by an impartial tribunal. Nowhere in the world are the rights of an accused so jealously guarded as in the United States. The case before us, however, presents an amazing paradox in jurisprudence. This Court says, through a majority of the Justices, that certain constitutional and legal guarantees such as immunity against self-incrimination, prohibition of hearsay, interdiction of ex parte and secret reports, all so zealously upheld in decisions from Alabama to Wyoming, are to be jettisoned in Pennsylvania when the person at the bar of justice is a tender-aged boy or girl.

The Majority is of the impression that the adjudication of delinquency of a minor is not a very serious matter because "No suggestion or taint of criminality attaches to any finding of delinquency by a Juvenile Court." This statement stamps the judicial imprimatur on the declaration in Section 19 of the Juvenile Court Act that: "No order made by any juvenile court shall operate to impose any of the civil disabilities ordinarily imposed by the criminal laws of the Commonwealth, nor shall any child be deemed to be a criminal by reason of any such order or be deemed to have been convicted of crime." These words are put together so as to form beautiful language but unfortunately the charitable thought expressed therein does not square with the realities of life. To say that a graduate of a reform school is not to be "deemed a criminal" is very praiseworthy but this placid bromide commands no authority in the fiercely competitive fields of every-day modern life.

A most disturbing fallacy abides in the notion that a Juvenile Court record does its owner no harm. The grim truth is that a Juvenile Court record is a lengthening chain that its riveted possessor will drag after him through childhood, youthhood, adulthood and middle age. Even when the ill-starred child becomes an old man the record will be there to haunt, plague and torment him. It will be an ominous shadow following his tottering steps, it will stand by his bed at night and it will hover over him when he dozes fitfully in the dusk of his remaining day.

It is equally a delusion to say that a Juvenile Court record does not handicap because it cannot be used against the minor in any court. In point of fact it will be a witness against him in the court of business and commerce, it will be a bar sinister to him in the court of society where the penalties inflicted for deviation from conventional codes can be as ruinous as those imposed in any criminal court, it will be a sword of Damocles hanging over his head in public life, it will be a weapon to hold him at bay as he seeks respectable and honorable employment. It is easy to say that the record will not be used in Court but it already has been introduced in this case against Joseph Holmes in the imperishable dockets of several Courts, it has been printed in the briefs which the world can read, and it will be published in the decisions of the Superior and Supreme Court.

It would not be kind to name the many figures in the world of sports, politics, entertainment and letters who have been embarrassed, harassed and encumbered because of a Juvenile Court record. And when I see how the intended guardian angel of the Juvenile Court sometimes nods at the time that the most important question of all — innocence or guilt — is being considered, I wonder whether some of these public figures may not have been unjustly tainted in their childhood.

Reading and studying the whole record in this case, it seems to me that a very erroneous idea pervades the reasoning of the judges throughout, namely, that a Juvenile Court hearing is simply an administrative procedure because its purpose eventually is to provide education, care and supervision over the subject of its jurisdiction. But when the minor is charged with what, (as against an adult), would be a felony, and the minor denies the charge, the resulting proceeding can only be a judicial *contest* to determine conflicting facts and contentions; and, being such, it is a *trial* in every sense of the word. It was well said in Hedden v. Hand, 90 N.J.Eq. 583, 107 A. 285, 291, 5 A.L.R. 1463, that "It is idle to entertain the thought for a single moment that the Legislature can change the nature of an offense by changing the forum in which it is to be tried."

The Majority of this Court, as well as the Courts below, have spoken almost feelingly of the great care that the State bestows on a juvenile after he has been adjudged a delinquent, pointing out that the State henceforth regards him not as a criminal but as a ward. But fairness and justice certainly recognize that a child has the right *not* to be a ward of the State, *not* to be committed to a reformatory, *not* to be deprived of his liberty, if he is innocent. The procedure for ascertaining the guilt or innocence of a minor may be designated a hearing or a civil inquiry, as the Majority says, but in substance and form it is a trial — a momentous trial which means even more than one which confronts an adult, because in the Juvenile Court trial the defendant's whole mature life still lies before him. And no matter how trained and experienced a Juvenile Court judge may be, he cannot by any magical fishing rod draw forth the truth out of a confused sea of speculation, rumor, suspicion and hearsay. He must follow certain procedures which the wisdom of centuries have established.

Although I do not agree with the conclusions reached by the Superior Court in this case, it certainly has pronounced the law accurately in declaring that the proceeding in a Juvenile Court hearing "is an action in a court of record, the court must have jurisdiction, its basic findings *must be supported by evidence and the rudiments of procedural due process and fair play must be observed. The record must be legally and factually adequate to sustain the findings of fact and order of commitment.* * * * The action of the juvenile court is always subject to appellate review and *correction for errors of law or abuse of discretion.*" 157 Pa. Super. 137, 103 A. 2d 454, 459. (Italics throughout mine, unless otherwise indicated.)

The distinguished Court of Appeals of New York State stressed as far back as November, 1932, that proceedings in Juvenile Courts (called Children's Court in New York) cannot ignore constitutional safeguards:

"There must be a reasonably definite charge. *The customary rules of evidence shown by long experience as essential to getting at the truth with reasonable certainty in civil trials must be adhered to.* The finding of fact must rest on the preponderance of evidence adduced under those rules. *Hearsay, opinion,*

gossip, bias, prejudice, trends of hostile neighborhood feeling, the hopes and fears of social workers, are all sources of error and have no more place in Children's Courts than in any other court." People v. Lewis, 260 N.Y. 171, 178, 183 N.E. 353, 355, 86 A.L.R. 1001.

The same Court said in the case of People v. Fitzgerald, 244 N.Y. 307, 155 N.E. 584, 588:

"Our activities in behalf of the child may have been awakened, but the fundamental ideas of criminal procedure have not changed. These require a definite charge, a hearing, competent proof, and a judgment. *Anything less is arbitrary power.*"

The concept that in Juvenile Court the State acts as *parens patriae* is being somewhat overdone. Even if the State assumes the parental role, this assumption does not prove that, by divine omniscience, it cannot be other than just. It is not impossible for a father, or even a mother, to be unreasonable with offspring. What a child charged with crime is entitled to, is *justice*, not a *parens patriae* which in time may become a little calloused, partially cynical and somewhat over-condescending. The child may not want to be treated parens patriaely, parens patriarchally, or parens patronizingly.

The argument is advanced throughout these entire proceedings that the State entertains no desire to punish a juvenile and, for that reason, some relaxation in strict court procedure is justified and even commendable. But informality may be at times carried to the point of confusion, sloppiness and unreliability. The appellee Commonwealth categorically declares in its brief that "commitment to an industrial school is not punishment." But it certainly does not come under the classification of pleasure. Calling a reformatory an "industrial school" does not mitigate its bleakness, loneliness and destitution of parental love and care.

What is punishment? It is the infliction of pain, sorrow, and grief. To take a child from the comfort of his home, the joy of his companions and the freedom of field, river and wood, and confine him to a building with whitewashed walls, regimented routine and institutional hours is punishment in the strictest sense of the word. To say, as the Commonwealth says, that this institutionalized incarceration is "for the care and treatment" of the juvenile does not make it any less abhorrent to the boy of spirit, health and energy.

The Commonwealth argues further in its brief that many constitutional restrictions against prosecuting authorities in a trial of adults in the criminal courts do not apply in Juvenile Court because the proceedings there do not constitute a criminal trial. From this it is argued that in Juvenile Court proceedings the rules of evidence may be relaxed. To say that the rules of evidence may be relaxed in Juvenile Court is like saying that during a surgical operation on a child the surgeon may relax the rules of precise hygiene. Hygienic precautions in the operating room are taken to keep out microbes and germs of infection in the same way that rules of evidence in Court erect barriers to bar the microbes of lies, the germs of prejudice and the infection of rumor.

The proceedings before us for review involve three different hearings: January 6, January 23 and March 6, 1953. The Majority points out in its Opinion that at the first hearing, Joseph Holmes was charged with stealing an automobile, operating an automobile without the owner's consent and operating a car without a driver's license. The Majority concedes that there was no evidence which connected Holmes with larceny of an automobile. Joseph denied all knowledge of the theft but he was adjudged a delinquent on the charge of operating a motor vehicle without a license.

On January 23, 1953, Joseph Holmes came before the Court on the very serious charge of participation in the robbery of a church. The so-called evidence presented to establish his participation in this robbery is so devoid of every symptom of competence that were a District Attorney to attempt to produce this same kind of testimony against an adult defendant in Criminal Court, he would properly earn for himself the censure of the Court. At this Juvenile Court hearing on January 23rd a detective by the name of Ashmore was allowed to testify orally to an alleged confession by a third person who, he reported, charged Holmes with participation in the robbery. The detective did not produce the confession, he did not produce the confessor, and the defendant Holmes was not given an opportunity to face the stranger who had supposedly implicated him. The Majority, which would undoubtedly condemn such sham testimony if presented in

a Criminal Court, accepts it implicitly here because it is introduced against a child in Juvenile Court. The Majority goes further. It even pays a tribute to hearsay testimony and says that, unless objected to, it may be received as direct evidence. The statement that hearsay may be utilized to strike down a child charged with the most reprehensible of crimes — robbery of a church — is to me appalling.

Hearsay is merely a legal term for unconfirmed rumor. Pouring rumored scandal into the bent ear of blabbering busybodies in a pool room or gambling house is no more disreputable than pronouncing it with clipped accent in a courtroom. Hearsay is not dross in one proceeding and gold in another. It is a deceptive commodity which should not be accepted in any market of freedom except under the most unusual circumstances which certainly are not present here.

If someone actually made a confession implicating Joseph Holmes in the alleged robbery of a church, why was that person not brought into court? The sheer legal nullity of the hearing of January 23rd, insofar as it attached culpability to Joseph Holmes, could not be better shown than by the fact that the to-be-accused Holmes was not even informed beforehand that he was to be charged with armed robbery. This startling omission offends against the most elemental standards of the most primitive trials.

The record of the entire hearing of January 23rd is scarcely recognizable as a responsible proceeding in an American court and especially a tribunal involving the liberty of a young citizen. Detective Ashmore testified:

"In regard to these two boys here, Holmes and Richard Hodges, one of the boys that was arrested here had given a signed confession and they implicated these two boys."

Ashmore then proceeded, as I indicated above, to give an oral description of the statement supposedly signed by one Widman. The Court, instead of demanding the exhibition of the confession or, more imperatively, the appearance of Widman himself, listened to this fantastic hearsay and then asked: "What did Hodges and Holmes actually do in the holdup?" This question was not only improper but it revealed a most serious lack of appreciation on the part of the Court as to its judicial duties. Ashmore had no knowledge of his own as to what Hodges and Holmes had done, he did not know whether Hodges and Holmes had participated in the holdup, and was in fact personally ignorant of facts as to whether there even was a holdup. The Court, brushing all this incompetence aside, and accepting Ashmore's ignorance as knowledge, his non-presence as presence and his irresponsibility as reliability, questioned this bearer of twice-told tales as follows:

"What did Hodges and Holmes do in the holdup?"

And then, the only questions put to Joseph Holmes on the grave accusation against him of armed robbery were the following:

"By the Court (to Joseph Holmes)
"Q. What about it, Joseph? A. He came to my house and picked me up. I had nothing to do with it.
"Q. You were in on the robbery? A. No, I haven't been identified by anybody. Skeets said he's going to tell you I had nothing to do with it."

Ashmore was now permitted to testify to more heterogeneous hearsay and then the Court summed up: "I heard enough." On this "evidence," the Court stripped Joseph Holmes of his liberty, deprived him of his home and parental care, and committed him to the melancholy shadows of a corrective, juvenile reformatory.

In justification of this incredible procedure, the Majority, as above indicated, says that it is proper to receive hearsay when it is admitted without objection. What did Joseph Holmes know about objections? He is a minor. He had no lawyer to represent him. No one informed him as to his rights. He was not told he could object. A child in a courtroom amid a throng of police officers, probation officers, court attendants and other officials, with a judge officiating from a podium, is not apt to summon the brashness, even if he possessed the knowledge, to lift his voice and cry out that what a police officer testified to was hearsay, even if he knew what hearsay meant. Children are usually brought up with the admonition that "they are not to speak unless spoken to." To convict a child of crime because he does not object to what a judge should never have allowed to be heard in the first place is, in my opinion, an unfairness that sheds none of its

repellence because approved by an appellate court.

But there is something more extraordinary about this affair that I have already indicated. At the third hearing (the one on March 6, 1954), the heretofore-missing Widman came into Court and repudiated the confession in which it was alleged he had implicated Joseph Holmes. But on this important disclosure the Majority makes the amazing observation: "Of course the judge was not obliged to believe his (Widman's) retraction." It cannot be denied that the Judge was not compelled to believe Widman. He was not obliged to believe anything that might be presented in exoneration of charges against Holmes. That is the prerogative of a Judge, and he needs to answer only to his conscience. But if a Judge chooses to close his ears to the words of the actual robber, it is difficult to understand why he should accept as gospel the erratic narrative of a third-handed listener of a distantly-told tale. But if, as the Majority suggests, the Juvenile Court judge could disbelieve Widman's retraction, he then could only go back to the credibility-riddled narrative of Widman whose knowledge of the holdup was zero.

The Majority says that "there is nothing in the record to indicate that the judge who presided in the Juvenile Court acted in the final disposition of appellant's case on the basis of any conclusion that appellant had in fact participated in the armed robbery of the church." The record reports the following:

"By the Court (To Joseph Holmes):
"Q. Joseph, you have been before us too many times for me just to disregard this. Highway robbery in 1949, burglary in 1951, highway robbery in 1952, discharged from Pennypack House two months later, and *now this*. A. I had nothing to do with it.
"The Court: I am sending you to White Hill."

What did the Judge mean by "and now *this*"? He could only mean the robbery of the church because that was the *only* offense then under discussion. Moreover, his reference to highway robberies in 1949 and 1952 and a burglary in 1951 was not only gratuitous but unjustified. If the proof of participation in the past robberies and burglary was no stronger than that presented in connection with the church robbery one could well fear that Holmes has received little of the protection for minors for which Juvenile Courts were created. In point of fact, Joseph Holmes was never proved guilty of the crimes referred to. The Majority makes that admission at the very beginning of its Opinion, when it says:

"In 1949, when he was 13 years of age, he was adjudged delinquent by the Juvenile Division of the Municipal Court of Philadelphia on a petition *alleging* that he was involved in a highway robbery * * *. He was later *accused* of participation in a burglary, but that offense *was not proved* * * and, in August, 1952, being *charged* with participation in a highway robbery and assault and battery, he was committed to Pennypack House."

One could almost be embarrassed in stating the question to be decided in this case. Candidly put, it is nothing less than:

"Are children entitled to the protection of the Constitution of the United States and the Constitution of Pennsylvania?"

It is almost like asking: Should children be fed, clothed and sheltered? And yet, this question (that is, the first one) has been answered in the negative by the Majority of this Court. We have apparently reached such a state of inevitable disputation in the law that one wonders if anything can ever be pronounced with juridical finality. We may yet hear a challenging of the law of gravitation, the law of cause and effect, and the law governing the planets as they swing through infinity in their appointed orbits in the universe.

Article 1, § 9 of the Constitution of Pennsylvania states categorically:

"In all criminal prosecutions the accused hath a right to be heard by himself and his counsel, to *demand the nature and cause of the accusation against him, to meet the witnesses face to face*, to have compulsory process for obtaining witnesses in his favor, and, in prosecutions by indictment or information, a speedy public trial by an impartial jury of the vicinage; *he cannot be compelled to give evidence against himself, nor can he be deprived of his* life, *liberty* or property, *unless by* the judgment of his peers or *the law of the land*."

On January 23, 1954, Joseph Holmes' constitutional rights were invaded in that he was brought to trial without being informed of "the nature and cause of the accusation against him," he was not allowed to meet his accusing "witnesses face to face," and he was deprived of

his liberty beyond "the law of the land." The constitutional provision quoted does not restrict the enumerated ironclad guarantees therein to accused *adults*. It says *accused* without limitation of any kind. By what authority, then, do we exclude children from this vast reservation of protection?

If we were to accept the utterly illogical proposition that a child is better guarded by denying him the security of the above-mentioned constitutional guarantees, why shouldn't we then throw the same defensive armor around women who are invariably regarded as being less able to fend for themselves than men? And if the extravagant supposition is accepted that children and women are in a superior position of vantage *outside* the Constitution, why not turn out of the State's tabernacle of inalienable rights the crippled, the mutilated, the aged and the blind? Certainly they are entitled to the same privileges which go to helpless children and women.

The Juvenile Court jurisdiction was originally limited to children up to the age of 16 years; it has now been extended to minors under 18 years of age. The interesting development then presents itself that if, instead of being tried on January 23, 1953, Holmes had been brought into court on May 7, 1954, (his 18th birthday), he would have been entitled to a jury trial. At a jury trial the Commonwealth could not possibly have sustained a conviction with the shamefully inadequate and incompetent so-called evidence presented in Juvenile Court on January 23rd. And with this irrefutable proposition before us, how can we accept the adjudication of delinquency in Juvenile Court when the evidence supporting it would have acquitted Holmes in Criminal Court? Is the good name of a citizen, to say nothing of his liberty, to depend on whether he is brought to trial sixteen months sooner or later?

The Majority contends that since "Juvenile Courts are not criminal courts, the constitutional rights granted to persons accused of *crime* are not applicable to children brought before them."[5]

What the Majority says here is that the protection assured the most penitentiary-hard-

---

[5] The Majority italicizes *crime* in its Opinion. Is armed robbery not a crime? Is it less a crime because allegedly committed by a minor?

ened adult criminal cannot be offered to children. Aside from the inhumanity embodied in such an observation it is subject to criticism for other reasons. In the first place, it is not true, for instance, that the constitutional immunity against self-incrimination is limited to Criminal Court trials. This immunity applies anywhere and everywhere; it applies to any proceeding which can conceivably end in a criminal prosecution. Practically every day the Fifth Amendment of the United States Constitution (in this respect the counterpart of Art. I. § 9 of the Pennsylvania Constitution) is invoked before legislative committees which are certainly not branches of a Criminal Court. The immunity against self-incrimination may be invoked in the civil law courts and equity courts if one is asked a question the answer to which may become a link leading to involvement in criminal prosecution. The immunity can be used as a barrier against being questioned in a Magistrate's court or before a Justice of the Peace. It can be employed anywhere except, according to the Majority, where it should, in all fairness, receive the highest sanction — in Juvenile Court. This Constitutional immunity is obviously intended to help those unjustly accused of wrongdoing. If then, it is handed to adults as a shield, why should it become a sword when the person accused is a child?

The Juvenile Court Act provides that if a minor is held for any offense (except murder) punishable by imprisonment in a state penitentiary, the Judge of the Juvenile Court may certify the case to the District Attorney. Although the Majority asserts that the minor is entitled to protection, it still will not make the bold statement that any self-incriminating evidence obtained from a child while still in Juvenile Court may not be used against him in any subsequent criminal proceedings. The farthest the Majority will go in guarding the interests of a child from whom self-incriminating evidence has been wrung, is to say that after a self-incriminating examination, a child's case "perhaps" should not be sent to the Criminal Court. "*Perhaps*" is a slender thread on which to suspend the constitutional rights of children obtained by their fathers and forefathers through hardship and sacrifice, not excluding the shedding of blood on the battlefields of the nation's wars. The District Attorney in his

able brief meets this situation quite objectively, and very candidly says:

"It may be that after questioning a child concerning his participation in a crime, the nature of the answers of the child may convince the Juvenile Court judge that the interest of the state require the prosecution of the case on an indictment. If the Juvenile Court judge uses these answers for this purpose, and certifies the case over to the District Attorney, then *there can be no question but that the child was required to incriminate himself, since the effect of his answers directly placed him in jeopardy of criminal prosecution.*"

The 14th Amendment to the Constitution of the United States guarantees to all citizens of the United States due process of law. No State law can abrogate this guarantee. It needs no citation of authority to establish that, included within due process of law, are the right to face one's accuser, to summon witnesses in one's defense, the immunity of self-incrimination, and to employ counsel. Leaving aside the question of a jury trial which this Court held, in the case of Commonwealth v. Fisher, 213 Pa. 48, 62 A. 198, was not required in Juvenile Court procedure, there is nothing in the Juvenile Court Act which deprives minors of the constitutional safeguards above indicated.

Armed robbery is a crime. The Legislature may not, by changing the name of armed robbery to "juvenile delinquency," strip from any citizen the constitutional guarantees which are his when he is tried for armed robbery. If the Legislature may, by a mere change in terminology, take away from a 17-year old boy the safeguards which the parent law of the land assures to him, then it can take it away from 18-year old boys and 25-year old men. Who is to decide the dividing line? I do not believe that the Pennsylvania Legislature ever planned by the Juvenile Court Act to make it easier to convict boys than to convict men. I cannot bring myself to accepting the self-revolting idea that the Legislature intended that children should be deprived of their liberty on evidence that would walk their grown-up elders triumphantly out of Criminal Court. If there is anything in the Juvenile Court Act which by fair interpretation sanctions this unconscionable thing, I must say that such an un-American proposition is unconstitutional and I would, therefore, declare it null and void. The scholarly jurist, Judge Crane of New York, in the case of

People v. Fitzgerald, 244 N.Y. 307, 155 N.E. 584, 587, spoke wisely, bravely and well when he said:

"Where, therefore, a child is arrested and charged with being a delinquent child because it has committed an offense which would be a crime in an adult, *that offense must be proved, and proved by competent evidence.*"

The Children's Bureau of the U. S. Department of Health, Education, and Welfare, in cooperation with the National Probation and Parole Association and the *National Council of Juvenile Court Judges*, has said in an authoritative pamphlet entitled, "Specialized Courts Dealing with Children," that:

"Rules of evidence calculated to assure proceedings in accordance with due process of law should be applicable to children's cases." (p. 7) Also:
"A juvenile court hearing is sometimes spoken of as 'informal.' Informality should not, however, mean that the court ceases to be a court or becomes merely a conference in the judge's chambers. *Still less should it mean that the court ignores rules of evidence or fails to establish procedures for its actions."* (p. 54)

No attorney appeared on the side of Joseph Holmes until the hearing (the third) of March 6, 1953. This attorney challenged, as he stated in his brief,

" * * * the right of the Court to determine delinquency and commit to White Hill in the absence of evidence that appellant's parents had been notified of or had attended the prior hearings or that the parents were unable or unwilling to afford the required and requisite care and in the absence of admissible evidence in support of all but a minor alleged act of delinquency, operating an automobile without a license, and finally, any and all other reasons which might be assigned after an inspection of the record, which had been denied."

All these objections were overruled by the lower court. Taking up the question of the parents' participation or non-participation in the Juvenile Court proceedings the Majority says that "The parents of a child involved in a Juvenile Court proceeding should certainly be notified in regard to what ought to be to them a matter of supreme importance," but it then goes on to say that: "Appellant's repeated derelictions are proof positive of the fact either that his parents were indifferent to his bad behavior

or were unable to control him." The majority's conclusions in this respect can scarcely be placed in the catalogue of impeccable logic. The absolute lack of trustworthy evidence to establish that Joseph Holmes ever committed robbery, burglary or any other serious crime, is now used to show that his parents were indifferent or unable to control him. If Joseph is a bad boy, this should not be reason for charging his parents with indifference. Court records do not carry the cardiograph tracings of the heartache of parents. And if Joseph is as bad as the Majority says he is, is the Juvenile Court, acting as *parens patriae*, to be charged with inability "to control him"?

In taking up the defense attorney's complaint that he was denied the opportunity to examine all the Juvenile Court records on Joseph Holmes, the Majority launches an encomium on out-of-court reports obtained for the purpose of helping judges to impose the proper kind of sentence. No one doubts the helpfulness of reports of this character. But the question here is: Why wasn't defense counsel allowed to see those reports? Information, data and memoranda obtained *ex parte* do not always represent the apogee of neutrality. Where is the person who by himself or through some relative has not at some time displeased a neighbor or crossed words with a business, scholastic or occupational superior or associate? Reports obtained at residential back doors or in outer business offices without the presence of an impartial referee or the adverse party in interest are always in danger of carrying prejudicial slants resulting from the aroma of feuds which have long smoldered in the dustbin of self-pitying memory or in the hothouse of imaginative hurts. For a judge to sentence on these secret reports without allowing the defendant's attorney to even see them for possible correction or explanation is to impose a sentence based on the utterances of phantoms. Our American traditions of fairness have always rebelled at secret reports, hearings or recommendations. The District Attorney well states this objective situation in his brief as follows:

"A sound and thorough inquiry into the needs of the child as well as the state would seem to require scrutiny by the child's counsel of the materials to be used by the court in the determination of ultimate disposition. Although at times information will be contained in the probation reports which for the child's sake should not be revealed to him, *trust will have to be placed in counsel* and officer of the court, not to betray the court's confidence or the welfare of the child * * *. Under our system of jurisprudence, *concealment of facts has never been recognized as an aid to justice."*

I have unstinted admiration for the Juvenile Court system. It has undoubtedly saved countless children from a life of crime. Under no circumstances must we ever go back to the archaic and cruel system which mingled children with hardened and coarse offenders in both the criminal courts and in the jails. I cannot help but express astonishment at the Majority's statement that the old English law was ever ready to make needy children wards of the State. Instead of citing the case of Shelley's children, I would refer to the writings of Charles Dickens (particularly Oliver Twist) in which the sheer brutality in the treatment of unfortunate children makes one truly wonder at the contents of the hearts of both judges and civil administrators in the "good old days."

The law has come a long way in its consideration of the welfare of children since the days of Oliver Twist, but that does not mean that perfection has been attained. In its laudable zeal to care for unfortunate children, the State must not become a universal mother. Loving parents in a house with the porch creaking and the paint cracking can still offer more happiness and guidance to children than the most highly trained reformatory superintendent. Before the State can take a child from its parents, it must be determined that he comes within the provisions of the statute enacted by representatives of the people for waifs, misguided minors and tattered children caught between the millstones of economic calamity. The filing of a delinquency petition does not of itself prove that the named minor needs or must have a *parens patriae.* A love of adventure, a careless weighing of possibilities, a mingling with strange playfellows can take an enthusiastic lad into a scrape and a confusion of circumstances which convey the appearance of a culpability not necessarily justified by the true facts. Hence, the imperative need for an inquiry which is organized, scientific and trustworthy, that is to say, a trial with all the safeguards which the centuries have proved to be essential in the business of finding the precious gem of truth.

The country today is plagued with consider-

able juvenile delinquency. The least effective way to solve that problem is to indiscriminately punish the guilty and the innocent. To charge a juvenile with armed robbery and then send him to a reformatory without legal proof that he has committed that heinous crime is to embitter not only him but all his companions who will feel that they no longer owe any loyalty to an unjust society.

The record of this case does not show that Joseph Holmes committed offenses which would justify the drastic treatment to which he has been subjected. The record clearly demonstrates that he was denied the due process of law which is the heritage of every American, regardless of age, color, sex or national derivation.

I would therefore require a re-hearing on all alleged offenses not constitutionally and legally proved.

78

State *v.* Christensen *

WOLFE, Chief Justice.

This is an appeal from a decree of the Juvenile Court in and for Sanpete County committing Lynn Lueorn Christensen to the State Industrial School, the court having previously adjudged him a delinquent child.

On February 21, 1950, Lynn, then a boy of fourteen years of age, appeared before the court below in a hearing on a petition alleging his delinquency. Specifically, it was alleged that he had entered a dressing room in the gymnasium of the Snow College in Ephraim and unlawfully taken money from the clothing of others and that he had unlawfully made a house-to-house canvass for funds which were purported to be for a school party. In addition, at that hearing one Calvin Kempf, a probation officer, reported to the court that he had found that Lynn had been molesting girls of the elementary grades and that he had attempted to take indecent liberties with a three-

---

* *State* v. *Christensen,* Supreme Court of Utah, 1951, 119 Utah 361, 227 P. 2d 760.

year-old girl. At the conclusion of the hearing, the court adjudged Lynn a delinquent child and ordered him committed to the State Industrial School until he reached the age of twenty-one or was sooner discharged. However, execution of the order of commitment was suspended until May 15, 1950 at which time the conduct of Lynn was to be reviewed. He was placed on probation under the supervision of Mr. Kempf, the probation officer, and Lynn's uncle, Ruel Christensen.

Subsequently, on May 11, 1950, Mr. Kempf petitioned the court for a rehearing of the case for a modification of its order. He alleged that Lynn had violated the order of probation in that he "did on May 10, 1950, and on several other occasions, steal a bicycle belonging to Beth Stewart of Ephraim, Utah; that he did damage the tires and the seat of said bicycle; that he had the bicycle without permission of Beth Stewart and her family; that during the past few weeks on several occasions, said child did unlawfully enter class rooms in the Jr. High School, even after being advised not to enter, said rooms were not school rooms in which said child has classes; that he has unlawfully on different occasions during the past few weeks, entered the girls dressing room unlawfully and that he has also on different occasions made indecent advances toward girls in the First, Second and Third Grade of Elementary School; that the above actions are similar to those of which said child has been accused during the past year and said child has been warned against continuing such action." At the hearing on the petition for rehearing and modification held on June 1, 1950, Lynn denied the commission of any of the acts with which he was charged in violation of the order of probation. The court found that he had violated his probation and ordered him committed to the State Industrial School.

It is urged by the appellant that it is error to commit a child to the State Industrial School simply because he has defective vision which retards his progress in school. Were that the reason for Lynn's commitment, we would have no difficulty in reversing it. However, Lynn's vision was at no time made an issue in the case and he was not committed because of poor vision. It appears that on April 15, 1950, while Lynn was on probation, he was taken to the State Training School by his father for a phys-

ical and psychological examination. Thereafter, Dr. H. H. Ramsey, superintendent of the Training School, in a letter addressed to the judge of the juvenile court, reported the results of the examinations given Lynn. Dr. Ramsey stated that the physical examination disclosed that Lynn was a healthy youth with no deformities, defects, or illness apparent and that "the only probable defect which I found was with reference to his vision which apparently has been corrected by glasses." This is the only reference in the evidence to Lynn's vision. No mention is made by the court in its findings of fact of Lynn's vision. It is clear that the court did not in any wise place its order of commitment upon that ground.

The court did not err in failing to place under oath, certain of the children who testified at the hearing on June 1st as to Lynn's deportment. At one point in the course of the hearing, counsel for the appellant asked the court: "Isn't the Court swearing these young witnesses?" The court replied: "Because of the young age, the Court feels they do not appreciate the meaning of an oath, but are of an age where they will state facts as they know them. For this reason, the other witnesses were not sworn. If you wish your witness sworn, the court will do so." Under the broad discretion given the juvenile courts of this state in regard to the manner and form of procedure to be followed in conducting hearings to inquire into the alleged delinquency of children, the court may, if it deems it advisable, allow children to testify without being sworn. In this regard, Sec. 14–7–25, Utah Code Annotated, 1943, provides, so far as is applicable here: "In all cases relating to the delinquency, neglect, dependency or other cases of children and their disposition the court shall be regarded as exercising equity jurisdiction. The court may conduct the hearing in an informal manner and may adopt any form of procedure in such cases which it deems best suited to ascertain the facts relating to such cases and to make a disposition in the best interests of such children and of the public. * * * The court may hear evidence in the absence of such children, and may compel children to testify concerning the facts alleged in the petition. * * * "

The appellant further assigns as error the admission into evidence of two letters sent to the judge of the court below, on the ground that the letters contained hearsay statements. One of these letters was written by Leland E. Anderson, Superintendent of the South Sanpete School District in which he reported the results of "Progressive Achievement Tests" given to Lynn. The other letter to which the appellant objects is the letter from Dr. Ramsey, heretofore mentioned, in which the results of a physical and psychological examination given Lynn are reported to the court. Section 14–7–25, U.C.A.1943, provides, in part, that: "The court shall inquire into the home environment, history, associations and general condition of such children, may order physical and mental examinations to be made by competent physicians, psychologists and psychiatrists, and may receive in evidence the *verified reports* of probation officers, physicians, psychologists or psychiatrists concerning such matters. . . ." The letter from Superintendent Anderson was verified but the letter from Dr. Ramsey contained no verification. While technically the court erred in admitting in evidence the letter from Dr. Ramsey because it did not comply with the above statute in regard to verification, counsel had not pointed out nor are we able to see how Lynn was prejudiced thereby. The letter from Dr. Ramsey reported that his examination of Lynn disclosed that he was in good physical condition, but that he was retarded mentally. As to Lynn's mental ability, the letter reported nothing that was not contained in the letter from Superintendent Anderson which was clearly admissible.*

It was not necessary, as contended by the appellant, that as a condition precedent to committing Lynn to the State Industrial School, the court should have found that Lynn's parents were unfit to have custody of him. As pointed out in the case of In re State, in Interest of Bennett . . . [page 477.—Ed.] 966, prior to 1919 the statutes of this state required a finding of unfitness of the parents before a child could be committed to the State Industrial School. However, in 1919 the legislature of this state repealed that requirement and since that time a child may be committed although his parents are fit to have his custody. In commenting on the amendment of 1919, this court in the Bennett case said: "It may well be that parents are generally fit to have

the custody of their children, and yet they may be unable to prevent one or more of their children from committing acts of delinquency and thus from becoming criminals and a menace to society. When it is made to appear that a parent or parents of a child know that said child is committing acts of delinquency and that they are unable to control such child and prevent him from further wrongdoing, the interest of the child as well as the protection of society may well demand that the parents surrender their custody of their child to the state so that, if possible, the child's evil tendency may be corrected and society protected. If, therefore, the parents, parent, custodian, or guardian of a delinquent juvenile are or is otherwise fit to have the control and custody of the juvenile, but cannot prevent him from wrongdoing, then and in such case the juvenile court may commit such juvenile to the industrial school when the best interests of the juvenile or the protection of society demand such commitment."

Section 14–7–31, U.C.A.1943, while giving parents a preferred right to custody of their children does not make a finding of unfitness of the parents a condition precedent to the commitment of a child to the State Industrial School. The lower court did find, however, that Lynn "is in need of specialized, supervised, treatment, and that from the experience of said child while on probation, he is not able to get such help in his home or in the community; it is therefore to the best interests and welfare of said child that he be committed to the State Industrial School until he reaches the age of twenty-one (21) or is sooner discharged by due process of law."

As a further ground for reversal, the appellant contends that the court erred in admitting in evidence testimony as to matters which were not embraced within the allegations of the petition for rehearing of the case and modification of the court's order. Assuming that the admission of such testimony was erroneous because it was outside of the allegations of the petition charging Lynn with violating the order of probation, the appellant cannot complain of that error on appeal because he failed to object to the admission of such testimony at the hearing. There is no error. Judgment affirmed.

WADE, LATIMER, McDONOUGH and CROCKETT, JJ., concur.

* *Cf. In re Smith*, ——— Okla. Cr, ———, 326 P2d 835 (1958).—*Ed.*

79

State *ex rel.* Shaw *v.* Breon *

MULRONEY, Chief Justice.

This is a juvenile case commenced upon the petition of Emma A. Shaw alleging under oath "that Frank Breon under the age of 18 years * * * is a delinquent child, for that the said Frank Breon as * * * petitioner is informed and believes is growing up in idleness and crime, contrary to the statutes of the State of Iowa, in such cases made and provided, and against the peace and welfare of the State of Iowa." The petition states the said Frank Breon was in the custody of his mother Myrtle Breon and notice was served upon her to the filing of the petition and that a hearing would be had thereon on September 15, 1951. It appears the father is in the state hospital for the insane at Mount Pleasant and the acting superintendent of that institution accepted service of the notice and attached petition but in his acceptance stated personal service of the same on the father would injuriously affect him.

Hearing was had before the court on September 15, 1951 without a court reporter. The petitioner was represented by the county attorney but defendant was not represented by counsel at this hearing. The judge's notes, made at the time of this hearing, state: "Defendant present in Court. Notice served on mother personally, and service accepted for father by Superintendent of Mt. Pleasant Hospital for Insane. Hearing proceeds. Evidence heard. The Court finds the defendant is a delinquent boy of the age of fifteen years and has been guilty of assaulting women. It is ordered that he be committed to the Industrial School for Boys at Eldora, Iowa as by law provided."

A few days later at the request of counsel then appearing for Frank Breon the court ordered the case "reopened and reheard on its merits." Hearings were then had on September 22nd and September 29, 1951 at which hearings witnesses testified and the court re-

porter reported all that transpired and all of the evidence at these hearings. At the conclusion of the hearing on September 29th, after both parties had rested, the court stated that he did not care to hear any arguments by counsel; that it was "quite clearly established this boy has been guilty, not only of drinking, but going into a place where he wasn't known and assaulting a woman apparently with intent to commit rape." Thereupon the court entered an order finding the boy "a delinquent child under the age of sixteen years and guilty of assaulting a woman with intent to commit rape" and ordering him "committed to the Industrial School for Boys at Eldora, Iowa as by law provided." Defendant appeals.

The evidence introduced by plaintiff shows the boy's actions on a single day, to wit, August 31, 1951. Frank, who was then 15 years old, had been working for a construction firm for about a week. There he had met another construction worker named Everett Scarlett who lived with his uncle, William Shaw, in the latter's apartment. Frank and Everett got off work about noon on Friday, August 31st and they bought six cans of beer and went down to the river bank and each drank three cans. Later that afternoon they bought eight more cans of beer and after drinking four they went to the Shaw apartment. Mrs. Shaw, her married daughter, and the daughter's year-old baby were in the apartment. Shortly thereafter Everett and Mrs. Shaw's married daughter left the apartment and went to a neighboring beer parlor. Frank asked if he could go with them but Everett told him to wait until they returned. Mrs. Shaw testified that while she and Frank were alone in the apartment, Frank seized her and attempted to have sexual intercourse with her. She testified at length as to her struggle with Frank and her screams for help and then said she managed to throw Frank behind the bed and escape and call the police. There is testimony that Frank was drunk or sick from the beer. He denied Mrs. Shaw's story about his attempted assault. He said he lay down on the bed and went to sleep. He was lying face down on the bed when the officers came. They said he wasn't asleep but he appeared "groggy, dopey." The barber who operates his shop under Mrs. Shaw's apartment heard no screams or any special noise in the apartment above him that afternoon. He said

---

* *State* ex rel. *Shaw* v. *Breon*, Supreme Court of Iowa, 1952, 244 Iowa 49, 55 N.W. 2d 565.

that generally he could hear noises in the apartment such as the crying of the baby.

There is no testimony showing Frank had ever before violated any law or in fact been guilty of any misconduct. Several witnesses who had known him all his life or for many years testified as to his prior good conduct. They said he was "always nice"; that he had "always been a fine boy." They described him as being "courteous" and very "pleasant to deal with." A grocer who had known him since he was born, and who had employed him in his store on Saturdays and evenings for most of the prior two-year period described him as "an awful good boy." Another neighbor for whom he did odd jobs described him as "eager to work." His teacher during the school year 1950–1951 described Frank as a "trustworthy boy." The teacher also said his intelligence test showed him to be average. Not a witness had ever heard him use bad or obscene language and none of them had ever heard of his being in any kind of trouble before.

As previously stated, the broad charge against Frank was that he was a "delinquent child." Section 232.3, Code 1950, I.C.A., states "the term 'delinquent child' means any child: 1. Who habitually violates any law of this state, or any town or city ordinance. 2. Who is incorrigible. 3. Who knowingly associates with thieves, or vicious or immoral persons. 4. Who is growing up in idleness or crime. 5. Who knowingly frequents a house of ill fame. 6. Who patronizes any policy shop or place where any gaming device is located. 7. Who habitually wanders about any railroad yards or tracks, gets upon any moving train, or enters any car or engine without lawful authority."

The petition narrowed the charge to No. 4 in that it alleged he was a delinquent child because he was growing up in idleness and crime. It can hardly be argued this record established the special charge made. As to the charge of idleness the record shows quite the contrary. And the phrase "growing up in crime" must be descriptive of a status or tendency toward crime. Evidence tending to establish a single violation of law would fall far short of showing an infant's growth in the direction of crime. Kahm v. People, 83 Colo. 300, 264 P. 718.

Under our early statutes the only commitments of children to the training schools were commitments of children charged with any crime except murder and found guilty. Section 2708, Code 1897. The statute gave the court discretion to order the child to the industrial school instead of entering the judgment of conviction. In 1904 the Thirtieth General Assembly enlarged the powers of the district court and authorized the commitment of children who were "delinquent." Chapter 11, Acts of the 30th G.A. This later act in section 2 defined the term "delinquent child" much as it appears today under section 232.3, previously quoted, except that No. 1 did not have the word "habitually" in it. The word "habitually" was added to No. 1 in the definition in 1924 by H.F. 84, section 352, Acts of the 40th Ex. G.A. (unpublished).

When the district court's power to commit children to the industrial schools was enlarged to include delinquents in 1904 as above noted, the statutes retained the provisions authorizing such commitments instead of judgments of conviction for children who were found guilty of crimes except those found guilty of crimes punishable by death or life imprisonment. Acts 30th G.A., Chap. 11, § 5 et seq., § 232.20, Code 1950, I.C.A. In 1924 when as previously pointed out, the legislature added the word "habitually" to No. 1 in its list of definitions of a delinquent in connection with violating laws or ordinances, it also gave the court discretion as to the course the proceeding against the child was to take. Section 365 of H.F. 84, Acts of the 40th G.A. (unpublished) added what is now Section 232.16, Code 1950, I.C.A. It gives the court discretion "In any case after an investigation of the facts and circumstances * * * cause the child to be charged" with an indictable or non-indictable offense. If the charge is an indictable offense the court is to hold a preliminary hearing and exercise the power of a magistrate. If the offense charged is not triable on indictment, the court proceeds to try the case before a jury of twelve. . . .

Where there is a charge of crime and a conviction of the child by plea of guilt or jury verdict the court may (if the punishment be not imprisonment for life, or death) instead of entering judgment of conviction, commit the child to the training school. Section 232.20, Code 1950, I.C.A. When there is a petition filed charging that the child is a delinquent, the court may, after an investigation, cause the charge to be changed to a charge of a specific crime. Section 232.16, Code 1950, I.C.A. If the charge is not changed and the matter proceeds to hearing on the petition charging the child is a delinquent the court may, if he finds the child is a delinquent as defined in section 232.3, Code 1950, I.C.A. previously quoted, commit the child to the training school.

The trial court is given discretion as to whether he shall cause the child to be charged with an offense or not. Section 232.16, Code 1950, I.C.A. But this does not mean the child can be tried for the offense without the charge. The discretion which the trial court must exercise is a choice of issues to be presented for trial. If the issue is to be the child's guilt or innocence of a certain offense the charge of that offense must be made and the case must proceed as other criminal prosecutions to the point where the child is found guilty or not guilty. If the issue is to be whether the child is delinquent as defined in Section 232.3, Code 1950, I.C.A. the court may proceed to try the case on the delinquency petition. The court is given no discretion to try and determine a criminal charge on a delinquency petition. We think the court would have discretion if the investigation shows both delinquency and probable commission of a crime, as to whether the cause should proceed on the delinquency petition or a charge of crime ordered. But if the investigation does not indicate delinquency as defined by statute but does show the probable commission of a crime the charge of commission of the crime must be made. If the child pleads guilty he can be sent forthwith to the training school without the entry of the judgment of conviction. If the child pleads not guilty no commitment to the training school can be made until a jury finds him guilty.

When we apply the above law to this case it is perfectly apparent the plaintiff sought to establish the alleged delinquency by proof of a specific crime. It is also apparent the boy was pleading not guilty to the crime. Upon plaintiff's uncorroborated testimony that Frank assaulted her with intent to commit rape, the trial court makes a finding that Frank is "guilty of assaulting a woman with intent to commit rape." He was entitled to a jury trial on that issue. There was not the slightest attempt on the part of plaintiff to establish that Frank was a delinquent child within any of the seven

definitions listed in section 232.3, Code 1950, I.C.A. All of plaintiff's evidence was directed toward establishing the assault, which Frank was denying. The police officers took him into custody on plaintiff's complaint of the alleged assault. While the charge of delinquency was made plaintiff proceeded as if the charge of assault with intent to commit rape had been made. The petition charging delinquency should only be made when there is no charge of specific crime. The delinquency statutes permit the administration of corrective and reformatory measures in a proper case *before the child commits a crime or at least without any charge of specific crime.* They were not designed as a substitute for a charge of a specific crime nor were they intended to deprive the child of his constitutional right to a jury trial when the only issue presented is whether the child did or did not commit a specific crime. The issue of Frank's guilt or innocence of the crime of assaulting Mrs. Shaw was not tendered by the delinquency petition. The trial court's finding of guilty of assault with intent to commit rape cannot be sustained. And his judgment of delinquency, so patently based on his finding that Frank was guilty of assaulting Mrs. Shaw with intent to rape, is reversed. . . .

All Justices concur.†

80

In re Mantell *

YEAGER, Justice.

The action out of which the proceeding for review here grew was one wherein Lawrence C. Krell filed a petition in the district court for Douglas County, Nebraska, juvenile division, charging that Anthony Mantell, a minor under the age of 18 years, was a delinquent, had

---

† Cf. *In re Glassbery,* 230 La. 396, 88 So. 2d 707 (1956), where judgment of delinquency was set aside because proof was not sufficient to support crime charged in petition although it could sustain a lesser offense. — *Ed.*

* *In re Mantell,* Supreme Court of Nebraska, 1954, 157 Neb. 900, 62 N. W. 2d 308.

been associating with vicious and immoral people, and that he had been guilty of immoral conduct.

In due form of law Mantell was brought before the court and a hearing was had at the conclusion of which the court found that the charges of delinquency against him were true; that he was a fit subject for commitment to the Boys' Training School at Kearney, Nebraska, and the care and custody of the Board of Control of the State of Nebraska; and accordingly committed him until he should arrive at the age of 21 years unless he was sooner paroled or otherwise disposed of according to law.

Mantell has brought this finding and judgment to this court for review by appeal. In the brief on appeal Lawrence C. Krell is designated as complainant and Anthony Mantell as defendant. These designations will be used for the further purposes of this opinion.

On the lodgment of the case here the complainant filed a motion for dismissal on the ground that this court is without jurisdiction to review the action of the district court on appeal. He contends this court has jurisdiction to review in a case such as this only on writ of error.

This question requires first consideration herein and upon the determination depends the question of whether or not the errors assigned by the defendant require consideration.

In support of his contention complainant relies on section 83–471, R.R.S.1943, as follows: "The proceedings before any county court or a justice of the peace may be reviewed on writ of error by the district court in the manner provided by law for reviewing criminal cases. Proceedings before any district court or judge thereof may be reviewed by the Supreme Court in the manner provided by law for reviewing criminal cases." This is a provision of what is commonly referred to as the State Industrial School Act.

The defendant has not briefed this question but we do not assume from this that the point is conceded. In this light it has been necessary to examine this provision together with its history and other related statutory provisions.

In 1879, by act of the Legislature, the Nebraska State Reform School for Juvenile Offenders came into existence. Laws 1879, p. 413. The act contained provisions relating to the commitment of children under the age of

16 years to the Reform School and the care of such children. It also contained procedural provisions which imposed duties upon courts in the treatment of such children. Nothing further need be said in this regard except that the act did not contain any provision relating to review of action in a legal proceeding.

This act was amended by chapter 74, Laws 1887. Section 10 of the act as amended contained the following: "The proceedings before any judge or the county court may be reviewed on writ of error by the district court, and proceedings before any district court or judge thereof may be reviewed by the supreme court in the manner provided by law for reviewing criminal cases in these courts." This language was carried into section 4180, Comp. St. 1899.

By chapter 51, Laws 1901, the name of the institution was changed to "State Industrial School." In the amended act the provision for appeal was carried forward without change. This same language was carried into the revision of 1913. Section 7378, Rev.St.1913. Likewise it was carried into the compilation of 1922. Section 7037, Comp.St.1922. Also it was carried into the compilation of 1929. Section 83–1108, Comp.St.1929.

The provision has never been repealed and it has never been specifically amended. It however has been revised and its substance came into the revision of 1943 as it now appears as section 83–471, R.R.S.1943.

It becomes clear that the review procedure in case of commitment of minors to the State Industrial School provided by the Industrial School Act has remained in all substantial respects the same since 1887.

Prior to 1887 it was clearly contemplated that a minor could not be committed except on conviction of a criminal offense. In 1887 power was granted for commitment not only on the basis of the conviction of a criminal offense but also in the case of a finding that a child was growing up in mendicancy and vagrancy, or was incorrigible. Laws 1887, c. 74, § 5, p. 592.

The provisions of the act of 1887 in this respect remained substantially the same until 1943. By the revision of 1943 the substance of the section was set forth in two sections. The first (section 83–465, R.R.S.1943) provides for commitment for conviction of a crime, except murder or manslaughter, in a court of record. The second (section 83–466, R.R.S. 1943) provides for commitment where it is found that a child is growing up in mendicancy or crime because of want of parental care or other cause.

There can be no doubt that in each instance where there has been a conviction in the district court of crime within the meaning of section 83–465, R.R.S.1943, or a finding that a child is growing up in mendicancy or crime within the meaning of section 83–466, R.R.S. 1943, and a commitment, and review is sought in this court, proceeding for review is provided by section 83–471, R.R.S.1943, that is in the manner provided by law for reviewing criminal cases. The method for review of all criminal cases by the Supreme Court is upon writ of error. Section 29–2306, R.S.Supp.,1951.

In the year 1905 the Legislature enacted what is commonly referred to as the Juvenile Court Act. Laws 1905, c. 59, p. 305. This was an entirely new body of law, the primary design of which was to set up administrative and judicial procedure for the care, control, protection, and correction of children who because of neglect or other circumstances, or individual propensities, needed attention. The act designated classifications or categories with general definitions within the general purview. One of the classifications was designated as "delinquent child." This is the classification which is of concern here.

The act made provision for the filing of complaint charging delinquency and it made provision, among other provisions, for, in case of finding of delinquency by the juvenile court, commitment in what is now the State Industrial School.

It was agreeable to this act in its present form Chapter 43, article 2, R.R.S.1943, that the defendant herein was complained against and after hearing committed to the State Industrial School.

The Juvenile Court Act contains no provision for review of a hearing had in the district court.

By the terms of section 25–1912, R.R.S. 1943, which is a provision of the Code of Civil Procedure, it is provided that the proceeding for review of judgments, decrees, or final orders of the district court shall be by appeal, except in case of judgments and sentences upon con-

victions for felonies and misdemeanors under the criminal code.

The proceeding here is not one under the criminal code and the complaint against the defendant is not a charge of felony or misdemeanor. It is a charge of delinquency under the Juvenile Court Act. Whether or not it is in the true sense a civil action we do not need to decide. It was clearly the intention of the Legislature to permit review on appeal in all cases not specifically excepted. Actions such as this are not excepted.

The intention of the Legislature in this respect being clear we hold that this action has come here properly by appeal. See Laurie v. State, 108 Neb. 239, 188 N.W. 110.

In the light of this conclusion it becomes necessary to examine the assignments of error urged as grounds of reversal.

The first assignment is that the court erred in admitting the unsworn hearsay testimony of the witnesses for the complainant over the objection of the defendant.

The assignment correctly reflects factually that which occurred at the hearing on which the defendant was committed as is disclosed by the bill of exceptions.

The case came on for hearing and at its commencement the following transpired: "Mr. Krell: This is a delinquency petition concerning Anthony Mantell, who is fifteen years old. Mr. Schrempp: Excuse me — Is there an arraignment here?" Mr. Schrempp was then and is now attorney for the defendant. "The Court: No. Just sit down and listen. Mr. Schrempp: Let the record show Warren C. Schrempp has been employed by the defendant and his parents to represent him in this hearing. The Court: Do you have a formal complaint? Mr. Krell: The petition says Anthony Mantell is delinquent, he has been associating with vicious and immoral people and has been guilty of immoral conduct." Then after an interchange of no importance here the following appears: "The Court: All right, proceed." Mr. Krell then proceeded to give a statement but was interrupted by objection of Mr. Schrempp, attorney for defendant, as follows: "Mr. Schrempp: At this time, Your Honor, we object to any unsworn testimony before the Court in this matter. The Court: Overruled. Go on. * * * Mr. Schrempp: May we have a continuing objection so we can keep the record straight? First we object to the petition, that it is not sworn testimony. The Court: You may have it shown that what is being said is what our Juvenile Court Records show, and what is being related is not evidence at the present time under oath. Mr. Schrempp: Then my objection to the statement of Mr. Krell at this time is based upon these grounds: First, that it is unsworn and consequently it is a relation of what is classified as hearsay testimony and in the nature of an admission against interest of any parties in this lawsuit. The Court: Your objection will go to all the matters which will now be related, and the same ruling will obtain."

Mr. Krell then proceeded to make a detailed statement with regard to the defendant not under oath all of which was clearly and admittedly hearsay. Others were allowed to make statements not under oath and which likewise were hearsay.

No witness was sworn and nothing except hearsay information was adduced at the hearing. It was at the conclusion of the hearing thus described that the order of commitment was rendered.

The claim of error embraced in this assignment or even of any assignment is not met by the brief of the county attorney who represents the complainant so we can only by conjecture arrive at a conclusion as to the basis upon which the court regarded the hearing conducted as one conforming to proper and legal processes.

The basis, if it may be regarded as a basis, of the court's conclusion is language appearing in section 43–206, R.R.S.1943, as follows: "* * * on the return of the summons or other process, or as soon thereafter as may be, the court shall proceed to hear and dispose of the case in a summary manner."

A child on being found to be a delinquent may be deprived of his liberty. Section 43–210, R.R.S.1943. The effect of the adjudication in this case was to deprive the defendant of his liberty.

Can it be that the Legislature by the quoted statement appearing in section 43–206, R.R.S. 1943, intended to destroy the traditional and constitutional safeguards of a trial? Can it be that it intended that trials should be had without the benefit of testimony of witnesses given under the sanction of oath or affirmation? Can

it be said that the Legislature intended that the liberty of a child had less sanctity than that of an adult? Even if it did so intend, could that intention be sustained? We think not.

This matter has not been previously considered here but it has been by other courts. The courts of New York and California have spoken in a manner which meets approval here.

In People v. Lewis, 260 N.Y. 171, 183 N.E. 353, 355, 86 A.L.R. 1001, it was said: "In the administration of Children's Court there is evidence of a tendency to confuse the procedure usual in mere dependency cases with that necessary in delinquency cases involving an issue of fact. To serve the social purpose for which the Children's Court was created, provision is made in the statute for wide investigation before, during and after the hearing. But that investigation is clinical in its nature. Its results are not to be used as legal evidence where there is an issue of fact to be tried. When it is said that even in cases of lawbreaking delinquency constitutional safeguards and the technical procedure of the criminal law may be disregarded, there is no implication that a purely socialized trial of a specific issue may properly or legally be had. The contrary is true. There must be a reasonably definite charge. The customary rules of evidence shown by long experience as essential to getting at the truth with reasonable certainty in civil trials must be adhered to. The finding of fact must rest on the preponderance of evidence adduced under those rules. Hearsay, opinion, gossip, bias, prejudice, trends of hostile neighborhood feeling, the hopes and fears of social workers, are all sources of error and have no more place in Children's Courts than in any other court."

In re Matter of Hill, 78 Cal.App. 23, 247 P. 591, 592, it was said: "The relations of parent and child should not be severed or disturbed, unless the facts justify it, and the interests of all parties concerned require that these facts be shown by evidence whose verity has been carefully and legally tested. And so, while the exact truth should be searched out, and all mere technicalities of procedure as distinguished from rules which protect substantial rights should be disregarded, the regular processes of the law provided to produce evidence, and the ordinary rules established to aid courts in testing and weighing it, are not scrapped because the proceeding is a summary one.

"In the instant case the process of the law was available to bring witnesses into court, and it should have been used for that purpose. If persons secretly informed the judge that the parents' home was not a fit place for this child, and if their information was reliable and of any value, these persons must have known facts which would warrant that conclusion. It was their duty to come forward and in a manly or womanly fashion give their testimony, so that this helpless infant might be withdrawn from danger and cruelty. But details whispered privately to a judge in chambers cannot be basis of a final order. The more serious the accusation the greater the need that it be carefully tested, and to that end that no one interested be denied the right of cross-examination." †

It must be said that the defendant was not accorded a legal hearing in the juvenile court.

This conclusion renders unnecessary consideration of the other assignments of error contained in the brief of defendant.

The judgment is reversed and the cause remanded for a new trial.

Reversed and remanded.

81

In re Lewis *

WILLIAM J. BRENNAN, Jr., J.

Shortly after six o'clock in the morning of August 22, 1951, a clear, dry day, appellant, then 17 years old, was driving a car west along Route 4, East Paterson, with four other youths, all of whom were asleep, as passengers. Mrs. Sarah Holms, on her way to her work, was standing near a telephone pole on the east corner of Elizabeth Avenue waiting for a bus. Mr. Walter Ruhren, also waiting for the bus, was standing in the middle of the block west of the intersection. He saw the car three blocks away approaching from the east "coming along in a

---

† See, also, *State v. Reister,* —— N.D. ——, 80 N.W. 2d 114 (1956). — *Ed.*

* *In re Lewis,* Supreme Court of New Jersey, 1953, 11 N. J. 217, 94 A. 2d 328.

normal manner" though "going pretty fast." When the car neared Elizabeth Avenue he saw it veer to the right, "he started toward the curb" "making a gradual turn right." The car jumped the curb close to the place where Mrs. Holms was standing, hit her and crushed her to death against the telephone pole. "The car bounced and made a turn," "flew across the street" "and hit the tree on the west corner of Elizabeth Avenue." One of the sleeping boys, Martin Head, was killed. The other boys, including appellant, were injured.

A minor under 18 who commits any act which is a misdemeanor when committed by a person of the age of 18 years or over may be adjudged guilty of an act of juvenile delinquency. N.J.S. 2A:4–14(1) (a), N.J.S.A. Complaint was made to the Bergen County Juvenile and Domestic Relations Court that the deaths of Mrs. Holms and Martin Head were caused by appellant's careless and heedless operation of the automobile in wilful or wanton disregard of the rights or safety of others, an offense constituted a misdemeanor by R.S. 2:138–9, since superseded by N.J.S. 2A:113–9, N.J.S.A. After trial the final judgment on appeal was entered. It adjudges appellant guilty of an act of juvenile delinquency and commits him to the Annandale Reformatory upon a finding that the deaths of Mrs. Holms and the Head boy were caused by appellant's driving of the car in the manner interdicted by R.S. 2:138–9. His appeal to the Appellate Division is here upon certification of our own motion.

The principal challenge is to the sufficiency of the proof to sustain the finding of the commission of the offense. The State on its brief concedes that the proof of the offense "should be at least as strong as would be required in ordinary criminal proceedings," but cf. State ex rel. Berry v. Superior Court, 139 Wash. 1, 245 P. 409, 45 A.L.R. 1530 (Sup.Ct.1926).

There was no direct testimony establishing exactly what appellant did or omitted to do to cause the car to leave the road. The evidence of his inculpatory conduct is entirely circumstantial. Circumstantial evidence of course suffices, indeed often is "more certain, satisfying and persuasive than direct evidence." State v. O'Connor, 134 N.J.L. 536, 539, 49 A.2d 45, 47 (Sup.Ct.1946); State v. Goodman, 9 N.J. 569, 89 A.2d 243 (1952). In view of the State's concession, the real question, cf.

State v. Goodman, supra, is whether the evidence, viewed in its entirety, was such that the trial judge could properly find therefrom, beyond reasonable doubt, that the deaths were the result of appellant's careless and heedless operation of the car in wilful or wanton disregard of the rights or safety of others. Our review of the testimony satisfies us that the proofs are sufficient to support the conclusion of the trial judge.

The offense condemned by R.S. 2:138–9 may be committed by the driver of a motor vehicle who causes the death of another when there inheres in his driving the high probability of causing harm because of conditions known to him which actually impair, or potentially have the capacity to impair, his faculties for vigilance and care. It is not necessary to show ill will toward, or a positive intent to injure, another in order to establish that a motor vehicle was driven in wilful or wanton disregard of the rights or safety of others. True, conduct which is wilful or wanton, unlike conduct which is merely negligent does import intent. 38 Am.Jur., Negligence, sec. 48, p. 692. However, the element of intent to harm is supplied by a constructive intention as to consequences, which entering into the intentional act which produces harm, namely, the driving of the vehicle, the law imputes to the actor, so that conduct which otherwise would be merely negligent becomes, by reason of reckless disregard of the safety of others, a wilful or wanton wrong. See King v. Patrylow, 15 N.J. Super. 429, 83 A.2d 639 (App.Div.1951). The emphasis is upon the reckless indifference to consequences of the intentional act of driving the motor vehicle in the face of known circumstances presenting a high degree of probability of producing harm. . . . [Citations omitted. — Ed.]

The five boys held summer jobs at a Catskill Mountain resort some 100 miles from New York City. Appellant had driven his companions down to the city after work the previous evening, arriving after midnight. His companions went separate ways after agreeing to meet him at Times Square at five a.m. for the return trip. They were due back at work about eight o'clock. Appellant testified that he spent the hours from two to five sleeping in the car. The other boys, however, apparently had no sleep at all. The car left Times Square about a quarter past five. They stopped for gasoline and a change of oil before leaving the city. One of the boys asked appellant at the service station, "How about me driving if you are tired" and appellant answered "No one drives this car but me."

The three in the back seat were asleep before the George Washington Bridge was reached. Appellant's fourth companion, Harry Call, sitting beside him in the front seat, stayed awake until after appellant had driven a few miles in New Jersey beyond the bridge. When they left Times Square the other boys had urged appellant to hurry so that they would get back to work on time. Call testified that nevertheless as they sped along "about 60 to 65" he said to appellant, "If you were tired, we were hurrying to get back to work, that is why we were going so fast, I said we could afford to slow down or pull over to the side for a while," — but appellant made no response. Call then fell asleep. Appellant testified that he had no recollection of Call's remark. He at first was positive in his denial that he had fallen asleep or dozed at the wheel, but finally said that he really did not know whether he did or not. Significantly, however, he testified that he had no memory whatever of any event or place after passing a boat house some distance before reaching the scene of the mishap.

Plainly it was open to the trial judge to conclude upon the evidence that appellant, knowing that he had once driven the car a long distance that night and lacked adequate sleep and rest, but feeling impelled to press on to get back to work on time, intentionally chanced driving the car at high speeds notwithstanding the evident risk that his senses were or would be so dulled as to leave him, as became clearly the case, without any appreciation or awareness of events or circumstances around him, and that it was his reckless folly in driving under those known conditions which brought about the deaths of Mrs. Holms and Martin Head. Appellant's proffered explanations that either the right front tire blew out or that he may have suffered a dizzy spell of the kind he had occasionally experienced after strenuous exercise, do not exculpate him. The first has no substance. A photograph in evidence taken immediately after the mishap shows the tire to be inflated. As to the second, while the suggestion of his seizure with a dizzy spell was pure conjecture on his part, if such was the case, he knew his tendency to such spells, and his driving, particularly at such high speeds, might certainly be considered an act of recklessness.

It is then urged that the commitment of appellant to Annandale Reformatory was un-justified and offends the spirit and purpose of the Juvenile and Domestic Relations Court Law "to secure for each child coming under the jurisdiction of the juvenile and domestic relations court such care, guidance and control, preferably in his own home, as will conduce to the child's welfare and the best interest of the state." N.J.S. 2A:4–2, N.J.S.A. It is argued that the revocation of appellant's driver's license and his placement upon probation would have sufficed to impress the boy "with the serious consequences of his unfortunate act or failure to act."

It is true that the statutory policy for the treatment of juvenile offenders is directed to their rehabilitation for useful citizenship through reformation and education and not to their punishment, even when the offense under-lying the adjudication of juvenile delinquency is of a kind which when committed by an older person would merit indictment, convic-tion and punishment. State v. Goldberg, 124 N.J.L. 272, 11 A.2d 299 (Sup.Ct.1940), af-firmed sub nom. State v. Goldberg, 125 N.J.L. 501, 17 A.2d 173 (E. & A.1940). The statute expressly saves the juvenile from the stigma of criminality by providing that he shall not be "deemed a criminal" and that his adjudication of juvenile delinquency shall not "operate to impose any of the civil disabilities ordinarily imposed by conviction," N.J.S. 2A:4–39, N.J.S.A.

However, the statute also grants discretion to the trial judge to determine whether the ob-jectives of the act will best be served in any case by substituting restraint and care by the public authorities for that which the child would usually receive from its parents; the judge "on proper cause shown" may commit the juvenile to a reformatory N.J.S. 2A:4–37, N.J.S.A. We cannot say in light of the cir-cumstances surrounding appellant's offense that proper cause is lacking for the instant judgment of commitment. Moreover, such a judgment is not ordinarily revisable by an appellate court

where the trial judge's discretion is exercised within the limits laid down by the statute. Cf. State v. Newman, 128 N.J.L. 82, 24 A.2d 206 (Sup.Ct.1942).

In compliance with R.S. 30:4–152, as amended by L.1951, c. 335, p. 1176, N.J.S.A., the court did not fix or limit the duration of appellant's commitment to the reformatory. Nor was the retention by the court of juris-diction over appellant stated in the order of commitment, and therefore, under Rule 6:7–13, such jurisdiction is relinquished. Accord-ingly, the board of managers of the reformatory may terminate appellant's term of service at a time of the board's selection in accordance with its formally adopted rules and regulations, but as provided by R.S. 30:4–152, N.J.S.A., may not detain appellant for a period in excess of the maximum term provided by law for the commission of an offense under R.S. 2:138–9.

Affirmed.

For affirmance: Chief Justice VANDERBILT and Justices HEHER, OLIPHANT, WACHENFELD, BURLING, JACOBS and BRENNAN — 7.

For reversal: None.

82

Garner v. Wood *

JENKINS, Justice.

1. The act of 1913 (Ga.L.1913, pp. 87, 90) as amended (Code, §§ 77–701, 77–704), establishing the Georgia Training School for Girls, and providing that the judges of the city and superior courts may in their discretion commit thereto "any girl under 18 years of age who has committed any offense against the laws of this State, not punishable by death or life imprisonment, or who habitually associates with vicious or immoral people, or who is in-corrigible to such an extent that she cannot be controlled by parent or guardian, there to be held until such girl reaches the age of 21, un-

---

* Garner v. Wood, Supreme Court of Georgia, 1939, 188 Ga. 463, 4 S.E. 2d 137.

less sooner discharged, bound out, or paroled under the rules and regulations of said Board of Control," with a right of jury trial if demanded, and a right of appeal, was not enacted with the "object * * * to punish for commission of crime, but to reclaim and rescue certain classes of females from a possible criminal career," and "to protect girls under the age of 18 years, during their minority, from the evil results of association with vicious or immoral people." Wingate v. Gornto, 147 Ga. 192, 195, 93 S.E. 206, 207. Since the welfare of female children is the primary purpose of this act; since the State, under its general power as *parens patriae*, has the right within reasonable limits to deprive children of their liberty, and their parents of their custody; since the reasonable classification of minors according to age is within the legislative power; and since due procedure with the right of jury trial whenever demanded, and with the right of appeal, are accorded, these statutes are not unconstitutional on the grounds that they violate art. 14, sec. 1, of the amendments to the constitution of the United States, U.S.C.A. (Code, § 1–815), or art. 1, sec. 1, par. 3, of the State constitution (§ 2–103), as depriving persons of liberty without due process of law, or art. 1, § 1, par. 2 (§ 2–102), as denying the equal protection of the laws; or that they violate art. 1, sec. 1, par. 17, of the State constitution (§ 2–117), as creating "involuntary servitude, save as a punishment for crime after legal conviction hereof"; or that they violate art. 1, sec. 4, par. 1, of the State constitution (§ 2–401), as a special law for which provision has been made by an existing general law, or as a law of general nature not having uniform operation throughout the State. State v. Cagle, 111 S.C. 548, 96 S.E. 291, 292; Whalen v. Olmstead, 61 Conn. 263, 23 A. 964, 15 L.R.A. 593, and note; 14 R.C.L. 273, 277; 31 C.J. 1101–1104, §§ 226–228; and citations.

2. A case against a female under the age of eighteen, under the Code, § 77–704, not being a "criminal proceeding," and no indictment or written accusation signed by a prosecuting attorney or the prosecutor being required (Wingate v. Gornto, supra; and see Williams v. Davidson, 147 Ga. 491, 94 S.E. 564, as to trials of delinquent minors under the juvenile-court act), the judge did not err in treating the in-

stant proceeding as civil rather than criminal, and accordingly in allowing jury strikes to the parties, swearing the jury, and charging the jury the rules of preponderance of evidence, all as applicable to civil cases, rather than in following the procedure and charging the rule of proof beyond a reasonable doubt as applicable to criminal cases.

3. A correct charge is not to be characterized as erroneous because of an omission by the court to charge in the same connection an additional pertinent legal proposition. But such an instruction should be in itself complete, accurate, and pertinent with reference to the particular legal rule stated; and where the judge undertakes to charge upon a certain subject, although it be one on which it is unnecessary, in the absence of a request, to instruct the jury, he must charge all the law upon that subject which is material to the facts of the case. Persons v. State, 27 Ga.App.592(3), 109 S.E. 533; Rome Ry. & Light Co. v. King, 33 Ga.App. 383 (3), 384, 126 S.E. 294, and citations. Accordingly, even though there was no request to charge, where, on the controlling jurisdictional fact in this case as to whether the defendant was under or over the age of eighteen, four witnesses testified in her favor and three to the contrary, and where "the court undertook to state the principles of the Code, § 38–107, as to how the preponderance of evidence should be determined, it was harmful error against the [defendant] to omit the final sentence of that section, that 'the jury may also consider the number of witnesses, though the preponderance is not necessarily with the greater number.'" Tucker v. Talmadge, 186 Ga. 798, 800(6), 198 S.E. 726; Farmers' State Bank v. Kelley, 166 Ga. 683, 144 S.E. 258; Gossett & Sons v. Wilder, 46 Ga.App. 651(5), 168 S.E. 903.

4. It was also error to admit, over proper objection, the evidence of a police officer, who sought to testify, not to the substantive fact as to the defendant's age or as to the general repute in the family with respect to the same, but merely that the defendant's mother told him at the time of the defendant's arrest that she was then seventeen years old. Such testimony was hearsay, and for that reason inadmissible. In so far as it might have been admissible to impeach the previous testimony

of the mother, no foundation had been laid for such purpose. . . . [Citations omitted. — Ed.]

5. The court erred in refusing a new trial for the reasons stated in the two immediately preceding paragraphs.

Judgment reversed.

All the Justices concur, except ATKINSON, Presiding Justice, who dissents from so much of the ruling in division four as holds that it was error to admit, over objection, testimony of the policeman as to a declaration of the mother of the defendant concerning the latter's age. This testimony is unquestionably hearsay, but it is of some evidentiary value, and it was not error to admit it.

83

In re Coyle, Coyle v. State *

WILTROUT, Judge.

Appellant was found to be a delinquent child and was ordered committed to the Indiana Boys' School until he shall attain the age of 21 years. He appeals, claiming that a number of errors were committed, to his prejudice.

It is claimed that the petition in this case is not a proper petition for the reason that it does not contain a proper prayer and does not charge an act of delinquency; that by reason thereof all proceedings taken by the court are void for lack of jurisdiction. We have carefully examined the petition. It is carelessly and inexpertly drafted, apparently having been drawn without much attention being paid to the exact provisions of the statutes involved. No objection was made to its infirmities, however, until after the trial and judgment of the court. We conclude from our examination of the petition that while it does not exactly conform to statu-

---

* In re Coyle, Coyle v. State, Appellate Court of Indiana, in Banc, 1951, 122 Ind. App. 217, 101 N.E. 2d 192.

tory requirements it is a sufficient petition to enable the court to assume jurisdiction in this case.

The only act of delinquency attempted to be set forth by the petition is that appellant "started a fire at the Superior Trailer Manufacturing Corporation, 2100 Fletcher Avenue, by pouring paint thinner over a pile of lumber and setting fire to it with a match."

The finding in this case rests entirely upon the uncorroborated confession or admission of appellant. Whether this evidence was properly admitted over the objection made or what its probative value might be we do not decide. It is sufficient to say that even if it were to be considered there is no evidence to support the particular act of delinquency charged. There is nothing in the evidence which shows that appellant had anything to do with a fire at the Superior Trailer Manufacturing Corporation, although there is a reference to a fire which, so far as the evidence shows, was at another place. The appellee in its brief makes no attempt to controvert appellant's statements and argument on this point. Rather, appellee says: "The appellee freely admits that the evidence given above, and the procedure followed in the hearing, would not be sufficient to safeguard appellant's rights, if he were being tried on a criminal charge; but appellant was not being so tried. Rather the court was simply making a determination as to whether or not the appellant's environment indicated that appellant's future training, and the best interests of the State would be best served by taking him from his home and placing him where proper training was available." We cannot agree with the latter part of appellee's statement. Juvenile court procedure has not been so far socialized and individual rights so far diminished that a child may be taken from its parents and placed in a state institution simply because some court might think that to be in the best interests of the state. "It is not the province of the courts to determine generally what conditions or exigencies will warrant the state in seizing the children of its citizens." Orr v. State, 1919, 70 Ind.App. 242, 123 N.E. 470, 473. Some specific act or conduct must be charged as constituting the delinquency and the truth of such charge must be determined in an adversary proceeding. State ex rel. Jones v.

Geckler, Judge, 1938, 214 Ind. 574, 16 N.E. 2d 875.*

Appellant also claims error in this case in that the judge acted as both judge and prosecuting attorney, and in that the prosecuting attorney was not called in to represent the state. It appears that the court conducted the entire examination of the witnesses for the state, offered and introduced documentary exhibits in evidence over objection of the appellant, and conducted the entire case on behalf of the state, thereby assuming the duties of the prosecuting attorney. Both parties in their briefs seem to assume that the prosecuting attorney was not present, and appellee argues that the present statute contains no requirement that the prosecuting attorney shall appear and therefore it was not proper for him to appear. We might point out that the Act of 1945, ch. 356, p. 1724, Burns' Stat. § 9–3201 et seq., which deals with the subject of delinquent children, provides that it is to be construed as being supplemental to and in furtherance of the laws affected thereby, and only repeals the laws and parts of laws which are in conflict therewith. Although the state is not designated as a party plaintiff in the title of the petition, Burns' Stat. § 9–3208, nevertheless "it is the state speaking to assert its paramount interest in the protection of society and infants even though it is not named in the petition." State ex rel. Johnson v. White Circuit Court, 1948, 225 Ind. 602, 77 N.E.2d 298, 302. However, the transcript of the record, which imports verity, states that an unnamed deputy prosecuting attorney was present at the hearing and at later stages of the proceedings, even though it also appears that at the hearing he was as silent as the bridegroom in Lochinvar. We do not pass upon the question as to whether proper objections were timely made as to the action of the court in view of the conclusion which we have reached that a new trial must be had. Such error will probably not be repeated at the new trial.

The decision of the court is not sustained by sufficient evidence and is contrary to law.

Judgment reversed, with instruction to sustain appellant's motion for a new trial.

---

* Petition must be sufficient to inform defendant but need only follow rules of *civil* procedure as to specificity. *Robinson* v. *State*, ——— Tex. Civ. ———, 204 S.W. 2d 981 (1947). — *Ed.*

84

In re Contreras *

WHITE, Presiding Justice.

This is an appeal by the above named minor and his mother, Maria Luisa Contreras, from an order of the Supreme Court sitting in separate session as a juvenile court, declaring the aforesaid minor a ward thereof and committing him to the Youth Authority of the State of California † and denying a motion to vacate and set aside the aforesaid order.

The original order declared said minor to be a person coming within the provisions of section 700(m) of the Welfare and Institutions Code in that, on March 19, 1951 he "committed an assault upon the person of Henry Davila with a deadly weapon or instrument or by means of force likely to produce great bodily injury."

The findings and judgment set forth that the alleged assault was committed in the following manner: "Minor participated in a gang fight, accompanied with other minors, in which said victim received a stab wound in the stomach inflicted by sharp-edged instrument, and also received several abrasions about the face and head as a result of being kicked and beaten."

After finding "that minor's welfare requires that his custody be taken from his mother," the judgment directed that said minor be committed to the Youth Authority of the State of California.

On this appeal it is contended that the evidence fails to support the judgment declaring the minor herein a ward of the juvenile court and committing him to the Youth Authority.

The record reflects that in this proceeding five boys, including the minor Lupe Cardenas Contreras, were charged with engaging in a "gang" fight during the course of which one Henry Davila was stabbed with a knife and otherwise set upon and beaten.

---

* *In re Contreras*, District Court of Appeal, Second District, Division 1, California, 1952, 109 Cal. App. 787, 241 P. 2d 631.

† See Article 106 of this book. — *Ed.*

It appears that at the hearing in the juvenile court, proceedings were first had as to Salvadore Gill, one of the boys accused with the minor herein. The proceedings were had outside the presence of the minor with whom we are here concerned. Gill gave no testimony involving Contreras, whereupon the mother of the former, and Probation Officer Sorkin advised the court that the witness was "afraid" and "reluctant" to testify. The judge then said to the minor Gill, "I am not going to tell any of these boys I got any information out of you. You don't need to worry about that. You can tell us anything you want to tell us. I also want you to know we already know what you told the officers, but we are not going to tell the rest of the boys that you told us anything. We are interested in finding out all we can about this matter so we can make sure we have the right guy and not the wrong fellows are accused in this difficulty. Let's get the record straight."

With these assurances, the witness continued but did not incriminate Contreras. Officer McAuliffe, however, testified that the witness Gill had theretofore told him, "He thought if anybody stabbed Davila, it was Contreras". Producing a miniature baseball bat, the officer further testified, "When Contreras was arrested * * * he had this. * * * I believe it was Salvadore (Gill) who saw somebody with something like this." Gill denied making this statement.

Contreras, the minor herein, denied any participation in the fracas, stating that on the night in question he was riding in an automobile with two boys, Richard Marques and Frank Chavez. Both of these boys corroborated this statement but admitted having told Probation Officer Sorkin to the contrary, contending that they did so because of threats made against them by other boys.

Henry Davila, victim of the assault, testified that eight or nine boys "jumped" on him as he was on his way to a drugstore. Salvadore Gill was the only one the victim recognized. With reference to the minor herein, the victim testified, "I know him by looks and everything, but I didn't see him that night. Maybe he was there, and maybe he was not; I don't know". (Emphasis added.)

Following this testimony Officer McAuliffe testified that the victim had previously told him, "I think Contreras (the minor herein) cut me, he was the one who used the knife * * * it was Contreras who was on top of me, I am pretty sure that he is the one that used the knife * * *. I'll get them when I get out." The officer also testified that "anyone that was mentioned by anybody was apprehended."

Section 736 of the Welfare and Institutions Code provides that "An order adjudging a person to be a ward of the juvenile court shall not be deemed to be a conviction of crime." In consonance therewith it has been held that issues presented to the juvenile court may be determined upon the preponderance of the evidence, Matter of Cannon, 27 Cal.App. 549, 553, 150 P. 794. In the instant proceeding the minor was not represented by counsel upon the hearing at which he was adjudged a ward of the court. A reading of the transcript of the testimony taken immediately suggests the probability that had the minor been represented by counsel considerable of the evidence given would have been excluded through timely objections.

While the juvenile court law provides that adjudication of a minor to be a ward of the court shall not be deemed to be a conviction of crime, nevertheless, for all practical purposes, this is a legal fiction, presenting a challenge to credulity and doing violence to reason. Courts cannot and will not shut their eyes and ears to everyday contemporary happenings.

It is common knowledge that such an adjudication when based upon a charge of committing an act that amounts to a felony, is a blight upon the character of and is a serious impediment to the future of such minor. Let him attempt to enter the armed services of his country or obtain a position of honor and trust and he is immediately confronted with his juvenile court record. And further, as in this case, the minor is taken from his family, deprived of his liberty and confined in a state institution. True, the design of the Juvenile Court Act is intended to be salutary, and every effort should be made to further its legitimate purpose, but never should it be made an instrument for the denial to a minor of a constitutional right or of a guarantee afforded by law to an adult. Regardless of the provisions of section 736 of the Welfare and Institutions Code, the fact remains that the minor herein was taken from the custody of his parents, deprived of his liberty and ordered confined in a state institution.

As was said in Re Hill, 78 Cal.App. 23, 27, 247 P. 591, 592, with reference to proceedings in the juvenile court: "And so, while the exact truth should be searched out, and all mere technicalities of procedure as distinguished from rules which protect substantial rights should be disregarded, the regular processes of the law provided to produce evidence, and the ordinary rules established to aid courts in testing and weighing it, are not scrapped because the proceeding is a summary one." In the instant case there can be no doubt that had the minor herein been an adult, an indictment or information filed against him, under the evidence here present, would have been set aside on motion under section 995 of the Penal Code.

Surely, a minor charged in the juvenile court with acts denounced by law as a felony does not have lesser constitutional statutory rights or guaranties than are afforded an adult under similar circumstances in the superior court. The record herein is barren of sufficient legal evidence to establish even reasonable or probable cause of the minor's guilt, and he should have been returned to his family, an institution that has ever been recognized as the foundation of society, and the sanctity of which the law has always upheld. A charge against a minor resulting in his removal from the custody of his parents cannot be regarded lightly, and such action is not justified unless facts be shown by evidence, the verity of which has been carefully and legally tested. We find nothing in the juvenile court law that attempts to impose any unlawful restraint upon personal liberty. In practically all of the cases affecting juvenile court proceedings that have come to our attention, the minor has admitted the charge lodged against him and the only problem presented to the court was how to best guide and control the minor with a view to his rehabilitation and further development. In the case at bar however, the minor emphatically and at all times denied his alleged delinquency. Under such circumstances his liberty should not be taken from him until his guilt of the charges lodged against him was established by legal evidence. That however praiseworthy, according to the viewpoint of the individual, may

be the motives of the juvenile court, that tribunal may not impinge upon the legal rights of one brought before it is emphatically set forth in Re Tahbel, 46 Cal.App. 755, 760, 761, 762, 763, 189 P. 804; in Re Hill, supra, 78 Cal.App. at pages 26, 27, 28, 247 P. 591; and in Re Rauch, 103 Cal.App.2d 690, 698, 230 P.2d 115. In the final analysis the juvenile court is a judicial institution.

If it be true, as some of the hearsay and legally inadmissible evidence indicates, that the minor herein may have been connected with the "gang" fight in question, and possibly unfortunate that a rehearing should be required, nevertheless, consequences fraught with far greater evil would inevitably result from the sanction of individual abuses of the character here presented.

Even though, as held in some of the cases, the quantum of proof necessary to sustain an order declaring a minor a ward of the juvenile court is not the same as in a criminal proceeding affecting an adult, In re Dargo, 81 Cal.App. 2d 205, 183 P.2d 282, and cases therein cited, it cannot seriously be contended that the constitutional guarantee of due process of law does not extend to minors as well as to adults.

When the motion to set aside the order committing the minor to the Youth Authority was made, several letters were presented attesting to his good character and reputation. These letters have been brought here on this appeal. One from the Principal of the school attended by the minor stated in part, "My principal contact with Lupe was on the playground during noon and after-school hours. Here he always exhibited good sportsmanship, good judgment and self control. He was honest and fair in all his dealings with fellow players, and was liked and respected by everyone. He showed definite leadership qualities and I confidently anticipated a successful future for the lad.

"I had a liking for Lupe and am very much surprised and concerned that he is involved in any kind of trouble."

Another letter from the school Vice-Principal contained the following: "Lupe's disciplinary record in my office shows that he had been sent in for minor class room disturbances only twice during the year and one half he was here.

"The following statements from two of his

teachers may also be significant as to Lupe's true character:

" 'Not a bad kid — worked well for me. He lacks initiative and followed the wrong crowd.' Phys. Ed. Teacher.

" 'Not a disciplinary case, but just not much work.' English Teacher.

"On the whole, I would say that we did not find Lupe to be a disciplinary problem at Garfield High School. I hope this letter may be of some value in helping Lupe."

Other similar and complimentary letters were written by a former teacher of the minor as well as by neighbors of his family.

We are persuaded that in denying the motion to vacate and set aside its order committing the minor herein to the Youth Authority of the State of California, the juvenile court abused its discretion. The motion should have been granted thereby enabling said minor, with the aid of counsel, to properly prepare and present a defense to the charges preferred against him.

For the foregoing reasons, the order of June 7, 1951 denying the motion to vacate and set aside the previous order declaring said minor a ward of the juvenile court and committing him to the Youth Authority of the State of California is reversed and the cause remanded with directions to the court below sitting in separate session as a juvenile court, to grant said motion.

DORAN and DRAPEAU, J.J., concur.

85

State *v.* Smith *

Appeal from Superior Court, McDowell County; Felix E. Alley, Judge.

Mann Smith, alias Hiawatha Smith, was convicted of rape, and he appeals.

Affirmed.

This is a criminal prosecution under a bill of indictment charging the defendant with

---

* *State* v. *Smith*, Supreme Court of North Carolina, 1938, 213 N. C. 299, 195 S.E. 819.

the commission of the capital felony of rape. The prosecutrix, a girl 13 years of age, was on her way home from school on March 31, 1937. When she walked she took a short cut by way of a path leading through woods. This path turned off at Black Bottom and led over the ridge. After she had gone some distance into the woods she saw the defendant standing by the path. There was evidence that he had seen her coming and had gone to this point to wait for her. When she got within a few steps of him the defendant told her to stop, and asked her if she wanted him to shoot her. He had his hands in his pocket; he then took her off the path in the woods and assaulted her and later took her further in the woods and again assaulted her, detaining the prosecutrix altogether about 2½ hours. There was a verdict of "guilty of rape as charged in the bill of indictment." From judgment of death by asphyxiation pronounced thereon, the defendant appealed.

BARNHILL, Justice.

The defendant offered no evidence, but rested his defense upon the contentions that: (1) He did not commit the crime; (2) the alleged confessions made by him were incompetent; and (3) that his age precluded his being sentenced to death.

To detail the evidence herein to any considerable extent would serve no good purpose. It is sufficient to say that there was ample evidence offered tending to show that the crime of rape was committed upon the person of the prosecutrix and to identify the defendant as the perpetrator of the crime. The prosecutrix testified to facts sufficient to constitute the offense and she was corroborated by the doctor who examined her, and others. The testimony was sufficient to be submitted to the jury for it to determine whether the threats made by the defendant and the circumstances surrounding the assault were sufficient to, and did, put the prosecutrix in fear and overcome her power of resistance. The prosecutrix likewise identified the defendant on the night following the assault in the afternoon. When the defendant was carried into the presence of the prosecutrix, immediately upon seeing her he said: "That's the girl." The evidence shows that this statement was spontaneous and was provoked only by the sight of the girl. The statements of the defendant offered as evidence of confessions likewise tend to prove both the commission of the offense and the identity of the perpetrator.

But the defendant stressfully challenges the competency of the evidence of statements made by the defendant by way of confession and likewise challenges the admission of this evidence, for that the court did not find the facts. Counsel for the defendant insists that at the time the alleged statements were made by the defendant he was suffering from abject fear. Even so, there is no evidence that the officers having him in charge, or any other person, made any threats against him, offered him any inducement, or held out any hope of reward in exchange for a statement from him. The mere presence of a number of officers at the time the statements were made is not sufficient to effect the competency of the evidence.

The prosecutrix had described the defendant and the clothes that he was wearing at the time of the assault. When he was arrested he did not have on the coat described. When the officers found the coat at his mother's and showed it to him he said that he was the man, and that he assaulted the prosecutrix twice. And then, as stated, when he was taken to the home of the prosecutrix, he spontaneously said: "That's the girl."

When the State offered the evidence of statements made by the defendant the defendant objected and asked permission to cross-examine the witness regarding the voluntariness of the statement. After some considerable cross-examination the defendant requested the court to find the facts regarding the alleged confession and to hold that any evidence regarding the same is incompetent. Thereupon the court asked the witness certain questions as to whether he made any promise, held out any hope, or did anything to put the defendant in fear, or to induce him to make the statement. The court made the following entry: "I hold, under the present evidence, that what he said was voluntary." The defendant excepted to the refusal of the court to find the facts regarding the alleged confession, as requested. The only finding the court was permitted to make, was made. In ruling upon the competency of this evidence the law required the court to make the preliminary finding, before admitting the evidence, that the statements were volun-

tary. A determination of the facts other than this is for the jury. It was not the duty of the court to find further facts. For the court to find facts other than that the statement was voluntarily made might be highly prejudicial to a defendant. The court below went as far in this respect as the law permits and there was no error in the refusal to find further facts. Likewise, there was no error in the admission of the testimony to which exception was entered.

The defendant contends here that he had the right to testify and offer witnesses in the absence of the jury in rebuttal, concerning the circumstances under which the alleged confession was procured from him. This is true if he asserts or requests the right at the time. However, when his counsel had completed his cross-examination of the witness in respect to the circumstances under which the confession was made, he did not tender any witnesses in rebuttal, but elected to request the court at that time to find the facts. It was not the duty of the court to call upon the defendant to offer evidence. It ruled upon the competency of the testimony when called upon to do so by the defendant. This gives the defendant no cause for complaint.

But the defendant further contends that, even if it be conceded that he was justly convicted in a trial free from error, the court was without power to impose the sentence of death. He contends that it was the duty of the court to commit him to a reformatory.

The juvenile courts created by the Legislature are without jurisdiction to try boys 15 years of age charged with a capital felony. State v. Burnett, 179 N.C. 735, 102 S.E. 711. The jurisdiction of such offenses was not taken from the superior court by the passage of the juvenile court act, C.S. § 5039 et seq. C.S. § 7322, which is section 11, chapter 509, P.L. 1907, creating the Stonewall Jackson Manual Training and Industrial School, relied on by the defendant, by its terms did not impose upon the judge below the duty to sentence this defendant to a reformatory. We cannot conceive that the Legislature by the terms of this act intended to require or permit the commitment of persons convicted of capital felonies to a reformatory. Even if this be conceded it would not avail the defendant. The statute provides that: "The judges of the superior courts * * * shall have authority, and it shall be their duty, to sentence to the school all persons under the age of sixteen years convicted in any court of this state of any violation of the criminal laws: provided, that such judge or other of said officers shall be of the opinion that it would be best for such person, and the community in which he may be convicted, that he should be so sentenced." It does not appear in this record that the court below was of the opinion that it would be best for the defendant and the community that he be sentenced to a reformatory. Nor does it appear that he was requested to make such finding. In the act creating the Morrison Training School for Negro Boys, the language providing for commitment of boys under the age of 16 years is permissive and not compulsory. C.S.Supp.1924, § 5912(d).

The age at which, and the circumstances under which, a child or youth becomes liable to criminal prosecution and subject to punishment for crime has been discussed in a number of cases in this court. State v. Pugh, 52 N.C. 61; State v. Sam, 60 N.C. 293, 300; State v. Yeargan, 117 N.C. 706, 23 S.E. 153, 154, 36 L.R.A. 196; State v. Hicks, 125 N.C. 636, 34 S.E. 247. State v. Yeargan, supra, is treated as one of the leading American cases on the subject. It is reported in 36 L.R.A 196, accompanied by an exhaustive and elaborate note on the English and American cases relating to the question. In this case Faircloth, C.J., states the rule which prevails in this jurisdiction as follows: "An infant under 7 years of age cannot be indicted and punished for any offense because of the irrebuttable presumption that he is doli incapax. After 14 years of age, he is equally liable to be punished for crime as one of full age. His innocence cannot be presumed. Between 7 and 14 years of age an infant is presumed to be innocent and incapable of committing crime, but that presumption, in certain cases, may be rebutted, if it appears to the court and jury that he is capable of discerning between good and evil, and in such cases he may be punished. The cases in which such presumption may be rebutted and the accused punished when under 14 years are such as an aggravated battery, as in maim or the use of a deadly weapon or in numbers amounting to a riot, or a brutal passion, such as unbridled lust, as in an attempt to commit rape, and the like. In such cases, if the

defendant be found doli capax, public justice demands that the majesty of the law be vindicated, and the offender punished publicly, although he be under 14 years of age; for malice and wickedness supply the want of age." This defendant was slightly over 15 years of age and there was no presumption that he was incapable of committing the crime charged. The presumption is to the contrary.

We conclude that the acts creating the juvenile courts and the several reformatories of the State for boys did not require the court below to impose any punishment other than that pronounced. If the youth of this defendant constitutes a mitigating circumstance and a just cause for relaxing the prescribed punishment as a matter of public policy in the relation of the State to its youth, it addresses itself to the discretionary power of commutation and parole possessed by the Governor of the State and not to this court. The jurisdiction of this court is limited to questions of law and legal inference.

In the trial below we find no error.

86

Appeal of Dattilo *

MALTBIE, Chief Justice.

This is an appeal from a decision of the Superior Court at a domestic relations session sustaining an order of the Juvenile Court denying an application to revoke the commitments of three children of the appellant. The only claim made by her which justifies any extended discussion is that the trial court had no right to consider certain reports made to the Juvenile Court by its investigators and sent to the Superior Court with the file of the case.

The rules of the Superior Court expressly provide, with reference to a hearing on an appeal from the Juvenile Court: "Such case histories and records of investigations as are in the possession of the juvenile court shall be ad-

---

* Appeal of Dattilo, Supreme Court of Errors of Connecticut, 1950, 136 Conn. 488, 72 A. 2d 50.

missible in evidence * * * and any party adversely interested may require the presence for cross-examination of any persons whose report is before the court. * * * " Practice Book, c. 26A, § 2(c). The trial court, acting under this rule, did consider the reports. We could dispose of the contention of the appellant on the ground that at the hearing of the case before the Superior Court not only did she not object to such action by the trial court, as the court has found, but, as an examination of the evidence made necessary by attacks on the finding shows, her attorney expressly stated that he had no objection. The question raised upon the appeal is, however, one of such general concern as regards appeals in juvenile cases that we have decided to consider it.

In the revision of the statutes consequent upon the adoption of the constitution of 1818, the Supreme Court of Errors was given power to make such rules of practice for the regulation of that court and of the Superior Court "as shall be deemed most conducive to the administration of justice." Statutes 1821, p. 137, § 5. The statute remained in force until 1855. Statutes 1854, p. 265, § 12. In 1855 the rule-making power was taken from the judges of the Supreme Court of Errors and vested in an assembly of the judges of the Superior Court; they were authorized to "make all necessary and proper rules, not contrary to law, for the trial of causes and other proceedings in said superior court"; and they were directed to make such rules "as shall promote dispatch in the business of said court, and secure, as far as possible, at every term, the completion of the business thereof." Public Acts 1855, c. 26, § 9, 13; See Public Acts 1859, c. 64, § 6. Except for the last clause, this provision was continued in effect until 1899. General Statute, Rev. 1875, p. 43, § 16; Rev. 1888, § 772. The Practice Act of 1879 contained a provision authorizing the judges at their annual or other meetings to make such order and rules as might be necessary "to give full effect to the provisions of this act." Public Acts 1879, c. 83, § 33. This provision was omitted from the Revision of 1888, apparently because the broader terms of § 772 in that revision were deemed sufficient to cover the matter. In 1899 an act was passed which in the first section gave the judges of the Superior Court authority at their annual meeting to make all orders

and rules necessary and proper to give full effect to the Practice Act and in the second section provided for their printing and distribution to attorneys. Public Acts 1899, c. 5. The act contained no repealing provision. In the Revision of 1902, however, the broad authority of the judges to make rules contained in § 772 of the 1888 revision was omitted and the provisions of the 1899 act were inserted, with the addition of authority to the judges to "make other rules for the dispatch of business in said court." General Statutes, Rev. 1902, § 467. That is the present statutory situation as regards the general rule-making power of the judges of the Superior Court. General Statutes, § 7655.

As used in the statute of 1855, the word "dispatch" was clearly intended to have the meaning of a speedy disposition of matters in the court. Webster's New International Dictionary (2d Ed.). The revisers in 1902 were confronted with two laws then on the statute books, § 772 of the Revision of 1888, and chapter 5 of the Public Acts of 1899. The first gave the judges of the Superior Court the power to "make all necessary and proper rules for proceedings in the Superior Court." The second gave them authority only to make rules to give effect to the Practice Act, with an added provision as to their printing and distribution. Apparently recognizing the limited extent of the power given in the latter statute as compared to the broader authority contained in the Revision of 1888, the revisers added to the provision of the 1899 act something not previously in it, the authority to "make other rules for the dispatch of business." It is presumed that revisers do not intend to change the law unless an intent to do so is apparent. *Bassett v. City Bank & Trust Co.*, 115 Conn. 393, 400, 161 A. 852; *Columbus Industrial Bank v. Miller*, 125 Conn. 313, 319, 6 A.2d 42. The intent of the words added in the 1902 revision was evidently to continue the broader rule-making power contained in the 1888 revision; and the word "dispatch" was clearly used with the significance "accomplishment." 3 Oxford Dictionary, Pt. 1, p. 479, "Dispatch" (5). In short, the statutes now give the judges of the Superior Court authority not only to make rules to carry out the provisions of the Practice Act but also, in the words of the 1855 act, to "make all necessary and proper rules, not contrary to law, for the trial of causes and other proceedings in said superior court."

Even if this were not so, it was within the power of the judges to make the particular rule in question. Apart from legislative authority, courts acting in the exercise of common-law powers have an inherent right to make rules governing procedure in them. *In re Hien*, 166 U.S. 432, 436, 17 S.Ct. 624, 41 L.Ed. 1066; *McDonald v. Pless*, 238 U.S. 264, 266, 35 S.Ct. 783, 59 L.Ed. 1300; *Woodbury v. Andrew Jergens Co.*, 2 Cir., 61 F.2d 736, 737; note, 110 A.L.R. 22; 14 Am.Jur. 355 *et seq.* That right is an inheritance from the common-law practice in England. *People v. Callopy*, 358 Ill. 11, 14, 192 N.E. 634. That the courts of this state, without any legislative authority, may make rules of procedure appears from a decision of the Supreme Court made in 1807. *Terry v. Capen*, 3 Day 495.

The statute authorizing an appeal to the Superior Court from a decision of the Juvenile Court does not state the nature and scope of the proceeding and contains only a single provision as to procedure. General Statute, § 2815. That provision authorizes the judge holding the session of the Superior Court at which such an appeal is heard to order an investigation to be made by a qualified probation officer or county investigator whose written report is admissible in evidence subject to the right of any party to require him to appear for cross-examination. The purpose of the provision clearly is to authorize the court, in an appeal which involves the custody of infants, to adopt a procedure which would not be proper in an ordinary court action; it was obviously intended to be an extension of, not a limitation upon, the power of the court in such cases. The provisions of the statute fall far short of establishing a procedure for the orderly disposition of such appeals. Even lacking statutory authority, it would be well within the inherent power of the judges of the Superior Court to make rules which would bring about an orderly, expeditious and just determination of the issues.

The appellant suggests rather than directly claims that the admission in evidence of reports of investigators which were before the Juvenile Court in itself violates basic principles of evidence. The Juvenile Court is required to make a broad investigation of relevant circumstances to determine what disposition of the case will best serve the welfare of the child, and in the case of a claim of delinquency the investigation is to be made by a probation officer. General Statutes, § 2811. The statute makes admissable in evidence on the hearing of an appeal by the Superior Court the reports of the investigations it directs to be made; General Statutes, § 2815; and the rule merely amplifies that provision to include reports of investigations made for the use of the Juvenile Court. The persons who made the investigations can be called as witnesses before the Superior Court, there to testify as to the facts they ascertained; the application of the rule saves time, trouble and expense in the disposition of the case, and at the same time protects the rights of the child and interested parties by the provision that they may require any investigator whose report is before the court personally to appear and subject himself to cross-examination. See *Wadell v. Board of Zoning Appeals*, 136 Conn. 1, 8, 68 A.2d 152. While we have found no case directly involving records of investigations of this nature, there is an increasing tendency to broaden the field of the admissibility of such reports. 5 Wigmore, Evidence (3d Ed.) p. 699; see General Statutes, § 4316; *State v. Levy*, 103 Conn. 138, 146, 130 A. 96. In the case of *People v. Lewis*, 260 N.Y. 171, 178, 183 N.E. 353, 86 A.L.R. 1001, relied upon by the appellant, the court was discussing the evidence which could be properly received in a children's court in deciding whether a child had committed a specific offense of a criminal nature on which a finding of delinquency could be based, not the broader considerations which are necessarily involved in determining whether the welfare of a child will best be served by leaving him with those who have custody of him or by placing him in the custodial care of some institution or other person. There is nothing contrary to any statute, unreasonable or violative of the rights of the parties in the rule in question.

The appellant attacks several paragraphs of the finding, but for the most part the ground of objection is that they are based upon the reports of investigations made for the Juvenile Court, and it follows from what we have said that these assignments of error cannot be sustained. The material paragraphs of the finding, not subject to correction present this situation:

The children in question, two boys and a girl, in 1943 and 1945 were committed to the New Haven County Temporary Home and they are now in that home or in foster homes. Subsequent to the commitments, the mother obtained a divorce from her husband. She has remarried. While the physical facilities of the home where she lives with her present husband are adequate to care for the boys, they are not for the girl. The children are properly cared for and well adjusted to their present living conditions. The present husband of the mother has a police record which dates back to 1916 and includes a variety of charges. He has quarrelled frequently with his wife and in 1947 was sent to jail as the result of one altercation. The mother is of mediocre intelligence and both she and her husband are of an excitable temperament. Neither appeared to the court qualified to supervise adolescent children, and the husband would not be a good influence

upon growing boys. The boys are easily led and require close supervision. We cannot find that the trial court was in error in concluding that the revocation of the commitments would not conduce to the best welfare of the children; and the appellant, as their mother, has no natural right to their custody which can prevail over such a disposition of the case as would serve their best interests. *Mullins v. Becker*, 113 Conn. 526, 529, 155 A. 705; *Hunt v. Hunt*, 116 Conn. 701, 702, 163 A. 608.

There is no error.

In this opinion the other Judges concurred.*

---

* For a thoroughgoing note on use of investigation reports, see "Employment of Social Investigation Reports in Criminal and Juvenile Proceedings," 58 Columbia L. R. 702, 715 (1958). See, also, B. Cheriff, "Correct Use of Background Reports in Juvenile Delinquency Cases," 5 *Syracuse* L. R. 67 (1953). — *Ed.*

Chapter 15

Problems of Disposition

87

State v. Myers *

BURKE, J. The appellant, Frank Myers, was adjudged a delinquent minor in juvenile court of Cass County and committed to the State Training School. Both he and his mother, Eva Myers, have appealed from the order of commitment and have asked a trial anew in this court upon the entire record in the case. Appellants' request for a trial de novo is a proper one. Section 27–1632, Rev. Code 1943, provides: "Any order made by this court (juvenile court) may be reviewed or appealed in the manner provided for the review of civil cases." . . .

There are two questions in the case. 1. Does the record establish that Frank Myers is delinquent in the degree which the statute requires as a jurisdictional basis for an order with respect to his custody? 2. The jurisdictional basis being established, was the order of commitment to the State Training School for the best interests of Frank Myers and the State of North Dakota?

The record discloses that Frank, who was 16 years old on November 7, 1945, is one of four sons of Eva Myers. When he was two years old the Myers' home was broken by divorce and Frank and his brothers were given into the mother's custody. Mrs. Myers worked as a cook in the Fargo Bus Depot and at other jobs. She kept her family together until 1941, when all four boys were committed to institutional care at the Lake Park Children's Home because of their mother's inability to provide for their support. In 1943, Mrs. Myers secured employment as a waitress in the Waldorf Liquor Store

---

* State v. Myers, Supreme Court of North Dakota, 1946, 74 N. D. 297, 22 N.W. 2d 199.

which has been described in the record and argument in the case as a "cocktail lounge" and "night club." She is still so employed. Her wages are twenty-five dollars a week and she testified that her tips average about the same amount.

In the spring of 1944, at the close of the school year, Frank left the Children's Home at Lake Park with the approval of all interested parties. He secured employment at Hope, N. D., as a farm hand. He worked the entire summer in this employment and earned $125.00. In the fall he came to Fargo to live with his mother. He entered the ninth grade at the Roosevelt Junior High School. After school hours he worked at odd employments including the setting of pins in bowling alleys. He completed his school work with satisfactory grades and was promoted to the tenth grade. As soon as school was out in the summer of 1945, he found employment doing odd jobs of yard work. In July and August he worked for the Northern States Power Company doing a man's work as an ordinary laborer. He worked an eight hour day and was paid 73½ cents an hour. His employer has testified to his ability and dependability. At the beginning of the current school year, he left this employment and entered the tenth grade at Fargo High School. In addition to his regular school work, he became a member of the football squad and continued to engage in gainful employment after school hours.

During all of the time after he left the Children's Home at Lake Park, Frank has purchased all of his clothes with his own earnings. At all times he has given his mother money to help defray their living expense and during the time he worked for the Northern States Power Company he paid her twenty dollars a month. At the time of the hearing in this case, on September 17, 1945, he had a balance of $185.00 in his saving account with the Northwestern Savings and Loan Assn., he had $200.00 in war bonds which he had purchased with his own savings and a $50.00 war bond which his mother had given him.

It appeared, however, that in March 1945, Frank was invited by two girl acquaintances to attend a party at the home of a Mrs. Selstrom, a place which later achieved scandalous notoriety. Frank attended this party and thereafter became one of a group of boys and girls who frequented this home. Mrs. Selstrom is a vicious woman. She is 24 years of age and while her husband was away in the army, made her home a rendezvous where boys and girls who were scarcely more than children might gather to engage in practices condemned both by the moral law and the law of the land. There they learned to drink intoxicating beverages purchased by Mrs. Selstrom for the most part with money they contributed for the purpose. There, some of them at least, learned and were afforded an opportunity to engage in sex delinquency. No doubt, their hostess was preceptress as well for she took one of the boys as her own paramour.

It is not contended that Frank was a participant in these immoral practices to the extent that others were. He stated that for the most part he just sat around and listened to the phonograph. He drank some of the whiskey and beer that were provided and on one occasion "loaned" Mrs. Selstrom two dollars with which she purchased intoxicating liquor. On another occasion he slept all night on the floor at the Selstrom home while Mrs. Selstrom and her particular friend occupied a bed in another room. The juvenile commissioner who investigated the affair thoroughly stated "as far as I know there is no question of sex delinquency in which he (Frank) was involved." Nevertheless, there is no question but that Frank was aware of what took place at the Selstrom home, and knowing it, he continued to go there until an automobile accident early in August 1945, focused official attention upon the disgraceful situation.

Section 27-1608, Rev. Code 1943, provides: "Except as otherwise provided by law, the court (juvenile) shall have original jurisdiction in all proceedings:

1. Concerning any child residing in or who is temporarily within the county:

a. . . . . b. . . . . c. Who habitually associates with dissolute, vicious, or immoral persons, or

who is leading an immoral or vicious life. . . ."

Clearly Frank's conduct was such as to bring him within the provisions of subjection c, supra, and the juvenile court therefore had jurisdiction to make an order with respect to his custody.

We thus reach the second question. Was the order committing Frank to the State Training School for his best interests and for the best interests of the State of North Dakota? The order of the juvenile judge makes it clear, that in reaching his decision he took into consideration the scandalous nature of the Selstrom affair as a whole, Frank's individual delinquency, the commitments that he had ordered in the cases of other participants in that affair who had been before him, the moral atmosphere of the City of Fargo, the fact that Frank's mother's working hours, which were from 6 o'clock p.m. until 1 o'clock a.m. made his supervision by her difficult, and the deterrent effect which the commitment would have upon other juveniles.

We realize that proper disposition of cases of juvenile delinquency requires a delicate balancing of mixed considerations and that even the most careful weighing of pertinent factors can only result in conclusions that are speculative to the extent that they attempt to predict the course of future events.* Confidence that a correct conclusion has been reached must of necessity rest upon hope founded in experience, rather than on certainty. We think therefore that the problem should be approached in a spirit of optimism and that drastic remedies should not be invoked where we can have reasonable hope that lesser ones will have an equal if not a complete success.

What then are the factors to be considered and what relative weight is to be given to each? To what extent is the welfare of an individual delinquent to be counterbalanced by the good of the state? In one sense, a decision, which will help quiet public indignation over a scandalous condition which has arisen in a community, or which, because of its severity, will act as a forbidding example to other youngsters, may be said to be for the good of the state. But we do not think that, as used in the juvenile act, the phrase can be given such a broad interpretation. Considerations of expediency, the satisfaction of public indignation, or example are

---

* See Articles 116–117 of this book. — Ed.

contrary to the whole spirit of the juvenile act. They are dependent on publicity to be effective for any purpose and all proceedings in juvenile court are declared by statute to be "confidential." Section 27-1606, Rev Code 1943. We therefore hold that the good of the State requires a child to be removed from a community only when his delinquency is such that he has become a danger to society either because of his own conduct or his influence upon others.

Whether Frank's influence will be detrimental to others depends largely upon what his future conduct will be. The question of what is best for the State is therefore inextricably intertwined with the question of what is best for Frank. The record shows that Frank has need for supervision. It also shows that he has not had proper supervision at home and that because of her working hours it will be difficult for his mother to give him the kind of supervision he needs. This situation, however, does not of necessity require a commitment to the State Training School. That institution is not without its disadvantages. Certainly if we can have reasonable hope that other measures will suffice, we should not resort to a commitment to the Training School. In this case we have that hope. The record does not disclose that Frank is incorrigible but rather that he has respect for parental authority. There is nothing in the record to indicate that Mrs. Myers, his mother, is not a fit person to exercise that authority. It is true, that in the past that authority was not sufficient to keep Frank from being led astray. But circumstances have changed. The source of Frank's contamination has been removed. His more vicious associates are no longer in Fargo. It is only at the State Training School that he could continue those associations. Mrs. Myers had not been aware of the nature of all of her son's activities. The evening he slept all night at the Selstrom home she thought that he was staying at the home of one of his school friends. It was not disclosed to her that his intimates were other than what they should be. Nevertheless, when he stayed out late nights she punished him by not permitting him to go out at all for a stated period. Now both Frank and his mother have undergone a difficult experience and we think the record shows them both to be people who will profit by that experience.

During the course of the argument considerable stress was laid upon a letter written by Frank to one of his acquaintances. This letter adds nothing to what we have already stated to be the nature of Frank's delinquency. In fact it is in his favor as well as it is against him, because it shows he was amenable to his mother's orders.

After a full consideration of all the evidence we have concluded that it is not for Frank's best interest to commit him to the State Training School. We think that he has demonstrated traits of character that entitle him to another chance to show he can accommodate himself to the normal healthy life society requires of a sixteen year old boy. We think this end may be obtained under the mother's supervision if she has the full and friendly cooperation of the juvenile authorities. The order committing Frank Myers to the State Training School is therefore reversed and the case remanded to the Juvenile Court of Cass County.

CHRISTIANSON, Ch. J., and NUESSLE and MORRIS, JJ., concur.

BURR, J. (concurring specially). The statement in the foregoing decision, regarding the acts of the juvenile concerned, is to say the least, as favorable to him as is warranted. But the serious situation in which this boy finds himself is a matter of his own choosing, as well as that of home and social environment. Thus this court, as well as the juvenile court, is convinced he is a delinquent.

The record shows that some of the others involved in the same transactions were committed to the training school by the juvenile court. He is not being singled out, though some others were not committed. The juvenile court which had the whole sordid matter before it — and it is a situation which the opinions herein do not adequately describe for reasons quite obvious — has not completed its adjustment.

There is intimation that disposition of some more seriously involved had not yet been determined. The problem here, however, is what to do with *this* boy. The juvenile court was confronted with a condition and not a theory — an extremely serious situation involving numerous people.

The boy is shown to be industrious and thrifty. The situation in which he is involved centers around drinking parties in which he participated, drinking associations and the consequent results that promote immorality. He is in bad company of his own choosing and with evidence, patent to him, which should have caused him to avoid it.

The record shows considerable effort to find a place where he could be sent for proper supervision. Nothing came of this, except, apparently, a choice between commitment to the training school, or of leaving the boy in the custody of his mother. These seem to have been the alternatives left to the juvenile court, and the court states the boy should not remain in Fargo.

The juvenile court, far better acquainted with the actual state of affairs that we, felt the mother was not a fit person to have supervision. I can not subscribe to the assumption in the opinion that he should be left under the influence of his mother. I see nothing in the record which suggests any improvement in him under her supervision. Confessedly she is engaged in the very business of promoting such a situation. For over two years she has been a barmaid in a liquor store serving intoxicating liquor to customers; and this very business of hers is an inducement for her son to do as others are doing. She seems to think that because she earns $25 a week with an average of $20 per week tips in addition, and is thus employed she said from "after supper" until 1 A. M. for six days in the week this shows she is capable of taking care of him and excuses the lack of good example and care.

The usual excuse "others are doing it" is given as justification of the mother's dereliction and of the boy's. When a mother engages in the very acts which are the cause of the downfall of her son and seems to think this is respectable, it is difficult for me to see how she can be considered a fit influence to direct his moral conduct. There is no indication in the record she intends to abandon the business in which she is engaged, and one can readily see how little good influence she would have with him when she herself is actively promoting the very situation which has contributed to her son's present state. The mother says the boy "is a very good student if he wants to work." She admits he did not do very well and gives as a reason, "I suppose he was running around at the Selstrom place and was not studying; that is what he told me himself."

The record shows definitely that arrangements had been made permitting him to enlist in the Merchant Marine. He has a brother in the Navy. In the record is the statement of his counsel that if the boy joined the Merchant Marine "he will receive four years of instruction and training which will train him for life if he wishes to stay in the Navy."

It does not appear the juvenile court gave any consideration to this possibility. While concurring in reversal and remand I believe it wise, before the boy is committed to the training school for the crucial years before him, to require the juvenile court to investigate this contingency, and make further efforts to find a proper place for this boy so that he be away from these evil influences which surround him.

88

In re Kroll *

RICHARDSON, Chief Judge.

Leroy Kroll, a sixteen year old minor, was found by the court to be "habitually beyond the control of his guardian" and was ordered "committed to the National Training School for Boys until twenty-one years of age." To review this ruling an appeal is prosecuted.

In an earlier proceeding initiated March 23, 1944, a petition was filed in Juvenile Court by a school attendance officer, charging that the boy, then aged fifteen, "is habitually truant from school." He was present with his mother at a hearing on March 29, 1944. Quoting him as "acknowledging the facts" the court ordered that he "be, and he is hereby, committed to the Board of Public Welfare."

The Board immediately placed him in the Industrial Home School.[1] A few weeks later he developed appendicitis. An operation was performed at a local hospital and while convalescing he was permitted to remain at the home of his parents.

On May 16, 1944, the parents petitioned the Juvenile Court to revoke the order of commitment. This was denied and the boy returned to the institution. A month later without per-

---

* In re Kroll, Municipal Court of Appeals for the District of Columbia, 1945, 43 A. 2d 706.
[1] Code 1940, § 32–501.

mission he went home; his parents returned him to the school. Shortly thereafter the parents unsuccessfully sought to secure his release by habeas corpus proceedings in the District Court of the United States for the District of Columbia. He was, however, permitted to remain with his parents for a few days on their promise to return him to the school. To avoid this he left Washington and went to Florida where he lived with an older brother.

In January, 1945, a few days before his sixteenth birthday, the age limit for compulsory school attendance, he returned to his parents' home in Washington. He was employed as an apprentice machinist at the Washington Navy Yard when, on March 7, 1945, he was taken into custody. The present proceeding was then initiated by a petition filed by one Robert S. Leonard, charging that he "is habitually beyond the control of his guardian." At a hearing on March 10, 1945, the foregoing facts were those offered in support of the petition.

The record contains a full transcript of the hearing, including the testimony of the boy and both parents. It shows, and this was not disputed, that except for his truancy and unauthorized departures from the custody of the Board of Public Welfare, his conduct had been good, he was obedient, and had had no trouble with police or neighbors. His parents expressed their urgent desire to retain him at home. He is the youngest of seven children. Three of his older brothers and sisters are in the armed services and three are employed in government bureaus in Washington. No lack of proper home surroundings or failure of the parents to properly supervise the boy were shown, except by such inferences as may be drawn from his truancy and failure to remain in custody of the Board. The father testified that his unwillingness to attend school was due to a nervous condition and that he had been advised by a physician to permit him to remain at home. From the father's testimony it would appear that while "truant" within the purview of the local statute [2] requiring children under sixteen to attend school, his absences were not without the knowledge or consent of his parents.

The boy's explanation of his leaving the Industrial Home School without authority and

failure to return was that he was mistreated there by other boys; that his legs were burned by lighted cigarettes; that he was beaten and struck in the stomach and that this had caused the attack of appendicitis; and that he could not report these things to the school authorities for fear of reprisals.

The issue here is whether there was sufficient evidence to support a finding that the boy's welfare or the safety and protection of the public required removal from the home of his parents. The Board of Public Welfare, in March, 1926,[3] succeeded to the powers of the Board of Children's Guardians, and was authorized "to have the care and legal guardianship of children who may be committed by courts of competent jurisdiction and to make such provision for their care and maintenance, either temporarily or permanently, in private homes or in public or private institutions, as the welfare of the child may require."

In Section 3 — 116 the classes of children over whom the Board shall have supervision are defined as follows:

"First. All children committed under section 32–209.[4]

"Second. All children who are destitute of suitable homes and adequate means of earning an honest living, all children abandoned by their parents or guardians, all children of habitually drunken or vicious or unfit parents, all children habitually begging on the streets or from door to door, all children kept in vicious or immoral associations, all children known by their language or life to be vicious or incorrigible whenever such children may be committed to the care of the board by the Juvenile Court of the District."

Section 3–160 places under the control of the Board various penal and other institutions of the District of Columbia, including Industrial Training Home School. The National Training School for Boys is a federal institution, under the control of the Attorney General of the United States, charged among other things with the detention and training, until twenty-one

---

[2] Code 1940, § 31–201.

[3] Code 1940, § 3–114.

[4] Under Section 32–209 the children referred to are those "subjected to cruel treatment, wilful abuse, or neglect, or any child under seventeen years of age found in a house of ill-fame."

years of age, of boys under seventeen convicted of crimes for which the penalty does not extend to life imprisonment.[5]

The Juvenile Court was given jurisdiction over minors under the age of eighteen years, including one:

"(2) Who is habitually beyond the control of his parents, custodian, or guardian; or

"(3) Who is habitually truant from school or home." [6]

In the chapter entitled "Juvenile Court" its "Purpose and basic aims" are defined in Section 11–902, Code 1940. We quote:

"The purpose of this chapter is to secure for each child under its jurisdiction such care and guidance, preferably in his own home, as will serve the child's welfare and the best interests of the state; to conserve and strengthen the child's family ties whenever possible, removing him from the custody of his parents only when his welfare or the safety and protection of the public cannot be adequately safe-guarded without such removal; and, when such child is removed from his own family, to secure for him custody, care, and discipline as nearly as possible equivalent to that which should have been given by his parents."

Sections 11–908 to 918 describe in detail procedure to be followed, and Section 11–915 authorizes the court, if it shall find that a child comes within the provisions of the Code, to proceed by order as follows:

"(1) Place the child on probation or under supervision in his own home or in the custody of a relative or other fit person, upon such terms as the court shall determine.

"(2) Commit the child to the Board of Public Welfare; or to the National Training School for Girls or the National Training School for Boys if in need of such care as is given in such schools * * *.

"(3) * * * That nothing herein shall be construed as authorizing the removal of the child from the custody of his parents unless his welfare and the safety and protection of the public can not be adequately safeguarded without such removal."

These provisions relating to the Juvenile Court were carefully considered in Re Stuart, 72 App.D.C. 389, 114 F.2d 825, 830. There, quoting from these sections of our statute, it was held that an order removing a child from the custody of his parent could not be sustained without substantial evidence to support a finding that "his welfare and the safety and protection of the public cannot be adequately safeguarded without such removal."

The objective of the law is rehabilitation, not punishment. We have quoted extensively from the statutes to emphasize the fact that this objective is manifest throughout our legislation dealing with juvenile offenders. As to them the same jealous care with which our civil courts seek the welfare of minors [7] has been in large measure substituted by Congress and by state legislatures for penal action. This thought variously expressed is found in many reported opinions.

"The very purpose of this law * * * is to provide for protection and care of juvenile offenders in a humanitarian effort to prevent them from becoming outcasts and criminals rather than to inflict punishment for their delinquencies." [8]

We find nothing in the record of these proceedings to justify the conclusion that the boy's "welfare and the safety and protection of the public can not be adequately safeguarded" without removing him from his home and parents. He testified that incident to his work he attends school at the Washington Navy Yard and we may take cognizance of the fact that a school is maintained there, where mathematics and other subjects are taught, which apprentice machinists are required to attend.

Counsel for appellee argues that the court having acquired jurisdiction by its commitment in the truancy case retains that jurisdiction until the subject is twenty-one years of age.[9]

---

[5] Huff v. O'Bryant, 74 App.D.C. 19, 121 F.2d 890; U.S.C.A. Title 5, § 133t, Plan No. II, Part 1, Sec. 3; Code 1940, § 32–815.

[6] Code 1940, § 11–906.

[7] As recently as June 11, 1945, the United States Court of Appeals for this district, in Boone v. Boone, 150 F.2d 153, a custody case, said: "The question for the trial court is the welfare of the children. This consideration overrides all others."

[8] Mattingly v. Com., 171 Ky. 222, 188 S.W. 370, 371. See also State ex rel. Berry v. Superior Court, 139 Wash. 1, 245 P. 409, 45 A.L.R. 1530 and annotation; 31 Am. Jur., Juvenile Courts and Offenders, Sec. 22.

[9] Code 1940, § 11–907 provides: "When jurisdic-

Had further orders as to custody been made in that case the argument may have been pertinent, but it completely disregards the fact that the order therein was set aside and that case has been dismissed; that the order here was based on a different charge, was made in a new and independent proceeding, and must find its justification in the record made therein.

We do not minimize the importance of enforcing our truancy laws. Education of the individual is reflected in the standard of intelligence of the citizen body as a whole, an essential element of successful republican government. But when this proceeding was brought the minor was beyond the age of compulsory education. His earlier truancy was past recall or cure. His disobedience to the lawful order of the court formed the basis of the proceeding. Though it was the ill-advised act of a fifteen and one-half year old boy, it should not have been condoned or passed unnoticed. But adults, presumably of mature judgment, may and frequently do show equal disregard for court orders. Usually a moderate fine or brief incarceration serves to remind that such acts may not be committed with impunity.

Will a child's development into a useful law abiding citizen be aided by taking him out of his home, away from respectable interested parents, from good associates and from a useful employment of his own choice, and placing him in a correctional institution where some of his associates, youths of his age or older, may be persons guilty of serious offenses and in some instances perhaps possessed of depraved or known criminal tendencies, and where he will be required to learn a trade for which he may have neither aptitude nor liking? Will respect for law and order be born of the natural resentment engendered by what he may well regard as punishment disproportionate to his offense against the law? As in Re Stuart, surpa, the Juvenile Court undoubtedly had jurisdiction under the terms of the statute, but, as in that case, the evidence here is insufficient to justify the severe order which was entered.

Reversed.

tion shall have been obtained by the court in the case of any child, such child shall continue under the jurisdiction of the court until he becomes 21 years of age unless discharged prior thereto."

89

In re Weiner *

HIRT, Judge.

On July 18, 1952 Aaron Weiner a thirteen-year old boy and his companion, John Spence, also known as John Wapner, were brought into the Juvenile Court on charges of delinquency. Nine burglaries had been committed within a period of two weeks; Aaron Weiner admitted that he had participated with Spence in seven of them. At the first hearing on August 8, 1952, the hearing judge stressed the importance of restitution to those whose property had been taken in Cheltenham Township, Montgomery County. At the suggestion of the court Abraham Weiner the father of one of the boys retired from the hearing room and discussed settlement with those present whose homes had been entered. But because witnesses as to two or three burglaries in Philadelphia County did not appear, the hearing judge stated: "* * * I will defer sentence until we can hear them. With respect to both boys, as to damage they did, I will take into consideration what adjustment is made with the prosecution, the people whose homes were burglarized. I will defer sentence, and both boys are to be held." An officer of the court reported that Aaron Weiner's father had deposited $185 with the "restitution department" of the court for the adjustment of the Cheltenham losses and the case was then continued to August 29, 1952 by the court; "Both defendants to be held in the House of Detention." At the hearing on August 29, 1952, the court stated to Abraham Weiner: "* * * you were here before and we told you to make some adjustment with the people whose homes were ransacked in Cheltenham" and referring to burglaries committed in Philadelphia the court said to the father of the boy: "I am placing Aaron on strict probation, restitution in the amount of $585 to be made before Aaron Weiner is released. Otherwise he will stand committed." The court indicated that Abraham Weiner was

* In re Weiner, Appeal of Weiner, Superior Court of Pennsylvania, 1954, 176 Pa. Super. 255, 106 A. 2d 915.

to pay that amount. And when he deposited $270 the court gave him until September 15, 1952 to pay the balance, and placed Aaron on probation in the custody of his father, apparently subject to some supervision by the Big Brother Association. The Spence boy was committed to Hawthorne Knolls School.

On November 17, 1952 Abraham Weiner again appeared in the Juvenile Court pursuant to notice. The hearing was addressed solely to the question of further payments by him. He had disregarded a recent demand of a Mr. Blank to pay him $62.50, the value of property taken from his house by the boys. Abraham Weiner stated to the court that he needed six months to pay off the loan by which he raised the $585 previously paid. And when he questioned his liability to pay the total amount of the losses, since there were two boys involved, the lower court found him guilty of contempt "for lack of cooperation." He was committed to the county prison but was released later when the court stated: "I will release him from the County Prison on the charge of contempt, but the restitution is to be paid, and probation is continued as to the boy."

Abraham Weiner again appeared in the lower court on November 24, 1952. He was summoned because he had failed to make restitution in still another case for property taken from owners in Elkins Park. The court again stressed the importance of restitution and said: "It is up to you to adjust this, with reference to this claim in Elkins Park."

All of the offenses were statutory burglaries committed in the daytime. The boys rode about on their bicycles and broke into houses which appeared to have been closed for some time. They stole a long list of articles — fishing tackle, guns and cameras and the like and committed serious acts of vandalism in some instances. The Weiner boy undoubtedly was led astray by his associate who had prior experience in similar delinquencies. Aaron had never been in trouble before and there is no suggestion that he has misbehaved since he was returned to his family. The orders of the court committing the Spence boy to an institution and returning Aaron Weiner on probation to his family concededly were appropriate and these orders are not questioned here.

The direction of the court on August 29, 1952 that Abraham Weiner make restitution in the sum of $585 amounted to an order of the court. This appeal is by Abraham Weiner from that order. He was not represented by counsel below and his numerous petitions subsequently filed were inartistically drawn. But in effect he complained of the restitution payments he was compelled to make and he sought a rehearing on the question of his liability. The court on December 30, 1953 denied a rehearing. The opinion of the court filed on February 11, 1954 assigns the failure of this appellant to comply with § 15 of the Juvenile Court Law of June 2, 1933, P.L. 1433, 11 P.S. § 257, in justification of the order. That section of the Act requires a petition for a rehearing within 21 days from an order "committing or placing any * * * delinquent child." On such petition the court is bound to grant a rehearing as a matter of right and an appeal lies only from the final order of the court after rehearing. Abraham Weiner's petitions apparently were not filed within 21 days from the date of the restitution order of August 29, 1952. But section 15 of the Juvenile Court Law has no application to this appellant. His appeal is before us for review, not as an appeal under the above 1933 Act, but as on certiorari questioning the jurisdiction of the court and the regularity of the proceedings in the restitution order imposed upon him by the lower court. Cf. Carroll's Appeal, 336 Pa. 257, 9 A.2d 407.

In Re Trignani's Case, 148 Pa. Super. 142, 24 A.2d 743, 745, we suggested that the function of a juvenile court is not to enforce satisfaction of civil damages, but " 'that evil tendencies may be checked' " by means of " 'such care, guidance and control as are essential to children in the formative period of life' " quoting from the preamble of the Act. 11 P.S. § 243. And in that case we recognized the power of the court to impose terms in placing a child on probation. But we held that the terms imposed in requiring restitution *by the juvenile*, must be wholly in the interest of the child, looking toward his reformation and not to make good the damages flowing from his illegal acts. Undoubtedly restitution by the parents of a delinquent child in some instances may be indicated to impress upon them their responsibility in the reformation of the child. But there is nothing in the Juvenile Court Law which authorizes the court to compel the parents to make restitution satisfying the civil demands of the victims of the child's delinquency and the juvenile court has no power by attachment to enforce such orders when made. The Municipal Court sitting as a juvenile court has only such jurisdiction as is given it by statute, and compelling restitution by the child's parents is not one of them.

Moreover, in general, there is no common law liability on a parent of a delinquent child to make restitution. The rule is thus stated in Condel v. Savo, 350 Pa. 350, 39 A.2d 51, 52, 155 A.L.R. 81: "At common law the mere relation of parent and child imposes upon the parent no liability for the torts of the child, but the parents may be liable where the act of the child is done as the agent of the parents or where the negligence of the parents makes the injury possible. The injury committed by the child must have been the natural and probable consequence of the parents' negligent act, that is, a consequence which, under the surrounding circumstances, might and ought reasonably to have been foreseen as likely to flow from such negligent act." Cf. Mendola v. Sambol, 166 Pa.Super. 351, 71 A.2d 827. Abraham Weiner the present appellant is in no sense chargeable with responsibility for his son's delinquencies and there is no common law liability for restitution on him.

The order of December 30, 1953 denying a rehearing did not extend the time of appeal; it had no bearing on that question. The appeal from the order of August 29, 1952 was properly taken, almost five months later, on January 11, 1954, since the court in making the order acted without authority. A final order entered by a court without jurisdiction may be questioned on appeal at any time. [Citation omitted. — Ed.]

The reversal in this case may be an empty victory for appellant since he complied with the order by making restitution as a condition to regaining custody of his child. But he nevertheless is entitled to be heard in the lower court and to such redress as is possible under the circumstances. Order reversed . . .

GUNTHER, Judge (dissenting).

Appellant was adjudged a delinquent by the Juvenile Division of the Municipal Court of Philadelphia. Two hearings were held, the second on August 29, 1952. The testimony established that the appellant committed a series of burglaries, most of which he admitted. He was placed on probation in the custody of a Jewish agency for placement in a home, after appel-

lant's father had agreed to make restitution to the victims of the burglaries. The father subsequently asked for a rehearing and for return of the money paid as restitution. He now appeals from the refusal, by the court below, of his petition for rehearing and from the order entered.

Appellant contends that the evidence is insufficient to establish that he committed the various burglaries for which he was charged and finally, that the values placed on the property stolen were greatly exaggerated. Examination of the record reveals more than sufficient competent evidence to sustain the findings and the decision of the court below. The appellant admitted his participation in most of the crimes. Two hearings were held, which afforded sufficient opportunity to elicit any testimony establishing appellant's innocence.

It is also contended that it was improper for the court to order restitution. It is clear from the record that the primary concern of the court was the welfare of the child. Restitution may be an entirely proper adjunct to an order regarding a delinquent, although it has been held improper in some instances. See In re Trignani's Case, 148 Pa.Super. 142, 24 A.2d 743. Here however, it is clear that the appellant and his father had the financial means to make restitution which the court ordered to be paid in a lump sum by a specified time. No burden was placed on the juvenile which might prove beyond his capabilities to perform. The main complaint, in truth, seems to be that the victims allegedly exaggerated their losses and were overpaid thereby. Had appellant's father wished to pursue the testimony in regard thereto he could have petitioned, as a matter of right, for a rehearing within twenty-one days of the final order of the court below. Having failed to do so, he must stand on the record, which I find, is sufficient to sustain the action of the court below.*

---

* See, also, *Lamro Independent Consol. School Dist.* v. *Cawthorne*, —— S. D. ——, 73 N.W. 2d 337 (1955) holding no parental liability for vandalism by son even in the face of a statute which appears to cover the situation. For recent attempts to impose punishment upon parents for the wrongs of their children, see Note 32, *Notre Dame Law Review* 155 (1956), "Criminal Law — Parental Responsibility for Juvenile Delinquents Imposed by New York Statute." Such statutes usually apply only after the juvenile court has taken jurisdiction and has issued instructions to parents. See, also, Chapter 30 of this book. — *Ed.*

90

Petition of Morin *et al.**

DUNCAN, Justice.

The proceedings which culminated in the committal of the plaintiff's minor child were instituted pursuant to the provisions of R.L. c. 132, relating to "Neglected and Delinquent Children." The plaintiffs contend that this act and in particular the provisions of § 2(II), defining "delinquent child" are unconstitutional. As understood, the argument is directed to the proposition that the statute provides for imprisonment of a minor child without requiring that the child be either charged with or convicted of a crime. By the statutory definition a child "who is wayward, disobedient or uncontrolled by his parent * * * or so deports himself as to injure or endanger the health or morals of himself or others" is a "delinquent child," as is one who "violates any law of this state or any city or town ordinance." § 2(II) supra. Under section 13 of the act a child found to be delinquent may be committed to the industrial school, or made subject to "such orders as to care, custody, and probation as justice and the welfare of the child require." The act provides that proceedings taken under it shall "not be deemed to be of a criminal nature," § 17, and that "no child shall be deemed a criminal by reason of an adjudication hereunder and such adjudication shall not be deemed a conviction." § 23. Under the provisions of R.L. c. 463, § 17, committal of a delinquent child to the industrial school is required to be for the term of his minority. The jurisdiction of the municipal court continues until the child reaches twenty-one, unless he is discharged by the court, or jurisdiction is released to the Superior Court. Laws 1945, c. 29.

We think it sufficiently plain that the act in question is designed to permit the exercise of the powers of the state as "parens patriae," for the purpose of rehabilitating minor children, and not of punishing them for the commission of a crime. "It is generally held that the purpose of such statutes is not penal, but protective. It is not that the child shall be punished for breach of a law or regulation, but that he shall have a better chance to become a worthy citizen." State v. Lefebvre, 91 N.H. 382, 384, 20 A.2d 185, 187. . . . [Some citations omitted. — *Ed.*] Similar statutes have been universally upheld over objections based upon constitutional grounds. . . . [Citations omitted. — *Ed.*]

The early decision of State ex rel. Cunningham v. Ray, 63 N.H. 406, 56 Am. Rep. 529, held unconstitutional a statute in no way comparable to the act before us. It permitted the court, in lieu of accepting a recognizance on binding over a minor charged with crime, to commit him to reform school without hearing, for the term of his minority. The case is not controlling here. Nor is People ex rel. O'Connell v. Turner, 55 Ill. 280, 8 Am.Rep. 645, persuasive. See In re Ferrier, 103 Ill. 367, 43 Am.-Rep. 10; McLean County v. Humphreys, 104 Ill. 378; Lindsay v. Lindsay, supra. There is no evidence to suggest that the industrial school is other than "a real school, not a prison in disguise" (Mack: The Juvenile Court, 23 Harv. Law Rev. 104, 114), or that committal to it is not a reasonably necessary restraint, rather than imprisonment. We conclude that R.L. c. 132 is constitutional.

The plaintiffs make no contention, if the act is constitutional, that the court did not obtain jurisdiction of their child in accordance with its provisions. The proceedings before the municipal court followed the course prescribed by the statute. There was a petition, § 3, notice to the child's parent, § 4, a hearing, § 9, and a finding of delinquency. § 13. It is apparently not questioned that the court, having thus obtained jurisdiction, in its discretion might have entered an order for committal forthwith. § 13. It is claimed however that because the order for committal followed an order for probation and was made without further notice or hearing, it violated constitutional and statutory rights, and therefore was invalid. As the cases previously cited indicate, constitutional guaranties applicable to criminal proceedings are inapplicable to proceedings such as these. Under the court's continuing jurisdiction, §§ 1, 13; Laws 1945, c. 29, deferred committal was as much within the Court's

---

* *Petition of Morin* et al., Supreme Court of New Hampshire, 1949, 95 N.H. 518, 68 A. 2d 668.

authority as was immediate committal. The order made was no more violative of constitutional requirements because it was deferred.

The particular statutory provision relied upon by the plaintiffs appears in the act by which the probation department was created. R.L. c. 379. It provides: "In case a probationer has violated any of the conditions of his probation any probation officer with or without a warrant, and any other officer with a warrant may arrest him, and the court, after summary hearing, may make such orders as justice requires." § 14. The Trustees assert that this provision is limited in its application to criminal cases, pointing out that the language of "arrest" is not the language applicable to juvenile cases arising under R.L. c. 132.

Whatever the intent of the legislature may have been with respect to the application of the probation act to proceedings authorized by the act relating to neglected and delinquent children, acts enacted within a week of each other, Laws 1937, cc. 143, 152, the application of the quoted provision to the instant case has not been established. The record contains no evidence of violation by the child of any condition of the probation imposed upon her. So far as appears, committal may equally as well have resulted from a purpose to protect her from influences beyond her control as from any voluntary misconduct on her part. The authority of the court to "make such orders as justice requires," § 14, c. 379, R.L., was not necessarily derived from the probation act requiring proof of violation of probation and a summary hearing. Section 13 of Chapter 132 provides that the court may "commit the child to the industrial school or continue the case with such orders as to care, custody, and probation as justice and the welfare of the child require." The provisions conferring continuing jurisdiction indicate the legislative intent that the alternative dispositions specified shall not be mutually exclusive, but that the requisite orders may be made from time to time during the child's minority. See In re Gomez, supra.

Whether the circumstances which prompted the order of committal in this case fairly called for its summary entry without notice or hearing is not disclosed by this record. Failure to provide such notice however cannot invalidate the order made, which was within the validly acquired, continuing jurisdiction of the tribunal which made it. Stoker v. Gowans, 45 Utah 556, 147 P. 911, Ann.Cas.1916E, 1025.

Though valid, the procedure followed is not necessarily beyond criticism. Even though the statute requiring summary hearing was not literally applicable, the better practice would have been to afford further notice and opportunity for hearing before committal. By operating to deprive a parent of custody, however restricted, and to take from a child the comparative liberty enjoyed upon probation, committal produces a drastic change in status which should not be imposed without good cause. Whether such cause exists can usually best be determined after hearing rather than before. If the delay incident thereto is thought to endanger the welfare of the child, suitable provision may properly be made for his detention pending hearing. R.L. c. 132, §§ 6, 7.

The refusal of the Superior Court on habeas corpus to invalidate the order was not error. Upon such an application, made for the purpose of determining the proper custody of a minor the Court is concerned not solely with the legality of the custody in which the child is found, but also with the question of what custody is most consistent with the future welfare of the child. Hanrahan v. Sears, 72 N.H. 71, 54 A. 702; Sheehy v. Sheehy, 88 N.H. 223, 226, 186 A. 1, 107 A.L.R. 635; Prendergast v. Titus, 95 N.H. 191, 60 A.2d 122. In the finding that the best interests of this child require that she remain in the custody of the defendants there was no abuse of discretion. See Commonwealth v. Ball, 259 Mass. 148, 156 N.E. 21. It follows that the petition was properly denied regardless of the possibility of irregularity in committal not affecting the jurisdiction of the committing court. State ex rel. Bethell v. Kilvington, 100 Tenn. 227, 45 S.W. 433, 41 L.R.A. 284; In re Turner, 94 Kan. 115, 145 P. 871, Ann.Cas.1916E 1022; Stoker v. Gowans, supra. See also Lowery v. Fayette County Children's Bureau, 306 Ky. 817, 209 S.W.2d 487.

So far as the plaintiff's exceptions rest upon a claim of insufficiency of the evidence to warrant the findings made, they are without merit. There was no evidence tending to establish fitness of the parents to resume custody. The fact of the marriage of the delinquent child after committal did not suspend operation of the law by which she was committed, nor did it entitle her to release from the defendants' custody.

Stoker v. Gowans, supra; In re Hook, 95 Vt. 497, 115 A. 730, 19 A.L.R. 610; note, 22 Minn.-L.Rev. 285; annotation 49 A.L.R. 402.

The petition was heard against a background of criminal prosecution of the minor's husband, State v. Lacoshus, now pending in this court. Both the Presiding Justice and plaintiff's counsel participated in that trial. While little of the evidence there received was introduced at the hearing on this petition, the Trial Court may properly have taken judicial notice of the pendency of the charge, as supporting the findings which were made.

We conclude that committal was by order of a court having jurisdiction to make it, and that there was no error in the finding or ruling that the welfare of the child required that there be no modification of the order.

Exceptions overruled.

KENISON, J., was absent; the other concurred.

91

In re Weintraub *

RHODES, President Judge.

This is an appeal from an order of the Municipal Court (Juvenile Division) committing the minor to the Pennsylvania Industrial School at White Hill.

The petition charged that he was a juvenile delinquent. As evidence of his delinquency the petition charged him with the destruction of personal property of others, with the possible commission of larceny, and with writing a threatening letter. The minor was born on November 25, 1933. Hearings were held before President Judge Boyle of the Municipal Court on September 8, 21, and 23, 1949, and a record made of 444 pages. Upon this record the Judge found that the minor was a delinquent, that he possessed serious abnormal sexual urges, that he is potentially and sexually dangerous, that, if he is permitted to remain at large, even upon probation, he would likely be a danger and a

menace to the community, and that for his own welfare and that of his family and the community at large he should be committed to an institution where he can receive psychiatric treatment. He thereupon made an order of commitment.

As provided by section 15 of the Act of June 2, 1933, P.L. 1433, 11 P.S. § 257,[1] a petition for review and rehearing was filed on behalf of the minor by his mother within twenty-one days after the order of commitment. The petition averred generally that the court erred in its findings of fact and in its conclusions of law, that the order of the court was improvidently and inadvertently made, that the court erred in refusing counsel for the minor the right to further cross-examine the witnesses, and that the commitment was illegal. The Commonwealth filed an answer, and a rehearing was held on October 19, 1949. At that time the testimony taken at the previous hearings on September 8, 21, and 23, 1949, was admitted as part of the record on the rehearing. Counsel for the minor was given opportunity to present further testimony and to sustain the averments of his petition. Counsel at the time stated that he did not challenge the finding of the court that the minor was a delinquent. His contention was that the rehearing on his petition was de novo and the equivalent of a new trial, and that all

---

* In re Weintraub, Superior Court of Pennsylvania, 1950, 166 Pa. Super. 342, 71 A. 2d 823.

[1] "Within twenty-one (21) days after the final order of any judge of the juvenile court, committing or placing any dependent, neglected or delinquent child, such child shall, as a matter of right, by his or her parent or parents or next friend, have the right to present to the court a petition to have his or her case or cases reviewed and reheard, if, in the opinion of such parent, parents, or next friend, an error of fact or of law, or of both, has been made in such proceedings or final order, or if the said order has been improvidently or inadvertently made.

"Upon the presentation of such petition, the court shall grant such review and rehearing as a matter of right. The testimony at such reviews and rehearing shall be taken down and transcribed by an official court stenographer, which testimony shall be duly made a part of the record in such case. From the final order of such court, in proceedings for such rehearings, and reviews, appeals shall lie as a matter of right to the Superior Court, upon the same terms and with the same regulations as are provided by law with respect to appeals from any decree of the orphans' court. In hearing such appeals, the Superior Court shall consider the testimony as a part of the record." Act of June 2, 1933, P.L. 1433, § 15, 11 P.S. § 257.

the witnesses for the Commonwealth should be recalled to establish again the facts to which they testified in order that he might be able to prove by further cross-examination, in addition to the testimony presented in defense on causation, what caused the minor to commit the acts for which he has been adjudged delinquent. No additional testimony being offered by counsel for the minor, the court refused his request that all the witnesses for the Commonwealth be recalled. After reviewing the record it entered the final order on November 2, 1949, affirming the commitment, from which this appeal has been taken.

The issues presented on this appeal are limited. The court did not classify the minor as a sexual psychopath or as a constitutional psychopathic inferior. The court found him to be a delinquent. Delinquency is admitted, and it is undisputed that he is abnormal sexually and requires treatment. Five psychiatrists testified, and the opinion of another was incorporated in the record. They all agreed that the minor required psychiatric treatment. The three engaged by the minor did not think that he should be placed in an institution. It was their opinion that the minor was not potentially dangerous, and that he could safely be permitted to be at large providing he received proper psychiatric treatment, he being kept under close observation during such time. The other three psychiatrists testified that the minor had a personality defect, that he was potentially dangerous, and that he should be given institutional treatment.

We are asked on this appeal to reverse the order of commitment with a rehearing de novo that there may be further cross-examination of Commonwealth witnesses as to causation. From our examination of the record it is clear to us that the judge allowed ample cross-examination on all matters relevant to the issues. The extent of cross-examination is ordinarily a question for determination by the trial judge. His action will not be reversed in the absence of an abuse of discretion. Tolomeo v. Harmony Short Line Motor Transportation Co., 349 Pa. 420, 423, 37 A.2d 511.

The court below has exclusive jurisdiction in the first instance in all proceedings affecting or concerning delinquent children under eighteen years of age. Act of July 12, 1913, P.L. 711, § 11(b), and amendments, 17 P.S. § 694;

Juvenile Court Law of June 2, 1933, P.L. 1433, § 2, 11 P.S. § 244(b). Section 1(4) of the Juvenile Court Law, 11 P.S. § 243(4), defines what constitutes delinquency. Section 8 of the Act of 1933, as amended by Act of June 15, 1939, P.L. 394, § 1, 11 P.S. § 250, further provides that after hearing the judge may determine whether the best interests and welfare of a child and the State require the care, guidance, and control of such child, and shall make an order accordingly; and that the court may, inter alia, place the child on probation or commit it to some suitable institution or industrial school. This section clearly implies that there is some discretion to be exercised by the court as to what shall be done with a delinquent child. "If a delinquent is found to be a proper subject for reformation the child remains within the jurisdiction of the juvenile court to be dealt with by it." In re Trignani's Case, 150 Pa.Super. 491, at page 493, 28 A.2d 702, at page 703.

An appeal from a final order of a juvenile court is a matter of right to the Superior Court, and shall be "upon the same terms and with the same regulations as are provided by law with respect to appeals from any decree of the orphans' court." Section 15 of the Act of 1933, 11 P.S. § 257. This Court shall consider the testimony as a part of the record on appeal from the final order in a proceeding for review and rehearing.

Section 22(b) of the Orphans' Court Act of June 7, 1917, P.L. 363, 20 P.S. § 2602, provides: "The Supreme and Superior courts of this Commonwealth shall, in all cases of appeal from the definitive sentence or decree of the orphans' court, hear, try and determine the same as to right and justice may belong, and decree according to the equity thereof; * * *."

In the exercise of its judicial discretion, the court committed the minor to White Hill where he could receive the psychiatric treatment indicated by all the psychiatrists. See Trignani's Case, supra, 150 Pa.Super. 491, 494, 28 A.2d 702. As the court below said: " * * * the dissatisfaction with the court's action had to do with the court's disposition of the minor after the delinquency was established." After referring to section 22(b) of the Orphans' Court Act, 20 P.S. § 2602, the Supreme Court, in In re Garrett's Estate, 335 Pa. 287, 292, 293, 6 A.2d 858, 860, said: "When the court has come to a conclusion by the exercise of its discretion, the party complaining of it on appeal has a heavy burden; it is not sufficient to persuade the appellate court that it might have reached a different conclusion if, in the first place, charged with the duty imposed on the court below; it is necessary to go further and show an abuse of the discretionary power. 'An abuse of discretion is not merely an error of judgment, but if in reaching a conclusion the law is overridden or misapplied, or the judgment exercised is manifestly unreasonable, or the result of partiality, prejudice, bias or illwill, as shown by the evidence or the record, discretion is abused.' " The court, in coming to the conclusion that the minor should be committed to an institution, gave careful consideration to the testimony and recommendations of the psychiatrists, and summarized their testimony as follows: "The psychiatrists on behalf of Paul, namely, Drs. Ornsteen, Spark and Winkelman, stated that in their opinion Paul was not and is not potentially dangerous; that he could safely be permitted to be at large, provided he received proper psychiatric treatment, and that he be kept under close observation during such time. * * * On the other hand, Dr. Stewart, a psychiatrist who has been on the staff of the Municipal Court for many years, states: 'He is a potentially dangerous boy whose personality defect is so fundamental that it will not respond to the usual course of psychiatric treatment. If permitted to remain at large he might well commit a serious sex crime. He is, therefore, in need of a long period of institutional training and should not be released until carefully re-evaluated. He should be committed to White Hill.' Dr. Stewart also stated: 'I think it would be far safer in an institution like White Hill. * * * We frequently send boys to White Hill and Huntingdon and after a few years they make a good adjustment. But I think it would be very dangerous to leave him at large at the present moment. * * * Paul is not feeble-minded nor mentally defective. * * * The associations in White Hill won't do him any harm * * * he will be supervised and controlled.' Dr. Drayton, another member of the staff of the Municipal Court, confirmed Dr. Stewart's opinion that Paul was potentially dangerous, stating that, 'He might injure some girl or some woman with his great sexual urge.' Dr. Davidson, who has observed this boy almost daily for about two months, stated that it was his opinion that Paul

should be 'restrained for some time' because Paul had abnormal sexual impulses and that such were always a danger to other people."

In the light of this testimony there was no abuse of discretion on the part of the court in making the final order of commitment. It declined to ignore the observations of the Commonwealth's medical experts. Moreover, it is to be borne in mind that an order in this type of case is never final. With a change of circumstances a petition on behalf of the minor may be presented asking for a revocation or modification of the existing order. Section 16, Act of 1933, 11 P.S. § 258. See, also, section 12 of the Act, 11 P.S. § 254.

We are of the opinion that there is no merit in appellant's contention that the rehearing on October 19, 1949, was not in accordance with section 15 of the Act of 1933, 11 P.S. § 257.

At the oral argument before this Court counsel for the minor contended that all witnesses for the Commonwealth who previously testified had to be recalled on such rehearing although there was no dispute as to the material facts — that the minor was a delinquent, and that he was abnormal requiring psychiatric treatment. Section 3 of the Act, 11 P.S. § 245, provides that all sessions of the juvenile court shall be held separate and apart from sessions of the court held for the purpose of its general, criminal, and other business; that the records shall be kept in a separate docket; and that they shall be withheld from indiscriminate public inspection. See, also, section 9 of the Act of July 12, 1913, P.L. 711, as amended, 17 P.S. § 692. Proceedings before a juvenile court are often informal, and at times the testimony taken at a hearing is not made a matter of record or reduced to writing. Under such circumstances, on an appeal from an order under the Act of April 23, 1903, P.L. 274, it was held that there was nothing before the appellate court for consideration other than the order of the court below. See Commonwealth v. Mountain, 82 Pa.Super. 523. The Act of June 1, 1915, P.L. 652, provided for a rehearing substantially as now provided by section 15 of the Act of 1933, 11 P.S. § 257. Such a rehearing assures a record which can be reviewed on appeal. In the present case the court granted a rehearing on the petition of the mother of the minor. The court gave to the appellant the opportunity to call witnesses to establish any material and relevant fact, and to point out any error of fact or law in the proceedings or order, or wherein the order had been improvidently or inadvertently made.

Where full hearing has been held and an order made, a "review and rehearing," as provided by section 15 of the Act, 11 P.S. § 257, is not in the nature of a new trial with the court's order vacated or set aside. The Act clearly indicates that the "review and rehearing" is for the correction of errors of fact or of law, or of both, which it is claimed the court had made in the proceeding or in its order, or for the disposition of an order improvidently and inadvertently made. On such rehearing the testimony presented "shall be taken down and transcribed by an official court stenographer, which testimony shall be duly made a part of the record in such case."

The Commonwealth at the rehearing in the present case could offer and rely on the record previously made. Appellant at the rehearing did not present any additional testimony or call any witnesses. The court thereupon reviewed the entire record and made its final order. Such record must be legally and factually adequate to sustain the findings of fact and order of commitment. A record destitute of any facts justifying the commitment of a minor would require a reversal. [Citation omitted. — Ed.]

In the present case we find no abuse of discretion, and the record contains no reversible error. Order is affirmed.†

92

In re Smith *

WYLEGALA, Judge.

Frieda Smith was duly committed by this court to Saint Anne Institute at Albany, N. Y., as a delinquent child on July 28, 1948. No appeal was taken and no application made for reconsideration of that commitment. Thereafter on the basis of reports from said Saint

---

† Examples of the broad discretion permitted the juvenile court judge will be found in In re Hartman, 93 Cal. App. 2d 801, 210 P2d 53 and State v. Smith, 11 N.J. 217, 94 A.2d 328 (1953). — Ed.

* In re Smith, Children's Court, Erie County, 1949, 92 N.Y. S. 2d 529.

Anne Institute, to the effect that Frieda could not benefit from their program, this court, without notice to the parents and without further hearing, amended the original order of commitment and had Frieda transferred to the New York State Training School for Girls at Hudson, New York, where she was accepted on May 17, 1949.

Application is now made for reconsideration of the commitment, with particular emphasis on the lack of notice to the parents that a change of place of commitment was contemplated.

Section 22, sub. c. of the Children's Court Act provides that when a child has been adjudicated to be delinquent, the court may

"commit the child to a suitable institution maintained by the state or any subdivision thereof, or subject to the further orders of the court to an authorized agency."

The New York State Training School is an institution maintained by the State, and commitments to it when accepted by it in conformity with the law, are not subject to any further order of the court. The release or discharge of the person so committed is controlled entirely by the institution. The court or committing judge has no control over the child.

Saint Anne Institute is an authorized agency and commitments to it are subject to the order of the court. Authorized agencies have the right to accept only such commitments as in their judgment can profit from their program, and may request the removal of a child, whenever such child fails to any longer profit from such commitment. It would seem that transfers of a child from one authorized agency to another should not require notice to parents or other interested parties.

In the instant case it has been argued that the parents of Frieda did not appeal from the ajudication of delinquency and the subsequent commitment, because they felt that as long as the commitment was subject to the further orders of the court her separation from her family would not be unduly prolonged; that they could by showing to the court that the home conditions have improved and that their control over Frieda would be improved, the court in its wisdom would return Frieda to them. They further argue that now, with their child in a State institution they are deprived of this possibility.

The instant case is the first of several such transfers made in this court during the past twelve years, where the court's power to make such transfer without notice to the parents is questioned. As far as I am able to find out the practice is general with the children's courts of our state, and has never been questioned.

After considerable deliberation on the subject I am convinced that when the change of place of commitment is from an authorized agency to a state institution the parent should receive notice and be given an opportunity to be heard. I therefore feel that the order amending the original commitment and transferring the child to the New York State Training School should be cancelled and the child returned to this court for further disposition.†

93

Ex parte S. H. *

HENRIOD, Justice.

Appeal from a denial of petition for habeas corpus. Affirmed, no costs awarded.

The divorced petitioner, mother of a 13-year-old, after time for appeal had expired, urged in her petition before the District Court, that the Juvenile Court erred in sending her son to the Industrial School because 1) he was too young, 2) there was no finding that she was unfit to have his custody and 3) that her son was returned to the School without a hearing after he had been allowed to return to his mother.

As to 1) and 2): These matters are reviewable on appeal, but do not go to the Juvenile Court's jurisdiction, and are not subject to review or collateral attack in habeas corpus proceedings.[1] As to 3): Under our statutes the Public Welfare Commission, and hence its agency, the Industrial School, has continuing jurisdiction over a committed child, and may expand and contract the walls of the institution as the welfare of the child dictates.[2] However, it could not be construed to operate as a device for oppression, and this court, in a proper case, would not hesitate to intercede if it faced a situation where the authorities had acted under the statute without good reason, capriciously or arbitrarily. There appears to be no proof of any such unreasonableness in the record here.

We do not believe that a child placed on probation, after having been committed to the School, is entitled to a hearing before being taken back into custody, but we do believe that once a child is allowed to leave the institution for rehabilitation or because he appears already to have been rehabilitated, the authorities must have good reason for returning him to the institution. The burden of proving lack of such good reason lies with him who contends it, and his proof should be not only more than preponderant, but something akin to that type of proof we ofttimes speak of as being clear and convincing.

Were the authorities unable to return a child released after commitment, without giving notice and without consulting a hearing, considerable mischief could result, the broad terminology of our statute would be somewhat meaningless, reasonable legislative control over domiciliaries would suffer at least partial emasculation, sovereign power over delinquents would be lessened and, as a practical matter, though it may not be seasoned with good legal reasoning, the School authorities naturally would be prone to hesitate in allowing a child his return to normal life, knowing the obstacles they would have to hurdle in returning him to the institution, — thus minimizing the chances for earlier redemption of many deserving children.

In this case an offer of proof was made with respect to the fitness of the mother, but none as to the unreasonableness of the School authorities' action, the petition having stated only in the form of a conclusion that the boy had been returned without a "legal hearing," and the matter having been made the subject of but a brief colloquy between court and counsel. Consequently, the trial court was justified in refusing to entertain jurisdiction in a habeas corpus

---

† Decisions vary on whether appearance in court constitutes waiver of notice, Compare In re Roth, 158 Neb. 789, 64 N.W. 2d 799 (1954) (parents present at order of commitment of boy) with Lazaros et al v. State, _____ Tex. Civ. _____, 228 S.W. 2d 972 (1950) (mother present at trial). — Ed.

* Ex parte S. H., Supreme Court of Utah, 1953, 1 Utah 2d 186, 264 P. 2d 850.
[1] U.S. v. Valante, 264 U.S. 563, 44 S.Ct. 411, 68 L.Ed. 850.
[2] Title 64–6–8, U.C.A.1953.

proceeding, to review the merits of the case before the Juvenile Court. There is no question but that the Juvenile Court has jurisdiction over children 13 years of age, and over the subject matter relating to parents' fitness to have custody. In truth, the Juvenile Court enjoys far wider jurisdictional and very well may commit a delinquent to the Industrial School for cause even though his parents are eminently fitted to have its custody.

Dehors the record we have learned that immediately following the habeas corpus proceedings the youngster here involved escaped, but that Mr. Beesley, his counsel, arduously worked, insisted and assisted in returning him to the School. We commend counsel's forthright attitude and ethical conduct.

McDonough and Wade, JJ., concur.

Crockett, J., concurs in result only . . .

94

Suarez v. Wilkinson *

Follmer, District Judge.

An application in forma pauperis for a writ of habeas corpus has been filed by the petitioner who is now serving his sentence at the United States Penitentiary, Lewisburg, Pennsylvania. He alleges that he

"was duly arrested on or about The (sic) seventh day of December, Nineteen and fifty one. (sic) On a Charge of violating the Federal Probation Act. By virtue of Civil proceding (sic) had in Court and was then and there, committed to the Federal Correctial (sic) Institution, at Englewood, Colorado for boys. The proceding (sic) being Civil Nature only and not Criminal, therefore the committment (sic) that holds Petitioner in the Northeastern Penitentiary at Lewisburg, Pennsylvania, is (Void). Being no committment (sic) at all."

A Rule to Show Cause issued in order that the record might be supplemented with the docket entries, information and judgment and commitment in the proceedings pursuant to which petitioner is now imprisoned.

* Suarez v. Wilkinson, United States District Court, M. D. Pennsylvania, 1955, 133 Fed. Supp. 38.

Having been arrested for having in his possession and having transported in interstate commerce an unregistered shotgun having a barrel less than eighteen inches in length he was brought before the United States District Court for the Western District of Missouri on an information charging him with having committed an act of juvenile delinquency. He consented to be prosecuted by information on a charge of juvenile delinquency and having plead guilty, on November 16, 1951, imposition of sentence was suspended and he was placed on probation for a period of two years. The opportunities of probation were apparently misconstrued by this petitioner since on December 10, 1951, a warrant of arrest issued to the Probation Officer and on January 11, 1952, the probation was revoked and he was "committed to the custody of the Attorney General or his authorized representative for imprisonment until he shall attain the age of twenty-one (21) years." He was originally committed to the Federal Correctional Institution at Englewood, Colorado, but it would appear that he still lacked the good common sense to avail himself of the opportunities for readjustment since it became necessary for the Attorney General to transfer him to a penitentiary.

It is his position that because 18 U.S.C. § 5032 provides:

"In such event the juvenile shall be proceeded against by information and no criminal prosecution shall be instituted for the alleged violation,"

the proceeding is civil in nature and bars his imprisonment in a penitentiary.

As was stated by Judge Yankwich in George v. United States, 9 Cir., 196 F.2d 445, 453,

" * * * Until the rise of juvenile delinquency and juvenile courts, minors everywhere were subjected to the penalties of all criminal statutes, even those relating to murder, * * *.

"Juvenile statutes allowing special treatment of offenders are a modern innovation. The first law creating a juvenile court was enacted by the Legislature of Illinois and went into effect on April 14, 1899. (Thorsten Sellin, in Foreword to 'Juvenile Delinquency', The Annals of the American Academy of Political and Social Science, No. 261, January 1949, pp. VII and VIII; Paul W. Tappan, Juvenile Delinquency, 1949, Chapter 8, pp. 167–194.) They were introduced into federal criminal jurisprudence by the Act of January 16, 1938, 52 Stat. 764, Chapter 486."

The original Juvenile Delinquency Act of 1938, 18 U.S.C. § 291 et seq., was incorporated in the 1948 codification, 18 U.S.C. § 5031 et seq. with some changes not material here. The purpose of this Act was to spare youths from having to bear the stigma of a criminal for the rest of their lives because of a violation of the law and to encourage such youths, by proper supervision and changed environment, to become law-abiding citizens. The Act was enacted with the realization that persons under the age of eighteen do not have mature judgment and may not fully realize the nature or consequences of their acts.[1] The right to the benefits of the Act is not absolute. The Act provides, inter alia, 18 U.S.C. § 5032,

"A juvenile alleged to have committed one or more acts in violation of a law of the United States not punishable by death or life imprisonment, and not surrendered to the authorities of a state, shall be proceeded against as a juvenile delinquent if he consents to such procedure, unless the Attorney General, in his discretion, has expressly directed otherwise."

Having been accorded the benefit of the Act he cannot dictate the Court's determination as to the proper remedy to be applied in his case. It is further provided by the Act, inter alia, 18 U.S.C. § 5034,

"If the court finds a juvenile to be a delinquent, it may place him on probation for a period not exceeding his minority, or commit him to the custody of the Attorney General for a like period.
"Such commitment shall not exceed the term which might have been imposed had he been tried and convicted of the alleged violation."

In the present case petitioner was originally placed on probation. It became necessary to revoke the probation in accordance with the provisions of the Probation Act, 18 U.S.C. § 3651 et seq. and he was then committed to the custody of the Attorney General. The Juvenile Delinquency Act does not take away from the Attorney General any of his discretion in connection with such commitment. It does add further discretionary powers in the provision that, 18 U.S.C. § 5034,

"The Attorney General may designate any public or private agency or foster home for the custody, care,

subsistence, education, and training of the juvenile during the period for which he was committed."

In order to provide as much flexibility as possible, correctional institutions and "training schools" have been provided for those juveniles who may benefit thereby. Custody is an essential feature in those cases where parole is not feasible and the nature of such custody, in line with the juvenile's reaction thereto, must necessarily be left to the discretion of those in charge of the problem of rehabilitation. The power of the Attorney General to designate the place of confinement[2] has not been abrogated in any respect by the Juvenile Delinquency Act.

Petitioner's application for a writ of habeas corpus must be denied.†

95

White v. Reid *

Laws, Chief Judge.

On May 26, 1952, while on probation from the Juvenile Court of the District of Columbia, petitioner, then sixteen years of age, was taken into custody on two charges of unauthorized use of an automobile. On August 15, 1952, he appeared before the Juvenile Court, acknowledged his participation in the alleged violations of law, and was committed to the National Training School for Boys until twenty-one years of age. On October 1, 1953, he was released on parole. On April 23, 1954, he was arrested on a charge of first degree murder and confined in the District of Columbia Jail. The Juvenile Court waived jurisdiction to this Court. Thereafter petitioner was indicted on a charge of misprision of felony in connection with the murder case. The indictment was dismissed on October 13, 1954. The next day a warrant, issued on April 28, 1954, and placed against him as a detainer by the Youth Division of the United

---

[1] United States v. Fotto, D.C.S.D.N.Y., 103 F.Supp. 430; United States v. Webb, D.C.W.D.Okl., 112 F.Supp. 950.

[2] See 18 U.S.C. § 4082.

† Compare Huff v. O'Bryan, 121 F. 2d 890 (1941) with White v. Reid, 125 F. Supp. 647 (1954); United States v. McCoy, 150 F. Supp. 237 (1957). — Ed.

* White v. Reid, U.S. District Court, District of Columbia, 1954, 125 F. Supp. 647.

States Board of Parole, was executed. Petitioner remains in custody of respondent, the Superintendent of the Jail, under authority of that warrant. To test the legality of his detention, he invokes the habeas corpus jurisdiction of this Court.

Respondent is represented by the Corporation Counsel of the District of Columbia, notwithstanding certain questions affecting the power of the Attorney General of the United States and of the United States Board of Parole are involved. The United States Attorney for the District of Columbia has been served with a copy of the writ of habeas corpus. Thus it appears the United States has had opportunity to appear.

The gravamen of petitioner's suit is that he was denied Constitutional rights in the proceedings and commitment of August 15, 1952, in that he was deprived of his liberty without due process of law and without presentment or indictment by a grand jury, contrary to the Fifth Amendment, and that he was not granted the right to public trial by jury, confronted with the witnesses against him, or accorded the right of compulsory process for obtaining witnesses in his favor or the right to assistance of counsel for his defense, in violation of the Sixth Amendment.

Proceedings against juveniles brought in the Juvenile Court are not criminal and penal in character, but are an adjudication upon the status of a child in the nature of a guardianship imposed by the state as *parens patriae* to provide the care and guidance that under normal circumstances would be furnished by the natural parents. Thomas v. United States, 1941, 74 App.D.C. 167, 121 F.2d 905; Richardson v. Browning, 1927, 57 App.D.C. 186, 18 F.2d 1008; Rule v. Geddes, 1904, 23 App.D.C. 31. "The fundamental philosophy of the juvenile court laws is that a delinquent child is to be considered and treated not as a criminal but as a person requiring care, education and protection. He is not thought of as 'a bad man who should be punished, but as an erring or sick child who needs help.'" Thomas v. United States, supra, 74 App.D.C. at page 170, 121 F.2d at page 908. Constitutional safeguards guaranteed one accused of crime therefore are not applicable. The proceedings in respect of petitioner having been in compliance with statutory requirements, there was no denial of due process of law. See 31 Am.Jur., Juvenile Courts and Offenders, § 6; 43 C.J.S., Infants, § 97.

As in all habeas corpus proceedings, the question before the Court is whether petitioner is being presently unlawfully restrained of his liberty. Although the Court may inquire into the validity of not only the fact of confinement but also the place of confinement, Miller v. Overholser, 1953, 92 U.S.App. D.C. 110, 206 F.2d 415, the Court will not speculate that petitioner may be transferred to the Federal Reformatory at Petersburg, Virginia, as orally suggested by counsel at the hearing of this case, but may only determine whether the District of Columbia Jail is a proper place for the continued detention of petitioner.

Petitioner having been committed under Juvenile Court proceedings, the test to be applied is whether the state is presently exercising a reasonable restraint as guardian *in loco parentis*, or whether petitioner is being confined as punishment for an offense. In upholding the Constitutionality of juvenile court acts, the Courts have emphasized not only that the proceedings are non-criminal, but also that the institution to which the delinquent is committed is not of a penal character. . . . [Citations omitted. — *Ed.*] This requirement is pointed up by decisions of the Supreme Court of New Hampshire. In State ex rel. Cunningham v. Ray, 1885, 63 N.H. 406, 56 Am.Rep. 529, the Court held unconstitutional a statute providing for commitment to reform school without jury trial, against the contention it was not punishment and the school was merely party of the state school system, the Court observing the school had always been regarded as a quasi penal institution, and detention there as involuntary, constrained and to some extent in the nature of punishment, with more or less of disgrace attached. Later, when a new statute had been enacted in no way comparable to this former act, its constitutionality was upheld in Petition of Morin, 1949, 95 N.H. 518, 68 A.2d 668, 670, the Court noting specifically there was no evidence to suggest the industrial school there was other than a "'real school, not a prison in disguise.'"

It is true that in both juvenile court and criminal proceedings a person may be deprived of his liberty. It is likewise true in the modern administration of penal institutions increasing emphasis has wisely been placed upon the rehabilitation and training of prisoners as essential elements in a program for crime prevention and correction. Therefore some of the features of penal institutions resemble those of educational, industrial and training schools for juvenile delinquents. The basic function and purpose of penal institutions, however, is punishment as a deterrent to crime. However broad the different methods of discipline, care and treatment that are appropriate for individual prisoners according to age, character, mental condition, and the like, there is a fundamental legal and practical difference in purpose and technique. Unless the institution is one whose primary concern is the individual's moral and physical well-being, unless its facilities are intended for and adapted to guidance, care, education and training rather than punishment, unless its supervision is that of a guardian, not that of a prison guard or jailor, it seems clear a commitment to such institution is by reason of conviction of crime and cannot withstand an assault for violation of fundamental Constitutional safeguards.

Respondent relies upon statute, 18 U.S.C. § 4082, as authority to detain petitioner pending transfer to another institution. In Huff v. O'Bryant, 1941, 74 App.D.C. 19, 121 F.2d 890, it was held a juvenile could not be transferred to Lorton Reformatory, since he was subject under then existing statutes to the orders of the Juvenile Court and not those of the Attorney General. While the decision was based upon statutory interpretation and not Constitutional issues, the Court observed that Lorton Reformatory was to all intents and purposes an institution of the penitentiary type, the place of confinement of hardened criminals, "repeaters" and the like. As a result of this decision, the statute was amended to confer authority on the Attorney General over custody and transfer of "all persons committed to the National Training School for Boys."

Respondent contends the amendment gives the Attorney General discretion as an administrative matter to detain any person committed to the National Training School for Boys for transfer to any federal institution without being subject to judicial review. If this were so, a juvenile committed by the Juvenile Court might be incarcerated under the statute at the United States Penitentiary

at Alcatraz, California, or Leavenworth, Kansas, where those convicted of crime are restrained.

In this jurisdiction, this Court and not the Juvenile Court is the Court of competent jurisdiction designated for trial of a felony. A Juvenile Court hearing in respect of a juvenile is not a criminal trial, and a commitment is not a conviction and punishment for a felony. To send a juvenile to the usual penitentiary where hardened criminals are kept in close confinement and under special types of strict discipline, where the juvenile would inevitably come into contact with them and suffer the same type of treatment as they do, would in effect stamp the case of the juvenile as a criminal case except insofar as his records would be protected from public disclosure. In such criminal prosecutions, Constitutional safeguards must be vouchsafed the accused.

It is a basic rule of statutory construction, however, that where legislation as drawn may be susceptible of two interpretations, by one of which grave and doubtful Constitutional questions arise, and by the other of which such questions are avoided, it is the Court's duty to adopt the latter construction. United States v. Rumely, 1953, 345 U.S. 41, 73 S.Ct. 543, 97 L.Ed. 770

In light of the history of the manner in which Congress has dealt with erring youths in the Juvenile Court Act, D.C.Code, § 11–901 et seq., indicating no purpose to stamp the juvenile with criminal conviction, D.C.Code, § 11–929, except in extreme cases where waivers are made by the Juvenile Court, D.C. Code, § 11–914, it is reasonable to interpret the Act of Congress conferring authority on the Attorney General to designate places of confinement as intended to be limited to those where special facilities are provided for training and care, somewhat comparable to those of the National Training School for Boys, but with closer supervision where necessary for those that may prove to be otherwise intractable. In the absence of evidence to the contrary, the Court must assume the Attorney General will follow this interpretation. The transfer of a youth committed by Juvenile Court to the Medical Center for Federal Prisoners at Springfield, Missouri, as in Riley v. Pescor, D.C.Mo.1945, 63 F.Supp. 1, may be justified under this view if the Center provides necessary medical facilities not otherwise available and special provision is made for training and treatment of the youth, if not physically incapacitated, similar to facilities available at the Training School. Cases such as Harwood v. State ex rel. Pillars, 1947, 184 Tenn. 515, 201 S.W.2d 672, holding a person committed by Juvenile Court to a State Vocational School may be transferred to the State Penitentiary, can only be reconciled on the theory that Juvenile Court proceedings there are criminal and penal in nature, since the statute there in question provided for transfer of any incorrigible girl over fifteen years of age "who was regularly convicted of a felony."

From what has been stated, the District of Columbia Jail is not a proper place for the continued detention of petitioner. His detention there from April 23 to October 13, 1954, was lawful, since it arose out of criminal charges preferred against him in this Court. Since October 13, 1954, he has been held under the parole violation warrant based on the commitment of August 15, 1952. While a juvenile properly held in jail for a time may be further held there pending determination of the institution to which he shall be transferred, the transfer must be made with reasonable dispatch.

Accordingly, the writ of habeas corpus will be discharged, without prejudice to its being renewed unless the Attorney General has within ten days designated that petitioner be transferred to the National Training School for Boys or transferred to an institution with similar facilities.*

---

* Petitioner was transferred to Federal Correctional Institution, Ashland, Ky., and claimed it was not a suitable place of confinement within court's earlier decision. It is a classification and treatment center for youthful offenders under Federal act; the program gives a full day of work and recreation and the facilities are equal or superior to those of National Training School. But disregarding this, "It must be decided whether a juvenile committed under civil or equitable proceedings may be sent to mingle with those convicted of crime." While Federal Youth Corrections Act is designed to rehabilitate youths who can be helped although they have been regularly convicted of crime, the Juvenile Court Act is guided by the spirit that the child's welfare is of prime importance. ". . . both Constitution and statute forbid the transfer of a youth committed under the Juvenile Court Act to any institution designed for the custody of persons convicted of crime, including the Federal Correctional Institution at Ashland, Kentucky, and the commingling of such juveniles with criminals. Because petitioner now has been held in jail for an undue length of time, the Court will order him released from custody, without prejudice to designation of the National Training School for Boys or a similar institution not designed as a place of confinement for those convicted of crime and where petitioner may not have contact or communication with those convicted of crime." White v. Reid, 126 Fed. Supp., 867, 871 (1954). — Ed.

Chapter 16

Custody, Neglect, Dependency

96

State in the Interest of Bennett *

ELIAS HANSEN, J.

The juvenile court of the Third judicial district in and for Salt Lake county, Utah, adjudged Ladrue Bennett, who is a minor of the age of 14 years, to be a delinquent, and ordered that he be committed to the state industrial school. He appeals. The acts of delinquency charged in the complaint in the juvenile court are:

"That on or about the 16th day of February, 1930, at the County of Salt Lake of Utah, said Ladrue Bennett, a child fourteen years of age, did become delinquent by reason of wilfully, knowingly and unlawfully taking and carrying away from the Post office in Midvale, Utah, from box rented to the Midvale State Bank, one letter addressed to said Midvale State Bank, containing $17,000.00 in cancelled checks; and by further reason that on February 21, 1930, he did then and there use a certain vehicle, to-wit: Chevrolet 1928 model * * *, being the property of Wm. E. and D. R. Palmer and General Motors Acceptance Corporation, without the consent of the owner thereof, contrary to the provisions of the Statutes of Utah in such cases made and provided."

The mother of appellant accepted services of notice of the time and place of the hearing upon the complaint. The father was not served with process nor did he enter an appearance in the cause. Various witnesses were examined at the hearing, including the father of the appellant. The juvenile court made written findings

---

* In re State, in Interest of Bennett, Supreme Court of Utah, 1930, 77 Utah, 247, 293 P. 963.

of fact wherein it was found that appellant was delinquent by reason of his having committed the acts alleged in the complaint together with other acts of delinquency not alleged in the complaint. The court also found "that Joseph Bennett and Minnie Bennett, parents of said juvenile, and each of them, by reason of their failure to control said juvenile and prevent said juvenile's act of delinquency aforesaid, are unfit to have and continue in custody of said juvenile Ladrue Bennett." The evidence is ample to support the finding that the appellant is a juvenile delinquent. No claim is made to the contrary. Complaint is made because the father of the appellant was not served with process; because the court found the parents of the appellant unfit to have and continue in his custody; and because appellant was committed to the state industrial school. The manner of procedure in the interest of a juvenile is provided for in title 21, c. 9, Comp. Laws Utah 1917 (sections 1814–1833), and the amendments thereto. It is there provided in section 1818 that:

"Upon filing such complaint, the clerk or court shall set the same for hearing; notice of said hearing shall be served by the probation officer, or sheriff or any peace officer, on the parents, parent, custodian, or legal guardian of said child residing within the state of Utah, which notice shall be substantially in the following form, to wit:
"(Title of court and cause.)
"To ———— (here designate relationship). You are hereby notified to appear within two days after the service of this notice upon you, if served within the county wherein the above proceeding is pending, otherwise within five days, and assert and defend any rights to custody, control, or guardianship you may have or claim over or in the above named child; otherwise your default will be entered and the court will proceed to hear and determine your said rights or supposed rights in accordance with the law and the evidence." *

---

* In the majority of jurisdictions, notice is required

This court held in the case of *Jensen* v. *Hinckley*, 55 Utah 306, 185 P. 716, that:

"Service of notice under Comp. Laws 1917, § 1818, or voluntary appearance amounting to waiver, is necessary to confer jurisdiction on the juvenile court to determine right to custody of a delinquent child, but not to confer jurisdiction, pursuant to section 1815, to determine delinquency," and "the mother of a minor son; against whom a delinquency complaint has been filed in the juvenile court pursuant to Comp. Laws 1917, § 1815; and not served with notice thereof, as required by section 1818, held not to have waived service of notice by appearing in court merely as a witness; 'waiver' being an intentional relinquishment of a known right."

The quotation is from the syllabus, which fairly reflects the principles of law announced in the opinion. The fact that the mother of the appellant in the instant case accepted service of notice upon herself cannot be said to have conferred jurisdiction on the juvenile court to determine the right of the father to the custody of his child. The right of the father to the custody of a minor child is co-extensive with that of the mother. The statute above quoted clearly contemplates that, where both parents are alive and reside within this state, each shall be served with notice. The rules of law announced in the case of *Jensen* v. *Hinckley*, supra, require a reversal of that part of the judgment appealed from whereby the appellant was ordered committed to the state industrial school and the father thus deprived of his right to his custody.

The evidence in this case, however, shows that the appellant is in need of vigilant supervision and guidance if he is to be reared to useful citizenship. The record before us does not justify a dismissal of the proceedings begun in his interest. It therefore becomes necessary to discuss other questions which are presented on this appeal for the guidance of the juvenile court in any further proceedings that may be had in this cause.

There is no evidence in this case which shows or tends to show that either of the parents of the appellant is unfit to continue to have his custody, unless it can be said that they are rendered unfit to have such custody because he committed acts of delinquency while in their custody. So far as appears, the parents are upright law-abiding citizens. They have provided the appellant with a good home, with food, clothing, and medical attention, and have required that he attend school regularly whenever his health has permitted.

It is the contention of appellant that a juvenile court may not deprive a parent of the custody of a minor child unless it is made to appear that such parent is unfit to have the custody of his child. The following cases lend support to such contention; *Mill* v. *Brown*, 31 Utah 473, 88 P. 609, 613, 120 Am. St. Rep. 935; *Stoker* v. *Gowans*, 45 Utah 556, 147 P. 911, Ann. Cas. 1916E, 1025; *Redford* v. *Anderson*, 56 Utah 287, 190 P. 775. In the case of *Mill* v. *Brown*, supra, it is said that:

"Before the state can be substituted to the right of the parent it must affirmatively be made to appear that the parent has forfeited his natural and legal right to the custody and control of the child by reason of his failure, inability, neglect, or incompetency to discharge the duty and thus to enjoy the right."

In the case of *Stoker* v. *Gowans*, supra, it was held that a juvenile court has jurisdiction to commit a juvenile to the state industrial school where its parent, after notice and a hearing, has been adjudged unfit to have its custody. In the case of *Bedford* v. *Anderson*, supra, it was held that the custody of a juvenile delinquent should remain with the mother until the juvenile court "upon due notice, and upon competent and sufficient evidence, determines that she is an unfit person to have the custody of said minor." The law creating juvenile courts and conferring upon them jurisdiction in cases relating to the custody, detention, and guardianship of delinquent children under the age of 18 years has been amended on various occasions since it was originally enacted. Some of those amendments were made between the time that *Mill* v. *Brown*, supra, was decided and the time that the opinion of *Bedford* v. *Anderson* was rendered. So far as material to a determination of the questions presented for determination in the instant case, the juvenile law is the same now as it was when the case of *Bedford* v. *Anderson* was determined. Pro-

---

in cases involving alleged fault of parents. In *Sinquefield* v. *Valentine* (1931), 159 Miss. 144, 132 So. 81, it was held that notice is required in neglect cases both under the due process clause of the state constitution and the fourteenth amendment to the Federal Constitution. — *Ed.*

vision is made in the act for the kinds of judgments or decrees that may be rendered by juvenile courts. Comp. Laws Utah 1917, § 1823, as amended by Special Session Laws Utah 1919, c. 5, 7, § 1, reads as follows:

"Upon the entry of such finding of fact, the court shall render a decree and judgment that the juvenile is a delinquent, and that the parents, parent, custodian, or guardian is or are fit or unfit to continue in control and custody of the juvenile in accordance with the fact. In case judgment is rendered that the parents, parent, custodian or guardian is or are fit to have control or custody of the juvenile, the court may commit the child to the care of the probation officer, allowing it to remain in its own home subject to the visitation of the probation officer, such child to report to the court or probation officer, as often as may be required and subject to be returned to the court for further proceedings whenever such action may appear necessary. In case it is adjudged and decreed that the parents, parent, custodian, or guardian is or are fit or unfit to have control and custody of the juvenile, the court may further adjudge and decree as follows:

"1. That the juvenile be committed to its own home under the care, control and visitation of a juvenile officer.

"2. That the juvenile be committed to any suitable family home open to the court for that purpose, subject to the care, control, and visitation of a probation officer.

"3. That the juvenile be committed to any institution within the state incorporated or organized for care, correction, or advancement of children.

"4. That the juvenile be committed to any institution that may be provided by the state or county for the care, correction, or advancement of children.

"5. That the juvenile be committed to the state industrial school.

"6. That the juvenile may be fined in any sum not exceeding $25.00.

"7. That in all cases where the juvenile is charged with the commission of a felony, the juvenile court shall act as a committing magistrate with the same jurisdiction as a justice of the peace sitting as a committing magistrate, and when it appears that a felony has been committed and that there is sufficient cause to believe the juvenile defendant guilty, to commit him to the district court of the county where the offense is committed, there to be prosecuted upon information or indictment as provided by law. In such cases the court shall not adjudge or decree that the parents, parent, custodian or guardian is or are fit or unfit to have control and custody of the juvenile.

"8. That the juvenile be disposed of in any other way except to commit it to jail or prison that may, in the discretion and judgment of the court, under all

the circumstances, be for the best interest of the child, to the end that its wayward tendencies shall be corrected and the child be saved to useful citizenship.

"No judgment or decree so entered shall operate after the child reaches the age of twenty-one years, and all orders, judgments, and decrees, except orders committing the juvenile to the state industrial school or to the district court, shall be under the control of the court and may be modified, amended, or recalled at any time until the child reaches the age of twenty-one years."

Prior to the amendment of 1919, the sentence which immediately precedes the enumeration of the judgments or decrees that may be entered by juvenile courts read thus:

"In case it is adjudged and decreed that the parents, parent, custodian, or guardian is or are unfit to have control and custody of the juvenile, the court may further adjudge and decree as follows."

It will be observed that the amendment of 1919 added the words "fit or" before the word "unfit" in the sentence above quoted. It would seem highly improbably that the Legislature intended by the amendment of 1919 that parents who are fit to have the custody of their child should be deprived of such custody where the parents are willing and able to correct the child's delinquency and rear it to useful citizenship. No institution can take the place of proper home influences in developing the character of a child. It has always been the policy of both the Legislature and the courts of the various states not to deprive or interfere with the important and sacred relation of parent and child unless absolutely necessary for the welfare of the child or for the protection of society. Such have been the purposes which have actuated the lawmaking power of this state in the enactment of the law creating juvenile courts and defining their powers, and such also have been the views entertained by this court whenever it has been called upon to construe that law. In the construction of a statute it is often necessary to enlarge or restrict the meaning of a word or phrase used therein in order to give effect to the purposes sought to be accomplished by the law-making power. It may well be that parents are generally fit to have the custody of their children, and yet they may be unable to prevent one or more of their children from committing acts of delinquency and thus from becoming criminals and a menace to society. When it is made to appear that a parent or parents of a child know that said child is committing acts of delinquency and that they are unable to control such child and prevent him from further wrongdoing, the interest of the child as well as the protection of society may well demand that the parents surrender their custody of their child to the state so that, if possible, the child's evil tendency may be corrected and society protected. If, therefore, the parents, parent, custodian, or guardian of a delinquent juvenile are or is otherwise fit to have the control and custody of the juvenile, but cannot prevent him from wrongdoing, then and in such case the juvenile court may commit such juvenile to the industrial school when the best interests of the juvenile or the protection of society demand such commitment. If the word "fit" as used in the amendment of 1919 is construed as indicated, the juvenile law as amended is in harmony with the aims and purposes evidently sought to be accomplished by the Legislature and is likewise in harmony with the decisions of this court. Otherwise the sentence last above quoted would be inconsistent with other provisions of the act and would offend against principles of natural justice.

Applying the law as thus construed to the facts in this case, can it be said that the parents should be deprived of the custody of appellant? There is no evidence whatsoever in the record that the parents are generally unfit to have the custody of the children. There is some evidence to the contrary. Both of the parents testified that they did not know of any delinquency of appellant until the filing of the complaint. In view of the fact that appellant's delinquencies covered only a short period of time, it may well be that the parents were ignorant of his wrongdoing until after these proceedings were begun. Under such circumstances it cannot be said that the parents are unable to correct the evil tendencies of the appellant, and they should not be deprived of his custody until they are first given a reasonable opportunity, with such assistance as may be rendered by the officers of the juvenile court, to bring about the desired reformation.

The judgment committing the appellant to the state industrial school is reversed, and this cause is remanded to the juvenile court of Salt Lake county for such further proceedings not inconsistent with the views herein expressed as may be deemed proper.

CHERRY, C. J., and STRAUP, EPHRAIM HANSON, and FOLLAND, JJ., concur.

97

Mill v. Brown *

FRICK, J.

This is an application to this court, in its original jurisdiction, for a writ of certiorari. The application is made under section 3631, Revised Statutes 1898, by Emil Mill (hereinafter styled applicant) as father of Albert E. Mill, a minor. The writ was duly issued by this court, directed to Willis Brown, as judge of the juvenile court of Salt Lake City, who made and filed his return by filing an answer in connection with what purports to be a transcript of the proceedings of the juvenile court which it is sought to have reviewed by this application. From the application and return it appears that Albert E. Mill is a minor of about the age of thirteen years; that a complaint in writing was duly filed in the juvenile court against him as a delinquent child under chapter 117, p. 182, Laws Utah 1905, entitled "Juvenile Courts"; that in such complaint he was charged with petit larceny for taking a box of cigars, was found guilty of that charge, and ordered committed to the Industrial School of the State of Utah as a delinquent child until he shall have attained the age of twenty-one years, unless sooner released by the board of control of said institution. The proceedings of the hearing and the judgment of the court are attacked upon various grounds, some of which will be noticed hereafter, and those presently noticed are: That chapter 117, aforesaid, is unconstitutional and void . . . While the record of the proceedings certified up is somewhat meagre and unsatisfactory, sufficient appears therefrom to warrant us in reviewing the essential parts of the proceedings. . . . [Discussion omitted concerning claim that judge does not

---

* *Mill* v. *Brown,* The Supreme Court of the State of Utah, 1907, 31 Utah 473, 88 P. 609.

have legal qualifications to act and was not lawfully appointed. — Ed.]

The order [sic] constitutional and legal objections respecting the right to trial by a jury, the want of arraignment and plea, the suspending of judgment or sentence, the manner of examination or trial, that the child is required to be a witness against himself, the want of notice to the parent, the dispensing with the warrant and arresting the child and bringing him before the court, and all like questions, are fully, learnedly and satisfactorily discussed and decided against the contentions of applicant in the following cases. . . . [Citations omitted. — Ed.] It would not only seem useless to enlarge upon the reasons in the foregoing cases why acts similar to chapter 117 do not contravene constitutional or substantial rights, except perhaps in the particulars above referred to, but it would smack of pedantry to attempt to do so. There is not a single argument presented by applicant in this case which is not considered and answered in the foregoing cases. . . . Such laws [regarding juvenile offenders] are most salutary and are in no sense criminal and not intended as a punishment, but are calculated to save the child from becoming a criminal. The whole and only object of such laws is to provide the child with an environment such as will save him to the state and society as a useful and law-abiding citizen, and to give him the educational requirements necessary to attain that end. To effect this purpose some restraint is essential. Such or similar restraint is, however, necessary in any institution of learning, however humble. Everywhere we are all met with restraint. Civilized society cannot exist without it, and no school can continue without discipline, and it is this discipline which is denominated restraint in schools such as are provided for juvenile offenders. We can see no valid reason for holding chapter 117 vulnerable to attack upon constitutional or other grounds, and therefore we cannot, for that reason alone, sustain the contentions of the applicant and set aside the judgment of the juvenile court.

The foregoing does not apply to section 7 of said chapter. By the provisions of said section the juvenile court deals directly with adult persons. While the provisions of section 7 are entirely germane to the principal object of the main act, the acts denounced in section 7 are made a misdemeanor, and are thus a crime

within the purview both of the Constitution and the Criminal Code of this state. As we have already pointed out, the proceedings of the juvenile court do not fall, nor are they intended to come, within what is termed criminal procedure, nor are the acts therein mentioned, as applied to children, crimes. To constitute the act under section 7 of an adult a crime, entitles such adult to the right of a trial as for any other crime. This right is denied by said section 7 and it cannot, therefore, be upheld. Quite true, some method is necessary to punish adults when interfering with children who may be held to be wards of the state, and no doubt it is proper for the Legislature to provide for their punishment. When such is done, however, trial must be provided for in the proper forum and in legal manner. Section 7 of the act, for the reason that it violates this elementary provision, so to speak, of criminal law and procedure, must, therefore, be held of no force or effect. This, however, in no way affects the other provisions or sections of the act. Section 7 was a mere excrescence, in one sense, on the principal provisions of the act, in no way connected with it so far as it affects the right to deal with children, and, as is clearly apparent, was not an inducement to the enactment of the other portions of the act. For these reasons, all other parts of the act may, and are permitted to, stand.

But there is another reason for which we think the judgment cannot be permitted to stand. By a careful examination of the cases above cited, it will be found that all the decisions rest upon the proposition that the state in its sovereign power has the right, when necessary, to substitute itself as guardian of the person of the child for that of the parent or other legal guardian, and thus to educate and save the child from a criminal career; that it is the welfare of the child that moves the state to act, and not to inflict punishment or to mete out retributive justice for any offense committed or threatened. In other words, to do that which it is the duty of the father or guardian to do, and which the law assumes he will do by reason of the love and affection he holds for his offspring and out of regard for the child's future welfare. The duty thus rests upon the father first. As the duty is imposed by the moral as well as the laws of society upon the father first, so it must likewise logically follow that he must be given the first right to discharge that duty. Indeed, the common law based the right of the father to have custody and dominion over the person of his child upon the ground that he might better discharge the duty he owed the child and the state in respect to the care, nurture, and education of the child. The right and duty are therefore reciprocal, and may be termed natural, as well as legal and moral. Before the state can be substituted to the right of the parent it must affirmatively be made to appear that the parent has forfeited his natural and legal right to the custody and control of the child by reason of his failure, inability, neglect, or incompetency to discharge the duty and thus to enjoy the right. Section 6 of the act defines the acts which constitute a child a delinquent and thus a fit subject to be brought before the juvenile court for examination. To bring the child before the court, the act provides that a complaint in writing must be filed, which was done in this case. But when a complaint is filed and one or more of the acts constituting delinquency are set forth the court only acquires jurisdiction of the child for the purpose of investigating into its condition or conduct. Quite true, in some states, a formal complaint in writing may not be an essential, but it is made so in this state, and hence must be observed. But when the court has investigated the matters set forth in the complaint and finds some or all of the charges to be true, it does not follow, from that fact alone, that the state should forthwith be substituted in place of the parent or legal guardian and take full control of the person of the child. All that the court has established so far is that the child is a delinquent in view of the provisions of the act. The question as to whether the parent has been derelict in respect to his duty, or whether he is a competent person or not to have charge of the child, and whether he has forfeited his natural and legal right to continue the relation, has not been touched upon, and no finding or adjudication of that fact has been made. There is nothing, therefore, up to this point, in the proceedings upon which a judgment can be based substituting the state as guardian of the person of the child in place of the parent. The whole fabric of the law, as is clearly shown by all the decisions cited, supra, rests upon this theory, and those laws are sustained by virtue of it. Until

something is made to appear that the child is not cared and provided for in respect to the matters involved, there exists no reason for the state to take charge of the person of the child, and hence no right exists to do so under the act. True, the parent need not be made a party to, or even have notice of, the proceedings against the child. The parent is not bound by the judgment against the child, and may at any time institute proper proceedings to obtain custody of him. But the matter now under consideration lies deeper than this; it is one of power to render judgment placing the child in charge of one guardian, the state, before determining or passing upon the qualifications of the natural guardian to have charge of the child. The court might as well enter up a judgment without any complaint or investigation whatever. The relative rights and duties of the father or mother are so well and thoroughly discussed in the case of *Nugent v. Powell*, 4 Wyo., at pages 189 to 199, 33 Pac. 23, 20 L. R. A. 199, 62 Am. St. Rep. 117, that we shall do no more than to refer to the discussion there presented. Moreover, in nearly all cases cited in this opinion, the fact of the dereliction, negligence, or incompetency of the parent is referred to as a ground for the exercise of the state of its right in respect to the child's custody. Indeed, in some of the cases it appears that this fact is made a part of the complaint and made a ground for the court to act, and in most of them the fact is found and adjudicated. While there is no express provision in chapter 117 requiring the juvenile court to find one way or the other in respect to the competency of the parent, still it appears from various portions of the act that the Legislature intended that the matter should be inquired into. It provides that the parentage should be investigated and reported upon to district courts by their probation officers in the state at large, and in cities of the first and second classes the juvenile judge and his probation officers, it is clearly implied, must do the same. Some of the acts constituting delinquency as defined by section 6 of the act are so trivial in themselves that any thoughtless boy might commit them and thus be adjudged a delinquent, and by a careless judge be sent to the industrial school when the parent was not only willing, but most competent, to have control of the child, and would offer it better surroundings and training than the state at best could give or afford. We are constrained to hold, therefore, that before a child can be made a ward of the state, at least two things must be found: (1) That the child is a delinquent within the provisions of chapter 117; and (2) that the parent or legal guardian is incompetent or has neglected and failed to care and provide for the child the training and education contemplated and required by both law and morals.

The foregoing conclusions are based upon what we conceive to be the true spirit and intent of the act itself. If it should be contended that nothing appears in the act requiring such a finding to be made, then we must still construe it in the light of other provisions of the law which may affect the relation of parent and child, and the rights of the parent, in view of such relation. Such a provision is found in section 82, Revised Statutes 1898, where it is expressly provided that a parent cannot be deprived of the custody of the child unless it is made to appear that he is unfit or incompetent to have such custody. We are doing no more, therefore, in requiring such a finding to be made, than is enjoined by positive law of this state. The act itself, where it is silent, must be construed in connection with other provisions upon the same subject. Unless, therefore, both the delinquency of the child and incompetency, for any reason, of the parent, concur and are so found, the court exceeds its power when committing a child to any of the institutions contemplated by the act. While we do not wish to be understood as holding that investigations before juvenile courts must be conducted as trials usually are, still these courts should not disregard all rules of procedure. The law requires a written complaint to be filed, hence there should also be an investigation of the matters set forth in the complaint and witnesses examined, under oath, with the right of cross-examination. Since there is no appeal, and can be none in these cases, there should be as thorough an examination into the matters complained of as the nature of the case admits, under all the circumstances. We desire to observe also that while the parent or guardian is not legally a necessary party to the proceedings, and should not, and cannot be bound by any judgment rendered in the juvenile court respecting his rights to the custody and control

of the child, yet, in view that he is affected, it perhaps were better that a formal notice of the hearing be served on him, if he can be found, to the end that all the facts may be elicited by the investigation. The whole proceedings should be conducted so as to subserve the rights and best interests of all, while in no way minimizing the beneficent purposes of the law itself. While, in the very nature of things, these courts cannot conform to the rigorous rules of criminal and law courts, their proceedings should still be conducted as a legal investigation.

From an inspection of the record in this case, meagre as it is, we are forced to the conclusion that the difficulties complained of are due far more to the respondent than to the law. To administer juvenile laws in accordance with their true spirit and intent requires a man of broad mind, of almost infinite patience, and one who is the possessor of great faith in humanity and thoroughly imbued with that spirit. Those who come, and are intended to be brought, before juvenile courts must be reached through love, not fear. The purpose in bringing them before the court is to lead them away from, and to destroy their propensities to, vice; to elevate, not degrade; to reform, not to punish them. Their parents likewise must be met and dealt with in the same spirit. They should be directed in a proper spirit, and not, as this record discloses, be met with defiance. The conditions surrounding them may be due as much to lack of information and misfortune as to viciousness. The judge of any court, and especially a judge of a juvenile court, should therefore, be willing at all times, not only to respect, but to maintain and preserve, the legal and natural rights of men and children alike. Respondent, as this record discloses, either has no regard for, or is uninformed in respect to, the rules that the experience of past generations has evolved for the purpose of safeguarding the rights of all. Like most laymen, but seemingly without their good judgment, respondent seems to regard these rules as mere technicalities to be brushed aside as obstructions in the pathway of what is usually termed "common-sense justice." He seems to be a willing convert to the theory that he is better, if not wiser, than both law and rules of procedure, and that he may thus disregard either or both at pleasure. While juvenile courts cannot, and are not expected to, be conducted as criminal or other courts usually are, the judge should still not wholly disregard all wholesome rules in an attempt to establish guilt which he suspects, or, worse yet, merely imagines. Most of the rules of evidence and procedure were established, and their observance is necessary, to curb the propensities of the inquisitor, and it would, no doubt, better subserve the best interests of all if the most important of these rules were observed by respondent in his investigations. The fact that the American system of government is controlled and directed by laws, not men, cannot be too often nor too strongly impressed upon those who administer any branch or part of the government. Where a proper spirit and good judgment are followed as a guide, oppression can and will be avoided.

It further appears from the record before us that either respondent, or some one for him, has devised a printed record to which all cases are made to conform. Printed formulas are well enough as guides, but to have a printed record only is too much of a temptation to make every case fit the record instead of making a record to fit the case. As we have already stated, the cases coming before the juvenile court are not criminal, and hence a criminal record does not fit those cases. Findings should be made in each case in conformity with the facts, and judgment rendered in accordance with the facts found.

Because a good and wholesome law has, in some instances, been abused, we are most earnestly implored to set aside the law. This we cannot do. The court may be reformed and the law amended, if, in the judgment of the Legislature, this is necessary. All good laws may be, and at times no doubt are, abused, but this is no reason why they should either be held bad or repealed. While it is neither the duty nor the province of this court to suggest what the laws should be, or who should administer them, we cannot silently pass by what seems to us a total disregard of wholesome rules. The juvenile court law is of such vast importance to the state and society that it seems to us it should be administered by those who are learned in the law and versed in the rules of procedure, to the end that the beneficent purposes of the law may be made effective and individual rights respected. Care must be exercised in both the selection of a judge and

in the administration of the law. When this is done, we have no doubt that most of the things complained of, and as they appear from the record, will be obviated. The juvenile law of this state is of too much importance to be hampered by or set aside for trivial or avoidable causes. All good citizens are interested in its proper administration and enforcement, and it is well worth the best efforts and patient care of those who, for the time being, are clothed with the power of administering such laws. If all governments are interested in the moral and educational welfare of those who in time will be called upon to discharge the duties of citizenship, how much greater should be that interest in a government like ours, where the citizen is the sovereign from whom emanates all the powers of government?

For the foregoing reasons, therefore, the judgment of the juvenile court committing Albert E. Mill to the Industrial School is set aside and annulled, and he is returned to the custody of Emil Mill, his father, until said Albert shall be legally adjudicated to be a ward of the state in accordance with the views herein expressed; neither party to recover costs. It is so ordered.

McCarty, C. J., and Straup, J., concur.†

98

In re Rinker, Appeal of Rinker *

Woodside, Judge.

This is an appeal from the order of the Court of Quarter Sessions of Huntingdon County sitting as a Juvenile Court in which it declared the appellant's three children neglected, and directed them committed to the care and custody of the Huntingdon County Child Welfare Services.

The mother, who has taken this appeal, questions the sufficiency of the evidence to warrant the action of the court.

A petition to have the children declared

---

† See, also, In re Barajas, 114 Cal. App. 2d 22, 249 P 2d 350. — Ed.

* In re Rinker, Appeal of Rinker, Superior Court of Pennsylvania, 1955, 180 Pa.Super. 143, 117 A. 2d 780.

"neglected" was filed in the Juvenile Court by a child welfare worker. The court ordered that the case be heard January 19, 1955 at which time the testimony of a number of witnesses was taken. After the hearing the learned Judge "determined" that the best interests of the children required their care, guidance and control and committed them to the care and custody of the Welfare Services.

As provided in section 15 of the Juvenile Court Law of June 2, 1933, P.L. 1433, 11 P.S. § 257, upon petition of the mother the court granted a review and rehearing. At the rehearing the court admitted the testimony taken at the previous hearing and heard additional witnesses.

There was no error in this procedure. Weintraub's Appeal, 1950, 166 Pa.Super. 342, 71 A.2d 923.

The procedure provided by the above section of the Juvenile Court Law for a rehearing is unusual, but its purpose is evident. To avoid the atmosphere and the formality of a courtroom the legislature established a separate court and procedure to deal with children. The informality of the procedure has much to do with its value, and this informality is generally followed by juvenile court judges and is encouraged both by the legislature and the appellate courts. This informality, however, makes it impossible to present to an appellate court a record that can be intelligently reviewed.

In order to provide a proper record for review when appeals are taken the legislature provided for the "review and rehearing" which the lower court *must* grant when requested within 21 days of the final order and which requires that the testimony be taken down and transcribed by an official court stenographer. The final order from which an appeal may be taken to this Court is based upon the record made at the rehearing.

In the instant case the mother was present at the first hearing; she was represented by counsel who examined and cross-examined witnesses; an official court stenographer took down and transcribed the testimony. Under these circumstances it was proper to admit the transcript of this testimony into evidence at the rehearing as a part of the record of the rehearing. Weintraub Appeal, supra. Both the petitioner, who was represented by the District Attorney, and the mother of the alleged neglected children had a right to offer additional testimony at the rehearing. Both did.

On the basis of the evidence thus submitted the court made certain findings of fact upon which it based its final order of June 22, 1955. The court found that the children were neglected, and that the mother neglected to provide the proper care necessary for the morals and well being of the children and it ordered them committed to the care and custody of the welfare agency. We are of the opinion that the evidence did not warrant this action.

Section 1 of the Juvenile Court Law, supra, 11 P.S. § 243, provides, inter alia, as follows:

"(5) the words 'neglected child' include:

* * * * * *

"(b) A child who lacks proper parental care by reason of the fault or habits of his or her parent, guardian, custodian or legal representative;

"(c) A child whose parent, guardian, custodian or legal representative neglects or refuses to provide proper or necessary subsistence, education, medical or surgical care, or other care necessary for his or her health, morals or well-being."

The family is an institution which preceded governments. Its sanctity was universally recognized before judges or statutes or constitutions or welfare organizations were known to man. The right of a child to a mother and a mother to a child are rights created by natural law. They are rights attributable to the nature of mankind rather than to the enactments of law.

It is a serious matter for the long arm of the state to reach into a home and snatch a child from its mother. It is a power which a government dedicated to freedom for the individual should exercise with extreme care, and only where the evidence clearly establishes its necessity. Yet, of course, there are cases where such authority must be exercised for the protection and welfare of children.

Under our system of government children are not the property of the state to be reared only where and under such conditions as officials deem best. On the other hand the state is interested in establishing a minimum standard of care for a child's physical, intellectual and moral well being. But this minimum standard must be viewed in the light of experience. Although there are many very good homes, there is no such thing as a "perfect home."

A child cannot be declared "neglected" merely because his condition might be improved by changing his parents. The welfare of many children might be served by taking them from their homes and placing them in what the officials may consider a better home. But the Juvenile Court Law was not intended to provide a procedure to take the children of the poor and give them to the rich, nor to take the children of the illiterate and give them to the educated, nor to take the children of the crude and give them to the cultured, nor to take the children of the weak and sickly and give them to the strong and healthy.

The power of the juvenile court is not to adjudicate what is for the best interests of a child, but to adjudicate whether or not the child is neglected. In re Rose Child Dependency Case, 1947, 161 Pa.Super. 204, 208, 54 A.2d 297.

Much of what we have said above was contained in the opinion of President Judge Himes of the lower court, some in almost the same language. Where we differ with the court below is not so much on the principles involved but in their application to the evidence.

The fact that the state is supporting the children does not take away from the mother any rights which she would have to the custody of the children were she supporting them from her own resources.

In habeas corpus cases involving the custody of children the contest is between two people usually parents or relatives. It seldom involves people who have not been at some time in a parental relationship to the child. In these cases the government acts as an arbiter between the parties and determines with whom the child's interests will best be served.

An action to have a child declared neglected is a contest between the state and the parent or person having custody of the child. The state becomes both arbiter and party. In order that justice may be done, it is necessary that juvenile court judges exercise their power with caution, for the restraint that is upon them is limited largely to self restraint.

It is because of this distinction between habeas corpus and neglected cases that the Supreme Court may have pronounced the apparently inconsistent rules of Commonwealth ex rel. Harry v. Eastridge, 1953, 374 Pa. 172, 97 A.2d 350; and Ciammaichella's Appeal, 1952, 369 Pa. 278, 85 A.2d 406.

In the Eastridge case the Supreme Court held that an appellate court is not free to nullify the fact-finding function of the hearing judge in a habeas corpus case, and that in such case the credibility of witnesses and the weight to be given to their testimony can best be determined by the judge before whom they appear.

In the Ciammaichella's Appeal the Supreme Court held that the Superior Court should not limit its review in a neglected case but should exercise its independent judgment after consideration of the entire record. "Obviously," it was there said, "its [the Superior Court's] scope extends to the fullest review consistent with equitable principles." 369 Pa. at page 281, 85 A.2d at page 408.

We perceive that as one of these cases was a habeas corpus and the other a neglected case, the rule relating to the scope of review in the Ciammaichella's Appeal was not reversed by the Eastridge case. But even if we were to limit our review in this case to the scope imposed upon us by the Eastridge case we would reach the same conclusion.

An examination of the record in this case shows that the evidence of the Commonwealth is not seriously disputed. The determination of this matter depends upon the inferences to be drawn from the evidence rather than the credibility of the witnesses.

The children in question Terry, 12, Harry, 10, and Nancy, 9, have been residing with their mother. The father's whereabouts are unknown, he having deserted his family seven years ago. The mother is receiving public assistance. During the fall of 1954 the mother became seriously ill and was under treatment in the hospital several months for an internal condition from which she probably has not recovered. There is no evidence to indicate that these children were neglected prior to their mother's confinement in the hospital.

Mr. and Mrs. Carl Edward Miller, in-laws of the appellant, had Terry for several years but the mother took him back to her home. While she was in the hospital the Millers kept all the children. Mr. Miller is a bartender at the Moose Hall; Mrs. Miller does not work; they have no children; they live in the country and own a television set; the children like it there. The learned trial judge considers them proper people to have custody of Terry.

When the mother was discharged from the hospital she took her children home. The evidence, even of the petitioner's or Commonwealth's witnesses, establishes that the mother kept the children clean, that they were in good health, that their school work and attendance was satisfactory, that they attended Sunday School and that through the mother's efforts Terry attended a Methodist Church Camp during at least two summers where he was a "good camper." Terry was also described as mannerly and dependable by a Commonwealth witness for whom he did odd jobs.

That does not sound like neglect by a mother who has been compelled to rear three small children on a public assistance allowance for seven years since her husband deserted her.

But the mother's conduct is not above reproach. Occasionally she gets drunk, and she accepts with impropriety the attentions of two married men. We shall examine the evidence as to these shortcomings.

This action seems to have been precipitated by the events which took place January 9, 1955. That night the mother had borrowed a car and went to a drinking establishment. There she met one of the men with whom she had been "keeping company." When she left, he got into the car with her. When she ordered him out he beat her severely, after which she drove away without him. Becoming ill she stopped along the road where she was found by the police who had been notified of her condition by a passing truck driver. So badly was she beaten that she was required to stay in the hospital several days.

There was some evidence that the children were late for school on several occasions, but from the Commonwealth's own witnesses it appears that this was not while the children were living with the mother, but while they were living with the Millers.

There was evidence at the first hearing that the cars of the two married men were frequently parked in the vicinity of the appellant's home, and that on several occasions one of the men became intoxicated in her home.

With the exception of the Millers, who had no complaints about the home, not one of the Commonwealth witnesses at the first hearing was ever in the appellant's house; not her sister Ann, who visited next door several times a week, drove by to see whether there were any cars parked near her home, and looked in the windows to see who was there; not the neighbor who saw the children playing in the alley, and who alone of all the witnesses, thought they were dirty; not the welfare worker who first learned of the case when she went to the hospital to get the mother to give the Millers more money for keeping the children while she was in the hospital.

There was very little testimony presented at the first hearing concerning the neglect of these children, and the learned trial judge did not declare the children neglected at that time. Although technically he had no jurisdiction to supervise the children without finding them neglected, he is not to be criticized for making an effort to assist the mother in providing a better home for the children by urging her to discontinue all improper conduct.

The week after the first hearing the probation officer called at the appellant's home at 6:30 in the evening, found her doing the dishes and the children playing in the kitchen. Two days later he called at 10:30 p.m., and found her asleep on a living room chair and the children in bed. In each succeeding week for a month he called and "found everything normal." On some occasions he went around the neighborhood looking for appellant's friends' cars and at least once looked in the window but did not stop. He found nothing improper or suspicious on any of these visits.

On March 18th he called at 10:30 a.m. He saw one of her male companions leave by the front door as he went into the house by the back door, and, because the appellant did not answer the knock promptly, he assumed she and her friend had been upstairs, and because it had snowed the previous night, and there was snow on the windshield of her friend's car he assumed he had been there all night. The appellant admitted her friend had been at her home the previous evening for a half hour, but said he had left and had come back the following morning.

On March 29th, the probation officer in response to a telephone call went to appellant's home and found the children in bed and alone. It developed, however, that before leaving that afternoon to visit a sick sister in Chambersburg the appellant arranged with another sister living next door to have the children fed and put to bed.

Attached to the brief of the district attorney is printed a statement of one of appellant's male companions taken not in open court but before the district attorney, a probation officer and a stenographer, only a few days before the argument. It is not a part of the record; it was not sworn to; it was not taken in the presence of the appellant or her counsel; the maker was not subject to cross-examination. It should not have been given to us, and we have not considered it.

One of the welfare workers testified to the remarks and stories of the neighbors. It was generalized hearsay gossip, which we are required to ignore.

The lower court admitted testimony of what the children had told other people, not "for the purpose of establishing the truth of existence of the matters stated by the children" but "to establish what was in the minds of the children, and the impact upon the children of the mother's conduct." Its use thus limited, the evidence was properly admitted at the Juvenile Court hearing.

If these children are to be found neglected it must be solely on the basis of the mother's use of alcohol to excess and her association with the two men to whom we have referred.

Although deserted more than seven years ago, the appellant is not divorced. The evidence creates a suspicion that she has committed adultery with one or both of her two friends. It is insufficient, however, to warrant a holding by the court that she has. Brower v. Brower, 1945, 157 Pa.Super. 426, 43 A.2d 422; Baxter v. Baxter, 1942, 147 Pa.Super. 207, 24 A.2d 15; Rech v. Rech, 1954, 176 Pa.Super. 401, 107 A.2d 601; Viale v. Viale, 1933, 109 Pa.Super. 560, 167 A. 437.

Even if she did commit adultery, that *alone* does not warrant taking her children away from her. Commonwealth ex rel. McMenamin v. McMenamin, 1952, 171 Pa.Super. 524, 90 A.2d 398; Commonwealth ex rel. Bock v. Bock, 1946, 159 Pa.Super. 159, 48 A.2d 133.

Of course, it is possible for a parent to establish such an immoral atmosphere about a home that it amounts to legal neglect. The morals of a child are affected by that which he is allowed to observe and hear as well as by that

which he is taught. In a neglect case the question is not whether a parent is a law violator or uses alcohol to excess, but whether intemperate and immoral conduct of the parent creates such deficiencies in the parental care of the child as to require separating him from his parent.

The appellant is unwise in the choice of her companions. They are married men and they beat her. Her children do not like them. Her conduct is not to be condoned, but under the evidence it does not warrant a finding that her children are neglected.

It is unfortunate that the mother uses intoxicating beverages to excess. She should not do it, and indirectly it is likely to have some demoralizing effect upon the children. There is no evidence, however, that while drinking she ever has abused or mistreated her children. Nor does the evidence show that it is a regular or frequent failing. There is no evidence that the children have ever seen her under the influence of liquor. There is no evidence that she was intoxicated during the months between the hearings.

There is an intimation that the children are neglected because the mother leaves them alone in the house while she goes to drinking places. The time the mother was beaten by her companion the children were being kept by her brother. There was evidence that she was not home over the lunch hour of the day before the first hearing. She went to see her lawyer and then went for a ride with one of her friends, returning in the afternoon by the time the children returned from school. She had asked her sister to care for the children over the noon hour. The time the probation officer was called at 10 o'clock at night the appellant had arranged with her sister, who lives on the other side of her double house, to give the children their supper and put them to bed. These three were the only specific incidents, when the children were home during the mother's absence, to which reference was made by the witnesses.

The appellant testified at the first hearing that since she had come home from the hospital she had been away from the house while the children were home not over a half dozen times.

Considering the way she was being watched by her sister, the welfare worker and the probation officer, as well as others, the probabilities are that her absence from the children after the hearing would have been quickly detected and reported. As a matter of fact the day she went to Chambersburg, her sister Ann, the probation officer and the welfare worker all knew before she returned home that she had been away.

As the record now stands there is no evidence of any specific time that she left the children alone without making provisions for their care.

It is our opinion that too much emphasis was placed upon the mother's conduct away from, and unrelated to, her relations with her children. Although there was some evidence to show the effect of her friends' visits upon the children, most of the evidence had to do with her conduct away from the home and the children.

There is evidence that the youngest child is below average mentally. Such child may need care beyond that required by a normal child. The legislature has recognized this in its definition of a neglected child in section 1 of the Juvenile Court Law, supra, which provides, inter alia: "The words 'neglected child' include: * * * (d) A child whose parent, guardian, custodian or legal representative neglects or refuses to provide the special care made necessary by his or her mental condition"; 11 P.S. § 243(5) (d). If the testimony should warrant it, the Juvenile Court could find that the youngest child is neglected and the other two are not.

Since the argument in this case, we have been informed that the appellant was sentenced for disorderly conduct arising out of her being intoxicated, and neither friend nor relative having paid her fine she was imprisoned. This came to the attention of this Court because a supersedeas had been issued and the District Attorney fearing the officials would be in contempt of this Court by placing custody of the children away from the mother while she was incarcerated, advised our President Judge of the situation.

We think there was insufficient evidence in this case to support a finding that the children are neglected. We are of the opinion, however, that we should not discharge the petition but should return the case to the lower court for further consideration.

The lower court may either discharge the

petition or take additional testimony relating to the neglect of the children. Evidence of events either before or subsequent to the last hearing may be admitted, and officially transcribed. If in the light of this opinion and any additional evidence which may be taken, the court finds that the children, or any of them, are neglected it may make an order accordingly. An appeal from such order would lie to this Court without the intervention of a rehearing.

The record is returned to the court below for action not inconsistent with this opinion.†

99

Rose Child Dependency Case *

PER CURIAM, July 17, 1947:

The Juvenile Court of Quarter Sessions of Westmoreland County made certain orders and decrees in regard to Maria Rose, alleged to be a dependent child, with a final order directing the officers to take the child from her home in Allegheny County and deliver her to the officers of the court below. There was also an order adjudicating in contempt the attorney for the persons having custody of the child in Allegheny County.

In this opinion we will chronologically develop the facts as and when they appeared on the record below. The first step was taken on February 28, 1946, when the juvenile court filed an order that "it having been called to the attention of the Court by the Juvenile Probation Officer that the above named child is dependent, *on due consideration it is . . . adjudged and decreed* that she . . . be and she is *hereby adjudged* to be a ward of the Juvenile Court of Westmoreland County, and is placed temporarily in the custody of the Catholic Welfare Association of Westmoreland County. . . ." The Juvenile Court Law of 1933 contains no provision for an adjudication that a child is a

---

† *Compare State v. Visser,* ——, Ia., ——, 88 N. W. 2d 925 (1958) *with State v. Greer,* —— Mo. App. ——, 311 S. W. 2d 49 (1958). — Ed.
* *Rose Child Dependency Case,* Grana and Leonard Appeals, Superior Court of Pennsylvania, 1947, 161 Pa. Super. 204.

"ward of the court." The court apparently meant that she was adjudged a dependent child. This order of court was void. The court had no jurisdiction of the subject matter, of the alleged dependent child, nor of any of the parties. The Juvenile Court Law (11 PS 243 et seq.) followed similar legislation for the protection of children and gives exclusive jurisdiction of proceedings affecting delinquent, neglected and dependent children to that court. But it provides that § 4 [1] that the powers of the court are to be exercised upon the petition of any citizen (or commitment by a magistrate). Until a petition was filed alleging that the child was neglected or dependent, the court had no power to act. Furthermore, the court could not make an *adjudication* on the petition until a full hearing had been had, and there could be no "due consideration" (in the language of the court) when there was no hearing. It is also true that it is an abuse of discretion for a court to go into such hearing and adjudication without notice to the persons having custody of the child, and without an opportunity for them to be heard, unless imperious reasons exist therefor. No such reasons existed here.

The void order of February 28, 1946, was followed by an amplified order of March 26, 1946, which recited that the interest of the child would be best served by placing her in the hands of her mother, and that the child was in need of medical treatment and should be near a hospital, and awarding custody of the child to the assistant probation officer of the

---

[1] "The powers of the court may be exercised —

"1. Upon the petition of any citizen, resident of the county, setting forth that (a) a child, giving his or her name, age, and residence, is neglected, dependent or delinquent, and is in need of care, guidance and control, (b) the names and residence of the parents, if any, or of his or her legal guardian if there be one, (c) the name and residence of the person or persons having control of the child, and (d) the name and residence of the nearest relative if no parent or guardian can be found.

"2. Upon commitment, by a magistrate, alderman or justice of the peace, of a child arrested for any indictable offense, other than murder, or for the violation of any other laws of this Commonwealth or the ordinance of any city, borough or township.

"3. There shall be no preliminary hearings in any cases affecting dependent, delinquent or neglected children under the age of sixteen years." 1933, June 2, P. L. 1433, § 4.

court. This order was also void for the same reasons, and also for the additional reason that the power of the juvenile court is not to adjudicate what is for the best interests of a child, but to adjudicate whether or not the child is neglected and dependent, and *if so*, to make orders in relief of the child.

On April 10 the attorney for Marco Grana and Bertha Grana, who had the custody of said child and lived in Allegheny County, applied for a "rehearing." Since the original and supplemental orders were void, and there never had been a hearing, such an application was superfluous, but was made because the custodians of the child believed (correctly) that the Juvenile Court of Westmoreland County had no jurisdiction. On April 11 the court made another order directing the Granas *and their attorney* to produce the child in open court on April 16 for a "rehearing." This order was void for the reasons already stated, and because the court had no power to direct the *attorney* for parties having custody to produce the child. In view of the facts developed at the hearing, and presumably known to the court at the date of the order, the court should not have directed the production of the child in court. There was no suspicion that the child was being mistreated, and the appearance of this infant nine months old in court could not aid in the determination of whether she was neglected or dependent; and the trial judge stated at the "rehearing" (and reaffirmed in his written opinion): "[There is] no dispute about the Grana home not being a proper home. . . . It is stipulated and agreed that the Grana home is a fit and proper home for the child." The only purpose of such an order was to get the child within Westmoreland County.

The "rehearing" was held April 16. The court, evidently advised by its own officers, "stipulated" that the child was in a good home. The unmarried mother of the child admitted that she had gone to the Roselia institution in Allegheny County to give birth to this child, and that she had signed a written paper, giving that institution the power to place the child for adoption. She admitted that the child had been placed with the Granas by the institution. The Granas therefore did not tortiously obtain custody. Even if a proper petition had been filed, the court at the conclusion of the testimony should have dismissed the proceeding. The child was admittedly not dependent and not neglected. She had a good home and was properly cared for. There was no evidence that she needed medical or hospital care.

The Granas, through their attorney, sought to convince the court that the child was not dependent; that since her custody by the Granas was by the written consent of the mother, the Juvenile Court of Westmoreland County had no jurisdiction, the child never having been in Westmoreland County, and that the purpose of the proceedings was merely to obtain custody. On all these scores the appellant was correct, for the mother herself stated in open court that her purpose was to "get back her child," and there was not the slightest evidence that she was neglected or dependent. Even though the mother claimed that her written consent to the Roselia institution to place the child for adoption was procured by what the judge called "a mild coercion," this still did not make the child dependent.

The hearing on April 11 was the first taking of any testimony, although the court had made an *adjudication* months before. On June 3 the court filed another order. It recited that a petition concerning the child had been presented to the court on May 1, 1946. No such petition was on that date in the files of the clerk of court. But such a petition, sworn to on May 1 by the mother, was filed on June 3. The order recited the prior "preliminary orders," and that the welfare of the child would be best served by granting the prayer of the petition, and therefore adjudged the child to be dependent, effective as of February 27, the date of the original order. No hearing had ever been had on this petition. The only testimony was taken on April 16, and that testimony clearly demanded the dismissal of the proceedings. The prayer of the petition was that the court "formally take jurisdiction over her said child, Maria Rose, *as* a dependent child in need of care, . . . and to . . . find a suitable foster home for the said child until . . . she [the mother] is able to care for her. . . ." (Emphasis supplied). No fact is averred in the nine paragraphs of the petition that the child *was* neglected or dependent. Its purpose was to secure custody. This order of the court cannot be sustained.

When made the court had indubitable evidence, and in fact had stated, that the child was in a good home, and she was neither neglected nor dependent.

On June 4 the court filed another order refusing to vacate the prior orders; and on June 5 ordered the state police to take the child by force from her home in Allegheny County and bring her to Westmoreland County. We are compelled to state that this order was an abuse of discretion under the evidence; and indeed under the rulings of the court itself, for the child was admittedly not dependent. It was also abuse of discretion for the court to make such an order directing the child to be forcibly taken from her home, unless clear and urgent reasons require the child to be rescued from present or imminent distress.

As to the contempt proceedings the first step was an order filed on June 18 and dated June 12 which recited that the attorney for the foster parents, by intimidation and force, prevented the court's probation officers from taking the child; that he ignored the order of court directing him to produce her, and had written an improper or impertinent letter to the president judge impugning the motives of the trial judge; and then adjudicating the attorney in contempt. This order and adjudication was likewise void, not only for all of the reasons heretofore recited, but because the court had no power to direct the attorney to produce the child unless the attorney had custody. As far as any advice or acts of the attorney having prevented the officers from taking the child from the Granas, such contempt was not committed in the presence of the court, and therefore no adjudication of contempt could be made without notice and hearing. We may also state that the attorney was quite right in doing everything in his power, short of the use of force, to dissuade the officers from taking the child. Although there was neither a petition, rule to show cause, notice nor evidence in the contempt matter, we have examined the letter written by the attorney to the president judge. As far as we can see there is nothing in the letter which is contemptuous, or which impugns the motives of the court. The letter stated what the mother–petitioner had told the attorney for the Granas. The repetition of this, if made out of proper motives, was not a contempt. On the whole subject matter, including the matter of motive, see *Commonwealth v. Sheasley*, 102 Pa. Superior Ct. 384.

We give full credit to the trial judge as to his sincerity of purpose and his desire to do right. The difficulty is that, however much the court believed it to be desirable, juvenile court proceedings, like adoption proceedings, are not a substitute for habeas corpus. This has often been decided (*Gard Appeal*, 356 Pa. 378, 52 A.2d 313) and the question of custody was the only thing that was ever sought to be determined in these proceedings.

We must make one other observation. No new proceedings can be entertained by the court below on a petition that avers this child is neglected or dependent unless the present situation changes so that the child is *actually* neglected. There is nothing in the proposition that a child is neglected if dependent on private charity, as alleged by the appellee. If the child is properly supported by her foster parents, the fact that possibly they cannot be compelled to support her in the future does not make the child dependent now. Any child may at some future time become dependent, but adjudication cannot be made until dependency actually occurs. The county seat of Westmoreland County is some thirty miles from the city of Pittsburgh, where sits a special and independent juvenile court of Allegheny County. Certainly that court will, if requested, have its officers investigate whether the child is properly cared for and nurtured. No more orders should be issued directing that this child be forcibly taken by the officers to Westmoreland County. It is both unnecessary and improper. If the child is in fact neglected and dependent (and nobody pretends that she is), complaint should be made to the Juvenile Court of Allegheny County, either by the mother or by the officers of the Juvenile Court of Westmoreland County. The question of custody must be adjudicated in Allegheny County.

The proceedings to No. 7 February Term, 1946, captioned in the Juvenile Court of Westmoreland County, relating to the custody of Maria Rose, alleged to be a dependent child, although initiated by the lower court with no doubt the best intentions, were pursued in a manner that cannot be sanctioned. The whole proceeding was nonjudicial, void in form and substance, and is ordered to be stricken from

the record. . . . As to the proceeding to No. 96 April Term, 1947, or the adjudication of contempt, since the alleged contempt is based upon violation of various orders of the court which were void in form and substance, and since the alleged contempt was not committed in the presence of the court, and no notice of hearing was ever given, the adjudication of June 12, 1946, by the Court of Quarter Sessions or the Juvenile Court of Westmoreland County, is also stricken from the record; costs to be paid by the county of Westmoreland.†

100

Lindsay v. Lindsay *

MR. JUSTICE FARMER delivered the opinion of the court:

This is a writ of error and was sued out in the name of Elizabeth Lindsay, William Lindsay, and Otoman Zar-Adusht Hanish to review a decree entered by a judge of the circuit court of Cook county sitting in the branch known as the juvenile court. Defendants in error filed a plea denying the right of all of plaintiffs in error to the writ and an issue of law was raised by a demurrer to said plea. At the last October term an opinion was filed holding that Elizabeth Lindsay was not entitled to the writ or to join in the assignment of errors but that the other two plaintiffs in error had a right to sue out the writ and have the decree reviewed. (*Lindsay* v. *Lindsay*, 255 Ill. 442.) Defendants in error have now joined in error and filed briefs on the merits of the case.

In the former opinion appears the following statement of the case:

"On December 15, 1911, defendant in error Charles R. Lindsay, Jr., filed in the juvenile branch of the circuit court of Cook county a petition charging that William Lindsay, a male child under seventeen years of age, was a dependent child and did not have proper parental care; that his father was dead and he was in the

---

† Compare *State* v. *Farrell*, 241 Mo. App. 234, 237 S. W. 2d 492 (1951) *with In re Belk*, 97 Ohio App. 114, 123 N. E. 2d 757 (1954). — *Ed.*

* *Lindsay* v. *Lindsay*, Supreme Court of Illinois, 1913, 257 Ill. 328. 100 N. E. 978.

care of his mother, Elizabeth Lindsay, and Otoman Zar-Adusht Hanish; that his mother had neglected and failed to properly care for the said child, and that she was an improper guardian and wholly unable to care for, protect, train and educate said child, by reason whereof he had become a dependent child. Summons was issued against the plaintiffs in error Elizabeth Lindsay and Hanish commanding them to appear before said court on the 4th day of January, 1912, and to have the said William Lindsay in open court. On the same day the petition was filed, December 15, 1911, the petitioner filed his affidavit stating that in his belief service of summons would be ineffectual to secure the presence of said child in court and that he should be taken into custody forthwith, 'as his immediate health and welfare are being jeopardized by his present care and custody.' A warrant was issued, and under and by virtue of it the boy was taken by officers to the Detention Home, where he was placed in confinement. Upon assurance being given that he would be brought into court at the time set for hearing, the boy was released and turned over to his mother and with her went to the home of a Miss Brauchmann, where they were staying at the time, and remained there until the 27th or 28th of December, when they disappeared. On the day of the hearing, January 4, 1912, Hanish filed an answer to the petition, stating under oath that he never had control or custody of said child or power to produce him in court, and had no knowledge of the place where the child was or in whose custody or control he might be. The court appointed an attorney to represent the child, and in the absence of Mrs. Lindsay and child proceeded to hear the testimony of witnesses upon the question whether or not the child was dependent or had proper parental care, and also as to the circumstances relating to the disappearance of Mrs. Lindsay and her boy. On January 24 the court entered a decree defaulting Mrs. Lindsay and William Lindsay, and finding that said William Lindsay was a neglected and dependent child, having no guardian of his person other than his mother, his natural guardian; that the father of said child died in Philadelphia in November, 1902, leaving an estate to his said son from which an income amounting to $1200 or $1500 per year is paid to his mother, to be expended in

his care, maintenance and education, by the Girard Trust Company of Philadelphia, guardian of the estate of said child; that Mrs. Lindsay was not a proper person to have the care and custody of said child and that he does not receive proper parental care. The decree further found that Hanish was the head of a religious organization to promote the Mazdaznan religion; that the said religion purports to be the teaching of oriental philosophy and religion; that Mrs. Lindsay was a believer in said religion and its teachings and recognized absolute spiritual and temporal power by Hanish over her religious beliefs, amounting to a religious fanaticism; that for a year last past she had been at divers places attending functions of said religion, had not kept the boy in school and had permitted him to reside and travel with said Hanish at different places in and through the United States and Canada, and that Hanish was not a proper person to have control over said child. The court appointed the petitioner and Ellwood C. Lindsay, of Philadelphia, Pa., guardians of William Lindsay, and authorized them to take him into their care and custody wherever he may be found, and to present to the proper court of Philadelphia a showing regarding the conditions surrounding said child when they shall have secured his custody, 'and abide by the orders of said court as to such care and custody.' The court adjudged Mrs. Lindsay in contempt of court for taking her child and leaving the jurisdiction of said court. To review this judgment a writ of error has been sued out of this court by Hanish and Mrs. Lindsay, and William Lindsay by his next friend."

The residence of the child, William Lindsay, was with his mother, in Pennsylvania or New York. It is not clear in which of those States they resided, but it is not disputed that they were not residents of this State but were in the State on a visit, or temporarily, when the proceeding was instituted in the juvenile branch of the circuit court.

Plaintiffs in error contend (1) that the act known as the Juvenile Court act is in violation of the Federal constitution and the constitution of this State; (2) that William Lindsay and his mother being residents of another State, temporarily stopping in this State, were not subject to the jurisdiction of the court in a proceeding under the Juvenile Court act; and

(3) that William Lindsay was not a dependent, neglected or delinquent child and his mother an unfit person to have custody and control of him.

The principal grounds urged against the validity of the act are: (1) It creates a new court, termed the "juvenile court"; (2) it denies the constitutional right of trial by jury; (3) it reduces the child to a state of involuntary servitude in cases other than as a punishment for crime; and (4) it deprives children and the parents of children of liberty, property and the right to the pursuit of happiness without due process of law. Particular objections made to specific sections of the act are unnecessary to a decision of this case and will therefore receive no discussion.

We entertain no doubt of the constitutional power of the legislature to pass an act of the character here involved, for the protection of dependent, neglected or delinquent children. Acts in many respects similar, in principle, for the protection of delinquent, neglected and dependent children have existed in some States for years, but acts like the one here being considered are of comparatively recent origin. This act was originally adopted in 1899, and is said by the editor of the eleventh and latest edition of Wharton's Criminal Law to be the first juvenile court act, as such acts are now generally known, adopted by any State. Similar acts have since been adopted by several other States and have been uniformly sustained as valid legislation, except in the State of Michigan, where the acts held invalid were subject to objections not found in our statute. Our statute and those of a similar character treat children coming within their provisions as wards of the State to be protected rather than as criminals to be punished, and their purpose is to save them from the possible effects of delinquency and neglect liable to result in their leading a criminal career. The purpose of such legislation is, we think, rightfully claimed to be unquestionably in advance of previous legislation dealing with children as criminals.

Our statute does not, as contended, create a new court unauthorized by the constitution. The decree which this writ of error is sued out to review was rendered by a judge of the circuit court of Cook county designated by the other judges of said court, pursuant to authority conferred by the act, to hear causes arising under said act. The judge so sitting is a circuit judge and the court in which the proceedings were held is a circuit court. The legislature of Pennsylvania passed an act defining the powers of the several courts of Quarter Sessions of the Peace with reference to the care, treatment and control of dependent, neglected, incorrigible and delinquent children under the age of sixteen years. The validity of the act came before the Supreme Court of that State, and one of the objections urged to it was that it provided for an unconstitutional tribunal. The Supreme Court said the act did not create a new court; that the court of quarter sessions was a constitutional court, and the legislature, recognizing it as an appropriate one upon which to confer jurisdiction in the care of neglected and unfortunate children recognized by the State as its wards and requiring its protection, had the constitutional power to confer such jurisdiction upon that court. (*Commonwealth* v. *Fisher*, 213 Pa. St. 48; 5 Am. & Eng. Ann. Cas. 92.) Our statute gives circuit and county courts concurrent jurisdiction in cases arising under it, and while it provides that the court exercising the powers and jurisdiction conferred by the act may for convenience sake be called juvenile court, it does not create a new court but delegates powers to constitutional courts already existing. The prerogative of the State arising out of its power and duty, as *parens patriæ*, to protect the interests of infants has always been exercised by courts of chancery. In *Wellesley* v. *Wellesley*, 2 Bligh, (N. S.) 142, Lord Beresford said the right of a chancellor to exercise such powers had not been questioned in one hundred and fifty years. This jurisdiction is by the Juvenile Court act conferred upon juvenile courts. *Witter* v. *County Comrs.* 256 Ill. 616.

Section 2 of the act under consideration authorizes a trial by a jury of six upon the demand of any person interested, or the judge may of his own motion order a jury of the same number to try the case. This, it is claimed, is not such a jury as the constitution guarantees. This contention of plaintiffs in error, and also the contention that the act deprives the child of his right to personal liberty, were decided contrary to the position of plaintiffs in error in *Petition of Ferrier*, 103 Ill. 367, and *County of McLean* v. *Humphreys*, 104 id. 378. In the *Ferrier case* Winifred Breen, a girl nine years old, was found to be a truant from school, without proper parental care and in imminent danger of ruin and harm. In a proceeding in the county court under "An act to aid industrial schools for girls," passed in 1879, she was committed to an industrial school for girls at Evanston and one of the vice-presidents of the school was appointed her guardian, in accordance with the provisions of the act. That act authorized a trial by a jury of six. It was contended in this court that the act violated the constitutional provision that no person should be deprived of liberty without due process of law. This court held that the jurisdiction conferred by the act upon the county court was the same character of jurisdiction exercised by courts of chancery over the persons and property of infants, having its foundation in the prerogative of the State flowing from its general power and duty, as *parens patriæ*, to protect those who have no other lawful protector. The court said: "The right to liberty which is guaranteed is not that of entire unrestrainedness of action. Civil government in itself implies an abridgment of natural liberty. 'Civil liberty, which is that of a member of society, is no other than natural liberty, so far restrained by human laws, and no farther, as is necessary and expedient for the general welfare.' (1 Blackstone's Com. 125.) It is not natural but civil liberty of which a person may not be deprived without due process of law. There are restrictions imposed upon personal liberty which spring from the helpless or dependent condition of individuals in the various relations of life, among them being those of parent and child, guardian and ward, teacher and scholar. There are well recognized powers of control in each of these relations over the actions of the child, ward or scholar, which may be exercised. These are legal and just restraints upon personal liberty which the welfare of society demands, and which, where there is no abuse, entirely consist with the constitutional guaranty of liberty. (See Cooley's Const. Lim. 339, 342.) We find here no more than such proper restraint which the child's welfare and the good of the community manifestly require and which rightly pertains to the relations above named, and find no such invasion of the right to personal liberty as requires us to pronounce this statute to be unconstitutional." On the trial of the case before the county court a jury of

twelve men was demanded and was denied. The statute, as we have said, provided for trial by a jury of six. Upon this question the court said: "The constitutional provision that 'the right of trial by jury, as heretofore enjoyed, shall remain inviolate,' does not apply. This is not a proceeding according to the course of the common law in which the right of a trial by jury is guaranteed, but the proceeding is a statutory one, and the statute, too, enacted since the adoption of the constitution. There was not, at the time of such adoption, the enjoyment of a jury trial in such a case. In reference to this subject, generally, Judge Cooley, in his work on Constitutional Limitations, (page 319), remarks: 'But in those cases which formerly were not triable by jury, if the legislature provide for such a trial now, they may doubtless create for the purpose a statutory tribunal composed of any number of persons, and no question of constitutional power or right could arise.'"

County of McLean v. *Humphreys, supra,* arose under the same act of 1879 and its validity was again attacked in this court. The court said: "It would be difficult to conceive of a class of persons that more imperatively demands the interposition of the State in their behalf than those we have just enumerated and for whose benefit the act under consideration was adopted, and it would be a sad commentary on our State government if it is true, as is contended, there is no constitutional power in the legislature to provide, by suitable legislation, for their education, control and protection. It is the unquestioned right and imperative duty of every enlightened government, in its character of *parens patriæ*, to protect and provide for the comfort and well being of such of its citizens as by reason of infancy, defective understanding, or other misfortune or infirmity, are unable to take care of themselves. The performance of this duty is justly regarded as one of the most important of governmental functions, and all constitutional limitations must be so understood and construed as not to interfere with its proper and legitimate exercise. We perceive no force in the objection that the act in question is an infringement upon the personal liberty of the citizen, as guaranteed by the constitution. The restraints which the act imposes are only such as are essential to the comfort and well being of the unfortunate class of persons who are brought within its provisions. All governmental and parental care necessarily imposes more or less wholesome restraint, and we see nothing in the act which looks beyond this. Assuming, then, as we do, the legislature has the right to provide for the education, support and control of these unfortunate beings, it clearly has the right also to provide the necessary instrumentalities or agencies for the accomplishment of these objects."

We have quoted extensively from those two cases because the principles involved in them are similar to those involved in this case, and we think they answer the objections here made to the Juvenile Court act.

Since 1899 several States have passed acts known as juvenile court acts. In Pennsylvania, Florida, Utah and Idaho the validity of such acts has been passed upon and sustained by the Supreme Courts of those States. . . . [Citations omitted. — Ed.] Acts of other States not known as juvenile court acts but authorizing the State to take the custody of neglected, abandoned and delinquent children and commit them to institutions established and maintained for their care, and authorizing them to be placed in good homes to be selected by those to whose custody they were committed, have been frequently before the courts and have almost uniformly been sustained. . . . [Citations omitted. — Ed.]

It is further contended the evidence does not sustain the finding of the decree that William W. Lindsay was a dependent child. The petition filed in this case alleged that William W. Lindsay was a dependent child in that he did not have proper parental care. It is further alleged that his father was dead and he was in the custody or control of his mother, Elizabeth Lindsay, and Hanish; that his mother had wholly neglected and failed to properly care for him; that she was an improper guardian and wholly unable to care for, protect, train and educate said child, by reason of which he had become dependent. Defendants in error do not contend that there is anything in the character or disposition of the boy that would make him amenable to the laws respecting delinquent children. The evidence shows that he is a modest, unassuming boy, twelve years of age, without any bad habits and no apparent evil tendencies, devoted to his mother and obedient to her wishes. His father died

when he was three years of age, and since that time he has been under his mother's care and has lived with her. He receives an income of from $1200 to $1500 per year from his father's estate, which is under the management of the Girard Trust Company of Philadelphia, the income being paid to Mrs. Lindsay for the boy's support and maintenance. Mrs. Lindsay and her boy have lived in various places since the death of the boy's father and have traveled to some extent abroad. In 1910, while residing in New York City, Mrs. Lindsay became a follower of Otoman Zar-Adusht Hanish and a member of the religious organization of which he was the leader. This organization maintains temples or places of worship in Los Angeles, New York City, Chicago, Lowell, Montreal, and in some foreign countries, and purports to teach what is called the Mazdaznan religion. It is the connection of Mrs. Lindsay with this religious society and the association of the boy with Hanish that afford basis for the allegation in the petition that she is an improper guardian of her boy. The evidence shows that while Mrs. Lindsay lived in New York City, and about six months after she became a member of the Mazdaznan religious society, Hanish stayed at her home about ten days. At the same time a Mrs. Hilton and daughters were residing with Mrs. Lindsay. Later Hanish spent three weeks at the home of Mrs. Lindsay, and during that time Miss Brauchmann and Mr. Hesbie were staying there also. The boy went on one occasion from New York City to Montreal to see Hanish, staying, while there, with a Mr. Malley, a member of the society, and from there went to Lowell, Mass., to attend services at the temple. In 1911, while Hanish was in California, the boy was sent to him, traveling alone. Together they visited San Diego, Los Angeles, San Francisco, Seattle, Salt Lake City, Portland, and then returned to Chicago. On part of the return journey they were accompanied by Maurice Clemens, a young man employed by Hanish in connection with his temple services. While on this trip, which occupied about seven weeks, Hanish and the boy sometimes occupied the same room and also slept together. The boy took no part in the services at the temple and was not employed by Hanish. On his travels over the country his expenses were paid by his mother. The evidence shows that Mrs. Lindsay attended the services at different times at the temples in Lowell, Montreal and New York City, and was on a visit to Chicago for that purpose when the petition was filed in this case. She appears to be a woman of culture and refinement and of more than ordinary intelligence. There is evidence showing that she has great faith in Hanish as the head of the Mazdaznan religion and is a firm believer in the doctrines taught by him, but aside from that there is no evidence that she is in any way an unfit or improper person to have the care and custody of her boy. She seems to be deeply attached to him and very solicitous in regard to his health and welfare. She may have been misguided in her religious views and mistaken as to the best method of educating and training her boy, but we search the record in vain for evidence that he lacked food, clothing or shelter or was being reared in immoral or indecent surroundings. Defendants in error introduced in evidence a book written and published under the supervision of Hanish, called "Inner Studies," — a philosophical and medical treatise on health and hygiene and the treatment of disease according to the tenets of the Mazdaznan religion, which, it is claimed, shows that its author is a man of perverted character and morally unfit to associate with a boy of the age of William W. Lindsay. A copy of this book was found in the room occupied by Mrs. Lindsay at the home of her sister, in New York City, about a year after she had used the room, but it is not shown that either Mrs. Lindsay or the boy had ever seen or read the book. The book certainly cannot be commended for perusal by anyone, but in the absence of evidence that its principles were being taught to the boy or that he had access to it, we would not be justified in concluding that association with its author would show such a lack of parental care as to make the boy dependent, within the meaning of this statute. These is no proof in the record that the Mazdaznan religion is an immoral religion or that Hanish himself is an immoral man or engaged in immoral practices. Nor is there any proof that in his relations with the boy or the boy's mother he was guilty of any conduct that rendered him an unfit associate.

The purpose of this statute is to extend a protecting hand to unfortunate boys and girls who, by reason of their own conduct, evil tendencies or improper environment, have proven that the best interests of society, the welfare of the State and their own good demand that the guardianship of the State be substituted for that of natural parents. To accomplish that purpose the statute should be given a broad and liberal construction, but it should not be held to extend to cases where there is merely a difference of opinion as to the best course to pursue in rearing a child. There should be evidence of neglect, abandonment, incapacity or cruelty on the part of the parent or that the child is being exposed to immorality and vice. The right of parents to the society of their offspring is inherent, and courts should not violate that right upon slight pretext nor unless it is clearly for the best interests of the child to do so. We do not so find the evidence in this case, and for that reason the decree of the circuit court is reversed.†

101

Matter of Knowack *

BARTLETT, J. This is a proceeding based upon a petition addressed to the Supreme Court of the state of New York by Charles Knowack and Johanna, his wife, praying that their four children, now in the custody of the Children's Aid Society of Rochester, be restored to their care and control.

At the time this petition was verified, on the 22d of December, 1897, the four children of the petitioners — the only issue of the marriage — were aged, respectively, Frank, twelve years; Gustave, eleven years; Emil, eight years, and Freddie, six years.

It appears that some two years before the present application was made, and on the fifth day of June, 1895, these children were committed by a police justice of the city of Rochester to the care of the Children's Aid Society, under section 291 of the Penal Code, on the

---

† Examples of evidence sufficient to sustain finding of "neglect": *In re Watson*, 177 Kan. 666, 281 P 2d 1116 (1955); *In re O'Beirne*, 194 Ore. 389, 241 P 2d 874 (1952); *In re Miller* 40 Wash. 2d 319, 242 P 2d 1016 (1952). — *Ed.*

* *Matter of Knowack*, New York Court of Appeals, 1899, 158 N. Y. 482, 53 N. E. 676.

ground of the intemperance and neglect of their parents.

Each child was committed by a separate commitment which was headed "Destitution Commitment," and recited that the child "was found not having any home or other place of abode, or proper guardianship, being in a state of want and suffering, and destitute of means of support, in violation of statute," etc. The child was to remain in charge of the society "until therefrom discharged in manner prescribed by law, not to exceed the period of its minority."

Section 291 of the Penal Code is contained in chapter III, entitled "Abandonment and other acts of cruelty to children."

This section is somewhat lengthy and provides that any child, actually or apparently under the age of sixteen years, who is found, under certain circumstances, may be duly committed.

Subdivision two states "not having any home or other place of abode or proper guardianship; or who has been abandoned or improperly exposed or neglected, by its parents or other person or persons having it in charge, or being in a state of want or suffering; or (subdivision three) destitute of means of support," etc.

So far as this record discloses the facts, the petitioners do not dispute the regularity of the original commitments, nor does the Children's Aid Society controvert the allegations in the petition and accompanying affidavits.

The petitioners aver that whatever ground might have existed on the fifth day of June, 1895, for the removing of the children from their care and custody, has been fully and absolutely removed; and that since the last-named day they have been sober, industrious, and have tried by all means possible to live honorable and respectable lives.

It further appears that the father and mother are both earning good weekly wages for persons in their position; that they are in comfortable financial circumstances and have a substantial bank account with the Rochester Savings Bank of the city of Rochester, and own good and valuable chattels and securities; that they are free from all debts and are in comparatively independent circumstances for persons in their station in life.

The petitioners further aver that they are in every way able, willing and desirous of car-

ing for their four children, who are now a charge upon the poor fund of the city of Rochester for their food, clothing and care, and that all the facts touching their willingness, ability and desire are more fully set forth and confirmed by the affidavits attached to the petition.

The petitioners further show that they have made frequent demands of the president and other officers of the Children's Aid Society for the return of their children, and that they even offered that the children be returned to them on trial, to be taken away again without resort to law, whenever the petitioners' conduct might seem to the officers of the society to justify such proceeding; but the officers have at all times refused to comply with these demands and requests.

It further appears that the children are all anxious and desirous of returning to the home of their parents.

Annexed to the petition are a number of affidavits of third parties corroborating in detail the allegations that the petitioners are sober, industrious and for a long time have been living honorable and respectable lives.

The truth of the allegations of the petition and affidavits is admitted, the Children's Aid Society in substance demurring to these facts.

It is claimed by the learned counsel for the society that persons committed by a final judgment of a court or magistrate of competent jurisdiction in a criminal proceeding cannot be discharged by the Supreme Court in the exercise of its general equitable powers.

Counsel further states that when a child is finally committed to a charitable institution under section 291 of the Penal Code, there is no way by which the institution can be deprived of its custody, except by the consent or in consequence of the misconduct of the institution itself, unless the commitment is directly and successfully attacked by appeal under section 749 of the Code of Criminal Procedure, or by a habeas corpus proceeding.

The main position of the society is based upon an erroneous conception of the situation now presented.

This is not a criminal proceeding; there is no prisoner and no crime has been committed.

We have already called attention to the fact that the section of the Penal Code (291) under which these commitments were made, is contained in the chapter (III) entitled "Abandonment and other acts of cruelty to children."

The state, as *parens patriæ*, by this legislation seeks to protect children who are destitute and abandoned by those whose duty it is to care for and support them.

To regard proceedings under this benign statute as criminal in their nature, and hedged about with all of those consequences that follow a judgment of conviction for crime, is to confound remedies.

The law relating to the commitment of minors to penal and charitable institutions is largely of American origin, and rests upon statutory provisions.

These commitments are naturally relegated into three classes, commitments as a punishment for crime, commitments where the proceeding is *quasi* criminal and commitments for care and guardianship. (30 Cent. Law J. 53.)

In the first class are cases of actual crime, where the proceeding often results in the commitment of the defendant to a reformatory by reason of his minority, rather than to send him to a penitentiary or state prison, where he would be thrown in contact with hardened criminals. Notwithstanding this consideration extended to the defendant, he stands in the attitude of a criminal duly convicted of crime.

The second, or *quasi* criminal class, may be illustrated by the case of a parent or guardian who makes application and complaint to a magistrate, asking the commitment of a minor child to some reformatory or charitable institution on the ground that he is incorrigible or beyond domestic control.

The main object of such a proceeding is to reform a child, if possible, and this commitment is governed by different rules than either of the other classes.

The third class, where the states intervenes to care for and protect the homeless and destitute child, is far more numerous and is the one that embraces the case at bar.

The single question presented by this appeal is whether the Supreme Court of the state of New York, having general jurisdiction in law and equity, and being vested with all the jurisdiction which was possessed and exercised by the Court of Chancery in England at the time of our separation from the mother country, except as modified by the Constitution and statutory provisions (Section 217, Code Civil Pro.),

has power to intervene in this case and restore these children to the custody and care of their parents.

It certainly is a most startling doctrine that a child, who is a public charge and has been committed for such reasons as are disclosed in this case, cannot be restored to parental care and control, where conditions have changed and are such that neither in law nor morals the separation of parent and child should be continued. We are not now called upon to decide what effect legal adoption in good faith by third parties would have on an application like this.

The Children's Aid Society stands in this proceeding upon the bald proposition of law already stated, that without its consent to their release these children are to remain in the custody of this institution during their minorities.

As the youngest child was only three and a half years of age when thus committed, it would be subjected to legal custody for a period of more than seventeen years.

This record fails to inform us as to the charter provisions of the Children's Aid Society.

Stripped of all form and technicality we have this situation: Intemperate parents are deemed to be unfit custodians of their children, and the state steps in and cares for and supports them for the time being. It now appears that the parents have reformed, are living honorable lives and are abundantly able to care for their children.

It seems self evident that public policy and every consideration of humanity demand the restoration of these children to parental control.

If the Court of Chancery can interfere and take the child from the custody of its parents, it can also intervene and restore it to their care in the exercise of the same discretionary power. . . . [Part of opinion omitted. — Ed.]

The leading case on this subject is *Wellesley v. Duke of Beaufort*, which went on appeal from Lord ELDON to the House of Lords, and in which the learned lord chancellor was unanimously affirmed. (2 Bligh's New Reports, 124; Schouler's Domestic Relations [fifth ed.], § 246.)

Lord REDESDALE, in a luminous opinion in the House of Lords, goes over the ground of the jurisdiction of the Court of Chancery in cases of infants. Speaking of the case before him he said: "Upon what ground is the court required to maintain these children out of their property and not at the expense of the father? It is because that father is an improper person to have the care of these children; and, as it is proposed that their maintenance and education should be put out of his control, it is, therefore, as he may refuse to afford them more than will supply them with their bare maintenance, which the law of the country would require from every person who had the means to maintain his children; it is for that reason that the court is to take upon itself, out of the property that those children have, instead of accumulating the income of their property for their benefit, till they should be capable of taking possession of it themselves, to apply a part of it for their maintenance and education."

It appears generally in this case that the father was a dissolute and abandoned character, and totally unfit to discharge the duties of a parent towards his children. It was under these circumstances that the Court of Chancery interfered and took the children from his custody and control.

It is such a power as is here disclosed that is now exercised by the Supreme Court of the state of New York; and, in a case where there has been interference by the court to protect and care for the child at the public's expense, that power seems only to be limited by the necessities of the case, having a due regard for the welfare of the infant.

This power is fully recognized in *Wilcox* v. *Wilcox* (14 N. Y. 576), where it was held that a court of equity has jurisdiction and authority to take a minor child from a guardian appointed by a surrogate on the death of its father and to deliver it to the care and custody of its mother where this is for the advantage of the child.

In the case cited the court was set in motion by a petition of the mother.

It appeared that the respondent and Nathan B. Wilcox, the son of the appellant, were married in 1838; they had two daughters, one nine and the other seven years of age; that after the birth of the first daughter her mother was in too feeble health to take care of her, and she was placed and taken care of in the family of her grandfather, where she afterwards continued to reside except during short intervals. Within a few years after the birth of the first child the father failed in business and became intemperate, and the respondent, with her other daughter, went to her father's and there resided with him until his death in 1852. The father was of large estate, and by his will made ample provisions for his daughter and the children. The father of the children died in 1854 without having made any legal disposition or guardianship of the eldest child. A few days after his death the grandfather was appointed by the surrogate the general guardian of the eldest child; the respondent was at this time temporarily absent from the state, and the appointment was made without notice to her or any other relatives.

It thus appears that the eldest daughter had been placed in the custody of the grandfather voluntarily and had remained there for years; and yet, when circumstances had changed, and the mother became possessed of ample means, the court intervened and restored the child to the custody of the mother, notwithstanding the relations that had grown up in the grandfather's family between the child and other relatives there residing and without regard to the letters of guardianship that had been duly issued to the grandfather.

While the decision in this case was rendered upon a divided court, there was no difference of opinion as to the main proposition that the court was possessed of this power. The only question upon which the judges were at variance was whether the power could be exercised at chambers or at a regular session of the Special Term.

In later cases it had been held that considerations affecting the health and welfare of a child may justify the court in withholding the custody of it temporarily even from the father acting as its legal guardian, and that they were so purely matters of discretion with the court of original jurisdiction that this court will not review the conclusion thereon unless some manifest error or abuse of power is made to appear. (*Matter of Welch*, 74 N. Y. 299; *People ex rel. Pruyne* v. *Walts*, 122 N. Y. 238.)

Many other cases might be cited, illustrating the general and ample powers of the Court of Chancery in the premises, but it is unnecessary.

It is urged on behalf of the petitioners and respondents that the restoration of these children can be effected under the general provisions of the Poor Law of the State (R. S. vol. 5 [Banks & Bros.' 9th ed.], p. 3373) on the ground that they have, since the fifth day of June, 1895, been a charge upon the poor fund of the city of Rochester.

Section two enacts: "A poor person is one unable to maintain himself; and such person shall be maintained by the town, city, county or state according to the provisions of this chapter."

Further on the section provides: "The town poor are such persons as are required by law to be relieved or supported at the expense of the town or city."

Section fifty-six provides in detail for the commitment of poor children under sixteen years of age.

Chapter four hundred and thirty-eight of the Laws of 1884, entitled "An act to consolidate the statutes of the state relating to the custody and care of indigent and pauper children by orphan asylums and other charitable institutions," is still in force. (See vol. 2 Birdseye's R. S. [2d ed.] p. 2308, where he inserts § 4 of this chapter as § 56d of the Poor Law.)

The section deals generally with the removal of children from one institution to another, and also provides for delivery of a child into the custody of the parent. It reads as follows: "But no parent of such pauper child, so in such asylum or other institution as in this section aforesaid, shall be entitled to the custody thereof, except in pursuance of a judgment or order of a court or judicial officer of competent jurisdiction, adjudging or determining that the interests of such child will be promoted thereby, and that such parent is fit, competent and able to duly maintain, support and educate such child."

We have here disclosed a statutory scheme in regard to the committal and subsequent discharge from custody of poor children that is practically in line with the general chancery powers of the Supreme Court.

In the case of *People ex rel. Inebriates Home for Kings County* v. *Comptroller of the City of Brooklyn* (152 N. Y. 399) Chief Judge Andrews while writing upon a kindred subject states, at page 407, as follows: "The duty of the state is discharged when it affords necessary relief to those whose support is cast upon the public, and it is plain that it should be given for such a length of time only as necessity demands. There is nothing more to be deprecated than encouragement to pauperism, or the extension of public aid to those who are able to support themselves, or the keeping of inmates in charitable institutions, whether children or adults, beyond the time that they can be self-supporting, or when they could be safely allowed to shift for themselves. Nor are institutions of charity subserving their proper function when they relieve friends or relatives of indigent persons, able and bound to maintain them, from the burden of their support."

It is true that the petition in this case is an appeal to the general equitable powers of the court and is not filed in the statutory proceeding, but it is evident that whether, in the Supreme Court, or based upon the statute, the questions controlling are the same, to wit, the best interests of the child and the ability of the parent, both moral and financial, to discharge his duty in the premises.

The order of the Appellate Division should be affirmed, without costs.

All concur.

Order affirmed.

102

Arizona State Department of Public Welfare *v.* Barlow *et al.* *

STRUCKMEYER, Justice.

Appellees, the parents of seventeen minor children, presented to this court five original petitions for writs of habeas corpus seeking to secure the custody of their children from the appellant Arizona State Department of Public Welfare. This court then being of the opinion that oral evidence would be required to sustain the averments of the petitions, directed that return be made to the Honorable Henry S. Stevens sitting in Division 8 of the Superior Court of Maricopa County, Arizona. After an

---

* *Arizona State Department of Public Welfare* v. *Barlow* et al., Supreme Court of the State of Arizona, 1956, 80 Ariz. 249, 296 P. 2d 298.

extensive hearing that court declared that the detention of the children by appellants was illegal and ordered their release to their respective parents. The present appeal followed.

On September 10, 1953, these children and others, all residents of Short Creek, Arizona, were determined by the Superior Court of Mohave County in juvenile hearings to be dependent and neglected within the meaning of Section 46–117, A.C.A.1939, as amended, now A.R.S. § 8–201, and were ordered placed in the custody of the Arizona State Department of Public Welfare. It was alleged in the applications for writs of habeas corpus that the Superior Court of Mohave County had denied certain fundamental rights to the parents, in violation of due process of law. No issue was framed either by the petition or the return nor was evidence offered or received concerning the fitness of petitioners to have custody of their children or whether it was to the children's best interest and welfare that they be detained in the custody of appellants. The Superior Court of Maricopa County found as a fact that petitioners were denied the active participation of their attorneys in the juvenile hearings in Mohave County. This finding is not challenged but the court's conclusions of law that the failure to permit the active participation of appellees' attorneys at the juvenile hearings denied basic constitutional safeguards are assigned as error. Appellants' argument on appeal is predicated on the premises (1) that appellees were not entitled to be represented by an attorney in the juvenile hearings in Mohave County as such hearings are by statute required to be informal and (2) that in any event since appellees were accorded all the essential elements of due process of law in the habeas corpus hearing, they could not complain of the denial thereof in the juvenile hearings.

Initially it should be emphasized that the questions presented do not embrace the rights of minors in juvenile hearings and accordingly this opinion is limited to a consideration of the rights of other persons who may be affected by the determination of custody. We recognize that a proceeding involving a dependent or delinquent juvenile is neither criminal nor penal in character and that the objective thereof is, as the case may be, the protection or rehabilitation of the child. Shioutakon v. District of Columbia, D.C.Mun.App., 114 A.2d 896. Be-

cause the child has attained a favored, beneficent status in our social and legal systems does not detract from the well-settled rule that the right of parents to the custody of minor children is both a natural and a legal right. Harper v. Tipple, 21 Ariz. 41, 184 P. 1005; in re Winn, 48 Ariz. 529, 63 P.2d 198. While the right to custody is not absolute because the parent may be deprived thereof by the state in the best interest and welfare of the child, Dickason v Sturdavan, 50 Ariz. 382, 72 P.2d 584; Fladung v. Sanford, 51 Ariz. 211, 75 P.2d 685, we are compelled to agree with the Court of Appeals of New York that "no court can, for any but the gravest reasons, transfer a child from its natural parent to any other person." *People* ex rel. *Portnov* v. *Strasser*, 303 N.Y. 539, 104 N.E.2d 895, 896. Moreover:

"The best of intentions and the greatest zeal to care for neglected, dependent, or delinquent children do not justify the violation of the constitutional provisions as to due process that are involved in removing a child from the custody of its parent. * * *" In re Godden, 158 Neb. 246, 63 N.W.2d 151, 156.

It has been repeatedly stated under a variety of circumstances that representation by one's duly constituted attorney is fundamental to our system of administration of justice. Powell v. State of Alabama, 287 U.S. 45, 53 S.Ct. 55, 77 L.Ed. 158; Roberts v. Anderson, 10 Cir., 66 F.2d 874; In re Tate, D.C., 63 F.Supp. 961; In re Hill, 78 Cal.App. 23, 247 P. 591; Arnold v. Fort Worth & D. S. P .R. Co., Tex.Civ. App., 8 S.W.2d 298; Camhi v. Camhi, Dom. Rel.Ct.N.Y., 25 N.Y.S.2d 559.

"What, then, does a hearing include? Historically and in practice, in our own country at least, it has always included the right to the aid of counsel when desired and provided by the party asserting the right. The right to be heard would be, in many cases, of little avail if it did not comprehend the right to be heard by counsel. * * * *If in any case, civil or criminal, a state or federal court were arbitrarily to refuse to hear a party by counsel, employed by and appearing for him, it reasonably may not be doubted that such a refusal would be a denial of a hearing, and, therefore, of due process in the constitutional sense.*" (Emphasis supplied.) Powell v. State of Alabama, supra, 287 U.S. 68, 53 S.Ct. 64.

"* * * It would seem necessarily to follow that if he is entitled to a hearing, he is likewise entitled to be represented by counsel, if he desires such representation; and that he also has the right to present evidence and adduce witnesses. Otherwise, the right to an appearance before the Board may be but a futile gesture. * * *" In re Tate, supra, 63 F.Supp. 962.

In our opinion the denial of the right to effective participation of counsel constitutes a denial of due process of law so gross as to lack a necessary attribute of a judicial determination. We hold that an order or judgment of a Superior Court which is predicated on a hearing in which a parent is denied the opportunity to be heard by counsel if requested is void. Cf. In re Frinzl, 152 Ohio St. 164, 87 N.E.2d 583; Phoenix Metal Corporation v. Roth, 79 Ariz. 106, 284 P.2d 645.

It is urged by applicants that the state, having an interest in the child as parens patriæ, should provide the kind of hearing which will be most conducive to the child's understanding — that the atmosphere of the hearing should approximate the kindly inquiry of a loving parent. This is a desirable end to be achieved. It conforms to the understanding of sociologists and psychologists in the era in which we live. In re Holmes, 379 Pa. 599, 109 A.2d 523. It is undoubtedly reflected in the language of the legislature of this state that "the hearing of any matter involving a child shall be informal * * *." R.S.A. § 8–229. However, we do not think the "informality," supra, may extend to the divesture of the fundamental right of the parent to be represented by counsel, if requested, when a substantial interest is dependent upon the outcome of the hearing. By the constitution, Article 6, § 6, the Superior Court is established as a court of general common law and equity jurisdiction. It is specifically empowered to determine proceedings affecting children under the age of eighteen years. While the constitution provides some distinctive procedure in juvenile matters, there is no language used from which an intention can be inferred to dispense with the fundamental rights of parents appearing before it when as a court of general jurisdiction it is exercising its constitutional powers in a juvenile matter. The informality referred to in A.R.S. § 8–229, supra, is simply legislative authorization for the court to disregard technical matters of procedure which do not affect the fundamental rights of litigants to due process of law.

As stated, appellants argue that since appellees had the right on habeas corpus to a determination of whether it was to the children's best interest and welfare to be returned to the custody of their parents, at which time they were accorded all the essential elements of due process of law, they could not complain of the denial thereof by the Mohave County Superior Court in the juvenile hearings. Ordinarily the sole function of the writ of habeas corpus is to determine the right to detain the individual of his liberty, Oswald v. Martin, 70 Ariz. 392, 222 P.2d 632. When the writ is used to invoke the court's equity powers to determine the custody of a minor child, it is not the personal liberty of the child but its welfare that is involved. In re Winn, supra.

In the present case the writ was not used to invoke the court's equity powers. The single issue presented to the Superior Court on habeas corpus was the legal right of the appellants to detain the children from their natural parents under the commitment of the Superior Court of Mohave County which, as we have shown, was void. Neither party submitted evidence as to whether it was to the best interest and welfare of the children that the parents be deprived of the custody. Since it is the legal presumption that an award of custody to a parent is to the best interest of the child, People ex rel. Yarmulnick v. Hoff, 323 Ill. App. 535, 56 N.E.2d 324; Paulson v. Windelow, 236 Iowa 1011, 20 N.W.2d 470; and since the burden is upon the party seeking to withhold a child from its natural parents or to deprive the natural parents of custody to establish that it is not to the best interest and welfare of the child for the parent to retain custody, Hale v. Henderson, 210 Ga. 273, 79 S.E.2d 804; People ex rel. Yarmulnick v. Hoff, supra; Ex parte De Castro, 238 Mo.App. 1011, 190 S.W.2d 949; Commonwealth ex rel. Human v. Hyman, 164 Pa.Super. 64, 63 A.2d 447; People ex rel. Portnoy v. Strasser, supra; Denessen v. Taylor, 198 Or. 347, 255 P.2d 148; Frazier v. Cowart, Tex. Civ.App., 191 S.W.2d 94, the Superior Court of Maricopa County did not err in directing that the children be returned to their natural parents.

Judgment affirmed.

LA PRADE, C. J. and UDALL, WINDES and PHELPS, JJ., concur.

103

Ripley v. Godden *

BOSLAUGH, J.

A petition was filed with the consent of the county attorney in the district court for Lancaster County by Dorothea W. Ripley, recited to be a reputable person, in which it was averred Michael Allen Godden was a dependent neglected child of the county without parental care and control. The child whose custody is the subject of this inquiry was 9 months of age. Appellant, his mother, who had his care and custody appeared with her counsel and made objections to and defense against the charge contained in the petition to the extent and within the limited time the district court permitted. The trial court found that Michael Allen Godden was dependent and neglected; that appellant was unfit to have his custody; that the family home was not an appropriate place for the child; and that it was for his best interest that his temporary custody be and it was given to the Child Welfare Department (Mrs. Helen Cox) for placement, supervision and boarding home care. The motion of appellant for a new trial was denied and she has brought this appeal.

Appellees argue that the law does not provide for an appeal to this court from any action of the district court in proceedings authorized by the Juvenile Court Act. §§ 43–201 to 43–227, R. R. S. 1943. A review of a finding and adjudication of the district court by authority of the Juvenile Court Act that a child is dependent and neglected, that his mother is not a suitable person to have his custody, and committing the child to the Child Welfare Department for placement, supervision, and boarding home care, may be had by an appeal to this court. Krell v. Mantell, 157 Neb. 900, 62 N. W. 2d 308. The argument of the appellees that the order of the district court in this case was not a final order and that by reason thereof this appeal is unauthorized may not be

accepted. The order was made in a special proceeding and it affects a substantial right. § 25–1902, R. R. S. 1943.

Appellant filed a written request that the court reporter be present and make a record of the proceedings and the matters offered as evidence at the hearing. The trial court announced before any proof was offered or received that this was a juvenile proceeding, a clinical hearing, and informal in character; that it was not a proceeding in which appellant was entitled to a record; and that there would be no record of anything that happened thereafter during the hearing of the case. The court did consent that appellant might, at her expense, have a record of the proceedings made. A court reporter is in Nebraska a state officer and an officer of the court. §§ 24–338, 24–341, R. R. S. 1943; § 24–339.01, R. S. Supp., 1953. See State ex rel. Carey v. Cornell, 50 Neb. 526, 70 N. W. 56. He is required by legislative mandate to make a stenographic report of oral proceedings had in the court for which he is appointed reporter "including the testimony of witnesses * * * and any further proceedings or matter when * * * requested by either party to said proceeding * * *." § 24–340, R. R. S. 1943. The duty the statute enjoins may not be disregarded by the reporter and the trial court has no authority or right to keep the reporter from performing his duty. A litigant is not obliged to make a request for a record by the reporter except in those situations where it is affirmatively required by the terms of the statute, otherwise a litigant may rely upon the reporter for a record of the proceedings. See Holland v. Chicago, B. & Q. R. R. Co., 52 Neb. 100, 71 N. W. 989. The office of court reporter is an important and responsible one. The duties of the office should be performed efficiently and with fidelity. In Home Fire Ins. Co. v. Johnson, 43 Neb. 71, 61 N. W. 84, it is said: "It is easily conceivable that a case of hardship might arise by a refusal of the character indicated, and if such hardship appeared, the judgment could not stand. Provision has been made for the use of stenographers as reporters, and to the proper administration of justice their services are very valuable, and they should be required to be in attendance, just as is required of any other officer of the court, when a trial is in progress." The court erroneously prevented the court reporter from making

---

* *Ripley* v. *Godden*, Supreme Court of Nebraska, 1954, 158 Neb. 246.

a record in this case. It improperly caused an expense to appellant as a condition of having the proceedings recorded. The error however was harmless because appellant, at her expense, provided a reporter who did what the court reporter should have done. If the appellant had sustained legal prejudice because of the ruling of the court it would have been reversible error. Home Fire Ins. Co. v. Johnson, *supra*; Coupe v. United States, 113 F. 2d 145.

The record does not show that any of the several persons referred to in the record as witnesses who appeared and gave information during the hearing of this case were administered an oath. It is certain that an oath was not taken by any of them. The court responded to a suggestion of appellant that an oath had not been administered to a person produced and who was about to be examined that "You are presumed to be under oath anyway." Section 25–1237, R. R. S. 1943, requires an oath to be administered to all witnesses and to be given in the manner "most binding upon the conscience of the witness." The exact language thereof is: "Before testifying, the witness shall be sworn to testify the truth, the whole truth, and nothing but the truth. The mode of administering an oath shall be such as is most binding upon the conscience of the witness." This provision of the law requires an oath of any witness. This proceeding was contested litigation involving a question of fact. It was a judicial search for the truth as a basis of deciding an issue affecting the right of a mother and her infant child. The failure to observe the plain mandate of the law is reversible error if objection is made and the omission is not waived. Fetty v. State, 119 Neb. 619, 230 N. W. 440; Krell v. Mantell, *supra*.

Appellant was not permitted an opportunity for an orderly and reasonable cross-examination of the persons examined in support of the charges made in the petition. The request of counsel for appellant to examine additional persons in support of her contentions that the claims made in the petition were untrue was refused by the court. The reason for this is clear from statements made by the court during the hearing that this was only a clinical proceeding; that the right of cross-examination did not exist; that it was not the kind of a proceeding where the credibility of a witness could be tested or questioned; that the rules of evidence were not applicable; and that a judgment was unnecessary.

The problem in this case was whether or not appellant was unfit to perform the duties of mother of the infant child or whether or not she had by wrongful acts or neglect forfeited the right to the custody of her child. It is firmly established in this state, and has been recently restated, that courts may not properly deprive a parent of the custody of a minor child unless it is shown that such parent is unfit to perform the duties of the relationship of parent and child and has forfeited the right to his custody. The custody of a child is to be determined by the best interest of the child with due regard to the superior rights of a fit and suitable parent. Lakey v. Gudgel, *ante* p. 116, 62 N. W. 2d 525. This case affects a 9-month-old infant who was in the custody of his mother. She and the father of the child had separated and the family home had been abandoned. The mother and the child were living in the parental home of the mother. An action for divorce and custody of the child was pending in the district court when this proceeding was commenced. The mother had the custody of the child and she is contesting to maintain her custody of him. There is probably no action known to the law more worthy of judicial consideration and careful determination than a proceeding affecting the custody of a little child. Claims of a parent should not be regarded in the removal of a child from the control of its parent if the parent is clearly unfit or has by misconduct forfeited his right to the custody of the child and if such drastic action is for the welfare of the child. However the devotion, care, and guidance of a normal parent are invaluable to his child and the relationship of parent and child should not be severed or disturbed unless the facts justify it. The interests of all parties concerned require, when the issue is contested in court, that the facts be shown by competent evidence. This should be accomplished by substantial observance of the rules of evidence and procedure that are usually considered essential to protect substantial rights in hearings without a jury had for the adjudication of issues of fact in civil cases in the district court. The essential processes, rules, and procedure of the law established and observed to aid courts in the investigation and adjudication of controversies and contested issues are not discarded or permitted to be disregarded because a pertinent statute refers to the proceeding as a summary one. If there is a contested issue of fact to be tried and determined in a proceeding by virtue of the statute concerning juvenile dependents or delinquents, as there is in this case, the result of an investigation ex parte and clinical in its nature may not be used as legal evidence in the trial of the contest, except insofar as it satisfies the requirements of the rules of evidence. It is sometimes said in delinquency cases involving very serious juvenile misconduct that constitutional safeguards and the procedures of the criminal law may be disregarded, but even in this there is no implication that a purely informal, hasty trial of a contested issue of fact may properly or legally be had with only scant regard to rules of evidence or of procedure. There must be a reasonably definite charge and customary rules of evidence essential to getting at the truth with reasonable certainty must be observed. Findings of fact must rest on preponderance of competent proof produced under such rules and an adjudication should be made in harmony with the findings. . . . [Citations omitted. — Ed.]

The best of intentions and the greatest zeal to care for neglected, dependent, or delinquent children do not justify the violation of the constitutional provisions as to due process that are involved in removing a child from the custody of its parent. The indispensable elements of due process are a tribunal with jurisdiction, notice of a hearing to the proper party, and an opportunity for a fair hearing according to applicable procedures. Appellant did not have an opportunity for or a fair hearing in this case.

Appellant complains that the court in its consideration and determination of this case considered not only the statements of unsworn persons examined during the hearing but many undisclosed reports made and communicated to the court by unnamed persons described as investigators from the police department and the Child Welfare Department. The record justifies the complaint of the appellant. The reports were not admissible in evidence. They were improper to be considered by the court in this case. If material competent information known to any of the persons who made the re-

ports was desired as evidence it should have been produced under oath with opportunity for cross-examination. Appellant could not meet matters contained in reports of which she had no knowledge or means of knowledge and the record in the case in this court on appeal could not present information contained in the reports and considered as a basis of the adjudication in the district court. Scherz v. Platte Valley Public Power & Irr. Dist., 151 Neb. 415, 37 N. W. 2d 721; Pope v. Tapelt, 155 Neb. 10, 50 N. W. 2d 352; Krell v. Mantell, *supra*. In State ex rel. Palagi v. Freeman, *supra*, the court said: "At most, the court had before it the ex parte reports of the probation officer above quoted, which were not legal evidence of even the facts therein set forth. As these matters must be set forth in the petition and charges made therein, those charges must be established by evidence, with the corresponding right of cross-examination." See, also, In re Matter of Hill, *supra*; People v. Lewis, *supra*.

This was a contested matter in the district court and the hearing should have been conducted with regard for established rules and procedures. State ex rel. Miller v. Bryant, 94 Neb. 754, 144 N. W. 804, decided that the act of the Legislature of 1905 (Laws 1905, c. 59, p. 305) in reference to dependent, neglected, and delinquent children, in essential particulars so far as applicable to this case the same as statutes now on the subject, did not create a new court or any court but only imposed new and additional powers on the district court. It is said therein: "By the act under consideration no new court was created, but the already existing district court was given new and additional powers and jurisdiction. That court is a court of general common law and equity jurisdiction, and it was clearly within the power of the legislature to require that court to exercise the powers and jurisdiction provided for by the juvenile court law." The Juvenile Court Act did not change the rules, practice, and procedure applicable to hearings without a jury of contested issues of fact in the district court.

The findings and adjudication of the district court should be and they are reversed and the cause is remanded for further proceedings.

REVERSED AND REMANDED.

Chapter 17

Suggested Procedural Reforms

THE ARTICLES IN THIS CHAPTER are extracts from published papers by former students of the Editor in his seminar on the Problem of Juvenile Delinquency given at the Harvard Law School. They are included not because the Editor necessarily agrees with the solutions proposed to the puzzling procedural problems which have developed in the course of administering juvenile court statutes but because they illustrate how difficult are the issues involved.

104

Determination of Delinquency in the Juvenile Court: A Suggested Approach *

J. J. Rappeport

Extracted from the *Washington University Law Quarterly* (1958), 123, 161–166.

The development of the juvenile court movement in the United States has stressed the harm done to the child during the process of trying him. There has been much concern with the detrimental aspects of what is assumed to be a "traumatic experience." As a matter of fact, a more formal, orderly, hearing, far from being "traumatic," may actually be a constructive factor in anticipatory preventive technique.[1] That is, the very formality of the hearing may

well have a sobering, educative effect on the child as well as his parents, acting as an effective deterrent to future delinquency.

However, assuming that some of the more rigid rules of criminal procedure may properly be eliminated from juvenile court proceedings, how may this be done while still affording basic protection? It has been asserted that constitutional safeguards ought to be provided only where necessary to assure fair treatment.[2] Under this approach, relevant factors are to be established, and the scope of judicial discretion regarding the necessity of a particular safeguard is to be delineated, by appellate decisions on a case-by-case basis. In addition to the obvious dangers that decisions which were intended to be limited to a particular fact situation may be regarded as binding in future cases, and that appellate courts have little control in these matters because so much depends upon the fact situation, there is a much more serious objection. The process could well be an empirical one because matters within the competence of the juvenile court are, by their very nature, certain to evoke conflicting emotions. Every judge has an ineradicable sociocultural background in these matters, which, subconsciously at least, might tend to color a decision left to his general discretion. In addition, since family matters are commonly experienced, and individual expertise is assumed to follow, there is likely to be a wide variance in the decisions.

---

* Used by permission of the author and the publisher. Some footnotes omitted; others renumbered. See, also, G. Geis, "Publicity and Juvenile Court Proceedings," 30 *Rocky Mountain L. R.* (1958), 1–26. — Ed.

[1] A detrimental aspect pointing up the need for counsel is that an infant untrained in the law and overawed by the presence of the court might be unable to conduct an intelligent and effective fight for

his freedom without proper advice. See In re Poff, 135 F. Supp. 224 (D.D.C. 1955).

[2] People v. Dotsen, 46 Cal. 2d 891, 895, 299 P.2d 875, 877 (1956).

If so, the familiar remark concerning undisciplined discretion in equity cases, to the effect
that equity was only as long as the chancellor's
foot, is relevant.[3]

To avoid delegating undefined discretion to
the courts, and to afford more clearly defined
rights to the juvenile offender, consideration
should be given to specific legislation which
would define, regularize, and record, the governing policy for all to know that it exists. Such
legislation would clearly differentiate between
the categories of causes which bring children
before the juvenile court. By a separation
rather than a consolidation of these causes, the
term "delinquency" would be applied exclusively in cases where a serious antisocial act was
alleged.[4] In cases of neglect and incorrigibility,
the constitutional safeguards and the probative
force of the evidence should be those required
in non-criminal proceedings.[5] To guard against

the abuse of power, even when exercised with
the loftiest of motives, and to ensure a proper
finding of guilt in delinquency cases, the same
constitutional safeguards and rules of procedure and evidence should be afforded the child
as are mandatory in the criminal trials of adults.
While the objectives of "individualized justice"
are recognized and approved, one must always
bear in mind that the child's status and rights,
as well as the rights of the parents, are involved.
Where an alleged violation of law might empower the court to deprive the child of liberty
and the parents of custody, the court must first
determine from competent evidence in a fair
hearing whether or not the child has, in fact,
committed an unlawful act. If a preponderance
of the evidence is thought to be more desirable
in delinquency proceedings than proof beyond
a reasonable doubt, then the authority of the
appellate courts in reviewing the evidence
should be substantially broadened.[6]

What is needed is a framework of formal-
ism designed solely for the protection of the
juvenile, within which there would be limited
flexibility. This flexibility would take the form
of modified courtroom formalities and an absence of those technicalities not essential to
justice which tend to confuse and intimidate
the child. In establishing proceedings which
are readily interpreted to a child and his parents,[7] it may also be desirable to eliminate
criminal law terminology.[8] The petition initiating the delinquency proceeding should be clear

---

[3] Selden, Table Talk 54 (1696): "Equity is according to the conscience of him that is Chancellor,
and as that is larger or narrower, so is Equity. 'Tis all
one as if they should make the standard for the
Measure, we call a Chancellor's Foot, what an uncertain measure this would be? One Chancellor has
a long Foot, another a short Foot, a third an indifferent foot; 'tis the same thing in the Chancellor's
Conscience."

[4] The tendency to consolidate was noted in note 2
supra. Contrast a recent case reasoning that child dependency or neglect arising not out of any conduct
or misconduct of the child, but from parental deficiency in providing the child with proper care, maintenance and support, is based on parental delinquency.
Hence, the same evidence which establishes parental
lack of fitness determines the child's status of dependency. However, "incorrigibility" may arise from
extrinsic sources, and the evidence establishing such
conditions may be wholly unrelated to the fitness of
the parent to perform his legal duties as a parent. In
re Welfare of Three Minors, 314 P.2d 423, 426
(Wash. 1957).

[5] In Evans v. Rives, 126 F.2d 633, 641 (D.C. Cir.
1942), the court reminded the juvenile court that the
social considerations underlying the Juvenile Court Act
and the informal procedures permitted under it are
not incompatible with the rights guaranteed by the
Constitution to one accused of crime. In re Poulin,
129 A.2d 672, 673 (N.H. 1957), the court said: "The
worthwhile objectives of the juvenile courts can be
accomplished without prohibiting the child or the
parent from obtaining the assistance of counsel."

We should keep complete and accurate records of
the proceedings in juvenile court, just as are kept in
criminal court and for use on appeal. Moreover, with
the granting of all procedural safeguards, the record
could be used for other desirable purposes, such as inquiring into the unchaste tendencies of complainants

in rape cases, and in imposing sentence under an "habitual offense" statute in any subsequent criminal proceeding. See Mass. Ann. Laws c. 119, § 60 (1957);
cf. note 34 supra [of original article. — Ed.]

[6] In re Hill, 78 Cal. App. 23, 247 Pac. 591 (1926)
(similar to the broader powers of the chancellor in
equity to review findings of fact as well as of law).
See text following note 111 supra [of original. — Ed.]

[7] See in re Sippy, 97 A.2d 455 (D.C. Munic. Ct.
App. 1953); In re Green, 123 Ind. App. 81, 108
N.E.2d 647 (1952); In re Coyle, 122 Ind. App. 217,
101 N.E.2d 192 (1951); Petition of O'Leary, 325
Mass. 179, 89 N.E.2d 769 (1950); Kahm v. People,
83 Colo. 300, 264 Pac. 718 (1928); State ex rel.
Palagi v. Freeman, 81 Mont. 132, 262 Pac. 168
(1927).

[8] E.g., summons, instead of warrant; petition on behalf of the child, as opposed to indictment or information; hearing to establish state's right to intervene
on behalf of the child, as opposed to trial. Cf. Bloch
& Flynn, Delinquency — The Juvenile Offender in
America Today 340–41 (1956).

and specific.[9] The court should explain the substance of the charge in simple language suitable to the child's age and understanding. Social investigation reports, psychological and psychiatric data should be prohibited as a source of information on which to determine the issue of delinquency.[10] Unless directed by the court, children should not be permitted in the courtroom, except when the proceedings are in relation to the child.[11] Even when so related, if the testimony being given relates to immoral conduct on the part of the child's parents, the child should be excluded. Where the juvenile is giving testimony relating to indecent conduct, the judge should have the power to clear the court of parties not directly concerned in the case.[12] If the child is called as a witness and does not understand the nature of an oath, then his unsworn testimony may be received if he understands the duty of speaking the truth.[13] The judge should ascertain a child's capacity as a witness by questioning the child and other necessary persons in the courtroom.[14] However, the unsworn testimony of a child should not be used as the basis for a conviction unless it is corroborated. In this connection it should be specified that the unsworn statement of one child is not corroborated by

the unsworn statement of another. Even if the child is testifying under oath, such natural drawbacks as an overactive imagination and undue nervousness when in court should be borne in mind and the judge should be required to instruct the jury of the risks involved in acting on the uncorroborated evidence of a child, even when given under oath.[15] If the child's attendance in court would seriously endanger his health, there should be a provision for taking his statement out of court. This might be accomplished by extending the present system of discovery depositions. However, if such a deposition is used as evidence, the same statute should provide for giving interested parties an opportunity to be present at the deposition and to cross-examine the child who is making it.[16] The trial should be open. However, if it is felt that publicity about the proceedings would harm the child, then the court in its discretion could restrict the revelation of any particulars which would lead to the identification of the child, as well as pictures of the child.[17]

An alternative solution would be to refer serious juvenile cases to criminal court for jury trial, with referral back to the juvenile court for sentencing after a finding of guilt. The advantages of this type of handling are: (1) juvenile courts often have superior clinical facilities for the individualized disposition of each case; (2) there is less tendency to use a social background investigation, including reports on school and general behavior, home and neighborhood surroundings, before an adjudication of status; (3) it would lessen the reluctance on the part of the court to dismiss the child when, even though the child may be adjudicated innocent, the court feels that treatment is necessary.

Implicit in the right to counsel to be guaranteed in all cases would be an offer of counsel and an implementation of that offer.[18] The argument that attorneys in juvenile proceedings

---

[9] In re Fisher, 184 S.W.2d 519 (Tex. Civ. App. 1944).

[10] This data would be proper if presented under oath and included first hand observations on parent–child relationships on issues of dependency and neglect. Even so, they are highly subjective interpretations of behavior, relevant only on questions of parental supervision, and should not be relied on without corroboration. Such reports should be offered for inspection by the child, his parent and their counsel, when proceedings begin. In re Godden, 158 Neb. 246, 63 N.W.2d 151 (1954); In re Mantell, 157 Neb. 900, 62 N.W.2d 308 1954); In re Contreras, 109 Cal. App. 2d 787, 241 P.2d 631 (1952). On the extent of use of background reports before hearing, see note 36 *supra* [of original article. — Ed.] and Note, Correct Use of Background Reports in Juvenile Delinquency Cases, 5 Syracuse L. Rev. 67 (1953).

[11] Mass. Ann. Laws c. 119, § 65 (1957) ("No minor shall be allowed to be present at any such hearing unless his presence is necessary either as a party or a witness."); S.C. Code § 15–1155 (1952).

[12] Children and Young Persons Act, 23 Geo. 5, c. 12, § 37 (1) (1933). [See, also, G. Geis, "Publicity and Juvenile Court Proceedings," 30 *Rocky Mountain L.R.* (1958), 1–26. — Ed.]

[13] *Id.* at § 38.

[14] Rex v. Reynolds [1950] 1 K.B. 606.

[15] If any child whose unsworn evidence is received wilfully gives false evidence, he should be liable to penalties, provided he would have been guilty of perjury had his evidence been given under oath.

[16] Children and Young Persons Act, 23 Geo. 5. c. 12, § 43 (1933).

[17] *Id.* at § 39.

[18] Assignment of counsel with adequate compensation, possibly through the Legal Aid Society. See Tappan, Delinquent Girls in Court 192 (1947); Ferguson v. Pottawattamie County, 224 Iowa 518, 278 N.W. 223 (1938).

are uniformed pettifoggers is often well-founded. It is recognized that a universal right to counsel will produce the desired result only after we have trained specialists in this field. However, pettifogging is a matter for control of the courts and adequate understanding of the aims and procedure of the juvenile courts is the responsibility of legal education.

Persons drafting such legislation must assume that standards will be implemented by competent personnel, and public efforts must be made to educate appointive agencies to the absolute necessity of appointing as juvenile judges people who are specially fitted for the position.

The possibilities suggested above certainly merit serious consideration in accommodating the various interests involved and striking a realistic and rational balance between the clinical and legalistic objectives of the juvenile court.[19]

105

Problems in the Structure of the Juvenile Court *

Henry Nunberg

If places of confinement are in reality prisons, the only criterion for commitment should be the magnitude of the offense. If, however, they are treatment centers designed to cure sick children and to protect the community, the standards for commitment should be based on

clinical diagnosis and the weighing of the rights of the child against the danger his actions present to the community. It has already been stated that the development of scientific methods of prediction will not eliminate the necessity for judicial decision. As Professor Sheldon Glueck has pointed out to the writer, a sick person has a right not to be treated; it is only when he becomes contagious that he may be quarantined. The same principle of social protection must be applied to the treatment of delinquent children. . . .

In the following pages, a proposal is set forth embodying a suggested solution to some of the problems presented in this paper. The proposal is in the form of a statute with comments appended to each section. Because of limitations of space, the statute and the comments have been abbreviated. More detailed commentary may be obtained by communication with the author. The statute is concerned exclusively with the delinquency jurisdiction of the juvenile court. It does not enter into a discussion of dependency or neglect; nor does it deal with the problems raised by "defective delinquents" and other children whose behavior is described in recognized categories of mental disease. The reason for omitting discussion of these aspects of the court's jurisdiction is the author's opinion that the function of the juvenile court in delinquency is in large part determined by the fact that the community must be protected from antisocial behavior. In this sense, the juvenile court in its delinquency aspect is similar to the criminal courts. Even under ideal conditions, therefore, the child and the community look upon the court, at least in part, as an agency of punishment. This orientation of the delinquency jurisdiction of the court, therefore, raises problems of a different nature than those of the neglect and dependency jurisdiction.

The proposal was drawn for the purpose of providing a system in which the outcome of each case would be conditioned by considerations both of a legal and of a clinical nature. Under the present Massachusetts system, the lawyer, expert in the evaluation of only one of these considerations, is alone responsible for disposition. Under a Youth Authority program, the judgment of the expert administrator prevails. The special skill of the administrator extends only to an evaluation of clinical data and

[19] Glueck, Crime and Justice 49–53 (1936). "But unbridled sentimentalism is also bad. Deep though our pity be, we cannot indulge in futile sentimentality while dangerous persons stalk the land. We must discipline our humane impulses with science and good sense. A head without a heart may lead to tyranny; a heart without a head may mean annihilation. . . . These two principles, then, the ethical and the scientific, must both be reckoned with." Id. at 6.

* Extracted from "Problems in the Structure of the Juvenile Court, 48 J. Crim L., Criminology and Police Science (1958), 500, 507–515. Used by permission of the author and the publisher. Some footnotes omitted; others renumbered. — Ed.

the application of treatment necessary to cure the disease. The expert is not trained in the delicate process of balancing the rights of the individual against the demands of the community. The training of the lawyer and the insights of the clinician are equally necessary in arriving at a disposition. Therefore, a system is needed under which the results of evaluation in each case will be the integrated expression of all the values that strive for recognition in the concept of the juvenile court. . . .

PROPOSAL FOR A PLAN RELATING TO THE CONTROL OF JUVENILE DELINQUENCY

I. Definitions

1. "Delinquent child" and "Wayward child"

   A. A Delinquent child is a child between the ages of seven and seventeen who violates any city ordinance or town by-law or commits any offense against the laws of the commonwealth, and who is adjudged to be in need of:

   a. treatment or supervision in order to prevent further outbreaks of illegal and antisocial behavior, or

   b. confinement, in order to protect himself or the community.

   B. A Wayward child is a child between the ages of seven and seventeen who:

   a. has engaged in a consistent pattern of serious antisocial behavior, (but has not violated any city ordinance or town by-law and has not committed any offense against the laws of the Commonwealth), and

   b. is in immediate danger of becoming a Delinquent child, or a criminal, unless he is subjected to preventive treatment, and

   c. is in need of, and will more probably than not benefit by, treatment or supervision without confinement.

Comment: Compare Mass. Anno. Laws, c. 119, sec. 52. The definition of "delinquent child" has been expanded so as to include children charged with capital crimes. Also, provision is made to permit the finding that a child has performed a delinquent act, but is not a delinquent child. If a finding is made that a child has performed a delinquent act, but that it is not necessary either for his own welfare or for the welfare of the community to subject him to

further state control, the child will not be found delinquent.

The definition of "wayward child" has been narrowed to provide a standard that is less vague than that in the present statute in Massachusetts. Compare Mass. Anno. Laws, c. 119, sec. 52. The section is intended to deal with those cases which appear to require attention by the state, but in which there has been no technical violation of law. It is to be noted that only supervisory, and not confinement, techniques may be used on children found to be "wayward."

II. Delinquency Control Areas

1. There shall be [X] Delinquency Control Areas in the Commonwealth.

[2. Establishment in each Area of a Court for the Disposition of Juvenile Cases, a Juvenile Court, and Facility of the Youth Service Board.]

Comment: This section establishes a regional system under a state-wide plan of organization to deal with problems of delinquency control. In each regional area, there is a complete set of institutions, including the regional courts which are provided for in later sections, and a regional office of the Youth Service Board.

III. The Juvenile Court

1. There shall be one Juvenile Court for each Delinquency Control Area in the Commonwealth.

2. Composition of the Juvenile Court; qualifications of the judge.

   A. The court shall consist of a judge, a clerk of the court, a court stenographer, and such administrative personnel as are required to keep the records of the court.

   B. The judge shall be a lawyer and a member of the Bar of the Supreme Judicial Court of the Commonwealth, and shall have engaged in the practice of law in the Commonwealth for [X] years.

[3. Powers, Duties, and Procedures. See Section VIII, subsection 1 below.]

4. Jurisdiction.

   A. The juvenile court shall have jurisdiction over all cases in which there is a petition of neglect or dependency in the case of a child under seventeen years of age.[1]

[1] Since this paper is devoted to the delinquency

B. The juvenile court shall have jurisdiction over all cases in which there is a petition of delinquency or waywardness, and to render decisions as hereinafter provided.

C. The juvenile court shall have jurisdiction over adults in cases in which contribution to delinquency, waywardness, neglect or dependency is charged.[2]

D. The juvenile court shall be a court of record of the Commonwealth.

5. Appointment of Judges to the Juvenile Courts; terms of office.

A. Judges of the juvenile courts shall be appointed by the Governor, upon the recommendation of the Board of Juvenile Court Judges.

The first appointments to the juvenile courts shall, however, be made by the Governor upon the recommendation of the Commissioners of Probation, Mental Health, Welfare and Corrections, the judge of the presently existing juvenile court of the City of Boston, the Youth Service Board and the Chief Justice of the Supreme Judicial Court.

[B. Term of Judge. Provision for an extended term of office for judge.]

6. Referees.

The judge of each court may appoint such referees as necessary to hear petitions coming before the court and to make findings, subject to the disapproval of the judge.

Comment: The main feature of this section is that it establishes a state-wide juvenile court system, as a substitute for the juvenile-sessions system now used in Massachusetts outside of the city of Boston. Since the courts are established on a regional basis, rather than one for each political subdivision of the state, it is thought that the plan would be feasible from a financial point of view.

---

jurisdiction of the juvenile court, for the reasons already discussed, there will be no further mention of the neglect and dependency jurisdiction of the court.

[2] It has been thought desirable to retain the jurisdiction over adults of the juvenile court, since frequently, it is necessary to treat the parents in order to effect a cure of the child. However, this is a question that the writer has not explored fully, and therefore, there will be no further discussion of it in this paper.

It is to be noted that no provision is made for a probation service attached to the court. The probation function is to be performed by the regional office of the Youth Service Board.

Formal qualifications for the position of juvenile court judge have been limited to legal education and experience. Until it becomes possible to develop a separate profession of juvenile court judge, as suggested by Sheldon Glueck,[3] it seems advisable to limit the statutory standards to those stated in this section. Moreover, subsection 5, paragraph A, provides a method through which men qualified to act as juvenile court judges may be chosen.

IV. *The Board of Juvenile Court Judges*

[Sections 1 and 2 establish the Board of Juvenile Court judges, and provide that it shall be composed of the judges of all the Juvenile Courts of the state.]

3. The board shall meet from time to time to discuss problems affecting the Juvenile Courts of the Commonwealth.

Upon the occurrence of any vacancy in any Juvenile Court, the Board shall present to the Governor a recommendation or recommendations as to candidates to fill the vacated office.

V. *The Court for the Disposition of Juvenile Cases*

1. There shall be a Court for the Disposition of Juvenile Cases (hereinafter known as the Court) in each Delinquency Control Area of the Commonwealth.

2. Composition.

A. Each Court shall be composed of a Chief Judge and two Special Judges.

(i) The Chief Judge shall be the Judge of the Juvenile Court of the Delinquency Control Area.

(ii) The Special Judges shall be experts in the diagnosis and treatment of delinquent children.

B. The Special Judges shall be chosen on the basis of their experience and training in the treatment and diagnosis of delinquent children.

(i) One Special Judge of each Court shall have received the degree of Doctor of Philosophy or the equiva-

---

[3] Sheldon Glueck, *The Sentencing Problem*, Address delivered at the Judicial Conference of the Third Circuit, United States Courts, at Atlantic City, N.J., September 12, 1956.

lent thereof, in clinical psychology, from an accredited university, and and shall have had at least [X] years of experience in the treatment of juvenile delinquency.

(ii) One Special Judge of each Court shall have received a degree of Master of Arts or Sciences, or the equivalent thereof, in sociology, psychology, or social work, from an accredited university, and shall have had [X] years of experience in social casework with juvenile delinquents.

3. Jurisdiction.

A. The Court shall have jurisdiction over all cases arising in its Areas in which a petition of delinquency or waywardness has been filed, and in which the judge of the Juvenile Court has made a finding:

(i) in the case of a petition of delinquency, that the child has committed a violation of law, as described in Section I, subsection A;

(ii) in the case of a petition of waywardness or delinquency that the child has engaged in a consistent pattern of serious antisocial behavior.

B. The Court shall have jurisdiction as a court of first instance over all cases arising in its Area in which it is alleged that the Youth Service Board has abused its powers. In all such cases, however, the Chief Judge alone shall render the decision of the Court; the Special Judges shall, however, advise the Chief Judge in those aspects of such cases which concern methods of treatment of delinquents and wayward children.

C. In all other cases, decisions of the Court shall be rendered by the Chief Judge with the concurrence of at least one of the Special Judges.

4. Powers, Duties, Procedures. — [See Section VIII subsection 2, below.]

5. Appointment of the Special Judges.

The special judges of each Court shall be appointed by the Governor, upon the recommendation of the Youth Service Board and the Commissioner of Mental Health.

Comment: The dispositions court is the central feature of this plan which distinguishes it

from other proposals which have been made for postadjudication procedure in determining the form that treatment is to take. It differs from the present plan in effect in Massachusetts in that it divests the judge of the juvenile court, sitting alone, of independent responsibility for disposition; it differs from the Model Youth Correction Authority Act and similar proposals in that it leaves the power of disposition in a judicial body, and gives the juvenile court judge a voice in determining disposition. The author is unaware of any other plan which provides for a sharing of ultimate responsibility by the court and the experts in determining the crucial question of what disposition will be made of a case that is before the juvenile court.

The proposal results from a consideration of the dilemma posed by the dispositions problem. On the one hand, it seems undesirable to leave ultimate responsibility for disposition in the hands of a lawyer-judge, who by training and often by temperament is not suited to make a decision that is in part a choice between therapeutic methods. On the other hand, since severe restraints upon the liberty of the individual may be imposed, it is equally unsatisfactory to place the dispositions function in an administrative body composed solely of experts on clinical method. The arguments of Bogen and Tappan concerning the undesirability of imposing what Tappan calls "anticipatory controls" upon an individual are relevant here as well. The underlying premise is the same: the interest of the individual to have the state not interfere in his life is the kind of interest that ought to be given the greatest possible protection.

Because both therapeutic and legal principles are integral parts of each decision as to disposition, provision should be made for their direct expression in the body that performs the disposition function. Therefore, even a system in which the judge makes his decision upon the recommendation of experts is unsatisfactory, for two reasons: First, the judge acting entirely upon the experts' recommendations, is little more than a puppet; the prestige and meaning of the court as a court of law stand in danger of becoming entirely submerged. On the other hand, the judge left free to decide by himself the best course of treatment to be followed, may act on a relatively uninformed basis. The dispositions court is suggested to provide a forum in which the lawyer and the expert can discuss each case and take joint responsibility for the results of their deliberations. Further, it provides an opportunity for expert and judge to work out together a policy of disposition to be followed, in different classes of cases. Individualization of justice and the legal requirement of adherence to precedent may thus, to a certain extent, be reconciled.

The dispositions plan is a way to stave off the abdication of the judges in determining what form treatment will take.

> The wise judge does not surrender the judging process to the specialist . . . It is his domain to pass their contributions through the alembic of his mind and distil them into a workable program that takes account of legal demands and social limitations, as well as clinical findings.[4]

In this body, the judge will still bear the burden of responsibility for taking into account "legal demands and social limitations"; the specialist will interpret the clinical findings. Each will contribute his own point of view; individual rights, community demands and clinical requirements will, of necessity, be considered in every disposition made by this court.

The proposal is unorthodox in that it provides for laymen to sit as judges in a court of law. This practice is seldom followed in the United States; there is, however, a precedent in the English practice of using lay magistrates extensively (sitting, incidentally, without a lawyer to share the bench with them) to hear and dispose of cases involving juvenile offenders.[5]

The plan is similar to the proposal of Professor Sheldon Glueck that judges of criminal courts sit on parole boards, in that it serves to acquaint the judge, through direct participation in their deliberations, with the considerations that enter into the decisions of experts in deciding how to treat offenders.

More study and thought are necessary to determine what the qualifications of the Spe-

cial Judges should be. The standards proposed in subsection 2B are thought to contain minimum educational requirements; however, it is possible that the fields of study designated as prerequisites for the office are not the most relevant ones. Considerable experience in practical work with antisocial children is, of course, essential.

The procedure of subsection 3B has been suggested because of the desire to emphasize the considerations that should govern the court's decision, and because it is felt that such cases will be directly concerned with questions of infringement of personal liberty. In such cases, the legal point of view should predominate. The reason that this jurisdiction is placed in the dispositions court rather than in the juvenile court is to remind the lawyer to consider the clinical necessities of the case. The adversary nature of our court system is thereby tempered, as it is in all juvenile courts. Although the Youth Service Board will have an opportunity to defend its actions, the presence of clinicians in the court will tend to create the understanding and coordination necessary to the proper functioning of the system.

The Youth Service Board has been made responsible for recommending to the Governor persons to act as Special Judges. It is hoped that this plan will serve to bring personnel of the Youth Service Board into the court system, and thereby provide a means of advancement for social workers, psychologists and others employed by the Board. It is also hoped that this method of selection will bring about a degree of cooperation between court and agency.

VI. *The Court of Juvenile Appeals*

1. There shall be a Court of Juvenile Appeals to hear all cases appealed from the Juvenile Court and the Court for the Disposition of Juvenile Cases.
2. The Court of Juvenile Appeals shall be composed of the members of the Board of Juvenile Court Judges.
3. The Chief Justice shall be the Judge of the Juvenile Court of the Boston (Metropolitan) Delinquency Control Area.
4. Appeals from the decisions of the Court of Juvenile Appeals shall be made directly to the Supreme Judicial Court, according to the rules of that Court.

---

[4] Sheldon and Eleanor Glueck, *1000 Juvenile Delinquents*, (Cambridge, 1943), p. 114.

[5] It has also come to my attention recently that in the Federal Republic of Germany the juvenile court of each district is composed of four unpaid lay magistrates who sit together with a stipendiary lawyer—magistrate to decide upon juvenile cases. Gordon Addam (1956) *Crim. L. Rev.* 401 (June 1956).

5. The Judge of the Juvenile Court of the Delinquency Control Area in which a case on appeal originated shall not participate in the deliberations of the Court of Juvenile Appeals concerning such a case.

Comment: . . . By providing for an appeal on the issue of *Treatment* . . . the law stultifies that tribunal which . . . is best qualified to pass on treatment matters.[6]

The specialized appellate court is suggested to eliminate the difficulties arising from juvenile appeals in the ordinary court system.[7]

VII. *The Youth Service Board*

1. Except as otherwise provided herein, and except as inconsistent with the provisions of this Act, Chapter 6, Sections 65 through 69A, and Chapter 120 of the General Laws of Massachusetts, are hereby incorporated into this Act.

2. The powers and functions of the Youth Service Board are hereby extended to include:
   A. Those functions formerly performed by the office of probation in juvenile cases, and
   B. Those functions formerly performed by clinics attached to the District Courts of the Commonwealth in juvenile cases, and
   C. Such other powers and functions as may be necessary to carry out the purposes of this Act.
   D. If a delinquent child has been committed to the custody of the Facility or its Delegate without confinement, as

---

[6] S. and E. T. Glueck, *op. cit.,* p. 24.

[7] The system of appeals in effect at present in Massachusetts is of such a nature that if it were used extensively it could destroy the juvenile court altogether. The trial on appeal is in the Superior Court; in effect, it is a proceeding *de novo.* If the appellant so desires, he may have a jury trial, since the case is to be determined as in a criminal trial. MASS. ANNO. LAWS, c. 119, sec. 56. The study by Alper of appeals from the Boston Juvenile Court from 1930–1935 demonstrates the damage that the juvenile court system can suffer from such an appeals system. B. S. Alper, *Juvenile Justice — A Study of Juvenile Appeals to Suffolk Superior Court,* Boston, 1930–1935, 28 J. Crim. L. and Crimin 340 (1937). The idea of a separate court to hear juvenile appeals is not original with the author; although I am unable to give citations, other writers have made similar proposals.

hereinafter provided, and the Director of the Facility or his Delegate deems it necessary for the safety of the child or of the community, the Director may:
   a. without notice to either the Juvenile Court or to the Court for the Disposition of Juvenile Cases, place the child in detention for a period not to exceed [X] hours, and
   b. if the Director deems it necessary to place the child in confinement for a longer period of time, he shall apply to the Juvenile Court for an order changing the status of the child from that of treatment or supervision (as defined in Section I, subsection 2, A & B) to that of confinement (as defined in Section I, subsection 2, C).
      Such an order of the Juvenile Court shall be subject to disapproval upon consideration by the Court for the Disposition of Juvenile Cases, under Section V, subsection 3, C.
   E. Section 6 of Chapter 120 of the General Laws is hereby repealed.

3. The Youth Service Board shall establish a Youth Service Board Facility (hereinafter referred to as the Facility) in each Delinquency Control Area.
   A. The Facility shall include a detention center, and
   B. Such other buildings and equipment as are necessary to enable it to conduct studies and administer programs of treatment, supervision and prevention of delinquency in the Area.

4. There shall be an Area Director of each Facility, and such other appropriately trained personnel as necessary shall be employed by the Youth Service Board in each Facility to carry out the functions provided for in this Act.

Comment: The purpose of this section is to integrate all forms of treating antisocial children. The new service will retain the functions of the present Youth Service Board; in addition, it will undertake the tasks now performed by the probation office. The Youth Service Board is intended to be separate from the court system, but integrated with it. The personnel and study centers of the Board are to aid the courts in reaching decisions as to the disposi-

tion of cases involving delinquency and waywardness.

VIII. *Proceedings before the Juvenile Court
and the Court for the Disposition of
Juvenile Cases*

1. Proceedings before the juvenile court.

    A. Upon a child being brought before the
juvenile court on a petition of delinquency or waywardness, a hearing shall
be held before the judge of the juvenile
court, in the presence of the child and
his parent or guardian.

        a. If the child has no parent or legal
guardian, the juvenile court shall appoint a guardian for the purposes of
the proceedings.

        b. A representative of the Facility of
the Youth Service Board of the Delinquency Control Area shall be
present at all proceedings before the
juvenile court.

    B. If the petition complains of delinquency
or waywardness, the juvenile court shall
determine:

        a. Whether the child has committed
the act complained of, and

        b. Whether, if it is determined that the
child has committed the act com-
plained of, the act constitutes a violation of any city ordinance, town by-
law or offense against the laws of the
Commonwealth, or

        c. Whether the child has engaged in a
consistent pattern of serious antisocial behavior.

    C. Upon the determination of the juvenile
court that a child has committed a violation of law as provided in subsection
B, paragraphs *a* and *b*, the judge shall
make a preliminary finding of probable
cause for an adjudication of delinquency.

        a. The judge shall thereupon continue
the case for a period of not less than
[X] days and not more than [X] days.

        b. The judge shall thereupon place the
child in the custody of a representative of the Youth Service Board Facility of the Delinquency Control
Area.

           (i) During the continuance, the Area
Facility shall undertake such
study as may be necessary to de-

termine final disposition of the
case, and

          (ii) Write a report containing the re-
sults of the study and recom-
mendations for disposition. Such
report shall be forwarded to the
Court for the Disposition of Juvenile Cases.

        c. If the juvenile court has reason to be-
lieve that the safety of the com-
munity demands that the child be
placed in detention during the continuance, it may of its own motion
order confinement of the child by the
Facility of the Youth Service Board.

        d. If the representative of the Youth
Service Board has reason to believe
that the welfare of the community or
of the child demands confinement of
the child during continuance, the
representative may make a motion
that the juvenile court order the confinement of the child for the period
of the continuance.

        Unless the juvenile court finds that
the motion of the representative is
not made with a reasonable belief
that confinement during continuance
is necessary for the welfare of the
child or of the community, it shall
grant the motion and issue the order
of confinement.

    D. Upon the determination of the juvenile
court that the child has engaged in a
consistent pattern of serious antisocial
behavior as provided in subsection B,
paragraph *c*, the judge shall make a preliminary finding of probable cause for
an adjudication of waywardness.

        a. The judge shall thereupon, continue
the case for a period of not less than
[X] days and not more than [X] days.

        b. The court shall thereupon place the
child in the custody of a representative of the Youth Service Board Facility of the Delinquency Control
Area.

           (i) During the continuance, the Area
Facility shall undertake such
study as may be necessary to
determine final disposition of the
case, and

          (ii) Write a report containing the results of the study and recommendations for disposition. Such report shall be forwarded to the Court for the Disposition of Juvenile Cases.

Comment: The purpose of this subsection is to set forth a procedure by which the judge may find the facts and the applicable law in cases of delinquency and waywardness. The juvenile court has then performed its function. Every case must be continued to provide an opportunity for the kind of study that the specialists deem necessary to arrive at an intelligent conclusion as to what should be done with the child. There is also a provision, in the case of children who have been charged with a violation of law, for the application of necessary restraints. There is no such provision in the case of wayward children. Again, this reflects the philosophy that a differentiation in treatment on the basis of "behavior circumstance," as some writers have called it, should properly be made in a legal proceeding.

2. Proceedings before the Court for the Disposition of Juvenile Cases.

A. Upon termination of the continuance, the case of a child in which the juvenile court has made a preliminary finding of probable cause for adjudication of delinquency or waywardness shall be brought before the court for the disposition of juvenile cases (for purposes of this subsection, referred to as the "Court").

B. If the juvenile court has made a preliminary finding of probable cause for adjudication of waywardness:

  (i) the Court shall determine whether the child:

    a. is in immediate danger of becoming a Delinquent child, or a criminal, unless he is subjected to preventive treatment, and

    b. is in need of, and will more probably than not benefit by, treatment or supervision without confinement.

  (ii) If the Court has found in the affirmative as to subparagraph (i) above, it shall adjudge the child Wayward, and remand him to the Youth Service Board Facility for

treatment or supervision without confinement for such period, not to exceed two years, as the Facility deems necessary.

C. If the juvenile court has made a preliminary finding of probable cause for adjudication of delinquency:

  (i) the Court shall determine whether the child is in need of treatment, supervision or confinement;

  (ii) if the Court determines that the child is in need of treatment, supervision or confinement, it shall adjudge the child Delinquent.

  (iii) The judgment of delinquency shall state that:

    a. the child is in need of treatment or supervision, or

    b. the child is in need of confinement.

  (iv) The Court shall remand the Delinquent to the custody of the Director of the Youth Service Board Facility or his representative, for such period as it deems necessary, or until the child shall have attained his 23rd birthday. The order of remand shall state that:

    a. the child is to be confined, or

    b. the child is to remain at liberty, under treatment or supervision, in the discretion of the Director of the Youth Service Board Facility.

    1. In the case of a child remanded with the direction that he is to remain at liberty, if thereafter it becomes necessary for the safety of the child or of the community, the Director of the Facility or his representative may, without obtaining an order from any court, confine the child in its detention home for a period not to exceed [X] hours.

    2. If the Director of the Facility deems it necessary to retain the child in confinement thereafter, it shall apply to the juvenile court

for an interim order of confinement. Such order shall be confirmed by the Court at its next regular session. Unless a question is presented of abuse of his powers by the Director of the Facility or his representative, the Court shall reach its decision in accordance with Section V, paragraph 2C. If such a question is presented, the decision shall be made in accordance with Section V, paragraph 2B.

    c. The Youth Service Board shall retain its powers, as enumerated in Chapter 120, section 12 of the Laws of Massachusetts, insofar as they concern children under confinement.

D. A representative of the Youth Service Board Facility shall be present at all hearings before the Court.

3. Right to Counsel.

The child shall have right to counsel at all hearings before the juvenile court and the Court for the Disposition of Juvenile Cases.

Comment: This subsection is spelled out in detail in order to define clearly the powers of the dispositions body. In its division between the permissible disposition of cases of delinquency and those of waywardness, the subsection is consistent with the philosophy that "behavior circumstances" should set limits on what kind of treatment may be administered.

The powers of the administrative agency to determine whether or not the child is to be at liberty or not, is circumscribed. As has already been stated in another connection, it cannot, without consulting the court, change a child's status from that of liberty to that of confinement.

The divestment of the Youth Service Board of its powers to change freely the status of a child from liberty to confinement is compensated for by the participation of clinicians in the body determining disposition. Therefore, the need to change the status of offenders should not occur too frequently. When it does occur, the Youth Service Board representative will have to go before the court to ob-

tain an order changing the status of the child. This procedure, while allowing the Board flexibility, protects the child from unnecessary infringements on his liberty.

From a therapeutic standpoint, the study required in every case and the composition of the disposition court provides a better system for determining the disposition of cases than exists at present. Under the system in force at this time, it is discretionary with the juvenile court whether or not it will order a complete study of the child before it; under this proposal, the personnel of the Youth Service Board Facility would determine what kind of study is necessary in each case. Under the present system, if a child is committed to the Youth Service Board, the decision as to liberty or confinement is made by a single three-man board, which must pass upon all cases committed from every court in the state. Under the proposed system, on the other hand, the regional dispositions court would make the preliminary decision on this important question. If a change in status were made subsequently, it would be subject to the approval of this body. The task presently performed on a state-wide basis by the Youth Service Board would be performed by this regional court, which would have a smaller case load, and hence, be able to give closer attention to each case that comes before it.

Therefore, both from the point of view of the therapist and from that of the lawyer, it would seem that this system is an improvement over the one presently in force.

IX. Appeals

1. All appeals from findings of the juvenile court and the Court for the Disposition of Juvenile Cases shall be taken to the Court of Juvenile Appeals.

2. Appeals shall be allowed from a preliminary finding of probable cause for adjudication of delinquency or waywardness by the juvenile court.

    Such appeals shall be limited to questions of law.

3. Appeals shall be allowed from a final order of the Court for the Disposition of Juvenile Cases.

    A. Such appeals shall be limited to questions of law.

    B. For purposes of this subsection, a "ques-

"tion of law" is defined as relating to a matter in which the decision of the Court for the Disposition of Juvenile Cases is rendered by the Chief Judge alone.

Comment: This section exists for the reasons given in the comment to Section VI . . .

A proposal has been made to replace the present system in Massachusetts with one that separates adjudication from treatment, and integrates the disposition function. Court hearings have been divided into two stages. In the first stage, the judge, sitting alone in the juvenile court, finds the facts and applies the law to the case before him. In the second stage, the judge and two clinicians, sitting as the Court for the Disposition of Juvenile Cases, determine upon the disposition of the case before them. The disposition is made in terms of a choice between permitting the child to remain at liberty, and ordering him into confinement. The determination is based in part upon "behavior circumstance." The court is divided into two stages so that the judge alone will perform the purely legal function, and to permit the clinician to participate with the judge in taking responsibility for disposition. The treatment function, however, is taken away from the court entirely. A state-wide administrative agency, with certain discretionary powers, is established to carry out treatment. The agency is organized on a regional basis. The court system is set up in a corresponding way. Provisions have been included to bring about cooperation between court and agency. Care has been taken, however, to avoid a fusion between the two organs.

The theory of the proposal is that there are three separate functions to be performed in the case of a delinquent before the court. The first, determining "behavior circumstance," is legal. The second, disposition, combines legal and clinical considerations. The third, treatment, is clinical. The proposal, therefore, is designed to provide a method whereby these three functions may be carried out separately. The purpose is to avoid slighting any one of them, and thereby to provide a system of delinquency control in which all three functions are adequately performed. . . . [Bibliography omitted. — *Ed.*]

Chapter 18

Youths Beyond Juvenile Court Age

YOUTHFUL OFFENDERS who are beyond the age limitations set by juvenile court statutes are ordinarily handled by traditional criminal law methods. Yet experience has suggested that the adolescent groups require special treatment from the time of arrest to the stage of their restoration to society.

In a few cities special "Boys' Courts" for offenders between juvenile court age and legal majority have been established as branches or parts of regular courts. While their procedures are intended to be somewhat less strict technically than those of traditional criminal courts, they tend to retain an atmosphere that makes them, in effect, criminal courts. So, also, special enactments have been made respecting "wayward minors."

The problem is highly complex, and requires, in all its ramifications, basic reform. To that end, in 1940, a committee of the American Law Institute drafted two bills which, the members hoped, would be enacted in many jurisdictions.[1] The first sets up a "Youth Court" of special personnel for metropolitan and large urban centers. It is, with certain exceptions, given exclusive jurisdiction to try youths within the requisite age spans. Its special judges are directed to appoint a "presenting" (not prosecuting) attorney and a special "counsel for the defense" in the nature of a public defender who is to represent defendants unable to employ regular counsel, and to establish special places of detention suitable for youths or approve other places for use in detention. In general, the judges are to improve pre-trial and trial procedures in respect to delinquent adolescents in the direction of greater understanding and protection as well as greater efficiency, including timely and proper interrogation, more effective liaison between police and prosecutor, employment of informal "information" for the initiation of proceedings instead of the more technical indictment, control of the prosecutor's power of *nolle prosequi*, etc.

The second bill is a greater departure from traditional attitudes and methods. It sets up a "Youth Correction Authority"[2] consisting of a specially qualified personnel, aided by experts representing relevant disciplines and techniques, to control and improve sentencing and treatment procedures as a unified, planned enterprise in each case. A number of states have adopted various modifications of this bill. However, as several studies have shown, the effect of the American Law Institute's proposed reforms has been rather to improve administrative and, to some extent, treatment procedures with *ordinary delinquents* than to make any basic contribution to the special class of young-adult offenders (under 21 but beyond juvenile court age) for whom the A. L. I. project was originally designed.

Few have given more intensive study to the problem than Professor Paul W.

---

[1] *Youth Correction Authority Act*, Official Draft, American Law Institute, Philadelphia, 1940.

[2] For a competent assessment of the Youth Authority Program as carried on, with considerable modification of the original A.L.I. bills, see B. M. Beck, *Five States*, 1951, Philadelphia, American Law Institute.

Tappan, author of the article in this chapter. Tappan adverts to the debate on the more recent draft code provisions of the A.L.I. for dealing with youthful offenders and presents the results of a first-hand study of what is perhaps the most advanced embodiment of the original Youth Correction Authority idea: that of California.

106

Young Adults Under the Youth Authority *

Paul W. Tappan

Since early 1952 the American Law Institute has been preparing tentative drafts of a Model Penal Code. One phase of this project is the development of provisions to deal with the sentencing and treatment of young adults over juvenile court age. Extended thought has been given to this subject both because of its intrinsic importance and because in 1940 the Institute had promulgated a Model Youth Correction Authority Act which proposed a novel structure and procedures for dealing with this group. A part of the task that confronted the Reporters on the project, therefore, was to determine whether, within the framework of a comprehensive Code dealing in detail with crimes, sentencing, and correction, the old Y.C.A.A. or some variation of it should be incorporated. Even before the Penal Code project was launched, the Institute had given a close scrutiny to the programs in several jurisdictions that had borrowed some of the policies and provisions of the Y.C.A.A.[1] Since 1952

these programs as well as other approaches that have developed to deal with young adults have been carefully reviewed and reconsidered. Many authorities who have worked with this age group in various states have been consulted in the effort to arrive at a policy that might result in a more effective rehabilitation, correction of youthful offenders and prevention of their offenses. As a consequence of all this the Institute printed in May of 1955 a set of tentative proposals for the sentencing and treatment of young adult offenders.[2] This draft incorporated the conclusion that the existing "youth authorities" have not focused specialized effort upon the young adult group, that the Y.C.A.A. has nowhere been followed at all closely, and that that Act ought not to be followed in the Model Penal Code. It was believed that a new effort should be made along different lines to secure a concentrated attention upon the treatment of young adults.

The failure to attempt again to promulgate the authority plan as a part of the Penal Code was not, of course, a repudiation of such excel-

---

* Reprinted from 47 J. Crim. L., Criminology and Police Science (1957), 629–646. Used by permission of the author and the publisher. For a recent discussion of the work of the Youth Division of the United States Board of Parole in connection with the paroling of youthful offenders, see The United States Board of Parole, Annual Report, 1957, 31–42. See, also, The Youthful Offender (a symposium), 2 NPPA Journal (1956). — Ed.

[1] The Model Youth Correction Authority Act provided for the establishment of an autonomous three-member Authority to determine and administer policies for the correctional treatment of serious offenders between the ages of 16 and 21. The Act empowered the Authority to establish and operate

new (but not existing) facilities for the treatment of such offenders; to submit its wards to probation; to release on parole, and discharge. It might maintain indefinite control over individuals considered dangerous to the public by making orders from time to time for such sustained control, subject to confirmation by court review. It was contemplated that, except for final discharge, most of these functions would be performed by subordinates, the Authority confining itself in the main to the administration of its policies. The "authority states" have deviated from the policy of the Model Act, inter alia, in focusing upon the juvenile rather than the young adult, in putting the existing juvenile correctional facilities under the direction of the authority or its director, and in making the board itself a multiple functional, rather than merely a policy making, agency. In these states the power to sentence to probation has been retained in the courts. For a detailed analysis of practice in certain of these jurisdictions, see Bertram Beck, 5 States, American Law Institute 1951. The present article is concerned primarily with the problems that may arise through vesting broad administrative as well as parole powers to deal with young adults in an autonomous authority and its director.

[2] Model Penal Code, Tentative Draft No. 3, A.L.I. 1954.

lent work as has been accomplished in a number of jurisdictions in the prevention and treatment of juvenile delinquency. Nor did the policy in the 1955 proposals fail to acknowledge the strides that have been made in some states in dealing specially with offenders over juvenile court age, progress that has been influenced in considerable part by the impetus that the Y.C.A.A. gave to efforts in behalf of this group. Indeed, the proposals that were formulated drew in large measure upon practices and programs that have developed in several jurisdictions in recent years, notably in New York, the Federal system, and in California. They reflected the considered judgment, however, that the administrative scheme proposed in the Y.C.A.A. and the variants adopted in a number of states in which a single board was given wide powers relative to sentencing, classification, correctional administration, parole, and community programs, was not the best arrangement for dealing with young adults under a new Model Code. These conclusions were given some currency in an article in which the author summarized briefly the tentative proposals of Draft No. 3.[3] This material provoked a spirited response from Mr. Justice Youngdahl[4] and critical reactions from some of the administrators in "authority" jurisdictions. The Institute concluded that before Code draft materials were developed it would be desirable to reconsider the current program and experience in California and the Federal systems. The writer, having observed again in 1956 the program in California, with the very generous cooperation of authorities there, and discussed its operation with various administrators, has set down some of the views and interpretations that emerged. He has been advised that it might be useful to publish them because of the general interest in the issues involved.

CALIFORNIA AND THE MODEL PENAL CODE

In considering the relevance of experience under the Youth Authority in California to policy and proposals of the Model Penal Code, several matters should be made clear at the

outset: First, the organization and procedures of government relating to the juvenile law violator do not come within the proposed scope of the Code. Therefore, policy and practice in California or elsewhere relating specifically to the juvenile age group have only quite limited significance for dealing with the young adult. Secondly, the Model Penal Code is not a "Uniform Code," proposed for adoption throughout the country. Indeed, it is not intended that Code policy or provisions should lead to change of practice in jurisdictions or in phases of criminal or correctional law where (as in the case of youth corrections in California) the existing legislation and procedures are found to function satisfactorily. On the contrary, recent experience in certain jurisdictions has highlighted the folly of attempting to superimpose a new set of legal provisions and a new administrative system upon a well established pre-existing structure with which they are incompatible, notably in Wisconsin's ill fated effort to establish a version of the youth authority and in the very limited development of that scheme in other jurisdictions. The Code purpose is, rather, to provide guidance to states where there is a recognized need for change in some area or areas of penal law and where the provisions of the Code appear to be adaptable to their requirements. It is quite clear that where change is sought there is no single design that is universally applicable: critical adaptation is required in accordance with the varying needs of different jurisdictions and, in particular, with the structure, practice and policy that they have previously employed.

Relative to the two points of emphasis above and with particular regard to California, perhaps it should be emphasized, though it is quite generally recognized, that this State has developed an exceedingly fine quality and variety of classification and treatment facilities under its particular Authority schemes. Against the background of a scandalized and impoverished correctional system that had existed there, California has gradually developed and since 1940 rapidly modified its institutions, programs, organizational structures and powers dealing with both juvenile and adult offenders. A number of special circumstances has influenced this development, such as the functions of the previously existing Board of Prison Terms and Paroles, the traditional limitations

[3] Tappan, "The Young Adult Offender under the American Law Institute's Model Penal Code," 19 Fed. Prob. 20, Dec., 1955.

[4] Youngdahl, "Give the Youth Corrections Program a Chance," 20 Fed. Prob. 3, March, 1956.

on the powers of the judiciary in sentencing and the long sentences established in the penal law. The result of employing a high calibre of personnel, particularly in administrative positions, and of a climate favorable to correctional development has been the establishment of experimental policies in treatment and a variety of institutional facilities that is impressive.

The California system of correctional administration, as it relates to young adults and their parole, appears awkward at some points to the foreign observer, as will be noted in some detail below. The Youth Authority system has been modified quite continuously through a succession of statutory and administrative changes, however, and further changes are contemplated. The present consequence is a correctional organization that appears to operate effectively as a progressive and experimental system that will continue to improve through the zeal and imaginativeness of its leaders. The rapid and steady progress there appears not to be the consequence of the particular administrative schemes of youth and adult corrections in operation, but rather a reflection of the personnel, budgets, and attitudes, referred to above.

One further limitation on the significance of California experience should be stressed. California is the second largest state in the United States with a rate of population growth (53.3 percent between 1940 and 1950) greater than that in any other state. Its crime rates and prisoner populations have increased even more rapidly, and only New York has a slightly larger prisoner population (16,530 as compared to 14,572 in 1955). Only one other additional state holds more than 10,000 prisoners in its institutions (Ohio) and there are only six other jurisdiction where more than 5,000 prisoners are contained in state institutions. The unique situation in California accounts in some part for the rapid increase and diversification of facilities there. Moreover, the size of the problems of crime and corrections in California suggests that administrative structures and methods appropriate to that state may be quite wrong elsewhere. In particular, where an authority scheme involving an autonomous board may arguably have merit for youth corrections in a state where there are roughly 1,000 committed offenders in the young adult age range (18 to 21), it may be quite inappropriate to a state where there are few of these ages.

CONTROL OVER JUVENILES AND YOUNG ADULTS IN CALIFORNIA

One of the major policy problems involved in the utilization of authority plans lies in the great power and the multiplicity of functions that are generally entrusted to authority boards. Extensive as were the functions proposed in the Model Youth Correction Authority Act, these have been enlarged considerably under the particular (and varying) versions of the Youth Authority that prevail in California and certain other jurisdictions. One major variation from the Model Act has been the extension of Board power to include children from the juvenile courts. While in most of the jurisdictions that have adopted some version of the authority plan, the boards and commissions involved have been charged exclusively with juveniles (in contrast with Model Act's specific exclusion of this group), the California board deals with the juvenile and youth groups. Its orientation is primarily toward the former. This is significant to the Model Penal Code, since as we have noted the Code does not propose to deal with the sentencing and treatment of juvenile delinquents.

Evidence that the orientation of the Youth Authority is primarily toward juveniles can be found in the official statistics. It will be observed from the data in Table 1 that the great majority (2,066, or 75.8 percent) of the 2,724 commitments to the Youth Authority in 1955 were of juveniles under the age of 18. Among those under 18 years of age, 2050, or 99.2 percent, were committed by juvenile courts. Of those over the age of 18 (658), 564, or 82.7 percent were committed by criminal courts. In fact, 97.2 percent of youths 19 or over committed to the Youth Authority were sentenced by the Superior Courts of criminal jurisdiction. Thus, it appears clear, while under the law juvenile courts may take jurisdiction of individuals up to the age of 21 in California, in actual practice most youths of 18 or over who are committed to the Youth Authority are dealt with by the courts as felons or misdemeanants,[5] while juvenile court commit-

---

[5] The Youth Authority is empowered to remove the felony status for those youths who have successfully completed parole.

Table **1**   *First Commitments Placed Under Authority Custody During 1955 by Committing Court* *

AGE	TOTAL		JUVENILE COURT		CRIMINAL COURT	
	Number	Per Cent	Number	Per Cent	Number	Per Cent
8	4	0.1	4	0.2		
9	6	0.2	6	0.3		
10	9	0.3	9	0.4		
11	28	1.0	28	1.3		
12	61	2.2	61	2.9		
13	151	5.6	151	7.0		
14	322	11.8	322	15.0		
15	491	18.0	491	22.9		
16	538	19.8	536	25.0	2	0.4
17	456	16.8	442	20.6	14	2.4
TOTAL 8–17	2,066	75.8	2,050	95.6	16	2.8
18	270	9.9	83	3.9	187	32.2
19	213	7.8	7	0.3	206	35.5
20	143	5.3	3	0.1	140	24.1
21	32	1.2	1	0.1	31	5.4
TOTAL 18–21	658	24.2	94	4.4	564	97.2
GRAND TOTALS	2,724	100.0	2,144	100.0	580	100.0

* Adapted from Delinquency and Probation in California, 1955, Table 7, p. 87.

ments to the Youth Authority are concentrated preponderantly in the range below 18 years of age at the time of offense. Not infrequently, however, juvenile courts maintain control and recommit individuals who have previously been under their jurisdiction after they reach 18.

Relative to the young adult group (aged 18 to 21) two circumstances prevail in California that are of special significance in their implications for Code consideration. First is the split pattern of criminal court commitment of these offenders. While juvenile court commitments are generally made to the Authority, the criminal courts may sentence in the alternative either to the Youth Authority or to the Director of Corrections (the adult correctional system, under which releases are at the discretion of the Adult Authority). It will be observed in the Table above that 658 youths over 18 were committed to the Youth Authority in 1955. In 1954, according to figures provided by the Bureau of Criminal Statistics 244 youths in this age range were committed to the Director of Corrections. It has been suggested by

some California authorities that the proportion of youth commitments to the Director would be larger were it not that the result would be unconscionably long sentences for these young offenders under the existing penal law there. [In this regard, see Table 5 and the discussion of the composition of the population and the release procedures at the Deuel Vocational Institution, below.]

Secondly, while juveniles in nearly all cases are committed to facilities that are under the administration of the Youth Authority, the 18 to 21-year-olds, even those committed to the Youth Authority, in most instances are processed through the reception-diagnostic facilities of the Department of Corrections and imprisoned in its institutions (both at Deuel Vocational Institution and at the several state prisons) where they are subject to the policy and programs of the adult Department. There appears to be a recognition that this group, and especially the behavior problems in the age range of 18 and over are better handled and treated within the adult correctional system, not

Table 2 Age of Admission to Institutions of Department of Corrections, Males Years Ending June 30, 1953, 1954 *

AGE IN YEARS	NUMBER	TOTAL PERCENT	1953	1954
Total	7,657	100.0	3,595	4,062
Under 20	198	2.6	89	109
20–24	2,128	27.8	999	1,129
25–29	1,926	25.2	903	1,023
30–34	1,172	15.3	547	625
35–39	749	9.8	363	386
40–44	583	7.6	266	317
45–49	393	5.1	184	209
50–54	240	3.1	108	132
55–59	130	1.7	61	69
60 and over	138	1.8	75	63
Median Age 28.7 years				

* From Department of Corrections, Biennial Report, 1953–1954, p. 68.

under a juvenile administration. Study of Table 3 below will reveal that out of 2,392 individuals of all ages sentenced to the Youth Authority during the year 1953–1954 (resident on June 30, 1954), 851, or more than 30 percent, were confined in facilities administered by the Department of Corrections. Comparison with the figures given above indicates the policy of placing young adults in institutions operated by the adult Department because they are too mature for juvenile facilities. Only in the Youth Authority forestry camps, fed primarily from the Deuel population and where the average offender age is a little more than 19, is there a significant number of young adults in facilities under the youth board. The camp groups are not large, however.

It may be clear from the tables and what has been said above that the population of the Deuel Vocational Institution and the exercise of powers there is of greatest significance so far as the young adult population is concerned. It is the primary facility for 18 to 21-year-olds. It would be difficult to find anywhere a nicer illustration of the awkward arrangements of function and power, reflecting at least in part, disparities in philosophy, that can emerge in dealing with this age group. At the present time some two-thirds (in round numbers, 800) of the D.V.I. population has been committed to the Youth Authority and one-third to the

Department of Corrections. The institution is administered, however, by the Department of Corrections. Assignments to Deuel come in part from the Department-operated Deuel Guidance Center, most of these criminal court commitments to the Youth Authority; in part from Department of Corrections reception centers at Chino and San Quentin, these in general commitments to the Director of Corrections; and in part from the Youth Authority Reception Centers at Perkins and Norwalk, mainly repetitive offenders who have previously spent time in the Youth Authority facilities or young serious offenders. It should be noted also that in recent years a considerable number (usually from 50 to 100 Youth Authority wards) have been transferred to San Quentin, generally because of their failure to adjust at Deuel, and some are allocated to Soledad Prison.

For obvious reasons the disparity in commitment provisions to the Deuel facility for young adults results in more or less serious inequity in the treatment of youths and may well confirm them in their antisocial attitudes. Offenders of similar age may be committed for the same crime (sometimes as criminal associates), one to the Youth Authority, another to the Director of Corrections, with very significant differences in their institutional retention as a consequence. Thus the Youth Authority

Table 3   *Youth Authority Resident Population,*
June 30, 1954 by Institution *

ASSIGNMENTS	AGE RANGE	POPULATION
Youth Authority Administration		
Fricot	8–15	146
Nelles	8–15	306
Paso Robles	14–17	235
Preston	15–21	570
Forestry Camps	16–21	242
Los Guilucos	8–16	138
Ventura	15–21	185
Waterman Reception	8–18	52
Northern Reception	8–18	115
Department of Corrections Administration		
California Medical Facility	18 up	7
Deuel Vocational	No specific limits	624
State Prisons	18 up	39
Reception Centers	18 up	181
County Jails		23

* Adapted from California Youth Authority, Biennial Report, 1953–1954, p. 45.

ward may be released after serving twelve to fifteen months (or, indeed, at any time) on a 1st degree robbery conviction while his partner under the Department of Corrections will be retained for two and a half or three years or longer before parole. The Youth Authority meets twice each month at Deuel, generally paroling its candidates at an early date. [See comment below relating to the apparent preoccupation of the Youth Authority with releasing inmates in order to make place for others awaiting entry.] The Adult Authority interviews young adult candidates for parole at Deuel once each month, and the average duration of retention of these Department of Corrections prisoners is significantly longer. Strictly comparable data on length of retention of Youth Authority as against Adult Authority cases at Deuel or other institutions of the State are not available. Tables 4 and 5 are informative, however, in showing average length of imprisonment of Youth Authority cases and of Department of Corrections prisoners. Note, in comparison to the short duration of the Y.A. commitments, the relatively long average terms spent by Department of Corrections offenders for the crimes prevalent among youths: burglary, theft, and auto theft. The Y.A. parolees are released to its field service officers, the A.A. parolees to agents of that Authority.

There appears to be little if any sound justi-fication for the parallel provisions of reception centers, parole agencies, and field service staffs for the largely repetitive and serious offenders of 18 to 21 who are sent to Deuel and to the state prisons. One sound and appropriate aspect of the system is the administration by the Department of Corrections of the excellent treatment and training facility at D.V.I. It is believed that the role of the Youth Authority there is uneconomical and confusing to the inmate population as a whole, regardless of any efforts which may be made to minimize the importance of the differences in the sentencing and release of the Youth Authority as against Department of Corrections prisoners.

It thus appears that except for parole, the Youth Authority in California does not deal with young adult offenders in any large sense. Therefore its experience bears little relation to Model Penal Code policy. This observer strongly questions the justification for its operation in the area of parole at Department of Corrections institutions.

POWERS AND FUNCTIONS OF THE YOUTH AUTHORITY IN CALIFORNIA

As we have previously observed, the statutory provisions and the day-to-day practices of the Youth Authority have changed rapidly since the original legislation was enacted in 1941.

Table **4** *Boys Released on Parole from Youth Authority Institutions During 1953 by Time in Institution (Months)* *

TIME IN INSTITUTION (MONTHS)	TOTAL		1ST RELEASE		OTHER RELEASE	
	Number	Percent	Number	Percent	Number	Percent
Total	2,666	100.0	2,011	100.0	655	100.0
Less than 3	57	2.1	24	1.2	33	5.0
3–5	302	11.3	210	10.5	92	14.0
6–8	633	23.8	455	22.6	178	27.2
9–11	832	31.2	662	32.9	170	26.0
12–14	537	20.1	412	20.5	125	19.1
15–17	205	7.7	169	8.4	36	0.5
18 and over	100	3.8	79	3.9	21	3.2
Median	9.8		10.0		8.9	
10th Percentile	4.9		5.2		3.8	
90th Percentile	15.0		15.2		14.2	

* From a Statistical Report of Youth Authority Activities, 1953 Annual Summary, p. 26.

Table **5** *Offense and Time Served Before Release: Men Paroled for First Time, 1953* *

OFFENSE	NUMBER	MEDIAN SENTENCE (YEARS)	MEDIAN TIME SERVED (MONTHS)	STATUTORY SENTENCE (YEARS)
Total	2,185	5	30	
Homicide				
Murder 1st	40	Life	144	Life
Murder 2d	39	12	65	5–Life
Manslaughter	55	6	36	0–10
Robbery				
Robbery 1st	278	6	41.5	5–Life
Robbery 2d	103	5	30	1–Life
Assault, deadly weapon	79	5	30	0–10
Burglary				
Burglary 1st	61	6	39	5–Life
Burglary 2d	383	5	27	1–15
Grand Theft, except auto	112	5	24	1–10
Auto Theft	112	4	26.5	1–10
Forgery and checks	421	5	24.5	0–14
Rape	49	7	45	0–50
Lewd and lascivious	57	7	50	1–Life
Narcotics	115	4	24	0–10
Escape from jail	38	4	21	0–10
Offense groups, less than 25 men	243			

* From Department of Corrections, Biennial Report, 1953–1954, p. 69.

Revisions have been made in 1943, 1945, 1947, 1949, and 1953. Currently a study of Youth Authority administration is being conducted by the Department of Finance. Some idea of the large volume of Youth Authority activities in 1952 when this was a board of only three members, including the Director, may be observed in the summary report of its activities published in 1953.[6] At that time the Director observed, "Such a load precludes opportunity for the careful consideration necessary for protection of society and for individualized treatment. The apparent solution is an increase in the membership of the Authority."[7] In response to this plea the board was enlarged to five members in 1953 and the Director was made specifically responsible for a number of administrative functions.

At the present time the Youth Authority Board as such is made responsible by law for the following major functions:

1. the acceptance or rejection of commitments
2. the designation of detention for its wards
3. classification, assignment and transfer of its wards to institutions or facilities
4. parole release or discharge from commitment; may petition court for extension of term up to the maximum term for the offense
5. determination of conditions of parole and release of its wards
6. orders for return to court for redisposition
7. orders of return of non-residents to places of residence
8. adoption of standards and qualifications of personnel
9. revocation or suspension of paroles and reconfinement or renewed release (may suspend or cancel parole without notice)
10. make examination and studies of its wards and reexamine them at least once each year to determine whether existing orders and dispositions should be modified.

The Director of the Youth Authority is made responsible for further important functions

which, however, he may delegate to subordinates:

11. transfer of wards
12. establishment of the classification, transfer, and discipline policies of the Department (in conjunction with the Board, the Director to have final authority)
13. establishment and operation of treatment and training services and other appropriate services
14. creation of administrative districts; the employment and discharge of personnel needed
15. establishment or assistance in the establishment of councils and committees and work with agencies for the prevention of delinquency
16. contracting with colleges and other organizations for research and training of workers
17. collection of statistics and information
18. deposit or investment of inmates' funds
19. inspection of all public institutions and agencies that Authority is using or is authorized to use
20. power to establish and operate places for detention, places for examination and study [operates two reception centers], places of confinement [operates six institutions and three forestry camps], educational institutions, hospital and other correction and segregative facilities, institutions and agencies
21. development of conservation work with state and federal divisions, growing and harvesting of crops and protection of natural resources
22. investigate, examine, and make reports on adult and juvenile probation; establish standards for performance of probation duties; on request make investigations and recommendations to probation officers and judges; on request establish standards for juvenile halls and detention facilities
23. require treatment of wards by vocational, physical, educational and corrective activities; require conduct and mode of life in preparation for release; employ other methods of treatment conducive to correction.

It will be observed that the Youth Authority Board as such is assigned tasks primarily of

---

[6] California Youth Authority Progress Report, 1948–1952, p. 19.

[7] California Youth Authority Progress Report, 1948–1952.

classification, parole release, revocation, and discharge. Except for determining the facility to which the offender should be sent or transferred (and this only in the case of its own wards, not youths committed to the Director of Corrections), the Board functions relating to juveniles and youths are similar to those of any parole board. In the tasks of the Director of the Youth Authority, on the other hand, are found substantial departures from the orthodox correctional pattern of separating the functions of institutional administration from parole. It is notable, however, that the 1953 legislation established these administrative functions as the special tasks of the Director, as distinct from the Board. It is in accord with sound administrative practice that the single executive should be charged with such functions as the administration of diagnostic and treatment facilities, and the partial splitting off of these functions from the Authority Board in California appears to have been a very considerable improvement. Moreover, the specialization of function has been greater than appears in the statutes. The Director is charged with such a number and variety of important duties relating to juveniles and youths that he has little time for Board functions as such and, in the impression of the writer, has tended increasingly to function like a director of corrections at the juvenile and youth levels. His representative does occasionally sit as a referee at hearings on classification and parole and, as opportunity permits, he does so himself, but there is decreasing occasion for this, in part because of the scope of his duties. Furthermore, it should be noted, the Director is assisted by Deputies in charge of Diagnosis and Treatment, of Field Services, and of Business Services, and by officers in charge of the more detailed phases of classification, training, parole field services, delinquency prevention and probation, etc. In major respects, the Department of the Youth Authority and its divisional staffs parallel the Department of Corrections *together with* the Adult Authority. However, whereas administrative duties and parole functions are strictly distinct at the adult level, they are in theory — and in some measure in fact — combined at the juvenile and youth level. What appears to be the normal and desirable separation of functions has been developing, however, both in the law and, to an even greater extent, in practice. This is a major and, it is believed, a desirable departure from the theory of the "authority plan." Perhaps it may reasonably be expected to continue to a point of complete severance.

Query: what will develop in relation to the young adult group between 18 and 21? They are now classified and assigned to institutions partly by the Department of Corrections, partly by the Youth Authority Board, and treated and supervised mainly in the diagnostic and correctional institutions of the Department of Corrections. They are released to the community by both the Youth Authority Board and the Adult Authority and supervised there by two different field staffs, one of which is responsible to the Director of the Youth Authority. A tradition of fifteen years development in California may either preserve some such splitting of powers and functions as this or conceivably even turn the treatment responsibility for the young adult group to the Youth Authority entirely. The trend, however, is toward the policy that prevails in other states, that is, to submit young adult offenders to a specialized treatment within an adult department of correction. This would seem reasonably to imply also the desirability of classification and release by the adult correctional and paroling agencies. The major barrier to this lies in the long terms provided under the California penal statutes (see Table 5): terms which can be avoided by Youth Authority commitments that result in shorter duration of retention. Except in the cases of youthful recidivists and murderers, however, the Adult Authority could release in most cases as early as the Youth Authority now does, if that were the objective of policy.

Whatever may be the future course of development in California in relation to the young adult, it is clear that the Youth Authority Board does not function even in relation to juveniles either in the fashion contemplated by the A.L.I. Model Bill or under earlier California Youth Authority legislation. We have noted that the role of the Director as administrator of a system of institutions and programs has been partially severed from the Board itself. Moreover, Board "meetings" and orders appear to have come to be largely the actions of single individuals or pairs who sit and determine at the time what will be the institutional classification or the parole plan or release date, or whether parole shall be revoked. "Meetings," as noted in the table below, are not Board meetings in the ordinary sense and decisions are not "Board decisions." Indeed, the Youth Authority Board is required to meet as a group under its rules, only bi-monthly and, while the members do sit as a board more frequently than this, the tendency has been for the action of the single member or referee to become the action of the Board.[8] This sort of phenomenon is common in parole board practices, of course, though it is dubious policy if decisions are intended to reflect group thinking. The result is to exaggerate the powers of the single board member over the life and liberty of the offender and over the security of the community, powers that are already very large. Put in general terms, it appears that, whereas the Youth Authority idea contemplated a Board formulation of general policies of reception, treatment and parole, with detailed instrumentation of these functions by agents of the Board specialized to deal with individual offenders, present practice imposes upon a single administrative director most of the broad policy making functions as well as the duty to administer juvenile correctional institutions (with the counsel, however, of the Youth Authority Board and, in a measure, the Board of Corrections) and the members of the Board make the individual case decisions.

The writer has previously expressed his opinion that the powers formally entrusted to the Youth Authority are too wide and varied. This belief has been strengthened by his further observations in California. That this has not proven to be a very serious problem may be explained by the fact that the Board does not

8 "The Youth Authority Act provides that members of the board may meet in panels, and two members constitute a quorum for the transaction of official business. Members hold weekly panel meetings at the two reception centers and the Los Angeles and Sacramento offices. The weekly San Francisco meeting is conducted by a single member of the board acting as referee. Referee findings must be confirmed by another member of the Board. Meetings are also held at the six Youth Authority schools, three forestry camps, and the Deuel Vocational Institution at least once each month. Members hold meetings every three months at Department of Corrections facilities housing Youth Authority wards. These include San Quentin Prison, California Medical Facility, and California Institution for Women." California Youth Authority, Biennial Report, 1953–1954, p. 5.

fully exercise the authority it possesses under the law and because there is close coordination of correctional and paroling agencies. The writer has observed a tendency of Board members to follow closely the recommendations, explicit or implicit, of institutional personnel in matters of classification and release. He is prepared to accept the view that the Board does not wield power as promiscuously at it might. But there appear to be two problems here: There should in fact be a specific allocation of responsibility for making decisions, whether in the individual case or on high levels of general policy. Moreover, some other board in this State or an analogous Board elsewhere might easily come to exercise its powers fully and unwisely. It is no easy feat to set up a board with the omnicompetence envisioned in the California Youth Authority law that would apply its powers in a restrained fashion and at the same time with appropriate, specialized functioning in each phase of the correctional processes.

There is another aspect of this problem that has not received the attention it merits. The youth authority idea, exemplified in California as well as other jurisdictions, is based upon a theoretical policy of vertical integration: a small board being entrusted with the entirety of powers and functions to deal with young offenders correctionally from start to finish (though, as we have noted, this is not the case in California so far as young adult offenders are concerned). This policy is based primarily upon a desire to achieve uniformity in diagnostic and treatment impact, "to individualize" handling of the offender through a single agency. The writer submits that this goal has not been and probably could not be achieved in fact. A board with nearly 2,500 wards in reception and treatment institutions and nearly 6,000 under its parole supervision, issuing from 20,000 to 30,000 orders each year, can not well individualize treatment in any very meaningful sense. It can do little more than review the decisions and recommendations of officers and agents employed at the various levels of the treatment process. Inspection of Table 6 should give some idea of the size and variety of the tasks performed, quite aside from the function of administering institutions and field parole services. This leads us to a comparison with the more orthodox pattern of horizontal integration in the handling of correction

Table **6** *Board Orders Issued by Youth Authority 1952 **

Court Referral Considered	2,776
Cases Accepted	2,680
Cases Rejected	96
Ancillary Orders	6,407
Referred to Parole for plans	1,226
Referred to Parole for out-of-state placement	247
Order of furlough	154
Progress report (institutional)	1,282
Progress report (parole)	2,583
Miscellaneous board orders	915
Classification, Segregation, Parole	9,369
Assignment of facility (transfer)	3,105
Released on parole	2,533
Restored to parole	1,015
Parole revoked	692
Parole suspended	2,024
Discharges	1,677
Total Orders Issued	20,229
Number of Meetings	289
Orders per Meeting	69
Miles traveled	47,545

* California Youth Authority Progress Report, 1948–1952, p. 20.

of young adults, systems under which reception, classification, and treatment functions are carried on within a Department of Correction. Thus, in New York State, for example, the Elmira Reception Center, the Reformatory, and camp are administered by the Director of Correction through a Deputy in charge of youth corrections. Parole release is by the State Board of Parole. (Only in two authority states is the parole of some young adults, as well as juveniles generally, determined and administered by a board distinct from the ordinary board of parole.) The conduct of parole field services is the responsibility of a parole executive or administrator, who is generally charged with administration of all parole supervision in the field.

There appear to be several distinct advantages in this form of horizontal organization: Most obvious, perhaps, though not the most important, is its relative *economy*. There appears little justification for having two paroling boards traveling each month to institutions to hold hearings on cases of young adults, two sets of field agents carrying on investigations in the community. Duplication in the administration of institutions is obviated, as we have seen, by putting young adults generally in institutions

under the Department of Corrections. The economic advantages of pooling in the fields of personnel, purchasing, and distribution are quite apparent, economies that are greatest under a system where young adult treatment is operated as a special phase of adult corrections. Furthermore, it should be apparent that where an autonomous agency is charged with the operations and budget of youth corrections, there may well result something less than an equitable distribution of state funds as between this group and others that require specialized correctional attention: first offenders, medical and psychiatric deviates, those requiring adult training or education, and other groups. It appears generally to be both more economical and fair to provide a single agency of institutional administration and a single parole board for dealing with young adults within a framework of adult correction.

It is apparent, too, that the orthodox hierarchal pattern of institutional administration — parole board release — parole field administration has the advantages of simplicity and specialization. Each agency is specialized functionally to perform its particular and limited correctional task. It may be argued that the administration of youth corrections is in some measure a different problem than the conduct of adult penology — and, indeed, it appears to be a major defense of the youth authority idea that specialization and integration may thus be achieved. However, where such diverse functions are involved as diagnosis and classification, institutional administration and discipline, parole release, field supervision, employee training, delinquency prevention, and research, it is highly dubious that any very real measure of specialization and integration could be achieved by a board, even if the same Authority members could follow the individual through from start to finish. In fact, however, panel composition varies under the circulation practices of the Authority. So far as youths from 18 to 21 are concerned, moreover, their correction is administered partly by adult, partly by juvenile authorities, and there are no discernible and reasonable lines of distinction.

It is submitted that the sounder pattern is commitment to an adult department of correction, classification by the department to an appropriate institution and release by the ordinary adult paroling agency. This should have the further advantage of greater uniformity and, therefore, a sense of more consistent justice. Conceivably the result might be a longer average duration of retention of young adults, though this is not necessarily so, and in any event policy in this matter should be determined by the needs of the individual and of the community, rather than by the contrasting philosophies of two paroling agencies. In this connection, it must be observed that the Youth Authority in California, in the writer's opinion, at least, has been too much impelled in its decisions on retention and release by a preoccupation, resulting from its interest in institutional administration, with making space for new inmates. This is a common phenomenon elsewhere where institutional administration and release functions are combined, very generally at the juvenile level, but is greatly to be deprecated in age levels of more serious and repetitive offenders.

Finally, but not least in importance, horizontal integration of corrections provides a better distribution of power at points where power relations are most trenchant in their impact on justice. Checks and balances are "built in" in a system of coordinated but semi-autonomous phases of correction where institutional administration can in large measure correct errors of original classification, where a parole releasing agency can utilize but where appropriate can overrule institutional counsel, where supervision in the field may be guided by but can modify appreciably the immense influence of a parole board. The writer does not doubt that self-imposed restrictions of the presently constituted Youth Authority in California results in a fine coordination and a properly limited exercise of power. He does not believe that this exemplary situation is the customary result where great authority is vested and where political considerations may come to intervene in appointments and in agency functioning. It is believed that there has been an extraordinarily fine quality of liaison in California between each of the two Authorities and the Department of Corrections, a coordination that has been quite essential, considering the zones of potential controversy as to jurisdiction and power under the authority legislation there. It is believed, however, that integration can be achieved in more natural and permanent channels horizontally, between the several functionally limited levels of correction, than under a system in which authorities are granted very wide powers in the exercise of which they may at times display considerable jealousy.

IMPLICATIONS FOR THE MODEL PENAL CODE OF EXPERIENCE IN OTHER JURISDICTIONS

It is even more difficult to generalize about the significance for the penal code of experiments in other jurisdictions that have in some measure followed the authority idea than from the experience in California. In general they have not followed the Model Youth Correction Authority Act in its focus on the youth group but have been established instead as boards to deal with juvenile delinquents. For the most part the variegated "authorities" set up in the several states have taken over from State boards of welfare or their equivalents the functions of operating juvenile institutions, of release and after-care, and of delinquency prevention programs. Wisconsin, where the previously existing board was sufficiently powerful and well-established, is a notable instance of a failure to accomplish this withdrawal of control. In other jurisdictions the change-over has been accomplished with some difficulty while in California, on the other hand, the development of the Youth Authority was hastened by the ignominious discrediting of the preceding administration. It was characterized by a crusading zeal to expand and improve facilities and services, though expansion was imperative in any case, what with the rapidly increasing population and offense rates there.

As the late Charles Chute and Marjorie Bell, long of the National Probation and Parole Association, have described the authorities in a recent publication:

"The result has been the passage of acts in seven states and by the Congress with some of the provisions of the original act, but in no case bearing a close resemblance to it. None of them have carried out its basic purpose, to require that convicted youths *above* the juvenile court age, with certain exceptions, must be committed by the courts to a state agency for disposition and treatment. State boards have been created in each of the seven states under varying names and with varying powers. Some of them are independent; others are attached to existing welfare or correctional departments. In every case commitment of youths as well as children is optional with the courts, and only a small percentage of juvenile delinquents and an even smaller percentage of youths have been so committed. . . . All of the state boards are concerned chiefly with two functions, neither of them contemplated in the original act: (1) dealing with children committed by juvenile courts for transfer to suitable institutions for delinquents, and (2) administering those institutions. All of them have become primarily state juvenile agencies. As such they have performed a greatly needed service in improving the training schools and their release programs. In California, the only state where it has been given sufficient funds for the purpose the Authority has been successful in opening new institutions, schools, and camps for delinquent children and youth." [9]

Other than California, only Minnesota has been a partial exception to the focus on juvenile delinquency. In Minnesota, however, as in California, the major facility serving young adults — the State Reformatory at St. Cloud — continues under the direction of the adult correctional department rather than the Youth Conservation Commission. The six-member Commission is in charge of the state training schools and of two small youth-service facilities, the reception center located at the St. Cloud

_____

[9] Chute and Bell, *Crime, Courts, and Probation,* pp. 160–161.

Reformatory, and a forestry camp. It does not have control over the program, discipline, or treatment of its reformatory wards; the situation is comparable to the Deuel institution in California. Also, as in California, two different parole boards release from the St. Cloud Reformatory. The Minnesota experience indicates a similar waste, duplication of effort, and morale problems of inmates serving disparate terms for similar crimes. It is on a smaller scale, but may be more serious in a sense in that funds for correctional staff are much more scarce there than in California.

The only modern legislation dealing specifically with young adult corrections is the Federal Youth Corrections Act of 1950, focused on offenders beyond juvenile court jurisdiction. The federal act is of special interest, moreover, because it represented the culmination of long extended efforts to adapt the authority idea to federal sentencing and specifically to youth corrections. Whether it should be considered an "authority plan" in any strict sense is a nice question of definition. More than elsewhere this legislation reflected a consensus derived from divergent conceptions of need and policy. It may be noted in passing that the 1955 proposals submitted for the Model Penal Code relating to the administrative structure of corrections for the young adult most closely resemble the provisions of this federal legislation. The Youth Corrections Act provides, at the discretion of the court, for shorter sentences for offenders up to the age of twenty-two who have been convicted of crimes, for reception-diagnostic study, for classification to and treatment in institutions and agencies administered by the Federal Bureau of Prisons, and for release and discharge by a youth division (the size of which is not determined by law) of the eight-member Board of Parole. It is the responsibility of the Director of the Bureau of Prisons to classify and transfer, to determine treatment, and to operate the institutions, though the youth division is empowered to "make recommendations of the Director with respect to general treatment and correction policies for committed youth offenders [those who have been committed specifically under the shorter terms provided by the law]." It is perfectly clear from the statute, however, that correctional treatment planning and administration remains in the Bureau of Prisons, as a specialized phase of its total operations. The youth division is in fact a part of the Board of Parole, charged with paroling and discharging youthful offenders. It is entirely clear to the writer from his experience with the Board and the Bureau that only this horizontal arrangement of liaison and of split powers is effective as a method of treatment administration and parole release: the Board is specialized in parole, the Bureau in institutional corrections, and their responsibilities are so allocated by law.[10] The American Law Institute reporters have drawn from this experience in recommending that young adult corrections should be within a Department of Correction and that release should be by an independent parole board.

It may be clear from what has been said in the previous pages that the correctional treatment of the young adult offender has continued to be a responsibility of the departments serving adults in every state. Relative to the group over juvenile court age the youth authorities, where they have any function at all, act in the main merely to release a selected group of offenders. As a specialized paroling agency, they generally duplicate the functions of the ordinary adult parole board, often with inconsistent as well as uneconomic consequences.

One further issue remains to be considered: the potential utility of the authority ideal in arousing enthusiasm for the worthy cause of specializing and extending correctional treatment resources for young adult offenders. California has rallied its forces under the authority model to strengthen its facilities for juveniles and for delinquency prevention. The major facilities for mature youths have been developed by the adult department of corrections, however, both there and in Minnesota. In the latter state the development of institutional

facilities has been very limited in any event, both before and since the creation of its youth commission.[11] During the same period when the juvenile authorities have emerged, other non-authority states have developed reception and classification centers, camps and forestry projects, prevention programs, professionalized paroling agencies, and other resources from which youth corrections has profited. New York, New Jersey, Michigan, Pennsylvania, and Ohio, as well as the federal system illustrate marked improvements in these areas without benefit of an autonomous and all-powerful board. Whether the "youth authority" as a slogan has power still today to stir the imagination of correctional authorities and generous impulses of legislators is a moot question. The reporter believes that any advantage which the authority ideal may be deemed to offer in this regard is outweighed by the general failure of the existing authorities to come to grips with those serious problems of the young adult offender with which the Institute was concerned when it developed the Model Youth Correction Authority Act in 1940. The quality and training of personnel, the variety and specialization of institutions, the vision and determination of administrators, the conduct of critical research: these are the elements of improved youth corrections, and it is submitted that they cannot be achieved either by a formal title or merely by providing wide powers to a small board.

What are the implications of the observations that have been made above for Model Penal Code policy? It is too early at this time to determine what will be the specific content of draft provisions for young adults. They remain to be formulated. It appears clear, however, that treatment and reception center administration for young adults should be in the hands of a department of correction and, where the scope of the problem justifies it, under a deputy in charge of this phase of the correctional program. Parole release should be entrusted to one board of parole, though there may be justification in some populous jurisdic-

---

[10] The testimony submitted to the Committees on the Judiciary prior to the enactment of the Federal Youth Corrections Act, as well as the terms of the statute itself, make it quite apparent that the traditional division of functions between parole board and correctional administration were to be maintained. See Hearings before Subcommittee No. 3 of the Committee on the Judiciary, House of Representatives, 78th Congress, 1st Session on H.R. 2139 and 2140, May 19 and June 10, 1943, Serial No. 4; Report from the Committee on the Judiciary, Senate, 81st Congress, 1st Session on S. 2609, October 17, 1949; and Public Law 865, 81st Congress, approved September 30, 1950.

[11] Minnesota has a reformatory for men opened in 1889; a reformatory for women opened in 1920; a prison established in 1851 and replaced by a new facility in 1913; two training schools, one founded in 1890, the other in 1911; a reception center started in 1948 at the Reformatory that accommodates 80 and a camp opened in 1951 for 60 male felons.

tions for a young adult panel of such a board to concentrate on the younger group. It is believed that special sentencing provisions should be made for young adults directed toward goals of rehabilitation and prevention of youth crime. Finally, while the material presented in this paper is not relevant to the point, it appears that the proposal for specialized courts of the Model Youth Court Act of the American Law Institute was basically sound. The establishment of specialized parts of the criminal courts will be recommended, therefore, to ad-

judicate cases of young adults in states where the volume of such cases may justify this measure of specialization. These proposals are drawn from the laws and practice of no single jurisdiction, obviously. They do not offer a simple formula to resolve the difficult problems of youthful offenses. They do rest upon the experience in a number of the states and the Federal jurisdiction where there has been a careful searching over the past generation for improved methods and policies.

Chapter 19

Intake, Detention, Clinical Examination, Investigation, and Hearing

How a delinquent or an endangered child comes to the attention of a juvenile court and what preliminary policy decisions must then be made comprise the important problem of "intake."

Police departments and juvenile aid bureaus have a basic "sifting" function in deciding which of numerous complaints of neighbors, railway guards and others can best be disposed of without taking the children involved to the juvenile court. The powers of the police in effecting an arrest of an adult without a warrant are strictly delimited. In the case of an endangered child, the police require broader authority; they must have power to take custody of a child preventively. At the same time the police must not abuse their power, and they must work cooperatively with the parents and teachers of endangered children. All this means that the police require good judgment, special training and sympathetic understanding of children's problems.[1] This can best be achieved through establishment of a specialized and professional delinquency prevention unit within the police department.[2]

In connection with the basic decisions, reliable predictive devices for distinguishing true pre-delinquents from children whose behavior has merely a nuisance value and is not indicative of any deep-lying tendency toward persistent delinquency, can be very valuable.[3]

An extract from the authoritative *Standards for Specialized Courts Dealing with Children* concerns the relationship of the police to the intake problem.

Once a child gets into court, however, there are further policy problems involving the sifting of cases. As has been shown in Chapter 11, in a number of courts, many cases are handled "informally" or "unofficially."

In respect to the problem of sifting the cases which should be formally considered by the court, there can be some conflict between the administrative policy concept of "intake" and the legal concept of "jurisdiction"; the former having its philosophy and source in social work, the latter in law. It should be pointed out that usually most matters of jurisdiction, law and proposed disposition of the case can be and are handled with considerable informality, since the parties to the proceedings do not ordinarily

---

[1] See *Police Services for Juveniles*, Children's Bureau, U. S. Department of Health, Education and Welfare, Washington, 1954.

[2] See J. E. Rinck, "Supervising the Juvenile Delinquent," and J. Chwast, "Casework Treatment in a Police Setting," Articles 184 and 185 of this volume. See, also, E. Lossing, "The Crime Prevention Work of the Berkeley Police Department," in S. and E. T. Glueck, *Preventing Crime*, New York, McGraw-Hill Book Co., 1936, 237–263.

[3] See Chapter 32 hereof.

insist on the observance of strictly technical forms. Where the alleged juvenile delinquent and his parents come into court with a lawyer, or where the juvenile and his parents claim that the facts are not as alleged in the petition for delinquency or neglect, issues arise which should be litigated formally, with the parties given every opportunity to rebut the allegations of the petition.

Unfortunately, there is room for improvement of intake policies and practices in many courts. A *sine qua non* is the appointment of a specialist who is trained both in social work and in the jurisdictional powers and duties of the court.

Both preceding a juvenile court hearing and during the stage between ascertainment of delinquency status and the initiation of a plan of treatment, it may be necessary to place the child in a temporary controlled environment other than his own home. Such detention facilities range all the way from cells in a jail for adult offenders to a homelike establishment that combines opportunities for social, psychologic and psychiatric study of the child with a warm and understanding attitude.

There is a tendency on the part of some persons to underestimate the possible traumatic effects of a bad detention facility by pointing out that it takes time for the influence of such institutions as the home and the school to become effective. While this is essentially sound, it overlooks the fact that even the brief contact that a child can have with such an institution as a detention home can mean a great deal in its future life. Here, as in so many other human problems, quality can mean more than quantity. As is pointed out in the first article in this series, the establishment of a relationship of empathy between the staff of the detention center and the children under care is important.

An extract from the *Standards for Specialized Courts Dealing with Children* concerns the problem of detention and shelter care, and the article by Norman is informative on what constitutes good practice in detention.

Two contributions — one by Birnbaum, the other by Schmidl — reflect some of the psychiatric techniques employed in the study of the child to develop a treatment plan.

The Editor would have liked to include Chapters VII and VIII of *One Thousand Juvenile Delinquents* [4] as indicative of the nature of the recommendations of a psychiatric clinic to a juvenile court, the extent to which such clinical advice was followed, and the reasons assigned for not complying with some of the recommendations; but limitations of space made this prohibitive. The student is invited to examine those chapters from a pioneering research regarding relationship of court and clinic.

The final item in this chapter deals with the judicial hearing. There are relatively few publications on the qualitative aspects of a juvenile court hearing.[5] Yet, as the article by Judge Schramm puts it, the court hearing can itself be a "part of the treatment process." Indeed, it can be the initiator of that rapport relationship that is indispensable if one wants to influence the behavior of another. On the other hand, the court hearing, despite the fact that it involves a juvenile court, can be a traumatic experience to the child.

The article by Judge Schramm was chosen because it reflects something of the flavor of a sympathetic court and an understanding judge. Couched in informal language, it breathes a spirit of that friendliness which a dedicated juvenile court judge tries to impart. The student should, however, bear in mind the legal decisions in prior chapters as a caveat that in the informality and friendliness of a hearing certain fundamental protections of the rights of the child and the parent should not be ignored.

---

[4] By S. and E. T. Glueck, Cambridge, Harvard University Press, 1934, 111–148.

[5] One of the best discussions of the hearing in a juvenile court is to be found in P. V. Young, *Social Treatment in Probation and Delinquency*, second edition, New York, McGraw-Hill Book Co., Inc., 1952, 174–206.

107

Intake *

CHILDREN'S CASES

The role of the police. Intake for the specialized court, particularly in relation to children involved in delinquency, generally begins within the local law enforcement agency. The importance of the role of the police in the prevention and control of delinquency is becoming increasingly recognized throughout the country. The police in many communities are aware of the specialized nature of this and have established special bureaus or divisions, particularly in large urban areas, to work with children and youth. As a result of this development, increased emphasis has been placed on special training for police officers. It is now generally accepted that basic training for all police officers should include some instruction in working with juveniles, and that the officers assigned to units specializing in this work should have intensive training. The courts in more and more communities are cooperating with law enforcement officials in establishing and developing training courses.

The conditions under which a child may be taken into custody should be set forth in the statute and should provide for his protection and at the same time permit the police to take reasonable action necessary to protect the community. Section 12 of A Standard Juvenile Court Act states: "If it appears that the child is in such condition or surroundings that his welfare requires that his custody be immediately assumed by the court, the judge may order, by endorsement upon the summons, that the officer serving the same shall at once take the child into custody." Section 15 of the act which states that "any child found violating any law or ordinance, or whose surroundings are such as to endanger his welfare is taken into custody . . ." seems to imply that the child may be taken into custody without a warrant

---

* Extracted from *Standards for Specialized Courts Dealing with Children*, Children's Bureau, U. S. Govt. Printing Office, 1954, 36–43. Used by permission of the publisher.

when such conditions exist. Many juvenile court laws contain this or a similar provision.

To restrict the police in taking into custody only those children "found violating a law or ordinance" is believed by many to be unrealistic. It is believed, therefore, that such statute should be amended also to permit the police to take into custody any child who, they have reasonable grounds to believe, has committed an act which would be a felony if committed by an adult.

A police officer who finds a child in a situation dangerous to himself or to others, or who finds a child who has committed a "delinquent" act, must decide whether the situation or the act is serious enough to bring to the attention of the court. This decision should be made on the apparent gravity of the situation or act, based on the investigation made by the police officer. Such decisions should not become a rule-of-thumb procedure by which children are always referred to the court for certain offenses or on the commission of a second offense.

If the officer does not believe that court action should be taken, he has a number of alternatives:

1. Referral of the situation to a social agency. This may be particularly applicable in cases of neglect, where an agency in the community is empowered by law to investigate situations of neglect and offer services in relation to them, or in a situation requiring public health care, or where a child is already under the care of an agency.

2. Advice to the child or parents, particularly as to the existence of community resources, welfare agencies, etc.

3. Warning or admonition.

4. Temporary arrangements for the child's safety, such as taking a child home, finding lodging for an older child at a YMCA or YWCA, referral to an emergency shelter operated by a social agency, or leaving a neighbor temporarily in charge of children left alone.

Consultation regarding such actions should be available to the police from the intake division of the court.

The police should not employ informal methods which involve penalties or restraint, such as placing the child on "informal probation," ordering restitution, or revoking a driving permit.

It should be the duty of the police officer to

locate the parent or parents, or other guardian or custodian of the child, as soon as possible after the child is found, and, if possible, before other action is taken. Until this is done, and for this time only, the child may be held temporarily by the police in the precinct or Juvenile Bureau office. Ordinarily, if the parent, guardian, or custodian cannot be located within one or two hours, the child should be taken to the place of detention or shelter designated by the court.

The holding of a child for a temporary period in a precinct or Juvenile Bureau office should only be permitted where an appropriate waiting room is provided which insures his not coming in contact with adults charged with a crime and under conditions which provide adequate supervision and physical care. When the parents are located, the officer may then either return the child to them with such advice or suggestions as may be necessary, or he may inform them that the child's and their presence may be required in court.

If the parents cannot be found within a reasonable period of time, or if they are found and after consulting with them, the officer is of the opinion that a petition should be filed in the court and that the interests of the child or the safety of the community warrant the child's being detained or provided with shelter care, the officer should take the child either to the court or to the place of detention or shelter designated by the court in accordance with agreed, written procedures. In such cases, the officer should (1) give written reasons, at the time the child is brought into detention or shelter care, why he decided not to leave the child in his own home and, (2) contact the intake worker of the court as soon as reasonably possible, but in any case within 24 hours, to consider filing a petition with respect to the child. The court should make it possible for such filing to be made on a Sunday or a holiday in instances where the child would otherwise be detained without a petition for more than 24 hours.

If further investigation is to be made by the police after the child is placed in detention or shelter care, the police should be given every opportunity to interview the child. It should be clear, however, that a police investigation is not the same as a social study made by the probation officer in that the police investigation involves securing the facts to determine whether or not a crime or a delinquent act has been committed or a neglect situation exists which may be necessary to sustain a petition in the court.

Because of the child's presumed immaturity, special safeguards should be thrown around a police officer's interview with a child in investigating a delinquent act. In certain situations, depending on the age of the child, and the act committed, waiver to criminal court may be a possibility. Moreover at the time of the interview, it is not known whether or not the court specializing in children's cases will retain jurisdiction over the case if a petition is filed, or will waive its jurisdiction and permit the child to be tried in a criminal court. Therefore, it cannot always be assumed that the police interview will lead only to a noncriminal proceeding.

Before being interviewed, the child and his parents should be informed of his right to have legal counsel present and to refuse to answer questions if he should so decide. In cases where waiver is possible, he should also be cautioned that if he answers, his answers may be used not only before the specialized court but possibly in a criminal court. Where a child has been questioned alone by a police officer, without having been given an opportunity to secure the presence of his parents, guardian, or counsel, his statements during such interview should be presumed to have been induced either by the child's immaturity or by the idea that they would be used only in the specialized court and they should, therefore, unless the presumption is overcome, be excluded from admission before a criminal court in which the child may be a defendant.

Whenever possible and especially in the case of young children, no child should be interviewed except in the presence of his parents or guardian. This should always be the policy when a child is being questioned about his participation or when formal statement concerning the child's participation in the alleged delinquent act is being taken. The presence of a parent during the interview may be helpful to the police as the parental attitudes shown under such circumstances may help the police decide whether the case should be referred to court or to another agency. This procedure, of course, would not apply when the matter being investigated involves the child's parents. In cases where the child has freely admitted his participation in the act to the police, there appears to be nothing improper about interviewing the child to secure background information of a social nature without the parents being present. It may be equally necessary to interview the parents without the child being present to secure social information for the purpose of making a referral.

When the child is brought to court the police report should include information which the police may have which would be helpful to the intake worker of the court, such as previous police contacts with the child in which no referral to court was made, the attitude of the child and his parents to the act and the attitude of the person against whom the act was directed or whose property was involved.

Fingerprints may be taken on authorization of the court if necessary to proper investigation of the act, but such prints afterwards should either be returned to the court for destruction or kept on a civil identification card. Such authorization should be granted by the court on an individual case basis, depending upon the factors in each specific situation. In every case where the court or the police find that the child is not involved in the act, the prints should be destroyed. If the prints are kept on a civil identification card, only the child's name and address should appear on the card. No information which might disclose the circumstances or reasons for taking the prints should appear on the card.

The police should not take pictures of a child except upon authorization of the court and then only for purposes of identification, for example, in the case of a runaway child. If taken, the negative and all prints should be returned to the court for destruction.

The police may give evidence in court necessary to the establishment of the court's jurisdiction and a finding as to the facts alleged in the petition. Frequently, though, this is not necessary. The child may have admitted his participation in the act, and the evidence may be such that no question of the validity of his admission is likely to arise. If there is a denial of participation or if the child's admission is questioned, the police officer concerned would, of course, be required to testify and to submit to cross-examination.

The role of the court intake worker. Intake in children's cases involving neglect or delinquency is essentially a screening and referral process which is necessary for efficient and effective court administration. It also helps citizens and agencies in the community to use constructively the authority and services of the court.

The intake worker should have considerable experience and be particularly skillful in short contact interviewing. He must be thoroughly familiar with court policies and procedures and the statutes under which the court operates. He should also be familiar with the functions and intake procedures of the agencies in the community which provide service and care for children.

Although the intake process is not designed to provide continuing treatment, every opportunity should be taken to make it a helping process. It should not become perfunctory.

It is generally agreed that a central intake unit is essential, especially in the larger courts. The organization and size of this unit, the duties performed, and the procedures followed will vary from court to court and from type of case to type of case. In children's cases involving neglect or delinquency, the basic function of the intake service is to make "a preliminary inquiry to determine whether the interests of the public or of the child require that further action be taken."[1] This preliminary inquiry should not be confused with the social study made by a probation officer for the purpose of helping the court arrive at a disposition, or with the investigation for determining facts which might sustain the petition. Matters which are determined at intake are typically as follows: Does the complaint or the action appear to be a matter over which the court may have jurisdiction? Can the interests of the child and the public be best served by court action (i.e., the filing of a petition) or by referral to another agency in the community? If by referral to another agency, what agency? If court action is indicated, what type of proceeding should be initiated? If the child is in detention, is continued detention care needed or should the child be released?

Generally, most of the facts upon which

---

[1] A Standard Juvenile Court Act, *op. cit.*, at p. 19, section 11. (See footnote 45, p. 33.)

these determinations are based can be secured from the complainant or can readily be obtained through office or telephone interviews. Typical illustrations of such facts in a delinquency case are — the nature of the complaint, the age of the child or children involved, the time the act took place, the number of times the child or other members of his family have been known to the court in the past, whether the child is active with another agency, the attitude of the child and his parents towards the situation.

The intake worker should have access to legal advice. There should be the right of appeal to the judge from any action or decision of the intake unit. Such decision should not, however, affect the right of any person to file a petition on a specific issue to which he is a party, such as adoption, paternity, application to be appointed *guardian of the person* of a child, proceedings for support, etc.

Where the complainant has sufficient evidence to file a petition and yet has reasonable grounds for believing that a child may be in such circumstances that he should be brought before a court, or where the complainant has sufficient evidence but is unwilling to take responsibility for filing a petition, the intake worker should refer the complainant or the complaint to an agency having statutory powers and responsibility to investigate such complaints and follow through by filing a petition where such action is deemed necessary.[2] In many communities the only agency having this statutory authority at present is the police.

2 Often the powers so claimed exist only as an agreement made in a Council of Social Agencies, or are assumed by virtue of a supposed professional responsibility to represent the interests of all children. See, for instance, Claire R. Hancock's "Protective Service in Practice" (New York: Child Welfare League of America, Inc., 1948, 24 pp.) where the agency relies on court sanction for its authority; Karl and Elizabeth de Schweinitz's "The Place of Authority in the Protective Function of the Public Welfare Agency" (*Bulletin* of Child Welfare League of America, Inc., 25: 1–6, 1946) in which reliance is placed both on a clause in an enabling Act and on the "inherent" authority of the agency; and such articles as Lionel C. Lane's "Aggressive" approach in prevention casework with children's problems (*Social Casework*, 33: 61–66, 1952) which affirms the responsibility of the agency to persist in offering service without legal authority and in the face of the parent's hostility.

Generally, the court should not accept such complaints for investigation by its own personnel. To do so would mean that the court, through the actions of its own representative, would be placed in the position of petitioner with the result that the court would be sitting in judgment on its own petition.

Although it is held that proceedings on petitions in behalf of children are "nonadversary" in nature, they are not necessarily accepted as such by the child or family. As an example, placing responsibility on the probation officer for investigating the act, filing the petition, and supporting the petition with the necessary evidence in court may in fact place him in an adversary position in the eyes of the child and family. The doubt and distrust thereby aroused in the minds of the child and parents hinders the development of the helping relationship which must be established if treatment is to be effective.

There are, however, certain situations where it may be desirable for the court to investigate complaints. Such situations may arise in cases where the court has already assumed jurisdiction and is providing service, for example, a complaint about a child on probation or a complaint by one parent against the other concerning the care children are receiving in nonsupport or contested custody cases.

ADULT CASES

In some courts the intake worker also has responsibility for authorizing the initiation of criminal proceedings against adults. If this practice is followed, the intake worker should either be well informed concerning the legal questions involved or have ready access to legal counsel. Placing this responsibility in intake is often defended on the grounds that the intake worker, having the social information, is in a better position to determine the social implications and possible effects of such action which, in a number of cases, may be the factors that determine whether or not criminal action should be initiated.

In other courts responsibility for authorizing the initiation of criminal proceedings rests in another person, for instance, the prosecuting attorney. When this procedure is followed, there should be an opportunity for intake workers to provide the prosecuting attorney with information concerning the social factors involved and to offer suggestions or recommendations as to the need for criminal action.

Failure to support a child is often the result of other unresolved problems facing one or both parents. Family disorganization, which may lead to delinquency and neglect, often may be prevented if the parents can be helped earlier to meet their problems. Because of the social factors involved and the need to secure certain social information for the court, and the possibility of effecting an adjustment or reconciliation, nonsupport actions against parents should undergo the same intake process as cases involving delinquency and neglect. The right, however, to file proceedings for support should not be denied by the intake worker.

108

Detention and Shelter Care *

Both detention and shelter care . . . involve a temporary limitation of the parent's or the child's rights. Both also involve difficult adjustments by a child to new living arrangements and to separation from his family at a time when he is likely to be otherwise upset and is facing court action. Therefore, care of either type should be resorted to only in cases of clear necessity and then only after very careful consideration of the facts and in accordance with sound procedures developed jointly by the court and the police department and other agencies. Police officers should place a child in detention or shelter care only after all other reasonable alternatives have been exhausted, should give written reason for so placing the child at the time of doing so, and should report the placement as soon as possible to the court.

Authority to place a child in detention or in shelter care without the consent of the parent or guardian should be vested only in the court, its probation staff, the police, or an administra-

tive agency having statutory powers to do so. A child should not be detained for a period longer than 24 hours without the filing of a petition to bring him before the court. This 24-hour rule should operate irrespective of Sundays or holidays. A child should not be detained for a longer time without a petition merely because he happens to be found on a Sunday or holiday, or on the day immediately preceding. In such cases, there should be procedures to permit the immediate filing of a petition upon call from the police.[1] There are certain situations where this rule would not necessarily apply; for example, where a child is already under the jurisdiction of the court and is on probation, or where a child is a runaway from a training school and is being temporarily held pending arrangements for his return.

If a petition is not filed or if the intake worker believes that continued detention or shelter care is not necessary, the child should be returned home at once. The placement of a child in detention or in shelter care should be promptly reported to the intake division of the court by the facility receiving him.

After a petition is filed, the decision as to whether the child is to continue in detention or is to be released should be made only by the judge or by a member of the probation staff (preferably the intake worker or his supervisor) to whom the judge delegates this responsibility. Written notification of the decision should be sent promptly to the facility. A hearing on the issue of detention or shelter care should be held on the request of the parent or on the court's own motion.

The primary purpose of detention is not continued treatment. However, should a child need detention, this period should always be used for observation, study, and treatment.

Detention should not be used for the convenience of personnel making a social study or a clinical examination. Detention should not be used as a disposition by the court, for example, as the local jail is used for the short-time

---

* Extracted from *Standards for Specialized Courts Dealing with Children*, Children's Bureau, U. S. Govt. Printing Office, 1954, 45–47. Used by permission of the publisher.

[1] Some persons working in the field believe that this rule would create serious administrative problems, particularly during the period of change from a previous procedure. To obviate this difficulty the court could be authorized to extend the period for an additional 24 hours by rule of court applicable to special types of cases.

sentence of an adult, nor should a probation officer place a child in detention without the intention of bringing the child before the court. Neither should detention be used as an interim placement facility by social agencies in the community.

Ordinarily, children who must be held as material witnesses either by a specialized or a criminal court should be held in shelter care and not in detention except in accordance with the above criteria.

Where an adequate detention facility exists, no child should be placed in jail. In the event that adequate detention facilities do not exist, children, who because of their behavior cannot be given shelter care, may have to be detained in a jail. This should never be done except on the express written authorization of the judge, and, if done, the child should be placed in a room or ward entirely separate from adults.

It should be the policy of the court to reduce the time a child spends in detention to the minimum compatible with his safety, the safety of the community and the court's determination of his case. The same principle should apply after disposition pending foster care plans by agencies, transportation to training schools, or other State or local institutions.

When children are placed in detention or shelter care, there is always a motive to protect the child, as well as to protect society. Therefore, bail should not be permitted.[2]

In some jurisdictions, however, the right to bail, provided for in the State constitution, may extend to cases of delinquency. Furthermore, many persons are of the opinion that to leave no avenue of release for the child is a denial of a basic right to which all persons are entitled.

Even those who favor this position do not believe that the release of a child should depend upon his or his family's ability to secure a bail bond. This all too often places an additional economic strain on families, a great number of which are already hard pressed. It is

also extremely difficult for a child to understand why he must remain in detention while his codelinquents are released because their families were able to secure bail bond.

Therefore, in those jurisdictions where constitutional or statutory provisions provide for the right of bail, the release should be made upon the personal recognizance of the parent, guardian, relative, or attorney representing the child or any other responsible person.

109

Detention Intake *

Sherwood Norman

To detain or not to detain children? That is the question asked from state to state, from county to county throughout the country. One county will detain nearly every child [1] picked up for delinquency, while another of comparable size and jurisdiction rarely holds a single child in custody pending disposition. Differing state laws, differing applications of the law from county to county, and the differing judg-

---

[2] Whether constitutional or statutory provisions regarding release on bail would be applicable to cases of delinquency in the specialized courts would depend upon harmonizing the statutes relating to such cases with the constitutional and statutory provisions. See discussion in "A Standard Juvenile Court Act," *op. cit.* at pp. 22–23. (See footnote 45, p. 33.) See also 160 A.L.R. 287 and 31 Am. Jur. 1951 supp., p. 68.

* Reprinted from *Crime Prevention through Treatment*, 1952 Yearbook, National Probation and Parole Association, 140–155. Used by permission of the author and the publisher. See, also, the following: R. Allaman, "Human Relations at the Detention Home," 16 *Federal Probation* (1952), 38–41; C. S. Antolina, "Principles of Intake Control," 1952 Yearbook, National Probation and Parole Association, 133–139; S. Burns, "The Detention Home School," 1953 Yearbook, National Probation and Parole Association, 155–158; R. N. Studt (Ed.), *Handbook for the Operation of Juvenile Halls*, California Youth Authority, Sacramento, State Printing Office, 1955; S. H. Kneisel, "Detention Home Programming," 1953 Yearbook, National Probation and Parole Association, 141–149; H. Palmieri, "Detention of the Youthful Offender," 1953 Yearbook, National Probation and Parole Association, 159–166; R. E. Walther, "The Detention Home Program," 1953 Yearbook, National Probation and Parole Association, 150–154. — *Ed.*

[1] The words *child* and *children* throughout this paper refer to boys and girls under juvenile court age whatever jurisdictional limit is set by the statutes in the various states.

ments of officials in our more than three thousand jurisdictions make for a hodge-podge of practices from which consistent principles are not easily drawn. Based on the wide experience of the National Probation and Parole Association's consultants in studying intake practices in every state in the union, this paper is an attempt to present the major problems of intake control and to recommend a practical program.

Detention is the temporary care of boys and girls, usually delinquent, who are under juvenile court jurisdiction and require secure care in a physically restricted facility pending investigation and disposition by the court. It should not be confused with shelter care, which is the temporary care of children, usually dependent or neglected, pending longer term foster care or return to their homes. Children under shelter care may or may not be held for the juvenile court. Detention care is exclusively a function of the juvenile court; shelter care is essentially a child welfare service administered not exclusively by the court but also by private agencies and other public welfare agencies in the community.

Satisfactory detention care requires a specially designed building and cannot be given by jails or jail-like facilities. On the other hand, shelter care purposes are best served by specially selected and subsidized foster family homes or institutions for temporary care, entirely separate from detention facilities.

At the point of detention, the child's relationship to organized society takes on a positive or a negative tone. Detention may intensify his resentment toward society, however cooperative he may appear to be on the surface. Or it may begin to change his attitude toward authority by helping him to come to terms with himself, to understand something of the nature of his underlying problem and thus to accept and profit by the probation or institutional treatment which lies ahead.

Far too little thought and planning have been given to court, probation, and detention intake practices. Limitations in staff and facilities are too often casually accepted instead of being made a public issue, one that merits precedence over the question of paved streets or public monuments. When the people of Seattle realized that the monkeys in their zoo received better care than the children in their juvenile court, they were willing to spend $2,500,000 for long-needed juvenile court and detention facilities. Unfortunately, it took a murder in the King County jail, the murder of a child by other youngsters, to set the wheels in motion.

After fifty years of operation, juvenile courts in all but a very few states are still using county jails and police lockups for the detention of children for periods ranging from a few hours to several months. In the whole state of Illinois, for example, there is only one detention home for the exclusive use of children requiring secure care pending court disposition, and even in the county where that lone facility is located the jail is still used extensively for children of juvenile court age.

Attempts have been made in a few communities to meet the problem by using temporary foster homes. But the special type of foster home required is hard to find, and in any case jail or jail-like facilities are still used for the more sophisticated youngsters, the very ones who need not repudiation of themselves and their problems, but the most skilled help available.

Other attempts to avoid the use of jails for children have resulted in the construction of lockup rooms with screened or barred windows. These lockups are located in a weird variety of facilities, including institutions for dependent and neglected children (often miscalled detention homes) and lockup rooms in courthouses, in hospitals, and even in homes for the aged. Such types of secure facility, it is true, make it unnecessary to rely on the adult jail, but they are to be condemned nevertheless as children's jails often medieval in character.

Recent studies of the detention of children in Michigan and other states have shown that even when juveniles are separated from adults, jails and jail-like detention and mass detention care make the hostile more hostile and the withdrawn more withdrawn, and actually push antisocial though treatable children beyond the reach of clinical treatment. Detention, as it exists throughout almost all of our country, plays a part in contributing to delinquency.

TYPES OF DETENTION HOMES

The legitimate detention home is a secure facility used exclusively for children with behavior problems who require secure care pending investigation and disposition by the court.

There are three general types of detention home, as follows:

1. The large city detention home which attempts to economize by herding groups of twenty, thirty, and even forty children under one supervisor. This is mass custodial care which can do little to help change the child's negative attitude toward authority.

2. The detention home which operates with small groups but offers custodial care only, leavened by a modicum of school and recreation activity.

Both of these types of detention home provide little more than storage, suspending the child's rehabilitation until the court makes its disposition. They stress conformity to routines and offer little toward understanding the child's problems.

3. The third type of detention home offers more than custodial care. Like the first two, it provides secure custody, but unlike them it offers to children full of anxieties and *tension* a staff and program which does a job of *detension*. In this home the process of rehabilitation begins when the child is detained. Sufficient staff is provided to assure a full school and recreation program and supervision in small groups. Personnel trained in casework help the child to understand his own problems, prepare diagnostic and prognostic information of value to the court, and provide in-service training to the staff.

This is the type of detention care recommended by the National Probation and Parole Association and a steadily increasing number of new detention-home buildings have been specially designed to make it possible. However, the great majority of detention homes, including many of the new ones, are still of the "custody only" type, and the county jail still serves as the only place of detention for most juvenile courts.

EXISTING INTAKE PRACTICES

Detention intake has to do with the use or misuse of detention facilities by police, probation officers, and courts. Children have been detained overnight and over weekends merely because the court office was closed and no one was authorized to release them. Others have been held for weeks and even months when secure custody was unnecessary in the first place. Often detention is used merely because it is a convenience to the police or the probation officer. In some counties police commonly detain and release children without even referring them to the court.

Perhaps the most startling proof of the need for standards in controlling detention admissions is the wide discrepancy in practice from court to court. Two juvenile courts may give you identical reasons for detaining children in the same type of facility — for example, "They might run away or commit further offenses" — yet one allows its law enforcement officers to detain nearly every child referred to the probation department, while the other will seldom admit to the detention facility more than 10 per cent of the children referred. The cause of this discrepancy appears to be variations in customary procedure in different jurisdictions rather than honest differences of opinion about well-defined professional standards or goals.

WHO SHOULD BE DETAINED?

Good standards of intake would take the emphasis off detention itself and place it on more intensive casework to the child and his parents in his own home, pending court disposition. Roughly three groups of children are referred to the court or to the probation department:

1. Children whose offenses *and* problems are so serious or whose parental relationships are so strained that they would be almost certain to run away or commit other offenses prior to court disposition, *even if intensive supervision were provided by a probation officer.*

2. Children whose offenses *and* problems are of such a nature that repeated offenses or running away from their own homes prior to court disposition *could be avoided by intensive supervision by a probation officer.*

3. Children whose offenses and problems appear to be of such a minor nature that *even without special supervision by a probation officer they would be unlikely to run away or commit further offenses pending court disposition.*

As a guide to detention intake, this grouping is different from and more valid than the policies generally followed. Needless to say, its effectiveness for classification depends on the casework skill and judgment of the probation officer at intake. It emphasizes the importance of beginning the casework process almost immediately after the child's apprehension.

Children placed into Group 1 after intake information is secured and interviews are held are relatively few in number. This is the group definitely in need of detention. Included in this group would be children held for other jurisdictions who could not be detained except in a secure facility.[2]

Children who fall into Group 2 do not need detention but are generally found in detention homes because the probation department is not sufficiently well staffed to provide intensive supervision prior to the hearing while the youngsters remain at home. The one or two interviews which a probation officer usually holds with a child during the pre-hearing period are primarily concerned with gathering facts for the social investigation; little intensive case-work is possible during these interviews.

Children in Group 3 should never be held in a detention facility. Although it is not likely that these youngsters will commit other offenses, many of them ought to be under supervision during the pre-disposition period. Where temporary care is called for because of physical or moral conditions in the home, or where relationships between child and parent are strained, a subsidized foster home or other place of shelter care should be used. Similarly, children held as material witnesses or who need protection from adults should be placed, if at all possible, in a temporary foster home or other shelter facility; they should not be subjected to confinement with disturbed delinquent children. One large city court has successfully placed such children in foster homes outside the county.

Should children be detained for purposes of observation and study? Certainly every child in Group 1 is in need of short term clinical observation and study for the simple reason that he has problems serious enough to place him in this group. Clinical observation and study are most effective when the detention home

---

[2] The holding of out-of-county children is not a simple problem. One solution is to hold the child in detention until it is known whether or not he is wanted by his local juvenile court and to remove him later to a shelter facility if delay in returning him appears likely. This procedure guarantees inter-court responsibility and avoids holding a youngster in a secure detention facility for long periods with sophisticated delinquents when his only offense may have been to run away from intolerable home conditions.

offers a full school, recreation, and case work program, and authorities must be alert to prevent such a detention facility from becoming a dumping ground for children in need of residential clinical study. The study function of a detention home must be necessarily limited in both scope and intake by the detention function. Residential clinical study for children who do *not* require secure custody should be provided by a study home under the direction of a child guidance clinic. Where, for lack of proper facilities in the community, the detention home is forced to serve other than legitimate detention purposes, this fact should be recognized and brought to public attention. Failure to do so in the past has given detention homes their reputation as dumping grounds for children.

COURT RESPONSIBILITY FOR INTAKE

The court's failure to assume full responsibility for detention intake has resulted in dual control: (*a*) by the law enforcement agency which places the child in detention following apprehension for delinquency; (*b*) by the court or probation department which at a later time either releases the child or authorizes his continued detention. One result of this practice is that some children have been detained who might better have been left in their own homes to begin with.

The typical picture of children held overnight and over holidays and week ends by the police and then released by the court or probation officer is a hangover from adult procedure; it is not in keeping with good juvenile court law and good juvenile court practice. While this short detention experience may not appear to harm some youngsters, it gives others, even in one of the better detention homes, the very delinquency status they crave and helps them to identify themselves with the more sophisticated. A boy with a dangerously short temper who had spent one night in a jail told his teacher later that he wouldn't repeat *all* he had learned there but that he did learn five easy ways to kill a man.

Unnecessary overnight and week-end detention is in large part caused by the interval between the relinquishing of police authority and the assumption of juvenile court jurisdiction. Faulty intake procedures and insufficient probation staff coverage are responsible for this gap. According to the current Standard Juvenile Court Act the court assumes jurisdiction at the time a child is taken into custody and the right of police to take him into custody is subject to juvenile court control. To close the gap between police and court jurisdiction and to achieve a more closely coordinated policy, it is necessary to provide convincingly effective probation service during the entire pre-disposition period, beginning at the earliest possible moment after the child's apprehension by the police.

When there is a juvenile or youth bureau in the city police or sheriff's department which handles not just minor cases but *all* offenses in which children are involved, it is possible to secure uniform procedures with children and more effective cooperation with the court. The child ought to be handled consistently throughout his experience with police, court, and detention home and not be passed around to agencies which disagree on the proper ways of handling children and selecting those who should be detained.

In one state the right of the police to hold children in custody for forty-eight hours before referral to the court has even been written into the statutes, with another twenty-four hours allowed before the court is required to act on the petition. With week ends and holidays intervening, five or more days may elapse before a child is released from detention. With different handling, he might have been released immediately. Thus two jurisdictions are set up. When the child is held in the detention facility operated by the court an incongruous situation arises in which the court has notice of referral by virtue of the child's presence in the detention facility but, having received no petition, does not act for fear of straining its relationship with the police agency.

In certain serious offenses it may be necessary for law enforcement officers to hold a child in order to make possible the apprehension of others involved with him, but such circumstances are not as frequent as some police practice would indicate. When they do occur, a cooperative working relationship between court and law enforcement agencies will guarantee the wise use of detention without violating the rights of the child.

The problem of detention control involves more than keeping admissions to a minimum.

Law enforcement authorities have a right to be disturbed when a child they have apprehended with some difficulty is released by the court and immediately commits another offense. To release a child pending hearing without coming to an understanding with him and his parents, and without some supervision or control by the probation officer, is as dangerous and stupid as detaining him unnecessarily. Leniency is easily misunderstood, and the child who has already lost respect for his parents is quick to carry over his disrespect to the court and to society and to show it by committing further offenses. Neither detention nor release without supervision should be used to close the gap between police and court functioning.[3]

The police, and the complainant, too, have a right to assurance that something constructive is being done by the court's probation department and that the child is not released to pursue his own ways without concern on the part of the court until the day of the hearing.

There are four typical methods of controlling court and detention intake. In all of these the only authority for removing a child from his home comes from the juvenile court even though the court may delegate that authority to its probation staff or other officials subject to the court's review.

TYPICAL INTAKE CONTROL PRACTICES

1. Control by the court clerk. When the court clerk handles detention admissions the decision to detain is often made on the basis of the offense alone and the child himself is not even seen. It is common practice for court clerks to leave in detention any child placed there by the police unless their parents come around to the court to try to get them out. This procedure, which we may call detention by default, is unsound for two reasons: first, because many parents assume they can do little about releasing a detained child until they hear from the court; second, because detention should be determined not by parental assent but by the likelihood (as gauged in intake interviews) that the child would evade the court's jurisdiction if allowed to return home. The

---

[3] Except in the case of children who fall into Group 3 of those referred to the court, and even a number of these may require pre-hearing supervision.

court clerk is not the proper person to control court and detention intake.

2. Control by preliminary hearing at a stated hour. The preliminary hearing conducted by the judge or referee at a stated hour each court day is another method for control of court and detention intake which is open to question when used without benefit of previous case work. Some juvenile courts with a narrowly legalistic view go so far as to consider it necessary to adjudicate the youngster or to hold a hearing in order to assume jurisdiction, before allowing the probation department to make a social investigation or do any casework. However, most courts consider it better to delegate the preliminary decision — to detain or not to detain — to a probation officer at intake, reasoning that this decision should rest on factors other than the child's offense, factors which may not be brought out in an initial interview before the judge or referee. They hold that subjecting the child to a preliminary hearing is unnecessary and may impair the values gained from building a case work relationship between the probation officer and the child and his family. Where parents request a hearing or when the probation officer considers that the appearance of the child before the judge could be especially helpful to the child and his parents, the casework and preliminary hearing method of intake is combined. However, the right to a preliminary hearing should always be made clear whether or not the child is detained and the judge should review all the reasons given for the detention of a child before signing the detaining order.[4]

One of the principal weaknesses of the preliminary hearing as the sole method of detention intake control is the fact that it usually occurs at a set hour each day. Thus the child apprehended just after the hearing period must be held in detention almost twenty-four hours before the court decides whether or not he should be released. NPPA studies have shown that most of the children so held could have been released immediately if intake and casework were initiated at the time they were taken into custody.

Frequently children are released from preliminary hearings and left free to pursue their delinquent behavior patterns without a clear understanding with them or their parents of exactly what is expected of them, including their responsibility to appear for a follow-up interview at a definite time within the next twenty-four hours. If the decision to detain a child is made at a preliminary hearing, a busy court has little time to brief the youngster, to help him understand and accept his forthcoming experience. Combining the judicial and casework functions of a court in a single preliminary hearing is not a good method of deciding whether or not a child should be detained.

3. Control by probation officers on all-day call in smaller communities. In smaller communities court and detention intake control by the chief probation officer on twenty-four hour call can effectively reduce the police use of detention after court office hours.[5] Where the court insists that police secure authorization for detention through the probation staff, the number of children unnecessarily detained becomes negligible, and the child receives what should be his right (comparable to the right of adults to bail) — immediate case work services from the court.

4. Control by intake divisions in larger courts. In a large court the probation department has an intake division which accepts children into the court's caseload or refers them to individuals and agencies in the community. A recent study of nine courts showed that all of them placed their most skilled workers in intake. In Wilmington, Delaware, for example, the minimum qualification for work in the intake division is a master's degree in social work; in addition, the supervisor must have had at least eight years of experience, including three years in supervision. An intake division makes it possible for children and their parents to be seen immediately, thus relieving them of anx-

---

[4] In avoiding criminal procedures for children, juvenile court law also by-passes the usual legal safeguards to individual rights. To compensate for this, the court must have adequate staff, trained in the best known methods of handling children with behavior problems. Children are robbed of their rights by the breadth of the juvenile court law if such staff is not available. It is a much overlooked fact that, without this safeguard, growing youngsters may be adversely affected by their police–detention–court experience.

[5] This is the method employed in Connecticut, which has a state juvenile court system and regional detention homes. There, for over ten years, no child under juvenile court jurisdiction has been held in a jail.

iety and uncertainty about what is going to happen and enabling them to use the court constructively.

INTAKE PROCEDURES

In jurisdictions with good court and detention intake practice, police bring children to the intake office of the probation department during the day, rather than detaining them first and then referring them to the court or probation department. But most referrals for detention occur at night when probation or court offices are closed. To offset the unnecessary detentions which occur at this time a number of probation departments, including those in Philadelphia, Cincinnati, and Houston, have extended their service to provide for sixteen continuous hours of court and detention intake control. Assigning one or more probation officers to duty after regular hours, these communities have reduced detention and have improved relationships with law enforcement agencies. If extended intake service is not provided beyond the usual court office hours by either an intake staff or an "on call" arrangement, it is all the more important to arrange periodic meetings with police agencies for the re-examination of detention intake policy.

Before the interview at intake, probation records should be checked not only for previous court appearances but for the latest available social information about the child and his family; the social service exchange should be reached by telephone and any agency active with the family should be called for whatever information it has about his current and past problems. Only after these preliminaries have been taken care of does the intake interview begin.

This kind of job cannot be done effectively at preliminary hearings because a number of separate as well as group interviews may be needed. Insight into the causes for commission of the offense is more important to the court than the details of the offense itself. Most important are the parents' attitude toward the child and the attitude of the child toward the offense, the school, and his general home situation. These must be considered before making the decision to detain, but they must also be evaluated in terms of the tensions created by the court referral. Will the parents and the child accept the temporary supervision

of the court if he is allowed to return home? If he returns home will he take up again with his former companions, will he keep late hours, will he truant from school? Will the parents as well as the child check with intake on these matters until the regular probation officer is assigned for social investigation?

As questions of this type are pursued, a situation which at first appeared to call for detention may turn out to be worth a calculated risk in release. It is unrealistic to expect 100 per cent cooperation from parents interviewed at intake and illogical to detain the child when they fail to show it. Attitudes of hostility and resentment on the part of some parents and children can often be changed by skilled workers to a desire to cooperate. On the one hand, with the reality of possible detention hanging over the youngster, requirements of school attendance, early hours, and frequent reporting take on an "either–or" aspect. On the other hand, the probation officer has an opportunity to build up a positive relationship to parent and child, helping them face the reality of the situation, offsetting tension-producing "blaming attitudes," and working out an immediate plan for living in lieu of detention. Most parents can be won over by a probation officer who has the time to prove his real concern and belief in the people with whom he is dealing.

Many courts incorrectly make a final decision to detain or not to detain, pending court disposition, on first interviews. Yet the behavior of the child, his relationship to his parents, and other factors may change during the pre-hearing period. When detention is used as part of the casework process its flexible use during the predisposition period can be effective. However, in removing a child from detention or allowing him to remain, the detention personnel should be consulted about the effect of the detention experience on him.

The decision to detain should be made only when the intake worker is convinced that the child is so beyond control that parents or guardians, even with the help of a caseworker, are unlikely to control behavior menacing to himself or the community. The court should review the reasons for detention and sign a court order within twenty-four hours.

So important is intake considered by the juvenile court at Indianapolis that the chief probation officer says that the four intake workers there "have as much time to devote to each matter called to their attention as the intake workers of any private agency in the state of Indiana. Each of the workers seldom has more than four cases a day and the average daily load is slightly under four."

A well-staffed intake department, through careful referrals to other agencies and skillful adjustment of those cases that do not require court attention, can pay for itself many times over. In Buffalo (Erie County), New York, three caseworkers are employed by the court to control detention intake. Whether or not the child is detained they are responsible for his whereabouts from the moment he is referred by the police to the final disposition by the court. A close working relationship between the detention and probation caseworkers strengthens the rehabilitative values inherent in the pre-disposition period. Only 17 per cent of the children apprehended by the police are detained.

LENGTH OF STAY

Length of stay in detention facilities should depend on the type of services offered by the detention home and the court. If the court staff is not equipped to make a thorough social investigation or if the detention facility is a jail or consists of lockup rooms in an "open" shelter, or if the staff and program are inadequate so that custodial care only is offered, then the rule is, "The shorter the detention, the better" — not more than three days, if possible.

Where the court staff is equipped to make thorough social investigations, where the facility is up to standard, where intake is well controlled so there are few overnight or week-end stays, and where the children are held in small groups and the staff and program of the detention home are adequate — even under these good conditions the average length of stay should seldom exceed ten days.

Extended lengths of stay (not exceeding four weeks) are recommended only in cases of children requiring short-term clinical study and observation during the detention period, provided only that the home has a full school and recreation program and is adequately staffed.

Of course there are always exceptional cases where modification of these criteria is justified. In any event, intake should be so controlled as to provide lengths of stays appropriate to the type of detention and probation service offered.

TWELVE GOALS FOR DETENTION INTAKE

In summary, twelve goals are recommended to achieve the proper use of detention and to offset our national lockup complex.

1. See that detention facilities are entirely separate from shelter facilities for dependent and neglected children and those delinquent children who must be removed from their homes but do not require secure care.

2. Except in extreme emergencies avoid the use of detention altogether when the detention facility offers only physical care or mass custody.

3. Abolish jail detention for children by developing state-operated regional detention homes for the use of counties which have too few children to detain to justify construction of their own specially designed buildings. Unless this is done, legislation forbidding the use of jails for detention of children is meaningless.

4. Change the custodial-type, "child storage" detention home to the kind that meets individual needs and provides professional information to the court about the child's potentialities and problems.

5. Encourage the development of a youth bureau in the city police department and the sheriff's office, to handle *all* police work with children and to effect closer coordination between the court and police so that methods of handling children and detaining children will be consistent.

6. Amend legislation where necessary to assure that the court assumes jurisdiction at the time a child is taken into custody and thus controls detention before, not after, he is detained by the police.*

---

* A recent letter to the Editor from Mr. Norman states that at the time his article was published, the statement here under goal number 6 conformed with the Standard Juvenile Court Act. Now the Standard Act Committee has approved a change in the wording so that goal number 6 would be more up-to-date if it read as follows: "Amend legislation where necessary to assure that the court assumes jurisdiction at the time a child is brought to a place of detention designated by the court; that full information as to the reason for detaining the child accompanies him and that policies and procedures be established by the court to screen children for detention when possible before they are detained." — *Ed.*

7. Arrange for law enforcement officers to bring children directly to the probation department when intake workers are on duty rather than to the detention facility, unless unusual circumstances warrant immediate detention and authorization for it is obtained from the probation department.

8. In smaller jurisdictions place responsibility for court and detention intake in the hands of the best probation officer and arrange for him to be on call to authorize all detentions by law enforcement agencies after court office hours. In large jurisdictions provide an intake staff and extend its service to at least sixteen hours. Hold regular conferences between probation and law enforcement agencies, and develop clearly understood written policies and procedures for court referral and for the detention of children after office hours when no probation intake worker is available.

9. After securing as full information as possible beyond the nature of the offense, determine detention or release, pending court disposition, with emphasis on the relationship of the child to his parents or those closest to him, his probable response to intensive supervision, and the likelihood of his running away or committing further offenses if he is returned to his home.

10. Assure the complainant that action is being taken and take advantage of the opportunity to explain to him the philosophy and function of the juvenile court.

11. In addition to conducting interviews for the social investigation, maintain frequent contact with all children pending court disposition and supervise those released in the custody of their parents.

12. Regardless of any hostility or resentment which may be displayed by the child or his parents, give them convincing evidence of the court's desire to understand and to help solve the problems underlying the child's antisocial behavior.

Let's get over the defeatist attitude that detention is a necessary evil. It's an *unnecessary* evil — an evil that can be corrected by properly controlling court intake, by improving the type of detention care offered, and, in most instances, by drastically reducing detention intake.

110

A Court Psychiatrist's View of Juvenile Delinquents *

Karl Birnbaum

Major problems in the handling of juvenile offenders in court are presented by cases that are not psychotic but plainly pathologic; they are diagnostically labeled mental defectives, defective delinquents, constitutional psychopaths, or sexual psychopaths.

The difficulties in these cases cannot be ascribed simply to the undeniable fact that the medicopsychiatric approach to the delinquent essentially differs from the legal and juridical one; for the practical work done in and by the juvenile court has sufficiently proved that these seemingly incompatible points of view can be very well reconciled in the best interest of both the child and the community.

The difficulties have to be sought rather in the nature of these pathological types themselves. Yet that does not at all mean that the factors which are of importance in understanding and appraising the average young offender can here be discarded. On the contrary, it is just the combination of the pathological and the "natural" factors that makes the picture of these pathological juveniles more complex and its interpretation more complicated. It therefore seems not superfluous to point here in advance to those two cardinal determinants which are found in every structural analysis of youthful delinquents: the immature mind from within and the environment influences from without.

The mental immaturity, or more specifically the immaturity of the personality, has to be considered a constant central element in each group of these pathological juveniles. The specific features of an incompletely integrated and organized personality structure may somewhat vary in the diverse phases of childhood, puberty, and adolescence; but unless the juvenile

* Reprinted from 261 *Annals* (1949), 53–63. Used by permission of the publisher.

is controlled and guided, his emotional instability, the lack of inner balance and self-control are sufficient to make him more or less unfit to find his way in a social world shaped by and adapted to the mentality of the adult.

Less easy to assess in pathological youth is the influence of the external factors such as commonly presented in the textbooks of criminology under the heading of economic, social, and cultural causes of delinquency. What difficulties may result in specific cases can easily be deduced from a single statement of a noted expert in this field: Cyril Burt lists more than 170 distinct conditions as adverse causes which may contribute to juvenile delinquency.

Individual Analysis

Even without further details, it then appears obvious that merely to offer a diagnostic label is not enough for the clarification of a pathological juvenile case. But to add simply a schematic enumeration of all the external factors involved would not suffice, either. Rather, a systematic, discriminating analysis of every individual picture is indispensable. It must not only show the special significance, position, and role which the various dynamic forces have in the complex interplay of factors, but also explain how these agents operate in the particular psychological configuration and sequence that finally lead to delinquent behavior and personality patterns.

This analytic procedure will thus clear up the points that matter most in pathological as well as in normal cases, namely, what the delinquency means to the young offender himself and what aims it serves in the dynamics of his inner life. In particular, it will become apparent what sort of personal needs and desires he seeks to satisfy by his delinquent acts, what obstacles or dangers he tries to escape, what inner or outer conflicts he strives to overcome, what frustrations or deprivations he attempts to compensate. All this together — but not the diagnosis alone — tells us what kind of offender the pathological youth really is, what we have to expect of him in the future, and what points of attack he offers to break down his antisocial propensities and build up a socialized personality.

Thus, indeed, a very worth-while task is set before the court psychiatrist. The trouble is that there are no ready patterns to be applied in every case, that every individual has psycho-logical dynamics of his own, and — what is worse — that for a full insight into these psychodynamic mechanisms and processes one is dependent on a branch of scientific psychology that only in the last decades has made the necessary inroads into long-neglected sectors of psychic life. All these general drawbacks play a part in the problems of the special types here to be dealt with.

The Mental Defective

The mental defective, in spite of his frequent appearance in court, is not too troublesome an object so long as one has to do with outspoken cases of lower and lowest grade. Idiots and imbeciles, for instance, can in most cases easily be disposed of by placing all the emphasis on the intellectual defect as a criterion that is readily discernible, fairly measurable, and capable of standardization. With the I. Q. at hand, giving general directions for proper handling, no further difficulties might come up except that a rigid admission policy of institutions, based too exclusively on fixed upper and lower limits of the I. Q., tends to cause placement difficulties.

The matter is different in cases in which the intellectual defect is not sufficiently marked to dominate the psychological picture and to explain the delinquent behavior. The figure of these mental defectives of borderline or slightly subnormal level would appear in a false perspective if seen in terms of intellectual deficiency to the exclusion of any other aspects. In these cases the fundamental fact has to be borne in mind that the arrested mental development which underlies the pathological condition is affecting all sectors of psychic life and thus entails temperament, emotions, will, and drives no less than memory, comprehension, judgment, and so forth. From this angle, the person with merely slight intellectual defect may be considered, as it were, a pathological variant of psychic immaturity, and, as such, requires focusing the attention on its particular character make-up.

In simple cases with a primitive personality, one may do sufficient justice to the mental defective by limiting the characteristics to a few basic elementary traits such as energetic or unenergetic, active or passive, steady or unstable, impressionable or irresponsive, and the like. But other cases of greater forensic significance resist such a simplification of the character picture. Apart from the general fact (to be elaborated in a later context) that every character, normal as well as pathologic, respresents a complex psychological structure with traits of diverse origin, it is the inevitable and hardly dissoluble combination of the natural, transient, mental traits of the developmental period and the persistent trends of pathological immaturity that confounds the picture of the mentally defective juvenile and easily misleads the examiner. With the normal traits of adolescence superimposed on and exaggerating those of the defective personality, the aspect of the delinquent youth may appear more serious and somber than the facts warrant. This erroneous view can sometimes be corrected only after many years of slow maturing, when the surprising part which the physiological immaturity had in the former delinquency picture ultimately becomes apparent.

THE DEFECTIVE DELINQUENT

In the center of forensic interest are, of course, those mental defectives who are characteristically named defective delinquents. They are singled out by law as particularly antisocial individuals who need confinement and training in specific institutions.

The question of what constitutes a defective delinquent has been and still is controversial, not merely because judges, psychiatrists, psychologists, and staff members of training schools look at him from different angles, but also because his nature itself is dubious. Certain it is (a merely negative statement) that the defective delinquent is not simply a defective who is delinquent or a delinquent who is mentally defective. But what are his positive criteria?

If one surveys the greater number of the inmates of institutions for defective delinquents as they appear in court before commitment or after discharge, one cannot find a uniform, clear-cut type. They vary not only in their intellectual equipment but even in those attributes which appear more relevant to the concept of the defective delinquent. Among them are first offenders as well as recidivists; individuals with a short or a long history of delinquency; active, aggressive types, and merely undisciplined, weak characters; boys whose delinquent inclinations seem to come directly from innate

personal qualities, and others whose antisocial tendencies mainly reflect acquired habits. What might here stand out as common traits — a defective mentality and an inferior personality as manifested in all kinds of social maladjustment to family, school, and community life — might at best suffice for a descriptive characterization but not for the recognition of a specific pathological type.

Now, no doubt the defective delinquent is not a genuine, scientifically well-established type, but a psychiatric–legal term; therefore one had better derive his specific properties from the underlying legal concept.

Taking as basis the Pennsylvania law and especially the respective articles of its Mental Health Act of July 11, 1923, we find as fundamental statements (a) that the defective delinquent is a mental defective but not insane and (b) that he has criminal tendencies.*

Criminal Tendency. Starting with the latter, more problematic, characteristic, the criminal tendency is explained as "the tendency to repeat offenses against the law or to perpetrate new ones as shown by repeated conviction — a tendency to habitual delinquency." According to this definition the diagnosis of a defective delinquent could and should be made only in cases of repeated offenses and convictions.

This, certainly, is for all practical purposes a very helpful suggestion, but can the court psychiatrist always strictly follow it? It would, for example, contradict the concept of a genuine criminal tendency if he ascribes this attribute to those emotionally disturbed children who, frustrated in the home in their natural desire for affection, belonging, or emotional security, time and again relapse into delinquent behavior. On the other hand, the examiner would probably not hesitate to recognize such a criminal tendency in a first offender if the picture of the delinquent youth or the delinquent act itself showed a marked preponderance of such specific "criminogenic" traits as aggressive drives, explosive temperament, coldness of feeling, and the like.

---

* For the serious legal and other practical difficulties which inadequate statutory definition of the concept of "defective delinquent" raises, see E. A. Gordon, and L. Harris, "An Investigation and Critique of the Defective Delinquent Statute in Massachusetts," 30 *Boston Univ. L. Rev.* (1950), 459–501. — *Ed.*

Of special importance in juvenile cases is another question: Should a true criminal tendency be attributed only to active, aggressive, antisocial individuals, inclined to serious crimes against person and property, or also to the more asocial–parasitic types — the shiftless, passive, weak-willed, habitual delinquents with their minor offenses of vagrancy, begging, petty larceny, and so forth? The present general practice in juvenile courts seems to be to consider both groups as suitable for training in an institution for defective delinquents, and, indeed, both types are to be found there, with the active antisocial type somewhat prevailing. One can admit in the first place that the active juveniles with inherent readiness for aggressive crimes require the specific training in this kind of institution, but that is no reason to exclude the others, whose weakness of moral resistance, of will and character, equally needs such disciplinary treatment.

Mental Deficiency. The other criterion of the defective delinquent, mental deficiency, gives occasion for special contemplations. The law demands as basis for the diagnosis the presence of both intellectual defect and criminal tendency; it does not require that an inner connection between both factors exist or be proved. As a matter of fact, mental deficiency is not inseparably connected with criminal propensities, nor is there any unequivocal correspondence between the grade of the mental defect and the seriousness of the delinquency. There are low-grade feeble-minded persons without any antisocial inclinations, and conversely there are persons who show a very moderate intellectual deficiency but an outspoken readiness for criminal actions.

The latter group leads directly, without demarcation line, to the individuals with normal dull or low average intelligence who could make a fair social adjustment were it not for their inferior character qualities, which constantly get them into trouble. Cases of this type may also appear more or less suitable subjects for institutions for defective delinquents, but they are not acceptable, since their I. Q. is too high. (An I. Q. of 75 is usually the upper limit.)

This dilemma raises the question if, from a practical angle, it would not be better to broaden the definition of the defective delinquent to include every individual who, on account of defective intelligence, defective character, or both, shows inherent criminal tendencies. Such a wider concept would not only eliminate useless controversies in cases with questionable intellectual defect, but would have the greater merit of taking care of the psychopathic juveniles, who seem to be somewhat unsatisfactorily handled, although they notably contribute to habitual criminality.

THE CONSTITUTIONAL PSYCHOPATH *

The court psychiatrist is usually in a quandary when the question of the juvenile psychopath comes up. There are many cases which are suspected to belong to this pathological type because the personality of the young defendant or the offense itself appears uncommon, exceptional, or otherwise psychologically conspicuous. Yet there are relatively few cases in which the diagnosis can be verified beyond any doubt. That is not due simply to the controversial concept of the constitutional psychopath, though that often complicates the matter. At any rate, for practical purposes one can apply a fairly plain and workable definition which states:

1. The psychopath belongs to the borderline group midway between the normal and the psychotic person.

2. His cardinal characteristics are to be found not in the intellectual sphere but in the province of the personality, in anomalies of temperament, instinctual drives, emotions, will, and character.

3. These abnormal traits are constitutional; that is, innate and (probably) hereditary.

But even with such a simplified concept at hand, one is not relieved of all difficulties in the individual case.

Personality Traits. First of all, looking at the personality picture, one finds not the innate traits in their original form and isolated from others, but complex psychological structures in which those constitutional, primary elements are combined and even amalgamated with secondary, acquired traits, or are presented in the special shape which external influences of the

---

* For a commendable scholarly attempt to clarify this concept, see W. and J. McCord, *Psychopathy and Delinquency*, New York, Grune & Stratton, 1956. — *Ed.*

life history have given them. Even in juveniles, with their character development still unfinished, it is not easy to discriminate between innate abnormal endowment and later reaction formations due to experiences during the formative years.

Apart from that, the external appearance itself as reproduced in the descriptive picture of the case does not aid as much as one might expect in ascertaining the diagnosis. The so-called psychopathic traits of character differ from the normal ones in degree and not in kind, and there is no way of exactly measuring whether a trait is within or without the limits of normalcy. From a practical standpoint, that means that, in general, personality traits, even if suggestive of psychopathic nature, give no absolutely reliable and cogent criteria.

This holds true especially in juvenile cases. There is, for instance, such a resemblance between specific psychopathic and typical adolescent traits that such findings as emotional imbalance, lack of self-control, or dominance of primitive impulses lead diagnostically to no useful result. Augmenting the difficulties, even the differences in degree become irrelevant, since some youngsters show the natural traits of juvenile immaturity in an exaggerated form without any indications of an underlying psychopathic constitution to account for it.

This similarity between psychopathic and juvenile traits is not surprising, since the psychopathic personality, after all, is likely to be a special pathological form of psychic immaturity, the outcome of a moderate developmental disturbance which affects not so much the basic intellectual elements of the mind but rather the subtler structure of the character. Be that as it may, in these dubious cases the court psychiatrist is faced with an alternative not to be disregarded, since the proper handling depends very much on whether transient traits of the adolescent period or permanent trends of a psychopathic constitution are involved.

Social Criteria. Admitting that the character traits in general are not specific enough to serve as criteria of a psychopathic personality, we can hardly expect more from the so-called social criteria, that is, those asocial or antisocial trends which traditionally are interpreted as reflections, if not proof, of the innate "vicious" tendencies of a constitutional psychopathic inferior. The forensic psychiatric practice de-

mands greater reserve in this respect. Take for instance one of those impressive cases in which we find an unusual combination of outspoken antisocial trends, early manifested in childhood; intensified and enlarged in adolescent age, with constant relapses in spite of previous experiences and no proper response at all to corrective measures. There always is an open question whether the whole picture has factually a mere constitutional foundation or rather is in the main acquired, resulting from all those various criminogenic influences in home, family, and neighborhood to which children of the underprivileged classes are often exposed during formative years.

Moral Qualities. No less caution should be observed in interpreting the moral qualities of a juvenile and especially in attributing to him that innate total lack of any moral feelings that marks him at once as prototype of a psychopathic antisocial personality, a kind of "born criminal." Not only is the proof of the innate nature of this alleged absolute moral defect mostly inconclusive, but even its actual presence is often not sufficiently demonstrated. As a fact, it is hardly possible to verify beyond doubt the absence not only of the higher socio-ethical sentiments but of so elementary and basic human traits as natural sympathetic feelings towards others. What commonly passes as proof, namely, the appearance of aggressive, destructive, brutal, cruel behavior in children, may be adequately explained in terms of natural childish traits such as carelessness, unorganized or misled overactivity resulting in reckless actions, thoughtless experimenting motivated by curiosity, and the like.

The Offense. Similarly questionable is the attempt to use the offense itself and its psychological and other concomitants as cogent evidence of a psychopathic perpetrator. However grave, strange, perverse, repulsive, and opposed to all normal feelings the criminal act and the subsequent behavior may appear, there should not be any recourse to the label "psychopath" as diagnostic makeshift unless all other motivations and causes are excluded. Impulsive discharge of strong drives, explosive relief of pent-up emotional energies, excessive after effects of emotionally overcharged experiences, uncurbed reactions to frustrated passions, and similar uncommon psychological occurrences are absolutely compatible with normal charac-

THE JUVENILE COURT AND THE LAW

ter make-up, though not the rule. To be sure, the crux of the matter is that these particular dynamic forces and mechanisms often enough operate just within the framework of a psychopathic constitution; they have grave consequences because of the pathological reaction tendencies of the psychopath.

Deceptive Attitudes. Finally, as a last complication, it should not be overlooked that the juvenile offender, subsequently exposed to the legal consequences of his doings and the psychological atmosphere of the court, may present an external aspect that is far from reflecting the real personality, not to speak of the basic innate traits. This surface picture, dominated by the momentary psychological reactions to the whole situation, may easily deceive the examiner unless he is looking for what is behind it.

There are in the first place the various forms of self-defense and self-protection which, consciously or instinctively set in motion, may suggest psychopathic trends. A defiant, antagonistic, aggressive attitude may be mistaken as expression of psychopathic antisocial inclinations. Cold indifference without any signs of remorse, compassion, or other emotional responses may appear as pathological lack of any natural human feelings, while in fact it is due to a psychogenic stupor, a temporary blocking of emotional reactions and expressions.

Further contributing to the distortion of the external picture of the personality are the diverse kinds of deceptive behavior which are used — partly intentionally — partly instinctively — to meet the forensic situation. All these reaction forms — telling lies, play acting, and, if need be, malingering — are found especially in psychopathic cases; they do not make it easier to ascertain what kind of person is hidden behind the false façade.

Diagnostic Caution. All these pitfalls should warn the court psychiatrist against too hasty and generous labeling of a juvenile delinquent as a constitutional psychopathic inferior, thus stamping him as an unreformable moral defective, a prospective habitual criminal, a potential murderer, and what else this ominous diagnosis seems to imply. If this caution is not observed, it may happen that the subsequent development refutes both the somber diagnosis and prognosis. After the stormy course of the

critical adolescent period, the individual may have ultimately, though belatedly, reached a stability, a dependability, and a maturity which no longer fit the previous picture.

But there is no cogent practical reason to enforce a diagnosis in doubtful cases. Even with the diagnosis left undecided, full justice can be done to these juvenile offenders. An exhaustive analysis, neither overdrawing nor disregarding the pathological elements, simply presents the personality, as it is, with its positive and negative sides, its assets and liabilities, and thus furnishes all the material for a constructive handling of the individual case.

THE SEXUAL PSYCHOPATH

The juvenile sex offender poses problems of a special kind, requiring separate consideration. They are, of course, in the main related to the particularities of the juvenile psychosexuality. But even the position of the sexual factor in the sociocultural life plays a part. The present-day overconsciousness and overawareness of sex compels the court psychiatrist to be very critical of the information related to him as so-called sexual misbehavior of children. The tendency to overrate and misinterpret juvenile behavior, however harmless, in a sexual sense sometimes furnishes monstrous pictures of youngsters, depicted as sexually overprecocious, excessively oversexed, and affected with all sorts of sex perversions, especially with homosexuality and sadism.

Sexual Immaturity. At the examination of the defendant himself, difficulties immediately arise if one loses sight of the basic fact that juvenile sexuality has a psychology of its own which does not admit of measurement, evaluation, and judgment of its manifestations in a way that might be appropriate to the sex behavior of adults. What in the sex conduct of children appears unnatural, perverse, abnormal, or psychopathic, mostly finds its full explanation in the very nature of their sexual immaturity.

This is doubtless true of sex misbehavior of younger children where sex play of any kind directly reflects natural infantile traits such as sexual curiosity, imitation of grownups, playful experimenting, and so forth. It is equally true of the more significant sex activities of adolescent sex offenders, where the whole range of sex delinquency, from indecent exposure to molesting little girls to sodomy and violent attempts at rape, can be traced back to the characteristics of a typically immature psychosexuality.

What this immature sexuality means can be made clear in a few words: The sex drive is not yet fully differentiated and organized; it still lacks the distinctive trends of the mature sex instinct, since its connection with the natural biological objects and ends is not yet firmly established; and finally — most important — the sex impulse is not yet integrated in the total structure of the personality; and therefore is not properly balanced and controlled by the regulating forces of reason and socioethical sentiments.

Most of these cases concern accidental sex offenses in which the causal connections are apparent, and the psychological configuration at once reveals the nonpathological origin of the delinquent act and — by implication — the sexual normality of the juvenile delinquent. In other cases the picture seems more complicated, since relapses and persistence in the deviant sex behavior seem to indicate a more deep-seated and inherent propensity. Yet here too, one can ascertain without difficulty that a natural psychological process has led to natural results, namely, to some kind of sex habit. The juvenile, if and when frustrated in the adequate gratification of his sex needs, is looking for and indulging in substitute or compensatory forms of sexual satisfaction. A follow-up soon proves that no constitutional pathology is involved. With advancing maturity and suitable sex opportunities available, the false patterns of sex behavior are abandoned and replaced by more natural and socially acceptable ones.

Pathologic Constitution. The true problems begin when the suspicion of an underlying psychopathic constitution compels the examiner to answer the question whether or not an individual is a sex psychopath. That happens especially when the juvenile, instead of following the natural course just mentioned, and giving up the apparent sex habit, continues acting at this immature, infantile level and ultimately incorporates the perverse tendencies as an integral part in the structure of his personality. Though on the surface it looks as if merely

external factors — in particular influences of early life which have left a lasting impression on the forming of the sexual personality — do account for the situation, closer analysis reveals rather that the real cause of these fixed sex deviations lies in a pathologic sexual constitution. It incapacitates the individual to outgrow the infantile stage of psychosexuality and to develop mature forms of sex functioning.

This persistence of an immature — undifferentiated and unorganized — sexuality belongs to the cardinal characteristics of the sex psychopath. It furnishes the proper subsoil in which, precipitated by suitable sex stimuli, sex perversion thrives. Among the pathological sex offenders, this type of sex psychopath stands out for its practical importance. Its representatives are to be found especially among the exhibitionists, the homosexuals, the bisexuals, and the individuals with sex propensity towards children.

Reserve Needed. The greatest reserve must be used when juveniles are charged with homosexual offenses. To attribute to a young person, without further proof, innate homosexual inclinations and accordingly mark him as a constitutional sex psychopath would contradict not only our general knowledge of juvenile sexuality but also our special experiences in the juvenile court.

Some justification for such an assumption may exist in exceptional cases. They show signs of a deviating physical organization, a female or intersexual type of bodily build, endocrine physical abnormalities, and the like, which seem to indicate that the sex perversion is at least organically founded and part of a general constitutional psychophysical pathology. But even in these cases a more plausible explanation would be that a constitutionally infantile psychosexuality has obtained a homosexual shape by specific environmental influences of the formative years.

Needless to say, a juvenile must not be called a sex psychopath merely because he shows traits suggestive of a psychopathic character and because these character traits (such as emotional instability, over-impressionability, psychic imbalance) are essential determining factors in his sex delinquency. That a juvenile psychopath on account of his general character make-up commits or has the tendency to commit sex offenses does not make him a sex psychopath.

A last problem may come up in certain serious cases of juvenile sex offenders under the influence of sensational publicity and excited public opinion. Should the youth be considered a "criminal sexual psychopathic person" in the sense this term is used in some criminal codes (e.g. Michigan or Illinois)? This special type of sex offender — analogous to the defective delinquent — has been singled out for specific handling, to meet more effectively the menace of certain abnormal individuals who seem to have an inherent disposition and tendency to commit sex crimes.

The question is not whether such a specially defined medicolegal type should be in general recognized, but whether it is needed in dealing particularly with sex offenders of juvenile age. This can be answered in the negative, for various reasons. Contrary to the common opinion and the lasting impression made by every single case, grave sex offenders are relatively infrequent among juvenile delinquents, and the probability of relapses is, as follow-up studies show, surprisingly slight.

Apart from this, the special provisions for handling all kinds of delinquents are so ample in the juvenile court and the judicial dispositions so flexible that proper care can also be taken of more serious sex cases. They seem in part to be suitable subjects for institutions for defective delinquents. Yet it shall not be denied that these juvenile sex offenders generally need a more psychiatrically oriented treatment than that accorded them up to now.

The question of proper treatment — not only of the sex delinquent but of every juvenile delinquent individually — remains open. It includes so many far-reaching problems that it could scarcely be touched in the context of this short paper. No ready-made answers can be given in these cases which altogether ask for individual solution. But since better understanding of the individual leads to more efficient practice, this attempt at an analytical clarification of dubious cases may serve as one of the preliminary steps for a constructive treatment of juvenile offenders.*

---

* For the related problem of children who are the victims of incest, see C. Greenland, "Incest," 9 *Brit. J. Delinquency* (1958), 62–64. — *Ed.*

111

Use of the Rorschach Personality Test *

Fritz Schmidl

The Rorschach personality test, developed by the Swiss psychiatrist Dr. Hermann Rorschach, is designed to reveal the structure of a personality. The subject is shown ten cards with certain standardized inkblot pictures to which he is asked to respond. On each card is an inkblot. Five of the ten cards are black and grey with many different shadings; two are black with some red spots; three are multi-colored. The inkblots show such a great variety of form, shading, and color that they allow for an indefinite number and variety of responses.

The test procedure is as follows: The subject is asked to say what the cards make him think of, that is, to project his own meaning into the inkblots. The responses are scored and evaluated by means of an elaborate system. The content of the answers is never as important as the elements of form, such as "location" and "determinants." Location is the place on the card where the subject sees a particular answer. For instance, a person may respond to the whole inkblot on a card. Or he may interpret a large detail of one of the blotches. Or he may pick out very tiny parts and protrusions and give interpretation for these portions. Determinants are those qualities of the inkblot picture that the subject uses in order to arrive at a certain response. He may, for instance, use the outline form of a blotch for the answer "two animals" to one of the cards, or the red color of a portion of the same card for the response "fire," or a combination of

---

* Reprinted from 27 *Focus* (1948), 133–137. Used by permission of the author and the publisher. See, also, F. Schmidl, "The Rorschach Test in Juvenile Delinquency Research," 17 *Am. J. Orthopsychiatry* (1947), 151–160, and F. Schmidl, "Psychological and Psychiatric Concepts in Criminology," 37 *J. Crim. L. and Criminology* (1946), 37–48. — *Ed.*

form and color for "green caterpillars," or a combination of form and movement for the answer "two waiters lifting a pot." Some responses are called popular because they appear very frequently. Rare answers are scored as original.

Clinical experience and statistical experiments have shown that the Rorschach test, if properly used and interpreted, gives a reliable picture of a person's basic personality. Rorschach himself developed the test mainly as a tool for psychiatric diagnosis although he mentioned that it could be useful in any other field where we deal with problems of personality. For about twenty-five years since the test was first published, psychologists have expanded the use of the test to many areas outside of psychiatry proper.

The Rorschach test is an objective method; its administration does not leave room for any subjective view on the part of the testing person. Since the subject has no way of knowing in which way his responses will be interpreted, he is unable to influence the outcome through an effort to show himself in a good light. A few years ago Dr. Irving A. Fosberg, a psychologist, made an experiment to inquire into the reliability of the test. Two groups of psychology students who did not know the Rorschach but had considerable experience with other test methods, were asked to take the Rorschach test. One group was asked to do everything in order to color the result as favorably as possible, the other one to try to fake in such a way that the final picture would be unfavorable. After the administration of the test all subjects were asked to indicate the means and ways in which they had tried to manipulate the outcome. Interpretation of the tests and study of the attempted methods to fake showed that not one subject had been able to influence the outcome efficiently, a result which is not too puzzling when one considers the fact that the ten inkblots are new to the subject and completely senseless, whereas the interpreter of the test has a thorough knowledge of the blots and the way different individuals react to them.

Testing the Delinquent

In the field of juvenile delinquency the Rorschach test can be used for two purposes: a) It helps to understand the personality of the

individual delinquent and to establish a differential diagnosis on which plans for treatment can be based; b) it is an important tool for research on psychological types of delinquents and their classification.*

In our work with the individual delinquent, be it in a detention home, in court or in an institution, we base our diagnostic findings on a number of data such as the child's social and health history, knowledge of his delinquency and of the particular way in which it was committed, study of his environment, etc. In addition to this information we use our impression and experience with similar types of delinquents to arrive at a decision on disposition of the case and treatment. There are situations in which the experienced practitioner feels fairly safe in making a decision on the grounds of such knowledge. However, in not too rare instances there is some room for doubt and in most instances confirmation of impressions and clinical findings will be welcome. The Rorschach test can be used as an additional tool for diagnosis be it to solve questions still open after thorough social study or to confirm relatively well established diagnoses. Some authors have compared the Rorschach test method with the X-ray technique in medicine. Like the X-ray picture the Rorschach "psychogram" offers a kind of cross-sectional view of the structure of a personality.

Without an attempt to give a comprehensive presentation we shall point out some typical situations in the field of juvenile delinquency exploration where the Rorschach test is particularly helpful.

Frequently it is difficult to decide whether some deviating behavior is due to the pressure of an environmental situation such as living in a delinquency area, poverty, absence from home or death of a parent, or whether we have to deal with a deep-rooted personality disturbance. Yet such decision may be very important for the establishment of a specific treatment plan. The Rorschach test is not influenced to any significant degree by any kind of environmental pressure. It therefore is an outstanding instrument for differential diagnosis of severe personality disorder, eventually serious mental

---

* For an outstanding illustration of the value of the Rorschach test, see S., and E. T. Glueck, *Unraveling Juvenile Delinquency*, New York, The Commonwealth Fund, Harvard University Press, 1950, pp. 209–240, 262–264, 363–385. — *Ed.*

disease, as compared with behavior problems mainly based on reaction to adverse external conditions.

Dr. Richard L. Jenkins in his article "A Psychiatric View of Personality Structure in Children," [1] has made a valuable distinction between the "over-inhibited," and "unsocialized aggressive" and the "pseudosocial" child. He has shown that these different types of delinquent children require different treatment. The attempt to diagnose a delinquent child in terms of one or another of these classifications frequently meets with great difficulties, especially when the decision on a treatment plan has to be made within a limited period of time. Here is an important field for the use of the Rorschach test as a diagnostic aid.

INCIPIENT MENTAL DISEASE

In some instances delinquent behavior is produced by an incipient mental disease such as schizophrenia. As long as the pathological process has not progressed very far, clinical diagnosis can be extremely difficult, but the Rorschach test is likely to show definite signs. Rorschach has shown that sometimes the indications in the test of a beginning psychosis are more obvious and outstanding than in a later more acute phase. The following two examples will give some idea as to the way the Rorschach test can be utilized with delinquents:

Marion came to the attention of a juvenile court shortly before her sixteenth birthday. She had truanted from school and in several instances had stayed out of her home late at night without any explanation as to where she spent her time. She was the second of three children. Unfortunately for her, her older brother Sam, as well as her kid sister Helen, were not only model students in school but also conforming children of parents who believed in bringing up youngsters "to be seen but not heard." The school did not think that the girl presented too serious a problem. Although her marks had never been very good, she always had made the grade. She was an uninteresting, frequently rather sullen girl. The arts and crafts teacher had observed that Marion during the last year frequently had become strangely confused when she had to do very simple work whereas she had been able to cope with some much more difficult jobs. The

school knew that Marion was discouraged because she never could live up to the successes of her brother and her sister.

The probation officer who prepared the case for the court saw the problem as mainly an environmental one. It seemed fairly obvious that the ambition of the parents was as much poison for this child as the competition of two brilliant siblings. The decision to have Marion tested was chiefly due to an interest to determine the kind of training that would prove most advantageous. It was felt that Marion needed to find a field of activity in which she too could be successful.

The girl's Rorschach test was a surprise to everybody who worked on her case, including the psychologist who had been asked to concentrate on vocational guidance. Marion encountered quite unusual difficulties in her attempts to interpret the inkblots and became utterly confused when reacting to one of them in which other subjects frequently see content of a sexual nature. The psychologist finished his detailed report on the test findings with the following sentences: "This girl's difficulties may have to be interpreted as signs of a beginning psychotic process. No recommendations as to occupational choices can be made. Marion should be seen by a psychiatrist."

The psychiatrist, after a few interviews with the girl and her parents, made the diagnosis of incipient schizophrenia. He felt that the early diagnosis would prove a definite asset for treatment.

Whereas in Marion's case the Rorschach test revealed a serious mental disturbance in a child who mainly seemed to suffer from difficulties in her environment, the outcome of testing Dolores, a twelve year old girl, showed that concern over hereditary disease had been unfounded. Dolores was brought to court because of a suspicion of sex delinquency. She and her sister Emanuela had been left with their father after the mother had been committed to a mental hospital when Dolores was seven. Although the father did not show any specific symptoms, he seemed to be so inefficient and at times erratic that there were doubts as to his mental health. The children grew up in an atmosphere where practically everybody feared that they might become affected by mental disease. This of course made a healthy development of the two youngsters impossible. They were neglected and tried to find on the streets the satisfaction which they missed at home. No wonder their behavior came to deviate from what is considered normal.

Here however the Rorschach test showed that Dolores' personality was not disturbed in the sense of serious mental pathology. She seemed to be much more emotionally impoverished than sick. The test results suggested that a change of environment through placement in a secure home might undo at least a considerable part of the harm that had been done to the child.

---

[1] *Delinquency and the Community in Wartime,* Yearbook of the National Probation Association, 1943, p. 199–217.

Distinguishing Sex Cases

The advantageous use of the Rorschach test in cases of sex delinquency deserves to be mentioned with particular emphasis. We are inclined to think of a sex delinquent as an impulsive, uncontrolled, "oversexed" individual. However, psychiatric examination and use of the Rorschach test show that in a considerable number of instances sex delinquencies are committed by rather inhibited persons who suffer from inability to form meaningful personal relations. Such subjects sometimes enter sexual relationships not because they enjoy the gratification of their instincts but because they do not find any other ways of contact with people. Often they are not far from a psychotic condition. Some signs in the Rorschach test indicate clearly whether a sex delinquent belongs in the impulsive uncontrolled group or in that of the impoverished personality with brittle relationships to people. It is obvious that each of the two types requires different treatment.

Elizabeth, sixteen, a pretty girl of average intelligence, was a severe problem at home, in school, and in an institution where she was placed after her parents had given up hope of coping with her behavior. She had been brought up in an extremely religious home. She did not present any particular problems until at fourteen she suddenly seemed to run wild. She practically stopped attending school and associated with a more than questionable group of young people who indulged in all kinds of sex activities. She became promiscuous, went from one boy to another; neither disciplinary measures nor friendly discussion seemed to have any influence on her. She seemed to be altogether a victim of her instincts which she apparently was completely unable to control.

The Rorschach test showed that Elizabeth was not at all a sensual type. On the contrary, there was even a lack of those emotional faculties which makes sex enjoyable to the normal person. According to the test results the girl's main difficulty was an extremely poor ability to develop sound relationships to other people. The psychologist felt that the girl had become a sex delinquent because sexual relationships seemed to her the only relationships to other human beings she could attain. Furthermore, it was obvious from the test that Elizabeth was unable to function normally in sex relationships. A great but largely unconscious anxiety permeated her personality. Her sex delinquency did not at all follow a pattern of gaining pleasure; she seemed to be driven from one to the next sex affair without any real enjoyment in any of them.

On the basis of the test results, plus history and clinical findings, the psychiatrist decided that this girl, although not really psychotic in a technical sense, was extremely sick and that a mere attempt to educate her or punish her would not suffice. It was felt that ways and means had to be found to protect this girl against her own self-destructive tendencies.

Olga, a girl of seventeen, seemed to be much better controlled than Elizabeth. She also was brought to the attention of the court because of sex delinquency. But in contrast to Elizabeth, she behaved very well in a home where she stayed pending court action and her quite solicitous parents thought that she was basically a good girl who only had fallen victim to the influence of bad company.

Here the Rorschach test showed some elements which suggested very serious delinquency: a combination of strong impulsiveness with a deep-rooted habit to conceal not only her actions but also her thoughts and feelings and to present a façade of superficial adjustment. In Olga's case the psychiatrist made the diagnosis "psychopathic personality."

In some instances the Rorschach test offers insight into a subject's intelligence which is much deeper than that offered by the conventional intelligence tests. The latter are a good instrument for measuring intellectual function. The Rorschach test, although not giving a measure of intelligence like an IQ, can reveal not only the level of a person's intellectual function, but also that of his frequently unused intellectual capacities.

Robert, a twelve year old Negro boy, was committed to a private institution because of stealing and some other delinquencies. He was an unattractive boy and it seemed no wonder that the other boys teased him by calling him "monkey." He seemed to be of low intelligence, did a poor job in school, but was no discipline problem in the institution. He showed one strange peculiarity: whenever his group had to do an unpleasant job he volunteered to do it.

When the school psychologist, in the course of a research study, administered the Rorschach test to Robert, he immediately saw that the boy was basically considerably more intelligent than he seemed to be. He produced four "human movement" responses, something only found in the Rorschach records of intelligent subjects. Subsequent psychiatric study showed that Robert was a case of "pseudodebility" and that a strong self-punishing tendency prevented him from using his native abilities. He was given considerable attention and when the institution released him about one and a half years after he had been tested, the psychiatrist's report on him said that eventually he may become college material.

In research on juvenile delinquency the main

problem is that of classification of types. The fact that a youngster breaks the law is a sociological and legal one. Psychologically the difference between one automobile thief and another often may be much more significant than the difference between a delinquent and a conforming child. For decades the students of delinquency have availed themselves of the help of the psychiatrist in order to learn about the inner dynamics of delinquency. However, the cooperation of criminologist and psychiatrist has not always been completely satisfactory. The psychiatrist as a physician usually deals with "patients," i.e., people who suffer, whereas the practitioner in the field of treating delinquents deals with persons who make others suffer. It may be due to this difference in basic attitudes that so many problems still wait to be solved. It can be expected that the Rorschach test will render an invaluable service in helping to arrive at a meaningful classification of juvenile delinquents.

However, in theoretical as well as in practical work it will be advisable to use the Rorschach test not as the only means of diagnosis or classification, but to supplement its findings with results of clinical examination, social study and eventually of other tests.

112

The Court Hearing as Part of the Treatment Process *

Gustav L. Schramm

One warm sunny day, as I was walking along the riverfront and saw the sunlight on the waters, I looked up at the high walls of the building in which I was to speak. There were

* Reprinted from *Matching Scientific Advance with Human Progress*, National Council of Juvenile Court Judges Journal, presented at the Pittsburgh Conference, May 1–3, 1950, 12–15. Used by permission of the author and the publisher. See, also, P. W. Alexander, "Of Juvenile Court Justice and Judges," *Redirecting the Delinquent*, 1947 Yearbook N.P.-P.A. (1948), 187–205. — Ed.

bars on the windows, and the lights were glaring from inside. I wondered what I, as one person, could do to meet such a tremendous power for evil as was symbolized by the walls of a penitentiary. I walked up the steps and the doors were thrown open. Apparently I was eligible for admission to a penitentiary. As I walked in, a guard came rushing up to meet me and shook hands vigorously, saying, "My boy is doing all right now." It all personified itself to me as I thought that this father might have had to meet his own boy at the gate of the penitentiary if you and I, if all of us working together, if the community, had not been able to help that boy in time.

Talking Back to a Judge

I was escorted to the platform of a large auditorium and looked down upon hundreds of men, sitting around in all sorts of poses, apparently not particularly thrilled by the prospect before them. Having so much time on their hands, I presume they thought they might as well attend. I told them that I had been asked to speak to them on the place of a child in the home and in the community. I told them I thought such a title too general a one. I would rather talk to them about my job. I asked them to tell me then, from their experience, how I might do a better job to keep boys and girls from growing up and going to such a place as they were in. I told them this was one time at least when they could talk back to a judge and that it wouldn't hurt them a bit. I could see smiles flitting across their faces. Some had talked back to a judge, and it hadn't been a very happy occasion. They took me at my word. I had a rather vigorous time. Many were rather sour and disillusioned. Life had been harsh. Here I was asking for it, and they were quit willing to let me have it.

Quickly, however, they sensed my challenge and wanted to give me the benefit of their experience and their thinking, so that the younger generation, through me, might benefit. I was much impressed with the thought expressed by one after the other that if there had been one person, at least one person, interested in them as a human being, they might not be where they were. Of course, this probably is an exaggeration; yet we do not have enough facilities to meet the problems of all persons, nor do we know enough about human nature to sense the problems that each person may have. However, I am quite convinced that in the great majority of cases these men could have been saved from a life of crime by the right contact at the right time. We are largely what we are by reason of the contacts we have had with other people, bringing out what is within us. If we look back in our own lives, I am sure each one of us will remember a parent, a teacher, a friend, or perhaps several people, if we're fortunate enough, of whom we say, "That person meant something to me," perhaps more than that person himself realized. We in turn are influencing the lives of others, perhaps more than we realize. Human conduct is to a large extent determined by human contact.

All of us want to have a sense of belonging to people who really care. We want some recognition for what we may be able to do well; and all of us must learn to play the game according to the rules. It is especially important that children during their immature, impressionable years be able to find themselves in relationship to the world about them. It is in the relationship of one with another that these elementary factors in human life become real and meaningful. Therefore we in the court set-up are trying to put into effect in our contacts what is fundamental in all human relationships.

Many people do not think of a court except as something cold and impersonal and punitive. In a juvenile court we are particularly directed to consider the needs of the individual child and the welfare of the community. As a juvenile court we are not a criminal court for children. We are not a criminal court at all but instead we are authorized to act *"in loco parentis,"* somewhat like a court of equity, in individualizing those who come before us.

Removing the Blindfold

Another way of illustrating it would be by considering Justice blindfolded holding a scale, allowing the facts in the case to tip the balance. Thus Justice is no respecter of persons and there is no one above the law. That is our ideal of justice in our adult world. However, with children we know that they are still in the formative period of life and we are, therefore, in a juvenile court directed to remove the blindfold, to see the child and to take him by the hand, so to speak, and lead him to firmer ground.

In such a court the judge has an unique opportunity to personify the interest of the community in the child, to compliment him for his good deeds, however minor, and to encourage him to correct his defects so that he may get along better and merit our increased approval. In other words, we have a chance to accentuate the positive and to help to learn that rules are reasonable and suitable for all of us and that we must play the game accordingly.

How can we as judges put into practice these objectives? Of course, we must have preparation for our contact with the child. It is important that a staff be organized to bring to the attention of the judge all the available information he may need concerning a child's family, his physical and mental condition, his school adjustment, his religious and community contacts — anything and everything that will distinguish him as a person. I like to receive the reports of the officer at least a day in advance of the hearing so that I may, the evening before, read over the reports calmly and thoughtfully without the pressure of time and people and consider what is basically the problem with this youngster.

The first time I asked for these reports, shortly after my induction into office, members of the staff in their tactful way attempted to point out to me how busy they were and how difficult it was to get the papers and reports ready in time for the hearing. I agreed with them but indicated that I was still anxious to have them before the hearing; and if necessary, we would postpone the hearing a day. They realized that I was serious about it, and we have had the reports accordingly on schedule. They have meant much to me in giving meaning to my contacts rather than going through a mere form with a lot of generalities. Youngsters are quick to see right through us; and unless we are prepared to do our part in accordance with what we say, the children will play us accordingly.

In opening our sessions we invite everyone present for hearing to come into the courtroom, where we repeat in unison the pledge of allegiance to the flag. This is for a two-fold purpose: first, it enables us to start our sessions on the proper patriotic and judicial note — justice for all. In the second place, it enables the people to come into the room to see what it looks like, and perhaps also to see what we look like, to relieve somewhat the tension of waiting hours, as it may be, until their turn arrives. As the pledge is completed, everyone again withdraws from the room except the clerk, the stenographer, and me. We are then ready for the first youngster's problem.

The probation officer comes into the room and discusses with me his report. It gives us a chance in a few brief moments to bring our thinking together. We usually then invite into the room those who are professionally interested, lawyer, clergyman, teacher, social worker, and others who are willing to consult with us. We always have a lawyer come in first and alone so that we may ask him to work with us as an officer of the court, as well as in his capacity of attorney for the child and his family, to reach a sound solution. We exchange information and approach the whole matter from an inquiry point of view. I am quite certain that lawyers respond wholeheartedly to such an approach as professional and civic-minded responsible members of the community. The attorney, if there is one present, then stays right with me throughout the balance of the hearing.

MAN TO MAN

After we have had a chance to consult with those who have come to the hearing on behalf of the child and the family, including those who have complaints to make, I find it suitable to leave the courtroom and to go to a small adjacent room where I may sit down alone with the child. To me that is the heart of the work. As we sit down together, very frequently the boy is surprised. I don't know what judges are supposed to look like, but obviously many boys are surprised when they see me. You know how youngsters are if you give them half a chance. I said to one boy who seemed so very much surprised, "Well, what did you expect?" "Oh," he said "I thought I'd see some old sourpuss," which I immediately accepted as a compliment.

Another boy leaned over to me very earnestly and said, "Let's talk man to man," which may sound very flippant but is exactly the idea when any one of us is in trouble; we like to sit down with another person and have a heart to heart talk and feel that the other person is really interested in us. In such a setting with a boy I can use language which he understands. There is no attempt at patronizing him or putting on a show. As each boy is a new challenge to me, I certainly have no feeling of boredom. If there were others present routinely and we came to talk about matters in a way that perhaps had been used before, there would be a subconscious relaxation and feeling, "Well, here comes that routine again." But with me as an active participant, there obviously cannot be such a feeling.

If, for example, a boy shows some hesitation to tell me the whole story, I can readily say to him, "When you are ill and go to see your doctor, do you try to fool your doctor?" Invariably, he expresses great surprise that anybody could be so foolish and says, "Of course not." I can then say to him, "Well, it's the same with us. You're young. We can help you more if you tell us everything than if you fool us." For just a moment I'm on trial. He looks me over. Can he trust me? If I can pass that test, it is one of the most humbling experiences to have a youngster just pour out his heart and tell me what he perhaps has not been able to tell anyone else before, not even his own father or mother. At such a time particularly, one wants to call upon the best within one's self and in the community to help that boy meet his problem.

A BOY'S FUTURE

Also in such a setting a boy can speak his own innermost thoughts without unpleasant distraction. I recall talking with a thirteen-year-old who had been a lookout for others in a burglary. As we were sitting there talking he told me, "You know, I didn't wait until the others came out. I went home." I said, "Yes?" He said, "You know, I got to thinking about it. Why, there's no future in this for me." If that boy had been in a room full of people I'm sure you will agree that there would have been a spontaneous reaction of smiles and perhaps laughter, and the boy might have thought to himself, "I said the wrong thing. They're laughing at me." He would have been hardened by such an experience. Instead, I could say to the lad, almost biting my tongue off, "You're right, son, there's no future in that for you," and encourage his naive expression of wanting to be on the right side and a member of the community's team. As we are talking together,

I can say to him again in his language, "Now, if you fumble the ball I can't pick it up for you." He quickly understands that while we are all on the same team he has a part to play, and no one else can play it for him. Very frequently he will smile and say, "I understand," which gives me a feeling of response that is often accentuated by a hand-clasp. Again in the boy's language, he will often say, "I won't let you down." He sees that we are in this thing together. If we have gauged accurately his ability as well as his desire to respond, we have stimulated a positive reaction which will, we hope, as time goes on, with the help of such others as the family, the probation officer, or the training school, complete the process of rehabilitation. We, as a symbol of society, have a chance to set the tone, to have the boy feel our interest in him. It isn't necessary to make a speech. The fact that we sat down alone with him when he knows that we are busy with many others as well must give him a feeling of significance, of belonging, and of individual worthiness.

Again, as we are talking I can compliment him on the good features of his adjustment. That often comes as a surprise because he has been more accustomed to negative comments. For example, parents will often say to me, "Did you give him a good scare?" — as though I could put on my fiercest expression and scare a youngster into behaving. I don't think it would last very long even if I tried. In fact, I have the impression at times that these youngsters have been scared by experts and that the competition would be too keen. Many of them do receive a pat on the back but only in one place; it isn't distributed enough. There isn't enough encouragement as well as correction. There is the example of the father who was surprised that his boy was in trouble. "Why," he said, "we just beat the life out of him every day."

Some time ago a woman called me on the telephone and asked me, "What happens to bad little boys?" Before I had much chance to reply, she rattled off a long list of things as though she were repeating from me and said, "Oh, thank you." I'm quite sure some little fellow was sitting near her, getting an awful idea as to what would happen to him if he ever got into our clutches.

The other day a little girl came into the juvenile court building carrying a bag of clothes. All she could tell us was that she was "bad." She couldn't even tell us her name or where she lived, until we got her quieted down enough to tell us how to reach her parents. Of course, by that time they were frantically running around trying to find her. They then told us that as they would pass our building from time to time with her they would point it out and say "You see, that's where you're going when you're bad," until at last I suppose she thought she might as well get it over with, and so she came in to see what we were like.

The negative approach may do much harm. I recall a chief of police (and I'm glad to say he's no longer a chief of police) in one of our communities who didn't represent at all the modern, progressive police point of view, who told me how he enjoyed putting youngsters in cells and seeing them turn white. He thought that was the universal cure!

As I sit talking with the boy, I am mindful that many of these lads have had the rules of the game changed on them in the midst of the game. Very often we find that the father has one set of rules and the mother another. The rules perhaps are different for Mary and for John. The rules may even vary from one time to another according to how the parent feels about the situation. Perhaps the most difficult thing for a child to understand is how a parent can say one thing and do another. Very often parents will say to me, "I didn't tell him to do that," and yet, by the parents' own behavior in breaking rules, the lad must have the impression that rules are a matter of convenience and desire, not applicable to all of us as we go through life.

In the "man to man" contact, we can point out again in his language how we are trying to make the best of our own abilities and yet live within a social order. At times a boy will tell me that he doesn't like to go to school, for instance. I may then say to him, "Well, there are a lot of things I don't like to do either; for example, when I'm driving my car and I come to a red light, very often I don't feel like stopping." And I'll say to him, "Would it be all right if I just went right through?" He usually is amazed at my suggestion and says, "Oh, no." And I ask him why not, and he says "Well, it might cause an accident. It's wrong." I say, "Would it be all right if the police officer standing there saw me go through and would say to himself, 'Oh, I suppose he doesn't want to stop today?' " The youngster's reaction is very amusing as he quickly senses that he has been going through red lights, as it were, and then will indicate that he wants to be a good sport and obey the rules. As I say, these are delicate moments that might enhance or harm, even by the tone of voice, the way in which the relationship is established and carried on. A child's future is at stake.

Parental Responsibilities

We, of course, will go back into the courtroom and talk with the parents and face them with their responsibilities as to their own part in the matter and their duty to the boy; but if we can avoid having weaknesses in the family dramatized in the boy's presence, we may help to build up family ties rather than to break them down. There are times when I feel it suitable and necessary to bring a boy into the courtroom to establish clearly in the minds of the parents and incidentally for our record, the facts of the boy's involvement, especially if there is the slightest question raised by the parent as to his knowledge of the facts. It is then a good precaution, although our usual difficulty in a juvenile court is not so much to establish facts but to find out the way and how to help. After we have talked with the boy and in our private conversations have reached a rapport, he is likely to respond even in the presence of his parents who may be somewhat defensive and protective. I have been amazed at the strength of children in sticking to the truth even though their parents may be implicitly or even directly urging them to be forgetful.

Fortunately, as a juvenile court acting as a court of equity and not as a criminal court, we may be flexible to meet the needs of individuals so far as procedure is concerned, keeping within the broad fundamental rules that govern any judicial procedure. It lies within the judge's power to understand these rules and to apply them to meet his great challenge and opportunity in serving the best interests of the child and the welfare of the community.

By these direct contacts with children the judge will also strengthen his belief in the essential soundness of human nature. Frequently my friends tend to sympathize with me because I have so many serious problems to deal with daily; and while I in no sense wish to minimize the heartbreaks and tragedies that do come to our attention in the lives of children who have been misguided and who may have made a mistake in the choice of their parents, I believe as well that a juvenile court judge has the best opportunity of seeing how children do want to respond properly if given half a chance, if we as adults are able to do our jobs well.

Let me tell you the story of "Grandpa." He was a fourteen-year-old boy in our detention home. Several days after his admission the other boys started calling him "Grandpa." He never smiled. He seemed so sad, as though he had the weight of the world upon his shoulders — an old man Atlas himself.

On a particularly warm day several of the boys had been helping the clothing department; and at the end of the day, the supervisor gave each of those boys a dime to go with him to the corner store to get an ice cream cone. As they were walking along one of them, a juvenile delinquent you might call him, slid up to the supervisor and said in a whisper, "Mr. Schmunk, if you don't mind, I'd rather not buy a dime cone. I don't like ice cream that much. I'd rather just buy a nickel cone and with the other nickel, if you don't mind, I'd like to buy a chocolate bar for 'Grandpa.' Nobody ever comes to see him, nobody ever brings him anything." This little fellow, who had very little himself, was willing to share his all with another who had less. When he did get his ice cream cone, it disappeared like magic. He liked ice cream but he liked even more to do something for another. Of these two, one was a white boy, the other a Negro boy.

Some time later I had my chance to talk with "Grandpa," and I asked him what he would like to have most of all, and in his very solemn way he turned to me and said, "a visitor," someone to come to see him, someone interested in him.

At the present moment in our detention home we have eight youngsters who are like Grandpa, without anyone interested in them. A group of young ladies has asked to visit the detention home regularly and to act as foster aunts, as it were, to youngsters in our building who otherwise do not have visitors. We shall be interested to see how that brightens the lives of these youngsters, so that when others have visitors they aren't standing by.

Our Opportunity

We are engaged in a great calling, the chance of serving humanity at a time when much can still be done, more certainly than at any later time. The pressure of time is always with us. As these youngsters grow older we know their habits will become more fixed, and it will be more difficult to help them if they turn on the wrong road.

Some time ago when I was in Washington at the headquarters of the FBI as a guest, I was shown the fingerprint department. It was well dramatized in having the total number of fingerprints on file at the moment shown on the wall like the number of your speedometer, and as a fingerprint is added the number changes right before your eyes. It made a vivid impression on me, so much so that I felt like running home to see whether I could not do more to keep boys and girls from growing up to be added to the criminal rolls of the country, knowing full well that when that record has been made they will be like water-soaked logs, sinking lower and lower, rarely able to rise to the surface again. There is much that all of us can do if we will only stimulate the community to recognize the needs of children. We must organize more effectively to meet those needs more adequately, and in that way

brighten the future for these children and for us all.

Some time ago I was out in San Francisco and saw Treasure Island. I'm sure many of you have seen it, that huge island created entirely by man in that great, swirling bay and connected by marvelous bridges with the mainland. Just a few years ago engineers would have said, "Impossible." Yet here it is. Seemingly, what man can dream in the scientific world he can do, whether it is the electric light, the telephone, the airplane, the radio, radar, the atomic bomb, television — who knows what next? But as you look around in that same bay out in San Francisco you see another island, Alcatraz, that pile of rock where some of our best-known citizens are making a permanent residence. You must wonder, "Is that the best we can do? Necessary today, yes; but can't we do better tomorrow?" In that respect, I am reminded of the words of the retired warden of Alcatraz, James Johnston, whom I admire and who is certainly no sentimentalist. As Mr. Johnston puts it, "I am interested in prisons. I want to see them humanized, modernized, made more efficient; but the finest prison we can ever build will be but a monument to neglected youth."

Let us have the courage and the vision to do early what we shall otherwise be obliged to do late — too late. As we join hands, one with the other, and look into the faces of troubled children, may we catch at least a glimpse of the divine unity of purpose behind it all.

Chapter 20

The Sentencing Process

PROBABLY THE MOST DIFFICULT and puzzling problem which a judge has to face is the determination of the sentence to be imposed. True, society has thus far provided a sentencing judge with but a relatively limited number of bottles of peno-correctional medicine — "straight" probation, probation accompanied by suspended sentence, commitment to an industrial school, sentence to a reformatory, a jail, a prison, and a few other specialized institutions, and fines. However, the judge is compelled to make a fundamental choice between these alternatives. A number of studies of the sentencing practices of judges in a single court dealing with similar cases over a considerable period of time (whether felonies or misdemeanors) have disclosed considerable erraticism in sentencing.[1]

It is no answer to claim that the wide variations in sentence for similar offenses among judges in the same court or the same level of jurisdiction can be attributed to "individualization"; for a just and scientific exercise of discretion in a large enough sample of cases ought, ultimately, to be reflected in a certain uniformity of dispositions at the sentencing level.

While certain candid judges have long ago urged that something constructive be done about the sentencing situation, others tend to minimize the significance of the wide variation in sentences.

Various reform measures have been suggested. One of these would strictly limit the exercise of discretion of judges by setting forth (as was done by the late Professor Enrico Ferri in his Italian Penal Code project) detailed "circumstances of greater dangerousness" and "circumstances of less dangerousness," each of which is given a certain time weight and which the judge must apply in assessing the exact length and type of sentence.[2] The difficulty with this solution of the problem of how to avoid erratic sentencing is that in making such detailed provisions to be automatically applied at the time of sentence by means of judicial arithmetic, the legislature has surrounded the judge with so clumsy an apparatus of control of discretion as to permit of but a poor counterfeit of scientific individualization.

Another device is the establishment of an appellate tribunal with the duty of reviewing, and as much as possible, equalizing sentences on appeal, as is done in a few American jurisdictions and by the English Court of Criminal Appeals. But it is doubtful whether a tribunal twice removed from the vital facts can do much to remedy erratic sentencing.

A third method is that suggested in the Model Penal Code of the American Law Institute; namely the establishment of certain "criteria" which the court may take into account (*e.g.*, no prior criminal record or the leading of a law-abiding life since the last offense, the criminal conduct having been "the result of circumstances unlikely to recur," the defendant's status as a professional criminal or a multiple offender, etc.).

---

[1] See S. Glueck, "The Sentencing Problem," 20 *Federal Probation* (1956), 15–25. For a pioneering study of sentencing practices in the London juvenile courts, see H. Mannheim, J. Spencer, and G. Lynch, "Magisterial Policy in the London Juvenile Courts," 8 *British J. Delinquency* (1957), 13–33, 119–138.

[2] Glueck, *op. cit.*, pp. 19–20.

But even this device of setting down in a code of "criteria" which the judge may be governed by if so inclined is inadequate. The difficulty is that the judge has no way of knowing how closely related to various types of post-sentence *behavior* are the criteria provided. The criteria of the American Law Institute Code are not such as have, by and large, been derived from follow-up investigations as a result of which traits and factors in the make-up and background of various types of offenders have been related to actual post-correctional conduct. The question is whether there is available, as an aid to scientific differentiation of treatment, an instrument that can help the judge in determining which influences have been demonstrated, by systematic analysis of past experience, to be truly *relevant* to the expectable behavior of various classes of offenders, and how much weight to give such factors in the type of case before the judge for sentence.

The problem is one of "individualization"; but individualization of sentence is easier said than done. To individualize, in the case of any specific offender, means, first, to differentiate him from other offenders in personality, character, sociocultural background, the motivation of his offense and his particular potentialities for reform or recidivism, and, secondly, to determine which, among a range of disciplinary, corrective, psychiatric and social measures, is best adapted to solve the special set of problems presented by that particular delinquent so as substantially to reduce the probability of his committing crimes in the future. A moment of reflection on what this process implies makes it evident that to speak glibly about "individualization" is one thing, and to be able to accomplish it is quite another.

Nor can the consultation by the judge of even the most thorough and detailed presentence investigation report (see Article 115 by Meeker in the present chapter), in itself, markedly improve the situation; the reason being that a single investigation report does not indicate, on the basis of organized past experience, the relative weights to be assigned to the items in such a report.[3] These can only be guessed at unless they are determined by comparison of the instant case, in respect to factors proved to be relevant to post-sentence behavior, with like factors in experience tables covering hundreds of similar and different cases.

In the Editor's view, the greatest aid that could be given to judges in individualization can come from *prediction* tables. Such devices, being based upon an analysis of results, would tend to induce judges to make their dispositional decisions in terms of objectified, systemized and relevant experience. This is far better than attempting to arrive at a decision from a mere reading of a presentence report, which covers a great deal of information without indicating which parts of it have been found, by systematic check-up, to be really relevant to subsequent behavior, or from checking off a list of unevaluated criteria presented in a code. In other words, the basic purpose of prediction tables is *to help the judge to marshal his experience more effectively*. While, of course, a judge should not follow these tables blindly or mechanically, he is bound, by consulting them, gradually to evolve a set of policies, principles and practices based not on "hunch" or "guess" or what can be (and often is) a mistaken conception of the kind of behavior expected from the particular delinquent involved, but on objectified experience with hundreds of other cases. The dispositions he makes in the light of such organized experience, as reflected in the tables, would, when focused on the presentence reports, tend to be not only more appropriate to the individual case but more consistent in the general run of cases than those under the present *ad hoc* method.

---

[3] This, in the Editor's opinion, is the only basic question that can be raised regarding the otherwise admirable little book, *Guides for Sentencing*, published by the Advisory Council of Judges of the National Probation and Parole Association, New York, 1957, and respecting the criteria presented by the American Law Institute in the draft of a modern penal code.

The sentencing problem points up a striking yet usually overlooked aspect of the history of penology and code drafting; namely, that all the reform devices of the present century — the juvenile court, probation, the indeterminate sentence, classification within institutions, parole — depend for their efficiency on the *reasonable predictability of human behavior under given circumstances.* Yet all these forward-looking additions to the apparatus of criminal justice were adopted long before this indispensable basis for their success — predictability — was available; and certain of their proponents and practitioners still ignore or minimize the crucial necessity of such systematic prognosis.[4]

Of course, the presentence report should include other factors than those embraced in the battery of predictive tables used by the court to distinguish probabilities of success or failure under the various corrective-treatment regimes, since details of a treatment plan require consideration of information correlative and supplementary to that of the basic factors in the prognostic instruments.

Students who are interested in the role of predictive techniques in sentencing and paroling are referred to the numerous books and articles written by the Editor and Dr. Eleanor T. Glueck on these topics.

This chapter opens with a perceptive article by Judge Gill in a recent valuable issue of the *NPPA Journal* dealing with juvenile institutions and aftercare. Every magistrate of any sensitivity, who is at all informed about the effect of an institutional regime on a young and growing personality, must experience doubt and heartache from time to time about his decision to commit a youngster to an industrial school or so-called reformatory. Gill lays bare the psychology of the conscientious judge. Wisdom is reflected in Gill's dictum that "authority, dependent as it is for its success upon lack of animus, cannot afford the crippling handicap of angry words." His discussion of the difference between the single overt act and the child's "over-all pattern of behavior," should be of value to other judges and their staffs. His insistence that clinical study of human behavior is no mere "frill" but indispensable to wise and just sentencing is reflected in his common-sense discussions of the role of inner and outer pressures in contributing to the development of different classes of delinquents, such as the emotionally distorted, in contrast with the inadequately socialized.

Gill's article is followed by an extract from the recently published *Guides for Juvenile Court Judges,* prepared by the Advisory Council of Judges of the National Probation and Parole Association in cooperation with the National Council of Juvenile Court Judges. This piece makes some astute observations on the practical considerations that should govern the sentencing process. Especially stimulative to thought are the five "mandates" basic to the disposition of delinquency cases.

Next follows a helpful discussion of the presentence investigation, by Meeker.

Finally, there is an extract from *Juvenile Delinquents Grown Up* which consists of cases illustrating the use of prediction tables involving juvenile delinquents [5] and a digest of the follow-up results of the application of these prediction tables to an entirely new series of juvenile delinquents (those studied in *Unraveling Juvenile Delinquency* [6]) with a view to determining the extent to which the forecasts indicated by the tables in the prior work have turned out successfully when applied to the cases of *Unraveling.*

In Chapter 32, the role of predictive techniques in a *preventive* program is indicated; the relevant items in the present chapter deal with predictive aids to sentencing.

---

[4] See S. Rubin, "Sentencing Goals: Real and Ideal," 21 *Federal Probation* (1957), 51–56. See, also S. Glueck, "Further Comments on the Sentencing Problem," 21 *Federal Probation* (1957).

[5] See S. and E. T. Glueck, *Juvenile Delinquents Grown Up,* New York, The Commonwealth Fund, 1940, for the entire study of which the materials in this book are an extract.

[6] S. and E. T. Glueck, *Unraveling Juvenile Delinquency,* New York, The Commonwealth Fund, 1950; and Cambridge, Harvard University Press, 1951.

Before closing this note, a few words should be said about a problem that has received scant attention in written works; namely, what to do with the incurable recidivist. The Glueck follow-up investigations have established that there are certain types of persons who do not respond acceptably to any form of existing peno-correctional treatment. Those of them who are persistently, aggressively dangerous — robbers, "muggers," rapists — should be subjected to some form of social quarantine to remove them from harm-dealing circulation. The policy should be similar to that employed, for example, with dangerous typhoid carriers. When society has given its available services without bringing about a stoppage of recidivism — even granting that those services can be greatly improved — it is time to remember that the best attention should be devoted to the most promising cases and that those who are persistently dangerous should be kept out of society. Just as there are hospitals for the chronically ill, so should there be institutions for delinquents who remain, despite a variety of attempts to improve them, aggressively dangerous. Here one is dealing with human dynamite, not with amiable eccentricities. The duty to protect society is obviously paramount, and such protection from clear and known danger is not something with which to be continuously experimenting. Only superficial sentimentality, which misunderstands the meaning and limitations of "permissiveness" and the shortcomings of existing therapeutic devices, can insist that dangerous offenders, approaching adulthood, be sent on a continuous round of clinics, schools and other such agencies while being allowed to carry on their depredations. As the Editor has said, on another occasion:

> Unbridled sentimentalism is also bad. Deep though our pity be, we cannot indulge in futile sentimentality while dangerous persons stalk the land. We must discipline our humane impulses with science and good sense. A head without a heart may lead to tyranny; a heart without a head may mean annihilation. These two principles, then, the ethical and the scientific, must both be reckoned with.[7]

Can such untreatable delinquents be adequately spotted before they have done too much damage?

The Editor is convinced that this is practicable. As a result of the completion of an elaborate prediction–treatment study made by Dr. Eleanor T. Glueck and the Editor, a research on which a report is at present in preparation, it has been possible to discover the characteristics of those delinquents who are very probably bound to fail under any of the existing correctional devices at present at the command of the typical juvenile court: probation, with or without suspended sentence, commitment to one or another correctional school, parole. Those boys whom we have labeled "untreatable" are the ones who had been predicted as having no more than one in ten chances of acceptable behavior during *extramural* forms of treatment and less than an even chance during *intramural*. On the basis of such a dichotomy, we were able, by relating 151 background factors of *Unraveling Juvenile Delinquency* (74 psychologic, psychiatric and Rorschach Test traits and 77 sociocultural factors) with the constellation of predicted results forecasting *all* forms of treatment, to construct a predictive device for use of clinicians, judges and others in determining, at the time of the first arrest of a youngster, whether he has the capacity to respond adequately to *any* of the current methods of "treatment" available to the average juvenile court. (This does not include individual and group psychotherapy.)

This important finding, resulting from a test of our series of juvenile court prediction tables constructed from the cases of 1,000 boys studied in *One Thousand Juvenile Delinquents* and *Juvenile Delinquents Grown Up*, upon an entirely different set of persistent delinquents in *Unraveling*, has resulted in a predictive cluster almost

---

[7] S. Glueck, *Crime and Justice*, Boston, Little, Brown and Company, 1936, 6.

identical with that previously derived in *Unraveling* for the purpose of identifying *potential* delinquents. This fundamental discovery would seem to indicate that *true* (as opposed to occasional or accidental) delinquents, as defined in *Unraveling*, are very difficult to treat successfully by the generally current methods employed by juvenile courts.[8] This vital fact should stimulate intensive experimentation with individual and group psychotherapy and other procedures in the case of children who are already frankly delinquent; and, if these too fail, it should justify the removal of aggressive offenders in their late teens from harm-dealing circulation.

Nevertheless, just as continuous experimentation in search of cures for obscure diseases goes on in the better establishments for the chronically ill, so is there a duty to continue to study the nature of the chronically recidivistic offender and to search for new methods of therapy. In this connection, researches have shown that the age-span of about 31 to 35 years is the Great Divide so far as reform or recidivism is concerned.

> This does not, however, mean that 31 to 35 years is *absolutely* the most likely age of reformation; for the percentage of non-criminalism in the 31–35 age group during the first follow-up period was only 14.7% while the highest incidence of non-criminalism (30.2%) had then occurred in the earlier 26–30 year span. There must therefore be a combination of influences involved. Tentatively, it is reasonable to assume, on the evidence, that these are: first, the age of the offender; secondly, the stage in the course of his criminalistic career at which he reaches a certain age, *i. e.*, whether he becomes 31 to 35 years old relatively early in his criminal career and is therefore, at 31 to 35, still close to the origins of his delinquency, or he reaches this age relatively late in his criminalistic career and therefore many years beyond the childhood beginnings of delinquency . . . The evidence . . . is strongly suggestive of the soundness of the conclusion tentatively arrived at in *Later Criminal Careers*: It was not achievement of any particular age, but rather the achievement of adequate maturation regardless of the chronologic age at which it occurred, that was the significant influence in the behaviour changes of our criminals. . . .
>
> We may, in other words, recognize two types of "reformed" ex-criminals; one type includes youths and men who, having achieved a socially requisite state of physical, mental, and emotional maturity and a socially requisite state of personality integration, have, as mental and not merely as physical adults, finally determined or been induced to abandon their criminalistic ways. The other type are the men whose abandonment of criminalism, or drift into milder, less aggressive and less daring forms of misconduct, was caused not by mature decision, or reflection on experience, or conscious inhibition, or other forms of adult-minded adaptation, but rather by the sheer slowing down or deterioration of the organism.[9]

Social quarantine of chronically dangerous offenders, until they have passed the peak of aggressiveness, would seem to be called for, with opportunity for periodic review of status as a matter of course. Perhaps establishments analogous to the forestry camps in some states, or the civilian conservation camps during the past war, and involving a regime which permits the expression of drives in harmless and constructive channels, but with a program of hard work and strict discipline, are indicated in such cases.

---

[8] See S. and E. T. Glueck, *Predicting Delinquency and Crime*, Cambridge, Harvard University Press, 1959.

[9] S. and E. T. Glueck, *After-Conduct of Discharged Offenders*, London, The Macmillan Company, 1946, 79, 81, 86–87.

113

When Should a Child Be Committed? *

Thomas D. Gill

Inevitably, an active juvenile court judge will be called upon with great frequency to consider the commitment of boys and girls to correctional institutions. Inevitably, too, no matter how lengthy his tenure of office, he will experience on each such occasion some resurgence of the misgivings which played so vivid a part in his first commitment. To some small degree, this is his reassurance, however trying, that he has not become a victim of judicial megalomania, that the humaneness and humbleness of spirit so essential to his administration of justice have survived both the numbing impact of long exposure to human shortcomings and the creeping arrogance so often implicit in unlimited authority. This quickening of anxiety and compassion is the judge's best evidence that he has not grown callous to the immense importance of the decision involved in abridging the most fundamental and perhaps the dearest of all human rights, the union between child and parent.

The judge's emotions, then, may well play a legitimate part in properly focusing for him the implications of his decision and perhaps to some degree may guide him in the manner in which he interprets that decision, but they must never become its chief concomitants. An emotionless judge will find it difficult to serve his office well — an emotional judge, impossible.

VISCERAL THINKING

Pity honors, even as anger discredits, its possessor, but both will and do betray the judge's efforts to protect the community and serve its youth. The blurred lens of pity can distort the fact that to place a youngster back

* Reprinted from 4 *NPPA Journal* (1958), 1–11. Used by permission of the author and the publisher.

in exactly the same circumstances which have repeatedly defeated him without either modifying the circumstances themselves or improving his ability to cope with them is neither kind nor understanding. Actually, it is hypocritical, for the judge is exacting from this youngster what he already knows he is incapable of giving. Although the child and his parents may be grateful for what seems to them a new opportunity, the judge knows the essential injustice of demanding the impossible of the child. He has granted the child and his family a lightning flash of happiness at a price which no one can accurately calculate, save that it will be beyond the youngster's ability to pay. Eventually, bearing additional scars from his new and needless encounters with an intolerable situation, and with a deepened sense of his own failure, this youngster will return for the judgment that should have taken place before.

The fact that anger or indignation should not intrude themselves into judicial deliberations does not, on occasion, prevent them from appearing, sometimes under circumstances so convincing and plausible that the judge can successfully rationalize that they played no part in his conclusions whatsoever. So often, as these circumstances facilely arrange themselves in the judge's mind, he is not in any sense getting back at the arrogant, indifferent youth who sits before him. He is merely teaching this young man that the realities of life include respect for the representatives of authority; it is, therefore, authority that is being upheld when such a boy is committed, rather than the wounded feelings of the judge. If the disposition so ordered seems inconsistent with all the prehearing investigative facts concerning the child's character and needs, it is naturally a tribute to the greater perspicacity of the judge that the errors of the report were discovered in time.

It may be true, as Bertrand Russell once stated, that "We never feel so good as when we are punishing someone," but the judge's judicial well-being cannot be built on the costly ingredient of anger; commitments so made inevitably leave to a perhaps applauding and impressed community a legacy of hostility and multiplying troubles. Authority, dependent as it is for its success upon lack of animus, cannot afford the crippling handicap of angry words. Once freed from visceral thinking, a judge has no need to wander in a judicial wilderness when confronted with the all-important question of whether in a given situation a commitment is a necessary and positive step. If the court over which he presides is a juvenile court in more than name only — that is, if its philosophy of individualizing the child is implemented by the skilled staff necessary to diagnose and treat children — he will have at his command information and resources which will make the answer to his query the scientific, objective solution it deserves to be.

In this article, four principles which appear to be inescapably a part of a decision involving commitment are considered. Implicit, of course, in such consideration, is the key assumption that the right of the court to make any disposition whatsoever has first been properly established by procedures completely consonant with due process of law.

1. THE YOUTH'S PATTERN OF BEHAVIOR AS EXEMPLIFYING HIS NEEDS

It would be idle to pretend that the overt act which brings a child to the juvenile court is of no particular significance in arriving at the nature of his disposition. Clearly, the overt act is important in the sense that it generally colors the attitude of the child and his parents toward the intervention of the court, even as it so often conditions and affects the reaction of the community toward the child. Yet the key to individualization is that the overt act must not become the sole determinant of the disposition. The judge must be able to distinguish between what the child has done which necessitated his referral and his over-all pattern of behavior, of which the specific act in question may or may not be an integral part. Only when a judge has trained himself to think in terms of this pattern will he be able to benefit fully from the skilled services which have been attached to his court and send to training schools and correctional institutions the type of youngster who may really benefit from their programs in the sense that they will find there some help for their particular needs and problems.

It is easy to oversimplify in dealing with the various types of delinquent behavior, but it is also possible to become so involved in the numerous refinements of conduct of delinquent children as to make it virtually impossible to arrive at reasonable and workable methods of classification. Probably no more forthright or common sense yardstick has been evolved for the practicing judge than that which may be fashioned from the Cambridge-Somerville studies on delinquency,[1] a yardstick which in its essence requires that each case be analyzed in terms of three essential criteria:

1. The frequency of antisocial behavior.
2. The seriousness of that behavior.
3. The child's attitude toward his actions, adults, and adult authority.

If a child persists in delinquent activity despite such assistance as the court can bring into his life through skilled supportive help, if these acts are intrinsically serious — measured by the degree to which they affect the rights of other people and consequently the attitude of these selfsame people toward the child, and if the child's attitude toward adult authority is one of continuing defiance or resistance, it can be assumed that here is a child who is advertising his inability to handle community responsibilities.

"One Shot" or Established Delinquency? This yardstick advances the judicial process one important step by making evident the difference between such a child and the casual "one-shot" delinquent who has blundered into trouble through his friends of the moment, the restlessness engendered by boredom, the familiar teen-age need for status and recognition, or other reasons divorced from deep-seated personality and environmental factors. When, however, it has been determined that this "established" delinquent cannot be assisted through the normal processes of probation because his areas of failure in the home, school, and community substantially outnumber those of his success, there still remains for determination the all-important question of how the additional structure so obviously required can best be obtained.

Inner Pressures. To answer this question, it is necessary to know whether the child whose pattern of activity presents him as an "established" delinquent has arrived at this pattern through inner conflicts or emotional disturbance, or because of environmental or

---

[1] Edwin Powers and Helen Witmer, *An Experiment in the Prevention of Delinquency: The Cambridge-Somerville Youth Study*, New York, Columbia University Press, 1951. [See, also, Article 186. — Ed.]

sociological pressures which have both taught and nurtured his delinquent behavior.

Representative of one of these two extremes of delinquent behavior is the emotionally upset child whose community difficulties stem from inner tensions generated by destructive personal relationships, usually within his own family circle. This is the child who presents basic problems of understanding and with whom no one usually has any effective or helpful relationship. Generally, he is a child who operates on impulse, is quickly changeable in mood, and cannot reconcile the wish to remain at home with a craving for excitement as the principal satisfaction of living.

For such troubled children, whipsawed by the emotions, the assets of the training school must generally fall short of positive help since the program presumes an ability to relate and persevere quite beyond the capacity of children as disturbed as these. They belong, whenever possible, in special treatment centers that can offer them the cushioned care, the carefully tailored routine, that their explosive personalities require. The judge has a responsibility to recognize and point out the fundamental differences in the patterns of this emotional delinquent and his social counterpart who will be presently discussed, and to crusade for facilities which will have a realistic chance of rehabilitating the former group rather than burdening the training schools with the frustrating and generally hopeless situations which stem from misplacement.

Outer Pressures. As contrasted with these emotionally upset children whose problems prove particularly challenging to judges because so many of them have not yet reached their teen years, there is the so-called "social" delinquent, generally a pseudo-sophisticated, somewhat aggressive adolescent living in or near the marginal areas of his community who either does not know or cannot recognize basic normal standards of behavior. This is the type of youngster who is generally associated in the public mind with the word "delinquent" and who, if he has taken on the pattern of the "established" delinquent, can be aided and helped by a training school. He is the child who has become thoroughly indoctrinated in the street corner point of view toward authority and restrictions, the child whose loyalty to friends has won out over loyalty to family, but who still has recognizable vestiges of fondness for his parents, is still approachable by adults not manifestly authoritative by profession, and possesses an essentially undamaged personality which is capable of learning the right as it has already absorbed the wrong. Generally, this type of youngster has not been short-changed in terms of affection by his parents — whose inadequacies have more often manifested themselves in the form of unsatisfactory and inconsistent guidance and direction.

This boy can be aided by the modern correctional school, although in the community he is temporarily unable to assume responsibility for himself through a complete loss of direction and blind adherence to curbstone standards; because of this, he requires protection from the situations his own inadequacies create. In essence, his personality permits of retraining.

Retraining the Social Delinquent. Among the reasons sustaining hope of a positive result, these might be noted:

In the training school it is often possible to give this poorly socialized child a taste of some of the rewards of acceptable behavior, the accolades that accompany success to which, of course, he was obliged to remain a stranger in the community since his activities there have consistently brought him condemnation instead of approval. The social delinquent has not been able to face up to the necessity of adapting himself to the rights of his fellow man, but in the persistent face-to-face relationships of the training school, there are real pressures upon the child to learn means of getting on with and respecting the rights of others, both adults and children; indeed the essential security of his day-to-day routines depends upon his doing so since he is denied the protective anonymity which he relied on as a member of the community. For normal socialization of a child and the development of an adequate conscience, there should be in his environment a relatively stable adult figure who can give him comradeship and understanding and serve as a pattern for his behavior. In his community living, the established "social" delinquent denied himself, or to some degree was denied, proper teachers, but within the school such denial is difficult. From involuntary exposure to a number of adequate adults, there is real hope for change.

Subject to the considerations discussed in

principles 3 and 4 below, the established "social" delinquent who has not responded to community treatment can be properly considered for a training school with real hope for favorable results if the school is genuinely dedicated to and capable of carrying out a rehabilitative program.

Without Facilities, What? For the unhappy judge who can expect virtually no help in determining the basic pattern of the child's behavior because of his court's lack of a trained staff, for the unfortunate jurist who knows that his state training school represents naked detention and nothing better, even perhaps something worse, there can be but one governing principle: to resolve every uncertainty in favor of the child and his home; to commit solely on the basis of unmistakable need for community protection. Lacking on the one hand the facts essential to accurate diagnosis and denied on the other a good training program for delinquents, the judge dares not assume that any beneficial results can accrue from his action save the protection of the community which enforced segregation guarantees. This does not minimize the importance which should be attached to this primary court responsibility, but makes certain that the inherent reasons underlying the decision to commit are understood by all, including the judge.

Even the contention that a commitment will have a deterrent effect on other children is highly suspect. Unfortunately, the confirmed delinquents who are, of course, the prospective candidates for commitment, whether their difficulties be social or emotional, remain blindly satisfied with their established patterns of activity, quite impervious to arguments and facts directed toward behavior changes. These delinquents, either mesmerized by group example or imprisoned by their own emotions, are dedicated to the maxim, "It can't happen to me." On the other hand, the children capable of absorbing the logic of the situation do not particularly need this type of teaching since they would never, in any event, become candidates for commitment. As to the one group, then, it becomes a lesson wasted; as to the other, a superfluous demonstration of the obvious.

How long such a judge and the community he serves must deny themselves the hope of truly helping children would depend on how long it takes to demonstrate to the citizens concerned that there is no magic, per se, in the Juvenile Court Act. Indeed, in some respects it is far more dangerous than no act at all, inducing as it easily may a sense of complacency concerning a program which, in fact, has never emerged from the statute books.

2. THE PROTECTION OF THE COMMUNITY

A judge of the juvenile court is in no sense negating the spirit of the law under which he operates by forthrightly acknowledging his duty at all times to protect the well-being of the citizens he serves. On the contrary, it is his responsibility to see to it that help and treatment for delinquent children shall be brought to them in a manner and under conditions consistent with the collective security.

Because the vast majority of children coming before the juvenile court are not seriously damaged in personality or irrevocably committed to the satisfaction of primary needs through antisocial behavior, the judge who is fortunate enough to be complemented by an adequately trained and supervised probation staff can be quite certain that in a very heavy majority of his cases probation will bring to the child concerned the "care, guidance, and discipline" he requires while insuring reasonable protection for the community.

There are those, however, who assume the community is in danger the moment "help," "treatment," and "probation" are mentioned; as they would have it, these terms are synonymous with the toleration of lawless conduct.

In time, there will be few to dissent concerning the essential wisdom of a method which preserves and utilizes the child's existing strength as the point from which to attack his weaknesses. Until, however, it has become accepted that it is illogical and unnecessary to resort to the uncertainties and dangers inherent in the total rebuilding job (which is commitment) when the remodeling afforded by probation can achieve the same end with far less risk, such criticism will continue. The informed judge will attempt to meet it forthrightly, not by equivocating concerning the efficacy of probation.

This particular statement as to the desirability of probation in a children's court seems worthy of reiteration here because of the dangers of distortion and overemphasis inherent in an article attempting to evaluate the reasons which make commitment the proper course in certain cases.

With the total picture thus in focus, it can now be stated that there are unquestionably cases where due consideration for the well-being of the community unmistakably requires that any help rendered the child shall be in a protective setting such as is typified by the training school. Fortunately, since one of the hallmarks of the "established" delinquent is ordinarily the demonstrated seriousness of his conduct as measured by its impact on the community, it is true that in many cases the needs of the delinquent and of the community complement rather than oppose each other. The same pattern which has posed a real threat to the peace and well-being of the community has likewise destroyed the child's ability to function within the nature orbit of his home, school, and neighborhood, and gives emphasis to his need for change. Thus, whichever approach is given the greater emphasis, whether the court gives expression to its concern for the child or the community, the indicated treatment remains the same — the need for restricted and structured living.

Self-damaging Delinquency. There is a group of cases, however, with which every judge is familiar. These children have a long history of rebellion against authority, but their pattern of conduct does not pose the obvious threat to the collective security generally implicit in the more common offenses against person and property. Youngsters in conflict with home or school authority (running away, truancy, improper friends and routines) are not generally so inherently dangerous to the community as to necessitate protective action for civic reasons alone. They can be and need to be judged against the particular intent of the governing delinquency statute. In almost every state, as in the Standard Juvenile Court Act, this was designed to and does bring before the court not only children who have done what, if committed by adults, would be considered criminal in nature, but also those whose behavior is prejudicial to their own present and future well-being. These children, basically in conflict with themselves rather than with their neighbors, have been brought within the court's jurisdiction because they need help with conduct both self-damaging and socially unacceptable, not because the community stands in

jeopardy from their acts. Knowing this, the judge will be particularly insistent that persuasive facts be adduced to show how conduct primarily self-destructive and non-criminal in nature challenges community safety.

This approach will encounter its greatest difficulty in the cases emanating from the public schools. As the American Dream of Education for All has expanded, it has asked educators to carry more and more children further and further along the highway of compulsory education without providing adequate exits for those intellectually and temperamentally ill-suited to the journey. Unable to provide the educational experience that the Dream in its present form demands, denied the right to grant to some faltering misfits the realistic succor of selected work experience, these harassed trustees of our state's educational ambitions turn to the court for deliverance from their problems. Because too often it is the only exit, the schools are compelled to try to squeeze through it many children that they and the courts know do not belong there.

As the guardian of this exit, the judge must see to it that the fault does not lie more in the demand than in the response. Some educational systems do not distinguish between a situation where a normal pupil has unreasonably and persistently revolted against equitable scholastic requirements and one where the fault lies more in unrealistic educational goals than in the bewildered student's shortcomings. In the first situation, due regard for the total well-being of the school should conceivably make commitment the proper course, for an ability to so conform is an essential prerequisite of citizenship in any group situation. In the latter case, justice to the child struggling beyond his educational depth would deny the school the relief that institutionalization might offer.

The judge should encourage school personnel to face and understand, as he must, the far-reaching implications of his decision for the child, which goes beyond the emergencies of today to the consequences of tomorrow. He should share with them what is the essence of the court's position, that there is often a wide divergence between what is theoretically and scientifically so and what is practically and humanely so, and that placement is never justified simply because children can physically be better provided for and more wisely treated as wards of the state. There are numerous cases where quite obviously the children's physical and educational needs would be better served outside their own home, but the state's power to challenge parental rights rests not on parents' failure to insure to their children a maximum of care, but upon their inability to provide the minimum.

There remains that most pitiful group of children who are committed with only the smallest likelihood that they personally will gain more than such benefits as accrue to them by virtue of being freed from some of the irritations of home, school, and neighbors which have perhaps served to ignite their volatile temperaments, or through being temporarily spared the continued condemnation which is the inevitable by-product of their anticommunity actions. These children are so placed by the judge because their activities have definitely hurt the community and there is "nothing else to do" which will insure an end to their damaging behavior — behavior of such danger as fire setting, unpredictable sex activity, and senseless property destruction. These are the children already referred to whose prolonged and firmly fixed patterns of delinquency stem from inner tensions quite beyond the reach of the present design of most training school programs. Regretfully, such commitments must and do take place in every jurisdiction because the treatment facilities, public and private, capable of meeting the challenge of this unhappy group are rarely available for more than a fraction of the group concerned. The judge can only assure himself that all conceivable possibilities for realistic help have been canvassed before he utilizes what is generally restraint without cure.

3. Timing and Interpretation as Prerequisites of Commitment

Human nature being what it is, the parties most directly affected by commitment — the child and his parents — are inevitably the last to accept it as a necessary, proper, and conceivably helpful answer to the challenge of delinquent conduct. Yet, it would be thoroughly unwise to pretend that there is not at all times a direct correlation between the effectiveness of the correctional school's work with a given child and the degree of understanding and acquiescence obtained from the child and his family at the time of the commitment hearing. To a very considerable extent, the stage is set at this point for the ultimate success or failure of the institutional program to follow. Ideally, therefore, such acquiescence and understanding must be an avowed objective of every commitment, no less candidly sought for in each instance because in some it will lie beyond judicial reach.

It is unfortunately true that the so-called "right moment" to commit is never granted a judge in a situation which finds the child so thoroughly alienated from his community by nature of his action as to permit of no other course, even though he be legally a first offender. Yet, beneath the panic of such a child and his parents, sometimes hidden by the surface resistance and noncooperation it so often engenders, lies real need for the reassurance that all is not actually lost, reassurance that the child is going to receive help and not punishment.

Every commitment hearing, therefore, is a judge's opportunity to salvage from an almost completely negative situation the seeds of positive action. A perfunctory order can crystallize despair; a humane explanation and interpretation can turn hostility to hope. Even where emotional confusion temporarily strips the listeners of their ability to comprehend the import of the spoken word, they will subsequently recall the consideration of the judge's manner, the sincerity of his interest, and the patience of his approach. These, far more than naked authority, are the prerequisites of a successful commitment hearing.

Unlike those situations in which the judge has little legal choice or none at all, there are many others where circumstances permit the court to select or reject commitment at a given time. In most, if not all of these, the child's and parents' acceptance should be a major — conceivably the controlling — determinant. Children whose persistent if not spectacular failures give unhappy augury of things to come might well warrant commitment at the earliest stage of their court contact to spare them the social and emotional scars that further community living will inevitably entail. Kindness to some of these children, as I have emphasized above, dictates that there be a forthright ending to their hapless struggle. But if they have not fully digested the inherent helplessness of their situations, if they and their parents wish to persist against the overpowering odds, *and if the subsequent events can be so structured by the court* as to reasonably insure recognition by them of their defeat upon the occasion of the next failure, there can properly be a postponement of the inevitable placement plan. It is unquestionably correct that some children need to get sicker before they can hope to get better.

Among such cases, judges will recognize boys and girls who, enveloped and smothered by unreasoning parental protection, have been denied an opportunity to measure their conduct against reality. They need a chance for such an introduction before commitment.

4. REALISTIC CLASSIFICATION

One of the persuasive arguments advanced on behalf of Youth Authority laws is the acknowledged need for proper study and classification of youthful offenders so that their rehabilitation may be undertaken at institutions where appropriate facilities geared to their actual needs exist. No less obligatory for the successful operation of a children's court and no less a part of its reason for being and its history is the scientific study of the child and an ensuing willingness on the part of the judge to utilize basic classification data. Criticism can properly attach to a court which shows little interest in whether the child brought before it is psychotic, feeble-minded, or otherwise so organically damaged as to make his presence in a correctional school a perversion of all the principles which presumably structure the court.

No Human Lottery. Even if the community fallaciously assumes the correct thing is being done for the rehabilitation of the child, the judge knows the unpleasant actualities; he knows not only that the child is being denied proper assistance, but that the school concerned, unreasonably harassed by the crippling burden of such a misplacement, is being seriously impeded in its efforts for those who really belong there. If a judge lacks the tools for proper study, then, as has been stated, he should make it understood that the court cannot properly protect the community until it knows the physical and mental make-up of the children it is dealing with. Too often, the demand for clinical service has emphasized its value to the individuals served rather than the patent fact that complete community protection and intelligent use of existing community resources must be predicated on the creation and employment of such service. Those who doubt the need for the study of human behavior, who regard it as an expensive "frill," should not be permitted to forget that if the individual gains through an objective scientific evaluation of his ability to function in society, so too does society itself necessarily find far more realistic protection.

A judge, if any there be, who fatalistically accepts the nonexistence of such service or who phlegmatically condones the absence of facilities for feeble-minded or psychotic children by committing them without protest to a correctional school, has done his office, the child, and the community a great disservice. He will, of course, find that no institution actually wants these signally unfortunate children. Doors are not readily opened to the dispiriting pattern presented by the union of organic handicaps with delinquent conduct. Yet, it is his responsibilty to see to it that such children are sent where their primary problems can be adequately dealt with — if it is retardation, then in a school for the feeble-minded; if psychosis, then in a hospital for those so afflicted.

When a juvenile court is unequivocally ready to individualize treatment of the child, it is automatically dedicating itself to the principles of classification, to the philosophy of matching the need with the treatment facility, an approach which has been basic to the operation of leading children's courts for many years before it was rediscovered with the creation of the Youth Authority acts. When the court is unable or unwilling to so individualize, its commitment policies can take on the hit-or-miss attributes of a human lottery.

THE LIMITS OF PRECEDENT

The juvenile court deals in human situations. These situations, characterized as they are by an infinite number of shadings and circumstances, do not lend themselves easily to definite rules. Even what has been set down here may seem to many presumptuously definitive. It was this conviction that prompted Judge Cardozo, in speaking of the duties of a juvenile court judge, to say: "He has to decide human questions which cannot be settled merely by citing old precedents. You cannot chart the future of a boy or girl or family by repeating what a learned judge said in a celebrated case." Therefore, though a judge of a juvenile court may turn with some assurance to the statutes and case law of his state for the answer to his inquiries concerning jurisdiction or procedure, he soon discovers that the cumulative wisdom of the law stops just where the area of his greatest responsibility and · decision begins. With the certain knowledge that this vast treasury of legal learning can avail him little, he must, for his own peace of mind, turn to and make welcome in his court the sciences of human behavior. For only out of their partnership with the law can come the principles of disposition which will truly serve justice in a children's court.

114

Disposition and Treatment *

PURPOSE OR GOAL OF DISPOSITION

The basic goals of the juvenile court are the protection of the community, the rehabilitation of the delinquent child and the protection of the neglected (or dependent) child. These goals are not antithetical. The commitment of a child to a training school does not constitute ultimate protection for the community unless treatment is provided for that child in the school preparing him for return. The threat to the peace and security of the community remains unless the underlying causes of the problem are treated and eliminated.

Once the judge has assumed jurisdiction in a given case, his purpose should be, not to set a penalty as in a criminal case, nor to settle a specific dispute between contending parties as in a civil case, but to order the

---

* Reprinted from *Guides for Juvenile Court Judges,* Advisory Council of Judges of the National Probation and Parole Association, in cooperation with the National Council of Juvenile Court Judges, New York, 1957, 69–82. Used by permission of the publisher.

available treatment which seems most likely to result in the eventual removal of the causes of this particular case of delinquency, neglect, etc. It is for this reason that juvenile court statutes give the judge unusual latitude. Unlike the criminal court judge, he is not limited by law to certain dispositions for particular offenses, but is allowed to base his disposition on what he judges to be the treatment needs of the particular offender, consistent with the protection of the public.

THE JUDGE'S RESPONSIBILITY

This latitude in choice of disposition imposes a tremendous responsibility upon the judge. It presupposes at least two conditions: first, that he will endeavor to ascertain the real causative factors of each case before him; and second, that his knowledge of available treatment facilities, both within and outside the court will enable him to select the disposition most likely to succeed. Well-trained probation officers can be of great help to him but it is the judge who must make the actual decision.

In the following discussion of dispositions, no attempt will be made to list or to discuss all of those available to the thousands of juvenile courts throughout the country. Rather, this discussion is geared to the jurisdiction of most courts and is intended to offer the judge guides to his thinking as he faces his day-to-day task of disposing equitably and constructively of each case coming before him.

DISPOSITION IN DELINQUENCY CASES

Under present conditions, the number of possible dispositions in delinquency cases will vary enormously from state to state and from community to community.

In many of the smaller communities the judge is often faced with the hard fact that he really has only two main choices; to commit the youngster to a state training school or to release him on a suspended commitment. The judge may call the suspended commitment "probation," but it is not really probation unless the child receives consistent and skilled help with his problems from a trained probation officer. These limitations will continue to prevail in the smaller communities until the judges themselves insist that they be furnished well-staffed probation services, preferably within the court itself or through a local or state agency equipped to administer such a program.

In the large communities the judge may be faced with an apparent embarrassment of riches: a well-staffed probation department, public and private casework agencies, psychiatric and psychological facilities for diagnosis and treatment, specialized social services in the school system, public and private vocational training facilities, public and private group work agencies, camping opportunities, well-selected foster homes, private character-training schools and so forth.

Regardless of the number of resources available, however, the judge's basic problem in deciding upon a disposition remains the same: how to insure that the disposition is realistically related to the causes of this youngster's behavior and not merely to the specific offense for which he is appearing in court.

Five mandates basic to the disposition of delinquency cases are:

1. *Individualize the child.* This is basic to all dispositions in the juvenile court, but particularly so for the delinquent child.

The judge must not lose sight of the basic principle that the juvenile, with rare exceptions, is answerable for the reasonable and natural consequences of his actions. However, it would be an obvious mistake to assume, for example, that every boy who "steals" a car needs the same treatment simply because the act of delinquency is the same in each case. A thorough social study might reveal, for instance, that one boy was a relatively normal youngster with a good record in school, an average family background and normally healthy associations, who had yielded to an urge to show off before his friends and had "borrowed" a car without the owner's permission but with no real idea of stealing it. It might reveal that a second boy, driven by the need to escape from an intolerable situation at home, had taken a car as a means of making his escape, but with no thought of the car as a thing of value in itself. It might also reveal that to a third youngster an automobile represented all the things he felt were lacking in his own life — prestige, economic security, power, etc., — and that he had taken a car as a kind of unconscious revenge on the society that denied these needs of his. In the public mind and to the owners of the cars involved, these three offenses might seem the same; but the discerning judge would recognize that he was dealing with three very different situations and that his disposition in each case must be determined by the problem underlying the act, and not by the act itself. He would also see that commitment to a training school would not alter the second boy's intolerable home conditions nor the third boy's feeling that the world was against him, and that suspended commitment without real probation would likewise do nothing to help either youngster. He might decide that warning the boy and his parents would be sufficient in the first case, but he would know that the second and third youngsters would require a great deal of skilled help with their emotional and social problems before they would be capable of making a normal adjustment in the community.

It is the judge's responsibility to know enough about each child appearing before him to fit the disposition to that particular youngster's problems, whether they be social, emotional, mental or other. But it is also the judge's moral if not legal responsibility to see that when he orders probation the child will receive the skilled help necessary to change faulty, antisocial attitudes and concepts, to improve weak or hostile family relationships, and to utilize the full resources of the community in the child's behalf. This is a kind of help that can best be obtained from trained, professional personnel.

The principle of "individualizing the child" as a prelude to the selection of the proper disposition is as basic for the judge as it is for the doctor to examine each individual patient before prescribing medical treatment.

2. *Have an awareness of how the child views himself.* The youngster who appears before the judge in a delinquency case may be a chronic failure — in the eyes of the community, as a member of his family, and more especially in his own thoughts and feelings. He is the child who makes poor grades in his school work and a poor impression on his teachers; he is a problem on the playground because his need for attention makes him obnoxiously aggressive and loud; at home he is disobedient, rude and prone to make unreasonable demands; he fights with his brothers and sisters in a never-ending contest for precedence and dominance, and bullies those who are smaller and weaker than he. In the privacy of his own thoughts

he admits that he is even worse than all the bad things that have been said of him by his parents, his teachers and associates of his own age. With no self-esteem to direct his choice between right and wrong and with an unfavorable reputation to live up to, he follows the only course he sees open and tries to force recognition through becoming the toughest kid on the block or the most skillful stealer of cars; or he tries to buy recognition by stealing money or goods and distributing the loot among his associates; and so on. He does gain a deal of recognition and attention through such behavior. His sense of failure is not relieved, however, when he is condemned, berated, and even beaten for his misconduct, but his conviction of his own worthlessness is further reinforced.

Faced with such a child, the judge's natural human reaction would be, except for one thing, to feel the same disgust and condemnation aroused by this youngster in everyone who has known him and to fall into the trap that has so often caught the general public — the belief that such cases can be handled only by a "get tough" policy. But the exception is that the judge has information and knowledge not available to the public. He knows how this youngster has suffered defeat time and time again. He also knows that the most belligerent child may be the most frightened and desperate one. He knows that this child who lacks faith in himself cannot change his behavior through his own efforts alone. Knowing these things, the judge would recognize the futility, even the cruelty, of returning him to the community with nothing more than a threat of dire consequences to follow further misbehavior, or a lecture on the error of his ways. He knows that commitment to a training school may appear to the child as final proof of his failure. Moreover, he would recognize that this youngster needs help from someone capable of gradually giving him recognition of his own worth, someone who could help him gain some understanding of how he constantly defeats himself, someone who could help him learn how to achieve recognition and acceptance in ways that are approved by society. Finally, the judge knows that it took years to make this child what he is today, and he would not expect miracles overnight. The judge anticipates relapses and would be prepared to deal patiently with such failures, recognizing them for what

they are and not seeing them as defiance of the court's authority.

3. *Weigh the past in terms of the future.* While there is often a tendency, especially in criminal law to deal with offenses on a cumulative basis, i.e., get tougher for each subsequent offense, this approach is not valid in any juvenile court.

This does not mean that the total past behavior of the youngster is not of tremendous importance in assessing the present situation. It does mean, however, that the number of times he has appeared before the court does not in itself supply a reliable yardstick for measuring the depth and extent of his problems at this time, and therefore that the number of these appearances cannot be used as a reliable basis for determining the present disposition. It does mean that time is needed to effect any changes in behavior and attitude, and that the longer the history of these problems, the more time may be needed to solve them. Arbitrary time limits cannot be set down as gauges for achieving certain changes in behavior. Thus a year on probation may not be sufficient in one case while it may be longer than necessary in another.

As said before, it takes time — often a great deal of time — for a treatment process to undo the damage that has been wrought over a number of years. During that period of time the child may relapse into his old pattern of behavior and commit additional delinquent acts. However, a child coming before the court for the third or fourth time may actually be a better risk and a more hopeful person than at the time of the first appearance. To commit such a child to a training school only because it is his third or fourth appearance without examining the present and previous patterns of behavior and attitude would defeat the whole purpose of the juvenile court. Each disposition should be determined not primarily by the record of past failure, but the prospect for future success.

4. *Do not tie your own hands with clichés like "probation is for first offenders only," or "only one chance on probation."* In considering a particular child before him, the judge should bear in mind that many delinquents coming to court are the victims of inconsistent or contradictory authority and their tendency is often to challenge the court's authority even

as they have already challenged and defeated the alleged authority of the home or the school. Such a child is not helped if authority, as exemplified by the court, seems to waver and contradict itself.

Yet everyone becomes more secure when he knows what standards of conduct are expected of him, when he knows who has established those standards, and what positive disciplinary action will be taken if he fails to meet them. The court can give the delinquent child that security by telling him just what is expected of him. One of the judge's problems, if he is to provide that security, is to avoid a situation where the court later contradicts itself or does not enforce its decisions or orders. To that end, decision as to disposition for some children might be reserved for a considerable period to leave the situation in an equivocal state and thus permit the court subsequently to render a disposition which is not too sharply at odds with what has gone before. To avoid inconsistency suspended commitment should not be used if the judge does not intend to put such a commitment in force in case of a new violation. This does not mean, however, that the court may never alter a decision once made.

Seeing every child as an *individual* to be understood and guided means that consistency is also called for in the entire period of the court–child relationship. This relationship is impaired when consistency is only the application of a general rule of thumb. True justice in the juvenile court is not to "treat 'em all alike," but to treat each child differently according to his needs. Consistency then implies change and modification of treatment as those needs arise.

5. *Determine the type and quality of treatment services available and select what is needed.* In general, and regardless of community resources, the dispositions available to the juvenile court in delinquency cases fall into four major classes or categories (exclusive of dismissals): *a*) probation, involving some kind of treatment program while the child remains in his own home or in a foster home (in some instances in a community other than the one in which he lives); *b*) commitment to an agency or institution for treatment under controlled living conditions; *c*) so-called "shock" dispositions, the goal of which is an immediate impact on the child and his family, which is not nec-

essarily correlated with a continuing program of treatment; and *d*) restitution.

a. For the vast majority of delinquency cases requiring judicial handling, a treatment program in the community is the wisest. The kind of treatment ordered may vary widely from case to case, depending upon the needs of the child and the resources available to the court. It may range from an intensive course of treatment in a psychiatric clinic, through a program of intensive case work with the child and his family, to relatively slight supervision in mild cases. Whether the child is in his own home (which should be the case whenever it is at all possible), in a relative's home, or in a foster home, and whatever the intensity of the treatment program, the great advantage in using this disposition is that the youngster receives help with his problems while living in the very community in which he must learn to get along. It tends to be less destructive to the child's self-respect, does not require the difficult adjustment to the abnormal living conditions of an institution or a camp, nor the readjustment to the community upon release, and does not further weaken already poor family relationships. To be fully effective, however, leaving a youngster in the community assumes that there is available to the court a probation officer or staff capable of giving or of procuring the kind of treatment that will enable the child to work through his problems and achieve a satisfactory adjustment.

When probation is used, the cooperation of the parents has an important place. As assessment of the family's strengths and their willingness to accept responsibility and to help their child will indicate the type of service the probation office must give them. The court, at the time of making the disposition, has an opportunity to emphasize the family role and to lay the background for close harmony between the family and the probation office.

b. Commitment to an agency or institution for treatment under controlled living conditions should imply that the judge is convinced that the youngster does not possess the resources to cope with the demands of community living, or that his aggressive impulses are so out of control that he constitutes a real and constant threat to the safety of the community. As a rule, a good social study will reveal the presence of either of these conditions.

The child for whom there is little hope of rehabilitation in the community is not easy to identify, but is usually characterized by the total deterioration of the relationships between himself and his parents or parent substitutes, often also of his teachers. Such a child frequently needs to be removed from his old, established associations and to have a chance to start all over again, as it were, to learn how to live with people. He often profits very considerably from a period of institutional life.

The child whose impulses are completely out of control is usually easy to identify by the violence and frequency of his acts of aggression. The impulse-ridden child may not profit too much from institutional life; but he is placed there in the first instance as a matter of protection to the community and while under the external controls of the institution may develop sufficient self-control to make possible return to the community under close supervision.

Commitment is not made in either case because these children are necessarily "worse" than those placed on probation; the choice is made because they need a kind of care that would not be possible if they were left at home or placed in a foster home. In fact, commitment is not a disposition of last resort, but should be deliberately chosen by the judge for those who need it. Some children may need this disposition at their first appearance in court.

A vital key in the use of commitment is the selection of the institution to be used. There are private institutions and schools as well as those operated by the county or state; moreover the institutions and schools vary both as to program and treatment offered and the type of delinquent who will be accepted there. Care is needed to select the proper institution or school. Thus it is axiomatic that a judge should know the various facilities that are available for commitment from his court. And the judge, in making his decision to commit a delinquent child, will have more assurance if he has visited each of those institutions, not only to see the building, but to acquaint himself with the program, equipment and personnel.

The child and his parents may consider commitment to be "cruel and unusual" punishment, but the judge must be guided by his conviction of what will ultimately be best for the child. Care should be taken not to indicate that the judge has "thrown his hands up" in disgust, or is "sending" the boy to a training school because he is convinced that the child "will never amount to anything." It is necessary to have both the child and his parents feel he is going to a treatment and training facility rather than to a place where all hope is abandoned.

Work with the family while the child is away is essential if there is to be any improvement in the home to which he will return, but all too often this is not done. Although not a specific responsibility for most courts, the judge can give the support of his office to the efforts of institutions and agencies who are attempting to develop this phase of their program.

c. In making dispositions some judges will use some device that will "shock" the child (and his family) and bring him up sharply to face the conditions and demands of community living. It cannot be overemphasized that this technique must be used with discrimination and always with people who are basically normal in personality and capable of meeting the normal demands of society.

A warning or lecture, for example, will serve to remind such a youngster of his obligations and responsibilities to society, but it assumes that he already recognizes and accepts such obligations and responsibilities in principle. A warning or lecture, on the other hand, will not change an individual character structure nor alter his personality. Thus, if the child's behavior is a symptom or result of serious emotional or social problems, or if it is an expression of a character warped by years of inadequate or faulty parental guidance, the warning or lecture will have no permanent effect on the child's behavior. Unfortunately, the temporary, even though completely sincere, contrition of a child in court is often confused with a true recognition of error and acceptance of responsibility and the judge is tempted to "let the child off with a warning." Such errors in judgment, although perfectly natural, can be very costly both to the child and to the community. They can be avoided when the judge has the benefit of a full social study and conference with his probation officer prior to making his decision.

The use of fines, in those states where they are permitted in juvenile cases, would have essentially the same limitations as warning lectures. Some feel that fines can be used constructively, if they are not too heavy and if the court allows the child to pay on the installment plan, thus giving him a periodic reminder over a period of several weeks that it does not pay to break the law. On the other hand, the child may feel he has "paid his debt" as soon as he pays his fine, and thus may develop a rather irresponsible attitude toward minor infractions of the law — an attitude which may eventually spread to more serious matters.

Probably the most effective of the shock dispositions is the removal of certain privileges, such as a driver's license, but even this method is effective only when used with the relatively normal youngster. It has, however, the advantages of a direct cause and effect relationship when the car was a factor in the delinquency, and it requires the boy to earn the restoration of the privilege.

Whether used as a separate disposition or as a condition of probation, restitution should always be part of but not in lieu of treatment. The court's chief concern is the change in behavior of the child and this can never be conclusively demonstrated by requiring payment of any sum of money. The change in behavior as well as the concern of the public, may call for restitution. (It should be noted that some judges believe restitution should not be required by the juvenile court but should be handled as a separate civil action by the party seeking restitution.)

Properly used, restitution emphasizes accountability for the natural and reasonable consequences of one's acts, and that one cannot have "fun" at the other fellow's expense. The court must make clear to the parents that restitution does not automatically guarantee the correction of any weakness in the child but that it does help the court in its understanding of the child in two ways. First, it gives a clearer indication of the sincerity of the child's regrets for what has taken place, and second, it helps clarify the degree of responsibility which the parents have concerning their child as they encourage him in his efforts to earn money for restitution. A delinquent child making restitution is forced to meet certain demands which may be therapeutic, but restitution by parents is not therapeutic treatment for a child.

Careful judgment must be used by the court in requiring restitution, particularly where it is made a condition of probation with a threat of commitment in case of failure to pay, for the commitment then becomes a matter of punishment because of such failure and not a judicial choice of treatment based on the child's current needs. Capacity and ability to pay varies and even the payment of five dollars a month may not be possible. Restitution, when used, must therefore be realistic and within the capacity and ability of the individual.

115

Analysis of a Presentence Report *

Ben Meeker

Federal Probation Editor's Note: The following presentation is the first of a series of analyses of presentence reports and chronological records to appear in FEDERAL PROBATION. The reports and records selected may or may not be examples of good case recording and presentence investigation reporting. They are selected primarily for their value in illustrating basic concepts in chronological recording and in the development of presentence investigation reports.

In approaching an analysis of the report presented herein, we first of all must have clearly in mind the purpose of a presentence report for the court and its potential value to the probation officer if probation supervision is decreed.[1] The primary function of a presentence report is to present the court with a concise, yet adequate, evaluation of all the factors which will influence the adjustment of an offender, either on probation or in confinement. The secondary function is to afford the probation officer a working knowledge of the problems and resources he will have to work with if the

---

* Reprinted from 14 *Federal Probation* (1950), 41–46. Used by permission of the author and the publisher.
[1] Such a report should be of value to institutional personnel if the defendant is sentenced to confinement.

defendant is placed on probation. At the same time, of course, throughout the process of assembling the information for the presentence report, an all-important beginning in the establishment of a relationship with the individual is being made.

There are, perhaps, two general areas to be explored by the probation officer in developing the investigation. In the first place, he must consider the individual offender's personality make-up; that is, his mental capacity, his emotional maturity, his attitudes toward himself and toward the community, his aptitudes, and his capacities. In evaluating this aspect of the individual's potential, the probation officer is attempting to discover the inner strengths, the stresses, and the limitations which the individual possesses in relation to himself and his external surroundings.

In the second place, the probation officer attempts to evaluate the total external economic and social milieu in which the offender moves in an effort to discover the nature of environmental conditions which exert influences, either for or against acceptable behavior in accordance with community standards. It is impossible to divorce the individual's personality from his external environment, since the development of personality is always a synthesis of each individual's biological and emotional demands *with* their modes of fulfillment. Modern research in human behavior tends to show that no exact line can be drawn between internal and external determinants of behavior since each tends to modify the other. Thus, a person's *conception* of the adequacy of his home may be more important in determining his reactions to that home than any objective impressions of the adequacy or inadequacy of such a home gained by a probation officer.

However, for practical purposes, it is perhaps helpful to separate the external and internal influences which appear significant in compiling the presentence report. If we apply this analysis to the following presentence report we find that a good deal of information is presented about the external social and economic environment from which this youth comes, but our knowledge of the boy's innermost feelings, his fears, his hopes, and individual limitations are, perhaps, not so well outlined.

The following presentence report is of a 16-year-old boy in a midwestern city who was charged with an offense against the National Motor Vehicle Theft Act (taking a stolen car across a state boundary). His case was heard under the provisions of the Federal Juvenile Delinquency Act.[2]

THE PRESENTENCE REPORT

I. OFFENSE:

This defendant, a juvenile, together with *three boys*, all of whom are juveniles, are charged as being juvenile delinquents in that they transported in interstate commerce from Central City *to a bordering state across the river*, and return, a stolen motor vehicle, to wit, a 1940 Chrysler sedan, well knowing said automobile to be stolen. Another defendant, *a boy age 20*, not a juvenile, is not charged at this time with these juveniles, but is awaiting Grand Jury action and is at present being held in the Clark County Jail.

The circumstances of the offense and this defendant's involvement therein, as taken from the reports of the Federal Bureau of Investigation and from interviews by this office, appear to be as follows: On the night of January 23, 1946, this defendant met and made the acquaintance of Charles. This meeting was in a theater near 7th and Central *in a neighboring town of an adjoining state*. Defendant and Charles came to Central City to a parking lot located at 325 Baltimore Street, at which place Charles had been previously employed, taking from this parking lot the automobile above described. Defendant and Charles drove the said automobile *across the river to the neighboring state* where they visited girl friends and took these girl friends for a ride at various places in the *immediate* vicinity. After returning their girl friends to their homes, defendant and Charles returned to Central City in said automobile and subsequently drove it to . . . , the home of Charles, and where he (Charles) remained.

Defendant returned the car to Central City where he kept possession of it for several days.

On the night of January 30, 1946, defendant and codefendants Brown, King, Cooper, and Carter, but not Charles, in the car above described, drove to a filling station at 12th and Vanderbilt Boulevard, Central City where, while defendant and Brown remained in the car, *the other three* burglarized said filling station taking therefrom four quarts of oil, a rubber hammer, and a hatchet. The group then drove said automobile to *a nearby town* where they broke into a drug store, obtaining cigarettes, chewing

---

[2] To protect the identity of the person studied, all identifying data, including names of persons and locations, have been altered. Italicized portions indicate slight changes in the language where reference is made to locations.

gum, a wrist watch, an electric razor, six or seven cigarette lighters, one box of cigars, and a cigarette case. This defendant swore that he did not enter the drug store but waited in the car, and it is presumed that he was acting as a lookout while the others burglarized the store. Thereafter, they drove to the vicinity of 18th and Central, *in the nearby city of the neighboring state*, thence to a point under the A. B. C. Bridge where the group slept in the car. The following day the group drove into the vicinity of *another neighboring town*. Here this defendant and Brown left the car to use a public restroom and while they were there the others, King, Cooper, and Carter, drove away deserting this defendant and Brown. This defendant and Brown are reported to have stolen and have admitted to the writer stealing a 1939 Chevrolet coupe at Smithville which they later abandoned in Parktown. *Three of the boys* were apprehended in the Chrysler automobile near 15th and Pine Streets, Central City, on the early morning of January 31, 1946. Brown was later arrested at his home, and this defendant surrendered himself at the local police station.

II. Prior Record:

Records of the Clark County Juvenile Court reveal that this defendant was arrested on December 2, 1942, for the theft of a 1941 Plymouth coupe. This car was taken from a parking lot at 14th and Wyman, and when it was recovered was in a partially wrecked condition. Defendant admitted his guilt and on December 4, 1942, was sentenced to the McCarthy Home until further orders of the court. The records further show that after a period of a few weeks the defendant ran away from the McCarthy Home and was not returned. Though the record does not record the fact, it is indicated by the Juvenile Probation Office that the defendant was thereafter returned to the Juvenile Court by his father and an understanding was had wherein the defendant was permitted to remain in his home, and to go to work.

III. Family History:

Defendant. — Defendant was born in Central City on September 18, 1929, the second of four children born to John and Mary Brown. Defendant has not been in school since he was 13 years of age but has worked and assisted in the support of the home, and for the past year has been unemployed much of the time.

Father. — Defendant's father was born in Central City in 1901. He received a third grade education. He has worked for various transfer companies here as a driver, and part of the time has operated for himself with a small truck. His earnings have always been limited and he has never made more than a bare living for his family. Since early 1945 he has been unemployed, maintaining that he is now in poor health.

In about 1928 he received a suspended prison sentence in . . . for an offense involving the theft of chickens and was placed on probation. His version of this offense is that he was hired to tow the car of the actual thieves and while doing so was arrested. He denies any part in the theft. His relationships with his home and family have not been good, and on a few occasions he has left the home. His wife and others have stated to the writer that for years he has carried on an affair with another woman and on occasions has lived with her. He is presently separated from the defendant's mother and living at 300 West 10th Street. He is presently unemployed.

Mother. — Defendant's mother was born in . . . in 1910. She states that she received an eighth grade education. As far as the writer can ascertain, she is a person of good moral reputation. She has been unable to live congenially with her husband, and asserts that this is largely due to his failure to support the family properly and the fact that he has at times associated himself with another woman.

Sisters. — Defendant's older sister is Elaine Ward whose husband is Irwin Ward. Elaine is 17 years old and was married to her husband when she was 13 years of age. She is the mother of two children, and as far as this writer can learn has never been involved in any difficulty.

Cathy is 15 years of age. In November 1944, she was in the Clark County Juvenile Court as a runaway child. She was not made a ward of the court but was carried unofficially for several months. She reported regularly to her probation officer and made very good progress in her home and school. On December 10, 1945, she was picked up in a tavern with three Mexicans. When she was brought to the attention of juvenile authorities she advised them that she did not care to return to her home and requested that they endeavor to find her a place away from her home. She suggested that she would like to go to the House of the Good Shepherd and on December 16, 1945, she was placed there. She frankly stated that conditions in her home were such that she did not care to return.

Marie, age 12, is living in the home of her mother at 3000 Washington. She attends school and has been involved in no difficulty.

IV. Home and Neighborhood:

Defendant's mother moved only a short time ago to 3000 Washington Avenue where she occupies a two-room apartment at a rental of $5 per week. Prior to that the family lived for approximately 2 years at 304 Madison Avenue; and prior to that at 502 Washington Avenue. The area in which the family lived was one in which living conditions are at a minimum, and in which the rate of juvenile delinquency is high. The home has rarely been above a subsistence level and at frequent intervals received assistance from state and local agencies. Defendant's mother is an obese, slovenly person and probably has been a poor housekeeper.

V. EDUCATION:

Defendant entered school in September 1934. The records show that he failed his first year's work, and again failed in grades 2-B and 5-B. His attendance during the time he was in school was good, and except for the fact that he was retarded in three grades, he made rather fair marks. The record shows that he was never at any time a discipline problem, and school authorities felt that in view of the defendant's abilities and the encouragement and assistance he had from his home, his school work could be considered satisfactory. Defendant's education terminated in the seventh grade and at the time he was committed to the McCarthy Home.

VI. RELIGION:

Defendant states that he is of Catholic faith, but has given little attention to his religious life. He states that at one time he did attend Sunday School at the City Union Mission. It is believed that the defendant's mother is of Catholic faith and a member of the Sacred Heart Church, though her attendance has been infrequent. Defendant's father is believed to be of Protestant faith, not a member of any congregation. There appears to have been little religious motivation in the life of this family.

VII. INTERESTS AND ACTIVITIES:

Defendant's chief recreation appears to have been in attending neighborhood picture shows. He states that he enjoys swimming, but is not active in other sports. He was, for a period, a member of the Beavers Club, a youth activity once active on the west side, but it appears to have failed in its purpose and is now closed. The defendant's employment has been for the most part as a truck driver, and he expresses an interest in mechanics, asserting that he desires to attend a school of this type.

VIII. HEALTH:

Physical. — Defendant is a 16-year-old white youth, 5 feet 10 inches in height, and weighing 185 pounds. He has blue eyes and light brown hair, and is of fair complexion. He does not give a history of any serious illnesses or diseases, and believes his present health to be good. The parents state that at the age of 3½ the defendant was struck by a car, at which time he suffered a skull fracture. They believe that the defendant recovered from this injury without impairment to his health or mental processes.

Mental and Emotional. — Defendant is a lad of rather good personality and has a very good use of the language. He was at ease during the interview and appeared to have a realization of his situation and talked freely with the writer. The Central City school records reveal that in 1942 defendant was administered an intelligence test, resulting in an intelligence quotient of 73. This score would place the defendant well below the average group and in the category of borderline intelligence.

IX. EMPLOYMENT:

In view of the defendant's youth, he presents a rather favorable record of employment. For a period of approximately one and one-half years, and to December 1944, defendant was employed by the Union Delivery Service where his record was quite satisfactory. From January to March 1945, defendant was employed by the Arnold Transfer Company as a driver, at the rate of 80 cents per hour. The company advises that the defendant's services were fairly satisfactory, considering his youth, and that he left of his own volition. From April 1945, through December 1945, defendant was employed by the Central Transfer Company where his work was regarded as satisfactory. For a period of three weeks in January 1946, defendant was employed by the National Transfer Company who report that his services were considered satisfactory, and that he was terminated when business became slack. Immediately prior to the date of the defendant's arrest in his instant offense, he was employed by the Northern Storage Company, his termination there being due to his arrest. The company reports that his work was good.

X. RESOURCES:

Defendant has no personal resources other than his clothing and immediate effects. In the event the defendant is considered for probation, the home of his mother is open to him. The defendant's father also expresses interest in assisting in a plan for subject should he be considered for probation. As has been stated, the defendant has for a period of approximately 1 year been the major support of the mother's home. A maternal aunt in . . . offers a home. Placement there away from the defendant's West Side environs and associates might be beneficial for a time.

XI. SUMMARY:

Defendant is a 16-year-old white youth charged as a juvenile delinquent in that he transported in interstate commerce a stolen automobile. Defendant also admits that while in the possession of this car he, together with others, burglarized a filling station in Central City and a drug store in *a nearby town.* Defendant also admits the theft of a 1939 Chevrolet automobile in . . . ., which was subsequently transported in interstate commerce. He has a record of one prior arrest which involved the theft of an automobile, but which it appears was not transported interstate. Defendant comes from a home which has been far from congenial and where, while the parents do not condone his antisocial behavior, they apparently have, through the life of the defendant, failed to set a pattern of good behavior for this subject to follow. Defendant's father is alleged to have neglected his home and his children, and the mother was likely unable to meet the entire responsibility of rearing this family. It seems pretty well established that the defendant has, for some time, been the support of the home.

ANALYSIS OF PRESENTENCE REPORT

Offense. Let us examine the statement concerning the offense. Here we find a 16-year-old boy who, together with four other boys, is involved in delinquency by the theft of an automobile and the burglarizing of at least two places of business. The record indicates that the other boys were apprehended but that this youth surrendered himself at the police station. Nothing is said about what his general attitude was toward the other boys with whom he was involved or the offense committed. To surrender oneself, though not uncommon, is not typical, and it perhaps would have helped in an understanding of this boy's behavior to have explored the reasons for his surrender.

Nor do we gain any indication of the boy's own reason for taking an automobile, though this pattern of behavior is apparently well established, since a juvenile court record indicates a previous auto theft at the age of 13. Automobile theft, of course, is recognized as one of the more persistently repeated offenses among juveniles seeking recognition, excitement, escape from dismal surroundings, or merely adventure.

Every probation officer is well aware of the distortion often present in the offender's account of his offense, which may not agree at all with the facts presented by the apprehending agents, and yet it has long been recognized that the offender's attitude toward his offense as he recounts the episode is frequently of great value in gaining an understanding of him.

Family History. Under the section on "Family History" we again find information about events and family make-up, but a dearth of information as to the attitudes and feelings of family members toward Johnny.[3] One discovers that the father has provided little

support for his family, having become involved with another woman. The record also indicates that the father received a prison sentence for theft of chickens but was placed on probation by the court. There is no description of the father, either from the standpoint of his appearance or of his attitude toward his son. However, the fact of separation from the mother is extremely significant in this case, and the probation officer might have found out a great deal about the mother — her attitudes, her limitations, as her husband sees them, however biased he may be — through an interview with him. There are always two sides to any separation, regardless of where the ultimate fault may reside, and it is important for a probation officer to get both sides of such questions.

Somewhat more information is presented about the boy's mother, yet we do not get any real feeling about her personality. We discover that she is 36 years of age, has an eighth-grade education, is believed to be a person of good moral reputation, but has been unable to live congenially with her husband. At one point the comment is made that she is an "obese, slovenly person and probably has been a poor housekeeper." Such comments reflect the human tendency of all of us to compare economically deprived, frequently poorly educated, and probably emotionally immature people to an absolute standard which may or may not have meaning in relation to the particular situation. We have no inkling of the boy's attitude toward his mother whom he may not regard as "obese, slovenly or a poor housekeeper," depending upon his own standards. To Johnny his mother may be attractive and neat enough, depending upon whether she comes up to the standards of the mothers of his friends. Nothing is said of her interest in her son, her feelings about his offense, or her knowledge of his good points. Although the external environment is important, the fact that most residents of deprived slum districts survive to become conforming, law-abiding citizens tends to indicate that the emotional involvements between parent and child are more significant in predisposing the child to engage in antisocial behavior than the external environment, though the latter may determine the kind of behavior an insecure child may engage in to compensate for feelings of inferiority, rejection, or hostility.

---

[3] Throughout most of the report the probation officer refers to Johnny as the "defendant." It may help to personalize the report if the name "Johnny" were used instead. This practice is especially recommended in juvenile cases.

The material concerning Johnny's sisters is again primarily descriptive in nature, with no documentation as to source. Even a sentence or two from the 17-year-old sister already married and the mother of two children, about her home and her feelings toward her brother would help in our understanding of this case. The fact that she married at the age of 13 is, of course, significant and probably indicated her need to escape an unbearable home situation. The 15-year-old sister, referred to the juvenile court as a runaway child, and at present living at the House of the Good Shepherd at her own request, preferred not to return home due to the conditions there but no additional clarification of these conditions she objected to is given. A 12-year-old sister is at home with the mother, but the only comment given is that she "has been involved in no difficulty."

Neighborhood. The report contains a number of generalizations about living conditions which convey the impression that the family lives in a blighted neighborhood where living standards are marginal and illiteracy rates are known to be high. No inkling is given, however, of the feelings of the mother or the boy toward the neighborhood in which they live. Does the mother blame the neighborhood for her son's delinquency?

Education and Religion. We gain a fairly complete descriptive picture of this boy's school attendance records, but very little about his attitude toward school or his reason for quitting school and nothing of his parents' attitude toward education. The fact that he appears to have been no problem in school is significant and would further tend to indicate that he is not an aggressive delinquent. As to religion, the record again presents an outline of events but little insight into the real place of religion in this family.

Interests and Activities. The presentence description of Johnny's interests and activities pictures him as a boy who finds his chief recreational outlet in the movies with some interest in swimming and erstwhile membership in a boys' club. We are no longer naive in our faith that a boys' group provides a cure-all for delinquency, but the value of group activity is known to be one of the tools which can be employed to encourage socially acceptable behavior and perhaps to develop wholesome,

leisure-time pursuits. Johnny also expresses a desire to receive some kind of vocational training, though whether this suggestion was given any serious consideration was not evident.

Health, Mental and Emotional Adjustments. We are here presented with a fine physical specimen, a 16-year-old boy nearly 6 feet in height and weighing 185 pounds. One can infer from this description that this youth is physically mature beyond his years, and we know the human tendency to confuse intellectual and emotional maturity with physical maturity. The fact that he left school early and was able to secure employment, although under age, is good evidence of his ability to get by on his physical appearance, and one might like to know how his unusual size and ability to work affected his parents' attitude toward him. Did they expect him to leave school and work? Was he burdened with too much responsibility too early merely because he looked mature?

The record reports that "he is a lad of rather good personality and has a good use of language . . . he is at ease during the interview." Thus, despite the fact that he was retarded in school and an old intelligence test administered by the city schools listed his I.Q. at 73, or borderline, he makes a far superior impression both physically and verbally than his intellectual capacity and emotional maturity would seem to indicate. Perhaps re-examination by a school psychologist or at a child guidance center might have revealed a better intellect than the older I.Q. record indicated.

Should we not also know something about Johnny's interest in girls? Nothing is contained in the record about his adjustment to girls, or his attitude toward sex matters. Yet we know that the average boy of 16 is very conscious of his sexual maturity and is experimenting with some sort of sexual expression.

Employment. Considering this boy's age and background, he presents an unusually favorable record of employment. His employers have found him satisfactory, and he has been a major source of support to his mother. One wonders whether he resented turning over so much of his income to her.

Resources. The home of his mother is presented as one resource and the father also appears to have offered a home. The home of a maternal aunt in a neighboring town is suggested as another. The concluding remark is that "placement there away from the defendant's West Side environs and associates might be beneficial for a time." Nothing is stated about the nature of the maternal aunt's home or her attitude toward the boy other than that she is willing to offer him a home, nor is any mention made of Johnny's attitude toward such placement. A change in his external surroundings may be indicated, but should any such plan be undertaken without first taking into consideration the boy's own desires, or at least exploring these desires and discussing them carefully with him? What are his hopes and fears, his hates and affections? What would he like to do, and how does he think probation can best help him? Is not too much reliance, perhaps, being placed upon a change of enviorns to effect a basic change in behavior?

What concrete services desired by this lad can be offered by the probation officer from community resources? Good casework meets concrete reality situations with practical services. Johnny has expressed an interest in vocational training which might prove a good beginning point. Does the probation officer know of a resource which might be of value here? How can he use this interest to further a relationship with this lad? The success of probation often is determined by the dynamic power of the relationship established between the probationer and the probation officer. Planning for a few definite services especially if they are strongly wanted by the probationer, may go far toward establishing a good working relationship at the outset of supervision. Likewise, the success of probation is greatly enhanced by utilizing the services of other agencies and in a community of this size there must be a number of good resources.

Can we conclude, therefore, that in this instance the probation officer has been preoccupied with the external environment without relating it adequately to the inner emotional feelings of the youth or his family? The information contained in the presentence report is impressive, but are the final conclusions drawn adequate? The capacities of this youth to adjust in the community at large are at best meager, and unless the community, including the aunt's home, offers a good many resources to challenge his interest, and unless

the probation officer sees a real opportunity to establish a relationship of mutual understanding, respect, and acceptance, the chances of probation success are indeed questionable.

OUTCOME OF THE CASE

(*Federal Probation Editor's Note:* At the time Mr. Meeker analyzed the presentence report presented herein, he had no knowledge of what disposition was made of the case nor the defendant's postsentence adjustment. The following statement was prepared by Mr. Meeker after this information was made available to him.)

On March 4, 1946, the court suspended execution of a 2-year sentence and placed Johnny on probation for 5 years with the stipulation that he live in the home of his aunt.

At the outset, the record shows that Johnny's adjustment was satisfactory, but before long he complained about the conditions of his aunt's home, stating that she and his sister, both widows, frequently remained out all night and that his grandmother gave him little attention. There also were some disagreements between Johnny and his aunt, and he accordingly was permitted to return home to live with his mother. During this period he continued to work as a truck driver and was the main support of his mother. The record shows that she became intensely involved in religious work, devoting virtually all of her time, day and night, to this activity and neglecting her home.

On January 6, 1947, Johnny, together with another youth, again stole a car and drove to Colorado. They were apprehended and Johnny subsequently received a 3-year sentence from the U. S. District Court at Denver. In view of this sentence he was discharged from further supervision in the original district.

This case dramatically illustrates the difficult problem so often presented by a probationer who returns to his former surroundings — which in this case became all the more involved because of the mother's abnormal religious preoccupation — while at the same time little insight into the probationer's inner emotional needs has been gained. A complete change of environment, freeing Johnny from financial responsibility of relatives, and providing opportunities for more satisfying activities might have spelled success. Greater assurance of success might have resulted from a combination of foster home placement and more exploration of Johnny's mental and emotional capacities, followed by some concrete plan which would have afforded him an opportunity to satisfy his needs for escape, adventure, independence, or accomplishment. Was the probation officer ever able to establish the kind of relationship with Johnny that fostered mutual confidence and provided Johnny with a feeling that he was a participant in planning as well as being held responsible for his activities?

Frequently, neither the time nor the resources for such thorough treatment are available, but such a case emphasizes the need to explore thoroughly the availability of other community services which might have rendered supplemental casework, vocational training, or other specific services. Certainly, if there was no alternative to placing Johnny in his old home, some plan for working more intensively with both him and his unstable mother was strongly indicated.

116

Cases Illustrating the Use of Prediction Tables *

Sheldon and Eleanor T. Glueck

In Chapters XII and XIX we presented prediction tables constructed on the basis of the materials of this research, showing the probable recidivism of offenders of the type represented by this group of juvenile delinquents, their

---

* Reprinted by permission of the publishers and The Commonwealth Fund from *Juvenile Delinquents Grown Up*, Sheldon and Eleanor T. Glueck, Cambridge, Mass.: Harvard University Press, Copyright, 1940, by The Commonwealth Fund. Chapter XX, pp. 216–234. Chapter, table, and page numbers within the text pertain to *Juvenile Delinquents Grown Up*. For further illustrations of the use of prediction tables, see Sheldon and Eleanor Glueck, *Predicting Delinquency and Crime*, Cambridge, Harvard University Press (in process of publication). See, also, the interesting No. 2, Vol. 6 of the *British J. of Delinquency*, 1955, which is concerned largely with prediction. — *Ed.*

probable age at reformation and at change from the commission of serious to minor offenses, and the probable behavior of such offenders during each of seven types of peno-correctional treatment and in the Army or Navy. Although these individual prediction tables are valuable at least in indicating the likelihood of ultimate good behavior or of good behavior during a particular treatment, to make full practical use of them a judge should know not only the type of treatment *during* which an offender is likely to behave well but also the type *following* which he gives the greatest promise of reformation. We are ready, therefore, to illustrate the practical use of prediction charts in improving the disposition practices of the courts within the framework of the present machinery for the administration of criminal justice.[1]

The reader of a work such as this is doubtless familiar with the present haphazard method of disposing of criminal cases. Random, trial-and-error procedures are the rule. Except for efforts to punish the crime — rather than the criminal — by penalties established by statute, there is no consistent approach to the disposition of cases. Courts waver between stringency and leniency, depending on their own or the community's mood or feeling about certain offenses or offenders. A rationale of punishment hardly exists. The typical case history of a criminal career is a series of fines, probations, commitments, paroles, more fines, recommitments, more probations, and so on and on through a maze of arrests, convictions, releases, nol-prosses. It is evident that offenders are constantly being resubjected to types of treatment to which they have already failed to respond, and until some means are found of subjecting an offender to the form of peno-correctional treatment that is most promising for his particular case, there can be no hope of better results than we are now getting. The disposition of cases by the use of prediction charts, which represent objectified and systematized experience with many cases similar to the particular one appearing before a judge or parole

---

[1] In *500 Criminal Careers, Later Criminal Careers*, and *Five Hundred Delinquent Women* we presented prediction tables indicating behavior following reformatory treatment, but the use of these charts is limited until we can study the behavior of the same or a like group of offenders during and following other forms of peno-correctional treatment.

board, offers an efficient method of selecting the treatment to which an offender is most likely to respond; for such charts are based on a consideration of many factors in an offender's history that are much more relevant to the conduct to be expected of him than is the offense itself.[2]

The reader is asked to bear in mind, however, that we are not proposing that judges use prediction charts to the exclusion of any other methods which have already shown themselves to be of value. A prediction table is, after all, only an instrument for the court's use, but it has, at least, a rational foundation and is not the result of vague notions about the presumably deterrent effect of this or that form of punishment, or a whim of the moment on the part of some judge, based on largely irrelevant but seemingly significant considerations — not to speak of pressure on the court for leniency or severity in a given case.

Let us assume that a judge has before him the eleven prediction charts presented in Chapters XII and XIX. These include: one indicating probable behavior of juvenile offenders during a fifteen-year span between the ages of fourteen and twenty-nine (Table 32, page 142), one indicating probable age at change from the commission of serious to the commission of minor offenses (Table 33, page 143), one indicating probable age at reformation (Table 34, page 145),[3] seven showing the probable behavior of offenders during specific types of peno-correctional treatment (Tables 70, 72, 74, 76, 78, 80, and 82, all in Chapter XIX), and one indicating probable behavior in the Army or Navy (Table 84, page 214). How would he be aided in disposing of an offender before him for sentence by the application of these predictive devices?

First, for every case appearing before him a judge would have to request a court officer to gather the necessary data on each of the fac-

tors used in the construction of the tables, as the basis for figuring the offender's scores. These scores determine his probable behavior during various forms of peno-correctional treatment and the likelihood of his ultimate reform. A glance at the prediction tables indicates that the number of factors about which information has to be gathered for each case is not large, because some of them are used in several tables. There is no doubt that a skilled investigator could assemble the necessary information and verify it in as short a time as is at present required by the court for the usual probation officer's investigation and report preliminary to an offender's sentence.

Once these data have been gathered, each offender can be scored. This process actually takes only a few minutes. With the scores made, the judge can see at a glance not only what the chances are of the particular offender's ultimate reformation, but also at what age he is likely to reform or, if he is not likely to reform, whether he has a reasonable chance at least of becoming a minor offender and at what age; also, he can determine during which form or forms of treatment the particular offender has the best chance of good behavior.

Consider a few illustrations. In Table 85 are shown, for a series of cases, post-treatment failure scores and chances of good behavior (reform) during the age-span fourteen to twenty-nine years under various forms of peno-correctional treatment and in the Army and Navy. Knowing an offender's chances of good behavior during particular treatments, and the chances of his ultimate reform, a judge examining such individual case charts could arrive rather quickly at a suitable disposition of the case.

Analyzing cases A, B, and C, to whom these tables can be applied because they actually were juvenile delinquents, let us put ourselves back in the juvenile court at the time when, as boys, these offenders first came before the judge, and see how he would have used the prediction tables. By consulting Table 32 in Chapter XII (page 142) he would first ascertain that as the youths score 98.3, 85.5, and 98.3, respectively, they are representative of a "treatment type" in which each has six chances in 10 of ultimate reformation, one and a half chances of remaining a serious offender, one and a half chances of becoming a minor of-

---

[2] See 500 *Criminal Careers*, p. 295–296.

[3] As we have shown earlier, this does not mean that arrival at any specific age is in itself a guaranty of reform, but only that arrival at a certain age by a person possessed of certain traits ("factors") will result in a certain kind of behavior. In these prediction tables, "age" is prognostically significant only as related to other factors. Persons scoring differently on the predictive factors will reform at different ages if at all.

fender, and less than one chance in 10 of erratic behavior (that is, not reforming but being occasionally a serious offender and occasionally minor). He would then ascertain from Table 34 (page 145) that with such scores, A, B, and C have only one and a half chances in 10 of reforming when less than fifteen years of age, five chances in 10 of doing so when between fifteen and twenty-one, and three and a half in 10 when twenty-one or over.

The judge might assume that because A, B, and C have equal chances of reforming, the same treatment is indicated in all three cases. But this is not so, as we shall see from an analysis of their chances of good behavior during various types of treatment. From the scoring made for each form of treatment we see that case A has four chances in 10 of behaving well during straight probation, only two in 10 of behaving well during probation that carries a threat of commitment to an institution, and only three in 10 of behaving well on parole after serving an institutional sentence. Obviously A is too great a threat to the general security to be allowed to remain at large. His chances of responding satisfactorily to treatment in institutions are better than during extramural supervision, for he has four and a half chances of satisfactory behavior in a correctional school, five and a half in a reformatory, six and a half in prison, and seven in jail.

But there is still another matter to be taken into account. Our judge's decision as to the disposition of this case would be determined finally by A's age at the time of the particular court appearance. If he is only thirteen years old, let us say, straight probation might well be indicated, in view of A's reasonably good changes of ultimate reformation and the fact that his antisocial behavior would probably not be serious at that age; if he does not respond satisfactorily to probation he can, on his next appearance in court, be committed to a correctional school. If, however, A, a former juvenile delinquent, is about twenty-one years old at the time of his appearance in an adult court, commitment to a reformatory would be wiser than placement on probation. But in view of the fact that A still has three and a half chances in 10 of reformation after the age of twenty-one, too long a sentence is not indicated (see Table 34, page 145). If A is between twenty-five and thirty at the time of court appearance,

the judge would choose between prison and jail, depending upon what opportunities A needs for vocational training, health supervision, or psychiatric attention; but subsequent parole would have to be applied with care, because of A's poor chance of good behavior during parole. The parole authorities would have to be particularly admonished to give A close and intensive supervision, or the judge would have to impose a longer sentence in order to avoid parole as long as possible.

As already pointed out, B has the same chance of ultimate reform as A, but his probable behavior during different forms of treatment does not resemble A's in all respects. Like A, he has four chances in 10 of behaving well during probation, but he has six chances (instead of A's two) of good behavior under suspended sentence. Unlike A who has but three chances, B has six and a half chances in 10 of behaving well during parole. Like A, he has four and a half chances of satisfactory behavior in a correctional school, but only three and a half chances of behaving satisfactorily in a reformatory, to A's five and a half. B has seven chances in 10 of behaving acceptably in prison or jail, which is about the same as A's.

In considering the best disposition of B's case, a judge would be likely to place him on probation under a suspended sentence if he was under twenty-one at the time of the particular court appearance; for his chances of good behavior on that form of treatment are greater than under straight probation or in a correctional school or a reformatory. If he is twenty-one or older he might be sent to prison or jail on a sentence which would provide early release on parole, for his score shows that he has six and a half chances in 10 of responding favorably to parole and there is, therefore, no need to keep him behind walls for any considerable length of time. In other words, the judge would see that B would do well on probation under a suspended sentence or under a short sentence to an institution (if commitment is indicated at all for any special reason, such as need of vocational training, medical care, or psychiatric attention) followed by a long period of parole, but that a correctional school or a reformatory should be avoided if possible.

It is of interest at this point to record what actually happened to B under the existing method of disposing of cases. He did finally

Table **85** *Illustrative Cases Showing Chances of Good Behavior During Age-Span Fourteen to Twenty-nine and During Specific Types of Peno-Correctional Treatment and in Army or Navy*

CASES	During Age 14-29	During Probation	During Probation Under Suspended Sentence	During Parole	In Correctional School	In Reformatory	In Prison	In Jail	In Army or Navy
Case A: Score	98.3	287.5	363.3	351.3	221.1	213.5	109.9	89.0	188.7
Chances of good behavior	6	4	2	3	4½	5½	6½	7	7
Case B: Score	85.5	273.1	327.4	341.1	225.4	222.4	128.7	95.4	214.9
Chances of good behavior	6	4	6	6½	4½	3½	7	7	7
Case C: Score	98.3	298.3	348.0	351.3	210.0	222.4	146.9	105.2	214.9
Chances of good behavior	6	4	2	3	6½	3½	7	7	7
Case D: Score	139.2	281.4	335.0	341.1	210.0	222.4	134.3	105.2	214.9
Chances of good behavior	3½	4	2	3½	6½	3½	7	7	7
Case E: Score	132.6	306.6	355.6	351.3	221.2	228.5	146.9	95.4	205.3
Chances of good behavior	3½	4	2	3	4½	3½	7	7	7
Case F: Score	120.0	252.2	296.0	312.0	210.0	206.8	128.7	78.2	188.7
Chances of good behavior	3½	6	5	3½	6½	6	7	7	7
Case G: Score	148.1	310.6	348.0	357.1	221.2	200.4	112.7	105.2	188.7
Chances of good behavior	3½	4	2	3	4½	6½	7	7	7
Case H: Score	145.3	318.4	348.0	371.1	210.0	209.3	127.4	88.0	195.5
Chances of good behavior	3½	4	2	3	6½	6	7	7	7
Case J: Score	168.4	318.4	348.0	351.3	210.0	209.3	162.3	105.2	195.5
Chances of good behavior	3½	4	2	3	6½	6	7	7	7
Case K: Score	184.3	318.4	383.1	364.9	227.4	213.5	130.2	88.0	222.2
Chances of good behavior	3½	4	2	3	4½	5½	7	7	7
Case L: Score	183.2	310.6	370.9	364.9	221.2	213.5	144.1	105.2	262.1
Chances of good behavior	3½	4	2	3	4½	5½	7	7	7
Case M: Score	183.2	310.6	383.1	364.9	195.8	222.4	144.1	68.1	222.2
Chances of good behavior	3½	4	2	3	7	3½	7	5	7

reform when he was about twenty-six years old, but meanwhile he had been placed on straight probation at the age of fifteen (instead of being given probation under suspended sentence under which, as his prediction chart indicates, his chances of good behavior were much greater than under probation). He soon ran away and when apprehended was committed to a correctional school (the chart indicates that he was not likely to respond well to this form of treatment). There he remained for fifteen months and proved to be very difficult and lazy. At the age of seventeen he was paroled, and for almost four years behaved quite well (his chart indicates a good chance of success on parole). At the age of twenty-two he again appeared in court, this time for non-support, and he was again placed on straight probation. He soon defaulted, however, and joined the Army where he remained for two years; he behaved exceedingly well and was given an honorable discharge (his prediction chart indicates likelihood of good behavior in the Army). Since his honorable discharge from the Army, B has given no trouble whatsoever. Whether he would have reformed earlier if given the kind of treatment during which he had a good chance of behaving well is of course an open question. Obviously, if throughout his career he had been given the kind of treatment during which he was likely to behave reasonably well, he would have avoided friction with the authorities, the public would have had greater protection from his depredations, treatment in his case would have been less wasteful, and possibly good adjustment would have carried over into his life in freedom.

As to case C, the judge would note that his chances of reformation are the same as A's and B's. A glance at his chart indicates that C, like A and B, has four chances in 10 of succeeding under probation; and like A but unlike B, he has very little chance of success either during probation under suspended sentence or during parole. He has, however, a better chance than either A or B of satisfactory conduct in a correctional school but as little chance as B of success in a reformatory, and as good a chance as A and B of adequate adjustment in prison or jail. If C happens to be under seventeen at the time of the particular court appearance, the judge might be inclined to try straight probation in his case. If probation has already

been tried and C has not done well, his small chance of succeeding under the more stringent probation accompanied by a suspended sentence to an institution makes it obvious that direct commitment to a correctional school is indicated, for C has six and a half chances in 10 of satisfactory behavior during this type of treatment. A wise judge would avoid sentencing this offender to a reformatory because his chances of satisfactory behavior there are clearly much lower than under the stricter regimes of prison or jail. If he sends C to an institution, it should be on a long rather than a short sentence, in the light of C's probably poor response to parole.[4]

What actually happened to C under the present system of disposing of cases is worth noting. At the age of twelve he was given probation under suspended sentence for the offense of burglary (which his chart indicates should not have been done, for he had but two chances in 10 of success). During this time he was arrested for stealing, the previous sentence was invoked, and he was committed to a correctional school, where his behavior was excellent (as his prediction chart indicates it was likely to be). He was paroled (as the prediction chart indicates he should not have been), and had to be returned to the correctional school because of consistent misbehavior. During a second, third, and fourth stay in the cor-

---

[4] The question whether an offender of this type should be released on parole involves a consideration of the entire philosophy of parole and the practical problem of balancing individual and social interests. If parole were implemented by a truly (i.e., wholly) indeterminate sentence the problem would be simple; given so high a risk, it would be the better part of wisdom to keep such an offender under strict institutional control, because the protection of society against aggression comes first and the individual's welfare second. Such a person might be released later in life, when he is no longer actively dangerous. However, existing "indeterminate" sentences are in a sense fixed sentences in that the upper and lower limits of a frequently narrow zone of years are set. As long as this is true, the paroling authority must cope with the puzzling problem of whether it is better, in the long run (a) to release all offenders at some time before the expiration of the maximum limit of sentence thereby affording them some supervision during the transition to absolute freedom but subjecting society to the risk of their committing new crimes during a period when they might have been safely in prison; or (b) to keep them incarcerated for the full term and release them at its conclusion without any supervision.

rectional school, C's behavior was excellent (as the chart indicates it was likely to be); while during a second, third, and fourth parole he seriously misbehaved (as the chart indicates he probably would). At the age of eighteen, during parole, he was arrested for larceny and placed on probation, during which he committed larcenies (his chart indicates only four chances in 10 of good behavior on probation). At the age of nineteen he was sent to a reformatory for larceny, and seriously misbehaved there (his chart indicates a very low chance of success in a reformatory). During parole from the reformatory he misbehaved and he was again sent to the reformatory where he again misbehaved; he was again placed on parole and misbehaved, and was again returned to the reformatory and misbehaved. At the age of twenty-three he was transferred from a reformatory to a jail, where he remained for a year and a half, and was then transferred to another jail for a year. While in jail his behavior was satisfactory (reference to the chart indicates that C had a very high chance of good behavior in jail). At the age of twenty-eight C is still a serious criminal. Although we cannot, within the present limited state of our knowledge, assert that, given the treatment indicated by the prediction chart, reformation, or minor rather than serious delinquency, would have resulted (it should be remembered that C's chances of ultimate reformation were six in 10), it is certainly reasonable to assume that C would at least have done much less damage along the way, and at less expenditure of public funds for rearrests, retrials, and the like, had he been given the treatment indicated.

It should be evident to the reader by now that although A's, B's, and C's chances of post-treatment reformation are the same, the peno-correctional treatments *during* which they had the best likelihood of good behavior are different.

We turn now to an application of the prediction charts to three other cases, D, E, and F (Table 85). Consultation of Table 32 (page 142) indicates that, unlike cases A, B, and C, who had six chances in 10 of reformation, D, E, and F, scoring 139.2, 132.8, and 120, respectively, have but three and a half chances in 10 of ultimately reforming, a like low probability of ultimately becoming minor offenders, almost two and a half chances of remaining

serious offenders, and less than one chance in 10 of being erratic offenders (that is, alternating between serious and minor delinquencies). A glance at Table 33 (page 143) shows further that D, E, and F have but two chances in 10 of becoming minor delinquents while still under twenty-one years of age, almost five in 10 when they are between fifteen and twenty-one, and three in 10 when they are twenty-one and over. In other words, there are about six and a half chances in 10 that they will become minor offenders when they are still under twenty-one, if they do not reform entirely or remain serious delinquents.

Despite the resemblance in the probable ultimate adjustment of cases D, E, and F, an examination of their scores for each form of peno-correctional treatment, as recorded in Table 85, again indicates certain differences in the way a court should dispose of these cases. For instance, F has a much better chance of succeeding on probation than D and E and likewise a much better chance of success on probation under suspended sentence. All three offenders have about a like chance of success on parole; but E has less of a chance of succeeding in a correctional school regime than D and F; while F has a much better chance of behaving well in a reformatory than D and E. All three offenders, however, have an equally good chance of conducting themselves acceptably in prison, in jail, or in the Service.

Examination of the chances of success of each one of these offenders *during* particular forms of peno-correctional treatment indicates that if probation fails in D's case, the correctional school regime gives promise of eliciting good behavior. A reformatory regime should be avoided, if possible, because D's chances of success there are low; prison or jail may be utilized with a good chance of satisfactory behavior, but parole should be avoided unless the strictest kind of supervision can be given, as D's chances of good behavior under this form of treatment are low.

In the case of E, on the other hand, a correctional school regime does not seem very promising, but if E is at the age where prison or jail could be considered, such regimes are more suitable for him. If probation is resorted to and fails and a correctional school is tried and he does not behave well there, this does not mean that E will not adjust himself to later intramural experiences; but if there appears to be no alternative treatment for him, probation and correctional school authorities would have to expend special effort to make the regime work successfully in E's case, and be on guard against his probable misbehavior.

In the case of F, as is readily seen from Table 85, there is a good chance of his success on straight probation or on probation under suspended sentence; not so good a probability of success on parole; but a good chance of adjusting satisfactorily in a correctional school, reformatory, prison, or jail. The judge has a wide variety of choices in prescribing treatment for F, and can be guided by the special facilities of the various institutions, by the call for a "deterrent punishment," or even by F's preferences.

Now a word as to what actually happened to D, E, and F under the present system of disposing of cases. D was placed on probation at the age of ten and did not respond well (his chart indicates four chances in 10 of good adjustment on probation). He was soon placed on probation again, but this time in a foster home where he was closely supervised. Here he behaved well, which would seem to indicate that probation under close supervision outside his home was indicated in his case. At the age of fifteen he was given probation under suspended sentence for the crime of larceny, and violated his probation by again committing larceny (his prediction chart indicates that he had but two chances in 10 of succeeding on probation under suspended sentence). Soon after, still at the age of fifteen, D was placed on probation in the home of an uncle where he was carefully supervised. There his behavior was excellent, as it had previously been while he was on supervised probation in a foster home. D did not ultimately reform (it will be remembered that his chances of reformation were but three and a half in 10), but he did become a minor offender approximately at the age of seventeen. Had the prediction chart been used in his case it is possible that his misconduct during periods of straight probation and probation under suspended sentence would have been avoided; or, if probation had been resorted to, very close extramural supervision, such as was provided in the foster home and in the home of an uncle, would have been given originally.

E and F each had but one period of probation, E at the age of twenty-five and F at the age of fourteen. They both behaved well during these periods. E, who was a minor offender, has remained such, and F reformed approximately at the age of fourteen. The question may well be asked whether the immediate use of the proper treatment for F did not hasten the reformation of this particular offender. This of course remains an academic question for the present. However, in the case of E, who had but one period of probation and then not till he was twenty-five years old, minor delinquencies continued. Is it possible that if probation or some other treatment to which he was likely to respond had been applied much earlier in his career, he might today be a non-delinquent rather than a minor delinquent?

We are now ready to consider the cases of G, H, and J whose probable behavior between the ages of fourteen and twenty-nine and during various peno-correctional treatments is indicated in Table 85. Their chances of ultimate reform, according to Table 85, are the same as of D, E, and F, that is, three and a half in 10; but unlike D, E, and F, who had but two in 10, they have almost four chances in 10 of remaining serious offenders; and further, unlike D, E, and F who had almost four in 10, they have only two chances in 10 of becoming minor offenders. A judge knowing the likelihood of the continuing serious delinquencies of G, H, and J would, for the sake of the public protection, no doubt be inclined to consider either very close extramural supervision or incarceration for them. He would use probation only with extreme caution. In the case of G, however, he might be more inclined at least to try probation during the juvenile court age, because G would have little more chance of successful behavior in a correctional school than on probation, and probation is cheaper; but H and J would have a better chance of adjustment in a correctional school than on probation. If the offenders were of reformatory, prison, or jail age at the time of a particular court appearance, the judge would be likely to resort to commitment to one of those institutions, without even attempting probation.

Under the present system of disposing of cases, G was put on probation when he was eleven years old, and he committed burglaries while on probation. Then commitment to a correctional school was attempted (the prediction chart indicates that G would have very little more chance of good behavior in a correctional school than on probation). He did not behave well during either this or any succeeding commitment to a correctional school, running away several times, committing malicious injury to property, being on one occasion discovered to have a hypodermic needle, assisting in the escape of another boy, and so on. During periods of parole from the correctional school his behavior was equally poor (that it was likely to be is evident from the prediction chart). When G was eighteen years old he was committed to a reformatory where his behavior, though better than in the correctional school, was still not entirely desirable (his chart shows six and a half chances in 10 of good behavior in a reformatory). When on parole from the reformatory, he was arrested several times for assault and battery and for burglary. At the age of twenty-one he was committed to prison where his poor behavior is reflected in several periods of solitary confinement (his chart shows seven chances in 10 of satisfactory behavior in prison). During periods of parole from prison, he was arrested on several occasions for burglary, for larceny, and for keeping and exposing liquor. On a recent commitment to prison, however, G's behavior has distinctly improved. At the present writing he is still incarcerated, but behaving well. He has until very recently seriously misbehaved throughout his career both in extramural and intramural periods, despite the fact that according to his prediction chart his chances of adjustment *during* certain intramural treatments are high. In view of this, the question may well be asked, whether, given especially good supervision in certain of the institutions, G might not have gotten along better. However, in a case like this, institutional authorities, guided perhaps by the findings in Chapter XV in which the reasons for failure to behave satisfactorily during intramural treatment are suggested, could determine the reasons in a case like G's, and perhaps give him more telling individualized guidance.

During a long criminal career, H has been placed on probation several times, has had suspended sentences, has been on parole on innumerable occasions, has served many times in correctional schools, and has served several sentences in a reformatory and in jails. Throughout his career, during extramural or intramural treatment and when free, he has committed many serious crimes including theft, burglary, assault to rob. Except during a brief term in jail, he has shown no tendency to good behavior. In view of his low chance of success during extramural treatment, such an offender should, for the sake of the public protection, certainly not be subjected to repeated periods of probation or parole. Since his chances for satisfactory behavior in institutions are high, every effort would have to be made by the penal authorities, as in the case of G, to bring about a good adjustment on his part.

J was placed on probation three times, and on each occasion seriously misbehaved. At the age of eighteen he enlisted in the Army, where he remained for eight years and behaved exceedingly well. He has been non-delinquent ever since his enlistment. It would appear that Army discipline "straightened him out." According to the prediction chart, his chances of ultimate reformation were no better than G's and H's; yet G and H continued to be serious offenders, while J apparently discovered for himself the very treatment to which he could respond well. Again the question arises, whether, given treatment during which the habit of good conduct becomes fixed, this habit is carried over into life in freedom.

We come, finally, to a consideration in Table 85 of cases K, L, and M. According to Table 32 (page 142), cases K, L, and M, with scores of 184.3, 183.2, and 183.2 respectively, each have three and a half chances in 10 of reformation, five and a half in 10 of remaining serious offenders, and less than one chance in 10 of becoming minor offenders. In view of the high probability of their continuing serious delinquency, it is unlikely that a judge would consider extramural supervision for such offenders. For K and L, however, he might be inclined to try probation during the juvenile court age, because their chances of good behavior in a correctional school are very little more than on probation; but if K and L were of the age when they could be sent to a reformatory, prison, or jail, such disposition would be made in preference to probation. In view of their slight chances of success on parole, however, the institutional sentences would have to be long.

A judge would hardly be inclined to attempt probation at all for M during the juvenile court age, as M's chances of good behavior in a correctional school are as high as seven in 10. The judge would avoid committing M to a reformatory, however, where the chances of the youth's success would be only three and a half in 10, and if restraint were called for, he would preferably send M to prison.

What actually happened to K, L, and M under the present system of disposing of cases may be illuminating at this point. L had periods of probation, was confined in correctional schools, reformatories, and prisons, and had several periods of parole in the course of his criminal career — eighteen treatment experiences in all. Until a very recent commitment to prison at the age of twenty-eight, he was a miserable failure. His first correctional treatment, probation, occurred when he was twelve years old, and from that time until he was fifteen he was on probation on four successive occasions, failing badly each time. Not until he was fifteen and the habit of delinquency was firmly established, was he placed in a correctional school where, according to his prediction chart, he should have behaved at least a little better than he would be likely to on probation. He actually did not behave well, however. The question to be raised in this case is whether a better result might not have been obtained in his case, at least in the form of better behavior inside walls, had commitment to an institution been applied early in his delinquent career, before his habits of delinquency became fixed.

As for M, he was placed on probation at the age of twelve and during this period committed larcenies (his score indicates four chances in 10 of good behavior on probation). Instead of being immediately sent to a correctional school (where, as his score indicates, he had seven chances in 10 of good behavior) he was again placed on probation, and continued to steal. Only then was he sent to a correctional school, and although in the beginning his conduct was not desirable, he soon settled into the routine, and during this and two successive commitments to a correctional school he behaved very well. While on parole from the correctional school, however, M got into serious difficulty (his prediction chart indicates only three chances in 10 of good behavior). At the age of nineteen, M was committed to a reformatory where he proved very troublesome (his chart indicates but three and a half chances in 10 of

good behavior in a reformatory). At the age of twenty-three he was sent to prison where his conduct was satisfactory (his chart indicates the high probability of seven chances in 10 of good behavior). Following his release from prison M was placed on parole, and during the next two years his conduct on parole was satisfactory. Is it possible that a substantial period of good behavior in prison contributed to his adjustment on parole, despite the fact that he failed during all previous parole periods and that his chart indicates but three chances in 10 of success on parole?

We want now to consider for a moment the case of K in contrast to L. The likelihood of continuing recidivism on the part of K is as high as L's, and as already indicated, both have exactly the same chances of good behavior during the various forms of peno-correctional treatment. Apparently, therefore, a judge using the prediction charts would handle both of these cases in just the same way. It is of interest at this point, therefore, to see what actually did happen to K and L under the present method of disposing of cases. On the occasion of his first court appearance at the age of sixteen, K was given a suspended sentence to a correctional school, which was imposed in less than a month's time because of failure on probation (his chart shows but two chances in 10 of good behavior on probation under a suspended sentence). He was in the correctional school for almost a year, and his behavior was very good (his chart shows four and a half chances in 10 of good behavior here). He was placed on parole at the age of seventeen and kept under parole supervision until he was twenty-one (his chart shows three chances in 10 of good behavior on parole). During this time his behavior was satisfactory, and he has since been a non-delinquent; and this despite the great probability of his recidivism.

As to L, it will be remembered that four periods on straight probation were attempted from the time he was twelve until he was fifteen years of age, before a correctional school was resorted to. His miserable failure throughout eighteen peno-correctional treatments, terminating in a life sentence to prison where his behavior now at the age of twenty-eight is fairly acceptable, is in sharp contrast to K's early good adjustment. We again venture the query: May not the fact of proper treatment in K's case almost immediately upon his first court appearance have contributed to his good adjustment not only during treatment but afterwards? Would not the delay in proper treatment in L's case furnish opportunity for the establishment of habits of delinquency which became hard to break?

However, our purpose in this chapter has not been to answer these and related questions, because they are unanswerable within the present state of our knowledge. We have attempted merely to show how treatment becomes more individualized with the use of prediction charts than it is without them.

117

Prediction of Success or Failure Under Various Forms of Treatment *

Sheldon and Eleanor T. Glueck

It is a familiar fact that until tables constructed from the correlation of background factors with behavior are tested on other samples of cases than the ones on which the tables were originally constructed, they should more correctly be regarded as summaries of experience rather than as definitive predictive instruments.

This fact has led us to follow up the careers of the 500 delinquents whose lives were originally studied in *Unraveling Juvenile Delinquency*. When these boys were originally examined (for a research comparing 500 persistent delinquents with 500 non-delinquents, previously matched, case by case, for age, intelligence, ethnic origin and residence in under-

privileged urban areas), the data necessary for predicting the behavior of the delinquents were systematically assembled for each boy. These predictions were set aside pending a long-term follow-up of the young offenders to see how closely their predicted behavior on straight probation, on probation with suspended sentence, in correctional schools, in reformatories, in prisons, on parole and at the end of five-year and fifteen-year follow-up spans after the treatment given by the juvenile court, turned out to be true to the subsequent facts.

This type of inquiry requires a great deal of skill and patience and the systematic consultation of a great many sources of material regarding the behavioral responses. An elaborate system of inquiry was established with the cooperation of the Trustees of the Massachusetts Training Schools, the Boys' Parole Division (now the Youth Service Board), the Massachusetts Board of Probation, the superintendents and certain staff members of the correctional schools (including psychologists, teachers and house-parents), the Massachusetts Department of Correction and Parole Board, the superintendents and other personnel of the Massachusetts Reformatory, the Massachusetts State Prison, State Prison Colony at Norfolk; the Massachusetts Bureau of Criminal Identification of the Department of Public Safety, and many out-of-state and Federal courts, institutions, and parole authorities.

The amount of effort expended, both within and outside of Massachusetts, may be surmised from the fact that during 1940–1956, complete reports were gathered on no fewer than 3,397 treatment periods.[1]

As soon as a boy was ready for follow-up, the Boys' Parole authorities would notify us promptly if the offender was paroled, rearrested, whether parole was revoked, whether a marked change had occurred in the offender's home, such as going to live with relatives, etc., whether the parole period was terminated. The institutional authorities also extended cooperation in ways that made it possible for us to obtain full reports promptly after treatment periods were completed. In order not to miss any treat-

---

* From "Prediction of Success or Failure under Various Forms of Treatment: Extracts from and Summary of Parts of Validation of Predictive Tables Involving Delinquents," *Predicting Delinquency and Crime*, (in process of publication) Chapter IV, Cambridge, Harvard University Press, Copyright by the President and Fellows of Harvard College. Used by permission of the publisher.

[1] Many more periods were in fact studied but where the data were found inadequate, these reports — behavior in jails and houses of correction, for example — were found to be too meagre to be used in the final analysis.

ment periods to which the 500 offenders might have been subjected, we annually cleared certain cases through the files of the Massachusetts Board of Probation, as well as through the fingerprint files of Massachusetts and elsewhere.

Progress charts were kept of the ever-increasing number of treatment periods. In this way the work yet to be carried out on each case was always in clear view.

As each case was completed, the data were summarized by Dr. Eleanor T. Glueck with some assistance from Richard E. Thompson on a special form designed for that purpose; the findings were coded and punched on I.B.M. cards to permit of tabulation and correlation with a view to determining the extent of *agreement between the predicted and the actual behavior*.

Four hundred and ninety-seven boys, whose behavior during various forms of peno-correctional treatment was followed from the onset of their criminal careers until their twenty-third birthday, had a total of 3,397 peno-correctional experiences of sufficient duration to be studied.

Details as to both methods and results are given in *Predicting Delinquency and Crime*.[2]

Regarding the number of types of treatment, ten offenders had experienced only one type; 53 had two; 156, three; 191, four; 76, five; and 11, six.

Two hundred and ninety-seven boys had 380 experiences on ordinary probation; 356 boys had 548 probations under suspended sentences; 488 boys had 1,055 correctional school experiences; 461 boys had 1,053 parole periods; 157 boys had 320 commitments to a reformatory, and 35 boys had experienced 41 prison terms.

In interpreting the following findings, it is necessary to take into account the fact that in our sample of cases the proportion of offenders predictable as *good risks* under each form of treatment is small; for these boys were true delinquents, rather than children who had committed one or two peccadilloes, when selected for inclusion in *Unraveling Juvenile Delinquency*.

With these preliminaries, the following findings are of the utmost significance:

(1) Regarding the various forms of extra-

mural treatment, it was found that of 286 delinquents predicted as having more than an even chance of *violating straight probation*, 94.4% actually committed serious, or persistent minor, offenses during probation. Of 344 offenders predicted as failures during *probation under suspended sentence*, 98% in fact turned out to be serious, or persistent minor, offenders; of 458 delinquents predicted as violating *parole*, 91% actually were later found to be parole violators.

(2) Turning now to intramural treatment, of 465 delinquents predicted as *not adapting well* to a *correctional school regime*, 78.7% proved to be serious, or persistent minor, offenders in correctional schools; of 39 boys predicted as not adapting well to a *reformatory regime*, 53.8% proved to be serious, or persistent minor, offenders, while in the reformatory. Although three of the four offenders predicted as not doing well in *prison* were found later to be serious, or persistent minor, offenders, the number involved is so small that no conclusion can be reached.

(3) Looking now at those few delinquents whom the tables predicted as adapting *well* in reformatories and prisons, a more cautious conclusion is necessary about these, because of the smallness of numbers of those predicted as behaving satisfactorily. Of 118 offenders predicted as adapting well to a *reformatory regime*, 67.8% proved to be non-offenders or to have committed only an isolated minor offense while in the institution; of 31 delinquents predicted as good risks in *prison*, 80.6% were in fact found to have been such. Those predicted as doing well in extramural treatment were too few in number to base definitive conclusions on.[3]

(4) We turn next to a consideration of the extent of agreement between the predicted and actual behavior during *each of the treatment periods* experienced by the offenders. Agreement between predicted and actual behavior is deemed to have occurred if an offender had been predicted as having *more than an even chance of delinquency* during a particular form of peno-correctional treatment and was actually found to have committed serious or persistent minor offenses while on such treatment; or, if

---

[2] *Op. cit.*, Chapter IV.

[3] See *Predicting Delinquency and Crime, op. cit.*, for details.

an offender was predicted as having *more than an even chance of non-delinquency* and was later found to be in fact a *non-offender*, or to have committed only an isolated minor offense such as violating traffic regulations.

(5) With this explanation, it was found that out of 380 *straight probation periods* the predicted and the actual behavior were in agreement in 92.1% of such periods; of 545 periods *of probation with suspended sentence*, agreement was found in 93.6%; of 1,053 *parole periods*, the predicted and the actual results were in accord in 91.9%; of 1,054 *correctional school experiences*, agreement occurred in 78.8%; and as to periods in *reformatories* and *prisons*, agreement was found in 73.1% and 75.6%, of the treatments respectively.

(6) The follow-up in question also disclosed that agreement between predicted and actual behavior becomes progressively lower as the youths grow older, ranging from 96.7% of those treatments occurring when the delinquents were under eleven years old, to 76.9% when they were 21 to 23 years of age. It was also discovered, in confirmation of our findings in other researches,[4] that as delinquents advance in age there is some decline in the total amount of recidivism.

(7) It was further found that, contrary to what some might expect, in a higher proportion of treatment periods of less than seven months' duration (83.1%), the unlawful behavior was serious, or persistent minor, in nature than in treatment periods of 25 months and over (73.6%). On the whole, the actual length of the treatment periods was found to have made very little difference in the proportion of those who had been serious, or persistent minor, offenders during such periods.

(8) Four hundred and thirty-five delinquents (98.6%) had been predicted as having more than an even chance of serious or persistent minor delinquency during the five-year span *after the end of the first treatment period*. Follow-up investigation disclosed that, actually, 419 of these 435 offenders (96.3%) turned out in fact to be serious, or persistent minor, offenders during the five-year post-treatment span.

The fact that the prediction tables constructed on one group of cases — boys who had appeared in the Boston Juvenile Court during 1917–22 — were later tested on boys who first appeared in juvenile courts throughout the greater Boston area (and some even in other cities and towns of Massachusetts) during the years 1938–40, makes it clear that it cannot be said that the Juvenile Court Prediction Tables discussed herein have only a very narrow applicability. It should be pointed out further that while the two sets of delinquents resemble each other in many respects, they also differ in various ways. *The fact that prediction tables constructed on one group of cases check so remarkably on another group, despite differences in the background of the two sets of delinquents, broadens the base of their usefulness.*[5]

From the foregoing results it would appear that the prediction tables for use in juvenile courts have met one stringent test of practical effectiveness as instrumentalities for aiding judges in forecasting the response of delinquents to the various traditional peno-correctional treatments prescribed by such courts.

---

[4] S. and E. Glueck, *Juvenile Delinquents Grown Up*, New York, The Commonwealth Fund, 1940, and S. and E. Glueck, *Criminal Careers in Retrospect*, New York, The Commonwealth Fund. 1943.

---

[5] See *Predicting Delinquency and Crime, op. cit.,* for details.

PART THREE

Treatment

Chapter 21

Forms of Treatment: Probation and Its Adjuncts

SOCIETY HAS THUS FAR FURNISHED but few alternatives to courts in the sentencing process: ordinary probation, probation with a suspended sentence, commitment to a reformative institution, imprisonment in a jail, house of correction or penitentiary, fine. Jail or house of correction imprisonment is of course not suitable to juveniles, and they are rarely subjected to a fine. In the present chapter one of the most frequently used devices — probation with or without suspended sentence to an industrial school or similar institution — is discussed. Subsequent chapters deal with the other types of disposition.

What is probation?

In any but a most superficial sense, this crime-treatment instrument consists of at least three indispensable elements: (1) retention of the offender in the community with or without a suspended sentence of imprisonment instead of his commitment to an institution; (2) the taking of such action only after study by the judge of a carefully prepared report that embodies the findings of an investigation into the offender's make-up, career, and probabilities of recidivism and reform; (3) and the resulting placement of the probationer under the sympathetic and understanding oversight of an adequately trained probation officer. These minimal requirements being absent, probation too often consists of just another "lenient disposition" of criminal cases without much discrimination on relevant grounds.

But why is probation administered by the court and the other forms of peno-correctional treatment by separate agencies?

It is a curious fact that in the various conferences and discussions conducted by professional groups concerned with improvement of juvenile court legislation and procedures, there is almost complete neglect of one basic question: Why should the authority to place a delinquent on probation — just as surely a form of correctional disposition and treatment as incarceration in an institution or release on parole — be retained in a court instead of being turned over to an administrative body specializing in *all* forms of correctional treatment? True, there is an historic reason for entrusting the power to suspend sentence to a court; but this does not apply to supervision of probationers, since the practice of placing persons who are on suspended sentence under supervision of an officer of the court is relatively recent.[1]

---

[1] See *John Augustus, First Probation Officer*, edited, with an Introduction, by S. Glueck, National Probation Association, 1939. *The Standards for Specialized Courts Dealing with Children* gives as a reason for retaining probation in the courts that probation is a "legal status," which "similar to the making of the social study, is so closely related to the judicial process in delinquency cases that it should be performed by personnel administratively under the direction of the court or responsible to the court." *Standards for Specialized Courts Dealing with Children*, prepared by Children's Bureau in cooperation with National Probation and Parole Association, and National Council of Juvenile Court Judges, Washington, U. S. Govt. Printing

In Massachusetts, children who are not granted probation are committed, under the statute, to the Youth Service Board. This agency conducts several detention and reception centers at which delinquents are studied psychiatrically, psychologically and sociologically during a period of remand. Thereafter the Board commits the children to one or another public or private agency which it deems most suitable for the special problems presented. It would seem more logical and efficient than the existing system for this type of board, instead of a court, to make the dispositional choice between allowing a child to remain at large under oversight and committing him to an institution or other therapeutic establishment. In fact, at present, a number of children who were denied probation by juvenile courts and committed to the Massachusetts Youth Service Board for study are shortly thereafter released on "parole" by the Board because intensive study at the reception center shows them to be favorable risks for extramural treatment — a finding which the necessarily more rapid examination by the investigative probation officer attached to the court had sometimes failed to make sufficiently clear.

Concentration of all treatment measures — extramural as well as intramural — in a specialized body with a wide range of clinical and therapeutic facilities would leave for the courts the function they are best suited to perform — the determination of delinquency status — and remove from them the function they are less suited to perform — the choice, planning and oversight of the treatment program, a process much more clinical than judicial in nature. Perhaps the best solution would be for the judge to participate with such a special disposition and treatment tribunal in determining the type of treatment best suited, after the clinic has given thorough study to the case.[2]

However, the existing practice is for the court to make the decision as between placing the delinquent on probation (with or without a suspended sentence) or committing him to an institution.

The materials in this chapter are designed to give a conception of the nature and practice of probation, one of the most promising yet, in its inception, simple devices for coping with persons who have been judicially declared to be delinquent.

The probation officer has a two-fold task: he is required to investigate the background, personality, and character of the offender as a basis for the judge's decision whether to permit the delinquent to remain in the community under some form of oversight or to commit him to one or another institution, or, in a few states, to some central administrative agency which, in turn, determines to which of several institutions the particular offender is to be committed. The second task of the probation officer is to furnish supervision and guidance, as well as a disciplinary oversight, to those delinquents whom the judge has permitted to remain in the community. When probation is decided upon, there is a wide range of existing practices from very superficial oversight (involving occasional visits of the probationer to the court to have his name checked off), through a practice of more or less infrequent visits of a "check-up" type to the home of the probationer, to (and the courts that have this last type of service are still relatively few) intensive social casework involving careful planning and the use of the social and psychiatric arts and related facilities.

Office, 1954, 13. The *Standards* states further that "Such action is especially warranted since it enables the same person who makes the study to continue the work with the child and parents during the probation period." *Ibid.* But (*a*) commitment to an institution, which may also result from the social study, is likewise a "closely related legal status," and (*b*) if the second point were crucial it would justify the court's staff also supervising institutional treatment. It should be pointed out that the provision of the American Law Institute's Model Youth Correction Authority Act removing probation from the court and placing it in a special administrative agency has not been accepted in the five states that have adopted the youth authority idea. Perhaps a basic reason for retention of probation in the courts is that judges do not like to surrender this authority. See B. M. Beck, *Five States*, American Law Institute, 1951, 8–10.

[2] See S. Glueck, "The Sentencing Problem," 20 *Federal Probation*, (1956), 25.

In the striving of some courts to bring probationary practices abreast of better case-work engaged in by social agencies, the fact that the court and its officers are "authoritarian" has come up as a frequent bone of contention.

The first article, by Reinemann, describes the organization, extent and various functions of the probation service, the selection and training of officers and the use of community resources. The second article, by Shipman, makes some thought-provoking observations regarding the need of considering the family as the focus of interest if headway is to be made with the delinquent child. In a striking passage at the outset, he sets the tone for his article: "It is not unusual for a probation officer to observe a family in which all the members should be on probation except possibly his client." His Family Institute suggestion deserves serious consideration.

In the next article Reeves argues against "the myth of inherent limitations" in the casework process when applied to the probation situation. He has some blunt and realistic things to say about the meaning and role of "authority" not only in relation to social work but in other aspects. Thus, he uses the fluctuations in educational philosophy and practice as a relevant example of the need to recognize the role of legitimate authority in improving character and conduct.

Taber, too, believes that modern casework practices can be reconciled with the "authoritarian setting." He brings out some relevant differences between, and similarities of, the authoritarian type of social work conducted by the better probation officer and casework procedures in other fields. He is convinced that penetrating casework practices are required in many instances; for "the moment we recognize the individual rather than the offense as the focus of attention we must also recognize the necessity of the probation officer's having insight into human behavior." And for this, not only native ability but social skills and insights are necessary "which can be used in a conscious and purposeful manner," and which can, through the self-discipline that comes from training, differentiate the probation officer's "own feelings and attitudes from those of his client." Taber is convinced that "Casework offers a realistic approach to a realistic problem. We cannot manipulate human beings and mold them to our own preconceived patterns. Nor can we endow them with intelligence and qualities which they do not possess. But we frequently can help them to reorganize and better use the capacities which they do possess," and "sharply define in a warm but objective manner the alternative which confronts a delinquent in order that he may redirect his behavior if he has the strength and will to do so."

The next item deals with an adjunct to probation that has as yet not spread sufficiently in the United States; namely, a structured form of supervision and treatment which requires regularity of attendance on the part of the probationer although permitting him to live at home. Two illustrations of this promising addition to the probation apparatus — one American (The Citizenship Training Group of Boston), the other English (The Probation Hostel in England) — are included in this chapter.

The last item in the present chapter deals with a camp as a facility used by the probation service. The use of camps has expanded, especially in California, to the point where such extramural establishments are employed not only as an adjunct to probation but as part of the institutional program under the Youth Authority. On pages 705–711, the California camp program is discussed from the point of view of the Youth Authority's classification and correctional procedures; the article in the present chapter is concerned with the use of the camp as a form of probational supervision.

118

Probation and the Juvenile Delinquent *

John Otto Reinemann

The establishment of juvenile courts, first created in Illinois half a century ago and since then introduced in all states of the Union and in its possessions, was a culmination of a movement which demanded a nonpunitive but rehabilitative treatment of child offenders. But a tribunal like the juvenile court, per se, could only be the framework in which cases of juvenile delinquents were to be handled. In order to translate into practice the underlying idea of the juvenile court, special devices were required. Probation has become one of its most important tools.

Historically, the beginnings of probation anteceded the creation of juvenile courts. In 1869 Massachusetts passed a law providing for the supervision of juvenile delinquents by a state agent. This was probably the direct outcome of the efforts and services of John Augustus, a Boston shoemaker, today recognized as the "first probation officer," who in the years 1841 to 1858 had befriended countless juvenile and other offenders.[1]

DEFINITION AND EXTENT OF PROBATION

Legally, in the case of an adult offender, probation is the suspension of sentence during a period of freedom, on condition of good behavior. In the case of a delinquent child, the juvenile court uses probation as a form of case disposition which allows the child to live at liberty in his own home or in the custody of a suitable person, be it a relative, a friend of the family, or a foster home, under supervision of an agent of the court and upon such conditions as the court determines. Socially, probation is a form of treatment administered by probation officers on a case-work basis.

The juvenile court laws in the forty-eight states and the territories make provision for probation by mentioning it as one of the possible case dispositions which are available to the juvenile court judge. In accordance with the noncriminal procedure of juvenile courts, some laws use the term "supervision" instead of "probation," because the word "probation" is an inadequate indication of social casework and is too strongly related to criminal court practices. However, the phrase "probation" is still preponderantly employed, both in theory and in practice.

What is the extent to which probation is being used as a proper approach to a delinquency situation? According to the "Juvenile Court Statistics for 1945," [2] published by the United States Children's Bureau and covering almost 115,000 cases reported from 374 juvenile courts throughout the country, probation was ordered in 30 per cent of the cases.

Another publication by the Children's Bureau states:

> The 20 per cent decrease from 1933 to 1945 in the number of children in institutions for delinquent children is significant also. In part it reflects the increased use of probation and parole as methods of supervision of delinquent children in the homes of parents or other relatives or in foster-family homes.[3]

PROBATION DEPARTMENT OF JUVENILE COURT

The great majority of juvenile courts are organized on the basis of county units, either as separate and independent courts or as special sessions, branches, or divisions of general courts. Probation is administered by the probation department, which is an adjunct to the juvenile court and consists of one or more probation officers and other clerical personnel, according to the size and population density of the county.

---

* Reprinted from 261 *Annals* (1949), 109–119. Used by permission of the author and the publisher. See, also, S. Glueck, *Probation and Criminal Justice*, New York, The Macmillan Company, 1933. — Ed.

[1] For details of this remarkable life history, see *John Augustus, First Probation Officer*, introduction by Sheldon Glueck, New York: National Probation Association, 1939.

[2] Supplement to the November 1946 edition of *The Child*.

[3] *Children Served by Public Welfare Agencies and Institutions 1945*, U. S. Children's Bureau Statistical Series No. 3, 1945.

The fact that the various state juvenile court acts provide for probation does not necessarily mean that there is a complete coverage of probation service in all counties throughout the United States. The National Probation and Parole Association reports that in 1947, out of a total of 3,071 counties, 1,610 counties did not have any such service for juveniles.[4] In many of these counties the lack may be attributed to the comparatively small number of children referred to the court. In other instances, however, it is due to an uninformed public opinion, to penny-pinching fiscal authorities, to judges without social vision; any one of these factors or all three combined may prevent the setting up of a probation program although it is vitally needed in the particular locality.

STATE PARTICIPATION

One of the ways of stimulating the establishment or the improvement of probation services on the local level is the active participation of state agencies in juvenile court work. Such state action might take various forms. There are only a few state-administered juvenile courts, as for instance in Connecticut, Rhode Island, and Utah. But in about half of the states, a state probation commission or a division of the state welfare department or department of correction has been given some kind of responsibility for the development and operation of probation services for children.

In California, the state Youth Authority grants probation to persons under 21 years of age committed to it by the local courts. In several states, examinations are given by state boards, commissions, or departments with the purpose of establishing eligibility lists from which probation officers are appointed locally (as for example in Indiana, Nevada, and Virginia); in others, probation officers are appointed by state agencies directly (in New Hampshire and Wyoming), or their appointment, though made locally, must be approved by a state agency (e.g. in North Carolina). In a number of states, county welfare agents, appointed by and operating under a state department of welfare or assistance, may be called upon by local juvenile court judges to render probation service. In West Virginia the Division of Child Welfare of the State Department of Public Assistance renders juvenile probation service through eight district offices, each administered by a child welfare supervisor.

In Virginia state aid is provided as a means of stimulating the establishment of probation service in local communities, by paying half of the salary of probation officers in juvenile courts in cities of over 10,000 population. In New York the Division of Probation of the State Department of Correction, headed by a director of probation, has general supervision of probation officers, both adult and juvenile, throughout the state. The director makes recommendations regarding administration of probation in children's courts, and adopts rules regarding methods and procedures in administration of probation throughout the state, except in New York City. There are also several states where the law authorizes a state agency in general terms to cooperate with the courts, to collect reports from probation officers on their case loads, or to give advisory service.

This list shows all possible varieties of state participation, from centralized administration to a merely advisory function. Unfortunately, too, as in the related fields of public health, welfare, and education, lack of funds and personnel has prevented several state departments from carrying out their assigned tasks. The new policy of the United States Children's Bureau, in effect since January 1, 1946, to collect juvenile court statistics directly from the state welfare or correction departments rather than from the hundreds of local juvenile courts, has at least forced all state departments to set up some machinery for the compilation of uniform statistical data within the confines of their respective states.

THE PROBATION OFFICER

The main prerequisite of a well-functioning probation program is an adequate staff. In the juvenile court, more than in any other judicial branch, the judge must rely on the work of court aides; these men and women are called probation officers, juvenile officers, or probation counselors. In the majority of instances they are appointed by the juvenile court judges, except where other provisions are made by law, as outlined before. Larger probation departments are headed by a chief probation officer.

[4] *Directory of Probation and Parole Officers in United States and Canada*, New York: National Probation and Parole Association, 1947.

On January 1, 1947 there were 3,681 probation officers for juveniles in the continental United States, appointed locally or as state employees. Many of them functioned in juvenile *and* adult cases, and in juvenile delinquency as well as child dependency and neglect situations. Not included in this figure were 267 Federal probation officers whose work is overwhelmingly concerned with adult offenders,[5] since Federal offenders of juvenile court age are often supervised by local juvenile court probation officers. Not all of the 3,681 probation officers are employed full time in this capacity; the other duties of part-time probation officers may include those of sheriff, bailiff, welfare worker, clerk of the court, attendance officer, or other.

The probation officer has two main assignments. First, prior to the court hearing, he makes social investigations covering the family and home environment, the school career, and all other pertinent data concerning the child's personality. He incorporates his findings in a report to the judge, often with his own evaluation and recommendation, so that it can be used as a guide for the disposition of the case. Second, he supervises the child who has been placed on probation by the judge; the details of this work will be presented later.

These tasks, entailing the probing and diagnosis of human behavior and the guidance of young, impressionable individuals, call for understanding and skill. Recent developments and new discoveries in the social and psychological sciences have greatly influenced the total child welfare program of which the probation service for youthful offenders constitutes a notable part. It is, therefore, more and more recognized that certain qualifications regarding educational background, training, and experience should be met by those desiring to enter the probation field.

Qualifications. A committee of the Professional Council of the National Probation and Parole Association,[6] consisting of leading authorities in the probation and parole field in 1945 formulated "Standards for Selection of Probation and Parole Officers," after consultation with many administrators in the correctional field throughout the country. These "Standards" suggest as minimum qualifications: a bachelor's degree from a college or university of recognized standing or its educational equivalent, with courses in the social sciences; one year of paid fulltime experience under competent supervision in an approved social agency or related field. As regards his personal qualification, a probation officer must possess a good character and a balanced personality. These traits are considered essential:

good health, physical endurance, intellectual maturity, emotional stability, integrity, tact, dependability, adaptability, resourcefulness, sincerity, humor, ability to work with others, tolerance, patience, objectivity, capacity to win confidence, respect for human personality, and genuine affection for people.

The educational qualifications are proposed as an entrance minimum for new appointees, and many probation departments strive to apply these principles when staff vacancies have to be filled. But the idea is still far from being universally adopted. Many state laws are silent regarding qualifications for probation officers; others couch them in such general terms that they can be met by any untrained person as long as he is a "discreet person of reputable character." Political influences, which as a rule have been successfully banned in the teaching profession, are still operating in the probation field and have prevented many states and local communities from adopting minimum requirements for the appointment of probation officers.

---

[5] Source for these figures, *Directory of Probation and Parole Officers in United States and Canada, op. cit.* note 4 *supra.*

[6] The National Probation and Parole Association is an organization exclusively engaged in the effort to extend and improve probation and parole services, juvenile and other specialized courts, for effective dealing with child and family problems. It conducts state, county, and city surveys, provides consultation services, holds conferences, publishes educational literature, and acts as a clearinghouse of information on all phases of probation and parole service in the United States. It is concerned with the co-ordination of probation, parole, and institutional work, and interested in all measures for constructive social treatment and the prevention of crime. On the state level, there are many associations of probation and parole officers which have as their aims the advancement of methods and standards in the probation and parole departments and the promotion of progressive legislation in the correction field.

As the introduction to the "Standards" emphasizes,

there are in many communities devoted and successful workers, qualified by self-education and assimilated experience, who have attained professional competence and who are in fact among our best workers. No suggestion to replace such competent workers is made, the standards refer only to the training and qualifications of future appointees.

Selection and Tenure. The method of selection of probation officers is closely related to the problem of qualification. The "Standards" suggests that appointments be made from eligibility lists resulting from competitive merit examinations. As has been mentioned before, some states have set up machinery for such examinations; in others, probation officers are appointed under the general state or local civil service regulations. Various progressive courts, even without specific legal requirements, have instituted a voluntary merit system.

A necessary complement to these provisions is the guarantee of reasonable tenure. This is of particular importance in view of the preponderant number of probation officers who are appointed by local judges whose office term is usually limited by statute and who often have to engage in political campaigns for re-election.

All these considerations — concerning qualification, selection, and tenure — point in the direction of making the public, the judges or other administrative bodies, and, last but not least, the probation officers themselves aware that probation service has become a profession.

Training. In order to promote this concept, special consideration must be given the training of probation officers. This includes pre-service training and in-service training.

Training prior to entrance into the probation career is determined by the adoption of the previously quoted educational and training requirements. The "Standards" states that "the best training for probation and parole work is in a graduate school of social work," but they realize that the previously mentioned educational requirement (bachelor's degree or equivalent, with courses in the social sciences) is probably as much as can at present be hoped for as a minimum in many parts of the country.

There is a difference of opinion whether casework training is a good preparation for proba-

tion work or not. Walter C. Reckless,[7] for instance, thinks that

the trained probation officer should have a good foundation in criminology and in the field of corrections, both juvenile and adult. He needs to take specially organized courses in probation and parole work which can give him a specific preparation rather than a casework preparation.

He is of the opinion that "the basic underpinning of probation and parole should not be casework and its allied psychiatric point of view, but rather criminology, corrections and social psychology." Reckless considers the schools of social work and the departments of sociology as the best places for the training of probation officers, but realizes that on the one hand "our schools of social work have been reticent about including courses in penology and corrections," while on the other hand "many departments of sociology have frowned disdainfully at the prospect of offering practical training."

In-service training has in recent years come to the fore in many branches of public administration; in the correctional field, in particular, it has gained widespread recognition and realization. In-service training cannot and should not be a substitute for adequate pre-service training. It will have its greatest value for probation officers who are at present employed as such and who did not have the benefit of professional schooling, and in those situations where probation departments feel that even for newly appointed staff members, professional pre-service training should not be required. However, in-service training should not be confined to these two groups; for the well-trained staff member, too, in-service training is a necessary tool for maintaining a high standard of job performance.

In-service Training Programs. Several types of in-service training programs have been successfully carried out in various parts of the country.

1. Many probation departments of juvenile courts have organized their own in-service instruction for their staff members by supervisory personnel or specially assigned instructors.

2. Another type is found, for instance, in Pennsylvania (among other states), where the

---

[7] Walter C. Reckless, "Training Probation and Parole Personnel," *Focus*, publication of the National Probation and Parole Association, March 1948, pp. 44 ff.

State Department of Public Instruction, using partly Federal funds appropriated on the basis of the George-Deen Act, has conducted in-service training courses for correctional workers on the local and state level for the past ten years, and where the probation administrators of the various courts have availed themselves of this opportunity by enrolling their staff members in these courses.[8]

3. A number of in-service training courses or institutes open to probation officers of the local courts have been conducted by universities, e.g. the University of California at Berkeley, the University of Southern California, the University of New Hampshire, the College of William and Mary in Virginia, the University of Minnesota, and others.[9]

Assignment of Cases. The assignment of cases to the probation officer should be guided by certain rules. Girls' cases should always be assigned to women probation officers; cases of boys under 12 years of age may be handled by women probation officers, but all cases of boys above that age should be assigned to men. To assign the probation officers according to geographical districts and have them handle all cases of children living in their respective territories is the most economical method; this does not preclude the assignment of special cases, for instance of sex delinquency, to officers who, due to training and experience, might be particularly qualified for this kind of work. Theoretically at least, it is generally agreed that not more than fifty cases should be under the supervision of one probation officer at any time; actually, however, this rule is far from being generally applied in practice.

VOLUNTEER PROBATION SERVICE

Volunteer service in the probation field can take the following two forms:

1. In small towns and sparsely populated rural areas an interested lay citizen may take over the supervision of a youngster placed on proba-

tion, as a neighborly sponsor. This volunteer worker should be well selected by the probation department of the county juvenile court and should be responsible to this department. Such an arrangement makes it possible to give supervision to children living in remote parts of the county who, due to the heavy case load and geographically extensive work area of the regular probation officer, would not receive the benefits of probation service.

There is, however, a danger that the services of volunteers (and this applies also in a certain degree to the previously mentioned use of part-time probation officers) are misused by protagonists of a false economy in preventing the employment of qualified, full-time probation officers where their services are vitally needed.

2. The volunteer can render valuable service in supplementing (rather than substituting for) the work of the regular probation officer, in both large and small communities.

He might be assigned as an individual or as a member of an organization to maintain frequent contacts with a child on probation and to collaborate closely with the probation officer in charge. It is considered good policy to hold each volunteer responsible for only one or two youngsters, and the type of case must be carefully selected.

In various cities members of the Big Brother and Big Sister organizations and similar youth service agencies carry out such a program. A good example of this kind of service is provided by the Juvenile Delinquency Clinics in Fayette County, Pennsylvania. Here, in the county seat (Uniontown) and several townships, business men, clergymen, and men in the professions have banded together for the purpose of giving supervision and counsel to boys assigned to them by the juvenile court upon the recommendation of the chief probation officer, to whom these lay workers are responsible and with whom they meet for frequent consultation.[10]

Beyond the service in individual cases there is another important asset in the utilization of volunteers in probation work; it provides a good channel to the public at large for the interpretation of the meaning of probation, the problems presented by delinquent conduct of children, and

---

[8] For more details on this program, see J. O. Reinemann, "Pennsylvania Experiments with Public Service Training," *National Municipal Review*, Oct. 1940, pp. 672 ff.

[9] See Helen D. Pigeon, "In-Service Training for Probation and Parole Officers," *Federal Probation*, July–Sept. 1941, pp. 8 ff.

[10] For further details about this project see Ruth W. Love, "Boys of Today — Citizens of Tomorrow," *Federal Probation*, Oct.–Dec. 1947, pp. 43 ff.

the need for community facilities for youth conservation and crime prevention.

SELECTION OF PROBATIONERS

The juvenile court judge places a child on probation after having studied the social case history, as compiled in the probation officer's investigation report, and the recommendations by the probation officer and the court psychiatrist; he has also taken into consideration the facts disclosed and impressions gained at the court hearing. In the majority of instances he orders probation as a kind of "middle of the road" disposition. These are cases in which the simple discharge or adjustment of the case, even with a reprimand by the judge, does not seem sufficient; on the other hand, these situations do not warrant the removal of the child from his home and his commitment into the controlled environment of an institution. Within these limits lie the range and the potentialities of probation.

More positively expressed, probation should be ordered whenever the following requirements are met: The home surroundings must appear sufficiently conducive to the proper upbringing of the child, and the adjustment of the boy or girl in an atmosphere of freedom, as the ordinary community life provides it, must be feasible, with the help of the court's supervisory authority. It follows from this that probation should not be "handed out" automatically, say, in all cases in which the child has committed his first serious offense or has been brought to court for the second or third time on any delinquency charge. Nor should probation be used, as happens all too frequently, though with misgivings, only because proper institutional facilities are lacking. The selection of probation as a proper treatment must be governed by all factors which are apparent in an individual case.

Attempts have been made to establish prediction tables, based on these various factors, as a guide for probation and parole selection. But, as Sanford Bates says, "the prognostic tables should never be a substitute for executive or judicial judgment, but will be a logical means of applying the accumulative experience of the past to the important problems of the future." [11]

Pauline Young adds to this, that "each institution, department, and community needs to develop its own experience tables and not rely upon those of other groups, which may strongly reflect unique elements in their peculiar situations." [12]

CONDITIONS OF PROBATION

Probation is predicated upon certain conditions. These may be general conditions applicable to all children placed on probation, or they may be especially determined by the court in the individual situation. The general conditions include obedience to parents, regular school attendance, keeping of early hours, following of instructions by the probation officer, notification to the court of changes of address, and staying away from undesirable companions and from disreputable places. Many of these conditions, often enumerated in a form letter which is given or sent to the parents, are full of negatives. In order to interpret the meaning of probation as a positive constructive measure, such a communication should include some kind of an opening and closing statement like the following sample:

WHAT DOES PROBATION MEAN?
Probation means that the court has confidence in the good character of your child.

Probation means that your child will remain in your home; you will continue to be responsible for your child.

The court through its probation officer will help you in supervising your child.

REMEMBER — everything that has been mentioned here is necessary for the WELFARE OF YOUR CHILD.

We, the Court, and you, the parents, want to see your child grow up into a fine American citizen, healthy in body, mind and spirit.[13]

Special conditions may consist of restitution for damages, living with a relative (due to inadequacy of the parental home), attendance at a special school, affiliation with an approved recreational agency, or carrying out of medical recommendations.

---

[11] Sanford Bates, *Prisons and Beyond* (New York: Macmillan, 1936), p. 120.

[12] Pauline Young, *Social Treatment in Probation and Delinquency* (New York: McGraw-Hill, 1937), p. 621.

[13] A form containing these statements has been recently adopted by the Municipal Court of Philadelphia.

SUPERVISION OF PROBATIONERS

Since probation is a treatment process, it is important that the probation officer at the beginning formulate some kind of treatment plan. In many instances, the probation officer already knows the child and his family from the investigation prior to court hearing. The probation officer should conceive his task of supervision as that of a counselor, a Big Brother or Big Sister. The probation officer will therefore strive to win the confidence of the child. In order to be successful he must also be accepted by the parents and other members of the family. Sometimes he has to break down an attitude of resistance on the part of the parents, who may consider the probation officer's interest and activity as an intrusion into their rights. He will have to interpret to them the real meaning of his assignment, namely, to help the child in his readjustment. The probation officer must be himself convinced that his is a positive and constructive task. No conscientious probation officer will be satisfied with merely keeping the child who is under his supervision out of another conflict with the law. As Lou, in his fundamental work on *Juvenile Courts in the United States*, points out:

to be really constructive, the plan must take into account not only the weak qualities of the probationer, but also his good qualities, upon which the desired superstructure of normal conduct and character may be built. It must be based upon an understanding of all the factors of the problem of the probationer, including his personality, his habits and reactions and the reasons for them, his mental life, his physical strength and weaknesses, the home influences, and the bearing of the school regime on the child's development.[14]

Method and frequency of contacts. The contacts of the probation officer with a child can be established either through home visits or through reporting of the child at the office of the probation department or a specially assigned room in a neighborhood settlement house.

In the home the probation officer sees the child as a part of the family; he wins an insight into the attitude of the parents toward the child, the child's relationship to his siblings, and the physical environment of home and neighborhood. The probation officer often finds himself undertaking reconstructive work with the whole family, since the child's behavior is frequently an outcome of unstable home conditions.

The reporting by the child to the probation department office or other designated place at regular intervals has its value in affording the probation officer an opportunity to converse with the child alone, unhampered by the presence of other members of the family and the frequently crowded conditions of the home. However, this form of reporting should be restricted to boys over 12 years of age.

There is, of course, no general rule regarding the frequency of contacts. Every individual case demands a different method. Some judges emphasize the need for very frequent contacts in specific cases, by placing the youngster on "strict probation." The Committee Report on Juvenile Court Standards [15] holds that "except in rare cases, home visits at least once every two weeks are essential to effective supervision, knowledge of the assets and liabilities of the family and correction of unfavorable conditions."

Use of community resources. One of the most important prerequisites for constructive probation work is the probation officer's intimate knowledge of the community resources. It is self-understood that the probation officer keeps himself informed of the child's progress in school. Frequent conferences are held with the principal or teacher and — in an increasing number of instances and with gratifying results — the school counselor or school social worker. School authorities are usually quite willing to co-operate with the probation department.

In the cases of older children on probation, the probation officer should assist and guide them in the choice of and preparation for a vocation. The probation officer must be familiar with existing health centers and family service agencies, and will collaborate with them. He must be fully acquainted with the various recreational and character-building groups to which he can refer his probationers. In certain cases of

---

14 Herbert H. Lou, *Juvenile Courts in the United States* (Chapel Hill: University of North Carolina Press, 1927), p. 153.

15 Juvenile Court Standards were formulated by a committee appointed by the U. S. Children's Bureau, and adopted by a conference held under the auspices of the Children's Bureau and the National Probation Association in Washington in May 1923, U. S. Children's Bureau Publication No. 121, reprinted 1947, Washington: Government Printing Office.

deep-rooted emotional disturbances he may utilize the services of child guidance clinics or similar facilities.

Use of casework principles. There has been considerable discussion regarding the use of casework principles within the authoritarian setting of the juvenile court and more particularly of probation. It is today recognized that the authority inherent in probation has a constructive role to play if it is used by a probation officer who is aware of his great responsibility and if it is interpreted to the probationer in an understandable way and therefore is accepted by him. The Panel Report on "Casework — Group Work" [16] summarizes this aspect of probation as follows:

During probation . . . case work has a contribution to make. In keeping with case work philosophy the delinquent and the probation officer must see probation as an experimental period of social adjustment. During the period, the individual must learn to live with authority. He must be helped to discover and develop his capacity to take responsibility for himself, as a member of the community, accepting its standards and rules of behavior (p. 18).

The probation officer should review the progress of probation with his supervisor from time to time and should modify the original plan if necessary. If a situation develops which threatens to impede the success of probation and which calls for a change of the court's order, the probation officer has not only the right but the duty to petition the judge for an amendment of his previous decision. This may result in continuance of probation in a different environment, for instance in a relative's home, or in commitment of the youngster to a foster home or an institution.

LENGTH AND TERMINATION OF PROBATION

In accordance with the individualistic character of probation, its length is dependent on the needs and requirements of each case. It is today customary in most juvenile courts not to limit probation in advance as to time. It is also recog-

nized that, with rare exceptions, short-term probation is of little value. The previously quoted Committee Report on Juvenile Court standards recommends a general minimum probation period of from six months to one year. The average length of probation for juveniles in the Municipal Court of Philadelphia, for instance, during recent years has been ten months.

Probation can be terminated in various ways. In those cases in which a definite time limit is set, it expires automatically; otherwise it is left to the probation officer to determine when the objectives of probation are met and consequently to petition the court for the discharge of the boy or girl from probation. Violations of probation may also lead to its termination. The commitment of a new offense is considered a violation of probation per se, while noncompliance with the conditions, general or specific, attached to probation is termed a technical violation. The probation officer has considerable discretion in determining whether the child and his parents are living up to the conditions imposed. In either instance the judge may decide to continue probation or to apply stricter measures, mostly institutional commitment.

Technically, probation of a juvenile may last until his twenty-first birthday. Most of the juvenile court laws of the various states, regardless of whether the upper juvenile court age limit is 18 (as in the majority of states) or lower or higher, contain provisions extending juvenile court jurisdiction to the age of majority, once it has attached in an individual case prior to the reaching of the upper juvenile court age limit of the respective state law.

EVALUATION OF PROBATION

Has probation been successful as a modern device of correctional treatment, especially in juvenile cases? To measure success of probation is difficult unless very detailed studies of individual cases with a follow-up over several years after termination of probation are undertaken. Otherwise, the purely negative yardstick of recidivism during the period of probation and within a certain time afterwards might be used. Austin H. MacCormick states:

Based on actual performances over a term of years, a good juvenile court and probation service, operating in a community with adequate social resources and utilizing them fully, can put as high as 90 per cent of its juvenile delinquents on probation the

---

[16] This is one of eighteen panel reports of the National Conference on Prevention and Control of Juvenile Delinquency held in Washington in November 1946 upon invitation by the U. S. Attorney General. The reports are available at the Government Printing Office, Washington.

first time around and 50 to 75 per cent the second or third time around, and get as high as 75 to 80 per cent successes.[17] *

Summarizing the positive values of probation in juvenile cases, the following points should be stressed: It is the most individualistic form of treatment; it applies the method of social case-work and uses the constructive values of authority; it leaves the child in its normal home surroundings; it enlists the help of community resources; it is not considered punitive and is therefore free of social stigma.

Recently a Sub-Committee on Probation of the Division of Social Activities of the United Nations, consisting of eleven probation administrators from various parts of the United States, met to prepare a statement on the basic principles and the application of probation for juvenile and adult offenders; this report, based on experiences in the United States, will be distributed to all member nations of the United Nations as a guide for the establishment of similar services in other countries. At the first meeting

---

[17] Austin H. MacCormick, "The Community and the Correctional Process," Focus, May 1948, p. 88.

* The Editor, on the basis of numerous, intensive follow-up studies, is convinced that MacCormick's estimate is too high. But compare The Results of Probation, A report of the Cambridge Department of Criminal Science, London, Macmillan, 1958, 2–4. The check-up on probation successes and failures is an extremely complex and difficult business. It entails intensive and extensive investigation of the crime record of probationers both in the jurisdiction in question and elsewhere. It cannot be based simply on the assumption that if a probationer in one court has not come to the attention of that court by a new arrest, he is necessarily not violating the conditions of probation or committing new offenses. For some idea of the difficulties involved in making reliable follow-up studies, see S. and E. T. Glueck, 500 Criminal Careers, New York, Knopf, 1930, 85–110, especially 98–100. Five Hundred Delinquent Women, New York, Knopf, 1934, 335–369, especially 335–356; One Thousand Juvenile Delinquents, Cambridge, Harvard University Press, 1934, 149–169. True, all the groups studied were not casual, first offenders; but these researches show how difficult it is to get at the true facts of recidivism. This does not mean that probation is not a very valuable instrument for the control of delinquent behavior. It does mean that the extent of its success should be founded on better information than has thus far been brought forward by those who claim 80% or 90% or better response to this form of supervision. — Ed.

of this group, a member of the United Nations Secretariat (not a United States representative) observed that probation, both in juvenile and adult cases, has progressed farthest in the United States of America. Such a statement should not cause us to be smugly proud of our achievements, but should rather make us realize our great responsibility in providing and maintaining adequate juvenile court and probation services everywhere in the United States on behalf of all children who require such community aids.

119

Probation and the Family *

Gordon Shipman

It is commonplace for social workers to emphasize family relationships as causative factors in delinquency and as obstacles to rehabilitation. In spite of this there is not a shred of legal philosophy leading us to view the family as a unit of delinquency or as a unit for incarceration. The one social invention which comes closest to applying methods of rehabilitation to the whole family is family case work. But my own experience in probation and parole leads to the conclusion that a new institution is required for family treatment, one that is something between probation and a prison.

It is not unusual for a probation officer to observe a family in which *all the members should be on probation except possibly his client.* These family complications may be centered on the juvenile probationer whose wholesome propensities have been warped by parents who are psychopathic or otherwise unadjusted, or on the adult probationer whose spouse is so unstable that the whole family is in a constant state of turmoil. Society has everything to lose in permitting such families to continue their demoralization. The only entering wedge is the authoritative control of one individual.

When the intelligence and stability of parents is average they are willing and anxious to cooperate with the probation officer to effect the

---

* Reprinted from 23 Probation (1944–45), 106–114. Used by permission of the author and the publisher.

rehabilitation of their delinquent child. When their deviations are more extreme they will hide their vices, fail to cooperate with the officer and nullify his efforts. When the probation officer takes the child out of such a home he is confronted with a host of problems which center about the building up of security in a substitute home, where the foster parents are somewhat reluctant to put up with a boy whose work or conduct does not satisfy them. The foster home often fails to provide the level of security which the delinquent child craves.

The types of parental influence upon delinquent children are baffling to juvenile courts. One is the subtle but persistent psychological abuse of children by parents who camouflage this abuse with a respectable social front. The other is the unfortunate example of low standards of parental conduct, the effect of which is insidious and potent. When a healthy child is subjected to such influences his so-called delinquent behavior is but the normal reaction of a normal child to an abnormal situation. More and more we are coming to see that while *juvenile delinquency* may be an appropriate term, *juvenile delinquent* is not.

The enthusiasts for probation have assumed that a complicated family problem which is a puzzle to the court is meat for the social worker who is a probation officer. This is erroneous. Probation is ill served by those who fail to recognize its limitations. The utility of probation cannot rise above the facilities at its disposal. There is not enough frankness on the inadequacy of those facilities; there is too much drivel about community resources. An officer may diagnose a family situation as to financial, cultural, recreational, medical, and psychological problems, but he cannot in serious cases fill the prescription for all members of the family within the time required for the rehabilitation of his one client.

While a probation officer corrects certain types of parental abuse and successfully treats many cases within or without the home, he is often confronted with family problems which baffle him into a sense of futility. The real significance of probation as a social invention is not what it is and does, but what it leads to. Among other things it points the way to an institution designed to treat therapeutically and simultaneously all members of a demoralized family. How much better to treat the worst families as a unit in a special institution than to experiment with a child on probation until revocation is necessary, then to commit the boy to an industrial school, and finally to send him home again to the same demoralizing environment on parole!

HARLEY AND ALTA

Let us now approach the family problem from the point of view of the adult probationer whose obstacle to rehabilitation is an unstable spouse. I illustrate with the case of Harley and Alta X. Harley came from a simple rural family where steady hard work was the rule. He entered a forced marriage at the age of twenty-four, and worked for a time on WPA. During the first two years of his probation period Harley made a fair adjustment as a farm laborer in spite of impoverished circumstances, but one day he lost his job because the employer was disgusted with Alta's instability. The family then moved some distance to a small city where Harley secured a job in a factory. All such changes of job and home are critical periods of adjustment for all impoverished families of weak character, but in Harley's case he had lost his car and some of his furniture to a finance company and the matter of getting established in a new home was attended with most distressing circumstances.

At this time Mrs. X was pregnant. She also proved to be neurotic, tuberculous, syphilitic, and badly in need of eyeglasses. She nagged constantly at her husband and screamed hysterically at her two small children. The household was dirty, disorderly and without ordinary facilities. In order to escape from this turmoil Harley spent more of his time and money with his drinking cronies until I pondered whether revocation was the best solution. Since Harley's delinquency was but a reaction to an impossible home situation I decided to refrain from sending him to prison and attempted to work on the family problem. This decision turned out to be unfortunate, but I rationalized that were I required to live with Mrs. X I would do something worse than drink quantities of beer.

It was obvious that the wife should be in an institution. At the moment, however, Alta could not be hospitalized because from the point of view of the dispensers of public relief her eyestrain was not unusual, her tubercular lesions not active, her pregnancy not advanced, her syphilis not contagious, and her nervous condition not psychotic. Neither could she be incarcerated in a penal institution, for however irritating her conduct, she had not committed a felony or even a misdemeanor. She was under no compulsion to follow the advice of her husband or of his probation officer. When she did apply for various types of assistance she invariably became so obnoxious to the authorities as to thwart the end in view. Another handicap to her applications for assistance was the fact that her husband was earning thirty-seven and one-half cents an hour.

MORE TROUBLE

When Alta's tuberculosis became active hospitalization was favorably considered. Then arose the question as to who would go into this household and care for two dirty, boisterous, undisciplined children. It was decided that Harley was to go to a boarding house, his wife to a sanitarium, and the children to a grandmother who was to receive a mother's pension for her services. Harley was to reimburse the agency as much as possible from his earnings. A month later a child was stillborn to Mrs. X. Shortly thereafter she returned to her husband, but since he had no home she went to live with her mother, who in the meantime had threatened to leave the children on the doorstep of the pension department. Then Harley was laid off and got behind financially before he secured another job. After the relief department set them up in housekeeping again Harley suddenly got a better job in a defense plant a hundred miles away whence he betook himself with his family in a trailer. To be cooped up in a few cubic yards of living space with a woman like Alta had its consequences. Harley spent his evenings in taverns. One night a female bar-fly encouraged his advances which she suddenly repelled. Harley was sent forthwith to prison for attempted rape with a one to twenty year sentence.

Then Alta really went to town. She consorted with a parolee in another jurisdiction and broke up his family. Two men of bad reputation lived in her apartment. She was brought into court and lectured for her bad conduct and for neglecting the children. When she was brought into court a second time the judge committed Alta to a tuberculosis sanitarium and the children to an orphanage. Alta was most unruly at the sanitarium and when the doctor suggested that she was pregnant she ran away. Next she turned up as a cook in a roadhouse,

and later in a metropolitan hospital where she gave birth to another child. Harley is now applying for parole but the family problem is no nearer solution with the prospect of parole than it was when he was on probation.

PIECEMEAL SERVICE

The handling of this family might be called extramural piecemeal social service. In a three year period the agencies which piddled with the case unsuccessfully included: three courts, two probation-parole officers, two relief departments, a pension department, two county nurses, a state nurse, two venereal clinics, a children's board, public officers, a sheriff's department, a county hospital, a foster home, an orphanage, two sanitariums, and a prison. After all this great effort the family situation is worse than at the beginning, and the outlook for the future still worse.

The main problem centered about the wife's condition. She needed simultaneous treatment for five different ailments in an institution where she would be temporarily freed from family responsibilities and yet close enough to her husband and children not to loosen family ties. The children and the husband had fewer but important requirements. If the various facilities of the above mentioned agencies could have been combined for the simultaneous treatment of the whole family in the beginning we might have done with minimum time and effort a commendable job of family rehabilitation. All the numerous agencies involved in the case had but a segment of jurisdiction. Each of them had but temporary jurisdiction over one member of the family at a time, and some of them only functioned with respect to one condition of one individual. Not a single agency was authorized to handle all the conditions of the wife or to handle her as a functioning unit. The need was for an agency which could treat not only each member as a functioning unit but also *the whole family as a functioning unit.*

The X family is but one of many. It is out of just such families that come our recidivists. They are the festering social foci of degeneracy. Every caseworker knows to what extent they remain an unsolved problem. How silly to mobilize our resources intermittently against an individual (or a segment of him) when all members of a family require therapy both individually and collectively. To rehabilitate them as a unit throughout a crisis is to strengthen family ties; to deposit them separately into reformatory, prison, and foster home is to weaken family ties so as to make chronic all their emotional disorders.

A New Institution

What are the requirements of an institution to handle the X families? How should we begin to establish what might be termed the Family Institute or the Family Refuge? We might begin with an administration building, a hospital, and a cluster of cottages in an isolated rural setting that has natural advantages. There should be many acres of good farm land and the necessary equipment for scientific farming. In due time there should be established facilities for processing dairy products, for slaughtering, freezing, canning, preserving, etc. There might be added small factories to better utilize female help, to preserve vocational skills, to facilitate occupational therapy, and to cut down the cost of operation. The hospital should be equipped to handle alcoholic, venereal, and psychopathic patients. There must be places of detention for men and women. The recreational and school program should cover the needs of the children and the adults with emphasis on group activity and self-expression. And finally there should be established a psychological laboratory.

How should problem families be referred to an institution? One is tempted to develop the idea that a delinquent family might be convicted as a unit and incarcerated as a unit, or that the head of the family might be incarcerated and the rest of the family permitted to follow him into the institution. One thing is certain: we cannot expect our jurisprudence to develop a concept of the family as an appropriate unit for criminal prosecution until we first invent an institution suitable for its incarceration. It may turn out that to put the institute on a voluntary basis will cover most cases appropriate for this type of treatment. If this is borne out by experience then legal procedure may never be necessary.

It is suggested that the Family Institute be considered as a facility of probation, parole, and the penal system generally. Referral would be appropriate when one or more members of the family are in the custody of a warden or of a probation or parole officer. Both the probationer and his family would enter the institute voluntarily with the written understanding that while they enjoyed the benefits of the institution they would abide by its regulations.

Getting the Family In

Would there be difficulty in getting a probationer to agree to take his family to such an institution? In times of crisis involving layoffs, evictions, garnishments, accidents, and illness, the Family Institute would seem like a Utopia to the distressed family. My experience in getting some of my probationers who are alcoholic to take treatment voluntarily at a state mental hospital is suggestive. As soon as an alcoholic released from jail is sober I advise him of the seriousness of his violation and the nature of his affliction. I explain that he must have treatment for this disorder and that he can get it in one of two state institutions: the prison (to which he has already been sentenced) or the state hospital for nervous diseases. I explain what work, recreational, and hospital facilities are at the prison and how long he must remain for treatment before he can apply for parole. I then explain what legal procedure is necessary to enter the state hospital as a voluntary patient either paying his own way or going at the expense of the country. He is told that the minimum treatment for alcoholism at the hospital is three months. Given his choice of institutions for treatment, invariably he chooses the hospital. I often take him there myself and give the physicians a history of the case. Before departing I explain to the probationer that he remains in my custody as a probationer while at the hospital and that he is not to leave until I come to take him home.

There would have been no hesitation on the part of Harley X in going to a Family Institute. He would have gone to any place that would take his sick and nervous wife out of earshot while he had a chance to work for his maintenance during the day and to play with his children in the evening. Mrs. X would have been more of a problem but she would not have turned down an opportunity to be cared for in a hospital away from the turmoil of her family, knowing that as soon as she was well enough she could rejoin them in a cottage that was adequately equipped.

The institute would be appropriate for the

vocational training of family men in prison who are ready for parole but who have neither skill, job, nor home. In these situations the institute would bring the family together and give them all a better start as a functioning unit. It is likely that the problem will not be one of commitment but of keeping down the waiting list, and of getting the rehabilitated families back into their own communities.

FLEXIBILITY OF TREATMENT

What are the advantages inherent in a Family Institute? The first advantage lies in providing flexibility of treatment. Any member of the family could be isolated from the rest and given special treatment in cell or hospital and then returned to the family circle at the proper moment or for limited periods each day. This cannot be done on probation except very crudely and without proper timing or sequence of treatment. A father could be called in from the fields if suddenly the mother had to be taken from the household. The children could at any moment be transferred to the nursery or cared for by an attendant at a critical moment. There can also be flexibility of treatment with respect to relatives who interfere and relatives who help. Certain large families involving grandparents, in-laws, or stepbrothers might be broken up to live in separate households, and remnants of broken families closely related might be brought together.

In addition to flexibility of treatment there is also the advantage of simultaneous treatment for each and all members of the family. Mrs. X could have treatment for all her five ailments at the same time; her husband could receive treatment for one chronic ailment, work full time on the job to get proper credit for maintenance of his family, and learn a new vocational skill in the evening school. The children meantime would have their adenoids removed, their teeth repaired, and at the same time be calmed down by the routine and discipline of the nursery school. Throughout all this activity the counselor or psychiatrist would iron out intrafamily problems. All this therapy would be carried out simultaneously and intensively and it would be done while keeping all healthy members of the family usefully employed and without destroying family ties by forced separation.

It is commonplace to observe that most delinquents have never learned how to play or to utilize their leisure time. It is just as commonplace to find that the rest of the family is no better off in this respect. It is important not only to teach all members of a demoralized family how to play, but also how to play together. The Family Institute would be in an advantageous position to encourage types of recreation that improve the family *esprit de corps*.

The institute would also teach those who need it most the responsibilities of husband and wife and the duties and responsibilities of parents. Some adults must be taught from the ground up how a spouse should be treated and how children should be trained. This cannot be done by social workers who drop in to lecture but one member of a family a few minutes each month. It could be done in a Family Institute which had the facilities of daily inspection, demonstration schools, and adult education classes.

PSYCHOTHERAPY

Another advantage would be to provide family counseling under circumstances most favorable both for the family and for the counselor. A counselor could accomplish far more in less time within this framework than he could in a clinic. The same would be true of the psychiatrist who would have an opportunity to study the psyche of the family as well as that of the individual. Psychological relationships within the family circle cannot be studied effectively in prison or hospital, but they could be studied advantageously in such a setup. Experience with probation and parole suggests that the family pattern is more significant in the etiology of crime than the personality pattern. This leads to speculation as to how much psychodiagnosis and psychotherapy could be speeded up by observing and treating several members of a family simultaneously. In any case the institute would provide a new opportunity for psychological research and the most favorable setting for certain types of psychotherapy.

This plan offers opportunity for intensive investigation of marital difficulties, those irritations between husband and wife which lead to divorce, desertion and to prison. I have had occasion during my experience as probation officer to effect reconciliations between estranged couples, especially in nonsupport cases. The job of helping to minimize irritations between the couple so that the family will continue to live together in reasonable peace remains after a reconciliation has been effected. Now an excessive reaction of irritation to an inconsequential habit of a spouse is in the nature of an emotional allergy. Such oversensitivity is more common among delinquents than nondelinquents, and an understanding of the source and nature of the sensitivity is important for all who profess to help the delinquent. For example, there is the family pattern in which a brute of a man maintains outward sullen calm while writhing internally when his wife flings accusations at him in a rasping voice. Many a man has gone to prison with a sense of relief because he thus avoids a sound that produces as much distress as does pollen in a hay fever victim. Conversely women may suffer when the male voice booms in anger. The sufferer from an emotional allergy is more or less inarticulate, and comprehends little of the psychological mechanisms involved.

The institute would be a great boon to local communities who are at a loss to handle delinquent families when the father is incarcerated. The sexual delinquency of wives of weak character which breaks forth when their husbands go to prison is well known. This is also the time when home discipline breaks down with disastrous consequences for the children. Whatever gains are being made in the rehabilitation of husbands and fathers in prison is offset by the demoralization of wives and children back home, and by the breaking of family ties that are so hard to mend again. Local authorities sometimes hesitate to prosecute and incarcerate the worst of women if they have a brood of small children clinging to their skirts. Establishment of the Family Institute would encourage local authorities to prosecute delinquent mothers, if such a serious step is necessary. It would also permit them to rid their community temporarily of multiple sources of delinquent contagion.

COMBINED TREATMENT

Such a device as the Family Institute is necessary to handle family problems that cannot be handled in any other way, to combine the advantages of probation treatment with those of institutional treatment, and to realize the advantages of treating delinquency from a family point of view. Experimentation with the Family Institute should be undertaken immediately so that our social and penal services will be better prepared to cope with family problems during the crisis of demobilization and the postwar era.

120

Administrative Procedures and Casework Services *

Elmer W. Reeves

Probation officer is an ugly term, so ugly that in some states probation officers are referred to as counsellors, as friends of the court, or are called by other euphemisms. Unfortunately but inevitably the term probation officer appears to set off in the minds of a certain group a sequence of thinking which culminates in the picture of a paunchy, cigar-smoking ward heeler equipped with gun and handcuffs who is solely interested in flashing a shield and drawing his monthly pay check.

Social work thinking has changed and developed during the past two or three decades. So has probation thinking. However, some caseworkers seem unwilling to keep pace with the developments in probation. This group, although quite willing to recognize that social work philosophy has traveled far from the days of almsgiving, is nevertheless persistent in viewing probation today as it was in the days of cashmere shawls and voluminous skirts, when horse-drawn buggies paraded down Beacon street and the first probation officer, the kindly John Augustus, encouraged his customers to bring to him their hopes and discouragements.

That this uninformed concept of probation does exist is evident not only from popular discussions but from so-called scientific investiga-

* Reprinted from "Administrative Procedures and Case Work Services," *Dealing with Delinquency*, 1940 Yearbook, National Probation Association, 180–192. Used by permission of the author and the publisher.

tions into the function and procedure of probation departments. These generally bring into sharp relief the following points which to us are untenable: (1) that the legal approach and the casework approach are at variance since the former is based upon the equality of all before the law, while the latter stresses the need for individualization; (2) that the law is concerned with protecting the community whereas casework sees the best interests of the community served through the appropriate treatment of the individual based on an understanding of his problem in relation to the rights of society; (3) that the law acts on authoritative prerogatives in its use of punishment for the protection of society whereas casework rests for the most part on the voluntary application of a client for services; (4) that under the law it is advantageous for the probationer to admit as little as possible whereas in a casework relationship the client can be helped only if he will share his problems with the caseworker.

Probation, as I know it is practiced, negates the specious reasoning that casework and probation, with its alleged legal limitations, are by their very nature inharmonious. The purpose of this paper is to demonstrate that there is nothing in the aims of probation and the machinery established for achieving them which is at variance with casework objectives and practices. That this fact is not generally accepted is partially due to probation's inability to find and develop vehicles for interpretation not only to the public but to the field of social work.

The erroneous ideas which some caseworkers have concerning probation stem mainly from contacts with probation departments which are not equipped to practice casework and do not claim to do so. However, the same situation can be found in the general field of social work wherein we also find agencies unable to conform to even minimal standards. With reference to private social agencies we sometimes find ourselves confronted with the same situation, even though in some schools of social thinking private agency is synonymous with casework agency, and public agency still symbolizes a blundering and futile group presumptuously clinging to the tail of the casework kite.

In considering whether or not probation

philosophy is at variance with casework philosophy it is imperative that we confine our discussion to probation departments which by virtue of standards, staff and finances are able to discharge properly their obligations to the individual and the community. It must also be recognized that in the delinquency area we deal with maladjustments which have assumed such grave proportions that they are inimical not only to the individual in his immediate situation but to the community as a whole. Because the community's well-being requires it we are at times compelled to assume responsibility for individuals who are unamenable to casework therapy. However, we also recognize that a few individuals at the other end of the distribution curve are not in need of casework services and are perfectly capable, with some little guidance, of working out a solution to their problems.

AUTHORITY IN CASEWORK

Only too widely does the thought exist that casework services are rendered ineffective in probation departments because of the presence of authority which brings with it its concomitant — enforced relationship. Authority reduced to its simplest terms is nothing more than an implement for orderliness. Authority may be divided into two categories. The first is that of natural law, or moral authority which is self-imposed. Call it conscience, censor, super-ego or what you will — all of us are subjected to it. The second is social authority. All of us are subjected to this too, for laws and social norms are the foundation of society and without them peaceful, productive life is impossible even among primitive peoples. It is neither authority nor restriction we resent, but the manner in which the authority is exercised; not the use but the abuse and misuse of authority is destructive. Each one of us is daily subjected to restrictions and if we understand the need for these restrictions we accept them. We rebel at the imposition of arbitrary, unreasonable conditions and so does the probationer. Thus the probation officer is confronted with the problem of interpreting the authoritative aspects of probation to the probationer, thereby relating treatment to the latter's capacity to profit from the planned use of authority.

We find the presence of authority in private agencies as well as in public. This authority is manifested in intake policy, in the closing of cases, and in the final analysis, in the need of having the client conform to the plan of treatment mutually developed by client and case worker. Authoritative controls exist in both the delinquent and non-delinquent fields. They stem from different sources, one from laws and social norms, the other from boards of directors; nevertheless they flow towards the same ultimate objectives.

A probation department has a dual function, protecting society and helping the individual probationer. The first function does not automatically remove the probation officer from the neutral position of the case worker. Probation recognizes that the best interests of society are served by the adjustment of the individual probationer. In any code of ethics for the social case worker may be found the statement that the caseworker's first duty is towards his client unless the performance of this duty jeopardizes the welfare of the community; with this no probation administrator has any quarrel.

The stereotype that probation is casework "with the punch of the law behind it" must be relegated to the limbo of outworn thoughts. In probation, as well as in other forms of social treatment, it is recognized that some persons are to be met with authority, some with gentleness, and all with an understanding individualized approach. It would appear axiomatic that before any permanent adjustment can take place the probationer or client must be helped to acquire habits of self-discipline. It may be that it is only through the use of planned but not necessarily legal authority that self-discipline can be acquired.

A good deal of time is ill-used if not wasted in discussions of the theoretical basis of the use and value of authority. When social work was struggling to have the public accept and respect its philosophy and function, probation with its legal background was welcomed. It was believed that with a legal background and an authoritative foundation, the field of social work could progress much further than the voluntary and haphazard relationships of those days could possibly permit in other types of casework. Is it true that the skills and techniques of social casework have become so perfected and standardized that the authoritive approach, formerly so welcome, can now be discarded entirely? If our treatment processes totally reject the use of authority, then our treatment processes are divorced from reality and we shall revert to the type of sentimentalism which formerly caused us to be regarded as incurable romanticists.

EDUCATION AND AUTHORITY

The field of education has provided us with an excellent object lesson if we are willing to accept it. More than a decade ago educators, rebelling against the overformalized curriculum of our school system, developed the so-called progressive schools in which all authority disappeared and free expression and uninhibited activity on the part of the child were stressed. The educational system is now reaping the rewards of the extremes of these natural schools; these uninhibited children find it extremely difficult to adjust to secondary and collegiate education; psychiatrists and educators recognize that this group reared on free expression will have to be reoriented before it can take its place in society as it is today. Utopia will perhaps be a place where everyone is uninhibited but educators recognize that the school's function is to train the child for society as it is today and will be tomorrow, and not for a nebulous golden age. Any realistic approach to problems of training and of adjustment must accept the presence of authority and utilize it upon a planned individualized basis.

Enforced relationship in the so-called authoritarian agency has been the subject of much discussion. A rational treatment of this question must be based upon the concept that all behavior reflects the needs of the individual. We all possess drives which in one form or another express basic needs. If we probe deeply and carefully we will find that the causes for crime are basically not different from the causes which result in applications for assistance to any social agency. Delinquent behavior and other forms of conflict are generally compensating substitutes for experiences and impulses which the individual fears to recognize and dares not express. The tension resulting creates frustration and fear. Whether or not the release takes the form of a criminal act is purely fortuitous and is dependent upon the attitudes and tensions operating at the time. Is the so-called voluntary client any more willing than the probationer to face or discuss the basic causes of his maladjustment?

If we accept the fact that the probation officer's work concerns itself with helping the man under supervision to bring to conscious expression his underlying emotional conflicts and thus rid these deep-seated unknown drives of their tension and potency, and if we recognize that the probationer's moral decisions must be his own, not the probation officer's, then is the generic problem of interpretation with which the probation officer is faced any different from that which must be met by the case worker?

FIRST CONTACTS

The statement is frequently made that the probation officer's first contact with his client, which may be in a prison cell, creates a situation wherein a casework relationship is next to impossible; that the physical surroundings and emotions experienced by the defendant may be so negative as to make impossible further service by a probation officer identified with that experience. May not the converse be true and may not the probation officer be gratefully identified as the person instrumental in effecting the defendant's release? Are not the psychological bars behind which a client shamefacedly and with the recognition of inadequacy seeks aid as strong as the physical bars of a cell? There are probationers who accept probation gladly and who have some concept of its meaning. Even with these the problem of interpretation remains.

Can we not disabuse ourselves of the idea that the first interview puts the fear of the law into the probationer, and that during subsequent interviews the officer is under a cloud of fear lest his probationer violates probation? The first interview is one of interpretation. Furthermore, probation officers are not blamed for violations. Probation administrators and judges are not so backward that they cannot understand that no man can be held responsible for another man's actions.

Why should the social worker assume that under planned probationary treatment the fear of jail is so tremendously operative especially when the probationer has already survived a detention period in jail? The average probationer is no more in fear of being returned to jail for a violation of probation than is the client of the private agency of having his case closed. The probationer to whom the service aspects of probation cannot be interpreted and who rejects them is the individual who is not amenable to probationary supervision and who will probably be returned for commitment. These probationers represent but a negligible percentage of cases. In the area of enforced relationship our problem, though possibly more difficult than that of the private agency, is still a problem of interpretation.

Conditions of probation are frequently regarded as additional barriers to the development of the casework relationship. Therapy in a private agency calls for conformance with a designated plan leading to wholesome social and family life. Conditions of probation are nothing else. They are standard rules of social behavior which you and I accept as everyday routine.

Reporting, sometimes regarded with horror as a kind of Frankenstein monster, is identical to the interview situation of the private agency. A probation department which has the respect and confidence of its judiciary and the community can easily establish a flexible procedure with respect to the number and occasion of reports. With a socialized judiciary, progressive administration, and a trained staff, supervision procedures lose their negative and irritant qualities and become positive and constructive forces in the treatment process. Is it possible that many of our difficulties in seeing eye to eye with some of our contemporaries in the field of social work resolve themselves into a matter of terminology?

The common thought that judges impose rigid restrictions upon the casework aspects of probationary supervision is erroneous. Where probation has attained its proper position it functions upon a basis which is about ninety-five per cent administrative discretion and five per cent legal and judiciary restriction. Can it not be argued that this allows for greater administrative freedom than is permitted to the private agency head whose policies are controlled by its board of directors, whose practices may be meddled with by its committee of patronesses, and whose freedom of action is often stringently limited by the terms of endowment or charter?

REJECTION AND COMMITMENT

Both the public and private agency in their casework processes are confronted with the problem of maladjustment. The area in which we all are interested is that of treatment. Maladjustment may result in the closing of the case or in commitment. In fact for purposes of therapy commitment of a probationer in some instances may be more desirable than the closing of a case by a private agency. A correctional institution, if it is a proper one, will continue to aim its efforts towards the eventual adjustment of the inmate. No matter how broad are plans or how effective is personnel, rejection of services by the client of a social agency inevitably brings with it rejection on the part of the agency.

Probation departments, like other casework agencies, upon finding treatment ineffective must close the case. Probation departments use commitment as an understanding parent who finds that all reasoning has failed resorts to stronger measures. It is recognized that such measures may not be too efficient and may be only temporary but they are our best answer to the needs of a situation which cannot be met in a more satisfactory way.

Commitment is desirable provided that institutionalization is used not because of the impatience, frayed nerves and lack of resourcefulness of the officer but as a rational solution to an apparent need. It may be advantageously utilized with venereally infected persons refusing treatment, potentially dangerous psychoneurotics and others who require a controlled environment. Unless we are willing to discard our entire system of jurisprudence and penal philosophy we must recognize that institutions may and do prepare inmates for community living.

When a probation department closes a case by discharging a probationer, either at the expiration of the probationary period or prior thereto, it recognizes that casework services are no longer necessary. If the statutory period of probation has expired and the probationer is still in need of services two channels are open. The probationer may be treated as a post-probation case or referred to another social agency for follow-up work. In probation departments which maintain adequate standards these courses are followed.

There is no question but that public agencies recognize their responsibilities in the treatment area. Possibly because they are responsible to the public they have developed not only standards but also criteria for evaluating the efficacy of their therapeutic processes. These evaluations are new and in some instances faulty, but the prevalence of efforts at scientific determination of crime causation, the development of prediction tables,* the critical evaluation of successes and failures, indicate a desire to meet problems on a realistic and self-critical level. Endeavors to determine the value and effectiveness of treatment appear today to be characteristic of the public agency of the future.

CONTROL THROUGH THE COURT

A mistaken impression has also developed with respect to the problem of intake. We hear it stressed that probation departments cannot be expected to utilize casework processes to the best advantage because of their lack of control over intake. There is a definite control and it is exercised by an individual who has been much maligned. In the field of probation intake is controlled by the judge aided by the chief probation officer.

The judge has been criticized by many people not adequately conversant with actual facts who continue to regard all judges as well-meaning ignoramuses or futile political hacks.

Charles L. Chute, executive director of the National Probation Association, has reached the core of the so-called intake problem in saying: "It has been demonstrated conclusively that by the thorough investigation of every case, including mental examination where called for, and with a probation staff of such high caliber that its recommendations are almost invariably followed by the judges, the granting of probation to unfit probationers, whether first or subsequent offenders, can be practically eliminated."

PERSONNEL

In any discussion of the problems of probation departments the ogre of unqualified per-

---

* See Articles 116–117, 171–173, *infra.* — *Ed.*

sonnel always raises its ugly head. At best, workers and executives in the private agency field are tolerant towards the less trained workers in the field of delinquency. Of course, on the basis of personal knowledge I can speak only for the state of New York, but here I can unequivocally say that the field of probation is now demanding and attracting a group of trained, enthusiastic men and women who are on the same level with the workers in any private agency. As a matter of fact most probation officers are now being recruited from private agencies with high standards.

The qualifications set by the chief probation officer in the Court of General Sessions of New York county for admission to a civil service examination to be given next month for the position of probation officer at a salary of $3000* are the following: (1) graduation from a college or university of recognized standing by which a bachelor's degree is granted, and in addition, graduation from an approved graduate school of social work or equivalent graduate education in the social sciences; or (2) graduation from a college or university of recognized standing by which a bachelor's degree is granted, with emphasis on studies in sociology, psychology and criminology, and in addition at least three years of satisfactory field work or supervisory experience (full time basis) in social work with an agency adhering to acceptable standards. These or similar requirements are undoubtedly being established in many states.

The query may well arise as to the presence on our staffs of the "old-timers" who have worked in the field for years but who cannot meet the foregoing or more rigorous requirements. Almost every agency, public or private, has such persons. The responsibility for meeting the educational needs of these workers rests with the administrator upon whom it is incumbent to develop in-service training programs which will stimulate the staff towards study and self-development.

Let us, however, approach this problem from another angle. Is it not true that there are executives in the private agency field as well as in the field of probation who lack the formal re-

quirements now necessary for field workers in their own agencies? This situation exists because we are still in a transitional stage in the field of social work. The administrator whose reputation is established is seldom criticized for his lack of formal training. Is it right to condemn the field worker who through long years of hard work has acquired the skills necessary to help people though he may not flaunt an involved terminology learned in a school of social work? Social work has not been ungrateful to its pioneers. Does it ask us to discard the men and women who struggled to make probation a reality?

The men and women in the field of probation have few illusions. We recognize that inherent in any dynamic field of endeavor are limitations which can be met only by constant struggle. We know that some judges may not be socially minded, that newspapers may distort public opinion, and that these distortions inevitably have repercussions on an elected judiciary; that some uninformed legislatures pass inadequate probation laws or harass us with statutory restrictions which make the problems of casework extremely difficult; that some penny-wise and pound-foolish budgeting authorities hamstring us; that some probation administrators lack vision and ability; that some probation departments are ineffective and politically controlled; that case loads are too high; and that probation officers generally are woefully underpaid.

These and more are obstacles with which we are confronted but they are being met and they are no more insurmountable than those which the pioneers in the broad field of social work successfully faced. Nor are they more grave than those which the private agency field must meet now in a period when they are confronted with the need of redefinition of function.

If there are unique limitations imposed upon casework services in the field of probation, they are not inherent in its basic philosophy but are present because we are in a period of expansion and development. If we can maintain our present pace, then the time is not far distant when the myth of inherent limitations will have been exploded and probation will take its legitimate place in the pattern of social treatment.

* Such salaries are probably outdated in the more advanced probation services. — *Ed.*

121

The Value of Casework to the Probationer *

Robert C. Taber

One question repeatedly raised in our discussions of the various aspects of probation proposes that the treatment function of the court might be more effectively administered if it were removed from its present authoritative setting and placed in the hands of other existing social agencies, either public or private. Although there can be no clear-cut answer which will hold for both urban and rural communities, an examination of the fundamentals underlying the treatment of delinquent behavior may throw some light on the question. If an authoritative setting is essential, and I firmly believe that it is, then the question may possibly reduce itself to the application of modern casework practice to probation rather than the transfer of the treatment function to other case-working agencies.

The application of casework to the field of probation has been gradual but its present extent gives promise of steady growth and development. The value of casework to the probationer cannot be measured in simple tangible terms but we have had the opportunity of observing its potentialities. When we stop to examine the delicate and highly complex nature of the responsibilities of a probation officer, we gain some insight into the validity of such an approach.

Three major factors appear to have hindered the widespread introduction of the recent developments of casework into the probation field. In the first place, the concept of delinquency and crime has been steeped in the tradition of punishment and restraint. The of-

fense has been the major concern and the offender has been punished in accordance with the type and seriousness of his delinquent act. A method of treatment which takes the individual into consideration frequently has been regarded as taking the edge off punishment and therefore defeating the very purpose of the judicial process. The extension of the juvenile court age from sixteen to eighteen years in Pennsylvania in September of 1939 has met with a series of criticisms which give evidence to the prevalence of the punishing attitude. A chief of police in a small community made a newspaper statement to the effect that the extended jurisdiction of the juvenile court had "hamstrung his police force" as these culprits now had to be taken before a "lollypop court." Others stated that it was a "crime to mollycoddle these adolescent criminals."

However, other recent developments, such as the widespread use of presentence investigations in criminal procedure, show recognition of the need for a socialized approach. The American Law Institute, whose purpose it is "to clarify and simplify the law, to better adapt it to social needs, to secure the better administration of justice, and to encourage scholarly and scientific work," gives momentum to the development of an enlightened approach in which the offender rather than the offense becomes the focus of attention.

Secondly, the community at large has been slow to accept the necessity of a career service for those engaged in the field of probation. The lack of experience and educational requirements, the low salaries, the uncertainty of tenure and the indifference to the size of case loads give evidence to the fact that probation has not as yet been accorded professional status. The result has been that probation in many communities is a mere gesture with heavy odds against any possibility of rehabilitation of the offender. On the other hand, the increasing use of merit systems for the appointment of probation personnel indicates recognition on the part of the community of the necessity of setting and maintaining standards.

THE USE OF AUTHORITY

Furthermore, casework practice, which has made such strides in the last decade, at first seemed irreconcilable with the exercise of au-

* Reprinted from "The Value of Case Work to the Probationer," *Dealing with Delinquency*, 1940 Yearbook, National Probation Association, 167–179. Used by permission of the author and the publisher.

thority. How could an individual confronted with the power of a court which was beyond his control, and which could arbitrarily deprive him of his freedom, make constructive use of a helping process? Would not any desire he might have to help himself be stymied by these forces imposed upon him from without? How could a court to which is delegated the duty of enforcing compliance with the normal restrictions of society employ a method which recognizes the individual's inner capacity as the key to his adjustment, and the necessity of his participating in the process of rehabilitation?

Backtracking over the history of probation we find that there has been a continuous struggle with the effective use of authority. At one moment the probation officer was wedded to authority and at another he was as completely divorced from it as he could possibly be. The punishing approach has probably been the more prevalent of the two extremes because of the general attitude that society must avenge itself against the offender. It was easily administered, as anyone could preach to the probationer or frighten him with the aid of an officer's badge. It was similar to the old remedy of sulphur and molasses which was administered on the slightest provocation. Needless to say, the punishing approach has been found wanting. The officer in effect became the law, and because of its personal basis the relationship frequently resolved itself into a battle of wills between the officer and the probationer. If the latter didn't rebel against this crude use of authority he was paralyzed with fright and his confusion and problem were only accentuated. This use of power might be compared to bandaging a festering wound without first examining and treating the wound itself. Extenuating circumstances and the personality of the individual were brushed aside with complete disregard for motivating factors, individual differences, and constructive measures. The offender had committed a delinquent act and the officer was interested only in keeping him in line by refreshing his memory of the dire consequences which would follow if the act were repeated.

THE SENTIMENTAL APPROACH

Equally blind and unrealistic was the sentimental approach in which the officer absolved the probationer of all responsibility. The of-

fender was told in effect that the past would be forgotten, that it was just too bad that he had been arrested as it was really society's fault and not his. It is probably this attitude which has justified the labels, "sob sister" and "mollycoddling." The primary concern of the officer was to win the probationer's confidence by any possible means with the thought that he might be bribed into being good. Again, needless to say, this sentimental approach was also found wanting. In the vast majority of cases of delinquency the offender has failed to exercise normal restraint and it is a false move to aid and abet him in placing the blame elsewhere. Such an attitude is only likely to lead him into further and more serious difficulties. Furthermore, if the officer overindulges in friendliness he will find himself on dangerous ground. For instance, when a child who has been told that he can count upon his probation officer as his friend in need, is subsequently involved in another infraction of the law, the officer is faced with the alternative of betraying the child's confidence by recommending further deprivation of freedom if such is warranted, or failing in his responsibility to both the child and the community by not holding him to account. Irresponsibility and utter disrespect for authority of any kind might easily be the end result.

THE CASEWORK APPROACH

An examination of the probation function indicates clearly that the modern practice of casework offers a positive and constructive process which I firmly believe can be reconciled with an authoritative setting. A social rather than a civil court has a dual function of protecting and preserving the welfare of the community and at the same time of helping the offender to make a satisfactory adjustment. In facing the task squarely we find that we have on the one hand the offender who is a human being possessed of all those intangible and unpredictable qualities which go to make up human behavior. On the other hand we have the community which is possessed of sanctions and laws so essential to its well-being. Probation, which has come to be an integral part of court procedure, must therefore provide an approach to delinquent behavior with a realistic acceptance of the need for authoritative rules and regulations as well as a realistic acceptance of the offender as an individual different from every other individual.

Probation implies that release is granted or sentence is suspended conditional upon satisfactory behavior. It is a trial period during which the convicted offender is given an opportunity to conduct himself in such a way that he will be acceptable to the community. Although probation is but one of the many dispositions which a court may make on the basis of a social investigation, its use will increase as it becomes a more effective method of treatment. Its potentialities have only begun to be realized; partly because unduly heavy case loads have forced the probation officer to spend the greater proportion of his time upon the investigation of new cases at the sacrifice of adequate supervision of probationers; and partly because we as probation officers have been confused as to how we should properly exercise our delegated authority. If probation is to have real meaning something new must be injected into the probationer's experience which will assist him in achieving a sense of equilibrium and harmony between himself and the community. Although probation has always employed an individualized approach it all too frequently lacks those vital but consciously directed forces which go to make up a constructive experience. Routine visits in the nature of a check-up, no matter how carefully recorded, give nothing more than a chronological chart of the course of behavior of the offender. It is a static kind of relationship — merely a period of observation or restraint which the individual may endure in a docile fashion as a means of earning his freedom, just as a prison inmate may seek an early parole by good behavior. It is a period of sufferance, a kind of blackout, in which the offender's attitude and outlook are not changed one iota. The offender in a sense remains on dead center during this period of time. Such probation is meaningless. Probation may even be a destructive influence, especially if the offender feels that his freedom actually has not been conditioned upon his own behavior. A haphazard relationship leaves the offender with the feeling that he has gotten away with something. This frequently is the tendency if the term of probation is definitely set by the court and has no relation to the kind or extent of adjustment that is necessary.

Probation, I firmly believe, can be set up within a framework which offers a helpful and constructive experience to the offender. To do so we accept the necessity of law and order and at the same time recognize that an individual cannot be forced to conform. We can assist him in helping himself but we cannot impose a new pattern of behavior upon him against his will. It is our function as probation officers to help the offender clearly understand his own situation and to assist him to make a satisfying adjustment to the circumstances which surround him without coming into conflict with society.

DEVELOPING RESPONSIBILITY

The authoritative setting of courts and probation is not mere happenstance. It plays a vital role in the entire court experience. The authority of the court may become one of the dynamic factors in the relationship between the offender and the officer. Perhaps for the first time the individual is confronted by this new kind of force which transcends anything which he has previously known. Although he has been aware of authority in many areas of his life such as parental and school authority, he is now face to face with a power which can deprive him of his freedom. He has not come to the court for help of his own volition. The very reality of this force sets into motion his fundamental reactions and attitudes. It represents a sharply defined and kaleidoscopic experience which serves as a kind of testing ground in which he has an opportunity to reorient himself. In a sense those intangible rules and regulations inherent in society suddenly become resolved into very tangible limitations in the form of the investigation, the hearing or trial, the necessity for reporting to the probation officer and observing the regulations governing probation. These limitations are symbolic of the limitations which exist for all of us in the community. How will he react to this new and critical experience? The responsibility for meeting this crisis is squarely upon his own shoulders. He may be utterly defiant or he may be irresponsible about keeping his appointments with the officer, or he may report regularly but present a tight-lipped barrier which the officer cannot penetrate. In this experience the probation officer has the opportunity, not only of observing the offender's behavior pattern and action, but of assisting him in clarifying his attitudes and feelings and in working together with him to find ways and means of satisfying his personal and social needs without coming into conflict with the law. A sound interpretation of what probation means without the use of threats gives the probationer an opportunity to decide for himself whether he will conform or continue to defy discipline. Whether it be a change in attitude or a change in circumstances, or both which may be required, the officer, if he is alert and understanding, is in a position to see the problem more clearly by reason of the fact that it is brought out in sharp relief. In short, the presence of authority serves to precipitate a reaction on the part of the offender and thereby provides a springboard, so to speak, for the relationship between the delinquent and the probation officer.

Although I firmly believe in the wisdom and necessity of referring cases to social agencies on the basis of a carefully defined and discriminating referral policy, I am convinced that it would be impractical for both courts and agencies to transfer the treatment function to other agencies in toto. The authority of the court offers a meeting ground on which the offender and the worker get together. It is the force which engages them, so to speak, and becomes a vital factor as a point of departure. Once the element of authority is removed, this springboard is lost.

This point is better understood when it is recognized that the delinquent as distinguished from the neurotic expresses his impulses in aggressive overt action rather than in repression of his desires and withdrawal into himself. No general statement is justified, but there is a tendency for the delinquent type to resolve his conflict in action and consequently he does not feel the need of help. The impetus in his case must come from without, whereas in the truly neurotic type the impulse to seek help comes from within because of the pressure of the conflict from within.

In addition to providing a sharply defined experience and a meeting ground, authority also serves to sustain the relationship between the worker and the delinquent, inasmuch as the delinquent does not come to the court of his own volition. The caseworking agency, divorced from this authoritative setting, has no other alternative but to close the case when his client does not take hold. The probation officer, on the other hand, offers help to the probationer with a clear understanding that his ultimate freedom is dependent upon his constructive use of the probation experience. Although the officer cannot control the use the probationer makes of this help, authority provides a limit which may help the offender to come to terms with himself and society.

Authority also provides a supporting quality, frequently enabling an individual to come to a decision which he is unable to make of his own volition. There are crises in life so overwhelming in their nature that the individual, lacking the strength within himself to meet the situation, finds support in an external force until such time as he can find it within himself. When it is recognized that delinquency reflects instability, the value of this support can be appreciated. It enables the probation officer to differentiate between a chronic instability growing out of inherent weakness or deficiency, as opposed to a temporary instability growing out of extenuating circumstances.

If this conception of probation as a possible period of growth and change growing out of a dynamic relationship is acceptable, we find that the two methods previously described are incapable of bringing about the desired result. The punishing approach ruled out the individuality of the offender by riding over him in a roughshod fashion with no recognition of his personal needs and conflicts or of his capacity for redirection. The approach was motivated entirely by the need for imposing social restrictions and it condemned the offender from the very outset. The sentimental approach on the other hand not only assumed that the offender was not responsible for his actions, but also ruled out the reality of and need for social restrictions.

CASEWORK PRINCIPLES

The basic principles of modern case work offer a method and content which can be applied to the probation function. Casework for our purposes may be defined as a process of attempting to understand the needs, impulses and actions of an individual and of helping him to reorganize these in a way that is satisfying to himself and yet in accord with the demands of social living. It is concerned with the release of individual capacities as well as the relieving of environmental pressures.

One of the basic concepts of social casework is that treatment cannot be forced upon another person. Domination or paternalism seldom if ever brings about effective results. To help another person we must accept him as he is with an honest respect for his capacity as well as regard for his need to solve his own problem with whatever help the worker can give him. The caseworker is concerned with assisting the individual to realize his own capacities to the fullest extent, as well as to orient him to the resources existing within his environment which will provide a satisfying outlet. In short, change to be effective depends upon the individual's willingness to help himself. A finely spun plan is utterly useless unless the probationer participates in making it and it becomes a part of him. He must be assisted in finding his own way at his own pace, otherwise a superstructure is imposed upon a foundation which cannot sustain it. A small degree of constructive change which is securely implanted within the individual will serve him far better than rapid change, which, when the support is removed, falls as does a house of cards.

UNDERSTANDING HUMAN BEHAVIOR

The moment we recognize the individual rather than the offense as the focus of attention we must also recognize the necessity of the probation officer's having specialized insight into human behavior. The worker's native ability is by far the more important factor, but to be helpful to others this native ability must be transformed into skills and insights which can be used in a conscious and purposeful manner by the worker. Self-discipline of the worker which enables him to differentiate his own feelings and attitudes from those of his client is essential. This self-discipline, acquired through supervised experience and specialized training, minimizes the possibility that the worker will impose his own ideas and prejudices on the person whom he is trying to help.

The necessity for continually expanding our knowledge and understanding of human behavior can readily be seen when we consider how lies and fabrications may have such different meanings. For instance, there is a striking difference between the child who indulges in a bit of fantasy and insists that there is a lion in his bed, and the adult who is suffering from paranoia and insists that he is continually seeing people pursuing him with a gun. A young lady told with great pride of having two jobs. Upon inquiry she stated that she and her father were directors of the State Hospital for the Insane. She said that she also trained all the policemen and firemen in the city of Philadelphia. At that point two policemen came into the building and she was asked if she trained these two men. She replied quickly: "Oh, those two sons of guns, they don't turn up for rehearsal." Contrast this with the case of a boy who, caught "red handed" by a policeman, absolutely denied having broken into a garage. Every phase of behavior has a different meaning for each individual, and treatment if it is to be effective must be differentiated according to the individual's need.

Casework offers a realistic approach to a realistic problem. We cannot manipulate human beings and mold them to our own preconceived patterns. Nor can we endow them with intelligence and qualities which they do not possess. But we frequently can help them to reorganize and better use the capacities which they do possess. There are no formulas which we can readily apply which will bring about the desired result, but we can sharply define in a warm but objective manner the alternatives which confront a delinquent in order that he may redirect his behavior if he has the strength and will to do so. We have long since recognized that there is no one cause of delinquency and that there can be no one solution. Surely an honest attempt to understand the individual and the factors contributing to his delinquency cannot be labeled as mollycoddling or as a lollypop attitude. If it is our responsibility to help reconcile the delinquent with the demands of social living, then it is only intelligent that we should learn as much as we can and develop a method which is constructive. Our task can be hindered or facilitated by our use of authority because it is a keen-edged instrument. It may be compared to the physician's scalpel which in skilful hands makes a clear-cut incision facilitating the easy removal of the diseased organ. The self-same scalpel in unskilful hands may result in nothing more than an ugly wound over a deeper disorder.

These very ramifications of the responsibilities attending the treatment of delinquent behavior prompted the Municipal Court of Philadelphia two years after its creation in 1913 to establish a medical department to throw further light upon the probation officer's investigation. Physical, psychological and psychiatric examinations have become an integral part of our procedure. The unusually broad jurisdiction of the court has made possible the gradual but steady application of this socialized approach which originated in the juvenile division, to the misdemeanants, domestic relations, criminal and adoptions divisions of the court. The very fact that this socialized approach has not been confined to the juvenile delinquent but has been applied to other branches of the court concerned with more serious offenses, bears evidence of its practicability and effectiveness as a sound method. Only through such a process of strengthening the probationer as an individual in relation to his environment can we hope to prevent the recurrence of delinquency and crime.

122

The Citizenship Training Program of the Boston Juvenile Court *

Louis G. Maglio

The Citizenship Training Group stands midway between the constant intensive supervision of the correctional institution on one hand and the periodic protective contacts on the other. The general plan of the program is that boys between the ages of 12 and 17 years placed on probation by the Boston Juvenile Court are required as a condition of their probation to attend the training program, immediately following their appearance in court. This attendance is for twelve weeks, five days a week, from 3:30 to 5:30 p.m. The boys on probation to the district courts of greater Boston are admitted at

* Reprinted from *Salute to American Youth*, National Council of Juvenile Court Judges *Journal*, presented at the Boston Conference, June 17–21, 1956. Used by permission of the author and the publisher.

the request of the presiding justice of the juvenile session of such courts.

PURPOSE

The purpose of the agency is to make good citizens of boys who made the wrong start: specifically to give training, counsel, and guidance to all boys who are ordered to attend by the court, and other boys who are in danger of becoming delinquent.

A factor which is frequently overlooked in many treatment programs is that the important step in any rehabilitation effort is to get the delinquent to accept the carefully planned decision on matters of conduct and future action. It is the delinquent's attitude, his acceptance or rejection of ideas and plans, which determines the ultimate success of treatment. A treatment program in common experience may look ideal; and yet if the boy will not accept it, we are all doomed to failure. We may have methods of drawing a boy in line with our plans, but this is merely a recognition of the truth that the boy has the final veto. The burden of the problem, therefore, is not merely to establish facts and arrive at conclusions, but to do this in a way which is acceptable and understandable to the individual, who is himself the final court of appeal.

While at the training program, the nature and scope of the boy's problem are studied from the standpoint of his personality and his specific reason for being in court, to prepare him to accept a subsequent treatment program. The program provides a twelve week educational experience, beginning immediately on the placement of a boy on probation. He accepts this as a condition of his probation. During this time he learns to accept responsibility, keep regular appointments in a schedule of training and physical reconditioning.

The curriculum of the Citizenship Training Group cannot be primarily scholastic as in the ordinary school, but must be rather a program of individual adjustment and retraining. Yet, certain requisites for success of the typical school and the Citizenship Training Group's curriculum are similar, since customary scholastic training has as its aim, not only the acquirement of knowledge, but also, though indirectly, character training, which is the most important objective of the activities of the training program.

The importance of physical conditioning cannot be underestimated. This phase of the program, consisting of three hours per week, is planned to interest the boys in muscular development and body hygiene as well as to provide the staff an opportunity for observation as well as treatment.

The crafts program is designed to help the boy to develop a high spirit of cooperation, to develop a sense of pride and self-discipline in his work, and to arouse in him an interest in activities related to those carried on in the crafts program. The most important aim, no doubt, is the development of a spirit of cooperation and respect for the rights of others. Two afternoons a week are provided for this activity. Although the projects attempted are of simple design and the resultant products are far from being expertly professional, the work has definite therapeutic value.

Quite often the delinquent boy resents meeting the type of abstract problems with which he is confronted in school. Nevertheless, the group discussions, twenty-four in all, held twice a week, have formed an important part of the training program. The boys are encouraged to talk openly, to tell what they think, to reveal what bothers them, and to straighten out in their minds their duties and responsibilities at home, in school, and in the community.

This procedure must be deftly handled. Delinquent boys are prone to boast, to lie, to ridicule, and to resent sound advice. Their attitude and personalities can be reshaped into wholesome patterns by a down-to-earth demonstration of the stupidity, the needless worry, and the uncomfortable consequences that not living up to rules of life involve.

SEEDS OF GOOD CITIZENSHIP

Trying to implant seeds of good citizenship in disorganized and recalcitrant youngsters is a task that challenges the best techniques of counseling and guidance. Other activities include dramatics, group singing and educational movies.

This program was adapted to meet the suggestion of Professor Robert Ulich, of the Harvard School of Education, who reviewed it as a member of the evaluation committee. In order to catch and hold the interest of many different types of boys, the program is flexible enough to meet the individual needs. Not only do these activities provide the boys opportunity to develop their interests and initiative, but they provide different types of settings in which the workers can get into close contact with the boys, and observe them both as individuals and as members of a group.

In the meantime, the skills of religion, medicine, psychology, psychiatry, and casework are utilized in trying to modify, so far as is possible, the boy's attitude and environment, in order to provide a more favorable atmosphere for his future living. We attempt retraining and rehabilitation with the boy without disturbing the normal routine of his life by removal from home or school. We work with the boys in groups and individually.

The staff, consisting of a director, caseworker, group workers, a psychiatrist, psychometrist, part-time teachers, and a secretary, functions directly under the judge of the Boston Juvenile Court. This arrangement permits its operation to be so controlled as to meet the special needs of the court. Headquarters are located in an old, well-established social agency, the Boston Young Men's Christian Union, which is located about a mile from the court. This agency has provided us with suitable quarters and complete maintenance since our inception in 1936.

INTRODUCTION

It is customary for the judge to refer delinquent boys to the Citizenship Training Group for study, guidance, training, and supervision, during the first 12 weeks of probation. During this time the responsibility for the boy is entirely in the hands of the department. In order to impress upon the boy and his parents the close relationship of this program with the court, he is introduced to a staff member of the department while still in the courtroom. An interview held with the boy and his parents, in an adjoining room, gives opportunity for a detailed explanation of the purpose of the program. Also discussed at this time is the degree of responsibility expected of the boy, as well as for the building of parental cooperation. Details are secured about the background and health of the boy on a medical form used by the Preventive Clinic of the Boston Dispensary. Parents sign formal permission for medical assistance, for it is required that all boys attending the training program must be given a thorough medical examination.

The importance of a sound and systematic medical examination to discover and correct physical defects is shown in the case of *Howard*, a thirteen-year-old boy who was sent to the Citizenship Training Group a short time ago by the Boston Juvenile Court. Howard was found delinquent on a larceny complaint. The medical examination at the Boston Dispensary revealed that Howard had a very bad eye — a serious strabismus. This condition had caused him much embarrassment. Children tauntingly referred to him as "cross-eye." Investigation revealed that his behavior seemed definitely traceable to his handicap. He is the sixth child of twelve children. The fact that nothing had been done previously about his eye must be explained by the suggestion that he was lost in the crowd.

The Citizenship Training Group set machinery in motion promptly. Following a recommendation of surgery by the Boston Dispensary, the caseworker was able to secure the parents' consent; the boy was admitted to the Boston City Hospital through its Social Service Department, and he was operated upon successfully. Eye glasses were recommended and supplied.

This treatment has done much for Howard physically and socially. After eight weeks of daily supervision, it can be said that he is a changed boy. An interesting sidelight is that Howard's next older brother voluntarily accompanies Howard to the Citizenship Training Group and takes part in the program. The two boys have always been very close in affection and interests, and it is hoped that the program will help both of them.

The fact that Howard is the only delinquent child in a family of twelve raises the age-old question of why one member of the family commits an offense and all the others remain law-abiding. The correction of Howard's physical handicap may be the solution to this question in this particular family.

Casework we believe is the heart of probation work with delinquent children. The Citizenship Training Group seeks to help its boys in developing a healthy attitude toward society by group work and casework processes.

TREATING THE "WHOLE" BOY

Dealing with the boy cannot be restricted to the particular problem that has brought him to the agency. His delinquent act may be only a symptom of still deeper difficulties which often are emotional. In all cases the worker must know the boy intimately — the "whole" boy: his environment, religious feelings, family, and family relations. The worker must be fully aware of the boy's past, his present mental and physical capabilities, and his attitudes toward himself and the community. The worker is then better able to aid with the problem which originally brought the youngster to the training program.

Much of the working out of the problem is left to the boy. He is encouraged to make his own effort in every phase of the program so that he may release his abilities which are dormant or restricted; but in order to do this, the boy must know himself and must understand how he, as an individual, forms a very vital part of the "whole family of relationships" which are a daily part of his life. Casework methods bring about a better relationship for the boy with his family, the Citizenship Training Group, and the court.

A complete social investigation of the home, each member of the immediate family, the boy's school and his church, as well as social agencies in the community to whom the family is known, is undertaken by the worker within a few days after the boy's arrival at the Citizenship Training Group. After several visits with either or both parents are made in their home, a good working relationship is usually established. All parties concerned are then aware of the function of the CTG and realize that this is not a punitive agency but one sincerely interested in assisting the boy as well as his family with their problems.

This material, together with an interest sheet prepared by the boy, and subsequent observations of the staff during training, is discussed in our staff conference (held every Thursday afternoon) in order to adapt the possibility of training and treatment to meet a boy's individual needs. Each boy's progress is evaluated at least four times during his training period. Although no great emphasis is placed on psychological testing, certain types of intelligence and school achievement tests are administered in all cases. Mr. Gallahue, our psychometrist administers the psychological tests while Dr. Selvig of the Judge Baker Guidance Center and consulting psychiatrist, reviews the material as each boy is considered in staff conference. Dr. Selvig sees the boy and his parents. On his judgment, the more difficult problems may be referred to the Judge Baker Guidance Center and other agencies for intensive treatment.

During the boy's 12-weeks' training period, he is encouraged to develop a healthy attitude towards the law, the family, and the institution under which he must live. He is instructed to develop insight into the motives of his own behavior. He is aroused so that he may make his own effort in every phase of the program. Activity, participation, and effort on his part are necessary in deciding the most appropriate form of treatment.

DIRECT DEALINGS

Our findings reveal that the one thing an adolescent boy demands is that we do business with him directly. He doesn't want the hearsay of the teacher or club leader or parents used as the basis of private discussion, however important this information may be. By giving the boy a chance to act in a variety of social situations, some of which demand strain, we have been able to develop fresh original material which we use directly with the boy. It has been our experience that a boy is willing to discuss a fight he has had in our locker room, but he resents discussing a fight he has had on the street if the details of the fight have been communicated to us by an outsider. The treatment or advantage of this can be seen nearly every day in our setup. If a boy blows up in a volleyball game, or makes a nuisance of himself in discussion, he can be taken aside immediately, and the whole matter discussed with him directly. Such instances, even though they may be violations of rules which involve discipline become mutual experience which the boys are ready to discuss.

The case of Tommy will illustrate what I mean: Tommy was referred to us as a result of a larceny complaint and was known to have a pugnacious manner which had previously put him into the court for assault and battery. His disposition to fight and quarrel eventually became evident in competitive games. After several misunderstandings with boys in the gymnasium, the matter was taken up directly with the boy on the basis of the incidents seen in our own presence. We did not have to refer to

an event, to draw our attention by the court record or by the probation officer. We had original, fresh, mutual incidents, which served as a basis for attacking the problem.

Regardless of the change of our own particular point of view, one conclusion is inevitable: A boy comes into court because he cannot get along with other people, because he cannot live successfully with others in those groups in which he finds himself. Specifically, the social side of this individual has not been developed to a point where he has learned to control his own personal impulses in the interest of happy group life. This has recently been pointed out by a study made by Dr. Fred Brown in Minneapolis. In three carefully selected groups of delinquents, protodelinquents, and non-delinquents, he found the developmental age of the non-delinquents in advance of both the other groups, clearly indicating a more infantile social behavior on the part of these boys who come into the court.

It has been said that living successfully with other people is a skilled occupation, and the acquisition of skill comes from persistent effort. No one ever succeeds in carrying the art of living to perfection, and to achieve even the minimum standard which society demands from its members requires a long apprenticeship. It is not easy to control our tempers, our desires, and our fears. It is hard to acquire singleness of purpose, to avoid taking selfish advantage, to look at things fairly, and without coloring them with our own self-interest. And yet these are the things a person must do, at least to a reasonable extent, if he is to live successfully with his neighbors. No one else can do them for him. Self-control comes only from self-discipline.

S. R. Slavson strikingly summarizes the value of group activity in developing maturity: "There are numerous boys who lack the most essential patterns of behavior in group relation: they do not possess elementary cultural tools for group life. These are the boys who have not acquired even rudimentary inhibitions. They hardly take in cognizance of the needs and conveniences of others. These young people have to be re-educated. They must learn the simple concepts and practices of human relationships. They have to be made into civilized persons. Group experience with a purpose and wholehearted interest is perhaps the most certain method of reaching such individuals, for they learn by experience rather than through abstract teaching. The group must therefore supply face-to-face contacts in an informal relation where conflicts, hostilities, friendships, and cooperation can concur and find expression; for it is well known that personality is modified through interaction and firsthand experience."

An Essential Goal

An essential goal of our work is, therefore, to help our boys develop a growing capacity for taking responsibility and to assist them in achieving a social maturity which will permit them to be successful, happy members in their homes, schools, and communities. To develop this skill in group living we can reasonably look to planned group activity, supervised by outstanding leadership as one of the promising treatment aids to be added to our present resources. Group activity as a treatment aid in probation depends upon an alliance with clinical psychology, education, medicine, and social casework.

From the treatment side we cannot hope to eradicate immediately long-established life patterns of behavior; but during the 12 weeks we have found it possible through group therapy to modify attitudes which hinder a healthy community adjustment. We do attempt in a preliminary way to initiate healthful, social, and personal habits by a special training program which includes the personal hygiene, working together, playing together, and discussing cooperatively problems of citizenship.

At the conclusion of the 12 weeks of training, a summary is drawn up which deals with the boy's problem from the standpoint of personality and delinquency. Specific recommendations are made to the judge of the court for the treatment of the boy's social, personal, and medical needs. At this time, the treatment program is agreed upon, and set into effect. If the boy satisfactorily completes his period of 12 weeks of training, it is then recommended upon his return to court that he be placed in the second stage of his probation period; that is, to report once a week for the next three months to the probation officer in charge of his district.

If at this time there is need for other specialized services, we have working agreements with psychiatric clinics, medical dispensaries, hospitals, placement agencies, religious organiza-

tions, and recreational or club centers, that carry out the service required for a boy.

If during the second period of his probation, the boy works out in a satisfactory manner, he is then placed in the third stage of his probationary period, by being on his own for the next three months. During this period he does not have to report. However, just before the case comes up again, a follow-up investigation is made; if all is satisfactory, the probation officer usually recommends that the boy's case be placed on file.

The Value of Group Work

This is a program in which we have attempted to utilize group-work methods in the study, guidance, and treatment of delinquents who are required to attend this department. When we speak about the value of group activity, we are clear in our minds that we do not mean mass activity. The groups must be small enough to insure individual care and to make individual relationships within the group important, effective and revealing. The ultimate value of what we are doing will directly depend upon the flexibility of our plan. There is no one cure. We must use the best tools at our disposal; we must be geared into the existing resources of the community; and we must do that which is the most difficult of all — the right thing at the right time.

While this program is affiliated with the Boston Juvenile Court and directly under the control of a Board of Trustees made up of outstanding public-spirited Boston people, it receives no city or state financial support. It is privately supported. I would like to pay tribute to the Rotary Club of Boston, the Charles Hayden Foundation, the Boston Junior Chamber of Commerce, the Committee of the Permanent Charity Fund, the Sarah A. Hyams Fund, and other funds who have so generously contributed to the financial support of this worthy and deserving program for delinquent boys.

Many people have asked about the success of this training program. Before giving you the statistical report, I would like to say that there were two criticisms directed to this program in its earlier days. The first was that we were assembling all of the delinquent boys under one roof, and if they were not delinquent when they arrived, they would soon be while in attendance. However, we have found that boys can be brought together in informal groups for short periods of time without contamination. Since 1936 when the program was organized, we do not know of a single instance in which a boy has been in subsequent trouble due to an association developed in this group. The 12-weeks' period proved to be too short a time to cement any new friendships. The 3:30 to 5:30 o'clock period has also been a fortunate hour for attendance, for the boys must hurry to get from their schools to our headquarters and must hurry at the conclusion of activities to get home for their evening meals.

CRITICISM

The second criticism was that our program was compulsory, and we were told when you compel someone to do something the results are almost always negative. My response to this remark is that there is a continuous voluntary return to the training program once boys have completed their training period. We have found that approximately nine out of every ten boys who have been through our setup return on a voluntary basis. Some come back to ask for additional help, some to tell about successes in jobs or schools. There are others who come back for program participation while some simply come in to talk but, who in the course of conversation, reveal problems which may need additional attention. What this seems to indicate is that there is a need for a point of reference to which a boy can turn when pressures and problems become annoyingly heavy. This point of reference must be available without red tape of appointments, and it must have the designation and reputation of a center which can be turned to when trouble is brewing. Only rarely do we act as a treating agency. We serve primarily as a reference point where boys may objectify problems and learn where special service is given. In probation we are dealing with boys who have many pressures and problems and it is important for them to have a place where they may clarify from time to time some of the difficulties which arise after probation supervision has terminated. We in the court, through our research project have just completed a 10-year study of the boys who have been through the training program. The results are that we have been able to restore 72.6

per cent of this group to decent and useful citizenship.

Delinquency, we have found, is not a fixed category by which boys can be classified. We have found delinquent behavior in all types of boys, regardless of station, race, culture or environment. This is seen in all ranges of the normal, pathological, and defective. We have also found that no particular skill has preeminence in the treatment of delinquent behavior. Insights from education, psychology, sociology, medicine, and religion all must be used in an adequate treatment program.

Delinquency is like tuberculosis. You cannot remove the disease. You must build up resistance to it, tone up the human system. There is deep in the heart of mankind an element of vigorous life that responds and quickens when it comes in contact with fine character. If conditions are to get better, it must be by personal influence, by the efforts of men and women of fine quality, integrity and devotion working together as a team in our unhealthy communities.

EDITOR'S NOTE: † The above paper was presented at the June 19 meeting of the Boston Conference held at Harvard Law School. As was noted in the October, 1956, *Journal*, the remarkable thing about the project is that it has not been copied more extensively over the country.

123

The Probation Hostel in England *

John C. Spencer and Tadeusz Grygier

PART I — FUNCTION AND ADMINISTRATION

John C. Spencer

The function of penal institutions is all too seldom subjected to scrutiny. Methods of punishment or of treatment become embodied in

---

† "Editor" here refers to the editor of the *Juvenile Court Judges Journal*.

* Reprinted from 31 *Focus* (1952), 165–172, by Institute for the Study and Treatment of Delinquency, London, England. Used by permission of the authors and the original publisher.

the penal system, and in the course of time are accepted as adequate and effective. Their success remains unquestioned and their rationale undiscussed. Indeed the mere passage of time is considered sufficient justification for their continuance. The function of the probation hostel is no exception. In England it appears to have grown almost imperceptibly since the end of World War I, and has come to be regarded as an integral part of the probation system. Yet little literature or research has appeared in examination of the problems involved.

The purpose of these two papers is to examine the place of the hostel in the penal system, and to assess some of its possibilities for therapy. Since the Criminal Justice Act of 1925 the expenditure of public money has been authorized to maintain probationers in these hostels, and as early as 1927 their extended use was recommended by the Young Offenders Committee. In 1936 the Departmental Committee on the Social Services in Courts of Summary Jurisdiction commented on their success, but pointed out that existing accommodation was inadequate for new demands. The committee suggested that hostels for the non-delinquent might also be employed. While the advantage to the delinquent of introducing him (or her) to a hostel for non-delinquents is obvious, the policy has never been adequately carried out.

A large part of the present system dates from the Criminal Justice Act of 1948 which resulted in important changes, perhaps the most significant relating to central inspection and control, finance, and length of stay. The initial inspiration and provision of the probation hostel has always been the work of voluntary bodies, some with religious affiliations, such as the Salvation Army or the Society of St. Vincent de Paul, and others of a secular character. Since 1948 the central authority, through the Home Office, has assumed responsibility for the general supervision of these hostels and for classification as "approved probation hostels." Inspection has been carried out jointly by the Probation Branch and the Children's Department.

Probation hostels had previously been financed by the voluntary body assisted by contributions from the central authority on a per capita basis. But under the new act financial responsibility was transferred to the Home Office assisted wherever possible by the voluntary bodies and by a per capita payment from the local authority,

so calculated as to divide the final cost of operation equally between the central and the local authority. This led to improvements in equipment and salaries though as regards the latter there is still room for very considerable improvement. The contribution made by the probationer himself is determined by a sliding scale, and varies according to his wages. Each boy or girl is allowed a minimum of 7s. pocket money, fares to work are guaranteed, and £2 from the weekly wages go to the hostel. Of the remainder, two-thirds is returned to the boy and one-third is saved for him until his discharge.

The initial decision to insert in the probation order a condition of residence in a hostel is made by the magistrates on the advice of their probation officer. The consent of the probationer is required, thus emphasizing the voluntary nature of the arrangement. The probation officer selects the hostel from personal enquiries assisted by a Home Office list. Not infrequently the probationer has to go to the only hostel with a vacancy and thus no real "choice" is involved. The maximum period for which the Home Office contribution is available was increased from six to twelve months. At the end of six months each case is reviewed by the court in whose area the hostel is located, and a decision is taken as to whether the full period of twelve months is required.

Supervision is by the local probation officer under the direction of the local magistrates court, adult or juvenile. If the probationer goes to a hostel outside his own district the court is obliged to transfer the case to the officer for the hostel area. Previous to the 1948 act transfer was unnecessary. The change has been the subject of frequent argument and also of a certain amount of evasion. In its favour it is argued that the supervision of delinquents by remote control, as it were, can seldom prove satisfactory, and a long journey may be imposed on the probation officer during his periodic visits. From the point of view of the hostel warden the present arrangement has the advantage of providing him with only one officer with whom to work for all the residents. On the other hand there is the argument that the essence of probation lies in individualization of treatment and if the probationer has to share the friendship of the probation officer with all the other hostel residents and also with the warden (a father or mother figure) he will lose some sense of this close relationship to his supervisor. The insecurity created by removal to a new environment will be increased.

In either case the relationship between warden and probation officer is a delicate one. While the probationer is in the hostel, responsibility for him rests with the warden rather than with the probation officer, who is perforce a visitor to the hostel, but responsibility to the court remains with the officer.

Secondly there is a strong case for improving the position and status of the hostel warden on whom so much depends, and for placing greater responsibility in his hands. It may well be that the warden should be given more direct responsibility to the court. Not infrequently he is seen by the court as a backroom figure. Moreover if the therapeutic value of the hostel is to be properly utilized, then a much better training of wardens in individual psychology as well as in group relationships is required.

At the present time there are twenty-one approved probation hostels for boys and eleven for girls. They are authorized to accept two age groups, fifteen to eighteen and seventeen to twenty-one. The total population averages 450 boys and 280 girls, mainly with a twelve month period of residence. This number includes the residents of five approved probation homes for boys and seven for girls. (The main difference between the home and the hostel relates to the place of work. In hostels the probationers go outside to work, whereas in homes the work is done inside.) Only about 2 per cent of the boys as compared with 40 per cent of the girls are sent under orders made by the juvenile court while acting in its non-criminal jurisdiction.

In what does the reformative value of the hostel lie? To say that the essence of the hostel is to be found in the training provided is to create a dilemma. The Departmental Committee agreed with the Young Offenders Committee when they said that "the functions of the probation system should be supervision in the open and that it would not be associated with institutional training in the strict sense." While accepting this principle, the question of how much and what kind of training still remains. Clearly the hostel ought to approximate the family situation as nearly as possible. It is certainly not an Approved School in miniature. Yet it is all too often expected to perform a

training for boys and girls for whom it is clearly unsuited. Above all it is restricted as regards length of stay by the fact that association in the young offender's mind of a period of hostel residence with "doing time" in an institution, or with any form of detention, would immediately create a feeling of injustice. The juvenile court is from time to time faced with the delinquent who does regard his hostel training in this light.

Interpretation by hostel wardens of what constitutes training varies. For some, training means little more than the keeping of regular hours; for others, the introduction of classes by instructors from the local education authority and by voluntary workers occupies a substantial part of the evening programme. Invitations to friends of the residents or of the staff in the evening is a valuable element in creating a homelike atmosphere. Making the hostel as little like an institution as possible is often encouraged. In girls' hostels boy friends may be invited to a weekly social, or a boys' club may be organized within a boys' hostel in an attempt to provide leisure activities in an informal setting. Or the residents may join a club in the neighbourhood, or go out to the cinema or to football matches during the weekend. Perhaps most precious of all is the visit by the probationer to his family, or by his family to him. From the point of view of training, a regular job can hardly be overestimated. The wise warden will do his utmost to prevent that chopping and changing of employment that provides so clear a signpost to a delinquent career.

Generally speaking, the hostel staff is not designed for any elaborate scheme of training; in fact it may be reduced to a minimum level owing to the participation of the residents in the domestic side of the hostel life. Such housework is sometimes regarded — perhaps too optimistically — as having an important reformative value. One may generally expect to find a warden (with his wife as matron in the case of boys' hostels), one or two assistants, and a small domestic staff.

The need for care in selection of residents can hardly be exaggerated. It is essential that magistrates should see the hostel as an integral part of the reformatory system and not as a dumping ground for delinquents for whom no other provision can be made. This latter category may include the homeless, the ex-Approved School or ex-Borstal boy or girl, or the young criminal whom the magistrates may hesitate to send to Borstal, for whom the hostel may be a useful expedient but for whom it is certainly not designed. A hostel can carry only a small number of young people with an institutional background, and it is a serious mistake for courts to send too many delinquents to hostels on the grounds of failure during after-care. The probation hostel is not intended for institutional failures. Nor should the period of residence be regarded merely as providing the probation officer with a useful breathing-space in which to plan further treatment.

At the same time there is a real need to exploit one of the main advantages of the hostel — the fact that the delinquent is still on probation. If the probationer is ultimately to return home, then one of the probation officer's main tasks is the preparation of the delinquent's family for his reception. It is one of the weaknesses of our system that there is often little family casework during the delinquent's residence in an institution, and that on his return home the family is no better prepared to receive him than when he left. The great advantage of hostel treatment is the availability of the probation officer to the family of the probationer. If this opportunity is neglected, then one of the most useful methods in the reformation of the delinquent is wasted.

Statistics of failure and success are at present inadequate for an accurate assessment of the value of hostel treatment. Enough, however, is known for us to be reasonably confident that it certainly can provide the necessary "half-way house to complete independence," as Margery Fry so aptly says in Arms of the Law, and in the process can help the delinquent to adjust himself to the demands of society.

Yet the probation hostel, by comparison with other methods of treatment, still has only inferior status. There is, therefore, a real need to raise the level of pay as well as the standards of recruitment and training in the hostel field. Ways have been suggested in which the hostel may be helped to become one of the major methods of treatment but much depends on a clearer recognition of its methods of training, and above all on a better understanding of the emotional needs of the boys and girls themselves.

PART II — PSYCHIATRIC CONSIDERATIONS
Tadeusz Grygier

The purpose of this part of the article is to present some aspects of hostel placement in the light of the experience gained at the Portman Clinic, established by the Institute for the Study and Treatment of Delinquency in 1933 for medical, social, and psychological examination and treatment of offenders. The clinic, which has been part of the National Health Scheme since 1948, continues to cooperate with the institute in matters of treatment, training and particularly research, and shares a building with it.

Offenders may be referred by any medical, legal or social agency, or may come voluntarily. The majority are sent by courts and probation officers. Each case is examined by one of the clinic's teams, composed of a physician, a psychiatrist, a psychologist, and a psychiatric social worker, and full data are obtained from school employers, relatives and other clinics where relevant. Recommended treatment is usually arranged at the clinic and is often made a condition of probation. Some offenders who live outside the London area are transferred to child guidance clinics or out-patient departments of mental hospitals which they can more easily attend. Some cases are placed in institutions, educational, correctional, or psychiatric. Some, requiring only social measures and environmental handling, are transferred elsewhere. Treatment nearly always involves an all-round approach by medical, psychiatric, educational and social measures with or without penal action by the court.

Most of these adolescent delinquents live with their parents or relatives; a few are in hostels when referred for psychiatric examination. Residence in the hostel is often made a condition of probation.

Boys and girls living in hostels in the London area have, generally speaking, two characteristics in common: a background of unstable, hostile, or broken homes, and a history of delinquency, mild or serious. They present a variety of clinical pictures, from minor behaviour disorders to psychopathic personalities and from mental defectives to cases of well above average intelligence. From the clinical point of view some of the hostel cases present very serious disorders. Examinations of clinical material for this paper aimed at distinguishing some personality factors or social influences which would make for success or failure in the hostel environment, in other words, at establishing indications and contra-indications for placement. In spite of the obvious limitations of the present inquiry it was possible to distinguish some broad categories into which the cases could be clearly and easily divided. We are grateful to the editors of *Focus* for stimulating this investigation which proved more rewarding than we had anticipated.

Short summaries of some case histories are presented on pages 644–645. Here are some general conclusions based on examination of these and many other case histories and on clinical experience. We are grateful to Dr. Denis Carroll, chairman of the staff of the Portman Clinic, and Dr. William Paterson-Brown, a psychiatric consultant to the clinic and a former medical inspector of the Home Office (Children's Branch), for their views and permission to quote the case histories.

1. Criminal record is not of great importance in determining success or failure in hostel environment. Some of the successes had long criminal records, some of the failures had none.

2. Within certain limits, the level of intelligence is equally unimportant. Only very low intellectual level combined with social immaturity is a contra-indication; in these cases specialized institutional treatment is necessary. With very high intelligence we also suspect difficulty in adjustment to hostel environment especially in those of higher cultural level, but our material is inadequate to form a definite conclusion.

3. In our material there was not one case in which the family background was favourable. A broken home, hostility between parents and the adolescent, friction and resentment caused by re-marriage of one parent, low moral standards — all of these factors are indications for hostel placement.

4. Bad school and work records, in particular truancy and absenteeism, are on the other hand contra-indications. They mean that the adolescent is not only unhappy at home but has been unable to adjust himself to any other environment; his personality requires a thorough rebuilding in a special institution, whether psychiatric or not, or possibly a good substitute family and intensive psychotherapy.

5. Good school and work records are definite indications. In these cases removal from the main source of frustration and friction with some psychiatric care and guidance, is usually sufficient. But in some of our cases the period of stay in a hostel is not long enough to be really effective. The hostel seemed to be an ideal solution and the adolescent undergoing treatment at the clinic was making real progress in social adjustment when his term of stay at the hostel was over. With the return to the old environment, relapse was inevitable, treatment was interrupted and new offences followed.

6. All serious disorders, whether intellectual, emotional or of the nature of a morbid process (neurosis or psychosis) form contra-indications. Not one youth of this type fully succeeded in spite of clinic treatment. Similar clinic cases treated in good family environment do often succeed.

7. The best prognostic criterion for hostel environment is the degree of emotional and social maturity. When clinical diagnosis or other findings included such terms as "immature, impulsive behaviour," "childish irresponsibility," "psychopathic personality with hysterical features," etc., improvement brought about by residence in the hostel and clinical treatment was not great enough for the outcome to be regarded as a success. The only exception was an emotionally immature girl who settled down at a hostel *after* having been successfully treated at the clinic; in this case a certain degree of stabilization, especially suitable employment, had already been achieved when hostel disposal was made. This does not always mean that placement in another environment would have succeeded: all our cases had already been treated in the family environment and failed, and some had been treated in institutions. Cases of psychopathy with hysterical features have poor prognosis whatever we do with them and even hospitalization has usually little effect. In another investigation undertaken by the present writer for the Royal Commission on Capital Punishment and based on 2079 consecutive cases treated at the Institute for the Study and Treatment of Delinquency and the Portman Clinic, 68 per cent of patients diagnosed as psychopathic did nevertheless succeed, and follow-up revealed "cure" or "considerable improvement"; but among the cases of psychopathy *and* hysteria or hysterical features not one could be regarded as a success though not all had com-

pletely failed. In other cases of hysteria and emotional immaturity psychiatric treatment backed by a stable family or an institution has often met with success, but apparently hostel environment requires some degree of maturity achieved before the placement is made. On the other hand psychopathic features alone are not a contra-indication.

8. The greatest weakness of hostels seems to be the strictly limited length of stay. The disturbed adolescent is supposed to achieve enough stability to navigate on his own within six months to one year. Most hostel cases treated at the Portman Clinic were very disturbed indeed. To suggest that six or even twelve months' stay in a hostel would solve their problems permanently is not realistic. In the end the majority of adolescents studied failed, even if hostel placement brought temporary improvement. The arrangement meant for most of them only temporary relief and a delay in solving their problems so the advantage from the point of view of their mental health was doubtful indeed. Provision should be made for hostel residence till the adolescent has reached full maturity or can come back to a rehabilitated family. This change would make provision for voluntary residence of adolescents who have ceased to be technically delinquent and whose probation orders have expired.

9. The scatter of hostel cases is, from the clinical point of view, too wide, and this makes impracticable establishing a regime which would be satisfactory for all inmates. The only solution seems to be classification of hostels according to the type of regime and the cases dealt with.

10. The suggested extension of stay would mean that young delinquents would remain in the same institution with those who had become technically non-delinquent. An immature boy put under the influence of older boys sophisticated in crime would be exposed to contagion, but it can only help when a young delinquent is influenced by a senior who has passed through the same stage of maladjustment and can act as a model of socialization and personality development.

11. Co-operation between the clinic and the wardens was, on the whole, satisfactory. However, linking the psychiatrist, the psychiatric social worker, the probation officer and the warden in one programme, requires tact and

skill, let alone good will, on the part of everybody concerned.

CASE HISTORIES
Failures:

1. *Mentally defective boy of eighteen*, IQ 57. Behaviour problem under probation supervision. An illegitimate child who had been placed with various foster parents, in children's homes and hostels. At the hostel from which he was referred to the clinic he showed immature and irresponsible behaviour, had a very bad work record and his leisure activities were at the level of a nine-year-old child. He was diagnosed as a certifiable mental defective and removal to an institution was recommended.

Comment: Too defective for handling in other than a specialized medical institution.

2. *Mental disorder in a boy of fifteen*, IQ 85. Several offences of stealing and truanting. Disturbed family background with early separations, parents divorced. Billeted in several places before the age of five, never with one family for more than a few years. At referral he was living with relatives who refused to keep him any longer, as he was stealing, lying and truanting persistently.

He was classified as a deeply neurotic individual requiring intensive psychotherapy. Placed in a hostel, he failed to settle down to any work. He was transferred to a psychiatric hospital.

Comment: Too neurotic for non-psychiatric residential care.

3. *Hysterical psychopathy in a girl of seventeen*, IQ 129. Stealing since the age of four. Rejected by both parents since early childhood. Under psychiatric care in several clinics and out-patient hospital departments. Poor school and work record, vagrancy, hysterical fugues, restless and impulsive behaviour with "love of excitement and general irresponsibility." She was living in a hostel when referred for treatment. She was diagnosed as a psychopathic personality with strong hysterical features. She discontinued clinic visits and several months later was again convicted for larceny.

Comment: Ceased treatment; very poor prognosis.

4. *Emotional immaturity in a girl of eighteen*, IQ 81. Charged with getting money under false pretences. This girl was spoilt at home by an hysterical mother, who frustrated

the father's efforts to introduce discipline. Bad work record, giving up jobs on the first day and not taking any further work for months. Childish, irresponsible behaviour, with few offences.

At the clinic she was found emotionally immature and diagnosed as "a dull, emotionally unstable hysteric," requiring residential medical treatment. In spite of this recommendation she was transferred to a hostel; there she was reported as craving attention, doing no work at the hostel or outside it, and behaving like a small child. She did not attend the clinic for treatment and was finally discharged as unimproved.

Comment: Too unstable for hostel regime.

5. *Girl of eighteen,* IQ 107. Offence larceny. An illegitimate child who was always reminded of her illegitimacy by her mother's relatives. Father an unstable individual, was killed in a gang fight. Mother rather dull, unable to control the girl who was brought up mainly in institutions, but lived with her mother or relatives from time to time. Much hostility and friction between the girl and her mother. Her work record was relatively steady, but her general behaviour was aggressive, uninhibited and childishly impulsive.

She was diagnosed as a behaviour problem, aggravated by hysterical make-up and friction with her mother. She was placed in a hostel, but she quarrelled so much with other girls that she had to be removed. She was eventually placed with a sympathetic landlady of a motherly disposition. A year later still in this home she was more settled, working and apparently happy. No further delinquency was reported.

Comment: Hostel regime too impersonal for such a girl.

Successes:

6. *Girl of sixteen,* IQ 100. "In need of care and protection." An extremely neurotic father and a dull and inefficient mother created an atmosphere full of tension and friction. Moral standards at home very low. When referred to the clinic the girl was running away from home, spending nights in undesirable company, in dance halls and night clubs. Her school record and work record had been good, but her work was affected by the home problem.

She was rather prematurely developed, with no signs of pathology, but with deep resentment directed against her parents.

Placed in a hostel and treated at the clinic, she gained more stability, her anxiety and tension decreased and general behaviour improved. When, however, she returned home after six months, her behaviour problems re-appeared and she ran away.

A year later she was traced to a different part of the country, where she was living in lodgings and working. No delinquency was reported, but she was known to the local police as mixing with individuals whose activities were not above suspicion.

Comment: Premature termination of stay in hostel and of treatment.

7. *Boy of fourteen,* IQ 101. Offence larceny. This boy spent several years in hospital and was evacuated without his parents during the war. Later on he failed to settle down at home and there was much friction with both parents; the antagonism between the boy and his mother increased to such an extent that he had to be removed from home.

Clinic examination revealed lack of warm affection, strong resentment, aggressiveness and delinquency, but no signs of emotional immaturity. His school progress was poor, but this was justified by poor health. He was diagnosed as having "character disturbance" due to early separation from his parents; hostel placement was recommended.

At the hostel his general behaviour improved greatly; there was no further delinquency; at school definite progress was made. After six months stay, and against the recommendation of the clinic, the boy returned home. A relapse followed. He was so upset that he said he would live in an Approved School or a Remand Home rather than his own home. Due to the joint efforts of the clinic, the probation officer and the headmaster of his school, he was allowed to return to the hostel on a voluntary basis. The London County Council provided financial help to enable the hostel to keep him till the age of eighteen. He has been taken off probation and discharged from the clinic as cured.

Follow-up a few years later revealed steady progress at school and subsequently at work, no further delinquency, and satisfactory adjustment, except for some unpopularity among his workmates.

Comment: An example of the benefits of stretching regulations to fit the case.

8. *Girl of eighteen,* IQ 139. Persistent stealing since the age of six at home, at school, and later on at the hostel. There was strong sibling jealousy in this case and constant friction between the girl and her mother. The girl had been under psychiatric care since early childhood without visible results. Her school record and work record were good. Each time it was stealing alone which created difficulties and brought about a change of school or place of work.

When referred for treatment she was living with her mother and stealing persistently. She was diagnosed as a case of obsessional stealing and a hostel was recommended. Treatment continued for a year while she was living in the hostel and working. Stealing stopped gradually; treatment was suspended indefinitely. She left the hostel after a year and took a room with another girl. Latest news (two years later): she is married, has a child, is happy; no further delinquency.

Comment: An illustration of the advantages of the combination of hostel and psychological treatment. The earlier failure was due to environment which was too bad to give treatment a chance.

124

California Camps for Delinquents *

O. H. Close

Camps for juvenile delinquents have been in operation in California for more than a quarter of a century. Like many other social movements, camps were born of necessity. The first forestry camp in California was started in Riverside County by Probation Officer C. W. Mathews

---

* Reprinted from *Social Correctives for Delinquency,* 1945 Yearbook, National Probation Association, 136–147. Used by permission of the author and the publisher.

in August, 1927. This camp was later abandoned, not because it was proving ineffective, but because of its cost during the depression years. Riverside County, in 1946, again established a forestry camp known as Twin Pines Ranch, which is one of the outstanding camp programs in the State.

In Los Angeles County, the first forestry camp opened in 1932 for the care and supervision of transient adolescent youths. During the depression years, transient youths came to California in greater numbers than ever before and the number that were committed to correctional institutions on account of delinquency increased to the point where there was no longer space for them in the State training schools. An experimental camp for transients was opened by the Los Angeles County Board of Supervisors. This camp, now known as Camp No. 10, proved so successful that Judge Samuel Blake, then juvenile court judge, recommended additional camps be started for local youthful offenders. From this beginning, Los Angeles County has greatly increased its camp program, and camps and ranch schools have been established in several other counties. The camp program of Los Angeles County was launched under the direction of Mr. Kenyon Scudder, then Chief Probation Officer, and was continued by his successor, Mr. Karl Holton.

LEGISLATION

In 1935, the State Legislature passed legislation providing for the establishment of forestry camps by Boards of Supervisors for the care of delinquent youths committed by juvenile courts for camp supervision. Under this legislation, boys committed to such camps may be required to labor on the buildings and grounds of the camps, on forestation and reforestation of public lands, or building of forest roads for fire prevention, making fire trails and fire breaks, for fire fighting or fire suppression, or to perform any other work or engage in any other duties or activities prescribed by the superintendent of the camp, subject to the approval of the Board of Supervisors. Boys in camp may receive wages for the work they do. Money earned may be paid in reparation for damages, or to parents or dependents of the boy, or to the boy, himself, in such manner as the court may direct.

In 1943, the Act was amended to permit the California Youth Authority to also establish camps in connection with its program of correctional schools of the State. The Youth Authority may establish camps to be operated independently or in cooperation with the Department of Natural Resources on such terms as may be agreed upon by the Youth Authority and the Director of the Department of Natural Resources. The law further provides for the establishment of county camps for girls and they may be required to perform such duties as prescribed or permitted by the Youth Authority. The Youth Authority may, on the State level, provide, in cooperation with the Department of Natural Resources, or otherwise, for the payment of wages to boys and girls for work they may do while housed in camps or juvenile homes; payment to be made in such manner and in such proportions as the Youth Authority may direct.

In 1945, the Legislature passed a measure providing for a subsidy by the State, through the Youth Authority, to counties operating juvenile homes, ranches, or camps, within or without the county, to which wards of the juvenile courts may be sent, who would otherwise be committed by the court to the Youth Authority. The law now provides, as subsequently amended in 1953, that a subsidy may be paid amounting to one-half of the cost of camp operation, but not to exceed $95 per month. The camps receiving this subsidy must not exceed 100 inmates in population. The programs and plants of the county camps are subject to inspection by the Youth Authority and must meet the minimum standards prescribed.

The California State Legislature, in 1957, further amended the law governing county camps and juvenile homes by passing legislation providing for matching funds for construction of county camps up to one-half the cost of the camp or homes, but not to exceed $3,000 per bed. This legislation was passed to further encourage counties to establish juvenile camps and homes. In order to make camp facilities available to small counties without camp facilities, through mutual agreement, youths may be committed to camps in other counties, by the committing counties paying the approximate cost per capita to the counties operating the camps. Camps may also be established jointly by two or more counties.

The county board of supervisors may, in order that school facilities be provided in camps, direct county superintendents of schools to establish and maintain public schools in juvenile homes and camps. The county board of supervisors must provide suitable buildings and equipment for such schools.

The camp subsidies paid to counties in the State of California by the Youth Authority now amount to over a million and a half dollars per year. The average monetary cost per capita for operation of camps is $233.54. This cost is in addition to the educational costs, which are borne by the county superintendent of schools under the regular average daily attendance program.

PROGRAM FOR GIRLS' CAMPS

The program for girls on the county level, although the law has provided for them, has been slow to develop in California. Los Angeles County established a camp type of school known as Broad Acres in 1949, but this camp was closed in 1951 due to administrative difficulties and excessive cost. A county school for girls has been established in Bakersfield, Kern County, in connection with another institution. The girls leave the institution to attend public school during the day. San Bernardino County has also recently established a camp for girls.

It is the writer's opinion that the problem of delinquent girls should, as far as possible, be treated in small groups at the county level with various phases of training programs and living conditions. Many girls sent to state training schools have serious difficulty in adjusting to the more regimented programs found in the state schools for girls.

ORGANIZATION

The California County Camps are under the direct supervision of the Chief County Probation Officers, except the Los Prietos Camp, which is operated jointly by Ventura and Santa Barbara Counties through a camp board of directors. This board consists of judges from Ventura and Santa Barbara Counties, a member of the Board of Supervisors of each county and the Chief Probation Officer from each county.

California county camps operate without custodial restraints and with a minimum amount of close supervision. Discipline in camps varies from loss of privileges to various

Table 1   *Chronological History of California Camps*

DATE	RANCH OR CAMP	TYPE	COUNTY	COMMENTS
Aug. 1927	Keen Camp	Boys' Camp	Riverside	Closed 1932
1932	Forestry Camp 10	Boys' Camp	Los Angeles	Renamed Camp Glenn Rocky
1936	Forestry Camp 8	Boys' Camp	Los Angeles	Renamed Camp No. 4
Dec. 1936	Mt. Woodson Sr. Camp	Boys' Camp	San Diego	Moved 1950 Rancho Del Campo
1937	Forestry Camp 3	Boys' Camp	Los Angeles	
1938	Camp Owen	Boys' Camp	Kern	
1939	Log Cabin Ranch	Boys' Camp	San Francisco	
1942	Mt. Woodson Jr. Camp	Boys' Camp	San Diego	Discontinued 1950
1943	Mt. Baldy Jr. Camp	Boys' Camp	Los Angeles	Discontinued 1950
1944	Los Prietos Camp	Boys' Camp	Santa Barbara and Ventura	
1945	La Tuna Camp	Boys' Camp	Los Angeles	Discontinued 1953
1947	Chabot Ranch	Boys' Camp	Alameda	
1948	Twin Pines Ranch	Boys' Camp	Riverside	
1949	Broad Acres Camp	School for Girls	Los Angeles	Discontinued 1951
May 1950	Verdemont	Boys' Camp	San Bernardino	
July 1950	San Benito School	Boys' Camp	San Benito	
July 1950	Oak Grove Camp	Boys' Camp	Los Angeles	
1951	Camp Hondo	Boys' Camp	Los Angeles	
1953	Wm. F. James Ranch	Boys' Camp	Santa Clara	
1955	Sonoma Mobile Camp	Boys' Camp	Sonoma	
July 1956	Prob. Recep. Camp 1	Boys' Camp	Los Angeles	Receiving Unit
Aug. 1956	Joplin Ranch	Boys' Camp	Orange	
Sept. 1956	Bar-O Ranch	Boys' Camp	Del Norte	Subsidized beginning July 1, 1957
Mar. 1957	Tulare County Camp	Boys' Camp	Tulare	
April 1957	Prob. Recep. Camp 2	Boys' Camp	Los Angeles	Receiving Unit
April 1957	Mary Lavers Home	School for Girls	Kern	
July 1957	Kenyon J. Scudder	Boys' Camp	Los Angeles	
1957	San Bernardino County Camp	Girls' Camp	San Bernardino	

extra duties that may be assigned to boys violating the rules and regulations. Boys who escape or commit other serious breaches of conduct are usually returned to court. These cases are generally then committed to the California Youth Authority for institutional placement. Camp placements, however, are not limited to mild cases and first offenders. Occasionally, boys are sent to camps, who, if they were adults, would probably receive prison sentences.

The length of stay in the camps varies from camp to camp. The earlier camp programs in this State were comparatively short, which averaged approximately sixteen weeks. The length of stay at the present time has been increased to seven and a half or eight months,

and in a few camps the stay is even longer.

When released from the camps, youths are placed under the supervision of probation officers, and most of the camps now have probation officers assigned directly to them to do liaison work between camps and probation departments.

PROGRAMS

Most of the county camps in California operate on a half-day school and half-day work basis. The school programs in the camps have teachers for approximately every fifteen students. The work program in some of the camps consists of forestry and kindred work in the county forestry departments. There is also industrial training and automotive work, arts programs, music, and hobby craft activities. The age range in most of the camps is from fourteen to seventeen years of age. In the larger counties, the younger boys are segregated into separate camps. A few of the county institutions are ranch type with limited farming activities. Three of the county camps have all-day programs in forestry work and fire suppression as the chief activities.

The three camps operated by the California Youth Authority in cooperation with the State Forestry Department are strictly work camps operating on an eight-hour basis with a very limited amount of handicraft training and classroom work. The boys in the California Youth Authority camps range from seventeen to twenty-one years of age and are carefully selected at the Guidance Centers and Clinics or sent out from the correctional institutions near the end of their period of institutional training.

The various camps of the State are constantly experimenting with new techniques and methods of treatment. A few of the county camps allow furloughs, weekends at home, and an effort is made on the part of all of the camps to prepare boys in every way possible for return to the community. One camp has set up a program known as Alumni Day when once each year the boys who have been released from camp may return with their families and friends, thereby displaying to the boys in residence that many of the boys who have been through the camp are now making a satisfactory adjustment in community life.

The tendency recently in some of the counties has been to establish camps with lower population — some as low as sixteen in number. These camps naturally are able to operate with a very relaxed program. It is believed by those observing their operations that the results of a smaller camp program are proving satisfactory. The expense of operating is approximately the same as the larger camps and it is the thought that for some types of boys the results obtained are more successful than in larger camps.

Appraisal of Camp Programs

On numerous occasions, the writer has visited both county-operated camps for juveniles and those operated by the California

Youth Authority on the State level. One of the notable features of the camps is the evident spontaneity and sense of freedom that prevails among the boys. This applies, not only to county camps for juvenile cases, but also to the camp populations of the California Youth Authority for older boys. There is less sense of restriction and regimentation in the camps, all of which operate with less than a hundred boys. Larger institutions must of necessity be more restricted and regimented because of the class of boys supervised. This greater sense of freedom in the camps, coupled with opportunities for individual counseling, plus the natural setting of most of the camps in the wooded mountain areas, provide a wholesome environment with positive therapeutic values.

Parents of the boys are generally very much pleased to have them placed in the camps in preference to the more routinized program of the training schools. Their reason, sometimes, is based upon the monetary aspects of the camp program, as boys in the camps receive some compensation, while lads in the training schools do not. But for the most part, parents are primarily concerned with the well-being of their boys and have the feeling that camp programs are less punitive in character.

It must be borne in mind that the success of the camps depends upon their operating in connection with more formal types of supervision and training offered at correctional training schools, as many boys require close custodial care and could not under any circumstances be placed in camps. Camps, furthermore, cannot provide very extensive vocational training programs. Boys who need a long period of detention and who are capable of making normal progress in academic and trades training programs, should generally be placed in training schools.

Camps, if properly operated, are no less expensive than training schools. They should not be looked upon as a means of reducing the cost of dealing with delinquent youths. Neither should the camps be considered merely as a means of securing cheap labor for the State to take care of fire-fighting, reforestation, road-building and other public works service. This work, in conjunction with camps in the foothills and mountains, should be so set up that it will be a part of a rehabilitative program. If camps for older boys are properly organized and the

right selection of youth is made for camp placement, the camps can be made profitable from a
labor and a rehabilitative standpoint. Habits of
work, improved health, and character development through counseling and guidance will be
the outcome of a well-balanced camp program.

It is the writer's opinion, based on twenty-
five years of experience in the operation of state
school programs for older boys, that fully 20
per cent of the boys that have passed through
this institution might have been effectively
cared for in camps, operated either by the counties or by the State. It is the writer's belief,
based on California's experience during the
past twenty-five years with juvenile camps, that
we shall see in the future many similar units in
various parts of the country, organized on a
permanent basis in our mountain forests, along
the shores of our lakes, in our valleys and in our
farming communities, where underprivileged
children may have the benefit of the kindness
of nature with all its healing potentialities, combined with the care and guidance of sympathetic and understanding counselors and teachers.

The ever rising tide of delinquency in our
country is viewed by those who understand the
problem with serious concern. We must develop new techniques and procedures in dealing with it, both as to prevention and treatment.
The small unit programs now gradually being
developed under the camp system in California
have passed from the experimental stages. The
success of these camps and ranch schools points
the way to a more normal and understanding
treatment of many of our juvenile offenders,
and constitutes a most valuable adjunct to probation and juvenile institutions.

Chapter 22

Forms of Treatment: Foster Home Care

PERHAPS THE MOST BAFFLING feature of attempts to cope constructively with delinquency is the fact that the family and home situation of the child is often so poor that, regardless of whether probation, institutional commitment or clinical psychotherapy is resorted to, the danger of the delinquent recidivating will be marked if he is sent back to the defeating under-the-roof culture which bred his antisocial attitudes and behavior in the first place. The individual delinquent needs to be strengthened, yes; but the familial environment can be, and often is, overwhelmingly destructive. Some interim (and, in some instances, more lengthy) milieu must be provided in such cases.

One device for coping with this situation is the foster home. The first article in this chapter, by Williams, gives a brief history of the substitute-home movement and describes the various forms that have evolved. Williams sets out the basic considerations that should govern the use of foster homes in different types of delinquency cases. (Incidentally, those who speak glibly about "the need for a typology of delinquents" will see how difficult it is to formulate "types," since, of course, the definition of type depends essentially on the particular purpose for which it is made; and one and the same child can belong to Type A for one purpose, Type B for another, Type C for still another, etc.) In discussing the ramifications of the foster-home problem, Williams considers the roles of the indispensable *dramatis personae:* the child, the foster parents and the natural parents, the social worker; and he has some practical things to say about the economics of the problem.

Beginning with another illustration of the history of foster homes, the next article, by Miss Gilpin, supplies further insight into the role of the social casework type of probation officer in helping to make the difficult placement decision. "The child and his family situation cannot fit into certain pigeonholes, predetermined and predestined for probation, foster-home care, or institution." Yet, she points out, "we seem to have built up a little scale of delinquency treatment, from probation to foster home and lastly to an institution." She goes on to define the responsibilities and techniques of the child-placing social worker. "It is no easy job to help [the child] take on a new family which is to become his by court order." The author has some thought-provoking observations on the nature and limitations of foster homes and foster parents, and regarding the difficult process most children go through in adjusting to a new family. Yet for large numbers — those from families broken by death, desertion or divorce, cruelty, neglect and illness — "foster home care supplies the essentials for a happy childhood and a healthy growing-up. These children find in foster homes the family life which no group living experience can attempt to provide."

The article by Dr. Gardner brings out, from an essentially psychoanalytic point of view, the significance, in home placement failure, of an ambivalent attitude of the child (especially prevalent in puberty) toward his true parents — "coexistent feelings of filial love and hate." Gardner suggests how this inconsistent child–parent attitude can be recognized, and points out that some fundamental change in the internal mental economy of the child, rather than mere manipulation of external environmental factors, is necessary. Typically, Gardner observes, the child who fails in placement expresses extreme hostility toward his own parents — usually the father — unwarranted by the reality situation. Experience shows that "the nearer any child's evaluation of his reality *does* coincide with the actual facts — however harsh it may really be — the better seem the chances for a successful placement."

Gardner gives many illustrations of the overt hostility symptoms directed at the parent. He unfolds and interprets the quite typical pattern of response to the foster-home placement: initial evident satisfaction of the child with the material advantages of his new home, but without indications of wholesome identification with the foster father; improved behavior, both in and out of school, followed by unfavorable reactions of alarm; unreal efforts to reciprocate affection at the stage when the child realizes that the foster parents are becoming fond of him; emergence of guilt feelings followed by the child's effort to destroy the relationship through antisocial behavior, motivated now by self-directed, instead of the prior, other-directed, hostility. This, Gardner observes, leads to a desire of the child to return to his own home and involves a flattering "secondary evaluation" of his own parents and expression of love for them. Thus the instinctual urges of love and aggression toward the child's own mother and father, with their consequent guilt and remorse, may be anticipated to express themselves also against the parental surrogates of the foster home. "The home they seem to desire and seem compelled to keep on seeking is one where their instinctual demands will not be reactivated in their present strength, or where external conditions are such as to give them the maximum help in repression of these drives." Dr. Gardner concludes that detection of extreme ambivalent feelings is a basic prerequisite to adequate choice of foster home as opposed to group placement and to deciding whether intensive psychotherapy is called for with a view to strengthening the child's ego to cope with the strongly activated pubertal drives.

125

Foster Homes for Juvenile Delinquents *

Herbert D. Williams

Can foster family homes be used for the rehabilitation of juvenile delinquents? If so, what kinds of homes are needed and where and how can they be found? What safeguards must be used to insure that efforts in this direction are successful? What experience have we to go on in the use of such homes? Which juvenile delinquents can be placed in foster homes? What kind of supervision is necessary for such placement? These are just a few of the questions which occur to anyone who is contemplating the use of foster homes for juvenile delinquents.

* Reprinted from 13 *Federal Probation* (1949), 46–51. Used by permission of the author and the publisher.

There has been an increasing acceptance of the importance of home life in social adjustment. Perhaps never before have the values of family life as determinants of the economic, social, civic, and other adjustments of adults been so generally recognized as now. At the same time there has been more understanding of the strengths and weaknesses of institutions and other forms of group care for juveniles. Better understanding of the personalities of delinquents as a result of the development of mental hygiene clinics, together with some research on the results of placement of children under various auspices also have helped to improve treatment methods of all kinds — the use of foster homes is one of these.

There are different types of foster home care: the adoption home, the boarding home, the wage home, the free or work home. In its early beginning foster home care was limited almost exclusively to the adoption home, the wage home, the free or work home. In general, there has been an increasing use of foster homes for children needing care away from their own homes. This has been particularly evident in the case of dependent and neglected children. In New York State, for example, only 31 per cent of all children in foster care in 1911 were to be found in foster family homes, and only 8 per cent were in boarding homes. In 1942, 58 per cent were being cared for in foster family homes and 49 per cent were in boarding homes.[1]

More recently the trend, as indicated above, has been in the direction of foster family boarding homes. For delinquents this is the most satisfactory type of home. The treatment and reclamation of the delinquent places an emphasis upon service under close supervision and requires more time and effort than is the case with less serious problems.

HISTORY OF FOSTER FAMILY CARE

As Thurston[2] points out, foster home care resulted from the breakdown of the feudal system in England. The first step in the process was the indenture of dependent children, based in part on the previous apprentice system. It had for its purpose making some person or family responsible for the care of a destitute child. The only difference between indenture for the dependent child and the method used for giving industrial training was that in the case of the dependent child some advance was made to the master until the child was able to work.

The first organized efforts to use foster family homes for the care of children was limited largely to the care of destitute, abandoned, and dependent children. About the middle of the nineteenth century there was developed in the United States an ambitious program of placing children in homes in the Middle West. Children were sent out in large groups and were selected by families upon arrival at designated points. This was in the form of informal indenture. The adults to whom the child was given agreed, in most instances, to send the child to school, feed him, clothe him, and give him training.

Undoubtedly, some of the children placed through this method were what would now be called delinquent children, but most of them would be classified as destitute children who had no relatives, or whose relatives could not provide for them in their own homes.

The most ambitious effort in the direction of placing children in free family homes or work homes was that of the Children's Aid Society of New York. From 1853 to 1879 this society placed out some 48,000 children in western and southern states. These placements were completely informal and were subject to abuses. These became known and ultimately brought about many improvements in child placing. Among these were more careful investigation of the prospective home, employment of staff to visit the home and children, and the development of standards of record keeping.

It was 1866 before there was any suggestion that some children needed to be placed with families to whom board should be paid. This suggestion was made about the same time by the Massachusetts State Board of Charities and by the Boston Children's Aid Society.[3] This society began to use boarding homes for children appearing in the courts charged with crime. From this early beginning Massachusetts continued to use foster care in families to a great extent. In those states which used institutions for the care of dependent and neglected children the movement toward the use of foster families for problem and delinquent children was retarded.

USE OF FOSTER FAMILY HOMES FOR PROBLEM AND DELINQUENT CHILDREN

The beginning of the twentieth century was marked by a tremendous upsurge in the manifested interest in children. The juvenile court movement began in 1899. This was followed by the establishment of Big Brother, Big Sister, Boy Scout, and other organizations interested in juveniles.[4] Public opinion had been outraged by reports of abuses of children and demanded that something be done for their protection, and the prevention of delinquency. There also was a growing skepticism regarding the value of institutional care for neglected children. The relative merits of home care and institutional care were being debated. This had happened before, in the last half of the nineteenth century, and a mighty effort to remove the children from the mixed almshouses had resulted in the establishment of orphan

[1] See Howard W. Hopkirk, *Institutions Serving Children*, New York: Russell Sage Foundation, 1944, p. 38.

[2] Henry W. Thurston, *The Dependent Child*, New York: Columbia University Press, 1930, pp. 1–18.

[3] *Ibid.*, pp. 164, 173.

[4] David M. Schnieder and Albert Deutsch, *History of Public Welfare in New York State, 1867–1940*, University of Chicago Press, 1941, p. 159.

asylums in this country. The results of placing children in these had been discouraging and again attempts were being made to discover more selective methods of treatment for different children. An appreciation of the need for "suiting the action to the needs of each child" which has been expressed by Birtwell [5] of the Boston Children's Aid Society in 1888, and accumulated experience indicated that a variety of resources would be required if the individual needs of the child were to be met.

Prior to 1900 the main reliance had been on institutional care for the juvenile offender who required care away from home. However, with the development of the juvenile court there was an increasing emphasis upon removing the stigma of crime from juvenile delinquents. Children were to be treated differently than adults. They were to be retrained. The state assumed the role of parent for this retraining. Every effort was to be made to keep the delinquent child from the adult criminal. This led to the establishment of juvenile detention homes and separate court buildings or courts for the juveniles.

Detention Homes Unsatisfactory for Most Part

The detention homes were at first mostly juvenile jails or wings of existing jails. They still are in many places. There has been an increasing concern about confining children in the same buildings with adult criminals, but, while in many states it is against the law, children still are confined in common jails. Detention homes, where they exist, are still for the most part unsatisfactory, both as to plant and as to program.[6] The opportunities for contagion, emotional upset, and the difficulties of developing any program for a large heterogeneous group of all ages and abilities, constantly changing, with varying periods of residence, have stimulated the search for a more constructive and satisfactory method of caring for children needing temporary detention care.

Many children who can be cared for in their own homes and do not need to be placed in confinement are placed in detention care where a detention home exists. It becomes a catch-all and destructive in its influence on children and on community attitudes toward children and their needs. Perhaps large cities need detention homes and can afford the costly type of care involved. But they need a number of varying types to fit the needs of the children requiring temporary care away from their own homes. For most cities and counties it is, in our opinion, an expensive and unsatisfactory way of meeting the situation. Several cities and counties[7] have demonstrated that foster family homes can be found for the detention care of most children who need it. These boarding homes reduce the number of children kept in detention, minimize the contagion between delinquents, alleviate the emotional upsets, and provide a more wholesome and normal environment for the child being separated from his home.

There always will be some older adolescent delinquents who cannot be contained in a regular foster family boarding home. They are the aggressive, gang-minded, excitement-seeking, chronic runaway types of individuals. In larger cities there will be several of these. In smaller communities the number will be very small. Because of the dramatic quality of their acts, they tend to overbalance the detention program in the direction of secure group custody — jail-like in type. It is surprising to find that most of the so-called "tough ones" respond to the warmth and acceptance of a good foster home. Where funds are limited it would seem better to provide foster homes for detention with not more than two beds in a home, spend the remainder on a more adequate child welfare program, locking children up only after they have demonstrated beyond the shadow of a doubt that such is required.

Evaluation of Foster Home Placement

It is a truism in the field of child welfare to say that the best place for a child is in his own home with his own parents unless the home is definitely destructive in its influence, and that

[5] Thurston, *op. cit.*, p. 185.

[6] See "Recommendations on Standards for Detention of Juveniles and Adults," compiled by the National Advisory Police Committee of the Federal Security Agency and approved by the National Sheriff's Association and the International Association of Chiefs of Police, U.S. Government Printing Office, Washington, D.C., 1945.

[7] See Victor B. Wylegala, *The Use of Foster Homes for Temporary Detention of Children,* Children's Court of Erie County, Buffalo, N.Y., p. 9.

he should not be removed from his home without every effort being made to develop whatever assets are present. The development of probation resulted from a recognition of this fact. It attempts to capitalize on the assets which exist in the home and in the individual to the end that adjustment to social living can be brought about in the environment in which the child will, in all likelihood, continue to live. For a long time it has been recognized that the best institutions fail to provide the best elements of a good home. They are artificial and, in the case of most institutions for delinquents, they operate in a vacuum so far as normal community contacts and living are concerned. This had led to the tentative use of foster family homes for some of the problem and delinquent children. With the development of mental hygiene clinics and better diagnostic facilities and techniques and with the development of more careful observation, supervision and recording, together with better evaluation of foster parents and families, the boarding home placement of children who present behavior problems or who have committed delinquent acts is fraught with less danger than was formerly the case.

The most ambitious undertaking in this field was, so far as we can learn, the efforts of the Children's Aid Association of Boston. The results of a study of 501 problem and delinquent children placed in foster family homes over a period of 10 years are reported in a book by Healy, Bronner, Baylor and Murphy.[8] They concluded that most delinquent children will make a better adjustment in carefully selected foster family boarding homes than in an institution, giving as a reason that the family life in a community setting offers a more natural environment and a better understanding of what society demands. They also emphasize the fact, substantiated by other experience, that a family home can be found for almost any child, regardless of his behavior problems or his offenses. Another emphasis which should be mentioned is that children do not fall into categories, such as dependent, neglected, truant, and delinquent. Careful study of children shows that

there are no really distinct lines of demarcation or distinction between these groups. They have much more in common than is implied by such labeling.

As a result of these studies the conclusion is reached that approximately 85 per cent of normal children who have been labeled as delinquent, because they have committed delinquent acts and have been brought to the attention of the authorities, make a satisfactory adjustment in foster family boarding homes and cease to be delinquents. Apparently the type of offense committed, or the fact that the delinquent has committed one or more different kinds of offenses, has little bearing on the rate of success or failure. The one significant factor that increased the rate of failure was the presence of abnormal mentality or personality. This led to the conclusion that mentally abnormal delinquents and those classified as psychopathic personalities show little promise of success in foster family boarding homes. One rather surprising result of this study was that for the normal, successful placement for the older group — those between 13 and 18 — was "only slightly less successful" than for those under 13. It is true that more abnormal personalities were found in the older group than among the younger group, but if these were excluded the results are as indicated above.

To sum up in the words of the authors:

First of all, we see plainly that delinquent children, even the severely delinquent, can be treated with great assurance of success through placing. For normal children, we have found no conditions or factors, whether of sex, age, heredity, or type of delinquency, that prove great obstacles to a favorable result. For normal personalities the chance of success is over five to one.

It is interesting to compare the results of this study with those of a study made by the State Charities Aid Association of New York.[9] This study covered the period from 1898 to 1922 so far as placements were concerned, and reported that 77.2 per cent of those whose capability was known were capable — that is, were law-abiding, managed their affairs with good

---

[8] William Healy, Augusta F. Bronner, Edith M. H. Baylor, and J. Prentice Murphy, *Reconstructing Behavior in Youth*, New York: Alfred A. Knopf, 1929, pp. 5, 12, 249, 253.

[9] *How Foster Children Turn Out*. A study and critical analysis of 910 children who were placed in foster homes by the State Charities Aid Association and who are now 18 years of age or over. By the State Charities Aid Association, 1924, pp. 25-26.

sense, and were living in accordance with good moral standards of their communities.

At least two of the state training schools for delinquent boys, the New York State Training School for Boys in 1937 [10] and the Illinois Training School for Boys, have tried using foster homes for the placement of certain children committed to them. Funds were made available to enable the school to place the child in a carefully selected foster family boarding home, instead of permitting him to return to a home which had proved to be destructive in its influence and which did not respond to the efforts of social workers while the child was in the training school. Sometimes the home was selected and the supervision was carried by a social agency, but in some instances, particularly in the case of the older child, the school found a suitable home and supervised the child and the home after the placement of the child. Both schools established divisions of foster home care in their social service or after-care departments. The difficulties of finding suitable homes and the extent of supervision required should not be minimized, nor should the valuable results achieved.

BASIC CONSIDERATIONS IN USE OF FOSTER HOMES

Perhaps the most basic consideration in the use of foster family homes for problem and delinquent children is the extent to which the personality and needs of the child are known. These can be determined only by a careful study of his life history up to the point where he is. Not only must his own actions and emotional life be studied, but the attitudes of the family toward him, his attitudes toward them, the kind of influences outside the home which have been playing on him and their effect on him; the kind of setting which brings out the behavior complained of, its psychogenesis, his relation to his father, mother, other relatives in the family. All are important. The child needs to be studied physically and mentally to determine his assets and liabilities, his interests, peculiarities, the content of his inner mental life, the specific causes of his malad-

justment. In other words, it is necessary to bring the whole child, with all that implies, into consideration before definite plans are made for his treatment. It may be determined that foster care should not be considered for this child because of his attitude toward his parents, or his need for group care in an institutional setting. There are still many problems to be solved in working out a more accurate set of criteria for the use of foster homes for delinquents as against institutional placement.*

In general, foster homes work best for those who have a need for affection, individualized attention, who require closer and more intimate relationships with adults and those whose personal habits and attitudes are not such as to make them too conspicuous in a community. Other factors which determine whether the delinquent child should be sent to the institution instead of a foster home are inherent in the community resources when contrasted with the institution. Some children are in need of special educational tutoring and remedial work which may not be available in the community where a suitable foster home is located, but the institution may have such specialized services. This is also true of the psychotherapy which may be needed in a particular case. Some children may need to be placed in an institution to get the psychotherapeutic treatment required. Some neurotic children do better in a foster home than in an institution if psychotherapy is also available. Children who do not respond to casework treatment are not ready for foster home placement, nor are those with strong aggressions against parent persons.

Another group of children who may need institutional treatment as a prelude to foster home placement are those delinquents who because of poor standards, indulgence, and neglect refuse to accept discipline. Delinquents whose mental imagery is preoccupied with thoughts of sex perversions and who have been indulging in perversions over a rather long period of time should be placed with caution, if at all, in boarding homes. This is also true of the delinquent who finds it impossible to accept or give affection and loyalty and who has been vari-

---

[10] See Helen P. Taussig and Alice Hyman, *A Demonstration of Foster Home Placement for Negro Delinquent Boys*, Child Welfare League of America Bulletin 18, June 1939, pp. 1–2, 5–7.

---

* Here is a field where carefully constructed prediction tables should be of great value. See Chapter 32 of this book. — *Ed.*

ously described as psychopathic, narcissistic, or an individuated delinquent. As a matter of fact, successful treatment of this group, either in an institution or out of it, has been rare. Foster home care is not indicated for the delinquents who have an organic pathology of the nervous system, or who are psychotic, or who fall into the classification of the defective delinquent. What has been said above emphasizes that the successful use of foster family boarding care for delinquents implies the use of scientific diagnosis as a prelude to placement.

It should be said that there are some exceptions to what has been said above. Some foster parents have accomplished miracles with most unpromising cases. So much depends upon the degree of involvement of the child in the directions indicated. So much depends, too, upon the patience, understanding, and strengths of the foster parents.

Another important factor which must be emphasized is the selection of foster homes in which delinquents are to be placed. This involves a careful study of each person in the home. Also to be considered are the location (preferably suburban or rural), community educational facilities, recreational facilities, clinics, personalities of the persons in the home, the atmosphere of the home, the arrangement of the home, etc. Experience in the use of a home is the best guide in determining whether it will be suitable for a given child. Some experience with problem children by the foster parents is almost a prerequisite for placement of delinquents in a home. Training school cottage parents sometimes make excellent foster parents for delinquent children, if they meet personality and attitude requirements. They will have shown their capacity to absorb deviations from the norm, will have demonstrated their patience, understanding, and the warmth of their acceptance. Not only should there be a careful study of the home as indicated above, but there should be careful preparation of the foster parents for work with problem children. Successful placement requires a continuing help to the foster parents.

It goes without saying that well-trained social workers are required to work successfully with delinquents. Not only must they have had formal training, but they must be fitted by personality and temperament to work with this more difficult group. Experience in work-

ing with children, including problem children, should precede work with delinquents. Above all, they must have patience, understanding, and an appreciation of the time required to overcome the attitudes and habits of long duration. They must be able to take disappointment and understand that progress toward the goal of social adjustment is filled with peaks and valleys of achievement. The social worker is perhaps the most important member of the team working toward the reclamation of the delinquent. She is the one continuing tie for the child throughout the process.

We have discussed the child, the foster parents and the social worker. The process of making them all work together is involved in the follow-up or supervision. The skill of the social worker will be expressed in the supervision which she gives to the situation. It is through her contact with the child and the foster parents that the attitudes and problems of the child become known. Her integrity and real interest will increase the likelihood of developing more meaningful relationships. The child's relationship to the social worker should be the same as that toward a good adult friend. He should not be reminded too much of the agency, nor should he think of himself as one of many cases. The social worker should be devoted to the child and his problems during the time of supervision. Frequent visits are necessary, especially in the beginning of the child's stay in a new foster home. Sufficient time should be allowed so that the social worker can follow through on any problems which present themselves. This means a small case load.

Conclusions

In an attempt to meet the needs of individual children, there has been increasing recognition of the necessity for developing various types of facilities. No longer is there insistence upon any one best method of taking care of all children presenting problems of social maladjustment. The conflict between the advocates of institutional care for all and advocates of foster home care for all has now given way to attempts to determine just what children need institutional care, for how long, what kind, and what children need foster care, what kind and how secured.

There has been an increasing use of boarding

home care for a number of children presenting special problems. This is also true of those labeled as delinquent. Foster family boarding home care has been used for them in lieu of institutional placement, before institutional commitment, as an interlude with institutional residence, and following institutional placement. Some training schools for delinquents have had more than a decade of experience with this type of boarding home care. The results have been gratifying, despite the fact that some of that period was during and after World War II when housing shortage was acute and conditions generally not conducive to finding foster homes and keeping them.

The use of subsidizing foster family boarding homes for detention care, for all except the largest cities, promises success, if properly supervised and subsidized. They are more economical, more normal, prevent contagion resulting from grouping all ages and problems together, give more individualized attention, and do less damage to the child. A few exceptional cases need more custodial care than can be given in any except specially modified homes. Careful selection of foster parents who have had experience with problem children, high grade supervision, and a small number of children in each home are essential for detention care.

The successful use of foster family boarding homes for problem and delinquent children requires that a careful study of the whole child be made and that placement be based upon a knowledge of the whole child and of the home in which he is to be placed. Some children cannot profit by placement in a boarding home, no matter how good. This should be recognized and the child should be given the type of care best suited to his needs. Some knowledge has been acquired as to the types of personalities which can benefit from foster family care. This should be used. But much more research is needed to develop the criteria which we should have in prescribing various types of care, including boarding home care.

What has been said about the selection of the child also applies to the selection of the home in which care is to be given. Skilled caseworkers can evaluate homes and match them with the children to some extent, but experience with the homes is still the best method of determining what kind of problems they can absorb. Here again we need to do more re-search before completely satisfactory criteria for placement can be known.

In the past two decades some real progress has been made in the development of supervisory skills in dealing with problem and delinquent children, but we still have many unanswered questions in this field. Temperament, training, and experience are the triad needed for success in this field. In addition, qualities of sympathy, understanding, and patience on the part of the social worker are essential. Working with foster parents, who work with problem and delinquent children, requires something extra in the way of qualifications. This should be recognized in the compensation given. It will be a good investment.

Foster parents working with problem and delinquent children are required to give more time and go to more trouble than is the case for children with less severe problems. There is a growing acceptance of the idea that foster parents who give extra service should be compensated for this. Helpless children, those who require special diets, crippled children, fall into this group. Some of the problem and delinquent children also would qualify for extra service. The New York State Training School for Boys at Warwick, beginning in 1938, paid slightly more than the rate for dependent and neglected children. Following the war this was increased considerably over what was being paid for dependent children.

Finally, some delinquent children of all ages can benefit from foster boarding home care. The number over 15 years of age will be less than those under that age, but the nature of the problem is more significant than the age of the child. It is easier to send a child to a detention home or to an institution than it is to take him home and make plans for him which include careful study and evaluation. Police authorities often have little patience with the length of time involved or with the process itself. Some social agencies prefer to accept good children who are not involved with the law and who do not present frequent emergencies. The problem and delinquent child has little respect for week-ends or for holidays, and sometimes interferes with regular office hours and routines. But, despite all this, it is possible to achieve gratifying results when careful selection of the home, the child, and the social worker is made.

126

Foster Home Care for Delinquent Children *

Ruth Gilpin

Young Spurrier was brought into court for attempting, with the help of a friend, to pick the pockets of passers-by. In the midst of the court hearing, the boy broke into a dance called the "double shuffle," much to the distress of a nearby police officer. According to Mr. Spurrier, who was questioned, this son of his was one of the worst thieves in the city. Mrs. Spurrier, on the other hand, testified that the boy had been a model child until he had met bad company on the streets at home and in the institution where he had stayed following a previous charge.

QUESTION OF DISPOSITION

What should become of the twelve-year-old Spurrier lad? The question happens not to be ours to answer. This boy lived in the city of London in the days of a young Victoria, and he has lived out whatever decision was made for him by the Lord Mayor who heard his case. But he was a delinquent child. He was a delinquent with parents and home and friends and inner needs not unlike those of the youngster of ours who is caught picking pockets on the streets of New York.

In the year 1848, when young Spurrier appeared in court,[1] there were people who were concerned, even as we are today, about him and the growing numbers of children like him. Some of these interested folks asked questions and sought to find answers. What will become of these children? Should they be put into jail? Should they be sent to industrial schools for young delinquents? Thomas Beggs, in 1849, raised yet another question. In his essay which

won second place in a £100 prize essay contest on Juvenile Depravity, he wondered whether there could not be some arrangement for these children other than police and schools.[2]

Today the judge of the juvenile court must try to answer some of these same questions as he faces the youngster who has picked the pockets of passers-by. With the advantage of one hundred years over Mr. Beggs and the Lord Mayor who heard the Spurrier case, our judge can choose from among various arrangements now available for children in trouble. The difficulty of inadequate care, which Mr. Beggs saw for children who, picked up by the police, were either dismissed or sent to institutions, is eased by these present-day arrangements.

But difficulties and additional questions, which Mr. Beggs could not foresee, have been uncovered. The judge can dismiss the child outright, he can place the child on probation, he can send the child to a foster home, or he can commit the child to an institution. How shall he decide what to do for a particular child? Shall the child remain at home? If he shall remain at home, shall he be put under probation to a worker from the juvenile court who can help child and parent around the problem which caused this court appearance? Shall the child be uprooted from his home? Shall he be sent to an institution? Shall he be sent to a large correctional institution, or to a small institution, or to a boarding school? Shall he be placed in a foster home? Shall he be placed in a specially run and subsidized boarding home for delinquent children?

THE CASEWORKER'S JOB

The judge of the juvenile court usually has the assistance of a caseworker, the man who is entrusted with the immediate experience of working with these youngsters in need of help. The caseworker in the juvenile court often has a job of dual responsibility. He begins the relationship of child and parent to the authority vested in the court and in himself as a representative of the court. He may also assist the judge in this decision which may involve a choice between foster home and institution for the child who can no longer remain in his own home.

As much as the caseworker might like to be

---

* Reprinted from 261 *Annals* (1949), 120–127. Used by permission of the author and the publisher.
[1] *Times*, London, April 6, 1848, as quoted by Thomas Beggs in *An Inquiry into the Extent and Causes of Juvenile Depravity* (London, 1849), p. 92.

[2] Thomas Beggs, *op. cit.* note 1 *supra*, p. 142.

able to establish definite and infallible criteria for the selection of a particular kind of care for a delinquent child (or any child), he has discovered that he can find none. It has not been possible to describe the child or the family situation which will fit into a static scheme of evaluation. For example, should the caseworker dare to operate on the theory that the child who is rejected at home is the one who can live comfortably in another's home, he would the very next day come upon the lad who, rejected at home, fights a continual battle to win love and recognition from his parents. A strange set of parents simply could not be a substitute. Always there will be the youngster and the family who defy and destroy, as humans do, any criteria which we might be foolish enough to set up as absolute. Then, what can be done to assure the rightness of the decision for the child who shall be removed from home and for the care which that child shall receive?

It is not enough for the caseworker to know how many children of a certain age have failed in foster home care or how many homes of certain qualifications have made the best homes. It is not enough for him to know whatever may be written about juvenile delinquency, its causes, and its cures. He must know how to put his knowledge into helpful operation for the child.

The caseworker must have the professional skill and the agency opportunity to initiate a process which will eventuate in a sound choice. He is the man who must help the child to find and move toward the spot best for him. He needs to believe in his agency, which is the court, in its authority, and in the way this authority can be used constructively by and for the child. He needs to recognize the difference between the functions of the institution and of the foster home agency, and he needs to be able to trust the care offered by such agencies as are resources to his community's children. He needs to have available to him the specialized services of medicine, psychology, and psychiatry. He needs to have an understanding of the developing personalities of young human beings and how they relate to those adults important to them.

The choice of care for a child must not be colored by personal feeling in one direction or another, as has happened in the past and some-times happens in the present. The child and his family situation cannot fit into certain pigeonholes, predetermined and predestined for probation, foster home care, or institution. Out of all the moving, changing factors in this situation, there must be found some stable point on which a worker can depend. He can rest on the function of his own agency, the court, and the requirements of the court prior to the hearing. In the brief prehearing time of usually a week, out of the experience he has with parents and child around these very court requirements, the caseworker must find the basis for the direction the child shall take next. Omitting probation, which is not pertinent here, ahead lie the known factors of the function of the institution for group living and the function of the foster home agency for family living.

FOSTER HOME AND INSTITUTION

A foster home for a child is a home in the full meaning of the word, yet it remains forever "foster." In the strict sense, the term "foster home" includes four different homes which are provided for children who must live away from their own homes. These four homes are the boarding home, the wage home, the free home, and the adoptive home. Of course, the boarding home is, and should be, the most frequently used for children not free for adoption.

Institutions cannot be disregarded in any discussion of foster home care, whether for the delinquent or the non-delinquent child. The battle which at one time raged between foster home and institution is well over, with both sides winning. Because family life has seemed the normal and natural way of life, the values of group living were eclipsed during the building of foster home programs. Now these values are being recognized as so important that the institution need be criticized only, as any agency might, on the basis of the effectiveness and the quality of its service.

Group living can very well be the kind of care needed by some children, by many delinquent children. Group living offers a child a group of his own contemporaries, a share in their interests, an identification with a larger whole. It offers the impersonality of rules established for the group and not for him alone. It offers staff and house parents interested in him but without need to ask for affection from him. These values of group living, and many others, are dependent, of course, upon the institution itself and the way in which it accepts its purpose and endeavors to fulfill it.

Placing the Child

If, out of the experience with child and parents, the court worker sees institutional care as the care needed by the child, and if the judge so orders, the child goes to an institution. The institutional authorities, trained in the institutional care of children, take over. If, on the other hand, foster home care seems to offer the best care for the child, it would seem to follow that a foster home agency with workers trained in child placing should take over. In some communities, however, the juvenile court maintains a child placing division of its own. Many of these courts are convinced of the soundness of such a program.

Other courts and communities have abandoned that way of working and have defined the court as an agency separate and distinct from either a placement agency or an institution. The judge and the caseworker in such courts are willing and eager for the specialists in child placing, usually within the public welfare department, to undertake the care of the child who needs a foster home. The court may retain custody of and ultimate responsibility for the child, while delegating the actual care to the child placing agency, with a minimum of control.

The Child Placing Worker

The child placing worker continues the process begun by the court caseworker. Here again, our young delinquent is entitled to a skilled casework service within an agency set up for the effective placing of children in foster homes. It is no easy job to help a child to move from his own home into a foster home and make the fullest use of what family life can give him. It is no easy job to help him take on a new family which is to become his by court order. On the child placing worker rests the selection of the foster family. On him rests the helping and sustaining of that foster family in the very difficult job of living with a troubled child who may approach them and live with them with noticeable reluctance.

The child placing worker must believe in foster home care and in the soundness of the de-

cision to use this care for this child. He must believe in this particular home and in its selection for this particular child. He must be willing to accept the authority which is his through his agency and through the court responsibility for this child. He must believe in the help which he can give to the child, to the child's parents, and to the foster parents through his agency and through his casework skill.

For the child placing worker, as for any caseworker, the amount of responsibility carried for another human being would appear too great to bear were it not that his agency's function and policies are at once his protection and his base of operation.

Casework is young as this world goes, and is still suffering from the growing pains of a young profession. Still, here and now, we can say with assurance that casework does work. Evidence of a goodly amount has been accumulated to show that casework, a process of helping based on clear and definite principles and carried out within the function of a social agency, can and does do what it professes to do — help people. It is a process of helping, dependent upon the caseworker's belief in the integrity of each individual and in the strength which each individual possesses to use the agency's service and the agency's limitations to move himself through his problem and on to a greater self-dependence. The opportunity of the delinquent child to reach a more satisfactory life adjustment is dependent in large measure upon his caseworker.

Change of Environment

While Thomas Beggs pondered the subject of juvenile delinquency and while young Spurrier picked pockets and danced, this foster home arrangement which they may have been seeking was about to be introduced in England and America. The placing of children in foster homes had been practiced for centuries in a casual way, but it began a reinvigorated and more organized life in the latter half of the nineteenth century. Already accepted was the theory of transportation for reform. A new land where criminals could begin a new life not only relieved the mother country of their presence, but also gave them a chance to reform themselves in the colonies. In a somewhat similar way, a new home in the wide spaces of pioneer states should give to children from the crowded streets of New York a chance for salvation in a home finer than their own.

Foster home care, its practice and its philosophy, has seen many changes since these first children were packed off to the West in 1853. In accounting for the century given to us, we would honestly admit at the outset that we have discovered foster home care to be no panacea for the ills of children, delinquent or not.

In the early days, foster homes for any and all children brought forth delighted approval which far outstripped the actual performance. The pioneers of modern child placing, with no experience to back them but with warm wishes to help children, could understandably make their desire appear as their fact. In the usual hard way of humans and at the expense of many children, we — the people professionally engaged in foster home care, then and now — had to learn that a change of environment does not necessarily mean a change in heart. We had to learn that some children do not live with any degree of comfort in a foster home which we think they should enjoy. We had to learn the extent of the responsibility which we take upon ourselves in providing a child with a stranger's home.

This kind of understanding has not lessened our belief in the deep and lasting values for children which our experience has shown to exist in foster home care. Indeed, our conviction about these values has deepened through the years. Only our increased knowledge and experience could allow us to admit, with equal conviction, that this type of care cannot be helpful to *all* children.

THE ASPECT OF PUNISHMENT

There are those among us today who say that all children needing placement should go to a foster home first, and if they fail there, they can always go to an institution. Strange it is to think of exclaiming about a youngster, not too different from the young Spurrier lad, "Oh, let's not send him to an institution. Let's give him a chance in a foster home first!" Off the boy then might go to what he wants and needs least of all — a foster home. The basis on which this young man's fate has been decided is that of personal feeling — hardly a valid basis at all. The personal belief that life in a family, any family, would be preferable to life in an institution may be behind the thinking.

More than that, we seem to have built up a little scale of delinquent treatment, from probation to foster home and lastly to institution. Degree of punishment may enter into and influence the building of this scale. The institution is severe punishment; the foster home is less severe, or no punishment.

A child in court, whether he is sent by the judge to an institution or to a foster home, must by the very order of banishment from home feel that he is being punished. Our telling each other that foster home care is treatment rather than punishment does not remove the aspect of punishment from the youngster's mind. Nor does this vocabulary really remove it from our own.

Perhaps it is punishment. Should we deny it to ourselves and to the child? Should we, rather, try to make use of the authority which is inherent in the situation to help the child to more comfort with life, in either a foster home or an institution, if he cannot remain in his own home to discover it? As long as we let ourselves become entangled with our own feelings, we cannot serve the child.

Too many times, our decision about a child's living rests wholly upon the available bed, wherever it may be — a fact which would entail a discussion of what the lack of money for facilities and personnel is doing to our children.

THE FOSTER HOME

The foster home is not a treatment center. Foster parents are not trained in psychology or psychiatry. Nor would we want them to be. They are parents. They are people who have achieved a successful living of their own lives and who want to share their lives and homes with a child.

Some of these foster parents are challenged by the thought of taking into their home the child who has found his way to juvenile court. Such foster parents probably have had experience with foster children and with the necessary sharing of responsibility for those children with a child placing agency. They need to be able to bear considerable hostile behavior, to expect a minimum of affectional response, and to call upon the inner reserves of their own security, understanding, and ingenuity. The treatment which the child receives from them is the treatment of family life itself.

The small amount of board which most agencies are able to pay to foster parents, and the clothing and medical care provided by the agencies, do not make the foster home less of a home, but rather a more secure and more responsible *foster* home. Because it is essentially a home, the foster home offers much to a child and also requires something in return. Home life at its best gives a child love, security, freedom within steadying limits, a place to laugh and a place to cry, a hand to comfort and a hand to spank.

The foster home asks, in return, an individual closeness. Parents, including foster parents, look for personal satisfactions from their children, including foster children. Their community is the child's community; their family is the child's family. As they offer the child their community, their family, and the individuals therein, they expect, to some extent, the child's appreciation of the group's value, of the individuals' worth. A variety of human relationships is set in motion the moment a child enters what can become for him his foster home.

ADJUSTMENT TO FOSTER HOME

For large numbers of children, foster home care supplies the essentials for a happy childhood and a healthy growing-up. These children find in foster homes the family life which no group living experience can attempt to provide. They are children whose own families have been broken through death, illness, desertion, neglect, and so forth. For the most part, they are young children who can respond warmly to a substitute family without giving up, in feeling, their own. Among these children can be included some of our young delinquents, those for whom a new family home can become a meaningful part of their lives and not just a house where they must serve out a sentence.

The adolescent child, placed in a foster home at a time when adolescents are beginning to pull away from, while at the same time depending upon, those family ties formed through the years, usually finds the going rough. The delinquent adolescent, with his adolescent problem heightened in both directions and his inner turmoil expressed in misbehavior, also usually finds foster home life very difficult. The struggle to define himself as separate from and yet a part of his own family, he may find

duplicated even more painfully in a foster family. Some of our young delinquents need neither family home nor large institution, and yet must live away from their own homes.

HOME-GROUP LIVING

Another arrangement, as Mr. Beggs might say, also called a foster home or a boarding home, is in present-day use for delinquent children. It is a home established and subsidized by an agency for the specific purpose of caring for a small number of difficult court-committed children. Conducted as a private home by a husband and wife, it differs from the true foster home in that the running of the home and the care of the children are the paid jobs of this man and woman. They may receive salaries, or a subsidy beyond the board rate for each child.

We know full well that being a good father or mother is a job in itself; but when the father and mother are paid to have a home and paid to look after children, a change occurs in the role which they play. These house parents are first of all employees. That very fact makes their relationship to the children different from that of foster parents, who are first of all parents. This difference is important for us to recognize and to acknowledge.

In establishing and paying for a boarding home unit for the care of a small number of these youngsters, we may be trying to find, not a second kind of boarding home, but rather a small piece of group living within the community. This so-called boarding or foster home can have many of the aspects of group living — in its house staff as employees of the agency, in its group of contemporaries among the children, in its limitations set up for the group, and in the fact that, though homelike, it is not a home, or even a foster home. At the same time, it offers the community church and school, the neighborhood boys and girls, the village movies. It also offers the warmth, understanding, helpfulness, and discipline of house parents who do not have too many children to supervise and who need feel no pull to become substitute parents.

Perhaps, somehow, these staff-member-run agency houses seem more respectable, more normal, more desirable when we call them by the term "foster homes" or "boarding homes" rather than by any word which would seem to connote a small institution. A name is important in its aid to definition. However, no matter what we may call this form of living, if it is group living, as it appears to be in contrast to our definition of foster home, we should admit its being so, define it as such, and strengthen it as such. It may, as such, have more possibilities as a resource for some of our delinquent youngsters than we have yet given it an opportunity to become.

In some communities the detention of children who cannot be left in their own homes prior to the court hearing has been given to just such a couple with just such a home. It takes the place of the old detention home, where the values of group living were lost in its regimented and punitive administration. These new house parents are employees of the public welfare department or the juvenile court, and are ready to take any children assigned to them by the agency, and to take the children at any time of the day or night.

These house parents know that they will have to keep within their small group children disturbed not only by their own inner problem but also by that problem aggravated by being detained against their will. The house parents know that they have a difficult job but a challenging one, and one which deserves adequate financial compensation. Sometimes they are assisted by visiting teachers of crafts and recreation. They are assisted by the caseworker whose work with the individual child is leading toward the court hearing and whatever decision is reached there.

Even though their group of children may number as low some days as two or three and never higher than seven or eight, these house parents know that they are not substitute parents, not foster parents, but that they are administering a tiny institution. With such an acceptance of their role, they can be clear about the service — as indeed they must be in order to discharge their duties — which they will offer to the troubled youngsters who come to them.

THE PARENTS

As we turn at last to the Mr. and Mrs. Spurriers, the children's parents, we follow the custom of the years. We should have begun our discussion here, and maybe one day, when we are clear about our services, we shall. Par-

ents have been badly neglected. They have gone through stages of being merely witnesses to their child's behavior, of being the inheritors of a cruel fate, common to them and to their child, and of being criminals responsible and punishable for their child's difficulties. They have never really been accorded a place which is truly theirs.

Those of us who have worked in courts and in social agencies from the time of Mr. Beggs have found parents difficult to understand. We have been somewhat loath to dismiss the last vestige of our theory that removal from home and parents is itself the cure for the child. We have become so engrossed in the child that we have overlooked the fact that any experience of a child is tied by him and for him to his parents. To deny parents a place in their child's life during any step on the way from own home to court, to foster home, is to invite failure for all that foster home care or institutional care or probation might mean. Parents should have a part in any process undertaken for their child, because at last we are beginning to realize that in order to help the child, we need the help of the parents.

The caseworker in the court and the caseworker in the foster home agency must discover the value of parents. It is difficult to think that the professional worker needs the help of inadequate, disinterested, even destructive, parents. Before such parents can be in a position to help, they themselves must change. Most likely they are wanting no change within themselves, and they are disclaiming any responsibility for their child's distress; yet most likely they are troubled people. They should have the opportunity to help their child by doing something about their own lives, which have evidently been found wanting.

Some way must be found in which these parents can become engaged in working with the agency which for the time being has the control of their child. The authority of the court — in the juvenile court and in the child placing agency — can have its part in work with these parents. Some requirements may be necessary, in interviews or board payments, for example, not as punishment, but as part of a process in which the parents may choose to win again the right to be actively responsible parents to their child.

Respect for these parents, their right to

their own decisions and their ability to change, is fundamental in helping them to help their child. Not a word in this paper would be valid if parents were dismissed as interested (or disinterested) spectators, relieved of their duty and privilege to become essential participants in a process affecting the life of their child.

127

Ambivalence as a Factor in Home Placement Failure *

George E. Gardner

In this communication it is hoped to call attention to and emphasize one of the factors that must be recognized, evaluated, and properly dealt with before and during foster home placement, namely, the possible existence of strong, unresolved, ambivalent feelings directed toward the parents, or toward a remaining parent if, because of death, divorce or desertion, the home is not intact. We ourselves carefully emphasize this factor as being but one factor that may contribute to the failure of foster home placement, knowing full well that when such a radical change in interpersonal relationships is demanded of the child, the subsequent success or failure may be determined by any one — or any constellation — of the many factors involved in individual and group adjustments.

Yet, in a number of our cases of failure we are struck particularly by the presence of these strong coexistent feelings of filial love and hate, and their marked prominence in those cases where placement was attempted in the pubertal years. Hence the case material which has thrown this factor into relief and is the basis for the present emphasis, has been contributed by boys of this age group whose repeated placement failures have seemed to the

* Reprinted from 12 *Am. J. Orthopsychiatry* (1942), 135–139. Used by permission of the author and the publisher.

placement agency to demand initial or additional psychotherapy before another placement was made. In each instance has been noted in the child's behavior leading to his failure, a certain bizarreness unjustified by the circumstances and experiences within the placement situation itself. We shall attempt to make no prediction as to the statistical appearance of this factor in a series of unselected cases of failures in this age group, but, on the contrary, are happy that our list of failures is not yet long enough to give you percentage figures. We are content at this time to cite the manner of emergence of this factor, the material that should lead the psychiatrist and the placement agency to suspect its presence, and its importance in the child's unsuccessful attempts at adjustment.

We may approach this problem by a detailed consideration of the changing and antithetical evaluations of the parents made by these children before and after placement failure, observing at the same time the varied behavior predicated thereon. To our mind a definite involuntary repetitive behavior pattern exists in these cases. As we observe the pattern unfolding, it is well to bear in mind that psychoanalysis has again and again emphasized that beneath such repeated inconsistencies, overexaggerations and fantasies, the truth is very carefully hidden. It should also be noted that an individual's interpretations and evaluations, not warranted by existent reality factors, are not changed or modified by the mere manipulation or elimination of those factors, but require some change in the individual himself. Let us review then the parental evaluations voiced by these children.

INITIAL EVALUATION OF PARENTS OR PARENT

As these children first relate their feelings for and opinion of their natural parents, we are struck by their exaggerated hostility and extreme hatred of and aggression toward one (usually the father) or both parents. It is charged by the child that harsh and unwarranted punishment is meted out for trifling misdemeanors; needlessly strict rules and regulations are enacted which prohibit enjoyment of all activities in which companions of their own ages engage. Parents have failed to provide even the barest necessities, food and clothing. They are guilty of excessive drinking, adultery, assaults on one parent by the other, or acts on the part of one parent are alleged to have directly or indirectly caused the death of the other. Where one parent is dead, there is an accompanied over-idealization of the deceased, regardless of his or her real character, plus a subtle identification with this parent and a consequent continuation of the intrafamilial struggles, the child playing the role of the dead parent. To be sure, all of us are acquainted with social service histories where such a harsh reality as outlined does in some part exist, but in these failure cases which I am trying to bring into focus today, the reality situation by no means warrants the interpretations and evaluations made by the child and, as will be seen later, he at some future date brings in his own denial or, at least, a drastic modification. It might be added here, parenthetically, that it would seem the nearer any child's evaluation of his reality *does* coincide with the actual facts — however harsh it may really be — the better seem to be the chances for a successful placement. But for us who are placed in a predictive role as to a possible successful placement, the important thing to note is that in the first instance — when markedly aggressive and antisocial behavior is at its height — the child denies, minimizes or offers substitutive evidence when confronted with extenuating circumstances or instances of parental good intent. When faced with these marked inaccuracies in the child's recital of reality as seen by him, we are led to suspect his production as a product of inner conflict, a mixture of fact and fantasy.

Examination of the child's overt aggressive behavior and his fantasies and dreams gives further clues of importance. The most common "complaints" or "charges" are running away, truancy, unmanageableness, or running away plus stealing money. The striking fact is, however, that many of these children steal money (in some instances, earn money) in order to run away from home, just as they steal and panhandle in order to stay away from home and, finally, they steal, earn or panhandle in order to run away from foster homes. In addition to these acts there are instances of assault or attempted injury of one parent (usually the father) by the child, and the almost joyous recital of falls and accidents suffered by them. Death-wish dreams, utopias, fantasies of vagabondage and the actual or fantasied change of name are common. Common also are strong doubts as to their real parentage; they attempt to substantiate adoption fantasies by reconsideration of alleged marriage dates of parents, their own birth dates and by misinterpretation of comments by relatives. They cite as further evidence the marked physical and personality differences between themselves and their siblings — differences noted by themselves and which, they say, are emphasized repeatedly by their parents. Finally, they are convinced by examples of sibling preference, that parents wish them "out of the house," "out of the way," or "dead."

All this, then, is the initial story before placement. If we carefully scrutinize the child's behavior and thoughts attendant upon his failure to adjust in previous placements, and if we may follow in treatment his voicing of this parental evaluation through his next placement, choose his foster home as best we know how with a view to offering a parental reality we sincerely believe he needs and from which he should derive those satisfactions which seem to have been denied him in his own home, what is the further unfolding of the pattern?

FOSTER HOME PLACEMENT RESPONSE

There is invariably an initial period of placement success, duration usually being a matter of some weeks or two or three months. During this period of success the child continually dwells upon his great fortune in being placed in such a good home, but always with the emphasis on the material benefits derived therefrom. He now gets good food and has new clothes; is not restricted in social activities; goes to the movies every Saturday; is granted an allowance of 50 cents a week; has his own room; may listen to the radio, etc. Discouragingly enough, there is rather perfunctory comment, or no comment at all, on the personalities or feelings of the foster parents, the child contenting himself with a recital of favors received as evidence that they are good to him. There is no evidence that the subtle process of identification with the foster father is taking place. It is enough for the child to contrast his present treatment with what he alleged was his lot at home. On the behavior side, too, there is improvement. He does not truant from school; he undertakes his school duties with some show of enthusiasm; he does not steal or run away because, according to him, there is no longer any necessity to do so.

Though one cannot predict the length of time in weeks or months that this successful adjustment will continue, one can with considerable accuracy date the beginning of placement failure as coincident with the realization on the part of the child that the foster parents are becoming genuinely fond of him, that their solicitude and affection are indications of real parental love.

When the child detects the existence of such feelings in the foster parents and identifies them by their emergence in conversations and motherly or fatherly acts, he becomes alarmed. He tries to reciprocate, but his attempts have the unreal quality of one acting the part of being in love. He intended to buy his foster mother a present, but forgot. He wanted to take her to the movies, but she appeared tired so he did not ask her. He enjoys being tucked in bed and kissed good-night, but he doesn't permit it because he is too old for that and only sissies allow such privileges. In one case the foster parents, though specifically warned not to shower too much affection on the boy while our study and treatment of him continued because of its disastrous effect in previous placements, allowed their enthusiasm for the boy's admittedly excellent qualities to get the better of them, and they confided to him that they would like to adopt him. The boy appeared at the clinic before it opened in the morning to tell me that he must be removed from his new home at once or he would have to run away, stating he could not stand being treated so well, that he was not "good enough" for that home. He carefully refrained, however, from making reference to the suggestion of possible adoption.

There follows a gradual emergence of definite guilt feelings in response to foster parents' continued proffer of love, attention and gifts, and behavior re-appears which seems definitely designed to destroy the situation in which the boy finds himself. But there is now a decidedly different quality to this resumption of his previous antisocial behavior. Whereas, before, his running away, truancy, stealing, etc., was accompanied by feelings of marked hostility, it is now motivated by such feelings directed in the main against himself. His productions are largely concerned with what he *himself* is *unable* to do to make his new home agreeable to him and only secondarily with what his foster parents do that is irksome. He has difficulty in justifying such

of his behavior as is directed against the foster parents or his visitor except as a means to cause his removal to some other home. If he has been placed in several homes, he usually states that at the time each of his impending failures became inevitable he convinced himself that each new home had been a better one than the last, and that eventually he would be placed in his fantasied ideal home.

As the child continues his discussion of his needs, it is soon apparent that the physical attributes of this "ideal home" which he fantasies, and the personalities with which he would like to surround himself, are not unlike those that he thinks could exist in his own home, and it is but a short step to frank statements that he wishes to be returned there. When we hint at the actual difficulties and shortcomings which led to his removal by the placement agency, a strikingly new and different evaluation of the parents emerges.

Secondary Evaluation of Parents

In this "secondary evaluation of the parents" the child begins a total repudiation of all material relative to the parents' alleged punishments, crimes, immorality or lack of understanding. They are pictured now as upright people misjudged by him and by the agency that thought placement a necessary step. He has wronged them by going away. We, of course, are acquainted with the actual inadequacies of the home, just as previously we knew of instances of good parental behavior, but the inadequacies are now non-existent for the child and he enforces this belief in their non-existence by detailed confessions to prove that he himself, by his wretched behavior, was the sole cause of family discord and friction.

There is for the first time portrayal of his feelings of love for his mother, and he produces memories that depict her feelings toward him. She took good care of him, bathed him, bought him new clothes, was ambitious for his future. Of all the siblings he probably was her favorite. His hatred of his father was unjustified. He cannot understand why he wished his father dead or out of the home. It was he himself who deserved such punishment. He fantasies his return as a self-sufficient hero who by his own labor and good works will provide for the home wherein henceforth he, his mother and siblings will live happily together. If his parents are estranged, he visualizes a reconciliation, particularly since he, who was one of the chief causes of their differences, is now a changed boy. As two boys stated, they would die or "go crazy" if they were not removed from their foster homes.

DISCUSSION

In discussion of these antithetical productions it seems unnecessary to emphasize that children depicting such strong ambivalent feelings as illustrated in this behavior and fantasy life cannot adjust to even the most carefully selected foster parents without psychiatric help before and, for an extended period, following placement. Their instinctual drives of love and aggression directed toward their own mothers and fathers, with attendant or subsequent feelings of guilt and remorse, are soon applied in unmodified fashion to the mother and father surrogates. Being unable to understand or accept the true meaning of these drives, they create of the home an unreality which justifies their intense feelings that they must get out of it at all costs. The home they seem to desire and seem compelled to keep on seeking is one where their instinctual demands will not be reactivated in their present strength, or where external conditions are such as to give them the maximum help in the repression of these drives. I would emphasize again the repetitive — compulsively repetitive — quality of these behavior patterns, a quality which is the hallmark of neurotic behavior. The emergence of compromise reactions in the form of various delinquencies is further

evidence of neurotic conflict, the basic instinctual elements of which are exposed in the dream and fantasy life.

That there is at puberty a definite resurgence of instinctual strivings with which the immature ego is unable to cope, has been stressed many times in the literature dealing with this particular age group. Our treatment in this critical period must, therefore, be directed primarily toward the modification of these intense feelings that only insight and self-understanding can bring about. It must be aimed at an exposure of the underlying fantasies that are making a true evaluation or acceptance of reality impossible. In short, it has as its object the strengthening of the child's ego.

Psychiatric study and treatment for all cases facing initial foster home placement is, of course, an impossibility. However, in conclusion, we may re-state our observation that our clinical material would seem to indicate that such study is particularly desirable before the initial placement of children in the early adolescent years (ages 11–14). The detection of extreme ambivalent feelings toward the parents in the material produced (as evidenced by unqualified condemnation, death fantasies, attacks) must be given proper consideration in (1) the choice of group placement as opposed to foster home placement, and (2) determining the need for intensive treatment *before*, or continued treatment *after*, placement, or both. Finally, psychiatric treatment seems definitely indicated in all placement failures in order that repeated costly and traumatic failures may be eliminated.

Chapter 23

Forms of Treatment: Institutional Care

COMMITMENT OF DELINQUENTS to institutions, although usually not as common as placing them on probation in the community, still plays a very important role. Although the constructive possibilities of guidance, counseling and psychotherapy of delinquents under probation in the community have not yet been adequately explored, and although many industrial and reform schools are not "reforming" (if not actually damaging) the children committed to their custody, institutions will always be required for a substantial proportion of delinquents. This is so because many children need a haven of refuge, as it were, from the storms of life in the slums; some require temporary incarceration to prevent them from damaging themselves or others; many need, temporarily, a controlled environment for the development of more acceptable habits, more conventional attitudes, more successful interpersonal relationships. Indeed, just as there have grown up hospitals for the chronically ill, so is there need for institutions for those delinquents who have not responded acceptably to the various extra-mural forms of discipline, education, guidance and psychotherapy thus far offered by society. Some of these dissocial or antisocial youngsters need to be carried over the more turbulent years of adolescence and will later develop sufficient stability and conventionality to be permitted to resume their life on the outside.

In a few states, notably California and Massachusetts, the choice of the institution to which a child will be sent is left to an administrative body rather than to the juvenile court judge. Thus, the child is given more intensive study and classification than is usually afforded in a court. But whether the decision to commit to incarceration is made by court or administrative agency, it is important to examine the history and regimes of institutions for delinquents.

That is the aim of the present chapter.

The first article, by Teeters, provides an historic survey of institutions for neglected and antisocial children, and indicates the gradual evolution of basic philosophy from imprisonment to education, reformation, rehabilitation and therapy. These modifications of aim are reflected in the fluctuations, historically, of the typical names of such institutions; *e.g.*, house of refuge, reform school, industrial school, training school, educational institution. Shrewd critiques of such familiar devices as inmate self-government, indenture and the cottage system are presented. The article ends with some wise observations regarding improvement in the correctional situation as part of a well rounded apparatus of therapy and rehabilitation.

The next article, by Blackburn, is an authoritative, up-to-date survey of basic aspects of institutions for delinquent juveniles. After some illuminative generalizations regarding a treatment program in such establishments, the author discusses problems of staff development, treatment emphasis, public relations, family relationships; the meaning of modification, as contrasted with mere control, of conduct; the dangers inherent in a too mechanical administration of security units; expansion and variation in facilities, especially the spreading use of forestry camps; administrative structures; personnel practices. The importance of various types of research, of value both administratively and as an addition to knowledge, is emphasized. The shortcomings of existing aftercare services are brought out and valuable suggestions are given for experimentation with new facilities, such as group homes and "halfway houses." Blackburn's survey should give the student a fair picture of the nation-wide situation with reference to institutions for delinquents.

The next item is the most recent and authoritative statement of general principles governing the role of the training school. It is part of a useful booklet, *Institutions Serving Delinquent Children: Guides and Goals*, prepared by the U. S. Children's Bureau in cooperation with the National Association of Training Schools and Juvenile Agencies. This piece, reflecting the thought and experience of many persons active in the correctional field, includes a discussion of the importance of a diversified program (co-educational training schools, forestry camps, objections to the use of the training school as a detention facility); the role of boards and advisory committees; the internal administration of the training school, the school in its relation to the community, the physical plant; various aspects of the treatment program (group-living principles and personnel), cottage activities; different types of intensive treatment services; the educational program; recreation and leisure time activities; disciplinary policy; and, especially important, methods of individualizing the program, and data regarding the problems met with in preparing the child for his return to the community. The entire booklet deserves careful reading by all those interested in delinquency.

A useful experiment in the special therapy of emotionally disturbed youngsters in a residential treatment unit within the more general setting of a state school for delinquents is described in the article by Coltharp and Weber. The authors set forth the difficulties in determining the selection of children especially suited to the type of psychiatric and psychologic approach involved, the definition of the aims of group and individual psychotherapy and their relationship to the academic and vocational education, work and play activities, and other aspects of the general program. Especially instructive is the discussion of the management of hyperactive aggressive and destructive youngsters and the modifications in attitudes and leadership that occur when more reflective, less destructive boys are introduced into the group.

Breed's article on the California Youth Forestry Camp Program indicates the activities, personnel, selection of the boys for the camp and their preparation for return to the community. It supplements the camp article presented in connection with probation.[1]

Dr. Pleune's article emphasizes his own clinical experience to the effect that most delinquents are ill in the sense of having recognizable signs of emotional pathology and that "normal delinquents" — those who are essentially undamaged from a psychologic point of view and can be aided through being "taught a lesson" by means of authoritarian restraint — are relatively few. On such a basis he adds confirmation to the McCords' findings that the traditional, strictly disciplinary training school, which fails to take account of the fact that *"true delinquency does not occur without disturbed interpersonal relationships,"* is bound to have little success in transforming delinquents into conventional and well balanced citizens. Pleune makes constructive suggestions for improving the correctional school atmosphere, regime and personnel. The essence of his article is the need of a conscious psychotherapeutic orientation in the institution for delinquents. Those who believe that most delinquents are the product of a special "delinquency subculture" or "differential association" would probably not go along with Dr. Pleune's emphasis.

The article by the McCords is a pioneering effort to compare the philosophy and results in terms of personality and behavioral modifications of two more or less opposite approaches to the treatment of delinquents: the traditionally authoritarian and the consciously permissive. While the findings are not conclusive, the McCords'

---

[1] Pp. 646–650 *supra*.

experiment points the way to more definitive explorations that should be made along similar lines.

Finally, the piece on the Massachusetts Youth Service Law is included to show the administrative organization of an agency whose function it is to investigate, detain, classify, educate and correct delinquents and develop delinquency prevention programs. It might have been included in Chapter 18, except that, as is true of most places which have been stimulated by the American Law Institute's Youth Correction Authority Act, it deals with delinquents rather than with (or in addition to) young-adult offenders.

128

Institutional Treatment of Juvenile Delinquents *

Negley K. Teeters

I. The Roots of the Reform School

To anyone familiar with institutional treatment of delinquent children in the United States, the crying need for a complete reorientation is apparent. This is particularly true of those schools that are wholly supported by taxation and known as "reform schools." There are usually two of these in each state, one for boys and one for girls although a few states operate a mixed school but with the sexes scrupulously segregated. In most of the southern states, moreover, there are special schools for Negro boys and girls. Approximately 22,000 children between the ages of six or seven and sixteen to eighteen, all committed by juvenile courts, are confined in these reform schools annually. In addition to state-supported schools there are many private and quasi-public institutions administered by agencies, lodges, churches, or by private individuals, some of which take only delinquent children while others accept only children from the courts who are labeled neglected, dependent or emotionally disturbed. These latter schools have their own intake policy and are thus more independent than the completely state-supported institutions.

* Reprinted from 29 *Nebraska L. Rev.* (1950), 577–604. Used by permission of the author and the publisher.

The public is all but ignorant of the complexity of institutionalism in the treatment of juvenile delinquency and a large segment of it takes the position that delinquent children need the sort of discipline traditionally attached to such schools. We are particularly concerned in this paper with the reform school, whether public or private. Later, after we have described and appraised this conventional institution we shall describe and evaluate another form of institution which is receiving favorable mention in recent times, namely, the forestry or other type of camp similar to those operated by the Youth Authority in California. Our first task is to sketch the history of the "institution complex" as we find it throughout the country today.

The segregation of wayward or delinquent children in the United States grew out of the apprentice system so prevalent in colonial times, and the orphanage, which is almost as old. While little is known of delinquency of children of tender years during colonial days, we do know that hundreds of youngsters were farmed out to masters or mistresses by their parents in order to learn a trade or, in the case of girls, how to become a good housewife. Children from impoverished homes, neglected and even depraved children, were usually pressed into an apprenticeship which was as binding on them as a contract between two adults. It was their parents who bound them over. In addition, many children were placed in the common county almshouses of the day.

Later, when the orphanage was established, the technique of apprenticing inmates to farmers, tradesmen, artisans or housewives continued. In fact, when special institutions for delinquent children were founded during the 1820's, this same system of indenture played a leading role.

Prior to the establishment of Houses of Refuge, which we shall describe below, many children were thrown into county jails, especially in our large cities. They were subjected to the crudest forms of treatment, usually not even segregated from adults who had been remanded for every conceivable crime or vice. The House of Refuge was founded as an attempt on the part of philanthropists and educators to bring to an end this benighted practice; thus their motives were above reproach despite their many shortcomings in understanding the juvenile personality.

The modern reform school, then, is a direct descendant of the orphanage and House of Refuge. Children sent to them were often more neglected than depraved. There has been great confusion throughout the years in rationalizing delinquency and dependency. Institutional treatment was perhaps logical a hundred years ago but it has about outlived its usefulness and, aside from a few cases of serious young offenders, should be abolished or radically reformed. It is the purpose of this paper to describe just how the modern reform school gained its strong position in the juvenile treatment field and to show what must be done by society to deal effectively with delinquent children if such institutions are to continue to be used for their rehabilitation.

Here are a few "firsts" so far as treatment of problem children is concerned: the first orphanage was established in New Orleans in 1729 and was known as the Ursuline Orphanage. In 1790 the Charleston Orphan home was opened in Charleston, South Carolina. In 1800 a quaint organization was founded in Philadelphia, carrying the title of Magdalen Society. Its purpose was to care for young girls who "in an unguarded hour have been robbed of their innocence and sunk into wretchedness and guilt." This is perhaps the first society in this country to grapple with incipient prostitution and the female sex problem.

Aside from the many orphanages that originated during the early nineteenth century, several child-saving agencies were also founded. One of the first of these was a lodging house for newsboys, opened in 1854 by that great friend of underprivileged children, Charles Loring Brace. He also founded the Children's Aid Society of New York the same year and began a movement which set the pace for children's organizations and institutions for many years.

Brace began taking children out of almshouses and placing them in foster homes in order to remove many of the abuses found in these old colonial catch-alls. The Massachusetts Board of Charities in 1868 began the practice of boarding out children at public expense. The first Society for the Prevention of Cruelty to Children was begun in 1875 in New York City and here again, children from homes where cruelty and abuse were present, were farmed out in foster homes.

Thus the concept of the foster home emerged, spread rapidly and today it is generally agreed that it meets the needs of dependent children more readily than any type of institutional care.

The early institutions for dependent and neglected children closely followed the "Lady Bountiful" type of charity. The dependent or delinquent child was to be "saved from the burning." While he was to be treated sympathetically, he was also to be handled with firmness. Inculcation of the homely virtues was of supreme importance and it was assumed that any child, if he wished, could become a model young citizen. It mattered very little that he lacked the capacity to make an abrupt adjustment to some new discipline. If he made a false slip from grace he was punished; if he persisted in his non-conformist tendencies he was punished more severely. Freedom of the will on the part of the child was excuse enough to determine the extent and degree of the punishment. This philosophy was also carried over to the administration of the Houses of Refuge.

The private organizations caring for children took on names that bring a smile today although many of them that survive still maintain these names: "Homes for Little Wanderers," "Children's Orphanages," "Sheltering Arms," or "Homes for Worthy Indigent Children." Until quite recently the Church of England maintained homes known as "Homes for Waifs and Strays."

The growth of private children's homes was so rapid that many of them were forced to use questionable methods of keeping up their intake. They begged state legislatures for subsidies for each inmate sent to them and were often guilty of shameless "log-rolling" tactics to insure the receipt of a subsidy. Parents were not only encouraged to send their children to them but often were warned that they were likely to become delinquent if they were not enrolled.

Since it was to the interest of administrators of these homes to have a large population in order to keep down the per capita cost, children were frequently kept much longer than necessary with little conscientious effort made to adjust the child to the free community.

II. THE HOUSES OF REFUGE

The first House of Refuge was opened in New York City in 1825. It was a barracks leased from the government and stood on Madison Square. Several forward-looking New York citizens were responsible for the movement. Perhaps the most famous of these men was John Griscom, Quaker school-teacher who had traveled widely in Europe and was impressed by the work of the great Pestalozzi in Switzerland. He and his professional friends organized a Society for Reformation of Juvenile Delinquents in 1823 and threw their resources into a battle to secure an institution which would translate their humanitarian ideals into active practice. The society received authority from the state to manage a school — an almost revolutionary departure from traditional methods of control — and with an initial subscription of $18,000 from private individuals, a Board of Managers was elected and the school opened January 1, 1825.

With impressive services this first House of Refuge opened with its first population composed of six boys and three girls gathered from the streets. The founders envisaged this institution as a "prison, manufactory and school." In fact the Rev. John Stanford, one of the founders, spoke thus to the nine little waifs:

"You are to look on these walls which surround the building, not so much as a prison, but as an hospitable dwelling, in which you enjoy comfort and safety from those who once led you astray. And, I may venture to say, that in all probability, this is the best home any of you ever enjoyed. You have no need for me to tell you, that the consideration of all these favors should stimulate you to submission, industry, and gratitude. You are not placed here for punishment, as to produce your moral development." [1]

In 1839 the House of Refuge gave up its makeshift set of buildings and moved to the site

now occupied by Bellevue Hospital; and in 1854, to Randall's Island. In 1932, when the New York State Vocational Institution was established at West Coxsackie, the House of Refuge was merged with it and came under the jurisdiction of the State Department of Correction. Since its opening in 1825, this institution has cared for some 35,000 boys and 5,000 girls.

In 1826 Boston opened its House of Refuge about two and a half miles from the city. It was known officially as the House of Reformation. But, apparently not satisfied with this institution, an "association of gentlemen of great respectability" purchased Thompson's Island, in Boston Harbor, in 1833, on which to erect a farm school for the "reformation of boys exposed to extraordinary temptations and who were in danger of becoming vicious and dangerous." In 1835 this new farm school merged with another private institution which had been previously organized under the name of the Boston Asylum to Care for Indigent Orphans. To this were sent boys who were not yet considered delinquent. It is interesting to note that Ralph Waldo Emerson worked out a system of education for this school but it was not received with any enthusiasm. But because its "broader institutional conception and its support by private philanthropy" possessed more meaning for child development than the House of Reformation, interest in the earlier school began to wane.

The third House of Refuge was opened in 1828 in the city of Philadelphia. Conferences between the guardians of the poor and the members of prison societies in that city dealing with their concern for young vagrants suggested recommendations for a "suitable place for the reception of all minors taken up by the watchmen . . . strolling the streets without homes, who are now committed to common prisons." Later, in 1828, the institution was opened.

The Philadelphia institution, little better than a prison, was moved to larger quarters in the 1850's and at the turn of the century, the boys' department migrated to the rolling hills of Delaware County and became known as Glen Mills School for Boys. Later, the girls' department moved to a site not far from that of the male establishment and has been known since as Sleighton Farms, one of the best known institutions of its kind in the country.

Despite the glowing language used in the

---

[1] B. K. Peirce, A Half Century with Juvenile Delinquents: The New York House of Refuge and Its Times, 377 (1869).

early reports of these three schools, they were little better than prisons. Neither in architecture nor in personnel did they differ much from the conventional prison. While it is true that the first superintendents were educators and men of some vision, little could be accomplished because of the type of children coming to them and the repression of the routine. The Boston and New York schools did develop a sort of crude self-government with a system of rewards and penalties which was unique and even revolutionary in those days. But it is quite probable that the boys or girls who finally worked their way into the top grade, through their industry and good deportment, were little better than prigs. And those who would or could not make the grade were probably not understood by the pious moralists who operated the establishments. The self-government systems in operation should be accepted now with considerable reservations. In the first place, we see them only on paper; and secondly, some of the features are no doubt open to criticism on the basis of good pedagogy. There were and are now different types of status and social approval in the world of young boys and girls and all children do not want the same kind. Many children repudiate the status that adults attempt to superimpose on them.

Let us take an example from the administration of Joseph Curtis, educator and first superintendent of the New York House of Refuge. He invented a self-government system, that on paper, sounds above reproach. Yet he was a stern disciplinarian. While at the table, the children were obliged to be silent, hold up a hand for water, a thumb for vinegar, three fingers for bread, and one finger for salt. He lasted only one year, and many children escaped during his regime.

The children were exposed to a long working day with little recreation. They divided their time between productive labor in the shops and educational classes. Many were indentured to merchants and artisans. The girls were sent out to do housework. In 1828 it is recorded that the New York school sent eight boys to Ohio to work on farms. We have little to go on in order to evaluate the product of these first reform schools. But there is one evaluation that bears recording. The French commissioners, de Beaumont and de Tocqueville, wrote the following concerning all the

children who had been released from the New York institution between 1825 and 1833:

"Of 427 male juvenile offenders sent back into society, 85 had conducted themselves well, and the conduct of 41 has been excellent; of 34 the information received has been bad, and of 24 very bad; of 37 among them the information is doubtful; of 24 rather good than otherwise, and of 14 rather bad than good.

Of 86 girls who have returned into society, 37 have conducted themselves well, 11 in an excellent manner; 22 bad, and 16 very bad; the information concerning 10 is doubtful; 3 seem to have conducted themselves rather well, and 3 rather bad than otherwise. Thus of 513 children who have returned from the house of refuge in New York into society, more than 200 have been saved from infallible ruin." [2]

The institution complex thus became solidified in the prisonlike Houses of Refuge and release followed the familiar pattern of indenture. The children remained under the control of the management until they reached their majority. While this specialized care for children is commendable, even as we glance backward, it was not without its critics at the time. Many large city magistrates continued to send children to county jails for infractions of the law, or as runaways from their apprenticeships, because they felt that a thirty-day stay in jail was far better for such children than several years' imprisonment in a House of Refuge.

III. The Cottage Type of Institutional Treatment

In 1854 a girls' reform school was opened at Lancaster, Massachusetts, and, coincidentally, four years later, a boys' school was opened at Lancaster, Ohio. Both featured the cottage or family plan. This idea of the small family unit is generally regarded as coming from the well-known school at Mettray, France, opened in 1839, by Judge Frederic Auguste Demetz. However, the family plan was conceived many years earlier by the members of the Philanthropic Society of London which, as early as 1788, conceived of child-saving in terms of small family units. Because of its historical interest in the cottage type of institution it is important that we set down here just what this organization accomplished:

"It distributed the children into families of twelve

[2] Homer Folks, The Care of Destitute, Neglected and Delinquent Children, 204 (1902).

in its modest dwellings, placing at the head of the whole group a general superintendent, and in the three families severally a gardener, a tailor, and a shoemaker, with their wives. It sought in this way to realize to the youthful objects of its charity the happiness and benefits of a home . . . One rubs his eyes in astonishment as he reads the reports of the Society — those for example, issued in 1788 and 1789." [3]

These reports envisaged agriculture as "the great source to which the Society looks for employment for its wards. Agriculture means natural life, and is the primary spring for health and happiness."

But Judge Demetz really got his inspiration for family units from Dr. Johann Heinrich Wichern, with his "Inner Mission" which established in 1833 the justly famous Rauhe Haus at Horn, near Hamburg, in Germany. He and his mother maintained that "if the Kingdom of Christ is again to be established . . . it is necessary among other things to found a house for the sole object of rescuing children from sin and disbelief." [4] Wichern sought out twelve of the worst boys he could find from the "lowest haunts of vice and misery" and took them to a "very rough farm" which he had secured for the purpose. While we do not know how ideal a place this school was — whether it was repressive or progressive — we do note in studying institutional treatment in those days that there was a universality of platitudinous, though sincere, remarks made by those who held the destiny of children in their hands. The children at Rauhe Haus were taught "wholesome learning, the truths of the Gospel, and honest labor." The "house father" and "house mother" were an integral part of the regime — a fact that appealed to Demetz who visited and studied the school.

Returning to France he opened his family school at Mettray, near Tours, with nine children selected from the prison at Frontrevault. By 1841 six houses and a small chapel were completed. Believing that agriculture is reformative, Demetz adopted as a motto, "the moralization of youth by the cultivation of the soil."

The program of the school was arduous. The founder believed in hard work on the farm. He and his staff sent his young charges to bed completely tired out, without so much as an evening's romp in the dormitories. As the school was based on the family unit, the boys were grouped according to their disposition and character and placed in separate cottages under special masters. Here we see a crude type of classification at a very early period. Each family was distinct and had no connection with the others, except at work, recreation, and divine services. The cottages were of three stories. On the ground floor was the workshop; on the first, the dining-room, school, and part of the dormitories; on the second floor were more dormitories. There was also a form of self-government. The boys selected two monitors or *frères aines* (older brothers) monthly, who worked out a system of rewards and discipline with the house father. The regime was military in nature which no doubt paved the way for this type of discipline being adopted by so many schools both in France and the United States. While the Mettray experiment met with almost universal favor it did have its critics. For instance, Prince Peter Kropotkin, the Russian humanitarian, described the system as most cruelly severe. Another criticism, aside from its great cost, was that the boys were intimidated by the constant threat that if they did not behave they would be returned to the penitentiary from which they had originally come.

But the cottage, or family type of institution was a distinct advance in the institutional treatment of delinquent and neglected children. As was stated above, the first two reform schools based on the family system to open in this country were the Massachusetts institution for girls at Lancaster (1854) and the Boys' Reform School at Lancaster, Ohio (1858). In the Ohio reform school, the first cottages were log cabins. Each housed forty boys. The custodians were known as "Elder Brothers." Each cottage was named for a river. Every effort was made to eliminate the characteristics of a prison, although the regime, like that at Mettray, was severe. The boys worked eight and a half hours on the farm each day, except Sunday. On this day their time was consumed with many religious services, "moral review of the week," and a "walk on the farm." Attempts to escape subjected the guilty ones to "degradation and to

---

[3] Enoch C. Wines, *State of Prisons and Child-Saving Institutions in the Civilized World*, 76 (1880).

[4] B. K. Peirce, *op. cit. supra* note 1, at 133.

confinement in a dark cell for two weeks, or to expulsion and transfer to the penitentiary." [5]

With these two reform schools as models — both along the lines of the cottage or family plan — many other states followed this pattern in establishing schools for delinquent boys and girls. In all fairness to this trend it must be stated that any innovation that departed from the old prison architecture with mass treatment of children is to be commended. The old Houses of Refuge set the stage for the specialized treatment of children as distinct from that of adults. The acceptance of the idea that children deserve a more humane type of imprisonment than do adults is also worthy of record. The House of Refuge inaugurated crude concepts of self-government and the cottage plan initiated a type of classification.

The cottage reform schools opened in the various states during the past century are generally attractively designed. They are usually built in isolated and even desolate areas and many make much of farming, especially for the boys. Some of these plants rival college campuses with their groves of shade trees, shrubbery, brick or stone cottages and tastefully arranged flower plots. The layman visiting any of these establishments is struck with their apparent beauty, is often misled by the surroundings and labels them as delightful places to send children. But few students of delinquency who possess any insight whatsoever can give a clean bill of health to any of these reform schools, even though they are referred to as educational institutions. While, as we stated above, they are an improvement over the older Houses of Refuge with their walls and cell blocks, there is enough criticism today coming from students of delinquency to question this type of institutional treatment for but a few youthful offenders.

It may be noted here that the names of the institutions vary. First they were Houses of Refuge and were just that, asylums for underprivileged children. Later the name was changed to "reform school" so there would be no element of doubt as to their intention. But in time children were stigmatized who had "served time" in a reform school. Since trade training

took on signal importance it was considered a happy thought to change the name to "industrial school." But even this name began to carry stigma and, conversely, it stigmatized boys and girls who were non-delinquent, who attended training schools on their own volition. Some schools developed a working arrangement with their state departments of education and thus took over the name of "educational institution." The latest trend is to name the schools after persons who have been active in the treatment of delinquents or in honor of early superintendents. Regardless of the name, they are still reform schools and those sent there by courts are stigmatized, whether they are rehabilitated or not.

In 1946 there were approximately 166 schools of this type under public auspices serving delinquent children. Of these, 115 were state and national schools and 51 were county and municipal institutions. During that year, the state and national institutions cared for an average of nearly 22,000 children of which approximately 16,000 were boys and 6,000 were girls. Taking into consideration the county and municipal institutions as well as the fairly large number of private or semi-official schools, the total average population has been estimated to exceed 30,000.[6]

Before we make an evaluation of institutional treatment for delinquents a word should be included concerning the Catholic institutions for delinquent children. The hierarchy maintains child welfare agencies and quite frequently juvenile judges refer cases to them, especially if the children belong to the Catholic faith. Boys are sent to "protectories" and girls to institutions operated by the Order of the Good Shepherd. The treatment in operation in both of these institutions is perhaps more highly regimented than in the state-supported schools although it is just as probable that excessive cruelty is less frequently detected than in state reform schools. Feelings of guilt are encouraged in the hope that children will see their error and thus reform. In other words, penitence or expiation is more often the rule in these schools than in state-supported reform schools.

Special institutions for the correction of truant children have been in existence also for some time. They are sometimes known as

---

[5] For a contemporary account of this first boys' cottage institution, see the *Journal of Prison Discipline and Philanthropy*, 153–168 (Oct. 1858).

[6] *Social Work Yearbook*, 282 (1949).

"parental schools" and have almost always been a part of the regular public schools, especially in the larger cities. The first parental schools were organized in Boston in 1896 and in Buffalo in 1897. The child is only placed in such an institution when his case of truancy is serious. Some of these schools have also been used for children who, in addition to truancy, have committed minor offenses around the school proper. A good example of such a school is the Shallcross School, a residential school for truant boys between the ages of 8 and 14½, operated by the Board of Public Education of Philadelphia.

IV. Criticism of Institutional Treatment for Delinquents

The criticism leveled against institutional treatment for the young offender is certainly not new. But within the past decade this criticism has reached a crescendo that makes it mandatory that judges of juvenile courts and others deeply concerned with the well-being of emotionally disturbed children, of which delinquent behavior is certainly one manifestation, appraise this technique of treatment. It is easy to send a child to such a school. "Out of sight, out of mind" seems to be the thesis of such a policy.

As far back as 1896 William Tallack, secretary of the Howard League of Penal Reform, of London wrote of the "Institution Craze" that reflected the thinking of mid-Victorians so far as the treatment of delinquents was concerned. Tallack's objections bear repeating even now. He voiced them in his book, *Penological and Preventive Principles,* as follows: first, institutional treatment shifts parental responsibility upon the state; second, lack of classification produces a collection of tender youth and more calloused delinquents which makes possible the training of sly and hardened criminals in such institutions; third, many children are sent back to depraved surroundings, including homes where no interim preparation has been effected. He speaks of the large training ships, to which many delinquent boys were sent, as "floating prisons" filled with all kinds of corruption; of reformatories where outbreaks, riots and fire-setting are the rule. While the above criticism is none too logical, it does demonstrate that the practice of institutional treatment was not considered a panacea even at that time.

The reform schools of this country have been caustically criticized by the Osborne Association of New York City, an organization that employs a trained staff of experts who are thorough and objective in their analysis of the plant, staff and training program of these schools. Through the past quarter century this organization has been bluntly outspoken in pointing up the many shortcomings of institutional treatment for delinquent children. Another source of criticism is Albert Deutsch, New York Journalist, whose earlier studies of the hospitals for the mentally diseased were received by the American people with horror. Mr. Deutsch made a survey of several of these schools and presented his shocking findings in the *Woman's Home Companion* for March 1948. The writer of this article can substantiate nearly everything Albert Deutsch has indicated in institutional treatment for children from his own observation of reform schools covering the past twenty years. Many of those who administer these schools live in an ivory tower, and retire to it in full knowledge that the reform school is a vested interest in the treatment of delinquency and thus will not be drastically uprooted or, for that matter, changed in any appreciable degree.

Before pointing out the serious shortcomings of institutional care, it is important to note that rarely, if ever, has a state-supported reform school asked voluntarily for an objective appraisal of its school by trained investigators There have been investigations of specific schools, such as that of the Fred C. Nelles School at Whittier, California, in 1940, the Ohio Reform School, at Lancaster in 1939 (the fifth since 1919) or a few other state schools. But these have come only after some scandal has occurred such as some brutal treatment of inmates, or a suicide of some boy or girl, or a wholesale escape or riot.

Many reports of reform schools present a bill of particulars regarding the inadequate physical plant, the decrepit buildings, the untrained staff or its frequent turnover, the poor food, poor sleeping arrangements, overcrowding, and other such results that accrue largely from a penurious fiscal policy of the state. Starving reform schools by state legislatures is all too common and is to be deplored. It is only fair that we mention their impoverishment before we point out shortcomings that inhere in the system of institutional care and administrative brutality. Even at their best, they are to be censured.

The reports of the Osborne Association have been devastating in their criticism yet they have been constructive in pointing out basic needs so far as physical plant or staff attitudes are concerned. Here and there a few schools merited some favorable comment; but the vast majority were found to be mediocre, and many downright repressive and inhumane in their treatment of the children. Here we find political domination, there we find old firetraps used for buildings; in this school we see a lack of many of the comforts and ordinary decencies we might reasonably expect where the care of children is the main objective; in that school we come upon untrained personnel with an attitude toward their work bordering on that of the average prison guard.[7]

The reports of this fact-finding organization reveal an almost utter bankruptcy of educational procedure and understanding so far as treatment of delinquency is concerned. The more recent investigations of Albert Deutsch during the year 1948 point out primarily the cruelty of staff officers in many of the schools and the indifference and apathy of the administration in most of the others he visited. Prefacing his articles, Mr. Deutsch makes this statement:

"The facts as I found them shock me profoundly. They add up to a black record of human tragedy, of social and economic waste, of gross brutality, crass stupidity, totalitarian regimentation and a corrupting monotony even deadlier for children's personalities than physical violence."

Allowing for a few notable exceptions where "staff members try to give kindly and intelligent guidance" he adds that "for the most part they are handicapped by public indifference, legislative penury and administrative inertia, or by the traditional view that juvenile offenders are miniature criminals and child reformatories are juvenile prisons." The truth is that the reform school embodies an outmoded philosophy in the light of the newer concepts of behavior problems.

It is not of much pertinence in such an article as this to dilate at length regarding the cruelty and inept handling of children in reform schools. There is plenty of clinical evidence through the years that demonstrates that it is almost impossible for institutions for children to maintain a decent healthy homelike atmosphere without repression of the worst sort. There are always infractions of the many rules of an institution and conventional types of punishment are invoked. When one punishment fails, another, more drastic, is administered. When this fails, a third, even more drastic, is evolved. Thus it goes. In time the most ingenious and sadistic penalties are dreamed up by the harassed and frustrated administrators. One significant feature of almost every investigation is that which deals with the brutal penalties practiced on the hapless children under the supervision of superintendents of these schools. The Deutsch investigation points up this sterility in the country's reform schools. In the next few pages we wish to discuss the problems of the reform school in order to see if some of them can be resolved to the ultimate well-being of delinquents sent to them.

V. Can the Institution Be Oriented Toward the Treatment of Delinquents?

Millions of dollars are tied up in buildings in each state; imprisonment as a philosophy is deeply rooted in the attitudes of legislators and the "good citizens" of our communities. There is little hope that we can actually abolish the reform school. But it is not out of the question to change it drastically. We are convinced that every effort must be made to keep children out of them through the use of probation and foster home placement. Mentally retarded children should be given specialized treatment in institutions or homes especially adapted to their needs. Psychiatric treatment should be extended to children in the public school who suffer from emotional problems. We are here concerned only with the treatment of those children who will eventually find their way into the reform schools.

It would seem, then, that the first major consideration confronting those who have the responsibility of dealing with delinquent children

---

[7] For criticisms of specific schools see the *Handbooks of American Institutions for Delinquents*, First edition, Vols. I (1938); II (1940); III (1940); IV (1943). The latest report (1943) sets up desirable standards for juvenile training schools.

is the policy of intake.* Just what type or types of boys and girls need institutional treatment? It is the studied judgment of many eminent people that each state should maintain small units, similar to those in operation in California and under the direction of the Youth Authority. Hundreds of boys may well profit from outdoor camp life, maturing for a year or two under a regime of training and counseling. Most boys taken from their homes by the juvenile court because there seems to be little in their home situations upon which to tie a meaningful preparation for life would profit from a camp experience. They would not abscond. They would find understanding counseling and a challenging program fruitful to them. It is not our purpose here to discuss the advantages of camps for delinquent boys but rather to explore the possibilities of the traditional reform school. Even the state of California finds it necessary to maintain the Fred

* The following is a recent statement of the intake policy of The Children's Village, Dobbs Ferry, New York:

"The Children's Village desires to serve English speaking boys between the ages of 10 and 15, boys who can profit from residential treatment and who need an environment in which planned living experiences based on clinical understanding are integrated with psychotherapy in one unified program. Generally, such youngsters fit into the following categories: (1) Children who cannot use close relationship with adults and for whom the security of various adult relationships and simple routinized living is a necessary experience in establishing mental health. (2) Children who must be removed from their homes in which the emotional disturbance has reached a degree in which separation of parents and child is necessary in order to reconstitute the home on a more wholesome basis and to rehabilitate the child sufficiently enough for his return. (3) Children with ego problems who need structured living, a sense of achievement, and belonging and relationships available at the time they are ready to involve themselves. (4) Children with poor super-egos who require vigorous relationships, opportunities for identification, and a chance to be dependent. (5) Children who do not respond to child guidance services on an out-patient basis because they require, in addition, controlled social living which is clinically oriented. We expect the boys we accept to be capable of achieving the minimum standards required for maintaining the group living we provide and that holding boys responsible and accountable for these requirements are reasonable and therapeutic. This would mean the boys must have the capacity for a degree of self-direction and initiative." Mimeographed statement furnished by Children's Village. — Ed.

C. Nelles School at Whittier for little boys and the Preston School of Industry for older youths.

It is the claim of the apologists of the reform school that it is because of these two reform schools still being maintained in that state, that a program of camp training is possible. The hardened and more "vicious" boys can still be sent to the schools and the more amenable boys given the camp training. This is doubtless true but the question is, what is the atmosphere of these reform schools? Both are dominated by the "lock psychosis" so familiar to such institutions. Fear of escape permeates them the same as in other states where we have little reason to expect a progressive policy of dealing with the delinquent boy. Of course a serious attempt has been made to install new personnel in these schools but thus far little optimism can be expressed. The older staff members are permeated with fear and, as they have tenure, cannot be replaced. In addition, they resist any indoctrination through in-service training. The Youth Authority program in California as well as in other states will thus be materially handicapped because of the reform school atmosphere. We shall now pass on to the reorientation of the reform school as we have known it.

Regardless of the function of the reform school it is necessary to survey some of the problems they have been shackled with for years. It is the belief of the writer that administrators of these schools, as well as legislators, must resolve these traditional problems. Only in their solution, can a reform school be of any value in treating delinquency.

First, then, we have the problem of intake. It is patently unfair to youngsters who have a normal intelligence, or who are not psychotic or pre-psychotic, or who are first offenders, to be sent to an institution where all kinds of children are sent. We are not here referring to states like California that already have a good screening program. It would seem most expedient then to use the institution either for those whose prognosis is good — or — to commit children who need specialized therapy. No institution can take care of both types and do an honestly good job. We have mentioned earlier that specialized institutions for defective delinquents and for seriously disturbed emotional types be developed. Regardless of what decisions are made relative to intake, nothing effective can be done if reform schools are to be merely catch-alls for all types of children. The insidious contagion of the modern reform school must be dissipated if a genuine type of treatment is to result. If the school is actually to reform, that is, re-educate for life, it must abound with normal stimuli to ordinary wholesome living.

Another question is whether it is to be surrounded or not by a fence. This seems academic to most persons since today no reform school feels such a restraint is necessary. But, unfortunately, what happens is that the "staff becomes the wall or fence." Responsibility for thwarting runaways is at present a serious part of the staff's duties. Thus we find repressions and regimentation, countings and checks. A survey of reform schools today would show, as part of regimentation, marching, often the boys with arms folded, counting off periodically throughout the day, inmates locked in their rooms before and after meals, and other prison-like restraints. Instead of a wholesome and rational cooperation between staff members and children we find resentments and antagonisms that drag down the already unwholesome atmosphere still further. This problem can only be met by admitting that some children will run away no matter how wholesome the program is. Thus, if walls and fences are to be absent from reform schools — and they should be — the program must be such that boys and girls will want to stay. That brings us to the third problem, that of the absconder.

It is a moot question as to just how serious absconding is. The reform school of the past and even of the present is characterized by the "lock psychosis" so familiar to adult prisons. It is assumed that superintendent and staff must keep their charges safely within bounds at all costs. One of the quaint methods used, aside from the more reprehensible routine of regimentation, is a so-called honor system. Let us see how this operates in a typical girls' reform school. After a child passes a period of time in a reception cottage she is then removed to an "honor" cottage where she is under group controls. These controls, superimposed initially by adults, are difficult for most children to conform to in a free society; how much more frustrating they must be to the type of child who is sent away for delinquency. Honest conduct, politeness, a high degree of morality, day in and day out, socially compelled by threats and moral

suasion often develop behavior in children at the opposite extreme from that intended. But we in America have the "honor" complex especially for growing children. Witness, as an example, the good turns daily of the Boy Scouts. The brilliant studies by Hartshorne and May, some years ago, show conclusively that we expect entirely too much from our children.[8] Honor systems as they are found in reform schools are doomed to fail because of two factors: (1) Most youngsters sent to these schools cannot absorb the type of honor pressed in on them by the administration because there has been little, if anything, in their experience upon which they can draw to be of help to them. An example of this may be found in a practice in operation in certain girls' schools: if a child runs away from her "honor" cottage, not only is she penalized when apprehended, but all the girls in that cottage have certain privileges withdrawn because they have failed in their responsibility. This calls for a very high degree of social insight that even children in a free society could not possibly assume. (2) Honor actually does not mean honor. It is usually diluted to such a degree and is so patently false that the inmates have no difficulty in seeing through the ruse. Thus they resent it. The reform school, for instance, which proudly boasts that its inmates are not locked up in their rooms at night rarely shows the metal enunciator placed in the jamb of the door which rings a bell in the matron's quarters if the occupant leaves her room; or, the administrator who tells visitors that inmates are free to come and go between cottages on regularly appointed tasks but who warn matrons or other staff members after the children are sent on their duties. These are practices that exist in many institutions that pose as "honor" schools. There can be no honor system unless the authorities are willing to accept breaches along with the positive.

Society must be willing to accept and support training schools that minimize runaways. True, everything honest must be done to inculcate principles of reliance and self-discipline into the inmates of these schools, but absconders must not be humiliated or punished in the traditional sense upon their apprehension. It takes skill

---

[8] Hartshorne and May, *Studies in the Nature of Character* (1928–30).

to know just how to penalize a child who absconds and is returned to the school.

A third problem is that of discipline. The reports of the Osborne Association and Albert Deutsch make sickening reading in their parade of sadistic punishments meted out to the nonconformist. It is a truism in penology that we are more brutal toward children than to adults. Many schools flog their inmates. In girls' schools it is not an uncommon practice for recalcitrant inmates to have their tresses shaved or to be given ice cold baths. Everyone denounces cruelty in institutions but yet it is quite widespread. Regimentation of the most rigid sort is found in many schools administered by "experts" who, in conferences of child workers, read papers fairly dripping with institutional soothing syrup. This is for public consumption. Upon their return they revert to their grim business of running their schools in a "workmanlike" manner. For example, it has been the practice in many boys' schools to discipline their charges with a strict military drill. The top boys known as cadet officers control the other boys; "delegated authority" it is called. In some schools these cadet officers often tend to become the meanest, toughest, and most sadistic inmates to be found in the school. Now this practice has been condoned in schools administered by well-known men who have made national reputations in the institutional field.

Let us see what the report of the Attorney General's National Conference on Prevention and Control of Juvenile Delinquency (held in Washington, D. C. in 1946) says about such practices: [9]

"Such disciplinary abuses are completely indefensible. Particularly vicious is the 'monitor' system which permits older, more aggressive children to exert authority over the more timid and less mature. Not only does such a program fail to develop the positive value of leadership but it encourages those very antisocial tendencies which the training school is attempting to correct."

The National Child Welfare Division of the conservative American Legion also condemns repressive discipline in reform schools. Culled

from its report we find the following: "Discipline should be firm but not tyrannical. Demerits should be given on the basis of punishment earned. The use of corporal punishment disregards the findings of scientific studies in the field of human endeavor, behavior and training." "Under no circumstances should such disciplinary methods as leg chains, irons, solitary confinement, stand-ups, lines, cells or bodily harm be used. Starvation, bread and water, etc., should be on the 'never used' list." "Runaways should be apprehended by duly constituted authorities only and no reward offered or paid to civilians for returning such children, a practice widely used by some of the 'better' schools. The use of sirens, bells, bloodhounds and the like should be forbidden." [10] Much has been written on discipline for children. Hundreds of conferences on children's problems have devoted a great deal of attention to this subject. The question that should be asked is: "What kind of discipline do we want?" Sheviakov and Redl, in an admirable little pamphlet, have answered this question as follows:

"1. We want discipline based on devotion to humanitarian principles and ideals such as freedom, justice, and equality or all rather than discipline based on a narrower, more egotistic affiliation of MY group.
"2. We want discipline which recognizes the *inherent dignity and rights* of every human being rather than discipline attained through humiliation of the undisciplined.
"3. We want *self-direction, self-discipline* rather than discipline based on obedience to a Führer.
"4. We want discipline based on understanding of the goal in view rather than discipline based on "taking someone else's word for it." [11]

Discipline, then, must have meaning for the child. It should be, in reality, a technique pointing toward the development of *self-discipline* rather than to regiment. Authority must be *personal* with an explanation of its relation to society.[12] The principles enunciated at the Attorney General's Conference on Juvenile De-

[9] Attorney General's National Conference on Prevention and Control of Juvenile Delinquency, Report No. 6, "Institutional Treatment of Juvenile Delinquents," Government Printing Office, Washington, D.C. (1947).

[10] *Building Asset Citizens, Recommended Objectives for Juvenile Training Schools*, (Revised Edition, June 1941–3), National Headquarters, American Legion, Indianapolis, Indiana.
[11] Sheviakov and Redl, *Discipline for Today's Children and Youth*, 7 (1947).
[12] Bromberg and Rogers, "Authority In the Treatment of Delinquents," *American Journal of Orthopsychiatry*, 672–85 (Oct. 1946).

linquency, mentioned above, square with what we have set down in discussing this subject.

There are those who suggest books of rules for institutional management setting down penalties so that all may see; others contend that the fewer rules there are the more fertile the field of growth in self-discipline. Relationships between inmates of an institution as well as between inmates and staff members may develop in a healthy manner only by the acceptance of the dignified status of the individual and through growth of self-respect and self-discipline. Whatever discipline there is should be handled by a committee of staff members rather than by a sole person. The committee members should rotate so that fixed rigid policies do not develop.

The fourth problem that must be handled honestly is the sex problem. Anyone who knows anything about American reform schools is aware of its existence. But it is pushed into the background. It is a problem that is never discussed at meetings of administrators yet it is the first question with which staff members greet outsiders who show any interest in administrative problems of their school. Deviational behavior is traditional in all reform schools, both for boys and for girls. Whatever control is suggested, it must be positive rather than negative. The child who pursues such acts should not be punished by shame or guilt feelings nor by corporal punishment. The solution, whatever it is, must flow from a healthy regime of treatment, understanding of adolescent problems, and by progressive concepts of sex on the part of the administration. For example, at the New York Training School for Girls at Hudson, New York, under the administration of Mrs. Fanny French Morse, some years ago, "crushes" were minimized. When the flirtations began to be "serious," the girls involved had their tasks changed without any mention made of the real reason or obstructions were tactfully placed so that the participants found it more difficult to carry on. A girl, thus involved, who had expressed a desire to take up some particular assignment was given that new task but no mention was made of *why* she was being changed. Ingenuity is called for in dealing with the problem of crushes or other overt homosexual acts. Methods that may work once may fail later; those used with profit in one school may not be the answer in another. The real thing is to study the problem in all its phases and experiment. So far as the writer knows there has never been any research or experimentation done among reform school administrators to see what can be done with the sex problem. They merely repress and condemn when confronted with its manifestations and complain that it is an ever-present situation to be dealt with on the punishment level.

A fifth problem of the reform school, much of which derives from the homosexual complex, is the "ganging up" of older or stronger boys, or girls, against the new or smaller inmates. This grim, relentless behavior persists in all schools. It is to cope with this internecine warfare that many of the most vicious punishments are resorted to by superintendents. The whole process is insidious because a deadly climate soon develops which stamps the institution for all time. This same tense atmosphere may be detected easily in juvenile detention quarters of our large cities and is carried over to the reform school. The moment it becomes apparent there is little hope for a healthy program to develop unless the administration has the courage to fight the tendency with courage — not by traditional punishments.

Thus we see that if a reform school is to be effective it must constantly accept the above-mentioned problems and resolve them. There is no room for sophistry. It calls for daring, resourcefulness, insight and a love for children, regardless of how difficult they may be.

It might be well at this point to take notice of the fact that there are no "reform" schools in England. Children committed by juvenile courts which, incidentally, are presided over by lay judges rather than paid jurists, are remanded to schools known as "Approved Schools." They derive their name from the fact that they are approved by the Home Office. Many of these institutions are privately operated by the churches of various denominations or have a long distinguished history running back to the eighteenth century and founded by philanthropists. They vary in size and in climate. Some are repressive but most of them are operated by intelligent persons who understand the delinquent and homeless child. Most of them take children who are either dependent or delinquent. In few of them is any differentiation made. The atmosphere in most of them is wholesome. The children do not wear any uniform garb and the Home Office provides car fare for vacations at home during the holidays, both in summer and at Christmas time. Cruelty is completely absent although some schools still persist in using the "cane" on obstreperous children. The approved school is certainly not free of fault but it is a much more progressive type of institution than most of our institutions in this country.

Let us look further at some of the *musts* if the correctional or reform school is to be accepted as a dignified integral part of the program of training for delinquent children. Some of the following suggestions are so obviously apparent that it seems redundant even to mention them. They are really a digest from the Report of the Attorney General's National Conference, already mentioned above. First, the institution should be in the country rather than a city; yet not so far out that staff members become isolated. Psychiatric services of a metropolitan area should be available as well as adequate hospital facilities for necessary operations and emergency medical treatment. As the National Conference report points out extreme isolation "makes it difficult to obtain and keep the services of good personnel, who will want to stay abreast of current developments in their field and take advantage of education and cultural opportunities."

The school should be of the cottage type with provision made for each child to have a room to himself. Most reform schools are cursed with dormitories, thus depriving children of any privacy whatsoever. They are under constant surveillance twenty-four hours each day. It is generally accepted by child experts that the human personality needs some privacy if it is to thrive and mature into a rational healthy individual. Thus it is imperative that individual sleeping rooms be provided in each school. While many girls' schools provide individual rooms, there are few boys' schools in this country that make such provision. It should not be necessary to call for fire-proof buildings, properly lighted and well heated in winter. As the National Conference states it: "Facilities provided in training centers for delinquents should include all the essential services of a well-organized small community." Each cottage should have its own kitchen and dining-room. The food should be ample, well-cooked and attractively served.

There should be an administrative center, a receiving or orienting unit, housing units in which should reside no more than 25 children, adequate residential facilities for house matrons and staff officers who must reside on the grounds, school buildings well equipped, medical and mental hygiene centers, a chapel, shops in boys' schools and training facilities in girls' schools. Farming should be an interesting part of the program, including animal husbandry, poultry and bee keeping, and if possible, a dairy herd.

Successful child adjustment is possible only through understanding personnel so it is essential that the best possible staff be assembled. Aside from adequate salaries, the staff should be encouraged to remain in the work by wholesome living quarters with an opportunity of getting away for relaxation and cultural pursuits. Pensions, sick leave, and tenure are also necessary.

An initial diagnostic interval, perhaps of one month's duration, is important if meaningful treatment is to be inaugurated. Facilities for diagnosis should be abundant and adequate. These services should include tests of various types which will eventually show what is needed for each child. These should include psychological, psychiatric, medical, vocational, social, and those dealing with personality. As the National Conference points out, relative to classification:

"Groupings within the institution should be the concern of the classification committee, which ought to include the cottage parents, counselors, and all others directly concerned with oversight and care. They will want to decide how to group the aggressive, antisocial leader; the submissive, easily led, easily dominated, suggestible, weak, inoffensive individual; the boy with neurotic symptoms, emotionally unstable, impulsive, and lacking in foresight; the child who becomes involved in difficulties because of an absence of acceptable patterns in his home and the presence of gang patterns on the street; the boy of superior or inferior intelligence, from a good home as well as from the slum area." [13]

As our states develop systems of treatment centers within institutions, camps, or hostels, as is now the case in California, a centralized diagnostic center should be provided, set apart from any of the specialized units.

---

[13] See note 9 *supra*, p. 681.

The educational program should envisage a full day for all children up to the age of 14 or 15 and preferably older. The program should be flexible, progressive and remedial. There should be adequate physical equipment and the school rooms should be attractively decorated; in keeping with the average or better schools within the state. The program should be challenging to all children, based on experiences in creative arts, in manual activities and in human relationships. Furthermore, the program should be legally and in reality an integral part of the state's educational system.

There should be provided as a part of the school program some experiences in group therapy under the supervision and direction of a trained therapist. Children should be presented an opportunity to verbalize their aggressions without fear of reprimand. Only in this manner and by this technique can there be any development in insight.

Instead of the sterile trade training that is so characteristic of boys' schools, there should be developed a meaningful program in vocational training geared to the best thought in this field. All boys sent to reform schools do not need a trade; many of them can never hope to learn or use a trade. Their emotional problems are much more important in setting up a program. Hobbies, manual skills, insight, are vastly more important than merely learning a trade. Of course there should be provision made for each boy's or girl's needs; provision made to impart to the child some values that have meaning to them. Aside from school and farming, auto mechanics, foundry, and the like could very easily be provided for the boys with domestic science, household arts, beauty culture, for the girls.

Nor should the religious life of the children be neglected. All creeds should be represented by ministers or chaplains who should be permitted to conduct services as well as to counsel the children. However, proselytizing should not be tolerated. If religion is to have any significance to the child, compulsion in attending church services should not be adopted.

Individual casework as well as group activities should be encouraged and developed by the administration wherever possible and needed. It is needless to point out that a well-rounded recreational program should be developed. While each child should be encouraged to

participate, he should not be forced into activities; nor should the inmates be "recreated" to the point of exhaustion each day as is done in many schools that are administered by persons who look upon physical exercise as the ultimate in treatment of delinquents. Recreation should be a joyful experience for the child, not a painful or obligatory chore. Hikes, swimming, athletics, trips to nearby cities to points of interest — all should be a part of the program.[14]

Frequent visits home should be a major innovation. Practically any child could be trusted to go home for a few days from time to time and especially so at Christmas and for a period during the summer. Visits to the children from their parents should also be encouraged. Certainly none of the above suggestions are difficult of attainment if only the boards and superintendents of our schools could assume a flexibility adequate of accepting them. In a few words, we can indict our country's reform schools in the statement that their atmosphere is little better than an adult penitentiary. In fact, in many instances, they are even more repressive than many prisons.

VI. Parole or After-Care

Parole or after-care of a child released from a reform school should also follow professional techniques found acceptable in the adult field. To release a child from institutional care where he has been strictly supervised, into a relatively free community life situation requires a particular type of guidance, sympathetic and tactful. It is imperative, therefore, that the child be prepared for this experience while he is in the institution. In addition there should be adequate investigation regarding home life and community resources which are to be used for his return. One of the greatest difficulties in the whole correctional field of treatment is encountered at this all-important juncture. Usually the child's home conditions have remained static, so far as his membership is concerned. If his family life has contributed to his delinquency there is reason to believe that nothing has been done to rectify it while the child has

[14] Costello, "Institutions for Juvenile Delinquents," 261 Annals, 166–218 (1949). This article shows what a *good* institution can do.

been absent. One of the unsolved problems in post-institutional treatment hinges around the family situation; that is, whether or not to return him to the same home atmosphere.

In many cases, the absence of the child may have produced a wholesome attitude on the part of parents toward their child and toward their own responsibilities in contributing to family morale. The institution, also, may have shaped the child's habits so that he is able to take his place more adequately in the family than prior to commitment. Adjustment, therefore, prior to release and adjustment after release are both serious phases of parole or after-care and obviously call for trained personnel.

Some institutions employ their own after-care staff. In some states the after-care staff is assigned by the juvenile court and in some other states, it is a state function. This latter situation is notably true in those states that have within the past few years developed the Youth Authority philosophy. The parole, or after-care work is carried on through regional offices although administratively all work is centralized in one state office.

No opinion can be expressed here as to the desirability of any one of the three after-care plans suggested above. All three types can and do work successfully in certain jurisdictions. In general, however, it has been found that in order to achieve high standards of performance, a centralized agency is best equipped to translate parole theory into efficient practice.

In many jurisdictions a sponsor, in addition to the parole officer, is required. This person may be a friend of the family, a minister, or anyone interested in child care. The main task of sponsoring is well stated by G. Howland Shaw as "simply the art by which an adult works out a constructive relationship with a youngster who has been or who is in trouble." [15] He continues by stating that sponsoring is not merely "sending a boy to a baseball game or having him to supper at one's home," important as these friendly gestures are.

While it is important that the released boy or girl have some understanding friends in the community, the crux of after-care is skillful supervision by a trained parole officer who, through his skill, is professionally competent

to bridge the gap between the vestigial aftermath of the institution experience and the potential warmth of community life. It is obvious that this task will be the more difficult because of the rigidity of the modern reform school. When this routinized establishment can become more socialized, the work of community adjustment will be more easily expedited.

Before passing on to a statement or two regarding other types of institutional treatment of delinquent children, it is of some significance that we append here a cogent remark that was made by the celebrated Hastings H. Hart in 1910 (forty years ago) concerning institutional treatment. It has considerable bearing on the status of the reform school today:

"The juvenile reformatory is not designed as a permanent institution in which to bring up children to manhood or womanhood. However good an institution may be, however kindly its spirit, however genial its atmosphere, however homelike its cottages, however fatherly and motherly its officers, however admirable its training, it is now generally agreed among those who are familiar with the needs of children of this class that institutional life is at the best artificial and unnatural, and that the child ought to be returned at the earliest practicable moment to the more natural environment of the family home — his own home if it is a suitable one, and if not, then some other family home." [16]

The children's institution, whether public, quasi-public or private, simply is not the answer to the problem of delinquency. It has failed and is still failing. It cannot match the normal environment of the family and the neighborhood. If the institution could make provisions for children to go home on frequent visits or provide those children who have no homes or inadequate families with friends who will serve in lieu of parents, this would have considerable merit.

We do not wish to take the space to discuss the many programs of privately supported institutions. In general, the many private schools scattered throughout the country are more wholesome than are those supported by states. Yet even in most of these establishments there is far too much repression, regimentation, moralizing and administrative apathy. The in-

[15] Shaw, "Sponsoring a Delinquent," *Federal Probation,* 13–15 (Dec. 1948).

[16] The Juvenile Reformatory, Preventive Treatment of Neglected Children 12 (Hart ed., 1910).

stitutional palsy has set in even with these much-publicized schools. The faults of the reform school, as enumerated above, are found to a lesser degree only in the privately sponsored schools. They, too, are to be indicted and condemned as unhealthy places to commit delinquent children except as a last resort.

VII. CAMP PROGRAMS

Perhaps the most significant as well as gratifying institutional movement of the present era is the establishment of forestry camps for delinquent boys as has been developed by the California Youth Authority. This procedure is similar to that of Britain where the small Borstal units have been developing during the past fifty years. California, through its Youth Authority, has gone one step further. It has set up several small camps for older youth and one small camp for younger boys (Fricot Ranch). For many years prior to the establishment of these state camps, Los Angeles and other counties had experimented with their own camps and found them successful in dealing with delinquent boys. It was but natural that the concept should be expanded on a state basis.

The work performed in the camps operated through the Youth Authority is in charge of the Department of Forestry but with supervision by the Authority. The work program includes fire fighting, trail blazing and parasite control, all of extreme importance to the welfare of the state. The camps are in the mountains and the boys live in open barracks. Treatment is in charge of trained guidance or counseling personnel. There is an extremely healthy atmosphere in the camps and few escapes are recorded. Visiting privileges are generous, food far superior to institutional fare, the recreational program geared to the type of boys enrolled, and the day's work program meaningful to adolescent boys. There are trips to nearby cities to attend movies and excursions to the beach for swimming are frequent. There is little authoritarian discipline and no cruelty whatsoever.

The Department of Forestry is enthusiastic about the work done by the boys in these camps. It contends that the training the boys receive makes them veteran fire fighters who take discipline in their stride when faced by emergencies. And the conservation work done by the boys is a valuable part of the program which saves the taxpayer money through the years.[17]

The state of California has adequately demonstrated that many delinquent boys committed by the juvenile courts can be given a constructive program of virile outdoors activity in forestry camps. Certainly a camp is an institution. Earlier the Federal government accomplished a similar work in the Civilian Conservation Corps. Camp life has an appeal to most boys of this age. The small camp unit has the distinct advantage of classifying various types so that the vicious contagion that permeates the reform school can easily be dissipated or at least significantly reduced. On this count, alone, the small camp unit has great merit. The concept could be easily expanded to include small shop units where certain types of boys could be sent to develop vocational skills. They, too, could live in barracks or small cottages out in the open. It is a happy idea that work or training supervision and direction shall be under some state agency other than correction. The development of trained guidance or counseling personnel is another significant advance made in California. There is danger, of course, that the case load may be too great for effective work. It is generally agreed that no counselor should be responsible for more than ten to fifteen boys.

The camp idea is fundamentally sound. The Federal government has established a camp for delinquent boys at Natural Bridge, Virginia, and has found it highly satisfactory. Says the *Handbook of Correctional Institution Design and Construction* issued by the Federal Bureau of Prisons (1950):

"Camps are especially well adapted to the reception and treatment of certain classes of juvenile delinquents: (1) those having some special need for outdoor life; (2) those requiring strong male relationships and guidance to insure complete rehabilitation and readjustment to normal, community life; and (3) those who may best be prepared for

---

[17] For further particulars regarding the California Youth Authority, see Ellingston, *Protecting Our Children from Criminal Careers* (1948); also the California Youth Authority Quarterly. [See, also, Articles 124, 132 of this book. — Ed.]

more or less immediate release by camp life . . . . there is little doubt that camps will be more widely utilized in the future for the custody and treatment of juvenile, as well as adult, delinquents." [C. IX]

In the opinion of the writer, there should be attached to each camp unit a few female staff members since their peculiar understanding can be of special value.

One should also mention that a wholesome camp program is far less expensive than the maintenance of reform schools. The per capita cost of keeping a boy or girl in the more rigid atmosphere of a reform school runs as high as $2,400 per year. Camp maintenance is not only cheaper but actually pays for itself; at least in part since the boys are productively employed. The future trend seems unmistakably away from the incarceration of most delinquents in the formalized institution, toward the strengthening of probation services and to a system of small units of the camp type. Institutionalization is no answer to the problem of delinquency.

The problem of dealing with the delinquent girl is more knotty. Obviously she is not adaptable to camp training although there is no reason to believe that some type of small outdoor units cannot be organized for her as well. Young girls do present peculiar problems but there is reason to believe that courageous and progressive steps may be taken to work out a wholesome program for them. Most girls sent to reform schools have been and are sex cases. Each girl needs special study in order to diagnose her difficulties and to effect a plan of treatment. Institutional treatment is no more healthy for her than for the boy. A program of domestic science, beauty culture and development of manual skills should be developed in small units and every effort to return the girls to their families or to some type of receiving home should be made; but always under careful supervision within the community.

The problem, then, of institutional treatment resolves itself about the will to develop programs that have meaning for the children enmeshed in the toils of the law. A scientific age such as ours is capable of more understanding techniques and concepts than are now in operation throughout this nation.

129

Institutions for Juvenile Delinquents *

Donald G. Blackburn

Approximately 350 institutions in the United States serve adjudicated delinquent children. This number includes the federal training school, 125 state training schools (60 for boys, 51 for girls, and 14 coeducational), about 35 county or city training schools, 11 state reception and diagnostic centers, 42 forestry camps, and about 135 training schools under private auspices.[1] It is estimated that on any one day the public institutions have 30,000 delinquent children and 12,500 employees,[2] and that the private training schools have 10,000 children and 4,000 staff members. In 1956 the national average per capita cost was approximately $1,850 a year in the public training schools alone. At least $56,000,000 of public funds is being spent annually for operational costs only, excluding capital expenditures for improvements and new facilities: the private institutions have an annual expenditure of about $20,000,000. Any way you look at it, caring for delinquent children in institutions has become "big business."

These institutions are attempting to provide services that are among the most difficult to administer of any in the entire child welfare field. Their unique role is complicated by variations in ages of the groups served, locations of the schools, qualifications of personnel, physical facilities, and their organizational structure. Even more basic differences are found in the behavioral and delinquency patterns of the children, philosophies and concepts

* Reprinted from "Institutions for Juvenile Delinquents, A Review of Recent Developments," 4 NPPA Journal (January, 1958), 12–21. Used by permission of the author and the publisher.
[1] Estimated from data used by the U.S. Bureau of the Census in its 1950 Census of Institutions.
[2] In 1953, there was, as a national average, a ratio of one full-time employee (including administrative, professional, and operational staff) to 24 children.

of treatment upon which the programs are based, community resources, and public understanding, support, and expectations.

Most people working in the field of juvenile delinquency believe that the training school program should provide the delinquent child with re-educative treatment geared to the development of a healthy personality and his successful return to society. They believe that through a new experience in community living the delinquent child can be led to realize that life holds many satisfactions for him which he can achieve by following socially accepted modes of behavior — not "because he must, but because he may." [3]

Despite their complex functions, our training schools are swinging slowly but surely into well-balanced treatment-oriented programs and away from programs which serve primarily as a means of maintaining custody.[*] Practically all training school children need a chance to develop and mature free from the warping influences in their homes or communities and to learn anew the values of, respect for, and experience in democratic living. Some may especially require remedial educational help; others, a period of controlled training. Some may need intensive clinical therapy; others, the experience of establishing a positive identification with a particular staff member; still others, relief from the demands of close personal relationships. Many need to acquire vocational skills to fit them for later livelihoods; many simply have to learn "to play by the rules."

Programs to meet these needs require the

selective use of experiences in group living; educational and vocational training; religious influences; recreational activities; constructive contacts in the outside community; and psychiatric, psychological, health, and social services. These facts not only emphasize the importance of flexibility in the training school program, but also suggest that each aspect of that program is a part of the treatment approach.

A treatment program cannot be carried out by any one particular discipline alone; it requires more than clinical services alone, or academic and vocational training alone, or custodial care alone. Each staff member is a member of the treatment team. No person should be engaged for maintenance work, for example, without thought given to how he will influence the social growth and development of the children. The mere fact that he is performing only maintenance operations does not mean that boys or girls may not identify themselves with him. Indeed, he may represent the only channel for reaching a particular child, for children frequently associate the work and skills performed by this group of employees with those performed by their own parents.

STAFF DEVELOPMENT

As schools recognize that each staff member is important as part of the treatment team, more attention is being given to selection of personnel and staff development. Work in training schools involves continuing guidance, direction, and staff training. The time-honored method of orienting new employees by the simple device of assigning them to work for a period of time with an experienced staff member is being broadened. Good job performance grows out of the employee's acceptance of certain concepts common to all staff. Time and effort are needed to teach this basic philosophy; one employee may in a very brief and limited contact undo the carefully planned work of many others.

Better supervision of personnel is being emphasized with the result that more administrative positions are being added to training school staffs. Good supervision is time-consuming; it consists of much more than a job-checking process. Regular staff conferences help each employee to evaluate his own job performance and to gain understanding of the

---

[3] "A few administrators see the training school primarily as a custodial agency, with treatment secondary. A few regard its basic function as educational and see the process of correction and rehabilitation as an educative process. But leading thinkers in the field believe that the main purpose of institutional placement today is treatment and that training schools must be essentially treatment institutions with an integrated professional service, wherein the disciplines of education, casework, group work, psychology, psychiatry, medicine, nursing, vocational rehabilitation, and religion all play an important role." *Institutions Serving Delinquent Children — Guides and Goals*, Children's Bureau Publication 360, U.S. Government Printing Office, Washington 25, D.C., 1957, p. 2.

[*] See the thoughtful article, "Three Postulates in Institutional Care," by D. G. Hardman and M. P. Hardman, 4 *NPPA Journal* (1958), 22–27. — Ed.

job and insight into his own reactions to its duties and responsibilities.

Only by the systematic and continuous use of various in-service training and special educational techniques designed to acquaint the staff with their important responsibilities and the dynamics of human behavior can institutional personnel be helped to be more effective during the comparatively short periods the children are in their charge.

The use of training schools as field placements for graduate students in schools of social work has proven mutually beneficial. Schools of social work have also contributed by sponsoring institutes for training school personnel.

TREATMENT EMPHASIS

Clinical service in the training school has made considerable headway. In some instances, this may be no more than a façade of psychiatry, psychology, and social work — window dressing good for the morale of the administration but too limited to help children resolve their basic conflicts. But these specialized services are becoming more generally accepted, the specialists are being given more opportunity to share in shaping the institution's policies, and their philosophy and therapeutic approach are beginning to filter through from the superintendent's office to the classroom and workshop and cottage.

Diagnosis without subsequent treatment is valueless; treatment not based on diagnosis is impossible. Clinically-trained personnel must be available to direct or put into action what is prescribed. Treatment of the delinquent child depends upon what is known about him as well as upon the proper use of this knowledge. Our training schools today have a greater need for diagnostic study of each youngster, made either just prior to his commitment or shortly after his admission. Most training schools now have special staff committees whose function is to determine a treatment program for each child, review his progress periodically, relate his length of stay to his individual needs, and consider his readiness for placement.

Group therapy or group counseling has been gaining general acceptance in a number of training schools. The use of the group to further the individual's understanding of his problems and to motivate him toward self-improvement and self-perception is the main characteristic of group therapy. The group session is an expediency in some institutions — where there is a shortage of professionally trained personnel, particularly caseworkers — but there is no denying the therapeutic advantages of small discussion groups, skillfully guided by qualified personnel.

The increased emphasis on treatment also means more flexible educational curricula with more concern about the remedial aspects of the academic program, particularly for those children who will re-enroll in public schools. Adaptations of each child's school work to a level at which he can achieve, increased prevocational try-out opportunities, and special arrangements for some youngsters to attend the public schools in nearby communities are becoming standard practices in more and more training schools.

PUBLIC RELATIONS

Among other developments leading toward more realistic and flexible training and treatment programs are the positive measures to break down the pattern of "isolation" that prevailed for many years. Recognizing that they need to be accepted as an integral part of the local community, training schools are establishing a freer give-and-take relationship with the larger community in which they are located.

They also are bringing more outside persons into contact with the program. In many instances volunteers are contributing to the recreational program as group leaders; or serving as Scout leaders, crafts instructors, and "big brothers" or "big sisters" to individual children; or playing vital roles in religious programs. The training schools are enlarging the opportunities for staff members to make contacts away from the schools and are forming good working relations with the public and the press. They are lending the use of some of their services and facilities to the community and calling upon the community for the use of some of its resources. Likewise, there is more participation by the students in off-campus activities, such as in summer camps, use of swimming pools, athletic contests and entertainments, religious services, trial home visits and extended vacations, and educational tours.

All of these help to make the training school program a part of life in the community.

The greater use of outside resources for vocational training has enlarged and enriched opportunities for such training by providing more realistic work experiences for older boys and girls. A few training schools permit boys and girls who are legally old enough and are able to benefit from such an experience to work in jobs away from the school.[4]

FAMILY RELATIONSHIPS

The family is being involved in planning for the child's care in the institution. Just as schools have come to realize that they cannot treat the child in isolation from the larger community, they also recognize that they cannot treat the child as a social entity separated permanently from his family group. The child brings his family ties and other close personal relationships along with him when he comes to the school, and these continue to exert a strong influence upon him while he is there.

The reaction of the parents to the child's commitment and their attitude toward the school and its program may reinforce or detract from efforts to help him. The importance of working with the child's family to develop better understanding of what is needed to effect his total readjustment, including contributions to his support, has led many training schools to give more attention to the development of constructive parental attitudes and coöperation.

MODIFICATION OF BEHAVIOR

Schools are growing in their understanding of the difference between the control of behavior and the permanent modification of behavior. This does not imply that control and modification are unrelated; on the contrary, they are related most intimately. The way in which behavior is controlled from day to day has a strong influence in shaping future conduct and changing a child's attitudes. Knowledge that behavior is affected by the individ-

---

[4] The Bureau of Employment Security of the U.S. Department of Labor (USES) has established cooperative agreements with about half of the state employment agencies for services aimed at providing specific assistance and vocational aids to training school graduates in job counseling, aptitude testing, and employment placements.

ual's attitude toward society and self has led training schools to a more careful evaluation of their methods used in maintaining controls. Penalties that humiliate the young person, diminish his self-respect, shake his self-confidence, or confirm his feeling that the adult world is a harsh, unfriendly place are giving way to methods that, though sometimes less effective in altering immediate behavior, build self-respect, self-control, and confidence in others.

Recognizing that a child's attitudes cannot be improved unless he feels liked and wanted and important has led training schools to wider efforts to make the youngsters feel the respect and dignity essential to mental health. This refers particularly to carefully planned reception and orientation procedures for new students, and student participation in program planning. These are not frills. Decent clothing, palatable and attractive food, pleasant surroundings, and courteous handling are essentials in a treatment program; each is a right, not merely a privilege, of every child in the United States.

SECURITY UNITS

Training school administrators are becoming concerned about the problem of the overly aggressive delinquent — the youngster who so often disrupts the program and takes a disproportionate amount of staff time and energy. As the pendulum swings from custody-centered institutions toward treatment-oriented schools this problem becomes more serious. There seems to be no ready answer to the question of how the increasing numbers of this type of delinquent should be handled in the typical training school program.

Certainly, a security unit is not the answer in itself. Of course some youngsters require temporary care in physically secure quarters; indeed, both the aims of treatment and the protection of other people sometimes require it. But youth who are so lacking in self-control that they are unmanageable in the open program are not helped to develop such control by the simple process of restricting their freedom to vent aggression on others or on their property. If such care is to be more than custodial isolation, the program within such a unit must be geared to meet the needs of seriously maladjusted personalities. Dangers to be guarded against are that one institution may be created within another, and that close and consistent supervision may be lacking.

In other words, constant precautions must be taken to keep the security unit from being used without purpose. Unless its use is planned carefully it becomes, like corporal punishment, a crutch that destroys resourcefulness and eliminates consideration of the cause of maladjustment. Without extreme care, security will tend to dominate the total program and become an abused substitute for treatment. As a matter of fact, runaway youngsters and those who are belligerent and incorrigible — those usually assigned to a segregated or security unit — are in special need of study and understanding. They should be brought nearer to the best supervision the school can offer, *not* removed from it.

PERSONNEL PRACTICES

The five-day, forty-hour work week, now standard in many training schools, has raised serious problems with respect to maintaining continuity of program, operating within the budget, and keeping staff at authorized strength. In numerous instances, it has resulted in a shift from the cottage parents plan, involving 24-hour responsibility, to the single counselor system, with its three changes daily. On the other hand, this work schedule is also helping to make training school jobs more attractive to higher caliber people.

Other general improvements in employee status and working conditions have occurred, including specific job descriptions and operational manuals, a gradual increase in salaries and fringe benefits, elimination of the requirement of living on campus, and more time off in the evenings and on weekends.

Educational qualifications of personnel are being raised, generally. Seventy-five per cent of ninety-three state training school superintendents who answered a questionnaire in 1953 had had some graduate education. Forty-one of them had graduate degrees (seventeen in social work, fourteen in education, and ten in other fields). Six out of ten schools employed full-time social workers and two-thirds of these had had some professional social work training. (These latter figures probably would be higher today.) At least thirty-four states provide some psychiatric services, even though quite limited, to their training schools.

EXPANSION OF FACILITIES

During the last fifteen years at least twenty new state facilities have been established, designed to care for a previously unserved group of youngsters or to reduce the load on existing facilities.[5] Two states have recently taken over the administration of existing county institutions for delinquents. Other facilities, particularly boys' ranches in the Southwest, have been created under private auspices. But the most significant expansion in recent years has been the increasing use of forestry camps as treatment resources in the state structure for the control and treatment of delinquency.

Forty-two camps or ranches to serve about 1,800 youngsters have already been established in at least twelve states — California, Illinois, Maryland, Minnesota, New Mexico, New York, Ohio, Oregon, Pennsylvania, Utah, Washington, and West Virginia — and by the federal government (in Virginia). California now has at least twenty-six camps operating (three state and twenty-three county camps under state subsidy); these alone have an enrollment of about 1,400 and an "alumni" list of over 14,000. Arizona, Michigan, South Carolina, Virginia, and Wisconsin are considering developing such facilities.

Evaluative study of these camps is needed, not only to document their effectiveness as a treatment resource but to analyze the comparative costs of care and the potential dangers of exploiting youngsters in a program where the conservation of natural resources involving hard physical labor has major emphasis.

For the eighth consecutive year national reports show a rise in juvenile delinquency greater in proportion than the increase in our juvenile population. This marked increase has been reflected in steadily increasing populations in the public training schools, most of which are filled beyond their designed capacity. Consequently, a considerable amount of new construction and expansion of facilities is going

---

[5] See *Institutions Serving Delinquent Children — Guides and Goals, supra,* p. 33. Six of ten state training schools, including both boys' schools and girls' schools, have populations of more than 150 children — the maximum capacity recommended by the Children's Bureau for an institution of this kind.

on today throughout the training school field. Emerging is a new type of architecture, attractive inside and out, which allows for a more flexible and constructive program of activities to replace enforced idleness and delinquency-breeding custody. This flexible, functional design provides for varied activity areas under visual control, with tempered glass-wall partitioning, individual rooms, and attractive yet durable furnishings and equipment. Today, we believe training schools should be planned to last a few decades rather than a century as formerly.

Although there is a definite trend toward building cottages for smaller groups of children, some schools are still planning for larger groups than the generally accepted standard of a maximum capacity of twenty children per cottage.[6] A few states, including Connecticut, Kansas, and Washington, are recognizing that even smaller groups — more nearly family-sized and family-like — are necessary in treatment, and they are providing cottages for twelve to fifteen children.

Five years ago the average length of stay in the training schools for boys was ten to eleven months and for girls fifteen to sixteen months; the trend now seems to be toward shorter training periods in the schools. Today's statistics indicate an average of eight to nine months for boys and twelve to fourteen months for girls in the more progressive schools. One reason for this is the pressure of increased commitments: practically all the state training schools are filled beyond their rated capacities; the result is reduction in length of stay in order to make beds available for new children as they arrive. Another reason is that improved clinical services and better diagnostic procedures are beginning to make a heavier treatment impact in a shorter period of time.

ADMINISTRATIVE STRUCTURES

In recent years a number of states have reorganized administrative structure and management of state services to delinquent children. This has had a direct bearing on training school programs. The general trend continues to be in the direction of establishing separate agencies to administer services for delinquent children and vesting legal custody of them in the central

administrative agency rather than committing children directly to the training school. In addition to the five youth authority states — California, Illinois, Massachusetts, Minnesota, and Texas — five other states now provide for this procedure (Delaware, Idaho, Ohio, Virginia, and Washington).

Advisory boards or committees for *each* training school, concerned only with that particular school's program and working directly with its administrator, have proven helpful in giving guidance to its program and in establishing and maintaining public understanding and support.

AGRICULTURAL PROGRAMS

There seems to be less emphasis in training schools today on the farm production program and more on vocational agricultural courses. Schools are taking a look at their expensive farm operations and the philosophy and policies behind them. They are recognizing that the principal value of an agricultural program lies in the vocational training and future job opportunities involved, rather than in the production of food for state institutions at the possible expense of exploiting training school youths.

RESEARCH

Training schools are learning the value of continuous study of the effectiveness — or the weaknesses — of their programs. Of the many interesting research projects now under way, space permits mention of only a few: measuring the effectiveness of after-care supervision of varying degrees of intensity, including efforts to determine the proper size of caseloads; contrasting the results obtained in a selected group of training school children having intensive casework services with those in a similar training school group to whom such services are not available; comparing the vocational interests and aptitudes of delinquents with non-delinquents to determine whether any significant differences exist; determining the motivations and social status strivings of the leaders, followers, and the isolates of a cross section of a large training school population; evaluating various treatment techniques, including the group therapy process; and studying the dynamics behind runaways, the roots of hostile-aggressive behavior disorders, the effects of mental re-

---

⁶ *Ibid.*, p. 43

tardation on behavior, and the relation of reading difficulties to delinquency.

The most ambitious research project to date in a training school deserves special mention. A five-man team of specialists (in group therapy, psychiatric social work, group work, and psychology) at the New York State Training School at Warwick has just completed a three-year study; it explored the question of how intensive professional consultation, embodying several disciplines, can produce an integrated institution program and at the same time improve what can be done by the regular staff. Through the services of the project staff, an attempt has been made to inject into the current treatment program a variety of procedures which would significantly widen its scope. Uniform statistical reporting procedures among training schools are rare, particularly with relation to per capita costs, AWOL's, and population movements. However, a national annual reporting program has been recently established by the Children's Bureau as one remedial measure.

AFTER-CARE SERVICES

Treatment is a continuous process that should not end until the youngster is successfully re-established in his community. This means that the entire task of rehabilitation cannot be done in the training school alone. The crucial phase of the rehabilitative process is the three-to-six-months period immediately after the child returns to his own community.

Although these principles are generally accepted, the placement and supervision of youngsters returning from training schools is still one of the weakest links in the rehabilitative chain. "What good does a training school program do a boy when he's sent back without adequate supervision to the home, community, or circumstances which led to his commitment?" The question is asked with irksome frequency but compelling justification, and it will continue to be asked as long as after-care services remain in their present condition. A tremendous need exists for expansion of field counselor staffs, for increased guidance and supervision, for boarding home funds to permit placement where advisable in other than the child's own home, for subsidized group homes and "halfway houses," and for additional consultation and statewide planning services so

that specialized resources and diversified services on the local level can be expanded and better coordinated. Family relationships, community attitudes, job opportunities, school readjustments, leisure-time facilities, guidance services — a weakness in any one of these may spell the difference between success and failure of the released youth.

Practically all state training schools now have available to them some sort of after-care service. However, these programs are operated in various ways and with widely varying degrees of efficiency and effectiveness. According to the questionnaire responses from 109 out of a total of 129 state training schools in the United States and its territories in 1953, after-care services were provided by the training school itself in twenty-five instances, by the probation department of the committing court in fourteen instances, by a state parole authority in eight instances, and by the state department of which the school was a unit in twenty-five instances. The remaining reported that the after-care programs were operated by various combinations of agencies: the training school with the probation department of the committing court, the state parole authority, the Youth Authority, or the local and state welfare departments; or by the probation department of the committing court with the state parole authority, the local and state welfare departments, or the state boards of control.

So many different plans of after-care supervision are operating with such varying degrees of success that any agreement on the best administrative structure for the provision of after-care is difficult to achieve. But the plan whereby the after-care services are provided by a statewide staff, regionally located, serving all state training schools, and directly responsible to the state agency administering them, has gained widest acceptance. "Experience has demonstrated that effective placement and after-care require continuous cooperation with the training school from the time of the child's commitment; this is so vital to success in rehabilitation that the placing and supervising worker must be a member of the treatment team and cannot discharge these tasks as an incident to county social work." [7]

---

[7] "The Control of Juvenile Delinquency in Maryland — Summary and Recommendations," re-

During the last twenty years training schools for delinquents have made many progressive advances, but they still have a long way to go. Many signs are encouraging; others are grim. Some critics claim that, generally, our public training schools are not meeting the treatment needs of many of our delinquent children. According to Dr. F. Gordon Pleune, "The authoritarian program of academic and vocational training and disciplined group living is suitable only for the minority of psychologically undamaged 'normal' delinquents. It does not sufficiently recognize and meet the needs of 'true' delinquents, many of whom not only fail to improve, but may be further damaged through their institutional experience. . . . Control and training by personal influence with more understanding tolerance and individual interest should replace much of the present authoritative control by rules, regulations, and punishment-discipline methods." [8]

The modern training school is no longer free to say that it can serve only the so-called "normal" delinquents. To fill their proper place in the state's network of child welfare services, training schools and their parent agencies must establish specialized services and develop a treatment program that meets the needs of the many children who are delinquent because of psychological factors or because of unhealthy personal relationships in their home settings.

Training school superintendents say that they are receiving a greater number of difficult and more seriously disturbed children than ever before — and a smaller proportion of fairly stable boys and girls who help to balance the group as a whole. Although their impact is not yet fully realized in the less urban states, we have little reason to expect a change of direction in this trend. This is due mainly to the improvement of community services whereby many of the more tractable children formerly sent to training schools are now being provided for by other services. The volunteer social

---

port of a study conducted by the American Law Institute; the Children's Bureau, U.S. Department of Health, Education, and Welfare; and the National Probation and Parole Association, 1953.

[8] F. Gordon Pleune, M.D., "Effects of State Training School Programs on Juvenile Delinquents," *Federal Probation*, March, 1957, p. 32. [Article 133 of this book. — *Ed.*]

agencies' services and the juvenile court probation programs, public school systems with their earlier case finding procedures, child guidance and diagnostic study centers — all these add up to more community services and a more careful screening process. Therefore, the youngster in trouble has available to him various resources for clearing up his problems and is less likely than before to be committed to a training school. The result is that the more seriously disturbed are the ones now coming to these institutions.

The steadily increasing number of births further complicates the situation. The Census Bureau predicts that by 1965 the population of children between the ages of ten and seventeen will have increased 44 per cent over the 1956 population of 20½ million children in this age group. Here the implications are quite clear. Not only do training school services have to be geared to a steadily mounting national population, but in many instances, they are going to have to be retooled and coordinated more closely with increased community services if their important and complex purposes are to be realized.

130

The Role and Contribution of the Training School [*]

INTRODUCTION

The philosophy of an institution, on which any detailed statement of program goals must be based, depends in turn on what the institution is expected to accomplish. In the case of training schools, different groups of people are likely to expect different accomplishments.

Most people working in the field of juvenile delinquency believe that a training school should provide re-educative treatment, geared to the development of a healthy, happy personality

---

[*] Reprinted from *Institutions Serving Delinquent Children*, prepared by the U.S. Dept. of Health, Education, and Welfare, Children's Bureau, in cooperation with the National Association of Training Schools and Juvenile Agencies, Washington, 1957, 1–7. Used by permission of the publisher. — *Ed.*

and a successful adjustment to society. They believe that through a new experience in community living the delinquent child can be led to realize that life holds many recognitions and satisfactions for him which he can achieve by following socially accepted modes of behavior.

The general public expects the training school to control the child for the period of commitment without a recurrence of delinquent conduct and to provide some type of training that will enable him to become a contributing rather than merely a consuming member of society. They assume that the institution will have honest, efficient management by capable, responsible personnel who understand children and enjoy working with them. But beyond this they are not seriously concerned, as a rule, with either the method or the means by which such a change in the individual is effected.

The value of the institution to the delinquent is that it offers a setting which combines controls, protection, and a totality of treatment which he has not experienced in his community. But the youngster committed to the training school usually is not aware of these values at first and has a very different expectation from that of the community which sends him. Despite the best interpretations of the community agencies, he generally views his commitment as punishment for wrong-doing and arrives at the school fearful, suspicious, and distrustful of its intentions toward him. Although he does not see the training school as a source of help in getting along in society, he may quickly recognize the need to conform so as to return home as soon as possible. The dominating factor in the new community, from the youngster's point of view, is that he has become a member of it by compulsion not from choice. This does not necessarily prevent acceptance of the situation, cooperation in retraining, and, in many cases, a real feeling of having benefited. But basically all students are conscious of compulsion and restraint, and their first objective is to get out.

Mindful of the community's expectations, and of the children's fears, and cognizant of the need for treatment, training, re-education and rehabilitation, training schools for delinquents are attempting to provide some of the most difficult services to administer in the entire child welfare program.

Community expectations and the necessity of

imposing controls frequently interfere with the institution's treatment function, which is to help a child develop controls within himself. If the outer controls are too rigid, the youngster has no opportunities for freedom of choice, self-direction and experimentation with self-control. These controls tend to increase some children's hostility toward all forms of authority; for others, they may have the effect of making them more withdrawn. At the same time, it is recognized that external controls can be effectively used to help a child develop self-control. How to create the relaxed environment that will enable children to develop normally while maintaining sufficient controls to protect them and the community is one of the major problems confronting training schools today.

Training school personnel must show the child that his commitment to the institution is an attempt to help him and not a form of punishment. This must be shown in everything they do. Simply to repress or suppress the delinquent behavior is not enough. They should seek to determine why each child has been unable to conform to the accepted standards of his community. To the fullest possible extent, they should try to provide experiences which will so meet a child's needs, alter his concepts, and improve his relationships that he will be able to achieve a satisfactory and satisfying social adjustment when he leaves the school.

A few administrators see the training school primarily as a custodial agency, with treatment secondary. A few regard its basic function as education and see the process of correction as an educative process. But leading thinkers in the field believe that the main purpose of institutional placement today is treatment and that training schools must be essentially treatment institutions with an integrated professional service, wherein the disciplines of education, casework, group work, psychology, psychiatry, medicine, nursing, vocational rehabilitation, religion, all play an important role. These disciplines are all directly related to human relations and personality development; and there should be no question of competition between them. The individual needs of the youngsters are sometimes best helped by an educator, sometimes by a psychiatrist, and sometimes by a minister.

If the premise is accepted that the goal of institutions for delinquents is to train, re-educate and rehabilitate the children under care and that the modern method of accomplishing this is the individualized application of an integrated treatment program — the recognition of the individuality of the child and the adaptation of his treatment program accordingly — the responsibilities of all training school personnel become much clearer. Then workers see their goals in terms of bringing these boys and girls to the point where, while living in a controlled environment, they learn to discipline themselves; where, through self-discipline and the acceptance of more and more responsibilties, they mature, because they have learned to seek status and recognition in a more socially acceptable manner. Such a treatment philosophy is based on modern psychological concepts of the motivations of human behavior and, more specifically, on the comparatively new concepts of the motivations of delinquents.

THE CHILDREN SERVED

"Delinquency" is a legal term, a finding by a court, generally as a result of the child's violation of a law. The term is not diagnostic and is not sufficient to classify the child. Chance sometimes determines whether a child is labeled delinquent, dependent, or neglected. Sometimes another term might easily have been used and the child given a different legal-social status. Nevertheless, only children who have been officially adjudicated "delinquent" should be committed to training schools for delinquents.

Although certain things are true of all delinquent children, it cannot be said too often that there is no uniform personality type to which all or most so-called "delinquent" children belong.[1] A successful rehabilitation pro-

gram must be based upon an understanding of the causes of the antisocial behavior and of how to deal with each individual case.

A child may become delinquent because his life lacks some of the elements necessary to healthy, normal growth. All boys and girls need homes where they are wanted, where there are parents they can depend on. They need a decent place to live, a chance to go to a school which has a curriculum geared to their individual interests and abilities, space enough to play, outlets for their healthy interests. They need adult guidance and supervision, to have their own rights respected, and to learn to assume some responsibility in the process. They need recognition at home, at school, and from their fellows. They need healthy bodies. They need community protection from undesirable influences. The period of adolescence introduces new elements, such as the tendency to form close associations outside the family circle, the strong desire to be accepted as a member of a group, the urgent need to conform to group standards, and the emergence of the sexual drives.

---

[1] Personality types associated with delinquency are discussed in:

(1) Aichhorn, August: *Wayward Youth.* The Viking Press, New York, 1939. 236 pp.

(2) Birnbaum, Karl: "A Court Psychiatrist's View of Juvenile Delinquents." The Annals of the American Academy of Political and Social Science, January, 1947. Vol. 261. *Juvenile Delinquency.* (pp. 55–63)

(3) Bloch, Donald A.: "The Delinquent Integration" *Psychiatry,* 15:297–303, August 1952.

(4) Cohen, Albert: *Delinquent Boys: The Culture of the Gang.* The Free Press, Glencoe, Illinois, 1955. 202 pp.

(5) Davis, Allison: "Socialization and Adolescent Personality." Swanson, Newcomb, and Hartley (Ed.): *Readings in Social Psychology.* Holt, New York, 1952. 680 pp. (pp. 520–530)

(6) Esman, Aaron H.: "Diagnostic Categories of 'Delinquency.'" *National Probation and Parole Association Journal,* October 1955. (pp. 113–117)

(7) Hirschberg, J. Cotter, and Joseph Noshpitz: "The Socio-Psychological Aspects of Juvenile Delinquency." *Disturbed Children,* 89:361–367. 1955.

(8) Jenkins, Richard L.: "Adaptive and Maladaptive Delinquency." *The Nervous Child,* October 1955. (pp. 113–117)

(9) Lourie, Norman V.: *Coordination of the Program of Institutional Care of Juvenile Delinquents in Pennsylvania,* Section III. A Report Prepared for the Department of Welfare, Commonwealth of Pennsylvania, by Government Consulting Service, Institute of Local and State Government, University of Pennsylvania. (pp. 60–81)

(10) Redl, Fritz: "Adolescent Changes as a Factor in Delinquency." *Probation and Parole Progress,* National Probation Association, 1941 Yearbook. (pp. 191–207)

(11) Redl, Fritz and David Wineman: *Children Who Hate.* The Free Press, Glencoe, Illinois, 1951. 250 pp.

(12) Witmer, Helen L. and Ruth Kotinsky: *New Perspectives for Research on Juvenile Delinquency.* Children's Bureau Publication No. 356; Government Printing Office, Washington, D.C., 1956. 92 pp. (pp. 51–74)

When these basic needs are not met, a child may become delinquent and seek his satisfactions in socially unacceptable ways. Other factors may also contribute to delinquency, such as identification with a particular gang, mental retardation, or brain damage.

Whatever the causes of their misbehavior, delinquents are likely to be immature, hostile, insecure, or badly frightened boys and girls. Most delinquent children believe that the world is essentially hostile, since this is what their experience of rejection and deprivation has taught them.

It follows that the therapeutic aim of the training schools for most of the children they serve is to alter their concepts of the world around them. Obviously, this cannot be achieved in an institution that is essentially punitive. Such institutions merely reinforce the delinquent's concept of the outer world and aggravate the problem they are attempting to meet.

What Is Treatment

Treatment can be defined in many different ways. In a limited sense, it refers to direct, individual or group psychotherapy. In the broader sense, it can be viewed as a suitable program for an individual based on a diagnostic evaluation of his or her particular needs. In this definition the proper utilization of the environment is a basic tool in treatment.

The word "treatment," as used in training schools today, means help given to the child — the total effort made by the school to rehabilitate the child and the after-care services in his home community. It denotes helping a child by providing a new and more satisfying experience in community living together with any special services that he may need. It includes a proper diagnosis of the child's problems and a plan of care based on that diagnosis. It implies providing an environment in which all activities are directed to getting the child ready for a successful return to community living. It covers every aspect of the child's institutional life and involves the total staff, as well as the neighboring community. Every staff member, including the cottage supervisor, teacher, clerk, maintenance man, cook, and nurse, has a definite and important contribution to make to treatment.

"Treatment" means more than "training."

As a rule, when we speak of "training" we think of establishing acceptable habits, teaching certain skills, and interpreting to the child the rules both of the school and society which govern acceptable behavior. By "treatment" we mean a great deal more than this. We mean discovering what has caused the child's trouble and, on the basis of this knowledge, attempting to correct his difficulties.

All children coming to a training school have learned to behave in ways that are unacceptable to the community. The training school is in a position to give these children a new community in which they can experience the satisfactions of socially acceptable behavior. Such experiences can stimulate and strengthen the child's maturing process and result in a major revision of his picture of the world around him and eventually of his concept of himself. This may occur without the child's being aware that anything is happening to him. For many children this aculturation process, sometimes called "milieu therapy," is the only treatment needed. For all children, it is the necessary base for any type of specialized treatment.

Making the relationship between the total environment and the child the crucial element of treatment does not discount the importance of special clinical services and program activities within the training school. On the contrary, it allows each aspect of institutional living to be viewed and used as a medium of treatment. Given the climate of treatment, the acquisition of new attitudes and skills, medical and psychological services, educational and vocational curricula, cottage life, and religious programs, will change the child's concept of himself and the world he lives in. These special services and activities provide necessary preparation for subsequent adjustment to community living. But they mean little in the absence of the kind of environment which develops within the child the feeling that adults are there to help, to understand, to persuade — and not to punish. It is only in such a climate that growth and learning can take place.

In some training schools treatment is seen as the responsibility of a department or division, functioning within an ongoing program devoted primarily to custody. Treatment cannot have its maximum effectiveness in such a setting. To be effective, clinical treatment must be supported by daily group living. This means that the institution must provide a team approach to the problems of the child. Only when each individual staff member — administrator, cottage worker, psychiatrist, psychologist, caseworker, group worker, teacher, nurse, and so on — has a genuine respect for the function and competence of the others will the children learn to trust and respect the adult world.

Training schools must place their greatest emphasis on the establishment of effective relationships between the institutional personnel and its student population. Such an effective relationship is noncombative and nonaggresive. It requires a healthy balance between acceptance and permissiveness on the one hand and the necessary controls on the other.

A positive, permissive atmosphere means a relaxed atmosphere and opportunities for choice and self-development, within the limits of the physical facilities and the readiness of the staff to help. Training schools should have as permissive an atmosphere as is consistent with the safety of the children under care. This does not mean a lack of controls. It means the application of positive methods to bring about positive results instead of reliance on custody or punitive practices to bring about conformity. Since permissiveness can also be harmful to some children, a child should have only as much liberty as he has shown himself capable of handling; but he should know that he can "lengthen the tether" as he proves himself able to use freedom properly. Only in this way can the child develop his individuality and learn to work toward a satisfactory resolution of his difficulties.

For treatment to be effective, clearly formulated goals and mature, sensitive, and understanding personnel are required. In order to help the youngster to live happily with adults and gain confidence in the adult world, it is essential that personal contacts with adults be purposefully planned so that the youngster's needs may be met in many different kinds of daily living situations.

It is the administration's responsibility to create and maintain an atmosphere wherein the desired changes can take place. Because of the effect of the administration on the human relationships under its influence, it can be said that the children often experience from the staff the same kind of relationships that the staff experience from the administration.

The primary requirement for an institutional treatment program is the proper personnel. The desirable worker is one who can establish warm, friendly and sensitive ties based upon a respect for the personality of each individual child and can elicit mutual respect and understanding in return. Only such a person can neutralize the necessarily restrictive routine of the training school which often appears to the child as punishment.

Obviously, persons whose own hostilities are easily stimulated and get out of hand cannot tolerate an expression of hostility on the part of the institutionalized youngster without some retaliation. Such staff members will utilize necessary restrictions as instruments of punishment. By the same token, persons who have a great need for affection and gratitude may ally themselves with the children in avoiding restrictions and be frustrated as they seek fulfillment of their needs by this kind of employment. Some persons cannot work helpfully with delinquent children no matter how well they are guided and supported. But many others are capable of good work if they are given administrative support and training.

131

A Residential Treatment Unit Within a State School for Delinquents: An Experiment *

Ralph W. Coltharp
and George H. Weber

It is only natural to find a heterogeneous population in a state school for delinquents which operates without a selective intake of

* Reprinted from 26 *Psychiatric Quar. Supp.* (1952), 149–160. Used by permission of the authors and the publisher. See, also, G. H. Weber and R. W. Coltharp, "Treatment Problems Facing a Boys' Industrial School," 24 *Psychiatric Quar. Supp.* (1950), 203–214.

students.[1] In this population, are an appreciable number of severely emotionally disturbed children who are not able to profit from what is generally known as "group living and experiences" in relatively large groups. Since there are practically no facilities for emotionally disturbed children in the state of Kansas to help meet this problem, or treat these children, a small treatment unit was set up as a pilot unit at the Kansas Boys' Industrial School (hereinafter referred to as KBIS) in October 1949.[2]

THE SETTING AND PERSONNEL

Since no extra funds were available and the demand for treatment was great, the space on hand was used — in this case the infirmary. It occupies a wing of one of the buildings and consists of seven rooms.

The infirmary was staffed with one nurse and two hospital attendants who assumed regular duties with the treatment unit; and one additional hospital attendant was hired. A psychiatrist and a psychologist (already on the staff) assumed responsibility for the unit as additional duties. The psychiatrist assumed the over-all supervision. The psychologist assisted the psychiatrist in planning and did much of the group work in the early months. The other members of the staff carried on various activities as well as the everyday management of the unit. Although a few of the workers had some training and experience in working with maladjusted children, no one had any experience with this type of unit.

SELECTION OF PATIENTS

Generally, admissions were accepted upon the recommendations of the clinical staff meetings. The boys were selected from the general population of the school on the basis of (1) the severity of illness, (2) inability to adjust in

given cottage groups, and (3) the need for more individual attention. It should be mentioned here that the selection was not controlled in a manner which would have been desirable, because, with a personnel somewhat better equipped than other units, and possessing some technical know-how, the writers often were obligated to take severely disturbed boys, as well as boys with special problems whom they were not prepared to manage or treat.

Originally it had been intended to treat only pre-adolescents (age 10 to 12) in the unit; but during the 18 months covered by this report, the focus shifted to treatment of adolescents (boys aged 13 to 16). This was mainly determined by the intense need of this age group.

The total capacity of the unit was 11; and over a period of 14 months, 21 boys were admitted. Of these seven were psychotic (five were schizophrenic, one was a juvenile paretic, and the other was a psychotic depressive). Of the schizophrenic group, two were aggressive and hyperactive, and three were paranoid and withdrawn. Of the remainder, five were borderline psychotics, and the rest were cases of character disorders with strong neurotic trends. In addition, five other boys were admitted to the unit for acute psychotic episodes from which they recovered and were returned to their units at the school without continued special care.

THE TREATMENT METHODS

The treatment methods were of necessity varied and attempted to meet the needs particular to the boys living in the unit and the problems which arose out of this particular social situation, as well as out of the general school environment. They consisted of systematizing the activities, attitudes and group discussions of the living-unit and co-ordinating some of the outside activities in the work assignments, academic and vocational school, and some recreation in the community. In some cases individual psychotherapy was also utilized. These methods were viewed as being techniques which would (1) permit a release for pent-up feelings; (2) re-channelize impulse, into more socially acceptable behavior; (3) build positive interpersonal relationships and encourage favorable identifications; and (4)

[1] Of 100 consecutive admissions during 1950, the conditions of the boys were classified as follows: 15 per cent psychotic, 29 per cent emotional maladjustment of adolescence, 29 per cent neurotic character disorder, 15 per cent psychopathic character disorder, 6 per cent mental deficiency, 1 per cent juvenile paresis, and 5 per cent undiagnosed.

[2] For information about the general Kansas Boys Industrial School program, see Ralph W. Coltharp, and George H. Weber: "The Kansas Boys' Industrial School Treatment Program." *Bull. Menninger Clin.*, 14:102–107, May 1950.

provide experiences from which the boy could gain some insight into his behavior.

THE EXPERIMENT

Although a wide variety of personalities were ultimately admitted to the unit, it was begun with the admission of five extremely active and aggressively destructive pre-adolescent boys. Prior to admission, several meetings were held with them and an effort was made to discusss in concrete terms their general adjustment problems and the probability that, with their responsible participation in a program of activities and discussions, their condition could be at least somewhat improved. Immediately, the change meant leaving their current living unit and moving into the hospital; leaving their cottage staff and relating to other staff members in the hospital; leaving their friends, except for associations in school and play activities around the grounds. Except for the initial reluctance of one boy, who had a close relationship to his cottage mother, the group enthusiastically, and generally irresponsibly, requested the move. The move was delayed for a short period of time with the hope that further discussions would clarify the program and gain more responsible acceptance on their part. This did not occur, and approximately two weeks after the initial discussion the move occurred. Although this orientation seemed to have very little immediate effect (because of the boys' inability to sustain attention and concentration), it was observed later that it did provide some basis for future understanding.

During the early months of their residence, these boys were severely disturbed and extremely destructive. Their destruction of the living unit was carried out in a variety of ways. Frequently they were sly and subtle, often the destructiveness occurred during rage outbursts, sometimes they were open and defiant in their manner. They broke windows, screens and light bulbs, knocked holes in the walls and knocked the transoms out above the doors, jammed locks, tore their mattresses, took their bed springs apart and used them to make steel darts and picks to open locks, removed some of the bed posts from their beds to use as steel clubs, plugged toilet seats and other drains, tore the insulation from steam pipes, disconnected radiators, removed knobs from doors and water faucets, broke tables and chairs, dis-mantled and destroyed a radio, piano and a phonograph, demolished all their Christmas gifts within several days, built fires in their rooms with papers and sometimes with their clothes, and carried metal objects into the living unit where they were "planted" for use in fights. They shunned washing, change of clothes, haircuts and grooming, but sometimes enjoyed playing in sewer water.

The eating activities of these boys were also illuminating. They devoured and gulped their food rapidly, frequently eating with their hands. They threw food at each other and put their hands into each others' food. And while they ate ravenously — and although they attempted to destroy everything else with which they came in contact — they always treated the refrigerator and stove of the living unit with great care.

Their initial group play in the living unit consisted of running up and down hallways and knocking each other down. Occasionally an individual would play with whatever was available. This play was primitive in that it amounted to pounding sticks or rolling rocks or pushing more formal toys around aggressively. This individual play was usually short-lived. If the individual did not stop spontaneously, other members of the group would interrupt the play. As these boys became less emotionally charged, and as they developed into a group, they did a great deal of spontaneous play-acting. This acting began without suggestion or encouragement and continued many times for several hours at a time. In the play area, they generally ignored the formal play equipment, frequently climbed tall trees, swung around in them with ropes attached to the limbs, and broke the dead limbs from the trees. Often they used the dead limbs for fights or fuel for unauthorized fires; sometimes they broke the limbs and spread them on the grass to jam lawn mowers. Rock fights occurred more than occasionally. Sometimes they climbed up the side of buildings, clinging to the down spouts as they ascended. When they reached the top they would run around on the roof and if asked to come down they frequently would curse, spit or urinate down at the staff member, as well as tear slate shingles from the roof and hurl them down at him. These boys also used their unusual quickness, nimbleness, alertness, and general agility to catch birds, pigeons and squirrels. They either would kill the animal immediately or profess a desire to retain it as a pet, only to kill it later when angry.

Efforts to hold group discussions with the boys were met by a whirl of shifting activity, e.g., constant rotation of the members participating in a card game; climbing up a steam pipe to the top of the room, spitting down on the group, and finally jumping down (often on other members of the group); running around the room; arguing, fighting, and shouting to other boys outside the building on the grounds. Sometimes a boy would crawl under the table to smoke. He soon would be joined by some of the other boys, and they would invariably begin fighting in several minutes over the division of the cigarette. Any efforts of the group leader even to introduce conversation were generally ignored. If a boy responded, the others would disrupt the communication by loud arguments and fights among themselves or against the interested boy. The discussion leader was frequently accused of "always wanting to talk," "always wanting to make trouble." Often a boy would playfully, yet aggressively, try to get the discussion leader involved in a scuffle.

Such activity would usually continue in these gatherings with increasing intensity until the boys were permitted to function in a broader environment. A broader environment did not change their behavior appreciably, it only provided more space and objects to absorb the energy.

More than occasionally the group would not follow its program, but became involved in destructive behavior about the grounds of the school. For example: One day the members got into the chapel of the school, which they turned upside down, urinating, defecating and spraying the contents of several fire extinguishers over the pews; at another time, they got into the tunnels that lead from building to building of the school and knocked out many of the light bulbs.

In the academic area, the group fared little better. The KBIS academic school which these boys attended emphasized individualized programs within a group framework, and the teachers offered a great deal of guidance and assistance. Yet these boys were frequently unable to make even a marginal adjustment in this adaptable program and returned to the living unit to function in a more limited environment.

In spite of their disturbed condition, supervised contacts with regular community life were provided. Difficulties presented themselves frequently; they cursed people, made sexual suggestions to girls and women, and stole.

Although nonpunitive restrictions were given, the boys' destructiveness, as well as some of their other behavior, was viewed as unacceptable in a matter-of-fact, firm, consistent, attitude. In other contacts, the staff approached them with an accepting, actively friendly attitude.

In an effort to assist the group constructively to control their destructive impulses, the supervision, guidance, activities and general planning were intensified. This increased planning, permitting very little free time, was too intensive and appeared to increase hyperactivity even though it did decrease destructiveness. With an allowance of approximately two hours of unscheduled time the boys seemed to slow down considerably. Initially they used this time mainly for sleeping, then fighting, and, finally more constructively, in individual building of model airplanes, kites, dog houses, etc. This slowdown could be attributed partly to the positive effects of the general environment.

Although the living unit provided regular arts, crafts, and recreational activities, many projects were planned from the cues given by the boys and the limitations of the setting. As a part of a project to make more play space available to them in the living unit, their services were enlisted to knock a hole in an eight-inch brick wall. Upon completion, this was used as an entrance to an adjoining room. The boys liked this type of activity so well that arrangements were made with the maintenance department to employ them when it needed to have something destroyed or wrecked. Old clocks and motors were given to them to "work on." This gave them something with which to tinker and eventually destroy. Their breaking of dead limbs from trees was organized so that dead limbs were systematically pulled off, and broken for fire wood, which was sawed and taken on camping trips. Hikes through wooded areas where the undergrowth was thick gave the boys an opportunity to use clubs to beat their way through the brush, and establish what they called the jungle trail.

Activities to satisfy their needs to destroy things, get dirty and find things of value were also arranged. Two boys requested and received a part-time work assignment of keeping the area close to the school incinerator clean. On this job, they enjoyed the scavenger activity of going through all the discarded junk, getting extremely dirty and salvaging articles which appealed to them. Smashing the refuse and assisting a staff member to burn some of the material also was thoroughly enjoyed.

In play activity, these needs were also met by difficult treasure hunts in which the boys had to dig, roll logs, climb trees, etc.

The initial treatment of animals improved — perhaps in part because of a project. One of the boys found a litter of puppies under a bush and a project of caring for them was planned. This included carrying food to them and building a house for them which first involved the tearing apart of packing crates and salvaging the lumber. The group became rather attached to these dogs.

In addition to these activities, finger painting, water coloring, soap carving, clay working, leather working, braiding and general arts and crafts were carried on regularly with the group. Although these activities proved helpful, it should be mentioned that many times the finger paint, and clay and water for water coloring were thrown at each other rather than used for more acceptable expressions. And the leather and braiding were used for whips.

In some of these situations, particularly when fighting each other, some of the boys' hostility and fear became sufficiently crystallized to give them enough concern to want help in the immediate situation. Although short, the resulting highly-charged discussions seemed helpful and prepared the way for more organized discussions in future.

The spontaneous play acting was encouraged, and efforts were made to have the boys increase the expression of their thoughts and feelings along with the acting. They enthusiastically recorded their play on a wire recorder, and they generally wanted to listen to the playback, even though it frequently made them anxious. This technique was used mainly for expression although some interpretive use was also made. The major themes of their play centered around disturbed family relationships and antisocial activity. Sex was one of their major themes, besides being included in many other themes. Physical aggression was always an important means of expression. When their play involved disturbed family relationships, it would frequently include a great deal of verbal and physical strife, particularly among the parent figures, as well as the other members of the family. Sexual approaches of the father to the mother would invariably follow parental quarreling and fighting. The antisocial play usually consisted of a suave, breezy, "tough" character burglarizing a place of business and "fighting it out" with the "cops." Initially all the boys wanted to play the prized role of the "crooks," and the action of the police was weak. However, as adjustment progressed, the role of the "crook" was less attractive, the "cops" becoming a stronger and a more effective force.

As they became better adjusted and were able to meet reality demands, the boys' acceptable behavior increased, firmer attitudes were used in reaction to their destructiveness and restrictions were invoked when they appeared appropriate and constructive.

After the unit had been functioning for several months, various staff members requested that additional boys be admitted. Some made their recommendations with a sincere hope that they would be helpful to the boys; others were only trying to pass very difficult problems along for their own convenience; and still others appeared to want to overload the unit to bring about its certain failure. Although not always possible, efforts were made to admit boys who could offset the extreme destructive nature of the original group. So some less impulsive and more reflective, as well as some withdrawn, adolescent boys were admitted. The admissions which followed were gradual. The new boys adapted themselves rather well to each other but generally held themselves aloof and took a superior attitude toward the younger, more openly aggressive, boys. Their aloof attitude later turned to one of condescension. The more reflective older boys exploited the more impulsive younger ones by having them carry out their own latent aggressive impulses.

In turn, the impulsive and openly aggressive boys affected the less aggressive boys in that they excited them into acting out some of their latent aggressive impulses, often stirring the withdrawn boys into rage outbursts. As these different boys became less mutually agitating and gained some group unity, the reflective boys assumed the intellectual leadership for the group, and the other boys gave force to or actually carried out their ideas.

During the early phases of the group's integration much of its activity was antisocial, and this found many devious expressions. The more intelligent and thoughtful leadership influenced the expressions from those of violence and destruction to those of conniving, shrewdness and scheming.

This more complex group made program work more difficult as it increased rivalry among the boys for adult attention, and seemingly increased the number and intensity of unhealthy love attachments among the boys. There were some positive aspects which came out of their associations. The more reflective boys, because of their generally calm and unruffled nature, many times slowed the tempo of the group and imparted a more thorough and thoughtful approach. Their broader range of constructive interests stimulated the total group; many times they assumed constructive and protective attitudes toward the other boys and sometimes even gave excellent counsel.

With the addition of the new boys to the unit, group discussion took on new meanings. With the aggressive boys, group discussions of the more usual type were not possible; however, with the addition of the more reflective boys they became one of the most effective approaches.

After the initial group meeting with the extremely disturbed boys, the group discussions were held three times weekly at the end of the day, with the psychiatrist or psychologist as the group leader. Free expressions of ideas were allowed, but the group leader discouraged fighting, encouraging instead group integration and reflection on the events of the day. Planning for the group was also encouraged, and an attempt was made to develop a "group conscience." Initially all that was possible was to tell the boys that the staff members would meet with them regularly to discuss the day-to-day problems, and would plan for their recreation. Also the boys were encouraged to participate in the discussion of discipline problems.

The group, after about two months of disorganized activity, began to depend upon the meetings and would feel hurt if the meetings were not held at the exactly appointed times. Simultaneously, they would ask for group meetings when emergencies arose, hoping to get some sort of group action. Shortly after this, some of the boys began to show evidence of assuming leadership and identifying with the group leader. In addition, some began to insist upon some order in the group where previously much had been bedlam.

In summary, the results of the meetings may be said to have been favorable in that they created group cohesiveness, group conscience, group morale, identification with the leader and served as media by which some difficult problems could be settled. Heated comments directed toward each other were utilized to encourage discussion along constructive lines. For instance one boy accused another of being a thief and asked that he be put out of the group. Another replied to this, "You guys ain't no damned good or you wouldn't be here." Such acute remarks were vehicles for discussions and helped create awareness of their social and personal problems. Remarks accusing one another unfairly were sometimes interrupted by the group leader; or if it appeared there was danger of a complete break-down of group discussion, the leader often assumed a very firm position. This seemed to relieve much anxiety.

Results — Evaluation

In evaluating experiences in establishing a unit for severely disturbed boys in a state institution for delinquents, the writers will consider the project in view of what happend to the boys in the unit, the boys outside the unit, the staff and the community.

Two of the unit's boys were returned to their regular units. One was much improved, the other unimproved. The latter needed a firmer environment, with boys his own age, and seemed to respond to a more suppressive management. Another boy was committed to the state reformatory after having escaped many times, and having committed many antisocial acts while away. Three boys were committed to the state hospital because they were of an older age group, and the writers had difficulty in maniging them in their own unit. Seven were released from the school to return home, having improved sufficiently to make satisfactory adjustments in the community. Of the remainder, all are making considerably improved adjust-ments as judged by their overt behavior and by their mental status. The gradual degree of relaxation after being in this unit, as well as their ease with adults, was striking. The shy, withdrawn boys brightened perceptibly. The faces of the schizophrenic boys showed gratify-ing changes from a pasty, flat expression to one of life and near-appropriate responses. Although the boys with character disorders were more difficult, some for whom, the writers had thought, there was little hope, showed good capacity for identification, creative activity and generally constructive development.

It would appear that these boys improved be-cause of more individual attention, less suppres-sion, group therapy, some individual therapy, educational and recreational facilities — in other words, a total approach — representing the combined effort of a number of people, avoiding the typical industrial school techniques.

Initially the other boys in the institution reacted with mixed feelings, some showing recognition of the boys' problems by calling them "nuts," "screw balls," "crazy," and the like, while others initially wanted to be admit-ted also. Since the unit started, over one-half of the boys in the school have requested admis-sion, presumably because of the smaller unit, relatively relaxed atmosphere, permissiveness, and enriched daily activity.

Although there was some preliminary orienta-tion, the staff of the school as a whole reacted with mixtures of approval, anxiety and hostility. Since this represented a frank break in the traditional management of boys within the school, house parents were threatened by what seemed to be undue permissiveness or by what, at other times, seemed to be outright approval of destructiveness. Also, since management was on the basis of psychological and social needs, it appeared to be incomprehensible to some; and others feared that this management would be foisted on them. They also feared, with justification, that juvenile aggressive activity would be contagious to their own groups. The considerable destruction of property and the concentrated number of severely disturbed boys aroused many latent problems among the per-sonnel. Although the unit was sometimes the subject of ridicule by cottage parents, they were always happy to transfer their more disturbed boys to it, rather than keep them as disturbing

influences to themselves and their own units.

The writers' own initial mistake was one of not being firm enough. This fact heightened the anxiety of the staff, as well as of the chil-dren. Often when the psychologist or psychi-atrist had to serve as the one to provide physical management, the writers found themselves as a result much more kindly disposed toward the cottage parents, of whom they had previously been critical. The writers heartily recommend that all professional personnel who would advise others in the management of disturbed children have some first-hand experience of this nature.

As a result of the establishment of this unit the community began to expect more services for psychotic children from the school, since many were helped and virtually no such facili-ties exist in the area.

DISCUSSION

The establishment of a special unit for se-verely emotionally-disturbed boys in an indus-trial school presents many problems. Not only should emotionally-disturbed children be sepa-rated from the general population of delin-quents, but they also should be further separated among themselves. A high ratio of well-trained personnel is essential. Adequate orientation and reasonable acceptance of the entire staff facili-tate operation; and, in the new setting, one should not be surprised at strong staff resistance. A near-indestructible physical plant is needed. There is likely to be a tendency toward being too permissive, and this is damaging, in that it increases the anxiety of the staff, as well as of the children. Establishment of this sort of unit, in which some professional personnel are utilized in the actual physical management of disturbed children, proves to be a valuable workshop for those who would guide others in such manage-ment. The use of group therapy, individual therapy and much on-the-spot counseling was most helpful. The unit created an awareness of the needs for such units by the boys, the staff and the community. Perhaps the most favorable aspect of such a unit is that it gen erally demonstrates techniques for management to the remainder of the institution, and helps increase the awareness of the public to the fact that juvenile delinquents do have emo-tional problems.

BOYS INDUSTRIAL SCHOOL
TOPEKA, KAS.

132

California Youth Authority Forestry Camp Program *

Allen F. Breed

Like so many social movements, the California Youth Authority camp program was born of necessity; this has been the history of the entire camp program in California.

The first camp was opened in Los Angeles County in 1931 to take care of transient delinquents until arrangements could be made to send them home to their legal residence. Judge Samuel R. Blake, then judge of the juvenile court of Los Angeles County, when confronted with crowded correctional schools and a marked increase in the number of transient delinquents, asked the board of supervisors to appropriate funds for an experimental camp. Boys were placed under the supervision of deputy probation officers and worked under the direction of the Los Angeles County Forestry Department. Lads were paid a small wage daily and the funds were saved for them until they had sufficient money to pay for a ticket to their legal residence.[1]

This experimental program was so successful that Los Angeles County soon opened a second camp. In 1935 the State legislature passed a measure providing for the establishment of juvenile forestry camps by boards of supervisors for the care of delinquent youths committed to the camps by the juvenile courts.

The success of these camps pointed the way to a more normal and understanding treatment of many juvenile offenders and constituted a most valuable adjunct to probation and juvenile institutions. The framers of the Youth Authority Act must have been cognizant of the early successes of the camp training program, for written into the Youth Authority Act, as amended in 1943, were definite stipulations to the effect that forestry camps could be es-

tablished. So, some 20 years after the first camp was established, California has 15 county camps operated with State subsidy, and 3 state camps administered directly by the California Youth Authority in cooperation with the Division of Forestry.

FIRST YOUTH AUTHORITY CAMP

The actual history of the Youth Authority camp program dates back to the time when in cooperation with the State Park Commission, 50 boys were transferred from county jails in 1943 to the Calaveras Big Trees Park where, under the supervision of skilled tradesmen, they built a camp of 100-boy capacity. They used portable buildings from the Benecia State Guard Camp, which were dismantled at Benecia and transported to the park. This was an expedient, and temporary in nature, but it did relieve some of the pressure on county jails and detention homes that existed at that time.

"In 1944 the Youth Authority entered into a contract with the U. S. Army for the establishment of two camps — one at Benecia Arsenal and the other at the Stockton Ordnance Depot — each with a boy population of 150. Boys were taken directly from county jails, staffs were recruited, and under joint supervision with the Army, the boys entered into the wartime program of varied, necessary, and vital production activity, working alongside civilian and military personnel." [2]

This camp program was successfully continued until after the cessation of hostilities when the need of the Army for camps declined and they were gradually closed.

Following the war, the Division of Forestry found itself faced with a real need for lookout stations, roads, firebreaks, telephone lines, and large fire suppression crews. There was also a backlog of real forestry work which included the replanting of burned areas, forestry nursery development, forest sanitation, check dam construction, and other similar projects. The need has long been there but the money and manpower had been difficult to acquire because of the magnitude of the job.

With the closing of the Youth Authority Army camps there was a critical need to acquire training facilities where the older delinquent boys committed to the Youth Authority could

---

* Reprinted from 17 *Federal Probation* (1953), 37–43. Used by permission of the author and the publisher.
[1] O. H. Close, *California Camps for Delinquents*, 1945, p. 1.

[2] *Ibid.*, p. 91.

be placed. The Youth Authority pattern of re-education and rehabilitation based upon individualized treatment could be well fulfilled in a forestry camp setting. Consequently, in July 1945 the Youth Authority entered into an agreement with the Division of Forestry of the Department of Natural Resources for the establishment of five permanent forestry camps to be located at strategic points throughout the State. Shortly thereafter, four camps were in operation. These were Whitmore, near Redding; Coarsegold, near Fresno; Pine Grove, near Jackson; and Ben Lomond, near Santa Cruz. With the exception of Camp Whitmore, all of these camps are still in operation at their original sites.

LOCALE OF THE CAMPS

The title "forestry camp" can be quite misleading, especially to one who might be accustomed to the dense evergreen growth of a typical mountain or forest area. A natural assumption would be that such an encampment would be hidden away in the bordering tall timbers of a luxuriant green forest. Such is hardly the case in the California Youth Authority forestry camps. In fact, circumstances are quite the contrary. Yet the need for such a fire prevention and suppression organization in the particular locales is hardly less emphatic. The country is generally rolling; the presence of timber is at a minimum in comparison with the wide expanse of thick grass and scrub growth; the altitude is around the 2,000-foot level, the dividing line between the broad open valleys and the higher, heavily wooded mountains. A normally short rainy season swells the many stream beds and the ensuing rapid growth of new green foliage lasts for only a short space of the year. Thus, it is brown and dry the major part of the year, an ideal condition for rapid spreading brush and grass fires.

So, here the camps were built. In these areas the first line of defense for the protection of our natural resources has been created. In these areas with the therapeutic influence of a forestry camp's natural setting, combined with a well-trained supervisorial staff and work projects in which the boy feels he is making a constructive contribution, a foundation has been erected upon which an effective program for the retraining of delinquent youths can be built.

NEED FOR CLEAR-CUT STATEMENT OF AGENCIES' RESPONSIBILITIES

Being an interdepartmental program it is necessary that the administrative structure of not only the Youth Authority but the Division of Forestry be clearly presented in order that the staffing patterns and lines of authority of the forestry camp itself can be understood. This organizational pattern can best be interpreted by a brief summary of the responsibilities and duties of the staff members concerned.

The Division of Forestry's responsibility for the operation of forestry camps is delegated by the state forester to a district deputy state forester. The District Deputy State Forester is responsible to the State Forester's office for the operation of the forestry camps located in his district.

A forestry work project supervisor is assigned to each forestry camp and he represents the District Deputy in all matters relating to Forestry interests in the home camp or spike camp affiliated with the home camp. Under the direction of the forestry work project supervisor is the forestry work project foreman. It is his responsibility to supervise work on projects and fires and to furnish technical skills and advice while so employed, to work closely with the boy's group supervisors so that each can assist the other in their primary responsibilities in order to keep the project moving in an efficient and orderly manner and to insure that proper consideration is given for the health, custody and discipline of the work crews. Although the exact numerical pattern of staff assignments by the Division of Forestry varies at the foreman level, it is usually the policy to assign four such work project foremen to each main camp operation and to assign two work project foremen to the operation of each spike camp.

The Supervisor of Youth Authority Camps working under the direction of the Chief of the Division of Training and Treatment is administratively responsible for the Youth Authority share of the forestry camp program.

To each camp is assigned a camp superintendent who, working under the direction of the supervisor of camps, is in charge of the Youth Authority camp program. He is primarily responsible for the health, safety, custody, religious, educational, and the recreational training of the wards. He is assisted in this operation at the administrative level by an assistant head boy's group supervisor who is primarily responsible for the business management of the camp operation. The Youth Authority staff members directly responsible for supervising of wards are designated as boy's group supervisors. They have varying degrees of responsibilities according to their shift assignments and this class is roughly broken into three categories: out-of-camp supervisors, in-camp supervisors, and night supervisors.

The Youth Authority has assigned to each main camp operation one superintendent, one assistant head boy's group supervisor, ten boy's group supervisors, two institution cooks, a part-time doctor, a part-time Catholic chaplain, and a part-time Protestant chaplain. At any spike camp operated from the main camp there are assigned five boy's group supervisors, one of whom is technically assigned the title of supervisor in charge.

In an article as brief as this one must be, it is impossible to list the many and varied duties of the various classes assigned to the forestry camp program. Suffice it to state that it is mandatory that each staff member understand not only his duties and responsibilities, but those of all other staff members of his class assigned to the program. Toward this end a very intensive in-service training program has been developed, not only to indoctrinate the new staff members assigned to the faculty, but to assist staff members already assigned to better understand their duties, responsibilities, and the philosophy of the department for which they work. It is clearly recognized that no program in any institution can be any better than the quality of its personnel. Likewise, no program can be successfully developed unless each member of the total staff is consciously aware of the major problems involved in the basic philosophy and operation of the institution. Therefore, it is important that every means possible be used to assist in helping those charged with the responsibility of the youths committed to the Youth Authority to more closely understand their duties and responsibilities.

The business management of the individual camps is under the direct supervision of the camps superintendent. It is necessary that he submit budget requirements for the operation of the camp. After the budgets have been processed by normal state procedure and approved by the State legislature, it is necessary that the camp establish fiscal control in order that it may operate within its financial limits. Although technical skills in the form of accounting and the submitting of bids for purchasing are handled by the State central office, it is necessary that the camp anticipate its needs, prepare requisitions, and receive and store supplies as needed.

It is the responsibility of the Youth Authority to provide adequate, suitable and palatable foods for boys and employees in Forestry Camps under its charge. The maintenance of a system whereby each camp will be assured of securing proper rations which have been developed on the basis of the recommended dietary allowances of the Food and Nutrition Board of the National Research Council for the type of ward or employee served is known as the food control.

The food control was developed and is adjusted by the Youth Authority food administrator and it is supervised by the camp administrative staff under the direction of the camp superintendent.

Although medical assistance is provided by the employment of a part-time doctor who makes weekly visits to the camp, it is necessary for the Youth Authority staff to be able to make preliminary diagnosis of medical needs and to properly refer medical cases for further treatment. All cases that cannot be handled at the weekly camp clinic held by the camp doctor are referred to one of the hospital units operated by the Youth Authority in one of their 24-hour school programs.

SELECTION OF BOYS FOR CAMPS

Boys for camp assignment are selected by the Youth Authority Board from wards committed to the Youth Authority by the juvenile and superior courts of the State of California. It is provided in Section 901 of the Welfare and Institutions Code that all boys selected for forestry camp assignment will have attained the age of 16 years and be physically able to perform the duties and tasks as would be necessary in such a placement.

There are roughly three principal sources of boy population: (1) Those who come to the camps directly from the Youth Authority Clinic after the conclusion of the diagnostic and classification process. Most people are obliged to work for a living. The type of work one does is determined to a very large extent by the kind and degree of training we are able to get. If the opportunity and experience for formalized training is limited, it is almost a certainty the class of work would be that of hard back-breaking manual labor. Even in this class of employment there is a great deal of opportunity for a man to find satisfaction if he can learn to do the task adequately and enjoy a degree of success. He must, however, be taught that there is dignity in hard work. A very large percentage of boys who come to the Youth Authority facilities fall into this group who, of necessity, will be relegated to vocations consisting of manual labor. There are those committed to the Youth Authority who cannot or will not profit by highly specialized trade training or formalized academic training. The typical correctional school program is geared mainly to its schedule of trade training or strictly academic training. There is little opportunity for the group who cannot or will not profit from such a training to find either satisfaction or success in such a schedule. There are those who are committed to the Youth Authority, particularly from the less sparsely populated communities, who would actually deteriorate from the formalized large institutional program. It is this type of boy who, after a thorough clinical study, is often transferred directly to a forestry camp placement where he will spend the entire period of training.

(2) Boys who have failed to adjust in a regular training program at one of the correctional schools operated by the Youth Authority. It is often found that boys who have been unable to adjust to a more or less regimented, formalized institutional program can often obtain a great deal of benefit from the experiences of an open honor type work program.

(3) Boys who have completed the training program at one of the correctional schools but who are not yet ready to be returned to society without further conditioning under a less regimented type program. It has been found advisable in many cases to use the forestry camp program as a bridge from the close custody of an institution to the relatively unsupervised environment of open society.

THE WORK PROJECT PROGRAM

During the period that a boy is assigned to a camp he undergoes a period of training in five separate yet well-integrated sections: (1) work program, (2) educational program, (3) recreational program, (4) religious training, and (5) individual and group counseling.

So far as the Division of Forestry is concerned, the principal justification for the forestry camp is naturally the accomplishment of the work program. Although for Forestry the camps are primarily operated for firefighting and fire prevention work, they do, however, have a variety of other projects which offer excellent training opportunities. Many of the projects carried on by the camps are necessarily similar. Thousands of man-hours are yearly expended for fire suppression, hazard reduction, road construction and maintenance, telephone line construction and maintenance, construction of new buildings, and the maintenance of buildings and stations already completed. There is, however, sufficient diversity to make each camp's program specialized to a degree. At one camp, where the State has taken over a large section of a redwood forest, the boys are utilized in projects of reforestation, nursery development, and general maintenance. In the accomplishment of this work, fallen redwoods are split up for fence posts, telephone pole stubs and shingle bolts, and the products thereof are utilized by the Division of Forestry in their stations throughout the State.

At another camp where raw materials are readily available, a pumice block plant has been established and the wards engage in the manufacturing of pumice blocks for the postwar building program of the Division of Forestry.

At still another camp, a vast nursery has been established and several million small trees are now under cultivation which will later be distributed for planting in the reforestation projects of the state.

It is interesting to note that at one camp during the calendar year of 1950, the Division of Forestry conservatively estimated the benefits to the State of California for the work accomplished by wards assigned to that camp as $206,217. For this same period, the total operating cost of that camp, including salaries, operating cost and equipment requirements, was approximately $150,000.

The budgetary procedure for the operation of the forestry camps in California is an interesting one. The Division of Forestry has agreed to pay to the Youth Authority at the beginning of each fiscal year $5.50 per boy per day in each operated camp provided this sum will be adjusted up or down at the close of the fiscal year depending upon actual expenditure experience.

To state that the program is self-sufficient is not enough. As an actuality, the wards assigned to these camps are a financial responsibility of the State of California. In actuality, not only does it cost less to keep a boy in a forestry camp for a year than 'it does in a State correctional school, but the State also benefits from the worth-while work accomplished by these boys while so assigned. Also, the people of the State of California reap great benefits from the work accomplishments of boys assigned to the forestry camps in the constant battle to preserve and protect the State's natural resources. Such a program should not be looked upon as a low-cost method of retraining delinquent youths. "Camps, if properly operated, are no less expensive than training schools. They should not be looked upon as a means of reducing the cost of dealing with delinquent youths. Neither should the camps be considered as a means of securing for the State cheap labor to take care of fire-fighting, reforestation, road-building and other public works service. This work, in conjunction with camps in the foothills and mountains, should be so set up that it will be a part of a rehabilitative program. If camps for older boys are properly organized and the right selection of youth is made for camp placement, the camps can be made profitable from a labor and rehabilitative standpoint." [3]

In addition to the work program the camps attempt to carry out a well-rounded leisure time activity program. The programs are built on a theory of voluntary cooperation rather than any form of forced participation. Staff ingenuity and interest are substituted for elaborate facilities and equipment. Without going into extensive details, the recreational program consists of the following: (1) Team sports — all camps' field teams in the accepted interscholastic team sports and through arrangements made with the California Interscholastic Federation are allowed to have practice games with local high schools. Competition, sportsmanship, and teamwork that are commonly associated with well-organized team athletics have been found to be as important in the rehabilitative process

as any other single attribute. Every attempt is made through extensive intramural sports to allow every boy to engage in some form of team participation. (2) Individual sports — recreational facilities provide for pingpong, boxing, shuffleboard, badminton, handball, croquet, pole ball, pool, snooker, and all the normal forms of indoor table games. Tournaments are frequently held and the boys are all encouraged to participate in some form of individual sport. Swimming trips, picnics, and snow parties are held as the season will allow and frequent visits are made to nearby places of historical importance or geographical beauty. It is difficult to determine where the recreational program ends and the educational program begins.

There is no stress laid on an academic curriculum as such, although through the assistance of the local high schools all the camps provide at least one class in remedial work. The remainder of the educational program, operated cooperatively with the local high school systems, consists of such leisure time programs as a camp newspaper, glee club, hobby shop, photography class, nature lore class and such other activities as will meet the specific needs and interests of the group. All who are in the correctional field know the importance of keeping children in custody as constructively busy as possible during the leisure time periods. In the forestry camps where the recreational and educational program has been placed on a voluntary participation basis, it has been discovered that the therapy derived through the leisure time program has a very definite carryover to the constructive use of leisure time of boys while they are on parole. Many boys have actually entered into a vocation from which they derived an interest in a camp recreational program. Many others, for the first time, have taken an active part in individual or group programs operated by YMCA's, Boy Scouts, and church and fraternity groups.

Religious services are provided by part-time chaplains and services are held at the camps once each week. Time does not provide the chaplains with any more than the opportunity to hold informal services and to provide some religious counseling for boys who have requested it or been recommended by the camp staff. All camps have solicited and receive the utmost cooperation from churches in nearby communities and have been provided with voluntary services

3 Ibid., p. 3.

of interested laymen and young people's groups. The social contacts received by religious groups visiting in the camps and by groups of boys visiting in the church communities have been found highly beneficial both to the wards assigned to the camps as well as the people in the community.

INDIVIDUAL COUNSELING IS STRESSED

Probably the most important single training aspect of the camp curriculum is the counseling program. The means of gaining insight into a boy's problems are varied. The total camp philosophy is aimed at simplicity. Since the population at any given camp is kept to a maximum of 70 boys, it is possible for each boy to become well acquainted with the entire staff, both Forestry and Youth Authority.

Each Youth Authority staff member is assigned a counseling load of approximately five boys on whom he is required to make a weekly written contact report. In addition, special emphasis is made to contact not only one's assigned counselees, but any boy who indicates a desire to relate or shows some symptom requiring individual attention. Every man–boy contact is in itself a form of hotspot counseling and this form of indirect informal counseling is being constantly practiced each day.

Through intensive in-service training, assigned reading, qualified outside lecturers, and day-by-day supervision of the administrative staff, the counselors are constantly developing new technique in assisting maladjusted boys to understand better their basic problems. If a counselor fails to gain any degree of rapport with a boy, changes in assignment are made at the weekly staff conferences. Full and detailed progress reports are prepared by the counselors in collaboration with the rest of the staff on all assigned counselees and these reports are presented to the Youth Authority Board. From these reports and concluding recommendations, the Youth Authority Board determines the future disposition of each boy's case.

Youth Authority camp staffs have taken tentative steps in the direction of group counseling. The initial experience has been favorable, but even though the process eventually develops into true group therapy it can never be a substitute for the individual staff–boy counseling relationships. The counselor holds a position of magnitude in that the trust placed in him by the boy

and the responsibility placed on him by the staff is of the highest.

The camps have no isolation unit or any method of placing a boy in security when emotionally disturbed. If the case is severe enough, it is within the prerogative of the superintendent to remove the boy to the closest county jail for safekeeping. This recourse is seldom used and the majority of the discipline is in the form of grading, restriction of privileges, or in the most severe cases the recommendation to the Youth Authority Board for an extension in the training period or return to the closer custody of one of the Youth Authority schools.

Each camp has a grading system by which all boys are rated daily for their conduct, work, and their social adjustment. Although great stress is laid on the importance of grades both to the staff who gives them and to the boys who receive them, a numerical or alphabetical grade, or for that matter any form of discipline, means little without the constant interpretation thereof that is given to the boy by his counselor. Because of this it is felt that the greatest single attribute of the California Forestry Camp program is the low staff-boy ratio and the informality of the program which allows each boy to relate directly with a man of his choice who is genuinely interested in helping him.

THE SPIKE (BRANCH) CAMPS

Another unique feature of the camp program was the establishment in the early days of small camps operated out of the main camps which are now referred to as spike camps. In the formative years of the camp program, it was often necessary, for the economical completion of a work project, to establish temporary camps at some great distance from the geographical location of the main camp. Such small camps were a definite hardship to those responsible for the custodial and administrative aspects of the program. It was soon discovered, though, that more was being accomplished in these small camps than the mere completion of the projects for the Division of Forestry. So, it has come that each main camp now operates one or more small spike camps of approximately 20 boys. It has been definitely established by correctional specialists that the smaller the group, without materially affecting the ratio of boys to staff, the more effective the training results. Establishing groups not to exceed 20 boys at geographical locations where constructive work is available has been found to be effective by both the Youth Authority and the Division of Forestry. The ratio of staff to boys has been kept to one staff member to each four boys with the administrative control and supervision being maintained out of the main camp. The therapeutic value of interesting and constructive projects, the "esprit de corps" created by a small group, and the even lower boys to staff ratio has more than made up for the loss of some specialized forms of educational and recreational activity.

RETURN TO THE COMMUNITY

After a boy has remained in the camp training program for such a period of time as prescribed by the Youth Authority Board, he again appears before the Youth Authority Board with such recommendations as the entire staff feels will meet the needs of the particular individual. If it is the staff's recommendation that the boy concerned is ready for parole, such a recommendation will be made to the Youth Authority Board. If this recommendation is concurred with, the Youth Authority Board makes an official order referring the boy to parole and continues his case for a period of approximately three months. During this period the placement section of the Youth Authority has the opportunity to make an evaluation of the parole possibilities and places these recommendations in the form of a placement report to the Youth Authority Board. During the same period the camp carries on an intensive pre-parole training program. This is carried on with the cooperation of the camp staff and an institutional parole officer, who is assigned to the camp on a part-time basis from the Youth Authority parole section. Although the entire period of training for the boy while he has been in camp has been in the direction of preparing him for parole, this last 3-month period is spent in individual and group sessions in which every realm of social and parole adjustment is discussed with the boy. At the completion of this period, if the boy's camp adjustment has continued to be satisfactory and if placement plans are in order, the Youth Authority Board makes an order of release and the boy concerned passes from the training program of the camp to a supervised program of parole.

133

Effects of State Training School Programs on Juvenile Delinquents *

F. Gordon Pleune

The magnitude of the delinquency problem and the unceasing flow of lay and professional literature have made restatements of it seem superfluous or even somewhat disagreeable to the frayed nerves of a worried public. Nor is it necessary to emphasize the conspicuous lack of success so far in treatment. Harris Peck [1] has pungently summarized this: "Up to now (our efforts in delinquency) might be described . . . as an attempt to arrest a national conflagration, fed by human and social wastage, with thimbles of therapeutic waters and a program of prevention which seems largely to consist of cleaning up the dead ashes so they will not litter up our community landscape."

Comparatively little is written by psychiatrists about the special problems of our state training schools for juvenile delinquents, where the largest, most difficult group of cases is being handled day by day. This is partly because institutional work is difficult and unattractive to most psychiatrists. The atmosphere is not conducive to research nor to careful, effective psychotherapeutic work. The psychiatric staff is usually a token force trying to keep abreast of a continuous flood of patients, none of which can be given the time and study they deserve. The realities of public institutional life are often discouraging, for not only the psychiatrist, but every staff member faces constant pressure to keep up with the daily routine and with new problems that demand immediate attention. These must be dealt with in the framework

---

* Reprinted from 21 *Federal Probation* (March, 1957), 24–32. Used by permission of the author and the publisher.
[1] "Psychodynamics of Child Delinquency, Further Contributions. Round Table," *American Journal of Orthopsychiatry*, 25:238–272, 1953.

of stringent budgets and limited resources of manpower, which creates inexorable pressure toward a machine-like routine in which practical necessity or expediency outweighs the desirable and ideal. In 1953 a New York State Supreme Court justice, the Honorable Francis Bergan, said of the treatment of delinquency and crime, "In no other field of human knowledge is there a wider discrepancy between what is accepted as desirable and worthwhile and what is actually done in practice." [2]

This opinion is shared by the author, who has worked as psychiatric consultant 1 day per week for 5 years at the New York State Training School for Delinquent Boys at Industry, New York. During this time over 1,000 court-committed children from 9 to 16 years old have been interviewed at least once. Some were studied in more detail in case discussions with their cottage staff, instructors, and administrative personnel. Six boys have been seen weekly for an hour and a half in a group therapy meeting from September 1955 to the present writing. These experiences, along with many informal contacts throughout the institution, provide the background for this discussion. My purpose is to examine the structure and operational methods of training schools from a psychological point of view.

Lag in Translating Knowledge into Action

I feel that despite the rapid growth of scientific knowledge about human behavior in the past few decades, and despite the remarkable interest and acceptance by the general public of modern psychiatric concepts, there continues to be a distressing lag in translating this knowledge into action at the level of institutional practice. While many institutions have subscribed to certain psychiatric protocol, the application of psychiatry is too often intellectual and theoretical. Psychiatric diagnoses, discussions, and recommendations at administrative levels are much more frequent than effective use of psychiatric knowledge in the daily interaction between delinquent child and institutional staff. There is a tenacious persistence of traditional patterns which often are ineffective at best, if not actually destructive to hopes of therapeutic success with delinquent children.

From the very beginning the training school has a most difficult problem. The frame of mind in which most children arrive is not an auspicious one for beginning treatment. Many of them are repeated offenders with chronic, well-entrenched delinquent patterns who have been rejected by their communities and families, having failed in other treatment plans in guidance clinics, foster homes, or private institutions. They are committed because they are not wanted or cannot be handled anywhere else. At the other extreme are mild, minimal offenders — committed on the theory that forceful, quick action will avoid future trouble. Occasionally there are hasty, ill-advised commitments resulting from a wave of indignant "get tough" policy after some especially shocking, well-publicized juvenile crime. Very frequently other circumstances over which the child has no control, such as desertion, illness or delinquency in his parents, may precipitate commitments that seem to him an unlucky and undeserved mishap. The usual beneficent assurance by the court that commitment is for his benefit is viewed with cynical disbelief as another piece of adult hypocrisy. Almost without exception they see the training school as a punitive agency, so that fear, distrust, and anger predominate in their conscious feelings. It is my reluctant opinion that too often the training period does little to change this mood, and that sometimes the institutional experience strengthens their pre-existing feeling that adult society is harsh, unfriendly and lacking in real understanding.

Chronic Delinquency Not Helped by Punishment–Discipline Approach

Historically, society has been much more concerned with their outward behavior than with their inner problems. Its attitude has been primarily authoritative, with emphasis on discipline, suppressive control, and forceful training. Training schools were established a century ago on the premise that delinquencies are "wrongful acts" by children who need "social and moral training and discipline" in order to "master their evil propensities." [3] This concept

---

[2] Frederick A. Moran Memorial Institute on Delinquency and Crime and St. Lawrence University, Canton, New York, 1953.

[3] 29,000 Boys — Centennial State Agricultural and Industrial School 1849–1949. Industry, New York, 1949.

has permeated our entire judicial and correctional structure for centuries, and only recently is there a reluctant, slow awakening to the fact that the punishment–discipline approach is an inadequate, bankrupt policy. Modern psychiatric knowledge has made impressive contributions toward understanding that socially deviant behavior is usually not a matter of stubborn disobedience or conscious intention and choice to do wrong. In 1931 Franz Alexander wrote: [4]

We owe to psychoanalysis the fact that we are now able to approach the crude asocial behaviour of these people without the usual evaluative, i. e. condemnative attitude, but with a sense of medical understanding to which we are accustomed in dealing with neurotic or organic symptoms. Their conduct arises from unconscious motives which are not directly accessible to their conscious personality. This fact justifies the contention that on principle such an individual is afflicted in his conduct in the same manner or sense that the man who has a neurotic or an organ complaint is afflicted with his symptom. Admonition, encouragement, or punishment coming from the environment is as useless as his own resolution, "I am beginning a new life tomorrow"; and his resolution is as useless as would be the attempt to cure oneself of diabetes by one's own will power. The impossibility of overcoming the tendency to act out neurotic impulses by a conscious effort of will, even when the tendency is condemned by the individual himself (and it might be added, by society), is the characteristic which it has in common with organic and neurotic conditions. . . . We are still accustomed to consider disease as something independent of the conscious will of the individual, as a vis a major which the sick person must endure. On the other hand, we are also accustomed to hold the personality of the individual accountable for all his apparently conscious acts, making exception only for those acts which are performed in a state of clouded consciousness (as, for instance, in paragraph 51 of the German Criminal Code). It is difficult to hold a man responsible for his gastric ulcer; it is much easier, as the experience of the war has shown us, to hold a man responsible for his hysterical symptom; and still easier to blame a man for his irresponsibility, his gambling and his incapacity to engage in serious work. To have the right to consider such people pathological, we should have to extend and redefine considerably our concept of disease.

This concept has gained increasing acceptance, so that now it is quite commonplace to speak of chronic delinquency as an illness. But it seems extraordinarily hard for society to proceed logically from this point toward more appropriate procedures in handling the problem. With our minds we profess to understand that delinquent children suffer from a disorder that needs special skillful treatment, but the attitude and actual behavior toward them in courts and training schools is still very much authoritarian and moralistic. Despite knowing they are psychologically troubled and in need of emotional support, personal guidance, and gratification, our training school programs are fundamentally disciplinary and demanding. The regime is characterized by forceful imposition of controls and insistent demand for conformance. We expect certain standards and deprive or punish when these standards are not met. We seem to emphasize the parental right and duty to enforce correct behavior, neglecting the other aspect of the parental role to *help* the child achieve this goal. Or else we mistakenly consider the academic, the vocational, and working assignments as the help which should ensure success in life — forgetting that it is the satisfaction of emotional needs in interpersonal contacts which enables children to become mature adults.

In my experience with 1,000 committed children, over 70 per cent show clinically significant emotional pathology. About 15 per cent have overt neurotic symptoms (mainly phobias, enuresis, sleep disturbances, headaches, dizziness, and various somatic anxiety symptoms); 2 or 3 per cent show prepsychotic symptoms — usually paranoid delusional trends, disorganized temper tantrums, and anxiety attacks. The remainder, over 50 per cent, were diagnosed as neurotic character disorders of various types. Usually a systematic history is available from the community agency or court, which describes the child's life experiences and interpersonal relationships and helps to give a better understanding of his social behavior. Unfortunately, scientific psychology essentially ceases here. The means for an effective, skillful psychotherapeutic approach to the problems that have been defined does not exist, and the child is per force turned over to a traditional "training process" whose aim is to alter his external behavior more than to heal his internal sickness. With grim determination to make good citizens out of delinquent children, the school tries to thrust

[4] "The Neurotic Character," *International Journal of Psycho-Analysis*, 11:292, 1930.

upon them the characteristics of good citizens — obedience, courtesy, respect for law, education, discipline, and work. Whatever its theoretical intentions or claims may be, it seems to me that training school regime in practice assumes that forcing a child to *act like* a normal person will cause him to become one; that delinquent children can and should respond to training like ordinary children do; and that correct behavior, no matter how it is achieved, is the training school's proper goal — an end in itself. The focus is on the external behavior — the symptom, which is vigorously attacked and suppressed — while the underlying illness, although acknowledged, is relatively unattended. This is in some ways comparable to giving icepacks and aspirin to a patient with fever while ignoring the disease that causes it. One must admit that this is better than nothing, and that sometimes illnesses become inactive or get better without anything more than suppressive symptomatic measures. This often happens with delinquents — especially with children who are called "normal delinquents." This group, which in my experience is a minority, consists of reasonably normal, psychologically undamaged children who are amenable to the imposition of authoritative control and can be "taught a lesson." Like an emotionally adequate soldier in the Army, they can successfully adapt to and benefit from traditional methods of vigorous discipline and training. In this type of child the training school often succeeds in providing what the family and community did not — a respect for and acceptance of society's restrictions and demands. But for the larger group of psychologically sick, "true" delinquents, the present approach in our training schools is unscientific, very often ineffective, and sometimes detrimental.

True Delinquency Does Not Occur without Disturbed Interpersonal Relationships

There are confusion, controversy, and multiple points of view as to the causes and proper treatment of delinquency. The origin, life history, and eventual outcome of the "delinquent process" is a vast and complicated story. Peck, Schmideberg, Kanner, and others [5] emphasize

that delinquency is not a clinical psychological entity, but rather a symptom complex with multiple determinants — a many-sided process from both etiological and therapeutic standpoints. Cultural and socioeconomic factors combine in varying degrees with internal emotional disturbance deriving from faulty interpersonal relationships to provide a bewildering array of considerations. Those with sociological orientation emphasize the effect of poor education, substandard economic status, crime movies, comics, drugs, and other social evils. While these things are unquestionably of importance, it seems to me that their influence is indirect and secondary. They promote, but in my opinion do not create the pathological process. Like a culture medium which nurtures but cannot conceive germs that grow within it, certain cultural and socioeconomic conditions foster the growth of delinquency. What I have called "true" delinquency, however, is spawned in interpersonal relationships and not by bad literature, poverty, or other characteristics of social and cultural environment. This is not philosophic reductionism, an attempt to reduce the entire problem of delinquency to a matter of psychopathology and psychotherapy. Such a point of view would be just as one-sided and ineffectual as the present overemphasis on morality and discipline. Nevertheless, in my experience the conclusion is inescapable that *true delinquency* does not occur *without* disturbed interpersonal relationships. This is the continuing source of trouble and improvement of this basic pathology in the *sine qua non* of successful treatment. Failing this, our program of enforced morality, education, and discipline builds a flimsy structure without foundation, which sooner or later tends to collapse.

In varying degrees all truly delinquent children [6] have experienced a lack of constructive, dependable loving relationships or they have experienced an excess of destructive aggression in their relationships with parent figures. Usually this pathogenic condition must have been fairly continuous and severe before a truly delinquent pattern appears. It happens when a child has suffered so much emotional injury that his personality is dominated by anger, fear, and distrust. He is intolerant of the tensions of so-

---

[5] "Psychodynamics of Child Delinquency, Further Contributions. Round Table," 1953. *American Journal of Orthopsychiatry*, 25:238–272.

[6] Excluding cases of mental defect, organic brain damage and constitutional deficiencies.

cial and interpersonal adjustment and he turns to, or remains at, immature levels of instinct gratification. He seeks immediate tension-relieving pleasure in stealing, truancy, sadistic aggression, etc., and seems to claim immunity from demands of reality. *The most logical, effective way of treating a truly delinquent child is through creating a situation in which corrective interpersonal relationships can occur. This should be the primary focus of the institutional program.* Unless the treatment period succeeds in arousing whatever capacity the child has to feel admiration, respect, affection, and desire to identify with emotionally healthy adults, it achieves little more than an increased fear and dislike of authority. He may conform to an authoritative program, but, as we so often see, it is a transient, symptomatic change lasting only so long as forcible controls from outside himself are present. Everyone agrees that in handling most delinquent children a rather rigid control must be maintained — that firm, authoritarian supervision is both necessary and therapeutically desirable. The training school realizes this and properly provides it. But without the nourishment of emotionally gratifying experiences with adults no child can develop a genuine acceptance of social requirements and a willingness to establish controls from within. If the treatment approach lacks therapeutic emotional experiences and the commitment turns out to be an exercise in enforced submission to impersonally applied demands, then it has not only failed, but has committed a further aggression. It has fostered the distrust and disillusionment the child has already experienced with adult society. There is an ancient admonition to the physician regarding his treatment of patients: *Primum non nocere —* "First of all, do nothing to harm." An unconstructive institutional experience may confirm a child's feeling that adults demand obedience without providing emotional satisfaction in return and that his conflict with society is irreconcilable.

TRAINING SCHOOLS URGENTLY IN NEED OF IMPROVEMENT

The remainder of this paper will briefly discuss some of the reasons for considering that our state training schools are in urgent need of improvement. Although this discussion deals mainly with negative factors and criticisms, it is not intended as an indictment of the particular institution where these observations were made. It is concerned with training school programs in general. In my opinion the New York State School at Industry is a good institution compared to others in its field. I have great respect and admiration for many sincere, capable members of its staff. These all-too-rare people, it seems to me, are faced with trying to perform major repairs on human lives without adequate therapeutic tools. They perform an enormously difficult task with limited resources and often with rather surprising success.

Here at Industry are nearly 500 boys from 9 to 16 years old, with an admission rate of about 350 per year. They live in 20 cottages rather widely scattered over a large tract of land. Each cottage houses about 25 boys and is managed by one married couple during the day and one supervisor alone through the evening and night. Aside from school teachers, vocational instructors, clinic staff and maintenance employees with whom some of the boys work, the major role in treatment is played by these cottage parents and supervisors. It is they who have the most immediate and continuous contact, and therefore the greatest influence with the boys. The cottage staff faces these most difficult problems in abnormal human behavior without the benefit of previous formal education in personality problems, emotional illness, or treatment techniques. When one stops to think it over, this is really a striking situation. In no other field (excepting, perhaps, politics) do we even allow, much less hire, untrained people to do a vital job requiring special knowledge and skill. In business, for example, or nursing or teaching one is not placed in a vital position until he has studied for years and demonstrated competence in the field. Surely the treatment of delinquent children is an important and difficult task. Since it is intimately concerned with human emotions and behavior, some knowledge and ability in psychological matters would seem to be a basic requirement. Yet here we depend upon people with no specific preparation. Aside from whatever native skill they possess, they must learn the job. The entire cottage staff of about 130 is under the direction of four administrative heads whose days are already overfilled with administrative work aside from the burden of training and supervising the staff. As a result, the important problem of on-the-job training becomes largely a matter of irregular and fairly infrequent contacts. The only systematic educational program for cottage parents consists of five or six meetings a year in the evening when a majority of staff is free to attend on their off-duty time. Any other planned meetings or unscheduled individual contacts between cottage personnel and their senior staff are concerned with matters of administrative procedures and policies or advice and disposition of some immediate problem of behavioral maladjustment in the institution. None of these are specifically designed for education in psychological knowledge and technique, nor are they attended by a psychiatrist.

OBSTACLES IN TREATMENT

Opportunities for the psychiatric clinic staff to participate in a clinical or educational role in the psychological life of the institution are so infrequent as to preclude any co-ordinated program of psychotherapeutic education or supervision. There are many reasons for this, some of which are simple and obvious: The first is a matter of statistics. At present there are three full-time social workers (although the table for organization provides for five, there have never been more than four at any one time in the past 5 years), one full-time psychologist and one visiting psychiatrist on 3 days of the week. This is the total professional psychiatric staff for an average census of nearly 500 boys with a yearly turnover of 70 to 75 per cent. At each visit the psychiatrist must read the history, interview, and write opinions and recommendations on four or five new cases. This occupies essentially the whole day, leaving little time for consultative meetings with clinic, cottage, or administrative staff, and no time at all for repeated treatment visits on any one case. The psychiatric attention given in these routine single visits is necessarily hasty and perfunctory — largely limited to diagnostic evaluation. The idea that professional psychotherapy exists at Industry is a complete misconception, yet many of the court commitment papers imply and even directly state their expectation of such treatment as they send increasing numbers of emotionally disturbed boys to Industry.

When a boy is not "adjusting" and disrupts the standard cottage program, the staff turns to the psychiatric clinic. Urgent requests for advice and help usually result in referral to the three overburdened social workers for counseling. Nonconformance to the program often dictates the choice of cases and demands the attention of the clinic more than psychiatric judgment as to which cases would be most amenable to counseling efforts. Meanwhile, the boys who do conform and whose psychological problems are therefore less obvious and troublesome command less attention and are not individually worked with by anybody. A conservative estimate would be that 75 per cent of cases proceed through their commitment term without any direct contact with psychiatric personnel except for the routine "intake" workup, and a brief interview called the "6-week review" to evaluate whether they are correctly assigned in their program. The psychiatric clinic is forced to expend most of its time in these routine nontherapeutic "workups" and in dealing with the disturbance-causing cases on a sort of stopgap emergency basis. This is a relatively ineffectual therapeutic effort. It is treating the program rather than the individuals. Even if it were more plentiful, we must realize that treatment in office interviews by psychiatric personnel cannot substitute for treatment within the basic framework of the institution's structure and program, i. e., in the cottages, shops, and school.

A second obstacle to any effective cooperation between psychiatric and cottage staff is the inability to arrange meetings during the working day. Because there are no replacements, because most of the house fathers have various daily jobs outside the cottage involving maintenance of the institution, while the housemothers are busy running the cottage household, they have to be continuously on duty. It is a very rare occurrence when any of them can or do come to the clinic for consultation. Somewhat less rarely a clinic staff member may put aside his office schedule and travel out to a cottage for a discussion. This means, however, interrupting his own and the cottage parents' work routine. This same difficulty contributes to the infrequency of contact between both cottage and clinic staff and the administration for purposes of discussion and study beyond the routine business of running the institution.

Lack of opportunity for learning through mutual stimulation and discussion makes psychological education and integration of staff well nigh impossible. It also fosters that greatest of all institutional problems — a feeling among the various departments of isolation, lack of status, and loss of morale with dull resignation to the routine.

Aside from lack of previous training, adequate supervision, and education on the job, a third and most important obstacle to the psychotherapeutic success of the training school is the very structure of the setting in which the cottage staff works. Average parents find it hard enough to supply three or four children with the emotional gratification they need. It is humanly impossible for any two people to be adequate parent substitutes to 25 boys at one time. There cannot be the intimate contact, the personal warmth and guidance that every adolescent should have. Commonsense knowledge tells us that delinquent children need this even more than normal ones — yet in institutional practice they get incomparably less of it. Close, affectionate relationships, with mutual regard and freedom of emotional interaction between adult and child are at a minimum. When 25 active boys are in the same room with one adult, it is inherent in the nature of things that the adult must become more a controlling authority than a companion. This is especially true when the total indoor living area is small and congested. In cottages at Industry, for example, the total first floor space (living room, dining room, and kitchen) is 1,315 square feet. Including space occupied by tables and sundry furniture, each of the 25 boys has about 50 square feet — an area 5 x 10 feet — to live in. The dormitory sleeping quarters total 1,089 square feet — an average space of 4 x 10 feet — in which to dress and sleep. Such physical compression promotes irritability and aggression, which requires additional restraint and regimentation. All the functions of living — washing, eating, coming, and going, and even relaxing — must be done on signal, under close supervision, and within rigid limits of behavior. Whereas the theoretical intention and claim of the cottage plan is to provide a constructive, corrective experience in family-like living, it becomes more like a prolonged exercise in group discipline. The cottage staff tends to be perceived as impersonal figures — proponents of discipline and reporters of conduct to higher levels from which a parole must be earned. Consider that the simple daily care and management of a household of 25 is a rather formidable task for any two parents even if the boys are normal cooperative ones. How much time and interest can a houseparent devote to understanding and guiding each one and how much can each boy feel that these houseparents are his personal helpers with an awareness of him as an individual with problems? The imperative need to maintain an orderly routine, and often a lack of psychological insight, result in a strong tendency to treat the child's behavior entirely as a moral problem and to try to correct it by exerting more and more control, pressure and punishment, which often only worsens the situation.

"You've Got To Stop This!"

A case in point is one tall, healthy 15-year-old white boy who attended the weekly group therapy meetings. He is of average intelligence, but academically weak, having been in an institution from age 7 to 12 and changing schools frequently thereafter, as he was shifted between his separated father and mother. For a year previous to commitment he lived with his mother and her Negro paramour in a large city where he encountered frequent ridicule and social rejection on this score. He is a fairly good-humored, but aggressive lad who has a considerable emotional investment in his physical strength and ability to fight. This was his trademark among his peers, and he admitted it was an enjoyable relief of inner tension and boredom to have a fight. This had led him into frequent difficulty at his cottage where he was usually deprived of cigarettes, made to polish the floor, or physically punished by the cottage staff for his aggressiveness. His 8-month report was critical and he was considered "in need of further training." This boy had been reticent but increasingly friendly in the group therapy sessions. In the 30th meeting the therapist asked him why he was so often in trouble with fighting. He replied with more emotion than he had ever shown before: "Cause I want to get my brains knocked out. I'm no good anyway. My mother always said I was stupid. All I can do is fight." Further discussion revealed how at the cottage one staff member in particular played into this neurotic self-destructive defense. The boy described how this man frequently said to him, "You're a dumb jerk, R., you're asking for it and unless you cut this out, some day you're really going to get your block knocked off."

Instead of understanding and trying to help the feelings of unworthiness and depression motivating this lad's delinquent behavior, it was met with criticism, punishment, and a vigorously authoritarian demand, "You've got to stop this." Such examples are not rare exceptions and could be cited many times over. If not typical they are at least much too frequent. Except in a few instances they are not due to sadistic aggression on the part of the staff. Rather, they reflect two basic deficiencies in training school programs: (1) Lack of therapeutic knowledge and a misguided idea that to enforce correct behavior is the substance of a training school's function, and (2) a lack of sufficient treatment personnel and facilities to structure the program as a primarily therapeutic process instead of a working and living routine. With 25 boys to manage, the cottage staff is forced to give precedence to establishing a workable equilibrium rather than to a constructive, corrective emotional interaction with them as foster children. Life becomes largely a system of automatic rewards and punishments based on external behavior, with little attention to the motives and feelings underlying it. Privileges are granted or taken away on the basis of obedience or infractions of rules. By being pressed into the service of group discipline and control, pleasurable activities lose much of their capacities for fostering healthy, positive relationship with adult staff. They become automatic payments for having complied with regulations, a quite depersonalized process in which there is little warmth or appreciation on either side. This promotes rather than cures their delinquency. It perpetuates and strengthens the main bastion of a delinquent child's psychology which is that since adults take such authoritative charge of his behavior, since they completely control what is permitted and what is restricted, and will punish him when he transgresses, he need not feel guilt or take responsibility for his actions. He can continue as before to seek pleasure and avoid punishment — a repetition of the delinquent way of life he has already learned in dealing with adults in the past.

LACK OF TRAINING AND PRESSURES OF WORK RESULT IN INABILITY TO MEET INDIVIDUAL NEEDS

One of the striking features of delinquent psychology is a tenacious projective defense — an uncanny ability to perceive and emphasize in adults any qualities of inconsistency, injustice, and lack of regard for others of which the delinquent himself is guilty. This was especially evident in the behavior of the six boys seen in group therapy over a 10-month period. They show an almost insatiable need to criticize, to depreciate and accuse the staff of insensitiveness to their needs as individuals and failure to provide a considerate, gratifying, understanding relationship. The therapist often realized with dismay that there is considerable reality to these claims. Oftentimes one is hard put to distinguish clearly between fact and fancy and to define wherein the claim is irrational, for there is in truth a distressing tendency to override therapeutic consideration of the individual in favor of the needs of the group and the institution. The training school expects certain ethical and moral standards, yet its program does not tend to foster whatever capacity a boy has to develop a sense of individual worth and dignity. It offers little opportunity to make decisions and choices for himself and to have a voice in his problems in an atmosphere of tolerance by his supervisors. This deadening of initiative and removal of responsibility for influencing his living conditions have an insidious and adverse effect in training school life. Unless someone has the time and the ability to relate to him with understanding as well as authoritativeness, with helpfulness as well as demands, he can only go on believing that the ideals and standards propounded by the training school are an unrewarding illusion. His pattern of projecting onto adults his own hostility remains unchanged, and he continues to evade any true sense of morality or motivation to acquire self-responsibility. He provocatively forces authority figures to make him do what *they* think is right and to prevent or punish him for what they think is wrong. It is their concern and burden, not his, and instead of learning through constructive interrelationships with cottage staff to establish controls within himself, he becomes further entrenched in the need for continued imposition of controls from without.

Countless times in early group therapy meetings when boys present problems or complaints of injustice relating to cottage life, I have asked whether they have discussed this with their houseparents or supervisors. Invariably they respond with disdainful surprise or disbelief, as if it were naive or ridiculous to think that this was practical. They put forth many obstacles:

(1) There is practically no time or place for private talks with cottage staff. They are always in a group and the staff member has to be tending to the group;

(2) The staff has to treat every boy the same, anyway. They cannot individualize or grant special consideration for certain needs and wishes. (Every cottage staff member I have talked with confirms these two points); and

(3) The boys fear being called "cheesers" if they attempt close, individual contact with staff. They feel it is not encouraged by the staff and will bring retaliation from their peers.

On occasion, when boys have complained of injustice or mistreatment, I have offered to arrange a meeting and go with them to talk out the problem with the staff member. They avoid this and openly fear that such frank approach would be resented by the staff member as insubordination and would directly or indirectly result in a disadvantage to themselves. Sometimes their reluctance is based on having misrepresented or exaggerated the facts to me, but on the one occasion when a boy did go with me to talk over a matter with his cottage staff, his fears were borne out. The discussion was accepted but resented, leaving him with the feeling that by voicing his opinions he had exposed himself to disapproval and suspicion.

These are not good conditions to promote emotional and social growth. They leave untouched the typical delinquent's feeling that since no one is really interested, helpful, and trustworthy anyway, he is justified in continuing his distrustful bitterness. An effective treatment process should not only permit but should actively take initiative to show a child that when he is in trouble he can expect a helpful, inquiring, receptive attitude from adults — that he can approach them with confidence instead of fear. As yet, the training school program does not sufficiently provide this. Its insistent emphasis on behavior promotes expectation of punishment as the only outcome of failure in performance. Too often, upon leaving its program they are still unencumbered by love and gratitude, undeterred by anything except fear of deprivation and punishment. I should like to emphasize again that in most instances the criticisms here expressed do not imply personal failure or disinterest on the part of the staff. A large majority of them do try to provide some home and parentlike touches to relieve the depressing institutional routine. On holidays many houseparents spend extra hours and money from their own resources to provide an unusually good meal or to decorate the cottage and have a party. The administration solicits funds to provide Christmas gifts and occasional extra benefits for those boys who are financially destitute. It carries on an excellent physical and recreational activities program within the limits of its resources and is constantly striving to enlarge these. Boy Scout activities, athletics, hobby crafts and, whenever possible, trips outside the institution in small groups to a circus, a movie, etc., are a constructive, useful part of the program. There is no lack of these typically American traditions. But physical exercise, recreation, and occasional benevolence are not therapy in themselves. They cannot prevent or repair the damage resulting from pathological, social, and personal relationships.

TRAINING SCHOOLS FOR JUVENILE OFFENDERS MUST BE PSYCHOTHERAPEUTICALLY ORIENTED

It is my conviction that to be more successful, state training schools for juvenile offenders must become more psychotherapeutically oriented. To transform the time-honored training regime into a better treatment process would involve far-reaching and expensive changes. It would necessitate having much smaller treatment groups and larger numbers of cottage personnel with a basic psychological orientation and training who can function as therapists rather than as working employees with the additional duty of trying to curb delinquency. It would involve having a larger maintenance and service staff so that the cottage personnel could devote themselves primarily to therapeutic relationships and to educational and consultative work with an enlarged psychiatric clinic staff.

It is realized that these are sweeping recommendations. It is a far cry from ideal recommendations to the pressing realities of the present. Those who have the burden of responsibility for administering and financing institutions such as Industry may impatiently call for something more "practical," which usually means something that would not cost too much. There is evidence, however, from other fields of scientific endeavor that good treatment, even though initially expensive, is practical and economically sound. Society has been willing to provide enormous budgets for research and treatment of tuberculosis, polio, heart disease, and other disabling illnesses, with results that are generally considered worth while. It is possible that our present policy in treating delinquency is "penny wise and pound foolish." Psychotherapeutic treatment is expensive, but it might in the long run cost no more than we now pay to protect ourselves from, to prosecute, and support in prisons many thousands of unrejuvenated boys and girls who now pass through our training schools. It is more economical to spend more in the beginning for good treatment than to take care of a person who does not get well for years and years afterward. It is sometimes said that the value of a so-called "psychotherapeutic approach" in training schools is doubtful since no one has proved it would produce a higher "success rate." "Success" is a difficult thing to measure in this type of work. If it means future avoidance of courts and prisons, it may be true that present "success rates" would be no higher with psychotherapeutic techniques. Since, however, to my knowledge no training school has ever been able to really try it, there is equally no proof that "success" as measured by court statistics would *not* be higher with a skillful psychotherapeutic approach. In either case this type of debating misses the main point. It is somewhat comparable to arguing that since just as many children will survive by drinking only water and not milk, why go to the trouble and expense of providing milk. In the first place, it is a doubtful claim, but even if true the final product is not likely to be as healthy (and successful). In dealing with human behavior, success is not (or should not be) measured by legal statistics alone, but by the contribution our efforts have made to developing a child's capacities for healthy emotional and social growth — admittedly a difficult thing to tabulate statistically.

In treating physical disease, if a type of therapy is scientifically sound, we do not hesitate to apply it because of knowing that in spite of it some patients will not recover. Nor do we make it conditional upon guarantees that the patient will never show the same symptom again. We consider it an ethical responsibility to do the best that is possible regardless. In this age of mental health hygiene it would hardly seem necessary to prove that emotionally satisfying, constructive, interpersonal relationships are more vital than group exercise, education, and discipline for the development of a mature, non-delinquent personality. Our training school programs should be refocused to emphasize repair of what psychological damage is reparable and to providing a better atmosphere for cultivating in its children whatever latent capacities they have for psychological growth. Our present, so-called practical, economical methods are no bargain. There is no shortcut to developing good citizens and no substitute for good treatment.

SUMMARY AND CONCLUSIONS

Our state training schools are not meeting the treatment needs of a majority of our delinquent children. The authoritarian program of academic and vocational training and disciplined group living is suitable only for the minority of psychologically undamaged "normal" delinquents. It does not sufficiently recognize and meet the needs of "true" delinquents, many of whom not only fail to improve, but may be further damaged through their institutional experience. More nearly family-sized and family-like treatment groups are needed. Control and training by personal influence with more understanding tolerance and individual interest should replace much of the present authoritative control by rules, regulations and punishment–discipline methods.

The present psychiatric facilities are inadequate. The clinic functions as a routine diagnostic service and is relatively isolated from active, effective participation in the total treatment program. It cannot provide specific psychiatric treatment nor an effective consultative liaison with cottage staff.

Enlargement and education of the treatment staff (especially cottage personal) in a psychological approach to understanding and handling of delinquent children are sorely needed.

A more psychotherapeutically oriented program would be initially expensive, but good treatment is in the long run economically sound.

134

Two Approaches to the Cure of Delinquents *

William and Joan McCord

I. INTRODUCTION

Boston's scholarly Dr. Harry Solomon often remarks to his younger, sometimes discouraged psychiatric colleagues, "The cure usually bursts upon the scene long before we can isolate, let alone explain, the causes of disease." Quinine stopped malaria dead in its tracks long before its responsible carrier, the anopheles mosquito, was trapped. Syphilis had been effectively treated by Paracelsus' mercury three centuries before the discovery of its causes. Today, modern medicine checks the devastation of cancer with radium while researchers still ponder the etiology of the ailment.

Solomon's sapient observations on the course of medical progress offer a modicum of hope for the younger, and in many ways, symbiont science of criminology. Slowly the devious origins of delinquency are giving way before the onslaught of scientific research. Recent studies by Sheldon and Eleanor Glueck, for example, have vanquished the plausible, but unsatisfactory, causative theories of differential association, constitutional types, † and neuroticism. As an epochal result of *Unraveling Juve-*

nile Delinquency, the family milieu emerges as the decisive factor in antisocial behavior.

A delinquency prediction scale developed by the Gluecks has proven 91 per cent accurate in startling corroborative studies by Richard Thompson,[1] Selma Glick and Bertram Black.[2] Nevertheless, the enlightening Glueck studies have not reached completion. Supported by a substantial grant from the Ford Foundation, the Gluecks are continuing their research in predictive scales and into the relation of the family to crime.

Eventually, Dr. Glueck's aim of "establishing the patterns of factors and interplays which almost inevitably make for delinquency and crime"[3] will reach fruition. Until that time, fragmentary studies may be of some value in establishing the relative efficacy of delinquent treatment.

Modern criminologists recognize the vital need for assessing the results of treatment. This paper, although of limited scope, attempts to distinguish the effects of two institutional regimes on the personalities of delinquents.[4]

II. AIM AND SETTING OF THE RESEARCH

Follow-up studies by objective investigators have clearly shown the disheartening failure of the modern juvenile reformatory. There is wide agreement that approximately 80 per cent of reformatory "graduates" recidivate after their release.[5] Old-fashioned training school administrators excuse this paucity of success by asking, "Can any treatment really change juvenile delinquents?"

This study attempts to give a tentative answer to that query by comparing a progressive

---

* Reprinted from 44 *J. Crim. L., Criminology and Police Science* (1944), 442–467. Used by permission of the authors and the publisher. See, also, W. and J. McCord, *Psychopathy and Delinquency*, New York, Grune and Stratton, 1956, 123–176; H. A. Weeks, *Youthful offenders at Highfield*, Ann Arbor, U. of Michigan Press, 1958. H. E. Freeman and H. A. Weeks, "Analysis of a Program of Treatment of Delinquent Boys," 62 *Am J. Sociology* (1956), 56–61. — Ed.

† But see Article 13 of this book. — Ed.

[1] Richard Thompson, *Journal of Criminal Law and Criminology*, "A Validation of the Gluecks' Social Prediction Scale," Vol. 43, Nov.–Dec. (1952), pp. 451–471.

[2] Selma Glick and Bertram Black, "Recidivism at Hawthorne-Cedar Knolls School," *Research Monogram* 2, Jewish Board of Guardians, New York (1952). [See, also, Articles 171–173 of this book. — Ed.]

[3] Sheldon and Eleanor Glueck, "What Do We Know About Delinquency?" in *Analyzing Social Problems*, John Nordskog et al., Dryden Press, New York (1950).

[4] The interviewers wish to express their sincere gratitude for the advice and help of Dr. Sheldon Glueck and for the full cooperation of the staffs of Wiltwyck and New England.

[5] See Gluecks, *Five Hundred Criminal Careers*, Knopf, New York. (1930).

private training school, the Wiltwyck School for Boys, and a typical public reformatory, the "New England School for Boys."[6]

Follow-up studies of the two schools reveal a significantly higher reformative rate for the Wiltwyck School (71 per cent) than for the New England School (53 per cent).[7] Both inquiries used the same criterion of failure (i.e., re-appearance in court). Therefore, the results seem indicative of the general efficacy of the two treatment programs. Wiltwyck's more rigorous study covered a five-year period. New England, however, investigated only the three-year parole period. Neither study can be accepted as a totally valid test of recidivism because superficial research failed to uncover undetected crimes and neglected to follow the boys into maturity.[8]

This study aims at uncovering the treatment processes at Wiltwyck that result in its relatively higher, albeit somewhat inaccurate, figure of success. Three specific questions guided the investigation:

Do meaningfully different patterns of leadership exist within the two reformatories?

Can personality differences be detected and traced to the two treatment programs?

Are the conscious values of Wiltwyck boys significantly different from those of the New England School?[9]

Before discussing the research methods, it is important to sketch in the settings of the two schools and to mark the distinguishing characteristics in the treatment programs, philosophies, and personnel.

A. *The Wiltwyck School — Consequences, Not Punishment.*

The Wiltwyck School, on the Hudson River near Poughkeepsie, New York, rests in a forested meadow of two hundred sixty acres. Clustered in an unwalled quadrangle are the living cottages, a classroom building, a gym-

nasium, a craft shop, an art room, and a dining hall. The main dormitories need repair, after sixteen years of use by emotionally maladjusted and confused children.

The boys range in age from eight to twelve. All are referred to Wiltwyck, a private institution, by New York courts. All are judged incorrigibly delinquent by their parents and their communities. Most of the boys have been previously rejected by other county homes and social agencies. In other words, Wiltwyck treats those boys considered most seriously delinquent.

Wiltwyck's philosophy emphasizes individual and group therapy. Four psychiatric social workers and a resident psychotherapist give each boy understanding counsel. An additional psychologist and an extra psychiatrist treat the more serious cases at Wiltwyck. Skilled workers guide music and art therapy sessions.

Wiltwyck recognizes the critical importance of the gang. Trained cottage counselors, each supervising ten youths, guide the boys in inter-racial group activities. Wiltwyck's one hundred students are urged to participate in their community affairs. An elected student council, a Food Committee, Job Committee, Canteen Committee, and Sports Committee cooperate with the staff in the discussion of common problems. Cottage living, student governments and weekly assemblies give the boys a chance to work out tensions, air hostilities, and train themselves in democratic procedure. Wiltwyck's dynamic executive director, Ernst Papanek, cogently summarized the school's therapeutic orientation:

Children who have never known understanding, social acceptance, prestige, friendship or love, or who have misinterpreted or misused them when offered in an over-protective and unchallenging way, would find (in Wiltwyck) a community of understanding grownups and children among whom they can gain security and status by social experience.[10]

Wiltwyck bases its healing techniques on a tenet of non-punishment. The children are allowed to express their pent-up bitterness and antagonism in a permissive atmosphere. No disciplinary cottages, no sadistic beatings, no disgruntled scoldings pervade Wiltwyck. In-

---

[6] The public reformatory studied in this research will not be named but will be referred to as the "New England School." Since the officials of the school have been informed of the results of this study, no professional benefit could result from a public unveiling of their problems.

[7] See Appendix 1 for summaries.

[8] Wiltwyck is currently conducting a more systematic ten-year follow-up study.

[9] Specific research techniques used to answer these questions are discussed in a later section.

---

[10] Ernst Papanek, "Training School — Program and Leadership," in *Federal Probation*, Washington (June, 1953).

stead, Papanek and his expert staff attempt to impress upon the child the true consequences of his acts. For example, an aggressive newcomer to Wiltwyck broke thirty-two windows in the school dining room. After waiting for the lad to "cool off," Papanek explained that some money would be deducted from the boy's weekly allowance to help pay for the damage. Three weeks later, the Director called the contrite boy to his office and quietly reinstated the full allowance. Thus Papanek soothed the boy's bitterness and taught him a fundamental lesson in social living. For the first time, the youth saw that authority can help an individual as well as hurt him.

Although all of its boys are toughened delinquents and 60 per cent are diagnosed as pre-schizophrenic, Wiltwyck runs smoothly along a course of loving guidance. Why does the "Consequence" method function effectively? Director Papanek explains:

Punishing teaches the child only how to punish; scolding teaches him how to scold. By showing him that we understand, we teach him to understand; by helping him, we teach him to help; by cooperating, we teach him how to cooperate.[11]

Wiltwyck recognizes the more formal aspects of education through the maintenance of an accredited school, under the direction of the New York City Board of Education. Teachers, skilled in the instruction of emotionally maladjusted children, conduct the ungraded classes.

The staff, under the direction of Papanek, consists of a psychiatrically trained resident director, an assistant director (social worker), four psychiatric social workers, the psychiatrist, ten counselors, six teachers, an art therapist, and a music therapist. All the staff members are college graduates and many have gone on for Masters' degrees in the behavior sciences. In-service training, weekly conferences, and classes, constantly enlarge their professional horizons.

The staff, representing several ethnic groups, promotes a spirit of tolerance within the school. One new boy with a Southern background complained of his distaste for his predominately colored cottage group. "The only really good guy in my whole cottage is the counselor. He's from the South and he understands about

11 Ibid.

Negroes." It was days before the boy admitted that his counselor, too, was Negro. The discovery that human love is not a white prerogative opened new paths of tolerance.

After an average residence of eighteen months, a boy returns to New York and Wiltwyck's after-care center in the city. There psychiatric social workers counsel parents and boy in the establishment of a new relationship. If the family situation remains hopeless, Wiltwyck leads the boy into a receptive foster home or private school.

Because of its emotionally healing environment, 70 per cent of Wiltwyck's boys do not return to court within five years after discharge.
B. *New England School — Discipline and Education.*

The New England School crowns a wooded hill near the Atlantic Coast. Financed by the state, the inter-racial, unwalled school offers vocational and academic education to its two hundred delinquents. The boys issue from a predominately Catholic, lower socioeconomic, slum background. Many inmates exhibit feebleminded, neurotic, and even psychotic symptoms. Ages of the inmates range from eight to sixteen.

The spacious campus of thirty-five buildings includes a school, an auditorium, a swimming pool, a roller-skating rink, individual dormitories, and a complete farm. The boys sleep and eat in separate cottages organized on the basis of age, with thirty-five boys and two counselors in each cottage.

The treatment program strongly emphasizes formal education. The school's "philosophy" demands inculcation of the "3 R's" in their traditional setting. Although the school conducts three ungraded classrooms for especially retarded children, the dominant attitude toward education is summarized by the principal:

I don't know whether you agree and I don't care. The real cause of juvenile delinquency is all the fol-de-rol of progressive education. Modern kids need firm discipline. Their social relations can take care of themselves.

New England officials give a nod of reluctant respect to psychological therapy but, unfortunately, fail to use it. The one trained psychologist of the school, an intelligent, well-educated young woman, is saddled with the administration of I.Q. tests to new comers. Personality diagnosis can be used with only the most disturbed cases. The psychologist holds a limited number of therapeutic sessions with one hundred and fifty of the year's population of six hundred. The largely untrained, seriously underpaid, cottage masters supposedly conduct "group therapy." In reality, the masters concern themselves with the maintenance of cleanliness and order among the boys.

The school puts full faith in a credit system. Each boy, upon admittance to the reformatory, receives a sentence of three thousand credits which he must work off by good conduct before his release. The "perfect" boy can check off four hundred and eighty credits per month (three hundred for good conduct in the cottage and one hundred eighty for an unblemished school record). However, when the school is overcrowded, credits are granted more freely. In some instances, credit requirements are raised. Since credit totals can be reshuffled, the boy's release date remains shrouded in mystery. Typically, each boy spends six months in the school.

When a boy escapes, as many do, he automatically receives one thousand additional credits plus a sentence in the disciplinary cottage, usually for three weeks.[12] During that period the boy is not permitted to work off credits. Consequently, an escapee acquires an additional sentence of nearly three months.

Boys are sentenced to the disciplinary cottage not only for escape but also for smoking, "stubbornness and disobedience," petty thievery, and sex offenses. The boys in the disciplinary cottage are forbidden to attend school, see movies, play games, or indulge in other social activities. They spend their days shoveling a "goodly crop" of manure at the farm. The discipline master maintains absolute silence at all times.

In addition to formal education and the credit system, the New England reformative process includes religious services and a work program in which the boys assist in the maintenance of the school. No student government exists. One teacher commented, "We don't give the boys authority because they always

start banging around. It especially goes to the heads of the colored boys." The good boys, those who roll off the monthly credits, are admitted to the Service Corps. This Corps entitles members to special privileges including office work, trips to football games, and leaves from the school.

The New England staff includes the Superintendent (a former public school administrator), the psychologist, sixteen teachers, the cottage masters, and a staff of maintenance workers. When questioned about the qualifications of cottage masters, the Superintendent replied, "We get the best we can. Most of them have finished high school." Technical knowledge about juvenile delinquency is practically non-existent. One school teacher showed the range of his understanding when he trumpeted, "Nobody can tell me a full moon doesn't affect these boys. Why, this school goes to pieces when a full moon comes up. It's no accident that the word 'lunatic' comes from the Latin name for the moon."

New England lacks an in-service training program for the staff. Consequently, the cottage masters oppose "snooping" by researchers. The school librarian spoke for his colleagues when he said, "Most of these criminologists — How do you say it? — should spend some time behind bars. Then they'd learn something. All these boys need is a father with a good strong razor strap!"

In 90 per cent of the cases, the New England graduate returns, upon release, to the same home environment that precipitated his antisocial acts. Supervision by an over-loaded staff of parole officers rounds out the boy's "reformative" experience.

Plagued by political influence, overcrowded, and hampered by a shallow philosophy, the New England School has stumbled through its one hundred year history. The miracle of the reformatory is that a handful of ardent staff members has presumably managed to reform 53 per cent of the boys. The New England School, neither better nor worse than the average American training school, typifies the methods (and success) of firm discipline.[13]

---

[12] Five boys from an original interviewing list of thirty-five attempted escape from New England in one week. The boys were replaced by new subjects. No one attempted escape from Wiltwyck during the interview period.

[13] A number of boys complained privately during the interviews about frequent beatings. Top officials forbid corporal punishment but apparently cannot control the cottage masters.

C. What's the Difference?

In Philosophy

Wiltwyck inculcates a new conscience by example and through use of the "consequence" method.

Wiltwyck focuses upon human relations, permissiveness, and child-centered therapy.

New England aims at remolding the child through discipline, the credit system, and the silent disciplinary cottage.

New England methods center around education and hard work.

In Treatment

Wiltwyck offers an intensive program of individual, group, and art therapy to all of its boys.

Wiltwyck supplements its therapeutic functions with instruction by trained teachers in ungraded classes.

Wiltwyck boys earn allowances by doing school chores under the direction of elected committees.

New England's one psychologist gives sporadic counseling to one third of the boys.

New England demands a traditional grounding in the formal studies, regardless of personality effects.

New England boys maintain the school's buildings under the direction of a staff of plumbers, painters, and carpenters.

In Staff

Wiltwyck's staff is composed of college graduates, skilled in the theory and practices of the behavior sciences.

Wiltwyck furnishes constant in-service training.

New England's staff is composed predominately of grade and high school graduates.

New England offers no in-service training.

In Practice

One counselor lives and plays with ten boys at Wiltwyck.

Wiltwyck boys elect representatives to manage current problems.

71 per cent of Wiltwyck's boys have made a successful adjustment to society.

Two counselors supervise thirty-five boys at New England.

New England officials rule the student activities without aid from the boys.

53 per cent of New England's boys have made a successful adjustment to society.

III. Research Procedure and Techniques

Do these startling differences in philosophy and treatment affect the leadership patterns,

personalities, and values of the delinquents? To answer these three vital points, the authors and school psychologists selected thirty-five boys from each school for intensive investigation.

The two groups included a proportional representation of severe personality problems in both schools. The sample represented 36 per cent of the Wiltwyck population and 18 per cent of the New England reformatory. The two groups were relatively homogeneous in age (nine to thirteen), ethnic origin, intelligence, socioeconomic status, and residential origin (New York's and Boston's slums). Wiltwyck I.Q.'s averaged 92 and New England's averaged 91.

Two criteria limited the sample. Boys with Stanford Binet I.Q.'s below 80 were excluded because of their possible misunderstanding of test questions. Boys who had not resided in the school for at least two months were also excluded. Measurement of the personality trends of newcomers would have been irrelevant since the study aimed at uncovering the effect of the treatment process.

The boys were individually (and privately) interviewed by the authors, who utilized several research aids.

A. *Sociogram.* Before beginning the interviews, each group of thirty-five was asked the question, "If permanent seats are assigned in the dining room, near which four people would you like to sit?" The interviewers tabulated the responses and included the leaders of each group in the interviewing schedule. The sociogram aimed at delineating the social patterns in the schools and the personal characteristics of the leaders.

B. *Adult-Child Interaction Test* (A.C.I.). The interviewers presented a series of eight provocative, but vague pictures of children and adults. The test, developed by Theron Alexander and based on the classic Murray style,[14] is designed to reveal "children's perceptions of adults, the forces in their world, their conceptions of themselves . . . and their own emotional composition."[15] The interviewers asked each child to tell a story about

---

[14] Henry A. Murray, *T.A.T. Manual*, Cambridge (1943).
[15] Theron Alexander, *Adult–Child Interaction Manual*, Florida State University (1952), p. 30.

each picture and then noted these responses as an indication of personality composition. Test scoring centered on two traits: anxiety and aggressiveness.

C. *Word Association Test.*[16] The interviewers read to every child a list of neutral and charged words, specifically constructed for this study. The child responded with the first word that came to his mind. The interviewers followed the Kent-Rosanoff technique and noted the reaction time for each word and the aggressiveness of response. The reaction time presumably indicated areas of anxiety.[17]

D. *Questionnaire on Authoritarianism* [18], *(Scale 1).* The interviewers read a list of fourteen statements to each boy. The sentences expressed such thoughts as, "What the child needs most is strict discipline," and, "Most of our problems would be solved if we could somehow kill off the crooked and dumb people." The boys could choose one of five responses ranging from "all correct" to "all wrong." The statements, based on the *Authoritarian Personality* scales, were simplified to fit a boy's world.[19] A high score indicates personality trends of punitiveness, authoritarian submission, stereotypy, and projectivity.[20]

E. *Questionnaire on General Prejudice and Hostility* [21], *(Scale 2).* A set of ten statements, again based on those used in the *Authoritarian Personality*, was designed to reveal the intensity of ethnocentrism and hostility toward outgroups in each boy.[22] The statements included, "If it weren't for the rich, the world would be headed toward peace and happiness by now," and, "Negroes have their rights but they should be kept in separate schools and districts." As in Scale 1, the boys chose one of five responses ranging from "all correct" to "all wrong." A high score indicated a general-

ized tendency to reject various outgroups such as Negroes, foreigners, Jews, and other minorities and to idealize corresponding ingroups.[23]

F. *Projective Personality Questions* [24], *(Scale 3).* This set of fourteen open-ended questions is fundamentally similar to other projective tests in that it brings to light the basic personality of the individual.[25] Most of the questions were designed by the Berkeley group and include such queries as, "What desires do you have difficulty controlling?" and, "What feelings are most unpleasant for you?" The responses of each boy were related to his A.C.I. record as an indication of anxiety and hostility.

G. *Conscious Values Questionnaire* [26], *(Scale 4).* Designed specifically for this project, Scale 4 consists of fourteen direct questions concerning the boys' conscious systems of morality, ego ideals, and views of the world. The questions ranged from, "What is Jesus' most important teaching about good and evil?" to, "Do you think that cheating is sometimes a good thing?"

H. *Leadership Patterns Questionnaire* [27], *(Scale 5).* The interviewers asked eleven questions designed to reveal the leadership patterns within the school and to determine the amount of "positive transference" between staff and boys. Typical questions were: "Who is the big shot in your cottage?" and, "Whom do you look up to most in the whole school?"

I. *Summary of Research Procedure.* Two groups of boys from Wiltwyck and New England Schools were intensively interviewed in an attempt to differentiate the characteristics peculiar to each group.

Leadership patterns were differentiated through sociograms and a questionnaire on leadership patterns.

Personality differences were assessed through use of the Adult–Child Interaction Test, a word association test, projective personality questions, a scale on authoritarianism, and a questionnaire on general prejudice and hostility.

Value differences were investigated through a questionnaire on morality.

---

[16] See Appendix 2 for a complete copy of the test.
[17] G. H. Kent and A. Rosanoff, "A Study of Association in Insanity," *American Psychiatric Journal,* issue 67 (1910), pp. 37–96.
[18] See Appendix 2 for complete copy of test and grading scale.
[19] Adorno, Frenkel-Brunswik, Levinson, and Sanford, *Authoritarian Personality,* Harpers, New York (1950), pp. 222–279.
[20] David J. Levinson, "Intergroup Relations Workshop," unpublished paper, Harvard (1952).
[21] See Appendix 2 for complete copy of test and grading scale.
[22] *Authoritarian Personality,* op. cit.

[23] Levinson, *op. cit.*
[24] See Appendix 2 for complete copy of questionnaire.
[25] *Authoritarian Personality,* op. cit.
[26] See Appendix 2 for complete copy of questionnaire.
[27] *Ibid.*

The specific research tests were chosen with three purposes in mind: objectivity, intensity, and scope. Except for the A.C.I. and the projective personality questions, the tests could be easily translated into numerical grades. This allowed objective comparisons of the results. The A.C.I. and the projective personality questions added depth to the analysis. Although not as easily standardized as the other techniques, these two tests did lend themselves to a rough categorization.

The questionnaires were chosen to cover the broad range of authoritarian trends, aggressiveness, anxiety, personal values, leader–follower relations, and out-group hostility. At all times the interviewers attempted to choose the techniques that were simplest and most objective, yet relevant to the study.

IV. RESEARCH RESULTS

A. *Leadership Patterns.*

Startling dissimilarities exist between the types of leaders chosen by the boys in the two schools. The sociogram at Wiltwyck revealed that one boy is overwhelmingly the most popular leader in the group. Only 6 per cent of the Wiltwyck boys emerged as "isolates," unchosen by their fellows. The Wiltwyck pattern of friendship roughly resembles a spoked wheel, gathered around the leader (see Figure 1).

The sociogram at New England showed a very different pattern. Two leaders, each surrounded by his own cohorts, dominate the group. In contrast to Wiltwyck, many trio friendships exist and more than 14 per cent of the New England boys are isolates (see Figure 2).

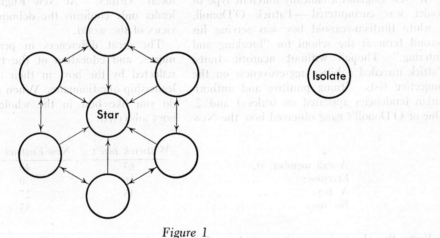

Figure 1

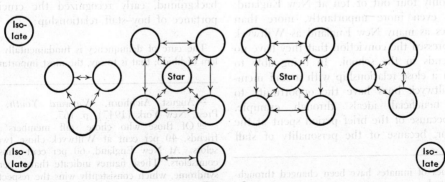

Figure 2

Since children absorb ideals from their leader, his character is of importance in their development.

John Lincoln,[28] Wiltwyck's Negro "star," came to the school seven years ago as an incorrigible delinquent who refused to talk to anyone. Because he exhibited schizophrenic tendencies, the Wiltwyck psychiatrist gave him a year of intensive psychotherapy. At the time of the research interview, thirteen-year-old John was making plans to return to New York to live with a married sister. On the personality tests he appeared well integrated, with little anxiety or hostility. On the questionnaires, he demonstrated a basic tolerance and egalitarianism by achieving the lowest scores of anyone at Wiltwyck. When queried about his values, John answered with a rational, optimistic view of the world. In other words, Wiltwyck officials could not have chosen a better example for their boys.

At New England a radically different type of leader was encountered — Patrick O'Donoll, a white thirteen-year-old boy was serving his second term at the school for "breaking and entering." Though without neurotic traits, Patrick unveiled a bitter aggressiveness on the projective tests. Strong punitive and authoritarian tendencies appeared on scales 1 and 2. One of O'Donoll's gang observed how the New

England leader controlled his cottage, "Two boys escaped yesterday from our cottage. They've spoiled our record. Boy, is O'Donoll going to smash their heads in when they're captured!"

Leaders like O'Donoll may aid the New England authorities in maintaining discipline, but they surely do nothing toward healing the basic insecurity and aggressiveness of their followers.

In his pioneering book, *Wayward Youth*, August Aichhorn, the Viennese educator observed:

The therapeutic work of the institution for re-education will be the more effective the more the grouping itself is utilized to relieve the delinquency.[29]

Undoubtedly much of Wiltwyck's reformative success stems from social osmosis. At Wiltwyck, the gang leader's example instills social "virtues." At New England, the gang leader only confirms the delinquents' punitive views of the world.

The great differences in personality, techniques, and education of the two staffs were reflected by the boys in their answers to the leadership questionnaire. When asked, "Whom do you like best in the whole school?" the boys answered:

	Wiltwyck perc't	New England perc't
A staff member: [30]	63	40
Everyone:	16	0
A boy:	15	27
No one:	6	33

From the above figures, it is evident that more than six out of ten boys at Wiltwyck respect and identify with staff members as against only four out of ten at New England. Perhaps even more importantly, more than five times as many New England as Wiltwyck boys expressed the conviction that they have no best friends in the school. In being able to establish a close relationship with a staff member, Wiltwyck boys have the opportunity to absorb beneficial ideals through example. Either because of the brief period spent at the school or, because of the personality of staff

members, most of the New England boys are denied this chance.

Aichhorn, drawing upon a psychoanalytic background, early recognized the crucial importance of boy–staff relationship:

The cure of delinquency is fundamentally a problem of libido; that is to say, the most important thing

---

[28] Names of inmates have been changed throughout the study.

[29] August Aichhorn, *Wayward Youth*, Viking Press, New York (1947), p. 167.

[30] Of those who chose staff members as best friends, 40 per cent at Wiltwyck chose two counselors. At New England, 60 per cent chose three counselors. These figures indicate that a personality syndrome, which consistently wins the respect of the boys, may exist.

is the child's feeling for the counsellor or, more generally for the people of his environment.[31]

To indicate the ideals absorbed by the boys from the staff, each interviewee was asked, "What type of person makes a good counselor or cottage master?" The boys described:

	Wiltwyck perc't	New England perc't
A *loving person:* (e.g., "understanding," "plays with the boys," "stands up for us," "puts group ahead of himself.")	54	21
A *disciplinarian:* (e.g., "hits you when you need it," "makes you obey.")	16	52
Unclear or don't know: (e.g., "a nice man," "well-educated.")	30	27

At Wiltwyck, the "male ego ideal" is seen as a loving person. At New England, the ideal is a disciplinarian. Once again, Aichhorn's experience offers an understandable explanation of Wiltwyck's success and New England's failure:

What helps the worker most in therapy with the dissocial? The transference! It is above all the tender feeling for the teacher that gives the pupil the incentive to do what is prescribed and not to do what is forbidden.[32]

Before passing on to the personality and value differences between the two schools, one interesting result should be noted. When asked whom they *disliked* the most at the school, 61% of the New England boys refused to answer. No one declined an answer at Wiltwyck. Such a striking contrast must be attributed to the New England atmosphere of discipline and restriction.

B. *Personality Differences.*

1. *Scoring system.* The Adult–Child Interaction Test was scored for only two variables: anxiety and aggressiveness. In order to make the two groups statistically comparable, the authors assigned one of three grades to each boy:

Anxiety	Aggressiveness
1-Little or no evidence of anxiety.	1-Little or no evidence of overt hostility.
2-Evidence in at least three pictures of some anxiety.	2-Evidence in at least three pictures of some hostility.
3-Evidence of very strong anxiety, neurosis, or psychosis.	3-Evidence of very strong overt hostility.

---

[31] Aichhorn, *op. cit.* p. 153.
[32] *Ibid.*, p. 235.

An independent judge checked the ratings of the original scorer and agreed with the judgments in 95% of the cases.

The Projective Question Test was marked on the same basis as the A.C.I. The independent judge reached 87.5% agreement with the ratings of anxiety and aggressiveness.

The Word Association Test, too, was scored for signs of anxiety and aggressiveness. Following the Kent-Rosanoff technique, the interviewers noted the number of long pauses and "don't know" responses as an indication of insecurity. Also, the interviewer listed the number of overtly aggressive replies as a mark of hostility. A response was considered aggressive only if it was directly hostile (e.g., to the word "neck," the boy responded, "I'll break that nigger's neck"). The independent judge agreed in 96 per cent of the cases.

On the Authoritarian Questionnaire, each boy could respond with one of five possible answers. The interviewer assigned a numerical grade for each phrase:

All right	plus 2
Mostly right	plus 1
Partly right and partly wrong	zero
Mostly wrong	minus 1
All wrong	minus 2

Since the statements were couched in authoritarian terms, any boy who achieved an average plus score presumably shows authoritarian trends. A minus average score, on the other hand, indicates "equalitarian" trends.

The interviewers graded the prejudice scale on the same basis as the authoritarian questionnaire. Possible averages ranged from plus two to minus two. A mean plus score shows ethnocentric and hostile tendencies; a minus score evidences tolerance of outgroups.

2. *Anxiety at Wiltwyck and New England.* On the three tests that measure anxiety (A.C.I., Word Association, and Scale 3), 29 per cent of the Wiltwyck boys showed definite signs of neurosis or psychosis. In the New England group, 21 per cent fell in that category.

In order to calculate the effect of school treatment in reducing anxiety and insecurity, the group scores were correlated with the number of months spent in the school. *On all three tests, anxiety of the Wiltwyck boys significantly decreased the longer the boy was exposed to the school program.*[33] *At New England, insecurity and inner conflict remained stable and even showed slightly increasing trends on some tests.*

At Wiltwyck, the average anxiety score on the Adult–Child Interaction Test significantly *decreased* from a mean of 2.7 for boys in residence two to six months to an average of 2.0 for boys in residence for two years or longer. At New England, however, anxiety as shown on the A.C.I. *increased* from 1.9 to 2.0 during the same period.

On the projective personality questionnaire (Scale 3), the Wiltwyck anxiety scores *decreased* with length of stay from 2.0 to 1.7. New England mean anxiety scores *increased* from 1.9 to 2.0.

On the word association test, the same trend occurred. At Wiltwyck, the number of "anxiety" responses per boy significantly *decreased* from 6.0 to 3.0. Although New England averages decreased from 5.0 to 3.6, this decrease is not statistically significant.

On all three measures, newcomers to Wiltwyck appeared to have a higher level of anxiety than do new inmates at New England. However, boys who had remained at Wiltwyck for twenty-four months showed lower anxiety than boys who remained at New England for the same period of time.

Wiltwyck's program of loving support and permissiveness evidently erases much of the basic insecurity and conflict of the delinquents. The New England program of "disciplined

---

[33] All "significant" personality differences mentioned are statistically significant at the 5 per cent level or better.

education" probably returns its boys to society with heightened anxiety and increased inner tensions.

3. *Aggressiveness at Wiltwyck and New England.* On the three tests which measured overt hostility, 8 per cent of the Wiltwyck group showed extreme aggressiveness compared to 10 per cent of the New England boys.

Aggressiveness did not decrease significantly with length of stay at either Wiltwyck or New England.

The three tests showed the following changes in aggressiveness:

Adult–Child Interaction Test:
    Wiltwyck aggressiveness decreased from 1.5 to 1.2.
    New England aggressiveness decreased from 1.3 to 1.2.
Projective question test:
    Wiltwyck hostility decreased from 1.7 to 1.4.
    New England hostility decreased from 1.5 to 1.2.
Word Association test:
    Wiltwyck aggressive responses per boy increased from 1.0 to 1.4.
    New England aggressive responses per boy increased from .85 to 1.0.

Although both schools apparently reduce aggressiveness, none of these variations are statistically significant at the 5 per cent level. Consequently, Wiltwyck's reformative success cannot be explained in terms of reduction in overt aggression.

Aggressiveness at New England usually reaches its greatest intensity during the six to twelve month interval. Since the school releases most of its boys during this critical period, it releases to society delinquents with uncurbed, if not increased, hostility.

4. *Authoritarian trends at Wiltwyck and New England.* Wiltwyck boys averaged plus .74 and New England boys averaged plus .98 on Scale 1. In other words, both groups showed an intense longing for support and care from a strong authority as well as marked tendencies toward punitiveness, stereotypy, projectivity.

Authoritarian tendencies among Wiltwyck boys decreased significantly with length of residence in the school. New England delinquents, too, evidenced a slight, but non-significant decrease.

5. *Prejudice at Wiltwyck and New England.*

Wiltwyck inmates achieved a mean score of plus .14 on the ethnocentrism scale. New England boys scored an average of plus .006. Both groups give evidence of hostility toward a variety of outgroups.

At Wiltwyck, the school treatment program, implemented by an inter-racial staff, effects a significant decrease in prejudice. At New England, however, prejudice increases with length of stay. Mean score at Wiltwyck decreased from plus .37 to minus .45. At New England, mean scores increased from plus .06 to plus .16.

6. Conclusions about personality differences. Wiltwyck orients its treatment around Aichhorn's dictum that "Dissocial behavior is the result of disturbed psychic patterns, of abnormal accumulation of affect." [34] Consequently, by attacking the "psychic" roots of behavior Wiltwyck's program soothes the basic insecurity of the delinquent, reduces his authoritarian tendencies, and alters his ethnocentric stereotypes.

At New England, the superficial triad of discipline, work, and school leaves the delinquent conflicts unresolved. The strict regimen does not touch (and may increase) anxiety, authoritarian tendencies, and ethnocentric trends.

Neither school conquers the overt aggressiveness of its boys. Aichhorn has noted, however, that the task of the training school is to "remove the cause rather than to eliminate the overt behavior." [35] In all probability, Wiltwyck's success stems from "removing the cause" and turning the unchanged delinquent aggressiveness to new goals.

Naturally, the small sample of seventy boys forbids rigid judgments on the personality differences. Nevertheless, the divergent trends seem to trace a significant pattern.

C. Value Differences.

The most important task of the training school lies in changing not only the personalities but also the ideals of delinquents. Through their answers to Scale 4 (the values questionnaire), the boys revealed startling value difference between Wiltwyck and New England.

1. View of the world. Wiltwyck boys more often judged the world as a happy environment where men are willing to be of service. New England boys more frequently looked at the world as an evil battleground where men fight for their own selfish interests.[36]

This contrast appeared in answer to, "Do you think the world is a bad place where men are mostly looking out for their own pocketbooks?"

	Wiltwyck perc't	New England perc't
World is good:	55	33
World is evil:	41	53
World is both good and evil:	0	10
Don't know:	4	4

The same differences emerged on the query, "Do you think that those who 'get ahead' in the world have to fight?"

	Wiltwyck perc't	New England perc't
Yes:	17	57
No:	60	32
Sometimes:	13	8
Don't know:	10	3

Such variant outlooks on their environment must reflect the boys' treatment within the schools.

2. Ego ideals: The delinquent's conception of himself, his parental image, and his hopes for the future seem vitally important in refor-

mation. As in their views of the world, the two groups showed highly significant differences that probably result from the teachings and atmospheres of Wiltwyck and New England.

---

[34] Aichhorn, op. cit. p. 41.

[35] Ibid., p. 39.
[36] All values differences mentioned are statistically significant at the 1 per cent level or better.

To the question, "If you could be anyone in the world, whom would you be?"

	Wiltwyck perc't answered:	New England perc't answered:
Myself:	50	22
Power Figure:	16	37
(e.g., Samson, God, president)		
Positive Ideal:	16	11
(e.g., Franklin, Carver, a counselor)		
Worst Enemy:	10	5
(e.g., "The guy who beats me")		
Don't Know:	8	25

These figures show that twice as many Wiltwyck boys expressed satisfaction with their own "egos" or were striving toward a positive ideal (66 per cent to 33 per cent). In categories revealing punitiveness and power seeking (i.e., Power Figure) and showing possible masochism (i.e., Worst Enemy), New England was nearly twice as numerous.

When asked, "What are good boys like?"

	Wiltwyck perc't answered:	New England perc't answered:
Positively:	40	5
(e.g., "kind" or "loving")		
Negatively:	55	76
(e.g., "doesn't steal" or "doesn't fight")		
Unclear:	5	19
(e.g., "healthy" or "nice")		

Once again, the Wiltwyck group showed a significantly clearer and more affirmative self-concept. Eight times as many Wiltwyck boys possessed consistent and verbalized image of the "good" boy (40 per cent to 5 per cent), though even at Wiltwyck less than half of the boys interviewed had a clear and positive concept of the "good" boy.

In an attempt to tap the boys' attitudes toward their families and their paternal images, the interviewees were asked, "What are good parents like?"

	Wiltwyck perc't answered:	New England perc't answered:
Loving Ideal:	55	23
(e.g., "Treats you good," "respects you")		
Disciplinarian Ideal:	40	54
(e.g., "Mother doesn't baby you when Father hits you")		
Unclear:	5	23
(e.g., "healthy," "rich")		

More than twice as many of the Wiltwyck boys possessed images of a kind and loving parent. Research by the Gluecks has shown the poor family relations of an overwhelming number of delinquents.[37] Therefore, it must be assumed that Wiltwyck's image of a "loving" parent stems from the school's atmosphere rather than from realistic memories.

In attempting to discover the future ideals (and the present fantasies) of the boys, the

[37] Unraveling Juvenile Delinquency, op. cit. pp. 108–133.

authors asked, "What do you want to be when you grow up?"

	Wiltwyck perc't answered:	New England perc't answered:
Realistically:	42	54
(e.g., carpenter, cop, machinist, house painter)		
Unrealistically:	25	26
(e.g., president, movie star) [38]		
Unclear:	12	15
(e.g., a man, a worker)		
Don't Know, Undecided:	21	15

Of those who answered realistically, two thirds of the 54 per cent at New England wanted to be a "cop" or a soldier; no one at Wiltwyck gave that response. Such an overwhelming preponderance of punitive desires might well be considered a result of New England's aggressive, authoritarian, and restrictive atmosphere.

To summarize: Wiltwyck boys seem to have absorbed clear and affirmative ego ideals and parental images from the care (and example) of the staff. Since the differences between the two groups are so distinctive, it can be assumed that Wiltwyck's therapeutic influence accounts for the startling improvements. In psychoanalytic terms, Wiltwyck's treatment not only integrates the boy's ego, but also furnishes him with a sturdier super-ego.

3. *Action orientations:* The delinquent's

	Wiltwyck perc't answered:	New England perc't answered:
Constructive Activities:	74	29
(e.g., sports, school work, read, work with horses)		
Destructive Activities:	11	48
(e.g., smoke, fight, steal)		
Neutral Activities:	15	23
(e.g., see movies, play marbles, fool around)		

The preoccupation of New England boys with smoking, fighting, and stealing reveals the ineffectiveness of firm discipline. New England's strict punishment fails to alter delinquent destructiveness and apparently increases the desire for "forbidden fruit."

When asked to verbalize ethical standards, both groups of delinquents indicated an abys-

quarrel with society centers around his destructive behavior. The training school must face the task of giving the boy new standards of action and some understanding of society's moral code. As in their views of the world and their ego ideals, Wiltwyck and New England showed highly significant differences to this aspect of re-education.

When the boys answered the question, "What do you like to do best in the school?" they replied with innocuous responses of, "play basketball," and, "go to school." When asked, "What do most of the boys in the school like to do best?" however, the delinquents partially lowered their inhibitive guards. The answers seem revelatory both of the actual conditions within the school and of the respondents' projected desires:

mal misunderstanding of the "accepted" moral code. To the question, "What is Jesus' most important teaching about good and evil?" [39]

---

[38] One boy at Wiltwyck said he wanted to be a girl and mentioned the "Christine Jorgensen case."

[39] At the time of the research no Jewish boys resided in either of the two schools.

	Wiltwyck perc't answered:	New England perc't answered:
Altruistic:	19	3
(e.g., "kindness," "Golden Rule")		
Authoritarian:	34	59
(e.g., "keep out of trouble," "obey your parents")		
Unclear or Don't Know:	47	38
(e.g., "attend mass," "be nice")		

The high percentage of authoritarian and unclear responses indicates that the delinquents do not comprehend, and often misinterpret, society's dominant Christian standards. Six times as many Wiltwyck boys, however, showed some understanding of Jesus' altruistic ethics (19 per cent to 3 per cent).

When asked, "What is your biggest problem?"

	Wiltwyck perc't answered:	New England perc't answered:
With Insight:	17	11
(i.e., concerned with personal, inner problems)		
With Avoidance:	50	65
(i.e., blamed others for problems, desired to leave the school)		
No Problems:	23	13
Don't Know:	0	11

Both Wiltwyck and New England boys show strong escapist tendencies. Nevertheless, a significantly higher proportion of the Wiltwyck boys have conscious insight into their emotional conflicts. The reformative rate of Wiltwyck "graduates" reflects this increased sensitivity.

4. *Conclusions about values.* Through personal kindness, example, and psychiatric therapy, the Wiltwyck staff molds the values of the delinquents. With the psychological roots of their behavior problems resolved, the Wiltwyck boys change their estimation of the environment, develop new self-ideals, and orient their action around constructive activities. Most of America's delinquents face life with a warped set of values — or with no set at all. Wiltwyck's healing treatment apparently results in the establishment of new values, acceptable to the greater society.

V. SUMMARY

Seventy delinquent boys were interviewed at the Wiltwyck and New England schools in an attempt to discover why Wiltwyck's program achieves a higher reformative rate. The Wiltwyck School emphasizes psychological therapy, non-punishment, and a loving environment. The New England School, typical of American training schools, centers around formal education, strict discipline, and vocational training.

A sociogram was secured from each school. The interviewers analyzed each delinquent through the use of projective personality tests and questionnaires on authoritarianism, prejudice, personal values, and leadership patterns.

Although the sample was small, statistically significant trends appear to differentiate the two schools.

The Wiltwyck boys chose exemplary student mentors whereas New England's charges followed punitive and authoritarian leaders. The Wiltwyck boys showed significantly greater affection toward and identification with the school counselors.

Wiltwyck's therapy decreases prejudice, anxiety, and authoritarianism. New England's program does not affect (or, actually increases) prejudice, anxiety, and authoritarian tendencies. Neither school significantly reduces aggressiveness.

The values of the Wiltwyck boys centered around constructive activities, affirmative ego ideals, and optimistic views of the world. The New England boys evidenced a preoccupation with destructive activities, negative and confused ego-ideals, and a punitive view of the world.

Wiltwyck's experience with seriously maladjusted youths shows that delinquents can be "cured." The school grounds its work on three axioms:

1. Delinquent behavior often springs from psychic roots: from unconscious guilt feelings, unintegrated traumas, pressing desires for love and recognition.

2. Delinquent behavior symptoms can be erased only when emotional conflicts are resolved. The essential ingredient in the treatment of the antisocial is "disciplined love" or psychoanalytically, a positive transference. As Aichhorn observed in 1925, "remedial treatment can begin only when the transference is established." [40]

3. Treatment of delinquents must focus on the consequences of action, not punishment; on democratic group living, not authoritarian supervision. Here again, Wiltwyck follows the path outlined by August Aichhorn:

Specific educational methods are far less important than an attitude which brings the child into contact with reality. We must give the pupils an experience which fits them for life outside and not for the artificial life of an institution. [41]

Wiltwyck's successful experiments in reformation bring new hope and, possibly, new directions to the training school movement.

Admittedly, this project has only scraped the surface in assessing institutional effects on delinquents. The interviewers hope to corroborate and extend the present research and hope, too, that this paper will serve as a stimulant to other investigators.

APPENDIX I
SUMMARY OF WILTWYCK FOLLOW-UP STUDY

The study, carried out by Lois Wiley of the New York School of Social Work, investigated court and social agency records in New York City in an attempt to trace the behavior of sixty-five Wiltwyck boys after five years of

---

[40] Aichhorn, op. cit., p. 167.
[41] Ibid., p. 201.

freedom. The study, completed in January, 1941, secured the following results:

> 43.2 percent (28 boys: complete successes. (No further court appearances occurred on any charge after the original remittance to Wiltwyck.)
>
> 27.6 percent (18 boys): partial successes. (Court appearances occurred in these cases for three reasons: boy requested return to Wiltwyck, boy ran away from home, or boy truanted irregularly.)

Total: 70.8 percent (46 boys): had benefited from Wiltwyck's program, had avoided antisocial behavior, and had made an adjustment to society.

> 29.2 percent (19 boys): complete failures. (This group had one or more appearances before court for severe delinquent behavior including assault, burglary, robbery, and sex offenses.)

The major faults of the study are:

1. Failure to investigate undetected crimes.
2. Failure to follow boy into maturity.
3. Failure to interview the boy or his family directly.
4. Failure to check with social agencies not registered with the Social Service Exchange.

Wiltwyck is currently conducting a ten-year follow-up study in an attempt to correct these deficiencies.

SUMMARY OF NEW ENGLAND FOLLOW-UP STUDY

In 1947, a citizen's committee undertook the investigation of former inmates of the New England School. The investigation, initiated at a time when the School's appropriation was before the legislature, unsystematically included former inmates of another school.

The study traced 228 boys through a three-year parole period after release from New England and showed the following results:

> 48.3 percent (110 boys): complete successes. (No further court appearances occurred during the three-year period and the boys were "honorably discharged" from parole.)
>
> 5.1 percent (12 boys): partial successes. (This group was "administratively discharged" from parole into the army. No attempt was made to discover their success within the army.)

Total: 53.4 percent (122 boys): were thought to have benefited from the school program and to have made an adjustment to society.

33.3 percent (76 boys): *complete failures.* (This group was currently serving sentence either in correctional institutions or in mental hospitals.)

13.3 percent (30 boys): *unknown outcomes.* (Three boys had died. The rest had disappeared, left the state or, for some other reason, were untraceable.)

The major faults of the study are:

1. Failure to extend the investigation beyond the three-year parole period.
2. Failure to investigate undetected crimes.
3. Failure to interview the boys or their families directly.
4. Failure to check with social agencies other than the courts and correctional institutions.
5. Failure to trace 13.3 percent of the boys.
6. Failure to follow "administratively discharged" boys.
7. Failure to check with agencies outside of Massachusetts.

APPENDIX II
WORD ASSOCIATION TEST

Time	Response	Time	Response
1. Dark		25. Home	
2. Red		26. Lie	
3. Sugar		27. Stool pigeon	
4. Table		28. Grind	
5. Mother		29. Smoke	
6. Teacher		30. Sissy	
7. Gang		31. Crazy	
8. Me		32. Cop	
9. Hate		33. Drunk	
10. Steal		34. Laugh	
11. Secure		35. (Name of superintendent)	
12. Power			
13. Fame		36. Alibi	
14. Love		37. Goy	
15. Leader		38. Guilt	
16. Man		39. Pen	
17. Money		40. Gun	
18. Sex		41. Jew	
19. God		42. Slug	
20. Fight		43. Neck	
21. Girl		44. Nigger	
22. Kill		45. Mugging	
23. Percy		46. Honest	
24. Swear		47. Kike	

SCALE 1

AUTHORITARIANISM

1. What the child needs most is strict discipline.
2. Some boys have ideas about doing things their own way, but as they grow up they ought to get over them and settle down.
3. Crimes such as murder deserve even more severe punishment than they get now.
4. Most of our problems would be solved if we could somehow kill off the crooked or dumb people.
5. The best teacher is the one who tells us just exactly what is to be done in every detail.
6. No decent person could ever think of hurting a close friend or relative.
7. More than anything else, it's good hard work that makes life worthwhile.
8. A child should never be allowed to argue with his parents or he will lose respect for them.
9. Any mother whose children are messy or noisy at all has failed in her duty as a mother.
10. If a child is different, his parents should get him to be more like other children.
11. A child should love and respect his parents, no matter what they do.
12. Those who fail, usually deserve to fail.
13. A person is usually right if he can win a fight or argument.

SCALE 2

GENERAL PREJUDICE AND HOSTILITY TOWARD OUTGROUPS

1. The worst danger to America has come from people who come from other countries.
2. Religions that do not believe in saluting the flag should be forced to carry out this patriotic act.
3. If it weren't for the rich, the world would be headed toward peace and happiness by now.
4. It is right for a person to feel that his country or religion is better than any other.
5. Foreigners should not be allowed to come to the United States because there will be less for Americans.
6. Anyone who lives in the United States and is not a real American in his thinking should be punished.
7. Negroes have their rights but they should be kept in separate schools and separate districts.

8. There may be some exceptions but in general, Jewish people are pretty much alike.
9. There are some exceptions, but most people are just trying to get more money in a crooked way.
10. It is somehow unnatural to place women in positions of leadership over men.

SCALE 3

PROJECTIVE PERSONALITY QUESTIONS

1. What feelings are most unpleasant for you?
2. What desires do you have difficulty controlling?
3. What great people do you admire most?
4. What might drive a person nuts?
5. What are your most embarrassing moments?
6. What do you think are the worst crimes?
7. If you knew you had only six months to live, how would you spend your time?
8. What gives you the greatest feeling of awe?
9. Do you think the world is a bad place where men are mostly looking out for their own pocket-books?
10. Which do you fear more — a bully or a cheater?
11. Have people ever been so mean to you that you could have killed them without good self-control?
12. If you could be anyone in the world, whom would you be?
13. What are good parents like?
14. What are good boys like?

SCALE 4

CONSCIOUS VALUES OF THE CHILD

1. Do you think that cheating is sometimes a good thing?
2. In order to have things you needed, did you sometimes have to steal?
3. Do you think tough guys should be punished strictly?
4. What do you like to do best in school?
5. What do most of the boys in the school like to do best?
6. Do you usually win in fist fights or gang fights?
7. What is your biggest problem? What caused it? Can it be solved?
8. What type of person makes a good counselor or cottage master?
9. What do you enjoy most about the school?

10. What do you like least?
11. If you were superintendent, how would you run the place?
12. What happens to a boy if he does something wrong? Is this right?
13. What do you want to be when you grow up?
14. What is Jesus' most important teaching about good and evil?
15. Do you think that those who "get ahead" in the world have to fight?

SCALE 5

LEADERSHIP PATTERNS

1. Whom do you like best in the whole school? Why? (Who is your best friend?)
2. Whom do you dislike most at the school? Why?
3. Which staff member do you like best?
4. Who is the "big shot" in the school? Who is the "big shot" in your cottage?
5. What person do you admire the most in the school? (Whom do you look up to most in the whole school?)
6. When you grow up, which person in the school would you most want to be like?
7. What is the main thing friends have to offer?

135

Service to Youth: The Story of the Youth Service Board *

THE YOUTH SERVICE LAW [1]

Enacted on May 13, 1948, the Youth Service Law (Ch. 310 of 1948) was the first major change in the State's approach to the juvenile

---

* Reprinted from a pamphlet published by the Commonwealth of Massachusetts, Division of Youth Service, March 1, 1955. Used by permission of the publisher.
[1] By Chapter 766 of the Acts of 1955, the Youth Service Act was amended, changing the method of appointing the Youth Service Board and the Advisory Committee, and increasing the duties and

delinquency problem since 1906, when the juvenile court system was created. Resulting from an upsurge in delinquency during and after World War II, the Youth Service Law is a Massachusetts adaptation of the Model Youth Correction Authority Act, originally proposed by the American Law Institute in 1940. The Massachusetts Law, like similar laws in other "Youth Authority" states, i.e. California, Wisconsin, Minnesota, Texas, and Illinois, is an attempt to incorporate the latest and most progressive ideas on delinquency prevention and treatment in one single legislative act.

In 1952, the Youth Service Act was amended (Ch. 605 of 1952) to provide a greater concentration of executive authority in the Board chairman. All facilities of the Board were placed in a Division of Youth Service in the State Department of Education "but not subject to its control." The Chairman of the Youth Service Board is ex-officio Director of the Division of Youth Service, and thus the real executive head of all Division activities. He is responsible for the formulation and execution of all policies, assisted by the other two Board members, who are Deputy Directors of the Division. The Director and the two Deputy Directors continue to function as a Board in all cases affecting classification, treatment, transfer, parole, and discharge of individual children.

The laws relating to the Division of Youth Service are codified in Massachusetts General Laws, Ch. 6. sec. 65–69, and Ch. 120.

As its central concept, the Massachusetts Youth Service Act places the responsibility for custody, diagnosis, care, and treatment of juvenile delinquents in a single specialized agency. The function of the juvenile court in determining the delinquency or non-delinquency of the juvenile is not disturbed by the Act; the court also retains its power to place a delinquent on probation. The court no longer may sentence a juvenile delinquent to a specific institution; instead, all commitments are made to the Youth Service Board, which, after intensive diagnostic study and individual consideration of each case, determines the appropriate course of treatment. This may include one of several of the following: re-education at a state training school,

placement in a foster home or private school, working placement, special medical or psychiatric treatment, or immediate release to the child's own home, if the committing court approves. The Division retains jurisdiction over a delinquent until he is 21 (in criminal cases until he is 23), but a child may be discharged from custody at an earlier time if it is felt that his adjustment is good and such discharge is consistent with the protection of the community. With court approval, the Division may retain jurisdiction of the offender even after he attains the maximum age limits, but this power has never been exercised to date.

Such a system insures fair and equitable treatment of all cases, wherever in the Commonwealth they may arise. It also provides that each delinquent will receive the treatment appropriate to his particular needs, as determined by intensive clinical study and social study of home and family.

The Division of Youth Service, in addition to prescribing the type of treatment for children committed to its care, was given full control of the existing state juvenile training schools at Westboro, Shirley, and Lancaster, and the parole branches. These facilities had been administered previously by an unpaid Board of Trustees in the State Department of Public Welfare. Since its creation, the Division of Youth Service has established additional facilities, including a Detention Center for boys in Boston, a Reception Center for boys at Westboro, a Detention-and-Reception Center for girls at Lancaster, the Institute for Juvenile Guidance at Bridgewater, and a Bureau of Research and Delinquency Prevention. A new Reception-Detention Center for Boys is being constructed in Boston.

THE ADVISORY COMMITTEE ON SERVICE TO YOUTH [2]

When establishing the Youth Service Board, the Legislature sought to divorce the new agency from political control, to provide it with the maximum degree of public cooperation and

---

[2] The Advisory Committee no longer has the responsibility of submitting to the Governor a list of nominees for membership on the Youth Service Board. Members of the Advisory Committee must henceforth be appointed in such a way as to provide geographical representation for all parts of the Commonwealth.

understanding, and to subject its activities and program to constant scrutiny and re-evaluation. The Youth Service Law, therefore, provided for an Advisory Committee on Service to Youth, consisting of fifteen members who are "influential citizens in their communities and recognized for their interest in youth"; they are appointed by the Governor, with the approval of the Executive Council, for six year terms, with the terms of five members expiring every two years. The Advisory Committee, which serves without compensation, elects its own chairman and meets at least six times each year.

The most important function of the Advisory Committee is to nominate candidates for membership on the Youth Service Board. For each vacancy that may occur on the Board, the Advisory Committee submits a list of three or more nominees, from which the Governor appoints one Board member. Other important duties of the Advisory Committee include the explanation of the Division's work to the public; recommendations to the Division and other public agencies in matters affecting the behavior, care or welfare of children or youth; and an annual report to the Legislature and Governor on such matters, including recommendations for legislation on youth matters.

THE YOUTH SERVICE BOARD [3]

The Youth Service Board is composed of three members who are required to devote their entire time to carrying out the work of the Division. Each member is appointed by the Governor, with the consent of the Council, from a list of nominees submitted by the Advisory Committee, and serves for a term of six years (originally five years); the terms of the members expire in different years, thus providing for a continuity of experience and policy. By law each member of the Board must have had "training and experience in the law, or in medicine, or in education, or in the handling of juvenile and youthful offenders, or in social work, or in planning and conducting programs for the prevention of delinquency and crime." One member of the Board must be a woman; non-residents of Massachusetts as well as residents are eligible for appointment.

The Governor, from time to time, designates one member of the Board as its Chairman and Director of the Division, at an annual salary of $9,000; the other members each receive a salary of $8,000 per year. The Chairman "who must have demonstrated superior administrative ability," has since 1952 been the ex-officio Director of the Division of Youth Service, with full executive control over the policy and operation of the Division's various institutions and programs; he may assign individual Board members, in their capacity as deputy directors of the Division, to perform various administrative and supervisory functions.

Acting as a Board in a quasi-judicial capacity, the three members are responsible for the classification of individual children committed to the Youth Service Board, as well as their placement and treatment, transfer between institutions, release under supervision, and discharge from custody. These responsibilities may not be delegated to an individual member or to any other person. Thus, the Board spends two or three full days each week at the reception centers and training schools in carrying out these most important functions. Decisions in each case are made after an interview with the child and a thorough review of the records, which include home and family study, reports from visitor-guardian and training school officials, psychological tests and other diagnostic studies made at detention and reception centers, training schools, and public and private agencies. The law also requires the Board to make periodic re-examinations at least once each year, of the cases of all boys and girls in its institutions.

BUREAU OF RESEARCH AND DELINQUENCY PREVENTION [4]

In addition to the main function of the Division of Youth Service of caring for and re-

---

[3] Henceforth, members of the Youth Service Board will simply be appointed by the Governor with the consent of the Council, and no nominations for appointment will be made by the Advisory Committee. The salary of the chairman has been raised to $12,000 per annum, and that of the members to $11,000 per annum (Sec. 2A, Chapter 730, 1955).

The Youth Service Board has been given the additional duty of visiting the three county training schools (Middlesex, Essex, and Hampden) for truants and school offenders, to coordinate their efforts with the Youth Service Board program, to advise and assist them, and to make recommendations in the public interest.

[4] This Bureau has been authorized to assist local communities, where requested or when the Board

habilitating children who have been committed to its custody by the courts, the Division also has special responsibilities in preventing delinquency.

"It shall be the function and duty of the Board to develop constructive programs to reduce and prevent delinquency and crime among youth, and to that end it shall cooperate with existing agencies and encourage the establishment of new agencies, both local and state-wide, having as their object the control of delinquency and crime; and the Division shall assist local authorities of any county or municipality, when so requested by the governing body thereof, in strengthening and coordinating its educational, welfare, health and recreational programs which have as their object service to youth." — Mass. Gen'l Laws, Chap. 6 — Sec. 67, Par. (1).

The Bureau of Research and Delinquency Prevention was formally established within the Division in August, 1953. Present staff includes a supervisor, four community consultants, and a stenographer. Funds are being requested to enlarge and extend the services of the Bureau to all communities in the Commonwealth.

The purpose of the Bureau is two-fold. First, it conducts research in all areas encompassed by the responsibilities of the Division of Youth Service, both in rehabilitation and prevention. This means both quantitative and qualitative research, reporting and evaluating the functions,

services, and effectiveness of the programs of the Division of Youth Service. Secondly, it works closely with local communities and private agencies in the prevention of juvenile delinquency, maintaining a consultation service which is available to any community in the Commonwealth through official request of its municipal government.

During the past six months, the Bureau has developed and emphasized several phases of its two-fold purpose. Statistics on court and police action are being collected and organized on a statewide basis, as well as statistics on the internal activities of the Youth Service Division; this will enable the Bureau to act as an information center regarding the trends and patterns of juvenile delinquency in Massachusetts. On-the-scene consultations with citizens' committees and community councils in planning prevention programs have been conducted and are carefully recorded so that methods and techniques may be evaluated and improved. An active public-speaking schedule is maintained to bring to community groups a better understanding of juvenile delinquency, its symptoms and causes, and appropriate measures for its prevention. Research studies have been initiated with the object of attaining more adequate legislation, policy, and procedure which will result in better understanding, treatment, and rehabilitation of all children in trouble.

DETENTION CENTER [5]

The establishment of a Detention Center by the Division of Youth Service was authorized in 1948 by the General Laws of the Commonwealth. The tremendous task of re-organizing the correctional training schools and their programs, the establishment of classification centers and the improvement of parole services, however, together with the difficulty of locating a suitable building, delayed the opening of a Detention Center for Boys until the Spring of 1951.

The Center, located in the Jamaica Plain section of Boston, offers its services of clinical study

---

deems it desirable, in establishing delinquency-prevention programs, and to set up districts for this purpose. The Bureau is presently employing community representatives to reside in such districts, and to provide technical assistance for the communities therein. Detached workers are also being employed to assist in the evaluation of delinquency situations and planning appropriate programs for prevention and control.

A major forward step in the state-wide delinquency-prevention program was the enactment of legislation (Chapter 696, 1955), providing state grants-in-aid to local school departments, to encourage the employment of "school adjustment counselors" for work in the primary and elementary grades. These counselors will provide casework services for maladjusted and emotionally disturbed children and their families, thus enabling the early detection and treatment of pre-delinquent children before they become serious problems to the community. The Director of the Division of Youth Service must approve the number of counselors in any school system, and the personal and professional qualifications of the counselors must be approved jointly by the Commissioner of Education and the Director of the Division of Youth Service.

[5] A new Reception-Detention Center for Boys, located in Roslindale, has replaced the former Boys Detention Center in Jamaica Plain and the temporary Boys Reception Center at Westborough. The new facility, which will accommodate 100 boys, is divided into separate reception and detention

and custody to the courts and police. Delinquent and wayward children are eligible for detention between the time of their arrest and the final disposition of their cases by the courts. The length of time spent in detention may range from a few hours to several weeks depending upon the reason for admission. The Center can accommodate 30 boys adequately.

The reasons for separate detention facilities for children are obvious and can be summarized as follows: —

Protecting juvenile offenders from contamination by hardened criminals in jails and lockups; providing a temporary home for those who have no home or whose home conditions are unwholesome and hazardous; safekeeping in cases where running away from judicial procedure and its consequences might be expected. The services in the Mass. Detention Center also include a clinical and social study of the child and family to assist the court in making a sound disposition of the case.

As a service to the courts, much consideration has been given to the practice of detaining children away from home for the sole purpose of diagnostic study. When the new Reception–Detention Center is completed and additional detention facilities are established in other parts of the Commonwealth, it is anticipated that diagnostic studies on an outpatient basis will be provided for those children who can safely be released in the custody of their parents.

---

units but is served by a single clinical and diagnostic staff.

The former Boys Detention Center in Jamaica Plain will be converted during 1956 into a combined Reception–Detention Center for Girls, replacing the temporary facilities now used at Lancaster.

As the result of a state-wide study of detention facilities, conducted by the Bureau of Research and Delinquency Prevention during the 1954 recess of the Legislature, the Division of Youth Service has been authorized to establish a detention unit in the Springfield area, to serve the children referred by courts and Police Departments of western Massachusetts (Chapter 573, 1955). It is anticipated that in future years similar units will be established to serve other areas of the Commonwealth.

Another result of the detention study was the enactment of new legislation (Chapter 609, 1955), further regulating the pre-trial detention of children, empowering the Division of Youth Service to inspect juvenile detention facilities of local Police Departments, and forbidding the use of sub-standard facilities.

The building is a well-equipped institution; personnel and programs are available to meet the individual needs of the child and to carry out the purpose of a detention center. The philosophy of the Detention Center is based on the feeling that through constructive experiences during the period of detention and through the design of living within the Center, initial shock at arrest and removal from home will be reduced; the child will be better prepared for appearance in court, and will accept more readily the court finding and any subsequent program for rehabilitation.

Facilities and services at the Detention Center include: — an ungraded classroom under direction of the Boston School Committee, arts and crafts, gymnasium, modern cafeteria for all, indoor and outdoor recreation areas, chapel, medical unit, and T.V.–movie room.

The professional staff includes a consulting psychiatrist, a psychologist, a psychometrist, two social workers, three counselors, a recreational director, two teachers, a nurse, and a part-time physician.

Clinical study includes psychological tests, social history, medical examination, appraisal of academic or vocational achievement, aptitude, and interest. The clinical summary with its diagnosis and evaluation of the child's problem and recommendation for action is submitted to the court to assist the judge in final disposition of the case. Parallel services in separate centers are provided for both boys and girls. More than a thousand boys and girls are processed in the detention centers each year.

RECEPTION CENTERS [6]

An outstanding feature of the legislation creating the Youth Service Board was the establishment of Reception Centers which serve as diagnostic and classification centers for all children committed to the Board. All children must be processed through the Reception Centers, undergoing complete medical, psychological, and, when necessary, psychiatric examination. Results of these examinations are summarized with reports of social history and interview with parents; a suitable plan of treatment or training is worked out for the individual child, and the Youth Service Board in its weekly classification meeting reviews each

---

[6] See footnote #5.

case presented and considers the recommendation.

Recommendations may include foster home placement, working placements, return home under supervision, out-patient therapy, placement in correctional training schools, or placement in private schools and institutions.

The study period at the Reception Center is usually three to five weeks; the activity program is complete with education, recreation, and religion. Parellel services in separate centers are offered to both boys and girls. Between 600 and 700 boys, and between 100 and 200 girls are committed to the Reception Centers each year.

TRAINING, EDUCATION, AND TREATMENT

The Division of Youth Service maintains three major units for training, education, and treatment of children for rehabilitation and prevention of further delinquencies. The programs of these schools are similar in many respects. Each is organized on the cottage plan and many activities are centered around the cottage units under the supervision of cottage personnel.

Week-end leaves are an important part of each school's program and have proved to be a good preparation for permanent release to the community. In addition, many activities in the communities are enjoyed by small groups of children from the schools through the invitation of individuals and organizations.

A brief summary of the schools is given below to describe the physical structure, program, and services of each.

THE LYMAN SCHOOL FOR BOYS [7]

Probably the oldest training school in America, the Lyman School for Boys was established

---

[7] A new dining commons is now in operation, providing cafeteria style meals for both boys and staff. Also in use is a recently-completed school building, completely modern in design and equipment, with ten classrooms, a library, a science room, and an arts and crafts room.

Recent improvements in the school program include the establishment of a Boy Scout Troop, affiliated with the national Scouting organization. Another program for older boys of special merit permits them to work in the local community on a day-to-day basis, thus providing an easier transition upon their release from the institution.

in 1846 from funds contributed jointly by the Commonwealth of Massachusetts and the Honorable Theodore Lyman, a former mayor of Boston. Like the other state training schools, it was operated by an unpaid Board of Trustees appointed by the Governor, until in 1949 the Division of Youth Service was given control of the institution.

For more than a century, the Lyman School has undergone constant transformation and development, both in plant and program. It is an "open" institution, without walls or fences, and during most of its existence has been operated on the cottage plan.

The school campus is located atop a plateau in the rolling countryside of Westborough, Massachusetts. Surrounding a central playground, there are ten cottages, each with a dormitory capacity of 28 boys. Prepared meals are delivered to the cottages from a central kitchen. In addition to the administration building, infirmary and staff residence, there is a twelve-room school building which also contains a gymnasium and a swimming pool. The auditorium building, which is used for religious services, movies, and dramatics, contains a roller-skating rink in the basement. Plans are underway for the construction of a completely modern school building, and a new cafeteria is nearing completion.

Prior to 1949, boys were committed directly to the school by the courts, and the maximum age limit was fixed by law at fifteen. While a statutory age limit no longer exists, the Division of Youth Service still uses the Lyman School for the rehabilitation of the younger boys, and the school program is geared to that age group. With the Division's increased emphasis on education, especially for the younger boys, the formal program at Lyman School is almost exclusively academic, and the once-extensive animal husbandry and agricultural program has been greatly curtailed. Boys receive instruction either in ungraded classes or formal academic training through the eighth grade, and thereafter may pursue the usual high school subjects through grade 10, if mentally qualified; vocational training in printing and carpentry is also provided. Recently, a beginning has been made in developing exploratory pre-vocational experiences. Generally, boys remain at the Lyman School for a period of eight to ten months. The average population ranges between 230 and 260.

THE INDUSTRIAL SCHOOL FOR BOYS [8]

Established in 1908, the Industrial School for Boys is located in a rural setting at Shirley, Massachusetts. Until the establishment of the Youth Service Board, the school was supervised by a Board of Trustees. The Industrial School is primarily used for the rehabilitation of boys over 15. Population of the I.S.B. is approximately 160 boys.

The Industrial School is an open institution on the cottage plan. The campus quadrangle is laid out on a sloping hillside, dominated by a large administration building on the summit. In addition to several offices, this structure contains a large chapel-auditorium, a fully equipped gymnasium, a swimming pool, library, arts-and-crafts shop, and several classrooms. The cottages, ten in number, are arranged around the quadrangle; each contains a recreation room, dining room, kitchen, and a dormitory for thirty boys. Prepared meals are delivered to the cottages from a central kitchen. The school also has an infirmary, several staff buildings, vocational-training shops, and farm buildings. Recreational facilities include a complete outdoor athletic area and field house. A new central cafeteria and a new building for both academic and vocational training are planned for the coming year.

In the past, the school program was primarily devoted to the practical teaching of various trades, including metalwork, carpentry, automotive repair, and masonry. The Division of Youth Service, however, is gradually putting into effect

---

[8] Plans are near completion for a new cafeteria and a new vocational building, to be built in 1956 and 1957 at a total cost of more than $1,000,000.

The academic needs of the boys are being met to an increasing degree through extension courses provided by the University of Massachusetts and credited throughout the Commonwealth toward high school diplomas. Ordinary classroom work is supplemented by field trips, remedial classes, vocational guidance, and a visual aid program, aided by the Fort Devens film library so that each boy may continue to receive a broad educational program fitting him for the problems of the everyday world.

A sports program is carried out on both the intramural and varsity level.

New treatment facilities include a cottage achievement plan, offering incentives for good citizenship, and a pre-parole cottage providing an opportunity for gradual preparation and adjustment to life in the community.

a full academic program on the high school level, as well as more modern methods and facilities for vocational training.

THE INDUSTRIAL SCHOOL FOR GIRLS [9]

The Industrial School for Girls is located at Lancaster and was founded in 1854. This school is the first "open" institution for girls established on the cottage plan in America or England.

At present the population consists of approximately 90 girls. The type and degree of emotional problems presented by these 90 children call for a well-rounded and flexible program to meet individual needs. Included in the activity program are: puppets, glee club and choir, sports, crafts, dramatics, and journalism. The school program begins with ungraded classes and offers courses at the high school level, in both a general and commercial preparation. The School staff includes one head teacher and eight staff teachers.

Complete clinical services are available through the consulting psychiatrist, physician, two social workers, and staff nurses.

The following summary statement by the Supt. of the I.S.G. illustrates the flexibility and versatility of program and personnel necessary to provide the therapeutic atmosphere essential in rehabilitation:

". . . the function of the School is to provide a healing, re-educative, living experience for the emotionally deprived or disturbed girl. The processes on all levels are therapeutic and teaching. The total program should be professionally directed and should be effected on all levels by persons of warmth, understanding and skill. The goal of the school is not primarily academic or vocational advancement, but rather the healing of emotional disorder and the stabilizing of personality, within the limits of capacity, through meaningful, satisfying relationships and experience. It is not possible to predict the time required for such accomplishment, as rates of growth are highly individual. Ideally, the girl

---

[9] This institution has expanded its pre-vocational training to include ceramic work in arts and crafts. A fully equipped grooming parlor not only provides training but emphasizes the importance of personal appearance and individual self-respect. A very complete music program, together with sports of all types helps to prepare a girl for adjustment as a member of society.

should remain in the school until a time of maximum gain, or until there can be a provision in the community which will satisfy her reasonable needs and which will encourage her in orderly living."

INSTITUTE FOR JUVENILE GUIDANCE [10]

On July 1, 1951, the Division of Youth Service officially opened its Institute for Juvenile Guidance at the Industrial School for Boys, Shirley, Massachusetts. A standard cottage was converted for security purposes by means of detention screening for both doors and windows. The staff consists of a Superintendent to administer the unit, a psychiatric social worker for guidance and counseling, and eight floor supervisors to provide adequate supervision of the boys on a twenty-four hour basis.

This unit was developed in order that the training schools could select and transfer their most seriously disturbed juveniles to the Institute. Treatment of the habitual runaway, who is a runaway because of his marked mental and/or emotional instability, is impossible under the rehabilitative program at the "open" schools. The clinical staff of the training schools make their selection for transfer and submit this list to the Youth Service Board for final approval.

When a boy is admitted to the Institute, the superintendent, with the assistance of his staff, formulates an academic, recreational, religious, and psychiatric program that would best fit the needs of the individual boy. To this end, the unit is provided with weekly church services, religious training classes, weekly movies, arts and crafts shop, library, and the use of the Industrial School swimming pool and gymnasium as well as medical and psychiatric services.

---

[10] This institution for boys unable to adjust in the open institution has two full-time teachers for remedial reading. University Extension courses are provided for all high school subjects, as well as on-the-job instruction in upholstery, carpentry and bookbinding. A unique music program, in which over half the boys are active participants, is carried on by a full-time instructor, providing a therapeutic as well as a recreational outlet.

Each boy has an individual room, and the presence of women as well as men on the supervisory staff helps the boys to establish proper adjustments and identifications. An honor section for pre-parole cases stresses individual initiative, responsibility and merit. The present population of the Institute is approximately 80 boys.

Initially, it was planned to maintain a population of 15 boys for a 3 to 6 month period and then to return them to the parent institution. As the experiment progressed, it became apparent that the complexity of the problem required a longer period of treatment. As the length of stay was increased, the population increased and the limitations of the physical plant and program made the problem more acute. After two years of operation, the Division of Youth Service was able to begin preliminary preparations for more adequate facilities.

As a result, the Division of Youth Service opened its new Institute for Juvenile Guidance at Bridgewater, Massachusetts, to replace the existing unit on October 23, 1954. The personnel and plant facilities are adequate to care for a larger group of seriously disturbed boys on an indefinite basis. Boys are selected from the following categories: character disorders, psychoneurotics, pre-psychotics, sexual deviates, habitual delinquents, and custodial problems.

The objectives of the Institute for Juvenile Guidance are:

1. To develop an academic, vocational, religious, and recreation program with adequate medical and psychiatric services into an intensive and extensive period of treatment for the rehabilitation of the seriously disturbed juvenile offenders.
2. To protect the individual boy from creating additional problems for himself as a result of running away.
3. To prevent injury and damage to the community caused by disturbed youngsters who habitually run away.
4. To facilitate the program of the training schools through selection and transfer of the most seriously disturbed juveniles.

The immediate objective of the Institute is to protect the rights of the community and its citizens by providing security measures to restrain selected individuals. The long-range objective is to provide an intensive therapeutic program necessary in the treatment and rehabilitation of deep-seated, aggressive, behavior problems.

PAROLE BRANCH [11]

At the outset, parole must be distinguished from probation. In probation the offender

---

[11] The Divisions' parole services have now been centralized under a single head in order to improve

is not committed to an institution, but is allowed to remain in the community under specific conditions, and under supervision of the court through its probation officer. In parole, the offender has been removed from the community and his home for an indefinite period of time under custody. When he appears able to adjust in the community and home, he is returned on parole under the supervision of the agency to which he has been committed, in this case, the Youth Service Board.

The Division of Youth Service maintains parole branches for boys and girls. Parole services extend to all parts of the State; 22 parole officers are assigned to the boys' branch and 9 workers to the girls.

Children committed to the Youth Service Board remain under the supervision of the Division until reaching the age of 21 years, or 23 years in some cases. Children may be discharged before this age limit if the Youth Service Board feels that the efforts at rehabilitation have been successful. They may be paroled from the Reception Center (although this is not the usual case), from a training school, or after specialized treatment elsewhere. The child may be paroled to his own home, foster home, private institution or school. Regardless of the type of placement or its location within the State, a parole officer (officially known as a visitor and guardian) will assume supervision of the child and support him in his adjustment to the community. Frequency of visits and interviews with children on parole depends a great deal on the stability and need of the child.

Expense of maintaining these children on parole to various foster homes and private institutions is often wholly paid by the Division of Youth Service and includes fees and tuitions,

clothing, medical and dental care, and special supplies, in addition to room and board. In other cases, parents or private agencies bear all or part of the cost.

As additional duties, the visitor–guardian attends all court proceedings involving parolees under his supervision, acts as a contact man between the Division and the local police and courts, and makes studies of home conditions for all new commitments to the Division from his locality. Approximately 1400 children are under the supervision of the Parole Branches.

THE SPECIAL RECESS COMMISSION ON JUVENILE DELINQUENCY

Greatly disturbed by the rapid increase of juvenile delinquency during World War II and the post-war years, the Massachusetts legislature in 1947 established an unpaid special commission to study the problems of delinquency prevention and the rehabilitation and treatment of delinquent children. The commission consisted of two senators appointed by the President of the Senate, three representatives appointed by the Speaker, and five persons appointed by the Governor.

In 1948, following an intensive study of the entire problem, the commission drafted the Youth Service Law and submitted it to the Legislature where it received approval so as to take effect on January 1, 1949. The Commission has continued in existence to the present time (1954) and has submitted other legislative proposals affecting juvenile delinquency. The most recent proposal, which was unsuccessful, would have created nine full-time courts devoted to juvenile business exclusively and serving the entire Commonwealth on a circuit basis.[12]

and make uniform the methods of parole supervision. A field supervisor and two more parole visitors for boys have been added to the staff of this branch.

[12] See, also, R. D. Patton, "The Illinois Youth Commission," 19 *Am. J. of Correction* (1957), 4–7; R. A. McGee, and H. G. Stark, "The California Department of Correction and the California Youth Authority, 18 *Am. J. of Correction* (1956), 20–28.

Chapter 24

Forms of Treatment: Hospital Care

EVEN THE MOST EXTREME psychiatrically oriented criminologist would not insist that a substantial proportion of delinquents requires hospitalization for the treatment of emotional and behavioral disorders. Nevertheless, there are delinquents who do.

The articles in this chapter are designed to give some conception of the treatment of such atypical cases.

The first article, by Warren, is an account of the methods of a psychiatric hospital in England for dealing with certain types of court and non-court delinquents. Taking as his point of departure the provision in the English Criminal Justice Act that a Court may, on medical evidence, require a probationer to submit to treatment if his "mental condition" requires this or suggests he may benefit from it, Warren discusses the question whether adolescents of this kind are different from other patients. He describes the regime, the variety of problems of those admitted, the nature of the diagnostic assessment and treatment, illustrating by case-history summaries. He points out, in connection with the setting up of diagnostic clinics in courts, that "some patients with difficult problems of diagnosis," require "a period of unhurried observation" in order to determine their suitability for psychiatric treatment; and also that since courts deal only with children charged with delinquency, they would not — even if they had clinical adjuncts — be in a position to take account of many other children with emotional–behavioral disorders.

Wolberg's article gives an account of the therapeutic measures employed — under great handicaps of personnel and resources — in dealing with emotionally disturbed youngsters, most of them with post-traumatic psychoses but including also some schizophrenics and children of limited intelligence evincing primary behavior disorders. Some illuminating insights are given into the psychologic mechanisms of the child whose troubles spring essentially from organic traumas, with emphasis in treatment being "not so much on the particular type of diagnostic category into which a patient fits, as upon his disturbances in operation as a social functional unit." It is pointed out that the removal of a child from a disturbed environment to a hospital does not, of itself, make his emotional disturbances and behavioral difficulties disappear. The importance of kindliness and controlled permissiveness in connection with discipline is emphasized. Methods of dealing with aggressiveness and with friction between juvenile and adolescent groups are described. The special problem created by disgruntled ward employees is discussed, and the qualifications of workers who contribute to the therapeutic situation are described. The process of growth to ego maturity is analyzed. A vivid description of the mental and behavioral responses of the emotionally distorted child is presented, together with the possibilities and limitations of "environmental correction." The mental mechanisms revolving around authority are indicated. Encouraging is the conviction, illustrated by a striking case history, that "in the dynamics of emotional disorder . . . a spontaneous driving force toward mental health exists, which is coordinate with the symptoms of a disturbed emotional state. Too often, one overemphasizes pathological elements in mental illness without realizing that even the most disturbed children show spontaneous tendencies toward remissions or cures."

The final article in this chapter, by Davis, Hulse, and Murphy, describes the results of an assessment of 200 unselected cases of dependent and neglected children. Characteristics of three basic categories of children — the moderately disturbed, the "difficult," and the extremely disturbed — are presented together with some practical suggestions for the treatment of these diagnostic categories.

136

Treatment of Youths With Behavior Disorders in a Psychiatric Hospital *

W. Warren

In 1949 a Ward Unit of sixteen beds was formed at the Bethlem Royal Hospital for the psychiatric investigation and treatment of adolescent boys. A review of the case histories of the first sixty-six patients admitted there shows that thirty-three (50 per cent) came in because of problems in their behaviour. This group, with conduct disorders predominant in the clinical picture, was not sharply delimited from the others who showed little or no disordered behaviour; there was a gradation between one extreme and the other. Patients of these age levels with any psychiatric disorders likely to benefit from the régime have been admitted; their clinical syndromes have been most heterogeneous, including sometimes organic conditions or psychotic developments; and in the majority a host of maladjustments, psychoneurotic reactions or personality disorders, with or without most types of conduct disorder. Thus, the psychiatric picture shown by each boy and the problems of his treatment were always unique.

The group of thirty-three patients singled out because of their behaviour disorders included twelve who were admitted at the request of the Court under the terms of the Criminal Justice Act of 1948. Two were admitted at the request of the Home Office, one from prison and the other from an Approved School. The other

* Reprinted from 3 *British J. Delinquency* (1952–53), 234–247. Used by permission of the author and the publisher.

nineteen, admitted at the request of their doctors, had in a few instances already appeared in Court, or subsequently were charged with some offence after discharge. A previous statistical investigation of children aged between five and fifteen under psychiatric treatment as outpatients because of behaviour disorders, had shown no significant differences of etiology and symptomatology as between those who had been charged in Court and those who had avoided this (Warren, W., 1951). Similarly, there appeared to be no clinical differences in etiology or symptomatology between Court and non-Court cases amongst the present group, although such small numbers do not allow statistical evaluation.

The Criminal Justice Act of 1948 directs that if a Court on medical evidence finds that the mental condition of an offender requires or may be susceptible to treatment, it may include in a Probation Order a requirement that the offender shall submit for such period not extending beyond 12 months to treatment with a view to the improvement of his mental condition. This may include in-patient treatment in a mental hospital as a Voluntary Patient. Norwood East (1950) in reference to this Act has stated "that an expert (at trial) can do no more than carefully select the material for treatment in the light of past experience. He cannot be sure that a particular offender will respond to treatment and he cannot foresee the accidental factors which may arise and neutralize his effort." It thus seems important to assess in practice how offenders may fare after admission as in-patients to a psychiatric hospital under the provisions of this Act; how they fit in with patients under treatment for other reasons; and whether their psychiatric problems are different from those of other patients or give rise to any special administrative or other difficulties.

These young patients with behavior disorders to be described in this paper, whether admitted under the provisions of this Act or otherwise, are considered typical of the kind of offender visualised in the Act as needing in-patient treatment. Experience gained in their handling may be helpful to those who select the material for such treatment. They are, however, of adolescent age, so that their characteristic unstable behaviour or sometimes turbulent reactions give rise to special problems; thus, any findings may not be applicable to those of more mature age.

RÉGIME

The régime and treatment undertaken in the unit have been fully described by the author elsewhere (Warren, W., 1952); it is sufficient to emphasise here that a full range of medical and psychiatric investigations and treatment is used and that there is opportunity for intensive individual psychotherapy if required. At the same time, the daily régime encourages a full programme of suitable activities, interests and education; but with enough control by the staff to promote security and an ordered routine, as it is necessary for each patient to conform within certain fairly wide limits. The unit is part of a psychiatric hospital; all patients are expected to observe the conventions usual in such a hospital, although the staff are well used to understanding and managing with success the anomalous, bizarre or acutely disturbed behaviour that may be found in psychiatrically ill patients. On the other hand, a psychiatric hospital is not equipped to deal with serious delinquent behaviour on the part of patients. Stealing from other patients or staff, breaking in or out, damage to property, or even fire-setting, are all possible with some youths exhibiting behaviour disorders; although, more often than not, these outbreaks with ordinary care are preventable by the staff. However, they can cause considerable difficulty in hospital if a delinquent boy is set on such conduct. He can be reasoned with, indeed the understanding and discussion of such impulses may be helpful towards furthering his treatment, but there can be no coercion or retribution. If these are necessary, they must be applied elsewhere and not by psychiatric personnel; in which case it may be impracticable to keep the patient.

Apart from the possibility of serious delinquent behaviour in hospital, any group of healthy teen-aged boys has a capacity for pleasurable mischief-making; they have not gained the self-control of adults. Those who are psychiatrically disturbed and in hospital have not lost such potentialities, unless they are so ill as to be out of touch with reality, or too withdrawn or crippled by their symptoms. In addition, their anxieties or aggressive qualities can be such as to make the group explosive, quick to react with unruly and provocative conduct. They need watchful and unremitting care to ensure their welfare. Thus the total of patients in the unit is kept to sixteen, a manageable number. The number of doctors, nurses and teachers forming the staff is, in proportion, high. Their intimate knowledge of each patient allows some prediction of his activities, and their direction when possible into reasonable channels, although with so varied a group all contingencies cannot be anticipated.

ADMISSIONS

As the result of practical experience a clearer assessment of the potentialities and limitations of the psychiatric unit for the care and treatment of cases with behaviour disorders has been reached. However, the exigencies of a hospital must influence, if not sometimes be decisive in, the choice for admission of a boy given to unruly and delinquent behaviour. Thus a number of requests for admission have been received for boys who were unsuitable, either because they were considered unlikely to benefit from the psychiatric treatment available, or because their behaviour or influence was likely to be too malign. Instances occurred when a boy was causing the authorities responsible for him considerable difficulties over his disposal; perhaps his instability or provocative qualities gave rise to objections to other placements; or perhaps psychiatric treatment elsewhere had failed. Constructive medical reasons for admission are essential to successful treatment, not merely the placement of some offender, seemingly undisposable because of his instability.

Timing of the admission of a patient is necessary for the tactful handling of the group. Experience has shown that more than three patients with active antisocial behaviour are likely to disorganise the ward; to admit more than one homosexual boy at one time may be regretted. A boy of sixteen or older is likely to lead others, and his influence on younger boys may be stabilizing or the reverse. Planning in the light of the current ward situation is continually necessary, and this is complicated by the uncertainty as to whether or not a boy will continue to behave in the same way as he did before admission. Some, whose management was a problem to their parents, have caused no anxiety to the staff on this score, others, admitted in a depressed or inhibited state, have become difficult as their mental state improved. Each prospective patient is studied in the light of these possible changes, and the date of his admission may be influenced to some extent by his probable impact on the ward group as a whole.

Once in the ward, a boy with a behaviour disorder, particularly if admitted from the Court, may react in various ways. He may settle down happily and be cooperative from the start, so that he is accepted by the other patients and fits in with them. He may, however, adopt a devil-may-care attitude, concealing his anxiety and unhappiness, or at first not regard himself as "ill," and so in need of hospital treatment. On the other hand, admission may be regarded as an easier alternative to an approved school, which recent sojourn in a Remand Home may have led him to expect; it may be a haven where he hopes to carry on his delinquent mode of life undisturbed. Or again there may be considerable resentment at what is regarded as an unnecessary waste of time (this attitude was shared by the parents in two Court cases). However, if suitable for admission in the first place, interviews with the therapist have usually dealt with these different attitudes, and the boy has then in most instances been prepared for the treatment that is necessary.

There was at first some uncertainty as to how patients with varied types of psychiatric syndrome would mix in the same ward. The disturbed psychotic is necessarily placed elsewhere, but the antisocial boy lives in hospital alongside the boy who shows a neurotic picture, and who has come, perhaps, from a very different background. In practice, it was found that socially normal boys are not corrupted by the antisocial; at these age levels it seems that the former have long developed standards of behaviour which are not seriously influenced by the latter. In addition, detailed knowledge of each other's background has not shown undue concern over these differences and they have accepted each other at face value. However, if a boy is antisocial or aggressive to others, then he is likely to become unpopular and be shunned.

If he is very difficult, all may find it hard to tolerate him; and so his anxieties and aggression may increase. He will then need considerable direct and indirect help from the staff, particularly from the therapist; on the one hand the difficulty may be successfully solved, with a consequent stimulus to the necessary "rapport" that needs to develop between therapist and patient; or on the other it may lead, for instance, to running away, so that treatment may become impracticable.

The following are examples of patients who proved themselves unsuitable for the hospital régime because of running away:

Case 1: aged 15. (Court Case. Released temporarily from prison for admission to the unit as a Voluntary Patient.)

This youth had a history of petty delinquencies (stealing) dating back to the age of two, and fifteen abscondings from remand homes and an approved school; he had started a two-year sentence of imprisonment. His background had been very disturbed, his father having after much quarrelling deserted his mother. The patient was fond of her, but he was later taken by his father to live with him and a 'stepmother' — a second unhappy ménage. Prior to admission repeated punishment had apparently led to further delinquencies, although it was reported that he had responded temporarily to active and friendly interest by adults. His delinquencies had been considered elsewhere to have a probable neurotic basis, and he was admitted with the full realisation of the high risk of failure.

In the ward, while at first superficially cooperative, he yet remained aloof and suspicious of everyone. He soon became overbearing and aggressive to other patients and stole repeatedly so that he was much hated by them. Many interviews with the therapist failed to help him with his difficulties. Three months after admission, he absconded after a quarrel and subsequently returned to prison. Follow up revealed that he remained there for a year, his record not being a good one. Efforts were made to place him in a job without success, and he was subsequently sent to Borstal, following further charges of stealing and housebreaking.

Case 2: aged 13. (Non-Court Case. Admitted at request of his school doctor.)

This boy had repeatedly truanted from school over two years, having previously been a model son. He was increasingly difficult at home and repeatedly stole money there. He had never been charged in Court. He had not improved with out-patient psychiatric treatment. He was of above average intelligence, clever with his hands, but sensitive and withdrawn. His mother was over-anxious and unable to cope with him; his father strict, quick-tempered and lacking in understanding.

When admitted to hospital, he promptly ran away. However, he settled down better in school after this experience. Six months later he was placed on probation for stealing; and finally joined the R.A.F. as a boy entrant and appears to be doing well.

INVESTIGATION AND TREATMENT

Examination of the case records emphasises the great variety of problems to be found amongst those with behaviour disorders. This was apparent in their etiology and in their symptoms, so that treatment had to be flexible. Their detailed analysis would serve little useful purpose; but some aspects can be emphasised and illustrated by further clinical examples.

Twenty-eight of this group remained in hospital for periods ranging from three weeks to fourteen months, with an average of five months. The other five either ran away or were removed by their parents after a period varying from a few hours up to three months. They have since remained out of this hospital for varying periods of time up to two and a half years. All have been followed up, and although no final assessment can be made it has been possible to ascertain whether they have remained reasonably stable, holding their own in work or school; or whether there have been further delinquencies or symptoms of disturbance.

Three of the group were investigated, and placed as soon as possible after assessment in a suitable institution; no further active treatment was attempted in hospital. These, with thirteen others who were given active treatment (48.5 per cent), appeared to have considerably benefited, as judged by their subsequent progress. The other seventeen (51.5 per cent) either did not improve in hospital, or were temporarily stabilized only to relapse after discharge. The proportion of those apparently helped was slightly higher in non-Court case than in Court cases, but the difference between them was not sufficient to be of significance.

The many factors that determined if a patient could be stabilized in hospital and remain so after discharge, included the general régime in the unit. A stable routine, during a crucial and turbulent time, may in itself lead, with further maturity, to increased integration, settling down and cessation of antisocial behaviour. In a small proportion it may alone have been

sufficient, but it is desirable to add what may not always be possible in institutional life, viz., the intimate knowledge of each boy by the staff and especially his therapist. His individual needs are studied, his feelings and reactions to the ward group appreciated, and at every stage of his stay he can discuss his difficulties with the therapist.

This careful attention to each boy in the total group appeared to be important, and has helped most whose behaviour and anxieties could otherwise have mounted until their stay would have been curtailed. It also helped the therapist towards the elucidation of the problems that led to admission in the first place.

Social factors. Another important factor that often needed attention during the patient's stay in hospital and afterwards was the home background.

As was to be expected, home circumstances either past or present were detrimental in the emotional sense in over two-thirds of the cases. The loss of a parent, unhappy relations between parents, and illegitimacy; rejection of the patient, or spoiling and over-solicitude, were very frequently recorded in the case histories. In nearly one-third the material circumstances at home were also detrimental, e.g., poverty, gross overcrowding, or lack of physical care through parents being absent or out at work. In a majority of instances considerable attention had to be paid to these factors; and the success of treatment could sometimes depend in part or wholly on what could be done to better them. If unalterable, the patient on leaving hospital might have to be placed elsewhere, unless he was old and stable enough to resist bad home influences. This placement was sometimes most difficult to effect; six of the patients who relapsed after discharge are believed to have done so in part because no suitable placement was possible. The following is an example: —

Case 3: aged 14. (Non-Court Case. Admitted at the request of his doctor.)

This patient was increasingly given to outbursts of temper, lying, stealing, truancy and minor sexual misdemeanors over a period of five years. He had never been charged. For a longer time he was enuretic by day and by night. His home had been grossly overcrowded, but had recently improved. Conceived before marriage, he had always been rejected by his mother; on the other hand, he lived in earlier years with his grandmother, who had spoilt and then nagged him. He was slow in development, and did not do well at school. Physically healthy, his I.Q. was 84.

After admission, he settled down at once, expressed pleasure at being away from home, and revealed himself as a rather boisterous, cheerful boy. His enuresis ceased within two days. No abnormal behaviour was observed, except that if frustrated or teased he quickly lost his temper; but with the growth of warm relationships with the staff this improved. Therapy was directed towards promoting security and sorting out with him his difficulties at home. Efforts were also made to improve the attitude of his parents towards him, but with little apparent success.

After three months he was discharged to his home, having been deemed maladjusted. It then became clear that the delay before transfer to a boarding school for maladjusted children would be so long that this course was not practicable. All his symptoms returned and he awaits placement in a hostel.

Constitutional factors. The investigation of each patient included an assessment of physical health, innate constitution, intelligence and educational attainments. All these had some bearing on the form and effectiveness of treatment. Bodily disease was comparatively rare. One patient had atrophied testicles and another undescended testicles needing physical treatment, and both these physical anomalies had considerable psychological concomitants.

Intelligence quotients ranged from 64 to 139, closely following the distribution curve found in a sample of the normal population. On the whole, those of high intelligence responded best to intensive individual psychotherapy. Thus of the seven patients with intelligence levels ranging between 109 and 139, five were considerably helped, but two did not respond because of deep-founded and apparently irreversible abnormalities of personality. A number of those of average intelligence and below were also helped, particularly one patient with an intelligence quotient of 97. We may assume therefore that factors other than the level of intelligence were more important in determining the outcome of psychotherapy. On the other hand, those with an I.Q. below 90 were, on the whole, more responsive to the general care and to the group influences of the ward than to formal psychological treatment.

The educational attainments of just under half were found to be considerably below the levels normal for their ages and intelligence quotients. Many had missed much schooling through truancy or other reasons, or were social failures at school, discouraged and wasting their time. While in hospital considerable efforts were made to help them educationally, but what could be achieved depended much on their ability to concentrate and their attitude to school lessons. To improve their educational attainments was believed to be an important factor in promoting self-esteem, in instilling the habit of regular attendance at school, or in helping towards more satisfying employment.

An electroencephalogram was made as a routine investigation. It was considered important to study in this way all patients who were not yet mature and especially those with behaviour disorders; but it was uncertain how far the readings could contribute to the total picture. They manifested a higher rate of abnormality than that found in adults or normal adolescents of the same age range. The majority of records were of the common, constitutional immaturity type, in that they showed an excess of activity in theta range. With some exceptions abnormalities did not appear to correlate closely with individual problems; but whereas only one-third of those without conduct disorders manifested them, just over one-half with conduct disorders did so. This agrees with the findings of a number of writers describing such disturbances in younger children. When an abnormality was found to be present, it was not necessarily a poor prognostic sign, and did not contra-indicate psychotherapy, since some responded well in spite of such a finding.

More specific findings amongst the group with behaviour disorders included one patient who showed unsuspected epileptic dysrhythmia. Another patient, aged 13 (a non-Court case), had foci in the temporal lobe, as in those patients described by Rey, Pond and Evans (1949). Others factors had contributed to his long-standing behaviour disorder, but it may have partly accounted for his vulnerability to detrimental influences. He slowly improved during seven months treatment in hospital, and was subsequently sent to a school for maladjusted children where the improvement continued. A further E.E.G. a year later was much nearer normal.

Two patients, with behaviour disorder of long standing, over-active and mischievous, with

whom little psychotherapeutic contact could
be made, and with abnormalities of the immaturity type in the electroencephalogram, responded to adequate doses of benzedrine. While
taking this (see Case 4) both were quieter,
less mischievous, more amenable and concentrated better. Other similar patients showed
no response, so that the drug is most uncertain but occasionally useful in such cases.

Case 4: aged 17. (Non-Court case. Admitted at
request of his doctor.)

This patient had a bad home background, with
an epileptic and intellectually dull mother and a
shiftless, ineffective father. Born before his parents'
marriage, he was dragged up in a very poor home in
an atmosphere of constant bickering. He showed
evidence of emotional disturbance as a child, failed
to gain any sense of responsibility, played with
younger children and had a quick and violent temper.
At twelve, he was psychiatrically treated and then
placed in a foster home. He was unmanageable, and
later, after being charged for the first time as beyond
control, went to an approved school for three years.
After leaving, he was repeatedly sacked from jobs for
petty pilfering and his failure to work. He avoided
further charges.

He was found to be physically immature and un-
dersized (I.Q. 97 per cent); his E.E.G. was abnormal
and of the constitutional immaturity type. He joined
with the younger boys and was either over-active,
cheerful and mischievous (although easily controlled), or quick-tempered and apt to burst into
tears. He failed to concentrate on anything constructive. Although ready to discuss his problems,
he seemed unaffected by a psychotherapeutic approach. 25 mgms. of Benzedrine a day gave a striking temporary response. He was more stable in mood,
less erratic, well behaved and was able to settle to
work. If the drug was stopped, he at once relapsed.
A year later the E.E.G. was unchanged. After discharge he failed to take the drug, and his continued
pilfering led later to a Borstal sentence.

It seems desirable, judging from these findings amongst a small group, that electroencephalographic examinations should be carried
out in young patients who show persistent behaviour disorders, and who are incorrigible in the
face of ordinary methods of correction. These examinations have been of service in providing
evidences regarding constitutional factors of
prognostic significance, but their interpretation calls for caution.

PSYCHOLOGICAL TREATMENT

A further important part of the investigation of each patient in hospital has been the
assessment of his suitability for individual psychotherapy. In the first place, whatever the
patient's personality make-up, and whether or
not he shows signs of psycho-neurosis, his general circumstances have had some influence,
favourable or otherwise on his suitability for
psychotherapy.

For treatment to be practicable, the patient
must be able to find some niche in the ward,
and to withstand what might be for him the
moderate stresses of its communal life, so that
he will at least stay. His behaviour also needs
to be within the limits that the hospital authorities could allow.

Constitutional factors, and especially the patient's intelligence, may be favourable or unfavourable, although seldom so detrimental as
to be an absolute bar to a psychotherapeutic approach. It has been emphasised, however, that
social factors can undo any help that may be
given him.

However, given a patient with reasonable
constitutional endowment and social circumstances, there are unusual opportunities for such
treatment in hospital compared with what may
be available outside. There is no set time limit
to his stay if it is likely to be of benefit to him;
and if necessary he can be interviewed daily
or at any time when a phase of treatment or
some crisis makes it necessary. The techniques
used have varied with the views and personality
of the therapist, but the intensity and length
of treatment have depended on the needs of
the patient.

It is well known that those with behaviour
disorders can be very difficult to treat by psychological means, and this has sometimes been
so in hospital. Some patients might not at
first regard themselves as having difficulties that
need such help. They were sometimes suspicious of any friendly contact with an adult,
who could be regarded as a hostile authority.
At the same time, there might be a strong desire
to repeat acts in hospital that had led before
to their being disliked and punished. Since they
are conditioned to such behaviour, considerable
patience is needed before an opportunity arises
to break through what had already become, be-

fore admission, a vicious circle of recrimination. It has sometimes required many interviews over a period of weeks before any significant relationship could be established, in which exploration of conflicts could begin. Some patients have a facility for provoking hostility, so that the personality of the therapist is important; and as a colleague remarked — "All seems to depend on whether one likes the patient." Considerable anxiety and aggression may be released once their protective armour has been pierced; this is reflected in their general behaviour, which requires careful handling, a task by no means easy even if the staff have full insight into the reasons for the behaviour.

Much depends on the relationship that can be established by the therapist with his patient. If the latter is not seemingly indifferent; feels unhappy and is anxious over his behaviour; recognises that he has worries over his relations at home; if there is some positive integration of his personality and some conscience formation; all these are pointers towards a successful outcome of psychotherapy. On the other hand, if no personal contact with other patients or staff develops except to satisfy immediate needs; if no relationship, positive or negative, springs up with the therapist; if anxieties and conflicts are so long buried as to remain hidden to the observer; if delinquent acts are constantly repeated with no accompanying emotion or apparent compunction; if the patient lies repeatedly until found out, and then shows no sense of guilt; then psychotherapy in the hospital setting is not as a rule effective.

In other words, it has appeared that patients with partly organised conduct disorders occurring as part of a psycho-neurosis, perhaps accompanied by other neurotic symptoms, or as part and parcel of difficulties typical of adolescence, are approachable by the psychotherapeutic means available, and with a fair chance of success. If, however, delinquent behaviour appeared to be deeply engrained in the personality, of very long standing or accompanied by little or no anxiety features, the chances of helping such a patient have been small. He may or may not have had a history of emotional traumata early in life, considered significant by Bowlby (1951) and others in forming the antisocial character; and it is debatable whether such a patient already has the hall marks of the psychopathic personality. However, it is also a matter of speculation whether more intensive and prolonged treatment in some setting without the limitations inherent in the hospital situation could have helped him further.

The following three patients are examples of patients with psychoneurotic difficulties who responded well to a psychotherapeutic approach in the ward setting:

Case 5: aged 16. (Court Case. Admitted under the terms of the Criminal Justice Act, 1948.)

The illegitimate son of an unstable woman, who married his stepfather when the patient was eighteen months old; the stepfather a morose, irritable man who severely nagged and beat the children. The family relationships were bad and little affection was shown. His early life was disturbed, but as a young child he was unnaturally good and quiet, failing to make any friends. Having a high intelligence — I.Q. 139 — he did well at school and won a scholarship. By eleven his resentment against his stepfather increased, especially when told of his illegitimacy. He truanted from school, failed to work and was expelled. Truancy continued with much petty pilfering and he failed to keep a job. Transfer to a hostel did not help matters and he was charged as beyond control.

When admitted he was depressed and anxious, covering up with a superior boastful façade. He took no part in any activities but spent his time reading and playing chess. At times he quarrelled and was generally uncooperative. After three or four months he became less anxious and depressed, established his position as the intellectual leader in the ward and was more helpful and better behaved. A therapeutic relationship was gradually possible, and his conflicts over his illegitimacy, his stepfather and mother were discussed and alleviated. After seven months he was discharged, still insecure, but free from anxiety and depression. Two years later, he was still living at home. Relationships there were much better and he was in steady work with one good friend. His chess had reached a very high standard.

This appeared to be an example of delinquency mostly on a basis of neurotic conflicts. His behaviour was always manageable in hospital, although treatment was slow and difficult.

Case 6: aged 16. (Court case. Admitted under the terms of the Criminal Justice Act, 1948.)

This patient had long shown neurotic symptoms including bed-wetting, and in addition since the age of eleven there had been episodic delinquency beginning with truancy from school, the theft of a bicycle and later one instance of breaking and entering, for which he was put on probation and placed in an Approved Probation Hostel. He ran away and lived by stealing, and it was following this charge that he was referred by the Court. An unwanted boy, he had been rejected by both parents. His early health had been poor and he was seclusive, easily provoked, and timid of other boys. There had been increasing rows with his parents and he had failed to keep his jobs. He had become anxious, discouraged and sullen. He was physically healthy and of average intelligence — I.Q. 97.

He resented admission, was sullen, aggressive and unpopular. He bullied the younger boys and went out of his way to show he was a 'bad boy.' This continued for some weeks and it was difficult to establish a relationship with him for the purposes of therapy. Improvement set in when he was given a job in the hospital kitchen, after which personal contact could be made; he was able to discuss his difficulties. He now steadily improved, his bed-wetting lessened, and he was discharged after four months. Efforts to get him into a hostel were without success and he returned home.

Two years later, he had remained in work and free from further offences, relationships at home were better and his enuresis had further improved.

This boy caused considerable disturbance in the ward by his behaviour, but he was manageable and he did not run away. His neurotic conflicts were clear, and once a relationship could be established, they were amenable to therapy. The Probation Officer helped considerably in ensuring his continued stability after discharge.

Case 7: aged 14. (Court case. Admitted under the terms of the Criminal Justice Act, 1948.)

An illegitimate boy, with an over-anxious, timid mother, who, when he was four, married a widower with three children. Further half-siblings were born. The patient's surname, however, was not changed. In his early life, he was passed from relative to relative; but after his mother's marriage his background became stabilized. He showed evidence of early emotional disturbance but later settled and did well at school. At twelve, he heard of his illegitimacy, became unhappy and restless and repeatedly truanted, when he lived by stealing. He also stole from both parents until charged as beyond control.

He had a high intelligence (I.Q. 120), and having settled down after admission remained cheerful, friendly and well-behaved. Therapy revealed much conflict and guilt over his parentage, aggression against his stepfather and ambivalence about his mother. His behaviour disorders were intimately associated with these difficulties. He was discharged

after two months, and sent to a naval training school. Eighteen months later, he remained stable and could be given considerable responsibility and privileges. When at home he was pleasant and happy both with his mother and stepfather.

This patient's conduct disorder also clearly had a neurotic basis and he proved an excellent subject for psychotherapy.

By way of contrast the following two patients are examples of those with severe personality disorders, who were not helped:

Case 8: aged 16. (Non-Court case. Admitted at the request of his doctor.)

This boy's father was inadequate, with a duodenal ulcer; his mother irritable, voluble and with frequent headaches. They were apt to quarrel and showed little overt affection for the patient. Two younger brothers were healthy. A few of his relatives showed considerable mental instability. He had a birth injury, was cyanosed for two days, then developed septicaemia and was a weakly baby. From the age of five, following the birth of his younger brother, he became disobedient, told lies, and showed neurotic traits for which he had some psychiatric treatment. He went to six schools, did badly and was unhappy in them, but behaved better when evacuated. At eleven, he had further psychiatric treatment without much effect following an illness lasting three months, in which he had fever and "lost his speech for a time." He was now said to be hypochondriacal, introspective, listless, swore a great deal and felt persecuted. So he remained, with outbursts of temper, mischievous, friendless and prone to tell fantastic lies. After leaving school, he lost six jobs, truanted and finally walked into a river as a dramatic gesture. His parents were anxious not to charge him in Court.

When admitted, he was found to be physically healthy and of average intelligence. An E.E.G. showed excess theta rhythm in the central area, of uncertain origin. He remained hypochondriacal, childish, unstable, unable to persist in any task, and apt to be mischievous, fantasying himself as a hero. In psychotherapeutic interviews, he aired his feelings of rejection, jealousy of his brother and fears of his own aggression; with no apparent benefit.

After five months he was discharged, and after failing follow-up appointments, has in two years appeared as an out-patient in two other hospitals, and been admitted to two more with the same symptoms.

This patient was not helped by admission, his personality was considered abnormal, and organic brain disease from birth injury or possible encephalitis at a later date was not excluded.

Case 9: aged 16. (Court Case. Referred under the Criminal Justice Act, 1948.)

An illegitimate boy, whose early history was unknown, except that from the first he was neglected and grossly ill-treated. At eight he was adopted by kind people but with a rigid moral code. He was at first cowed and anxious, but later seemed polite and well-behaved although much given to lying. He sought adult company, tended to curry favour and failed to make friends. At thirteen he began to steal repeatedly and to truant. He lost a number of jobs from this and was involved in homosexual activities. He was plausible and furtive, with rationalisations and no expression of guilt over his misdemeanours. He was finally charged for the first time with stealing.

When admitted he was found to be of above average intelligence; and from the first, showed a smooth, ingratiating manner, explained away his offences and although ready to discuss himself at length, allowed no psychotherapeutic progress to be made. He continued to steal and made homosexual advances to other patients, until after five months he was brought back to Court and referred to an approved school. Nine months later, no fundamental change in his behavior had yet taken place.

This boy was considered to have deep founded abnormalities in his personality, and psychotherapeutic efforts in hospital failed to help him. His behaviour in the ward precluded a longer stay.

Conclusions

The admission of these boys with behaviour disorders has always involved investigation in the full socio-psycho-biological sense. Kennedy (1949) described how diagnostic centres might be set up in connection with Courts, where such investigations could be carried out. Some patients with difficult problems of diagnosis would require a period of unhurried observation; their suitability for psychotherapy, for instance, may not be quickly determined. Those who require further psychiatric treatment would need to be transferred to such a centre as that described here.

Such a preliminary sorting out might have saved some of the inevitable wastage that occurred amongst this small group after admission. Such Court diagnostic centres could only help offenders. They would not deal with the many children with behaviour disorders who are not

on charge, and who are normally assessed in psychiatric out-patients' departments.

Experience of the treatment of behaviour disorders in hospital is yet small. It is important to test its value in many types.

References

Bowlby, J. (1951). "Maternal Care and Mental Health." Geneva: World Health Organization, 179.

East, Norwood (1950). "Medical Aspects of the Criminal Justice Act, 1948." *J. Crim. Sci.*, 2, 90.

Kennedy, Alexander (1948). "Discussion: Juvenile Delinquency with special reference to Remand Homes." *Pro. R. Soc. Med.*, 41, 197.

Rey, Pond & Evans (1949). "Clinical and Electroencephalographic Studies of Temporal Lobe Function." *Pro. R. Soc. Med.*, 42, 891.

Warren, W. (1951). "Conduct Disorders in Children Aged Five to Fifteen Years." *Brit. J. Delinq.*, I, 164.

Warren, W. (1952). "In-patient Treatment of Adolescents with Psychological Illnesses." *Lancet*, I, 147.

137

Child Institutionalization as a Psychotherapeutic Procedure *

Lewis R. Wolberg

This paper deals with experiences in the care of mentally and emotionally disturbed children at the children's unit of Kings Park State Hospital. Specifically, it deals with the effect of the hospital environment on the child, apart from such procedures as play techniques, art projects and kindred psychotherapies.

The children's unit was established in 1924 to care for juvenile patients suffering from

* Reprinted from 18 *Psychiatric Quar. Supp.* (1944), 167–178. Read at a symposium on child psychotherapy under the auspices of the Association for the Advancement of Psychotherapy, Steinway Hall, New York, N.Y., March 24, 1943. Used by permission of the author and the publisher. See, also, F. Clothier, "The Need of New Facilities for the Care of Disturbed Children," 34 *Mental Hygiene* (1950), 97–105. — *Ed.*

postencephalitic disorders as a sequel of the epidemic of that period. The unit was designed primarily for custodial care and for habit training. Gradually, children suffering from mental disorders other than the postencephalitic variety were admitted. Most of these belonged to the organic group. There were juvenile paretics, cases of post-traumatic psychoses and various types of organic brain disease. Mental defectives and epileptics with psychoses or with severe behavior disorders were also represented. There were a few schizophrenics and an occasional case of primary behavior disorder. In the years that followed, the incidence of postencephalitic admissions dropped; and the proportion of children admitted with primary behavior disorders and other functional conditions increased. At the present time, for example, out of an average population of 50, approximately one-third are patients with primary behavior disorders, one-third behavior disorders associated with mental deficiency, and one-third organic mental conditions. Most of the children in the unit possess borderline or a dull–normal intelligence. This is because behavior disorders in children with normal or superior intelligence are usually treated at other children's groups in the State, such as the Rockland State Hospital.

Reasons for hospitalization are approximately the same in all three groups of patients. Among these, conduct disorders — in the form of truancy, delinquency, fire-setting, runaway tendencies, sex offenses, and uncontrollable outbursts of violence and cruelty — are the most common. Here, the child constitutes a community problem, and his hospitalization is a last resort in a long series of attempts at adjustment in his own home or in a foster home. A smaller group of children is referred because of deterioration in habits or interests, as in the organic and schizophrenic psychoses. Epileptic children are often brought in for drug therapy, and juvenile paretics are referred for malarial and arsenical treatment. Occasionally, enlightened parents or guardians recognize a not too severe behavior disorder as an illness and apply to the hospital for help in adjusting the child.

Facilities for formal psychotherapy are limited, because no funds have been made available for this purpose. The children's unit is, furthermore, handicapped by an absence of trained personnel, such as child psychologists, art instructors and teachers trained to deal with behavior problems or with special mental disabilities. As a result, it has been necessary to utilize whatever resources were available or could, without too great cost, be converted. On April 8, 1938, the boys were moved from cottages condemned because of their age to a ward that had previously been used for the care of senile and infirm patients. Although the building was far from ideal, it was clean and airy and proved adequate. A space behind the building was fenced in as a play yard. No school facilities were available, but, through the cooperation of the occupational therapy department, an old bakery was equipped as a school with whatever materials could be found or could be obtained as gifts from neighboring town schools.[1] The occupational therapy department supplied a physical trainer and two workers to act as teachers, one to instruct the smaller children in formal school subjects up to the third grade level, the other to work with the older children in various occupational projects. A charge nurse and male and female attendants supervise the children on the ward and introduce them to a routine which involves as much self-care as is possible, considering the handicaps of the children.

Attempts are made to surround the child with kindness from the start and to inculcate in him the attitude that he has done nothing particularly wrong or bad. Most children when they first come to the hospital are very much confused about what constitutes "good" and "bad." They look upon their behavior at home as "bad"; and they are convinced that they are patients when they are not reprimanded for their past misconduct or for rebelling at some aspects of the ward routine.

Discipline is reduced to a minimum. At Kings Park, the first efforts were directed toward depriving a recalcitrant child of certain privileges such as the movies; but it was soon found that, instead of evoking a more wholesome future response, this actually provoked the child into greater exhibitions of aggression. Most of the children have an uncompromising hostility toward all forms of correction and have run the gamut of disciplines from bribery to brutality

---

[1] Gertrude Vink: "The Little Red Schoolhouse at Kings Park State Hospital," *Psychiat. Quart. Suppl.,* 13: 171–174, 1939.

without the slightest effect on their behavior disorders. As a matter of fact, some children seem to use aggression to precipitate a crisis with authority in a struggle for control or as a means of gaining punishment to purge themselves of guilt. Unwisely used discipline may, therefore, play into the hands of the compulsive drives of a child and help perpetrate his neurotic problems.

It was discovered that the best way to deal with aggressive and hostile children is on the basis of personal talks with the physician in which no trace of condemnation is injected. An attempt is made to convince the child that his doctors are trying to understand why he becomes upset and that they wish to help him if they can. Frequently, the patient will ask spontaneously that a certain privilege be kept from him as a result of his misbehavior. Where the discipline that the child prescribes for himself is not out of proportion to the infraction, it has been followed without demonstrable hostility being stirred up in the patient. With a technique such as this, the problem of disturbed behavior on the ward has been materially reduced. The results speak for themselves; and in the past two years, the unit has used no mechanical restraint or seclusion and very few sedative drugs.

Occasionally, the unit admits a child whose power drive and aggression flourishes rather than abates in spite of all efforts to help him feel that he is secure and loved in his new environment. The same diminutive super-ego appears to exist in this type of patient as in the psychopathic personality; and hospitalization is associated with little improvement in his relationships with people. Such children have proved foci of great anxiety for the other patients, and their transfer to adult wards has been found the only possible way of restoring peace.

Another great probelm has been the friction that develops between the adolescent and the juvenile groups. The older boys resent associating with smaller children, and the younger patients often utilize the older ones as adult substitutes. The adolescents are unable to handle the exorbitant demands and the aggression of the younger boys without becoming personally involved. Much tension has developed as a result. Because the unit is so understaffed, it has been found necessary to transfer children over 13 or 14, unless they are physically and emotionally immature, to a different ward.

By far the most common cause of difficulty is a disgruntled or hostile ward employee who seeks to flaunt his authority or to impose what he considers the proper kind of discipline for "bad boys," namely, a whipping. The children soon become intimidated, even to the point of refusing to divulge the fact that they are being abused for fear that they will be severely beaten. Instead, they work out their hostility on each other and on the ward furniture; and they become tremendously upset and insecure. Needless to say, such an employee is immediately discharged on discovery; but the damage wrought persists for a long time. Frequently, attendants who dislike children or whose personality problems are precipitated in their contacts with aggressive or sexually curious children use a less forceful — and perhaps deadlier — approach in a carping, nagging attitude. It is obvious that a dissatisfied attendant who feels he is being punished by being put on a ward with children is no fit person to supervise and care for emotionally disturbed youngsters. The greatest asset of the ward has been found to be an emotionally stable adult who is genuinely fond of children and who uses his authority in a directive rather than in a controlling manner. Knowledge and intelligence do not compensate for an inability to give affection, and it is impossible to feign a liking for children if one does not feel love. Even the mental defectives are able to see through pretense.

The objective, although not entirely realized, has been to provide for the child an environment in which he can obtain those elements essential to mental health. Much as the physical body requires certain essential ingredients, as foodstuffs and favorable temperature, for optimum growth, so an ego structure consonant with mental health develops on the bedrock of gratification of vital psychological needs. An atmosphere of security is indispensable, and this involves a feeling that one's impulses and pleasure strivings are respected and are capable of being satisfied. It includes a conviction that one is not going to be abandoned to pain or to catastrophic helplessness. It embraces a sense of knowing what is expected of one and the ability to live up to these expectations. It involves a sense of belonging and of being wanted. Bound up with the child's security, is the feeling that he is loved and the experience of real warmth and affection in his relationship with adults. He must feel that he is loved unstintedly, that he is loved for himself rather than for what he does and that he is not threatened with the withdrawal of love for his acts or impulses. Furthermore, opportunities must be provided for him where he can assimilate his environment and express his curiosity, where he can utilize to the full his native capacities and acquired skills, where he can learn to develop self-confidence and self-esteem. Yet an environment fulfilling all these requirements is not in itself sufficient. It must include a means of developing the character structure of the child, providing techniques for him that can mediate in an efficient manner his relationships with others. In short, the ultimate goal is toward a personality sufficiently plastic to effect a harmonious balance between the child's biological impulses and cultural demands.

An environment that contains even a modicum of these ideals can liberate strivings toward ego maturity that have been seriously thwarted in the impoverished atmosphere in which many problem children have been reared. There are children admitted to the hospital who are the product of broken homes, parental drunkenness and gross immorality. Many have been rejected, frightened and robbed of their self-respect. Others have been exposed to severe physical deprivation, abuse and cruelty. There are those who have been subjected to unfair demands, to unfavorable comparisons, to crippling oversolicitudes on the part of neurotic mothers. Some are brought up like wild sheep without restraint or discipline and seek by sheer force to bend the world to their tiny might. Some are raised in the shadow of authoritarian fear, and avoid hurt by trekking a rigid pathway of conformity, shrinking from life's pleasures and from self-fulfillment.

Occasionally, a simple change of environment, with a removal of the child from hampering or destructive influences, releases the floodgates of self-development. Very young children and those whose emotional problems have not been structuralized in the form of neurotic disorders or character disturbances may blossom and go ahead to fairly adequate personality evolutions.

Unfortunately, however, by the time a child has come to the hospital, the impact of inimical pressures already has produced a widespread character disorder with neurotic strivings that perpetuate themselves in spite of his new setting. Indeed, every child reacts to the new environment of the hospital with all the machinery of his character structure. He may be peculiarly oblivious to the kindnesses or considerations given him. He may retreat from any gesture of friendliness and feel threatened when he starts reaching out for companionship. He may cling compulsively to a nurse or attendant and abase himself in an appeal for affection or aid. He may resent bitterly any efforts expected of him and feel exploited by the attendants or fellow-patients in spite of any attempts they may make to treat him fairly. He may strive to outdo others and to win approval by shining in recreation and activities. He may strive for admiration and ruthlessly seek all kinds of praise. He may yield to a need to dominate or to terrorize others. He may periodically explode in hostile and aggressive behavior without any apparent cause, or exhibit masochistic tendencies by seeking to be hurt, humiliated or beaten.

Thus, simple environmental correction — in which the child is made to feel secure, in which positive demonstrations of affection are given to him, in which he is encouraged to express his self-strivings — does not usually suffice in itself to correct the child's difficulties, even though these are manifestly the result of a limited upbringing. The emotionally-ill child needs an environment with further requirements, perhaps the chief one being that he be permitted to express his neurotic character drives as far as is feasible without fear of punishment or threat of the loss of love. The child's impulses, vicarious as they seem, are tremendously important to him and serve the dynamic function of protecting him from helplessness and from fears of a menacing world. It is often difficult for hospital personnel to realize this and to understand the meaning of the child's unprovoked outbursts. One of the most important conflicts of the child is the fear that he will be hurt or rejected or humiliated when he expresses certain drives that he cannot willfully control. The ideal environment is one, therefore, in which the child can express his strivings, neurotic as they are, in an atmosphere of understanding rather than condemnation.

This brings up the subject of authority. A

great many of the problems of the emotionally-ill child are oriented around a disturbed relationship to authority. Originally vested in the child's conditionings and experiences with his parents, his attitudes toward authority are soon projected outward toward the world at large. Furthermore, his inner system of moral restraint is patterned in the light of these attitudes, and he experiences the same disquietudes and anxieties in regard to his impulses as if these were under direct surveillance of his parents. Rejected children, those who have been overprotected or subjected to excessive domination, organize their behavior to avoid injury or the loss of love. Because self-assertiveness, aggressiveness and sexual curiosity are so frequently prohibited, an inhibition of these functions is mandatory to the retention of the good will of the parent. Hostility is inevitable and usually contributes to the problem, for the expression of hostility, too, is fraught with danger. On the basis of an attitude which conceives of authority as destructive or fearful, the child is blocked in his strivings for security, for self-expressiveness, for love, for satisfactions in play and for the attainment of creative growth in accordance with his capacities and aptitudes. As long as the child regards authority as a harbinger of destruction, he will be unable to express the basic biological and social needs which are essential to normal personality growth.

Ego development, therefore, presupposes a reorientation in the child's attitudes toward authority to a point where he is able to express his basic strivings without fear of injury. Many of the child's character drives are subterfuges to win security in a vicarious manner, in accordance with his particular experiences. Detachment from people, ingratiation with them, compulsive clinging are a few of the patterns that protect the child. These compulsive drives eventually alienate him from people and from his own biological impulses. Until his attitudes toward authority are straightened out, he will be unable to relinquish his neurotic strivings, and he will be incapable of fulfilling needs that are necessary to his physical and psychic well-being.

While the child seeks desperately to express his needs, he will naturally withdraw when these expose him to a more intimate relationship with another being in which he may be hurt. It is a slow process whereby the child's attitudes to authority eventually are changed to a point where

he is able to express his impulses without fear of injury. It is necessary, therefore, for adults to bear with the child while he works out his relationships with authority in the more tolerant setting of the hospital. Many of his reactions are in the nature of tests to convince himself that adults are not to be trusted. For example, the child in the presence of an affectionate attendant, may experience feelings of love. He may then be tremendously threatened by these feelings as they emerge and feel very hostile toward the attendant for evoking feelings in him which involve possibilities of being hurt in an interpersonal relationship. The overt expression of his conflict may, therefore, be an aggressive act toward the attendant. Where the attendant bears with the patient, is kindly toward him and does not punish him, the patient may arrive at the discovery that his concept of people as universally dangerous is not a truth. Eventually he may even overtly express his feelings of love toward the attendant and extend this gradually to other people.

A child of five was admitted to the hospital in a tense, sullen state, exhibiting a fearful shrinking attitude whenever approached and whenever attempts were made to get him to participate in any of the activities on the ward. The boy was an illegitimate child of a psychopathic mother who had apparently accepted him to some extent when he was an infant, but had abandoned him to the care of her parents when he was two years of age. The grandparents themselves were hostile and maladjusted people who subjected the child to cruel treatment of an almost inhuman nature. The child was kept locked in a cellar and often tied when he remonstrated. Social agencies intervened at the complaints of neighbors, and it was discovered that the boy had been exposed to severe beatings. On one occasion, he had even been locked out of the house overnight and had, as a result, suffered frostbite resulting in gangrene of two of his toes. On the ward, the boy withdrew from all contacts; and whenever an attempt was made to get close to him, he exhibited manifest symptoms of anxiety. It was almost as if he regarded any attempt to treat him with kindness and consideration as a trap. It was months before he would respond to demonstrations of interest in him. But having advanced this far, the patient gradually extended his interest in his fellow-patients. He participated more and more in games and other activities, and soon he spontaneously greeted the attendants with gestures of friendship. As the months went by, one could almost see him develop from a retarded, detached individual to one of the most likable little chaps on the ward. Foster home placement was successful and the patient was entered in school where he progressed successfully.

The case illustrates an important point in the dynamics of emotional disorder, namely, that a spontaneous driving force toward mental health exists, which is coordinate with the symptoms of a disturbed emotional state. Too often, one overemphasizes pathological elements in mental illness without realizing that even the most disturbed children show spontaneous tendencies toward remissions or cures. The motivating forces that drive the patient forward toward better relationships with the world are perhaps his unfulfilled biological and social promptings that ceaselessly strive for gratification. When a reasonable chance is given, the child will actively enter into relationship situations as if he desperately seeks to reorient himself to the world.

As the child enters into a new life on the ward, one may see him cautiously — always with the expectation of imminent catastrophe — expressing the very impulses that have at home been subjected to repression. The ability to express these impulses without the fear of retaliatory punishment, to express aggression or hostility without counter-hostility, is one of the most potent means of altering the child's attitude toward authority as potentially destructive and toward his own impulses and needs as completely bad and worthless.

An example may illustrate this point. A boy of 13 was admitted to the children's ward with a history of difficulties since the age of seven. He was the only child of a neurotic mother who would not permit him to leave the house unless she accompanied him, because she feared that he might be run over or attacked by other children. The mother was an extremely domineering individual whose own love life had resulted in disappointment and who apparently was compensating for her lack of interests by concentrating completely on her child. The patient was very submissive, timid, never lost his temper and was absolutely obedient to his mother. He was never known to raise his voice.

Whenever he became fretful or tense, he would tear his own clothing or his handkerchief. At school, he developed an uncontrollable tendency to laugh explosively to the amusement of the pupils and the annoyance of his teacher.

Shortly after he reached the age of seven, he began to express a wish to be a girl, and he refused to cut his hair, attempting to talk and behave like a girl. He would spend hours in front of a mirror combing his hair, and he would ask for rouge, lipstick and mascara. He had night terrors and expressed fears of dark ominous animals. He was taken to several mental hygiene clinics, but the mother never made a concerted effort to obtain treatment for him.

At the age of 12, he began to act more peculiarly; and finally he insisted that he was not the son of his mother. He was really, he declared, a French boy who had been kidnaped and brought up by the woman who posed as his mother. He developed the conviction that if he ate the dandruff from French peoples' hair or the wax from their ears he would become reconverted into a French boy. There were other peculiarities with a schizophrenic tinge. On admission to the hospital the patient was extremely timid, self-centered, submissive and obsequious. He had an affected feminine manner, asked for lipstick, curled his hair and constructed a doll out of a handkerchief. When approached by the other boys, he would shrink away in a corner. He was very "cowardly" and never quarrelled. Whenever interviewed, he was overly courteous, always trying to create a good impression. The more aggressive children teased and tormented him about his feminine interests.

As the months went by, he gradually interested himself in activities that were more in accord with boyish proclivities. Coincident with his "opening up" to people, his aggression became more and more pronounced. His anxiety, apparently invoked by his aggression, came more and more under his control as he found he could express himself. Soon, he discovered that he could stand up to the other boys whenever they approached him or picked on him. The turning point in his development was a fist fight in which he emerged victorious. The change that occurred in the boy was little short of miraculous. He abandoned his strivings for femininity and appeared to lose all his previous delusional ideas. When questioned regarding his interest in becoming a Frenchman, he laughed at the statements he had made, saying he could not comprehend why he had acted this "crazy" way.

An interesting sidelight is that when he was taken home by his mother, he insisted upon being permitted to smoke, upon going outside and playing with the boys and upon staying out as late as they did at nighttime. When his mother forbade him to do these things, he did them anyway. The mother was manifestly disturbed by this change in the boy's conduct and admitted that she really preferred to have him the other way even though he was "a little off." It was apparent that she, herself, was in need of considerable treatment before the boy could be returned to her home. While no claim of permanency in mental cure is made, his improvement was definitely seen to be related to his experiences on the ward.

There should be a word about organic disturbances. In general, the principles of handling the child with structural brain damage are approximately the same as in the functional behavior disorders. The organically handicapped child responds explosively to errors in handling or to disturbed conditions at home; and his reactions may be quantitatively greater, though qualitatively similar, to those of the child with functional disorders. Every organic condition represents a fusion of reactions symptomatic of the destructive influence of the disease as well as of the result of pressures exerted on the child by his environment. Often, the child is expected to come up to the standards of other children in his age group, and his own self-esteem may suffer disastrously when he fails. His tolerance of frustration, and his abilities to repress pleasure strivings, may be impaired; and he may be unable to elaborate adequate techniques of dealing with his tension. As a consequence, he will be at the mercy of feelings of helplessness and overwhelmed by fears of authority.

A case in point is the hyperkinetic postencephalitic child. Often, against his will, the latter will yield to impulses of an unrestrained or destructive nature. In those children with a hypertrophied super-ego these reactions will be associated with intense anxiety, on the basis that they will be unloved or punished for acts that they know are wrong, but which they are unable to control. The suffering in some of these children is intense and frequently results in an elaboration of defenses against the ex-

ternalization of aggression in the form of a turning of hostility inward, with self-recriminations and self-injury. In some cases, there is a development of a compulsive–obsessive type of reaction, apparently as a means of neutralizing hostile wishes. It is obvious that the development in the child of a new attitude toward authority and toward his own impulses has a markedly ameliorative effect on the symptom picture. The organic condition remains, of course, but the child becomes a healthier and happier child and is frequently enabled to contribute something of value to the group.

Emphasis in treatment, therefore, is not so much on the particular type of diagnostic category into which the patient fits, as upon his disturbances in operation as a social functional unit. The handling of the child is essentially the same, regardless of whether one is dealing with an organic mental condition or with a functional behavior disorder. Specific therapeutic measures, if these are indicated for the organic condition, must of course be utilized; but the behavior problems of the child, the difficulties that he has in social functioning, are handled best by an approach that strives to reorient him in his relationships with people.

SUMMARY

It does not follow that because a child is removed from a disturbed environment his behavior problem or emotional difficulty will of necessity vanish. As a general rule, the emotionally sick child carries over, in his own character structure, attitudes toward authority, toward the world and toward himself that perpetuate themselves in his new setting. When institutionalized, for instance, he may actively create situations that seem to bear out his particular philosophies of life. Change is wrought, not by the passive influence of a beneficial environment, but rather follows his ability to reorient himself actively in his relationships with people.

Placement in a hospital, by removing the child from discordant elements at home, materially lessens tension and anxiety. Where the personality difficulty has not become too deeply structuralized, a spontaneous drive for development may stimulate ego growth in the direction of mental health. The child with the more severe problems, though clinging to his neurotic drives for a much longer time than the child with lesser difficulties, has, in his new environment, a better chance of substituting more gratifying techniques in his adjustments to life — techniques which will eventually enable him to function free from anxiety.

The security of the child is bound up with his interpersonal attitudes, and it is essential to regard his drives — whether they consist of inordinate dependency, submissiveness, detachment, masochistic surrender, aggression or power strivings — in the light that they serve the dynamic function of protecting him from helplessness and from his fears of the world. It is essential also to understand that while his drives have a vicarious safety value, they isolate him from other persons and divert him from the gratification of vital biological and social needs. The object in the hospital treatment of the child is to reintegrate him in his attitudes toward authority, toward himself and toward his impulses to a point where his abnormal drives serve no useful purpose.

An atmosphere of security is a prime requirement, and an effort must be made to convince the child that the adults who surround him do not consider him a bad or a vicious person because he has certain impulses and drives. Rather, he must be shown that his wishes and feelings are respected and that other persons like him and are genuinely interested in him. At the same time that he learns that he is not rejected or threatened for his symptoms, he must be shown that they are against his best interests. In aggressive reactions for example, the mere abreaction of hostility in itself is not so important as the fact that the child learns, from the way his aggression is handled, new attitudes toward authority whereby he does not automatically feel punished for feelings of hate. The sanction of aggressive behavior on the ward is without value unless it is followed up by insight in the child into the fact that aggression serves no particular function in his new setting. The more wholesome attitudes that the patient develops in his hospital contacts are the nucleus around which he can rebuild patterns of behavior capable of mediating harmonious relationships with others and eventuating in a gratification of his basic strivings in conformity with the mores of the culture.

The most important factor in the hospital treatment of the child is the kind of adult with whom he associates and lives. It is essential to surround the child with emotionally stable adults whose own personality problems do not handicap them in their relationships with children. An ideal adult is one with a genuine liking for children who is threatened neither by their hostility nor sexual curiosity, who does not pander to a child's compulsive drives nor reject him for them. Success is so directly bound up with the character of the personnel that this remains the chief consideration in the organization of a children's unit.

CHILDREN'S UNIT
KINGS PARK STATE HOSPITAL
KINGS PARK, N. Y.

138

Social Background and Social Integration of the Psychiatrically Ill Child in Congregate Temporary-Shelter Care *

William S. Davis,
Wilfred C. Hulse,
and John J. Murphy

This paper is concerned with the emotionally ill child who needs psychiatric service in a congregate temporary shelter. The 200 unselected cases discussed here were in residence at the Children's Center of the Department of Welfare of the City of New York. This institution is a non-sectarian, interracial, publicly operated shelter for dependent and neglected children between the ages of two and sixteen years. It has accommodations for 356 children, and there

---

* Reprinted from 38 *Mental Hygiene* (Oct., 1954), 556–564. Used by permission of the authors and the publisher. See, also, "Preliminary Report on a Psychiatrically Focused Program of a Temporary Shelter for Dependent and Neglected Children," by J. J. Murphy, J. A. Simmons, W. C. Hulse, and M. C. Vargara, 2 *J. Child Psychiatry* (1952), 285–301. — Ed.

is an annual population turnover of approximately 1,780 children. However, because of difficulties in securing appropriate foster care, nearly two-thirds of the children in residence remain beyond a temporary period of care, some for as long as two or three years.

At the center, a child is referred for psychiatric examination by the social-service department if disturbed behavior is observed by the social worker, the children's counselor, the teacher, the recreation worker, or the pediatrician. Other children are seen when significant facts about their emotional disturbances are known before their admission to the center.

The orthopsychiatric personnel at Children's Center consists of one chief psychiatrist, 10 hours per week; one associate psychiatrist, 10 hours per week; one director of social services, full time; seven psychiatric caseworkers, full time; one director of psychological services, 10 hours per week; one clinical psychologist, 10 hours per week; and three clinical psychologists in training giving a total of 45 hours per week. In addition, a child-guidance team from the Manhattan State Hospital, engaged in a special experimental and training program, was in attendance two half-days per week in 1951 and 1952.

In New York City, during the year 1952, there was a daily average of 1,157 dependent and neglected children in temporary-shelter care. All 15 shelter-care agencies in New York City, except Children's Center, are operated under private voluntary auspices, and their intake can be controlled. Children's Center, as a public agency, cannot refuse shelter to a child in need. As a result, most of the children who present psychiatric problems at the time they are referred for temporary-shelter care are admitted to the center. The only exceptions are those children who have been diagnosed as acutely psychotic, or who are grossly defective. It should be noted that until January 1, 1953, the residential-treatment facilities for seriously disturbed children in New York City were extremely limited and, as a consequence, the psychiatrically ill child at the center remained in temporary-shelter care for excessively long periods of time.

The 200 cases are evaluated according to reasons for reference, past history, symptomatology, and diagnosis.

This paper is concerned with the types of psychiatric disturbance found in a congregate children's shelter and the backgrounds of the children that contributed to those disturbances. The specific difficulties of shelter care for the emotionally ill child and the difficulties in placement are discussed. Suggestions are made for a more adequate placement of children of these types.

Case Material. Of the 200 children included in the study, 108 were boys and 92 girls. This distribution conforms to that of the general population of the center, wherein the number of boys was slightly higher than the number of girls.

The reasons for referring children for psychiatric study were: (1) an unusual amount of aggressive, hostile behavior — *e.g.*, gross acting out, such as stealing, running away, fighting, and open sex play; (2) manifestations of withdrawal or depression; (3) numerous physical complaints without medical confirmation; and (4) unrealistic and bizarre behavior.[1]

Past history pointed to some interesting data which are presented in the following tables:

Of the 200 cases selected at random, 44 had had previous psychiatric histories; 37 of them had been diagnosed as psychoneurotic, primary behavior disorder, character disorder, and so forth.

According to diagnosis, the 200 cases were grouped into the categories shown in Table 4:

The low number of psychotic, organically ill,

Table 1   *Prolonged Absence of One or Both Parents* *

REASONS FOR ABSENCE	NUMBER OF INSTANCES
Separation (incompatibility)	59
Death	51
Illegitimacy	51
Mental illness	51
Severe physical illness (TB, cancer, etc.)	49
Long-term imprisonment	8

* Parents were living together in only 13 out of the 200 cases. There were frequently several reasons for parental absence.

[1] See " 'On the Spot' Psychotherapy in a Children's Institution," by W. C. Hulse, R. Whitfield, and M. C. Vargara. *Psychiatric Quarterly Supplement,* Vol. 28, 1953.

Table 2   *Asocial Behavior in Parents*

ASSOCIATED BEHAVIOR	NUMBER OF INSTANCES
Alcoholism	57
Neglectful father or mother (court adjudicated)	37
Promiscuity or prostitution in mother	26
Criminality	8
Other asocial behavior	7

Table 3   *Age-Group Distribution of Children*

AGE GROUP	NUMBER OF CHILDREN
Pre-school	5
6–10	77
11–13	66
14–17	52
TOTAL	200

Table 4   *Diagnostic Categories*

DIAGNOSIS	NUMBER OF CASES
Psychoneuroses	85
Primary behavior disorders	71
Character disorders	23
No gross psychopathology	10
Organic illness	5
Psychoses	4
Mental deficiency	2
TOTAL	200

and mentally defective patients can be attributed to the fact that cases of these types are usually weeded out early for hospitalization or other institutional placement. When they are clinically identified at the point of admission, they are not retained at the center.

The cases in our study fall into the following I.Q. groupings:

Illustrative case material is herewith presented to show types of family background and behavior problem in the cases that come to the Children's Center. These are typical examples.

Case 1. Alvin, a six-year-old boy whose behavior varied from a very lovable, coöperative attitude to a violent, aggressive one, was subject to frequent temper tantrums in which he screamed, kicked, bit, and attempted to destroy anything within his reach. He was referred for a psychiatric work-up. His tantrums were extremely upsetting and frightening to the children in his group.

A., with his siblings — R., five, and H., three — all of illegitimate birth, were referred to the children's court by the Society for the Prevention of Cruelty to Children, which initiated a neglect petition that was adjudicated by the court. The children's mother had separated from the father because of his excessive drinking, only to take up another illicit relationship with another alcoholic who, under the influence of liquor, was abusive to wife and children.

This mother had been surrendered for adoption when only a few months old, had been placed in an adoptive home, but had been returned to the institution, only to be subsequently placed in two adoptive homes, six boarding homes, and two institutions in New York State. Coming to New York City in 1943 at the age of sixteen, she went to a girls' resident club, but was so disturbed that she was sent to Bellevue Hospital and later to Rockland State Hospital with a diagnosis of "psychopathic personality with psychosis." She had

Table 5   *Intelligence Grouping of Children **

RETARDED	NUMBER	NORMAL OR ABOVE	NUMBER
I.Q. below 60	2	I.Q. 90– 99	42
" 60–69	9	" 100–119	12
" 70–79	31	" 120–130	2
" 80–89	47	Above 130	2
	89		58

* In 53 cases no data were available on intelligence as the children left the center before psychometrics could be completed or were too disturbed to be properly evaluated.

remained at Rockland State Hospital until July, 1944. Out on parole and receiving public assistance, she had lived with different men. She was unable to assume proper care of children and home. Before the neglect petition was finally instituted in 1951, she had conceived again in an out-of-wedlock affair with another alcoholic man.

The mother, a white woman, was very ambivalent toward Alvin, who had been born of a Negro father. The boy's developmental history was not significant except that he was always described as being "hyperactive."

Case 2. Barbara, a thirteen-year-old girl, was referred because she had made a poor adjustment to the center and to the "outside" school. She was described as having wide swings in moods — alternately quiet and withdrawn, and impudent and indolent. She was a truant, quarrelsome, disobedient, and subject to temper outbursts. In addition, she had disabilities in reading and arithmetic. The older of two girls, B. had been exposed to constant social, economic, and emotional deprivation. The father had deserted when she was a small child. Her mother and grandmother, with whom she had always lived, were alcoholic and engaged in other forms of asocial activity. The mother was subsequently committed to a mental institution, and placement in temporary shelter for the children was effected, pending placement in foster care.

Case 3. Charles, a sixteen-year-old boy, was referred because he had begun to show signs of restlessness and expressed a desire to be alone. He resented being with a group after having spent six and one-half years in another institution for boys. Anxiety about his academic difficulties was evinced. He had become quick to anger, and would fight at the slightest provocation. C. was the older of two siblings. The mother had divorced her first husband after one year because of infidelity. Seven years later she had married Mr. X. (C.'s father), but after one year had separated from him because of his drinking. Three years later, she had taken up a common-law relationship with Mr. Y., who had met a violent death by stabbing some eight years later.

After C.'s birth, Mrs. X had suffered a depression and had been picked up by police when she had attempted suicide by trying to jump into the Harlem River. She had been admitted to a state hospital and released the same year as improved. She had returned to her legal husband, Mr. X., and given birth to a second child. Eleven years later she had sought placement for the children, saying that she was having a "nervous breakdown." Two months later she had committed suicide by turning on the gas in her apartment.

Case 4. Dolores, a twelve-year-old girl, was referred because she appeared tense and restless, was unable to relate to adults, was unkempt in her personal appearance, was unable to converse with her mother when she visited, and showed difficulty in functioning in the group.

The mother was negligent of the children and an alcoholic. She had had seven out-of-wedlock children. She had once married, but had separated after two years. The children were aware that the mother's paramour had killed her brother. One sibling had actually witnessed the slaying by this man, with whom the mother continues to have a relationship. Charges against the paramour were dismissed by the court.

Case 5. Edward, an eight-and-a-half-year-old boy, was referred for a psychiatric evaluation because he was unable to relate either to adults or to his peers. He was excessively withdrawn, appeared unhappy, and was given to thumb-sucking, nail-biting, and daydreaming.

His father and two siblings, ages seventeen and nineteen, visited him infrequently, because of work schedules and distance. His mother had been confined to a state hospital for chronic tuberculosis for three years. During this period, he has never visited his mother, but has been shifted from one relative to another.

Our case material shows uniformly severe neglect by parents who are seriously disturbed and unable to maintain for themselves and their families even a minimum of social standards. They are disorganized, violent, delinquent, and physically or mentally ill people who are unable to care for themselves and are, therefore, incompetent to bring up children. The five case histories given high-light this common background of the group of 200 children discussed.

All 200 cases presented severely disturbed and traumatized backgrounds. We feel that this material is significant on the basis of experiences gained at Children's Center. Such experiences have not been high-lighted elsewhere.

The general population of the center has been further investigated by four studies entitled, *A Survey of Problems Presented by Dependent and Neglected Children in Residence at Children's Center.* Identical methodology was used in all four studies. One of the ten specific problems identified in the studies was the seriously disturbed child for whom psychiatric care is recommended. On May 9, 1951, there were 68 (18.9 per cent) such children in residence at the center; on November 28, 1951, there were 80 (24.2 per cent); on May 14, 1952, there were 82 (22.7 per cent); and on November 12, 1952, there were 87 (26.1 per cent).

The majority of the seriously disturbed children identified in the four studies have suffered from lack of proper family care due to severe physical or mental illness or delinquent behavior in the parents. They should, therefore, not be returned to their parents until adequate rehabilitation of the parental home has been achieved. In most instances, the parents presented severe psychopathology in their own lives. On the other hand, most foster-care agencies are reluctant or unable to accept children who are emotionally disturbed, particularly if these children have excessive educational disabilities.

In an attempt to make available to all seriously disturbed children the facilities of Children's Center, these children were classified into three broad categories for the purpose of screening and selecting them according to their treatment needs and their probable response to environmental manipulation and orthopsychiatric disciplines. For the 87 children identified as seriously disturbed, for whom psychiatric care had been recommended in the November 12, 1952, study, the following categories were established:

A. *Moderately disturbed* (39 children). This type of child can respond to a carefully directed and psychiatrically oriented group-living situation, requires a minimum of regimentation, and can be integrated into the community life of school, church, and leisure-time activities away from the institution. This child can respond to individualized care given by a counselor who is warm, intelligent, understanding, and able to absorb aggressive behavior. Integration of the child into the total program is achieved through close liaison between the counselor and the psychiatric social worker. Individual psychotherapy is *desirable*, but *not absolutely necessary* for this type of child.

B. *Difficult* (37 children). These are children whose needs are such that they cannot be completely met in day-to-day group living. This type of child requires, in addition to the setting described in "A," special individual, psychiatric treatment. The process used at Children's Center is as follows: The child is seen regularly, once a week or more often if necessary, for individual psychotherapy sessions of from 45 to 60 minutes duration, by a professional person (psychiatrist, psychiatric social worker, or clinical psychologist) who works with the child under the supervision of the chief psychiatrist, generally over a period of three months, but often for a period of from six to ten months. The cases of all the children under treatment are reviewed regularly in conference with the director of social services, the director of psychological services, and the chief psychiatrist. The therapist, caseworker, psychologist, and psychiatrist remain in close liaison with the institutional staff and school, in order to coördinate the psychotherapeutic and environmental management.

C. *Extremely disturbed* (11 children). A child of this type requires frequent temporary restriction and constant close supervision in the group-living situation. Regular control is necessary at all times and all program activities have to be confined to the limited area of the institution proper. Control is required as an adjunct to the therapeutic procedures described in "A" and "B."

At Children's Center there is a firm belief in the concept of a balanced population. We apply this concept not only to the three above described categories, but to all children in residence. Experience has taught us that within the generic description of congregate temporary-shelter care, the children need not be of the same sex, the same race, the same intellectual capacity, the same background, or the same type of behavior pattern. We do not presume to assess arithmetical percentages as to how a balanced population should be achieved. Each facility will have to make an analysis of its own resources and construct its own formula to fit the particular set of circumstances inherent in its total program.

In consequence, we feel that the emotionally disturbed child can be absorbed into a total group-living experience, providing the total program has an orthopsychiatric focus in which the specialized services are used in consultative capacities and for the orientation of the total staff. We came to this conclusion as a result of careful evaluation of controlled surveys.

At Children's Center, there is a recognition of the practical reality of operative problems, such as lack of control over intake, limited facilities for diagnostic work-ups, insufficient services for the number of children who require psychotherapy, and a lack of proper balance in both primary and interest grouping of children. However, despite these limitations, Children's Center has tried to demonstrate that all group-living facilities can admit and accommodate seriously disturbed children if they can provide adequate orthopsychiatric disciplines. We hope that our experiences will encourage those institutions that are now hesitant to admit emotionally disturbed children to open their doors to a limited number of such children and to adjust their total program to the needs of these children.

To summarize, a survey of 200 children who came to the attention of the psychiatric services at Children's Center, Department of Welfare, City of New York, shows that 93.5 per cent came from broken families, in which rehabilitation of sound and adequate family living appeared impossible in the foreseeable future. While the diagnostic categories and the distribution of intelligence among this group of children do not show any unusual features, their behavior creates management problems in an open shelter for neglected and dependent children. Children's Center has developed a psychiatrically oriented program focused on the integration of all disciplines. This program has been described in a previous paper.[1] The present paper focuses on another stage in the development of a psychiatrically oriented program — namely, the integration of emotionally disturbed children in the general population of a congregate temporary shelter.

In an attempt to meet the needs of all seriously disturbed children with the facilities available within Children's Center, the children were classified into three broad categories for the purpose of screening and selecting each child according to his treatment needs and his probable response to environmental manipulation and orthopsychiatric disciplines. It is hoped that other group-living facilities which at the present moment are hesitant to accommodate seriously disturbed children will be encouraged to provide orthopsychiatric disciplines as developed in Children's Center.

---

[1] See Murphy, Simmons, Hulse, and Vargara, op. cit.

Chapter 25

Institutional Personnel

WHEN ALL IS SAID AND DONE, it is people — rather than institutions, buildings, organization-charts and like paraphernalia — on whom reliance must be placed in the treatment of delinquency, as in the management of almost any social problem. During the past few decades, it has been generally conceded that aberrations of personality and conduct require for their understanding and therapy a trained mind — the knowledge and techniques of the psychiatrist, the psychologist, the psychiatric social worker. And yet there are instances in everyone's experience where the insight and warmth of a layman has done more to help a twisted or unhappy personality than have the techniques of the scientifically equipped specialist. In every walk of life there are a few persons whom nature has blessed with the gift of healing. If some method could be devised for the early recognition of such *therapeutic personalities* and their guidance into areas of work where their natural competence could be used to best advantage, two great values would be supplied: first, the marked shortage of technical expertise would be lessened, and, secondly, a substantial ingredient of sympathetic insight, warmth and dedication would be added to the efforts of specialists.

On the other hand, the ignorant and rigid non-professional, who is so unintelligent as to scoff at the special competence of the technically equipped worker, can counteract the basic theories and plans behind a treatment program.

How can the contributions of the two groups be maximized, and misunderstanding and friction be minimized? This is a crucial question in all institutions.

In this connection, there is a tendency toward misunderstanding and even occasional conflict between the "professional staff" of an establishment for coping with aberrant emotion and behavior and the "non-professional staff," such as cottage parents, vocational supervisors and maintenance workers. It is being recognized more and more, however, that it is the *total human environment* of an institution — including the sympathy and understanding of even the maintenance staff — that plays its part for weal or woe.[1]

The articles in the present chapter deal with the personnel problem. The first two are concerned with general ideas of the roles to be assigned to each type of worker in an institution for delinquents.

Beginning with a brief résumé of the history of residential treatment for delinquents and basing their discussion on a wide variety of institutions, Lourie and Schulman, in the first article, give a panorama of the type of arrangements and duties of various members of an institution staff, in the light of theories of treatment. They point to the passage from custodial and punitive governing ideas in institutions for delinquents to the introduction, through the influence of psychoanalytic theories of child development, of the goal of stimulating the child's normal growth by means of relevant casework and psychiatric skills. It is recognized that the entire staff must be therapeutically oriented, and that "the essence of residential treatment lies in the milieu — in the complement of adult–child relationships and experiences which can be

---

[1] See S. Glueck, "Two International Criminologic Congresses: A Panorama," 40 *Mental Hygiene* (1956), 384–405, 599–630, at 623.

clinically manipulated and controlled in the interests of therapy." The authors indicate that the problems of children who require intramural care — children of depriving, rejecting, or cruel familial backgrounds, who have "run the gamut of institutions, clinics, boarding schools, or foster homes and who have exhausted the ability of all concerned to find ways of caring for them" — need much more than psychotherapy. The problems involve fundamental damage to personality structure, aggressiveness, destructiveness, extreme anxiety, bizarre behavior, truancy and other serious manifestations which cannot be tolerated in the ordinary school situation. "Residential treatment offers to these children, unable to face the demands of reality living, the opportunities for processed or diluted living experiences and relationships." The authors, like so many other writers in this field, emphasize the basic need of tolerance, affection, non-punitive attitudes on the part of all adults dealing with such children, to enable them to rebuild ego strength. "Out of planned use of resident staff comes the atmosphere, the therapeutic milieu, which is the tool of residential treatment," and which results in "tempered reality." One would like to have illustrations of the mechanisms involved in carrying out the authors' optimistic conception that "relationships can be diluted or concentrated, experiences can be juggled: to create anxiety, to lessen anxiety, to protect . . . [the child] from, or project him into reality, to create situations which accelerate or give impetus to the child's individual therapy."

The authors point to the skilful use of house-parents not only for taking care of the child's physical needs and routines of daily living, but for other parental functions, such as shopping for the child, granting him permission to carry out certain forms of recreation, etc. — all designed to provide a "framework of order, the external force which protects the child from his own impulsive drives." The authors discuss the role of the counselor and the nurse or attendant under various arrangements of individual and group therapy. Summarizing a variety of institutional provisions, Lourie and Schulman conclude that the only basic difference in the approach to the use of the resident staff among various institutions is that in one type the staff works integratedly with the individual therapist so that the daily living of the child is more or less clinically planned and directed, while in the other the residential person is the chief therapist, "in effect a residential or environmental therapist." The first type predominates in most residential treatment centers.

The next piece, by Weber, is concerned with conflicts between professional and lay members of an institutional staff. It is an instructive article based on long experience in two private and three public institutions for delinquents. Weber illustrates how the value orientations and the varied conceptions of status and role among professionals and non-professionals working under the same roof lead to misunderstandings and friction; and he makes some recommendations to relieve such conflicts.

The remaining articles in this chapter deal specifically with one or another specialist in the institutional personnel.

The first, also by Weber, describes the role of the psychologist in the training school for delinquents. Weber recounts the experience of a group of progressive educators in developing a therapeutic program in an industrial school for boys which had previously used a military approach to delinquents. He describes the work of the clinical psychologist not merely in the assessment of the boy upon his entrance but in developing an individualized program and in participating in counseling, psychotherapy and other aspects. Both intelligence- and personality-testing are provided, and added evaluations are made by special test techniques where prior findings indicate their need. Weber gives a case-history illustration of the nature of the material developed by the comprehensive testing process. Varieties of counseling and individual and group psychotherapy in which the psychologist participates are described. The expansion of the opportunity of the clinical psychologist to develop into a therapist is pointed out.

Rev. J. L. Cedarleaf discusses the role of the chaplain with delinquent boys in an institution. Pointing out that in the past it was customary to assign retired or misfit clergy to institutional chaplaincies, he says that in more recent years ministerial work in this field has been recognized as important and challenging, largely "because of the revelation through dynamic psychology." He recounts the work of the Council for Clinical Training in providing seminarians and clergy with clinical experience in problems of interpersonal relationships and in the role of religion and pastoral care in alleviating the problems. By means of case summaries he shows how the chaplain plays an important part, as a member of the institutional team, in the diagnostic and therapeutic processes. He indicates the possible relationship of emphasis by the child of one or another Biblical story to various deep-lying personality involvements. Not only basic religious problems, but sexual values, attitudes and ethical concepts are taken into account in the diagnostic assessment; and an attempt is made to discover the association between religious and cultural values and libidinal drives. The subject's attitude toward God — whether he conceives the Diety anthropomorphically as a sort of "supermanipulator" or more maturely — is related to the therapeutic potentials. "If a patient is basically concerned about his ultimate relationships, then dealing with these as oedipal, neurotic, or character problems is of little therapeutic avail." On the other hand, "if the patient is primarily concerned with the finite issue and the counselor attempts to deal purely with the ultimate concerns, failure is certain to take place." The author draws a distinction, in the therapeutic process, between neurotic faith and creative faith. In respect to treatment, Mr. Cedarleaf is of the opinion that "it is the distinct kind of transference that occurs in relation to the chaplain that makes him a unique person on the team." In that connection, he refers to difficulties that arise in subject–clergyman relationships, particularly regarding the stereotyped role of the chaplain as a father and the complications it leads to in the therapeutic relationship. Finally, Mr. Cedarleaf has some inspiring things to say about the redemptive power of "understanding-love" in the relationship of the chaplain to the human being he is trying to aid.

The last article in this chapter, by Konopka, deals with the role of the group worker in an institution. (Elsewhere,[2] there are accounts of the group work procedure in other connections.) She tells of her experience under a research grant designed to study the contribution that a trained group worker might make in the life of an institution for young delinquents. She points out that the strictly imposed routine of so many schools for delinquents achieves a superficial conformity without fundamentally relieving anxiety or allowing a youngster to express his real self. The article is illustrated by several extracts from records of a one-month experiment with a "natural subgroup" chosen after brief contact "as the core of the group" with which she worked. Konopka aimed to use a methed "that takes into account the understanding of individual and group behavior, that allows for a large amount of freedom and that is based on respect for the individual." She recounts certain basic principles of group work, describes the organization of discussion groups, and gives a summary of her conclusions from the brief experiment, with special reference to the sort of group-work person who should be part of the institutional therapeutic team and the type of technique that can take advantage of group dynamics in an institution.

---

[2] Chapter 28.

139

The Role of the Residential Staff in Residential Treatment *

Norman V. Lourie and Rena Schulman

To review completely the history of residential treatment would be outside the scope of this paper; but a brief review is called for since it may serve to show how residential treatment developed and how the experiences of its antecedents contributed to its development — particularly how the clinical usages of resident staff seem to have emerged.

Although institutional care for children goes back thousands of years, it is in the Middle Ages that we find the first organized attempts to collect children in institutions. These were most often under church auspices and dealt chiefly with orphaned and foundling children.

Later, with the development of public welfare concerns, came poorhouses and almshouses where children were congregated together with indigent adults, the sick, the feebleminded and the insane. Food, physical care and education were meager. Work was the major program for children.

More recently, particularly in the last century, the history of child welfare services reveals changes which recognized the need for special types of care for different children. The first move was from the almshouses to institutions designed only for children. This move from the unclassified populations of the almshouses came as public opinion made itself felt in behalf of more humanitarian services to children. In succession, the orphaned, dependent and neglected children, the so-called delinquents, and the feebleminded youngsters were delivered from the poorhouses; the first, into orphanages and asylums; the delinquents, into

* Reprinted from 22 *Am. J. Orthopsychiatry* (1952), 798–808. Used by permission of the authors and the publisher. Bibliography omitted. See, also, G. H. Weber, "The Use of the Conference Method in the In-service Training of Cottage Parents," 3 *Int. J. of Soc. Psychiatry* (1957), 49–61. — Ed.

industrial or training schools; and the feebleminded children, into specially designed institutions. Segregation in mental hospitals of the psychotic child or adolescent came much later. Here segregation was generally done without the introduction of any specially designed program for children.

Parenthetically we must note that there is still no full swing of the pendulum. Alongside of our modern child care and resident treatment programs we find, in many parts of the country, archaic programs with substandard care with children still kept in almshouses and jails.

The original orphan asylums, or orphanages, were generally under church or sectarian group auspices; and, as children's laws were written, the spirit of the American religious democracy was maintained so that public authorities were required to place children in institutions of their own faith wherever practicable. Religious precepts and moral training were an essential part of the program. Child care was handled by a staff, predominantly of women, who were selected mainly for their domestic abilities. The attitudes and practices of staff were accidental and not the result of training; dependent on their individual qualities as human beings was the amount of warmth and affection they gave their charges. The fiction of earlier days often pictured the cruel treatment of the young inmates of the orphan homes who were described as poorly fed, overworked, apprenticed to exploiting families, and frequently beaten. This was the popular conception of life in the orphan asylum, not always true, of course, but revealing as a reflection of the pattern of the times. The limited professional literature of the day — reports of superintendents and boards — describes high educational, moral and religious motives. The intent of the managing boards and administrations of the institutions was to provide a home, physical care, the advantages of sound education, and moral upbringing to render the child a good citizen. These attitudes reflected, at least, the beginning of a philosophy that the responsibility of children's institutions was to provide maternal and familial care for children deprived of their own families, or in need of more responsible care than their own families might afford, within the framework of what we now describe as Victorian concepts of child rearing.

The role of those who lived with children in the days of the early institution has been described as custodial, with a general overseeing of their activities and habit-training through precept, work, and sometimes the birch. As child-rearing theories broadened with the times, the educational needs of the child were emphasized. "School" and "Home" often replaced the terms "Asylum" and "Orphanage." These new designations did convey some of the new approaches to child care, as the attempt was made to render institutions into homelike and educational settings. This brought a new view of the child care institution as a place where many skills and areas of service were united to contribute to the child's normal development, a concept basic to modern institutional child care. With this development came the replacement of congregate buildings by cottage type institutions, offering a more familial atmosphere with adults acting as substitute parents.

This change came in the same period as the beginning trend toward foster home care, with the stress on the importance of relationships and family life for normal child development, and understanding of the effects of maternal deprivation. The impetus for this trend came as the development of the mental hygiene movement and progressive education had its effects on the child care field. This stress on maintaining children in their own homes or in foster homes, the idea that poverty alone should never be the reason for breaking up a home and placing children, the growing public welfare and social security programs, and casework services — all served to influence the type of care given in children's institutions and the character of the institutional populations.

Orphan homes no longer contained orphans. Homes were less frequently broken by death and economic distress. Children came into the care of foster homes and institutions for reasons having to do mainly with inadequate parents. As we learned more about the effects of parental neglect and maternal deprivation, we recognized this residue of children in care as presenting a wide variety of personality disturbances. It has been recognized, really only quite recently, that children in care by reason of upset familial situations cannot be merely described as dependent children in need of substitute homes; but, rather, that all of them in some degree present personality problems which have to be dealt with in a variety of ways.

The impact of modern psychiatry, psychoanalytic theories of child development, and the mental hygiene movement was reflected in this understanding of the problems of children and the type of care they needed. The more advanced children's institutional programs showed an increasing use of casework and psychiatry to help in the understanding of the needs of the child who remained in institutional care and in the diagnosis and treatment of his problems. Studies reveal that where foster home programs are highly developed, the residue of children in institutions represent the most damaged children who could not use a home atmosphere constructively.

It is from this residue of severely damaged children that the residential treatment populations are mainly drawn. An examination would probably reveal that most of the children presently in resident treatment programs were exposed to some form of child care program at one time or another. Thus residential treatment centers often came out of institutional programs for dependent or delinquent children, as part of the search for more helpful methods of caring for the children whose real problems had become recognized. Some came into being as small study homes or treatment centers related to child guidance clinics or child care agencies, often set up initially as observation places to determine the best mode of treatment, and often turning into treatment centers as it was discovered what the most effective treatment for these children might be and that the existing child care programs were not the answer.

Other centers evolved in medical settings, sometimes out of child guidance clinics and pediatric services, and sometimes out of a mental hospital program for children. Only to a limited degree has the impetus for resident treatment come out of the psychiatric hospital. In the last few years there has been a heartening development of interest in resident treatment within some state hospital and state welfare programs.

We would define residential treatment as therapeutically directed institutional or group care for emotionally disturbed children in which all possible ways of helping — casework, education, recreation, planned group life, and psychotherapy — are utilized and integrated into a clinically oriented and directed treatment plan for the individual child. It is not merely the removal of the child to a benign environment where he is available for psychotherapeutic interviews. The essence of residential treatment lies in the milieu — in the complement of adult–child relationships and experiences which can be clinically manipulated and controlled in the interests of therapy.

Residential treatment institutions exist today in a variety of forms and settings. They may be called schools, centers, study homes, hospital wards, etc. They have originated in many different ways out of the recognition of a need for a new form of treatment for disturbed children. Many of the variations in structure and form have been determined by the origin of the specific program and the actual physical setting.

Despite the variations in treatment centers, they all have certain features in common. They all emphasize the importance of daily living experiences, the structure and organization of the child's life, the various forms of occupation and recreation and creative experiences. They all utilize education therapeutically, whether on the premises or off, and some form of psychotherapeutic effort; and all of them utilize staff in the direct handling of children for relationships or experiences of a therapeutically helpful nature.

The problems presented by children needing intramural care are such that they cannot usually be met by the use of psychotherapy alone or even by psychotherapy in ordinary placement. These are generally children who have not been able to cope with their life situations in the community or who have to be removed from community living. They are often children with deprived, neglectful backgrounds who have run the gamut of institutions, clinics, boarding schools, or foster homes and who have exhausted the ability of all concerned to find ways of caring for them. Outpatient treatment may have been attempted, but with little success. They may be children who are unable to function in groups, in the school, in community activities, and who alienate their peers as well as adults. They are children who have developed deviant modes of behavior, of lesser or greater extreme, and who may present some danger to themselves or to the community.

Some of these children are unable to remain in school. They may truant, do not learn, or, because of their aggressive, destructive or bizarre behavior, cannot be tolerated in the ordinary school situation. They are children whose symptoms may be presented in their own homes, in distorted relationships with parents, in regressive patterns of behavior, or whose conflicts express themselves in symptoms of withdrawal, strangeness, or infantilism.

It is not possible to give a minute description of all the types of children who might benefit from treatment in residence. They represent a variety of diagnostic categories; even the same symptoms may represent a variety of meanings and, therefore, a variety of clinical entities. In some, the behavior may represent a low threshold of resistance, severe personality impairment or defect, or a severe neurotic conflict. The diagnosis may range from behavior disorder to psychosis. Inevitably, they are children in whom physical and emotional deprivations have produced changes in personality structure. They are children who are frightened, fearful of relationships, children who have not experienced the gratification of positive accomplishments necessary to their healthy growth. They may be impulsive, unable to tolerate anxiety, frustration or competition, and may react with withdrawal, or aggression, or other defensive mechanisms against their real feelings of inadequacy and insecurity. They may be anxiety-ridden children who have never known the security of consistent framework and control. They are children who have experienced too little love or too much neglectful indulgence. Though many come from broken homes, they are homes broken not by poverty essentially, but more often by irresponsibility of the parents, by their emotional problems and through their inability to cope with the demands of parenthood.

Many of these children have had little stability or continuity in their significant relationships, or they have been brought up by rejecting or hostile parents, too threatening to permit normal identifications to develop. They may be children who, because of their chaotic relationships, cannot be treated while they are living with their own parents. Their needs cannot be met, usually, in a foster home or in the average children's institution.

In the treatment of these children, they must

be exposed to a variety of relationships among children and adults; to constructive experiences and activities in which there can be accomplishment and a sense of gratification; in which they can have a feeling of being wanted and loved; in which there can be routine and framework and the kind of consistent regime or controls they need. Residential treatment offers to these children, unable to face the demands of reality living, the opportunities for processed or diluted living experiences and relationships. And it is the resident staff who must be utilized as the core of planned living experiences for the child.

With this kind of program, the entire staff must be oriented in the direction of therapy — the people who live with the children and give physical care — the house parents, the cook, the maintenance staff, teachers, recreational workers. They should be people who can control and regulate their own attitudes, feelings, and handling of children; who can accept psychiatric and casework concepts as they are translated into ideas of living, and are able to work as part of a treatment team.

Residential treatment institutions operate today in a variety of ways, based on different approaches to treatment. However, despite theoretical differences, there seems to be a basic consistency of approach concerning the place of residential staff in the programs. Though each residential treatment center may have its own unique concept of staff, its own term to apply to this function, and distinct engineering of the milieu in a different fashion, each gives to the resident staff a place in the treatment of the child. They are the persons who represent in the daily life of the child in residence an auxiliary aid to treatment, around which are developed the planned and therapeutic relationships and experiences in the course of daily living. Essentially, the job of the resident staff calls for the conscious care of children in the emotional as well as the physical sense. They go through the routines of daily life — waking, bathing, feeding, sleeping, help with schoolwork, recreation, and may deal with controls, limits, permissions or disciplines.

Placing a damaged child with an uncrystallized personality in a setting where he has opportunity for normal growth experiences is in itself treatment. Real experience and real relationships come out of the process of daily living as it may be planned and directed in accordance with the therapeutic needs of the case. The resident staff is the medium for the reality which is set up for the child. Acceptance, tolerance, love, relationships with non-punitive, non-retaliatory adults, experiences which in their repetition may test out the new reality — these help him to give up his older modes of relating to the world, to try out and confirm new expectations from himself and others.

The resident staff are the people who relate themselves to the child as he is, not only to his pathology and illness, but mainly to the remnants of healthy or wholesome aspects of his personality. Constructive experiences which can provide gratification are essential in the rebuilding of the child's ego, and the residential treatment setting must permit the opportunity for constructive and gratifying experiences at the level on which the child is capable of using them. The residential staff provides for the child those non-compulsory relationships which are necessary for his regrowth.

Out of the planned use of resident staff comes the atmosphere, the therapeutic milieu, which is the tool of residential treatment. This results in what we call "tempered reality." While the concept of reality which is presented to the child differs in many programs, it is our own belief that helpfulness to the child comes out of presenting to him a framework of reality living, but a reality which is trained down to a consistency which he can absorb somewhat like a prepared baby food. It is reality tempered in the sense that the adult's response to the child's hostility, destructiveness, anger, bizarre behavior, ambivalence or withdrawal, while varying according to the treatment approach, is not the same kind of response which he received from the significant adults in his earlier life.

The therapist can use the environment in planning the child's reality to afford him the kinds of experiences which seem necessary for him at any stage of his treatment. He can accomplish this by modifications, change of pace and emphasis in experiences and relationships which are possible. Relationships can be diluted or concentrated, experiences can be juggled: to create anxiety, to lessen anxiety, to protect him from, or project him into reality, to create situations which accelerate or give impetus to the child's individual therapy. The relationships which can be developed with the resident staff can be effectively utilized in individual therapeutic sessions. These controlled experiences may enable the child to test out his new or changing modes of reaction, new relationships and new strengths. Through repetition, they may serve to convince the child that adults do not react as in his own distorted concept of the world he has always expected them to react.

For the children who are fearful of relationships, who must react with hostility and destructiveness, relationships can be provided in diluted form. The relationship with the resident staff is one which is shared, usually with a group, in which responsiveness by the child to warmth and giving by the adult is neither expected nor demanded. When it is safer for the child, opportunity for peer relationships of some sort may be presented before demanding relationships with adults.

Such therapeutic use of the environment and resident staff can be possible only with the constant interchange of information and the thorough integration which are part of the core of residential treatment.

A review of the specific use of residential staff in several of the existing programs reveals that people are used differently in the resident role, and their places in the treatment program are defined differently. These variations include the use of cottage parents or house parents, the counselor or counselor-therapist, group leader, group therapist, nurse-attendant on the children's psychiatric wards, house staff, resident worker, housemother, housefather, or professional social worker. To a single person or a couple may be assigned a specific group of children for whose total daily living they are partly or completely responsible in a physical and emotional sense. Or, there may be no specific assignment of child to adult, but merely the presence of several adults from among whom the child may choose one or more persons according to his needs.

In many settings, the people who live with the child are called house parents. They may not only take care of the physical needs of the child and the routines of daily living, but may also be invested with considerable authority in the child's life. It is they who give permissions and make decisions about day-to-day events. It is sound and helpful that the people who live with the child shall also be the ones who get him socks when needed and permit him to go to the movies. It is this use of adults which offers a framework of order, the external force which protects the child from his own impulsive drives. They offer stability and security in their management of the events of daily living. They may supply the child with an emotional experience through relationships if the child is accessible to them or the availability of relationships when he is ready for them. They may serve wholly or in part in the parental sense if it supplies the child's need.

When married couples are used, it is felt that the couple supplies a certain amount of reality to the situation, providing a combination of mother and father figures through which the child may act out therapeutically his conflicts with his own parents. The action of both male and female influences on the child's growth is even more essential. The presence of a married couple offers this in a formal conventional sense. The experience of living with a happily married couple in which man and woman play their respective roles in a normal fashion can be most helpful to children who are working out in individual therapy their own confusion as to male and female roles, and whose concept of the marital relationship is one only of discord and friction.

These same values may of course be provided where single persons are used as housemothers and housefathers. Often a housemother may be assigned to a group for the care of the child in his daily living and hers is essentially a mothering role. The male influences and relationships may come from others in the program, often a recreational worker or teacher. The elements of parental relationship are usually present without the semifamilial structure provided by house parents. It is found that the child most often couples off for himself the people in his environment.

The single house parent or counselor, as she is often termed, is differently defined and used. She may be seen not as a house parent, but as a group leader or sometimes a group therapist. In one center, it is emphasized that the adults do not represent familial figures at all and the group interaction and group life are seen as the main therapeutic force. The group leader's role here is to provide creative leadership, to permit the most constructive group relationships and activities to develop. However, though the emphasis is on the group leader role, the giving of physical care to the child by the adult and his involvement in the daily sequence of living sets up relationships with the child which are little different from the child's relationship to the house parent. Though group relationships are important to the child and some children may relate first to their peers and utilize what has been termed the anonymity of the group, at some point, if treatment is engaged in, the child moves toward experiences with adults.

In one small center, the role of the counselor has been related to that of a group therapist. His role in interaction with the group, the group life itself and the structure of the group, as well as the living out of experiences with a therapeutic person, are the planned essentials of the treatment process. In this setting, individual psychotherapy in the classical sense is not used. It is believed that these children are not able to use such treatment because of their basic hostility and distrust of adults. The group living and milieu treatment process, with its resultant changes in the child's personality, may make him available for individual therapy later if it is indicated. We feel that in an actual living situation, the process takes on other aspects and that what is described is not actually group therapy.

As described in one setting, the resident staff is used in a counselor–therapist role. The child lives his daily life with one or more counselors in a small group and the residential staff is used as the experiential medium for therapy. It is with the counselor–therapist that the child acts out and works out his conflicts, and therapy takes place in a medium of guided relationships and the processes of daily life. This may be accompanied by occasional individual therapeutic sessions with the counselor or with a therapist who is not the child's own counselor; but most often, the verbalization of conflict and interpretation takes place at appropriate points in daily living and on-the-spot therapy.

Resident treatment centers in hospitals use nurses, attendants, and counselors, or combinations of these as resident staff. The nurses, as well as all other ward personnel, occupational or recreational therapists, and teachers are used as relationship figures for the children and as staff who give program and activities rather than typical ward care. They usually do not wear hospital uniforms and an attempt is made to develop a nonhospital-like atmosphere. The child may relate himself to any one of a number of people who may become his key relationship figures. The management person in his life may be the nurse or the doctor or, as in one setting, may be the social worker who relates himself to the specific realities of the child's life.

In this kind of situation there are usually several people who deal with the child's living experiences. One may put him to bed, another eats with him, another gives him clothing and permissions. One might question the therapeutic effects and possible confusions of so many adult figures who walk in and out of the child's life, with one putting him to bed and another eating with him, and another giving approval or disapproval. Much of the therapeutic usefulness of the resident staff under these circumstances is susceptible to dilution or loss.

Only in one setting is the resident staff described specifically as having no element of parental or familial relationship. There it is held that this should not be an element in the residential treatment process. Actually, treatment is seen as coming about chiefly through separation from the home and through individual psychotherapy. Emphasis is placed on separation of therapy from the practical realities, involvements and consequences of daily behavior which are handled realistically by the resident staff. The resident staff person is influenced in what he does and in his decisions by the therapist, but unbeknown to the child. The resident staff person is not called a house parent because this would imply a substitution of the parent person in the child's life. However, even in this setting, the person who lives with the child assumes the role of authority in the child's life and is apparently used consciously to assist the therapist in steering the child's problems to his therapy sessions. It seems obvious that an element of relationships and interaction between the child and adult must be present in any situation where the child lives in close intimacy with the adult. One would wonder if the difference does not lie only in the interpretation and use rather than in what takes place qualitatively between the child and the adult.

There has been growing interest in the use of professionally trained persons as resident staff. In one center, in addition to other house staff, the people in direct charge of the child's care are trained psychiatric social workers. This is related to the concept that though residence is auxiliary to therapy, therapy should be continued in the living situation. The professional resident staff can function on a colleague level with the therapist and can carry out in a more disciplined, understanding, and controlled fashion their role as prescribed by the child's therapist. Living is an extension of therapy both in the process of daily life and also in the discussion of the child's problems which may be carried out of the interview room and brought into his life at appropriate points where the child's behavior or activity relates very specifically to his problem. The trained worker can pick up cues and carry along the treatment of the child in the bathtub or at bedtime while carrying out the mothering role.

In summary, we believe that despite all of the described variations there is only one real difference in the approach to the use of resident staff. In one we see the resident staff working in an integrated way with the individual therapist and the daily living of the child in a greater or lesser degree clinically planned and directed. The resident staff is used as an adjunctive treatment aid. The nature of the relationship with adults, the organization and structure of daily life, the group interaction, the group relationships and their integration into the total treatment of the child by the individual therapist make up the whole of residential treatment.

In the other approach, we see the residential person as the basic therapist, in effect residential or environmental therapist. It is the actual living out experiences which produce the correct measures enabling the child to change. The environmental or residential therapist may or may not use individual interviews, and most often these are of an informal nature. There is emphasis on the concept of group milieu treatment and the direct handling of the child's conflicts and distortions as they appear in living.

In most residential treatment centers today, it is the first approach that predominates. There may be differences of opinion as to the exact nature of the role of the resident staff worker, how he should be used, under how much prescriptive direction or control, and by whom; what his responsibilities should be and who should best be utilized. The most controversial aspect, perhaps, is the extent of parental relationships implied in the role. However, despite our constant denial that these are substitute parents, we cannot deny existence in some degree of the familial aspects of these relationships. Disturbed children see every adult in some distorted fashion and it is most often the child's attitudes toward his own parental persons that are projected onto all other adults. This is not only a concomitant of the living process, but a desirable aspect; for we do not believe the child can be successfully treated if he is insulated from the disturbing aspects of his interpersonal relationships.

There is much that remains to be learned about the way that resident staff may be used and integrated into residential treatment. The literature is still quite limited and research of a basic nature is called for. It is encouraging that the Child Welfare League of America, with the help of the Field Foundation, is presently studying residential treatment programs. Also, the Children's Bureau is carrying out an examination of existing programs. From their examinations, we should get the first complete inventory, program descriptions, and method analysis. From there we, hopefully, will find clues for ways to study scientifically the residential treatment process and to isolate out the treatment values inherent in the current methods and usages.

140

Conflicts Between Professional and Non-Professional Personnel in Institutional Delinquency Treatment *

George H. Weber †

In an effort to provide better diagnostic and treatment services for juvenile delinquents committed to their care, many institutions, in recent years, have added people from a number of professions to their staffs. These usually include social workers, teachers in special education, psychologists, psychiatrists and recreational therapists. In institutions, these people are frequently known as the "professional staff." They are employed for the study and treatment [1] of delinquents, and the consultation with and guidance of other staff members.

In this latter function, the professionals may be asked by the administration to advise those workers who supervise and manage the everyday living experiences of the delinquents, such as getting up, going to bed, personal hygiene, eating, playing and working. Within the institutions, these workers are commonly known as the "non-professional staff" (as differentiated from the professional staff) [2] and usually include cottage parents, vocational and work supervisors, and maintenance workers.

This division of work, with its theoretical consistency and its apparent applicability, would seem to be acceptable to both groups as it is consistent with the currently accepted principles of delinquency treatment, personnel practice and education. It is a plan which should allow the professionals an opportunity to increase their practical knowledge of delinquency and to apply the specific skills of their work to the delinquents and the institution. It is a plan which should also give the non-professionals an opportunity to increase their theoretical knowledge of delinquency and to receive some specialized help with some of their difficult problems.

In actual practice, however, this plan may encounter sharp difficulties in acceptance and functioning. Conflicts may emerge when professionals and non-professionals attempt to bring their specialties together. Value orientations, statuses and roles and ideas of delinquency causation and treatment, undoubtedly, will differ in each group. Problems are likely to arise from the conceptions that each group have of themselves and each other in each of these different areas.

The material for this paper was secured from two private and three public institutions for delinquents and was gathered over a period of three years. The method of the study was that of participation and observation. The data were gathered by four people, including the writer, who worked in these institutions in either a professional or non-professional job. The institutions varied in the number of delinquents in residence from about thirty to nearly four hundred. The proportion of professionals to non-professionals varied from two per cent to thirty-seven per cent. With the exception of two institutions, the non-professionals preceded the professionals in the setting.

In all institutions studied, conflicts were in evidence. In some, the conflicts were more intense, continuous and dramatic than others. In all the institutions, some cooperation transpired between the professionals and non-profes-

* Reprinted from 48 *J. Crim. L.*, *Criminology and Police Science* (1957), 26–43. Used by permission of the author and the publisher. See, also, S. Glueck, "Two International Criminologic Congresses: A Panorama," 40 *Mental Hygiene* (1956), 623. — Ed.

† I wish to thank Dr. Melville Dalton for his guidance and suggestions in the prosecution of the research on which this paper is based. — G. H. W.

[1] "Treatment," as used in this paper, denotes all the systematic efforts which are carried on within an institutional setting to assist in the rehabilitation of the delinquent. This includes general environmental arrangements, as well as individual and group treatment.

[2] The titles "professional" and "non-professional" accentuate the differences between the two groups and appear to facilitate conflict rather than cooperation. It is an unfortunate differentiation. For an analysis of the difficulties in defining a profession, see M. L. Cogan, "Toward a Definition of Profession," *Harvard Educ. Rev.*, 23 (Winter, 1953), pp. 33–50.

sionals and the author does not wish to imply that all these conflicts occurred to the same degree in every institution or that they were continuous. However, conflicts were a significant aspect of the relationships existing between the professional and the non-professional in all the institutions studied.[3]

VALUE ORIENTATIONS

The professionals and non-professionals held different values regarding their own and the other's work. The professionals often stressed humanitarianism and service. They thought of themselves as primarily providing a service to the delinquents and they believed that when they went into a particular case or group for study, they should assume full responsibility for it within their specialty. The professionals thought of themselves as cooperative, as sharing and exchanging information and ideas, as respecting the integrity of others and the right of others to express themselves. Keen observations and a reflective and critical approach to problems were held in high regard by them. Formal education and training, as such, were also respected by this group.

The professionals saw the non-professionals as holding two sets of values. One view regarded the non-professionals as being a hardworking, simple group of people, usually generous and kind to the delinquents in their care, and good-intentioned in their relationships and dealings with the other staff members. They saw them as valuing sincerity, friendliness, courage, simplicity and industry. The other view regarded the non-professionals as strict disciplinarians who demanded hard work and obedience from the delinquents. They thought that they were rigid in their viewpoints, antagonistic toward professionals, and reluctant to take any suggestions concerning their work. Here they regarded the non-professionals as valuing formal and restrained behavior, compliance and authoritarianism. In both of these conceptions,

the professionals saw the non-professionals as having very little importance in working with problems concretely and had little regard for a theoretical approach to these problems. A psychiatrist alluded to several of these points when he was discussing a cottage mother's management of a boy:

> Mrs. S. wants Bobby punished for his stealing, immediately. She isn't interested in studying it more fully. She says that "if he did it, he should be punished and then he has paid his debt." If anyone expresses any other ideas on it, she feels her position is seriously threatened. If pressed on the matter, she'll take her feelings out on the boy.

On another occasion a psychologist, referring to the uncritical methods of the non-professional, said:

> It seems that many of the cottage parents have worked out rather simple schemes for dealing with behavior problems. It apparently makes them more comfortable, even though it may be harmful to the boys. It's difficult to approach them about these things because you are apt to break down whatever relationship you have.

The non-professional emphasized kindness, firmness, the ability to get along with people, and hard work as necessary qualities for work with delinquents. They viewed the immediate, the concrete, the practical, and action — the "getting something done" — as important. Broad experience and intimacy with the problems of working with delinquents were considered indispensable by them. The non-professionals considered themselves responsible for the general development and welfare of all the boys.

The non-professionals regarded the professionals as generally pseudo-intellectual and theoretical. They also regarded the professionals as valuing material wealth and education. The non-professional often pointed to the higher salaries given to the professionals for work they believed was "easier." They believed that the professionals valued leisure and comfort for themselves above that of the delinquents and that they tended to be authoritarian in their relationships with others. The apparent leisure and comfort of the professionals was referred to by a cottage parent when she said:

> It's fine and easy for you people working up in the administration building to come at eight o'clock, leave at five, and have a half-day off on Saturday,

---

[3] Carl R. Doering describes some similar professional and non-professional conflicts in a penal system in Foreword to A *Report on the Development of Penological Treatment at Norfolk Prison Colony in Massachusetts*, edited by Carl R. Doering, New York, Bureau of Social Hygiene, Inc., 1940. For conflicts between psychologists, psychometrists and social workers on the one hand and the house officers on the other, see particularly pages XI and XII.

but we cottage parents are with the boys all the time. If we aren't, one of our helpers is.

Another comment by a vocational supervisor illustrates this situation:

We don't feel they (the professionals) understand or appreciate our job. It's easy enough for them to sit up in the main office in a nice soft chair and behind a fancy desk. They only have to deal with one boy at a time and he is putting his best foot forward most of the time when he is up seeing them. He knows they have a lot to do with the paroles.

The non-professionals charged the professionals with confusing "book learning" with workable knowledge, and of ranking such learning above the non-professional's practical experience. They contended this theoretical background and professional training while important to the professional actually hindered their grasp of the total situation at times.[4] This was being considered by a maintenance worker when he remarked:

That guy who calls himself a psychologist is so busy studying what he calls psychopathology and working in therapy that he doesn't know the rest of the world the kid lives in. The way he is going about things, it doesn't look like he's going to have much chance to learn about it.

A psychologist, reflecting on this point, commented:

The psychologist trained primarily in the psychology of the individual, the social worker trained mainly for casework, and the psychiatrist trained primarily in the diagnosis and treatment of the individual patient are not prepared to deal with the complex problems which the therapeutic management of groups presents. This is no reflection against them, unless they assume they are specialists in something they obviously are not.

Although many non-professionals saw the professional as emphasizing a theoretical background and professional training for work with delinquents in practice, the non-professionals

viewed some as smooth operators without "real know-how," hiding their ineptness and, at times, some hostility behind good manners and the prestige conferred by schooling.[5] They also saw the professionals as placing power and status over democratic practices. A maintenance worker's comment illuminates the non-professional's view of some aspects of the professionals' relations to others.

These professional people talk about democratic practices and group processes, and that we have just as much to say about things as they do but I haven't seen it operate that way. Not only do they try to tell us what to do, but the caseworkers and the others are right next to the superintendent's office and they're telling him what to do. They have been off to school and while they haven't learned much, they have learned how to operate. When you give them a tough kid to deal with, they can't tell you what to do that's of much account — saying nothing about taking the kid on themselves.

Conflicts of values between professionals and non-professionals may be further illustrated by an episode in the parole planning for a delinquent. It shows that these conflicts can have a detrimental influence on the adjustment of the delinquents.

Don was a fifteen-year-old boy who had been committed to the "Boys' Training School" for petty stealing. His father had died and his mother had deserted him. While he had been severely deprived of parental love and childhood friendships, his maladjustment was not extreme. His development at the school during his year of residence was excellent. His major activities included study in the academic school where he excelled in the sciences, and work in the school infirmary as an orderly.

Don had been offered two placement plans. One placement was in the home of a dentist and his wife, who were interested in adopting the boy and giving him educational opportunities to the limit of his capacity and interest. The other placement was in the home of a farm family, who could offer him a good home but could not give him the education or the material advantages of the dentist's home.

After discussing these possibilities with the so-

---

[4] The specialist's limitations have been described by others: Harold J. Laski, "The Limitations of the Expert," Harpers, 162 (December, 1930), pp. 102–106; Robert K. Merton, "The Machine, The Worker and The Engineer," Science, 105 (January 24, 1947), pp. 79–81; Wilbert E. Moore and Melvin M. Tumin, "Some Social Functions of Ignorance," American Sociol. Rev., 14, (December 1949), pp. 788–789.

[5] This problem raises several questions: 1) Was the professional's education, on which he leaned for support in his work, relevant to and adequate for carrying out his assignments? 2) Was the web of conflicts so complex that the education could not be utilized?

cial worker, Don also talked about it with his science teacher, cottage mother and a nurse. The teacher encouraged him to accept placement with the dentist emphasizing the educational opportunities. The nurse encouraged him to do the same. She emphasized the possible material advantages of the dentist's home, the opportunity of making the right kind of friends, as well as the educational opportunities. The cottage mother, however, thought that he should choose the farm family because it was her opinion that they really wanted him and would love him more than the dentist and his wife. She also expressed the opinion that farm life was good and would present fewer temptations than life in the city.

When Don attempted to reconcile these different points of view with his own ambivalence about any type of placement, he became anxious, tense and restless. He went to see the social worker about his confusion; she accepted his indecision and said it was unfortunate that he had been given so much advice.

After this conference Don talked with some boys who overheard a heated argument between the nurse and his cottage mother. They informed Don that the nurse had flatly informed the cottage mother that her own preference, as well as that of the science teacher, was for his placement in the dentist's home. The boys also told Don several other things: that the nurse insisted that the farm family only wanted to exploit him as a laborer; that the cottage mother had denied this, and pointed out that while he would have to do his share of the work, they had excellent farm machinery and some hired help and that the cottage mother had countered that the dentist only wanted the boy as a show piece to follow in his footsteps.

Don became increasingly uneasy and confused. That night he ran away.

The teacher and nurse, as members of the professional group which valued education, social and economic status, favored the dentist's home for Don. The non-professional, in this case the cottage mother, attached the values of honesty and independence of rural life and favored the farm placement. This conflict in values, with Don caught in the middle, had damaging results for him.

CONCEPTIONS OF STATUS AND ROLE

The professionals thought of themselves as being primarily responsible for the study of delinquents for diagnostic and planning purposes. While they acknowledged the value of the non-professionals' diagnostic observations and opinions for institutional and post-institutional planning, the professionals maintained that this area of responsibility was essentially theirs.

In addition to their diagnostic studies and planning duties, the professionals believed that they should devote a large portion of their time to treatment. For example, they gave suggestions for structuring the delinquent's environment to the non-professionals or offered some form of individual or group treatment to the delinquents. If they aided the delinquent by structuring his environment, the professionals usually worked with other professionals and non-professionals; if they offered some form of treatment, they worked immediately with the individual delinquent or group of delinquents.

The professional's conception of their work also included assisting the delinquent to bridge the gap between the institution and outside world by proper orientation upon entry, by communication with relatives and officials during his stay, and follow-up studies with parole agencies after he left.

The professionals thought of the non-professionals as primarily guiding and supervising the delinquents. They thought the non-professionals were: 1) too restrictive with the delinquents, 2) did not try to understand the delinquents, and 3) resisted the professional's ideas and recommendations. While the professionals recognized that the non-professionals had some duties in connection with diagnostic studies and program planning, they regarded such duties as minor. The idea that the non-professionals were too restrictive is exemplified by the remark of a social worker.

That's what's the matter with these people, they are too hard on the kids. They want to make them follow a rigid and exact pattern which is their idea of being good. They don't want to hear what we have to say about management of the boys because so often it goes against their whole way of doing their job.

The rejections of the professionals' recommendations by the non-professionals was pinpointed by a psychiatrist when he said:

I have been working with the D's (cottage parents) for approximately a year. I don't believe they have any intention of modifying their cottage management. I don't believe they ever will. We used to get open resistance from them; now it's passive resistance. For example, the strap was used openly, but now you never see a strap around; however, anyone who has anything to do with their cottage knows it's still being used.

A social worker commented further on this problem:

I sincerely believe that we cannot move any faster in creating a good treatment program for the boys than some of the staff (non-professionals) are willing and able to move. I also believe in helping them to move forward but after a while, it seems a little foolish to try to help some of these people become good rehabilitative workers.

On the other side of the picture, the non-professionals saw themselves as the backbone of the institution. Their constant intimate relationship with the delinquent was believed to be the major part of the delinquent's institutional program and they felt responsible for the boy's total welfare while in the institution. They believed that their duties in this connection were performed in an interested, definite, firm and consistent manner. A typical attitude was reflected by a cottage parent who said:

We ran this institution well for many years. I'm pretty sure that we did a better job with the boys than is done now with all this high-priced help. We are still doing a good job; if it weren't for us, this place couldn't run.

Whether a staff member is married and/or has reared a family seems to play a role in the staff conflict over the care and treatment of delinquents.[6] A non-professional's comment shows this:

I ought to know something about this. I raised

6 In one institution where this was a point of conflict, fifty percent of the professionals were, or had been married, while ninety-seven percent of the non-professionals are, or had been, married. In another institution it was forty-two percent of the professionals and eighty-four percent of the non-professionals.

The age differences also appeared to be important in the conflict between the two groups. In one institution the average age of the professionals was thirty years while that of the non-professionals was forty-one years. In another institution the average age of the professionals was thirty-four and that of the non-professionals was forty-six. Statistically, these are highly significant differences. Together with the other data, they suggest that age differences and experiential disparities in family and parental roles were very important factors in the dissimilar orientations of the two groups toward the delinquents.

five kids of my own and they are all doing all right. That is more than you can say for some of those young fellows up there in the office who are passing out the word.

On this same point a professional remarked:

The trouble with our cottage parents and vocational supervisors is that they think they can treat these delinquents like they treated their own youngsters. They don't realize that these boys may be quite different. Nor do they recognize that, by thinking of these boys as they thought of their own children, they may get quite personally involved.

Occasionally some non-professionals saw themselves as having even broader duties, and they assumed responsibility for the delinquent's welfare outside the institution. This took the form of unofficial parole planning and, at times, unofficial parole supervision. In one institution, after a cottage mother had unofficially written to the relatives of a boy asking them to come and get him, as he was ready for placement, she said:

Social work is fine, I guess, but there is too much red tape to it, or they make it that way. There's no reason to keep a boy waiting six weeks when he is ready to go and his relatives are ready to take him, just to make a lot of agency referrals. These referrals are for the purpose of studying the home to see whether it is all right or not, but what difference does it make? If it is all right, fine. If it isn't, they can seldom find another place for an "adolescent delinquent," as they say. So the boy is ready and waiting. If he doesn't get some satisfaction about placement, he soon will go downhill fast and all the good we have done for him will go, too.

There are some similarities in the way in which the professionals view their duties and the way in which non-professionals view them. For their part, the non-professionals considered the professional's duties as centering around: (1) the delinquent's admission into the institution; (2) initial diagnostic and planning activities; (3) communication with relatives and outside agencies; (4) considerable counseling on situational problems and limited special treatment work with delinquents; (5) some consultation work with staff members; (6) planning with the administration; (7) planning the parole of the boy and (8) liaison work with the parole authorities after the delinquent leaves the institution.

The non-professionals formally conceded the diagnostic duties to the professionals but they believed that diagnosis has only general implications in shaping a boy's program and probably very little significance for them in their areas of work.

A cottage parent's statement makes this clear:

I like to talk with others about the boys and plan for them because there is always a lot one person misses or fails to do. I do not appreciate having some person push an opinion of a boy's character and intelligence on me that they may have formed in a few hours' time. I've worked with some of these boys a long time and I think I know them, too. I've tried different ways with them (professionals), now I just listen and then go ahead and do it my own way.

The necessity of having the professional's diagnosis was questioned by the non-professionals. The professionals' means of communication was criticized.

A farmer of an institution had this to say:

I work with boys all day long, every day. I know a boy, what he is like and what he's not like, what he can do and can't do. Just the other day, without me saying a thing, a boy told me all about his home and he cried. I can't put it in the language that those people in the administration building can — that is, put it up so that nobody but them can understand it — but I know this boy. That outfit up at the administration sees a boy for a few hours and they think they know the whole story and then want to tell us in language we can't understand. And besides the kids come back to us all upset about these tests they give 'em.

The non-professionals were reluctant to concede the advisory or consultation role to the professionals. While there was some overt harmony, underlying negative feelings were strong. This underlying resentment was pointed out by a vocational supervisor who said:

I wouldn't mind this long-haired bunch up in the offices who have their education, but when they feel like they have been called on to give it to me too, I don't want it.

The superintendent of one of the institutions of this study who himself was a professional remarked:

The ordinary run-of-the-mill professional clings to his theory too much, and unfortunately, theory is frequently too abstract to be directly applicable to concrete problems. As a result, the cottage parents and others do not have too much confidence or respect for them.

In considering this problem, a social worker talked about professional workers without experience:

People with some professional education bring valuable knowledge to their job, but they would be better off if they could appreciate themselves a little more realistically. You know, they haven't really learned what is needed to do their job, and all that it implies. Unfortunately, many of them feel compelled to give advice and suggestions. I guess they feel they have to justify their existence on the staff.

The work of the professionals which involved the delinquent's admission into the institution was generally accepted by the non-professionals; however, the cottage parents thought that considerable orientation and intake work needed to be done with the delinquents once they reached the cottage. They also accepted the role of the professionals in communicating with relatives and outside agencies, but some difficulties arose in this connection because the cottage parents would give different information to visiting parents than the social workers and other professionals did.

The non-professionals were troubled by the part professionals played in planning the institution's treatment program. They felt left out.[7]

---

[7] Status and role conflicts of the professionals are not limited to these institutional settings. Ruth Emerson, writing on "Standards in Medical Social Work," an article in *The Hospital in Modern Society*, a symposium edited by A. C. Bochmeyer, New York, 1943, The Commonwealth Fund, p. 346, says, "That there is too great a diversity of opinion among executives as to the nature of the return to the hospital, which should be expected from the activities of the social service department, seems indubitable. To some, the social worker is a glorified, and yet not altogether satisfactory, bill collector. She is sent on miscellaneous errands and asked to perform various institutional tasks for which there is no provision in the personnel of the hospital budget. Her position in some institutions is to be classed somewhere between that of the cash girl in a department store and the telephone clerk at the information desk."

Further, in this regard, the professional–nonprofessional conflicts of this study bear many similarities to the staff–line conflicts of industrial organizations reported by Melville Dalton in "Conflicts Between Staff and Line Managerial Officers," *Amer. Sociol. Rev.* 15 (June 1950) pp. 342–351.

In an unreported research by the author on fifty

The non-professionals also felt they were by-passed when it came to parole planning and actual placement. They thought their ideas did not receive adequate consideration. They also complained about delays in placing a boy once he was given parole.

Many conflicts occurred over these divergent ideas of statuses and roles.[8] Those stemming from the diagnosis and treatment of the boys were also found to be serious.

John had been in the Training School for approximately two weeks. During this period, his time had been largely taken up by his orientation program and diagnostic studies of him by the staff. The cottage parents had been orienting him to institutional and cottage life and had been observing him in a variety of situations. The psychologist had given him several tests. He had been seen by the psychiatrist, physician, dentist and social worker.

At the end of these two weeks, a staff meeting was called and each member who had contact with John came with a report of his findings. A professional chaired the meetings and the other professionals consumed the majority of the period with their discussion and recommendations. This was particularly so with the psychologist and psychiatrist, who became involved in a discussion about the nature and extent of the boy's anxiety and the defenses he had available for its control. The social worker raised the point of the historical development of this anxiety and its significance for programing.

After these lengthy discussions, the conference progressed to the point of concrete program planning. John was brought into the group at this time to participate in the planning. While he previously

---

psychiatric aides, similar status and role conflicts were observed between the aides on the one hand and the physicians and particularly the nurses on the other.

[8] One of the most important components of a healthy and vigorous staff morale is the opportunity the staff has to express their ideas and to contribute suggestions concerning the institutional program, particularly on those matters which involve them. For evidence of the motivational effects of group decision, see Kurt Lewin, "Group Decision and Social Change" in T. M. Newcomb and E. L. Hartley, Eds., *Readings in Social Psychology*, New York, Henry Holt and Company, 1947, pp. 330–345; D. McGregor, "Conditions for Effective Leadership in the Industrial Situation," *Jour. of Consult. Psychol.*, VIII, March–April, 1945, pp. 55–63, and Robert Tannenbaum and Fred Massarik, "Participation by Subordinates in the Managerial Decision-making Process," *Canad. Jour. of Econ. and Pol. Sci.*, 16, (August, 1950) pp. 408–418.

discussed his desires and wishes regarding his institutional program with his social worker, his inclusion here was an effort to have him share more directly in matters concerning his future. John expressed his interests and wishes to the staff. He said he wanted to be assigned to the tailor shop because he wanted to learn the trade.

John left the group and his cottage mother questioned assigning him to Mrs. F. at the tailor shop because she did not believe John was especially interested in tailoring and she knew that the disciplinary control of the boys in the tailor shop was poor. She said she thought he had been attracted to tailoring by reports from the grapevine that this shop allowed more freedom than some others. She acknowledged John's anxiety but emphasized his aggressive behavior in the cottage and urged that he be considered for a work placement that offered more disciplinary control.

The professionals listened to her, respectfully, but no one responded to her ideas. Rather, they discussed other aspects of John's program.

John's case was summarized by the chairman, and his assignment to the tailor shop was included without comment. John's staff conference was finished; everyone returned to his place of work.

Several days later, the woman in charge of the tailor shop reported that John had not reported to the shop as assigned and she wondered what had happened. John's absence was investigated. It appeared that the complete rejection of the cottage mother's proposal and the lack of further discussion of it at the staff meeting had made her angry; she had deliberately sent John to another assignment.

When the cottage mother attempted to participate in the planning for John's program she indicated that she conceived of herself as having responsibilities for planning delinquent's programs. The professionals, reserving this role for themselves, rejected the cottage mother's participation. The cottage mother retaliated by ignoring the job assignment for John that the professionals arranged.

The Concepts of Delinquency and Delinquency Treatment

Generally, the professionals viewed delinquency as deviant behavior resulting from the interaction of etiological, predispositional factors with situational variants. They saw this behavior as emerging from the interplay of many elements in which the boy's conscious activity was only one of these involved. They believed that institutional treatment stemming from a constructive institutional milieu, as well as individual and group treatment, provides the boys with rehabilitative experiences and would help them modify their behavior.

The professionals were found to hold the delinquent responsible for his behavior, within a certain framework, but they did not morally evaluate it. Rather, they tried to understand the motivations for this behavior and if some appropriate therapeutic measures were available, they would recommend them. If the professionals thought it was indicated, they would participate in the treatment.

To the non-professionals, the professionals seemed inconsistent in their thinking about treatment. The professionals talked about many of the delinquents being activity and action-oriented rather than thoughtful and verbal in their behavior and thus the major way of treating them was to provide a variety of constructive everyday corrective environmental experiences for them. Yet the professionals continued to see boys in office interview situations. When this was explained to the non-professionals on the basis of diagnostic and special treatment work for selected cases, the non-professionals countered with: 1) weren't the factors of comfort, easiness, and simplicity entering the professional's decisions, 2) if their (the non-professionals) environmental treatment was the most effective approach to the delinquents, why the salary, status and other differentials between themselves and the professionals.

Many non-professionals assumed that all similar surface behavior had the same dynamics or meaning. Thus they were confused when the professionals recommended dissimilar attitudes and activities for what the non-professionals thought were like delinquents.

The criteria for selecting boys for individual or group therapy seemed confusing to the non-professionals, thus such questions as: "If good for some boys, why not for others? I've got a couple over in my shop that need something. I don't see why they weren't included." With little insight as to what the professionals were attempting to accomplish, the non-professionals were skeptical, suspicious and at times opposed to therapy.

The majority of the non-professionals had not formalized their thinking about delinquency causation; however, many of them believed that delinquent behavior was historically and situationally determined. They believed that present situations and past experiences played an important part in bringing about delinquent behavior, but that once institutionalized, the delinquent would become penitent, see the error of his ways, and of his own free will choose socially constructive goals despite his present obstacles and past experiences.

To the professionals, the non-professionals appeared inconsistent and ambiguous in their thinking about treatment. The non-professionals talked of past experiences and the current situation as factors in behavior but said that if only the delinquent "would make up his mind, he could do what is right, because after all, he knows right from wrong. If he doesn't know right from wrong, then punish him because a child always learns to leave a hot stove alone after he has been burned often enough." At times, they assumed that "if a boy has been mistreated, all you have to do is be nice to him and treat him right, and he will be O. K." In this instance, they viewed treatment as being synonymous with kindness. Some of these inconsistencies are apparent in the case of Jim.

Jim was transferred to the "Boys Training School" from the state orphanage because he was "incorrigible." Following the orientation and study period, the staff met to discuss the results of these findings and to plan for his stay at the school. The professionals generally agreed that the boy was suffering from an insidiously developing schizophrenic condition, that his controls over his intense anxiety and hostility were crumbling and that his contact with reality was weak and intermittent. They viewed his judgment as severely impaired and anticipated bizarre hostile behavior from him. Their general recommendations included an environment of acceptance, security and supportive psychotherapy.

The cottage-father listened to these analyses and proposals. He appeared to have difficulty with the terminology but understood it well enough to disagree in principle. He went on to describe several concrete episodes of Jim's behavior in which Jim had torn some plastic tile from the floor of the hall and had collected all the dirty socks he could find and put them in his locker. He further pointed out that when he had confronted Jim with this "nonsense" that he could stop it if he wanted to, especially if there was some penalty attached to such behavior, Jim agreed. The house-father commented that while the medical diagnosis might be "true" he still regarded Jim's behavior as rising from a wish to be "ornery" and that it could be changed "if people would put their foot down on him."

Some bizarre behavior borders on the normal. To the untrained observer, it is frequently difficult to determine where one stops and the other starts. Although Jim's cottage parent could understand the schizophrenic condition of Jim in theory, he could not recognize or accept it as it occurred in Jim's daily living. Perhaps he had known many boys who did some of the very things Jim had done, and they were relatively normal.

He was intimately aware of Jim's actions, but he did not have a diagnostic frame of reference that he could bring to bear on this behavior and thus was unable to understand Jim's condition as being anything else than simple orneriness.

Some Negative Effects of the Conflicts[9]

These conflicts had significant detrimental effects on the system of social relationships as a whole as well as on the groups and individual involved.[10]

In some of the institutions, conflicts between these groups resulted in the system of social relationships becoming so disorganized that constructive interaction among the staff was nearly impossible. For example, some of the institutions required all the professionals and non-professional people working with a particular delinquent to attend his staff meetings; however, many of the non-professionals could not "find time" to attend the meetings even though their work load or schedule of duties had not noticeably increased. In other institutions, the professionals and non-professionals avoided meeting each other informally, as in the cafeteria and the staff recreation rooms.

Both professional and non-professional

groups were disturbed by internal frictions. At times, dissensions pitted the vocational teachers and maintenance workers against the cottage parents and the social workers against the psychologists and psychiatrists.

In all of the institutions, a varying number of staff members set up devices to protect themselves and withdrew from some of the normal and expected activities. This, of course, reduced constructive interaction. In one institution the professionals spent much of their time in research although this was not included in the duties of their job. At another institution, the professionals tended to ignore the organizational problems, and discussed instead the theory of their various fields. At several institutions, the professionals carried on exhaustive discussions regarding individual cases of delinquents and the institution's problems, but they rarely advanced beyond diagnosis of a delinquent or criticism of the administration and the non-professionals.

The non-professionals also had a variety of protective devices. Only one cottage parent would work when both were scheduled to work; the other would be upstairs resting. They would force particularly difficult boys into recreational activities outside the cottage rather than follow the professional's recommendations for providing activities for them at the cottage where the situation at the time was expected to be less complex.

Staff members, in their efforts to work in these situations and adapt to them, may become maladjusted. Anxiety, feelings of discouragement, aggressive and psychosomatic reactions were not uncommon responses among many of the workers in these institutions.

Situationally, these reactions appeared related to the staff conflicts as well as to the nature and intensity of the children's behavior.[11]

Some staff members sought "one sided" solutions outside of the institution by feigning cooperation with the institution's efforts to achieve cooperation. For example, in one institution a group of dissatisfied non-professionals

---

[9] This is not to imply that only negative and destructive phenomena are associated with conflict although this is the focus here. For a theoretical discussion of the positive as well as the negative aspects of conflict see, George Simmel, as translated by Albion W. Small, "The Sociology of Conflict," *Amer. Jour. of Sociol.*, Vol. 9, 1903–1904, pp. 490–525.

[10] As in society, there were those who took difficulties and conflicts in their stride; however, frustration, anxiety and other reactions were widespread. Some of these problems in society are characterized by Karen Horney, *The Neurotic Personality of our Time*, New York, W. W. Norton and Company, 1937.

[11] Information was given about these points in a paper entitled, "The Emotional Reactions of People Working with Emotionally Disturbed and Delinquent Children" by Ralph W. Coltharp and George H. Weber, presented at the 1951 Mid-Continent Psychiatric Association, Kansas City, Missouri.

appealed directly to the commissioner of the institution's administration concerning their complaints. In several institutions, a powerful cadre of non-professionals worked undercover for a change of administration through special interest groups. They wanted to be rid of the present administration and many of the professionals. This group complained about the professionals "meddling with our discipline." In another institution, the professionals, thinking that the administration failed to support their ideas and recommendations, worked secretly to gain a change in the administration.

Further along this web of subterfuge, the "acting out" of certain staff members worked against the institutions' goals. For example, at several schools, the professionals left work early, commenting "What's the use of staying? We can't get any cooperation anyway." Yet they always accepted full-time pay. In another institution, a few of the professionals appropriated books from the library rationalizing that "I might as well get something out of this job," and "You couldn't get anyone around here interested in learning about this." [12] A farmer at one institution was highly critical of administrative laxness concerning inter-group conflicts. He declared vehemently that people should be made to "toe the line or get out." Gradually his criticism waned and he would sarcastically remark, "I'm running my own little playhouse now, I expect others to run theirs. That's the only way a guy can get along here." A short time later he was caught stealing some livestock from the school.

As a result of these staff conflicts, the delinquent is frequently damaged rather than helped. Many delinquents came to these institutions from homes with extremely disturbed family situations where their needs for a secure and stable family life were ignored or where the parents were highly inconsistent. As a result, many delinquents developed devious means of satisfying their needs. They very shrewdly evaluated the social situations about them. They detected weaknesses, and they exploited and manipulated the situation for their personal ends. This behavior-attitude had played a

strong role in their delinquency in the first place and was one of the behavioral tendencies that the institution tried to modify. Yet this was quite impossible if the delinquent was exposed to an institutional environment where the surroundings were similar to those which had contributed to his unhealthy condition.

John, a delinquent at a Training School, was denied a holiday pass to his home by his cottage parent because he had persistently been intimidating younger boys and, whenever possible, beating them. Aware that there were differences of opinion regarding treatment methods between the social worker and the cottage parent, John went to see the social worker, complaining that he was restricted from his pass unfairly and that the cottage parent was "down on him" and that "he had just been playing with the other fellows." The social worker was sympathetic and after the boy left, she discussed it with the chief social worker. He took it to the superintendent who, in turn, asked to see the cottage parent. The cottage parent, threatened by this apparent display of power by the professionals, said that "he thought maybe a pass would be the thing to help him." Later, in talking with his associates, the cottage parents bitterly denounced the professionals.

Many delinquents are shrewd and devious in their actions. John was such a boy. By manipulating some staff members, who fell unwittingly into his trap, he got his pass. The conflict of status and role here between the professionals and non-professionals is evident again; a conflict over treatment methods is also indicated. Jim was aware of these conflicts and cleverly exploited them to his own advantage, and continued his delinquent way of dealing with the world.

SOME RECOMMENDATIONS TO RELIEVE THESE CONFLICTS

Education is obviously not a cure-all but the professionals might profit from training programs that provided them with a broader frame of reference, and sensitized them to the practical functioning of an organization. If properly administered, such training should help them empathize with a greater variety of people. While the colleges do teach the professionals many things, there is a lot that the institution itself can do to add to this teaching process. In-service training, internships and residences

---

[12] For a discussion of this problem on a broader scale, see Lawrence S. Thompson, *Notes on Bibliokleptomania*, New York, The New York Public Library, 1944.

at institutions for delinquents would be of considerable help.[13]

In order for the professional to understand the role of the non-professional, it might be well for him to work as a participant–observer in the various non-professional jobs during the early period of his employment. However, such a procedure would probably be difficult for many professionals to accept. In one of the institutions studied, the administration and the heads of professional departments agreed to provide this type of experience for the newly hired professionals. At first it was intimated to the professionals that one week's close sharing of cottage life would aid greatly in their orientation. Later they were told that such a period of observation and participation was expected, and that as soon as they were ready the process would begin.

Of the nine professionals to whom this opportunity was extended, three began it and only one completed the activity. When those who did not attempt it or failed to complete it were faced with their failure to participate, various excuses were made.

"I was too busy with other activities."
"After all, I'm not studying to be a cottage parent."
"Just how do you conceive of my role here?"
"My wife needed me at home at night."
"I can learn just as much by testing a boy as I can by watching him in a cottage."

This procedure and reasons for the expected participation had been previously explained to them.[14]

---

[13] The current program of the Training Branch, Juvenile Delinquency Service, United States Children's Bureau, is important in this respect. Under their leadership special training in the field of corrections is being planned to assist various specialists working in the field of delinquency control. For example, a program has been offered to university teachers and prospective teachers of social work at the University of California, Berkeley, in the summer of 1956. See "Projects and Progress," *Children*, Vol. 3 No. 1, January–February, 1956, p. 37.

[14] The theoretical bases for the importance of being able to take the role of the other in interpersonal relations is set forth in George H. Mead, *Mind, Self and Society*, Chicago, University of Chicago Press, 1934, pp. 360–376. For the practical application of this idea to training in industry see Alex Bavelas, "Role Playing and Management

Concomitant with the experience of being a participant–observer in a variety of non-professional jobs the professional should meet with the non-professional of each job to learn of the activities and problems of the job from the standpoint of the non-professional. In such arrangements the professional would, of course, profit from constructive departmental and administrative leadership.

The total institution should be made aware of a new staff member's arrival in advance along with the position he is to fill and the role he is expected to play. Upon arrival he should be introduced to the other staff members, including non-professionals. Many times the new staff member needs some early reassurance, support and friendly guidance in his efforts to work himself into the institution. In several of the organizations, efforts were made in this direction but in the others, very little was done. Such procedures are as necessary for the non-professional as they are for the professional.[15]

The non-professionals need systematic frames of reference to use in shaping their experiences and first-hand familiarity with delinquents into an organized repertoire of knowledge and skills which provide them with new vantage points from which to view and work with the delin-

---

Training," *Sociatry*, 1:2: 183–190, June 1947. The work that has been done to improve the relationships between supervisors and workers in industry is suggestive in regard to improving the relationships between the professionals and non-professionals in institutions for delinquents. N. R. F. Maier, *Principles of Human Relations*, New York, John Wiley and Sons, 1952, describes how supervisors are taught to consider problems from the worker's point of view, to look at the various possible motives underlying the worker's behavior, to encourage the worker's self-expression and to develop solutions to problems with the work group. The effects of employee participation in decision making on production, in industry are presented by Lester Coch and J. R. P. French, Jr., "Overcoming Resistance to Change," *Human Relations*, 1948 I, pp. 512–532.

[15] The importance of incorporating the new worker into an organization is described by Delbert C. Miller and William H. Form, in *Industrial Sociology*, New York, Harper and Brothers, 1951, pp. 676–697 and Edwin E. Ghiselli and Clarence W. Brown in *Personnel and Industrial Psychology*, New York, McGraw-Hill Book Company, Inc., 1955, pp. 378–410, and Margaret L. Newcomb, Eleanor Gay, and Barry L. Levin, "A Training Program for Social Work Students in a Psychiatric Clinic," *Social Case Work*, Vol. XXXIV, No. 5, May 1953, pp. 204–211.

quents. This might be provided by in-service training.[16]

The non-professionals may need to take part in regularly scheduled classes in connection with their work. The classes should be small and carried on by conference and discussion, rather than by lecture. The subject matter of these classes should be focused on the personality of the delinquents and the behavior of groups in an institutional setting. Also, the non-professional worker should become familiar with some of the terminology and theoretical background that professional people use in approaching the problem of delinquency. This does not mean that the non-professional must be trained as a theorist but that he must have some understanding of this as it relates to his job.

The institutions need to refine and intensify their recruitment, selection and orientation procedures for both the professionals and non-professionals. In many cases this means that in addition to sponsoring various programs to increase the efficiency of these procedures, the institutions must also raise wages and improve working conditions.[17]

Within the institutions, the administration as well as the professional and non-professional staff must always strive to keep the various channels of communication functioning. Administrative–department head conferences and departmental, along with interdepartmental, meetings can facilitate this. Various institutional service committees, e.g., staff recreation and library committees, might prove effective vehicles. An institutional planning board made up of equal numbers of professionals and non-professionals could help in planning the overall policies of the school and might have some value in decreasing the number and intensity of conflicts between the two groups.[18]

In addition to these attempts to structure situations that would be conducive to harmonious staff relationships, the institution must provide regular procedures through which conflicts can be managed. Different conflicts would require different types of action. Sometimes administrative action would be clearly indicated, as in the case of pay and hours, or unsatisfactory working conditions. In many cases, however, it would appear that the people with conflicts need an opportunity to meet, discuss and try to "work through" their differences and problems, either individually or in groups, with an experienced, capable institutional worker who has a broad grasp of the situation.[19]

It should be remembered, however, that the routine employment of in-service training, conferences, or committee meetings will not insure the resolution or prevention of conflicts. None of these are a "package approach" to all situations. Rather, they provide several ways to work toward these ends. It takes a sympathetic and interested administration and some desire on the part of employees to improve staff relationships. Excellent leadership on the part of those working directly with the conflicts is required if any of these means are to be realized at their fullest potential.[20] Hostilities,

---

[16] In respect to the general problems of training non-professionals for training schools see Susanne Schulze and Morris Fritz Mayer, "Training for House-parents and Kindred Personnel in Institutions for Juvenile Delinquents," pp. 44–71, in *Training Personnel for Work with Juvenile Delinquents*, Children's Bureau Publication No. 348, 1954. The work of Bernard H. Hall, *et al.*, "Psychiatric Aide Education," New York, Grune and Stratton, 1952, is significant in a related field with similar problems.

[17] This is particularly true for the non-professional. For the house-parent's problems in this connection see Morris F. Mayer, "The House-parents and the Group Living Process," pp. 97–117 in Susanne Schulze, Ed., *Creative Group Living in a Children's Institution*, New York, Association Press, 1951.

[18] The position of one side cannot possibly be clearly understood by those on the other side unless frequent communication occurs. For a vivid illustration of this truism see Alexander H. Leighton, *The Governing of Men*, Princeton, Princeton University Press, 1946. For the importance of communication for effective integration of any group see Fritz J. Roethlisberger, *Management and Morale*, Cambridge, Harvard University Press, 1941, pp. 62–63.

[19] Should the spontaneous, informal day-to-day efforts of the staff to resolve their conflicts prove ineffective, administrators would undoubtedly find procedures of voluntary conciliation more acceptable to the members of the professional and non-professional groups than compulsory measures. In the area of labor and management it is interesting to note that most members of the Minnesota "fact-finding" commissions favored voluntary as opposed to compulsory arbitration in regard to labor relations problems. The "fact-finding" commissions are appointed under the Minnesota Law to place certain limitations on strikes, see Jack Stieber, "Minnesota Labor Relations Acts — An Opinion Survey," *Harvard Business Rev.*, 27, 1949, pp. 665–667.

[20] For discussions of leadership see Chester I. Barnard, *The Functions of the Executive*, Cam-

anxieties, suspicions, resistances and negativisms are involved in any of these approaches if they are employed intensively.[21]

In one institution, a cottage mother expressed her hostility toward a teacher by criticising her teaching methods. Actually, the teacher's methods were good but the cottage mother was jealous of the friendly feelings and loyalty that the boys from her cottage were expressing to the teacher. This problem grew until each worker was openly criticising the other. The psychologist was asked by the superintendent to work this out with them. In that institution, he assumed this role at times.[22]

The psychologists talked with each individual for approximately an hour on two different occasions about these problems. After these talks, it appeared that a meeting including both workers could help in the resolution of this matter. Each agreed that such a meeting might be helpful. The meeting took place at a mutually convenient time and place. It progressed well until the school teacher pointed out one too many critical things about the cottage mother's attitude to her boys. In spite of the psychologist's efforts to help the cottage mother express her thoughts and feelings regarding this problem, she left the meeting in a defensive rage.

In retrospect, a number of critical considerations can be raised. Was the joint meeting premature? Had the psychologist moved too quickly in his effort to have the two people talk

bridge, Harvard University Press, 1938, George C. Homans, *The Human Group*, New York, Harcourt Brace and Company, 1950, pp. 415–440 and Leon H. Richman, "Sound Administration: The Key That Unlocks," pp. 18–34 in Susanne Schulze, Ed., *Creative Group Living in a Children's Institution*, New York, Association Press, 1951.

[21] Though outside of the framework of this discussion it should be recognized that many times the problem of conflict between professionals and non-professionals in institutions serving delinquents cannot be resolved by dealing only with the groups or individuals who experience the problems. In addition, determinants of conflict outside of the institution such as economic or political conditions must be included in this problem-solving process. HAROLD L. SHEPPARD, in an article, "Approaches to Conflict in American Industrial Sociology," presented at the Congress of International Sociological Association, Liege, Belgium, 1953, stresses this point in respect to industrial conflict.

[22] For the general rationale underlying this psychologist's approach to the workers, see NATHANIEL CANTOR, *Employee Counseling*, New York, McGraw-Hill, 1945, pp. 73–131, CARL R. ROGERS, *Client-Centered Therapy*, New York, Houghton Mifflin Company, 1951, pp. 19–64, and ELLIOTT JAQUES, Ed., "Social Therapy," *Jour. of Soc. Issues*, Vol. III, No. 2, 1947.

over their mutual problem? Should he have tempered the teacher's remarks? Instead of encouraging the cottage mother to express her feelings, should the psychologist have used different techniques in coping with the cottage mother's reaction? For example, should he have supported her in this crisis? Or should he have focused the discussion more on facts than on the thoughts and feelings of the cottage mother and teacher?

The psychologist then saw the cottage mother the following morning. At first she was defensive and self-righteous. Following this, she began to express some guilt about her "walking out." The psychologist listened and accepted her expressions and then purposely focused the discussion on the more immediate problem. After another meeting with the cottage mother and the teacher individually in which each vented considerable hostility toward the other, a joint meeting was tried again. This meeting was a success in the sense that they were able to express their ideas and feelings and could accept those of the other in working out their mutual responsibilities and relationships to the boys.

The overt and readily apparent aspects of any institutional problems have their deeper counterparts in the personal problems of the staff members. Often the institutional problems of anxiety, jealousy, hostility and competitive feelings stem in part from the personal and individual feelings of the staff members and are aggravated by them. The institutions for delinquents, because of their social structure and delinquent population, were fertile battlegrounds upon which the individuals brought their personal tendencies into play. Thus, this problem has both the individual as well as the institutional aspects.[23]

A case in point is that of Mr. M., who was a rigid, caustic, and driving trades instructor. He was often officious about administrative unfairness.

[23] See in this connection the special symposia, AMER. JOUR. OF SOC., XLII, May 1937 and XLV, November, 1939, SIGMUND FREUD, GROUP PSYCHOLOGY AND THE ANALYSIS OF THE EGO, London, The Hograth Press, and The Institute of Psychoanalysis, 1948 and FRITZ REDL, *Group Psychological Elements in Discipline Problems*, AMER. JOUR. OF ORTHOPSYCHIATRY, XII, 1943, pp. 77–81.

Also, he was ambivalent in his attitudes towards people in positions of leadership and authority. Mr. M., did his best work and seemed most comfortable when he was given encouragement and support by his supervisor. Under optimum institutional conditions, the approach was enough to offset his tendencies to be overly critical of people in superior positions.

Shortly after Dr. H., joined the staff of this institution as a psychologist, he attended a meeting of department heads. Mr. M.'s supervisor was one of those in attendance. Techniques of supervision were considered by the group during this meeting. Mr. M.'s supervisor asked Dr. H., what caused people to be "hard-headed." Without questioning the supervisor further, Dr. H., replied, "Sometimes people do that to defend themselves against their real feelings." The supervisor accepted this without question and then proceeded to discuss another subject. Several days after this department head's meeting Mr. M. became irritable, critical and uncompromising with his boys. His supervisor, in talking with Mr. M., commented that Mr. M's attitude must be caused by something else — perhaps anger toward the boys of this class.

This interpretation made Mr. M. angry and he replied sarcastically that it sounded like a psychological idea. At lunch and after school that day he was very outspoken against all of the professionals as he talked with others. Some of what he had to say had its contagious effect and was carried to the school's administration. Following this, the superintendent talked with Dr. H. and the supervisor to learn more about the situation and how to correct it. Mr. M. learned of this meeting and suspicioned that plans were being made against him. As a result he became more defensive and exceedingly critical of others.

The general procedure used to attack these problems will influence the techniques used by the individuals who cope with a particular problem. However, the skill and knowledge of the person who works with the problems will probably be the dominant factors in determining the choice of procedures.

However, whatever the procedure or technique may be, the groups and individuals must be helped to recognize and face some of the more important conflicts. They must be shown how to explore those conflicts and learn about their causes including their own contributions to them, and they must work these problems through to a better level of understanding and work relationships.

141

Psychologist in the Training School *

George H. Weber

In recent years the function of a clinical psychologist has been greatly extended in the various settings in which he works. This has occurred with 1) the extension of the psychological examination from tests designed primarily to determine an intelligence quotient or aptitudes, to tests which give data relevant to the structure and functioning of the "total" personality; 2) the inclusion of counseling and psychotherapy in the domain of the psychologist; 3) expansion from the traditional experiments concerned with the simpler processes of consciousness to experimental investigations concerned with the psychological dynamics of human behavior. One setting where the psychologist has developed functionally is the training school for delinquents. The writer's experience has been in a state school for boys in the midwest. The Kansas Boys Industrial School dates back to 1879 when it was established as a "state reform school" to care for dependent, neglected and delinquent boys. Many programs have been initiated to carry out the objective of "reform." Immediately preceding the present program, the school was operated on a rigid military basis. However we have been developing, for approximately the last five years, a program objective, treating the delinquent by meeting his psychological, social and physical needs. The principles of a dynamic and military approach are obviously opposed and even though the entrenchment of the previous military program has sometimes made progress difficult, we can see advances. The work was begun by a group of progressive educators and the staff has been gradually increased by the addition of social workers, psychologists, and finally psychiatrists. To provide an in-

* Reprinted from 31 Focus (January 1952), 7–10. Used by permission of the author and the publisher.

tegrated program, all the services have been organized into four departments; clinical (which includes social service and institutional home life), educational, religious, and business management. Psychology naturally falls into the clinical department and the psychologist provides services in the examination and treatment of the boys. He also provides certain services in connection with the institution's personnel program.

For the first six weeks after admission every boy participates in a tentative program based on interviews, case-history information, educational and vocational testing. During this interval the boy is given a complete diagnostic examination — medical, neurological, psychiatric, psychological, educational, vocational and social. The information gained from these different approaches is pooled at a clinical staff meeting held at the end of this period. The boy is present; a more definite program is outlined, which, in addition to participation in institutional group life, usually includes counseling or psychotherapy, medical corrective measures, vocational and educational work, religious and recreational participation. After a boy has been in residence seven and one-half months, his progress is reviewed in the light of recommendations of the caseworker and the clinical services director.

The psychologist uses various well-known tests in his efforts to understand the individual. After admission each boy is routinely given the Wechsler Bellevue Intelligence Scale to get data about his intellectual functioning and some information concerning his personality. If the boy is too young to take this or if he is severely retarded, he is given one of the Binet forms, from which we learn about his intelligence. More recently the Wechsler Intelligence Scale for Children has been used for the younger boys. The Rorschach (inkblot) test reveals the boy's personality structure, and enables the psychologist to estimate his endowment and get a picture of the relationships of affects and anxieties to endowment and efficiency of mental functioning. Actual thought content, attitudes, and feelings of the boy are made available by the various apperception tests. Standard educational achievement and diagnostic tests provide leads for his educational program. If data from any of the tests suggest the presence of thought disorder, a sorting test and a word as-

sociation test are given to check the boy's conceptual thinking and perceptual and associative processes, respectively. Lastly, Bender's Visual Motor Gestalt Test is used if organic brain damage is suspected. Although standard educational achievement tests are given periodically to measure school progress, retesting of intelligence and personality even for re-evaluation purposes is seldom done because of other work demands.

The following test report of R. B., committed to Kansas Boys Industrial School from a large city in Kansas for burglary, is an example of the kind of information that is made available by psychological diagnostic testing. The test reports are based only on the test data without any case-history material or collaboration with other workers.

PSYCHOLOGICAL TEST REPORT

Name. R. B.
Age. Sixteen years
Date. March 5, 1950
Tests Given. Wechsler Bellevue Intelligence Scale, Word Association Test, Rorschach Test, Thematic Apperception Test, and B.R.L. Sorting Test.

R. is suffering from a severe emotional maladjustment which overshadows an underlying character disorder of moderate severity. Extreme free-floating anxiety, latent hostile feelings, confusion and fear concerning sexual and religious conflicts seem to be the paramount problems facing a boy whose behavior in superficial relationships may appear to be hesitatingly friendly, usually cooperative, somewhat indecisive and generally passive.

His extreme free-floating anxiety causes impairment of immediate memory functioning and interferes with concentration to the extent that he becomes confused under conditions of moderate stress. Under intense anxiety-arousing situations he is apt to "block" completely and temporarily withdraw.

The latent feelings of hostility in R. are intense and are apt to find expression in a "hot temper," veiled negativism, infrequent quarreling, disobedience, and aggressive self-assertion. Antisocial behavior seems to be a means of expressing his latent hostile feelings. The great emphasis placed on money and material things suggests that this aggressive antisocial behavior is prone to find its expression in stealing.

The problems concerning sex are complex, involving 1) an underlying intense "love relationship" with his mother, 2) some latent confusion concerning his own sexual identity, and 3) strong underlying homoerotic impulses pressing for expression.

Although religion seems to be a comfort and support to him generally, doubt and concern regarding his faith are sufficiently strong to give him some discomfort.

In spite of his many problems and severe impairments, the boy presents numerous positive qualities which suggest a relatively good prognosis provided he has professional help. He is puzzled and concerned about his antisocial behavior and is aware that there is something abnormal about this behavior. He is capable of real sensitivity of feeling and he desires help. R. possesses a relatively good sense of social justice; he has many social aspirations and strivings in the way of education, work and family living. He has a need for friends and possesses an ability to form interpersonal relationships. However there are some early signs of a breakdown of thought processes and if the present maladjustment should go untreated, there are indications that schizophrenia is almost certain to develop.

The boy achieved a total IQ of 100, a verbal IQ of 94 and a performance IQ of 105, all IQs falling into the average intelligence range. Certain test indicators suggest intellectual retardation, probably due to poor cultural and educational background and impairment of intellectual functioning due to emotional maladjustment. The boy, without this intellectual retardation and impairment, could perhaps achieve an IQ in the bright normal intelligence range.

Diagnostic psychological testing elicits from the subject samples of behavior which reflect the different aspects and levels of the subject's personality. In the case of R. the tests indicated how he might generally appear, think, feel and act in everyday life as well as under special conditions of stress. Some underlying factors for his behavior were suggested; severe impairments and special assets were revealed. Current intellectual functioning was expressed as being the result of a number of interacting influences, several of the major influences being the natural endowment for intellectual development, the effects of the environment with its restricting or stimulating character, the schooling and special interests with their expanding or constricting nature and the effects of any emotional disturbance.

TREATMENT SERVICES

Every boy at the school receives some counseling or psychotherapy. The amount and intensity vary, depending upon the needs of the boy and the time and training of the particular social worker, psychologist or psychiatrist. Staff members are supervised by case supervisors, the school psychiatrist, or a staff member of the Menninger Foundation. A few boys are treated as out-patients in the children's division of the Menninger Foundation. Some group psychotherapy is being carried on with hyperaggressive, withdrawn, enuretic and retarded boys.

The psychologist has an opportunity to work with the boys in both individual and group treatment situations under supervision of a psychiatrist. While the boys who are in individual treatment with the psychologist live in the regular school quarters, four hyper-aggressive and destructive boys with whom the psychologist works as a group live in the school hospital and are in an experimental project in the residential group treatment of this type of youngster.

Since the school's staff is relatively small, numbering between seventy and eighty employees, a personnel department is not warranted, and various people assume additional duties in a personnel program. The psychologist is the chairman of the personnel selection committee which is composed of the superintendent, the director of the clinical services department and the head of the particular department needing a new worker. The committee function includes job analysis, and the evaluation and selection of applicants. Specifically, the psychologist is responsible for the job analysis, testing the applicants, and obtaining opinions concerning the applicant from other committee members.

Thus the function of a psychologist in a state delinquency treatment institution has been extended along with the general growth of the field of psychology. The development of diagnostic tests of intelligence, of concept formation, ideational content and personality has provided the psychologist with effective tools for eliciting information useful in the diagnosis and treatment of delinquents. The door is now open to a psychologist interested in doing therapy and if he is trained and supervised (supervision depending on extent of training) he can make a contribution. Through the application of his skills to personnel work he can be particularly helpful in the selection of personnel to work with the delinquents in various respects.

142

The Chaplain's Role with Delinquent Boys in an Institution *

Rev. J. L. Cedarleaf

While religious ministry to institutionalized persons has been traditional throughout the history of institutions, the usual practice was to install retired clergymen or a parish misfit in this ministry. In a sense, this probably reflected, on the one hand, the lack of real concern by the church for the sick in body and spirit and, on the other hand, the lack of knowledge by the church in the interrelationship of body and spirit. The last 25 years have seen a decided awakening of interest in this ministry. Largely because of the revelation through dynamic psychology has the church become alert to a much deeper and significant responsibility to institutionalized people.

In the Protestant tradition the rise of the clinical training movement has been of major importance to the institutional ministry. This movement had its roots in the personal exploration of the inner world by Anton Boisen.[1] It became organized into the Council for Clinical Training and has expanded and matured so that it now provides many seminarians and clergymen with a clinical experience in various institutional centers. This training has been defined as: "a firsthand learning experience under accredited supervision which provides theological students and clergymen with opportunities for intensive clinical study of problems in the field of interpersonal relationships, and which seeks to make clear to the student in understanding and practice the resources, methods, and meanings of religion so they are expressed through pastoral care." [2] The Council carries on its functions through individuals whose primary work is that of chaplain on the institutional staff. These ministers constantly engage in the problem of making clear to the patients, other professional people, and themselves the distinctive function of the minister of religion. This paper will largely concern itself with a description of this type of religious ministry to juvenile delinquents as carried on at St. Charles, where there has been a clinically trained chaplain on the staff since 1940. It will specifically describe the present chaplain's work at St. Charles from 1948 to 1953.

The institution maintains full-time Catholic and Protestant chaplains and part-time Jewish chaplaincy service. The chaplains are considered by the administration to be part of the clinical team, which has social workers, psychologists, psychiatrists, physician, and dentist as other members. The administrative position of each of the team members is equal, though obviously their function differs in terms of their training and service rendered. This means that the chaplains participate in diagnostic conferences, and the general treatment program, as well as carry out their specific religious ministry. I shall elaborate on the services rendered in these areas.

THE CHAPLAIN'S ROLE IN THE DIAGNOSTIC PROCESS

It is a common practice in institutions and clinics to have a diagnostic team made up of a social worker, psychologist, and psychiatrist. At St. Charles the chaplain has been added to the team. In adding the chaplain, it was expected that he would prepare and present diagnostic material and information which can be useful in planning a treatment program for the patient; yet to produce and present this material from a specific point of view. In other words,

---

* Reprinted from 18 Federal Probation (1954), 40–45. Used by permission of the author and the publisher.
[1] Anton Boisen, Exploration of the Inner World. Willet and Clark, 1936.

[2] Standards: Council for Clinical Training, Inc.

if the chaplain merely duplicated the social worker's history, his contribution would be of little significance.

The initial religious interview has been developed to meet this need. It is conducted with every new boy who enters the institution. While the interview is basically diagnostic, it also serves as a method for helping the chaplain become acquainted with the newly admitted patient and to assure the patient of his interest and the availability of his services. In order to clarify this diagnostic procedure, some detailed comments need to be made on it. The following is a sample of a diagnostic interview from the chaplain:

Personal Religious History: — John states that he attended the . . . Church quite regularly for the past year. Previous to that time he had attended a Protestant church in an area which he cannot specify. He has received correspondence from the pastor of the . . . Church and they know each other quite well. He states that he has not been confirmed nor baptized. He recall's the story of God feeding a multitude of people and the account of Noah and the Ark. He thinks of God in relationship to his remaining at the institution. He stated that he had had the urge to run and then commented that he prayed to God to help him stay here. He feels that God loves him and also states that God is like a father. He refers to his stealing of a car as sinful activity and then very anxiously went on to state that he really wound up here because he had run away from Parental School. He had been picked up by the police on suspicion of being involved in a shooting at a gas station in Chicago. He was originally sent to Parental for stealing a car and in discussing this incident he mentioned that he had a good deal of anxiety about driving and actually hadn't known how to drive until he had taken this car with some other boys. With this he associated that his father had told him that he should have let him know about his urge to drive and he would have made arrangements to get him a car. At times when he was involved in trouble he claimed that his conscience bothered him. He discussed girl friends and commented to the chaplain that he had a regular girl friend before he came here, but he doesn't know if she is still interested in him now. He denies sexual activity with girls and says that masturbation was a disturbing practice. In discussing marriage, he says that he doesn't think he will marry now but he does not commit himself in the future. The subject of dreams was raised. He commented that at night he is often afraid of the dark and after having seen scary pictures he does have frightening

dreams. However, the specific content of these dreams he cannot state.

Family Religious History: — John stated that his mother had started to attend church only since he got into trouble. He told of his mother being ill and said that she has a bad heart. He went on to talk about a friend telling him that at a doctor's visit this meant his mother was going to die. In discussing this further, he felt that his mother's heart condition was somehow related to her having to worry. He mentioned that his mother is not particularly rigid with him and that he feels very badly when he gets mad at her, stating, "she's right most of the time." His father died about 4 years ago from a heart condition. He was in his late forties at the time. John was uncertain about the nature of his work and stated that he was only an occasional attender at church. For the past 3 years there has been a stepfather in the home. He works as a crane operator and is occasional in attendance at church. John states that he likes him fairly well. He is the oldest of six children in this family, the youngest of whom is a girl 18 months.

Reactions of the Boy in the Interview: — John was somewhat anxious, but cooperative, in the interview with the chaplain. He tended to relate quite well, but seemed to have an anxious cast about him. A bit of a tremble was noted in much of the conversation. He talked very warmly about his identification with the religious group. Some anxiety and pressure was noted in the discussion of the mother. In talking about the deceased father, a tendency to block and be tense was present. The stepfather was discussed in a fairly open mood. As we discussed the concept of God, he tended to become quite dependent and in some ways rather flat. Concern was present in the discussion of the aggressive activity. Rather warm feelings appeared as he discussed the idea of a girl friend. Some anxiety was present in the discussion of sexual activity.

An analysis of this report reveals the distinctive approaches in this interview. Religious affiliations and practices are explored. In this area information is gathered on the denomination to which he belongs, the church he attended, and the extent of that attendance. It also includes information on the parents' attendance and interest. Inquiry is also made into baptism and confirmation.

What can this information contribute to the diagnostic understanding? If we refer to the interview, we notice that John had a history of rather scattered church attendance. He cannot recall specific instances of early attendance. The history does, however, show increased interest in the recent past. Furthermore, the history reveals that the mother only recently became interested in church and this in connection with his difficulties. Little or nothing is stated about his father and stepfather in relation to church attendance. From this one would conclude that the family had little or no active interest in activity that represented "good" society, but they were aware of the church as a resource when trouble was brewing.

In the interview, we notice that John comments that he prays for help to control himself. This indicates some need for the guiding influence of a father or authority figure.

The second major area covered by the initial religious interview is that of uncovering the patient's personal values, goals, and ethical relationships. Recollections of religious or Biblical stories are used, as well as dreams and feelings about sin.

In the interview it will be noticed that John recalls the story of the Feeding of the Multitude and Noah and the Ark. Alone they cannot be relied on for a diagnostic opinion in the framework under discussion, but when coupled with other material, they are often clearly diagnostic. It appears that the recollection of the stories of the Feeding of the Multitude and Noah and the Ark would represent either a strong necessity to rely on the miraculous or the presence of strong dependent needs. Other material will have to corroborate this.

Boys who have difficulties in assuming a masculine role will often recall the story of David and Goliath. Problems with the mother are often reflected in the story of Samson and Delilah. It is important here that the interviewer let the patient tell his own story. The patient could easily recall a story the interviewer suggests. Such a response would have little diagnostic value.

John expresses a fear of darkness. This suggests anxiety over aloneness. Thus we have seen the anxiety over separation and independence is present.

He tends to consider his delinquent activity as sinful. There is thus some concern about values. However, the subtle expressions of mood need to be utilized to determine the depth of this concern. For instance, if activity is discussed as sinful in a bland, open mood, we suspect that the words are said for the interviewer.

If, however, the discussion evokes a depth of feeling and concern, a tendency to block, or a show of concern, this suggests the penetrations of values into the depths of his personality.

Sexual values, attitudes, and ethics are considered. If he accepts and follows the cultural and religious pattern, little anxiety is noted. If, however, he conforms, but has impulses in an opposite direction, a great deal of concern and hesitancy shows in this area. The equation of his religious values with regard to impulses can be observed rather easily. Exploration in this area reveals the harmonization or tension between the religious cultural values and the libidinal drives. The chaplain's exploration of this area aids greatly in evaluating these dynamic aspects of the patient's personality.

The final area of investigation here concerns the basic religious or theological problems. This is an exploration into his relationship to God or the depth of his existence. Does the patient have concern beyond the usual finite structures of life? Does the patient view his existence in any kind of ultimate context? Evidence on this is gathered from his spontaneous productions to the clergyman as a symbol, his attitudes on God, as well as the content and mood of dreams. What does this interview show in relation to this area? God is viewed primarily in relation to the tangible human situation. In his fear of the dark, there is a suggestion that he may have some anxiety about the deeper meaning of existence. His fear of isolation is probably to some degree a concern about his deeper meaning in life. The evidence thus indicates problems on both finite and ultimate levels of existence.

If the patient tends to view God totally in an anthropomorphic sense or as supermanipulator, this suggests that the problems are largely on the finite level and he is unaware of concern in the framework of the infinite. The problems and concerns that do arise here need to be seen clearly. If a patient is basically concerned about the ultimate relationships, then dealing with these as oedipal, neurotic, or character problems is of little therapeutic avail. This is often the error of the psychiatrist. The reverse, however, is also true. If the patient is primarily concerned with the finite issue and the counselor attempts to deal purely with the ultimate concerns, failure is certain to take place. This is often the error of the clergyman.

A further word needs to be said here. Often an individual uses theological systems and attitudes as a neurotic defense system. This is seen in the person who has "faith" in order to avoid internal or external conflict. Such a "faith" always hinders growth, and is in contrast to creative faith which is a way to a broadening and deepening of existence. The chaplain's training and sensitivity in this area can contribute significantly to the diagnostic understanding of the patient.

As a member of the team, he presents his material along with other disciplines. It is as all these approaches are combined that a true diagnostic picture emerges.

SPECIFIC RELIGIOUS PRACTICES AND RESOURCES

The second major area of religious ministry in an institution is the utilization of the historical and traditional forms of the church. These practices have existed through the ages, and through them many have found their way out of darkness. These forms and practices do, however, need to be adapted to the individual needs, as well as to the institution in which the chaplain ministers. Thus, even in these traditional practices, the diagnosis is taken into account. The following are some of the resources and practices the training school chaplain uses.

Worship. For the delinquent, the worship service offers the opportunity to participate in creative activities, in contrast to the former destructive group activity. Further, the worship service is a concrete demonstration of God's concern for man. One time a boy of 12 said to me: "I'm a different boy because I've gone to chapel; even my cottage father says it is the only thing that has helped me."

The chaplain who is alert to the needs of delinquents will be able to use the worship service to arouse creative tensions. But to do this the chaplain must be an active member of the team, and his efforts must be integrated with the total program.

Prayer. This is a much misused resource of religion. All too often in our institutions we have made it a forced formal practice that leads to conformity rather than creativity. The saying of table grace tends to be an advertisement as well as a means of control by conformity. Prayer is used to express inhibited, unachievable, or unrealistic desires. As such it is removed from the stream of reality. By the chaplain's use of prayer in worship and in personal relationships, a feeling of harmony between the individual and his larger world should be the result. Prayer is a way of expressing significant creative feelings, rather than the formal or magical formula that so often it is. The value of prayer is really in direct proportion to the level of maturity in a person.

The Communion Service. In the various Christian traditions the concepts of this communion service vary widely. I can only tell you about our specific service. At the Training School at St. Charles, in the Protestant service, we have a communion service the first Sunday of every month. The mood of this service is that God accepts us and wants to be one with us. For many of the boys this becomes an anchoring point in an otherwise drifting life. As these boys come to the altar rail, they are aware of a large oil painting above the altar. With its religious symbols, primarily the idea that God is light, it is a source of help to the delinquent.

The above practices and resources used by the chaplain are not a complete list. A particular religious tradition such as the Roman Catholic, Lutheran, or Episcopal would have additional resources to offer in the restoration of delinquents to creative living.

INDIVIDUAL TREATMENT RELATIONSHIPS

Probably the most significant function that the chaplain has on the treatment team is the unique personal relationship that he has with boys. In the boy's mind the chaplain generally is a symbol of God or of a father. The important thing at this point is how the boy considers the chaplain. Initially what we as chaplains think of our role is less important than what a particular boy thinks of it. This, of course, does not hold true for the total course of treatment. We cannot proceed therapeutically without being aware of the meaning the boy attaches to the role.

Psychoanalysts have demonstrated the force of transference in treatment. It is the distinct kind of transference that occurs in relation to the chaplain that makes him a unique person on the team. This does not imply that other disciplines do not have unique functions. As suggested, this aspect of the boy's relationship to the chaplain is primarily determined by the boy. As such it is subject to his individual distortions, and thus many variations exist in the relationship to the chaplain. To this the chaplain has to be alert. Probably the most helpful ally here is the accurate diagnosis.

The following case illustrates the problem of the boy's conception of the chaplain and its effect on his relationship to the chaplain. Riley Rollins is a 14-year-old boy who has been committed to our training school. In the interview with the chaplain he told of extensive contacts with various clergymen and regular attendance at church camps. He indicated a strong desire to spend time with the chaplain. This seemed to be a good idea, and the chaplain suggested to the diagnostic staff that he be the counselor. Upon very careful consideration of this boy from psychiatric and psychological points of view, as well as the history of his previous contacts with clergy, it was quite clear what Riley sought was a subtle kind of homosexual gratification from clergymen. In the past such relationships had only served to intensify some of his fundamental problems, rather than clarify them. It was evident from the diagnostic point of view that the chaplain was not the individual to deal with this particular boy; in fact, it was pointed out that the fewer contacts he had with the chaplain, the better would be his chances of becoming reconstructed. After his basic conflicts were clarified, the chaplain would then be in a position to offer him constructive counsel and leadership in a creative rather than regressive direction.

I owe you a further word on this case. Our staff consideration revealed that this boy regarded clergymen as asexual objects, who would not mutually engage in direct homosexual relatedness. For this reason it was easy for him to relate with intense fantasy preoccupation on his part, to the extent that he used clergymen almost purely as the fantasy object of his sexual impulses, and he could not relate on any other level. This material has been incorporated to show how the relationship to the minister, and the conception of his role, is initially determined almost completely by the boy. Where the above type of relationship is constructed by the boy, a creative interpersonal relationship is generally ruled out.

I have suggested that the chaplain is frequently considered in the role of a father. This is encouraged directly in the Roman Catholic tradition. Simply stated, this means that the boy at the beginning of the relationship sees in the chaplain characteristics of his father as well as God. Thus he tends to feel toward him as he felt toward his father or God. This may either be a positive or a negative kind of emotional relatedness. Most of the time this is not a simple transfer of feelings. For instance, a boy may have strong negative feelings toward his real father, and yet he has inner images of the ideal-father (God). Then the relatedness to the minister in all likelihood will be of a mixed nature, and as the relationship progresses, this may confuse the chaplain. However, where the internal pattern of hostility is fixed, along with few fantasy ideations, the chaplain can be almost certain that the pattern of hostility will be transferred rather directly to him. It is important, therefore, for the chaplain to know the nature of the relationship toward the father. Usually this is not a simple one-dimensional situation, but is multidimensional and somewhat unpredictable in its manifestations. Cultural factors play a significant role here as well. The further the chaplain is removed from the culture of the father and the boy, the less likely are we to get the transferred father relatedness that is useful in treatment.

Here is an illustration of this. A series of about 35 interviews were held with a very likeable and friendly boy whom we shall call Steve J. Diagnostic interviews revealed him to be an intelligent and fairly well-integrated boy who had been involved in minor difficulty. He had mixed feelings toward his father, who was then incarcerated in a penitentiary for having incestuous relationships with his daughter. This was, however, strongly denied by Steve. It was felt that the chaplain would be able to provide this boy with a consistent and meaningful father relationship which would enable him to clarify his feelings toward his own father. During the interviews the boy seldom expressed any feelings about his own father. He resisted the identifying process. He ran away on several occasions and missed interviews whenever he could. This was especially true toward the end of his stay. What went on can only be understood in the context of our discussion about the role of the chaplain as a father. In the relationship to the chaplain Steve became aware of his hostile feelings toward his own father. This threatened to separate him from his own father, and he had not been able to enter into the new relationship because he felt a distinct cultural distance between the new father figure — the chaplain — and his own father. To enter totally into the new relatedness was to admit separation from his own and his father's culture. This he was unable to do even though it was apparent that he had resources and skills which would have enabled him to move beyond his present cultural orientation. On one runaway he secured a job on a river boat which was his father's original occupation. As the chaplain became aware of this, focus was shifted to the boy's culture and interest, rather than developing the relationship to the chaplain. This case illustrates the factors that play into the relationship of a boy to the chaplain.

LOVE AS A REDEMPTIVE FORCE

As treatment progresses, the chaplain's personal faith and philosophy become of major importance. The chaplain regards all men as sons of God, by birth. It is true that many seem to have surrendered such a birthright by uncreative and destructive activity. This, however, primarily affects the individual's relatedness to God; not God's relatedness to the individual. To Him they still are His children, even though they may have strayed far away. As Our Lord tells us in the parable of the lost sheep, the one which has strayed the farthest is still His lost sheep. The chaplain by his acceptance demonstrates to every boy whom he counsels that God always loves, no matter how far he may have wandered from the fold. God wants the boy to know that He never stops loving him, because the boy is always His child. Thus the chaplain approaches his client with an attitude of redemptive and accepting love, and not with condemnation. This means that he does not engage in moralizing or condemning, but shows acceptance and concern.

Then the chaplain holds that the major redemptive force is love, and that by giving of love growth and redemption occur. It is necessary to say something about love at this point. On no subject does there seem to be more confusion. I prefer the term "understanding-love" rather than "love." That is, this is love with a certain distinct quality. We find that some love is without direction and only sentiment. Often love implies such things as coddling, overprotection, sexuality, and the like.

This kind of love inhibits growth. Understanding can be cold and mechanical; this is clearly seen in parents who raise their children according to rather strict science. For instance, they "coddle a child for 15 minutes before bedtime." To them it is not the coddling that is important; it is the 15 minutes at the proper interval.

A mother once came to me and said, "I've done everything for my boy. I brought him up according to the book on child care. I've talked to caseworkers and psychiatrists and have followed their advice in detail. Why, I've used all the best methods. Why he is like he is, I cannot understand." Her boy, who was sent to our training school, was a seriously disturbed youth, afraid of almost everyone, and completely dependent. His only spontaneous acts were his delinquent acts. Despite the mother's talk, she was a harsh cold intellectual who manifested subtle hostility and no real warmth. It thus becomes evident that understanding needs to have the warmth of love, and love needs the guidance of understanding. Understanding-love is really the kind of love that God has for us. It is his Agape!

This should be the love that the chaplain shares with the delinquent boy whom he counsels. The effectiveness of this love will be determined by two things. One is the receptivity of the boy toward it, and the other is the ability of the chaplain to share this love without personal qualification. The extent to which he is able to do this is in direct proportion to his personal maturity, and his understanding of humanity. The only qualification then, in this love, is in the acceptance of it, not in the giving of it. In the treatment relationship the chaplain's philosophy and demonstration of love is the central core, from his point of view.

It is possible that the reader's reaction at this point is that I am talking about social work and not religion. If this is the objection, it had better be faced. I am aware of the absence of typical religious procedure in the final section of the paper. However, I do feel that the treatment relationships described are fundamentally of a deeply religious quality. We know that a mature religious personality is not suddenly achieved by saying words or going through some rituals. In fact mechanically or defensively going through such activity can create deep defense systems rather than open up and free the creative energies in a person. In those instances religion, rather than aiding growth, adds immovable boulders or sticky clay. It is my contention that in order to help a delinquent become a mature religious personality we often have to engage in major plowing and cultivation for a long period on the finite level before seeds can be planted that will spring up into an abundant eternal harvest. The chaplain at the training school works with boys in whom there are serious interpersonal problems and perplexing social relationships, and not with young people whose creative powers are flowing freely. It is because the chaplain deals with boys whose problems are largely finite that he must utilize treatment processes which are designed by psychology and social work, in order that a solid foundation may be laid, from which the boy can build with the help of others, a secure and abiding faith in God, that will give him courage [3] to face the most serious and disturbing concerns of his existence.

143

The Group Worker's Role in an Institution for Juvenile Delinquents *

Gisela Konopka

In the summer of 1948 the University of Minnesota gave me a research appointment to study the contribution that a trained group worker can make in an institution for juvenile delinquents. In many out-patient settings, such as child guidance clinics, we have realized in the past years the value of supplementing individual treatment with therapeutic group work. We have a beginning of the use of this method in

---

[3] Paul Tillich, *The Courage To Be.* New Haven: Yale University Press, 1952.

* Reprinted from 15 *Federal Probation* (1951), 15–23. Used by permission of the author and the publisher.

several psychiatric hospitals, but we have thus far badly neglected the institutions for delinquent youngsters. Our "training schools," or whatever name is given to them, are in most cases "detention facilities."

The establishment of youth commissions in different parts of the country is a step forward in recognizing the youthful offender as a person in need of help rather than punishment. In 1948 Minnesota created its Youth Commission and the first reception centers under its auspices with the explicit purpose of helping in "diagnosis and treatment of the juvenile delinquent." Because of lack of funds, those reception centers were established in the existing state training schools, used the existing staff, and in many ways had to conform to the routine of the training schools. Such a reception center was used for the experiment.

A Routine Day at the Reception Center

At the time of my arrival about 70 boys were living in the cottage. It was a quickly changing group. New boys were continually brought in, and others left after the Youth Commission had made a decision regarding further plans. The boys were sent to the training school, put on probation at home, or sent to a foster home.

It is easily understood that the atmosphere in the reception center, therefore, was filled with anxiety, extreme insecurity, defiance, and real fear. Here youngsters lived together in a strange environment after having been pulled out of their home environment usually after a difficult encounter with police, jails, and court. A routine day in the institution and at the reception center follows:

The boys got up at 6:00 o'clock, made their beds, had breakfast. To avoid contact with the boys regularly committed to the training school, meals were taken in the large dining room before the other boys came in. The boys always marched in formation from one building to another.

After breakfast some of the boys helped with cleaning, while others were in the basement — this was the shower and locker room in which the boys were asked to stay when they were not on duty. From about 9:00 to 11:00 a.m. they did some chores such as cleaning up the grounds, cutting beans for canning, etc. After 11:00 a.m. they were again in the basement for about a half hour to clean up for the noon meal. After the noon meal they were in the basement, and at 1:00 o'clock they marched to the library of the training school.

The library is a very pleasant room with a great variety of books and some handicraft material. The boys chose their books and were allowed to take out books. During this hour they sat around tables and on the floor. At 2:00 o'clock the boys had gym if no other work had to be done. From 3:00 to 5:00 the boys were either in the basement or outside on the playground, usually playing ballgames. At around 5:00 o'clock they had supper. After this they returned to the basement or played for about an hour out-of-doors and then went to bed. They were allowed to listen to the radio or to read for about an hour. They slept in large locked dormitories.

This routine was sometimes interrupted by a visit from their families, by a visit to the hospital for a check-up, or by conferences with the caseworker, the probation officer, or the visiting psychiatrist. The boys never crossed the campus by themselves without a guard except for a few boys who had the confidence of the staff and who could be recognized by wearing a special belt. Strict conformity was required. Punishment consisted mainly of "standing on line." The boys would stand with crossed arms, not being allowed to sit down, or speak, or do anything else. Often the whole "company" had to stand "on line," if one of the boys had done something more serious such as running away. Punishment sometimes consisted in beating but this was definitely forbidden by the management of the training school and the Youth Commission, and members of staff were continually admonished to "keep hands off."

This quite drab routine was livened up by the human attitude of some of the staff members and the sincere efforts of the supervisor to create a more therapeutic atmosphere.

STRICT ROUTINE DOES NOT RELIEVE ANXIETY

I think it is self-evident that such strict routine does little to relieve anxiety and therefore open the way to any kind of treatment. It also makes diagnosis almost impossible. It struck me that not only aggressive but also withdrawn behavior was repressed this way. Conforming meant to act exactly the way everyone else acted and the way it was safest to live through this experience without being punished

or prolonging the stay. There was no room for self-determination, and little room for showing anything of the true self. It seems to me that this basically explains so many of our failures with youngsters who behaved so well in the protected setting, but fell back into delinquency the moment they left the institution. Not only did they not receive help, but they were never allowed to show their real self. There simply was no way for them to act the way they really felt and, therefore, no way was open for the observer to see them and to give help.

To make diagnosis possible we must find a way to create a climate that allows the youngster to express his likes and dislikes, his fears and wishes, his resentment and his affection. That means that the experience of being segregated from the rest of the community, from his friends, his gang, and his usual environment must change into an experience of acceptance by contemporaries and adults, by some belief in one's own value and own strength. Certainly each delinquent is different and there are individual problems, but we must realize that in forcing them to live together we have created for them a group situation which must be used in the most skillful way to help toward better adjustment.

In addition to the fact that there is a given group situation we know that the group means a great deal to the adolescent:

> To earn the right to belong he (the child) will adopt whatever code of behavior the gang or group prescribes regardless of how much it conflicts with society.[1]

Since we could conduct the experiment for one month only, we were sure that no final results could be achieved. All we could do was to try the value of a method that takes into account the understanding of individual and group behavior, that allows for a large amount of freedom and that is based on respect for the individual.

Detailed process records were kept and I want to present a few of them.

NATURAL SUBGROUP IS SOUGHT FOR STUDY

It was clear that individual attention could not be given in a group of 70 boys. The group had to be broken down into smaller groups.

---

[1] John R. Ellingston, *Protecting Our Children from Criminal Careers.* New York, 1948, p. 35.

How should this be done? We knew from previous experience how important good grouping is for purposes of therapy. Little was known about the individual boy. There was usually only a juvenile court record giving the reason for detention, but nothing else. In a few cases there was a case history available at the time of arrival. Some knowledge of the boy was gained through an initial interview by the caseworker and in some instances psychological examinations had been given. The grouping therefore could not be done very systematically. The group worker decided to observe the boys for one day, get acquainted with them, and choose a natural subgroup as the core of the group with which she would work.

I will read the record of this first contact.[2]

Arrived at reception center around 1:30 p.m. The boys, about 60 of them, were scattered over the playground waiting for visitors. The first Sunday of each month is visiting day.

Supervisor introduced W. first to Arne. . . . Told him that W. would be around for the month of August and probably later would take on a group of boys but that W. would like to know all the boys if possible. Several boys sitting close by were interested and volunteered their names. One of them, Ralph, said his only when another nudged him, and seemed quite disgruntled. Supervisor also introduced W. to Bob who during the rest of the day kept very close to W. We kidded first some about names and how hard they are, etc., to become a little acquainted with each other. More and more boys crowded around. They spontaneously told from where they came.

Bob very quickly related to W. and was apparently hungry for such contact. He said sadly that nobody would come for him. His parents are divorced and, "I am on my own since I was 6 months old." He said if somebody only cared for him he might not be here now, and "if they would let us little kids work." He is "in" for "armed robbery." W. said that he did not look terribly "tough" and he said he wished now he had not done it. He hoped he would get into a boarding home. He repeated twice, "Miss S. thinks this is not the place for me." He pointed several boys out to W. and took his task to "introduce" W. very seriously.

Ralph was sitting on the bench, often staring into

[2] Case record excerpts appearing in this article are reprinted from *Therapeutic Group Work With Children* by Gisela Konopka (copyright 1949), by permission of the University of Minnesota Press.

space as if he hardly saw anyone. Some boys teased him, said he was telling on others. Ralph said, "Nobody likes me here, they say one of the boys was sent to the training school because I told on him." Bob said with feeling, "I like you, Ralph, and he would have been sent there anyway."

Some other boys came to the bench. They asked what W. would do, whether W. would go with her group off the grounds. There was an apparent interest in something "new." A handsome boy with the name of Ted joined the group several times. He was lively, seemed something like a link between the older and the younger boys.

There was some talk about the candy some of the boys were getting and how some would not want to share and how they just take the candy away from them. There was much mentioning of the "Commission" and how they wanted to get before it and know what would happen to them.

Each boy also mentioned that three boys had "drifted" (run away) the previous day. They said that because of this they will have to stand in line all day for 15 days with hands folded and were not allowed to play with the exception of Sunday and when they worked. They said that one boy wanted to sit down but the attendant hit him. Mr. N. is smarter, they said. When he had to leave he said that they could sit down, because he knew that they would do it anyhow when they were alone.

W. caught a ball of one of the boys and soon about six of the younger boys and one older one (about 17) and W. were engaged in a long and fast ball game. One of the boys, Ferd, was especially intent on making W. lose. It was clear that he enjoyed trying to defeat an adult, but that he could do it in an almost friendly, acceptable way. A young blond boy, Walter, sat restlessly and dejectedly around saying sadly that nobody came for him. W. told him that it was only 3:00 o'clock and there might be a good chance that they yet might come. He suggested that he join the game. He did so, and while we laughed and ran and caught the ball he forgot the time and was happily surprised when his family finally arrived.

At around 4:00 o'clock the boys went inside. Two boys, Al and Leo, were on duty with the visitors. Both of them gave the impression of being especially friendly, sensitive boys. Al told W. that he really is on probation but it might take a long time until they find a farm where he can be. He would like to do farming. He said, "The hardest thing is to tell people that the time is up for a visit, but you have to do it." The other boy, Leo, asked W. with great interest and intelligence what W. would do. He said it would be good if somebody is around who can make things a bit more pleasant —

"Sometimes you don't know *what* to do." Then he added, "I saw you playing with the kids. You are the first adult I have seen playing with them."

W. went downstairs where the boys stay about an hour before supper. It is a large empty room with benches at the walls. The older boys were in one group together smoking and talking. Some of the older boys sat in smaller groups playing cards. The younger ones sat around doing nothing, as far as W. could see. Only Ralph was working on some handicraft.

W. sat down beside Ralph on one side and Harry, the only colored boy in the whole group. On the playground the boys had pointed Harry out to W. and had said that he can get "real mad." W. wondered whether that does not happen to anybody once in a while and that started Bob out to tell how he got mad at the county school and threw a billiard ball and others told how they got mad. W. asked Harry whether he had had any visitors and he said that he did, and that he hoped to go home soon. He says everything with a solemn, hesitant manner. Arne came over and was very affectionate with several of the boys sitting on their laps and holding them.

The boys said that they were not allowed to have a show this week because of the drifters. W. wondered whether they might like to put on their own show some time, and they seemed very enthusiastic. They wondered whether they could use the auditorium.

The time and the place seemed especially boring. We talked about other things to do, such as clay work, and everything was taken up with enthusiasm. W. had some pieces of paper and a pencil in her pocketbook and started some writing games. W. never thought that one could make such a hit. Harry, Bob, Ted, and Ralph played very intensely. If W. had had more paper many would have played. Bob showed a considerable amount of intelligence and skill in the games, Harry and Ted were average, Ralph was slow but wanted badly to be in on it. When W. told stories and drew pictures he became especially interested and tried to imitate more as a smaller child would do. In this group activity was also the youngest boy, Ed. He kept more by himself than some of the others.

While many boys stood around there was again talk about hearings before the Commission. Several mentioned their birthdays. Leo said, "A sad place to celebrate your birthday."

(W. wonders whether birthdays should not be celebrated somehow? They mean a lot to boys.)

There was again talk about W.'s "group." Several of the boys, Harry, Bob, Ralph, Ferd and an older boy, begged W. to take them into the group. W. said that we did not have to decide right away anyhow.

The boys went to supper.

W. met the boys after supper on the playground. A whole bunch greeted W. right away, stood around ready to talk or to do something. It was obvious that they waited for some initiative coming from W. W. wondered who knew a good game. The same boy who had spoken so intelligently about the need of doing something suggested a running game, and about 10 boys and W. played this game with a lot of laughter until W. was exhausted.

W. taught them a new game that is played sitting down. Bob and Ralph showed again their great need for attention, because they always wanted to be "it." Interestingly enough, the other boys seemed very tolerant of this need.

Several of the boys questioned whether W. would be around.

SOME BASIC PRINCIPLES OF GROUP WORK

We see in this record the group worker using several principles of group work:

1. Start where your group is. To do this you must know where your group is and you must learn to know the members of your group as quickly as possible. We see the observation and the detailed recording of each boy who stands out as an individual. There is emphasis on observation of nonverbal material, so important in children, as in the case of Ralph "staring into space," Ferd's way of playing a game, or Arne's being affectionate with other boys.

2. Establish an informal, relaxed, friendly relationship. The group worker — and here he differs in his role often from the caseworker and psychiatrist — works indirectly with the problem of the group member. His contribution to an all-around treatment situation lies in working with the strength of the client, with the part that is healthy, making him feel comfortable in the knowledge that there *is* something healthy in him, that he is in some ways *not* different from other people. The group worker is at the same time aware of the sickness, too, and might at times work with it, but his specific task is to relax the emotionally upset person. We see this informal approach in the kidding about names, the spontaneous ball game *in which the worker takes part*, the running game, the sitting down with the boys in a place they especially dislike, such as the basement.

3. Material or some kind of program should be used as a helpful means to better mental

health. Program is an important tool in group activity therapy. We see a beginning here in drawing Walter into the game to help him overcome his fear of rejection by his family, and in the writing game in the basement.

A group of about 15 boys was formed, most of them around the age of 14 and 15 years. The reasons for their referral to the Youth Commission were various. In most cases it was their second or third "offense" which had brought them to the reception center. In most cases the "offense" consisted of stealing.

At the beginning of the group meetings, the boys showed the same conforming behavior that was requested of them in the institution. These meetings lasted 2 hours in the morning and 2 hours in the afternoon. Very soon the "group climate" changed. There were fights among the boys and reconciliations; complaints against treatment received; initiative in asking for some specific work; etc.

In this loosening-up process some of the boys showed considerable fear of this greater freedom. For the first time they were able to show their insecurity. They needed to make a greater effort when they had to make their own decisions, instead of doing what they were told. It was necessary to give them support and reassurance, while continuing to encourage them to express their feelings.

STRENGTHS AND WEAKNESSES EMERGE

Now individuals with their strengths and weaknesses emerged.

Ray, for instance, a 14-year-old, handsome, strong boy was known to all the attendants only as an insignificant, rather conforming boy who caused "no trouble." In this group Ray showed more and more the qualities of a gang leader. Other boys followed him willingly even if he handled them roughly. He was often charming toward adults and youngsters alike, but he also showed a mocking attitude as if he wanted to say that really nobody mattered much. He showed little concern for anybody. Some of his remarks directed at other boys were cruel, yet the boys never challenged him. At the same time Ray showed a real talent for drawing which he hid first behind a great deal of smearing, until he felt more secure. Slowly he drew excellent cartoons and did some very good clay modeling.

The important point is that under the restricting circumstances in the institution Ray could not be seen the way he really was. There was also no way to help him to turn some of the strength that made him a gangleader into more constructive use.

The help given to him in the group had to be threefold. He had to learn (1) that he could gain recognition for a more acceptable kind of behavior; (2) to gain confidence in at least one adult; and (3) that he could continue being respected by his contemporaries even if he was not abusing them. Point one was partially satisfied by the recognition he got through his drawing and also through his skill in games. On point two I would like to quote from the record:

There was a scuffle around the pool table. W. had assigned Ralph to play, not realizing that it was not yet his turn. Ray had pushed him. Ralph sat on a chair doubled up as in agony and crying. Ray said he is a cry baby. W. said he might be really hurt and what was it all about? The boys explained and W. said to Ray that it was really her fault, was it not, and next time he should hit W. for that, not the other boy. His face looked blank, then he smiled — for the first time, W. thought, warmly without his usual irony — and said twice, "I am sorry, Ralph."

Ray was startled by an adult accepting the responsibility for a mistake made and this was the beginning of some change in him. On point three, the boys had talked once about elections. I quote again from the record.

Ray clamored for the election. W. suggested that we could at least start it and go on tomorrow. W. wondered whether he would write down the different offices. He did, asked a lot about spelling.

W. tried to call the boys together and calm them, which seemed like an impossible task. Ray again became the leader in the rough way of the gang leader who knows "how to handle them." He would pull boys and push little Ed into the circle. Ed hit back, etc. Arne sulked in a corner, said that he did not want any office anyway.

Ray suggested: one mayor, one judge, two policemen, three from the jury, one probation officer and one sheriff. The list of "government" officials certainly is indicative.

W. asked who wanted to run for mayor. Ray and Charles volunteered. When asked about election speeches, Ray became tongue-tied, murmured about giving good government and sending the kids to the judges and probation. Charles was less embarrassed, said that he would run the city well.

After the voting the record continues:

Only a short time after every boy had started "office," Ray made definite positive contribution to the group. As the mayor, he started to count his "citizens" which helped to check on the presence of everybody. Yet he did this in a friendly, non-authoritarian manner.

Here we see the beginning of a change from the rough gang leader to a real leadership personality.

The gang leader plays a great role in the whole formation of juvenile gangs. If we can learn how to recognize and work with him, we will be a great step forward in our work with delinquents. For much too long a time we have only isolated or disregarded the gang leader.

After some time of observation in the group the group worker pointed out in her summary of Ray to the Youth Commission his leadership potentialities and suggested a closer relationship with a man since it seemed that he needed the identification with a strong male person. The case history, received later, bore out this tentative diagnosis. When Ray was 7 years old his parents were divorced and he stayed with his mother and three siblings. His father remarried, but soon moved with his second family into the house of the first family.

The case history shows in the following years constant disorganization of the family. Father deserted, returned, deserted again, etc. Ray was sent away to relatives, was called back and sent away again. He finally burglarized a school, was put on probation, but broke probation by stealing several cars. The case history points out the lack of identification with a father person.

Group workers who work in neighborhood houses and other youth serving agencies are constantly in the position of working with emotional difficulties in children without the benefit of case histories. Clues come from individual behavior and relationship to the group. This skill will be needed badly in our institutions since we cannot expect to receive good case histories in each case because of lack of professional personnel in the communities from where the youngsters come and often work must be begun with a youngster a long time before case histories can be received.

Because of lack of time and space this paper cannot go more into all the aspects of working out inter-relationships in the groups. One question that is often asked is how difficult situations among easily excitable youngsters can be handled. Again most training schools will ask for restrictions and punishment when fights occur. To this question there is no general answer, but only the application of a general principle; even the difficult situation must be handled from the point of view of treatment, and not of retaliation.

The worker being with a group of youngsters under the trying circumstances of confinement in an institution must understand that often tempers flare up because of the close living together, the anxiety, and the accumulation of many unstable youngsters in one place. The freer the atmosphere the less conflict there will be. In many instances the worker will "feel" the rising conflict before it breaks out, and may open up channels early enough so that it does not turn into a tempest. Yet outbursts will not always be avoided. I am quoting from the record to give an example of such an incident:

. . . It was a hot day and the wind was blowing without any relief. This weather seems to make itself felt with everyone. The boys were restless.

Things went all right until Ed and Larry got into a fight. Both boys had no self control, but Larry had a real fit and was dangerous. He threw stones, took the scissors or a large pole. He is not very fast so W. could get hold of him. W. held his two arms, talking in a soothing voice until he relaxed under her hands. The difficulty was that Ed did not let him alone but provoked him. Larry's rage mounted again, and beside physical force he used terrible language. Again he reacted upon the holding and the soothing words like somebody coming out of a trance. He then lay down on the ground, perfectly exhausted, sweat standing on his brows. When he was rested a little W. asked him whether he wanted to draw and write out all his anger. He was perfectly willing to do this. Ed immediately asked for paper too.

The important point in this situation is that despite his tantrum the boy felt that the worker was not angry at him. The worker did not let him "just release," which is one of the dangerous concepts in therapeutic work, when it is carried to the extreme. She certainly limited him, but he could feel at the same time that she was not fighting him. We must also know that this event did not occur in a vacuum. The worker was not alone with those two boys. Fifteen other boys were present. Yet the fight was not carried over to the others. If the worker had reacted with violence, I am convinced that this would have involved violent reactions from others in the group. This way the conflict was isolated.

Discussion Groups Are Organized

Besides those activity meetings, discussion groups with a smaller number of boys were conducted. In the discussion groups the focus was on a very tangible problem. Indirectly this helped the boys to realize something about themselves, and their own reactions to their environment.

The first discussion group consisted of five boys, 14 years of age, who had their hearing before the Youth Commission and were told that they would go on probation the moment suitable placement was found for them. All four boys knew the worker through the informal activity meetings and therefore felt free in her presence.

The second discussion group consisted of four boys, 15 years of age, who had only recently come to the reception center and who seemed most disturbed, bitter and forlorn. These boys knew the worker from at least one meeting in the activity group. This method of introducing seems especially helpful to me since otherwise discussions often are strained and the boys need a much longer time to feel free and confident.

Here is the record of the second discussion meeting with the first group of boys:

W. wondered whether there were other difficulties they would have to face after leaving the Center. Arne said it would be the people at home who would ask so many questions, where they had been, etc. Bob, Dale, and Walter were reasonably sure that they would not get into the same environment, but they all agreed that people might ask them at the new place too and anyhow, they hoped to visit at home. They all agreed that it was a tough problem to face people. W. asked, "Why?" Bob slowly said, "Because it is a disgrace." Harry added, "It is, and they always think that it is your mother's fault." Arne said, "I have older brothers and they feel disgraced."

Worker: Let us think for a moment what that means. What is really the disgrace? To be here?

Dale: Oh, really the things we have done, but people think differently.

W. suggested to stick first to what we thought.

Walter said that this was really a place which wanted to help them to get along better. W. said that they knew that this was not a jail. They understood, they said, but Arne said with feeling that they were closed up anyhow and beaten, and people don't always understand. W. suggested to the boys that this time we should stick to our difficulties and talk about the problems we would have when leaving here.

Arne: Yes, let's do that. Now, for instance, there is a man in a drugstore at the corner. I don't know whether he likes me and is interested in me or if he is mean and wants to tease me. Every time I come back he right away asks me where I have been, why I went there, etc. It makes me mad.

Worker: What do you answer, Arne?

Arne: It is none of your business.

Walter: Well, that will make him really mad at you.

Worker: What would you answer, Walter?

Walter: I was at the Y.C.C. because I got into trouble and now I know better and will get along.

Worker: What do the others think?

Harry: That won't make him so mad, but he will ask more.

Worker: Let's think for a moment why the man and others might ask such questions.

Arne: He wants to know.

Dale: He is jealous.
The others laugh, "What should he be jealous about?"

Dale: I can't explain, it just seems to me. . . .

Worker: Maybe Dale has something there — wait a minute. And what do others think?

Bob: He is curious.
The others agreed with the latter.

Worker: Have you ever seen what people do when they see a soldier coming home with one arm?

Bob: Sure, they always ask questions. And the soldier might not want to talk about it either.

Arne: They are not really mean, they are just curious.

Worker: Sure, see, people are that way. Your drugstore man probably too. And a friendly answer does help. But what about Dale? He said jealous. You know people always like to get some attention and you boys get it, even if it is not pleasant. The man probably does not know it, but maybe he likes some attention too.

Bob: So it is better to give some friendly, steady answer.

Worker: Do you think you boys can try now?

Arne: I think I can, but it is tougher with the kids. They really tease you.

Harry: Sure, they make you feel miserable. They ask, where have you been, what did you do? What do they do to you? Do they beat you? Do you get enough to eat? Tell us all about it.

Arne: Harry knows; Harry went through it once.

Worker: Why do you think the boys ask?

Dale & Bob: Oh, they are curious too.

Arne: And it sounds exciting.

Worker: Sure, they like adventure and it is like an adventure story to them. What do you do when they tease you?

Arne: Oh, I get mad, really mad.

Walter: That won't help, Arne.

Worker: Let's try it. One of you teases the other and he answers. (The boys all refused to be the teaser, fearing the other would really get mad at him.)

Worker: O.K., I will tease Arne and he will answer.

W. does not recall this game verbally, but she repeated the things the boys had said, such as where have you been and you good-for-nothing, etc. Arne always answered defiantly, getting more and more angry until he got to a "you . . . you . . ." W. stopped at this point and asked what would come next? They all shouted that now a fight would come. One of them added, "and being on probation, that might end badly for you, Arne."

W. asked whether someone else would like to try. Walter was willing. This time Arne was the teaser. This dramatization was unusually realistic. Arne used every mean device. After he had asked the usual questions, he started with a dry "Well, you won't go straight. Started little and you will get worse. You will end in the penitentiary anyhow."

Walter stuck with an amazing calm to his guns. He always answered clearly. He gave a good interpretation of Y.C.C. He said he *tried* to go straight. On the penitentiary attack he said, "Maybe, but I will try not to." At another point he said, "I have been out for three weeks and I am still all right" after Arne had attacked him with, "I bet you can't go straight for three days."

Arne: Oh, three weeks. Your parents probably kept you at home all the time. You are only good when you are in bed.

Walter: I went to school, didn't I?

Arne: Your poor mother — What she has to take!

Walter: We are getting along all right now.

W. stopped the dramatic play at this point. The others discussed it, saying that it was helpful to get it so clearly. They would try to act as Walter in the play. W. said that she knew it would be harder when the teasing was real, but she hoped it helped to have thought it through a little and maybe, in the middle of the teasing, they might remember our discussion.

Preceding these discussions there was often first an outburst about conditions in the institution. This was very helpful because it made the boys free to come back to discuss their own difficulties.

A preparation for "life outside" seems to me especially important. We have had a great deal of literature about the returning soldier and how to help him make the change from a confined life with many restrictions and constant living with many men to a civilian life, but we have not given much thought to the youngster who has spent a short or a long time under even more restricted circumstances at a very impressionable age. We send him out "on probation" without preparing him for all the difficulties he will encounter. One interview certainly may not help. One group discussion alone will not give much help either. Yet it is a beginning of their knowing that they are not alone in facing the difficult problem of returning to an often hostile environment.

The beginning of the discussion with the new boys was more difficult, because they did not know the worker so well. I quote from the first record:

The group sat outside around the table and W. told the boys that she has asked them to come for an hour discussion because she thought they had a lot of questions on their mind. W. said that we could be very frank with each other here, that the more openly we discussed things the more helpful it would be. After today they could decide themselves whether they wanted more of this.

Gus started the ball rolling by asking what W.'s group was all about. W. explained in as simple terms as possible that we thought it helpful not to have the large group together all of the time; that W. also had found that it was good to have a few hours where the boys could decide on their own activity, make some of their own decisions. They would have to do this later on too. W. asked them whether they would like to do something specific. W. would try to provide it, if possible. Suggestions came fast from all five of the boys, mainly in terms of handicraft. Lastex work and making rings out of plastic were on the top of the list. W. was interested in the real need for such work that was expressed. W. asked whether there were other things in which they needed help. Roy said hesitantly that he would like to know what "YCC" meant, why they were here. Herb joined in, said he did not understand the whole thing. W. asked whether anyone had explained to them the Youth Commission set-up. Their faces were blank. Had the judges not told them? W. asked each one what the judge had said when he had suggested their coming to the YCC Reception Center. The answers can be summarized by Herb's answer: "He looked at some magazines and he looked at a big book and he said, YCC, and I was brought here."

(It was perfectly possible that the judges gave a much more detailed explanation. It only shows how upset the boys are at this point and how more often they need information.)

W. explained that Youth Commission means how the new law tries to help youngsters like them, how this is just a period of trying to learn to know them and then make a decision as to what would be best for them. Roger and Herb asked why, since this was not a punishment, they were allowed to be beaten by the attendants and why they were constantly locked in and watched. The others joined in on this, said how terrifying the locking in at night was especially. W. said that beating was not allowed, that they should let Miss S. know when it happened. The locking up, W. said, is mainly because of the fear that some would run away. W. said that she and everybody else working here do not think that everything is perfect, but that W. thought they were old and intelligent enough to know that things do not always work the best way. W. explained how young YCC was, explained about the lack of funds. It was interesting that the boys listened attentively, sometimes nodding assent.

Joe suddenly said in a bitter tone of voice that the whole thing was nonsense anyhow, they would all go to the Training School, and even if they are put on probation they all would be back some day. W. asked Joe why he thought this. In the same bitter tone he said that they all were no good anyhow, that they will do the same things they did before, he knows. He will do it too. (Joe's bitterness was pathetic. He is one of the most intelligent boys and apparently very hurt. He needs much help.)

The other boys, especially Herb, objected, "No, we will not do it again."

Gus: Sometimes you do those things because you had a raw deal.

Worker: Hm, there *are* reasons why we do these things. What happened to you, Gus?

Gus: Well, everything would be O.K. now, I would have a new family if I had not been caught. You know, I ran away from Boy's Town and I got along all right. I slept on the roofs and I met Arthur in a movie. Arthur is such a swell boy.

And he took me home and his family would have adopted me.

Worker: Do you know anything about your parents, Gus?

Gus: (Apparently relieved that he can talk more about himself, pouring out his whole story). No, I don't know my father. But I have a mother, I have a mother. But I lived in a convent. And the Sisters said I had set fire, but I did not. I wished they don't say things. I did not set the fire. I ran away from the convent and later I ran away from Boy's Town.

Roger: He did have a raw deal. He has no parents. I have parents. I did not have a raw deal, but I stole a car. Lots of boys do, only I got caught.

Worker: If you were not caught, then the car stealing would be all right, Roger?

Roger: I don't know.

Worker: Would you like it if you had a car that somebody stole from you?

Joe: I would, if I had insurance. I would be glad if somebody stole it.

Herb: You are crazy Joe. He might have to go somewhere fast and the car is gone. And it is wrong anyhow. You should not steal. (Here Roy, who usually was very quiet, nodded.)

Herb: I surely will never take a car again. Only I am so worried about my mother. She had intended to move to California and now she can't because I am here. What will happen to us?

Boys Relax and Gain Insights

The third meeting shows how they have relaxed more and how they gain some insight.

Roger: I stole a car. Funny, all of us have taken a car or so. Most kids would not be here if it were not for cars.

Worker: That *is* interesting, Roger, is it not? It would help us to understand why we do this. When did you start thinking of taking a car?

This question was put to all four boys and they all said about when they were 13 years old.

During all this Roy sat silently, looking very unhappy. He said he would never tell why he came here. W. said this was all right. Did he want to leave the group? No, he wanted to stay, but he did not want to talk. He was told that this was all right.

W. said to the boys that it was interesting that they all started around the same age. They nodded thoughtfully. W. then explained in very simple terms about adolescence, without using the word. W. said that at that age both boys and girls get somewhat restless. Things change. They are not really children anymore. And because they are restless, they want to do a lot of things, "and go fast" added Roger. W. said he had hit it on the head. And going fast and having adventure was now connected with cars. W. said that it might be, also, that they wanted to impress a girl. Herb said with astonishment, "How did *you* know?" W. said it was not so unusual, we all, at that age, like to impress the other sex. Herb said the girls want a fellow with a car, and he felt so lonely. He again mentioned his parents' divorce. W. said that she knew it was hard feeling lonely. Gus said he was all alone, but he wanted to find a girl who did not need a car to love him (he said this very seriously) and Roger said he knew one who did not mind a fellow without a car, but he felt sometimes alone too. Joe said it was tough when your father is dead. . . .

These boys who usually pretend being "tough," especially Joe and Roger, could now frankly admit that they often felt lonely and scared.

W. said that being lonely makes you do things sometimes which you later regret. Maybe we could help find things and people who help you over such times. Herb said, maybe these days had helped him a little, he understood things better. He added, "And I will go back to my mother. I know now that I can't have both of my parents."

Conclusions Drawn from Experiment

We were able to draw some conclusions from this experiment:

1. There is the need of a person, or several persons, on the staff of an institution who can handle a group situation in an informal, releasing way; who understands enough about dynamics of individual behavior to react in a therapeutic way; who understands the meaning of behavior; and who is able to make an intelligent report to other professional people on the staff.

2. We recognized that the more rigid the group climate, the less hope there is for accurate diagnosis.

3. We learned something about spontaneous grouping, knowledge of which is greatly needed to do better group work. Some of the principles of grouping we observed are:

(a) The more rigid the group climate, the smaller the group cohesion. In the rigid climate we find a great deal of fighting, "telling on each other," distrust. The more relaxed the group climate the more real "esprit de corps." There was genuine "we-feeling" in the selected group of boys.

(b) Spontaneous grouping did not occur according to the clinical difficulty of the boys, but more according to social maturity. Age was important mainly in terms of status. Being older meant being stronger; having had more adventures; being allowed to smoke, knowing girls. Similar reactions toward the adult created subgroups. The boys who were more secure with adults than others formed a definite subgroup.

4. We learned that, as in most groups, work with the indigenous leader is important. Only in the presence of an accepting adult will this leader reveal himself. Help in working with him comes from direct work with him and from strengthening the rest of the group members so that they are able to get along without depending on him.

5. Group discussions are most helpful when they are preceded by some informal group meeting with the worker. The great contribution of the informal group meetings lies in their relaxing influence, in the feeling transmitted to the youngsters that they are not *all* bad, not *all* different from any other youngster in society. It is a strengthening of the ego by strengthening the *healthy* parts of it. In the group discussion the youngster is forced to focus on his problem. He will do it more frankly and with greater security in the presence of an adult with whom he has had a pleasant contact.

Institutions for delinquent youngsters should be staffed with teams similar to child guidance clinics. Since the youngsters live in close group associations the professional group worker is an essential part of this team. For too long a time we have either neglected our institutions for delinquents, or we have thought that an hour interview of an expert will help the youngsters. Professional services of psychiatrists, psychologists, caseworkers are indispensable, but they will be lost if the people who work daily and hourly with the boys are not directed toward the basic therapeutic aim of restoring in the youth a feeling of self-respect and a warmth toward other human beings.

Chapter 26

Techniques of Treatment: Casework

THE ART OF SOCIAL CASEWORK can be of great importance in transforming ordinary probation, parole or institutional confinement into constructive experiences that go behind the surface of personality and character. The carrying forward of the process of "individualization" begun at the sentencing stage requires a continuous adaptation of social and psychologic means to the end of stimulating internal personality integration and accommodation of the person to social groups and codes. In this process, external compulsion or threat have little effect. As stated by Pray, in the first and extraordinarily perceptive article in the present chapter, the treatment process, from the point of view of modern social work, "loses all semblance of control or manipulation of one person by another," depending, instead, "upon a relationship between worker and client within which the client may, if he is able and willing, ask, receive, and use help in clarifying his own wants and purposes, in relation to the resources available to him, and in mustering his own powers to achieve his chosen ends."

This does not mean, however, the absence of authority and discipline. The difficulties inherent in the dilemma that, in the case of delinquency, it is the community, through its laws, judges and officers, that seeks to change the individual rather than the delinquent's own seeking of aid are persuasively discussed. The student may well ask whether the traditional casework approach is incurably incompatible with the authoritarian necessities of courts, probation offices and institutions, — a topic encountered in this book in other connections. How far the caseworker can go in risking the community's safety by refusing to take sufficiently into account the fact that not a few youthful offenders are not only non-responsive to the familiar techniques of his profession and to psychotherapy but are openly, flagrantly and aggressively dangerous to life and limb is an issue that has become especially acute with the burgeoning of socially offensive, violent gangs in the large cities of the country. Pray expresses his confident belief that "the true principles of social casework are not only applicable — they are indispensable — to the administration of any effective program of treatment of the delinquent."

To this view, the Editor would subscribe; but he is convinced that a system of *priorities* must be worked out in coping with delinquents, which will emphasize the early and more therapeutically responsive stages of antisocial habituation, and that there comes a time when it is both wasteful and dangerous to continue to give the costly aid of casework and psychiatric therapy to persons upon whom a great deal of effort has already been expended without adequate results and who continue to carry on their antisocial aggressions. Every agency concerned with criminal justice and related problems must draw such a line; for, first and foremost, is the necessity of protecting society against actively dangerous offenders, just as it is necessary to protect it by means of quarantine against typhoid carriers or other active spreaders of disease.

Regarding the philosophy of the caseworker with delinquents, Pray, after exposing certain misconceptions in respect to social casework and "individualization," reminds the worker that he "must start from the one common premise that the basic purpose of delinquency treatment is the protection of the community. That is the only reason we enter the lives of these people at all. Its concern for the individual, wherever and however expressed, is as a member of the community." He wisely reminds the reader that all life requires a framework of discipline. "Social adjustment and readjustment consist of the acceptance and use of real limitations upon our absolute freedom." It is high time that all concerned with the education and the behavioral problems of children recall the role of self-discipline and external discipline in the process of growing up; for the "combination of freedom and authority is the very essence of democratic life for all of us." Pray then gives illustrations of the value of realistic social casework at various stages in the administration of criminal justice, beginning with the police. Especially significant is his emphasis on the use of the presentence investigation as a means of building a constructive relationship with the delinquent and his family, through making the investigative experience a cooperative process. He stresses the importance of the social casework art in institutions as well as in probation and parole. A wise discussion of Pray's article by Charlotte Towle, and a supplementary comment by Pray, conclude this exchange of ideas.

The second article in the present chapter is by the late Hans Weiss, whose untimely death in an automobile accident was a tragic loss to social work in the field of delinquency. Although Weiss's contribution is not recent, it still submits vital words of wisdom. It is still relevant, for example, to point to the possibility that the "technique of the social worker is in danger of becoming so over-developed and standardized that it impairs free and creative action in the work." Weiss shows the similarity in the evolution of practices from mass treatment to individualization in social work and in probation. In both, "real influence springs from understanding the personality of the individual, from recognizing the difficulties with a sympathetic mind and from exercising wise guidance over a sufficiently long period of time." While there is a difference in the type of symptom which brought the client to the attention of the worker and in the kind of social agency called upon, there is no essential difference between "the social worker's problems, tasks and goals and those of the probation officer."

Using extracts from case histories, Weiss offers convincing illustrations of the approach of the probation officer to the client and of the subsequent stages in the process of casework as it involves delinquents. Beginning with the need to establish relationships of confidence and rapport, between probationer and judge and probation officer, Weiss presents in simple but convincing terms the psychology of constructive social intercourse as a basis for effective client–worker relationships. He shows how interviews leading to friendship are conducted. He points to a fact too often overlooked that "approach" cannot be readily learned but is rather "an outgrowth of the worker's philosophy of life." How sound, from a mental hygiene point of view, is this wise probation officer's suggestion that although the "worker may feel the need of being stern, strict, particularly patient or kind, the undertone should always be the same keynote of interest and sympathy"! Even experienced probation officers can profit from Weiss's analysis of the three stages of the social worker's technique: investigation, diagnosis and treatment, "scientific terms for very simple and logical processes," and of the interrelated methods of eliciting relevant information from the client and other sources, diagnosing or thinking about the problems presented by the individual delinquent and his family, and planning the treatment program in such a way as to bring about the adjustments and improvisations which the currents in the life stream make necessary.

Weiss discusses the authoritarian aspect of the probation officer's approach to social work, a problem it will be recalled also dealt with in Pray's article. He concludes with some discerning observations on the meaning and opportunities of probation as "not a substitute for punishment" but an opportunity to help the probationer to "rebuild his life in the community," on the qualifications of a competent probation officer, and on the qualities of a wise juvenile court judge.

144

The Place of Social Casework in the Treatment of Delinquency *

Kenneth L. M. Pray

It is necessary, I think, to face candidly at the outset of this discussion the fact that the assumption underlying this topic — namely, that social casework does certainly have some place in the treatment of delinquency — is itself still debatable. Not only is it obviously true, as we all know, that many of those primarily responsible for determining and administering treatment of delinquents are not committed to the use of social casework — to put it mildly — it is also true that social caseworkers themselves are by no means of one mind as to the possibility of applying the principles and methods of social casework to the treatment of these particular problems.

We face, as a matter of fact, the very interesting paradox that social workers, after struggling for a generation to establish and fortify the validity of the assumption that social casework is an essential instrument in the adequate handling of this problem, sometimes appear to be retreating from that position, just at a time when some public authorities, originally very skeptical of social casework, are beginning to see and use some of the values in it.

This paradox arises, of course, out of the development that has taken place both in social work and in the penal system. Thirty years ago, when modern social casework and modern

---

* Reprinted from "The Place of Social Case Work in the Treatment of Delinquency," by Kenneth L. M. Pray, 19 *Social Service Review* (1945), 235–248, by permission of The University of Chicago Press. Copyright 1945 by the University of Chicago Press, all rights reserved. ["This paper and the following discussion were presented at a meeting held in Chicago under the auspices of the Central Howard Association. Some parts of Mr. Pray's paper are appearing simultaneously in the April-June issue of *Federal Probation* (Vol. IX, No. 2). — Editor" (of *Social Service Review*). Editor's footnote, page 235.] — Ed.

penal treatment were both in their infancy, social workers could confidently assure themselves and the rest of the world that their service was not only applicable but indispensable to the adequate scientific treatment of delinquents. For social casework in those days was still definable only in most general terms, as individualized social treatment, and the concept of individualization of treatment was then coming to represent, also, the very core of modern penal reform.

Judges and penal administrators, however, were then equipped, on the whole, only with the tools of mass treatment — for instance, relatively fixed statutory sentences, based on the nature of the offense rather than on the offender, and congregate institutions, geared principally to the maintenance of secure custody. It was not surprising, therefore, that in those early times judges and administrators did not quickly recognize the possibility of introducing into this structure so new and so radical a concept as individualized social service. As time passed, however, the established program of treatment of delinquents came to minimize more and more completely its ancient strictly punitive purpose and to substitute more and more thoroughly the objective of reform and rehabilitation, with the individual delinquent rather than the specific delinquency as the focus of effective treatment. This working philosophy and method conformed perfectly with that which dominated social casework. For in social casework, as in other aspects of the penal program, individual treatment was directed largely to the manipulation of environmental factors, on the one hand, and to moral and intellectual instruction and suasion, on the other. It was the worker's chief business to find out what was wrong with the individual, to devise a remedy, and then to apply his superior understanding and his powerful influence to the fulfilment of this chosen plan of rehabilitation. Consciously or unconsciously, subtly or frankly, the worker assumed a large measure of responsibility for remolding the life of the individual client — whether delinquent or other — into conformity with community standards or, even more often, with the personal standards of the worker himself, who was regarded almost as a free agent, charged with personal accountability for the success of the chosen plan. Judges and penal administrators could come quite readily to an understanding and acceptance of this additional means of direct corrective influence upon individual delinquents. And they have done so.

But our present dilemma appears in the fact that social casework has largely abandoned this original concept of its own task and of the nature of the individual worker's responsibility. Drawing upon the advancing sciences of human behavior, as well as upon the critically analyzed outcomes of its own accumulating experience, social casework has undergone a fundamental change of philosophy and practice. Its new position rests upon the conviction — indeed, upon the absolute knowledge — that change enforced upon an individual from outside is, in all truth, no change at all. He will change himself and his social attitudes and behavior only to satisfy himself. He will, in the end, do only what he himself genuinely wants to do, from his own motivations, to achieve his own satisfactions. Social caseworkers, therefore, no longer believe that they can successfully take upon themselves the role of compelling, persuading, or cajoling individuals to make a different and better social adjustment, to satisfy standards outside themselves. They can only help individuals to discover and face the alternatives open to them, to make responsible voluntary choices of their own from among those alternatives, and then to accept responsibly the consequences of their own judgments and decisions. The helping or treatment process, from this viewpoint, loses all semblance of control or manipulation of one person by another. It depends, rather, upon a relationship between worker and client within which the client may, if he is able and willing, ask, receive, and use help in clarifying his own wants and purposes, in relation to the resources available to him, and in mustering his own powers to achieve his chosen ends.

When one tries to relate this type of service to the situation in which the delinquent finds himself and to the general purpose expressed in the community's total plan for the treatment of delinquency, the potential conflict is obvious and the assumption that the two belong together is far from axiomatic. The judge and the penal administrator are now, as they were in the beginning, representatives of the community, which, through law, in specific terms, has established certain standards of behavior,

to which it requires all its citizens to conform if they are to participate as free individuals in the community. They are charged with the specific responsibility of upholding those standards in the lives of particular individuals who have been held to account by the community for violation of those standards. Individual delinquents come under this influence not because they have expressed or consciously felt a voluntary desire for help in conforming to community standards or in changing their own but because the community has compelled them to subject themselves to this new relationship. It is the community's will, not the individual delinquent's, that initiates and sanctions whatever service or treatment is rendered. It is the community's general purpose, in reality, to change the individual.

To deny or to belittle the deep significance of the apparent difference between these two concepts is to be blind to reality. The reality of this difference is being expressed right now both by social workers and by judicial and penal administrators. There is, for instance, an influential movement among professional social workers, including some of those who are in positions of leadership and authority in the field of delinquency control, to bring about the ultimate separation of the so-called "casework functions" from the authoritative operations of agencies like the courts or correctional institutions, because the two functions are deemed inherently incompatible. While this movement is now directed chiefly to the limitation of the juvenile court to its strictly judicial role, through the transfer of its so-called casework tasks to other administrative child welfare agencies, the basic hypothesis underneath the movement certainly denies, by implication, the validity of a casework approach to the handling of adult delinquents as well. The similar viewpoint of some judges and administrators, approaching the problem from a different angle, is expressed in the recent articles in the *Atlantic Monthly* by Judge Perkins of Boston, who presides over one of the oldest and best juvenile courts in the country and who now contends that the preoccupation of the social caseworker with the interests of the individual — the caseworker's apparent willingness to risk the community's safety, at times, in order to permit the individual delinquent to develop and use his own powers and to realize his own purposes — runs contrary to sound social principles and stands in the way of effective administration of the law.

It seems to me that the time has come to face this issue squarely. Until we do, we cannot claim for social casework, nor will it possibly achieve, a real place in the treatment of delinquency. For myself, I affirm my profound conviction that this alleged conflict between social casework and other essential authoritative processes in the treatment of delinquency is only apparent, not real; that the true principles of social casework are not only applicable — they are indispensable — to the administration of any effective program of treatment of the delinquent; that the alleged conflict is based on a misconception or misinterpretation of both social casework and these other aspects of treatment.

The dominating misconception of social casework is twofold, and it has been unfortunately fostered by certain social caseworkers themselves. First, is the tendency in some quarters to limit the meaning of the term "social casework" to a presumably intensive therapeutic process, set up within the relationship between worker and client, which is addressed directly to effecting deep personality change in the client. From this point of view the simple, practical, day-to-day services that usually initiate, always accompany, and often wholly sustain the helping relationship may be useful and necessary in opening avenues of access to the inner personality of the client, but these services in themselves do not involve social casework. They are believed to be beneath the level of truly professional skill and dignity, because they do not necessarily enlist the whole self of the client in changing himself. They are external trappings, so to speak, behind which we should conduct our real professional operations.

The second misconception of social casework, necessarily involved in this first one, is the tendency to abstract the client from his social setting as the object of effort.* The social worker's alleged preoccupation with the inner life and being of the individual, with the personality problem, if you please — the effort to respond to the client's own personal need, without limit or definition — seems to leave

out of account, as Judge Perkins asserts, the community's stake in its own protection against individual violation of its own proper and necessary rules.

The misconception of the true nature of modern individualization of treatment in other aspects of the delinquency problem is also twofold. First, is the assumption that flexible individual programs of treatment — the separation of the individual out from the mass, for any purpose whatever — is somehow a means of relaxing or easing the authority exerted by the community, a form of leniency. Second, necessarily involved in this same concept, is the tendency to regard any exercise of firm authority, therefore, as an evidence of failure in the use of a more subtle professional skill. Since the exercise of authority is inherent in the operation of court, of institution, of probation and parole, the relationship between worker and client comes to be regarded as inherently unprofessional — not a helping, but an exclusively controlling, relationship.

It is necessary, I believe, to reject, explicitly and finally, all these misconceptions. We must start from the one common premise that the basic purpose of delinquency treatment is the protection of the community. That is the only reason we enter the lives of these people at all. Its concern for the individual, wherever and however expressed, is as a member of the community. Individualized treatment — whether by social casework or otherwise — is justified, if at all, only because the protection of the community against crime is best achieved in that fashion; that is, by affording the offender opportunity, incentive, and help to live *within* community standards rather than outside or in opposition to them. Those standards and limitations remain in full force and effect under a program of individualized treatment as under any other program; they are not abrogated or denied; they are not relaxed in the slightest degree; they are accepted and used.

It is within this framework that social casework, like every other part of the treatment process in relation to delinquency, must operate, if it is to find its place in that process. The vital question must then be answered, "Can social casework operate within this framework?" Can it accept this kind of limitation upon the freedom of the individual to be fully responsible for himself, to choose his own

* See, also, S. Hofstein, "Social Factors in Assessing Treatability," 4 *Children*, 48–53. — Ed.

ends, and to find his own way to the attainment of those ends? Is this acknowledgment of the rightful authority of the community to establish and maintain its own standards incompatible with the concept, underlying social casework, of the way in which human beings change their patterns of behavior and their social relationships?

Not only is there room, in the practice of social casework, for such limitations upon individual freedom; there is positive, unavoidable need for just such limits. They constitute the framework within which, alone, real freedom, real movement and change, is possible to anybody. There is no absolute freedom for any of us in this life. Life itself consists of a constant process of adjustment to the limitations that surround humankind. There are limitations of physical strength and capacity in ourselves, with which each of us must come to terms. There are limitations of mental ability. There are also social limitations — not only those of law and custom, but of ordinary human intercourse. In some measure each of us pays for the recognition, respect, and comradeship we seek from others, by accepting and respecting the conditions imposed by others with whom we want to associate.

These limitations are not only ineradicable facts of life to which, willy-nilly, we are bound to adjust. They are, in fact, the very basis upon which we discover our own capacities, for we must have something to struggle and measure ourselves against, in order to find ourselves, to achieve selfhood with all its satisfactions, at all. Without those limits we are lost in a tidal wave of surging impulses, none of which is better, more satisfying, than any other. It is profoundly true, as the psychologists tell us, that it is conflict between our impulses, some barrier to realization of some of them, that makes us think at all. Social adjustment and readjustment consist of the acceptance and use of real limitations upon our absolute freedom. They consist of making one's own, taking into one's self, a share of the social authority that sanctions these inherent limitations upon individual life, so that we can use them constructively and stop fighting them vainly.

The function of social casework in facilitating social adjustment is not, therefore, to free the individual from all limitations; it is not to assist him to achieve, without let or hindrance, any or all of the ends to which he might aspire, but rather it is to help him to face, to understand, to accept, and to deal constructively and responsibly with certain realities of his own situation — his own capacities and also the facts of his social setting. The individual social worker is, furthermore, not a free agent, responding freely to every need of the client. He works within an agency setting, which not only accepts community standards as the basis of its own service — whether it be a public or a private agency — but which sets up conditions of its own, to which the client must conform if the service is to be available to him. Agency function, structure, and policy, represented by the worker, become a part of the limits within which the client must learn to operate if he is to attain the personal satisfaction he seeks.

Now, it is peculiarly true of the delinquent that social readjustment must be founded upon the recognition and acceptance of the inherent, rightful, essential social authority that underlies social living. He has rejected or violated that authority in the past. He has to learn anew, through painful experience, that those social limits, like those of his own personal capacities, are inviolable and that his real satisfactions are to be found only within them. It is obvious that he cannot learn the values of those standards to him, if he does not find them upheld in practice, as he struggles to come to new terms with the community. They must be an integral part of the framework within which and against which he tests himself but with which in the end he must come to terms by his own will, if he is to resume free, independent life in the world outside. To assume or to contend, therefore, that social casework with delinquents, if it is to have any place at all in the process of their treatment, must be separated from authority, must be divorced from all enforced limitations, is to rob the service of its most important dynamic — a vital, candid facing of reality — and it is to frustrate, in advance, its primary objective — namely, to help the individual delinquent to accept and to deal responsibly with the whole of that reality, including its inviolable limitations.

There are only two essential conditions for the practice of social casework within this authoritative setting. The first is that the authority involved shall be not arbitrary and personal, not an expression of the individual worker's particular will but a true expression of the social will, controlling both worker and client. This requires that the agency, whether public or private, which the worker serves and represents shall, in its own definition of purpose and of policy, define, express, and sustain the conditions which the worker applies, the limits within which both worker and client operate. The second condition is that within the limits thus prescribed there shall still be room, there shall still be obligation and opportunity, for the individual delinquent to exercise freedom, to make really vital choices of his own, to face his own problem, and to accept responsibility for dealing with it. This combination of freedom and authority is the very essence of democratic life for all of us, at every level, and in every circumstance. Wherever this combination really exists, social casework — that is, the art of helping individuals through the offer of specific services to find the strength to face reality, to muster the power to make responsible choices, and to accept for themselves the consequences of those choices — can find a congenial and a fruitful sphere of service.

Before following through the implications of this conception into a few of the practical places at which it can be applied, I must revert for a moment to a consideration of that narrower definition of social casework to which I referred in passing — that is, the concept of its task which set it somewhat apart from the meeting of the simple, practical, immediate needs of the client and which focused it in a so-called therapeutic relationship, directed to the discovery, the interpretation, and the redirection of the deep personal forces that presumably underlie the overt immediate problems. There is something extremely plausible and alluring about that concept. It has in it an apparent effort to get at and remove underlying causes rather than to deal with superficial symptoms in behavior. But it has serious defects.

In the first place, of course, if social caseworkers follow this definition of professional function, they are likely to find themselves perilously entangled with the functions and prerogatives of another profession — psychiatry,

for instance — which is devoted to precisely this purpose and which is far more qualified, on the whole, to pursue it effectively. But there are other more compelling considerations, already presented, which invalidate this concept of social casework. It tends to sacrifice, both theoretically and practically, the reality limits which are so essential an element in the effort of the client, with the help of the worker, to come to terms with his problem. It is precisely in the concrete needs which he feels now, in relation to concrete services available, under specific conditions, that the delinquent faces the necessity of meeting, in its full force, and finding a way to master, the present problem of finding a new way of adjusting to life. If he can escape facing these practical immediate issues, even by collaborating in an exploration of his past, or by disregarding, for a time, his immediate problems, because they are presumably less important than hidden causes, he can easily continue to evade immediate responsibility for dealing with present reality. By the same token, the worker, faced with the endless catacombs of mixed feeling and purpose, imbedded in the shadowy depths of the individual's personality, may easily find himself lured into an illimitable labyrinth of problems, without chart or compass or destination. Without some firm basis, in the need of the moment for present commitment in decision and action and for responsible, considerate, effectual choices and judgments, the controls and the goals that are essential for both taking and giving help, in a social casework relationship, are lacking.

Furthermore, every expression of real need, every offer of real service, within the relationship between these two, client and social worker, affords an opportunity for pin-point focus upon the attitudes and feelings, the will and the purpose, which are decisive at this moment. In the smallest detail of daily living — a change of address, a change of job, a desire for a new suit of clothes, a fear of writing home, a reluctance to report to the authorities, or to meet regular appointments — is imbedded the whole problem which the individual finds in relating freedom to authority, dependence to independence, and in taking responsibility or evading it. To overlook or to minimize the significance of these opportunities for service, to deny their validity and their supreme importance as factors in the social casework process, is to be blind to the very essence of professional responsibility and opportunity.

And so, to answer, at last, the question implied in our topic — "What Is the Place of Social Case Work in the Treatment of Delinquency?" — I affirm: The place of social casework is at every point in the whole system of treatment at which the individual finds difficulty in relating and reconciling his personal feelings and wants with the demands of his social situation, including the authority inherent in it. It is a means of individualizing the impact of the social forces that bear down upon him, of helping him to discover their meaning to him, their effect upon him, and of helping him to choose a course of action that sustains his own individuality and integrity, while yielding enough of his old self to accept the limits these social forces represent.

What are some of the points at which these problems appear with the most vital force? I shall leave out of account, for this occasion, those moments during the individual's life — in the family, at school, at work, at play — when, as the forces of confusion and growth, of change and disintegration, beset him, the clear, objective help of a social caseworker might mean the actual prevention of the first overt steps to ultimate delinquency.

I cannot elaborate, or even enumerate, more than a few of those particular occasions upon which, as delinquency does develop, social casework may be a peculiarly appropriate and helpful tool. I can only mention, in passing, for instance, the possibilities of its fruitful application in relation to the function of the police, bizarre as that association may at first glance appear. Yet, in the activities of so-called policewomen and some crime-prevention units, at least a primitive kind of social casework has gained a tiny toehold, even there. But this fairly novel idea does illustrate, with special vividness, perhaps, the basic problems to which social casework can address itself with considerable confidence and clarity. Consider, for instance, the disillusionment, the shock of fear and shame, that may come — does certainly come — to many a person who, for the first time, or without warning, faces arrest for crime. Guilty or innocent, hard-boiled or unsophisticated, novice or expert, the individual at that moment turns frantically in one direction or another for help in facing the terrifying unknown that lies just ahead. Is it too much to expect that a skilful professional practitioner of social casework, alertly sensitive to what this occasion means to the individual and his family, identified in feeling and understanding both with the community that has suddenly imposed its naked force upon him and with the individual who has suddenly lost direction of his own life, could help to avert either heedless and futile rebellion, on the one hand, or complete abdication of self-respect and personal responsibility, on the other?

There are other spots, long after this moment, in which social casework has already found far more common acceptance. The presentence investigation in the court is one. Indeed, this, I think, often seems to the court and to the public to be the typical, if not the only specific, purpose to which social casework can profitably be applied. Social casework has been generally identified with this investigative process since the days of Mary Richmond's *Social Diagnosis* a generation ago, and this process is still the hallmark of social casework in many minds. And even this aspect of it is not to be minimized in importance. As an aid to the truly scientific and socially sound treatment of the delinquent, within the function of the court, it has an enormous value, for the technical skill of the social worker in discriminating, economical, sure-footed discovery and weighing of hidden, as well as surface, facts can have a respectable and decisive part in achieving real justice. But it should be added, I believe, that in this investigative process it is not always the external, mechanical technique which is of first importance and value. It is rather the disciplined capacity of the worker to begin and to carry on, throughout this investigative process, the building-up of a relationship with the individual delinquent and with those with whom he is involved, through which they can, from the first, face their problems and responsibilities with somewhat greater freedom and clarity and can find in the whole experience something more than the destruction of all their normal strengths and hopes. The investigation can be, in a measure, a co-operative process, which enlists the responsible participation of those to whose ultimate treatment it is addressed. It is this kind of investigation that really counts in the long run, and I know of no specialist more adept in this skill than the social caseworker.

I shall pass hurriedly over the next step at which social casework is most commonly and confidently invoked — the period of probation. It is obvious that in this relationship of mutual and continual responsibility between worker and delinquent, over a considerable period of time, all we have said of the scope and nature of the art of social casework is applicable down to the last letter and comma. It need only be supplemented by this repetitive note of warning. If social casework is to be effective here — as it can and should be — two conditions must be regarded. To the court, release upon probation cannot be viewed as a form of leniency, in which the authority of the court is relaxed or abdicated. It must be understood by court, delinquent, and probation officer alike, that this is an experimental period of social adjustment, during which the individual is expected and helped to learn to live with authority. It is a testing time to discover and develop his capacity to take responsibility for himself, as a member of the community, within its framework of rules and with all its deficiencies and limitations. Unless the social worker accepts his own responsibility in the same terms; unless he himself can accept and use the authority inherent in his own functions; unless, at the same time, he has the insight, the patience, the faith, to give help when it is needed but never to relieve the client of his own full responsibility — this process can be an empty series of motions, valuable neither to the court, to the community, nor to the delinquent himself.

There is one additional service to which, I believe, social casework may be far more widely and confidently dedicated in the future than in the past. This is in the administration of a correctional institution. The enormous strides that have been taken in recent years to convert these dark and dismal structures from places of exile and punishment into scenes of constructive labor and community life, centers of a deliberately planned rehabilitative program, are admirable in purpose and often in effect. But it seems to me that it is necessary to remind ourselves and the community that just to the degree that the normal conditions, opportuni-

ties, and incentives of social living are introduced into the institution, just to the degree that the normal, universal social institutions devoted to work, play, education, health, comradeship, and intercourse become part and parcel of institutional life — just to that same degree do the customary problems of social conflict and social adjustment, which characterize social living on any level and at any place, appear upon the scene. They are, indeed, intensified by the perpetual, uninterrupted contact with comparative strangers and by the unnatural isolation from the stabilizing forces of family, neighborhood, and other normal group associations. It seems to me axiomatic that if, in the free community which we all know, there is need for the service of competent professional social workers to help individuals and families to relate themselves comfortably and constructively to the frictions and frustrations that beset human beings in their living together, there is vastly more need and more certain usefulness in making that kind of individualized helping available to those who are torn from their familiar settings and set down by no will of their own in an artificial, rigid, inherently disagreeable social setting. In relating to institution rules and authorities, in relating to fellow-inmates, in relating to the families and friends they have left behind, in looking forward to the problem of resuming responsible living after a period of complete dependency, in learning to use positively and purposefully the time they are to spend in this particular way and place — some of these human beings, indeed many, perhaps most of them, will find a way to use, for their own good and for the good of the community to which they return, the understanding help of a skilful social caseworker if it is available to them. I can assert out of specific personal observation, and from the demonstrable results of such service where it has been tried, that they can and will do so. And I venture to predict that one of the outstanding developments of the next ten years in our penal system will be the steady expansion of social casework services in correctional institutions all over the country.

I need not more than mention the obvious value — indeed, the imperative necessity — of following through with this same kind of help and guidance when the prison door finally opens and the former convict walks out into the free world to begin life anew. The official parole service and the voluntary prisoners' aid society, with this essential ingredient of professional social casework service at its command, has the overwhelming responsibility, the almost illimitable opportunity, and along with these, the indescribable satisfaction, of putting into this crucial experience a meaning and a quality that can have inestimable value for the individual and for the community.

I must close with the very emphatic assurance — which I hope has been implicit in all I have said — that social casework is no panacea for crime, nor is it a magic and mysterious key to all the intricate problems of crime prevention or treatment, nor can it always succeed. I contend only that it must be a part — not by any means the whole, but a significant part — of any program in this field. For it has in it — in its philosophy, in its method, in its objective, in its outcome — that profound faith in men, that respect for the inherent dignity and worth of every human personality, that repudiation of crude power as a factor in human life, coupled with a real appreciation of the necessity and the value of social structure and limitation, which is the essence of the democratic spirit, the true foundation of just and effective law, and the basis of orderly, stable, progressive social life.

PENNSYLVANIA SCHOOL OF SOCIAL WORK

DISCUSSION BY CHARLOTTE TOWLE

Mr. Pray has presented the problem which confronts the caseworker who must work with the individual in a situation in which his services are imposed rather than sought. He has emphasized the fact that we cannot fulfil our dual function — that of safeguarding the community and of helping the individual — by identifying with him against the authoritative system responsible for his supervision. Instead we must help the individual in such a way that the demands of society, as conveyed through a correctional agency, may become sufficiently desirable that he himself regulates his behavior.

We have learned that, just as this end is not attained by identifying with the offender versus the law, it likewise is not attained by such a complete identification with the authoritative system that we are not able to see its defects and limitations and to understand what the individual is feeling, as he must submit to the drastic restrictions involved in imprisonment and to society's mistrust as expressed in supervised parole. It is probably true that much of our ineffectual work in authoritative systems has been due to an extreme alignment on the side either of the individual or of the correctional agency. It is clear that we must accept and maintain our identity as representatives of the law and at the same time extend to the individual help which may become desirable to him because he feels our kindly purpose, our understanding, and our respect for him as a person who has an identity other than that of the offender. This seems so obvious that we might well wonder why caseworkers in general have not functioned this way to a greater extent than they have. Time does not permit discussion of the many factors which may have operated against our relating ourselves both to the correctional system and to the individual. I shall mention only those that seem to me to be particularly significant.

Workers as human beings have had strong feelings which have led to marked alignments and which have determined their thinking and their action. Many of us have come to adulthood with intense feelings about offenders. These feelings have ranged, varying with the offense, from mild distaste to extreme repugnance and from mild anxiety to extreme fear. The very feelings which in part enabled us to inhibit our own unsocial impulses operate, *warningly*, to make us condemn their enactment by others. Any acceptance or understanding of antisocial behavior may be reacted to with the fear that we are condoning and thereby perhaps lowering our own standards. These feelings gradually give way in many workers as they experience professional education. In some instances, however, vestiges may remain. Feelings of condemnation may give way to sympathy and understanding, as workers study human behavior. This may occur as they come to know the effects of frustrating and hurtful relationships, as they become acquainted with the effects of adverse social and economic conditions on family life and of the effects of disturbed family life on the individual. They see the individual not as having sinned so much as having been sinned against. At this point there may come a marked swing away from their former attitudes. There may emerge as strong an identification with the individual against the law as formerly there was with the law against the individual.

At this point there may come also through study of human behavior and through knowledge of the mechanisms operating in some instances of antisocial behavior an appreciation of the need of these individuals for supportive moral judgments and for help given by consistent discipline and understanding authority. When workers see this, they are less fearful of identifying with the correctional agency. They may then come to use the authority of the agency and the supportive judgments of society objectively and effectively because they use them now in response to the individual's need rather than from their own need to punish and condemn. But right here, at a time of psychological readiness to represent the law-enforcing agency and to help the individual incorporate its dictates, they are driven back by the very nature of some institutional programs either into alignment with the individual or into a defensive alliance with the agency. In so far as case workers care mightily what happens to people and in so far as they truly understand the factors and forces which shape men to unsocial ends and which undermine possibilities for their rehabilitation, they find it difficult indeed to accept the programs and the administrative procedure of some correctional agencies. When these regimes are destructively restrictive, caseworkers are driven either to reject or to defend *blindly* the agencies which theoretically they should be able to use in the confident, resourceful, and creative way described by Mr. Pray. This occurs, almost inevitably, in systems which are administered by people who are harshly punitive and who lack respect for the individuals they serve, that is, when everything is done to defeat rather than to attain the aims of a rehabilitation program. Until many correctional institutions are corrected, it is probable that caseworkers will find it difficult if not impossible to work constructively within their authoritative framework. The creative use of this framework which Mr. Pray's stimulating discussion envisages presupposes an acceptable regime, administered by reasonably well-qualified personnel, oriented to human needs and to the import of their work. When these conditions are not present, it is important that we not become blindly worshipful of restrictive and depriving systems on the assumption that in and

of themselves and even by reason of these qualities the caseworker can help the individual make constructive use of them. It is important to remember that in some instances institutional reform is prerequisite to effective casework service. If social workers put first things first, they will make known the need for program change rather than assume that in their skilled hands a poor instrument may be wielded effectively.

Within a well-planned and constructively administered correctional system we would do well to note the therapeutic possibilities inherent in helping the individual learn to live within social limits. In some instances this may come about in so far as the individual finds in the caseworker a person who understands his anger and his frustration, who at the same time helps him to understand the purpose of the social demands, who values his efforts at fitting in, and who through trusting him shows confidence in his ability to modify his behavior. As he is thus understood and encouraged, he may come to feel different about authority and he may move into identification with the worker's attitudes toward social restrictions, gradually making them his own apart from the worker. This will occur when the individual has considerable capacity for relationship, considerable capacity to endure denial, and a relatively active conscience — in short, a character structure which enables him to come to grips with reality. Little other than sometimes a temporary "institution cure" may take place in such instances as the adult offender with a markedly infantile character. This is particularly true when his inability to inhibit his unsocial impulses stems from life-long deprivation and from the lack of sufficiently meaningful relationships to have developed a normal conscience. The juvenile offender when behavior is on this same basis may experience through imposed authority more lasting ability to inhibit his unsocial impulses, providing conformity and consideration for others gives him new patterns for relating to others which are more gratifying than the old ones. Socially acceptable behavior will be more firmly intrenched, however, if within the institution the young person is afforded meaningful relationships through which he develops genuine feelings of love and hence of obligation to others. Benefits to the individual through the use of imposed authority may not occur in those instances of adult or juvenile offenders where the delinquency is a solution for some deep neurotic conflict, as, for example, when it serves the purpose of obtaining punishment, or of punishing others, etc. Many adult offenders and some juvenile delinquents are persons who may not be able to make use of imposed limits without help other than has been described. Their irrational strivings, that is, their inability to think, has derived from an excess of deprivation, of frustration, and of measuring and bruising themselves against limiting circumstances. For some of these individuals direct psychotherapeutic help will be indicated. Institutional regimes which are permissive rather than restrictive in character also will be needed in some instances.[1]

It is true that caseworkers sometimes have undertaken direct psychotherapeutic work inadvisedly. In my opinion more often than not these abortive attempts have not derived from a lack of respect for usual casework measures. Instead these attempts have been motivated by the case worker's comprehension of the individual's need and his lack of realization of the full extent of knowledge and skill demanded for competent service of this nature. We would all agree with Mr. Pray that the sick delinquent is a large order for the average caseworker, and we would not recommend ambitious efforts at direct treatment for which he lacks adequate preparation.

It is important, however, that case workers focus on understanding what purpose delinquent behavior serves the individual in a given instance; also on what the correctional experience is meaning to the person in relation to the needs expressed in his delinquency. Finding the answers to these questions will imply history-taking, that is, exploration of the past for light on the present problem and the present experience which we are trying to help him use constructively. As the trained worker attains skill through experience, his inquiries will become differential. They will not be a random collection of facts useless in the present problem of determining what help the individual needs and can use. Nor will these inquiries be used blindly as an escape to the past or unjustifiably as an excuse for not coming to terms with the present reality, if there is evidence of capacity for facing

that reality. They may be used, however, as a safeguard against misguided hopes and mistaken assumptions as to the benefits of imposed limitations. They may serve also as a basis for referring individuals to available psychiatrists and as a safeguard against overambitious attempts at direct treatment. Finally, it is as we understand in the purpose served by the delinquent behavior as well as the meaning of the correctional experience in relation to that behavior, that we may see possibilities for that more effective use of the authority, the discipline, the limiting realities — in short, the use of the "social will" expressed in the institutional regime and parole procedure.

We are indebted to Mr. Pray for a thought-provoking discussion, one which should stimulate us to careful evaluation of our casework efforts and of our correctional programs. He has reinforced our long-standing conviction as to the importance of good institutions and of adequate parole supervision as a framework for effective social casework in the treatment of delinquency.

UNIVERSITY OF CHICAGO

SUPPLEMENTARY COMMENT BY MR. PRAY

Miss Towle's discriminating and penetrating discussion has raised extremely significant questions that go to the very heart of social casework philosophy and practice. I am happy to have this opportunity to clarify my own point of view upon some of these basic issues.

Miss Towle points out three dangers:

First, that the social caseworker's identification with, and use of, agency function and policy which, especially in the field of delinquency, often represent very imperfect and even potentially destructive standards and practices — may threaten the integrity of both worker and client by condoning and perpetuating indefensible limitations that prevent, rather than promote, the client's sound social adjustment;

Second, that the emphasis placed upon the maintenance and use of such specific limits, as decisive factors in the helping process, tends to place upon many clients more responsibility for facing and dealing with the realities of their situations than they can be expected to carry and tends to underestimate the responsibility which the worker must carry for protective help

---

[1] See August Aichhorn, *Wayward Youth* (New York: Viking Press, 1935).

in some cases and for direct psychotherapeutic help in others;

Third, that this extensive responsibility of the social caseworker necessitates greater reliance upon history-taking and "diagnosis" in the usual sense, than appears in the social casework function and practice which I have described.

It is undeniably true, as Miss Towle asserts, that "in some instances institutional reform is prerequisite to effective casework service." Unless a given program has constructive values for the individual and unless within the program the individual has sufficient freedom, opportunity, and incentive to discover and realize those values for himself — and unless the social caseworker has conviction on that point and has sufficient freedom to help the individual use the program for his own benefit — there is no place for social casework in such a program. Furthermore, one must agree wholeheartedly with the concept that social workers, "who do care mightly what happens to people," should accept a full share of responsibility for helping to substitute constructive for destructive conditions, policies, and methods, whether they are working inside or outside the institutional system.

The crux of the question, however, is this: Given a program which has a sound purpose, with which the social worker can be identified, because it has constructive elements in it — though it is not perfect by any standard — can the social worker's responsibility be best discharged by helping the individual to come to terms with the actual limitations in his social situation, through the offer of specific service, available within these fixed limits, or is it necessary for the worker to offer help on the basis of her own individual judgment of the individual's need and capacity and her own appraisal of the validity of community demands or of agency policy?

It is my contention merely that since social life is social and is never subject to individual control alone, real social adjustment is facilitated by a helping process that rests on the acknowledgment and use, rather than the denial or evasion, of the limitations inherent in social living. This does not mean that the social worker must defend, either to himself or to the client, all the limitations within which they operate. These are facts, which bind both worker and client while they exist. The worker

can accept the client's feeling about them — may, indeed, share it — but it is the worker's business to see to it, so far as possible, that this feeling, however rational and justifiable in itself, does not prevent either of them from facing the realities and from examining the alternatives that are actually available in the premises. I assert that this solid framework of functional limitations and conditions of service protects both client and worker against arbitrary and capricious judgments and decisions and holds them both to the task of reconciling, practically and effectually, the individual and the social interests at stake.

It is true, as Miss Towle implies, that this way of helping places heavy responsibilities upon the client. That is its keystone. It approaches the client as a person who is expected to manage his own life, who presumably has the strength to do so, and whose present need is for help in clarifying his own problem, in facing courageously the alternatives open to him, and in mustering his own powers to choose a course of action and to accept the consequences of that decision responsibly. It rejects the concept that social casework is primarily for the dependent person who has to be protected against his own weakness; who, therefore, must be treated as a patient, so to speak, and who must be permitted to accept only so much responsibility as the worker thinks he can carry at a given time. It is obviously true that not everyone to whom a social caseworker offers service has equal capacity for accepting responsibility in these terms. Everyone is entitled, however, to face his own responsibilities and to do what he can with them, and there is overwhelming evidence of the amazing capacity of human beings, however battered and bruised by circumstances, to find their own way to reasonably adequate self-organization and reorganization, in a relationship with a professional person who respects their strength, who leaves them free to feel and express all the conflicting elements in their struggle toward a new self, and who yet steadily and firmly offers service on terms which are acceptable to the community and which the client must by his own will accept or reject.

It is also true, of course, as Miss Towle says, that there are clients whose disorganization is so deep-seated as to involve far-reaching disturbance of the total personality structure. Psychotherapy in some form is certainly called for in such cases if the delinquent can accept and use it. Social caseworkers must, by all means, have the basic training which enables them to recognize these needs and to help the individual to take advantage, where possible, of psychotherapeutic services. Some case workers will be associated with agencies whose functions are addressed to these special needs and will be able to participate in this process. But this does not impose upon social case workers, in general, a function and a practice based upon these exceptional and specialized problems. The social caseworker's primary task is to help individuals who do have the strength to use specific social services to meet specific problems and, in that process, to move toward such reorganization of their own lives as to find a constructive relation to the realities of their social setting.

And this brings us to the third point — history-taking and diagnosis. Again it is undeniably true that the individual's present capacity to deal with reality is the expression and culmination of his whole experience, and that insight into the nature and meaning of that experience may have great value in helping the client to understand and deal with certain aspects of his present problem. It is in the concept of the relative value and the practical use of such history that difference of viewpoint appears. Is the history to be gathered as the basis of an advance "diagnosis," like that to which the medical practitioner first devotes himself, and upon which the social caseworker is to build a "plan of treatment" through the development of a working relationship? It is clear that this viewpoint tends to maximize the responsibility of the worker for arriving at a solution that conforms, presumably, to the worker's judgment of the client's capacity to accept responsibility, and so to minimize the responsibility of the client for dealing with his own problem.

A contrary view, which I hold, values history primarily for the present meaning it has for the client in dealing with his own present problem. A sensitive alertness to this meaning as expressed here and now, in dealing with present reality, does not require in the worker or the client a complete grasp of all that has transpired in the past. It requires, only, that as the relationship unfolds, and as the client, with the worker's help, explores the present, the worker shall not fail to encourage and help the client to face and examine, for himself, whatever mean-

ing any elements of the past may have as factors in his present practical predicament, or as guides to alternative actions. This makes of history not a first step, not a static, absolute thing, not a specific tool in itself, but a relative, developing factor, to be used, like all else in the relationship, by the client himself, according to his own need and capacity for using it. And by the same token, "diagnosis" is not a specific prerequisite step toward a specific plan of "treatment"; it is not a specific "picture of a personality," defined for the guidance of the worker in determining what services she shall make available to the client. It is a developing process, worked out by the client himself, as he uses the agency service made available by the worker and as he tests his own capacities and needs in accepting or contesting the conditions and responsibilities he faces in using that service and so in dealing with his own problem.

Every social caseworker worthy of the name must, of course, be sensitive to all the factors Miss Towle mentions; must be keenly aware, as a result of thorough study and training, of the personality factors that inevitably operate in individualized forms in every client's handling of his problem and in every client–worker relationship. To be sensitive to all these elements and still to leave the client free to face them and deal with them himself, within the limits of a defined service relationship, is the essence of the caseworker's professional discipline.

PENNSYLVANIA SCHOOL OF SOCIAL WORK

145

The Social Worker's Technique and Probation *

Hans Weiss

I

In this age of the machine on water and land, in the air and under water, of the machine in form of some concrete object as a tool of man

---

* Reprinted from *Probation and Criminal Justice,*

or as the crystallization of some abstract idea expressed in terms of organizations, the word "technique" has slipped into our everyday language as if it were of good old Anglo-Saxon origin. We have a technique of building houses, bridges and roads; we have a technique of advertising chewing gum, of selling thumb tacks and of breathing correctly; we have a technique of training boxers, of studying the human soul and of preaching sermons. In short, we have a technique of everything; and the power which one attributes to this magic term resembles that of a mysterious goddess. Most people wish to express by it the mechanism which makes a thing go, the well-organized process of reaching results. They believe that it is something one can learn, as one may, after some honest effort, master the Morse alphabet or memorize the catechism. To them, the essence of technique is rigidity, the static element, that which stays firm in the process of crystallization; and that, because of its static nature, it can be acquired and possessed like a well fitting coat.

It is to be deplored if the meaning of "technique" should become fixed in this distorted mask; for, its origin is a noble and beautiful one. In ancient Greece, "technique" (*technae*) meant art; not art as the product of a creative effort, but art as the creative effort itself. "Technique" was the process of making something beautiful, so that it was in harmony with the laws of beauty. To know this original meaning is of extreme importance when one speaks of "technique" in relation to methods of dealing with human beings. The creative process which we call "art" is anything but static. It is the most dynamic thing which exists in this world. The dynamic power born of the creative impulse to give life to something which is beautiful contains another element of equal importance: freedom. The two are inseparable. To be sure, in order to create one must have knowledge of the material, of the use of tools and of certain laws of physics, of harmony, of symmetry, or of discord and of the grotesque. But this equipment is merely the foundation which one acquires for being able to give free play to the creative forces wishing to find adequate expression. The process itself must be dynamic

edited by S. Glueck, New York, The Macmillan Company, 1933, 165–196. Used by permission of the publisher.

and free if the result is to be a truly happy solution.

This moving away from technique, as the skillful art of creating, to technique, as a well-organized and almost conventional method of doing things, may be one among many other and perhaps stronger reasons, why the average probation officer looks down on the social worker. Though it is primarily the element of authority which makes the probation officer feel superior, he cannot get over the impression that his haphazard way of dealing with people may, after all, still be preferable to the clients and to himself than the more systematic and planful method of the trained social worker. No matter how superficial and crude such thinking may be called, there is an element of truth in it. The technique of the social worker is in danger of becoming so over-developed and standardized that it impairs free and creative action in the work.

No method can be examined and understood as such. It is always part of a whole which consists of two poles: the problem, as the starting point, and the goal toward which the method should lead. All technique is, therefore, related to the problem and to the goal, in the individual case as well as in general. Though one may work out a technique involving a set of general principles, the application of this technique should be something of a new discovery in each individual case because each case is individual.

II

The social worker is dealing with human beings "in trouble." The problems are as varied and manifold as life itself. The denominator common to all of these problems is the fact that the individual in question has run up against social difficulties in his life which he is unable to disentangle by himself. The social worker is supposed to be the magician who knows the formula which will bring relief in a complex situation. Isn't the probation officer facing the same task?

There was a time when social workers believed that methods of mass treatment such as giving relief, arranging for free medical care, sending clients to employment agencies, or conducting courses on Americanization, hygiene and the like would naturally and by themselves lead people to make the adjustments they seemed to need. Today, every intelligent social worker knows that no case can be dealt with successfully on the basis of "mass prescription" and that these measures, though they may be of value, merely lie on the periphery of the problem. No matter how much of a "chance" an individual "in trouble" is given, he will not ordinarily find his way out of the labyrinth of difficulties unless he is helped to understand the causes and effects of his own maladjustment with his social environment. That a person is poor, ill, mentally deficient, delinquent or criminal, without a job or without the proper training as a worker and citizen are important facts to know; but they fail to penetrate to the core of his maladjustment. There·are a great many people in similar situations, and yet they know how to help themselves. They are not a liability to society. These facts are only symptoms and the real reasons lie deeper. There must be other factors which explain why some people cannot get along with their fellow men.

When we ask ourselves what it is that makes us feel content or maladjusted, we begin to think of people around us rather than of things which we do not like. One can always change situations to some extent, but our relationships with others around us are a far more delicate matter. It is the interplay of our personality with that of others which exercises such a great influence on our emotional well-being. If our personality gains emotional satisfaction out of our human relationships, we are able to go a long way even with discouraging and annoying situations in our life. On the other hand, emotional starvation, repulsion on the part of those whose affection we wish to win, overbearing and possessive attitudes displayed by those with whom our life is closely bound up, may either lead us to the point where other things in life begin to move on a downward path, or give these outside factors real destructive force. It follows that the combination of maladjusted personal relationships and environmental difficulties depends to a very large extent on our personality. To the extent that we succeed in bringing our personality into tune with our environment we are succeeding in making a successful adjustment.

This is precisely the conclusion which through years of thinking and accumulated experience has been reached in social work. The personality of the individual and of the persons who make up a social group such as the family have become the center of attention. The wise social worker is primarily concerned with influencing the personality of his clients in directions which will make them use the assets of their personality and environment constructively. These efforts are called "social casework." In line with this concept of social work is Mary Richmond's definition: "Social casework consists of those processes which develop the personality through adjustments consciously effected, individual by individual, between men and their social environment." [1]

What is the probation officer's goal? Are there essential differences which demand some other orientation? Would it offend some of those probation officers who still harbor misgivings toward social work if, without their knowing the origin of the above definition, one would substitute the term "probation work" for "social casework?"

The treatment of delinquency and crime, as far as methods of reconstruction are concerned, has been undergoing very much the same changes as other forms of social work. When criminology began to advocate the idea of re-educating the criminal, first as part of the penal system and later by trying to replace punishment by education, the efforts, put into practice along these lines, bore the signs of "mass prescriptions." Probation in the early days — and unfortunately still in so many courts of today — was a vague measure of "giving the poor fellow another chance." It seemed to be common belief that the generous act of forgiving a man's sins when one could have punished him was enough of a stimulus to make him go straight. He was quasi-bound by contract to make good. The results failed to satisfy, and the tendency has been a steadily increasing attention to the individual as a human being and a member of social groups. It has been recognized that unless the personality of the delinquent is somehow reached, profound changes cannot be expected. When judges or probation officers sermonize to the offenders before them, it is because this conviction has become part of their working knowledge. They

---

[1] Mary Richmond, *What Is Social Case Work?* Russell Sage Foundation, New York, 1922, pp. 98–99.

fail to see, however, that a sermon is not a very fortunate approach and that much more than a sermon is needed to help a human being to change his course in life. Real influence springs from understanding the personality of the individual, from recognizing the difficulties with a sympathetic mind and from exercising wise guidance over a sufficiently long period of time. Thus the efforts of the progressive group of probation officers, as well as those of social workers in other fields, consist of "those processes which develop the personality through adjustments consciously effected, individual by individual, between men and their social environment."

We see, then, that *there is no essential difference between the social worker's problems, tasks and goals and those of the probation officer.* The difference lies merely in the type of agency and in the kind of symptom which brought to light the fact that the individual in question was in need of help.

III

What then, is the technique of the social worker? It has to be viewed from two angles, one being the *approach* to the client and the other the *stages* to be followed through in the process of casework.

No constructive work can be done with human beings without creating the psychological basis for it. In the parable of the Sower we learn that only part of the seed will fall on fertile soil; and this soil has to be prepared for it. We cannot expect any one to accept our leadership unless we have been able to develop a relationship of confidence which builds a bridge of common understanding and of joint effort between the worker and the client. The Church recognized this centuries ago, and it has made it a matter of dogma that the Father Confessor be the one to whom the faithful may turn for relief in trouble. The Church has considered this element of such great importance that, by its divine authority, in a wholly impersonal sense, the believer *must* have confidence in the Father Confessor. In this way, the Church has eliminated efforts which would have to be spent on the kind of approach that would create confidence. Psychiatry has given equally careful attention to this question. The psychiatrist knows he cannot hope to make progress with his analysis, before the patient shows signs

of having confidence in his leadership; and success is in direct proportion to the degree of confidence which the psychiatrist has been able to build up in the patient. This relationship between analyst and patient is called "rapport." If these two greatest leaders in influencing human behaviour, the Church and the science of psychiatry, have grown to consider the winning of confidence as the key to constructive work with the individual, it seems only wise that workers in other fields dealing with human conduct should follow these teachers. The social worker has done this. If it was not the Church and the psychiatrist, it was experience that pointed the way; and *the building-up of a relationship of confidence between worker and client has become one of the fundamental aims in casework.*

Confidence is based largely on emotional values. It is a matter of attitudes. When human beings meet, a sensitive interplay of forces begins to create situations which open or close the doors to constructive intercourse. If we like a person, we are willing to listen to suggestions and we feel the desire to reveal ourselves. The social worker, or any one else who wishes to help, should know the art of making himself liked by his client. This should not be misunderstood to mean an effort at indulgence; dignity, sympathy and purposeful leadership are the qualities which attract. There are definite elements in methods of approach conducive to an attitude of response by the client. First of all, the worker should radiate a spirit of sympathetic understanding (we would like to call it *love* — if the word had not suffered so much abuse), an interest apt to create an undercurrent of well-being which will set the client free to speak frankly and which will lead him to disclose thoughts and actions of a more intimate nature. For it is information of this type which throws light on the mental processes of the individual. The worker should not try merely "to find out"; he should try to find out *because he wants to help.* This presupposes a willingness on the part of the worker to listen patiently and with real — not feigned — interest to whatever the client wishes to say. Through occasional questions, if put skillfully, the worker may "steer" the conversation to some extent. But he should not press for information or force a point. Any one who has been successful with "people in trouble," knows from experience that patient listening always pays, even when the person seems to drift far from the point. It is just the direction indicated by such drifting that very frequently is most illuminating on what is going on in a person's mind. In addition, the chance to talk, and to be listened to, often has a liberating effect. It may relieve the client and, at the same time, may be the corner stone for that relationship of confidence that is so essential to guidance.

Approach is not a thing to be learned or accepted easily. It is an outgrowth of a more fundamental attitude toward the work, an outgrowth of the worker's philosophy of life. If a social worker believes that negroes are humanly inferior, she cannot help displaying this belief toward a colored client. If a probation officer speaks of "hopelessly lost girls" or of "tough kids" who need a "strong hand," she will rarely succeed in learning a single thing about the inner life of her charges. If a boys' worker wishes to work only with "good boys," he can never expect to be fair to a delinquent boy. An Americanization worker who considers the immigrant as an inferior being, will only be able to "Americanize" a poor type of immigrant; the more refined type with some education will shun him. *Our personal ideas on questions of race, nationality, immigration, delinquency, ethics, economics and similar problems are bound to influence our attitudes toward clients.* We cannot cherish private "pet-ideas" without having them color our thoughts and attitudes in our work. The broader and more unprejudiced the personal philosophy of a social worker or probation officer is, the more will he be able to develop an approach which opens people's hearts and prepares them for accepting the leadership they need.

A fourteen-year-old boy was in court for a long list of serious delinquencies. His father listened to the hearing in a sulky mood, openly showing that he didn't expect anything from any court. He had a long court record himself and had served several terms in reformatories and jails. After the hearing, the judge had a talk with the father alone. The judge began in a calm, objective, but kind tone: "I have here your record before me. You have gone through what your boy may have to go through, if he continues on his way. You are the one who knows what this means far better than anyone else. I wish to get some help from you, not only for your boy, but for the many boys of other fathers whom

I see here every day. I would greatly appreciate it, if you were willing to tell me something of your experiences, of how you got started on this way, of how you felt about those who were trying to prevent you from going on, of what you think of courts, reform schools and jails. What do you think a judge could do for a boy to help him? What do you feel might have helped you or would help your boy now? I am sure, it was not an easy road for you, and you must have been doing a lot of thinking about it," etc. The expression on this man's face had changed from plain discontent to vivid interest and eager cooperation. He braced himself up and sketched in brief strokes the history of his life, his impressions of the prevailing penal treatment and its effects upon him. He was convinced that institutional care would not help his boy, but admitted that drastic steps were necessary, and he was ready to collaborate in any plan which the court might suggest. Further discussion developed a very comprehensive picture of the family situation. When he came out of the court room, the father remarked to the probation officer, that this had been the first time in his life he had had a chance to discuss his experience with an understanding and sympathetic person. The judge's approach prepared the ground for constructive treatment with the boy and his family.

Approach is not a thing of the moment. One might think of a colorful mosaic in which the work of art consists of many small pieces put together according to a planned design conforming to laws of symmetry and color. Every interview and contact with the client should be in harmony with previous contacts. The worker may feel the need of being stern, strict, particularly patient or kind; the undertone should always be the same keynote of interest and sympathy. People are far more sensitive to these undertones, to the conviction lying back of a worker's attitude, than we might imagine.

An adolescent boy, who was finally committed to the reform school, expressed his feelings on this in commenting on the judge: "He is stiff and I don't like what he did to me this time; I never was really afraid of him, though, because I kind of felt that he always means well by you."

A fifteen-year-old colored boy who had run away from a large city, where he had been on probation twice, was brought before the juvenile court of the city where he was apprehended. While he was waiting to be sent back (it was on a Saturday afternoon), the probation officer took the boy to his room instead of holding him at the police station. The boy couldn't take his eyes off of an instrument on the wall and the probation officer allowed him to pass the time trying to play it. Suddenly, the boy looked up and asked: "Say, are you a probation officer?" "Yes," was the answer. "Well, you don't look like one. A probation officer makes me think of somebody far away, kind o' high up, who asks you a couple of questions and calls it a day. They don't speak to you as if you was somebody." This boy did not complain of unkindness, but the thing which was engraved in his mind was the undertone, *the fundamental attitude* which the probation officers whom he had met before, had continuously displayed in their approach.

IV

The working plan of the social worker's technique consists of three stages: *investigation, diagnosis* and *treatment*. These are scientific terms for very simple and logical processes. If we retranslate them into everyday language, we see that to follow these stages is mere common sense. In order to do anything with or for a person we must *understand* him. This implies that we *find out* what it was within him and outside of him that made him the individual with whom we are dealing (investigation). If we wish to utilize what we have thus discovered, we must do some *thinking* about the situation (diagnosis); and if this thinking is to be of benefit to our client, we should work out a comprehensive *plan of action* (treatment).

The process of finding out involves inquiries in three directions. They are identical with our sources of information. We learn facts about the client and his environment from himself, from those who know him and from studying the setting in which he moves.

By far the most important source is the client himself. He is frequently also the most difficult source. He may consider it to his interest to give a misleading picture. Besides, there are very few people who know themselves. Here is the real test of a social worker's or probation officer's skill in the art of understanding and dealing with human nature. The extent to which a person reveals himself is in direct proportion to the degree of confidence which the social worker or probation officer succeeds in developing in his client. Most workers are content if the client relates experiences and actions of his; and they believe they have penetrated deeply into the mental life of a client if he reveals hitherto unknown facts which could be used against him. While this may be il-

luminating in many ways, real insight begins when the client is willing to discuss his ideas, his beliefs, his relationships to others and his outlook on life. This may throw light on some of the causes of his behavior, which, after all is the most essential thing to know.

An eighteen-year-old boy was before court for stealing. He was in the graduating class of high school and his parents had done everything to give him a good education. In court he denied his delinquency until he had entangled himself so far that he had to admit the theft. The parents were shocked and heartbroken. Though he was supernormal mentally, his school record was poor and he had been truant very often. It took four weeks of patient dealing with the boy before he was willing to face the situation. He then revealed a number of earlier delinquencies which led one to think that he might have drifted into this path through companions. The probation officer was not satisfied. The career of the boy seemed in no proportion to the apparent wholesome background and the sensible, intelligent personality of the boy. He did not like to talk about his father. The probation officer sensed that the difficulty might lie in that direction, and yet the boy denied having had any serious friction with his father. One night, after several months of probation, the probation officer made a late call and found father and boy engaged in a veritable battle. The situation was such that the probation officer placed the boy in a temporary foster home the same night. On the way, the probation officer drove to a quiet place, and the boy had a chance to talk about his relationship with his father. A very decent feeling of pride and loyalty had prevented him from doing this before. His father was an immigrant who had resented all his life that he had never been able to get an education. The only way he could realize his dream to some extent was to give it to his oldest son. From the first grade of grammar school he began to drive the boy. He limited his time for play and recreation, he watched with incessant eagerness his progress in school. When the boy was in the second year of high school he hated everything that smacked of learning and schoolwork. George expressed his reaction in these words: "Do you know the saying about the drops of water dripping on a stone? That is the way I have felt for years when my father asked me about my schoolwork." The father, who was a devout Catholic, justified his attitude by stating to the judge the following day: "Education means as much to me as religion." And now, the boy began to open up about the underlying causes of his delinquences. He had developed a regular complex of hatred against his father. On one occasion, when his father did not allow him to go to the movies,

George took the money out of the father's pockets and spent it on something else. This gave him a strange sense of satisfaction. He repeated it. This led to his stealing from other people. Though he had a bad conscience, he felt at the same time that discovery would hurt his father more than anything else, and he went on. His truancy had the same origin. This is a comparatively simple explanation, but the difficulty was, to reveal it. From that moment on, progress was made with the boy. The point of attack for treatment was now clear and much could be done in improving the situation between father and son. The boy's schoolwork began to rise in proportion. No matter how much the boy had told the probation officer about his delinquent career before, nothing had hitherto been gained in understanding his personality, and the true difficulties in the situation only came to light later.

To tap the second source of information — that outside the offender himself — requires tact in approach and an intelligent sense of selection. Running down a scheme of sources in a more or less mechanical way is like turning on the same record on a victrola. A thoughtless method of "collecting information" may be worse than no investigation at all. There are some principles of selection which the good social worker bears in mind. He may proceed along two lines. Every person is known by other people with whom he is connected in some definite capacity: members of his family, teachers, employers, landlords (and more or less communicative landladies), etc. These may be consulted for information as a matter of routine. *The problem which every social worker and probation officer faces, is to obtain as many illuminating facts as possible without arousing discrimination against the client.* Some probation officers are overconscientious in this respect. In a case, in which a man was on probation on a charge based on the illegitimate child act, the probation officer prided himself in his report on record in court that he had met the man's parents and sister without disclosing his capacity of probation officer and without mentioning his probationer's court case, although these parents were partly supporting their son. The parents did not know either (nor did this probation officer) that the man was on probation at the same time in another court for nonsupport of his wife and child. In fact, the man had committed adultery and thereby had an illegitimate child. That no worthwhile probation work can be done on this basis, is evident.

As to some persons who are being consulted for information it is not only poor policy to approach them under disguise (we know a probation officer who appears in the role of an insurance agent when he does not wish to disclose his identity) but they have a positive right to know the facts of the case. "Tact" and "discretion" should not be exercised on the basis of concealment; the criterion should be: how much should be disclosed in order to state the truth without hurting the cause of the client?

This is especially difficult with employers. Many probation officers have been overanxious about the dangers of consulting employers. In the great majority of these cases, the employer turns out to be a most valuable source of information and of real help in the treatment later on; and no harm comes to the client if he has any standing at all in his work. However, extreme caution should be exercised in this regard.

The other principle of selection is based on the kind of relationship that exists between the individual and those around him. We either like or hate people or we feel indifferent toward them. This is the dynamic nature of our environment. It is surely of value to take this factor into consideration when we approach for information individuals belonging to the client's immediate environment. Especially when the dynamic differences are very pronounced and the client harbors strong feelings for or against members of his family, is it essential that both sides be heard, including those who claim to keep aloof. It may also be said that family members are biased or given to concealment because of their very closeness to the situation. Only through a comparison of the information obtained from members of the environment who express different attitudes toward the client will one be able to gain some light on the personality of the client and on the situation as it is seen by those who have known him over long periods of his life.

Much can be learned by an intelligent observer from studying the setting in which the individual lives. What are the standards of his home? What responsibilities are his and how does he fill them? What is his work, his professional standing and what are his professional possibilities? Where does he spend his spare time and what kind of recreation does he prefer? What kind of people are his friends and companions, and what is his role among them? Does he lead or follow, and in what direction? Such an environmental study gains in significance *to the degree that the facts are collected in their relation to the client.*

These inquiries, called the "investigation," should give a comprehensive picture of the individual's own world: of his personality, his relationships to others, his immediate environment as seen in relation to him. We should now know something of his likes and dislikes, his desires and hopes, his disappointments and failures, his ambitions and plans, his shortcomings and disabilities, his qualities and assets, and, above all, the possibilities of getting him on his feet.

Diagnosis is *thinking* about the case. Dr. Richard Cabot, in his introduction to *Case Teaching in Medicine* expressed the difference in the functions of investigation and diagnosis very vividly when he said: "After a student has learned how to open his eyes and see, he must learn to shut them and think."

The emphasis on this part of the social worker's technique is of extreme importance because so much "casework" is being done without real thinking. It means that the worker must concentrate on sifting his material, on comparing contradictory information, on evaluating his facts and on considering them in their relation to each other. Based on this, he should inquire in his mind for the probable causes which have created the maladjustment. This analytical thinking should be followed by synthetic thinking, that is, by a process of viewing the knowledge gained on the case in the light of a constructive plan which will help the individual to become again a self-reliant, self-respecting, independent citizen.

There are cases in which such thinking cannot be done successfully alone. The situation may suggest problems which require the assistance of experts. The science of psychiatry, which — in plain terms — is the science of human nature, should be called upon whenever a client is struggling with personality difficulties to such an extent that they interfere with his response to constructive plans. A personality study by a good psychiatrist can be of inestimable value in aiding decisions on methods of treatment.

Carrying out plans made in the effort of helping the individual toward an adjustment is called *social treatment.* But, actual treatment takes place only partly within the frame-work of a plan. Our whole attitude toward the client, whatever else we do and fail to do in relation to him, has its effect. In addition, there are always a great many factors influencing the situation over which we have no control. Life is far too vast a power to be guided by any human being. Life is never static; it is moving, it is flowing like a great river. Rigid adherence to plans will, therefore, never yield happy solutions; and one of the most essential faculties of a good caseworker is sensitive alertness to the changing needs of the individual, combined with ingenuity and resourcefulness ready to meet those needs. The value of a plan of treatment lies in the discipline of planning and in the thinking done for it. The principle is purposeful action instead of hit-and-miss decisions called for because things were left to drift toward the stage of emergency.

What has been said is true of the relationship between the three stages of the social worker's technique. Investigation, diagnosis and treatment are not strictly separate functions, as so many social workers and probation officers seem to think. Such classifications are theoretically useful by giving the caseworker lines along which to proceed; they are useful practically in the organization of the work. But, they should never be looked upon in a concrete case as stages which follow each other like "morning, noon and night." The approach during the investigation is already the beginning of treatment, for, if serious mistakes are made during the first contacts with the client, their effects will be carried into the treatment just as the throwing of a stone into a quiet pond ruffles the entire surface. The judge who was able, by his masterly approach, to win the confidence of that father with a long criminal record laid the foundations to successful treatment at the very first hearing on the case. Our experience with George shows that in spite of a very careful investigation at the beginning which told us all the surface facts about his family, his career in school, his recreation and even his delinquencies unknown to others, the essential facts were discovered only after several months of attempted treatment, and the diagnosing had to be done all over again. The three processes should fit into each other like the parts of a Chinese puzzle. They should go along hand in hand, and even though the functions might be separated among several workers for administrative reasons, these workers should see to it that such separation does not interfere with viewing the case in its totality at all times. What unfortunate situations may arise when social workers or probation officers violate this principle is beautifully demonstrated by the following case:

A man with a long court record for forgery having served sentences in several states, father of three young children, was on probation in two courts at the same time. Probation Officer A of Court X learned of a number of new larcenies; since they were committed within the jurisdiction of Court Y, he assumed that Probation Officer B of that court who was also to supervise the man, was taking care of the matter. Probation Officer B heard of these new offenses a few days later, when the Chief Probation Officer of that court had assigned another probation officer specializing in investigating to investigate the new cases. Probation Officer B happened to make one of his monthly home calls, failed to meet the man at home but learned from his wife that he was still around. He added to his routine entry on record that he had not taken any steps in the matter of the new offenses as this was the task of the special investigating probation officer. When this special officer found time to look for the man, he was gone. He was found nearly a year later serving a sentence of one year in another state.

This concept of probation work — dividing the stages of technique, the functions and responsibilities, like slices of an apple pie — is not only detrimental to the work but also wholly unintelligent. And yet, this extreme case is merely an illustration of what happens every day in a less drastic way in a great many courts and social agencies, simply because the work is mechanically so "well organized" that a case is only viewed in pieces and the clients either suffer or profit by it — but, both at the expense of the community.

The technique of investigation and treatment involves wise and efficient utilization of existing social facilities. In the interest of the work and in the interest of the community, which supports social work (and also the courts), the social worker cannot afford to play the role of the lone wolf. Our large American communities are socially well organized and there is no excuse for waste of effort and time caused by the failure to consult other social agencies

which are or have been familiar with the family of the client.[2]

V

We have seen that there exists no fundamental difference between social workers and probation officers as to the problems and goals they are facing with their clients. Both are dealing with human beings "in trouble" who need the assistance of some one who should be able to guide them on the strength of a wide and fruitful experience in dealing with human nature; both are trying to do as good as possible a job at reconstruction. The social worker's technique as developed above should, therefore, also be the technique of the probation officer, unless there are other differences of such unique nature that the application of the technique of one group seems impossible in the work of the other.

The main difference, as pointed out previously, lies in the type of agency and in the kind of symptom which bring the individual to the attention of the agency or of the court. The probation officer is in a different position than the social worker. The client, as a rule, comes to the social agency by his own free will *asking* for assistance. The offender is brought before the court by the police and the only choice he has is between imprisonment, fine and probation; and even as to these, the choice is essentially with the court. The social worker can advise her client, she can make plans with him, but her power is limited to methods of persuasion. The client may follow these suggestions, or he may refuse at any time to have anything further to do with the social agency. The probation officer can order his probationer to follow a certain plan, he can surrender him to the court. In short, he has power over the individual in his charge.

Are these distinctions fundamental enough,

2 This description of the social worker's technique is merely a very brief and rough sketch of what might fill a volume if it were to be done adequately. For the systematic study of the scientific treatment of the subject we wish to refer to Mary Richmond's able books: *What Is Social Case Work?* and *Social Diagnosis*, which contain a vast and carefully selected mass of case material and illustrations. The purpose herein was to outline in broad strokes the fundamentals of social case work for comparison with the needs of probation work.

as far as the work is concerned, to necessitate a different approach and a different technique?

Many probation officers believe that the probation officer's position of power embodies a great many advantages over that of the social worker. True enough, when friction arises between worker and client, it is much easier to dictate than to make an effort at hard thinking in order to guide the client by reason and similar approaches. And again it is true that with some offenders power is necessary to achieve any results. But the dangers involved in its use are immense. In fact, the psychological situations for constructive work and for a relationship of confidence between worker and individual is exceedingly more difficult for the probation officer than for the social worker. The very fact that the probationer enters into a relationship with the officer under a system of coercion (the order of the court) makes it necessary for the probation officer to break down the wall of force between him and his probationer before he can hope to reach the latter's personality. The whole process of gaining insight into the mental life of the probationer and of building on the constructive elements discovered is rendered extremely difficult by the very fact that the supervising agent is a probation officer. There was a time — and we still find many people clinging to the belief — when we believed that "Authority" and the "Law" are forces which in themselves carry the magic power of influencing people effectively. But we no longer live in the age of the medicine man, and we have discovered that far more real wisdom and skill is required to assist a human being in changing his course in life. We have grown very humble about it all.

If we look at this situation with frankness and with the firm desire to do constructive work with offenders in spite of these greater difficulties, we will realize that only the very best methods of dealing with human nature are "just good enough" for probation work. The ways of reaching the personalities of others and the response wished for are fundamentally the same for all those engaged in the work of influencing human nature and conduct — be it minister, psychiatrist, social worker or probation officer. The difference is largely one of emphasis. If the social worker's technique grew out of the experiences of leaders who have been successful in the "art of helping people out of

trouble," its wise application in probation work is bound to produce results also. But, because of the spirit of force which can never entirely be banned from probation work (and we admit that there may be justification for force to some extent on account of the imperfection of our wisdom and of the values which society wishes to protect at any cost), the social technique of the probation officer should not only be equal to that of the social worker, but even finer, the worker's faith should be stronger, and the quality of his leadership should be greater. Only then will he be able to penetrate the wall between him and his probationer; he uses his power wisely by using it only when he has to submit to the failure of his efforts.

For the consideration of those probation officers who still make reservations — secretly or openly — to the use of the social worker's technique in probation work, we wish to describe two illustrative cases. The first one is that of a juvenile, the second that of an adult.

(1) *Edward* was nine years old when he appeared before the Juvenile Court for the first time. The police had known him for at least two years as a troublesome youngster. He was caught stealing in department stores rather frequently, and from time to time he was brought to the police station after midnight, when he was found to be still on the streets in the downtown section. He would sell the things which he stole and, being quite generous, he would invite younger and older boys to join him on trips to amusement places out of town, paying for everything with the profits he had made. The police were so very "kind" to him because of his wistful appearance, his polite manners and his glib and plausible explanations. At one time, he claimed that his father was a musician who was traveling from town to town with a well-known orchestra. At other times, he explained that his mother was ill and he had to go to a drug store at night to get some medicine.

Investigation by the probation officer disclosed that Edward's parents lived separated — the father on the ground that the mother was a prostitute and the mother because she called the father cruel, abusive and alcoholic. The facts were, that the father was conceited, not interested in his children, that he drank a good deal and was never home when the family still lived together. The mother had a court record as a prostitute, but was now living with her mother who was supported by a man to whom she was not married. There was a two-year-old sister and a brother of twenty. This older brother had been in correctional institutions five times; he had been released just recently from prison, after having served a six months' sentence for stealing. No one knew his whereabouts, but two months later he committed suicide in the cell of the police station to avoid being sent to prison again.

The mother was working during the day, as she did not receive any support from the father. The home was extremely poor and in a bad section of the city. Edward went to school very irregularly, but had a good record of scholarship. The teacher found him very restless, nervous, talkative, boastful, obstinate and rather difficult to handle. He did not go to church at all. His recreation consisted of stealing and selling his loot to people at the entrances of cinemas and other amusement places. The rest of his time he spent at the pictures, where he loved hair-raising adventure films, and in cheap amusement places.

The clinic reported that Edward was an exceptionally bright boy with an extraordinary capacity for inventing stories. It was very difficult to know just how many of his statements were true, since he seemed suspicious of adults and his confidence could not be gained easily. He had derived a great deal of pleasure out of his escapades, and he knew more about the seamy side of life than many an adult. He was so nervous that he could not sit still for a moment, and he stammered considerably in talking. He was easily frightened, felt inferior to boys older and bigger than himself, and his generosity was entirely a selfish desire to gain power over others whom he could not win otherwise. All his attitudes toward others were motivated by the thought of how much he could get out of them. Only with his mother he seemed to have a strong bond of affection. He had no interests of any kind beyond those developed during his street life. He disliked athletics because he was delicate, and this made him feel that he could not compete with other boys successfully.

Edward did not want to leave his mother. He declared this emphatically to the judge. The mother refused to cooperate in any plan because "courts were only against the poor people," and all the court wanted to do "was to take her boy away from her." However, during two weeks, the probation officer spent considerable time with Edward, and took the boy with him on two trips when he visited boys in the country. Edward began to look at the plan differently, and his mother seeing the interest taken in her boy, agreed to have him placed in a private foster-home if she could visit him from time to time, which was granted. The father stated that he would pay for the boy's board and clothing, but that his responsibility did not go beyond that. Edward was finally placed with a family which had been successful with diffi-

cult court boys. The school in this town had also cooperated freely with the court.

Things went fairly well for two months. Then Edward began to steal from stores in town, took trips to the city and truanted from school. The probation officer arranged for an interview of boy and mother with the judge. The mother was quite upset, as she liked the foster-home well. Edward seemed to feel sorry and began to show improvement again. This time, it lasted for ten weeks. Suddenly, his attitude changed completely. He destroyed things in the foster-home, and was cruel to younger children in the street. The foster-parents refused to keep him any longer. In the meantime, his mother had moved to a different part of the city, to meet the request of the court that she should no longer stay with her mother. In the new home, a woman in the same house who was kindly and felt sympathy with her struggle, took care of Edward's younger sister during the day, and was also willing to look after Edward if he was allowed to stay with the mother. The court decided to try this plan, but for an entirely different reason. It was felt that a more thorough personality study should be made by the clinic, which required many visits of the boy to the clinic.

In addition, it was more important to win this mother's confidence in the court completely than to protect the boy against further failures just at this point. If boy and mother came to the conclusion that Edward could not possibly succeed at home they would, then, cooperate in any plan which court and clinic might work out in the future. For a few weeks, things went well again. However, the temptations of the city and the old associations proved too strong for Edward and he was finally brought into court again by the police for new escapades of stealing and staying away from home.

In the meantime, the probation officer arranged that the psychiatrist work steadily with the boy, seeing him twice a week. After much labor, a new clue was discovered. Edward wondered why his father took no interest in him. He was so ashamed of it that he always evaded any attempt that might lead to a discussion of his relationship with his father. Whenever this subject came up, the boy evidently struggled to hide his emotions and refused to talk. Finally, the probation officer went to see the father and explained the situation. The father agreed to meet the boy at the clinic. When he came he brought the boy a little present. Edward was so moved that he wept. Just after this, the boy was brought before the court on the charge of several new offences.

This time, the child-placing agency recommended the home of an educated woman who had made it her interest in life to take care of children with serious behavior problems. Her husband did some farming and the place was ideal for boys. There were many things boys could do during their spare time, and there was also a good school in town. The father agreed to visit Edward from time to time if he went there. The other five boys in this home were all older and were sufficiently adjusted there, so that they would be rather a help than a handicap to Edward. The foster-mother was well informed of the boy's past history.

Edward did not make a better start in this foster-home than he had done in the previous one. However, by a patient process of giving the boy the confidence that he could really do better if he only tried, and by making him feel that it was worth while to try, Edward began to improve; the lapse of time from one outbreak to the next one grew steadily larger and after two years he had given up stealing and similar delinquencies altogether. His father also did his share by showing a real interest in him. Today, he is fourteen. He has a little garden which he takes care of himself, he has a nice stamp collection of several hundred different pieces, he is a member of a scout troop and, last summer, he won a number of "badges" at the camp for excellent work and conduct. He is a happy youngster with a fine record in school and devoted to his foster-mother, who believed in him when he did not seem to deserve it. He is still fond of his own mother whom he visits at regular intervals. He shows a fine sense of loyalty toward his probation officer with whom he is still in correspondence, though probationary supervision has ceased long ago. No one would suspect in him a former delinquent.

From the tragic end of his brother, who came from the same soil — but was dealt with by the commonly known methods of correctional treatment — one dreads to think what might have happened to this lovely and intelligent youngster if he hadn't had a court and probation officer who applied the modern technique of the social worker.

(2) *John M*—— had been in court four times, once for larceny, twice for drunkenness and the fourth time on two complaints of larceny in two different courts at about the same time. The larceny case in the first court involved approximately $250 while the one in the second consisted of a number of thefts totalling nearly $1,000. The case in the first court was continued until a decision was reached in the second.

The investigation of the probation officer in Court B disclosed the following situation: John M—— was a mechanic of normal intelligence with a good working record and high pay for his trade. He came from a home with the usual standards of a laborer's family of the better type. At the age of twenty-five he married a girl of his nationality and faith, of whom he was extremely fond. Her family had been less harmonious and she was spoiled especially by her father who did not get along with her mother. At first, things went fairly well. During the second year of this marriage, the young wife began to make excessive demands on her husband for clothing and amusement. When she failed to get her way she would leave the house and spend the evening with friends. This continued even after children were born to the couple. The children were fonder of their father than they were of the mother. Frequent scenes about money, about neglecting the children and on many other subjects led things from bad to worse. John began to drink, neglected his family and paid a bill on his car with a forged check. He lost his job, failed to steady himself enough to keep another one, and, having been dishonest once before, he made a desperate attempt to avoid a complete crash by meeting pressing debts with forged checks. When things became too hot for him, he disappeared to a distant city with money he had taken from his last employer. He was brought back by the police and turned over to the court. His family had been supported by a social agency.

This information, with many more details, was collected by the probation officer from John himself, from his parents, from his wife and her father, from two previous employers and from three social agencies to whom the family was known. John's parents blamed the wife, and John's father-in-law blamed him for the whole situation. One employer spoke well of him, while the other one (not the one from whom he took the money) claimed that he was sulky, unreliable and inefficient as a worker. Two of the social agencies had nothing good to say for him; the third, which had made a rather careful analysis of John's background and which was supporting his family during his desertion, felt that the whole catastrophe would never have happened if John had been well adjusted with a wife who would have been more sensible and would have understood how to guide him.

The probation officer had several long interviews with John, and went over the whole situation with him. His childhood and youth were discussed, and so were his marital life and his professional career. At first, John blamed his tough luck, his wife, his employers and even his parents for not having sent him through high school. He resented the fact that his probation officer, who was asking him so many questions, happened to be a woman. He then began to reason what might have happened if this thing or that thing had been different in his life. The probation officer led him on, and the next step of his analysis was that he began to ask himself what would have been the result if *he* had done a few things differently. He ended by feeling truly sorry over it all and by being greatly discouraged.

At this point, the probation officer did her most intensive thinking. Had he the stuff in him to make good, or was his attitude of remorse merely a temporary mood? Was he essentially weak or did he have qualities in him on which one could build? Was it possible that these years of unhappiness could so completely cover up those qualities, or did they not exist in him at all? If they did exist, what were they? His children were fond of him; he had been a good worker at one time; he had tried to please his wife; he had been a good son to his parents. But this had been years ago; could these qualities revive under wise guidance? The probation officer remembered having seen in the back yard of John's house a skillfully constructed aquarium with a miniature amusement park around it; the oldest boy pointed at it with pride and said: "Daddy done this for me." The work of art was of fairly recent date. The probation officer weighed all this against the crushing mass of unfavorable facts. She decided to take the risk though she was fully aware of the grave responsibility involved. She claimed later that, very probably, the aquarium had given her the courage to try it.

From the moment she had made this decision, the probation officer changed her course. The process of finding out became of secondary importance; the main point in the diagnosis had become clear, and the attention was now focused on treatment. The final decision would still depend on John's response to the first steps of treatment.

She began by trying to build up his courage. Then, she spoke of the children, how they needed their father and how much he had to make up toward them. His relationship with his wife was not touched upon at this point, but John was asked to work out a plan of how he could repay the money which he had taken. During the next two interviews, concrete plans were discussed so that John could see his way out, and when he began to take the attitude that all he needed was courage and a "chance" from the judge, probation was recommended after the continuance of two weeks had elapsed. The court agreed with this plan.

The work of reconstruction had to be attacked step by step. The social agency agreed to give John a small loan (not as much as it would have cost the community if John had been sent to jail) to set up a small business as a plumber. The wife who had been ill was sent to a convalescent home for two months, and the children were placed with John's parents. After six months, John had paid up most of his restitution, whereupon his father paid the rest. A year later, John moved the family into a suburban bungalow, bought a secondhand truck for his business and had some savings in the bank. The probation officer's most difficult job, after John had regained his self-confidence concerning his work,

was to win the cooperation of his wife. The worst crisis was reached when she bought an expensive set of furniture on the instalment plan without consulting her husband. The probation officer succeeded in persuading the company to take the set back without any loss to John. The result was the last great scene by Mrs. M. From that point on, she began to make progress also. After three years of probation, the situation was sufficiently stable for supervision to be discontinued.

To do probation work of this kind, some of the now customary concepts of probation will have to be changed. Probation is not a substitute for punishment. It is an attempt at helping the offender to rebuild his life in the community. Probation cannot be meted out on the basis of the seriousness of the offense. A chronic alcoholic may be a far less suitable subject for probationary treatment than a burglar or a "thief." The length of the probation period cannot depend on the value of the stolen property, nor is it intelligent to fix the term of probation mechanically for six months, for a year or whatever it may be, with the idea of ending probation if the probationer has not been brought before the court for a new offense in the meantime. Short terms of probation are wholly valueless and are, in fact, identical with placing the case "on file." The period of probation can intelligently be measured only on the progress which the probationer is able and willing to make. Routine investigations and a mechanical type of supervision consisting of periodic home calls and thoughtless "reporting" at the court house are of less value than no probation at all, because the latter practice, at least, does not bring probation into disrepute in the eyes of offenders and public. Probation work without enlisting the cooperation of social agencies, where such cooperation might help the probationer and the court, is, in fact, a waste of time and money. The community has created both the social agencies and the courts, and it is supporting both; it is only logical that the community wants them to cooperate in every single case where such cooperation means more efficient work and better results. The practice of basing surrender of the offender to the court on the commission of a new offense (as is the custom in so many courts) means throwing the entire burden of responsibility on the probation officer. If difficulties arise and the probationer fails to cooperate, it is the judge's duty to do his share and to take the offender to task. To wait until a new offense has come to the knowledge of the court is certainly affording poor protection to the community. And, finally, no individual should ever be released from probation (within the limits of the law) unless he or she is in the position of showing definite results in terms of conduct and achievements.

No offender has to accept probation, and no judge is obliged to "give" probation. It is a responsibility which should be faced with care and apprehension. Probation can be the most constructive and most hopeful method of all the measures of penal treatment. Probation is destructive to the offender and to the community if allotted to a man not ready for it. If, from the first, probation had been used wisely, constructively and with intelligent discretion, the saying "to get off with probation," which is now so common, would never have been coined.

That the personality and the training of the probation officer are factors of fundamental importance seems self-evident. It takes a person of exceptional qualities of leadership, combined with a sensitive and broad understanding of human nature, to make a probation officer equal to his task. A good educational background followed by thorough training in the technique of social case work are an essential part of a probation officer's equipment. There should, for instance, be some knowledge of psychiatry and of biology. And yet, the average probation officer of today is drawn from almost every walk of life, and, altogether too often, such an appointment is sought (and obtained) by people who consider it a "safe job" for the rest of their life. No one will deny that the social and professional standing of the probation officer is below that of a physician, lawyer or the average business man. At the same time, we know that social ills are far more difficult to cure than physical ills or than to plead a case successfully

before a court. Has the community ever considered what it means in terms of money and insecurity when it entrusts the care of the majority of its beginning offenders to a group of people so many of whom are not equipped for the task?

Good probation work is possible, in the long run, only with a judge who is socially minded and who knows at least as much about the art of approach as he knows about the law. Modern criminology makes far greater demands on the knowledge of psychological factors than it does on the knowledge of the law. The very meaning of the legal structure of society is protection and security. Modern criminology has introduced methods which make the proper application of the law *insecure* if it is done in disregard of psychological factors. Mere compliance with the letter of the law no longer suffices. The judge's power — and with it his responsibility — is so great that he cannot afford to exercise it without taking most carefully into consideration those factors which explain the offender as a personality with assets and liabilities, with emotions, with a certain mental equipment, with a past and with a future. Society cannot eliminate the offender, it must prepare him for rehabilitation. That is why social and psychologic factors are of prime importance in the criminal court of today.

America is haunted by periodic "crime waves." The newspapers are doing their share to exploit them. When the public is aroused it demands swift action. Special funds are granted for combating crime. Police cars are equipped with radio and machine guns. These efforts are like trying to extinguish a contagious disease by segregating the patients without reaching the germs. No real progress will be made until the community demands judges and probation officers who are equal to their task in the psychological and social fields as well as in the legal, and unless it is willing to furnish the funds and the equipment for adequate probationary service.

Chapter 27

Techniques of Treatment: Individual Psychotherapy

THERE CAN BE LITTLE DOUBT that a substantial proportion of delinquents might be better understood and aided if there were available many more facilities for psychotherapy than exist at present. The literature on the techniques of psychotherapy in the diagnosis and treatment of behavior problems is extensive. The aim of the Editor was to include in this chapter a few articles, written in a style understandable to the intelligent non-expert, which involve some of the principal approaches of the therapeutic process.

The first article, by Szurek, is an essay on the child therapy procedures of the Illinois Institute for Juvenile Research. It recounts the history and evolution of the techniques employed in child guidance institutes from those involving largely environmental manipulations in home and school to more penetrating psychoanalytically-influenced diagnosis and therapy. With candour and insight, the author describes the vicissitudes of "play therapy" with children, and points to the rather unreflective carryover of Freudian hypotheses into the treatment of youngsters, through equating child and adult. This has resulted in "overindulgent permissiveness and overidentification," in an implication that the parent is the child's enemy, in a vague concern with the possible future mental illness of the child more than with his present capacity to tolerate prohibitions. Finally it was found that the crux of the clinical problem is "not the child's behavior, or his symptoms nor yet the complaints of the parent about him but the nature of the parent–child integration. More inclusively the total family unit and the nature of the interpersonal relations within it were not only the proper objects of study for the explanation of the child's personality reactions or disorder but also the entity to be considered for therapy." It has been confirmed that Freud's fundamental insight is true "that neurosis and character disorder of the child [are] an expression of the great importance of the parent's personality in the development of the self of the child." This has led to the treatment of parents, particularly the mother, as an indispensable part of child therapy, a process which, because of the shortage of psychiatrists, is frequently carried out by social workers. The article gives details about the assignment of the various aspects of therapy to different types of worker, including a situation where two psychiatrists are simultaneously involved in a single parent–child problem. The rest of the article deals with treatment of severer mental disorders of children in a hospital situation, with particular reference to the parental roles reflected by nurses and attendants, and to the aid afforded by various play and recreational measures in the entire therapeutic program.

The next piece, by Topping, deals with the "pseudosocial" or gang boy, "who may be said to be socialized" but "within a delinquent group." After discussing many desirable traits of such boys, the author describes the superficial self-adjustment of this type of lad in an industrial school setting (the New York State Training School), with an eye to early release on parole as a "model student." She describes the attitude and behavior of such boys while on parole and gives some revealing insights regarding the compensatory mechanisms involved, and the effect of various types of parent–child relationships. The author is of opinion that while intensive psychotherapy might help in uncovering the basic problems involved in such cases, "the task frequently becomes one of helping large numbers to adjust at a relatively simple level rather than attempting deep therapy with a few"; and she wisely advances the thesis that "with the pseudosocial boy the effort must be not to wean him from his code, but to win him to its wider application." She points to the frequently ignored fact that the clinical cliché about each case being "individual," tends to obscure "the methods of science, which continually seek formulation and classification;" and she is of opinion that, in fact, "conditions and techniques directed toward more conscious levels are not so essentially different . . . from those commonly employed at a less conscious level." But the major difficulty with the pseudosocial boy is the establishment of rapport to a sufficient degree to influence his attitudes and behavior. She gives illustrations of the methods of taking advantage of "unexpected openings" in the protective armor (leading, ultimately, to a boy's discussion of more personal problems) and of the ways of penetrating the shield of the obdurately silent type of boy. She describes various methods of achieving rapport through "accepting" techniques. The author also gives useful hints about the placement of the pseudosocial boy with a view to fitting the particular child to the type of cottage father with whom he can achieve rapport. This practical article concludes with some shrewd "dont's."

In a suggestive article on the factors determining antisocial "acting out" and, more complexly, perverse behavior on the part of delinquents in whom the basic etiologic pressures cannot be attributable to general societal or cultural forces, Giffin, Johnson and Litin develop the clinically-determined thesis that delinquency is, in certain cases involving super-ego defects, "unconsciously initiated, fostered and sanctioned by the parents." Such parents vicariously achieve gratification of their own poorly integrated forbidden impulses through their child's antisocial behavior. One or both parents also "unconsciously experience gratification for their own hostile and destructive wishes toward the child who is repeatedly destroyed by his behavior." Thus this article might have been included in the section on causation; but it is more valuable here in describing the processes of psychotherapy with individuals who, as a group, comprise a family. Especially illuminating are the case-history extracts reflective of parent–child emotional and behavioral involvements and how these are dealt with by "collaborative therapy," a procedure of "dynamic psychotherapy in which the individual treatment hours of each patient are reviewed in great detail, hour by hour, among all the psychiatrists acting as therapists." If anything were needed to bring out the fact that one typical cultural explanation of delinquency — "the confusion which accompanies transition from puritanic mores of a culture to greater individualization" — is inadequate and to demonstrate the crucial and protean influence of the parents' own problems and attitudes on the antisocial tendencies of the child, this article supplies that need.

Rosenheim's article is a persuasive account of the formation, diagnosis and treatment of the "rejected child." The author presents in detail a psychoanalytically oriented case history illustrating the dynamic processes of cause and therapy in the case of a young boy. The skill and patience of the therapist are reflected in the case history.

By way of contrasting technique, the last article, by Newkirk, deals with a form of psychotherapy which has not been in too high repute in America — hypnotic suggestion. Freud's rejection of hypnosis in favor of psychoanalysis is well known; but hypnotic suggestion remains, nevertheless, a real phenomenon whose possibilities have not yet been sufficiently explored either in or outside the delinquency field. Newkirk presents a few case-history illustrations of the technique and its results. He is of opinion that "average juvenile delinquents are neither more nor less suggestible than non-delinquents," but that suggestibility is "not merely a constitutional and fixed quality of mind," since persons longing for relief from physical and emotional suffering are much more accessible to suggestive psychotherapy than are those who participate merely for experimental purposes. He then describes two psychologic extremes: those who are less than normally, and those who are more than normally, suggestible. He states that because only the highly suggestible group are amenable to this form of psychotherapy, a prerequisite to its employment is psychiatric diagnosis and classification. Hypnotic tests should reveal if the subject is suggestible and whether he carries out post-hypnotic orders. The author raises the question whether, lawfully, inmates of institutions can be subjected to this form of treatment. While not claiming that the basic personality structure can be altered by hypnosis, the author says that "there is no reason why psychotherapeutic control should not be continued for years and in some cases even to the limit of the maximum sentence. This would practically mean reformation, because it is known that juvenile criminals do not relapse readily after the thirty-fifth year." [1] The author concludes with a plea that "suggestive psychotherapy be given a chance to prove its usefulness in the management of juvenile delinquents of the psychoneurotic type."

146

Child Therapy Procedures *

Stanislaus A. Szurek

Child psychiatry as a special branch of the general field of psychiatry is so comprehensive in its scope that a brief discussion of the subject might perhaps be most fruitfully limited to a summary review of some of the methods of practice peculiar to this relatively young discipline. The more recent experiences of the staff of the Illinois Institute for Juvenile Research, one of the oldest psychiatric clinics for children — or child guidance clinics, as some still prefer to call them — forms the basis of this brief résumé. The Institute, as the Illinois State Child Guidance Clinic, serves the community as a whole. In addition to rendering out-patient clinical services, the Institute has had under its direction for the past year and a half a ward in the Illinois Neuropsychiatric Institute for observation and study of fourteen severely disturbed children ranging in age from 3 to 11 years.

Not so many years ago, treatment in this clinic for children consisted chiefly of recommendations to parents, or their substitutes, regarding methods of management of particular symptoms or specific behavior disturbances. After the anamnestic study, physical examination, psychometric testing, and the psychiatric interview with the child, and often with the parent, the diagnostic results obtained from this four-fold approach were evaluated in a conference of the examining team composed of psychiatrist, psychologist, psychiatric social worker, and sometimes a pediatrician, and the therapeutic measures agreed upon. These were often conveyed by reporting letters of advice, and if possible, specific suggestions. Now and then the social worker was entrusted with executing referrals to appropriate clinics for medical attention to defects uncovered, or to social agencies for placement in foster home or institution, or to other agencies supplying economic assistance, legal advice, recreational facilities or employment. Not infrequently the social worker visited the home at intervals or brought the child to the clinic or other agency. Sometimes the school was visited in an effort to obtain some adjustment of the curriculum. During such casework the psychiatrist might have an occasional interview with either the child or the parent. More rarely, he might have several

---

[1] The author perhaps refers here to the findings in the various Glueck follow-up studies regarding the role of age and maturation in recidivism. See pp. 994–1002 *infra*, and S. and E. T. Glueck, *After-Conduct of Discharged Offenders*, New York, The Macmillan Company, 1945, pp. 76–90, and prior works therein cited.

* Reprinted from 7 *Psychiatry* (1944), 9–14. Used by permission of the author and the publisher. An essay on the therapeutic methods in a psychiatric clinic and hospital for children presented as part of a Symposium on Neuropsychiatry at the March, 1943, meeting of the Illinois Neuropsychiatric Institute, Chicago. Reprinted by permission of The William Alanson White Psychiatric Foundation, Inc.; copyright 1944, by The William Alanson White Psychiatric Foundation, Inc. — *Ed.*

840   TREATMENT

interviews with the child, often to give lectures on sex physiology.

Naturally, the numerical pressure of such diagnostic studies was a factor in precluding more intensive direct therapy and in recognizing, through follow-up studies, the high percentage of relatively inconsequential results from such measures. That there was dissatisfaction with the effectiveness of their efforts on the part of the clinicians is undoubted, and continued self-critical questioning kept the staff keenly searching for improved methods and for more basic theoretical principles for their application.

There came a period when psychoanalytic theory, practice and training began to interest more and more of the child psychiatrists and psychiatric social workers. Students of Anna Freud — and of Aichhorn — returned from their training with the fund of child psychoanalysis and began teaching in this country. Since classical analytic techniques — especially the frequency of sessions with the child — were not easily applicable to the clinic's facilities, which continued to be overburdened by demands for large numbers of diagnostic studies, modifications in the use of play and playrooms, especially with pre-adolescent children, were soon discussed and much in vogue.[1] Jessie Taft[2] and other followers of Otto Rank gave further impetus to attempts at direct therapy of children in playrooms with sessions at weekly intervals. Excellent descriptions of these experiences, published as well as presented in seminars, increased the enthusiasm of the clinicians, sometimes to degrees which were rather unrealistic in their optimism. These techniques were obviously meeting not only real needs for progress but also some rather personal feelings of inadequacy. The psychiatrist or social worker with experience in play methods came somehow to be invested with the somewhat esoteric glamour which surrounded the child analysts, who labored as patiently and as intensively as their colleagues interested in adult psychoneurotics.

In these efforts, the differences in the intensiveness of child analyses and play therapy, and the differences between the adult and the child tended, on the one hand, to become obscured and, on the other, exaggerated. The almost complete transfer of Freudian hypotheses, especially in regard to sexuality,[3] from the adult to the child and a rather tacit assumption that similar results even with less frequent contacts between therapist and child were to be expected, were, in part, the reasons for the equation of child and adult. In some instances it seemed as if the natural sympathy of the adult therapist for the child led to a general attitude of such overindulgent permissiveness and over-identification that discussions seemed almost to imply that the parent was not only the enemy of the child but also of all who wished to "cure" him. The child's actual capacity to tolerate prohibitions or restrictions disappeared in the therapist's vague concern about his sanity in the future. Occasionally, the ideal of more or less completely non-authoritative, non-judgmental and benevolent passive acceptance of all the child did came into sharp conflict with the therapist's natural resentment at being hurt by dart guns or soiled by water, paint, or other products of playroom destruction.

Such reliance on the classically described "passive attitude" of the analyst indicated failure to recognize the immaturity of the child, especially of his conscience development. Parenthetically, one might insert here that this is an impossible attitude for the analyst of even the adult psychoneurotic in regard to the infantile trends and impulses of the patient emerging from repression. The lack of relief from symptoms such as enuresis, soiling, and other provocative behavior in the world outside the playroom was sometimes taken as evidence either that this was still a neurotic conflict unresolved by the therapy or that the child was being even more deprived by the increasingly envious or hostile parent. Other reasons were found for the reactions of the parent to such playroom treatment of the child. It was "unconscious sabotage" of the treatment if the parent did not see to it that the child appeared regularly for his session in the playroom. Or, if the increasing defiance of the child was met with

---

[1] Section on Play Therapy, American Orthopsychiatric Association, 1938 Meeting, Chicago.

[2] Jessie Taft, *The Dynamics of Therapy,* New York, Macmillan, 1933 (xi and 296 pp.).

[3] Harry Stack Sullivan, "Conceptions of Modern Psychiatry," *Psychiatry* (1940) 3:1–117. See, especially, Lecture 3; pp. 28–33.

punishments and deprivations, the essential "parental rejection" of the child was thus uncovered. If the parent became curious and wanted to discuss the child's behavior with the therapist, his wish to interfere was even more obvious. Naturally, in many instances this was true.

A social worker might have been asked to keep the parent somehow at bay through conversations while the all-important play sessions continued without interruption or without contact of the therapist with anyone else while the child was in the clinic. Now and then therapists have shown a rather excessive concern about arousing the child's envy. Thus, they took great precautions that two patients of the same therapist did not meet. Gifts to the child patient on his birthday — a legitimate method of expressing the therapist's feelings about the patient — grew to such importance that gifts were offered on many other occasions, such as Christmas, Valentine's Day, or graduation day. Much effort was expended on getting just the gift the child desired and getting it to him on time. Care about contact with the child led therapists to remember to send postal cards during vacations or whenever, for any other reasons, the therapist and child were unable to meet. With individual patients these are, of course, the methods of choice in reaching the child's feelings and in establishing therapeutic rapport. The duration of such treatment, when the parent did not interrupt it, tended to continue for a year and sometimes longer with varying degrees of success.

Such experiences, and the lively exchanges of opinions about them, led gradually to clearer recognition of the simple fact that the problem presented to the clinicians was not the child's behavior or his symptoms, nor yet the complaints of the parent about him, but the nature of the parent–child integration. More inclusively the total family unit and the nature of the interpersonal relations within it were not only the proper objects of study for the explanation of the child's personality reactions or disorder but also the entity to be considered for therapy. Thus, child guidance clinics' psychiatrists tended to come full circle to the fundamental insight of Freud that neurosis and character disorder of the child was an expression of the great importance of the parent's personality in the development of the self of the child.

As a result of all these converging experiences, the techniques of therapy of the clinic are logical — and aetiologically oriented — attacks upon any aspect of the situation which promises to be either most easily available or modifiable with the therapeutic facilities at hand, or, given adequately trained staff and time, that aspect aetiologically most closely connected. In this clinic this varies from treatment of the most anxious parent alone — especially when the child is relatively young and only acutely and recently disturbed — through therapy of both parents and child, to treatment of the child alone, particularly when he is adolescent and relatively more independent of the parent. When the child is brought or referred to the clinic by others than his own parents, guardians, foster home placement agencies, school authorities, the concern or anxiety of these is also a legitimate object of therapeutic attention. All the professional resources of the clinic — psychiatric social workers, psychologists, recreational therapists, as well as the psychiatrists themselves — may be utilized in the treatment program each alone or, more commonly, in a collaboration between them which brings its own special problems.[4]

Chiefly because of their availability, even in these times, social workers of the clinic staff are perhaps most frequently used especially in the treatment of the parents, particularly the mother, in weekly or bi-monthly interviews. These are held either at the clinic or less often — now that tires are valuable — at the home of the patient. The child, too, may be dealt with by the social worker most often by means of repeated recreational trips in which relatively little attempt is made at exploration, but confidences are accepted as they appear. In these types of treatment there are often two workers assigned to a case — one for the parent and one for the child. Pre-adolescent and adolescent children have been found rather difficult to treat by this measure when the worker is of the opposite sex. Male workers with boys of the early teen ages have obtained encouraging results. The behavior disorders, that is, moder-

---

[4] Stanislaus A. Szurek, Some Problems in Collaborative Therapy, News Letter Amer. Assn. Psychiatric Social Workers (1940) 9: 1–7.

ately severe failures in conscience formation about particular impulses, such as disobedience, stealing, hyperaggressiveness, or malintegration with coevals, are apt to be most responsive to these techniques, especially if the parental anxiety and disturbance is not too severe and capable of amelioration.

The social worker has also for a long time undertaken work with the parent when the psychologist attempts remedial tutoring treatment for school disabilities or speech therapy, or when the psychiatrist makes an effort to administer direct psychotherapy to the neurotically inhibited and fearful child in the playroom session or interview. From modern researches it is now clear why in these collaborative efforts success has been only partial — the neurosis or character problem of the parent is too often a major psychotherapeutic task beyond the training or competence of the social worker. Attempts by social workers at therapy of delinquents by means of prolonged, intensive treatment, with periodic supervisory conferences with the psychiatrist, are methods which have been rather successful but need further study. All such treatment is subject to periodic and regular review in conferences over which psychiatrists preside.

The role of the psychiatrist in the clinic may well be left to the last. The well-trained child psychiatrists, in addition to their thorough general training in psychiatry and in psychoanalysis, are likely to be those of the age most desired by the armed forces. This has progressively decreased the possibility of carrying forward promising experimental attempts in collaborative techniques in which two such psychiatrists are engaged in treating a single, severe, parent–child problem — one with the parent and one with the child. These attempts have already been recorded.[5] Their promise of increased efficiency in therapeutic efforts, as well as in major contributions to fundamental problems of the genesis of personality traits and disorders must await happier times.

The problems of treatment in a hospital situation of severe psychiatric disorders of chil-

dren deserve separate attention and discussions from those of children treated extramurally or in an out-patient clinic. The Children's Service of the Institute for Juvenile Research has the facilities of a whole floor in one wing of the Illinois Neuropsychiatric Institute. This comprises a five and a two bed ward for each sex; a two bed ward for younger children; an isolation room for children suffering from infectious illnesses and for initial study to exclude contagious diseases; a lounge; a dining room; living and playrooms; and doctors' and nurses' offices. In addition, there is a schoolroom with connecting library in the nearby building occupied by the Institute for Juvenile Research where the children come five days a week for school work with the educational therapist; and a special playwork room under the direction of the recreational therapist.

After more than a year's experience with the Children's Service, the staff of the clinic has learned much about the problems of full-time care and treatment of juvenile patients. The methods used in this effort may be conveniently and arbitrarily divided under four categories: provision of medical service; maintaining educational and psychological facilities; attending to recreational and occupational needs; and, supplying specific and general psychiatric service.

The Children's Service has been fortunate in receiving excellent cooperation from all the special departments of the University of Illinois Colleges of Medicine, Dentistry, and of its general hospital. In addition to the routine physical examinations and special tests for contagious diseases and tuberculosis administered by the resident psychiatrist upon admission, the children have had the benefit of routine examinations and care from the Department of Pediatrics and the children's Dental Clinic. As the occasion arose, the Roentgenological, Neurological, Ophthalmological, Dermatological, and Surgical Departments have been consulted and their response has been uniformly helpful. All necessary routine and special laboratory diagnostic work is available and provided. All patients, without exception, have gained in weight and on the whole have remained in a generally good state of health or have improved markedly.

The organization of the clinical staff permits

---

[5] Stanislaus A. Szurek, Adelaide Johnson, and Eugene Falstein, "Collaborative Psychiatric Therapy of Patient–Child Problems." *Am. J. Orthopsychiatry* (1942) 12:511–516.

study and treatment of many more of the ætio-
logical factors in specific or general educational
disabilities of children than is possible in the
ordinary school system. Contributing parental
anxieties, their extraordinary demands for
achievement, or their indifference can be dealt
with more adequately by the combined efforts
of the various specialists in the case of patients
in the clinic. In the hospital service there is
even a greater opportunity for such an integrated approach. The observations and work
of the educational therapist and psychologists
are always a part of every staff conference.
Several remarkable results from such interchange of information and from this communal
approach have already been observed.

Recreation is an avenue "par excellence" of
approach to the child's feelings of self-regard.
This means is so important that the previously
mentioned therapeutic methods are based upon
it. The general recreation activities are under
supervision of a trained recreational therapist
who is also an integral member of the clinical
staff. In addition to regular play and occupational periods in a special play and workroom
where various games, music, dancing, hand-
crafts, cooking facilities and pets are provided,
the patients have regular periods for walking,
swimming, shopping and the playing of outdoor
games in season. The nursing staff participates
in these activities, conducting outings to movies,
theatres, parks, and other points of interest.
Regular weekly parties with refreshments and
movies, supervised rhythm band practice, drama,
pantomime and skit performances, music on
special holidays, and birthday parties further
fulfill the recreational needs of the children
and provide opportunities for group and individual amusement, achievement, and development of responsibility, as well as opportunities
for staff study of individual and group behavior.
For the school and recreational activities, the
children are usually divided into appropriate
age groups, although the entire group participates on some occasions.

Among psychiatric services, that of the nursing staff is one of the most important.[6] Super-

vising the daily routine of nutrition, rest, cleanliness and giving general physical care, the
nurses and attendants have contact with the
children more of the time than any other portion of the staff personnel. Their experiences
reported in staff conferences often supply invaluable clues to the distorted personality dynamisms of the individual patient. Conversely,
the participation of the nurses and attendants
in such general discussion at staff conferences
increases the possibility of greater uniformity
of attitudes toward given problems. They are
considered an extremely important therapeutic
facility of the service. The fact that the children attach themselves to a particular nurse
or attendant, calling her "mother" or "mom,"
as well as choose them as objects of their hostility, indicates their importance in the total therapeutic process.

The resident and the attending psychiatrist,
when these are men, are quickly cast in the
father role by the patients themselves. Towards them and against them the children direct
various impulses of submission and defiance or
they frequently and very obviously seek to identify with them. Agreement, therefore, in regard
to basic disciplines is especially important to
achieve between the psychiatrists and the nurses.
Special weekly or daily conferences do much
to attain this goal. It is particularly important
that this relation is not merely one of authoritative prescription and written orders by the physician to a rigidly disciplined passively accepting
underling, but one infused with mutual confidence, trust, and friendly collaboration. Similar relationship between all members of the
working staff is, to their minds, a *sine qua non*
of effective hospital therapeutics.

As a concluding note, one may add that the
other techniques of individual direct therapy
of the child in play sessions, or interviews by
other psychiatrists of the clinic staff are an
added instrument in frequent use. The greater
availability of the child permits the direct treatment to be more intensive than in the case
of the out-patient clinic. Concomitant therapy
of parental attitudes by psychiatrists or social
workers, as well as close consultations with social agency workers, completes the total integrated, collaborative approach now characteristic
of this service.

[6] Ruth Gilbert, and Helen Sutton, "A Children's
Psychiatric Service," Am. J. Nursing (1943) 43:
570–572.

147

Treatment of the Pseudosocial Boy *

Ruth Topping

The pseudosocial or "gang" boy, vividly portrayed in "Dead End Kids," is here used to designate the boy who may be said to be socialized within a delinquent group. While his attitude toward society is not dissimilar to that of the asocial or unsocialized boy, he differs from him in that he adheres to a well-defined code which gives him obligations chiefly to a highly selected few contemporaries of similar outlook who share in exploits calculated to furnish thrills, money, loot.

Loyalty undoubtedly is the cardinal virtue of such boys. This implies considerably more than "honor among thieves" or not "ratting," as they call informing. It more nearly approximates the spirit of the immortal Musketeers, "One for all and all for one." Concomitant virtues are generosity, daring, self-reliance, initiative, and resourcefulness. Members of this group are often characterized by extreme love of independence, a wish "to live their own lives." As a corollary, they are openly rebellious toward parents, school, and other authority. Usually they are sticklers for their rights. Loudly and logically they emphasize their wrongs. Impatient, impulsive, they want what they want when they want it and brook delay poorly. Some will go almost any length to evade or overcome restraint, regardless of the probable consequences. Theirs seems to be a philosophy of a short life and a merry one; or, "Have your fun until you are 16, when you can get a job and won't have to steal"; or, "After 16

---

* Reprinted from "Treatment of the Pseudo-Social Boy," 13 Am. J. Orthopsychiatry (1943), 353–360. Used by permission of the author and the publisher. Presented at the 1942 meeting. The concepts here expressed were largely developed at the New York State Training School for Boys, Warwick, N.Y. Cf. Jenkins' and Hewitt's article, pp. 101–108 supra. — Ed.

(in New York State) you will get a record so you'll stop stealing."

Thus we see this specially socialized boy at the opposite extreme from the asocial "lone wolf" youngster. Midway between we have the average, normal or typical adolescent. The pseudosocial boy further is likely to be especially characterized by youthful ardor, love of excitement and adventure, reckless daring, rebelliousness, striving toward maturity, thirst for independence — traits commonly ascribed to the adolescent stage of development. The pseudosocial adolescent is rebellious at *adult* control, not in isolation as is the asocial boy, but as a participating member of a social group with most exacting demands and the most severe and intolerant social control. Socialization seen in the smaller group centers around organization for behavior which is antisocial with respect to the larger group. The pseudosocial may be regarded as a cultural minority group adopting a way of life which is parasitic and predatory upon our culture. This group appears to say in effect, "We build our own world." Among themselves its members may be said to be more highly socialized than are average adolescents.

With the pseudosocial boy, important differences are found also in the limited range of his attachments. Usually there is less "homesickness" than longing for "the block," the gang, the old familiar haunts and hangouts. Furthermore, one senses in this group an absence of the "puppy-love" stage, the embarrassed uncertainties and indecisions classically portrayed in Booth Tarkington's *Seventeen*. Girls there are on a simple sex basis or to enhance status with the gang. But all loyalty, altruism, need for response, are seemingly taken up by boys.

Boys who are committed to a training school, while not necessarily "hardened offenders," usually have extensive contact with police, courts, probation officers, foster homes or private institutions for dependent or delinquent children. Their first court appearances may have been on petitions of neglect. Later ones, in the case of the pseudosocial boy, often arose from truancy, home desertion, petty stealing; and, with the onset of adolescence, bolder forms of stealing, not uncommonly involving assault, burglary, and wild "get-aways" in stolen cars. A sizeable proportion of those who finally reach the training school come on transfer from some private institution which claims that the boy's influence has been deemed detrimental to the group. Such boys appear well versed in "cop-and-court" lore and "know the ropes."

It has proved relatively easy to recognize the pseudosocial boy; the usual earmarks are aloofness, cool self-possession or assumed nonchalance, tight-lipped silence, furtively watchful glances, thinly veiled hostility. When afforded an opportunity to ask questions about the training school, he may shrug his shoulders or break his silence enough to say that there is nothing he wants to know. Sometimes he will ask for a particular shop assignment, inquire about some friend at the school or want to know how long he must stay.

This type of boy frequently makes a model adjustment from the day he is placed in the training school program. He seems fully resolved, as coached by friends, to "do as the man says" and "take the rap." Most often he presents no disciplinary problem and often by meritorius conduct succeeds in earning various special privileges. This model behavior is clearly motivated by one wish only, to get out as quickly as possible.

Other members of the group settle down superficially, while pursuing a policy of watchful waiting. Still others run away at the first favorable opportunity, usually taking others with them. If caught and returned, they quickly renew the attempt. To effect their escape they may overpower a supervisor, steal a car from the grounds or from some nearby point and not hesitate to break into homes, stores or gas stations. Naturally they may become involved in serious auto accidents. Their depredations too often gain for the training school unenviable repute in the community.

This rebellious element often proves an undermining influence in the institution in less apparent ways. Their rejection of the school as a constructive force sometimes adversely affects the better disposed boys who, through fear of losing status with other boys, are deterred from conforming to requirements of making adequate effort in school, shop, or cottage. Such boys naturally create acute administrative problems. They may reduce their supposed training to mere custodial care, unless some approach adapted to their peculiar needs can be devised.

At the New York State Training School, each boy's case is considered at the end of two months and reviewed at about six-month intervals by a committee which considers treatment program and the question of release. This committee usually recognizes the superficial quality of the "model" adjustment of some of these boys, realizing that inner changes have not taken place and if the boy were released, he would most likely resume his delinquencies.

At the review after eight months a decision for a second review six months later invariably comes as a severe jolt to these model-behavior boys. They view it as grossly unfair and scornfully demand, do they have to be "bad" in order to be sent home? Some actually proceed on that assumption. Some become particularly resentful and compare their fate with that of a "worse" boy who was released. Not without logic and a certain shrewdness they hammer away, point by point, at the other boy's delinquencies prior to commitment, his misconduct in the training school, in contrast to their own showing. It is probably safe to assume (and it is only an assumption) that the majority of pseudosocial boys who are in training or correctional schools are receiving or responding to little more than custodial care. They are simply "serving time."

At this point it is important to take into account still another factor in the pseudosocial boy's attitude toward length of commitment and his angry reaction to postponement of parole in the face of blameless conduct. Theirs is a well-ingrained crime–punishment philosophy, adhered to in their circles. These traditional attitudes are rooted in centuries of folk-thought, feeling and experience. So it is not surprising that boys refer again and again to "serving their time," "learning their lesson," or ask whether "time" in the detention home "counts."

The relatively recent concepts or procedures dealing with the indeterminate sentence and individual treatment of the delinquent have not as yet penetrated these circles. Nor do committed boys understand them, however simply interpreted. The minimum "term" for the maximum of good behavior is what most of them want to know. It is in this conflict of opposed philosophies that a program directed toward individual treatment meets its severest challenge.

On parole, the pseudosocial boy sometimes upsets the prediction of an unfavorable outcome. A number find and hold jobs and become law-abiding. On the other hand, professional criminals are largely recruited from the ranks of the pseudosocial. The basis for this difference of outcome remains a matter of speculation. Perhaps it is too superficial to suggest that with some the removal of the necessity of attending school with its corollary, a chance to work and earn, is a factor in favorable adjustment; or that time and the maturing process itself, deserve credit for successful outcome; or that recognition of graver consequences for the older offender serves as a deterrent; or that crumbling of the gang organization or the success of an older friend or a brother offers an incentive. The training school experience may after all have had more of a stabilizing effect than was apparent at the time.

From much of the foregoing material it can readily be seen that the pseudosocial boy represents a serious menace in the community; more frequently than not he proves a disrupting influence as well as a definite menace in institutions; through predatory exploits while on runaway he often becomes a menace to surrounding localities; not uncommonly continues his delinquencies or crimes following release; constitutes a substantial element in the ranks of future criminals and probably spends a good portion of his life in and out of penal or correctional institutions. When all this is thought of in terms of cost to the taxpayer, as well as loss, damage or injury to individuals, there is little danger of exaggerating the seriousness of the problem presented by such a group.

This paper so far has dealt with the external characteristics and behavior of the pseudosocial boy and less with the underlying motivations and mechanisms which have contributed to the personality structure. Here again, speculation outruns actual knowledge.

The weak "pretty boy" appearance of many pseudosocial boys, their frequent poor school achievement, strongly suggests an attempt on their part to overcompensate for a sense of effeminacy, or physical or mental inadequacy. It is not unusual to find him dependent and immature in relation to the mother and indifferent to or resentful of the father. There is a curious absence of warm, wholesome attachment to members of the family and, as suggested elsewhere, the affectional life appears to be centered on comrades of their own sex, though this may not necessarily express itself emotion-

ally. There appears to have been enough family acceptance for fundamental socialization, followed by lack of supervision and effective adult influence, and by incorporation into a delinquent gang. Some believe that the pseudosocial boy comes from larger families, while the asocial may come from smaller.

Leaders in this group are usually far more aloof and uncompromising than are the followers. They successfully maintain their hostile, suspicious, and defiant attitude and usually develop no relationship with adults in the institution.

Unlike the neurotic, who has solved his problem through insulating conflicting elements of his personality, the pseudosocial boy has externalized his difficulties and thus is at peace with himself. As one boy aptly phrased it, "My stealing is a problem to others, not to me."

Such boys are not self-consumed by the doubts and indecisions which beset the neurotic, yet unlike the asocial boy or the psychopath, are capable of moving in a social direction. They judge everything from the framework of their special code and follow a course of logic which may seem curious indeed, unless viewed from the angle of their own underlying assumptions. One such boy exclaimed fervently, "I am good here to be bad outside. Keeping me here can do me no good. It is what I think in my own mind. Keeping me here can't change my mind." Occasionally they are ready to cancel their "debt to society," but to prolong their stay, for treatment, is remote from their thinking. Hence, from a casework point of view they lack the *sine qua non* for treatment, that is, a sense of need and a wish for help in changing their life adjustment. All the help they want is to get out of the place. The boy's need for group approval easily outweighs any desire for help with his problems, even were he aware of their existence. Personality problems at a deep level he may have, but these can hardly be treated effectively without working through his armor. His whole adjustment on a pseudosocial basis seems to fend off awareness of inner conflict. Hence these problems are not near enough to consciousness to disturb him.

Ideally, one might wish treatment of such boys to persist to the point where deeper rapport might lead to the uncovering of basic needs or problems. Several sessions a week over a prolonged period might conceivably serve such an end, yet we must be doubtful even of this, and we may well wonder, in terms of our experience with these boys, whether such treatment if effective would not be understandable more in terms of ordinary close human influence than in terms of deeper-level psychotherapeutic techniques. In any case, the professional services usually available in a training school for several hundred boys, practically precludes such an expenditure of time on one individual. This does not mean that some form of treatment should not be attempted. The task frequently becomes one of helping larger numbers to adjust at a relatively simple level rather than attempting deep therapy with a few.

With the pseudosocial boy the effort must be not to wean him from his code, but to win him to its wider application. His capacity for loyalty, his other good qualities and his fundamental socialization here become important assets in treatment. The effort should be to divert his drive into socially acceptable channels rather than to uncover deep-seated conflicts.

This, it may be stated, is treating symptoms rather than seeking to get at the underlying causes. Still, the multiplicity and complexity of the causative factors underlying behavior sometimes divert attention from the comparatively limited range of those mechanisms which the individual employs in the struggle to adapt to his environment. This suggests that, while treatment directed toward uncovering causes necessarily must be individual, treatment procedures which seek to utilize the adaptive mechanisms may be formulated and generalized and applied to persons who show similar types of adaptation. The latter endeavor, in one sense, is individual in that it seeks, by listening closely to what the subject says, to learn his particular attitudes, feelings, tricks or grooves of thinking, and use this knowledge in making comments or suggestions to which it appears he most likely can respond. The frequent clamor that "each case is individual" is in danger of obscuring the methods of science, which continually seek formulation and classification.

Conditions and techniques directed toward more conscious levels are not so essentially different, however, from those commonly employed at a less conscious level. With our pseudo-social boy, however, one major difficulty is in establishing rapport to a degree where it is possible to draw him out and in time suggest modifications of outlook in keeping with his general viewpoint, yet useful as a basis for social adjustment. The difficulty of establishing rapport arises from characteristics and attitudes previously mentioned. The caseworker is at the further disadvantage of operating within an authoritative set-up.

Sometimes, however, the boy gives unexpected openings. In his eagerness to know, for example, in which cottage or shop he will find a particular buddy, a newly admitted boy will ask the caseworker. After naming the assignments, the worker makes some appreciative comment about the friend. This usually prompts other queries. On one occasion, where a new boy referred spontaneously to one of our parolees, the worker remarked that at the training school he had seemed such a game youngster and with little occasion for feeling handicapped by his diminutive size. She wondered whether he had carried out his intention of becoming a jockey. Thus encouraged, the new boy talked freely about this and other friends. Soon he was happily discussing their escapades, his own participation and revealing unconsciously much about himself. Such boys derive keen pleasure in discussing with an uncritical listener, their gang and "the block." In time they will proceed to discuss more personal aspects of their own lives, even though it often is at a superficial level. They like to complain and are past masters in picking the social structure to pieces, citing injustices and inconsistencies, usually as a means of self-justification. In this need to justify himself the pseudosocial boy is sharply distinguishable from the asocial. One such boy maintained, "Everyone steals, even if it's only a pencil," he continued, "Or, in the country, maybe the housewife has set a few pies out to cool; a child sees them and takes one. That is the way it is with some boys and a car. They just want to have some fun with it and put it back when they're through. It's what you don't have that you want." He discussed administrative policies as freely, saying that he was sure many a runaway would have been prevented if boys who were homesick, boys who had never spent a day of their lives away from home, were given "little breaks." "What are these psychiatrists paid for," he suddenly exclaimed, "if they can't figure out what is in a boy's mind!"

With obdurately silent boys, a beginning can sometimes be made by the worker showing awareness of some of the boy's thoughts and accepting them as natural. A certain newly admitted boy was known to be a member of a notorious gang which had engaged in a series of car thefts and burglaries. He had escaped several times from a private correctional school. On the last runaway, he had enlisted in the CCC and was still wearing their uniform, although he had deserted the camp because he became bored with exterminating the gypsy moth. In the initial interview he had offered nothing spontaneously, until after the worker had observed good-naturedly that it was clear he intended his stay to be brief. She assured him that it was not difficult to run away and asked, why shouldn't he? He had been doing this successfully for some time and seemingly had little trouble in maintaining himself while out on his own. She did wonder if he had been as happy as he wished, whether the sense of someone looking for him was a bother, etc. She told him frankly that a number of boys had made successful runaways. The boy then offered a few spontaneous remarks and began to ask questions. He managed to drop his suspicious watchfulness and readily acknowledged his intention to leave. He had not done so at the time of last news about him. Special pains were taken at the start to introduce him to the director of recreation and to others of a strongly masculine type which he clearly admired. This seemed to please him and led him to a measure of acceptance of the training school. He was placed with supervisors known for their skill in dealing with this sort of boy. The approach in this instance was clearly one of showing the boy that his thoughts were apparent, despite his silence. He was able to see that the worker was unconcerned over his harboring ideas out of keeping with the institutional scheme of things and that she could admire his resourcefulness. This paved the way for later interviews, where doubts of the wisdom of his course, in terms of his own ultimate satisfaction, could be suggested and the boy thus aided in re-evaluating his experience.

Mildly provocative tactics sometimes succeed with the stubbornly silent boy where other measures have failed. After repeated runaways,

for example, the sponsor sometimes has acknowledged herself puzzled that such a liberty-loving youth persists in defeating his own ends and needlessly prolongs his stay by escapes or other acts of insubordination. This may invite an expression of views, usually in a negative direction — a tirade against the training school, courts, or the whole social order — and lead by a different route to the voicing of sentiments similar to those just cited. At this stage it seems well to employ passive tactics, quietly acknowledging that there is of course a lot in what he is saying. The discovery that an adult will listen and not become argumentative is in itself astonishing. There is response also to the interest shown and the apparent wish of the listener to understand his point of view. After unburdening much of his hostility, he may become interested in his immediate situation and seek to know about conditions of release. One boy thought it particularly silly to keep him after he had decided for the first time in his life to stop stealing and go to work. It was possible for the worker to assure him of her personal belief in his good intentions and ability to carry them out, while pointing out at the same time that the reviewing committee would have to be shown first by his adjustment in the training school that he was ready for parole.

Even with these pseudosocial boys, therefore, rapport can be achieved through the usual "accepting" techniques, friendly comment, expression of interest, appeal to love of fair play, sense of humor, and flair for logic. It helps to give the boy an occasional "inside tip" and thus outsmart the boys who are his usual sources of information. Another aid in developing rapport is doing legitimate favors, attending to reasonable requests promptly. He appreciates a personal letter in answer to his inquiries. This tangible evidence of one's interest in his welfare gives him, as no words can, a gradual conviction that the worker is *for* him. It is important above all to accept this type of boy on terms of equality as an adult well entitled to his viewpoint. Such an approach succeeded beyond expectation when a particularly rebellious youth of superior intelligence explained to the worker: "You and I are two very stubborn people. We could talk all day and neither of us change our opinion."

Through the pseudosocial boy's discussion of his friends we are afforded an excellent opportunity also for introducing other ways of looking at the matters under discussion. With care not to criticize the friend, thus arousing antagonism or evoking a defensive attitude, the boy is able to regard the friend's attitudes and behavior more objectively, and unconsciously to apply to himself some of the viewpoints indirectly suggested. He may even advance these newer viewpoints as his own in later talks with his friend. There are obvious risks, of course, in employing such methods and they should be used with the utmost caution and then only after considerable rapport exists.

Again, treatment organized around the boy's patterns of thinking, rather than delving into causative factors, is indicated. It is needful to keep in mind as he talks, his points of emphasis and line of reasoning as clues for future use, when he seems ready to listen.

Treatment in the broader sense embraces techniques extending beyond the clinic into the general program of the training school. Care in assignment to the cottage is seen as especially important. The pseudosocial boy, in particular, needs to be placed with a cottage father with whom he can readily identify. This often proves to be our best hope of winning the boy to a wider application of his code. Certain of the personnel at the training school have been found to deal particularly competently with such lads. One cottage father was especially effective in that he furnished in his own physique and personality a striking masculine ideal. He was an ex-army officer. He liked boys, tried to be fair, and promptly recognized and rewarded meritorious conduct. He was vivid, witty without being sarcastic, and severe when occasion demanded. He trusted his boys (sometimes in the face of disillusionment) and spent some of his own time and money on them. He willingly helped them with their personal problems. Once thoroughly convinced that a boy had changed, that he could "make the grade," he backed him with all his power, as zealously as a lawyer might battle for a client. The boys would comment, "That guy's sure on the level." This cottage father, by virtue of these qualities, captured that loyalty which these boys show in such abundance, yet generally reserve for contemporaries only. His

boys might run away or "breeze" as they call it, but they wouldn't "breeze on him." One such boy wrote, concerning a similar supervisor in another institution: "He was a square guy. All the other boys liked him. He told you when you were wrong and punished you for it . . . Tell him for me, I never met a more squarer, good guy. Tell him I want to thank him for giving me my experience in auto mechanics. Yes sir, he was one square guy."

Some "don'ts" in treatment of these boys would seem to be: don't shoot too high; don't attempt deep-level therapy unless there are exceptional facilities in the number of skilled personnel; don't focus on seeking to develop insight. On the other hand, under suitable conditions, treatment at a deeper level would be interesting from an experimental and research point of view.

In conclusion it may be said that the fundamental socialization of the pseudosocial boy and his capacity for loyalty provide the ace cards for a wider adjustment. The maturing process, the treatment the boy receives, and the influence of other persons upon him may largely determine whether he will swell the ranks of crime, find himself in the ranks of labor, or enrolled in such groups as the CCC or the armed forces of the country.

148

Specific Factors Determining Antisocial Acting Out *

M. E. Giffin, A. M. Johnson,

and E. M. Litin

Delinquency is unquestionably on the increase in this country. The individuals involved in such behavior, if unassociated with any gang

* Reprinted from a 1954 symposium, "Antisocial Acting Out," by M. E. Giffin, A. M. Johnson, E. M. Litin, Sections of Neurology and Psychiatry, Mayo Clinic and Mayo Foundation (Graduate School, University of Minnesota), Rochester, Min-

group, can be treated, but only with the enormous expenditure of energy by highly trained people. Successful therapy of children at home can be accomplished only by intensive collaborative treatment of parents and child. Successful treatment of the average *neurotic* adolescent is a simple task, by contrast.

For treatment to be rational, etiology must be explicit. Arrival at our understanding of clinical evidence for etiology has necessitated drastic changes in our previous understanding of traditional psychoanalytic theory. Psychoanalysts' first interest was in the neuroses, and with few exceptions research has been concerned largely with this aspect of psychopathology. In understanding the neuroses one conceives of a too-punitive superego. Until recently, pathology of the superego was viewed only in terms of its being too punishing to patients. For years any antisocial acting out was explained in terms of a patient's being excessively guilty about conflicts or being driven by constitutionally unmanageable instinctual drives. The reflected preventive attitude for all patients has been "Do not repress the child so drastically or he will become neurotic or act out."

Therapists, as well as parents, have become greatly confused, thinking that prohibitions in all forms lead to too much guilt and thus, neurosis. Some therapists have unwittingly permitted and fostered acting out in, especially, the sexual sphere. Prohibitions in themselves do not lead to unhealthy guilt; rather, they are an important aspect of security. So far as the prevention of neurosis is concerned, the prohibition of antisocial activity merely requires the presence of a parent sufficiently well integrated to accept in legitimate ways the hostility expressed by the child over the limit-setting that society demands.

It has become increasingly clear that many parents, particularly those with poorly integrated impulses, have become uneasy about setting limits, even concerning matters which are specifically destructive to society, such as stealing, sexuality or even murderous intent. Yet it is evident that certain specific things, such as stealing, fire-setting, murder and sexual destructiveness, cannot be countenanced in our society

— they must be prohibited completely and definitively. As most of us clearly recognize, there is, then, specific behavior, the expression of which should arouse guilt in everyone. The guilt alone is not unhealthy. Neurosis need be feared only if great rage has been repressed, along with the prohibition of such antisocial activity.

Our concern in this paper is with the development of that form of pathologic super-ego which permits antisocial behavior. Clinical evidence shows it to be lacunar, weak in some respects, punitive in some and normal in still other areas.

Many people have strong latent antisocial impulses, yet never act out such fantasies. We are concerned with defining the specific stimulus to the acting-out behavior. We shall first consider the problems of the direct acting out of forbidden antisocial impulses; namely, stealing, truancy, fire-setting and direct sexual acting out. Later in the paper, we shall consider the problems found in those *structurally* more complicated cases in which acting out is associated with perversions.

Since the early work of Szurek and one of us (Johnson) (7), collaborative studies on antisocial acting out have continued. From the initial studies emerged the thesis that antisocial acting out in a child is unconsciously initiated, fostered and sanctioned by the parents, who vicariously achieve gratification of their own poorly integrated forbidden impulses through a child's acting out. One or both parents in addition unconsciously experience gratification for their own hostile and destructive wishes toward the child, who is repeatedly destroyed by his behavior. It is possible in every case adequately studied to trace the specific conscience defect in the child to a mirror image of similar type and emotional charge in the parent. The focus of these observations has been not on the activities of the kind seen among deprived and other sociologically determined gang groups, but rather among individual children of poor or of privileged class, frequently from families of "good" reputation and high social standing.

The super-ego defects in these children are frequently in only one or two areas and are rarely widespread. A child may steal, but never be truant. Another may set fires and do nothing else that is antisocial. In another, only the sexual sphere will be implicated through the acting out. To be sure, like other people, these pa-

nesota, 24 Am. J. Orthopsychiatry (1954), 668–684. Used by permission of the authors and the publisher. See, also, A. M. Johnson and S. A. Szurek, "Parental Sanction of Delinquency," 34 Focus (1955), 44–49. — Ed.

tients have neuroses with conflict and guilt, but they have also the super-ego weakness in one or more areas, permitting discharge of tension.

There is frequently confusion regarding the use of the phrase "acting out." The expression "acting in the transference" was first used recurrently by Freud to refer to the phenomenon which was seen during psychoanalytic therapy in which the neurotic patient repeated in the transference, without insight, certain salient episodes of his earlier life.

Eduardo Weiss (13) aptly described it in the following way: "By acting-out is meant the behavior of a person who repeats without insight an unconscious psychic situation out of his past in terms of current reality. A man, for instance, repeats intense feelings of hostility towards his brothers and sisters by quarreling with his fellow workers."

Weiss continued, "Freud considered transference as a form of acting-out. According to Freud one acts out instead of remembering. However, psychoanalytic experience teaches us that patients in analysis often act out emotional situations which they have already remembered." Weiss stated that "Freud's formulation can be modified by saying that one acts-out instead of remembering fully with the appropriate attending emotions." He continued, "While acting-out is a substitute for recall, it does not have the therapeutic effect of the latter. The patient who acts out has still to acknowledge that *his present behavior is a reproduction of past experiences*." Weiss concluded, "I agree fully with Anna Freud who says that the patient who acts-out *exclusively* cannot be analyzed."

In more recent years the phrase "acting out" has come to be used almost exclusively in referring to that behavior against authority which is specifically forbidden by our society. Actually, except for the moral issue, there is no sharp line of demarcation between the acting in the transference and the kind of phenomenon expressed by the unconscious acting-out problems with which we are here dealing. This is in keeping with the view commonly held today: That ego and super-ego are not separate entities, but merge imperceptibly on the spectrum of reality testing. At one end are observed highly moral aspects of the ego; here there can be no alternatives to conforming morally. Proceeding to the opposite end of the spectrum, increasingly complicated alternatives and choices become obviously permissible, since ethics is not involved; it is more in this latter area that acting out during analysis occurs.

The provocative contributions of Reich (10), Alexander and Healy (2), Healy and Bronner (5), Schmideberg (11), Gardner (4) and many others have been extensively reviewed in our previous communications. It was Aichhorn (1) whose contributions first unquestionably moved delinquency out of the nihilistic depths of constitutional inheritance, into the realm of dynamic understanding. Every worker in the field of childhood and adolescent acting out has been stimulated by and greatly indebted to this man who genuinely understood delinquents.

We follow the emphasis of Szurek (12), who as early as 1942 described the psychopathic personality as being only a delinquent grown older, as an individual defective in personality organization, specifically in the individual's conscience. Szurek distinguished those individuals from the sociologically stimulated gang lawbreakers, and presented one of the earliest contributions to the dynamic understanding of these problems. He wrote, "Clinical experience leaves the impression that the definition of psychopathic personality is no greater mystery than other syndromes in psychopathology. Almost literally, in no instance in which adequate psychiatric therapeutic study of both parent and child has been possible has it been difficult to obtain sufficient evidence to reconstruct the chief dynamics of the situation. Regularly, the more important parent, usually the mother, although the father is always in some way involved, has been seen unconsciously to encourage the amoral or antisocial behavior of the child."

It is impossible to understand the dynamic concepts behind the behavior of these individuals unless one has clearly in mind the development of the normal super-ego. One must understand the reaction of the well-integrated parent, and the subtle conscious and unconscious ways in which this behavior directs the development of the child's super-ego. Identification with the parent consists of more than incorporation of the *manifest* behavior of the parent; it necessarily involves inclusion of the subtleties of the parent's conscious and unconscious image of the child. The healthy parent fantasies his child as capable of becoming law abiding. The well-integrated, mature mother does *not* immediately check on a child following an order or request; she unconsciously assumes that the order will be carried out. The neurotic mother, who immediately checks or warns that if the job is not done dire consequences will follow, merely conveys to the child that an unstated alternative exists in the mother's mind. It is frequently with this alternative image in the mother's thoughts that the child more strongly identifies. This is true because the child senses the peculiar parental emotional need conveyed in the anxious, vacillating tone of the parent's expression.

The child internalizes, then, not only the positive, socially consistent attitudes of the parent, but also the frequently unexpressed, ambivalent antisocial feelings. We cannot agree with those who state that the child identifies only with idealized aspects of the parent. The child identifies with all facets of the parent — to be sure, repressing those parental characteristics which cause conscious confusion, anxiety and shame.

The patients with whom we are specifically concerned in this paper are those manifesting what are frequently called "super-ego lacunae." The apparent "punched-out" aspect of this kind of super-ego is misleading except from the point of view of society. From the point of view of the patient there is a positive, undeniable drive toward acting in the manner in which the parent unconsciously wishes, even though it be antisocial in direction. The conception of a deficit within the super-ego structure must be elaborated to include the overwhelming parentally determined dynamic push toward antisocial behavior which the child senses and with which he necessarily complies. Although we are not here concerned with sociologically delinquent gang members, there is frequently overlapping of the individuals who act out antisocially, these latter often moving into gangs.

If our thesis is correct that parents unconsciously initiate and foster antisocial behavior in order to experience gratification for themselves, accurate documentary evidence must be defined in answer to two basic questions:

1. How is sanctioning communicated to the child?

2. Why is one child implicated in a family in which all the other children are quite conforming?

Not only is it possible by careful questioning and observation to define the process by which a specific child is chosen and the dynamic factors behind the choice of a particular form of socially disapproved behavior, but it is also possible to detect the highly personal technique by which the parent transmits the double talk, interest, permissive tone or structured situation by which the activity is fostered.

During the process of definitive treatment, it is clearly seen why one child becomes emotionally chosen to be the outlet of expression for these forbidden impulses. An adopted child, whose behavior can be blamed on heredity, becomes a natural victim through whom to express antisocial trends, with simultaneous expression of hostile feelings in the parent toward this child. Sometimes the only son of a woman who is disturbed by unresolved hostile dependent problems with her own father, and permitted by her own mother to carry on petty stealing, may become the means of expressing both her unconscious anger and her poorly integrated stealing impulses through her fostering such socially destructive activities in her child.

Proper understanding of case material is impossible unless one is aware of the many innuendoes of communication which occur without conscious awareness between parents and child. Such communications are by all conceivable means of approach sometimes errors of omission, frequently ones of frank commission. Knowing *what* to listen for, and *how*, the diagnostician gradually defines these operations from direct quotations, double talk, facial expressions, and often through histrionic portrayal by some parents who dramatize the actual interchange between themselves and the child. In the more subtle cases the casuistic, disingenuous rationalizations of these parents can reduce the whole spirit of an ethical principle to a quibbling absurdity.

The specific manner in which, for instance, the truancy from home was handled on a particular day must be obtained; frequently, when this is done, one finds that the mother met the girl with the comment, "If you don't like us and our house, find another; we can get along without you." If this mother is merely asked for adjectival descriptions of the relationship between herself and Jennie she will, without realizing it, forget to indicate this kind of response.

The entranced parental facial expression apparent to the child describing a stealing episode, a sexual misdemeanor, or a hostile attitude toward a teacher conveys to the child that the parent is achieving some pleasurable gratification. No amount of subsequent punishment will act as a deterrent against the recurrences of the acting out. A child wishes to do the thing which he senses gives the parent pleasure, even though he may be punished. We frequently see parents who describe the child's delinquent behavior with obvious pleasure. Suspicious questioning often conveys the parents' unconscious wish that the child comply by doing the thing *verbally* warned against.

Frequently, parents verbalize evasion and deceptions such as, "Here is an extra quarter, but don't tell your father"; "You can get into the movie for half-price, since you certainly don't look twelve years old"; "Fires are dangerous, but if you must get it out of your system, then we'll set some in the yard."

A mother can make such a suggestion, yet she would never recommend that her child take a trial run in front of cars on the street. The mother of a 14-year-old girl was not genuinely interesting in prohibiting her child's stealing; she said to her daughter, "Why did you take the money from your *aunt's* purse instead of from mine?"

Children hear their parents gloating about shortchanging the grocer; naturally they sense the parental pleasure. Some parents do not follow through when the facts of stealing are perfectly clear. For instance, they hesitate to go with the child to the dime store to make proper restitution for a stolen trinket. A mother who has poorly integrated prohibitions concerning her own hostile sexual impulses may fantasy that her eight-year-old daughter will "get into sexual difficulties" as adolescence approaches. With her provocative warnings accompanied by anxiety she is a predictable stimulus to vacillating sexual behavior in such a child.

We frequently have patients whose parents tell the child to ask the physician for permission to do something they already well understand to be forbidden. Parents complain of *children's* breaking family rules when the parents themselves consciously or unconsciously break rule after rule and promise after promise without apology or comment.

The process of vicarious gratification now becomes clearer. The antisocial behavior of the implicated child becomes a means of parental expression by which poorly integrated antisocial impulses of the parent are expressed through the child. As Emch (3) lucidly stated it, the child is "acting-out the caricatured reproduction of past parental behavior." In addition to this use as a mode of expression for parental impulses, such a child is the recipient of a hostile destructive drive in the parent; in close relationship lie vicarious gratification through the child and the wish to destroy this same child. Such family behavior in the end is destructive to both the parent's ego organization and that of the child.

For purposes of research, particularly, but also for the proper controlled therapy of non-residential acting-out patients, collaborative therapy is the only adequate technique. There continues to be misunderstanding about the actual procedure, and it must therefore be pointed out that the term "collaborative therapy," as we use it, refers to that particular form of dynamic psychotherapy in which the individual treatment hours of each patient are reviewed in great detail, hour by hour, among all the psychiatrists acting as therapists. It is not the task of a social work follow-up, nor is it concomitant therapy in which two individuals of the same family unit are undergoing therapy during the same period of time; it is a form of highly specialized therapy in which the individual treatment is intensive and the interchange between therapists is regular and frequent. The availability of each physician to the other must be immediate. Material pertinent to the current problem is discussed openly between therapists and with the patients, as it may be useful to them. Transference problems arising from such interchange of timely material are actively analyzed. The purpose and advantage lie in the convenient interchange of information between therapists, material which helps the understanding of each patient and hastens the treatment of all. By means of it, adequate and suitably timed limit-setting is possible, long before its need might be apparent in individual therapy.

ANTISOCIAL ACTING OUT: ILLUSTRATIVE CASES

Scientific proof of causation is not satisfied merely by demonstrating the invariable presence of the suspected cause (unwitting parental permissiveness) whenever the effect (antisocial behavior of children) is observed. In addition, it must also be shown that whenever the suspected cause is present, the effect is also seen. Our first case demonstrates the factors that must be satisfied for scientific proof of causation.

Stealing. Ten years ago one of us was asked to treat a young single woman of 22 years who was depressed. Her married sister, the only relative in that city, came to give some family history and assist with medical arrangements. At that interview, this sister, in commenting on the personalities of her *own* three children, said of her only son, 9-year-old Mark, "He runs circles around us all — he is so brilliant that schoolwork is no challenge to him. I often wish he had been born more dumb so he would be forced to work hard. I tell him that since his schoolwork requires no effort, he will never learn how hard it is to make an honest living. He has not stolen yet, that I know of, but I cannot see him working hard to make an honest living."

We were very interested at the time in recording these exact words because they indicated a hostile wish and image that the boy not be a straightforward citizen. In the course of 2½ years' treatment of Mark's 22-year-old maternal aunt, it was observed that her oldest brother, Bob, a brilliant fellow, was always permitted by his parents to cut corners to the point of frank cheating and stealing. Although his parents ostensibly favored him over the girls by this sanctioning, they were literally destroying him, and the law finally intervened. He was imprisoned for a few years, to the bitter humiliation of our patient and Mark's mother.

By the time Mark was 12 years old his parents came to see us because he had been caught with another boy stealing four jackknives from a sporting-goods store. Needless to say, when questioned closely the parents had absolute evidence of stealing from the mother's purse for at least a year; the only punishment for such transgressions had been a casual remark, which is now so familiar to us, "You are just Uncle Bob over again." In brief, when that mother became our patient, it was unmistakably clear that all Mark's life she had identified him with her hated brother and conveyed this image to the boy in countless ways.

The most alarming attitudes were those expressed quite unconsciously in the diagnostic interview with the parents as they related the episode of the stolen jackknives. When the parents were asked if they had any ideas as to why the child had stolen the knives, the mother immediately answered, *and* to the father's great discomfort, "Children don't realize it, but grownups know that stealing and

cheating are on the short route to seriously injuring someone."

The husband burst out angrily, "Jean, your wild ideas run away with you. What do you mean? Mark has never hurt anyone. You've always had him so scared stiff of you that he won't even play a little baseball, let alone hurt anyone."

To this the wife responded angrily, "You don't listen to me — I've been telling you that for the past year when I slap him his eyes blaze with anger — there's terrible temper there, even if he does not *say* anything." Later in her treatment the mother's fantasies that this boy could steal and murder *"if driven to it"* had to be actively dealt with as a manifestation of her own fantasies. The normal parent neither anticipates impending disaster nor dismisses monetary or other transgressions as trivial.

When one discovers the presence of stealing in one family member, its occurrence in at least one other is predictable. Such a relationship is also true of fire-setting, truancy and direct hostile or sexual acting out. A case of the last is appropriate.

Direct murderous acting out. Very attractive, prominent parents in a large city came with their 14-year-old adopted son for study. There were three older sisters, and one older brother, all unadopted. The parents' only concern was that sexually their son might not be developing normally — that his slight plumpness might be an endocrine problem. Fortunately, this boy was away in a private school from the age of 10 years, yet when he came home on vacations the mother bathed him, cleaned his penis thoroughly and felt of his testes, ostensibly to ascertain if they were firm and large enough. She laughingly spoke of her amusement when her son called her by the name of a currently enticing actress as she herself strutted about in the nude. She complained bitterly of how defiant her boy was, yet when questioned by her husband, she could not describe any real naughtiness. The boy did surreptitiously take out anger in mild ways on colleagues — yet never had he dared an open battle. When this mother was alone with us, without the father's being present, she described fantasies which aptly reflect her image of her son's future. We could hardly believe the material spontaneously given by this well-dressed, intelligent, attractive woman.

"He is very affectionate — he hugs and kisses me. The school wanted his eyes checked for blinking. I wanted his male organs checked — they seem too small. His brother's seem bigger and firmer. He says I'm prettier than he — nicer in the breasts. We like our baths together. I'm afraid to turn him loose with boys for what he might do — a bad blow — afraid for him to have a gun. I worry he might rape or butcher someone — not just sexually. There are cases of boys who carved up people's organs, heads and faces. I have the feeling that an attraction to a girl would develop in him a wish to mutilate her — stab her in the back, slice her throat, cut her from head to foot."

When the father was seen alone, he was, of course, not told of the mother's fantasies given to us, but in relating the family history he described his wife's background. Her father was brutal to her mother when he was drunk, a condition which was habitual. He was always kindly to our patient and she adored him. When she was 6 years old she saw her intoxicated father beat up the mother and throw her cruelly across the room. The 20-year-old son in the family picked up a bat and crushed his father's skull, killing him. This son, the maternal uncle of our 14-year-old patient, was imprisoned for a time. Our unfortunate parent, bewildered at what could happen and indeed did happen before her eyes as a child, had no capacity within herself to believe in her own son's control. It was not surprising that the mother, however, implicated the adopted son's heredity.

The boy himself, attractive and well built, showed the most rigid compulsive defensive attempt at inner control associated with considerable depression. His unconscious fantasy life was filled with murder, retribution, and "then everyone lived happily in the end."

In the foregoing case we see the poorly integrated seductive and hostile components of the mother's personality tragically coercing her son into mounting rage over the seduction, rage completely frightening in view of *her* concept of how anger is handled. These are truly terrifying cases, and often initially in treatment, for safety's sake, the child is treated best by removal to the medical floor of a hospital. The apparent mystery of adolescent homicides can be quickly dissipated if adequate background material is available.

Treatment of Antisocial Acting Out

Since our concepts of etiology are relatively new, we cannot detail the therapeutic procedures employed with any finality. The broad outlines of therapy, however, may be indicated. Most of our treatment has dealt with the adolescent who comes to the clinic and lives at home — this has permitted more adequate focus on etiology, research which has necessitated close study of the parents as well as of the child. In this communication we must restrict ourselves to the mention of basic tenets. It should be remembered that the task is prodigious. One adolescent girl and her parents now in treatment under the three authors' care involve a minimum of 12 hours a week, and this for months and years.

Frequently, the child with acting-out problems is brought to treatment only after a series of pressures from neighbors, teachers and often the law. At times a younger child is brought at the insistence of one parent who is better integrated than the other. Implicit in these situations is the fact that motivation for treatment is often superficial and ambivalent. Obviously, a parent who receives gratification, albeit unconscious, is not anxious to remove his source of supply, and a child attempting to satisfy parental wishes is not driven to seek help which will separate him from a needed parent. Frequently, however, by the time an *adolescent* comes to treatment he is frightened by the increasing discrepancy between parental and social standards, and he appears as a sullen, distraught and confused child.

No area in psychoanalysis involves the possibility of greater intensity of countertransference problems than the realm of delinquency. Disruption of treatment frequently follows inadequate resolution of such problems. A few aspects of this problem can be discussed.

1. The use of collaborative therapy in the handling of any psychiatric problem involves the proper resolution of countertransference problems. All collaborative therapy is based on the premise that we are dealing with family pathology; a therapist's overidentification with his patient, and narcissistic competitive complications arising from such overidentification create chaos. It must not matter *which* patient gets well first; the goal of successful collaborative therapy is the recovery of *all* members of the family.

2. The problem of limit-setting, even though dynamically timed, is disturbing to some therapists. The resorting to the historical concept of the analyst as utterly noninterfering may well be used as a rationalization for some vicarious gratification on the part of the therapist, achieved through the acting out. Brian Bird has elaborated extensively and with very apt illustrations on this point in his discussion of this paper.

3. It must be remembered that even healthy

parents are not omnipotent; actually they do make mistakes. Therapists who cannot face these facts develop such contempt for erring parents and such overidentification with the child that they cannot casually and directly point out a lie, deception, or confusing corruption in a parent, and deal with the immediate hostility. Every good therapist grows with each patient he treats; likewise, every parent has the right to grow with his child in treatment.

4. Just as in the treatment of a neurosis in which the patient may relapse or become more disturbed, so in the treatment of acting-out problems, the mature therapist does not become discouraged or contemptuous when some complicated re-educational measure has not taken hold as yet, or when some hitherto unrecognized pressure leads to recurrence of acting out.

We shall mention a few rules relative to the treatment of the child, followed by generalizations about therapy of the parents. Treatment of the child must take into account the following:

1. As many have recognized, the patients most successfully treated on a clinic basis are those who are able to develop early some positive feelings for the therapist.

2. Any initiation of interviews by asking a child to give an account of misdemeanors only pushes him into further falsification.

3. We are aware that the normal super-ego develops through identification with a parent who unconsciously assumes that the child will learn to be as honest as the parent; we assume that similar identification is possible, in time, with these delinquent children if they are able to make some contact with us. We indicate that in time, as we know each other, the adolescent will find himself handling these troublesome matters more and more easily. This is a detailed meticulous re-education process, in which the therapist assumes that the child has capabilities eventually to learn a new mastery of impulses heretofore unconsciously given free rein.

4. Since for a long time the child has known consciously or unconsciously that his antisocial behavior was ambiguously condoned at home, he has developed a pattern of expectation that adults will overlook misdemeanors. The therapist's own corruptibility is immediately tested, since the child automatically responds in his usual pattern. When we are positive of the facts, we catch little things early, so that the child does not commit greater misdemeanors and then feel betrayed when we interfere with only a large issue.

5. We certainly do *not* begin by asking a child why he acted out. He does not yet know that this behavior is in keeping with the parent's wish that he comply in this fashion. We shall see how this comes about in treatment.

6. The initiation of dynamic therapy, associated with limit-setting, the core of re-education, comes about in the following way.

All therapists watch for the first current evidence showing unmistakably that parents themselves are acting out with the child. For instance, when all three therapists agree that such an act is a fact, then each takes it up with the patients involved. A short illustration will make this more clear.

The seductive father of an adolescent girl who was acting out sexually finally confessed, with considerable anxiety, that he had called his daughter an "s.o.b." and a "whore." The father's therapist helped him understand that his regret would be meaningful to his daughter, should she know from her therapist of her father's real concern and remorse about the outburst.

For some time the child's therapist had known that this girl was overwhelmed by some very disturbing comment from her father, whom at one time she had loved very much. She had been unable, however, to mention the distressing names. When the therapist told the child that her father had expressed great remorse about having used these epithets, the child reflected amazement, followed by a pathetic inquiry, "You mean he really told *that?*"

This was the first evidence of real anxiety and conflict in the girl, and it was followed by a rather dramatic deepening of attachment to the therapist.

Again, when the mother broke a very definite rule that had been established between the three patients, this was called to her attention at once. When this was discussed with the daughter, it had truly dynamic merit in making her more consciously aware of her previous *automatic* compliance with the mother's uninhibited behavior. If parents break rules continuously with evasions, the child automatically does the same. The collaborator treating the child can tactfully discuss with the child any matter about which the family has confusion and of which they had been unaware.

Treatment of the parents is probably a more formidable and prolonged procedure than that of the child. Therapists differ in their views as to the means of successful enlistment into treatment of parents of any child, neurotic or delinquent. Every therapist must handle this in the manner which works most successfully for him. We have some definite views on this matter, ideas which have been elaborated in another communication (6). Detecting the clues of unconscious permission as they operate between parents and child, and bringing this to the parent's awareness, naturally arouses anxiety and anger. This must be dealt with very actively, and the anger must be absorbed by the therapist, who maintains his stand with society on the corrupting issue. The parents unconsciously try every artifice and perfidy to engage the therapist in condoning the forbidden issue in question. After hours of accepting the anger, but with no capitulation on the moral issue, one can begin to see better integration within the parent. This, however, is achieved only by active analysis of all transference indications of mounting tension related to the parental neurotic equilibrium that is now being disturbed by the limit-setting.

Many therapists seriously question the wisdom of helping the child to recognize the manner in which the parents unwittingly operate. These skeptics maintain that such recognition detracts from the parents' esteem and mobilizes unmanageable guilt in both parents and child. However, therapy cannot be a swindle; the problems recognized unconsciously by all participants must be made conscious. Hilde Bruch, in her discussion, emphasizes that confidentiality between patient and therapist becomes a mockery when a patient unconsciously feels he is engaging his therapist in a contract of secret misrepresentation. When we call a deception to the patient's awareness with no contempt on our part, but with firmness and friendliness, absorbing the anger, the patient can then begin to deal with the real issues. It is remarkable to observe the almost revelatory experience with which the parent suddenly becomes conscious for the first time of his own deceptive heritage.

Problems of Sexual Aberration

As with the direct activities of stealing and fire-setting, so with the perversions: One can invariably detect, with proper study, the interdigitation of parent-and-child conflicts. These are dynamically more complicated cases because of the additional regressive step which will be elaborated. Many individuals become aware, particularly during the course of psychotherapy, of strong latent homosexual, transvestite or exhibitionistic trends, yet it never occurs to them to act out such fantasies, just as many neurotics show tendencies to set fires or steal, yet never act out such desires. We are here concerned with evaluating the specific stimuli to the overt behavior.

The etiology of perverse behavior follows a similar, but more complicated, pattern to that of direct acting out. With proper means of research it is possible to define: 1) the specific details of a confused and unsatisfactory parental relationship; 2) evidences of pathologic seduction of a particular child, with condoning by the other parent; 3) a pattern of genital frustration following the initial pattern of seduction; 4) the impetus from the parent toward an abnormal pattern of sexual behavior.

As in antisocial acting out, the choice of the specific child in terms of the parents' background and neurosis is similarly definable. This is a very simplified statement of the factors entering into the acting out of aberrant sexuality. One must keep in mind that this is no simple one-to-one relationship, but rather, a relationship which depends upon all of these factors' interrelating with the total intrapsychic life of the patient.

It is necessary to understand that by the term "seduction," we are referring to a pathologic form of a parental sexual temptation which is completely inappropriate temporally for the child. Under the guise of tenderness, it confronts the child with an ambivalent, genital passion which he cannot understand or begin to integrate. Faced with what is overtly parental love, he becomes unconsciously aware of the hostile parental feelings; in incest or with genital frustration the hostile guilty, shameful feelings of the parent are absorbed by the child, who experiences in himself confusion, guilt, fear of detection and anxiety. Out of the parents' own guilt another form of personally acceptable sexual expression must be defined. Unconsciously, this has been previously emphasized by the parent during the polymorphous sexual period of the child.

How is the defining of a permitted regressed (perverse) outlet to the tension *generated* by seduction and frustration? Here we must observe the very early pregenital behavior of the child and mother, beginning with the ambivalence of the oral dependency on up to the genital struggles. In these cases of perversion we always see overstressing of at least one aspect of polymorphous sexual behavior of the young child, such as to lead to unusual selective hypertrophy. Although at such an early age there is no orgasm, and therefore this cannot be called a "perversion," still the hypotrophy can be so *profound* and *organized* that we cannot accept this as just the unorganized sexuality of the polymorphous perverse child. We shall not include here a report on a child of this age; a case in which extreme transvestitism began in a child at 2½ years is now in press (9).

We shall present only one case of adolescent perversion, that of exhibitionism.

A 17-year-old boy was apprehended by the police while exhibiting himself to three young women in a park. Investigation revealed that although the boy's transgressions never had been brought to the attention of the police before, certain neighbors had complained of his behavior to his parents for the three years preceding the incident in question. Medical help was not spontaneously sought by the moderately wealthy parents, both of whom were active in civic organizations.

Both parents were seen separately and together diagnostically. The father was humiliated and filled with rage and contempt toward the boy.

"I've been telling his mother for years that that kid would come to a bad end with her coddling and drooling over him like a spoiled pup. I despise her youngest brother, who was pampered and coddled by his mother — he isn't worth a darn. Of course, I admit his father never paid an hour's attention to him in his life, and then probably only to pull a few strings with politicians to bail him out of jams. I know my wife has been ashamed a hundred times of her brother, but she gets furious if I say one word of truth about the bum."

The mother was first interviewed by a man. The interviewer was immediately aware of her frank, rather intimate, seductive approach. No sign of anxiety was apparent in this woman.

When asked what she thought about the immediate problem, she said, "I don't understand Don — we have always been completely frank with each other about everything, but when I try to talk to him about this, he won't talk."

When the interviewer remained silent, she went on, "He is our only son and so many terrible mistakes were made with my youngest brother that I vowed to keep things friendly and frank with our boy. I've answered all his questions and he has told me everything until now. I admit he didn't tell me about these other things with women, and I didn't talk to him because I knew he would tell me in due time — my husband was so angry that I wouldn't let him talk to Don, but I can't trust my husband — he gets so angry and rigid with the child."

At this point the psychiatrist asked the mother if she could give some elaboration of how frank and confidential the boy had been with her. This opened a recital of wholly unconscious tragic seduction and unhealthy intimacy between this mother and Don. There were no restrictions on nudity, or the bathroom, and talk was endless about sexual matters. The mother went into great detail with the boy about her own sexual life, to the point of revealing frequency of intercourse, her husband's hostile demands, and her rearing concerning the duties of a wife.

The 15-year-old daughter, from 7 years on, would have none of this frankness; she demanded privacy in the bathroom and would not be lured into sexual discussions.

The father frequently rebuked the mother for carrying on her "long harangues" with the boy and shouted that he would be better off "learning stuff the hard way on the streets," as he did.

There is no need to include the boy's great detail in describing his mother's appearance, her breasts and other anatomic attributes; these attitudes of her son were given by the mother with a dreamy, pleasurable expression. She herself expanded at length about her son's fine physique, including what she called his "beautiful masculine endowment." The seduction between mother and son was obvious to any listener.

But how did this boy come to choose exhibitionism as a means of discharging his rage and sexual drive? The mother fostered and showed the keenest interest in exhibiting herself and in looking at the nude boy from his earliest years. Until Don was 13 he and the mother often showered together, especially when the father was away on trips. The mother commented, "Loneliness brings one closer to a child."

The boy hated his father; as this mutual dislike mounted, Don and the mother became even closer. Subsequent interviews with the mother revealed a most unhappy marriage, the husband being engrossed in business as well as openly flirtatious with other women; the mother was humiliated, but unable, because of her own background and conflicts, truly to enter a love relationship with her husband.

Don, a handsome, strongly built boy, was barely defending himself against murderous feelings toward both parents. His identifications with them were so confused as to suggest that no treatment was safe without his initial removal from home.

Intensive therapy for Don, his mother and father was necessary.

TREATMENT OF PERVERSIONS

We shall give only the briefest summary of basic ideas concerning the collaborative therapy of a case of perversion. More detailed material is now in press.

In this group of cases it is imperative to have preliminary interviews with parents before the child is ever seen, since these children are even more withdrawn, sullen and uncommunicative than many of the other delinquents. The initial contacts divulge the basic clinical data, exposing unconscious seduction and unwitting condoning of the perverse outlet. Such material is used as the steppingstone to the therapy of parents and child as well, making possible the enlistment into treatment of a child who might otherwise be lost.

During the interviews with the parent it is possible to define two sets of clues; the first, seductive; the second, permissive. The first include incidents and conversations which reveal current, unconscious, ambivalent seduction, such as sleeping with the child, nudity or excessive freedom in the bathroom. The second group of clues consists of evidences of parental permissiveness, distinguishing the special form of permitted perversion or abnormal sexuality. With the interpretation of specific examples of unconscious seduction and unconscious permission, the dynamic therapy of parent and child begins.

These are in part acting-out problems between all participants. Early limits must be set with parents and child about the current ambivalent seduction, whether it be sleeping together, bathing together, mutual bathroom gratifications or nudities. From the child's point of view, when such seduction ceases he does not have so strongly the original need to act out through the perverse outlet. From the parents' point of view, as soon as a limit is set on the parents' seductive behavior toward the child, great tension will develop in the parent stemming from his own poorly integrated sexual drives and the associated hostility. This must be very actively analyzed in the transference. Usually, the first evidence of the tension in the transference is acute anger of the parent toward the therapist. As this is absorbed by the therapist in a manner quite different from the par-

ents' experience with their own parents, the transference deepens, and analysis of the distorted genital and pregenital life of the patient is under way.

As treatment progresses, if the child continues perverse acting out, it means either that seduction has transpired at home or that the child's therapist has appeared as a seductive threat. In the first instance, information from the combined treatment hours permits more definite limit-setting. In the second, transference material must be more actively analyzed. With etiology more explicit, experimental technical modifications in the treatment of adult overt homosexuals have been presented in a paper now in press (8).

When the acting out then seems well controlled in all patients, analysis proceeds as in any complicated neurosis, with intensive therapy for the resolution of all the complex pregenital fixations inherent in these disorders.

SUMMARY

In this communication we have discussed the etiology of individual antisocial acting out, and of sexual aberrations. Latent unconscious impulses to steal, set fires and murder, as well as fantasies about such practices as homosexuality and transvestitism, are frequently seen in many patients. We have been concerned with defining the specific stimuli to their becoming overt.

Antisocial acting out is seen as a super-ego defect which stems from unconscious parental initiation and fostering because of poorly integrated forbidden impulses in the parents. These impulses, and their permission to be acted upon, are communicated usually unconsciously to the child. In his acting out the child affords to the parents vicarious gratification for their own forbidden impulses, and concomitantly satisfies parental destructive feelings toward the child. Such behavior is destructive toward both the child's and parent's ego organization, as well as toward society, unless adequate collaborative therapy is instituted.

Sexual aberrations are seen to develop as a result of ego adaptation to highly specific, often unconscious, family attitudes impinging on the child; these attitudes subtly coerce and distort the child's psychosexual development. The parent, because of his own problems, unconsciously seduces the child, then sets *genital* limits and unwittingly defines the direction for regressed perverse outlets.

The emphasis of this paper has been on factors in etiology. The basic tenets important in intensive collaborative therapy of parents and children stem from a more rational concept of etiology. Our thesis necessitates the early establishment of definite limits to behavior, the timing of which varies with the case. As has been seen, the concepts emerging in this paper place the emphasis in acting-out problems on a pathologic super-ego which is weak in certain specific areas; this is in contrast to the neurotic super-ego, which is too punitive.

It is the responsibility of psychiatrists to resolve the confusion in the treatment of individuals with weak super-ego structure. To be sure, we are cognizant of the confusion which accompanies transition from puritanic mores of a culture to greater individuation. But it is not alone this transition which has led to many improper treatment plans, and far too permissive, ill-defined, so-called preventive psychiatric suggestions to parents. With clearer definition of etiologic factors in this group of patients, we are in a better position to be definitive about when we should be permissive of anger in order to offset neurosis, and when we must be prohibitive of amoral impulses in order to prevent acting out. No one should give tacit consent to behavior which acts against the individual's best interests in our society. Parents increasingly can be helped to absorb and to channel in constructive fashion the child's hostilities when society's prohibitions are imposed emphatically. When psychiatrists achieve greater clarity, parents, educators and those executing the law will function with less confusion.*

REFERENCES

1. AICHHORN, AUGUST. Wayward Youth. (Transl. from 2nd German ed.) Viking Press, New York, 1935.

2. ALEXANDER, FRANZ, and WILLIAM HEALY. Roots of Crime. Knopf, New York, 1935.

3. EMCH, MINNA. "On the 'Need to Know' as Related to Identification and Acting Out." Internat. J. Psa., 25: 13–19, 1944.

4. GARDNER, GEORGE E. Personal communication to the authors.

5. HEALY, WILLIAM, and AUGUSTA F. BRONNER. New Light on Delinquency and its Treatment. Yale Univ. Press, New Haven, 1936.

6. JOHNSON, ADELAIDE M. "Collaborative Psychotherapy: Team Setting," in Psychoanalysis and Social Work (Marcel Heiman, Ed.), pp. 79–108. Internat. Univ. Press, New York, 1953.

7. JOHNSON, ADELAIDE M., and S. A. SZUREK. "The Genesis of Antisocial Acting Out in Children and Adults." Psa. Quart., 21: 323–343, 1952.

8. KOLB, L. C., and ADELAIDE M. JOHNSON. "Etiology of Overt Homosexuality and the Need for Therapeutic Modification." Psa. Quart., in press.

9. LITIN, E. M., MARY E. GIFFIN, and ADELAIDE M. JOHNSON. "Parental Influence in Unusual Sexual Behavior in Children." Psa. Quart., in press.

10. REICH, WILHELM. Der triebhafte Charakter. Internat. Psa. Verlag, Vienna, 1925.

11. SCHMIDEBERG, MELITTA. "The Mode of Operation of Psychoanalytic Therapy." Internat. J. Psa., 19: 314, 1938.

12. SZUREK, S. A. "Notes on the Genesis of Psychopathic Personality Trends." Psychiatry, 5: 1–6, 1942.

13. WEISS, EDUARDO. "Emotional Memories and Acting Out." Psa. Quart., 11: 477–492, 1942.

149

Character Structure of a Rejected Child *

Frederick Rosenheim

Cases of children who lacked love in the early years of their lives, though with varying degrees of severity, are common in every child guidance clinic. In general, the nature of the disturbance produced is well known. These individuals have never been loved and have never learned to love; they lack ability to establish relationships with people; there is a lack of real responsiveness and affection. In an essential sense they are unapproachable, though this may not always seem to be the case on the surface. Consequently, it is very difficult to modify them. It is hoped that this account of the analysis of a boy who was not loved will present a fuller picture of the character dis-

* Discussions of this article have been omitted. They will be found in 24 Am. J. Orthopsychiatry (1954), 685–696. — Ed.

* Reprinted from 12 Am. J. Orthopsychiatry (1942), 486–494. Presented at the 1942 meeting. Used by permission of the author and the publisher.

turbance and of what the process of modification of this really involves.

HISTORY

When the analysis was begun, after a year of unsuccessful psychotherapy, James was 13 years old. For some time prior to his birth his mother had been ill and had been advised not to become pregnant. She did so, nevertheless, because of her desire to have a girl. When our patient was born she was disappointed and would not look at him. Her illness became aggravated, and for three years she remained an invalid at home, spending most of her time in bed. The boy saw her only rarely. He was scarcely permitted to remain in the house because of the need for quiet.

We lack the details of his developmental history. He was not breast fed. A good deal of his care was in the hands of a next door neighbor in whose house he spent much time.

The father was very bitter to this boy who was the cause of his wife's ill health and unhappiness. Severe with the boy, he often whipped and scolded him.

When James was three, his mother died. For the next nine years a succession of housekeepers appeared on the scene, none of whom was in any way satisfactory. It seems extraordinary that the father succeeded in picking women who were abnormal and completely lacking in any capacity to be affectionate with James. One housekeeper seduced him into sexual play, one stole, one drank, one became psychotic and finally committed suicide. During these years the father spent little time at home and continued in his blustering, severe manner toward the boy. Attempting to teach James to swim, he threw him into a pond. James looked upon this as an attempt on his life.

When James was twelve years old, his father remarried. The stepmother was an intelligent, understanding, capable woman with a sincere desire to help James. She, herself, was helped tremendously by her numerous sessions with the social worker. During the analysis when the father repeatedly threatened to have the boy sent away, it was only the stepmother's firmness that prevented this.

The Problem. When James began the analysis, he was in good health, of average intelligence, rather slim, with sharp features, somewhat unprepossessing because of moderately severe acne, but more so because of a hard, grim look. There were numerous complaints about him from almost every source — that he did not do his work in school, was inattentive, deceitful, a pest, always in minor difficulties of one kind or another, such as petty stealing. He was always irritable, moody, extraordinarily unreasonable, defiant, and quarrelsome. He had no hobbies, no special interests, no special ability at any games. He was friendless. Everyone who knew him was markedly impressed by his disagreeableness. His father wanted him out of the home, the principal and teachers would have wanted him out of the school. He never smiled.

The Hater. James spent the first six months of analysis in hating. Everyone was against him, everyone was always wrong and he was always right. He never budged the slightest from his position of complete justification at all times. He would never confess any of his thefts no matter how strong the evidence was against him. On the contrary, he would indignantly complain of the injustice of the accusations of his stealing. He was very unreasonable, would neglect his work and then complain that the teachers didn't do their work properly. He was almost like a paranoiac, persecuted by all and in turn hating everyone. He talked about his wishes to kill and shoot and murder; often felt like shooting up the world. His only prized possessions were a dozen or so toy guns of different descriptions, which he sometimes brought to the clinic. He would make figures of different people in drawings or clay — Hitler, his teacher, his principal — then viciously attack them with BB rifle, hammer, knife, scissors. With relish and venom he would cut a clay figure apart, slicing the head off, gouging the eyes out, chopping it, squashing it, throwing it violently around the room. He would have me join him in some of these games on a competitive basis in which the loser was to die. The figure would be set up as a target, and the winner was the one who scored the most hits. He would burn a pencil or an eraser, shoot at a lighted candle with a water-pistol. He brought fire-crackers to the clinic to blow it up, chemicals to make poison gas, and referred to himself as a demon. He often interrupted his play to go to the toilet. Frequently he exhibited a deliberate stutter best described as a biting of words. He was always grim, hard, rigid and unsmiling.

He showed several reactions to his hostile feelings. As already indicated, they were justified. He saw himself as a small edition of Hitler, a really reasonable man who only wanted what had been taken away from him and whom no one would let live in peace. Though much of his hostility was a reaction to his having been so deprived, it was more than that. It was necessary for him to hate. The fuller elaboration of this, however, must be reserved for later. Also, he reacted with guilt, expressed in a variety of ways. Not being tall enough to grasp the strap in the subway easily, he carried a handle with him which he used to grasp the strap. He once made an offhand remark that this was a nice invention to hang himself, immediately after many expressions of hatred and desires to kill people. On several occasions when dismembering a clay figure, he cut his hand. There was considerable fear of retaliation. A typical expression was in his immobilizing me with a ray gun. The hostility had a protective quality, too. He told a story of the skunk who automatically reacted to the approach of any human being by emitting his terrible odor to keep himself protected.

No one was exempt from his expression of hate. He hated his stepmother and father. When they married, James felt that instead of his having gotten a mother, his father had gotten a wife. He elaborated a long story of a boy whose mother had died, and who lived on with his father for some years until eventually the boy married, and not the father — the opposite of what had occurred in reality. Many of the figures he killed in fantasy were father-figures — Hitler, Stalin, Mussolini, Roosevelt.

Insight. Only after this preliminary six month period was some of his rigidity broken down, and for the first time he expressed an awareness of a problem and of a need to have something worked out. He told many stories of projects of his which always failed. An airplane model would crash, for example. He complained that he had no talents, that he couldn't do anything well so that other kids did not like him and did not want him to join them in play. "Wherever I go, I make a poor impression. I do everything wrong, I steal in school, I do everything wrong in church. I strike out

in the baseball game in gym. Even here I do everything wrong. (Referring to a ceiling light he had accidentally broken by throwing a ball.) You must think I'm a louse." Nevertheless, his expressions of hostility did not cease. He even told a story of the Martian whose interests in some way had been damaged by something which had accidentally occurred on the earth, but who nevertheless devoted himself to the pursuit of destroying the earth.

It became possible for the first time to offer him interpretations on the basis of material he brought in, especially about his desire to have his stepmother's interest, attention and affection, and his resentment when these were given to his father. He did not express appreciation when his father and stepmother made arrangements for him to go to summer camp. Instead he looked upon it as an unloving act in which he was being pushed out. On some occasions when the family went on a picnic, he made himself very disagreeable by annoying behavior. It was easy to show him from his acts that he wished to come between stepmother and father. At times some improvement was noted in his behavior, and he had the experience unusual for him, of having the principal commend him. On the whole, however, he remained as disagreeable and annoying as ever. His parting from me at the beginning of the summer was a casual one. During the summer he got along very well. No complaints whatsoever were made regarding his behavior.

The Oedipus Complex. The analysis was resumed after the summer, and in the course of the next month the oedipus situation was clearly revealed. He had a variety of fantasies about his father: he should work in some distant town, be able to come home only weekends, should join the army or the Foreign Legion and, finally, father should die, be struck by lightning or killed by an assassin, and James could then have stepmother for himself. This was also expressed in the transference situation. Curiosity was expressed about my wife, whether she was pretty, and a fantasy of punching me in the nose, knocking me down and rendering me dead to the world for three hours. He showed very marked reaction to the emergence of this material. There was fear of retribution. Suffering from a slight cold, he was afraid that it might progress to pneumonia and cause his death. He misinterpreted a telephone conversation I had, thought that I was communicating with his parents to reveal what he had expressed. He made all kinds of attempts at denial, that I twisted everything, that I misinterpreted things.

I told a story of a moving picture he had seen about "Mr. Average Man," who was used as a tool by an unscrupulous individual who tried to find out what Mr. Average Man's likes, dislikes, and opinions were in order to capitalize on these with advertisers, manufacturers, and so on. The unscrupulous individual even arranged a mock bombing to see how Mr. Average Man would react to the outbreak of war. The picture ended with the unscrupulous man receiving his just deserts, incarceration in the psychopathic ward, while Mr. Average Man happily married his sweetheart. It was his way of accusing me of distorting things, and his way of reassuring himself and minimizing things. After all, he was only an average boy, there wasn't anything wrong. The moving picture had been comical and he could make a joke of it. Even the hostility was not true; it had only been simulated and, after all, was a product of my mind and not his.

He hid his hostility toward his father behind the hostility toward his stepmother. The latter hostility he could justify to himself — stepmother was mean. Everyone knew that a stepmother was mean, and it was only right to wish her dead. He could not accept, however, the wish to have his father die in order to have stepmother for himself. It was harder for him to justify that; to lose the justification for hating implied the undermining of his whole pattern of life. He had to hate, and it was easy to see from much of his behavior that he provoked aggression and hostility in others in order to justify his attitude. To lose some of his justification for hating meant the temptation to stop hating and to attempt human relationships, which we shall see, was fraught with anxiety. When he could not altogether disclaim some hostility toward his father, he attempted to put it on another basis, a justifiable one. For example, that his father refused to allow him to play his radio at night. He told me of a vaudeville actor who had appeared at the school assembly and who answered questions put to him by singing appropriate songs. He had answered the question, "Did you commit the murder?" by singing, "No, no, a thousand times, no, I'd rather die than say yes." He projected his evil intent; it wasn't that he wanted father to die so that he could have stepmother for himself, but that stepmother wanted him to die so that she could have father for herself.

As time went on he began to recognize this hostility within himself for what it was and tried to cast it out. He went through a period of housecleaning in which he fixed up his room at home and the drawer in my office in which he kept his belongings. Among these was an electric light bulb he had stolen a long time ago in a subway train, of which he now rid himself. He brought me candy and gifts, and proposed at a class meeting that a cake should be given the principal on his birthday. He joined the church where he read the Scriptures and worked hard to win a Sunday School prize. He was praised by the minister and rewarded with a ticket to the Rodeo. He spoke of inventions he contemplated making to render harmless, guns, bullets, torpedoes. All wars would stop at once because his invention would render harmless all the terrible implements of warfare. There would be only good feelings between people. He even contemplated a machine which would do away with bad feelings There would be no wars, no gangsters, no police, no locks and, incidentally, no psychiatrists.

During the entire period in which this material was worked out, one of his most frequent games with me was a guessing game in which he tried in every way to outwit me.

Infantile Omnipotence. At this point in the analysis, about the fourteenth or fifteenth month, a definite change in James was noted. His character had taken on a softer, less rigid quality; he became more reasonable. He talked a lot about a moving picture he had seen called, "Love Thy Neighbor." When the pupils of his school organized a strike, he refused to join. For the first time in his life he told jokes and laughed. He began to approach me in a warmer, more intimate way. When I had to go away for a few days, he was very much interested, wanted to know if I would take my children. He showed his disappointment and resentment at my leaving him by misbehaving during the time I was away. His approach to a human being for the first time now definitely presented itself to him as a temptation, but a temptation that aroused a great deal of anxiety. He had hated, for one reason, to keep himself from this temptation. After all, he had been born into a hostile world, and from his standpoint all human beings were dangerous. His position was much like that of Robinson Crusoe on his desert island, yearning in his loneliness for human companionship, but fleeing in terror from the humans who had come to the island because they were dangerous cannibals.

It was fascinating to watch his approach to me, calling upon all his infantile powers to protect himself. He brought in rubber bands with which he would shoot paper wads around the room and at me; he would bring in longer and longer elastics, tying many rubber bands together. Instead of paper wads he used canvas slugs and shot from all positions. Finally he would bend down and shoot out the wads from behind. Often he interrupted his shooting to go to the toilet to defecate. He would also bend down and throw clay balls from behind. He called himself the human slingshot. Sometimes he put the elastic between his teeth and would shoot out that way. He indulged in a lot of biting of words and belching. From clay he made a long water chute which became his magic water-gun and would kill whoever was touched by the water. As he played this game, he would cry out, "Watch my magic." This was his new hobby, magic. He became a great magician, would come to the office with his pockets loaded with all kinds of magic tricks he had bought, illusions of all kinds, disappearing coin tricks, and many others. He showed his prowess, his invulnerability, his magic, his omnipotence. In all the games we played he had to overcome me and actually succeeded in many. He exhibited all kinds of feats of strength and power. He thought he could lift my desk, an extremely heavy one, with one hand; believed he had a means of lifting a chair with one finger. He would throw a ball of clay in the air, then as it came down, hit it back up into the air again with his fists. Now he was Superman, stopping a bomb by catching it and throwing it back at the plane from which it had fallen. He became the Lone Ranger and often shouted, "Heigh-ho, Silver," as a sign of his invulnerability. The Lone Ranger, too, is a kind of great magician who can extricate him-self from all kinds of dangerous situations. An interesting bit of acting out occurred at home. Alone in the house one afternoon, he set something to cook on the stove and then went upstairs to the toilet where he read stories about Superman, defecating in the meantime. He remained in the toilet a long time, long enough for the water in the pot to evaporate and the house to fill with smoke and odor.

We begin now to get a better picture of just what was this boy's position. Deprived of warmth and affection, he hated. His hostile wishes, through fear of retaliation, only made him fear his environment all the more. His growing hate induced guilt feelings. He felt responsible for some of the hostility shown him in that in some way he had been partly responsible for his mother's death. He had eventually to provoke hostility in others to justify his own feelings which otherwise would have become insupportable. The provocation of hostility in others which brought about punishment satisfied a need resulting from his guilt. More than all this, his hating, like the skunk's mechanism, was a means of keeping people away and of keeping himself from being tempted to approach anybody. He did not wish to be tempted into friendliness. To be reminded always that people hated him, he insured by his own conduct. To the little child, mother is a source not only of love, but of protection; she is the source of the child's strength. Lacking this and, even worse, mother being a source of hostility rather than protection, it is no wonder that James isolated himself behind the protecting barrier of his infantile armamentarium. So, in his omnipotence, he dwelt alone. This could be seen clearly in his approach to me. He showed me his weapons, his number one gun, his number two gun, his teeth. He was the Lone Ranger, Superman, the human slingshot, the maker of poison gas, the magician.

With all this he continued his approach to me. At the end of one hour, as we walked to the door together, he made an affectionate gesture toward me for the first time — he put his arm on my shoulder. It was only a tentative gesture and aroused anxiety. He quickly withdrew his arm to show me a jiu jitsu hold. Again he had a need to become invulnerable and all-powerful. During this same period he had me help him make a plane and on many occasions would revert to baby talk. In asking me to hand him a tool, for example, he would say, "Pass the honey, sugar," and "pretty please." Extraordinary expressions indeed from a boy who had been such an intense hater. He showed a definite exuberance, and it was reported by the others in the clinic that he showed a definite change. Previously he would spend his time in the waiting-room reading comic books. Now he talked, joked, smiled, and was friendly. It is of interest that only in this phase, where his deepest anxieties were aroused, did he come late to appointments.

The Bid for Affection. There now occurred a very interesting phase in which he became the auctioneer. Before almost every hour he would go to auction places nearby and watch proceedings with great interest. He told me with pleased enthusiasm how much he learned there: to sell, to auction, to make people like and want and offer a lot for what you have. He acted this out successfully by bringing magazines to the clinic and selling them to people there. In his hours with me he would play the auctioneer game and eagerly ask, "What am I bid?" I would always answer appropriately that he was worth a great deal. He would jokingly play the auction game in foreign languages, pretending he was able to speak them. It was as though he were grandiloquently announcing that he was able to put himself across in any language; in other words, that he was accepted and desired anywhere and everywhere, a kind of universal acceptance. Several times he sang a song:

There'll be a change in the weather,
There'll be a change in the sky,
There'll be a change in the sea,
There'll be a change in me.

Evidently the change in him was manifested outside, too, because he would tell me with satisfaction to how many places he had been invited and of the friends he made, including a girl. Our previous separation for the summer vacation had brought about no reaction in him whatever. Now, when I had to leave him for a week, he showed marked reaction. When I returned, he said he did not want to come back and had all sorts of bad news for me; father had threatened to put him out of the house, he had almost been expelled from

school, had been put off the neighborhood playground. He did not express these complaints with hatred and resentment, but rather in a pathetic, appealing kind of way — he had felt himself deserted by me. He wanted to know again, for example, whether I had taken my children on the trip.

The stories he brought in to the hours were of significance. There was a book called *The Story of Hitler, the Man of Hate,* and he spoke about how wonderful it would be to cure Hitler. He enjoyed reading love stories. For quite a time he would bring a book and have me spend the whole hour reading it to him, bringing his chair close to mine. The book he had me read for him hour after hour, *The Medico of Painted Springs,* was the story of a young doctor who tries to bring about peace between sheep herders and cattle men in a Western community.

Just before the next summer vacation began he showed his feelings very strongly at the impending separation. In the fall, a little less than two years after I had begun my work with him, he expressed a desire to come in not more than once a week. In part, perhaps, this was resistance, but in part, too, it represented his ability to participate in various activities with which the analysis would have interfered. The analysis was not continued, but he has since been seen occasionally. Six months have elapsed; general reports are quite satisfying. His mark in conduct in school had always been the lowest possible. In the last six months of the analysis his conduct mark had gradually gotten better until, at promotion time, he received an A. He spent the summer in camp, first as a camper, and then because he did so well, was given a job as swimming counselor. When his father and stepmother visited him, they were agreeably surprised because he seemed so much more mature; he was generous, offered them little things, foregoing them himself. He became interested in a girl at camp and then in the Fall developed normal adolescent interests in swing music, dances, bowling, and hockey.

Though the contrast in his character is very marked, I cannot feel that he has become fully normal. Perhaps it is safe enough to say that without the help afforded him by the analysis he might have developed the most serious kind of disturbance, perhaps permanent, in his adolescence. The important point is how he will respond to events that occur in the future. Perhaps he will continue on the healthful road and increase his capacity to sustain sincere relationships with human beings, or there may always remain some limitation in this regard, and perhaps it may even be rather severe. I have already had opportunity to observe his reaction to several crises; once a girl friend suddenly refused to see him any more because she had heard stories of how crazy he used to act in school. I could follow his temporary regression. He would come in and twist my gooseneck lamp, talk about his ability to twist iron and steel, and about being a magician again, but this passed. He did not lose his confidence and soon found new friends. It is important that his attitude toward what had happened was a reasonable one. He was resentful, but didn't become a hater again, nor did he fail to acknowledge that his behavior in the past had been bad. He continued to live in the same household with a father who may at the slightest provocation spill over all his still existing rage against the boy, so that unfortunately his home situation is still an unpleasant one.

In a brief and very condensed presentation of a great deal of material it is inevitable that some distortions should occur and that much relevant and significant material should be omitted. It is perhaps easier to understand now why the prognosis in these cases is so poor and why it is so difficult to modify them. We can understand, for example, why the efforts of well intentioned people to help these children with love, affection and kindness are met only with rebuffs and perhaps even worse demonstrations of misconduct. Psychotherapy fails very often because in a sense that is also a kindness, an interest, a token of affection which must often be spurned by increased demonstration of hatred. We have seen from this study that this particular type of child is struggling against temptation to become friendly with anyone, and that he reacts to the friendly approaches of others with manifestations of anxiety, increased use of defensive measures, and a further retreat. This case only confirms the well known impression of the difficulties involved in treatment, but it makes this clearer and perhaps indicates that with a great deal of effort some amelioration is still possible.

150

Psychotherapy on Juvenile Delinquents *

P. R. Newkirk

Psychiatric cooperation at reformatories and penitentiaries is on the increase. The task of the psychiatrist at a penal institution consists however, of classification mainly. This paper will try to prove that there is a definite place for therapy within the scope of penology: therapy here means psychotherapy. There are many methods of psychotherapy and to make my point clear, I am forced to say something about the history of my endeavor in this field.

Originally active in research work, I took up internal medicine. After 1920, I also became interested in psychotherapy. Orthodox psychoanalysis did not fit into my general practice, but I found that a short analysis followed by suggestive methods, particularly post-hypnotic suggestion, was a practical and effective treatment of many neuroses. I even became convinced that suggestion is the main active principle of all psychotherapy; no psychotherapeutic method can achieve anything without the influence of one mind on the other. For six years I taught psychotherapy within the scope of internal medicine at a European Medical School. It so happened that prosecuting attorneys and lawyers referred incriminated subjects for examination and treatment before the case was taken into court. Kleptomaniacs, sex offenders, and forgers were prevalent. Therapeutically, I could not find much difference between delinquent and non-delinquent neurotics although incriminated delinquents were generally more accessible to suggestive treatment than other groups.

* Reprinted from 34 J. Crim. L. and Criminology (1943–44), 100–105. Used by permission of the author and the publisher. See, also, P. R. Newkirk, "Psychopathic Delinquents," 14 Diseases of the Nervous System (1953); and P. R. Newkirk, "Psychopathic Traits Are Inheritable," 18 Diseases of the Nervous System (1957). — Ed.

In this country I found a surprising prejudice against suggestive methods. Hypnosis seemed to be abhorred by the medical profession. Its abuse by fakers and quacks, silly publicity, and perhaps disinclination against imposing one's will power on another subject, seemed motives for this antagonism. In fact, it is quite possible that ruthless hypnotists may take material and even emotional advantage of their medium. All these objections, however, are irrelevant if suggestive therapy is applied to delinquents at an institution by a psychotherapist who is at the full-time service of the State and acts under the eyes of the authorities.

It cannot be denied that innumerable neurotics have been treated successfully by suggestive methods since ancient times and certainly during the last one hundred years since adequate methods have been developed by Braid, Charcot, Liébault, and Forel.

Incidents of crime among juveniles of the same stock are, in the United States, several times higher than in Scandinavia. This high juvenile criminality in the United States is due to the unfavorable influence of poor neighborhoods, bad company, and broken homes on the subjects. If this is true, part of the delinquents at least, should be accessible to counter-suggestions.

During two and one-half years at the Northern State Hospital at Sedro-Woolley, Washington, and some observations at a reformatory, I came to the conclusion that after elimination of morons, severe psychopaths, and other constitutionally antisocial individuals, there remain about ten to fifteen percent of juvenile delinquents who could be prospective candidates for psychotherapy. Intelligence, suggestibility and personal confidence are the requirements. Two examples may show what psychotherapy can achieve:

A: Under suspended sentence
B: After minimum sentence has been passed

First Case

This seventeen-year-old boy, G. J., was referred for observation to the Northern State Hospital on March 5, 1941, by the Court, after having committed numerous homosexual acts, some of them bordering on male prostitution. Although this boy may have a constitutional homosexual trend, his perversion was started by seduction at the age of six by an older boy. There is no indication of endocrine abnormality in this case. The boy's sister was a paroled patient of this hospital and had been admitted in 1926, age 13, because of kleptomania and sexual promiscuity. When re-examined, she confirmed the rule that all such female delinquents are abnormally suggestible. So her brother was experimentally subjected to hypnotic examination and treatment, also. He was found to be an even better medium than his sister. During a period of three months at the hospital he obeyed post-hypnotic orders with the greatest precision. Given the suggestion not to leave his ward without the special permission of the psychotherapist, he disobeyed all orders of other persons, to pass the door of the ward for any purpose whatsoever. He stole small coins and chewing gum several days after pertinent suggestions. He confessed, and made excuses after having received new hypnotic orders. After receiving pertinent suggestions he became nauseated when the word "sodomy," was mentioned, and questions such as "Do you have many friends?" made him terminate the conversation angrily. After he had been tested thoroughly it was proposed to the Court that this minor be paroled to the farm of his parents under the condition that, (a) he keep away from his former town of residence; (b) abstain from all abnormal sexual actions and that, (c) he appear at the hospital at regular intervals for treatment.

The Court's sentence was one to ten years in the reformatory but the sentence was suspended under the condition that he would live up to the above enumerated directions. No complaints have been heard for one year and a half. As the community is comparatively small and the boy well-known to all police officers and many other persons, it can be assumed as proven, that he has not associated with male persons outside of his family. He has a girl friend with whom he has been seen frequently by unprejudiced observers, and he is planning on marriage.

Thus far, I have not met anyone who claimed that the same result would have been obtained under standard management. The method applied was the following:

1. The delinquent was isolated at his farm home with gradually increasing privileges, such

as visiting movies in the vicinity but not in his former residence.

2. He was kept at work — first on his father's farm; later at a plant.

3. Follow-up suggestions were given, at first every two, later every four weeks. Theoretically, psychotherapy could be continued to the limit of the maximum sentence of ten years. According to the sentence, the case will be expunged from the record after five years of good behavior.

SECOND CASE

The second case, W. H., is the 'black sheep' of his reputable family. Up to the second year of high school, he seemed quite normal. He was good natured, easily influenced by others. Lack of will power was noticed by his mother, his school principal, and his first employer. He was sentenced to the reformatory in 1937 and served two years for forgery and carnal knowledge. After his parole, he resumed the practice of writing bad checks and on December 6, 1941, was sentenced to twenty years in the penitentiary. From there he was re-transferred to the reformatory on May 15, 1942. At the reformatory, W. H. complained of various intestinal ailments. He ate little; lost weight; was deeply depressed and on August 18, 1942, he was transferred to the Northern State Hospital for observation and incidental treatment. No organic changes were discovered. A psychiatric examination revealed all his ailments to be the somatic expression of despair and despondency because of his ruined life. This diagnosis justified the application of psychotherapy which was effective immediately. W. H. recovered rapidly and began helping the attendants on his ward. This was encouraged by suggestions. His work and endeavor were excellent. Secondary suggestions were never to leave the ward without personal permission of his physician and never to write his name in longhand but to print it only. The work which he did, meant no coddling of the delinquent: he cleaned and bedded untidy mental patients and he helped the charge attendants at first without enjoying any privileges. Later on he had ground parole. He never failed to return on the minute after his hour's walk.

The state hospitals in Washington are open to committed psychotics, and to observation cases for a period of ninety days only. Because of these rules, W. H.'s treatment had to be terminated after ninety days and he was returned to the reformatory. The work that he did at the hospital was successful and to his liking and he could have continued with this for years while being under psychotherapeutic control and permanent observation of fellow-employees. It is easy to predict that at the reformatory, this boy will, under the suggestive influence of energetic fellow-prisoners, remain what he is now, — a recidivist.

Psychotherapy cannot be effective on subjects who are serving fixed sentences at a penal institution. Suggestive psychotherapy must cooperate with a regime granting the subject increasing liberty and opportunity to prove his reformation. There is practically no danger of escape. Persons, well tested under this kind of therapy, are acting as though on an invisible leash. Physical restraint is replaced by more humane suggestive restraint.

A number of young men and boys were tested with regard to their suggestibility. Two of them had been transferred to the Northern State Hospital for observation in 1940, because of prison neurosis. All prison neurotics are highly suggestible because prison neurosis is the result of auto-suggestion while under emotional strain. Both were excellent mediums. After the termination of their observation they had to be returned to the reformatory and contact with them was lost. They are behaving well at the reformatory and would be candidates to test the psychotherapeutic parole method which I am recommending.

Experimental work seems to prove that the average juvenile delinquents are neither more nor less suggestible than non-delinquents. Suggestibility is, however, not merely a constitutional and fixed quality of the mind. Persons who suffer physically or emotionally and long for relief are much more accessible to psychotherapy than individuals who undergo suggestion for experiment's sake. Even the initial proposition of psychotherapeutic treatment to a delinquent is most revealing. Those who have a genuine desire to reform are eager to be helped and are immediately ready to cooperate. Others, like alcoholics and addicts, hesitate and make excuses. Without being able to prove this statistically, I found that among juvenile delinquents, there are two psychological extremes:

Those who are less than normally and those who are overly suggestible.

The first group acts antisocially because they follow their own pattern of life. The second group of juveniles, if growing up in a decent environment, may not cause any trouble or at least not come to the attention of the court. If they are products of divorced marriages or living under conditions of poverty among amoral companions, they are prone to become delinquents.

Only the highly suggestible group is accessible to suggestive psychotherapy. The prerequisite for psychotherapy is therefore psychiatric diagnosis and classification. Morons, schizoids, antisocial psychopaths, and a-suggestibles should be eliminated. Forgers, automobile thieves, alcohol and sex delinquents are the most promising groups, but good prospective subjects are found among juvenile–hold-up men, too. The type of crime is not as important as the finding of the psychiatric examination. Hypnotic tests must then reveal whether the subject is not only suggestible but whether he executes post-hypnotic orders. I admit that this kind of work calls for psychiatric as well as psychological experience and that its basis is careful diagnosis. The preliminary tests should be performed within an institution. All subjects are given hypnotic orders not to talk about the treatment and are forbidden to accept hypnotic orders from anyone except their physician. It is the general experience in psychotherapy, that both these orders are obeyed.

The obstacles to planned psychotherapy on juvenile delinquents are neither to be found in difficulties of technique nor does the method meet with opposition from the delinquents. The difficulties are due to laws and regulations based originally on theories of punishment and determent. Psychotherapy does not agree with standardized imprisonment, but it calls for free occupation under psychotherapeutic guidance and in the morally best environment that can be found under the circumstances. An ideal solution, for example, is work at a mental institution where gentle treatment of helpless patients and work on the ward under discipline, are helpful towards the aim of re-education. A practical plan could be: All juvenile delinquents pass an observation clinic conducted by a psychiatrist in cooperation with a sociologist. The recommendation of this unit should carry weight with the judge and the parole board.

Individuals found accessible to psychotherapy, would be tested thoroughly and should then receive a suspended sentence, like G. J. After termination of observation they could live with their family or at a home, or as workers at a state hospital. They should appear for psychotherapy as ordered. Their liberty must be restricted by suggestive orders. In case of disobedience, arrest and transfer to the reformatory would be the consequence. It is my experience that psychotherapy is accepted readily under the natural fear of the law. In other cases several months at a reformatory would raise the individual's willingness to accept foreign suggestion for his own benefit. Parole should be granted only after a period of psychotherapeutic treatment.

The legal question might be raised whether juvenile delinquents may be held under foreign influence: All who undergo treatment are informed of its nature before the treatment is started. They take the first step voluntarily. If someone has as little will power as W. H., a boy who achieved nothing in life but a maximum sentence of twenty years in a reformatory, then it seems quite permissible to give him a loan from another person's will power, if this serves the purpose of converting a shiftless young criminal into a useful member of society. The same is quite as true for offenders like G. J.

It is not claimed that basic qualities of the personality can be changed but there is no reason why psychotherapeutic control should not be continued for years and in some cases, even to the limit of the maximum sentence. This would practically mean reformation, because it is known that juvenile criminals do not relapse readily after the thirty-fifth year.

The method is practicable. It takes some time and effort to give the first treatment and to accomplish observation. The follow-up treatment, however, in the case of G. J., takes about fifteen minutes at intervals of one month.

It is generally admitted that the present management of juvenile delinquents is not satisfactory. Dr. Richard C. Cabot's foreword to S. and E. Glueck's "500 Criminal Cases," stresses the small percentage of reforms achieved. He says: "So far as I have seen such reforms or heard of them from others, there has been at least one necessary condition; that someone should come to know and understand the man in so intimate and friendly a way that he comes to a better understanding of himself and to a truer comprehension of the world he lives in." It goes without saying that psychotherapy as described, creates such an atmosphere of confidence. I consider the case of W. H. as a test case and I conclude in raising the question:

After careful examination and three months of observation, I claim that a man like W. H.

can be rehabilitated for all practical purposes if paroled and put to work under psychotherapy. This cannot be achieved under the existing laws. This suggestible individual will serve his fixed minimum sentence in company of harder delinquents and will remain what he is, a recidivist.

I plead that suggestive psychotherapy be given a chance to prove its usefulness in the management of juvenile delinquents of the psychoneurotic type.

Chapter 28

Techniques of Treatment: Group Therapy

THREE MAJOR CURRENTS of influence may be detected in the development of the group therapy method for coping with personality and behavioral distortions. One is the practical consideration that there are not and never can be enough trained personnel to cope with the ever mounting problems of mental aberration and antisocial behavior; hence a more economical method must supplement individual psychotherapy and guidance. A second influence derives from the recognition among psychologists and sociologists of the phenomenon of group inducement on the thinking and emotional expression of individuals. A third and related influence springs from the fact that American criminologists have largely been concerned with group phenomena in delinquency, as expressed in the great interest in the gang, the "delinquency area," and, more recently, the "delinquent sub-culture" existing largely, it is claimed, among children of the working class, whose formation into gangs is attributed to their being judged and treated, in school and elsewhere, by middle-class standards.[1]

Something of the promise of group therapeutic techniques is suggested in the collection of materials in this chapter. The materials are divided into three parts. The first set of articles deals with group therapy as a recognized professional technique, the second is concerned with a modified approach involving boy gangs, and the final part deals with the camp as a group experience. It may perhaps have been preferable to put these three types of group treatment in separate chapters; but despite the more specific techniques of group therapy proper, the three forms of joint guidance have certain underlying social–psychologic phenomena in common.

A. *Group Therapy Proper.* Sohn's article is valuable as giving something of the history of group psychotherapy and indicating, by case summaries, some of the dynamics involved in the treatment of delinquents by this method. The relationship of the insights and methods used to psychoanalytic theory is exemplified, and is the theme of the group experience as a "reliving" of the child's early connections with the most important adults in his world. The role of group psychotherapy as a prelude to individual therapy is emphasized, with especial reference to the carrying over into individual guidance of the "transference" situation developed in the group experience, to the fact that group dynamics tend to deal more with external than internal conflicts, and to the fact that the reenactment of the "family drama" is facilitated in that, in the parent-substitute situation provided by the therapist, the individual child is more on terms of equality with, rather than subordination to, the parental surrogate. An interesting account is given of the beginnings and the development of the attitudes of various types of individuals as they gradually become absorbed in the group exercises. An assessment of follow-up results is presented.

The article by Konopka is not concerned with group treatment as a form of therapy by the psychiatrist but presents the issues from the point of view of the social worker engaged in activities with groups. She calls attention to the fact that not only are

---

[1] For example, F. H. Thrasher, *The Gang,* Chicago, University of Chicago Press, 1927; C. Shaw, *Delinquency Areas,* Chicago, University of Chicago Press, 1927; A. K. Cohen, *Delinquent Boys: The Culture of the Gang,* Glencoe, Ill., The Free Press, 1955; see, also, R. K. Merton, "Social Structure and Anomie," in *Social Theory and Social Structure,* Glencoe, Ill., The Free Press, 1949.

other methods of coping with delinquency not supplanted (but rather supplemented) by group work, but that the underlying assumptions and techniques of group work itself vary with the disciplines represented by the various types of workers who practice the method. She analyzes effectively a number of basic group mechanisms, sets forth a list of thought-provoking principles of social group work as "guidelines" for practitioners, and spells out their application to the special problem of delinquents. She takes account of the internal inconsistency — restriction versus treatment — in the two basic functions of a correctional institution, yet makes practical suggestions regarding techniques for bringing about identification of the delinquent with socially sanctioned goals. The *Leitmotif* of her paper is to be found in these words: "The specific skill of the social group worker lies in helping the individual to find his full satisfaction as well as to relate to others"; and she points to such practical devices involving the central goal as giving the inmate a choice of associations where possible, assuring him a balance between privacy and interaction, providing him with occasions for the exercise of independent judgment, allowing outlets for hostility, aggression, adventure within safe bounds — the whole program geared to the ultimate goal of preparing the inmate for constructive living on his release.

The piece by Brother Aquinas Thomas deals with "deductive" group psychotherapy, a more formalized and intellectualized type of approach to the problem of intragroup dynamics.

On the basis of his general theory of group therapy, in which he has been a pioneer, Slavson considers the management of aggression in the therapeutic situation and delineates the various types of aggressive reaction as well as the relationship of each to the indicated therapeutic approach. He points out that aggression as such cannot be treated, since it is merely symptomatic of more pervasive and deeper-lying character malformations and neurotic drives; the different forms of aggression are, however, tangible indices of the more general affective situation which can be approached through the avenue afforded by aggression.

Further hints on the relationship of group to individual therapy are given in the article by Patterson, Schwartz and Van der Wart. Their aim is to assess the varied contributions made by group therapy as compared to individual therapy, both diagnostically and from the point of view of treatment. The children are younger than those usually dealt with in the experiments described in the prior articles, being in the "latency period," [2] and the therapeutic process involves activities rather than discussion. The basic mechanisms of aggression, frustration, the need to compete with others, and the wellsprings of anxiety and rage are involved. Gratification of the child's "social hunger," a sense of identification with the group, the winning of the approval of his peers, the solution of problems of relationship with others — these are some of the signs of improvement. The role of the group therapist in manipulating the resources available is indicated. The importance to the assessment of ego-strengths of watching the child's behavior in a group situation is shown as is also the role of the group in aiding the child to select the types of self-expression and to learn the limits of acceptable behavior. The therapeutic implications of the sibling-rivalry situation in group therapy are indicated. It is pointed out that the inter-child

---

[2] According to psychoanalytic theory the basic roots of personality and typical modes of reaction to be expected in adulthood have already been laid down during the period of infancy — birth to about six years. Already the child's energies and emotions are involved in the complex and difficult physiologic–psychologic task of "genitalization of the libido," and, thereafter, in the attachment of libidinous energy to an object (for a boy, the mother; for a girl, the father), this to be followed by the task of repression of desire for the parent of the opposite sex. After this stage comes the period of relative sexual *latency*, which extends from about the sixth year to the pre-pubertal period. In the pre-pubertal and pubertal stages that follow, much of the effort of the individual goes into keeping the burgeoning sex energy in check, sublimating and directing it into socially acceptable channels.

relationships are often more important in therapy than is the role of the therapist himself. Especially illuminative is the discussion of the ways in which the group therapist tempers the reality stresses of the child and the need for a skillful use of the processes of identification, reality testing, and interpretation of the behavior to the child. Suggestive hints as to the types of children best suited to individual or to group therapy are given.

"Delinquent Parents Anonymous," by Barbara Casey, describes a promising experiment in explaining to mothers the nature of their delinquent children's problems and aiding the parents themselves to cope with their emotional stresses. The process might be deemed a form of group therapy, yet it is not as rigidly guided by a special psychologic theory. It is the sort of process that can be initiated to good advantage by any probation officer of intelligence and warm-heartedness.

B. *Work With Gangs.* Starting the series on work with gangs, Dumpson reports on the Central Harlem Street Clubs Project for coping with the gang situation in a large urban region. After analyzing the underlying causes of gang formation, he presents a series of objectives of the project designed to involve the total community and its resources. The process of establishing relationship with aggressively antisocial gangs and the methods of bringing about acceptance of the area worker are described. The organization and officers of the gang and the various types of gangs are delineated, as is the economic and cultural milieu in which gangs tend to originate. The development of legitimate ways for achieving status in the community and devices for assimilation of desirable value systems are also outlined. The setting of the project in the wider and deeper arena of community living is shown. A research adjunct and a tentative evaluation of the project are presented in terms of the boys' increased use of leisure constructively, reduction of certain forms of antisocial behavior, capacity of the boys to form a relationship with a mature and sympathetic and accepting adult, democratization of the intragroup processes, greater use by the boys of legitimate community facilities, and acceptance of the techniques worked out in the Central Harlem Street Clubs Project by other agencies.

Delany's article describes in detail the method of establishing relations with antisocial gangs and the internal structure and leadership dynamics of such groups. A commentary by John C. Spencer calls attention to the gang phenomenon in certain foreign countries.

C. *Camp Work.* In respect to using the camp situation therapeutically, the article by Young, Miller, and Verven describes an experiment in the use of a children's camp as a treatment agency for emotionally disturbed boys, by employing both group therapeutic techniques and psychodrama. The authors expound their four guiding principles: a psychodynamic orientation (as a means of understanding the roots of irritating behavior), permissiveness (as a means of assuring free self-expression without fear of retaliation or rejection), warm relationship of the children with the counselors (as a means of modifying the boys' aberrant ego mechanisms for coping with adults), and adequate explanation to the campers of the therapeutic as well as recreational aims of the camp (as a means of creating a favorable "mental set"). The relationship of the counselor to the boys is discussed in terms of the processes involved in group psychotherapy, notably anxiety leading to hostility. The basic aim is to give the boys insight into interpersonal situations and the emotions thereby activated, the leader being the original target of the group's hostility until this is redirected. The article is also of value in showing how the process of clarification of the emotional roots of the boys' behavior operates both individually and in group discussions. The authors explain the use of psychodrama as a means of plumbing the more unconscious depths of personality and bringing about catharsis. Psychodrama is conceived of as a process designed to complement the group therapeutic technique which deals essentially with ego involvements.

The article by Hallowitz seeks to define the values inherent in the camping experience that could be of special significance to the disturbed child and to indicate how these can be marshalled for the special benefit of such a youngster. A basic aim is to provide an environment in which stress and strain — under which disturbed children have had to live while in the home — are kept at a minimum. Apart from the enhancement of ego strength through the acquisition of skills, the child experiences, in the informed counselor, an adult who is sympathetic and understanding; and, by reliving to some extent his prior experiences in the family setting, he learns to develop more acceptable patterns of attitude and behavior. The author shows how the potent urge to be accepted by one's fellow-campers, as well as other needs, can be employed therapeutically. The use of the case history prepared by the social agency caseworker in grouping the children and in understanding the basic problems of the individual child and the role of a camp psychiatric caseworker are discussed. Reasons are specified why disturbed children, youngsters with "sick personalities," cannot be given adequate treatment in ordinary camps but must be provided for in a therapeutically oriented camp. The roles of authority and punishment in an essentially permissive milieu are indicated. Basic problems arising in the planning of a special camp for disturbed children are considered.

151

Group Therapy for Young Delinquents *

Leslie Sohn †

GROUP INFLUENCES

Group psychotherapy, that is to say the conscious and deliberate use of group influence in the treatment of mental disorder has only recently been applied to young delinquents; its use as a general therapeutic method dates back only some forty-five years. The first recorded reference to the visible improvement of patients under positive group influences, as contrasted with patients under the same régime but without the group influences — i.e. patients in a

* Reprinted from 3 *British J. Delinquency* (1952), 20–33. Used by permission of the author and the publisher.

† I wish to thank Dr. K. Cameron, Physician-in-Charge, Children's Department, Maudsley Hospital, for his help and encouragement in connection with this work and for permission to publish this paper; also the Psychiatric Social Work Department for their assistance with the parents and the later follow-up. — Leslie Sohn.

large ward contrasted with patients of similar type, but probably more opulent, treated in private rooms — appeared in 1904 in Camus and Pogniez's 'Isolement et Psychothérapie.' The existence of a reciprocal influence between the group as a whole and the individual patient was not recognized.

The first conscious and directed use of the principles of group psychotherapy was, however, made in the treatment of tuberculous patients. A group meeting in Boston, under Dr. J. H. Pratt, were given instructions in personal hygiene and their records were checked. They enjoyed the social stimulus of such meetings and felt encouraged; so that Pratt extended the method to include patients with other chronic diseases. Emerson, in 1908, started similar class meetings for groups of badly under-fed children in Boston, and enlisted the aid of social workers to enquire into the home background of these underprivileged children. The classes involved 'talks' and instruction about hygiene, diet and food values. The children were supplied with a competitive motive for gaining weight; they were seated in the classroom according to the amount of weight they had gained. A game was thus made out of the weight problem, in which each child had a stake, and the results achieved helped to remove phobias and anxieties about food and weight-gaining systems.

Following Emerson's good results, classes were organized for diabetics, cardiac cases, patients in need of corrective exercise, and others. Buck reported on his good results in the treatment of a group of patients with essential hypertension, and reports followed of treatment of groups of patients with peptic ulcers. In 1911 in Vienna, Dr. Moreno began working with children by his method of psychodrama, in which the children were encouraged to act and play out their fantasies, which were normally on a primitive fairytale level.

Dr. E. W. Lazell, at St. Elizabeth's Hospital in Washington, developed the idea of delivering a series of lectures to patients, particularly to those inaccessible to individual psychotherapy. Lazell states: "The effect was remarkable: silent, dreamy boys suddenly became interested and drank in every word, realizing that here was someone who understood their problems — troubles they had considered peculiar to themselves. They were greatly relieved when told that all mankind has to contend with the same emotions that had broken them down." Lazell devised a series of lectures based on psychoanalytical psychology, in language simple enough for the average patient to understand. The results were apparently gratifying.

In 1927, Trigant Burrow began to try out his new method of group psychoanalysis on himself and his associates. His therapeutic aim was to undermine the authority of artificial social demands which are foisted on the individual and which he feels obliged to accept, thereby hindering his individual adjustments.

In 1935, Slavson commenced group therapy classes with problem children in New York with a double aim — diagnosis and treatment.* He admitted the non-complementary nature of such therapy but also stressed its individual and specific value. Slavson felt that the child should actually experience real situations within the group and in that way achieve a new group orientation. The children chosen were those rejected by their parents or school, also children interfered with by prolonged coddling and parental over-solicitude. The therapist kept in the background as merely a shadowy presence and only rarely tendered any interpretation, took direct part in the group activities or interfered in any way.

---

* For the application of some of Slavson's ideas to the treatment of aggression in children, see Article 154 *infra.* — Ed.

Autonomy within the group is the cardinal principle, a permissive atmosphere being the means to this end. Slavson's summing up is that the great use of group experience in character formation is that it modifies or eliminates egocentricity and psychological insularity. He seeks to convince the children of the genuineness of the relationship to the therapist by giving them "unconditional love"; antisocial or asocial behavior in the group is accepted by the therapist. If a child refuses to eat, eats with his fingers or helps himself to another child's portion, the therapist does not interfere, but works towards the eventual development of group formation which will bring about an equilibrium; each child will participate and in so doing will achieve the process of social adaptation which is in part the aim of therapy. One principle underlying this is that the child's super-ego is derived from fear of punishment or a fear of rejection — both negative values. If the therapist were to enforce restraints and prohibitions, he would immediately be identified with the negative adults of the child's experience and so be unable to relieve the child's tensions and hostilities, which must invariably be accepted.

Whereas Slavson's group leaders take great pains to remain passive and shadowy, Redl believes that children's groups are far more tolerant of active adult leadership than is generally held, and views a purely permissive atmosphere without overt activity as potentially dangerous, once more because of the problem of the child's super-ego formation. The aim may be passivity, but this can be achieved only to the extent that the child will permit it; permissiveness may threaten super-ego formation or create anxiety and guilt feelings; and the group situation may demand not passivity but observation and reactivity if it is to be given sufficient ego support. Redl finds that interpreting some behavior on the spot is advantageous.

DYNAMICS

As Burrow indicates, many of the disturbances seen in our patients are difficulties in adaptation to social conventions and demands. The individual psychotherapeutic setting may be regarded as an artefact in that it does not give a direct outlet to this most important part of the patient's trouble and so gives rise to resistances. This was particularly true of our delinquent patients, since they were all referred to us from the courts via the probation officers. We were automatically identified with these punishing legal figures, and this increased the hostile resistance of these disturbed children.

Group psychotherapy with such children permits the reliving of early relationship to their first significant adults, within a setting which is not felt to be so artificial as in the individual interview. It can prepare the patients for later individual psychotherapy and the transference occurring within the group can be carried over into the individual sessions. Group dynamics are more specifically adapted to "externalized" than to "internalized" patterns of conflict, i.e. those conflicts in which the struggle is played out between the person and his environment rather than those contained within the psyche. It fosters a living-out of emotional experience and tends to release tensions on a motor level.

There occurs inter-patient transference — a reliving of inter-sibling transference in the family which must reinforce transference to the therapist. This transference is real enough for my young patients to see one another outside and to refer during sessions to their extra-mural mutual activities. It breaks down the early "psychological insularity" (cf. Slavson) and helps extravert the patient.

In the group a re-enactment of the family and social drama occurs; but the patient finds himself on terms of equality with the parent-substitute (therapist) in the permissive atmosphere.

In this connection, Redl's types of therapeutic leader which he treats as analogous with types of schoolmaster are interesting. First the Patriarchal Sovereign type where the supervision is of a stern but not unfriendly nature. He stands for discipline and order, making that fact quite clear to the children. The children accept his values without question; their feelings about him are compounded of love and admiration, intermixed, however, with an anxious sense that their security is dependent on their adoption of his code.

Secondly, the Leader type — usually young, standing for work and discipline and getting this without outward pressure. He plays a dual rôle in that he is identified with the requirements of the school or organization and at the same time is aware of and sympathetic with the emotional drives of the young members; i.e. he represents both the group's strivings and the demands of society. If he succeeds in combining these func-

tions, the children will feel secure and content; if not they will become anxious and frightened, either of him or of their own drives.

Here we may note that according to Klapman "the group leader appeals to the love impulses as well as the narcissistic tendencies of the children." The leader is put in the place of the children's ego-ideal; they wish to be like him and they become a group because they incorporate the leader's personality into their ego-structure and on that basis develop group emotions towards each other.

In Redl's opinion the greatest danger to the group emotional and therapeutic atmosphere is not the patient who creates physical disturbance, but he who tries to obtain a more intense transference from the therapist. Such a one is my patient L., of far higher I.Q. than my other boys, who attempts to deviate from the general course of conversation, and frequently informs us during the sessions of his intention to go to Cambridge to read medicine or law. All the others have strong desires to be apprenticed to various trades. Frequently he attempts to monopolize the conversation.

Redl's third type of leader is the so-called "Tyrant"; one usually bound to apply a certain pattern of discipline to the children. There is always an imposition of some capricious "order" or discipline; nor is this ever effected quietly. Despite it, and the expectation that there should be a healthy hatred of the teacher with a reactive refractoriness to supervision, the children submit. Here, too, there appears to be an identification with the teacher, and usually the rebel child has not only the teacher but all the other children to contend with. The children become afraid of the rebel and grow angry. In this situation, emotional relationships within the group are less intense. Displaying little camaraderie, the boys appear to be afraid of each other, and possibly too much intra-group intimacy might endanger the repression of the hostility felt towards the leader. The identifications occurring here are based on fear, not love, incorporating the leader's super-ego because of fear of the aggressor.

Relatively easy catharsis in groups is due to the catalytic effect patients exert upon each other. They stimulate one another by removing the bars to self-revelation. At first the material is not very significant, but later more personal material is divulged in the course of general conversation. Wolf, discussing the composition of groups, expresses the opinions that schizoids are amazingly helpful as adjunct-analysts of fantasies and dreams and of the latent meaning of behavior in the group; having access to the unconscious material comprising the world in which they live, they can often clarify material which baffles everyone else. The utilization of this factor was stressed by Rosen in his handling of schizophrenics and in his use of cured patients as nurses.

Of resistance to joining a group, I, in my limited experience, have found no evidence; my little group welcomed its inception enormously. This reaction, too, is open to interpretation. We have not yet had the experience of having a new member join the group, though we have discussed this on some few occasions at which all expressed indifference to such a possibility. This indifference would, however, appear to be a definite reaction formation, since the topic frequently recurred. Two members in particular raised the matter in individual sessions attended during the course of the group formation.

THE ORIGIN OF THE GROUP

The group was formed during November, 1950. Its formation followed a particularly slow and static situation that arose in my individual therapeutic relationship with these boys. They resented me very strongly, were intensely hostile and resistant to having to attend, regarding it as an unnecessary and unreal part of their being on probation,* they were never weary of reiterating in chorus that they only saw their Probation Officer about once a month — why should they see me so often? and anyway, they weren't looney and I was just a Nosey-Parker. There was a further implication that I was a bit "filthy and bloody-minded."

Their sessions consisted, for the most part, of hostile silences punctuated by monosyllabic evasive replies and frequent references to the dire effect their having to attend would have on their schooling. Indeed this was the only real form of spontaneous articulation they offered. I therefore decided to suggest to them the possibility of their forming a group. I indicated the

nature of the group, stressing that it did not mean any violation of their confidences and pointing out that it lay with them to prohibit any such breach themselves. I introduced them to one another as all being under probation and asked them what they thought of the idea. The response was unanimous and we started immediately.

MEMBERS OF THE GROUP

The boys varied in age from twelve to fourteen. To start with the youngest: T.E., aged twelve, was referred to us for stealing bicycles and on charges of habitual truancy. He was brought by a paternal aunt who knew very little of his personal development. His father and mother are divorced, and since the divorce T. had been living alternately with mother and father. He resented having to stay with his mother, who it seemed almost completely rejected the boy, and the delinquencies all occurred during a more recent stay with her. The father lived some few streets away, and the boy waited breathlessly for his daily contact with him. During the previous year he had been reported to be becoming less and less interested at school, with repeated truancy; and the bicycle which he was actually caught stealing was apparently taken in order to ride to his grandfather some fifteen miles off. He is now living with an aunt. During this last year he had repeated colds and nose-bleeding, but repeated physical examination and investigation revealed nothing abnormal.

T. was the least hostile of the group. He was at the initial meeting a mildly depressed, intelligent boy, who was uninterested and dubious about our ability to help him; in his initial interviews he discussed in detail visits to the Science Museum and his desire to be a laboratory technician. He was beginning to make a good relationship and because of this was introduced into the group to encourage the development of intra-group transferences and because of his contrast with the other potential members. T. was a cherubic, ginger-haired little boy, and would be described as "nice." At the moment his father is living in the same house as he, with a common-law wife. T. is doing well under this arrangement.

The second case, B.H., was sent to us by the probation officer. He is twelve years and some months old, and was referred with the story of

---

*Compare this type of approach to probationers with that of the Citizens' Training Group in Boston, Article 122 *supra*. — Ed.

having, in company with another boy slightly older, raped a girl of eleven. B. was apparently the active raper and had stuffed the girl's mouth with grass. The other boy had apparently only played the rôle of expectant onlooker when they were interrupted. B. had never been suspected of any abnormality and showed no evident anti-social trends; although his parents gradually volunteered that he had of late become somewhat sullen. His birth and early development were apparently normal and he manifested no difficulties in early adaptation at school or at home. There were four siblings, an elder sister of fourteen or fifteen and three younger brothers; the family was happy and well integrated, without financial worries. The father is a successful street trader and within their own environment he and the boy's grandfather have some social standing — their ownership of stables, horses and carts, which they hire out to other traders, stamps them as outstandingly successful in their district. The mother is an inadequate, anxious little woman who is convinced that the whole story is a pack of lies and that B. is incapable of such behavior; she finds his sullenness and occasional outbursts of aggression disturbing, but attributes all that to his being a "growing boy." She, like the boy, was at first hostile to his attending the clinic, as was the father; but from the time of B.'s ready acceptance of his visits the family have become somewhat reconciled to the situation.

B.'s original visits, when he was seen by my predecessor, were somewhat chaotic; he was extremely sullen, hostile and resentful, and terminated interviews either by walking out, threatening not to return, or by refusing to speak. When I saw him individually on a few occasions he was a tense, anxious, resentful pre-adolescent, sitting on each occasion with tightly folded arms and tightly compressed lips, looking for all the world like an unhappy caricature of a more mature, street-corner lounger. He affected the peculiar haircut characteristic of this type. On the second visit he cried and rushed out of the room when I spoke to him about masturbation; he later returned, or was returned by his mother. He said he cried because he wanted to "bash me in." B. welcomed the formation of the group.

The next case, L.F., was an attractive, talkative, highly intelligent boy of thirteen and a half. He was referred to us by the probation officer for stealing stamps from a shop. This was the fourth time he had been before the Juvenile Court on a similar charge. I never really ascertained the details of these offences but they seemed to involve the technique of the confidence trickster and there was usually a stooge directed by the master-mind of L. The first delinquent episode had occurred at the age of eight. L. is the eldest of three children, the son of intelligent but embittered parents. He had a normal birth, a rapid, precocious development and gained a scholarship to a Public School, from which, however, he was expelled on account of the charge. L. was said to be an excitable, restless boy with a passion for stamp-collecting and noting engine numbers. He developed numerous passionate but transient friendships. On the first interview, although manifestly tense, unhappy and troubled he was glib and verbose and rationalized freely. It seemed that he was more anxious about his father's reaction than about the offence or the possible court decision. His father was a tense, obsessional perfectionist, working as a clerk at £7 a week, an intelligent, aggressive type, bitterly disappointed about his own social and financial position. He was full of plans for his son's future and indulged in long discussions with the boy, principally about these plans and about politics. Concurrently with this amiable course of conduct, Mr. F. was, however, repeating the pattern of his own relationship with his father, a strict disciplinarian. He frequently practised a sneering sarcasm and aggression towards the boy. This attitude was manifested first when the father returned from almost six years' army service; prior to that there had been an unquestioning mutual idolization. L.'s identification with this vacillating father varied a good deal, but he also presented a façade of intense admiration and approval of him. L. was a disapproving, defaulting, uninterested attender at the clinic, and the first few months were rightly devoted to finding the appropriate educational environment for this intelligent boy. During his interviews he embarked on condescending, apologetic discussions of some of his superficial difficulties, and no progress was noted. I saw him on a few occasions and invited him to join the group. He was fascinated by the prospect and when I outlined the procedure his only question was whether we could discuss politics.

The fourth boy, D.W., aged fourteen, was referred by the probation officer for masturbating publicly in a park. The description of the occurrence given to us was characteristic of exhibitionism: as soon as he had seen a woman and child approaching he had exhibited his penis and commenced masturbating. D. denied the exhibitionistic aspect but said that he had been in the park where he frequently went to masturbate. He denied any special gratification at being seen masturbating. D. had a normal birth and development and was one of seven siblings, ranging from nine to twenty-three years of age. He had no overt difficulties during or after evacuation, which had occurred in company with the whole family. His father, a master builder, is a shadowy figure whom D. would not discuss until a private interview took place, after some ten group sessions. It then came out that the father is an atheistic Irishman who drinks rather heavily, is argumentative, and is not much interested in the boy. The mother is a reasonably intelligent, affectionate woman, primarily concerned with her large family. The brother born after D. was blind from the age of twelve months. D. was particularly attached to him and learned Braille with him. The brother left home to go to a boarding school some three weeks before the offence, and D. wrote and read the family letters to and from this boy. D. was not sexually unsophisticated; he had apparently twice had sexual intercourse with a young girl two years his senior and enjoyed both occasions. They had been fellow-members of a social club. Although enjoying intercourse he had recently not wanted it; he had developed a good deal of general anxiety which was possibly due in part to a fear of syphilis; and he began to avoid this girl and changed his club. D. hated attending the Clinic; his sessions were unproductive and unhappy. He occasionally referred to his masturbation anxieties and asked me if his mother knew that he masturbated in bed at night. His masturbation fantasies were apparently conventional, about nude women. He offered the rationalization that he needed no treatment because he merely masturbated — that wasn't abnormal, was it? D., like the others, was pleased about the group formation.

Group Reactions and Material

The first group meeting occurred in conventional style: the boys sat around in chairs of their own choice in my room, and each looked eagerly around for somebody to open the conversation. This occurred in unusual fashion. B. had been sitting in a more relaxed position than usual, but kept tapping his feet on the ground and beating time with his thumb and forefinger on his knee. D. looked at him and asked why he was tapping, "Oh," said B., "I do this for hours — I can sit at home and keep on doing this. Don't you ever do anything like this?" "Yes," said D., "I whistle without whistling." Everyone looked surprised. D. explained that he pursed his lips and went through all the motions of whistling without making a sound, but keeping the tunes in his mouth. T. then said apologetically that he did the same, and that he also played the piano in the air for "hours," whistling to it all the while. He named the tunes he liked playing, and wondered if he would ever be as great a pianist as he believed himself to be during his own private "sessions." T.'s mentioning one particular tune reminded L. and B. simultaneously of hearing it over the radio; and they were soon busy discussing their favourite radio programmes. In this connection I might add that radios and radio programmes play an important part in these boys' lives and are frequently referred to in group sessions. An interesting episode occurred at the second session when they were again discussing radio and radio plays and serials, and the long duration of some serials. I was asked my opinion of serials but pleaded ignorance of them. However, the boys came to the unanimous conclusion that they didn't like long-drawn-out episodic plays, waiting around for something else to happen; they far preferred the whole thing to be finished in one long "do." I interpreted this for the group and indicated their hostilities to prolonged treatment and to me. They giggled — B. laughed, which was the first positive demonstration from him.

Incidentally the radio is also utilized by these boys in other ways, e.g. in attempts to bring me within the orbit of current discussions by frequent questions as to what I think of such and such. I have to lie unashamedly and must appear to these youngsters a peculiarly unsophisticated listener. Radio is also used to indicate and introduce their intra-familial hostilities and disappointments which would further indicate their desire to introduce me as an enthusiastic listener. They discuss those members of the family who don't want to listen, or have the radio turned up louder, which they all interpret as being indifferent to their interests. They express disappointment at parental lack of enthusiasm, usually paternal. This lack of enthusiasm they equate with age, though no actual age has yet been indicated.

Radio has also permitted the introduction of group fantasies. A play — a serial about Australian bushrangers — permitted B. to introduce the topic of his grandfather's horses. He told us how much time he spends in the stables and how he utilizes these carthorses for Wild West fantasies. He frequently goes direct from the stables to the neighbouring cinema where he stays for the cowboy film and leaves without seeing the other film, a point to which I shall have occasion to return. Once B. had touched on his daydreams all the others were stimulated to produce similar material. Two of them think continually about going to South Africa and ranching there. The daydreams described by L. were all on a "higher" plane. He spoke of going to Cambridge and becoming a barrister, but openly questioned whether he had the brain for it. Nobody reassured him, but this intrusion of reality into the daydream discussion stimulated T. to recall that someone had told him how unwelcome he would be in South Africa; and he supposed he would return to the other wish and dreams, concerning the Science Museum. They proceeded to blame school teachers for not telling the truth about far-away places. This particular session they concluded by long tirades against the "school teacher."

We exchanged our room for the more comfortable setting of a large consulting room; the boys were all suitably impressed by the surroundings and stared at the pictures — one in particular, about which there was considerable argument whether it was a man or woman, or whether a sailor or soldier. Opinion was pretty evenly divided. This was followed by a prolonged discussion of why the two halves of the picture were painted in different colours. They all accepted L.'s view that it was to depict different sides of the soldier, sailor, man-woman-figure's character, good and bad, or unhappy and happy; but they couldn't decide which colour meant which; only L. and T. projected themselves into this situation and saw themselves as being of two sides and two colours; but nothing further developed.

This session was interesting because towards the end T. was most unhappy, squirming around in his seat and continually fidgeting, and finally rushed to ask me where the lavatory was. Some time after the session was concluded he was seen leaving the lavatory. The next session I myself asked T. why he hadn't got up earlier and gone to the lavatory. T. replied: "I was too interested to worry"; and then added spontaneously, "I enjoy both so much, being here and not going to the lavatory, and I also enjoy going to the lavatory more afterwards." L. tut-tutted and invoked the biology master, who had apparently lectured to them on the dangers of withholding urine and fæces; but added, "I did it before he told us, but only with my water; I kept it in for hours." L. then returned to the theme of the previous week about good and bad and wondered about the utilization of bad for good — i.e. enjoying holding in the water and enjoying the discomfort. D. took part in the discussion, saying that he remembered when he was an evacuee holding in his fæces, and being frightened into abandoning the habit by somebody's threats that he would become encopretic — he thinks the "somebody" was his mother (this in answer to a direct question of mine). B. remained silent through all this. Then there was a short general silence, and D. suddenly said: "It's the same with tossing, you stop, and wait, and then you go on — it is the same, isn't it?" B. was the only one who became overtly disturbed at this disclosure — he reddened and became visibly uncomfortable and kept muttering "No." D. and I together asked him what the "No" referred to. He relaxed and said just "No." We all unanimously decided that the "No" indicated a taboo on the introduction of the topic of masturbation. This session then resolved into a semi-class-lecture on masturbation and the popular legend of its dangers.

The next meeting occurred on a particularly cold day. The boys wondered if it was going to snow. I remarked "Isn't it too cold to snow?" The group then turned on me like one man and proceeded to ridicule my remark. A long dissertation on the formation of sleet, snow and hail, and moons and tides followed. They relished this enormously and were all greatly pleased with their display of knowledge. During the next session someone mentioned that he now visited his probation officer only once a month and that at the new club to which his probation officer had introduced him, they had dancing. B. remarked how pleased he was with his new-found prowess in dancing: "Wait till you dance with a girl," said D. B. said he didn't like dancing with boys but D. felt he preferred it and hadn't danced with girls yet; he was too shy, he said. L. didn't like dancing; he had other things to do. T. also infinitely preferred dancing with boys (it is apparently quite common for boys to dance together in these clubs, and dancing in boys' clubs is standard procedure).

At this point they began teasing each other about being scared to dance with girls, but nothing emerged from this, except that B.'s girl partners were only his sister and a cousin. I noted at this stage that B. had changed a good deal physically; moreover, he had adopted an ordinary haircut, his tie was no longer outside his pullover, nor was it of the previous "spiv" shape and size. He walked differently, without his hands in his pockets, and his chin didn't keep jutting out as aggressively as before.

The approach of the General Election provided the next few sessions with material but nothing definite emerged until one evening L. arrived a few minutes late and said he had questioned a speaker about his attitude to wars, and he had not received much of a reply. L. then proceeded to berate me about Mr. Churchill and warmongering. He kept referring to me as "you Tories," identifying me with Mr. Churchill, and then developed his theme about wars — how fathers had to go away during wars; how their protective influence was removed, which led to "boys getting into trouble." L. invited the others to agree with him, but they only decided that they wanted Labour to win. They wanted jobs, they said, and Labour was going to look after them.

During the next session, which took place on the day before the Election, D. was describing the general excitement when B. said "I don't like war or fighting," and went on to report how he leaves the cinema if he knows people are going to get killed. He admits that killing in cowboy pictures is different: "You know they're not really dead." But fighting and killing "like in other pictures" he didn't want to see. He then added rather shyly that he walked out on "soppy kissing" as well. All except D. expressed conventional dislike for kissing films and a strong preference for slap-stick comedy. T. said he didn't mind it on the radio, during a pro-gramme. Everyone agreed. All the three non-aggressive boys enjoyed screen violences in any form, and said so.

More recent sessions have been less productive. The last one was concerned with aspirations; L.'s desire to "continue learning" caused astonishment and amusement in the other three; there was obvious disapproval and resentment of his continual references to scholarships and Cambridge.

RESULTS

At the time of writing I have now been seeing these boys for about five months, during which time there has been continued progress. They look forward to sessions — attend regularly and enjoy them. They have lost their hostile and resentful reactions to the hospital. I have lost my policeman's uniform and we are reliving numerous conflict situations, which, within the permissive friendly group atmosphere, are losing their previous traumatic character. We have not worked through very much, but the process has been started positively and can now continue.

These boys have improved in more ways than one. The non-recurrence of delinquencies by itself is meaningless, but in association with the improvement of "physical tone" can be viewed as the relaxation of a particularly persistent neurotic symptom. Moreover I was able to report from personal observation of the parents that they responded favourably to the change in the rebellious boy who previously "performed" each time mother sent him to the "policeman."

To have carried on seeing these children individually in weekly interviews would, in view of their hostility, certainly not have produced the conspicuously gratifying result that these bi-weekly group sessions produced in them. At the same time it is quite evident that the true underlying pattern of neurotic maldevelopment and delinquent behaviour is not as well understood by the therapist or the child from group as from individual sessions. As a result of release of tension, diminution of internal hostility and improvement of well-being, these children were able to feel free enough on a few occasions to ask for individual sessions. I felt they were in need of this and readily agreed. These individual sessions invariably dealt with feelings of anxiety concerning their behaviour in the group and certain minor events at home.

The group created for them a situation which they are well able to carry over into individual sessions. One can envisage such a group as being a very useful preliminary to more intensive individual investigation and treatment, but the difficulties occurring in a busy children's department prevent such intensive interviews as would facilitate a working through of the problems of these disturbed children.

FOLLOW-UP

A follow-up study of these four boys, carried out for about a year after the cessation of treatment by a social worker who was in close touch with the parents and the families of these children throughout their treatment, produced an interesting picture. Three of the boys — B., the aggressive raper, D., the exhibitionist, and the youngest one, T., have all done well; they have concluded their probation period and have not got into trouble; and reports from the local Care Committee, from Schools and from parents all substantiate the appearance of improvement in these children. In addition, they are adapting well to their home situation and are apparently happy. The fourth boy, L., however, who throughout the group sessions was always noticeably different, garrulous and somewhat effusive, has had repeated breakdowns. He has been expelled from his school as a result of repeated charges of petty theft; he is once again on probation and is now receiving individual treatment. His breakdowns, of course, have served to increase the intense hostility that existed between this boy and his father, and it is now obvious that a combined approach is required. Both the boy and his father need individual treatment.

REFERENCES

Burrow, T. J. "Social Images versus Reality," J. Abnorm. Soc. Psychol., 1924, 19, 230–5.

Klapman, J. "Group Psychotherapy." London: William Heinemann Ltd., 1948. Pp. 332.

Lazell, E. W. "The Group Psychiatric Treatment of Dementia-Præcox by Lectures in Mental Re-education," Psychoanal. Rev., 1921, 8, 168–79.

Redl, F. "Group Emotion and Leadership," Psychiatry, 1942, 5, 573–96.

Redl, F. "Group Psychological Elements in Discipline and Problems," Amer. J. Orthopsychiat., 1943, 13, 77–88.

Slavson, S. R. "Group Therapy," Mental Hygiene, 1940, 24, 36–49.

Slavson, S. R. "Current Practices in Group Therapy," Mental Hygiene, 1944, 28, 414–22.

Wolf, A. "The Psychoanalysis of Groups" (Part II), Amer. J. Psychother., 1950, 4, 16–50.

152

The Social Group Work Method: Its Use in the Correctional Field *

Gisela Konopka

With the recent interest in juvenile delinquency and the whole field of corrections a controversy over the use of methods is too often expressed in sharp accusations: "punitive sadists" on the one hand, or "soft mollycoddlers" on the other hand. In a field which deals with human beings of every age, intelligence level, background, and motivation, it seems childish that we consider this problem in such simplified ways. It will be helpful to acquire a calmer research attitude, and to allow for thoughtful experimentation under controlled enough circumstances so that we know at the end whether the method used was helpful or not. Without question, methods in correctional work must be highly diversified. No professional skill alone will achieve success. When I discuss in this article the possible use of the social group work method in relation to corrections, I want to make it clear from the beginning that I do not consider it a panacea, that I cannot conceive the group work method as the only method used with offenders, and that I would wish that we test its effectiveness as rigorously as we would test any new medication.

We will be able to test it only if we clarify what we mean by the social group work method, what specific goal we hope to achieve, and on

* Reprinted from 20 Federal Probation (1956), 25–30. Used by permission of the author and the publisher. See, also, L. W. McCorkle, "Group Therapy in the Treatment of Offenders," 16 Federal Probation (1952), 28–32. For a recent important experiment in "group interaction" in a short-term, non-custodial residential center, see H. A. Weeks, Youthful Offenders at Highfield, Ann Arbor, University of Michigan Press, 1958. — Ed.

what premises we are making our claim. There recently has been a wide use of the group approach in correctional and therapeutic settings. Those approaches have been varied, have been carried on by people trained in different professions who based their methods on different assumptions. I am sure many of those attempts are very valuable and others are probably not helpful because they are carried on in an amateurish way. It is quite conceivable that different group methods will prove equally sound and helpful. For some highly intellectual adults, for instance, group therapy sessions which demand a high degree of verbal interaction will be appropriate. For others who have labored all their lives with their hands and who have done little introspection such sessions will be completely useless.

Before we go into any specific applications of group methods, let us clarify what we mean by the *social group work method*.

Social group work is a part of social work. As such it cannot be understood as a technique alone, but as a method dealing with human beings based on a framework of values, a certain conception of individuals and society, and principles growing out of those premises.

The *framework of values* of the social group worker can be shortly summarized by four basic tenets:

1. The belief in the dignity and worth of each individual.
2. The right of each individual to full development of his capacities.
3. The responsibility of each individual not to harm or misuse others.
4. The responsibility of each individual to contribute to the common welfare — in the limits of his capacities.

CONCEPT OF THE INDIVIDUAL

The social group worker sees the individual human being as a whole — that means one cannot separate mind, body, and emotions. He recognizes that human beings are social beings, that they are interdependent and that we cannot understand an individual separated from his human and physical environment. He has the conviction that every human being has a capacity to grow and change even if there have been disruptions, blocks, and interference in his development. He understands that behavior is only a surface expression of many underlying motives and that to understand a human being one must be able to look beneath this surface. He recognizes that values influencing human behavior are strongly formed by the primary group, the family, but that there are many secondary groups which also help to form those values. The older a person is the more importance those other groups will have on his value system. To a teen-ager, the values of other teen-agers or the values of a gang or those of any youth group are important. The adult may acquire new values through professional or vocational associations. The social group worker believes that the maturing process is really the process of learning how to love, to become concerned with others, and to act even for others when it limits one's own comfort.

CONCEPT OF SOCIETY

We have learned about the great influence of general cultural values on the individual. Because one of the characteristics of social work is the individualization of people, the social worker will constantly try to find out how a specific individual relates to his culture. He must not stereotype an individual's behavior.

He recognizes the function of social institutions in society and knows that they can be changed — but usually slowly — because they grew out of historical necessities. He therefore regards the legal framework as a given, yet a dynamic, reality. He recognizes the importance of economic and social environment. They are not the sole determinants of an individual's behavior. Yet they are as significant as inner-emotional forces and human relationships.

CONCEPT OF THE GROUP PROCESS

In addition to trying to understand the individual and society the social group worker concerns himself with the group process. In this area he learns much from sociologists as he has learned from psychiatrists and anthropologists in other areas. Because of the interdependence of human beings group life has an enormous importance. Here, actually, lies the strength and the security of human beings, here is the testing ground of their capacities to get along with others and yet to stand on their own. Here are the opportunities for a highly constructive work as well as for the most destructive action. In understanding groups the social group worker must sensitize himself to many aspects of group behavior. He must understand and learn about the strength of the bond among the group. He must know on what this bond is founded, whether it is built around allegiance to a strong leader or to a cause or to fear or hatred. He must be able to understand why some people in the group are especially accepted and why some are members of the group and yet rejected. He must get to know the subgroups and the complicated reasons for an individual's isolation. He cannot take for granted that an individual is an isolate because of his specific incapacity to relate to the group. This might be the case but it also may be that he is in a kind of group which cannot accept his difference. I remember a very lively example of this in an institution for delinquent boys. Every deviation from societal standards was accepted by the boys. Only the one homosexual in the group was shunned and rejected, in spite of his desperate efforts of wanting to belong.

The group worker must understand the strange phenomenon of scapegoating which is a form of group projection. He must learn to understand when group contagion is high and when it is low. He must accept conflict as a part of group life which can become constructive if a group learns how to deal with such tensions but which is not constructive when it is suppressed or when it is never solved.

Principles of Social Group Work

Out of this framework of values, out of the conception of man, society, and man's interaction with each other, grow certain principles and guidelines for those using the group work method. I purposely use the word "guidelines" because they are not fixed rules of conduct. In a profession the most important skill of a person is to be able to observe facts carefully, to diagnose a situation or an individual, and to use his judgment. It is only the dull and unimaginative person who is looking for rules which are unchangeable. Some of the principles of social group work are:

1. The function of the social group worker is a helping or enabling function. He must help the members of the group to move toward greater independence and capacity to direct themselves.

2. In determining his way of helping, the group worker uses the scientific method: fact finding (observation), analyzing, diagnosis in relation to the in-

dividual, the group, and the social environment, and finally treatment.

3. The group worker must form purposeful relationships with group members. This includes a conscious focusing on the needs of the members and on the purpose of the group as expressed by the members and as expected by the sponsoring agency. It is different from a casual unfocused relationship.

4. To form meaningful relationships the group worker needs self-knowledge and discipline in relationships without the loss of warmth and spontaneity.

5. Acceptance of people without accepting all their behavior. This means a sympathetic understanding of individuals as well as the incorporation of societal demands. This requires high flexibility and abundance of warmth in the social group worker as well as identification with values and knowledge.

6. Starting where the group is. The capacity to let groups develop from their own point of departure.

7. The constructive use of limitations: They must be used judiciously in relation to individual and group needs and agency function. The group worker will mainly use himself, program materials, interaction of the group, and awakening of insight in the group members.

8. Individualization: It is characteristic of the group work method that the individual is not lost in the whole, but that he is helped to feel as a unique person who can contribute to the whole.

9. Use of the interacting process: The group worker must help balance the group, must allow conflict when necessary and prevent it when harmful. His help to the isolate consists in giving him individual attention, also in relating him to other members.

10. Understanding and conscious use of nonverbal as well as verbal material. The group worker must be able to use many media to help individuals. He must know when discussions or activities are most appropriate. He must be able to conduct interviews related to the group endeavor and to help group members with their problems.

What has all this to do with our work with the offender? In an unpublished paper Elliot Studt defined the correctional field as:

that group of agencies in American Society which have a common responsibility of providing for the offender a social environment different from that of the nonoffender in that he is circumscribed and supervised.

Russell G. Oswald named an additional function:

treatment directed toward the rehabilitation of the individual to the end that he may be restored to the community as one capable of developing a personally satisfactory method of living as a constructive, productive member of the community (*Social Work Yearbook*, 1954, p. 135).

We see, therefore, that our work with the offenders is determined by two goals which seem to be in opposition. The one is keeping them restricted and the other is to develop a personality who can find a satisfactory method of living as a constructive productive member of the community. It seems to me that we increasingly understand the great importance of both purposes. The "circumscription and supervision" are necessary because of the needs of society and at times because of the need of the individual who has committed the offense. We also want to help this person to become a productive member of the community who feels satisfied and happy. We must learn to recognize and reconcile the two goals. One of the great contributions social group work can make to the correctional field is the fact that most group workers have experience in the rough and tumble reality of neighborhood life around settlement houses and community centers. All through the history of social group work great stress has been laid not only on help toward a satisfying life for the individual but also on the importance of social goals. The most recent definition of social group work says:

The group worker enables various types of groups to function in such a way that both group interaction and program activity contribute to the growth of the individual and the achievement of desirable social goals. The objectives of the group worker include provision for personal growth according to the individual's capacity and need, the adjustment of the individual to other persons, to group and to society; the recognition by the individual of his own rights, limitations, and abilities as well as his acceptance of the rights, abilities, and differences of others (*Social Work Yearbook*, 1954, p. 480).

Definitions are nothing but a summary of what has grown out of long observation and experience. It might reassure the harassed prison official and the superintendent of a training school that a profession has developed such clear conception of the interrelationship of "the individual's own rights, limitations and abilities as well as his acceptance of the rights, abilities, and differences of others."

We see two main reasons why the social group work method is so essential in working with offenders: (1) the dynamics of the offender himself and (2) the specific institutional setting in which he finds himself.

CONFLICT IN INTERPERSONAL RELATIONS

All offenders, for whatever reason they have been committed to an institution and whatever their individual differences, have come in conflict with the law presented by society which means there are conflicts in interpersonal relations. Certainly the range of disturbance is very great. We know that in the adolescent group approval or rejection is often far more important than adult approval or rejection. Sontag pointed out among other factors of delinquent behavior the following:

1. Strong identification with an already delinquent individual. Identification yields a feeling of being a part of another individual, a sense of acquiring some of the individual's power or strength and at the same time preventing the destructive potentialities of that power from being used against the identifying one. It means also the adoption of this method of expressing hostility.

2. Identification with a delinquent group or gang. In this instance, the same factors are operative, plus the fact that delinquent behavior elicits peer approval from the group.

3. The existence of a subculture in which delinquent behavior is acceptable. In some slum districts a substantial part of the population is more or less emotionally allied against the "law" and the privilege which it seems to represent. Delinquency here is acceptable in the home as well as by the gang (Roundtable at the 1953 meeting of the Orthopsychiatric Conference, "Psychodynamics of Child Delinquency," *American Journal of Orthopsychiatry*, January 1953).

The group has not such strong meaning to the adult and we find many more offenses committed by an adult alone than we find in juvenile gangs. Yet, the adult, too, is very dependent on the status he receives from others. We often find much distrust but also much yearning to be accepted. It is because of those needs that the group work method becomes essential in closed institutions. The goals of the group should be:

1. A strengthening of the security of the individual in the framework of the group so that he does not feel alone and helpless, but also moves toward not being wholly dependent on it.

2. The strengthening of the individual's independence by helping him actually to *participate* in group

decisions, not to submit to a gangleader or a powerful subgroup.

3. The introduction of an adult who represents the values of a society the offender rejects, but who because of his accepting attitude represents adult security and love. The delinquent can meet this adult in a group while still feeling the support of his contemporaries and relating in different degrees of intensity.

4. The opportunity of gaining satisfactions in the need for adventure and experimentation in ways that are accepted by society.

5. An opportunity for some catharsis under the protection of an adult and for gaining insight with the help of an adult and with trusted contemporaries.

6. An opportunity to gain inner resilience and status with the group through accomplishment in activities accepted by society.

For the adult we would add here an increased acceptance of insight into his own problems through learning that others have similar problems, and also the awakening and the exercise in interests which can fulfill inner needs in a constructive way. A feeling of inner worth never comes only through talking, but through *experience* of a constructive activity which helps the individual to gain status. I like to underline this latter thought because too often group treatment in correctional institutions has been understood exclusively as occurring in discussion meetings. It is very important that we see also activities in recreation or in education or in art as essential for a feeling of importance.

INDIVIDUAL AND SOCIETY CANNOT BE SEPARATED

The goal of correctional institutions as expressed in their dual role of restriction and treatment gives another reason for the importance of the use of the group work method. We said previously that those goals seem to be in conflict but actually it resolves itself when we accept the basic tenet of a democratic society:

We understand individualism not as an apartness of the whole, but as a contribution to the whole. (Mary Follett)

Actually, individual and society cannot be separated. There is no "complete freedom from restraint" and rights invariably include responsibilities. Laws restrain the individual for his own protection as well as those around him. There is no question they are not perfect; they are often hangovers from history where basic democratic philosophy had not permeated the structure of law, and in applying the law we find human errors and the expression of community hostility. The same applies to the forms in which the law is carried out in many correctional institutions. The remedy of those misuses lies largely in the area of social reform and belongs to a wide variety of professions. Yet given none of those abuses, the philosophical base of the democratic society includes the restraint of those who will harm other members and the dual goal of the institution remains.

The social worker in the correctional institution must, therefore, accept *both* goals and cannot set himself outside either of them. Unfortunately I have seen both: The social worker who accepted only the treatment goal smuggled letters from an inmate to the outside against the rules of the institution. Another social worker who had worked for years in the institutional setting told me that the only way to deal with delinquents was "to watch them all the time, make them do things all the time, keep them in large bunches for better observation." Here the treatment goal was lost.

In relation to this dual goal the group work method seems especially appropriate. It is inherent in the demands of small group interaction (not mass activity) that the rights of each individual must be considered, that there is a learning of balance between the fulfillment of one's own needs and the recognition of the needs of others, and that there are limitations growing out of this. In addition to this natural functioning of the group process the specific skill of the social group worker lies in helping the individual to find his full satisfaction as well as to relate to others. He uses a method which has implicitly stated the use of constructive limitations. (This distinguishes it basically from some other methods which insist on the nondirective or neutral approach.) It is therefore suited to combine the "restrictive" as well as the "treatment" goal of the correctional institution.

Another aspect of the institution is the fact that many people must live together who have not chosen such communal living. This would be a strain on any person, but is especially hard on those who have difficulties in relationships, as the offender. The group living situation, therefore, should give opportunity for a balance between privacy and interaction. One of the specific group purposes of formed groups inside the institutional setting should be the opportunity of *choice of association* excepting where this choice is harmful to the individual's own needs or to somebody else.

CONFORMITY VERSUS INDEPENDENT JUDGMENT

In institutional living a certain amount of conformity is unavoidable. Yet the rehabilitative goal demands the individual be helped to incorporate standards and to use judgment on his own in accordance with demands of society. Again, the daily living situations, the school hours, the working hours, etc., should consciously include occasions for *exercise of independent judgment*. Formed groups in the institution must incorporate this as a specific goal for the purpose of better observation (and following diagnosis) as well as for direct preparation for life outside of the institution.

As long as the purpose of confinement was exclusively the protection of society from the offender and locks were strong, treatment methods were quite unimportant. With the addition of the treatment goal, namely, the goal to *return* the offender to the community with a capacity to accept the limits of the law, method became important. As limited as our knowledge of dynamics is, the one thing we know is that the breakdown is not exclusively in the intrapersonal area, but mostly in interpersonal relationships. Very simply stated the demand of society is: "When you release him or her, they should be able to get along with other people without harming them." Certainly this goal cannot be achieved with everybody, the same way we cannot heal all sickness. Yet the moment we do not keep people in institutions for life, this function is clear. Purely custodial care or purely individual treatment actually violates the very task which society has given to the institution. The delinquent — the inmate — must be helped to learn to *constructively relate to others*.

The general living situation therefore must not be allowed to be a mass situation with natural stratification according to old and delinquent patterns and hierarchy related to brutal power or the best way of "putting something over on the administration." It must be a guided and structured group experience allowing for *break-up of such patterns*, for *gratification through positive group associations*, for *emergence of leadership in relation to construc-*

tive goals, for *participation in administrative questions as to* begin *identification with a sanctioned institution of society*. Formed groups must include the same opportunity for such experience as well as the reflection on *inner forces* resisting such constructive participation and on clear perception of forces in the environment which are detrimental to "getting along." From the first day of entering the institution all efforts must be related to keeping the individual in the institution for the time being, but preparing him for living outside of it. Since the crucial goal is the functioning in the social situation, the present *social situation* must be used as a tool for help.

SOME CONSIDERATIONS IN GROUP PROGRAMMING

What are some of the practical groups that will be helpful in institutional settings? Because of the high incidence of impulsive aggressiveness, especially in the juvenile delinquent, groups usually must be small. Program media will be as varied as in all groups. Some specific considerations will be that they must allow for outlet of the adventure spirit (and stay in the frame of a closed institution). They must allow for outlet of hostility, and yet not seduce the group to unacceptable behavior. Programing will allow at times for the individual need of withdrawal by letting a group member do something for himself without feeling guilty that he does not participate, but help him feel accepted by letting him stay in the group. Program should not be handled only for the convenience of the worker or stereotyped notions, such as "all boys want sports," "girls do not do woodwork," "fingerpainting is therapeutic," or — to quote Fritz Redl — "the ridiculous use of the punching-ball theory."

Besides helping with the outlet of feelings the program should include opportunity for real achievement, for some acquisition of skill and property, and opportunity to do for others. It should strike a balance between more individual and more cooperative projects, according to the readiness of the group members. It should allow for pure enjoyment and aesthetic satisfaction. There is hardly anything more "freeing" than moments of real happiness. I participated in a discussion with the staff of an institution for delinquent girls who were concerned whether five girls who had started a near riot should participate in the Christmas festivities. It was remarkable how the staff worked themselves through to the realization that participation was not "candy" offered to the girls, but a therapeutic measure. One of the teachers remarked, "I can't imagine anything more helpful to Marge than to carry her previously assigned role of Mother Mary — after this experience. Some guilt might be aroused (but guilt is in itself not always detrimental), but also a feeling of importance and beauty and peace." The others added with a sense of humor what it would mean to those girls who had just almost interrupted institutional life to represent "angels." The actual experience — combined with discussions helping the girls with insight — bore out the effectiveness of this approach to program.

Since every inmate, whether youngster or adult, has experienced a loss of status, all program activities that prove to him and let him genuinely experience his own worth are important. An interesting example of this is the group of men chosen as Civilian Defense watchers in one of the men's reformatories. In the three years of the existence of this program none of these men had to be reminded of his duty, nor did anyone try to misuse it. Those were selected men, yet the guard especially charged with this responsibility reported that he had also observed an increased self-confidence and calm in them. A parallel to this was the experience in a women's prison to which a unit of feebleminded children was attached. No feebleminded child in any other institution received as much love and gentle care as those children. The warden of the reformatory reported increased responsible behavior on the part of the women. This was a program that allowed for actual contribution and a feeling of self-worth.

The use of the group as a tool in correctional work has been recognized more and more. There are several authorities in the field who consider it the coming and most crucial treatment tool. Lloyd W. McCorkle, who has done a great deal of group therapy in correctional institutions for adults, says:

The guided group interaction technique can serve as a sort of spearhead around which many activities

of the institution are organized in an effort to get at the inner life of the person ("Group Therapy in Correctional Institutions, FEDERAL PROBATION Vol. XIII, No. 2, p. 34).

The need for social group work services was recognized by the National Conference on Prevention and Control of Juvenile Delinquency in 1946. It appeared in several of their reports. They stated:

Group work services should be provided for those apprehended for delinquent behavior, for those in institutions for detention, and for long-term treatment of juvenile delinquency (Section on Case Work-Group Work, p. 38).

The social group worker carries this responsibility by doing direct work with formed groups and by helping the staff, house parents, or counselors or guards to carry through some of the basic principles of the social group work method. In present-day practice social group workers have only begun to enter the correctional field. Where they have practiced, the conviction has grown that they are playing an increasingly vital part in correctional institutions. Whether this is so will depend on the understanding of administrators in the correctional field, but especially on the clarity and precision of the presentation of the method by group workers themselves, on their skill in using it, on their willingness to enter a field with a definite restricting component, on their courage to expose themselves and their method to testing, and above all on their genuine concern for those with whom they work. The people are more important than any theory:

Never settle down within the theory you have chosen, the cause you have embraced; know that another theory, another cause exists, and seek that. The enhancement of life is not for the comfort-lover. As soon as you succeed — real success means something arising to overthrow your security.[1]

Their conviction is based on Mary Follett's beautiful insight: "Who then are free? Those who win their freedom through fellowship."[2]

[1] Mary Follett, The New State, Group Organization the Solution of Popular Government. New York: Longmans, Green and Company, 1918 (Rev. 1934, p. 54).
[2] Ibid.

153

Deductive Group Psychotherapy with Adolescent Delinquents *

Brother Aquinas Thomas, F.S.C.

On more than a few occasions I have been asked to explain why I refer to the work I have been engaged in as deductive group psychotherapy. In what way is it different or unique? What is some of the thinking behind this group process? It is the answer to these basic questions that I shall attempt to make clear.

At the outset I feel that I should express my position in relation to the work of the fathers of group psychotherapy, and to show to what extent I subscribe to or differ with their principles.

My group therapy sessions are by no means the activity group sessions after the pattern of Slavson. While there is a totally permissive atmosphere, allowing for a free-flowing mood, there are basic restrictions as to movement and deportment within the group. We do appeal to oral wishes by providing cigarettes, candy, cookies and occasional drinks. These are available within respectable limitations dictated by politeness and good manners. By that I mean that one fellow can't take all of the goodies or pocket all of the butts, to the exclusion of the others. To maintain a proper perspective there are many times when the group supplies its own cigarettes and goes without food.

We agree with Slavson that it is erroneous to talk about group emotion. We do feel, however, that it is a service to the group if the therapist maintains a group tone among the members predicated upon mutual respect. Since the members of the group are volunteers who elect to participate, we as the therapists feel responsible to prevent the generation of currents of hostility so charged that any one lad becomes

the "scapegoat" as illustrated in the writings of Dr. Irving Schulmann.

We cannot applaud the therapist who would allow for the disintegration of a group by permitting such uncontrolled acting out as to contribute to the deterioration of the group. Schulmann pictured this when he wrote of Mary, who "rubbed stick cologne on the therapist's suit and how by the end of the session all five (delinquent) girls had managed to coat the therapist with many odors of cheap cologne."

In the Warwick experiment with group therapy Girard H. Franklin described as a technique his permissive atmosphere when he wrote: "Nor did the therapist place any restrictions on the behavior other than to forbid destruction of institutional property and physically destructive behavior toward each other. Members are thus free to withdraw from discussions in such ways as lying on the floor, making noise or retiring to the adjoining bathroom; but they could leave the session completely only if their intention was to withdraw permanently from the group."

We feel that too much of this sort of performance is being tolerated and finding its way into our literature as technique under the aegis of group therapy. If I understand correctly the connotation of the word technique, I feel that it implies methodology and the details of procedure essential to expertness of execution in any science. The boundless recording and recitation of the aimless antics of unbridled kids is not technique and it is not science, according to my manner of thinking concerning group psychotherapy.

Perhaps, as I unfold the details of the method I have developed, I should at the outset borrow from etymology. Thus I shall more clearly define the terms I employ as I set my title within a framework. I should also avoid the gibberish of coined words that becloud much of the literature on group therapy, to the detriment of those who are seeking to learn.

We consider our method one of deductive group psychotherapy. We have heard many say, What does he mean by that preface "deductive?"

We presume that we are all of the same mind on the definition of our common tool, psychotherapy, through which one mind has an influence on another in an individual or a group

* Reprinted from 3 J. Social Therapy (1957), 89–96. Used by permission of the author and the publisher.

setting. If that influence extends itself to the point of change, re-education, a healing or a cure, then only do we respect the process as therapy. It is not therapy if it is ventilation for ventilation's sake. It is not therapy if it is unbridled babbling in belligerent bull sessions. That is almost entirely feeling.

We call upon reason in our deductive process as well as feeling. We endeavor to lead, to draw out, to help trace the course, as implied by the Latin root "ducere." We as the therapist help the group reason, from the general or the universal to the individual or the particular. Of special note it is that we endeavor to stimulate the group to move in the direction of a conclusion.

We have found it necessary to develop this method because of the fact that our subjects have been primarily delinquent boys. Conventional group therapy procedures did not prove efficacious or fruitful after many years of experimentation, so we decided to develop our own technique.

One conclusion that we came to as a result of our intimate living contact with delinquent boys for more than a decade was the following. Delinquents are essentially people motivated by expediency in contrast with the nondelinquent, who is more likely to be a person motivated by principle.

It logically followed in our thinking about means of improvement that, if we wanted to avoid anything that might resemble the blind leading the blind in our group sessions, we would have to call upon logic and reason. We felt that this could be encompassed through the process of deduction if our group sessions were to effect any carry-over in behavior alteration, change in attitudes or in a strengthening of the will.

At this juncture I probably should make clear my contention that the usual adolescent delinquent is motivated by expediency. This follows logically upon the accepted premise that these boys are products of faulty or deficient habit training; also that their powers of volition have not been strengthened by practice. It can then be seen that they are filled with the spirit of the Latin root expidire-exiditus (to be free of foot as in ex-pedis), or in another sense free of impediment or obstacle. Hence their attitude is often noted to be free, light, easy, handy or convenient. They find themselves doing things for kicks. Their movement can be predicted upon a feeling tone, "let's have fun."

On this fleet-footed base they build up a sense of practical wisdom which takes the place of moral suasion. Their frame of mind is often salted with an attitude of "don't giv'a damitas." They see only immediate advantage and present conditions. In this circumstance they act, often impulsively. Their ulterior motive is self-interest.

Can we not then see that, if a boy is moved by expediency, he is often opposed to what is right and proper? This implies that his choice is influenced by temporal ends. Propriety would be determined by principle. The expedient lad sees only the immediate practical viewpoint with the attitudinal tone best expressed by "What'll I get out'a it?." His strategy is determined by pleasure. He is fundamentally hedonistic. He lives a life dedicated to the gratification of the sense appetites. He makes no distinction between happiness and pleasure. He is so much lost in the fog of delectation that he finds quietude upsetting. He must live in a whirl of continuous activity. This phase of noisy motion produces one stimulus upon another. In the feeling tone of the delinquent it is best described as "living it up."

The most effective sedative to reduce this overcharged emotional tone is the introduction of reason. One can note the tranquilizing effect upon these hyperactive youngsters as we help them think by means of the process of deductive logic. They do, through this, learn much about the psychology of adolescent development or, as one of the lads put it, "I'm loining a lotta sicologee — that helps me see how I'm wired up and why I blow a fuse when my feelings get short-circuited."

The group setting in which the process of deductive psychotherapy is employed affords these lads just such an opportunity to learn as they slow down.

In the formulation of a group we do it by invitation. When the groups are operating, we are more bothered with rejects than with invitations, for the boys become the best salesmen. Numerous lads ask to get in a group.

Essential to this process is that the same therapist have the boy in individual therapy as well as in the group setting.

The first step is to explain the group process to an individual boy and learn if he wants to talk over his problems with a small group of boys who have the same problems. If his interest has been stimulated, we then point out the next step: that of screening so that we can find the boys with the same problems.

The most useful tool in screening is to employ the Science Research Associates, Youth Inventory. By this each boy will be able to draw up his own profile. To do this the youngster hand-checks the 298 statements in the inventory. (This requires about thirty minutes.) Then, by following the simple directions, he plots his profile on the graph provided. Most all of the boys are encouraged by the directional note, which indicates that they will be comparing themselves to 15,000 other teen agers when plotting their profile. They are reassured by the statement in the directions that problems are the rule, not the exception, in the case of teenagers. It must be remembered that through the use of this inventory we are finding the boys who say that they have problems, and also that they are asking for help with these problems through group discussion.

In possession of these profile plottings, the therapist is able to assemble boys in groups according to the similarity of their problems. It can be noted through these profiles that the boys cluster around particular problem areas, such as getting along with others, home and family, boy meets girl etc.

When the group of no more than seven boys is first assembled, the initial discussions are about the test, the profile and the plan of attack upon these problems. In subsequent sessions the boys are shown random samples of the "Look in the Mirror" cards. These cards are 146 in number. They outline numerous aspects of personality and behavior problems. They are built upon the philosophy that no one of us sees himself as well as our neighbor sees us. Let's look in the mirror and see how they look upon us. The cards and the "Look in the Mirror" process provide the therapist with a most essential element in therapy, the stimulation of hostility. The therapeutic results can well be measured in direct ratio to the amount of hostility generated and the degree of abreaction produced.

In these initial sessions the cards and their use are explained. It is well to note that from the outset the tape recorder should be in evidence. Along with talk about the cards and their use, it is well to have the boys talk about the recorder and their feelings about going on tape. It has been found valuable to employ the machine for demonstration purposes when the group is engaged with an indifferent topic, such as the discussion pertaining to the use of the cards or the recorder. It is well to allow the boys the opportunity for playbacks so that they will know how they sound on tape. It is important to be certain that the boys understand the reasons behind the use of the tape. The tape is very frequently played back at the beginning of succeeding sessions so as to insure continuity if one session carries over to the next. Often a playback session will be held in which the boys analyze the arguments presented in the previous session.

Let us presume that the group of seven boys we are at this time concerned with have identified with each other on the profile peak No. 4 — "Getting along with others."

The therapist, because of his extramural knowledge of these boys, is aware of how they fit into the institutional population. He examines the question. Are they the bullied or the bullies? From his knowledge of the case histories, the therapist has additional objective evidence supplied by the clinical data. Through this he knows the schizoid and the paranoid personality types, along with many of the other classifications. He can thus eliminate the psychopaths as not amenable to therapy.

The therapist, with all of his background data, carefully structures his group according to a predetermined plan. For example, he may place two bullies in a group with five of the bullied. This being set up, how do we get the sessions rolling without our purpose appearing too obvious. We may pick from any one of the thirteen cards covering group influence. Let us, for the sake of illustration, dwell upon card No. 10 which covers the specific topic, Belligerence. Each of the boys in the group is issued a copy of card No. 10. They are asked to read the statements on the card with a view to identifying with one of the five statements. More than likely some of the boys will select statements which reveal that they never get mixed up in fights, or that they do not like to see boys fight. On the other hand, there is the probability that some of the group members will assume the opposite pole and say that they enjoy seeing boys fight.

To the eye of the experienced therapist this is a highly desirable situation for a starting point. As the discussions on the part of the boys proceed, we can note these undercurrent dynamics beginning to flow. The more timid lads are gratified at their ability to express openly that they do not like to fight because they are physically afraid. There is a great deal of reassurance in being able to hear others say what one has felt all the time. A feeling of empathy begins to generate as some of the anti-fighters call to question the logic of some of the pro-fighters. These are the fellows whose bluster, and belligerence would never be challenged outside of the therapy session.

The alert therapist aware of the dynamic — that bullies are almost always afraid and that they usually cover up their own fear by feigning bravery — can at a point interject a well-structured question. This question may bring out the reason why a bully feels he has to act so hard-boiled, why such a boy compensates by being loud or aggressive. In the discussion that flows the boys, with the help of the therapist, begin to recognize that fundamental to belligerence is fear and inferiority feelings. The therapist works them in the direction of understanding that when one is faced with fear some of us meet it by attack while others meet it by retreat. The therapist helps them see that the loud guy is often just as scared as the quiet guy, for he often fears that his bluff will be called.

Through this process the therapist has helped the group move by deductive logic from a universal consideration, that of belligerence (which is a surface or management problem) to the particular dynamic element — a discussion of fear and inferiority feelings.

As the group moves in the direction of a conclusion the therapist might ask the fighters to suggest to the non-fighters what they would recommend to avoid being picked upon, or perhaps what to do when next challenged — how to face up to a bully if he tries to dominate.

The therapist might high-point some of the dynamic elements that have flowed from the therapy session by way of brief review. For example, he might indicate that we came to the point of understanding that fear and inferiority feelings are essentially the undercurrent in all fights; that the timid fellow is primarily afraid of body hurt; that he must be willing to suffer some pain or sport a black eye in order to increase his self-respect; that the aggressive fellow fears not body pain but carries a chip on his shoulder as a cover-up because he does not consider himself as good as the other fellow; that he attacks by word or fist against those who cannot retaliate before they see through him, and because of this he fails to make real and fast friends. Finally, both of these types so much in need of ego building can gain strength and insight by helping each other in the therapy sessions, now that they begin to feel some advantage by talking things out.

This recitation of one small illustration is without doubt an oversimplification. It has to be because of time limitations. It might, however, lead us to see how this same process is possible in dealing with the many aspects of personality and behavior covered by each of the numerous "Look in the Mirror" cards.

Through this method of deductive group psychotherapy we have been able to assist delinquent adolescent boys to see and understand themselves better. It is quite revealing to the therapist to watch the change in a delinquent boy who begins to understand that he has been victimized by the virus of human respect; a victim to the extent that he always did what the other fellow wanted because he hated to be considered a deuce-out, a chicken or a punk. It is not always the easiest task, but it is most enlightening to observe the lads when they begin to talk about those punk and chicken feelings. It is quite telling to note their reaction and their arguments when they begin to analyze the therapist's statement. "Is not the mind of the mob that of the lowest of its members?" When these boys, through a discussion of a lead statement such as this, can be helped to see some of the structural dynamics of mob composition, they are on the way to splintering gang solidarity and the force of negative identification.

This same kind of awakening is the by-product of deductive reasoning in group discussion as the boys begin to learn about negativistic behavior, peer identification, emancipation, security, responsibility, facing reality, the relationship of frustration to maladjustment, the inferiority syndrome, invidious comparison, to mention only a few teen-time problems. These are but a few of the aspects of human nature that frequently become the psychological booby-traps that ensnare many of our boys who, because of their inability to handle these growing pains, often become delinquents.

These sessions are very cathartic. Through them many boys are able to unburden themselves of disturbing pressures. These sessions afford a stage for abreaction through which to gain relief from these pressures. The therapist can often note an acceleration of reaction as the sessions act as a catalyst and stimulate the boy to seek individual help.

In the light of the fact that the therapist also carries the boy in individual therapy, understanding and relief are not too far removed. These provoked reactions are more usually remote than immediate. The lad will ordinarily seek personal contact with the therapist within the next few days rather than just after the session.

Summing up, we feel the "Look in the Mirror" process of deductive group psychotherapy adds to the established practice in group therapy. In addition to the usual dynamic factors of insight, catharsis, ego building, reality testing and transference, this procedure offers methodology. It channelizes thought and at the same time stimulates the process of reason and the will.

154

The Treatment of Aggression Through Group Therapy *

S. R. Slavson

Before elaborating on the treatment of aggression through group therapy, it may be helpful to clear up several basic points. First, we need to come to some understanding concerning the meaning of the term aggression as I think of it. Numerous acts leading to survival

---

* Reprinted from 13 Am. J. Orthopsychiatry (1943), 419–427, part of a symposium on aggression. Used by permission of the author and the publisher. See, also, L. Bender, Aggression, Hostility and Anxiety in Children, Springfield, Ill., C. C. Thomas, 1953. A. B. Abramovitz, "Treating Delinquency through Pleasure," 23 Probation (1944–45), 8–14. — Ed.

by man and the lower animals — and to some extent also by plants — involve aggression against the environment. The needs of life make it necessary that we manipulate, control, direct, and subject things and people to our will. The intensity of these mechanisms varies with the character of the individual, the type of relations he has with people, the special setting in which he operates, as well as the total cultural atmosphere. The hunter, for example, in the act of hunting is constantly aggressive against shrubs and bushes, as well as the animals. By comparison the laboratory scientist may seem to be less aggressive, but actually he is equally so intellectually. Each of us functions aggressively as we sell and buy, make our way socially, gain status, and in other such everyday activities. The therapist, however, is not concerned with these manifestations of aggression. Rather he is preoccupied with aggression that is excessive to meet the needs of a given situation, when it is diffuse and uncanalized, and when it is hostile.

Aggression as differential from other activity, is directed activity, having definite *purposes, direction and object*. The object (or recipient) may in some cases be the aggressor himself, characteristic of some neuroses and psychoses. In abnormal or pathological aggression the factor of hostility enters in a purely unconscious form, but its presence is recognized by the fact that the aggressor aims to provoke, injure or destroy the object or recipient. It seems to me that there is an error involved when we say that frustration leads to aggression. Frustration *may* lead to aggression, but more often frustration begets hostility. The fact remains, however, that within limits and to the extent to which it serves the ends of survival and creative effort, aggression is a normal form of behavior. Only when it is excessive, uncontrolled, hostile, destructive, does it come within the purview of the therapist.

A second point to clear up is the difference between aggression and hostility, which will be only briefly mentioned here. Strictly speaking there is no such entity as aggression. There are aggressive acts and it is through such acts that we observe aggression. Hostility, on the other hand, is an *emotional state* which may or may not manifest itself in overt behavior. It is rather a motivation and an emotional quality that accompanies behavior. It may, however, remain unexpressed as in passive resistance, pathological withdrawal, excessive passivity, non-cooperation. In the neurotic it is often manifested as symptoms.

Third, in judging aggressiveness in patients, it is necessary that we evaluate behavior in terms of the specific culture in which the individual has his roots and by which his character has been shaped. What may be considered excessive aggressiveness in a person in one cultural group may be quite acceptable in his own milieu. Unacceptable table manners in one group or neighborhood are quite acceptable and normal in another. Personal manners of children who come to us for treatment, their food anxieties and similar behavior patterns may shock us, but they become quite acceptable if considered in relation to their background. This principle must also be applied to their attitudes and behavior toward each other and toward adults. The clients' directness, indiscretion, "disrespect," and boisterousness may not be at all pathological viewed in terms of the total cultural environment and early background. Everyone around them, including parents, behave in a similar way. They have been "brought up" to such behavior. In fact, were these youngsters different, they would not be acceptable to their neighborhood peers. They would be stigmatized as weak and sissy, become scapegoats, and generally be socially maladjusted in their surroundings. Thus, the needs of survival in certain sections of a large city require a degree of aggressiveness which may be considered undesirable elsewhere.

Another point requiring clarification as preparation to the main thesis of this paper is the nature and practices of group therapy. The group therapy to which we specifically refer consists of treatment of socially maladjusted and personally disturbed children in which the therapeutic agents are the group situations, the interaction of the personnel of the group, the activities that grow out of the setting, the expanding reality to which they are exposed, the complete freedom of expression, and the growing restraints emanating from the situation.

A therapy group consists of a maximum of eight children within a two-year age range and having fairly equated social maturation, psychosocial development, physical size and other similar factors. The group is provided with arts and crafts materials, toys and games to which there is free access for use at will by the members. They also have free access to each other, and there is communication, interchange, combat, quarrels, friendships, and whatever else spontaneously arises. The children eat together at the end of each meeting and frequently go out on trips, excursions, to the theatre and restaurants. The adult is a neutral person, and for a long period strives to remain passive.

Because children in these groups are permitted to act out their difficulties freely and unrestrainedly, their latent problems, anxieties and preoccupations, as well as their true characters, are revealed. In fact, in a group under the stimulation of other children, these are brought out vividly even in those cases where they are withheld or disguised in individual treatment. As a result of observation of some eight hundred children, we were able to relate types of aggression (and their treatment) to specific characteristics. A full discussion of our findings in the area of character formation is reserved for future publication. I shall confine this discussion to the treatment of aggression as such, omitting etiology, manifestations and other elements. Group treatment of nine types of aggression which we have been able to identify is briefly outlined.

1. *Aggression emanating from prolonged infancy.* A child who has been over-protected and pampered at home tends to continue his infantile behavior in other relations as well. He is playful, provocative, annoying; he demands attention, cajoles, begs, wheedles, and demands. The other members of the group usually reject this behavior and the infantile child finds himself excluded or harassed by his contemporaries. The social maladjustment of such children is quite intense even though in some instances they get along well at home. However, in most cases, the parents, who are largely responsible for this state of their child, become impatient, annoyed and rejecting. A therapy group offers to these children many possibilities for maturing. First, the therapist (the substitute parent), while accepting the client's behavior, is at the same time objective and restraining in his manner. At first he does not react to the childish cajoling, wheedling and annoyance; neither does he seek to exploit the child for his emotional needs, as is the

case with the parent. He does not feed the child's craving to continue in a state of infancy by telling him he is "cute," or by being amused. He rather lets the client navigate on his own and make the necessary adaptations acceptable to the group. If the child wishes to be accepted, which is the basic assumption in group therapy, he will make these adaptations. He will check himself and behave in a way that would cause the group to accept him.

The group therapist does not always remain neutral and inactive in the case of the infantile child. As the child becomes secure, the therapist restrains him in kindly but firm fashion, and encourages constructive activity whenever he shows any inclination for it. In almost all instances these children initiate projects largely because the other children are actively occupied. Another therapeutic element in a group is the presence of other children (substitute siblings) with whom the adult, the tools, materials, food and privileges must be shared. If he wishes to survive in the group, he cannot be the preferred or only child. This is a disturbing reality which he must accept and grow up to. In a group such as we have described, the client has the incentive to change, and models after whom he can pattern himself. The more mature and more constructive members are busily occupied and make things that are freely praised. They become objects of identification and sources of ego-ideals.

The group is exposed as a part of the treatment procedure to progressively extended reality through trips, excursions, limitations and constantly changing situations planned by the therapist. As the child adapts to these and becomes more self-reliant and better self-controlled, his reactions become more mature and more realistic. Our observations show that the non-threatening but constructive atmosphere of the therapy group and the restrictions that grow out of group living in the presence of an accepting but non-seductive and non-exploiting adult, help the child mature and his uncontrolled aggression gradually disappears. This is especially true if treatment is undertaken early in the child's life.

2. *Aggression as a means of attention-getting.* This type of behavior is a manifestation of complex intrapsychic mechanisms. For the sake of brevity this discussion is confined to children who feel inferior and as a result seek attention from people around them, the objective of their aggression. A child who feels inadequate may either completely withdraw or develop patterns of self-maximation and impose himself upon others, since he needs to feel important, strong and powerful. To overcome a basic feeling of weakness, helplessness and impotence, he feels the need to be the center of things and claim the attention of everyone around him. Ordinarily, children with these feelings start projects but do not finish them. They flit from one activity to another and need help in this area from the adult. To finish a job may mean to the child that he will be judged. This he seeks to prevent, since *he expects an unfavorable response.* Some children in this category do not finish jobs also because of early experiences in the home, school and other relationships when they were made to feel weak and helpless. They therefore expect failure and are afraid to finish a job lest their expectation of failure is not confirmed.

For children with attention-getting aggression because of inferiority feelings, the group is an exceedingly effective method of treatment. Particularly is this true of those children who happen to have some special talent. They work in clay, paints, and other media. They make plaques, pieces of furniture and similar objects that bring praise from the therapist, from the other members of the group, and later from teachers and parents as well. They are encouraged to participate with the others in games in which they are helped to succeed. Unless the attention-getting mechanism is complicated by serious personality malformations, it yields to group treatment. We must always keep in mind, however, that in attention-getting there may be the element of infantilism, neurosis, psychopathy, and even psychosis. At this point we are discussing the common variety of attention-getting aggression resulting from a feeling of inferiority or inadequacy.

With such children, the group therapist is actively encouraging. He helps the child over difficult places in his work and protects him against the impact of the group. This is done subtly, for obvious protection and helpfulness by the adult would not only create tension in the group, but would also emphasize the client's inadequacy and confirm his feelings of worth-lessness about himself. Group therapy has evolved strategies and techniques by which the therapist can meet the child's needs without aggravating the problems.

3. *Aggression as a release of organic tension.* This form of behavior is often described as hyperkinetic and may be caused by one of several conditions or a combination of these. It may originate in organic tensions; it may be a symptom of neurotic disorder; it may also result from repressed energies. Where constitutional factors are present, medical treatment may be indicated. We are concerned here with aggressive acts that emanate from suppressed physical and mental drives. The reaction to frustration may have the appearance of neurotic behavior, but actually it is a result of suppressed drives for normal, wholesome activity. We have found, for example, that talented "problem" children become normalized when they have the opportunity to work in fields that fit their special talents. Because they find fulfillment through expression and gain social recognition and status through achievement, they grow poised and happy. They no longer need to express their cravings through substitutive and divertive aggression. Suitable activity for these children is libido-binding.

Children and young people who are repressed physically may act as though they are neurotic or emotionally disturbed but, as the suppressions are removed, they behave quite normally. The neuro-muscular craving for function and activity must be satisfied, thereby establishing equilibrium essential to poise and social adjustment. Canalization of energy is important for humans, and group therapy is valuable here. It not only supplies opportunities for free, unimpeded activity, but helps the child discover latent abilities and directs him toward constructive occupations and interests.

Regulating and sublimating aggression of this type should really be the concern of education in the home and in the school. One gains the impression that homes and schools rather activate aggression through their rigidity, discipline, frustrations and suppression of normal activity drives. The substitution with young children of intellectual learning for muscular and esthetic experience is undoubtedly a major cause for the persistence of this type of ag-

gression. Anxiety about success and failure in school further contributes to an emotional tension relieved by hyperactivity and aggression. Frustration of essential motor activity, however, begins long before school age. Very young children are inhibited by their parents and nurses for their own comfort and as protection for the furniture. Congestion in the home and street, the absence of play space, and unsympathetic supervision are among the many elements that serve to inhibit the young child. These result in cumulative tensions, relieved through hyperactivity.

We omit for the present a discussion of the concomitant emotional tensions which build up attitudes and feeling-tones in the growing child. Prohibitions and limitations which counter the natural development of powers and expression-drives constitute to the child rejection and hatred. As the adult applies restrictions and metes out punishments which seem "reasonable" enough to him, the child perceives them as hostile acts. In psychotherapy we must deal with these attitudes and they form the basic reasons that the group therapist is permissive and neutral, and the children are permitted to release tension through free, unimpeded activity.

4. *Aggression as acting out of neuroses.* The anxieties characterizing neuroses are so varied and so deeply laden with unconscious meaning and latent content that the therapist must proceed cautiously. To begin with, children with intense neuroses are unable to enter into a relation with other children, cannot share the therapist, and are frightened by the manifestation of aggression and hostility on the part of the other members in the group. In fact, many of these clients can not bear the presence of others. They can face life only in isolation or under conditions which they set. Some are unable to accept love and kindness and are frightened by attention and praise. Such clients require individual treatment to a point when they can participate in a group of low pressure or permissive environment.

Children who act out their hostilities in the group must be permitted to do so without restraint or control. In fact, it is of the utmost importance that they be placed in a "mild" group, *i.e.*, a group where the other members will not be rejecting or punitive toward them. The largest number of children, especially in the younger age groups, are not definitely neurotic. They may have neurotic trends or neurotic traits, yet can participate in group activity such as we supply for them. However, our present view is that in all children with neurotic constellations, group therapy can serve only as supplementary to individual psychotherapy.

The value of a free group experience lies in the fact that the client can act out his problems without fear of retaliation, punishment or criticism. He can behave as he wishes and reveal himself as he really is without incurring the disfavor of the adult or children. As a result, his guilt is allayed and his conflicts reduced. He discovers that other children too have problems similar to his own and that he is not as different from others as he had felt. Feelings of loneliness, guilt, and worthlessness are thus supplanted by a more hopeful outlook. Through free activity in a group the client is released, and group therapy under these conditions serves as *release therapy*. Our observations prove that such clients become more productive in individual treatment through this release. They become more communicative and improvement is not only accelerated by group therapy but is also more thorough.

5. *Aggression resulting from maturity phantasies*. Although most infantile children have a fundamental fear of growing up, we have observed a number who, though possessed by this fear, have phantasies and exaggerated strivings to be grown up. Their early identifications with parents of the opposite sex are faulty. A boy whose father is weak, altogether absent, or rejects his wife intensely, may phantasy himself the protector of his mother and assume (or act as though he assumes) responsibility for her. The normal striving to be worthy of the mother is intensified and prolonged in these cases. Such attitudes are especially intense where the mother is seductive, dependent, and exploits the child for her emotional needs or as a weapon against the father. In many instances the boy is sexually overstimulated and is disoriented in this area also.

The form of aggression in such children is both interesting and difficult to deal with in a group. It is interesting because these children act as adults, quite the opposite of what one usually finds in the treatment of children. The disharmony lies in the fact that the child is socially maladjusted because he can not function on the level of other children of his own age — he is *too old* for them. This disharmony also expresses itself in relations with other members of the family, especially the father, in school, and with playmates. The difficulty in group therapy lies in the fact that the aggression is directed toward the other children in a form that would generally meet with the approval of society. They dominate the group, but along lines of maturity, responsibility, and economy. They insist on good behavior and self-control by the others. They are inhibitors, miniature "witch hunters," tyrants and, as we term them, the "group's super-ego." As a result, the accepting, releasing and permissive atmosphere and relations upon which we rely for therapy are blocked or vitiated.

The tyrannical and self-righteous attitudes toward group-mates is supplemented by a subtle and indirect aggression against the therapist. Such children render him impotent by taking over responsibilities for, and the administration of, the group. They check on materials and tools, buy and prepare food, and settle conflicts in the group. They not only seek to possess the adult but also *strive to be* the adult. In one instance a boy of fifteen whom we classified in this category actually asked the therapist to leave the room, so that he could handle a conflict between two other boys.

A major treatment need of such a child is to re-direct identifications from adults to his peers. This is accomplished in most instances by careful and well-planned group placement. Boys and girls who manifest strivings to be prematurely grown-up are detrimental to the others whom they dominate and frustrate, while they are themselves unable to submit to the will of others. Group placement must be with the view of making it possible for the client to make friends with at least one child through whom he can make his way into the group. In this we apply the principle of the *supportive ego*. The group therapist can not deny himself, use authority, or in any way frustrate these clients without the risk of losing them.

6. *Aggression resulting from effeminacy*. When early identifications are not in accord with the requirements of "normal" development in our particular culture, or where either one of the parents, especially the mother, is over-dominant, boys may develop a character aptly described as the effeminate (castrated) character. Such a character is also found among

only boys in families of many sisters, where the total atmosphere is feminine and the boy must fit himself into it. Many become submissive and compliant, lack initiative and are unassertive. However, considerable hostility may underlie this façade. Many who fall within this classification become actively aggressive, with marked arrogance and provocativeness. They behave as though they seek to activate the aggression of the other members of the group. With weaker children they can be quite hostile and even sadistic. This is considered a character disturbance which can be treated successfully only if the clients come to us when very young. It can only be treated by exposing the child to a living situation in which he can take on masculine characteristics. Intimate relations with boys and a non-exploiting adult are very effective in the treatment of these effeminate boys.

These clients are among our most successful cases. Aggression disappears because there is general improvement in character structure. Due to past effeminizing influence they had built up phantasies of the danger and evil of masculinity, and some responded with exaggerated reactive behavior. That boys act as boys in the group, play boys' games, wrestle and fight, and engage in manual activity characteristic of boys in our present culture, gives such clients security concerning their own masculinity. Forming friendships in a group extends their identifications with male images. The fact that the therapist, despite his masculinity, is non-threatening and non-destructive, also helps the client develop security in relation to his potential masculinity. As his behavior gradually becomes normal and he is accepted by other boys and plays with them, the need for the compensatory arrogance and provocativeness is lessened or disappears.

7. "*Deflective aggression*" is an interesting phenomenon. This type of behavior is found in a great many groups of children and adults, as well as among larger groups, even nations. When a child is afraid of possible attack from a very aggressive boy in a group, he becomes anxious and uses the following strategy, both to resolve his anxiety, and to re-direct the possible attack. He attacks a third child, one probably weaker than himself, and through various strategies involves the potential aggressor with him in attack. The two combine to

torment their victim whom they persecute, beat and otherwise make uncomfortable. Thus the child fearing possible aggressiveness against himself saves himself from his peril. This may become a permanent relation of the three boys. Frequently the boy chosen first as a protective object of attack also becomes a scapegoat for other members of the group.

The aim of treatment is to build security and self-reliance, so the fearful child may have courage to face the attack. This is difficult to do in a group situation where alignments have already been created. Subgroups tend to become strongly entrenched and are difficult to deal with after they have been formed. They result from an erroneous original grouping of clients and once the mistake has been made in the group personnel, it may not be possible to work out the problem. It is therefore necessary to withdraw either the child who is a menace or the one who is menaced and place him in a group offering more suitable therapeutic relations.

8. *Oral aggression*, we have found, is the most difficult type of all to deal with in groups. This is found in individuals whose relationships with other people seems to consist of incessant verbal attack, screaming, and cursing. They almost constantly quarrel with other members of the group; criticize, order their groupmates about, find fault with them, and generally make their presence known through screaming and verbal attack against those around them. Most behavior of this nature is not associated with sadism; indeed, it is not even hostile. It is rather a form of social contact which seems to proceed from early fixation on an oral level. It can be described as the lowest primitivism of social behavior and, so far as we can see at present, is probably untreatable; certainly it does not respond to group therapy. The giving and nurturing atmosphere of a therapy group does not quench the psychological insatiability of these children. To permit the acting out of oral aggression in no way alters the need for imposing upon people and dominating them; these individuals continue in their imperious, querulous, gossipy practice.

Oral aggression, as here described, is seldom found among boys, and when it is, exists only in a very slight degree. Aggressiveness in boys has other outlets in our culture; they can fight, physically attack the environment, and sublimate through various types of physical activity. Our oral aggressive girls have special physical characteristics; they are plump, of good complexion, good-natured, and voracious eaters. We have found it necessary to eliminate all such cases from our groups.

9. *Aggression that proceeds from hostility.* Aggressive acts which serve to act out a client's crystallized hostile drives for destructiveness and sadism obviously can not be tolerated in a group. We may be dealing with very intense behavior disorders, psychopaths, neurotic personalities or a combination of these and other trends. When sadism motivates aggressiveness, we face the problem of protecting others of the group against the onslaughts of the sadistic individual. When hostility has already become very deeply entrenched in character and the youngster's drives are dominated by destructiveness, a free group environment is obviously unsuitable and such children must be removed. Treatment of these clients would have to be suited to the particular problem and intrapsychic condition.

It is to be noted that accepted psychiatric categories were not employed in this discussion. It is useful to classify clients in such categories as primary behavior disorders, character disorders, neurotics, and psychopaths, but for the purpose of group treatment it is necessary to consider the nature of the nuclear problem of the client, his intra-psychic dynamics and the goals which he aims to achieve through his behavior. Some of the groupings used in this paper fall into these categories. However, the nature of the child's goals and the propelling forces within his personality may be different from others in the same diagnostic category. We can state with some degree of certainty that intense psychopaths can not be treated by our type of group therapy. They need groups of high pressure with considerable discipline and authority to restrain their behavior as well as develop relationships. Neurotic personalities also can not be included in our groups. We feel, however, that accessibility of clients is rather a matter of degree and intensity of the problem than the nature of the problem itself. We have therefore found it of greater value to describe our clients along the lines used in this paper. This approach helps us in prognosis as to outcome of treatment, determining the suitability of the client for group therapy, and

grouping children in such a way that they would have therapeutic effect upon each other.

Since the group is our treatment instrument, it must be so constructed that it will have therapeutic value for all the members. We must have a group constellation in which the clients' problems will not be intensified. Improper grouping may traumatize some children. A classification such as we employ helps greatly in preventing mistakes in constructing the therapeutic groups.

Finally, the point must be briefly made that aggression as such cannot be treated either through groups or individually. In psychotherapy we are concerned with correcting the character malformations and neurotic drives — of which aggression is a symptom. When we speak of the treatment of aggression, we really have in mind the total psychological syndrome of the client and his characterological states producing the aggressive manifestations. The aim of therapy is not to treat a symptom, but rather to correct personality defects which produce pathological and diffuse behavior. It seems to the writer that we cannot rightly discuss treatment of aggression apart from the total personality of the client.

155

The Integration of Group and Individual Therapy *

*Gerald Patterson, Rene Schwartz,
and Esther Van der Wart*

The use of group therapy with children in psychiatric settings has been in effect for some time. Papers and books have been published on the practical steps necessary to set up group programs, the effectiveness of group therapy, and some of its underlying assumptions.

* Reprinted from 26 *Am. J. Orthopsychiatry* (1956), 618–629. Used by permission of the authors and the publisher.

Group therapy has been a part of the Amherst H. Wilder Child Guidance Clinic services since 1949. Its effectiveness has been demonstrated. But as with any service, once you know it is good, the next step is to determine where it fits in. How do you make optimum use of it so as to enhance the total network of services?

In this paper we shall consider the following: What is the particular contribution which group therapy makes to diagnosis and treatment? How is it different from the contribution which is made by individual interviews? How can we capitalize upon these differences?

Our general plan is to outline briefly what we see as the similarities and differences in individual and group therapy. Although the similarities are greater, we are stressing the differences. We feel we make the most effective use of the two types of treatment by capitalizing upon these differences. We are oversimplifying in describing these two forms of therapy. However, group therapy will be described more specifically since it is newer and less well known in clinical treatment.

It might be well to indicate briefly the type of group and individual treatment being carried out at Wilder Clinic. Our over-all orientation is of the analytic type in which we use analytic principles as the basis for our formulations. However, a good percentage of our children are not severely psychoneurotic. We seldom deal directly in treatment with unconscious material but focus mainly upon ego mechanisms and conflicts. Length of treatment may range from a few months to a few years, with the majority of children probably seen about nine or ten months.

Children worked with in individual therapy are usually seen once a week. The approach is eclectic, making use of a wide range of expressive media such as paintings, clay, dolls, fantasy play, as well as direct discussion of problems.

The group program follows the general orientation of the clinic. The groups are composed of from four to seven children within a two-year age span. Most of these children are in the latency years. They meet once a week in one-and-a-half-hour sessions. These are activity groups as opposed to discussion groups. They are activity groups with a main focus on helping the children to work through their problems by dealing with the current experience in the group. The group therapists at this clinic are social workers with a specialization in group work.

Keeping the description of this clinic in mind, let us first approach a comparison of individual and group therapy by looking at the situation in which the child finds himself. The child's entrance into the group is marked by his immediate awareness of the presence of four or five other members with whom he must effect some kind of adjustment. Pressures are created which may be closely akin to the life pressures which have been so upsetting to him in the past. He must, for instance, face the necessity to compete, to share, to handle aggression or frustration. As he does this, he must struggle with his own feelings — of sibling rivalry perhaps, of rage, of fear, of overwhelming incompetence in relation to others. Not only are group pressures activating his conflicts, but he is rewarded with acceptance by the other children in relation to how he behaves. In a sense the group becomes continuation of the child's usual reality. This is a partial truth. To capture the entire spirit of the group, one almost has to tell at the same moment what else is so obviously present for the child in the group. At the same time that he experiences the pressures of this reality situation, he also warms up to its gratifications, which are of a very real nature. The group room is very much a child's world. All kinds of toys and materials are free for the using. He need not talk with an adult, but can play. Other children not only frustrate him but interest and stimulate him. Whether he can get along well with them or not, he wishes that he could, and positive overtures that do come to him from peers mean much to the child whose social hunger is great. An adult is there, to give help, to find new toys, but is not so uncomfortably near when you don't want him. As the child goes on in the group, the gratifications issuing from the room and the specific toys form a backdrop for the greater importance of finding gratification through relationships. New things become important — a sense of identity with the others, fears mastered, problems of relationship solved.

The social pressures which make the child uncomfortable at times in the group are not necessarily negative factors. They offer a tool for treatment. The pressures placed upon the child by the group are not static or unchanging. They are open to manipulation by the group therapist, whom we have chosen for the moment to leave out of the picture. As we shall discuss later, the crux of our group treatment comes through the manipulation and modification of the social situation so that the child can utilize it for change.

In individual therapy, the child may also perceive his first interviews as threatening. Initially here, he feels called upon to come up with some type of social response. Here also he must handle whatever negative responses and conflicts are mobilized as he reacts to the adult. However, this reaction fades as the therapist sets up for the child a special situation, not typical of any other part of his life. Whatever his behavior, whatever his personality, the child finds basic acceptance. The child comes to realize that in individual interviews he does not have to produce, to prove himself, in order to earn affection. The primary threat of non-acceptance which issues from the other children in the group is absent. Equally important is the feeling which the therapist transmits to the child of total concentration on him and of all-encompassing understanding. Early comments of the therapist are often aimed less at helping the child to gain understanding of himself and more at building in him a confidence that the therapist deeply understands him.

Not only is the general climate different, but the child's means of communication is different in group and individual therapy. In the group the child's energies are largely spent in responding to and manipulating the immediate social environment. He is not talking about his problems but is right in there acting them out with other group members. His central medium for communication in the group is action within the immediate living situation.

In individual therapy, other means of communication are put at the child's command. The child is helped to explore his world of fantasy, to bring out his concerns through dream material, doll play, fantasy stories or other projective or unstructured media. A child's view of this symbolic communication was summarized after an hour of puppet play as, "Boy, this is just like dreaming." This is but one part of the interview content. Often the child can sit down and directly discuss his problems, not only his general feelings but his specific practical difficulties. However, as the child describes these situations, they are not really happening and he is dealing with the residual feelings or memories which he may have.

We find that we are prone, because of the differences described, to get at different aspects of the child in each setting. From seeing the child in the group, we get a rather striking opportunity to assess his ego strengths. As he responds to the pressures and stimulation which issue from the group, we get a picture of his ability to postpone satisfactions, of his response to frustrations. We see how accurately he perceives the responses of others and how realistically he evaluates himself. As he is forced to react quickly and impulsively, we also get a view of the emergency mechanisms he uses for defense.

The child reveals himself in the group not only in relation to felt pressures but also because the group offers him a particular kind of safety. The child can stand aside and watch the other children less inhibited than he act out feelings which he has as yet been unable to express. He recognizes that others survive undamaged the expression of feelings which he has been forced to contain. He may find the needed support to express himself in the knowledge that others also are having a difficult time adjusting. In addition, he can see the worker react to the disturbed behavior of others in a non-judgmental manner and thus envision his own negative behavior as safer.

There is an additional safety factor in the group. The child is offered the opportunity to reveal himself and yet avoid any direct response by the worker, through an escape into activities or into involvement with other children. For example, one rather constricted child, always respectful of his individual therapist, was first able to strike out against the adult by calling the group therapist names and brandishing a cardboard sword at him — then dashing back to play with some children at the opposite end of the room.

The child expresses himself in the group because of these pressures and safety factors. However, the group may limit the extent of expression. Unless the child is very sick, the social demands of the members' responses to one another are ever present. At some point they become a signal to the child: go no further lest you invite ridicule or other rejection. Every group demands a degree of intact functioning from its members. These demands vary according to the kinds of youngsters in the group, but at some point the child will limit his expression in anticipation of the reactions of the other children.

The group may thus offer a particular kind of safety to the child, but it can never offer the total safety which can eventually be found in individual therapy. Here the unconditional acceptance and understanding of the therapist create an atmosphere which encourages the child to explore more fully expressions which would evoke negative reactions in a group situation. In addition, because he has opportunity to mull over, to reflect, to reach into the past, he may go more thoroughly into any one area.

Material may appear in group therapy and not in individual therapy, or the reverse, depending upon the type of safety factors most necessary to the child. We get a graphic picture of the child's pathology from what we see of his ability to give and take in relationships in the group. In individual interviews we get another view of pathology through the production of fantasy material, dream material, or the response of the child to specific questions dealing with feelings about his problems and his current life situation.

We have tried to outline the differences in climate, means of communication, and the resultant differences in the material obtained. We should like now to attempt to indicate what we feel are a few of the important differences in the actual treatment processes in group and individual therapy.

In discussing the treatment process in group and individual therapy, we have broken down the treatment of the child into two broad facets — living through a corrective emotional experience and developing self-understanding. More specifically we are thinking of the roles played by relationship and interpretation in therapy with children.

Dealing first with relationships, it is obvious that both therapists can offer the child the experience of an accepting and understanding adult figure, against whom he may project and work through his conflicts and from whom he may derive a different self-image. The difference is mainly in terms of the kind of relationship the therapists can offer the child.

As we have mentioned, in individual therapy the child experiences the therapist's total attention, love and understanding and can be, for the hour, the only, the preferred child. In group therapy the child is constantly faced with the necessity of sharing the love of the therapist, of being a sibling among other siblings who are projecting similar needs. Obviously there are components of this in individual therapy also, as witnessed in the problems that many children have with the fact that the therapist sees other children. In the group, however, the experience of being a sibling is ever present and more intense. Many times the child who is as yet unable to share a parental figure may either avoid a relationship with the therapist or he may destroy his relationships with the other children as he battles them as rivals for the adult. The necessity to share the adult in the group may work as an asset in treatment. As the child is able to experience a new family constellation in which he is not on the short end of the shared relationship, he may come to realize that sharing love does not mean less love for him.

The necessity for sharing is not the only factor which differentiates the child's relationships with the two therapists. A second factor is the fluidity of role which can be assumed by either therapist. As was mentioned, the figure of the individual therapist is a rather ambiguous one which the child more or less creates to fulfill his own needs. If it be important, child and therapist may transform themselves into little baby and parent person.

In group therapy, while the child also projects meanings onto the therapist, the atmosphere in itself does not allow for this complete departure from social dimensions. The other children are constantly defining the reality role of the therapist. In addition, the group therapist's choice of roles is more limited. Allowing a child to assume a needed intense dependent relationship to him may throw another child into a panic or may bring the hostility of the group down upon the child. The group therapist must consider how his actions with one child affect the total group. In assuming a role which is helpful to the total group, the therapist may limit the meaning which he might have to any one child.

These limitations on the group therapist's role are eased as the members become increasingly aware of the treatment focus of the group.

Then they come to understand the therapist's role as related to the differing needs and problems of the various members. They begin to understand that the therapist limits one child where he encourages another in aggressive expression. However, even at this point in treatment, the group therapist is not free to offer the child any relationship which would set off intolerable conflicts in other children.

In this comparison of the two adult relationships, the limitations in the group therapist's role would seem to be a treatment handicap. But treatment responsibility in group therapy is not carried solely by the therapist; the relationships between the children are a major and usually a more important aspect of treatment. In the children's relationships to each other we find the same processes of support through acceptance, possibilities for identification, and for safe expression and mastery of conflicts. The acceptance and support which the child gains from his relationships to other group members is not a duplication of what the therapist can accomplish. It has a particular and different meaning to the child.

We have already mentioned the conflicts which the children create for each other. Of course our groups are not all-loving, nor would we wish it this way. However, the group members do become quite accepting and supportive, able to use consciously acceptance and rejection in the group as a basis for modification.

In part the ability of the group members to offer each other acceptance grows out of a tempering of the reality stresses for them. This is effected in many ways.

1. The love of the worker provides a cushion for the child in group therapy. No matter how painful the group may become for the child at a given moment, rejection is never complete since the child at all times has the worker to fall back upon. This was expressed rather graphically by an eight-year-old boy who said, "I was trying but I just didn't know how . . . but every time I got all messed up or knocked down, that lady was there." The worker not only provides a cushion for individual children, but affects the members' responses to one another. As the children see that their feelings are accepted by the worker, they become better able to tolerate each other and to assume some of the worker's attitudes.

2. Programming is an important means used by the group therapist to modify the total climate and to facilitate relationships. The group therapist uses the program to control frustrations and to create opportunities for achievement and gratification. For instance, a whole group session may be devoted to cooking and eating, which satisfy the children's oral needs and reduce tensions. The group therapist also uses the program to contain, redirect or encourage expression of feelings. One meeting may consist of setting up a fantasy situation — a rocket ship perhaps — in which several of the children can experiment with expression of aggression in fantasy which they are not yet ready to express openly. Through programming the therapist moves the group together in proportion to the amount and intensity of personal contact for which they are ready. The same cooking session may become an initial experience for the children working together. Later, the therapist uses the program to reintroduce frustrations and even to encourage conflict as the children become strong enough to deal successfully with this.

3. The children's understanding of the treatment function of the group also modifies their reactions to each other. Each child comes to realize that he is in the group for help with specific problems. He also begins to relate the other children's behavior to their problems. This comes about as the group therapist explains the over-all function of the group and as he deals directly with the problems of individual children within the group. One passive boy was teased by other members because he was a sissy. As the others began to understand that his fear of fighting was part of a problem which made him unhappy, they decreased their teasing and eventually gave him approval for any slight steps he could take toward being more courageous.

No one who has worked with groups underestimates the value of the acceptance which these children give to each other. To recognize the importance of this we need only stop and reflect for a moment upon how in our culture personal success is equated with social popularity and upon how miserably most of our children have failed in this area. Difficulty in peer relationships is certainly symptomatic of core difficulties. However, putting aside the resolution of the core conflict for a moment, the finding of a friend, especially in light of past failures, can be a big achievement for the child.

Our children have not only felt social isolation but have also felt different and separate from the rest of the world because of their problems and because of the necessity for treatment. A group of boys discovered that they all happened to be non-readers. Their first look of wonderment changed to one of relief as they realized that others whom they had not thought dumb also shared this problem. The therapist may reassure the child that others feel as he does, but it is never the same as finding out firsthand from other children.

Relationships between the children are also important in offering the child several sources for identification. The passive or fearful youngster may gain strength through his identification with the aggressiveness of another member. He may try on the role for size with the model at hand for close observation. Or the impulsive child may gain strength through identification with a more controlled group member. The child is also afforded a variety of children to relate to. The fearful child may first reach out through the next most fearful child and then, only when ready, go on to more aggressive members.

Thus far in discussing the impact of the children's relationships with each other we have emphasized the positives. When experiencing some measure of acceptance they are also able to make use of negative criticism from each other, particularly when the therapist is at hand both to give support and to help them spot the real source of the temporary rejection. Children can register their disapproval in quite vivid and blunt ways and often offer the attacked child real motivation for change. Thus the child can use the group as a ground for discovering what part of his behavior elicits approval and what part disapproval. He can also begin to sort out his depreciating attitudes toward himself from his real inadequacies when he has some peers right at hand to demonstrate that they do not always reject him as he perhaps feels they do. Again the therapist is present to help him to recognize the distortions in his perception of the children's reactions to him.

The child not only evaluates his behavior by the responses of others to him, but also by seeing how the behavior of other children is received. He not only suffers when he begins grabbing things from others, but he also sees another child bask in group approval for his ability to share. This use of other children for

reality testing is important all the way through treatment, from the child's first recognizing both negatives and positives in his behavior through his testing out new patterns of behavior, to his evaluating the gains which he is making in treatment. Along with giving motivation for change the group also gives support for change, particularly when a child's progress makes the group experience a more livable one for all concerned.

Summarizing the differences in relationships in group and in individual therapy: in the group the child experiences a shared relationship to the therapist and a new family constellation. The role of the group therapist is less flexible since his role is defined by consideration for the total group. The relationships of the children to each other are of different and special importance to the child, offering him strength through cutting into his sense of social isolation and his feelings of difference. The members provide the necessity and the motivation for change, and the media for self-evaluation. Individual therapy provides the child with an exclusive relationship in which the therapist can alter his role in keeping with the needs of the child. Through the unconditional love and understanding of the therapist, the child may change his perception of himself and receive strength through identification with the therapist, and motivation for change.

Just as individual and group therapy provide different possibilities for relationships, so they provide different opportunities for the child to develop self-understanding. In the context of this paper we shall use the word "interpretation" to mean explaining that which is not immediately known to the child. This does not refer necessarily to unconscious material. It may be something as obvious as helping the child to see the connection between anger and striking out.

A large share of the interpretation in group therapy is aimed at helping the child gain the understanding which will facilitate his relationships to the other children. Although interpretation starts in pointing up for the child the results of his current behavior, it does not necessarily stop here. It may continue to tie up current behavior with the child's basic feelings and conflicts which have their source in the child's personal life.

The greatest asset to interpretation in the group is the fact that the conflict being dealt with is currently activated. This is behavior which has just occurred and the child still retains all the intense feeling attached to it. Individual therapy can also structure situations so that the behavior being interpreted is just as immediate and just as graphic. Conflicts around the therapist's being late, receiving phone calls, setting limits, provide opportunities for on-the-spot interpretation; but quite naturally the group provides a much greater range of such material in a more spontaneous fashion.

There is another aspect to interpretation in group therapy which creates a powerful impact on the child. Interpretations come not only from therapist to child, but also from children. Our children can be quite perceptive. A nine-year-old boy once told another youngster, "You know, you are not mad at John because he's a sissy. You're mad at him because you're afraid to fight yourself."

The limitations on interpretation in the group should also be considered. There is the matter of the therapist's not having time to follow up interpretations in a continuous fashion with six children. A more important limitation is that the child's conflicts may be of such a personal nature that he may not want them exposed in front of other children. For instance, one boy spent session after session in individual therapy discussing intensely with his therapist what his father's death meant to him. At the same time he was unwilling to get into this personal area in the group, where he did not even casually mention the death of his father for a year and a half. Moreover, although the one child may be willing to discuss his conflicts in the group, other members may be too threatened to tolerate discussion of particular conflicts except for brief intervals, if at all. For example, discussion of extremely effeminate behavior on the part of one child would perhaps stimulate enough anxiety in other members so that this could not be attempted. It is possible, however, to discuss thoroughly areas which the group members see as common problems. Such problems include expression of aggression, competition, sibling rivalry, and conflicts with authority.

In individual therapy, on the other hand, the therapist is able to give the child his total attention. He uses this opportunity to ask questions, to refer back to earlier points made, to pursue far more extensively the matter at hand. For his part, the child may be more willing to undertake personal discussion with this adult who has proven so understanding and accepting. In individual therapy, the child through verbal or other symbolic media may bring out his conflicts more directly. This is not an indirect expression through behavior, but an actual discussion of how he feels and what he has experienced in the past. Thus the individual therapist has the material and the opportunity for a broader and a deeper exploration of a particular conflict.

We have discussed several aspects of the two kinds of therapy, including climate, material obtained, relationships, and means of furthering understanding. The logical ending for this paper would be a statement of what kinds of children work out best in individual or group treatment. We devoted considerable time to this subject but did not come up with any over-all meaningful categories. However, we do have a few random impressions from our experience.

We have found that the child with an extremely tenuous hold on reality does not work out well in our groups. As stated, our groups demand at least a minimally adequate reality functioning, often impossible for the borderline or psychotic child. Our children are often too threatened by the bizarreness of this type of child to tolerate him.

We have had some children who have deeply repressed their conflict while manifesting a smooth peer adjustment. The group here was ineffectual. The children had a delightful time in the group, which often interfered with treatment since they often used the group as another defense against facing their problems. Frequently after a period of individual treatment in which the child comes to acknowledge his problems, he can make effective use of the group to experiment with his increased understanding.

With the child who is particularly suspicious or fearful of adults or who has been generally hostile toward the clinic, as with children who have felt forced into coming, the group is an effective beginning. The opportunity for a diluted relationship with the adult and the opportunities for the child to test the situation through other children have been effective aids. In some cases children have changed their feelings about individual therapy through discussions with other children who have felt positively toward this experience.

We realize this cuts across many types of

problems, but the group can be particularly effective with the child who needs help in establishing self-control. The group makes this child's problem its concern because of the discomfort which he causes, and the group can exert effective pressures and rewards for increased control.

Most often the child is seen individually and in the group throughout the course of treatment. When a case is accepted, our general practice is to see the child both individually and in group therapy in order to capitalize on the different material which can be obtained. At the conclusion of the study, a team conference is held in which the findings are presented and treatment direction outlined. By this time, some of the children will have shown us quite clearly that they are setting out to make use of one or the other type of treatment. The passive child may have started to move out more assertively in response to the support given him by group members or the child may have brought out some of his concerns in the individual interview. More frequently, however, at the beginning stage of treatment, the child has not yet demonstrated a beginning ability to work on his problem and we are unable to predict by his early response how he will make use of the two forms of treatment. In such cases assignment to group therapy may rest upon the child's having difficulty with peer relationships. Or, a child may be assigned to individual treatment if he has demonstrated some ability to communicate with the therapist in a verbal or symbolic manner or has expressed some need for this particular relationship. Usually we are confronted with the child in whom some elements of his problem need individual therapy for resolution and expression, and whose problem is also manifesting itself in an inability to form adequate relationships which can be dealt with effectively in group therapy. Our problem here becomes that of making a differentiated use of the two forms of treatment. Fortunately, a child's making a differentiated use of the two types of treatment does not come solely from our efforts toward coordinated planning. The child himself will react to the inherent differences in the two situations. Often after the initial conference in which the general treatment plan is made, the therapists individually develop specific techniques, each relying upon what he feels the child needs from his form of therapy, with the major

communication between them coming from reading the case material. At times the results of this approach are effective. At other times, we fear we are wasting many opportunities to exploit our differences and similarities by failing to plan specific treatment approaches together.

We usually find ourselves getting together for close planning at the point where the child has brought in new diagnostic material or a new response to some specific aspect or technique of treatment as we try to decide how this new development should be followed up and by whom. At times, we are also driven to joint consideration of our techniques by the hopeless feeling that we have just been marking time with the child. Whatever the immediate push that brought us together in planning, as we begin to sort out what the child is and is not responding to in treatment, we begin to consider jointly many questions.

1. We may consider whether the anxiety which the child is currently experiencing in therapy should be mobilized or alleviated and by whom. Often we have achieved good results simply through a planned change in timing of appointments. We have found cases in which the child was exhibiting his conflicts openly in the group and denying them in individual therapy. By having the child's interview follow the group session, the child, because of the anxiety felt in the group, became more productive in individual therapy. Either form of therapy can give the child support to handle the anxiety being stimulated in the other.

2. We consider in what ways we can mutually reinforce specific gains which the child is making. For example, one child had begun to express his fears related to aggression in individual therapy. The group was able to provide him with the first important safe opportunity to move out aggressively. This had a circular effect. The child then discussed the results of his achievement in the group with the individual therapist, and fortified with more understanding, had added strength to try again in the group with more success.

3. We consider how group and individual therapy can focus on different areas with the child. As an example, in one case the individual therapist allowed dependent expression at the same time that the group focus was on encouraging more mature expression.

Obviously these are but a few of the practical considerations in integrating the two types of treatment. As we go along in this work, we are more and more impressed with the possibilities opened up by having these two types of treatment for the child. The opportunities for presenting the clinician with a wider range of treatment approaches would pose this as a practical clinical problem. We know for ourselves that we have just made a start in recognizing the potentials.

156

Delinquent Parents Anonymous *

Barbara Casey

If necessity is the mother of invention, frustration may well be the midwife. For many years as a probation officer I realized that the irritation expressed against their parents — particularly their mothers — by the girls under my supervision was, in many instances, justified. Many of their mothers *were* unreasonable, did not know how to help their daughters, antagonized them when support and understanding were necessary, ignored them when they needed attention, and so on. I also knew that the daughters' behavior was bewildering and unpredictable and often frightening.

I felt that I could help the girls more if I could do something constructive with and for their parents — but there was the rub, for in the regular course of work I wasn't able to see the parents more than once in a great while. I asked myself why I should expect the girls to assume all the responsibility for change in behavior just because I could not get around to seeing their mothers often enough.

THE NEED FOR COMMUNICATION

I had thought of gathering some of the mothers together in a small group for a weekly meet-

* Reprinted from 32 *Focus* (1953), 178–182. Adapted from an article in the California Youth Authority Quarterly, Summer, 1953. Used by permission of the author and the publisher.

ing but had shied away from the idea whenever it reared its head. But my dilemma stayed unresolved and finally, about a year ago, my growing frustration and desperation helped me to rationalize away my fear of the "group psychotherapy" concept. I reasoned that Alcoholics Anonymous has proved to be valuable because it gives the participants an opportunity to share their fears, failures, and successes, and because it gives them emotional support which eventually strengthens their belief in themselves. Surely, then, a bewildered, guilt-oppressed, or hostile mother of a delinquent or pre-delinquent daughter could find some release from concern and worry by sharing her feelings, could find some comfort through realizing she was not alone. Even though I do not have a great fund of psychiatric knowledge I felt sure I could use what I do know. I was aware that self-growth and the lessening of tension and anxiety come through a personal desire to find a better way, through an understanding of motivations, through the realization that others have worries which have been resolved, through subjecting feelings to the test of expression and examination, and through group understanding and acceptance rather than judgment. New personal insights would unquestionably improve family relationships. Improved family relationships would lessen the need for probation department authority and hasten the move toward normality. My personal concern for the girls would diminish as their parents' concern became expressed through positive action based on understanding rather than emotional reaction. Parents of delinquent girls would then feel and be less delinquent themselves.

One of my motives, therefore, was to find a tool which would relieve me of the constant need to be authoritarian. By helping only the girls toward better self-understanding and control I was, in some cases, broadening the gap between mother and daughter because the girls were growing emotionally faster than the mothers could understand or handle, which added to the mothers' sense of failure. They do not like to be deprived of their rights and yet I was in a sense helping them to resent the probation department's expropriation of their role. Therefore I had to find a way to help both mothers and daughters, a way to prove my belief in the mothers' ability to solve their own problems, a way to prove to the mothers my genuine interest in their daughters, a way to help the parents understand their family relationships in order to eliminate the need for wardship. I knew from experience that a mother would continue to be anxious until the probation department dismissed her daughter, who "could not possibly have done what she was accused of," or was always a little rebellious, or refused to go to school, or was boy-crazy, or had brought shame and disgrace on the family by her arrest, and so on and on. There were as many different reasons for anxiety as there were mothers.

TRIAL AND ERROR

I began this experiment with a group of four mothers who met with me once a week after dinner.

1. A mother whose youngest daughter felt her to be unsympathetic and who had run away from home to escape her and an alcoholic father. The girl felt inferior because she was extremely underweight and her mother considered her stupid. (You might guess that the older sister was "smart.")

2. A mother whose son had shown some signs of instability but has now leveled off, whose older daughter was delinquent but never a formal case, and whose younger daughter (twelve years old) threatened to leave home and finally did run away — to Juvenile Hall.

3. A mother of nine — eight boys and a girl. None of the boys was difficult for her to handle or understand. She complained that "the girl did not act like the boys."

4. A stepmother who has been divorced from the girl's father for ten years. The girl has recently been returned to her care by the father; two months later she went on on extended hitch-hiking trip through Arizona and Texas.

Two of these girls had been sexually promiscuous and were known as excessive drinkers.

Fluctuating attendance proved that evening was a poor meeting time and we changed to Thursday mornings at 9:30, for a period of one and a half to two hours. At about this time three other mothers were added to the group.

5. An Indian-Mexican mother of five children whose sixteen-year-old girl had been drinking and running around without her parents' knowledge for three years.

6. A widow whose daughter had been arrested for indecent exposure, having been caught with her boy friend completely unclothed in his car. This mother recently had a hysterectomy and could not return to the group for some time. Her worry over the im-

pending operation and the physical strain caused by her condition contributed somewhat to her daughter's delinquency.

7. A stepmother with one daughter. The girl resented both her and her father and expressed her hostility by becoming infatuated with a man much older than herself and later by running away from home.

Our first few meetings were, as you might well guess, dominated by the leader. I was overanxious, afraid of silences, unsure of just how this technique should work. I desperately wanted the mothers to appreciate the meetings as an "opportunity." I knew the process could be helpful, and I also knew it could fail if there were too much "I."

Two of the "charter members" of the group continued to attend. They came at first because of their anxiety and they have returned again and again because they feel the meetings are worthwhile. At these early sessions I asked these two to express recognition of the benefits they were deriving from attendance, and they came through with testimonials in fine style. Rationalizing, I said to myself that I did this to stimulate other mothers to a perception of the group's value and thus insure their return. Later, when I had gained enough confidence in the group technique to be honest with myself, I realized that I had encouraged this audible support to get positive proof of the benefits of the process and thus ease my own anxiety about it.

At first I felt that the meeting had to have a definite form and a predetermined content, but my own experience and that of skilled and authoritative group leaders have taught me that this is not necessary. The leader of a new group may find a plan helpful, but if he becomes too devoted to it he will find himself ignoring the participant's spontaneous contributions. The more plan, the less spontaneity and interest. I had to learn the hard way that one does not need to guide group discussion toward what the leader believes the group should learn. There are unexpected satisfactions for all to be derived from the small revelations which come from increasing self-awareness, from the challenging questions and answers of the members themselves, and from the suspense we all share as one or another mother gets her worries off her mind.

On the other hand, the group leader should take notes, mentally if possible, on the information implicit in the comments or statements offered. This information can then be synthesized and restated to help each mother toward a better understanding of her daughter's behavior in particular and her family's interrelationships in general. I try to make use of information drawn from my reading and experience by imparting it at appropriate spots in the discussion. Most of these mothers have read very little and their intellectual understanding of adolescence is meager. Usually the dynamics of teen-age behavior are recognizable throughout the discussion. My job is to help with such recognition, to supplement and elaborate with additional facts or observations, as well as to recognize and rephrase the elements of personal relationship which are so much a part of the mother's position, attitudes, or anxieties. In some respects I am a part of the group. In others I am looked to as the leader or the authority.[1]

CONTENT OF THE DISCUSSIONS

"But," you ask, "without a planned program, what do these mothers talk about?" They talk about their daughters. This is their common problem. This is why I brought them together. This is why they are having a first or second or third experience with the probation department. As long as the daughters' behavior keeps the mothers worried, frightened, restless, angry, shamed, or feeling guilty, they continue to chronicle things which have happened. As they become more relaxed, more at ease in the group, they begin to talk about themselves. "Things are so much happier at home now." "My husband and I are getting along better; we talk together more." "I'm not worried about Sue anymore; it's little Joe I am worried about now." Mothers who had asserted that nothing was wrong in the family, who could not understand why a daughter would run away from their "happy home," who placed all the blame on their daughters for the delinquent behavior, who were so anxious to succeed that they didn't realize they were afraid to fail — these mothers are now, after weeks, beginning to say such

things as, "I think the whole trouble was that I just didn't pay enough attention to Sally. I didn't realize how self-conscious she was about her figure." (I also try to see each girl every week and I find the threat they first feel about their mother's attendance wanes as soon as the mother's tension and anxiety lessen.)

The mother whose daughter annoyed her because she did not react as her eight sons did is now a "mother of nine." She had been literally leaving this daughter out of her positive feelings because she could not understand her. At first she resented us, her daughter's behavior, and any implication that anything was wrong with anyone but the girl. She could not express any feelings of guilt or failure but, almost weekly, she did admit her insecurity by dragging herself to the meetings. I worked hard to convince this mother of my friendship. I hoped that she would grow by contact with the group, even if she did not participate actively. I knew there was absolutely no chance of her accepting the responsibility for getting help through the mental hygiene clinic or a family service agency. To my great surprise, and I believe that of the other mothers, she finally discovered that she had many things to say and she wasn't afraid to say them. As she talked more she thought more; as she thought more she talked with her husband more; as she talked with her husband more she found ways to help her daughter understand him. As they all began to think together, "peace broke out" in the family.

I am now comfortable in defining my responsibility toward parents, in telling one mother she must come to the meetings or in inviting another mother or in accepting the refusal of still another whose home problems I know are not acute. I am sure of the value of this group process and more certain of my own ability to employ it. I have found it most valuable with from five to ten participants, but it can be effective even if only two or three attend.

Worry has been discussed in the group and will be again. We came to the conclusion that worry is usually fear or concern over the unknown. The participants found that all mothers worry, but to different degrees and about very different things. No one in the group vowed to stop worrying, but our discussion eased some of the worry about worry.

I visited with Mrs. L, the little Indian-Mexican mother whose sixteen-year-old daughter had

---

[1] The meetings are held in my office. Physically it is impossible to arrange the room in any way other than chairs facing around my desk. I cannot, therefore, step out of the role of leader as is possible in other groups. Furthermore, the responsibility for deciding who should attend is entirely mine.

been drinking and keeping bad company for three years without her parents knowing anything about it. When I invited her to join the group she told me over and over that nothing was wrong at home. Her nineteen-year-old son was a quiet chap who never went out on dates. Why would her daughter, a shy girl, go out drinking? It was extremely difficult for her to face the fact of the girl's two arrests, which made her want to crawl further inside her house, so ashamed that she felt she could never face anyone again. She said she had vowed to be a good mother, the kind who stayed at home, and she had kept this vow. She had never left her children in others' care and didn't see how she could do so now to attend a meeting downtown. She was told, kindly, that she *had* to find a way to come to the meetings, that it would be good for her and the children to be apart a little while. I told her we needed her (which was true). She finally agreed to come, but with much doubt and fear. "What will I talk about? I will not be able to talk because I'll be thinking of my children. I'm shy around people."

Mrs. L came, frightened but all dressed up. She talked, with *little* urging. She decided it was good for her to get away from home for a few hours, and she eagerly plans to return each week. She was proud of the family's interest in what was for her a great adventure. She began to think that perhaps it was her passivity that encouraged her husband to take her for granted these many years and she released her resentment for having been so long regarded by him as only a mother, not as a woman. She developed confidence, courage, and a firm notion of what her role should be. The insights she grasped at the meetings were applied at home and she is more content now that her husband's attitude has changed for the better. The daughter, needless to say, has not been arrested again. She accepts more gracefully the limits established for her gently but firmly by her parents, and gradually she is telling her mother more of how she feels, although she still resents our supervision. Mrs. L. is likewise slowly finding meaning in her daughter's comments because she is looking for meaning, and she is enjoying the growing friendship with her. She now realizes the influence of her daughter's shyness and feelings of social insecurity and I think she could, today, tell me why the girl had run around with ruffians and indulged in wine.

One of the new members is a woman who has been a stepmother for ten years and in all that time has been trying, subconsciously and unsuccessfully, to prove that she is perfect in comparison with the girl's real mother, who was "no good." She found the going in the group a little rough at first and she comes in to talk with me privately and in greater detail. Both she and the girl are now under less tension and as she gains insight into some of her anxieties she will be better able in the group meeting to freely admit her errors without fear of recrimination and to face the necessity of changing the habits and attitudes which almost lost her her daughter. She is unsure, frank, sincere, and scared. I hope I will succeed in promoting a self-referral to the mental hygiene clinic. But even if I do not, at least we all have the satisfaction of knowing she is interested in improvement.

THE GROUP AS A RESOURCE

I have found this group a convenient resource for mothers of new probation department referrals. The amount of anxiety felt by the mother seems to determine how quickly she will accept a group situation. I have not found that mothers of different cultural backgrounds have any particular difficulty in fitting into the group, nor have the older members made it hard for a new person to join. I make an attempt to draw out individuals who tend to passivity, and I try to refer to the mental hygiene clinic or the Family Service Agency anyone who I believe has the kind of personal problem that we cannot cope with successfully in the group.

It eases my concern about a ward to know how her mother's attitudes are changing. What I learn about the mother's attitudes is valuable in my contacts with the girl, and vice versa. We have never had the problem in the group of a mother's asking for information divulged by a daughter. No mother has been reticent in the group about her daughter's delinquent behavior, nor has any been afraid that another member would gossip outside. They have the comfortable feeling of sharing common problems which will be respected by all.

I hope that this article has conveyed to you my sense of satisfaction in this work. It was written with that in mind, not as a sales talk for the group psychotherapy technique, and I have no bibliography to recommend. If you are seriously interested in using the technique I would suggest that you yourself make a point of participating in a continuing group situation under the guidance of an experienced and skilled leader. Such an experience, if you bring to it a knowledge of the dynamics of human behavior, will teach you much. As your interest in group work increases you will become familiar with the work of certain university professors who are recognized authorities in this field and in whose sessions at institutes and conferences you will want to participate — John Milner, Mary Duren, Donald McNassor, Gordon Hearn, and George Sheviakov, to name only a few in California; there are others in every part of the country.

Everyone needs to share; everyone has anxieties; everyone strives for inner security; everyone enjoys a situation in which no one dominates; everyone can learn from others. As a group leader I have found that providing an opportunity for meeting the needs of mothers also meets many of my needs. The gulf narrows between the parent and the probation department, understanding deepens, respect grows, self-pity disappears, pride develops, hostility is released or tempered. It is satisfying for all!

157

An Approach to Antisocial Street Gangs *

James R. Dumpson

One of the concomitant phenomena of the social and economic disruption of the recent war was the marked rise of delinquent behavior on the part of teen-age youth in this country. Particularly in our urban communities, a dra-

matic and disturbing series of outbreaks of warfare was observed among teen-age groups or clubs disdainfully called gangs. During 1945 and 1946 in New York City, violence among "conflict gangs" reached an all-time high. From September 10 to September 19, 1946, a nine-day period, three youngsters were killed in gang warfare in one neighborhood of the city.

Action was deemed imperative to protect the community and its members. The Prison Association of New York called on the Welfare Council of New York City as the central planning and coordinating social agency in New York to "formulate a definite program of action" for the amelioration of antisocial activity by gangs. Despite considerable discussion about the cases of juvenile delinquency, few efforts had been made to examine empirically the methods being used to prevent and control delinquency. The Council called together a committee of experts in the field of youth services, and after months of careful analysis and study, the committee recommended the operation of an experimental project with street gangs designed to formulate methods for developing and extending suitable programs of treatment. The project was to operate for a three-year period in two of the most seriously affected areas of the city. Limitation of funds confined the effort to one area, and in the spring of 1947, the Central Harlem Street Clubs Project was set up.

In reporting on the Central Harlem Street Clubs Project, the writer, at the outset, wishes to acknowledge the contribution of the entire staff of the project in the presentation of the material on which this paper was based. However, the writer personally takes responsibility for the form in which it is presented, and particularly for the evaluations that are set forth.

Basic Assumptions and Objectives

There are multiple causative factors underlying individual delinquent behavior, and an examination of causation of antisocial group behavior similarly indicates many contributing factors. The degree to which any one factor contributes to antisocial behavior, whether individual or group, may be negligible. As stated by Shulman, "It is the cumulative impact of a large number of these factors that constitute the multiple causation pattern and, at the same time, the complex treatment problem of the

* Reprinted from 13 *Federal Probation* (1949), 22–29. Used by permission of the author and the publisher. See, also, E. G. Beier, "Experimental Therapy with a Gang," 30 *Focus* (1951), 97–102; W. B. Miller, "The Impact of a Community Group Work Program on Delinquent Corner Groups," 31 *Social Service Review* (1957), 390–406. — *Ed.*

delinquent situation." [1] The aggression and hostility of the delinquent reflects his neglect, his lack of affection, his rejection by his family, neighborhood or community. Devastating economic and social conditions play a major role in the breakdown of the family which in turn results in emotional deprivations and frustrations that drive the individual to behavior which we call delinquent. Racial, religious, and class prejudice, topped off by a stereotyped and depersonalized school experience, contribute further to his feelings of rejection and to the influences of unsatisfying interpersonal relations in a home that frequently is emotionally demoralized.

The Committee on Street Clubs, in its analysis, defined the following as causal factors in the antisocial club behavior which they studied: (a) the glorification of violence and "commando" tactics during the war years; (b) the tension resulting from an intensified emphasis placed on racial differences; and (c) the deep-seated frustrations as the result of political, social, and economic discrimination on racial, religious and nationality basis in our country or city.

The recreation and leisure-time agencies in the area were not equipped, either by stated function or structure, to cope with the street gang situation. A survey revealed that not more than 10 per cent of the total adolescent age group in the area studied were participating in adult-sponsored leisure-time activities. Even where attempts had been made to reorganize programs in an effort to attract a greater proportion of the teen-age group, it has not been possible to integrate into total agency programs those autonomous street gangs which already had developed patterns of aggressive antisocial behavior. The complex cultural and socioeconomic factors underlying the street gang pattern dictate that an approach to the situation cannot be anchored in a recreation program. No amount of adaptation of services on the part of leisure-time agencies alone can prevent or control juvenile delinquency. To seek the answer in recreation is to deny the subjective meaning of antisocial behavior. The prevention and treatment of delinquent behavior requires the utilization and coordination of *every* available and known resource of the community. It must use effectively the knowledge and skills of every discipline that relates to man in society. It must be a total community approach.

We have learned that punitive and repressive methods will not control the street gang situation. Such methods on the part of the police and other community agents have tended to heighten existing tensions and to increase hostile activity. Authority has its proper place in treatment and control, but must be used as part of a total plan which is geared to the individual and his needs. Brutality and ruthlessness on the part of the police merely fan the flames of hostility of gang members and serve to strengthen the unity of the group out of its felt-need for protection and retaliation.

The committee agreed that existing approaches were not meeting the needs of street gang members. Experimentation with an approach that would involve in a positive manner the total community and all of its resources seemed indicated. The approach used recognized that the street gang is a normal expression of the needs of adolescents to emancipate from adults and to establish themselves as independent individuals. By its very nature, the street gang has constructive potentialities. It is a medium through which the adolescent can gain a security which arises from acceptance by one's social group and also one through which capacities for group loyalties, leadership, and community responsibility can be developed.

The objectives and goals of the project as set forth by the Committee on Street Clubs may be stated as follows:

1. Reduction of antisocial behavior among street gangs through redirecting antisocial behavior into socially constructive channels.

2. The development of a local area committee composed of persons having an active interest in the area and concerned about our problems. The purposes of this committee would be to sponsor the project at the area level, be responsible for developing and utilizing local resources for meeting the needs of the street gangs, and to stimulate further community action toward the removal of forces acting as hindrances to wholesome living in the neighborhood.

3. The determination of the validity of the

---

[1] Harry Manuel Shulman, "The Family and Juvenile Delinquency," *The Annals of the American Academy of Political and Social Science*, January, 1949, p. 21.

project method as an approach which may be adaptable for use by other areas.

In order to achieve these goals, it is necessary to structure a process that provides a dynamic relationship between the boys and the workers. The project must help the people of the area to focus their interest and constructive efforts on the problems which adversely affect wholesome living, and to provide them with skill in finding ways of solving these problems. Finally, if the project method is valid, the techniques employed should be defined for use by other areas and communities faced with the street gang problem.

Working directly with the various street gangs in the neighborhood are five area workers, one of whom is a woman, who are responsible for direct contact with a gang and who, through the skills and understanding of casework, group work, and community organization, attempt to help the gangs and their members to find satisfaction in socially acceptable club activities. The research director has the responsibility of recording the operations and of evaluating the results of the project. The area director, working with the Council's Consultant on Correction and Delinquency and the Committee on Street Clubs of the Welfare Council, provides the administrative direction of the entire project. The woman worker devotes her skills and efforts to the girls who are directly related to the boys in the clubs.

THE STREET GANG STRUCTURE

During the two years of the project's existence, relationship has been established with four of the area's most aggressive, antisocial gangs and contact has been established with the girls related to them. Each of these gangs has a history of violent gang warfare, weapon carrying, stealing, rape, and the use of narcotics. Truancy, drinking, and tangles with the police have been prevalent among the boys, whose age group is from 11 to 23, and many of whom have been in one or more correctional institutions.

Except during mobilization for gang warfare, the structure of the gangs is generally loose and organized for a face-to-face relationship and the protection of its members. The largest gang has approximately 100 members; the smallest about 35 members. However, the boys travel in groups of two or three and it is unusual to see more than 10 or 15 members together at any one time

or place. Basically autocratic, the gangs can be divided into two distinct groups: leader and leadership clique consisting of five or six boys, and the members. The gang is broken up into various special interest groups for activities, and while membership in these gangs varies, there is a tendency for the leadership clique to play a dominant role in them and to determine the nature of most of their activities. The gangs also have what the boys call "divisions." These usually are based on age groupings, have their own organizational structure, and serve, by a kind of vertical mobility, to perpetuate the gangs. The club officers' titles are functionally descriptive and seem to indicate the roles their holders have in gang warfare. Usually there is a "president," "vice-president," and war counselor, assistant war counselor, and occasionally a "light up" man. This latter boy usually carries the pistols and initiates the war by "shooting up" the rival gangs.

Newspaper and magazine articles and recent glorified films on the gang have given a distorted picture of the frequency of the groups' participation in antisocial behavior. The experience of the project indicates that only a small part of the boys' time is spent in such activities. Participation in sports, attendance at the movies, parties, dances, "be-bop" sessions, and "bull sessions" take up a much larger part of their time. Just "hanging around" and visiting their girl friends are important activities of all the gangs.

The so-called "street gang" may be one of three types: (1) A group whose principal activities are antisocial. This is the "criminal gang" whose sole function and activity is antisocial in nature. (2) A group which occasionally engages in antisocial activities. This is a normal social unit of adolescents. Under appropriate external stimuli, it may engage in antisocial activity. (3) A group which, as a unit, does not engage in antisocial activities although individual members of the gang may follow a confirmed pattern of delinquent behavior. Although our experience during the two-year period has been with four of the city's most notorious gangs, it is my judgment that the so-called "street gang" is a combination of the last two types.

THE PROJECT AREA

The section of New York in which the project is working is one of the most depressed, underprivileged areas in the city. It is an area of inadequate health, educational, and recreational facilities; overcrowding; poor housing; and low economic status. The people, for the most part, react to segregation and racial discrimination with hostile and tense feelings which underlie many of their attitudes toward the value system of the community at large. The violation of conduct norms among adults is an ever-present reality. Charges and countercharges of bribery by the police and of police brutality are part of the daily flow of events. The setting for the average child is one of poverty, value conflict, bitterness, anxiety, fear, and antisociality. However, there has been no evidence of any sympathetic attitudes on the part of adults toward inter-club warfare among the teen-age groups. Indeed, in most instances, most of the adults have characterized the boys involved in gang warfare as "trouble-making hoodlums," and this has been of real concern to many of the boys. As the boys have come to engage in constructive social activities, there has been an increasing measure of cooperation on the part of the adults. Their mixed feelings about the community, and the realities of segregation and discrimination present a real problem for effective organization for local community action.

Relations with Street Gangs

The operation of the project began officially with the appointment of the area director on April 14, 1947. For the first three months, the director's work consisted largely of a survey of the cultural, ethnic, economic and social aspects of the neighborhood; charting the movement and respective areas of operation of individual gangs; and establishing a relationship with the leadership of the gangs and the indigenous adult leadership in the neighborhood.

The approach in establishing a relationship has been informal and no attempt has been made to interfere with the boys' accustomed ways of carrying out their activities. In fact, identification was built up through able participation by the area workers in those activities which had special meaning for the boys. It was found helpful to have an extra package of cigarettes on hand as the boys were always "bumming" them from each other. Acceptance of the director by the gang can be noted by the following type of incident which is quoted from an area worker's process record:

When one of the boys would ask if he got the cigarette from the director, frequently the answer would be "Yeah, man. He is a citizen," or by the statement, "No, man, he ain't no cop . . . we cased him."

The relationship with the first gang, the Royal Counts,[2] was sufficiently established to enable the director to obtain their cooperation in fixing up the project office. Throughout the cleaning period, questions were asked of the director as to how the place was to be operated. The presence of office furniture seemed to have motivated many of these questions. They were answered frankly and directly, and the aims and purposes of the project were discussed freely. After the confidence and interest of this group had been secured, the boys were transferred to the first area worker at the end of three months. Through utilization of similar techniques, another area worker was able to establish a relationship with the Lords. In this case, the worker formed a close relationship with the janitor who cleaned the project office and who had been purposely selected to do this job because of his thorough knowledge of the neighborhood. Through the janitor, the worker was introduced to a key member of the Lords. Their interest in the Dodger baseball team, a picture at the neighborhood theatre, and invitations by the worker to accompany him on errands, laid the foundations for at least a beginning relationship. It paved the way for casual visits by the worker to their hang-out. Here he usually found the boys either boxing or sparring. He decided that their expressed interest in baseball was an attempt to please him or may have been a reflection of his anxiety to rush the job of acceptance. In order to extend the relationship, therefore, he attempted to use the medium of boxing instead of baseball.

A third worker made his contacts in a block where the existence of a street gang had been established. The worker was in need of housing and asked many people on the block for help in finding a place to live. In this way, he became acquainted with people of all ages. As was the practice with the previous workers, after just "hanging around," drinking coffee, playing the juke box, this worker became known as "one of the boys." He was included in con-

---

[2] Pseudonyms are used in all references to the names of gangs and gang members.

versations and challenged to pitch pennies, and to play football with the boys. Through these contacts, which were purposefully initiated by the worker, he gradually gained the acceptance of the members of the street gang. The following excerpt from his process records gives a picture of the background and atmosphere in this particular situation:

Edward [the candy store proprietor] had a small juke box in his store, and I have played it quite often, frequently as a means of extending my stay. On four occasions, I asked the fellows to help me choose some decent numbers. After that they changed the numbers I punched to play records of their own choice. They don't do this secretly, but openly and with good humor. They stand around the juke box and talk about dates and dances — but I seldom, if ever, see them with a girl. They are usually together. Even on Saturdays and Sundays. When they enter the store and I am there, they greet me along with anyone else in the store whom they know. On the several occasions that I have entered the store to find them there, they continued talking or doing whatever they were engaged in. On one occasion, one of the fellows asked me for a cigarette and on another occasion they approached me en masse and asked if I did not want to hear "Let Me Love You Tonight," — I laughed and played the record for the umpteenth time.

The workers experienced numerous frustrations and anxieties in developing relationship with the boys. Although constantly assured that there were no "deadlines" to meet and no rigid schedules to which they must adhere, they always looked eagerly for the first signs of real acceptance. But these signs, at least in the minds of the area workers, were painfully slow in appearing. Sometimes, in the midst of a conversation which had all the opportunity to deepen the relationship, the boys suddenly would move away leaving the worker alone. The worker might approach a group hoping to join in the conversation, and the boys would become silent. Months later, the boys would tell the workers that they originally suspected them of being policemen or similar representatives of the law. They had watched carefully for any clues that might confirm their suspicions. Finally, through real acceptance of the boys and their group, a conviction about the constructive potentiality of the club,[3] and through his un-

derstanding, warmth, skill, and unending patience, the worker was able to establish a relationship in varying degrees with members of the club.

WORKER'S ROLE

What to do with the relationship has presented one of the most difficult questions in the project, for we are learning that this relationship has been structured differently from the usual casework relationship. We are only now beginning to define the quality of this relationship and to distill the area worker's role in its dynamics.

In working with the boys, the workers usually follow the initiative of the boys. They participate in games, bull sessions, block parties, "bebop jumps," card-playing, or just "hanging around." Recently, boys of several former conflict groups have gone on weekend camping trips, and other similar intergroup activities are planned. The workers see club members almost every day, usually in the afternoon and evening, and spend from 12 to 25 hours a week with them. Usually, they see from 4 to 12 boys in a contact. Sometimes they see only one boy in a contact; sometimes as many as 50. The contacts take place wherever the boys hang out — the street, the candy store, the pool room, at the boys' homes, and now, with growing frequency, at the project office.

We do know that the area worker's role varies with the needs of the group. At times the boys ask them to arbitrate a dispute, to give help in securing a job, or advice on personal problems. The worker's word is not law and the boys freely accept or reject the worker's opinion as they see fit without being rejected by the worker. In a discussion of antisocial behavior, the worker's role also varies. Frequently the worker will listen without expressing approval or disapproval. Sometimes he will disapprove openly of their behavior and give his reasons. If the total situation warrants, the worker may initiate a group discussion and utilize group interaction. Or he may await an opportunity to discuss the situation with an individual boy in terms of that particular boy and his ability to use more intensive help. The area of antisocial behavior is the most difficult to handle. The worker must use great skill in defining his difference from the boy and at the same time maintain a horizontal relationship with him.

---

[3] The term "club" is used hereafter in reference to the street gang with which a working relationship has been established with the area worker.

Skillfully, he must determine the motivations of the boys' behavior, determine the leadership in the situation, and manipulate the situation so as to provide substitute satisfactions for the real goal of the antisocial behavior. In all of this, however, his identification with the boys and their needs must never blind him to his responsibility to the larger community. While he can never betray the confidence of the boys he constantly must interpret to the schools, the police, and to the entire community constructive ways of meeting the needs and frustrations and hostility which their behavior represents. The worker must recognize and accept his own limitations in the helping process and assist a boy to move on to the use of specialized services in the community when the need is recognized and the boy is ready to use it. Gradually, very gradually, he must help the boys make the fullest use of the facilities in the community and at the same time help the agencies understand and accept this boy. Many of the leisure-time agencies are having to accept the hit-and-miss kind of participation by the boys as they test and retest the realness of their place in the agency after they have accepted the worker's suggestion that they use the agency's facilities.

The worker is called upon to assume responsibilities which other club members are unable or unready to assume. When the boys show an interest in some project, the worker usually helps in the planning and takes on responsibilities just as any other club member. He helps get equipment, permits for block parties, and secures tickets and passes from the police for events that the boys previously had rejected. Gradually the worker transfers responsibilities to individuals in the group, and himself takes on fewer and fewer responsibilities. To illustrate, one area worker writes in describing a second block party:

A significant change that is apparent is the contrast between the amount of responsibility that the boys took upon themselves at the first block party and at this block party. At the first block party I had to get my hand into a great many things and the boys waited for me to do things before they would start. This time they took on responsibilities without waiting for me. I just had to carry out my duties as a member of the group rather than as the supervisor. At this block party, Fred took the responsibility for running the record machine; Leon asked the fellows

not to shoot fire crackers; he had signed the permit for the party and therefore felt a keen responsibility for conducting it without unhappy incident with the law. Harry took chief responsibility for drawing up a list of the refreshments to be purchased, making the purchases, and supervising all of the boys who helped to prepare and sell the refreshments. Spike's feeling of responsibility was exhibited in his helping out where needed and checking up on all phases of the activity. Jim, an older boy, got a number of his friends to assist the boys in selling raffle tickets and took the responsibility for borrowing a large lamp from the owner of the barber shop and setting it up to provide light for the party.

The worker suggests new ways of doing things that are leading to a greater democratization of the clubs. The boys are experiencing the satisfactions of successful efforts and cherish the "rep" they are achieving in the community, which gives them the status they previously sought in daring and dangerous antisocial activities.

COMMUNITY SELF-HELP

One of the unique objectives of the project is to offer assistance to the community in dealing with the problems of the area and meeting the needs of the boys. Chiefly, this involves the development of resources and the stimulation of local community action toward the removal of hindrances to wholesome living in the area. Not only has it been necessary for the staff to gain the acceptance of the boys in the clubs. The adults in the community were as suspicious and mistrustful of the area workers as the boys were. During the first 18 months' operation, the staff had to build the kind of relationship with the people in the area that would allow them to use the skills it has in community organization. Efforts are being made to develop an area committee — parents, interested local citizens, and representatives of the four clubs with which the project is in contact. The area committee will attempt, on a local level, to engage in social action designed to effect changes in the neighborhood that contribute to juvenile delinquency. It will attempt to create an atmosphere in which the boys and the potential constructive value of the street club are accepted. It will set in motion the creation of a spirit of cooperation between the boys and the adults and a feeling on the part of the boys that they are "somebody," that they are valuable as individuals and in groups and have a worthwhile contribution to make to the local community. The area committee receives guidance and direction from the staff using, however, whatever indigenous leadership there is in the neighborhood. It will receive the full support of the influential Committee on Street Clubs as programs are developed in matters of housing, police activities, health and welfare facilities, employment opportunities, educational facilities, and the elimination of adult criminal activity in the neighborhood. Progress in this area is painfully slow and considerable interpretation and support is necessary.

A professional advisory committee, made up of representatives of agencies and organizations in the local community, is attempting to supply services that are needed and to assist the agencies in meeting the needs of the boys and community as defined by the project staff. Plans are being considered by the committee as to how the techniques developed by the project may best be used by existing agencies after the project has terminated in 1950. The regional division of the Welfare Council of New York is working with the project staff, the area committee and the professional advisory committee in an effort to achieve the fullest coordination and the best arrangement of existing services, and to identify areas of unmet need.

RESEARCH

Space does not permit a detailed exposition of the research plan. The answers to two basic problems were assigned originally to the research director: (1) Is the area project effective? (2) Why is the project effective or ineffective?

Evaluating the effectiveness of the project involves a determination of the extent to which desired changes occurred in club members and the extent to which these changes can be attributed alone to the project's influence. Determination of the answers to the second question involves the formulation of the methodology developed in working with street clubs during the three-year operation of the project. It will be necessary to define the methods which were followed by positive change, negative change, or no change at all. We shall want to compare those club members who change most with those who change least. It is hoped that re-

search will indicate the extent to which such environmental influences as the socioeconomic conditions of the area, police practices, etc., seem to influence club members. And finally, we hope to be able to define the personal qualities and professional equipment necessary for an effective area worker. The area worker records his contacts by means of chronological process records. Following this, he answers an interpretation questionnaire designed to help him think through the significance of his experience in preparation for the next contact. He also prepares a review of his records each month as an aid to judging his progress, the effectiveness of his methods, and the most appropriate procedures for the future. Volumes of process records are being analyzed by the research director in order to provide an analysis of various change categories, an evaluation of the workers' techniques, and the boys' response to them. From this material, research is able to provide a current evaluation out of which the staff is able to refine and reformulate techniques and methods of operation. Research also will allow us to state the success or failure of this approach to street gangs and help determine its usability in other communities facing a similar situation in the control of juvenile delinquency.

PRELIMINARY EVALUATION

Any assessment of accomplishments of the project must, of necessity, be tentative. Even now, we have not perfected the tools for measuring the effectiveness of this project approach to antisocial street gangs. And when this is done, we will be faced with the limitation that is set by not having any precise accounting of the extent to which the boys engaged in various activities at the beginning of the project. Nor can we be sure that we are securing now a complete picture of their activities. Even though the boys tell the area workers a great deal, we cannot be sure that they can and do "tell all." Finally, change is a gradual process. If the workers are putting into their relationship with the boys a content that allows the boys to experience a reorganization of any part of themselves, we may not be able to measure the full effectiveness of the project for some time yet to come.

Despite these limitations, we are able to make certain tentative judgments about change in the clubs and to isolate positive results in several of the change categories:

1. The boys are spending increasingly more time in constructive and satisfying activities. Behind these activities are hours of joint planning and sharing. Through these activities, we have helped the boys release much of their potential initiative, leadership, and resourcefulness in socially acceptable and individually satisfying endeavors. They have gained some status in the group and in the community from these activities which they formerly sought in antisocial behavior. They have begun to gain a sense of individual worth and are developing an interdependent relationship with the adults in the community including the heretofore despised policemen.

2. Certain forms of antisocial behavior have decreased. Since the beginning of the project none of the clubs has engaged in interclub warfare although there have been incidents in other sections of the city. Concomitantly, there has been a marked decrease in intergang warfare among the gangs which occupy territory immediately adjacent to that of our clubs. There has been less measurable decrease in the use of narcotics, sex activities, individual stealing, truancy, and drinking. It may very well be that these forms of antisocial behavior for some of the boys are symptomatic of deep personality disorders and are not amenable to the approach of the project. However, there is evidence that the boys have a greater awareness of a new value system and, in individual instances, are consciously striving to identify with the value system of the area worker.

3. The ability of these boys to establish a relationship with a mature, warm, accepting adult has been unquestionably established. This accomplishment augurs well for their use of the only medium through which help may be offered to these boys in order to effect any substantial change.

4. Relations within the group have improved. The leaders are less autocratic and the opinions of the club members are more consistently sought. There is evidence that intragroup dynamics are beginning to operate in a broader democratic framework.

5. The boys have been helped to recognize the availability of facilities in the community which more satisfactorily meet their needs. Their use of the facilities of the Police Athletic League, the gymnasia of public schools, camping facilities, and their willingness to test their acceptance by the group work and leisure-time agencies indicates that success is being realized in broadening the boys' horizons and enriching their day-to-day experiences.

6. Here and there existing recreational agencies have been helped to accept these autonomous groups and to gear their programs to the boys' interests and needs. Considerable reorientation needs to be done in this area before the boys are ready to use the agencies and before the agencies are prepared to accept the boys.

7. Finally, several agencies in the city have begun to adopt this project's approach for their program in an effort to reach groups of boys similar to those in the project. In one instance, a group of extension workers from a group work agency is working with street gangs in the immediate area of the agency. In another instance, two recreational workers in the public schools have been released from the after-school program to work with two street gangs that recently caused the death of one boy and seriously injured another. A project in still another area of the city, under one of our regional councils, using the approach of the Central Harlem Project, has been completed successfully and the report is now being written. The program of the New York City Youth Board to prevent and control delinquency will include a group of workers who will use the approach of this project in working with street gangs in various parts of the city.

We are convinced, at this point, of the soundness of this approach. There remain many limitations to overcome and many problems to work through. As yet, we have not fully defined the function of the area worker, the specific equipment he needs to bring to the job, and the extent to which the area worker must use the disciplines of casework and group work. There yet remains the task of isolating, in a demonstrable way, the various techniques used by the area workers, testing the effectiveness of each of these with the various types of boys in the street gangs and the motivations of their participation in the antisocial activities of the gang. Then we will need to find ways of adapting these techniques for use in existing or new agencies as a way of working with antisocial street gangs.

Finally, if we are to prevent, control, and treat delinquency, we must all find a way to use, in every appropriate setting, the knowledge and skills we have concerning human behavior. We have not begun, as a profession nor as a society, to use all that we know about mental hygiene, social improvement, and change in our efforts to meet the challenge of juvenile delinquency. More than new agencies, more than new techniques, more than greater emphasis on psychiatry and sociology, group work, recreational facilities, or additional institutions, is our need to develop a broad, comprehensive program of child welfare in every community that utilizes every bit of knowledge and skill presently at our command. We shall need constantly to test and retest the things we do in that program. As we develop research in every phase of child welfare, we shall have a valid basis for change in experience and practice. Then, and only then, shall we meet the needs of children at home, in school, and in other areas of community activity. Then we shall effectively prevent and control the individual and group expressions of juvenile delinquent behavior.

158

Establishing Relations With Antisocial Groups and an Analysis of Their Structure *

Lloyd T. Delany

This paper is in two parts. Part I proposes to describe how relations are established with street gangs.[1] Part II describes the internal

---

* Reprinted from "Establishing Relations with Antisocial Groups and an Analysis of Their Structure," 5 *British J. Delinquency* (1954), 34–42. Used by permission of the author and the publisher.

[1] The term gang is never used by members of such groups or by people working with them. The term club is used by both members and workers. In this paper, group, street club, and for purposes of clarity, gang, are used interchangeably.

structure and leadership functions of anti-social groups.

PART I

Street fighting is a by-product of gang life. In the early '40s and probably related to the fact that a world war was then raging, teen-age warfare took a new and more serious direction in the United States. Simultaneously throughout the country, adolescent groups in our large cities began to use lethal weapons. Some were home-made, fashioned out of wood, small piping and rubber bands. Others, of a more standard make, were acquired from older brothers and friends returning with "war souvenirs." In the span of a few years gang activity was taking a serious toll in the lives of its members. The "Zoot Suit" riots of 1943 in Los Angeles received nation-wide attention (11). As a result of these and other incidents, certain segments of social work, psychological services, and other allied fields were spurred to re-examine past attempts at working with teen-age clubs. Out of these studies, an approach evolved that has at varying times been described as "area work, detached work, or street club work" (2, 7 p. 100–101, 3, 11). Basic to the approach is the requirement that the practitioner spend most of his time working with the group in its own setting, that is, its local candy store hang-out, street corner, or cellar club room.

ESTABLISHING THE RELATIONSHIP

There are generally three stages involved in building a working relationship with an anti-social street group (3). The first is locating the specific hang-out spots of the gang; the second is establishing actual contact; the third and most important is gaining the gang's confidence and acceptance.

Locating the Gang. Location of the street club requires an extensive and exhaustive survey of the community in which the gang is reported to operate. Although much information about the operations of antisocial groups is available from the police, district attorney's office, and other public agencies, it is important to supplement this information by visits to local schools, social agencies, business establishments, churches, playgrounds, etc., etc. Names of groups and their members are carefully copied from walls of buildings. Many hours are spent walking up and down avenues and streets observing adolescent grouping in the area. Eventually one or two specific places are selected and the attempt to contact the group is initiated.

Contacting the Gang. Contacting the gang can be done in several ways (2, 11, 13). If the group is using a community centre, the worker may assume the character of a "volunteer." In this approach it is important that the gang's attitude towards the centre should be an accepting one. Using the agency as a starting point, it is possible gradually to spend more and more time with the street club in its street hangouts. Most antisocial groups avoid established centres, or use them so sporadically that establishing contact within the agency is impossible. In fact this is one of the major reasons why the far more difficult "area approach" and what is known as the "hanging around" method came into use (2, p. 3). Using this method, the starting place is a candy store, pool room, or street corner. The time is varied from early afternoon and evening to late at night and week-ends. The aim is to become a familiar part of the group's surroundings. Conversations are initiated with the more friendly and receptive boys. Sports is a safe noncommittal topic; the "juke box" is frequently a useful device in establishing contact (8). It provides common experiences with the group, and gives a pretext for remaining in the stores, etc., without appearing too conspicuous. There are times when contact cannot be established with an overtly suspicious gang. On these occasions, friendly contact can sometimes be established with an affiliated but less antisocial street club. Eventually, opportunity occurs to work directly with the gang by virtue of having associated with the affiliated group.

Gaining the Gang's Acceptance. In the early stages of establishing contact most street gang members regard the worker as a threat. Invariably they think of him and accuse him of being a cop, narcotics man, or FBI agent. This attitude of deep suspicion persists in spite of all reassurances; it is indeed understandable. As Johnson reports, "Personality-wise, almost without exception, their individual life histories reveal failure to obtain adequate stability, security, from essential parental figures; neglect and rejection have played large rôles in their lives . . ." (6, p. 2). The detective is an authority figure, who in their perception is destructive. It is inconceivable to them that any adult could really have a sincere interest in knowing and working with them. When a group reacts to friendly overtures with suspicion and hostility, it is really saying: "Why are you interested in us? You are going to harm us. Most adults have. We won't give you the chance." Mere denials of the accusation cannot change these attitudes. Hence it is necessary to deal with the distorted perceptions on their real, not manifest level. Change in perception may be started by accepting the concern, communicating awareness of the group's anxiety, and then interpreting its behaviour; one can say, for example: "I know you have had lots of hard times with adults, and when you meet someone new, especially if you don't know who they are and what they do, you probably think they are out to give you a hard time. Maybe that's why you think I'm a cop." An interpretation on this level gives the group an opportunity to understand some of the forces underlying its suspicion. It may well be the first step in the re-educative process in the group.

None of the above is meant to imply that words alone can bring about acceptance. To do this, it is necessary to act out much of what is verbalized to the group. This is best accomplished through concrete service, such as helping members obtain jobs, acting as advisers to their social clubs, or finding a place for the basketball team to practise. These and other similar actions provide *functional* definition of rôle, and thus dissipate much of the early distrust.

There are certain indications that the group's confidence and acceptance have been achieved. For example, spontaneous invitations to members' homes or the "club room" are positive signs of acceptance. Recounting specific information about present and past antisocial activities is also indicative of progress. Other indications of acceptance are the freedom with which gang members are willing to discuss personal difficulties about home, problems in their sex life, their ambition in life, etc. The group worker, caseworker, or psychologist functions in an agency setting. Their clients come with some awareness of the services to be rendered, as well as some desire to be helped. In contrast to this, the practitioner with a street gang is a stranger entering the lives of these boys unasked; they neither ask for his help nor think they need it. In working with the street club all may well depend on how the help is offered. The full acceptance of the group is only achieved if the gang maintains relationship with the practitioner *after* understanding who he is and what he wants. The establishment of a working relationship with an antisocial street group under these conditions usually takes from three to seven months.

PART II

As the pattern of inter-group conflict changed with the introduction of the pistol into gang warfare, so certain changes evolved concomitantly in the internal structure and leadership functions of the antisocial group.

The Internal Structure of Antisocial Groups. There are as many variations in the internal structure of antisocial groups as there are gangs. In spite of this, certain basic patterns exist. Three related but independent patterns of organization have evolved; the antisocial structure, the social structure, and the clique.

The Antisocial Structure. There are three variations of the antisocial structure. The most common pattern is the *vertical* type (3). In this variation the gang is subdivided into what the members call divisions (2). Each division is an integral part of the gang, yet functions in many respects as an autonomous group. For example, it is possible for one division to wage club war without involving the other divisions of the gang. Generally, in these situations they fight divisions of other gangs comparable in age. As long as the older divisions do not interfere, this limited warfare can go on indefinitely; but usually one group or the other makes the accusation that an older division of the enemy is giving unauthorized assistance, and this becomes the occasion for full fledged warfare involving the entire gang. Each division has its own set of officers and tends to involve boys of a particular age range, such as 14–15, or 18–20. The oldest division, generally known as the "seniors," is at the top of the gang hierarchy. The others descend in order of age category, with the youngest, known as "tims," at the bottom. Movement from one division to another is based on age. Often, however, a particularly popular member of one of the younger divisions may become the "mascot" of an older division. A younger member who has achieved widespread reputation because of his skill and daring in club fighting may be permitted to "join" an older division. A constant flow of members comes into the gang and moves up through the structure. While this is the primary method by which the structure is maintained, there are occasions when an entire group is incorporated into a gang. It may then constitute a division or the greater part of one. This latter method of getting members is more common among the "newer" gangs which are still growing in size and reputation. As a particular group gains in status, other neighbourhood groups may seek affiliation with the up and coming gang. Sometimes mergers occur as a result of club warfare. Temporarily aligned groups become permanently incorporated divisions. This process was once described to me by a member of a gang in New York City. He was describing the growth of his particular group. "We started out as the Jolley men, there was eight of us in the club and we changed our name to the Sabers. We had a couple of rumbles with the Dukes and the Eastside Cobras. They also was rumbling with the Knights. So we joined up with the Knights and first we called ourselves the Saber Knights, but later we changed it to just Knights. Altogether we got about fifty guys in our club now." Even defeated groups have been known to be incorporated as divisions of the victorious group.

The second variation of the antisocial structure is known as the *horizontal type* (3). As the name implies, the relationships among the divisions are contemporary rather than on age differentials. This variation is actually a federation-like organization of a number of antisocial clubs in a particular neighbourhood. It is especially common in Philadelphia. As in the vertical type of division, there is a great deal of autonomy. The horizontal divisions also have independent officers and other functionaries. Nevertheless, a complete and real identification with the over-all gang exists. The division in the horizontal variation that has the highest status is generally the one from which the original gang came.

The third variation is *a combination of the horizontal and vertical forms* of organization; that is, some of the horizontal divisions will have vertical divisions. An example of this is the Commandos, a group that operated in New York City. The Commandos have a Green Street division, a Front Street division, and Siken Avenue division, with seniors, cubs, and tims, and a Second Street division with a cubs and tims division. Obviously, only the larger street gangs could have this type of organization.

The evolvement of such a complicated antisocial structure in the street gang occurs over a period of time. To a greater extent it was the result of forces acting from without rather than of conscious effort on the part of the members of gangs. A young adult in Philadelphia, who was once a member of a gang, describes the process by which he and his group became involved in antisocial behaviour, and evolved a structure similar to the horizontal type described above. "A group of us fellows use to hang around on Nevins Street, we had a little basketball team too. We was playing for a little money, well when we won, they didn't want to get up off the money so we told them, 'man, ain't gonna be no stuff like that around here,' so we took our money. They said they'd be back. So that night the fellows was standing on the corner, waitin'. Man, about twenty of them cats came down, but we was waitin' for 'em. We had our sticks and bottles stashed away. We started to mix it with them cats, and man, the next thing we knew them cats was shootin' at us. That was the first time I ever heard a gun . . . we didn't have nothin' so we cut out. The next day, the fellows got together and said that if that's the way they want it, it's okay with us. We went around Apple Street, and we told the guys around there what happen', that some guys from crosstown came over with guns. We knew the guys on Apple Street, but we didn't hang out with them much. We said we was gonna get some stuff and go cross town tonight, did they want to come? They said yeh. One of the fellows in the club said he knew how to make a homemade, so from then on the mess was on. Cats went wild, and soon everybody had homemades and then some cats even got real guns, man many a head was broken . . . I'm telling you. Cats was gettin' stabbed and shot all over the place, it wasn't safe to walk the streets alone any more. Our club was one of the baddest [2] around here, we had guys from Apple Street, Davis Street and Nevins, most of us started hangin' around on Davis Street, 'cause Nevins got too hot."

[2] Used in this sense, the word means tough. It carries no connotation of bad in the usual sense of the word.

The Social Structure. Practically every gang participates to some extent in social activities. When there is at least minimal involvement a social structure evolves in the form of teams and social clubs. The social structure tends to follow age ranges in groups that have a vertical type of organization in the antisocial structure, and geographic location in groups that have the horizontal pattern. Yet the social structure is by no means identical with the antisocial structure. The pattern of inter-relationships in the social structure is different. The athletic teams and social clubs frequently cut across the divisional lines to get a "better player" or a "nice guy" who "knows a lot of girls" for the social club. Many boys who participate in the antisocial activities do not take an active rôle in the social structure; boys who are not members of the gang may sometimes participate in its social activities, but never in its antisocial ones.

The social structure, along with that of the clique, is the everyday functioning structure. If an observer were to study the gang, he would recognize the social structure first. Not but that antisocial activities would be easily observed, but the intricate structure around antisocial behaviour is clearest in times of crisis. Members seldom discuss their participation in antisocial activities and the concomitant relationships in the presence of outsiders. Moreover, in their daily lives and for the greater portion of their time, gang members associate within the social and clique structure, though they are continually aware of the antisocial structure, and this is the most important set of relationships from the status point of view. This is an interesting feature of antisocial groups, for almost all the status a member enjoys, both within the group and from without, is in terms of his participation and position in the antisocial structure. This is true in spite of the fact that he spends comparatively little time in gang warfare. The intensity of emotional involvement is very high. Powers (10) makes this same observation in his work with delinquents.

The Clique Structure. The clique structure is the most pervasive and cuts across the antisocial and the social structure. The clique is the smallest sub-grouping in the gang and is based completely on personal preferences. All the members of a clique are members of the same division in the antisocial structure and grouping (if they participate in social activities) in the social structure. The clique is the informal grouping in the street club. It is the one group in which there is complete freedom of operation and acceptance for the individual member. There are no rules governing participation, and acceptance in the clique is as completely personal as is possible in human society.

Leadership Functions in the Antisocial Structure. Each division has its own leaders. Each generally has a president, vice-president, war counsellor, and assistant war counsellor. War counsellors are charged with the responsibility for arranging alignments, setting up rules of conduct during warfare, signing truces and peace pacts. In time of conflict they are in actual command of the gang. War counsellors in many instances decide when and where the gang is to fight and when they are to stop. Other groups have specific members designated as "light up men." As few gangs have enough guns to go round, certain boys are charged with the responsibility of carrying the pistols and "lighting up" [3] the rivals' hang-outs when they arrive. Some groups no longer use these particular designations, but their functions are continued. One group in Philadelphia (9) was recently reported as having twelve distinct officers with such descriptive titles as vice-president of war, chief of armament, chief of war intelligence, spokesman, and commander of tactical operations. This is an unusual case, but there is no question that members of street gangs are given specific functions to implement the conducting of warfare among rival gangs.

Leadership Functions in the Social Structure. Here leadership functions take on a more familiar pattern: teams have captains, social clubs presidents etc. It will be asked whether the same boys hold leadership positions in both the social and antisocial structures. This will depend on the importance attributed to the social activities of the gang. There is a tendency for leadership functions in the social structure to be held by boys who also hold high status positions in the antisocial structure. This is modified by several factors. Leadership in the social structure is based on ability to function in that area. An expert club fighter is not necessarily a skilled basketball player. Secondly, leadership in the social structure tends to be ar-

rived at more democratically. When social activities are lightly regarded, as they generally are in the more aggressive groups, leadership in the social structure is carried on by lower status members. The level of the gang's interest in social activities can frequently be measured by observing who is leading the activity.

Leadership Functions in the Clique Structure. Cliques follow the status relationships operating in the over-all gang. Members gravitate into cliques according to their relationships within the gang structure. Within the clique, leadership is informal and carried on through the mechanism of prestige suggestions and opinions, which clique members accept or reject solely according to their individual perceptions of the member making the suggestion. Since clique members are close to one another in terms of their status positions in the gang, there is a great deal of fluidity in leadership functions within the clique. The relationship important here is the relationship among the cliques rather than within them.

PSYCHE- AND SOCIO-GROUP PROCESSES OPERATING IN THE GANG

An interesting frame of reference for analysing the internal structure of antisocial groups can be found in Jennings' (4, 5) formulation of "psyche" and "socio" groups. This formulation has been elaborated in other places (1, 12).

The socio-group is one in which participation and association are based on a "collective criterion" (4). In the socio-group, as Coffey (1) indicates, there are structure, established rules, and regulations. Membership is both voluntary and involuntary. There is greater heterogeneity of membership with more crystallized and explicit goals. On the other hand, the psyche-group is described as one in which the individuality of the member is the basic component, where mutual relations and association are very personal matters (4).

The antisocial and social structure of the street gang, while possessing some psyche-group processes, is more nearly representative of socio-group processes. There are rules and regulations governing an individual's functioning within the social and antisocial structure. Membership is voluntary to a certain extent; but since many boys are members of gangs through fear and need for protection, in this sense membership is not voluntary. There is also much hetero-

geneity in terms of age, rôle and status; much
of this is handled through the mechanism of
divisions in the antisocial structure, and teams
or clubs in the social structure. (It was to
handle the growing work orientation of the
gang that the antisocial and social structure
evolved.) The gang also has a vivid and real
purpose — for example, the protection of its
members (through the antisocial structure),
the purchase of jackets, or production of a dance
in the social structure.

The psyche-group process operates to its fullest extent in the clique structure. Membership
is entirely voluntary. (A boy may need to be
identified with the gang, but does not need to
associate intimately as in the case of the clique.)
There are no rules or regulations in the clique,
and it is homogeneous in terms of age, rôle and
status in the gang. The clique has no purpose
except the emotional support that comes from
close accepting inter-personal relations.

The importance of psyche-group processes
cannot be over-estimated. It was from this
original kind of grouping that the other structures in the gang evolved. It is still the main-
stay of the gang, and that aspect of participation
from which a deep sense of "belongingness" is
developed.

REFERENCES

1. Coffey, H. (1952). Socio and Psyche Group
Process: Integrative Concepts. *Journal of Social
Issues*, **8**, 75–80.

2. Crawford, P., Malamud, D., Dumpson, J.
(1950). Working With Teen-Age Gangs. New
York: Welfare Council.

3. Delaney, L. (1951). Principles of Street Club
Work. *Paper read at New York City Youth Board
Conference, Brooklyn, N.Y. in February.*

4. Jennings, H. (1947). Leadership and Socio-
metric Choice. *In Newcomb and Hartley (ED) Readings in Social Psychology; New York, Henry Holt*
407–412.

5. Jennings, H. (1950). Leadership and Isolation
(2nd Edition), New York, Longmans Green.

6. Johnson, H. (1952). Working Together in a
High Delinquency Area. *Paper read at Youth Board
Conference, New York, in October.*

7. McCarthy, J. (1952). Re-Directing Teen-Age
Gangs (Reaching the Unreached). *New York City
Youth Board.*

8. Marshall, K. (1951). Working with a Street
Gang. *Paper Read at Youth Board Conference,
Brooklyn, N.Y. in February.*

9. Philadelphia Daily News (1953), April 10th.

10. Powers, E. (1950). Some Reflections on Juvenile Delinquency, *Federal Probation*, December, **14**,
21–25.

11. Robinson, D. (1949). Chance to Belong, New
York, Woman's Press.

12. Thelen, H. (1950). Educational Dynamics:
Theory and Research, *Journal of Social Issues*, **VI**,
19–22.

13. Whyte, W. (1943). Street Corner Society,
Chicago: The University of Chicago Press.

COMMENTARY

John C. Spencer (Bristol). In his article
Mr. Delany is concerned with gang behaviour
in America, but he raises a subject of considerable importance to workers in this country in
the youth service and the juvenile court. The
extent and nature of gang violence have at all
times been difficult to assess. It is certainly
no new phenomenon and it is always sure of a
ready press and a public eager to read of aggression and destruction caused by the gang.
Since the end of the second world war the antisocial gang has been the focus of attention in
both Europe and America. In this country
during the winter of 1950–51 and again more
recently, there have been reports of further
outbursts. A club leader, reflecting on thirty
years' experience in South London, has suggested that attacks on the club in which rival
gangs "compete in destruction, even to stealing
everything, bursting pipes, and flooding the
place, and a host of meaningless acts of destruction" had developed largely since the war.[1] In
Liverpool a revival in gang activity was noted
by the chief probation officer in his report for
1953. The members belong largely to the age-
group between 16 and 21. "They roam a set
area, frequently resorting to physical violence if
their demands are refused." [2]

In the occupied countries during the postwar years the opportunities for gang behaviour
due to the effects of under-nourishment and the
presence of the allied forces were considerable.
M. Chazal, the Children's Magistrate of the

[1] *The Times*, March 4th, 1954.
[2] *The Times*, March 11th, 1954.

Seine Court, has described a gang of boys between 12 and 14 who used to snatch women's handbags at rush-hours in the Paris Underground and spend the proceeds on sumptuous meals in .black-market restaurants.[3] In Italy the "shoe-shiners," and indeed the whole problem of vagrant youth organized very often in bands, presented serious difficulties in rehabilitation. Though less organized than the New York gangs which Mr. Delany describes, the groups of vagrant children, stealing from supply dumps and cadging from the troops, presented a ready source of exploitation at the hands of criminals. Indeed, their very lack of organization made the work of rehabilitation the more difficult, providing no framework through which the agency might work.

In Paris this re-educative work has been done by squads (*équipes d'amitié*) in a manner not dissimilar from the American experience which has been mentioned above. It was realized that a gang member could only be helped through the helping of the gang itself. Each of the squads dealt with a particular gang and often assumed the name of the street from which the gang originated, rue Morand squad, Ménilmontant squad and so on. Their object was to convert an antisocial gang into a more social group, giving it sufficient stability for the friendship which united it to extend its range beyond the limits of the group. The worker made his contact with the gang in various ways, while at play in the street, or in a game of football, or by giving the members a book of photographs. His approach was informal. In the work of these squads probation officers have played a leading part and the opportunities of help and friendship have been accepted by the gang.

In an area of East London the experience has been similar. One club, initially built up around an antisocial group, has depended very much on the local knowledge and contacts of a probation officer whose sincerity has been understood by the members but whose official position in the juvenile court has not proved an insuperable obstacle to his own club work.

The principle is an important one — concentration on the group or on the individual adolescent alone is an inadequate approach to rehabilitation. *Both* are the concern of an agency setting out to assist in the rehabilitation of the antisocial gang. In Hoxton the work has been materially assisted by the knowledge of individual boys and their families gained by the probation officers through their casework but used also in the club. In Paris, M. Chazal has pointed out how impossible it is for his probation officer, when dealing with the adolescent, to make an arbitrary division of the various problems he presents. It was therefore no accident that in the work of the *équipes d'amitié* probation officers were closely concerned. In the Central Harlem Street Club in New York, described in a book to which Mr. Delany has already referred,[4] the authors emphasize the value that could have been derived from supervisors trained in psychiatric social work.

In his second part, Mr. Delany describes the internal structure of the gang. He comments on the many variations in this structure. At the U.N.E.S.C.O. Conference (1949) also, it was observed how varied their structure may be. According to one authority on the situation in Rome not only did the gangs have an inter-city organization, but at that time a firm internal organization as well, adjusted to their particular purposes. Independent bands of children were often exploited and directed by an adult — either a man or a woman. On the other hand, another experienced worker, the Director of the "Don Bosco's Boys" village, stated that these gangs were seldom organized according to rank, and hardly ever acknowledged an official leader. Certain boys became *de facto* leaders by reason of their superior skill, physical strength, or astuteness; the remainder submitted to the influence of the more resourceful and took part in gang operations without any prior arrangement of tasks.

The latter view contrasts noticeably with the elaborate organization into divisions described by Mr. Delany, whether of a vertical or a horizontal pattern, to use his own phraseology. In England the pattern is equally varied, the main distinction being between the small face-to-face group based on the local street, tene-

---

[3] Conference of Experts and Directors of Children's Communities on the problems of the Education of Vagrant Children. U.N.E.S.C.O. 1949.

[4] P. Crawford, D. Malamud, and J. Dumpson, *Working with Teen-Age Gangs*, N.Y., 1950.

ment, or ice-cream parlour, and the much larger gang, sub-divided into small groups, owing allegiance to an adult or based on a local meeting place, a fairground for example, a prominent road junction, or a park.

The gang's aggressiveness has been the subject of frequent comment and observation.[5] In the underprivileged areas of large cities the emotional deprivation of many of its members and the inadequate opportunities for constructive and exciting leisure pursuits contribute jointly to the search for an enemy against whom hostility may be directed. Mr. Delany has described some of the methods employed in inter-gang warfare, a type of behaviour with which social workers in Glasgow have long been familiar. One recent observer on the activity of London gangs has commented on the unwelcome attention paid by the gang to the youth club, though it is a subject on which reports are unreliable. In actual fact the extent of damage is often much less than press reports suggest.

Traditionally the centre of hostility has been the presence of rival gangs with territorial bonds of association, e.g., street or tenement, or of adults in the neighbourhood classified as "authority." The more recent appearance of the youth club as a focus of attack is less easy to explain. From a study of gang behaviour in East London it seems probable that in several cases individual members of the gang have previously been members of the club or have been unsuccessful in their attempts at joining. There is no clear line of demarcation in the membership of the two groups. The emphasis in the antisocial gang is frequently on aggressive rather than on delinquent behaviour.

The issues raised by Mr. Delany's article are of practical rather than theoretical significance. Our methods of analysis and measurement in the field of gang behaviour are inadequate and our observations still insufficient for theoretical study. The fact is, however, that public opinion on this matter remains so widely inaccurate, both as regards causation as well as therapy, that continued emphasis must be placed on those methods of re-education which use the gang itself as the foundation of further work.

159

Treatment Techniques in a Therapeutic Camp [*]

Robert A. Young, Lovick Miller, and Nicholas Verven

Organized camping has for many years been considered a desirable adjunct to childhood experience. Early emphasis was on health and recreation. With the gradual realization that for some children the camp experience could also provide an opportunity for emotional growth, attention was focused on attempting to understand why it was that some children became less timid and fearful and learned to get along more adequately with their contemporaries, or in other ways showed that they were better able to cope with day-to-day living problems. This led to a re-examination of the camp program and to a consideration of the dynamics of personality development. Workers became aware that personality changes were due as much to meeting the emotional needs of the child through the interpersonal relationships as to the gratifications gained through physical facilities and activities.

Profiting from this increased knowledge as to what constitutes the most favorable environment for psychologically healthy development, camps became more aware of the needs of the difficult child. This awareness led to the belief that many behavior problems could be dealt with in the framework of the summer camp, despite the fact that camps were organized primarily for groups with few disturbed children. In order to cope with deviant behavior problems some camps added psychiatrically trained personnel to their staffs, either as counselors or consultants.

A few camps were established solely for children with neurotic or behavior disorders re-

[*] Reprinted from 21 Am. J. Orthopsychiatry (1951), 819–826. Presented at the 1951 annual meeting. Used by permission of the authors and the publisher.

quiring extensive therapy. For a number of years one of us directed such a camp (1), in connection with a psychiatric clinic, in which encouraging results were obtained. We felt, however, that positive results fell far short of what could be accomplished if a more integrated and intensive program of therapy could be worked out. This paper is a preliminary report of an attempt to put into practice a therapeutic camp program with group therapy and psychodrama. Our purpose is to indicate the therapeutic possibilities of combining these three techniques into a single integrated and intensive program.

The present camp, from which this study was made, was organized in 1949 as an outgrowth of recommendations made by the Committee on Case Work and Group Work Services of the Greater Boston Community Council.[1] The purpose of the camp is the "treatment of emotionally disturbed children in a camp setting, training of professional people in the dynamics and therapy of problem children, and research which will contribute to a better understanding of these children and their problems" (2). Approximately thirty boys between the ages of 9 and 13 are accepted each year. Referrals are made mainly through social agencies. Children with severe physical disabilities, psychotic-like behavior, or so disturbed that they could require constant individual attention are not accepted.

We believe the camp proper to be of prime importance as a therapeutic implement. The physical set-up was typical of the usual boys' camp. Situated in an isolated wooded area on a lake, it afforded facilities for a wide variety of activities associated in a boy's mind with the enjoyment of camping — archery, boating, swimming, fishing, riflery, crafts, nature study, sleeping-out trips, and many others. Besides the opportunity for pleasure gratifications which serve as a firm foundation for the therapeutic process we consider four principles to be essential to a therapeutic camp: (1) a psychodynamic orientation, (2) a permissive attitude, (3) a close relationship between the boy and a mature, understanding adult, and (4) ade-

[1] The study was made possible through financial grants from the Charles H. Hood Dairy Foundation, the Committee of the Permanent Charity Fund, and the Sarah A. Hyams Fund, Inc.

quate preparation of the child and the parents for the therapeutic program.

Only with a psychodynamic point of view is it possible to understand the behavior manifestation of a faulty or inadequate ego structure. Obviously a counselor cannot act intelligently unless he has some idea of what the behavior means to the camper in terms of past life experiences. Living and working in close association with a group of disturbed children twenty-four hours a day puts a strain on even the most mature of adults. The difficulty and the importance of maintaining an objective attitude should not be underestimated, for these children have amazing capacities for irritation and often have a need to provoke, to the point of exasperation, campmates and staff alike. Understanding the source of the behavior, as well as being personally divorced from this source, is conducive to helping the staff member to respond to the behavior therapeutically.

Our second principle, permissiveness, has come to be an accepted therapeutic principle, for it creates greater freedom for self-expression without the child's needing to fear adult retaliation or rejection. It is not to be confused with passivity, however. Within the camp, permissiveness did not refer simply to toleration of deviant behavior. It became a working principle not only for the interpersonal relationship between staff and camper but for the program as a whole. For example, there was little or no pressure put upon the individual to attend any group activities, and all verbalizations were accepted and encouraged. In general the whole camp was geared to the expression of the needs of the individual camper with the respect for and tolerance of these expressions which this attitude implies.

The third aspect of the camp program is the relationship which the campers could form with counselors who maintained the attitudes discussed above. Each counselor was assigned to a cabin containing six boys. This became "his cabin" and the boys "his boys." He ate, slept, worked, and lived with these boys for two months. This situation permitted constant and close relationships to be formed between counselor and boys and among the boys themselves. Within it the campers began to realize that in this environment many of their ways of dealing with adults and peers were no longer necessary, since they found that not all adults reacted to them as the significant adults of their childhood had — in a way which had originally made some type of faulty ego mechanism necessary. This realization was a strong force in causing a reorientation of their perception of the world and enabled the campers to work through and alter many of their misperceptions based upon infantile experiences in a neurotic family pattern.

In order to prepare the camper for accepting the therapeutic program, we attempted to create a favorable mental set by explaining to each boy, prior to camp, that the purpose of the camp was not only to afford him a good time, but also to help him work out some of the problems and fears which brought him to his agency. We further explained that every other boy in the camp was also there for a definite purpose and that we would try to help them all by some special activities in which we hoped they would be willing to participate. There was no doubt that this attempt to get them to accept their problems and the treatment program created a much greater tolerance for their own difficulties as well as those of other people. As a result of this preparation we heard boys who we knew were very much ashamed of their symptoms discussing them quite openly in a healthy manner. This in no way interfered with the enjoyment of the general camp experience.

We feel that these four principles, the permissive and the psychodynamic attitudes, an opportunity for close relationships with adults who maintain these attitudes, and a favorable mental set help explain changes which took place within our first summer camp, which had no formal therapeutic techniques.

When devising the therapeutic program we had as one of our possibilities the utilization of individual therapy within the camp. However, early in the program we decided that treatment in the group should be group treatment, that is, that any individual work would be directed toward getting the boy to profit from the constructive forces within the group. Therefore, in developing our program, we assumed that the group was the central therapeutic unit and that all therapeutic attempts should intermesh so as to form a smooth-working group process.

As Slavson (3) states, group therapy refers specifically to planned small groups with members chosen in accordance with their suitability to each other. It has as its aim at least a minimum degree of permanent modification within the personality itself. This reduces anxiety, hostility and aggression which originally caused the individual either to withdraw or defensively to attack people. The aim is achieved because the group permits acting out of instinctual drives so that release and catharsis are constantly taking place. The ego defenses are reduced; transference is greatly facilitated and intensified, particularly in its negative phases. Transference in groups is also intensified on its positive levels when there is sibling rivalry and the patients make a bid for the love of the therapists.

The group therapy at camp was of two types, interview and modified activity. In evaluating the two types, we felt that the activity groups were more suitable for our age range since the discussion groups did not offer the immediate gratification which younger boys seem to require. Therefore, we intend to concentrate on activity groups in our future program planning. Our discussion will concern mainly group therapy of this type.

As Slavson (3) discusses group therapy, it is difficult to differentiate it from the process which goes on within camp. Here we have groups of six boys each, living with an adult who attempts to be neutral and to permit the children free expression of their instinctual drives. The primary difference between what Slavson describes as group therapy and our cabin groups seems to lie in the fact that the counselor is not only everything that the group therapist is, but he is much more. Because of his living with the child, the counselor represents reality much more than does the therapist. For example, the cabin must be cleaned up at times, and there must be opportunity for the eating of meals without the anxiety and hostility which the indiscriminate throwing of food would produce. The counselor reduces anxiety by external control and thereby not only becomes the object of the boy's transference, but a father surrogate as well. Whether his additional role as the substitute father differentiates the cabin counselor from the group therapist is a theoretical question, but certainly many of the same therapeutic phenomena take place within the cabin groups and in group therapy, such as catharsis, reduction of ego defenses, toleration of others' difficulties, and transference.

Since we thought that the cabin groups were fulfilling about the same needs as Slavson's activity groups, we felt that a duplication of his techniques would be repetitious in our program. Furthermore we have a somewhat different theoretical orientation, which will be discussed later. The structure of our groups, was similar to the classical activity group. We met for one hour a day, five days a week, in a room known as the clubroom. Within the room we provided crafts material, a fireplace, water, and other play media. At the end of each meeting we had a simple snack for the boys. The members were encouraged to express themselves freely and to work out their own interpersonal problems which arose.

The role of the therapist in our groups differed considerably from that of the therapist described by Slavson. Our point of departure is the observation that anxiety is a natural and universal phenomenon whenever a group of people are assembled. One of the easiest and most frequent mechanisms employed to handle this anxiety is hostility, which, if it is expressed at random, can result in the dissolution of the group; but if it is repressed, it can result in a lack of solid group cohesion, which prevents the constructive forces of the group from coming into play. The problem of the therapist is to permit the expression of hostility so as to use this powerful force for therapeutic purposes, but at the same time to redirect the hostility which arises between members by channeling it in another direction so that it does not destroy the group. Therefore, one of the primary roles of the therapist is to become the object of the group's hostility. This procedure enables the individuals to become a group, since they need not fear their mutual aggression because it is directed against the therapist. Once this working unit is established the therapist encourages the group to find other means of handling the hostility than merely focusing it upon the leader.

We considered that insight into interpersonal situations was a major therapeutic goal and that it was the role of the therapist to help the campers gain this insight. This was accomplished by the therapist's clarifying the interpersonal situations which arose among the group members. The clarifier becomes the natural object of hostility since few people enjoy having the reasons for their irrational acts pointed out.

Clarifications were of two types, those made to individuals and those made to the group. An example of the former occurred when no explanations would keep a camper from taking the fire outside of the therapy room. This was behavior which we could not permit because of the danger. The therapist interpreted this behavior to the camper, in the light of his previous expressions of fear of fire, as an attempt to prove to himself and to others that he was not afraid of the fire. After this interpretation he ceased, for the most part, to play with the fire dangerously.

Group clarification was employed when a group ganged up against one of the members and drove him raging from the room. When the therapist pointed out to them what they had done they turned on him, becoming terribly destructive, but also quite anxious. The therapist was then able to verbalize for the group how angry they were at him for pointing out what had occurred. He realized that they were angry but preferred that they tell him about it instead of being destructive. There followed a tremendous outburst of feeling expressed by cursing, jeering and yelling. Over the tumult could be heard such comments as, "The club is lousy," "The leader ought to get in his car and go away," "All this is crap," "The leader minds everyone else's business." Finally the leader was able to say, "You boys don't like the club." "We hate it and we hate you too. We'd like to have a club with our name on our shirts and play other cabins in soft ball." All threatened not to return. "Jeez, you'd think he's your mother and father." "I won't have you for my father." When the time was up, one asked if the leader were really going to leave, as the boys had requested. This outburst not only created a solid group unity, but formed a framework within which the therapeutic process continued.

Psychodrama is the final technique to be discussed. Unlike camp activities and group therapy, which aim largely at strengthening the ego, psychodrama is oriented to the unconscious and therefore rounds out the therapeutic program.

The aim of psychodrama is to stimulate the free expression of feelings in order to achieve an emotional discharge or catharsis. This expression occurs while the boy is participating in a dynamic reproduction of a real-life situation. He is brought to a point where he can duplicate on the psychodramatic stage the conditions and key situations of his own life. A basic assumption is that this re-enactment brings with it a realization of his life's problems and enables him to gain insight into his emotional conflicts. At the same time the catharsis frees him from his deep-lying anxiety, leaving him better able to cope with the difficulties arising in day-to-day living. Spontaneity and deep emotional involvement in the dramatic event are fundamental to release and development of self-awareness.

Psychodrama sessions were held one hour every other day for each cabin group. The psychodramatist was not the same as the group therapist. The techniques used were based on the work of Moreno (4).

In general the psychodrama program was divided into three stages: (1) relationship and free play, (2) role playing, and (3) situations of personal relevance. During the first stage the problem was to win the boys over to "dramatics," as this period was called. This was done rather effectively by allowing the first few sessions to be relatively undirected free play, in which the therapist remained principally an observer. From time to time he would make suggestions as to what games the boys might play. When they showed definite evidence that they liked this play, they were ready to move into the next stage, that of helping them to develop the necessary skills in role taking and spontaneity. For example, they were asked to tell and then to act out the kind of people they would like to be some day. Once these skills were developed, the boys were encouraged to act out simple camp situations, for example, a counselor trying to manage an uncooperative camper. The boys enjoyed doing this and we found that many camp problems could be worked out within the drama situation. However, this was only preparation for the real therapeutic attempt, since it was only after these skills were learned and the boys were sufficiently motivated that they could be induced into the third stage, in which personally relevant situations could be acted out. For this activity the therapist drew from the case histories information concerning problems of the individual boys and built up drama situations

around them. As the play was introduced, no hint was given to the boy or to any member of the group that the scene had been taken from anyone's actual experience. However, on most occasions when a play of this sort was done, both actors and audience gave significant indication that they were completely wrapped up in the action. Nervousness and quiet laughter were common responses and, contrary to the previous stages, no one tried to disrupt the play.

Following is an illustration of how one boy responded therapeutically to the psychodrama. Ed, a round, chubby, morose boy, was inclined to identify himself with the counselors and to dominate the smaller boys of his cabin. He usually withdrew from the dramatic sessions and openly expressed contempt for them. During one session the therapist had the group act out a problem situation which was personally relevant to Ed. At the beginning of the period Ed was reclining on the bench farthest from the stage and away from all the others. As the play progressed, he became interested and gradually moved from bench to bench, coming closer to the stage. At first he limited himself to making sarcastic remarks about the action. As he became absorbed in the play he supported the hero. When the boy's father was punishing him, Ed cried out: "Why don't you leave him alone, you big jerk?" His comments which followed indicated that the hero's experiences had fundamental meaning for him: "Yeah, I know just how he feels," and "That kinda thing happens to me too." At one point when the boy was being interviewed by a psychiatrist (played by a camper) Ed accepted an offer to be in the play in the role of the hero's only friend. He played the role as if he were the hero of the play and responded aggressively toward the psychiatrist, or father figure.

Ed worked himself into the role without realizing it. He willingly took the role of the boy's friend, as he strongly identified with him, and then suddenly he found himself playing his own role unwittingly. When it was finished he still did not realize that the play had really been about him. He did remark, however, that the boy was a lot like him.

This demonstrates that unconscious material can be reached through psychodrama. We consider that this technique was not only therapeutically helpful to certain boys, but that it was adaptable to our treatment program and also made a real contribution to the camp as a whole.

Of the many technical difficulties which we encountered in this program, we shall mention only two. Because of scheduling problems the therapy groups were the same as the cabin groups, which meant that the therapeutic process did not begin and end with a given therapeutic hour, but continued during the twenty-four hours. Within two days after the groups began, the camp, which had been running relatively smoothly, suddenly became chaotic. The anxiety and its resulting hostility were carried back to the cabins, to the dining halls, to swimming, and to games. This created a problem not only for the boys but for the staff. Our experience showed that the effects of constant groups, while making the work more difficult, were not necessarily detrimental, however, for they tended to hasten as well as to intensify the therapeutic process. We realize that this is purely qualitative judgment, since we have no objective measures, but we did notice a "speed-up" of group cohesion over previous years.

Another difficulty which we could not avoid was the lack of balanced groups. Once a boy had been admitted to camp there was very little we could do if he were not suited to group work except to send him home, which we were reluctant to do. Furthermore, we knew of no device which would enable us to select those boys who would be suitable for our program. Consequently, we found we had a few boys who would normally be rejected for group work. The problem was further complicated by the fact that if the boy were a disrupting factor in the group we had no way to segregate him, for we did not have the necessary staff. We had to work with the boy within the group. Since we could not make ideal group placements we rearranged the cabin groups on the basis of the boys' behavior in camp. This meant shifting the boys after they had become attached to their groups, which in itself is anxiety-producing, but which, in the long run, proved beneficial for the group and in turn for the boys.

In conclusion, we wish to emphasize that this is a preliminary report of an intensive therapeutic program carried out in a camp setting with disturbed children. There are many problems to be solved before a final analysis can be made as to what constitutes the best type of therapeutic program — problems of the most efficient therapeutic procedures, the personalities most suited for treatment and the selection and training of staff workers. Our limited experience, however, justifies our conviction that therapeutic changes are enhanced by these formal techniques and that this is a rich field for further exploration.

REFERENCES

1. Robert A. Young, "A Summer Camp as an Integral Part of a Psychiatric Clinic," *Ment. Hyg.*, **23**: 241–256, April 1939.

2. Report to the Trustees of Guidance Camps Trust on the Treatment Camp, Summer, 1950. November 1, 1950.

3. S. R. Slavson (Ed.), *The Practice of Group Therapy*, Internat. Univ. Press, New York, 1947.

4. J. L. Moreno, *Psychodrama*, Vol. I., Beacon House, New York, 1946.

160

Camping for Disturbed Children *

Emanuel Hallowitz

Many articles, pamphlets, and books, published over the years, have contributed to our appreciation of the values of camping for children. These reports have dealt with various aspects of the problem — program, staff, supervision, administration — and as a result of this pooling of knowledge and experience, camping to-day is a much more worth-while activity than it was.

But this is true chiefly for the average camp or rather for the camp that deals with "normal" children. Camping as a tool for helping emotionally disturbed children is a comparatively new field and there is a paucity of literature on the subject. Exchanging views, examining

* Reprinted from 34 *Mental Hygiene* (1950), 406–422. Used by permission of the author and the publisher.

the approaches of others, and even subjecting our own ideas to a critical evaluation are absolute essentials to the development of this special area of camping.

This paper deals with the experiences of a child-guidance agency in attempting to help its clients through a camping program.

Integration of Camp and Agency. Camp Ramapo is affiliated with the Jewish Board of Guardians, a child-guidance agency. While it is theoretically independent, operating under a separate budget and board of directors, there is a very close connection between the two organizations. The Jewish Board of Guardians acts as the parent organization of the camp. The director of the camp, while employed by the camp board, is also responsible to and is supervised by the executive of the agency. The boys served by the camp are undergoing psychiatric treatment in the agency. The camp, so far as its purpose is concerned, may be viewed as another arm of the Jewish Board of Guardians.

Over the years, there has been much movement toward integrating the camp program and objectives into the total agency program and practices. An increasing number of caseworkers are recognizing camp as more than just a vacation for their clients. They see it as potentially a real positive force in the child's life, of value in furthering the treatment goals of the case. Some workers have used camp in such a way that the child feels it to be an extension of the agency, another tool by which his worker is helping him to overcome his problems. In such cases a thorough discussion is held with the child as to why he is being sent to camp. This discussion is related to his particular problem. The child knows that not only will he be having a good time, but that he will also have an opportunity to work out some of his difficulties in group relationships in an atmosphere that is different from the one he has at home. He is helped to see that at camp he will have a chance to test out the new insight he has gained into his own behavior. He can try new patterns of adaptation and he will find people who are interested, tolerant, and willing to help him in these new attempts to adjust.

A written summary is submitted by the caseworker on each child who is sent to camp. This information is used for grouping children and as a source of reference which the "camp case-worker" employs in his discussions with the counselors in individual cases.

Further to integrate camp into its treatment function, the agency provides a trained psychiatric caseworker as consultant to the camp. This person is responsible for the education of the camp staff in mental-hygiene principles, the interpretation of difficult youngsters to the counselors, and the handling of those problem situations with children which the staff has not the capacity to deal with. In addition, he is responsible for aiding counselors in writing reports of the child's adjustment during the camp season.

In brief, the supervision of the camp director by the executive director of the agency, the preparation of the client by his social worker for the camping experience, the use of the summary for grouping and consultation, the use of a caseworker as resident consultant to the camp, and the camp's reports on the child's adjustment, all tend to bring about a closer integration of camp and agency and make possible a more effective use of camp as a treatment tool.

Development of Camp Philosophy. In planning for camp, two important questions are raised. What are the values inherent in camping that have special significance to the disturbed child? How can we assure these benefits to our children?

Camping, it is felt, provides an excellent opportunity for ego building. The acquisition of new skills — learning to play baseball, to swim, to row, to make a bow and arrow, or to fashion an elephant or a dog out of clay — helps children to get a more realistic sense of their powers and worth, to say nothing of the entrée these new skills give them into relationships with their peers.

Providing new experiences for these children through camp and the camping program is another valuable aid in building the child's ego. Hikes in the woods, trips off camp grounds to neighboring farms, communities, and places of interest, cooking their meals over a fire they themselves have built, climbing a tree, a moonlight swim, are only a few of the experiences that broaden a child's perspective and enrich his emotional life. Hikes, trips, cook-outs, and so on, have added value in that they help a child to overcome his fears of new situations — travel, darkness, the woods, insects, and small animal life. In addition, such activities also serve to develop a child's resourcefulness and initiative.

Inherent in the very nature of camping is the separation of the child from the family. While separation is fraught with danger, it has some very valuable aspects for the child who is ready for such an experience. For four weeks or more, a child can be free from the tensions and pressures in the home and the community. For this brief period, he can be "on his own," free from a nagging, rigid parent who usually makes him toe the mark, or from an overindulgent one who so infantilizes him that growth is impossible. Our children come from all kinds of home and family constellation, and each one is fraught with some form of tension or pressure that has been detrimental to the child. In many cases, the mere removal of a child to camp is enough to bring about a most remarkable change in his adjustment. One of our aims, therefore is to provide these children with an experience in an environment in which stress and strain are kept at a minimum, an environment that is not repressive, but in which the child will feel free to be himself and which will encourage growth.

By far the greatest value that camping has for our children lies in the communal life. The child at camp has an opportunity to experience a new and different kind of family. The analogy of the bunk unit to the family, with the counselor acting as a parent surrogate, is not new. The bunk group has many elements in common with the family. Here eight children and an adult live together in a cabin, sleeping in adjoining beds, sharing closet space and clean-up responsibilities, eating at the same table, and, even better, participating as a unit in the day's program. We know that children bring to this situation the same patterns of behavior and adaptation as they present in their own family setting.

Can this situation, which is inherent in camp life be utilized to further the treatment of the child? The answer is yes. If the child's behavior and needs are understood, and if he meets with tolerance, warmth, and encouragement from the counselor, he will soon realize that this adult is different from his own parent. Old patterns of adjustment will no longer be necessary. New ones will come to the fore. Healthy and mature responses can be encour-

aged and infantile and unwholesome patterns discouraged. The counselor becomes the parent and the child has an opportunity to relive those early, formative years in which the parent's love or denial of love is so important in his training. The child now begins to make appropriate responses and to exercise control over his asocial impulses, not through fear of punishment, but in order to please and gain the love of the parent (counselor). While at first these new patterns are created just to please some one outside himself, later they are incorporated and become part of his own demands on himself.

The influence of the other children in the bunk group aids this growth process. The building and strengthening of masculine or feminine identification through close association with his or her peers is for the child a very important derivative of group living. The child who can see other children act out their hostilities and aggressions without being punished will begin to make tentative steps in that direction. The need to be accepted and liked by one's peers is another strong determinant in creating a desire to be like them. When a child is told by his peers that he is acting like a baby, it has much more meaning and value then were he to hear this from the lips of an adult. This intense desire for acceptance by other children becomes a compelling motive for change.

The acquisition of new skills and the improvement of old ones, the positive relationships that the child develops with the adults and other children at camp go a long way toward changing his feelings about himself. He gains a new perception of himself; he is no longer unworthy, inferior or inadequate. He can achieve! People can like him! The world is not such a bad place to live in, after all.

Camp can serve the agency's purpose in still another way. Very often the picture of the child who is in treatment is not complete. The mother or the child may state that he has no friends. Why not? Nobody clearly knows. Or problems may exist in the child of which he or his parents either are not aware, or are, as yet, not ready to share with his therapist. At camp, we have an opportunity to observe a child twenty-four hours a day for twenty-eight days in real life situations. Symptoms only dimly perceived are now seen in sharp outline. Observations made of a child's behavior patterns help the caseworker to gain a more complete picture of the total child which contributes to more precise understanding and treatment.

This, then, was what we were striving for. Since these values are inherent in most camps, why not send our children to camps already in existence? The answer was fourfold:

First, our children could not adjust to a "normal" camp, for this kind of a camp is not interested in the treatment of sick personalities, but rather in helping average, stable children make maximum use of their abilities and develop their interest and skills. Of necessity, many demands are placed on the children for conformity to an outlined routine and program. These are flexible, but only to a point. They are suitable for children who can accept limits, who already can function in groups and are capable of adapting themselves to a group code. Our children, in such a setting, stand out like sore thumbs. They are not happy in such an atmosphere and, in one way or another, they become disruptive influences.

Secondly, our agency has no control over the kinds of experience the children are exposed to in such a camp. It has no voice in the selection of personnel, policy, philosophy, and so on. In addition, the number of our children who could use a camping experience is greater than can be handled by existing facilities.

More important than all of this is the fact that, in operating a camp, the Jewish Board of Guardians, by virtue of its special and particularized knowledge of pathology and personality dynamics, can make a positive contribution to the treatment of the emotionally disturbed child.

Implementation of Philosophy. It is recognized, then, that Ramapo, because it deals with sick personalities, has to be a different kind of camp. Our focus is upon helping the child through corrective emotional experiences. Expert drama productions, art work, perfection in any form, is not the goal. Meeting a child's needs for expression; offering suitable outlets for his pent-up aggression and hostility; providing experiences that will counteract fear, build self-confidence, and increase feelings of self-worth; giving understanding, tolerance, and warmth so that the child can slowly readapt himself and give up immature and unhealthy patterns of adjustment — these are the goals. To achieve these goals, special attention is paid

to the child–counselor relationship, the daily program, and the role of the caseworker.

Since for the most part our children are not capable of accepting many limits or demands, few are imposed. Only the most necessary limits are applied, and even these with flexibility and a light hand. We expect a certain degree of conformity in such matters as getting to meals on time, cleaning up, and going to bed on time. These few things are emphasized, and by and large are accepted by the children. We recognize that as the relationship between a child and his counselor develops, there will also be a growing desire on the part of the child to please the counselor, making him more capable of responding to the counselor's requests. As time goes on and in accordance with the needs of individual children and the strength of the child–counselor relationship, the children are asked to assume more responsibility for curbing their asocial impulses and adopting more mature behavior.

In this child–counselor relationship, one of the most ticklish questions is that of discipline. Whatever rules or limits are established, we can be certain that there will be violations. We do not want the child to look upon his counselor as an authoritarian or as a policeman. We feel that the relationship between the child and the counselor is our most important therapeutic tool and that this must be fostered and protected wherever possible. Our attitude toward rules and regulations is, therefore, governed not only by the needs of the children, but also by our desire to eliminate areas of possible friction between the child and his counselor.

The use of punishment or authority by the counselor is discouraged. He uses his authority as little as possible and only when he is certain that it will be heeded and will not destroy his relationship with the child or the group or when it is felt that a particular child needs this kind of approach. A counselor's command that a child do something is a perfect invitation to refusal. The counselor is directly challenged and there is no way out but to meet the challenge, and a battle of wills ensues. The counselor may win his point, but in the long run he has lost. When any one is forced to submit, hostility is a natural consequence and the child will find some way to get even. Certainly the positive feeling for the counselor is diminished and the desire to please him is gone.

If the child is to go swimming, for example, and refuses, the counselor will try to encourage or to persuade him, but will not make a burning issue of it — will not threaten "or else." If personal persuasion fails, the counselor may say, "Well, I guess you know what you want, but we will miss you," and leave it at that. The counselor then informs either the head counselor or the caseworker that Johnny does not want to go with his group. Depending on the child and the meaning of his refusal, the incident may be ignored or acted upon. If it is felt that Johnny should go and an authoritative approach is called for, this will be supplied by the head counselor. The hostility the child will feel at being forced will be directed toward the head counselor. The latter becomes the "bad guy," and the child's relationship with his own counselor is preserved.

This is not to say that the counselor never exercises any authority. There are times when a child, or the entire group, will be testing him. They are trying to find out whether he is permissive because he is weak, or whether he is really strong and lets them be themselves because he loves them. In such cases a strong positive stand, free from hostility, is necessary. Punishment or authority, when used wisely and with discrimination, for the purpose of helping the child and not for giving vent to one's own feelings, is beneficial. Through planned use of disciplines and through a clear definition of the counselor's role, the child–counselor tie is strengthened. This becomes another compelling motive for change.

Our daily program at camp is geared to the needs of the children. We avoid hustle and bustle. More than sufficient time is allotted for going from one activity to another. Children returning from swimming do not have to run back, jump into their clothes, and be at lunch all in fifteen minutes. They have time to talk to their bunk mates, play mumblety-peg, or even to read a comic book. This provides an atmosphere of ease, freedom, and relaxation.

Many, if not all, of our children have difficulty in functioning in groups. To function adequately as part of a group, it is necessary for the individual to give up part of himself for the sake of a group code or ideal. Functioning in a group implies a give-and-take relationship with others, an awareness of others' needs, and a willingness and ability to forego individual pleasure for group satisfactions. Our children do not get along in groups because they are unable to give of themselves. They are still functioning on an infantile, narcissistic level. They cannot stand much frustration, and they are not able to forego for any length of time immediate pleasure for future satisfactions. At camp, then, it would be futile to emphasize group programing, planning, and organization. Rather, we attempt to provide a limited or modified group experience for these youngsters. Instead of scheduling an entire day's activities by bunk units, we do this only for the morning activities, leaving the afternoon for the pursuit of individual choices. We try to give the children an experience of a group process under conditions that we feel are favorable to their participating in it and gaining from it.

In the morning the bunk group acts as a unit. They play baseball, go to arts and crafts, hike, have photography, and so on, as a group. Bunk projects may be undertaken during this period, and each child is asked to be with his group. If he does not like the activity, he does not have to participate — he just attends. Only in rare cases will an exception be made. It may be asked, if a child does not like baseball, why can't he go to arts and crafts, which he prefers? This was allowed at first, but we found from experience that if it is permitted both in the morning and in the afternoon, there is a great deal of difficulty in keeping groups together. It also breaks down the need for compromise and accommodation within the group when it comes to planning and deciding a group activity. Two children want arts and crafts, one wants baseball, one wants photography, and the remaining four want to work on the bunk's lean-to. If each can go where he wants to, whenever he wants, there is no motivation for group decision. There is still another difficulty involved. Groups that are functioning well at a group activity could easily be disrupted by the advent of children from other groups into the activity. The child who does not like a particular activity is free to sit on the side lines, but what happens most often is that he is soon drawn into the activity.

We found from experience that a group activity that requires close coöperation and sustained interest, and in which the results and satisfactions are not immediate, are beyond the capacity of our children. Their interest span is short. If a dramatic production is being contemplated, each has to be the star; or on a work project each has to wield an axe or to feel that his task is the most important of all. Activities that do not call for a high degree of organization seem to go off best. Walks in the woods combined with hide-and-seek or ring-o-leavio, a photography hunt, nature hunts, arts and crafts work, swimming, cook-outs, are some of the more popular choices.

The afternoon program is devoted to a free choice. Nine or ten different activities are available and each child can select whatever activity interests him most. This idea of being able to go wherever they wish appeals a great deal to the children. They feel that they are their own masters. In a way it plays in with their narcissistic impulses of wanting to do what they want when they want. In the past when we attempted a full day of scheduled activity, we found children demanding free choice, and it made for much conflict in the group life.

Needless to say, this kind of free-choice program produces wanderers. Some children don't know what they want to do; they haven't been sufficiently motivated, or they are so dependent that when they are thrown on their own, they can't act, but need adult direction. Counselors specifically assigned to this problem try to interest these children in one of the activities. They also cover the activity areas in order to pick up children who are flitting from one activity to another and try to help them get settled. It should be noted that when a child does not wish to participate either with his group or in the free-choice program, he is not just dropped or left on his own. The camp recognizes that supervision of children is important and during group and activity periods counselors are assigned to cover specific areas, such as the cabins, the athletic field, and the frog-hunting area. In this way the whereabouts of each child is known, and the child himself gains a certain degree of strength and security from the fact that an adult is close by and on call.

One of the important things we have to consider is how easily our children get bored. Changes in activities and games have to be introduced frequently into the program. An activity will catch on for a week and then only a handful of children will select it. Some of the new games and activities have been music hour, clock golf, science talks, game room (which includes bowling, shuffleboard, box hockey, and ping-pong) and three-day camp-out. Even in the more regular activities, such as arts and crafts, new media and new ways of presenting the work have to be constantly devised or else interest will begin to wane.

The camp caseworker, by virtue of his special skill and knowledge, is called upon to handle situations that are beyond the capacity of the counselor. Specifically, he is responsible for helping the individual child to adjust and integrate himself into the camp life. This requires direct work either with counselors, with the children, or with both. This may include staff meetings, individual conferences with the bunk counselor, conferences with the specialists on their activity programs, and participation in the planning and administrative meetings of the key personnel. As the representative of the agency's clinical-treatment program, the caseworker is also instrumental in the development of the camp philosophy and practice. He holds regularly scheduled weekly conferences with each counselor. These interviews are concerned not only with the progress of the children, but also with areas of group-work supervision. While the latter was not at first contemplated as part of the caseworker's function, it soon became apparent that a child could not be discussed in isolation. The total functioning of the group had also to be considered. Since we are attempting to help these children in large measure through the group-work process, attention to the counselor's handling of the group is essential. This emphasis on individual and group progress was found to be very necessary if the philosophy and objectives of the camp were to be realized.

Basic Problems to be Considered in the Planning of a Camp for Disturbed Children. The more qualitative the job that a camp undertakes, the more consideration and thought must be expended on all phases of its organization and operation. In some respects the camp for disturbed children has still not found answers to problems that confront all camps; in other respects we have borrowed organizational and administrative traditions from the "normal" camp with insufficient evaluation of their applicability to the new situation; and in still other cases, new problems have emerged out of the differences in techniques and goals. Some of the more salient problems include choice of staff, the nature of the physical plant, size of groups, selection and grouping of children, and preparation of the child for a camp experience.

Probably the most important tool in any camp is the counselor staff. Regardless of how advanced and developed our camping philosophy may be, in the last analysis, it is the staff that will have to execute, implement, and strive for these goals. The age-old camping problem of a staff adequate both in numbers and in qualifications becomes even more important and more striking when the goals are high and not easily attainable.

The counselor staff at Camp Ramapo were mostly college students interested in social work or allied professions. Though interested in the work and with suitable personal qualities, their lack of experience and limited knowledge of personality and group dynamics were felt to be handicaps. To meet this problem, the director, the head counselor, and the caseworker, acting as a team, planned and conducted orientation meetings and frequent individual conferences with the counselors both before and during the camp season. These meetings and conferences were necessary not only to give the counselors some elementary skills in dealing with our children, but also to work through their natural biases and resistances. While in some cases there was real growth and development of basic skills and attitudes, this type of supervision and training is not a substitute for a well-trained, experienced staff. In fact, this program should also be employed, but on a more intensive level, even with more mature and experienced personnel.

It need hardly be emphasized that a well-trained, experienced staff is essential, particularly in a camp that is trying to give more than a fresh-air vacation to their children. Greater inducement has to be offered, not only to attract a more qualified staff, but also to insure their return during subsequent summers. The use of camp as a training center for graduate social-work students, with course credit plus salary offered, merits further exploration.

The physical set-up of a camp also plays an important rôle in its effective functioning. If the water front is too far from the camp proper, it imposes a burden that will be reflected in many areas of a camp's program. For children who are not too anxious to be in the water, another obstacle is placed in the way of their getting there. On the other hand, those who love water may go there when no one is present to supervise them. Problems may also arise on the long walk to and from the water.

Inadequate facilities for washing and bathing create problems of health and cleanliness. Crowded cabins make for added friction and tension. Inadequate play space for rainy weather results in boredom and short tempers, and taxes the ingenuity and patience of the most stable counselor.

When a camp is set up to deal with "problem children," all these little things take on added importance. The child has enough difficulty in adjusting under the best of circumstances, without inconveniences that only add to his sense of frustration and bewilderment.

At Ramapo the physical plant compares favorably with that of any other camp. Ramapo boasts some very nice features: a large ball field, a recreation hall for rainy weather, a clear spring-fed lake, one-half mile in diameter, a stage room, a shower building, a large infirmary, and so on, all conveniently located. In addition, there is enough property to allow for blazing trails through the woods, and having lean-tos and overnight hikes without going off the camp grounds. It also has workshops — arts and crafts, photography, nature, and so on. There are, however, some areas that create difficulties and make the job so much the harder.

There are six cabins set in a line a few yards apart, housing from 14 to 16 children per cabin. Each cabin is shared by two bunk groups with a token partition (three feet high) separating the groups. In reality there are from 14 to 16 children sharing one cabin, living in close proximity to one another. There is provision for clothes, but it is inadequate, with the result that many of the children live out of barracks bags, or their clothes are jammed up underneath their beds in a most sloppy and disorganized way. Also, the close proximity makes for continual friction and tension. The timid, fearful child cannot help but get in the way of the very aggressive child. For the children with whom we are dealing, space to move around in and freedom to withdraw and be on the side lines are very important. These children are not able to stand much frustration or inconvenience; they react to it in an infantile fashion. Two children get into an argument and one pushes the other so that he falls on a third's bed. We now have three in on one fight and it does not take much to get the others involved. The counselor soon finds himself acting as a referee and policeman. The fact that the cabins are set so close together adds to these difficulties, for children are free to roam into neighboring cabins.

The inadequacies of the Ramapo cabins have been recognized and though there are no definite plans, there has been talk of increasing the size of the cabins by adding porches. In the meantime, the placing of fewer children in each cabin seems to have alleviated some of the difficulties. Our experience with camping for disturbed children makes us feel that the traditional camp set-up, in which buildings are grouped close together to simplify such problems as sanitation and supervision, is not adequate. New design is necessary to eliminate possible elements of friction and frustration.

Another tradition that we need to break away from is that of having eight or even more children in a bunk unit. In the past at Ramapo there have been eight children in a bunk group, headed by one counselor. While this ratio is not unusual in most camps, it is a difficult one when it is considered that each of the children is a "problem child" in his own right. Each of these children needs individual and special attention. When a counselor has responsibility for so many children, it is difficult for him to be fully aware of individual differences and needs, and it limits what he can do about them. The writer recognizes that to limit units to six children to a counselor might mean that fewer children would be served and that operating expenses per capita would be higher. The desire to give every child a camp experience is a worthy one, but we who deal with psychiatric problems must be aware that quality rather than quantity should be the goal.[1]

[1] For the 1950 season, Camp Ramapo has instituted a ratio of six campers per counselor. Also rearrangement of bunk interiors will provide more living space for the children.

While the camp was organized to deal with the emotionally disturbed child, we found that certain types of child, because of the dynamics of their particular pathology, are not suitable for a camp experience. Some children need a more controlled and repressive environment; others suffer from too close an association with members of the same sex; and still others are too disturbing to their fellows, so that while they may benefit from the experience, they minimize or even destroy whatever benefits the other children might receive.

One such case was John G. John had been diagnosed as psychoneurotic — anxiety hysteria. This in itself does not mean too much. More important was the fact that John had strong homosexual tendencies. Living with other children in very close proximity, sleeping in adjoining beds, watching them dress and undress, and so on, increased the child's anxiety about his homosexual desires. As a result, John was not only very irritable and hard to manage, but he also began to indulge in behavior that was very upsetting to the other children. His language was sexually provocative; in play he would grab other boys' genitals, and also in play, would go into other boys' beds at night and at times jump on another boy, going through the motions of sexual intercourse. This behavior finally culminated in an attempt to have another boy commit felatio with him.

There was also the case of Myron S. He was an artist in getting other boys to beat him up. Intuitively he sensed the weak spots of others and would taunt and tease until, without fail, the other child would beat him. Myron was beaten three times a day regularly, and seemed insatiable in his desire for physical punishment.

Then there was the case of Jimmy L., who wanted to do whatever pleased him at the moment. He could not accept any limits, could not relate himself to other children or to adults.

These are only a few examples. There were other such children at camp. These children were not ready for a group experience, and as a result were continual sources of conflict and tension in their bunk group and in the camp at large. Not only did they derive little benefit from camp for themselves, but they prevented the other children from achieving the maximum benefit from the camp experience.

Why are these children sent to camp? The writer, after the last camp season, held discussions in the various clinics of the agency and found that caseworkers and therapists had little concept of what camp life really involved. Workers tended to think only in terms of the individual child. They did not see the broader problem of the effect that their particular child would have on the other children, or how the other children would react to their child. They sent children to camp for any number of reasons, most of them very valid from the point of view of the child, such as to begin a separation of mother and child; to give the child a preplacement experience; to provide a respite from destructive family life; to strengthen his ego through the acquisition of new skills; and so on. Only once, however, did any one talk of sending the child to camp because of the group experience inherent in the camp set-up.

During the last season, there was much discussion among the clinic staffs in order to give them a greater understanding of camp, its program and its philosophy and practices, so that they would have a clearer idea of how to select children for this kind of experience.

While no specific criteria for the selection of children have been worked out, what has been emphasized is that the main purpose of camp is to provide a limited group experience. With this in mind, it becomes clear that only those children who are able to remain away from their families for at least a month's time without undue anxiety, who are able to accept some frustration and limitation, and who have the capacity and the desire for relationships with their contemporaries, should be sent to camp. It has also become clear that in a camp situation certain kinds of children cannot be handled adequately, such as the very aggressive child, the masochistic child, the homosexual child, and so on.

In addition to the screening of children for camp, there is the preparation of the child for this experience. Too often a worker accepts a child's request to go to camp as a real indication of his desire to separate himself from his family and to share in a group experience. These requests must be examined more closely. Does the child really know what is involved in camp or does he want to go to camp merely because a friend of his is going and he is afraid he is missing out on something? In other words, we must understand the full meaning that going to camp has for a child, and then evaluate this meaning in terms of whether it is neurotically determined or is an expression of a positive drive toward health. In the same way a child's resistance to this experience must be understood and, where possible, resolved so that he can attain the maximum benefit of the camp experience. As we have said, some workers now tie up camp with the total-treatment plan for the child. The child thus gets a feeling that camp is not merely a vacation, but another way in which the worker is trying to help him through his difficulties.

These are the major problems now confronting Ramapo and other camps of a similar nature. In addition to working on these problems, all camps must constantly reëxamine their philosophy and practices in order to modify or change them so that they can best serve the interests of their client group. This writer cannot overemphasize that if a camp for disturbed children is to be run effectively, there can be no stinting, either in money or in planning and thought.

Chapter 29

After-Care

THE PROCESS OF REINTRODUCTION of a delinquent into the community after he has spent a period in an institution, while not as difficult and heartrending to the young person as is the case of an adult returning "home" from prison, is still a delicate one. The youthful ex-prisoner may be hailed by his gang as a returning hero; or he may suffer the humiliation arising out of unsympathetic attitudes and lack of understanding on the part of his parents, siblings, teachers and fellow pupils.

The transitional period between incarceration and freedom is therefore of great importance in determining the future fate of the delinquent.

While much has been written about the parole of adult offenders and important follow-up studies have been made of the post-parole behavior of mature offenders, relatively little sound material has been published about the processes of reintroduction into society of ex-prisoners of institutions for young delinquents.

The first article in the present chapter, by Betz, presents the results of a questionnaire study of release practices from training schools for delinquents. Indicating at the outset the great variety of establishments for delinquents, of the statutes under which they operate, and of the institutional programs, Miss Betz discusses the findings regarding the term "parole" as applied to children's institutions, the variation in the techniques of preparation for parole, pre-release investigation, "trial parole" or temporary community placement, determination of eligibility for release, the structure and techniques of the releasing authority, supervisory practices, placement resources, pre-release requirements and termination of parole. For all these, Miss Betz suggests what she believes to be the best practices.

Miss Rappaport's article deals with after-care supervision given by the Baltimore Department of Public Welfare. There is an unusual arrangement in Baltimore, whereby the after-care children of that city who have been released from the State of Maryland's four training schools and two forestry camps are given oversight and aid by the Protective Services Division of the municipality's Department of Public Welfare on the basis of a court order issued by the Circuit Court of Baltimore, Division for Juvenile Causes. Miss Rappaport recounts, with sympathetic insight yet with firm realism, both what difficulties the released delinquent will meet on his return to the community and what can be done constructively by the social worker to render that return helpful to the ex-prisoner and his family and fundamentally protective to society. The author puts the issue in these words: "The problem for the After-Care Supervision social worker is to find the balance between tight supervision and help which will make it possible for this troubled youth to take over more and more responsibility for his own behavior."

The article by Wogahn, Sommer, and Larsen describes Wisconsin's experiment with the use of small group homes, each licensed to care for six children, as part of the post-institutional program with delinquents. This experiment with small-group homes might well be taken up by other jurisdictions; for, as the authors state, "A number of the youngsters who had failed in numerous previous placements have adjusted very well in the group homes," and there are children who are not able to relate to the typical foster-home parents. The type of group parents sought is described; the nature of the physical facilities is taken into account in selection of group homes as is also the location of the homes convenient to the offices of the Division of Corrections of the State's Department of Public Welfare. Intake policies are clearly discussed, with an account of why it was found advisable to centralize intake decisions in the agents supervising the homes for administrative and for casework purposes. The skillful placement of individuals to bring out the best resources of the group is described; the roles of discipline and rules are indicated; home visit practices and the levels of leadership in the group situation are discussed. The article ends with an assessment of costs and such evaluation of results as is possible in an experiment that has been going on for a relatively short time. The authors point out that the idea of small-group homes for children who could not succeed in foster homes arises naturally out of the fact that the group situation is more acceptable because it is more of a "neutral setting" with fewer emotional demands on the child, it provides a socializing milieu, it presents a situation permitting a ready transition into another form of treatment, and it is sometimes used as a temporary placement facility for purposes of observation and planning for more permanent placement. It will be very interesting to see how the Wisconsin experiment develops; for among the most urgent needs in coping with delinquency is greater flexibility and more experimentation with new treatment methods.

The final piece in this chapter is by Zimmermann and Wendell and covers a frequently overlooked, if incidental, aspect of the supervision of delinquents — interstate oversight. It presents the relevant terms of an interstate compact to govern out-of-state supervision.

161

Release from Training Schools *

Elizabeth A. Betz

For several months I have studied, under the sponsorship of the National Probation and Parole Association and the United States Children's Bureau, release practices from training schools. The material collected covers a wide variety of categories, beginning with terminology and covering such aspects of parole as preparation, eligibility, organization of the releasing authority, the hearing, parole conditions, placement in the community, supervision, duration, revocation, and supervisory personnel.

* Reprinted from a thesis for the Master of Arts degree, New York University, in *Advances in Understanding the Offender*, 1950 Yearbook, National Probation and Parole Association, 75–88. Used by permission of the author and the publisher. See, also, E. Borenstein, "Release of the Child from the Institution," in *Dealing with Delinquency*, 1940 Yearbook, National Probation Association, 3–23. — Ed.

Before presenting some of the more important findings of the survey, it may be well to consider that parole has different meanings for different people depending upon varying practices in the training school field. In one state for instance a child committed to a training school is treated on a casework basis until he is discharged from all supervision. At the other extreme, the statute of another state provides that all committed children must be fingerprinted. Elsewhere a child who is a behavior problem in the training school may be transferred to an adult penal institution for discipline, but the statute mercifully makes it clear that "in no event shall the girl or boy be confined or placed in any sweat box." One training school determines eligibility for parol on "recommendations of the mental hygiene clinic and completion of certain educational and training requirements on an individual basis." In another school a child earns one credit a week for conduct and effort, and may be paroled when he has fifty-two of them. Thirty days stay is added for a child caught smoking in one school, while in another older children are allowed to smoke. In one school parole plans are made only a few days before release. In better schools parole planning begins the day the child enters.

Within one state or even within one city

may be found courts with widely opposing attitudes towards children's cases. One judge makes it his business to understand the program offered in the training school and attempts to find out whether a particular child would benefit by commitment, or whether probation or some other plan might be more effective. Another judge with a distaste for a juvenile assignment conducts hearings in a perfunctory manner and makes commitments without discrimination.

In the strict sense parole is conditional release from an institution, and in this discussion it will apply to the juvenile training school. But with such a variety of practices it is obvious that the full meaning of the word will be dependent upon the processes involved in the philosophy of any particular jurisdiction. To function effectively, each process in the total picture must be dependent upon the other. Thus a school in a particular state has a poor training program, so a child to be paroled has not been fundamentally changed or re-educated for community living. Even if he has good supervision in the community, he may do poorly on parole for lack of institutional training. These two factors, variations of meaning in the term parole, and the necessity of effective functioning of the various processes involved, are of fundamental importance, yet a survey such as this cannot bring out these qualitative findings.

This study was based mainly upon questionnaires which were returned from 88 public training schools for juvenile delinquents, representing the District of Columbia, the federal government, Hawaii, and all of the states except Mississippi and North Dakota. Study of the statutes to some extent supplemented the material from the questionnaires. Some conclusions which could not be drawn from the collected data were reached by conference with authorities in the field, from literature, and from the writer's personal experience in training schools in several states.

THE WORD PAROLE

Before discussing institutional practices we may consider briefly the reaction of administrators to the word parole. It was found that the majority of training schools use it to describe the process of release. Other terms include placement, discharge, after-care, trial place-

ment, release, furlough. Only a small number prefer parole, and the majority indicate that some other expression should be used.

Opposition to the term is significant but it is impossible from our findings to suggest a better one. Various people have stated that parole has a penal connotation and has more meaning in reference to adult release procedures. Such comments as these came in: "We do not use the term 'parole' or 'sentence' because any concept of the penal has no place in the life of any youngster." "Parole is a general term for prisons and prisoners and we have tried to stay away from prison terms." "No one under sixteen who is classified as a juvenile is considered a criminal and therefore a 'parolee.'" Before a more fitting term is found it will probably be necessary to define more clearly the whole process in light of advances in this field. Perhaps when this time comes a phrase will evolve which will be acceptable to everyone. For convenience the word parole is used in the ensuing discussion.

PREPARATION

Inquiry in regard to techniques of preparation for release revealed that in the majority of schools pre-parole classes were not held. The interview as the only formal preparation is used in most schools. Where there is no formal preparation some schools indicated that the day to day program is so regarded, and that this starts with admission. It should be noted that while special preparation such as classes and personal interview have a place, they should be integrated into the whole process.

All but seven of the schools in this study stated that investigation is always made before the child is released. These seven indicated that it is sometimes made. Investigations, usually by those who have the responsibility of supervision after release, are made three months or less before the child leaves the training school in 51 of the 88 schools. It is encouraging to point out that in 18 schools planning for parole begins at or soon after the child's admission, although one school stated that the investigation was not made far enough in advance of the release date, sometimes two days, sometimes two weeks.

In a majority of schools preparatory work is done with the family while the child is in the school. It is impossible to know the extent of this, but since most children are released to families or relatives, preparation of the family to receive the child should be incorporated into the release program.

How many training schools have some form of gradual release or try temporary community placement? It was found that day to day parole for employment is used by 39 of the 76 schools reporting on this practice, a technique which can be valuable in the total training program and an aid to parole if it is well regulated and precaution is taken to avoid exploitation of the child. A majority of schools allow children weekend or vacation visits home. One reported that the boys can go home for holidays, or if there is illness or death in the family. Another said that girls were allowed to go home for weekends or vacations on a "casework treatment basis." A third permits visits after three months of good behavior.

Over half of the 78 schools supplying information on visits reported some method of trial placement. Thus the child may be allowed to go home as a trial of adjustment. In one school this is considered a visit and release is granted if the adjustment is good. A child may be placed in the community during the day and return to the school at night. One school stated that boys are given trial parole for one to three months to check on their progress before final release. If a child is afraid to leave the school, placement can be made on a visiting basis at first. Programs of gradual release may be one process in the re-education of the child, and a stepping stone to his return to community life.

The next step in the process is the determination of eligibility for release. It would be necessary to study individually and intensively the methods of the schools to present a truly realistic picture of this aspect. There are probably as many methods of determining when a child is ready for placement as there are training schools. However, in analysis of our data general patterns emerged. A majority of schools reported that satisfactory adjustment in the institution determines eligibility for parole. This gauge may be applied by such groups as classification committees, boards, case conferences, etc. Adjustment may be judged solely on completion of training, or on training in conjunction with other factors. Or placement possibilities may be considered along with satisfactory

institutional behavior and other factors. Some replies were less specific, with phrases such as "when the child seems rehabilitated," and "rehabilitation complete to succeed in society," or "progress in rehabilitation and definite improvement."

Another method for determining eligibility is the credit or marking system. Nine schools use this device solely and nine others use it in conjunction with such factors as satisfactory adjustment in the school, attitude, review by case committee, etc. A child must earn 360 points, one a day with a monthly bonus for a good record in one institution. In another the child earns one credit a month, and must earn 15 before release. A third school comments that a star or credit is awarded each week for acceptable conduct and effort, and 52 credits are required. Three schools stipulate a minimum length of stay, and three report individual progress as the sole determinant.

Most training schools, in contrast to adult institutions, have opportunity for greater flexibility in decision as to release. It is encouraging to find that only a small number use such mechanical devices as credit systems or minimum required time. Obviously the child's readiness for parole should be determined on a casework basis. It is improbable that any training school now has or could have in the near future complete individualization of treatment. The size of the school tends to defeat the personal approach. Complete individualization requires money and staff not available for most of these public institutions. Many are hampered by the court's lack of discrimination in the commitment of children unsuited to the program offered. So in urging eligibility on an individual rather than a stereotyped basis we must face present limitations. Two factors should be watched: 1) we must not apply the term where procedures do not even approximate this concept, and then, because the term is used, assume that the process is taking place; 2) because individualization does not in fact exist, we must not therefore excuse haphazard, loose methods in determining eligibility.

It is possible to approximate determination on an individual basis. Training schools can establish classification systems to plan each child's program to suit his needs. They can aim to increase their personnel and to improve its quality. They can urge the need of clinical services, or increase those they have already. These are only a few suggestions among many possible ones.

Of prime importance are the actual structure of the releasing authority and its dynamic functioning, although in a survey of this kind it is impossible to judge the operation qualitatively. Four principal authorities were found: 1) the superintendent of the training school either with or without the aid of others; 2) boards of managers or trustees which could operate with or without advice of other agencies or individuals; 3) independent bodies such as youth authorities, boards of education; 4) committing courts. Most frequently the superintendent with the aid of other groups or individuals had the authority to parole.

With the releasing authority rests a dual responsibility: decision in the best interest of the child, and protection of the community. The release of a child may be an unjustified risk, or the community may not be ready to accept him. Herein lies a dilemma hard to resolve.

What kind of releasing authority can provide the best service to both the child and the community? With such complex questions as this authority must consider, it would seem that training in the field of child welfare and related disciplines would be requisite. Objectivity, thorough knowledge of the school program and of what is involved in supervision after release are called for. The releasing authority should keep abreast of changes in the field and should be free from political control and influence. It would seem logical that no one person could meet all of these demands and that no one person should have sole responsibility for the final decision.

It is doubtful whether release by an institutional board is the best method. This is not to say that such systems cannot or are not at this time operating effectively. But too many variables occur in the board system for an ideal plan.

The committing court is less often the paroling authority. It would seem that the regular duties of the court are extensive enough without adding the time of this function which demands so much outside of the court's knowledgeable area.

A separate board of well-paid people who have specialized in work with children would seem to be the most suitable authority. The school personnel, with their day by day knowledge of the progress the child has made, would be in a position to make recommendations to the board which should work in close cooperation with them. Success of a board such as this would depend upon the quality, training and ability of its personnel, and of course upon the treatment given the child before and after release. The additional expense of such a system would appear to be warranted by the later adjustment of the child.

REGULATIONS GOVERNING PAROLE

Opinion is divided in regard to giving the child definite written rules of parole. Of the 85 schools reporting on this practice, 42 indicated that printed rules are given children on release, and 43 reported negatively. In 37 schools printed conditions are given to all children, and in the remaining five discretion is used on this point. Is the child required to promise in writing to observe the conditions? A majority of schools indicated that a written promise is not required, and some that do ask it, use no printed rules. The child's signature is taken to show that he understands the requirements which have been explained to him orally. The printed rules studied contained general stipulations governing change of residence, marriage, legal requirements, reporting (both to the school and the parole officer), friendships, activities, use of automobiles, contracts, revocation of parole, etc.

Printed rules reveal two extremes: those written in a formal, legalistic style, and those which are informal in wording and general form. Such words and phrases as "must," "shall not," "it is the order of the board that you shall comply," "you will not be permitted," "do not" and so forth are scattered throughout most of those studied. The more formal type begins like this: "Know All Men By These Presents, That the Board of ...., desiring to test the ability of ...., a ward of the state, to lead an honorable and useful life, does by virtue of the authority conferred upon it by law hereby parole him and allows him to leave the .... School . . ." Following is a brief sample of the rules:

"He shall in all respects conduct himself honestly, obey the law and refrain from use of all intoxicants, tobacco and narcotic drugs. He shall not leave the place of parole without permission from the parole agent, but shall endeavor to lead an industrious life, obedient to those in authority and self-respecting in his habits. He shall avoid all idle and evil companions and all places where such resort; public billiard or poolrooms and public dances. He shall especially avoid the continuance of friendship with those who have been companions in wrongdoing and shall avoid making such friendships in the future."

A few sections of a different statement of parole conditions illustrate the approach which is still quite authoritative and restrictive.

"It will be better for you and for other Training School girls if you will not try to keep your School friendships, and would try to make new friends entirely.

"You will not be permitted to correspond with the girls in the School, so please do not attempt to do so.

"You must not have over two dates a week and they must be with someone of whom the person you are paroled to thoroughly approves.

"You must never stay out after eleven o'clock at night.

"Dress conservatively."

An illustration, in part of a parole agreement which while containing restrictions and implying authority, is somewhat more positive in its general tone, is next given:

"The staff of the .... school is interested in you and your future welfare. We feel that you are now ready to leave the School and you are capable of making a good adjustment in society. If, however, at any time you have bad luck, get into trouble or have problems that are bothering you, we will be happy to have you come in and discuss these things with us, or you may consult your placement supervisor. We are confident that you will exert your best efforts to make good."

Such conditions as these follow:

"I fully understand that my placement is dependent upon my conduct and good behavior; that any violation of the law or of my placement rules may cause my return to the school.

"I will be careful in the selection of my companions and will, during conferences with my placement supervisor, discuss the type of individual I am associating with.

"I will first obtain the permission of my placement supervisor before leaving the state or going on an extended trip."

Whether printed rules are given or conditions are informally imparted to the child, he should be familiar with what is expected of him well in advance of his release, not suddenly confronted with a set of rules just before he leaves. The whole tone of these necessary conditions should be positive, but friendly so that the child will react favorably to them. Such phrases as "Listen to and follow the advice of your parole officer," or "See your parole officer whenever you are in any kind of trouble or have a serious problem," were found in the parole conditions of one state; they imply a positive relationship between the child and his supervisor.

PLACEMENT

The possibilities for placement of the child are varied. The three most frequent types of placement were with parents or relatives, in work homes, and in foster homes. Seventy-seven of the 88 schools indicated, not surprisingly, that parents or relatives were their first choice. This finding points to the importance of preparing the home for the child's return. It is not necessary to restate the importance of this except to say that the positive gains from the training school program will be of little consequence unless constructive work has been done in the family.

Forty-three of the 88 schools do not require a child of working age to have a job before he leaves, but 36 do demand it, though exceptions are occasionally made in some of them. In one school an exception is made if the child is being paroled to his family. Some schools with no job requirement make an effort to find employment for the parolee. It was interesting to find that when the child is paroled with a job in prospect, 61 of the schools state that the employer is told of his status, and 14 indicated that the employer is told in some cases. Only three schools have a policy of withholding this information. It would seem that telling the employer would give him a better understanding of the child in their mutual relationship and would eliminate the likelihood of his learning the child's history from other sources. Two schools emphasize the importance of giving general information, but point out that details of the child's offense should not be discussed.

SUPERVISION

This study reveals that throughout the country the types of supervision are extremely varied and complex, showing no definite pattern except that the great majority of schools do claim some form of supervision. Five main operative types of supervision can be classified as: 1) supervision by the staff of the institution; 2) through a central parole agency; 3) by state or local public welfare agencies; 4) by juvenile or adult probation workers; 5) by other community agencies such as peace officers, family or other private agencies, and volunteers. In this study only four schools out of the 88 reported that at times there was no supervision at all.

In eleven schools parole officers or social workers attached to the institution are the sole supervisors, and one school uses the superintendent or another staff member in this capacity. Five report that the state parole authority is used exclusively, six use welfare departments only, and two use probation departments. None use volunteers or peace officers only. In a survey of this kind it is impossible to show how these methods of supervision actually operate.

It seems reasonable that supervision of the child should have some connection with the training school, preferably through field staff, perhaps providing liaison service between the institution and the welfare department, probation department or other supervising agency if the institution does not supervise directly. Parole implies some relationship to the institution, and for it to be successful a connecting link should exist.

While 43 schools use reporting by mail, no school indicated this as the sole contact between the child and the supervising personnel. A slight majority of schools reported the use of sponsors in some cases. Only 16 used them regularly to supplement official supervision. Children are released to other states on parole by many schools, and usually the receiving state is asked to supervise.

Some general recommendations on supervision may be made:

1. A central agency within each state system should set up definite policies for those carrying out supervision.

2. Personnel must be of the highest possible quality, with specialized training in work with children.

3. The extent and intensity of supervision should be based on the child's needs; no limits of time or attention can be applied to all children.

4. Discriminating use of sponsors in addition to trained personnel can be of value.

TERMINATION OF PAROLE

In nearly half of the schools the authority to terminate parole rests with personnel in the training schools, such as the superintendent, the caseworker or a case committee. The remainder of the schools reported that authority to revoke rested with outside agencies, usually those having the task of supervision. Generally speaking, the supervising agency is in the best position to decide whether the child should be returned to the training school. If supervision is by some authority or department not related to the school, the decision should result from a pooling of opinions of the two agencies. In this study it was found that a majority of schools do not hold a formal hearing on the parole revocation. Of the 74 answering the question as to revocation when conditions of parole have not been violated, one-half stated that the child could be returned and the other half that he could not. It would seem that returning under such circumstances has a proper place in the parole program. It is not always possible for the parole officer to anticipate difficulties which may arise when the release plan is put into operation. Conflicts may develop which could not have been foreseen. Death or illness in the family may radically alter a given situation. Or it may be obvious that the child is in need of further institutional training, although no violation of the specific conditions has occurred. Sometimes the school is the only place where a child can receive convalescent care or extended medical treatment for serious illness, though this should not be the case.

Some comments illustrate this return practice. One school reports that a girl may be brought back "for placement in some other situation as a preventive measure, . . . for medical care or further training." Another states that a boy may be returned "at his request or for his protection as in the case of improper placement." In another jurisdiction boys and girls may be returned "if . . . further treatment is indicated or . . . the child is unable to adjust satisfactorily."

It has been necessary to discuss all these aspects of juvenile parole briefly, and only the more important points have been touched. It can be seen that a wide variety of practices exist. If this research had been more intensive, even greater variations would undoubtedly have been revealed.

In individual states the variations in policy have a haphazard appearance. The statutes relating to these practices seem for the most part to be vague and casual. Probably the most significant finding is the present confusion of ideas and motives. We probably all agree that the aim of parole is to provide the child with the chance to live a normal life in the community. But the specialized process of parole does not and cannot stand by itself. It must be integrated into the total program of any particular jurisdiction. A clear-cut, realistic philosophy must underlie the whole program for delinquent children. This philosophy should be widely accepted and understood so that the goal can be the greatest possible service to the child as well as protection for the public.

To accomplish three major aims — formulation of realistic policies, coordination of the elements of the total program relating to delinquent children, education of the public and enactment of better laws — we need to know what we want. We should define our goals in the most realistic way possible in the light of our present knowledge, always learning more by research, by keeping abreast of changes that are constantly taking place, and by sifting out what is worthwhile from that which is unimportant.

162

The Possibility of Help for the Child Returning from a State Training School *

Mazie F. Rappaport

". . . . . . It has been so ever since, and with ordinary children of men no rebirth is ever wholly clear and sure. A man's essential pattern does not change and that is what makes his rebirth seem uncertain. But if he makes the best of the present moment he will seem to be continually in birth, which is perhaps as near as he can approach a wholly fresh beginning. To sense this upward inner drift is the work of a great judge, and it is a work of art that forwards the progress of the race directly, since the world will always be a reflection of what men are within themselves."

Bok, Curtis, *I, Too, Nicodemus*, p. 333, Knopf, 1946.

No juvenile delinquent has ever been helped by being made to remember and look back. Real help for him must come from hope and belief in him — belief that he can make a better and more satisfying life for himself. And in doing this he will need help. An effective program for boys and girls returning home from state training schools must be as modern and functional as the new bridges and buildings our communities are building. Such an After-Care Supervision program is the bridge back towards community living, the opportunity for the delinquent child to make "a fresh beginning," "to make the best of the present moment" towards rebirth.

It is understandable that a community might feel relief when one of its recalcitrant youths — a juvenile delinquent — goes off into protective custody elsewhere. But like parents, no community is totally relieved of its responsibility for its citizens — no matter how delinquent they may have been. While he is in a training school, the community has only tem-

* Revised by the author from her original article in *J. of Social Work Process* (1954). Used by her permission and that of the publisher. — *Ed.*

848

porary respite from its delinquent youth's anti-social acts — respite which should be used in planning for his return. Communities, however, do not usually welcome back those who have gone away — even to the institutions for the sick: the tuberculous, the mentally ill. With even greater reluctance do they accept back those who have been "sent away" to penal institutions and training schools. A proud American community is ashamed and resentful of its failures and those who go off do represent failure — failure in prevention and in rehabilitation within the community. While pity may be mixed with apprehension for the arrested tuberculosis patient or the "cured" mentally ill man, there is usually only undiluted rejection and fear of the "released" man or boy who has rebelled against law and order. While there has been a shift in attitude from purely punitive to rehabilitative methods of dealing with the offender, "an eye for an eye" and deep conviction that heavy penalties deter others still are widely accepted as proper and useful ways of dealing with delinquency and crime. This feeling in the community against the "returnee" has a deep base in guilt — the guilt of not having given more and provided better for its citizens, guilt for having to "put people away" and then the awful guilt of really not wanting them back.

In most communities the delinquent boy or girl is sent to a training school only as a last resort. Other "things" have been tried or, perhaps, there were no other "things" to try. And so the community has little hope that he will be different when he returns; he has been bad, and by many he is thought to still be bad; adults' standards frequently are held out as proper for him to meet as the community wonders if he had learned his lesson. The training school boy is, indeed, still a "marked boy" in most communities.

Closer examination of attitudes reveals little actual information as to what the juvenile delinquent is like. There is not much knowledge of the difference between the delinquent who can be helped to take more responsibility for himself and the one who cannot. There is a growing trend toward excusing the behavior of all delinquents as that of "emotionally disturbed" children, without facing the fact that there is risk in this simple and ready explanation — the risk of relaxing from discovering

new and more effective methods of helping many delinquent children to become happier young citizens while they still live in the community. Some — indeed most — delinquent children are not emotionally disturbed but are anti-social boys and girls who can learn another way — a better way — of living. Why some unhappy children become delinquent while others become physically ill or neurotic is beyond the scope of this paper in which I want, rather, to describe a method of helping one group of delinquent boys and girls — those returning from the training schools to their homes.

Delinquency is the legal term used to describe the antisocial behavior of the young offender — the child or youth who comes into conflict with the standards of behavior set by the community. Delinquency and crime frequently begin when family and community fail to meet their respective responsibilities by holding realistically to what is theirs to give and to expect in living, thereby helping their children learn to be responsible for their own behavior. Delinquency can begin when giving and taking are far out of balance, when there is denial rather than affirmation of self, when the individual blames and demands of the other but expects not of himself. For the unhappy child delinquency is one way of responding to the situation at hand. It can become a way of living for a child, destructive to himself and to those about him. Usually he can be stopped only by something stronger than he — something which finally commands his respect and engages him in more satisfying and constructive activity.

The delinquent child represents a challenging and exciting opportunity for the social worker, for community concern — even its pessimism — provides the framework for creative effort to meet this problem. This is an area in which the traditionalist can no longer survive; the old way has not worked; new and different methods must be evolved.

What can a social agency do to help a child as he returns from a training school? How does the caseworker[1] begin with him as he

[1] For the sake of clarity I use the feminine gender throughout this paper for the caseworker and the masculine for the delinquent, except where I am citing a particular case. In the Protective Services Division

leaves such a highly structuralized setting to come back into an "open" community — his own community in which he failed once before? What is the problem for him and the community? Why is this such a difficult service to give?

What must be faced first of all is that these boys and girls are adolescents with all of the problems of the "normal" adolescent plus the fact that they have been adjudicated to be delinquents. They come to us as delinquents *once removed from* their delinquent acts but still under the jurisdiction of the Juvenile Court *because* of their antisocial behavior. And now they must make the shift from the protection of the hated training school, a place in which they were protected and controlled — to the open community. And as they do this they are afraid that their parents do not want them and sometimes they are correct in this assumption. But these boys and girls both want and do not want their parents in the way that is typical of adolescence. And then they feel that the community does not trust them and this, too, may be true. What the delinquent adolescent cannot know at the point of his return is how little he trusts anyone — even himself. Trust is something which is earned and won, and this he must learn through help from those who care what is happening to him and who will not desert him as he tries himself out in his newly regained freedom.

The cardinal principle for the social agency in working with the delinquent is that no one can take over for or from him what he must be responsible for now and forever more in his life — his own behavior. This responsibility will vary in amount from infancy through childhood, adolescence and adulthood, but the willingness to learn to be responsible for his own acts must begin early. That another person cannot do this for the delinquent in terms of taking the blame for his own antisocial act is hard for even the social worker to learn and accept, but in just such ratio as the social worker does learn and accept this will she be able to help the delinquent who, indeed, needs a great deal of help. Whether or not the delinquent can use this help will depend on a great many factors,

one of the most important of which is the steadiness of the helper who knows what it will take, has deep respect for the delinquent as he struggles but moves not one whit from holding him to his own part in this struggle. That the delinquent often wants to change and be less burdened with hate and guilt comes out over and over again as the skilled social worker works with him.

Evasion and hopelessness in dealing with the problem of delinquency are implicit in the fear of many social agencies to call the boy on probation or in a training school what he really is — a juvenile delinquent. No help for the person even the young child in trouble can come from this. It will yield no success in working with him. The *only* way in which a delinquent of any age can be helped is for him to be held responsible for what he has been doing — in this case his own antisocial behavior. Only as he knows and feels from those in authority — parents, teachers, judges, or social workers in courts and authoritative settings — that what he has been doing is unacceptable, will he have the framework in which to deal with his own problem. Only as the skillful caseworker helps him struggle with whether he can possess his own delinquent act can he find a point of departure, a spot from which to shift and move. And only as he takes hold of the fact that he may not go on as he has been, can he then begin to know and feel that his past behavior is not what he wants for himself.

The problem for the After-Care Supervision social worker is to find the balance between tight supervision and help which will make it possible for this troubled youth to take over more and more responsibility for his own behavior. The question for the social worker is how to help a youth to hold the gains he made while in the training school, how to help his parents carry their rightful responsibility during this very difficult period — difficult for both the boy and his parents — in such a way that he may truly have a second chance. It is the function of the After-Care Supervision service which I will describe to do just that — to protect both the boy and the community and to make it possible for him to find something within himself on which he can depend during the years ahead.

In the State of Maryland, Baltimore City boys and girls leaving the four state training

---

actually many of the caseworkers are men, and about 10–15% of the clients in After-Care Supervision are girls.

schools and the two forestry camps come to the Protective Services Division of the Baltimore City Department of Public Welfare. This service, known as After-Care Supervision, works with youngsters under sixteen years of age for one year following release; with youths over sixteen years, for six months or until their eighteenth birthday. The service also works with the parents of all the boys and girls under sixteen, with parents on a voluntary basis if the youth is over sixteen. The basis for After-Care Supervision is a formal court order issued by the Circuit Court of Baltimore City, Division for Juvenile Causes, which specifically gives to the Protective Services Division the responsibility of helping the child refrain from further delinquency. The length of the period of supervision has been determined by the Protective Services Division and not by the Court and is in relation to the differences in community activity and family living for those under and over sixteen years of age. It also is based on the period of time the agency can afford to give intensive supervision.

The Order of Supervision does not carry responsibility for custody, nor is it probation in a Juvenile Court or parole from a training school. It is supervision by the community's public social agency which gives this specific kind of help to the training school releasees in readjusting back into their community. In the procedure in the Circuit Court for Juvenile Causes on the day of the boy's release, custody is returned to his family, and by this transfer they, the people who are naturally responsible for him in the community, will now take back their parental roles. While this Court Order gives the Protective Services the right and responsibility of trying to help the boy use what his family and the community are now providing for him, he is held by the Court to demonstrating his willingness to try to live within the community's laws. If he cannot or will not use this help, the Protective Services Division must call this to the attention of the Court by letter, petition or warrant.[2]

In working in After-Care Supervision we have experimented with schedules, time limits and assigning different workers to the boy and his parents, having some workers carry both the parent and the boy in After-Care Supervision. At the present time the boys and girls in After-Care Supervision have their own workers and their parents have a separate worker. This seems a sound way to begin since the boy and his parents, though now living together, were still quite separated when we began. His parents began with their worker while he was still in the training school, and he often feels that their worker is identified with them and will be for them. Certainly the older adolescent cannot bear to have as his social worker a person who seems to him to be his parent's worker.

The skill here in helping the boy is in helping him accept his young adult responsibilities while at the same time helping his parents to affirm or reaffirm their parental responsibilities by releasing him into the world with their support but also with their love and trust. The two workers so assigned "keep together" and we hope the child and his parent will come together through this joint effort. Memos go to and from workers following each interview when the boy or his parent is deeply engaged in some specific struggle, less frequently if there is no need for such careful exchange of information. Conferences are arranged when there is need for them. Wherever possible the same supervisor carries both the boy's worker and the parent's worker.

Everything which the Protective Services Division had previously learned, used, and tested out in working with the adult sex delinquent and in working with negligent parents has some application in the After-Care Supervision. We have had to learn, however, how to adapt our method to working simultaneously with both

---

[2] A letter to the Court is used to report some significant change for better or worse. Also, the progress report required at the end of each six months After-Care Supervision goes to the Court. A petition is used to place a charge against either the boy or his parent if the boy seems to be violating the terms of supervision. This petition initiates a formal hearing

in the Circuit Court for Juvenile Causes during which the agency must substantiate its charge and the boy and his family are given an opportunity to present their "case." "The right to a day in court" is a precious right and the agency tries to help even the boy it is petitioning against to use this right. The Protective Services Division and a parent may co-file charging that the boy is violating supervision and is beyond parental control. A warrant issued by the Court is used to apprehend the boy who either refuses to respond to the court summons or whose whereabouts are unknown.

the delinquent youth and his parent who has failed.

As we begin with such a boy, we begin with what we know, that both he and the community have great question about his ability to make good. How can we help him to "carry his own weight" with so much that will be different now? There is a real area for helping him move from the protective controlled group setting of the training school to the open, unrestricted community to which he is now returning. This difference is too great for the boy — even with the help of his family — to bear alone. His fear usually comes out in stubborn insistence that he has "served his time" and should now be on his own. He often makes it clear that he wants no part of any more social workers. What he wants is to be away from the institution and away from family restriction. He is vocal about wanting a chance to try himself out in his own way — on his own terms. And since it cannot and should not be that way, to the delinquent adolescent it can seem that so much is put on him, that he must do so much. As one thirteen-year-old Negro boy, Willie Andrews, said, after some months of supervision, "You gotta do too much around here." What was going on inside of Willie came out one afternoon when he seemed unusually burdened with the difficulties of being under supervision. After several attempts to discover what was wrong his worker (a man) moved in with "Willie, *what* is wrong? You seem so mad and upset today." To this Willie retorted with an angry "You gotta do too much here." "Like what?" "Just too much." Again came the worker's question, "Like what?" Willie exploded with "I gotta get up in the morning; I gotta wash and I gotta brush my teeth, I gotta get dressed and I even gotta eat breakfast; I gotta go to school, I gotta come here!" Here the worker (who was a man) broke in with "I've gotta do things, too, Willie," to which came Willie's angry retort, "Oh, yeah, like what?" "Well, Willie, I've gotta get up in the morning, I've gotta wash, brush my teeth, shave, eat breakfast and get here to work. . . ." It was Willie who interrupted this time with "You do?" "Sure I do. Why do you ask?" Then came Willie's surprising reply, "*Because I thought you owned the joint.*" To Willie it seemed that too many things have "to be done" by the boy who has been bad. And the worker

needs to be sensitive to this as the requirements are put in — requirements which are the simple stuff of living.

The boy's return to the community after release from one of the state's training schools comes about through an orderly process which begins about two months before he is ready to leave the institution. At that point the training school notifies the Department of Public Welfare *and* the boy's parents that he is being considered for release. In effect the training school is saying that this boy has achieved something important for himself. He was committed to the school as a delinquent, a boy who could not live safely in the community. After eight to ten months, the training school now believes he should try once again to live in a less controlled setting; he will be ready to leave in about two months. Because a child's own home is the best possible place in which a boy or girl can live, the Protective Services always begins with parents — or any other relatives — if there is the slightest chance that they can help their child.

The Protective Services acknowledges the training school's referral by writing directly to the child (with a copy to his training school social worker) and to his family, setting an appointment for both to be seen in our offices within the coming week. At the time of the appointment the child and his parents visit a little before they are interviewed separately. In beginning to work with his parents we ask several questions. Do they, as parents, want their once delinquent boy back with them? Will they take him back as he is now — having been helped in the training school — or will they receive him as he was a year ago, when they could not control him? How do they feel about their inability to control him then? Or about what he did to them — for that is the way a child's delinquency feels to most parents. What makes them feel that it will be different now? How do they feel about the training school experience being finished, the Juvenile Court holding jurisdiction and the Protective Services Division having responsibility for the supervision of their child for one year? Will they be able to use the Protective Services' help for their child? And then we explain that there will not be the Court Order to hold them for *they* will not be on probation. They are the parents of a child who will be under Court Order and we will expect them to do everything that is humanly possible to help their child come back to his home and the community. We go on to say to these parents that something must have gone wrong — pretty badly wrong — for this to have happened and we do need to discuss with them what can be different now that their child is coming back. We will be working with their child to hold his newly found strength, his gain while in the training school. We know that their child needs warm but firm parental love and strength. We explain, too, that this is not the only alternative open to these parents. They can help their child to live elsewhere — in an agency foster home, with other relatives, in an independent boarding home or perhaps in another kind of institution. All that we, as a responsible social agency, can require is that they help their child come into the community with some known and sound plan worked out. And we believe that *every* child returning from a training school needs After-Care Supervision.

We do not focus our work with parents on their marital or other problems, but, rather, on those problems which they, as parents have in relation to the care of their child who will be under After-Care Supervision. After-Care Supervision is not a marriage or parent–child counselling service, but is help for them with anything which can make their child's return a more satisfying one to him and to them. Their child has been in a training school; they are expected to help him now that he is ready to come out; if he gets into further difficulty, the judge will want to know what *they* have done to help him stay out of trouble. This they know from us right from the start.

Most parents begin with us as do any other people in trouble: some feel guilty, some are defiant, some seem not to care. Some parents have never visited their child during the time he has been in the training school; there are parents able to pay for their children's care who have not paid anything to the training school which has provided food, clothing, shelter, and many special services for their child. Some of the parents who come to us are so alcoholic or psychotic that they cannot be held to any responsible planning for themselves or their children. But as we have worked with many, many hundreds of parents and relatives during the past ten years, we have found many among

them who for the first time have claimed or reclaimed the rewards as well as the responsibilities of parenthood and have done this well. The use they made of this casework service is not too unlike that made by negligent parents when their children have been committed as neglected. The parents of these training school children often have to face for the first time their own behavior, their own unwillingness to give and "do" for their children when they come into direct contact and conflict with the requirements set up by the agency. When a parent is required to accompany his fourteen-year-old boy to the Department of Labor and Industry in connection with an after-school job, when he is expected to get to the principal or visiting teacher about his child's progress in school, he must begin to shift some other things in his own life. The agency does not expect him to take over responsibilities which his child should be assuming or to so dedicate his life to his child that neither can individuate himself from the other; it does expect him to know where his twelve-year-old son is at 10 P.M. or where his sixteen-year-old daughter works. It expects him to help his boy through some of the hazards to which all boys are exposed, to help him live within rather than outside the law. As a parent he cannot always do this alone, but he can usually do it within the framework which an agency which knows how to help can set up for him.

Recently we "battled it out" with a mother who strongly resisted help from the Protective Services. We had said that her seventeen-year-old daughter could not leave the city without permission while she was under our supervision. This mother who less than two years ago had filed the delinquency petition which put her daughter into the training school was now insisting on taking her to a nearby resort city where they had both found night employment, the mother in a night club, the daughter in a boardwalk restaurant. Only our requirement that Jane remain in Baltimore helped this mother struggle through giving up her job and bringing her daughter back to Baltimore. While we made it clear that Mrs. Green did not have to return, we were emphatic that if Jane had not come back within forty-eight hours, we would be filing a petition against Jane for violating supervision and against Mrs. Green as contributing to the delinquency of her daughter.

One of the first requirements we set up for parents is that they visit the training school before their child's release, to let their child know from them that he is wanted back, to talk with the social worker at the training school, to find out firsthand what his problem is, and how they, as parents, can help most when he comes back. We say, too, that we will be visiting their home before their child returns so that we will know how they live as a family. If there are two parents, we see them both even though they may be separated or divorced. We know, too well now, that there is too much estrangement between parents and their delinquent children. We know, too, that unhappy and unable parents may be shifting the responsibility onto each other, that fathers sometimes feel that they have done enough if and when they bring home a pay envelope. For them it may seem too hard or to be too much trouble to have to come to the Protective Services offices for regular appointments. Our answer to this can only be that it *cannot* be too much trouble when their child is in trouble.

And of the boy the Protective Services Division also asks some questions: How does he feel as he comes out? Does he believe that he will be followed and watched? Will he worry about the threat of return to the training school? How does he feel about having a worker of his own? Or about his parents also coming to the Protective Services Division and having their own worker? Will he be able to test himself out during the year, trying the things he must try out to see if he can manage himself in this newly regained freedom? Will he test out his family and his social worker to see what they will do? What is he going to do about reinstating himself in his home?

It is harder to set up specific structure for working with a child under supervision than it is with an adult on probation. The child is part of a family group; less can be expected of him in relation to the concrete and ordinary things in living, but there are several practical requirements which can be and are set up immediately by our service. He is expected to go to school if he is within the compulsory attendance age, which is to the sixteenth birthday in Maryland. He is expected to get himself to our office for his appointments on time and without "pals" or other distractions; he knows from us that he may not leave the city without our permission; if he is sixteen and does not wish to remain in school he must try with our help to secure a job and try to keep it. We say to him that we will be holding him to attending school regularly or to getting a job in a safe and allowable industry. We set up a period of time for getting himself into the school which the training school and the Special Services Division of the Department of Education have selected as the place in which he can learn best. If it is work which is to be considered with a boy who is sixteen years of age, we will be requiring of him that he go about getting this in an orderly and legal manner. He goes first accompanied by a parent to the Department of Labor and Industry, where he shows our card, introducing him to a special information clerk who explains the Maryland Law for the employment of minors. She tells him which jobs are permitted, explaining the obligation of both the employee and of the employer and gives him a folder in which this is explained in simple terms so that he may re-read and use this as he needs to. If he is able to accomplish this much he then goes to a specially assigned counselor in the Special Services Division of the Maryland Employment Service. And this he does alone — since a boy cannot find a job *for himself* if his parent is along. After his first interview if he has not been sent out on a job *and* secured it, we will expect him to report to the employment counselor early every morning to go out on the jobs to which he is referred and if he is not placed in a job, then he is expected to search for work "on his own" during the rest of the day. The Child Labor Law of Maryland rules out certain jobs for boys under 18 years of age, because of the physical risk involved and the Protective Services Division rules out still others for these boys and girls from 12–18 years of age, who have been in trouble. We do not permit a delinquent boy to take a job around carnivals, race tracks, poolrooms "arabing carts," etc., where the opportunities for getting into trouble are so plentiful. Nor will we permit him to take a "self-employment" job such as being a shoe-shine boy, a newsboy, etc., where there is no supervision, where he controls his own earnings rather than getting a pay envelope from which withholding taxes, etc. have been deducted. We say to girls coming out of Montrose and

Barrett Schools that they may not be bar-maids, waitresses, entertainers, etc. The jobs with tips, irregular hours and casual supervision are too hazardous for these adolescents who have been in trouble.

The boy in After-Care Supervision is expected to work out with his family the hours he will be coming in on week nights and over week-ends. And, most of all what he is doing at home, in school or work and with us, must add up to showing that he is trying to stay out of trouble. To do this he must have taken a hold of the need to change something — and in his case "this something" is his previously unacceptable behavior. It is with this that the boy usually has the most trouble with his worker, for now it is *he* who must bring in the "evidence": and while this is something which he may understand intellectually, it is also what he can resist with all of his will, protesting that "I haven't done anything wrong," or "You can't prove I've been in trouble." What we want from him, articulated in his own way, is what *he has done* that is different from what he was doing before. Can he tell us of one thing that he is doing differently now? If he can identify it we will help him to affirm it and possess it so that he can move on to the next important piece of living.

What is the choice then for the youngster, for this adolescent, as he begins his supervision? It is that he can either use the help we have to offer or he can refuse to try to use it. What this means in concrete terms is that we will be requiring certain specific things of him — those things which we have explained, things which we believe to be within his capacity to accomplish and things we will help him to do. But the agency will not be requiring these changes without offering the help necessary for their achievement.

A youth's struggle with himself in After-Care Supervision is full of fear and he must go through much as he shifts from "getting by" to taking on a way of living in which getting by is not only not good enough for the community, but *is no longer acceptable to him*. As we see it, the question in working with the delinquent is not how bad the boy had been or is, but what he can do about his past behavior, what parents do with his badness, and what an agency does with the parent and child in relation to this. A child and his parents need each other and as

we work with those returning boys and girls what we must test is whether these parents and this child can tolerate each other. Where there is hate, there can only be violence and destruction; and where there is only rejection, there is not enough comfort and affection for a child to flourish in. Competition between parent and child or between parent and social worker over the child, bears only frustration and failure; it is the social worker's responsibility in the After-Care Supervision service not to separate the child from his parent — even from a somewhat unable parent, but rather to work with and try to develop and preserve the human values of the person who should be in intimate care of the young delinquent wherever possible. We believe these persons to be those whom a boy or girl wants most — his parents and relatives.

Skill in working with the delinquent adolescent comes in expecting and requiring him to try to do a few things well, developing some identifiable competence in staying with and seeing at least one accomplishment which is really his own. It matters not whether this be in relation to school attendance, hunting a job, coming to grips with what time he will come in at night, working out how he will keep his appointment in the agency or any other problem which is important to him. He cannot manage everything, but he can feel more adult if he is trusted in some important matters. What must be kept in balance is that he is not yet an adult and he needs to be picked up and brought back as he begins to fail — before be becomes too deeply involved in trying to blame others, trying to evade assumption of responsibility for his own acts. The fact that he is not yet able to make adult decisions does not, however, keep him from wanting to be and feel like an adult. This is illustrated by a boy in After-Care Supervision, Bill Bernard, who knows himself as a man!

Bill Bernard was a handsome sixteen-year-old Negro boy, an only son, an illegitimate child. Coming back to his mother's home was hard. She was on public assistance because of a bad back, but Bill could not be included in the grant because he was 16, out of school and employable. He "fooled around" for the first few weeks, relaxing from the routine of Boys' Village, testing out our service's requirement that he try to get a job immediately. When the fourth week of Bill's unemployment came around, his worker uttered an ultimatum — either Bill get himself over to the Maryland State Employment Service to try to get a job or the worker would be taking him back to Court. Bill seemed to have taken in the seriousness of this, but the next week he appeared dressed as a drape — long checked coat, oversized necktie, peg trousers. Even his hair seemed longer as he had it brushed in the back. He had been growing a mustache and this seemed to have come "of age" with his acquisition of his bizarre clothing. Altogether Bill had presented himself ready to "argue it out."

The worker met Bill with a statement as bold as Bill's costume. He said simply but firmly that he could not come here in those clothes. They weren't good enough for what we have to do here. And then the worker gave him exactly one more week in which to get a job. No job next week — no more supervision! Bill who had expected an argument or at least some question as to how he had purchased his bizarre clothing was left with nothing to defend. To the worker's next question expressing doubt about Bill's ability to do much more and wondering whether he would even get in for next week's appointment, Bill muttered an invective followed by "I'll show *you!*" and left.

Next week Bill was dressed in his "regular" clothes. With a glint in his eye he announced that he had been working part-time, and with that he rattled some change in his trouser pocket. While he had not gone to the Maryland State Employment Service, he had found part-time work in a grocery in his neighborhood. The worker took this as it was — not pressing this important omission in relation to the Maryland State Employment Service, but instead asked Bill how it felt to have money in his "jeans." "Fine." Now he has money for taking out some girls. "Like the girls?" the worker asked. "Sure" — then after a pause — "some for talking to, some for loving." Bill

stopped, then firmly said, "A guy ain't a man 'til he's loved a girl!" "And you're telling me that you are a man?" "Yes," replied Bill expansively. "OK, fellow, then behave like one! In our society a man goes to work and takes care of himself and his family." In this example of staying with the problem which brought the client and worker together — his need to get a job if he is to stay in After-Care Supervision, the worker does not get involved in other things, no matter how relevant they might be to his behavior. If Bill is ever to meet the agency's requirement that he get a job, he has to be recognized as what he is saying he is — a man — and then expected to be just that.

Recently a sixteen-year-old Negro boy in his final interview with his worker was showing the usual fear of ending something which had become quite important to him. "I figure 'advice' isn't the right word for what you helped me with," he said. And then, "It has made me feel a part of something," and "When you write to the Judge, please tell him that my mother has been of extra special help to me during this whole year." Louis agreed to his worker's saying that he knew that he had done well. Then he ended on his own unique note, "I tried. I know now that the only thing you can do in life is to try. Maybe it will come out, maybe it won't, but at least you know you have tried."

To help young delinquents coming back from the training school "to make the best of the present moment" to try to make a new beginning, the Protective Services Division of the Baltimore Department of Public Welfare is committed. To paraphrase what Louis said to his worker: Maybe for some of these delinquents it will come out, maybe for some it won't, but at least we will know that we have tried. This, then, can be for them the rebirth, the being "continually in birth," which is perhaps as near as they can approach to a wholly fresh beginning.

163

An Experiment
in Group Placement
of Juvenile Parolees *

Lester E. Wogahn, Edith Sommer,
and Lawrence Larsen

For the past couple of years the Division of Corrections of the Wisconsin State Department of Public Welfare has been experimenting with the use of small group homes for the placement of selected juvenile parole cases. Each of these homes is licensed by the department to care for six youngsters. We have been the supervising agents in two of the homes, and we propose in this article to describe the experimental program and to share with others some of the things we have learned thus far. It should be emphasized, however, that we speak only for ourselves and not for the entire Division of Corrections.

Juvenile parole in Wisconsin is administered within the state's integrated correctional system. At any one time, six to seven hundred persons between the ages of twelve and twenty-one are on parole from our two juvenile institutions, the Wisconsin School for Boys at Waukesha and the Wisconsin School for Girls at Oregon. For some time it has been apparent that some type of placement other than the parent's home, a job, or even a foster home was required in the post-institutional treatment of these youngsters. Too many of them have been (and still are) returned to the same homes which were instrumental in their delinquency in the first place. Those placed elsewhere have usually had to be put where a home was available at the moment, rather than according to their needs. This has been a matter not of choice but of necessity, born of a lack of funds. Funds for foster homes for the juvenile parolee be-

came available in Wisconsin only about five years ago.

Even then, however, there were still certain cases which needed a type of placement experience different from what we are able to provide. We then began to think about the possibilities of group care; we believed that a substantial number of youngsters could profit from this type of placement but could not succeed in a foster home.

This belief has been strengthened by our experience with group homes thus far. A number of the youngsters who had failed in numerous previous placements have adjusted very well in the group homes. Some of them did not have the capacity to relate to "foster parents"; the very phrase "foster home" was a threat to them. The group situation has been found to be much more acceptable: it provides (1) a neutral setting in which fewer emotional demands are made of them; (2) a socializing process to help them work out their place in society with the aid of the security derived from being part of a group; (3) a transition for the youngster who will later be able to move into some other type of situation; (4) a temporary placement facility when time is needed for observation or for planning with a youngster for a more permanent placement.

THE GROUP PARENTS

Numerous considerations went into the selection of the two homes which we have supervised in this program. Of primary importance, of course, were the couples chosen to act as group parents. Certain characteristics were set down and have been confirmed as desirable attributes for group parents. They should be observant and intelligent enough to be able to recognize and cope with problem situations as they arise. They should be old enough to be capable of forming effective relationships with the youngsters in their home. They should have a basic understanding of young people and an accepting attitude toward the problems young people often present. They should be emotionally stable; if they are not, they cannot supervise the emotionally unstable youngster. They should be secure enough to be able to accept supervision and to proceed with confidence on their own.

We felt that experienced foster parents who had already demonstrated their interest and

* Reprinted from 4 *NPPA Journal* (January, 1958), 66–73. Used by permission of the authors and the publisher.

ability in working with problem youngsters would be the best prospects for group home parents. Previous experience would make them less likely to be overwhelmed by the rather awesome responsibility to be placed on them.

We do not think, however, that all successful foster parents can be successful group parents. Unlike foster parents, the group parents must be willing to leave the selection of the youngsters to be placed in their homes entirely up to the agent, and they must be able to accommodate a new youngster at any time. Then, too, dealing effectively with six adolescent youngsters of diverse backgrounds and problems is much more difficult than dealing with one or two at a time. Indeed, it sometimes seems that each addition to the size of the group increases the problems geometrically instead of arithmetically. The group parents must therefore have an intense desire to work with young people and a willingness to give unselfishly of themselves, often with very little expression of thanks in return. Theirs is a 24-hours-a-day responsibility. The average foster parents would simply not measure up to the demands of the group situation.

We were very fortunate in finding two couples who possessed enough of the attributes to make good group parents and at the same time were willing to undertake this difficult role.

The E. home for boys was the first of our two group homes to be set up. Mr. and Mrs. E. were sixty-four and sixty-three years old, respectively, at the time. Both are college graduates. Mr. E. is a retired businessman and farmer; Mrs. E. had taught school for eleven years prior to her marriage. They have been married for over thirty years and are well adjusted to each other. They have raised two children of their own, a boy and a girl, both grown and married. In addition, their home had been used as a work placement and foster home for our cases in the past. We knew they were very much interested in young people, though their motives in becoming group parents were not entirely philanthropic. Originally their motive was partially a desire to supplement their income; it was definitely subordinate, however, to their interest in working with young people.

The second group home which we are dealing with is the C. home for girls. Mr. and Mrs. C. were fifty-eight and fifty-six years old, re-

spectively, when their home was licensed as a group home. Neither of them had an extensive formal education, but they are capable, intelligent, and understanding. They have been married for thirty-six years. They have had no children of their own, but they have had a hand in rearing several nieces and nephews. Prior to becoming group parents they had demonstrated remarkable success as foster parents and had boarded as many as three girls in their home at one time. They became interested in the group home program mostly out of a desire to do something worthwhile for more young people. Mr. C. is regularly employed outside the home and financial gain is not a primary motive in their serving as group parents.

PHYSICAL FACILITIES

A second consideration evaluated in the search for our group homes was the actual building which the prospective group parents had available. At first we thought that group parents must own their own homes, but we have found that while this is an advantage, it is not necessarily an essential qualification. The chief difficulty in renting, of course, lies in the fact that many landlords do not want to rent their property for use as a group home for delinquent youngsters.

The home for our purposes must, of course, be fairly large since it must house at least eight people. We do not feel that individual rooms for the youngsters are necessary, however, and are inclined to think that sharing a room with others has been a constructive experience for them. Perhaps much of the value of the group living experience would be lost if individual rooms were provided. We have tried, though, to make some provision for privacy for each youngster, even if this has been only in the form of bureau drawers for his exclusive use.

Sanitation and safety were other items to be considered. Every community has standards which apply to private dwellings and which are not difficult to meet. (There was, in addition, an important initial question in Wisconsin — whether the home might be classed as an institution, thus becoming subject to other rigid regulations which obviously most private homes could not meet. If such regulations had been ruled to apply, this program would never have come into being.)

The two dwelling units which house our

958TREATMENT

groups are quite different in many ways, but each has proven satisfactory in most respects.

The E. home for boys is a farm home. Mr. and Mrs. E. own the farm (but rent out the land). There is ample space for outdoor recreation and there is a river about a quarter of a mile away. The house is a 25-year-old two-story frame structure in good condition, attractively decorated, and with all modern conveniences. In addition to a full basement, an enclosed porch, and a bathroom, there are seven good-sized rooms, four of which are bedrooms (on the second floor). The boys have two of these bedrooms and sleep in bunk beds, three to a room. Closet and drawer space is adequate.

The C. home for girls is in the city. Mr. and Mrs. C. rent a comfortably furnished apartment over a grocery store in a residential neighborhood, across the street from the high school which the girls attend. The grocery store on the ground floor is operated by the landlord, who is interested in the program and willing to cooperate in every possible way. In addition to two porches and two bathrooms, the apartment consists of six rooms, four of which are bedrooms. Three of the bedrooms are for the girls; one has three single beds, another has two single beds, and the third is used as a single room. Each girl has her own closet and drawer space.

LOCATION

A third consideration in establishing these group homes was location. Our preference was for homes in or very near the communities where our offices are located. We obtained this in one instance, but not in the other, and the effect of the location of the home has thus been demonstrated very clearly.

The C. home for girls is located in the city in which the supervising agent has her office. This has proved to be a great advantage since it makes the agent available whenever a situation arises that demands her attention. She is able to be in the home every day, if necessary. This is important because there are many problems which the group parents cannot be expected to handle alone and because the settling of some of these problems cannot always be safely postponed until the agent's regularly scheduled visit. Of course, the danger of "oversupervising" must not be ignored and too much dependence on the agent should not be fostered,

but this is a danger which a capable agent knows how to avoid.

The E. home for boys is located about thirty miles from the supervising agent's office. A lot of time is consumed in traveling to and from the home, and the agent has found it necessary to set aside one afternoon each week for a visit. Of course, he is on call at all times if a major problem arises that demands his attention, but the tendency is for everyone concerned to "save up" things during the rest of the week for that one afternoon. This means that the youngsters and group parents may have had to nurse problems for several days before having an opportunity to discuss them with the agent; it means that important matters are sometimes ignored simply because the agent is not available; and it means that on the agent's regular day in the home so many things have to be discussed that none of them receives the thorough attention it deserves.

Another disadvantage in the E. home location pertains to school arrangements. The bus goes right by the home but the school the boys must attend is a small one, located in a town of about 2,000 population. We have not been able to win acceptance of our program in the school, which is not big enough to absorb these boys without their being identified as "delinquents" from the outside. We suspect that much the same problem would be encountered in many communities of this size. We have not been faced with this problem in the large school attended by the girls in the C. home. There the school administration has cooperated and the girls are less conspicuous.

Transportation is a problem not only for the agent, but also for the group parents in a rural home. Having a group of youngsters in their home means that the group parents must make countless trips into town which they wouldn't otherwise make. The boys ordinarily have no way of getting around unless the group parents take them. Of course, this has its advantages, since it pretty well eliminates the problem of too much chasing around. Rural location also, as mentioned above, provides ample space for wholesome outdoor recreation; on the other hand, work opportunities are limited, a vocational school program is not possible, and participation in many worthwhile church, school, and organizational activities is difficult if not impossible.

INTAKE, SUPERVISION, AND TERMINATION

Definite intake policies were established immediately to screen all referrals. Responsibility for intake decisions was centralized in the agents supervising the homes for both administrative and casework reasons. Administrative chaos would result if more than one person made placement plans in these homes because only the group home agents know at all times how many openings are available and what the plans are for filling existing vacancies. From a casework standpoint, too, the group home agents are in the best position to decide whether a particular case will fit into one of these homes. The referring agent may be in a better position to evaluate the strengths and weaknesses of the youngster being considered, but the group home agent is in the only position to evaluate the group as it is then composed. This is an important point, for a particular case might well fit into a group home at one time but not at another.

Extreme care in screening is indispensable. Not every youngster can profit by this type of experience, not every youngster can adjust to this type of environment, and not every youngster would be acceptable to the rest of the group. We think that the group home can be effective with some very difficult cases, but it should not be used as a dumping ground for them simply because they are difficult to place elsewhere. It is no place for the psychotic, the epileptic, the incendiary, or the homosexual. It is not the place for the youngster whose disturbances and problems require intensive individual attention. A misplaced youngster in this type of setting is more likely to disturb the others than to be helped by them.

Intake of cases into these group living situations should be staggered to achieve the most effective use of the strengths of the group. The structure of the group home can be most useful to the newly placed youngster if there are some members in the group who have been there for some time. These "veterans" give continuity to the program and are invaluable in the acclimation of the new member and in providing the proper kind of leadership. Excessive turnover makes for unstable composition of the group and reduces opportunity for a climate of conformity and a healthy esprit de corps.

Like intake, supervision of the cases in the group home also must be the responsibility of one agent. The home is used primarily and mostly for long-term care and it would be confusing to everyone to have several agents working with the youngsters. Therefore, complete responsibility for supervision as well as intake has been centralized in the group home agent. This has provided continuity of supervision and planning.

It follows naturally that termination of the placement should also be the responsibility of the group home agent. He is able to observe closely the readiness of each youngster for a different plan and can proceed accordingly. In a few cases revocation and return to the institutional setting has been necessary; in others, an individual foster home placement has been arranged when it appeared that such a plan would better meet a youngster's needs. One of the boys was able to enter the armed forces, and jobs have been obtained for other youngsters who were ready to become self-supporting and independent. Marriage or discharge from custody might be other reasons for termination.

DISCIPLINE AND RULES

Firm discipline and certain formalized rules are essential. Young people want discipline and a reasonable set of rules which they are expected to follow. They sometimes give the impression of rebelling against both; actually they rebel not against discipline and rules per se but against the extremes of these things. The effect of unreasonable demands and of no demands at all in the etiology of delinquency is too well known to belabor here, but it might be well to remind ourselves that a just system of discipline and rules, with the assurance of both punishments and rewards when they are deserved, provides structure and contributes to a sense of security which cannot be given in any other way.

The rules in our group homes are as few and simple as possible, and they have been found to be necessary and helpful. They are not exactly the same in the two homes because the problems presented by boys and girls are not the same and because the locations are different; in general, they pertain to hours, activities, school attendance, home visits, work assignments, etc.

It usually takes a few days for the newly placed youngsters to fit into the routine of these rules. During that time he tests them, attempting to gain concessions and exceptions. He quickly learns, however, that the rules apply to everyone and he soon accepts them. Though some interpretation of the rules by the agents is necessary, the most effective interpretation usually comes from the other youngsters in the group.

Disciplinary action for violation of the rules has been no more severe than necessary, but it has been firm and as certain as we have been able to make it. Minor violations have usually been handled by the group parents. More serious violations of the rules and all violations of parole regulations have received the personal and immediate attention of the agents. This has been essential in order to maintain control, which, once lost, can be extremely hard to regain.

Occasionally, however, it has been unnecessary for either the group parents or the agents to take disciplinary action for offending behavior. The groups sometimes have their own effective and acceptable ways of dealing with a member who does something which adversely affects the others or which outrages their sense of propriety. An example of this happened in the E. home shortly before Christmas, 1956. The boys had saved some money from their weekly allowances to buy Mr. and Mrs. E. a gift. The money was then given to one boy to make the purchase. Instead of buying a gift, however, he spent the money on himself. The other boys took care of the matter very effectively themselves by seeing to it that the money was repaid from the culprit's allowance and by excluding him from all group activities until it was repaid.

Of course, this sort of thing must be watched to prevent it from getting out of hand. Youngsters cannot responsibly police themselves in all matters, though perhaps they can do a better job than adults sometimes give them credit for.

HOME VISITS

Space does not permit an exploration of all the other problems of group homes, but one of considerable importance is visits by the youngsters to their own homes.

We have followed the policy of permitting such visits except where they would be definitely harmful in a particular case. The homes and parents of some of these youngsters may be grossly unfit, but the youngsters still idealize them and usually look forward to an opportunity to visit them. These visits have been closely controlled, however, and have been allowed only on special occasions. They usually result in the temporary loss of some of the progress which a youngster has made, but a few days after his return from such a visit he is back in the routine of the group home again. The problems resulting from refusal to let a youngster visit his parents are often more severe and of longer duration than those resulting from such visits. Thus far the youngsters have returned pretty much on time and without having become involved in any serious trouble during their absence.

We have encouraged visits from those parents who live fairly close to the group homes. This has usually resulted in their increased cooperation. Perhaps partly as a result of our visiting policies we have had almost no interference from the parents.

LEADERSHIP

Numerous forms and levels of leadership interact in group home situations. First of all there is the leadership exerted by the group parents. They are the ones who are doing the day-to-day supervising of the youngsters' activities. It is from their acceptance, understanding, patience, and wisdom and from the good examples which they set that the youngsters entrusted to their care will benefit.

A second form of leadership present in these homes is that which is exerted by the youngsters themselves. If this leadership is bad, the whole group is affected adversely; if it is good, the whole group will benefit. We have kept this in mind at intake and have attempted always to have in each home at least one or two youngsters able to exert a positive influence on the others. Likewise, we have attempted to keep out the youngsters who would be likely to lead the others astray.

A third form of leadership is that exerted by the supervising agents. It does not consist of autocratic direction, but it has sometimes had to be more direct than subtle. In exerting this leadership the agents use many standard principles and techniques of social work. They form purposeful relationships, define limits, lend support, and give encouragement and recognition. Their role cannot always be that of the mere "enabler," however. They must keep in mind the function of their agency and their position of authority and responsibility. They represent the demands and expectations of society. They are charged with the responsibility of planning, coordinating, and administering treatment plans to achieve the re-education of these youngsters, not only to enable them to lead better lives but also to protect society from further delinquencies on their part. They are the key to the operation of the program.

Costs

The Wisconsin State Department of Public Welfare pays the group parents in this program a subsidy of $15 per bed per month, which amounts to $90 a month in each home, since each is licensed for the care of six youngsters. This sum is paid every month even if the homes are not always filled to capacity. In addition, a board rate of $2.50 per day per child is paid. An initial wardrobe of whatever clothing is necessary is furnished at the time of placement, and thereafter a clothing allowance of $8.50 per month is included in the budget of each youngster. In addition, a $10 per month personal allowance is granted each child. Necessary medical and dental care is paid for by the department.

The cost of this program is fairly high, probably double the cost of placing the same number of youngsters in individual foster homes — but less than the price of institutional care.

A comparison of costs, however, is meaningless without considering other values as well. Equally important is the question of which type of placement is likely to be most effective in the re-education of a youngster. We do not advocate group home placement for all delinquents, but only for certain selected cases. If such a placement can contribute more effectively to the readjustment of certain young offenders than can other placements, then the additional cost is not a very big item.

Evaluation

The program has now been in operation on a rather limited basis for about two years. It is still in an experimental stage, and we have not dealt with enough cases to be able to present an imposing or significant set of statistics. Our experience thus far has been heartening, however, and we think the program has a useful place in the over-all plan of delinquency treatment in Wisconsin.

We have witnessed in the group homes the success of cases which we feel certain would have failed in a different setting. Quite a number were considered exceptionally "tough" — youngsters who were difficult to place or who had failed in previous placements and were referred to us as a final alternative to return to the institution from which they were paroled. Nevertheless, our success rate has been as good as, if not better than, the success rate for all juvenile parole cases in Wisconsin.

We see possibilities for a more extensive use of this type of placement facility in the future. If this should come about, we hope that some statistically valid studies will be made to determine more accurately the effectiveness of the program.

164

Interstate Compacts *

Frederick L. Zimmermann
and Mitchell Wendell

. . . For some time it had seemed anomalous that adult parolees and probationers should be able to receive out-of-state supervision in those

* Reprinted from XI *The Book of the States* (1956–57), 15–16. Used by permission of the authors and the publisher. See, also, "Interstate Compacts," XII *The Book of the States* (1958–59), 216: "Other examples of crime control compacts are the Out-of-State Incarceration Amendment to the Interstate Compact for the Supervision of Parolees and Probationers and the Interstate Compact on Juveniles which, although primarily considered as social welfare legislation, also has crime control significance to the extent that it provides for out-of-state supervision of juvenile parolees and probationers. Both the Incarceration Amendment and the Compact on Juveniles received additional enactments during the period covered by this article." — *Ed.*

cases where it would assist in their rehabilitation, while similar benefits were not available to juvenile offenders. The situation has been even more unfortunate than might appear to the casual observer, because restrictions placed on the juvenile parolee or probationer often affect the movements and mode of living of his family unit, as well as that of the juvenile himself, in a way that is not necessary when the offender is an adult, able to establish his own place of abode as circumstances may require. The adult parole and probation compact is only available to persons who have been convicted of crime. Consequently, the special non-convict status for juvenile offenders, although inspired by humane and praiseworthy considerations, has, until now, barred them from the benefits of out-of-state supervision and the improved opportunities for rehabilitation frequently made possible by it.

From time to time other interstate juvenile problems also have received some recognition. In some instances these may be even more serious than the absence of inter-jurisdictional parole and probation. Notably, there has been a need to develop regular legal machinery for the expeditious return of children who simply run away from home and who are found in another state. Also, it has been thought that some types of problem juveniles might benefit from treatment in specialized institutions. But the provision of such facilities has lagged because of heavy financial burdens involved in their establishment and maintenance. Finally, procedures for returning juvenile escapees from institutional confinement have been uncertain, because juvenile delinquency is technically not a crime. As a result, the constitutional remedy of extradition is not available.

The new Interstate Compact on Juveniles provides means for handling all four of the situations discussed above. Its parole and probation provisions parallel those of the adult compact. The escapee return provisions accomplish the same result as extradition, but in simplified fashion. Procedures for the return of runaways emphasize and authorize voluntary, informal methods of return in all those cases where the factual situation permits, but also provide for compulsory process where necessary. The problem of institutional treatment of juveniles is handled through enabling provisions. One of the compact articles provides for supplementary agreements with regard to joint or cooperative use of institutions for juveniles. A number of specific standards for the making and the contents of such agreements are spelled out, but the actual negotiation and entry into force of any arrangements for joint or cooperative institutions are left to administrative determination in the various states, in accordance with specific needs.

The Interstate Compact on Juveniles was the result of a painstaking drafting process during most of 1954. The final draft was approved at an interstate conference in New York City on January 20 and 21, 1955. This was after most of the state legislatures had begun their sessions. Nevertheless, at the conclusion of the 1955 sessions eleven states and Hawaii had enacted the compact.

Since the juvenile compact does not call for the exercise of any powers which impinge on the constitutional province of the national government, it does not require consent of Congress to become effective as among the states which so far have enacted it. Nevertheless, legislation for such consent is before Congress. The principal reason for this is that the compact envisages participation by the territories and possessions, the Commonwealth of Puerto Rico, and the District of Columbia. Hawaii, as noted, already has enacted it. Congressional consent probably will be necessary to include these jurisdictions. To date, the only other instance in which a territory has become a party to a compact is that of Alaska's recent ratification of the Western Education Compact. . . .

Chapter 30

Punishment, or Treatment, of Parents of Delinquents

IN A MOOD OF DESPERATION, a number of authorities have in recent years recommended that courts "get tough" with parents of delinquents. Their attitude, they believe, is justified by recent reliable research which shows that of all the complexes of factors involved in the end-product of delinquency, the lack of intelligence, care, affection, and responsibility on the part of parents is the most penetrating and pervasive. Nevertheless, to pass from this fact to a policy of punishing parents is to indulge in a foolish and dangerous *non sequitur*. If we are to have a causal attitude toward child delinquency, we cannot inconsistently ignore the search for reasons and the need for aid when it is the parent who is delinquent. Moreover, punishment of the parent by fine or imprisonment only tends to aggravate the familial situation. Still, something constructive is needed where parents are concerned. Indeed, much of the material in this book points to the need of treating the family, rather than the individual delinquent, as the unit of therapeutic effort.

By way of illustration of a statute designed to hold parents responsible for the delinquency of their children, a recent New Hampshire enactment is included in this chapter. The reader is referred, in this connection, to the case of *Mill* v. *Brown* (Article 97) in Chapter 16, a decision that spells out the court's duty in respect to determining the fitness of parents for custody of a child charged with being a delinquent.

Gladstone's article recites the early legislation providing for the prosecution and punishment of parents found guilty of acts of commission or omission contributing to the delinquency of their children. The pros and contras of such statutes are presented as the result of a check-up on opinions of judges, public welfare officials, prosecutors, school authorities, psychiatrists, and editors.

Judge Smyth, an experienced magistrate who has long been in the forefront of those who regard the philosophy and aims of the juvenile court as essentially therapeutic, shares some reflections out of his rich experience on this troublesome matter of what to do about delinquent parents of delinquent children. He mentions the fact that one object of the investigative case history in the juvenile court is to throw light on parental attitudes and behavior that may have contributed to the child's antisocial malaise. He emphasizes the inseparability of the problems of child and parents. Recognizing realistically the limitations of resort to prosecution of parents, he points out that broad and deep social casework with the family, backed by the authority of the court, is the most promising approach to recalcitrant, unintelligent, or irresponsible parents. Illustrating the types of objectionable parents and parental misconduct, Judge Smyth lays the basis for sound policy suggestions.

The article by Buchmueller and Gildea describes a more constructive method of dealing with parents of problem children than resort to prosecution and punishment. Using a form of group therapy, the authors describe their techniques of coping with maladjusted youngsters through therapeutic endeavors with their parents. They include the results of a follow-up investigation.

Szurek, Johnson, and Falstein describe an experiment in concomitant therapeutic efforts by two psychiatrists, one of whom deals with the significant parent, the other with the child. The philosophy here is that "the behavior of the child is to be understood fundamentally only in the context of the intrafamilial interpersonal relations," and that "pathological relationships between mother and father and child play a great role in helping to maintain the distorted and unintegrated tendencies in the child."

165

New Hampshire Statutes, Chapter 214 *

169:32 Contribution to Delinquency. Any parent or guardian or person having custody or control of a child found to be delinquent, or anyone else, who shall knowingly or wilfully encourage, aid, cause, or abet, or connive at, or has knowingly or wilfully done any act to produce, promote, or contribute to the delinquency of such child, may be punished by a fine of not more than five hundred dollars or by imprisonment for not more than one year or both. The court may release such person on probation, subject to such orders as it may make concerning future conduct tending to produce or contribute to such delinquency, or it may suspend sentence, or before trial, with his consent, it may allow him to enter into a recognizance, in such penal sum as the court may fix, conditioned for the promotion of the future welfare of the child, and the said case may be placed on file. The fact that a child has been found more than once to be delinquent on account of conduct occurring while in the custody or control of his parent or parents, guardian, or any other person, shall be presumptive evidence that such person is responsible for his last adjudged delinquency.

169:33 Procedure. If any child is found to

be delinquent by the court, the court may, upon complaint of the county solicitor or any other reputable person, or upon its own motion, issue a warrant commanding any parent, guardian or person having custody or control of the child found to be delinquent to be brought before the same court in which the finding of delinquency was made.

169:34 Court Orders. If the court finds, after a hearing, that the parent, guardian or person having custody or control of the child has failed to exercise reasonable diligence in the control of such child to prevent him from becoming guilty of juvenile delinquency as defined by statute, or from becoming adjudged by the court to be in need of the care and protection of the state as defined by statute, it may make such orders specifying future conduct as are designed to reasonably prevent the reoccurrence of delinquency and to promote the future welfare of the child. Such order shall remain in effect for a period of not more than one year, to be specified by the court, and said order may be extended or renewed by the court. Before issuing any such order the court shall advise such parent, guardian or other person of his right to have the reasonableness thereof immediately reviewed and in this connection the superior court is vested with jurisdiction to summarily determine the reasonableness of any question of law or fact relating to such written specifications and to make such further orders upon review thereof as justice may require.

169:35 Criminal Contempt. Wilful violation of any provision of such order shall constitute criminal contempt out of the presence of the court. The persons so charged shall be notified thereof and have a reasonable time to make a defense. The trial of such proceedings shall take place before a judge other than the one who issued the written order. Punishment for such contempt may be by fine not exceeding two hundred and fifty dollars or by imprisonment not exceeding thirty days, in the discre-

---

* Reprinted from *New Hampshire Statutes: An Act to Determine the Responsibility for the Intentional or Negligent Contribution to the Delinquency of a Minor.* The American Law Institute is considering a proviso of its new penal code making it a misdemeanor for a parent knowingly to endanger a child's physical or moral welfare through violation of a legal duty of care, protection, or support, or knowingly to cause, encourage, or permit the child to engage in criminal activity prohibited by the code. — *Ed.*

tion of the court. In case the child is found to be delinquent during the time such orders are in effect, the finding of delinquency shall be presumptive evidence of responsibility of such parent, guardian or other person for that delinquency. In addition to the summary hearing and orders issued pursuant thereto the court may, after a hearing, require the parent to compensate any injured party for damages done to persons or property by the child in the last act of delinquency, or for a portion thereof provided such liability does not exceed five hundred dollars. . . . [1]

166

Spare the Rod and Spoil the Parent *

Irving A. Gladstone

Anxious parents are becoming increasingly aware of a modern theory of punishment designed as a shortcut to the solution of the problem of juvenile delinquency. Although the shock-absorbing area classically reserved for children is not affected by this 20th century legal concept, parental pocketbooks are in fact threatened. Moreover, the head of the family found guilty of breaking this law may find himself contemplating its effects from behind prison bars, with no exception made for mothers.

In Richmond, Texas, for example, a 35-year-old mechanic is serving a 6-month jail term because he could not keep his 8-year-old son out of trouble. In passing sentence on the

---

[1] For an excellent analysis of statutory responsibility of parents and others for a child's delinquency, see F. J. Ludwig, *Youth and The Law*, Brooklyn, Foundation Press, 1955, 153–167. — *Ed.*

* Reprinted from 19 *Federal Probation* (1955), 37–41. Used by permission of the author and the publisher. See, also, W. Herzog, "And What About the Parents of Juvenile Delinquents?" 19 *Federal Probation* (1955), 17; F. J. Ludwig, "Delinquent Parents and the Criminal Law," 5 V*and. L. Rev.* (1952), 719; S. Rubin, "Should Parents Be Held Responsible for Juvenile Delinquency?" 34 *Focus* (1955) 35–49; H. L. Witmer, "Parental Responsibility for Delinquency," *Ibid.*, 50–57; P. W. Alexander, "What's This About Punishing Parents?" 12 *Federal Probation* (1948), 23–29. — *Ed.*

father, whose son was caught breaking into a barber shop, the judge remarked, "Maybe it will teach other parents a lesson." This jail sentence ended the first case under a new local law making parents responsible for the delinquency of their children.

Moving northeast across the country to New England, we note that parents of East Hartford, Connecticut, are becoming familiar with an ordinance enacted last year which sets penalties ranging to fines of $500 and jail terms of 6 months for parents who fail to exercise reasonable diligence in the control of their children.

In New York City parents are reading press reports of new efforts to revive a local law (twice defeated in the City Council by a tie vote) fining parents for acts of vandalism committed by their children. The obvious alternative to paying the fine is a jail term for the parent.

What will come as a surprise to most parents is the fact that this shortcut solution to juvenile delinquency has been legally enacted in this country since the turn of the century. In the past 50 years most of our states, including the District of Columbia and Hawaii, have adopted such laws. Consequently, the recent crop of city ordinances making news are usually mere local repetitions of statewide statutes long in the books.

There is no question that this novel approach is likely to upset American parents who themselves have been brought up in varying degrees of paddling on, "spare the rod and spoil the child." According to a recent survey, the majority of parents are maintaining their family tradition by literally applying this maxim in rearing their own children. Since psychiatric analysis is known to be lengthy as well as costly, we will not seek here to plumb the emotional reactions of individual parents to the startling situation created by this law. Instead, an effort will be made to furnish the answer to several obvious questions certain to be asked collectively by parents.

WHERE DID IT START?

Punishing parents for the delinquency of their children appears to be a native American product, because no trace of it can be found either in the old English common law or in the various ancient legal codes with which lawyers are familiar. Judge Ben B. Lindsey is father of the first law of this kind enacted in Colorado in

1903 and significantly named the "Adult Delinquency Law."

The underlying idea of this legal innovation appeared to have a compelling logic for legislators here and abroad. Plainly, parents have the duty to take care of their children and keep them out of trouble. What could be simpler than to make this moral duty of parents a legal responsibility, punishable by fine or imprisonment? The Colorado statute served as a model for similar laws in our states and abroad. Local pride is reflected in an early decision of Colorado's highest court which noted that the novel law met at once with the approval of those actively engaged in bettering the conditions of children and was cordially welcomed by the bench, bar, pulpit, and press as a long step in advance in treating the indiscretions of youth.

WHAT DOES IT MEAN?

The early Colorado law provided that a parent encouraging, causing, or contributing to the delinquency of a child shall be guilty of a misdemeanor and subject to fine or imprisonment. Most of the states that subsequently adopted this law, however, made it very clear that parents would be held accountable for acts of *omission*, as well as *commission*; for what they failed to do, as well as what they *did* do. The New York State statute, for example, made it a misdemeanor for a parent to *omit* to exercise due diligence in preventing his child from becoming delinquent.

Fortunately, cases of parents deliberately encouraging their children to be delinquents are rare indeed. We are hard pressed to recall instances of a parent coaching his child in the technique of stealing or otherwise encouraging him to break the law. A search of court records happily reveals a dearth of such cases.

It should be noted, moreover, that in those unusual cases where the parents deliberately contribute to the delinquency, the legal problem is no different from that presented by any other crime. No special adult contributory law is needed in this category of cases because these parents, as accessories to the illegal act, would be guilty under our law just as any stranger to the juvenile would be guilty under the same circumstances.

Obviously, in practically all cases parents are linked to juvenile delinquency by acts of omis-

sion rather than commission, by failure somehow to prevent their children from getting into difficulty with the law, rather than through any actual encouragement or overt act. These are the parents who fail to give children the love they want; who fail to correct children without hurting, shaming, or confusing them; who fail to let the children grow up with increasing responsibility and freedom as they become adolescent; who fail to provide a home where children have something to believe in and work for because their parents have sincerely lived up to their ideals and religious faith. While this appears to be a large order, millions of American homes have adequately met it; many, alas too many, have failed to do so.

Although, as has been noted, the contributory law is very clear and simple in its provision for punishing parents who have failed to prevent delinquency, actual enforcement of this purpose is far from easy. Prosecution of a parent under this law is a criminal proceeding and, as such, is subject to all the rigid formalities and technical safeguards which American criminal law affords all defendants. The defendant–parent must be presumed innocent until he is proved guilty, and this beyond a reasonable doubt. Moreover, such guilt must be established not by inference, guesswork, or a zealous wish to solve the problem of juvenile delinquency, but by competent legal evidence.

WHAT ARE THE PROS AND CONS?

Searching for the answer to this question, the writer polled authorities concerned with the welfare of children. Opinions were sought of all judges presiding in the children's courts of New York State; all commissioners of public welfare, district attorneys, and superintendents of schools in the cities of New York State; all editors of newspapers in this State with daily average circulation of more than 100,000; 60 psychiatrists practicing in this State; and all directors of welfare societies in New York City. The authorities were asked whether they favored or opposed enforcement of the law punishing parents for contributing to the delinquency of their children. They were also called upon to state their reasons for such opinion. A majority of the authorities responded generously to the inquiry.

It is noteworthy that about one-third of these authorities opposed enforcement of the law;

one-third favored enforcement, and about one-third qualified their endorsement of the law.

From their reasoning the following arguments were gleaned:

Pro 1. Parents are the greatest causal factor of juvenile delinquency: It is the quality of home life which determines whether a child will become delinquent. If his family life is adequate, the chances are only 3 in 100 that he will turn out to be a delinquent, whereas if his family situation is poor, the likelihood of his becoming delinquent is 98 out of 100. The kind of relationships that exist between the child and his family has far more to do with delinquency than whether he lives in a slum area, or comes from a large family where there was much ill health, or has a high or low I.Q. Parental indifference and irresponsibility set the pattern for delinquent behavior because in parent–child relations are to be found the crucial roots of character which make for acceptable or unacceptable adjustments to the realities of life in society.

Con 1. Parental inadequacy may contribute unintentionally to juvenile delinquency but so do many other factors: The causes of delinquency are so deep rooted and far reaching that it is logical to speak only of factors of causation. Nobody should be taken seriously who blames anything as complicated as delinquency "on parents" or any one cause, except that a lot of harm may be done by this oversimplification.

Although the most significant single influence on the character and personality of a child is his family life, maintaining a good home is obviously the most difficult problem for many parents with the very best intentions.

Imprisoning the breadwinner of the family might of itself be a factor contributing to delinquency of the child.

Pro 2. Parents must be charged with criminal responsibility for juvenile delinquency: By natural law parents have a prime right and responsibility for the education of their children, including the mental, moral, physical, social, and emotional aspects of such training. The school, the church, and the community, possessing secondary rights with respect to children, may be generally regarded as deputies for parents.

In recognition of the fact that the child's mind is insufficiently mature to comprehend the seriousness of his act, our law is ever being modified to extend leniency to children. If leniency is extended to the child, the responsibility must remain in the parent.

Parents are now slowly but surely losing their former sense of responsibility concerning the welfare of their children. The stakes are too high to allow parents to disclaim responsibility for correctly rearing their children. Criminal law charges parents with an initial responsibility which they may not shirk.

Con 2. Parents may be morally accountable for juvenile delinquency but they should not be charged with criminal responsibility: Parents should not be held criminally responsible for the behavior of their children because they have only a relative responsibility. On the same basis we indict the parent we may indict society for the engendered insecurity, its failure to teach its youth a sense of morality and moral obligations. The child becomes delinquent in his total environment.

Blaming parents when young people are in trouble is as destructive an attitude as "Let's find out what is wrong and do something useful" is constructive. Progress will be made in preventing delinquency when all the resources of the community are utilized to help the child and the parents.

Pro 3. The law is fair to parents: There is no intention to punish parents who are doing all in their power to guide and control their children. Guilt on the part of parents does not automatically follow in each case of delinquency because each case is tried on its own facts. Because of the heavy burden of proof in the prosecution of criminal cases, parents will be protected from circumstances beyond their control.

We must have confidence in the integrity of our judges with respect to this law as well as other laws. Juvenile delinquency is found in all economic strata; poor parents are no worse off under this law than they are under other laws.

It is simple justice to punish a parent whose failure to assume moral parental responsibility has contributed to the delinquency of his child.

Con 3. The law is unfair to parents: Even a well-meaning parent can make mistakes with children, as many parents will vouchsafe.

This law is open to abuse because some judges are punishment-minded and make arbitrary decisions in interpreting criminal negligence which is vague and indefinite.

The possibility of miscarriage of justice is greatest among the poor and underprivileged. While there are widespread maladjustments among children of all economic levels, they show themselves differently at various levels. In the middle class there is a widening amount of neurosis and incipient neurosis shown in the behavior of emotionally disturbed children who do not break laws but who constitute severe disciplinary problems. In the lower economic classes this kind of behavior is likely to express itself in acts of outright delinquency.

A basic principle of law is the inequity of punishing people for the crimes of others. This principle obtains even if those others be the children of the punished.

Pro 4. Enforcement of the law will deter parents contributing to delinquency: Human beings are afraid of punishment. Its influence arrests acts and, if properly administered, teaches non-repetition.

If more parents knew they were going to be prosecuted, they would be more vigilant in the care of their children. A few publicized examples would bring about better control of parents over their children's actions.

Even opponents of punishment concede that threat of punishment is sometimes effective. How can there be threat of punishment without the law which provides for such punishment? Of what use is it to threaten punishment unless the court can actually resort to such punishment where threats fail?

Con 4. Enforcement of the law would constitute a discharge of anger on the part of society toward the parents of delinquent children but it would fail as a deterrent: This law reflects the attempt on the part of the community to assuage its guilt for permitting such a state of affairs to develop by finding a scapegoat in the person of these parents. We must recognize within us an unfortunate tendency to live according to the law of talion, for only in recognizing it can we avoid acting according to it.

Threat of punishment will merely frighten parents to the point of dumping their children into the courts for placement for fear that they themselves will be punished for their children's acts over which they have no control. It is

locking the stable door after the horse has been stolen, since there is little a parent can do once the child has reached the point where he is in conflict with the law.

Pro 5. The difficulty of proving parental contribution to delinquency can be alleviated: It is not unusual to encounter difficulty in obtaining criminal conviction. This very difficulty serves to protect innocent parents. Extraordinary difficulty, however, should be met by responsible authorities exercising even greater diligence in enforcing the law.

An efficacious means of alleviating the difficulty would be the addition to our law of a provision contained in the statutes of Minnesota to the effect that there is a presumption of the parent's guilt when more than one adjudication of delinquency has been made. This is considered a rule of evidence rather than law. The prosecution needs only to show two convictions, and then the burden of proceeding rests upon the defendant. Because of this presumption the defendant is almost compelled to show that he did not contribute to the delinquency of the child.

Con 5. The legal proof required to establish that a parent has contributed to delinquency makes the statute unenforceable for all practical purposes: Our norms of behavior as adults in the community are not so established that we can decide that the adult individual who happens to be a parent is not living up to our social and legal norm of the responsibility of adults toward children.

There are so many intangibles involved in family relationships that it is most difficult to prove beyond a reasonable doubt a direct cause and effect between the parental conduct and the delinquency. It would be almost impossible, for example, to obtain legal evidence of parental contribution during early childhood when the foundation for adjustment is laid.

The horrifying effect of the Minnesota statute is to saddle a defendant with the burden of proving that he is innocent of a crime committed by another.

Pro 6. This law is essential to the efficiency of the children's court: The court cannot deal effectively with children unless it has adult jurisdiction which includes punishment of parents who contribute to delinquency. Where the parent is refractory and resists the casework approach, actual punishment is needed to bring about cooperation.

Con 6. The law defeats its own purpose by impairing the efficiency of the children's court: The function of the children's court is not to punish the child, but to treat and rehabilitate him. The cooperation of the parent is essential in accomplishing this purpose. This cooperation cannot be gained by punishing the parent, a course of action which creates friction between the court and parent, as well as between the parent and the child.

Pro 7. Because of non-enforcement this law has never been adequately tried: The principle reasons for the infrequent use of this law include:

(1) The general lack of understanding on the part of those responsible for its enforcement of how such enforcement would help improve social conditions.

(2) Police officers generally have too little understanding of the social value of such action to put themselves out to gather the necessary evidence. District attorneys and other prosecutors do not like to trouble themselves with such "trivia" and use the difficulty of obtaining convictions as an excuse. Authorities usually find it much easier to commit a child to an institution than to invoke this law.

(3) Social workers, even graduates with certificates and degrees from schools of social work, learn very little substantive law along these lines and much less about procedure.

Con 7. Punishing parents does not succeed: Since 1903 this law has been either a dead letter or a failure in both the criminal courts and children's courts of our states.

The one recorded success with punishing parents related by Judge Ben B. Lindsey in Denver 50 years ago is open to serious doubts. Furthermore, it is at variance with the experience of Toledo, Ohio, in punishing parents over a period of 10 years. Judge Paul W. Alexander reported in 1948 that the law in Toledo "accomplishes very few, if any, of the things claimed for it except revenge."

Sporadic attempts to enforce this law on a local basis have shocked the public conscience. An example is the widely publicized campaign inaugurated by the New York City Police Department in 1947, ending with the jailing of an impoverished, miserable, psychotic mother.

MAYBE

A small percentage of the authorities who opposed the law conceded that *maybe* parents would be more diligent in the care of their children if the law were enforced.

IF

Most of the authorities who qualified their endorsement thought they would favor the law *if* it could be enforced.

CHARGE TO THE JURY

Your questions regarding the 20th century concept, "Spare the Rod and Spoil the Parent," have been answered. Authorities have testified on the "pros, cons, maybe, and if" of punishing parents for the delinquency of their children.

Fundamental to your evaluation of the law holding parents criminally responsible for juvenile delinquency must be its promise of success in curbing or preventing such delinquency.

It is important, therefore, that you do not oversimplify juvenile delinquency. Conceive of juvenile delinquency as a complex, recalcitrant problem centered in a maze of roads possibly leading to its solution. Remember that because juvenile delinquency is society's problem, *everybody* will have to travel these paths sensibly before our problem can be ultimately solved. We have no doubt regarding the value of negotiating some of these roads; for example, those marked: "Better Understanding of Mental Hygiene"; "Education for Wise Use of Leisure Time"; and "Greater Religious Faith and Higher Moral Standards."

We are here concerned, however, with only one such way, that of punishing parents for the delinquency of their children. On the basis of the evidence presented, you are asked to mark this road with one of the following verdicts:

1. "Road Open — Short Cut"
2. "Proceed Carefully — Danger"
3. "Road Closed — Dead End"

Punishment as a method of control of that great bulk of delinquent parents whose contributing consists mainly of acts of omission — failure to teach, train, and supervise the child from the cradle on up — is so impracticable as to be worthless, and it appears quite useless to attempt it.

— *Judge Paul W. Alexander.*

167

The Juvenile Court and Delinquent Parents *

George W. Smyth

The general philosophy of the juvenile court rejects the theory that we are engaged basically in the enforcement of the criminal law. Primarily these courts were created to shield children from criminal court surroundings; to bring them into new tribunals where they might be considered not as criminals, but as children in need of aid, protection, and guidance; tribunals in which a new type of individualized justice might be practiced, dependent not upon the offense committed, but upon the needs of the child; [1] tribunals where programs of education and social work designed for the rehabilitation of homes would supplant time-dishonored sentencing of children and the further breakdown of the home.

The entire emphasis was placed upon the integration of moral training, education, social work, and physical and mental hygiene in the court or authoritative setting. A new concept appeared — the concept of a legal tribunal wedded to the social sciences; a combined sociolegal institution. We still call it a court, perhaps properly and necessarily because it represents the power of the state, and the word court conveys that meaning to the lay mind. But the juvenile court is or should be an institute of family relations with the force of the law behind it.

Into this clinic come parents and children. The purpose of the court in working with children is to endeavor to understand the problems which have caused them to become in need of the care and protection of the state, to alleviate adverse conditions as far as possible, and to bring understanding and guidance to the children who have become delinquent, as well as to those verging on delinquency because of neglect. To serve these social purposes, the court is permitted to make wide investigation before, during, and after the hearing. These investigations which are clinical in their nature, have been endorsed and approved by our highest courts.[2] They include a broad study of the child's home and other environment, careful physical examinations, testing by the psychologist, and studies of the child and frequently of the parents by the psychiatrist in order that the court may be informed with respect to their mental attitudes and trends of thought toward their social, civic, and religious duties and responsibilities. Being thus informed, the court attempts to show the children that their conduct is harmful to themselves and society, and why it should be avoided, at the same time attempting to ameliorate the unfavorable factors in the home, and to bring the children into association with constructive character building influences, directing them to higher standards of living and personal conduct.

The same studies through which we endeavor to understand and to bring understanding in children's cases, reveal to us the nature and extent of the contributions which the parents have made toward delinquency or neglect. They also indicate the modifications which are desirable in home surroundings and parental attitudes, in order that the children may experience, in the future, better example and guidance. While inspiring the child to seek for higher standards, we also try to teach the parents how the lack of parental guidance has combined with unfavorable elements of leadership and example outside the home, to cause the children to become in need of our care and protection.

PROBLEMS OF CHILDREN AND PARENTS INSEPARABLE

The problems of the parents and children are inseparable. No problem of a neglected or delinquent child can be treated successfully without also considering the attitudes and actions of the parents. We find that an element of oversight, carelessness, disinterest, or ineptitude in the discharge of parental duties appears in

---

* Reprinted from 13 *Federal Probation* (1949), 12–17. Used by permission of the author and the publisher. See, also, the informative article by P. W. Alexander, "What's This About Punishing Parents?" 12 *Federal Probation* (1948), 23–29. — *Ed.*

[1] Roscoe Pound, National Probation Association Yearbook, 1946.

[2] *People* v. *Lewis*, 260 N.Y. 171. (See Article 55 of this book. — *Ed.*)

almost every case. In some we find wilful fault such as abandonment or failure to provide support or supervision, commission of crimes such as carnal abuse and impairing morals, misconduct on the part of parents such as drunkenness or immoral personal example, and active or passive encouragement in delinquency. In any case, the basic problem for the court remains the same; namely, to alleviate the neglect and to forestall the further growth of delinquency. To that end we strive to gain the cooperation of the parents, for without it we have little chance of succeeding with the children. We need not only to open the eyes of those who slumber, but to change the thinking of those who consciously commit wrongs against children.

The only authoritative approach to the parents is through the law which confers upon the juvenile court a measure of criminal jurisdiction over parents who neglect or contribute to the delinquency of their children. Our objectives cannot be achieved through literal adherence to the statutes, but rather through persuasion, with occasional recourse to the authoritative powers we possess. All parents who contribute to the neglect or delinquency of children technically are guilty of misdemeanors and therefore subject to prosecution. Indeed, in New York the law goes so far as to provide "that a parent who omits to exercise reasonable diligence in the supervision of a child to prevent him from becoming delinquent or in need of the care and protection of the State," is guilty of a misdemeanor. The difficulty of prosecuting parents in such cases may be gleaned from the fact that no reported case under that section [3] has appeared, although it has been on the books since 1910, except where the neglect has been wilful. The court of Appeals, in *Cannon* v. *Cannon*, 287, N.Y. 425, very aptly remarked: "The law which imposes on parents the duty to support and discipline a minor child and prescribe a course of conduct designed to promote his health, education, and recreation accords to the parents a wide discretion, and in the exercise of that discretion and the performance of duties imposed by law through no choice by the parents, they are held to no higher standard of care than the measure of their own physical, mental, and financial abilities to provide for the well being of their child." The imponderables in

this situation render it particularly difficult to place responsibility. On the other hand there are many cases reported in which parents have been guilty of wilful neglect or of wilfully contributing to the delinquency of their children, as distinguished from mere errors of judgment.

METHOD OF TREATING PARENTS

In the great majority of cases, whether based on conscious or unconscious fault, we find that if we are able to gain the confidence of the parents they will cooperate readily and willingly with those who represent the court in its endeavors to improve parental supervision and home conditions. Sometimes we encounter reluctance or failure to carry out the instructions of the court. Often the very fact that the court possesses power is sufficient to secure compliance. But in a considerable percentage we meet with ignorance, continued carelessness, or active opposition on the part of parents. It serves no useful purpose to prosecute a parent and convict him or her of the commission of a misdemeanor and to grant a suspended sentence, or to hold the threat of jail over his head, and thus try to operate through fear. We must do something more constructive than that. We must bring to these parents, whether wittingly or unwittingly at fault, a type of constructive social service which challenges our maximum ability to understand and guide human conduct and human relationships. The suspended sentence must be accompanied by probation. Whether probation is denominated casework or something else, I agree with both Professor Meeker and Miss Marilyn A. Blake who discussed the question in the June, 1948, issue of *Federal Probation*. The work to be done with parents and children in these cases, involving as it does the reconstruction of human lives in the authoritative setting of the juvenile courts, is one which calls for expert skill equaling and probably exceeding that which is required in any other field of social work. Probation has been called the right arm of the juvenile court without which the court would be nothing more than one of minor criminal jurisdiction. The experience of the years has taught us how true that is, how absolutely dependent we are upon probation, and how little we can accomplish in dealing with parents except through the broadest and most competent social work backed by the authority of the court. We speak of it as

---

[3] Section 494 Penal Law.

probation, and it is carried on by people called probation officers. The title is most misleading and should be changed. They should be called probation counselors, for that term is so much more truly descriptive of the attributes they should possess and the work they should do. Ideally they should have knowledge and experience in children's problems, child psychology, and the methods of solving human problems by various means. They should be sympathetic with those in misfortune and kind, yet firm when necessary, in dealing with the parents and children. They require real understanding of the physical and mental health of children and parents, and should be able to interpret and carry out the recommendations of the psychiatrist. They should acquaint themselves with the institutions and resources which are available in the community to minister to the sick and mentally ill among children and parents, to secure relief from grinding poverty, and to afford opportunities for stimulating leadership for children during their out-of-school hours. They should associate themselves with those who give spiritual leadership in the community that their clients may receive the guidance and succor which is so essential to them in their hours of trouble. All of these and many more services the probation counselor representing the court should be able to marshal for the benefit of parents as well as the children.

Those who have directed the most respected juvenile courts, where probation has reached its highest stage of development, freely admit how far short of the ideal we fall and how much still remains to be done in the way of educating probation counselors through colleges and in-service training. But despite limitations, great progress has been achieved.

Although the successful development and practice of this persuasive service enlists the cooperation of most parents, some always will remain deaf to persuasion. The law, therefore, wisely empowers the court to deal authoritatively with these recalcitrant parents. Obviously this power should never be invoked for the purpose of blind punishment. We are conducting children's courts. Our jurisdiction over adults is merely incidental to the work we do with children. We are concerned in the use of criminal law merely as an aid in salvaging the delinquent and protecting the neglected, and in prescribing such penalties as may be reasonable

or necessary to right wrongs committed, and to secure compliance on the part of obdurate parents, with the general objectives of our socio-legal services. Exclusion of the offending parent from the home may be necessary in some cases and fines or imprisonment for reasonable periods in others, not as vindication, nor as a deterrent to others, but to check misconduct and to bring about reformation and permanent improvement. Probation should continue during the period of exclusion from the home and after the return of the offending spouse to the home when the period of exclusion terminates. It should also be resumed after a prison sentence terminates, in order that in either case the probation service may be constant and persistent, so long as hope remains of salvaging the individual offender or of rehabilitating the home. Thus we justify the disciplining of parents in the privacy of juvenile courts, and avoid the "lurid accounts of all the goings on" in the press, which my good friend Judge Alexander so rightly found objectionable in cases heard in open court.[4]

TYPES OF DELINQUENT PARENTS

Let us consider the practical application of the principle above stated:

Father who is guilty of incest. A father was found guilty of attempting immoral practices with his young daughters when he sometimes returned home drunk after they were in bed. He was placed on probation for the maximum period, ordered to leave the home and contribute a specified amount weekly to the support of the family. Thus the immoral conditions were ended, support continued, and the social service essential to both individual and family was initiated. This man is still on probation. In a similar case a few years ago, the conditions were permanently relieved and the defendant, in due time, because of the guidance he received, was restored to his family as a dependable member.

Parents who leave child at home unattended. Two college graduates were parents of a two-year-old child. Neighbors complained that he was seen at the windows at night crying while the parents were off to the movies, having left

---

[4] "What's This About Punishing Parents?" *op. cit.*

him alone. They were prosecuted for neglect. Under probation they were helped to realize their mistake and became devoted parents.

Mother who loses three unattended children by fire. A woman lost three children in a fire because she left them unattended. She received a suspended sentence and probation. A few years later the lives of her subsequently born children were endangered in a similar manner. This time she was committed. True, the family was broken up and the children were placed. But it was a necessary step. Fortunately the reformatory, under the superintendency of one of our foremost social workers, is teaching her a great deal about parental responsibility, housekeeping, and child care. If she returns to her children eventually, all will experience the benefit derived from her stay at the institution.

Mother who refuses to send child to school. A mother stubbornly refused to send her child to school. He was placed in a foster home but she encouraged him to run away. Each time he went home she concealed him from the authorities. Finally she was charged with the misdemeanor of contributing to delinquency. Instead of a jail sentence, she, on conviction, was placed in the Psychiatric Institute and in due time emerged improved in bodily and mental health and became a firm friend of the court. Johnny continued under supervision and became a well-adjusted boy.

Mother who is alcoholic. Several mothers have been found to be alcohol addicts. Sometimes the children have been removed to foster homes; sometimes they have been left in their own homes. In either case the mother has been placed on probation, and with the aid of the psychiatric institutes or clinics, private sanitariums or Alcoholics Anonymous, improvement has been achieved in many cases. Imprisonment has been ordered only as a protection of the woman. I have never known it to effect a cure of alcoholism.

Father who lives in open adultery. Many different problems may be brought to light in one case. A 15-year-old boy who had been adjudged a juvenile delinquent because of burglary failed to respond to probation and was placed in a correctional school. Eventually he was paroled but again was brought to court a few months later on the charge of indecently exposing himself to a nine-year-old girl. Our social studies revealed that his father was then living in open adultery with a young woman in the very home he maintained for the boy; that he also had adulterous relations with the mother of a 15-year-old girl to whom he also was making improper advances; that these two adults took the child riding in his automobile, indulged in indecent language and conduct in her presence, and flaunted their improper relations before her. The girl was also before us as a neglected child because of the improper guardianship and because of budding sexual delinquency. The causal connection between the delinquency of these children and the immoral conduct of the boy's father and the girl's mother is abundantly clear. The treatment to be attempted in each case must be molded to the accomplishment of our basic responsibility of salvaging children through protection and guidance and discipline of the offending parents. Probation will play a major role, for even though it seemed advisable to remove the children, it is inevitable that they will in time return. For their sakes, as well as for the sake of other children, re-education of the adults through probation must be attempted.

Mother who has disreputable associations with other men. Mothers desert their children, usually going off with members of the opposite sex for varying periods and eventually returning. Their conduct is wilful and wrongful. Technically they are guilty. Looking beneath the surface we find unhappiness, discouragement, despair, human weaknesses, and mental or emotional unbalance. Imprisonment is not the answer. The constructive therapy of probation may help.

Father who deserts. Fathers desert their families, going off to distant points and leaving the families to be rescued through public relief. They are guilty, may be extradited, brought back, and imprisoned. But the adoption of reciprocal laws among the various states, as advocated by the State of New York (see Laws of 1947, Chapter 790) would provide a more effective remedy.

Mother who encourages daughter to engage in prostitution. Mothers with daughters use their homes for purposes of prostitution. The daughters might be taken away with consequent traumatic results. Experience proves that with the aid of pastors and other community services the immoral conditions in the home can be eliminated and the ties of affection which exist even in such cases can be appealed to as a powerful incentive to improvement.

Parents who condone child's thefts. Not many Fagins are found (at least in the area where I work), but occasionally parents wink the other eye when children bring home stolen bicycles or other articles, and sometimes encourage them in shoplifting and other dishonest practices. I have never found it necessary to sentence a parent in such case, but through good probation counseling have succeeded in achieving the objective of the juvenile court.

DAMAGES OR RESTITUTION

There are some forms of juvenile delinquency with which we find difficulty, either because probation seems too mild or commitment too severe, or because complete justice cannot be rendered through existing law. I refer to automobile stealing (joy-riding), driving without a license, habitual truancy, and violation of child labor laws. In these cases my experience proves that the parents are principally at fault and will continue to be so unless they receive a sharp lesson. I have found that charging the parent with the misdemeanor of contributing where the facts warrant such charge, and upon conviction imposing a stiff fine, is very effective. Well-placed publicity concerning the fine stopped an epidemic of automobile stealing.

In cases of stealing and malicious mischief involving damage to property we find that the law does not hold the parents responsible for restitution or damages. Probably if it did the parents would be more interested in preventing such conduct, but if it only resulted in causing parents to carry insurance the injured parties would at least be able to secure restitution or damages.

PREVENTION OF DELINQUENCY THROUGH ALLEVIATING NEGLECT

Another effective approach to the parents of neglected and potentially delinquent children is found in many jurisdictions through the wise use of laws such as Article 3a of the Children's Court Act of the State of New York, and similar sections of the law governing the Court of Domestic Relations of the City of New York. Under these statutes the court is granted the power to hear and determine proceedings to compel the support of a child or stepchild, and the support of the wife, if pregnant, or if the support of the minor child or stepchild is involved. In order to secure an award the petitioner is not required to prove that the dependent for whom support is desired would otherwise be likely to become a public charge. The amount awarded shall be such, "as justice requires having due regard to the circumstances of the respective parties." Thus we have a statute which authorizes a specialized court to grant adequate support to dependent wives and children, in a civil as distinguished from a criminal proceeding, although, as we shall see, the proceeding does at a later stage assume a quasi-criminal character. This has proved to be one of the most salutary and useful of all the court's powers. Many cases are brought before us on the complaint of mothers to the effect that the defendant husbands have failed and neglected to support their wives and children in accordance with their means and the needs of the family. Our social studies in these cases reveal that nonsupport is only one of the many forms of neglect to which children in the families are exposed, ranging all the way from simple neglect to provide, to drunkenness, abuse and cruel conduct, obscene and indecent language, immoral practices, desertion, and all the ills which arise from divorce and remarriage of persons having inadequate incomes to warrant their indulging in that marital pastime. The law provides not only that orders of support may be made, but permits social service of the most complete nature, and authorizes orders of the protection to be granted setting forth conditions of behavior to be observed for a specified time, which shall be binding upon husbands or wives as circumstances may require. Such orders may direct either spouse to stay away from the home or from the other spouse or children, may permit such spouse to visit the children at stated periods, may require a husband or wife to abstain from offensive conduct against the other or against the children and to give proper attention to the care of the home, and to refrain from acts of commission or omission which tend to make the home not a proper place for the other spouse or the children. The offending spouse may be placed on probation, and these conditions may also be incorporated in the order of probation. Ample power is granted to deal with those who prove to be defiant or stubborn in their opposition to the court's efforts to improve the family situation. Undertakings for support may be required, and those who wilfully fail to obey the support order may be committed to the penitentiary for reasonable terms. At this point the proceeding acquires a somewhat quasi-criminal aspect although it still continues to be regarded as a civil proceeding. Commitment or service of the sentence does not, however, terminate the liability for support, and the support order is revived and probation is resumed after the sentence has been served. Psychiatric and medical examinations are authorized and are enforceable, and, in short, the court is given complete power, within reasonable bounds, to control and rearrange the lives of the offending parent or parents in such manner that the interests of the children may be advanced, and the home cleansed of the conditions which have caused it to be an undesirable place for the children. Constructive work may be carried on with the ultimate goal of strengthening and reuniting the families wherever that may appear to be a possibility. The amounts recovered for the support of mothers and children are large, but the boon to the mothers and children in alleviating conditions inimical to the health and moral welfare of the children is greater than any financial consideration.

The principles to be observed in the treatment of these cases follow closely the methods which are employed in the other types of cases to which I have referred. After a complete social investigation including psychiatric diagnosis has been made, the most competent type of probation counseling is employed. The helpful social, educational, religious, and scientific resources which the community affords are marshalled in the manner most effective for the rehabilitation of the individual or family before the court. Understanding and sympathy are coupled with firmness and discipline.

SUMMARY

First, the juvenile courts are concerned primarily with service to children. Limited jurisdiction is granted over adults pursuant to the criminal law for the purpose of dealing with parents who neglect or contribute to the delinquency of children.

Second, these powers should not be used principally for the purpose of vindication nor as a deterrent to others, but as an aid in securing compliance on the part of obdurate parents, with the broad objectives of the juvenile courts.

Third, imprisonment, threats, and fear are neither effective nor desirable. Understanding guidance which is offered through the court and its probation counselors for the purpose of alleviating harmful conditions, and strengthening the moral and ethical concepts and conduct of both children and parents is the most constructive method of dealing with offending parents.

Fourth, it is therefore necessary that the probation service in all our courts which deal with social and moral problems involving children and parents be raised to the highest possible degree of efficiency, for the task is so great that it requires our maximum efforts.

Fifth, finally, while progress has been made in many of our courts, we must still look to our colleges and in-service training for the still greater improvements which must occur if we are to meet this challenge successfully.

168

Group Therapy for Parents of Behavior Problem Children in Public Schools *

A. D. Buchmueller

and Margaret C.-L. Gildea †

The authors have worked for the past seven years in the St. Louis area † to develop a concept of comprehensive community care for emotionally disturbed children, and to implement it with services. There are four general types of services, each designed to meet the problems of a special group of children.

The first of these is a program of mental health education, now operated by the St. Louis Mental Health Association, a Community Chest

* Reprinted from 1 *International J. Social Psychiatry* (1955), 51–56. Used by permission of the authors and the publisher.

† The authors are indebted to Dr. John C. Glidewell, Research Director of St. Louis County Mental Health Program, for the figures in this analysis.

Agency. Briefly, the program consists of a series of discussion groups led by lay discussion leaders who have received training in leadership methods in a workshop course. These discussions are focused around a film showing or the presentation of a skit, and are offered primarily to parent groups, usually through Parent–Teacher Associations, Mothers' Clubs or similar organizations. The target of this program is the parent of normal or Group 1 children. These numerical designations are used as a means for the preliminary classification of children; to assign them and their parents to the services best fitted to help them. The Group 1 children are those who exhibit behavior disorders of a transient nature in reaction to environmental stress, or exhibit minor problems which are not severe enough to interrupt for long the usual processes of growth in personal and social maturation and education. The educational method described above is usually enough to help parents to understand the children's problems, and to help the children back on to the pathway of normal development.

The Group 2 children are those whose problems have persisted for a longer time, and who manifest these problems in school. They are those whose disturbance threatens to disrupt their school and social lives, and whose problems become evident to teachers and other school personnel. The method for this category is group therapy with the parents. This school-centered group therapy program with parents of behavior problem children was developed in St. Louis city schools, was supported by the St. Louis Council for Parent Education, and is now merged into the St. Louis Mental Health Association. Parents of children showing fixed behavior disorders are referred to the school-assigned worker. Suitable parents, after screening, are invited to take part in groups, and, in this setting, following an extended period of group experience, are able to modify themselves and the home environment sufficiently to improve the behaviour of their children.

Group 3 children are those who do not respond to the group therapy method, and whose problems disrupt their school lives either through school failure or phobias. This may be associated with severe aggressive or withdrawn behavior of a persistent nature, which it is impossible to deal with effectively in a school-centered program. For this the team approach of the Child Guidance Clinic is necessary.

Group 4 children are those whose problems are so severe or whose homes are so disrupted that they need to live in a treatment center for emotionally disturbed children. Most psychotic children will fall into the Group 4 classification.

This paper is concerned with the Group 2 children and the school-centered program designed to serve them. Earlier papers reviewed experiences and reported successful operations in a number of city schools, but failed in a Negro school. The program has now operated in St. Louis County for three years.

The county is a large area adjacent to the city, composed of ninety-one incorporated municipalities. There are urban, suburban, semi-rural and rural areas, with large sections of unincorporated farming country and woodland. There has been a very rapid expansion of population since the war. There is a wide economic range, from extremely wealthy suburbs to areas of low income; but true poverty exists in a much smaller degree than in the adjacent city.

The present program which is a service of the St. Louis County Health Department, was begun in the fall of 1951. The Mental Health Division of the Health Department was established at that time, with two major units of service, the Child Guidance Clinic for those children in the community who fall into the category of Group 3 described above, and the School Mental Health Service. The latter program is established in three school districts under contract between the School Administration and the Health Department. A professional worker is assigned to each school to confer with school personnel and parents of children who may be referred. The classroom teacher is the case finder, although other school personnel such as the principal, the school guidance worker or the nurse, may also refer children to the worker. As a rule the teacher is the first adult person outside the family to have a sustained, significant relationship with the child and is also usually the first adult to observe the child functioning in a group of his peers.

Three factors influence success or failure of the program of group therapy with mothers. (1) The background, training and personality of the worker. (2) The nature of the school personnel, with special reference to their general understanding of basic mental health concepts, and their willingness to accept an outsider representing another discipline. (3) The character of the population which the school serves. Other significant factors are the geographical distribution of the population, the social and economic levels, the acceptance of mental health principles and the willingness to accept this kind of help.

The program had previously met with success in five city schools for white children. Four different white workers from varied backgrounds had all been successful. Two were psychiatric social workers, another a clinical psychologist with an M.A., and the fourth was a middle-aged woman, a college graduate who had studied child psychology, had had some casework experience, and had raised children of her own. There was no difficulty in forming and maintaining groups of parents. In two different Negro school districts, however, groups failed to get going, although two workers used here were two of the successful white women workers with graduate degrees. Thinking a Negro worker might be more successful with Negro parents, a Negro psychiatric social worker was used; but she did not meet with any more success than the two white workers. The failure of this program was clearly not caused by the worker.

The attitudes of school personnel have markedly influenced the formation of groups. Previously, the attitude of the principals in the Negro schools combined superficial acceptance with passive resistance. The teachers reflected this attitude. Few referrals were made and many of these were of families too disturbed to benefit from this kind of help. Passive resistance on the part of the principal was shown by breaking or delaying appointments with the worker, by not being available for discussion of the cases and by not making referrals.

In the present program school personnel showed varying degrees of acceptance. Some were eager to participate and cooperate. Others were resistant and fearful at first, feeling that the presence of the worker in the school implied some incompetence on their part; but as the program continued their defensiveness greatly diminished. In a few cases, initial resistance and defensiveness were not overcome. However, in the two schools reported here, one

school in each of the two districts, the principals and the majority of the teachers understood the purpose of the program and cooperated well. Nevertheless, in one school (B) it has not been possible to establish a mothers' therapy group, while in the second (L) the program has been successfully carried on.

In the B School District there was relative failure to get a parents' group going. During the year 1952–53 there were 32 referrals, of which nine mothers were considered good group material, but only four of them attended any group meetings, and their attendance was erratic to such a degree that after six weeks the group was disbanded. Follow-up inquiry on each of these cases revealed the following reasons for not attending: lack of transportation, illness in the family, inability to make plans for the care of pre-school children at home, pressure of work, and belief that the child's problems were not severe enough to warrant the effort to attend group meetings. Three workers failed to establish a group in this school, two women and one man, all psychiatric social workers who had conducted successful groups in other schools. In this district, as stated, the principal was understanding and cooperative, and all workers had good relations with school personnel.

Of the nine potential candidates for the mothers' group in B school, seven of the children referred were boys and two were girls. Their grade placement ranged from the first through fourth grade, the age range being from six to ten. Four of the boys were referred because of aggressive, hyperactive, immature behaviour; three of them because of poor school work, shyness, and withdrawn behaviour. One of the girls was characterized as a "show-off," hyperactive and excessively demanding. The other was shy, withdrawn, friendless and a stutterer.

In the first interview each of the mothers showed a good deal of defensiveness, resistance and difficulty to the idea that her child had any problem for which she needed help. However, in consultation with the worker, each agreed to become a member of the group.

Four mothers attended the first scheduled meeting. All had children in the third grade. Two were the mothers of the girls, one was the mother of an immature, aggressive boy with temper outbursts, while the other's child was a shy, friendless, thumb-sucker. Only two mothers attended the second meeting, one the next, two the next, and only one the fifth and sixth meetings. One mother, whose boy was the shy thumb-sucker, came in regularly for the six weeks. She continued to see the counsellor periodically, was grateful for the experience, and said the boy had improved considerably in his social adjustment.

Follow-up contact of the other three revealed two reported transportation difficulties and recurrent illnesses in the family, and one refusal to recognize the existence of a problem. Attempts were also made to contact each of the mothers who did not show up for any meetings. Three of them pleaded lack of transportation and considerable illness of pre-school children; one said she was too ill and nervous to attend, and one was forbidden to come by her husband who refused to admit that his son had any problem. None of these mothers was an active member of a parents' organization, and their contact with the school personnel was most superficial.

One session of the group which all four mothers attended was characterized by a quite lively and animated discussion. After introductions were made, the worker explained that the purpose of the group was the full discussion of whatever problems came up. Although all of the mothers had children in the same class room, none of them knew each other very well and only two were slightly acquainted. But discussion soon began with questions to the worker such as, "What can I do with my child when he does such and such?" As these questions were redirected back to the group, there was an increasing give and take between them, with the mothers exchanging experiences in dealing with their children. In the worker's opinion each of the mothers gained some satisfaction from the experience, and she was surprised when the group died out, though some did say they "would have difficulty coming in regularly."

In the L School District the group therapy program had been relatively successful. During the year 1952–53 there were 19 referrals made, of which eleven mothers were selected to form a group. All eleven attended two or more meetings of the group, six attending most of the meetings with only an occasional absence. The group met on a regular weekly basis for about an hour and a quarter. As in the B District the principal was cooperative and satisfactory, and satisfactory relationships were established with the school personnel.

Of the eleven referrals, eight were boys and three were girls. Their grade placement ranged from kindergarten through fifth grade, while the age range was from five to ten years. Five of the boys were referred because of aggressive, hyperactive, behavior, including two who were suspected of petty stealing; three of them because of immature, shy, passive, dependent behavior. Two of the girls were referred because of hyperactivity, aggressiveness, and "nervousness" and the other because of shyness and infantilism. Six of them, two girls and four boys, were reported as doing poor school work or failing at it.

In the beginning there was considerable resistance by most of the mothers, with the usual projection of blame on the school. However, this was quickly worked through by the group, as at least three of the mothers tended to blame themselves for their children's problems. For the most part, the mothers welcomed the opportunity to discuss any problems they wished in order to try to understand their children and themselves better, and so help the children to a more satisfactory adjustment.

Six of the mothers who attended most regularly were also the most active participants; of these, four had hyperactive, aggressive boys, and there was the mother of a girl who was hyperactive, aggressive and "disobedient," while the sixth was the mother of a girl who was described as shy, immature, and doing poor school work. Generally speaking these six mothers were deeply concerned about their children's problems, and tried to do something about them.

There were approximately 20 meetings of the group, the largest number in attendance at one time being eleven, the smallest three, while the average was six to seven. The meetings were held in the school building during school hours, and coffee and cookies were usually served. Soon after the meetings began, a good group feeling developed about their common interests in the problems of their children. As a result the discussion was usually lively and spontaneous with strong feelings often expressed. Discussion generally centered around the children and the parents and the problems of their feelings and relationships. At first there was considerable reliance on the leader for answers, but this gradually changed to an interaction between the mothers themselves, each raising questions and offering suggestions to each other. At the end of the year school personnel and parents agreed that the children had made considerable improvement in adjustment. Three children, all previously hyperactive had become "normal" according to their teachers.

The B School District is consolidated, and the children come by bus. It consists largely of a semi-rural area, with a few scattered, recently developed subdivisions of small, medium-priced houses. The population consists mainly of second and third generation Americans born of German ancestry. Occupations range from small truck farming to skilled, semi-skilled and common labour, with only a few professional and small business people. There are no large industries, though many of the people work in industry in the city of St. Louis. There is no large shopping or major business center in the district and homes are scattered over a fairly wide area and some distance from the school. There is "open country" in the immediate

vicinity of the school buildings and public transportation is very poor and irregular. The organized parents' groups, Mothers' Club and P.-T.A. have not been very active. For instance, some children have gone through 12 grades without any participation on the part of their parents. In other cases, parents have never been to school at all.

The L District is a more concentrated housing area and the socioeconomic level is somewhat lower than in B District. There is a much greater density of population in a smaller geographic area. The school buildings are in the middle of a concentrated housing area, with most children and parents needing to walk only a few blocks to the school. Occupations of parents are skilled, semi-skilled, and common labourers, with a fairly high number of construction and factory workers, but only a few professional and small business owners. The population consists mainly of first and second generation (and a few third) families of mixed extraction. Many have moved to the city from rural areas to obtain industrial work. There is a good deal of neighborly feeling, and the Mothers' Club of the school is active and meetings are well attended.

The following tabulation shows some of the difference in the two school districts:

Table 1   *School Census Data, 1952-3*

SCHOOL	ACRE-AGE	POP. OF CHILDREN	TOTAL SCHOOL ENROLL-MENT	% POP. OF CHIL-DREN ENROLLED	AV. DAILY SCHOOL ATTEN.	% AVERAGE DAILY ATTENDANCE OF		SCHOOL COST PER PUPIL	% OF POP. WITH 8TH GRADE OR LESS EDUCATION
						Pop.	Enrollment		
B Consolidated Unsuccessful	26.9	1,326	767	57%	652	49%	85%	313.78	56%
L Successful	8.4	2,186	1,726	78%	1,548	71%	90%	203.20	67%

These two districts are adjacent. The acreage of L is about ⅓ that of B, but there are 2½ times more children in L schools than in B schools. It costs the citizens of B District ⅓ more per pupil to run their schools than in L District. Four times as many B pupils enroll in college as do pupils from the L District,

so a considerably larger proportion of the population in L has less than eighth grade education (67 per cent in L, 56 per cent in B). Study of school census data comparing the two shows that in the successful (L) Districts there is a 71 per cent average daily attendance of pupils. While in the unsuccessful (B) district, average daily attendances are only 49 per cent. In the consolidated B District, a smaller percentage of the child population attends the public schools, and there is more absenteeism. The widely scattered population of B District and the many new subdivisions contribute to a lack of community solidarity. In the L District, with the closer settlement of families in older established neighborhoods, there is more of a community spirit and a stronger bond between the people and their schools.

SUMMARY

Reviewing successes and failures in the seven years of this work, it appears that the group therapy program with parents operates most smoothly in a lower-middle to upper-lower class area where there is a degree of social uniformity and there are no unusual minority or discriminatory sentiments. Consolidated districts increase the difficulties, as parents do not have easy access to the school or any comfortable familiarity with it. A scattered population creates transportation problems which increase the strangeness parents feel about the school. Where there is a lack of community spirit and neighborliness it is more difficult to form a cohesive and workable group.

REFERENCES

1. Brashear, E. L., Kenney, E. T., Buchmueller, A. D., and Gildea, M. C.-L. "A Community Program of Mental Health Education, Using Group Discussion Methods, Led by Volunteer Work-shop Trained Discussion Leaders." Am. J. Orthopsychiat. XXIV, 4, July, 1954.

2. Buchmueller, A. D. and Gildea, M. C.-L. "A Group Therapy Project with Parents of Behavior Problem Children in Public Schools." Am. J. Psychiat., 106:46, July, 1949.

3. Buchmueller, A. D., Porter, Frances, and Gildea, M. C.-L. "A Group Therapy Project with Parents of Behaviour Problem Children in Public Schools — Paper 2. A Comparative Study of Behavior Problems Occurring in Two School Districts, with Discussion of Etiological Factors, Treatment Methods and Results." The Nervous Child, Vol. 10, No. 3–4, 1954.

4. Kahn, Jane, Buchmueller, A. D., and Gildea, M. C.-L. "Group Therapy for Parents of Behavior Problem Children in Public Schools — Paper 3. Failure of the Method in a Negro School." Am. J. Psychiat., Vol. 108, No. 5, November, 1951.

169

Collaborative Psychiatric Therapy of Parent–Child Problems *

Stanislaus Szurek, Adelaide Johnson, and Eugene Falstein

This paper describes a technique for psychiatric treatment and research in the behavior problems and psychoneurotic disorders of children in which concomitant therapeutic efforts are made by two psychiatrists, one of whom deals with the significant parent and the other directly with the child. Although the rationale of the approach has been indicated by Lowrey, and at times even explicitly stated in the literature by Almena Dawley, Greig, Anna Freud, Silberpfennig, and Rogers, people who are clearly aware of the importance of the parental neuroses in the treatment of children, it seems that the type of procedure which has been elaborated in this clinic might be of interest to record, not only because of its therapeutic value, but also because of its research possibilities.

There is an increasing awareness on the part of clinicians dealing with children that the behavior of a child is to be understood fundamentally only in the context of the intrafamilial interpersonal relations. Pathological relationships between mother and father and child play a great role in helping to maintain the distorted and unintegrated tendencies in the child.

It is unnecessary here to refer to the many years of excellent and successful collaborative work that has been done with the psychiatric social worker seeing the mother and the psychiatrist seeing the child in treatment disorders that are not too firmly crystallized. Such collaborations between psychiatrist and social worker will continue to constitute the predominant method of treatment in a child guidance

* Reprinted from 12 Am. J. Orthopsychiatry (1942), 511–516. Footnotes and bibliography omitted. Used by permission of the authors and the publisher.

clinic (7). This paper deals exclusively with those severely distorted child–parent relationships where the techniques of two psychiatrists well trained in dynamic psychiatry seem to be necessary for alleviation of the presenting problems.

Because it had been impossible to treat severe school phobias by treatment of the child alone, in this clinic the mother, or the more significant parent, and the child were each treated by a psychiatrist concomitantly and, as it seemed, more successfully. Such collaborative therapy has been expanded in treating many behavior problems and other severe neuroses. Experience over a period of about three years with this technique has led the writers to the impression that: (1) many severe cases cannot be treated at all without the use of it; (2) it becomes a valuable tool in carrying research further in the study of interpersonal relations; and (3) many cases, where child or mother might be successfully treated alone, still seem to progress more rapidly when the two are treated concomitantly.

Probably the most fundamental requirement of such therapy is that the competitiveness of the psychiatrists involved in treatment shall be at a minimum. A psychiatrist treating the mother, for example, with unconscious rivalrous attitudes toward the other therapist, may quite unwittingly block the mother's expression of jealousy and hostility toward the child's therapist. Such complications can become manifold. A competitive therapist may unconsciously fail to give all of his available information to the other therapist for discreet use, or may ignore as superfluous what the other therapist could make available to him. Thorough training may reduce the problem, but a long training in dynamic psychiatry may not entirely resolve the sources of these competitions.

The writers do not draw too sharp a line between the neuroses and behavior problems, but there are certain quantitative distinguishing characteristics. The provocative or self-frustrating activities of the child with the behavior disorder seem to stem from the fact that there has been less warmth and support in the environment, and therefore less guilt about his greater tendency to direct seeking of gratification of impulses in an ungenerous and unsympathetic milieu.

In addition, there appears to be in these children as much wish to punish the hostile environment as to punish themselves, if not more. The self-punishing element has usually been more stressed in the literature. Because of these considerations it is difficult at times to know what is the more basic motive in the provocative behavior of such a child. Sometimes, the psychiatrist working alone with the child, sees only the child's guilt, anxiety and resentment, and not the provocation from the parent. Two psychiatrists in such a situation can observe better than one how mutually gratifying to all involved is the particular mode of interpersonal behavior, no matter how distorted or disguised the symptom or technique may be. It is as inaccurate to say that the mother alone fosters the behavior in the child, as to say that the child on his own stimulates certain responses in the mother. It is a mutual exchange, built of techniques slowly evolved between them. A few brief examples follow.

Elaine, IQ 150, a middle child with two brothers, in a very moralistic, respectable family, at age 12 suddenly began stealing and revealed to her mother that she had had intercourse many times with a high school boy. The mother was horrified and brought the child for treatment. It soon became obvious that this behavior was in defiance of and designed to injure the mother. The child only became guilty and depressed after she became aware of her mother's reactions. The mother, in treatment at the same time, gradually became aware of impulses and attitudes toward the child that were thoroughly hostile and designed to provoke situations where Elaine would be confronted with some impasse. She had no such feelings toward the sons, but was over-identified with the daughter who was named after her. Elaine was in treatment a brief time and was relieved of anxiety and depression, whereas the mother continued for a long period. No further difficulty arose with Elaine. The mother saw how she pushed the child into the father's lap, so to speak, and then reacted to the child with intense jealousy. She recalled episodes in her own early life of an attachment to her father about which she had great guilt and she was fearful of seeing the same reaction develop in Elaine. At the same time, however, by unconsciously fostering such an attitude in Elaine, she derived vicarious gratification of her own unintegrated infantile impulses.

Another mother, whose boy was extremely sadistic toward her, revealed with tears during her treatment that she had derived real gratification from his having twisted and hurt her arm. She wondered why she had permitted him to do it. Her own masochistic tendencies led her unconsciously to foster sadism in her son.

In this clinic, collaboration between psychiatrists in treating so-called behavior problems and neuroses has raised a number of significant hints about the matter of "choice of symptom." This term implies too much of conscious volition. The symptom itself is an on-going process expressing interplay of unconscious tendencies. How does a child, and later an adult, happen on a certain type of behavior such as stealing books or fire setting, or tearing the clothes, or promiscuity? How does a child evolve enuresis, vomiting, or a reading inhibition as one symptom of his neurotic disorder? In the following instance it was possible to see that one factor directing the child's expression of her tensions was the specific neurotic anxiety of the mother.

Doris, 13, suddenly set the family apartment on fire. The child has never destroyed with fire before, although she enjoyed bonfires very much. When the mother came into treatment, she revealed with considerable anxiety the deep hostility between her and Doris, an exact repetition of the rage existing between the mother and her sister after whom Doris was named. Three weeks before the fire-setting the mother told her own therapist that she had gone to a fire several blocks away. While at the fire she thought, "My own apartment will be the next to burn and Doris will be the one to start the fire." The mother went home and told Doris and her father about it, saying children had set the fire, although of this she was not at all sure. On the day she heard that her apartment was on fire she knew instantly that Doris was responsible. Also, when she came into treatment she was horrified by the fact that ever since the fire she had had the firm conviction that Doris would be struck by an automobile. The violent feelings felt by this woman toward her own mother and sister were projected onto Doris and unconsciously the mother fostered the acting out of her own frightening, forbidden feelings which dealt with years of hostile death wishes against her family by burning. For a few days before Doris set the fire, the mother

had been extremely hostile and provocative, as she later told her therapist.

Another example in a family studied in detail was David's mother who "had a horror of a stealing child." In handling David she was vacillating and uncertain when it came to advising him firmly of property rights. Further discussion with the mother gradually revealed her own early stealing tendencies, the conflict about which had not been resolved.

In another family James promptly became a party to an interesting reaction manifest in his mother during his and her treatment. The mother said in discussing her own problems that she "could not stand bedwetting in a child." A week later she returned and reported that for the first time in his life 13-year-old James had wet the bed four nights in a row.

These symptoms of pathological techniques become complicated when several family members are involved. For example, in the case of Marion who was extremely provocative with her mother it was found that the father fostered much of the child's acting out because of the vicarious gratification he derived from seeing his wife injured.

The behavior of parent and child in relation to their two therapists is illustrated by a brief incident in the treatment of Robert and his mother. Robert had almost recovered from his school phobia when suddenly be became much worse and his mother called the boy's male therapist. He at once referred the mother to her own therapist, a woman, and in the following interviews it became quite clear that the mother's need to see the boy's male therapist was in part an expression of her own unresolved oedipal conflicts. It was obvious that she provoked Robert, making him much worse, and thus felt she now had sufficient excuse to talk to Robert's therapist herself. This was one of numerous efforts on her part not to work through her own difficulties with her therapist but to "seek advice" from the boy's therapist.

On the basis of 22 cases studied in detail and illustrated by these brief excerpts it seems clear that in some instances the parent unconsciously gives the child a cue. It may be an expression of a specific fear, as in the fire-setting, or an ambivalent anxious reaction to some behavior or symptom of the child. This combination of events has seemed to fix the form of the clinical picture through which the parent's own unintegrated and forbidden impulses are afforded vicarious gratification.

Although it is frequently easier to see the forbidden impulse vicariously fostered by the significant adult in the behavior problems, there are also strong hints of the presence of the same factors in the more disguised pathologic formations of the neuroses.

We have had occasion to study several sets of identical twins, which material will be reported in greater detail in a later communication. In these studies one could see the mother, and at times the father, splitting off their acceptable tendencies from the forbidden. They fostered the unacceptable trends in one twin and the acceptable in the other. One mother brought her normal boy for treatment and for a long period was protective and secretive about the really sick boy who represented for her gratification of certain tendencies in herself which she had great difficulty in facing and giving up.

Since its reactions are gratifying somehow to the parent, the child is not brought for treatment until the secondary gains or gratifications of the child exceed those of the mother or father, when the latter speaks of *complaints*. At that time, too, the excess is usually sufficient to cause anxiety in the parent to bring the child for treatment but not to accept treatment for himself. Getting the parent into treatment depends upon such factors as the skill of the therapist, and the anxiety of and gratification to the parent.

From the experience of this clinic impressions concerning treatment of behavior problems and neuroses differ somewhat. These impressions may be summarized as follows.

1. Almost no serious behavior problem regardless of the child's age can be treated unless the significant parent is in treatment. 2. Any serious neurotic adjustment between parent and child necessitates the treatment of both parent and child with the following possible exceptions: (a) an adolescent neurotic child, not too bound by the parent, can often be successfully treated without treatment of the parent, if the child is old enough to be able possibly to identify with the therapist toward a satisfactory emancipation; (b) treatment of the parent alone with a child under 4 or 5 may be satisfactory; (c) intensive treatment of the child of 5 or under, suffering from a neurosis of recent origin, may be suffi-

cient occasionally. Levy has reported the successful treatment of this type of conflict.

The logical outcome of such collaborative experiences is that it would seem better in treatment to avoid, on the whole, giving much in the way of advice. The educability of parents bringing children as disturbed as is seen in this clinic is rather limited. In other words, it is not suggested that a mother "show more restraint" or "give more love," for she would have done this if she could have, and she may regard the advice as criticism. It does little good to urge a parent to give a stealing child an allowance without understanding the parent's own deeper attitudes about giving and stealing. For instance, Mrs. A. clearly indicated as her treatment progressed that although she had given Ted an allowance according to earlier advice of a therapist, she deeply envied the boy and begrudged him his allowance. The boy sensed her attitude and stopped stealing only when her own conflicts over envies had been resolved.

Often out of anxiety or hostility, parents may become very demanding for concrete advice. The skillfull therapist will see beyond this device and deal with the anxiety back of the demand. For the same reason it is not very helpful in training the young social worker or beginning psychiatrist to "advise" that they never give advice to demanding, hostile parents. In other words, the young therapist must deal with his own feelings in the situation and do the best he can. Even the experienced psychiatrist at times finds himself giving advice. He may tell parents he can do no more for their boy until they relax their pressure on the child for achievement, but the psychiatrist soon finds he has only shifted responsibility and has not done therapy. Parents, out of guilt, may try to lighten their pressure, but the child senses the artificiality and anxiety, and feels less assurance as to where he stands. Through some measure of reliving early unresolved conflicts with their permissive therapist the hostility beneath the anxiety in the parents is lessened with the gaining of some insight.

Workers interested in the socially delinquent child have had some hope that these collaborative psychiatric techniques would be effective in treatment. It is apparent that such children, in very little conflict with their social group, possess a defect in conscience with regard to the larger community. Such children cannot develop guilt and self-restraint in relationship to the larger community without much more warmth and firmness than can be offered in the weekly psychiatric interviews. At times these aims can be attained by the warm, consistently firm and basically friendly foster-parent with whom the child lives, or in the institution properly staffed for such treatment, such as Aichhorn's. As for getting the parents of the child in for collaborative treatment they usually are unavailable for the same reasons as apply to the child, i.e., they usually cannot be won by the brief psychiatric interview.

In conclusion, it would seem that a collaborative approach by two psychiatrists is frequently necessary and more rapidly effective in treatment of most behavior problems and the more severe neuroses. It is recognized that facilities for such studies are sometimes not available. But beyond the clinical advantages, and really of more fundamental importance, are the research opportunities made possible by this direct participant observation of the dynamic interplay between parent and child. Out of such observations have come rather clear impressions that the unconscious gratifications parents derive from their unintegrated tendencies, is a powerful stimulus in fostering certain behavior or determining a neurotic symptom in a child. It is apparent that for the complete study of the genetics of so-called "symptom choice" or pathologic formations in children, one must know the meaning of such manifestations to the parent. Such collaborative techniques make it possible to observe something of the genesis of behavior and, eventually, of character traits.

It seems this method permits direct empirical observations bearing on these questions instead of depending upon speculations and reconstructions from studies of adult neurotics or from the study of the neurotic child alone. It affords a further avenue of inquiry before retreating to such concepts as "constitutional tendencies."

Chapter 31

Post-Treatment Behavior

THERE ARE VERY FEW reliable check-ups on the after-conduct of delinquents who have gone through a juvenile court and associated facilities. A frequently cited study of this kind is *One Thousand Juvenile Delinquents*,[1] which analyzed the relationship of the Boston Juvenile Court to its affiliated clinic, the Judge Baker Foundation. This was followed by a further check-up on the delinquents involved, to determine their behavior during three successive five-year test periods after their appearance in the Boston Juvenile Court. The substance of the present chapter is an extract from this latter study, *Juvenile Delinquents Grown Up.*[2]

It has been claimed that the cases involved in the two works in question are "atypical," since not all boys who appeared in the Boston Juvenile Court were sent to the Judge Baker Foundation clinic for study. However, a later check-up on a "run-of-the-mill" sample of cases by Doctors William Healy and Augusta Bronner, who were then the directors of the clinic in question, aided by Myra Shimberg, showed that the recidivism rate was quite similar to that found among the boys who were studied in *One Thousand Juvenile Delinquents*. This check-up was significantly entitled "The Close of Another Chapter in Criminology." [3]

It is preferable for a neutral party to discuss the controversy that arose upon the publication of *One Thousand Juvenile Delinquents*. To that end, the Editor quotes from a well-recognized textbook on delinquency by Teeters and Reinemann:

> The Gluecks found that of approximately one thousand cases (actually 905)[4] handled by the Judge Baker Clinic and the Boston Juvenile Court, 798 (88.2 per cent) had committed additional delinquencies during the five-year period following diagnosis by the clinic. Two-thirds of the 905 boys were arrested for serious offenses. The average number of arrests for each of the groups who repeated (recidivated) was 3.6. The conclusion reached by the authors was that "the treatment carried on by the Clinic, Court, and associated community facilities had very little effect in preventing recidivism." [5]
>
> This statement, coming from careful investigators, gave the critics of child-guidance clinics the opportunity to bolster up their prejudice against such agencies and to state that delinquent children were being coddled by advocates of these scientific techniques. The wave of vociferous discussion that was stimulated by the publication of the Gluecks' study eventually simmered down so that definite conclusions could be drawn.[6] It has been pointed out in defense of the court and clinic

---

[1] S. and E. T. Glueck, Cambridge, Harvard University Press, 1934.

[2] S. and E. T. Glueck, New York, The Commonwealth Fund, 1940.

[3] W. Healy, A. Bronner, and M. Shimberg, "The Close of Another Chapter in Criminology," 19 *Mental Hygiene* (1935), 208–282. See, also, 1934 Yearbook, the National Probation Association, 63–103.

[4] Reliable follow-up data were obtained as to 923 of the thousand cases; but 18, though not delinquent, had no opportunity (because of death or incarceration throughout the first five-year follow-up period) to commit further offenses. Of 784 boys who had a treatment period, 47% were non-delinquent and 53% were delinquent *during* the treatment period as compared to the small incidence of 12% of non-delinquency opposed to 88% of recidivism during the five-year *post-treatment* period.

[5] Harvard University Press, 1934, p. 233.

[6] See *Yearbook*, NPPA, 1934, pp. 63–103; see, also, Healy, Bronner, and Shimberg, "The Close of Another Chapter in Criminology," *Mental Hygiene*, April, 1935, pp. 208–282.

that the Judge Baker Foundation was at that time only a diagnostic center and had not yet embarked on a treatment program; that in only 21 per cent of the cases were all the recommendations made by the clinic for the treatment of the boys carried out,[7] and that what would have happened to these boys had they been sent to a reform school or prison might have been far worse.

The results of this study stimulated the friends of both court and clinic to check on their methods and to integrate the work of both more closely. The Gluecks themselves come to the conclusion that both the court and clinic must be retained, since these agencies provide much more satisfactory treatment than did the old criminal court procedure of an earlier period. Moreover, they decided that the clinic "furnishes not only a scientifically valid attitude and a source of needed adult education, but very tangible immediate assistance to the Court." [8,9]

The results in *One Thousand Juvenile Delinquents* followed a combination of influences, including court appearance, diagnosis of the case by the clinic, efforts of various official and non-official agencies, and other factors that may have entered into the situation. The authors pointed out that better results were obtained where the recommendations of the clinic to the court were followed. They concluded that "it is not alone the presence of reform-favoring factors that is responsible for non-delinquency in the post-treatment period, but also the carrying out of the clinical recommendations." [10] However, it was evident that the carrying out of the recommendations plays a less significant part than might be assumed.

An unfortunately phrased subheading of *One Thousand Juvenile Delinquents*, "Their Treatment by Court and Clinic," occasioned misunderstanding. What the authors meant by the word "treatment" — and this was obvious from the contents of the book — was such efforts of a clinical nature and of the court (and associated agencies) as were in fact given. So far as the clinic was concerned, these efforts were largely diagnostic rather than therapeutic. A book subsequently published by Healy and Bronner, involving the work of the Judge Baker clinic with 400 cases (non-court, as well as court, delinquents) in which treatment was given over a period of almost three years for "personality or behavior problems," [11] reports that the outcomes on 323 (81 per cent) were regarded as "favorable." In 39 of these there was reported "unexpectedly rapid or unexpectedly good response and continued success," and in 174 the problems were "solved, less rapidly but with steady improvement." [12]

In this matter of assessing the effectiveness of courts and clinics it has seemed to the Editor and his co-worker in follow-up researches that the surest yardstick of "success" is non-commission of further crimes; and of "failure," or recidivism, — the repetition of one or more crimes during a reasonable test period. There is room for stages of improvement in personality and character that fall between the limits of success (no criminal behavior) and failure (recidivism).[13] Such intermediate stages are, however, very difficult to assess and the basic aim of a juvenile court is the reduction of recidivism.

---

[7] See Benedict Alper, "Forty Years of the Juvenile Court," *Am. Sociological Review*, April, 1941, pp. 235–236.

[8] *Ibid.*, p. 239. See Chap. XIII of their work for recommendations.

[9] Negley K. Teeters and John Otto Reinemann, *The Challenge of Delinquency*, "Causation, Treatment and Prevention of Juvenile Delinquency," pages 603–604, copyright 1950 by Prentice-Hall, Inc., Englewood Cliffs, N.J. Reprinted by permission of the authors and the publisher.

[10] *One Thousand Juvenile Delinquents, op. cit.,* p. 182.

[11] "These children, of course, are not true delinquents as we have defined the term earlier, but they do represent the stuff out of which overt delinquency stems." *The Challenge of Delinquency, op. cit.,* p. 93.

[12] Cited by Teeters and Reinemann in *The Challenge of Delinquency, op. cit.,* p. 606. The Editor has used a secondary source, because the copies of the Healy-Bronner study, *Treatment and What Happened Afterward*, were not available in the Harvard Law Library when the above was written.

[13] For example, Healy and Bronner report among the 323 cases of favorable outcome in 30 cases, "Main problem solved, but some undesirable personality traits persisting."

The following extract from *Juvenile Delinquents Grown Up* is from an intensive and extensive follow-up study of the after-conduct of the approximately one thousand boys who had been previously studied in *One Thousand Juvenile Delinquents*. While the trend of conduct during three successive follow-up periods of five years each is not too encouraging in respect to the efforts of the sociolegal mechanism set up in one State for coping with delinquents, it is informative and reliable. No good can come from refusing to look the facts in the face, and the promise of improvement in practices presupposes sound factual information. There is also one encouraging finding; namely, the steady increase in the percentage of those delinquents who abandoned their criminalistic activities in quantity and seriousness with the passage of time. Included also is a chapter from *Juvenile Delinquents Grown Up* which re-enforces a prior finding, involving another sample of offenders — youths and young adults — regarding the important role of the maturation process in reducing the incidence of delinquency.

170

Trend of Conduct *

Sheldon and Eleanor T. Glueck

In the four preceding chapters we have described the behavior of our juvenile delinquents from childhood through three successive five-year periods after their contact with the Boston Juvenile Court and its affiliated community agencies. It will be recalled that these lads were of an average age of nine years and seven months when they showed the first signs of delinquency; we have traced their criminal careers from these early years until their age averaged twenty-nine years. The method of comparing their behavior in each of the three five-year periods with that in the period immediately preceding it has given us some idea of these changes, but we cannot clearly define the *trend* in their conduct until we compare their behavior during the three five-year periods with their conduct before they appeared in the Boston Juvenile Court.

* Reprinted by permission of the publishers from *Juvenile Delinquents Grown Up*, by Sheldon and Eleanor T. Glueck, 1940: Chapters 7 and 8, pp. 75–106; Cambridge, Mass., Harvard University Press, Copyright, 1940, by The Commonwealth Fund. Some footnotes have been omitted, others renumbered in sequence. — *Ed.*

TREND OF ARRESTS

The average age of the group at the time of the arrest for which they were brought before the Boston Juvenile Court was thirteen and a half years. Some two-thirds of the lads (62.5 per cent) had been apprehended one or more times prior to that particular arrest. The proportion arrested reached its peak during the first follow-up span, at which time 79.8 per cent were arrested. At the end of that period our youths were of an average age of nineteen years, almost three-fourths of them (70.8 per cent) being still under twenty-one. In the second follow-up period, there was a drop to 66.1 per cent in the proportion of those arrested, and a still further drop to 57.9 per cent in the third five-year period, by the end of which the men were an average age of twenty-nine years.[1]

The increase in the proportion of youths arrested during the first follow-up period over those arrested prior to their Court appearance was accompanied by an increase in the average number of arrests among those arrested, from 2.3 arrests in the earlier years to 3.4 during the first follow-up period. Despite the fact that there was a decline in the proportion of youths arrested thereafter, the average number of arrests among those actually apprehended in the successive periods was about the same as in the first follow-up span — 3.7 in both the second and third follow-up periods.

However, these increases in the proportion arrested and in the average number of arrests

[1] . . . Doubtless the decrease is due partly to increasing facility in avoiding arrest.

were not accompanied by any rise in the frequency of arrests among those who were apprehended more than once. The average frequency of arrests in the pre-court period was one in 10.5 months, as compared with one arrest in 14 months during the first follow-up period. After that, however, there was a slight increase in the average frequency of arrests among those apprehended more than once, from one arrest in 14 months in the first five-year period to one in 13 months in the second and one in 12.5 months in the third. This seems to indicate that, although fewer of the men were arrested as they grew older, those who continued to come into conflict with the law were intensifying their antisocial behavior.

The passing of the years has also witnessed a marked change in the nature of the offenses committed by our youths. This is shown in the reasons for their arrests. The most notable change is a decrease in the proportion of arrests for property crimes (larceny, pick-pocketing, burglary, and similar offenses), the decline being from 62.9 per cent of all arrests before the Juvenile Court appearance to 48.7 in the first follow-up period, to 24.6 in the second, and down to 18.2 in the third. On the other hand, a marked rise took place in the proportion of arrests for drunkenness. There were none at all in the earlier years, 9.3 per cent during the first follow-up period, 29.0 in the second, and 43.0 in the third. Time has thus clearly defined the chronic alcoholics.

Because of the smallness of numbers involved, other changes in the nature of arrests which have occurred with the passing of the years may be regarded as of relatively minor significance. For example, sex crimes increased from .3 per cent in the early years to 2.6 during the third five-year period; offenses against the family (neglect or non-support) rose from none in the early years to 3.3 percent in the third five-year period; arrests for drug using from none in the early years to .6 percent in the third follow-up period; crimes against the person (mainly assault and battery) from 2.5 per cent previous to the appearance of the boys in the Boston Juvenile Court to 6.8 during the third follow-up period. The proportion of arrests for crimes against the public welfare, such as violation of license laws, traffic laws, and liquor laws, gaming, and vagrancy, has remained about stationary. Naturally, a marked drop occurred in distinctly juvenile offenses such as truancy, stubbornness, unmanageableness, and malicious mischief.

Turning now from a consideration of the changes in the nature of the offenses for which our youths were arrested to the changes in the proportion of youths arrested for each particular offense, we find a sharp reduction in the proportion apprehended for property crimes. In the early years, 76.6 per cent of the original group of juvenile delinquents were arrested for crimes against property, and almost a like proportion, 74.8 per cent, continued to be arrested for such crimes during the first follow-up period. However, there was a falling off during the second follow-up period to 50.9 per cent, and during the third to but 42.4 per cent.

This decrease is largely offset by the rising proportion arrested for drunkenness, from none in the early years to 13.4 per cent during the first follow-up period, up to 35.3 during the second, and to 46.3 during the third. The decrease in the ratio of property offenders was further offset by a steady rise in the percentage of youths apprehended for the commission of sex offenses of one sort or another — .6 per cent in the early years, 4.7 in the first follow-up period, 7.9 in the second, and 9.6 in the third. These sex offenses ranged from fornication or adultery to rape and pathological sex crimes. There also occurred a steady rise in the proportion of men arrested for neglect or non-support of their wives or children, the increase being from none in the early period to .9 per cent in the first five years (when a few of them were old enough for marriage), to 6.0 during the second, and to 8.8 in the third.

From their early years until the end of the second follow-up period, when the group averaged twenty-four years of age, an increasing proportion of those arrested were apprehended for offenses against the public welfare, 32.7 per cent in the early years, 43.7 during the first follow-up period, and 58.8 during the second. However, there was a slight decline during the third five years, when 50.2 per cent of all those arrested were apprehended for crimes against the public welfare. A similar trend is to be seen in the proportion of youths arrested for crimes against the person (mainly assault and battery). In the early years, 4.8 per cent of the young delinquents were apprehended for such offenses, 12.4 per cent during the first follow-up period, and 24.3 per cent during the second, followed by a slight reduction, to 21.2 per cent, during the third five-year period. Considered in the light of the sharp decrease in property crimes, this may be indicative of a general quieting down in the turbulence and aggressiveness of the offenders, probably attributable to temperamental and other changes due to increasing age and to growing experience.

All in all, therefore, it is evident that the peak of arrests in this group of juvenile delinquents was reached roughly during the average age span fourteen to nineteen years. And the commission of property crimes, characteristically begun in their early years, extended with about uniform vigor through an average age of nineteen years, after which there was a sharp decline in this type of offense. This drop has been largely absorbed by a rise in the proportion of those arrested as drunkards, vagrants, and offenders against the person. However, although the drunkards among our group are still on the increase, offenders against the public welfare and against the person appear to have reached their peak in the age span nineteen to twenty-four years.

TREND OF DISPOSITIONS BY COURTS

With the passing of the years, a considerable change has occurred in the dispositions made by the courts of the offenses for which our men were arrested. Before the appearance of our 1,000 juvenile delinquents in the Boston Juvenile Court, only 7.6 per cent of all their arrests had resulted in commitments to peno-correctional institutions; but during the first follow-up period 30.6 per cent of all the arrests ended in commitments. Apparently judges were most inclined to send our youths to institutions when the boys were in the average age span of fourteen to nineteen years; for during the second five-year follow-up period, when they averaged nineteen to twenty-four years, the proportion of all the arrests that were followed by commitments to peno-correctional establishments dropped to 20.2 per cent and remained about the same, 22.0, during the third follow-up period.

As was to be expected, when our youths first showed signs of delinquent behavior, judges were inclined to place them on probation

rather than to incarcerate them. This is evidenced by the fact that, in the period prior to the appearance of the boys in the Boston Juvenile Court, 44.6 per cent of all their arrests resulted in probation; in the first five-year follow-up period the use of probation declined to 17.4 per cent, during the second follow-up period to 8.7, and during the third to 6.2.

In the earlier stages of the delinquent careers of our youths, likewise, judges obviously resorted more frequently to the filing of cases, perhaps on the theory that their early offenses were of an "accidental" character, for which there was, therefore, no need to impose severe punishment; for prior to the appearance of these boys in the Boston Juvenile Court, 27.8 per cent of all their arrests had resulted in the filing of the charges against them without further action. This proportion dropped to 16.6 per cent of all arrests during the first follow-up period, and remained about the same throughout the later years — 13.9 during the second follow-up period and 15.9 during the third.

In earlier years before the contact of the boys with the Boston Juvenile Court, only a very small percentage of arrests (5.2) resulted in the payment of fines. There was an increasing resort with the passing of the years to this mild form of punishment: for during the first follow-up period 13.9 per cent of all the arrests resulted in fines, and during the second, 27.5. However, in the third five-year follow-up period the incidence dropped to 19.8 per cent.

Comparatively, the use of probation under suspended sentence has been limited as a disposition of the arrests of our group of delinquents. In the time preceding their appearance before the Boston Juvenile Court, only 6.3 per cent of all the arrests were thus disposed of; during the first follow-up period 9.4, during the second 5.4, and during the third 7.0. There was also only a very slight recourse to the nol-prossing of cases: .2 per cent in the early years, .7 during the first follow-up period, and 2.0 during both the second and third follow-up periods. There was, likewise, relatively little resort to a finding of "No bill": none in the early years, .6 per cent during the first follow-up period, 1.9 during the second, and 1.5 during the third.

A rise in the proportion of arrests for drunkenness that resulted in the release of the offender by a probation officer without court appearance, from none in the early years to 9.3 per cent in the third period, is of course explainable by the increasing number of arrests for drunkenness with the passing of the years.

Perhaps the growing ratio of arrests resulting in a finding of "Not guilty" was due to more experience on the part of these offenders with court methods and to the greater use of lawyers to defend them; for in the early years and during the first follow-up period slightly over 8 per cent of the arrests among the juvenile delinquents resulted in a finding of "Not guilty" (or non-delinquent), while during the second follow-up period, 15.9 per cent of all arrests resulted in acquittals, and in the third five-year period 16.3.

By and large, therefore, it can be said that in the years prior to the contact of these boys with the Boston Juvenile Court, the courts attempted constructive extramural treatment in the form of probation. During the first follow-up period they turned more to incarceration, largely in correctional schools, reformatories, and prisons. Thereafter they tended more toward disposing of arrests by fining or release.

Considering, now, the dispositions of all arrests in the three successive periods, from the point of view of the number of youths undergoing each type of sentence rather than on the basis of the dispositions of individual arrests, we see more clearly the changes that occurred with the passing of the years. During the period prior to the appearance of these youths in the Boston Juvenile Court, 11.2 per cent of the group were committed to peno-correctional institutions (new sentences only). During the first follow-up period the proportion increased markedly, rising to 49.3 per cent. This ratio has been steadily maintained: during the second follow-up period 41.2 per cent of the youths received one or more new sentences to peno-correctional institutions and during the third 43.7 per cent. There was a sharp progressive decline, however, in the proportion of offenders placed on straight probation (without suspended sentence), from 63.0 per cent in the early years to 42.5 during the first follow-up period, to 26.4 during the second, and to 21.2 during the third.

In their early years, somewhat over a tenth of these youths, 11.9 per cent, were placed on probation with suspended sentence of imprisonment. This proportion increased markedly during the first follow-up period, when 25.6 per cent of the youths were given this form of treatment. Far fewer offenders had their arrests disposed of in this way during the second five-year period, however, when only 15.9 per cent of all those arrested were placed on probation under suspended sentence. The third follow-up period saw a slight rise, to 20.2 per cent.

Only 9.6 per cent of the young offenders were fined in the early part of their delinquent careers, while during the first follow-up period 26.8 per cent had their cases disposed of in this way. The proportion increased very sharply, to 51.9 per cent, during the second follow-up period, but dropped to 40.6 per cent during the third. The proportion of delinquents whose cases were disposed of by a filing of charges against them remained about the same throughout the years: 32.4 per cent in the period prior to the appearance of the boys before the Juvenile Court, 38.1 during the first follow-up period, 36.7 during the second five years, and 39 during the third.

There was a steady rise over the years in the proportion of delinquents released by the probation officer (without formal court appearance) on charges of drunkenness, and also in the proportion found "Not guilty." In the earlier period of their delinquent careers none of the boys had been released by the probation officer, for the obvious reason that none of them had been arrested for drunkenness at that time. During the first follow-up period, 4.5 per cent of the delinquents were released by a probation officer, and this percentage rose to 12.2 during the second follow-up period, and to 20.8 during the third. "Not guilty" (or not delinquent) was the verdict obtained by 14.9 per cent of the group during the early years. This percentage rose to 22.4 during the first follow-up period, to 36.7 during the second, and to 39.4 during the third.

There was an increase, also, up to the end of the second five-year follow-up period, in the proportion of offenders whose cases were nol-prossed or disposed of by a finding of "No bill," but a slight dropping off in the third period. Less than one per cent had charges against them nol-prossed in the early years of their delinquencies. The percentage rose to 2.1 during the first five-year period and to 7.6 in the second and dropped to 6.9 per cent in the third.

Because of the non-criminal procedure in juvenile courts none of the young delinquents had his case disposed of by a finding of "No bill" during the early years; in the first follow-up period 2 per cent of the youths had their cases so disposed of, this proportion rising to 7.1 per cent during the second five-year span, and dropping to 4.7 during the third.

An interesting related finding is the shift which occurred as the years passed in the type of court disposition most often experienced by those who committed crimes. During the early days of their delinquent careers, the largest proportion of offenders, 63 per cent, were placed on probation; while during the first follow-up period the major proportion, 49.3 per cent, received new sentences to peno-correctional institutions, mostly truant and correctional schools. During the second five-year period the highest ratio of offenders, 51.9 per cent, had their cases disposed of by fines; while during the third follow-up span the largest proportion of offenders, 43.7 per cent, were in the group who were given new sentences of imprisonment. It should be remembered in this connection that, with the increasing proportion of drunkards, a rise occurred in short-term jail sentences. This partly accounts for the fact that commitment holds first place among all possible dispositions of arrests in the third follow-up period.

The proportion of convictions following arrests has remained fairly stationary throughout the delinquent careers of our youths. In the years prior to their contact with the Boston Juvenile Court, 93.2 per cent of all their arrests resulted in convictions or findings of delinquency; during the first follow-up period 97.9 per cent resulted in convictions, during the second 92.9 per cent, and during the third 91 per cent.

The average number of convictions among those arrested one or more times rose from 2.2 in the early years to 3.1 during the first follow-up period, and remained about the same during the second follow-up period (3.3), and during the third (3.2). However, the average frequency of convictions among those arrested more than once dropped from one in 11.4 months in the earlier years to one in 15.1 months during the first follow-up span, and has remained about the same throughout the subsequent years, one conviction in 15.4 months occurring in the second follow-up period, and one in 15 months during the third.

TREND OF PENO-CORRECTIONAL EXPERIENCES

Considering next the changes which have occurred with the passing of the years in the incidence and nature of the peno-correctional experiences and in the amount of time spent behind walls, we note first that 7 per cent of our group were in correctional institutions during their early years. This proportion mounted to 45 per cent during the first follow-up period, dropped to 34.4 during the second, and further to 30 during the third.

The average number of peno-correctional experiences among these youths in their early years was 1.7. It rose to 2 during the first five-year period and has remained the same. It should be noted, of course, that while fewer of our youths have been incarcerated with the passing of the years, the average number of peno-correctional experiences among those who were imprisoned has remained constant.

The passing of the years did, however, slightly increase the average number of months spent by the offenders in peno-correctional institutions. In the earlier years and through the first and second follow-up periods, the average was 18 to 19.5 months; during the third follow-up span it rose to 23 months.

There was a marked change over the years in the nature of the peno-correctional experiences of our youths, which is readily explainable on the ground of age. In the early years, for example, when the boys were thirteen and a half years on the average, 95.7 per cent of all their commitments were to truant and correctional schools. During the first follow-up period, this figure dropped to 76.4 per cent. A fifth (21.9 per cent) of all commitments during this period were served in reformatories; 21.2 per cent in jails, houses of correction, or state farms; and 6.9 per cent in prisons. During the second follow-up period a still further change occurred in the nature of the peno-correctional experiences: there was a drop to 14 per cent in truant or correctional school experiences, an increase to 31.3 per cent in terms spent in reformatories, and an increase to 52.4 per cent in commitments to jails, houses of correction, or state farms. A marked increase, to 23.1 per cent, also occurred in the proportion of terms served in prisons. In the third five-year follow-up period, there was a drop to 18.3 per cent in the proportion of reformatory incarcerations; but a continuing increase to 41.2 per cent in terms served in prisons, as well as an increase to 61.5 per cent in those spent in jails. Naturally, in the third five-year period there were no commitments or revocations to truant or correctional schools, because by that time our youths were all too old for such commitments.

Before summarizing the trend in the behavior of our young men, it should be pointed out that in the pre-court period 93.2 per cent of them were not imprisoned and did not spend any time in mental hospitals or in hospitals for the chronically ill. The same may be said of 54.6 per cent of the youths during the first follow-up period, of 64.6 per cent during the second, and of 69.5 per cent during the third. The number of months spent at large (that is, not in prisons or hospitals for the mentally diseased or chronically ill) by those who were not resident in the community throughout each five-year period decreased from an average of 41.5 during the first five-year period, to 39.1 during the second, and to 35.7 during the third.

TREND OF DELINQUENCY AND CRIMINALITY

After this review of the changes that occurred in the arrests, convictions, and peno-correctional experiences of our offenders from their early years to the time when they averaged twenty-nine years of age (at the end of the third five-year follow-up period), it should be helpful to summarize briefly the chief features of the trend in their conduct.

First should be recalled the encouraging finding of *a steady increase in the proportion of those who abandoned their criminalistic activities altogether.* Thus, during the first follow-up period, only 14.6 per cent of the entire group could be classified as non-offenders (which means that they did not commit either official or unofficial offenses); by the second follow-up span this percentage had risen to 26.8, and by the third to 36.6.

Secondly, *even among the men who remained criminalistic throughout the years, there was a notable and on the whole favorable change in the character of their offences.* It will be recalled that the differentiation made for the purposes of this research between "serious" and "minor" offenders is essentially one between

felons and misdemeanants. There was a decrease in the proportion of serious offenders among those who continued to violate the criminal laws throughout the years, from 77.4 per cent of all delinquents during the first follow-up period, to 56.6 during the second, and to 47.8 during the third; and an increase in minor offenders from 22.6 per cent of all the delinquents during the first follow-up span, to 43.4 during the second, and to 52.2 during the third.[2]

The change in the predominant character of the delinquencies of our offenders with the passage of time is significant. Property crimes, for example, were the typical offenses of 71.1 per cent of all our young delinquents before their appearance in the Boston Juvenile Court. During the first follow-up period this proportion dropped to 65.5 per cent; while during the second period only 39.2 per cent of the youths committed offenses, mainly against property; and the ratio was still further reduced to 31.5 per cent during the third five-year period. There was also a marked decrease in such offenses as running away from home, truanting, malicious mischief, stubbornness, and like offenses, which are of course distinctly juvenile acts. Sex offenses increased only slightly as typical and characteristic forms of misbehavior. But in the characteristic commission of offenses against the public welfare, safety, and policy (such as vagrancy, being present at gaming, violation of liquor laws, violation of license laws, and the like), and of drunkenness, there was a marked increase with the passing of the years. For only 2.2 per cent of our juvenile delinquents had been mainly offenders against the public welfare during their early years, but the proportion rose to 10.7 per cent during the first follow-up span, and to 22.6 during the second, with but a slight drop, to 19.9, during the third five-year period. Drunkenness as a predominant offense rose from no incidence during the early years to being the characteristic offense among

---

[2] It should be noted that except for the period prior to the appearance of these boys in the Boston Juvenile Court, when the delinquencies of 63.3 per cent of the group were based on actual arrests or on other "officially" recognized misbehavior (such as dishonorable discharge or escape from institutions), some 93 per cent of the offenders in each of the three five-year follow-up periods were judged delinquent because of the commission of crimes that were given official cognizance by agencies of the law.

4.2 per cent of all offenders in the first follow-up period, 16.6 in the second, and 23.7 in the third.

In view of the fact that so large a proportion of these youths were predominantly offenders against property before their appearance in the Boston Juvenile Court, it is worth noting that 35.2 per cent of the property offenders had become non-delinquent by the beginning of the third follow-up period, 12.5 per cent had become predominantly offenders against the public welfare, 15.5 developed into drunkards, 2.6 evolved into offenders against the family, 1.4 into sex delinquents, 1.4 into offenders against the person, .4 (2 men) into drug addicts, 5.8 into "varied" offenders. Only 25.2 per cent of the original group of early offenders against property continued to commit such offenses during the third five-year follow-up period.

Nevertheless, *only 109 of the original group of 1,000 were non-delinquents throughout the three follow-up spans, while 226 were serious offenders, and 88 were minor offenders throughout the fifteen years.* Further, 67 of the entire original group were serious delinquents during the first and second five-year periods and minor offenders during the third; 95 were serious offenders during the first five-year period and minor delinquents during the second and third; 40 were minor offenders during the first follow-up period and non-delinquents during the second and third; 23 were minor offenders during the first and second five-year spans and non-delinquents during the third; 67 were serious criminals during the first follow-up period but non-offenders during the second and third; 36 of the 1,000 youths were serious criminals during the first five-year span, minor offenders during the second, and non-delinquents during the third; and 27 were serious offenders during the first and second periods, and non-offenders during the third. In addition, there are 40 youths whom we have termed "erratic" in their behavior in that they did not progress from more to less serious delinquency, or to non-delinquency.[3]

The above enumeration accounts for the behavior of 818 youths whose delinquencies were known throughout the three five-year follow-up periods. In 155 of the 1,000 cases it was not possible, for one reason or another (unknown, "inapplicable," dead), to describe the behavior of the youths in all the three follow-up periods, although their conduct was ascertainable in one or another of them. In only 27 cases out of the 1,000 was the behavior of our youths entirely unknown throughout the three follow-up periods.

AGE AT WHICH CONDUCT CHANGES OCCURRED

It is important to know at approximately what age the youths changed from the commission of serious to the commission of minor offenses, and likewise at what age delinquent behavior was abandoned entirely. Of 293 youths who were originally serious offenders but became minor delinquents before the end of the fifteen-year span (and it was possible to determine at what age), 34.8 per cent were still under seventeen years old when they began to commit minor offenses, 32.6 per cent were between seventeen and twenty-one, 21.5 per cent were between twenty-one and twenty-five, and 11.3 per cent were twenty-five or older. Their average age at change from the commission of serious to the commission of minor offenses was 18.86 ($\pm$.16) years.

There were 312 youths who were definitely non-delinquent by the beginning of the third follow-up period, and 6 more who became non-delinquent after the beginning of the third period. In 6.0 per cent reformation occurred when they were still under twelve years old, in 13.8 per cent between twelve and fifteen, in 23.6 per cent between fifteen and eighteen, in 22.6 per cent between eighteen and twenty-one, in 18.2 per cent between twenty-one and twenty-four, in 12.9 per cent between twenty-four and twenty-seven, and in 2.9 per cent between twenty-seven and thirty. The average age of reformation of these 318 youths was 18.49 ($\pm$.17) years.

The major and most encouraging finding of this chapter is that with the passing of the

---

[3] Two of this group, for example, were non-delinquents during the first and second five-year periods, but serious offenders in the third; 2 were minor offenders during the first, serious delinquents during the second, and non-delinquents in the third period; 6 were serious offenders in the first five years, minor offenders in the second, and again serious offenders in the third; 4 were minor delinquents during the first and second five years, but serious offenders in the third, and so on.

years there was, among our original group of 1,000 delinquents, *both a decline in criminality and a decrease in the seriousness of the offenses of those who continued to commit crimes*. How account for these changes in behavior? What roles have age and its accompaniments played in influencing improvement in the conduct of these offenders? To this and related questions we shall turn our attention in the next four chapters.

AGE, MATURATION, AND CHANGES IN CONDUCT

In the previous chapters we described the changes that occurred in the extent and nature of the delinquency of our 1,000 offenders from the onset of their criminal careers in childhood until they arrived at an average age of twenty-nine years. These changes are in the direction not only of less delinquency in the group as a whole, but of less serious crime among those who have continued their criminal careers.

In this chapter our first question is whether arrival at a particular age-span has any relation to the conduct of delinquents. Our next concern, related to the first, is whether there is in this research any evidence that maturation (regardless of the age when it occurs) plays a major role in behavior changes, as was suggested in *Later Criminal Careers*. In that work, which was a follow-up study of the careers of male Reformatory graduates originally reported on in *500 Criminal Careers*, it was ascertained from a correlation of 63 factors reflecting every aspect of the lives of these men with the changes in their behavior, that in the factor of maturation through aging lies the most significant explanation of these changes. It was further discovered that mental abnormalities were largely responsible for a blocking or retarding of the natural process of maturation, and hence for persisting misconduct. The interested reader

is referred to Chapters IX, X, and XI of *Later Criminal Careers* for a full statement of the findings, which suggests not only that the natural process of maturation mainly accounts for the improvement in respect to criminal conduct, but that a very close relationship exists between such improvement and improvement in respect to other major activities of the offenders, such as industrial adjustment, use of leisure, family life, and the like.

Because, in connection with *One Thousand Juvenile Delinquents*, we limited our inquiry to the tracing of their antisocial behavior and omitted from consideration their economic status, family relationships, employment history, use of leisure, and the like, we did not have the data from which, in the present work, directly to determine the reasons for the changes in conduct with the passage of the years.[4] However, there is indirect evidence — some of which will be presented in the latter portion of this chapter and the rest in the three succeeding chapters — that the maturation of the human organism which, in varying degrees, accompanies aging, when aided by certain favorable factors, largely accounts for the improvement which has occurred in the conduct of our offenders.

DELINQUENCY AND CHRONOLOGICAL AGE

Adverting now to the first concern of this chapter — namely, whether arrival at a particular age span is closely related to the conduct changes of delinquents — we shall examine the behavior of our 1,000 offenders in relation to their ages. But first it will be well to have before us in Table 1 the transformations in the behavior of the group as a whole

---

[4] The reasons for the above-mentioned limitation will be found in *One Thousand Juvenile Delinquents*, p. 4, note 3.

Table 1 Degree of Criminality in First, Second, and Third Follow-up Periods (Percentages)

OFFENDERS	FIRST PERIOD	SECOND PERIOD	THIRD PERIOD
Non-criminals	14.6	26.8	36.6
Minor offenders	19.3	31.8	33.1
Serious offenders	66.1	41.4	30.3

Note. Derived from Appendix C, 20.

Table 2 *Comparison of Criminality in Age Span Sixteen to Twenty Years, in First and Second Follow-up Periods (Percentages)*

OFFENDERS	FIRST PERIOD	SECOND PERIOD
Non-criminals	12.9	31.7
Minor offenders	19.4	26.8
Serious offenders	67.7	41.5

which have occurred with the passing of the years.

The question which is naturally raised at this point is whether youths who arrived at a specific age span (say, sixteen to twenty years) during the first follow-up period showed the same proportions of criminality and non-criminality as youths who did not reach a like age span until the second five-year follow-up period.[5] The answer should throw light on whether the behavior changes that occurred are to any significant extent related to the characteristics generally accompanying any particular age span. Attention is directed to such a comparison in Table 2, from which it is clear that youths who were sixteen to twenty years old during the first five-year period did not resemble in behavior youths who, having begun their delinquencies earlier in life, did not arrive at the age of sixteen to twenty years until the second follow-up period. Moreover, comparison of Table 2 with Table 1 indicates that much the same general improvement occurred with the passage of five years among those who were sixteen to twenty years old in the first and second periods, respectively, as occurred in the entire group, regardless of age. The same phenomenon is noted in Table 3, which deals with those of our delinquents who became twenty-one to twenty-five years old during each of the three successive follow-up periods. The lack of relationship between arrival at a specific age span and change in conduct is confirmed in Table 3; for those of the original 1,000 juvenile delinquents who were twenty-one to twenty-five years old in each successive follow-up period did not resemble each other in incidence of criminal conduct. And, again, with the passing of the years, the same changes in behavior occurred within this particular age span as among the 1,000 offenders as a whole regardless of age.

5 No comparison could be made with youths of this age during the third five-year follow-up period because, of course, none of our group were still within this low age span by the time the third follow-up period was reached.

Table 3 *Comparison of Criminality in Age Span Twenty-one to Twenty-five Years, in First, Second, and Third Follow-up Periods (Percentages)*

OFFENDERS	FIRST PERIOD	SECOND PERIOD	THIRD PERIOD
Non-criminals	18.1	25.4	38.0
Minor offenders	23.4	33.0	31.6
Serious offenders	58.5	41.6	30.4

Table 4 *Comparison of Criminality in Age Span Twenty-six to Thirty Years, in Second and Third Follow-up Periods (Percentages)*

OFFENDERS	SECOND PERIOD	THIRD PERIOD
Non-criminals	27.3	36.5
Minor offenders	32.1	32.4
Serious offenders	40.6	31.1

Note. Since only two youths were within this age span during the first five-year follow-up period, they were omitted from consideration.

Still further evidence on this point is presented in Table 4 which shows behavior of the youths who were twenty-six to thirty years old during the second follow-up period and those who did not enter this age span until the third. As in Tables 2 and 3, we note that offenders of like ages (now the twenty-six to thirty-year-olds) did not resemble each other in behavior.

With the passing of the years, regardless of their age span, there occurred the same general upward trend in their conduct as took place in the group of 1,000 offenders as a whole.

All the above evidence tends to establish the point that, at least so far as these particular offenders are concerned, the tendency to settle down or become less aggressive in antisocial behavior is not attributable to arrival at any particular chronological age span. Not only does the internal evidence of this particular research show this to be true, but it is confirmed by a comparison, in Table 5, of the behavior of our 1,000 juvenile delinquents in the age-span twenty-four to twenty-nine years with another sample of offenders — the 500 male criminals reported on in *Later Criminal Careers* — when they were in the *same age span*. Little resemblance between them in conduct is shown.

If arrival at any particular chronological age were of crucial significance in changing the conduct of offenders, there ought to be greater similarity between these two groups at similar ages. There appears to be no question, therefore, that the characteristics of particular age spans do not bear a significant or direct relationship to the behavior changes which have occured in our offenders.

DELINQUENCY AND MATURATION

If the factor of age does not satisfactorily account for the change in behavior with the passage of time, what other factors do? We next turn our attention to evidence in Table 6, which is indirectly confirmative of the finding

Table 5 *Comparison of Criminality of Juvenile Court Group and Reformatory Group in Age Span Twenty-four to Twenty-nine Years (Percentages)*

OFFENDERS	JUVENILE COURT GROUP *	REFORMATORY GROUP †
Non-criminals	36.6	21.5
Minor offenders ..	33.1	31.6
Serious offenders	30.3	46.9

* Derived from Appendix C, 20.
† Derived from *Later Criminal Careers*, Appendix D, Table 54. Actually this group was twenty-five to thirty years old.

Table 6 *Comparison of Criminality of Juvenile Court Group in Age Span Twenty-four to Twenty-nine Years and in Reformatory Group in Age Span Thirty to Thirty-five Years (Percentages)*

OFFENDERS	JUVENILE COURT GROUP *	REFORMATORY GROUP †
Non-criminals	36.6	32.1
Minor offenders ..	33.1	33.9
Serious offenders	30.3	34.0

* Derived from Appendix B, 74.
† Derived from *Later Criminal Careers*, Appendix C, Table 2–51a.

in *Later Criminal Careers* that, not arrival at any particular age, but rather the *achievement of adequate maturation regardless of the chronological age at which it occurs, is the significant factor in the behavior changes of criminals.*

After discovering that the offenders reported upon here and those described in *Later Criminal Careers* (which groups have been studied with like care and by the same method) did not resemble each other in behavior in similar age spans, we found that there was, however, a close resemblance between the conduct of the former juvenile delinquents during their average age span of *twenty-four to twenty-nine years* [6] and the ex-inmates of the Reformatory in their average age span of *thirty to thirty-five years.* [7] This resemblance is shown in Table 6. Clearly, there was practically the same distribution of non-criminals, minor offenders, and serious offenders within the two groups, though there was a *five-year average age difference between them.* This finding must be interpreted in the light of the facts that the two groups of offenders were drawn from different parts of Massachusetts (the juvenile delinquents originally came entirely from Boston, and the ex-inmates of the Reformatory from cities and towns all over Massachusetts); and that both groups had, since the onset of their criminal

[6] The juvenile delinquents were in this age span in the third five-year follow-up period.
[7] The adult criminals were in this age span during the second five-year follow-up period.

careers, scattered to different areas [8] and had been subjected to many different forms of peno-correctional treatment in different parts of Massachusetts and in other states.

This close resemblance becomes even more significant in the light of the following facts: Not only was there a five-year difference in the average ages of the two groups of offenders at the time of this resemblance in their conduct, but there was a difference of some five years in the average age at which each group *first became delinquent*: the juvenile delinquent group were of an average age of nine years and seven months when they first showed signs of antisocial behavior,[9] while the ex-inmates of the Reformatory were fourteen years and nine months old at the first manifestations of delinquency.[10] Moreover, there was a difference of about seven years in the average age at which those in each group who reformed actually became non-offenders. The 318 juvenile delinquents who became non-offenders before the end of a third five-year follow-up period did so when they were of an average age of 18.5 years; while the 118 Reformatory graduates who became non-delinquent before the end of a second five-year follow-up period did so when they were of an average age of 25.85 years. It will be seen that the difference in their average ages at the time of reformation is little more than the difference in the actual ages of the two groups at the time when they so closely resembled each other in delinquent conduct.

To summarize, at a point of resemblance in their criminal conduct,

(1) there is a five-year difference in the average ages of the two groups of offenders;

(2) there is a difference of about five years in the average age at which the two groups first showed signs of antisocial behavior;

(3) there is an average difference of seven years in the age at which those in each group

who actually reformed became non-criminal.

In the light of the facts already stated that these two groups of offenders were drawn from different parts of Massachusetts and were subjected to a different variety of peno-correctional treatments over the years, the basic explanation for their resemblance in conduct at different age spans seems to lie in the fact that both groups have the characteristics of being approximately *the same distance away from the onset of their delinquent behavior and, in the case of those in each group who reformed, of being, at the time of abandonment of their criminalistic conduct, approximately the same distance away from the onset of their antisocial behavior.*

Since the conduct of the two groups of offenders, who were drawn from different places, at different times, at different levels in society's official apparatus for coping with criminality (i.e., juvenile court and young-adult reformatory), and who were studied entirely independently one of the other, was so much alike at a time in their lives when the two groups were found to be approximately the same average distance away from the onset of their criminal careers, we may reasonably conclude that, despite the varying influences to which these two groups must have been subjected, there is some underlying process in the lives of criminals related to their growth or development from the time of onset of their delinquent behavior which seems to play a basic role in the evolution and devolution of their criminal careers. A further check on this finding is the fact that the two groups of offenders resembled each other in conduct not only in the age spans twenty-four to twenty-nine and thirty to thirty-five, respectively, but when five years younger — in the age spans nineteen to twenty-four and twenty-five to thirty, respectively.[11]

[11] As shown by the following table:

OFFENDERS	JUVENILE DELINQUENT GROUP AT 19–24 *	REFORMATORY GROUP AT 25–30 †
Non-criminals ...	26.8	21.5
Minor offenders	31.8	31.6
Serious offenders	41.4	46.9

* Derived from Appendix C, Table 20, Period II.
† Derived from *Later Criminal Careers*, Appendix D, 54, Period I.

[8] For whereabouts of juvenile offenders at the end of the third five-year follow-up period, see Chapter XXI, p. 235; and of Reformatory group, see *Later Criminal Careers*, Appendix C, 2–H81b.

[9] See *One Thousand Juvenile Delinquents*, Appendix H, 57; and page 95.

[10] See *Later Criminal Careers*, Appendix C, 49. See also *500 Criminal Careers*, page 143. Since the same degree of care and intensity was used in tracing down the earliest delinquencies of the two groups, the difference in the ages at first delinquency is a real one.

Our analysis leads to the significant conclusion, therefore, that *not age per se, but rather the acquisition of a certain degree of what we have called "maturation," regardless of the age at which this is achieved among different groups of offenders, is significantly related to changes in criminalistic behavior once embarked upon.* Some implications of this finding are discussed in Chapter XXII [of *Juvenile Delinquents Grown Up*].

In an effort to glean some clues as to which factors facilitate or hamper this underlying basic one of biologic maturation, we turn our attention in the next three chapters to comparisons, *regardless of age*, between (a) those juvenile offenders who reformed and those who continued to be delinquent, (b) those among the reformed juvenile delinquents who abandoned their criminal conduct when still under twenty-one and those who were older when they became non-criminals, and (c) those who became minor offenders and those who remained serious offenders.

Before turning to the next chapter, however, it will be well to pursue the comparison of the juvenile delinquents and the Reformatory graduates in various aspects of their criminal activities, because it bears out the close resemblance of the two groups at a time equidistant from the onset of their criminal careers. The reader is again reminded that all the following comparisons of the juvenile delinquents and the Reformatory graduates refer to the behavior of the first group when they were of an average age of twenty-four to twenty-nine years, and of the latter when they were thirty to thirty-five years old; and, as just stated, at a stage when the two groups were approximately the same average distance away from the time of the onset of their delinquent careers.

Considering first, in Table 7, the nature of the offenses of both groups as reflected in the reasons for their arrests, we find that the only difference between them that may be of any importance is the proportion of arrests for drunkenness, which was greater in the Reformatory group (51.3 per cent against 43.0 per cent). This is obviously explainable by the fact that this group was older and, therefore, more likely to indulge in drinking because the men had more time to acquire the habit of alcoholism and because they had already passed the peak of maturation and were therefore drifting into less aggressive and less energetic forms of criminality.

There are further significant similarities between the two groups in average number and frequency of arrests, average number of convictions, dispositions of arrests, and average number of penal experiences among those having such experiences; but there is a marked difference in the nature of their peno-correctional experiences which is clearly due to statutory limitations on the commitment of offenders of certain chronological ages to certain institutions.

During the respective periods in their lives

Table 7 *Nature of Arrests of Juvenile Court Group in Age Span Twenty-four to Twenty-nine Years, and of Reformatory Group in Age Span Thirty to Thirty-five Years (Percentages)*

OFFENSES	JUVENILE COURT GROUP *	REFORMATORY GROUP †
Offenses against property	18.2	17.3
Offenses against chastity	2.6	1.8
Offenses against family and children	3.3	4.1
Offenses against public peace, morals, welfare, etc.	22.5	17.2
Drunkenness	43.0	51.3
Drug selling	.6	1.2
Offenses against the person	6.8	4.3
Other	3.0	2.8
Number of arrests	2,195	955

* Derived from Appendix B, 60.
† Derived from *Later Criminal Careers*, Appendix C, Table 2–H125.

that are under comparison, a like proportion of the juvenile delinquents and Reformatory graduates (57.9 per cent of the former and 55.1 per cent of the latter) were arrested. We note this striking resemblance not only between the proportion of offenders in each group who were arrested, but also in the average number of their arrests. Our 1,000 juvenile delinquents were apprehended an average of 3.78 ($\pm$ .07) times in the age span twenty-four to twenty-nine; while our Reformatory graduates were arrested an average of 3.71 ($\pm$ .12) times in the age span thirty to thirty-five. There is a further striking resemblance between the two groups of offenders in the average frequency of arrests among those who were arrested more than once during the periods in question. Our juvenile delinquents were arrested an average of once every 12.58 months ($\pm$ .27), while our Reformatory graduates were arrested once in 12.5 months ($\pm$ .45).

Turning to a comparison of the frequency of convictions among juvenile offenders in the twenty-four to twenty-nine-year span and the Reformatory graduates in the thirty to thirty-five-year span, we find a further striking resemblance between the two groups. Although this, and the next factor of dispositions (convictions and sentences), reflects not the offenders' conduct but the action of courts toward such conduct, the close resemblance in the handling of their cases is significant in that it further confirms the recognition of a strong similarity in the behavior of the two groups at the respective periods in their lives which are under comparison.

First, among the juvenile delinquents who were arrested more than once, the average frequency of convictions was once in 15.07 ($\pm$ .29) months; while among the Reformatory graduates one conviction occurred every 15.65 ($\pm$ .48) months. Second, as Table 8 shows, there is a strong resemblance between the two groups in the dispositions, by courts, of the arrests of the Juvenile Court group in the age span twenty-four to twenty-nine and of the ex-inmates of the Reformatory in the age span thirty to thirty-five, when, as already emphasized, both groups of offenders were the same average distance away from the onset of their antisocial behavior. This resemblance is doubly significant because, as already stressed, the juvenile group were originally drawn from Boston while the Reformatory graduates came from various parts of the state of Massachusetts; the court's recognition of this resemblance is confirmed by the similarity of the sentences imposed on the two groups. The only difference of any significance is the higher proportion of institutional commitments in the older group of offenders. The differences in the chronological ages (as opposed

Table **8** *Dispositions of Arrests of Juvenile Court Group in Age Span Twenty-four to Twenty-nine Years, and of Reformatory Group in Age Span Thirty to Thirty-five Years (Percentages)*

DISPOSITIONS OF ARRESTS	JUVENILE COURT GROUP *	REFORMATORY GROUP †
Imprisonment (including recommitment on revocation of parole)	22.0	30.7
Probation (including probation under suspended sentence)	13.2	13.6
Fine (including commitment for non-payment of fine and restitution)	19.8	20.7
File	15.9	14.8
Release by probation officer following arrest for drunkenness	9.3	5.4
Nol-pros	2.0	1.2
No bill	1.5	.7
Not guilty or released	16.3	12.9
Number of known dispositions	2,154	920

* Derived from Appendix B, 64.
† Derived from *Later Criminal Careers*, Appendix C, Table 2–H126.

to what might be called "maturation ages") of the two groups probably accounts for this, for proportionately more of the older group were committed to institutions on short-term sentences following drunkenness and proportionately fewer were released by the probation officer.

Comparison of the peno-correctional experiences of our juvenile delinquents in the age span twenty-four to twenty-nine years with the Reformatory graduates in the age span thirty to thirty-five years indicates a further close resemblance between them: 30 per cent of the juvenile delinquents and 36.8 per cent of the Reformatory graduates were in peno-correctional institutions during the period in question. The slightly higher proportion in the Reformatory group is obviously accounted for by the difference in the chronological age of the two groups. The older offenders experienced more jail sentences, as is seen from Table 9, owing to the fact that they were to a greater extent drunkards and vagrants.

There is a difference, but only a small one, between the groups in the average number of penal experiences — 2.14 (± .05) among the juvenile delinquents and 2.72 (± .12) among the Reformatory graduates — and in regard to the average number of months spent in penal institutions: the juvenile delinquents were incarcerated for an average of 23.26 (±.74) months, and the Reformatory graduates for an average of 24.26 (±1.05) months.

Coming now to a comparison of the institutional experiences of the two groups of offenders as shown in Table 9, we note a marked dif-

ference in the nature of the institutional treatment of the two groups, obviously due in large measure to the difference in their chronological ages. This is due partly to a belated diagnosis of mental defect in the older group and is also related to age limitations in commitment laws. The large proportion of commitments to institutions for mental defectives among the older group and in commitments to reformatories in the younger group are clearly attributable to the two influences mentioned above. On the other hand, the high percentage of jail commitments among the older men, with a corresponding decrease in prison commitments, is partially attributable to the "settling down" or deteriorative effect of aging beyond the peak of maturation, which all persons sooner or later experience.

In the foregoing analysis we have answered, at least partially, the query whether it is primarily arrival at a particular age span or achievement of a requisite degree of maturation, regardless of the specific age level at which this occurs, that explains the significant improvement in the conduct of offenders with the passing of the years.[12]

Apparently abandonment of criminal conduct does not occur at any specific chronologic age level, but rather after the passage of a certain length of time from the point of first expression of definite delinquent trends. On the

[12] Not all factors significant in original propensity to delinquency are necessarily significant in determining at what stage criminality will be abandoned. This distinction has been alluded to in our previous works.

Table 9 Institutional Experiences of Juvenile Court Group in Age Span Twenty-four to Twenty-nine Years, and of Reformatory Group in Age Span Thirty to Thirty-five Years (Percentages)

INSTITUTIONAL EXPERIENCES	JUVENILE COURT GROUP *	REFORMATORY GROUP †
Schools for feebleminded and institutions for defective delinquents	3.2	7.4
Reformatories	15.1	1.7
Prisons	31.1	23.3
Jails	50.6	67.6
Number of penal experiences	312	421

* Derived from Appendix B, 68.
† Derived from Later Criminal Careers, Appendix C, Table 2–H139.

whole, if the acts of delinquency begin very early in life, they are apparently abandoned at a relatively early stage of manhood, provided various mental abnormalities do not counteract the natural tendency to maturation that brings with it greater powers of reflection, inhibition, postponement of immediate desires for more legitimate later ones, the power to learn from experience, and like constituents of a mature personality. If, on the other hand, the acts of delinquency begin in adolescence, the delinquent tendency seems to run its course into a later stage of adulthood, again provided the natural maturation process is not interfered with. In both instances, distribution of the delinquents into comparable proportions of persistent offenders and non-offenders occurs not at any particular age level but rather during a quite definite period beyond the age when delinquent impulses first express themselves in antisocial acts. In both instances, it appears that if the offenders are to reform at all before the wasting effects of age have intervened, their improvement in conduct occurs after they have "gotten delinquency out of their systems," as it were, that is, after the antisocial impulses have run their course; and this process seems to take about the same length of time regardless of whether delinquent conduct first occurs in childhood or during adolescence.

Obviously, many questions are raised by these findings, answers to which the materials obtainable for this research cannot give. Why is it, for example, that one group of offenders begin their criminal careers later than others? Do differences in ethnic origins, in intelligence, in temperament account for this? [13] Or may the

explanation be found in other differences? Much exploration would be necessary to arrive at the answers. But it seems evident from even the brief sampling reflected in footnote 13 that there are significant differences between the two groups. It may well be that such differences in make-up account for the variation in average age at which these two groups first embarked upon delinquent careers. The important points are, however, that with these differences in the characteristics of the two groups, their behavior, once they have embarked on delinquency, follows a pattern largely determined by the underlying process of maturation,[14] and that this pattern is uniform, being somehow related to the span of time intervening between the average age of offenders at the origin of their delinquency and the passage of a certain number of years thereafter. Two series of offenders, quite different in make-up and background and significantly different in the fact that one began to be delinquent (on the average) five years before the other, have been shown to resemble each other strikingly in conduct, *not at similar ages, but rather at a similar distance removed from the time they began to be delinquent.* This would seem to indicate that what may be called, after Quételet,[15] the propensity to crim-

---

[13] A comparison of the nativity of the parents of the two groups indicated that twice the proportion of parents of the Reformatory group as of the Juvenile Court group were native born (27.2 per cent and 13.2 per cent). (Derived from 500 *Criminal Careers*, p. 118, and *One Thousand Juvenile Delinquents*, p. 303, Table 2.)

Further, a comparison of the intelligence of the two groups shows a higher proportion of persons of normal intelligence among the Juvenile Court group (41.6 per cent against 33 per cent) and a lower proportion of definitely feeble-minded (13.1 per cent against 20.6 per cent). (Derived from *One Thousand Juvenile Delinquents*, p. 102, and *500 Criminal Careers*, p. 156.)

A comparison of the mental condition of the two groups as ascertained in their early years shows the presence of mental disease or personality distortions

of one sort or another among a lower proportion of the Juvenile Court group than among the Reformatory graduates (55.7 per cent and 72.7 per cent). (Derived from *One Thousand Juvenile Delinquents*, p. 310, Table 37, and *Later Criminal Careers*, p. 276, Table 70.)

[14] To avoid clumsiness of phraseology, we have not used the expressions "maturation–disintegration" or "maturation–settling down." Such expressions, however, more accurately express the processes involved; for it is not only the achievement of a certain degree of physical-intellectual-emotional maturity and integration that leads to abandonment of criminality or change to less aggressive and less serious forms of misbehavior on the part of former offenders, but the gradual loss of such qualities as initiative, recklessness, daring, and physical health. This matter is discussed in Chapter XXII.

[15] M. A. Quételet, *A Treatise on Man and the Development of His Faculties*, translated from the French, 1842, p. 82. "Supposing men to be placed in similar circumstances, I call the greater or less probability of committing crime, the propensity to crime. . . . I have said that the circumstances in which men are placed ought to be similar, that is to say, equally favourable, both in the existence of objects likely to excite the propensity and in the facility of committing the crime. It is not enough that a man may merely have the intention to do evil, he

inality" has a more or less definite life span regardless of the age at which delinquent behavior actually begins. Of course, it may be that as the two groups approach old age they will tend more and more to resemble each other in behavior, not at the same distance from the delinquent starting point, but rather at the same chronological age levels. But certainly in the segment of the life cycle so far analyzed, it seems clear that it is not arrival at a certain age that determines the nature of delinquency, but rather arrival at a certain distance from the age at which delinquency began.

Under such a theory, the age (on the average) at which delinquency begins is significant as fixing the point at which the symptoms of abnormal functioning of the maturation process first manifest themselves in the form of delinquent conduct of a kind serious and consistent enough to be called to the attention of the authorities. Given a sufficient period of time, plus an equipment not unfavorable, it may be expected that a significant proportion of such offenders will abandon their criminality either because they have achieved sufficient integration to seek more legitimate goals for their

desires or to inhibit or sublimate their antisocial impulses or because they have passed the stage in which they had the energy and daring to commit crimes. Some who never achieve a sufficient degree of maturation until they have finally lapsed into those forms of antisocial behavior which require less and less energy, planfulness, and daring, such as drunkenness and vagrancy, will not abandon a life of crime. But those who do reform will do so after an adequate maturation time has elapsed since the first signs of delinquency, and this regardless of whether they were first delinquent at around nine years of age (on the average) or around fifteen.[16] We shall discuss this concept further in Chapter XXII [of *Juvenile Delinquents Grown Up*].

---

must also have the opportunity and the means. Thus the propensity to crime may be the same in France as in England, without, on that account, the *morality* of the nations being the same."

[16] The special class of offenders who do not really commit their first crimes until they are men of twenty-five or more are unrepresented in the two series under discussion; and they probably represent quite a different type of person and different problems of criminogenesis and reform.

Prevention
of Delinquency

Prevention
of Delinquency

SECTION I
EARLY RECOGNITION OF POTENTIAL DELINQUENTS

Chapter 32
Prediction of Delinquency

IT CANNOT BE DENIED that in any fundamental program to prevent juvenile delinquency it is necessary to identify and reach *potential* delinquents as early as possible. In this connection it might be pointed out that among the delinquents involved in *Unraveling Juvenile Delinquency* [1] various forms of school misbehavior first occurred at an average age of 9.5 years (a third of the group having been but eight years old or less when first indulging in school misconduct). By contrast, evidences of classroom misbehavior showed up as early as 9.5 years of age in less than a tenth of the very few nondelinquents who had misbehaved in school, their average age at first classroom misconduct having been 12.5 years.

When, to this early age of school misbehavior is added the early age of first delinquent behavior outside the school (almost half the delinquents were under eight years old at their first delinquencies and nine-tenths were under eleven), it becomes crystal-clear that the signals of probable persistent delinquency flash their warnings before puberty. Since gang formation comes much later, whatever the role of gang membership may be in consolidating the tendency to misbehave, it cannot be said that such group influence accounts for the *origins* of delinquent behavior.

This means that the elementary schools are in a strategic position to discover *potential* persistent delinquents before the trends of maladapted behavior become too fixed. The relationship of this task to the work of the juvenile court is brought out by one of the more significant findings in *One Thousand Juvenile Delinquents*: namely, that where a boy was brought to the court and examined by the clinic immediately or shortly after the onset of his misbehavior, the curbing of his antisocial tendencies was more likely to be accomplished than where the boy's misconduct was not dealt with until it had long endured.[2]

Character prophylaxis — the testing of children early and periodically to discover beginnings of malformations of emotional development and habit formation at a stage when the twig can still be bent — is as necessary as are early and periodic medical or dental examinations. In other words, a crying need is a *preventive medicine of personality and character*. Youngsters who, unaided, face a career of storm and stress should be discovered as early as possible and given adequate therapy long before the law's label of juvenile delinquency is affixed to them or before they develop serious mental illnesses. In an enlightened educational system the school might function as the litmus paper of personality and character maladaptation.

However, when a child first begins to display signs of maladaptation, it is very

---

[1] S. and E. T. Glueck, New York, The Commonwealth Fund, 1950.
[2] S. and E. T. Glueck, Cambridge University Press, 1934, 180–181.

difficult to say whether these are true danger signals of persistent delinquency in the offing or merely transient evidences of the youngster's trying of his wings. Bits of aberrant behavior at the age of five or six are not necessarily prognostic of future persistent delinquency. It therefore becomes of prime importance to devise a method of distinguishing, very early in life, those children who, unaided, are probably headed for delinquent careers, in order that therapeutic intervention may be timely and effective.

Such a device has been developed in three prediction tables presented in *Unraveling Juvenile Delinquency*.

When first published, these prediction tables were subjected to criticism by certain reviewers on the ground that while, in the general population, the proportions of delinquents to non-delinquents are supposedly only 5, 10, or 15 to 100, the Glueck tables are constructed on the basis of a 50–50 proportion, that is, of equal numbers of delinquents and non-delinquents.[3] These critics have re-computed the Glueck tables to take account of the presumed influence on the results of the differences in the proportions of delinquents and non-delinquents in the general community as compared to the samples in the Glueck research. For example, Reiss has presented a table that he recomputed according to his views and through which he found the original Glueck table to show very little predictive capacity when his adjustments were made.[4]

In the Editor's opinion, Reiss and the other critics of the Glueck tables are in error both theoretically and practically. They are wrong theoretically because, by saying that the Glueck tables should have been adjusted as indicated, they are confusing differences in the size of two statistical "universes" with differences in the size of the *samples* drawn from those two universes for comparison. By so doing, they beg the very question at issue, which is: Will the predictive factors embodied in the Glueck tables forecast delinquency and non-delinquency with a high degree of accuracy irrespective of other influences, including the difference in the size of the universes from which their samples were drawn, or will such other influences be found, *by actual experience*, to invalidate the tables when these are subjected to the practical test of application to new samples of cases? To have made the "adjustment" suggested by Reiss and similar critics would have spoiled the experiment for validation purposes; for it would have made it impossible to say whether the outcomes in subsequent validation tests were due essentially to the proportion of delinquents to non-delinquents assumed in the adjustment or to the predictive efficacy of the factors involved.

The theoretical error involved in the reasoning of these critics can be simply illustrated:

Suppose a public health official were testing the bacterial and chemical content of two samples of water drawn from two lakes, and suppose that Lake No. 1 were only a tenth the size of Lake No. 2. Now assume he found that in Lake No. 1 the sample drawn shows the water to be non-drinkable, but in Lake No. 2 it is safely drinkable, while a mixture of the two is potable or not depending on the proportion of water from each of the samples mixed together. Would the fact that one lake is much smaller than the other make any serious difference in his ability to predict whether subsequent samples of water drawn from each of these lakes, or various combinations thereof, would be drinkable or not? Only if each of the original *samples* were clearly

---

[3] See A. Reiss, "Unraveling Juvenile Delinquency, II: An Appraisal of the Research Methods," 57 *Am. J. of Sociology* (1951), 115–120.

[4] "It can be seen in Table 2 that, so far as prediction of delinquency or non-delinquency is concerned, the table has a low predictive efficiency when the rate of delinquency is estimated at 10 per cent. For example, in the score group 250–99 the chances of delinquency were 63.5 in the Gluecks' table, while the chances are only 16.2 per hundred in the table which assumes a rate of 10 per cent habitual delinquency." *Ibid.*, 119.

and markedly not representative of the respective lakes from which they were drawn.

In *Unraveling Juvenile Delinquency* the Gluecks made clear the nature and composition of the samples of 500 persistent delinquents and 500 non-delinquents under comparison. They first matched the cases in pairs — each delinquent with his opposite number, the non-delinquent — in respect to age, general intelligence (I.Q.), ethnical-racial derivation (an Irish delinquent with an Irish non-delinquent, an Italian delinquent with an Italian representative of the control group, etc.) as well as to residence in economically and culturally underprivileged areas of Greater Boston. They then compared the two groups in respect to the incidence of the sub-categories of over 400 factors — anthropologic, neurologic, psychiatric, characterial (Rorschach Test), psychologic (constituents of global intelligence, as determined by the Wechler-Bellevue Test) and sociocultural (home, school, neighborhood conditions). They used, in the three prediction tables they developed, five factors derived from each of the psychiatric, Rorschach and social (family relations) areas in which the differences in incidence between the delinquents and controls had been found to be very marked.

Nobody has yet attempted to test the psychiatric and Rorschach tables; but the Glueck Social Prediction Table has been tried out on several different samples of cases by various workers.

This leads to the second point made at the outset — that the critics of the Glueck tables are in error pragmatically as well as theoretically; for, *uniformly and without exception,* irrespective of the nature of the samples involved — whether in various parts of the United States, in Japan, or in France — the Social Prediction Table has shown a very high degree of effectiveness in prediction.[5] Moreover, the percentage distributions between delinquents and non-delinquents which have actually emerged when this table was applied by various investigators, at different places and times and to a wide variety of samples of cases other than the ones on which it was constructed, do not follow the percentages embraced in the critics' suggested adjustment of the Glueck table, but do essentially conform to the percentages published in the original table in *Unraveling Juvenile Delinquency.*[6]

The evidence accumulated until recently is set forth in this chapter in the article by Dr. Eleanor T. Glueck. The various validations discussed in that article are "retrospective," that is, they check on the incidence of the predictive sub-categories of the five factors involved in the case of children already delinquent. This should make little difference, provided the validations have been properly made — as they most assuredly have been. However, the New York City Youth Board has recently published an interim report[7] which gives strong indication that the Glueck Social Prediction Table in fact does *prospectively* distinguish, from among first-grade school children, which ones will later become delinquent and which will remain non-delinquent.

It should be pointed out, further, that these strikingly effective outcomes of the validation experiments occurred in such a variety of places and times that it can be reasonably assumed that the proportions of delinquents to non-delinquents varied. In New York, for example, the teachers in the public schools involved in the validation

---

[5] Reiss opines that "unless this [50%] is the actual rate in a similar population for which predictions are made, the tables will yield very poor prediction." *Ibid.,* 118. In the light of experience, Reiss's confident prediction as to the poor predictability of the Glueck tables turns out to be a far worse prediction than the tables have been demonstrated to be able to make.

[6] Incidentally, the validation studies also dispose of the guesses of Reiss and others about the inability to predict delinquent behavior at the early age of six and about the prime etiologic importance of the gang (some 90 per cent of the boys in *Unraveling* were clearly delinquent at 10 years of age or less, 48.4 per cent at 7 or less — long before the "gang age.").

[7] *An Experiment in the Validation of the Glueck Prediction Scale,* Progress Report from November, 1952, to December, 1956, New York City Youth Board, Research Department, July, 1957. Relevant parts of this report are set forth on pp. 1031–1050 *infra.*

experiment claimed that about a third of the children were delinquent — a fact borne out essentially by the validation check-up — instead of the 10:90 proportion adopted by Reiss as the basis for his "adjustment" of the prediction tables. Yet, as indicated, the outcomes in some 90 per cent of the new cases to which the Social Prediction Table was applied were essentially such as the table had predicted. Professor Edwin B. Wilson, the eminent biostatistician was, in this respect, wiser than the critics; for, recognizing the possible influence of the proportion of delinquents to non-delinquents on the prediction tables, he nevertheless took no dogmatic stand. He said [8]:

> ... The problem of prediction, therefore, becomes necessarily statistical, to be stated in terms of probabilities or even in terms of ranges of probability. As such, it is a group affair. In any particular instance, the phenomenon will or will not occur and in that particular instance great misfortune or injustice may arise from the application of the appropriate probability to the disposal of the case.
>
> That the Gluecks realize all these difficulties is manifest throughout their writings; but they have not been deterred thereby from setting up prediction tables. And in respect to a table in an earlier book, namely, one which predicted behavior of civilian delinquents in the armed forces, they had a noteworthy success *a posteriori* in showing that of 200 military offenders who had been civilian offenders about 85 per cent would have been so predicted to be. The proof of this pudding came in the eating.
>
> In their present work, after a long and careful analysis of a large number of physical, psychological and social characters attributable to 500 delinquents and to an equal number of controls (non-delinquents matched pairwise with the delinquents in respect to age, ethnic origin, intelligence and type of area of residence), the Gluecks set up a series of proposed prediction tables (c. 20) based on attributes common among delinquents and uncommon among the controls, or vice versa. I do not see how they could have done better, but the proof of the pudding can come only with its eating.
>
> There is one respect in which this pudding seems to me different from that already eaten with such satisfaction. The table involving military offenses by those who were civilian delinquents was based on the records of a considerable set of such delinquents of whom half had committed military offenses and half had not. Thus, when the resulting prediction table was applied to the new series of 200 military offenders who had been civilian offenders, what was proved was that the new series behaved like the series from which the table was constructed. This was decidedly worth while as showing that the table was more than a statistical description of the series on which it was based — that it was competent of some generalization — that probably it would be valuable for future inductions.
>
> The comparable use of the prediction tables of Chapter 20 would be to a new series of delinquents and controls similarly set up — and that would be a worthwhile investigation to make. Science advances by broadening the base upon which empirical uniformities are established; indeed, it is only by this broadening that we come to know that the descriptions of our sample are uniformities. This is not a new pudding, only just another one, in respect to such a usage, and I should expect it would prove quite satisfactory to eat.

The following findings of the New York City Youth Board's experiment with the Glueck Social Prediction Table are of basic interest:

(a) Including *serious school problems* in the "observed delinquency group," of the 220 cases thus far predicted, 88.9 per cent turned out as predicted.

(b) Of the 53 cases of white boys thus far predicted, 90 per cent are reacting as predicted.

---

[8] From "Prediction" by Edwin Bidwell Wilson, in "A Symposium on *Unraveling Juvenile Delinquency*," 64 *Harvard Law Review* (1951), 1040–1041. (Footnote omitted.) Copyright 1951 by the *Harvard Law Review* Association. Used by permission of the author and the publisher.

(c) Of the 130 Negro children thus far predicted, 85 per cent are reacting as predicted.

(d) Of the 37 Puerto Rican children thus far predicted, 91 per cent have turned out as predicted.

It should be pointed out in this connection that the Glueck table was constructed largely on the basis of English-American, Irish and Italian boys, including no Negroes and Puerto Ricans.[9]

The age-range of the children at the time their future behavior was predicted by the New York City Youth Board on the basis of the five factors involved (discipline of boy by father, supervision of boy by mother, affection of father for boy, affection of mother for boy, family cohesiveness) was 5½ to 6½ years. By the time of the interim follow-up report these children had become 8½ to 9½ years of age; but, since the Glueck tables were built on data regarding children of an average age of 12½, the investigation still has several years to run. However, it would be surprising indeed if it were later found that the present clear indications are not correctly casting their shadows before them.

It would seem that the evidence of the numerous follow-up investigations on a wide variety of samples constitutes a satisfactory refutation of the views of the critics of the table [10] and, incidentally, of those other critics who have engaged in the facile game of criticizing the "typicality" of the sample without indicating in exactly which relevant respects the sample is atypical. If the factors which have been demonstrated to be so highly predictive on such a variety of samples examined by various investigators in different places were not in fact directly or indirectly strongly criminogenic they never would have had the prognostic potency they have in fact been shown to possess.

Needless to add, the prediction tables are designed to be servants, not masters; they are intended to aid the clinician, social worker and police officer to exercise discretion more meaningfully than would otherwise be possible, by bringing to bear, on decisions respecting the individual case, the organized results of prior experience with numerous other cases, thereby reducing a tendency to act impressionistically or on the basis of "hunch."

The materials in this chapter include the prediction tables presented in *Unraveling Juvenile Delinquency* and a summary of the results of various validations of the Social Prediction Table.

---

[9] Only 2 per cent of the boys in the Glueck sample were Jewish, compared to 43.4 per cent of the boys in the New York City Youth Board's validation experiment.

[10] It has been found that the probable effectiveness of the three tables from *Unraveling Juvenile Delinquency* (psychiatric, Rorschach and social) is quite similar, as determined by a comparison of the three tables individually and when used in conjunction with each other. "It does not appear that the increment in efficiency (when combinations of factors involving all three tables are used) is great enough to warrant a recommendation that Rorschach tests and psychiatric skills be used in 'screening' or 'spotting' potential delinquents." S. and E. T. Glueck, "Early Detection of Future Delinquents," 47 *J. Crim. L., Criminology and Police Science* (1956), 174–182.

171

Prediction of Delinquency *

Sheldon and Eleanor T. Glueck

Having established the resemblances of and differences between the delinquents and non-delinquents in each area of the investigation, we now turn our attention to the utilization of some of the marked differences for the purpose of constructing predictive instrumentalities on the basis of which it should be possible to differentiate between potential juvenile offenders and non-offenders very early in life, preferably at school entrance.

The selection of potential delinquents at the time of school entrance or soon thereafter would make possible the application of treatment measures that would be truly crime preventive. To wait for the certain manifestations of delinquency before applying therapy is to close the barn door after the horse has been stolen. Reliance on symptomatic behavior to select pre-delinquents is also a dubious procedure.

Alexander and Staub point out: "The human being enters the world as a criminal, i.e., socially not adjusted. During the first years of his life, the human individual preserves his criminality to the fullest degree. His actual social adjustment begins . . . during the so-called latency period. . . . This period begins between the ages of four and six, and ends at puberty. It is at this period that the development of the criminal begins to differentiate itself from that of the normal. The future normal individual succeeds (mostly in the latency period) in partly repressing his genuine criminal instinctual drives, and thus cuts them out of motor expression, and partly in transforming them into socially acceptable striving; the future criminal more or less fails in carrying out this adjustment." [1]

If stealing, for example, marks the beginning

* Reprinted by permission of the publishers and The Commonwealth Fund from *Unraveling Juvenile Delinquency*, Sheldon and Eleanor T. Glueck, Cambridge, Mass.: Harvard University Press, Copyright, 1950, by The Commonwealth Fund. Pages 257–271.

of a habitual tendency to this form of antisocial behavior, it must indeed be taken seriously. If, however, it is soon discarded as the child passes safely through the latency period, it has very little, if any, significance. As for other danger signals of delinquent behavior such as truancy, destructive mischief, stubbornness, running away, stealing rides, temper tantrums, disobedience, sex play, stealing junk, gambling, using vile language, begging, staying out late at night, sneaking admissions, and lying, we know that these too characterize some non-delinquent children prior to puberty. A fourth of the 500 non-delinquents in this research showed danger signals that might easily have been misinterpreted: 22.8 per cent smoked at a very early age; 23.8 per cent hopped trucks; 24.5 per cent stole once or twice from five-and-ten-cent stores; 9 per cent gambled; 10 per cent sneaked into movies; 10.6 per cent truanted from school occasionally; 9.6 per cent were stubborn; 6.8 per cent kept late hours; 4.6 per cent used vile language; and so on. Therefore, to depend on these early evidences of what on the surface resembles antisocial behavior may lead to the labeling of some children as delinquents who are not really such, and, on the other hand, to the possible neglect of other children who are potentially persistent offenders; and to wait until delinquent conduct has come to the official attention of the formal judicial and peno-correctional agencies of a community is to make far more difficult, if not almost impossible, the task of curbing the further development of a delinquent career.

The 500 delinquents were found, in retrospect, to have been a little over eight years of age on the average when the first signs of their maladaptive behavior either in or out of school became evident (Table IV-1). Actually, about half of them were under eight at the first clear signs of misbehavior, while all but 12.4 per cent were under eleven. But they had already reached the average age of twelve and a half by the time of their first court appearance, were almost thirteen when first placed on probation, and nearly fourteen when first committed to a correctional institution. The earliest clear signs of maladaptive behavior in school manifested themselves among 478 delinquents at nine and a half years, and at twelve and a half years among the 86 non-delinquents who showed behavioral difficulty in school. At the time the former were in the fourth grade, on the average, and the latter, in the seventh grade (Tables XII-23 and XII-24); in fact, a third of the delinquents had shown signs of delinquency in the first and second grades. The first indications of school maladjustment took the form of truancy among three-fourths of the 478 delinquents and half of the 86 non-delinquents (Table XII-25).

Although misconduct either prior to or after school entrance may cause real concern to parents and teachers, their recognition of true danger signals of delinquency for the purpose of applying preventive and early corrective measures is not to be expected; and it certainly cannot be determined in advance of the onset of external signs of maladjustment whether a particular child is a potential delinquent or merely evidencing emotional growing pains. Even an experienced clinician generally cannot ascertain until the beginning of puberty whether certain kinds of aberrant behavior mark the beginning of a delinquent career.

It therefore becomes of crucial importance to develop prognostic instrumentalities that can be applied to children at the point of school entrance, without waiting for the actual appearance of serious and persistent antisociality. (There are undoubtedly persons who will be skeptical about the possibility of predicting behavior as early as six years. To them we point out that Dr. Arnold Gesell, former Director of the Clinic of Child Development at Yale University, has developed a method of rating infants as "highly favorable, favorable, or unfavorable risks" for adoption, by the use of psychological tests which he has especially devised for this purpose.) [2] With such an aid to the clinician and teacher, there is a greater likelihood that the development of delinquency can be curbed than is possible under the present haphazard system. The success of such a preventive endeavor would naturally be dependent upon the expert clinical insights and resources available in school and community for the treatment of children found to be potential offenders.[3] The school has the function not only of teaching the "three R's" but of discovering and remedying those distortions of personality that are brought to the surface by the child's first attempts to adjust to the codes and authority imposed by adults outside the home. This stage in the child's contact with the adult world affords the acid test of his social adaptability; and if fundamental psychiatric, psychologic, educa-

tional, and social measures are not taken at this stage, subsequent remedial action becomes proportionately more difficult.[4]

SELECTION OF FEASIBLE PREDICTIVE DEVICES

In reviewing the findings of this research, we decided not to use as a basis for predictive instrumentalities the factors of differentiation emerging from the somatic data (physique and health) or from the psychological tests.

As regards physique, we are dealing with a discipline as yet highly controversial because physical anthropologists have not yet answered a major question, namely, whether or not the somatotype remains constant and, if it does, whether, in the formative years of growth around the age of six or seven, when children normally enter school, the physique type is as yet reliably distinguishable. For this reason we did not utilize the differential findings in the comparison of the physique of the delinquents and non-delinquents for predictive purposes. As for the health of the delinquents and non-delinquents, the reader will recall that there are no very marked differences between the two groups. Therefore, or at least until more deep-probing studies are made which may reveal subtler and greater health differences than have come to light in this inquiry, it is not feasible to construct a predictive instrumentality based on health data.

The possibility of a predictive device to be applied at school entrance derived from the differential findings of the Wechsler-Bellevue and Stanford Achievement tests was also ruled out, because Dr. Wechsler had suggested to us "that the scale not be used with children under ten years and, indeed, to avoid its application, I have omitted giving IQ tables for chronological ages below this year." Moreover, because the boys were matched originally on total intelligence quotient, there is necessarily not as much difference between the delinquents and non-delinquents in the components of their intelligence as in those areas of comparison in which no such controls were applied. For this reason alone, a predictive device from the psychological data of this study could not possibly be as sound an instrumentality as that stemming from other aspects of the research.

From the other data — the social background of the boys, the Rorschach Test, and the psychiatric findings — it seemed entirely feasible to construct predictive tables that would mark-edly differentiate between potential delinquents and potential non-delinquents, provided that factors were selected from among those that were already in effect at school entrance. Clearly some factors do not become operative until the boys are older.

METHOD OF CONSTRUCTING A PREDICTION TABLE

Readers familiar with the prediction tables developed in connection with our other re-searches will recall that each is constructed on the basis of five differentiating factors. Experi-ence has shown that such a number is adequate for prediction purposes. In our prior studies such factors distinguish between reformed of-fenders and recidivists, and between offenders who respond well to certain specific forms of peno-correctional treatment and those who do not. In the present investigation the factors serve to differentiate between boys who are po-tential delinquents and those who are not.

Although in several earlier publications we have described our method of constructing a prediction table,[5] it may be well to review the technique for readers who are unfamiliar with it.

As already indicated, the particular tables about to be presented were derived from among those factors that clearly differentiate the de-linquents and non-delinquents in this research. Since we are interested primarily in prediction tables on the basis of which it would be possible to identify potential delinquents upon or soon after school entrance, selection of the factors had, as already indicated, first to be narrowed to those already operable in the lives and make-up of the boys prior to school entrance. From among all such possibly applicable factors, those in which the greatest difference existed between the delinquents and non-delinquents had then to be determined. Next, we had to consider whether or not these factors were mu-tually exclusive and, if possible, to select those that were more likely to be independent of one another. To find five highly differentiating and mutually exclusive factors was not always pos-sible. However, we have learned from experi-ence that even if there is some overlapping of the factors, the value of the resulting instru-mentality for predictive purposes is not im-paired.

Another consideration in selecting the factors is related to the practical matter of the ease or difficulty of gathering the data by those who would be charged with the task. This consid-eration, however, can be applied only if there is a sufficient choice among the factors; and it did not apply, for example, to the selection of traits for a prediction table derived from the Rorschach Test, because to determine any one of them requires the highly specialized skills of a person who has been well trained in the in-terpretation of the test.

In the light of the above considerations, we selected five highly differentiative factors for the construction of each prediction table. In respect to each of these five significant factors of a particular table, we then set down the per-centages of sub-class incidence of delinquency. For example, among the five factors selected for the construction of the table from among the factors of social background of the boys, is the factor, discipline of boy by father (see Table XX-1). Distribution of all the cases (non-de-linquent as well as delinquent) shows that of the boys whose discipline by the father was *lax*, 59.8 per cent were in the delinquent group; of those who had the benefit of *firm but kindly* disci-pline, only 9.3 per cent were delinquents. Ex-amination of the two sub-categories, *overstrict* and *erratic* shows them to be so close in per-centage distribution that for purposes of scoring the individual cases the two can be combined, with the result that of all the boys whose pa-ternal discipline can be described as *overstrict* or *erratic*, 71.8 per cent were among the delin-quent group. The percentage of delinquents in each sub-category of the factor, discipline of boy by father, thus constitutes the weighted failure score.

The next step was to determine what were the highest and the lowest failure scores which it was possible for a boy to obtain on the basis of a summation of the individual weighted fail-ure scores. By adding all the lowest percentages of the sub-categories of the five factors, we ob-tained the lowest possible total failure score; by summating the highest percentages, we derived the highest possible total failure score. Score classes in narrow intervals between these limits were next established. Each of the boys, de-linquents and non-delinquents, was then scored on the five factors and placed in his appropriate score class. The resulting numbers of delinquents and of non-delinquents falling into each score class were then translated into percentages, this yielding the chances per hundred of potential delinquency and potential non-delinquency.

The distribution of such percentages was then examined in order to determine what combinations of the detailed failure score classes would provide the sharpest differentiating predictive instrumentality between the delinquents and non-delinquents, and the detailed failure score classes were combined accordingly.

PREDICTION TABLE CONSTRUCTED FROM FACTORS OF SOCIAL BACKGROUND

A review of the factors of differentiation emerging from the family and personal history of the delinquents and non-delinquents made it clear that those that were probably operable in their lives prior to school entrance were largely in the area of interpersonal relations in the family group, specifically those dealing with the relationship between the boy and his parents. For this reason, for example, we excluded from consideration the factor, gang membership, because few boys as young as six are already members of gangs; and the factor, broken home, which, though differentiating sharply between the delinquent and non-delinquent group somewhat later in their lives, was, at the point of school entrance, as yet an incompleted factor. (The reader is reminded that the boys ranged in age from eleven to seventeen when selected for study.)

The following are the five factors (with their sub-categories and failure scores) that we finally selected for inclusion in a prediction table

Table **XX—1** Discipline of Boy by Father

DISCIPLINE	DELINQUENTS		NON-DELINQUENTS	
Sub-category	Number	Per Cent *	Number	Per Cent
Lax	122	59.8	82	40.2
Overstrict	120	75.0	40	25.0
Erratic	191	69.9	82	30.1
Firm but kindly	26	9.3	255	90.7

* Weighted failure score.

Table **XX—2** Detailed Prediction Table from Five Factors of Social Background

WEIGHTED FAILURE SCORE CLASS	NUMBER OF DELINQUENTS	CHANCES OF DELINQUENCY (PER HUNDRED)	NUMBER OF NON-DELINQUENTS	CHANCES OF NON-DELINQUENCY (PER HUNDRED)
Under 150	5	2.9	167	97.1
150–199	19	15.7	102	84.3
200–249	40	37.0	68	63.0
250–299	122	63.5	70	36.5
300–349	141	86.0	23	14.0
350–399	73	90.1	8	9.9
400 and over	51	98.1	1	1.9
TOTAL	451		439	

constructed from the social background of the boys:

SOCIAL FACTORS	WEIGHTED FAILURE SCORE
1. Discipline of Boy by Father [6]	
Overstrict or erratic	72.5
Lax	59.8
Firm but kindly	9.3
2. Supervision of Boy by Mother [7]	
Unsuitable	83.2
Fair	57.5
Suitable	9.9
3. Affection of Father for Boy [8]	
Indifferent or hostile	75.9
Warm (including over-protective)	33.8
4. Affection of Mother for Boy [9]	
Indifferent or hostile	86.2
Warm (including over-protective)	43.1
5. Cohesiveness of Family [10]	
Unintegrated	96.9
Some elements of cohesion	61.3
Cohesive	20.6

Summation of the lowest possible score and the highest possible score that might be obtained in any one case on all five factors resulted in a failure-score range of 116.7 — 414, which was then divided into seven class intervals. By assigning to each delinquent and non-delinquent, concerning whom information was available on all five factors, his score on each, summating the scores, and distributing the cases into the appropriate score classes, we arrived at the detailed prediction table (Table XX-2) above, after translating the number of cases in each sub-class into a per cent of the total number in each score class. These then became the chances out of a hundred of potential delinquency and non-delinquency.

Inspection of Table XX-2 suggested that a reduction of the seven failure-score classes into four would provide a suitable predictive instrumentality, as shown in Table XX-3.

Further contraction into a three-class table appeared feasible (Table XX-4).

An even further contraction of the score classes into two was made (Table XX-5). Since the chances of delinquency of those falling into the mid-group, namely, the failure score class, 250 — 299, are well over fifty in a hundred, cases scoring within this range might be combined with those scoring in the range 300-and-

Table **XX–3**   Four-Class Prediction Table from Five Factors of Social Background

WEIGHTED FAILURE SCORE CLASS	CHANCES OF DELINQUENCY (PER HUNDRED)	CHANCES OF NON-DELINQUENCY (PER HUNDRED)
Under 200	8.2	91.8
200–249	37.0	63.0
250–299	63.5	36.5
300 and over	89.2	10.8

over. The resulting prediction table differentiates very sharply the likelihood of potential delinquency between those scoring under 250 and those scoring 250 and above. Those with a score under 250 have only sixteen chances out of a hundred (one and a half chances in ten) of becoming delinquent, while those scoring 250 and over have 79.1 chances in a hundred (eight in ten) of becoming delinquent.

In applying the prediction table derived from the social background of the boys, some scorers may for various reasons prefer to use the four or the three rather than the two score-class table.

It should be pointed out that a boy's discriminative total score is predictive regardless of its separate ingredients. For example, Boy A's total failure score of 250 or over may comprise the following sub-categories of the five social factors: discipline of boy by father: *firm but kindly* (9.3); supervision of boy by mother: *unsuitable* (83.2); affection of father for boy: *warm* (33.8); affection of mother for boy: *in-*

Table **XX–4**   Three-Class Prediction Table from Five Factors of Social Background

WEIGHTED FAILURE SCORE CLASS	CHANCES OF DELINQUENCY (PER HUNDRED)	CHANCES OF NON-DELINQUENCY (PER HUNDRED)
Under 250	16.0	84.0
250–299	63.5	36.5
300 and over	89.2	10.8

Table **XX—5** Two-Class Prediction Table from Five Factors of Social Background

WEIGHTED FAILURE SCORE CLASS	CHANCES OF DELINQUENCY (PER HUNDRED)	CHANCES OF NON-DELINQUENCY (PER HUNDRED)
Under 250	16.0	84.0
250 and over ..	79.1	20.9

different or hostile (86.2); and cohesiveness of family: *unintegrated* (96.9). This results in a total failure score of 309.4. Among these scores are two factors that might have placed the boy among the potential non-delinquents, namely, the firm but kindly discipline of the boy by his father and the warm affectional relationship of the father toward the boy. However, the over-all score places him among the potential delinquents. Boy B's total failure score of under 250 (which means that he is not a potential delinquent) may, on the other hand, contain certain unfavorable factors, for example, discipline of boy by father: *overstrict* (71.8); but if in regard to the remaining four factors he falls into the more favorable categories, the chances of his becoming a persistent delinquent are well below the crucial level.

PREDICTION TABLE CONSTRUCTED FROM CHARACTER TRAITS DETERMINED IN THE RORSCHACH TEST

As regards the construction of a prediction table on the basis of character traits revealed by the Rorschach Test, any five sharply differentiating factors might be used. Since it is generally assumed that character structure is on the whole quite well solidified by the sixth year, there seems to be no reason why it would not be possible to determine the traits at this early age. Dr. Schachtel points out that "Rorschach Tests have been given from the age of two years upward. They certainly can be given at six years. However, in my not-very-wide experience with Rorschach Tests of preschool children I have found that it is possible in only certain cases to get a clear view of character structure in children so young; in others it is not possible. The more intelligent and cooperative the child is, the more one will be able to see, as a rule. One can quite often see marked disturbances at this early age, but not as often can one get a clear view of character structure. The possibility of seeing something about character structure is greater when other methods of observation are used in addition to the Rorschach. I have found the Mosaic Test useful and I know that Dr. Lois Murphy's Miniature Life Toy technique is often very illuminating." Few Rorschach experts have explored the application of the test to young children. Dr. Anna Har-

Table **XX—6** Detailed Prediction Table from Five Character Traits of Rorschach Test

WEIGHTED FAILURE SCORE CLASS	NUMBER OF DELINQUENTS	CHANCES OF DELINQUENCY (PER HUNDRED)	NUMBER OF NON-DELINQUENTS	CHANCES OF NON-DELINQUENCY (PER HUNDRED)
Under 205	21	14.7	122	85.3
205–229	51	37.8	84	62.2
230–254	28	41.2	40	58.8
255–279	32	64.0	18	36.0
280–304	36	80.0	9	20.0
305–329	32	97.0	1	3.0
330–354	31	86.1	5	13.9
355–379	22	91.7	2	8.3
380 and over	2	100.0	0	0.0
TOTAL	255		281	

toch Schachtel, associated with this study from 1939 to her death in 1944, was one of those most successful in such work.

Obviously much experimentation has to be carried out in the use of the Rorschach Test for this specific purpose. In addition to the problem of modifying the Rorschach Test to fit various age levels (for example, pre-latency period, latency period, early puberty, puberty, adolescence, or other divisions which will be disclosed by experimentation), there is the practical problem of furnishing adequately trained administrators and interpreters of the Rorschach Test. Our present concern is merely to provide such a possible predictive instrumentality as a basis for further exploration.

The five selected factors, with their sub-categories and weighted failure scores, are as follows:

RORSCHACH CHARACTER TRAITS [11]	WEIGHTED FAILURE SCORE
1. Social Assertion [12]	
Marked	75.9
Slight or suggestive	63.8
Absent	39.7
2. Defiance [13]	
Marked	91.0
Slight or suggestive	76.7
Absent	34.9
3. Suspicion [14]	
Marked	67.3
Slight or suggestive	47.3
Absent	37.5
4. Destructiveness [15]	
Marked	77.7
Slight or suggestive	69.9
Absent	35.7
5. Emotional Lability [16]	
Marked	75.2
Slight or suggestive	65.0
Absent	40.0

The failure-score range was found to be 187.8–387.1. A distribution of the delinquents and non-delinquents, about whom information was available on all five factors, into nine detailed score classes resulted in Table XX-6.

Tables XX-7, XX-8, and XX-9 present contractions of the nine failure-score classes into four, three, and two score classes, respectively.

Here again, the choice of using a four, three, or two score-class table would depend entirely on the preference of those charged with carrying out the scoring. It would seem to us that

Table **XX–7**   *Four-Class Prediction Table from Five Character Traits of Rorschach Test*

WEIGHTED FAILURE SCORE CLASS	CHANCES OF DELINQUENCY (PER HUNDRED)	CHANCES OF NON-DELINQUENCY (PER HUNDRED)
Under 205	14.7	85.3
205–254	38.9	61.1
255–279	64.0	36.0
280 and over	87.9	12.1

for practical purposes it again makes little difference whether the chances of potential delinquency are six and a half in ten, or about nine in ten, because a boy falling into either score class would have to be looked upon as a potential offender for the purposes of preventive therapy. The only significance that the finer classifications would have is in calling the clinician's attention to the individual factors making up the total failure score, thereby indicating the specific problems on which therapy (mental, educative, social) might profitably concentrate.

PREDICTION TABLE CONSTRUCTED FROM PERSONALITY TRAITS DETERMINED IN PSYCHIATRIC INTERVIEW

The value of a prediction table constructed from the personality traits of the boys as revealed in the psychiatric interview lies in the fact that in a relatively brief time (an hour or less) an experienced clinician should be able

Table **XX–8**   *Three-Class Prediction Table from Five Character Traits of Rorschach Test*

WEIGHTED FAILURE SCORE CLASS	CHANCES OF DELINQUENCY (PER HUNDRED)	CHANCES OF NON-DELINQUENCY (PER HUNDRED)
Under 255	28.9	71.1
255–279	64.0	36.0
280 and over	87.9	12.1

to derive the necessary data; while a Rorschach Test requires at least an equal amount of time for administration, plus some six hours for interpretation by a skilled analyst.

Only certain of the factors included in the psychiatric interview can be uniformly derived at the point of school entrance (see Chapter XIX). Inspection of all the factors indicated to us that we could safely use the following five personality characteristics (all subsumed under the general category, Deep-Rooted Emotional Dynamics) in the construction of a prediction table:

PSYCHIATRIC PERSONALITY TRAITS	WEIGHTED FAILURE SCORE
1. Adventurous [17]	
Present in marked degree	75.3
Not prominent or noticeably lacking	35.4
2. Extroverted in Action [18]	
Present in marked degree	66.5
Not prominent or noticeably lacking	37.8
3. Suggestible [19]	
Present in marked degree	69.4
Not prominent or noticeably lacking	35.5
4. Stubborn [20]	
Present in marked degree	83.4
Not prominent or noticeably lacking	39.0
5. Emotionally Unstable [21]	
Present in marked degree	62.0
Not prominent or noticeably lacking	26.5

The range of failure scores was 174.2–356.6. Distribution of the delinquents and non-delin-

Table **XX–9** Two-Class Prediction Table from Five Character Traits of Rorschach Test

WEIGHTED FAILURE SCORE CLASS	CHANCES OF DELINQUENCY (PER HUNDRED)	CHANCES OF NON-DELINQUENCY (PER HUNDRED)
Under 255	28.9	71.1
255 and over	81.6	18.4

quents into eight detailed score classes resulted in Table XX-10.

Contractions of the eight score classes of Table XX-10 into four, three, and two score classes are shown in Tables XX-11, XX-12, and XX-13.

COMPARISON OF PREDICTION TABLES DERIVED FROM SOCIAL, RORSCHACH AND PSYCHIATRIC DATA

Examining the three detailed prediction tables that emerged from the social background of the boys (Table XX-2), their basic character structure as determined by the Rorschach Test (Table XX-6), and their personality traits as revealed by a psychiatric interview (Table XX-10), we were impressed with the fact that they are of approximately similar predictive range. Also, the more contracted tables (the four-class, three-class, and two-class) showed a very similar incidence of chances of delinquency and non-delinquency. Although this in itself would seem to indicate the validity of all three instru-

Table **XX–10** Detailed Prediction Table from Five Personality Traits Derived in Psychiatric Interview

WEIGHTED FAILURE SCORE CLASS	NUMBER OF DELINQUENTS	CHANCES OF DELINQUENCY (PER HUNDRED)	NUMBER OF NON-DELINQUENTS	CHANCES OF NON-DELINQUENCY (PER HUNDRED)
Under 195	4	4.5	85	95.5
195–219	30	12.6	209	87.4
220–244	74	43.0	98	57.0
245–269	51	63.0	30	37.0
270 294	159	82.4	34	17.6
295–319	78	94.0	5	6.0
320–344	45	91.8	4	8.2
345 and over	29	93.5	2	6.5
TOTAL	470		467	

Table **XX–11**   Four-Class Prediction Table from Five Personality Traits Derived in Psychiatric Interview

WEIGHTED FAILURE SCORE CLASS	CHANCES OF DELINQUENCY (PER HUNDRED)	CHANCES OF NON-DELINQUENCY (PER HUNDRED)
Under 220	10.4	89.6
220–244	43.0	57.0
245–269	63.0	37.0
270 and over ...	87.4	12.6

mentalities, we sought a way of subjecting them to further testing. We therefore decided to compare the predictive value of the tables in the case of the 424 boys (205 delinquents and 219 non-delinquents) about whom we had weighted failure scores on all three sets of data, and thereby to ascertain the extent of agreement between each two of the tables.

At the beginning of this comparison, we used the four-class prediction tables (Tables XX-3, XX-7, and XX-11), the failure-score classes of which we now can designate as classes A, B, C, D. The results revealed clearly that many boys falling into Class A or Class B (representing the low chances of delinquency) on one of the prediction tables often fell into either Class A or B of each of the other two prediction tables. The same was found to be true in regard to boys

Table **XX–12**   Three-Class Prediction Table from Five Personality Traits Derived in Psychiatric Interview

WEIGHTED FAILURE SCORE CLASS	CHANCES OF DELINQUENCY (PER HUNDRED)	CHANCES OF NON-DELINQUENCY (PER HUNDRED)
Under 245	21.6	78.4
245–269	63.0	37.0
270 and over ...	87.4	12.6

falling into the last two of the four failure-score groups, Class C and Class D (in both of which there is a high chance of potential delinquency). For example, a boy whose total failure score on the five social prediction factors placed him in Class A (chances of delinquency less than one in ten) was frequently in Class B (chances of delinquency three and a half to four in ten) on the basis of the five Rorschach or five psychiatric prediction factors; while a boy whose total failure score placed him in Class D (chances of delinquency eight in ten) on the basis of the five social factors often appeared in Class C (chances of delinquency a little over six in ten) on the Rorschach or psychiatric prediction tables; and vice versa.

Profiting from this discovery, we decided to use the two-class tables (Tables XX-5, XX-9, and XX-13) for our comparison of the extent of agreement between each two of the three prediction tables. The predictive power of these two-class tables is summarized in Table XX-14. Boys scoring less than 250 on the five social factors, less than 255 on the five Rorschach factors, and less than 245 on the five psychiatric factors, and therefore showing low chances (one and a half to three in ten) of being offenders, are designated as Class I; those scoring higher and therefore having a great likelihood (approximately eight out of ten chances) of being potential offenders are designated as Class II.

Table **XX–13**   Two-Class Prediction Table from Five Personality Traits Derived in Psychiatric Interview

WEIGHTED FAILURE SCORE CLASS	CHANCES OF DELINQUENCY (PER HUNDRED)	CHANCES OF NON-DELINQUENCY (PER HUNDRED)
Under 245	21.6	78.4
245 and over ...	82.8	17.2

Table XX-15 presents the extent to which each pair of prediction tables (social–Rorschach, social–psychiatric, psychiatric–Rorschach) agree in placing the 424 boys into Class I or Class II. The social and Rorschach prediction tables place 65.1% of the 424 boys in the same pre-

Table **XX–14**   Comparison of Chances of Potential Delinquency as Derived from Social, Rorschach, and Psychiatric Prediction Tables

CLASS	SOCIAL Chances of Delinquency (per hundred)	RORSCHACH Chances of Delinquency (per hundred)	PSYCHIATRIC Chances of Delinquency (per hundred)
I (low chance of potential delinquency)	16.0	28.9	21.6
II (high chance of potential delinquency)	79.1	81.6	82.8

dictive class — 157 in Class I, and 119 in Class II. The social and psychiatric tables show agreement in 67.9% — 152 boys being placed in Class I and 136 in Class II. The psychiatric and Rorschach tables show 69.8% agreement — 192 boys being placed in Class I and 104 in Class II by both predictive instruments.

We have given considerable thought to the possible reasons for the placement of a boy in a high failure-score category on one table and in a low failure-score category on another. The explanation, it seems to us, hinges very largely on the fact that "prophetic infallibility is beyond the reach of social scientists"; [22] in other words, that, since we are in the realm of probabilities, there is always some chance that a boy placed in the category of low potential delinquency really belongs in the opposite group, and vice versa. It is evident from Table XX-14 that there are anywhere from one and a half to three chances in ten that those placed in the group of potential non-delinquents are really potential delinquents, and about two chances in ten that those placed among the potential delinquents are really potential non-delinquents. For this reason alone, the placement of a boy in the same predictive category by any two of the three tables can hardly be any higher than approximately 65% to 70%, which is the result that we have actually attained.

Having made these bivariate comparisons of each pair of prediction tables, we decided to take still another step in comparing the extent of agreement among the tables: namely, by determining those instances among the 424 boys in which (1) all three tables properly identify them as delinquents or non-delinquents, (2) two of the three tables properly identify them,

(3) two of the three tables do not properly identify them, and (4) all three tables incorrectly identify them as delinquents or non-delinquents.

From Table XX-16 we see that all three tables place a boy in his proper predictive category in 49% of the cases, while in an additional 37.8%, two of the three tables do so, making a total of 86.8% of the 424 boys concerning whom two or all three of the tables are in correct agreement as to the predictive category in which they belong. In 2.4% of the cases all three tables incorrectly identify delinquents as non-delinquents and vice versa, while in an additional 10.8% two of the three tables do so, making a total of only 13.2% in which two or all three of the tables place a boy in the wrong predictive category.

FURTHER EXPLORATION

The extent of agreement, one with the other, of the prediction tables presented above indicates to us that they are ready for experimental application. As in our prior writings on predictive instrumentalities, we must emphasize, however, that we are not recommending the use of such tables to the exclusion of all other data. We are in agreement with the statement: "We would guess that no matter how substantial are the advances of scientific psychology, the best series of predictions of individual careers — apperception operating as it does — will involve the play of experienced intuitions, the clinical hunch, products of unconsciously perceived and integrated symptomatic signs. The assessment of men . . . is the scientific art of arriving at sufficient conclusions from insufficient data." [23]

Table **XX–15**   *Summary of Bivariate Classifications of Low Chances (Class I) and High Chances (Class II) of Delinquency Derived from Social–Rorschach, Social–Psychiatric, and Psychiatric–Rorschach Prediction Tables*

SUMMARY	SOCIAL AND RORSCHACH		SOCIAL AND PSYCHIATRIC		PSYCHIATRIC AND RORSCHACH	
	Number	Per Cent	Number	Per Cent	Number	Per Cent
Agreement:						
Both in Class I	157	37.0	152	35.8	192	45.3
Both in Class II	119	28.1	136	32.1	104	24.5
Disagreement:						
One in Class I, one in Class II	148	34.9	136	32.1	128	30.2
TOTAL	424	100.0	424	100.0	424	100.0

Detailed Bivariate Classifications Showing Result of Comparison of Prediction Tables

SOCIAL AND RORSCHACH					SOCIAL AND PSYCHIATRIC					PSYCHIATRIC AND RORSCHACH				
	Social					Social					Psychiatric			
RORSCHACH	Class	I	II	TOTAL	PSYCHIATRIC	Class	I	II	TOTAL	RORSCHACH	Class	I	II	TOTAL
	I	157	110	267		I	152	93	245		I	192	75	267
	II	38	119	157		II	43	136	179		II	53	104	157
	TOTAL	195	229	424		TOTAL	195	229	424		TOTAL	245	179	424

Our concern at this stage is not so much in expressing caution in the use of these predictive devices — obviously they must be in the hands of highly experienced persons, and the necessary prediction scores must be derived from absolutely accurate data — but rather in suggesting to those who may use the tables that if two or three of them are applied in an individual case, the likelihood of placing a boy in his proper predictive category is thereby increased.

It has occurred to us that if a boy has a high chance of potential delinquency as determined by the factors of his social background, but a low chance as derived from the factors of his basic character structure (Rorschach) or the dynamics of his personality (psychiatric), this would indicate that the chances of early preventive treatment are excellent, if the necessary attention is directed toward improving the conditions revealed by the social data (family interrelations). It would seem, in such a situation, that we are dealing essentially with an environmental offender, and that the environmental stimuli to delinquency have been so recent or superficial that their impact has not

reflected itself in basic personality or character structure. If the opposite is true, namely, that the boy's chances of delinquency are low in accordance with the social prediction table, but high in accordance with either or both the Rorschach and psychiatric prediction tables, it should indicate to the therapist that he may be dealing with a very recalcitrant individual, the prevention of whose delinquent career might be extremely difficult and involve nothing short of a basic reorganization of his character structure and temperamental constitution. Here it is probable that the difficulties are deeply rooted, perhaps genetically, perhaps in the very first few years of the parent–child emotional interchange.

A matter requiring further exploration is whether it is possible to use other psychological tests in place of the Rorschach Test, which is not only very time-consuming but requires exceptional skill in administration and interpretation, in order to derive more readily the factors in the basic character structure that have been shown to be sharply differentiating between delinquents and non-delinquents. If a simpler and less time-consuming test could

Table **XX–16**   *Extent of Agreement among Social, Rorschach, and Psychiatric Prediction Tables in Placing 424 Boys (205 Delinquents and 219 Non-Delinquents) in Their Proper Predictive Category*

DESCRIPTION	NUMBER	PER CENT
Three tables correctly identify boy as delinquent	86	20.2
Three tables correctly identify boy as non-delinquent	122	28.8
Two of the three tables correctly identify boy as delinquent	80	18.9
Two of the three tables correctly identify boy as non-delinquent	80	18.9
Two of the three tables incorrectly identify boy as delinquent	31	7.3
Two of the three tables incorrectly identify boy as non-delinquent	15	3.5
Three tables incorrectly identify boy as delinquent	8	1.9
Three tables incorrectly identify boy as non-delinquent	2	0.5
TOTAL	424	100.0

Detailed Trivariate Classifications Showing Results of Comparison of Social, Rorschach, and Psychiatric Prediction Tables

SOCIAL	RORSCHACH	PSYCHIATRIC	DELINQUENTS	NON-DELINQUENTS	TOTAL
I	I	I	8	122	130
I	II	I	3	19	22
I	I	II	7	20	27
I	II	II	14	2	16
II	I	I	21	41	62
II	II	I	24	7	31
II	I	II	42	6	48
II	II	II	86	2	88
TOTAL			205	219	424

be developed to bring out the presence or absence of the particular Rorschach traits shown to be most differentiative of potential delinquents from non-delinquents, it would be a powerful aid to those clinics, schools, courts, and institutions that do not have the trained personnel or cannot take the time to administer and interpret the entire test. Of course, there is the danger of such a procedure degenerating into a mechanical routine imitation of the true testing and interpreting procedure. However, a beginning in the direction of simplifying the administration of the Rorschach Test has already been made by giving it to groups, through projection of the Rorschach cards onto a screen, or to individuals who can administer it themselves.[24]

The same question arises in connection with the personality characteristics that form the basis of the psychiatric prediction table. Psychiatric services are both expensive and difficult to obtain. If psychiatric social workers and psychologists could derive the necessary data by simpler methods with acceptable skill, the application of the psychiatric prediction table could then be extended.

As for the use of the social factors, certainly trained caseworkers could readily gather and interpret the materials. From a practical point of view, the five factors in the social background can be more easily and widely obtained than the factors of the other two prediction tables, simply because there are many more persons skilled in gathering social data than there are in securing and interpreting Rorschach and psychiatric data.

In this volume we have not gone beyond the development of prediction tables that can be applied at or soon after school entrance. It would be possible to construct some additional tables from the social data, which, though not applicable at the point of school entrance, could be used at later stages in the school career.

School systems will not be able and ready to use these predictive instrumentalities on all children. It is suggested that a beginning might be made in cases in which maladaptive behavior is already present and school authorities wish to determine whether or not the boy in question is really a potential delinquent. In an enlightened educational system, the school could function as the litmus paper of personality maladaptation, reflecting the acid test of the child's success or failure in his first attempts to cope with the problems of life posed by a restrictive, impersonal society and code. In such a system the best psychiatric, psychologic, social, medical, and other facilities would be focused to cope with problems of personality distortion and maladaptive behavior at a critical point in the development of the child.

Finally, it should again be emphasized that these prediction tables should not be used mechanically and as a substitute for clinical judgment. They are designed to aid the clinician in the always difficult task — mentioned so trippingly on the tongue — of individualization. They are intended to help him see the individual in the perspective of organized experience with hundreds of other boys who in many crucial respects resemble the boy before him. As to some factors the child remains unique; but the dimensions and depths of his problems can be much more accurately assessed by seeing them in the light of the total picture of hundreds of other children, than they can be if the investigator or therapist relies exclusively on his clinical hunch. If a psychiatrist, utilizing a prognostic instrument for different combinations of symptoms as an aid to treatment, were to follow such a table blindly, he would soon find himself and his patient in trouble. Such a device can only furnish support to the clinician's reason and experience; it is not a substitute for either.

NOTES AND REFERENCES

1. F. Alexander and H. Staub, *The Criminal, the Judge, and the Public*, tr. by G. Zilboorg, New York, Macmillan, 1931, p. 34. It should be borne in mind that "the formation of personality — the basis for the individual's habitual modes of reaction — occurs during the period of infancy (birth to about six years of age). . . . If the parents are mature individuals, their attitudes enable the child to pass through this stage and enter the period of sexual latency. This extends from about the sixth year to the pre-pubertal period. . . . During the period of latency the child enters two new situations in which he has to depend on himself — at school and with playmates. . . . His reaction to the teacher who stands for authority (the father) and whose favors must be shared with other children (the mother) will depend entirely on the modes of behavior he has developed through his relations with his parents and how these relations have enabled him to handle his desires, loves, jealousies, and other manifestations of the sex instinct." O. S. English, and G. H. J. Pearson, *Common Neuroses of Children and Adults*, New York, Norton, 1937, pp. 44-45.

2. See A. Gesell and C. S. Amatruda, *Developmental Diagnosis*, New York, Harper, 1941; and A. Gesell, *Biographies of Child Development*, New York, Hoeber, 1939.

3. Clinicians are beginning to recognize the great value inherent in a scientific prediction instrument as an aid to clinical judgment. See H. A. Murray, "Problems in Clinical Research, Round Table, 1946," *American Journal of Orthopsychiatry*, XVII (1947), 208–209. Dr. Murray stresses "the great merit (for the education of the psychiatrist and psychologist) of making explicit predictions of events to come; and . . . the necessity of establishing truly satisfactory criteria for the final evaluation of clinical judgments or of test procedures . . . that psychiatrists test their hypotheses by predicting the forms of behavior which will be exhibited . . . finally, that psychiatrists in clinics undertake repeated systematic studies of the validity of their interpretations and predictive judgments, employing for this purpose the statistical analysis of variants." *Ibid.*, p. 209.

4. "Public schools are usually classed among delinquency-prevention institutions, although it is sometimes difficult to understand why this designation should be made. The formal curriculum of academic subjects does not present much opportunity for character training, personality study, or remedial work." R. S. Cavan, *Criminology*, New York, Crowell, 1948, p. 353. See also D. R. Taft, *Criminology*, New York, Macmillan, 1942, pp. 650 ff.

5. *500 Criminal Careers*, Chapter XVIII; *One Thousand Juvenile Delinquents*, Chapter XI; *Five Hundred Delinquent Women*, Chapter XVII; *Later Criminal Careers*, Chapter XII; *Juvenile Delinquents Grown Up*, Chapter XIX; *Criminal Careers in Retrospect*, Chapters XIV–XVI.

6. *Discipline of Boy by Father*. For original tabular presentation, see Table XI–22. Refers to usual discipline of the boy. *Lax:* Father is negligent, indifferent, lets boy do what he likes. *Overstrict:* Father is harsh, unreasoning, demands obedience through fear. *Erratic:* Father varies between strictness and laxity, is not consistent in control. *Firm but kindly:* Discipline is based on sound reason which the boy understands.

7. *Supervision of Boy by Mother*. See Table X–10.

Suitable: If mother does not work outside the home and is not ill, she personally keeps close watch on the boy or provides for his leisure hours in clubs or playgrounds. If she is ill or out of the home a great deal, there is a responsible adult in charge. *Fair:* Mother, though at home, gives only partial supervision to boy. *Unsuitable:* Mother is careless in her supervision, leaving the boy to his own devices without guidance, or in the care of an irresponsible child or adult.

8. *Affection of Father for Boy.* See Table XI–13. *Warm:* Father is sympathetic, kind, attached, even, in some cases, overprotective. *Indifferent:* Father does not pay much attention to boy. *Hostile:* Father rejects boy.

9. *Affection of Mother for Boy.* See Table XI–14. See footnote 8 for definition.

10. *Cohesiveness of Family.* See Table X–14. *Cohesive:* There is a strong "we-feeling" among members of the immediate family, as evidenced by cooperativeness, group interests, pride in the home, affection for each other. "All for one and one for all." *Some elements of cohesion:* Even if the family group may not be entirely intact (because of departure of one or more members), the remaining group of which the boy is a part has at least some of the characteristics of the cohesive family. *Unintegrated:* Home is just a place to "hang your hat"; self-interest of the members exceeds group interest.

11. *Marked* indicates that the trait is clearly present in the character structure. *Slight or suggestive* indicates that the presence of the trait in the character structure, though not conclusive, is suggestive or indicated in degree. *Absent* means that the trait does not play a relevant or significant role in the character structure. (These definitions and those in footnotes 12–16, which follow, were supplied by the Schachtels.)

12. See Table XVIII–2. *Social assertion:* (unlike self-assertion which is usually based on the development of a genuine and spontaneous self) refers to the more superficial quality of expressing will and ambition in relation to the environment.

13. See Table XVIII–3. *Defiance:* aggressive self-assertion born out of deep insecurity or weaknesses and therefore often indiscriminate in its aims and means.

14. See Table XVIII–23. *Suspicion:* indiscriminate or exaggerated mistrust of others, not warranted by the objective situation. The individual is generally unaware of being unduly suspicious, believing that he is merely cautious, or realistic, or being persecuted, and so on. Suspicion often accompanies hostility and fear of hostility.

15. See Table XVIII–24. *Destructiveness:* the tendency to destroy, to hurt, to be negativistic. This tendency may be directed against others and against oneself; usually both trends run parallel, often one being more manifest and the other more suppressed.

16. See Table XVIII–37. *Emotional lability or impulsiveness:* qualities in the affective reactions of a person which permit inner drives, urges, feelings to take their course, allow tensions to explode, and which thus lead to certain actions and moods more or less regardless of consequences and of the objective requirements of the situation. The term "emotional

lability" refers to the way in which affectivity is discharged, and not to the general "lability" or "stableness" of a person.

17. See Table XIX–1. *Adventurous:* impulse for change, excitement, or risk. (This definition and those in footnotes 18–21 were supplied by Dr. Moulton.)

18. See Table XIX–1. *Extroverted in action:* free expression in activity.

19. See Table XIX–1. *Suggestible:* easily swayed by appeal to his feelings even though against his better judgment.

20. See Table XIX–1. *Stubborn:* resistive or persistent but not in a freely expressed drive; probably the result of thwarted dynamic qualities.

21. See Table XIX–1. *Emotionally unstable:* unharmonious and inappropriate feeling reaction, conflict of feeling tendencies. Not to be confused with lability of emotion.

22 *Assessment of Men*, compiled and written by the Office of Strategic Services Assessment Staff, New York, Rinehart, 1948, p. 8.

23. *Idem.*

24. M. R. H. Erickson, and M. E. Steiner, *Large Scale Rorschach Techniques: A Manual for the Group Rorschach and Multiple Choice Test*, Springfield, Ill., Thomas, 1945.

172

Spotting Potential Delinquents: Can It Be Done? *

Eleanor T. Glueck

In *Unraveling Juvenile Delinquency*[1] Professor Sheldon Glueck and I presented three tables on the basis of which we believe it should be possible to select in a first grade school population those children who will prob-

---

[1] The Commonwealth Fund, New York, 1950, Chap. XX.

* Reprinted from 20 *Federal Probation* (1956), 7–13. Used by permission of the author and the publisher. See, also, E. T. Glueck, "Identifying Juvenile Delinquents and Neurotics," 40 *Mental Hygiene* (1956), 24–43, and "Body Build in the Prediction of Delinquency," 48 *J. Crim. L., Criminology and Police Science* (1958), 577–579. For a recent account of American prediction experiments, see E. D. Monachesi, "The Prognosis of Recidivism: American Studies," 20 *Sociologist* (1957), 1–7. For an account that includes English studies on predic-

ably become persistent delinquents unless timely and effective intervention diverts their predicted course of maladapted behavior into socially acceptable channels. One of these tables, which has come to be known as the Glueck Social Prediction Table, is based on five interpersonal family factors that have been found sharply to differentiate the 500 delinquents from the control group of 500 non-delinquents who were the subjects of *Unraveling Juvenile Delinquency* (*supervision of boy by mother, discipline of boy by father, affection of mother for boy, affection of father for boy,* and *cohesiveness of the family*); a second on five traits of character structure derived from the Rorschach Test (*social assertion, defiance, suspiciousness, destructiveness,* and *emotional lability*); and a third on five traits of temperament as determined by psychiatric interviews (*adventurousness, extroversion* and *emotional instability*). These tables show a high association between the relevant factors and the likelihood of delinquency or non-delinquency — a potentiality that in the case of the Social Prediction Table is already being converted into a high probability through a series of retrospective checks on other samples of cases.

These three tables represent only a very small segment of a series of 51 such devices constructed over 30 years, the first one appearing in 1930 in *500 Criminal Careers* [2] and the most recent ones in a paper of the author's entitled "Identifying Juvenile Delinquents and Neurotics," [3] directed toward finding in a population of school children the neurotic delinquents and distinguishing them in turn from potential delinquents who are healthy emotionally. Some concept of the range of the 51 tables can be given briefly here, but the interested reader is

referred to another article of the author's in which the entire series of tables is listed. [4]

Our first prediction table, which appeared in *500 Criminal Careers*, [5] was directed toward determining the possibilities of recidivism of young adult male offenders during 5 years after completion of parole from a reformatory. In *Five Hundred Delinquent Women* [6] there are tables of a similar nature concerned with the probable recidivism of young adult female offenders, and also, with their probable behavior on parole from a reformatory.

Certain other prediction tables that we have made concerning adult offenders stem from the volumes *Later Criminal Careers* [7] and *Criminal Careers in Retrospect*. [8] These studies encompass further followups of the men originally reported in *500 Criminal Careers*. The resulting prediction table from *Later Criminal Careers* [9] deals with the recidivism of young male offenders during 10 years following parole from a reformatory. In *Criminal Careers in Retrospect*, which represents a third followup of the same men and covers a period of 15 years after the completion of a reformatory sentence, there is a series of tables dealing not only with probable recidivism over a span of 15 years after the completion of a reformatory sentence, but also with behavior during the various existing forms of extramural and intramural penocorrectional treatment. In this series of tables we have also made an attempt to determine the difference in behavior of adult offenders in various age spans. Thus, for example, there is a table on the recidivism of young adult male offenders during probation when under 27 years of age; and one in the age span 27–32; and still a third in the age span 32 years and older. In other words, we have in these tables not only a means for determining the probable response to probation of young adult male offenders, but also their response to it during

tion, see H. Mannheim and L. T. Wilkins, *Prediction Methods in Relation to Borstal Training*, London, H. M. Stationery Office, 1955. For a discussion of the Minnesota Multiphasic Personality Inventory (MMPI) as a predictive instrument for older school children, see E. D. Monachesi, "The Personalities of Predelinquent Boys," 48 *J. Crim. L., Criminology and Police Science* (1957), 149–163. See, also, W. C. Kvaraceus, *KD Proneness Scale and Check List*, Manual of Directions, Yonkers, World Book Co., 1950. See, especially, S. and E. T. Glueck, *Predicting Delinquency and Crime*, Cambridge, Harvard University Press, 1959. — Ed.

² Sheldon and Eleanor Glueck. New York: Alfred A. Knopf, 1930.

³ *Mental Hygiene*, January 1956, pp. 24–43.

⁴ Eleanor T. Glueck, "Status of Glueck Prediction Studies," *Journal of Criminal Law, Criminology, and Police Science*, May–June 1956.

⁵ *Op. cit.*, Table 112, p. 285.

⁶ Sheldon and Eleanor T. Glueck. New York: Alfred A. Knopf, 1934, Table 9, p. 290; Table 10, p. 292.

⁷ Sheldon and Eleanor Glueck. New York: The Commonwealth Fund, 1937.

⁸ Sheldon and Eleanor T. Glueck. New York: The Commonwealth Fund, 1943.

⁹ *Op. cit.*, Table 32, p. 141.

various age levels. This series therefore constitutes a refinement of the more crude tables
which we prepared in connection with the volumes *500 Criminal Careers* and *Five Hundred
Delinquent Women*. In *Criminal Careers in
Retrospect* there are 33 prediction tables, at
least some of which should be subjected to careful checking against other samples of cases,
because these tables, together with those in *500
Criminal Careers* and *Later Criminal Careers*,
could, if validated, provide peno-correctional
authorities who deal with young adult offenders
a possible means for more effective disposition
and treatment, regardless of whether or not an
adult offender had been a juvenile delinquent.

The series of tables dealing with the prediction of recidivism and of behavior during various forms of peno-correctional treatment (probation, probation with suspended sentence, correctional institution, reformatory, prison, jail,
and parole), has a purpose quite apart from
that of the tables published in *Unraveling Juvenile Delinquency* which are designed to make
possible the "spotting" of potential delinquents
at a stage in life when it can be theorized that
suitable intervention will stay the development
of a criminal career.

PREDICTION TABLES IN "UNRAVELING JUVENILE DELINQUENCY"

As this article is not directed to those who
might wish to construct prediction devices but
rather to those who want to understand their
practical implications, this is not the place to
describe the method of constructing the tables,
which is fully reported in *Unraveling Juvenile
Delinquency* (Chapter XX), as well as in our
other works,[10] beyond pointing out that the
five factors comprising each of the three tables
in *Unraveling Juvenile Delinquency* were initially selected from among those showing the
widest range in difference in incidence between

the 500 delinquents encompassed in *Unraveling
Juvenile Delinquency* and their 500 matched
non-delinquents. The per cent of delinquents
among the 1,000 boys actually occurring in each
sub-category of a factor, provided the basis for
constructing a "total weighted score" derived
from summating the individual scores on the
sub-categories of all five factors on each boy.
The tables themselves were derived from separately distributing all the delinquents and all
the non-delinquents (for whom their status on
all five factors was known) into "weighted score
classes." Assuming validation on other series
of cases, the incidence of the delinquents and
non-delinquents within each "weighted score
class" expresses the likelihood of delinquency
for individuals falling within that "score class."
Whether such a table has applicability to
samples of different composition had, of course,
to await practical demonstration.

For present purposes, the discussion will be
confined to the Social Prediction Table. We
can lay aside any consideration of two of the
tables in *Unraveling Juvenile Delinquency*,
namely the ones constructed from Rorschach and
psychiatric data, because from a practical point
of view their application would be limited to
Rorschach and psychiatric experts, while the
Social Prediction Table can be applied by welfare workers, probation and parole officers, psychiatrists, psychologists, teachers, and ministers.
This does not mean that special skills are not
required, but many more persons have or can
acquire them than can administer Rorschach
and psychiatric examinations.

But there is an even more telling reason for
confining the discussion to the Social Prediction Table, which is that standing alone it
would (if completely validated) do as good a
job of selecting potential delinquents as either
of the other two tables or as any combination
of the 15 factors in all three tables. Although
some combinations of the 15 factors involved
result in a very slightly greater predictive capacity, that of the Social Prediction Table is
already so high that there is no reason to urge
the use of the other tables except as supplementary aids.[11]

---

[10] *500 Criminal Careers, op. cit.*, pp. 278–296;
Glueck, S. and E. T., *One Thousand Juvenile Delinquents*, 1934, Harvard University Press, Cambridge,
pp. 185–190; *Five Hundred Delinquent Women, op.
cit.*, pp. 284–298; *Later Criminal Careers, op. cit.*,
pp. 134–144; Glueck, S. and E. T., *Juvenile Delinquents Grown Up*, 1940, New York, The Commonwealth Fund, pp. 199–234; *Criminal Careers in
Retrospect, op. cit.*, pp. 215–283; Glueck, S. and
E. T., *After-Conduct of Discharged Offenders*, 1945,
New York and London, Macmillan Co., pp. 63–73.

---

[11] See Sheldon and Eleanor Glueck, "Early Detection of Future Delinquents: A Comparison of the
Total Discriminative Capacity of Various Combinations Among Fifteen Factors Significantly Differenti-

Likelihood of Persistent Delinquency
(Derived from status on five interpersonal family factors)

SCORE CLASS	LIKELIHOOD OF PERSISTENT DELINQUENCY	
	Percentage of delinquents occurring in this score class	Likelihood of delinquency
Under 200	8.2	Negligible
200–249	37.0	Low
250–299	63.5	More than an even chance
300 and over	89.2	High

THE SOCIAL PREDICTION TABLE

The Social Prediction Table has already been considerably publicized, not only in articles which Professor Glueck and I have written but also in several popular articles; but perhaps this discussion of its possible uses would be facilitated by its presentation here.

FIVE FACTORS COMPRISING SOCIAL PREDICTION TABLE WITH "DELINQUENCY SCORE" OF EACH SUB–CATEGORY [12]

DISCIPLINE OF BOY BY FATHER [a]   SCORE
Overstrict or erratic 72.5
Lax 59.8
Firm but kindly 9.3

SUPERVISION OF BOY BY MOTHER [b]
Unsuitable 83.2
Fair 57.5
Suitable 9.9

AFFECTION OF FATHER FOR BOY [c]
Indifferent or hostile 75.9
Warm (including overprotective) 33.8

AFFECTION OF MOTHER FOR BOY [d]
Indifferent or hostile 86.2
Warm (including overprotective) 43.1

COHESIVENESS OF FAMILY [e]
Unintegrated 96.9
Some elements of cohesion 61.3
Cohesive 20.6

ating Delinquents From Non-Delinquents," *Journal of Criminal Law, Criminology and Police Science*, July–August 1956.

[12] Those who wish to apply the Table are asked to note that the determination of the particular category

The uninitiated reader is no doubt bewildered by this Table and is trying to understand how to apply it to a particular child. Before he can do this, he must have before him the five factors comprising the Table, with their sub-categories and definitions and their scores (which represent the percentage of delinquents among the 1,000 cases of *Unraveling Juvenile Delinquency* who were actually found in a particular sub-category of a factor).

into which a case falls is based on the situation generally prevailing in a child's life up to the point at which the prediction is made. In cases in which one or another parent has left or been removed from the home before a child was 3 years old, and there is no parent surrogate (stepparent, foster parent), discipline of the missing parent is graded as "lax," affection as "indifferent," and supervision as "unsuitable." But if there has been a substitute parent, at least since the child was 3 years old, the discipline, affection, and supervision of the parent substitute is rated.

In regard to cohesiveness of the family, it is usually rated *fair* in a situation in which one of the parents is for any reason not living in the home, providing the remaining family group, of which the particular child is a part, is a "cohesive" unit. If, however, the absence of one parent from the home does not reflect his or her indifference to the family but is rather the result of unavoidable circumstances, such as illness, the family unit is regarded as cohesive if all the other elements that enter into this judgment would normally have designated the family as cohesive.

[a] DISCIPLINE OF BOY BY FATHER
    Overstrict: Father is harsh, unreasoning, demands obedience through fear;
    Erratic: Father varies between strictness and laxity, is not consistent in control;
    Lax: Father is negligent, indifferent, lets child do what he likes;
    Firm but kindly: Discipline is based on sound reason which the child understands and accepts as fair.

For example, if it has been determined that a particular youngster is harshly disciplined by his father, he would be scored 72.5 (because of all the 1,000 boys in *Unraveling Juvenile Delinquency* whose fathers were always or sometimes overstrict in their discipline, 72.5 were actually delinquent boys). To continue the illustration, as to supervision of the boy by his mother, she leaves him to his own devices, allows him to run about the streets, and does not know what he does or where he goes. On this factor he is therefore scored 83.2. Regarding paternal affection, the father dislikes the boy, expressing his hostility in no uncertain terms. The score here is 75.9. In respect to maternal affection, the mother is indifferent to her son, with little warmth of feeling for him. This score is 86.2. As regards the cohesiveness of the family, this has to be regarded as unintegrated because the mother spends most of the day away from home, giving little if any thought to the doings of the children, and the father, a heavy drinker, spends most of his leisure in

b SUPERVISION OF BOY BY MOTHER

Unsuitable: Mother is careless in her supervision, leaving the child to his own devices without guidance, or in the care of an irresponsible person;

Fair: Mother, though home, gives only partial supervision to child;

Suitable: If mother does not work outside the home and is not ill, she personally keeps close watch on the child or provides for his leisure hours in clubs or playgrounds; if she is ill or out of the home a great deal, there is a responsible adult in charge;

c AFFECTION OF FATHER FOR BOY
d AFFECTION OF MOTHER FOR BOY

Indifferent: Father (or mother) does not pay much attention to child; relationship is neither warm, overprotective or hostile;

Hostile: Father (or mother) rejects child;

Warm (including overprotective): Father (or mother) is sympathetic, kind, attached, even overprotective;

e COHESIVENESS OF FAMILY

Unintegrated: Home is just a place to "hang your hat"; self-interest of the members exceeds group interest;

Some elements of cohesion: Even if the family group may not be entirely intact (because of absence of one or more members), the remaining group has at least some of the characteristics of the cohesive family;

Cohesive: There is a strong "we" feeling among members of the immediate family as evidenced by cooperativeness, group interests, pride in the home, affection for each other.

bars and cafes with his own friends. The boy is therefore scored 96.9. Addition of the scores results in a grand total of 414.7. The prediction table places this boy in the group whose chances of delinquency are very high — in fact, preventive treatment is urgently indicated.

The reader cannot be asked to accept the Social Prediction Table as a useful device without evidence that it applies to samples of cases different from the one on which it was constructed. In *Unraveling Juvenile Delinquency*, 500 proved delinquents ranging in age from 11 to 17 years, were matched with 500 proved non-delinquents, by age, ethnic derivation, intelligence level, and residence in the congested and low-income regions of Boston. The delinquents were selected from a population of correctional school boys, the non-delinquents from the public schools.

It has been argued by critics of the Social Prediction Table that factors derived in a study of boys in the 11–17 age group would not apply to boys at the age of 6 and before they necessarily show any outward signs of antisocial behavior. But such critics have lost the point about the selection of the particular factors entering into the Table; for out of a range of choices presented to us in the many factors in *Unraveling Juvenile Delinquency* that markedly distinguished the delinquents from the non-delinquents, we deliberately selected, five (experience in constructing such tables having shown that five factors are a sufficient basis for the tables) which would be in operation and clearly ascertainable by the time a child was six years old. Secondly, if *Unraveling Juvenile Delinquency* is what we think it is, namely a study of persistent delinquents (largely boys who steal and burglarize) as measured against a control group of non-delinquents (even though 25 per cent of the latter actually had committed occasional peccadilloes not followed by a pattern of antisocial conduct), the factors found to distinguish such delinquents from non-delinquents should be "universal," i.e., should be found in any sample of persistent juvenile delinquents and in those headed for such careers.

Our first problem after the publication of *Unraveling Juvenile Delinquency* was to encourage application of the Table to samples of juvenile delinquents different in makeup from those on which it had been constructed. Would they, too, be found to have the cluster of factors in their interpersonal family relations that were found among the delinquents in *Unraveling Juvenile Delinquency?* Next, if the Table were applied to boys at an early age, say at 6 years, before most of them showed signs of persistent antisocial behavior, would it be found that the "potential delinquents" and the "potential non-delinquents" would actually prove in large measure to be such?

"RETROSPECTIVE" VALIDATIONS OF THE SOCIAL PREDICTION TABLE

Since the publication of the Social Prediction Table in *Unraveling Juvenile Delinquency* in 1950, there have come to our personal attention several applications of the Table to samples of delinquents differing in one way or another from the cases on which the table was initially constructed. As some of these have already been reported in published articles, only the briefest references will be made to them.

The first study — made by Bertram J. Black and Selma J. Glick of the Jewish Board of Guardians in New York City — appeared in the spring of 1952.[13] The table was applied to a group of 100 Jewish boys confined in the Hawthorne-Cedar Knolls School in New York State, with a view to determining the extent to which it would have been possible years earlier to have identified them accurately as potentially serious delinquents. Black and Glick ascertained that 91 per cent of the group would have been thus identified. It is of especial significance that although the Social Prediction Table was compiled on the basis of underprivileged Boston boys largely of English, Italian, and Irish descent and of Protestant and Catholic religions, it was found to operate so satisfactorily on a sample of New York Jewish boys.

Another study, by Richard E. Thompson,[14] establishes the Social Prediction Table as a valid instrumentality for distinguishing from among children already showing behavioral difficulties those who are true delinquents and those whose maladapted behavior is probably temporary. It shows that among a representative group of 100 boys, included originally in a research in Massachusetts known as the Cambridge-Somerville Youth Study,[15] it would have been possible (as in the study by the Jewish Board of Guardians) to identify accurately 91 per cent of all the boys as either potential delinquents or as true non-delinquents. The discriminative potential of the table was found to be considerably greater than that of three clinicians (psychiatrist, psychologist, and criminologist) who had been initially charged with selecting the boys for the Cambridge-Somerville Youth Study. Thompson reports that in the light of the actual behavior of the boys subsequent to their selection for the study, the clinicians (as determined by the staff of the study) had correctly identified 65 per cent as true pre-delinquents or true non-delinquents, in comparison with 91 per cent correctly identified by the Social Prediction Table.[16] In this inquiry, as in that made by the Jewish Board of Guardians, the table reveals a capacity for usefulness on boys of status and background different from that of the boys on whom it was originally constructed, for its power was maintained among the boys in the Cambridge-Somerville Study who were younger than the boys in *Unraveling Juvenile Delinquency*; on those who were of different ethnic origin; on those who were of higher intelligence; on those of better economic status; and on those who grew up in neighborhoods that were not as disadvantaged as those in which the boys in *Unraveling Juvenile Delinquency* were reared.[17]

Still another check on the Social Prediction Table was published in April, 1955. This is a study made by the New Jersey Department of Institutions and Agencies in which the Table was applied to 51 delinquent boys who were on parole. "It will be observed," says the report, "that the closeness of the findings on the basis of the New Jersey data with the original findings in the study of *Unraveling Juvenile Delinquency* is rather noteworthy, since the New Jersey boys were selected at random, and no attempt was made to match the individual characteristics of the New Jersey delinquent

[13] "Predicted vs. Actual Outcome for Delinquent Boys," New York, Jewish Board of Guardians, 1952.

[14] "A Validation of the Glueck Social Prediction Scale for Proneness to Delinquency," *Journal of Criminal Law, Criminology and Police Science*, November–December, 1952.

[15] Edwin Powers and Helen Witmer, *An Experiment in the Prevention of Delinquency*, New York: Columbia University Press, 1951. [See Article 186 *infra.* — Ed.]

[16] See p. 464 *et seq.* of Thompson's article.

[17] *Ibid.*, pp. 467–469.

boys with the delinquent boys included in the Harvard Law School Study." [18]

In addition to these published studies, there are several other checks on the Table, some of which are now being prepared for publication.

Thompson, in an as yet unpublished study, applied the Social Prediction Table to 50 boys appearing before the Boston Juvenile Court in 1950 who averaged 13.1 years of age (compared with an average age of 14.6 years of the boys in *Unraveling Juvenile Delinquency*). In retrospect, he found that had the Table been applied when these boys were 6 years old it would have been possible to determine that 92 per cent, barring therapeutic intervention, would become delinquents. These boys also differed in some ways from the original sample of cases on which the table had been constructed — not only were they younger, but half of them had no prior court appearances (all the delinquent boys in *Unraveling Juvenile Delinquency* had been in court before). The religious distribution of these boys was also different, a higher proportion being Protestants than in the group studied in *Unraveling Juvenile Delinquency*; they were less retarded in school; in a higher proportion of cases they were the sons of two native-born parents; and, in a far higher proportion, one or both parents had attended high school.

Another opportunity to test the validity of the Social Prediction Table came in 1954 when the Douglas A. Thom Clinic for Children in Boston (a psychoanalytically oriented clinic) applied the Table to 57 boys ranging in age from 6 to 12 years who had been treated for aggressive, destructive, antisocial behavior. The scorings made by the clinic psychologist indicated that 82.3 per cent of these boys would have been clearly identified by the table at the age of 6 as potential delinquents. [19]

Thompson also applied the Table to 50 girls committed as delinquents to the Division of Youth Service of the Massachusetts Department of Education (better known as The Youth Service Board) over a 7-month period, from November 1954 to May 1955. The application of the Table to girl delinquents is the second such attempt, the first being one by Selma Glick and Catherine Donnell of the Jewish Board of Guardians in 1953 on 150 unmarried mothers, in which it was found that 81 per cent of the girls would have been identified as potential delinquents had the Table been applied to them at the age of 6.

The result of the application of the Table by Thompson to girl offenders seems quite phenomenal in that *all of the 50 girls would have been identified as potential delinquents.* This is a finding which we can explain only by the fact that Thompson's analysis indicates that there is much more social pathology in the background of the delinquent girls than in that of the delinquent boys to whom the Table has thus far been applied. This is clearly reflected in the categorization of this group of girl offenders on the five social factors that comprise the prediction table, as compared with the boys of *Unraveling Juvenile Delinquency*, on whom the Table was constructed. For example, as regards laxity of discipline by their fathers, this was found in 75.6 per cent of the girls as contrasted with 26.6 per cent of the boys in *Unraveling Juvenile Delinquency*; the fathers of the girls were indifferent or hostile to them in 87.5 per cent of the cases, as compared with 59.8 per cent of the fathers of the boys in *Unraveling Juvenile Delinquency*. As regards the affection of the mothers, they were indifferent or hostile to the girls in 80.6 per cent of the cases, as compared with 27.9 per cent of the mothers of the boys. The families of 76 per cent of the girls did not comprise a cohesive unit, as contrasted with 25.7 per cent of the families of the boys of *Unraveling Juvenile Delinquency*. It is, to our minds, this greater social pathology which accounts for the 100 per cent result in the application of the Social Prediction Table to the 50 girl offenders.

An application of the Social Prediction Table to 150 delinquent boys in upper income groups ($7,500 and thereabouts) by Selma Glick of the Jewish Board of Guardians is still in process. Thus far, work has been completed on applying the Table to 81 boys and Selma Glick has reported informally that the Social Prediction Table would accurately have identified 89 per cent of these boys as delinquents. It is to be

---

[18] "Predicting Juvenile Delinquency," *Research Bulletin* No. 124, April 1955, published by the State Department of Institutions and Agencies, Trenton, N. J.

[19] Eveoleen N. Rexford, M.D., Maxwell Schleifer, and Suzanne Taets Van Amerongen, M.D., "A Follow-Up of a Psychiatric Study of 57 Antisocial Young Children," *Mental Hygiene*, April 1956, pp. 196–214.

noted, of course, that the income level of the boys in *Unraveling Juvenile Delinquency,* on whom the Table was constructed, was much lower, and also that the groups were far different in ethnic distribution — the current sample being entirely Jewish.

Even to those readers who would consider that these evidences (and there are others I have not taken the space to mention) of the "workability" * of the Social Prediction Table are not conclusive, these findings can at least be accepted as "straws in the wind" which are blowing in the right direction. (Incidentally, the fact that the validations of the Social Prediction Table are so consistently encouraging should dispel any doubts about the samples of delinquents and non-delinquents in *Unraveling Juvenile Delinquency* on which the Table is based.)

"Prospective" Validations of the Social Prediction Table

It would appear to be a reasonable assumption that if various groups of delinquents are found to resemble each other in their interpersonal family relations, as evidenced by the checking of the Social Prediction Table on groups of juvenile offenders differing in one way or another from the 500 delinquents of *Unraveling Juvenile Delinquency,* such factors appearing in the background of children not yet delinquent are danger signals of budding criminal careers. However, this must be put to a rigid test by applying the Social Prediction Table to a sufficient group of children, preferably in a public school setting, when they enter first grade, and following them over a period of several years, in order to determine whether the predicted results actually occur. Two such studies are in progress, one in New York City and one in Washington, D. C. The first experiment is being carried out by the New York City Youth Board,[20] applying the Table to about 250 boys in the first grade of two public

schools in high delinquency areas in the Bronx. This experiment has been in process since 1953 and is in midstream. The boys' behavior in school is being followed and it is planned to extend the followup to home and community. It will be several years before the results are definitive. At the present writing, however, only 8.3 per cent of those predicted as having very little likelihood of delinquency are showing signs of overt antisocial behavior in the classroom in contrast to 50 per cent of the boys predicted as almost certainly potential delinquents. It is to be remembered that these youngsters are as yet only between 8 and 9 years old.*

Another application of the Social Prediction Table to first grade children is being carried on in Washington, D. C., under the sponsorship of the Commissioners' Youth Council of Washington, D. C., and known as the Maximum Benefits Project, that has as its objective a "multidisciplinary study of pre-delinquency with a threefold clinical–demonstration–research mission." It is set up in two elementary schools in high delinquency areas in Washington. The Social Prediction Table is being used to identify the potential delinquents among the group of children reported by teachers as having "behavior difficulties." Of such a group, 75 per cent were rated as true pre-delinquents. They are being followed up and some of them (as in the New York City Youth Board Study) are under treatment. It is, of course, too soon to speak of any "results." †

Varied Uses of Social Prediction Table

Because of the nature of the factors included in the Social Prediction Table, it can be applied at any age level ranging from 6 to 16 years. The question it is designed to answer is simply: "Is the particular child about whom I am concerned probably a persistent juvenile delinquent or likely to become one?" Such checks of the Table as have been made to date would appear to substantiate the efficacy of the Table for this purpose. Its efficacy when applied *before* the onset of overt evidence of maladapted behavior, however, is as yet to be determined, but findings so far made are promising. The answer to this will come from the New York City Youth

---

* A report has recently reached us of the successful validation of the Glueck Social Prediction Table in Japan by Tokuhiro Tatezawa, Family Court Probation Officer, Yokohama Family Court, Japan. However, the numbers involved in this pilot study are small — 30 delinquents, 30 non-delinquents. — *Ed.*

[20] Ralph W. Whelan, "An Experiment in Predicting Delinquency," *The Journal of Criminal Law, Criminology and Police Science,* November–December 1954.

* See Article 173 *infra.* — *Ed.*

† A recent report on this experiment confirms once again the efficacy of the Glueck Social Prediction Table in identifying potential delinquents. — *Ed.*

Board Study and the Washington, D. C., Maximum Benefits Project. True, it is somewhat more difficult to arrive at the exact score in the case of a child of 6 because, for example, although there is to a skilled inquirer evidence of a trend toward the disintegration of a family, the parents may still be living together and some semblance of unity is being maintained. Such a case would have to be categorized as showing *some elements of cohesion* (with a score of 61.3); while later on the categorization would be *"unintegrated"* (with a score of 96.9). However, as all the factors refer to the entire period from birth of the child up to the point at which the Prediction Table is actually applied, it is the *usual* or the most prevalent condition with which we are concerned and not with a small segment of it.

As regards uses of the Table once signs of maladapted behavior are clear, the reader is reminded of Thompson's findings in applying the Table to the Cambridge-Somerville Youth Study cases. The boys in this group were all "behavior problems" to their teachers; but the Table correctly distinguished (in the light of subsequent follow-up) 90 per cent of those who were true delinquents from those who were really non-delinquents. This means that if a child is showing signs of what appears to a teacher, or social worker, or police officer, to be evidence of true pre-delinquency, the Table would be helpful in arriving at a decision in the matter.

And at the clinical level, it has its uses in distinguishing from among a group of children referred for "behavior difficulties," those who are likely to "act them out" to the detriment of society. We have had more than gleanings of this not only from the findings in the Cambridge-Somerville Study but from the experience of the Thom Clinic for Child Guidance in Boston, as well as from other sources.

What of the uses of the Social Prediction Table in a juvenile court? Not all children with some prior record of offenses are necessarily headed for persistent careers of delinquency. And some children, though labeled "minor offenders" may be serious delinquents.

The Social Prediction Table applied here would certainly serve as an aid to juvenile court judges and probation officers in separating minor from serious offenders.

Much more could be said about the possible uses of the Table. Only its further experimental application will reveal its full potential. Of even more importance, however, than the practical one of determining how and where the Social Prediction Table works is the dissection by clinicians and others of the factors comprising the Table in order to determine what their meaning is in the dynamics of delinquency. Such research is actually going forward in the Thom Clinic for Child Guidance in Boston.

There will always be some skeptics who remind us that "no two human beings are alike" and "such different elements enter into their conduct." But this overlooks the reality that people are far more alike than they are different. Prediction tables are not to be applied mechanically as a substitute for clinical judgment. Such tables, however, should help the teacher, the social worker, the clinician, the juvenile court judge, and the probation officer to evaluate a particular child in the perspective of organized experience with hundreds of other children who, in many crucial respects, are like the one in question. Used properly, this instrumentality can open the way for dealing more directly with the root causes of delinquent behavior than has thus far been possible. We forsee its extensive application as a screening device in "public health" programs for the prevention and treatment of delinquency.

The home is the cradle of human personality. Each person, from the moment of birth, is deeply influenced by the people around him. The baby is born not knowing *what to think* or *how to feel* about life, but ready to learn, and learn he does, willy nilly. From a warm, loving, stable family, the child learns that people are friendly, worth knowing, and can be depended upon. When a family is cold, despairing, rejecting, or neglectful the child learns distrust, hostility, or downright hatred of people. Such families are to be found in all economic, cultural, racial, national, and educational backgrounds.
— *National Conference on Prevention and Control of Juvenile Delinquency, 1946.*

173

New York City
Youth Board Validation *

I. BACKGROUND OF THE STUDY

The New York City Youth Board, in accordance with its mandate to develop ways of detecting and treating delinquent children, has followed with intense interest the detailed researches of Doctors Sheldon and Eleanor T. Glueck in the field of juvenile delinquency prediction. The publication of *Unraveling Juvenile Delinquency*,[1] and the prediction tables presented therein, provided the means for this agency to test an instrument designed to prognosticate early in a child's life the probability of future delinquent behavior.

The thinking of the Youth Board in selecting this project as one of its major research investigations has been adequately covered in a previous publication.[2] It may be well, however, to restate the salient research decisions made in setting up the prediction–validation study and to review the methodological procedures employed to date.

The findings of the Gluecks and the three predictive or diagnostic tables which were evolved from their study represent some ten years of extensive and intensive study of two matched groups, consisting of 500 persistently delinquent boys selected from a correctional school population and 500 non-delinquent boys selected from the public school population in high delinquency areas of a large city. The variables on which the groups were matched were age, intelligence, ethnic derivation, and neighborhood conditions.

Working with the Gluecks were a staff of social investigators, psychologists, a physician, psychiatrist, and physical anthropologist. From this listing, the range of potentially "causal" factors studied in the two groups can be gleaned: social background factors including intrafamily relationships (what the Gluecks call "under-the-roof culture"), physical, physico-anthropological, psychiatric and psychological characteristics were covered. In all, data concerning 402 factors were gathered, verified, and checked on the 1,000 youths, and the two groups were compared factor by factor.

Three predictive tables were constructed using those factors which (1) most sharply differentiated between the two groups; and (2) were also presumed to operate in a young childhood population (*e.g.*, at the point of entry into school) and were, therefore, most suitable for predictive purposes. One table was based on differences in basic character traits as derived from the Rorschach protocols; another table was based on differences in personality traits as derived from the psychiatric interview; and a third table was based on the most significant social factors. Each table is made up of the five weighted factors that differentiate most clearly between the delinquents and non-delinquents and a youngster can be scored on each factor (the Gluecks call these *weighted failure scores* and they were derived from the percentage incidence of delinquents in each sub-category of a table). Then a total class score is summed. It is from the total score that the probability of delinquency is derived. It is the last table, called the Social Factors Prediction Table, that the Youth Board is testing in the present investigation. The details of the construction of the prediction tables and the statistical methodology employed are presented in *Unraveling Juvenile Delinquency*.

A recent paper [3] compares the effectiveness

---

* Reprinted from *An Experiment in the Validation of the Glueck Prediction Scale: Progress Report from November, 1952, to December, 1956*, New York City Youth Board, Research Department, July, 1957, 7–36; Research Staff of Study: Maude M. Craig, director; Freeda Taran, supervisor; Isabel Baughn, Julius Guttenplan, Elinore Nemovicher, research assistants; Barbara Wood, home interviewer for new sample; Ruth M. Smith, statistician; Selma J. Glick and Mrs. Marion S. Shute (former project supervisor), raters; Josephine McAbee, secretary. Mr. Pendleton Rogers was the first project supervisor. Footnotes renumbered. Used by permission. — *Ed.*

1 Sheldon and Eleanor T. Glueck, *Unraveling Juvenile Delinquency*, The Commonwealth Fund, New York, 1950.

2 Ralph W. Whelan, "An Experiment in Predicting Juvenile Delinquency," *The Journal of Criminal Law, Criminology and Police Science*, Vol. 45, No. 4, November–December, 1954.

3 Sheldon and Eleanor T. Glueck, "Early Detection of Future Delinquents," *Journal of Criminal Law, Criminology and Police Science*, Vol. 47, No. 2, July–August, 1956.

of the three tables (based on Rorschach, psychiatric and social data) individually and when used in conjunction with each other on the group reported upon in *Unraveling Juvenile Delinquency*. Combinations of selected factors from the three tables were found to yield only slightly better efficiency in predicting of delinquency than that attained by the three sets of data without intercorrelation or by the Social Factors Prediction Table alone. The conclusion reached is: "It does not appear that the increment in efficiency (when combination of factors involving all three tables are used) is great enough to warrant a recommendation that Rorschach tests and psychiatric skills be used in 'screening' or 'spotting' potential delinquents." The Youth Board thus feels secure that the earlier decision to use the Social Factors Prediction Table alone has essentially been a sound one.

II. THE YOUTH BOARD STUDY

Retrospective studies of the Social Factors Prediction Table,[4] had already yielded results which were encouraging and suggestive of the value of working further with this predictive instrument. No investigator, however, had applied the table to a group of children prior to the onset of overt symptoms of delinquency. The Youth Board was in a position, both by the nature of its functions and the availability of its resources, to initiate such a prospective prediction study. Thus, the agency set forth in the fall of 1952 to test the validity of the instrument which was made available by the Gluecks.

A. *Sample.* The first group of cases consisted of the *total* first grade male population in two public schools in New York City (schools not identified), which are located in a high delinquency area. All boys entering the first grade classes in these two schools during the academic year 1952–1953 were candidates for inclusion in the study. The age range was 5½-6½ years.

---

[4] Bertram J. Black, and Selma J. Glick, *Recidivism at Hawthorne — Cedar Knolls School*, Predicted Versus Actual Outcome for Delinquent Boys, Research Monograph No. 2, Jewish Board of Guardians, New York, 1952.

Richard E. Thompson, "Validation of the Glueck Social Prediction Scale for Proneness to Delinquency," *The Journal of Criminal Law, Criminology and Police Science*; Vol. 43: November–December, 1952.

Table 1   *Number and Per Cent of Boys by Ethnic Grouping (1952–53)* *

ETHNIC GROUP	NUMBER	PER CENT
All boys	224	100.0
White	53†	23.7
Negro	131	58.5
Puerto Rican *	40	17.8

* For the purposes of this study, children of Puerto Rican parentage were classified separately and have not been included either as white or Negro.

† Twenty-three or 43.4% of these are of Jewish parentage.

Starting with a pool of 236 names, the sample was decreased to 224. The principal reason for this decrement was the removal of families from the school district. In only two cases did the parents refuse to cooperate. There were three additional boys who were "dropped" because the "cooperation" of the parent interviewed was so limited that the final data were completely inadequate for purposes of scoring.

Table 1 presents the distribution of Negro, white, and Puerto Rican boys in this Sample I group of 224 boys.

In selecting the total first grade population, the study by design included Negro and Puerto Rican children. The preponderance of Negroes in this sample, however, led to a reconsideration of certain methodological issues. It was evident that the sample was markedly different from the group studied by the Gluecks which included neither of these two populations and only a negligible number of Jewish boys (2% of the Glueck sample).

The major question raised concerned the validity of applying the prediction table to boys of different racial and cultural backgrounds from those on whom it had been devised. To make the Board sample more comparable to the Glueck group, it was decided to increase the number of white non-Jewish boys. Each academic year, therefore, for the two succeeding years, the two cooperating public schools were asked to submit the names of entering first grade students who were white, non-Puerto Rican and non-Jewish. Sampling increments for these two years yielded 32 additional cases (Sample II Group) with the resultant distribution of the total sample as follows: White —

84; Negro — 132 [5]; Puerto Rican — 40 [6] for this new total of 256 boys. The objective of appreciably narrowing the differences in ethnic origins between the two groups had thus not been achieved.

In view of the differential in age between the Sample I boys and the more recent additions to the study and the problems in data analysis that would ensue if annual increments to the sample continued to be made, a major decision regarding further increases in sampling was made in the spring of 1956. It was decided to make the final increase in the sample at this time by including two other schools in an area which also had a high delinquency rate and which was adjacent to the one in which the original schools were located. To achieve the desired objective, the older kindergarten children who met our criterion (white, non-Puerto Rican and non-Jewish) were added to the first grade boys eligible for inclusion. This yielded a total of 47 additional boys [7] and comprised the Sample III group.

The final distribution by ethnic origin for the total group of 303 boys is shown in Table 2. It may be observed that the final racial distribution is such that more interesting comparisons may eventually be made with the Glueck study boys than would have been the case if the Board study was confined to Group I boys alone.

However, it should be noted that the ethnic origin of the boys in the Youth Board study group is much *more varied* than and *differs considerably* from that of the Glueck study group in which there were no Negroes or Puerto Ricans and in which English, Irish and Italian parentage was dominant — (69 percent of the total). This agency has felt from the outset that unless the scale is predictive for a much broader group than a primarily white Anglo-Saxon and

Table **2**　*Number and Per Cent of Boys by Ethnic Grouping (Total Sample)* *

ETHNIC GROUP	NUMBER	PER CENT
All boys	303	100.0
White	130†	42.9
Negro	132	43.6
Puerto Rican	41	13.6

* For the purpose of the study, children of Puerto Rican parentage were classified separately.

† The percentage of Jewish boys in the white population now becomes 17.7%.

Italian population, its usefulness will be limited, particularly in the City of New York.

B. Area characteristics. A comprehensive study was made of the area from which the two schools draw their pupils. School selection had stemmed from the decision to choose one school which housed a child guidance clinic under the combined auspices of the Youth Board and Board of Education (for treatment purposes) and the need to match this school with a school located in a neighborhood with analogous socioeconomic characteristics. Thus, the second school selected was characterized by its proximity to the first school and the similarity of the school population and environmental factors.

The area study included data regarding the boundaries, physical characteristics of the neighborhoods, population characteristics, vital statistics, housing conditions, economic status and community resources in the two school districts.[8] In addition, two workers were sent into the neighborhoods to chart on a block-by-block basis the neighborhood characteristics and population composition. On the basis of these data, the two districts finally approved appeared to be sufficiently similar in their socioeconomic constellations to warrant their selection. The following are some of the salient features of the analysis.[9]

---

[5] The increase of one in the number of Negroes is the result of the reclassification of one boy submitted as white who was later found to have a Negro grandparent. The classification of Negro used includes persons of mixed white and Negro parentage.

[6] In cases of mixed Puerto Rican and non-Puerto Rican parentage, it was decided to accept the birthplace of the father for this classification.

[7] Fifty-three names were submitted by the teachers in the four schools. Of these, two families refused to participate and four families moved out of the city before home visits were made. One of the forty-seven boys accepted was later discovered to be of Puerto Rican parentage.

---

[8] Tables derived from this study are presented in an unpublished manuscript of the Research Department, New York City Youth Board, dated December 1953.

[9] The limitations of the available indices on which these findings are based were recognized.

1. Approximately 35 per cent of the children in each of the two schools were considered "problem youth" by the administrative staffs of the two schools.
2. Both areas are characterized by a decline and a rapid change in the population composition. Both areas are characterized by a large influx of Negro and Puerto Rican populations. The rate of influx in both districts varies slightly but the pattern of population change is fundamentally the same.
3. Considerable portions of both these districts are zoned for industry and/or commerce.
4. There are no supervised playstreets or playgrounds in either of these school districts except in the schools themselves.
5. The populations are served by the same kind of community resources.

The considerations which led to an increase in the sample size have already been discussed. When the decision as to the ultimate sample size was made in 1956, an ideal objective was seen as an increase of 100 boys in the white group. The achievement of this goal would have necessitated the selection of cases from a different area, probably from another borough. Weighed against this was the desirability of securing the sampling increase from the same geographical area as earlier to keep constant such variables as socioeconomic and neighborhood conditions. The latter decision, with a consequent smaller increment in the sampling, was seen as the most tenable choice.

Conferences were held with the Assistant Superintendent of Schools, responsible for schools in the same area of the City.[10] The decision to add the schools adjacent to those first selected was made upon the advice that school conditions and neighborhood characteristics are congruent in these four school districts. The decision not to expand beyond this point was based on the further advice that we would border on areas where neighborhood conditions become perceptibly better.

C. Data gathered. Data on the boys and their families were obtained from three

sources: interviews with mothers (and some fathers) conducted in the homes; interviews with teachers; and collateral information from those social agencies who had served these families.

1. Home interviews:

A structured form was devised as a guide for obtaining family relationship data [11] and the workers who secured the information were oriented in using it. The importance of specific factual data particularly concerning predictive factors being evaluated, in contrast to primarily "impressionistic" and "diagnostically" oriented statements, was stressed. Each schedule was reviewed when received in the research office and workers informed when further family data was needed for scoring purposes. At times, fathers were interviewed in an effort to supplement inadequate, equivocal or ambiguous statements about their roles. Unfortunately, this was achieved less frequently than an ideal situation would warrant, and the mother served as interpreter of the father's role in most of the families interviewed.

Home interviewers were obtained to work part-time from the staffs of the Youth Board Referral Units, the Youth Board — Board of Education clinic, and the Youth Board Research Department.[12] In all, over thirty persons were involved in one or more home interviews. Despite periodic group meetings for the training of workers and an attempt to schedule individual conferences with them, the size of the group of interviewers and the dispersion of their primary responsibilities constituted a procedural limitation in this study. For this reason, one full-time interviewer was employed for a four-month period to do the group of forty-seven interviews which constitute the last sampling increase. This made a more intensive training period possible; introduced less variability in interviewing techniques; and hopefully, resulted in a sustained high level performance.

Our experience in interviewing parents in a pre-test group consisting of eight cases resulted

---

[10] We wish to acknowledge our gratitude to the Board of Education, its administrators, teachers and other personnel who have offered maximal cooperation in all phases of the study since its inception.

[11] See Appendix A. [Appendix not included. — Ed.]

[12] This group consisted of trained caseworkers with a minimum of three years of experience. Supervisors assigned to this project have been social workers whose casework training has been supplemented by research experience.

in the decision to make unannounced home visits. It was found that letters caused parents to react suspiciously, and to assume that their boy had been misbehaving. Emotional reactions on the part of parents, it was felt, could be handled more effectively "on the spot" by the social worker and misinterpretations dealt with as they arose. Various experienced researchers believed, too, that there was an advantage in viewing the home situation informally.

One important preparation was a discussion of the project at general PTA meetings of the two schools. Despite small attendance at these meetings, they served as a lever even in securing the cooperation of parents who did not attend since it established the connection of the study with the school and provided the official auspices for the study. Parents who attended the meeting passed the information along to their neighbors and friends.

Workers introduced themselves as representatives of the New York City Youth Board, an agency interested in children. A general statement was made to the effect that the study evolved from an interest in knowing more about the boys and following their progress during their school careers. It was, of course, important to emphasize that the agency was interested in *all* first grade boys. This served to reassure parents whose knowledge of Youth Board activities associated this interest with the stigma of deviant behavior. Parents were further reassured by telling them that their cooperation was on a purely voluntary basis and the confidentiality of the data they supplied was stressed.

2. School interviews:

A structured form was devised as a guide for obtaining data on the boy's adjustment in school.[13] This was to serve as part of a permanent yearly record of the child's school behavior in terms of conduct, relationships, academic attitudes and achievement. The first year's report was used only as an adjunct in scoring the case, since the major emphasis was perforce placed on the family relationship material and social agency data.

3. Social agency data:

All cases were cleared through the Social Ser-

vice Exchange, and relevant agency reports were obtained. This served as an important supplement to the family picture presented during the home interview and was used as a corrective in evaluating information provided by the family. For those families who have not been known to any social agencies, there may be certain subtle factors missed by the interviewer or carefully concealed by the family. (Follow-up data clearly indicate that certain families tried to create a "halo" effect in the presentation of information.)

D. Delinquency prediction scores. The supervisor[14] of the project served as one of the two raters in the assignment of scores in accordance with the Glueck Social Factors Prediction Table. All cases were scored independently by another qualified rater. "In 90 percent of the cases, the two raters placed the boy in the same predictive score class. For one half of the remaining cases, differences in predictive score class did not extend beyond the limits of the delinquent or non-delinquent range"[15] (see Table 4 and text which follows for an explanation of the cut-off point between delinquency and non-delinquency). All cases on which the raters differed in regard to predictive score class were submitted to Dr. Eleanor Glueck for a third rating.

The following table presents the five categories of the Social Factors Prediction Table, with the sub-categories and weighted failure scores, used for prediction purposes.

The definitions (revised 6/4/53 in cooperation with Dr. Eleanor Glueck) for each social factor and the sub-categories are as follows.

1. Discipline of boy by father:

Overstrict or erratic — Father is harsh, unreasoning, demands obedience through fear; or varies between strictness and laxity, is not consistent in control.

Lax — Father is negligent, indifferent, lets boy do what he likes. Or boy has not lived with father at all.

Firm but kindly — Discipline is based on

---

[13] See Appendix A. [Appendix not included. — Ed.]

[14] There was a change in supervisors in the early phase of the study. The second appointee served as one of the raters in the majority of the cases.

[15] Ralph W. Whelan, "An Experiment in Predicting Juvenile Delinquency," *op. cit.*

Table **3**   Social Factors Prediction Table

FACTORS	WEIGHTED FAILURE SCORE
1. Discipline of Boy by Father	
Overstrict or erratic	71.8
Lax	59.8
Firm but kindly	9.3
2. Supervision of Boy by Mother	
Unsuitable	83.2
Fair	57.5
Close or suitable	9.9
3. Affection of Father for Boy	
Indifferent or hostile	75.9
Warm (including over- protective)	33.8
4. Affection of Mother for Boy	
Indifferent or hostile	86.2
Warm (including overprotective)	43.1
5. Cohesiveness of Family	
Unintegrated	96.9
Some elements of cohesion	61.3
Cohesive	20.6

sound reason which the boy understands and accepts as fair.

2. Supervision of boy by mother:

Unsuitable — Mother is careless in her supervision, leaving boy to his own devices without guidance or in the care of an irresponsible child or adult.

Fair — Mother, though at home, gives or provides only partial supervision to boy.

Close — If mother does not work outside the home and is not ill, she personally keeps close watch on the boy or provides for his leisure hours in clubs or playgrounds or if she is ill or out of the home a great deal, there is a responsible adult in charge.

3. Affection of father for boy:
            and
4. Affection of mother for boy:

Indifferent — Parent does not pay much attention to boy, but is not outwardly hostile.
Hostile — Parent obviously rejects boy.

Warm — Parent is outwardly sympathetic, kind, attached, even though in some cases overprotective.

5. Cohesiveness of family:

Unintegrated — Home is just a place to "hang your hat"; self interest of the members exceeds group interest. This applies especially to the parents and to the older siblings.

Some elements of cohesion — Even if the family group may not be entirely intact (because of departure of one or more members for purely selfish reasons), the remaining group of which the boy is a part has at least some of the characteristics of the cohesive family.

Cohesive — There is a strong "we-feeling" among members of the immediate family as evidenced by cooperativeness, group interests, pride in the home, affection for each other, "All for one and one for all." This applies even if one parent, usually the father, has never been a part of the family group.

Table 4 presents the four-class breakdown of total weighted failure scores used in the Youth Board Study [16] and the associated probability of delinquency for each class.

On the basis of the four predictive score classes, as shown above, boys with total failure scores under 200 are classified as having 8.2 chances of delinquency per hundred; those with scores between 200 and 249 in the group having 37 chances of delinquency per hundred; those with scores between 250 and 299 in the group having 63.5 chances of delinquency per hundred; and those with scores of 300 and over in the group having 89.2 chances of delinquency per hundred. The score of 250 has been considered by the Gluecks as the cut-off point between potential delinquency and potential non-delinquency. Table 5 will present the final classification of the sample of 224 children by weighted failure scores and the probability of delinquency.

It became apparent that we need to look at the ratings assigned to the Sample I group of cases and to attempt to "iron out" any question-

---

[16] See Sheldon and Eleanor T. Glueck, *Unraveling Juvenile Delinquency*, The Commonwealth Fund, New York 1950, p. 261–262, for other class breakdowns.

Table 4

WEIGHTED FAILURE SCORE	CHANCES OF DELINQUENCY	CHANCES OF NON-DELINQUENCY
Under 200	8.2) Low probability	91.8
200–249	37.0) or non delinquent	63.0
250–299	63.5) High probability	36.5
300 and over	89.2) or delinquent	10.8

able scoring at this stage of the experiment. Accordingly, the present supervisor read critically the case material used in the rating of these 224 cases. It was feared, for example, that in the earlier phases of the study before criteria for rating had been evolved in a more final form, rating judgments may have been more variable and less standardized than at a later point. In addition, there was a small number of cases in which no consensus between two raters had been achieved and a compromise rating had been accepted. An occasional case had received only one rating. There were, too, a few cases that had originally been formally characterized by the rater as rated with a low degree of confidence.

A group of 40 cases was selected from 224 cases and submitted for rescoring on the five factors of the Social Factors Prediction Table. No information pertinent to the later behavior of the boy and his family was provided to the re-raters. The criteria for re-rating and procedures are described in Appendix B. [Appendix not included. — Ed.] The results of the re-rating and a comparison with the original rating assigned are presented in the following table.

The over-all picture presented by the final ratings is not markedly different from the former ratings except that a slightly larger number of cases fall into the "non-delinquent" category (69.6 percent as compared with 67.9 percent.) The general shift has been in the direction of decreasing the failure scores and probability of delinquency with the greatest shift into the 200–249 score class. There has been a reduction in both the 250–299 class and the 300 and over group. A total of sixteen changes in rating was involved with seven coming from a group of cases in which there had not originally been a consensus of two raters. An eighth case was changed because new more valid data had become available regarding the child's living arrangements and this replaced the earlier data.

For comparative purposes the classification of the 47 Sample III cases (rated in 1956) is presented below [on the following page. —Ed.].

A little more than one-third (⅓) of the cases are concentrated above the score of 250 (potential delinquency) in the Sample III (47 cases), whereas somewhat less than one-third (⅓) of the cases are found above this cut-off point in Sample I (224 cases).

Table 5 — Classification of 224 Children by Probability of Delinquency Revised Scoring (Sample 1: 1952–53)

WEIGHTED FAILURE SCORE	PROBABILITY OF DELINQUENCY	REVISED RATING		ORIGINAL RATING	
		Number	Per Cent	Number	Per Cent
Total		224	100.0	224	100.0
Under 200	8.2	111	49.5	114	50.9
200–249	37.0	45	20.1	38	17.0
250–299	63.5	49	21.9	50	22.3
300 & over	89.2	19	8.5	22	9.8

Table **6** *Classification of 47 Children by Probability of Delinquency*

WEIGHTED FAILURE SCORE	PROBABILITY OF DELINQUENCY	NUMBER	PER CENT
Total		47	100.0
Under 200	8.2	25	53.2
200–249	37.0	6	12.8
250–299	63.5	12	25.5
300 & over	89.2	4	8.5

The entire matter of scoring will warrant further evaluation at a later date. There are several components integrated into the scoring procedure and it is recognized that a weakness in any one aspect will modify the validity of a given score.

In the first instance, there may have been inaccuracies and inadequacies in information secured in what was for the most part a one-interview operation. Some distortions may have stemmed from deliberate falsification of the family situation, whereas in others, the limitations of parental comprehension and awareness (either through dullness or emotional factors) may constitute a source of error. An understandable tendency on the part of many parents is to "protect" the child.

An ever-present difficulty stemmed from the hardship that many mothers [17] had in focusing their observations on the specific child at issue, since they tended to offer data more characteristic of the total family situation. This difficulty is, of course, enhanced in dealing with the more limited parents. In addition, there are many subtle factors in intrafamily relationships which may be operating at a level that would not be apparent in a family study such as this.

Several potential weaknesses may also be reviewed in the actual scoring process. For example, the many changes and fluctuations in family relationships that may occur during the first 6 years of the child's life create difficulty in evaluating these cases. Sometimes the role of a father substitute in the form of a grandfather, uncle, mother's boy-friend, or the entrance of a stepfather into the picture, may present a rating problem due to elements of ambiguity in the data or some falsification of the role of such persons. The rater must decide how stable the new relationships seem to be. The following case illustrates the point at issue:

Willie, an out-of-wedlock child of Negro parentage, lived with his maternal grandmother in a southern town until his mother married in New York City and he became part of the new family unit. At the time of the home interview, Willie had been a part of this new group for only six months but such a unified picture in the mother's home was presented, that three raters evaluated the family as showing maximum cohesion (20.6). The passage of time has revealed, however, that the mother and stepfather separated two years later at which time he allegedly beat her and she defended herself with a knife (Domestic Relations Court Report). Subsequently, the child was returned to his grandmother with a later return to New York City to his mother.

Another area of potential weakness grows out of limitations in the raters' knowledge of the influence of certain cultural factors. This was pointed up in the Puerto Rican group and raters felt a lesser degree of confidence in rating this group as a whole. Another illustration is the Maltese family which required special consideration since culturally these fathers consider it a sign of weakness to demonstrate any overt affection toward children (e.g. kiss them only when they sleep) and fairly rigid disciplinary measures are the rule.

The area of judgment involved in rating some of the situations such as those cited above is self-evident. Only one case, however, has been left with a "compromise" rating. This situation will be summarized here since it sharpens some of the issues discussed concerning ratings.

Milton's family, at the time of rating, consisted of his parents and four siblings. Family had come North after the birth of two children and Milton was the

---

[17] As already noted, the mother or mother substitute was the usual parent interviewed.

first born in New York City. Both parents were employed, the father as a laborer (in an industry in which seasonal unemployment was recurrent) and the mother in a factory. It was noted that the father was polite but very shy and never answered questions directly. The interviewer observed that the child responded when the father gave him a firm command, in contradistinction to his disregard of the mother's commands. Mother stated that a neighbor looks after the children while she is at work but children appeared poorly cared for and dirty. Further indication of lack of care was noted in the statement that the boy sometimes forgot until he went to bed that he had not eaten. So far as the relationship with his father is concerned, mother stated that the father takes the boy out in the car with him occasionally, but does very little at home other than sleep.

A Department of Welfare report contributed the following: "Mr. Z is illiterate and seems retarded. He finds it very difficult to find his way around town, since he can't read. He is also difficult to place". This note was dated two years after the family's arrival in N.Y.C. at the time of reapplication for relief due to loss of employment (place of employment had burned down). It was noted that the wife seemed more intelligent than her husband. The agency record is replete with entries about unemployment and reemployment. In one entry it is noted that Mr. Z cannot tell the investigator anything about household expenses or past maintenance and that even his age is uncertain.

Originally the case was scored as follows by two raters:

Discipline:	9.3
Supervision:	57.5
Affection of father:	33.8
Affection of mother:	43.1
Cohesiveness of family:	20.6
Total	164.3
Chances of Delinquency:	8.2

This case was re-rated on the basis of the current supervisor's impression that there was sufficient evidence to indicate mental retardation in the father. She therefore questioned whether such a father could perform his function as a father at this optimal level. (It should be noted, however, that the interviewer did observe that the child obeyed his father's firm commands. This, undoubtedly, influenced the scores assigned to the case).

The case was submitted for rescoring to three persons, one of whom had originally rated the case. She maintained the same rating of 8.2 chances of delinquency. A second rater (rating the case for the first time) scored it as having 63.5 chances of delinquency (commenting in relation to the sections on the father: "mentally defective"),[18] and a third rater (also rating for the first time) scored it as having 37.0 chances of delinquency (commenting that if the father of the boy is defective, the rating would be higher but that on the basis of the data as given, she cannot feel assured of the mental status of the father).

A conference in regard to these scorings was held with each rater elaborating on the judgment used in rating. Rater I (low score) stated that her rating was influenced by cultural factors; e.g., she did not consider it unusual for an adult Negro born in the South to be illiterate and therefore seem retarded. Rater II (high score) stressed heavily the fact that the father is illiterate, was very unresponsive during the interview (and also sleeps much of the time), and is unable to find his way around the city; therefore could not function as a "good" father. Rater III (middle score) stressed the fact that the data are equivocal and one could suspect serious limitations in the father, but the facts are not sufficiently clear to validate this assumption.

E. Treatment experiment. This project was designed to include a study of the effectiveness of treatment for a group scored as potentially delinquent boys (more than a 50 per cent chance of becoming delinquent). Thus the high scoring groups attending one school were referred for treatment to the school clinic. This constituted approximately one-half of the total high scoring boys.

There has been a constant process of attrition in the size of the treatment group. School mobility is high in this area and a sizeable number of children had already moved before a diagnostic evaluation could be completed.

The treatment group will warrant full-scale evaluation at a later date. An attempt will be made to match cases which have received treatment with a comparable untreated group.

It is hoped that the treatment study will make a significant contribution to the understanding of pre-delinquency and delinquency in its incipient stages.

---

[18] Raters were encouraged to make comments when re-rating for the purpose of providing material for a manual of definitions which is being planned.

F. *Follow-up procedures.* The research design called for an intensive and comprehensive follow-up procedure for each of the boys in the study. It was anticipated that this would include an annual school interview, annual home visits, periodic reclearances through the Social Service Exchange and the Police Department.[19]

School interviews were given precedence in view of the need to complete them within a specified academic period. It was during the process of carrying on this assignment and in reclearing the cases, that the expense of this type of follow-up became apparent to the agency. Up to this point, the staff assigned to this project simultaneously carried out responsibilities in connection with other research studies. Thus the follow-up procedures to date have been limited primarily to annual reports on the behavior patterns and social adjustment within the school setting. It is noteworthy, however, that many of the difficulties involving the child and family are known to school personnel and information such as that concerning police contacts, official and unofficial, with the boys has come to our attention through the school interviews.

To make possible full-time supervision and the necessary research assistance to carry out more intensive follow-up procedures, the Ford Foundation approved a grant of $105,300 for additional staff needed for a four-year period of continuation. The Youth Board agreed to continue its support of the staff already assigned to the project.

To sum up, the follow-up procedures to date have consisted of annual school interviews, reclearance with the Social Service Exchange, reports from registered social agencies and clearance with the files of the Police Department.

One of the problems encountered in the follow-up process has been locating the children included in the study. Mobility in these families is extremely high. The following table indicates the dispersion of the boys in the first three samples as of July 1956.

Written reports are requested on all out-of-town residents. An intensive effort is made to locate any child who moves out of town. As

Table 7 School Geographical Distribution of 256 Boys in Prediction Study: July 1956

SCHOOL LOCATION	NUMBER OF BOYS	NUMBER OF DIFFERENT SCHOOLS
Total	256	89
Two original schools	144	2
Bronx	59	35
Brooklyn	6	6
Manhattan	11	10
Queens	10	10
Richmond	2	2
Out-of-City	24	24
In New York State	(12)	—
Other States	(12)	—

of July 1956, 4 children were missing, one in South Carolina and three in Puerto Rico. An effort is still being made to locate these through local social agencies.[20]

III. PRESENT STATUS OF BOY'S BEHAVIOR

In response to a marked interest in the findings and present status of this investigation, it was decided to examine and present at this time, data descriptive of the boys' behavior as of the end of the academic year, 1955–56, four years after the start of the project. An analysis was made of the behavior status of the oldest boys in the study, age range 9½–10½ years, who had finished four years of grade schooling. The analysis was based on school and social agency data for this period and court or police (Juvenile Aid Bureau) records, through 1956.

It must be emphasized in the beginning that *the study has not yet reached the stage where definitive results might be anticipated.* The criterion measure in this study is *persistent delinquency* and the oldest children being studied are at an age level when the incidence of delinquency would expectedly be low. The Gluecks based their findings on a group of children ranging in age from eleven to seventeen years with a median age of somewhat over 14.5 years. The average age of the first court appearance was 12.4. Slightly over one-fourth of the boys

[19] We are grateful for the cooperation of Commissioner Robert J. Mangum and his record room staff for making the Juvenile Aid Bureau, Police Department files available to us.

[20] During the writing of this report, two of the three Puerto Rican children were relocated in New York City and will be followed-up again.

fell below the age of eleven years; 45.8 percent were in the age range of eleven to thirteen years; and another 25.8 percent were fourteen through sixteen years of age at the time of their first court appearance.[21]

We have drawn heavily for this analysis upon the school reports, and much of the information is described in terms of classroom behavior and situations. The limitations of teachers' reports as a source of data are more than compensated for by the continued availability of this source of data and the universality of the school society as a setting within which all children are expected to learn to function in a variety of areas.

A classification system was devised which is descriptive, rather than diagnostic, of each boy's reported behavior patterns, "symptoms" and traits. These groupings cover a range of behavior starting with those which were presumed to be the farthest removed from pre-delinquent behavior to those already established as delinquents.

The assumptions implicit in the classifications are as follows: By definition, we are primarily interested in the children who have already become delinquent; and those, too, who are indulging in "unofficial" delinquent behavior. In addition, it would seem that the children who show evidence of an antisocial character formation have a base which has been found related to "latent" delinquency. A child's failure to conform to more or less generally accepted standards of behavior and an indulgence in a positive rebellion against these standards, would seem to us, on the basis of the literature, to be exhibiting precursory symptoms of potentially delinquent behavior.

The definition of delinquency used by the Gluecks has been applied to the boys in the Youth Board study.

"Delinquency refers to repeated acts of a kind which when committed by persons beyond the statutory juvenile court age of sixteen are punishable as crimes (either felonies or misdemeanors) — except for a few instances of persistent stubbornness, truancy, running away, associating with immoral persons, and the like. Children who once or twice during the period of growing up in an excitingly attractive milieu steal a toy in a ten cent store, sneak into a subway or

motion picture theatre, play hooky, and the like and soon outgrow such peccadilloes, are not true delinquents even though they have violated the law." [22]

An eight-category classification scheme was established. A case-by-case evaluation was made by two or more members of the staff (all cases were evaluated by the director of research and the project supervisor). The judgments were made independently of the knowledge of the delinquency ratings. They may be considered impressionistic and subjective except in those situations where findings of persistent delinquent behavior are noted. We tried to achieve a reasonably consistent level of performance and anchored our judgments to case illustrations by means of which other staff members reviewed the decisions. There are some borderline cases in each category which "borrow" characteristics of another grouping. In such cases, a final decision had to be made with a lesser degree of confidence than we would have liked to achieve.

It is axiomatic that delinquency covers a wide variety of personality structures. At this point, we are not attempting to label these children as already indelibly delinquent, or irrevocably nondelinquent. Some of them may conceivably become followers of more aggressive leaders at a later stage and some may form a part of the group of neurotic delinquents. It should be remembered, too, that some of these children are active treatment cases and this will in some measure determine the final outcome of some cases.

The following sections describe the classification groupings used and provide a case illustration. Additional illustrations will be found in Appendix C. The reader should refer to Tables 8 and 9 for the behavior classifications of the boys in relation to their predicted behavior.

1. Essentially normal behavior for age and IQ and including mild behavior disorders and deviations. Group I cases range in behavior from the well-adjusted to the group evaluated as showing mild behavior difficulties. At one end of the continuum we find children who are well-ordered, cooperative, and highly motivated. At the other end we find those who show some evidence of withdrawing and immature behavior or evidence of assertive and mild acting-out be-

---

[21] Sheldon and Eleanor T. Glueck, *Unraveling Juvenile Delinquency*, The Commonwealth Fund, New York, 1950.

[22] S. and E. T. Glueck, *Unraveling Juvenile Delinquency*, The Commonwealth Fund, New York, 1950, p. 13.

havior, or a fluctuation of behavior within acceptable limits.

They are not the children who present serious disciplinary difficulties to their teachers and cause little concern in the classroom situation. With minor deviations, they comply with the requirements of the school setting in academic performance and behavior. They are not all necessarily prototypes of the best mental health adjustment, however.

Children who show behavior which appears to be temporary maladaptive behavior (markedly different from previous years and oftentimes associated with some environmental circumstance) have generally been included in Group I.

There are some children in this category who have been guilty of an isolated small theft, an isolated truancy episode, or have thrown rocks on occasion, but such complaints neither reoccurred nor seemed characteristic of the child's basic pattern.

Some children in this classification are inattentive, show intermittent elements of aggression (within moderate limits) and need to be prodded to perform. Some are characterized by one or two symptoms (speech defects or nervous mannerisms, etc.). On the whole, they seem to improve in their relationships and skills with the length of stay in school. In the evaluation of children with a low level of intelligence, their intellectual limitations were taken into consideration in their assignment to this category.

Only one of the 110 children in this group was known to the Juvenile Aid Bureau; at the age of seven he was throwing stones (comment — "no intent to damage").

Rivers was described as a really dependable boy, although he was inclined to be aggressive and restless when he entered school. He later showed an inclination to cry, to offend extremely easily and to be among the shyer, more timid children in the class. He seemed to be outgrowing these patterns by the fourth year of school. The teacher was able to be open in her "criticism" of him. At this point he was becoming better liked, participated actively in group projects and was coming closer to realizing his better than average intellectual endowment.

2. *Children with emotional symptoms (essentially neurotic-like behavior)*. Children in this category showed a considerable number of symptoms as well as predominant patterns of withdrawing behavior. Symptoms found were varied: thumbsucking, tics, marked daydream-

ing, urinary frequency (or enuresis), nervous mannerisms, effeminate tendencies, inappropriate or odd behavior, and vague physical complaints. Some of these are children who are not absorbing academically although they seriously make an effort to do so; others are immobilized when presented with anything new.

Only one of the 34 children in Category II was known to the Juvenile Aid Bureau. He was found playing in the vicinity of a railroad yard when he was seven years old and was throwing cardboard boxes.

Martin is a perfectionistic high-strung fearful child, so easily upset by trifles that he is unable to cope with ordinary school problems. Easily moved to tears in his earlier years, he continued to be shy and a block in his reading performance has developed.

3. *Behavior problems: Aggressive–disruptive school behavior.* We have included in this group the children who present evidence of disruptive school behavior and are essentially troublesome in the school setting. Among them are the highly energetic, hyperactive, non-conforming, mischievous children. At the less troublesome end of the continuum they may be teasing in a competitive or cowardly fashion pushing their peers and "taking" their belongings. They often relate poorly to either peers or teachers because of their extreme attention-getting devices. At the more serious end of the continuum they indicate a resentment of authority and/or controls and are aggressive (fighting) and quarrelsome with their peers. Among these latter, we may find an admixture of neurotic-like traits with the predominating acting-out (aggressive) trends.

The majority show little or no interest in school work, are inattentive and definitely not functioning up to capacity. There are only a few attendance problems in this group, other than occasional tardiness which occurs because of fooling around and mischievous behavior on the way to school.

We have called this category our "suspended judgment" group, anticipating that some of these children may develop increasingly aggressive patterns, whereas others will manage to stay out of any serious difficulty.

Three children out of the 45 in this category have single Juvenile Aid Bureau offenses. One boy, at age 8, was known for stealing (misdirected play — taking a neighbor's car keys), another was picked up as a truant, and a third was reported for a "farebeat."

Richard is an excitable, bold noisy boy. He wastes the class time, causes confusion in the room and is antagonistic to his classmates. He fights, jokes and is non-conforming in an attention-getting way. When younger, he would throw himself on the floor and use bad language which, too, according to the teacher was seen as an attention-getting device. He is, however, better liked by his 4th year teacher and is seemingly more interested in school now, despite a lower-than-expected academic performance.

Categories IV and V have been defined as covering a group of boys who seemed nearer to becoming delinquent. On the basis of this judgment, we grouped them together under the general rubric of a Potentially Delinquent Group.

4. *Delinquent traits.* This group encompasses those children whose behavioral patterns and constellation of traits have frequently been associated with pre-delinquent behavior. No serious delinquent act has been reported and they are not the most aggressive children in the study. In this they differ from the more hostile, belligerent and assaultive children put into Category V.

A number of children in IV started their school careers as either quiet or frightened children or presented a strange intermeshing of fearful and aggressive acts (*e.g.*, is frightened and fights; fights and is nervous; is whiny and rebellious). Their acting out is more focused toward specific areas of school requirements, often a rebellion versus academic and/or school attendance requirements. It is here that we find the children who are considered serious attendance problems, persistently come to school late, or associate with the predelinquent ringleaders in the school. We note such teacher comments as: "He puts a wall around him;" "Impossible to reach."

It should be pointed out that the incidence of clear-cut truancy in our group as a whole is extremely small. There are, however, a number of attendance problems in boys whose absences are over and above any reasonable expectation. At times the apathy of the parents has become the apathy of the child (or vice versa); or the mother persistently keeps the boy at home on various pretexts of her own. Frequently, the teacher suspects that truancy has been covered up and official truancy record has been established. It is not infrequent for many of their parents to overlook absence notes routinely.

Three Juvenile Aid Bureau referrals and two police contacts have been found for children in this group of 12 boys. The Juvenile Aid Bureau offenses cover: a farebeat (and truancy); throwing stones at a child (at age 10½); allegedly took $5.00 (boy stated he found the money after wrestling with the owner).

Burt's first year report portrayed him as a responsive child with a mind of his own. On the negative side, he was "fairly" aggressive, always late and tended to associate with the aggressive boys. Frequent absences became characteristic of his pattern, and he began to do poorly in his academic tasks. Later years indicated emerging aggression and sullenness intermingled with a tendency to daydream. He finally was described as belligerent, jumpy, insolent, and taking off from school for the P.M. session. He has also truanted when he refused to do his spelling assignment. Burt is known to ride the "El" and was picked up for a "farebeat" while truanting.

5. *Antisocial behavior patterns or character.* This group represents the severe behavior disorders; the children who have come into serious conflict with the school society. Essentially hostile and severely attacking behavior prevail. To our knowledge, they have not committed any serious delinquent acts.

Three out of the six children classified in this group have had one Juvenile Aid Bureau offense: throwing stones (see below); beating a boy with clenched fists while truant; a farebeat.

William has demonstrated what one teacher called an "untamed quality" both in his handling of people and objects. An immature, disruptive first grader, he already chased and poked the children, threw blocks at them and took their belongings. He graduated to the stage of throwing books and pencils, and in his 4th year resorted to uncontrolled hitting, and sticking them with pins. Parents refused to have their offspring seated near him. Understandably, William is in constant trouble, is uncontrollable and has no friends. He was accused of stealing one year but the teacher found no tangible evidence of this. He frequently comes to school late (plays in the park) and his school achievement is almost nil.

(At the age of seven, William was known to the Juvenile Aid Bureau for throwing stones at trains.)

6. *Unofficial delinquency.* The five children in this group have either committed a specific act equivalent to an officially delinquent act or been involved in delinquent-like behavior. They

have not necessarily received any official handling in relation to their behavior.

Scott, a boy with a limited intellectual endowment, has been unduly aggressive from the first year of school; bold, fighting, destructive, and using vile language. He later began to bite the children, throw himself on the floor, and roam around the room. Nervous mannerisms were also noted and his rocking back and forth was assumed to be related to his mental retardation. Scott takes many things that don't belong to him and, on one occasion, stole $25.00 from the teacher's purse. He assaulted a classmate with a key dangling from a strap. Teacher evaluates his academic ability as above the level at which he tested and it had been thought that his poor behavior, in some measure, influenced his performance during the psychometric testing.

7. *Diagnosed mental illness.* There are 4 children on whom a psychiatric diagnosis of mental illness had been established. It may suffice to note that these children were aggressive, disruptive and extremely difficult to handle. One of these children was committed to a state hospital.

8. *Adjudicated delinquency or persistent delinquencies involving several police (JAB) and/or court contacts.* The delinquency status of the four boys found in this group is briefly presented here.

Carlos has been our first persistent delinquent. Three court petitions have been brought because of Carlos' persistence in breaking into parking meters and into a truck where he removed several articles. There was an earlier JAB contact, also for breaking into parking meters.

Robert's first court appearance was due to his running away from home which resulted in a wayward minor petition being brought by his mother (incorrigible, ungovernable, a runaway 15 times). Earlier, the JAB had known Robert for throwing stones at a skylight and stealing from the mails. In the school setting, he very early appropriated school supplies and brought to school a trinket stolen from the ten cent store.

Robert accumulated three later JAB offenses: (runaway, farebeat, disorderly conduct) and one unregistered police contact for truancy.

Michael's delinquent career reveals the following listing of offenses: Farebeat, Breaking and Entering and stealing property valued at $15.00 — (arrested and referred to the Children's Court), Shoplifting.

Jonathan has 2 (JAB) offenses on his roster: putting slugs in the turnstile and stealing a bicycle. This constitutes only a fraction of the difficulties in which he has been involved. His school record is replete with incidents of assaultive attacks on others. It was said that he fought as though "dealing out retribution." He both stole and extorted money from his classmates as early as his second year in school and appeared with Board of Education property not obtainable in his school. His "bad moods" increased and during his fourth school year, he was suspended as a danger to the children (broke one child's tooth; raised welts on another child's face, etc.). He is awaiting placement in an institutional setting.

Table 8 presents the relationship between the behavior classifications (which were described previously) and the delinquency ratings assigned to each boy. Findings are presented on 220 out of the 224 boys in the oldest group. Data on four (4) boys, were not available at the time of analysis.

In view of the small number of cases in some of the categories a summarization of Table 8 is presented in Table 9. Categories I and II, presumed to be the farthest removed from delinquent patterns of behavior have been merged. Category III is presented separately, whereas Categories IV-VIII (the "problem" boys) have been combined.

The most prominent feature in Table 8 is the fact that the four persistent delinquents (Category VIII) were rated as having more than a 50% chance of becoming delinquent (one case was rated with a 63.5% probability and three were rated with a 89.2% probability of becoming delinquent). The number of persistent delinquents is still small (as was anticipated due to the age level of this group) but the concentration of this small number of cases in the group with a higher probability of becoming delinquent is evident. Equally important at the present stage of the analysis is the finding that 68% of the children rated as having only 8.2% chances of becoming delinquent, are classified as belonging in Category I. Very few of these children are found in Categories IV-VIII (none in Category VII or VIII).

In inspecting vertically the last column of Table 9, it is seen that 31 boys are involved in the combined "problem" grouping (Categories IV-VIII). Of these twenty-four (24) boys were rated as having more than a 50% chance of becoming delinquent. Conversely seven were scored as having less than a 50% chance of becoming future delinquents.

The summarized table presents another verti-

Table 8 Behavior Classification in Relation to Delinquency Rating December 1956 (220 Boys)

CHANCES OF DELINQUENCY	TOTAL		NORMAL I		NEUROTIC II		SCHOOL BEHAVIOR PROBLEMS III		DEL. TRAITS IV		ANTI-SOCIAL V		UNOFF. DEL. VI		MENTAL ILLNESS VII		OFFICIAL DEL. VIII	
	No.	%	No.	%	No.	%	No.	%	No.	%	No.	%	No.	%	No.	%	No.	%
Total	220	100	110	50	34	15	45	21	12	5	6	3	5	2	4	2	4	2
8.2	109	100	74	68	12	11	18	16	1	1	2	2	1	1	1	1	—	—
37.0	45	100	20	45	9	20	14	31	2	4	—	—	—	—	—	—	—	—
63.5	47	100	13	27	11	24	11	24	4	9	3	6	2	4	2	4	1	2
89.2	19	100	3	15	2	11	2	11	5	27	1	5	2	11	1	5	3	15

Table **9**   *Summary of Table* 8

CHANCES OF DELINQUENCY	TOTAL		NORMAL AND NEUROTIC I and II		SCHOOL BEHAVIOR PROBLEMS III		DELINQUENCY TRAITS, ETC. IV–VIII	
	No.	%	No.	%	No.	%	No.	%
Total	220	100	144	65	45	21	31	14
8.2	109	100	86	79	18	16	5	5
37.0	45	100	29	65	14	31	2	4
63.5	47	100	24	51	11	24	12	25
89.2	19	100	5	26	2	11	12	63
Police Contacts	16		2		3		11	

Including "school problems" as failures 89% are reacting as predicted.

cal distribution which is interesting, namely that found in Category III, the so-called suspended judgment group in which more than half of the boys (25 out of 45) came from the middle range of the rating score distribution. This concentration of "equivocal" cases (in terms of classifying present behavior) in the middle range will bear scrutiny in terms of the later development of these boys. Related to this is the observation (seen in Table 8) that the majority of boys in Category II (20 out of the total of 34), the children with neurotic-like behavior, are also concentrated in the middle group.

This raises the hypothesis that the future trends in groups rated with 37.5% and 63.5% chances of becoming delinquent will provide valuable clues about the development of various types of deviant behavior. We have been impressed by the fact that the extreme cases (at both ends of the distribution) are easily identified, whereas characteristics are less clear-cut in this middle range of cases. A further complication stems from the fact that a case scored with a "high" 37.5% chance of becoming delinquent may receive an arithmetical score very close to the cut-off point for the group scored with a 63.5% chance of becoming delinquent (*e.g.* a 248.1 score versus a 250 point score).[23]

We may summarize this data by saying that in terms of this classification scheme, the boys assigned the least chance of becoming delin-

quent (8.2% rating) constitute the majority of the group presenting no serious problems, whereas the group that already meets the criterion of *persistent delinquent behavior*, come from the high probability group. The data also suggest there is a greater concentration of the serious problems (Categories IV-VII) in the high probability group.

We consider these data as only suggestive due to the small number of cases found in Categories IV-VIII.

IV. FUTURE PLANS

1. Home interviews. Careful follow-up of cases through home visits had been anticipated as a routine aspect of the study. At this mid-way point in the study a decision to do home visits on those children residing within or near the metropolitan area was made. For cases known to treatment agencies, a report or agency conference may be substituted for a home visit. This decision would be made on an individual basis in consultation with the agency.

The primary objective of these visits will be to learn in detail as much as possible about the child's adjustment in the home and in the community, as well as to record any changes in the family circumstances which may influence or "explain" changes in the child's behavior. It may be possible also to learn of other antisocial activities of the children which have not been officially known.

The next step in relation to this phase is to refine a schedule for areas to be covered in the home interview. A decision has to be made

---

[23] See pages 1036 *et seq.* (a discussion of delinquency prediction scores).

Table 10   *Evaluation of Behavior by Score Classification by Ethnic Group —
White (24.1% of Total Sample)*

CHANCES OF DELINQUENCY	TOTAL		NORMAL AND NEUROTIC I–II		SCHOOL BEHAVIOR PROBLEMS III		DELINQUENCY TRAITS, ETC. IV–VIII	
	No.	%	No.	%	No.	%	No.	%
Total	53	100.0	44	83.0	5	9.4	4	7.6
8.2	37	100.0	33	89.2	3	8.1	1	2.7
37.0	7	100.0	6	85.7	1	14.3	—	—
63.5	6	100.0	4	66.6	1	16.7	1	16.7
89.2	3	100.0	1	33.3	—	—	2	66.7

Including "school problems" as failures 90% are reacting as predicted.

Negro (59.1% of Total Sample)

CHANCES OF DELINQUENCY	TOTAL		NORMAL AND NEUROTIC I–II		SCHOOL BEHAVIOR PROBLEMS III		DELINQUENCY TRAITS, ETC. IV–VIII	
	No.	%	No.	%	No.	%	No.	%
Total	130	100.0	76	58.5	32	24.6	22	16.9
8.2	51	100.0	36	70.6	11	21.6	4	7.8
37.0	31	100.0	18	58.1	11	35.5	2	6.4
63.5	35	100.0	18	51.4	9	25.7	8	22.9
89.2	13	100.0	4	30.8	1	7.7	8	61.5

Including "school problems" as failures 85% are reacting as predicted.

Puerto Rican (16.8% of Total Sample)

CHANCES OF DELINQUENCY	TOTAL		NORMAL AND NEUROTIC I–II		SCHOOL BEHAVIOR PROBLEMS III		DELINQUENCY TRAITS, ETC. IV–VIII	
	No.	%	No.	%	No.	%	No.	%
Total	37	100.0	24	64.9	8	21.6	5	13.5
8.2	21	100.0	17	81.0	4	19.0	—	—
37.0	7	100.0	5	71.4	2	28.6	—	—
63.5	6	100.0	2	33.3	1	16.7	3	50.0
89.2	3	100.0	—	—	1	33.3	2	66.7

Including "school problems" as failures 91% are reacting as predicted.

Table **11** *Formula for Figuring Per Cent Who Are Presently Behaving as Predicted*

WEIGHTED FAILURE SCORE	NUMBER IN GROUP	PROBABILITY OF BECOMING DELINQUENTS	EXPECTATION OF DELINQUENCY [24]	OBSERVED DELIN-QUENCY	ABSOLUTE DIFFERENCE BETWEEN EXPECTATION AND OBSERVATION	PER CENT OF CHILDREN NOT REACTING AS EXPECTED [26]
Total	220	——	72.38	76	24.50 [25]	11.1%
Under 200	109	8.2	8.94	23	14.06	12.9
200—249	45	37.0	16.65	16	0.65	1.4
250—299	47	63.5	29.84	23	6.84	14.6
300 & over	19	89.2	16.95	14	2.95	15.5

Note: Per cent of children acting as predicted, 88.9%. The school problems are included in "observed delinquency group."
[24] Expectation = Probability × Number in Class
[25] Sum of Absolute Differences
[26] Per cent of children *not* behaving as predicted = Sum of Absolute Differences ÷ Number in Group

about the size of the group that will be reinterviewed and one of the alternatives being considered is the use of a sampling procedure for the large group of low score children who are doing well. Follow-up home visits will begin in the fall–winter of 1957.

2. *Reclearance of cases through the social service exchange.* This will be continued on a biannual basis and appropriate agencies will be contacted. Cases will also be cleared annually through the files of the Juvenile Aid Bureau of the Police Department.

3. *Continuation of annual school interviews.* Emphasis will continue to be placed on securing adequate and full reports from the teacher. Careful attention will be paid to the child's attendance record since deviant behavior often begins with problems in attendance.

One of the uses of this school data will be to check schedules covering each year along qualitative continua in several areas of the child's behavior and functioning: Aggressive and destructive behavior, attitude toward adult authority and control, non-disruptive–disruptive activity, relationship to other children in the school, attendance record, symptomatic behavior and personality traits, parental behavior, attitude toward school work, academic achievement, unofficial delinquency, or official delinquency known to the school.

From an analysis such as this we hope to determine the point at which the vulnerable chil-

dren clearly present emerging delinquent patterns.

4. *Evaluation of treatment.* A detailed, comprehensive evaluation of the treatment cases will be undertaken at a later point, when the boys have been under treatment for a longer period of time and have reached an age when a more stable evaluation of their adjustment can be made. The treated group will be matched as closely as possible with an untreated group.

5. *Rescoring of cases in Sample II (1953–54) and Sample III (1954–55).* The same scrutiny in regard to the need for rescoring is planned for the group of cases, which constitute the sampling increments in these two years, as was used for Sample I. The criteria used for the latter group will be applied in selecting the cases that warrant rescoring and they will be presented to the same raters.

6. *Manual of scoring definitions and criteria used in rating cases.* It is anticipated that the writing of such a manual, covering a broad range of complex factors which confront case raters, will be possible. This would undoubtedly be of value to investigators whom we hope will undertake validation studies on other samples as well as provide the Youth Board research staff with more objective criteria for any future discussion or consideration of scores assigned to cases in the study.

We have tried to indicate as fully as possible the methodological problems and limitations found in the procedures used in the study thus far. We have already observed areas in which the scale may need refinement if its application is to become widespread. Some changes were made early in the study in cooperation with the Gluecks and these investigators continue to look to our experiment as a source of further refinement for this scale. Undoubtedly other factors will emerge as the study progresses.

In addition to the theoretical aspects which may emerge from this research, the practical considerations are also of tremendous significance should the scale prove to be valid. Early identification and treatment are prime goals in the field of juvenile delinquency.

A counterpart of this present experiment is the relationship it bears to areas which are suggested by other Youth Board Research. One of the most important of these areas is that of the study of the multi-problem family and the attendant failures in family functioning. From these two avenues of approach, that of the child in relation to his family, and that of the family in relation to the child, may come new horizons for the use of sensitive and effective instruments of prediction.

SUMMARY

The New York City Youth Board has undertaken this study in line with its mandate to conduct a research program bearing upon the prevention and treatment of juvenile delinquency. It is based on the work of the Gluecks, of Harvard University, whose researches in the area of delinquency prediction have been among the most significant in the field. These investigators described and compared the delinquent boy and his family with that of the non-delinquent boy.

In their publication, *Unraveling Juvenile Delinquency*, they translated this description into mathematical terms by developing a Prediction Table based on the five social relationship factors which were statistically the most significant in differentiating delinquent and non-delinquent boys:

1. Discipline of boy by father
2. Supervision of boy by mother
3. Affection of father for boy
4. Affection of mother for boy
5. Cohesiveness of family

The Youth Board in 1952 selected the testing of the validity of this scale as one of its major research investigations. The experiment was begun in two schools situated in comparable high delinquency areas in New York City. The families of *all of the boys* entering the first grade in these schools in the fall of 1952 were interviewed (224 boys). The interview material relating to the five social factors cited above was scored by two independent raters, and in accordance with the Glueck Social Factors Prediction table the scores were assigned. Agreement between two raters was required before a probability score was considered final. The chances of delinquency were divided into a four-class breakdown: 8.2, 37.0, 63.5, or 89.2 out of 100. These boys scoring 63.5 and 89.2 were considered as potential delinquents since they had more than a 50% chance of becoming delinquent.

Follow-up procedures consisted of annual school interviews with teachers and data from social agency and police records. Data covering behavior for the four-year period since the study was begun were classified into an eight category behavior classification according to their current involvement or noninvolvement in delinquent or pre-delinquent behavior. This report relates the behavior of 200 of the 224 boys to the scores assigned to them four years ago. These boys are now between 9½–10½ years of age. *The findings at this point reveal that the majority of the boys are behaving in accordance with the prediction made when they entered school. The majority of those who were rated with a low probability of becoming delinquent are currently presenting no serious community problem. The majority of those who are already showing delinquent or pre-delinquent tendencies were assigned a high probability of becoming delinquent.* *

It should be noted that 45 of the 220 boys are presenting *school behavior problems*. Children in this group give evidence of disruptive school behavior and are essentially troublesome in the school setting. The majority show little or no interest in school work, are inattentive and definitely not functioning to capacity. It is this

---

* Recent information from the New York Youth Board reports that additional cases, in the fourth year of follow-up, have been added since the above; and the predictive outcomes remain as before. — Ed.

group that no doubt will alter the results each year. We have called this category the "suspended judgment" group, anticipating that some of these children may develop increasingly aggressive patterns, whereas others will manage to stay out of any serious difficulty.

This is a longitudinal study in which the final criterion of *persistent delinquency* will be related to the prediction score. It is of particular significance that these boys are now only between the ages of 9½–10½ years, whereas the incidence of official delinquency becomes accelerated between 12–13 years of age.

Approximately half (33) of the high score children in this first sample were referred for treatment. These will be matched with a group not treated to obtain clues regarding the effect of casework in the prevention of delinquent behavior.

If the Youth Board study indicates that the scale has validity, we would hope that other research groups in New York and other cities would also test its validity, particularly with groups unlike those from which the scale was built. When these steps have been taken, further research will be needed to determine the types of treatment required to prevent delinquency among these children.

Chapter 33

Preventive Philosophy, Programs, and Devices

IT IS A FAMILIAR FACT that researchers in delinquency, who feel themselves on quite solid ground in spinning out a "theory" or "testing an hypothesis" regarding the cause of antisocial behavior, find it most difficult when they are asked to "be practical" and to recommend measures designed to prevent or "cure" delinquency. Despite their adherence to some favorite theoretical construct, they know full well that the etiologic wellsprings are in fact so widespread, so deep, and so ramified that programs based on some single theory are doomed, at best, to the yielding of results which fall far short of roseate anticipations.

Nevertheless, the delinquency problem is both serious and urgent; and if "something must be done," it is best that efforts be directed at relatively well-defined targets. It is not hard to suggest the need of broad, general programs for the abolition of poverty, for better housing, for improvement of "the status of the working class," for application of the lessons drawn by some persons from genetics, etc. The famous European criminologists of the past — Lombroso, Ferri, Garofalo, Aschaffenburg, and others — tended to couch their suggestions for crime-preventive efforts in terms so general as to amount to little more than baffling clichés. Thus, Aschaffenburg concluded that "every measure that helps to make the people physically, mentally, and economically healthier is a weapon in the struggle against the world of crime." [1] Ferri, though somewhat more specific and concrete, still emphasized broad-ranging reforms, suggesting "penal substitutes" such as free trade, reduction in hours of labor and in consumption of alcohol, and the like.[2] Socialistic criminologists, convinced that practically all crime is due to the private-profit system, argue that crime would virtually disappear under a socialistic economy. On the other hand, some eugenists contend that delinquency would be eliminated at the source, or at least greatly reduced, through birth-control measures.

Even certain modern criminologists, enticed by some favorite theory, resort, when confronted with the call to implement their theory as a basis for crime-preventive efforts, to such vague generalizations as to contribute little of value to practical effort. Thus, a frequently used textbook on criminology tells us "that control of delinquency lies principally in the personal groups within the local community . . . that the factor in these local and personal groups which had the greatest significance was the definition of behavior as desirable or undesirable," that "the closest approximation to a formula for the control of delinquency that can be made at present is that delinquency must be defined as undesirable by the personal groups in which a person participates," that "the local community must be the active agency in reducing its own delinquency.

---

[1] G. Aschaffenburg, *Crime and Its Repression*, Modern Criminal Science Series, No. 6, Boston, Little, Brown, and Company, 1913, p. 228.

[2] E. Ferri, *Criminal Sociology*, Modern Criminal Science Series, No. 9, Boston, Little, Brown, and Company, 1917, pp. 246 *et seq.*

The personal groups can be modified through the efforts of local organizations such as the school, the church, the police, welfare agencies and civic groups; they also can be modified through the efforts of laymen." [3] All this, it is submitted, is not very helpful in any practical sense.

Another, more recent propounder of a theory, contributes the following sage, but not too helpful, remarks:

> From a diagnosis of a social ill, even a correct one, the "right" solution does not leap to the eye in any direct and obvious way. Compare delinquency with malaria.[4] . . . Now consider delinquency. In this volume we have set forth some rather specific ideas about the causation of the delinquent subculture. We have not explained this subculture as a consequence of some particular concrete circumstance but as the consequence of whole webs and chains of circumstances. We have mentioned a number of things which may be considered aspects of the "cause" in the sense that, were they different, the outcome would be different. It follows that, if we want to change the outcome, these are the things we might want to control.
>
> However, as in the case of malaria, this is only the beginning. Of these various circumstances and features of our social system which are involved in the production of the delinquent subculture, which are subject to deliberate control? . . . How, for example, can we enable the working-class male to compete more effectively for status in a largely middle-class world or, if we want to cut into the web of causation at another point, how can we change the norms of the middle-class world so that his working-class characteristics do not relegate him to an inferior status? . . . . In any case, the formulation of policy is a matter of choosing among alternatives and our choices must involve not only technical considerations but the balancing of social values.
>
> Drawing inferences for policy from a theory about the causes of delinquency is, then, a complex and difficult affair and entails a certain social responsibility. It calls for reasoning as careful and disciplined as an inquiry into causes, and a sensitivity to the diverse values which may be at stake.[5]

Now, there can be little quarrel with broad prescriptions or cautious generalizations, except that it cannot be claimed that they are, usually, either very original or very helpful in the management of the delinquency problem, or even that they flow logically and exclusively from the theoretical constructs confidently advanced to "explain"

---

[3] E. H. Sutherland, *Principles of Criminology*, 5th Ed., revised by D. R. Cressey, J. B. Lippincott Co., 1955, pp. 609–610. For a critique of the well-known Sutherland-Cressey point of view, see Article 41 *supra*.

[4] Cf. pp. 1058 *infra*.

[5] A. Cohen, *Delinquent Boys: The Culture of the Gang*, Glencoe, III., The Free Press, 1955, 176–177. Cohen's elaboration of a theory that status frustration and attendant seeking of self-esteem by children of the working class sub-culture through their drawing together into gangs are basic to an understanding of delinquency fails to take into account the findings of *Unraveling Juvenile Delinquency*. That research disclosed marked relevant differences between numerous factors of the anthropologic, psychologic, and social fabrics of a fair sample of 500 true (*i.e.,* persistent) delinquents and 500 true non-delinquents, *all* of whom came from families of the "working-class." (See, especially, Chaps. VIII–XII of *Unraveling*.) Furthermore, almost 90 per cent of the boys were found to have been committing delinquencies before the age of 11, long before the gang-age. Moreover, the theory in question ignores a familiar chapter of American urban history: the rise of very many economically submerged members of working-class sub-cultures out of their status as immigrants in the slums into successful business and professional status instead of their resorting to criminal activity. Furthermore, in a recent study of the "multi-problem family" the New York City Youth Board "estimated that such families constitute less than 1 per cent of the City's two million families," yet "these families produce at least 75 per cent of the juvenile delinquents." — "Focus on the Multi-Problem Family," 9 *Youth Board News* (May, 1957), 3. In Cohen's theorizing, as well as that of the "delinquency area" and "differential association" specialists, there is a tendency to overlook the fact that the numbers on which the speculations are based comprise but a small fraction of the total number of boys in a region, plus a tendency to ignore solid research findings which raise issues contrary to the theories in question.

criminogenesis. They are the sort of generalizations which almost any piece of criminologic research, as well as common sense, might suggest. Moreover, while there is a partial truth of a sort in all such generalizations, solid evidence exists which justifies greater specificity both in explaining delinquency and coping with it.

Intensive analysis of thousands of delinquent and criminal careers (and comparison with non-delinquents) must force upon the careful student of delinquency a skeptical but informed eclecticism as to both cause and prevention, as well as a frankly experimental trial-and-error point of view when it comes to implementing the research findings by therapeutic and preventive measures. This is the attitude that has governed the Editor. In the contributions contained in the following pages, a variety of quite practical suggestions, related to antecedent research findings, is presented. The contributors of the following articles are, of course, not unaware of the broader and deeper cultural currents involved; but since little can be done about these, they are content to see what immediately useful results can be obtained through cultivation of their own corners of the vineyard; to do as much good as lies within immediately manageable territory.

Before considering these contributions, it may perhaps be helpful to reproduce what was said in a prior work on crime prevention, in order to achieve a workable perspective:

> It is worthy of note that in the field of medicine much good was accomplished before the causal problem had been solved. Until Edward Jenner's discovery of smallpox vaccination in 1798, smallpox took a heavy toll in disfiguration and death. Jenner's great contribution gave a method of controlling that disease, even though the specific etiology of smallpox has to this day not been definitely established. Similarly, the efficacy of quinine in the treatment of fever was known to the Peruvian Indians for centuries before the significance of the connection was determined. Cinchona bark was introduced into Europe by the Jesuits in 1632. Soon thereafter it was used by Sydenham, enabling him to differentiate malarial from non-malarial fevers on the basis of the therapeutic response to treatment with quinine. Yet the cause of malaria was not known until 1880, when the French army surgeon, Laveran, discovered and described the malarial parasites in the red blood cells. Thus, during a period of some two and a half centuries, the treatment of malaria by cinchona bark and its derivatives was based exclusively upon empirical clinical evidence. To cite still another example, although the discovery by the Yellow Fever Commission of the United States Army that yellow fever is transmitted by a species of the mosquito resulted in the virtual eradication of that disease from the world, its exact etiologic agent remains unknown to this day. The search for the real villain in the piece resulted, in our own time, in the tragic death of the great Noguchi.
>
> Obviously, therefore, exact knowledge of etiology need not always precede successful control.
>
> On the oher hand, there are certain diseases in which the etiologic agents and epidemiologic factors are quite well known — tuberculosis, gonorrhea, and syphilis, for example — yet control and eradication are still far from complete.
>
> The analogy to medicine . . . [is] of course imperfect and should not be pushed too far. But the urgencies and reasoning that govern preventive efforts in these fields are not dissimilar to the ones involved in fighting crime.[6]

Effective measures are, then, possible, without awaiting the discovery of the ultimates in delinquency causation.

---

[6] By permission from *Preventing Crime* by S. and E. T. Glueck. Copyright, 1936. McGraw-Hill Book Co., Inc., New York, pp. 4–5. The discovery of such antibiotic means of therapy as penicillin, for example, since the above was written, may have brought about more specific treatment for one or more of the above-mentioned diseases; but the example remains unimpaired as an illustration of the point at issue.

Following these preliminary observations, it is appropriate to give a brief digest of the materials included in the present chapter.

The first item, "Paths to Prevention," is from *Delinquents in the Making*,[7] which, in turn, is a condensation of *Unraveling Juvenile Delinquency*.[8] It sketches the limits of effective preventive action and makes some suggestions growing out of a detailed comparison of representative samples of delinquents and non-delinquents of a depressed urban area. Emphasis is laid on specific targets of preventive effort as these have emerged from analysis of the findings of the works in question. The suggestions pertain to the delinquent's characteristics, to family life, to the school and to leisure-time activities.

The second item in the present chapter is derived from *Physique and Delinquency*,[9] and indicates the qualifications that might usefully be made in general delinquency-preventive programs to take account of the different psychologic tendencies of the various typical physical constitutions — mesomorphic, ectomorphic, endomorphic, and balanced types of delinquents.

The next item in the present chapter, although somewhat dated, is still, in the Editor's opinion, a very helpful chart and compass for a delinquency prevention program. It comprises a Report of the Committee on Crime Prevention of the American Prison Association (now the American Correctional Association) which contains specific illustrations of efforts related to findings regarding causal factors. The piece by Kvaraceus is useful as a terse guide to a preventive enterprise.

The article by Carr is valuable in laying down a design for organized community activity in crime control. It discusses delinquency-preventive efforts in different parts of the country. This is followed by the report of a citizens' committee (of Cincinnati) outlining the scope and ramifications of a municipal program designed to cope with youthful misconduct. It is included to show how the citizenry of a community can go about planning and carrying out an organized effort in the control of delinquency.

Then comes Whelan's sketch of a large city project (that of The New York City Youth Board) for striking at the manifold problems of youthful antisocial behavior.

Turning next to certain specialized activities in the crime-preventive field, Cox's piece on the role of the school counselor shows how this type of guidance personnel can be of practical aid in coping with the early "distress signals" of impending delinquency from the point of view of work with the types of child for whom "school is a trying experience." While not underestimating the value of technical training of a kind enjoyed by clinicians, it would seem, from the illustrations she gives, that old-fashioned human sympathy, common sense, and native psychologic insight are also important. A brief critique is given of "special classes," and assessment is made of the role of the counselor in explaining to parents the likely sources of a great variety of childhood maladjustments brought out in the proving-ground of the school. Illustrations are given of different etiologic syndromes as reflected in individual case summaries and of the relationship of the counselor's work to that of remedial clinics and other resources, as well as of his "special task of creating a bond between parents and the school."

Cox's article is followed by Stullken's piece on Chicago's Special School for Social Adjustment. The work of the Montefiore School is well known.[10] It has long been an important adjunct of the Chicago school system, in coping with "unadjusted children,

[7] By S. and E. T. Glueck, New York, Harper and Brothers, 1951.

[8] *Op. cit.* For an appreciation of the value of these contributions, see B. M. Beck, *Five States*, Philadelphia, American Law Institute, 129–131.

[9] By S. and E. T. Glueck, New York, Harper and Brothers, 1956.

[10] See, for example, E. H. Stullken, "Montefiore Special School for Problem Boys," in S. and E. T. Glueck, *Preventing Crime, op. cit.*, pp. 197–212.

truants, incorrigibles, behavior deviates, etc., who are more vulnerable than others to delinquency" because of intellectual, affective, or behavioral idiosyncrasies; exceptional children who cannot compete satisfactorily in the ordinary school routine and who, in turn, are a disturbing influence on the other children. Stullken's article describes the curriculum of the special school, the characteristics of its pupils and of the families from which they spring, the family–school relationships and the post-school adjustment. After presenting a case from the points of view of diagnosis and preventive therapy, he points to the great need of "securing earlier recognition and diagnosis of problem children," and of school provision "for an early identification and diagnosis of children who are maladjusted" — crucially important disiderata to which Chapter 32 of the present work, on predictive devices, is devoted.

A pilot program for dealing with teen-age "conflict groups" or gangs is next described by Whelan in his article on the New York City Youth Board's Council of Social and Athletic Clubs. Prior articles in this volume have dealt with gang formation and, to some extent, with psychologic and social work with gangs.[11] Whelan's piece recounts the experiences and techniques of "detached workers," operating from a settlement house "but working outside its structured setting." He points out that "the underlying assumption upon which the Street Club Project is based is that teen-age group association is a natural part of growing up," and that "members seek in the gang fulfillment of all their fundamental needs for recognition, affection, status, new experience and security." Whelan stresses the importance of setting the specialized work with gang members in the matrix of "the welfare of the community as a whole," the Council and the Athletic Clubs, for example, working closely with the Police Department and letting the boys know that impending crimes will have to be reported. By winning the confidence of gang members in their familiar haunts, through the rendering of services and signs of friendship, such as helping them to get jobs, the worker becomes recognized "as an enabling adult" who, "although he accepts them as individuals . . . does not accept their antisocial behavior." An important aspect of the work is the prevention of gang warfare, the worker acting as "the voice of reason and of caution" in an excitable atmosphere.

Rinck's article discusses the role of a police department in crime-preventive activities. Starting with the complications involved in the definition of delinquency,[12] she defines the role of the police department in the over-all community program of stopping delinquency at the source. These center on around-the-clock preventive patrolling, informed use of social and other agencies, the exerting of leadership in community planning for delinquency control. As to patrolling, the point of view is well expressed by the statement: "No amount of spot maps or statistics can substitute for the knowledge of a district that comes only with long association." In speaking of the relationship of police work to social work, the emphasis is placed on the need of "adjustment of a child's problems so that he may become a happy and useful member of society," both through single interviews (in the case of most simple situations) and through more persistent situations requiring use of the social service exchange (a central file of social agency contacts) as a basis for proper referrals. Certain difficulties arising out of the policies and attitudes of private and public social agencies toward the police are discussed. The need for a collaborative plan with the schools is emphasized. Limitations of the police in serving as substitutes for probation officers or taking over the provision of recreation for youth are pointed out, as is also the valuable role the police department, through its strategic means of gaining relevant information, can play in community planning and in integrating the efforts of various governmental agencies to focus on socially pathologic regions of the city. "Information can shape a specific program and cut down aimless generalizations about the horrors of modern youth.

11 See Articles 157, 158, *supra.*   12 Cf. Articles 1 and 2, *supra.*

Police can, with little trouble, show a need for service for children aged ten to fourteen years at the corner of X Street and Y Avenue at 7:00 P.M." Keen observations are made regarding the recruitment, training, and supervision of police crime prevention personnel.

The advantages, disadvantages, and special problems of "aggressive casework" in an "authoritarian agency" are illustrated by Chwast with the aid of case-history summaries from the Juvenile Aid Bureau of the New York City Police Department. The special techniques used, such as making initial contact with the delinquent, are discussed and illustrated. Special policies involving the relationship of the police agency, with its authoritarian status, to various types of treatment resources are discussed. Some of the techniques have evidently been discontinued since Chwast wrote his article, but they are still of interest.

The chapter concludes with an article by Powers describing the well-known Cambridge–Somerville (Massachusetts) youth experiment in the prevention of delinquency. The results of the work of the counselors involved, as is well known in criminologic circles, were on the whole disappointing. A recent, as yet unpublished, follow-up of the cases involved in the original Cambridge–Somerville project, by W. and J. McCord, shows that with the passage of time the picture became even more disappointing. Yet, to the scientist, negative results are just as important as positive. We know one thing now: that the type of effort involved in that historic experiment does not yield acceptable results. New approaches, guided by new concepts and executed by sounder methods, are required. Let us, in the meantime,

Still achieving, still pursuing,
Learn to labour and to wait.

174

Paths to Prevention *

Sheldon and Eleanor T. Glueck

A fundamental value of the research on which this book is based is the fact that certain *specific* traits and characteristics in the background, constitution, and early experiences of the boys involved have been shown markedly to differentiate delinquents as a group from non-delinquents, in depressed urban areas. Assuming such differentia to be quite typical of a general situation in such regions (and their nature and internal consistency render this probable), we have a considerable array of suggestive clues to action designed to ameliorate criminogenic conditions. We have at least a partial basis for de-

signing preventive programs which will be pointedly directed to the things that count most, instead of haphazardly relying upon some favorite "cause," "cure," or "preventive," or galloping in all directions at once in the vain expectation of arriving at a desirable goal. Programs of delinquency prevention that are buttoned into the specific needs and conditions suggested by sound research are not likely to be wasteful, because they deal with what has been found to be *probably relevant*.

Some of the clues brought out by our investigation have been discerned in other researches; [1]

---

* Reprinted from *Delinquents in the Making*, New York, Harper and Brothers, 1952, 188–210. Used by permission of the publisher.

[1] Without exhausting the notable contributions to the study of the causation of delinquency, one must mention the books of Healy and Bronner, especially *New Light on Delinquency and its Treatment*, New Haven, Yale University Press, 1936, and Healy's classic, *The Individual Delinquent*, Boston, Little, Brown, and Company, 1915; C. L. Burt, *The Young Delinquent*, New York: Appleton-Century-Crofts, 1933; C. Shaw, especially, *Delinquency Areas*, Chicago, University of Chicago Press, 1929; R. Lindner, *Rebel Without a Cause*, New York, Grune & Stratton, 1945; J. Slawson, *The Delinquent Boy*, Boston, Badger, 1926. See P. S. de Q. Cabot, *Juvenile Delinquency, A Critical Annotated Bibliography*, New York, H. W. Wilson, 1946, for other studies.

but there has previously been no systematic comparison of a sufficiently large, carefully defined sample of persistent delinquents matched with a large, carefully defined group of non-delinquents, and compared in respect to so many verified factors in so many areas. But even this study requires a great deal more supplementation to get at deeper meanings through detailed intercorrelations of the findings in each area of the research. We are at work on that project. In the meantime there are enough specific clues for action to enable communities to begin on a program of reorientation of preventive efforts with the aim of more pointed and relevant attacks on crucial factors.

The specific factors that distinguish persistent delinquents from non-delinquents have been found to be numerous. The precise, detailed manner of their interplay in raising the tendency to antisocial behavior from a possibility inherent in all to a very high probability cannot be determined without a great deal more investigation and analysis. The tracing of intimate connections of "mental mechanisms" [2] is rather the task of the clinician dealing therapeutically with the individual than that of the planner of general prophylactic programs based on mass phenomena. The two methods complement each other in shedding light on the causal process, but the clinical method of intensive study of the individual and the drawing of judgments about causal interplay is not indispensable to either the study of causation or the designing of efficient programs of prevention. Indeed, the method of intercorrelational study of delinquents and non-delinquents en masse can illumine the clinical technique in helping the psychiatrist, psychologist, and social investigator to determine which among numerous factors emerging from examination of the individual child and his background are probably *relevant*.

---

[2] See W. Healy, *The Individual Delinquent, op. cit., Mental Conflicts and Misconduct*, Boston, Little, Brown, and Company, 1917; F. Alexander and W. Healy, *Roots of Crime: Psychoanalytic Studies*, New York, A. Knopf, 1935; Lindner, *Rebel Without a Cause, op. cit.*, B. Karpman, *The Individual Criminal: Studies in the Psychogenetics of Crime*, Washington, Nervous and Mental Disease Publishing Co., 1935; E. Powers and H. Witmer, *An Experiment in the Prevention of Delinquency*, New York, Columbia University Press, 1951.

The fact that comparison of the two closely matched sets of boys discloses that each of numerous factors unquestionably differentiates large groups of persistent delinquents from non-delinquents in a way that cannot be attributable to mere chance, and the further fact that they evidently lead to a very high potential of antisocial behavior, furnish specific pathways to preventive measures.

NEED FOR A REALISTIC APPROACH

Before we take the reader along these pathways, let us not forget that we must approach the problem of delinquency prevention with a realistic attitude. There are no "pink pills" that will "cure" delinquency; nor is there a general prophylactic agent that will prevent it in the sense that the stamping out of the mosquito-breeding swamps will prevent malaria. If the reader reflects on the multiplicity, variety, and subtlety of the factors which combine in varying ways and weights to induce persistency in social maladjustment, he will concede that the task of prevention has many ramifications; that it implicates fields of science in which knowledge is as yet far from complete; and that it touches upon almost all social institutions. It is, in a word, a highly complicated affair.

This is not a counsel of despair or pessimism; it is merely a call for the application of common sense and non-deceptive judgment to the results of our quest for solid facts and promising measures of prevention.

One point about which we must be realistic in planning a program of delinquency prevention is that there are limits to effective action laid down by the general sociocultural situation. Children have to live in the world as it is; fundamental changes cannot be effectuated in a short space of time — too many special interests, prejudices, and values are involved. Nor can children be made good by removing evil out of their experience. Character is not built that way. For example, one does not get at the basic problems presented by the energetic, adventure-thirsty, mesomorphic lad by taking movies or comics away from him. If he has a need for such outlets he will somehow get to them; and deprivation is no cure. Direct police action against obvious evils, such as the peddling of drugs to children, is, of course, necessary. But, to the extent that general cultural pressures and disharmonies of our civilization may be involved in the background of antisocial behavior, we are confronted with a tremendous problem that can be managed only by society in general and an over-all social policy. This is difficult to achieve and would take years to evolve.

As one illustration of the immensity and difficulty of the general problem, we repeat what we said in 1930 in our first published work in this field, *Five Hundred Criminal Careers:*

After studying the careers of these five hundred young men and their families one is impelled to the . . . conclusion that a critical evaluation of contemporary American ideals is necessary as a basis for the more intelligent moral guidance of our future citizens. That the uninteresting reiteration of moral precepts appears to be a failure in building character is becoming more and more clear. If we would build character in our youth and moor it to socially valuable ideals, something much more vital is needed. The youth of today can only be convinced and influenced by something that not only goes deeper, but is more appealing, than the ordinary church or Sunday-school routine. What that something is we do not know. Here is a field of research wherein social philosophers, the clergy educators, social workers, and psychiatrists can join in fruitful and much needed study.[3]

When the above was written, most of the delinquents and young criminals of today were infants. It cannot be said that there has been much progress in improving that aspect of the general culture with which the above passage is concerned. And this is but one example of the slowness of cultural change in fundamentals.

But this fact need not make us pessimistic. For in the ultimate analysis, prevention of delinquent careers, as our findings suggest, is also dependent upon something more specific than the manipulation of the general cultural environment. It entails structuring of *integrated personality and wholesome character during the first few formative years of life; and this, fortunately, is accomplished largely in the home.* Although basic modifications in the general system of habits and values that permeate our culture are bound to be slow, we can take advantage of the oft-neglected fact that parents are to a great extent not only the bearers, but also the *selective filters,* of the general culture. The same is true of school-teachers, with whom children spend much of their time during the most impressionable and formative stages of life. Thus,

there is both realism and promise in taking more direct and specific steps to improve the *under-the-roof culture* in home and school.[4]

TYPES OF PREVENTIVE PROGRAMS

Programs of delinquency prevention are classifiable into (1) those dealing with very general socioeconomic conditions that affect an entire culture and are therefore but remotely related to delinquency; (2) those which, though not organized chiefly to cope with delinquency, still have a natural, albeit indirect and incidental, relationship to the problem; and (3) those which are set up to deal specifically with the conditions that presumably make for delinquency.

European criminologists have generally recommended the first type of attack, couching their suggestions for crime-preventive measures in general terms. But while there can be little quarrel, for example, with such a generalization as that "Every measure that helps to make the people physically, mentally, and economically healthier is a weapon in the struggle against the world of crime," [5] it is too remote from the factors specifically involved in the social evil of delinquency and crime to be of much practical value.

As for the second type of crime-preventive activity, although it is much closer to the operative details of the problem, it is still not specially designed to cope with it. It has been pointed out by Lukas, who has given much study to the problem, that "Except for the police, children's courts, and reformatory institutions, public and private agencies are not organized primarily for the prevention of crime and delinquency. That function is considered to be an adjunct to or a by-product of their other related purposes. Direct services, designed mainly as crime preventives, are few; the indirect services are many." [6]

---

[3] New York, Alfred A. Knopf, 1930, pp. 337–338.

[4] We do not of course deny the value of community efforts at crime control; these can be improved by a better definition of specific goals derived from differentiative traits of delinquents and non-delinquents.

[5] G. Aschaffenburg, *Crime and Its Repression,* Boston, Modern Criminal Science Series, No. 6, 1913, p. 228.

[6] E. J. Lukas, "Prevention of Crime," in V. C. Branham and S. B. Kutash, *Encyclopedia of Criminology,* New York, Philosophical Library, p. 333. This thoughtful article can be of help to all who contemplate preventive programs.

He adds that since such "fairly typical indirect preventive services" as wholesome recreation, good housing, good schools, and the like "can contribute a vital and significant force in the lives of everyone," they have "justifiably had claimed for them the function of contributing to delinquency . . . prevention." [7] While this is true, the data of the present study indicate how much more pointed the approach to the problem of prevention must be. That socioeconomic measures for general improvement of the lot of the underprivileged are desirable cannot be gainsaid; but their exact contribution to the prevention of delinquency is hard to assess; the same underprivileged status in which the families of our delinquents found themselves was also the lot of the non-delinquents' families.

The third type of delinquency-preventive program is designed, specifically, to cope with the problems of discovering and dealing with the forces and situations, inside and outside the child, that are commonly found associated with pre-delinquency and delinquency.

The specific clues to prevention disclosed in the preceding chapters suggest clearly defined targets at which to aim specific programs to supplement that shotgun attack on general socioeconomic evils which is made with a hope and a prayer that, as regards the prevention of delinquency, a few of the pellets will somehow hit the right spots.

SPECIFIC TARGETS OF DELINQUENCY PREVENTION

In reflecting upon the major findings of the foregoing chapters, it is evident that the primary focus of interest must be on (a) the traits and characteristics of the delinquent himself, (b) the family life, (c) the school, and (d) the employment of leisure time.

(a) *The delinquent himself.* What can be done, specifically, about the constitution, traits, and characteristics that distinguish delinquents as a group from non-delinquents?

The greater incidence of mesomorphic constitutional physique among delinquents, and the "growth spurt" of these boys at thirteen to fourteen years, provide targets for specific action. The excess of mesomorphy among delinquents as a class ought to suggest to all persons and agencies intimately concerned with

the guidance of youth — parents, teachers, community recreational agencies, and others — that special allowance must be made in all major channels of self-expression for the greater energy output of certain boys, if their drives are not to take antisocial expression. The days of "winning the West," of the whaling ship, and of other fields of action for energetic, adventure-hungry youth are no more. To supply legitimate substitutes is a challenge to the ingenuity of schools, recreational authorities, and vocational guides. There is obviously a need for greater variety in curriculum patterns, in leisure-time programs and in vocational opportunities, and a more specific fitting of types of boys into areas of activity.

The greater inclination of the delinquents to the practical, concrete forms of mental activity and their disinclination to abstract, verbalistic intellectual processes furnish specific targets for designers of school curricula. In regard to such qualitative intellectual traits as incapacity for objective interests, unrealistic thinking, lack of "common sense," and unsystematic approach to mental problems, those who plan curricula need to consult with experts in clinical psychiatry and psychology, because such traits are especially entangled with emotional tendencies.

In weighing the characteristics of delinquents as derived from the Rorschach Test and psychiatric interview, school and clinic have the greatest opportunity for action directed toward specific goals. These are so clearly of a nature to interfere with a satisfactory taming of primitive impulses and to facilitate uncontrolled, unthinking antisocial self-expression, that they furnish specific targets for preventive activities on the part of family clinics and school agencies. Among them, it will be recalled, are assertiveness, defiance of or ambivalence to authority; excessive feelings of hostility, suspiciousness, destructiveness; unconventionality in ideas and behavior; oral–receptive and sadistic–destructive trends; marked emotional impulsiveness, and defective self-control; sensuality and acquisitiveness; deficiency in conscientiousness and self-criticism; preponderance of extroversive trends and/or the tendency to resolve emotional conflicts by an impulsive "acting out."

Such traits tell their own story as to why it is that so frequently the efforts of juvenile courts and other agencies dealing with delinquents,

---

[7] *Ibid.*

devoted and intelligent as they often are, can accomplish so little in changing a course of habitual antisocial conduct. The deep-seated nature of the temperamental and character traits found to differentiate persistent delinquents from non-delinquents, and the extremely early age at which delinquents first manifest marked difficulties in adjustment as expressed in misbehavior, should make us realize how absolutely essential it is for schools, particularly, to be equipped to discover *potential* delinquents before the trends of maladaptive behavior become too fixed. For the schools are in a strategic position to note such marked deviations and difficulties of adaptation at the age of around six when the child first enters grade school. *Character prophylaxis* — the testing of children early and periodically to detect malformations of emotional development at a stage when the twig can still be bent — is as necessary as are early and periodic medical examinations. A crying need of the times in this field is a *preventive medicine of personality and character*.

(*b*) *Family life.* Many crucial differences were found between the parents of the delinquents and those of the other boys — the greater intellectual and emotional abnormalities of the delinquents' grandparents (and other distant relatives) and parents, the higher incidence of alcoholism and criminalism in the families in which the parents of the delinquent boys had themselves been reared; their more extensive physical, intellectual, and emotional handicaps, as well as drunkenness and criminalism; their greater dependence on various social welfare agencies. All this suggests that the community must somehow break the vicious circle of character-damaging influences on children exerted by parents who are themselves the distorted personality products of adverse parental influences. This can be done only through intensive instruction of each generation of prospective parents in the elements of mental hygiene and the requisites of happy and healthy family life. It calls for a tremendous multiplication of psychiatric, social, religious, educational, and other community resources for improving the basic equipment of present and prospective parents in the assumption of a wholesome parental role. For there cannot be the slightest doubt, in the light of the facts marshaled in the preceding pages, that it is

futile to treat the child, delinquent or otherwise, apart from the family that contributes much to make him what he is. Without concentration on the family, particularly the parents, we may set up boys' clubs, recreational centers, clinics, and the like, and we may inveigh against the movies, comics, and crime-suggesting toys; but we shall still be trying to sweep back the tide of childhood maladjustment and delinquency with pitifully inadequate brooms.

Parents are not born with a knowledge of how to bring up children; if they were, there would be far less delinquency. Under modern conditions of city life, especially in the underprivileged areas, what used to be a problem that tended to take care of itself in rural and semi-rural America, when families were large, cultural ideas and ideals more uniform, and life simpler, has become difficult and perplexing. It is obvious that little progress can be made in the prevention of juvenile delinquency until family life is strengthened through a large-scale, pervasive, continuous program designed to bring to bear all the resources of mental hygiene, social work, education, and religious and ethical teaching upon this central issue.

The differentiative traits of the parents of our boys lead to the conclusion that all the community's agencies for the guidance of young people in the proper selection of mates and in preparation for marriage — agencies specializing in marital problems, church groups, family welfare organizations — need to enlarge and enrich their techniques.

The evidences of disruption in the family life of delinquents are specific targets at which to aim. To cite but one illustration — if agencies interested in the recreational movement, boys' clubs, and other agencies for constructive use of leisure were to formulate their plans and activities around a working principle of encouraging recreations that would engage the interest of the family as a unit, this one principle alone might serve to counteract the tendency to family disintegration. Beginning with the cementing influence of family-group recreation, the path might be opened to improvement in other constituents of the unhealthy family pattern.

It will be recalled that certain other unwholesome parent–child relationships, apart from those already noted, were found strikingly to differentiate the family atmosphere of delinquents and non-delinquents. Far more of their homes were broken; far more of the mothers of the delinquents allowed their children to shift for themselves during leisure hours; far fewer of their fathers evinced sympathy and affection for their boys; and while there was much more warmth on the part of the mothers generally, fewer of the delinquents' mothers had a healthily affectionate relationship to the boys. Far fewer of the delinquents were, in turn, warmly attached to their fathers and mothers; a far lower percentage of the delinquent boys accepted their fathers as desirable models for emulation; to a greater extent the former believed that neither of the parents was genuinely concerned for their welfare; and the disciplinary practices of the parents of the delinquents were far less adequate.

Here is a dynamic area of intrafamily cross-currents that in large measure accounts for the persistent maladjustment of the boys who became delinquent. Again we have a situation which, though highly involved and complex, might be attacked by concentrating on a series of specific constituents of the entire emotion-laden area. If, for example, there were community agencies to instruct parents systematically in regard to the emotional significance of various disciplinary practices and to demonstrate to them how behavior situations usually improve when discipline is fair and firm and unaccompanied by anger, they might learn to adopt such practices with socializing effect on their children. Again, if parents were systematically taught simple elements of the dynamics of parent–child relationships, of the struggle the young child must go through in adjusting his instinctual drives and their emotional accompaniments in relation to mother, father, and brothers and sisters; of the role of the father as the first "ego-ideal," and, in general of the great part played by early parent–child experiences in the crystallization of the child's basic personality and character traits which will be carried into adulthood and become more difficult to modify with the passage of time, some headway might be made in rendering intrafamily life more hygienic and happy.

The problem is enormous in scope. It calls for the widespread cooperative endeavor of child-guidance clinics, school-teachers, family welfare agencies, church and other communal resources. In most communities it will be found that there are not enough facilities, such as clinics, and that the effort of public and private agencies is not planfully articulated so as to give the most economical results.

(c) *The school.* A great deal of time, and at a very impressionable age, is spent by children in schools. Our findings have shown that much more goes on in the intraschool situation than the mere commerce in ideas about "readin', writin', and 'rithmetic," and that what does transpire is of an essentially emotional nature. On the part of the teacher, she cannot altogether get rid of her own emotional problems through the channel of drilling students in the curriculum. On the part of the little pupils, they do not, when they enter the classroom, leave behind their emotional freight, their worries about parental anger, neglect, drunkenness, criminalism.

We have seen that delinquent boys largely possess certain temperamental and personality traits and special abilities and disabilities which distinguish them from the general run of non-delinquents. We have also seen that because of the poor parent–child relationships predominating in delinquents' families the boys have difficulty in finding an emotionally sympathetic adult as a symbol for emulation around whom ideals and standards of behavior can be woven to form the core of character. Such facts — and there are other relevant ones — suggest that fundamental changes in school curricula and teacher training must be made.

Forcing certain types of children into the traditional mold results in increasing tension, frustration, revolt, and delinquency. Much greater flexibility in school curricula is called for; a rich variety of satisfying school experiences must be devised which will enlist the interests of different types of children.

To supply teachers with the necessary "know-how" for coping with the emotional problems of childhood, teacher training will have to be modified to include liberal elements of dynamic psychology and opportunities to participate in clinical conferences. Practice teaching of the various subjects in the curriculum cannot replace the need for an understanding of the troubles and tensions of children as they wrestle with the problem of adjusting to the taming restraints of the adult world.

More important, school authorities will have to recognize the role of teachers as parent-substitutes and ego-ideals in the case of many children. Perhaps young-adult male teachers are needed in greater number, even in the kindergarten and elementary grades. Perhaps husband–wife teams of teachers would provide a more natural and wholesome emotional climate in the classroom. At all events, experiments are needed to test out various patterns of teacher–child relationships from the point of view of their effect on the dynamics of temperament and emotion and the formation of integrated personality and acceptable character.

The existing great shortage of teachers presents a serious social problem in itself; to attract the kind of teachers who will be skilled in coping with the emotional difficulties of childhood, a far higher social evaluation of the role of the teacher will have to be brought about.

The marked differences between the delinquent boys and their non-delinquent counterparts again afford specific targets at which to direct preventive action in this area: Among the delinquents as a group there was more school retardation, poorer scholastic achievement, greater dislike of school, less academic ambition, greater preference for adventurous activities. But these traits are not essentially chargeable to a difference in general intelligence, for the two groups were similar in average I.Q. Their true roots are apparent from the other differentiative traits and behavior manifestations in which the delinquents were different from the other lads: They did not adjust themselves as well to their schoolmates; almost all the delinquents, compared to but 86 of the other lads, indulged in all forms of misconduct in school, ranging from defiance, stubbornness, lying, and persistent inattention to truancy, stealing, and sexual misconduct. It will be recalled further, that while such misbehavior occurred at eight or less among a third of the delinquents (their average age at first school misbehavior having been 9.5 years), it occurred as early as this among less than a tenth of the few non-delinquents who had misbehaved in school (their average age at first misconduct in school having been 12.5 years).

These facts suggest not only that a boy's school misconduct as a harbinger (and sometimes an accompanier) of misconduct in the general community is not merely of emotional origin, but that the emotional difficulties are deep-rooted, reaching into the most tender years. When, to the early age of first school misconduct is added the early age of first antilegal behavior (almost half the delinquents were only eight at the time), it becomes clearer than ever that the evidences of persistent delinquency arise essentially before puberty and that the elementary school therefore stands in the front line of attack on the problem.

In an enlightened educational system the school could function as the litmus paper of personality and character maladaption, reflecting early in the child's growth the acid test of his success or failure in his first attempts to cope with the problems of life posed by a restrictive society and code of behavior. In such a system, the best psychiatric, psychologic, medical, social, and other facilities would then be focused on the specific traits shown to be most largely related to personality distortion and maladapted behavior at a critical point in the child's development when character and habit are still sufficiently plastic for effective therapeutic intervention.

The intricacies of the problem of early recognition and treatment of delinquency, and a chief reason why so little has been accomplished toward its solution, is shown by the simple fact that when a child first begins to display signs of maladaptation it is very difficult to say whether these are true danger signals of persistent delinquency to come or are merely transient phenomena of the youngster's trying of his wings. Bits of maladapted and even antisocial behavior at this early stage are not necessarily symptomatic of future delinquency. It therefore becomes of prime importance to devise a method of distinguishing, very early in life, those children who are headed for delinquent careers in order that therapeutic measures may be timely and effective.

Is there a sufficiently reliable instrumentality for making this crucially important distinction between the potentially delinquent child and the child who will probably soon outgrow his difficulties of adaptation? * . . .

If the reader will review some of the other distinguishing but less differentiative factors in the family background, he will see that it is

* At this point, the prediction tables of *Unraveling Juvenile Delinquency* were discussed. See previous chapter. — *Ed.*

possible to construct other prognostic tables, even though it would probably require the cumulative weight of more than five such factors to yield as high a predictive power as those afforded by the five we have used. This is an illustration of a fundamental idea discussed in the preceding chapter: the concept of multiple causation. In other words, it is not merely one syndrome of the five most highly differentiative social (or any other) factors that yields the greatest prognostic possibility because of high causal weight, but also other syndromes or patterns. We have here a sort of interchangeable "coin of the realm" of causation, in which a certain number of external and/or internal pressures of one kind may just as readily incline a boy to delinquency as a larger (or smaller) number of pressures of another kind. It is the task of the therapist in the individual case to uncover and remove or modify as many of these pressures as possible in order to permit the particular child to function on a relatively even keel without, on the one hand, becoming too neurotic or, on the other, becoming a persistent delinquent.

Prognostic tables similar to the one above described were also prepared on the basis of five of the most differentiative character traits brought out by the Rorschach Test and five temperamental traits revealed through the psychiatric examinations. Use of all three types of tables would enhance prognostic power; but these latter, of course, require technically trained psychologists and psychiatrists to administer the examinations and apply the predictions, while teachers and social workers can more readily apply the table based on family background factors.

Prognostic tables should, of course, not be used mechanically, automatically, or as a substitute for sound clinical judgment. They are merely intended to help in considering the problems of an individual child in the perspective of organized experience with hundreds of other boys who in many respects resemble or differ from the lad under consideration. As to some factors, each child of course remains unique; but such qualities, and their significance in the total situation, are exceedingly difficult to determine and assess. The dimensions and depths of each child's problems can be much more accurately appraised by seeing them in the light of the background picture of hundreds of other children, than they can be if the investigator or therapist relies exclusively on "good guesses" or "clinical hunch."

The prognostic tables should not be used even by clinical experts until they have been tested on other samples of children than those embraced in this research. As a distinguished authority on biometrics, statistics, and public health has put it, "A priori argument [as to the value or validity of such prognostic instrumentalities] will not get far, howsoever it be extended. What one needs is trial and observation." [8]

(d) *Leisure time.* In their life on the city streets, as well as in the other respects noted, we have seen that the delinquent boys are worse off than the non-delinquents: These families moved about more frequently, interfering with whatever stabilizing influences there are in attachment and loyalty to a definite community. To a greater extent than the non-delinquent lads, the delinquents worked in street trades where they were subject to the hazards of unsupervised employment at an impressionable age. Their recreational as well as work preferences were for risky and adventurous energy outlets, reflected not only in excessive truck hopping, keeping late hours, bunking out, running away from home, destroying property, and the like, but also in seeking out play places at a considerable distance from their homes, and other enticing locales of risk and adventure such as railroad yards and waterfronts. These tendencies are also shown in the greater extent to which the delinquents had serious street accidents and even (vicariously) in their much more frequent movie attendance. Most of the delinquents became gang members, and many preferred companions older than themselves. There is also strong evidence that the delinquents disliked the confinement of playgrounds, supervised recreations, or attendance at clubs or other centers which they rarely joined of their own desire. Finally, they were more neglectful of church attendance than the non-delinquents.

Here we have a series of behavior manifestations that unquestionably suggest that settlement houses, school community centers, church

[8] Edwin Bidwell Wilson, "Prediction," book review in "A Symposium on *Unraveling Juvenile Delinquency*," *Harvard Law Review*, 1951, pp. 1022, 1041.

centers, boys' clubs, and other agencies must take into account the preferences of these adventure-thirsty boys who dislike intensive supervision and tend to turn to delinquency as a congenial way of life. Such agencies should experiment with various means of attracting and guiding youngsters of this type into at least socially harmless, if not positively constructive, channels. In a busy, exciting, urban community of individualists "on the make," these boys drift among the general population unattached by loyalties except to those of similar energy drive and consuming interest. There is obviously a crying social need for coping with this problem through well-planned community action, based upon careful surveys of local conditions, liabilities, facilities, and needs. A number of communities have made promising beginnings in this direction.[9]

Throughout the foregoing analysis our purpose has been to emphasize fundamental ideas — the better aiming of preventive efforts at more specific targets. We have not attempted to go into detail about techniques to be used in boys' clubs, other social agencies, juvenile courts, probation, and the like.

Nor have we found it feasible to pigeonhole the relevant targets for action into those which the school should *exclusively* be charged with, those which are the sole responsibility of the church, those which are the private domain of the clinic, those which some other community agencies should alone deal with. Reflection upon the nature of the problem shows that, while each of the agencies has a job to do, the specific traits and characteristics to be coped with do not neatly fall into institutional compartments. All that can be said is that the school or the clinic or some other agency should be charged with a leading, if not the primary, responsibility in this or that area; but just as the separate identity of each factor or target does not destroy the organic unity of the person-situation,[10] so the specialization of each agency in one group of factors does not eliminate the harmonious participation of all community agencies in a well-conceived general plan of attack.[11]

We have not attempted in this book to make detailed suggestions as to how a community should go about the task of organizing clinics, establishing and improving premarital and marital guidance centers, and the like. There are some useful publications which the interested citizen can consult for such practical matters. To name but a few, we may refer to *Preventing Crime*,[12] a symposium of some of the more promising programs in different parts of the United States organized under the headings of "Coordinated Community Programs," "School Programs," "Police Programs," "Intramural Guidance Programs," "Extramural Guidance Programs," "Boys Clubs," and "Recreational Programs"; the "Report of the Committee on Crime Prevention of the American Prison Association, 1942" [Article 176 of this volume — Ed.];[13] Carr's well-documented guidebook on *Delinquency Control*,[14] with the very useful part on "Social Action," which gives a blueprint and clearly defined ideas regarding organization, procedure, and division of labor;[15] the reports of the National Conference on Prevention and Control of Juvenile Delinquency held in Washington in the fall of 1946;[16] the publications of the White House Conference on child welfare, the various Yearbooks of the National Probation and Parole

---

[10] A leading pioneer in the study of crime long ago pointed to a basic truism: "The criminal act in every instance is the resultant interaction between a particularly constituted personality and a particular environment." — Bernard Glueck, *First Annual Report of the Psychiatric Clinic, Sing Sing Prison, Mental Hygiene*, Vol. 2, 1918, p. 12.

[11] See Lukas, *op. cit.*, p. 334, on the value of coordination of the efforts of all community agencies.

[12] Edited by Sheldon and Eleanor Glueck, New York, McGraw-Hill Book Company, Inc., 1936.

[13] American Prison Association, 135 East Fifteenth St., New York. There are other valuable publications of the Association.

[14] Revised Edition, New York, Harper and Brothers, 1950.

[15] Compare, also, Carr's method of predicting juvenile delinquency with ours. *Op. cit.*, pp. 163 *et seq.*

[16] Publications are available from the Superintendent of Documents, Government Printing Office, Washington, D.C.

---

[9] See Glueck and Glueck (Editors) *Preventing Crime*, New York, McGraw-Hill Book Company, Inc., 1936; "Report of the Committee on Crime Prevention of the American Prison Association," New York, American Prison Association, October, 1942 [Article 176 of this volume. — Ed.]; P. W. Tappan, *Juvenile Delinquency*, New York, McGraw-Hill Book Company, Inc., 1949, pp. 490 *et seq.*; L. J. Carr, *Delinquency Control*, New York, Harper and Brothers, 1950, Part IV.

Association; [17] and the more recent, thoughtful textbooks on criminology, such as Taft's *Criminology, A Cultural Interpretation* [18] and Tappan's *Juvenile Delinquency*. [19] This list by no means exhausts the sources of sound practical advice related to findings of fact; it is merely a guide to the reader who is interested in the strategy and tactics of community effort for delinquency control.

But let us once more caution that delinquency cannot be coped with through prejudices about this or that "ology" or "cause," or through purblind faith in some simple nostrum. Nor is it likely that some inspired researcher will soon come up with a brilliant yet simple idea in the manner of Archimedes' sudden inspiration in the bathtub. Yet we trust that those who see this problem in the true perspective of its immense perplexity and its tangled ramifications will not despair. There is soundly based hope in the fact that persistent delinquency is usually not inevitable. There has been much futile argument throughout the ages about the puzzle of freedom of will versus determinism. The argument has largely misfired because it has dealt with the question in the abstract: Does Man have freedom of will, or is he the slave of deterministic forces? The practical issue is the extent to which the particular *individual* under consideration has capacity for purposive self-direction. Individuals differ in this, largely on the basis of the limits laid down genetically and their potentialities under favorable environmental circumstances. It is the function of parents, teachers, clinicians, and others who have to do with children to remove as many of the stifling "deterministic" ashes as possible so that the spark of "freedom" in the above sense may be achieved by the particular individual to the fullest extent of his genetically anchored potentialities. Except in the most extreme cases, it should be possible to modify character and the environmental pressures that distort character, if early, relevant, and sufficiently patient measures are taken.

In the meantime, we have one source of comfort that should stimulate research and experi-

mentation. Determinism does not mean fatalism; it refers to the observed fact that nature presents a routine series of events linked together in what we call causal sequence. This does not mean that we are unable to intervene to change a familiar sequence by therapeutic and prophylactic methods that "hit the bull's eye." In other words, *in delinquency we are dealing not with predestination but with destination.* And experiments have demonstrated that there is a probability that in many cases destination can be redirected by pointed and specific early intervention.

If we recognize that this problem is not merely one of "bad" boys needing to be punished to make them "good," or even of misled boys needing to be treated kindly to make them "reform," [20] but rather of disorders of temperament, personality, and character with an even more complex causative system than exists in many diseases, we will at least approach the problem with an *attitude* and an *insight* that give every promise of the ultimate achievement of effective remedies and preventive programs.

Such an attitude and such an insight may be summed up simply in the recognition that in the eyes of science there are no "good boys" or "bad boys," but only children who need less help in growing up and those who need more.

175

Physique and the Management of Juvenile Delinquency *

Sheldon and Eleanor T. Glueck

INTRODUCTORY

What do our findings suggest regarding the more effective management of juvenile delinquency? Incomplete as are the data of this

---

[17] Such as *Dealing with Delinquency*, 1940 (Edited by Marjorie Bell), New York, The National Probation and Parole Association, 1790 Broadway.

[18] Revised Edition, New York, The Macmillan Company, 1950.

[19] New York, McGraw-Hill Book Company, 1949.

[20] On this type of approach see the thoughtful analysis of results of an experiment in preventive therapy, in E. Powers, and H. Witmer, *An Experiment in the Prevention of Delinquency*, New York, Columbia University Press, 1951. [See, also, Article 186 of this volume. — Ed.]

* Reprinted from *Physique and Delinquency*, New York, Harper and Brothers, 1956, 249–266. Used by permission of the publisher.

analysis, there is certainly evidence that differences in bodily morphology are not only implicated in the genesis of delinquency, but must also be taken into account in its management. Although it is quite apparent that physique alone does not adequately explain delinquent behavior, it is nevertheless clear that, in conjunction with other forces, it does bear a relationship to delinquency.

The current inquiry has led us to three major conclusions:

(1) The basic morphologic differentiation of the physique types is accompanied by differences in the incidence among them of certain traits, some of which are actually associated with delinquency, others potentially so.

(2) Differences in the physical and temperamental structure of body types bring about some variation in their response to environmental pressures.

(3) Differences in the incidence of certain traits among the physique types, as well as divergences in their reactions to the environment, are reflected in certain differences in the etiology of delinquency among the body types.

Thus, even if other researchers should confirm our finding that 60 per cent of delinquents (at least in disorganized urban areas) are of the mesomorphic body type, thereby suggesting a focus in prophylactic and therapeutic endeavors on the mesomorphs in the child population, the special characteristics of the other physique types point to the need of some *diversity* of approach to the prevention and treatment of antisocial behavior in boys of different body structures. There is enough evidence of differences in clusters of traits and sociocultural factors that have a selective influence on the delinquency of the body types to warrant taking into account variations in bodily structure in the planning of general programs of prevention and control and in applying therapeutic measures for individualized treatment of delinquents.

NEED FOR NEW APPROACHES

There are no nostrums or "pink pills" that will "cure" delinquency; nor, from the fact of the multiplicity and complexity of the influences that have been shown to be involved, can there be any general prophylactic agent which will prevent delinquency, as the stamping out of mosquito-breeding swamps will prevent malaria.

The task of coping with antisocial behavior not only has many ramifications but is dependent on fields of science in which knowledge is as yet very imperfect, and involves almost all our social institutions.

We must move forward, however, because there is no assurance that the methods now employed in coping with delinquency either curb or "cure" it in substantial measure. Individual counseling, supportive psychotherapy, psychoanalysis, hypnoanalysis, chemotherapy, group therapy, play therapy, psychodrama, and family casework have not been adequately tested to evaluate their effectiveness; but there is already evidence to suggest that, by and large, many of the measures in use have not as yet produced sufficiently encouraging results in the very difficult task of rebuilding character.[1] A crying need is for carefully designed experiments directed toward improving existing practices and toward the discovery of new methods of prophylaxis and therapy; and in this connection certain ideas arising out of the current inquiry may be helpful.

There are four major areas in which efforts in the direction of better management of delinquency are suggested by the present work: (a) *Family Life*, (b) *Schooling*, (c) *Use of Leisure*, and (d) *Clinical Practices*.

Before offering a few suggestions (intended merely as illustrative of how application of the knowledge gleaned in this inquiry might be relevant to the prevention and treatment of juvenile delinquency), it will help if we keep in mind a condensed formulation of the most distinguishing features of each body type as determined in this inquiry:

Mesomorphs (the bone-and-muscle physique) present a portrait of an essentially sturdy physical and nervous and emotional structure, with a tendency to express impulse in action.

Endomorphs (the soft, round physique) are less sturdy, less energetic, and less dynamic

---

[1] See S. and E. T. Glueck, *One Thousand Juvenile Delinquents*, Cambridge, Harvard University Press, 1934; E. Powers and H. Witmer, *An Experiment in the Prevention of Delinquency*, New York, Columbia University Press, 1951; and H. L. Witmer and E. Tufts, *The Effectiveness of Delinquency Prevention Programs*, Children's Bureau Publication, Number 350, Washington, D.C., U.S. Department of Health, Education, and Welfare, Social Security Administration, 1954. [See, also, Article 186 of this volume. — *Ed.*]

than the mesomorphs, and are more inhibited and conventional in their ideas and behavior.

Ectomorphs (linear, fragile body type) have less sturdiness and are more delicately organized than mesomorphs and present a more sensitive and aesthetic exterior to the world. They are more tense, inhibited, and conflict-ridden, bottling up their impulses and their destructive–sadistic trends.

Balanced physique. The only trait found to distinguish boys of this body type from all the others is that they are less fearful of failure and defeat. Otherwise, a clear picture does not emerge. They appear to have some characteristics of each physique.

It is the personality as a whole that is involved in behavior, not independent and dissociated fragments. Therefore suggestions regarding the management of delinquency should take account of bodily morphology with special reference to those traits found in the present work to yield a varied delinquency *potential* to each of the physique types, those traits and sociocultural factors demonstrated to exert an *excessive* criminogenic impact on one or another of the body types, and those traits and sociocultural influences which, although not shown to vary in impact on the physique types, are nevertheless criminogenic (see Chapters XI, XII, XIII, XIV *).

FAMILY LIFE

A striking finding from the current inquiry is the considerable association to the delinquency of *ectomorphs* of such adverse conditions as absence of the mother from the home, careless personal oversight of the boy by the mother, indifference or hostility of mother and siblings to boy, emotional illness of father, unsuitable discipline of boy by father, incompatibility of parents, disunited families, families having low standards of behavior, homes lacking in cultural refinement, broken homes, rearing by parent substitutes.

On the basis of this knowledge, preventive and rehabilitative efforts can be improved, for example, by a recognition of the excessive effect on *ectomorphs* of deprivation of a confidence-inspiring father figure, so necessary for the achievement of integration and a balanced attitude toward authority. Although this is a seri-

ous handicap to any boy, it is even more crucial to ectomorphic youngsters, probably because this sensitive physique type requires more reassurance of love and security than, say, the mesomorphs. In handling ectomorphs who are potential delinquents or already frankly delinquent, it may, for example, be even more necessary than in the case of other body types to include their parents in psychotherapy, teaching them what is involved from a mental hygiene point of view in their attitudes and practices, and, if necessary, even to provide parental adjuncts whom nature has endowed with therapeutic personalities.[2]

In respect to the delinquency of *mesomorphs*, on the other hand, we have found that growing up in disorderly households where family group recreations are lacking and play facilities are meager has a greater bearing on the delinquency of mesomorphs than on other body types. In dealing with mesomorphic boys, therefore, stress has to be placed on means of making their homes less expulsive and of providing vigorous, exciting, but socially acceptable, avenues of recreation for them in order to forfend antisocial escapades to which boys of this body build might otherwise be attracted in seeking outlets for their natural vigor and dynamism.

---

[2] We have long believed that there is a great deal of natural talent in dealing with human beings that is going to waste. It is well known that certain persons are so endowed with "personal magnetism" or warmth, or strength of character, as to be able to exert an influence on children, without necessarily being equipped with technical knowledge of child psychology. It has been found that certain social workers and probation and parole officers have a better success rate than others, without necessarily having a better technical education. In police departments, in school systems, and in other fields, perhaps 5–10 per cent of the personnel have this precious "X" quality. Because of the great shortage of psychiatrists and psychiatric social workers, systematic effort should be made to discover such persons and guide them into work with pre-delinquent and delinquent children. Perhaps it will be possible to evolve a series of projective and other tests through which the basic constituents can be defined and which could then be used by civil service agencies to help select and place persons naturally qualified to guide youth. Many a young police officer, for example, is better endowed to influence youth than to guide traffic. Upon selection of the men and women possessing the *therapeutic personality*, they could be given in-service training in the elements of mental hygiene and other disciplines that might make them understand their work better without dampening their natural abilities.

---

* Of *Physique and Delinquency.* — Ed.

As regards *endomorphs*, the *lesser* influence on their delinquency than on that of the other body types of such conditions as careless household routine, working mother, incompatibility of parents, lack of family group recreations, meager recreational facilities in the home, might well be kept in mind in order to avoid a stress on conditions and influences that do not have too great a bearing on the delinquency of endomorphs. The only aspect of the family life of endomorphs (within the compass of the present inquiry) that appears to have a *greater* association with their delinquency (in contrast with boys of balanced type) is a lack of a close attachment to them of the other children in the family. This would seem to suggest that they are in particular need of warmth and affection from their peers. On the whole, in dealing with pre-delinquent or delinquent *endomorphs*, those sociocultural factors that were found to be *generally* criminogenic (see Chapter X, "Common Ground of Criminogenesis") are the ones to which attention must be largely directed.

As is true of endomorphs, so of boys of *balanced type*, the sociocultural factors that are *generally* criminogenic must be taken into account in dealing with them, since there is evidence that some of the factors that have a special bearing on the delinquency of one or more of the other physique types exert *less* of an influence on the delinquency of boys of balanced type (low conduct standards in the family, incompatibility of parents, and lack of attachment of brothers and sisters).

These few suggestions are meant only as illustrations of the need for sharpening preventive and therapeutic efforts in the light of the special needs of each physique type.

However, in keeping in mind the special needs of boys of the different physiques, we must not overlook the pervasive criminogenic influences that have a similar impact on *all* the body types and the general preventive measures which they suggest. Many crucial differences were found in *Unraveling* between the family life of the delinquents and non-delinquents which call for constructive efforts to improve family life. Since in *Unraveling Juvenile Delinquency*[3] and *Delinquents in the Making*,[4]

we have already discussed their implications for the management of juvenile delinquency, there is no need to repeat them here, except to reemphasize that little progress can be expected in the prevention of delinquency until family life is strengthened and enriched by a large-scale, continuous, and pervasive program designed to bring to bear all the resources of mental hygiene, social work, education, and religious and ethical instruction upon the cradle of character, the home. Experimentation must be directed to the discovery of means to break the vicious circle of character-damaging influences on children exerted by parents who are themselves the distorted personality products of pathogenic parental influences. A tremendous multiplication of psychiatric, social, pastoral, and educational resources to improve the basic equipment of present and prospective parents for assumption of a wholesome parental role is indispensable to the control of delinquency.

Schooling

What do the findings of the current inquiry suggest as regards the need for reorienting school programs to meet the special needs of boys of the different body types? The facts derived from *Unraveling Juvenile Delinquency*[5] suggest that emotional disturbance rather than intellectual deficiency is the fundamental root of maladaptation to school life, expressing itself in a disharmony of relationship between the boy and the small society of the school which often continues into the larger society whose code is the law. Because of the early age of onset of delinquency, it becomes clear that the school stands in the front line of a community-wide attack on antisocial behavior, especially in the opportunity for its early recognition.

Our current findings suggest a need for (a) some re-emphasis in teacher training programs; (b) adaptation of school curricula to meet the special needs of youngsters of the different body types; and (c) experimentation with screening devices that take into account the variations in the influence of certain traits and sociocultural factors on the development of antisocial behavior in the different body types.

Training of Teachers. It would seem of value to create an awareness in teachers and

---

[3] Chap. XXII.
[4] Chap. XVI.

[5] Chap. XII.

school counselors of fundamental divergencies in the temperamental equipment of children of the various body types. For example, because of the excessive sensitivity of *ectomorphs*, teachers and counselors might unwittingly cause particular damage to them unless alerted to the special needs of children of this physique and temperament. Because of the pathologic parent–child relationships prevailing in most families of delinquents, such youngsters have difficulty in finding in their own fathers an affectionate, sympathetic, and understanding adult around whom to weave the ideals, values, and standards of behavior that are incorporated in them through identification with and emulation of parents — a process that is at the core of character and of respect for authority.*

We have elsewhere suggested that perhaps young adult male teachers are needed in greater numbers, even in the kindergarten and early grades; perhaps husband-wife teams of teachers would provide a more natural and warm emotional climate in the classroom.[6]

Adaptation of Curricula. In the light of differences in the characteristics of boys of the various body types and of their selective response to certain delinquency-inducing sociocultural influences, it becomes evident that forcing all types of children into a single academic mold is likely to result in increased tension, frustration, and revolt. To cite but a few of the traits in which each of the body types differs from one or more of the others (see Chapters XI, XII, XIII, XIV†) the need for diversification of school activity is suggested by the strength and uninhibited motor response to stimuli of mesomorphs; the greater submissiveness, sensuousness, and conventionality of endomorphs; the greater aestheticism, feeling of inadequacy, and emotional instability of ectomorphs. If the school is to function in the network of crime preventive agencies, obviously a broader range of curricula must be devised to enlist the interest and take into account the distinctive needs of boys of the various body types.

As regards the management of boys already delinquent, the flexibility of school programs is also important. For example (see Exhibit 19), although delinquents in general are far more behind grade for their age than non-delinquents, *mesomorphic* delinquents are found to be clearly more so than delinquents of balanced type and probably than endomorphs; and although many delinquents want to leave school as early as possible, *mesomorphs* are found to be much more eager to do so than endomorphs or ectomorphs.

More intensive study of other aspects of school activities would no doubt disclose other distinctive inclinations and needs of the different physique types.

Screening of delinquents. The importance of identifying pre-delinquents before they are fully embarked on delinquent careers is gaining recognition. In the application of screening devices the school is in the "front line," because, by and large, it is in a position to reach all children before maladapted behavior expresses itself overtly or, if already in evidence, before it becomes too deeply rooted. A prime need, therefore, is to distinguish at school entrance between those children who are headed for delinquency and those who are not likely to embark on criminal careers; and also to distinguish true forerunners of delinquency from merely transient phenomena of healthy experimentation with reality. Bits of maladapted behavior during the first few years of life are not necessarily symptomatic of future delinquency.

Our pioneer effort in the construction of three screening devices [7] and several validations of one of them [8] encourages us to recommend experimentation with such instrumentalities as a basis for a wide and comprehensive prophylactic attack on the growing scourge of juvenile delinquency. It therefore becomes pertinent to

---

* A good illustration of sound advice to teachers written in non-technical language is R. H. Ojemann, *Personality Adjustment of Individual Children*, 1954, Department of Classroom Teachers, American Educational Research Association of the National Education Association, Washington, D.C. — *Ed.*

[6] *Delinquents in the Making*, New York, Harper and Brothers, 1952, pp. 200–201. [Article 174 of this voulme. — *Ed.*]

† Of *Physique and Delinquency*. — *Ed.*

[7] *Unraveling*, Chapter XX.

[8] Sidney Axelrad and Selma J. Glick, "Application of the Glueck Social Prediction Table to 100 Jewish Delinquent Boys," *The Jewish Social Quarterly*, Vol. 30, No. 2 (1953), pp. 127–136; Richard E. Thompson, "A Validation of the Glueck Social Prediction Scale for Proneness to Delinquency," *The Journal of Criminal Law, Criminology and Police Science*, Vol. 43, No. 4 (Nov.–Dec., 1952), pp. 451–470. [See Article 171–173 of this volume. — *Ed.*]

Exhibit **19** *School History of Delinquents*

PHYSIQUE TYPES	Percentages of the Respective Physique Type Totals			
	WANTS TO LEAVE SCHOOL		TWO OR MORE YEARS RETARDED	
	Number	%	Number	%
Total	206	43.2%	202	40.8%
Mesomorphs	144	50.0	135	45.1
Endomorphs	16	28.1	18	30.5
Ectomorphs	19	27.9	30	42.2
Balanced	27	42.2	19	28.8
Significance of Differences between Physique Types				
Meso-Endo		.05		—
Meso-Ecto		.02		—
Meso-Balanced		—		.05
Endo-Ecto		—		—
Endo-Balanced		—		—
Ecto-Balanced		—		—

raise the question as to whether, and how, the newly established dimension of physique type in the patterning of delinquency modifies and/or enhances the development and usefulness of screening devices.

How does the knowledge gained in the current inquiry regarding the role of physique in delinquency assist, if at all, in identifying pre-delinquents? Examination of the traits found in *Unraveling Juvenile Delinquency* to be highly associated with delinquency reveals that by and large these do not vary significantly in their impact on the delinquency of the body types. In the screening device based on the five traits of character structure derived from the *Rorschach Test* — social assertiveness, defiance, suspiciousness, destructiveness, and emotional lability — only *destructiveness* varies in association with the delinquency of the physique types, being much more criminogenic when occurring in mesomorphs than in ectomorphs. Of the five traits of temperament based on *psychiatric findings* — adventurousness, extroversiveness, suggestibility, stubbornness, and emotional instability — only *emotional instability* varies in its influence on the delinquency of the physique types, it also being more likely to result in delinquency when occurring in mesomorphs than in ectomorphs.

In contrast to these findings, however, of the five *sociocultural* factors in *Unraveling* which comprise a screening device for distinguishing pre-delinquents from non-delinquents — discipline of boy by father, supervision of boy by mother, affection of father for boy, affection of mother for boy, and family cohesiveness — only one, *lack of affection of father for boy*, was *not* found in the present inquiry to be more largely associated with the delinquency of one body type than of the others. It is to be noted that all four of the sociocultural factors which do play a selective role in the delinquency of the body types have more to do with impelling *ectomorphs* to delinquency than mesomorphs and/or endomorphs (see Tables 95, 98, 103, and 104).

Thus it will be seen that the efficacy of the first two of the three screening devices developed in connection with *Unraveling* is largely independent of body build, but that the third table would appear to have an even *greater* prognostic power in the case of ectomorphic boys than when applied to boys irrespective of body build.

Although the above findings point to the likelihood of enhancing even further the usefulness of the screening instrumentality as regards boys of ectomorphic physique beyond its already quite satisfactory power, there would appear to be no particular urgency for this,[9] especially in view of the fact that the added problem of somatotyping children as a preliminary to screening them for their delinquency potential might discourage its use. However, once a pre-delinquent has been identified, the additional knowledge that certain sociocultural factors exert an even more harmful influence on ectomorphs than on other body types should serve to diversify prophylactic and therapeutic efforts in accordance with the special vulnerabilities of each body type.

Were it to appear desirable, however, there are some additional findings in the current inquiry that might serve as a basis for developing separate screening devices for boys of each physique type, designed to establish their vulnerability to delinquency even more accurately than do the prediction tables in *Unraveling Juvenile Delinquency*.* For example, in the case of mesomorphs, we have found a cluster of three traits (feeling of inadequacy, emotional instability, and emotional conflicts) which, more markedly than any other pattern of traits within the compass of the current inquiry, distinguish delinquent from non-delinquent mesomorphs (90.5%:9.5%). In addition to this are two aspects of the home environment (careless household routine and lack of family group recreations) which in combination most sharply differentiate delinquent from non-delinquent mesomorphs (78.1%:21.9%). (See Appendix E.)

As regards ectomorphs, there appears to be a combination of two traits more sharply distinguishing delinquent from non-delinquent ectomorphs — extreme restlessness in early childhood and receptive trends (85.7%:14.3%); and a cluster of four sociocultural factors — rearing in homes of low conduct standards, in homes lacking cultural refinement, in families lacking cohesiveness, and by fathers whose discipline of the boy is other than firm and kindly — that in combination more sharply distinguish

delinquent from non-delinquent ectomorphs than any other cluster of sociocultural factors within the compass of the present inquiry (91%:9%). (See Appendix E.)

As regards endomorphs and boys of balanced type, there is *no specific* cluster of traits that significantly differentiates endomorphic delinquents from non-delinquents; and no pattern of sociocultural factors that significantly distinguishes delinquent from non-delinquent endomorphs. (See Appendix E.)

Although it does not appear to be too necessary to organize the findings concerning the mesomorphs and ectomorphs into formal screening instrumentalities, school personnel and others should find the trait and factor clusters suggestive in designing preventive and therapeutic services.

USE OF LEISURE

In *Unraveling Juvenile Delinquency* differences in the use of leisure among delinquents as compared with non-delinquents were revealed. The recreational preferences of delinquents are for risky and adventurous energy outlets, reflected not only in excessive truck-hopping, keeping late hours, bunking out, but also in seeking play places at a considerable distance from their homes, and hunting for exciting locales of risk and adventure such as railroad yards and waterfronts. These tendencies are also reflected in the greater extent to which the delinquents have serious street accidents and, vicariously, in their much more frequent movie attendance. Most of the delinquents run around in gangs or crowds, and many prefer companions older than themselves. There is also strong evidence that delinquents dislike the confinement of playgrounds, supervised recreations, or attendance at boys' clubs or community centers, which they rarely join of their own volition.

Apart from this, what do our current findings suggest about the special recreational needs of the different physique type? A few examples will illustrate the point (see Exhibit 20): Although delinquents in general tend to have more companions than non-delinquents, a breakdown by physique type reveals that *mesomorphs* and boys of *balanced* physique are more likely than endomorphs and ectomorphs to have many playmates. Such constitutional preferences need to be taken into account in

---

[9] At least, until the experiment now going on in New York City under the auspices of the New York City Youth Board has been completed. See article by Ralph Whelan, *Journal of Criminal Law and Criminology*, Vol. 45, No. 4 (Nov.–Dec., 1954), pp. 432–441, describing this experiment.
* See E. T. Glueck, "Body Build in the Prediction of Delinquency," 48 *J. Crim. L., Criminology and Police Science* (March–April, 1958), 577–579. — Ed.

Exhibit **20** *Leisure Time Activities of Non-delinquents*

	TOTAL		MESO-MORPHS		ENDO-MORPHS		ECTO-MORPHS		BALANCED	
ACTIVITIES	No.	%	No.	%	No.	%	No.	%	No.	%

Percentages of the Respective Physique Type Totals

ACTIVITIES	No.	%	No.	%	No.	%	No.	%	No.	%
Runs Around with a Crowd	215	44.4%	76	51.0%	23	31.9%	76	39.8%	40	55.6%
Enjoys Competitive Sports	130	28.4	56	38.6	12	17.9	37	21.3	25	35.2
Dislike of Supervised Recreations	178	62.7	52	61.9	30	61.2	74	69.2	22	50.0
Prefers Adventuresome Activities	45	9.8	20	13.8	3	4.5	17	9.8	5	7.0
Steals Rides/Hops Trucks	116	24.0	42	28.2	10	13.9	44	23.0	20	27.8
Seeks Recreations in Distant Neighborhoods	69	14.3	27	18.1	5	6.9	30	15.7	7	9.7
Plays on Waterfronts	76	15.8	28	18.8	6	8.3	25	13.1	17	23.6

Significance of Differences between Physique Types

ACTIVITIES	MESO—ENDO	MESO—ECTO	MESO—BALANCED	ENDO—ECTO	ENDO—BALANCED	ECTO—BALANCED
Runs Around with a Crowd	.05	—	—	—	.05	—
Enjoys Competitive Sports	.05	.05	—	—	.10	—
Dislike of Supervised Recreations	—	—	—	—	—	—
Prefers Adventuresome Activities	.10	—	—	—	—	—
Steals Rides/Hops Trucks	.05	—	—	—	—	—
Seeks Recreations in Distant Neighborhoods	.10	—	—	—	—	—
Plays on Waterfronts	—	—	—	—	.05	—

the planning of recreational programs. To push ectomorphs and endomorphs into group activities would obviously "go against the grain." Although delinquents have somewhat *less* interest in competitive sports than non-delinquents, boys of *mesomorphic* and *balanced* physique are found in general to have greater preference for such activities than do ectomorphs and endomorphs. This is also illustrative of the need for tailoring recreational activities to meet the special needs of the different body types.

Youngsters in today's culture have ample leisure; and unless channels of legitimate energy-outlet are provided it is natural that uninhibited drive-tendencies may result in delinquency. Especially in the case of *mesomorphs*, opportunities need to be created not only in the home or in school, but in the community, for adventuresome yet socially harmless physical activity in the company of other boys, as diversions from antisocial expression of the strong drives of this body type, keeping in mind that mesomorphic boys typically "live by action." [10]

---

[10] Sheldon's striking expression for "the energetic characteristic" of "Somatotonia." See W. H. Sheldon

A basic need in preventing antisocial aggression in mesomorphs is the provision of "moral equivalents" for the acts of aggressive energy which are especially easy, congenial, satisfying, and even *necessary* to boys of this vigorous physique.

Some boys prefer quieter and less aggressive recreational outlets. For example, *endomorphs* have less need for adventuresome activities than mesomorphs. This is evidenced by the lower proportion who have the urge to steal rides and hop trucks, by their less frequent seeking of recreations in neighborhoods distant from their homes, and by less playing on waterfronts. And *ectomorphs* have more dislike of *supervised* recreations than do boys of balanced physique.

In planning their programs, boys' clubs, camps, settlement houses, and other recreational agencies obviously need to take into account divergencies of preference related to differences in basic constitutional nature; and to educate the boys themselves to appreciate that there are varieties of recreational preferences related to temperamental needs and physical and mental abilities.

CLINICAL PRACTICES

Psychotherapists also might well incorporate into their treatment of pre-delinquents and delinquents some of the findings of this and similar research.

It has been shown that the delinquency potential of *mesomorphs* is especially high in that (compared to one or more of the other physique types) they possess some traits (e.g., physical strength, social assertiveness, uninhibited motor response to stimuli) which if improperly channeled might lead to delinquency and criminalism. This has to be taken into account not only by all those engaged in broad preventive efforts, but by therapists dealing with individual pre-delinquents and delinquents.

Clinically, in the treatment of *mesomorphs* already delinquent, it should be helpful, together with other data relevant to the understanding and treatment of socially maladapted children, to consider the characteristics especially impelling mesomorphs to delinquency. That susceptibility to contagion, low verbal in-

telligence, feelings of not being taken care of, destructiveness, destructive–sadistic trends, feelings of inadequacy, emotional instability, and emotional conflicts play a special criminogenic role *in a physique habitus where they do not usually occur in excess* is an important source of insight that should help clinicians to understand what they and their associates must take into account in the treatment of mesomorphic delinquents in order to provide satisfying emotional support and physical outlets for them.

Endomorphs, also, present some special problems for the clinician. Because of lower vitality than that possessed by mesomorphs, a lesser tendency to resolve their tensions in action, greater conventionality, and greater submissiveness to authority, their delinquency potential is not nearly as great as that of mesomorphs. But certain traits found in fact to have an excessive criminogenic impact on endomorphs need to be taken into account by those called upon to treat them for distortions of personality, character, or conduct. Among the influences especially related to the delinquency of endomorphs are cyanosis, ambivalence to authority, feeling of not being able to manage one's own life. The first of these is a reflection of some neurologic disturbance and is therefore a medical concern; of the other two traits, the first may require psychiatric attention, and both need constructive channeling.

Ectomorphs, too, require specialized clinical attention. Their sensitiveness, their excessive inclination to emotional conflicts, their tendency to keep their affective tensions bottled up, and the relative deficiency among ectomorphs generally of an outflowing motor tendency, gives them a far lower delinquency potential than mesomorphs. To lessen the chances of this potential becoming actual may often require intensive psychotherapy and special instruction to the parents and teachers of ectomorphs. Clinically, a history of extreme restlessness in early childhood, dermographia (skin sensitivity), and receptive (oral) trends must be noted as particularly related to delinquency in this body type. On the other hand, the delinquency of ectomorphs is not especially associated with those traits that operate with excessive force on mesomorphs.

Boys of *balanced type* possess some of the characteristics of each of the other physiques, the only trait found to differentiate them from

---

with the collaboration of S. S. Stevens, *The Varieties of Temperament,* New York and London, Harper and Brothers, 1942, p. 51.

all the other body types being a lesser fear of failure and defeat. Since they are less acquisitive, more stable emotionally, and have less tendency to emotional conflicts than ectomorphs, and are less likely to seek outlets for tensions in action than are mesomorphs, they too present a relatively low delinquency potential. Clinically, it is well to take into account the traits having an especial impact on the delinquency of this body type: e.g., susceptibility to contagion, strong hand grip, high performance intelligence, lack of fear of failure and defeat, marked dependence on others, and sensuousness. Some or all such traits, operating with the generally etiologic ones, exert a sufficient pressure to impel boys of the balanced type in the direction of delinquency.

CONCLUSION

We wish it were possible to speak with as much confidence regarding the prevention and "cure" of delinquency as we do regarding the traits and reactions of delinquents, incomplete as our findings are as to these. In the management of emotional and behavioral disorders, it is a far cry from diagnosis to therapy. A basic difficulty is, of course, the relative imperfection of the psychiatric and behavioral disciplines. Another difficulty (established in *Unraveling Juvenile Delinquency*) is that the tendency to maladaptation originates very early in life. A striking finding in that work was that half the delinquents showed persistent evidence of antisocial behavior when still under the age of eight, and nine-tenths when under the age of eleven. Therefore, it is clear that a major focus must be on the early years.

The foregoing discussion indicates that although many preventive and therapeutic indications flow from differences in the personality and temperamental makeup of boys of the different body types and require consideration in the effective management of delinquency, we must not lose sight of the *permeative* criminogenic influences that must needs be dealt with. It is particularly necessary to be realistic about the fact that there are limits to effective prophylactic action laid down by the general sociocultural situation. Our mores and widespread social influences are slow to change. In the meantime, children have to live in the world as it is; nor can they be made good by removing evil out of their experience. Character is not built that way and strength of character comes out of coping with evils, temptations, and problems to the best of one's ability. There is no doubt of the need of direct, repressive action against obvious evils, such as the peddling of drugs to children. But there are general cultural pressures and disharmonies and contradictions in our civilization involved in the broad and deep background of antisocial behavior that are difficult to change and can only be modified by an over-all social policy framed and projected over a long period of time by civic, political, and religious leaders.

As in *Unraveling Juvenile Delinquency*, and in *Delinquents in the Making* based thereon, we have not attempted to go into detail about techniques to be employed in coping with the antisocial conduct of children. Our aim has been simply to give some illustrations of the relevancy of physique type and constitutional psychology to the problem. We must leave to social practitioners the task of more fully implementing the indications of this inquiry if they find them challenging.

The evidence of the present research, added to that of *Unraveling*, does not lead us to the pessimistic conclusion that persistent delinquency springs largely from the germ plasm and is inevitable. We repeat what we have previously said: [11] *In delinquency we are dealing not with predestination but with destination.* We believe that imaginative and intensive experimentation with prophylactic and therapeutic measures, providing it is timely and thorough, should produce evidence that the destination of children toward delinquency is capable of change in a substantial proportion of instances. At the same time, we cannot escape the conclusion that differences in body structure can no longer be ignored in assessing the causal involvements of delinquency, and in shaping measures to cope with it.

In the final chapter we present a few etiologic hypotheses or theories in the confidence that they are worthy of further exploration.

---

[11] *Unraveling*, p. 289; *Delinquents in the Making*, p. 210.

176

Report of the Committee
on Crime Prevention of the
American Prison Association *

I. INTRODUCTORY

At the last (August, 1941) meeting of the Association in San Francisco, the following resolution was adopted:

The American Prison Association recognizes that through unanimity of planning and systematized methods on a national basis, control of delinquency and crime through preventive processes can be more effectively accomplished.

In the light of our own experience and the experiences of other organizations concerning themselves with the problem of delinquency and crime prevention, it becomes apparent that, in contrast to the effective and objective community programs now in existence, there are many so-called crime prevention bureaus coming into existence which are poorly planned, unscientifically operated and superficial in function, and

It is our conviction that the individual community is the basic unit in which comprehensive programs of crime prevention may be employed, and that such community programs will in many cases be rendered more effective if operating under a competent State authority:

Therefore, Be it Resolved, That this Association establish a proper study committee, whose membership shall consist of a comparatively small number of outstanding leaders in recognized fields of welfare who will be willing to serve and devote their best efforts toward a proper appraisal and evaluation of community programs now operating in this country, and

That this shall be a continuing committee whose purpose it shall be to ultimately produce a manual of standards and procedures for the information and guidance of those who seek advice upon the subject of prevention of crime and delinquency on a community basis, and that this manual shall be issued

by and with the approval of the American Prison Association.[1]

In pursuance of this resolution, your President invited Prof. Sheldon Glueck of the Harvard Law School to be Chairman of this Committee, and the following additional members were appointed: Mr. Saul Alinsky, Dr. Eleanor T. Glueck, Mr. Leonard V. Harrison, Mr. E. L. Johnstone, Mr. Morris Ploscowe, Prof. Frederic M. Thrasher and Mr. August Vollmer. . . .

It is true that detailed and accurate statistics covering the entire country and comparing the incidence of established juvenile misconduct for the past few years do not yet exist; and therefore any conclusive estimate of the amount of increase and differences in the nature of the offenses that have undergone a rise cannot yet be made. But it would amount to criminal negligence in a double sense not to take note of the fact that the sample probings here and there in different parts of the nation constitute a warning signal more significant for the future than any air-raid siren could be. . . .

II. CRIME PREVENTION IN NORMAL TIMES

On this subject of *basic* crime-preventive programs, your Committee has so far taken three steps: (1) It has made a sample analysis of crime prevention articles during the period between the publication, in 1936, of *Preventing Crime* [2] (edited by Sheldon and Eleanor Glueck), the first volume to be devoted exclusively to this subject, and December, 1941. (2) Your Committee has written to the various experts who had contributed articles to the volume, *Preventing Crime,* to obtain information on what changes, if any, had occurred since its publication. (3) It has held a meeting at the offices of the Association in New York, to discuss some of the implications of a really thorough attack on the problem of crime prevention. As the result of these three lines of exploration of the problem, your Committee presents the following conclusion:

A truly efficient program of crime prevention requires a much more thorough knowledge of causal influences than we as yet possess; but much more

---

* Presented at the 72nd Annual Congress of Correction, sponsored by the American Prison Association in Asheville, North Carolina, October 18–23, 1942. [Certain parts have been omitted and footnotes renumbered. Used by permission of the American Correctional Association. — *Ed.*]

[1] Proceedings of the Seventy-First Annual Congress of the American Prison Association, 1941, pp. 501–502.

[2] Glueck and Glueck (Editors), *Preventing Crime,* McGraw-Hill Book Company, Inc., 1936.

progress in preventing or diminishing juvenile delinquency and adult recidivism than has so far been made is nevertheless possible.

As is well known, there are differences in emphasis, if not fundamental disagreements, among those who have given serious study to the intricate problem of crime causation. These differences range from a markedly biologic orientation to a markedly sociologic one. Now, theoretically, in order to set up a program of prophylaxis or prevention, one should have very specific and proved knowledge of the causal agencies; only in this way can the exactly fitting instruments for attack upon causes be designed and used.

However, just as preventive medicine has often had to act in the emergencies of an epidemic without possessing full and accurate knowledge of exactly which causal agencies it was attacking — something true, for example, of influenza — so those concerned with the control and reduction of delinquency and recidivism must act without completely adequate knowledge. This means, of course, that programs set up for coping with these social ills will be more wasteful and less successful than they would be if specific and demonstrable causal forces were attacked. It is the difference between the shotgun approach, with its widespread and rather wasteful attack based on the hope that a few of the pellets will hit the target, and the approach with a gun that shoots businesslike bullets aimed at a very specific bull's-eye.

Our state of ignorance regarding the *specific mechanisms* of crime causation and the reasons for recidivism can, however, be exaggerated just as markedly as the extent and quality of our knowledge can be overestimated. There are certain statements regarding crime causation, or at least the more intimate surrounding circumstances of delinquency and recidivism, about which there ought to be very little disagreement even among experts of extremist points of view; and it is upon an attack on these that we shall have to place our faith in the efficacy of crime prevention programs in our time.

Among these statements about which there can be little cavil, we may list the following:

1) That in a very high proportion of instances, adult criminals are persons who had been maladjusted and delinquent children;

2) That at least a small percentage of children who become delinquent are mentally defective;

3) That a larger percentage of them suffer from personality distortion, mental tensions and conflicts, and faulty habits;

4) That an appreciable proportion of them come from either definitely broken homes, or those in which the parents, by virtue of their mental makeup or conduct, are hardly competent to carry out successfully the duties of parenthood in modern society;

5) That many delinquent children are to be found among those who had left school at a too early age, and had achieved neither sufficient academic education nor training in honest and useful trades or occupations;

6) That in correctional institutions it is usually discovered that large proportions of young-adult offenders have never established even rudimentary habits of continuous and efficient work, correlated with periods of constructive or healthily relaxing recreation;

7) That the highest proportion of delinquent children spring from communities in which processes of deterioration and disintegration are marked, manifesting themselves (a) in certain cultural standards different from and in conflict with the standards followed by the majority of persons; (b) in conditions of poverty, undernourishment, overcrowding and squalor; (c) in inadequate social provision for wholesome (or at least not antisocial) recreational outlets; (d) in the presence of centers of antisocial attitude and behavior, such as gambling joints, poolrooms, improperly supervised dance halls and movie theatres, and the like;

8) That the failure of the legitimate world to lend an understanding mind, a sympathetic heart, and a helping hand to ex-prisoners from the "half-world" and the underworld has much to do with their recidivism;

9) That inadequate therapeutic programs — in probation, parole and institutional treatment — also have much to do with recidivism.

Other factors of this kind which very probably have some causal hook-up with delinquent and criminal behavior, although that connection is not always clear, might be mentioned. But the above list is sufficiently concrete and represents conditions found often enough to serve at least as a *large target* at which we can direct our preventive shotgun, if not as a small clean-cut bull's-eye, toward which we might shoot our preventive bullets with greater skill and confidence of success.

Now, considering the situation realistically, what instruments of crime prevention are being used? Examination of a bibliography of some 100 articles from 1936 to December, 1941, from a search of *Readers' Guide, International Index to Periodical Literature* and other *Indexes* to more technical journals,[3] has led your Committee to the conclusion that very few *new* crime-preventive techniques have been reported in current periodicals, since the publication of *Preventing Crime* in 1936. No single article indicates any promising fundamental or sweeping change over the practices advocated some five or six years ago in that volume. However, from the large amount of exhortation — serious and gaseous — to be found among these 100 articles, it seems safe to assume that several regions are attempting crime prevention in some organized manner without as yet reporting on either techniques or results. Perhaps more recent publications report, specifically, on these matters. . . . We shall later summarize a few of the more interesting approaches found in the literature or uncovered in response to inquiries. In the meantime, it seems fair and useful to retain, until further developments make changes indispensable, the following classification of major crime-preventive activities throughout the country, as originally published in *Preventing Crime*:

a) Coordinated Community Programs
b) School Programs
c) Police Programs
d) Intramural Guidance Programs
e) Extramural Guidance Programs
f) Boys' Clubs and Recreational Programs

As to (a) "Coordinated Community Programs," *Preventing Crime* had commented as follows:

Those who stress a coordinated community approach to the problems of crime prevention are inclined to the view that preventive activity should be predicated upon the recognition of the community or neighborhood or "area" as a more or less natural cultural entity. Since the forces that make for juvenile demoralization pervade entire regions, it would seem that a community-wide program is called for. Such a program involves consideration of the entire network of culture-generating and culture-transmitting forces in a neighborhood or city; its destructive and constructive agencies, its public and private institutions, its means of work and play, its gangs, its citizens' groups, its ethnic and language problems, its prejudices, and the like. The essence of a coordinated community

program seems to be the recognition of the inter-relationship of the various elements in community life, their reformulation according to some desirable standard of communal soundness, the strengthening of constructive elements and weakening of others, and the guidance of the community's growth, under appropriate leadership, toward the realization of wholesome values in the lives of the community and its denizens.

"This [says Thrasher] is the sociological, as contrasted with the individualistic, approach to the problem of crime prevention. It is the community, as contrasted with the institutional attack on the problem. The failure of the programs of educational, welfare, and recreational agencies to prevent crime may be summed up best by the term "institutional mindedness." This is the collective individualism which puts the supposed success of institutional programs ahead of the community program. Vested interests undoubtedly enter the picture at this point, but whatever the explanation, the fact remains that community planning for crime prevention and consequent coordination and integration of pertinent activities into a well-rounded program is well-nigh impossible under these conditions."

Among the outstanding features of this approach to the problems involved in a crime-prevention program are the following: (1) A preliminary survey of the region to be served, to determine its problems and criminogenic influences; (2) the canvassing of the community's constructive resources — both institutional and human — and of the possibility of their more widespread and intensive employment under guidance; (3) the determining of the scope of activity of existing social-welfare organizations and the extent of their cooperation and overlapping in the solution of the community's problems; (4) the providing of an organization (such as the coordinating council described by Scudder [4] or the means developed by Thrasher [5]) for the better collaboration of existing agencies and extension of their services, as well as those of such institutions as schools, churches, playgrounds, play streets and the like; (5) the education of the public in the aims and methods of a cooperative effort to reduce delinquency and crime and enrich the material and spiritual resources of the community; (6) the liberal use of citizens' groups, civic organizations, and individuals in planning and carrying on the various elements of an interwoven program of crime prevention and community welfare.[6]

---

[3] The Committee is indebted to Benjamin B. Ferencz, a third-year student at the Harvard Law School, for aid in digesting this material. — S. G.

[4] K. J. Scudder, "The Los Angeles County Coordinating Council Plan," in S. and E. T. Glueck, Editors, *Preventing Crime*, New York, 1936, pp. 24–25.

[5] F. F. Thrasher, "The Lower West Side Crime Prevention Program, New York City," in *Id.*, pp. 68–76.

[6] S. and E. T. Glueck, *Preventing Crime, op. cit.*, pp. 13–14.

Under the general head of "Coordinated Community Programs," *Preventing Crime* had included such somewhat varied programs as those of The Los Angeles County Coordinating Council Plan, The Lower West Side Crime Prevention Program of New York City, The Foundation for Youth of Columbus, Indiana, and The Director-at-Large Plan of the San Francisco Recreation Commission. Some of these interesting experiments have, since 1936, either expanded or contracted their activities; others have closed shop for financial, personnel or other reasons. However, your Committee's analysis of the literature, as well as the personal knowledge of some members of your Committee, impels the following observations upon existing activities that might today be subsumed under the above heading of "Coordinated Community Programs":

1) *The Chicago Area Project:* Beginning in 1932 as an outgrowth of the well-known "delinquency area" studies of Clifford Shaw and his colleagues, this project has spread to include six local communities in Chicago, ranging in size from 10,000 to 40,000 residents. All these communities ranked relatively high in the rate of delinquency during some four previous decades. The researches of the Chicago sociologists have tended to demonstrate that the high rates of delinquency in certain communities were due to the disorganization of community life, the breakdown of traditional forms of control, the confusion of social and moral values and the concomitant development of boy gangs and strong criminalistic organizations. This being the diagnosis, the therapeutic aim was to re-build the solidarity of attitude, sentiment and values in the communities, through engaging the efforts of the residents in a collective attack on this common problem.

This Chicago Area Project differs from the typical "coordinating" (or "community") council approach in that responsibility for planning and operating programs is vested in a committee of local residents of the region rather than one comprised essentially of professional workers who often do not reside in the community in question and do not sufficiently reflect the basic needs, interests and sentiments of the people. Nevertheless, professional guidance, furnished through personnel provided by the State Department of Public Welfare through its Institute for Juvenile Research, is involved, although it aims to remain in the background.

As an indication of the nature of the local committees may be mentioned the fact that the officers of the West Side Community Committee are an automobile dealer, a truck driver, a garage attendant, a priest, a physician, a certified public accountant, an attorney, an office clerk.

The various committees operate on the basis of their own budgets and in relation to the Chicago Community Fund, also, however, raising funds locally from individuals and firms in the neighborhood.

The Area Project differs from such enterprises as social settlements, neighborhood centers, Y. M. C. A.s, boys' clubs, and the like, in that, generally speaking, the ordinary local residents to be served by such institutions have little voice in the management of these latter agencies in respect to budgets, programs, and the like; while in the Area Project control is originally vested and remains throughout in the residents of the Area. So, also, publicity for specific accomplishments in the community gives credit to local residents, and reports on accomplishments are, likewise, to be made by the local residents themselves. Nevertheless, in developing the work in each area, the local committee of residents is encouraged to seek the cooperation of churches, schools, recreation centers, labor unions, industries, and other resources in the effort to bring about coordinated attack.

It will be seen at once, that whatever may ultimately be the results of the Chicago Area Project in reducing delinquency, it is to be credited with operating in the true democratic tradition. Moreover, there are certain valuable by-products of the integrated neighborhood approach that may turn out to be at least as significant as is the major aim of preventing boys and girls from *becoming* delinquent, as is shown in the following statement by Mr. Shaw: "We can present evidence that the work of the citizens' committees has been effective in reorganizing the lives of individual delinquents and adult offenders. In the case of adult parolees the local residents not only give aid in securing employment, but also take the parolees into their own organization and give them a chance to establish new and constructive relationships with their neighbors."

Finally, Mr. Shaw and the other originators of the Chicago Area Project are to be commended for having recognized the need of some legitimate methods of evaluation of results. Space does not permit going into these methods further than to say that yearly records are kept of truants, boys and girls who have been handled by the police, and those taken into the juvenile court on delinquency petitions, so that changes in trend can be compared with neighboring "control areas." [7]

[7] Data culled from letter from Mr. Clifford R. Shaw and articles and other materials submitted by him. Above is a summary of selected data; it is not a complete analysis and certainly not a definitive evaluation of the Area Project work. The same may be said in regard to the other programs herein described. Careful field studies and follow-up investigations are indispensable to final judgments on these enterprises. — S. G.

2) Similar in general conception regarding the larger forces that make for delinquency and recidivism, but stressing the deepest socioeconomic and cultural roots and differing from the Area Project in certain fundamental approaches of technique, is the work of the "*Industrial Areas Foundation*," also in Chicago, but recently spreading its activities to include other cities. Here again we find an expression of protest against the mere "coordination" of professional agencies, "which are, first, superimposed upon the community and, second, play a superficial role in the life of the community." [8]

This work was initiated by Mr. Saul D. Alinsky and has a distinguished panel of supporters behind it. Its best-known enterprise is the "Back of the Yards" Neighborhood Council, operating in a region close to the stock yards. A community council was formed, including the two basic institutions of the area, organized religion and organized labor, but also less important interests and "action groups." In an abstract to an article describing his approach to the problems involved, Mr. Alinsky says: "'Back of the Yards' Neighborhood Council is an experimental demonstration of a community organizational procedure predicated upon a functional conception of the character of a community and its problems. On the local scene the council has operated a successful program. It has brought about not only a tangible improvement in the way of life of the local residents of Back of the Yards but has also resulted in the development of an unusual sympathy and understanding between organizations which previously had been in opposition and conflict. This Council has not confined its efforts to the local scene but has also addressed itself to the task of coping with those larger socioeconomic issues which converge upon the local scene to establish the plight of Back of the Yards. The Council is aiding other industrial areas to organize in a similar manner in the hope that the combined strength of many such community councils will be sufficient to deal effectively with these major destructive forces.[9]

Here is an attempt to bring about greater community solidarity through a systematic breaking down of the barriers of class and religious misunderstanding. It therefore has implications far beyond the mere problem of delinquency and crime, and far beyond the period before or during the present war; for it is at least one beacon pointing the way to a realistic, instead of a self-deceptive, attack upon those basic ills of an industrial age — poor housing, widespread malnutrition and disease, unemployment and other dark members of the "Kingdom of Evils" — whose preoccupations are not only delinquency and crime

but the whole realm of human ills. Including active participants of the church, both types of labor unions, the local Chamber of Commerce, the American Legion post, the leading businessmen, the social, ethnic, fraternal and athletic organizations formed by the denizens of "Back of the Yards," and utilizing leaders who come from the community itself, it seems to offer considerable promise. For a major task of America's coming of age is that recognized in this enterprise; namely, that capital and labor, Jew and Gentile, Greek, Italian and English-born American — we all have a "common stake" in maintaining the privileges of the American way of life, in multiplying its opportunities, in supplying civilized care to its handicapped, in destroying its wasteful and mentally unhygienic prejudices.

Your Committee is distinctly in favor of both types of effort just described, and it urges communities to study the *Chicago Area* and the *Back of the Yards* projects as means of bringing about that greater understanding, unity and wholesomeness of community life that are needed to strengthen the sinews of Uncle Sam. . . . At the same time your Committee is of opinion that much of the promising work of the Coordinating Council movement is worthy of encouragement; for it is after all one step in the right direction of a closer knitting of community resources, albeit its major stimulus and guidance come from the professionals "on top." Your Committee, therefore, brings to the attention of the members of the Association the various publications of the National Probation Association, Mr. Kenyon Scudder and others on the subject of Coordinating Councils.

But however much we may stress the neighborhood or community approach, it must not be forgotten that a social segment operates through well-defined organs and agencies — the school, the police department, various types of institutions and camps, mental and guidance clinics, boys' clubs and others. These have a more direct and specific role to play in the prevention of delinquency, than do the generalized programs. It is therefore necessary for your Committee to bring to the attention of the Association some of these special institutions and agencies that are the instruments of, or supplement, community effort.

As to (b) "School Programs," *Preventing Crime* commented as follows:

The contributions . . . by school authorities throw much light on specific ways in which educational

---

[8] S. D. Alinsky, "Community Analysis and Organization," *Am. J. of Soc.*, Vol. XLVI (May, 1941), p. 797.

[9] *Op. cit.*

systems and individual schools — both ordinary and special ones — can engage in activities helpful to the prevention of antisocial and delinquent conduct. . . . The [schools enjoy a] strategic position . . . in having children under control during their most impressionable years. . . . And yet . . . the schools have on the whole been slow to make the most of their rare opportunities for discovering and counteracting dissatisfactions and maladjustments that may lead to misconduct.

Among the significant features of the schools' attack upon delinquency are the following: (1) Discovery of children mentally or physically handicapped and children presenting behavior or other special problems; (2) provision of special classes or schools for the intensive study and individualized treatment of such children, for making curricula more attractive, and for otherwise counteracting the mass-treatment tendency of schools; (3) employment of visiting teachers or other social workers in bridging the gap between the school and the home; (4) collaboration of the school system with other community organizations and agencies.[10]

Tentative exploration of the field has produced few new or highly significant experiments by schools in addition to the following reported on in 1936 in *Preventing Crime:* namely, the late Dr. Nathan Peyser's "character building" program as conducted by him in Public School 181, Brooklyn, New York, with the aim of preventing various maladjustments including delinquency; the Bureau of Special Service in the Jersey City school system, under direction of Dr. Thomas W. Hopkins; the visiting teacher movement, as illustrated by the one conducted by Miss Ethel Reynolds in the Cincinnati Public Schools; the school clinic for the diagnosis and treatment of maladjusted children, as evidenced by the one carried on in Detroit by Dr. Harry J. Baker and the one conducted in Newark by the late Dr. Meta L. Anderson; and the special schools for "problem children," such as the Montefiore Special School for Problem Boys carried on in Chicago by Edward H. Stullken.* There are probably other worthwhile experiments conducted by schools or under the auspices of school systems which have not come to the attention of your Committee. But the above mentioned contributions to *Preventing Crime* in themselves contain much theoretical wisdom and practical suggestion; and

they should be consulted by both professional and lay persons interested in an attack upon delinquency or pre-delinquency that focuses its efforts upon that theatre of thought and action in which the growing child first meets high hurdles which he often finds difficult to jump, with the result that failures, frustrations, conflicts and defeats may not unnaturally lead to other maladjustments, including delinquency, and to difficulties of adjustment to the responsibilities of adulthood.

As to (c) "Police Programs," *Preventing Crime* commented as follows:

. . . Under informed guidance, a police crime-preventive unit furnishes not only the protective and repressive aspects of preventive work, but many of the others which are normally [in other regions] carried on by other agencies. Its chief activities are the supervision of the "plague spots" of delinquency (commercial poolrooms, dancehalls, and the like); the granting of advice to parents and others regarding children in danger of becoming delinquent; the arrest of adults endangering the morals or health of youth; the teaching of children to respect the law and its officers; the putting of pre-delinquent and delinquent children and parents in touch with community-welfare and health organizations and related activities. But . . . the presence in a police department of a crime-preventive unit serves the further purpose of re-interpreting, in a socially desirable manner, the entire range of tasks of the police in the modern community. . . . Crime-preventive efforts by a police department can reflect the philosophy and technique of the trained social worker without interfering with the efficiency of the traditional branches of a metropolitan police organization.

Effective work on the part of a crime-preventive unit in a police department is dependent not only on the specific activities of the unit, but upon its intimate collaboration with other constructive community agencies.[11]

The above observations indicate that a police crime preventive program limited to traditional police methods and facilities is bound to be ineffective. How necessary it is to integrate police understanding and techniques into a community approach is shown in two articles to be found in *Preventing Crime:* "The Crime Prevention Bureau of the New York City Police Department," by Henrietta Additon, and Elizabeth Lossing's "The Crime Prevention Work of the Berkeley Police Department."

---

[10] S. and E. T. Glueck, *op. cit.,* pp. 14–15.
* See Article 182, *infra.* for a recent account of the Montefiore School program. — *Ed.*

[11] S. and E. T. Glueck, *op. cit.,* pp. 15–16.

Police organizations are in more recent years beginning to recognize that they have a duty in crime prevention which transcends either total ignoral of the preventive problem or the limiting of police activity to such dramatically publicized gadgets as "junior police," or "Christmas parties in precinct stations." This is shown by the efforts of such organizations as the Crime Prevention Bureau of Richmond, Virginia, the Juvenile Aid Bureau of the New York City Police Department, the Juvenile Division for Boys of the Police Department of Detroit, the Big Brother Division of the San Francisco Police Department, the Juvenile Aid Bureau of the Miami Police Department, the Juvenile Crime Prevention Bureau of Glendale, California, and others.*

This roster of crime-preventive efforts on the part of police departments in recent years is an impressive indication that there are chiefs of police who are beginning to recognize that prevention of crime at the source is at least as important a part of the work of a modern police organization as is patrolling a beat, doing detective work or regulating traffic. This is a far cry from the not so distant days of active service of Police Commissioner Arthur Woods, who was indeed a prophet crying in the wilderness! Perhaps the day is near when the following admonition and prophecy by Col. Woods will be fully heeded and realized:

The preventive policeman is the policeman of the future. However faithfully he does it, he can no longer fully justify himself by simply "pounding the beat." The public will look to him to prevent crime, and to prevent from falling into crime those who may be under temptation, be they children, or drug users, or defectives, or normal human beings who already bear the convict mark, or who are pushed to the wall in the battle of life.[12]

As to (d) "Intramural Guidance Programs," *Preventing Crime* includes some illustrations of the work of private institutions which give full-time supervision to problem children over a period of a few months to several years; and concludes that "not only problem children . . .

but many normal ones might benefit by some of the guidance techniques utilized in these institutions," of which the following are illustrations: Longview Farm, in Acton, Massachusetts, a former experiment in the intensive care of especially difficult problem children, conducted by Leslie B. Blades; the Children's Village at Dobbs Ferry, as described by the late George C. Minard;[13] the citizenship training program of the George Junior Republic, as detailed by Donald T. Urquhart; and the summer camp for delinquent boys at Greenwood Lake, Delaware, Ohio, as described by Irving A. Wagner.*

Little can be added to what was said in *Preventing Crime* in estimating the chief conceptions of intramural guidance programs. Such enterprises operate on the belief that education is broad and deep; on the conviction that its chief goal is preparation for the realities of life; on the educational philosophy of "learning by doing"; on the assumption that every experience and personal contact contributes to make children better or worse and that therefore those who furnish such experiences and contacts should think twice before subjecting children to some of them.

In the case of certain children, education thus broadly conceived necessitates a controlled environment for a time long enough to permit of readjustment of habits and attitudes in the chief activities of life; such an environment, under professional guidance, is supplied by establishments like the Republic and Village.[14]

In this as in other crime-preventive approaches, your Committee makes no claim to any total or even relatively complete listing, much less appraisal, of all programs. It does recognize, however, that in any well-rounded attack upon the problems of maladjusted youth, special institutions must play their role, since some children require removal from the stresses, strains and temptations of the ordinary environment for a time sufficient to permit of their observation and of the inculcation of desirable habits and points of view. In saying this, how-

---

* See Articles 184 and 185 of this volume. — *Ed.*
[12] A. Woods, *Preventing Crime*, Princeton, 1918, p. 123. Despite his opposition because of membership on this Committee, I cannot refrain from mentioning, on my own responsibility, the splendid pioneer efforts of August Vollmer. — S. G.

[13] Too late for inclusion in this report, we have been notified by Harold F. Strong, now executive director of the Children's Village, of certain changes in the program of the Village, looking to its improvement. — S. G.
* See Articles 159 and 160 of this volume. — *Ed.*
[14] S. and E. T. Glueck, *op. cit.*, p. 17.

ever, your Committee at the same time warns against the prevailing evil in so many walled or partly-walled establishments, — the institutionalization of both inmates and attendants. While a period of "quarantine" from society may be "indicated" in specific instances, the aim from the moment the offender arrives at the institution should always be the preparation of the child or adult to resume his life in free society as soon as possible and with better equipment in self-understanding, in attitude, skill and habit than he brought with him when he entered.

Under this general head your Committee should also mention the experiments in the nature of forestry camps. We have been impressed with published articles regarding the forestry camps for youths established in some parts of the country.[15] However, the members of your Committee caution against the excessive enthusiasm expressed, not only among the laity but in quarters that ought to know better, for this approach as a "solution for crime." There are no palliatives in the control of delinquency and criminalism; and those who know the subject thoroughly can point to numerous blasted hopes and wrecked cure-alls along the tortuous pathway of criminology. At the conclusion of this report your Committee has something to say about needed check-ups on all alleged crime-preventive or crime-curative enterprises as a basis for an objective evaluation and for the giving of sound advice to the public.

As to (e) "Extramural Guidance Programs," *Preventing Crime* presented four illustrations of part-time guidance and recreational work with children. One of these, The Alfred Willson Children's Center of Columbus, Ohio, described by Miss Bertha Fulton, is a place where not only diagnosis and customary clinical treatment, but most of the other elements of an organic program

for dealing with predelinquent and delinquent children, are centralized under unified control. As Fulton puts it, "The purpose was to provide a place to which all children's problems could be brought for diagnosis, and from which would radiate the facilities for the solution of these problems." Not only is the case diagnosed, but all medical and social work necessary is carried out and paid for by the Center. "There is no scattering of service, since it radiates from the Center. This method has been found to give a unity of purpose which is invaluable to the child." The implications of such an approach may perhaps be inferred from the nature of the Center's staff, which includes, besides the customary physicians, psychologists and social workers, camp and recreational directors. Another significant feature of this program is its commitment to the policy that when a case is accepted for supervision, it is taken with the idea of long-time service.[16]

Among other activities included under the general head of "Extramural Guidance Programs" are the Worcester Child Guidance Clinic, typical of, yet somewhat different from, the various children's psychiatric clinics that have sprung up in different parts of the country since the pioneer clinics of Doctors William Healy and Augusta Bronner in Chicago and Boston and of Dr. Bernard Glueck in New York.

These clinics are of great importance to delinquency-preventive efforts in at least two ways: first, they are the only agencies that consciously examine and deal with the *nexus* of organic impulses and environmental pressures making for maladjustment of human beings in a highly complex civilization; secondly, they are educators of children, parents, teachers, community social workers, and police officers. It is no fatal criticism of such clinics to say that the disciplines of psychology and psychiatry are as yet far from perfect. Physicians have long had to deal with diseases about which our knowledge of cause and cure is still very hazy. Mental clinicians are specialists focusing their thought upon the crucial problems of internal conflict, tension, and distress as these influence one's attitudes and behavior toward the self and others. In children's clinics, many simple patterns of unhygienic mental habits can be pointed out to all concerned, and simple methods of therapy can thereby bring about the reduction or elimination of much unhappiness and misconduct.

As to (f) "Boys' Club and Recreation Pro-

---

[15] H. G. Stark, "Forestry Camps for Delinquent Boys," 1937 Yearbook, the National Probation Association, pp. 357–361; "Boys Rebuilt," Christian Science Monitor, March 2, 1940; Kiwanis Magazine, Oct., 1940. In this connection your Committee might also mention the Berkshire Industrial Farm of the New York School for Delinquent Boys, in which training in agriculture for some two years and placement on farms at low wages was found, by a follow-up study, not to have obtained as good results as had been expected. See G. E. Speer, "Social Value of Agricultural Training for Delinquent Boys," *Social Service Review*, Vol. 12 (1938) pp. 640–50.

[16] S. and E. T. Glueck, *op. cit.*, pp. 18–19.

grams," *Preventing Crime* had the following to say:

The boys' club is the typical illustration of an essentially (though not exclusively) group-work method of supervising the leisure time of children. . . . It is of course recognized by the workers in this field that recreation is not the exclusive interest of childhood and is certainly not the sole gateway to prevention. However, the absorption of the energies of youth in harmless or constructive pursuits not only takes up much of the time that might otherwise be put to vicious and antisocial uses, but is an entering wedge to winning the confidence of youth and exerting an influence for good in other than recreational activities.

Programs of boys' clubs are well known and need not here be rehearsed. It will suffice to call attention to a number of special features. . . . The first . . . is the growing recognition that boys' clubs should concern themselves more generally with "difficult" or "problem" or "queer" or even downright delinquent boys, as well as normal ones. Instead of opening their doors merely to boys who have the interest, curiosity, and initiative to partake of their facilities, boys' clubs are coming to feel obligated to go out into the community and draw in boys who in the past were neglected. . . . Particularly is this true in respect to boy gangs which, under skillful guidance, can be transformed into healthy play groups.

A second point is the growing emphasis on the value of a survey of neighborhood conditions and boy life as a prerequisite to the establishment of boys' clubs and the definition of their programs. Related to this is the growing recognition of the need of the boys' clubs' striking root in the community.[17]

The revealing reports of boys' club aims and methods by Armstrong, Keltner, Scudder and Thompson to be found in *Preventing Crime* need not be reviewed. That boys' clubs are indirectly contributing to the reduction of prospective juvenile delinquency seems a reasonable conclusion, however difficult to prove. In some regions, too, they definitely aid in constructive probation and parole work by a systematic relationship with courts and industrial schools. But boys' clubs are not primarily concerned with such aims, nor can they be expected to bear more than a reasonable share of the work of crime prevention. The discovery of an excessive juvenile delinquency rate in a community has frequently been used as the incentive to the creation of sufficient interest for the establishment of a boys' club. Your Committee feels

obliged to warn that the mere establishment of a boys' club where none had existed before is not a cure-all for delinquency or crime. Nor is the task of coping with juvenile delinquency merely one of supplying more recreational facilities for youth. Boys' clubs and recreational outlets are valuable constituents of a more general and varied program of attack on these problems.

Among the more interesting and promising experiments in group work with pre-delinquent and delinquent youth which are different from traditional boys' club approaches may be mentioned the following:

1) On the theory that individual treatment within group activity is a valuable tool in re-conditioning a delinquent to acceptable social living, Harry M. Shulman has conducted an interesting experiment in his "sheltered play group" for maladjusted children, carried on in established recreational centers in New York. The use of manipulative activities (arts and crafts, games) gives the boy who is backward only in verbal skills a chance to recognize his equality in other respects. Normal children are mingled with the "problem children" to give the constructive experience in association with them. Leaders are trained in social work and are not told which are the problem children.[18]

2) On the theory that group therapy must be instituted along with individual diagnosis and treatment, the Boston Juvenile Court has established a "Citizenship Training Department" of the Court, at which boy probationers are given a twelve-week training in citizenship, from 4 to 6 P.M., five days a week. After his problems are appraised, each boy works with a small group on a program of individual interviews, personal hygiene, physical training, vitalized class work, crafts, recreation, etc. This is then a therapeutic and observation period; and at its close, the delinquent is put in touch with various social agencies in his community (churches, clinics, camps, Y. M. C. A., foster homes, etc.) best suited to help him solve his problems.* Since intensive individual therapy is practically impossible for a Court, owing to the great expense, this combination of individual with group approaches appears to be economical as well as probably effective.[19]

---

17 S. and E. T. Glueck, *op. cit.*, pp. 20–21.

---

18 H. M. Shulman, "Group Work — A New Program for Probation," 1939 Yearbook, National Probation Association, pp. 116–129.

* See Article 122 of this volume. — *Ed.*

19 K. I. Wollan and G. K. Gardner, "A Group-Clinic Approach to Delinquency," *Mental Hygiene*, Vol. 22 (1938), pp. 567–584; K. I. Wollan, "The Use of Group Activity in Probation Work," 1938 Yearbook, the National Probation Association, pp. 240–255; "The Citizenship Training Department of

3) Of a different nature are a few more recent experiments by local bar associations stressing the inculcation "in the minds of children [of] respect for law and the institutions which enforce our laws."[20] A leader in this movement has been Mr. Harold H. Krowech, Chairman of the Juvenile Crime Prevention Committee of the California State Bar. It is his view that "Education in observance and respect for law has been sadly neglected in the United States. Our schools have not met this need on the part of youth. The child has been allowed to remain in ignorance of the law, learning by trial and error, by guess, by curbstone hearsay, by what the other fellow does. It is an admitted fact that youth acting in ignorance of the possible consequences of his behavior is in danger of invading and violating the restrictions or compulsions of the law." [21]

Lack of space prevents any detailed discussion of the program of the State Bar of California to meet this need. It may be briefly summarized in Mr. Krowech's own words: "The Bar has discarded the old axiom, 'ignorance of the law excuses no one,' in its application to children and has substituted the more enlightened phrase that 'to know the law is to respect it.' The legal profession has undertaken the responsibility of bringing the law to the child instead of the child to the law. This has been done effectively by making available to the principals of the public school system, attorney speakers qualified in legal guidance activity. Each County Bar Association has assumed the responsibility of furnishing speakers to its local school district. Thirty-seven Bar Associations are now [summer of 1942] engaged in this endeavor in California. The program is conducted by means of talks given by attorneys before entire student bodies and before small class groups. Open forum sessions are also held to give the children an opportunity to ask questions. . . . Legal guidance objectives to meet the needs of juveniles in under-

standing the processes of the law have been formulated by the Bar. Primarily, the objectives are to develop respect for the law; to give the child a better understanding of the mechanics involved in the administration of justice; to familiarize the child with the duties and problems of law-enforcement officers; to explain modern day specialization in apprehension technique employed by law enforcement agencies; to explain and caution youth with respect to criminal involvements; to give children rules and guides to measure and judge the conduct of those persons seeking to engage them in criminal activity; to demonstrate by the use of actual court cases the exorbitant price paid for the commission of a crime; to dispel the idea that a crime can be committed without eventually "getting caught"; to reconcile imaginative ideas of juveniles respecting the law in accord with fact and to give youth an appreciation of the duties confronting the judge, district attorney, probation officer, and law-enforcement officials.

Further, to explain the public policy underlying the law; to develop a concept that violation of law is equal to lack of loyalty to our government; to single out those areas in which crimes occur most frequently; to do away with the popular conception that intoxication is considered in mitigation of a public offense; to demonstrate to youth that expediency is not a justification for the commission of a crime; to acquaint children with the pertinent provisions of the California Penal Code regulating their conduct; to encourage a spirit of cooperation on the part of children in law observance; to explain the mysteries of legal terminology; to point out the "danger signals" of the precipitating causes of crime; to explain the meaning of circumstantial evidence; to interpret human behavior in terms of legal consequences; to give youth an opportunity to "ask the lawyer" the question troubling him and finally, to demonstrate the idiocy of criminal activity.[22]

Your Committee can only wish the Crime Prevention Committee of the State Bar of California, and similar bar association committees, the best of success in the almost Herculean task they have undertaken. It must be remembered, however, that involved in the commission of antisocial acts are not only the intellectual but the emotional–volitional aspects of personality, and that unfortunately the latter frequently rule the former in the affairs of life. However, there can be no doubt that any improvement of knowledge of the law, why it must and should be obeyed by youth, and of its aims and methods, should the better equip many of them to lead

---

the Boston Juvenile Court," (pamphlet, no author's name), November, 1941. Judge John F. Perkins of the Boston Juvenile Court, writes: The Citizenship Training Department "was an idea developed from long discussions by the whole staff of the Juvenile Court and by discussions with social workers, and interested individuals like Dr. Stanley Cobb and Dr. Walter Beck. The plan was a gradual evolution which finally took form and was put into operation by the Boston Juvenile Court and the City Wide Boys' Workers Conference jointly. After the plan was worked out Dr. Wollan was secured as its first director and its successful development was largely due to his ability and insight. But he did not establish it. And neither did I." — Letter to Dr. E. T. Glueck, October 16, 1942.

[20] H. H. Krowech, "Legal Guidance in Crime Prevention," *Federal Probation,* Vol. VI, No. 2, (April–June, 1942), p. 33.

[21] *Id.*

[22] *Id.*, pp. 34–35. See also H. H. Krowech, "Crime Prevention Digest," The State Bar of California, Vol. I, No. 8, July, 1942.

a law-abiding life.[23] At the very least it should help to bring about a greater unity of culture and therefore of behavior, in communities which before the war were undergoing progressive disintegration and conflict regarding many social values and standards, including the criminal law.

In the opinion of your Committee, the California Bar Association, the Florida Bar Association [24] (under the leadership of Judge Walter H. Beckham of the Juvenile and Domestic Relations Court of Miami), and several others deserve commendation for making the prevention of delinquency and crime one of their specific and major aims, and taking steps to implement such aim.

Lack of space prohibits the discussion of numerous other projects and programs in crime prevention throughout the country. These are of every conceivable kind, some bordering on the bizarre. It is exceedingly difficult if not impossible to evaluate such projects and programs without personal investigations in the field; and even this is not enough without a sound follow-up enterprise to check on results achieved. . . .

There is considerable ferment and some good local guidance in crime prevention, in many parts of the country. The American Prison Association, either alone or in collaboration with other nation-wide organizations interested in crime prevention, might well assemble reports on all these enterprises. Your Committee knows of no completely adequate clearinghouse of crime-preventive information. . . .

[The section on Crime Prevention in War Time has been omitted. — Ed.]

III. CONCLUSIONS

In conclusion, your Committee wishes to point out that the mandate given it by the Association in the Resolution quoted at the beginning of this report is "a large order." The job is not one that can be done by a Committee composed of very busy people who are already overloaded. Your Committee therefore recom-

mends that it be transformed into an Advisory Committee to give counsel to a staff of full-time experts who can devote themselves to the task envisaged by the resolution.

Your Committee recommends that there be established, in the offices of the Association, a Bureau of Crime Prevention, in charge of a full-time, trained executive; that he be assisted by at least one full-time field investigator and a secretary; that the job of this staff should be, first, to establish a clearinghouse of information on crime prevention activities throughout the country; secondly, to make field investigations to check up on the methods and efficacy of the most promising crime-preventive enterprises; thirdly, to prepare a biennial directory of crime-preventive agencies; fourthly, to prepare a handbook of instructions regarding the establishment of different types of crime-preventive organizations.

Respectfully submitted:

Saul Alinsky, Eleanor T. Glueck, Leonard V. Harrison, E. L. Johnstone, Morris Ploscowe, Frederic M. Thrasher, August Vollmer, and Sheldon Glueck, *Chairman*.

October, 1942.

177

Preventing and Treating Juvenile Delinquency: Some Basic Approaches *

William C. Kvaraceus

The juvenile delinquent is a perennial conversation piece. Like discipline, progressive education, or the Brooklyn Dodgers, delinquency can always evoke a good argument or a bad editorial. Nevertheless, the best data [1] (nothing

---

[23] The Boston Juvenile Court's Citizenship Training Department takes this into account.

[24] See Report of Committee on Juvenile Courts and the Prevention of Juvenile Delinquency, *Florida Law Journal*, April, 1942, pp. 109–110. Your Committee has had considerable valuable correspondence with Judge Beckham.

* Reprinted from 63 *School Review* (1955), 477–479. Used by permission of the author and the publisher, University of Chicago Press.

[1] a) *Some Facts about Juvenile Delinquency*, United States Children's Bureau Publication No. 340, Washington, Government Printing Office, 1953.

b) *News Notes on Juvenile Delinquency*, United

can spoil a good argument like a few facts) on current trends of juvenile population and delinquency, if grasped in terms of their full significance, would chill any parent or any probation officer. "The facts, ma'am, are these."

The tidal wave of child population which now engulfs the elementary school will reach the secondary school by 1960 and increase the enrollment by about 32 per cent over the enrollment in 1949–50. This will give us a "normal" or "natural" increase (32 per cent) in the incidence of juvenile misconduct. It is pertinent to note that the increase in juvenile delinquency during the past few years has been more than four times the population increase and that this upward trend is continuing. Present figures, although somewhat incomplete, point to the fact that 1954 (the last year for which data are coming in) seems to have produced 475,000 court cases, or almost half a million delinquent children. Using 1948 as a base, the number of juvenile delinquency cases in 1954 shows a 58 per cent increase against a corresponding 13 per cent increase in child population. If these ratios of increase continue to spiral upward, the 1,000,000 delinquents recently predicted by Benjamin Fine may soon become an awesome reality.

But these figures tell only the story of officially noted delinquent behavior. Research [2] on hidden or unrecorded delinquent behavior has revealed that in a given community as few as 1.5 per cent of infractions for which children could be apprehended actually culminate in official or legal action, even when the infractions are labeled as serious. As inadequate as the delinquency figures are, they must be taken as minimal estimates of the size of this over-all problem.

PRINCIPLES OF COMMUNITY ACTION

What can the community do about it? This is a many-sided question to which there is no single or simple answer. The question involves all members of the community, lay and professional, juvenile and adult. The community can answer that it is doing something about the situation if those persons and agencies that come in close contact with children and youth make a systematic effort to (1) identify and refer those children who are vulnerable, prone, or exposed to the development of undesirable behavior; (2) study and diagnose pre-delinquent and delinquent children's behavior; and (3) utilize all community resources in an individualized and scientific treatment program based on prior study of needs. Again, this is not the job of any one agency. It is the cooperative responsibility of all community groups.

Let us consider more specifically what is to be included in the three essential phases of a comprehensive approach to treating and preventing delinquency.

Identification and Referral. Is it possible for parents and youth workers today to spot those children who are prone, exposed, or vulnerable to the development of delinquent behavior patterns before they actually get into serious difficulty? The answer to this question must come from the research literature. The growing bibliography on this subject is promising in its implication that a large fraction, though not all, of the children who are finally to come into contact with child-welfare agencies, police, and courts can be identified early and screened off as those who will need help and assistance. On this step depends the community's preventive effort.

A careful survey of the literature indicates that the following instruments or techniques appear to have sufficient experimental data behind them to warrant further study and trial use to aid in the early detection of the child highly susceptible to delinquent adaptation in behavior:

Personal Index of Problem Behavior [3]
Minnesota Multiphasic Personality Inventory [4]

States Children's Bureau, Washington, Government Printing Office, 1955, 1.

c) Benjamin Fine, *1,000,000 Delinquents*, Cleveland, Ohio, World Publishing Co., 1955.

[2] Fred J. Murphy, Mary M. Shirley, and Helen L. Witmer, "The Incidence of Hidden Delinquency," *American Journal of Orthopsychiatry*, XVI (October, 1946), 686–96. [Article 2 of this volume. — *Ed.*]

[3] *a*) Graham C. Loofbourow and Noel Keys, The Personal Index, Minneapolis,, Educational Test Bureau, 1933.

b) Winifred C. Riggs and Arnold E. Joyal, "A Validation of the Loofbourow-Keys Personal Index of Problem Behavior in Junior High Schools," *Journal of Educational Psychology*, XIX (March, 1938), 194–201.

[4] *a*) Starke R. Hathaway and C. Charnley McKinley, The Minnesota Multiphasic Personality Inventory, New York, Psychological Corporation, 1943.

Porteus Maze Test [5]
Washburne Social-Adjustment Inventory [6]
Glueck Prediction Tables [7]
Behavior Cards: A Test-Interview for Delinquent Children [8]
K D Proneness Scale and Check List [9]

While no one of these techniques has been shown to be infallible, it is not unlikely that several of them will soon be able to identify the potentially delinquent child as well as present-day intelligence tests identify the high or low achiever in the classroom.

Child Study and Diagnosis. The second phase of a community program of delinquency prevention and control must include the processes of child study and diagnosis on which to plan an individualized treatment program. This raises the question of the adequacy of facilities for scientific study of the child and of the many outside forces that impinge on his development. Until certain basic child-study resources (including such workers as guidance personnel in the schools, pediatricians, psychologists, psychiatrists, social workers) are easily accessible to the individual child in need, little hope can be held out for real aid to delinquent children. Both delinquency prevention with the exposed or vulnerable child and delinquency control with the habitual offender postulate an understanding of *why* the child shows the particular form of aggressive–adjustive behavior that bothers the dominant elements in our society. Unless the community is successful in unlock-

ing the meaning of a child's behavior, through the effective use of all modern techniques of child study, little can be done to rehabilitate or re-educate the pre-delinquent or delinquent child.

Specially planned treatment. A systematic and scientific program of delinquency prevention and control must culminate in the third phase: treatment specially planned to meet the personal, social, and environmental needs of the child as revealed in the study and diagnostic phase of the community's effort. Very frequently the processes of child study, diagnosis, and treatment will continue simultaneously or even blend into one operation. Here all community forces can be, and should be, brought into play for the benefit of the child, including the home and family, the school, the medical center, the churches, the YMCA, the "4-H" club, the Boy Scout troop, the playground center, settlement house, Boys' Club, and the like. The core of the community's program must always include the individually planned therapy program based on careful diagnosis of the child's needs. Treatment must be accompanied by a co-ordination of community effort to insure the particular service for the individual child at the strategic moment of need.

Corollaries of the Principles. Several corollaries stem from these three principles. They include the following: (1) Coordination of all community resources which are in close contact with children and their families must be such as to result in a smooth meshing of community facilities. (2) Child-study, diagnostic, and treatment resources cost money and require a sizeable budget; there are no dime-store solutions to a fifteen-billion-dollar crime problem. (3) Community practices and adaptations for delinquency prevention and control must always be based on proved knowledge and must reflect research at the local level as well as the findings of research elsewhere.

EVALUATION OF COMMUNITY PROGRAMS

To aid the local community to inventory its efforts in the direction of prevention and control, a Scale for Appraisal of Community Progress in Delinquency Prevention and Control [10]

b) Starke R. Hathaway and Elio D. Monachesi, *Analyzing and Predicting Juvenile Delinquency with MMPI*, Minneapolis, University of Minnesota Press, 1953.

[5] S. D. Porteus, *Qualitative Performance in the Maze Test*, New York, Psychological Corporation, 1942.

[6] *a*) J. W. Washburne, Washburne Social-Adjustment Inventory, Yonkers-on-Hudson, New York, World Book Company, 1938.

b) J. W. Washburne, "An Experiment on Character Measurement," *Journal of Juvenile Delinquency*, XIII (January, 1929), 1–8.

[7] Sheldon Glueck and Eleanor Glueck, *Unraveling Juvenile Delinquency*, New York, Commonwealth Fund, 1950. [See Articles 171–173 of this volume. — Ed.]

[8] Ralph M. Stogdill, Behavior Cards: A Test-Interview for Delinquent Children, New York, Psychological Corporation, 1949.

[9] W. C. Kvaraceus, K D Proneness Scale and Check List, Yonkers-on-Hudson, New York, World Book Company, 1953.

[10] W. C. Kvaraceus, *The Community and the Delinquent*, Yonkers-on-Hudson, New York, World Book Co., 1954, 168–84.

has been developed and refined by the author. This observation instrument enables the community to measure its progress in seven areas on a five-point scale ranging from "Progressive and scientific" to "Neglected and backward." The seven areas include:

I. Initiating, Planning, and Co-ordinating a Program
II. Identifying and Reducing Danger Factors
III. Educational Standards and Practices
IV. Recreation and Group Work
V. Discovery and Referral of Problem Cases: Apprehension of Offenders
VI. Detention and Adjudication
VII. Social Treatment and Readjustment

Such an appraisal, if carried on with the co-operation of lay and professional workers in the community, including youths themselves, can alert the community to its strengths and weaknesses in the prevention and control of juvenile delinquency.

DEFINITION OF JUVENILE DELINQUENT

Our discussion has sidestepped the crucial and difficult question: "Who is the juvenile delinquent?" — the subject of our discussion. Answering *legally* (and much too simply), the juvenile delinquent is the child of seven to seventeen (the age will vary according to state and frequently according to local residence) who violates any city ordinance or town by-law or commits an offense generally not punishable by death. But such a definition serves us poorly since it tells us little or nothing about the meaning of the child's behavior. *Clinically* the delinquent is a child who habitually resolves his personal–social problems through overt aggressive behavior, which society finds bothersome and contrary to its value identifications. For the juvenile this delinquency–aggression is purposive and adjustive; from the point of view of society, it constitutes an irritating maladaptation.

Studies of delinquents and non-delinquents have frequently uncovered only a few significant differences between the young offender and his more law-abiding counterpart. We can say that the delinquent is any boy on any street in any community. He is singular because he is the one who is usually putting up a fight in an effort to solve or work out his own problems. In so doing, he gives us more than a hint of his

need of help — if we are alert enough to take the hint and do something about it.

178

Organization for Delinquency Control *

Lowell J. Carr

At least three phases can be discerned in the development of juvenile delinquency control in the United States: first, a pioneer-rural, primary-group phase; second, an urban, specialized, individual-treatment phase; and third, a statewide, organized prevention phase.

ACCENT ON THE INDIVIDUAL

In the pioneer-rural, primary-group phase which lasted from the beginnings of settlement till the rise of cities in the nineteenth century, and still persists in some isolated parts of the country — in this phase the integration of the oncoming generation into the adult community was brought about largely by the spontaneous, unplanned, face-to-face experiences in the home, in the natural play group, and in the simple neighborhood. Under ordinary conditions the child simply accepted adult behavior patterns and social values as a matter of course. Such cases of deviant behavior as did occur were attributed to innate wickedness or to the Devil. Serious offenses beyond "the age of discretion" were, of course, punished by the criminal law.

With the growth of cities in the nineteenth century, there gradually supervened a second phase characterized by the appearance of private and public agencies devoted to protecting and aiding individual children in trouble: orphanages, the juvenile court, private case-

---

* Reprinted from 261 *Annals* (1949), 64–76. Used by permission of the author and the publisher. Also, by permission of Harper & Brothers, publisher of Carr's *Delinquency Control*. This piece is, in a narrow sense, "dated"; but, in essentials, it is still very timely. — *Ed.*

work agencies, and the like. It was now recognized that the old spontaneous socializing process of pioneer and rural America was no longer working very well under urban conditions. Special organizations were now needed to do the work of those processes, or to supplement them where they still continued to function.

But these special organizations reflected the individualism of the period: they tended to focus attention mainly on individual children. Even group work agencies had no commission to concern themselves with anything except their own selected groups of individuals. When guidance clinics began to appear in the early years of the new century, they followed this trend: they seldom concerned themselves with causal factors outside the immediate family. From the rise of modern social work till well into the twentieth century, the major emphasis of public and private agencies alike rested on the individual. The task, it seemed was to understand the individual, to protect or reform him — later to "adjust" him; in short, to do consciously and a bit clumsily for the individual child what good and capable families had formerly done quite as a matter of course.

THE DELINQUENT AS AN END PRODUCT

However, as city slums continued to grow, developing not only sub-cultures of their own but antisocial cultures as well, and as research slowly revealed the social as well as the psychological complexities of causation, new needs of control began to be felt. For one thing, it had by now become fairly clear that the juvenile courts and the guidance clinics were not really dealing merely with individuals, much less with sporadic individual acts without a past. They were dealing with the end products of a long chain of events that had begun to shape the end products months and years before. Every case in court or clinic now came to be viewed as the end product of a kind of psychosocial assembly line. This line never stopped, and it never ran out of material. Moreover, on this line nobody could pull a switch and then send a delegation in to argue with the boss about the speed-up. This line just kept them coming all the time.

The implications of that idea were far-reaching. For one thing, what good did it do to keep attention focused on the *end* of the line so long as the *line itself* kept right on working? Of course, it was still important to salvage as many of the end products as possible; to tinker up as many of the finished models as could be kept off the scrap heap. And from that point of view the tragedy of the whole juvenile court movement right down to date has been the failure of most communities to equip their courts with the facilities and the personnel needed for the salvage job. About nine-tenths of our juvenile courts are not yet equipped even to mend a tire! Yet even those that are doing a passable job of salvage are doing just that. The assembly line keeps right on delivering the wrong kind of goods!

WIDENING THE HORIZON

It took the work of a good many men over a good many years to make the public even dimly aware that the juvenile court was not enough. Healy, Shaw, the Gluecks, the guidance clinic movement, the accumulating experience of schools and social agencies — all these had a part in widening the horizon of control. One significant symptom was the rise of the co-ordinating council movement which began in California in the twenties and spread into other states during the thirties. The plight of youth during the depression alerted another portion of the public. Then came World War II, with something of a newspaper furor about the increase in delinquency near the camps and in the war-production cities. A number of state governments, notably in California, New York, and Michigan, took action to supplement the work of the juvenile courts.

The end of the war found the uneasiness spreading. Additional states followed California's lead or set up study commissions to prepare the way for later action.

Three years after V–J Day, signs were multiplying that a few states, at least, were moving into a state-wide, organized prevention phase of delinquency control. Courts and social agencies were still treating individuals, but more and more state governments and social work leaders were talking about prevention on a state-wide basis.

Three characteristics had already appeared to mark this phase off from the others that had gone before. In the first place, the emphasis was not only on prevention — the nature of the case; some preventive work had been carried on in Phase 2 also. It was on *comprehen-*

sive, all-inclusive prevention — prevention on a state-wide level, utilizing many different programs and agencies. In the second place, there was appearing more interest in *better articulation and closer integration* of the different programs and agencies with one another. And in the third place, a few states were beginning to *spend public money for prevention*, and one at least was spending it at a rate approaching one million dollars a year.

PROGRAMS IN CALIFORNIA AND MICHIGAN

State-wide prevention was clearly the goal of carefully organized programs in six states, with a seventh taking steps in the same direction. In its State Youth Authority, California in 1943 had set a pattern for centralizing responsibility for state-wide prevention and for controlling the treatment of delinquents beyond the level of local probation. Minnesota and Wisconsin set up similar bodies in 1947 and Massachusetts in 1948.

As California was setting up its State Youth Authority, Michigan created a State Youth Commission and enlarged its technical services by increasing its state-supported guidance clinics to ten and providing state aid for local visiting teachers. By 1948 there were ninety visiting teachers employed in Michigan communities. Since the richer communities could match the state grants more easily than could the poorer ones, most of these school social workers had been added to urban systems. With a change of administration, however, the legislature changed its mind about a centralized agency for planning prevention, and abolished the Youth Commission, which had never had an adequate budget in the first place. The result three years after V–J Day was the curious spectacle of a state spending upwards of half a million dollars annually on delinquency prevention services of one kind or another without any guiding, over-all philosophy of delinquency prevention, and without any central agency capable of drafting one or of applying it if one existed. All this, of course, in striking contrast to the situation in California, Minnesota, Wisconsin, and Massachusetts, and especially in contrast to the situation in New York.

NEW YORK'S PROGRAM

New York's state government reacted to the wartime need of prevention at about the same time as the state governments in California and Michigan, but with somewhat less haste. Governor Dewey appointed a study committee in 1943, and on the basis of this committee's report in 1945 approved the creation of a "temporary" State Youth Commission to expire July 1, 1950. This commission, with very explicit powers of spending state money to release local money for preventive purposes, has proceeded to develop what is perhaps the most comprehensive plan for the control of juvenile delinquency yet proposed in the United States.

Standing, of course, on the technical services provided by the public and private social agencies and law enforcement bodies of the richest state in the Union, this plan is aimed at stimulating local communities to help themselves. During its first year the New York commission expended more than $300,000 of state money which in turn released more than $500,000 from local municipalities outside of New York City, a grand total of more than $800,000. For what? Mainly for three things: (1) the establishment of local Youth Bureaus for young people; (2) recreation projects; and (3) educational projects which include guidance clinics. In 1948 this program was working through eleven Youth Bureaus and three new traveling child guidance clinics added to the state's previous eight. There were also 520 recreation projects under way.

Such a statement, however, conveys no idea of the comprehensive scope of the Youth Commission's approach. In *Prevention in Action*, published in July 1946, the commission sketched a program which, pivoting on the Youth Bureaus and the special projects, is designed to articulate and co-ordinate the entire educational, clinical, law enforcement, and public relations agencies in the state. One of its most significant lines of attack is the early discovery of maladjusted children in the school.

Guided by successful studies made in Columbus, Ohio, in 1942 and in New York City in 1944, the Youth Commission's psychologists have developed a screening technique for selecting those children who are inadequately adjusted to the school situation.[1]

Within a few months of its creation the commission had the schools of ten communi-

---

[1] New York State Youth Commission, *Prevention in Action*, Albany, 1946, 45.

ties evaluate over 5,000 school children, and drew this tentative conclusion:

The available evidence indicates that all but a negligible number of our current delinquents could have been detected in the early stages of their maladjustments, and that remedial action by the schools will now decrease materially the incidence of delinquency in the future.[2]

Growth of Public Action

Up to June 1948 no other state had duplicated the New York program in either its comprehensiveness or its cost, but prevention had emerged in the public consciousness as something for public bodies to undertake. In California, Minnesota, Wisconsin, and Massachusetts this function was explicitly in the hands of central agencies. That it was apparently high time somebody took some interest in that function is revealed in the report of the Wisconsin investigating committee on the basis of which Wisconsin set up its Youth Service Division.

At Waukesha [correctional school] they found boys who were there primarily for truancy — simply because they did not like, and could not get along in, school. It caused members of the committee to wonder about the inconsistency in our laws which require boys and girls to attend school until they are 18, while at the same time other laws say in effect, if our schools do not offer a program that is challenging enough or adapted to the particular needs of our boys and girls, then we will legislate them into our reformatories and industrial schools.[3]

Apparently a wave of mild skepticism concerning old practices and old child welfare and juvenile court laws was running through a number of states in 1948. In June, out of 39 states on which data were available either from Children's Bureau reports or from special questionaire returns, 23 had more than 27 official agencies of one kind or another either to supplement the work of the juvenile courts, to try to forestall delinquency itself, to draft new children's codes, or merely to study the problem. Seven of these states also had private organizations at work in the prevention or control field, i.e., in the field of publicity, co-ordination, or cooperation with official bodies. In eight other

states the private organizations were working without any official help. Seven states out of the 39 reported that there were no organizations of this kind within their borders. In nine states — Arizona, Delaware, Indiana, Iowa, New Mexico, Pennsylvania, South Dakota, Utah, and Vermont — no information on delinquency prevention organization was available.

Table 1 identifies the states on which information was available either through the Children's Bureau or from questionaires returned by their respective welfare departments or special youth agencies. It also indicates roughly the functions assigned to these various official bodies. Three of them were purely advisory; 6 had co-ordinating or educational functions to perform; 5 were drafting new children's codes for their states; 9 were merely studying child welfare and delinquency problems and existing legislation; 4 — the ones in California, Massachusetts, Minnesota, and Wisconsin — were organized as state youth authorities to give central direction to prevention in their states and also to control the formal treatment of juvenile offenders beyond the stage of local probation. In one state — New York — there was a central state agency not charged with administering treatment at any stage, but set up to plan and administer a broad and comprehensive program of co-ordination and prevention.

Increased Public Attention

It is perhaps worth while to pause at this point to call attention to the contrast between all this stir and bustle about delinquency problems in some 23 states and public behavior after World War I. In the Gay Twenties, it will be recalled, while the intelligentsia bemoaned the fate of the "lost generation," The Best People went blithely ahead devoting more attention to their bootleggers than to their own children. This time nobody is selling the younger generation short. Moreover, a respectable number of respectable people seem actually to be worrying about the impacts of a topsyturvy culture on the young. After having marked time for nearly two generations in the comfortable illusion that the juvenile court, pinch-hitting for modern parents, would control delinquency for them, more and more Americans three years after V–J Day were apparently waking up to the need of groping forward to new conceptions.

---

[2] *Ibid.*, 46.
[3] Wisconsin Youth Service Division, "The New Youth Service Program," mimeographed.

METHODS OF ATTACK

It would be straining the evidence to infer that even in the most advanced states there was any very clear recognition of the added effectiveness to be gained by using consciously, comprehensively, and according to plan the four major "weapons" which society is forced to take up when the primary-group processes of integration and control fail. These weapons are scientific research, skilled techniques, social action, and social organization.

Obviously, all through the phase of urban individual treatment, some use was made of each of these weapons. As a matter of fact, it was the growth of skilled techniques of treatment that made the individual-treatment phase possible. And it was largely on the basis of facts revealed by the individual-treatment agencies, public as well as private, that research was able to function in this field and that social action and social organization developed as they did. The individual-treatment phase was apparently necessary to open the way for more basic methods of attack. But in the individual-treatment phase these weapons were used piecemeal, grudgingly, without effective co-ordination, and without covering the total front.

More basic methods of attack mean four things: (1) deliberate planning from the local community to the nation to mobilize all four of these weapons at the same time and place; (2) equipping every county and important community at least with the full complement of skilled services necessary for the job from the discovery of predelinquents to the handling of institutional parolees; (3) raising the level of function of individual agencies toward the level of best practice in each field; and (4) articulating and co-ordinating the policies and practices of schools, police, courts, clinics, social agencies, and all the other organized bodies in every community.

THE PIECEMEAL EFFORT

The central agency states and obviously New York were planning, true enough, but their planning had one serious defect. In all these states there was no adequate provision for mobilizing research, along with skilled techniques, social action, and social organization. We will consider the role of research in the delinquency prevention efforts of 29 states in a moment. Meanwhile it is necessary to observe that, so far as the evidence goes, no state is facing the problem of a total attack on delinquency, an attack utilizing everything we know. No state is even getting ready to make a total attack on a limited front, i.e., in one county or in one community. No state government seems to have any plans for equipping any community with all the techniques known for combating juvenile delinquency.

New York and California have come closest to grasping the concept of "total war" on delinquency, but even in those states there are no reported plans for an all-out attack anywhere. As a matter of fact, one prevention commission in another state epitomizes a point of view not entirely outgrown in California and New York. That commission in its published literature emphasizes its "experimental approach," the fact that it is "moving slowly," "not attempting too much."

This seems to be one of the growing pains inherent in the difficult transition from the second control phase to the third. The commission is not really experimental in a scientific sense. It is merely attacking piecemeal again and it is moving slowly because politically the state is still in the second phase of control, the individual-treatment phase. From the point of view of control theory, as it would appear in the third, or state-wide organized prevention phase, the commission's piecemeal attack is about as logical as a piecemeal attack, soldier by soldier, would have been on the German lines in France. If we are to have prevention, we must have prevention *all along the line*; not here and there and once in a while.

That the technical requirements for this kind of prevention may not be politically attainable at the start is one reason why social action — publicity, education, propaganda, influence — has to be mobilized along with the skilled techniques that are needed. *Part of the job of delinquency control is to raise the limits of the politically possible.*

In 1948 the general pattern of readjustment on the part of state governments seemed to be to appoint a study commission when the problem reached a certain degree of urgency. The study commission usually handpicked existing programs and came up with recommendations that happened to appeal to influential persons. No state program to date combines the best

Table 1   *Delinquency Prevention and Control Organizations (Exclusive of Juvenile Courts and Technical Agencies)*

STATE	SPONSOR		NO ORGANIZATION IN STATE	STATE-SPONSORED FUNCTIONS						NO DATA
	State	Private		Advisory	Co-ordinating, Educational	Draft Child Code	Study	Prevention, Administration	Organized Prevention	
Alabama	x			x	x	x				
Arizona										x
Arkansas	x*						x			
California	x									
Colorado	x*	x*								
Connecticut	x							x		
Delaware										x
Florida	x*					x		x		
Georgia	xx	x					x			
Idaho			x							
Illinois	x	x					x			
Indiana										x
Iowa										x
Kansas	x*	x*				x				
Kentucky			x							
Louisiana	D					D				
Maine			x							
Maryland	x						x			
Massachusetts	x									
Michigan		x								
Minnesota	x*							x		
Mississippi	xx			x		x				
Missouri		x*								
Montana	x									
Nebraska	x						x			
Nevada		x*								
New Hampshire		x*								
New Jersey	x			x						
New Mexico										x
New York	x									
North Carolina	xx				x		x			
North Dakota	x*									
Ohio		x								
Oklahoma	x*					x				
Oregon	xx				x			x		
Pennsylvania			x							
Rhode Island			x							
South Carolina			x							
South Dakota										x
Tennessee			x							
Texas										x
Utah										x
Vermont										x
Virginia					x					
Washington			x							
West Virginia			x							
Wisconsin	x							x		
Wyoming	x				x					
TOTALS	27	15	7	3	6	5	9	4	1	9

x = as of June, 1948. D = completed in 1947, not included in totals. * = data from Children's Bureau. Total states on which data available in June, 1948 = 39. xx = two or more state organizations counted here as two.

points of all programs. California, for example, has a network of local organizations working on prevention, 284 co-ordinating councils. No matter what professional social workers may think about such councils from the technical point of view, there can be no doubt whatever that *politically* they are an asset to the delinquency prevention program. No other state is duplicating that effort. Michigan's program of state provision of technical services, supplemented by the technical services provided by socialized wealth in the state, particularly the work of the Children's Fund of Michigan and of the Kellogg Foundation — all this hangs in the air without any organized local support and without any centralized planning agency to direct it.

UNUSED KNOWLEDGE

What is even more significant, all those states that have taken any action at all up to three years after V–J Day, have ignored some of the most promising methods of delinquency control yet developed. Slum clearance, for example, is not on any prevention program. Neither is the kind of program developed by Clifford Shaw in his Area Projects in Chicago, probably the most hopeful program yet developed for attacking the root causes of delinquency in slum areas. Why? Do they cost too much? Do they challenge too many vested interests? In short, are such methods still in the class beyond the politically possible? So what!

Apparently the transition from the second control phase to the third involves political growing pains as well as technological readjustments. If we really intend to make a serious effort to control juvenile delinquency, perhaps it would be just as well to face up to the implications of the task in an urban America shot through with racial conflicts, class differences, and all the rest.

State approaches to prevention as reported in the summer of 1948 did not quite seem to be doing that. Or possibly the fumbling and groping that was going on was going on precisely because some of the implications were beginning to register. In any event, trial and error rather than planned, comprehensive "total war" dominated the picture.

In this process of trial and error (a) the role of research, (b) the level of current practice in public and private agencies affecting delinquents, (c) the amount of supplementary technical service provided to forestall delinquency or to assist the juvenile courts, (d) the extent of organization for social action to aid the courts and the technical agencies, and (e) the opinions of responsible and technically competent officials about the most immediately needed action to improve the whole system — all these varied from state to state.

WHAT 30 STATES ARE DOING

What follows is a summarized analysis of the returns from state welfare departments or specially constituted youth bodies in 29 states which were circularized in May 1948. Nineteen state boards failed to answer,[4] but data on one of these states, Michigan, were available from other sources.

RESEARCH

No state reported plans for duplicating the Ohio Bureau of Juvenile Research or the famous Illinois Institute for Juvenile Research. While this does not mean that no research is going on in the 28 states that have no such plans, it does mean that those state governments feel no need of science as a partner in their prevention and control programs. While industry and the federal government are spending billions of dollars each year on scientific research to improve products and to advance our knowledge of the atom, 28 of the most important state governments in the union cannot find anything but pocket money and not much of that to advance our knowledge of juvenile delinquency and what to do about it. Yet most of them are "going slow" precisely because they *don't* know what to do.

---

[4] Welfare departments or other agencies in the following states cooperated in supplying the information which is summarized in this article: Alabama, California, Connecticut, Georgia, Idaho, Illinois, Kentucky, Louisiana, Maine, Massachusetts, Mississippi, Montana, Nebraska, Nevada, New Jersey, New York, North Carolina, Ohio, Oklahoma, Oregon, Rhode Island, South Carolina, Tennessee, Texas, Virginia, Washington, West Virginia, Wisconsin, Wyoming. Certain data on Michigan were supplied by the author. Exceedingly valuable aid was also received from the Children's Bureau, Washington, and from the National Probation Association, New York.

The four prevention and treatment commissions — California, Minnesota, Wisconsin, and Massachusetts — were all interested in research in a kind of small, retail way. The California Youth Authority had for several years allocated some money to research workers at the University of Southern California, and had made 26 county-wide youth-service surveys in five years. An advisory committee appointed by the governor had also secured funds for special studies of detention, transient youth, and community organization. In Wisconsin the Youth Service Division was planning to develop research through the University of Wisconsin. No estimates are available as to how much money is actually being spent in any of these states to determine the causes of delinquency, area by area, but it is a safe guess that the amount is considerably less than the same states are spending on studies of traffic and highway transport problems.

Yet a good deal of fact-finding for administrative purposes is going on. We have already mentioned the problem-child surveys instigated by the New York State Youth Commission.

Among agencies on the firing line, perhaps the most significant projects reported were in New Jersey and Illinois. The New Jersey State Welfare Department was continuing its study of community vulnerability to social breakdown, and, in cooperation with a number of local municipal youth guidance councils and boards of education, was starting a five-year test of plans for the early identification of vulnerable children — the same sort of action as that promoted by the New York commission. One of the New Jersey probation departments was cooperating with Rutgers University in a study of probation outcomes.

Illinois reported a number of administrative studies of a similar type, but among them was one of somewhat broader significance, namely, a study of social conditions and law enforcement methods in selected counties that had made no commitments to reform schools for ten years or more.

In Ohio the Ohio Welfare Council was trying to find out the needs of children referred to local agencies.

Connecticut, Louisiana, Mississippi, Nebraska, Oregon, Wisconsin, and Wyoming all reported special studies for administrative or

legislative action, either under way or recently completed.

CURRENT PRACTICE

Asked to indicate the most hopeful examples of social work practices in the state relative to the prevention and control of delinquency, most welfare departments or youth bodies answered in generalities, or called attention to current improvements in the understanding of modern social work methods on the part of juvenile court officials and the public in their states. New Jersey and Ohio were more specific.

The New Jersey department pointed to the Passaic and Jersey City experiments in the coordination of schools and the social work and law enforcement agencies; to the New Jersey Welfare Council — Department of Institutions and Agencies Joint Committee for the Extension of Case Work Service; to the newly established Arthur Brisbane Child Study Center, a new state facility for the psychiatric treatment of emotionally disturbed children; and to the Menlo Park Diagnostic Center for the psychiatric study of court, school, and social agency referrals.

In Ohio, requirements for probation officers and welfare workers throughout the state were being raised. The 1946 legislature had provided for increases in social services for children on the county level. Meanwhile, in Columbus the police department had recently employed a number of graduates from the Ohio State University School of Social Administration as police officers in the Juvenile and Social Welfare Bureau.

SUPPLEMENTARY TECHNICAL SERVICES

It is very difficult to gauge the extent of state supplementary services merely on the basis of brief answers to such a question as was asked of these official bodies: "Other than the juvenile courts and the correctional institutions, what special personnel, or special facilities such as guidance clinics, visiting teacher programs, etc., are available as preventive or treatment agencies *at public expense* on the state level and on the local level?"

Some respondents listed all public welfare agents and the programs of other state departments such as the departments of health and education. Others confined themselves to special adjustive services only, such as guidance clinics and visiting teachers. On the local level some even included school attendance officers, while others did not.

Only very broad generalizations seem indicated. One is that, as in so many other things so also in the provision of supplementary services of this kind, the more populous and more industrialized states of the east and north and of the Pacific coast provide more services than do the southern and interior states. New York, Massachusetts, Connecticut, New Jersey, Ohio, Illinois, and California listed considerably more than did the others. Eight states — Idaho, Kentucky, Louisiana, Nevada, Oklahoma, South Carolina, Virginia, and West Virginia — specifically mentioned that there were no supplementary services at all within their borders on the state level; and five of these — Idaho, Nevada, Oklahoma, South Carolina, and West Virginia — failed to specify any on the local level.

So one generalization that seems indicated is, the richer the state — and by analogy, the community — the richer is likely to be its complement of preventive services and agencies. Economic factors may not be the only ones involved. Various supplementary services may be diffusing differently in different parts of the country. Nebraska, for example, reported only one state psychiatric clinic, and that was less than a year old. Another was expected to open July 1. At the other extreme, such states as Massachusetts and New Jersey had literally scores of clinics, and most of them had been operative for years. The biggest state of all, Texas, reported only three clinics operating and a fourth in prospect. In other words, in many states such as Nebraska and Texas, clinical services were rudimentary and very new.

That suggests a second generalization: Different states seem to be in different stages of development of supplementary services. From the fact that all services do not develop uniformly in any given state, it follows that the same services will be in different stages of development in different states at any given time. This means, for example, that Michigan will have ninety visiting teachers while California reports visiting teacher programs as "almost non-existent in California." California will provide consultant service and a field staff to help in problems of probation, detention, forestry camps, community councils, youth center, and juvenile police bureaus, while Michigan, in turn, will have nothing of the kind.

Of equally serious significance is the fact that in practically all states, even the best, whatever supplementary services are provided are by no means universally available to the individuals and the communities that need them. In most states, only a few communities have any supplementary services at all. Michigan's ten guidance clinics could be multiplied by two and still not be able to meet the needs of the 30,000 or more problem children in the schools. New York's program, despite its comprehensiveness, still leaves many communities short of some or of all services.

The conclusion emerges inescapably that if supplementary services are to be allowed to spread as they have in the past, it will be a long time indeed before all states are pulling their share of the load and all areas within each state are getting their share of the help.

ORGANIZATION FOR SOCIAL ACTION

To the question, "Is there a state organization of any kind similar to the Mental Hygiene Society but devoted to education, agitation, political pressure, etc., for the prevention and control of juvenile delinquency?" 12 respondents answered Yes, 15 No, and 3 were noncommittal. States with organizations functioning in that way — but often not specifically organized for that purpose — were: Alabama, California, Connecticut, Georgia, Illinois, Michigan, Mississippi, Montana, New Jersey, Ohio, South Carolina, and Texas. The ones reporting no such organizations were: Idaho, Kentucky, Louisiana, Maine, Massachusetts, Nebraska, Nevada, North Carolina, Oregon, Rhode Island, Virginia, Washington, West Virginia, Wisconsin, and Wyoming. Noncommittal or failing to answer were New York, Oklahoma, and Tennessee.

Did these organizations in the 12 active states have any connection at all with the Continuing Committee of the 1946 National Conference for the Prevention and Control of Juvenile Delinquency that met in Washington?

Seven of the 12 states reporting active organizations answered Yes, 4 answered No, and one failed to answer. The states with active contacts were: California, Connecticut, Georgia, Illinois, Michigan, New Jersey, and South Carolina. The states without such active contacts: Mississippi, Montana, Ohio, Texas. Alabama failed to answer.

One other development should be credited to the National Conference: a lone local council organized by the Rhode Island juvenile court as a result of the Washington meeting.

Each state body was also asked, "What is the extent and vitality of the co-ordinating council movement in your state? How does this compare with its extent and vitality before the way? Are the councils growing or declining in numbers and effectiveness?

Twenty-nine out of 30 states reported the co-ordinating council movement of negligible proportions within their borders. California was the exception. California reported 284 councils, praised the effectiveness of most of them, and regarded the movement as definitely growing. No other state reported more than "several" or "a few," except Illinois. But the Illinois report specifically pointed out that most of the 163 organizations with which the department had made contact during the preceding year were community councils, recreation committees, and neighborhood projects, "which bore little resemblance to co-ordinating councils as a national movement."

Only 13 of the 30 states reported any councils at all. They were: Alabama, California, Georgia, Illinois, Michigan, Mississippi, Nebraska, New Jersey, Rhode Island, South Carolina, West Virginia, Wisconsin, and Wyoming. Seven out of the 13 — California, Georgia, Illinois, Mississippi, New Jersey, West Virginia, and Wisconsin — thought that the organizations in their states were growing. Four thought such organizations weak and ineffective: Nebraska, Rhode Island, South Carolina, and Wyoming.

NEEDED ACTION

"What organized action would you regard as desirable to improve the effectiveness of delinquency prevention and control in your state now? (For example, by the juvenile court judges as a group, by the state Rotary or Kiwanis Clubs, by the League of Women Voters, by the superintendents of schools, etc.)"

The California Youth Authority and like bodies in states with similar legislation, as well as the New York State Youth Commission, mostly stressed better co-ordination of local agencies as immediately desirable. Illinois thought all state agencies and organizations ought to support community projects more strongly. The Kentucky, Nebraska, and Ohio departments felt the need of a unified state plan of prevention and a central prevention agency — a state youth authority. Georgia, Idaho, Louisiana, Nevada, and New Jersey wanted further legislation, and New Jersey had numerous and detailed suggestions on the point. North Carolina and Tennessee emphasized the need of improving the level of social work, as had Connecticut's Public Welfare Council in a report to the 1947 General Assembly. The departments in Maine, Mississippi, Montana, Rhode Island, North Carolina, Virginia, Washington, and West Virginia recommended more united action by various official and civic bodies. Texas emphasized the need of more educational work through conferences and the like.

It is obvious that conditions varied widely in different states, and opinions likewise. On the whole, the recommendations of some 29 official representatives called mainly for "next steps" rather than for any far-reaching, all-inclusive planning.

SUMMARY

1. Having passed through a pioneer-rural, primary-group phase of delinquency control and having become somewhat aware of shortcomings in the second, or urban, specialized, individual-treatment phase, a number of American states in 1948 seemed to be on the way to a third phase which will apparently be characterized by the state-wide orientation of control efforts and by the inclusiveness of social organization for control.

2. As evidenced by official prevention bodies in five states — California, Massachusetts, Minnesota, New York, and Wisconsin — and by official emphasis on technical services in a sixth, Michigan, some awareness of the value of purposeful mobilization of scientific research, skilled techniques, social action, and social organization seemed to have appeared. But as yet this

awareness seemed to be weak, confined to a few states, and was poorly implemented even in those states.

3. Out of 39 states on which data were available 23 had set up special bodies of some kind — 5 central planning bodies; 6 co-ordinating and educational bodies; and 12 commissions whose functions ranged from advice to the drafting of new children's codes. This seemed to indicate a wide-spread feeling that something needed to be done either to strengthen the juvenile court or to supplement it with additional services.

4. Of the four basic "weapons" in the delinquency fight — scientific research, skilled techniques, social action, and social organization — the first seemed to be the one that was most neglected and least used.

5. The richer a state, the richer are likely to be the preventive services available in it.

6. Different states are in different stages of the development of supplementary services for prevention.

7. The same services are in different stages of development in different states.

8. Services are unevenly distributed within states.

9. Without planned preventive effort deliberately organizing and distributing services to equalize inequalities, it will be a long time before all states are pulling their share of the load and all areas within each state are getting their share of the help.

10. Organizations carrying on social action in the delinquency field were reported from twelve states. Fifteen states reported none. The 1946 National Conference for the Prevention and Control of Juvenile Delinquency has had lasting effects in seven out of the twelve states reporting active organizations. The co-ordinating council movement seems of insignificant importance outside of California, where it seems to be flourishing.

11. Recommendations for immediate action coming from responsible officials call for "next steps" rather than inclusive planning.

12. In general, in June 1948 most of the American state governments that were reacting to public uneasiness about juvenile delinquency seemed to be groping ahead by trial and error. Only five had set up central bodies to plan and supervise somewhat comprehensive prevention programs.

179

Extract from Report of Citizens Committee on Juvenile Delinquency, Cincinnati, Ohio *

CONCLUSION

The basic position which this committee takes is that existing resources for the education, recreation, and guidance of families and youth, and for the detection, diagnosis, and treatment of their problems do not have sufficient impact or sufficient focus to prevent an increasing number of our young people from developing unacceptable and antisocial patterns of behavior. There are unmet needs which can be identified. There are groups and individuals and neighborhoods which require fresh approaches if we are to have any hope of reducing what is apparently a major threat to a healthy society in this city and throughout the United States.

We do not believe that the situation outlined above can be alleviated, cured, or even intelligently attacked by limited and narrow means which involve only improved treatment for that minority of youngsters who become juvenile delinquents. While such treatment is important, it involves working with the symptoms rather than the cause of the disease which afflicts society. In doing this it completely neglects all those youngsters who don't get caught but who are going to become adults in our society with attitudes and behavior patterns developed in youth. In this report, we have, therefore, advocated a much broader, a more comprehensive, and a more difficult approach to our community's problems with youngsters who seem to be developing unacceptable attitudes of mind and unconstructive patterns of behavior.

If this community adopts our suggestion for a revitalizing of all services which have an impact on young people through a city-financed

---

* Submitted to City Council, December, 1955. Used by permission of the Citizens Committee.

organization, it is important that certain basic assumptions be clear. First among these is the idea that we cannot remake today's society so that young people can grow up without the pressures and problems which now confront them. These things we have to accept. Our objective must be so to fortify our vulnerable youth that they will be able to cope with their environment and their problems according to sound principles. It is more intelligent and more economical to deal with youth's problems as a normal part of growing up than to wait and deal with them as problems of delinquency or crime.

A second major point to be kept in mind is that, as we try to build sound principles, healthy attitudes, and balanced emotions into today's young people, we must not create an undue emphasis on conformity. Certainly no social or religious institution should have a preferred position in determining what ethical principles should guide us all. There is a danger that in thinking about all our young people as a group we may lean toward the view that it is important to strive for an integrated, unified community with a minimum of social differences. Our committee would assert the belief that most differences are healthy and that a large portion of the vigor and the potential of American society springs from its diversity. In planning for youth in a community as varied as ours, the job to be done involves the statement and emphasis of those principles which are common to all individuals and groups in our society. There are certain basic assumptions regarding the rights of individuals, the rights of groups, the rights of property, and the interrelationships among these rights which should be common to all people in our community. We cannot presume to state these things in this brief report, but for an excellent statement of them we refer the reader to several publications issued by the Cincinnati Public Schools: *Schools and the Means of Education* and *Foundation Values of American Life.*

There is a wide belief that one effective weapon against juvenile delinquency is that of removing demoralizing influences on youth. Books, magazines, television programs, movies, etc., in fact all the mass media, have come under attack in recent years as causes of juvenile delinquency. The restriction of public presenta-

tions via these media is a complicated problem which is closely bound up with the fundamental rights of individuals in our society. Our committee has not presumed to enter into the legal aspects of this matter. We are, of course, sympathetic to sensible and legal restrictions on materials which obviously have a degenerate influence, and we have had some sensational examples of such materials presented before the committee. At the same time, we are aware that the extremists on both sides of this issue present dangers for our society. It is easy in the name of righteousness and clean living to emasculate art, literature, social criticism, and freedom of expression. It is equally possible in the name of individual rights to expose young people to unwarranted stimulation of emotions, to unbalanced development of social attitudes, and to a great deal of bad taste. The difficult task our society faces as it concerns itself with young people is to steer a balanced course between these dangers. As it does so it must be particularly careful to avoid accepting the opinions of some one group as valid for everyone. Our committee can make one assertion on this matter of the mass media. We believe that, if all the movies, comic books, magazines and television shows which children see were suddenly concerned only with virtuous people in ideal families, there would still be a lot of juvenile delinquency. We can't prove this, but we assert it because our investigations on this problem have led us to the conviction that any youngster's delinquency is the product of his total environment, personality, and emotional make-up. The cases in which influences like those here discussed are the determining factor in developing delinquency will probably not represent a major portion of the delinquency in this or any other city. This does not mean, however, that we should not attempt to remove the causes of these cases in a legal and intelligent manner. In working on this problem every little bit helps. Positive programs which attempt to make many aspects of the environment healthier have more to offer than approaches which see an answer to the whole problem in the removal of one influence.

With these basic ideas in mind our committee has developed the plan of attack which is outlined in the previous chapters of this report. We recapitulate briefly here.

A. OUR PLAN OF ATTACK

(1) *Give youth status and recognition.* The committee arrived at the feeling that the vulnerable children are SEEN, they are instructed, preached at, exhorted, criticized, harangued, guided, and exploited, but they are seldom HEARD. As consultants reported on their interviews with young people, we concluded that many Cincinnati youth feel practically anonymous. They are treated like a mass — seldom individualized. This seems to be particularly true in the most vulnerable neighborhoods or groups. This is indeed an "adult-controlled" world, and some of the adults don't have any respect for kids.

The committee heard reports of comments by young people such as "Even my home room teacher has a student call the roll. She hasn't said my name yet." "You know those kids up in Juvenile Court. They ride up there so that when they go back people will talk — use their names. We want our names spoken." As one youngster summed it up, "You get into the city and you're nobody."

Just as industry and business have found that involving personnel in decisions which concern them gives them incentive for better work, we believe that in tackling the problem of juvenile delinquency we cannot do without the voice of the youth and the help of young people in developing their own sanctions. It seems important also that young people, particularly those needing social adjustment, should have opportunities to know and emulate community leaders who work hard for the good of the community. It may be that by exposing them to this good example where they are treated with respect we can offset some of the confusion of the world they see around them.

(2) *Know the facts about youth problems and understand how our youth and their families feel about the environment to which we ask them to conform.* It was with somewhat of a shock that the committee heard comments of youngsters when they talk of how difficult it was to live in Cincinnati. This is a comment reported from a series of group interviews conducted for the committee: "A lot of getting along when you come into Cincinnati is sheer luck. It just depends on where you land. Anyone landing on Sixth Street can't pull out of

it". A neighborhood center worker reported on his interview with older boys:

I've found that if I talk to them on a man to man basis it eventually boils down to "Can you find me a job?" . . . Their attitude seems to be one of suspicion toward those who come to them saying they want to help them. They almost feel that they are not wanted by any one. They want money and yet they are not able to compete in the open market. They make sporadic visits to the employment center but they never seem to get anything there. Some of the boys are beginning to wonder if they are being discriminated against so far as color is concerned when it comes to finding jobs. There may be a tendency there to make some of them bitter. Meanwhile, they are spending their time just hanging around. Sometimes, we find that a lot of boys don't go to school. They'll report in the morning and leave school and stay out for the rest of the day. . . . The greatest need is to find out more about these fellows. They are a great potential for delinquency. They're desperate, they want money, and they are ripe for suggestions from anyone who can tell them how to get it.

Remarks like these indicate that there are some real problems to be looked into among the young people of Cincinnati. We are in the paradoxical position of having a great deal of information, but not knowing very much about delinquency, delinquents, or children with problems in Cincinnati:

(*a*) We need to identify specific youth problems contributing to delinquency and do some research on these problems in our community.

(*b*) We need to identify particular geographic neighborhoods which have unusual problems in connection with juvenile delinquency.

(*c*) We need to inform ourselves about groups of youngsters who seem especially vulnerable.

(*d*) We need to provide information for planning the identification of individual youngsters not receiving needed services.

(*e*) We need to keep abreast of scientific investigation on delinquency conducted in other areas and develop ways of applying them to our local situation.

(3) *Mobilize our community defenses against delinquency.* Every indication is that the citizens of Cincinnati want to mobilize their resources for the purpose of preventing and modifying the delinquent behavior pattern and reclaiming these vulnerable youngsters to useful citizenship.

It is impossible for the committee to be

specific in all detail, but as we see it, the job to be done is:

(*a*) To open many kinds of opportunities for youth to gain status and recognition in the community and to become working partners with adults on community projects.

(*b*) To seek out children and young persons with behavior and personality difficulties which may lead to delinquency and who are not now being served.

(*c*) To determine what kind of help they need to treat their problems or prevent them from worsening.

(*d*) In accordance with their individual needs, to obtain for them — and their parents, if necessary — appropriate educational or recreational opportunities, spiritual advice or social services.

(*e*) To help expand and create new treatment services in *those localities where current needs are not being met*, wherever possible through existing tax-supported or voluntary services.

(*f*) To demonstrate and develop new, more effective ways of treating and preventing juvenile delinquency.

(*g*) In the interest of delinquency prevention, to develop and expand programs of wholesome community activities, with special emphasis on organized recreation, self-governing youth groups, and civic activities which develop neighborhood leadership and spirit.

(*h*) In connection with all preventive work, to cooperate in co-ordination and improvement of the quality, amount, and distribution of services for children and youth in general wherever necessary.

In order to get this plan of attack into operation our committee has made a recommendation for the creation of an organization charged with the responsibility of bringing these objectives and purposes into being as a part of our community life. We have called this The Mayor's Committee on Youth, and we have described it in detail in Chapter II and in the Appendix of this report. We see no other alternative. Certainly, we do nothing constructive about juvenile delinquency as a community problem by studying it and then putting the study aside without follow-up action. We have the feeling that this problem has been studied to death in Cincinnati. In December of 1937 a study committee especially appointed to look into juvenile delinquency presented its extensive mimeographed report to the City Manager, the Judge of the Juvenile Court, the Superintendent of Schools, the Executive Vice-chairman of the Community Chest, and the Director of Catholic Charities. These gentlemen were then known

as "The Sponsoring Committee for the Prevention of Juvenile Delinquency." Here is a quotation from that report:

The social agencies of this community, particularly those dealing with this problem, have been studied and surveyed to the point of diminishing returns. Your Committee feels that the time has come to move forward from a period of study into one of administrative action.

It is now eighteen years later, and we are a different committee. But we still feel the same way.

In April of 1944, a *Report with Recommendations* was submitted by the Committee on Juvenile Welfare Problems of the Council of Social Agencies. It is an excellent report, and it should become a part of the background of any broad community efforts on juvenile delinquency since many of its recommendations are still to be acted upon. There are two paragraphs we would like to quote from it:

(1) The Committee believes that the city administration, in view of its responsibility for making and enforcing laws, should give direct and positive attention to the problems which are its concern, and in so planning for action, to be cognizant of the many available facilities in the community which can be interrelated in the interest of children. It is rather overwhelmingly clear that the city is not taking sufficient responsibility for revision of old laws or adoption of new ones to meet new conditions; it is not making available a sufficient number of qualified persons in a juvenile crime prevention program; it is not meeting public recreational requirements; and it should be assured that its activities, as existent or as may be planned, dovetail with those of the Juvenile Court and other community agencies.

(2) That the city administration review its responsibilities as suggested in the report, and reach a determination to the extent to which those responsibilities can be undertaken in the interest of juvenile delinquency prevention.

These were good points in 1944. We believe that they are still good.

We believe that the whole history of our approach to juvenile problems in Cincinnati gives evidence in the lives of our growing numbers of delinquents that we have done "too little too late." It seems to us that the current trend, if it continues here and elsewhere, can well become a serious threat to our way of life. We strongly advocate that this community give of its time, energy, and resources to institute some program to guarantee more effectively than we do now that each youngster among us will develop fully the unique potentialities which are his.

So, then, to every man his chance — to every man, regardless of his birth, his shining, golden opportunity — to every man the right to live, to work, to be himself, and to become whatever thing his manhood and his vision can combine to make him — this, seeker, is the promise of America.

— Thomas Wolfe, *You Can't Go Home Again.*

APPENDIX

SUGGESTED ARTICLES OF INCORPORATION
OF
THE CINCINNATI MAYOR'S COMMITTEE
ON YOUTH

The undersigned, all of whom are citizens of The State of Ohio and of the United States, desiring to form a corporation not for profit under The General Corporation Law of Ohio, do hereby certify:

FIRST: The name of said corporation shall be:

THE CINCINNATI MAYOR'S
COMMITTEE ON YOUTH

SECOND: The place in this state where the principal office of the corporation is to be located, is Cincinnati, Hamilton County, Ohio.

THIRD: The purpose or purposes for which said corporation is formed are:

The effective prevention of juvenile delinquency and the encouragement of more effective treatment for young people who become delinquents. To this end, the following purposes are to be its responsibility:

1) To keep the Mayor and the members of the Cincinnati City Government informed about the problems related to the youth of the city and to keep them informed about and aware of developing State and Federal programs with which this city might cooperate to reduce the incidence of juvenile delinquency.

2) To cooperate with those organizations, departments, and agencies in this area which have relationships with the problems of youth in order to encourage coordinated efforts for the reduction of juvenile delinquency.

3) To provide skilled and professional leadership in the following endeavors:

a) The promotion of research and the accumulation of statistics relating to the problem of juvenile delinquency in Cincinnati.

b) The securing of information about and financial support for special projects in the interests of youth.

c) The development, initiation, and carrying through of experimental programs which seem to offer hope of reducing juvenile delinquency in Cincinnati.

4) To develop a community wide awareness of what must be done in Cincinnati to solve the juvenile delinquency problem.

5) To evaluate the effectiveness of endeavors in Cincinnati to reduce juvenile delinquency.

6) To identify and call attention to what seem to be the city's most pressing problems as far as young people are concerned and to suggest solutions for them in cooperation with others.

7) To act as a center for information for people who are working on or interested in the problem of juvenile delinquency.

8) To keep abreast of developments in other cities in Ohio and throughout the United States so that Cincinnati will get the benefit of significant progress made elsewhere.

180

New York City's Approach to the Delinquency Problem *

Ralph W. Whelan

Shortly after Pearl Harbor delinquency rates began to skyrocket in most American communities. This trend was not confined to the large metropolis; few were the cities, towns, or villages whose children and youth did not reflect in their behavior the profound social and emotional disturbances which accompanied World War II.

New York City, of course, was not exempt from this trend, nor were the various upstate

---

* Reprinted from 17 *Federal Probation* (1953), 19–25. Used by permission of the author and the publisher. See, also, R. P. Capes, "New York State's Blueprint for Delinquency Prevention," 8 *Federal Probation*, 45–50. — Ed.

communities. Because of widespread concern about the delinquency trends, the State Legislature in 1945 passed the State Youth Commission Act. This has served to help New York City release and better utilize in behalf of its youth a good deal of professional energy and community resources which might otherwise have been untapped.

As a result, the past five years have seen the development in New York City of a program which has attracted national and international attention because of the universality of the delinquency problem as well as the general applicability of the principles on which the New York City Youth Board program is based.

YOUTH BOARD PURPOSES

The Youth Board was established in 1947 under the New York State Youth Commission Act and by resolution of the New York City Board of Estimate. The Youth Board is a public agency with five major functions in conformity with the statute creating the State Youth Commission. These functions are: to coordinate the activities of public, private, and religious agencies; to make studies and analyses of the problems of youth guidance and the prevention of juvenile delinquency; to seek to remove the causes of juvenile delinquency; to disseminate information on the prevention, treatment, and causes of delinquency; and to approve applications for financial aid to public and private agencies for the operation of recreation and youth service projects. As is readily apparent, these functions are so broad that the Youth Board has a relationship — actual or potential — to practically every agency in the City of New York providing services to children and youth under 21 years of age who are potential or actual delinquents.

The Youth Board comprises 13 persons: 7 public officials, who are ex-officio members, and 6 lay members appointed by the Mayor, who are representative of the various cultural, civic, and welfare interests in the community. The ex-officio members are the heads of those public agencies most vitally concerned with our youngsters: the Domestic Relations Court, the school system, the City Housing Authority, and the Departments of Health, Parks, Police, and Welfare.

To carry out its responsibilities the New York City Youth Board receives from the Board of Estimate of the city of New York each year an appropriation totaling $1,185,645. This money is matched by the State of New York through the Youth Commission, upon the latter's approval of the total Youth Board program. Thus, almost $2½ million is available to carry out our program. However, that is not a large sum of money when it is considered that there are in New York City nearly 2½ million children and youth under 21.

When the Youth Board first began to survey the problem in New York City, three things became apparent:

First, that it would be necessary to concentrate the Youth Board program in areas of highest delinquency if the program were to have effective impact.

Second, that it would be imperative to develop a method of locating or detecting children with incipient behavior problems and getting them to needed services promptly.

Third, that it would be particularly important to develop ways and means of reaching those children and their families who present serious social pathology and who have in the past resisted the services of social agencies.

Regarding the selection of areas for concentration, the Board, in order to insure a maximum return on the expenditure of its funds, focused the program on eleven identified areas of high delinquency. This means that there are large sections of the city where the Youth Board does not operate at all. It also means that in those areas where it does have a program it is sufficiently intensive to produce what are hoped will be lasting results. Each of the high delinquency areas has a population of two hundred thousand or more persons. Together, they produce almost three out of every five known delinquents in the city, although they contain only about one-half of the child population.

REFERRAL AND TREATMENT

The hub of the entire Youth Board program is the referral unit. One such unit has been established in each of the 11 high delinquency areas. The purposes of the referral unit are: to act as a detection center for the location of child problems in their incipient stages; to study and diagnose these situations; to locate appropriate community resources to treat these individual problems; and then to prepare families or adolescents for referral to these services. The

Youth Board allocates about $360,000 annually for the referral unit program.

Since the school is one agency that comes in contact with practically the whole child population, the Youth Board contracted with the Division of Child Welfare of the Board of Education to operate nine of the referral units in public and parochial schools. Although financed by the Youth Board, policies and procedures are established jointly by the Board of Education and the Youth Board. Each unit is staffed with a highly qualified casework supervisor and four trained caseworkers who have had at least 3 years of professional experience. While it is closely tied in with the schools, the referral unit works also with all other agencies in the community in an effort to locate children whose problems, if untreated, might lead to serious consequences.

These questions probably arise at this point: Since most of the existing youth guidance and family services are already overburdened with work, what is the advantage of detecting still more problems? Where can suitable treatment be found for the children whom the referral units have been able to identify as the actual or potential delinquents? The Youth Board meets this problem by providing funds for existing social agencies to employ additional staff and thereby increase the services they can offer. The Youth Board has entered into a contract with 17 casework agencies and child guidance clinics to provide treatment for children and their families who are referred to them by the referral units. Reimbursement for services rendered is made monthly. To keep such expenditures within budgetary limits there is a maximum up to which each contract treatment agency can bill the Youth Board within the year. The maximum is usually set in units of $5,700, which is roughly equivalent to keeping 20 families under continuous treatment for 1 year.

In signing a contract to serve Youth Board referrals, the treatment agencies must agree to certain basic stipulations. These do not deal with the quality of service. This is assumed; if it were not so, the agency is not offered a contract in the first place. The terms of the contract deal rather with the agency's approach and what the Youth Board calls the "reaching out" philosophy. The families referred by the Youth Board have not in most instances sought help

on their own initiative. They have been "prepared" by the referral unit so that they will accept referral and verbalize a willingness to cooperate with a treatment agency. However, to involve them in treatment it is often necessary for the casework agencies to meet them halfway. Youth Board agreements therefore provide that referrals be picked up promptly, or at least within 7 days, that agencies follow up their first letters of appointment if the clients do not respond, and that they extend themselves in every way possible to engage and hold a reluctant client in treatment.

Initially, many agencies were resistive to this kind of approach. When the Youth Board program was first developed it was necessary to deal with the resistive agency and the resistive worker, as well as the resistive parent. For many years during the development of the social work profession the emphasis has been, and properly so, on the refinement of techniques and concern about accomplishments. There has been an inclination for the profession to turn its back on situations which are difficult and which experience showed were least likely to respond to the skills thus far developed. By such standards, reaching out to resistive families in trouble was considered relatively unproductive, difficult, costly, and uneconomical. But it is shortsighted economy which asks for an immediate return on our service dollar; it was possible to convince the agencies that they would not profit in the end if they applied their efforts exclusively and selectively to those receptive clients who are ready for their help and could use to full advantage what they had to offer. Such receptive youngsters and families are likely to secure help in one way or another on their own. They are not, by and large, the boys and girls who will become the costly misfits and the hardened criminals of tomorrow.

ACTIVE "REACHING OUT"

After five years of working together it can be stated with truth that most agencies have been won over to the Youth Board's philosophy of reaching out and are modifying their practices to incorporate it as part of their ongoing routine. They have demonstrated an increasing willingness to accept responsibility for the adjustment of the children referred to them, whether or not their parents are willing to cooperate. The agencies make home visits when a client refuses to keep office appointments and are willing to work with a situation, often for considerable periods of time, on almost any constructive basis, such as help with health and environmental problems until they can involve the client in more subtle and intangible treatment relationships.

However, Youth Board experience also demonstrated that even with the full cooperation of the casework agencies, approximately one-third of the cases coming to the attention of the referral units still do not respond and fail to involve themselves in treatment. These are families who are too confused, too upset, too damaged, often too disorganized to be able to use, in the beginning, anything but supportive help. Their situations often involve both physical and emotional neglect. They are the "unreached." Their children, also "unreached," continue to present problems in the school and the community. Badly in need of assistance, but unable to accept what help is offered them, they move on through progressively serious delinquencies to adult criminal careers.

As a first step in getting assistance to these discouraged, troubled, and hard-pressed clients, the Youth Board set up a new project. In cooperation with the Bureau of Child Welfare of the Department of Welfare there was established a program known as Casework Service for Families and Children, a nondescript but neutral title for a dynamic program of outgoing, "aggressive" service.

In this project the usual role of the social worker is reversed. He goes to the client instead of the client coming to him. The social worker goes out more "aggressively" to meet the client than most existing agencies would be able or willing to do. This aggressive approach was adopted because the Youth Board believed that the community has not only the *right* to protect children, but also the *responsibility to take action in their behalf* when their behavior in any serious way reflects a destructive process. The only alternative is to wait until neglect or delinquency reaches the point of court action or removal of the child from his own home. To adopt a laissez faire response to children's needs would not only repudiate the statutory intent of the Youth Board program but also represent an abdication of the Board's responsibility as citizens and representatives of the public interest.

However, to careful students of social work history, the approach is not as novel as it seemed at first glance. One outstanding family service agency executive recently made the following comment:

The Youth Board has dared, if you please, to look back on some methods and practices which were common to social work some fifteen or twenty years ago, and determined that for some types of clientele they still appear to have merit even though essentially abandoned as current practice.

The worker takes some of his techniques from the unpopular but industrious salesman. He has had to learn that doors slammed in his face are not an obstacle. As a matter of fact, some of these social workers have sometimes used the "foot-in-the-door" technique. There has been an instance of a worker standing 15 minutes outside the door waiting for admission — and he finally got in. Another worker went through this ordeal and finally succeeded in getting a discouraged, harrassed mother to sit down and talk to him. During the interview one of the children in the overcrowded tenement climbed to the top of the bureau and pointing two toy guns at the worker cried, "bang, bang, you're dead." The mother said in a tone of resignation, "There's no point in trying to kill him off because if you do another will come and take his place." Various interpretations might be put on this episode, but actually it was the turning point in getting help to a sorely pressed, discouraged mother who finally responded to the worker as one who really cared enough about her to keep on trying.

At the beginning of the project there was a deep conviction not only about responsibility to these families and children, but also that the method would prove therapeutically successful. Today the Youth Board *knows* that it works. There are case records and the experience gained from over 2 years of application of this program to prove that aggressive casework has been helpful to most of the families who have been served by it.

To summarize briefly the individual treatment aspects of the program, the Youth Board has a referral unit in each of its 11 areas acting as the pivotal agency. Around it are treatment services provided by voluntary agencies through contract with the Youth Board; in several of the areas there is also the Casework Services for Families and Children project which is administered by the Department of Welfare with Youth Board funds.

GROUP WORK AND RECREATION

The Youth Board's group work and recreation program is also concentrated in the 11 highest delinquency areas in accordance with the Board's principle of saturation to the limit of its financial ability. One fact encountered from the outset was the universal one, that the membership of most youth serving agencies is heavily weighted with the more conforming, relatively dependent young people. Group workers, like their colleagues in casework, have accepted the groups considered "ready to utilize a group experience," and have turned away from the hard-to-reach groups; the loose-end teen-age clubs, the preadolescents who "horse around" creating havoc by being in and out of many activities and a part of none, the shy forlorn youngsters who are groping to find their place in life, the new neighbors, especially Puerto Ricans and Negroes, as well as the aggressive, fighting street gangs. In attempting to cope with this problem the Board had to come to grips with the concerns of the agencies and their workers. Agencies were fearful that working with groups whose behavior patterns presented one or more of the following characteristics of the turmoil of growing up — occasional destructiveness, aggression toward other groups, hostility toward authority, precociousness in boy-girl relationships, and experimentation with drinking, gambling, and occasional narcotics — would discourage the participation of more conforming teen-agers.

In helping agencies to reach a truer cross section of teen-agers as well as to reach the harder-to-reach groups, the Youth Board has done several things in developing its group work program. The Board set forth criteria for practice in a statement entitled "The Definition and Criteria for Group Work Services." This statement, in the judgment of the best practitioners in the field, represented a pioneering step in that it attempted to clarify and standardize group work practice for the first time in New York City. It established a set of standards of practice which all of the widely diverse agencies cooperating with the Youth Board were expected to meet. Particu-

larly significant to the subject of serving hard-to-reach groups is the fact that the criteria require the employment of a trained group worker to work directly with groups. For many agencies, this represented their first opportunity to provide skilled professional service for direct work with membership.

NEIGHBORHOOD CENTER EXPERIMENT

But the Board did not stop at that point. It undertook, through direct operation of a demonstration community center, to develop a body of experience which it could share with other agencies. Fortunately, at the time that the Board was considering this plan a large building which previously had been used as a settlement became available in one of the city's most underserved neighborhoods. Although the Board originally conceived of the operation of the community center as a laboratory for the development of experimental techniques in the field of social group work, after a few months of exploration and actual experience in the neighborhood the dire need for group work and recreation services caused the Board to modify its original objective. To meet the needs of the neighborhood it was necessary to develop a basic recreation and group work program with selected experimentation related to actual needs. Particularly significant in the work of the center was the fact that top priority was given to work with teen-agers, and that antisocial street clubs were served within the center as an integral part of the program.

Many of the groups which used the center were known gangs with a history of violent conflict. Through intensive work with these groups — at many points actually living around the clock with them; going to the hospital with individuals injured in street fights, going to the police department with those arrested, hanging around candy stores and bars frequented by the members — the staff was able not only to encourage the participation of the gangs in the total agency program, but also to contain street fights or "rumbles" through a process of mediation and the settlement of disputes between individuals by supervised boxing matches. While the focus of work with these street clubs was on a group basis, as with the other teen-age clubs, effective service required an extensive amount of activity with individuals. Demanding though the task was, this experience indicated that effective work with street gangs can be done within the framework of a regular youth-serving agency, provided the agency has an accepting, reaching-out attitude toward its hard-to-reach groups and has sufficient staff, both qualitatively and quantitatively, to cope with this problem.

However, the Youth Board recognized that for many agencies this kind of job is not possible. Handicapped by traditional methods of operation, committed to goals projected with the Board, and limited in terms of staff by lack of funds and a limited job market, existing agencies are unable to cope with the problems presented by street clubs. In some instances, protection of the community has necessitated police action. Because the function of the police is primarily focused toward community protection and not geared to the rehabilitation of gangs and their members, from the long view it has been unproductive. The seriousness of the problem in New York City coupled with the lack of success of traditional methods fostered the Youth Board's experimentation with new approaches.

What the Youth Board did was to establish a project called the Council of Social and Athletic Clubs which reached out to the hard-to-reach group as the aggressive casework project reaches out to the hard-to-reach individual and family.

Working with Gangs

In setting up the project the Youth Board was guided by certain underlying assumptions. First of all, in spite of the antisocial patterns developed by such groups, participation in a street club, like participation in any natural group, is part of the growing-up process and such group associations possess potentialities for positive growth and development.

Second, regarding those groups which have developed patterns of antisocial behavior, experience has indicated that many of their members are young people who are deprived in various ways — deprived of a satisfying family life, deprived of opportunities for education, employment and recreation, and deprived of a feeling that they count in their community.

Thirdly, they are responsive to a sympathetic, understanding worker who has the ability to function comfortably in the group's own setting. This third factor was later found to be

so important that project workers were selected from a wide variety of backgrounds, including bartending, athletic coaching, bell-hopping as well as the graduate schools of education, psychology, and social work. All are under the supervision of extremely well-qualified, trained supervisors who offer in-service training as well as individual supervision. All are continuing their formal education.

A fourth important principle is that effective work with gangs must be applied on a saturation basis; namely, all antisocial gangs in contact with each other in a given geographical area must be worked with simultaneously.

The project operates in three neighborhoods where the problem had been acute. It reaches out to these antisocial groups on the basis of what is understood to be their real need; their need for meaningful activities, their need for vocational activity, and their need for status — without fixed ideas concerning program. The workers go out and associate with the gangs in their own hang-outs — on the street corners, in the poolrooms, and in the candy stores. They make friends with the boys, get to know their leaders, gain their confidence, and eventually achieve the ability to redirect their activities when they finally win the boys. An important aspect of their work is the containment of street fighting, or "rumbles," by developing ways and means of settling intergang conflict.

Two methods have proved useful: One is mediation — a discussion between representatives of warring groups conducted by an impartial arbitrator; the second, the "fair-one" — supervised boxing matches between individual representatives from each group. The project has had to work with not only the groups as such, but with their members as individuals. In working with these groups the street club workers manage to give such services as personal guidance, help with family troubles, and getting jobs. To these ends various community resources are utilized.

At this point it can be restated that Youth Board confidence in the reaching-out principle has again been rewarded. Gang fights over the past years have diminished, democratic self-government has taken the place of petty tyrannizing within the group. Well-organized dances have replaced sex forays. Athletic events are supplementing gang fights and violence.

The work of the Youth Board with these groups has been very absorbing: it has had its humorous as well as its tense moments. One such occasion combined both elements.

A prominent attorney served as arbitrator for a conference which was called to mediate a "rumble," or fight between gangs. During the conference tempers flared and one of the boys produced a loaded revolver. After fast action on the part of some of the more level-headed young people and the Youth Board workers, the commotion subsided, the boy gave up his gun, and the meeting was ready to be resumed. At that point, however, it was necessary to summon the lawyer, the arbitrator of the meeting, from under the conference table where he had retired in haste at the first draw of the gun.

"PREVENTIVE" RECREATION

Also of note is the Youth Board's cooperative program with the Bureau of Community Education of the Board of Education. For many years this bureau had been providing necessary and valuable recreation services for children and adults in the City of New York. However, it had long known the need for full-time community center operation for children and youth. Therefore, in developing a program for the expansion of recreation services through this bureau the Board made funds available for full-time teams to staff certain centers in the high delinquency areas. Each team includes a center director; a recreations worker, a group worker, and a secretary–registrar. Because these teams operate on a full-time basis, they get to know their neighborhoods, build a bridge between the home and the community's leisure time program, provide continuity of service, and develop mutual confidence between families, neighborhoods, and the full school program.

A very important part of this cooperative program is the introduction of the group worker into the recreation setting. The group worker makes it possible to work with small groups and with individuals who experience difficulty in adjusting within the recreation setting. The group worker also contributes to the enrichment of the over-all program and the involvement of young people in the determination of center program and policy. Several of the centers

operated as a part of this program are utilizing not only the facilities of the school but of nearby housing projects as well.

In the words of Mark A. McCloskey, Director of the Bureau of Community Education, the cooperative experience of the Bureau and the Youth Board has established beyond doubt that children and young people "fare better and fall out less" because of the meshing of services provided by the full-time center team made possible by the Youth Board program.

The fundamental respect for the individual and his latent potentialities, regardless of how obscure, which motivated the Youth Board's activities on behalf of individuals and families, the respect for the constructive potentials of groups and their indigenous leadership, regardless of how much they are tied up in resentment and hostility which guided our efforts with hard-to-reach groups, has been carried over to Youth Board activities in the field of community organization.

On a neighborhood basis, planning meetings were held in each of the 11 areas of greatest need where community services were to be expanded and supplemented. They were attended by both lay and professional persons and it was jointly determined with Youth Board staff how the program could best be carried out in each neighborhood.

The Board had a further experience in working with indigenous leadership in the neighborhoods where the Council of Social and Athletic Clubs is operating. Local leaders were involved in this project on three levels: exploration and planning, policy-making, and programming. In terms of planning and as a supplement to the collection and analysis of pertinent statistical data by the Youth Board's Research Department, several staff members moved directly into the area to determine firsthand through face-to-face contact with the people, the urgent needs which fell within the function of the Youth Board. They ate in neighborhood restaurants. They had their hair cut by local barbers and talked and listened to them. They got chummy with teen-agers in candy stores and on street corners. In addition, local priests, ministers, and doctors, as well as school principals and local agency directors, were visited and involved in the growth and development of the project through an advisory committee. This committee shares with staff and membership the responsibility for policy-making and programming.

By democratically involving those who live with the problems, the New York City Youth Board has been trying to bring about a fusion of citizens and their government into a dynamic partnership with meaningful services to those people who really need them. While it is not claimed that the agency has fully achieved this goal, there are clear indications that it has made a beginning.

181

The School Counselor's Contribution to the Prevention of Delinquency *

Rachel Dunaway Cox

Now and then in any city a spectacular juvenile delinquency shocks the public and draws skeptical or even hostile attention to the community's youth-serving agencies. We who work in such agencies feel dismay no less than others, but the shock comes closer home. What, we ask ourselves, have we done that we should not have done? What should we have done that we lacked the wisdom to do at the proper time, that we thought ourselves too busy to do, that we had not the courage to do?

We cannot expect to prevent all delinquencies and avert every youthful indiscretion. But by accepting our professional assignment we have made ourselves responsible both to the community at large and to the children in it. Recognizing the responsibility, we must ask ourselves what we can do as counselors to forestall the outbursts that bring boys and girls into conflict with society. How can we reduce the number of spoiled and scarred lives?

---

* Reprinted from 14 *Federal Probation* (1950), 23–28. Used by permission of the author and the publisher.

SPRINGS OF DELINQUENT BEHAVIOR

Delinquency springs from the interaction of the individual's needs or drives and factors in his environment. It does not strike as a sudden, unforeseen misfortune. It almost never erupts in the well-adjusted, effectively-functioning individual who is achieving recognition, success, and satisfaction. A study of the delinquent's situation reveals the circumstances that preceded the overtly hostile act. You know them: economic stress, a broken or breaking home, intelligence below the competitive level in the child's particular group, an unsatisfactory adjustment to school.

A recently published study [1] compares delinquents and non-delinquents from the same neighborhood. Both groups are distributed over a common socioeconomic range. They attend the same schools. They have access to the same educational, recreational, and religious facilities.

The investigation found that whereas two-thirds of the delinquents come from marginal homes, (homes living from day to day on current earnings without any accumulation against a rainy day), only half of the non-delinquents come from such homes. Twenty-two per cent of the delinquents come from families on relief as against 17.3 per cent of the non-delinquents. At the other end of the scale, 31.5 per cent of the non-delinquent children have comfortable homes, whereas 11.5 per cent of the delinquents do. More than half the delinquents have homes broken by death, divorce, or separation; only a quarter of the non-delinquents have broken homes. The proportion of non-delinquents who enjoy their homes is nearly twice that of the delinquents.

The delinquents preferred social activities that were less creative than those favored by non-delinquents. They wanted passive rather than active sport participation and were less likely to seek relaxation in reading. In their leisure they characteristically sought diversion with groups of people.

I.Q.'s of 70 or below are more than four times as common among the delinquents as among the non-delinquents. Another published report showed an average I.Q. of 85 for 1,731

---

[1] Maud A. Merrill, *Problems of Child Delinquency*, Boston, Houghton Mifflin Company, 1947.

delinquents; only 21 per cent had I.Q.'s of 100 or over. Remember that the average I.Q. for unselected children is 100 and that about 50 per cent can be expected to make more than 100.

A thread of consistency runs through these patterns. In every way the delinquent tends to be less fortunately placed than the non-delinquent — less adequately equipped to meet the demands of school and society, less happy with his family, more in need of external stimulation, and less able to rely upon his own inner resources. It is noteworthy that many non-delinquents struggle successfully with the same untoward life circumstances. Note that 25 per cent of the non-delinquents come from broken homes; that 36 per cent are not in good rapport with their families. Why do these people make an adjustment at least good enough to stay beyond the censure of the law? We need much more research into the problem.

No Single Cause of Delinquency

One answer may lie in the fact that for the delinquent disadvantageous factors tend to occur not singly but in combination. Children who break into conflict with society have fewer points of rest, fewer areas of satisfaction. Delinquency is aggressive, and aggression is one response to frustration. The more areas in which the individual meets frustration, the less opportunity he will have for a socially acceptable expression of his inner drives and the more likely he will be to release the tension through unacceptable behavior.

Court records suggest that the more bitter and extensive the frustration is, the greater will be the anger and the concomitant aggression. They make it clear that delinquency is multiple-caused. The causal factors do not merely overlap. They are not merely coincidental. They interact mutually. School counselors may well be disheartened by the complexity of any predelinquent child's circumstances. Even when we "see it coming" we may feel helpless before the impending disaster.

Yet, paradoxically, in the very multiplicity of causes lies one of the hopes for prevention. A court psychiatrist has expressed the opinion that before a child turns to delinquency he usually exhausts the resources within himself, in his family, and in his community. At least, he exhausts the resources to which he as an un-

guided child has ready access. It is out of an intense unhappiness, says the psychiatrist, that he performs acts hurtful to the community, to his parents, and to himself.

It is reasonable, then, to believe that the school counselor often can prevent delinquency without relieving all the disturbing elements in the child's life. A much more modest program offers great hope. Give the troubled youth one or two areas of competence, one or two avenues along which he can find status and security, and he may not seek release in defiant and destructive acts.

If this be true, in what directions may we in the schools push our preventive work with promise of success? In what areas is the child not finding success? When we have identified them, which ones can the school do something about?

Does the counselor with his school-centered function really have a chance to work with the predelinquent on his problems? A recent study [2] answers this question. Out of 347 consecutive cases examined in the records of a county juvenile court, two-thirds had been school conduct problems, truants, or had disliked school. Another study [3] of 65 cases indicates that when those whose grade placement shows retardation are added in, approximately 75 per cent of the delinquents have had some sort of difficulty in school.

Who are the children for whom school is a trying experience? Who are the children who in one way or another send up distress signals in the school? Primarily they are the ones who have difficulty in learning. We should never forget that the learning task is one of the school child's most pressing reality problems. Of the 347 children mentioned above, only 28 per cent have I.Q.'s of 100 or above; the rest ranged downward from that point, 20 per cent were from 90-100, 17 per cent from 80-90, and 34 per cent were below 80. We educators like to think that school nurtures and heals, not that it creates problems. Yet, when school confronts a child with situations in which he cannot succeed, which find him never quite as good as most of those around him, he inevitably

[2] From unpublished study in the Juvenile Court of Delaware County, Pa., by Elisabeth S. Cantarow, psychologist of the Court.

[3] From unpublished study by the author.

seeks to escape. If we block his escape by compulsory education, we put him in a situation that an adult would not tolerate for himself.

SOME CHILDREN IN CONSTANT FEAR OF HUMILIATION

Gordon Allport has pointed out that:

When an adult undertakes to perform a task he generally places his goal at a level not so far above his abilities that he will suffer embarrassment and humiliation if he fails, not so far below his abilities that he will feel ineffectual and cheap upon accomplishing the task. He undertakes that amount and kind of labor which will keep his self-esteem at a maximum.[4]

This choice the child is not free to make. Unless very special provision is made for him the school child with an I.Q. under 100 lives in constant fear of humiliation; and he can change no important objective circumstance in his situation. Small wonder that anger and defiance grow.

Jack B. found himself in just such a situation. At 15, having reached the eighth grade chiefly by courtesy, he could read at fifth-grade level and handle number concepts at sixth-grade level. His I.Q. was 90. He was failing three out of four major subjects. He was no athlete and had a slight lisp. His father drank heavily. From what the school could learn, the mother seemed to be a weak and ineffectual person. When he first came to the counselor's attention he was on probation for stealing automobile tools from a locked garage.

He begged the counselor to have him placed in the special education class. He believed he could do the work there. The discussion in the regular classes where the "brains" showed off, was wholly beyond Jack's grasp. He frequently had skipped school even before the stealing incident. It was, in fact, on one of his truant days that he fell in with two other boys who asked him to climb through the garage window and hand the tools out to them. He knew it was risky; but these boys accepted him as an equal and asked him to do something he was able to do. He found comradeship in the enterprise.

In talking of it, however, he saw very clearly that the trouble in which it had landed him

---

[4] From *Personality: A Psychological Interpretation,* p. 169, New York, Henry Holt, Inc. 1936.

sprang directly from the truancy and that truancy had been his way of escaping from a hopeless school situation. He did not want more trouble and saw the special education class as the solution. Jack was above the legal limit for special class, but fortunately a special roster could be arranged. Later, in response to the cry for help from such boys, this particular school system set up self-contained classrooms at the junior high level. In these rooms academic offerings are on the level of the learner. Other school activities are shared with the rest of the junior high pupils. The counselor, through her earnest insistence upon the need for such a measure, has made a contribution to the prevention of delinquency in her community.

SPECIAL CLASSES — A BULWARK AGAINST TROUBLE

Well-taught special education classes, if they do not slip imperceptibly into mere disciplinary uses, go far toward helping the lowest grades of educable children to find opportunity and satisfaction. And yet, despite the fact that they meet a need realistically, a casework job may need to be done with the children themselves and with their parents around the acceptance of special class placement. As Albert Binet long ago pointed out, membership in these classes is not usually considered an honor. But if parents understandingly accept the measure, the child himself is likely to do so. He will indeed find in it the deliverance and the opportunity it is meant to be. Counselors have an opportunity, an obligation, to help parents grow into this acceptance.

Special education classes as designed for the lower I.Q. do not help the middle-grade children who often have the hardest time in our educational system today. Their need is most severe at seventh- and eighth-grade levels, for before and after these grades there is a flexibility that serves them to a degree. But most junior high programs are too rigid, make too little provision for individual difference. This is especially true of small and medium-sized high schools. Here is a job of curricular revision that calls for imagination, originality, and conviction. It lies outside the counselor's function, but she can fire the enthusiasm of the teachers and administrators whose task it is.

Another group of unhappy school children

whose unhappiness may be fertile ground for delinquency are those who are deficient in a fundamental school skill such as reading, spelling, or numbers. Reading is the commonest cause of serious school trouble. Reasons for failure in mastering this educational tool are legion, and like delinquency they rarely exist singly. A child of eight years or more who cannot read fluently almost always has an emotional problem too; but which is cause and which is effect is not easily determined. Let us not overlook the fact that failure to learn causes emotional disturbance quite as surely as emotional tension blocks learning. And of course the two factors interact in a vicious round robin. The mean I.Q. of reading-problem children is, to be sure, lower than the mean I.Q. of children who read without difficulty. But even here the overlap is so great that the I.Q. is not, except at the extremes, predictive of reading failure or of success. Many a bright child's school experience is poisoned by a reading deficiency that creates a conviction that he is really dull. The child will believe it; his parents fear it; and even his teachers become convinced of it. The habit of failure becomes fixed and weakens the structure of character and personality.

When the counselor sets out to find remedial help for such a child, her job does not end after referral is arranged. She still has to help the child accept and use the service. This may be a disheartening undertaking, for often by the time we get to him he is a chronically defeated child.

Ronny was such a case. He was in grade 6B at 12 years, having repeated 1A, and came to the counselor of his own volition, saying reading especially bothered him. The counselor told him he could join a remedial reading class, but to do so he would have to give up Saturday morning play, late sleep, and weekend trips to the country with his brothers. By way of reward, if he learned to read he would have a very helpful and satisfying accomplishment. The counselor suggested that he think it over and let her know. If he decided on the reading clinic, she would give him a card for his mother to sign.

Ten days later he came back for the card saying he had made the hard decision to give up Saturday morning play. Before the appointment for the first clinic session came around Ronny fell and hurt his foot so that he had to be on crutches for 3 weeks. During the delay this caused, Ronny's resolution weakened. A rainy day prevented his keeping his appointment at the clinic; a taxi failed to come on another day; he had to go to the hospital on a third Saturday. It began to seem that the relaxation of failure was more attractive than the struggle, sacrifice, and possible defeat involved in another effort. At this point the counselor told Ronny that if he did not go to the clinic the following Saturday their counseling contact would have to end. When Ronny expressed dismay, the counselor explained that children did not come to the counselor for a social visit — that the school expected some help to be given. Her firmness made it possible for Ronny to undertake that difficult first trip to the clinic.

The following Monday he returned to the counselor all smiles. He was delighted with the clinic. There had been a party at his house on Friday night that kept him up until 1 o'clock; but he had gotten up and gone anyway. Ronny gained steadily at the clinic at least until the midyear when he was promoted and sent on to junior high school and dropped out of the counselor's orbit.

THE UNWANTED, FORGOTTEN CHILD

Court records tell us that it is not usually the high school class president or the belle of the junior prom who find themselves in conflict with established law and social custom. Occasional escapades yes, and once in a while a serious lapse. But not as a general thing. It is the unwanted, unsupported individual who is likely to get into difficulty. In the social sphere also, the counselor may find an opportunity to forestall delinquency. For successful experience on an athletic team, in a club, or in a social group may be the sustaining factor in an otherwise bleak existence.

Robert's father was a semiskilled mechanic in a community where most of the fathers were professional men or executives. About average in intelligence, awkward, inclined to obesity, Robert was the youngest of the family that included several stepbrothers and sisters by the father's previous marriage. The family, torn by dissension between the mother and her stepchildren, received a patronizing kindness from the community. One brother had gone to reform school.

Robert was a behavior problem from kindergarten onward. His large size and aggressiveness made him the bane of the children in his grade. His spicy language, rough manners, and inferior social status made him an unwelcome playmate in most homes. His teachers tried hard, but Robert remained a problem. In the sixth grade he was picked up by the police for petty theft. The town awaited his adolescence with trepidation.

Then Robert reached seventh grade and the junior high counselor who had known Robert by reputation suggested that he join the school band, for which the school provided instruments and uniforms. She kept in touch with him, enlisted the special interest of his teachers and the bandmaster. Robert became better than passable on the saxophone; and now for the first time he had found a secure place in his school. When the band goes to out-of-town athletic contests he goes with them. When the team wins, he marches with them down the main street. When they stand to play the school hymn, he stands with them, giving himself to a group experience, fused with his fellows at last in a common loyalty. The school band and the school counselor have not solved all Robert's problems; but they have given him something no other experience ever brought him — a bond with his fellows. Perhaps it is not too wishful to hope — because it is certainly true that Robert is not much trouble anymore.

For Robert, as for every other child, few burdens are as heavy as social isolation. Insecure youth may rush into social activity to escape it and, as James Plant pointed out, no activity except marriage is as social as delinquency. The delinquent's very deviate acts — as in Jack's case — may be an effort to prove his acceptability. By timely guidance the counselor can help him find the reassurance he needs through legitimate social channels.

Home Relationships and Delinquency

Poor home environment, family disorganization, neglect, and rejection or rigidity in the family also are factors in delinquency which can be placed second to none. The counselor with her school-centered function may not quite see how to make a vital contribution to the child's home relationships. This is true especially at the secondary level. The large

size and impersonal atmosphere of the modern high school do not offer much opportunity to parents and educators for the growth of mutual knowledge, respect, and trust which develop chiefly through personal contacts and cooperation. And even counselors, who carry the special task of creating a bond between parents and the school, find that effective work with the parents of troubled children calls for a higher degree of skill and professional confidence than almost any area of their work. The simplest home problem may require referral to any of a dozen agencies. To refer properly, the counselor must know community resources and how to clear cases through the social service exchange. Work with parents often consumes much time, and it requires good judgment, wisdom, and restraint at every step. Work with parent–child relationships demands a sensitive awareness of the meaning of such a relationship to both the child and the parent and a clear understanding by the counselor of the proper limitation to his sphere of operations. Undertaking too much may do more damage than undertaking too little. The extent of the responsibility often will depend upon the condition of the home and upon the responsiveness and capabilities of the parents. Yet even in this flexible framework the counselor's function will need to be held within clearly defined limits. Beyond this point the referral facilities of the community will be used.

Parents Need Insight and Understanding

Sometimes parents need only to have the school share with them its knowledge and concern about the child's problems. Parents' absorption in their own affairs, oversolicitude, spoiling, or preconceived goals and standards may be creating a situation in which delinquency will take root. Not infrequently parents may be blindly hoping for the best, assuring themselves there is really nothing to worry about. The counselor can help them face the truth, and either work the problem through with them or refer them to appropriate sources of help.

It takes no mean degree of insight, courage, and skill to help parents face painful truths. They may have to accept the fact that the boy who was to take over his father's medical practice is not equipped for that role. They may need to recognize the effects of immaturity, egocentricity, or insecurity in their own lives upon the child's development. They may respond quickly, once they have been made aware of the need. Indeed, it is in family situations of this sort that juvenile courts often make striking contributions, though the school counselor ought to render it before there has occurred the traumatic collision with the law.

Sometimes, unfortunately, the parental response is not good, and only by being pulled up short can they be helped to give the child minimal nurture. They are too weak or inadequate to stand on their own strength alone. Donald's family was of that sort. Donald, an intermittent truant at 12 years, lived with his mother in a poor district of a large city. His father had been killed in an automobile accident 2 years previously, and his mother now worked. She left home at 7:30 every morning while Donald was still asleep. The boy often did not go to school at all, but roamed the streets, hanging around stores and on street corners, and had had a minor brush or two with the police. The school psychologist found him to be alert, personable, loquacious, demanding much attention. His conversation was bright but flighty; his interests were unstable. His I.Q. was 108, but his reading and spelling were at second-grade level, his arithmetic at third-grade. Donald's older brother Tom had some influence with the boy but had married since the father's death and was struggling to get his own home started.

About this time the school medical officer referred Donald for glasses, which the school supplied. Because of his truancy he was summoned to the attendance office. His brother Tom accompanied him. The mother's health had become precarious; she had given up her job and was receiving public assistance. Tom was disturbed by Donald's trouble and worried about his mother's health. He said Donald has his way in everything at home. The mother takes him to midnight movies and then allows him to sleep late. An aunt and uncle in a nearby community wanted to take Donald but his mother did not want this.

For about a month after the visit to the attendance officer Donald had a perfect record. Then he was picked up by the police for taking reflectors from cars parked around a school near his home. He was very much upset by this. He wanted to know where the police would take him and whether his mother would have to be told. Would he have to tell the priest at confession? He was taken to the police station where his mother came for him at 4:30 the same afternoon. Less than 2 months later Donald took a fountain pen from another classroom because he "wanted things." The counselor arranged to have the pen returned.

During all this time the counselor was unable to see the mother, who ignored notes requesting her to come to the school and was never at home when the counselor visited. A week after the second stealing episode the brother came to the counselor's office. He said with much feeling that Donald needed supervision and repeated his wish that the boy might be placed.

In about a month accusations of sexual advances to girls both in and out of the school were made against Donald. The mother came this time in response to a summons from the school but ignored the issues of stealing and sex difficulty, demanding to know when the school would replace the glasses Donald had lost some weeks previously. The counselor finally terminated the interview by a request that Tom come to see her. Tom was much shocked by his little brother's trouble but seemed helpless to effect any change.

After further difficulties the counselor, having consulted with her supervisor, recommended that the school administration ask the juvenile court to provide protective service to this family; i.e. give periodic supervisory checks on family regime. It is too soon to know what the outcome will be, but it is believed that the authoritative functioning of the court may bring order and responsibility into a chaotic family situation and give Donald the limits his mother has been unwilling, or unable, to set up for him.

COUNSELOR'S CONTINUING RESPONSIBILITY FOR CHILD THROUGHOUT HIS STAY IN SCHOOL

Another special opportunity in delinquency prevention lies in the counselor's continuing responsibility for the individual child. The child makes a more or less discontinuous grade-to-grade and teacher-to-teacher movement through school. The counselor is one school official who is readily accessible to the child throughout his stay in a school. Moreover, she is on the scene early. Court probation workers lament the lateness of their entry upon the delinquent's progress. Prevention should begin long before bitterness and restlessness culminate the illegally aggressive act. The school counselor's part in prevention can begin when the youngster with a low or dull normal intellect enters school, when the socially inept or immature child meets his earliest rejections on the playground, when the second grade child fails in reading, when the child of any age gives us reason to believe that his home offers an insecure base.

This means that counseling should begin in the elementary school, where the fundamental personality patterns are laid down.

As counselors and school social workers we are members of a team both in and outside the school who share responsibility for the child's welfare. The counselor alone cannot meet all the needs of a troubled child. We must rely upon the parent and upon his ability and willingness to change. We must depend upon the flexibility, skill, and good will of the teacher. We must know how to make the best use of social agencies and of the medical and psychiatric resources in the community. Most of all, perhaps, we must rely, in this baffling enterprise, upon the child himself — upon his capacity to make his own way, with some direction and support, toward wholesome adjustment.

182

Chicago's Special School for Social Adjustment *

Edward H. Stullken

The Montefiore Special School was established as a part of the public school system of Chicago in September 1929. It was organized as a result of a nationwide survey made by the writer who was authorized by the superintendent

of schools and the Board of Education of Chicago to study what other metropolitan school systems were doing to help prevent juvenile delinquency.

The Montefiore School was established to care for unadjusted children, truants, incorrigibles, behavior deviates, etc., who are more vulnerable than others to delinquency. The Montefiore School and its girls' branch care for cases of maladjustment and behavior problems among children with which teachers need help from specialists.

In every large school system there will be found a sizable number of these severe problem children who, because of emotional disturbances or social maladjustment, fail to respond to the work of the best teachers, the most modern school programs, and the efforts of specialized workers provided by a school system to help teachers prevent maladjustment. One reason is that the symptoms of their disturbances are too severe or too upsetting to other children. The regular school can do little for the maladjusted and disturbed child who rarely attends classes. Nor can he be helped by specialists working in regular schools when he cannot be reached by their services.

Another reason some children cannot be retained in regular grades is because schools must operate with 35 or 40 and even more pupils per teacher. No teacher has the right to take from the great majority of his pupils an unreasonable amount of time which may be necessary to deal with an extremely difficult child in his room. Many problem children cannot profit from regular class activities until they have undergone a personal reorientation through counseling, psychotherapy, or remedial work done in small groups.

For such children as these the Montefiore Special School is provided. While at first thought it might seem that the behavior problems of such children would be intensified by a transfer to a special school, it has been the experience at Montefiore that serious types of misbehavior are diminished. Moreover, segre-

* Reprinted from 20 Federal Probation (1956), 31–36. Used by permission of the author and the publisher. See, also, E. H. Stullken, "The Schools and the Delinquency Problem," 43 J. Crim. L.,

Criminology, and Police Science (1952–53), 563–574; W. C. Kvaraceus, "The Role of the School in a Delinquency Prevention and Control Program," 11 Federal Probation (1947), 9–12; S. M. Brownell, "The Unique Position of the Schools in the Prevention and Control of Delinquency," 19 Federal Probation (1955), 14–16. — Ed.

gation as commonly defined is not applicable to the special education of these children because many problem children are much more harmfully segregated when kept in regular classes which cannot meet their needs than when transferred to the special school which does meet their needs far better. This is due, no doubt, to the fact that the Montefiore School concentrates on remedial measures, gives careful attention to physical and mental health, and maintains a competent staff of special teachers, social workers, psychologists, and other workers. The special educational program is adapted to the individual needs of the pupils enrolled, with emphasis upon activities that have proved an effective antidote for emotional disturbances. The Montefiore makes it possible for many maladjusted pupils to enjoy success in school work instead of experiencing the accumulation of feelings of failure which characterized their work in the regular schools where their unusual needs could not be met.

MONTEFIORE'S CURRICULUM

Pupils are transferred to the Montefiore on a simple school transfer rather than commitment by a court. Placement in the Montefiore is not to be considered as punishment, but rather as a decision by school authorities that such placement will be of material benefit to the child by virtue of the fact that the special school can give him the particular attention he needs. The Montefiore School makes curriculum modifications, provides special equipment, gives medical and dental clinical care, and keeps adequate cumulative records of the work and interests of the pupils enrolled.

Academic work is given in reading, English, mathematics, science, and social studies. Courses in woodwork, general metal work, electric shop, shoe repairing, printshop, crafts laboratory, mechanical drawing, and general mechanics are offered for the boys. Homemaking, hairdressing, personal grooming, sewing, cooking, and typing are offered in the girls' branch. Other courses found in both boys' and girls' branches are music, art, and physical training and play activities. Teachers have special training, special qualifications, and exceptional abilities, and are carefully selected. Special provisions are also made for educational, personal, and vocational guidance. Psychological, social worker, dental and some psychiatric services are given.

In fact, the school is in reality a combination of a special school and a child guidance clinic. The Montefiore School also provides a free noonday hot lunch for all pupils enrolled and carfare for all living more than a mile from the school.

SOME FACTS ABOUT MONTEFIORE'S PUPILS

School Grade and Age. During the past year the Montefiore cared for a total of 1,336 boys and 526 girls in its two day-school branches. Grades three through eleven were represented in this enrollment. Among the boys there were more elementary school pupils (grades 3–8) than high school pupils (grades 9–12) but among the girls the proportion was reversed. The ages of the pupils vary from 9 years through 16. The median age of elementary school boys enrolled last year was 13 years, 11 months, and that of elementary school girls, 13 years, 8 months. The median age of high school boys enrolled last year was 15 years, 4 months and that of high school girls, 15 years, 3 months. These figures indicate that the proportion of older pupils is entirely too high to give the special school the time required to rehabilitate maladjusted individuals before they reach the age of 16 when compulsory school attendance ceases.

Intelligence Quotient. The school psychologists report that the median intelligence quotients for elementary school boys and girls last year was 85.4 and for high school boys and girls 94. Studies by the psychologists and others indicate that many of the Montefiore pupils belong to the dull–normal group who cannot compete with their fellows on equal terms in ordinary school work. Without a sense of success and with only feelings of failure these children too often seek relief in truancy from regular schools or in attempts to gain recognition by committing overt acts of misbehavior.

Reading and Arithmetic Levels. — A complete battery of educational tests is given by the psychologists to all Montefiore pupils at the time of their enrollment. Results of these tests indicate that elementary school pupils are retarded in reading almost five years below their chronological age expectancy, slightly more than three years below mental age expectancy, and slightly less than three years below the grade placement they had while still in the regular schools. For the high school groups the reading retardation was three years, two months as based on chrono-logical age; two years, one month on the basis of mental age expectancy; and two years, two months according to the grade placement given by the transferring school. In arithmetic ele-mentary school pupils usually score higher than they do in reading, while high school pupils score higher in reading than in arithmetic. Ap-parently after enrolling in high school, prob-lem boys and girls find experiences and stimula-tion to maintain their reading level, while they lose the more advanced arithmetical skills that they acquired in the upper elementary grades.

Mechanical Aptitude. The average me-chanical age for the pupils in the Montefiore School, as determined on tests for mechanical aptitude, exceeds their verbal ability as de-termined by the various types of standardized tests. In fact, the average problem boy enrolled in the Montefiore often exceeds his chronologi-cal age expectancy in mechanical ability. In art and music Montefiore boys do not show either the aptitude or interest which they have for mechanical work. Girls on the other hand do show more aptitude and much more interest in the fine arts.

Personality Traits. The use of the California Test of Personality indicates that Montefiore pupils show greater disability in traits measured by the personality test than in any other facet of their characters. The correlation between intelligence and personality rating scores has been found to be very slight. Pupils scoring very low on the personality rating scales, pupils exhibiting rebellious and antisocial behavior, or pupils who give other evidence of serious emo-tional instability are referred to the school psychiatrist for diagnosis and treatment. How-ever, if the pupil is or has been known to any mental hygiene clinic, he is urged to continue or renew his contacts with such agency.

Progress Shown. All pupils who have been in the Montefiore School for a semester or more are given tests in the basic skill subjects. The amount of gain made in the Montefiore School varies widely among the pupils and among the different classes. While it is evident that certain teachers are able to obtain consistently higher progress ratings in the classes that come to them than other teachers, regularity of attendance appears to be one of the most important factors in effecting progress. On the whole, the duller pupils always make a greater gain than the

brighter pupils when their expected rate of gain is based on their intelligence quotients. The most gratifying gains are made by the pupils in the remedial reading groups. The great retarda-tion in reading below the pupil's ability probably makes possible a rapid rate of gain until this wide discrepancy is diminished.

Family-School Relationships. As indicated above, the Montefiore School employs case-workers, and school social workers who attempt to bring about a better understanding between the home, the child, and the school. These workers are concerned with problems of regular school attendance, problems of health and wel-fare, personality adjustment, and family and school relationships. The caseworkers suggest the use of community facilities for out of school activities for pupils and often recommend adult facilities available to the parents. In addition they contact the social agencies of the city and last year 83 different agencies were consulted in making referrals for 363 different pupils. Many of these referrals were made to hospitals and clinics in an attempt to keep the pupils in a good healthy physical condition. Dental care is made possible through the Chicago Health Department which maintains a dental clinic in the Montefiore school building.

Home Conditions. Last year the seven case-workers made 3,691 visits to the homes of Montefiore boys and girls and also held numer-ous office conferences with parents, children, and teachers. They have found that approxi-mately 55 per cent of the Montefiore pupils came from broken homes — homes having only one parent, or from homes of relatives, or from foster homes. Slightly more than 35 per cent of the mothers of these pupils were employed outside of the home in order to keep the family intact. In approximately half of the cases it was found that the father was dead or had deserted or left the home. Over 50 per cent of the pupils or their families were known to the Family Court of Chicago before the pupils were enrolled at the Montefiore School. Only 21 per cent came to the attention of the Court after enrollment. Of this 21 per cent, about one-third were cases where the contact between the pupil and the court had been made previous to his enrollment in the special school and such contact was renewed or continued after enrollment. The actual number of Montefiore pupils taken into court by the Montefiore

School is less than 15 per cent of those enrolled.

Family Contacts with Social Agencies. The caseworkers also have found that almost 90 per cent of all pupils in the Montefiore School were known to one or more social agencies before their transfer to the Montefiore. The average is 3.5 agencies per pupil. This fact has particular significance because it indicates that in spite of the efforts of agency workers it was necessary to transfer the child to the special school, although it must be pointed out that agency workers often request a transfer to the Montefiore for one of their clients in order that the child may profit from the special facilities of the Montefiore.

Post-school Adjustment. Approximately one half of the pupils enrolled in the Montefiore School leave school at the age of 16 to find employment. In other words, the Montefiore must provide terminal education for these who do not continue in school at either the special or regular schools of the city. Studies indicate that approximately 60 per cent of them keep out of difficulty after they leave the special school. Of those who are returned to the regular schools of the city approximately 70 per cent make good records in the schools to which they are returned.

MANY FACTORS AFFECT BEHAVIOR

The foregoing paragraphs indicate that the Montefiore tries to make provisions for the rehabilitation of its pupils. It studies the variety of causative factors that produce maladjustment and tries to provide for their re-entry in a regular school within the normal life of society. Much attention is given to working with clinics, agencies, and courts to secure proper diagnosis and remedial measures. All cases are cleared through the Social Service Exchange of the Welfare Council of Metropolitan Chicago. The school believes that it is successful in dealing with approximately 70 per cent of its enrollment if they receive them in time, that is, before they are too old or before bad habits have •been too firmly established.

Study of the needs of the socially maladjusted children enrolled in the Montefiore indicates that there are many factors which affect their behavior. It is the combination of many factors within and without the child's individual personality, with the interplay and reaction of those factors on the life of the individual that produce the socially maladjusted and delinquent child. The earlier years, particularly, are of great significance in determining his later social adjustment.

Very often the problem child is one who feels unwanted, unloved, discriminated against, unjustly condemned or punished, and unrecognized as an individual having rights and needs. The school must therefore project itself into the life situations of maladjusted boys and girls, not only during school hours, but outside of the school and in the family life and community environment of the children if it is to help them. This cannot be done by the ordinary school with 35 or more pupils per teacher. It can be done only by those workers who are especially qualified in education and social work and versed in clinical procedures not found in the work of regular schools. The special school with its smaller groups, its clinical facilities, and its social workers can make compensations for the deficiencies in the life of a problem child. These facts raise the question whether schools are providing adequate facilities to meet the problem.

A CASE ILLUSTRATION

The case of one boy who received special instruction at the Montefiore School is presented to show progress and its effect upon educational adjustment and personality. The case has been selected from among those who have been studied for a time long enough to allow an evaluation of the results of teaching.

Jack, age fourteen years, two months, had many behavior difficulties when he first enrolled in Montefiore Special School from a Chicago Elementary School, grade 6B. Jack's School Problem Report indicated "poor work production, poor adjustment to the group, caused classroom disturbances, was aggressive toward his peers, refused to take teacher-direction. Outside of school he was a neighborhood menace; damaged property by breaking windows, pulling down fences, etc., terrified people passing by on the street by hanging out third floor windows; walking the porch rail." Many of the facts in the case antedated the educational deficiencies and were problems for psychological and psychiatric study.

Montefiore Special School records reveal that Jack started in first grade at a private day school and continued there through third grade. He then was placed in a private boarding school for problem boys where he remained three and a half years. It is reported that during the time at boarding school "Jack made little progress in his studies and had difficulty adjusting to the students and the staff. He appeared to be a very lonely, immature boy. . . . His attempts to make friends were unsuccessful and he was demanding of attention.

After three and a half years at boarding school, Jack returned to the private day school where he remained briefly and then transferred to Chicago Public Schools. In order to circumvent his difficulties, Jack transferred back and forth from private schools to public schools for 2 years. He was subsequently provided Special School placement.

Before Jack enrolled in the Montefiore School he was given a Revised Stanford Binet Form L examination by the school psychologist. An I. Q. of 94, indicating an average rating, was obtained. The findings were considered minimal, however, because of limited amount of cooperation on Jack's part and lack of confidence in his own ability.

Psychiatric and physical examinations were undertaken. Physical findings were essentially negative except for one carious tooth. Jack's health was such that he might be expected to participate in the usual activities at a public school. Interviews with Jack and his parents revealed that "the boy comes from a complete home where apparently there have been health, financial, and drinking problems, crowded living quarters, and a number of younger siblings apparently consuming a great deal of time and effort, especially of the mother, so that Jack may not have been able to receive the amount of supportive encouragement from the home that he has needed."

Some time after Jack enrolled at Montefiore, further tests were administered. The Wechsler Bellevue Intelligence Scale for Adolescents and Adults was administered. Jack earned an I. Q. of 113 on the Full Scale, indicating a higher than average rate of learning and mental age grade expectancy adequate for high school materials. An I. Q. of 112 was obtained on the Verbal Scale and 113 I. Q. on the Performance Scale. The psychologist believed that part of the discrepancy between the two tests was due to relief of tension and apprehension which permitted the boy to do himself greater justice in dealing with test materials than at the first test. These later findings were believed to be a better rating of the boy's capacities.

On the Mechanical Comprehension Test — G. K. Bennett (administered by adjustment teacher, Montefiore Special School) Jack's rating was 75th Percentile which is considered an excellent rating for a Montefiore boy of Jack's age and grade placement.

On the California Test of Personality — for Grades 7–10, Form AA, administered by the adjustment teacher (Jack was given help with reading test items), Jack's rating was: 50th Percentile — Personal Adjustment: 90th Percentile — Social Adjustment.

Jack's responses indicated that he had a grasp of social situations but he was not entirely self-reliant. It is to be noted that on the self-adjustment side Jack's ratings were rather low in the components, self-reliance, sense of personal worth, sense of belonging.

Academic testing by the school psychologist revealed that despite the behavior problem, the ability in arithmetic was in accordance with grade placement, 6B; reading and spelling fell on 3B level.

A diagnosis of reading disability revealed that Jack was right-handed, but he preferred his left eye in sighting. He had great difficulty in forming visual-auditory associations and in blending sounds in word-building. He was never sure in recognition of complex word patterns although he recognized the individual letters of words easily. There was indication of reversal of letter sequence in writing words. (This tendency to reversal might have been more marked earlier.)

At first, in the special reading class, there was a pronounced behavior reaction. Despite previous counseling, Jack believed himself to be defective and was resistant to teaching. Because of his resistance to school work Jack was given much individual attention and kindly supportive management in the special reading class. In the arithmetic classroom, Jack was given recognition for his ability. In the gym and playroom he was given encouragement and trials as leader. Teachers of content subjects gave attention to his needs. Within ten months Jack made three years gain in reading and spelling. Within another nine-month period, his reading achievement indicated eighth grade; spelling, seventh grade; arithmetic, adequate for high school. Ability in content subjects appeared sufficient for high school materials. In line with Jack's personality, it is interesting to note that his taste in reading in the school library ran to adventure stories of highly imaginative type.

With improvement in school work there has been a general improvement in the boy's behavior and social adjustment, although excitability persists and he does not always act in a responsible manner. His attendance is now quite regular with few absences due to illness.

Jack has graduated from 8A. He is very anxious to enroll in a regular high school and probably will be given that opportunity.

There has been no radical change in the home situation but it has been modified as a result of psychiatric counsel and guidance by the school social worker of the Montefiore Special School. Presently, Jack has supervised outside activities and he does some outside reading. He has an educational plan, it seems; also, vocational interest (mechanical). However, when all the factors in this case have been taken into consideration, we feel that there is the possibility that Jack may find adjustment difficult in the regular high school where classes are large and individual

attention to his needs as well as the close supervision afforded him at Montefiore Special School will not always be forthcoming. Jack will need help from the high school personnel and the parents will probably need guidance in directing the boy. It seems advisable, therefore, that the high school adjustment teacher and guidance officer follow up on the case. Jack should be referred from time to time to the high school psychologist. High school classroom teachers should make every effort to give Jack encouragement in order to further instill self-confidence, and shop teachers to create opportunities for praising Jack for ability in manipulative and spatial media.

Jack's case, complicated as it was by many problems, illustrates the necessity of a combined approach from school personnel — school principal, psychiatrist, psychologist, adjustment teacher, and social caseworker working with Special School teachers. With such cooperative treatment, a more satisfactory educational adjustment has been made by a boy who presented difficult personality and behavior problems as well as specific disabilities in reading. Since reading is basic in school subjects, Jack was seriously handicapped in school work required of him previous to enrollment in the Montefiore Special School.

Work at Montefiore indicates the necessity for securing earlier recognition and diagnosis of problem children and of effecting their transfer to a special school before they have so nearly reached the end of compulsory school age, and before they have had habits so firmly established.

Need for Specially Trained Staff

Another problem faced by the Montefiore School for social adjustment is that of securing adequately qualified personnel. The school needs the best trained psychologists, and the best trained school social workers. One step that could be taken would be to free the special schools from the regular rules, regulations, and procedures now affecting the transfer of teachers in regular schools. Another step would be to set up separate and well worked out qualifications for teachers of socially maladjusted children.

Every activity in special education usually involves the problem of financing the work which must be done. The education of the socially maladjusted is no exception and its costs must be considered. The state recognizes its obligation by providing for the excess cost of educating socially maladjusted children over and above the cost of educating normal children. For over 20 years the state has reimbursed local school districts up to $190 per year per child in aver-

age daily attendance in special classes and special schools for truant, delinquent, and incorrigible children. At the Montefiore it costs approximately $700 per year per child and the $190 does not provide anywhere near the amount spent per child in these schools over and above the amount spent per child in regular schools. Consequently the state should increase its allotment for excess cost of educating socially maladjusted children because the cost of educating these children has increased just like the costs in other branches of special education.

Socially maladjusted and delinquent children are entitled to the advantages of a special educational and clinical program that will give them a real equal educational opportunity with all other children. These children must have the right to develop into self-respecting, useful citizens by the process of public education, and that right must not be abridged by a handicap of any kind which can be eliminated or mitigated through the facilities of special schools and special services.

Schools Should Be Responsible for Social Adjustment of Their Pupils

School administrators must maintain a balance between the interests of pupils needing placement in special schools and the interests of the great majority of the school population. While these interests often conflict, the conflict must be resolved for the best interests of all concerned. In general, placement of a child in a special group should not be made if that child may receive as good or better training in a normal group, even though it may be necessary to give additional services over and above those which are usually provided. The exception to this rule is found whenever the detriment to the normal pupils and the time taken from them outweighs the benefits to the maladjusted individual from his association with the regular group. This principle needs study because too many problem children are retained in regular schools too long and with detriment to too many normal individuals as well as harm to the maladjusted child.

The program for educating socially maladjusted and delinquent children should fit into the general program of the schools. It should be considered as an educational program — not a punitive program. Moreover, the time has come when a school system should assert its

right to protect its investment in the social adjustment of all children from the inimical influences to which the child may be subjected outside the school. It appears that through the services of special schools for socially maladjusted children a school system must venture into the field of social and clinical services to protect this investment.

No program for socially maladjusted children is sound unless it recognizes the special needs of this group and meets those needs more fully than they can be met in regular schools. All schools like the Montefiore need to have adequate follow-up service.

Schools should provide for an early identification and diagnosis of children who are maladjusted.* School children become problem cases as a result of experience and at a much younger age than is often thought to be the case. Unless such children are identified and given an opportunity in a special school early, it becomes impossible to correct habits in the time remaining before most of them leave school. Furthermore, no special school can correct habits and difficulties in adjustment in a few months' time when the habits and difficulties have existed over a period of years. The education of socially maladjusted children requires a broader basis than that of mere intellectual development. Educational programs for meeting the needs of the socially maladjusted should be subjected to a minimum of regimentation, their curricula should be enriched and not curtailed, and the program of education should be complemented by the services of psychology, medicine, psychiatry, and social work. These auxiliary services are most effective when a part of the special school's program. The whole program should be a unit, the services should all be centered at the school where the maladjusted child meets the teacher. Unless the demands of society upon the problem child are unified, further disintegration of his personality results.

Finally, the program of education for the socially maladjusted and delinquent in the schools will be conditioned by the selection of properly trained and qualified personnel, both those who work in the program and those

who administer and direct the program of special education.

183

The New York City Youth Board's Council of Social and Athletic Clubs *

Ralph W. Whelan

The Council of Social and Athletic Clubs, popularly known as the Street Club Project, has since 1951 been an integral part of the New York City Youth Board's program for the prevention of juvenile delinquency. The project grew out of the community's increasing concern with the problem of antisocial teenage gangs. Such conflict groups, although not an entirely new phenomenon, occasioned more serious reflection since World War II because of the increasing availability of weapons to gang members and because of the younger age of participation in fighting gangs. Conflict among these groups became more widespread and destructive in nature and often resulted in the death or serious injury not only of the participants but of bystanders as well.

The community's regular leisure-time resources and facilities such as settlement houses and community centers found themselves unequipped to deal adequately with the aggressive acting-out young person, particularly when he was involved in an antisocial gang. When the agencies attempted to bring these youngsters into their on-going program, the result had not only been failure but often proved damaging to the total program.

Originally the Youth Board sought to meet this situation by contracting with settlement houses to provide workers for assignment to street club groups in their neighborhoods. These workers, under settlement house supervision but working outside its structured setting, were known as "detached workers." In

---

New York, however, this plan did not prove successful because the worker had to divide his energies and attention between the needs of the conflict group to which he was assigned and the day-to-day problems of the agency for which he was working. As a result, more often than not, the youngsters whom the worker reached, although members of unaffiliated groups, were not members of a hard-core street gang.

This early program revealed the importance, also, of saturating a neighborhood, of assigning a worker to each key fighting gang within that area on a co-ordinated basis. Complete coverage is necessary, for to work with only one group in a neighborhood in which there are several conflict groups constitutes work in a vacuum.

Because of this experience and drawing on experience gained in projects initiated by the Welfare Council of New York City in Central Harlem and others, the Council of Social and Athletic Clubs came into being. Initially, this project, which provided centralized administration and systematic coverage, worked with gangs in two Brooklyn areas. Currently, it is functioning in ten city areas, is serving 60 fighting gangs directly and is in contact with 15–20 others.

The Street Club Project gives service on a seven day, twenty-four hour basis. Its fundamental purpose is the containment, prevention, and eventual elimination of gang conflict, the resolution of individual and group problems, and, ultimately, the redirection into wholesome channels of the activities and energies of anti-social gangs.

In the course of service, the street club worker works with the members of the gangs individually around their own problems in the home and community as well as with the frustrations and conflicts of the groups as a whole. He utilizes all community resources. Where indicated, he makes referral to treatment, group work, health, housing, and other services to meet the individual or group needs.

The underlying assumption upon which the Street Club Project is based is that teen-age group association is a natural part of growing up. Young people everywhere seek each other's company, join in clubs, fraternities, sororities, cliques, etc. The groups with which the Youth

Board works are not a source of concern because they have joined together, but because of the direction their group activities have taken. It is also recognized that, unlike members of other teen-age groups, their members seek in the gang fulfillment of all their fundamental needs for recognition, affection, status, new experience, and security. It is the worker's job to help them discover that these needs can better be satisfied in normal relationships and help them recognize their own individuality and that of others. This project serves as a bridge between these young people and the interest and resources of the community from which they have cut themselves off.

In all the work of the Street Club Project the welfare of the community as a whole is never lost sight of. This means that neither active nor passive support is given to the anti-social, destructive, illegal acts of the gangs and that, at all times, the Council of Social and Athletic Clubs works closely with the Police Department.

Within this philosophical framework, the fundamental technique of the Street Club Project consists of sending skilled workers into the hangouts of the teen-age gangs — in the candy stores, luncheonettes, and poolrooms and on the streets. The street club worker seeks the confidence of the gang members and leaders through service and gradually, as he is accepted by them, begins to use his relationship with the group to turn them away from their destructive activities and to guide them into more socially acceptable pursuits. The street club worker uses this relationship in such a way that the gang comes to view him as an interested, enabling adult rather than as a member of the gang. An important step in establishing this relationship with the group is the worker's interpretation to the boys of the fact that, although he accepts them as individuals, he does not accept their antisocial behavior. He is an understanding adult concerned with their welfare. He makes it very clear to them that if he learns of an impending "rumble", illegal possession of weapons, or the "pushing" of narcotics, he will take immediate action to assure that the police are notified.

An essential part of redirecting the gang is the provision of constructive alternatives for the excitement the members receive from their participation in conflict and antisocial behavior. Athletics, camping, dances, bus trips to parks in the vicinity of the city are all an important part of the Council's program. It is the experience of the project's workers that the horizons of the gang members are very narrow and their capacities undeveloped. Often they have never been outside of the few crowded blocks of the neighborhoods in which they live. Many are afraid to participate in sports or in social activities because of their fear of failure. On the other hand, they feel that they can find "status" only in fighting.

In several areas of the city, meeting rooms have been established where, under close and intensive supervision, members of several gangs can participate in social and recreational activities without conflict. This setting offers the street club workers with each of the groups served an unusually good opportunity to observe the members and to give them individual attention.

Jobs would do much to increase the stability of many gang members, but employment is usually difficult for them to find. Standing in the way of obtaining and holding good jobs is not only the gang members' lack of education and training, but their negative, rejecting attitude toward work as well as their unrealistic desire for immediate gratification. Street club workers often find that helping the boys to develop sounder work attitudes and assisting them to get jobs is an important way of demonstrating their interest and winning the gang's confidence as well as a valuable step in combating antisocial behavior. In finding employment for such youngsters, the Council utilizes the resources of the community and the services of vocational testing and placement agencies in contract with the Youth Board.

Since participation in violent conflict is the criterion by which gangs are selected for service by the Street Club Project, workers are constantly faced with the problem of dealing with situations which carry with them the threat of a "rumble." Among these gangs very little is required to trigger serious and destructive fights. A few insulting words, a dirty look, the presence of newcomers in the neighborhood or the mere appearance of the members of a rival gang on a block which the group considers its "turf" is sufficient irritation. Rumors spread quickly, often with the encouragement of

troublemakers in the gang or of neighborhood girls hoping for excitement. The worker functions in these situations as the voice of reason and of caution. Is the rumor true, he asks, and even if it is, do you want to risk death, injury, or imprisonment because some boys from the next block "looked funny" at some of your fellow gang members? Usually, no matter what they may verbalize, the individual gang members are not at all eager to risk their lives. The great majority of them, in fact, have a deep fear of physical hurt resulting from fighting. However, the code by which the gang lives prevents it from "punking out," from ignoring what it considers an insult and a challenge. The Street Club Project, recognizing the gangs' need to find a way of avoiding fights without losing status or "face," arranges for mediation meetings in which representatives of rival gangs face each other across a conference table and exchange words rather than trading shots across a crowded street. The agreements which the gangs arrive at during such mediations bind only their respective members, not the Youth Board or any other agency working in the community. Often these mediations are directly responsible for halting or preventing violent and deadly gang wars.

As the street club worker increasingly demonstrates his genuine interest in the gang members and their problems, the relationship between him and the gang gains strength, and positive results begin to be manifested. Often the boys begin to emulate his dress, his mannerisms, his interests, and, little by little, they come to accept his attitudes toward street fighting, drugs, promiscuity, and the like. As this happens, they gradually draw away from antisocial behavior and begin to develop more worth-while interests. One reason for this is that the street club worker is often the first adult to show a continuing interest in and regard for them as individuals, to concern himself in a helpful way with their problems and to demonstrate a willingness to listen to their points of view.

The process is a slow one, in most instances requiring many months of patient effort, with set-backs and disappointments along the way. There is a continuing give-and-take, for the gang members are constantly seeking ways of testing the worker, of seeing just how far he can be pushed. He must be on guard against attempts to exploit him in ways which will diminish his prestige with the gang or to make him appear an easy mark at the same time that he is demonstrating that he can always be counted on for help. His immediate goal, in the context of a gang situation which continues to hold the potential for serious conflict, must be containment, checking the spread of antisocial activities to new groups and areas. But never out of sight is his ultimate goal of helping each of the gang members to develop his capacity for constructive, contributing, adjusted membership in the community.

In two of the four city boroughs in which the project operates, it works closely with Technical Advisory Committees composed of representatives of the social agencies, schools, law enforcement authorities and various other interests in the community. These committees, which are chaired by the borough's respective District Attorneys, are invaluable in identifying needs, problems and resources in the areas in which the Council of Social and Athletic Clubs functions. It is also through these committees that widespread community cooperation and support for the project is aroused.

It is the aim of the Youth Board, once the existing antisocial gangs have all been covered and their activities brought under control, to move on to the defensive and unattached groups of teen-agers which, in the absence of positive guidance and direction, often drift into antisocial behavior. In this way, it is hoped eventually to cut off a principal source of membership in the fighting gangs.

The approach of the Council of Social and Athletic Clubs is not and does not claim to be a panacea to the problem of juvenile delinquency or of teen-age gangs. Without the presence of a comprehensive and coordinated battery of services of the entire community, this project could not hope for success. However, within the bounds of the specific and important goals which the Street Club Project has set for itself, its method offers, we believe, the best answer yet developed to the problem of antisocial teen-age gangs.*

---

* See, also, Articles 157 and 158 of this book. — Ed.

184

Supervising the Juvenile Delinquent *

Jane E. Rinck

Any specialized police approach to the juvenile problem is necessarily limited to the small minority of American forces enjoying a numerical strength that is sufficient to staff and support the operation. Such devices prove far beyond the resources of the vast majority of police establishments, which must deal with all offenders through their general, unspecialized personnel. That in itself implies no inferiority as to either methods or results, since experience shows that results obtained through mere inauguration of a so-called specialized unit can fall far short of those secured through more general means.

In practically all major cities and in some small communities, police have established special bureaus for the purpose of dealing with the problem of juvenile delinquency. These special bureaus are relatively new; most have been established within the last twenty years. The activities of the juvenile bureaus differ widely from city to city. Activities include sponsorship and administration of recreation programs, organization of neighborhood councils, patrol of areas that harbor juvenile offenders, guarding school crossings, extensive casework advice and counseling, referral to other social agencies, community education through public speaking programs, use of volunteer counselors, "gang workers" to tame street gangs, and search for missing persons.

No one bureau does all of these things. In

---

* Reprinted from 291 Annals (1954), 78–86. Used by permission of the author and the publisher. See, also, S. and E. T. Glueck, Preventing Crime, New York, McGraw-Hill Book Company, Inc., 1936, 215–237; R. J. Milliken, "The Police and Children in Trouble," 18 Federal Probation (1954), 35–40; J. B. Nolan, "Police and Youth," 43 J. Crim. L., Criminology, and Police Science (1952–53), 339–345. — Ed.

fact, considerable disagreement may be found as to the activities that are most valuable and those that should not be performed at all. Some bureaus, for example, never patrol; others rely mainly on patrol. Some carry on extensive recreation programs; others make no attempt to conduct such programs.

In addition to these special bureaus, which generally emphasize a sociological approach to prevent delinquency, some large police departments have youth squads attached to detective bureaus. The squads deal with young offenders in a manner more in line with usual police methods. They tend to deal with young criminals, whereas juvenile bureaus tend to deal with children who have not advanced so far on the road to crime. Differences in the methods employed by the two units can be a source of trouble, and the allocation of cases correspondingly hard to make.

CONFUSING FEATURE

The very words "juvenile delinquent" cause confusion.* They now serve as a large receptacle into which all kinds of young human problems are tossed at random; problems of case-hardened junior criminals, of high-spirited offenders who will never do it again and who never do, and of small children who persist in running away. In addition, a special category has been devised called the "pre-delinquent," for children who will probably turn delinquent unless somebody does something. What the "something" is may also be debatable. Furthermore, since no one wants to tack an unfavorable label on a child, much double talk has been indulged in to avoid the use of precise definitions to describe a child's misdeeds or problems.

To compound the difficulty, various agencies and private individuals struggle with this problem. The result is that the identical misbehavior which would be subject to official action and official recording in one part of a city may be settled by private individuals or families in another part of the city, with no records to assist and guide later investigations. Even in the same neighborhood, differences arise according to the person or agency that happens to be concerned about the child. Private agencies or public departments of welfare may carry some cases which are indistinguishable from those carried by probation officers. Some school principals are exceedingly defensive concerning the reputations of their schools, and so settle or attempt to settle major difficulties in their own offices. Juvenile courts add to the hazy picture by handling some cases on an unofficial basis. Hence it is very difficult to count heads or to measure the success or failure of a given type of program in curbing or preventing delinquency.

Police have the task of holding a course though buffeted by confused seas and shifting winds. It need scarcely be emphasized that cities vary, that counties and towns may have quite different problems. Fortunately, not all of the problems arise in one place. Yet, despite many differences, some general truths for the operation of police programs for supervising juvenile delinquents seem to be emerging.

THE ROLE OF THE POLICE

Police should enforce the law. If police do not do it, no one else will. If the police department turns into just one more social agency, the community and its children have lost a valuable asset. No one wants police to be rough with children or ignorant of what little has been learned about delinquency. On the contrary, police should know more about delinquency than any other organization in the community.

When police concentrate on doing a good job of law enforcement for children as well as adults, they help to set a standard of acceptable conduct that becomes both vivid and helpful to children. This means stopping children who are violating laws, taking them home when it is apparent that they are getting into trouble. Day and night, endlessly, police need to explain the law and the trouble that comes through its violation. Children need this kind of curbstone schooling.

A program for law enforcement for children includes three main duties: (1) thorough patrol, (2) intelligent use of social and other agencies to aid individual children, and (3) police leadership in community planning for delinquency control.

PATROL AS A FOUNDATION FOR A JUVENILE PROGRAM

In those cities with specialized juvenile bureaus, the staff often is comparatively small;

---

* See Chapter 1 of this volume. — *Ed.*

therefore patrol has to be somewhat selective. Special attention is usually given to such trouble spots as bus terminals, railway stations, all-night movies, parks, and hotels. When patrol duty is performed during school hours, it is likely to duplicate work of attendance officers; therefore it is a less rewarding use of time. Delinquent acts increase when school lets out, and finally taper off at dawn. Saturdays and Sundays also bring extra opportunities for trouble. A nine-to-five schedule, five days a week, does not meet problems when they are still urgent. As with other police patrol, the juvenile patrol must be round the clock, with emphasis on the leisure and night hours.

Some bureaus attempt to get along without performing any patrol duty, and depend upon referrals from other branches of the force. This cannot provide adequate coverage, since other branches are usually tied up with traffic control or investigations of adult offenses. No matter how willing the regular patrol force may be to interest itself in children, members cannot take time to visit licensed premises, cannot leave their beats, and are not always free to escort children home.

Juvenile officers are not usually assigned to particular patrol sectors. Each one tries to cover the whole city or a very large section of it. Often an officer will cover a different section each night. No juvenile officer has a territory of his own for which he is definitely responsible. Hence he has no opportunity to become fully acquainted with people who can give him leads about where trouble may lie. No amount of spot maps or statistics can substitute for the knowledge of a district that comes only with long association. Other branches of police service rely heavily on this kind of localized knowledge. Juvenile bureaus should be so organized that they can assign a particular officer to a particular area.

As a valuable by-product, localized patrol can help to keep the juvenile bureau staff in close working association with the rest of the force. A staff that sits it out in a warm downtown office is readily forgotten, and if not forgotten, may earn some disfavor. Patrol work keeps the bureau personnel in touch with the regular stream of police work, and with the youth squads in particular. Patrol work can break up easily developed unprofessional habits of dealing only with nice children.

REFERRALS TO OTHER AGENCIES

A major police function of most juvenile work is to refer children who have been picked up on patrol to the agency or organization best able to help the child. This should entail a brief study by the officer of the child's situation and a reasonably rapid decision as to what should be done. The emphasis of most bureaus is placed not on arrest and prosecution, but rather on the adjustment of a child's problems so that he may become a happy and useful member of society. Not all cases are referred. The majority seem to be simple matters handled in a single interview. Experience indicates that most cases involve only one offense, or at most two offenses of minor significance. But when real trouble is brewing, other social agencies are called in. Most juvenile bureaus use the social service exchange in order to learn what other agencies may be acquainted with the child or his family.

On the surface, this seems like a simple matter; but it is not. In establishing a referral service, the police department is immediately and inextricably involved in all problems which confront social workers, in all the difficulties arising from gaps in welfare services, the shortcomings of juvenile courts, and the tribulations of social agencies.

Of all these problems, the one which is most baffling is the refusal of some private social agencies to accept cases referred by police unless the child or his parent physically appears at the agency and verbally and specifically asks for advice and counseling service. Many private agencies do not go out into the field, but rather write letters assigning time for an office interview. Rarely can children meet such conditions, particularly delinquent children. Private social agencies justify their policies by citing limitations of funds and staff. They do not want to be so burdened with following up people who have not asked for help that they have to refuse help to those who ask for it. However, they secure their funds through heartwarming appeals which do not jibe with such laissez faire policies. Some modification of policies should be possible more nearly to meet the broad responsibilities of a community agency.

Public welfare departments, no less than private social agencies, have established working methods that do not always help a child who has gotten into trouble. Public welfare agencies have been preoccupied with the granting of public assistance and the intricacies of investigation of need. Public *child* welfare agencies have tended to concentrate time on children who need placement outside their own homes. Children who happen to need such service may receive a great deal of careful consideration, understanding, and thorough medical care. The unfortunate child who is delinquent but who remains at home receives little if any attention from the public agency. Whether or not a child receives help from a public child welfare agency is therefore largely accidental and without any rational basis.

The textbook idea of a juvenile court as a place where a child receives the attention of experts is sometimes a reality, but often only partially true. At its worst, the court has become a placement agency for state institutions and is called upon only when such placement is needed. The quality of the institutions thereafter determines the value of the court. If the juvenile courts were all that they should be, many problems might be more easily solved. At present, some police go to considerable lengths to bypass the juvenile courts. A high-quality probation service could lift much of the burden now carried by police.

Schools. A plan for true collaboration between the schools and the police is essential. A child's world centers around the school, and when the child fails in school or quits too early with no developed skills to assist in the transition, police and the social agencies can never quite patch up gaps that appear. Police can sometimes find out about a child's trouble even before the school authorities, for some children apparently get along well in school but are in serious trouble outside of school hours. Minor adjustments of school program and extra attention by the teacher may help.

Some schools have rather elaborate guidance services, with staffs of psychiatrists, psychologists, and trained visiting teachers. Some guidance services will accept referrals only through classroom teachers, and so are not readily available to police. That policy does not take into account the total needs of the child, and may exclude the very children most in need of expert help. Thus, rigid intake policies go a long way toward destroying co-operation among the various government services. Even though guidance services are short of staff in some communities, selection of cases should be governed by the needs of the child rather than the source of the referral.

The regular staff of a school system can be a great source of help. Many school principals are alert to the problems of their neighborhoods and are well able to give intelligent and useful guidance to their students. Some teachers are leaders of the community and have an unmatched interest in the well-being of their pupils. Police can easily find these people and enlist their support.

Complicating factors. The relative strength or weakness of community agencies is only one aspect of the problem of referral. Police must also contend with other problems. Of no small import is the prejudice against police officers among social workers. The concepts of law and order, restraint and punishment, do not fit neatly into the psychological theories which form the basis of casework treatment.

Unfortunately, in this matter it has become necessary to state and restate the obvious; that ours is a government of law; that laws were passed with serious intent; that laws must be administered and applied with equality. We do not have one set of laws for clients of social agencies and another for the rest of our citizens. The two professions of police and social work alike are bound to comply with the provisions of law. Neither has any choice. This being the case, the two professions might just as well resolve their differences and each strive to appreciate the other's unique contributions to social living. Social workers do not want to be robbed or murdered; police do not want to clap little children into jail.

A further problem in referral is this: sometimes no one knows what to do. All the caseworkers, police officers, psychiatrists, teachers, and others cannot help. Everyone does his best and we still lose. By a frank acknowledgment of the fact that we still have not found all the solutions, we can keep the way open for further explorations. The professional insistence that it knows all the answers can obstruct us all in getting results.

POLICE SHOULD NOT BE PROBATION OFFICERS

Where police have found that large gaps

in services for children greatly hampered their efforts to prevent delinquency, they have developed programs of continuous supervision, a casework treatment service comparable to that of social agencies or probation departments. Programs of this kind include weekly or bi-weekly visits by police officers to children's homes, many conferences with parents, study of children's background to learn the sources of trouble, employment placement, and use of medical and psychiatric services.

In spite of laudable motives, continuous supervision of this kind constitutes a misuse of police authority. Though most officers are not uniformed when doing this work, police authority is present whatever the informality or disguise. Police enter homes and extract a measure of co-operation when social agencies cannot. Parents of delinquent or near-delinquent children are likely to consider themselves in no position to protest: the alternative may be institutional placement for their children. Some may not realize that they have a right to ask the officer to leave, so their ignorance is exploited.

Continuous supervision of parents by police would be intolerable. It is no less so for children. The police department may call it "social treatment in an authoritarian setting," but it is nothing more or less than probation without adjudication.* It is a violation of our system of justice.

It is not recommended here that children needing supervision should be abandoned by government services. Far from it. Police also need a few days to investigate and determine whether or not a child needs referral, and if so, where he should be referred. However, the public funds now used to pay for police "probation" work should be reallocated into regular probationary channels. In regular probationary work, authority is exerted openly, the police are not set up as judges, and children are not denied their right to treatment with a scrupulous regard for their substantial rights.

POLICE CAN LEAD SOME PARTS OF COMMUNITY PLANNING

Of all the governmental or private organizations in a community, the police department is the one that should know the most about juvenile delinquency and the effectiveness with which the problem is being handled. A well-informed police administrator can know exactly where his trouble spots lie, at what hours, with what age groups of children. He can know which social agencies are able to work in this field, and which ones cannot. He can know very readily and exactly what facilities are lacking to meet precise needs. Furthermore, he can make some very accurate predictions of the fate of many unfortunate children known to his department.*

All too often this information does not get out into the daylight where it can be of some use. People doing community planning underestimate the perceptiveness of the police department. For its part, the police department does not publicize its information so that it can be understood by those who are less well informed. Information that is pulled together in some form can help to direct the efforts of the well-intentioned and ever present committees on juvenile delinquency. Information can shape a specific program and cut down aimless generalizations about the horrors of modern youth. Police can, with little trouble, show a need for service for children aged ten to fourteen years at the corner of X Street and Y Avenue at 7:00 P.M.

The police could use the same information to pull together many different governmental services to help clean up particularly troublesome areas. A glance at a spot map of residences of delinquent children will reveal that there are clusters of spots in particular neighborhoods. Within an entire area that is well seeded with delinquency, some streets will be much worse than others, with troubles piling up in well-defined centers. A regular drive on these clusters by all agencies of government — public welfare, sanitation, housing, health, school attendance officers, and others — might serve to clean them up. Such areas need more than run-of-the-mill service. They need direct and co-ordinated action.

Concentrated attention is also needed for the small minority of children known to be growing up into full-fledged criminals. Police, as well as anyone else, can distinguish between the casual, happy-go-lucky lawbreakers and the children who are in serious difficulty. The lat-

---

* See Articles 49 and 50 of this volume. — Ed.

* Cf. Articles 171–173 of this volume. — Ed.

ter are now filed away alphabetically with casual offenders. Their records grow longer and longer. One after another the social workers take a turn, and finally give up and close the case. The police never really close their case. All the people who have struggled to help the particular child never or only rarely get together to compare notes, to lay out a plan, to review what they have done, or to analyze why they have failed. With the present lack of co-ordination, communities are doomed to repeat mistakes.* If the city has no effective council of social agencies to call case consultations, this task could fall to the police. Regardless of the auspices, it should be done.

PROVIDING RECREATON IS NOT A TASK FOR POLICE

In their earnest desire to halt juvenile delinquency, many police departments have initiated recreation programs for children. Such programs are intended to do double duty by creating public good will towards police. Police do not want to be considered tough thief catchers, and the recreation program probably gives them some affirmative publicity from time to time. But as they actually work out, police recreation programs are obsessed by many delusions. A police force that does its job efficiently, courteously, and with high professional standards will receive freely all the public good will that it thus earns. It will have no need to prove that "police are human" by conducting police softball tournaments or soapbox derbies, or by teaching boxing. If the department is not doing a good job of promoting public safety, the public will not be fooled by games with children. If it is doing a good job, it does not need the publicity.

Other departments of government should be able to conduct recreation programs better than police. Recreation is a full-time, lifetime profession with many men and women. Its techniques have no relation to the kinds of skills taught in police academies. Public recreation programs can be full of color and variety, can appeal to all ages, can make use of city-owned facilities. The know-how of an experienced, qualified recreation leader can bring into being city-wide programs almost by magic, certainly

with professional ease. Such people can avoid many of the problems that arise in controlling large programs.

The inadequacy of some public and private recreation programs is cited by police as a reason for police sponsorship. Even though true, the problem is not properly solved by setting up a new, duplicating, and perhaps competing program in the police department. Recreation will always be an auxiliary function, outside the main purpose of the police task. Recreation policies are inevitably guided by higher police officers who, also inevitably, are amateurs in organized recreation.

In some communities, police collect or sponsor the collection of funds to support the recreation program. When police collect and handle such funds, public misunderstanding is certain to arise. Police are able to collect money from private sources when other privately sponsored recreation fails. The plain fact is that many people will not refuse a policeman. Even though no one intends extortion, the objective manifestations are identical. The worthiness of the cause is no excuse. Police should not collect money for any purpose, from anyone, under any circumstances.

Those who work with children who already are well along the road to delinquency and adult crime express considerable doubt as to the effectiveness of recreational programs in helping these children. Such children will not participate; or if they do, they break the place up. Many private agencies definitely do not welcome hefty and destructive adolescents. Cure through referral to a recreation center is not automatic. The child must be fitted into a suitable group and must be accepted by the group. The recreation leader has to make a special effort to help. When delinquency arises from serious personality disorders, it may be quite unreasonable to expect a child to fit in at all.

In any event, a recreation program that is founded on the negative idea of preventing trouble is founded on a distorted conception. Most children are not delinquent and never will be, even in the worst of our slum areas. The majority of children are reasonably well behaved, have a healthy interest in sports, and enjoy lawful fun. If the community provides well for these children, plenty of room will be left to handle the small minority of delinquents.

---

* See Article 178 of this volume. — *Ed.*

It is not a part of the police job to provide recreation for all.

The positive interest of police in working with groups of children should, however, be preserved and cultivated. On an off-duty basis, away from official sponsorship, much good can be done. As in police probation work, abandonment of needed recreation programs is not suggested, but rather a transfer to other auspices.

THE JUVENILE BUREAU IS NO BETTER THAN ITS PERSONNEL

The effectiveness of the juvenile program is determined in large measure by methods of personnel selection, training, and supervision. It is not practical to pin a new title on a man or woman and expect a qualified performance that fits the title. Nor can the police administrator rely solely on fixed educational qualifications or the results of intelligence tests to make his selection for him. Some units have tried both, and the results are not good.

Usually a basic qualification for a male juvenile officer is membership on the force. Two or three years of experience are often required. He must have proved himself a reliable officer who can be called for other duty in an emergency.

Since women cannot be recruited from within the force, other qualifications are needed. The day of the hard-boiled police matron has passed, and nothing should be allowed to recall it. Matrons are still needed, but should not be confused with women police officers. College education and some work experience are usable minimum requirements. Since women also do detective work, their adaptability for this service must be considered. Stringent physical requirements are necessary to ensure that a woman can stand the wear and tear of patrol duty. Basic training along with men recruits is essential.

Juvenile officers, both men and women, must have a genuine liking for children. This qualification is so obvious that sometimes it is overlooked. It is a quality that can be observed readily, and its absence is a categorical imperative for removal to other duty. Other personal qualifications of tact, judgment, and mental balance are required for all police work, and in equal measure in juvenile bureau work.

Training and supervision. Juvenile officers need training beyond regular police work. Some departments have developed their own training courses, some depend wholly on supervisory conferences to train, and some have sponsored the pursuit of advanced degrees at schools of social work. Training should help to develop skillful interviewers and bring some understanding of children and the reasons why they get into trouble. Training can give the officer something to work with, tools that are more useful than monotonous warnings to be "good."

Training has to include precise information regarding the social agencies in the community and the state. In small communities this is not a great chore, but in larger cities the list of available agencies may be very long. These agencies are the tools of the trade, and the juvenile officer must know not only the avowed policies of the agencies, but also their actual working policies. The better the officer knows the agency staff, the more likely he is to receive good service.

Furthermore, the officer can develop unofficial contacts that can be useful for individual children. Some church workers can be of great help. Most areas have leading citizens who in effect act as guardians for certain children in the neighborhood. These people can be discovered if sought; it may be the postman, the keeper of a drugstore, the editor of the neighborhood newspaper, or a housewife with an exceptionally warm and understanding heart.

Despite good training, personnel will not be effective without supervision. In new units, sergeants, lieutenants, and captains who may be able supervisors of regular police services can find themselves somewhat baffled by the problem of supervising a unit with functions that are not clearly defined. As a result, the atmosphere of a soft berth can develop, disguised however as a noble purpose, and trimmed with academic degrees.

The supervisor has to know what he wants. If it is patrol work, are his people patrolling, shopping, in the movies, or at home? Where do they go? Where does he want them to go? If it is referrals, are they referring all the cases to one or two agencies? Do most of the referrals bounce back? Are decisions made, or do cases dangle? Does the staff follow his policy, or is each man and woman his own mentor? Are the records in order? What is the staff doing with children and with children's problems?

Promotion. The juvenile bureau will not be a good place to work unless some provision is made for promotion, either within the bureau or to other departments of the force. A large bureau may provide satisfactory promotion within the four corners of juvenile work. In such instances some preference should be given to those who have experience and special training in the bureau and its work. If this is not done, the fieldworkers will always know more than the supervisors — an unwholesome situation. Small bureaus of two or three persons cannot provide such opportunities, and so promotions must be made to other branches of the force. If the bureau demands extra training and stiff standards of performance, additional salary opportunities should be part of a promotion system.

. . . . .

The time has long since passed for expressions of pride in our methods of tackling the problem of delinquency. Adult crime furnishes tragic proof of the fact that what is being done is by no means the answer. Police are newcomers in the field of juvenile delinquency. They have started out in every direction at once. But they have a fresh zeal that should be welcomed; and they do not give up easily.

185

Casework Treatment in a Police Setting *

Jacob Chwast

The doubts regarding the effectiveness of casework treatment in an authoritative setting have been steadily diminishing. We have long known that the delinquent should benefit from modern casework methods. Delinquents generally are unwilling clients and the ordinary social agency is not geared to meet them at their level of functioning. Even if the social worker of such an agency succeeds in making a slight dent in the armor of this type of client, he is almost invariably ill-equipped to deal with the kind of intense problems which create anxiety, guilt, and lead to acting-out disturbances. The entirely permissive nature of the relationship between client and caseworker usually ends with the delinquent's staying away with the inevitable result that he will get into trouble again.

This problem is of prime importance to the Juvenile Aid Bureau which is a branch of the New York City Police Department designated to work toward the prevention of juvenile delinquency and the rehabilitation of youth in trouble. It is staffed by policemen and policewomen, specially selected and trained for its particular work, who are distributed to 12 field units throughout the City. The field units receive annually about 19,000 reports of juveniles who have committed delinquent acts of one kind or another. These cases are screened in terms of the problems which they present and are then disposed of in such a manner as to bring about the appropriate solution to the difficulties which are unearthed.

Another group of cases are those where court action alone can insure the acquisition of help necessary to meet the needs of the juvenile offender or his situation. In the vast majority of cases an admonitory letter or discussion and clarification with the client and his parents is sufficient. A residual group remains unsuited for court action where an urgent need for casework assistance exists but cannot be secured by referral for a variety of reasons. These constitute the cases which are considered by our agency for more extended social treatment. Each year they number about four to five hundred. The Juvenile Aid Bureau attempts to refer as many of these cases as it can to outside agencies. For all of the others, casework treatment is provided by our own staff.*

FLEXIBILITY OF APPROACH

From its inception the Juvenile Aid Bureau clearly saw the paramount significance of reach-

* Reprinted from 18 *Federal Probation* (1954), 35–40. Used by permission of the author and the publisher.

* I am not certain of the present extent of this type. — *Ed.*

ing out to the client in fulfilling its objectives. This meant that the casework relationship need not be confined to verbal material developed within an interview room. If the client could not for one reason or another come to the unit office serving his area, the field worker would automatically make every effort to see the client at home, the community center, school, or elsewhere. This approach which has in many ways been taken over by other agencies which attempt to treat delinquents is essentially what has become known as "aggressive casework."[1]

THE ADVANTAGE OF THE AUTHORITATIVE SETTING

The worker within a police setting — police caseworker if you will — has, however, distinct advantages in making an initial contact with a client in this regard. Our experience in numerous cases has shown that an authoritative background has not interfered with establishing therapeutic rapport with our clients. A trained police caseworker is almost always able to enter through the front door to carry through the exploratory and feeling-out phases of the casework contact. The case of Dolores describes this in action.

Dolores was reported to us by several neighbors for having hit younger girls. We were warned that the girl's mother would not cooperate. Our caseworker, a policewoman of eight years' experience in the Juvenile Aid Bureau, had no difficulty in getting into the house and found that the girl's mother who was a widow was happy to have somebody she could trust help her. She resented the neighbors' interference but showed she was genuinely concerned with her daughter's difficulties. The woman, nervous and frail, felt protected and secure by the fact that our worker was connected with the Police Department. This first interview initiated a fruitful relationship for some time with both the girl and the mother who were helped greatly.

At the outset, it may be true that the handicap with which the police worker must contend is the client's distrust of him. This distrust, however, is mixed with sufficient respect to enable the officer at least to meet with the client and establish a personal relationship. The many conspicuously positive outcomes of treatment by superior officers assigned to such work in military rehabilitation centers and the excellent work of many parole and probation officers attest to this point of view independently of our own findings. Likewise, an important function of the courts as seen by a large portion of the professional community is that of providing adequate treatment facilities to offenders, especially delinquents, by the use of its authority.[2] One need not here discuss the effectiveness of specific techniques in the treatment of delinquents by courts, but it is nevertheless clear that authority per se is required for this purpose. The misuse of authority has perhaps often produced a misunderstanding as to its potentially tremendous utility. The requisite competence can be acquired by the police caseworker who has had the opportunity to test out the limits and consequences of the use of his authority under many and varied circumstances. Authority developed in this fashion is finely attuned to the everchanging patterns of feelings and attitudes appearing during the course of a dynamic interpersonal relationship.

The non-police worker who attempts to meet the delinquent for the first time is probably in the more difficult position. Whereas the policeman represents an awesome but known quantity with whom the delinquent or his parents must come to terms, the other is entirely unknown and hence may be treated with far greater suspicion or contempt. His inability to put his foot in the door is ofttimes in sharp contrast to the relative facility with which the police worker gains access to the client.

Just as every discipline develops its own traditions and methods in solving the problems which constitute its daily work, so is it true in the case of the policeman. An accepted practice in police work is to be available at any hour of the day or night. This reflects itself in the case of the Juvenile Aid Bureau worker by his making appointments to see his client at such times as are suitable to him, be it at the office or at the client's home. This procedure sharply differs from typical case-

[1] Lionel C. Lane, "Strengthening the Child's Own Home — Application of 'Aggressive Casework' in Protective Services to the Family and Children in Their Own Homes." Presented at the New York State Conference of Social Welfare, November 12, 1951.

[2] Alex C. Sherriffs, "The Authority Aspect of the Worker–Client Relationship: Asset or Liability?" *Federal Probation*, June 1953, pp. 22–25.

work hours of availability which are almost universally confined to the daytime.

Frequently we meet with parents such as Mrs. Smith, the mother of fourteen-year-old Henry, who had been reported to us for stealing flashlight batteries from the 5 and 10 cents store. An attractive woman, Mrs. Smith also had three other children whom she had to support with her meager earnings from a hat factory. The worker casually recalled that he had expected to see her about 5 o'clock. At this, Mrs. Smith stated bluntly she could not come at that hour because she had to work. She was the sole breadwinner of the family. The plain truth is that we are dealing with clients whose daily lives confront them with acute problems for survival and they are not willing to make further sacrifices. When the worker pointed out to Mrs. Smith that he could be seen at her convenience after she had finished work, she was very much pleased.

THE RELATION OF SOCIAL AGENCIES TO THE DELINQUENT

One can speak freely about the resistance of the delinquent and his family coming to the counseling agency to see the caseworker, but should we also not ask ourselves this question: Do not the vast majority of our agencies systematically and quite thoroughly resist coming to this type of client? Treatment, we feel, should not place additional hardships upon the client such as worrying about the loss of income. The current practice of keeping open one night a week for working parents is a step in the right direction but as far as we can see it is not sufficient. We have found that the best hours to meet with our clients usually begin about 3:30 p.m. and continuing through the evening. Our policy, accordingly, has been to schedule office appointments or home visits evenings, including Saturdays and Sundays. The bulk of our caseload is handled at these times. This procedure is followed not because we think the client should not put himself out but rather because this is a more realistic policy. One of the reasons why a police agency can undertake visiting clients residing in poorly lighted, foreboding neighborhoods is the familiarity of the police worker with such conditions. Furthermore, as a policeman he is better prepared to deal with unforeseen hazards which may arise.

EVOLUTION OF THEORETICAL APPROACH

The Juvenile Aid Bureau, as it evolved during the course of the years, has benefited considerably from its background of police thinking which rightly emphasizes the necessity for direct, concrete action in meeting the needs of its clients. In order to obtain the requisite training in carrying out our highly specialized work, our staff attended professional schools such as the New York School of Social Work and the Fordham School of Social Service, in addition to our own in-service training program. They have concentrated upon learning and using modern casework techniques.

In the beginning much of the casework of the Juvenile Aid Bureau fell to its lot because no facilities were available elsewhere. Confronted with numberless situations demanding immediate help, it became necessary to develop our own facilities for handling such cases. The Bureau has always been and still is willing to send such cases to any other community resource which could render adequate assistance. We do believe, however, that most such cases would require authoritative intervention very similar to the work done by ourselves in many cases. It is our belief that authority expertly used can be of primary therapeutic significance.

MAKING CONTACT WITH THE DELINQUENT

Treatment as seen by the Juvenile Aid Bureau is a process which is set into motion immediately upon the initial contact with the client. Even in those situations which only require ordinary police action, the Bureau worker always retains awareness of the delinquent as an individual: his personality and social environment as it bears upon his potential for rehabilitation. The offense in many ways determines the course of action available to the worker, setting limits to what he can or cannot do on behalf of the client. However, the worker, very mindful of these prescribed limits, attempts as much as he possibly can to maintain a friendly, warm, insightful relationship with the child. It cannot be denied that sometimes the force of police intervention creates a block to the development of a cordial ongoing beneficial contact. We have found nonetheless, despite the belief held by many working in non-authoritative agencies, that such blocks are not inevitable but, on the contrary, can be managed therapeutically by the worker depending upon his sensitivity, maturity, and skill in functioning as an agent of authority. In some cases it has even been possible for us to reactivate casework with a client whom we may formerly have been required to take into court.

An illustration of this is seen in the case of Ralph M. Since he was twelve years old, a dozen complaints had been lodged against him ranging from disorderly conduct to robbery and felonious assault. Although he appeared to come from a relatively stable and economically secure family in which he was the second of three siblings, the boy early developed a hatred for authority. At home rivalry with his siblings was acute; at school he was aggressive and abusive. When thirteen, the boy was sent to a state training school where he was said to have adjusted well and he was released on parole. At this time Ralph was picked up again for malicious mischief. The Juvenile Aid Bureau worker who investigated the offense consulted with his parole officer who decided that it would be best for the boy to return to serve out the remainder of his sentence in a "controlled environment." About two years later, Ralph's parents got in touch with the Bureau because they believed that he had become addicted to drugs and thought that we might be able to help them. The worker who was assigned discussed the problem with Ralph who agreed to voluntarily enter Bellevue Hospital for medical treatment. After he came out of the hospital free of physiological dependence upon drugs, Ralph returned to see his worker who succeeded in helping him obtain necessary psychiatric treatment for his severe personality problems.

This case illustrates the difficult situations with which we must contend. It shows the hardships we must sometimes overcome in establishing a casework relationship. Despite his obvious abnormality, we made every effort to continue working with the boy throughout the vicissitudes of his delinquent career. Our policy is to assign another worker to handle the casework aspects with a client when another of our staff may have had to resort to repressive police action.

As we see it at the present time treatment and rehabilitation fit into the Bureau's program in four different ways. They are as follows:

1. To refer for treatment to another agency.
2. To use authority to bring into treatment by another agency or professional person.
3. To use authority to help maintain in treatment by an outside agency or other professional person.
4. To undertake social casework treatment where it is not possible to obtain this elsewhere.

REFERRING FOR TREATMENT TO ANOTHER AGENCY

In common with the practices employed by the vast majority of social work agencies, the Juvenile Aid Bureau in its early meetings with the client attempts to assess what his needs are, the extent to which they are being met, and the manner in which his unfulfilled needs, if these lead to maladjustment, can be met. If it is at all possible to obtain the help necessary to accomplish the latter, the field worker tries to refer the case to any accredited agency or professional person who is available. Referral is not considered an information-giving procedure but a process which may entail considerable preparation of both the client and the appropriate agency. It is often overlooked that an effective referral can itself be of therapeutic value to the client and also, in many cases, demands the same positive orientation essential in good casework or psychotherapy. From the very moment of his first contact with the client, the worker starts to lay the foundation for a referral. A number of our cases are successfully referred to other agencies in this fashion.

An illustration of this can be seen in the case of Hannah C., a thirteen-year-old girl apprehended the first time for shoplifting. The girl, who had a voracious appetite for sweets, had already been involved in petty pilfering for some time. Her two younger sisters appeared to be somewhat prettier than Hannah and were favored by the parents. A bright girl, Hannah's mental ability seemed conspicuously to exceed her motor development especially in her younger years. This took the form of clumsiness which prevented her from successfully competing with girls of her own age and making her feel anxious and frustrated. At school the girl was doing poorly.

After several interviews our caseworker helped the girl and her parents to recognize the need for help with their mutual interpersonal problems. The mother accepted the responsibility for initiating the necessary steps which led the family to maintain a lengthy contact with a family counseling agency.

USING AUTHORITY TO BRING INTO TREATMENT BY ANOTHER AGENCY OR PROFESSIONAL PERSON

Often the usual permissive casework attitudes are totally inadequate in attempting referrals to other agencies in the manner which has been described above. While the family may not interfere with our carrying out the exploratory phase of the contact by our caseworker, they frequently fail to heed our suggestions about going for help. The fact is that many of the more serious delinquent offenders are involved in situations wherein it is necessary to insist that they go for treatment. This is the only sure way of knowing that this will be done. The argument that the client must willingly appear before the treatment resource under his own power is totally unrealistic when it comes to cases of this type. We feel, and this has been confirmed by the contention of other authorities in the field of delinquency treatment, that professionals to whom we refer such clients must possess specialized and newer methods in approaching the offender.[3] We can definitely say that we have found surprising success in effecting referrals of this kind.

Consider the case of Robert M., first reported to us when thirteen years of age for peeping through windows. He was a handsome and intelligent boy who came from a family background that superficially did not appear wanting. A year later repetition of the same offense resulted in our successfully bringing the family into contact with a family casework agency.

Several years later, however, Robert again was accused of voyeurism but the complainant refused to press the charge. The caseworker assigned recognized from the boy's nervous mannerism, generalized timidity, and inhibition that he was in need of some form of psychiatric assistance. Upon this he contacted an agency specializing in the treatment of the offender which agreed to assume responsibility for the case. Inasmuch as Robert had not accepted opening feelers that he might be willing to receive such assistance, the worker flatly insisted that the boy must go for therapy and told him

that he would see to it that he went. Of course, our worker appreciated that he could not implement his ultimatum from a legal standpoint. He did, however, skillfully gauge the full psychological impact of authoritarian display at this point in helping the boy make up his mind. In consequence the boy did appear for his initial interview for psychotherapy. Our check-up at the end of two months revealed that he was deeply involved in the therapeutic process.

USING AUTHORITY TO HELP MAINTAIN IN TREATMENT WITH AN OUTSIDE AGENCY OR PERSON

Ideally speaking, sound casework procedures are based upon the principle that maximum cooperation be elicited from all persons or agencies professionally concerned with a given client. Further, it is necessary to co-ordinate their activities so as to insure that no conflict will result but, on the contrary, that necessary measures will be undertaken optimally. This, of course, represents consistent work on behalf of the client from different sources, each of which contribution fits into a total treatment plan. Because of the heterogeneity of approaches to helping the client, not only among social workers but with other professional persons, such an ideal integration of therapeutic forces can seldom be aligned.

Although lack of such co-ordination may not necessarily prove fatal to movement and constructive change in the case of the average agency client, it is crucially imperative when working with the offender. Whether he is adult or juvenile, we have found in our considerable experience with delinquents over the course of many years that the vast majority of agency failures in the treatment of the delinquent have resulted from complete inability to understand the role of authoritativeness and the extent to which it should be used for treatment purposes. Conventional social work practices today frown upon multiple transference situations. Agencies to whom we refer cases usually insist that the Juvenile Aid Bureau withdraw its interest. On the other hand if they do see fit to call upon us, it is usually only for punitive measures. The latter may occur when a social worker or therapist feels threatened and wants to use the Juvenile Aid Bureau worker to gratify his own unconscious needs to punish the client.

Recently, however, we have been finding an

---

[3] Melitta Schmideberg, M.D., "Some Practical Problems in the Treatment of Delinquents," *Psychiatric Quarterly Supplement*, Part 2, 1949.

increasing desire by persons engaged in the treatment of delinquents to use us with consistency and real effect. The therapist has learned that the most difficult problems with offenders arise in the establishment of therapeutic contact and rapport, and in its continuance.[4] Since the delinquent is usually too unstable to face up to the requirements of a therapeutic relationship the Bureau worker must give him support.

The therapist is made to feel perfectly free to call upon the Juvenile Aid Bureau worker and discuss with him pertinent problems which have arisen during the course of treatment in such instances as when the patient stops coming or when complex practical problems arise. Sometimes depending upon the circumstances, he may help to erase a misunderstanding by the client concerning the therapeutic experience, or he may act in a strictly supervisory manner — sort of checking on the client's attendance.

UNDERTAKING SOCIAL CASEWORK TREATMENT [*]

The Juvenile Aid Bureau provides long-range casework services for children who are not acceptable to other social agencies and for whom a court appearance is not indicated. It also sees clients on a short-term basis where the offense is not of a serious nature. The effectiveness of a brief contact of this type which meets emergent crises immediately and practically on the spot has been too often underestimated by professional people in non-police circles. They simply have never been in the position of meeting cases of this type.

In essence, the worker in such short-contact cases calls the child and his parents into the field office. In a firm yet understanding way, he holds the child to account for his misdeeds and if necessary does likewise with the parents. The worker, at such times, scrupulously avoids allying himself with either parent, child, or complainant, presenting himself as an objective individual whose job it is to find out the facts and to face these parties with the realities of the situation. Authority forthrightly used in this manner depends upon a rapid, accurate evaluation of the case which has in such in-

stances precluded the necessity of setting up the type of relationship requiring a closer, warmer rapport for sustained casework contact. To give some idea of the degree of flexibility used in this approach, the worker may behave as a stern, interested authority figure or at the other extreme as the proverbial "Dutch uncle." The client and members of his family in such cases are seen one, two, or three times at most.

The long-range casework approach is far different from the above as the worker meets his client. Since he is about to start a more extended relationship during the course of which significant tangible change in the client and his situation will be sought, the worker tries to relate with as much acceptance and permissiveness as is possible under the circumstances. He lets the client know who and what he is and how far he can go with him. This he relays gradually in terms of the developing rapport. The measure of success which the worker obtains depends upon his own security in acting in the very difficult joint capacity as a permissive caseworker and, also, as an agent of authority. The blending of these two components in the practice of authoritative casework demands of the worker intelligence, maturity, and sensitivity of the highest order. Not only must the worker be well-versed in the techniques of social casework but he must also have had considerable experience as a policeman in learning how to use authority non-punitively and constructively.

Take the case of Arlene J., a pretty, slender fifteen-year-old girl who was apprehended by a uniformed policeman in the act of setting fire to a car at three o'clock in the afternoon. The manner in which she tried to do this, by stuffing the exhaust pipe with newspapers and rags which she then ignited, and the reason she gave, which was to get even with her former school teacher, raised a suspicion of mental disturbance. This was later reinforced when interviewed at the field unit office by her display of infantile negativism and the discordance of her feelings as related to her intellectual processes. The unit worker quickly perceived the necessity of referring this apparently disturbed youngster to some agency providing psychiatric assistance. After a little time, Arlene's initial guardedness was overcome enough to ascertain her fears about seeing a "brain doctor." A later discussion with school

[4] Melitta Schmideberg, M.D., and Jack Sokol, "The Function of Contact in the Psychotherapy of Offenders," Social Casework, November, 1953.
[*] Long-range casework services recently discontinued.

authorities revealed that this girl and her sisters had been fighting out a feud with the school which had started with the mother years before. It was also learned that efforts had been made time and again by school authorities and other persons to enjoin the mother to take up her problem with a counseling agency. This met with no success. The mother expressed to the worker her antagonism toward social agencies and her unwillingness to go to them for help. In view of these facts, the field worker asked her whether she would object to one of our own people continuing with her. The mother shrugged her shoulders indifferently as if to imply, "Well, that's your business."

The new caseworker first assigned found her reception to be one of annoyed tolerance. However, she persisted in returning and after about three visits, her genuine non-threatening interest coupled with the strength and conviction of her manner made the mother realize that she was dealing with somebody who could be trusted. The worker consulted with her supervisor upon several occasions and realized that her primary objective with this family would be to get them to accept the necessary counseling for the mother and intensive psychotherapy for Arlene.

As of now, several months since the initial contact, probably the most significant outcome in this case has been the new experience for this woman and her family in learning that someone is available who can try to help them meet their difficulties in life. Now at least they know that the whole world is not against them. How much more can be accomplished only time will tell. At least we can see in this case that a worker coming from a police setting has not only been able to put his foot in, then enter through the door, but has also been offered a chair.

The Juvenile Aid Bureau of the Police Department of the City of New York over the years has fitted itself into the total repertory of treatment facilities available to the delinquent and pre-delinquent child in the community. Other aspects of the work of the Juvenile Aid Bureau have not received attention in this paper. The Bureau is in the full-time business of coping with the delinquent problem. It will continue to assist and stimulate in every way that it possibly can such persons and organizations who can help accomplish this objective. The Bureau feels that it is doing a pioneer job in an uncharted and extremely difficult area of social treatment. To meet this challenge it has had to forge many of its tools empirically. The policy of the present leadership has been to incorporate into its operation so far as possible knowledge and skills provided by the related scientific disciplines.

186

An Experiment in Prevention of Delinquency *

Edwin Powers

More public and private funds are pouring into crime prevention programs every year, and yet it is currently reported that youthful criminals are increasing in numbers and in the seriousness of their offenses. To account for this perverse condition one has a choice of a wide variety of explanations, depending upon whether one's frame of reference is psychiatric, sociological, or religious. Can delinquency be prevented? Has research an answer?

Numerous statistical studies have demonstrated the close association of overt delinquent behavior with specific personal and environmental factors. Relatively few reports, however, have highlighted the effectiveness or ineffectiveness of methods of prevention. Such reports as have been written are generally based on nothing more than faith or bold assertion, buttressed by illustrative cases.

THE CAMBRIDGE–SOMERVILLE YOUTH STUDY

Dr. Richard C. Cabot relatively early in life won a reputation in medical research as the "greatest contributor to cardiology in our gener-

* Reprinted from 261 Annals (1949), 77–88. Used by permission of the author and the publisher. For a detailed discussion of the Cambridge–Somerville experiment, see E. Powers and H. Witmer, An Experiment in the Prevention of Delinquency, New York, Columbia University Press, 1951. — Ed.

ation." [1] In his later years he was equally well known and respected in the fields of social service and social ethics. He was keenly aware of the discrepancy in method between the laboratory technician and the social scientist who seldom had available adequate measures of evaluation by which to check his practice. In his presidential address to the National Conference of Social Work in 1931 he asserted:

Many of us are now forced to base our opinions of the value of any given piece of social work largely on the character, experience, and expertness of those in charge of it. But even persons of the highest value may be doing work of far less value than they and others think, unless it can be shown to measure up reasonably to the standards which it sets for itself. [He looked forward to] the much-to-be-desired epoch when we shall control our results by comparisons with a parallel series of cases in which we did nothing.[2]

A few years later Dr. Cabot established a ten-year research project in delinquency prevention utilizing, perhaps for the first time in history, a carefully constructed control group.[3] To each of six men and four women, trained in social work or allied professional fields, were assigned a number of boys, usually 30 to 35, all under the age of twelve (with an average age of ten and one-half), in the hope that by wise and friendly counsel supplemented by social casework techniques, these young children might be encouraged to make the most of their

potential assets and become useful, law-abiding citizens. About half of the group were already showing definite signs that pointed to a delinquent career.

The plan called for an evaluation by comparing 325 T boys at the end of a contemplated ten-year program with a C group [4] similar in numbers and in all other relevant respects but receiving no help or guidance from the study, the hypothesis being that if the two groups were similar at the outset, then any significant behavioral differences between them at the end of the program could reasonably be attributed to the major variable in the picture — the counselor's treatment.

LENGTH OF PROGRAM

Work was started at the end of 1937 with five selected boys. Seventy-one additional boys were placed in the program in 1938, and work with the remainder was commenced during the first half of 1939. After two or three experimental years, 65 boys, or 20 per cent of the total group, were dropped from the program because they presented no special problems and were definitely non-delinquent.

The remaining 260 boys, including both the delinquency-prone and the non-delinquent, were retained for varying periods of time. Death of a few, removal of some of the boys from the local area, the loss of staff due to the demands of World War II, and the departure of some of the older boys for war service or enlistment in the Merchant Marine made it impossible for the counselors to continue with all of the 260 boys. Close associations were maintained and casework continued with 113 boys for an average period of four years and two months; with 72 boys for an average of five years and eleven months; and with 75 boys for an average of six years and nine months. For none did the treatment program, which closed on December 31, 1945, last more than eight years and one month, although many of the counselors still keep in touch with the boys assigned to them.

WHERE THEY ARE NOW

More than a decade has now elapsed since the study's first acquaintance with these boys and their families. The group's average age is

[1] Dr. Paul D. White, "Richard Clarke Cabot, 1868–1939," *The New England Journal of Medicine*, Vol. 220 (1939), pp. 1049–52.

[2] National Conference of Social Work, *Proceedings*, 1931, 3–24.

[3] This project, located in Cambridge, Massachusetts, was called the Cambridge–Somerville Youth Study, as it embraced in its operations the city of Cambridge and the adjacent city of Somerville. It was supported entirely by funds contributed by the Ella Lyman Cabot Foundation, a charity incorporated in Massachusetts in 1935. Dr. Richard C. Cabot and Dr. P. Sidney de Q. Cabot were the original co-directors of the project until the death of the former in May 1939, when Dr. P. Sidney de Q. Cabot became the sole director. On his resignation on January 1, 1941, the author became the director of the project until its termination. During the course of the treatment program a total of approximately 75 people were employed, half of them on a part-time schedule. Approximately 22,000 pages of records have been compiled relating the story of what happened in the lives of these boys over a crucial period of their existence.

[4] T and C in this article refer to the treatment and control groups.

now twenty — the oldest twenty-two and eight months. A number of these youngsters who were in the lower grades of the elementary public schools when first known to the study are now married and fathers of a second generation. Some are earning good incomes, some are unemployed, some are officers or enlisted men in the Army or the Navy, a few are still in school, while others are in reformatories or prisons.

The study, over the years has seen boys become delinquent in spite of its best preventive efforts, and it has likewise seen others, who seemed less promising at the outset, achieve considerable success. Take the case of Dick, for example. A counselor became Dick's friend and visited him at frequent intervals but utterly failed to prevent him from expressing his assaultive tendencies, which led him in his later adolescent years into robbery and eventually into State Prison. Assisting in the treatment plan were a psychiatrist, numerous school teachers, and two social workers from another agency called into the picture by the study. Three foster homes, though temporarily apparently successful, had no real deterrent effect on the boy.

Or there is the case of Tony, a persistent truant. The social workers, cooperating with the schools and the attendance officers, using all techniques available to them, supplemented by psychiatric advice and the counsel of a clinical psychologist, watched helplessly as this boy developed into a sly thief and was committed to a county training school for truancy and subsequently to three different correctional institutions before he reached his nineteenth birthday.

On the other hand, we see John, well on his way toward a delinquent career when first known to his counselor, now a law-abiding citizen with a good job. If his counselor had not shown a friendly interest in him, he tells us, he would today be confined in a prison or reformatory.

The fathers of these boys, too, were often appreciative of the work done for the child or for the entire family. At the end of the treatment program Joe's father wrote the counselor a letter of warm appreciation for keeping the family together and giving him the courage and confidence to carry on in spite of most adverse circumstances.

The picture of what happened in treatment — how many boys became delinquent and how many did not — will be more meaningful if the research structure is first briefly described.

THE EXPERIMENTAL DESIGN

As the project was essentially a study in the prevention of boy delinquency, it called for the selection of boys under 12 who had not yet become delinquent but who might some day constitute part of the prison population. Who were these hypothetical youngsters, and where did they live? That was the first problem. Secondly, it was necessary to balance this group of pre-delinquents with boys who showed no such signs of early delinquency, for one aspect of the project was to study a wide variety of boys and to note later what kind became delinquent and what kind did not. Furthermore, for practical reasons it was necessary to include a group of presumed non-delinquents, for to deal solely with boys who would be labeled "pre-delinquent" would be unfair to the boys and impractical of accomplishment.

Teachers in the Cambridge and Somerville public schools and the Cambridge parochial schools submitted on request the names of many boys whom they regarded as "difficult" (in the study's scheme this meant "probably pre-delinquent") and many others whom they considered normal or "average" boys. All referrals were subsequently classified in accordance with the delinquency prognostic scale as described below. Approximately 1,500 names of boys under 12 were submitted by the schools. [5] At this point neither the boy nor his family knew that his name had been submitted.

Social agencies in the locality were also requested to submit names of "difficult" boys known to them. Court records were examined and police and probation officers were interviewed in order to include all boys in both cities who at an early age were considered troublesome or likely to become delinquent.

---

[5] The original plan called for boys between the ages of 6 and 7. It was soon learned that boys in this age group were not well known by the schools, and because of their tender years were referred far less frequently than the older boys. It was necessary, therefore, in order to get the desired number of boys of pre-delinquent tendencies, to shift the upper age limit to 11 and later to 12 when delays in starting the program were encountered.

From these supplementary sources 450 names (with some duplications) were received.

Thus, at the end of a two-year search, there were on file at the study the names of all boys in both cities (with the exception of boys attending private schools or the Somerville parochial schools) who were believed destined to become delinquent, plus an equal number who were thought to be non–pre-delinquent.

How Each Boy Was Studied

A comprehensive picture of the boy, his family, and his social environment was obtained from a variety of sources. Social workers were sent to the homes for interviews with one or both of the boy's parents. Information concerning the boy's developmental history, his habits, his recreation, his attitudes toward school, his religion, and his personality was obtained and recorded. Basic information relating to the parents' education, employment history, social activities, and so on, was also sought. The boy's potentialities as well as the total impact of forces upon him were described by the social workers with their own interpretations and numerous rating scales. Although they went to the boys' homes unannounced and without previous notification to the parents, they were, in most cases, cordially received. They reported that in three-quarters of the homes they were received in a very friendly spirit, while in only eight cases out of 839 homes visited did the parents definitely refuse to be interviewed in the first instance.

Extensive information was then obtained from each boy's teacher through long personal interviews conducted by a member of the staff, supplemented by the checking by the teacher of rating scales and cards listing personality traits. The teacher was also asked to give a brief personality description of the boy.

Staff psychologists gave each boy tests to measure his mental ability and school achievement, and the boy's grade placement was recorded. Dr. Richard C. Cabot himself gave the physical examinations, noting at the same time the general impressions made upon him by the child. He was assisted by a staff nurse who independently recorded her own impressions and interviews with the boys. Official reports about delinquency or criminality of boys or parents were obtained from the State Board of Probation, from the local courts, and from the police and probation officers of the two cities, all of whom were very cooperative. Information was also obtained from those agencies listed in a central Social Service Index as acquainted with the families. The neighborhoods in which the boys lived were studied and rated in terms of the probable good or bad influences on a boy living in each locality. Delinquency "spot maps" constructed on the basis of a survey of all official court records for the two cities over a four-year period assisted in establishing the neighborhood ratings. A small school photograph of each boy was also available.

Separating Good from Bad Prognoses

The plan called for 650 boys to be divided equally into an experimental and a control group. Almost three times that number had been referred. A selection and screening process was necessary to assure the study group of boys about equally balanced between the pre-delinquent and the non–pre-delinquent. The policy was adopted of not eliminating any boy who showed obvious pre-delinquent traits, provided he met the other necessary requirements of age, residence, and school attendance.

To determine which boys might reasonably be labeled pre-delinquent and which non–pre-delinquent was the next problem. Reliance could not be placed on the teachers' referral alone, for the teachers were not acquainted with the great variety of facts pertaining to the boy and his family that were available to the study. A committee of three individuals experienced in dealing with both youthful and adult delinquents made a thorough study of the comprehensive data assembled in each case, although they had no opportunity for personal interviews with the boys.*

This committee consisted of one psychiatrist and two prison caseworkers. With a prognostic scale that ranged from plus five, indicating the greatest probability that the boy would *not* develop a delinquent career, through zero, the mid-point, to minus five, indicating the greatest probability that the boy *would* develop a delinquent career, they were able to classify the 782 boys who had survived the preliminary screening process. Judgments of the committee members were independently arrived at,

---

* See p. 1028 of this volume. — *Ed.*

group judgments being invoked in cases of initial disagreement. Thus, all 782 boys were finally scored on an eleven-point scale for probable delinquency.[6]

CREATION OF TWO MATCHED GROUPS

Out of the 782 cases available, two staff psychologists created two matched groups consisting of 325 boys each. A method of matching boy with boy, combining a statistical study of more than 100 relevant variables with a clinical interpretation of the personality as a whole, divided the 650 boys into two similar groups. Two boys were considered a well-matched pair if the configurational pattern of the most important variables showed them to be psychologically similar. A coin was tossed to determine which boy of a given pair was to be placed in the treatment group and which in the control group, thus eliminating any possible "constant error" after a pairing had been made.

The most important variables, in addition to age and prediction rating (which within each pair showed little, if any, variation) were health, intelligence and educational achievement, personality, family factors, and environment. Emphasis was placed on the relationship of the variables, on the profile or "contour" of the personality, rather than on the presence or absence of a large number of independent factors. It was subsequently found that the T-C group differences in the arithmetic means of 20 selected variables were extremely small — so small as to be almost negligible. Thus, the study was provided with controls that adequately served the purpose of comparing quantitative data later ascertained for each group.

THE TREATMENT PROGRAM

The 325 T boys were then assigned to ten counselors. The younger boys, as a rule, were assigned to the four women counselors. During the course of the program nine additional counselors were engaged to meet the unanticipated turnover of personnel due to the war demands.[7]

Treatment consisted of the application of whatever skills each counselor was capable of applying. The essence of the relationship between the boy and his counselor was personal intimacy and friendship. "What is it that keeps any of us straight unless it is the contagion of the highest personalities whom we have known?" asked Dr. Cabot in an earlier talk.[8]

Each counselor was left largely to his own resources. The agency policies, instead of being predetermined, as in most other social work agencies, were gradually evolved during the course of treatment. To social workers the "friendship" emphasis may have seemed old-fashioned and paternalistic; in practice, counselors were permitted and encouraged to utilize any of the modern techniques of social work with which they were familiar.

Although some counselors considered the job to be that of an orthodox social caseworker, others did not. One counselor, for example, believed that genuine, personal friendship was of greater value to a boy than all the technical skills that a more objective social worker could bring to the case. Inspiration, practical help, and persuasion were more commonly used by this counselor than was the traditional method of searching for the basic causes of the maladjustment. Others believed that the skill of the psychiatric social worker was indispensable in treating delinquency as a symptom of the boy's maladjustment. Certainly no one point of view prevailed, either as to therapy or as to interpretation of the concepts used.[9]

entire program to four or five different counselors; another third to three; while the remaining third were not reassigned more than once. Of the nineteen counselors, eight were professional social workers, six had completed part of the academic requirements for a degree in social work, two were experienced boys workers, one was a trained nurse, and two were psychologists. The counselors represented a wide distribution of ages, with an average of approximately 31 years. Three of them were about the same age as the boys' parents; nine were under 30.

[8] In an address called "The Consecration of the Affections," given before the American Social Hygiene Association, February 3, 1911.

[9] It became increasingly evident that the concept "delinquent boy" was misleading. A single act (minor or serious) might make a boy delinquent in the legal sense, but one could not draw valid generalizations about a group of boys who were similar in respect to a legal judgment but who differed among themselves

---

[6] An analysis of the variables noted and a description of the method of prediction has been published in an article by Donald W. Taylor.

[7] Only two of the original ten served during the entire treatment period, from 1937 to 1945. It was necessary, therefore, to assign approximately one-third of the 75 boys who were carried through the

Attention was given to each boy individually. Many visits were made to his home and to his school. Group work was seldom used. Sometimes the boy was taken on trips or to the counselor's home, or (particularly in the later years of the study) to the office of the study for scheduled interviews with the counselor. Some boys were seen two or three times a week for long periods of time; most of them at less frequent intervals. An important feature of the program was its coordination with available resources and agencies in the community.[10]

Areas of emphasis. Treatment comprised a wide variety of activities. An analysis of the records at the end of the program showed that major emphasis had been placed on the boy's adjustment to school. The cooperation of the school officials was good throughout the history of the study. Counselors continually visited each school to seek information or to enlist the cooperative efforts of the teachers in treatment planning. Frequently it was important to interpret to the teachers the boy's difficulties and to acquaint them with the conditions in the boy's home which so frequently were unknown to them.

So many of the boys in trouble were retarded in school that the staff employed special tutors, who had had public school teaching experience, to give individual attention to 93 of the boys during or after school. Special attention was given to reading difficulties commonly found among retarded children.

---

in almost every conceivable way, each responding to a different combination of forces. The medical analogy that a delinquent boy is a "sick" boy leads one further astray. The evidence seems to show that delinquent behavior, as a rule, is more likely to be related to a normal, impulsive response to a particular culture or specifically to the restrictions of that culture, or the yielding to the adolescent's urge for exciting adventure, rather than to any serious emotional conflict or abnormality. Most delinquents become relatively law-abiding after the age of 18. Those who persist in their antisocial behavior constitute a highly selected group. Generalizations might be made with greater validity about the persistent delinquent who, on the whole, seems to be neurotic and unhappy.

[10] For a brief case study demonstrating the coordination of the services of the school and other local agencies, see Margaret G. Reilly, R.N., and Robert A. Young, Ed.D., "Agency-Initiated Treatment of a Potentially Delinquent Boy," *The American Journal of Orthopsychiatry,* Vol. XVI, No. 4, October, 1946.

Another area of treatment constantly receiving the attention of the counselors was the boy's health. The counselors arranged for more thoroughgoing physical examinations for the boys, and many of them were taken to clinics or hospitals or were treated by the staff pediatricians. For eight summers camping was made available through local camping associations or other youth organizations. Two hundred and four boys were sent to camps for two-week periods or longer. Counselors, too, frequently took the boys on overnight or week-end camping trips. They guided them to recreational opportunities and in some cases obtained for them scholarships or memberships in various organized youth groups. Boys were encouraged to develop their own religious ties.

The study initiated the placement of twenty-four boys in foster homes; sent ten to private schools, the expenses being underwritten by the study if the families could not meet all the costs. Much family casework was called for to gain the cooperation and understanding of the parents and to assist them in dealing with their own or their children's problems. In fact, the counselors realized that winning and retaining the friendship and confidence of the parents was essential.

Professional services. During the last three or four years of the program there were available for consultation a pediatrician, a psychiatrist, and a clinical psychologist. During the early days of the study the counselors were not supervised by a trained social worker, although for a period of a little over a year an experienced social worker and director of a local children's agency was available once a week for consultation on especially difficult problems. During the last four years of the study the Director placed the entire treatment program under the supervision of a clinical psychologist who had had long experience in dealing with boys' problems. A counselor with special skills in dealing with family problems supervised that aspect of the work for a period of four years.

In brief, it can be said that the treatment program, utilizing some of the best professional advice obtainable, comprised an unusually wide diversity of special services to boys and their families, from removing nits from the boys' heads (and their siblings' heads, too!) to preparing them for higher education.

DISTINGUISHING FEATURES OF THE STUDY

It is so unusual for one to carry on research with boys with whom one is at the same time attempting treatment that the project was faced with a number of unprecedented situations. As there has not been, to the writer's knowledge, any other research project comparable to the study, some of its unique aspects may be pointed out.

Aid unsought. Boys receiving guidance from the study had not asked for it. The counselor's first visit to the boy and his family occasioned surprise in some cases, while in others it was taken as a matter of course, the assumption being that the counselor came from the school. Would a boy or his family profit by help if they were not motivated to seek it in the first place? The answer was "yes" and "no." Experience showed that in a few cases the offer of help was received with polite tolerance. In these instances casework was not possible. In a great majority of cases, however, a friendly relationship was very easily and early established. The personality of the worker seemed to be the determining factor.

If rapport were achieved, then the boy usually expressed his most obvious needs. If there were no need, expressed or even implied, over a long period of time, the case was usually dropped. It is evident that boys of eight to eleven in need of help do not ordinarily turn to a social agency. Their names do not come to the attention of social workers, as a rule, until something of an emergency nature has happened. There is some advantage, therefore, in becoming acquainted with the boy before a problem arises. It cannot be denied, however, that the plan of offering unsolicited help was financially extravagant.

Not linked to special need. The closing of a case did not follow upon the solution of a specific problem, as is usually true in social agencies. Most boys, in fact, had not been referred because of the existence of an acute problem. The casework relationship was, then, generally maintained beyond or in disregard of any special need, and in this respect was more akin to friendship than to conventional social work. The counselor stood by the boy "for better or for worse."

Before the act. Most studies of delinquents are made only after a boy has been in court or committed to an institution. The study was in the unusual position of observing the development of delinquent behavior in boys who, when first known, were not overt delinquents and in some cases not even considered pre-delinquents.

Non-problem boys. The facilities of the study were not limited to those who were in need, but included a wide variety of boys, both "good" and "bad." The inclusion within the T group of boys whose problems were the normal problems of an average boy (or whose parents were adequate to meet any problem that arose) occasionally left the counselors in a state of confusion. It was frequently stated in case conferences that "the boys without problems are our greatest problems." Although there were obvious research advantages in including within the T group, for observation at least, all kinds of boys, the trained social workers were not eager to develop a relationship that seemed, from a professional point of view, to have no point. Nevertheless, the project probably would not have been able to develop good public relations if it had not included "all kinds of boys." However, 18.7 per cent of the "non-problem" boys were carried through the entire treatment period.

Objectivity. Ordinarily, the very existence of an agency depends upon convincing a board of directors that its money has been well spent. Under such circumstances one is sometimes blinded to failure and is thus denied the benefit of searching self-criticism. The study, on the other hand, had ten years to go — and no longer — regardless of its effectiveness in preventing delinquency. It was trying to test, not to prove, the hypothesis that delinquency might be prevented by an intensive, enduring, personal, friendly relationship. It insisted only on doing what was best for the boy, on the keeping of accurate records, and on a fair evaluation. It is now in a position to give its first report on its successes and failures.

DID THE C.S.Y.S. PREVENT DELINQUENCY?

Looking at the record at the end of the treatment program *without reference to the C group*, the counselors could point to several very satisfying reports:

The treatment group: 1. There are 70 T boys who are now well past the age of 17 whose careers have been closely followed and who, as boys under 12, appeared to the predictors to be more likely than *not* to develop delinquent careers. That is, they had been rated on the "minus" side of the prediction scale. After these boys had been through the treatment program, not more than one-third (23 boys) committed serious or repeated delinquent acts, while 31 of them proved not to be delinquent at all.

2. There are 163 T boys who, when under 12, were rated on the "minus" side of the prediction scale as "probable" predelinquents. How many of these boys in the ensuing years committed delinquent acts that led to their commitment to a correctional institution? [11] Inspection of the registers of the two Massachusetts correctional institutions for juveniles, the reformatory for older offenders and the House of Correction for the county in which Cambridge is located, shows that only 23 had been committed as of March 1, 1948. This rate, of 14.1 per cent, seems a surprisingly low figure in view of the fact that the study, it was believed, included practically all boys in the two cities, with a combined population of 213,000, who showed early signs of future delinquency.

3. Counselors' opinions were sought — an unusual research procedure, and yet who would be in a better position to know the effect of their own treatment on their own boys? Each counselor, during the middle period of the program, was asked on three or four different occasions to list all T boys who he or she thought had been "substantially benefited by their contact with the study." Of the 255 boys then in the program, 166, or about two-thirds, were so listed. About half of the 166 were recorded by the counselors as having been "outstanding" in respect to benefit received.

4. Let us turn to the T boys themselves. They are much older now. They are in a position to look back upon their years of association with the study and to evaluate the experience with some insight. One hundred and twenty-five boys who in 1946 and 1947 were still in the Cambridge–Somerville area and who were available for a personal interview were questioned by special (non-staff) investigators who had had no prior information about the study. The boys were asked direct questions concerning the part the study may have played in their lives. More than half (62 per cent) of this large, unselected sample stated that the study had been of value to them. Jim's declaration that "they helped me keep out of trouble" was typical of many of the replies. Henry summed up the impact of the study upon his life by saying, "I used to be backward but they snapped me out of it and got me interested in so many different things and finally I got to college."

By such evidence alone, one might reasonably conclude that the study had been successful in preventing delinquency. Many illustrative cases could be given to "prove" the point in the traditional manner. Such evaluation, though of the customary type, is inconclusive.

The control group: At the core of the plan was the *control group*. What had happened to boys who had received *no* help at all from the study during the years in question? Had they become delinquent with greater or less frequency and seriousness than the T boys? We now look at the record.

1. The records of the Crime Prevention Bureau, established in 1938 by the police department in the city of Cambridge, reveal some interesting facts relating to the T and C boys who lived in Cambridge. Practically all boys who are reported by citizens or officials for minor offenses come to the attention of this bureau. Some recorded offenses were relatively trivial, such as "upsetting bags of ashes" or "taking rope from a flagpole"; others were serious enough to be referred to the local court for disposition.[12] Without differentiating degrees of seriousness, a tabulation of offenses from 1938 to 1945 (while treatment was in progress) lists the names of 267 T boys but only 246 C boys. It appears, at first sight, that treatment was ineffectual.

---

[11] About nine out of every ten of these boys are now over seventeen; a few over twenty-one. Most of the remaining are sixteen, the youngest fifteen years and five months.

[12] Many boys, of course, who committed delinquent acts were not known to the police. An estimate was made from the records of the study of the number of unlawful acts committed by boys that did not result in an official complaint, for one reason or another. A study based on the records of 114 boys showed that there were approximately 4,400 minor offenses. Less than 1 per cent of these were prosecuted. See Fred J. Murphy, Mary M. Shirley, and Helen L. Witmer, "The Incidence of Hidden Delinquency," *American Journal of Orthopsychiatry*, Vol. XVI, No. 4, October, 1946. [See Article 2 of this volume. — Ed.]

2. Two evaluations were made, also while treatment was in progress, by comparing samples of T boys with their paired controls. Comparisons of scores on a wide variety of tests, questionnaires, and rating scales pertaining to character, personality, social behavior, and achievements showed that while, as a general rule, the T boys excelled the C boys, the group differences were uniformly so small that they could be attributed to chance.

3. Studying the records of the 68 C boys who have passed the age of 17 and who were characterized as predelinquents in their early years (that is, they had been rated "minus" on the prediction scale in the same manner as the 70 T boys above referred to) but who were not subjected to the study program, we find that an almost equal proportion had refrained from serious delinquency. The record shows that 27, or 39.7 per cent, of the older C boys had become more or less serious delinquents, compared to 23, or 32.9 per cent, of the comparable group of T boys. The difference of 6.8 per cent in favor of the T boys is obviously not great.

4. Taking the 165 C boys who had been predicted on the "minus" side (in the same manner as the 163 T boys above referred to) we find on an inspection of the registers of the same correctional institutions where we sought the names of our T boys, that 22, or 13.3 per cent, of the C boys had been committed for delinquent behavior — about 1 per cent *less* than the percentage of committed T boys.

5. A comparison can also be made of the frequency of delinquent offenses that brought the T or the C boys to the attention of the court (although court appearance may not have led to an institutional commitment). The State Board of Probation that compiles data recording the appearance of boys in any court of the state discloses the following facts:

Of the 325 T boys, 76 are listed as having a court appearance for a relatively serious offense, compared to 67 of the 325 C boys.

If we include minor offenses, along with the serious, the score stands: 90 T boys, 85 C boys.[13]

---

[13] By "minor offense" is meant: traffic violations, breaking glass, using profane language, hopping a ride on a streetcar, or the like. The Board of Probation records were cleared as of July 1, 1947.

FIRST CONCLUSION

A T–C comparison of official records made within a few years after the termination of the treatment program shows that the special work of the counselors was no more effective than the usual forces in the community in preventing boys from committing delinquent acts.

The utilization of a control group thus casts a sharply revealing beam of light on the record. The effectiveness of the professional staff in preventing delinquency was clearly below anticipations, although it must be conceded that the difficulties of carrying out a well-planned and consistent program were considerable, in view of the impact of the war and the resulting turnover of personnel.[14]

Before we conclude that the treatment program was completely ineffectual, let us look deeper. There is evidence to suggest that, given a further lapse of time, greater differences between T and C groups in the seriousness of official offenses may appear in favor of the T boys. It begins to look as though the C boys are the more serious and the more persistent offenders. We find, for example:

1. The Crime Prevention Bureau statistics show that the C boys are more frequently brought in for repeated violations.

2. The records of correctional institutions show that more C boys (eight in number) have been sent to more than one institution than T boys (four in number).

3. Eight of the more serious offenders were

---

[14] Although relatively meager records were kept relating to the behavior of the C boys, it might be deduced from the T–C comparison what was happening to the predelinquents in the C group. If counselors were successful in preventing some boys from becoming delinquent, then it would be reasonable to infer from our statistics that certain deterrent forces in the community were operating with equal effectiveness on the C group during the same period of time. One is prone to overlook the strengthening influences of the home, the church, the school, and the public and private agencies in combating the forces of evil. It is reasonable to assume that without such influences the entire group of 165 predelinquent C boys might be developed into serious offenders. Seldom do we hear the question — "Why is there not more delinquency?" Seldom does one know or appreciate the great extent of preventive work constantly going on. Indeed, there is less need for concern over the fact that there is so much delinquency than there is reason for optimism over the fact that there is so little, in the face of so many adverse circumstances.

committed to the Massachusetts Reformatory, an institution for older male criminals between the ages of seventeen and thirty. Seven of these were C boys.

4. Again, in comparing the number of boys who had committed more than four serious offenses (known to the authorities), we find the names of five T boys and nine C boys.

5. In a list of the 108 relatively serious offenses (arson, sex offenses, burglary, assault with a dangerous weapon, robbery, and manslaughter), 46 were committed by T boys, 62 by C boys.

SECOND CONCLUSION

Though the counselors were unable to stop the rapid advance of young boys into delinquency with any greater success than the usual deterrent forces in the community, some of the boys were evidently deflected from delinquent careers which, without the counselors' help, might have resulted in continued or more serious violations. Thus, the evidence seems to point to the fact that though the first stages of delinquency are not wholly averted when starting treatment at the 8-to-11-year level, the later and more serious stages are to some degree curtailed.

This conclusion must, of course, be subject to a further check at a later time.

These facts, based on group statistics, do not necessarily imply that the counselors were not helpful in individual cases. Furthermore, delinquency was not the whole story. The making of good citizens — "social adjustment" in the language of the social worker — was the broader objective on which the study was based. An examination of the records and interviews with the boys themselves offers evidence that in many cases, even in the lives of many of the delinquent boys, emotional conflicts were alleviated, practical problems were dealt with successfully and boys were given greater confidence to face life's problems.

An analysis of the less tangible effects of treatment is now being made. The Ella Lyman Cabot Foundation is planning a series of publications to include a complete account of the treatment program and a more extensive evaluation of it. Answers will be attempted to such questions as — "What types of treatment were most effective?" "What kinds of boys were responsive — what kinds unresponsive to the counselors' services in general and to specific types of treatment measures?" "Can delinquency be predicted?" "Do delinquent boys come from 'delinquent areas'?" "From this experiment, what implications for social work can be drawn?" Case studies will describe how some boys became delinquent in spite of treatment and how other boys were helped to build constructive lives, emphasis being put on factors in the boys' lives and in treatment measures that differentiated these two types.*

---

* Dr. William McCord has recently furnished the following brief summary of a forthcoming book recording a further follow-up of the cases involved in the Cambridge–Somerville study:

"In 1956, eleven years after the completion of the project, the clinical records of the subjects were followed up. Analysis indicated that those boys who received treatment committed the same number of crimes and the same kind of crimes as the boys in the control group. This finding held true regardless of the intelligence, character, or background of the boys in the treatment group. No counselor was more successful than the others. There were only two indications that the treatment might have had a favorable effect: (1) A smaller portion of treatment boys than control boys had served time in jail; (2) those boys who received the most intensive, psychologically sophisticated treatment had a better general record than boys who received only counseling. Unfortunately, neither of these trends was statistically significant at a high level." The title of the forthcoming work is *The Genesis of Crime: A Later Study of the Cambridge–Somerville Experiment*, Columbia University Press. — *Ed.*

CONTRIBUTORS

BALISTRIERI, JAMES J. Clinical psychologist. Currently a junior at Marquette Medical School working toward an M.D. degree. Prior to re-entering school, worked as a clinical psychologist at Wood V.A. Hospital in Milwaukee, Wisconsin.

BANDER, EDWARD J. Librarian of the United States Court of Appeals for the First Circuit, Boston. Formerly in the Dept. of Research and Statistics, Cuyahoga County Juvenile Court; asst. ref. librarian, Harvard Law School Library. A.B., LL.B., Boston U., 1949, 1951; M.S. in Library Science, Simmons College, 1956.

BEELEY, ARTHUR L. Dean of the Graduate School of Social Work and chairman of dept. of sociology, U. of Utah. Formerly served on the faculty of the Universities of Chicago, Minnesota and S. California; for several years a research associate on staff of the late Dr. Herman M. Adler, Illinois State Criminologist. Author of many studies in criminology, notably *The Bail System in Chicago* (University of Chicago Press, 1927). Fellow of the American Orthopsychiatric Assn. Ph.D., U. of Chicago; L.L.D., U. of Utah. Member of numerous professional societies.

BETZ, ELIZABETH ANNE Presently employed by the United Nations in the Bureau of Social Affairs, Section of Social Defence. Prior to obtaining M.A. degree, worked for several years in various state training schools for juvenile delinquents in the United States; Ph.D. in sociology, N.Y.U., 1956.

BIRNBAUM, KARL Now deceased, Dr. Birnbaum was formerly a member of the psychiatric department of the Municipal Court of Philadelphia; lectured at the New School for Social Research, New York City; was professor of psychiatry at the University of Berlin and supt. of the Berlin Municipal Hospital for mental diseases at Buch. Author

of *The Psychopathic Criminal, Criminal Psychopathology,* and *Biopsychological Criminology,* as well as other books in clinical, social, and forensic psychiatry.

BLACKBURN, DONALD G. Executive director, Delaware Youth Services Commission, Wilmington. Formerly Institutions Consultant, Div. Juvenile Delinquency Service, Children's Bureau, U.S. Dept. of Health, Education and Welfare; Dean of Boys, Boys' Industrial School, Lancaster, Ohio; Supt. Cleveland Boys School, Dobbs Ferry, New York; M.S.S., Western Reserve, 1946.

BLAU, ABRAM Attending psychiatrist, Mt. Sinai Hospital since 1953. Formerly instructor in psychiatry, N.Y.U., 1936–1939, asst. clin. prof., 1939–1951; chief psychiatrist, N.Y.U. Clinic, 1937–1949; asst. alienist, Bellevue Psychiatric Hospital, 1934–1937; asst. neuropsychiatrist Univ. Hosp., N.Y.U., 1949–1951; school psychiatrist, Bur. Child Guidance, N.Y.C. Board of Education, 1940–1946; served as Lt. Commdr., M.C., U.S.N.R., 1944–46. Author of articles in medical journals. Fellow of the A.M.A., Am. Orthopsychiatric Assn., N.Y. Acad. of Medicine, Am. Psychiatric Assoc., Am. Academy Child Psychiatry, and others. B.Sc., 1927; M.Sc., 1929; M.D., C.M. 1931, McGill U.

BREED, ALLEN F. Supervisor of Camps, Youth Authority, State of California. Since late 1952, supt. of Fricot Ranch School for Boys, the California Youth Authority Institution for the most immature boys committed to State care.

BROTHER AQUINAS THOMAS, F.S.C. Christian Brother and psychiatric social worker. Received his training at Manhattan College, Fordham, New York and Columbia Universities. Has worked intimately with delinquents for two decades, both in institutions and in mental hygiene clinics; has taught in the educational field, from the grades through graduate courses at Manhattan College in New York City. Frequent contributor to professional journals and author of the "Look-in-the-Mirror Test," a device for group therapy. Member of various professional societies.

BUCHMUELLER, A. D. Executive director, Child Study Association of America. Formerly on staff of the Washington U. Medical School, dept of psychiatry; from 1940 to 1957, member of faculty of School of Social Work of Washington U. as instructor of psychiatric casework; in 1947, directed a four-year experimental program of group therapy with mothers of children with behavior problems, sponsored by St. Louis Council for Parent Education; former consultant to the St. Louis Mental Health Assn. and Pupil Welfare Division of the St. Louis City School Administration; from 1951 to 1957, director of the Mental Health Service Division of the St. Louis County Health Department. Author of many published papers. Member of the Nat'l Assn. of Social Workers, Psychiatric Social Work Section; American Orthopsychiatric Assn., American Public Health Assn., and St. Louis Society for Neurology.

CANTOR, NATHANIEL Professor, dept. sociology and anthropology, U. of Buffalo. Formerly visiting professor of sociology, Columbia U., 1954; consultant for the U.S. Foreign Operations Adm. in Western Europe during 1955; consultant to the Am. Tel. & Tel. Co. and other corporations in Management Development. Author of books on criminology and education. A.B., LL.B., Ph.D. (in anthropology), Columbia U. Member of New York State Bar.

CARR, LOWELL J. Visiting professor, U. of Miami, since 1955. Formerly at U. of Michigan, from 1925 until retirement in 1956 as emeritus professor; Director, Michigan Child Guidance Institute, from its inception in 1938 until its abolition in 1943; state editor of Detroit Free Press for many years. Author of several works in sociology, social work and delinquency. A.B., U. of Mich., 1920; Ph.D., U. of Mich., 1924; studied with Hobhouse, U. of London.

CASEY, BARBARA (Mrs. Wallace) Re-tired probation officer. Taught in elementary schools; after two years in New York in the visual education field, became a probation officer in Imperial County, California; asst. prob. officer, Santa Barbara County, 1948. Active in local Mental Hygiene Society, Council of Social Work, and California Prob. and Parole Assn. B. Ed., U.C.L.A.

CEDARLEAF, JOHN LENNART Since 1954, chaplain of Northern Reception Center and Clinic of the Cal. Youth Authority. Graduated from North Park Theological Seminary, Chicago, 1944; ordained as minister in the Presbyterian Church; graduate work, Northwestern U., Garrett Biblical Institute, and Chicago Psychoanalytic Institute Child Care Program. After serving as parish minister, became associate chaplain of Wesley Memorial Hospital, Chicago, chaplain of Cook County Hospital in Chicago, and served as research associate of the Federal Council of Churches; in 1948, became chaplain of the Illinois State Training School for Boys at St. Charles, and from 1952–54, served as director of clinical services for this institution. Clinical training at Elgin State Hospital, Wesley Memorial Hospital, Cook County Hospital; appointed supervisor for the Council for Clinical Training. Co-author (with Paul Maves) of *Older People and the Church*, and various articles.

CHWAST, JACOB Director, Planning and Training, Juvenile Aid Bureau, New York City Police Dept., staff and supervising psychologist since 1949. Formerly clinical psychologist, Brooklyn Jewish Hospital, 1946–49; consultant, Assoc. for Psychiatric Treatment of the Offender; certified psychologist, New York State Dept. of Mental Hygiene, 1952; instructor, St. Lawrence U., Frederick A. Moran Inst. of Crime and Delinquency, 1954; lecturer on occasion at various educational institutions. Member of various committees dealing with delinquency. Author of articles and reviews on delinquency. B.A., 1937, M.S. in Education, 1941, Ph.D., 1946.

CLINARD, M. B. Professor, sociology dept., U. of Wisconsin, since 1946. Formerly member of sociology department, U. of Iowa and Vanderbilt U.; from 1941 to 1942, chief, Criminal Statistics, U.S. Bureau of Census;

from 1942 to 1945, chief, Analysis and Reports Branch and principal statistician, Enforcement Dept., Office of Price Adm., Wash., D.C. Author, *The Black Market: A Study of White Collar Crime*, 1952; *Sociology of Deviant Behavior*, 1957; and articles in the fields of delinquency, criminology, and group therapy. During 1954–55, Fulbright Research Professor in Sweden, investigating delinquency and crime. B.A., M.A., Stanford U.; Ph.D., U. of Chicago, 1941.

CLOSE, O. H. Member of Calif. Youth Authority since 1941; member of Calif. State Board of Corrections, since 1944. Principal of San Juan High School, Fair Oaks, Calif., 1914–1920; served in World War I; supt. Preston School of Industry, Ione, Calif., 1920–1945; chairman, Delinquency Section of Commonwealth Club, San Francisco, 1935–37; president, Nat'l Conf. of Juvenile Agencies, 1940; chairman of Youth Authority Board, 1942–45; president, Western Prob. and Parole Assn., 1957. A.B., M.A., Stanford U.; graduate work in education, U. of California.

COLTHARP, RALPH W. Deceased. Formerly clinical director, Boys Industrial School, Topeka, Kansas, and director, Child Guidance Clinic, Dallas, Texas. Diplomate, American Board of Psychiatry and Neurology (1949); fellow, Menninger School of Psychiatry. B.A., U. of Texas, 1938, and M.D. in 1942.

COX, RACHEL D. Director, Child Study Institute and professor of psychology and education, Bryn Mawr College, Pa. Formerly education director, West Side Y.W.C.A., N.Y.C.; hospital caseworker, American Red Cross at Walter Reed Hospital, 1944. Member of American Psychological Assn., American Personnel and Guidance Assn., Society for Projective Techniques, and other professional organizations. B.A., U. of Texas; M.A., Columbia U.; Ph.D., U. of Penn.

DAVIS, WILLIAM S. Formerly chief psychiatrist, Children's Center, Bureau of Child Welfare, Dept. of Welfare, N.Y.C. M.D.

DELANY, LLOYD Clinical psychologist; consultant to The Educational Alliance,

N.Y.C.; staff psychologist of the Children's Court, N.Y.C. and on a joint research project sponsored by the Yorkside Center for Child Development and the Board of Education, N.Y.C. His experience has been with schizophrenic children in a treatment center conducted by the Jewish Board of Guardians, with antisocial groups for the N.Y.C. Youth Board, and in various experiments dealing with group therapy. M.A., New School for Social Research, N.Y.U.; now completing work for Ph.D. at N.Y.U.

DUMPSON, JAMES R. Since 1950, part-time faculty member of Graduate School of Public Adm. and Social Service, N.Y.U.; director, Bureau of Child Welfare, Dept. of Welfare, N.Y.C. since 1955. Formerly public school teacher; supervisor, Dept. of Public Assistance, Philadelphia; caseworker and director of Brace Farm School for Boys and Residence for Adolescents, Children's Aid Society of New York; asst. child care consultant and consultant on corrections and delinquency, Welfare Council, N.Y.C.; adm. supervisor, Central Harlem Street Clubs Project (for work with delinquent gangs); exec. sec., Committee on Narcotics among Teen-Age Youth; consultant, Child Care Planning Board, Federation of Protestant Welfare Agencies; U. N. advisor and chief of training in social welfare to Government of Pakistan. Author of various articles on social work, delinquency and street gangs, and narcotics addiction, and co-author (with Malamud and Crawford) of *Working with Teen-Age Gangs*. B.S., Penn. State Teachers College, 1932; B.A., N.A., New School of Social Research, 1947, 1950; Do. Soc. Sc. (Hon.), U. of Dacca, 1953.

EISENSTADT, S. N. Head of department of sociology, Hebrew U., Jerusalem; fellow, Center for Advanced Study in the Behavioral Sciences. Author of "Absorption of Immigrants," 1954, and papers in professional journals. M.A., Ph.D., Hebrew University.

FALSTEIN, EUGENE I. Clinical professor of psychiatry, Chicago Medical School; chief of child and adolescent care, Inst. for Psychosomatic and Psychiatric Research and Training, Michael Reese Hospital Medical Center,

Chicago; attending psychiatrist, Div. of Neuro-psychiatry, Michael Reese Hospital.

FERRERO, GINA LOMBROSO Daughter of Cesare Lombroso, Italian physician and criminologist. Author.

GARDNER, GEORGE E. Director, Judge Baker Guidance Center, Boston; psychiatrist-in-chief, Children's Medical Center, Boston; clinical professor of psychiatry, Harvard Medical School; lecturer, Department of Social Relations, Harvard University. Author of numerous articles on mental hygiene, psychotherapy, and delinquency.

GIFFIN, MARY Consultant in psychiatry at the Mayo Clinic; assistant professor of psychiatry of the U. of Minn. Graduate of Johns Hopkins Medical School, training in psychoanalysis at Chicago Institute of Psychoanalysis.

GILDEA, MARGARET C.-L. Asst. clinical professor of psychiatry, Washington U. School of Medicine since 1949; psychiatric consultant, St. Louis Mental Health Assn. and Mental Health Div. of St. Louis County Health Dept. since 1952. Formerly asst. in psychiatry, Yale U. School of Medicine and asst. attending physician, New Haven Hospital and Dispensary (1938–1942); medical director, Waterbury Society for Mental Hygiene (1939–1942) and New Britain Society for Mental Hygiene (1942); instructor in psychiatry, Wash. U. School of Medicine (1942–1949); former president and vice-pres. of Missouri Assoc. for Mental Hygiene; chairman, Committee of Child Psychiatry, Am. Psychiatric Assn. (1952–54). Member, Am. Psychiatric Assn., American Orthopsychiatric Assn., and various other professional organizations. B.S., U. of Chicago, 1923; M.D., Yale U. School of Medicine, 1936; medical externship and psychiatric internship at New Haven Hospital.

GILL, THOMAS D. Presiding judge, Connecticut Juvenile Court since 1943; chairman, Governor's Child Study Home Commission; trustee, Good Will Boys' Club; director and vice-president, Hartford, Conn., County Y.M.C.A.; board member of numerous other organizations. Former Judge of the Connecti-cut Juvenile Court, Third District. Member, Nat'l Probation and Parole Assn., N.Y.C., Committee of Judges; consultant, U.S. Children's Bureau and U.S. Senate Committee on Delinquency. Admitted to the Connecticut Bar in 1932 and practiced law in Hartford. Graduate of Yale University and Yale Law School.

GILPIN, RUTH Associate professor of social work, U. of North Carolina. Formerly, asst. prof. social casework, U. of Penn.; lecturer, Salem College, Winston-Salem, where she was exec. sec. of the Family and Child Service Agency; caseworker and supervisor, Children's Aid Society of Pennsylvania.

GLADSTONE, IRVING Since 1927, teacher and supervisor, Board of Education, N.Y.C.; principal, P.S. 186, Brooklyn; lecturer, Brooklyn College, since 1952. U.S. Army and Reserve (Major), 1944–1954. Member, New York Bar. LL.B., St. Lawrence U., 1930; Ph.D., N.Y.U., 1953.

GLUECK, BERNARD Psychiatrist and psychoanalyst; director, Stony Lodge Foundation, Ossining-on-Hudson, N.Y. Formerly member of staff of Govt. Hospt. for Insane; mental examiner of immigrants, Port of New York, 1913; director of psychiatric clinic, Sing Sing Prison, 1915–18; director of mental hygiene department, New York School of Social Work and Bureau of Child Guidance, 1918–23; Capt. Medical Corps, U.S. Army, 1918. Member, A.M.A., Am. Psychiatric Assn., Am. Psychopathol. Assn., Am. Psychoanalytic Assn., N.Y.Soc. Psychopathology and Psychotherapy. Author of Studies in Forensic Psychiatry as well as articles on psychiatry and psychoanalysis; lecturer at New School for Social Research. M.D., Georgetown U., 1909; studied at U. of Munich and Berlin, 1911.

GLUECK, ELEANOR T. Research Associate in Criminology, Harvard Law School. Formerly in dept. of social ethics; research in criminology, Harvard U.; research asst., Harvard Law School Crime Survey, 1928–30; research asst. and co-director, research in criminology, Harvard Law School, since 1930; trustee, Judge Baker Guidance Center; member Am. Assn. Social Workers, Am. Assn. University Women (Boston branch); Mass. Conf. Social Work. Author (with Sheldon Glueck) of many books including *500 Criminal Careers, One Thousand Juvenile Delinquents, Unraveling Juvenile Delinquency, Physique and Delinquency*; author *The Community Use of Schools, Evaluative Research in Social Work* and of numerous articles on delinquency. A.B., Barnard College, 1920; Diploma, N.Y. School of Social Work, 1921; Ed.M., Ed.D., Harvard U. Grad. School of Education, 1923, 1925; D.Sc. (hon.) Harvard U., 1958.

GLUECK, SHELDON Roscoe Pound Professor of Law at Harvard Law School and Director of Research in Juvenile Delinquency and Criminology. Formerly instructor in criminology and penology, dept. social ethics, Harvard U.; asst. prof. criminology, Harvard Law School, 1929–31. Official Delegate of U.S. Govt. to International Prison Congress, Prague, 1930 and Paris, 1950; member, Advisory Com. on Rules of Criminal Procedure, Supreme Court of U.S.; Am. Law Inst. for Youth Correction Authority Model Bill and for Model Penal Code; adviser to Justice Robert H. Jackson on law governing war crime trials at Nuremberg. Served with A.E.F., World War I. Author of several books, including *Mental Disorder and the Criminal Law, Crime and Justice, War Criminals, Their Prosecution and Punishment, Crime and Correction; The Nuremberg Trial and Aggressive War*; with L. Hall: *Cases on Criminal Law,* 1939, 1940, 1951, 1958; with E. T. Glueck: *500 Criminal Careers, After-Conduct of Discharged Offenders, One Thousand Juvenile Delinquents, Unraveling Juvenile Delinquency, Physique and Delinquency*; author of numerous articles on delinquency, crime and law in professional journals. Student at Georgetown U. Law School, 1914, 1915; A.B., George Washington U., 1920; LL.B., LL.M., Nat. Univ. Law School, 1920; student, Harvard Law School, 1926; A.M., Harvard U., 1922; Ph.D., Harvard, 1924; LL.D. (hon.) U. of Thessaloniki (Greece), 1948; D.Sc. (hon.) Harvard University, 1958. Member of American Bar Assn. and New York State Bar.

GORING, CHARLES Deceased. Formerly Deputy Medical Officer at Parkhurst Prison, England, and at Brixton Prison; Class I

Medical Officer to Manchester Prison, England. B.S., University College, London, 1895; M.D., 1903. He gained the Entrance Medical Exhibition and was John Stuart Mill Scholar of Philosophy; later elected a Fellow of the College. In 1914, he received the Weldon Prize Medal of the University of Oxford.

GRYGIER, TADEUSZ Senior psychologist, Dept. of Clinical Psychology and Research, Banstead Hospital, Surrey, England. Before the war, engaged in research at the Institutes of Criminology and Forensic Psychiatry at the U. of Warsaw, and member of Bar; from 1949 to 1952, Research Fellow of the Institute for the Study and Treatment of Delinquency; in 1952, recipient of a Rockefeller Fellowship. Author of *Oppression: A Study in Social and Criminal Psychology* and other works. Educated at Universities of Cracow and Warsaw; B.Sc., LL.M.; Ph.D., London School of Economics, 1950.

HALLOWITZ, EMANUEL District director, Community Service Society of New York; consultant on group therapy, Family Service of New Haven and Jewish Board of Guardians, New York City. Formerly director of vacation services, Community Service Society of New York.

HEWITT, LESTER E. Professor of sociology, Ball State Teachers College, Muncie, Indiana. Member, Governor's Youth Council, Indiana; formerly research associate, Michigan Child Guidance Institute. Co-author (with R. L. Jenkins) of *Fundamental Patterns of Maladjustment* (1946). Ph.D., U. of Michigan, 1945.

HULSE, WILFRED C. Consultant psychiatrist, Children's Center, Bureau of Child Welfare, New York City. Formerly chief psychiatrist at the center.

JENKINS, RICHARD L. Psychiatrist; director of psychiatric evaluation project, U.S. Veterans Adm., Washington, D.C. Formerly psychiatrist at New York State Training School for Boys, Warwick, and at Michigan Child Guidance Institute, Ann Arbor; chief psychiatrist, Institute for Juvenile Research, Chicago; acting director, assoc. prof., and acting head of dept. of criminology, social hygiene, and medical jurisprudence, U. of Ill. College of Medicine. With Lester E. Hewitt, author of *Fundamental Patterns of Maladjustment: The Dynamics of Their Origin*, State of Illinois Monograph, 1946. His book, *Breaking Patterns of Defeat*, deals in part with the problems of delinquency, and he has published a number of articles relating to delinquency.

JOHNSON, ADELAIDE M. M.D., professor of psychiatry, Mayo Foundation, Graduate School, U. of Minnesota; consultant, dept. of psychiatry at Mayo Clinic and head of child psychiatry. Adult and child psychoanalyst, particularly interested in research in juvenile delinquency and sexual deviations. Much of her early work on delinquency was done with Dr. S. A. Szurek of the Langley Porter Clinic, San Francisco.

KILLIAN, FREDERICK W. Assoc. prof. of sociology, Clark U.; consultant and member of numerous official and private organizations in the fields of delinquency, crime and law. Formerly Asst., Circuit Court of Appeals for the Second Circuit, N.Y., and managing clerk in law offices, 1921–27; practice of law, N.Y.C., 1927–30; asst. prof. of sociology (acting) at Oberlin College, 1938–39; atty. for the National Labor Relations Board, Review Division; lecturer in sociology, C.C.N.Y. and Wharton School, U. of Penn.; legal consultant, Nat'l Prob. and Parole Assn., N.Y.; director, Family Court for New Castle County, Delaware. Author of articles on sociology and criminology. Two years at Washington Square College, N.Y.U., before entering N.Y.U. Law School; LL.B., N.Y.U. Law School, 1925; member, New York Bar; B.A., Dana College, 1934; graduate work in sociology and public law, N.Y.U. Graduate School, 1934–38 under Fairchild; one year at Columbia U. Graduate Faculty working with Prof. Robert M. Mac-Iver; in 1949–50, Graduate Fellow at Yale Law School.

KONOPKA, GISELA Professor of social work, School of Social Work, U. of Minn. Studied in Berlin and Hamburg and worked there in progressive schools and an institution for delinquents. When the Nazis came to power she joined the forces against them in-

side Germany and was put in a concentration camp in 1936–37. After release from the camp, she worked with children in Vienna and briefly studied its excellent nursery school and kindergarten work. After the invasion of Austria, she escaped to France, arriving in the U.S. in 1941. Studied social work at the School of Social Work, U. of Pittsburgh, and received doctorate from Columbia U. From 1943 until 1947, she did therapeutic group work in the Pittsburgh Child Guidance Center, supervising students in psychiatric group work at Pittsburgh and lecturing at the schools of social work at the U. of Pittsburgh and Carnegie Tech. Member of NASW, Nat'l Conf. of Social Work, and various professional societies. Author of articles on group work, group therapy, and understanding of children, and of *Therapeutic Group Work with Children* and *Social Group Work in the Institution*.

KVARACEUS, WILLIAM C. Professor, Boston University School of Education; currently engaged in a three-year research project on prediction of juvenile delinquency sponsored by U.S. Office of Education, Dept. of Health, Education and Welfare. Formerly, director of guidance, research, and curriculum in Brockton, Mass., Schools; asst. supt. of schools, Passaic, N.J.; head of Passaic Children's Bureau and a consultant to the U.S. Children's Bureau; from 1952–53, in an advisory and teaching capacity to the Ministry of Education at the request of the Turkish Government, helped to establish the first center for the study and treatment of juvenile delinquents in Turkey. Author of several books and articles and of the KD Proneness Scale and Check List. Graduate of Boston College; Ph.D., Harvard University.

LARSEN, LAWRENCE C. Supervisor of field department, Kent County Juvenile Court, Grand Rapids, Michigan. From 1952 to 1957, Probation and Parole Agent in Division of Corrections, Wisconsin State Dept. of Public Welfare. B.A., U. of Iowa, 1950; M.A.S.A., Ohio State University, 1952.

LITIN, EDWARD Consultant in psychiatry, Mayo Clinic. Graduated in medicine, U. of Minnesota. Has been in training in psychoanalysis at Chicago Institute of Psycho-analysis and has done a great deal of work at Mayo Clinic on the problem of delinquency and sexual deviation.

LOURIE, NORMAN V. Deputy secretary for social welfare, Penn. Dept. of Welfare. Organized and was first director of the Psychiatric Social Work Section in the Army School of Military Neuropsychiatry. Formerly director, Assoc. for Jewish Children, Philadelphia; consultant, Institute of Local and State Government, U. of Penn.; director, Madison House Settlement, Lower East Side, New York; assistant director, Bronx House Settlement, Bronx, New York; research associate, Russell Sage Foundation, Greater New York Fund, and New York City Health and Welfare Council; practitioner in casework and group work; asst. prof., Adelphi College, School of Social Work, Long Island, New York; guest lecturer, Cornell U., U. of Penn., Columbia U., N.Y.U.; co-ordinator, Training Bureau for Communal Service, N.Y.C. Member of various professional organizations and public and private committees in the field of social work. Author of articles in professional journals. Studied at Cornell U., N.Y.U. School of Education, Columbia U., and School of Clinical Psychology, U.S. Army; graduate, New York School of Social Work.

MAGLIO, LOUIS G. Executive director and probation officer, Citizenship Training Group, Inc., affiliated with the Boston Juvenile Court. Formerly Director of Boys Work as well as Camp Director, East Boston Social Centers; instructor, Boston U. School of Education, 1952–53; supervisor, in-service training program for prospective probation officers, and field work training, social work students; Major, U.S. Army Active Reserve. Member of various professional organizations and community services. Contributor of articles on delinquency and probation. B.S. and Ed.M., Boston University.

McCORD, JOAN Co-director of the Stanford Study on Alcoholism. Has been associated with her husband, William McCord, in a number of research studies dealing with social problems. Author (with her husband) of *Psychopathy and Delinquency*.

McCORD, WILLIAM Assistant professor of sociology and Assistant Dean of Humanities and Sciences, Stanford U. Formerly Woodrow Wilson Fellow and Instructor in Social Psychology at Harvard U. Has been a psychologist at San Quentin Prison, Norfolk Prison, and the Wiltwick School. Author of books and articles on delinquency.

McKAY, HENRY D. Supervising sociologist at the Illinois Institute for Juvenile Research and the Chicago Area Project. Formerly teacher of sociology at U. of Illinois and U. of Chicago and more recently lecturer at the Cook County Training School for Nurses and Roosevelt College. Co-author, with Clifford R. Shaw, of *Social Factors in Juvenile Delinquency* and *Juvenile Delinquency in Urban Areas* and collaborator on several other books and articles dealing with criminals and the community.

MEEKER, BEN S. Chief U.S. Probation Officer, Northern District of Illinois; director, Federal Probation Training Center; lecturer, University of Chicago. From 1946–50, member of faculty of the School of Social Work, Indiana U.; prior to the war, employed in Oklahoma Public Welfare Service (1933–1938), and on the Federal Probation staff in Chicago (1939–1941); U.S. Navy (1942–46), attached to Navy Disciplinary Barracks program; consultant on probation and parole, German Federal Republic, Bonn, 1954. Author of articles on probation. M.A., School of Social Service Adm., U. of Chicago, 1940.

MILLER, LOVICK Currently associated with the Judge Baker Guidance Center, Guidance Camp Section, Boston.

MURPHY, FREDERICK J. Probation officer, working with juveniles, Malden District Court, Mass. Formerly associated with Citizenship Training Department of Boston Juvenile Court, Massachusetts; S.P.C.C.; New England Home for Little Wanderers; Cambridge–Somerville Youth Study; and Judge Baker Guidance Center Camp, Boston. B.S., in Social Science, Massachusetts State College, 1936; 1940–1946, Boston U. Graduate School of Social Work.

MURPHY, JOHN J. Executive director, Children's Center, Bureau of Child Welfare, Dept. of Welfare, City of New York.

NEWKIRK, PAUL R. Clinical director and staff psychiatrist, Northern State Hospital, Sedro Woolley, Washington. From 1923 to 1933, professor of internal medicine at Medical School in Dusseldorf; eight years in practice in New York. Author of numerous papers on physiological and pharmacological subjects. Graduated from Heidelberg U. Medical School, Germany, in 1909, summa cum laude.

NORMAN, SHERWOOD Director of detention services for the National Probation and Parole Association, N.Y.C., and full-time national consultant on the care of children awaiting juvenile court hearings. After ten years of teaching in public and private schools, became superintendent of a Southern institution used for the detention of children by the juvenile court. Lack of recognized standards for the proper use and operation of detention homes led the National Probation and Parole Association to ask Mr. Norman to make a survey of juvenile detention throughout the country. Author of *Detention for the Juvenile Court, Design and Construction of Detention Homes,* and *New Goals for Juvenile Detention,* as well as surveys and articles on detention. Graduated from Antioch College; has done graduate work in the fields of psychology, education, and social work.

NUNBERG, HENRY At present studying for degree of Doctor of Medicine at Albert Einstein College of Medicine, New York; graduated from Harvard College in 1954; LL.B., Harvard Law School, 1957.

PARMELEE, MAURICE Professor of sociology, economics, anthropology, successively, at Universities of Kansas, Missouri, Minnesota, and College of City of New York, 1909–19; formerly special asst. to Sec. of State; economist consultant, Berlin, Germany, 1920–23; economist, Dept. of Agr., 1934–36; sr. economic analyst, Treasury Dept., 1939–40; chief of research, U.S. Railroad Retirement Board since 1942; awarded Grant Squires prize for sociological research by Columbia U., 1915. Fellow A.A.A.S.; mem. Inst. International de

Sociologie. Author of books and articles on anthropology, sociology, economics and criminology. A.B., 1904 and A.M., 1908, Yale University; Ph.D., Columbia U., 1909.

PATTERSON, GERALD Psychologist, Nebraska Psychiatric Institute, U. of Nebraska College of Medicine. Formerly psychologist, Wilder Child Guidance Clinic. Ph.D in psychology, U. of Minnesota.

PERLMAN, I. RICHARD Chief, Juvenile Delinquency Statistics Section, U.S. Children's Bureau; analyst (statistician) in child welfare and delinquency statistics with Children's Bureau since 1942. Supervisor of educational research projects, Work Projects Adm., 1935–1941. Member, Nat'l Assoc. of Social Workers and Committee on Social Research and Social Studies, Nat'l Conf. on Social Welfare. B.S. (1934) and M.S. (1937), College of City of New York.

PIHLBLAD, C. TERENCE Professor of sociology, U. of Missouri, since 1930. Formerly associate professor of sociology, Wittenberg College, Springfield, Ohio; major fields of interest, criminology and population study; for some time advisor to Missouri State Department of Corrections and to State Board of Probation and Parole; Fulbright fellowship to Norway at the U. of Oslo, 1953 to 1954 to study effect of development of heavy industry on internal migration; continued study with grant from Population Council, 1957. Author of articles in various sociologic and criminologic journals. A.B., Bethany College, 1917; Ph.D., U. of Missouri, 1925.

PLEUNE, F. GORDON Asst. professor of psychiatry since 1954, U. of Rochester School of Medicine. Graduate of U. of Rochester Medical School, 1943; internship in surgery and obstetrics, 1943–1944; after 21 months in military service overseas, asst. residency, Residency in Neurosurgery, Strong Memorial Hospital; residency training in psychiatry, 1947–1949, U. of Rochester, dept. of psychiatry, Strong Memorial and Rochester Municipal Hospitals. Member of American Board of Psychiatry and Neurology and graduate of the Chicago Institute for Psychoanalysis.

PODOLSKY, EDWARD Practicing psychiatrist, in Brooklyn, N.Y.; psychiatric staff, Kings County Hospital; clinical instructor in psychiatry, State University of New York, Downstate Medical Center; consultant to National Association for Mental Health. Fellow, American Psychiatric Association; member of Society of Medical Jurisprudence and American Academy of Forensic Sciences. Author of many articles dealing with the psychiatric aspects of criminal behavior.

POWERS, EDWIN Deputy commissioner for personnel and training, Massachusetts Department of Correction, since 1956. Formerly director of research and correctional education for the United Prison Association of Massachusetts; director of the Cambridge–Somerville Youth Study; instructor in English at Robert College, Istanbul, Turkey; and instructor and assistant professor of psychology at Dartmouth College. Co-author, with H. Witmer, of *An Experiment in the Prevention of Delinquency* and author of other books and articles.

PRAY, KENNETH L. M. Deceased. Formerly director of Pennsylvania School of Social Work, Philadelphia. Author of articles for professional journals.

RAPPAPORT, MAZIE F. Division supervisor in the Department of Public Welfare, Baltimore, Protective Services Division (which she created and developed). Much previous experience in medical social work, work with delinquent girls and women, with negligent parents, and with delinquent youth in general. Ph.B., U. of Chicago; M.S.W., U. of Pennsylvania School of Social Work.

RAPPEPORT, JACK J. Assistant professor of law, U. of Pittsburgh School of Law; member of the Florida Bar; member of the Florida Bar Committee on Family Law. Formerly assistant professor of law and law librarian at Stetson U. College of Law (1956–57); in U.S.M.C. (active duty) 1943–1946; U.S. Atomic Energy Commission, security officer, 1947–1951. Contributor to professional journals of articles on family law and delinquency. B.S., Cornell U., 1948; attended U. of Arizona College of Law; LL.B., Stetson U. College of Law, 1955; LL.M., Harvard U. Law School,

1956; S.J.D. candidate at Harvard Law School and Ford Foundation Fellow, 1958.

REEVES, ELMER W. Deputy chief probation officer, Court of General Sessions, New York; vice-president, Professional Council, Nat'l Probation and Parole Assn. Former chairman, Corrections Section, Welfare Council, N.Y.C.; guest lecturer, N.Y.C. Police Academy.

REINEMANN, JOHN OTTO Director of probation, Municipal Court of Philadelphia, since 1934. Formerly City Solicitor, Welfare Adm., City of Berlin, Germany; Doctor of Jurisprudence, U. of Frankfurt-am-Main, Germany, 1926. Co-author (with Dr. Negley K. Teeters) of textbook, *The Challenge of Delinquency*, and author of numerous articles in professional journals on juvenile courts, probation, and parole.

RINCK, JANE Member of the New Jersey Bar. Formerly community planning associate in councils of social agencies and research analyst with Institute of Public Adm. and Princeton Surveys. M.S., Columbia U.; LL.B., N.Y.U.

ROSENHEIM, FREDERICK J. P. Psychoanalyst and professor of psychiatry at Boston College School of Social Work. Formerly co-director of Judge Baker Guidance Center, Boston; assistant professor of psychiatry at Boston U. School of Medicine; and professor of psychiatry at Boston College School of Social Work. Member of Massachusetts Medical Society, Am. Orthopsychiatric Assn., Am. Psychoanalytic Assn., and Boston Psychoanalytic Society. B.A., 1926, and M.D., 1929, Columbia.

RUGGIERI, BARTHOLOMEW ALBERT Diplomate, American Board of Pediatrics; fellow, American Academy of Pediatrics; member, American Orthopsychiatric Assn. A.B., M.D., M.S. in Pediatrics.

SCHMIDL, FRITZ Assistant chief social worker, Vet. Adm. Regional Office, Seattle; instructor, Psychoanalytic Training Center, Seattle. Fellow, Rorschach Institute. Published articles in psychiatric and psychoanalytic journals. Dr. Juris, U. of Vienna; M.S., New York School of Social Work, Columbia U.

SCHRAMM, GUSTAV L. President judge, Juvenile Court of Allegheny County, Pennsylvania. Elected, 1933, for ten-year term; reelected for third term, 1953. Served two terms as President, Nat'l Council of Juvenile Court Judges; formerly chairman, Committee on Problems of Juvenile Delinquency of the American Bar Assn.; Board of Trustees of the Nat'l Juvenile Court Foundation; director, Children's Service Committee of the R. W. Grand Lodge, F. & A.M. of Pennsylvania. Member of faculty of U. of Pittsburgh, 1918–1953; Attorney-in-charge of the Legal Aid Society of Pittsburgh, 1924–1934. Since 1948, instructor on faculty of the FBI National Police Academy, Washington, D.C. LL.B., Ph.D., LL.D.

SCHULMAN, RENA Clinical supervisor, Madeleine Borg Child Guidance Institute of the Jewish Board of Guardians, New York. Formerly supervisor of clinical services, Hawthorne Cedar Knolls School. B.A., Hunter College; M.S.S., Columbia University.

SCHWARTZ, RENE M. Social group worker at the Amherst H. Wilder Child Guidance Clinic, St. Paul, Minn. M.S.W., U. of Minn.

SCHWARZ, BERTHOLD ERIC Diplomate, American Board of Psychiatry and Neurology; fellow, American Psychiatric Assn.; member American Electroencephalographic Society. A.B., M.D., M.S. in psychiatry.

SHAW, CLIFFORD R. Deceased. Former sociologist and head of the department of research sociology and director of the Chicago Area Project, Institute for Juvenile Research. Author of many books and articles dealing with criminals and the community, including *Delinquency Areas*.

SHIPMAN, GORDON D. Chairman, dept. of sociology and anthropology, U. of Wisconsin. Formerly professor of sociology, Wisconsin State College, Milwaukee; head of social science dept., Shurtleff College; state probation–parole agent, State Dept. of Public Welfare, Wisconsin Rapids; director, Rent Dept., Oshkosh, Relief Commission; teacher at Osh-

kosh Normal School, U. of Arkansas, U. of Nebraska, and high school. Member of professional societies and contributor of articles to sociologic, psychologic and popular journals. Graduate, Oshkosh State Normal School; B.A., M.A., Ph.D., U. of Wisconsin (political science, sociology, modern European history); graduate work, Columbia U. (Carnegie Fellowship).

SHIRLEY, MARY Deceased. Formerly with U.S. Children's Bureau, Washington, D.C.

SHULMAN, HARRY M. Associate professor of sociology, dept. of sociology and anthropology, City College of New York. Responsible for department's offerings in criminology, penology, juvenile delinquency, and correctional casework. For some years, director of the Community Service Division of the college; for two-and-a-half years previously, on leave as First Deputy Commissioner of Corrections of the City of New York, a post from which he returned to the college in 1956.

SLAVSON, S. R. Committee chairman, International Aspects, American Group Psychotherapy Association, Inc., N.Y.C. Formerly on teaching staff of N.Y.U. and Springfield College. Founder of American Group Psychotherapy Association and International Council on Group Psychotherapy as well as founder and editor of *International Journal of Group Psychotherapy*. Author of numerous books in fields of psychotherapy, education, and sociology; contributor to scientific journals in the United States and abroad.

SMYTH, GEORGE W. Lawyer, White Plains, New York. Former Judge of Children's Court, Westchester County, New York; president of Nat'l Probation and Parole Association, 1949–1956; past president, New York State Association of Children's Court Judges and charter member of Nat'l Council of Juvenile Court Judges. Participant in White House Conferences. LL.B., New York Law School, 1906. Admitted to the Bar of the State of New York, 1907.

SOHN, LESLIE Psychoanalyst. Formerly senior registrar, Maudsley Hospital, London;

senior registrar and psychiatrist, Cassell Hospital, Richmond, London; ass. member, British Psycho-Analytical Society; member, British Psycho-Analytical Society. Contributor of medical papers to professional journals. M.B., Ch.B., U. of Cape Town, 1943.

SOMMER, EDITH Probation and parole agent, Div. of Corrections, Wisconsin State Dept. of Public Welfare since 1953, and at the present time, successfully operating two group homes. Formerly social worker at Central Baptist Children's Home, Lake Villa, Illinois; social worker at St. Mary's Home for Children, Chicago, Illinois; child welfare worker for county court of Waukesha County, Waukesha, Wisconsin. B.A., Northwestern University; three semesters (part-time), Graduate School of Social Work, Loyola U., Chicago.

SPENCER, JOHN C. Director, Bristol Social Project and research fellow in social studies at the University of Bristol, England. Formerly lecturer in social science, London School of Economics and magistrate in the Metropolitan Juvenile Courts. Author of *Crime in the Services*, 1954, and articles in the *British Journal of Delinquency* and other professional journals.

STULLKEN, EDWARD H. Principal, Montefiore Special School, Chicago. Formerly high school teacher and principal of elementary schools, organizer of Montefiore School, and conductor of educational surveys. Co-author of books and contributor to professional journals in the fields of school administration, education, and child development. A.B., Central Wesleyan, 1917; A.M., U. of Chicago, 1928.

SZUREK, S. A. Director, Children's Service, Langley Porter Clinic, San Francisco. professor, U. of Cal. School of Medicine; councilor, Amer. Assn. Psychiatric Clinics for Children, 1947–49; member of Amer. Psychoanalytic Assn. and several other organizations; diplomate, Am. Bd. Psychiatry and Neurology; Lt. Comdr., USNR, MC, 1943–46; consultant, VA Hosp., Palo Alto, Calif., 1946–47, and VA Mental Hygiene Clinic, San Francisco, 1947–51; member of numerous professional societies.

B.S., 1927; M.S., 1929; U. of Chicago; M.D., Rush Medical College, 1932. Resident physician, Chestnut Lodge Sanitarium, Rockville, Md., 1934.

TABER, ROBERT C. Director, Div. of Pupil Personnel and Counseling, Philadelphia Board of Education since 1942. Formerly boys' worker, U. Settlement House; director of social service, Christian Assn. of U. of Penn. (1932); exec. sec. of Boys' Club and Settlement House Committee, Council of Social Agencies, Philadelphia (1933–1938). Member of Pennsylvania Governor's Committee on Children and Youth since 1949, Youth Services Board, National Child Labor Committee, and others. Contributor of articles to professional journals. B.S., Wharton School of Business, U. of Penn., 1931; M.S.W., Penn. School of Social Work, U. of Penn., 1936.

TAPPAN, PAUL W. Professor of sociology and law, New York University; associate reporter, Model Penal Code project, American Law Institute; technical consultant on various public penologic projects. Formerly chairman, U.S. Board of Parole. Member of the New York Bar; author of several volumes in the fields of criminology and delinquency, including *Comparative Survey on Juvenile Delinquency, North America* (United Nations), *Delinquent Girls in Court, Juvenile Delinquency, The Habitual Sex Offender*; co-author of *Social Problems*; editor, *Contemporary Correction*; author of numerous articles in professional journals of law, criminology, psychiatry, sociology and social work. M.A., Ph.D., U. of Wisconsin; LL.B., N.Y.U.; Jur. Sc.D., Columbia.

TEETERS, NEGLEY K. Professor and chairman of department of sociology, Temple University, Philadelphia, since 1948. Formerly instructor, Minn. State Teachers College (with Temple University since 1927); consultant, Prison Industries Sect., W.P.B., 1944; member, Pa. Joint State Govt. Commission of Gen. Assembly to revise penal code, 1945–1947; member, Governor's Commission on Correctional Matters since 1955; member, American Prison Assn., American Assn. U. Profs., and others. Author of numerous books including *The Challenge of Delinquency* (with

J. O. Reinemann), and contributor to professional journals. A.B., Oberlin College, 1920; A.M. (1925), Ph.D. (1931), Ohio State University.

THOMAS, BROTHER AQUINAS (see Brother Aquinas Thomas)

TOPPING, RUTH   Executive director, Chicago Home for Girls; member of American Association of Residential Treatment Centers. Lived in Germany, 1912–14, and while there was English correspondent of American Chamber of Commerce. Formerly librarian of General Education Board; participant in several social studies with Bureau of Social Hygiene. Extension courses at Columbia University and Pennsylvania School of Social Work; Rand School of Social Science; New School of Social Research. Author and co-author of reports on social studies, including *Specialized Courts Dealing with Women Delinquents* (with G. E. Worthington).

VAN DER WART, E. (Now Mrs. Yanai) Social group worker at Amherst H. Wilder Child Guidance Clinic, St. Paul, Minn. M.S.W., U. of Minn.

VERVEN, NICHOLAS   Currently associated with the Judge Baker Guidance Center, Guidance Camp Section, Boston.

WAITE, EDWARD F.   Deceased. Former judge of Municipal Court and Juvenile Court, Minneapolis; special asst. to U.S. Atty. Gen. for hearing cases of conscientious objectors in Minnesota; asst. city atty., Minneapolis; supt. of police, Minneapolis (1902–03); lecturer, dept. of sociology, U. of Minn. (1926–34). Author of many articles in sociological and legal journals. A.B., Madison U. (now Colgate), 1880; LL.B., George Washington U., 1883; LL.M., 1884.

WALDNER, PAUL F.   Executive secretary of the Catholic Charities of the Diocese of Galveston, Houston, Texas. Referee, Lucas County Juvenile Court, Toledo, Ohio (1947–51); director of Welfare Dept. and Juvenile Dept., Oak Ridge, Tenn. (1944–47); Counter Intelligence Corps, U.S. Army (1942–46); Probation Department, Cuyahoga County

Juvenile Court (1941–42). A.B., John Carroll U., 1939; M.S.W., Western Reserve U. School of Applied Social Sciences, 1942.

WARREN, WILFRED   Physician to the Bethlem Royal Hospital and the Maudsley Hospital (Institute of Psychiatry), London, England; medical director, Brixton Child Guidance Unit, London. He shares with Dr. Kenneth Cameron the responsibility for a residential unit for the treatment of adolescent patients in the Bethlem Royal Hospital. M.A., M.D., D.P.M.

WATTENBERG, WILLIAM W.   Faculty member at Wayne State U. Since 1947, has worked in cooperative research programs with the Youth Bureau of the Detroit Police Department and acted as the Bureau's research consultant to discover predictive factors. Co-author, with Fritz Redl, of *Mental Hygiene in Teaching*; author of *The Adolescent Years*. Ph.D., Teachers College, Columbia, 1936.

WEBER, GEORGE H.   Director, Div. of Diagnosis and Treatment, Minn. Youth Conservation Commission, St. Paul. Formerly assistant G-I officer in charge of enlisted personnel, Marine Corps Air Base, Cherry Point, N.C. (1944–46); vocational advisor and psychometrist, V.A., Council Bluffs, Iowa (1946); psychological interne, Winter V.A. Hospital and Menninger Foundation, Topeka, Kansas (1946–48); clinical psychologist and later consultant, Kansas Boys' Industrial School, Topeka (1948–51); clinical psychologist, Bert Nash Mental Health Clinic, Lawrence, Kansas (1953–54). Consultant to professional and public agencies. Author of numerous articles and monographs in psychology and delinquency. B.S. in Education, Northern State Teachers College, 1943; A.B. with a major in social work, U. of S. Dakota, 1943; M.A. in psychology, 1949, and Ph.D. in sociology and human relations, 1954, U. of Kansas.

WEINBERG, S. KIRSON   Professor of sociology and chairman of the Committee on Social Psychology, Roosevelt University. Formerly visiting professor of sociology, U. of Minn.; co-director of a study of the social structure and functions of a mental hospital; has made intensive researches into schizophrenia, the deviant group, and the comparative forms of social disorganization in folk and urban societies and has been a psychologist in the military services. Member of various professional societies and the executive committee of the Illinois Academy of Criminology. Author of *Society and Personality Disorders, Incest Behavior, Culture and Personality,* and various articles.

WEISS, HANS Deceased. One of the most imaginative and dedicated juvenile court probation officers in America. He came to Boston Juvenile Court (1923–1930) from Switzerland. His untimely accidental death has left a real void in the ranks of the more progressive probation officers.

WENDELL, MITCHELL Associate professor of political science, American International College; research consultant, New York State Joint Legislative Committee on Interstate Cooperation; legal consultant, Parole and Probation Compact Administrators Association. Author, *Relations Between the Federal and State Courts.* Co-author, with Frederick L. Zimmermann, of "The Interstate Compact Since 1925."

WHELAN, RALPH W. Executive director, N.Y.C. Youth Board. Formerly executive director, Youth Counseling Service, Archdiocese of New York; assistant secretary, Nat'l Conf. of Catholic Charities; field investigator, Glueck Research Program, Harvard Law School; social worker, Highland Heights, New Haven, Conn.; member, Fordham School of Social Service Faculty, 1944–47. Member of various professional organizations, boards and committees. Author, *God's Rascals,* 1943; editor of monographs on Catholic social work; contributor to various professional social welfare journals. A.B., Boston College, 1935; M.S.S.W., Boston College School of Social Work, 1938.

WILLIAMS, HERBERT D. Director of the Juvenile Welfare Board of Pinellas County, Fla., for the past six years counseling in the areas of marriage and the family as a preventive service to insure a good emotional climate for growing children. He has found that conflict between parents provides the soil in which delinquency and mental illness get

their start. Formerly director of a child guidance clinic, superintendent of a boy's training school, director of social service in an institution for boys and girls, and referee in a court of domestic relations. He has spent most of his life working with people in trouble. During the early part of his life, he taught in the public school system of Georgia and later at Tulane, Northwestern, Ohio State, and New York University. Training in psychology and social work. Ph.D. in psychology, specializing in abnormal psychology, State U. of Iowa.

WITMER, HELEN Director, Division of Research, Children's Bureau, Dept. of Health, Education and Welfare, Washington, D.C. Formerly professor, School of Social Welfare, U. of Calif.; Director of Fact-Finding, White House Conference on Children and Youth, 1949–1951; editor, Smith College Studies in Social Work, 1929–1949; asst. prof. Dept. of Sociology, U. of Minnesota, 1926–27; statistician, Division of Corrections, Commonwealth of Massachusetts, 1925. A.B., Dickinson College, 1919; M.A., U. of Wisconsin, 1923; Ph.D., U. of Wisconsin, 1925; Social Science Research Council Fellow, London School of Economics, 1927–29. Author of numerous books and articles on child guidance and delinquency.

WOGAHN, LESTER E. District supervisor of the Eau Claire District, supervising corrections program in twenty-one Wisconsin counties. Formerly probation and parole agent with the Division of Corrections, State Department of Public Welfare, with area responsibility in Milwaukee County. Practiced law in Milwaukee for ten years. LL.B., Marquette University Law School, 1933.

WOLBERG, LEWIS ROBERT Psychiatrist (analysis and hypnosis); associate clinical professor and clinical professor of psychiatry, New York Medical College. Formerly medical director, Postgraduate Center for Psychotherapy; consultant, State Dept. of Vocational Rehabilitation, New York; diplomate, American Board of Psychiatry. Graduate of Tufts College, 1930; internship, Vassar Bros. Hospital, Poughkeepsie, N.Y., 1931; Los Angeles County Hospital,

1932; resident, Boston Psychopathic Hospital, 1932. Postgraduate training, Kings Park State Hospital, New York, 1933–1945; New York Psychoanalytic Institute and American Institute of Psychoanalysis, 1939–1943. Member of several professional associations, including American Orthopsychiatric Assn. Author of books and articles on psychiatry, psychology, psychoanalysis and medical hypnosis.

YOUNG, ROBERT A. Assistant director of Judge Baker Guidance Center, Boston; director of Camp Wediko (treatment camp); faculty member, Boston University, since 1936, and assistant professor of clinical psychology, Boston University School of Social

Work and the Graduate School. Formerly staff psychologist of Judge Baker Guidance Center; director of child guidance clinic at the N. H. Children's Aid Society (1947–57); faculty member, Smith College School of Social Work (1945–53). Member of various professional societies. Author of articles for professional journals. Ed.D., Harvard U.

ZIMMERMAN, FREDERICK L. Associate professor of political science, Hunter College, New York. Research Director of the New York State Joint Legislative Committee on Interstate Cooperation. Co-author, with Mitchell Wendell, of "The Interstate Compact Since 1925."

INDEX

Hooton, E. A., 44, 47n
Hoover, J. E., 368
Hopkins, T. W., 1081
Hopkirk, H. W., 653n
Horney, K., 786n
Hospital(s):
  admissions to, 748-749
  care for delinquents, 746-762
  care for probationers, 621
  discipline in, 756
  investigation of cases in, 750
  regime of, 748
  treatment of cases in, 750
Hostility of children in group, 896-897, 899
Houses of Refuge, 673-674
Howard Association, Central, Chicago, 812n
Howell, John C., ix
Hulse, W. C., 89, 112, 113n, 114n, 746, 762, 762n, 763n, 767n, 1153
Humiliation, fear of, 1112
Hyams, Sarah R., Fund, 638
Hyman, A., 656n
Hypnosis, 99, 838, 866-870
Hypoglycemia, and crime, 70
Hysteria, 97

I

Id, 94, 96n, 101
Identification:
  early, of maladjusted and delinquent children ("screening"), 156, 160, 1005, 1023-1051, 1063-1064, 1070-1072, 1087-1088, 1091
  of supposed delinquent by witnesses, 418-422
  psychologic process of:
    and delinquency, 252, 851
    and group therapy, 873
Illinois Institute for Juvenile Research, 837, 839n
  juvenile court statute of (1899), 255
  State Penitentiary, 244n
Imbalance between expressive and repressive forces, in delinquency, 228, 235
Immigrant families and delinquency, 202, 218
Imprisonment, selection for:
  of delinquents, 346
  of physically and mentally inferior, 50
Impulses, primitive, 94, 101
Incidence of delinquency, 3
Indemnification of victim of criminal, 47
Indeterminate sentence, 596n
India, delinquency in, 212
Indictment, in juvenile cases, 474
Individual and mass (group) in social casework, 814, 817, 837-838, 883, 886-887, 899-907
Individualistic societies, 203
Individual, study of, supplementary to study of culture, 219
Individualization: 178, 272, 355, 508, 552, 568, 569, 574, 581, 609, 810, 1031
  and classification, 579

Individualization (cont.)
  and human differences, 272, 1031
  cliché of, 838, 847, 1031
Industrial Areas Foundation, Chicago, 1080
Industrial schools for delinquents, 323, 323n, 393, 425, 427, 444, 459, 459n
Industrialization and urbanization, and delinquency, 212
Infant, as egocentric, narcissistic creature, 90
Infantile omnipotence, 863
Informal and private procedures in Norway Child Welfare Councils, 314
Information, as basis of proceeding against delinquent:
  in Federal court, 472
  instead of indictment, in A.L.I. Youth Court Act, 520
Inhibitions, internal, 101-102
"Inmate," of industrial school, being, as basis for jurisdiction of criminal court, 394-397
"Innate depravity": 407
  proneness to delinquency, 215
In-service training, 613-614, 724
Instability of delinquent youth groups in Israel, 204, 205
Instinct:
  and delinquency, 118, 217, 234
  and social institutions, 235
  sexual, 235
Instinctual equipment, taming and socialization of, 91, 94, 127
Institute for the Study and Treatment of Delinquency, 270n
Institutional care, in Norway, 316
Institutions Serving Delinquent Children: Guides and Goals, 670, 688n, 694n
Institutions, social, 182, 235
Intake practices of juvenile court: 268, 277, 280, 291, 333, 536-537, 538-551
  and adult cases, 541-542
  and court responsibility, 546-547
  and detention, 542, 545
  and jurisdiction of court, 279-280, 536-537
  and social work training, 280-281, 537
  officers of court, charged with, 537, 540-541
  police and, 536, 538-540, 542
  procedures, 549
  twelve goals of detention, after, 550-551
  typical controls of, 547-549
Intelligence, general:
  and age, 84
  and emotional dynamics, 87
  and recidivism, 83-84
  and offense, 82
  and socio-economic status, 81
  and type of offense, 82-83
  of children in New York City Shelter, 764
  of juvenile delinquents, 78-81
  mechanical, and delinquency, 85
  performance intelligence, 86
  social, and delinquency, 84-85

Intelligence, general (cont.)
  testing of, 76-78
  verbal, 86
Interactants, position of, in social relationships, 223
Interdependence of causal influences, 248-249
Interdisciplinary approach, 248
Interests, adjustment of by law, 274n
International Association of Chiefs of Police, 11n
Interpersonal relations and delinquency, 154
Interstate compacts for supervision of probationers and parolees, 944, 961-962
Interstimulation and interresponse in causation, 41
"Interstitial areas," 35-36, 97n, 215, 241
Interviews with children in detention, 539-540
Intramural guidance programs and prevention, 1078, 1082-1083
Introjection, 94n, 164, 166
Investigation of delinquent:
  before or after adjudication of status, 285, 291, 295, 327, 340, 342, 412, 435, 441, 454-455, 509, 811
  by police, 538-539
  by probation officer, 238, 411, 412, 413, 608, 627
  by psychiatrist, 412, 413, 435
  in Norwegian Child Welfare Council procedure, 314
  preliminary, to determine if petition should be filed, 354
Investigation reports: 563
  as guide to finding of delinquency, 327
  as guide to sentence, 560
  consultation of, by parents, 327n
I.Q., 552, 1111
Isolation, social, 904
Israel, delinquency group formation in, 168, 201-209
Italian penal code project (Ferri), 568

J

Jaques, E., 790n
Jenkins, R. L., 88, 89, 101, 101n, 171, 176, 284n, 560, 696n, 844n, 924, 1153
Jenner, E., 1054
Jewish Board of Guardians, New York City, 932, 1028
Job changes, 619
Johnson, A. M., 144n, 147n, 149n, 838, 842n, 849, 849n, 850, 850n, 860, 963, 1154
Johnson, H., 924
Johnston, J., 567
Johnstone, E. L., 1076, 1086
Jones, E., 97
Jones et al. v. Commonwealth, 297n, 418
Jones, Matter of, v. Rochester S.P.C.C., 415-416
Jones v. Geckley, State ex rel., 390-391